ANTHOL

An Introduction to Literature

Cover picture, "Fighting Téméraire," by JOSEPH MALLORD WILLIAM TURNER.
Reproduced by courtesy of the Trustees, the National Gallery, London.

ANTHOLOGY

An Introduction to Literature

FICTION · POETRY · DRAMA

Lynn Altenbernd

UNIVERSITY OF ILLINOIS
AT URBANA–CHAMPAIGN

Macmillan Publishing Co., Inc.

NEW YORK

MACMILLAN PUBLISHING CO., INC.
866 Third Avenue, New York, New York 10022

Library of Congress Cataloging in Publication Data

Main entry under title:

Anthology, an introduction to literature.

Includes index.
1. Literature—Collections.   I. Altenbernd, Lynn.
PN6014.A62   808.8   76–12104
ISBN 0-02-301960-3

Printing: 2 3 4 5 6 7 8   Year: 8 9 0 1 2 3

ACKNOWLEDGMENTS

"The Great Baker Street Bank Raid" from the London *Times*, 13–17 September 1971. Reproduced from *The Times* by permission.

"The Darling" by Anton Chekhov. Reprinted with permission of Macmillan Publishing Co., Inc. from *The Darling and Other Stories* by Anton Chekhov. Translated from the Russian by Constance Garnett. Copyright 1916 by Macmillan Publishing Co., Inc., renewed 1944 by Constance Garnett.

"Roman Fever" (copyright 1934 *Liberty Magazine*) is reprinted by permission of Charles Scribner's Sons from *The Collected Short Stories of Edith Wharton*.

"Saint Emmanuel the Good, Martyr" by Miguel de Unamuno. Translated by Anthony Kerrigan. Reprinted by permission of Henry Regnery Company.

"The Bull That Thought," copyright 1924 by Rudyard Kipling from *Debits and Credits*. Reprinted by permission of Doubleday & Company, Inc.

"Disorder and Early Sorrow" by Thomas Mann. Copyright 1936 and renewed 1964 by Alfred A. Knopf, Inc. Reprinted from *Stories of Three Decades*, by Thomas Mann, translated by H. T. Lowe-Porter. Reprinted by permission of the publisher.

"I Want to Know Why" by Sherwood Anderson. Reprinted by permission of Harold Ober Associates Incorporated. Copyright © 1919 by Sherwood Anderson. Copyright renewed.

"Sex Education" by Dorothy Canfield Fisher. Copyright 1945 by Dorothy Canfield Fisher; renewed 1973 by Sarah Fisher Scott. Reprinted from *A Harvest of Stories* by Dorothy Canfield, by permission of Harcourt Brace Jovanovich, Inc.

"The Celestial Omnibus" by E. M. Forster. From *The Collected Tales of E. M. Forster*. Published 1947 by Alfred A. Knopf, Inc. Reprinted by permission of the publisher.

"The Dead" from *Dubliners* by James Joyce. Copyright © 1967 by the Estate of James Joyce. All rights reserved. Reprinted by permission of Viking Penguin, Inc.

"A Hunger Artist" by Franz Kafka. Reprinted by permission of Schocken Books Inc. from *The Penal Colony* by Franz Kafka. Copyright © 1948 by Schocken Books Inc.

"The Blind Man" from *The Complete Short Stories of D. H. Lawrence*, Vol. II, by D. H. Lawrence. Copyright 1922 by Thomas B. Seltzer, Inc., copyright renewed 1950 by Frieda Lawrence.

"The Body of the Crime" by William Daniel Steele. Copyright 1931, 1958 by William Daniel Steele, reprinted by permission of Harold Matson Co. Inc.

"The Fig Tree" by Katherine Anne Porter. Reprinted by permission of Joan Daves. Copyright © 1960 by Katherine Anne Porter.

"In a Grove" is reprinted from *Rashomon and Other Stories* by Ryūnosuke Akutagawa, translated by Takashi Kojima, with the permission of Liveright Publishing Corporation. Copyright 1952 by Liveright Publishing Corporation.

"The Jelly-Bean" (copyright 1920 Metropolitan Newspaper Syndicate; renewal copyright 1948 Frances Scott Fitzgerald Lanahan) is reprinted by permission of Charles Scribner's Sons from *Tales of the Jazz Age* by F. Scott Fitzgerald.

"Barn Burning" by William Faulkner. Copyright 1939 and renewed 1967 by Estelle Faulkner and Jill Faulkner Summers. Reprinted from *Collected Stories of William Faulkner*, by permission of Random House, Inc.

"The Undefeated" (Copyright 1927 Charles Scribner's Sons) is reprinted by permission of Charles Scribner's Sons from *Men Without Women* by Ernest Hemingway.

"Joining Charles" by Elizabeth Bowen. Reprinted by permission of Curtis Brown Ltd.

"Tlön, Uqbar, Orbis Tertius," Jorge Luis Borges, translated by James E. Irby, *Labyrinths*. Copyright © 1962 by New Directions Publishing Corporation. Reprinted by permission of New Directions Publishing Corporation.

"The Destructors" from *Twenty-one Stories* by Graham Greene. Copyright 1954 by Graham Greene. Reprinted by permission of Viking Penguin, Inc.

"Of This Time, Of That Place" by Lionel Trilling. Copyright by The Estate of Lionel Trilling. Reprinted by permission.

"Big Boy Leaves Home" in *Uncle Tom's Children* by Richard Wright. Copyright 1936 by Richard Wright; renewed 1964 by Ellen Wright.

"Keela, the Outcast Indian Maiden" by Eudora Welty. Copyright, 1941, renewed, 1969, by Eudora Welty. Reprinted from her volume, *A Curtain of Green and Other Stories*, by permission of Harcourt Brace Jovanovich, Inc.

"Miss Muriel" by Ann Petry. Copyright © 1971 by Ann Petry. Reprinted by permission of the publisher Houghton Mifflin Company.

"The Swimmer" by John Cheever. Reprinted by permission; © 1964 John Cheever. Originally in *The New Yorker*.

The Last Mohican" from *The Magic Barrel* by Bernard Malamud. Copyright © 1958 by Bernard Malamud. Reprinted with the permission of Farrar, Straus & Giroux, Inc.

"Between the Porch and the Altar" from *The Collected Stories* by Jean Stafford. Copyright 1945 by Jean Stafford, copyright renewed 1973 by Jean Stafford. Reprinted with the permission of Farrar, Straus & Giroux, Inc.

"Christmas Every Day" by Heinrich Böll. Reprinted by permission of Joan Daves. Copyright © 1957 by Heinrich Böll.

"Previous Condition" excerpted from *Going to Meet the Man* by James Baldwin copyright © 1948 by James Baldwin. Originally published in *Commentary*. Reprinted by permission of The Dial Press.

"Good Country People" from *A Good Man Is Hard to Find and Other Stories*, copyright © 1955 by Flannery O'Connor. Reprinted by permission of Harcourt Brace Jovanovich, Inc.

"Flight" by John Updike. Copyright © 1962 by John Updike. Reprinted from *Pigeon Feathers and Other Stories*, by John Updike, by permission of Alfred A. Knopf, Inc. Originally appeared in *The New Yorker* in another version.

"Where Are You Going, Where Have You Been" by Joyce Carol Oates. Reprinted from *The Wheel of Love* by Joyce Carol Oates by permission of the publisher, Vanguard Press, Inc. Copyright © 1970, 1969, 1968, 1967, 1966, 1965 by Joyce Carol Oates.

"Success Is Counted Sweetest," "I Taste a Liquor Never Brewed," "There's a Certain Slant of Light," "The Soul Selects Her Own Society," "I'll Tell You How the Sun Rose," "A Bird Came Down the Walk," "Much Madness Is Divinest Sense," "I Died for Beauty," "Because I Could Not Stop for Death," "Presentiment—Is That Long Shadow," "I Stepped from Plank to Plank," "A Narrow Fellow in the Grass,"

"Tell All the Truth," by Emily Dickinson. Reprinted by permission of the publishers and the Trustees of Amherst College from *The Poems of Emily Dickinson*, edited by Thomas H. Johnson, Cambridge, Massachusetts: The Belknap Press of Harvard University Press, © 1951, 1955 by the President and Fellows of Harvard College.

"After Great Pain," "My Life Had Stood—a Loaded Gun," by Emily Dickinson. Copyright 1929 by Martha Dickinson Bianchi. Copyright 1957 by Mary L. Hampson.

"Hap," "Neutral Tones," "Drummer Hodge," "The Darkling Thrush," "The Man He Killed," "Ah, Are You Digging on My Grave," "Channel Firing," by Thomas Hardy. Reprinted with permission of Macmillan Publishing Co., Inc. from *Collected Poems* by Thomas Hardy. Copyright 1925 by Macmillan Publishing Co., Inc.

"Loveliest of Trees," "When I Was One-and-Twenty," "On the Idle Hill of Summer," "On Wenlock Edge," "To an Athlete Dying Young," "1887" by A. E. Housman. From "A Shropshire Lad"—Authorized Edition—from *The Collected Poems of A. E. Housman*. Copyright 1939, 1940, © 1965 by Holt, Rinehart and Winston. Copyright © 1967, 1968 by Robert E. Symons. Reprinted by permission of Holt, Rinehart and Winston, Publishers.

"The Way Through the Woods," copyright 1910 by Rudyard Kipling from *Rudyard Kipling's Verse: Definitive Edition*. Reprinted by permission of Doubleday & Company, Inc.

"The Lake Isle of Innisfree" by William Butler Yeats. Reprinted with permission of Macmillan Publishing Co., Inc. from *Collected Poems* by William Butler Yeats. Copyright 1906 by Macmillan Publishing Co., Inc., renewed 1934 by William Butler Yeats.

"The Wild Swans at Coole" by William Butler Yeats. Reprinted with permission of Macmillan Publishing Co., Inc. from *Collected Poems* by William Butler Yeats. Copyright 1919 by Macmillan Publishing Co., Inc., renewed 1947 by Bertha Georgie Yeats.

"The Second Coming" by William Butler Yeats. Reprinted with permission of Macmillan Publishing Co., Inc. from *Collected Poems* by William Butler Yeats. Copyright 1924 by Macmillan Publishing Co., Inc., renewed 1952 by Bertha Georgie Yeats.

"Sailing to Byzantium," "Leda and the Swan," by William Butler Yeats. Reprinted with permission of Macmillan Publishing Co., Inc. from *Collected Poems* by William Butler Yeats. Copyright 1928 by Georgie Yeats, renewed 1956 by Bertha Georgie Yeats, Michael Butler Yeats, and Anne Yeats.

"Crazy Jane Talks with the Bishop" by William Butler Yeats. Reprinted with permission of Macmillan Publishing Co., Inc. from *Collected Poems* by William Butler Yeats. Copyright 1933 by Macmillan Publishing Co., Inc., renewed 1961 by Bertha Georgie Yeats.

"Beautiful Lofty Things," "Hound Voice," by William Butler Yeats. Reprinted with permission of Macmillan Publishing Co., Inc. from *Collected Poems* by William Butler Yeats. Copyright 1940 by Georgie Yeats, renewed 1968 by Bertha Georgie Yeats, Michael Butler Yeats, and Anne Yeats.

"Luke Havergal" and "Richard Cory" are reprinted by permission of Charles Scribner's Sons

from *The Children of the Night* by Edwin Arlington Robinson.
"How Annandale Went Out" (Copyright 1910 Charles Scribner's Sons) is reprinted from *The Town Down the River* by Edwin Arlington Robinson.
"The Dark Hills," "The Mill," by Edwin Arlington Robinson. Reprinted with permission of Macmillan Publishing Co., Inc. from *Collected Poems* by Edwin Arlington Robinson. Copyright 1920 by Edwin Arlington Robinson, renewed 1948 by Ruth Nivison.
"Mr. Flood's Party" by Edwin Arlington Robinson. Reprinted with permission of Macmillan Publishing Co., Inc. from *Collected Poems* by Edwin Arlington Robinson. Copyright 1921 by Edwin Arlington Robinson, renewed 1948 by Ruth Nivison.
"The Listeners," "Silver," "The Dreamer," "Peace," by Walter De La Mare. Reprinted by permission of the Literary Trustees of Walter De La Mare and The Society of Authors as their representatives.
"A Line-Storm Song," "The Road Not Taken," "Birches," "Stopping by Woods on a Snowy Evening," "For Once, Then, Something," "The Onset," "Spring Pools," "Desert Places," "Design," "The Silken Tent," by Robert Frost. From *The Poetry of Robert Frost* edited by Edward Connery Lathem. Copyright 1916, 1923, 1928, 1934, © 1969 by Holt, Rinehart and Winston. Copyright 1936, 1942, 1944, 1951, © 1956, 1962 by Robert Frost. Copyright © 1964, 1970 by Lesley Frost Ballantine. Reprinted by permission of Holt, Rinehart and Winston, Publishers.
"Chicago," "Fog," "Nocturne in a Deserted Brickyard," from *Chicago Poems* by Carl Sandburg, copyright, 1916, by Holt, Rinehart and Winston, Inc.; renewed, 1944, by Carl Sandburg. Reprinted by permission of Harcourt Brace Jovanovich, Inc.
"Skyscrapers Stand Proud," copyright © 1960 by Carl Sandburg. Reprinted from his volume *Honey and Salt* by permission of Harcourt Brace Jovanovich, Inc.
"Cool Tombs" from *Cornhuskers* by Carl Sandburg, copyright, 1918, by Holt, Rinehart and Winston, Inc.; renewed, 1946, by Carl Sandburg. Reprinted by permission of Harcourt Brace Jovanovich, Inc.
"Domination of Black," "The Snow Man," "The Death of a Soldier," by Wallace Stevens. Copyright 1923 and renewed 1951 by Wallace Stevens. Reprinted from *The Collected Poems of Wallace Stevens*, by permission of Alfred A. Knopf, Inc.
"A Postcard from the Volcano" by Wallace Stevens. Copyright 1936 by Wallace Stevens and renewed 1964 by Holly Stevens. Reprinted from *The Collected Poems of Wallace Stevens*, by permission of Alfred A. Knopf, Inc.
"Study of Two Pears" by Wallace Stevens. Copyright 1942 by Wallace Stevens and renewed 1970 by Holly Stevens. Reprinted from *The Collected Poems of Wallace Stevens*, by permission of Alfred A. Knopf, Inc.
"The House Was Quiet and the World Was Calm" by Wallace Stevens. Copyright 1947 by Wallace Stevens. Reprinted from *The Collected Poems of Wallace Stevens*, by permission of Alfred A. Knopf, Inc.
"Dawn," "The Poor," "Spring and All," "The

Yachts," from William Carlos Williams, *Collected Earlier Poems*. Copyright 1938 by New Directions Publishing Corporation. Reprinted by permission of New Directions Publishing Corporation.
"Raleigh Was Right" from William Carlos Williams, *Collected Later Poems*. Copyright 1944 by William Carlos Williams. Reprinted by permission of New Directions Publishing Corporation.
"Landscape with the Fall of Icarus" from William Carlos Williams, *Pictures from Brueghel and Other Poems*. Copyright © 1960 by William Carlos Williams. Reprinted by permission of New Directions Publishing Corporation.
"Gloire de Dijon," "Piano," "Snake," "Bavarian Gentians," from *The Complete Poems of D. H. Lawrence*, edited by Vivian de Sola Pinto and F. Warren Roberts. Copyright © 1964, 1971 by Angelo Ravagli and C. M. Weekley, Executors of the Estate of Frieda Lawrence Ravagli. All rights reserved. Reprinted by permission of Viking Penguin Inc.
"To the Stone-Cutters" by Robinson Jeffers. Copyright 1924 and renewed 1952 by Robinson Jeffers. Reprinted from *The Selected Poetry of Robinson Jeffers*, by permission of Random House, Inc.
"Shine, Perishing Republic" by Robinson Jeffers. Copyright 1925 and renewed 1953 by Robinson Jeffers. Reprinted from *The Selected Poetry of Robinson Jeffers*, by permission of Random House, Inc.
"Hurt Hawks" by Robinson Jeffers. Copyright 1928 and renewed 1956 by Robinson Jeffers. Reprinted from *The Selected Poetry of Robinson Jeffers*, by permission of Random House, Inc.
"The Eye" by Robinson Jeffers. Copyright 1941, 1944 and renewed 1969, 1972 by Donnan Jeffers and Garth Jeffers. Reprinted from *Selected Poems*, by Robinson Jeffers, by permission of Random House, Inc.
"Original Sin" by Robinson Jeffers. Copyright 1948 by Robinson Jeffers. Reprinted from *Selected Poems*, by Robinson Jeffers, by permission of Random House, Inc.
"Carmel Point" by Robinson Jeffers. Copyright 1954 by Robinson Jeffers. Reprinted from *Selected Poems*, by Robinson Jeffers, by permission of Random House, Inc.
"Poetry," "To a Steam Roller," by Marianne Moore. Reprinted with permission of Macmillan Publishing Co., Inc. from *Collected Poems* by Marianne Moore. Copyright 1935 by Marianne Moore, renewed 1963 by Marianne Moore and T. S. Eliot.
"The Steeple-Jack" by Marianne Moore. Reprinted with permission of Macmillan Publishing Co., Inc. from *Collected Poems* by Marianne Moore. Copyright 1951 by Marianne Moore.
"Granite and Steel" from *Complete Poems* by Marianne Moore. Copyright © 1966 by Marianne Moore, originally appeared in *The New Yorker*. Reprinted by permission of Viking Penguin, Inc.
"The Love-Song of J. Alfred Prufrock," "Journey of the Magi," "Eyes that Last I Saw in Tears," "The Wind Sprang Up at Four O'Clock," from *Collected Poems 1909–1962* by T. S. Eliot, copyright, 1936, by Harcourt Brace Jovanovich, Inc.; copyright © 1963, 1964, by T. S. Eliot. Reprinted by permission of the publishers.
"The Harlem Dancer," "America," "Flame-Heart," from *Selected Poems of Claude McKay;*

copyright 1953 by Twayne Publishers and reprinted with permission of Twayne Publishers, A Division of G. K. Hall & Co.

"in Just- spring," "a wind has blown the rain away," by e. e. cummings. Copyright 1923, 1951, by E. E. Cummings. Reprinted from his volume, *Complete Poems 1913–1962*, by permission of Harcourt Brace Jovanovich, Inc.

"next to of course god america i" by e. e. cummings. Copyright 1926, by Horace Liveright; renewed, 1954, by Marion Morehouse Cummings. Reprinted from his volume, *Complete Poems 1913–1962*, by permission of Harcourt Brace Jovanovich, Inc.

"anyone lived in a pretty how town" by e. e. cummings. Copyright, 1940, by e. e. cummings; renewed, 1968, by Marion Morehouse Cummings. Reprinted from his volume, *Complete Poems 1913–1962*, by permission of Harcourt Brace Jovanovich, Inc.

"Repose of Rivers," "Proem: To Brooklyn Bridge," by Hart Crane. Poems reprinted from *The Complete Poems and Selected Letters and Prose of Hart Crane* with the permission of Liveright Publishing Corporation. Copyright 1933, © 1958, 1966 by Liveright Publishing Corporation.

"The Negro Speaks of Rivers," "The Weary Blues," "Dream Variation," "I, Too," by Langston Hughes. Copyright 1926 by Alfred A. Knopf, Inc. and renewed 1954 by Langston Hughes. Reprinted from *Selected Poems*, by Langston Hughes, by permission of the publisher.

"Theme for English B" by Langston Hughes from *Montage of a Dream Deferred*. Reprinted by permission of Harold Ober Associates Incorporated. Copyright 1951 by Langston Hughes.

"Listen," copyright 1940 by Ogden Nash; "Very Like a Whale," Copyright 1934 by Ogden Nash; "The Germ," copyright 1935 by Ogden Nash from *Verses from 1929 On*, by Ogden Nash, Reprinted by permission of Little, Brown and Company.

"Come Live with Me and Be My Love," "Newsreel" by C. Day Lewis, from *Collected Poems 1954* by C. Day Lewis. Reprinted by permission of the Executors of the Estate of C. Day Lewis and of the publishers, Jonathan Cape Ltd and the Hogarth Press.

"Almost Human," by C. Day Lewis, from *Pegasus and Other Poems* by C. Day Lewis. Reprinted by permission of the Estate of C. Day Lewis and of the publisher, Jonathan Cape Ltd.

"Who's Who" by W. H. Auden. Copyright 1937 and renewed 1965 by W. H. Auden. Reprinted from *Collected Shorter Poems 1927–1957*, by W. H. Auden, by permission of Random House, Inc.

"Lullaby," "Musée des Beaux Arts," "The Unknown Citizen," by W. H. Auden. Copyright 1940 and renewed 1968 by W. H. Auden. Reprinted from *Collected Shorter Poems 1927–1957*, by W. H. Auden, by permission of Random House, Inc.

"The Shield of Achilles" by W. H. Auden. Copyright 1952 by W. H. Auden. Reprinted from *Collected Shorter Poems 1927–1957*, by W. H. Auden, by permission of Random House, Inc.

"Moss-Gathering," copyright 1946 by Editorial Publications; "My Papa's Waltz," copyright 1942 by Hearst Magazines, Inc.; "Elegy for Jane," copyright 1950 by Theodore Roethke;

"The Waking," copyright © 1958 by Theodore Roethke; "I Knew a Woman," copyright 1954 by Theodore Roethke; "In a Dark Time," copyright © 1960 by Beatrice Roethke as Administratrix of the Estate of Theodore Roethke from the book *The Collected Poems of Theodore Roethke*. Reprinted by permission of Doubleday & Company, Inc.

"The Man-Moth," "The Sandpiper," by Elizabeth Bishop. Reprinted with the permission of Farrar, Straus & Giroux, Inc. from *The Complete Poems* by Elizabeth Bishop, Copyright © 1962, 1969 by Elizabeth Bishop.

"On Inhabiting an Orange" by Josephine Miles. Reprinted by permission of the author. "Belief," "Reason," from *Poems 1930–1960* by Josephine Miles. Copyright © 1960 by Indiana University Press. Reprinted by permission of the publisher.

"The Ballad of Sue Ellen Westerfield," "Runagate Runagate," by Robert Hayden from *Selected Poems*. Copyright © 1966 by Robert Hayden. Reprinted by permission of October House.

"Auto Wreck" by Karl Shapiro. Copyright 1942 and renewed 1970 by Karl Shapiro. Reprinted from *Selected Poems*, by Karl Shapiro, by permission of Random House, Inc.

"Drug Store" by Karl Shapiro. Copyright 1941 and renewed 1969 by Karl Shapiro. Reprinted from *Selected Poems*, by Karl Shapiro, by permission of Random House, Inc.

"The Leg" by Karl Shapiro. Copyright 1944 by Karl Shapiro. Reprinted from *Selected Poems*, by Karl Shapiro, by permission of Random House, Inc.

"The Force That Through the Green Fuse," "When All My Five and Country Senses See," "In My Craft or Sullen Art," "Fern Hill," from *The Poems of Dylan Thomas*. Copyright 1939, 1946 by New Directions Publishing Corporation. Reprinted by permission of New Directions Publishing Corporation.

"We Real Cool," copyright © 1959 by Gwendolyn Brooks; "The Chicago *Defender* Sends a Man to Little Rock," copyright © 1960 by Gwendolyn Brooks. "Way-Out Morgan," copyright © 1968 by Gwendolyn Brooks Blakely. From *The World of Gwendolyn Brooks* by Gwendolyn Brooks. By permission of Harper & Row, Publishers, Inc.

"The Mouth of the Hudson," "For the Union Dead," by Robert Lowell. Reprinted with the permission of Farrar, Straus & Giroux, Inc. from *For the Union Dead* by Robert Lowell, Copyright © 1960, 1964, by Robert Lowell. "Grandparents," by Robert Lowell. Reprinted with the permission of Farrar, Straus & Giroux, Inc. from *Life Studies* by Robert Lowell, Copyright © 1956, 1959 by Robert Lowell.

"Make Love Not War," "The Town Dump," by Howard Nemerov. Copyright by Howard Nemerov. Reprinted by permission of the author.

"Digging for China," "Mind," by Richard Wilbur. From *Things of This World*, copyright © 1956 by Richard Wilbur. Reprinted by permission of Harcourt Brace Jovanovich, Inc.

"The Pardon" by Richard Wilbur. From *Ceremony and Other Poems*, copyright 1948, 1949, 1950 by Richard Wilbur. Reprinted by permission of Harcourt Brace Jovanovich, Inc.

"Advice to a Prophet" by Richard Wilbur. Copyright © 1957 by Richard Wilbur. Reprinted viii]

ACKNOWLEDGMENTS

from his volume, *Advice to a Prophet and Other Poems*, by permission of Harcourt Brace Jovanovich, Inc. First published in *The New Yorker*.

"The Heaven of Animals," "The Beholders," by James Dickey. Copyright © 1961, 1962 by James Dickey. Reprinted from *Poems 1957–1967* by permission of Wesleyan University Press. First appeared in *The New Yorker*.

"A Supermarket in California" from *Howl & Other Poems* by Allen Ginsberg. Copyright © 1956, 1959 by Allen Ginsberg. Reprinted by permission of City Lights Books.

"My Sad Self" from *Reality Sandwiches* by Allen Ginsberg. Copyright © 1963 by Allen Ginsberg. Reprinted by permission of City Lights Books.

"A Presentation of Two Birds to My Son," "A Blessing," by James Wright. Copyright © 1957, 1961 by James Wright. Reprinted from *Collected Poems*, by permission of Wesleyan University Press. "A Blessing" first appeared in *Poetry*.

"Unknown Girl in the Maternity Ward," "Ringing the Bells," from *To Bedlam and Part Way Back*. Copyright © 1960 by Anne Sexton. Reprinted by permission of the publisher, Houghton Mifflin Company.

"The Knight," reprinted from *Snapshots of a Daughter-in-Law*, Poems, 1954–1962, by Adrienne Rich. By permission of W. W. Norton & Company, Inc. Copyright © 1956, 1957, 1958, 1959, 1960, 1961, 1962, 1963, 1967, by Adrienne Rich Conrad.

"The Trees," reprinted from *Necessities of Life*, Poems, 1962–1965, by Adrienne Rich. By permission of W. W. Norton & Company, Inc. Copyright © 1966 by W. W. Norton & Company, Inc.

"Diving into the Wreck," reprinted from *Diving into the Wreck*, Poems, 1971–1972, by Adrienne Rich. By permission of W. W. Norton & Company, Inc. Copyright © by W. W. Norton & Company, Inc.

"Morning Song," copyright © 1961 by Ted Hughes; "Tulips," copyright © 1962 by Ted Hughes; "Little Fugue," "The Arrival of the Bee Box," copyright © 1963 by Ted Hughes. From *Ariel* by Sylvia Plath. By permission of Harper & Row, Publishers, Inc.

"Ka 'Ba," "A Poem for Black Hearts," by Imamu Amiri Baraka. From *Black Magic Poetry 1961–1967*, copyright © 1969, by LeRoi Jones, reprinted by permission of the publisher, The Bobbs-Merrill Company, Inc.

"Preface to a Twenty Volume Suicide Note" by Imamu Amiri Baraka. Copyright © 1961 by LeRoi Jones (Imamu Amiri Baraka). Reprinted by permission of The Sterling Lord Agency, Inc.

"Song of the Thrush" by Laurence Lieberman.

Reprinted with permission of Macmillan Publishing Co., Inc. from *The Osprey Suicides* by Laurence Lieberman. Copyright © 1971 by Laurence Lieberman. Originally appeared in *The Yale Review*.

"Inside the Gyroscope" by Laurence Lieberman. Reprinted with permission of Macmillan Publishing Co., Inc. from *The Osprey Suicides* by Laurence Lieberman. Copyright © 1971 by Laurence Lieberman. Originally appeared in *The Saturday Review*.

The Antigone of Sophocles: An English Version by Dudley Fitts and Robert Fitzgerald, copyright, 1939, by Harcourt Brace Jovanovich, Inc.; renewed, 1967, by Dudley Fitts and Robert Fitzgerald. Reprinted by permission of the publishers.

CAUTION: All rights, including professional, amateur, motion picture, recitation, lecturing, performance, public reading, radio broadcasting, and television are strictly reserved. Inquiries on all rights should be addressed to Harcourt Brace Jovanovich, Inc., 757 Third Avenue, New York, New York 10017.

A Doll's House by Henrik Ibsen. From *The Oxford Ibsen*, Volume V, translated and edited by James Walter McFarlane. © Oxford University Press 1961. Reprinted by permission.

Arms and the Man by Bernard Shaw. Copyright 1898, 1913, 1926, 1931, 1933, 1941, George Bernard Shaw. Copyright 1905, Bretano's. Copyright 1958, The Public Trustee as Executor of the Estate of George Bernard Shaw. Reprinted by permission of Dodd, Mead & Company and The Society of Authors for the Estate of George Bernard Shaw.

The Hairy Ape by Eugene O'Neill. Copyright 1922 and renewed 1950 by Eugene O'Neill. Reprinted from *Selected Plays of Eugene O'Neill*, by permission of Random House, Inc.

Mother Courage and Her Children by Bertolt Brecht. Reprinted by permission of Grove Press, Inc. Copyright © 1955, 1959, 1961, 1962, 1963, 1966 by Eric Bentley.

Death of a Salesman by Arthur Miller. Copyright 1949 by Arthur Miller. All rights reserved. Reprinted by permission of Viking Penguin, Inc.

A Raisin in the Sun by Lorraine Hansberry. Copyright © 1958, 1959 by Robert Nemiroff as executor of the Estate of Lorraine Hansberry. Reprinted by permission of Random House, Inc.

Picnic on the Battlefield by Fernando Arrabal. Reprinted by permission of Grove Press, Inc. Copyright © 1967 by Calder & Boyars, Ltd., London.

PREFACE

Anthology: An Introduction to Literature is designed for an introductory course in literature. Although the reader will undoubtedly find many unfamiliar selections in a book of this size, the "introduction" is not so much to more works of literature as to ways of looking at literature. The study of literature at the advanced secondary and beginning college levels provides valuable opportunities for summarizing the literary experiences of past years and for gathering strength and equipment for further exploration. This is a fitting time to examine literary form and to consider the relationships of genres, historical periods, and individual genius. It is a time to confirm the rudiments of critical taste. It is a time to read widely and to discover the realm of literature in all its richness and diversity and seriousness and hilarity.

The selections in *Anthology: An Introduction to Literature* are as diverse in form, subgenre, technique, period, theme, and complexity as the exceptionally liberal dimensions of the book allow. The range of techniques within the traditional genres permits the student to study the elements of fiction, poetry, and drama with an increasing understanding of diction, imagery, structure, characterization, and allusion. The modern interpretation of the classification "literature" has further expanded the variety of forms; our inclusion of science fiction and the detective story, for example, reflects a broad view. Roughly half the content is twentieth-century work, yet the traditions that have helped form the present are thoroughly represented. Poetry and drama, having longer histories than prose fiction, show a proportionately greater selection from the past. Although the themes represented are numerous and diverse, we deliberately emphasize certain motifs, such as *coming of age and initiation, ways of knowing* (the tensions of experience, knowledge, and belief), *alternative forms of existence* (what Wordsworth in *The Prelude* calls "unknown modes of being"), *marriage and family relations*, and, above all, the tension between *Apollonian and Dionysian impulses*—between, that is, spirit and flesh, polity and wilderness, creativity and destructiveness, intellect and emotion. Finally, the selections vary in sophistication and subtlety. Everyone can find a connection with past adventures in reading, and all will find new roads to travel. Thus we hope without clouding the delight of youthful experience to encourage the fascination and engagement with the most vital human concerns that mark thoughtful reading.

The arrangement of material is traditional and convenient, by genres, and within genres in an approximately chronological order. The study of a genre opens the way to the broader study of literary form. Similarly the historical context provided by chronology contributes to our understanding of a work, although we are by no means exclusively concerned with development and progression. But the arrangement of the collection is not intended as the design for a course. That plan should arise out of the needs and interests of a particular class as it pursues its most important goal—an understanding of the interaction of form and meaning.

To provide ready access to the texts and to encourage concentration on matters of theme and form, we have modernized and Americanized spelling throughout, with a very few exceptions: we have respected the expressed wishes of copyright holders, we have permitted Spenser his deliberate archaism, and we have avoided tampering with sound values in poetry. The "Glossary of Literary Terms" has been prepared with care to see that necessary elements are included and that they are presented with comprehensive explanation and with illustration where necessary. We have supplied generous footnotes according to a principle easily defined, but difficult to apply. The notion that leafing through a dictionary builds character is out of date; it is more important for the reader to stay with the primary text in uninterrupted application than to go trudging about the library for handbooks of biography, mythology, literature, history, and art. Hence we have provided most information a student is unlikely to possess, though we have left a number of items unglossed—deliberately at times, and no doubt inadvertently elsewhere —to permit the student to learn and practice all phases of the art of explication. We have refrained from stating, or even implying, the import of the information given, on the ground that the student must apply, interpret, and understand. We hold with Dr. Johnson, "I have found you an argument; I am not obliged to find you an understanding." Or more gently, we might note that only the understanding the student seeks out is absorbed and retained, even though he or she finds it in the company of a classroom.

As often before I find myself indebted to many people, sometimes in subtle and intangible ways, for understanding, advice, and encouragement. In two instances the support was sustained and thoroughly tangible: Anthony English of Macmillan has given counsel and practical help beyond normal expectations, and my wife has shared the labor and the delight even more fully than usual in this enterprise.

L. A.

CONTENTS

◇

FICTION

◇

xi

❖

POETRY

❖

THE MIDDLE AGES

THE SIXTEENTH CENTURY

THE EIGHTEENTH CENTURY

THE ROMANTIC PERIOD

THE VICTORIAN AGE

THE MODERN PERIOD

◊

DRAMA

◊

Fiction

Nathaniel Hawthorne
1804–1864
MY KINSMAN, MAJOR MOLINEUX

AFTER the kings of Great Britain had assumed the right of appointing the colonial governors, the measures of the latter seldom met with the ready and general approbation which had been paid to those of their predecessors, under the original charters. The people looked with most jealous scrutiny to the exercise of power which did not emanate from themselves, and they usually rewarded their rulers with slender gratitude for the compliances by which, in softening their instructions from beyond the sea, they had incurred the reprehension of those who gave them. The annals of Massachusetts Bay will inform us, that of six governors in the space of about forty years from the surrender of the old charter, under James II,[1] two were imprisoned by a popular insurrection; a third, as Hutchinson inclines to believe, was driven from the province by the whizzing of a musket-ball; a fourth, in the opinion of the same historian, was hastened to his grave by continual bickerings with the House of Representatives; and the remaining two, as well as their successors, till the Revolution, were favored with few and brief intervals of peaceful sway. The inferior members of the court party, in times of high political excitement, led scarcely a more desirable life. These remarks may serve as a preface to the following adventures, which chanced upon a summer night, not far from a hundred years ago. The reader, in order to avoid a long and dry detail of colonial affairs, is requested to dispense with an account of the train of circumstances that had caused much temporary inflammation of the popular mind.

It was near nine o'clock of a moonlight evening, when a boat crossed the ferry with a single passenger, who had obtained his conveyance at that unusual hour by the promise of an extra fare. While he stood on the landing-place, searching in either pocket for the means of fulfilling his agreement, the ferryman lifted a lantern, by the aid of which, and the newly risen moon, he took a very accurate survey of the stranger's figure. He was a youth of barely eighteen years, evidently country-bred, and now, as it should seem, upon his first visit to town. He was clad in a coarse gray coat, well worn, but in excellent repair; his under garments were durably constructed of leather, and fitted tight to a pair of serviceable and well-shaped limbs; his stockings of blue yarn were the incontrovertible work of a mother or a sister; and on his head was a three-cornered hat, which in its better days had perhaps sheltered the graver

[1] in 1686

brow of the lad's father. Under his left arm was a heavy cudgel formed of an oak sapling, and retaining a part of the hardened root; and his equipment was completed by a wallet, not so abundantly stocked as to incommode the vigorous shoulders on which it hung. Brown, curly hair, well-shaped features, and bright, cheerful eyes were nature's gifts, and worth all that art could have done for his adornment.

The youth, one of whose names was Robin, finally drew from his pocket the half of a little province bill of five shillings, which, in the depreciation in that sort of currency, did but satisfy the ferryman's demand, with the surplus of a sexangular piece of parchment, valued at three pence. He then walked forward into the town, with as light a step as if his day's journey had not already exceeded thirty miles, and with as eager an eye as if he were entering London city, instead of the little metropolis of a New England colony. Before Robin had proceeded far, however, it occurred to him that he knew not whither to direct his steps; so he paused, and looked up and down the narrow street, scrutinizing the small and mean wooden buildings that were scattered on either side.

"This low hovel cannot be my kinsman's dwelling," thought he, "nor yonder old house, where the moonlight enters at the broken casement; and truly I see none hereabouts that might be worthy of him. It would have been wise to inquire my way of the ferryman, and doubtless he would have gone with me, and earned a shilling from the Major for his pains. But the next man I meet will do as well."

He resumed his walk, and was glad to perceive that the street now became wider, and the houses more respectable in their appearance. He soon discerned a figure moving on moderately in advance, and hastened his steps to overtake it. As Robin drew nigh, he saw that the passenger was a man in years, with a full periwig of gray hair, a wide-skirted coat of dark cloth, and silk stockings rolled above his knees. He carried a long and polished cane, which he struck down perpendicularly before him at every step; and at regular intervals he uttered two successive hems, of a peculiarly solemn and sepulchral intonation. Having made these observations, Robin laid hold of the skirt of the old man's coat, just when the light from the open door and windows of a barber's shop fell upon both their figures.

"Good evening to you, honored sir," said he, making a low bow, and still retaining his hold of the skirt. "I pray you tell me whereabouts is the dwelling of my kinsman, Major Molineux."

The youth's question was uttered very loudly; and one of the barbers, whose razor was descending on a well-soaped chin, and another who was dressing a Ramillies wig,[2] left their occupations, and came to the door. The citizen, in the mean time, turned a long-favored countenance upon Robin, and answered him in a tone of excessive anger and annoyance. His two sepulchral hems, however, broke into the very center of his re-

---

[2] an eighteenth-century style having a pigtail tied with bows

buke, with most singular effect, like a thought of the cold grave obtruding among wrathful passions.

"Let go my garment, fellow! I tell you, I know not the man you speak of. What! I have authority, I have—hem, hem—authority; and if this be the respect you show for your betters, your feet shall be brought acquainted with the stocks by daylight, tomorrow morning!"

Robin released the old man's skirt, and hastened away, pursued by an ill-mannered roar of laughter from the barber's shop. He was at first considerably surprised by the result of his question, but, being a shrewd youth, soon thought himself able to account for the mystery.

"This is some country representative," was his conclusion, "who has never seen the inside of my kinsman's door, and lacks the breeding to answer a stranger civilly. The man is old, or verily—I might be tempted to turn back and smite him on the nose. Ah, Robin, Robin! even the barber's boys laugh at you for choosing such a guide! You will be wiser in time, friend Robin."

He now became entangled in a succession of crooked and narrow streets, which crossed each other, and meandered at no great distance from the water-side. The smell of tar was obvious to his nostrils, the masts of vessels pierced the moonlight above the tops of the buildings, and the numerous signs, which Robin paused to read, informed him that he was near the center of business. But the streets were empty, the shops were closed, and lights were visible only in the second stories of a few dwelling houses. At length, on the corner of a narrow lane, through which he was passing, he beheld the broad countenance of a British hero swinging before the door of an inn, whence proceeded the voices of many guests. The casement of one of the lower windows was thrown back, and a very thin curtain permitted Robin to distinguish a party at supper, round a well-furnished table. The fragrance of the good cheer steamed forth into the outer air, and the youth could not fail to recollect that the last remnant of his traveling stock of provision had yielded to his morning appetite, and that noon had found and left him dinnerless.

"Oh, that a parchment three-penny might give me a right to sit down at yonder table!" said Robin, with a sigh. "But the Major will make me welcome to the best of his victuals; so I will even step boldly in, and inquire my way to his dwelling."

He entered the tavern, and was guided by the murmur of voices and the fumes of tobacco to the public-room. It was a long and low apartment, with oaken walls, grown dark in the continual smoke, and a floor which was thickly sanded, but of no immaculate purity. A number of persons—the larger part of whom appeared to be mariners, or in some way connected with the sea—occupied the wooden benches, or leather-bottomed chairs, conversing on various matters, and occasionally lending their attention to some topic of general interest. Three or four little groups were draining as many bowls of punch, which the West India trade had long since made a familiar drink in the colony. Others, who had the appearance of men who lived by regular and laborious handicraft, preferred the insulated bliss of an unshared potation, and became more taciturn under its influence. Nearly all, in short, evinced a predilection for the Good Creature in some of its various shapes, for this is a vice to which, as Fast Day sermons of a hundred years ago will testify, we have a long hereditary claim. The only guests to whom Robin's sympathies inclined him were two or three sheepish countrymen, who were using the inn somewhat after the fashion of a Turkish caravansary; they had gotten themselves into the darkest corner of the room, and heedless of the Nicotian atmosphere, were supping on the bread of their own ovens, and the bacon cured in their own chimney-smoke. But though Robin felt a sort of brotherhood with these strangers, his eyes were attracted from them to a person who stood near the door, holding whispered conversation with a group of ill-dressed associates. His features were separately striking almost to grotesqueness, and the whole face left a deep impression on the memory. The forehead bulged out into a double prominence, with a vale between; the nose came boldly forth in an irregular curve, and its bridge was of more than a finger's breadth; the eyebrows were deep and shaggy, and the eyes glowed beneath them like fire in a cave.

While Robin deliberated of whom to inquire respecting his kinsman's dwelling, he was accosted by the innkeeper, a little man in a stained white apron, who had come to pay his professional welcome to the stranger. Being in the second generation from a French Protestant, he seemed to have inherited the courtesy of his parent nation; but no variety of circumstances was ever known to change his voice from the one shrill note in which he now addressed Robin.

"From the country, I presume, sir?" said he, with a profound bow. "Beg leave to congratulate you on your arrival, and trust you intend a long stay with us. Fine town here, sir, beautiful buildings, and much that may interest a stranger. May I hope for the honor of your commands in respect to supper?"

"The man sees a family likeness! the rogue has guessed that I am related to the Major!" thought Robin, who had hitherto experienced little superfluous civility.

All eyes were now turned on the country lad, standing at the door, in his worn three-cornered hat, gray coat, leather breeches, and blue yarn stockings, leaning on an oaken cudgel, and bearing a wallet on his back.

Robin replied to the courteous innkeeper, with such an assumption of confidence as befitted the Major's relative. "My honest friend," he said, "I shall make it a point to patronize your house on some occasion, when"—here he could not help lowering his voice—"when I may have more than a parchment three-pence in my pocket. My present business," continued he, speaking with lofty confidence, "is merely to inquire my way to the dwelling of my kinsman, Major Molineux."

There was a sudden and general movement in the room, which Robin interpreted as expressing the eagerness of each individual to become his guide. But the innkeeper turned his eyes to a written paper on the wall, which he read, or seemed to read, with occasional recurrences to the young man's figure.

"What have we here?" said he, breaking his speech into little dry fragments. " 'Left the house of the subscriber, bounden servant, Hezekiah Mudge,—had on, when he went away, gray coat, leather breeches, master's third-best hat. One pound currency reward to whosoever shall lodge him in any jail of the province.' Better trudge, boy; better trudge!"

Robin had begun to draw his hand towards the lighter end of the oak cudgel, but a strange hostility in every countenance induced him to relinquish his purpose of breaking the courteous innkeeper's head. As he turned to leave the room, he encountered a sneering glance from the bold-featured personage whom he had before noticed; and no sooner was he beyond the door, than he heard a general laugh, in which the innkeeper's voice might be distinguished, like the dropping of small stones into a kettle.

"Now, is it not strange," thought Robin, with his usual shrewdness,— "is it not strange that the confession of an empty pocket should outweigh the name of my kinsman, Major Molineux? Oh, if I had one of those grinning rascals in the woods, where I and my oak sapling grew up together, I would teach him that my arm is heavy though my purse be light!"

On turning the corner of the narrow lane, Robin found himself in a spacious street, with an unbroken line of lofty houses on each side, and a steepled building at the upper end, whence the ringing of a bell announced the hour of nine. The light of the moon, and the lamps from the numerous shop-windows, discovered people promenading on the pavement, and amongst them Robin hoped to recognize his hitherto inscrutable relative. The result of his former inquiries made him unwilling to hazard another, in a scene of such publicity, and he determined to walk slowly and silently up the street, thrusting his face close to that of every elderly gentleman, in search of the Major's lineaments. In his progress, Robin encountered many gay and gallant figures. Embroidered garments of showy colors, enormous periwigs, gold-laced hats, and silver-hilted swords glided past him and dazzled his optics. Traveled youths, imitators of the European fine gentlemen of the period, trod jauntily along, half dancing to the fashionable tunes which they hummed, and making poor Robin ashamed of his quiet and natural gait. At length, after many pauses to examine the gorgeous display of goods in the shop-windows, and after suffering some rebukes for the impertinence of his scrutiny into people's faces, the Major's kinsman found himself near the steepled building, still unsuccessful in his search. As yet, however, he had seen only one side of the thronged street; so Robin crossed, and continued the same sort of inquisition down the opposite pavement, with stronger hopes than the philosopher seeking an honest man, but with no better fortune. He had arrived about midway towards the lower end, from which his course be-

gan, when he overheard the approach of some one who struck down a
cane on the flag-stones at every step, uttering, at regular intervals, two
sepulchral hems.

"Mercy on us!" quoth Robin, recognizing the sound.

Turning a corner, which chanced to be close at his right hand, he hastened to pursue his researches in some other part of the town. His patience
now was wearing low, and he seemed to feel more fatigue from his ram-
bles since he crossed the ferry, than from his journey of several days on
the other side. Hunger also pleaded loudly within him, and Robin began
to balance the propriety of demanding, violently, and with lifted cudgel,
the necessary guidance from the first solitary passenger whom he should
meet. While a resolution to this effect was gaining strength, he entered
a street of mean appearance, on either side of which a row of ill-built
houses was straggling towards the harbor. The moonlight fell upon no
passenger along the whole extent, but in the third domicile which Robin
passed there was a half-opened door, and his keen glance detected a
woman's garment within.

"My luck may be better here," said he to himself.

Accordingly, he approached the door, and beheld it shut closer as he
did so; yet an open space remained, sufficing for the fair occupant to observe the stranger, without a corresponding display on her part. All that
Robin could discern was a strip of scarlet petticoat, and the occasional
sparkle of an eye, as if the moonbeams were trembling on some bright
thing.

"Pretty mistress," for I may call her so with a good conscience,
thought the shrewd youth, since I know nothing to the contrary,—"my
sweet pretty mistress, will you be kind enough to tell me whereabouts I
must seek the dwelling of my kinsman, Major Molineux?"

Robin's voice was plaintive and winning, and the female, seeing nothing to be shunned in the handsome country youth, thrust open the door,
and came forth into the moonlight. She was a dainty little figure, with a
white neck, round arms, and a slender waist, at the extremity of which
her scarlet petticoat jutted out over a hoop, as if she were standing in a
balloon. Moreover, her face was oval and pretty, her hair dark beneath
the little cap, and her bright eyes possessed a sly freedom, which triumphed over those of Robin.

"Major Molineux dwells here," said this fair woman.

Now, her voice was the sweetest Robin had heard that night, the airy
counterpart of a stream of melted silver; yet he could not help doubting
whether that sweet voice spoke Gospel truth. He looked up and down the
mean street, and then surveyed the house before which they stood. It was
a small, dark edifice of two stories, the second of which projected over
the lower floor, and the front apartment had the aspect of a shop for
petty commodities.

"Now, truly, I am in luck," replied Robin, cunningly, "and so indeed is my kinsman, the Major, in having so pretty a housekeeper. But

I prithee trouble him to step to the door; I will deliver him a message from his friends in the country, and then go back to my lodgings at the inn."

"Nay, the Major has been abed this hour or more," said the lady of the scarlet petticoat; "and it would be to little purpose to disturb him tonight, seeing his evening draft was of the strongest. But he is a kind-hearted man, and it would be as much as my life's worth to let a kinsman of his turn away from the door. You are the good old gentleman's very picture, and I could swear that was his rainy-weather hat. Also he has garments very much resembling those leather small-clothes. But come in, I pray, for I bid you hearty welcome in his name."

So saying, the fair and hospitable dame took our hero by the hand; and the touch was light, and the force was gentleness, and though Robin read in her eyes what he did not hear in her words, yet the slender-waisted woman in the scarlet petticoat proved stronger than the athletic country youth. She had drawn his half-willing footsteps nearly to the threshold, when the opening of a door in the neighborhood startled the Major's housekeeper, and, leaving the Major's kinsman, she vanished speedily into her own domicile. A heavy yawn preceded the appearance of a man, who, like the Moonshine of Pyramus and Thisbe, carried a lantern, needlessly aiding his sister luminary in the heavens. As he walked sleepily up the street, he turned his broad, dull face on Robin, and displayed a long staff, spiked at the end.

"Home, vagabond, home!" said the watchman, in accents that seemed to fall asleep as soon as they were uttered. "Home, or we'll set you in the stocks by peep of day!"

"This is the second hint of the kind," thought Robin. "I wish they would end my difficulties, by setting me there tonight."

Nevertheless, the youth felt an instinctive antipathy towards the guardian of midnight order, which at first prevented him from asking his usual question. But just when the man was about to vanish behind the corner, Robin resolved not to lose the opportunity, and shouted lustily after him,—

"I say, friend! will you guide me to the house of my kinsman, Major Molineux?"

The watchman made no reply, but turned the corner and was gone; yet Robin seemed to hear the sound of drowsy laughter stealing along the solitary street. At that moment, also, a pleasant titter saluted him from the open window above his head; he looked up, and caught the sparkle of a saucy eye; a round arm beckoned to him, and next he heard light footsteps descending the staircase within. But Robin, being of the household of a New England clergyman, was a good youth, as well as a shrewd one; so he resisted temptation, and fled away.

He now roamed desperately, and at random, through the town, almost ready to believe that a spell was on him, like that by which a wizard of his country had once kept three pursuers wandering, a whole winter night, within twenty paces of the cottage which they sought. The streets lay before him, strange and desolate, and the lights were extinguished in almost every house. Twice, however, little parties of men, among whom Robin distinguished individuals in outlandish attire, came hurrying along; but, though on both occasions they paused to address him, such intercourse did not at all enlighten his perplexity. They did but utter a few words in some language of which Robin knew nothing, and perceiving his inability to answer, bestowed a curse upon him in plain English and hastened away. Finally, the lad determined to knock at the door of every mansion that might appear worthy to be occupied by his kinsman, trusting that perseverance would overcome the fatality that had hitherto thwarted him. Firm in this resolve, he was passing beneath the walls of a church, which formed the corner of two streets, when, as he turned into the shade of its steeple, he encountered a bulky stranger, muffled in a cloak. The man was proceeding with the speed of earnest business, but Robin planted himself full before him, holding the oak cudgel with both hands across his body as a bar to further passage.

"Halt, honest man, and answer me a question," said he, very resolutely. "Tell me, this instant, whereabouts is the dwelling of my kinsman, Major Molineux!"

"Keep your tongue between your teeth, fool, and let me pass!" said a deep, gruff voice, which Robin partly remembered. "Let me pass, I say, or I'll strike you to the earth!"

"No, no, neighbor!" cried Robin, flourishing his cudgel, and then thrusting its larger end close to the man's muffled face. "No, no, I'm not the fool you take me for, nor do you pass till I have an answer to my question. Whereabouts is the dwelling of my kinsman, Major Molineux?"

The stranger, instead of attempting to force his passage, stepped back into the moonlight, unmuffled his face, and stared full into that of Robin.

"Watch here an hour, and Major Molineux will pass by," said he.

Robin gazed with dismay and astonishment on the unprecedented physiognomy of the speaker. The forehead with its double prominence, the broad hooked nose, the shaggy eyebrows, and fiery eyes were those which he had noticed at the inn, but the man's complexion had undergone a singular, or, more properly, a two-fold change. One side of the face blazed an intense red, while the other was black as midnight, the division line being in the broad ridge of the nose; and a mouth which seemed to extend from ear to ear was black or red, in contrast to the color of the cheek. The effect was as if two individual devils, a fiend of fire and a fiend of darkness, had united themselves to form this infernal visage. The stranger grinned in Robin's face, muffled his particolored features, and was out of sight in a moment.

"Strange things we travelers see!" ejaculated Robin.

He seated himself, however, upon the steps of the church-door, resolving to wait the appointed time for his kinsman. A few moments were consumed in philosophical speculations upon the species of man who had just left him; but having settled this point shrewdly, rationally, and satisfactorily, he was compelled to look elsewhere for his amusement. And first he threw his eyes along the street. It was of more respectable appearance than most of those into which he had wandered; and the moon, creating, like the imaginative power, a beautiful strangeness in familiar objects, gave something of romance to a scene that might not have possessed it in the light of day. The irregular and often quaint architecture of the houses, some of whose roofs were broken into numerous little peaks, while others ascended, steep and narrow, into a single point, and others again were square; the pure snow-white of some of their complexions, the aged darkness of others, and the thousand sparklings, reflected from bright substances in the walls of many; these matters engaged Robin's attention for a while, and then began to grow wearisome. Next he endeavored to define the forms of distant objects, starting away, with almost ghostly indistinctness, just as his eye appeared to grasp them; and finally he took a minute survey of an edifice which stood on the opposite side of the street, directly in front of the church-door, where he was stationed. It was a large, square mansion, distinguished from its neighbors by a balcony, which rested on tall pillars, and by an elaborate Gothic window, communicating therewith.

"Perhaps this is the very house I have been seeking," thought Robin.

Then he strove to speed away the time, by listening to a murmur which swept continually along the street, yet was scarcely audible, except to an unaccustomed ear like his; it was a low, dull, dreamy sound, compounded of many noises, each of which was at too great a distance to be separately heard. Robin marveled at this snore of a sleeping town, and marveled more whenever its continuity was broken by now and then a distant shout, apparently loud where it originated. But altogether it was a sleep-inspiring sound, and, to shake off its drowsy influence, Robin arose, and climbed a windowframe, that he might view the interior of the church. There the moonbeams came trembling in, and fell down upon the deserted pews, and extended along the quiet aisles. A fainter yet more awful radiance was hovering around the pulpit, and one solitary ray had dared to rest upon the open page of the great Bible. Had nature, in that deep hour, become a worshipper in the house which man had builded? Or was that heavenly light the visible sanctity of the place,—visible because no earthly and impure feet were within the walls? The scene made Robin's heart shiver with a sensation of loneliness stronger than he had ever felt in the remotest depths of his native woods; so he turned away and sat down again before the door. There were graves around the church, and now an uneasy thought obtruded into Robin's breast. What if the object of his search, which had been so often and so strangely thwarted, were all the time moldering in his shroud? What if his kinsman should glide through yonder gate, and nod and smile to him in dimly passing by?

"Oh that any breathing thing were here with me!" said Robin.

Recalling his thoughts from this uncomfortable track, he sent them over forest, hill, and stream, and attempted to imagine how that evening of ambiguity and weariness had been spent by his father's household. He pictured them assembled at the door, beneath the tree, the great old tree, which had been spared for its huge twisted trunk and venerable shade, when a thousand leafy brethren fell. There, at the going down of the summer sun, it was his father's custom to perform domestic worship, that the neighbors might come and join with him like brothers of the family, and that the wayfaring man might pause to drink at that fountain, and keep his heart pure by freshening the memory of home. Robin distinguished the seat of every individual of the little audience; he saw the good man in the midst, holding the Scriptures in the golden light that fell from the western clouds; he beheld him close the book and all rise up to pray. He heard the old thanksgivings for daily mercies, the old supplications for their continuance, to which he had so often listened in weariness, but which were now among his dear remembrances. He perceived the slight inequality of his father's voice when he came to speak of the absent one; he noted how his mother turned her face to the broad and knotted trunk; how his elder brother scorned, because the beard was rough upon his upper lip, to permit his features to be moved; how the younger sister drew down a low hanging branch before her eyes; and how the little one of all, whose sports had hitherto broken the decorum of the scene, understood the prayer for her playmate, and burst into clamorous grief. Then he saw them go in at the door; and when Robin would have entered also, the latch tinkled into its place, and he was excluded from his home.

"Am I here, or there?" cried Robin, starting; for all at once, when his thoughts had become visible and audible in a dream, the long, wide, solitary street shone out before him.

He aroused himself, and endeavored to fix his attention steadily upon the large edifice which he had surveyed before. But still his mind kept vibrating between fancy and reality; by turns, the pillars of the balcony lengthened into the tall, bare stems of pines, dwindled down to human figures, settled again into their true shape and size, and then commenced a new succession of changes. For a single moment, when he deemed himself awake, he could have sworn that a visage—one which he seemed to remember, yet could not absolutely name as his kinsman's—was looking towards him from the Gothic window. A deeper sleep wrestled with and nearly overcame him, but fled at the sound of footsteps along the opposite pavement. Robin rubbed his eyes, discerned a man passing at the foot of the balcony, and addressed him in a loud, peevish, and lamentable cry.

"Hallo, friend! must I wait here all night for my kinsman, Major Molineux?"

The sleeping echoes awoke, and answered the voice; and the passenger, barely able to discern a figure sitting in the oblique shade of the steeple, traversed the street to obtain a nearer view. He was himself a gentleman in his prime, of open, intelligent, cheerful, and altogether pre-possessing countenance. Perceiving a country youth, apparently homeless and without friends, he accosted him in a tone of real kindness, which had become strange to Robin's ears.

"Well, my good lad, why are you sitting here?" inquired he. "Can I be of service to you in any way?"

"I am afraid not, sir," replied Robin, despondingly; "yet I shall take it kindly, if you'll answer me a single question. I've been searching, half the night, for one Major Molineux; now, sir, is there really such a person in these parts, or am I dreaming?"

"Major Molineux! The name is not altogether strange to me," said the gentleman, smiling. "Have you any objection to telling me the nature of your business with him?"

Then Robin briefly related that his father was a clergyman, settled on a small salary, at a long distance back in the country, and that he and Major Molineux were brothers' children. The Major, having inherited riches, and acquired civil and military rank, had visited his cousin, in great pomp, a year or two before; had manifested much interest in Robin and an elder brother, and, being childless himself, had thrown out hints respecting the future establishment of one of them in life. The elder brother was destined to succeed to the farm which his father cultivated in the interval of sacred duties; it was therefore determined that Robin should profit by his kinsman's generous intentions, especially as he seemed to be rather the favorite, and was thought to possess other necessary endowments.

"For I have the name of being a shrewd youth," observed Robin, in this part of his story.

"I doubt not you deserve it," replied his new friend, good-naturedly; "but pray proceed."

"Well, sir, being nearly eighteen years old, and well grown, as you see," continued Robin, drawing himself up to his full height, "I thought it high time to begin the world. So my mother and sister put me in handsome trim, and my father gave me half the remnant of his last year's salary, and five days ago I started for this place to pay the Major a visit. But, would you believe it, sir! I crossed the ferry a little after dark, and have yet found nobody that would show me the way to his dwelling; only, an hour or two since, I was told to wait here, and Major Molineux would pass by."

"Can you describe the man who told you this?" inquired the gentleman.

"Oh, he was a very ill-favored fellow, sir," replied Robin, "with two great bumps on his forehead, a hook nose, fiery eyes; and, what struck me as the strangest, his face was of two different colors. Do you happen to know such a man, sir?"

"Not intimately," answered the stranger, "but I chanced to meet him a little time previous to your stopping me. I believe you may trust his word, and that the Major will very shortly pass through this street. In the mean time, as I have a singular curiosity to witness your meeting, I will sit down here upon the steps and bear you company."

He seated himself accordingly, and soon engaged his companion in animated discourse. It was but of brief continuance, however, for a noise of shouting, which had long been remotely audible, drew so much nearer that Robin inquired its cause.

"What may be the meaning of this uproar?" asked he. "Truly, if your town be always as noisy, I shall find little sleep while I am an inhabitant."

"Why, indeed, friend Robin, there do appear to be three or four riotous fellows abroad tonight," replied the gentleman. "You must not expect all the stillness of your native woods here in our streets. But the watch will shortly be at the heels of these lads and"—

"Ay, and set them in the stocks by peep of day," interrupted Robin, recollecting his own encounter with the drowsy lantern-bearer. "But, dear sir, if I may trust my ears, an army of watchmen would never make head against such a multitude of rioters. There were at least a thousand voices went up to make that one shout."

"May not a man have several voices, Robin, as well as two complexions?" said his friend.

"Perhaps a man may; but Heaven forbid that a woman should!" responded the shrewd youth, thinking of the seductive tones of the Major's housekeeper.

The sounds of a trumpet in some neighboring street now became so evident and continual, that Robin's curiosity was strongly excited. In addition to the shouts, he heard frequent bursts from many instruments of discord, and a wild and confused laughter filled up the intervals. Robin rose from the steps, and looked wistfully towards a point whither people seemed to be hastening.

"Surely some prodigious merry-making is going on," exclaimed he. "I have laughed very little since I left home, sir, and should be sorry to lose an opportunity. Shall we step round the corner by that darkish house, and take our share of the fun?"

"Sit down again, sit down, good Robin," replied the gentleman, laying his hand on the skirt of the gray coat. "You forget that we must wait here for your kinsman; and there is reason to believe that he will pass by, in the course of a very few moments."

The near approach of the uproar had now disturbed the neighborhood; windows flew open on all sides; and many heads, in the attire of the pillow, and confused by sleep suddenly broken, were protruded to the gaze of whoever had leisure to observe them. Eager voices hailed each other from house to house, all demanding the explanation, which not a soul could give. Half-dressed men hurried towards the unknown commotion, stumbling as they went over the stone steps that thrust themselves into the narrow foot-walk. The shouts, the laughter, and the tuneless bray, the antipodes of music, came onwards with increasing din, till scattered individuals, and then denser bodies, began to appear round a corner at the distance of a hundred yards.

"Will you recognize your kinsman, if he passes in this crowd?" inquired the gentleman.

"Indeed, I can't warrant it, sir; but I'll take my stand here, and keep a bright lookout," answered Robin, descending to the outer edge of the pavement.

A mighty stream of people now emptied into the street, and came rolling slowly towards the church. A single horseman wheeled the corner in the midst of them, and close behind him came a band of fearful wind-instruments, sending forth a fresher discord now that no intervening buildings kept it from the ear. Then a redder light disturbed the moon-beams, and a dense multitude of torches shone along the street, conceal-ing, by their glare, whatever object they illuminated. The single horse-man, clad in a military dress, and bearing a drawn sword, rode onward as the leader, and, by his fierce and variegated countenance, appeared like war personified; the red of one cheek was an emblem of fire and sword; the blackness of the other betokened the mourning that attends them. In his train were wild figures in the Indian dress, and many fantastic shapes without a model, giving the whole march a visionary air, as if a dream had broken forth from some feverish brain, and were sweeping visibly through the midnight streets. A mass of people, inactive, except as ap-plauding spectators, hemmed the procession in; and several women ran along the sidewalk, piercing the confusion of heavier sounds with their shrill voices of mirth or terror.

"The double-faced fellow has his eye upon me," muttered Robin, with an indefinite but an uncomfortable idea that he was himself to bear a part in the pageantry.

The leader turned himself in the saddle, and fixed his glance full upon the country youth, as the steed went slowly by. When Robin had freed his eyes from those fiery ones, the musicians were passing before him, and the torches were close at hand; but the unsteady brightness of the latter formed a veil which he could not penetrate. The rattling of wheels over the stones sometimes found its way to his ear, and confused traces of a human form appeared at intervals, and then melted into the vivid light. A moment more, and the leader thundered a command to halt: the trumpets vomited a horrid breath, and then held their peace; the shouts and laughter of the people died away, and there remained only a uni-versal hum, allied to silence. Right before Robin's eyes was an uncovered cart. There the torches blazed the brightest, there the moon shone out like day, and there, in tar-and-feathery dignity, sat his kinsman, Major Molineux!

He was an elderly man, of large and majestic person, and strong, square features, betokening a steady soul; but steady as it was, his ene-mies had found means to shake it. His face was pale as death, and far more ghastly; the broad forehead was contracted in his agony, so that his eyebrows formed one grizzled line; his eyes were red and wild, and the foam hung white upon his quivering lip. His whole frame was agitated by a quick and continual tremor, which his pride strove to quell, even in those circumstances of overwhelming humiliation. But perhaps the bitterest pang of all was when his eyes met those of Robin; for he evidently knew him on the instant, as the youth stood witnessing the foul disgrace of a head grown gray in honor. They stared at each other in silence, and Robin's knees shook, and his hair bristled, with a mixture of pity and terror. Soon, however, a bewildering excitement began to seize upon his mind; the preceding adventures of the night, the unexpected appearance of the crowd, the torches, the confused din and the hush that followed, the specter of his kinsman reviled by that great multitude,— all this, and, more than all, a perception of tremendous ridicule in the whole scene, affected him with a sort of mental inebriety. At that moment a voice of sluggish merriment saluted Robin's ears; he turned instinctively, and just behind the corner of the church stood the lantern-bearer, rubbing his eyes, and drowsily enjoying the lad's amazement. Then he heard a peal of laughter like the ringing of silvery bells; a woman twitched his arm, a saucy eye met his, and he saw the lady of the scarlet petticoat. A sharp, dry cachinnation appealed to his memory, and, standing on tiptoe in the crowd, with his white apron over his head, he beheld the courteous little innkeeper. And lastly, there sailed over the heads of the multitude a great, broad laugh, broken in the midst by two sepulchral hems; thus, "Haw, haw, haw—hem, hem,—haw, haw, haw, haw!"

The sound proceeded from the balcony of the opposite edifice, and thither Robin turned his eyes. In front of the Gothic window stood the old citizen, wrapped in a wide gown, his gray periwig exchanged for a nightcap, which was thrust back from his forehead, and his silk stockings hanging about his legs. He supported himself on his polished cane in a fit of convulsive merriment, which manifested itself on his solemn old features like a funny inscription on a tombstone. Then Robin seemed to hear the voices of the barbers, of the guests of the inn, and of all who had made sport of him that night. The contagion was spreading among the multitude, when all at once, it seized upon Robin, and he sent forth a shout of laughter that echoed through the street,—every man shook his sides, every man emptied his lungs, but Robin's shout was the loudest there. The cloud-spirits peeped from their silvery islands, as the congregated mirth went roaring up the sky! The Man in the Moon heard the far bellow. "Oho," quoth he, "the old earth is frolicsome tonight!"

When there was a momentary calm in that tempestuous sea of sound, the leader gave the sign, the procession resumed its march. On they went, like fiends that throng in mockery around some dead potentate, mighty no more, but majestic still in his agony. On they went, in counterfeited pomp, in senseless uproar, in frenzied merriment, trampling all on an old man's heart. On swept the tumult, and left a silent street behind.

"Well, Robin, are you dreaming?" inquired the gentleman, laying his hand on the youth's shoulder.

Robin started, and withdrew his arm from the stone post to which he had instinctively clung, as the living stream rolled by him. His cheek was somewhat pale, and his eye not quite as lively as in the earlier part of the evening.

"Will you be kind enough to show me the way to the ferry?" said he, after a moment's pause.

"You have, then, adopted a new subject of inquiry?" observed his companion, with a smile.

"Why, yes, sir," replied Robin, rather dryly. "Thanks to you, and to my other friends, I have at last met my kinsman, and he will scarce desire to see my face again. I begin to grow weary of a town life, sir. Will you show me the way to the ferry?"

"No, my good friend Robin—not tonight, at least," said the gentleman. "Some few days hence, if you wish it, I will speed you on your journey. Or, if you prefer to remain with us, perhaps, as you are a shrewd youth, you may rise in the world without the help of your kinsman, Major Molineux."

Edgar Allan Poe
1809–1849

THE FALL OF THE HOUSE OF USHER

Son coeur est un luth suspendu;
Sitôt qu'on le touche il résonne.[1]
—DE BÉRANGER

DURING the whole of a dull, dark, and soundless day in the autumn of the year, when the clouds hung oppressively low in the heavens, I had been passing alone, on horseback, through a singularly dreary tract of country, and at length found myself, as the shades of the evening drew on, within view of the melancholy House of Usher. I know not how it was—but, with the first glimpse of the building, a sense of insufferable gloom pervaded my spirit. I say insufferable; for the feeling was unrelieved by any of that half-pleasurable, because poetic, sentiment with which the mind usually receives even the sternest natural images of the desolate or terrible. I looked upon the scene before me—upon the mere

[1] His heart is a suspended lute; As soon as one touches it, it resounds.

house, and the simple landscape features of the domain—upon the bleak
walls—upon the vacant eye-like windows—upon a few rank sedges—and
upon a few white trunks of decayed trees—with an utter depression of
soul which I can compare to no earthly sensation more properly than to
the after-dream of the reveller upon opium—the bitter lapse into everyday life—the hideous dropping off of the veil. There was an iciness, a
sinking, a sickening of the heart—an unredeemed dreariness of thought
which no goading of the imagination could torture into aught of the sublime. What was it—I paused to think—what was it that so unnerved me
in the contemplation of the House of Usher? It was a mystery all in-
soluble; nor could I grapple with the shadowy fancies that crowded
upon me as I pondered. I was forced to fall back upon the unsatisfactory
conclusion, that while, beyond doubt, there *are* combinations of very simple natural objects which have the power of thus affecting us, still the
analysis of this power lies among considerations beyond our depth. It
was possible, I reflected, that a mere different arrangement of the particulars of the scene, of the details of the picture, would be sufficient to
modify, or perhaps to annihilate its capacity for sorrowful impression;
and, acting upon this idea, I reined my horse to the precipitous brink of a
black and lurid tarn that lay in unruffled lustre by the dwelling, and
gazed down—but with a shudder even more thrilling than before—upon
the remodelled and inverted images of the gray sedge, and the ghastly
tree-stems, and the vacant and eye-like windows.

Nevertheless, in this mansion of gloom I now proposed to myself a
sojourn of some weeks. Its proprietor, Roderick Usher, had been one of
my boon companions in boyhood; but many years had elapsed since our
last meeting. A letter, however, had lately reached me in a distant part
of the country—a letter from him—which, in its wildly importunate nature, had admitted of no other than a personal reply. The MS. gave evidence of nervous agitation. The writer spoke of acute bodily illness—of
a mental disorder which oppressed him—and of an earnest desire to see
me, as his best and indeed his only personal friend, with a view of attempting, by the cheerfulness of my society, some alleviation of his
malady. It was the manner in which all this, and much more, was said—
it was the apparent *heart* that went with his request—which allowed me
no room for hesitation; and I accordingly obeyed forthwith what I still
considered a very singular summons.

Although, as boys, we had been intimate associates, yet I really knew
little of my friend. His reserve had been always excessive and habitual.
I was aware, however, that his very ancient family had been noted, time
out of mind, for a peculiar sensibility of temperament, displaying itself,
through long ages, in many works of exalted art, and manifested, of late,
in repeated deeds of munificent yet unobtrusive charity, as well as in a
passionate devotion to the intricacies, perhaps even more than to the
orthodox and easily recognizable beauties, of musical science. I had
learned, too, the very remarkable fact, that the stem of the Usher race,

all time-honored as it was, had put forth, at no period, any enduring branch; in other words, that the entire family lay in the direct line of descent, and had always, with very trifling and very temporary variation, so lain. It was this deficiency, I considered, while running over in thought the perfect keeping of the character of the premises with the accredited character of the people, and while speculating upon the possible influence which the one, in the long lapse of centuries, might have exercised upon the other—it was this deficiency, perhaps, of collateral issue, and the consequent undeviating transmission, from sire to son, of the patrimony with the name, which had, at length, so identified the two as to merge the original title of the estate in the quaint and equivocal appellation of the "House of Usher"—an appellation which seemed to include, in the minds of the peasantry who used it, both the family and the family mansion.

I have said that the sole effect of my somewhat childish experiment—that of looking down within the tarn—had been to deepen the first singular impression. There can be no doubt that the consciousness of the rapid increase of my superstition—for why should I not so term it?—served mainly to accelerate the increase itself. Such, I have long known, is the paradoxical law of all sentiments having terror as a basis. And it might have been for this reason only, that, when I again uplifted my eyes to the house itself, from its image in the pool, there grew in my mind a strange fancy—a fancy so ridiculous, indeed, that I but mention it to show the vivid force of the sensations which oppressed me. I had so worked upon my imagination as really to believe that about the whole mansion and domain there hung an atmosphere peculiar to themselves and their immediate vicinity—an atmosphere which had no affinity with the air of heaven, but which had reeked up from the decayed trees, and the gray wall, and the silent tarn—a pestilent and mystic vapor, dull, sluggish, faintly discernible, and leaden-hued.

Shaking off from my spirit what *must* have been a dream, I scanned more narrowly the real aspect of the building. Its principal feature seemed to be that of an excessive antiquity. The discoloration of ages had been great. Minute fungi overspread the whole exterior, hanging in a fine tangled web-work from the eaves. Yet all this was apart from any extraordinary dilapidation. No portion of the masonry had fallen; and there appeared to be a wild inconsistency between its still perfect adaptation of parts, and the crumbling condition of the individual stones. In this there was much that reminded me of the specious totality of old woodwork which has rotted for long years in some neglected vault, with no disturbance from the breath of the external air. Beyond this indication of extensive decay, however, the fabric gave little token of instability. Perhaps the eye of a scrutinizing observer might have discovered a barely perceptible fissure, which, extending from the roof of the building in front, made its way down the wall in a zigzag direction, until it became lost in the sullen waters of the tarn.

Noticing these things, I rode over a short causeway to the house. A servant in waiting took my horse, and I entered the Gothic archway of the hall. A valet, of stealthy step, thence conducted me, in silence, through many dark and intricate passages in my progress to the studio of his master. Much that I encountered on the way contributed, I know not how, to heighten the vague sentiments of which I have already spoken. While the objects around me—while the carvings of the ceilings, the somber tapestries of the walls, the ebon blackness of the floors, and the phantasmagoric armorial trophies which rattled as I strode, were but matters to which, or to such as which, I had been accustomed from my infancy—while I hesitated not to acknowledge how familiar was all this —I still wondered to find how unfamiliar were the fancies which ordinary images were stirring up. On one of the staircases, I met the physician of the family. His countenance, I thought, wore a mingled expression of low cunning and perplexity. He accosted me with trepidation and passed on. The valet now threw open a door and ushered me into the presence of his master.

The room in which I found myself was very large and lofty. The windows were long, narrow, and pointed, and at so vast a distance from the black oaken floor as to be altogether inaccessible from within. Feeble gleams of encrimsoned light made their way through the trellised panes, and served to render sufficiently distinct the more prominent objects around; the eye, however, struggled in vain to reach the remoter angles of the chamber, or the recesses of the vaulted and fretted ceiling. Dark draperies hung upon the walls. The general furniture was profuse, comfortless, antique, and tattered. Many books and musical instruments lay scattered about, but failed to give any vitality to the scene. I felt that I breathed an atmosphere of sorrow. An air of stern, deep, and irredeemable gloom hung over and pervaded all.

Upon my entrance, Usher arose from a sofa on which he had been lying at full length, and greeted me with a vivacious warmth which had much in it, I at first thought, of an overdone cordiality—of the constrained effort of the *ennuyé*[2] man of the world. A glance, however, at his countenance convinced me of his perfect sincerity. We sat down; and for some moments, while he spoke not, I gazed upon him with a feeling of pity, half of awe. Surely, man had never before so terribly altered, in so brief a period, as had Roderick Usher! It was with difficulty that I could bring myself to admit the identity of the wan being before me with the companion of my early boyhood. Yet the character of his face had been at all times remarkable. A cadaverousness of complexion; an eye large, liquid, and luminous beyond comparison; lips somewhat thin and very pallid, but of a surpassingly beautiful curve; a nose of a delicate Hebrew model, but with a breadth of nostril unusual in similar formations; a finely molded chin, speaking, in its want of prominence, of a

[2] bored

want of moral energy; hair of a more than web-like softness and tenuity; these features, with an inordinate expansion above the regions of the temple, made up altogether a countenance not easily to be forgotten. And now in the mere exaggeration of the prevailing character of these features, and of the expression they were wont to convey, lay so much of change that I doubted to whom I spoke. The now ghastly pallor of the skin, and the now miraculous luster of the eye, above all things startled and even awed me. The silken hair, too, had been suffered to grow all unheeded, and as, in its wild gossamer texture, it floated rather than fell about the face. I could not, even with effort, connect its Arabesque expression with any idea of simple humanity.

In the manner of my friend I was at once struck with an incoherence —an inconsistency; and I soon found this to arise from a series of feeble and futile struggles to overcome an habitual trepidancy—an excessive nervous agitation. For something of this nature I had indeed been prepared, no less by his letter, than by reminiscences of certain boyish traits, and by conclusions deduced from his peculiar physical conformation and temperament. His action was alternately vivacious and sullen. His voice varied rapidly from a tremulous indecision (when the animal spirits seemed utterly in abeyance) to that species of energetic concision—that abrupt, weighty, unhurried, and hollow-sounding enunciation—that leaden, self-balanced, and perfectly modulated guttural utterance, which may be observed in the lost drunkard, or the irreclaimable eater of opium, during the periods of his most intense excitement.

It was thus that he spoke of the object of my visit, of his earnest desire to see me, and of the solace he expected me to afford him. He entered, at some length, into what he conceived to be the nature of his malady. It was, he said, a constitutional and a family evil, and one for which he despaired to find a remedy—a mere nervous affection, he immediately added, which would undoubtedly soon pass off. It displayed itself in a host of unnatural sensations. Some of these, as he detailed them, interested and bewildered me; although, perhaps, the terms and the general manner of their narration had their weight. He suffered much from a morbid acuteness of the senses; the most insipid food was alone endurable; he could wear only garments of certain texture; the odors of all flowers were oppressive; his eyes were tortured by even a faint light; and there were but peculiar sounds, and these from stringed instruments, which did not inspire him with horror.

To an anomalous species of terror I found him a bounden slave. "I shall perish," said he, "I *must* perish in this deplorable folly. Thus, thus, and not otherwise, shall I be lost. I dread the events of the future, not in themselves, but in their results. I shudder at the thought of any, even the most trivial, incident, which may operate upon this intolerable agitation of soul. I have, indeed, no abhorrence of danger, except in its absolute effect—in terror. In this unnerved—in this pitiable condition—I feel that the period will sooner or later arrive when I must abandon life and reason together, in some struggle with the grim phantasm, F EAR."

I learned, moreover, at intervals, and through broken and equivocal hints, another singular feature of his mental condition. He was enchained by certain superstitious impressions in regard to the dwelling which he tenanted, and whence, for many years, he had never ventured forth—in regard to an influence whose suppositious force was conveyed in terms too shadowy here to be re-stated—an influence which some peculiarities in the mere form and substance of his family mansion had, by dint of long sufferance, he said, obtained over his spirit—an effect which the *physique* of the gray walls and turrets, and of the dim tarn into which they all looked down, had, at length, brought about upon the morale of his existence.

He admitted, however, although with hesitation, that much of the peculiar gloom which thus afflicted him could be traced to a more natural and far more palpable origin—to the severe and long-continued illness—indeed to the evidently approaching dissolution—of a tenderly beloved sister, his sole companion for long years, his last and only relative on earth. "Her decease," he said, with a bitterness which I can never forget, "would leave him (him, the hopeless and the frail) the last of the ancient race of the Ushers." While he spoke, the lady Madeline (for so was she called) passed slowly through a remote portion of the apartment, and, without having noticed my presence, disappeared. I regarded her with an utter astonishment not unmingled with dread; and yet I found it impossible to account for such feelings. A sensation of stupor oppressed me, as my eyes followed her retreating steps. When a door, at length, closed upon her, my glance sought instinctively and eagerly the countenance of the brother—but he had buried his face in his hands, and I could only perceive that a far more than ordinary wanness had overspread the emaciated fingers through which trickled many passionate tears.

The disease of the lady Madeline had long baffled the skill of her physicians. A settled apathy, a gradual wasting away of the person, and frequent although transient affections of a partially cataleptical character were the unusual diagnosis. Hitherto she had steadily borne up against the pressure of her malady, and had not betaken herself finally to bed; but on the closing in of the evening of my arrival at the house, she succumbed (as her brother told me at night with inexpressible agitation) to the prostrating power of the destroyer; and I learned that the glimpse I had obtained of her person would thus probably be the last I should obtain—that the lady, at least while living, would be seen by me no more.

For several days ensuing, her name was unmentioned by either Usher or myself: and during this period I was busied in earnest endeavors to alleviate the melancholy of my friend. We painted and read together, or I listened, as if in a dream, to the wild improvisations of his speaking guitar. And thus, as a closer and still closer intimacy admitted me more unreservedly into the recesses of his spirit, the more bitterly did I perceive the futility of all attempt at cheering a mind from which darkness, as if an inherent positive quality, poured forth upon all objects of the moral and physical universe in one unceasing radiation of gloom.

I shall ever bear about me a memory of the many solemn hours I thus spent alone with the master of the House of Usher. Yet I should fail in any attempt to convey an idea of the exact character of the studies, or of the occupations, in which he involved me, or led me the way. An excited and highly distempered ideality threw a sulphureous luster over all. His long improvised dirges will ring forever in my ears. Among other things, I hold painfully in mind a certain singular perversion and amplification of the wild air of the last waltz of Von Weber.[3] From the paintings over which his elaborate fancy brooded, and which grew, touch by touch, into vaguenesses at which I shuddered the more thrillingly, because I shuddered knowing not why;—from these paintings (vivid as their images now are before me) I would in vain endeavor to educe more than a small portion which should lie within the compass of merely written words. By the utter simplicity, by the nakedness of his designs, he arrested and overawed attention. If ever mortal painted an idea, that mortal was Roderick Usher. For me at least, in the circumstances then surrounding me, there arose out of the pure abstractions which the hypochondriac contrived to throw upon his canvas, an intensity of intolerable awe, no shadow of which felt I ever yet in the contemplation of the certainly glowing yet too concrete reveries of Fuseli.[4]

One of the phanatasmagoric conceptions of my friend, partaking not so rigidly of the spirit of abstraction, may be shadowed forth, although feebly, in words. A small picture presented the interior of an immensely long and rectangular vault or tunnel, with low walls, smooth, white, and without interruption or device. Certain accessory points of the design served well to convey the idea that this excavation lay at an exceeding depth below the surface of the earth. No outlet was observed in any portion of its vast extent, and no torch or other artificial source of light was discernible; yet a flood of intense rays rolled throughout, and bathed the whole in a ghastly and inappropriate splendor.

I have just spoken of that morbid condition of the auditory nerve which rendered all music intolerable to the sufferer, with the exception of certain effects of stringed instruments. It was, perhaps, the narrow limits to which he thus confined himself upon the guitar which gave birth, in great measure, to the fantastic character of his performances. But the fervid facility of his impromptus could not be so accounted for. They must have been, and were, in the notes, as well as in the words of his wild fantasias (for he not unfrequently accompanied himself with rhymed verbal improvisations), the result of that intense mental collectedness and concentration to which I have previously alluded as observable only in particular

---

[3] Carl Maria von Weber, 1786–1826, German romantic composer
[4] Henry Fuseli (Johann Heinrich Füssli), 1741–1825, Swiss-born British painter of "The Nightmare"

moments of the highest artificial excitement. The words of one of these rhapsodies I have easily remembered. I was, perhaps, the more forcibly impressed with it as he gave it, because, in the under or mystic current of its meaning, I fancied that I perceived, and for the first time, a full consciousness on the part of Usher of the tottering of his lofty reason upon her throne. The verses, which were entitled "The Haunted Palace," ran very nearly, if not accurately, thus:

I

In the greenest of our valleys,
By good angels tenanted,
Once a fair and stately palace—
Radiant palace—reared its head.
In the monarch Thought's dominion—
It stood there!
Never seraph spread a pinion
Over fabric half so fair.

II

Banners yellow, glorious, golden,
On its roof did float and flow
(This—all this—was in the olden
Time long ago)
And every gentle air that dallied,
In that sweet day,
Along the ramparts plumed and pallid,
A winged odor went away.

III

Wanderers in that happy valley
Through two luminous windows saw
Spirits moving musically
To a lute's well-tunéd law,
Round about a throne, where sitting
(Porphyrogene!) [5]
In state his glory well befitting,
The ruler of the realm was seen.

IV

And all with pearl and ruby glowing
Was the fair palace door,
Through which came flowing, flowing,
*   flowing*
And sparkling evermore,

[5] born to the purple

A troop of Echoes whose sweet duty
Was but to sing,
In voices of surpassing beauty,
The wit and wisdom of their king.

V

But evil things, in robes of sorrow,
Assailed the monarch's high estate;
(Ah, let us mourn, for never morrow
Shall dawn upon him, desolate!)
And, round about his home, the glory
That blushed and bloomed
Is but a dim-remembered story
Of the old time entombed.

VI

And travelers now within that valley,
Through the red-litten windows see
Vast forms that move fantastically
To a discordant melody;
While, like a rapid ghastly river,
Through the pale door,
A hideous throng rush out forever,
And laugh—but smile no more.

I well remember that suggestions arising from this ballad, led us into a train of thought, wherein there became manifest an opinion of Usher's which I mention not so much on account of its novelty, (for other men have thought thus,) as on account of the pertinacity with which he maintained it. This opinion, in its general form, was that of the sentience of all vegetable things. But, in his disordered fancy, the idea had assumed a more daring character, and trespassed, under certain conditions, upon the kingdom of inorganization. I lack words to express the full extent, or the earnest *abandon* of his persuasion. The belief, however, was connected (as I have previously hinted) with the gray stones of the home of his forefathers. The conditions of the sentence had been here, he imagined, fulfilled in the method of collocation of these stones—in the order of their arrangement, as well as in that of the many fungi which overspread them, and of the decayed trees which stood around—above all, in the long undisturbed endurance of this arrangement, and in its reduplication in the still waters of the tarn. Its evidence—the evidence of the sentience—was to be seen, he said (and I here started as he spoke), in the gradual yet certain condensation of an atmosphere of their own about the waters and the walls. The result was discoverable, he added, in that silent yet importunate and terrible influence which for centuries had molded the destinies of his family, and which made *him* what I now saw him—what he was. Such opinions need no comment, and I will make none.

Our books—the books which, for years, had formed no small portion of the mental existence of the invalid—were, as might be supposed, in strict keeping with this character of phantasm. We pored together over such works as the *Ververt et Chartreuse* of Gresset; the *Belphegor* of Machiavelli; the *Heaven and Hell* of Swedenborg; the *Subterranean Voyage* of Nicholas Klimm of Holberg; the *Chiromancy* of Robert Flud, of Jean D'Indaginé, and of De la Chambre; the *Journey into the Blue Distance* of Tieck; and the *City of the Sun* of Campanella. One favorite volume was a small octavo edition of the *Directorium Inquisitorum*, by the Dominican Eymeric de Gironne; and there were passages in Pomponius Mela, about the old African Satyrs and Ægipans, over which Usher would sit dreaming for hours. His chief delight, however, was found in the perusal of an exceedingly rare and curious book in quarto Gothic— the manual of a forgotten church—the *Vigiliæ Mortuorum secundum Chorum Ecclesiæ Maguntinæ.*[6]

I could not help thinking of the wild ritual of this work, and of its probable influence upon the hypochondriac, when, one evening, having informed me abruptly that the lady Madeline was no more, he stated his intention of preserving her corpse for a fortnight, (previously to its final interment,) in one of the numerous vaults within the main walls of the building. The worldly reason, however, assigned for this singular proceeding, was one which I did not feel at liberty to dispute. The brother had been led to his resolution (so he told me) by consideration of the unusual character of the malady of the deceased, of certain obtrusive and eager inquiries on the part of her medical men, and of the remote and exposed situation of the burial-ground of the family. I will not deny that when I called to mind the sinister countenance of the person whom I met upon the staircase, on the day of my arrival at the house, I had no desire to oppose what I regarded as at best but a harmless, and by no means an unnatural, precaution.

At the request of Usher, I personally aided him in the arrangements for the temporary entombment. The body having been encoffined, we two alone bore it to its rest. The vault in which we placed it (and which had been so long unopened that our torches, half smothered in its oppressive atmosphere, gave us little opportunity for investigation) was small, damp, and entirely without means of admission for light; lying, at great depth, immediately beneath that portion of the building in which was my own sleeping apartment. It had been used, apparently, in remote feudal times, for the worst purposes of a donjon-keep, and, in later days, as a place of deposit for powder, or some other highly combustible substance, as a portion of its floor, and the whole interior of a long archway

---

[6] These are all actual works of metaphysical speculation and occultism, ranging in date from the Middle Ages to nearly contemporary times.

through which we reached it, were carefully sheathed with copper. The door, of massive iron, had been, also, similarly protected. Its immense weight caused an unusually sharp grating sound, as it moved upon its hinges.

Having deposited our mournful burden upon trestles within this region of horror, we partially turned aside the yet unscrewed lid of the coffin, and looked upon the face of the tenant. A striking similitude between the brother and sister now first arrested my attention; and Usher, divining, perhaps, my thoughts, murmured out some few words from which I learned that the deceased and himself had been twins, and that sympathies of a scarcely intelligible nature had always existed between them. Our glances, however, rested not long upon the dead—for we could not regard her unawed. The disease which had thus entombed the lady in the maturity of youth, had left, as usual in all maladies of a strictly cataleptical character, the mockery of a faint blush upon the bosom and the face, and that suspiciously lingering smile upon the lip which is so terrible in death. We replaced and screwed down the lid, and, having secured the door of iron, made our way, with toil, into the scarcely less gloomy apartments of the upper portion of the house.

And now, some days of bitter grief having elapsed, an observable change came over the features of the mental disorder of my friend. His ordinary manner had vanished. His ordinary occupations were neglected or forgotten. He roamed from chamber to chamber with hurried, unequal, and objectless step. The pallor of his countenance had assumed, if possible, a more ghastly hue—but the luminousness of his eye had utterly gone out. The once occasional huskiness of his tone was heard no more; and a tremulous quaver, as if of extreme terror, habitually characterized his utterance. There were times, indeed, when I thought his unceasingly agitated mind was laboring with some oppressive secret, to divulge which he struggled for the necessary courage. At times, again, I was obliged to resolve all into the mere inexplicable vagaries of madness, for I beheld him gazing upon vacancy for long hours, in an attitude of the profoundest attention, as if listening to some imaginary sound. It was no wonder that his condition terrified—that it infected me. I felt creeping upon me, by slow yet certain degrees, the wild influences of his own fantastic yet impressive superstitions.

It was, especially, upon retiring to bed late in the night of the seventh or eighth day after the placing of the lady Madeline within the donjon, that I experienced the full power of such feelings. Sleep came not near my couch—while the hours waned and waned away. I struggled to reason off the nervousness which had dominion over me. I endeavored to believe that much, if not all of what I felt, was due to the bewildering influence of the gloomy furniture of the room—of the dark and tattered draperies, which, tortured into motion by the breath of a rising tempest, swayed fitfully to and fro upon the walls, and rustled uneasily about the decorations of the bed. But my efforts were fruitless. An irrepressible tremor gradually pervaded my frame; and, at length, there sat upon my very heart an incubus of utterly causeless alarm. Shaking this off with a gasp and a struggle, I uplifted myself upon the pillows, and, peering earnestly within the intense darkness of the chamber, hearkened—I know not why, except that an instinctive spirit prompted me—to certain low and indefinite sounds which came, through the pauses of the storm, at long intervals, I knew not whence. Overpowered by an intense sentiment of horror, unaccountable yet unendurable, I threw on my clothes with haste, (for I felt that I should sleep no more during the night,) and endeavored to arouse myself from the pitiable condition into which I had fallen, by pacing rapidly to and fro through the apartment.

I had taken but few turns in this manner, when a light step on an adjoining staircase arrested my attention. I presently recognized it as that of Usher. In an instant afterward he rapped, with a gentle touch, at my door, and entered, bearing a lamp. His countenance was, as usual, cadaverously wan—but, moreover, there was a species of mad hilarity in his eyes—an evidently restrained hysteria in his whole demeanor. His air appalled me—but anything was preferable to the solitude which I had so long endured, and I even welcomed his presence as a relief.

"And you have not seen it?" he said abruptly, after having stared about him for some moments in silence—"you have not then seen it?—but, stay! you shall." Thus speaking, and having carefully shaded his lamp, he hurried to one of the casements, and threw it freely open to the storm.

The impetuous fury of the entering gust nearly lifted us from our feet. It was, indeed, a tempestuous yet sternly beautiful night, and one wildly singular in its terror and its beauty. A whirlwind had apparently collected its force in our vicinity; for there were frequent and violent alterations in the direction of the wind; and the exceeding density of the clouds (which hung so low as to press upon the turrets of the house) did not prevent our perceiving the life-like velocity with which they flew careering from all points against each other, without passing away into the distance. I say that even their exceeding density did not prevent our perceiving this—yet we had no glimpse of the moon or stars—nor was there any flashing forth of the lightning. But the under surfaces of the huge masses of agitated vapor, as well as all terrestrial objects immediately around us, were glowing in the unnatural light of a faintly luminous and distinctly visible gaseous exhalation which hung about and enshrouded the mansion.

"You must not—you shall not behold this!" said I, shuddering, to Usher, as I led him, with a gentle violence, from the window to a seat. "These appearances, which bewilder you, are merely electrical phenomena not uncommon—or it may be that they have their ghastly origin in the rank miasma of the tarn. Let us close this casement;—the air is chilling and dangerous to your frame. Here is one of your favorite romances. I will read, and you shall listen;—and so we will pass away this terrible night together."

The antique volume which I had taken up was the *Mad Tryst* of Sir Launcelot Canning; but I had called it a favorite of Usher's more in sad jest than in earnest; for, in truth, there is little in its uncouth and un-imaginative prolixity which could have had interest for the lofty and spiritual ideality of my friend. It was, however, the only book immedi-ately at hand; and I indulged a vague hope that the excitement which now agitated the hypochondriac, might find relief (for the history of mental disorder is full of similar anomalies) even in the extremeness of the folly which I should read. Could I have judged, indeed, by the wild over-strained air of vivacity with which he hearkened, or apparently heark-ened, to the words of the tale, I might well have congratulated myself upon the success of my design.

I had arrived at that well-known portion of the story where Ethelred, the hero of the *Tryst*, having sought in vain for peaceable admission into the dwelling of the hermit, proceeds to make good an entrance by force. Here, it will be remembered, the words of the narrative run thus:

"And Ethelred, who was by nature of a doughty heart, and who was now mighty withal, on account of the powerfulness of the wine which he had drunken, waited no longer to hold parley with the hermit, who, in sooth, was of an obstinate and maliceful turn, but, feeling the rain upon his shoulders, and fearing the rising of the tempest, uplifted his mace out-right, and, with blows, made quickly room in the plankings of the door for his gauntleted hand; and now pulling therewith sturdily, he so cracked, and ripped, and tore all asunder, that the noise of the dry and hollow-sounding wood alarumed and reverberated throughout the forest."

At the termination of this sentence I started and, for a moment, paused; for it appeared to me (although I at once concluded that my excited fancy had deceived me)—it appeared to me that, from some very remote portion of the mansion, there came, indistinctly, to my ears, what might have been, in its exact similarity of character, the echo (but a stifled and dull one certainly) of the very cracking and ripping sound which Sir Launcelot had so particularly described. It was, beyond doubt, the coincidence alone which had arrested my attention; for, amid the rattling of the sashes of the casements, and the ordinary commingled noises of the still increasing storm, the sound, in itself, had nothing, surely, which should have interested or disturbed me. I continued the story:

"But the good champion Ethelred, now entering within the door, was sore enraged and amazed to perceive no signal of the maliceful hermit; but, in the stead thereof, a dragon of a scaly and prodigious demeanor, and of a fiery tongue, which sate in guard before a palace of gold, with a floor of silver; and upon the wall there hung a shield of shining brass with this legend enwritten—

Who entereth herein, a conqueror hath bin;
Who slayeth the dragon, the shield he shall win.

And Ethelred uplifted his mace, and struck upon the head of the dragon, which fell before him, and gave up his pesty breath, with a shriek so horrid and harsh, and withal so piercing, that Ethelred had fain to close his ears with his hands against the dreadful noise of it, the like whereof was never before heard."

Here again I paused abruptly, and now with a feeling of wild amazement—for there could be no doubt whatever that, in this instance, I did actually hear (although from what direction it proceeded I found it impossible to say) a low and apparently distant, but harsh, protracted, and most unusual screaming or grating sound—the exact counterpart of what my fancy had already conjured up for the dragon's unnatural shriek as described by the romancer.

Oppressed, as I certainly was, upon the occurrence of this second and most extraordinary coincidence, by a thousand conflicting sensations, in which wonder and extreme terror were predominant, I still retained sufficient presence of mind to avoid exciting, by any observation, the sensitive nervousness of my companion. I was by no means certain that he had noticed the sounds in question; although, assuredly, a strange alteration had, during the last few minutes, taken place in his demeanor. From a position fronting my own, he had gradually brought round his chair, so as to sit with his face to the door of the chamber; and thus I could but partially perceive his features, although I saw that his lips trembled as if he were murmuring inaudibly. His head had dropped upon his breast —yet I knew that he was not asleep, from the wide and rigid opening of the eye as I caught a glance of it in profile. The motion of his body, too, was at variance with this idea—for he rocked from side to side with a gentle yet constant and uniform sway. Having rapidly taken notice of all this, I resumed the narrative of Sir Launcelot, which thus proceeded:

"And now, the champion, having escaped from the terrible fury of the dragon, bethinking himself of the brazen shield, and of the breaking up of the enchantment which was upon it, removed the carcass from out of the way before him, and approached valorously over the silver pavement of the castle to where the shield was upon the wall; which in sooth tarried not for his full coming, but fell down at his feet upon the silver floor, with a mighty great and terrible ringing sound."

No sooner had these syllables passed my lips, than—as if a shield of brass had indeed, at the moment, fallen heavily upon a floor of silver— I became aware of a distinct, hollow, metallic, and clangorous, yet apparently muffled, reverberation. Completely unnerved, I leaped to my feet; but the measured rocking movement of Usher was undisturbed. I rushed to the chair in which he sat. His eyes were bent fixedly before him, and throughout his whole countenance there reigned a stony rigidity. But, as I placed my hand upon his shoulder, there came a strong shudder over his whole person; a sickly smile quivered about his lips; and I saw that he spoke in a low, hurried, and gibbering murmur, as if unconscious of my presence. Bending closely over him, I at length drank in the hideous import of his words.

"Not hear it?—yes, I hear it, and *have* heard it. Long—long—long—many minutes, many hours, many days, have I heard it—yet I dared not—oh, pity me, miserable wretch that I am!—I dared not—I *dared* not speak! *We have put her living in the tomb!* Said I not that my senses were acute? I *now* tell you that I heard her first feeble movements in the hollow coffin. I heard them—many, many days ago—yet I dared not—I *dared not speak!* And now—tonight—Ethelred—ha! ha!—the breaking of the hermit's door, and the death-cry of the dragon, and the clangor of the shield!—say, rather, the rending of her coffin, and the grating of the iron hinges of her prison, and her struggles within the coppered archway of the vault! Oh whither shall I fly? Will she not be here anon? Is she not hurrying to upbraid me for my haste? Have I not heard her footstep on the stair? Do I not distinguish that heavy and horrible beating of her heart? MADMAN!"—here he sprang furiously to his feet, and shrieked out his syllables, as if in the effort he were giving up his soul—"MADMAN! I TELL YOU THAT SHE NOW STANDS WITHOUT THE DOOR!"

As if in the superhuman energy of his utterance there had been found the potency of a spell, the huge antique panels to which the speaker pointed threw slowly back, upon the instant, their ponderous and ebony jaws. It was the work of the rushing gust—but then without those doors there DID stand the lofty and enshrouded figure of the lady Madeline of Usher. There was blood upon her white robes, and the evidence of some bitter struggle upon every portion of her emaciated frame. For a moment she remained trembling and reeling to and fro upon the threshold, then, with a low moaning cry, fell heavily inward upon the person of her brother, and in her violent and now final death-agonies, bore him to the floor a corpse, and a victim of the terrors he had anticipated.

From that chamber, and from that mansion, I fled aghast. The storm was still abroad in all its wrath as I found myself crossing the old causeway. Suddenly there shot along the path a wild light, and I turned to see whence a gleam so unusual could have issued; for the vast house and its shadows were alone behind me. The radiance was that of the full, setting, and blood-red moon, which now shone vividly through that once barely discernible fissure, of which I have before spoken as extending from the roof of the building, in a zigzag direction, to the base. While I gazed, this fissure rapidly widened—there came a fierce breath of the whirlwind—the entire orb of the satellite burst at once upon my sight—my brain reeled as I saw the mighty walls rushing asunder—there was a long tumultuous shouting sound like the voice of a thousand waters—and the deep and dank tarn at my feet closed sullenly and silently over the fragments of the "HOUSE OF USHER."

Mark Twain

1835–1910

WHAT STUMPED THE BLUEJAYS

ANIMALS talk to each other, of course. There can be no question about that; but I suppose there are very few people who can understand them. I never knew but one man who could. I knew he could, however, because he told me so himself. He was a middle-aged, simple-hearted miner, who had lived in a lonely corner of California, among the woods and mountains, a good many years, and had studied the ways of his only neighbors, the beasts and the birds, until he believed he could accurately translate any remark which they made. This was Jim Baker. According to Jim Baker, some animals have only a limited education, and use only very simple words, and scarcely ever a comparison or a flowery figure; whereas, certain other animals have a large vocabulary, a fine command of language and a ready and fluent delivery; consequently these latter talk a great deal; they like it; they are conscious of their talent, and they enjoy "showing off." Baker said, that after long and careful observation, he had come to the conclusion that the bluejays were the best talkers he had found among birds and beasts. Said he:

"There's more *to* a bluejay than any other creature. He has got more moods and more different kinds of feelings than other creatures; and, mind you, whatever a bluejay feels, he can put into language. And no mere commonplace language, either, but rattling, out-and-out book-talk—and bristling with metaphor, too—just bristling! And as for command of language—why, *you* never see a bluejay stuck for a word. No man ever did. They just boil out of him! And another thing: I've noticed a good deal, and there's no bird, or cow, or anything that uses as good grammar as a bluejay. You may say a cat uses good grammar. Well, a cat does—but you let a cat get excited, once; you let a cat get to pulling fur with another cat on a shed, nights, and you'll hear grammar that will give you the lockjaw. Ignorant people think it's the *noise* which fighting cats make that is so aggravating, but it ain't so; it's the sickening grammar they use. Now I've never heard a jay use bad grammar but very seldom; and when they do, they are as ashamed as a human; they shut right down and leave.

"You may call a jay a bird. Well, so he is, in a measure—because he's got feathers on him, and don't belong to no church, perhaps; but otherwise he is just as much a human as you be. And I'll tell you for why. A jay's gifts, and instincts, and feelings, and interests, cover the whole ground. A jay hasn't got any more principle than a Congressman. A jay will lie, a jay will steal, a jay will deceive, a jay will betray; and four times out of five, a jay will go back on his solemnest promise. The sacredness of an obligation is a thing which you can't cram into no bluejay's head. Now, on top of all this, there's another thing: a jay can outswear any gentleman in the mines. You think a cat can swear. Well, a cat can; but you give a bluejay a subject that calls for his reserve powers, and where is your cat? Don't talk to *me*—I know too much about this thing. And there's yet another thing; in the one little particular of scolding—just good, clean, out-and-out scolding—a bluejay can lay over anything, human or divine. Yes, sir, a jay is everything that a man is. A jay can cry, a jay can laugh, a jay can feel shame, a jay can reason and plan and discuss, a jay likes gossip and scandal, a jay has got a sense of humor, a jay knows when he is an ass just as well as you do—maybe better. If a jay ain't human, he better take in his sign, that's all. Now I'm going to tell you a perfectly true fact about some bluejays.

"When I first begun to understand jay language correctly, there was a little incident that happened here. Seven years ago, the last man in this region but me moved away. There stands his house—been empty ever since; a log house, with a plank roof—just one big room, and no more; no ceiling—nothing between the rafters and the floor. Well, one Sunday morning I was sitting out here in front of my cabin with my cat, taking the sun, and looking at the blue hills, and listening to the leaves rustling so lonely in the trees, and thinking of the home away yonder in the States, that I hadn't heard from in thirteen years, when a bluejay lit on that house, with an acorn in his mouth, and says, 'Hello, I reckon I've struck something!' When he spoke, the acorn dropped out of his mouth and rolled down the roof, of course, but he didn't care; his mind was all on the thing he had struck. It was a knot-hole in the roof. He cocked his head to one side, shut one eye and put the other one to the hole, like a possum looking down a jug; then he glanced up with his bright eyes, gave a wink or two with his wings—which signifies gratification, you understand—and says, 'It looks like a hole, it's located like a hole—blamed if I don't believe it *is* a hole!'

"Then he cocked his head down and took another look; he glances up perfectly joyful this time; winks his wings and his tail both, and says, 'Oh, no, this ain't no fat thing, I reckon! If I ain't in luck!—why it's a perfectly elegant hole!' So he flew down and got that acorn, and fetched it up and dropped it in, and was just tilting his head back with the heavenliest smile on his face, when all of a sudden he was paralyzed into a listening attitude, and that smile faded gradually out of his countenance like breath off'n a razor, and the queerest look of surprise took its place. Then he says, 'Why I didn't hear it fall!' He cocked his eye at the hole again, and took a long look; raised up and shook his head; stepped around to the other side of the hole, and took another look from that side; shook his head again. He studied a while, then he just went into the *de*tails—walking round and round the hole, and spied into it from every point of the compass. No use. Now he took a thinking attitude on the comb of the roof, and scratched the back of his head with his right foot for a minute, and finally says, 'Well, it's too many for *me*, that's certain; must be a mighty long hole; however, I ain't got no time to fool around here, I got to 'tend to business; I reckon it's all right—chance it, anyway!'

"So he flew off and fetched another acorn and dropped it in, and tried to flirt his eye to the hole quick enough to see what become of it, but he was too late. He held his eye there as much as a minute; then he raised up and sighed, and says, 'Consound it, I don't seem to understand this thing, no way; however, I'll tackle her again.' He fetched another acorn and done his level best to see what become of it, but he couldn't. He says, 'Well, *I* never struck no such a hole as this before; I'm of the opinion it's a totally new kind of hole.' Then he begun to get mad. He held in for a spell, walking up and down the comb of the roof, and shaking his head and muttering to himself; but his feelings got the upper hand of him presently, and he broke loose and cussed himself black in the face. I never see a bird take on so about a little thing. When he got through he walks to the hole and looks in again for half a minute; then he says, 'Well, you're a long hole, and a deep hole, and a mighty singular hole altogether—but I've started to fill you, and I'm d——d if I *don't* fill you, if it takes a hundred years!'

"And with that, away he went. You never see a bird work so since you was born. He laid into his work like a nigger, and the way he hove acorns into that hole for about two hours and a half was one of the most exciting and astonishing spectacles I ever struck. He never stopped to take a look any more—he just hove 'em in, and went for more. Well, at last he could hardly flop his wings, he was so tuckered out. He comes a-drooping down, once more, sweating like an ice-pitcher, drops his acorn in and says, '*Now* I guess I've got the bulge on you by this time!' So he bent down for a look. If you'll believe me, when his head come up again he was just pale with rage. He says, 'I've shoveled acorns enough in there to keep the family thirty years, and if I can see a sign of one of 'em, I wish I may land in a museum with a belly full of sawdust in two minutes!'

"He just had strength enough to crawl up on to the comb and lean his back agin the chimbly, and then he collected his impressions and begun to free his mind. I see in a second that what I had mistook for profanity in the mines was only just the rudiments, as you may say.

"Another jay was going by, and heard him doing his devotions, and stops to inquire what was up. The sufferer told him the whole circumstances, and says, 'Now yonder's the hole, and if you don't believe me, go and look for yourself.' So this fellow went and looked, and comes back and says, 'How many did you say you put in there?' 'Not any less than two tons,' says the sufferer. The other jay went and looked again. He couldn't seem to make it out, so he raised a yell, and three more jays come. They all examined the hole, they all made the sufferer tell it over again, then they all discussed it, and got off as many leather-headed opinions about it as an average crowd of humans could have done.

"They called in more jays; then more and more, till pretty soon this whole region 'peared to have a blue flush about it. There must have been five thousand of them; and such another jawing and disputing and ripping and cussing, you never heard. Every jay in the whole lot put his eye to the hole, and delivered a more chuckled-headed opinion about the mystery than the jay that went there before him. They examined the house all over, too. The door was standing half-open, and at last one old jay happened to go and light on it and look in. Of course, that knocked the mystery galley-west in a second. There lay the acorns, scattered all over the floor. He flopped his wings and raised a whoop. 'Come here!' he says, 'Come here, everybody; hang'd if this fool hasn't been trying to fill up a house with acorns!' They all came a-swooping down like a blue cloud, and as each fellow lit on the door and took a glance, the whole absurdity of the contract that the first jay had tackled hit him home and he fell over backwards suffocating with laughter, and the next jay took his place and done the same.

"Well, sir, they roosted around here on the house-top and the trees for an hour, and guffawed over that thing like human beings. It ain't no use to tell me a bluejay hasn't got a sense of humor, because I know better. And memory too. They brought jays here from all over the United States to look down that hole, every summer for three years. Other birds too. And they could all see the point, except an owl that came from Nova Scotia to visit the Yo Semite, and he took this thing in on his way back. He said he couldn't see anything funny in it. But then, he was a good deal disappointed about Yo Semite, too."

Henry James
1843–1916
THE REAL THING

I

W HEN the porter's wife, who used to answer the house-bell, announced "A gentleman and a lady, sir," I had, as I often had in those days—the wish being father to the thought—an immediate vision of sitters. Sitters my visitors in this case proved to be; but not in the sense I should have preferred. There was nothing at first however to indicate that they mightn't have come for a portrait. The gentleman, a man of fifty, very high and very straight, with a moustache slightly grizzled and a dark gray walking-coat admirably fitted, both of which I noted professionally—I don't mean as a barber or yet as a tailor—would have struck me as a celebrity if celebrities often were striking. It was a truth of which I had for some time been conscious that a figure with a good deal of frontage was, as one might say, almost never a public institution.

A glance at the lady helped to remind me of this paradoxical law : she also looked too distinguished to be a "personality." Moreover one would scarcely come across two variations together.

Neither of the pair immediately spoke—they only prolonged the preliminary gaze suggesting that each wished to give the other a chance. They were visibly shy; they stood there letting me take them in—which, as I afterwards perceived, was the most practical thing they could have done. In this way their embarrassment served their cause. I had seen people painfully reluctant to mention that they desired anything so gross as to be represented on canvas; but the scruples of my new friends appeared almost insurmountable. Yet the gentleman might have said "I should like a portrait of my wife," and the lady might have said "I should like a portrait of my husband." Perhaps they weren't husband and wife— this naturally would make the matter more delicate. Perhaps they wished to be done together—in which case they ought to have brought a third person to break the news.

"We come from Mr. Rivet," the lady finally said with a dim smile that had the effect of a moist sponge passed over a "sunk" piece of painting, as well as of a vague allusion to vanished beauty. She was as tall and straight, in her degree, as her companion, and with ten years less to carry. She looked as sad as a woman could look whose face was not charged with expression; that is her tinted oval mask showed waste as an exposed surface shows friction. The hand of time had played over her freely, but to an effect of elimination. She was slim and stiff, and so well-dressed, in dark blue cloth, with lappets and pockets and buttons, that it was clear she employed the same tailor as her husband. The couple had an indefinable air of prosperous thrift—they evidently got a good deal of luxury for their money. If I was to be one of their luxuries it would behoove me to consider my terms.

"Ah Claude Rivet recommended me?" I echoed; and I added that it was very kind of him, though I could reflect that, as he only painted landscape, this wasn't a sacrifice.

The lady looked very hard at the gentleman, and the gentleman looked round the room. Then staring at the floor a moment and stroking his moustache, he rested his pleasant eyes on me with the remark: "He said you were the right one."

"I try to be, when people want to sit."

"Yes, we should like to," said the lady anxiously.

"Do you mean together?"

My visitors exchanged a glance. "If you could do anything with *me* I suppose it would be double," the gentleman stammered.

"Oh yes, there's naturally a higher charge for two figures than for one."

"We should like to make it pay," the husband confessed.

"That's very good of you," I returned, appreciating so unwonted a sympathy—for I supposed he meant pay the artist.

A sense of strangeness seemed to dawn on the lady. "We mean for the illustrations—Mr. Rivet said you might put one in."

"Put in an illustration?" I was equally confused.

"Sketch her off, you know," said the gentleman, coloring.

It was only then that I understood the service Claude Rivet had rendered me; he had told them how I worked in black-and-white, for magazines, for story-books, for sketches of contemporary life, and consequently had copious employment for models. These things were true, but it was not less true—I may confess it now; whether because the aspiration was to lead to everything or to nothing I leave the reader to guess—that I couldn't get the honors, to say nothing of the emoluments, of a great painter of portraits out of my head. My "illustrations" were my pot-boilers; I looked to a different branch of art—far and away the most interesting it had always seemed to me—to perpetuate my fame. There was no shame in looking to it also to make my fortune; but that fortune was by so much further from being made from the moment my visitors wished to be "done" for nothing. I was disappointed; for in the pictorial sense I had immediately *seen* them. I had seized their type—I had already settled what I would do with it. Something that wouldn't absolutely have pleased them, I afterwards reflected.

"Ah you're—you're—a—?" I began as soon as I had mastered my surprise. I couldn't bring out the dingy word "models": it seemed so little to fit the case.

"We haven't had much practice," said the lady.

"We've got to *do* something, and we've thought that an artist in your line might perhaps make something of us," her husband threw off. He further mentioned that they didn't know many artists and that they had gone first, on the off-chance—he painted views of course, but sometimes put in figures; perhaps I remembered—to Mr. Rivet, whom they had met a few years before at a place in Norfolk where he was sketching.

"We used to sketch a little ourselves," the lady hinted.

"It's very awkward, but we absolutely *must* do something," her husband went on.

"Of course we're not so *very* young," she admitted with a wan smile.

With the remark that I might as well know something more about them the husband had handed me a card extracted from a neat new pocket-book—their appurtenances were all of the freshest—and inscribed with the words "Major Monarch." Impressive as these words were they didn't carry my knowledge much further; but my visitor presently added: "I've left the army and we've had the misfortune to lose our money. In fact our means are dreadfully small."

"It's awfully trying—a regular strain," said Mrs. Monarch.

They evidently wished to be discreet—to take care not to swagger because they were gentlefolk. I felt them willing to recognize this as something of a drawback, at the same time that I guessed at an underlying sense—their consolation in adversity—that they *had* their points. They certainly had; but these advantages struck me as preponderantly social; such for instance as would help to make a drawing-room look well. However, a drawing-room was always, or ought to be, a picture.

In consequence of his wife's allusion to their age Major Monarch observed: "Naturally it's more for the figure that we thought of going in. We can still hold ourselves up." On the instant I saw that the figure was indeed their strong point. His "naturally" didn't sound vain, but it lighted up the question. "*She* has the best one," he continued, nodding at his wife with a pleasant after-dinner absence of circumlocution. I could only reply, as if we were in fact sitting over our wine, that this didn't prevent his own from being very good; which led him in turn to make answer: "We thought that if you ever have to do people like us we might be something like it. *She* particularly—for a lady in a book, you know."

I was so amused by them that, to get more of it, I did my best to take their point of view; and though it was an embarrassment to find myself appraising physically, as if they were animals on hire or useful blacks, a pair whom I should have expected to meet only in one of the relations in which criticism is tacit, I looked at Mrs. Monarch judicially enough to be able to exclaim after a moment with conviction: "Oh yes, a lady in a book!" She was singularly like a bad illustration.

"We'll stand up, if you like," said the Major; and he raised himself before me with a really grand air.

I could take his measure at a glance—he was six feet two and a perfect gentleman. It would have paid any club in process of formation and in want of a stamp to engage him at a salary to stand in the principal window. What struck me at once was that in coming to me they had rather missed their vocation; they could surely have been turned to better account for advertising purposes. I couldn't of course see the thing in detail, but I could see them make somebody's fortune—I don't mean their own. There was something in them for a waistcoat-maker, an hotel-keeper or a soap-vendor. I could imagine "We always use it" pinned on their bosoms with the greatest effect; I had a vision of the brilliancy with which they would launch a table d'hôte.

Mrs. Monarch sat still, not from pride but from shyness, and presently her husband said to her: "Get up, my dear, and show how smart you are." She obeyed, but she had no need to get up to show it. She walked to the end of the studio and then came back blushing, her fluttered eyes on the partner of her appeal. I was reminded of an incident I had accidentally had a glimpse of in Paris—being with a friend there, a dramatist about to produce a play, when an actress came to ask him to be entrusted with a part. She went through her paces before him, walked up and down as Mrs. Monarch was doing. Mrs. Monarch did it quite as well, but I abstained from applauding. It was very odd to see such people apply for such poor pay. She looked as if she had ten thousand a year. Her husband had used the word that described her: she was in the London current jargon essentially and typically "smart." Her figure was, in the same order of ideas, conspicuously and irreproachably "good." For a woman of her age her waist was surprisingly small; her elbow moreover had the orthodox crook. She held her head at the conventional angle, but why did she come to *me?* She ought to have tried on jackets at a big shop. I feared my visitors were not only destitute but "artistic"—which would be a great complication. When she sat down again I thanked her, observing that what a draftsman most valued in his model was the faculty of keeping quiet.

"Oh *she* can keep quiet," said Major Monarch. Then he added jocosely: "I've always kept her quiet."

"I'm not a nasty fidget, am I?" It was going to wring tears from me, I felt, the way she hid her head, ostrich-like, in the other broad bosom.

The owner of this expanse addressed his answer to me. "Perhaps it isn't out of place to mention—because we ought to be quite business-like, oughtn't we?—that when I married her she was known as the Beautiful Statue."

"Oh dear!" said Mrs. Monarch ruefully.

"Of course I should want a certain amount of expression," I rejoined.

"Of *course!*"—and I had never heard such unanimity.

"And then I suppose you know that you'll get awfully tired."

"Oh, we *never* get tired!" they eagerly cried.

"Have you had any kind of practice?"

They hesitated—they looked at each other. "We've been photographed—*immensely*," said Mrs. Monarch.

"She means the fellows have asked us themselves," added the Major.

"I see—because you're so good-looking."

"I don't know what they thought, but they were always after us."

"We always got our photographs for nothing," smiled Mrs. Monarch.

"We might have brought some, my dear," her husband remarked.

"I'm not sure we have any left. We've given quantities away," she explained to me.

"With our autographs and that sort of thing," said the Major.

"Are they to be got in the shops?" I enquired as a harmless pleasantry.

"Oh yes, *hers*—they used to be."

"Not now," said Mrs. Monarch with her eyes on the floor.

2

I could fancy the "sort of thing" they put on the presentation copies of their photographs, and I was sure they wrote a beautiful hand. It was odd how quickly I was sure of everything that concerned them. If they were now so poor as to have to earn shillings and pence they could never have had much of a margin. Their good looks had been their capital, and they had good-humoredly made the most of the career that this resource marked out for them. It was in their faces, the blankness, the deep intellectual repose of the twenty years of country-house visiting that had given them pleasant intonations. I could see the sunny drawing-rooms, sprinkled with periodicals she didn't read, in which Mrs. Monarch had continuously sat; I could see the wet shrubberies in which she had walked, equipped to admiration for either exercise. I could see the rich covers the Major had helped to shoot and the wonderful garments in which, late at night, he repaired to the smoking-room to talk about them. I could imagine their leggings and waterproofs, their knowing tweeds and rugs, their rolls of sticks and cases of tackle and neat umbrellas; and I could evoke the exact appearance of their servants and the compact variety of their luggage on the platforms of country stations.

They gave small tips, but they were liked; they didn't do anything themselves, but they were welcome. They looked so well everywhere; they gratified the general relish for stature, complexion and "form." They knew it without fatuity or vulgarity, and they respected themselves in consequence. They weren't superficial; they were thorough and kept themselves up—it had been their line. People with such a taste for activity had to have some line. I could feel how even in a dull house they could have been counted on for the joy of life. At present something had happened—it didn't matter what, their little income had grown less, it had grown least—and they had to do something for pocket-money. Their friends could like them, I made out, without liking to support them. There was something about them that represented credit—their clothes, their manners, their type; but if credit is a large empty pocket in which an occasional chink reverberates, the chink at least must be audible. What they wanted of me was to help to make it so. Fortunately they had no children—I soon divined that. They would also perhaps wish our relations to be kept secret: this was why it was "for the figure"—the reproduction of the face would betray them.

I liked them—I felt, quite as their friends must have done—they were so simple; and I had no objection to them if they would suit. But somehow with all their perfections I didn't easily believe in them. After all they were amateurs, and the ruling passion of my life was the detestation of the amateur. Combined with this was another perversity—an innate preference for the represented subject over the real one: the defect of the real one was so apt to be a lack of representation. I like things that appeared; then one was sure. Whether they *were* or not was a subordinate and almost always a profitless question. There were other considerations, the first of which was that I already had two or three recruits in use, notably a young person with big feet, in alpaca, from Kilburn, who for a couple of years had come to me regularly for my illustrations and with whom I was still—perhaps ignobly—satisfied. I frankly explained to my visitors how the case stood, but they had taken more precautions than I supposed. They had reasoned out their opportunity, for Claude Rivet had told them of the projected *édition de luxe* of one of the writers of our day—the rarest of the novelists—who, long neglected by the multitudinous vulgar and dearly prized by the attentive (need I mention Philip

Vincent?) had had the happy fortune of seeing, late in life, the dawn and then the full light of a higher criticism; an estimate in which on the part of the public there was something really of expiation. The edition preparing, planned by a publisher of taste, was practically an act of high reparation; the wood-cuts with which it was to be enriched were the homage of English art to one of the most independent representatives of English letters. Major and Mrs. Monarch confessed to me they had hoped I might be able to work *them* into my branch of the enterprise. They knew I was to do the first of the books, "Rutland Ramsay," but I had to make clear to them that my participation in the rest of the affair—this first book was to be a test—must depend on the satisfaction I should give. If this should be limited my employers would drop me with scarce common forms. It was therefore a crisis for me, and naturally I was making special preparations, looking about for new people, should they be necessary, and securing the best types. I admitted however that I should like to settle down to two or three good models who would do for everything.

"Should we have often to—a—put on special clothes?" Mrs. Monarch timidly demanded.

"Dear yes—that's half the business."

"And should we be expected to supply our own costumes?"

"Oh no; I've got a lot of things. A painter's models put on—or put off—anything he likes."

"And you mean—a—the same?"

"The same?"

Mrs. Monarch looked at her husband again.

"Oh she was just wondering," he explained, "if the costumes are in *general* use." I had to confess that they were, and I mentioned further that some of them—I had a lot of genuine greasy last-century things—had served their time, a hundred years ago, on living world-stained men and women; on figures not perhaps so far removed, in that vanished world, from *their* type, the Monarchs', *quoi!*[1] of a breeched and bewigged age. "We'll put on anything that *fits*," said the Major.

"Oh I arrange that—they fit in the pictures."

"I'm afraid I should do better for the modern books. I'd come as you like," said Mrs. Monarch.

"She has got a lot of clothes at home: they might do for contemporary life," her husband continued.

"Oh I can fancy scenes in which you'd be quite natural." And indeed I could see the slipshod rearrangements of stale properties—the stories I tried to produce pictures for without the exasperation of reading them—whose sandy tracts the good lady might help to people. But I had to return to the fact that for this sort of work—the daily mechanical grind—I was already equipped: the people I was working with were fully adequate.

[1] what!

"We only thought we might be more like *some* characters," said Mrs. Monarch mildly, getting up.

Her husband also rose; he stood looking at me with a dim wistfulness that was touching in so fine a man. "Wouldn't it be rather a pull sometimes to have—a—to have—?" He hung fire; he wanted me to help him by phrasing what he meant. But I couldn't—I didn't know. So he brought it out awkwardly: "The *real* thing; a gentleman, you know, or a lady." I was quite ready to give a general assent—I admitted that there was a great deal in that. This encouraged Major Monarch to say, following up his appeal with an unacted gulp: "It's awfully hard—we've tried everything." The gulp was communicative; it proved too much for his wife. Before I knew it Mrs. Monarch had dropped again upon a divan and burst into tears. Her husband sat down beside her, holding one of her hands; whereupon she quickly dried her eyes with the other, while I felt embarrassed as she looked up at me. "There isn't a confounded job I haven't applied for—waited for—prayed for. You can fancy we'd be pretty bad first. Secretaryships and that sort of thing? You might as well ask for a peerage. I'd be *anything*—I'm strong; a messenger or a coal-heaver. I'd put on a gold-laced cap and open carriage-doors in front of the haberdasher's; I'd hang about a station to carry portmanteaux; I'd be a postman. But they won't *look* at you; there are thousands as good as yourself already on the ground. *Gentlemen*, poor beggars, who've drunk their wine, who've kept their hunters!"

I was as reassuring as I knew how to be, and my visitors were presently on their feet again while, for the experiment, we agreed on an hour. We were discussing it when the door opened and Miss Churm came in with a wet umbrella. Miss Churm had to take the omnibus to Maida Vale[2] and then walk half a mile. She looked a trifle blowsy and slightly splashed. I scarcely ever saw her come in without thinking afresh how odd it was that, being so little in herself, she should yet be so much in others. She was a meager little Miss Churm, but was such an ample heroine of romance. She was only a freckled cockney, but she could represent everything, from a fine lady to a shepherdess; she had the faculty as she might have had a fine voice or long hair. She couldn't spell and she loved beer, but she had two or three "points," and practice, and a knack, and mother-wit, and a whimsical sensibility, and a love of the theater, and seven sisters, and not an ounce of respect, especially for the *h*. The first thing my visitors saw was that her umbrella was wet, and in their spotless perfection they visibly winced at it. The rain had come on since their arrival.

"I'm all in a soak; there *was* a mess of people in the 'bus. I wish you lived near a stytion," said Miss Churm. I requested her to get ready as quickly as possible, and she passed into the room in which she always

---

[2] a middle-class area in London

changed her dress. But before going out she asked me what she was to get into this time.

"It's the Russian princess, don't you know?" I answered; "the one with the 'golden eyes,' in black velvet, for the long thing in the *Cheapside*."[3]

"Golden eyes? I *say!*" cried Miss Churm, while my companions watched her with intensity as she withdrew. She always arranged herself, when she was late, before I could turn round; and I kept my visitors a little on purpose, so that they might get an idea, from seeing her, what would be expected of themselves. I mentioned that she was quite my notion of an excellent model—she was really very clever.

"Do you think she looks like a Russian princess?" Major Monarch asked with lurking alarm.

"When I make her, yes."

"Oh if you have to *make* her—!" he reasoned, not without point.

"That's the most you can ask. There are so many who are not makeable."

"Well now, *here's* a lady"—and with a persuasive smile he passed his arm into his wife's—"who's already made!"

"Oh I'm not a Russian princess," Mrs. Monarch protested a little coldly. I could see she had known some and didn't like them. There at once was a complication of a kind I never had to fear with Miss Churm.

This young lady came back in black velvet—the gown was rather rusty and very low on her lean shoulders—and with a Japanese fan in her red hands. I reminded her that in the scene I was doing she had to look over some one's head. "I forgot whose it is; but it doesn't matter. Just look over a head."

"I'd rather look over a stove," said Miss Churm; and she took her station near the fire. She fell into position, settled herself into a tall attitude, gave a certain backward inclination to her head and a certain forward droop to her fan, and looked, at least to my prejudiced sense, distinguished and charming, foreign and dangerous. We left her looking so while I went downstairs with Major and Mrs. Monarch.

"I believe I could come about as near it as that," said Mrs. Monarch.

"Oh you think she's shabby, but you must allow for the alchemy of art."

However, they went off with an evident increase of comfort founded on their demonstrable advantage in being the real thing. I could fancy them shuddering over Miss Churm. She was very droll about them when I went back, for I told her what they wanted.

"Well, if *she* can sit I'll tyke to bookkeeping," said my model.

"She's very ladylike," I replied as an innocent form of aggravation.

"So much the worse for *you*. That means she can't turn round."

---

[3] a popular magazine of the late nineteenth century

"She'll do for the fashionable novels."

"Oh yes, she'll *do* for them!" my model humorously declared. "Ain't they bad enough without her?" I had often sociably denounced them to Miss Churm.

3

It was for the elucidation of a mystery in one of these works that I first tried Mrs. Monarch. Her husband came with her, to be useful if necessary—it was sufficiently clear that as a general thing he would prefer to come with her. At first I wondered if this were for "propriety's" sake—if he were going to be jealous and meddling. The idea was too tiresome, and if it had been confirmed it would speedily have brought our acquaintance to a close. But I soon saw there was nothing in it and that if he accompanied Mrs. Monarch it was—in addition to the chance of being wanted—simply because he had nothing else to do. When they were separate his occupation was gone and they never *had* been separate. I judged rightly that in their awkward situation their close union was their main comfort and that this union had no weak spot. It was a real marriage, an encouragement to the hesitating, a nut for pessimists to crack. Their address was humble—I remember afterwards thinking it had been the only thing about them that was really professional—and I could fancy the lamentable lodgings in which the Major would have been left alone. He could sit there more or less grimly with his wife—he couldn't sit there anyhow without her.

He had too much tact to try and make himself agreeable when he couldn't be useful; so when I was too absorbed in my work to talk he simply sat and waited. But I liked to hear him talk—it made my work, when not interrupting it, less mechanical, less special. To listen to him was to combine the excitement of going out with the economy of staying at home. There was only one hindrance—that I seemed not to know any of the people this brilliant couple had known. I think he wondered extremely, during the term of our intercourse, whom the deuce I *did* know. He hadn't a stray sixpence of an idea to fumble for, so we didn't spin it very fine; we confined ourselves to questions of leather and even of liquor—saddlers and breeches-makers and how to get excellent claret cheap—and matters like "good trains" and the habits of small game. His lore on these last subjects was astonishing—he managed to interweave the station-master with the ornithologist. When he couldn't talk about greater things he could talk cheerfully about smaller, and since I couldn't accompany him into reminiscences of the fashionable world he could lower the conversation without a visible effort to my level.

So earnest a desire to please was touching in a man who could so easily have knocked one down. He looked after the fire and had an opinion on the draft of the stove without my asking him, and I could see that he thought many of my arrangements not half knowing. I remember telling him that if I were only rich I'd offer him a salary to come and teach me how to live. Sometimes he gave a random sigh of which the essence might have been: "Give me even such a bare old barrack as *this*, and I'd do something with it!" When I wanted to use him he came alone; which was an illustration of the superior courage of women. His wife could bear her solitary second floor, and she was in general more discreet; showing by various small reserves that she was alive to the propriety of keeping our relations markedly professional—not letting them slide into sociability. She wished it to remain clear that she and the Major were employed, not cultivated, and if she approved of me as a superior, who could be kept in his place, she never thought me quite good enough for an equal.

She sat with great intensity, giving the whole of her mind to it, and was capable of remaining for an hour almost as motionless as before a photographer's lens. I could see she had been photographed often, but somehow the very habit that made her good for that purpose unfitted her for mine. At first I was extremely pleased with her ladylike air, and it was a satisfaction, on coming to follow her lines, to see how good they were and how far they could lead the pencil. But after a little skirmishing I began to find her too insurmountably stiff; do what I would with it my drawing looked like a photograph or a copy of a photograph. Her figure had no variety of expression—she herself had no sense of variety. You may say that this was my business and was only a question of placing her. Yet I placed her in every conceivable position and she managed to obliterate their differences. She was always a lady certainly, and into the bargain was always the same lady. She was the real thing, but always the same thing. There were moments when I rather writhed under the serenity of her confidence that she *was* the real thing. All her dealings with me and all her husband's were an implication that this was lucky for *me*. Meanwhile I found myself trying to invent types that approached her own, instead of making her own transform itself—in the clever way that was not impossible for instance to poor Miss Churm. Arrange as I would and take the precautions I would, she always came out, in my pictures, too tall—landing me in the dilemma of having represented a fascinating woman as seven feet high, which (out of respect perhaps to my own very much scantier inches) was far from my idea of such a personage.

The case was worse with the Major—nothing I could do would keep *him* down, so that he became useful only for the representation of brawny giants. I adored variety and range, I cherished human accidents, the illustrative note; I wanted to characterize closely, and the thing in the world I most hated was the danger of being ridden by a type. I had quarrelled with some of my friends about it; I had parted company with them for maintaining that one *had* to be, and that if the type was beautiful—witness Raphael and Leonardo—the servitude was only a gain. I was neither Leonardo nor Raphael—I might only be a presumptuous young modern searcher; but I held that everything was to be sacrificed sooner than character. When they claimed that the obsessional form could easily *be* character I retorted, perhaps superficially, "Whose?" It couldn't be everybody's—it might end in being nobody's.

After I had drawn Mrs. Monarch a dozen times I felt surer even than before that the value of such a model as Miss Churm resided precisely in the fact that she had no positive stamp, combined of course with the other fact that what she did have was a curious and inexplicable talent for imitation. Her usual appearance was like a curtain which she could draw up at request for a capital performance. This performance was simply suggestive; but it was a word to the wise—it was vivid and pretty. Sometimes even I thought it, though she was plain herself, too insipidly pretty; I made it a reproach to her that the figures drawn from her were monotonously (*bêtement*,[4] as we used to say) graceful. Nothing made her more angry; it was so much her pride to feel she could sit for characters that had nothing in common with each other. She would accuse me at such moments of taking away her "reputytion."

It suffered a certain shrinkage, this queer quantity, from the repeated visits of my new friends. Miss Churm was greatly in demand, never in want of employment, so I had no scruple in putting her off occasionally, to try them more at my ease. It was certainly amusing at first to do the real thing—it was amusing to do Major Monarch's trousers. They *were* the real thing, even if he did come out colossal. It was amusing to do his wife's back hair—it was so mathematically neat—and the particular "smart" tension of her tight stays. She lent herself especially to positions in which the face was somewhat averted or blurred; she abounded in ladylike back views and *profils perdus*.[5] When she stood erect she took naturally one of the attitudes in which court-painters represent queens and princesses; so that I found myself wondering whether, to draw out this accomplishment, I couldn't get the editor of the *Cheapside* to publish a really royal romance, "A Tale of Buckingham Palace." Sometimes however the real thing and the make-believe came into contact; by which I mean that Miss Churm, keeping an appointment or coming to make one on days when I had much work in hand, encountered her invidious rivals. The encounter was not on their part, for they noticed her no more than if she had been the housemaid; not from intentional loftiness, but simply because as yet, professionally, they didn't know how to fraternize, as I could imagine they would have liked—or at least that the Major would. They couldn't talk about the omnibus—they always walked; and they didn't know what else to try—she wasn't interested in good trains or cheap claret. Besides, they must have felt—in the air—that she was amused at them, secretly derisive of their ever knowing how. She wasn't a person to conceal the limits of her faith if she had had a chance to show them. On the other hand Mrs. Monarch didn't think her tidy; for why else did she take pains to say to me—it was going out of the way, for Mrs. Monarch—that she didn't like dirty women?

---

[4] stupidly   [5] hidden profiles

One day when my young lady happened to be present with my other sitters—she even dropped in, when it was convenient, for a chat—I asked her to be so good as to lend a hand in getting tea, a service with which she was familiar and which was one of a class that, living as I did in a small way, with slender domestic resources, I often appealed to my models to render. They liked to lay hands on my property, to break the sitting, and sometimes the china—it made them feel Bohemian. The next time I saw Miss Churm after this incident she surprised me greatly by making a scene about it—she accused me of having wished to humiliate her. She hadn't resented the outrage at the time, but had seemed obliging and amused, enjoying the comedy of asking Mrs. Monarch, who sat vague and silent, whether she would have cream and sugar, and putting an exaggerated simper into the question. She had tried intonations—as if she too wished to pass for the real thing—till I was afraid my other visitors would take offense.

Oh they were determined not to do this and their touching patience was the measure of their great need. They would sit by the hour, uncomplaining, till I was ready to use them; they would come back on the chance of being wanted and would walk away cheerfully if it failed. I used to go to the door with them to see in what magnificent order they retreated. I tried to find other employment for them—I introduced them to several artists. But they didn't "take," for reasons I could appreciate, and I became rather anxiously aware that after such disappointments they fell back upon me with a heavier weight. They did me the honor to think me most *their* form. They weren't romantic enough for the painters, and in those days there were few serious workers in black-and-white. Besides, they had an eye to the great job I had mentioned to them—they had secretly set their hearts on supplying the right essence for my pictorial vindication of our fine novelist. They knew that for this undertaking I should want no costume-effects, none of the frippery of past ages —that it was a case in which everything would be contemporary and satirical and presumably genteel. If I could work them into it their future would be assured, for the labor would of course be long and the occupation steady.

One day Mrs. Monarch came without her husband—she explained his absence by his having had to go to the City. While she sat there in her usual relaxed majesty there came at the door a knock which I immediately recognised as the subdued appeal of a model out of work. It was followed by the entrance of a young man whom I at once saw to be a foreigner and who proved in fact an Italian acquainted with no English word but my name, which he uttered in a way that made it seem to include all others. I hadn't then visited his country, nor was I proficient in his tongue; but as he was not so meanly constituted—what Italian is?— as to depend only on that member for expression he conveyed to me, in familiar but graceful mimicry, that he was in search of exactly the employment in which the lady before me was engaged. I was not struck with him at first, and while I continued to draw I dropped few signs of interest or encouragement. He stood his ground however—not importunately, but with a dumb dog-like fidelity in his eyes that amounted to innocent impudence, the manner of a devoted servant—he might have been in the house for years—unjustly suspected. Suddenly it struck me that this very attitude and expression made a picture; whereupon I told him to sit down and wait till I should be free. There was another picture in the way he obeyed me, and I observed as I worked that there were others still in the way he looked wonderingly, with his head thrown back, about the high studio. He might have been crossing himself in Saint Peter's. Before I finished I said to myself "The fellow's a bankrupt orange-monger, but a treasure."

When Mrs. Monarch withdrew he passed across the room like a flash to open the door for her, standing there with the rapt pure gaze of the young Dante spellbound by the young Beatrice. As I never insisted, in such situations, on the blankness of the British domestic, I reflected that he had the making of a servant—and I needed one, but couldn't pay him to be only that—as well as of a model; in short I resolved to adopt my bright adventurer if he would agree to officiate in the double capacity. He jumped at my offer, and in the event my rashness—for I had really known nothing about him—wasn't brought home to me. He proved a sympathetic though a desultory ministrant, and had in a wonderful degree the *sentiment de la pose*. It was uncultivated, instinctive, a part of the happy instinct that had guided him to my door and helped him to spell out my name on the card nailed to it. He had had no other introduction to me than a guess, from the shape of my high north window, seen outside, that my place was a studio and that as a studio it would contain an artist. He had wandered to England in search of fortune, like other itinerants, and had embarked, with a partner and a small green hand-cart, on the sale of penny ices. The ices had melted away and the partner had dissolved in their train. My young man wore tight yellow trousers with reddish stripes and his name was Oronte. He was sallow but fair, and when I put him into some old clothes of my own he looked like an Englishman. He was as good as Miss Churm, who could look, when requested, like an Italian.

4

I thought Mrs. Monarch's face slightly convulsed when, on her coming back with her husband, she found Oronte installed. It was strange to have to recognize in a scrap of a lazzarone[6] a competitor to her magnificent Major. It was she who scented danger first, for the Major was anecdotically unconscious. But Oronte gave us tea, with a hundred eager confusions—he had never been concerned in so queer a process—and I think she thought better of me for having at last an "establishment."

---

[6] idler or beggar (Italian)

They saw a couple of drawings that I had made of the establishment, and Mrs. Monarch hinted that it never would have struck her he had sat for them. "Now the drawings you make from *us*, they look exactly like *us*," she reminded me, smiling in triumph; and I recognized that this was indeed just their defect. When I drew the Monarchs I couldn't anyhow get away from them—get into the character I wanted to represent; and I hadn't the least desire my model should be discoverable in my picture. Miss Churm never was, and Mrs. Monarch thought I hid her, very properly, because she was vulgar; whereas if she was lost it was only as the dead who go to heaven are lost—in the gain of an angel the more.

By this time I had got a certain start with "Rutland Ramsay," the first novel in the great projected series; that is I had produced a dozen drawings, several with the help of the Major and his wife, and I had sent them in for approval. My understanding with the publishers, as I have already hinted, had been that I was to be left to do my work, in this particular case, as I liked, with the whole book committed to me; but my connection with the rest of the series was only contingent. There were moments when, frankly, it *was* a comfort to have the real thing under one's hand; for there were characters in "Rutland Ramsay" that were very much like it. There were people presumably as erect as the Major and women of as good a fashion as Mrs. Monarch. There was a great deal of country-house life—treated, it is true, in a fine fanciful ironical generalized way—and there was a considerable implication of knickerbockers and kilts. There were certain things I had to settle at the outset; such things for instance as the exact appearance of the hero and the particular bloom and figure of the heroine. The author of course gave me a lead, but there was a margin for interpretation. I took the Monarchs into my confidence, I told them frankly what I was about, I mentioned my embarrassments and alternatives. "Oh, take *him*!" Mrs. Monarch murmured sweetly, looking at her husband; and "What could you want better than my wife?" the Major inquired with the comfortable candor that now prevailed between us.

I wasn't obliged to answer these remarks— I was only obliged to place my sitters. I wasn't easy in mind, and I postponed a little timidly perhaps the solving of my question. The book was a large canvas, the other figures were numerous, and I worked off at first some of the episodes in which the hero and the heroine were not concerned. When once I had set *them* up I should have to stick to them—I couldn't make my young man seven feet high in one place and five feet nine in another. I inclined on the whole to the latter measurement, though the Major more than once reminded me that *he* looked about as young as any one. It was indeed quite possible to arrange him, for the figure, so that it would have been difficult to detect his age. After the spontaneous Oronte had been with me a month, and after I had given him to understand several times over that his native exuberance would presently constitute an insurmountable barrier to our further intercourse, I waked to a sense of his heroic capacity. He was only five feet seven, but the remaining inches were latent. I tried him almost secretly at first, for I was really rather afraid of the judgment my other models would pass on such a choice. If they regarded Miss Churm as little better than a snare what would they think of the representation by a person so little the real thing as an Italian street-vendor of a protagonist formed by a public school?[7]

If I went a little in fear of them it wasn't because they bullied me, because they had got an oppressive foothold, but because in their really pathetic decorum and mysteriously permanent newness they counted on me so intensely. I was therefore very glad when Jack Hawley came home: he was always of such good counsel. He painted badly himself, but there was no one like him for putting his finger on the place. He had been absent from England for a year; he had been somewhere—I don't remember where—to get a fresh eye. I was in a good deal of dread of any such organ, but we were old friends; he had been away for months and a sense of emptiness was creeping into my life. I hadn't dodged a missile for a year.

He came back with a fresh eye, but with the same old black velvet blouse, and the first evening he spent in my studio we smoked cigarettes till the small hours. He had done no work himself, he had only got the eye; so the field was clear for the production of my little things. He wanted to see what I had produced for the *Cheapside*, but he was disappointed in the exhibition. That at least seemed the meaning of two or three comprehensive groans which, as he lounged on my big divan, his leg folded under him, looking at my latest drawings, issued from his lips with the smoke of the cigarette.

"What's the matter with you?" I asked.

"What's the matter with *you?*"

"Nothing save that I'm mystified."

"You are indeed. You're quite off the hinge. What's the meaning of this new fad?" And he tossed me, with visible irreverence, a drawing in which I happened to have depicted both my elegant models. I asked if he didn't think it good, and he replied that it struck him as execrable, given the sort of thing I had always represented myself to him as wishing to arrive at; but I let that pass—I was so anxious to see exactly what he meant. The two figures in the picture looked colossal, but I supposed this was *not* what he meant, inasmuch as, for aught he knew to the contrary, I might have been trying for some such effect. I maintained that I was working exactly in the same way as when he last had done me the honor to tell me I might do something some day. "Well, there's a screw loose somewhere," he answered; "wait a bit and I'll discover it." I depended upon him to do so: where else was the fresh eye? But he produced at last nothing more luminous than "I don't know—I don't like your types." This was lame for a critic who had never consented to discuss with me

[7] in England, what is called a private school in America

anything but the question of execution, the direction of strokes and the mystery of values.

"In the drawings you've been looking at I think my types are very handsome."

"Oh they won't do!"

"I've been working with new models."

"I see you have. *They* won't do."

"Are you very sure of that?"

"Absolutely—they're stupid."

"You mean *I* am—for I ought to get round that."

"You *can't*—with such people. Who are they?"

I told him, so far as was necessary, and he concluded heartlessly: "Ce sont des gens qu'il faut mettre à la porte."[8]

"You've never seen them; they're awfully good"—I flew to their defense.

"Not seen them? Why all this recent work of yours drops to pieces with them. It's all I want to see of them."

"No one else has said anything against it—the *Cheapside* people are pleased."

"Every one else is an ass, and the *Cheapside* people the biggest asses of all. Come, don't pretend at this time of day to have pretty illusions about the public, especially about publishers and editors. It's not for *such* animals you work—it's for those who know, *coloro che sanno*[9]; so keep straight for *me* if you can't keep straight for yourself. There was a certain sort of thing you used to try for—and a very good thing it was. But this twaddle isn't *in* it." When I talked with Hawley later about "Rutland Ramsay" and its possible successors he declared that I must get back into my boat again or I should go to the bottom. His voice in short was the voice of warning.

I noted the warning, but I didn't turn my friends out of doors. They bored me a good deal; but the very fact that they bored me admonished me not to sacrifice them—if there was anything to be done with them—simply to irritation. As I look back at this phase they seem to me to have pervaded my life not a little. I have a vision of them as most of the time in my studio, seated against the wall on an old velvet bench to be out of the way, and resembling the while a pair of patient courtiers in a royal ante-chamber. I'm convinced that during the coldest weeks of the winter they held their ground because it saved them fire. Their newness was losing its gloss, and it was impossible not to feel them objects of charity. Whenever Miss Churm arrived they went away, and after I was fairly launched in "Rutland Ramsay" Miss Churm arrived pretty often. They managed to express to me tacitly that they supposed I wanted her for the low life of the book, and I let them suppose it, since they had attempted

---

[8] These are the sort of people that you have to put out the door. (French)

[9] those who know (Italian)

to study the work—it was lying about the studio—without discovering that it dealt only with the highest circles. They had dipped into the most brilliant of our novelists without deciphering many passages. I still took an hour from them, now and again, in spite of Jack Hawley's warning: it would be time enough to dismiss them, if dismissal should be necessary, when the rigor of the season was over. Hawley had made their acquaintance—he had met them at my fireside—and thought them a ridiculous pair. Learning that he was a painter they tried to approach him, to show him too that they were the real thing; but he looked at them, across the big room, as if they were miles away; they were a compendium of everything he most objected to in the social system of his country. Such people as that, all convention and patent-leather, with ejaculations that stopped conversation, had no business in a studio. A studio was a place to learn to see, and how could you see through a pair of feather-beds?

The main inconvenience I suffered at their hands was that at first I was shy of letting it break upon them that my artful little servant had begun to sit to me for "Rutland Ramsay." They knew I had been odd enough —they were prepared by this time to allow oddity to artists—to pick a foreign vagabond out of the streets when I might have had a person with whiskers and credentials; but it was some time before they learned how high I rated his accomplishments. They found him in an attitude more than once, but they never doubted I was doing him as an organ-grinder. There were several things they never guessed, and one of them was that for a striking scene in the novel, in which a footman briefly figured, it occurred to me to make use of Major Monarch as the menial. I kept putting this off, I didn't like to ask him to don the livery—besides the difficulty of finding a livery to fit him. At last, one day late in the winter, when I was at work on the despised Oronte, who caught one's idea on the wing, and was in the glow of feeling myself go very straight, they came in, the Major and his wife, with their society laugh about nothing (there was less and less to laugh at); came in like country-callers—they always reminded me of that—who have walked across the park after church and are presently persuaded to stay to luncheon. Luncheon was over, but they could stay to tea—I knew they wanted it. The fit was on me, however, and I couldn't let my ardor cool and my work wait, with the fading daylight, while my model prepared it. So I asked Mrs. Monarch if she would mind laying it out—a request which for an instant brought all the blood to her face. Her eyes were on her husband's for a second, and some mute telegraphy passed between them. Their folly was over the next instant; his cheerful shrewdness put an end to it. So far from pitying their wounded pride, I must add, I was moved to give it as complete a lesson as I could. They bustled about together and got out the cups and saucers and made the kettle boil. I know they felt as if they were waiting on my servant, and when the tea was prepared I said: "He'll have a cup, please—he's tired." Mrs. Monarch brought him one where he stood, and he took it from her as if he had been a gentleman at a party squeezing a crush-hat with an elbow.

Then it came over me that she had made a great effort for me—made it with a kind of nobleness—and that I owed her a compensation. Each time I saw her after this I wondered what the compensation could be. I couldn't go on doing the wrong thing to oblige them. Oh it *was* the wrong thing, the stamp of the work for which they sat—Hawley was not the only person to say it now. I sent in a large number of the drawings I had made for "Rutland Ramsay," and I received a warning that was more to the point than Hawley's. The artistic adviser of the house for which I was working was of opinion that many of my illustrations were not what had been looked for. Most of these illustrations were the subjects in which the Monarchs had figured. Without going into the question of what *had* been looked for, I had to face the fact that at this rate I shouldn't get the other books to do. I hurled myself in despair on Miss Churm—I put her through all her paces. I not only adopted Oronte publicly as my hero, but one morning when the Major looked in to see if I didn't require him to finish a *Cheapside* figure for which he had begun to sit the week before, I told him I had changed my mind—I'd do the drawing from my man. At this my visitor turned pale and stood looking at me. "Is *he* your idea of an English gentleman?" he asked.

I was disappointed, I was nervous, I wanted to get on with my work; so I replied with irritation: "Oh my dear Major—I can't be ruined for *you!*"

It was a horrid speech, but he stood another moment—after which, without a word, he quitted the studio. I drew a long breath, for I said to myself that I shouldn't see him again. I hadn't told him definitely that I was in danger of having my work rejected, but I was vexed at his not having felt the catastrophe in the air, read with me the moral of our fruitless collaboration, the lesson that in the deceptive atmosphere of art even the highest respectability may fail of being plastic.

I didn't owe my friends money, but I did see them again. They reappeared together three days later, and, given all the other facts, there was something tragic in that one. It was a clear proof they could find nothing else in life to do. They had threshed the matter out in a dismal conference—they had digested the bad news that they were not in for the series. If they weren't useful to me even for the *Cheapside* their function seemed difficult to determine, and I could only judge at first that they had come, forgivingly, decorously, to take a last leave. This made me rejoice in secret that I had little leisure for a scene; for I had placed both my other models in position together and I was pegging away at a drawing from which I hoped to derive glory. It had been suggested by the passage in which Rutland Ramsay, drawing up a chair to Artemisia's piano-stool, says extraordinary things to her while she ostensibly fingers out a difficult piece of music. I had done Miss Churm at the piano before

—it was an attitude in which she knew how to take on an absolutely poetic grace. I wished the two figures to "compose" together with intensity, and my little Italian had entered perfectly into my conception.
The pair were vividly before me, the piano had been pulled out; it was
a charming show of blended youth and murmured love, which I had only
to catch and keep. My visitors stood and looked at it, and I was friendly
to them over my shoulder.

They made no response, but I was used to silent company and went on
with my work, only a little disconcerted—even though exhilarated by
the sense that *this* was at least the ideal thing—at not having got rid of
them after all. Presently I heard Mrs. Monarch's sweet voice beside or
rather above me: "I wish her hair were a little better done." I looked
up and she was staring with a strange fixedness at Miss Churm, whose
back was turned to her. "Do you mind my just touching it?" she went
on—a question which made me spring up for an instant as with the instinctive fear that she might do the young lady harm. But she quieted me
with a glance I shall never forget—I confess I should like to have been
able to paint *that*—and went for a moment to my model. She spoke to her
softly, laying a hand on her shoulder and bending over her; and as the
girl, understanding, gratefully assented, she disposed her rough curls,
with a few quick passes, in such a way as to make Miss Churm's head
twice as charming. It was one of the most heroic personal services I've
ever seen rendered. Then Mrs. Monarch turned away with a low sigh
and, looking about her as if for something to do, stooped to the floor with
a noble humility and picked up a dirty rag that had dropped out of my
paint-box.

The Major, meanwhile had also been looking for something to do,
and, wandering to the other end of the studio, saw before him my break-
fast-things neglected, unremoved. "I say, can't I be useful *here?*" he
called out to me with an irrepressible quaver. I assented with a laugh that
I fear was awkward, and for the next ten minutes, while I worked, I
heard the light clatter of china and the tinkle of spoons and glass. Mrs.
Monarch assisted her husband—they washed up my crockery, they put
it away. They wandered off into my little scullery, and I afterwards
found that they had cleaned my knives and that my slender stock of plate
had an unprecedented surface. When it came over me, the latent eloquence of what they were doing, I confess that my drawing was blurred
for a moment—the picture swam. They had accepted their failure, but
they couldn't accept their fate. They had bowed their heads in bewilderment to the perverse and cruel law in virtue of which the real thing could
be so much less precious than the unreal; but they didn't want to starve.
If my servants were my models, then my models might be my servants.
They would reverse the parts—the others would sit for the ladies and
gentlemen and *they* would do the work. They would still be in the studio
—it was an intense dumb appeal to me not to turn them out. "Take us
on," they wanted to say—"we'll do *anything*."

My pencil dropped from my hand; my sitting was spoiled and I got rid of my sitters, who were also evidently rather mystified and awe-struck. Then, alone with the Major and his wife I had a most uncomfortable moment. He put their prayer into a single sentence: "I say, you know—just let *us* do for you, can't you?" I couldn't—it was dreadful to see them emptying my slops; but I pretended I could, to oblige them, for about a week. Then I gave them a sum of money to go away, and I never saw them again. I obtained the remaining books, but my friend Hawley repeats that Major and Mrs. Monarch did me a permanent harm, got me into false ways. If it be true I'm content to have paid the price—for the memory.

Sarah Orne Jewett
1849–1909

A WHITE HERON

I

THE WOODS were already filled with shadows one June evening, just before eight o'clock, though a bright sunset still glimmered faintly among the trunks of the trees. A little girl was driving home her cow, a plodding, dilatory, provoking creature in her behavior, but a valued companion for all that. They were going away from the western light, and striking deep into the dark woods, but their feet were familiar with the path, and it was no matter whether their eyes could see it or not.

There was hardly a night the summer through when the old cow could be found waiting at the pasture bars; on the contrary, it was her greatest pleasure to hide herself away among the high huckleberry bushes, and though she wore a loud bell she had made the discovery that if one stood perfectly still it would not ring. So Sylvia had to hunt for her until she found her, and call Co'! Co'! with never an answering Moo, until her childish patience was quite spent. If the creature had not given good milk and plenty of it, the case would have seemed very different to her owners. Besides, Sylvia had all the time there was, and very little use to make of it. Sometimes in pleasant weather it was a consolation to look upon the cow's pranks as an intelligent attempt to play hide and seek, and as the child had no playmates she lent herself to this amusement with a good deal of zest. Though this chase had been so long that the wary animal herself had given an unusual signal of her whereabouts, Sylvia had only laughed when she came upon Mistress Moolly at the swamp-side, and urged her affectionately homeward with a twig of birch leaves. The old cow was not inclined to wander farther, she even turned in the right direction for once as they left the pasture, and stepped along the road at a good pace. She was quite ready to be milked now, and seldom stopped

to browse. Sylvia wondered what her grandmother would say because
they were so late. It was a great while since she had left home at half past
five o'clock, but everybody knew the difficulty of making this errand a
short one. Mrs. Tilley had chased the hornéd torment too many summer
evenings herself to blame any one else for lingering, and was only thankful as she waited that she had Sylvia, nowadays, to give such valuable
assistance. The good woman suspected that Sylvia loitered occasionally
on her own account; there never was such a child for straying about out-
of-doors since the world was made! Everybody said that it was a good
change for a little maid who had tried to grow for eight years in a
crowded manufacturing town, but, as for Sylvia herself, it seemed as if
she never had been alive at all before she came to live at the farm. She
thought often with wistful compassion of a wretched dry geranium that
belonged to a town neighbor.

   " 'Afraid of folks,' " old Mrs. Tilley said to herself, with a smile,
after she had made the unlikely choice of Sylvia from her daughter's
houseful of children, and was returning to the farm. " 'Afraid of folks,'
they said! I guess she won't be troubled no great with 'em up to the old
place!" When they reached the door of the lonely house and stopped to
unlock it, and the cat came to purr loudly, and rub against them, a deserted pussy, indeed, but fat with young robins, Sylvia whispered that
this was a beautiful place to live in, and she never should wish to go home.

The companions followed the shady woodroad, the cow taking slow
steps, and the child very fast ones. The cows stopped long at the brook
to drink, as if the pasture were not half a swamp, and Sylvia stood still
and waited, letting her bare feet cool themselves in the shoal water, while
the great twilight moths struck softly against her. She waded on through
the brook as the cow moved away, and listened to the thrushes with a
heart that beat fast with pleasure. There was a stirring in the great
boughs overhead. They were full of little birds and beasts that seemed
to be wide-awake, and going about their world, or else saying goodnight
to each other in sleepy twitters. Sylvia herself felt sleepy as she walked
along. However, it was not much farther to the house, and the air was
soft and sweet. She was not often in the woods so late as this, and it made
her feel as if she were a part of the gray shadows and the moving leaves.
She was just thinking how long it seemed since she first came to the farm
a year ago, and wondering if everything went on in the noisy town just
the same as when she was there; the thought of the great red-faced boy
who used to chase and frighten her made her hurry along the path to
escape from the shadow of the trees.

   Suddenly this little woods-girl is horror-stricken to hear a clear whistle
not very far away. Not a bird's whistle, which would have a sort of
friendliness, but a boy's whistle, determined, and somewhat aggressive.
Sylvia left the cow to whatever sad fate might await her, and stepped
discreetly aside into the bushes, but she was just too late. The enemy had

discovered her, and called out in a very cheerful and persuasive tone, "Halloa, little girl, how far is it to the road?" and trembling Sylvia answered almost inaudibly, "A good ways."

She did not dare to look boldly at the tall young man, who carried a gun over his shoulder, but she came out of her bush and again followed the cow, while he walked alongside.

"I have been hunting for some birds," the stranger said kindly, "and I have lost my way, and need a friend very much. Don't be afraid," he added gallantly. "Speak up and tell me what your name is, and whether you think I can spend the night at your house, and go out gunning early in the morning."

Sylvia was more alarmed than before. Would not her grandmother consider her much to blame? But who could have foreseen such an accident as this? It did not appear to be her fault, and she hung her head as if the stem of it were broken, but managed to answer "Sylvy," with much effort when her companion again asked her name.

Mrs. Tilley was standing in the doorway when the trio came into view. The cow gave a loud moo by way of explanation.

"Yes, you'd better speak up for yourself, you old trial! Where'd she tuck herself away this time, Sylvy?" Sylvia kept an awed silence; she knew by instinct that her grandmother did not comprehend the gravity of the situation. She must be mistaking the stranger for one of the farmer-lads of the region.

The young man stood his gun beside the door, and dropped a heavy game-bag beside it; then he bade Mrs. Tilley good-evening, and repeated his wayfarer's story, and asked if he could have a night's lodging.

"Put me anywhere you like," he said. "I must be off early in the morning, before day; but I am very hungry, indeed. You can give me some milk at any rate, that's plain."

"Dear sakes, yes," responded the hostess, whose long slumbering hospitality seemed to be easily awakened. "You might fare better if you went out on the main road a mile or so, but you're welcome to what we've got. I'll milk right off, and you make yourself at home. You can sleep on husks or feathers," she proffered graciously. "I raised them all myself. There's good pasturing for geese just below here towards the ma'sh. Now step round and set a plate for the gentleman, Sylvy!" And Sylvia promptly stepped. She was glad to have something to do, and she was hungry herself.

It was a surprise to find so clean and comfortable a little dwelling in this New England wilderness. The young man had known the horrors of its most primitive housekeeping, and the dreary squalor of that level of society which does not rebel at the companionship of hens. This was the best thrift of an old-fashioned farmstead, though on such a small scale that it seemed like a hermitage. He listened eagerly to the old woman's quaint talk, he watched Sylvia's pale face and shining gray eyes with ever growing enthusiasm, and insisted that this was the best supper he had eaten for a month; then, afterward, the new-made friends sat down in the doorway together while the moon came up.

Soon it would be berry-time, and Sylvia was a great help at picking. The cow was a good milker, though a plaguey thing to keep track of, the hostess gossiped frankly, adding presently that she had buried four children, so that Sylvia's mother, and a son (who might be dead) in California were all the children she had left. "Dan, my boy, was a great hand to go gunning," she explained sadly. "I never wanted for pa'tridges or gray squer'ls while he was to home. He's been a great wand'rer, I expect, and he's no hand to write letters. There, I don't blame him, I'd ha' seen the world myself if it had been so I could.

"Sylvia takes after him," the grandmother continued affectionately, after a minute's pause. "There ain't a foot o' ground she don't know her way over, and the wild creatur's counts her one o' themselves. Squer'ls she'll tame to come an' feed right out o' her hands, and all sorts o' birds. Last winter she got the jay-birds to bangeing[1] here, and I believe she'd 'a' scanted herself of her own meals to have plenty to throw out amongst 'em, if I hadn't kep' watch. Anything but crows, I tell her, I'm willin' to help support,—though Dan he went an' tamed one o' them that did seem to have reason same as folks. It was round here a good spell after he went away. Dan an' his father they didn't hitch,—but he never held up his head ag'in after Dan had dared him an' gone off."

The guest did not notice this hint of family sorrows in his eager interest in something else.

"So Sylvy knows all about birds, does she?" he exclaimed, as he looked round at the little girl who sat, very demure but increasingly sleepy, in the moonlight. "I am making a collection of birds myself. I have been at it ever since I was a boy." (Mrs. Tilley smiled.) "There are two or three very rare ones I have been hunting for these five years. I mean to get them on my own ground if they can be found."

"Do you cage 'em up?" asked Mrs. Tilley doubtfully, in response to this enthusiastic announcement.

"Oh, no, they're stuffed and preserved, dozens and dozens of them," said the ornithologist, "and I have shot or snared every one myself. I caught a glimpse of a white heron three miles from here on Saturday, and I have followed it in this direction. They have never been found in this district at all. The little white heron, it is," and he turned again to look at Sylvia with the hope of discovering that the rare bird was one of her acquaintances.

But Sylvia was watching a hop-toad in the narrow footpath.

"You would know the heron if you saw it," the stranger continued eagerly. "A queer tall white bird with soft feathers and long thin legs. And it would have a nest perhaps in the top of a high tree, made of sticks, something like a hawk's nest."

---

[1] loafing about (New England dialect)

Sylvia's heart gave a wild beat; she knew that strange white bird, and had once stolen softly near where it stood in some bright green swamp grass, away over at the other side of the woods. There was an open place where the sunshine always seemed strangely yellow and hot, where tall, nodding rushes grew, and her grandmother had warned her that she might sink in the soft black mud underneath and never be heard of more. Not far beyond were the salt marshes and beyond those was the sea, the sea which Sylvia wondered and dreamed about, but never had looked upon, though its great voice could often be heard above the noise of the woods on stormy nights.

"I can't think of anything I should like so much as to find that heron's nest," the handsome stranger was saying. "I would give ten dollars to anybody who could show it to me," he added desperately, "and I mean to spend my whole vacation hunting for it if need be. Perhaps it was only migrating, or had been chased out of its own region by some bird of prey."

Mrs. Tilley gave amazed attention to all this, but Sylvia still watched the toad, not divining, as she might have done at some calmer time, that the creature wished to get to its hole under the doorstep, and was much hindered by the unusual spectators at that hour of the evening. No amount of thought, that night, could decide how many wished-for treasures the ten dollars, so lightly spoken of, would buy.

The next day the young sportsman hovered about the woods, and Sylvia kept him company, having lost her first fear of the friendly lad, who proved to be most kind and sympathetic. He told her many things about the birds and what they knew and where they lived and what they did with themselves. And he gave her a jack-knife, which she thought as great a treasure as if she were a desert-islander. All day long he did not once make her troubled or afraid except when he brought down some unsuspecting singing creature from its bough. Sylvia would have liked him vastly better without his gun; she could not understand why he killed the very birds he seemed to like so much. But as the day waned, Sylvia still watched the young man with loving admiration. She had never seen anybody so charming and delightful; the woman's heart, asleep in the child, was vaguely thrilled by a dream of love. Some premonition of that great power stirred and swayed these young foresters who traversed the solemn woodlands with soft-footed silent care. They stopped to listen to a bird's song; they pressed forward again eagerly, parting the branches,—speaking to each other rarely and in whispers; the young man going first and Sylvia following, fascinated, a few steps behind, with her gray eyes dark with excitement.

She grieved because the longed-for white heron was elusive, but she did not lead the guest, she only followed, and there was no such thing as speaking first. The sound of her own unquestioned voice would have terrified her—it was hard enough to answer yes or no when there was need of that. At last evening began to fall, and they drove the cow home together, and Sylvia smiled with pleasure when they came to the place where she heard the whistle and was afraid only the night before.

2

Half a mile from home, at the farther edge of the woods, where the land was highest, a great pine-tree stood, the last of its generation. Whether it was left for a boundary mark, or for what reason, no one could say; the woodchoppers who had felled its mates were dead and gone long ago, and a whole forest of sturdy trees, pines and oaks and maples, had grown again. But the stately head of this old pine towered above them all and made a landmark for sea and shore miles and miles away. Sylvia knew it well. She had always believed that whoever climbed to the top of it could see the ocean; and the little girl had often laid her hand on the great rough trunk and looked up wistfully at those dark boughs that the wind always stirred, no matter how hot and still the air might be below. Now she thought of the tree with a new excitement, for why, if one climbed it at break of day, could not one see all the world, and easily discover whence the white heron flew, and mark the place, and find the hidden nest?

What a spirit of adventure, what wild ambition! What fancied triumph and delight and glory for the later morning when she could make known the secret! It was almost too real and too great for the childish heart to bear.

All night the door of the little house stood open, and the whippoorwills came and sang upon the very step. The young sportsman and his old hostess were sound asleep, but Sylvia's great design kept her broad awake and watching. She forgot to think of sleep. The short summer night seemed as long as the winter darkness, and at last when the whippoorwills ceased, and she was afraid the morning would after all come too soon, she stole out of the house and followed the pasture path through the woods, hastening toward the open ground beyond, listening with a sense of comfort and companionship to the drowsy twitter of a half-awakened bird, whose perch she had jarred in passing. Alas, if the great wave of human interest which flooded for the first time this dull little life should sweep away the satisfactions of an existence heart to heart with nature and the dumb life of the forest!

There was the huge tree asleep yet in the paling moonlight, and small and hopeful Sylvia began with utmost bravery to mount to the top of it, with tingling, eager blood coursing the channels of her whole frame, with her bare feet and fingers, that pinched and held like bird's claws to the monstrous ladder reaching up, up, almost to the sky itself. First she must mount the white oak tree that grew alongside, where she was almost lost among the dark branches and the green leaves heavy and wet with dew; a bird fluttered off its nest, and a red squirrel ran to and fro and scolded pettishly at the harmless housebreaker. Sylvia felt her way easily. She had often climbed there, and knew that higher still one of the oak's upper branches chafed against the pine trunk, just where its lower boughs were set close together. There, when she made the dangerous pass from one tree to the other, the great enterprise would really begin.

She crept out along the swaying oak limb at last, and took the daring step across into the old pine-tree. The way was harder than she thought; she must reach far and hold fast, the sharp dry twigs caught and held her and scratched her like angry talons, the pitch made her thin little fingers clumsy and stiff as she went round and round the tree's great stem, higher and higher upward. The sparrows and robins in the woods below were beginning to wake and twitter to the dawn, yet it seemed much lighter there aloft in the pine-tree, and the child knew that she must hurry if her project were to be of any use.

The tree seemed to lengthen itself out as she went up, and to reach farther and farther upward. It was like a great main-mast to the voyaging earth; it must truly have been amazed that morning through all its ponderous frame as it felt this determined spark of human spirit creeping and climbing from higher branch to branch. Who knows how steadily the least twigs held themselves to advantage this light, weak creature on her way! The old pine must have loved his new dependent. More than all the hawks, and bats, and moths, and even the sweet-voiced thrushes, was the brave, beating heart of the solitary gray-eyed child. And the tree stood still and held away the winds that June morning while the dawn grew bright in the east.

Sylvia's face was like a pale star, if one had seen it from the ground, when the last thorny bough was past, and she stood trembling and tired but wholly triumphant, high in the tree-top. Yes, there was the sea with the dawning sun making a golden dazzle over it, and toward that glorious east flew two hawks with slow-moving pinions. How low they looked in the air from that height when before one had only seen them far up, and dark against the blue sky. Their gray feathers were as soft as moths; they seemed only a little way from the tree, and Sylvia felt as if she too could go flying away among the clouds. Westward, the woodlands and farms reached miles and miles into the distance; here and there were church steeples, and white villages; truly it was a vast and awesome world.

The birds sang louder and louder. At last the sun came up bewilderingly bright. Sylvia could see the white sails of ships out at sea, and the clouds that were purple and rose-colored and yellow at first began to fade away. Where was the white heron's nest in the sea of green branches, and was this wonderful sight and pageant of the world the only reward for having climbed to such a giddy height? Now look down again, Sylvia, where the green marsh is set among the shining birches and dark hemlocks; there where you saw the white heron once you will see him again; look, look! a white spot of him like a single floating feather comes up from the dead hemlock and grows larger, and rises, and comes close at last, and goes by the landmark pine with steady sweep of

wing and outstretched slender neck and crested head. And wait! wait!
do not move a foot or a finger, little girl, do not send an arrow of light
and consciousness from your two eager eyes, for the heron has perched
on a pine bough not far beyond yours, and cries back to his mate on the
nest, and plumes his feathers for the new day!

The child gives a long sigh a minute later when a company of shouting
cat-birds comes also to the tree, and vexed by their fluttering and law-
lessness the solemn heron goes away. She knows his secret now, the wild,
light, slender bird that floats and wavers, and goes back like an arrow
presently to his home in the green world beneath. Then Sylvia, well
satisfied, makes her perilous way down again, not daring to look far below the branch she stands on, ready to cry sometimes because her fingers
ache and her lamed feet slip. Wondering over and over again what the
stranger would say to her, and what he would think when she told him
how to find his way straight to the heron's nest.

"Sylvy, Sylvy!" called the busy old grandmother again and again, but
nobody answered, and the small husk bed was empty, and Sylvia had
disappeared.

The guest waked from a dream, and remembering his day's pleasure
hurried to dress himself that it might sooner begin. He was sure from the
way the shy little girl looked once or twice yesterday that she had at
least seen the white heron, and now she must really be persuaded to tell.
Here she comes now, paler than ever, and her worn old frock is torn and
tattered, and smeared with pine pitch. The grandmother and the sportsman stand in the door together and question her, and the splendid moment
has come to speak of the dead hemlock-tree by the green marsh.

But Sylvia does not speak after all, though the old grandmother fret-
fully rebukes her, and the young man's kind appealing eyes are looking
straight in her own. He can make them rich with money; he has promised it, and they are poor now. He is so well worth making happy, and
he waits to hear the story she can tell.

No, she must keep silence! What is it that suddenly forbids her and
makes her dumb? Has she been nine years growing, and now, when the
great world for the first time puts out a hand to her, must she thrust it
aside for a bird's sake? The murmur of the pine's green branches is in
her ears, she remembers how the white heron came flying through the
golden air and how they watched the sea and the morning together, and
Sylvia cannot speak; she cannot tell the heron's secret and give its life
away.

Dear loyalty, that suffered a sharp pang as the guest went away disappointed later in the day, that could have served and followed him and
loved him as a dog loves! Many a night Sylvia heard the echo of his
whistle haunting the pasture path as she came home with the loitering
cow. She forgot even her sorrow at the sharp report of his gun and the

piteous sight of thrushes and sparrows dropping silent to the ground, their songs hushed and their pretty feathers stained and wet with blood. Were the birds better friends than their hunter might have been,—who can tell? Whatever treasures were lost to her, woodlands and summertime, remember! Bring your gifts and graces and tell your secrets to this lonely country child!

Joseph Conrad
1857–1924
YOUTH

THIS could have occurred nowhere but in England, where men and sea interpenetrate, so to speak—the sea entering into the life of most men, and the men knowing something or everything about the sea, in the way of amusement, of travel, or of bread-winning.

We were sitting round a mahogany table that reflected the bottle, the claret-glasses, and our faces as we leaned on our elbows. There was a director of companies, an accountant, a lawyer, Marlow, and myself. The director had been a *Conway* boy,[1] the accountant had served four years at sea, the lawyer—a fine crusted Tory, High Churchman, the best of old fellows, the soul of honor— had been chief officer in the P. & O.[2] service in the good old days when mail-boats were square-rigged at least on two masts, and used to come down the China Sea before a fair monsoon with stun'-sails set alow and aloft. We all began life in the merchant service. Between the five of us there was the strong bond of the sea, and also the fellowship of the craft, which no amount of enthusiasm for yachting, cruising, and so on can give, since one is only the amusement of life and the other is life itself.

Marlow (at least I think that is how he spelt his name) told the story, or rather the chronicle, of a voyage:—

"Yes, I have seen a little of the Eastern seas; but what I remember best is my first voyage there. You fellows know there are those voyages that seem ordered for the illustration of life, that might stand for a symbol of existence. You fight, work, sweat, nearly kill yourself, sometimes do kill yourself, trying to accomplish something—and you can't. Not from any fault of yours. You simply can do nothing, neither great nor little—not a thing in the world—not even marry an old maid, or get a wretched 600-ton cargo of coal to its port of destination.

"It was altogether a memorable affair. It was my first voyage to the East, and my first voyage as second mate; it was also my skipper's first

---

[1] one who has served on the frigate *Conway*, a training ship for sailors
[2] The Peninsular and Oriental Company

command. You'll admit it was time. He was sixty if a day; a little man, with a broad, not very straight back, with bowed shoulders and one leg more bandy than the other, he had that queer twisted-about appearance you see so often in men who work in the fields. He had a nut-cracker face—chin and nose trying to come together over a sunken mouth—and it was framed in iron-gray fluffy hair, that looked like a chin-strap of cotton-wool sprinkled with coal-dust. And he had blue eyes in that old face of his, which were amazingly like a boy's, with that candid expression some quite common men preserve to the end of their days by a rare internal gift of simplicity of heart and rectitude of soul. What induced him to accept me was a wonder. I had come out of a crack Australian clipper, where I had been third officer, and he seemed to have a prejudice against crack clippers as aristocratic and high-toned. He said to me, 'You know, in this ship you will have to work.' I said I had to work in every ship I had ever been in. 'Ah, but this is different, and you gentlemen out of them big ships; . . . but there! I dare say you will do. Join tomorrow.'

"I joined tomorrow. It was twenty-two years ago; and I was just twenty. How time passes! It was one of the happiest days of my life. Fancy! Second mate for the first time—a really responsible officer! I wouldn't have thrown up my new billet for a fortune. The mate looked me over carefully. He was also an old chap, but of another stamp. He had a Roman nose, a snow-white, long beard, and his name was Mahon, but he insisted that it should be pronounced Mann. He was well connected; yet there was something wrong with his luck, and he had never got on.

"As to the captain, he had been for years in coasters, then in the Mediterranean, and last in the West Indian trade. He had never been round the Capes. He could just write a kind of sketchy hand, and didn't care for writing at all. Both were thorough good seamen of course, and between those two old chaps I felt like a small boy between two grandfathers.

"The ship also was old. Her name was the *Judea*. Queer name, isn't it? She belonged to a man Wilmer, Wilcox—some name like that; but he has been bankrupt and dead these twenty years or more, and his name don't matter. She had been laid up in Shadwell basin for ever so long. You may imagine her state. She was all rust, dust, grime—soot aloft, dirt on deck. To me it was like coming out of a palace into a ruined cottage. She was about 400 tons, had a primitive windlass, wooden latches to the doors, not a bit of brass about her, and a big square stern. There was on it, below her name in big letters, a lot of scrollwork, with the gilt off, and some sort of a coat of arms, with the motto 'Do or Die' underneath. I remember it took my fancy immensely. There was a touch of romance in it, something that made me love the old thing—something that appealed to my youth!

"We left London in ballast—sand ballast—to load a cargo of coal in a northern port for Bangkok. Bangkok! I thrilled. I had been six years at sea, but had only seen Melbourne and Sydney, very good places, charming places in their way—but Bangkok!

"We worked out of the Thames under canvas, with a North Sea pilot on board. His name was Jermyn, and he dodged all day long about the galley drying his handkerchief before the stove. Apparently he never slept. He was a dismal man, with a perpetual tear sparkling at the end of his nose, who either had been in trouble, or was in trouble, or expected to be in trouble—couldn't be happy unless something went wrong. He mistrusted my youth, my common sense, and my seamanship, and made a point of showing it in a hundred little ways. I dare say he was right. It seems to me I knew very little then, and I know not much more now; but I cherish a hate for that Jermyn to this day.

"We were a week working up as far as Yarmouth Roads, and then we got into a gale—the famous October gale of twenty-two years ago. It was wind, lightning, sleet, snow, and a terrific sea. We were flying light, and you may imagine how bad it was when I tell you we had smashed bulwarks and a flooded deck. On the second night she shifted her ballast into the lee bow, and by that time we had been blown off somewhere on the Dogger Bank. There was nothing for it but go below with shovels and try to right her, and there we were in that vast hold, gloomy like a cavern, the tallow dips stuck and flickering on the beams, the gale howling above, the ship tossing about like mad on her side; there we all were, Jermyn, the captain, every one, hardly able to keep our feet, engaged on that gravedigger's work, and trying to toss shovelfuls of wet sand up to windward. At every tumble of the ship you could see vaguely in the dim light men falling down with a great flourish of shovels. One of the ship's boys (we had two), impressed by the weirdness of the scene, wept as if his heart would break. We could hear him blubbering somewhere in the shadows.

"On the third day the gale died out, and by and by a north-country tug picked us up. We took sixteen days in all to get from London to the Tyne! When we got into dock we had lost our turn for loading, and they hauled us off to a tier where we remained for a month. Mrs. Beard (the captain's name was Beard) came from Colchester to see the old man. She lived on board. The crew of runners had left, and there remained only the officers, one boy and the steward, a mulatto who answered to the name of Abraham. Mrs. Beard was an old woman, with a face all wrinkled and ruddy like a winter apple, and the figure of a young girl. She caught sight of me once, sewing on a button, and insisted on having my shirts to repair. This was something different from the captains' wives I had known on board crack clippers. When I brought her the shirts, she said: 'And the socks? They want mending, I am sure, and John's—Captain Beard's—things are all in order now. I would be glad of something to do.' Bless the old woman. She overhauled my outfit for me, and meantime I read for the first time *Sartor Resartus*[3] and Burnaby's *Ride to Khiva*.[4] I didn't understand much of the first then; but I remember I preferred the soldier to the philosopher at the time; a preference which life has only confirmed. One was a man, and the other was either more—or less. However, they are both dead and Mrs. Beard is dead, and youth, strength, genius, thoughts, achievements, simple hearts—all die. . . . No matter.

"They loaded us at last. We shipped a crew. Eight able seamen and two boys. We hauled off one evening to the buoys at the dockgates, ready to go out, and with a fair prospect of beginning the voyage next day. Mrs. Beard was to start for home by a late train. When the ship was fast we went to tea. We sat rather silent through the meal—Mahon, the old couple, and I. I finished first, and slipped away for a smoke, my cabin being in a deck-house just against the poop. It was high water, blowing fresh with a drizzle; the double dock-gates were opened, and the steam-colliers were going in and out in the darkness with their lights burning bright, a great plashing of propellers, rattling of winches, and a lot of hailing on the pier-heads. I watched the procession of head-lights gliding high and of green lights gliding low in the night, when suddenly a red gleam flashed at me, vanished, came into view again, and remained. The fore-end of a steamer loomed up close. I shouted down the cabin, 'Come up, quick!' and then heard a startled voice saying afar in the dark, 'Stop her, sir.' A bell jingled. Another voice cried warningly, 'We are going right into that barque, sir.' The answer to this was a gruff 'All right,' and the next thing was a heavy crash as the steamer struck a glancing blow with the bluff of her bow about our fore-rigging. There was a moment of confusion, yelling, and running about. Steam roared. Then somebody was heard saying, 'All clear, sir.' . . . 'Are you all right?' asked the gruff voice. I had jumped forward to see the damage, and hailed back, 'I think so.' 'Easy astern,' said the gruff voice. A bell jingled. 'What steamer is that?' screamed Mahon. By that time she was no more to us than a bulky shadow maneuvering a little way off. They shouted at us some name—a woman's name, Miranda or Melissa—or some such thing. 'This means another month in this beastly hole,' said Mahon to me, as we peered with lamps about the splintered bulwarks and broken braces. 'But where's the captain?'

"We had not heard or seen anything of him all that time. We went aft to look. A doleful voice arose hailing somewhere in the middle of the dark, '*Judea* ahoy!' . . . How the devil did he get there? . . . 'Hallo!' we shouted. 'I am adrift in our boat without oars,' he cried. A belated water-man offered his services, and Mahon struck a bargain with him for half-a-crown to tow our skipper alongside; but it was Mrs. Beard that

---

[3] "The tailor re-patched"—a work of romantic philosophy by Thomas Carlyle
[4] Frederick Gustavus Burnaby, 1842–1885, was primarily a cavalry officer and only incidentally a writer.

came up the ladder first. They had been floating about the dock in that mizzly cold rain for nearly an hour. I was never so surprised in my life.

"It appears that when he heard my shout 'Come up' he understood at once what was the matter, caught up his wife, ran on deck, and across, and down into our boat, which was fast to the ladder. Not bad for a sixty-year old. Just imagine that old fellow saving heroically in his arms that old woman—the woman of his life. He set her down on a thwart, and was ready to climb back on board when the painter came adrift somehow, and away they went together. Of course in the confusion we did not hear him shouting. He looked abashed. She said cheerfully, 'I suppose it does not matter my losing the train now?' 'No, Jenny—you go below and get warm,' he growled. Then to us: 'A sailor has no business with a wife—I say. There I was, out of the ship. Well, no harm done this time. Let's go and look at what that fool of a steamer smashed.'

"It wasn't much, but it delayed us three weeks. At the end of that time, the captain being engaged with his agents, I carried Mrs. Beard's bag to the railway-station and put her all comfy into a third-class carriage. She lowered the window to say, 'You are a good young man. If you see—John—Captain Beard —without his muffler at night, just remind him from me to keep his throat well wrapped up.' 'Certainly, Mrs. Beard,' I said. 'You are a good young man; I noticed how attentive you are to John—to Captain—' The train pulled out suddenly; I took my cap off to the old woman: I never saw her again. . . . Pass the bottle.

"We went to sea next day. When we made that start for Bangkok we had been already three months out of London. We had expected to be a fortnight or so—at the outside.

"It was January, and the weather was beautiful—the beautiful sunny winter weather that has more charm than in the summertime, because it is unexpected, and crisp, and you know it won't, it can't, last long. It's like a windfall, like a godsend, like an unexpected piece of luck.

"It lasted all down the North Sea, all down Channel; and it lasted till we were three hundred miles or so to the westward of the Lizards[5]: then the wind went round to the sou'west and began to pipe up. In two days it blew a gale. The *Judea*, hove to, wallowed on the Atlantic like an old candle-box. It blew day after day: it blew with spite, without interval, without mercy, without rest. The world was nothing but an immensity of great foaming waves rushing at us, under a sky low enough to touch with the hand and dirty like a smoked ceiling. In the stormy space surrounding us there was as much flying spray as air. Day after day and night after night there was nothing round the ship but the howl of the wind, the tumult of the sea, the noise of water pouring over her deck. There was no rest for her and no rest for us. She tossed, she pitched, she stood on her head, she sat on her tail, she rolled, she groaned, and we had

---

[5] Lizard Point in southwest Cornwall

to hold on while on deck and cling to our bunks when below, in a constant effort of body and worry of mind.

"One night Mahon spoke through the small window of my berth. It opened right into my bed, and I was lying there sleepless, in my boots, feeling as though I had not slept for years, and could not if I tried. He said excitedly—

" 'You got the sounding-rod in here, Marlow? I can't get the pumps to suck. By God! it's no child's play.'

"I gave him the sounding-rod and lay down again, trying to think of various things—but I thought only of the pumps. When I came on deck they were still at it, and my watch relieved at the pumps. By the light of the lantern brought on deck to examine the sounding-rod I caught a glimpse of their weary, serious faces. We pumped all the four hours. We pumped all night, all day, all the week—watch and watch. She was working herself loose, and leaked badly—not enough to drown us at once, but enough to kill us with the work at the pumps. And while we pumped the ship was going from us piecemeal: the bulwarks went, the stanchions were torn out, the ventilators smashed, the cabin-door burst in. There was not a dry spot in the ship. She was being gutted bit by bit. The long-boat changed, as if by magic, into matchwood where she stood in her gripes. I had lashed her myself, and was rather proud of my handiwork, which had withstood so long the malice of the sea. And we pumped. And there was no break in the weather. The sea was white like a sheet of foam, like a caldron of boiling milk; there was not a break in the clouds, no—not the size of a man's hand—no, not for so much as ten seconds. There was for us no sky, there were for us no stars, no sun, no universe—nothing but angry clouds and an infuriated sea. We pumped watch and watch, for dear life; and it seemed to last for months, for years, for all eternity, as though we had been dead and gone to a hell for sailors. We forgot the day of the week, the name of the month, what year it was, and whether we had ever been ashore. The sails blew away, she lay broadside on under a weather-cloth, the ocean poured over her, and we did not care. We turned those handles, and had the eyes of idiots. As soon as we had crawled on deck I used to take a round turn with a rope about the men, the pumps, and the mainmast, and we turned, we turned incessantly, with the water to our waists, to our necks, over our heads. It was all one. We had forgotten how it felt to be dry.

"And there was somewhere in me the thought: By Jove! this is the deuce of an adventure—something you read about; and it is my first voyage as second mate—and I am only twenty—and here I am lasting it out as well as any of these men, and keeping my chaps up to the mark. I was pleased. I would not have given up the experience for worlds. I had moments of exultation. Whenever the old dismantled craft pitched heavily with her counter high in the air, she seemed to me to throw up, like an appeal, like a defiance, like a cry to the clouds without mercy, the words written on her stern: '*Judea*, London. Do or Die.'

"O youth! The strength of it, the faith of it, the imagination of it! To me she was not an old rattletrap carting about the world a lot of coal for a freight—to me she was the endeavor, the test, the trial of life. I think of her with pleasure, with affection, with regret—as you would think of someone dead you have loved. I shall never forget her. . . . Pass the bottle.

"One night when tied to the mast, as I explained, we were pumping on, deafened with the wind, and without spirit enough in us to wish ourselves dead, a heavy sea crashed aboard and swept clean over us. As soon as I got my breath I shouted, as in duty bound, 'Keep on, boys!' when suddenly I felt something hard floating on deck strike the calf of my leg. I made a grab at it and missed. It was so dark we could not see each other's faces within a foot—you understand.

"After that thump the ship kept quiet for a while, and the thing, whatever it was, struck my leg again. This time I caught it—and it was a saucepan. At first, being stupid with fatigue and thinking of nothing but the pumps, I did not understand what I had in my hand. Suddenly it dawned upon me, and I shouted, 'Boys, the house on deck is gone. Leave this, and let's look for the cook.'

"There was a deck-house forward, which contained the galley, the cook's berth, and the quarters of the crew. As we had expected for days to see it swept away, the hands had been ordered to sleep in the cabin—the only safe place in the ship. The steward, Abraham, however, persisted in clinging to his berth, stupidly, like a mule—from sheer fright I believe, like an animal that won't leave a stable falling in an earthquake. So we went to look for him. It was chancing death, since once out of our lashings we were as exposed as if on a raft. But we went. The house was shattered as if a shell had exploded inside. Most of it had gone overboard—stove, men's quarters, and their property, all was gone; but two posts, holding a portion of the bulkhead to which Abraham's bunk was attached, remained as if by a miracle. We groped in the ruins and came upon this, and there he was, sitting in his bunk, surrounded by foam and wreckage, jabbering cheerfully to himself. He was out of his mind; completely and forever mad, with this sudden shock coming upon the fag-end of his endurance. We snatched him up, lugged him aft, and pitched him headfirst down the cabin companion. You understand there was no time to carry him down with infinite precautions and wait to see how he got on. Those below would pick him up at the bottom of the stairs all right. We were in a hurry to go back to the pumps. That business could not wait. A bad leak is an inhuman thing.

"One would think that the sole purpose of that fiendish gale had been to make a lunatic of that poor devil of a mulatto. It eased before morning, and next day the sky cleared, and as the sea went down the leak took up. When it came to bending a fresh set of sails the crew demanded to put back—and really there was nothing else to do. Boats gone, decks swept clean, cabin gutted, men without a stitch but what they stood in, stores spoiled, ship strained. We put her head for home, and—would you believe it? The wind came east right in our teeth. It blew fresh, it blew continuously. We had to beat up every inch of the way, but she did not leak so badly, the water keeping comparatively smooth. Two hours' pumping in every four is no joke—but it kept her afloat as far as Falmouth.

"The good people there live on casualties of the sea, and no doubt were glad to see us. A hungry crowd of shipwrights sharpened their chisels at the sight of that carcass of a ship. And, by Jove! they had pretty pickings off us before they were done. I fancy the owner was already in a tight place. There were delays. Then it was decided to take part of the cargo out and caulk her topsides. This was done, the repairs finished, cargo reshipped; a new crew came on board, and we went out—for Bangkok. At the end of a week we were back again. The crew said they weren't going to Bangkok—a hundred and fifty days' passage—in a something hooker that wanted pumping eight hours out of the twenty-four; and the nautical papers inserted again the little paragraph: '*Judea*. Bark. Tyne to Bangkok; coals; put back to Falmouth leaky and with crew refusing duty.'

"There were more delays—more tinkering. The owner came down for a day, and said she was as right as a fiddle. Poor old Captain Beard looked like the ghost of a Geordie[6] skipper—through the worry and humiliation of it. Remember he was sixty, and it was his first command. Mahon said it was a foolish business, and would end badly. I loved the ship more than ever, and wanted awfully to get to Bangkok. To Bangkok! Magic name, blessed name. Mesopotamia wasn't a patch on it. Remember I was twenty, and it was my first second-mate's billet, and the East was waiting for me.

"We went out and anchored in the outer roads with a fresh crew—the third. She leaked worse than ever. It was as if those confounded shipwrights had actually made a hole in her. This time we did not even go outside. The crew simply refused to man the windlass.

"They towed us back to the inner harbor, and we became a fixture, a feature, an institution of the place. People pointed us out to visitors as 'That 'ere barque that's going to Bangkok—has been here six months—put back three times.' On holidays the small boys pulling about in boats would hail, '*Judea*, ahoy!' and if a head showed above the rail shouted, 'Where you bound to?—Bangkok?' and jeered. We were only three on board. The poor old skipper mooned in the cabin. Mahon undertook the cooking, and unexpectedly developed all a Frenchman's genius for preparing nice little messes. I looked languidly after the rigging. We became citizens of Falmouth. Every shopkeeper knew us. At the barber's or tobacconist's they asked familiarly, 'Do you think you will ever get to Bangkok?' Meantime the owner, the underwriters, and the charterers

---

⁶ a collier-boat

squabbled amongst themselves in London, and our pay went on. . . .
Pass the bottle.

"It was horrid. Morally it was worse than pumping for life. It seemed
as though we had been forgotten by the world, belonged to nobody,
would get nowhere; it seemed that, as if bewitched, we would have to
live for ever and ever in that inner harbor, a derision and a byword to
generations of long-shore loafers and dishonest boatmen. I obtained three
months' pay and a five days' leave, and made a rush for London. It took
me a day to get there and pretty well another to come back—but three
months' pay went all the same. I don't know what I did with it. I went to
a music-hall, I believe, lunched, dined, and supped in a swell place in Re-
gent Street, and was back in time, with nothing but a complete set of
Byron's works and a new railway rug to show for three months' work.
The boat-man who pulled me off to the ship said: 'Hallo! I thought you
had left the old thing. *She* will never get to Bangkok.' 'That's all *you*
know about it,' I said scornfully—but I didn't like that prophecy at all.

"Suddenly a man, some kind of agent to somebody, appeared with full
powers. He had grog-blossoms all over his face, an indomitable energy,
and was a jolly soul. We leaped into life again. A hulk came alongside,
took our cargo, and then we went into dry dock to get our copper
stripped. No wonder she leaked. The poor thing, strained beyond endurance by the gale, had, as if in disgust, spat out all the oakum of her
lower seams. She was recaulked, new coppered, and made as tight as a
bottle. We went back to the hulk and reshipped our cargo.

"Then, on a fine moonlight night, all the rats left the ship.

"We had been infested with them. They had destroyed our sails,
consumed more stores than the crew, affably shared our beds and our
dangers, and now, when the ship was made seaworthy, concluded to
clear out. I called Mahon to enjoy the spectacle. Rat after rat appeared
on our rail, took a last look over his shoulder, and leaped with a hollow
thud into the empty hulk. We tried to count them, but soon lost the tale.
Mahon said: 'Well, well! don't talk to me about the intelligence of rats.
They ought to have left before, when we had that narrow squeak from
foundering. There you have the proof how silly is the superstition about
them. They leave a good ship for an old rotten hulk, where there is nothing to eat, too, the fools! . . . I don't believe they know what is safe or
what is good for them, any more than you or I.'

"And after some more talk we agreed that the wisdom of rats had
been grossly overrated, being in fact no greater than that of men.

"The story of the ship was known, by this, all up the Channel from
Land's End to the Forelands, and we could get no crew on the south
coast. They sent us one all complete from Liverpool, and we left once
more—for Bangkok.

"We had fair breezes, smooth water right into the tropics, and the old
Judea lumbered along in the sunshine. When she went eight knots everything cracked aloft, and we tied our caps to our heads; but mostly she

strolled on at the rate of three miles an hour. What could you expect? She was tired—that old ship. Her youth was where mine is—where yours is—you fellows who listen to this yarn; and what friend would throw your years and your weariness in your face? We didn't grumble at her. To us aft, at least, it seemed as though we had been born in her, reared in her, had lived in her for ages, had never known any other ship. I would just as soon have abused the old village church at home for not being a cathedral.

"And for me there was also my youth to make me patient. There was all the East before me, and all life, and the thought that I had been tried in that ship and had come out pretty well. And I thought of men of old who, centuries ago, went that road in ships that sailed no better, to the land of palms, and spices, and yellow sands, and of brown nations ruled by kings more cruel than Nero the Roman, and more splendid than Solomon the Jew. The old bark lumbered on, heavy with her age and the burden of her cargo, while I lived the life of youth in ignorance and hope. She lumbered on through an interminable procession of days; and the fresh gilding flashed back at the setting sun, seemed to cry out over the darkening sea the words painted on her stern, '*Judea*, London. Do or Die.'

"Then we entered the Indian Ocean and steered northerly for Java Head. The winds were light. Weeks slipped by. She crawled on, do or die, and people at home began to think of posting us as overdue.

"One Saturday evening, I being off duty, the men asked me to give them an extra bucket of water or so—for washing clothes. As I did not wish to screw on the fresh-water pump so late, I went forward whistling, and with a key in my hand to unlock the forepeak scuttle, intending to serve the water out of a spare tank we kept there.

"The smell down below was as unexpected as it was frightful. One would have thought hundreds of paraffin-lamps had been flaring and smoking in that hole for days. I was glad to get out. The man with me coughed and said, 'Funny smell, sir.' I answered negligently, 'It's good for the health they say,' and walked aft.

"The first thing I did was to put my head down the square of the midship ventilator. As I lifted the lid a visible breath, something like a thin fog, a puff of faint haze, rose from the opening. The ascending air was hot, and had a heavy, sooty, paraffiny smell. I gave one sniff, and put down the lid gently. It was no use choking myself. The cargo was on fire.

"Next day she began to smoke in earnest. You see it was to be expected, for though the coal was of a safe kind, that cargo had been so handled, so broken up with handling, that it looked more like smithy coal than anything else. Then it had been wetted—more than once. It rained all the time we were taking it back from the hulk, and now with this long passage it got heated, and there was another case of spontaneous combustion.

"The captain called us into the cabin. He had a chart spread on the table, and looked unhappy. He said, 'The coast of West Australia is near, but I mean to proceed to our destination. It is the hurricane month, too; but we will just keep her head for Bangkok, and fight the fire. No more putting back anywhere, if we all get roasted. We will try first to stifle this 'ere damned combustion by want of air.'

"We tried. We battened down everything, and still she smoked. The smoke kept coming out through imperceptible crevices; it forced itself through bulkheads and covers; it oozed here and there and everywhere in slender threads, in an invisible film, in an incomprehensible manner. It made its way into the cabin, into the forecastle; it poisoned the sheltered places on the deck, it could be sniffed as high as the mainyard. It was clear that if the smoke came out the air came in. This was disheartening. This combustion refused to be stifled.

"We resolved to try water, and took the hatches off. Enormous volumes of smoke, whitish, yellowish, thick, greasy, misty, choking, ascended as high as the trucks. All hands cleared out aft. Then the poisonous cloud blew away, and we went back to work in a smoke that was no thicker now than that of an ordinary factory chimney.

"We rigged the force-pump, got the hose along, and by and by it burst. Well, it was as old as the ship—a prehistoric hose, and past repair. Then we pumped with the feeble head-pump, drew water with buckets, and in this way managed in time to pour lots of Indian Ocean into the main hatch. The bright stream flashed in sunshine, fell into a layer of white crawling smoke, and vanished on the black surface of coal. Steam ascended mingling with the smoke. We poured salt water as into a barrel without a bottom. It was our fate to pump in that ship, to pump out of her, to pump into her; and after keeping water out of her to save ourselves from being drowned, we frantically poured water into her to save ourselves from being burned.

"And she crawled on, do or die, in the serene weather. The sky was a miracle of purity, a miracle of azure. The sea was polished, was blue, was pellucid, was sparkling like a precious stone, extending on all sides, all round to the horizon—as if the whole terrestrial globe had been one jewel, one colossal sapphire, a single gem fashioned into a planet. And on the luster of the great calm waters the *Judea* glided imperceptibly, enveloped in languid and unclean vapors, in a lazy cloud that drifted to leeward, light and slow; a pestiferous cloud defiling the splendor of sea and sky.

"All this time of course we saw no fire. The cargo smoldered at the bottom somewhere. Once Mahon, as we were working side by side, said to me with a queer smile: 'Now, if she only would spring a tidy leak—like that time when we first left the Channel—it would put a stopper on this fire. Wouldn't it?' I remarked irrelevantly, 'Do you remember the rats?'

"We fought the fire and sailed the ship too as carefully as though nothing had been the matter. The steward cooked and attended on us.

Of the other twelve men, eight worked while four rested. Everyone took his turn, captain included. There was equality, and if not exactly fraternity, then a deal of good feeling. Sometimes a man, as he dashed a bucketful of water down the hatchway, would yell out, 'Hurrah for Bangkok!' and the rest laughed. But generally we were taciturn and serious—and thirsty. Oh! how thirsty! And we had to be careful with the water. Strict allowance. The ship smoked, the sun blazed. . . . Pass the bottle.

"We tried everything. We even made an attempt to dig down to the fire. No good, of course. No man could remain more than a minute below. Mahon, who went first, fainted there, and the man who went to fetch him out did likewise. We lugged them out on deck. Then I leaped down to show how easily it could be done. They had learned wisdom by that time, and contented themselves by fishing for me with a chain-hook tied to a broom-handle, I believe. I did not offer to go and fetch up my shovel, which was left down below.

"Things began to look bad. We put the long-boat into the water. The second boat was ready to swing out. We had also another, a 14-foot thing, on davits aft, where it was quite safe.

"Then, behold, the smoke suddenly decreased. We redoubled our efforts to flood the bottom of the ship. In two days there was no smoke at all. Everybody was on the broad grin. This was on a Friday. On Saturday no work, but sailing the ship of course, was done. The men washed their clothes and their faces for the first time in a fortnight, and had a special dinner given them. They spoke of spontaneous combustion with contempt, and implied *they* were the boys to put out combustions. Somehow we all felt as though we each had inherited a large fortune. But a beastly smell of burning hung about the ship. Captain Beard had hollow eyes and sunken cheeks. I had never noticed so much before how twisted and bowed he was. He and Mahon prowled soberly about hatches and ventilators, sniffing. It struck me suddenly poor Mahon was a very, very old chap. As to me, I was as pleased and proud as though I had helped to win a great naval battle. O! Youth!

"The night was fine. In the morning a homeward-bound ship passed us hull down—the first we had seen for months; but we were nearing the land at last, Java Head being about 190 miles off, and nearly due north.

"Next day it was my watch on deck from eight to twelve. At breakfast the captain observed, 'It's wonderful how that smell hangs about the cabin.' About ten, the mate being on the poop, I stepped down on the main-deck for a moment. The carpenter's bench stood abaft the mainmast: I leaned against it sucking at my pipe, and the carpenter, a young chap, came to talk to me. He remarked, 'I think we have done very well, haven't we?' and then I perceived with annoyance the fool was trying to tilt the bench. I said curtly, 'Don't, Chips,' and immediately became aware of a queer sensation, of an absurd delusion,—I seemed somehow to be in the air. I heard all round me like a pent-up breath released—as if a thousand giants simultaneously had said Phoo!—and felt a dull concussion which made my ribs ache suddenly. No doubt about it—I was in the air, and my body was describing a short parabola. But short as it was, I had the time to think several thoughts in, as far as I can remember, the following order : 'This can't be the carpenter—What is it?—Some accident—Submarine volcano?—Coals, gas!—By Jove! we are being blown up—Everybody's dead—I am falling into the afterhatch—I see fire in it.'

"The coal-dust suspended in the air of the hold had glowed dull-red at the moment of the explosion. In the twinkling of an eye, in an infinitesimal fraction of a second since the first tilt of the bench, I was sprawling full length on the cargo. I picked myself up and scrambled out. It was quick like a rebound. The deck was a wilderness of smashed timber, lying crosswise like trees in a wood after a hurricane; an immense curtain of soiled rags waved gently before me—it was the mainsail blown to strips. I thought, The masts will be toppling over directly; and to get out of the way bolted on all-fours towards the poop-ladder. The first person I saw was Mahon, with eyes like saucers, his mouth open, and the long white hair standing straight on end round his head like a silver halo. He was just about to go down when the sight of the main-deck stirring, heaving up, and changing into splinters before his eyes, petrified him on the top step. I stared at him in unbelief, and he stared at me with a queer kind of shocked curiosity. I did not know that I had no hair, no eyebrows, no eyelashes, that my young moustache was burnt off, that my face was black, one cheek laid open, my nose cut, and my chin bleeding. I had lost my cap, one of my slippers, and my shirt was torn to rags. Of all this I was not aware. I was amazed to see the ship still afloat, the poop-deck whole—and, most of all, to see anybody alive. Also the peace of the sky and the serenity of the sea were distinctly surprising. I suppose I expected to see them convulsed with horror. . . . Pass the bottle.

"There was a voice hailing the ship from somewhere—in the air, in the sky—I couldn't tell. Presently I saw the captain—and he was mad. He asked me eagerly, 'Where's the cabin-table?' and to hear such a question was a frightful shock. I had just been blown up, you understand, and vibrated with that experience,—I wasn't quite sure whether I was alive. Mahon began to stamp with both feet and yelled at him, 'Good God! don't you see the deck's blown out of her?' I found my voice, and stammered out as if conscious of some gross neglect of duty, 'I don't know where the cabin-table is.' It was like an absurd dream.

"Do you know what he wanted next? Well, he wanted to trim the yards. Very placidly, and as if lost in thought, he insisted on having the foreyard squared. 'I don't know if there's anybody alive,' said Mahon, almost tearfully. 'Surely,' he said, gently, 'there will be enough left to square the foreyard.'

"The old chap, it seems, was in his own berth winding up the chronometers, when the shock sent him spinning. Immediately it occurred to

him—as he said afterwards—that the ship had struck something, and he
ran out into the cabin. There, he saw, the cabin-table had vanished somewhere. The deck being blown up, it had fallen down into the lazarette[7]
of course. Where we had our breakfast that morning he saw only a great
hole in the floor. This appeared to him so awfully mysterious, and impressed him so immensely, that what he saw and heard after he got on
deck were mere trifles in comparison. And, mark, he noticed directly
the wheel deserted and his bark off her course—and his only thought
was to get that miserable, stripped, undecked, smoldering shell of a ship
back again with her head pointing at her port of destination. Bangkok!
That's what he was after. I tell you this quiet, bowed, bandy-legged, almost deformed little man was immense in the singleness of his idea and
in his placid ignorance of our agitation. He motioned us forward with a
commanding gesture, and went to take the wheel himself.

"Yes; that was the first thing we did—trim the yards of that wreck!
No one was killed, or even disabled, but everyone was more or less hurt.
You should have seen them! Some were in rags, with black faces, like
coal-heavers, like sweeps, and had bullet heads that seemed closely
cropped, but were in fact singed to the skin. Others, of the watch below,
awakened by being shot out from their collapsing bunks, shivered incessantly, and kept on groaning even as we went about our work. But
they all worked. That crew of Liverpool hard cases had in them the right
stuff. It's my experience they always have. It is the sea that gives it—the
vastness, the loneliness surrounding their dark stolid souls. Ah! Well!
we stumbled, we crept, we fell, we barked our shins on the wreckage, we
hauled. The masts stood, but we did not know how much they might be
charred down below. It was nearly calm, but a long swell ran from the
west and made her roll. They might go at any moment. We looked at
them with apprehension. One could not foresee which way they would
fall.

"Then we retreated aft and looked about us. The deck was a tangle
of planks on edge, of planks on end, of splinters, of ruined woodwork.
The masts rose from that chaos like big trees above a matted undergrowth. The interstices of that mass of wreckage were full of something
whitish, sluggish, stirring—of something that was like a greasy fog. The
smoke of the invisible fire was coming up again, was trailing, like a poisonous thick mist in some valley choked with dead wood. Already lazy
wisps were beginning to curl upwards amongst the mass of splinters.
Here and there a piece of timber, stuck upright, resembled a post. Half
of a fiferail had been shot through the foresail, and the sky made a patch
of glorious blue in the ignobly soiled canvas. A portion of several boards
holding together had fallen across the rail, and one end protruded overboard, like a gangway leading upon nothing, like a gangway leading over
the deep sea, leading to death—as if inviting us to walk the plank at once

[7] a storeroom between decks

and be done with our ridiculous troubles. And still the air, the sky—a ghost, something invisible was hailing the ship.

"Someone had the sense to look over, and there was the helmsman, who had impulsively jumped overboard, anxious to come back. He yelled and swam lustily like a merman, keeping up with the ship. We threw him a rope, and presently he stood amongst us streaming with water and very crestfallen. The captain had surrendered the wheel, and apart, elbow on rail and chin in hand, gazed at the sea wistfully. We asked ourselves, What next? I thought, Now, this is something like. This is great. I wonder what will happen. O youth!

"Suddenly Mahon sighted a steamer far astern. Captain Beard said, 'We may do something with her yet.' We hoisted two flags, which said in the international language of the sea, 'On fire. Want immediate assistance.' The steamer grew bigger rapidly, and by and by spoke with two flags on her foremast, 'I am coming to your assistance.'

"In half an hour she was abreast, to windward, within hail, and rolling slightly, with her engines stopped. We lost our composure, and yelled all together with excitement, 'We've been blown up.' A man in a white helmet, on the bridge, cried, 'Yes! All right! all right!' and he nodded his head, and smiled, and made soothing motions with his hand as though at a lot of frightened children. One of the boats dropped in the water, and walked towards us upon the sea with her long oars. Four Calashes pulled a swinging stroke. This was my first sight of Malay seamen. I've known them since, but what struck me then was their unconcern: they came alongside, and even the bowman standing up and holding to our mainchains with the boat-hook did not deign to lift his head for a glance. I thought people who had been blown up deserved more attention.

"A little man, dry like a chip and agile like a monkey, clambered up. It was the mate of the steamer. He gave one look, and cried, 'O boys—you had better quit.'

"We were silent. He talked apart with the captain for a time,—seemed to argue with him. Then they went away together to the steamer.

"When our skipper came back we learned that the steamer was the *Somerville*, Captain Nash, from West Australia to Singapore *via* Batavia with mails, and that the agreement was she should tow us to Anjer or Batavia, if possible, where we could extinguish the fire by scuttling, and then proceed on our voyage—to Bangkok! The old man seemed excited. 'We will do it yet,' he said to Mahon, fiercely. He shook his fist at the sky. Nobody else said a word.

"A noon the steamer began to tow. She went ahead slim and high, and what was left of the *Judea* followed at the end of seventy fathom of tow-rope,—followed her swiftly like a cloud of smoke with mast-heads protruding above. We went aloft to furl the sails. We coughed on the yards, and were careful about the bunts. Do you see the lot of us there, putting a neat furl on the sails of that ship doomed to arrive nowhere? There was not a man who didn't think that at any moment the masts would topple over. From aloft we could not see the ship for smoke, and they worked carefully, passing the gaskets with even turns. 'Harbor furl—aloft there!' cried Mahon from below.

"You understand this? I don't think one of those chaps expected to get down in the usual way. When we did I heard them saying to each other, 'Well, I thought we would come down overboard, in a lump—sticks and all—blame me if I didn't.' 'That's what I was thinking to myself,' would answer wearily another battered and bandaged scarecrow. And, mind, these were men without the drilled-in habit of obedience. To an onlooker they would be a lot of profane scallywags without a redeeming point. What made them do it—what made them obey me when I, thinking consciously how fine it was, made them drop the bunt of the forsail twice to try and do it better? What? They had no professional reputation—no examples, no praise. It wasn't a sense of duty; they all knew well enough how to shirk, and laze, and dodge—when they had a mind to it—and mostly they had. Was it the two pounds ten a-month that sent them there? They didn't think their pay half good enough. No; it was something in them, something inborn and subtle and everlasting. I don't say positively that the crew of a French or German merchantman wouldn't have done it, but I doubt whether it would have been done in the same way. There was a completeness in it, something solid like a principle, and masterful like an instinct—a disclosure of something secret—of that hidden something, that gift of good or evil that makes racial difference, that shapes the fate of nations.

"It was that night at ten that, for the first time since we had been fighting it, we saw the fire. The speed of the towing had fanned the smoldering destruction. A blue gleam appeared forward, shining below the wreck of the deck. It wavered in patches, it seemed to stir and creep like the light of a glowworm. I saw it first, and told Mahon. 'Then the game's up,' he said. 'We had better stop this towing, or she will burst out suddenly fore and aft before we can clear out.' We set up a yell; rang bells to attract their attention; they towed on. At last Mahon and I had to crawl forward and cut the rope with an axe. There was no time to cast off the lashings. Red tongues could be seen licking the wilderness of splinters under our feet as we made our way back to the poop.

"Of course they very soon found out in the steamer that the rope was gone. She gave a loud blast of her whistle, her lights were seen sweeping in a wide circle, she came up ranging close alongside, and stopped. We were all in a tight group on the poop looking at her. Every man had saved a little bundle or a bag. Suddenly a conical flame with a twisted top shot up forward and threw upon the black sea a circle of light, with the two vessels side by side and heaving gently in its centre. Captain Beard had been sitting on the gratings still and mute for hours, but now he rose slowly and advanced in front of us, to the mizzen-shrouds. Captain Nash hailed: 'Come along! Look sharp. I have mail-bags on board. I will take you and your boats to Singapore.'

" 'Thank you! No!' said our skipper. 'We must see the last of the ship.'

" 'I can't stand by any longer,' shouted the other. 'Mails—you know.'

" 'Ay! ay! We are all right.'

" 'Very well! I'll report you in Singapore. . . . Good-bye!'

"He waved his hand. Our men dropped their bundles quietly. The steamer moved ahead, and passing out of the circle of light, vanished at once from our sight, dazzled by the fire which burned fiercely. And then I knew that I would see the East first as commander of a small boat. I thought it fine; and the fidelity to the old ship was fine. We should see the last of her. Oh, the glamor of youth! Oh! the fire of it, more dazzling than the flames of the burning ship, throwing a magic light on the wide earth, leaping audaciously to the sky, presently to be quenched by time, more cruel, more pitiless, more bitter than the sea—and like the flames of the burning ship surrounded by an impenetrable night.

"The old man warned us in his gentle and inflexible way that it was part of our duty to save for the underwriters as much as we could of the ship's gear. Accordingly we went to work aft, while she blazed forward to give us plenty of light. We lugged out a lot of rubbish. What didn't we save? An old barometer fixed with an absurd quantity of screws nearly cost me my life: a sudden rush of smoke came upon me, and I just got away in time. There were various stores, bolts of canvas, coils of rope; the poop looked like a marine bazaar, and the boats were lumbered to the gunwales. One would have thought the old man wanted to take as much as he could of his first command with him. He was very, very quiet, but off his balance evidently. Would you believe it? He wanted to take a length of old stream-cable and a kedge-anchor with him in the long-boat. We said, 'Ay, ay, sir,' deferentially, and on the quiet let the things slip overboard. The heavy medicine-chest went that way, two bags of green coffee, tins of paint—fancy, paint!—a whole lot of things. Then I was ordered with two hands into the boats to make a stowage and get them ready against the time it would be proper for us to leave the ship.

"We put everything straight, stepped the long-boat's mast for our skipper, who was to take charge of her, and I was not sorry to sit down for a moment. My face felt raw, every limb ached as if broken, I was aware of all my ribs, and would have sworn to a twist in the backbone. The boats, fast astern, lay in a deep shadow, and all around I could see the circle of the sea lighted by the fire. A gigantic flame arose forward straight and clear. It flared fierce, with noises like the whirr of wings, with rumbles as of thunder. There were cracks, detonations, and from the cone of flame the sparks flew upwards, as man is born to trouble, to leaky ships, and to ships that burn.

"What bothered me was that the ship, lying broadside to the swell and to such wind as there was—a mere breath—the boats would not keep astern where they were safe, but persisted, in a pig-headed way boats have, in getting under the counter and then swinging alongside. They were knocking about dangerously and coming near the flame, while the ship rolled on them, and, of course, there was always the danger of the masts going over the side at any moment. I and my two boat-keepers kept them off as best we could, with oars and boat-hooks; but to be constantly at it became exasperating, since there was no reason why we should not leave at once. We could not see those on board, nor could we imagine what caused the delay. The boat-keepers were swearing feebly, and I had not only my share of the work but also had to keep at it two men who showed a constant inclination to lay themselves down and let things slide.

"At last I hailed, 'On deck there,' and someone looked over. 'We're ready here,' I said. The head disappeared, and very soon popped up again. 'The captain says, All right, sir, and to keep the boats well clear of the ship.'

"Half an hour passed. Suddenly there was a frightful racket, rattle, clanking of chain, hiss of water, and millions of sparks flew up into the shivering column of smoke that stood leaning slightly above the ship. The cat-heads had burned away, and the two red-hot anchors had gone to the bottom, tearing out after them two hundred fathom of red-hot chain. The ship trembled, the mass of flame swayed as if ready to collapse, and the fore top-gallant-mast fell. It darted down like an arrow of fire, shot under, and instantly leaping up within an oar's-length of the boats, floated quietly, very black on the luminous sea. I hailed the deck again. After some time a man in an unexpectedly cheerful but also muffled tone, as though he had been trying to speak with his mouth shut, informed me, 'Coming directly, sir,' and vanished. For a long time I heard nothing but the whirr and roar of the fire. There were also whistling sounds. The boats jumped, tugged at the painters, ran at each other playfully, knocked their sides together, or, do what we would, swung in a bunch against the ship's side. I couldn't stand it any longer, and swarming up a rope, clambered aboard over the stern.

"It was as bright as day. Coming up like this, the sheet of fire facing me was a terrifying sight, and the heat seemed hardly bearable at first. On a settee cushion dragged out of the cabin Captain Beard, his legs drawn up and one arm under his head, slept with the light playing on him. Do you know what the rest were busy about? They were sitting on deck right aft, round an open case, eating bread and cheese and drinking bottled stout.

"On the background of flames twisting in fierce tongues above their heads they seemed at home like salamanders,[8] and looked like a band of desperate pirates. The fire sparkled in the whites of their eyes, gleamed on patches of white skin seen through the torn shirts. Each had the marks

[8] a mythical creature believed capable of living unharmed in fire

as of a battle about him—bandaged heads, tied-up arms, a strip of dirty rag round a knee—and each man had a bottle between his legs and a chunk of cheese in his hand. Mahon got up. With his handsome and disreputable head, his hooked profile, his long white beard, and with an uncorked bottle in his hand, he resembled one of those reckless sea-robbers of old making merry amidst violence and disaster. 'The last meal on board,' he explained solemnly. 'We had nothing to eat all day, and it was no use leaving all this.' He flourished the bottle and indicated the sleeping skipper. 'He said he couldn't swallow anything, so I got him to lie down,' he went on; and as I stared, 'I don't know whether you are aware, young fellow, the man had no sleep to speak of for days—and there will be dam' little sleep in the boats.' 'There will be no boats by-and-by if you fool about much longer,' I said, indignantly. I walked up to the skipper and shook him by the shoulder. At last he opened his eyes, but did not move. 'Time to leave her, sir,' I said quietly.

"He got up painfully, looked at the flames, at the sea sparkling round the ship, and black, black as ink farther away; he looked at the stars shining dim through a thin veil of smoke in a sky black, black as Erebus.[9]

" 'Youngest first,' he said.

"And the ordinary seaman, wiping his mouth with the back of his hand, got up, clambered over the taffrail, and vanished. Others followed. One, on the point of going over, stopped short to drain his bottle, and with a great swing of his arm flung it at the fire. 'Take this!' he cried.

"The skipper lingered disconsolately, and we left him to commune alone for a while with his first command. Then I went up again and brought him away at last. It was time. The ironwork on the poop was hot to the touch.

"Then the painter of the long boat was cut, and the three boats, tied together, drifted clear of the ship. It was just sixteen hours after the explosion when we abandoned her. Mahon had charge of the second boat, and I had the smallest—the 14-foot thing. The long-boat would have taken the lot of us; but the skipper said we must save as much property as we could—for the underwriters—and so I got my first command. I had two men with me, a bag of biscuits, a few tins of meat, and a breaker of water. I was ordered to keep close to the long-boat, that in case of bad weather we might be taken into her.

"And do you know what I thought? I thought I would part company as soon as I could. I wanted to have my first command all to myself. I wasn't going to sail in a squadron if there were a chance for independent cruising. I would make land by myself. I would beat the other boats. Youth! All youth! The silly, charming, beautiful youth.

"But we did not make a start at once. We must see the last of the ship. And so the boats drifted about that night, heaving and setting on the

---

[9] in Greek myth the gloomy region on the approach to Hades

swell. The men dozed, waked, sighed, groaned. I looked at the burning ship.

"Between the darkness of earth and heaven she was burning fiercely upon a disc of purple sea shot by the blood-red play of gleams; upon a disc of water glittering and sinister. A high, clear flame, an immense and lonely flame, ascended from the ocean, and from its summit the black smoke poured continuously at the sky. She burned furiously; mournful and imposing like a funeral pile kindled in the night, surrounded by the sea, watched over by the stars. A magnificent death had come like a grace, like a gift, like a reward to that old ship at the end of her laborious days. The surrender of her weary ghost to the keeping of stars and sea was stirring like the sight of a glorious triumph. The masts fell just before daybreak, and for a moment there was a burst and turmoil of sparks that seemed to fill with flying fire the night patient and watchful, the vast night lying silent upon the sea. At daylight she was only a charred shell, floating still under a cloud of smoke and bearing a glowing mass of coal within.

"Then the oars were got out, and the boats forming in a line moved round her remains as if in procession—the long-boat leading. As we pulled across her stern a slim dart of fire shot out viciously at us, and suddenly she went down, head first, in a great hiss of steam. The unconsumed stern was the last to sink; but the paint had gone, had cracked, had peeled off, and there were no letters, there was no word, no stubborn device that was like her soul, to flash at the rising sun her creed and her name.

"We made our way north. A breeze sprang up, and about noon all the boats came together for the last time. I had no mast or sail in mine, but I made a mast out of a spare oar and hoisted a boat-awning for a sail, with a boat-hook for a yard. She was certainly over-masted, but I had the satisfaction of knowing that with the wind aft I could beat the other two. I had to wait for them. Then we all had a look at the captain's chart, and, after a sociable meal of hard bread and water, got our last instructions. They were simple: steer north, and keep together as much as possible. 'Be careful with that jury-rig, Marlow,' said the captain; and Mahon, as I sailed proudly past his boat, wrinkled his curved nose and hailed, 'You will sail that ship of yours under water, if you don't look out, young fellow.' He was a malicious old man—and may the deep sea where he sleeps now rock him gently, rock him tenderly to the end of time!

"Before sunset a thick rain-squall passed over the two boats, which were far astern, and that was the last I saw of them for a time. Next day I sat steering my cockle-shell—my first command—with nothing but water and sky around me. I did sight in the afternoon the upper sails of a ship far away, but said nothing, and my men did not notice her. You see I was afraid she might be homeward bound, and I had no mind to turn back from the portals of the East. I was steering for Java—another blessed name—like Bangkok, you know. I steered many days.

"I need not tell you what it is to be knocking about in an open boat. I remember nights and days of calm, when we pulled, we pulled, and the boat seemed to stand still, as if bewitched within the circle of the sea horizon. I remember the heat, the deluge of rain-squalls that kept us baling for dear life (but filled our water cask), and I remember sixteen hours on end with a mouth dry as a cinder and a steering-oar over the stern to keep my first command head on to a breaking sea. I did not know how good a man I was till then. I remember the drawn faces, the dejected figures of my two men, and I remember my youth and the feeling that will never come back any more—the feeling that I could last for ever, outlast the sea, the earth, and all men; the deceitful feeling that lures us on to joys, to perils, to love, to vain effort—to death; the triumphant conviction of strength, the heat of life in the handful of dust, the glow in the heart that with every year grows dim, grows cold, grows small, and expires—and expires, too soon, too soon—before life itself.

"And this is how I see the East. I have seen its secret places and have looked into its very soul; but now I see it always from a small boat, a high outline of mountains, blue and afar in the morning; like faint mist at noon; a jagged wall of purple at sunset. I have the feel of the oar in my hand, the vision of a scorching blue sea in my eyes. And I see a bay, a wide bay, smooth as glass and polished like ice, shimmering in the dark. A red light burns far off upon the gloom of the land, and the night is soft and warm. We drag at the oars with aching arms, and suddenly a puff of wind, a puff faint and tepid and laden with strange odors of blossoms, of aromatic wood, comes out of the still night—the first sigh of the East on my face. That I can never forget. It was impalpable and enslaving, like a charm, like a whispered promise of mysterious delight.

"We had been pulling this finishing spell for eleven hours. Two pulled, and he whose turn it was to rest sat at the tiller. We had made out the red light in that bay and steered for it, guessing it must mark some small coasting port. We passed two vessels, outlandish and high-sterned, sleeping at anchor, and, approaching the light, now very dim, ran the boat's nose against the end of a jutting wharf. We were blind with fatigue. My men dropped the oars and fell off the thwarts as if dead. I made fast to a pile. A current rippled softly. The scented obscurity of the shore was grouped into vast masses, a density of colossal clumps of vegetation, probably—mute and fantastic shapes. And at their foot the semi-circle of a beach gleamed faintly, like an illusion. There was not a light, not a stir, not a sound. The mysterious East faced me, perfumed like a flower, silent like death, dark like a grave.

"And I sat weary beyond expression, exulting like a conqueror, sleepless and entranced as if before a profound, a fateful enigma.

"A splashing of oars, a measured dip reverberating on the level of

water, intensified by the silence of the shore into loud claps, made me
jump up. A boat, a European boat, was coming in. I invoked the name of
the dead; I hailed: *Judea* ahoy! A thin shout answered.

"It was the captain. I had beaten the flagship by three hours, and I was
glad to hear the old man's voice again, tremulous and tired. 'Is it you,
Marlow?' 'Mind the end of that jetty, sir,' I cried.

"He approached cautiously, and brought up with the deep-sea lead-
line which we had saved—for the underwriters. I eased my painter and
fell along-side. He sat, a broken figure at the stern, wet with dew, his
hands clasped in his lap. His men were asleep already. 'I had a terrible
time of it,' he murmured. 'Mahon is behind—not very far.' We conversed in whispers, in low whispers, as if afraid to wake up the land.
Guns, thunder, earthquakes would not have awakened the men just then.

"Looking round as we talked, I saw away at sea a bright light traveling in the night. 'There's a steamer passing the bay,' I said. She was not
passing, she was entering, and she even came close and anchored. 'I
wish,' said the old man, 'you would find out whether she is English. Perhaps they could give us a passage somewhere.' He seemed nervously anxious. So by dint of punching and kicking I started one of my men into a
state of somnambulism, and giving him an oar, took another and pulled
towards the lights of the steamer.

"There was a murmur of voices in her, metallic hollow clangs of the
engineroom, footsteps on the deck. Her ports shone, round like dilated
eyes. Shapes moved about, and there was a shadowy man high up on the
bridge. He heard my oars.

"And then, before I could open my lips, the East spoke to me, but it
was in a Western voice. A torrent of words was poured into the enig-
matical, the fateful silence; outlandish, angry words, mixed with words
and even whole sentences of good English, less strange but even more
surprising. The voice swore and cursed violently; it riddled the solemn
peace of the bay by a volley of abuse. It began by calling me Pig, and
from that went crescendo into unmentionable adjectives—in English.
The man up there raged aloud in two languages, and with a sincerity in
his fury that almost convinced me I had, in some way, sinned against the
harmony of the universe. I could hardly see him, but began to think he
would work himself into a fit.

"Suddenly he ceased, and I could hear him snorting and blowing like a
porpoise. I said—

" 'What steamer is this, pray?'

" 'Eh? What's this? And who are you?'

" 'Castaway crew of an English bark burnt at sea. We came here
to-night. I am the second mate. The captain is in the long-boat, and
wishes to know if you would give us a passage somewhere.'

" 'Oh, my goodness! I say. . . . This is the *Celestial* from Singapore
on her return trip. I'll arrange with your captain in the morning, . . .
and, . . . I say, . . . did you hear me just now?'

" 'I should think the whole bay heard you.'

" 'I thought you were a shore-boat. Now, look here—this infernal lazy scoundrel of a caretaker has gone to sleep again—curse him. The light is out, and I nearly ran foul of the end of this damned jetty. This is the third time he plays me this trick. Now, I ask you, can anybody stand this kind of thing? It's enough to drive a man out of his mind. I'll report him. . . . I'll get the Assistant Resident to give him the sack, by . . . ! See—there's no light. It's out, isn't it? I take you to witness the light's out. There should be a light, you know. A red light on the—'

" There was a light,' I said, mildly.

" 'But it's out, man! What's the use of talking like this? You can see for yourself it's out—don't you? If you had to take a valuable steamer along this God-forsaken coast you would want a light, too. I'll kick him from end to end of his miserable wharf. You'll see if I don't. I will—'

" 'So I may tell my captain you'll take us?' I broke in.

" 'Yes, I'll take you. Good-night,' he said, brusquely.

"I pulled back, made fast again to the jetty, and then went to sleep at last. I had faced the silence of the East. I had heard some of its language. But when I opened my eyes again the silence was as complete as though it had never been broken. I was lying in a flood of light, and the sky had never looked so far, so high, before. I opened my eyes and lay without moving.

"And then I saw the men of the East—they were looking at me. The whole length of the jetty was full of people. I saw brown, bronze, yellow faces, the black eyes, the glitter, the color of an Eastern crowd. And all these beings stared without a murmur, without a sigh, without a movement. They stared down at the boats, at the sleeping men who at night had come to them from the sea. Nothing moved. The fronds of palms stood still against the sky. Not a branch stirred along the shore, and the brown roofs of hidden houses peeped through the green foliage, through the big leaves that hung shining and still like leaves forged of heavy metal. This was the East of the ancient navigators, so old, so mysterious, resplendent and somber, living and unchanged, full of danger and promise. And these were the men. I sat up suddenly. A wave of movement passed through the crowd from end to end, passed along the heads, swayed the bodies, ran along the jetty like a ripple on the water, like a breath of wind on a field—and all was still again. I see it now—the wide sweep of the bay, the glittering sands, the wealth of green infinite and varied, the sea blue like the sea of a dream, the crowd of attentive faces, the blaze of vivid color—the water reflecting it all, the curve of the shore, the jetty, the high-sterned outlandish craft floating still, and the three boats with the tired men from the West sleeping, unconscious of the land and the people and of the violence of sunshine. They slept thrown across the thwarts, curled on bottom-boards, in the careless attitudes of death. The head of the old skipper, leaning back in the stern of the long-boat, had fallen on his breast, and he looked as though he would never wake.

Farther out old Mahon's face was upturned to the sky, with the long white beard spread out on his breast, as though he had been shot where he sat at the tiller; and a man, all in a heap in the bows of the boat, slept with both arms embracing the stem-head and with his cheek laid on the gunwale. The East looked at them without a sound.

"I have known its fascination since; I have seen the mysterious shores, the still water, the lands of brown nations, where a stealthy Nemesis lies in wait, pursues, overtakes so many of the conquering race, who are proud of their wisdom, of their knowledge, of their strength. But for me all the East is contained in that vision of my youth. It is all in that moment when I opened my young eyes on it. I came upon it from a tussle with the sea—and I was young—and I saw it looking at me. And this is all that is left of it! Only a moment; a moment of strength, of romance, of glamor—of youth! . . . A flick of sunshine upon a strange shore, the time to remember, the time for a sigh, and—good-bye!—Night—Good-bye . . . !"

He drank.

"Ah! The good old time—the good old time. Youth and the sea. Glamor and the sea! The good, strong sea, the salt, bitter sea, that could whisper to you and roar at you and knock your breath out of you."

He drank again.

"By all that's wonderful it is the sea, I believe, the sea itself—or is it youth alone? Who can tell? But you here—you all had something out of life: money, love—whatever one gets on shore—and, tell me, wasn't that the best time, that time when we were young at sea; young and had nothing, on the sea that gives nothing, except hard knocks—and sometimes a chance to feel your strength—that only—what you all regret?"

And we all nodded at him: the man of finance, the man of accounts, the man of law, we all nodded at him over the polished table that like a still sheet of brown water reflected our faces, lined, wrinkled; our faces marked by toil, by deceptions, by success, by love; our weary eyes looking still, looking always, looking anxiously for something out of life, that while it is expected is already gone—has passed unseen, in a sigh, in a flash—together with the youth, with the strength, with the romance of illusions.

Sir Arthur Conan Doyle
1859–1930
THE RED-HEADED LEAGUE

I HAD called upon my friend, Mr. Sherlock Holmes, one day in the autumn of last year and found him in deep conversation with a very stout, florid-faced, elderly gentleman with fiery red hair. With an apology for my intrusion, I was about to withdraw when Holmes pulled me abruptly into the room and closed the door behind me.

"You could not possibly have come at a better time, my dear Watson," he said cordially.

"I was afraid that you were engaged."

"So I am. Very much so."

"Then I can wait in the next room."

"Not at all. This gentleman, Mr. Wilson, has been my partner and helper in many of my most successful cases, and I have no doubt that he will be of the utmost use to me in yours also."

The stout gentleman half rose from his chair and gave a bob of greeting, with a quick little questioning glance from his small, fat-encircled eyes.

"Try the settee," said Holmes, relapsing into his armchair and putting his finger-tips together, as was his custom when in judicial moods. "I know, my dear Watson, that you share my love of all that is bizarre and outside the conventions and humdrum routine of everyday life. You have shown your relish for it by the enthusiasm which has prompted you to chronicle, and, if you will excuse my saying so, somewhat to embellish so many of my own little adventures."

"Your cases have indeed been of the greatest interest to me," I observed.

"You will remember that I remarked the other day, just before we went into the very simple problem presented by Miss Mary Sutherland, that for strange effects and extraordinary combinations we must go to life itself, which is always far more daring than any effort of the imagination."

"A proposition which I took the liberty of doubting."

"You did, Doctor, but none the less you must come round to my view, for otherwise I shall keep on piling fact upon fact on you until your reason breaks down under them and acknowledges me to be right. Now, Mr. Jabez Wilson here has been good enough to call upon me this morning, and to begin a narrative which promises to be one of the most singular which I have listened to for some time. You have heard me remark that the strangest and most unique things are very often connected not with the larger but with the smaller crimes, and occasionally, indeed, where there is room for doubt whether any positive crime has been committed. As far as I have heard it is impossible for me to say whether the present case is an instance of crime or not, but the course of events is certainly among the most singular that I have ever listened to. Perhaps, Mr. Wilson, you would have the great kindness to recommence your narrative. I ask you not merely because my friend Dr. Watson has not heard the opening part but also because the peculiar nature of the story makes me anxious to have every possible detail from your lips. As a rule, when I have heard some slight indication of the course of events, I am able to guide myself by the thousands of other similar cases which occur to my memory. In the present instance I am forced to admit that the facts are, to the best of my belief, unique."

The portly client puffed out his chest with an appearance of some little pride and pulled a dirty and wrinkled newspaper from the inside pocket of his great-coat. As he glanced down the advertisement column, with his head thrust forward and the paper flattened out upon his knee, I took a good look at the man and endeavored, after the fashion of my companion, to read the indications which might be presented by his dress or appearance.

I did not gain very much, however, by my inspection. Our visitor bore every mark of being an average commonplace British tradesman, obese, pompous, and slow. He wore rather baggy gray shepherd's check trousers, a not over-clean black frock-coat, unbuttoned in the front, and a drab waistcoat with a heavy brassy Albert chain, and a square pierced bit of metal dangling down as an ornament. A frayed top-hat and a faded brown overcoat with a wrinkled velvet collar lay upon a chair beside him. Altogether, look as I would, there was nothing remarkable about the man save his blazing red head, and the expression of extreme chagrin and discontent upon his features.

Sherlock Holmes's quick eye took in my occupation, and he shook his head with a smile as he noticed my questioning glances. "Beyond the obvious facts that he has at some time done manual labor, that he takes snuff, that he is a Freemason, that he has been in China, and that he has done a considerable amount of writing lately, I can deduce nothing else."

Mr. Jabez Wilson started up in his chair, with his forefinger upon the paper, but his eyes upon my companion.

"How, in the name of good-fortune, did you know all that, Mr. Holmes?" he asked. "How did you know, for example, that I did manual labor? It's as true as gospel, for I began as a ship's carpenter."

"Your hands, my dear sir. Your right hand is quite a size larger than your left. You have worked with it, and the muscles are more developed."

"Well, the snuff, then, and the Freemasonry?"

"I won't insult your intelligence by telling you how I read that, especially as, rather against the strict rules of your order, you use an arc-and-compass breastpin."

"Ah, of course, I forgot that. But the writing?"

"What else can be indicated by that right cuff so very shiny for five inches, and the left one with the smooth patch near the elbow where you rest it upon the desk?"

"Well, but China?"

"The fish that you have tattooed immediately above your right wrist could only have been done in China. I have made a small study of tattoo marks and have even contributed to the literature of the subject. That trick of staining the fishes' scales of a delicate pink is quite peculiar to

China. When, in addition, I see a Chinese coin hanging from your watch-chain, the matter becomes even more simple."

Mr. Jabez Wilson laughed heavily. "Well, I never!" said he. "I thought at first that you had done something clever, but I see that there was nothing in it, after all."

"I begin to think, Watson," said Holmes, "that I make a mistake in explaining. '*Omne ignotum pro magnifico*,'[1] you know, and my poor little reputation, such as it is, will suffer shipwreck if I am so candid. Can you not find the advertisement, Mr. Wilson?"

"Yes, I have got it now," he answered with his thick red finger planted halfway down the column. "Here it is. This is what began it all. You just read it for yourself, sir."

I took the paper from him and read as follows:

To THE RED-HEADED LEAGUE:
On account of the bequest of the late Ezekiah Hopkins, of Lebanon, Pennsylvania, U.S.A., there is now another vacancy open which entitles a member of the League to a salary of £4 a week for purely nominal services. All red-headed men who are sound in body and mind, and above the age of twenty-one years, are eligible. Apply in person on Monday, at eleven o'clock, to Duncan Ross, at the offices of the League, 7 Pope's Court, Fleet Street.

"What on earth does this mean?" I ejaculated after I had twice read over the extraordinary announcement.

Holmes chuckled and wriggled in his chair, as was his habit when in high spirits. "It is a little off the beaten track, isn't it?" said he. "And now, Mr. Wilson, off you go at scratch and tell us all about yourself, your household, and the effect which this advertisement had upon your fortunes. You will first make a note, Doctor, of the paper and the date."

"It is *The Morning Chronicle* of April 27, 1890. Just two months ago."

"Very good. Now, Mr. Wilson?"

"Well, it is just as I have been telling you, Mr. Sherlock Holmes," said Jabez Wilson, mopping his forehead; "I have a small pawnbroker's business at Coburg Square, near the City. It's not a very large affair, and of late years it has not done more than just give me a living. I used to be able to keep two assistants, but now I only keep one; and I would have a job to pay him but that he is willing to come for half wages so as to learn the business."

"What is the name of this obliging youth?" asked Sherlock Holmes.

"His name is Vincent Spaulding, and he's not such a youth, either. It's hard to say his age. I should not wish a smarter assistant, Mr. Holmes; and I know very well that he could better himself and earn twice what I am able to give him. But, after all, if he is satisfied, why should I put ideas in his head?"

---

[1] Everything unknown is thought to be splendid. (Tacitus)

"Why, indeed? You seem most fortunate in having an employee who comes under the full market price. It is not a common experience among employers in this age. I don't know that your assistant is not as remarkable as your advertisement."

"Oh, he has his faults, too," said Mr. Wilson. "Never was such a fellow for photography. Snapping away with a camera when he ought to be improving his mind, and then diving down into the cellar like a rabbit into its hole to develop his pictures. That is his main fault, but on the whole he's a good worker. There's no vice in him."

"He is still with you, I presume?"

"Yes, sir. He and a girl of fourteen, who does a bit of simple cooking and keeps the place clean—that's all I have in the house, for I am a widower and never had any family. We live very quietly, sir, the three of us; and we keep a roof over our heads and pay our debts, if we do nothing more.

"The first thing that put us out was that advertisement. Spaulding, he came down into the office just this day eight weeks, with this very paper in his hand, and he says:

"'I wish to the Lord, Mr. Wilson, that I was a red-headed man.'

"'Why that?' I asks.

"'Why,' says he, 'here's another vacancy on the League of the Red-headed Men. It's worth quite a little fortune to any man who gets it, and I understand that there are more vacancies than there are men, so that the trustees are at their wits' end what to do with the money. If my hair would only change color, here's a nice little crib all ready for me to step into.'

"'Why, what is it, then?' I asked. You see, Mr. Holmes, I am a very stay-at-home man, and as my business came to me instead of my having to go to it, I was often weeks on end without putting my foot over the door-mat. In that way I didn't know much of what was going on outside, and I was always glad of a bit of news.

"'Have you never heard of the League of the Red-headed Men?' he asked with his eyes open.

"'Never.'

"'Why, I wonder at that, for you are eligible yourself for one of the vacancies.'

"'And what are they worth?' I asked.

"'Oh, merely a couple of hundred a year, but the work is slight, and it need not interfere very much with one's other occupations.'

"Well, you can easily think that that made me prick up my ears, for the business has not been over-good for some years, and an extra couple of hundred would have been very handy.

"'Tell me all about it,' said I.

"'Well,' said he, showing me the advertisement, 'you can see for yourself that the League has a vacancy, and there is the address where you should apply for particulars. As far as I can make out, the League was founded by an American millionaire, Ezekiah Hopkins, who was very peculiar in his ways. He was himself red-headed, and he had a great sympathy for all red-headed men; so when he died it was found that he had left his enormous fortune in the hands of trustees, with instructions to apply the interest to the providing of easy berths to men whose hair is of that color. From all I hear it is splendid pay and very little to do.'

" 'But,' said I, 'there would be millions of red-headed men who would apply.'

" 'Not so many as you might think,' he answered. 'You see it is really confined to Londoners, and to grown men. This American had started from London when he was young, and he wanted to do the old town a good turn. Then, again, I have heard it is no use your applying if your hair is light red, or dark red, or anything but real bright, blazing, fiery red. Now, if you cared to apply, Mr. Wilson, you would just walk in; but perhaps it would hardly be worth your while to put yourself out of the way for the sake of a few hundred pounds.'

"Now, it is a fact, gentlemen, as you may see for yourselves, that my hair is of a very full and rich tint, so that it seemed to me that if there was to be any competition in the matter I stood as good a chance as any man that I had ever met. Vincent Spaulding seemed to know so much about it that I thought he might prove useful, so I just ordered him to put up the shutters for the day and to come right away with me. He was very willing to have a holiday, so we shut the business up and started off for the address that was given us in the advertisement.

"I never hope to see such a sight as that again, Mr. Holmes. From north, south, east, and west every man who had a shade of red in his hair had tramped into the city to answer the advertisement. Fleet Street was choked with red-headed folk, and Pope's Court looked like a coster's[2] orange barrow. I should not have thought there were so many in the whole country as were brought together by that single advertisement. Every shade of color they were—straw, lemon, orange, brick, Irish-setter, liver, clay; but, as Spaulding said, there were not many who had the real vivid flame-colored tint. When I saw how many were waiting, I would have given it up in despair; but Spaulding would not hear of it. How he did it I could not imagine, but he pushed and pulled and butted until he got me through the crowd, and right up to the steps which led to the office. There was a double stream upon the stair, some going up in hope, and some coming back dejected; but we wedged in as well as we could and soon found ourselves in the office."

"Your experience has been a most entertaining one," remarked Holmes as his client paused and refreshed his memory with a huge pinch of snuff. "Pray continue your very interesting statement."

"There was nothing in the office but a couple of wooden chairs and a deal table, behind which sat a small man with a head that was even redder

---

[2] a vendor of fruits or vegetables from a street stand or cart

than mine. He said a few words to each candidate as he came up, and then he always managed to find some fault in them which would disqualify them. Getting a vacancy did not seem to be such a very easy matter, after all. However, when our turn came the little man was much more favorable to me than to any of the others, and he closed the door as we entered, so that he might have a private word with us.

" 'This is Mr. Jabez Wilson,' said my assistant, 'and he is willing to fill a vacancy in the League.'

" 'And he is admirably suited for it,' the other answered. 'He has every requirement. I cannot recall when I have seen anything so fine.' He took a step backward, cocked his head on one side, and gazed at my hair until I felt quite bashful. Then suddenly he plunged forward, wrung my hand, and congratulated me warmly on my success.

" 'It would be injustice to hesitate,' said he. 'You will, however, I am sure, excuse me for taking an obvious precaution.' With that he seized my hair in both his hands, and tugged until I yelled with the pain. 'There is water in your eyes,' said he as he released me. 'I perceive that all is as it should be. But we have to be careful, for we have twice been deceived by wigs and once by paint. I could tell you tales of cobbler's wax which would disgust you with human nature.' He stepped over to the window and shouted through it at the top of his voice that the vacancy was filled. A groan of disappointment came up from below, and the folk all trooped away in different directions until there was not a red head to be seen except my own and that of the manager.

" 'My name,' said he, 'is Mr. Duncan Ross, and I am myself one of the pensioners upon the fund left by our noble benefactor. Are you a married man, Mr. Wilson? Have you a family?'

"I answered that I had not.

"His face fell immediately.

" 'Dear me!' he said gravely, 'that is very serious indeed! I am sorry to hear you say that. The fund was, of course, for the propagation and spread of the red-heads as well as for their maintenance. It is exceedingly unfortunate that you should be a bachelor.'

"My face lengthened at this, Mr. Holmes, for I thought that I was not to have the vacancy after all; but after thinking it over for a few minutes he said that it would be all right.

" 'In the case of another,' said he, 'the objection might be fatal, but we must stretch a point in favor of a man with such a head of hair as yours. When shall you be able to enter upon your new duties?'

" 'Well, it is a little awkward, for I have a business already,' said I.

" 'Oh, never mind about that, Mr. Wilson!' said Vincent Spaulding. 'I should be able to look after that for you.'

" 'What would be the hours?' I asked.

" 'Ten to two.'

"Now a pawnbroker's business is mostly done of an evening, Mr. Holmes, especially Thursday and Friday evening, which is just before pay-day; so it would suit me very well to earn a little in the mornings. Besides, I knew that my assistant was a good man, and that he would see to anything that turned up.

" 'That would suit me very well,' said I. 'And the pay?'

" 'Is £4 a week.'

" 'And the work?'

" 'Is purely nominal.'

" 'What do you call purely nominal?'

" 'Well, you have to be in the office, or at least in the building, the whole time. If you leave, you forfeit your whole position forever. The will is very clear upon that point. You don't comply with the conditions if you budge from the office during that time.'

" 'It's only four hours a day, and I should not think of leaving,' said I.

" 'No excuse will avail,' said Mr. Duncan Ross; 'neither sickness nor business nor anything else. There you must stay, or you lose your billet.'

" 'And the work?'

" 'Is to copy out the *Encyclopædia Britannica*. There is the first volume of it in that press. You must find your own ink, pens, and blotting-paper, but we provide this table and chair. Will you be ready to-morrow?'

" 'Certainly,' I answered.

" 'Then, good-bye, Mr. Jabez Wilson, and let me congratulate you once more on the important position which you have been fortunate enough to gain.' He bowed me out of the room, and I went home with my assistant, hardly knowing what to say or do, I was so pleased at my own good fortune.

"Well, I thought over the matter all day, and by evening I was in low spirits again; for I had quite persuaded myself that the whole affair must be some great hoax or fraud, though what its object might be I could not imagine. It seemed altogether past belief that anyone could make such a will, or that they would pay such a sum for doing anything so simple as copying out the *Encyclopædia Britannica*. Vincent Spaulding did what he could to cheer me up, but by bedtime I had reasoned myself out of the whole thing. However, in the morning I determined to have a look at it anyhow, so I bought a penny bottle of ink, and with a quill-pen, and seven sheets of foolscap paper, I started off for Pope's Court.

"Well, to my surprise and delight, everything was as right as possible. The table was set out ready for me, and Mr. Duncan Ross was there to see that I got fairly to work. He started me off upon the letter A, and then he left me; but he would drop in from time to time to see that all was right with me. At two o'clock he bade me good-day, complimented me upon the amount that I had written, and locked the door of the office after me.

"This went on day after day, Mr. Holmes, and on Saturday the manager came in and planked down four golden sovereigns for my week's work. It was the same next week, and the same the week after. Every morning I was there at ten, and every afternoon I left at two. By degrees Mr. Duncan Ross took to coming in only once of a morning, and then, after a time, he did not come in at all. Still, of course, I never dared to leave the room for an instant, for I was not sure when he might come, and the billet was such a good one, and suited me so well, that I would not risk the loss of it.

"Eight weeks passed away like this, and I had written about Abbots and Archery and Armour and Architecture and Attica, and hoped with diligence that I might get on to the B's before very long. It cost me something in foolscap, and I had pretty nearly filled a shelf with my writings. And then suddenly the whole business came to an end."

"To an end?"

"Yes, sir. And no later than this morning. I went to my work as usual at ten o'clock, but the door was shut and locked, with a little square of cardboard hammered on to the middle of the panel with a tack. Here it is, and you can read for yourself."

He held up a piece of white cardboard about the size of a sheet of note-paper. It read in this fashion:

The Red-Headed League

is

Dissolved.

October 9, 1890.

Sherlock Holmes and I surveyed this curt announcement and the rueful face behind it, until the comical side of the affair so completely overtopped every other consideration that we both burst out into a roar of laughter.

"I cannot see that there is anything very funny," cried our client, flushing up to the roots of his flaming head. "If you can do nothing better than laugh at me, I can go elsewhere."

"No, no," cried Holmes, shoving him back into the chair from which he had half risen. "I really wouldn't miss your case for the world. It is most refreshingly unusual. But there is, if you will excuse my saying so, something just a little funny about it. Pray what steps did you take when you found the card upon the door?"

"I was staggered, sir. I did not know what to do. Then I called at the offices round, but none of them seemed to know anything about it. Finally, I went to the landlord, who is an accountant living on the ground-floor, and I asked him if he could tell me what had become of the Red-headed League. He said that he had never heard of any such body. Then I asked him who Mr. Duncan Ross was. He answered that the name was new to him.

" 'Well,' said I, 'the gentleman at No. 4.'

" 'What, the red-headed man?'

" 'Yes.'

" 'Oh,' said he, 'his name was William Morris. He was a solicitor and was using my room as a temporary convenience until his new premises were ready. He moved out yesterday.'

" 'Where could I find him?'

" 'Oh, at his new offices. He did tell me the address. Yes, 17 King Edward Street, near St. Paul's.'

"I started off, Mr. Holmes, but when I got to that address it was a manufactory of artificial kneecaps, and no one in it had ever heard of either Mr. William Morris or Mr. Duncan Ross."

"And what did you do then?" asked Holmes.

"I went home to Saxe-Coburg Square, and I took the advice of my assistant. But he could not help me in any way. He could only say that if I waited I should hear by post. But that was not quite good enough, Mr. Holmes. I did not wish to lose such a place without a struggle, so, as I had heard that you were good enough to give advice to poor folk who were in need of it, I came right away to you."

"And you did very wisely," said Holmes. "Your case is an exceedingly remarkable one, and I shall be happy to look into it. From what you have told me I think that it is possible that graver issues hang from it than might at first sight appear."

"Grave enough!" said Mr. Jabez Wilson. "Why, I have lost four pound a week."

"As far as you are personally concerned," remarked Holmes, "I do not see that you have any grievance against this extraordinary league. On the contrary, you are, as I understand, richer by some £30, to say nothing of the minute knowledge which you have gained on every subject which comes under the letter A. You have lost nothing by them."

"No, sir. But I want to find out about them, and who they are, and what their object was in playing this prank—if it was a prank—upon me. It was a pretty expensive joke for them, for it cost them two and thirty pounds."

"We shall endeavor to clear up these points for you. And, first, one or two questions, Mr. Wilson. This assistant of yours who first called your attention to the advertisement—how long had he been with you?"

"About a month then."

"How did he come?"

"In answer to an advertisement."

"Was he the only applicant?"

"No, I had a dozen."

"Why did you pick him?"

"Because he was handy and would come cheap."

"At half-wages, in fact."

"Yes."

"What is he like, this Vincent Spaulding?"

"Small, stout-built, very quick in his ways, no hair on his face, though he's not short of thirty. Has a white splash of acid upon his forehead."

Holmes sat up in his chair in considerable excitement. "I thought as much," said he. "Have you ever observed that his ears are pierced for earrings?"

"Yes, sir. He told me that a gypsy had done it for him when he was a lad."

"Hum!" said Holmes, sinking back in deep thought. "He is still with you?"

"Oh, yes, sir; I have only just left him."

"And has your business been attended to in your absence?"

"Nothing to complain of, sir. There's never very much to do of a morning."

"That will do, Mr. Wilson. I shall be happy to give you an opinion upon the subject in the course of a day or two. Today is Saturday, and I hope that by Monday we may come to a conclusion."

"Well, Watson," said Holmes when our visitor had left us, "what do you make of it all?"

"I make nothing of it," I answered frankly. "It is a most mysterious business."

"As a rule," said Holmes, "the more bizarre a thing is the less mysterious it proves to be. It is your commonplace, featureless crimes which are really puzzling, just as a commonplace face is the most difficult to identify. But I must be prompt over this matter."

"What are you going to do, then?" I asked.

"To smoke," he answered. "It is quite a three pipe problem, and I beg that you won't speak to me for fifty minutes." He curled himself up in his chair, with his thin knees drawn up to his hawk-like nose, and there he sat with his eyes closed and his black clay pipe thrusting out like the bill of some strange bird. I had come to the conclusion that he had dropped asleep, and indeed was nodding myself, when he suddenly sprang out of his chair with the gesture of a man who has made up his mind and put his pipe down upon the mantelpiece.

"Sarasate[3] plays at the St. James's Hall this afternoon," he remarked. "What do you think, Watson? Could your patients spare you for a few hours?"

"I have nothing to do today. My practice is never very absorbing."

"Then put on your hat and come. I am going through the City first, and we can have some lunch on the way. I observe that there is a good deal of German music on the program, which is rather more to my taste than Italian or French. It is introspective, and I want to introspect. Come along!"

We traveled by the Underground as far as Aldersgate; and a short walk took us to Saxe-Coburg Square, the scene of the singular story which we had listened to in the morning. It was a poky, little, shabby-

---

[3] Pablo de Sarasate, 1844–1908, Spanish composer and concert violinist

genteel place, where four lines of dingy two-storied brick houses looked out into a small railed-in enclosure, where a lawn of weedy grass and a few clumps of faded laurel-bushes made a hard fight against a smoke-laden and uncongenial atmosphere. Three gilt balls and a brown board with "JABEZ WILSON" in white letters, upon a corner house, announced the place where our red-headed client carried on his business. Sherlock Holmes stopped in front of it with his head on one side and looked it all over, with his eyes shining brightly between puckered lids. Then he walked slowly up the street, and then down again to the corner, still looking keenly at the houses. Finally he returned to the pawn-broker's, and, having thumped vigorously upon the pavement with his stick two or three times, he went up to the door and knocked. It was instantly opened by a bright-looking, clean-shaven young fellow, who asked him to step in.

"Thank you," said Holmes, "I only wished to ask you how you would go from here to the Strand."

"Third right, fourth left," answered the assistant promptly, closing the door.

"Smart fellow, that," observed Holmes as we walked away. "He is, in my judgment, the fourth smartest man in London, and for daring I am not sure that he has not a claim to be third. I have known something of him before."

"Evidently," said I, "Mr. Wilson's assistant counts for a good deal in this mystery of the Red-headed League. I am sure that you inquired your way merely in order that you might see him."

"Not him."

"What then?"

"The knees of his trousers."

"And what did you see?"

"What I expected to see."

"Why did you beat the pavement?"

"My dear doctor, this is a time for observation, not for talk. We are spies in an enemy's country. We know something of Saxe-Coburg Square. Let us now explore the parts which lie behind it."

The road in which we found ourselves as we turned round the corner from the retired Saxe-Coburg Square presented as great a contrast to it as the front of a picture does to the back. It was one of the main arteries which conveyed the traffic of the City to the north and west. The road-way was blocked with the immense stream of commerce flowing in a double tide inward and outward, while the foot-paths were black with the hurrying swarm of pedestrians. It was difficult to realize as we looked at the line of fine shops and stately business premises that they really abutted on the other side upon the faded and stagnant square which we had just quitted.

"Let me see," said Holmes, standing at the corner and glancing along the line, "I should like just to remember the order of the houses here.

It is a hobby of mine to have an exact knowledge of London. There is Mortimer's, the tobacconist, the little newspaper shop, the Coburg branch of the City and Suburban Bank, the Vegetarian Restaurant, and McFarlane's carriage-building depot. That carries us right on to the other block. And now, Doctor, we've done our work, so it's time we had some play. A sandwich and a cup of coffee, and then off to violin-land, where all is sweetness and delicacy and harmony, and there are no red-headed clients to vex us with their conundrums."

My friend was an enthusiastic musician, being himself not only a very capable performer but a composer of no ordinary merit. All the afternoon he sat in the stalls wrapped in the most perfect happiness, gently waving his long, thin fingers in time to the music, while his gently smiling face and his languid, dreamy eyes were as unlike those of Holmes, the sleuth-hound, Holmes the relentless, keen-witted, ready-handed criminal agent, as it was possible to conceive. In his singular character the dual nature alternately asserted itself, and his extreme exactness and astuteness repre-sented, as I have often thought, the reaction against the poetic and con-templative mood which occasionally predominated in him. The swing of his nature took him from extreme languor to devouring energy; and, as I knew well, he was never so truly formidable as when, for days on end, he had been lounging in his armchair amid his improvisations and his black-letter editions. Then it was that the lust of the chase would sud-denly come upon him, and that his brilliant reasoning power would rise to the level of intuition, until those who were unacquainted with his methods would look askance at him as on a man whose knowledge was not that of other mortals. When I saw him that afternoon so enwrapped in the music at St. James's Hall I felt that an evil time might be coming upon those whom he had set himself to hunt down.

"You want to go home, no doubt, Doctor," he remarked as we emerged.

"Yes, it would be as well."

"And I have some business to do which will take some hours. This business at Coburg Square is serious."

"Why serious?"

"A considerable crime is in contemplation. I have every reason to be-lieve that we shall be in time to stop it. But today being Saturday rather complicates matters. I shall want your help tonight."

"At what time?"

"Ten will be early enough."

"I shall be at Baker Street at ten."

"Very well. And, I say, Doctor, there may be some little danger, so kindly put your army revolver in your pocket." He waved his hand, turned on his heel, and disappeared in an instant among the crowd.

I trust that I am not more dense than my neighbors, but I was always oppressed with a sense of my own stupidity in my dealings with Sherlock Holmes. Here I had heard what he had heard, I had seen what he had seen, and yet from his words it was evident that he saw clearly not only what had happened but what was about to happen, while to me the whole business was still confused and grotesque. As I drove home to my house in Kensington I thought over it all, from the extraordinary story of the red-headed copier of the *Encyclopædia* down to the visit to Saxe-Coburg Square, and the ominous words with which he had parted from me. What was this nocturnal expedition, and why should I go armed? Where were we going, and what were we to do? I had the hint from Holmes that this smooth-faced pawnbroker's assistant was a formidable man—a man who might play a deep game. I tried to puzzle it out, but gave it up in despair and set the matter aside until night should bring an explanation.

It was a quarter-past nine when I started from home and made my way across the Park, and so through Oxford Street to Baker Street. Two hansoms were standing at the door, and as I entered the passage I heard the sound of voices from above. On entering his room I found Holmes in animated conversation with two men, one of whom I recognized as Peter Jones, the official police agent, while the other was a long, thin, sad-faced man, with a very shiny hat and oppressively respectable frock-coat.

"Ha! our party is complete," said Holmes, buttoning up his pea-jacket and taking his heavy hunting crop from the rack. "Watson, I think you know Mr. Jones, of Scotland Yard? Let me introduce you to Mr. Merryweather, who is to be our companion in tonight's adventure."

"We're hunting in couples again, Doctor, you see," said Jones in his consequential way. "Our friend here is a wonderful man for starting a chase. All he wants is an old dog to help him to do the running down."

"I hope a wild goose may not prove to be the end of our chase," observed Mr. Merryweather gloomily.

"You may place considerable confidence in Mr. Holmes, sir," said the police agent loftily. "He has his own little methods, which are, if he won't mind my saying so, just a little too theoretical and fantastic, but he has the makings of a detective in him. It is not too much to say that once or twice, as in that business of the Sholto murder and the Agra treasure, he has been more nearly correct than the official force."

"Oh, if you say so, Mr. Jones, it is all right," said the stranger with deference. "Still, I confess that I miss my rubber. It is the first Saturday night for seven-and-twenty years that I have not had my rubber."

"I think you will find," said Sherlock Holmes, "that you will play for a higher stake tonight than you have ever done yet, and that the play will be more exciting. For you, Mr. Merryweather, the stake will be some £30,000; and for you, Jones, it will be the man upon whom you wish to lay your hands."

"John Clay, the murderer, thief, smasher, and forger. He's a young man, Mr. Merryweather, but he is at the head of his profession, and I would rather have my bracelets on him than on any criminal in London. He's a remarkable man, is young John Clay. His grandfather was a royal duke, and he himself has been to Eton and Oxford. His brain is as cunning

as his fingers, and though we meet signs of him at every turn, we never
know where to find the man himself. He'll crack a crib in Scotland one
week, and be raising money to build an orphanage in Cornwall the next.
I've been on his track for years and have never set eyes on him yet."

"I hope that I may have the pleasure of introducing you tonight. I've
had one or two little turns also with Mr. John Clay, and I agree with you
that he is at the head of his profession. It is past ten, however, and quite
time that we started. If you two will take the first hansom, Watson and
I will follow in the second."

Sherlock Holmes was not very communicative during the long drive
and lay back in the cab humming the tunes which he had heard in the
afternoon. We rattled through an endless labyrinth of gas-lit streets until
we emerged into Farringdon Street.

"We are close there now," my friend remarked. "This fellow Merryweather is a bank director, and personally interested in the matter. I
thought it as well to have Jones with us also. He is not a bad fellow,
though an absolute imbecile in his profession. He has one positive virtue.
He is as brave as a bulldog and as tenacious as a lobster if he gets his
claws upon anyone. Here we are, and they are waiting for us."

We had reached the same crowded thoroughfare in which we had
found ourselves in the morning. Our cabs were dismissed, and, following
the guidance of Mr. Merryweather, we passed down a narrow passage
and through a side door, which he opened for us. Within there was a
small corridor, which ended in a very massive iron gate. This also was
opened, and led down a flight of winding stone steps, which terminated
at another formidable gate. Mr. Merryweather stopped to light a lantern,
and then conducted us down a dark, earth-smelling passage, and so, after
opening a third door, into a huge vault or cellar, which was piled all round
with crates and massive boxes.

"You are not very vulnerable from above," Holmes remarked as he
held up the lantern and gazed about him.

"Nor from below," said Mr. Merryweather, striking his stick upon
the flags which lined the floor. "Why, dear me, it sounds quite hollow!"
he remarked, looking up in surprise.

"I must really ask you to be a little more quiet!" said Holmes severely. "You have already imperilled the whole success of our expedition. Might I beg that you would have the goodness to sit down upon
one of those boxes, and not to interfere?"

The solemn Mr. Merryweather perched himself upon a crate, with a
very injured expression upon his face, while Holmes fell upon his knees
upon the floor and, with the lantern and a magnifying lens, began to examine minutely the cracks between the stones. A few seconds sufficed to
satisfy him, for he sprang to his feet again and put his glass in his pocket.

"We have at least an hour before us," he remarked, "for they can
hardly take any steps until the good pawnbroker is safely in bed. Then

they will not lose a minute, for the sooner they do their work the longer time they will have for their escape. We are at present, Doctor—as no doubt you have divined—in the cellar of the City branch of one of the principal London banks. Mr. Merryweather is the chairman of directors, and he will explain to you that there are reasons why the more daring criminals of London should take a considerable interest in this cellar at present."

"It is our French gold," whispered the director. "We have had several warnings that an attempt might be made upon it."

"Your French gold?"

"Yes. We had occasion some months ago to strengthen our resources and borrowed for that purpose 30,000 napoleons[4] from the Bank of France. It has become known that we have never had occasion to unpack the money, and that it is still lying in our cellar. The crate upon which I sit contains 2,000 napoleons packed between layers of lead foil. Our reserve of bullion is much larger at present than is usually kept in a single branch office, and the directors have had misgivings upon the subject."

"Which were very well justified," observed Holmes. "And now it is time that we arranged our little plans. I expect that within an hour matters will come to a head. In the meantime, Mr. Merryweather, we must put the screen over that dark lantern."

"And sit in the dark?"

"I am afraid so. I had brought a pack of cards in my pocket, and I thought that, as we were a *partie carrée*,[5] you might have your rubber after all. But I see that the enemy's preparations have gone so far that we cannot risk the presence of a light. And, first of all, we must choose our positions. These are daring men, and though we shall take them at a disadvantage, they may do us some harm unless we are careful. I shall stand behind this crate, and do you conceal yourselves behind those. Then, when I flash a light upon them, close in swiftly. If they fire, Watson, have no compunction about shooting them down."

I placed my revolver, cocked, upon the top of the wooden case behind which I crouched. Holmes shot the slide across the front of his lantern and left us in pitch darkness—such an absolute darkness as I have never before experienced. The smell of hot metal remained to assure us that the light was still there, ready to flash out at a moment's notice. To me, with my nerves worked up to a pitch of expectancy, there was something depressing and subduing in the sudden gloom, and in the cold dank air of the vault.

"They have but one retreat," whispered Holmes. "That is back through the house into Saxe-Coburg Square. I hope that you have done what I asked you, Jones?"

"I have an inspector and two officers waiting at the front door."

[4] about \$120,000   [5] a party of four

"Then we have stopped all the holes. And now we must be silent and wait."

What a time it seemed! From comparing notes afterwards it was but an hour and a quarter, yet it appeared to me that the night must have almost gone, and the dawn be breaking above us. My limbs were weary and stiff, for I feared to change my position; yet my nerves were worked up to the highest pitch of tension, and my hearing was so acute that I could not only hear the gentle breathing of my companions, but I could distinguish the deeper, heavier in-breath of the bulky Jones from the thin, sighing note of the bank director. From my position I could look over the case in the direction of the floor. Suddenly my eyes caught the glint of a light.

At first it was but a lurid spark upon the stone pavement. Then it lengthened out until it became a yellow line, and then, without any warning or sound, a gash seemed to open and a hand appeared; a white, almost womanly hand, which felt about in the center of the little area of light. For a minute or more the hand, with its writhing fingers, protruded out of the floor. Then it was withdrawn as suddenly as it appeared, and all was dark again save the single lurid spark which marked a chink between the stones.

Its disappearance, however, was but momentary. With a rending, tearing sound, one of the broad, white stones turned over upon its side and left a square, gaping hole, through which streamed the light of a lantern. Over the edge there peeped a clean-cut, boyish face, which looked keenly about it, and then, with a hand on either side of the aperture, drew itself shoulder-high and waist-high, until one knee rested upon the edge. In another instant he stood at the side of the hole and was hauling after him a companion, lithe and small like himself, with a pale face and a shock of very red hair.

"It's all clear," he whispered. "Have you the chisel and the bags? Great Scott! Jump, Archie, jump, and I'll swing for it!"

Sherlock Holmes had sprung out and seized the intruder by the collar. The other dived down the hole, and I heard the sound of rending cloth as Jones clutched at his skirts. The light flashed upon the barrel of a revolver, but Holmes's hunting crop came down on the man's wrist, and the pistol clinked upon the stone floor.

"It's no use, John Clay," said Holmes blandly. "You have no chance at all."

"So I see," the other answered with the utmost coolness. "I fancy that my pal is all right, though I see you have got his coat-tails."

"There are three men waiting for him at the door," said Holmes.

"Oh, indeed! You seem to have done the thing very completely. I must compliment you."

"And I you," Holmes answered. "Your red-headed idea was very new and effective."

"You'll see your pal again presently," said Jones. "He's quicker at climbing down holes than I am. Just hold out while I fix the derbies."[6]

"I beg that you will not touch me with your filthy hands," remarked our prisoner as the handcuffs clattered upon his wrists. "You may not be aware that I have royal blood in my veins. Have the goodness, also, when you address me always to say 'sir' and 'please.'"

"All right," said Jones with a stare and a snigger. "Well, would you please, sir, march upstairs, where we can get a cab to carry your Highness to the police-station?"

"That is better," said John Clay serenely. He made a sweeping bow to the three of us and walked quietly off in the custody of the detective.

"Really, Mr. Holmes," said Mr. Merryweather as we followed them from the cellar, "I do not know how the bank can thank you or repay you. There is no doubt that you have detected and defeated in the most complete manner one of the most determined attempts at bank robbery that have ever come within my experience."

"I have had one or two little scores of my own to settle with Mr. John Clay," said Holmes. "I have been at some small expense over this matter, which I shall expect the bank to refund, but beyond that I am amply repaid by having had an experience which is in many ways unique, and by hearing the very remarkable narrative of the Red-headed League."

"You see, Watson," he explained in the early hours of the morning as we sat over a glass of whisky and soda in Baker Street, "it was perfectly obvious from the first that the only possible object of this rather fantastic business of the advertisement of the League, and the copying of the *Encyclopædia*, must be to get this not over-bright pawnbroker out of the way for a number of hours every day. It was a curious way of managing it, but, really, it would be difficult to suggest a better. The method was no doubt suggested to Clay's ingenious mind by the color of his accomplice's hair. The £4 a week was a lure which must draw him, and what was it to them, who were playing for thousands? They put in the advertisement, one rogue has the temporary office, the other rogue incites the man to apply for it, and together they manage to secure his absence every morning in the week. From the time that I heard of the assistant having come for half wages, it was obvious to me that he had some strong motive for securing the situation."

"But how could you guess what the motive was?"

"Had there been women in the house, I should have suspected a mere vulgar intrigue. That, however, was out of the question. The man's business was a small one, and there was nothing in his house which could account for such elaborate preparations, and such an expenditure as they were at. It must, then, be something out of the house. What could it be? I thought of the assistant's fondness for photography, and his trick of

[6] handcuffs

vanishing into the cellar. The cellar! There was the end of this tangled clue. Then I made inquiries as to this mysterious assistant and found that I had to deal with one of the coolest and most daring criminals in London. He was doing something in the cellar—something which took many hours a day for months on end. What could it be, once more? I could think of nothing save that he was running a tunnel to some other building.

"So far I had got when we went to visit the scene of action. I surprised you by beating upon the pavement with my stick. I was ascertaining whether the cellar stretched out in front or behind. It was not in front. Then I rang the bell, and, as I hoped, the assistant answered it. We have had some skirmishes, but we had never set eyes upon each other before. I hardly looked at his face. His knees were what I wished to see. You must yourself have remarked how worn, wrinkled, and stained they were. They spoke of those hours of burrowing. The only remaining point was what they were burrowing for. I walked round the corner, saw that the City and Suburban Bank abutted on our friend's premises, and felt that I had solved my problem. When you drove home after the concert I called upon Scotland Yard and upon the chairman of the bank directors, with the result that you have seen."

"And how could you tell that they would make their attempt to-night?" I asked.

"Well, when they closed their League offices that was a sign that they cared no longer about Mr. Jabez Wilson's presence—in other words, that they had completed their tunnel. But it was essential that they should use it soon, as it might be discovered, or the bullion might be removed. Saturday would suit them better than any other day, as it would give them two days for their escape. For all these reasons I expected them to come tonight."

"You reasoned it out beautifully," I exclaimed in unfeigned admiration. "It is so long a chain, and yet every link rings true."

"It saved me from ennui," he answered, yawning. "Alas! I already feel it closing in upon me. My life is spent in one long effort to escape from the commonplaces of existence. These little problems help me to do so."

"And you are a benefactor of the race," said I.

He shrugged his shoulders. "Well, perhaps, after all, it is of some little use," he remarked. "'L'homme c'est rien—l'œuvre c'est tout,'[7] as Gustave Flaubert wrote to George Sand."

---

[7] The man is nothing; the work is all. Flaubert and Sand were nineteenth-century French novelists.

The Times (London)

1785–

THE GREAT BAKER STREET BANK RAID[1]

13 SEPTEMBER 1971: *Radio ham tunes in to £½m robbery talk*

An amateur radio enthusiast yesterday picked up a conversation between two bandits believed to be robbing a bank of £500,000. Last night Scotland Yard detectives were checking every bank within a ten-mile radius of Marylebone in central London to find the men.

The operation, mounted in great secrecy, was launched after a man overheard the conversation on his shortwave radio set early yesterday. He heard the two men discuss the robbery. They spoke of sandwiches and flasks of tea and then one of them said: "We are sitting on £500,-000."

The man told the Post Office, who alerted Scotland Yard.

Detectives believe the two bandits were communicating with each other using shortwave radios. With the aid of Post Office technicians they narrowed down the hunt to within a ten-mile radius of Marylebone.

14 SEPTEMBER 1971: *Bank raiders get thousands after radio ham warning and police check*

By CLIVE BORRELL

Scotland Yard, bank security staff and the Post Office last night disputed responsibility for the failure to prevent a weekend raid at the Baker Street branch of Lloyds Bank in London. One million pounds could be involved.

At least four men and probably a woman escaped with the contents of private safety deposit boxes worth possibly £1m, or even more. Cautious first estimates put the figure no higher than several thousand pounds.

It is thought that soon after the bank closed on Friday night the thieves entered the tradesmen's entrance of SAC, a leather goods shop next door but one. This shop had been closed for nearly two weeks but had in its front window a sign saying "Open again Sept 14."

The thieves are thought to have carried several hundredweights of equipment inside the shop without setting off an alarm. Among their gear were several oxygen cylinders, steel rods required for thermic lances, two-way radio sets and receivers, torches, hammers and chisels, and sandwiches and flasks of tea.

The gang took their equipment into the shop cellars and began a forty-foot tunneling operation under a restaurant next door.

They handed back plastic buckets full of earth and brickwork to be

---

[1] Reproduced from *The Times* by permission.

dumped in the back yard of the shop. After chipping away for forty feet they ran into difficulty. Below was a well; less than ten feet above was the floor of the bank.

Then two other members of the gang were called in by two-way radio. One man on the roof of a building overlooking the bank sent a message to a woman acting as "controller" in a building, probably about a mile away. The lookout told "control" they had burrowed their way through to a well below.

Police officers believe that tubular steel extending ladders were passed along the tunnel, followed by thermic lance equipment.

It is thought that an expert, wearing a mask and being passed oxygen cylinders and steel rods, began burning through more than three feet of reinforced concrete into the floor of the bank vault.

After that had been successfully completed police believe they first received their tip-off.

On the two-way radio the man inside the vault said that he was suffering from the fumes caused by the burning. He called for sandwiches and a flask of tea and said he wanted a rest. This message was relayed by shortwave radio to the lookout, who passed it to the woman at control.

At that moment Mr. Robert Rowlands, aged 32, of Wimpole Street, St. Marylebone, a radio "ham," picked up the conversation between the gang inside the bank and those outside. He heard them talk of "sitting on half a million" and other remarks.

By 2 A.M. on Sunday Mr. Rowlands, who had been catching snatches of the conversation, reported to the police his fears that the radio frequency on 27.15 megacycles was being used by criminals.

Earlier, I understand, Mr. Rowlands had been trying to tell the police of his fears but was unable to speak to a senior officer.

By 2 A.M. Commander Robert Huntley of Scotland Yard had decided to take Mr. Rowlands's information seriously. Post Office radio detector vans were called in. They toured an area of about ten miles around Wimpole Street and Baker Street for several hours but the trail was dead.

Meanwhile Scotland Yard had been told of the conversations picked up by Mr. Rowlands. Officers began a systematic search of 750 banks in the inner London area. Double checks were done on 150 banks within a mile of Baker Street and Wimpole Street.

At 3:30 P.M. on Sunday bank security officers and detectives searched Lloyds Bank at the corner of Baker Street. There were no obvious signs of entry. The vaults were found to be intact. The doors are fifteen inches thick and showed no signs of being tampered with.

The detectives believe that the thieves might have been behind the vault's doors but were keeping quiet after a tip-off from the lookout man using his two-way radio.

Soon afterwards, it is thought, the gang escaped with the contents of hundreds of deposit boxes. A bank official told me last night that the whole of the vaults were wired up to alarms except the floors "which we thought were foolproof."

A senior Yard officer said: "There is going to be an almighty row about this."

Lloyds Bank said last night that customers who left articles in the bank's deposits were advised to insure them. The bank did not guarantee liability.

14 SEPTEMBER 1971: *Yard inquiry into "let down" over bank raid*

Scotland Yard last night called for an inquiry into "disturbing aspects" of police handling of events in connection with the weekend raid at Lloyds Bank, Baker Street, London. Complaints had been voiced that they were slow to follow up information supplied to them by an amateur radio operator, or "ham." The report is likely to be passed to Sir John Waldron, the Commissioner of Metropolitan Police, after inquiries have been made by senior Yard men.

The Yard men say that they were let down by the security staff of Lloyds Bank. The bank staff say that they were assured that their alarms were foolproof. The Post Office complains that it could have caught the gang if the information about the radio ham's activities had been given to it earlier.

The inquiry will want to know the answer to two main questions: Why the Post Office detector service was not called until midday on Sunday, ten hours after the ham had reported to the police, when the Post Office said it was too late for it to do anything; and Why an empty shop two doors away from the bank was not checked when police went to the premises. If they had checked, it is suggested, they would have found a tunnel leading straight into the bank's strongroom forty feet away.

Lloyds Bank is expected to carry out a full review of its security arrangements. The strongroom floor was clearly not wired to the main alarm circuit.

Scotland Yard was cautious last night about questions on whether it had handled the tracking operation efficiently. It stated that it did not know why the Post Office was not told earlier and that this point would be investigated.

Asked why the empty shop was not searched, a Scotland Yard official said: "One has to remember that police were engaged in trying to check a very large number of premises in a very short time."

The inquiry is likely to want to know whether the first report from the radio ham, Mr. Robert Rowlands, in Wimpole Street, about the conversations he heard between the bank thieves was taken seriously enough.

Scotland Yard maintained that a news blackout on radio messages was imposed because they thought publication of the details would prejudice inquiries and attempts to catch the thieves.

"We suppose it could be argued that if publication had been authorized and details had been reported on radio and in the newspapers there is the possibility that the raiders would have panicked and abandoned their attempt. But this is hindsight," the Yard said.

Questions that may arise are how Scotland Yard thought it would trace the bank concerned without calling in the Post Office. The detector vans have some of the most sophisticated equipment available in the world for tracing the source of a radio signal, but it is a long and complicated task.

The police appear to have been misled by the bank security men when they called at the Baker Street premises on Sunday. They were told that if the strongroom door was shut and the circuit was not broken then everything must be all right.

They were informed, too, that if they wanted to check the inside of the strongroom they would have to go through a complicated, and necessary, procedure of obtaining permission from a senior bank official. With that assurance they left, after standing only a few feet from the raiders.

Lloyds Bank said yesterday: "It is a little unusual for raiders to come up through the floor."

From Sunday evening the radio messages were flashing back and forwards between members of the gang, estimated to number six or seven and to include a woman.

The raiders were inside the strongroom when the bank security men arrived on the scene and sat tight.

The police, it is suggested, could perhaps have got a good "fix" on the radio signal location if they had enlisted the aid of other radio hams. They could have done this by calling them up on another wave band and asking them to tune in to the conversation.

They could have reported back the strength of the signal. A compass and a map are then needed to pinpoint the signal. It should be found to be coming from where the lines of the various signal points meet.

Police said that the tunnel driven under a restaurant from the shop to the bank was a professional job. "It was obviously made by someone with experience of tunneling and probably with knowledge of the layout of this street," an officer said.

"It would have been very easy to have chosen a point where the tunnel would have been blocked by gas or electricity cables, but it was a straight, clear course."

Mr. Rowlands said on Independent Television News last night that he picked up the gang's conversation because "I just happened to change the frequency." He added, "I was fortunate. It was a pure fluke."

He said that he had told the police he estimated the transmissions were coming from within half a mile of where he was. The Post Office had later confirmed this. Mention of a waiter in the raiders' conversation suggested that an hotel was in the vicinity.

14 SEPTEMBER 1971: *Ethereal dialogue from a fume-filled vault*

The *Evening Standard* yesterday printed what it claimed to be a conversation between the bank raid thieves in Baker Street, London, as picked up by a radio amateur. It read as follows:

First voice: Are you receiving me?

Second voice: Loud and clear.

First voice: Right, well listen carefully. We want you to mind for one hour from now until approximately one o'clock and then to go off the air, get some sleep and come on the air with both radios at six o'clock in the morning.

Second voice: This is not a very good pitch during the day, you know that, don't you? It's all blowing about and everything.

First voice: Are you sure you will be on the street tomorrow?

Second voice: I suggest we carry on tonight, mate, and get it done with.

First voice: Look, the place is filled with fumes where we was cutting. And if the Security come in and smell the fumes we are all going to take stoppo and none of us have got nothing. Whereas this way we have all got 300 grand to cut up when we come back in the morning. And if Security have loused it up for us, well at least we have got something.

Second voice: I've heard you. Let me alone and let me have a think for a second.

The radio reception at that point was distorted but the second man seemed to have said that if he left he could return in the morning and go up through a back window.

First voice: What happens if you are sighted?

Second voice: Sighted? These back stairs are not half so bad as these front. I can only be booked from one way. I should think I've a good chance of not being sighted.

First voice: Well, they join; they all say that you should stay there.

Second voice: Well the difference is they don't all feel like . . . my eyes are like organ stops, mate. I'm not going to be any good tomorrow anyway. I can hardly see now unless I don't do something.

First voice: But you can go to sleep tonight.

Second voice: How am I going to sleep tonight? For a start off I won't wake up. It's a certainty that, and I am not going to sleep away up to ten am I?

First voice: You'll have to stay up there. How can you guarantee getting in in the morning? Cor . . . the noise upstairs; you've got to hear and witness it to realize how bad it is.

Second voice: You have got to experience exactly the same position as me, mate, to understand how I feel. My eyes are so bad they are blurred and I've been using bins [cockney slang for spectacles or binoculars] all night.

First voice: You can have eight hours' sleep.

Second voice: Where am I going to sleep, mate? Who wakes me up?

First voice: If you don't wake up after eight hours you are not a normal person are you? Listen, it is not a bad rate of pay, is it? It's thirty and probably another thirty to come or more.

Second voice: What time do you plan to start tomorrow?

A woman's voice: About half eight to nine.

After more argument another voice came into the conversation. It also complained of the fumes and went on: "We have done 90 per cent of the easy ones and we now face the hard ones. If you are worried about waking up put the ear plugs in your ear and go to sleep. We will call you up. It will be like an alarm call. We are in a rough state ourselves."

In the morning a voice asked: "How's everything?"

Second voice: Everything's fine. No intruders whatsoever.

The first voice then thanked him for the work he had done and said they would all be leaving early that afternoon (Sunday). Later, referring to the security men, the first voice said: "They're in here somewhere now so pay absolute attention."

Second voice: The guy from next door has just looked in our window. He has gone back now. It's not the normal guy, it's a waiter.

Some time later something was said which may have been the signal that the job was over.

14 SEPTEMBER 1971: *The Times Diary:*

Police investigating the "Great Baker Street Bank Raid" might find an ironic parallel in the Sherlock Holmes story, "The Red-Headed League." In that story Jabez Wilson, a struggling pawnbroker, has his attention drawn by his assistant, Vincent Spaulding, to an advertisement seeking red-headed men for four hours office work a day, between 10 A.M. and 2 P.M.

Wilson, whose shop is next door to the Coburg branch of the City and Suburban Bank, gets the job which consists of copying out *Encyclopædia Britannica* from start to finish. However, the ever-watchful Holmes, who had seen the advertisement and recognized Spaulding as having a criminal record, began to linger in the area of the bank.

By tapping the pavement with his stick he realized there was a hollow underneath and when the bank robbers eventually broke into the strong-room from the pawnbroker's shop, Holmes was there to meet them—unlike the police over the weekend who were apparently checking the bank premises while the robbers were in the strongroom.

16 SEPTEMBER 1971: *Yard seek man who warned them of bank robbery*

BY CLIVE BORRELL

An underworld informant who warned them 12 months ago that Lloyds Bank in Baker Street was to be robbed was being sought last night by Scotland Yard detectives.

For several months Flying Squad officers kept day and night observation on the premises. Nothing happened and eventually the police guard was called off. . . .

At least £1m in cash and valuables is believed to have been stolen from 215 deposit boxes in the raid. . . .

Armed detectives were keeping a watch last night on a house in the south of England where a man, believed to have put up the money to finance the raid, is living. A similar watch was being kept on a flat frequented by a woman associate.

The Yard were told a year ago that the gang would tunnel under the bank from a shop nearby. The informant then described exactly how the robbery would and in fact did take place.

Detectives are examining their earlier files. They fear that their original informant may now be in danger of his life.

[*We break off the* Times *account just beyond the point at which the Sherlock Holmes adventure and the actual events of more than eighty years later diverge. In justice to Scotland Yard we should add that as a result of long, patient detective work of the kind mentioned in our last* Times *item the Yard finally apprehended all members of the gang and secured their conviction in 1973.*]

Anton Chekhov

1860–1904

THE DARLING

OLENKA, the daughter of the retired collegiate assessor, Plemyanniakov, was sitting in her back porch, lost in thought. It was hot, the flies were persistent and teasing, and it was pleasant to reflect that it would soon be evening. Dark rainclouds were gathering from the east, and bringing from time to time a breath of moisture in the air.

Kukin, who was the manager of an open-air theater called the Tivoli, and who lived in the lodge, was standing in the middle of the garden looking at the sky.

"Again!" he observed despairingly. "It's going to rain again! Rain every day, as though to spite me. I might as well hang myself! It's ruin! Fearful losses every day."

He flung up his hands, and went on, addressing Olenka:

"There! that's the life we lead, Olga Semyonovna. It's enough to make one cry. One works and does one's utmost, one wears oneself out, getting no sleep at night, and racks one's brain what to do for the best. And then what happens? To begin with, one's public is ignorant, boorish. I give them the very best operetta, a dainty masque, first rate music-hall artists. But do you suppose that's what they want! They don't understand anything of that sort. They want a clown; what they ask for is vulgarity. And then look at the weather! Almost every evening it rains. It started on the tenth of May, and it's kept it up all May and June. It's simply awful! The public doesn't come, but I've to pay the rent just the same, and pay the artists."

The next evening the clouds would gather again, and Kukin would say with an hysterical laugh:

"Well, rain away, then! Flood the garden, drown me! Damn my luck in this world and the next! Let the artists have me up! Send me to prison! —to Siberia!—the scaffold! Ha, ha, ha!"

And next day the same thing.

Olenka listened to Kukin with silent gravity, and sometimes tears came into her eyes. In the end his misfortunes touched her; she grew to love him. He was a small thin man, with a yellow face, and curls combed forward on his forehead. He spoke in a thin tenor; as he talked his mouth worked on one side, and there was always an expression of despair on his face; yet he aroused a deep and genuine affection in her. She was always fond of some one, and could not exist without loving. In earlier days she had loved her papa, who now sat in a darkened room, breathing with difficulty; she had loved her aunt who used to come every other year from Bryansk; and before that, when she was at school, she had loved her French master. She was a gentle, soft-hearted, compassionate girl, with mild, tender eyes and very good health. At the sight of her full rosy cheeks, her soft white neck with a little dark mole on it, and the kind, naïve smile, which came into her face when she listened to anything pleasant, men thought, "Yes, not half bad," and smiled too, while lady visitors could not refrain from seizing her hand in the middle of a conversation, exclaiming in a gush of delight, "You darling!"

The house in which she had lived from her birth upwards, and which was left her in her father's will, was at the extreme end of the town, not far from the Tivoli. In the evenings and at night she could hear the band playing, and the crackling and banging of fireworks, and it seemed to her that it was Kukin struggling with his destiny, storming the entrenchments of his chief foe, the indifferent public; there was a sweet thrill at her heart, she had no desire to sleep, and when he returned home at daybreak, she tapped softly at her bedroom window, and showing him only her face and one shoulder through the curtain, she gave him a friendly smile. . . .

He proposed to her, and they were married. And when he had a closer view of her neck and her plump, fine shoulders, he threw up his hands, and said:

"You darling!"

He was happy, but as it rained on the day and night of his wedding, his face still retained an expression of despair.

They got on very well together. She used to sit in his office, to look after things in the Tivoli, to put down the accounts and pay the wages. And her rosy cheeks, her sweet, naïve, radiant smile, were to be seen now at the office window, now in the refreshment bar or behind the scenes of the theater. And already she used to say to her acquaintances that the theater was the chief and most important thing in life, and that it was only through the drama that one could derive true enjoyment and become cultivated and humane.

"But do you suppose the public understands that?" she used to say. "What they want is a clown. Yesterday we gave 'Faust Inside Out,' and almost all the boxes were empty; but if Vanitchka and I had been producing some vulgar thing, I assure you the theater would have been packed. Tomorrow Vanitchka and I are doing 'Orpheus in Hell.' Do come."

And what Kukin said about the theater and the actors she repeated. Like him she despised the public for their ignorance and their indifference to art; she took part in the rehearsals, she corrected the actors, she kept an eye on the behavior of the musicians, and when there was an unfavorable notice in the local paper, she shed tears, and then went to the editor's office to set things right.

The actors were fond of her and used to call her "Vanitchka and I," and "the darling"; she was sorry for them and used to lend them small sums of money, and if they deceived her, she used to shed a few tears in private, but did not complain to her husband.

They got on well in the winter too. They took the theater in the town for the whole winter, and let it for short terms to a Little Russian company, or to a conjurer, or to a local dramatic society. Olenka grew stouter, and was always beaming with satisfaction, while Kukin grew thinner and yellower, and continually complained of their terrible losses, although he had not done badly all the winter. He used to cough at night, and she used to give him hot raspberry tea or lime-flower water, to rub him with eau-de-Cologne and to wrap him in her warm shawls.

"You're such a sweet pet!" she used to say with perfect sincerity, stroking his hair. "You're such a pretty dear!"

Towards Lent he went to Moscow to collect a new troupe, and without him she could not sleep, but sat all night at her window, looking at the stars, and she compared herself with the hens, who are awake all night and uneasy when the cock is not in the hen-house. Kukin was detained in Moscow, and wrote that he would be back at Easter, adding some instructions about the Tivoli. But on the Sunday before Easter, late in the evening, came a sudden ominous knock at the gate; someone was hammering on the gate as though on a barrel—boom, boom, boom! The drowsy cook went flopping with her bare feet through the puddles, as she ran to open the gate.

"Please open," said someone outside in a thick bass. "There is a telegram for you."

Olenka had received telegrams from her husband before, but this time for some reason she felt numb with terror. With shaking hands she opened the telegram and read as follows:

"Ivan Petrovitch died suddenly today. Awaiting immate instructions fufuneral Tuesday."

That was how it was written in the telegram—"fufuneral," and the utterly incomprehensible word "immate." It was signed by the stage manager of the operatic company.

"My darling!" sobbed Olenka. "Vanitchka, my precious, my darling! Why did I ever meet you! Why did I know you and love you! Your poor heart-broken Olenka is all alone without you!"

Kukin's funeral took place on Tuesday in Moscow. Olenka returned home on Wednesday, and as soon as she got indoors she threw herself on her bed and sobbed so loudly that it could be heard next door, and in the street.

"Poor darling!" the neighbors said, as they crossed themselves. "Olga Semyonovna, poor darling! How she does take on!"

Three months later Olenka was coming home from mass, melancholy and in deep mourning. It happened that one of her neighbors, Vassily Andreitch Pustovalov, returning home from church, walked back beside her. He was the manager at Babakayev's, the timber merchant's. He wore a straw hat, a white waistcoat, and a gold watch-chain, and looked more like a country gentleman than a man in trade.

"Everything happens as it is ordained, Olga Semyonovna," he said gravely, with a sympathic note in his voice; "and if any of our dear ones die, it must be because it is the will of God, so we ought to have fortitude and bear it submissively."

After seeing Olenka to her gate, he said goodbye and went on. All day afterwards she heard his sedately dignified voice, and whenever she shut her eyes she saw his dark beard. She liked him very much. And apparently she had made an impression on him too, for not long afterwards an elderly lady, with whom she was only slightly acquainted, came to drink coffee with her, and as soon as she was seated at table began to talk about Pustovalov, saying that he was an excellent man whom one could thoroughly depend upon, and that any girl would be glad to marry him. Three days later Pustovalov came himself. He did not stay long, only about ten minutes, and he did not say much, but when he left, Olenka loved him—loved him so much that she lay awake all night in a perfect fever, and in the morning she sent for the elderly lady. The match was quickly arranged, and then came the wedding.

Pustovalov and Olenka got on very well together when they were married.

Usually he sat in the office till dinnertime, then he went out on business, while Olenka took his place, and sat in the office till evening, making up accounts and booking orders.

"Timber gets dearer every year; the price rises twenty per cent," she would say to her customers and friends. "Only fancy we used to sell local timber, and now Vassitchka always has to go for wood to the Mogilev district. And the freight!" she would add, covering her cheeks with her hands in horror. "The freight!"

It seemed to her that she had been in the timber trade for ages and ages, and that the most important and necessary thing in life was timber; and there was something intimate and touching to her in the very sound of words such as "baulk," "post," "beam," "pole," "scantling," "batten," "lath," "plank," etc.

At night when she was asleep she dreamed of perfect mountains of planks and boards, and long strings of wagons, carting timber somewhere far away. She dreamed that a whole regiment of six-inch beams forty feet high, standing on end, was marching upon the timber-yard; that logs, beams, and boards knocked together with the resounding crash of dry wood, kept falling and getting up again, piling themselves on each other. Olenka cried out in her sleep, and Pustovalov said to her tenderly: "Olenka, what's the matter, darling? Cross yourself!"

Her husband's ideas were hers. If he thought the room was too hot, or that business was slack, she thought the same. Her husband did not care for entertainments, and on holidays he stayed at home. She did likewise.

"You are always at home or in the office," her friends said to her. "You should go to the theater, darling, or to the circus."

"Vassitchka and I have no time to go to theaters," she would answer sedately. "We have no time for nonsense. What's the use of these theaters?"

On Saturdays Pustovalov and she used to go to the evening service; on holidays to early mass, and they walked side by side with softened faces as they came home from church. There was a pleasant fragrance about them both, and her silk dress rustled agreeably. At home they drank tea, with fancy bread and jams of various kinds, and afterwards they ate pie. Every day at twelve o'clock there was a savory smell of beet-root soup and of mutton or duck in their yard, and on fastdays of fish, and no one could pass the gate without feeling hungry. In the office the samovar was always boiling, and customers were regaled with tea and cracknels.[1] Once a week the couple went to the baths and returned side by side, both red in the face.

"Yes, we have nothing to complain of, thank God," Olenka used to

---

[1] hard biscuits

say to her acquaintances. "I wish every one were as well off as Vassitchka and I."

When Pustovalov went away to buy wood in the Mogilev district, she missed him dreadfully, lay awake and cried. A young veterinary surgeon in the army, called Smirnin, to whom they had let their lodge, used sometimes to come in in the evening. He used to talk to her and play cards with her, and this entertained her in her husband's absence. She was particularly interested in what he told her of his home life. He was married and had a little boy, but was separated from his wife because she had been unfaithful to him, and now he hated her and used to send her forty roubles a month for the maintenance of their son. And hearing of all this, Olenka sighed and shook her head. She was sorry for him.

"Well, God keep you," she used to say to him at parting, as she lighted him down the stairs with a candle. "Thank you for coming to cheer me up, and may the Mother of God give you health."

And she always expressed herself with the same sedateness and dignity, the same reasonableness, in imitation of her husband. As the veterinary surgeon was disappearing behind the door below, she would say:

"You know, Vladimir Platonitch, you'd better make it up with your wife. You should forgive her for the sake of your son. You may be sure the little fellow understands."

And when Pustovalov came back, she told him in a low voice about the veterinary surgeon and his unhappy home life, and both sighed and shook their heads and talked about the boy, who, no doubt, missed his father, and by some strange connection of ideas, they went up to the holy ikons, bowed to the ground before them and prayed that God would give them children.

And so the Pustovalovs lived for six years quietly and peaceably in love and complete harmony.

But behold! one winter day after drinking hot tea in the office, Vassily Andreitch went out into the yard without his cap on to see about sending off some timber, caught cold and was taken ill. He had the best doctors, but he grew worse and died after four months' illness. And Olenka was a widow once more.

"I've nobody, now you've left me, my darling," she sobbed, after her husband's funeral. "How can I live without you, in wretchedness and misery! Pity me, good people, all alone in the world!"

She went about dressed in black with long "weepers,"[2] and gave up wearing hat and gloves for good. She hardly ever went out, except to church, or to her husband's grave, and led the life of a nun. It was not till six months later that she took off the weepers and opened the shutters of the windows. She was sometimes seen in the mornings, going with her cook to market for provisions, but what went on in her house and how she lived now could only be surmised. People guessed, from seeing her drink-

---

[2] a badge of mourning, probably the widow's black veil

ing tea in her garden with the veterinary surgeon, who read the newspaper aloud to her, and from the fact that, meeting a lady she knew at the
post office, she said to her:

"There is no proper veterinary inspection in our town, and that's the
cause of all sorts of epidemics. One is always hearing of people's getting
infection from the milk supply, or catching diseases from horses and
cows. The health of domestic animals ought to be as well cared for as
the health of human beings."

She repeated the veterinary surgeon's words, and was of the same
opinion as he about everything. It was evident that she could not live a
year without some attachment, and had found new happiness in the lodge.
In any one else this would have been censured, but no one could think ill
of Olenka; everything she did was so natural. Neither she nor the veterinary surgeon said anything to other people of the change in their relations, and tried, indeed, to conceal it, but without success, for Olenka
could not keep a secret. When he had visitors, men serving in his regiment, and she poured out tea or served the supper, she would begin talking of the cattle plague, of the foot and mouth disease, and of the munici-
pal slaughterhouses. He was dreadfully embarrassed, and when the guests
had gone, he would seize her by the hand and hiss angrily:

"I've asked you before not to talk about what you don't understand.
When we veterinary surgeons are talking among ourselves, please don't
put your word in. It's really annoying."

And she would look at him with astonishment and dismay, and ask
him in alarm: "But, Voloditchka, what *am* I to talk about?"

And with tears in her eyes she would embrace him, begging him not to
be angry, and they were both happy.

But this happiness did not last long. The veterinary surgeon departed,
departed for ever with his regiment, when it was transferred to a distant
place—to Siberia, it may be. And Olenka was left alone.

Now she was absolutely alone. Her father had long been dead, and his
armchair lay in the attic, covered with dust and lame of one leg. She got
thinner and plainer, and when people met her in the street they did not
look at her as they used to, and did not smile to her; evidently her best
years were over and left behind, and now a new sort of life had begun for
her, which did not bear thinking about. In the evening Olenka sat in the
porch, and heard the band playing and the fireworks popping in the
Tivoli, but now the sound stirred no response. She looked into her yard
without interest, thought of nothing, wished for nothing, and afterwards,
when night came on she went to bed and dreamed of her empty yard. She
ate and drank as it were unwillingly.

And what was worst of all, she had no opinions of any sort. She saw
the objects about her and understood what she saw, but could not form
any opinion about them, and did not know what to talk about. And how
awful it is not to have any opinions! One sees a bottle, for instance, or the
rain, or a peasant driving in his cart, but what the bottle is for, or the

rain, or the peasant, and what is the meaning of it, one can't say, and could not even for a thousand roubles. When she had Kukin, or Pustovalov, or the veterinary surgeon, Olenka could explain everything, and give her opinion about anything you like, but now there was the same emptiness in her brain and in her heart as there was in her yard outside. And it was as harsh and as bitter as wormwood in the mouth.

Little by little the town grew in all directions. The road became a street, and where the Tivoli and the timber-yard had been, there were new turnings and houses. How rapidly time passes! Olenka's house grew dingy, the roof got rusty, the shed sank on one side, and the whole yard was overgrown with docks and stinging-nettles. Olenka herself had grown plain and elderly; in summer she sat in the porch, and her soul, as before, was empty and dreary and full of bitterness. In winter she sat at her window and looked at the snow. When she caught the scent of spring, or heard the chime of the church bells, a sudden rush of memories from the past came over her, there was a tender ache in her heart, and her eyes brimmed over with tears; but this was only for a minute, and then came emptiness again and the sense of the futility of life. The black kitten, Briska, rubbed against her and purred softly, but Olenka was not touched by these feline caresses. That was not what she needed. She wanted a love that would absorb her whole being, her whole soul and reason—that would give her ideas and an object in life, and would warm her old blood. And she would shake the kitten off her skirt and say with vexation:

"Get along; I don't want you!"

And so it was, day after day and year after year, and no joy, and no opinions. Whatever Mavra, the cook, said she accepted.

One hot July day, towards evening, just as the cattle were being driven away, and the whole yard was full of dust, some one suddenly knocked at the gate. Olenka went to open it herself and was dumbfounded when she looked out: she saw Smirnin, the veterinary surgeon, gray-headed, and dressed as a civilian. She suddenly remembered everything. She could not help crying and letting her head fall on his breast without uttering a word, and in the violence of her feeling she did not notice how they both walked into the house and sat down to tea.

"My dear Vladimir Platonitch! What fate has brought you?" she muttered, trembling with joy.

"I want to settle here for good, Olga Semyonovna," he told her. "I have resigned my post, and have come to settle down and try my luck on my own account. Besides, it's time for my boy to go to school. He's a big boy. I am reconciled with my wife, you know."

"Where is she?" asked Olenka.

"She's at the hotel with the boy, and I'm looking for lodgings."

"Good gracious, my dear soul! Lodgings? Why not have my house? Why shouldn't that suit you? Why, my goodness, I wouldn't take any rent!" cried Olenka in a flutter, beginning to cry again. "You live here and the lodge will do nicely for me. Oh dear! how glad I am!"

Next day the roof was painted and the walls were whitewashed, and Olenka, with her arms akimbo, walked about the yard giving directions. Her face was beaming with her old smile, and she was brisk and alert as though she had waked from a long sleep. The veterinary's wife arrived —a thin, plain lady, with short hair and a peevish expression. With her was her little Sasha, a boy of ten, small for his age, blue-eyed, chubby, with dimples in his cheeks. And scarcely had the boy walked into the yard when he ran after the cat, and at once there was the sound of his gay, joyous laugh.

"Is that your puss, auntie?" he asked Olenka. "When she has little ones, do give us a kitten. Mamma is awfully afraid of mice."

Olenka talked to him, and gave him tea. Her heart warmed and there was a sweet ache in her bosom, as though the boy had been her own child. And when he sat at the table in the evening, going over his lessons, she looked at him with deep tenderness and pity as she murmured to herself:

"You pretty pet! . . . my precious! . . . Such a fair little thing, and so clever."

" 'An island is a piece of land which is entirely surrounded by water,' " he read aloud.

"An island is a piece of land," she repeated, and this was the first opinion to which she gave utterance with positive conviction after so many years of silence and dearth of ideas.

Now she had opinions of her own, and at supper she talked to Sasha's parents, saying how difficult the lessons were at the high schools, but that yet the high school was better than a commercial one, since with a high-school education all careers were open to one, such as being a doctor or an engineer.

Sasha began going to the high school. His mother departed to Harkov to her sister's and did not return; his father used to go off every day to inspect cattle, and would often be away from home for three days together, and it seemed to Olenka as though Sasha was entirely abandoned, that he was not wanted at home, that he was being starved, and she carried him off to her lodge and gave him a little room there.

And for six months Sasha had lived in the lodge with her. Every morning Olenka came into his bedroom and found him fast asleep, sleeping noiselessly with his hand under his cheek. She was sorry to wake him.

"Sashenka," she would say mournfully, "get up, darling. It's time for school."

He would get up, dress and say his prayers, and then sit down to breakfast, drink three glasses of tea, and eat two large cracknels and a half a buttered roll. All this time he was hardly awake and a little ill-humored in consequence.

"You don't quite know your fable, Sashenka," Olenka would say, looking at him as though he were about to set off on a long journey. "What a lot of trouble I have with you! You must work and do your best, darling, and obey your teachers."

"Oh, do leave me alone!" Sasha would say.

Then he would go down the street to school, a little figure, wearing a big cap and carrying a satchel on his shoulder. Olenka would follow him noiselessly.

"Sashenka!" she would call after him, and she would pop into his hand a date or a caramel. When he reached the street where the school was, he would feel ashamed of being followed by a tall, stout woman; he would turn round and say:

"You'd better go home, auntie. I can go the rest of the way alone."

She would stand still and look after him fixedly till he had disappeared at the school-gate.

Ah, how she loved him! Of her former attachments not one had been so deep; never had her soul surrendered to any feeling so spontaneously, so disinterestedly, and so joyously as now that her maternal instincts were aroused. For this little boy with the dimple in his cheek and the big school cap, she would have given her whole life, she would have given it with joy and tears of tenderness. Why? Who can tell why?

When she had seen the last of Sasha, she returned home, contented and serene, brimming over with love; her face, which had grown younger during the last six months, smiled and beamed; people meeting her looked at her with pleasure.

"Good-morning, Olga Semyonovna, darling. How are you, darling?"

"The lessons at the high school are very difficult now," she would relate at the market. "It's too much; in the first class yesterday they gave him a fable to learn by heart, and a Latin translation and a problem. You know it's too much for a little chap."

And she would begin talking about the teachers, the lessons, and the school books, saying just what Sasha said.

At three o'clock they had dinner together: in the evening they learned their lessons together and cried. When she put him to bed, she would stay a long time making the Cross over him and murmuring a prayer; then she would go to bed and dream of that far-away misty future when Sasha would finish his studies and become a doctor or an engineer, would have a big house of his own with horses and a carriage, would get married and have children. . . . She would fall asleep still thinking of the same thing, and tears would run down her cheeks from her closed eyes, while the black cat lay purring beside her: "Mrr, mrr, mrr."

Suddenly there would come a loud knock at the gate.

Olenka would wake up breathless with alarm, her heart throbbing. Half a minute later would come another knock.

"It must be a telegram from Harkov," she would think, beginning to tremble from head to foot. "Sasha's mother is sending for him from Harkov. . . . Oh, mercy on us!"

She was in despair. Her head, her hands, and her feet would turn chill, and she would feel that she was the most unhappy woman in the world.

But another minute would pass, voices would be heard: it would turn out to be the veterinary surgeon coming home from the club.

"Well, thank God!" she would think.

And gradually the load in her heart would pass off, and she would feel at ease. She would go back to bed thinking of Sasha, who lay sound asleep in the next room, sometimes crying out in his sleep:

"I'll give it you! Get away! Shut up!"

Translated by Constance Garnett

Edith Wharton
1862-1937
ROMAN FEVER

FROM the table at which they had been lunching two American ladies of ripe but well-cared-for middle age moved across the lofty terrace of the Roman restaurant and, leaning on its parapet, looked first at each other, and then down on the outspread glories of the Palatine and the Forum, with the same expression of vague but benevolent approval.

As they leaned there a girlish voice echoed up gaily from the stairs leading to the court below. "Well, come along then," it cried, not to them but to an invisible companion, "and let's leave the young things to their knitting"; and a voice as fresh laughed back: "Oh, look here, Babs, not actually *knitting*—" "Well, I mean figuratively," rejoined the first. "After all, we haven't left our poor parents much else to do . . ." and at that point the turn of the stairs engulfed the dialogue.

The two ladies looked at each other again, this time with a tinge of smiling embarrassment, and the smaller and paler one shook her head and colored slightly.

"Barbara!" she murmured, sending an unheard rebuke after the mocking voice in the stairway.

The other lady, who was fuller, and higher in color, with a small determined nose supported by vigorous black eyebrows, gave a good-humored laugh. "That's what our daughters think of us!"

Her companion replied by a deprecating gesture. "Not of us individually. We must remember that. It's just the collective modern idea of Mothers. And you see—" Half guiltily she drew from her handsomely mounted black handbag a twist of crimson silk run through by two fine knitting needles. "One never knows," she murmured. "The new system has certainly given us a good deal of time to kill; and sometimes I get tired just looking—even at this." Her gesture was now addressed to the stupendous scene at their feet.

The dark lady laughed again, and they both relapsed upon the view, contemplating it in silence, with a sort of diffused serenity which might have been borrowed from the spring effulgence of the Roman skies. The luncheon-hour was long past, and the two had their end of the vast terrace to themselves. At its opposite extremity a few groups, detained by a lingering look at the outspread city, were gathering up guidebooks and fumbling for tips. The last of them scattered, and the two ladies were alone on the air-washed height.

"Well, I don't see why we shouldn't just stay here," said Mrs. Slade, the lady of the high color and energetic brows. Two derelict basket-chairs stood near, and she pushed them into the angle of the parapet, and settled herself in one, her gaze upon the Palatine. "After all, it's still the most beautiful view in the world."

"It always will be, to me," assented her friend Mrs. Ansley, with so slight a stress on the "me" that Mrs. Slade, though she noticed it, wondered if it were not merely accidental, like the random underlinings of old-fashioned letter-writers.

"Grace Ansley was always old-fashioned," she thought; and added aloud, with a retrospective smile: "It's a view we've both been familiar with for a good many years. When we first met here we were younger than our girls are now. You remember?"

"Oh, yes, I remember," murmured Mrs. Ansley, with the same undefinable stress.—"There's that head-waiter wondering," she interpolated. She was evidently far less sure than her companion of herself and of her rights in the world.

"I'll cure him of wondering," said Mrs. Slade, stretching her hand toward a bag as discreetly opulent-looking as Mrs. Ansley's. Signing to the head-waiter, she explained that she and her friend were old lovers of Rome, and would like to spend the end of the afternoon looking down on the view—that is, if it did not disturb the service? The head-waiter, bowing over her gratuity, assured her that the ladies were most welcome, and would be still more so if they would condescend to remain for dinner. A full-moon night, they would remember. . . .

Mrs. Slade's black brows drew together, as though references to the moon were out of place and even unwelcome. But she smiled away her frown as the headwaiter retreated. "Well, why not? We might do worse. There's no knowing, I suppose, when the girls will be back. Do you even know back from *where?* I don't!"

Mrs. Ansley again colored slightly. "I think those young Italian aviators we met at the Embassy invited them to fly to Tarquinia for tea. I suppose they'll want to wait and fly back by moonlight."

"Moonlight—moonlight! What a part it still plays. Do you suppose they're as sentimental as we were?"

"I've come to the conclusion that I don't in the least know what they are," said Mrs. Ansley. "And perhaps we didn't know much more about each other."

"No; perhaps we didn't."

Her friend gave her a shy glance. "I never should have supposed you were sentimental, Alida."

"Well, perhaps I wasn't." Mrs. Slade drew her lids together in retrospect; and for a few moments the two ladies, who had been intimate since childhood, reflected how little they knew each other. Each one, of course, had a label ready to attach to the other's name; Mrs. Delphin Slade, for instance, would have told herself, or any one who asked her, that Mrs. Horace Ansley, twenty-five years ago, had been exquisitely lovely—no, you wouldn't believe it, would you? . . . though, of course, still charming, distinguished. . . . Well, as a girl she had been exquisite; far more beautiful than her daughter Barbara, though certainly Babs, according to the new standards at any rate, was more effective—had more *edge*, as they say. Funny where she got it, with those two nullities as parents. Yes; Horace Ansley was—well, just the duplicate of his wife. Museum specimens of old New York. Good-looking, irreproachable, exemplary. Mrs. Slade and Mrs. Ansley had lived opposite each other—actually as well as figuratively—for years. When the drawing-room curtains in No. 20 East 73rd Street were renewed, No. 23, across the way, was always aware of it. And of all the movings, buyings, travels, anniversaries, illnesses—the tame chronicle of an estimable pair. Little of it escaped Mrs. Slade. But she had grown bored with it by the time her husband made his big *coup* in Wall Street, and when they bought in upper Park Avenue had already begun to think: "I'd rather live opposite a speakeasy for a change; at least one might see it raided." The idea of seeing Grace raided was so amusing that (before the move) she launched it at a woman's lunch. It made a hit, and went the rounds—she sometimes wondered if it had crossed the street, and reached Mrs. Ansley. She hoped not, but didn't much mind. Those were the days when respectability was at a discount, and it did the irreproachable no harm to laugh at them a little.

A few years later, and not many months apart, both ladies lost their husbands. There was an appropriate exchange of wreaths and condolences, and a brief renewal of intimacy in the half-shadow of their mourning; and now, after another interval, they had run across each other in Rome, at the same hotel, each of them the modest appendage of a salient daughter. The similarity of their lot had again drawn them together, lending itself to mild jokes, and the mutual confession that, if in old days it must have been tiring to "keep up" with daughters, it was now, at times, a little dull not to.

No doubt, Mrs. Slade reflected, she felt her unemployment more than poor Grace ever would. It was a big drop from being the wife of Delphin Slade to being his widow. She had always regarded herself (with a certain conjugal pride) as his equal in social gifts, as contributing her full share to the making of the exceptional couple they were: but the difference after his death was irremediable. As the wife of the famous corpora-

tion lawyer, always with an international case or two on hand, every day
brought its exciting and unexpected obligation: the impromptu entertaining of eminent colleagues from abroad, the hurried dashes on legal
business to London, Paris or Rome, where the entertaining was so handsomely reciprocated; the amusement of hearing in her wake: "What,
that handsome woman with the good clothes and the eyes is Mrs. Slade
—*the* Slade's wife? Really? Generally the wives of celebrities are such
frumps."

Yes; being *the* Slade's widow was a dullish business after that. In living up to such a husband all her faculties had been engaged; now she had
only her daughter to live up to, for the son who seemed to have inherited
his father's gifts had died suddenly in boyhood. She had fought through
that agony because her husband was there, to be helped and to help; now,
after the father's death, the thought of the boy had become unbearable.
There was nothing left but to mother her daughter; and dear Jenny was
such a perfect daughter that she needed no excessive mothering. "Now
with Babs Ansley I don't know that I *should* be so quiet," Mrs. Slade
sometimes half-enviously reflected; but Jenny, who was younger than
her brilliant friend, was that rare accident, an extremely pretty girl who
somehow made youth and prettiness seem as safe as their absence. It was
all perplexing—and to Mrs. Slade a little boring. She wished that Jenny
would fall in love—with the wrong man, even; that she might have to be
watched, outmaneuvered, rescued. And instead, it was Jenny who
watched her mother, kept her out of drafts, made sure that she had taken
her tonic. . . .

Mrs. Ansley was much less articulate than her friend, and her mental
portrait of Mrs. Slade was slighter, and drawn with fainter touches.
"Alida Slade's awfully brilliant; but not as brilliant as she thinks,"
would have summed it up; though she would have added, for the enlightenment of strangers, that Mrs. Slade had been an extremely dashing
girl; much more so than her daughter, who was pretty, of course, and
clever in a way, but had none of her mother's—well, "vividness," some
one had once called it. Mrs. Ansley would take up current words like
this, and cite them in quotation marks, as unheard-of audacities. No;
Jenny was not like her mother. Sometimes Mrs. Ansley thought Alida
Slade was disappointed; on the whole she had had a sad life. Full of failures and mistakes; Mrs. Ansley had always been rather sorry for
her. . . .

So these two ladies visualized each other, each through the wrong end
of her little telescope.

2

For a long time they continued to sit side by side without speaking.
It seemed as though, to both, there was a relief in laying down their somewhat futile activities in the presence of the vast *memento mori*[1] which

---

[1] reminder of death

faced them. Mrs. Slade sat quite still, her eyes fixed on the golden slope of the Palace of the Caesars, and after a while Mrs. Ansley ceased to fidget with her bag, and she too sank into meditation. Like many intimate friends, the two ladies had never before had occasion to be silent together, and Mrs. Ansley was slightly embarrassed by what seemed, after so many years, a new stage in their intimacy, and one with which she did not yet know how to deal.

Suddenly the air was full of that deep clangor of bells which periodically covers Rome with a roof of silver. Mrs. Slade glanced at her wrist-watch. "Five o'clock already," she said, as though surprised.

Mrs. Ansley suggested interrogatively: "There's bridge at the Embassy at five." For a long time Mrs. Slade did not answer. She appeared to be lost in contemplation, and Mrs. Ansley thought the remark had escaped her. But after a while she said, as if speaking out of a dream: "Bridge, did you say? Not unless you want to. . . . But I don't think I will, you know."

"Oh, no," Mrs. Ansley hastened to assure her. "I don't care to at all. It's so lovely here; and so full of old memories, as you say." She settled herself in her chair, and almost furtively drew forth her knitting. Mrs. Slade took sideway note of this activity, but her own beautifully cared-for hands remained motionless on her knee.

"I was just thinking," she said slowly, "what different things Rome stands for to each generation of travelers. To our grandmothers, Roman fever; to our mothers, sentimental dangers—how we used to be guarded! —to our daughters, no more dangers than the middle of Main Street. They don't know it—but how much they're missing!"

The long golden light was beginning to pale, and Mrs. Ansley lifted her knitting a little closer to her eyes. "Yes; how we were guarded!"

"I always used to think," Mrs. Slade continued, "that our mothers had a much more difficult job than our grandmothers. When Roman fever stalked the streets it must have been comparatively easy to gather in the girls at the danger hour; but when you and I were young, with such beauty calling us, and the spice of disobedience thrown in, and no worse risk than catching cold during the cool hour after sunset, the mothers used to be put to it to keep us in—didn't they?"

She turned again toward Mrs. Ansley, but the latter had reached a delicate point in her knitting. "One, two, three—slip two; yes, they must have been," she assented, without looking up.

Mrs. Slade's eyes rested on her with a deepened attention. "She can knit—in the face of *this!* How like her. . . ."

Mrs. Slade leaned back, brooding, her eyes ranging from the ruins which faced her to the long green hollow of the Forum, the fading glow of the church fronts beyond it, and the outlying immensity of the Colosseum. Suddenly she thought: "It's all very well to say that our girls have done away with sentiment and moonlight. But if Babs Ansley isn't out to catch that young aviator—the one who's a Marchese—then I don't know

anything. And Jenny has no chance beside her. I know that too. I wonder
if that's why Grace Ansley likes the two girls to go everywhere together? My poor Jenny as a foil—!" Mrs. Slade gave a hardly audible
laugh, and at the sound Mrs. Ansley dropped her knitting.

"Yes—?"

"I—oh, nothing. I was only thinking how your Babs carries everything before her. That Campolieri boy is one of the best matches in
Rome. Don't look so innocent, my dear—you know he is. And I was
wondering, ever so respectfully, you understand . . . wondering how
two such exemplary characters as you and Horace had managed to produce anything quite so dynamic." Mrs. Slade laughed again, with a touch
of asperity.

Mrs. Ansley's hands lay inert across her needles. She looked straight
out at the great accumulated wreckage of passion and splendor at her
feet. But her small profile was almost expressionless. At length she said:
"I think you overrate Babs, my dear."

Mrs. Slade's tone grew easier. "No; I don't. I appreciate her. And
perhaps envy you. Oh, my girl's perfect; if I were a chronic invalid I'd—
well, I think I'd rather be in Jenny's hands. There must be times . . .
but there! I always wanted a brilliant daughter . . . and never quite
understood why I got an angel instead."

Mrs. Ansley echoed her laugh in a faint murmur. "Babs is an angel
too."

"Of course—of course! But she's got rainbow wings. Well, they're
wandering by the sea with their young men; and here we sit . . . and
it all brings back the past a little too acutely."

Mrs. Ansley had resumed her knitting. One might almost have imagined (if one had known her less well, Mrs. Slade reflected) that, for her
also, too many memories rose from the lengthening shadows of those
august ruins. But no; she was simply absorbed in her work. What was
there for her to worry about? She knew that Babs would almost certainly
come back engaged to the extremely eligible Campolieri. "And she'll
sell the New York house, and settle down near them in Rome, and never
be in their way . . . she's much too tactful. But she'll have an excellent
cook, and just the right people in for bridge and cocktails . . . and a
perfectly peaceful old age among her grandchildren."

Mrs. Slade broke off this prophetic flight with a recoil of self-disgust.
There was no one of whom she had less right to think unkindly than of
Grace Ansley. Would she never cure herself of envying her? Perhaps
she had begun too long ago.

She stood up and leaned against the parapet, filling her troubled eyes
with the tranquilizing magic of the hour. But instead of tranquilizing her
the sight seemed to increase her exasperation. Her gaze turned toward
the Colosseum. Already its golden flank was drowned in purple shadow,
and above it the sky curved crystal clear, without light or color. It was
the moment when afternoon and evening hang balanced in mid-heaven.

Mrs. Slade turned back and laid her hand on her friend's arm. The gesture was so abrupt that Mrs. Ansley looked up, startled.

"The sun's set. You're not afraid, my dear?"

"Afraid—?"

"Of Roman fever or pneumonia? I remember how ill you were that winter. As a girl you had a very delicate throat, hadn't you?"

"Oh, we're all right up here. Down below, in the Forum, it does get deathly cold, all of a sudden . . . but not here."

"Ah, of course you know because you had to be so careful." Mrs. Slade turned back to the parapet. She thought: "I must make one more effort not to hate her." Aloud she said: "Whenever I look at the Forum from up here, I remember that story about a great-aunt of yours, wasn't she? A dreadfully wicked great-aunt?"

"Oh, yes; Great-aunt Harriet. The one who was supposed to have sent her young sister out to the Forum after sunset to gather a night-blooming flower for her album. All our great-aunts and grandmothers used to have albums of dried flowers."

Mrs. Slade nodded. "But she really sent her because they were in love with the same man—"

"Well, that was the family tradition. They said Aunt Harriet confessed it years afterward. At any rate, the poor little sister caught the fever and died. Mother used to frighten us with the story when we were children."

"And you frightened *me* with it, that winter when you and I were here as girls. The winter I was engaged to Delphin."

Mrs. Ansley gave a faint laugh. "Oh, did I? Really frightened you? I don't believe you're easily frightened."

"Not often; but I was then. I was easily frightened because I was too happy. I wonder if you know what that means?"

"I—yes . . ." Mrs. Ansley faltered.

"Well, I suppose that was why the story of your wicked aunt made such an impression on me. And I thought: 'There's no more Roman fever, but the Forum is deathly cold after sunset—especially after a hot day. And the Colosseum's even colder and damper.'"

"The Colosseum—?"

"Yes. It wasn't easy to get in, after the gates were locked for the night. Far from easy. Still, in those days it could be managed; it *was* managed, often. Lovers met there who couldn't meet elsewhere. You knew that?"

"I—I daresay. I don't remember."

"You don't remember? You don't remember going to visit some ruins or other one evening, just after dark, and catching a bad chill? You were supposed to have gone to see the moon rise. People always said that expedition was what caused your illness."

There was a moment's silence; then Mrs. Ansley rejoined: "Did they? It was all so long ago."

"Yes. And you got well again—so it didn't matter. But I suppose it struck your friends—the reason given for your illness, I mean—because everybody knew you were so prudent on account of your throat, and your mother took such care of you. . . . You *had* been out late sight-seeing, hadn't you, that night?"

"Perhaps I had. The most prudent girls aren't always prudent. What made you think of it now?"

Mrs. Slade seemed to have no answer ready. But after a moment she broke out: "Because I simply can't bear it any longer—!"

Mrs. Ansley lifted her head quickly. Her eyes were wide and very pale. "Can't bear what?"

"Why—your not knowing that I've always known why you went."

"Why I went—?"

"Yes. You think I'm bluffing, don't you? Well, you went to meet the man I was engaged to—and I can repeat every word of the letter that took you there."

While Mrs. Slade spoke Mrs. Ansley had risen unsteadily to her feet. Her bag, her knitting and gloves, slid in a panic-stricken heap to the ground. She looked at Mrs. Slade as though she were looking at a ghost.

"No, no—don't," she faltered out.

"Why not? Listen, if you don't believe me. 'My one darling, things can't go on like this. I must see you alone. Come to the Colosseum immediately after dark tomorrow. There will be somebody to let you in. No one whom you need fear will suspect'—but perhaps you've forgotten what the letter said?"

Mrs. Ansley met the challenge with an unexpected composure. Steadying herself against the chair she looked at her friend, and replied: "No; I know it by heart too."

"And the signature? 'Only *your* D.S.' Was that it? I'm right, am I? That was the letter that took you out that evening after dark?"

Mrs. Ansley was still looking at her. It seemed to Mrs. Slade that a slow struggle was going on behind the voluntarily controlled mask of her small quiet face. "I shouldn't have thought she had herself so well in hand," Mrs. Slade reflected, almost resentfully. But at this moment Mrs. Ansley spoke. "I don't know how you knew. I burned that letter at once."

"Yes; you would, naturally—you're so prudent!" The sneer was open now. "And if you burnt the letter you're wondering how on earth I know what was in it. That's it, isn't it?"

Mrs. Slade waited, but Mrs. Ansley did not speak.

"Well, my dear, I know what was in that letter because I wrote it!"

"You wrote it?"

"Yes."

The two women stood for a minute staring at each other in the last golden light. Then Mrs. Ansley dropped back into her chair. "Oh," she murmured, and covered her face with her hands.

Mrs. Slade waited nervously for another word or movement. None came, and at length she broke out: "I horrify you."

Mrs. Ansley's hands dropped to her knee. The face they uncovered was streaked with tears. "I wasn't thinking of you. I was thinking—it was the only letter I ever had from him!"

"And I wrote it. Yes; I wrote it! But I was the girl he was engaged to. Did you happen to remember that?"

Mrs. Ansley's head drooped again. "I'm not trying to excuse myself . . . I remembered. . . ."

"And still you went?"

"Still I went."

Mrs. Slade stood looking down on the small bowed figure at her side. The flame of her wrath had already sunk, and she wondered why she had ever thought there would be any satisfaction in inflicting so purposeless a wound on her friend. But she had to justify herself.

"You do understand? I'd found out—and I hated you, hated you. I knew you were in love with Delphin—and I was afraid; afraid of you, of your quiet ways, your sweetness . . . your . . . well, I wanted you out of the way, that's all. Just for a few weeks; just till I was sure of him. So in a blind fury I wrote that letter . . . I don't know why I'm telling you now."

"I suppose," said Mrs. Ansley slowly, "it's because you've always gone on hating me."

"Perhaps. Or because I wanted to get the whole thing off my mind." She paused. "I'm glad you destroyed the letter. Of course I never thought you'd die."

Mrs. Ansley relapsed into silence, and Mrs. Slade, leaning above her, was conscious of a strange sense of isolation, of being cut off from the warm current of human communion. "You think me a monster!"

"I don't know. . . . It was the only letter I had, and you say he didn't write it?"

"Ah, how you care for him still!"

"I cared for the memory," said Mrs. Ansley.

Mrs. Slade continued to look down on her. She seemed physically reduced by the blow—as if, when she got up, the wind might scatter her like a puff of dust. Mrs. Slade's jealousy suddenly leaped up again at the sight. All these years the woman had been living on that letter. How she must have loved him, to treasure the mere memory of its ashes! The letter of the man her friend was engaged to. Wasn't it she who was the monster?

"You tried your best to get him away from me, didn't you? But you failed; and I kept him. That's all."

"Yes. That's all."

"I wish now I hadn't told you. I'd no idea you'd feel about it as you do; I thought you'd be amused. It all happened so long ago, as you say; and you must do me the justice to remember that I had no reason to think

you'd ever taken it seriously. How could I, when you were married to
Horace Ansley two months afterward? As soon as you could get out of
bed your mother rushed you off to Florence and married you. People
were rather surprised—they wondered at its being done so quickly; but
I thought I knew. I had an idea you did it out of pique—to be able to say
you'd got ahead of Delphin and me. Girls have such silly reasons for
doing the most serious things. And your marrying so soon convinced me
that you'd never really cared."

"Yes. I suppose it would," Mrs. Ansley assented.

The clear heaven overhead was emptied of all its gold. Dusk spread
over it, abruptly darkening the Seven Hills. Here and there lights began
to twinkle through the foliage at their feet. Steps were coming and going
on the deserted terrace—waiters looking out of the doorway at the head
of the stairs, then reappearing with trays and napkins and flasks of wine.
Tables were moved, chairs straightened. A feeble string of electric
lights flickered out. Some vases of faded flowers were carried away, and
brought back replenished. A stout lady in a dust-coat suddenly appeared,
asking in broken Italian if any one had seen the elastic band with her
stick under the table at which she had lunched, the waiters assisting.

The corner where Mrs. Slade and Mrs. Ansley sat was still shadowy
and deserted. For a long time neither of them spoke. At length Mrs.
Slade began again: "I suppose I did it as a sort of joke—"

"A joke?"

"Well, girls are ferocious sometimes, you know. Girls in love especially. And I remember laughing to myself all that evening at the idea
that you were waiting around there in the dark, dodging out of sight,
listening for every sound, trying to get in—. Of course I was upset when
I heard you were ill afterward."

Mrs. Ansley had not moved for a long time. But now she turned slowly
toward her companion. "But I didn't wait. He'd arranged everything. He
was there. We were let in at once," she said.

Mrs. Slade sprang up from her leaning position. "Delphin there? They
let you in? Ah, now you're lying!" she burst out with violence.

Mrs. Ansley's voice grew clearer, and full of surprise. "But of course
he was there. Naturally he came—"

"Came? How did he know he'd find you there? You must be raving!"

Mrs. Ansley hesitated, as though reflecting. "But I answered the
letter. I told him I'd be there. So he came."

Mrs. Slade flung her hands up to her face. "Oh, God—you answered!
I never thought of your answering. . . ."

"It's odd you never thought of it, if you wrote the letter."

"Yes. I was blind with rage."

Mrs. Ansley rose, and drew her fur scarf about her. "It is cold here.
We'd better go . . . I'm sorry for you," she said, as she clasped the fur
about her throat.

The unexpected words sent a pang through Mrs. Slade. "Yes; we'd better go." She gathered up her bag and cloak. "I don't know why you should be sorry for me," she muttered.

Mrs. Ansley stood looking away from her toward the dusky secret mass of the Colosseum. "Well—because I didn't have to wait that night."

Mrs. Slade gave an unquiet laugh. "Yes; I was beaten there. But I oughtn't to begrudge it to you, I suppose. At the end of all these years. After all, I had everything; I had him for twenty-five years. And you had nothing but that one letter that he didn't write."

Mrs. Ansley was again silent. At length she turned toward the door of the terrace. She took a step, and turned back, facing her companion.

"I had Barbara," she said, and began to move ahead of Mrs. Slade toward the stairway.

Miguel de Unamuno
1864–1936
SAINT EMMANUEL THE GOOD, MARTYR

> If with this life only in view we have had hope in Christ, we are of all men the most to be pitied.
> —SAINT PAUL: I Cor. 15:19

NOW THAT the bishop of the diocese of Renada, to which this my beloved village of Valverde de Lucerna belongs, is seeking (according to rumor), to initiate the process of beatification of our Don Manuel, or more correctly, Saint Emmanuel the Good, who was parish priest here, I want to state in writing, by way of confession (although to what end only God, and not I can say), all that I can vouch for and remember of that matriarchal man who pervaded the most secret life of my soul, who was my true spiritual father, the father of my spirit, the spirit of myself, Angela Carballino.

The other, my flesh-and-blood temporal father, I scarcely knew, for he died when I was still a very young girl. I know that he came to Valverde de Lucerna from the outside world—that he was a stranger— and that he settled here when he married my mother. He had brought a number of books with him: *Don Quixote*, some plays from the classic theater, some novels; a few histories, the *Bertoldo*, everything all mixed together. From these books (practically the only ones in the entire village), I nurtured dreams as a young girl, dreams which in turn devoured me. My good mother gave me very little account either of the words or the deeds of my father. For the words and deeds of Don Manuel, whom she worshipped, of whom she was enamored, in common with all the rest of the village—in an exquisitely chaste manner, of course—had obliterated the memory of the words and deeds of her husband; him she commended to God, with full fervor, as she said her daily rosary.

Don Emmanuel I remember as if it were yesterday, from the time when I was a girl of ten, just before I was taken to the convent school in the cathedral city of Renada. At that time Don Emmanuel, our saint, must have been about thirty-seven years old. He was tall, slender, erect; he carried himself the way our Buitre Peak carries its crest, and his eyes had all the blue depth of our lake. As he walked he commanded all eyes, and not only the eyes but the hearts of all; gazing round at us he seemed to look through our flesh as through glass and penetrate our hearts. We all of us loved him, especially the children. And the things he said to us! Not words, things! The villagers could scent the odor of sanctity, they were intoxicated with it.

It was at this time that my brother Lazarus, who was in America, from where he regularly sent us money with which we lived in decent leisure, had my mother send me to the convent school, so that my education might be completed outside the village; he suggested this move despite the fact that he had no special fondness for the nuns. "But since, as far as I know," he wrote us, "there are no lay schools there yet,— especially not for young ladies—we will have to make use of the ones that do exist. The important thing is for Angelita to receive some polish and not be forced to continue among village girls." And so I entered the convent school. At one point I even thought I would become a teacher; but pedagogy soon palled upon me.

At school I met girls from the city and I made friends with some of them. But I still kept in touch with people in our village, and I received frequent reports and sometimes a visit.

And the fame of the parish priest reached as far as the school, for he was beginning to be talked of in the cathedral city. The nuns never tired of asking me about him.

Ever since early youth I had been endowed, I don't very well know from where, with a large degree of curiosity and restlessness, due at least in part to that jumble of books which my father had collected, and these qualities were stimulated at school, especially in the course of a relationship which I developed with a girl friend, who grew excessively attached to me. At times she proposed that we enter the same convent together, swearing to an everlasting "sisterhood"—and even that we seal the oath in blood. At other times she talked to me, with eyes half closed, of sweethearts and marriage adventures. Strangely enough, I have never heard of her since, or of what became of her, despite the fact that whenever our Don Manuel was spoken of, or when my mother wrote me something about him in her letters—which happened in almost every letter—and I read it to her, this girl would exclaim, as if in rapture: "What luck, my dear, to be able to live near a saint like that, a live saint, of flesh and blood, and to be able to kiss his hand; when you go back to your village write me everything, everything, and tell me about him."

Five years passed at school, five years which now have evanesced in memory like a dream at dawn, and when I became fifteen I returned to my own Valverde de Lucerna. By now everything revolved around Don Emmanuel: Don Emmanuel, the lake and the mountain. I arrived home anxious to know him, to place myself under his protection, and hopeful he would set me on my path in life.

It was rumored that he had entered the seminary to become a priest so that he might thus look after the sons of a sister recently widowed and provide for them in place of their father; that in the seminary his keen mind and his talents had distinguished him and that he had subsequently turned down opportunities for a brilliant career in the church because he wanted to remain exclusively a part of his Valverde de Lucerna, of his remote village which lay like a brooch between the lake and the mountain reflected in it.

How he did love his people! His life consisted in salvaging wrecked marriages, in forcing unruly sons to submit to their parents, or reconciling parents to their sons, and, above all, of consoling the embittered and the weary in spirit; meanwhile he helped everyone to die well.

I recall, among other incidents, the occasion when the unfortunate daughter of old aunt Rabona returned to our town. She had been in the city and lost her virtue there; now she returned unmarried and castoff, and she brought back a little son. Don Emmanuel did not rest until he had persuaded an old sweetheart, Perote by name, to marry the poor girl and, moreover, to legitimize the little creature with his own name. Don Emmanuel told Perote:

"Come now, give this poor waif a father, for he hasn't got one except in heaven."

"But, Don Emmanuel, it's not my fault. . . !"

"Who knows, my son, who knows. . . ! And besides, it's not a question of guilt."

And today, poor Perote, inspired on that occasion to saintliness by Don Emmanuel, and now a paralytic and invalid, has for staff and consolation of his life the son he accepted as his own when the boy was not his at all.

On Midsummer's Night, the shortest night of the year, it was a local custom here (and still is) for all the old crones, and a few old men, who thought they were possessed or bewitched (hysterics they were, for the most part, or in some cases epileptics) to flock to the lake. Don Emmanuel undertook to fulfill the same function as the lake, to serve as a pool of healing, to treat his charges and even, if possible, to cure them. And such was the effect of his presence, of his gaze, and above all of his voice—the miracle of his voice!—and the infinitely sweet authority of his words, that he actually did achieve some remarkable cures. Whereupon his fame increased, drawing all the sick of the environs to our lake and our priest. And yet once when a mother came to ask for a miracle in behalf of her son, he answered her with a sad smile:

"Ah, but I don't have my bishop's permission to perform miracles."

He was particularly interested in seeing that all the villagers kept themselves clean. If he chanced upon someone with a torn garment he would send him to the church: "Go and see the sacristan, and let him mend that tear." The sacristan was a tailor, and when, on the first day of the year, everyone went to congratulate him on his saint's day—his holy patron was Our Lord Jesus Himself—it was by Don Emmanuel's wish that everyone appeared in a new shirt, and those that had none received the present of a new one from Don Emmanuel himself.

He treated everyone with the greatest kindness; if he favored anyone, it was the most unfortunate, and especially those who rebelled. There was a congenital idiot in the village, the fool Blasillo, and it was toward him that Don Emmanuel chose to show the greatest love and concern; as a consequence he succeeded in miraculously teaching him things which had appeared beyond the idiot's comprehension. The fact was that the embers of understanding feebly glowing in the idiot were kindled whenever, like a pitiable monkey, he imitated his Don Emmanuel.

The marvel of the man was his voice; a divine voice which brought one close to weeping. Whenever he officiated at Solemn High Mass and intoned the prelude, a tremor ran through the congregation and all within sound of his voice were moved to the depths of their being. The sound of his chanting, overflowing the church, went on to float over the lake and settle at the foot of the mountain. And when on Good Friday he intoned "My God, my God, my God, why hast Thou forsaken me?" a profound shudder swept through the multitude, like the lash of a northeaster across the waters of the lake. It was as if these people heard the Lord Jesus Christ himself, as if the voice sprang from the ancient crucifix, at the foot of which generations of mothers had offered up their sorrows. And it happened that on one occasion his mother heard him and was unable to contain herself, and cried out to him right in the church, "My son!" calling her child. And the entire congregation was visibly affected. It was as if the mother's cry had issued from the half-open lips of the Mater Dolorosa—her heart transfixed by seven swords—which stood in one of the chapels of the nave. Afterwards, the fool Blasillo went about piteously repeating, as if he were an echo, "My God, my God, my God, why hast Thou forsaken me?" with such effect that everyone who heard him was moved to tears, to the great satisfaction of the fool, who prided himself on this triumph of imitation.

The priest's effect on people was such that no one ever dared to tell him a lie, and everyone confessed themselves to him without need of a confessional. So true was this that on one occasion, when a revolting crime had been committed in a neighboring village, the judge—a dull fellow who badly misunderstood Don Emmanuel—called on the priest and said:

"Let us see, Don Manuel, if you can get this bandit to admit the truth."

"So that afterwards you may punish him?" asked the saintly man. "No, Judge, no; I will not extract from any man a truth which could be the death of him. That is a matter between him and his God. . . . Human justice is none of my affair. 'Judge not that ye be not judged,' said our Lord."

"But the fact is, Father, that I, a judge . . ."

"I understand. You, Judge, must render unto Caesar that which is Caesar's, while I shall render unto God that which is God's."

And, as Don Emmanuel departed, he gazed at the suspected criminal and said:

"Make sure, only, that God forgives you, for that is all that matters."

Everyone went to Mass in the village, even if it were only to hear him and see him at the altar, where he appeared to be transfigured, his countenance lit from within. He introduced one holy practice to the popular cult; it consisted in assembling the whole town inside the church, men and women, ancients and youths, some thousand persons; there we recited the Creed, in unison, so that it sounded like a single voice: "I believe in God, the Almighty Father, Creator of heaven and earth . . ." and all the rest. It was not a chorus, but a single voice, a simple united voice, all the voices based on one on which they formed a kind of mountain, whose peak, lost at times in the clouds, was Don Emmanuel. As we reached the section "I believe in the resurrection of the flesh and life everlasting," the voice of Don Emmanuel was submerged, drowned in the voice of the populace as in a lake. In truth, he was silent. And I could hear the bells of that city which is said hereabouts to be at the bottom of the lake—bells which are also said to be audible on Midsummer's Night —the bells of the city which is submerged in the spiritual lake of our populace; I was hearing the voice of our dead, resurrected in us by the communion of saints. Later, when I had learned the secret of our saint, I understood that it was as if a caravan crossing the desert lost its leader as they approached the goal of their trek, whereupon his people lifted him on their shoulders to bring his lifeless body into the promised land.

When it came to dying themselves, most of the villagers refused to die unless they were holding on to Don Emmanuel's hand, as if to an anchor chain.

In his sermons he never inveighed against unbelievers, Masons, liberals or heretics. What for, when there were none in the village? Nor did it occur to him to speak against the wickedness of the press. On the other hand, one of his most frequent themes was gossip, against which he lashed out.

"Envy," he liked to repeat, "envy is nurtured by those who prefer to think they are envied, and most persecutions are the result of a persecution complex rather than of an impulse to persecute."

"But Don Emmanuel, just listen to what that fellow was trying to tell me . . ."

"We should concern ourselves less with what people are trying to tell us than with what they tell us without trying . . ."

His life was active rather than contemplative, and he constantly fled from idleness, even from leisure. Whenever he heard it said that idleness was the mother of all the vices, he added : "And also of the greatest vice of them all, which is to think idly." Once I asked him what he meant and he answered : "Thinking idly is thinking as a substitute for doing, or thinking too much about what is already done instead of about what must be done. What's done is done and over with, and one must go on to something else, for there is nothing worse than remorse without possible relief." Action! Action! Even in those early days I had already begun to realize that Don Emmanuel fled from being left to think in solitude, and I guessed that some obsession haunted him.

And so it was that he was always occupied, sometimes even occupied in searching for occupations. He wrote very little on his own, so that he scarcely left us anything in writing, even notes; on the other hand, he acted as scrivener for everyone else, especially mothers, for whom he composed letters to their absent sons.

He also worked with his hands, pitching in to help with some of the village tasks. At threshing time he reported to the threshing floor, to flail and winnow, meanwhile teaching and entertaining the workers by turn. Sometimes he took the place of a worker who had fallen sick. One day in the dead of winter he came upon a child, shivering with the bitter cold. The child's father had sent him into the woods to bring back a strayed calf.

"Listen," he said to the child, "you go home and get warm, and tell your father that I am bringing back the calf." On the way back with the animal he ran into the father, who had come out to meet him, thoroughly ashamed of himself.

In winter he chopped wood for the poor. When a certain magnificent walnut tree died—"that matriarchal walnut," he called it, a tree under whose shade he had played as a boy and whose fruit he had eaten for so many years—he asked for the trunk, carried it to his house and, after he had cut six planks from it, which he put away at the foot of his bed, he made firewood of the rest to warm the poor. He also was in the habit of making handballs for the boys and a goodly number of toys for the younger children.

Often he used to accompany the doctor on his rounds, adding his presence and prestige to the doctor's prescriptions. Most of all he was interested in maternity cases and the care of children; it was his opinion that the old wives' sayings "from the cradle to heaven" and the other one about "little angels belong in heaven" were nothing short of blasphemy. The death of a child moved him deeply.

"A child stillborn," I once heard him say, "or one who dies soon after birth, is the most terrible of mysteries to me. It's as if it were a suicide. Or as if the child were crucified."

And once, when a man had taken his own life and the father of the suicide, an outsider, asked Don Emmanuel if his son could be buried in consecrated ground, the priest answered:

"Most certainly, for at the last moment, in the very last throes, he must certainly have repented. There is no doubt of it whatsoever in my mind."

From time to time he would visit the local school to help the teacher, to teach alongside him—and not only the catechism. The simple truth was that he fled relentlessly from idleness and from solitude. He went so far in this desire of his to mingle with the villagers, especially the youth and the children, that he even attended the village dances. And more than once he played the drum to keep time for the young men and women dancing; this kind of activity, which in another priest would have seemed like a grotesque mockery of his calling, in him somehow took on the appearance of a holy and religious exercise. When the Angelus would ring out, he would put down the drum and sticks, take off his hat (all the others doing the same) and pray: "The angel of the Lord declared unto Mary: Hail Mary . . ." And afterwards: "Now, let us rest until tomorrow."

"First of all," he would say, "the village must be happy; everyone must be happy to be alive. To be satisfied with life is of first importance. No one should want to die until it is God's will."

"I want to die now," a recently widowed woman once told him, "I want to be with my husband . . ."

"And why now?" he asked. "Stay here and pray God for his soul."

One of his well-loved remarks was made at a wedding: "Ah, if I could only change all the water in our lake into wine, into a dear little wine which, no matter how much of it one drank, would always make one joyful without intoxicating . . . or, if intoxicating, would make one joyfully drunk."

Once upon a time a band of poor acrobats came through the village. The leader—who arrived on the scene with a gravely ill and pregnant wife and three sons to help him—played the clown. While he was in the village square making all the children, and even some of the adults, laugh with glee, his wife suddenly fell desperately ill and had to leave; she went off accompanied by a look of anguish from the clown and a howl of laughter from the children. Don Emmanuel hurried after, and, a little later, in a corner of the inn's stable, he helped her give up her soul in a state of grace. When the performance was over and the villagers and the clown learned of the tragedy, they came to the inn, and there the poor bereaved clown, in a voice choked with tears, told Don Emmanuel, as he took his hand and kissed it: "They are quite right, Father, when they say you are a saint." Don Emmanuel took the clown's hand in his and replied before everyone:

"It's you who are the saint, good clown. I watched you at your work and understood that you do it not only to provide bread for your children, but also to give joy to the children of others. And I tell you now that your wife, the mother of your children, whom I sent to God while you worked to give joy, is at rest in the Lord, and that you will join her there, and that the angels, whom you will make laugh with happiness in heaven, will reward you with their laughter."

And everyone present wept, children and elders alike, as much from sorrow as from a mysterious joy in which all sorrow was drowned. Later, recalling that solemn hour, I have come to realize that the imperturbable joyousness of Don Emmanuel was merely the temporal, earthly form of an infinite, eternal sadness which the priest concealed from the eyes and ears of the world with heroic saintliness.

His constant activity, his ceaseless intervention in the tasks and diversions of everyone, had the appearance, in short, of a flight from himself, of a flight from solitude. He confirmed this suspicion: "I have a fear of solitude," he would say. And still, from time to time he would go off by himself, along the shores of the lake, to the ruins of the abbey where the souls of pious Cistercians seem still to repose, although history has long since buried them in oblivion. There, the cell of the so-called Father-Captain can still be found, and it is said that the drops of blood spattered on the walls as he flagellated himself can still be seen. What thoughts occupied our Don Emmanuel as he walked there? I remember a conversation we held once in which I asked him, as he was speaking of the abbey, why it had never occurred to him to enter a monastery, and he answered me:

"It is not at all because of the fact that my sister is a widow and I have her children and herself to support—for God looks after the poor —but rather because I simply was not born to be a hermit, an anchorite: the solitude would crush my soul; and, as far as a monastery is concerned, my monastery is Valverde de Lucerna. I was not meant to live alone, or die alone. I was meant to live for my village, and die for it too. How should I save my soul if I were not to save the soul of my village as well?"

"But there have been saints who were hermits, solitaries . . ." I said.

"Yes, the Lord gave them the grace of solitude which He has denied me, and I must resign myself. I must not throw away my village to win my soul. God made me that way. I would not be able to resist the temptations of the desert. I would not be able, alone, to carry the cross of birth . . ."

I have summoned up all these recollections, from which my faith was fed, in order to portray our Don Emmanuel as he was when I, a young girl of sixteen, returned from the convent of Renada to our "monastery of Valverde de Lucerna," once more to kneel at the feet of our "abbot."

"Well, here is the daughter of Simona," he said as soon as he saw me, "made into a young woman, and knowing French, and how to play the piano, and embroider, and heaven knows what else besides! Now you must get ready to give us a family. And your brother Lazarus; when does he return? Is he still in the New World?"

"Yes, Father, he is still in the New World."

"The New World! And we in the Old. Well then, when you write him, tell him for me, on behalf of the parish priest, that I should like to know when he is returning from the New World to the Old, to bring us the latest from over there. And tell him that he will find the lake and the mountain as he left them."

When I first went to him for confession, I became so confused that I could not enunciate a word. I recited the "Forgive me, Father for I have sinned," in a stammer, almost a sob. And he, observing this, said:

"Good heavens, my dear, what are you afraid of, or of whom are you afraid? Certainly you're not trembling now under the weight of your sins, nor in fear of God. No, you're trembling because of me, isn't that so?"

At this point I burst into tears.

"What have they been telling you about me? What fairy tales? Was it your mother, perhaps? Come, come, please be calm; you must imagine you are talking to your brother . . ."

At this I plucked up courage and began to tell him of my anxieties, doubts and sorrows.

"Bah! Where did you read all this, Miss Intellectual. All this is literary nonsense. Don't succumb to everything you read just yet, not even to Saint Theresa. If you need to amuse yourself, read the *Bertoldo*, as your father before you did."

I came away from my first confession to that holy man deeply consoled. The initial fear—simple fright more than respect—with which I had approached him, turned into a profound pity. I was at that time a very young woman, almost a girl still; and yet, I was beginning to be a woman, in my innermost being I felt the juice and stirrings of maternity, and when I found myself in the confessional at the side of the saintly priest, I sensed a kind of unspoken confession on his part in the soft murmur of his voice. And I remembered how when he had intoned in the church the words of Jesus Christ: "My God, my God, why hast Thou forsaken me?" his own mother had cried out in the congregation: "My son!"; and I could hear the cry that had rent the silence of the temple. And I went to him again for confession—and to comfort him.

Another time in the confessional I told him of a doubt which assailed me, and he responded:

"As to that, you know what the catechism says. Don't question me about it, for I am ignorant; in Holy Mother Church there are learned doctors of theology who will know how to answer you."

"But you are the learned doctor here."

"Me? A learned doctor? Not even in thought! I, my little doctress, am only a poor country priest. And those questions, . . . do you know who whispers them into your ear? Well . . . the Devil does!"

Then, making bold, I asked him pointblank:

"And suppose he were to whisper these questions to you?"

"Who? To me? The Devil? No, we don't even know each other, my daughter, we haven't met at all."

"But if he did whisper them? . . ."

"I wouldn't pay any attention. And that's enough of that; let's get on, for there are some people, really sick people, waiting for me."

I went away thinking, I don't know why, that our Don Emmanuel, so famous for curing the bedeviled, didn't really even believe in the Devil. As I started home, I ran into the fool Blasillo, who had probably been hovering around outside; as soon as he saw me, and by way of treating me to a display of his virtuosity, he began the business of repeating—and in what a manner!—"My God, my God, why hast Thou forsaken me?" I arrived home utterly saddened and locked myself in my room to cry, until finally my mother arrived.

"With all these confessions, Angelita, you will end by going off to a nunnery."

"Don't worry, Mother," I answered her. "I have plenty to do here, in the village, and it will be my only convent."

"Until you marry."

"I don't intend to," I rejoined.

The next time I saw Don Emmanuel I asked him, looking straight into his eyes:

"Is there really a Hell, Don Emmanuel?"

And he, without altering his expression, answered:

"For you, my daughter, no."

"For others, then?"

"Does it matter to you, if you are not to go there?"

"It matters for the others, in any case. Is there a Hell?"

"Believe in Heaven, the Heaven we can see. Look at it there"—and he pointed to the heavens above the mountain, and then down into the lake, to the reflection.

"But we are supposed to believe in Hell as well as in Heaven," I said.

"That's true. We must believe everything believed and taught by our Holy Mother Church, Catholic, Apostolic, and Roman. And now, that will do!"

I thought I read a deep unknown sadness in his eyes, eyes which were as blue as the waters of the lake.

Those years passed as if in a dream. Within me, a reflected image of Don Emmanuel was unconsciously taking form. He was an ordinary enough man in many ways, of such daily use as the daily bread we asked for in our Paternoster. I helped him whenever I could with his tasks, visiting the sick, his sick, the girls at school, and helping, too, with the church linen and the vestments; I served in the role, as he said, of his deaconess. Once I was invited to the city for a few days by a school friend, but I had to hurry home, for the city stifled me—something was missing, I was thirsty for a sight of the waters of the lake, hungry for a sight of the peaks of the mountain; and even more, I missed my Don Emmanuel, as if his absence called to me, as if he were endangered by my being so far away, as if he were in need of me. I began to feel a kind of maternal affection for my spiritual father; I longed to help him bear the cross of birth.

My twenty-fourth birthday was approaching when my brother Lazarus came back from America with the small fortune he had saved up. He came back to Valverde de Lucerna with the intention of taking me and my mother to live in a city, perhaps even Madrid.

"In the country," he said, "in these villages, a person becomes stupefied, brutalized and spiritually impoverished." And he added: "Civilization is the very opposite of everything countryfied. The idiocy of village life! No, that's not for us; I didn't have you sent away to school so that later you might spoil here, among these ignorant peasants."

I said nothing, though I was disposed to resist emigration. But our mother, already past sixty, took a firm stand from the start: "Change pastures at my age?" she demanded at once. A little later she made it quite clear that she could not live out of sight of her lake, her mountain, and, above all, of her Don Emmanuel.

"The two of you are like those cats that get attached to houses," my brother muttered.

When he realized the complete sway exercised over the entire village —especially over my mother and myself—by the saintly priest, my brother began to resent him. He saw in this situation an example of the obscurantist theocracy which, according to him, smothered Spain. And he commenced to spout the old anti-clerical commonplaces, to which he added anti-religious and "progressive" propaganda brought back from the New World.

"In the Spain of sloth and flabby useless men, the priests manipulate the women, and the women manipulate the men. Not to mention the idiocy of the country, and this feudal backwater!"

"Feudal," to him, meant something frightful. "Feudal" and "medieval" were the epithets he employed to condemn something completely.

The failure of his diatribes to move us and their total lack of effect upon the village—where they were listened to with respectful indifference—disconcerted him no end. "The man does not exist who could move these clods." But, he soon began to understand—for he was an intelligent man, and therefore a good one—the kind of influence exercised over the village by Don Emmanuel, and he came to appreciate the effect of the priest's work in the village.

"This priest is not like the others," he announced. "He is, in fact, a saint."

"How do you know what the others are like," I asked. To which he answered:

"I can imagine."

In any case, he did not set foot inside the church nor did he miss an opportunity to parade his incredulity—though he always exempted Don Emmanuel from his scorning accusations. In the village, an unconscious expectancy began to build up, the anticipation of a kind of duel between my brother Lazarus and Don Emmanuel—in short, it was expected that Don Emmanuel would convert my brother. No one doubted but that in the end the priest would bring him into the fold. On his side, Lazarus was eager (he told me so himself, later) to go and hear Don Emmanuel, to see and hear him in the church, to get to know him and to talk with him, so that he might learn the secret of his spiritual hold over our souls. And he let himself be coaxed to this end, so that finally—"out of curiosity," as he said—he went to hear the preacher.

"Now, this is something else again," he told me as soon as he came from hearing Don Emmanuel for the first time. "He's not like the others; still, he doesn't fool me, he's too intelligent to believe everything he must teach."

"You mean you think he's a hypocrite?"

"A hypocrite . . . no! But he has a job by which he must live."

As for me, my brother undertook to see that I read the books he brought me, and others which he urged me to buy.

"So your brother Lazarus wants you to read," Don Emmanuel queried. "Well, read, my daughter, read and make him happy by doing so. I know you will read only worthy books. Read even if only novels; they are as good as the books which deal with so-called 'reality.' You are better off reading than concerning yourself with village gossip and old wives' tales. Above all, though, you will do well to read devotional books which will bring you contentment in life, a quiet, gentle contentment, and peace."

And he, did he enjoy such contentment?

It was about this time that our mother fell mortally sick and died. In her last days her one wish was that Don Emmanuel should convert Lazarus, whom she expected to see again in heaven, in some little corner among the stars from where they could see the lake and the mountain of Valverde de Lucerna. She felt she was going there now, to see God.

"You are not going anywhere," Don Emmanuel would tell her; "you are staying right here. Your body will remain here, in this land, and your soul also, in this house, watching and listening to your children though they do not see or hear you."

"But, Father," she said, "I am going to see God."

"God, my daughter, is all around us, and you will see Him from here, right from here. And all of us in Him, and He in all of us."

"God bless you," I whispered to him.

"The peace in which your mother dies will be her eternal life," he told me.

And, turning to my brother Lazarus: "Her heaven is to go on seeing you, and it is at this moment that she must be saved. Tell her you will pray for her."

"But—"

"But what? . . . Tell her you will pray for her, to whom you owe your life. And I know that once you promise her, you *will* pray, and I know that once you pray . . ."

My brother, his eyes filled with tears, drew near our dying mother and gave her his solemn promise to pray for her.

"And I, in heaven, will pray for you, for all of you," my mother responded. And then, kissing the crucifix and fixing her eyes on Don Emmanuel, she gave up her soul to God.

"Into Thy hands I commend my spirit," prayed the priest.

My brother and I stayed on in the house alone. What had happened at the time of my mother's death had established a bond between Lazarus and Don Emmanuel. The latter seemed even to neglect some of his charges, his patients and his other needy to look after my brother. In the afternoons, they would go for a stroll together, walking along the lake or toward the ruins, overgrown with ivy, of the old Cistercian abbey.

"He's an extraordinary man," Lazarus told me. "You know the story they tell of how there is a city at the bottom of the lake, submerged beneath the water, and that on Midsummer's Night at midnight the sound of its church bells can be heard . . ."

"Yes, a city 'feudal and medieval' . . ."

"And I believe," he went on, "that at the bottom of Don Emmanuel's soul there is a city, submerged and inundated, and that sometimes the sound of its bells can be heard . . ."

"Yes . . . And this city submerged in Don Emmanuel's soul, and perhaps—why not?—in yours as well, is certainly the cemetery of the souls of our ancestors, the ancestors of our Valverde de Lucerna . . . 'feudal and medieval'!"

In the end, my brother began going to Mass. He went regularly to hear Don Emmanuel. When it became known that he was prepared to comply with his annual duty of receiving Communion, that he would receive when the others received, an intimate joy ran through the town, which felt that by this act he was restored to his people. The rejoicing was of such nature, moreover, so openhanded and honest, that Lazarus never did feel that he had been "vanquished" or "overcome."

The day of his Communion arrived; of Communion before the entire village, with the entire village. When it came time for my brother's turn, I saw Don Emmanuel—white as January snow on the mountain, and moving like the surface of the lake when it is stirred by the northeast wind—come up to him with the holy wafer in his hand, which trembled violently as it reached out to Lazarus's mouth; at that moment the priest had an instant of faintness and the wafer dropped to the ground. My brother himself recovered it and placed it in his mouth. The people saw the tears on Don Emmanuel's face, and everyone wept, saying: "What great love he bears!" and then, because it was dawn, a cock crowed.

On returning home I locked myself in with my brother; alone with him I put my arms around his neck and kissed him.

"Lazarus, Lazarus, what joy you have given us all today; the entire village, the living and the dead, and especially our mother. Did you see how Don Emmanuel wept for joy? What joy you have given us all!"

"It was for that reason that I did what I did," he answered me.

"For what? To give us pleasure? Surely you did it for your own sake, first of all; because of your conversion."

And then Lazarus, my brother, grown as pale and tremulous as Don Emmanuel when he was giving Communion, bade me sit down, in the very chair where our mother used to sit. He took a deep breath, and, in the intimate tone of a familiar and domestic confession, he told me:

"Angelita, the time has come when I must tell you the truth, the absolute truth, and I shall tell you because I must, because I cannot, I ought not, conceal it from you, and because, sooner or later, you are bound to intuit it anyway, if only halfway—which would be worse."

Thereupon, serenely and tranquilly, in a subdued voice, he recounted a tale that drowned me in a lake of sorrow. He told how Don Emmanuel had appealed to him, particularly during the walks to the ruins of the old Cistercian abbey, to set a good example, to avoid scandalizing the townspeople, to take part in the religious life of the community, to feign belief even if he did not feel any, to conceal his own ideas—all this without attempting in any way to catechize him, to instruct him in religion, or to effect a true conversion.

"But is it possible?" I asked in consternation.

"Possible and true. When I said to him: 'Is this you, the priest, who suggests I dissimulate?' he replied, hesitatingly: 'Dissimulate? Not at all! That is not dissimulation. "Dip your fingers in holy water, and you will end by believing," as someone said.' And I, gazing into his eyes, asked him: 'And you, celebrating the Mass, have you ended by believing?' He looked away and stared out at the lake, until his eyes filled with tears. And it was in this way that I came to understand his secret."

"Lazarus!" I cried out, incapable of another word.

At that moment the fool Blasillo came along our street, crying out his: "My God, my God, why hast Thou forsaken me?" And Lazarus shuddered, as if he had heard the voice of Don Emmanuel, or of Christ.

"It was then," my brother at length continued, "that I really understood his motives and his saintliness; for a saint he is, Sister, a true saint. In trying to convert me to his holy cause—for it is a holy cause, a most holy cause—he was not attempting to score a triumph, but rather was doing it to protect the peace, the happiness, the illusions, perhaps, of his charges. I understood that if he thus deceives them—if it *is* deceit—it is not for his own advantage. I submitted to his logic—and that was my conversion.

"I shall never forget the day on which I said to him: 'But, Don Emmanuel, the truth, the truth, above all!'; and he, all a-tremble, whispered in my ear—though we were all alone in the middle of the countryside— 'The truth? The truth, Lazarus, is perhaps something so unbearable, so terrible, something so deadly, that simple people could not live with it!'

" 'And why do you show me a glimpse of it now, here, as if we were in the confessional?' I asked. And he said: 'Because if I did not, I would be so tormented by it, so tormented, that I would finally shout it in the middle of the plaza, which I must never, never, never do . . . I am put here to give life to the souls of my charges, to make them happy, to make them dream they are immortal—and not to destroy them. The important thing is that they live sanely, in concord with each other,—and with the truth, with my truth, they could not live at all. Let them live. That is what the Church does, it lets them live. As for true religion, all religions are true as long as they give spiritual life to the people who profess them, as long as they console them for having been born only to die. And for each people the truest religion is their own, the religion that made them . . . And mine? Mine consists in consoling myself by consoling others, even though the consolation I give them is not ever mine.' I shall never forget his words."

"But then this Communion of yours has been a sacrilege," I dared interrupt, regretting my words as soon as I said them.

"Sacrilege? What about the priest who gave it to me? And his Masses?"

"What martyrdom!" I exclaimed.

"And now," said my brother, "there is one more person to console the people."

"To deceive them, you mean?" I said.

"Not at all," he replied, "but rather to confirm them in their faith."

"And they, the people, do they really believe, do you think?"

"About that, I know nothing! . . . They probably believe without trying, from force of habit, tradition. The important thing is not to stir them up. To let them live from their thin sentiments, without acquiring the torments of luxury. Blessed are the poor in spirit!"

"That then is the sentiment you have learned from Don Emmanuel. . . . And tell me, do you feel you have carried out your promise to our mother on her deathbed, when you promised to pray for her?"

"Do you think I *could* fail her? What do you take me for, sister? Do you think I would go back on my word, my solemn promise made at the hour of death to a mother?"

"I don't know. . . . You might have wanted to deceive her so she could die in peace."

"The fact is, though, that if I had not lived up to my promise, I would be totally miserable."

"And . . ."

"I carried out my promise and I have not neglected for a single day to pray for her."

"Only for her?"

"Well, now, for whom else?"

"For yourself! And now, for Don Emmanuel."

We parted and went to our separate rooms. I to weep through the night, praying for the conversion of my brother and of Don Emmanuel. And Lazarus, to what purpose, I know not.

From that day on I was fearful of finding myself alone with Don Emmanuel, whom I continued to aid in his pious works. And he seemed to sense my inner state and to guess at its cause. When at last I came to him in the confessional's penitential tribunal (who was the judge, and who the offender?) the two of us, he and I bowed our heads in silence and began to cry. It was he, finally, Don Emmanuel, who broke the terrible silence, with a voice which seemed to issue from the tomb:

"Angelita, you have the same faith you had when you were ten, don't you? You believe, don't you?"

"I believe, Father."

"Then go on believing. And if doubts come to torment you, suppress them utterly, even to yourself. The main thing is to live . . ."

I summoned up courage, and dared to ask, trembling:

"But, Father, do you believe?"

For a brief moment he hesitated, and then, mastering himself, he said: "I believe!"

"In what, Father, in what? Do you believe in the after life? Do you believe that in dying we do not die in every way, completely? Do you believe that we will see each other again, that we will love each other in a world to come? Do you believe in another life?"

The poor saint was sobbing.

"My child, leave off, leave off!"

Now, when I come to write this memoir, I ask myself: Why did he not deceive me? Why did he not deceive me as he deceived the others? Why did he afflict himself? Why could he not deceive himself, or why could he not deceive me? And I want to believe that he was afflicted because he could not deceive himself into deceiving me.

"And now," he said, "pray for me, for your brother, and for yourself —for all of us. We must go on living. And giving life."

And, after a pause:

"Angelita, why don't you marry?"

"You know why I do not."

"No, no; you must marry. Lazarus and I will find you a suitor. For it would be good for you to marry, and rid yourself of these obsessions."

"Obsessions, Don Emmanuel?"

"I know well enough what I am saying. You should not torment yourself for the sake of others, for each of us has more than enough to do answering for himself."

"That it should be you, Don Emmanuel, who say this! That you should advise me to marry and answer for myself alone and not suffer over others! That it should be you!"

"Yes, you are right, Angelita. I am no longer sure of what I say. I am no longer sure of what I say since I began to confess to you. Only, one must go on living. Yes! One must live!"

And when I rose to leave the church, he asked me:

"Now, Angelita, in the name of the people, do you absolve me?"

I felt pierced by a mysterious and priestly prompting and said:

"In the name of the Father, the Son and the Holy Ghost, I absolve you, Father."

We quitted the church, and as I went out I felt the quickening of maternity within me.

My brother, now totally devoted to the work of Don Emmanuel, had become his closest and most zealous collaborator and companion. They were bound together, moreover, by their common secret. Lazarus accompanied the priest on his visits to the sick, and to schools, and he placed his resources at the disposition of the saintly man. A little more zeal, and he would have learned to help celebrate Mass. All the while he was sounding deeper in the unfathomable soul of the priest.

"What manliness!" he exclaimed to me once. "Yesterday, as we walked along the lake he said: 'There lies my direst temptation.' When I interrogated him with my eyes, he went on: 'My poor father, who was close to ninety when he died, was tormented all his life, as he confessed to me himself, by a temptation to suicide, by an instinct to self-destruction which had come to him from a time before memory—from birth, from his *nation*, as he said—and was forced to fight against it always. And this fight grew to be his life. So as not to succumb to this temptation he was forced to take precautions, to guard his life. He told me of terrible episodes. His urge was a form of madness,—and I have inherited it. How that water beckons me in its deep quiet! . . . an apparent quietude reflecting the sky like a mirror—and beneath it the hidden current! My life, Lazarus, is a kind of continual suicide, or a struggle against suicide, which is the same thing. . . . Just so long as our people go on living!' And then he added: 'Here the river eddies to form a lake, so that later, flowing down the plateau, it may form into cascades, waterfalls, and torrents, hurling itself through gorges and chasms. Thus does life eddy in the village; and the temptation to suicide is the greater beside the still waters which at night reflect the stars, than it is beside the crashing falls which drive one back in fear. Listen,

Lazarus, I have helped poor villagers to die well, ignorant, illiterate
villagers, who had scarcely ever been out of their village, and I have
learned from their own lips, or divined it when they were silent, the real
cause of their sickness unto death, and there at the head of their death-
bed I have been able to see into the black abyss of their life-weariness.
A weariness a thousand times worse than hunger! For our part, Lazarus,
let us go on with our kind of suicide of working for the people, and let
them dream their life as the lake dreams the heavens.'

"Another time," said my brother, "as we were coming back, we spied
a country girl, a goatherd, standing erect on a height of the mountain
slope overlooking the lake and she was singing in a voice fresher than
its waters. Don Emmanuel took hold of me, and pointing to her said:
'Look, it's as though time had stopped, as though this country girl had
always been there just as she is, singing in the way she is, and as though
she would always be there, as she was before my consciousness began,
as she will be when it is past. That girl is a part of nature—not of history
—along with the rocks, the clouds, the trees, and the waters.' He has such
a subtle feeling for nature, he infuses it with spirit!

"I shall not forget the day when snow was falling and he asked me:
'Have you ever seen a greater mystery, Lazarus, than the snow falling,
and dying, in the lake, while a hood is laid upon the mountain?' "

Don Emmanuel had to moderate and temper my brother's zeal and his
neophyte's rawness. As soon as he heard that Lazarus was going about
inveighing against some of the popular superstitions he told him force-
fully:

"Leave them alone! It's difficult enough making them understand
where orthodox belief leaves off and where superstition begins. It's hard
enough, especially for us. Leave them alone, then, as long as they get
some comfort. . . . It's better for them to believe everything, even
things that contradict one another, than to believe nothing. The idea that
someone who believes too much ends by not believing in anything is a
Protestant notion. Let us not protest! Protestation destroys contentment
and peace."

My brother told me, too, about one moonlit night when they were returning to town along the lake (whose surface a mountain breeze was
stirring, so that the moonbeams topped the whitecaps), Don Emmanuel
turned to him and said:

"Look, the water is reciting the litany and saying: *ianua caeli, ora pro
nobis*: gate of heaven, pray for us."

Two evanescent tears fell from his lashes to the grass, where the light
of the full moon shone upon them like dew.

And time went hurrying by, and my brother and I began to notice that
Don Emmanuel's spirits were failing, that he could no longer control

completely the deep rooted sadness which consumed him; perhaps some treacherous illness was undermining his body and soul. In an effort to rouse his interest, Lazarus spoke to him of the good effect the organization of a type of Catholic agrarian syndicate would have.

"A syndicate?" Don Emmanuel repeated sadly. "A syndicate? And what is that? The Church is the only syndicate I know. And you have certainly heard 'My kingdom is not of this world.' Our kingdom, Lazarus, is not of this world . . ."

"And of the other?"

Don Emmanuel bowed his head:

"The other is here. Two kingdoms exist in this world. Or rather, the other world. . . . Ah, I don't really know what I'm saying. But as for the syndicate, that's a vestige from your days of 'progressivism.' No, Lazarus, no; religion does not exist to resolve the economic or political conflicts of this world, which God handed over to men for their disputes. Let men think and act as they will, let them console themselves for having been born, let them live as happily as possible in the illusion that all this has a purpose. I don't propose to advise the poor to submit to the rich, nor to suggest to the rich that they subordinate themselves to the poor; but rather to preach resignation in everyone, and charity toward everyone. For even the rich man must resign himself—to his riches, and to life; and the poor man must show charity—even to the rich. The Social Question? Ignore it, for it is none of our business. So, a new society is on the way, in which there will be neither rich nor poor, in which wealth will be justly divided, in which everything will belong to everyone—and so, what then? Won't this general well-being and comfort lead to even greater tedium and weariness of life? I know well enough that one of those chiefs of what they call the Social Revolution has already said that religion is the opium of the people. Opium . . . Opium . . . Yes, opium it is. We should give them opium, and help them sleep, and dream. I, myself, with my mad activity, give myself opium. And still I don't manage to sleep well, let alone dream well. . . . What a fearful nightmare! . . . I, too, can say, with the Divine Master: 'My soul is weary unto death.' No, Lazarus, no; no syndicates for us. If *they* organize them, well and good—they would be distracting themselves in that way. Let them play at syndicates, if that makes them happy."

The entire village began to realize that Don Emmanuel's spirit was weakening, that his strength was waning. His very voice—that miracle of a voice—acquired a kind of quaking. Tears came into his eyes for any reason whatever—or for no reason. Whenever he spoke to people about the other world, about the other life, he was compelled to pause at frequent intervals, and he would close his eyes. "It is a vision," people would say, "he has a vision of what lies ahead." At such moments the fool Blasillo was the first to break into tears. He wept copiously these days, crying now more than he laughed, and even his laughter had the sound of tears.

The last Easter Week which Don Emmanuel was to celebrate among us, in this world, in this village of ours, arrived, and all the village sensed the impending end of tragedy. And how the words did strike home when for the last time Don Emmanuel cried out before us: "My God, my God, why hast Thou forsaken me?"! And when he repeated the words of the Lord to the Good Thief ("All thieves are good," Don Emmanuel used to tell us): "Tomorrow shalt thou be with me in Paradise.". . . ! And then, the last general Communion which our saint was to give! When he came to my brother to give him the Host—his hand steady this time—, just after the liturgical ". . . in vitam aeternam,"[1] he bent down and whispered to him: "There is no other life but this, no life more eternal . . . let them dream it eternal . . . let it be eternal for a few years . . ."

And when he came to me he said: "Pray, my child, pray for us all." And then, something so extraordinary happened that I carry it now in my heart as the greatest of mysteries: he bent over and said, in a voice which seemed to belong to the other world: ". . . and pray, too, for our Lord Jesus Christ."

I stood up, going weak as I did so, like a somnambulist. Everything around me seemed dream-like. And I thought: "Am I to pray, too, for the lake and the mountain?" and next: "Am I bewitched, then?" Home at last, I took up the crucifix my mother had held in her hands when she had given up her soul to God, and, gazing at it through my tears and recalling the "My God, my God, why hast Thou forsaken me?" of our two Christs, the one of this earth and the other of this village, I prayed: "Thy will be done on earth as it is in heaven," and then, "And lead us not into temptation. Amen." After this I turned to the statue of the Mater Dolorosa—her heart transfixed by seven swords—which had been my poor mother's most sorrowful comfort, and I prayed again: "Holy Mary, Mother of God, pray for us sinners, now and in the hour of our death. Amen." I had scarcely finished the prayer, when I asked myself: "Sinners? Sinners are we? And what is our sin, what is it?" And all day I brooded over the question.

The next day I presented myself before Don Emmanuel—Don Emmanuel now in the full sunset of his magnificent religiosity—and I said to him:

"Do you remember, my Father, years ago when I asked you a certain question you answered: 'That question you must not ask me; for I am ignorant; there are learned doctors of the Holy Mother Church who will know how to answer you'?"

"Do I remember? . . . Of course. And I remember I told you those were questions put to you by the Devil."

---

[1] in eternal life

"Well, then, Father, I have come again, bedeviled, to ask you another question put to me by my Guardian Devil."

"Ask it."

"Yesterday, when you gave me Communion, you asked me to pray for all of us, and even for . . ."

"That's enough! . . . Go on."

"I arrived home and began to pray; when I came to the part 'Pray for us sinners, now and at the hour of our death,' a voice in me asked: 'Sinners? Sinners are we? And what is our sin?' What is our sin, Father?"

"Our sin?" he replied. "A great doctor of the Spanish Catholic Apostolic Church has already explained it; the great doctor of *Life Is a Dream* has written 'The greatest sin of man is to have been born.' That, my child, is our sin; to have been born."

"Can it be atoned, Father?"

"Go and pray again. Pray once more for us sinners, now and at the hour of our death. . . . Yes, at length the dream is atoned . . . at length life is atoned . . . at length the cross of birth is expiated and atoned, and the drama comes to an end. . . . And as Calderón[2] said, to have done good, to have feigned good, even in dreams, is something which is not lost."

The hour of his death arrived at last. The entire village saw it come. And he made it his finest lesson. For he would not die alone or at rest. He died preaching to his people in the church. But first, before being carried to the church (his paralysis made it impossible for him to move), he summoned Lazarus and me to his bedside. Alone there, the three of us together, he said:

"Listen to me: watch over these poor sheep, find some comfort for them in living, and let them believe what I could not. And Lazarus, when your hour comes, die as I die, as Angela will die, in the arms of the Holy Mother Church, Catholic, Apostolic, and Roman; that is to say, of the Holy Mother Church of Valverde de Lucerna. And now, farewell; until we never meet again, for this dream of life is coming to an end . . ."

"Father, Father," I cried out.

"Do not grieve, Angela, only go on praying for all sinners, for all who have been born. Let them dream, let them dream . . . O, what a longing I have to sleep, to sleep, sleep without end, sleep for all eternity, and never dream! Forgetting this dream! . . . When they go to bury me, let it be in a box made from the six planks I cut from the old walnut tree —poor old tree!—in whose shade I played as a child, when I began the dream. . . . In those days, I did really believe in life everlasting. That is to say, it seems to me now that I believed. For a child, to believe is the same as to dream. And for a people, too. . . . You'll find those six planks I cut at the foot of the bed."

[2] Pedro Calderón de la Barca, 1600–1681, Spanish dramatist

He was seized by a sudden fit of choking, and then, composing himself once more, he went on:

"You will recall that when we prayed together, animated by a common sentiment, a community of spirit, and we came to the final verse of the Creed, you will remember that I would fall silent. . . . When the Israelites were coming to the end of their wandering in the desert, the Lord told Aaron and Moses that because they had not believed in Him they would not set foot in the Promised Land with their people; and he bade them climb the heights of Mount Hor, where Moses ordered Aaron stripped of his garments, so that Aaron died there, and then Moses went up from the plains of Moab to Mount Nebo, to the top of Pisgah, looking into Jericho, and the Lord showed him all of the land promised to His people, but said to him: 'You will not go there.' And there Moses died, and no one knew his grave. And he left Joshua to be chief in his place. You, Lazarus, must be my Joshua, and if you can make the sun stand still, make it stop, and never mind progress. Like Moses, I have seen the face of God—our supreme dream—face to face, and as you already know, and as the Scripture says, he who sees God's face, he who sees the eyes of the dream, the eyes with which He looks at us, will die inexorably and forever. And therefore, do not let our people, so long as they live, look into the face of God. Once dead, it will no longer matter, for then they will see nothing . . ."

"Father, Father, Father," I cried again.

And he said:

"Angela, you must pray always, so that all sinners may go on dreaming, until they die, of the resurrection of the flesh and the life everlasting . . ."

I was expecting "and who knows it might be . . ." But instead, Don Emmanuel had another attack of coughing.

"And now," he finally went on, "and now, in the hour of my death, it is high time to have me brought, in this very chair, to the church, so that I may take leave there of my people, who await me."

He was carried to the church and brought, in his armchair, into the chancel, to the foot of the altar. In his hands he held a crucifix. My brother and I stood close to him, but the fool Blasillo wanted to stand even closer. He wanted to grasp Don Emmanuel by the hand, so that he could kiss it. When some of the people nearby tried to stop him, Don Emmanuel rebuked them and said:

"Let him come closer. . . . Come, Blasillo, give me your hand."

The fool cried for joy. And then Don Emmanuel spoke:

"I have very few words left, my children; I scarcely feel I have strength enough left to die. And then, I have nothing new to tell you, either. I have already said everything I have to say. Live with each other in peace and contentment, in the hope that we will all see each other again some day, in the other Valverde de Lucerna up there among the nighttime stars, the stars which the lake reflects over the image of the reflected mountain. And pray, pray to the Most Blessed Mary, and to our Lord. Be good . . . that is enough. Forgive me whatever wrong I may have done you inadvertently or unknowingly. After I give you my blessing, let us pray together, let us say the Paternoster, the Ave Maria, the Salve, and the Creed."

Then he gave his blessing to the whole village, with the crucifix held in his hand, while the women and children cried and even some of the men wept softly. Almost at once the prayers were begun. Don Emmanuel listened to them in silence, his hand in the hand of Blasillo the fool, who began to fall asleep to the sound of the praying. First the Paternoster, with its "Thy will be done on earth as it is in heaven"; then the Ave Maria, with its "Pray for us sinners, now and in hour of our death"; followed by the Salve, with its "mourning and weeping in this vale of tears"; and finally, the Creed. On reaching "The resurrection of the flesh and life everlasting" the people sensed that their saint had yielded up his soul to God. It was not necessary to close his eyes even, for he died with them closed. When an attempt was made to wake Blasillo, it was found that he, too, had fallen asleep in the Lord forever. So that later there were two bodies to be buried.

The village immediately repaired en masse to the house of the saint to carry away holy relics, to divide up pieces of his garments among themselves, to carry off whatever they could find as a memento of the blessed martyr. My brother preserved his breviary, between the pages of which he discovered a carnation, dried as in a herbarium and mounted on a piece of paper, and upon the paper a cross and a certain date.

No one in the village seemed able to believe that Don Emmanuel was dead; everyone expected to see him—perhaps some of them did—taking his daily walk along the side of the lake, his figure mirrored in the water, or silhouetted against the background of the mountain. They continued to hear his voice, and they all visited his grave, around which a veritable cult sprang up, old women "possessed by devils" came to touch the cross of walnut, made with his own hands from the tree which had yielded the six planks of his casket.

The ones who least of all believed in his death were my brother and I. Lazarus carried on the tradition of the saint, and he began to compile a record of the priest's words. Some of the conversations in this account of mine were made possible by his notes.

"It was he," said my brother, "who made me into a new man. I was a true Lazarus whom he raised from the dead. He gave me faith."

"Ah, faith . . ."

"Yes, faith, faith in the charity of life, in life's joy. It was he who cured me of my delusion of 'progress,' of my belief in its political implications. For there are, Angela, two types of dangerous and harmful men: those who, convinced of life beyond the grave, of the resurrection of the flesh, torment other people—like the inquisitors they are—so that they will despise this life as a transitory thing and work for the other life; and then, there are those who, believe only in this life . . ."

"Like you, perhaps . . ."

"Yes, and like Don Emmanuel. Believing only in this world, this second group looks forward to some vague future society and exerts every effort to prevent the populace finding consoling joy from belief in another world . . ."

"And so . . ."

"The people should be allowed to live with their illusion."

The poor priest who came to the parish to replace Don Emmanuel found himself overwhelmed in Valverde de Lucerna by the memory of the saint, and he put himself in the hands of my brother and myself for guidance. He wanted only to follow in the footsteps of the saint. And my brother told him: "Very little theology, Father, very little theology. Religion, religion, religion." Listening to him, I smiled to myself, wondering if this was not a kind of theology, too.

I had by now begun to fear for my poor brother. From the time Don Emmanuel died it could scarcely be said that he lived. Daily he went to the priest's tomb; for hours on end he stood gazing into the lake. He was filled with nostalgia for deep, abiding peace.

"Don't stare into the lake so much," I begged him.

"Don't worry. It's not this lake which draws me, nor the mountain. Only, I cannot live without his help."

"And the joy of living, Lazarus, what about the joy of living?"

"That's for others. Not for those of us who have seen God's face, those of us on whom the Dream of Life has gazed with His eyes."

"What; are you preparing to go and see Don Emmanuel?"

"No, sister, no. Here at home now, between the two of us, the whole truth—bitter as it may be, bitter as the sea into which the sweet waters of our lake flow—the whole truth for you, who are so set against it . . ."

"No, no, Lazarus. You are wrong. Your truth is not the truth."

"It's my truth."

"Yours, perhaps, but surely not . . ."

"His, too."

"No, Lazarus. Not now, it isn't. Now, he must believe otherwise; now he must believe . . ."

"Listen, Angela, once Don Emmanuel told me that there are truths which, though one reveals them to oneself, must be kept from others; and I told him that telling me was the same as telling himself. And then he said, he confessed to me, that he thought that more than one of the great saints, perhaps the very greatest himself, had died without believing in the other life."

"Is it possible?"

"All too possible! And now, sister, you must be careful that here, among the people, no one even suspects our secret . . ."

"Suspect it?" I cried in amazement. "Why even if I were to try, in a fit of madness, to explain it to them, they wouldn't understand it. The people do not understand your words, they understand your actions much better. To try and explain all this to them would be like reading some pages from Saint Thomas Aquinas[3] to eight-year-old children, in Latin."

"All the better. In any case, when I am gone, pray for me and for him and for all of us."

At length, his own time came. A sickness which had been eating away at his robust nature seemed to flare with the death of Don Emmanuel.

"I don't so much mind dying," he said to me in his last days, "as the fact that with me another piece of Don Emmanuel dies too. The remainder of him must live on with you. Until, one day, even we dead will die forever."

When he lay in the throes of death, the people of the village came in to bid him farewell (as is customary in our towns) and they commended his soul to the care of Don Emmanuel the Good, Martyr. My brother said nothing to them; he had nothing more to say. He had already said everything there was to say. He had become a link between the two Valverde de Lucernas—the one at the bottom of the lake and the one reflected in its surface. He was already one more of us who had died of life, and, in his way, one more of our saints.

I was desolate, more than desolate; but I was, at least, among my own people, in my own village. Now, having lost my Saint Emmanuel, the father of my soul, and my own Lazarus, my more than carnal brother, my spiritual brother, now it is I realize that I have aged. But, have I really lost them then? Have I grown old? Is my death approaching?

I must live! And he taught me to live, he taught us to live, to feel life, to feel the meaning of life, to merge with the soul of the mountain, with the soul of the lake, with the soul of the village, to lose ourselves in them so as to remain in them forever. He taught me by his life to lose myself in the life of the people of my village, and I no longer felt the passing of the hours, and the days, and the years, any more than I felt the passage of the water in the lake. It began to seem that my life would always be thus. I no longer felt myself growing old. I no longer lived in myself, but in my people, and my people lived in me. I tried to speak as they spoke, as they spoke without trying. I went into the street—it was the one highway—and, since I knew everyone, I lived in them and forgot myself (while, on the other hand, in Madrid, where I went once with my brother, I had felt a terrible loneliness, since I knew no one, and had been tortured by the sight of so many unknown people).

Now, as I write this memoir, this confession of my experience with saintliness, with a saint, I am of the opinion that Don Emmanuel the

---

[3] one of the greatest of the medieval Scholastic theologians; lived 1226–1274

Good, my Don Emmanuel, and my brother, too, died believing they did not believe, but that, without believing in their belief, they actually believed, with resignation and in desolation.

But why, I have asked myself repeatedly, did not Don Emmanuel attempt to convert my brother deceitfully, with a lie, pretending to be a believer himself without being one? And I have finally come to think that Don Emmanuel realized he would not be able to delude him, that with him a fraud would not do, that only through the truth, with his truth, would he be able to convert him; that he knew he would accomplish nothing if he attempted to enact the comedy—the tragedy, rather—which he played out for the benefit of the people. And thus did he win him over, in effect, to his pious fraud; thus did he win him over to the cause of life with the truth of death. And thus did he win me, who never permitted anyone to see through his divine, his most saintly, game. For I believed then, and I believe now, that God—as part of I know not what sacred and inscrutable purpose—caused them to believe they were unbelievers. And that at the moment of their passing, perhaps, the blindfold was removed.

And I, do I believe?

As I write this—here in my mother's old house, and I past my fiftieth year and my memories growing as dim and blanched as my hair—outside it is snowing, snowing upon the lake, snowing upon the mountain, upon the memory of my father, the stranger, upon the memory of my mother, my brother Lazarus, my people, upon the memory of my Saint Emmanuel, and even on the memory of the poor fool Blasillo, my Saint Blasillo—and may he help me in heaven! The snow effaces corners and blots out shadows, for even in the night it shines and illuminates. Truly, I do not know what is true and what is false, nor what I saw and what I merely dreamt—or rather, what I dreamt and what I merely saw—, nor what I really knew or what I merely believed true. Neither do I know whether or not I am transferring to this paper, white as the snow outside, my consciousness, for it to remain in writing, leaving me without it. But why, any longer, cling to it?

Do I really understand any of it? Do I really believe in any of it? Did what I am writing about here actually take place, and did it take place in just the way I tell it? Is it possible for such things to happen? Is it possible that all this is more than a dream dreamed within another dream? Can it be that I, Angela Carballino, a woman in her fifties, am the only one in this village to be assailed by far-fetched thoughts, thoughts unknown to everyone else? And the others, those around me, do they believe? And what does it mean, to believe? At least they go on living. And now they believe in Saint Emmanuel the Good, Martyr, who, with no hope of immortality for himself, preserved their hope in it.

It appears that our most illustrious bishop, who set in motion the process for beatifying our saint from Valverde de Lucerna, is intent on writing an account of Don Emmanuel's life, something which would serve as a guide for the perfect parish priest, and with this end in mind he is gathering information of every sort. He has repeatedly solicited information from me; more than once he has come to see me; and I have supplied him with all sorts of facts. But I have never revealed the tragic secret of Don Emmanuel and my brother. And it is curious that he has never suspected. I trust that what I have set down here will never come to his knowledge. For, all temporal authorities are to be avoided; I fear all authorities on this earth—even when they are church authorities.

But this is an end to it. Let its fate be what it will . . .

How, you ask, did this document, this memoir of Angela Carballino fall into my hands? That, reader, is something I must keep secret. I have transcribed it for you just as it is written, just as it came to me, with only a few, a very few editorial emendations. It recalls to you other things I have written? This fact does not gainsay its objectivity, its originality. Moreover, for all I know, perhaps I created real, actual beings, independent of me, beyond my control, characters with immortal souls. For all I know, Augusto Perez in my novel *Mist*[4] was right when he claimed to be more real, more objective than I myself, who had thought to have invented him. As for the reality of this Saint Emmanuel the Good, Martyr—as he is revealed to me by his disciple and spiritual daughter Angela Carballino—of his reality it has not occurred to me to doubt. I believe in it more than the saint himself did. I believe in it more than I do in my own reality.

And now, before I bring this epilogue to a close, I wish to recall to your mind, patient reader, the ninth verse of the Epistle of the forgotten Apostle, Saint Judas—what power in a name!—where we are told how my heavenly patron, St. Michael Archangel (Michael means "Who such as God?" and archangel means archmessenger) disputed with the Devil (Devil means accuser, prosecutor) over the body of Moses, and would not allow him to carry it off as a prize, to damnation. Instead, he told the Devil: "May the Lord rebuke thee." And may he who wishes to understand, understand!

I would like also, since Angela Carballino injected her own feelings into her narrative—I don't know how it could have been otherwise—to comment on her statement to the effect that if Don Emmanuel and his disciple Lazarus had confessed their convictions to the people, they, the people, would not have understood. Nor, I should like to add, would they have believed the pair. They would have believed in their works and not their words. And works stand by themselves, and need no words to back them up. In a village like Valverde de Lucerna one makes one's confession by one's conduct.

And as for faith, the people scarce know what it is, and care less.

---

[4] an actual novel of Unamuno, published 1914

I am well aware of the fact that no action takes place in this narrative, this *novelistic* narrative, if you will—the novel is, after all, the most intimate, the truest history, so that I scarcely understand why some people are outraged to have the Bible called a novel, when such a designation actually sets it above some mere chronicle or other. In short, nothing happens. But I hope that this is because everything that takes place happens, and instead of coming to pass, and passing away, remains forever, like the lakes and the mountains and the blessed simple souls fixed firmly beyond faith and despair, the blessed souls who, in the lakes and the mountains, outside history, in their divine novel, take refuge.

Translated by Anthony Kerrigan

Rudyard Kipling
1865–1936

THE BULL THAT THOUGHT

W ESTWARD from a town by the mouths of the Rhône, runs a road so mathematically straight, so barometrically level, that it ranks among the world's measured miles and motorists use it for records.

I had attacked the distance several times, but always with a Mistral[1] blowing, or the unchancy cattle of those parts on the move. But once, running from the East, into a high-piled, almost Egyptian, sunset, there came a night which it would have been sin to have wasted. It was warm with the breath of summer in advance; moonlit till the shadow of every rounded pebble and pointed cypress wind-break lay solid on that vast flat-floored waste; and my Mr. Leggatt, who had slipped out to make sure, reported that the road-surface was unblemished.

"*Now*," he suggested, "we might see what she'll do under strict road-conditions. She's been pullin' like the Blue de Luxe all day. Unless I'm all off, it's her night out."

We arranged the trial for after dinner—thirty kilometers as near as might be; and twenty-two of them without even a level crossing.

There sat beside me at table d'hôte an elderly, bearded Frenchman wearing the rosette of by no means the lowest grade of the Legion of Honor, who had arrived in a talkative Citroën. I gathered that he had spent much of his life in the French Colonial Service in Annam and Tonquin.[2] When the War came, his years barring him from the front line, he had supervised Chinese woodcutters who, with axe and dynamite, deforested the center of France for trench-props. He said my chauffeur had told him that I contemplated an experiment. He was interested in cars—

---

[1] a harsh northern wind in the south of France   [2] Indo-China

had admired mine—would, in short, be greatly indebted to me if I permitted him to assist as an observer. One could not well refuse; and, knowing my Mr. Leggatt, it occurred to me there might also be a bet in the background.

While he went to get his coat, I asked the proprietor his name. "Voiron—Monsieur André Voiron," was the reply. "And his business?" "Mon Dieu! He is Voiron! He is all those things, there!" The proprietor waved his hands at brilliant advertisements on the dining-room walls, which declared that Voiron Frères dealt in wines, agricultural implements, chemical manures, provisions and produce throughout that part of the globe.

He said little for the first five minutes of our trip, and nothing at all for the next ten—it being, as Leggatt had guessed, Esmeralda's night out. But, when her indicator climbed to a certain figure and held there for three blinding kilometers, he expressed himself satisfied, and proposed to me that we should celebrate the event at the hotel. "I keep yonder," said he, "a wine on which I should value your opinion."

On our return, he disappeared for a few minutes, and I heard him rumbling in a cellar. The proprietor presently invited me to the dining-room, where, beneath one frugal light, a table had been set with local dishes of renown. There was, too, a bottle beyond most known sizes, marked black on red, with a date. Monsieur Voiron opened it, and we drank to the health of my car. The velvety, perfumed liquor, between fawn and topaz, neither too sweet nor too dry, creamed in its generous glass. But I knew no wine composed of the whispers of angels' wings, the breath of Eden and the foam and pulse of Youth renewed. So I asked what it might be.

"It is champagne," he said gravely.

"Then what have I been drinking all my life?"

"If you were lucky, before the War, and paid thirty shillings a bottle, it is possible you may have drunk one of our better-class *tisanes*." [3]

"And where does one get this?"

"Here, I am happy to say. Elsewhere, perhaps, it is not so easy. We growers exchange these real wines among ourselves."

I bowed my head in admiration, surrender, and joy. There stood the most ample bottle, and it was not yet eleven o'clock. Doors locked and shutters banged throughout the establishment. Some last servant yawned on his way to bed. Monsieur Voiron opened a window and the moonlight flooded in from a small pebbled court outside. One could almost hear the town of Chambres breathing in its first sleep. Presently, there was a thick noise in the air, the passing of feet and hooves, lowings, and a stifled bark or two. Dust rose over the courtyard wall, followed by the strong smell of cattle.

"They are moving some beasts," said Monsieur Voiron, cocking an

[3] A light champagne

ear. "Mine, I think. Yes, I hear Christophe. Our beasts do not like automobiles—so we move at night. You do not know our country—the Crau,
here, or the Camargue?[4] I was—I am now, again—of it. All France is
good; but this is the best." He spoke, as only a Frenchman can, of his
own loved part of his own lovely land.

"For myself, if I were not so involved in all these affairs," he pointed
to the advertisements—"I would live on our farm with my cattle, and
worship them like a Hindu. You know our cattle of the Camargue, Monsieur. No? It is not an acquaintance to rush upon lightly. There are no
beasts like them. They have a mentality superior to that of others. They
graze and they ruminate, by choice, facing our Mistral, which is more
than some automobiles will do. Also they have in them the potentiality
of thought—and when cattle think—I have seen what arrives."

"Are they so clever as all that?" I asked idly.

"Monsieur, when your sportif chauffeur camouflaged your limousine
so that she resembled one of your Army lorries, I would not believe her
capacities. I bet him—ah—two to one—she would not touch ninety kilometers. It was proved that she could. I can give you no proof, but will
you believe me if I tell you what a beast who thinks can achieve?"

"After the War," said I spaciously, "everything is credible."

"That is true! Everything inconceivable has happened; but still we
learn nothing and we believe nothing. When I was a child in my father's
house—before I became a Colonial Administrator—my interest and my
affection were among our cattle. We of the old rock live here—have you
seen?—in big farms like castles. Indeed, some of them may have been
Saracenic. The barns group round them—great white-walled barns, and
yards solid as our houses. One gate shuts all. It is a world apart; an administration of all that concerns beasts. It was there I learned something
about cattle. You see, they are our playthings in the Camargue and the
Crau. The boy measures his strength against the calf that butts him in
play among the manure-heaps. He moves in and out among the cows,
who are—not so amiable. He rides with the herdsmen in the open to shift
the herds. Sooner or later, he meets as bulls the little calves that knocked
him over. So it was with me—till it became necessary that I should go to
our Colonies." He laughed. "Very necessary. That is a good time in
youth, Monsieur, when one does these things which shock our parents.
Why is it always Papa who is so shocked and has never heard of such
things—and Mamma who supplies the excuses? . . . And when my
brother—my elder who stayed and created the business—begged me to
return and help him, I resigned my Colonial career gladly enough. I returned to our own lands, and my well-loved, wicked white and yellow
cattle of the Camargue and the Crau. My Faith, I could talk of them all
night, for this stuff unlocks the heart, without making repentance in the
morning. . . . Yes! It was after the War that this happened. There was

[4] a region in southern France which includes the delta of the Rhône

a calf, among Heaven knows how many of ours—a bull-calf—an infant indistinguishable from his companions. He was sick, and he had been taken up with his mother into the big farmyard at home with us. Naturally the children of our herdsmen practised on him from the first. It is in their blood. The Spaniards make a cult of bull-fighting. Our little devils down here bait bulls as automatically as the English child kicks or throws balls. This calf would chase them with his eyes open, like a cow when she hunts a man. They would take refuge behind our tractors and wine-carts in the center of the yard: he would chase them in and out as a dog hunts rats. More than that, he would study their psychology, his eyes in their eyes. Yes, he watched their faces to divine which way they would run. He himself, also, would pretend sometimes to charge directly at a boy. Then he would wheel right or left—one could never tell—and knock over some child pressed against a wall who thought himself safe. After this, he would stand over him, knowing that his companions must come to his aid; and when they were all together, waving their jackets across his eyes and pulling his tail, he would scatter them—how he would scatter them! He could kick too, sideways like a cow. He knew his ranges as well as our gunners, and he was as quick on his feet as our Carpentier.[5] I observed him often. Christophe—the man who passed just now—our chief herdsman, who had taught me to ride with our beasts when I was ten—Christophe told me that he was descended from a yellow cow of those days that had chased us once into the marshes. 'He kicks just like her,' said Christophe. 'He can side-kick as he jumps. Have you seen, too, that he is not deceived by the jacket when a boy waves it? He uses it to find the boy. They think they are feeling him. He is feeling them always. He thinks, that one.' I had come to the same conclusion. Yes—the creature was a thinker along the lines necessary to his sport; and he was a humorist also, like so many natural murderers. One knows the type among beasts as well as among men. It possesses a curious truculent mirth—almost indecent but infallibly significant—"

Monsieur Voiron replenished our glasses with the great wine that went better at each descent.

"They kept him for some time in the yards to practise upon. Naturally he became a little brutal; so Christophe turned him out to learn manners among his equals in the grazing lands, where the Camargue joins the Crau. How old was he then? About eight or nine months, I think. We met again a few months later—he and I. I was riding one of our little half-wild horses, along a road of the Crau, when I found myself almost unseated. It was he! He had hidden himself behind a wind-break till we passed, and had then charged my horse from behind. Yes, he had deceived even my little horse! But I recognized him. I gave him the whip across the nose, and I said: 'Apis,[6] for this thou goest to Arles! It was un-

[5] Georges Carpentier, French boxer; world's light heavyweight champion, 1920–1922

[6] the bull-god of the ancient Egyptians

worthy of thee, between us two.' But that creature had no shame. He went away laughing, like an Apache. If he had dismounted me, I do not think it is I who would have laughed—yearling as he was."

"Why did you want to send him to Arles?" I asked.

"For the bull-ring. When your charming tourists leave us, we institute our little amusements there. Not a real bull-fight, you understand, but young bulls with padded horns, and our boys from hereabouts and in the city, go to play with them. Naturally, before we send them we try them in our yards at home. So we brought up Apis from his pastures. He knew at once that he was among the friends of his youth—he almost shook hands with them—and he submitted like an angel to padding his horns. He investigated the carts and tractors in the yards, to choose his lines of defense and attack. And then—he attacked with an *élan*,[7] and he defended with a tenacity and forethought that delighted us. In truth, we were so pleased that I fear we trespassed upon his patience. We desired him to repeat himself, which no true artist will tolerate. But he gave us fair warning. He went out to the center of the yard, where there was some dry earth; he kneeled down and—you have seen a calf whose horns fret him thrusting and rooting into a bank? He did just that, very deliberately, till he had rubbed the pads off his horns. Then he rose, dancing on those wonderful feet that twinkled, and he said: 'Now, my friends, the buttons are off the foils. Who begins?' We understood. We finished at once. He was turned out again on the pastures till it should be time to amuse them at our little metropolis. But, some time before he went to Arles—yes, I think I have it correctly—Christophe, who had been out on the Crau, informed me that Apis had assassinated a young bull who had given signs of developing into a rival. That happens, of course, and our herdsmen should prevent it. But Apis had killed in his own style—at dusk, from the ambush of a wind-break—by an oblique charge from behind which knocked the other over. He had then disembowelled him. All very possible, *but*—the murder accomplished—Apis went to the bank of a wind-break, knelt, and carefully, as he had in our yard, cleaned his horns in the earth. Christophe, who had never seen such a thing, at once borrowed (do you know, it is most efficacious when taken that way?) some Holy Water from our little chapel in those pastures, sprinkled Apis (whom it did not affect), and rode in to tell me. It was obvious that a thinker of that bull's type would also be meticulous in his toilette; so, when he was sent to Arles, I warned our consignees to exercise caution with him. Happily, the change of scene, the music, the general attention, and the meeting again with old friends—all our bad boys attended—agreeably distracted him. He became for the time a pure *farceur*[8] again; but his wheelings, his rushes, his rat-huntings were more superb than ever. There was in them now, you understand, a breadth of technique that comes of reasoned art, and, above all, the passion that arrives after

---

[7] dash   [8] practical joker

experience. Oh, he had learned, out there on the Crau! At the end of his little turn, he was, according to local rules, to be handled in all respects except for the sword, which was a stick, as a professional bull who must die. He was maneuevred into, or he posed himself in, the proper attitude; made his rush; received the point on his shoulder and then—turned about and cantered toward the door by which he had entered the arena. He said to the world: 'My friends, the representation is ended. I thank you for your applause. I go to repose myself.' But our Arlesians, who are—not so clever as some, demanded an encore, and Apis was headed back again. We others from his country, we knew what would happen. He went to the center of the ring, kneeled, and, slowly, with full parade, plunged his horns alternately in the dirt till the pads came off. Christophe shouts: 'Leave him alone, you straight-nosed imbeciles! Leave him before you must.' But they required emotion; for Rome has always debauched her loved Provincia with bread and circuses. It was given. Have you, Monsieur, ever seen a servant, with pan and broom, sweeping round the baseboard of a room? In a half-minute Apis has them all swept out and over the barrier. Then he demands once more that the door shall be opened to him. It is opened and he retires as though—which truly, is the case—loaded with laurels."

Monsieur Voiron refilled the glasses, and allowed himself a cigarette, which he puffed for some time.

"And afterwards?" I said.

"I am arranging it in my mind. It is difficult to do it justice. Afterwards—yes, afterwards—Apis returned to his pastures and his mistresses and I to my business. I am no longer a scandalous old *sportif* in shirtsleeves howling encouragement to the yellow son of a cow. I revert to Voiron Frères—wines, chemical manures, *et cetera*. And next year, through some chicane which I have not the leisure to unravel, and also, thanks to our patriarchal system of paying our older men out of the increase of the herds, old Christophe possesses himself of Apis. Oh, yes, he proves it through descent from a certain cow that my father had given his father before the Republic. Beware, Monsieur, of the memory of the illiterate man! An ancestor of Christophe had been a soldier under our Soult against your Beresford, near Bayonne.[9] He fell into the hands of Spanish guerrillas. Christophe and his wife used to tell me the details on certain Saints' Days when I was a child. Now, as compared with our recent war, Soult's campaign and retreat across the Bidassoa—"

"But did you allow Christophe just to annex the bull?" I demanded.

"You do not know Christophe. He had sold him to the Spaniards before he informed me. The Spaniards pay in coin—douros of very pure silver. Our peasants mistrust our paper. You know the saying: 'A thousand francs paper; eight hundred metal, and the cow is yours.' Yes,

---

[9] in 1811, during the Peninsular War

Christophe sold Apis, who was then two and a half years old, and to
Christophe's knowledge thrice at least an assassin."

"How was that?" I said.

"Oh, his own kind only; and always, Christophe told me, by the same
oblique rush from behind, the same sideways overthrow, and the same
swift disembowelment, followed by this levitical[10] cleaning of the horns.
In human life he would have kept a manicurist—this Minotaur.[11] And so,
Apis disappears from our country. That does not trouble me. I know in
due time I shall be advised. Why? Because, in this land, Monsieur, not a
hoof moves between Berre and the Saintes Maries without the knowledge
of specialists such as Christophe. The beasts are the substance, and the
drama of their lives to them. So when Christophe tells me, a little before
Easter Sunday, that Apis makes his début in the bull-ring of a small Cata-
lan town on the road to Barcelona, it is only to pack my car and trundle
there across the frontier with him. The place lacked importance and
manufactures, but it had produced a matador of some reputation, who
was condescending to show his art in his native town. They were even
running one special train to the place. Now our French railway system is
only execrable, but the Spanish—"

"You went down by road, didn't you?" said I.

"Naturally. It was not too good. Villamarti was the matador's name.
He proposed to kill two bulls for the honor of his birthplace. Apis, Christophe told me, would be his second. It was an interesting trip, and that
little city by the sea was ravishing. Their bull-ring dates from the middle
of the seventeenth century. It is full of feeling. The ceremonial too—
when the horsemen enter and ask the Mayor in his box to throw down
the keys of the bull-ring—that was exquisitely conceived. You know, if
the keys are caught in the horseman's hat, it is considered a good omen.
They were perfectly caught. Our seats were in the front row beside the
gates where the bulls enter, so we saw everything.

"Villamarti's first bull was not too badly killed. The second matador,
whose name escapes me, killed his without distinction—a foil to Villamarti. And the third, Chisto, a laborious, middle-aged professional who
had never risen beyond a certain dull competence, was equally of the
background. Oh, they are as jealous as the girls of the Comédie Fran-
çaise, these matadors! Villamarti's troupe stood ready for his second
bull. The gates opened, and we saw Apis, beautifully balanced on his
feet, peer coquettishly round the corner, as though he were at home. A
picador—a mounted man with the long lance-goad—stood near the barrier on his right. He had not even troubled to turn his horse, for the
capeadors—the men with the cloaks—were advancing to play Apis—to
feel his psychology and intentions, according to the rules that are made
for bulls who do not think. . . . I did not realise the murder before it

---

[10] The Book of Leviticus includes the laws for ritual cleansing.
[11] a monster of Greek myth, half man and half bull

was accomplished! The wheel, the rush, the oblique charge from behind, the fall of horse and man were simultaneous. Apis leaped the horse, with whom he had no quarrel, and alighted, all four feet together (it was enough), between the man's shoulders, changed his beautiful feet on the carcass, and was away, pretending to fall nearly on his nose. Do you follow me? In that instant, by that stumble, he produced the impression that his adorable assassination was a mere bestial blunder. Then, Monsieur, I began to comprehend that it was an artist we had to deal with. He did not stand over the body to draw the rest of the troupe. He chose to reserve that trick. He let the attendants bear out the dead, and went on to amuse himself among the capeadors. Now to Apis, trained among our children in the yards, the cloak was simply a guide to the boy behind it. He pursued, you understand, the person, not the propaganda—the proprietor, not the journal. If a third of our electors of France were as wise, my friend! . . . But it was done leisurely, with humor and a touch of truculence. He romped after one man's cloak as a clumsy dog might do, but I observed that he kept the man on his terrible left side. Christophe whispered to me: 'Wait for his mother's kick. When he has made the fellow confident it will arrive.' It arrived in the middle of a gambol. My God! He lashed out in the air as he frisked. The man dropped like a sack, lifted one hand a little towards his head, and—that was all. So you see, a body was again at his disposition; a second time the cloaks ran up to draw him off, but a second time, Apis refused his grand scene. A second time he acted that his murder was accident and—he convinced his audience! It was as though he had knocked over a bridge-gate in the marshes by mistake. Unbelievable? I saw it."

The memory sent Monsieur Voiron again to the champagne, and I accompanied him.

"But Apis was not the sole artist present. They say Villamarti comes of a family of actors. I saw him regard Apis with a new eye. He, too, began to understand. He took his cloak and moved out to play him before they should bring on another picador. He had his reputation. Perhaps Apis knew it. Perhaps Villamarti reminded him of some boy with whom he had practised at home. At any rate Apis permitted it—up to a certain point; but he did not allow Villamarti the stage. He cramped him throughout. He dived and plunged clumsily and slowly, but always with menace and always closing in. We could see that the man was conforming to the bull—not the bull to the man; for Apis was playing him towards the center of the ring, and, in a little while—I watched his face— Villamarti knew it. But I could not fathom the creature's motive. 'Wait,' said old Christophe. 'He wants that picador on the white horse yonder. When he reaches his proper distance he will get him. Villamarti is his cover. He used me once that way.' And so it was, my friend! With the clang of one of our own Seventy-fives,[12] Apis dismissed Villamarti with

[12] a famous French artillery piece

his chest—breasted him over—and had arrived at his objective near the barrier. The same oblique charge; the head carried low for the sweep of the horns; the immense sideways fall of the horse, broken-legged and half-paralyzed; the senseless man on the ground and—behold Apis between them, backed against the barrier—his right covered by the horse; his left by the body of the man at his feet. The simplicity of it! Lacking the carts and tractors of his early parade-grounds he, being a genius, had extemporised with the materials at hand, and dug himself in. The troupe closed up again, their left wing broken by the kicking horse, their right immobilized by the man's body which Apis bestrode with significance. Villamarti almost threw himself between the horns, but—it was more an appeal than an attack. Apis refused him. He held his base. A picador was sent at him—necessarily from the front, which alone was open. Apis charged—he who, till then, you realise, had not used the horn! The horse went over backwards, the man half beneath him. Apis halted, hooked him under the heart, and threw him to the barrier. He heard his head crack, but he was dead before he hit the wood. There was no demonstration from the audience. They, also, had begun to realize this Foch[13] among bulls! The arena occupied itself again with the dead. Two of the troupe irresolutely tried to play him—God knows in what hope!—but he moved out to the center of the ring. 'Look!' said Christophe. 'Now he goes to clean himself. That always frightened me.' He knelt down; he began to clean his horns. The earth was hard. He worried at it in an ecstasy of absorption. As he laid his head along and rattled his ears, it was as though he were interrogating the Devils themselves upon their secrets, and always saying impatiently: 'Yes, I know that—and that—and that! Tell me more—more!' In the silence that covered us, a woman cried: 'He digs a grave! Oh, Saints, he digs a grave!' Some others echoed this—not loudly—as a wave echoes in a grotto of the sea.

"And when his horns were cleaned, he rose up and studied poor Villamarti's troupe, eyes in eyes, one by one, with the gravity of an equal in intellect and the remote and merciless resolution of a master in his art. This was more terrifying than his toilette."

"And they—Villamarti's men?" I asked.

"Like the audience, were dominated. They had ceased to posture, or stamp, or address insults to him. They conformed to him. The two other matadors stared. Only Chisto, the oldest, broke silence with some call or other, and Apis turned his head towards him. Otherwise he was isolated, immobile—somber—meditating on those at his mercy. Ah!

"For some reason the trumpet sounded for the *banderillas*—those gay hooked darts that are planted in the shoulders of bulls who do not think, after their neck-muscles are tired by lifting horses. When such bulls feel the pain, they check for an instant, and, in that instant, the men step gracefully aside. Villamarti's banderillero answered the trumpet me-

[13] Ferdinand Foch, 1851–1929, marshal of France during World War I

chanically—like one condemned. He stood out, poised the darts and stammered the usual patter of invitation. . . . And after? I do not assert that Apis shrugged his shoulders, but he reduced the episode to its lowest elements, as could only a bull of Gaul. With his truculence was mingled always—owing to the shortness of his tail—a certain Rabelaisian abandon, especially when viewed from the rear. Christophe had often commented upon it. Now, Apis brought that quality into play. He circulated round that boy, forcing him to break up his beautiful poses. He studied him from various angles, like an incompetent photographer. He presented to him every portion of his anatomy except his shoulders. At intervals he feigned to run in upon him. My God, he was cruel! But his motive was obvious. He was playing for a laugh from the spectators which should synchronise with the fracture of the human morale. It was achieved. The boy turned and ran towards the barrier. Apis was on him before the laugh ceased; passed him; headed him—what do I say?—herded him off to the left, his horns beside and a little in front of his chest: he did not intend him to escape into a refuge. Some of the troupe would have closed in, but Villamarti cried: 'If he wants him he will take him. Stand!' They stood. Whether the boy slipped or Apis nosed him over I could not see. But he dropped, sobbing. Apis halted like a car with four brakes, struck a pose, smelt him very completely and turned away. It was dismissal more ignominious than degradation at the head of one's battalion. The representation was finished. Remained only for Apis to clear his stage of the subordinate characters.

"Ah! His gesture then! He gave a dramatic start—this Cyrano[14] of the Camargue—as though he was aware of them for the first time. He moved. All their beautiful breeches twinkled for an instant along the top of the barrier. He held the stage alone! But Christophe and I, we trembled! For, observe, he had now involved himself in a stupendous drama of which he only could supply the third act. And, except for an audience on the razor-edge of emotion, he had exhausted his material. Molière[15] himself—we have forgotten, my friend, to drink to the health of that great soul—might have been at a loss. And Tragedy is but a step behind Failure. We could see the four or five Civil Guards, who are sent always to keep order, fingering the breeches of their rifles. They were but waiting a word from the Mayor to fire on him, as they do sometimes at a bull who leaps the barrier among the spectators. They would, of course, have killed or wounded several people—but that would not have saved Apis."

Monsieur Voiron drowned the thought at once, and wiped his beard.

"At that moment Fate—the Genius of France, if you will—sent to assist in the incomparable finale, none other than Chisto, the eldest, and, I should have said (but never again will I judge!) the least inspired of all; mediocrity itself but, at heart—and it is the heart that conquers always,

[14] grandiloquent hero of Edmond Rostand's neo-Romantic play, *Cyrano de Bergerac*, 1897

[15] French dramatist, 1622–1673

my friend—at heart an artist. He descended stiffly into the arena, alone and assured. Apis regarded him, his eyes in his eyes. The man took stance, with his cloak, and called to the bull as to an equal : 'Now, Señor, we will show these honorable caballeros something together.' He advanced thus against this thinker who at a plunge—a kick—a thrust— could, we all knew, have extinguished him. My dear friend, I wish I could convey to you something of the unaffected bonhomie, the humor, the delicacy, the consideration bordering on respect even, with which Apis, the supreme artist, responded to this invitation. It was the Master, wearied after a strenuous hour in the atelier, unbuttoned and at ease with some not inexpert but limited disciple. The telepathy was instantaneous between them. And for good reason! Christophe said to me : 'All's well. That Chisto began among the bulls. I was sure of it when I heard him call just now. He has been a herdsman. He'll pull it off.' There was a little feeling and adjustment, at first, for mutual distances and allowances.

"Oh, yes! And here occurred a gross impertinence of Villamarti. He had, after an interval, followed Chisto—to retrieve his reputation. My Faith! I can conceive the elder Dumas[16] slamming his door on an intruder precisely as Apis did. He raced Villamarti into the nearest refuge at once. He stamped his feet outside it, and he snorted : 'Go! I am engaged with an artist!' Villamarti went—his reputation left behind for ever.

"Apis returned to Chisto saying : 'Forgive the interruption. I am not always master of my time, but you were about to observe, my dear confrère[17]. . . ?' Then the play began. Out of compliment to Chisto, Apis chose as his objective (every bull varies in this respect) the inner edge of the cloak—that nearest to the man's body. This allows but a few millimeters clearance in charging. But Apis trusted himself as Chisto trusted him, and, this time, he conformed to the man, with inimitable judgment and temper. He allowed himself to be played into the shadow or the sun, as the delighted audience demanded. He raged enormously ; he feigned defeat ; he despaired in statuesque abandon, and thence flashed into fresh paroxysms of wrath—but always with the detachment of the true artist who knows he is but the vessel of an emotion whence others, not he, must drink. And never once did he forget that honest Chisto's cloak was to him the gauge by which to spare even a hair on the skin. He inspired Chisto too. My God! His youth returned to that meritorious beef-sticker—the desire, the grace, and the beauty of his early dreams. One could almost see that girl of the past for whom he was rising, rising to these present heights of skill and daring. It was his hour too—a miraculous hour of dawn returned to gild the sunset. All he knew was at Apis' disposition. Apis acknowledged it with all that he had learned at home, at Arles and in his lonely murders on our grazing-grounds. He flowed round Chisto like a river of death—round his knees, leaping at his shoul-

---

[16] Alexandre Dumas (Dumas père), 1802–1870, French novelist and playwright
[17] colleague

ders, kicking just clear of one side or the other of his head; behind his back hissing as he shaved by; and once or twice—inimitable!—he reared wholly up before him while Chisto slipped back from beneath the avalanche of that instructed body. Those two, my dear friend, held five thousand people dumb with no sound but of their breathings—regular as pumps. It was unbearable. Beast and man realized together that we needed a change of note—a *détente*. They relaxed to pure buffoonery. Chisto fell back and talked to him outrageously. Apis pretended he had never heard such language. The audience howled with delight. Chisto slapped him; he took liberties with his short tail, to the end of which he clung while Apis pirouetted; he played about him in all postures; he had become the herdsman again—gross, careless, brutal, but comprehending. Yet Apis was always the more consummate clown. All that time (Christophe and I saw it) Apis drew off towards the gates of the *toril*[18] where so many bulls enter but—have you ever heard of one that returned? *We* knew that Apis knew that as he had saved Chisto, so Chisto would save him. Life is sweet to us all; to the artist who lives many lives in one, sweetest. Chisto did not fail him. At the last, when none could laugh any longer, the man threw his cape across the bull's back, his arm round his neck. He flung up a hand at the gate, as Villamarti, young and commanding but *not* a herdsman, might have raised it, and he cried: 'Gentlemen, open to me and my honorable little donkey.' They opened—I have misjudged Spaniards in my time!—those gates opened to the man and the bull together, and closed behind them. And then? From the Mayor to the Guarda Civile they went mad for five minutes, till the trumpets blew and the fifth bull rushed out—an unthinking black Andalusian. I suppose some one killed him. My friend, my very dear friend, to whom I have opened my heart, I confess that I did not watch. Christophe and I we were weeping together like children of the same Mother. Shall we drink to Her?"

[18] the stall where the bull awaits his entrance into the bullring

H. G. Wells

1866–1946

THE COUNTRY OF THE BLIND

THREE hundred miles and more from Chimborazo, one hundred from the snows of Cotopaxi, in the wildest wastes of Ecuador's Andes, there lies that mysterious mountain valley, cut off from the world of men, the Country of the Blind. Long years ago that valley lay so far open to the world that men might come at last through frightful gorges and over an icy pass into its equable meadows; and thither indeed men came, a family or so of Peruvian half-breeds fleeing from the lust and tyranny of an evil Spanish ruler. Then came the stupendous outbreak of Mindo-bamba,[1] when it was night in Quito for seventeen days, and the water was boiling at Yaguachi and all the fish floating dying even as far as Guayaquil; everywhere along the Pacific slopes there were land-slips and swift thawings and sudden floods, and one whole side of the old Arauca crest slipped and came down in thunder, and cut off the Country of the Blind for ever from the exploring feet of men. But one of these early settlers had chanced to be on the hither side of the gorges when the world had so terribly shaken itself, and he perforce had to forget his wife and his child and all the friends and possessions he had left up there, and start life over again in the lower world. He started it again but ill, blind-ness overtook him, and he died of punishment in the mines; but the story he told begot a legend that lingers along the length of the Cordilleras of the Andes to this day.

He told of his reason for venturing back from that fastness, into which he had first been carried lashed to a llama, beside a vast bale of gear, when he was a child. The valley, he said, had in it all that the heart of man could desire—sweet water, pasture, and even climate, slopes of rich brown soil with tangles of a shrub that bore an excellent fruit, and on one side great hanging forests of pine that held the avalanches high. Far over-head, on three sides, vast cliffs of gray-green rock were capped by cliffs of ice; but the glacier stream came not to them but flowed away by the farther slopes, and only now and then huge ice masses fell on the valley side. In this valley it neither rained nor snowed, but the abundant springs gave a rich green pasture, that irrigation would spread over all the valley space. The settlers did well indeed there. Their beasts did well and multi-plied, and but one thing marred their happiness. Yet it was enough to mar it greatly. A strange disease had come upon them, and had made all the children born to them there—and indeed, several older children also—blind. It was to seek some charm or antidote against this plague of blind-ness that he had with fatigue and danger and difficulty returned down the gorge. In those days, in such cases, men did not think of germs and in-fections but of sins; and it seemed to him that the reason of this affliction must lie in the negligence of these priestless immigrants to set up a shrine so soon as they entered the valley. He wanted a shrine—a handsome, cheap, effectual shrine—to be erected in the valley; he wanted relics and such-like potent things of faith, blessed objects and mysterious medals and prayers. In his wallet he had a bar of native silver for which he would not account; he insisted there was none in the valley with something of the insistence of an inexpert liar. They had all clubbed their money and ornaments together, having little need for such treasure up there, he said, to buy them holy help against their ill. I figure this dim-eyed young mountaineer, sunburnt, gaunt, and anxious, hat-brim clutched feverishly,

---

[1] The volcano appears to be fictitious, but the other place names are actual.

a man all unused to the ways of the lower world, telling this story to some keen-eyed, attentive priest before the great convulsion; I can picture him presently seeking to return with pious and infallible remedies against that trouble, and the infinite dismay with which he must have faced the tumbled vastness where the gorge had once come out. But the rest of his story of mischances is lost to me, save that I know of his evil death after several years. Poor stray from that remoteness! The stream that had once made the gorge now bursts from the mouth of a rocky cave, and the legend his poor, ill-told story set going developed into the legend of a race of blind men somewhere "over there" one may still hear today.

And amidst the little population of that now isolated and forgotten valley the disease ran its course. The old became groping and purblind, the young saw but dimly, and the children that were born to them saw never at all. But life was very easy in that snow-rimmed basin, lost to all the world, with neither thorns nor briars, with no evil insects nor any beasts save the gentle breed of llamas they had lugged and thrust and followed up the beds of the shrunken rivers in the gorges up which they had come. The seeing had become purblind so gradually that they scarcely noted their loss. They guided the sightless youngsters hither and thither until they knew the whole valley marvelously, and when at last sight died out among them the race lived on. They had even time to adapt themselves to the blind control of fire, which they made carefully in stoves of stone. They were a simple strain of people at the first, unlettered, only slightly touched with the Spanish civilization, but with something of a tradition of the arts of old Peru and of its lost philosophy. Generation followed generation. They forgot many things; they devised many things. Their tradition of the greater world they came from became mythical in color and uncertain. In all things save sight they were strong and able, and presently the chance of birth and heredity sent one who had an original mind and who could talk and persuade among them, and then afterwards another. These two passed, leaving their effects, and the little community grew in numbers and in understanding, and met and settled social and economic problems that arose. Generation followed generation. Generation followed generation. There came a time when a child was born who was fifteen generations from that ancestor who went out of the valley with a bar of silver to seek God's aid, and who never returned. Thereabouts it chanced that a man came into this community from the outer world. And this is the story of that man.

He was a mountaineer from the country near Quito, a man who had been down to the sea and had seen the world, a reader of books in an original way, an acute and enterprising man, and he was taken on by a party of Englishmen who had come out to Ecuador to climb mountains, to replace one of their three Swiss guides who had fallen ill. He climbed here and he climbed there, and then came the attempt on Parascotopetl, the Matterhorn of the Andes, in which he was lost to the outer world. The story of the accident has been written a dozen times. Pointer's narrative is the best. He tells how the little party worked their difficult and almost vertical way up to the very foot of the last and greatest precipice, and how they built a night shelter amidst the snow upon a little shelf of rock, and, with a touch of real dramatic power, how presently they found Nunez had gone from them. They shouted, and there was no reply; shouted and whistled, and for the rest of that night they slept no more.

As the morning broke they saw the traces of his fall. It seems impossible he could have uttered a sound. He had slipped eastward towards the unknown side of the mountain; far below he had struck a steep slope of snow, and plowed his way down it in the midst of a snow avalanche. His track went straight to the edge of a frightful precipice, and beyond that everything was hidden. Far, far below, and hazy with distance, they could see trees rising out of a narrow, shut-in valley—the lost Country of the Blind. But they did not know it was the lost Country of the Blind, nor distinguish it in any way from any other narrow streak of upland valley. Unnerved by this disaster, they abandoned their attempt in the afternoon, and Pointer was called away to the war before he could make another attack. To this day Parascotopetl lifts an unconquered crest, and Pointer's shelter crumbles unvisited amidst the snows.

And the man who fell survived.

At the end of the slope he fell a thousand feet, and came down in the midst of a cloud of snow upon a snow slope even steeper than the one above. Down this he was whirled, stunned and insensible, but without a bone broken in his body; and then at last came to gentler slopes, and at last rolled out and lay still, buried amidst a softening heap of the white masses that had accompanied and saved him. He came to himself with a dim fancy that he was ill in bed; then realized his position with a mountaineer's intelligence, and worked himself loose and, after a rest or so, out until he saw the stars. He rested flat upon his chest for a space, wondering where he was and what had happened to him. He explored his limbs, and discovered that several of his buttons were gone and his coat turned over his head. His knife had gone from his pocket and his hat was lost, though he had tied it under his chin. He recalled that he had been looking for loose stones to raise his piece of the shelter wall. His ice-axe had disappeared.

He decided he must have fallen, and looked up to see, exaggerated by the ghastly light of the rising moon, the tremendous flight he had taken. For a while he lay, gazing blankly at that vast pale cliff towering above, rising moment by moment out of a subsiding tide of darkness. Its phantasmal, mysterious beauty held him for a space, and then he was seized with a paroxysm of sobbing laughter. . . .

After a great interval of time he became aware that he was near the lower edge of the snow. Below, down what was now a moonlit and practicable slope, he saw the dark and broken appearance of rock-strewn turf. He struggled to his feet, aching in every joint and limb, got down painfully from the heaped loose snow about him, went downward until he was on the turf, and there dropped rather than lay beside a boulder, drank deep from the flask in his inner pocket, and instantly feel asleep. . . .

He was awakened by the singing of birds in the trees far below.

He sat up and perceived he was on a little alp at the foot of a vast precipice, that was grooved by the gully down which he and his snow had come. Over against him another wall of rock reared itself against the sky. The gorge between these precipices ran east and west and was full of the morning sunlight, which lit to the westward the mass of fallen mountain that closed the descending gorge. Below him it seemed there was a precipice equally steep, but behind the snow in the gully he found a sort of chimney-cleft dripping with snow-water down which a desperate man might venture. He found it easier than it seemed, and came at last to another desolate alp, and then after a rock climb of no particular difficulty to a steep slope of trees. He took his bearings and turned his face up the gorge, for he saw it opened out above upon green meadows, among which he now glimpsed quite distinctly a cluster of stone huts of unfamiliar fashion. At times his progress was like clambering along the face of a wall, and after a time the rising sun ceased to strike along the gorge, the voices of the singing birds died away, and the air grew cold and dark about him. But the distant valley with its houses was all the brighter for that. He came presently to talus, and among the rocks he noted—for he was an observant man—an unfamiliar fern that seemed to clutch out of the crevices with intense green hands. He picked a frond or so and gnawed its stalk and found it helpful.

About midday he came at last out of the throat of the gorge into the plain and the sunlight. He was stiff and weary; he sat down in the shadow of a rock, filled up his flask with water from a spring and drank it down, and remained for a time resting before he went on to the houses.

They were very strange to his eyes, and indeed the whole aspect of that valley became, as he regarded it, queerer and more unfamiliar. The greater part of its surface was lush green meadow, starred with many beautiful flowers, irrigated with extraordinary care, and bearing evidence of systematic cropping piece by piece. High up and ringing the valley about was a wall, and what appeared to be a circumferential water-channel, from which the little trickles of water that fed the meadow plants came, and on the higher slopes above this flocks of llamas cropped the scanty herbage. Sheds, apparently shelters or feeding-places for the llamas, stood against the boundary wall here and there. The irrigation streams ran together into a main channel down the center of the valley, and this was enclosed on either side by a wall breast high. This gave a singularly urban quality to this secluded place, a quality that was greatly enhanced by the fact that a number of paths paved with black and white stones, and each with a curious little curb at the side, ran hither and thither in an orderly manner. The houses of the central village were quite unlike the casual and higgledy-piggledy agglomeration of the mountain villages he knew; they stood in a continuous row on either side of a central street of astonishing cleanness; here and there their parti-colored façade was pierced by a door, and not a solitary window broke their even frontage. They were parti-colored with extraordinary irregularity, smeared with a sort of plaster that was sometimes gray, sometimes drab, sometimes slate-colored or dark brown; and it was the sight of this wild plastering first brought the word "blind" into the thoughts of the explorer. "The good man who did that," he thought, "must have been as blind as a bat."

He descended a steep place, and so came to the wall and channel that ran about the valley, near where the latter spouted out its surplus contents into the deeps of the gorge in a thin and wavering thread of cascade. He could now see a number of men and women resting on piled heaps of grass, as if taking a siesta, in the remoter part of the meadow, and nearer the village a number of recumbent children, and then nearer at hand three men carrying pails on yokes along a little path that ran from the encircling wall towards the houses. These latter were clad in garments of llama cloth and boots and belts of leather, and they wore caps of cloth with back and ear flaps. They followed one another in single file, walking slowly and yawning as they walked, like men who have been up all night. There was something so reassuringly prosperous and respectable in their bearing that after a moment's hesitation Nunez stood forward as conspicuously as possible upon his rock, and gave vent to a mighty shout that echoed round the valley.

The three men stopped, and moved their heads as though they were looking about them. They turned their faces this way and that, and Nunez gesticulated with freedom. But they did not appear to see him for all his gestures, and after a time, directing themselves towards the mountains far away to the right, they shouted as if in answer. Nunez bawled again, and then once more, and as he gestured ineffectually the word "blind" came up to the top of his thoughts. "The fools must be blind," he said.

When at last, after much shouting and wrath, Nunez crossed the stream by a little bridge, came through a gate in the wall, and approached them, he was sure that they were blind. He was sure that this was the Country of the Blind of which the legends told. Conviction had sprung upon him, and a sense of great and rather enviable adventure. The three stood side by side, not looking at him, but with their ears directed towards him, judging him by his unfamiliar steps. They stood close together like men a little afraid, and he could see their eyelids closed and sunken, as though the very balls beneath had shrunk away. There was an expression near awe on their faces.

"A man," one said, in hardly recognisable Spanish—"a man it is—a man or a spirit—coming down from the rocks."

But Nunez advanced with the confident steps of a youth who enters upon life. All the old stories of the lost valley and the Country of the

Blind had come back to his mind, and through his thoughts ran this old proverb, as if it were a refrain—

"In the Country of the Blind the One-eyed Man is King."

"In the Country of the Blind the One-eyed Man is King."

And very civilly he gave them greeting. He talked to them and used his eyes.

"Where does he come from, brother Pedro?" asked one.

"Down out of the rocks."

"Over the mountains I come," said Nunez, "out of the country beyond there—where men can see. From near Bogota, where there are a hundred thousands of people, and where the city passes out of sight."

"Sight?" muttered Pedro. "Sight?"

"He comes," said the second blind man, "out of the rocks."

The cloth of their coats Nunez saw was curiously fashioned, each with a different sort of stitching.

They startled him by a simultaneous movement towards him, each with a hand outstretched. He stepped back from the advance of these spread fingers.

"Come hither," said the third blind man, following his motion and clutching him neatly.

And they held Nunez and felt him over, saying no word further until they had done so.

"Carefully," he cried, with a finger in his eye, and found they thought that organ, with its fluttering lids, a queer thing in him. They went over it again.

"A strange creature, Correa," said the one called Pedro. "Feel the coarseness of his hair. Like a llama's hair."

"Rough he is as the rocks that begot him," said Correa, investigating Nunez's unshaven chin with a soft and slightly moist hand. "Perhaps he will grow finer." Nunez struggled a little under their examination, but they gripped him firm.

"Carefully," he said again.

"He speaks," said the third man. "Certainly he is a man."

"Ugh!" said Pedro, at the roughness of his coat.

"And you have come into the world?" asked Pedro.

"*Out* of the world. Over mountains and glaciers; right over above there, half-way to the sun. Out of the great big world that goes down, twelve days' journey to the sea."

They scarcely seemed to heed him. "Our fathers have told us men may be made by the forces of Nature," said Correa. "It is the warmth of things and moisture, and rottenness—rottenness."

"Let us lead him to the elders," said Pedro.

"Shout first," said Correa, "lest the children be afraid. This is a marvelous occasion."

So they shouted, and Pedro went first and took Nunez by the hand to lead him to the houses.

He drew his hand away. "I can see," he said.

"See?" said Correa.

"Yes, see," said Nunez, turning towards him, and stumbled against Pedro's pail.

"His senses are still imperfect," said the third blind man. "He stumbles, and talks unmeaning words. Lead him by the hand."

"As you will," said Nunez, and was led along, laughing.

It seemed they knew nothing of sight.

Well, all in good time he would teach them.

He heard people shouting, and saw a number of figures gathering together in the middle roadway of the village.

He found it tax his nerve and patience more than he had anticipated, that first encounter with the population of the Country of the Blind. The place seemed larger as he drew near to it, and the smeared plasterings queerer, and a crowd of children and men and women (the women and girls, he was pleased to note, had some of them quite sweet faces, for all that their eyes were shut and sunken) came about him, holding on to him, touching him with soft, sensitive hands, smelling at him, and listening at every word he spoke. Some of the maidens and children, however, kept aloof as if afraid, and indeed his voice seemed coarse and rude beside their softer notes. They mobbed him. His three guides kept close to him with an effect of proprietorship, and said again and again, "A wild man out of the rocks."

"Bogota," he said. "Bogota. Over the mountain crests."

"A wild man—using wild words," said Pedro. "Did you hear that— *Bogota?* His mind is hardly formed yet. He has only the beginnings of speech."

A little boy nipped his hand. "Bogota!" he said mockingly.

"Ay! A city to your village. I come from the great world—where men have eyes and see."

"His name's Bogota," they said.

"He stumbled," said Correa, "stumbled twice as we came hither."

"Bring him to the elders."

And they thrust him suddenly through a doorway into a room as black as pitch, save at the end there faintly glowed a fire. The crowd closed in behind him and shut out all but the faintest glimmer of day, and before he could arrest himself he had fallen headlong over the feet of a seated man. His arm, outflung, struck the face of someone else as he went down; he felt the soft impact of features and heard a cry of anger, and for a moment he struggled against a number of hands that clutched him. It was a one-sided fight. An inkling of the situation came to him, and he lay quiet.

"I fell down," he said; "I couldn't see in this pitchy darkness."

There was a pause as if the unseen persons about him tried to understand his words. Then the voice of Correa said: "He is but newly formed. He stumbles as he walks and mingles words that mean nothing with his speech."

Others also said things about him that he heard or understood imperfectly.

"May I sit up?" he asked, in a pause. "I will not struggle against you again."

They consulted and let him rise.

The voice of an older man began to question him, and Nunez found himself trying to explain the great world out of which he had fallen, and the sky and mountains and sight and such-like marvels, to these elders who sat in darkness in the Country of the Blind. And they would believe and understand nothing whatever he told them, a thing quite outside his expectation. They would not even understand many of his words. For fourteen generations these people had been blind and cut off from all the seeing world; the names for all the things of sight had faded and changed; the story of the outer world was faded and changed to a child's story; and they had ceased to concern themselves with anything beyond the rocky slopes above their circling wall. Blind men of genius had arisen among them and questioned the shreds of belief and tradition they had brought with them from their seeing days, and had dismissed all these things as idle fancies, and replaced them with new and saner explanations. Much of their imagination had shriveled with their eyes, and they had made for themselves new imaginations with their ever more sensitive ears and finger-tips. Slowly Nunez realized this; that his expectation of wonder and reverence at his origin and his gifts was not to be borne out; and after his poor attempt to explain sight to them had been set aside as the confused version of a new-made being describing the marvels of his incoherent sensations, he subsided, a little dashed, into listening to their instruction. And the eldest of the blind men explained to him life and philosophy and religion, how that the world (meaning their valley) had been first an empty hollow in the rocks, and then had come, first, inanimate things without the gift of touch, and llamas and a few other creatures that had little sense, and then men, and at last angels, whom one could hear singing and making fluttering sounds, but whom no one could touch at all, which puzzled Nunez greatly until he thought of the birds.

He went on to tell Nunez how this time had been divided into the warm and the cold, which are the blind equivalents of day and night, and how it was good to sleep in the warm and work during the cold, so that now, but for his advent, the whole town of the blind would have been asleep. He said Nunez must have been specially created to learn and serve the wisdom they had acquired, and that for all his mental incoherency and stumbling behavior he must have courage, and do his best to learn, and at that all the people in the doorway murmured encouragingly. He said the night—for the blind call their day night—was now far gone, and it behooved every one to go back to sleep. He asked Nunez if he knew how to sleep, and Nunez said he did, but that before sleep he wanted food.

They brought him food—llama's milk in a bowl, and rough salted bread—and led him into a lonely place to eat out of their hearing, and afterwards to slumber until the chill of the mountain evening roused them to begin their day again. But Nunez slumbered not at all.

Instead, he sat up in the place where they had left him, resting his limbs and turning the unanticipated circumstances of his arrival over and over in his mind.

Every now and then he laughed, sometimes with amusement, and sometimes with indignation.

"Unformed mind!" he said. "Got no senses yet! They little know they've been insulting their heaven-sent king and master. I see I must bring them to reason. Let me think—let me think."

He was still thinking when the sun set.

Nunez had an eye for all beautiful things, and it seemed to him that the glow upon the snowfields and glaciers that rose about the valley on every side was the most beautiful thing he had ever seen. His eyes went from that inaccessible glory to the village and irrigated fields, fast sinking into the twilight, and suddenly a wave of emotion took him, and he thanked God from the bottom of his heart that the power of sight had been given him.

He heard a voice calling to him from out of the village.

"Ya ho there, Bogota! Come hither!"

At that he stood up smiling. He would show these people once and for all what sight would do for a man. They would seek him, but not find him.

"You move not, Bogota," said the voice.

He laughed noiselessly, and made two stealthy steps aside from the path.

"Trample not on the grass, Bogota; that is not allowed."

Nunez had scarcely heard the sound he made himself. He stopped amazed.

The owner of the voice came running up the piebald path towards him. He stepped back into the pathway. "Here I am," he said.

"Why did you not come when I called you?" said the blind man. "Must you be led like a child? Cannot you hear the path as you walk?"

Nunez laughed. "I can see it," he said.

"There is no such word as *see*," said the blind man, after a pause. "Cease this folly, and follow the sound of my feet."

Nunez followed, a little annoyed.

"My time will come," he said.

"You'll learn," the blind man answered. "There is much to learn in the world."

"Has no one told you, 'In the Country of the Blind the One-eyed Man Man is King'?"

"What is blind?" asked the blind man carelessly over his shoulder.

Four days passed, and the fifth found the King of the Blind still incognito, as a clumsy and useless stranger among his subjects.

It was, he found, much more difficult to proclaim himself than he had supposed, and in the meantime, while he meditated his *coup d'état*, he did what he was told and learnt the manners and customs of the Country of the Blind. He found working and going about at night a particularly irksome thing, and he decided that that should be the first thing he would change.

They led a simple, laborious life, these people, with all the elements of virtue and happiness, as these things can be understood by men. They toiled, but not oppressively; they had food and clothing sufficient for their needs; they had days and seasons of rest; they made much of music and singing, and there was love among them, and little children.

It was marvelous with what confidence and precision they went about their ordered world. Everything, you see, had been made to fit their needs; each of the radiating paths of the valley area had a constant angle to the others, and was distinguished by a special notch upon its curbing; all obstacles and irregularities of path or meadow had long since been cleared away; all their methods and procedure arose naturally from their special needs. Their senses had become marvelously acute; they could hear and judge the slightest gesture of a man a dozen paces away—could hear the very beating of his heart. Intonation had long replaced expression with them, and touches gesture, and their work with hoe and spade and fork was as free and confident as garden work can be. Their sense of smell was extraordinarily fine; they could distinguish individual differences as readily as a dog can, and they went about the tending of the llamas, who lived among the rocks above and came to the wall for food and shelter, with ease and confidence. It was only when at last Nunez sought to assert himself that he found how easy and confident their movements could be.

He rebelled only after he had tried persuasion.

He tried at first on several occasions to tell them of sight.

"Look you here, you people," he said. "There are things you do not understand in me."

Once or twice one or two of them attended to him; they sat with faces downcast and ears turned intelligently towards him, and he did his best to tell them what it was to see. Among his hearers was a girl, with eyelids less red and sunken than the others, so that one could almost fancy she was hiding eyes, whom especially he hoped to persuade. He spoke of the beauties of sight, of watching the mountains, of the sky and the sunrise, and they heard him with amused incredulity that presently became condemnatory. They told him there were indeed no mountains at all, but that the end of the rocks where the llamas grazed was indeed the end of the world; thence sprang a cavernous roof of the universe, from which the dew and the avalanches fell; and when he maintained stoutly the world had neither end nor roof such as they supposed, they said his thoughts were wicked. So far as he could describe sky and clouds and stars to them it seemed to them a hideous void, a terrible blankness in the place of the smooth roof to things in which they believed—it was an article of faith with them that the cavern roof was exquisitely smooth to the touch. He saw that in some manner he shocked them, and gave up that aspect of the matter altogether, and tried to show them the practical value of sight. One morning he saw Pedro in the path called Seventeen and coming towards the central houses, but still too far off for hearing or scent, and he told them as much. "In a little while," he prophesied, "Pedro will be here." An old man remarked that Pedro had no business on path Seventeen, and then, as if in confirmation, that individual as he drew near turned and went transversely into path Ten, and so back with nimble paces towards the outer wall. They mocked Nunez when Pedro did not arrive, and afterwards, when he asked Pedro questions to clear his character, Pedro denied and outfaced him, and was afterwards hostile to him.

Then he induced them to let him go a long way up the sloping meadows towards the wall with one complacent individual, and to him he promised to describe all that happened among the houses. He noted certain goings and comings, but the things that really seemed to signify to these people happened inside of or behind the windowless houses—the only things they took note of to test him by—and of these he could see or tell nothing; and it was after the failure of this attempt, and the ridicule they could not repress, that he resorted to force. He thought of seizing a spade and suddenly smiting one or two of them to earth, and so in fair combat showing the advantage of eyes. He went so far with that resolution as to seize his spade, and then he discovered a new thing about himself, and that was that it was impossible for him to hit a blind man in cold blood.

He hesitated, and found them all aware that he had snatched up the spade. They stood alert, with their heads on one side, and bent ears towards him for what he would do next.

"Put that spade down," said one, and he felt a sort of helpless horror. He came near obedience.

Then he thrust one backwards against a house wall, and fled past him and out of the village.

He went athwart one of their meadows, leaving a track of trampled grass behind his feet, and presently sat down by the side of one of their ways. He felt something of the buoyancy that comes to all men in the beginning of a fight, but more perplexity. He began to realize that you cannot even fight happily with creatures who stand upon a different mental basis to yourself. Far away he saw a number of men carrying spades and sticks come out of the street of houses, and advance in a spreading line along the several paths towards him. They advanced slowly, speaking frequently to one another, and ever and again the whole cordon would halt and sniff the air and listen.

The first time they did this Nunez laughed. But afterwards he did not laugh.

One struck his trail in the meadow grass, and came stooping and feeling his way along it.

For five minutes he watched the slow extension of the cordon, and then his vague disposition to do something forthwith became frantic. He stood up, went a pace or so towards the circumferential wall, turned, and went back a little way. There they all stood in a crescent, still and listening.

He also stood still, gripping his spade very tightly in both hands. Should he charge them?

The pulse in his ears ran into the rhythm of "In the Country of the Blind the One-eyed Man is King!"

Should he charge them?

He looked back at the high and unclimbable wall behind—unclimbable because of its smooth plastering, but withal pierced with many little doors, and at the approaching line of seekers. Behind these others were now coming out of the street of houses.

Should he charge them?

"Bogota!" called one. "Bogota! where are you?"

He gripped his spade still tighter, and advanced down the meadows towards the place of habitations, and directly he moved they converged upon him. "I'll hit them if they touch me," he swore; "by Heaven, I will. I'll hit." He called aloud, "Look here, I'm going to do what I like in this valley. Do you hear? I'm going to do what I like and go where I like!"

They were moving in upon him quickly, groping, yet moving rapidly. It was like playing blind man's buff, with everyone blindfolded except one. "Get hold of him!" cried one. He found himself in the arc of a loose curve of pursuers. He felt suddenly he must be active and resolute.

"You don't understand," he cried in a voice that was meant to be great and resolute, and which broke. "You are blind, and I can see. Leave me along!"

"Bogota! Put down that spade, and come off the grass!"

The last order, grotesque in its urban familiarity, produced a gust of anger.

"I'll hurt you," he said, sobbing with emotion. "By Heaven, I'll hurt you. Leave me along!"

He began to run, not knowing clearly where to run. He ran from the nearest blind man, because it was a horror to hit him. He stopped, and then made a dash to escape from their closing ranks. He made for where a gap was wide, and the men on either side, with a quick perception of the approach of his paces, rushed in on one another. He sprang forward, and then saw he must be caught, and *swish!* the spade had struck. He felt the soft thud of hand and arm, and the man was down with a yell of pain, and he was through.

Through! And then he was close to the street of houses again, and blind men, whirling spades and stakes, were running with a sort of reasoned swiftness hither and thither.

He heard steps behind him just in time, and found a tall man rushing forward and swiping at the sound of him. He lost his nerve, hurled his spade a yard wide at his antagonist, and whirled about and fled, fairly yelling as he dodged another.

He was panic-stricken. He ran furiously to and fro, dodging when there was no need to dodge, and in his anxiety to see on every side of him at once, stumbling. For a moment he was down and they heard his fall. Far away in the circumferential wall a little doorway looked like heaven, and he set off in a wild rush for it. He did not even look round at his pursuers until it was gained, and he had stumbled across the bridge, clambered a little way among the rocks, to the surprise and dismay of a young llama, who went leaping out of sight, and lay down sobbing for breath.

And so his *coup d'état* came to an end.

He stayed outside the wall of the valley of the Blind for two nights and days without food or shelter, and meditated upon the unexpected. During these meditations he repeated very frequently and always with a profounder note of derision the exploded proverb: "In the Country of the Blind the One-Eyed Man is King." He thought chiefly of ways of fighting and conquering these people, and it grew clear that for him no practicable way was possible. He had no weapons, and now it would be hard to get one.

The canker of civilization had got to him even in Bogota, and he could not find it in himself to go down and assassinate a blind man. Of course, if he did that, he might then dictate terms on the threat of assassinating them all. But—sooner or later he must sleep! . . .

He tried also to find food among the pine trees, to be comfortable under pine boughs while the frost fell at night, and—with less confidence —to catch a llama by artifice in order to try to kill it—perhaps by hammering it with a stone—and so finally, perhaps, to eat some of it. But the llamas had a doubt of him and regarded him with distrustful brown eyes, and spat when he drew near. Fear came on him the second day and fits of shivering. Finally he crawled down to he wall of the Country of the-Blind and tried to make terms. He crawled along by the stream, shouting, until two blind men came out to the gate and talked to him.

"I was mad," he said. "But I was only newly made."

They said that was better.

He told them he was wiser now, and repented of all he had done.

Then he wept without intention, for he was very weak and ill now, and they took that as a favorable sign.

They asked him if he still thought he could "*see*."

"No," he said. "That was folly. The word means nothing—less than nothing!"

They asked him what was overhead.

"About ten times ten the height of a man there is a roof above the world—of rock—and very, very smooth.". . . He burst again into hysterical tears. "Before you ask me any more, give me some food or I shall die."

He expected dire punishments, but these blind people were capable of toleration. They regarded his rebellion as but one more proof of his general idiocy and inferiority; and after they had whipped him they appointed him to do the simplest and heaviest work they had for anyone to do, and he, seeing no other way of living, did submissively what he was told.

He was ill for some days, and they nursed him kindly. That refined his submission. But they insisted on his lying in the dark, and that was a great misery. And blind philosophers came and talked to him of the wicked levity of his mind, and reproved him so impressively for his doubts about the lid of rock that covered their cosmic casserole that he almost doubted whether indeed he was not the victim of hallucination in not seeing it overhead.

So Nunez became a citizen of the Country of the Blind, and these people ceased to be a generalized people and became individualities and familiar to him, while the world beyond the mountains became more and more remote and unreal. There was Yacob, his master, a kindly man when not annoyed; there was Pedro, Yacob's nephew; and there was Medina-saroté, who was the youngest daughter of Yacob. She was little esteemed in the world of the blind, because she had a clear-cut face, and lacked that satisfying, glossy smoothness that is the blind man's ideal of feminine beauty; but Nunez thought her beautiful at first, and presently the most beautiful thing in the whole creation. Her closed eyelids were not sunken and red after the common way of the valley, but lay as though they might open again at any moment; and she had long eyelashes, which were considered a grave disfigurement. And her voice was strong, and did not satisfy the acute hearing of the valley swains. So that she had no lover.

There came a time when Nunez thought that, could he win her, he would be resigned to live in the valley for all the rest of his days.

He watched her; he sought opportunities of doing her little services, and presently he found that she observed him. Once at a rest-day gathering they sat side by side in the dim starlight, and the music was sweet. His hand came upon hers and he dared to clasp it. Then very tenderly she returned his pressure. And one day, as they were at their meal in the darkness, he felt her hand very softly seeking him, and as it chanced the fire leapt then and he saw the tenderness of her face.

He sought to speak to her.

He went to her one day when she was sitting in the summer moonlight spinning. The light made her a thing of silver and mystery. He sat down at her feet and told her he loved her, and told her how beautiful she seemed to him. He had a lover's voice, he spoke with a tender reverence that came near to awe, and she had never before been touched by adoration. She made him no definite answer, but it was clear his words pleased her.

After that he talked to her whenever he could take an opportunity. The valley became the world for him, and the world beyond the mountains where men lived in sunlight seemed no more than a fairy tale he would some day pour into her ears. Very tentatively and timidly he spoke to her of sight.

Sight seemed to her the most poetical of fancies, and she listened to his description of the stars and the mountains and her own sweet white-lit beauty as though it was a guilty indulgence. She did not believe, she could only half understand, but she was mysteriously delighted, and it seemed to him that she completely understood.

His love lost its awe and took courage. Presently he was for demanding her of Yacob and the elders in marriage, but she became fearful and delayed. And it was one of her elder sisters who first told Yacob that Medina-saroté and Nunez were in love.

There was from the first very great opposition to the marriage of Nunez and Medina-saroté; not so much because they valued her as because they held him as a being apart, an idiot, incompetent thing below the permissible level of a man. Her sisters opposed it bitterly as bringing discredit on them all; and old Yacob, though he had formed a sort of liking for his clumsy, obedient serf, shook his head and said the thing could not be. The young men were all angry at the idea of corrupting the race, and one went so far as to revile and strike Nunez. He struck back. Then for the first time he found an advantage in seeing, even by twilight, and after that fight was over no one was disposed to raise a hand against him. But they still found his marriage impossible.

Old Yacob had a tenderness for his last little daughter, and was grieved to have her weep upon his shoulder.

"You see, my dear, he's an idiot. He has delusions; he can't do anything right."

"I know," wept Medina-saroté. "But he's better than he was. He's getting better. And he's strong, dear father, and kind—stronger and kinder than any other man in the world. And he loves me—and, father, I love him."

Old Yacob was greatly distressed to find her inconsolable, and, besides —what made it more distressing—he liked Nunez for many things. So he went and sat in the windowless council-chamber with the other elders and watched the trend of the talk, and said, at the proper time, "He's better than he was. Very likely, some day, we shall find him as sane as ourselves."

Then afterwards one of the elders, who thought deeply, had an idea. He was the great doctor among these people, their medicine-man, and he had a very philosophical and inventive mind, and the idea of curing Nunez of his peculiarities appealed to him. One day when Yacob was present he returned to the topic of Nunez.

"I have examined Bogota," he said, "and the case is clearer to me. I think very probably he might be cured."

"That is what I have always hoped," said old Yacob.

"His brain is affected," said the blind doctor.

The elders murmured assent.

"Now, *what* affects it?"

"Ah!" said old Yacob.

"*This*," said the doctor, answering his own question. "Those queer things that are called the eyes, and which exist to make an agreeable soft depression in the face, are diseased, in the case of Bogota, in such a way as to affect his brain. They are greatly distended, he has eyelashes, and his eyelids move, and consequently his brain is in a state of constant irritation and distraction."

"Yes?" said old Yacob. "Yes?"

"And I think I may say with reasonable certainty that, in order to cure him completely, all that we need do is a simple and easy surgical operation—namely, to remove these irritant bodies."

"And then he will be sane?"

"Then he will be perfectly sane, and a quite admirable citizen."

"Thank Heaven for science!" said old Yacob, and went forth at once to tell Nunez of his happy hopes.

But Nunez's manner of receiving the good news struck him as being cold and disappointing.

"One might think," he said, "from the tone you take, that you did not care for my daughter."

It was Medina-saroté who persuaded Nunez to face the blind surgeons.

"*You* do not want me," he said, "to lose my gift of sight?"

She shook her head.

"My world is sight."

Her head drooped lower.

"There are the beautiful things, the beautiful little things—the flowers, the lichens among the rocks, the lightness and softness on a piece of fur, the far sky with its drifting down of clouds, the sunsets and the stars. And there is *you*. For you alone it is good to have sight, to see your sweet, serene face, your kindly lips, your dear, beautiful hands folded together. . . . It is these eyes of mine you win, these eyes that hold me to you, that these idiots seek. Instead, I must touch you, hear you, and never see you again. I must come under that roof of rock and stone and darkness, that horrible roof under which your imagination stoops. . . . No; you would not have me do that?"

A disagreeable doubt had arisen in him. He stopped, and left the thing a question.

"I wish," she said, "sometimes—" She paused.

"Yes," said he, a little apprehensively.

"I wish sometimes—you would not talk like that."

"Like what?"

"I know it's pretty—it's your imagination. I love it, but *now*—"
He felt cold. "*Now?*" he said faintly.
She sat quite still.
"You mean—you think—I should be better, better perhaps—"
He was realizing things very swiftly. He felt anger, indeed, anger at
the dull course of fate, but also sympathy for her lack of understanding
—a sympathy near akin to pity.
"*Dear*," he said, and he could see by her whiteness how intensely her
spirit pressed against the things she could not say. He put his arms about
her, he kissed her ear, and they sat for a time in silence.
"If I were to consent to this?" he said at last, in a voice that was very
gentle.
She flung her arms about him, weeping wildly. "Oh, if you would,"
she sobbed, "if only you would!"

For a week before the operation that was to raise him from his servitude and inferiority to the level of a blind citizen, Nunez knew nothing
of sleep, and all through the warm sunlit hours, while the others slumbered happily, he sat brooding or wandered aimlessly, trying to bring
his mind to bear on his dilemma. He had given his answer, he had given
his consent, and still he was not sure. And at last work-time was over,
the sun rose in splendor over the golden crests, and his last day of vision
began for him. He had a few minutes with Medina-saroté before she
went apart to sleep.
"Tomorrow," he said, "I shall see no more."
"Dear heart!" she answered, and pressed his hands with all her
strength.
"They will hurt you but little," she said; "and you are going through
this pain—you are going through it, dear lover, for *me*. . . . Dear, if a
woman's heart and life can do it, I will repay you. My dearest one, my
dearest with the tender voice, I will repay."
He was drenched in pity for himself and her.
He held her in his arms, and pressed his lips to hers, and looked on her
sweet face for the last time. "Good-bye!" he whispered at that dear
sight, "good-bye!"
And then in silence he turned away from her.
She could hear his slow retreating footsteps, and something in the
rhythm of them threw her into a passion of weeping.
He had fully meant to go to a lonely place where the meadows were
beautiful with white narcissus, and there remain until the hour of his
sacrifice should come, but as he went he lifted up his eyes and saw the
morning, the morning like an angel in golden armor, marching down the
steeps. . . .
It seemed to him that before this splendor he, and this blind world in
the valley, and his love, and all, were no more than a pit of sin.
He did not turn aside as he had meant to do, but went on, and passed

through the wall of the circumference and out upon the rocks, and his eyes were always upon the sunlit ice and snow.

He saw their infinite beauty, and his imagination soared over them to the things beyond he was now to resign for ever.

He thought of that great free world he was parted from, the world that was his own, and he had a vision of those further slopes, distance beyond distance, with Bogota, a place of multitudinous stirring beauty, a glory by day, a luminous mystery by night, a place of palaces and fountains and statues and white houses, lying beautifully in the middle distance. He thought how for a day or so one might come down through passes, drawing ever nearer and nearer to its busy streets and ways. He thought of the river journey, day by day, from great Bogota to the still vaster world beyond, through towns and villages, forest and desert places, the rushing river day by day, until its banks receded and the big steamers came splashing by, and one had reached the sea—the limitless sea, with its thousand islands, its thousands of islands, and its ships seen dimly far away in their incessant journeyings round and about that greater world. And there, unpent by mountains, one saw the sky—the sky, not such a disc as one saw it here, but an arch of immeasurable blue, a deep of deeps in which the circling stars were floating. . . .

His eyes scrutinized the great curtain of the mountains with a keener inquiry.

For example, if one went so, up that gully and to that chimney there, then one might come out high among those stunted pines that ran round in a sort of shelf and rose still higher and higher as it passed above the gorge. And then? That talus might be managed. Thence perhaps a climb might be found to take him up to the precipice that came below the snow ; and if that chimney failed, then another farther to the east might serve his purpose better. And then? Then one would be out upon the amber-lit snow there, and half-way up to the crest of those beautiful desolations.

He glanced back at the village, then turned right round and regarded it steadfastly.

He thought of Medina-saroté, and she had become small and remote.

He turned again towards the mountain wall, down which the day had come to him.

Then very circumspectly he began to climb.

When sunset came he was no longer climbing, but he was far and high. He had been higher, but he was still very high. His clothes were torn, his limbs were blood-stained, he was bruised in many places, but he lay as if he were at his ease, and there was a smile on his face.

From where he rested the valley seemed as if it were in a pit and nearly a mile below. Already it was dim with haze and shadow, though the mountain summits around him were things of light and fire. The mountain summits around him were things of light and fire, and the little details of the rocks near at hand were drenched with subtle beauty—a vein of green mineral piercing the gray, the flash of crystal faces here and there, a minute, minutely-beautiful orange lichen close beside his face. There were deep mysterious shadows in the gorge, blue deepening into purple, and purple into a luminous darkness, and overhead was the illimitable vastness of the sky. But he heeded these things no longer, but lay quite inactive there, smiling as if he were satisfied merely to have escaped from the valley of the Blind in which he had thought to be King.

The glow of the sunset passed, and the night came, and still he lay peacefully contented under the cold clear stars.

Thomas Mann

1875–1955

DISORDER AND EARLY SORROW

THE PRINCIPAL dish at dinner had been croquettes made of turnip greens. So there follows a trifle, concocted out of one of those dessert powders we use nowadays, that taste like almond soap. Xaver, the youthful manservant, in his outgrown striped jacket, white woolen gloves, and yellow sandals, hands it round, and the "big folk" take this opportunity to remind their father, tactfully, that company is coming today.

The "big folk" are two, Ingrid and Bert. Ingrid is brown-eyed, eighteen, and perfectly delightful. She is on the eve of her exams, and will probably pass them, if only because she knows how to wind masters, and even headmasters, round her finger. She does not, however, mean to use her certificate once she gets it; having leanings towards the stage, on the ground of her ingratiating smile, her equally ingratiating voice, and a marked and irresistible talent for burlesque. Bert is blond and seventeen. He intends to get done with school somehow, anyhow, and fling himself into the arms of life. He will be a dancer, or a cabaret actor, possibly even a waiter—but not a waiter anywhere else save at the Cairo, the night-club, whither he has once already taken flight, at five in the morning, and been brought back crestfallen. Bert bears a strong resemblance to the youthful manservant Xaver Kleinsgutl, of about the same age as himself; not because he looks common—in features he is strikingly like his father, Professor Cornelius—but by reason of an approximation of types, due in its turn to far-reaching compromises in matters of dress and bearing generally. Both lads wear their heavy hair very long on top, with a cursory parting in the middle, and give their heads the same characteristic toss to throw it off the forehead. When one of them leaves the house, by the garden gate, bareheaded in all weathers, in a blouse rakishly girt with a leather strap, and sheers off bent well over with his head on one side; or else mounts his push-bike—Xaver makes free with his employers', of both sexes, or even, in acutely irresponsible mood, with the Professor's own—Dr. Cornelius from his bedroom window cannot, for the life of him, tell whether he is looking at his son or his servant. Both, he thinks, look like young moujiks.[1] And both are impassioned cigarette-smokers, though Bert has not the means to compete with Xaver, who smokes as many as thirty a day, of a brand named after a popular cinema star. The big folk call their father and mother the "old folk"—not behind their backs, but as a form of address and in all affection: "Hullo, old folks," they will say; though Cornelius is only forty-seven years old and his wife eight years younger. And the Professor's parents, who lead in his household the humble and hesitant life of the really old, are on the big folk's lips the "ancients." As for the "little folk," Ellie and Snapper, who take their meals upstairs with blue-faced Ann—so-called because of her prevailing facial hue—Ellie and Snapper follow their mother's example and address their father by his first name, Abel. Unutterably comic it sounds, in its pert, confiding familiarity; particularly on the lips, in the sweet accents, of five-year-old Eleanor, who is the image of Frau Cornelius's baby pictures and whom the Professor loves above everything else in the world.

"Darling old thing," says Ingrid affably, laying her large but shapely hand on his, as he presides in proper middle-class style over the family table, with her on his left and the mother opposite: "Parent mine, may I ever so gently jog your memory, for you have probably forgotten: this is the afternoon we were to have our little jollification, our turkey-trot with eats to match. You haven't a thing to do but just bear up and not funk it; everything will be over by nine o'clock."

"Oh—ah!" says Cornelius, his face falling. "Good!" he goes on, and nods his head to show himself in harmony with the inevitable. "I only meant—is this really the day? Thursday, yes. How time flies! Well, what time are they coming?"

"Half past four they'll be dropping in, I should say," answers Ingrid, to whom her brother leaves the major rôle in all dealings with the father. Upstairs, while he is resting, he will hear scarcely anything, and from seven to eight he takes his walk. He can slip out by the terrace if he likes.

"Tut!" says Cornelius deprecatingly, as who should say: "You exaggerate." But Bert puts in: "It's the one evening in the week Wanja doesn't have to play. Any other night he'd have to leave by half past six, which would be painful for all concerned."

Wanja is Ivan Herzl, the celebrated young leading man at the Stadt-theater. Bert and Ingrid are on intimate terms with him, they often visit

[1] Russian peasants

him in his dressing-room and have tea. He is an artist of the modern school, who stands on the stage in strange and, to the Professor's mind, utterly affected dancing attitudes, and shrieks lamentably. To a professor of history, all highly repugnant; but Bert has entirely succumbed to Herzl's influence, blackens the lower rim of his eyelids—despite painful but fruitless scenes with the father—and with youthful carelessness of the ancestral anguish declares that not only will he take Herzl for his model if he becomes a dancer, but in case he turns out to be a waiter at the Cairo he means to walk precisely thus.

Cornelius slightly raises his brows and makes his son a little bow—indicative of the unassumingness and self-abnegation that befits his age. You could not call it a mocking bow or suggestive in any special sense. Bert may refer it to himself or equally to his so talented friend.

"Who else is coming?" next inquires the master of the house. They mention various people, names all more or less familiar, from the city, from the suburban colony, from Ingrid's school. They still have some telephoning to do, they say. They have to phone Max. This is Max Hergesell, an engineering student; Ingrid utters his name in the nasal drawl which according to her is the traditional intonation of all the Hergesells. She goes on to parody it in the most abandonedly funny and lifelike way, and the parents laugh until they nearly choke over the wretched trifle. For even in these times when something funny happens people have to laugh.

From time to time the telephone bell rings in the Professor's study, and the big folk run across, knowing it is their affair. Many people had to give up their telephones the last time the price rose, but so far the Corneliuses have been able to keep theirs, just as they have kept their villa, which was built before the war, by dint of the salary Cornelius draws as professor of history—a million marks, and more or less adequate to the chances and changes of post-war life. The house is comfortable, even elegant, though sadly in need of repairs that cannot be made for lack of materials, and at present disfigured by iron stoves with long pipes. Even so, it is still the proper setting of the upper middle class, though they themselves look odd enough in it, with their worn and turned clothing and altered way of life. The children, of course, know nothing else; to them it is normal and regular, they belong by birth to the "villa proletariat." The problem of clothing troubles them not at all. They and their like have evolved a costume to fit the time, by poverty out of taste for innovation: in summer it consists of scarcely more than a belted linen smock and sandals. The middle-class parents find things rather more difficult.

The big folk's table-napkins hang over their chair-backs, they talk with their friends over the telephone. These friends are the invited guests who have rung up to accept or decline or arrange; and the conversation is carried on in the jargon of the clan, full of slang and high spirits, of which the old folk understand hardly a word. These consult together meantime about the hospitality to be offered to the impending guests. The Professor displays a middle-class ambitiousness: he wants to serve a sweet—or something that looks like a sweet—after the Italian salad and brownbread sandwiches. But Frau Cornelius says that would be going too far. The guests would not expect it, she is sure—and the big folk, returning once more to their trifle, agree with her.

The mother of the family is of the same general type as Ingrid, though not so tall. She is languid; the fantastic difficulties of the housekeeping have broken and worn her. She really ought to go and take a cure, but feels incapable; the floor is always swaying under her feet, and everything seems upside down. She speaks of what is uppermost in her mind: the eggs, they simply must be bought today. Six thousand marks apiece they are, and just so many are to be had on this one day of the week at one single shop fifteen minutes' journey away. Whatever else they do, the big folk must go and fetch them immediately after luncheon, with Danny, their neighbor's son, who will soon be calling for them; and Xaver Kleinsgutl will don civilian garb and attend his young master and mistress. For no single household is allowed more than five eggs a week; therefore the young people will enter the shop singly, one after another, under assumed names, and thus wring twenty eggs from the shopkeeper for the Cornelius family. This enterprise is the sporting event of the week for all participants, not excepting the moujik Kleinsgutl, and most of all for Ingrid and Bert, who delight in misleading and mystifying their fellow-men and would revel in the performance even if it did not achieve one single egg. They adore impersonating fictitious characters; they love to sit in a bus and carry on long lifelike conversations in a dialect which they otherwise never speak, the most commonplace dialogue about politics and people and the price of food, while the whole bus listens openmouthed to this incredibly ordinary prattle, though with a dark suspicion all the while that something is wrong somewhere. The conversation waxes ever more shameless, it enters into revolting detail about these people who do not exist. Ingrid can make her voice sound ever so common and twittering and shrill as she impersonates a shop-girl with an illegitimate child, said child being a son with sadistic tendencies, who lately out in the country treated a cow with such unnatural cruelty that no Christian could have borne to see it. Bert nearly explodes at her twittering, but restrains himself and displays a grisly sympathy; he and the unhappy shop-girl entering into a long, stupid, depraved, and shuddery conversation over the particular morbid cruelty involved; until an old gentleman opposite, sitting with his ticket folded between his index finger and his seal ring, can bear it no more and makes public protest against the nature of the themes these young folk are discussing with such particularity. He uses the Greek plural: "themata." Whereat Ingrid pretends to be dissolving in tears, and Bert behaves as though his wrath against the old gentleman was with difficulty being held in check and would probably burst out before long. He clenches his fists, he gnashes his teeth, he shakes from head to foot; and the unhappy old gentleman, whose intentions had been of the best, hastily leaves the bus at the next stop.

Such are the diversions of the big folk. The telephone plays a prominent part in them: they ring up any and everybody—members of government, opera singers, dignitaries of the Church—in the character of shop assistants, or perhaps as Lord or Lady Doolittle. They are only with difficulty persuaded that they have the wrong number. Once they emptied their parents' card-tray and distributed its contents among the neighbors' letter-boxes, wantonly, yet not without enough impish sense of the fitness of things to make it highly upsetting, God only knowing why certain people should have called where they did.

Xaver comes in to clear away, tossing the hair out of his eyes. Now that he has taken off his gloves you can see the yellow chainring on his left hand. And as the Professor finishes his watery eight-thousand-mark beer and lights a cigarette, the little folk can be heard scrambling down the stair, coming, by established custom, for their after-dinner call on Father and Mother. They storm the dining-room, after a struggle with the latch, clutched by both pairs of little hands at once; their clumsy small feet twinkle over the carpet, in red felt slippers with the socks falling down on them. With prattle and shoutings each makes for his own place: Snapper to Mother, to climb on her lap, boast of all he has eaten, and thump his fat little tum; Ellie to her Abel, so much hers because she is so very much his; because she consciously luxuriates in the deep tenderness—like all deep feeling, concealing a melancholy strain—with which he holds her small form embraced; in the love in his eyes as he kisses her little fairy hand or the sweet brow with its delicate tracery of tiny blue veins.

The little folk look like each other, with the strong undefined likeness of brother and sister. In clothing and haircut they are twins. Yet they are sharply distinguished after all, and quite on sex lines. It is a little Adam and a little Eve. Not only is Snapper the sturdier and more compact, he appears consciously to emphasize his four-year-old masculinity in speech, manner, and carriage, lifting his shoulders and letting the little arms hang down quite like a young American athlete, drawing down his mouth when he talks and seeking to give his voice a gruff and forthright ring. But all this masculinity is the result of effort rather than natively his. Born and brought up in these desolate, distracted times, he has been endowed by them with an unstable and hypersensitive nervous system and suffers greatly under life's disharmonies. He is prone to sudden anger and outbursts of bitter tears, stamping his feet at every trifle; for this reason he is his mother's special nursling and care. His round, round eyes are chestnut brown and already inclined to squint, so that he will need glasses in the near future. His little nose is long, the mouth small— the father's nose and mouth they are, more plainly than ever since the Professor shaved his pointed beard and goes smooth-faced. The pointed beard had become impossible—even professors must make some concession to the changing times

But the little daughter sits on her father's knee, his Eleonorchen, his little Eve, so much more gracious a little being, so much sweeter-faced than her brother—and he holds his cigarette away from her while she fingers his glasses with her dainty wee hands. The lenses are divided for reading and distance, and each day they tease her curiosity afresh.

At bottom he suspects that his wife's partiality may have a firmer basis than his own: that Snapper's refractory masculinity perhaps is solider stuff than his own little girl's more explicit charm and grace. But the heart will not be commanded, that he knows; and once and for all his heart belongs to the little one, as it has since the day she came, since the first time he saw her. Almost always when he holds her in his arms he remembers that first time: remembers the sunny room in the Women's Hospital, where Ellie first saw the light, twelve years after Bert was born. He remembers how he drew near, the mother smiling the while, and cautiously put aside the canopy of the diminutive bed that stood beside the large one. There lay the little miracle among the pillows: so well formed, so encompassed, as it were, with the harmony of sweet proportions, with little hands that even then, though so much tinier, were beautiful as now; with wide-open eyes blue as the sky and brighter than the sunshine—and almost in that very second he felt himself captured and held fast. This was love at first sight, love everlasting: a feeling unknown, unhoped for, unexpected—in so far as it could be a matter of conscious awareness; it took entire possession of him, and he understood, with joyous amazement, that this was for life.

But he understood more. He knows, does Dr. Cornelius, that there is something not quite right about this feeling, so unaware, so undreamed of, so involuntary. He has a shrewd suspicion that it is not by accident it has so utterly mastered him and bound itself up with his existence; that he had—even subconsciously—been preparing for it, or, more precisely, been prepared for it. There is, in short, something in him which at a given moment was ready to issue in such a feeling; and this something, highly extraordinary to relate, is his essence and quality as a professor of history. Dr. Cornelius, however, does not actually say this, even to himself; he merely realizes it, at odd times, and smiles a private smile. He knows that history professors do not love history because it is something that comes to pass, but only because it is something that *has* come to pass; that they hate a revolution like the present one because they feel it is lawless, incoherent, irrelevant—in a word, unhistoric; that their hearts belong to the coherent, disciplined, historic past. For the temper of timelessness, the temper of eternity—thus the scholar communes with himself when he takes his walk by the river before supper—that temper broods over the past; and it is a temper much better suited to the nervous system of a history professor than are the excesses of the present. The past is immortalized; that is to say, it is dead; and death is the root of all godliness and all abiding significance. Dr. Cornelius, walking alone in the dark, has a profound insight into this truth. It is this conservative instinct of his, his sense of the eternal, that has found in his love for his little daughter a way to save itself from the wounding inflicted by the times. For father love, and a little child on its mother's breast—are not these timeless, and thus very, very holy and beautiful? Yet Cornelius, pondering there in the dark, descries something not perfectly right and good in his love. Theoretically, in the interests of science, he admits it to himself. There is something ulterior about it, in the nature of it; that something is hostility, hostility against the history of today, which is still in the making and thus not history at all, in behalf of the genuine history that has already happened—that is to say, death. Yes, passing strange though all this is, yet it is true; true in a sense, that is. His devotion to this priceless morsel of life and new growth has something to do with death, it clings to death as against life; and that is neither right nor beautiful—in a sense. Though only the most fanatical asceticism could be capable, on no other ground than such casual scientific perception, of tearing this purest and most precious of feelings out of his heart.

He holds his darling on his lap and her slim rosy legs hang down. He raises his brows as he talks to her, tenderly, with a half-teasing note of respect, and listens enchanted to her high, sweet little voice calling him Abel. He exchanges a look with the mother, who is caressing her Snapper and reading him a gentle lecture. He must be more reasonable, he must learn self-control; today again, under the manifold exasperations of life, he has given way to rage and behaved like a howling dervish. Cornelius casts a mistrustful glance at the big folk now and then, too; he thinks it not unlikely they are not unaware of those scientific preoccupations of his evening walks. If such be the case they do not show it. They stand there leaning their arms on their chair-backs and with a benevolence not untinctured with irony look on at the parental happiness.

The children's frocks are of a heavy, brick-red stuff, embroidered in modern "arty" style. They once belonged to Ingrid and Bert and are precisely alike, save that little knickers come out beneath Snapper's smock. And both have their hair bobbed. Snapper's is a streaky blond, inclined to turn dark. It is bristly and sticky and looks for all the world like a droll, badly fitting wig. But Ellie's is chestnut brown, glossy and fine as silk, as pleasing as her whole little personality. It covers her ears —and these ears are not a pair, one of them being the right size, the other distinctly too large. Her father will sometimes uncover this little abnormality and exclaim over it as though he had never noticed it before, which both makes Ellie giggle and covers her with shame. Her eyes are now golden brown, set far apart and with sweet gleams in them—such a clear and lovely look! The brows above are blond; the nose still unformed, with thick nostrils and almost circular holes; the mouth large and expressive, with a beautifully arching and mobile upper lip. When she laughs, dimples come in her cheeks and she shows her teeth like loosely strung pearls. So far she has lost but one tooth, which her father gently twisted out with his handkerchief after it had grown very wobbling. During this small operation she had paled and trembled very much. Her cheeks have the softness proper to her years, but they are not chubby; indeed, they are rather concave, due to her facial structure, with its somewhat prominent jaw. On one, close to the soft fall of her hair, is a downy freckle.

Ellie is not too well pleased with her looks—a sign that already she troubles about such things. Sadly she thinks it is best to admit it once for all, her face is "homely"; though the rest of her, "on the other hand," is not bad at all. She loves expressions like "on the other hand"; they sound choice and grown-up to her, and she likes to string them together, one after the other: "very likely," "probably," "after all." Snapper is self-critical too, though more in the moral sphere: he suffers from remorse for his attacks of rage and considers himself a tremendous sinner. He is quite certain that heaven is not for such as he; he is sure to go to "the bad place" when he dies, and no persuasions will convince him to the contrary —as that God sees the heart and gladly makes allowances. Obstinately he shakes his head, with the comic, crooked little peruke, and vows there is no place for him in heaven. When he has a cold he is immediately quite choked with mucus; rattles and rumbles from top to toe if you even look at him; his temperature flies up at once and he simply puffs. Nursy is pessimistic on the score of his constitution: such fat-blooded children as he might get a stroke any minute. Once she even thought she saw the moment at hand: Snapper had been in one of his berserker rages, and in the ensuing fit of penitence stood himself in the corner with his back to the room. Suddenly Nursy noticed that his face had gone all blue, far bluer, even, than her own. She raised the alarm, crying out that the child's all too rich blood had at length brought him to his final hour; and Snapper, to his vast astonishment, found himself, so far from being rebuked for evil-doing, encompassed in tenderness and anxiety—until it turned out that his color was not caused by apoplexy but by the distempering[2] on the nursery wall, which had come off on his tear-wet face.

Nursy has come downstairs too, and stands by the door, sleek-haired, owl-eyed, with her hands folded over her white apron, and a severely dignified manner born of her limited intelligence. She is very proud of the care and training she gives her nurslings and declares that they are "enveloping wonderfully." She has had seventeen suppurated teeth lately removed from her jaws and been measured for a set of symmetrical yellow ones in dark rubber gums; these now embellish her peasant face. She is obsessed with the strange conviction that these teeth of hers are the subject of general conversation, that, as it were, the sparrows on the

---

[2] paint mixed with egg white

house-tops chatter of them. "Everybody knows I've had a false set put in," she will say; "there has been a great deal of foolish talk about them." She is much given to dark hints and veiled innuendo: speaks, for instance, of a certain Dr. Bleifuss, whom every child knows, and "there are even some in the house who pretend to be him." All one can do with talk like this is charitably to pass it over in silence. But she teaches the children nursery rhymes: gems like:

> *Puff, puff, here comes the train!*
> *Puff, puff, toot, toot,*
> *Away it goes again.*

Or that gastronomical jingle, so suited, in its sparseness, to the times, and yet seemingly with a blitheness of its own:

> *Monday we begin the week,*
> *Tuesday there's a bone to pick.*
> *Wednesday we're half way through,*
> *Thursday what a great to-do!*
> *Friday we eat what fish we're able,*
> *Saturday we dance round the table.*
> *Sunday brings us pork and greens—*
> *Here's a feast for kings and queens!*

Also a certain four-line stanza with a romantic appeal, unutterable and unuttered:

> *Open the gate, open the gate*
> *And let the carriage drive in.*
> *Who is it in the carriage sits?*
> *A lordly sir with golden hair.*

Or, finally that ballad about golden-haired Marianne who sat on a, sat on a, sat on a stone, and combed out her, combed out her, combed out her hair; and about bloodthirsty Rudolph, who pulled out a, pulled out a, pulled out a knife—and his ensuing direful end. Ellie enunciates all these ballads charmingly, with her mobile little lips, and sings them in her sweet little voice—much better than Snapper. She does everything better than he does, and he pays her honest admiration and homage and obeys her in all things except when visited by one of his attacks. Sometimes she teaches him, instructs him upon the birds in the picture-book and tells him their proper names: "This is a chaffinch, Buddy, this is a bullfinch, this is a cowfinch." He has to repeat them after her. She gives him medical instruction too, teaches him the names of diseases, such as infammation of the lungs, infammation of the blood, infammation of the air. If he does not pay attention and cannot say the words after her, she stands him in the corner. Once she even boxed his ears, but was so ashamed that she stood herself in the corner for a long time. Yes, they are fast friends, two souls with but a single thought, and have all their adventures in common.

They come home from a walk and relate as with one voice that they have seen two moollies and a teenty-weenty baby calf. They are on familiar terms with the kitchen, which consists of Xaver and the ladies Hinterhofer, two sisters once of the lower middle class who, in these evil days, are reduced to living "*au pair*"[3] as the phrase goes and officiating as cook and housemaid for their board and keep. The little ones have a feeling that Xaver and the Hinterhofers are on much the same footing with their father and mother as they are themselves. At least sometimes, when they have been scolded, they go downstairs and announce that the master and mistress are cross. But playing with the servants lacks charm compared with the joys of playing upstairs. The kitchen could never rise to the height of the games their father can invent. For instance, there is "four gentlemen taking a walk." When they play it Abel will crook his knees until he is the same height with themselves and go walking with them, hand in hand. They never get enough of this sport; they could walk round and round the dining-room a whole day on end, five gentlemen in all, counting the diminished Abel.

Then there is the thrilling cushion game. One of the children, usually Ellie, seats herself, unbeknownst to Abel, in his seat at table. Still as a mouse she awaits his coming. He draws near with his head in the air, descanting in loud, clear tones upon the surpassing comfort of his chair; and sits down on top of Ellie. "What's this, what's this?" says he. And bounces about, deaf to the smothered giggles exploding behind him. "Why have they put a cushion in my chair? And what a queer, hard, awkward-shaped cushion it is!" he goes on. "Frightfully uncomfortable to sit on!" And keeps pushing and bouncing about more and more on the astonishing cushion and clutching behind him into the rapturous giggling and squeaking, until at last he turns round, and the game ends with a magnificent climax of discovery and recognition. They might go through all this a hundred times without diminishing by an iota its power to thrill.

Today is no time for such joys. The imminent festivity disturbs the atmosphere, and besides there is work to be done, and, above all, the eggs to be got. Ellie has just time to recite "Puff, puff," and Cornelius to discover that her ears are not mates, when they are interrupted by the arrival of Danny, come to fetch Bert and Ingrid. Xaver, meantime, has exchanged his striped livery for an ordinary coat, in which he looks rather rough-and-ready, though as brisk and attractive as ever. So then Nursy and the children ascend to the upper regions, the Professor withdraws to his study to read, as always after dinner, and his wife bends her energies upon the sandwiches and salad that must be prepared. And she has another errand as well. Before the young people arrive she has to take her shopping-basket and dash into town on her bicycle, to turn into provisions a sum of money she has in hand, which she dares not keep lest it lose all value.

[3] with board and lodging, but no salary

Cornelius reads, leaning back in his chair, with his cigar between his middle and index fingers. First he reads Macaulay[4] on the origin of the English public debt at the end of the seventeenth century; then an article in a French periodical on the rapid increase in the Spanish debt towards the end of the sixteenth. Both these for his lecture on the morrow. He intends to compare the astonishing prosperity which accompanied the phenomenon in England with its fatal effects a hundred years earlier in Spain, and to analyse the ethical and psychological grounds of the difference in results. For that will give him a chance to refer back from the England of William III, which is the actual subject in hand, to the time of Philip II and the Counter-Reformation,[5] which is his own special field. He has already written a valuable work on this period; it is much cited and got him his professorship. While his cigar burns down and gets strong, he excogitates a few pensive sentences in a key of gentle melancholy, to be delivered before his class next day: about the practically hopeless struggle carried on by the belated Philip against the whole trend of history: against the new, the kingdom-disrupting power of the Germanic ideal of freedom and individual liberty. And about the persistent, futile struggle of the aristocracy, condemned by God and rejected of man, against the forces of progress and change. He savors his sentences; keeps on polishing them while he puts back the books he has been using; then goes upstairs for the usual pause in his day's work, the hour with drawn blinds and closed eyes, which he so imperatively needs. But to-day, he recalls, he will rest under disturbed conditions, amid the bustle of preparations for the feast. He smiles to find his heart giving a mild flutter at the thought. Disjointed phrases on the theme of black-clad Philip and his times mingle with a confused consciousness that they will soon be dancing down below. For five minutes or so he falls asleep.

As he lies and rests he can hear the sound of the garden gate and the repeated ringing at the bell. Each time a little pang goes through him, of excitement and suspense, at the thought that the young people have begun to fill the floor below. And each time he smiles at himself again—though even his smile is slightly nervous, is tinged with the pleasurable anticipations people always feel before a party. At half past four—it is already dark—he gets up and washes at the wash-stand. The basin has been out of repair for two years. It is supposed to tip, but has broken away from its socket on one side and cannot be mended because there is nobody to mend it; neither replaced because no shop can supply another. So it has to be hung up above the vent and emptied by lifting in both hands and pouring out the water. Cornelius shakes his head over this basin, as he does several times a day—whenever, in fact, he has occasion

---

[4] Thomas Babington Macaulay, 1800–1859, English historian and statesman
[5] William of Orange, King of England, 1689–1702. Philip II, King of Spain, 1556–1598. Counter-Reformation: movement of reform within the Roman Catholic Church following the Protestant Reformation

to use it. He finishes his toilet with care, standing under the ceiling light to polish his glasses till they shine. Then he goes downstairs.

On his way to the dining-room he hears the gramophone already going, and the sound of voices. He puts on a polite, society air; at his tongue's end is the phrase he means to utter: "Pray don't let me disturb you," as he passes directly into the dining-room for his tea. "Pray don't let me disturb you"—it seems to him precisely the *mot juste;*[6] towards the guests cordial and considerate, for himself a very bulwark.

The lower floor is lighted up, all the bulbs in the chandelier are burning save one that has burned out. Cornelius pauses on a lower step and surveys the entrance hall. It looks pleasant and cosy in the bright light, with its copy of Marées over the brick chimney-piece, its wainscoted walls — wainscoted in soft wood—and red-carpeted floor, where the guests stand in groups, chatting, each with his teacup and slice of bread-and-butter spread with anchovy paste. There is a festal haze, faint scents of hair and clothing and human breath come to him across the room, it is all characteristic and familiar and highly evocative. The door into the dressing-room is open, guests are still arriving.

A large group of people is rather bewildering at first sight. The Professor takes in only the general scene. He does not see Ingrid, who is standing just at the foot of the steps, in a dark silk frock with a pleated collar falling softly over the shoulders, and bare arms. She smiles up at him, nodding and showing her lovely teeth.

"Rested?" she asks, for his private ear. With a quite unwarranted start he recognizes her, and she presents some of her friends.

"May I introduce Herr Zuber?" she says. "And this is Fräulein Plaichinger."

Herr Zuber is insignificant. But Fräulein Plaichinger is a perfect Germania, blond and voluptuous, arrayed in floating draperies. She has a snub nose, and answers the Professor's salutation in the high, shrill pipe so many stout women have.

"Delighted to meet you," he says. "How nice of you to come! A classmate of Ingrid's, I suppose?"

And Herr Zuber is a golfing partner of Ingrid's. He is in business; he works in his uncle's brewery. Cornelius makes a few jokes about the thinness of the beer and professes to believe that Herr Zuber could easily do something about the quality if he would. "But pray don't let me disturb you," he goes on, and turns towards the dining-room.

"There comes Max," says Ingrid. "Max, you sweep, what do you mean by rolling up at this time of day?" For such is the way they talk to each other, offensively to an older ear; of social forms, of hospitable warmth, there is no faintest trace. They all call each other by their first names.

A young man comes up to them out of the dressing-room and makes

[6] exactly the right word

his bow; he has an expanse of white shirt-front and a little black string tie. He is as pretty as a picture, dark, with rosy cheeks, clean-shaven of course, but with just a sketch of side-whisker. Not a ridiculous or flashy beauty, not like a gypsy fiddler, but just charming to look at, in a winning, well-bred way, with kind dark eyes. He even wears his dinner-jacket a little awkwardly.

"Please don't scold me, Cornelia," he says; "it's the idiotic lectures." And Ingrid presents him to her father as Herr Hergesell.

Well, and so this is Herr Hergesell. He knows his manners, does Herr Hergesell, and thanks the master of the house quite ingratiatingly for his invitation as they shake hands. "I certainly seem to have missed the bus," says he jocosely. "Of course I have lectures today up to four o'clock; I would have; and after that I had to go home to change." Then he talks about his pumps, with which he has just been struggling in the dressing-room.

"I brought them with me in a bag," he goes on. "Mustn't tramp all over the carpet in our brogues—it's not done. Well, I was ass enough not to fetch along a shoe-horn, and I find I simply can't get in! What a sell! They are the tightest I've ever had, the numbers don't tell you a thing, and all the leather today is just cast iron. It's not leather at all. My poor finger"—he confidingly displays a reddened digit and once more characterizes the whole thing as a "sell," and a putrid sell into the bargain. He really does talk just as Ingrid said he did, with a peculiar nasal drawl, not affectedly in the least, but merely because that is the way of all the Hergesells.

Dr. Cornelius says it is very careless of them not to keep a shoe-horn in the cloak-room and displays proper sympathy with the mangled finger. "But now you *really* must not let me disturb you any longer," he goes on. "*Auf wiedersehen!*" And he crosses the hall into the dining-room.

There are guests there too, drinking tea; the family table is pulled out. But the Professor goes at once to his own little upholstered corner with the electric light bulb above it—the nook where he usually drinks his tea. His wife is sitting there talking with Bert and two other young men, one of them Herzl, whom Cornelius knows and greets; the other a typical "Wandervogel"[7] named Möller, a youth who obviously neither owns nor cares to own the correct evening dress of the middle classes (in fact, there is no such thing any more), nor to ape the manners of a gentleman (and, in fact, there is no such thing any more either). He has a wilderness of hair, horn spectacles, and a long neck, and wears golf stockings and a belted blouse. His regular occupation, the Professor learns, is banking, but he is by way of being an amateur folk-lorist and collects folk-songs from all localities and in all languages. He sings them, too, and at Ingrid's command has brought his guitar; it is hanging in the dressing-room in an oilcloth case. Herzl, the actor, is small and slight, but he has a

[7] bird of passage

strong growth of black beard, as you can tell by the thick coat of powder
on his cheeks. His eyes are larger than life, with a deep and melancholy
glow. He has put on rouge besides the powder—those dull carmine high-
lights on the cheeks can be nothing but a cosmetic. "Queer," thinks the
Professor. "You would think a man would be one thing or the other—
not melancholic and use face paint at the same time. It's a psychological
contradiction. How can a melancholy man rouge? But here we have a
perfect illustration of the abnormality of the artist soul-form. It can
make possible a contradiction like this—perhaps it even consists in the
contradiction. All very interesting—and no reason whatever for not
being polite to him. Politeness is a primitive convention—and legitimate.
. . . Do take some lemon, Herr Hofschauspieler[8]!"

Court actors and court theaters—there are no such things any more,
really. But Herzl relishes the sound of the title, notwithstanding he is a
revolutionary artist. This must be another contradiction inherent in his
soul-form; so, at least, the Professor assumes, and he is probably right.
The flattery he is guilty of is a sort of atonement for his previous hard
thoughts about the rouge.

"Thank you so much— it's really too good of you, sir," says Herzl,
quite embarrassed. He is so overcome that he almost stammers; only his
perfect enunciation saves him. His whole bearing towards his hostess
and the master of the house is exaggeratedly polite. It is almost as though
he had a bad conscience in respect of his rouge; as though an inward
compulsion had driven him to put it on, but now, seeing it through the
Professor's eyes, he disapproves of it himself, and thinks, by an air of
humility toward the whole of unrouged society, to mitigate its effect.

They drink their tea and chat: about Möller's folk-songs, about
Basque folk-songs and Spanish folk-songs; from which they pass to the
new production of *Don Carlos*[9] at the Stadttheater, in which Herzl plays
the title-rôle. He talks about his own rendering of the part and says he
hopes his conception of the character has unity. They go on to criticize
the rest of the cast, the setting, and the production as a whole; and Cornelius is struck, rather painfully, to find the conversation trending towards his own special province, back to Spain and the Counter-Reformation. He has done nothing at all to give it this turn, he is perfectly
innocent, and hopes it does not look as though he had sought an occasion
to play the professor. He wonders, and falls silent, feeling relieved when
the little folk come up to the table. Ellie and Snapper have on their blue
velvet Sunday frocks; they are permitted to partake in the festivities up
to bedtime. They look shy and large-eyed as they say how-do-you-do to
the strangers and, under pressure, repeat their names and ages. Herr
Möller does nothing but gaze at them solemnly, but Herzl is simply
ravished. He rolls his eyes up to heaven and puts his hands over his

---

[8] court actor
[9] opera by Giuseppe Verdi about the tangled love affairs of the son of Philip II

mouth; he positively blesses them. It all, no doubt, comes from his heart, but he is so addicted to theatrical methods of making an impression and getting an effect that both words and behavior ring frightfully false. And even his enthusiasm for the little folk looks too much like part of his general craving to make up for the rouge on his cheeks.

The tea-table has meanwhile emptied of guests, and dancing is going on in the hall. The children run off, the Professor prepares to retire. "Go and enjoy yourselves," he says to Möller and Herzl, who have sprung from their chairs as he rises from his. They shake hands and he withdraws into his study, his peaceful kingdom, where he lets down the blinds, turns on the desk lamp, and sits down to his work.

It is work which can be done, if necessary, under disturbed conditions: nothing but a few letters and a few notes. Of course, Cornelius's mind wanders. Vague impressions float through it: Herr Hergesell's refractory pumps, the high pipe in that plump body of the Plaichinger female. As he writes, or leans back in his chair and stares into space, his thoughts go back to Herr Möller's collection of Basque folk-songs, to Herzl's posings and humility, to "his" Carlos and the court of Philip II. There is something strange, he thinks, about conversations. They are so ductile, they will flow of their own accord in the direction of one's dominating interest. Often and often he has seen this happen. And while he is thinking, he is listening to the sounds next door—rather subdued, he finds them. He hears only voices, no sound of footsteps. The dancers do not glide or circle round the room; they merely walk about over the carpet, which does not hamper their movements in the least. Their way of holding each other is quite different and strange, and they move to the strains of the gramophone, to the weird music of the new world. He concentrates on the music and makes out that it is a jazz-band record, with various percussion instruments and the clack and clatter of castanets, which, however, are not even faintly suggestive of Spain, but merely jazz like the rest. No, not Spain. . . . His thoughts are back at their old round.

Half an hour goes by. It occurs to him it would be no more than friendly to go and contribute a box of cigarettes to the festivities next door. Too bad to ask the young people to smoke their own—though they have probably never thought of it. He goes into the empty dining-room and takes a box from his supply in the cupboard: not the best ones, nor yet the brand he himself prefers, but a certain long, thin kind he is not averse to getting rid of—after all, they are nothing but youngsters. He takes the box into the hall, holds it up with a smile, and deposits it on the mantel-shelf. After which he gives a look round and returns to his own room.

There comes a lull in dance and music. The guests stand about the room in groups or round the table at the window or are seated in a circle by the fireplace. Even the built-in stairs, with their worn velvet carpet, are crowded with young folk as in an amphitheater: Max Hergesell is there, leaning back with one elbow on the step above and gesticulating with his free hand as he talks to the shrill, voluptuous Plaichinger. The floor of the hall is nearly empty, save just in the center: there, directly beneath the chandelier, the two little ones in their blue velvet frocks clutch each other in an awkward embrace and twirl silently round and round, oblivious of all else. Cornelius, as he passes, strokes their hair, with a friendly word; it does not distract them from their small solemn preoccupation. But at his own door he turns to glance round and sees young Hergesell push himself off the stair by his elbow—probably because he noticed the Professor. He comes down into the arena, takes Ellie out of her brother's arms, and dances with her himself. It looks very comic, without the music, and he crouches down just as Cornelius does when he goes walking with the four gentlemen, holding the fluttered Ellie as though she were grown up and taking little "shimmying" steps. Everybody watches with huge enjoyment, the gramophone is put on again, dancing becomes general. The Professor stands and looks, with his hand on the door-knob. He nods and laughs; when he finally shuts himself into his study the mechanical smile still lingers on his lips.

Again he turns over pages by his desk lamp, takes notes, attends to a few simple matters. After a while he notices that the guests have forsaken the entrance hall for his wife's drawing-room, into which there is a door from his own study as well. He hears their voices and the sounds of a guitar being tuned. Herr Möller, it seems, is to sing—and does so. He twangs the strings of his instrument and sings in a powerful bass a ballad in a strange tongue, possibly Swedish. The Professor does not succeed in identifying it, though he listens attentively to the end, after which there is great applause. The sound is deadened by the portière that hangs over the dividing door. The young bank-clerk begins another song. Cornelius goes softly in.

It is half-dark in the drawing-room; the only light is from the shaded standard lamp, beneath which Möller sits, on the divan, with his legs crossed, picking his strings. His audience is grouped easily about; as there are not enough seats, some stand, and more, among them many young ladies, are simply sitting on the floor with their hands clasped round their knees or even with their legs stretched out before them. Hergesell sits thus, in his dinner jacket, next the piano, with Fräulein Plaichinger beside him. Frau Cornelius is holding both children on her lap as she sits in her easy-chair opposite the singer. Snapper, the Bœotian,[10] begins to talk loud and clear in the middle of the song and has to be intimidated with hushings and finger-shakings. Never, never would Ellie allow herself to be guilty of such conduct. She sits there daintily erect and still on her mother's knee. The Professor tries to catch her eye and exchange a private signal with his little girl; but she does not see him.

[10] a nation regarded as dull witted

Neither does she seem to be looking at the singer. Her gaze is directed
lower down.

Möller sings the "joli tambour":

> Sire, mon roi, donnez-moi votre fille—[11]

They are all enchanted. "How good!" Hergesell is heard to say, in
the odd, nasally condescending Hergesell tone. The next one is a beggar
ballad, to a tune composed by young Möller himself; it elicits a storm of
applause:

> Gypsy lassie a-goin' to the fair,
> Huzza!
> Gypsy laddie a-goin' to be there—
> Huzza, diddlety umpty dido!

Laughter and high spirits, sheer reckless hilarity, reigns after this
jovial ballad. "Frightfully good!" Hergesell comments again, as before.
Follows another popular song, this time a Hungarian one; Möller sings
it in its own outlandish tongue, and most effectively. The Professor ap-
plauds with ostentation. It warms his heart and does him good, this out-
cropping of artistic, historic, and cultural elements all amongst the
shimmying. He goes up to young Möller and congratulates him, talks
about the songs and their sources, and Möller promises to lend him a
certain annotated book of folk-songs. Cornelius is the more cordial because all the time, as fathers do, he has been comparing the parts and
achievements of this young stranger with those of his own son, and being
gnawed by envy and chagrin. This young Möller, he is thinking, is a
capable bank-clerk (though about Möller's capacity he knows nothing
whatever) and has this special gift besides, which must have taken talent
and energy to cultivate. "And here is my poor Bert, who knows nothing
and can do nothing and thinks of nothing except playing the clown, without even talent for that!" He tries to be just; he tells himself that, after
all, Bert has innate refinement; that probably there is a good deal more
to him than there is to the successful Möller; that perhaps he has even
something of the poet in him, and his dancing and table-waiting are due
to mere boyish folly and the distraught times. But paternal envy and
pessimism win the upper hand; when Möller begins another song, Dr.
Cornelius goes back to his room.

He works as before, with divided attention, at this and that, while it
gets on for seven o'clock. Then he remembers a letter he may just as
well write, a short letter and not very important, but letter-writing is
wonderful for the way it takes up the time, and it is almost half past
when he has finished. At half past eight the Italian salad will be served;
so now is the prescribed moment for the Professor to go out into the
wintry darkness to post his letters and take his daily quantum of fresh

---

[11] Sire, my King, give your daughter to me.

air and exercise. They are dancing again, and he will have to pass through the hall to get his hat and coat; but they are used to him now, he need not stop and beg them not to be disturbed. He lays away his papers, takes up the letters he has written, and goes out. But he sees his wife sitting near the door of his room and pauses a little by her easy-chair.

She is watching the dancing. Now and then the big folk or some of their guests stop to speak to her; the party is at its height, and there are more onlookers than these two: blue-faced Ann is standing at the bottom of the stairs, in all the dignity of her limitations. She is waiting for the children, who simply cannot get their fill of these unwonted festivities, and watching over Snapper, lest his all too rich blood be churned to the danger-point by too much twirling round. And not only the nursery but the kitchen takes an interest: Xaver and the two ladies Hinterhofer are standing by the pantry door looking on with relish. Fräulein Walburga, the elder of the two sunken sisters (the culinary section—she objects to being called a cook), is a whimsical, good-natured sort, brown-eyed, wearing glasses with thick circular lenses; the nose-piece is wound with a bit of rag to keep it from pressing on her nose. Fräulein Cecilia is younger, though not so precisely young either. Her bearing is as self-assertive as usual, this being her way of sustaining her dignity as a former member of the middle class. For Fräulein Cecilia feels acutely her descent into the ranks of domestic service. She positively declines to wear a cap or other badge of servitude, and her hardest trial is on the Wednesday evening when she has to serve the dinner while Xaver has his afternoon out. She hands the dishes with averted face and elevated nose—a fallen queen; and so distressing is it to behold her degradation that one evening when the little folk happened to be at table and saw her they both with one accord burst into tears. Such anguish is unknown to young Xaver. He enjoys serving and does it with an ease born of practice as well as talent, for he was once a "piccolo."[12] But otherwise he is a thorough-paced good-for-nothing and windbag—with quite distinct traits of character of his own, as his long-suffering employers are always ready to concede, but perfectly impossible and a bag of wind for all that. One must just take him as he is, they think, and not expect figs from thistles. He is the child and product of the disrupted times, a perfect specimen of his generation, follower of the revolution, Bolshevist sympathizer. The Professor's name for him is the "minute-man," because he is always to be counted on in any sudden crisis, if only it address his sense of humor or love of novelty, and will display therein amazing readiness and re-source. But he utterly lacks a sense of duty and can as little be trained to the performance of the daily round and common task as some kinds of dog can be taught to jump over a stick. It goes so plainly against the grain that criticism is disarmed. One becomes resigned. On grounds that appealed to him as unusual and amusing he would be ready to turn out of

[12] serving-boy

his bed at any hour of the night. But he simply cannot get up before eight in the morning, he cannot do it, he will not jump over the stick. Yet all day long the evidence of this free and untrammelled existence, the sound of his mouth-organ, his joyous whistle, or his raucous but expressive voice lifted in song, rises to the hearing of the world above-stairs; and the smoke of his cigarettes fills the pantry. While the Hinter-hofer ladies work he stands and looks on. Of a morning while the Professor is breakfasting, he tears the leaf off the study calendar—but does not lift a finger to dust the room. Dr. Cornelius has often told him to leave the calendar alone, for he tends to tear off two leaves at a time and thus to add to the general confusion. But young Xaver appears to find joy in this activity, and will not be deprived of it.

Again, he is fond of children, a winning trait. He will throw himself into games with the little folk in the garden, make and mend their toys with great ingenuity, even read aloud from their books—and very droll it sounds in his thick-lipped pronunciation. With his whole soul he loves the cinema; after an evening spent there he inclines to melancholy and yearning and talking to himself. Vague hopes stir in him that some day he may make his fortune in that gay world and belong to it by rights—hopes based on his shock of hair and his physical agility and daring. He likes to climb the ash tree in the front garden, mounting branch by branch to the very top and frightening everybody to death who sees him. Once there he lights a cigarette and smokes it as he sways to and fro, keeping a look-out for a cinema director who might chance to come along and engage him.

If he changed his striped jacket for mufti, he might easily dance with the others and no one would notice the difference. For the big folk's friends are rather anomalous in their clothing: evening dress is worn by a few, but it is by no means the rule. There is quite a sprinkling of guests, both male and female, in the same general style as Möller the ballad-singer. The Professor is familiar with the circumstances of most of this young generation he is watching as he stands beside his wife's chair; he has heard them spoken of by name. They are students at the high school or at the School of Applied Art; they lead, at least the masculine portion, that precarious and scrambling existence which is purely the product of the time. There is a tall, pale, spindling youth, the son of a dentist, who lives by speculation. From all the Professor hears, he is a perfect Alad-din. He keeps a car, treats his friends to champagne suppers, and showers presents upon them on every occasion, costly little trifles in mother-of-pearl and gold. So today he has brought gifts to the young givers of the feast: for Bert a gold lead-pencil, and for Ingrid a pair of ear-rings of barbaric size, great gold circlets that fortunately do not have to go through the little ear-lobe, but are fastened over it by means of a clip. The big folk come laughing to their parents to display these trophies; and the parents shake their heads even while they admire—Aladdin bow-ing over and over from afar.

The young people appear to be absorbed in their dancing—if the performance they are carrying out with so much still concentration can be called dancing. They stride across the carpet, slowly, according to some unfathomable prescript, strangely embraced; in the newest attitude, tummy advanced and shoulders high, waggling the hips. They do not get tired, because nobody could. There is no such thing as heightened color or heaving bosoms. Two girls may dance together or two young men—it is all the same. They move to the exotic strains of the gramophone, played with the loudest needles to procure the maximum of sound: shimmies, foxtrots, one-steps, double foxes, African shimmies, Java dances, and Creole polkas, the wild musky melodies follow one another, now furious, now languishing, a monotonous Negro program in unfamiliar rhythm, to a clacking, clashing, and strumming orchestral accompaniment.

"What is that record?" Cornelius inquires of Ingrid, as she passes him by in the arms of the pale young speculator, with reference to the piece then playing, whose alternate languors and furies he finds comparatively pleasing and showing a certain resourcefulness in detail.

"*Prince of Pappenheim*: 'Console thee, dearest child,' " she answers, and smiles pleasantly back at him with her white teeth.

The cigarette smoke wreathes beneath the chandelier. The air is blue with a festal haze compact of sweet and thrilling ingredients that stir the blood with memories of green-sick pains and are particularly poignant to those whose youth—like the Professor's own—has been over-sensitive. . . . The little folk are still on the floor. They are allowed to stop up until eight, so great is their delight in the party. The guests have got used to their presence; in their own way, they have their place in the doings of the evening. They have separated, anyhow: Snapper revolves all alone in the middle of the carpet, in his little blue velvet smock, while Ellie is running after one of the dancing couples, trying to hold the man fast by his coat. It is Max Hergesell and Fräulein Plaichinger. They dance well, it is a pleasure to watch them. One has to admit that these mad modern dances, when the right people dance them, are not so bad after all—they have something quite taking. Young Hergesell is a capital leader, dances according to rule, yet with individuality. So it looks. With what aplomb can he walk backwards—when space permits! And he knows how to be graceful standing still in a crowd. And his partner supports him well, being unsuspectedly lithe and buoyant, as fat people often are. They look at each other, they are talking, paying no heed to Ellie, though others are smiling to see the child's persistence. Dr. Cornelius tries to catch up his little sweetheart as she passes and draw her to him. But Ellie eludes him, almost peevishly; her dear Abel is nothing to her now. She braces her little arms against his chest and turns her face away with a persecuted look. Then escapes to follow her fancy once more.

The Professor feels an involuntary twinge. Uppermost in his heart is

hatred for this party, with its power to intoxicate and estrange his darling
child. His love for her—that not quite disinterested, not quite unexcep-
tionable love of his—is easily wounded. He wears a mechanical smile,
but his eyes have clouded, and he stares fixedly at a point in the carpet,
between the dancers' feet.

"The children ought to go to bed," he tells his wife. But she pleads
for another quarter of an hour; she has promised already, and they do
love it so! He smiles again and shakes his head, stands so a moment and
then goes across to the cloak-room, which is full of coats and hats and
scarves and overshoes. He has trouble in rummaging out his own coat,
and Max Hergesell comes out of the hall, wiping his brow.

"Going out, sir?" he asks, in Hergesellian accents, dutifully helping
the older man on with his coat. "Silly business this, with my pumps,"
he says. "They pinch like hell. The brutes are simply too tight for me,
quite apart from the bad leather. They press just here on the ball of my
great toe"—he stands on one foot and holds the other in his hand—"it's
simply unbearable. There's nothing for it but to take them off; my
brogues will have to do the business. . . . Oh, let me help you, sir."

"Thanks," says Cornelius. "Don't trouble. Get rid of your own tor-
mentors. . . . Oh, thanks very much!" For Hergesell has gone on one
knee to snap the fasteners of his snow-boots.

Once more the Professor expresses his gratitude; he is pleased and
touched by so much sincere respect and youthful readiness to serve. "Go
and enjoy yourself," he counsels. "Change your shoes and make up for
what you have been suffering. Nobody can dance in shoes that pinch.
Good-bye, I must be off to get a breath of fresh air."

"I'm going to dance with Ellie now," calls Hergesell after him. "She'll
be a first-rate dancer when she grows up, and that I'll swear to."

"Think so?" Cornelius answers, already half out. "Well, you are a
connoisseur, I'm sure. Don't get curvature of the spine with stooping."

He nods again and goes. "Fine lad," he thinks as he shuts the door.
"Student of engineering. Knows what he's bound for, got a good clear
head, and so well set up and pleasant too." And again paternal envy rises
as he compares his poor Bert's status with this young man's, which he
puts in the rosiest light that his son's may look the darker. Thus he sets
out on his evening walk.

He goes up the avenue, crosses the bridge, and walks along the bank
on the other side as far as the next bridge but one. The air is wet and
cold, with a little snow now and then. He turns up his coat-collar and
slips the crook of his cane over the arm behind his back. Now and then
he ventilates his lungs with a long deep breath of the night air. As usual
when he walks, his mind reverts to his professional preoccupations, he
thinks about his lectures and the things he means to say tomorrow about
Philip's struggle against the Germanic revolution, things steeped in melancholy and penetratingly just. Above all just, he thinks. For in one's
dealings with the young it behooves one to display the scientific spirit,

to exhibit the principles of enlightenment—not only for purposes of mental discipline, but on the human and individual side, in order not to wound them or indirectly offend their political sensibilities; particularly in these days, when there is so much tinder in the air, opinions are so frightfully split up and chaotic, and you may so easily incur attacks from one party or the other, or even give rise to scandal, by taking sides on a point of history. "And taking sides is unhistoric anyhow," so he muses. "Only justice, only impartiality is historic." And could not, properly considered, be otherwise. . . . For justice can have nothing of youthful fire and blithe, fresh, loyal conviction. It is by nature melancholy. And, being so, has secret affinity with the lost cause and the forlorn hope rather than with the fresh and blithe and loyal—perhaps this affinity is its very essence and without it it would not exist at all! . . . "And is there then no such thing as justice?" the Professor asks himself, and ponders the question so deeply that he absently posts his letters in the next box and turns round to go home. This thought of his is unsettling and disturbing to the scientific mind—but is it not after all itself scientific, psychological, conscientious, and therefore to be accepted without prejudice, no matter how upsetting? In the midst of which musings Dr. Cornelius finds himself back at his own door.

On the outer threshold stands Xaver, and seems to be looking for him.

"Herr Professor," says Xaver, tossing back his hair, "go upstairs to Ellie straight off. She's in a bad way."

"What's the matter?" asks Cornelius in alarm. "Is she ill?"

"No-o, not to say ill," answers Xaver. "She's just in a bad way and crying fit to bust her little heart. It's along o' that chap with the shirt-front that danced with her—Herr Hergesell. She couldn't be got to go upstairs peaceably, not at no price at all, and she's b'en crying bucketfuls."

"Nonsense," says the Professor, who has entered and is tossing off his things in the cloak-room. He says no more; opens the glass door and without a glance at the guests turns swiftly to the stairs. Takes them two at a time, crosses the upper hall and the small room leading into the nursery. Xaver follows at his heels, but stops at the nursery door.

A bright light still burns within, showing the gay frieze that runs all round the room, the large row of shelves heaped with a confusion of toys, the rocking-horse on his swaying platform, with red-varnished nostrils and raised hoofs. On the linoleum lie other toys—building blocks, railway trains, a little trumpet. The two white cribs stand not far apart, Ellie's in the window corner, Snapper's out in the room.

Snapper is asleep. He has said his prayers in loud, ringing tones, prompted by Nurse, and gone off at once into vehement, profound, and rosy slumber—from which a cannon-ball fired at close range could not rouse him. He lies with both fists flung back on the pillows on either side of the tousled head with its funny crooked little slumber-tossed wig.

A circle of females surrounds Ellie's bed: not only blue-faced Ann is there, but the Hinterhofer ladies too, talking to each other and to her. They make way as the Professor comes up and reveal the child sitting all pale among her pillows, sobbing and weeping more bitterly than he has ever seen her sob and weep in her life. Her lovely little hands lie on the coverlet in front of her, the nightgown with its narrow lace border has slipped down from her shoulder—such a thin, birdlike little shoulder —and the sweet head Cornelius loves so well, set on the neck like a flower on its stalk, her head is on one side, with the eyes rolled up to the corner between wall and ceiling above her head. For there she seems to envisage the anguish of her heart and even to nod to it—either on purpose or because her head wobbles as her body is shaken with the violence of her sobs. Her eyes rain down tears. The bow-shaped lips are parted, like a little *mater dolorosa's*,[13] and from them issue long, low wails that in nothing resemble the unnecessary and exasperating shrieks of a naughty child, but rise from the deep extremity of her heart and wake in the Professor's own a sympathy that is well-nigh intolerable. He has never seen his darling so before. His feelings find immediate vent in an attack on the ladies Hinterhofer.

"What about the supper?" he asks sharply. "There must be a great deal to do. Is my wife being left to do it alone?"

For the acute sensibilities of the former middle class this is quite enough. The ladies withdraw in righteous indignation, and Xaver Kleingutl jeers at them as they pass out. Having been born to low life instead of achieving it, he never loses a chance to mock at their fallen state.

"Childie, childie," murmurs Cornelius, and sitting down by the crib enfolds the anguished Ellie in his arms. "What is the trouble with my darling?"

She bedews his face with her tears.

"Abel . . . Abel . . ." she stammers between sobs. "Why—isn't Max—my brother? Max ought to be—my brother!"

Alas, alas! What mischance is this? Is this what the party has wrought, with its fatal atmosphere? Cornelius glances helplessly up at blue-faced Ann standing there in all the dignity of her limitations with her hands before her on her apron. She purses up her mouth and makes a long face. "It's pretty young," she says, "for the female instincts to be showing up."

"Hold your tongue," snaps Cornelius, in his agony. He has this much to be thankful for, that Ellie does not turn from him now; she does not push him away as she did downstairs, but clings to him in her need, while she reiterates her absurd, bewildered prayer that Max might be her brother, or with a fresh burst of desire demands to be taken downstairs so that he can dance with her again. But Max, of course, is dancing with Fräulein Plaichinger, that behemoth who is his rightful partner and has

13 Our Lady of Sorrows

every claim upon him; whereas Ellie—never, thinks the Professor, his heart torn with the violence of his pity, never has she looked so tiny and birdlike as now, when she nestles to him shaken with sobs and all unaware of what is happening in her little soul. No, she does not know. She does not comprehend that her suffering is on account of Fräulein Plaichinger, fat, overgrown, and utterly within her rights in dancing with Max Hergesell, whereas Ellie may only do it once, by way of a joke, although she is incomparably the more charming of the two. Yet it would be quite mad to reproach young Hergesell with the state of affairs or to make fantastic demands upon him. No, Ellie's suffering is without help or healing and must be covered up. Yet just as it is without understanding, so it is also without restraint—and that is what makes it so horribly painful. Xaver and blue-faced Ann do not feel this pain, it does not affect them—either because of native callousness or because they accept it as the way of nature. But the Professor's fatherly heart is quite torn by it, and by a distressful horror of this passion, so hopeless and so absurd.

Of no avail to hold forth to poor Ellie on the subject of the perfectly good little brother she already has. She only casts a distraught and scornful glance over at the other crib, where Snapper lies vehemently slumbering, and with fresh tears calls again for Max. Of no avail either the promise of a long, long walk tomorrow, all five gentlemen, round and round the dining-room table; or a dramatic description of the thrilling cushion games they will play. No, she will listen to none of all this, nor to lying down and going to sleep. She will not sleep, she will sit bolt upright and suffer. . . . But on a sudden they stop and listen, Abel and Ellie; listen to something miraculous that is coming to pass, that is approaching by strides, two strides, to the nursery door, that now overwhelmingly appears. . . .

It is Xaver's work, not a doubt of that. He has not remained by the door where he stood to gloat over the ejection of the Hinterhofers. No, he has bestirred himself, taken a notion; likewise steps to carry it out. Downstairs he has gone, twitched Herr Hergesell's sleeve, and made a thick-lipped request. So here they both are. Xaver, having done his part, remains by the door; but Max Hergesell comes up to Ellie's crib; in his dinner-jacket, with his sketchy side-whisker and charming black eyes; obviously quite pleased with his rôle of swan knight and fairy prince, as one who should say: "See, here am I, now all losses are restored and sorrows end."[14]

Cornelius is almost as much overcome as Ellie herself.

"Just look," he says feebly, "look who's here. This is uncommonly good of you, Herr Hergesell."

"Not a bit of it," says Hergesell. "Why shouldn't I come to say good-night to my fair partner?"

[14] Shakespeare, Sonnet 30

And he approaches the bars of the crib, behind which Ellie sits struck mute. She smiles blissfully through her tears. A funny, high little note that is half a sigh of relief comes from her lips, then she looks dumbly up at her swan knight with her golden-brown eyes—tear-swollen though they are, so much more beautiful than the fat Plaichinger's. She does not put up her arms. Her joy, like her grief, is without understanding; but she does not do that. The lovely little hands lie quiet on the coverlet, and Max Hergesell stands with his arms leaning over the rail as on a balcony.

"And now," he says smartly, "she need not 'sit the livelong night and weep upon her bed'!" He looks at the Professor to make sure he is receiving due credit for the quotation. "Ha ha!" he laughs, "she's beginning young. 'Console thee, dearest child!' Never mind, you're all right! Just as you are you'll be wonderful! You've only got to grow up. . . . And you'll lie down and go to sleep like a good girl, now I've come to say good-night? And not cry any more, little Lorelei?"

Ellie looks up at him, transfigured. One birdlike shoulder is bare; the Professor draws the lace-trimmed nighty over it. There comes into his mind a sentimental story he once read about a dying child who longs to see a clown he had once, with unforgettable ecstasy, beheld in a circus. And they bring the clown to the bedside marvelously arrayed, embroidered before and behind with silver butterflies; and the child dies happy. Max Hergesell is not embroidered, and Ellie, thank God, is not going to die, she has only "been in a bad way." But, after all, the effect is the same. Young Hergesell leans over the bars of the crib and rattles on, more for the father's ear than the child's, but Ellie does not know that—and the father's feelings towards him are a most singular mixture of thankfulness, embarrassment, and hatred.

"Good night, little Lorelei," says Hergesell, and gives her his hand through the bars. Her pretty, soft, white little hand is swallowed up in the grasp of his big, strong, red one. "Sleep well," he says, "and sweet dreams! But don't dream about me—God forbid! Not at your age— ha ha!" And then the fairy clown's visit is at an end. Cornelius accompanies him to the door. "No, no, positively, no thanks called for, don't mention it," he large-heartedly protests; and Xaver goes downstairs with him, to help serve the Italian salad.

But Dr. Cornelius returns to Ellie, who is now lying down, with her cheek pressed into her flat little pillow.

"Well, wasn't that lovely?" he says as he smooths the covers. She nods, with one last little sob. For a quarter of an hour he sits beside her and watches while she falls asleep in her turn, beside the little brother who found the right way so much earlier than she. Her silky brown hair takes the enchanting fall it always does when she sleeps; deep, deep lie the lashes over the eyes that late so abundantly poured forth their sorrow; the angelic mouth with its bowed upper lip is peacefully relaxed and a little open. Only now and then comes a belated catch in her slow breathing.

And her small hands, like pink and white flowers, lie so quietly, one on the coverlet, the other on the pillow by her face—Dr. Cornelius, gazing, feels his heart melt with tenderness as with strong wine.

"How good," he thinks, "that she breathes in oblivion with every breath she draws! That in childhood each night is a deep, wide gulf between one day and the next. Tomorrow, beyond all doubt, young Hergesell will be a pale shadow, powerless to darken her little heart. Tomorrow, forgetful of all but present joy, she will walk with Abel and Snapper, all five gentlemen, round and round the table, will play the ever-thrilling cushion game."

Heaven be praised for that!

Translated by H. T. Lowe-Porter

Sherwood Anderson
1876–1941
I WANT TO KNOW WHY

WE GOT up at four in the morning, that first day in the East. On the evening before, we had climbed off a freight train at the edge of town and with the true instinct of Kentucky boys had found our way across town and to the race track and the stables at once. Then we knew we were all right. Hanley Turner right away found a nigger we knew. It was Bildad Johnson, who in the winter works at Ed Becker's livery barn in our home town, Beckersville. Bildad is a good cook as almost all our niggers are and of course he, like everyone in our part of Kentucky who is anyone at all, likes the horses. In the spring Bildad begins to scratch around. A nigger from our country can flatter and wheedle anyone into letting him do most anything he wants. Bildad wheedles the stable men and the trainers from the horse farms in our country around Lexington. The trainers come into town in the evening to stand around and talk and maybe get into a poker game. Bildad gets in with them. He is always doing little favors and telling about things to eat, chicken browned in a pan, and how is the best way to cook sweet potatoes and corn bread. It makes your mouth water to hear him.

When the racing season comes on and the horses go to the races and there is all the talk on the streets in the evenings about the new colts, and everyone says when they are going over to Lexington or to the spring meeting at Churchill Downs or to Latonia, and the horsemen that have been down to New Orleans or maybe at the winter meeting at Havana

in Cuba come home to spend a week before they start out again, at such
a time when everything talked about in Beckersville is just horses and
nothing else and the outfits start out and horse racing is in every breath
of air you breathe, Bildad shows up with a job as cook for some outfit.
Often when I think about it, his always going all season to the races and
working in the livery barn in the winter where horses are and where men
like to come and talk about horses, I wish I was a nigger. It's a foolish
thing to say, but that's the way I am about being around horses, just
crazy. I can't help it.

Well, I must tell you about what we did and let you in on what I'm
talking about. Four of us boys from Beckersville, all whites and sons of
men who live in Beckersville regular, made up our minds we were going
to the races, not just to Lexington or Louisville, I don't mean, but to the
big Eastern track we were always hearing our Beckersville men talk
about, to Saratoga. We were all pretty young then. I was just turned
fifteen and I was the oldest of the four. It was my scheme. I admit that,
and I talked the others into trying it. There was Hanley Turner and
Henry Rieback and Tom Tumberton and myself. I had thirty-seven dollars I had earned during the winter working nights and Saturdays in
Enoch Myer's grocery. Henry Rieback had eleven dollars and the others,
Hanley and Tom, had only a dollar or two each. We fixed it all up and
laid low until the Kentucky spring meetings were over and some of our
men, the sportiest ones, the ones we envied the most, had cut out. Then
we cut out too.

I won't tell you the trouble we had beating our way on freights and all.
We went through Cleveland and Buffalo and other cities and saw Niagara Falls. We bought things there, souvenirs and spoons and cards and
shells with pictures of the falls on them for our sisters and mothers, but
thought we had better not send any of the things home. We didn't want
to put the folks on our trail and maybe be nabbed.

We got into Saratoga as I said at night and went to the track. Bildad
fed us up. He showed us a place to sleep in hay over a shed and promised
to keep still. Niggers are all right about things like that. They won't
squeal on you. Often a white man you might meet, when you had run
away from home like that, might appear to be all right and give you a
quarter or a half dollar or something, and then go right and give you
away. White men will do that, but not a nigger. You can trust them.
They are squarer with kids. I don't know why.

At the Saratoga meeting that year there were a lot of men from home.
Dave Williams and Arthur Mulford and Jerry Myers and others. Then
there was a lot from Louisville and Lexington Henry Rieback knew but
I didn't. They were professional gamblers and Henry Rieback's father
is one too. He is what is called a sheet writer and goes away most of the
year to tracks. In the winter when he is home in Beckersville he don't
stay there much but goes away to cities and deals faro. He is a nice man

and generous, is always sending Henry presents, a bicycle and a gold watch and a boy scout suit of clothes and things like that.

My own father is a lawyer. He's all right, but don't make much money and can't buy me things, and anyway I'm getting so old now I don't expect it. He never said nothing to me against Henry, but Hanley Turner and Tom Tumberton's fathers did. They said to their boys that money so come by is no good and they didn't want their boys brought up to hear gamblers' talk and be thinking about such things and maybe embrace them.

That's all right and I guess the men know what they are talking about, but I don't see what it's got to do with Henry or with horses either. That's what I'm writing this story about. I'm puzzled. I'm getting to be a man and want to think straight and be O.K., and there's something I saw at the race meeting at the Eastern track I can't figure out.

I can't help it, I'm crazy about thoroughbred horses, I've always been that way. When I was ten years old and saw I was growing to be big and couldn't be a rider I was so sorry I nearly died. Harry Hellinfinger in Beckersville, whose father is Postmaster, is grown up and too lazy to work, but likes to stand around in the street and get up jokes on boys like sending them to a hardware store for a gimlet to bore square holes and other jokes like that. He played one on me. He told me that if I would eat a half a cigar I would be stunted and not grow any more and maybe could be a rider. I did it. When Father wasn't looking I took a cigar out of his pocket and gagged it down some way. It made me awful sick and the doctor had to be sent for, and then it did no good. I kept right on growing. It was a joke. When I told what I had done and why, most fathers would have whipped me, but mine didn't.

Well, I didn't get stunted and didn't die. It serves Harry Hellinfinger right. Then I made up my mind I would like to be a stableboy, but had to give that up too. Mostly niggers do that work and I knew Father wouldn't let me go into it. No use to ask him.

If you've never been crazy about thoroughbreds, it's because you've never been around where they are much and don't know any better. They're beautiful. There isn't anything so lovely and clean and full of spunk and honest and everything as some race horses. On the big horse farms that are all around our town Beckersville there are tracks, and the horses run in the early morning. More than a thousand times I've got out of bed before daylight and walked two or three miles to the tracks. Mother wouldn't of let me go, but Father always says, "Let him alone." So I got some bread out of the breadbox and some butter and jam, gobbled it and lit out.

At the tracks you sit on the fence with men, whites and niggers, and they chew tobacco and talk, and then the colts are brought out. It's early and the grass is covered with shiny dew and in another field a man is plowing and they are frying things in a shed where the track niggers sleep, and you know how a nigger can giggle and laugh and say things that make you laugh. A white man can't do it and some niggers can't, but a track nigger can every time.

And so the colts are brought out and some are just galloped by stable-boys, but almost every morning on a big track owned by a rich man who lives maybe in New York, there are always, nearly every morning, a few colts and some of the old race horses and geldings and mares that are cut loose.

It brings a lump up into my throat when a horse runs. I don't mean all horses, but some. I can pick them nearly every time. It's in my blood like in the blood of race track niggers and trainers. Even when they just go slop-jogging along with a little nigger on their backs, I can tell a winner. If my throat hurts and it's hard for me to swallow, that's him. He'll run like Sam Hill when you let him out. If he don't win every time it'll be a wonder and because they've got him in a pocket behind another or he was pulled or got off bad at the post or something. If I wanted to be a gambler like Henry Rieback's father I could get rich. I know I could and Henry says so too. All I would have to do is to wait till that hurt comes when I see a horse and then bet every cent. That's what I would do if I wanted to be a gambler, but I don't.

When you're at the tracks in the morning—not the race tracks but the training tracks around Beckersville—you don't see a horse, the kind I've been talking about, very often, but it's nice anyway. Any thoroughbred, that is sired right and out of a good mare and trained by a man that knows how, can run. If he couldn't, what would he be there for and not pulling a plow?

Well, out of the stables they come and the boys are on their backs and it's lovely to be there. You hunch down on top of the fence and itch inside you. Over in the sheds the niggers giggle and sing. Bacon is being fried and coffee made. Everything smells lovely. Nothing smells better than coffee and manure and horses and niggers and bacon frying and pipes being smoked out of doors on a morning like that. It just gets you, that's what it does.

But about Saratoga. We was there six days and not a soul from home seen us and everything came off just as we wanted it to, fine weather and horses and races and all. We beat our way home and Bildad gave us a basket with fried chicken and bread and other eatables in, and I had eighteen dollars when we got back to Beckersville. Mother jawed and cried, but Pop didn't say much. I told everything we done, except one thing. I did and saw that alone. That's what I'm writing about. It got me upset. I think about it at night. Here it is.

At Saratoga we laid up nights in the hay in the shed Bildad had showed us and ate with the niggers early and at night when the race people had all gone away. The men from home stayed mostly in the grandstand and betting field and didn't come out around the places where the horses are kept except to the paddocks just before a race when the horses are saddled. At Saratoga they don't have paddocks under an open shed as at Lexington and Churchill Downs and other tracks down in our country, but saddle the horses right out in an open place under trees on a lawn as smooth and nice as Banker Bohon's front yard here in Beckersville. It's lovely. The horses are sweaty and nervous and shine and the men come out and smoke cigars and look at them and the trainers are there and the owners, and your heart thumps so you can hardly breathe.

Then the bugle blows for post and the boys that ride come running out with their silk clothes on and you run to get a place by the fence with the niggers.

I always am wanting to be a trainer or owner, and at the risk of being seen and caught and sent home I went to the paddocks before every race. The other boys didn't, but I did.

We got to Saratoga on a Friday, and on Wednesday the next week the big Mullford Handicap was to be run. Middlestride was in it and Sunstreak. The weather was fine and the track fast. I couldn't sleep the night before.

What had happened was that both these horses are the kind it makes my throat hurt to see. Middlestride is long and looks awkward and is a gelding. He belongs to Joe Thompson, a little owner from home who only has a half dozen horses. The Mullford Handicap is for a mile and Middlestride can't untrack fast. He goes away slow and is always 'way back at the half, then he begins to run and if the race is a mile and a quarter he'll just eat up everything and get there.

Sunstreak is different. He is a stallion and nervous and belongs on the biggest farm we've got in our country, the Van Riddle place that belongs to Mr. Van Riddle of New York. Sunstreak is like a girl you think about sometimes but never see. He is hard all over and lovely too. When you look at his head you want to kiss him. He is trained by Jerry Tillford who knows me and has been good to me lots of times, lets me walk into a horse's stall to look at him close and other things. There isn't anything as sweet as that horse. He stands at the post quiet and not letting on, but he is just burning up inside. Then when the barrier goes up he is off like his name, Sunstreak. It makes you ache to see him. It hurts you. He just lays down and runs like a bird dog. There can't anything I ever see run like him except Middlestride when he gets untracked and stretches himself.

Gee! I ached to see that race and those two horses run, ached and dreaded it too. I didn't want to see either of our horses beaten. We had never sent a pair like that to the races before. Old men in Beckersville said so and the niggers said so. It was a fact.

Before the race, I went over to the paddocks to see. I looked a last look at Middlestride, who isn't such a much standing in a paddock that way, then I went to see Sunstreak.

It was his day. I knew when I see him. I forgot all about being seen myself and walked right up. All the men from Beckersville were there and no one noticed me except Jerry Tillford. He saw me and something happened. I'll tell you about that.

I was standing looking at that horse and aching. In some way, I can't tell how, I knew just how Sunstreak felt inside. He was quiet and letting the niggers rub his legs and Mr. Van Riddle himself put the saddle on, but he was just a raging torrent inside. He was like the water in the river at Niagara Falls just before it goes plunk down. That horse wasn't thinking about running. He don't have to think about that. He was just thinking about holding himself back till the time for the running came. I knew that. I could just in a way see right inside him. He was going to do some awful running and I knew it. He wasn't bragging or letting on much or prancing or making a fuss, but just waiting. I knew it and Jerry Tillford his trainer knew. I looked up, and then that man and I looked into each other's eyes. Something happened to me. I guess I loved the man as much as I did the horse because he knew what I knew. Seemed to me there wasn't anything in the world but that man and the horse and me. I cried and Jerry Tillford had a shine in his eyes. Then I came away to the fence to wait for the race. The horse was better than me, more steadier and, now I know, better than Jerry. He was the quietest and he had to do the running.

Sunstreak ran first of course and he busted the world's record for a mile. I've seen that if I never see anything more. Everything came out just as I expected. Middlestride got left at the post and was 'way back and closed up to be second, just as I knew he would. He'll get a world's record too some day. They can't skin the Beckersville country on horses.

I watched the race calm because I knew what would happen. I was sure. Hanley Turner and Henry Rieback and Tom Tumberton were all more excited than me.

A funny thing had happened to me. I was thinking about Jerry Tillford the trainer and how happy he was all through the race. I liked him that afternoon even more than I ever liked my own father. I almost forgot the horses thinking that way about him. It was because of what I had seen in his eyes as he stood in the paddocks beside Sunstreak before the race started. I knew he had been watching and working with Sunstreak since the horse was a baby colt, had taught him to run and be patient and when to let himself out and not to quit, never. I knew that for him it was like a mother seeing her child do something brave or wonderful. It was the first time I ever felt for a man like that.

After the race that night I cut out from Tom and Hanley and Henry. I wanted to be by myself and I wanted to be near Jerry Tillford if I could work it. Here is what happened.

The track in Saratoga is near the edge of town. It is all polished up and trees around, the evergreen kind, and grass and everything painted and nice. If you go past the track you get to a hard road made of asphalt for automobiles, and if you go along this for a few miles there is a road turns off to a little rummy-looking farmhouse set in a yard.

That night after the race I went along that road because I had seen Jerry and some other men go that way in an automobile. I didn't expect to find them. I walked for a ways and then sat down by a fence to think. It was the direction they went in. I wanted to be as near Jerry as I could. I felt close to him. Pretty soon I went up the side road—I don't know why—and came to the rummy farmhouse. I was just lonesome to see Jerry, like wanting to see your father at night when you are a young kid. Just then an automobile came along and turned in. Jerry was in it and Henry Rieback's father, and Arthur Bedford from home, and Dave Williams and two other men I didn't know. They got out of the car and went into the house, all but Henry Rieback's father who quarreled with them and said he wouldn't go. It was only about nine o'clock, but they were all drunk and the rummy-looking farmhouse was a place for bad women to stay in. That's what it was. I crept up along a fence and looked through a window and saw.

It's what give me the fantods. I can't make it out. The women in the house were all ugly mean-looking women, not nice to look at or be near. They were homely too, except one who was tall and looked a little like the gelding Middlestride, but not clean like him, but with a hard ugly mouth. She had red hair. I saw everything plain. I got up by an old rose-bush by an open window and looked. The women had on loose dresses and sat around in chairs. The men came in and some sat on the women's laps. The place smelled rotten and there was rotten talk, the kind a kid hears around a livery stable in a town like Beckersville in the winter but don't ever expect to hear talked when there are women around. It was rotten. A nigger wouldn't go into such a place.

I looked at Jerry Tillford. I've told you how I had been feeling about him on account of his knowing what was going on inside of Sunstreak in the minute before he went to the post for the race in which he made a world's record.

Jerry bragged in that bad woman house as I knew Sunstreak wouldn't never have bragged. He said that he made that horse, that it was him that won the race and made the record. He lied and bragged like a fool. I never heard such silly talk.

And then, what do you suppose he did! He looked at the woman in there, the one that was lean and hard-mouthed and looked a little like the gelding Middlestride but not clean like him, and his eyes began to shine just as they did when he looked at me and at Sunstreak in the paddocks at the track in the afternoon. I stood there by the window—gee!—but I wished I hadn't gone away from the tracks, but had stayed with the boys and the niggers and the horses. The tall rotten-looking woman was between us just as Sunstreak was in the paddocks in the afternoon.

Then, all of a sudden, I began to hate that man. I wanted to scream and rush in the room and kill him. I never had such a feeling before. I was so mad clean through that I cried and my fists were doubled up so my fingernails cut my hands.

And Jerry's eyes kept shining and he waved back and forth, and then he went and kissed that woman and I crept away and went back to the tracks and to bed and didn't sleep hardly any, and then next day I got the other kids to start home with me and never told them anything I seen.

I been thinking about it ever since. I can't make it out. Spring has come again and I'm nearly sixteen and go to the tracks mornings same as always, and I see Sunstreak and Middlestride and a new colt named Strident I'll bet will lay them all out, but no one thinks so but me and two or three niggers.

But things are different. At the tracks the air don't taste as good or smell as good. It's because a man like Jerry Tillford, who knows what he does, could see a horse like Sunstreak run, and kiss a woman like that the same day. I can't make it out. Darn him, what did he want to do like that for? I keep thinking about it and it spoils looking at horses and smelling things and hearing niggers laugh and everything. Sometimes I'm so mad about it I want to fight someone. It gives me the fantods. What did he do it for? I want to know why.

Dorothy Canfield Fisher
1879–1958
SEX EDUCATION

IT WAS THREE TIMES—but at intervals of many years—that I heard my Aunt Minnie tell about an experience of her girlhood that had made a never-to-be-forgotten impression on her. The first time was in her thirties, still young. But she had been married for ten years, so that to my group of friends, all in the early teens, she seemed quite of another generation.

The day she told us the story, we had been idling on one end of her porch as we made casual plans for a picnic supper in the woods. Darning stockings at the other end, she paid no attention to us until one of the girls said, "Let's take blankets and sleep out there. It'd be fun."

"No," Aunt Minnie broke in sharply, "you mustn't do that."

"Oh, for goodness' sakes, why not!" said one of the younger girls, rebelliously, "the boys are always doing it. Why can't we, just once."

Aunt Minnie laid down her sewing. "Come here, girls," she said, "I want you should hear something that happened to me when I was your age."

Her voice had a special quality which, perhaps, young people of today would not recognize. But we did. We knew from experience that it was the dark voice grownups used when they were going to say something about sex.

Yet at first what she had to say was like any dull family anecdote; she had been ill when she was fifteen; and afterwards she was run down, thin, with no appetite. Her folks thought a change of air would do her good, and sent her from Vermont out to Ohio—or was it Illinois? I don't remember. Anyway, one of those places where the corn grows high. Her mother's Cousin Ella lived there, keeping house for her son-in-law.

The son-in-law was the minister of the village church. His wife had died some years before, leaving him a young widower with two little girls and a baby boy. He had been a normally personable man then, but the next summer, on the Fourth of July when he was trying to set off some fireworks to amuse his children, an imperfectly manufactured rocket had burst in his face. The explosion had left one side of his face badly scarred. Aunt Minnie made us see it, as she still saw it, in horrid detail: the stiffened, scarlet scar tissue distorting one cheek, the lower lip turned so far out at one corner that the moist red mucous-membrane lining always showed, one lower eyelid hanging loose, and watering.

After the accident, his face had been a long time healing. It was then that his wife's elderly mother had gone to keep house and take care of the children. When he was well enough to be about again, he found his position as pastor of the little church waiting for him. The farmers and village people in his congregation, moved by his misfortune, by his faithful service and by his unblemished character, said they would rather have Mr. Fairchild, even with his scarred face, than any other minister. He was a good preacher, Aunt Minnie told us, "and the way he prayed was kind of exciting. I'd never known a preacher, not to live in the same house with him, before. And when he was in the pulpit, with everybody looking up at him, I felt the way his children did, kind of proud to think we had just eaten breakfast at the same table. I liked to call him 'Cousin Malcolm' before folks. One side of his face was all right, anyhow. You could see from that that he *had* been a good-looking man. In fact, probably one of those ministers that all the women—" Aunt Minnie paused, drew her lips together, and looked at us uncertainly.

Then she went back to the story as it happened—as it happened that first time I heard her tell it. "I thought he was a saint. Everybody out there did. That was all *they* knew. Of course, it made a person sick to look at that awful scar—the drooling corner of his mouth was the worst. He tried to keep that side of his face turned away from folks. But you always knew it was there. That was what kept him from marrying again, so Cousin Ella said. I heard her say lots of times that he knew no woman would touch any man who looked the way he did, not with a ten-foot pole.

"Well, the change of air did do me good. I got my appetite back, and ate a lot and played outdoors a lot with my cousins. They were younger than I (I had my sixteenth birthday there) but I still liked to play games. I got taller and laid on some weight. Cousin Ella used to say I grew as fast as the corn did. Their house stood at the edge of the village. Beyond it was one of those big cornfields they have out West. At the time when

I first got there, the stalks were only up to a person's knee. You could see over their tops. But it grew like lightning, and before long, it was the way thick woods are here, way over your head, the stalks growing so close together it was dark under them.

"Cousin Ella told us youngsters that it was lots worse for getting lost in than woods, because there weren't any landmarks in it. One spot in a cornfield looked just like any other. 'You children keep out of it,' she used to tell us almost every day, '*especially you girls*. It's no place for a decent girl. You could easy get so far from the house nobody could hear you if you hollered. There are plenty of men in this town that wouldn't like anything better than—' she never said what.

"In spite of what she said, my little cousins and I had figured out that if we went across one corner of the field, it would be a short cut to the village, and sometimes, without letting on to Cousin Ella, we'd go that way. After the corn got really tall, the farmer stopped cultivating, and we soon beat down a path in the loose dirt. The minute you were inside the field it was dark. You felt it as if you were miles from anywhere. It sort of scared you. But in no time the path turned and brought you out on the far end of Main Street. Your breath was coming fast, maybe, but that was what made you like to do it.

"One day I missed the turn. Maybe I didn't keep my mind on it. Maybe it had rained and blurred the tramped-down look of the path. I don't know what. All of a sudden, I knew I was lost. And the minute I knew that, I began to run, just as hard as I could run. I couldn't help it, any more than you can help snatching your hand off a hot stove. I didn't know what I was scared of, I didn't even know I *was* running, till my heart was pounding so hard I had to stop.

"The minute I stood still, I could hear Cousin Ella saying, 'There are plenty of men in this town that wouldn't like anything better than—' I didn't know, not really, what she meant. But I knew she meant something horrible. I opened my mouth to scream. But I put both hands over my mouth to keep the scream in. If I made any noise, one of those men would hear me. I thought I heard one just behind me, and whirled around. And then I thought another one had tiptoed up behind me, the other way, and I spun around so fast I almost fell over. I stuffed my hands hard up against my mouth. And then—I couldn't help it—I ran again—but my legs were shaking so I soon had to stop. There I stood, scared to move for fear of rustling the corn and letting the men know where I was. My hair had come down, all over my face. I kept pushing it back and looking around, quick, to make sure one of the men hadn't found out where I was. Then I thought I saw a man coming towards me, and I ran away from him— and fell down, and burst some of the buttons off my dress, and was sick to my stomach—and thought I heard a man close to me and got up and staggered around, knocking into the corn because I couldn't even see where I was going.

"And then, off to one side, I saw Cousin Malcolm. Not a man. The minister. He was standing still, one hand up to his face, thinking. He hadn't heard me.

"I was so *terrible* glad to see him, instead of one of those men, I ran as fast as I could and just flung myself on him, to make myself feel how safe I was."

Aunt Minnie had become strangely agitated. Her hands were shaking, her face was crimson. She frightened us. We could not look away from her. As we waited for her to go on, I felt little spasms twitch at the muscles inside my body. "And what do you think that *saint*, that holy minister of the Gospel, did to an innocent child who clung to him for safety? The most terrible look came into his eyes—you girls are too young to know what he looked like. But once you're married, you'll find out. He grabbed hold of me—that dreadful face of his was *right on mine*—and began clawing the clothes off my back."

She stopped for a moment, panting. We were too frightened to speak. She went on, "He had torn my dress right down to the waist before I— then I *did* scream—all I could—and pulled away from him so hard I almost fell down, and ran and all of a sudden I came out of the corn, right in the back yard of the Fairchild house. The children were staring at the corn, and Cousin Ella ran out of the kitchen door. They had heard me screaming. Cousin Ella shrieked out, 'What is it? What happened? Did a man scare you?' And I said, 'Yes, yes, yes, a man—I ran—!' And then I fainted away. I must have. The next thing I knew I was on the sofa in the living room and Cousin Ella was slapping my face with a wet towel."

She had to wet her lips with her tongue before she could go on. Her face was gray now. "There! that's the kind of thing girls' folks ought to tell them about—so they'll know what men are like."

She finished her story as if she were dismissing us. We wanted to go away, but we were too horrified to stir. Finally one of the youngest girls asked in a low trembling voice, "Aunt Minnie, did you tell on him?"

"No, I was ashamed to," she said briefly. "They sent me home the next day anyhow. Nobody ever said a word to me about it. And I never did either. Till now."

By what gets printed in some of the modern child-psychology books, you would think that girls to whom such a story had been told would never develop normally. Yet, as far as I can remember what happened to the girls in that group, we all grew up about like anybody. Most of us married, some happily, some not so well. We kept house. We learned— more or less—how to live with our husbands, we had children and struggled to bring them up right—we went forward into life, just as if we had never been warned not to.

Perhaps, young as we were that day, we had already had enough experience of life so that we were not quite blank paper for Aunt Minnie's frightening story. Whether we thought of it then or not, we couldn't have failed to see that at this very time, Aunt Minnie had been married for ten years or more, comfortably and well married, too. Against what she tried by that story to brand into our minds stood the cheerful home life in that house, the good-natured, kind, hard-working husband, and the children—the three rough-and-tumble, nice little boys, so adored by their parents, and the sweet girl baby who died, of whom they could never speak without tears. It was such actual contact with adult life that probably kept generation after generation of girls from being scared by tales like Aunt Minnie's into a neurotic horror of living.

Of course, since Aunt Minnie was so much older than we, her boys grew up to be adolescents and young men while our children were still little enough so that our worries over them were nothing more serious than whooping cough and trying to get them to make their own beds. Two of our aunt's three boys followed, without losing their footing, the narrow path which leads across adolescence into normal adult life. But the middle one, Jake, repeatedly fell off into the morass. "Girl trouble," as the succinct family phrase put it. He was one of those boys who have "charm," whatever we mean by that, and was always being snatched at by girls who would be "all wrong" for him to marry. And once, at nineteen, he ran away from home, whether with one of these girls or not we never heard, for through all her ups and downs with this son, Aunt Minnie tried fiercely to protect him from scandal that might cloud his later life.

Her husband had to stay on his job to earn the family living. She was the one who went to find Jake. When it was gossiped around that Jake was in "bad company" his mother drew some money from the family savings-bank account, and silent, white-cheeked, took the train to the city where rumor said he had gone.

Some weeks later he came back with her. With no girl. She had cleared him of that entanglement. As of others, which followed, later. Her troubles seemed over when, at a "suitable" age, he fell in love with a "suitable" girl, married her and took her to live in our shire town, sixteen miles away, where he had a good position. Jake was always bright enough.

Sometimes, idly, people speculated as to what Aunt Minnie had seen that time she went after her runaway son, wondering where her search for him had taken her—very queer places for Aunt Minnie to be in, we imagined. And how could such an ignorant, homekeeping woman ever have known what to say to an errant willful boy to set him straight?

Well, of course, we reflected, watching her later struggles with Jake's erratic ways, she certainly could not have remained ignorant, after seeing over and over what she probably had; after talking with Jake about the things which, a good many times, must have come up with desperate openness between them.

She kept her own counsel. We never knew anything definite about the facts of those experiences of hers. But one day she told a group of us—all then married women—something which gave us a notion about what she had learned from them.

We were hastily making a layette for a not-especially welcome baby in a poor family. In those days, our town had no such thing as a district-nursing service. Aunt Minnie, a vigorous woman of fifty-five, had come in to help. As we sewed, we talked, of course; and because our daughters were near or in their teens, we were comparing notes about the bewildering responsibility of bringing up girls.

After a while, Aunt Minnie remarked, "Well, I hope you teach your girls some *sense*. From what I read, I know you're great on telling them 'the facts,' facts we never heard of when we were girls. Like as not, some facts I don't know, now. But knowing the facts isn't going to do them any more good than *not* knowing the facts ever did, unless they have some sense taught them, too."

"What do you mean, Aunt Minnie?" one of us asked her uncertainly.

She reflected, threading a needle, "Well, I don't know but what the best way to tell you what I mean is to tell you about something that happened to me, forty years ago. I've never said anything about it before. But I've thought about it a good deal. Maybe—"

She had hardly begun when I recognized the story—her visit to her Cousin Ella's Midwestern home, the widower with his scarred face and saintly reputation and, very vividly, her getting lost in the great corn-field. I knew every word she was going to say—to the very end, I thought.

But no, I did not. Not at all.

She broke off, suddenly, to exclaim with impatience, "Wasn't I the big ninny? But not so big a ninny as that old cousin of mine. I could wring her neck for getting me in such a state. Only she didn't know any better, herself. That was the way they brought young people up in those days, scaring them out of their wits about the awfulness of getting lost, but not telling them a thing about how *not* to get lost. Or how to act, if they did.

"If I had had the sense I was born with, I'd have known that running my legs off in a zigzag was the worst thing I could do. I couldn't have been more than a few feet from the path when I noticed I wasn't on it. My tracks in the loose plow dirt must have been perfectly plain. If I'd h' stood still, and collected my wits, I could have looked down to see which way my footsteps went and just walked back over them to the path and gone on about my business.

"Now I ask you, if I'd been told how to do that, wouldn't it have been a lot better protection for me—if protection was what my aunt thought she wanted to give me—than to scare me so at the idea of being lost that I turned deaf-dumb-and-blind when I thought I was?

"And anyhow that patch of corn wasn't as big as she let on. And she knew it wasn't. It was no more than a big field in a farming country. I was a well-grown girl of sixteen, as tall as I am now. If I couldn't have found the path, I could have just walked along one line of cornstalks—*straight*—and I'd have come out somewhere in ten minutes. Fifteen at the most. Maybe not just where I wanted to go. But all right, safe, where decent folks were living."

She paused, as if she had finished. But at the inquiring blankness in our faces, she went on, "Well, now, why isn't teaching girls—and boys, too, for the Lord's sake don't forget they need it as much as the girls—about this man-and-woman business, something like that? If you give them the idea—no matter whether it's *as* you tell them the facts, or as you *don't* tell them the facts, that it is such a terribly scary thing that if they take a step into it, something's likely to happen to them so awful that you're ashamed to tell them what—well, they'll lose their heads and run around like crazy things, first time they take one step away from the path.

"For they'll be trying out the paths, all right. You can't keep them from it. And a good thing too. How else are they going to find out what it's like? Boys' and girls' going together is a path across one corner of growing up. And when they go together, they're likely to get off the path some. Seems to me, it's up to their folks to bring them up so when they do, they don't start screaming and running in circles, but stand still, right where they are, and get their breath and figure out how to get back.

"And anyhow, you don't tell 'em the truth about sex" (I was astonished to hear her use the actual word, taboo to women of her generation) "if they get the idea from you that it's all there is to living. It's not. If you don't get to where you want to go in it, well, there's a lot of landscape all around it a person can have a good time in.

"D'you know, I believe one thing that gives girls and boys the wrong idea is the way folks *look!* My old cousin's face, I can see her now, it was as red as a rooster's comb when she was telling me about men in that cornfield. I believe now she kind of *liked* to talk about it."

(Oh, Aunt Minnie—and yours! I thought.)

Someone asked, "But how *did* you get out, Aunt Minnie?"

She shook her head, laid down her sewing. "More foolishness. That minister my mother's cousin was keeping house for—her son-in-law—I caught sight of him, down along one of the aisles of cornstalks, looking down at the ground, thinking, the way he often did. And I was so glad to see him I rushed right up to him, and flung my arms around his neck and hugged him. He hadn't heard me coming. He gave a great start, put one arm around me and turned his face full towards me—I suppose for just a second he had forgotten how awful one side of it was. His expression, his eyes—well, you're all married women, you know how he looked, the way any able-bodied man thirty-six or -seven, who'd been married and begotten children, would look—for a minute anyhow, if a full-blooded girl of sixteen, who ought to have known better, flung herself at him without any warning, her hair tumbling down, her dress half unbuttoned, and hugged him with all her might.

"I was what they called innocent in those days. That is, I knew just as little about what men are like as my folks could manage I should. But I was old enough to know all right what that look meant. And it gave me a start. But of course the real thing of it was that dreadful scar of his, so close to my face—that wet corner of his mouth, his eye drawn down with the red inside of the lower eyelid showing—

"It turned me so sick, I pulled away with all my might, so fast that I ripped one sleeve nearly loose, and let out a screech like a wildcat. And ran. Did I run? And in a minute, I was through the corn and had come out in the back yard of the house. I hadn't been more than a few feet from it, probably, any of the time. And then I fainted away. Girls were always fainting away; it was the way our corset strings were pulled tight, I suppose, and then—oh, a lot of fuss.

"But anyhow," she finished, picking up her work and going on, setting neat, firm stitches with steady hands, "there's one thing, I never told anybody it was Cousin Malcolm I had met in the cornfield. I told my old cousin that 'a man had scared me.' And nobody said anything more about it to me, not ever. That was the way they did in those days. They thought if they didn't let on about something, maybe it wouldn't have happened. I was sent back to Vermont right away and Cousin Malcolm went on being minister of the church. I've always been," said Aunt Minnie moderately, "kind of proud that I didn't go and ruin a man's life for just one second's slip-up. If you could have called it that. For it *would* have ruined him. You know how hard as stone people are about other folks' letdowns. If I'd have told, not one person in that town would have had any charity. Not one would have tried to understand. One slip, *once*, and they'd have pushed him down in the mud. If I had told, I'd have felt pretty bad about it, later—when I came to have more sense. But I declare, I can't see how I came to have the decency, dumb as I was then, to know that it wouldn't be fair."

It was not long after this talk that Aunt Minnie's elderly husband died, mourned by her, by all of us. She lived alone then. It was peaceful October weather for her, in which she kept a firm roundness of face and figure, as quiet-living country-women often do, on into her sixties.

But then Jake, the boy who had had girl trouble, had wife trouble. We heard he had taken to running after a young girl, or was it that she was running after him? It was something serious. For his nice wife left him and came back with the children to live with her mother in our town. Poor Aunt Minnie used to go see her for long talks which made them both cry. And she went to keep house for Jake, for months at a time.

She grew old, during those years. When finally she (or something) managed to get the marriage mended so that Jake's wife relented and went back to live with him, there was no trace left of her pleasant brisk freshness. She was stooped and slow-footed and shrunken. We, her kins-people, although we would have given our lives for any one of our own children, wondered whether Jake was worth what it had cost his mother to—well, steady him, or reform him. Or perhaps just understand him. Whatever it took.

She came of a long-lived family and was able to go on keeping house for herself well into her eighties. Of course we and the other neighbors stepped in often to make sure she was all right. Mostly, during those brief calls, the talk turned on nothing more vital than her geraniums. But one midwinter afternoon, sitting with her in front of her cozy stove, I chanced to speak in rather hasty blame of someone who had, I thought, acted badly. To my surprise this brought from her the story about the cornfield which she had evidently quite forgotten telling me, twice before.

This time she told it almost dreamily, swaying to and fro in her rock-ing chair, her eyes fixed on the long slope of snow outside her window. When she came to the encounter with the minister she said, looking away from the distance and back into my eyes, "I know now that I had been, all along, kind of *interested* in him, the way any girl as old as I was would be, in any youngish man living in the same house with her. And a minister, too. They have to have the gift of gab so much more than most men, women get to thinking they are more alive than men who can't talk so well. I *thought* the reason I threw my arms around him was because I had been so scared. And I certainly had been scared, by my old cousin's horrible talk about the cornfield being full of men waiting to grab girls. But that wasn't all the reason I flung myself at Malcolm Fairchild and hugged him. I know that now. Why in the world shouldn't I have been taught *some* notion of it then? 'Twould do girls good to know that they are just like everybody else—human nature *and* sex, all mixed up to-gether. I didn't have to hug him. I wouldn't have, if he'd been dirty or fat and old, or chewed tobacco."

I stirred in my chair, ready to say, "But it's not so simple as all that to tell girls—" and she hastily answered my unspoken protest. "I know, I know, most of it can't be put into words. There just aren't any words to say something that's so both-ways-at-once all the time as this man-and-woman business. But look here, you know as well as I do that there are lots more ways than in words to teach young folks what you want 'em to know."

The old woman stopped her swaying rocker to peer far back into the past with honest eyes. "What was in my mind back there in the corn-field—partly anyhow—was what had been there all the time I was living in the same house with Cousin Malcolm—that he had long straight legs, and broad shoulders, and lots of curly brown hair, and was nice and flat in front, and that one side of his face was good-looking. But most of all, that he and I were really alone, for the first time, without anybody to see us.

"I suppose, if it hadn't been for that dreadful scar, he'd have drawn me up, tight, and—most any man would—kissed me. I know how I must have looked, all red and hot and my hair down and my dress torn open. And, used as he was to big cornfields, he probably never dreamed that the reason I looked that way was because I was scared to be by myself in one. He may have thought—you know what he may have thought.

"Well—if his face had been like anybody's—when he looked at me the way he did, the way a man does look at a woman he wants to have, it would have scared me—some. But I'd have cried, maybe. And probably he'd have kissed me again. You know how such things go. I might have come out of the cornfield halfway engaged to marry him. Why not? I was old enough, as people thought then. That would have been nature. That was probably what he thought of, in that first instant.

"But what did I do? I had one look at his poor, horrible face, and started back as though I'd stepped on a snake. And screamed and ran.

"What do you suppose *he* felt, left there in the corn? He must have been sure that I would tell everybody he had attacked me. He probably thought that when he came out and went back to the village he'd already be in disgrace and put out of the pulpit.

"But the worst must have been to find out, so rough, so plain from the way I acted—as if somebody had hit him with an ax—the way he would look to any woman he might try to get close to. That must have been—" she drew a long breath, "well, pretty hard on him."

After a silence, she murmured pityingly, "Poor man!"

E. M. Forster

1879–1970

THE CELESTIAL OMNIBUS

T HE BOY who resided at Agathox Lodge, 28, Buckingham Park Road, Surbiton,[1] had often been puzzled by the old sign-post that stood almost opposite. He asked his mother about it, and she replied that it was a joke, and not a very nice one, which had been made many years back by some naughty young men, and that the police ought to remove it. For there were two strange things about this sign-post: firstly, it pointed up a blank alley, and, secondly, it had painted on it, in faded characters, the words, "To Heaven."

"What kind of young men were they?" he asked.

"I think your father told me that one of them wrote verses, and was expelled from the University and came to grief in other ways. Still, it

---

[1] a suburb of London

was a long time ago. You must ask your father about it. He will say the same as I do, that it was put up as a joke."

"So it doesn't mean anything at all?"

She sent him upstairs to put on his best things, for the Bonses were coming to tea, and he was to hand the cake-stand.

It struck him, as he wrenched on his tightening trousers, that he might do worse than ask Mr. Bons about the signpost. His father, though very kind, always laughed at him—shrieked with laughter whenever he or any other child asked a question or spoke. But Mr. Bons was serious as well as kind. He had a beautiful house and lent one books, he was a churchwarden, and a candidate for the County Council; he had donated to the Free Library enormously, he presided over the Literary Society, and had Members of Parliament to stop with him—in short, he was probably the wisest person alive.

Yet even Mr. Bons could only say that the signpost was a joke—the joke of a person named Shelley.

"Of course!" cried the mother; "I told you so, dear. That was the name."

"Had you never heard of Shelley?" asked Mr. Bons.

"No," said the boy, and hung his head.

"But is there no Shelley in the house?"

"Why, yes!" exclaimed the lady, in much agitation. "Dear Mr. Bons, we aren't such Philistines as that. Two at the least. One a wedding present, and the other, smaller print, in one of the spare rooms."

"I believe we have seven Shelleys," said Mr. Bons, with a slow smile. Then he brushed the cake crumbs off his stomach, and, together with his daughter, rose to go.

The boy, obeying a wink from his mother, saw them all the way to the garden gate, and when they had gone he did not at once return to the house, but gazed for a little up and down Buckingham Park Road.

His parents lived at the right end of it. After No. 39 the quality of the houses dropped very suddenly, and 64 had not even a separate servants' entrance. But at the present moment the whole road looked rather pretty, for the sun had just set in splendor, and the inequalities of rent were drowned in a saffron afterglow. Small birds twittered, and the bread-winners' train shrieked musically down through the cutting—that wonderful cutting which has drawn to itself the whole beauty out of Surbiton, and clad itself, like any Alpine valley, with the glory of the fir and the silver birch and the primrose. It was this cutting that had first stirred desires within the boy—desires for something just a little different, he knew not what, desires that would return whenever things were sunlit, as they were this evening, running up and down inside him, up and down, up and down, till he would feel quite unusual all over, and as likely as not would want to cry. This evening he was even sillier, for he slipped across the road towards the sign-post and began to run up the blank alley.

The alley runs between high walls—the walls of the gardens of "Ivanhoe" and "Belle Vista" respectively. It smells a little all the way, and is scarcely twenty yards long, including the turn at the end. So not unnaturally the boy soon came to a standstill. "I'd like to kick that Shelley," he exclaimed, and glanced idly at a piece of paper which was pasted on the wall. Rather an odd piece of paper, and he read it carefully before he turned back. This is what he read:

S. and C. R. C. C.

Alteration in Service.

Owing to lack of patronage the Company are regretfully compelled to suspend the hourly service, and to retain only the

Sunrise and Sunset Omnibuses,

which will run as usual. It is to be hoped that the public will patronize an arrangement which is intended for their convenience. As an extra inducement, the Company will, for the first time, now issue

Return Tickets!

(available one day only), which may be obtained of the driver. Passengers are again reminded that *no tickets are issued at the other end,* and that no complaints in this connection will receive consideration from the Company. Nor will the Company be responsible for any negligence or stupidity on the part of Passengers, nor for Hailstorms, Lightning, Loss of Tickets, nor for any Act of God.

For the Direction

Now he had never seen this notice before, nor could he imagine where the omnibus went to. S. of course was for Surbiton, and R.C.C. meant Road Car Company. But what was the meaning of the other C.? Coombe and Malden, perhaps, or possibly "City." Yet it could not hope to compete with the South-Western. The whole thing, the boy reflected, was run on hopelessly unbusiness-like lines. Why no tickets from the other end? And what an hour to start! Then he realized that unless the notice was a hoax, an omnibus must have been starting just as he was wishing the Bonses good-bye. He peered at the ground through the gathering dusk, and there he saw what might or might not be the marks of wheels. Yet nothing had come out of the alley. And he had never seen an omnibus at any time in the Buckingham Park Road. No: it must be a hoax, like the sign-posts, like the fairy tales, like the dreams upon which he would wake suddenly in the night. And with a sigh he stepped from the alley— right into the arms of his father.

Oh, how his father laughed! "Poor, poor Popsey!" he cried. "Diddums! Diddums! Diddums think he'd walky-palky up to Evvink!" And his mother, also convulsed with laughter, appeared on the steps of Agathox Lodge. "Don't Bob!" she gasped. "Don't be so naughty! Oh, you'll kill me! Oh, leave the boy alone!"

But all the evening the joke was kept up. The father implored to be taken too. Was it a very tiring walk? Need one wipe one's shoes on the door mat? And the boy went to bed feeling faint and sore, and thankful for only one thing—that he had not said a word about the omnibus. It was a hoax, yet through his dreams it grew more and more real, and the streets of Surbiton, through which he saw it driving, seemed instead to become hoaxes and shadows. And very early in the morning he woke with a cry, for he had had a glimpse of its destination.

He struck a match, and its light fell not only on his watch but also on his calendar, so that he knew it to be half-an-hour to sunrise. It was pitch dark, for the fog had come down from London in the night, and all Surbiton was wrapped in its embraces. Yet he sprang out and dressed himself, for he was determined to settle once for all which was real: the omnibus or the streets. "I shall be a fool one way or the other," he thought, "until I know." Soon he was shivering in the road under the gas lamp that guarded the entrance to the alley.

To enter the alley itself required some courage. Not only was it horribly dark, but he now realized that it was an impossible terminus for an omnibus. If it had not been for a policeman, whom he heard approaching through the fog, he would never have made the attempt. The next moment he had made the attempt and failed. Nothing. Nothing but a blank alley and a very silly boy gaping at its dirty floor. It *was* a hoax. "I'll tell papa and mamma," he decided. "I deserve it. I deserve that they should know. I am too silly to be alive." And he went back to the gate of Agathox Lodge.

There he remembered that his watch was fast. The sun was not risen; it would not rise for two minutes. "Give the bus every chance," he thought cynically, and returned into the alley.

But the omnibus was there.

2

It had two horses, whose sides were still smoking from their journey, and its two great lamps shone through the fog against the alley's walls, changing their cobwebs and moss into tissues of fairy-land. The driver was huddled up in a cape. He faced the blank wall, and how he had managed to drive in so neatly and so silently was one of the many things that the boy never discovered. Nor could he imagine how ever he would drive out.

"Please," his voice quavered through the foul brown air, "Please, is that an omnibus?"

"Omnibus est," said the driver, without turning round. There was a moment's silence. The policeman passed, coughing, by the entrance of the alley. The boy crouched in the shadow, for he did not want to be found out. He was pretty sure, too, that it was a Pirate; nothing else, he reasoned, would go from such odd places and at such odd hours.

"About when do you start?" He tried to sound nonchalant.

"At sunrise."

"How far do you go?"

"The whole way."

"And can I have a return ticket which will bring me all the way back?"

"You can."

"Do you know, I half think I'll come." The driver made no answer. The sun must have risen, for he unhitched the brake. And scarcely had the boy jumped in before the omnibus was off.

How? Did it turn? There was no room. Did it go forward? There was a blank wall. Yet it was moving—moving at a stately pace through the fog, which had turned from brown to yellow. The thought of warm bed and warmer breakfast made the boy feel faint. He wished he had not come. His parents would not have approved. He would have gone back to them if the weather had not made it impossible. The solitude was terrible; he was the only passenger. And the omnibus, though well-built, was cold and somewhat musty. He drew his coat round him, and in so doing chanced to feel his pocket. It was empty. He had forgotten his purse.

"Stop!" he shouted. "Stop!" And then, being of a polite disposition, he glanced up at the painted notice-board so that he might call the driver by name. "Mr. Browne! stop; O, do please stop!"

Mr. Browne did not stop, but he opened a little window, and looked in at the boy. His face was a surprise, so kind it was and modest.

"Mr. Browne, I've left my purse behind. I've not got a penny. I can't pay for the ticket. Will you take my watch, please? I am in the most awful hole."

"Tickets on this line," said the driver, "whether single or return, can be purchased by coinage from no terrene mint. And a chronometer, though it had solaced the vigils of Charlemagne,[2] or measured the slumbers of Laura,[3] can acquire by no mutation the double-cake that charms the fangless Cerberus[4] of Heaven!" So saying, he handed in the necessary ticket, and, while the boy said "Thank you," continued: "Titular pretensions, I know it well, are vanity. Yet they merit no censure when uttered on a laughing lip, and in an homonymous world are in some sort useful, since they do serve to distinguish one Jack from his fellow. Remember me, therefore, as Sir Thomas Browne."[5]

"Are you a Sir? Oh, sorry!" He had heard of these gentlemen drivers. "It *is* good of you about the ticket. But if you go on at this rate, however does your bus pay?"

"It does not pay. It was not intended to pay. Many are the faults of my equipage; it is compounded too curiously of foreign woods; its cushions tickle erudition rather than promote repose; and my horses are nourished

---

[2] Frankish king, 768–814, and also a figure of legend
[3] the beloved of Francesco Petrarch, 1304–1374, Italian poet
[4] the three-headed dog that guarded the entrance to Hades
[5] English prose writer, 1605–1682, who quotes himself here

not on the evergreen pastures of the moment, but on the dried bents and clovers of Latinity. But that it pays!—that error at all events was never intended and never attained."

"Sorry again," said the boy rather hopelessly. Sir Thomas looked sad, fearing that, even for a moment, he had been the cause of sadness. He invited the boy to come up and sit beside him on the box, and together they journeyed on through the fog, which was now changing from yellow to white. There were no houses by the road; so it must be either Putney Heath or Wimbledon Common.

"Have you been a driver always?"

"I was a physician once."

"But why did you stop? Weren't you good?"

"As a healer of bodies I had scant success, and several score of my patients preceded me. But as a healer of the spirit I have succeeded beyond my hopes and my deserts. For though my drafts were not better nor subtler than those of other men, yet, by reason of the cunning goblets wherein I offered them, the queasy soul was ofttimes tempted to sip and be refreshed."

"The queasy soul," he murmured; "if the sun sets with trees in front of it, and you suddenly come strange all over, is that a queasy soul?"

"Have you felt that?"

"Why yes."

After a pause he told the boy a little, a very little, about the journey's end. But they did not chatter much, for the boy, when he liked a person, would as soon sit silent in his company as speak, and this, he discovered, was also the mind of Sir Thomas Browne and of many others with whom he was to be acquainted. He heard, however, about the young man Shelley, who was now quite a famous person, with a carriage of his own, and about some of the other drivers who are in the service of the Company. Meanwhile the light grew stronger, though the fog did not disperse. It was now more like mist than fog, and at times would travel quickly across them, as if it was part of a cloud. They had been ascending, too, in a most puzzling way; for over two hours the horses had been pulling against the collar, and even if it were Richmond Hill they ought to have been at the top long ago. Perhaps it was Epsom, or even the North Downs; yet the air seemed keener than that which blows on either. And as to the name of their destination, Sir Thomas Browne was silent.

Crash!

"Thunder, by Jove!" said the boy, "and not so far off either. Listen to the echoes! It's more like mountains."

He thought, not very vividly, of his father and mother. He saw them sitting down to sausages and listening to the storm. He saw his own empty place. Then there would be questions, alarms, theories, jokes, consolations. They would expect him back at lunch. To lunch he would not come, nor tea, but he would be in for dinner, and so his day's truancy

would be over. If he had had his purse he would have bought them presents—not that he should have known what to get them.

Crash!

The peal and the lightning came together. The cloud quivered as if it
were alive, and torn streamers of mist rushed past. "Are you afraid?"
asked Sir Thomas Browne.

"What is there to be afraid of? Is it much farther?"

The horses of the omnibus stopped just as a ball of fire burst up and
exploded with a ringing noise that was deafening but clear, like the noise
of a blacksmith's forge. All the cloud was shattered.

"Oh, listen, Sir Thomas Browne! No, I mean look; we shall get a
view at last. No, I mean listen; that sounds like a rainbow!"

The noise had died into the faintest murmur, beneath which another
murmur grew, spreading stealthily, steadily, in a curve that widened but
did not vary. And in widening curves a rainbow was spreading from the
horses' feet into the dissolving mists.

"But how beautiful! What colors! Where will it stop? It is more like
the rainbows you can tread on. More like dreams."

The color and the sound grew together. The rainbow spanned an enormous gulf. Clouds rushed under it and were pierced by it, and still it
grew, reaching forward, conquering the darkness, until it touched something that seemed more solid than a cloud.

The boy stood up "What is that out there?" he called. "What does it
rest on, out at that other end?"

In the morning sunshine a precipice shone forth beyond the gulf. A
precipice—or was it a castle? The horses moved. They set their feet
upon the rainbow.

"Oh, look!" the boy shouted. "Oh, listen! Those caves—or are they
gateways? Oh, look between those cliffs at those ledges. I see people! I
see trees!"

"Look also below," whispered Sir Thomas. "Neglect not the diviner
Acheron."[6]

The boy looked below, past the flames of the rainbow that licked
against their wheels. The gulf also had cleared, and in its depths there
flowed an everlasting river. One sunbeam entered and struck a green
pool, and as they passed over he saw three maidens rise to the surface of
the pool, singing, and playing with something that glistened like a ring.

"You down in the water—" he called.

They answered, "You up on the bridge—" There was a burst of music. "You up on the bridge, good luck to you. Truth in the depth, truth
on the height."

"You down in the water, what are you doing?"

[6] the river beyond which lies the underworld of Greek myth

Sir Thomas Browne replied: "They sport in the mancipiary posses-sion[7] of their gold"; and the omnibus arrived.

3

The boy was in disgrace. He sat locked up in the nursery of Agathox Lodge, learning poetry for a punishment. His father had said, "My boy! I can pardon anything but untruthfulness," and had caned him, saying at each stroke, "There is *no* omnibus, *no* driver, *no* bridge, *no* mountain; you are a *truant*, a *gutter snipe*, a *liar*." His father could be very stern at times. His mother had begged him to say he was sorry. But he could not say that. It was the greatest day of his life, in spite of the caning and the poetry at the end of it.

He had returned punctually at sunset—driven not by Sir Thomas Browne, but by a maiden lady who was full of quiet fun. They had talked of omnibuses and also of barouche landaus. How far away her gentle voice seemed now! Yet it was scarcely three hours since he had left her up the alley.

His mother called through the door. "Dear, you are to come down and to bring your poetry with you."

He came down, and found that Mr. Bons was in the smoking-room with his father. It had been a dinner party.

"Here is the great traveler!" said his father grimly. "Here is the young gentleman who drives in an omnibus over rainbows, while young ladies sing to him." Pleased with his wit, he laughed.

"After all," said Mr. Bons, smiling, "there is something a little like it in Wagner.[8] It is odd how, in quite illiterate minds, you will find glim-mers of Artistic Truth. The case interests me. Let me plead for the cul-prit. We have all romanced in our time, haven't we?"

"Hear how kind Mr. Bons is," said his mother, while his father said, "Very well. Let him say his Poem, and that will do. He is going away to my sister on Tuesday, and will cure him of this alley-sloping." (Laughter.) "Say your Poem."

The boy began. " 'Standing aloof in giant ignorance.' "[9]

His father laughed again—roared. "One for you, my son! 'Standing aloof in giant ignorance!' I never knew these poets talked sense. Just de-scribes you. Here, Bons, you go in for poetry. Put him through it, will you, while I fetch up the whisky?"

"Yes, give me the Keats," said Mr. Bons. "Let him say his Keats to me."

So for a few moments the wise man and the ignorant boy were left alone in the smoking-room.

[7] holding in trust
[8] German composer, 1813–1883, noted chiefly for his cycle of operas, *The Ring of the Nibelungen*
[9] John Keats, "To Homer"; see p. 778.

" 'Standing aloof in giant ignorance, of thee I dream and of the Cyclades, as one who sits ashore and longs perchance to visit—' "

"Quite right. To visit what?"

" 'To visit dolphin coral in deep seas,' " said the boy, and burst into tears.

"Come, come! why do you cry?"

"Because—because all these words that only rhymed before, now that I've come back they're me."

Mr. Bons laid the Keats down. The case was more interesting than he had expected. "*You?*" he exclaimed. "This sonnet, *you?*"

"Yes—and look further on: 'Aye, on the shores of darkness there is light, and precipices show untrodden green.' It *is* so, sir. All these things are true."

"I never doubted it," said Mr. Bons, with closed eyes.

"You—then you believe me? You believe in the omnibus and the driver and the storm and that return ticket I got for nothing and—"

"Tut, tut! No more of your yarns, my boy. I meant that I never doubted the essential truth of Poetry. Some day, when you have read more, you will understand what I mean."

"But Mr. Bons, it *is* so. There *is* light upon the shores of darkness. I have seen it coming. Light and a wind."

"Nonsense," said Mr. Bons.

"If I had stopped! They tempted me. They told me to give up my ticket—for you cannot come back if you lose your ticket. They called from the river for it, and indeed I was tempted, for I have never been so happy as among those precipices. But I thought of my mother and father, and that I must fetch them. Yet they will not come, though the road starts opposite our house. It has all happened as the people up there warned me, and Mr. Bons has disbelieved me like every one else. I have been caned. I shall never see that mountain again."

"What's that about me?" said Mr. Bons, sitting up in his chair very suddenly.

"I told them about you, and how clever you were, and how many books you had, and they said, 'Mr. Bons will certainly disbelieve you.' "

"Stuff and nonsense, my young friend. You grow impertinent. I—well—I will settle the matter. Not a word to your father. I will cure you. Tomorrow evening I will myself call here to take you for a walk, and at sunset we will go up this alley opposite and hunt for your omnibus, you silly little boy."

His face grew serious, for the boy was not disconcerted, but leaped about the room singing, "Joy! Joy! I told them you would believe me. We will drive together over the rainbow. I told them that you would come." After all, could there be anything in the story? Wagner? Keats? Shelley? Sir Thomas Browne? Certainly the case was interesting.

And on the morrow evening, though it was pouring with rain, Mr. Bons did not omit to call at Agathox Lodge.

The boy was ready, bubbling with excitement, and skipping about in a way that rather vexed the President of the Literary Society. They took a turn down Buckingham Park Road, and then—having seen that no one was watching them—slipped up the alley. Naturally enough (for the sun was setting) they ran straight against the omnibus.

"Good heavens!" exclaimed Mr. Bons. "Good gracious heavens!"

It was not the omnibus in which the boy had driven first, nor yet that in which he had returned. There were three horses—black, gray, and white, the gray being the finest. The driver, who turned round at the mention of goodness and of heaven, was a sallow man with terrifying jaws and sunken eyes. Mr. Bons, on seeing him, gave a cry as if of recognition, and began to tremble violently.

The boy jumped in.

"Is it possible?" cried Mr. Bons. "Is the impossible possible?"

"Sir; come in, sir. It is such a fine omnibus. Oh, here is his name— Dan some one."

Mr. Bons sprang in too. A blast of wind immediately slammed the omnibus door, and the shock jerked down all the omnibus blinds, which were very weak on their springs.

"Dan . . . Show me. Good gracious heavens! we're moving."

"Hooray!" said the boy.

Mr. Bons became flustered. He had not intended to be kidnapped. He could not find the door-handle, nor push up the blinds. The omnibus was quite dark, and by the time he had struck a match, night had come on outside also. They were moving rapidly.

"A strange, a memorable adventure," he said, surveying the interior of the omnibus, which was large, roomy, and constructed with extreme regularity, every part exactly answering to every other part. Over the door (the handle of which was outside) was written, "Lasciate ogni baldanza voi che entrate"[10]—at least, that was what was written, but Mr. Bons said that it was Lashy arty something, and that baldanza was a mistake for speranza.[11] His voice sounded as if he was in church. Meanwhile, the boy called to the cadaverous driver for two return tickets. They were handed in without a word. Mr. Bons covered his face with his hands and again trembled. "Do you know who that is!" he whispered, when the little window had shut upon them. "It is the impossible."

"Well, I don't like him as much as Sir Thomas Browne, though I shouldn't be surprised if he had even more in him."

"More in him?" He stamped irritably. "By accident you have made the greatest discovery of the century, and all you can say is that there is more in this man. Do you remember those vellum books in my library, stamped with red lilies, This—sit still, I bring you stupendous news!— *this is the man who wrote them.*"

[10] Abandon all arrogance, you who enter here—a revision of the inscription over the gate of hell in Dante's *Inferno*

[11] hope

The boy sat quite still. "I wonder if we shall see Mrs. Gamp?" he asked, after a civil pause.

"Mrs.—?"

"Mrs. Gamp and Mrs. Harris. I like Mrs. Harris. I came upon them quite suddenly. Mrs. Gamp's bandboxes have moved over the rainbow so badly. All the bottoms have fallen out, and two of the pippins off her bedstead tumbled into the stream."

"Out there sits the man who wrote my vellum books!" thundered Mr. Bons, "and you talk to me of Dickens and of Mrs. Gamp?"

"I know Mrs. Gamp so well," he apologized. "I could not help being glad to see her. I recognized her voice. She was telling Mrs. Harris about Mrs. Prig."[12]

"Did you spend the whole day in her elevating company?"

"Oh, no. I raced. I met a man who took me out beyond to a race-course. You run, and there are dolphins out at sea."

"Indeed. Do you remember the man's name?"

"Achilles. No; he was later. Tom Jones."

Mr. Bons sighed heavily. "Well, my lad, you have made a miserable mess of it. Think of a cultured person with your opportunities! A cultured person would have known all these characters and known what to have said to each. He would not have wasted his time with a Mrs. Gamp or a Tom Jones. The creations of Homer, of Shakespeare, and of Him who drives us now, would alone have contented him. He would not have raced. He would have asked intelligent questions."

"But, Mr. Bons," said the boy humbly, "you will be a cultured person. I told them so."

"True, true, and I beg you not to disgrace me when we arrive. No gossiping. No running. Keep close to my side, and never speak to these Immortals unless they speak to you. Yes, and give me the return tickets. You will be losing them."

The boy surrendered the tickets, but felt a little sore. After all, he had found the way to this place. It was hard first to be disbelieved and then to be lectured. Meanwhile, the rain had stopped, and moonlight crept into the omnibus through the cracks in the blinds.

"But how is there to be a rainbow?" cried the boy.

"You distract me," snapped Mr. Bons. "I wish to meditate on beauty. I wish to goodness I was with a reverent and sympathetic person."

The lad bit his lip. He made a hundred good resolutions. He would imitate Mr. Bons all the visit. He would not laugh, or run, or sing, or do any of the vulgar things that must have disgusted his new friends last time. He would be very careful to pronounce their names properly, and to remember who knew whom. Achilles did not know Tom Jones—at least, so Mr. Bons said. The Duchess of Malfi[13] was older than Mrs.

---

[12] comic low-life characters in Charles Dickens's *Martin Chuzzlewit*, 1843. Mrs. Harris exists only in Sairy Gamp's imagination.

[13] title character of a play, *c.* 1614, by John Webster

Gamp—at least, so Mr. Bons said. He would be self-conscious, reticent, and prim. He would never say he liked any one. Yet, when the blind flew up at a chance touch of his head, all these good resolutions went to the winds, for the omnibus had reached the summit of a moonlit hill, and there was the chasm, and there, across it, stood the old precipices, dreaming, with their feet in the everlasting river. He exclaimed, "The mountain! Listen to the new tune in the water! Look at the camp fires in the ravines," and Mr. Bons, after a hasty glance, retorted, "Water? Camp fires? Ridiculous rubbish. Hold your tongue. There is nothing at all."

Yet, under his eyes, a rainbow formed, compounded not of sunlight and storm, but of moonlight and the spray of the river. The three horses put their feet upon it. He thought it the finest rainbow he had seen, but did not dare say so, since Mr. Bons said that nothing was there. He leaned out—the window had opened—and sang the tune that rose from the sleeping waters.

"The prelude to Rhinegold?" said Mr. Bons suddenly. "Who taught you these *leit motifs?*" [14] He, too, looked out of the window. Then he behaved very oddly. He gave a choking cry, and fell back on to the omnibus floor. He writhed and kicked. His face was green.

"Does the bridge make you dizzy?" the boy asked.

"Dizzy!" gasped Mr. Bons. "I want to go back. Tell the driver."

But the driver shook his head.

"We are nearly there," said the boy. "They are asleep. Shall I call? They will be so pleased to see you, for I have prepared them."

Mr. Bons moaned. They moved over the lunar rainbow, which ever and ever broke away behind their wheels. How still the night was! Who would be sentry at the Gate?

"I am coming," he shouted, again forgetting the hundred resolutions. "I am returning—I, the boy."

"The boy is returning," cried a voice to other voices, who repeated, "The boy is returning."

"I am bringing Mr. Bons with me."

Silence.

"I should have said Mr. Bons is bringing me with him."

Profound silence.

"Who stands sentry?"

"Achilles."

And on the rocky causeway, close to the springing of the rainbow bridge, he saw a young man who carried a wonderful shield.

"Mr. Bons, it is Achilles, armed."

"I want to go back," said Mr. Bons.

The last fragment of the rainbow melted, the wheels sang upon the living rock, the door of the omnibus burst open. Out leapt the boy—he

---

[14] in Wagner's music drama, a musical theme associated with a particular character

could not resist—and sprang to meet the warrior, who, stooping suddenly, caught him on his shield.

"Achilles!" he cried, "let me get down, for I am ignorant and vulgar, and I must wait for that Mr. Bons of whom I told you yesterday."

But Achilles raised him aloft. He crouched on the wonderful shield, on heroes and burning cities, on vineyards graven in gold, on every dear passion, every joy, on the entire image of the Mountain that he had discovered, encircled, like it, with an everlasting stream. "No, no," he protested, "I am not worthy. It is Mr. Bons who must be up here."

But Mr. Bons was whimpering, and Achilles trumpeted and cried, "Stand upright upon my shield!"

"Sir, I did not mean to stand! something made me stand. Sir, why do you delay? Here is only the great Achilles, whom you knew." [15]

Mr. Bons screamed, "I see no one. I see nothing. I want to go back." Then he cried to the driver, "Save me! Let me stop in your chariot. I have honored you. I have quoted you. I have bound you in vellum. Take me back to my world."

The driver replied, "I am the means and not the end. I am the food and not the life. Stand by yourself, as that boy has stood. I cannot save you. For poetry is a spirit; and they that would worship it must worship in spirit and in truth."

Mr. Bons—he could not resist—crawled out of the beautiful omnibus. His face appeared, gaping horribly. His hands followed, one gripping the step, the other beating the air. Now his shoulders emerged, his chest, his stomach. With a shriek of "I see London," he fell fell against the hard, moonlit rock, fell into it as if it were water, fell through it, vanished, and was seen by the boy no more.

"Where have you fallen to, Mr. Bons? Here is a procession arriving to honor you with music and torches. Here come the men and women whose names you know. The mountain is awake, the river is awake, over the race-course the sea is awaking those dolphins, and it is all for you. They want you —"

There was the touch of fresh leaves on his forehead. Some one had crowned him.

ΤΕΛΟΣ[16]

From the *Kingston Gazette*,
Surbiton Times,
and *Raynes Park Observer*.

The body of Mr. Septimus Bons has been found in a shockingly mutilated condition in the vicinity of the Bermondsey gas-works. The deceased's pockets contained a sovereign-purse, a silver cigarcase, a bijou pronouncing dictionary, and a couple of omnibus tickets. The unfortunate gentleman had apparently been hurled from a considerable height. Foul play is suspected, and a thorough investigation is pending by the authorities.

[15] See Tennyson, "Ulysses," line 64, p. 825.
[16] the end—with overtones of "the goal"

James Joyce
1882–1941
THE DEAD

LILY, the caretaker's daughter, was literally run off her feet. Hardly had she brought one gentleman into the little pantry behind the office on the ground floor and helped him off with his overcoat than the wheezy hall-door bell clanged again and she had to scamper along the bare hallway to let in another guest. It was well for her she had not to attend to the ladies also. But Miss Kate and Miss Julia had thought of that and had converted the bathroom upstairs into a ladies' dressing-room. Miss Kate and Miss Julia were there, gossiping and laughing and fussing, walking after each other to the head of the stairs, peering down over the banisters and calling down to Lily to ask her who had come.

It was always a great affair, the Misses Morkan's annual dance. Everybody who knew them came to it, members of the family, old friends of the family, the members of Julia's choir, any of Kate's pupils that were grown up enough and even some of Mary Jane's pupils too. Never once had it fallen flat. For years and years it had gone off in splendid style as long as anyone could remember; ever since Kate and Julia, after the death of their brother Pat, had left the house in Stoney Batter and taken Mary Jane, their only niece, to live with them in the dark gaunt house on Usher's Island, the upper part of which they had rented from Mr Fulham, the corn-factor on the ground floor. That was a good thirty years ago if it was a day. Mary Jane, who was then a little girl in short clothes, was now the main prop of the household for she had the organ in Haddington Road. She had been through the Academy and gave a pupils' concert every year in the upper room of the Antient Concert Rooms. Many of her pupils belonged to the better-class families on the Kingstown and Dalkey line. Old as they were, her aunts also did their share. Julia, though she was quite grey, was still the leading soprano in Adam and Eve's, and Kate, being too feeble to go about much, gave music lessons to beginners on the old square piano in the back room. Lily, the caretaker's daughter, did housemaid's work for them. Though their life was modest they believed in eating well; the best of everything: diamond-bone sirloins, three-shilling tea and the best bottled stout. But Lily seldom made a mistake in the orders so that she got on well with her three mistresses. They were fussy, that was all. But the only thing they would not stand was back answers.

Of course, they had good reason to be fussy on such a night. And then it was long after ten o'clock and yet there was no sign of Gabriel and his wife. Besides they were dreadfully afraid that Freddy Malins might turn up screwed. They would not wish for worlds that any of Mary Jane's pupils should see him under the influence; and when he was like that it was sometimes very hard to manage him. Freddy Malins always came late but they wondered what could be keeping Gabriel: and that was what brought them every two minutes to the banisters to ask Lily had Gabriel or Freddy come.

—O, Mr Conroy, said Lily to Gabriel when she opened the door for him, Miss Kate and Miss Julia thought you were never coming. Goodnight, Mrs Conroy.

—I'll engage they did, said Gabriel, but they forget that my wife here takes three mortal hours to dress herself.

He stood on the mat, scraping the snow from his goloshes, while Lily led his wife to the foot of the stairs and called out:

—Miss Kate, here's Mrs Conroy.

Kate and Julia came toddling down the dark stairs at once. Both of them kissed Gabriel's wife, said she must be perished alive and asked was Gabriel with her.

—Here I am as right as the mail, Aunt Kate! Go on up. I'll follow, called out Gabriel from the dark.

He continued scraping his feet vigorously while the three women went upstairs, laughing, to the ladies' dressing-room. A light fringe of snow lay like a cape on the shoulders of his overcoat and like toecaps on the toes of his goloshes; and, as the buttons of his overcoat slipped with a squeaking noise through the snow-stiffened frieze, a cold fragrant air from out-of-doors escaped from crevices and folds.

—Is it snowing again, Mr Conroy? asked Lily.

She had preceded him into the pantry to help him off with his overcoat. Gabriel smiled at the three syllables she had given his surname and glanced at her. She was a slim, growing girl, pale in complexion and with hay-coloured hair. The gas in the pantry made her look still paler. Gabriel had known her when she was a child and used to sit on the lowest step nursing a rag doll.

—Yes, Lily, he answered, and I think we're in for a night of it.

He looked up at the pantry ceiling, which was shaking with the stamping and shuffling of feet on the floor above, listened for a moment to the piano and then glanced at the girl, who was folding his overcoat carefully at the end of a shelf.

—Tell me, Lily, he said in a friendly tone, do you still go to school?

—O no, sir, she answered. I'm done schooling this year and more.

—O, then, said Gabriel gaily, I suppose we'll be going to your wedding one of these fine days with your young man, eh?

The girl glanced back at him over her shoulder and said with great bitterness:

—The men that is now is only all palaver and what they can get out of you.

Gabriel coloured as if he felt he had made a mistake and, without looking at her, kicked off his goloshes and flicked actively with his muffler at his patent-leather shoes.

He was a stout tallish young man. The high colour of his cheeks pushed upwards even to his forehead, where it scattered itself in a few formless patches of pale red; and on his hairless face there scintillated restlessly the polished lenses and the bright gilt rims of the glasses which screened his delicate and restless eyes. His glossy black hair was parted in the middle and brushed in a long curve behind his ears where it curled slightly beneath the groove left by his hat.

When he had flicked lustre into his shoes he stood up and pulled his waistcoat down more tightly on his plump body. Then he took a coin rapidly from his pocket.

—O Lily, he said, thrusting it into her hands, it's Christmas-time, isn't it? Just . . . here's a little. . . .

He walked rapidly towards the door.

—O no, sir! cried the girl, following him. Really, sir, I wouldn't take it.

—Christmas-time! Christmas-time! said Gabriel, almost trotting to the stairs and waving his hand to her in deprecation.

The girl, seeing that he had gained the stairs, called out after him:
—Well, thank you, sir.

He waited outside the drawing-room door until the waltz should finish, listening to the skirts that swept against it and to the shuffling of feet. He was still discomposed by the girl's bitter and sudden retort. It had cast a gloom over him which he tried to dispel by arranging his cuffs and the bows of his tie. Then he took from his waistcoat pocket a little paper and glanced at the headings he had made for his speech. He was undecided about the lines from Robert Browning for he feared they would be above the heads of his hearers. Some quotation that they would recognise from Shakespeare or from the Melodies would be better. The indelicate clacking of the men's heels and the shuffling of their soles reminded him that their grade of culture differed from his. He would only make himself ridiculous by quoting poetry to them which they could not understand. They would think that he was airing his superior education. He would fail with them just as he had failed with the girl in the pantry. He had taken up a wrong tone. His whole speech was a mistake from first to last, an utter failure.

Just then his aunts and his wife came out of the ladies' dressing-room. His aunts were two small plainly dressed old women. Aunt Julia was an inch or so the taller. Her hair, drawn low over the tops of her ears, was grey; and grey also, with darker shadows, was her large flaccid face. Though she was stout in build and stood erect her slow eyes and parted lips gave her the appearance of a woman who did not know where she was or where she was going. Aunt Kate was more vivacious. Her face, healthier than her sister's, was all puckers and creases, like a shrivelled red apple, and her hair, braided in the same old-fashioned way, had not lost its ripe nut colour.

They both kissed Gabriel frankly. He was their favourite nephew, the son of their dead elder sister, Ellen, who had married T. J. Conroy of the Port and Docks.

—Gretta tells me you're not going to take a cab back to Monkstown[1] tonight, Gabriel, said Aunt Kate.

—No, said Gabriel, turning to his wife, we had quite enough of that last year, hadn't we. Don't you remember, Aunt Kate, what a cold Gretta got out of it? Cab windows rattling all the way, and the east wind blowing in after we passed Merrion. Very jolly it was. Gretta caught a dreadful cold.

Aunt Kate frowned severely and nodded her head at every word.

—Quite right, Gabriel, quite right, she said. You can't be too careful.

—But as for Gretta there, said Gabriel, she'd walk home in the snow if she were let.

Mrs Conroy laughed.

—Don't mind him, Aunt Kate, she said. He's really an awful bother, what with green shades for Tom's eyes at night and making him do the dumb-bells, and forcing Eva to eat the stirabout.[2] The poor child! And she simply hates the sight of it! . . . O, but you'll never guess what he makes me wear now!

She broke out into a peal of laughter and glanced at her husband, whose admiring and happy eyes had been wandering from her dress to her face and hair. The two aunts laughed heartily too, for Gabriel's solicitude was a standing joke with them.

—Goloshes! said Mrs Conroy. That's the latest. Whenever it's wet underfoot I must put on my goloshes. Tonight even, he wanted me to put them on, but I wouldn't. The next thing he'll buy me will be a diving suit.

Gabriel laughed nervously and patted his tie reassuringly while Aunt Kate nearly doubled herself, so heartily did she enjoy the joke. The smile soon faded from Aunt Julia's face and her mirthless eyes were directed towards her nephew's face. After a pause she asked:

—And what are goloshes, Gabriel?

—Goloshes, Julia! exclaimed her sister. Goodness me, don't you know what goloshes are? You wear them over your . . . over your boots, Gretta, isn't it?

—Yes, said Mrs Conroy. Guttapercha[3] things. We both have a pair now. Gabriel says everyone wears them on the continent.

—O, on the continent, murmured Aunt Julia, nodding her head slowly.

Gabriel knitted his brows and said, as if he were slightly angered:

—It's nothing very wonderful but Gretta thinks it very funny because she says the word reminds her of Christy Minstrels.[4]

—But tell me, Gabriel, said Aunt Kate, with brisk tact. Of course, you've seen about the room. Gretta was saying . . .

---

[1] a prosperous residential suburb of Dublin
[2] oatmeal porridge   [3] a material resembling rubber
[4] black-face entertainers imitating Negro songs and jokes

—O, the room is all right, replied Gabriel. I've taken one in the Gresham.

—To be sure, said Aunt Kate, by far the best thing to do. And the children, Gretta, you're not anxious about them?

—O, for one night, said Mrs Conroy. Besides, Bessie will look after them.

—To be sure, said Aunt Kate again. What a comfort it is to have a girl like that, one you can depend on! There's that Lily, I'm sure I don't know what has come over her lately. She's not the girl she was at all.

Gabriel was about to ask his aunt some questions on this point but she broke off suddenly to gaze after her sister who had wandered down the stairs and was craning her neck over the banisters.

—Now I ask you, she said almost testily, where is Julia going? Julia! Julia! Where are you going?

Julia, who had gone half way down one flight, came back and announced blandly:

—Here's Freddy.

At the same moment a clapping of hands and a final flourish of the pianist told that the waltz had ended. The drawing-room door was opened from within and some couples came out. Aunt Kate drew Gabriel aside hurriedly and whispered into his ear:

—Slip down, Gabriel, like a good fellow and see if he's all right, and don't let him up if he's screwed. I'm sure he's screwed. I'm sure he is.

Gabriel went to the stairs and listened over the banisters. He could hear two persons talking in the pantry. Then he recognised Freddy Malins' laugh. He went down the stairs noisily.

—It's such a relief, said Aunt Kate to Mrs Conroy, that Gabriel is here. I always feel easier in my mind when he's here. . . . Julia, there's Miss Daly and Miss Power will take some refreshment. Thanks for your beautiful waltz, Miss Daly. It made lovely time.

A tall wizen-faced man, with a stiff grizzled moustache and swarthy skin, who was passing out with his partner, said:

—And may we have some refreshment, too, Miss Morkan?

—Julia, said Aunt Kate summarily, and here's Mr Browne and Miss Furlong. Take them in, Julia, with Miss Daly and Miss Power.

—I'm the man for the ladies, said Mr Browne, pursing his lips until his moustache bristled and smiling in all his wrinkles. You know, Miss Morkan, the reason they are so fond of me is—

He did not finish his sentence, but, seeing that Aunt Kate was out of earshot, at once led the three young ladies into the back room. The middle of the room was occupied by two square tables placed end to end, and on these Aunt Julia and the caretaker were straightening and smoothing a large cloth. On the sideboard were arrayed dishes and plates, and glasses and bundles of knives and forks and spoons. The top of the closed square piano served also as a sideboard for viands and sweets. At a smaller side-board in one corner two young men were standing, drinking hop-bitters.

Mr Browne led his charges thither and invited them all, in jest, to some ladies' punch, hot, strong and sweet. As they said they never took anything strong he opened three bottles of lemonade for them. Then he asked one of the young men to move aside, and, taking hold of the decanter, filled out for himself a goodly measure of whisky. The young men eyed him respectfully while he took a trial sip.

—God help me, he said, smiling, it's the doctor's orders.

His wizened face broke into a broader smile, and the three young ladies laughed in musical echo to his pleasantry, swaying their bodies to and fro, with nervous jerks of their shoulders. The boldest said:

—O, now, Mr Browne, I'm sure the doctor never ordered anything of the kind.

Mr Browne took another sip of his whisky and said, with sidling mimicry:

—Well, you see, I'm like the famous Mrs Cassidy, who is reported to have said: *Now, Mary Grimes, if I don't take it, make me take it, for I feel I want it.*

His hot face had leaned forward a little too confidentially and he had assumed a very low Dublin accent so that the young ladies, with one instinct, received his speech in silence. Miss Furlong, who was one of Mary Jane's pupils, asked Miss Daly what was the name of the pretty waltz she had played; and Mr Browne, seeing that he was ignored, turned promptly to the two young men who were more appreciative.

A red-faced young woman, dressed in pansy, came into the room, excitedly clapping her hands and crying:

—Quadrilles! Quadrilles!

Close on her heels came Aunt Kate, crying:

—Two gentlemen and three ladies, Mary Jane!

—O, here's Mr Bergin and Mr Kerrigan, said Mary Jane. Mr Kerrigan, will you take Miss Power? Miss Furlong, may I get you a partner, Mr Bergin. O, that'll just do now.

—Three ladies, Mary Jane, said Aunt Kate.

The two young gentlemen asked the ladies if they might have the pleasure, and Mary Jane turned to Miss Daly.

—O, Miss Daly, you're really awfully good, after playing for the last two dances, but really we're so short of ladies tonight.

—I don't mind in the least, Miss Morkan.

—But I've a nice partner for you, Mr Bartell D'Arcy, the tenor. I'll get him to sing later on. All Dublin is raving about him.

—Lovely voice, lovely voice! said Aunt Kate.

As the piano had twice begun the prelude to the first figure Mary Jane led her recruits quickly from the room. They had hardly gone when

Aunt Julia wandered slowly into the room, looking behind her at something.

—What is the matter, Julia? asked Aunt Kate anxiously. Who is it?

Julia, who was carrying in a column of table-napkins, turned to her
sister and said, simply, as if the question had surprised her:

—It's only Freddy, Kate, and Gabriel with him.

In fact right behind her Gabriel could be seen piloting Freddy Malins
across the landing. The latter, a young man of about forty, was of Gabriel's size and build, with very round shoulders. His face was fleshy and
pallid, touched with colour only at the thick hanging lobes of his ears and
at the wide wings of his nose. He had coarse features, a blunt nose, a
convex and receding brow, tumid and protruded lips. His heavy-lidded
eyes and the disorder of his scanty hair made him look sleepy. He was
laughing heartily in a high key at a story which he had been telling Gabriel on the stairs and at the same time rubbing the knuckles of his left
fist backwards and forwards into his left eye.

—Good evening, Freddy, said Aunt Julia.

Freddy Malins bade the Misses Morkan good-evening in what seemed
an offhand fashion by reason of the habitual catch in his voice and then,
seeing that Mr Browne was grinning at him from the sideboard, crossed
the room on rather shaky legs and began to repeat in an undertone the
story he had just told to Gabriel.

—He's not so bad, is he? said Aunt Kate to Gabriel.

Gabriel's brows were dark but he raised them quickly and answered:

—O, no, hardly noticeable.

—Now, isn't he a terrible fellow! she said. And his poor mother made
him take the pledge on New Year's Eve. But come on, Gabriel, into the
drawing-room.

Before leaving the room with Gabriel she signalled to Mr Browne by
frowning and shaking her forefinger in warning to and fro. Mr Browne
nodded in answer and, when she had gone, said to Freddy Malins:

—Now, then, Teddy, I'm going to fill you out a good glass of lemonade just to buck you up.

Freddy Malins, who was nearing the climax of his story, waved the
offer aside impatiently but Mr Browne, having first called Freddy Malins' attention to a disarray in his dress, filled out and handed him a full
glass of lemonade. Freddy Malins' left hand accepted the glass mechanically, his right hand being engaged in the mechanical readjustment
of his dress. Mr Browne, whose face was once more wrinkling with
mirth, poured out for himself a glass of whisky while Freddy Malins
exploded, before he had well reached the climax of his story, in a kink of
high-pitched bronchitic laughter and, setting down his untasted and overflowing glass, began to rub the knuckles of his left fist backwards and
forwards into his left eye, repeating words of his last phrase as well as his
fit of laughter would allow him.

. . . .

Gabriel could not listen while Mary Jane was playing her Academy piece, full of runs and difficult passages, to the hushed drawing-room. He liked music but the piece she was playing had no melody for him and he doubted whether it had any melody for the other listeners, though they had begged Mary Jane to play something. Four young men, who had just come from the refreshment room to stand in the doorway at the sound of the piano, had gone away quietly in couples after a few minutes. The only persons who seemed to follow the music were Mary Jane herself, her hands racing along the key-board or lifted from it at the pauses like those of a priestess in momentary imprecation, and Aunt Kate standing at her elbow to turn the page.

Gabriel's eyes, irritated by the floor, which glittered with beeswax under the heavy chandelier, wandered to the wall above the piano. A picture of the balcony scene in *Romeo and Juliet* hung there and beside it was a picture of the two murdered princes in the Tower[5] which Aunt Julia had worked in red, blue and brown wools when she was a girl. Probably in the school they had gone to as girls that kind of work had been taught, for one year his mother had worked for him as a birthday present a waistcoat of purple tabinet,[6] with little foxes' heads upon it, lined with brown satin and having round mulberry buttons. It was strange that his mother had had no musical talent though Aunt Kate used to call her the brains carrier of the Morkan family. Both she and Julia had always seemed a little proud of their serious and matronly sister. Her photograph stood before the pierglass. She held an open book on her knees and was pointing out something in it to Constantine who, dressed in a man o'-war suit, lay at her feet. It was she who had chosen the names for her sons for she was very sensible of the dignity of family life. Thanks to her, Constantine was now senior curate in Balbriggan and, thanks to her, Gabriel himself had taken his degree in the Royal University. A shadow passed over his face as he remembered her sullen opposition to his marriage. Some slighting phrases she had used still rankled in his memory; she had once spoken of Gretta as being country cute and that was not true of Gretta at all. It was Gretta who had nursed her during all her last long illness in their house at Monkstown.

He knew that Mary Jane must be near the end of her piece for she was playing again the opening melody with runs of scales after every bar and while he waited for the end the resentment died down in his heart. The piece ended with a trill of octaves in the treble and a final deep octave in the bass. Great applause greeted Mary Jane as, blushing and rolling up her music nervously, she escaped from the room. The most vigorous

---

[5] Edward V, Prince of Wales, and Richard, Duke of York, were murdered in 1483 in the Tower of London, presumably on the orders of their uncle, King Richard III.
[6] a fabric of silk and wool

clapping came from the four young men in the doorway who had gone away to the refreshment-room at the beginning of the piece but had come back when the piano had stopped.

Lancers[7] were arranged. Gabriel found himself partnered with Miss Ivors. She was a frank-mannered talkative young lady, with a freckled face and prominent brown eyes. She did not wear a low-cut bodice and the large brooch which was fixed in the front of her collar bore on it an Irish device.

When they had taken their places she said abruptly :

—I have a crow to pluck with you.

—With me? said Gabriel.

She nodded her head gravely.

—What is it? asked Gabriel, smiling at her solemn manner.

—Who is G. C.? answered Miss Ivors, turning her eyes upon him.

Gabriel coloured and was about to knit his brows, as if he did not understand, when she said bluntly :

—O, innocent Amy! I have found out that you write for *The Daily Express*. Now aren't you ashamed of yourself?

—Why should I be ashamed of myself? asked Gabriel, blinking his eyes and trying to smile.

—Well, I'm ashamed of you, said Miss Ivors frankly. To say you'd write for a rag like that. I didn't think you were a West Briton.

A look of perplexity appeared on Gabriel's face. It was true that he wrote a literary column every Wednesday in *The Daily Express*, for which he was paid fifteen shillings. But that did not make him a West Briton surely. The books he received for review were almost more welcome than the paltry cheque. He loved to feel the covers and turn over the pages of newly printed books. Nearly every day when his teaching in the college was ended he used to wander down the quays to the second-hand booksellers, to Hickey's on Bachelor's Walk, to Webb's or Massey's on Aston's Quay, or to O'Clohissey's in the by-street. He did not know how to meet her charge. He wanted to say that literature was above politics. But they were friends of many years' standing and their careers had been parallel, first at the University and then as teachers : he could not risk a grandiose phrase with her. He continued blinking his eyes and trying to smile and murmured lamely that he saw nothing political in writing reviews of books.

When their turn to cross had come he was still perplexed and inattentive. Miss Ivors promptly took his hand in a warm grasp and said in a soft friendly tone :

—Of course, I was only joking. Come, we cross now.

When they were together again she spoke of the University question and Gabriel felt more at ease. A friend of hers had shown her his review

[7] a kind of quadrille

of Browning's poems. That was how she had found out the secret: but she liked the review immensely. Then she said suddenly:

—O, Mr Conroy, you will come for an excursion to the Aran Isles[8] this summer? We're going to stay there a whole month. It will be splendid out in the Atlantic. You ought to come. Mr Clancy is coming, and Mr Kilkelly and Kathleen Kearney. It would be splendid for Gretta too if she'd come. She's from Connacht,[9] isn't she?

—Her people are, said Gabriel shortly.

—But you will come, won't you? said Miss Ivors, laying her warm hand eagerly on his arm.

—The fact is, said Gabriel, I have just arranged to go—

—Go where? asked Miss Ivors.

—Well, you know, every year I go for a cycling tour with some fellows and so—

—But where? asked Miss Ivors.

—Well, we usually go to France or Belgium or perhaps Germany, said Gabriel awkwardly.

—And why do you go to France and Belgium, said Miss Ivors, instead of visiting your own land?

—Well, said Gabriel, it's partly to keep in touch with the languages and partly for a change.

—And haven't you your own language to keep in touch with—Irish? asked Miss Ivors.

—Well, said Gabriel, if it comes to that, you know, Irish is not my language.

Their neighbours had turned to listen to the cross-examination. Gabriel glanced right and left nervously and tried to keep his good humour under the ordeal which was making a blush invade his forehead.

—And haven't you your own land to visit, continued Miss Ivors, that you know nothing of, your own people, and your own country?

—O, to tell you the truth, retorted Gabriel suddenly, I'm sick of my own country, sick of it!

—Why? asked Miss Ivors.

Gabriel did not answer for his retort had heated him.

—Why? repeated Miss Ivors.

They had to go visiting together and, as he had not answered her, Miss Ivors said warmly:

—Of course, you've no answer.

Gabriel tried to cover his agitation by taking part in the dance with great energy. He avoided her eyes for he had seen a sour expression on her face. But when they met in the long chain he was surprised to feel his hand firmly pressed. She looked at him from under her brows for a mo-

---

[8] group of islands at the entrance to Galway Bay on the west coast of Ireland
[9] a province in the northwest of Ireland

ment quizzically until he smiled. Then, just as the chain was about to start again, she stood on tiptoe and whispered into his ear:

—West Briton!

When the lancers were over Gabriel went away to a remote corner of the room where Freddy Malins' mother was sitting. She was a stout feeble old woman with white hair. Her voice had a catch in it like her son's and she stuttered slightly. She had been told that Freddy had come and that he was nearly all right. Gabriel asked her whether she had had a good crossing. She lived with her married daughter in Glasgow and came to Dublin on a visit once a year. She answered placidly that she had had a beautiful crossing and that the captain had been most attentive to her. She spoke also of the beautiful house her daughter kept in Glasgow, and of all the nice friends they had there. While her tongue rambled on Gabriel tried to banish from his mind all memory of the unpleasant incident with Miss Ivors. Of course the girl or woman, or whatever she was, was an enthusiast but there was a time for all things. Perhaps he ought not to have answered her like that. But she had no right to call him a West Briton before people, even in joke. She had tried to make him ridiculous before people, heckling him and staring at him with her rabbit's eyes.

He saw his wife making her way towards him through the waltzing couples. When she reached him she said into his ear:

—Gabriel, Aunt Kate wants to know won't you carve the goose as usual. Miss Daly will carve the ham and I'll do the pudding.

—All right, said Gabriel.

—She's sending in the younger ones first as soon as this waltz is over so that we'll have the table to ourselves.

—Were you dancing? asked Gabriel.

—Of course I was. Didn't you see me? What words had you with Molly Ivors?

—No words. Why? Did she say so?

—Something like that. I'm trying to get that Mr D'Arcy to sing. He's full of conceit, I think.

—There were no words, said Gabriel moodily, only she wanted me to go for a trip to the west of Ireland and I said I wouldn't.

His wife clasped her hands excitedly and gave a little jump.

—O, do go, Gabriel, she cried, I'd love to see Galway again.

—You can go if you like, said Gabriel coldly.

She looked at him for a moment, then turned to Mrs Malins and said:

—There's a nice husband for you, Mrs Malins.

While she was threading her way back across the room Mrs Malins, without adverting to the interruption, went on to tell Gabriel what beautiful places there were in Scotland and beautiful scenery. Her son-in-law brought them every year to the lakes and they used to go fishing. Her son-in-law was a splendid fisher. One day he caught a fish, a beautiful big big fish, and the man in the hotel boiled it for their dinner.

Gabriel hardly heard what she said. Now that supper was coming near he began to think again about his speech and about the quotation. When he saw Freddy Malins coming across the room to visit his mother Gabriel left the chair free for him and retired into the embrasure of the window. The room had already cleared and from the back room came the clatter of plates and knives. Those who still remained in the drawing-room seemed tired of dancing and were conversing quietly in little groups. Gabriel's warm trembling fingers tapped the cold pane of the window. How cool it must be outside! How pleasant it would be to walk out alone, first along by the river and then through the park! The snow would be lying on the branches of the trees and forming a bright cap on the top of the Wellington Monument. How much more pleasant it would be there than at the supper-table!

He ran over the headings of his speech: Irish hospitality, sad memories, the Three Graces, Paris, the quotation from Browning. He repeated to himself a phrase he had written in his review: *One feels that one is listening to a thought-tormented music.* Miss Ivors had praised the review. Was she sincere? Had she really any life of her own behind all her propagandism? There had never been any ill-feeling between them until that night. It unnerved him to think that she would be at the supper-table, looking up at him while he spoke with her critical quizzing eyes. Perhaps she would not be sorry to see him fail in his speech. An idea came into his mind and gave him courage. He would say, alluding to Aunt Kate and Aunt Julia: *Ladies and Gentlemen, the generation which is now on the wane among us may have had its faults but for my part I think it had certain qualities of hospitality, of humour, of humanity, which the new and very serious and hypereducated generation that is growing up around us seems to me to lack.* Very good: that was one for Miss Ivors. What did he care that his aunts were only two ignorant old women?

A murmur in the room attracted his attention. Mr Browne was advancing from the door, gallantly escorting Aunt Julia, who leaned upon his arm, smiling and hanging her head. An irregular musketry of applause escorted her also as far as the piano and then, as Mary Jane seated herself on the stool, and Aunt Julia, no longer smiling, half turned so as to pitch her voice fairly into the room, gradually ceased. Gabriel recognised the prelude. It was that of an old song of Aunt Julia's—*Arrayed for the Bridal.* Her voice, strong and clear in tone, attacked with great spirit the runs which embellish the air and though she sang very rapidly she did not miss even the smallest of the grace notes. To follow the voice, without looking at the singer's face, was to feel and share the excitement of swift and secure flight. Gabriel applauded loudly with all the others at the close of the song and loud applause was borne in from the invisible supper-table. It sounded so genuine that a little colour struggled into Aunt Julia's face as she bent to replace in the music-stand the old leather-bound songbook that had her initials on the cover. Freddy Malins, who had listened with his head perched sideways to hear her better, was still applauding when everyone else had ceased and talking animatedly to his mother who nodded her head gravely and slowly in acquiescence. At last, when he could clap no more, he stood up suddenly and hurried across the room to Aunt Julia whose hand he seized and held in both his hands, shaking it when words failed him or the catch in his voice proved too much for him.

—I was just telling my mother, he said, I never heard you sing so well, never. No, I never heard your voice so good as it is to-night. Now! Would you believe that now? That's the truth. Upon my word and honour that's the truth. I never heard your voice sound so fresh and so . . . so clear and fresh, never.

Aunt Julia smiled broadly and murmured something about compliments as she released her hand from his grasp. Mr Browne extended his open hand towards her and said to those who were near him in the manner of a showman introducing a prodigy to an audience:

—Miss Julia Morkan, my latest discovery.

He was laughing very heartily at this himself when Freddy Malins turned to him and said:

—Well, Browne, if you're serious you might make a worse discovery. All I can say is I never heard her sing half so well as long as I am coming here. And that's the honest truth.

—Neither did I, said Mr Browne. I think her voice has greatly improved.

Aunt Julia shrugged her shoulders and said with meek pride:

—Thirty years ago I hadn't a bad voice as voices go.

—I often told Julia, said Aunt Kate emphatically, that she was simply thrown away in that choir. But she never would be said by me.

She turned as if to appeal to the good sense of the others against a refractory child while Aunt Julia gazed in front of her, a vague smile of reminiscence playing on her face.

—No, continued Aunt Kate, she wouldn't be said or led by anyone, slaving there in that choir night and day, night and day. Six o'clock on Christmas morning! And all for what?

—Well, isn't it for the honour of God, Aunt Kate? asked Mary Jane, twisting round on the piano-stool and smiling.

Aunt Kate turned fiercely on her niece and said:

—I know all about the honour of God, Mary Jane, but I think it's not at all honourable for the pope to turn out the women out of the choirs that have slaved there all their lives and put little whippersnappers of boys over their heads. I suppose it is for the good of the Church if the pope does it. But it's not just, Mary Jane, and it's not right.

She had worked herself into a passion and would have continued in defence of her sister for it was a sore subject with her but Mary Jane, seeing that all the dancers had come back, intervened pacifically:

—Now, Aunt Kate, you're giving scandal to Mr Browne who is of the other persuasion.

Aunt Kate turned to Mr Browne, who was grinning at this allusion to his religion, and said hastily:

—O, I don't question the pope's being right. I'm only a stupid old woman and I wouldn't presume to do such a thing. But there's such a thing as common everyday politeness and gratitude. And if I were in Julia's place I'd tell that Father Healey straight up to his face . . .

—And besides, Aunt Kate, said Mary Jane, we really are all hungry and when we are hungry we are all very quarrelsome.

—And when we are thirsty we are also quarrelsome, added Mr Browne.

—So that we had better go to supper, said Mary Jane, and finish the discussion afterwards.

On the landing outside the drawing-room Gabriel found his wife and Mary Jane trying to persuade Miss Ivors to stay for supper. But Miss Ivors, who had put on her hat and was buttoning her cloak, would not stay. She did not feel in the least hungry and she had already overstayed her time.

—But only for ten minutes, Molly, said Mrs Conroy. That won't delay you.

—To take a pick itself, said Mary Jane, after all your dancing.

—I really couldn't, said Miss Ivors.

—I am afraid you didn't enjoy yourself at all, said Mary Jane hopelessly.

—Ever so much, I assure you, said Miss Ivors, but you really must let me run off now.

—But how can you get home? asked Mrs Conroy.

—O, it's only two steps up the quay.

Gabriel hesitated a moment and said:

—If you will allow me, Miss Ivors, I'll see you home if you are really obliged to go.

But Miss Ivors broke away from them.

—I won't hear of it, she cried. For goodness sake go in to your suppers and don't mind me. I'm quite well able to take care of myself.

—Well, you're the comical girl, Molly, said Mrs Conroy frankly.

—*Beannacht libh,*[10] cried Miss Ivors, with a laugh, as she ran down the staircase.

Mary Jane gazed after her, a moody puzzled expression on her face, while Mrs. Conroy leaned over the banisters to listen for the hall-door. Gabriel asked himself was he the cause of her abrupt departure. But she did not seem to be in ill humour: she had gone away laughing. He stared blankly down the staircase.

At the moment Aunt Kate came toddling out of the supper-room, almost wringing her hands in despair.

—Where is Gabriel? she cried. Where on earth is Gabriel? There's everyone waiting in there, stage to let, and nobody to carve the goose!

---

[10] Blessings upon you.

—Here I am, Aunt Kate! cried Gabriel, with sudden animation, ready to carve a flock of geese, if necessary.

A fat brown goose lay at one end of the table and at the other end, on a bed of creased paper strewn with sprigs of parsley, lay a great ham, stripped of its outer skin and peppered over with crust crumbs, a neat paper frill round its shin and beside this was a round of spiced beef. Between these rival ends ran parallel lines of side-dishes: two little minsters of jelly, red and yellow; a shallow dish of blocks of blancmange and red jam, a large green leaf-shaped dish with a stalk-shaped handle, on which lay bunches of purple raisins and peeled almonds, a companion dish on which lay a solid rectangle of Smyrna figs, a dish of custard topped with grated nutmeg, a small bowl full of chocolates and sweets wrapped in gold and silver papers and a glass vase in which stood some tall celery stalks. In the centre of the table there stood, as sentries to a fruit-stand which upheld a pyramid of oranges and American apples, two squat old-fashioned decanters of cut glass, one containing port and the other dark sherry. On the closed square piano a pudding in a huge yellow dish lay in waiting and behind it were three squads of bottles of stout and ale and minerals, drawn up according to the colours of their uniforms, the first two black, with brown and red labels, the third and smallest squad white, with transverse green sashes.

Gabriel took his seat boldly at the head of the table and, having looked to the edge of the carver, plunged his fork firmly into the goose. He felt quite at ease now for he was an expert carver and liked nothing better than to find himself at the head of a well-laden table.

—Miss Furlong, what shall I send you? he asked. A wing or a slice of the breast?

—Just a small slice of the breast.

—Miss Higgins, what for you?

—O, anything at all, Mr Conroy.

While Gabriel and Miss Daly exchanged plates of goose and plates of ham and spiced beef Lily went from guest to guest with a dish of hot floury potatoes wrapped in a white napkin. This was Mary Jane's idea and she had also suggested apple sauce for the goose but Aunt Kate had said that plain roast goose without any apple sauce had always been good enough for her and she hoped she might never eat worse. Mary Jane waited on her pupils and saw that they got the best slices and Aunt Kate and Aunt Julia opened and carried across from the piano bottles of stout and ale for the gentlemen and bottles of minerals for the ladies. There was a great deal of confusion and laughter and noise, the noise of orders and counter-orders, of knives and forks, of corks and glass-stoppers. Gabriel began to carve second helpings as soon as he had finished the first round without serving himself. Everyone protested loudly so that he compromised by taking a long draught of stout for he had found the carving hot work. Mary Jane settled down quietly to her supper but Aunt Kate and Aunt Julia were still toddling round the table, walking on each other's heels, getting in each other's way and giving each other unheeded orders. Mr Browne begged of them to sit down and eat their suppers and so did Gabriel but they said there was time enough so that, at last, Freddy Malins stood up and, capturing Aunt Kate, plumped her down on her chair amid general laughter.

When everyone had been well served Gabriel said, smiling:

—Now, if anyone wants a little more of what vulgar people call stuffing let him or her speak.

A chorus of voices invited him to begin his own supper and Lily came forward with three potatoes which she had reserved for him.

—Very well, said Gabriel amiably, as he took another preparatory draught, kindly forget my existence, ladies and gentlemen, for a few minutes.

He set to his supper and took no part in the conversation with which the table covered Lily's removal of the plates. The subject of talk was the opera company which was then at the Theatre Royal. Mr Bartell D'Arcy, the tenor, a dark-complexioned young man with a smart moustache, praised very highly the leading contralto of the company but Miss Furlong thought she had a rather vulgar style of production. Freddy Malins said there was a Negro chieftain singing in the second part of the Gaiety pantomime who had one of the finest tenor voices he had ever heard.

—Have you heard him? he asked Mr Bartell D'Arcy across the table.

—No, answered Mr Bartell D'Arcy carelessly.

—Because, Freddy Malins explained, now I'd be curious to hear your opinion of him. I think he has a grand voice.

—It takes Teddy to find out the really good things, said Mr Browne familiarly to the table.

—And why couldn't he have a voice too? asked Freddy Malins sharply. Is it because he's only a black?

Nobody answered this question and Mary Jane led the table back to the legitimate opera. One of her pupils had given her a pass for *Mignon*. Of course it was very fine, she said, but it made her think of poor Georgina Burns. Mr Browne could go back farther still, to the old Italian companies that used to come to Dublin—Tietjens, Ilma de Murzka, Campanini, the great Trebelli, Giuglini, Ravelli, Aramburo. Those were the days, he said, when there was something like singing to be heard in Dublin. He told too of how the top gallery of the old Royal used to be packed night after night, of how one night an Italian tenor had sung five encores to *Let Me Like a Soldier Fall*, introducing a high C every time, and of how the gallery boys would sometimes in their enthusiasm unyoke the horses from the carriage of some great *prima donna* and pull her themselves through the streets to her hotel. Why did they never play the grand old operas now, he asked, *Dinorah, Lucrezia Borgia?* Because they could not get the voices to sing them: that was why.

—O, well, said Mr Bartell D'Arcy, I presume there are as good singers today as there were then.

—Where are they? asked Mr Browne defiantly.

—In London, Paris, Milan, said Mr Bartell D'Arcy warmly. I suppose Caruso,[11] for example, is quite as good, if not better than any of the men you have mentioned.

—Maybe so, said Mr Browne. But I may tell you I doubt it strongly.

—O, I'd give anything to hear Caruso sing, said Mary Jane.

—For me, said Aunt Kate, who had been picking a bone, there was only one tenor. To please me, I mean. But I suppose none of you ever heard of him.

—Who was he, Miss Morkan? asked Mr Bartell D'Arcy politely.

—His name, said Aunt Kate, was Parkinson. I heard him when he was in his prime and I think he had then the purest tenor voice that was ever put into a man's throat.

—Strange, said Mr Bartell D'Arcy. I never even heard of him.

—Yes, yes, Miss Morkan is right, said Mr Browne. I remember hearing of old Parkinson but he's too far back for me.

—A beautiful pure sweet mellow English tenor, said Aunt Kate with enthusiasm.

Gabriel having finished, the huge pudding was transferred to the table. The clatter of forks and spoons began again. Gabriel's wife served out spoonfuls of the pudding and passed the plates down the table. Midway down they were held up by Mary Jane, who replenished them with raspberry or orange jelly or with blancmange and jam. The pudding was of Aunt Julia's making and she received praises for it from all quarters. She herself said that it was not quite brown enough.

—Well, I hope, Miss Morkan, said Mr Browne, that I'm brown enough for you because, you know, I'm all brown.

All the gentlemen, except Gabriel, ate some of the pudding out of compliment to Aunt Julia. As Gabriel never ate sweets the celery had been left for him. Freddy Malins also took a stalk of celery and ate it with his pudding. He had been told that celery was a capital thing for the blood and he was just then under doctor's care. Mrs Malins, who had been silent all through the supper, said that her son was going down to Mount Melleray in a week or so. The table then spoke of Mount Melleray, how bracing the air was down there, how hospitable the monks were and how they never asked for a penny-piece from their guests.

—And do you mean to say, asked Mr Browne, incredulously, that a chap can go down there and put up there as if it were a hotel and live on the fat of the land and then come away without paying a farthing?

—O, most people give some donation to the monastery when they leave, said Mary Jane.

[11] Enrico Caruso, 1873–1921, perhaps the greatest of Italian tenors

—I wish we had an institution like that in our Church, said Mr Browne candidly.

He was astonished to hear that the monks never spoke, got up at two in the morning and slept in their coffins. He asked what they did it for.

—That's the rule of the order, said Aunt Kate firmly.

—Yes, but why? asked Mr Browne.

Aunt Kate repeated that it was the rule, that was all. Mr Browne still seemed not to understand. Freddy Malins explained to him, as best he could, that the monks were trying to make up for the sins committed by all the sinners in the outside world. The explanation was not very clear for Mr Browne grinned and said:

—I like that idea very much but wouldn't a comfortable spring bed do them as well as a coffin?

—The coffin, said Mary Jane, is to remind them of their last end.

As the subject had grown lugubrious it was buried in a silence of the table during which Mrs Malins could be heard saying to her neighbour in an indistinct undertone:

—They are very good men, the monks, very pious men.

The raisins and almonds and figs and apples and oranges and chocolates and sweets were now passed about the table and Aunt Julia invited all the guests to have either port or sherry. At first Mr Bartell D'Arcy refused to take either but one of his neighbours nudged him and whispered something to him upon which he allowed his glass to be filled. Gradually as the last glasses were being filled the conversation ceased. A pause followed, broken only by the noise of the wine and by unsettlings of chairs. The Misses Morkan, all three, looked down at the tablecloth. Some one coughed once or twice and then a few gentlemen patted the table gently as a signal for silence. The silence came and Gabriel pushed back his chair and stood up.

The patting at once grew louder in encouragement and then ceased altogether. Gabriel leaned his ten trembling fingers on the tablecloth and smiled nervously at the company. Meeting a row of upturned faces he raised his eyes to the chandelier. The piano was playing a waltz tune and he could hear the skirts sweeping against the drawing-room door. People, perhaps, were standing in the snow on the quay outside, gazing up at the lighted windows and listening to the waltz music. The air was pure there. In the distance lay the park where the trees were weighted with snow. The Wellington Monument wore a gleaming cap of snow that flashed westward over the white field of Fifteen Acres.

He began:

—Ladies and Gentlemen.

—It has fallen to my lot this evening, as in years past, to perform a very pleasing task but a task for which I am afraid my poor powers as a speaker are all too inadequate.

—No, no! said Mr Browne.

—But, however that may be, I can only ask you tonight to take the

will for the deed and to lend me your attention for a few moments while
I endeavour to express to you in words what my feelings are on this occasion.

—Ladies and Gentlemen. It is not the first time that we have gathered
together under this hospitable roof, around this hospitable board. It is
not the first time that we have been the recipients—or perhaps, I had
better say, the victims—of the hospitality of certain good ladies.

He made a circle in the air with his arm and paused. Every one laughed
or smiled at Aunt Kate and Aunt Julia and Mary Jane who all turned
crimson with pleasure. Gabriel went on more boldly:

—I feel more strongly with every recurring year that our country has
no tradition which does it so much honour and which it should guard so
jealously as that of its hospitality. It is a tradition that is unique as far as
my experience goes (and I have visited not a few places abroad) among
the modern nations. Some would say, perhaps, that with us it is rather a
failing than anything to be boasted of. But granted even that, it is, to my
mind, a princely failing, and one that I trust will long be cultivated among
us. Of one thing, at least, I am sure. As long as this one roof shelters the
good ladies aforesaid—and I wish from my heart it may do so for many
and many a long year to come—the tradition of genuine warm-hearted
courteous Irish hospitality, which our forefathers have handed down to
us and which we in turn must hand down to our descendants, is still alive
among us.

A hearty murmur of assent ran round the table. It shot through Gabriel's mind that Miss Ivors was not there and that she had gone away
discourteously: and he said with confidence in himself:

—Ladies and Gentlemen.

—A new generation is growing up in our midst, a generation actuated
by new ideas and new principles. It is serious and enthusiastic for these
new ideas and its enthusiasm, even when it is misdirected, is, I believe, in
the main sincere. But we are living in a sceptical and, if I may use the
phrase, a thought-tormented age: and sometimes I fear that this new
generation, educated or hypereducated as it is, will lack those qualities of
humanity, of hospitality, of kindly humour which belonged to an older
day. Listening tonight to the names of all those great singers of the past
it seemed to me, I must confess, that we were living in a less spacious
age. Those days might, without exaggeration, be called spacious days:
and if they are gone beyond recall let us hope, at least, that in gatherings
such as this we shall still speak of them with pride and affection, still
cherish in our hearts the memory of those dead and gone great ones
whose fame the world will not willingly let die."

—Hear, hear! said Mr Browne loudly.

—But yet, continued Gabriel, his voice falling into a softer inflection,
there are always in gatherings such as this sadder thoughts that will recur
to our minds: thoughts of the past, of youth, of changes, of absent faces

that we miss here tonight. Our path through life is strewn with many such sad memories: and were we to brood upon them always we could not find the heart to go on bravely with our work among the living. We have all of us living duties and living affections which claim, and rightly claim, our strenuous endeavours.

—Therefore, I will not linger on the past. I will not let any gloomy moralising intrude upon us here tonight. Here we are gathered together for a brief moment from the bustle and rush of our everyday routine. We are met here as friends, in the spirit of good-fellowship, as colleagues, also to a certain extent, in the true spirit of *camaraderie*, and as the guests of—what shall I call them?—the Three Graces[12] of the Dublin musical world.

The table burst into applause and laughter at this sally. Aunt Julia vainly asked each of her neighbours in turn to tell her what Gabriel had said.

—He says we are the Three Graces, Aunt Julia, said Mary Jane.

Aunt Julia did not understand but she looked up, smiling, at Gabriel, who continued in the same vein:

—Ladies and Gentlemen.

—I will not attempt to play tonight the part that Paris[13] played on another occasion. I will not attempt to choose between them. The task would be an invidious one and one beyond my poor powers. For when I view them in turn, whether it be our chief hostess herself, whose good heart, whose too good heart, has become a byword with all who know her, or her sister, who seems to be gifted with perennial youth and whose singing must have been a surprise and a revelation to us all tonight, or, last but not least, when I consider our youngest hostess, talented, cheerful, hard-working and the best of nieces, I confess, Ladies and Gentlemen, that I do not know to which of them I should award the prize.

Gabriel glanced down at his aunts and, seeing the large smile on Aunt Julia's face and the tears which had risen to Aunt Kate's eyes, hastened to his close. He raised his glass of port gallantly, while every member of the company fingered a glass expectantly, and said loudly:

—Let us toast them all three together. Let us drink to their health, wealth, long life, happiness and prosperity and may they long continue to hold the proud and self-won position which they hold in their profession and the position of honour and affection which they hold in our hearts.

All the guests stood up, glass in hand, and turning towards the three seated ladies, sang in unison, with Mr Browne as leader:

[12] three beautiful young women, Aglaia, Euphrosyne, and Thalia, attendants to Aphrodite, goddess of love

[13] Zeus appointed Paris to award a golden apple marked "For the Fairest" to one of three claimants. Paris awarded it to Aphrodite and incurred the enmity of Athena and Hera.

For they are jolly gay fellows,
For they are jolly gay fellows,
For they are jolly gay fellows,
Which nobody can deny.

Aunt Kate was making frank use of her handkerchief and even Aunt Julia seemed moved. Freddy Malins beat time with his pudding-fork and the singers turned towards one another, as if in melodious conference, while they sang with emphasis:

Unless he tells a lie,
Unless he tells a lie.

Then, turning once more towards their hostesses, they sang:

For they are jolly gay fellows,
For they are jolly gay fellows,
For they are jolly gay fellows,
Which nobody can deny.

The acclamation which followed was taken up beyond the door of the supper-room by many of the other guests and renewed time after time, Freddy Malins acting as officer with his fork on high.

.   .   .   .

The piercing morning air came into the hall where they were standing so that Aunt Kate said:

—Close the door, somebody. Mrs Malins will get her death of cold.

—Browne is out there, Aunt Kate, said Mary Jane.

Browne is everywhere, said Aunt Kate, lowering her voice.

Mary Jane laughed at her tone.

—Really, she said archly, he is very attentive.

—He has been laid on here like the gas, said Aunt Kate in the same tone, all during the Christmas.

She laughed herself this time good-humouredly and then added quickly:

—But tell him to come in, Mary Jane, and close the door. I hope to goodness he didn't hear me.

At that moment the hall-door was opened and Mr Browne came in from the doorstep, laughing as if his heart would break. He was dressed in a long green overcoat with mock astrakhan cuffs and collar and wore on his head an oval fur cap. He pointed down the snow-covered quay from where the sound of shrill prolonged whistling was borne in.

—Teddy will have all the cabs in Dublin out, he said.

Gabriel advanced from the little pantry behind the office, struggling into his overcoat and, looking round the hall, said:

—Gretta not down yet?

—She's getting on her things, Gabriel, said Aunt Kate.

—Who's playing up there? asked Gabriel.

—Nobody. They're all gone.

—O no, Aunt Kate, said Mary Jane. Bartell D'Arcy and Miss O'Callaghan aren't gone yet.

—Someone is strumming at the piano anyhow, said Gabriel.

Mary Jane glanced at Gabriel and Mr Browne and said with a shiver:

—It makes me feel cold to look at you two gentlemen muffled up like that. I wouldn't like to face your journey home at this hour.

—I'd like nothing better this minute, said Mr Browne stoutly, than a rattling fine walk in the country or a fast drive with a good spanking goer between the shafts.

—We used to have a very good horse and trap at home, said Aunt Julia sadly.

—The never-to-be-forgotten Johnny, said Mary Jane, laughing.

Aunt Kate and Gabriel laughed too.

—Why, what was wonderful about Johnny? asked Mr Browne.

—The late lamented Patrick Morkan, our grandfather, that is, explained Gabriel, commonly known in his later years as the old gentleman, was a glue-boiler.

—O, now, Gabriel, said Aunt Kate, laughing, he had a starch mill.

—Well, glue or starch, said Gabriel, the old gentleman had a horse by the name of Johnny. And Johnny used to work in the old gentleman's mill, walking round and round in order to drive the mill. That was all very well; but now comes the tragic part about Johnny. One fine day the old gentleman thought he'd like to drive out with the quality to a military review in the park.

—The Lord have mercy on his soul, said Aunt Kate compassionately.

—Amen, said Gabriel. So the old gentleman, as I said, harnessed Johnny and put on his very best tall hat and his very best stock collar and drove out in grand style from his ancestral mansion somewhere near Back Lane, I think.

Everyone laughed, even Mrs. Malins, at Gabriel's manner and Aunt Kate said:

—O, now, Gabriel, he didn't live in Back Lane, really. Only the mill was there.

—Out from the mansion of his forefathers, continued Gabriel, he drove with Johnny. And everything went on beautifully until Johnny came in sight of King Billy's[14] statue: and whether he fell in love with the horse King Billy sits on or whether he thought he was back again in the mill, anyhow he began to walk round the statue.

Gabriel paced in a circle round the hall in his goloshes amid the laughter of the others.

—Round and round he went, said Gabriel, and the old gentleman, who

[14] King William III of England

was a very pompous old gentleman, was highly indignant. *Go on, sir!
What do you mean, sir? Johnny! Johnny! Most extraordinary conduct! Can't
understand the horse!*

The peals of laughter which followed Gabriel's imitation of the incident was interrupted by a resounding knock at the hall-door. Mary Jane
ran to open it and let in Freddy Malins. Freddy Malins, with his hat well
back on his head and his shoulders humped with cold, was puffing and
steaming after his exertions.

—I could only get one cab, he said.

—O, we'll find another along the quay, said Gabriel.

—Yes, said Aunt Kate. Better not keep Mrs Malins standing in the
draught.

Mrs Malins was helped down the front steps by her son and Mr
Browne and, after many manoeuvres, hoisted into the cab. Freddy Malins
clambered in after her and spent a long time settling her on the seat, Mr
Browne helping him with advice. At last she was settled comfortably
and Freddy Malins invited Mr Browne into the cab. There was a good
deal of confused talk, and then Mr Browne got into the cab. The cabman
settled his rug over his knees, and bent down for the address. The confusion grew greater and the cabman was directed differently by Freddy
Malins and Mr Browne, each of whom had his head out through a window of the cab. The difficulty was to know where to drop Mr Browne
along the route and Aunt Kate, Aunt Julia and Mary Jane helped the discussion from the doorstep with cross-directions and contradictions and
abundance of laughter. As for Freddy Malins he was speechless with
laughter. He popped his head in and out of the window every moment, to
the great danger of his hat, and told his mother how the discussion was
progressing, till at last Mr Browne shouted to the bewildered cabman
above the din of everybody's laughter:

—Do you know Trinity College?

—Yes, sir, said the cabman.

—Well, drive bang up against Trinity College gates, said Mr Browne,
and then we'll tell you where to go. You understand now?

—Yes, sir, said the cabman.

—Make like a bird for Trinity College.

—Right, sir, said the cabman.

The horse was whipped up and the cab rattled off along the quay amid
a chorus of laughter and adieus.

Gabriel had not gone to the door with the others. He was in a dark
part of the hall gazing up the staircase. A woman was standing near the
top of the first flight, in the shadow also. He could not see her face but
he could see the terra-cotta and salmon-pink panels of her skirt which
the shadow made appear black and white. It was his wife. She was leaning on the banisters, listening to something. Gabriel was surprised at her
stillness and strained his ear to listen also. But he could hear little save

the noise of laughter and dispute on the front steps, a few chords struck on the piano and a few notes of a man's voice singing.

He stood still in the gloom of the hall, trying to catch the air that the voice was singing and gazing up at his wife. There was grace and mystery in her attitude as if she were a symbol of something. He asked himself what is a woman standing on the stairs in the shadow, listening to distant music, a symbol of. If he were a painter he would paint her in that attitude. Her blue felt hat would show off the bronze of her hair against the darkness and the dark panels of her skirt would show off the light ones. *Distant Music* he would call the picture if he were a painter.

The hall-door was closed; and Aunt Kate, Aunt Julia and Mary Jane came down the hall, still laughing.

—Well, isn't Freddy terrible? said Mary Jane. He's really terrible.

Gabriel said nothing but pointed up the stairs towards where his wife was standing. Now that the hall-door was closed the voice and the piano could be heard more clearly. Gabriel held up his hand for them to be silent. The song seemed to be in the old Irish tonality and the singer seemed uncertain both of his words and of his voice. The voice, made plaintive by distance and by the singer's hoarseness, faintly illuminated the cadence of the air with words expressing grief:

> *O, the rain falls on my heavy locks*
> *And the dew wets my skin,*
> *My babe lies cold . . .*

—O, exclaimed Mary Jane. It's Bartell D'Arcy singing and he wouldn't sing all the night. O, I'll get him to sing a song before he goes.

—O do, Mary Jane, said Aunt Kate.

Mary Jane brushed past the others and ran to the staircase but before she reached it the singing stopped and the piano was closed abruptly.

—O, what a pity! she cried. Is he coming down, Gretta?

Gabriel heard his wife answer yes and saw her come down towards them. A few steps behind her were Mr Bartell D'Arcy and Miss O'Callaghan.

—O, Mr D'Arcy, cried Mary Jane, it's downright mean of you to break off like that when we were all in raptures listening to you.

—I have been at him all the evening, said Miss O'Callaghan, and Mrs Conroy too and he told us he had a dreadful cold and couldn't sing.

—O, Mr D'Arcy, said Aunt Kate, now that was a great fib to tell.

—Can't you see that I'm as hoarse as a crow? said Mr D'Arcy roughly.

He went into the pantry hastily and put on his overcoat. The others, taken aback by his rude speech, could find nothing to say. Aunt Kate wrinkled her brows and made signs to the others to drop the subject. Mr D'Arcy stood swathing his neck carefully and frowning.

—It's the weather, said Aunt Julia, after a pause.

—Yes, everybody has colds, said Aunt Kate readily, everybody.

—They say, said Mary Jane, we haven't had snow like it for thirty years; and I read this morning in the newspapers that the snow is general all over Ireland.

—I love the look of snow, said Aunt Julia sadly.

—So do I, said Miss O'Callaghan. I think Christmas is never really Christmas unless we have the snow on the ground.

—But poor Mr D'Arcy doesn't like the snow, said Aunt Kate, smiling.

Mr D'Arcy came from the pantry, fully swathed and buttoned, and in a repentant tone told them the history of his cold. Everyone gave him advice and said it was a great pity and urged him to be very careful of his throat in the night air. Gabriel watched his wife, who did not join in the conversation. She was standing right under the dusty fanlight and the flame of the gas lit up the rich bronze of her hair which he had seen her drying at the fire a few days before. She was in the same attitude and seemed unaware of the talk about her. At last she turned towards them and Gabriel saw that there was colour on her cheeks and that her eyes were shining. A sudden tide of joy went leaping out of his heart.

—Mr D'Arcy, she said, what is the name of that song you were singing?

—It's called *The Lass of Aughrim*, said Mr D'Arcy, but I couldn't remember it properly. Why? Do you know it?

—*The Lass of Aughrim*, she repeated. I couldn't think of the name.

—It's a very nice air, said Mary Jane. I'm sorry you were not in voice tonight.

—Now, Mary Jane, said Aunt Kate, don't annoy Mr D'Arcy. I won't have him annoyed.

Seeing that all were ready to start she shepherded them to the door, where good-night was said:

—Well, good-night, Aunt Kate, and thanks for the pleasant evening.

—Good-night, Gabriel. Good-night Gretta!

—Good-night, Aunt Kate, and thanks ever so much. Good-night, Aunt Julia.

—O, good-night, Gretta, I didn't see you.

—Good-night, Mr D'Arcy. Good-night, Miss O'Callaghan.

—Good-night, Miss Morkan.

—Good-night, again.

—Good-night, all. Safe home.

—Good-night. Good-night.

The morning was still dark. A dull, yellow light brooded over the houses and the river; and the sky seemed to be descending. It was slushy underfoot; and only streaks and patches of snow lay on the roofs, on the parapets of the quay and on the area railings. The lamps were still burning redly in the murky air and, across the river, the palace of the Four Courts stood out menacingly against the heavy sky.

She was walking on before him with Mr Bartell D'Arcy, her shoes in a brown parcel tucked under one arm and her hands holding her skirt up from the slush. She had no longer any grace of attitude but Gabriel's eyes were still bright with happiness. The blood went bounding along his veins; and the thoughts went rioting through his brain, proud, joyful, tender, valorous.

She was walking on before him so lightly and so erect that he longed to run after her noiselessly, catch her by the shoulders and say something foolish and affectionate into her ear. She seemed to him so frail that he longed to defend her against something and then to be alone with her. Moments of their secret life together burst like stars upon his memory. A heliotrope envelope was lying beside his breakfast-cup and he was caressing it with his hand. Birds were twittering in the ivy and the sunny web of the curtain was shimmering along the floor: he could not eat for happiness. They were standing on the crowded platform and he was placing a ticket inside the warm palm of her glove. He was standing with her in the cold, looking in through a grated window at a man making bottles in a roaring furnace. It was very cold. Her face, fragrant in the cold air, was quite close to his; and suddenly he called out to the man at the furnace:

—Is the fire hot, sir?

But the man could not hear with the noise of the furnace. It was just as well. He might have answered rudely.

A wave of yet more tender joy escaped from his heart and went coursing in warm flood along his arteries. Like the tender fire of stars moments of their life together, that no one knew of or would ever know of, broke upon and illumined his memory. He longed to recall to her those moments, to make her forget the years of their dull existence together and remember only their moments of ecstasy. For the years, he felt, had not quenched his soul or hers. Their children, his writing, her household cares had not quenched all their souls' tender fire. In one letter that he had written to her then he had said: *Why is it that words like these seem to me so dull and cold? Is it because there is no word tender enough to be your name?*

Like distant music these words that he had written years before were borne towards him from the past. He longed to be alone with her. When the others had gone away, when he and she were in their room in the hotel, then they would be alone together. He would call her softly:

—Gretta!

Perhaps she would not hear at once: she would be undressing. Then something in his voice would strike her. She would turn and look at him. . . .

At the corner of Winetavern Street they met a cab. He was glad of its rattling noise as it saved him from conversation. She was looking out of the window and seemed tired. The others spoke only a few words, pointing out some building or street. The horse galloped along wearily under the murky morning sky, dragging his old rattling box after his heels, and

Gabriel was again in a cab with her, galloping to catch the boat, galloping to their honeymoon.

As the cab drove across O'Connell Bridge Miss O'Callaghan said:

—They say you never cross O'Connell Bridge without seeing a white horse.

I see a white man this time, said Gabriel.

—Where? asked Mr Bartell D'Arcy.

Gabriel pointed to the statue, on which lay patches of snow. Then he nodded familiarly to it and waved his hand.

—Good-night, Dan, he said gaily.

When the cab drew up before the hotel Gabriel jumped out and, in spite of Mr Bartell D'Arcy's protest, paid the driver. He gave the man a shilling over his fare. The man saluted and said:

—A prosperous New Year to you, sir.

—The same to you, said Gabriel cordially.

She leaned for a moment on his arm in getting out of the cab and while standing at the curbstone, bidding the others good-night. She leaned lightly on his arm, as lightly as when she had danced with him a few hours before. He had felt proud and happy then, happy that she was his, proud of her grace and wifely carriage. But now, after the kindling again of so many memories, the first touch of her body, musical and strange and perfumed, sent through him a keen pang of lust. Under cover of her silence he pressed her arm closely to his side; and, as they stood at the hotel door, he felt that they had escaped from their lives and duties, escaped from home and friends and run away together with wild and radiant hearts to a new adventure.

An old man was dozing in a great hooded chair in the hall. He lit a candle in the office and went before them to the stairs. They followed him in silence, their feet falling in soft thuds on the thickly carpeted stairs. She mounted the stairs behind the porter, her head bowed in the ascent, her frail shoulders curved as with a burden, her skirt girt tightly about her. He could have flung his arms about her hips and held her still for his arms were trembling with desire to seize her and only the stress of his nails against the palms of his hands held the wild impulse of his body in check. The porter halted on the stairs to settle his guttering candle. They halted too on the steps below him. In the silence Gabriel could hear the falling of the molten wax into the tray and the thumping of his own heart against his ribs.

The porter led them along a corridor and opened a door. Then he set his unstable candle down on a toilet-table and asked at what hour they were to be called in the morning.

—Eight, said Gabriel.

The porter pointed to the tap of the electric-light and began a muttered apology but Gabriel cut him short.

—We don't want any light. We have light enough from the street.

And I say, he added, pointing to the candle, you might remove that handsome article, like a good man.

The porter took up his candle again, but slowly for he was surprised by such a novel idea. Then he mumbled good-night and went out. Gabriel shot the lock to.

A ghostly light from the street lamp lay in a long shaft from one window to the door. Gabriel threw his overcoat and hat on a couch and crossed the room towards the window. He looked down into the street in order that his emotion might calm a little. Then he turned and leaned against a chest of drawers with his back to the light. She had taken off her hat and cloak and was standing before a large swinging mirror, unhooking her waist. Gabriel paused for a few moments, watching her, and then said:

—Gretta!

She turned away from the mirror slowly and walked along the shaft of light towards him. Her face looked so serious and weary that the words would not pass Gabriel's lips. No, it was not the moment yet.

—You looked tired, he said.

—I am a little, she answered.

—You don't feel ill or weak?

—No, tired: that's all.

She went on to the window and stood there, looking out. Gabriel waited again and then, fearing that diffidence was about to conquer him, he said abruptly:

—By the way, Gretta!

—What is it?

—You know that poor fellow Malins? he said quickly.

—Yes. What about him?

—Well, poor fellow, he's a decent sort of chap after all, continued Gabriel in a false voice. He gave me back that sovereign I lent him and I didn't expect it, really. It's a pity he wouldn't keep away from that Browne, because he's not a bad fellow at heart.

He was trembling now with annoyance. Why did she seem so abstracted? He did not know how he could begin. Was she annoyed, too, about something? If she would only turn to him or come to him of her own accord! To take her as she was would be brutal. No, he must see some ardour in her eyes first. He longed to be master of her strange mood.

—When did you lend him the pound? she asked, after a pause.

Gabriel strove to restrain himself from breaking out into brutal language about the sottish Malins and his pound. He longed to cry to her from his soul, to crush her body against his, to overmaster her. But he said:

—O, at Christmas, when he opened that little Christmas-card shop in Henry Street.

He was in such a fever of rage and desire that he did not hear her come from the window. She stood before him for an instant, looking at him strangely. Then, suddenly raising herself on tiptoe and resting her hands lightly on his shoulders, she kissed him.

—You are a very generous person, Gabriel, she said.

Gabriel, trembling with delight at her sudden kiss and at the quaintness of her phrase, put his hands on her hair and began smoothing it back, scarcely touching it with his fingers. The washing had made it fine and brilliant. His heart was brimming over with happiness. Just when he was wishing for it she had come to him of her own accord. Perhaps her thoughts had been running with his. Perhaps she had felt the impetuous desire that was in him and then the yielding mood had come upon her. Now that she had fallen to him so easily he wondered why he had been so diffident.

He stood, holding her head between his hands. Then, slipping one arm swiftly about her body and drawing her towards him, he said softly:

—Gretta, dear, what are you thinking about?

She did not answer nor yield wholly to his arm. He said again, softly:

—Tell me what it is, Gretta. I think I know what is the matter. Do I know?

She did not answer at once. Then she said in an outburst of tears:

—O, I am thinking about that song, *The Lass of Aughrim.*

She broke loose from him and ran to the bed and, throwing her arms across the bed-rail, hid her face. Gabriel stood stock-still for a moment in astonishment and then followed her. As he passed in the way of the cheval-glass he caught sight of himself in full length, his broad, well-filled shirt-front, the face whose expression always puzzled him when he saw it in a mirror, and his glimmering gilt-rimmed eyeglasses. He halted a few paces from her and said:

—What about the song? Why does that make you cry?

She raised her head from her arms and dried her eyes with the back of her hand like a child. A kinder note than he had intended went into his voice.

—Why, Gretta? he asked.

—I am thinking about a person long ago who used to sing that song.

—And who was the person long ago? asked Gabriel, smiling.

—It was a person I used to know in Galway when I was living with my grandmother, she said.

The smile passed away from Gabriel's face. A dull anger began to gather again at the back of his mind and the dull fires of his lust began to glow angrily in his veins.

—Someone you were in love with? he asked ironically.

—It was a young boy I used to know, she answered, named Michael Furey. He used to sing that song, *The Lass of Aughrim.* He was very delicate.

Gabriel was silent. He did not wish her to think that he was interested in this delicate boy.

I can see him so plainly, she said after a moment. Such eyes as he had: big, dark eyes! And such an expression in them—an expression!

—Oh, then, you were in love with him? said Gabriel.

—I used to go out walking with him, she said, when I was in Galway.

A thought flew across Gabriel's mind.

—Perhaps that was why you wanted to go to Galway with that Ivors girl? he said coldly.

She looked at him and asked in surprise:

—What for?

Her eyes made Gabriel feel awkward. He shrugged his shoulders and said:

—How do I know? To see him, perhaps.

She looked away from him along the shaft of light towards the window in silence.

—He is dead, she said at length. He died when he was only seventeen. Isn't it a terrible thing to die so young as that?

—What was he? asked Gabriel, still ironically.

—He was in the gasworks, she said.

Gabriel felt humiliated by the failure of his irony and by the evocation of this figure from the dead, a boy in the gasworks. While he had been full of memories of their secret life together, full of tenderness and joy and desire, she had been comparing him in her mind with another. A shameful consciousness of his own person assailed him. He saw himself as a ludicrous figure, acting as a penny-boy for his aunts, a nervous well-meaning sentimentalist, orating to vulgarians and idealising his own clownish lusts, the pitiable fatuous fellow he had caught a glimpse of in the mirror. Instinctively he turned his back more to the light lest she might see the shame that burned upon his forehead.

He tried to keep up his tone of cold interrogation but his voice when he spoke was humble and indifferent.

—I suppose you were in love with this Michael Furey, Gretta, he said.

—I was great with him at that time, she said.

Her voice was veiled and sad. Gabriel, feeling now how vain it would be to try to lead her whither he had purposed, caressed one of her hands and said, also sadly:

—And what did he die of so young, Gretta? Consumption, was it?

—I think he died for me, she answered.

A vague terror seized Gabriel at this answer as if, at that hour when he had hoped to triumph, some impalpable and vindictive being was coming against him, gathering forces against him in its vague world. But he shook himself free of it with an effort of reason and continued to caress her hand. He did not question her again for he felt that she would tell him of herself. Her hand was warm and moist: it did not respond to his touch but he continued to caress it just as he had caressed her first letter to him that spring morning.

—It was in the winter, she said, about the beginning of the winter when I was going to leave my grandmother's and come up here to the convent. And he was ill at the time in his lodgings in Galway and wouldn't be let out and his people in Oughterard were written to. He was in decline, they said, or something like that. I never knew rightly.

She paused for a moment and sighed.

—Poor fellow, she said. He was very fond of me and he was such a gentle boy. We used to go out together, walking, you know, Gabriel, like the way they do in the country. He was going to study singing only for his health. He had a very good voice, poor Michael Furey.

—Well; and then? asked Gabriel.

—And then when it came to the time for me to leave Galway and come up to the convent he was much worse and I wouldn't be let see him so I wrote him a letter saying I was going up to Dublin and would be back in the summer and hoping he would be better then.

She paused for a moment to get her voice under control and then went on:

—Then the night before I left, I was in my grandmother's house in Nuns' Island, packing up, and I heard gravel thrown up against the window. The window was so wet I couldn't see so I ran downstairs as I was and slipped out the back into the garden and there was the poor fellow at the end of the garden, shivering.

—And did you not tell him to go back? asked Gabriel.

—I implored of him to go home at once and told him he would get his death in the rain. But he said he did not want to live. I can see his eyes as well as well! He was standing at the end of the wall where there was a tree.

—And did he go home? asked Gabriel.

—Yes, he went home. And when I was only a week in the convent he died and he was buried in Oughterard where his people came from. O, the day I heard that, that he was dead!

She stopped, choking with sobs, and, overcome by emotion, flung herself face downward on the bed, sobbing in the quilt. Gabriel held her hand for a moment longer, irresolutely, and then, shy of intruding on her grief, let it fall gently and walked quietly to the window.

.   .   .   .

She was fast asleep.

Gabriel, leaning on his elbow, looked for a few moments unresentfully on her tangled hair and half-open mouth, listening to her deep-drawn breath. So she had had that romance in her life: a man had died for her sake. It hardly pained him now to think how poor a part he, her husband, had played in her life. He watched her while she slept as though he and she had never lived together as man and wife. His curious eyes rested long upon her face and on her hair: and, as he thought of what she must have been then, in that time of her first girlish beauty, a strange friendly pity for her entered his soul. He did not like to say even to himself that her face was no longer beautiful but he knew that it was no longer the face for which Michael Furey had braved death.

Perhaps she had not told him all the story. His eyes moved to the chair over which she had thrown some of her clothes. A petticoat string dangled to the floor. One boot stood upright, its limp upper fallen down: the fellow of it lay upon its side. He wondered at his riot of emotions of an hour before. From what had it proceeded? From his aunt's supper, from his own foolish speech, from the wine and dancing, the merry-making when saying good-night in the hall, the pleasure of the walk along the river in the snow. Poor Aunt Julia! She, too, would soon be a shade with the shade of Patrick Morkan and his horse. He had caught that haggard look upon her face for a moment when she was singing *Arrayed for the Bridal.* Soon, perhaps, he would be sitting in that same drawing-room, dressed in black, his silk hat on his knees. The blinds would be drawn down and Aunt Kate would be sitting beside him, crying and blowing her nose and telling him how Julia had died. He would cast about in his mind for some words that might console her, and would find only lame and useless ones. Yes, yes: that would happen very soon.

The air of the room chilled his shoulders. He stretched himself cautiously along under the sheets and lay down beside his wife. One by one they were all becoming shades. Better pass boldly into that other world, in the full glory of some passion, than fade and wither dismally with age. He thought of how she who lay beside him had locked in her heart for so many years that image of her lover's eyes when he had told her that he did not wish to live.

Generous tears filled Gabriel's eyes. He had never felt like that himself towards any woman but he knew that such a feeling must be love. The tears gathered more thickly in his eyes and in the partial darkness he imagined he saw the form of a young man standing under a dripping tree. Other forms were near. His soul had approached that region where dwell the vast hosts of the dead. He was conscious of, but could not apprehend, their wayward and flickering existence. His own identity was fading out into a grey impalpable world: the solid world itself which these dead had one time reared and lived in was dissolving and dwindling.

A few light taps upon the pane made him turn to the window. It had begun to snow again. He watched sleepily the flakes, silver and dark, falling obliquely against the lamplight. The time had come for him to set out on his journey westward. Yes, the newspapers were right: snow was general all over Ireland. It was falling on every part of the dark central plain, on the treeless hills, falling softly upon the Bog of Allen and, farther westward, softly falling into the dark mutinous Shannon waves. It was falling, too, upon every part of the lonely churchyard on the hill where Michael Furey lay buried. It lay thickly drifted on the crooked crosses and headstones, on the spears of the little gate, on the barren thorns. His soul swooned slowly as he heard the snow falling faintly through the universe and faintly falling, like the descent of their last end, upon all the living and the dead.

Franz Kafka

1883–1924

A HUNGER ARTIST

DURING these last decades the interest in professional fasting has markedly diminished. It used to pay very well to stage such great performances under one's own management, but today that is quite impossible. We live in a different world now. At one time the whole town took a lively interest in the hunger artist; from day to day of his fast the excitement mounted; everybody wanted to see him at least once a day; there were people who bought season tickets for the last few days and sat from morning till night in front of his small barred cage; even in the nighttime there were visiting hours, when the whole effect was heightened by torch flares; on fine days the cage was set out in the open air, and then it was the children's special treat to see the hunger artist; for their elders he was often just a joke that happened to be in fashion, but the children stood open-mouthed, holding each other's hands for greater security, marveling at him as he sat there pallid in black tights, with his ribs sticking out so prominently, not even on a seat but down among straw on the ground, sometimes giving a courteous nod, answering questions with a constrained smile, or perhaps stretching an arm through the bars so that one might feel how thin it was, and then again withdrawing deep into himself, paying no attention to anyone or anything, not even to the all-important striking of the clock that was the only piece of furniture in his cage, but merely staring into vacancy with half-shut eyes, now and then taking a sip from a tiny glass of water to moisten his lips.

Besides casual onlookers there were also relays of permanent watchers selected by the public, usually butchers, strangely enough, and it was their task to watch the hunger artist day and night, three of them at a time, in case he should have some secret recourse to nourishment. This was nothing but a formality, instituted to reassure the masses, for the initiates knew well enough that during his fast the artist would never in any circumstances, not even under forcible compulsion, swallow the smallest morsel of food; the honor of his profession forbade it. Not every watcher, of course, was capable of understanding this; there were often groups of night watchers who were very lax in carrying out their duties and deliberately huddled together in a retired corner to play cards with great absorption, obviously intending to give the hunger artist the chance of a little refreshment, which they supposed he could draw from some private hoard. Nothing annoyed the artist more than such watchers; they made him miserable; they made his fast seem unendurable; sometimes he mastered his feebleness sufficiently to sing during their watch for as long as he could keep going, to show them how unjust their suspicions were. But that was of little use; they only wondered at his cleverness in being able to fill his mouth even while singing. Much more to his taste were the watchers who sat close up to the bars, who were not content with the dim night lighting of the hall but focused him in the full glare of the electric pocket torch given them by the impresario. The harsh light did not trouble him at all. In any case he could never sleep properly, and he could always drowse a little, whatever the light, at any hour, even when the hall was thronged with noisy onlookers. He was quite happy at the prospect of spending a sleepless night with such watchers; he was ready to exchange jokes with them, to tell them stories out of his nomadic life, anything at all to keep them awake and demonstrate to them again that he had no eatables in his cage and that he was fasting as not one of them could fast. But his happiest moment was when the morning came and an enormous breakfast was brought them, at his expense, on which they flung themselves with the keen appetite of healthy men after a weary night of wakefulness. Of course there were people who argued that this breakfast was an unfair attempt to bribe the watchers, but that was going rather too far, and when they were invited to take on a night's vigil without a breakfast, merely for the sake of the cause, they made themselves scarce, although they stuck stubbornly to their suspicions.

Such suspicions, anyhow, were a necessary accompaniment to the profession of fasting. No one could possibly watch the hunger artist continuously, day and night, and so no one could produce first-hand evidence that the fast had really been rigorous and continuous; only the artist himself could know that; he was therefore bound to be the sole completely satisfied spectator of his own fast. Yet for other reasons he was never satisfied; it was not perhaps mere fasting that had brought him to such skeleton thinness that many people had regretfully to keep away from his exhibitions, because the sight of him was too much for them, perhaps it was dissatisfaction with himself that had worn him down. For he alone knew, what no other initiate knew, how easy it was to fast. It was the easiest thing in the world. He made no secret of this, yet people did not believe him; at the best they set him down as modest, most of them, however, thought he was out for publicity or else was some kind of cheat who found it easy to fast because he had discovered a way of making it easy, and then had the impudence to admit the fact, more or less. He had to put up with all that, and in the course of time had got used to it, but his inner dissatisfaction always rankled, and never yet, after any term of fasting—this must be granted to his credit—had he left the cage of his own free will. The longest period of fasting was fixed by his impresario at forty days, beyond that term he was not allowed to go, not even in great cities, and there was good reason for it, too. Experience had proved that for about forty days the interest of the public could be stimulated by a steadily increasing pressure of advertisement, but after that the town began to lose interest, sympathetic support began notably to fall off; there were of course local variations as between one town and another or one country and another, but as a general rule forty days marked the limit. So on the fortieth day the flower-bedecked cage was opened, enthusiastic spectators filled the hall, a military band played, two doctors entered the cage to measure the results of the fast, which were announced through a megaphone, and finally two young ladies appeared, blissful at having been selected for the honor, to help the hunger artist down the few steps leading to a small table on which was spread a carefully chosen invalid repast. And at this very moment the artist always turned stubborn. True, he would entrust his bony arms to the outstretched helping hands of the ladies bending over him, but stand up he would not. Why stop fasting at this particular moment, after forty days of it? He had held out for a long time, an illimitably long time; why stop now, when he was in his best fasting form, or rather, not yet quite in his best fasting form? Why should he be cheated of the fame he would get for fasting longer, for being not only the record hunger artist of all time, which presumably he was already, but for beating his own record by a performance beyond human imagination, since he felt that there were no limits to his capacity for fasting? His public pretended to admire him so much, why should it have so little patience with him; if he could endure fasting longer, why shouldn't the public endure it? Besides, he was tired, he was comfortable sitting in the straw, and now he was supposed to lift himself to his full height and go down to a meal the very thought of which gave him a nausea that only the presence of the ladies kept him from betraying, and even that with an effort. And he looked up into the eyes of the ladies who were apparently so friendly and in reality so cruel, and shook his head, which felt too heavy on its strengthless neck. But then there happened yet again what always happened. The impresario came forward, without a word—for the band made speech impossible— lifted his arms in the air above the artist, as if inviting Heaven to look down upon its creature here in the straw, this suffering martyr, which indeed he was, although in quite another sense; grasped him round the emaciated waist, with exaggerated caution, so that the frail condition he was in might be appreciated; and committed him to the care of the blenching ladies, not without secretly giving him a shaking so that his legs and body tottered and swayed. The artist now submitted completely; his head lolled on his breast as if it had landed there by chance; his body was hollowed out; his legs in a spasm of self-preservation clung close to each other at the knees, yet scraped on the ground as if it were not really solid ground, as if they were only trying to find solid ground; and the whole weight of his body, a featherweight after all, relapsed onto one of the ladies, who, looking round for help and panting a little—this post of honor was not at all what she had expected it to be—first stretched her neck as far as she could to keep her face at least free from contact with the artist, then finding this impossible, and her more fortunate companion not coming to her aid but merely holding extended on her own trembling hand the little bunch of knucklebones that was the artist's, to the great delight of the spectators burst into tears and had to be replaced by an attendant who had long been stationed in readiness. Then came the food, a little of which the impresario managed to get between the artist's lips, while he sat in a kind of half-fainting trance, to the accompaniment of cheerful patter designed to distract the public's attention from the artist's condition; after that, a toast was drunk to the public, supposedly prompted by a whisper from the artist in the impresario's ear; the band confirmed it with a mighty flourish, the spectators melted away, and no one had any cause to be dissatisfied with the proceedings, no one except the hunger artist himself, he only, as always.

So he lived for many years, with small regular intervals of recuperation, in visible glory, honored by the world, yet in spite of that troubled in spirit, and all the more troubled because no one would take his trouble seriously. What comfort could he possibly need? What more could he possibly wish for? And if some good-natured person, feeling sorry for him, tried to console him by pointing out that his melancholy was probably caused by fasting, it could happen, especially when he had been fasting for some time, that he reacted with an outburst of fury and to the general alarm began to shake the bars of his cage like a wild animal. Yet the impresario had a way of punishing these outbreaks which he rather enjoyed putting into operation. He would apologize publicly for the artist's behavior, which was only to be excused, he admitted, because of the irritability caused by fasting; a condition hardly to be understood by well-fed people; then by natural transition he went on to mention the artist's equally incomprehensible boast that he could fast for much longer than he was doing; he praised the high ambition, the good will, the great self-denial undoubtedly implicit in such a statement; and then quite simply countered it by bringing out photographs, which were also on sale to the public, showing the artist on the fortieth day of a fast lying in bed almost dead from exhaustion. This perversion of the truth, familiar to the artist though it was, always unnerved him afresh and proved too much for him. What was a consequence of the premature ending of his fast was here presented as the cause of it! To fight against this lack of understanding, against a whole world of nonunderstanding, was impossible. Time and again in good faith he stood by the bars listening to the impresario, but as soon as the photographs appeared he always let go and sank with a groan back on to his straw, and the reassured public could once more come close and gaze at him.

A few years later when the witnesses of such scenes called them to mind, they often failed to understand themselves at all. For meanwhile the aforementioned change in public interest had set in; it seemed to happen almost overnight; there may have been profound causes for it, but who was going to bother about that; at any rate the pampered hunger artist suddenly found himself deserted one fine day by the amusement seekers, who went streaming past him to other more favored attractions. For the last time the impresario hurried him over half Europe to discover whether the old interest might still survive here and there; all in vain; everywhere, as if by secret agreement, a positive revulsion from professional fasting was in evidence. Of course it could not really have sprung up so suddenly as all that, and many premonitory symptoms which had not been sufficiently remarked or suppressed during the rush and glitter of success now came retrospectively to mind, but it was now too late to take any countermeasures. Fasting would surely come into fashion again at some future date, yet that was no comfort for those living in the present. What, then, was the hunger artist to do? He had been applauded by thousands in his time and could hardly come down to showing himself in a street booth at village fairs, and as for adopting another profession, he was not only too old for that but too fanatically devoted to fasting. So he took leave of the impresario, his partner in an unparalleled career, and hired himself to a large circus; in order to spare his own feelings he avoided reading the conditions of his contract.

A large circus with its enormous traffic in replacing and recruiting men, animals and apparatus can always find a use for people at any time, even for a hunger artist, provided of course that he does not ask too much, and in this particular case anyhow it was not only the artist who was taken on but his famous and long-known name as well; indeed considering the peculiar nature of his performance, which was not impaired by advancing age, it could not be objected that here was an artist past his prime, no longer at the height of his professional skill, seeking a refuge in some quiet corner of a circus; on the contrary, the hunger artist averred that he could fast as well as ever, which was entirely credible; he even alleged that if he were allowed to fast as he liked, and this was at once promised him without more ado, he could astound the world by establishing a record never yet achieved, a statement which certainly provoked a smile among the other professionals, since it left out of account the change in public opinion, which the hunger artist in his zeal conveniently forgot.

He had not, however, actually lost his sense of the real situation and took it as a matter of course that he and his cage should be stationed, not in the middle of the ring as a main attraction, but outside, near the animal cages, on a site that was after all easily accessible. Large and gaily painted placards made a frame for the cage and announced what was to be seen inside it. When the public came thronging out in the intervals to see the animals, they could hardly avoid passing the hunger artist's cage and stopping there for a moment, perhaps they might even have stayed longer had not those pressing behind them in the narrow gangway, who did not understand why they should be held up on their way towards the excitement of the menagerie, made it impossible for anyone to stand gazing quietly for any length of time. And that was the reason why the hunger artist, who had of course been looking forward to these visiting hours as the main achievement of his life, began instead to shrink from them. At first he could hardly wait for the intervals; it was exhilarating to watch the crowds come streaming his way, until only too soon—not even the most obstinate self-deception, clung to almost consciously, could hold out against the fact—the conviction was borne in upon him that these people, most of them, to judge from their actions, again and again, without exception, were all on their way to the menagerie. And the first sight of him from the distance remained the best. For when they reached his cage he was at once deafened by the storm of shouting and abuse that arose from the two contending factions, which renewed themselves continuously, of those who wanted to stop and stare at him—he soon began to dislike them more than the others—not out of real interest but only out of obstinate self-assertiveness, and those who wanted to go straight on to the animals. When the first great rush was past, the stragglers came along, and these, whom nothing could have prevented from stopping to look at him as long as they had breath, raced past with long strides, hardly even glancing at him, in their haste to get to the menagerie in time. And all too rarely did it happen that he had a stroke of luck, when some father of a family fetched up before him with his children, pointed a finger at the hunger artist and explained at length what the phenomenon meant, telling stories of earlier years when he himself had watched similar but much more thrilling performances, and the children, still rather uncomprehending, since neither inside nor outside school had they been sufficiently prepared for this lesson—what did they care about fasting?—yet showed by the brightness of their intent eyes that new and better times might be coming. Perhaps, said the hunger artist to himself many a time, things would be a little better if his cage were set not quite so near the menagerie. That made it too easy for people to make their choice, to say nothing of what he suffered from the stench of the menagerie, the animals' restlessness by night, the carrying past of raw lumps of flesh for the beasts of prey, the roaring at feeding times, which depressed him continually. But he did not dare to lodge a complaint with the management; after all, he had the animals to thank for the troops of people who passed his cage, among whom there might always be one here and there to take an interest in him, and who could tell where they might seclude him if he called attention to his existence and thereby to the fact that, strictly speaking, he was only an impediment on the way to the menagerie.

A small impediment, to be sure, one that grew steadily less. People grew familiar with the strange idea that they could be expected, in times like these, to take an interest in a hunger artist, and with this familiarity the verdict went on against him. He might fast as much as he could, and he did so; but nothing could save him now, people passed him by. Just try to explain to anyone the art of fasting! Anyone who has no feeling for it cannot be made to understand it. The fine placards grew dirty and illegible, they were torn down; the little notice board telling the number of fast days achieved, which at first was changed carefully every day, had long stayed at the same figure, for after the first few weeks even this small task seemed pointless to the staff; and so the artist simply fasted on and on, as he had once dreamed of doing, and it was no trouble to him, just as he had always foretold; but no one counted the days, no one, not even the artist himself, knew what records he was already breaking, and his heart grew heavy. And when once in a time some leisurely passer-by stopped, made merry over the old figure on the board and spoke of swindling, that was in its way the stupidest lie ever invented by indifference and inborn malice, since it was not the hunger artist who was cheating; he was working honestly, but the world was cheating him of his reward.

Many more days went by, however, and that too came to an end. An overseer's eye fell on the cage one day and he asked the attendants why this perfectly good cage should be left standing there unused with dirty straw inside it; nobody knew, until one man, helped out by the notice board, remembered about the hunger artist. They poked into the straw with sticks and found him in it. "Are you still fasting?" asked the overseer. "When on earth do you mean to stop?" "Forgive me, everybody," whispered the hunger artist; only the overseer, who had his ear to the bars, understood him. "Of course," said the overseer, and tapped his forehead with a finger to let the attendants know what state the man was in, "we forgive you." "I always wanted you to admire my fasting," said the hunger artist. "We do admire it," said the overseer, "but why shouldn't we admire it?" "Because I have to fast, I can't help it," said the hunger artist, lifting his head a little and speaking, with his lips pursed, as if for a kiss, right into the overseer's ear, so that no syllable might be lost, "because I couldn't find the food I liked. If I had found it, believe me, I should have made no fuss and stuffed myself like you or anyone else." These were his last words, but in his dimming eyes remained the firm though no longer proud persuasion that he was still continuing to fast.

"Well, clear this out now!" said the overseer, and they buried the hunger artist, straw and all. Into the cage they put a young panther. Even the most insensitive felt it refreshing to see this wild creature leaping around the cage that had so long been dreary. The panther was all right. The food he liked was brought him without hesitation by the attendants; he seemed not even to miss his freedom; his noble body, furnished almost to the bursting point with all that it needed, seemed to carry freedom around with it too; somewhere in his jaws it seemed to lurk; and the joy of life streamed with such ardent passion from his throat that for the on-lookers it was not easy to stand the shock of it. But they braced them-selves, crowded round the cage, and did not want ever to move away.

Translated by Willa and Edwin Muir

D. H. Lawrence

1885–1930

THE BLIND MAN

ISABEL PERVIN was listening for two sounds—for the sound of wheels on the drive outside and for the noise of her husband's foot-steps in the hall. Her dearest and oldest friend, a man who seemed almost indispensable to her living, would drive up in the rainy dusk of the closing November day. The trap had gone to fetch him from the station. And her husband, who had been blinded in Flanders, and who had a disfiguring mark on his brow, would be coming in from the outhouses.

He had been home for a year now. He was totally blind. Yet they had been very happy. The Grange was Maurice's own place. The back was a farmstead, and the Wernhams, who occupied the rear premises, acted as farmers. Isabel lived with her husband in the handsome rooms in front. She and he had been almost entirely alone together since he was wounded. They talked and sang and read together in a wonderful and unspeakable intimacy. Then she reviewed books for a Scottish newspaper, carrying on her old interest, and he occupied himself a good deal with the farm. Sightless, he could still discuss everything with Wernham, and he could also do a good deal of work about the place—menial work, it is true, but it gave him satisfaction. He milked the cows, carried in the pails, turned the separator, attended to the pigs and horses. Life was still very full and strangely serene for the blind man, peaceful with the almost incompre-hensible peace of immediate contact in darkness. With his wife he had a whole world, rich and real and invisible.

They were newly and remotely happy. He did not even regret the loss of his sight in these times of dark, palpable joy. A certain exultance swelled his soul.

But as time wore on, sometimes the rich glamor would leave them. Sometimes, after months of this intensity, a sense of burden overcame Isabel, a weariness, a terrible ennui, in that silent house approached be-tween a colonnade of tall-shafted pines. Then she felt she would go mad, for she could not bear it. And sometimes he had devastating fits of de-pression, which seemed to lay waste his whole being. It was worse than depression—a black misery, when his own life was a torture to him, and when his presence was unbearable to his wife. The dread went down to the roots of her soul as these black days recurred. In a kind of panic she tried to wrap herself up still further in her husband. She forced the old spontaneous cheerfulness and joy to continue. But the effort it cost her was almost too much. She knew she could not keep it up. She felt she would scream with the strain, and would give anything, anything, to escape. She longed to possess her husband utterly; it gave her inordinate joy to have him entirely to herself. And yet, when again he was gone in a black and massive misery, she could not bear him, she could not bear herself; she wished she could be snatched away off the earth altogether, anything rather than live at this cost.

Dazed, she schemed for a way out. She invited friends, she tried to give him some further connection with the outer world. But it was no good. After all their joy and suffering, after their dark, great year of blindness and solitude and unspeakable nearness, other people seemed to them both shallow, rattling, rather impertinent. Shallow prattle seemed presumptuous. He became impatient and irritated, she was wearied. And so they lapsed into their solitude again. For they preferred it.

But now, in a few weeks' time, her second baby would be born. The first had died, an infant, when her husband first went out to France. She looked with joy and relief to the coming of the second. It would be her salvation. But also she felt some anxiety. She was thirty years old, her husband was a year younger. They both wanted the child very much. Yet she could not help feeling afraid. She had her husband on her hands, a terrible joy to her, and a terrifying burden. The child would occupy her love and attention. And then, what of Maurice? What would he do? If only she could feel that he, too, would be at peace and happy when the child came! She did so want to luxuriate in a rich, physical satisfaction of maternity. But the man, what would he do? How could she provide for him, how avert those shattering black moods of his, which destroyed them both?

She sighed with fear. But at this time Bertie Reid wrote to Isabel. He was her old friend, a second or third cousin, a Scotchman, as she was a Scotchwoman. They had been brought up near to one another, and all her life he had been her friend, like a brother, but better than her own brothers. She loved him—though not in the marrying sense. There was a sort of kinship between them, an affinity. They understood one another instinctively. But Isabel would never have thought of marrying Bertie. It would have seemed like marrying in her own family.

Bertie was a barrister and a man of letters, a Scotchman of the intellectual type, quick, ironical, sentimental, and on his knees before the woman he adored but did not want to marry. Maurice Pervin was different. He came of a good old country family—the Grange was not a very great distance from Oxford. He was passionate, sensitive, perhaps over-sensitive, wincing—a big fellow with heavy limbs and a forehead that flushed painfully. For his mind was slow, as if drugged by the strong provincial blood that beat in his veins. He was very sensitive to his own mental slowness, his feelings being quick and acute. So that he was just the opposite to Bertie, whose mind was much quicker than his emotions, which were not so very fine.

From the first the two men did not like each other. Isabel felt that they *ought* to get on together. But they did not. She felt that if only each could have the clue to the other there would be such a rare understanding between them. It did not come off, however. Bertie adopted a slightly ironical attitude, very offensive to Maurice, who returned the Scotch irony with English resentment, a resentment which deepened sometimes into stupid hatred.

This was a little puzzling to Isabel. However, she accepted it in the course of things. Men were made freakish and unreasonable. Therefore, when Maurice was going out to France for the second time, she felt that, for her husband's sake, she must discontinue her friendship with Bertie. She wrote to the barrister to this effect. Bertram Reid simply replied that in this, as in all other matters, he must obey her wishes, if these were indeed her wishes.

For nearly two years nothing had passed between the two friends. Isabel rather gloried in the fact; she had no compunction. She had one great article of faith, which was, that husband and wife should be so important to one another, that the rest of the world simply did not count. She and Maurice were husband and wife. They loved one another. They would have children. Then let everybody and everything else fade into insignificance outside this connubial felicity. She professed herself quite happy and ready to receive Maurice's friends. She was happy and ready : the happy wife, the ready woman in possession. Without knowing why, the friends retired abashed, and came no more. Maurice, of course, took as much satisfaction in this connubial absorption as Isabel did.

He shared in Isabel's literary activities, she cultivated a real interest in agriculture and cattle-raising. For she, being at heart perhaps an emotional enthusiast, always cultivated the practical side of life and prided herself on her mastery of practical affairs. Thus the husband and wife had spent the five years of their married life. The last had been one of blindness and unspeakable intimacy. And now Isabel felt a great indifference coming over her, a sort of lethargy. She wanted to be allowed to bear her child in peace, to nod by the fire and drift vaguely, physically, from day to day. Maurice was like an ominous thunder-cloud. She had to keep waking up to remember him.

When a little note came from Bertie, asking if he were to put up a tombstone to their dead friendship, and speaking of the real pain he felt on account of her husband's loss of sight, she felt a pang, a fluttering agitation of re-awakening. And she read the letter to Maurice.

"Ask him to come down," he said.

"Ask Bertie to come here!" she reechoed.

"Yes—if he wants to."

Isabel paused for a few moments.

"I know he wants to—he'd only be too glad," she replied. "But what about you, Maurice? How would you like it?"

"I should like it."

"Well—in that case—But I thought you didn't care for him—"

"Oh, I don't know. I might think differently of him now," the blind man replied. It was rather abstruse to Isabel.

"Well, dear," she said, "if you're quite sure—"

"I'm sure enough. Let him come," said Maurice.

So Bertie was coming, coming this evening, in the November rain and darkness. Isabel was agitated, racked with her old restlessness and indecision. She had always suffered from this pain of doubt, just an agonizing sense of uncertainty. It had begun to pass off, in the lethargy of maternity. Now it returned, and she resented it. She struggled as usual to maintain her calm, composed, friendly bearing, a sort of mask she wore over all her body.

A woman had lighted a tall lamp beside the table and spread the cloth. The long dining room was dim, with its elegant but rather severe pieces of old furniture. Only the round table glowed softly under the light. It had a rich, beautiful effect. The white cloth glistened and dropped its heavy, pointed lace corners almost to the carpet, the china was old and handsome, creamy-yellow, with a blotched pattern of harsh red and deep blue, the cups large and bell-shaped, the teapot gallant. Isabel looked at it with superficial appreciation.

Her nerves were hurting her. She looked automatically again at the high, uncurtained windows. In the last dusk she could just perceive outside a huge fir-tree swaying its boughs: it was as if she thought it rather than saw it. The rain came flying on the window panes. Ah, why had she no peace? These two men, why did they tear at her? Why did they not come—why was there this suspense?

She sat in a lassitude that was really suspense and irritation. Maurice, at least, might come in—there was nothing to keep him out. She rose to her feet. Catching sight of her reflection in a mirror, she glanced at herself with a slight smile of recognition, as if she were an old friend to herself. Her face was oval and calm, her nose a little arched. Her neck made a beautiful line down to her shoulder. With hair knotted loosely behind, she had something of a warm, maternal look. Thinking this of herself, she arched her eyebrows and her rather heavy eyelids, with a little flicker of a smile, and for a moment her gray eyes looked amused and wicked, a little sardonic, out of her transfigured Madonna face.

Then, resuming her air of womanly patience—she was really fatally self-determined— she went with a little jerk towards the door. Her eyes were slightly reddened.

She passed down the wide hall and through a door at the end. Then she was in the farm premises. The scent of dairy, and of farm-kitchen, and of farm-yard and of leather almost overcame her: but particularly the scent of dairy. They had been scalding out the pans. The flagged passage in front of her was dark, puddled, and wet. Light came out from the open kitchen door. She went forward and stood in the doorway. The farm-people were at tea, seated at a little distance from her, round a long, narrow table, in the center of which stood a white lamp. Ruddy faces, ruddy hands holding food, red mouths working, heads bent over the tea-cups: men, land-girls, boys: it was tea-time, feeding-time. Some faces caught sight of her. Mrs. Wernham, going round behind the chairs with a large black teapot, halting slightly in her walk, was not aware of her for a moment. Then she turned suddenly.

"Oh, is it Madam!" she exclaimed. "Come in, then, come in! We're at tea." And she dragged forward a chair.

"No, I won't come in," said Isabel. "I'm afraid I interrupt your meal."

"No--no—not likely, Madam, not likely."

"Hasn't Mr. Pervin come in, do you know?"

"I'm sure I couldn't say! Missed him, have you, Madam?"

"No, I only wanted him to come in," laughed Isabel, as if shyly.

"Wanted him, did ye? Get up, boy—get up, now—"

Mrs. Wernham knocked one of the boys on the shoulder. He began to scrape to his feet, chewing largely.

"I believe he's in top stable," said another face from the table.

"Ah! No, don't get up. I'm going myself," said Isabel.

"Don't you go out of a dirty night like this. Let the lad go. Get along wi' ye, boy," said Mrs. Wernham.

"No, no," said Isabel, with a decision that was always obeyed. "Go on with your tea, Tom. I'd like to go across to the stable, Mrs. Wernham."

"Did ever you hear tell!" exclaimed the woman.

"Isn't the trap late?" asked Isabel.

"Why, no," said Mrs. Wernham, peering into the distance at the tall, dim clock. "No, Madam—we can give it another quarter or twenty minutes yet, good—yes, every bit of a quarter."

"Ah! It seems late when darkness falls so early," said Isabel.

"It do, that it do. Bother the days, that they draw in so," answered Mrs. Wernham. "Proper miserable!"

"They are," said Isabel, withdrawing.

She pulled on her overshoes, wrapped a large tartan shawl around her, put on a man's felt hat, and ventured out along the causeways of the first yard. It was very dark. The wind was roaring in the great elms behind the outhouses. When she came to the second yard the darkness seemed deeper. She was unsure of her footing. She wished she had brought a lantern. Rain blew against her. Half she liked it, half she felt unwilling to battle.

She reached at last the just visible door of the stable. There was no sign of a light anywhere. Opening the upper half, she looked in: into a simple well of darkness. The smell of horses, and ammonia, and of warmth was startling to her, in that full night. She listened with all her ears but could hear nothing save the night, and the stirring of a horse.

"Maurice!" she called, softly and musically, though she was afraid. "Maurice—are you there?"

Nothing came from the darkness. She knew the rain and wind blew in upon the horses, the hot animal life. Feeling it wrong, she entered the stable and drew the lower half of the door shut, holding the upper part close. She did not stir, because she was aware of the presence of the dark hind-quarters of the horses, though she could not see them, and she was afraid. Something wild stirred in her heart.

She listened intensely. Then she heard a small noise in the distance— far away, it seemed—the chink of a pan, and a man's voice speaking a brief word. It would be Maurice, in the other part of the stable. She stood motionless, waiting for him to come through the partition door. The horses were so terrifyingly near to her, in the invisible.

The loud jarring of the inner door-latch made her start; the door was opened. She could hear and feel her husband entering and invisibly pass-ing among the horses near to her, darkness as they were, actively inter-mingled. The rather low sound of his voice as he spoke to the horses came velvety to her nerves. How near he was, and how invisible! The darkness seemed to be in a strange swirl of violent life, just upon her. She turned giddy.

Her presence of mind made her call, quietly and musically:

"Maurice! Maurice—dea-ar!"

"Yes," he answered. "Isabel?"

She saw nothing, and the sound of his voice seemed to touch her.

"Hello!" she answered cheerfully, straining her eyes to see him. He was still busy, attending to the horses near her, but she saw only dark-ness. It made her almost desperate.

"Won't you come in, dear?" she said.

"Yes, I'm coming. Just half a minute. *Stand over—now!* Trap's not come, has it?"

"Not yet," said Isabel.

His voice was pleasant and ordinary, but it had a slight suggestion of the stable to her. She wished he would come away. Whilst he was so utterly invisible, she was afraid of him.

"How's the time?" he asked.

"Not yet six," she replied. She disliked to answer into the dark. Pres-ently he came very near to her, and she retreated out of doors.

"The weather blows in here," he said, coming steadily forward, feel-ing for the doors. She shrank away. At last she could dimly see him.

"Bertie won't have much of a drive," he said, as he closed the doors.

"He won't indeed!" said Isabel calmly, watching the dark shape at the door.

"Give me your arm, dear," she said.

She pressed his arm close to her, as she went. But she longed to see him, to look at him. She was nervous. He walked erect, with face rather lifted, but with a curious tentative movement of his powerful muscular legs. She could feel the clever, careful, strong contact of his feet with the earth, as she balanced against him. For a moment he was a tower of darkness to her, as if he rose out of the earth.

In the house-passage he wavered and went cautiously, with a curious look of silence about him as he felt for the bench. Then he sat down heavily. He was a man with rather sloping shoulders, but with heavy limbs, powerful legs that seemed to know the earth. His head was small, usually carried high and light. As he bent down to unfasten his gaiters and boots he did not look blind. His hair was brown and crisp, his hands were large, reddish, intelligent, the veins stood out in the wrists; and his thighs and knees seemed massive. When he stood up his face and neck were surcharged with blood, the veins stood out on his temples. She did not look at his blindness.

Isabel was always glad when they had passed through the dividing door into their own regions of repose and beauty. She was a little afraid of him, out there in the animal grossness of the back. His bearing also changed, as he smelt the familiar indefinable odor that pervaded his wife's surroundings, a delicate, refined scent, very faintly spicy. Perhaps it came from the potpourri bowls.

He stood at the foot of the stairs, arrested, listening. She watched him, and her heart sickened. He seemed to be listening to fate.

"He's not here yet," he said. "I'll go up and change."

"Maurice," she said, "you're not wishing he wouldn't come, are you?"

"I couldn't quite say," he answered. "I feel myself rather on the *qui vive*."

"I can see you are," she answered. And she reached up and kissed his cheek. She saw his mouth relax into a slow smile.

"What are you laughing at?" she said roguishly.

"You consoling me," he answered.

"Nay," she answered. "Why should I console you? You know we love each other—you know *how* married we are! What does anything else matter?"

"Nothing at all, my dear."

He felt for her face and touched it, smiling.

"*You're* all right, aren't you?" he asked anxiously.

"I'm wonderfully all right, love," she answered. "It's you I am a little troubled about, at times."

"Why me?" he said, touching her cheeks delicately with the tips of his fingers. The touch had an almost hypnotizing effect on her.

He went away upstairs. She saw him mount into the darkness, unseeing and unchanging. He did not know that the lamps on the upper corridor were unlighted. He went on into the darkness with unchanging step. She heard him in the bathroom.

Pervin moved about almost unconsciously in his familiar surroundings, dark though everything was. He seemed to know the presence of objects before he touched them. It was a pleasure to him to rock thus through a world of things, carried on the flood in a sort of blood-prescience. He did not think much or trouble much. So long as he kept his sheer immediacy of blood-contact with the substantial world he was happy, he wanted no intervention of visual consciousness. In this state there was a certain rich positivity, bordering sometimes on rapture. Life seemed to move in him like a tide lapping, lapping, and advancing, enveloping all things darkly. It was a pleasure to stretch forth the hand and meet the unseen object, clasp it, and possess it in pure contact. He did not try to remember, to visualize. He did not want to. The new way of consciousness substituted itself in him.

The rich suffusion of this state generally kept him happy, reaching its culmination in the consuming passion for his wife. But at times the flow would seem to be checked and thrown back. Then it would beat inside him like a tangled sea, and he was tortured in the shattered chaos of his own blood. He grew to dread this arrest, this throw-back, this chaos inside himself, when he seemed merely at the mercy of his own powerful and conflicting elements. How to get some measure of control or surety, this was the question. And when the question rose maddening in him, he would clench his fists as if he would *compel* the whole universe to submit to him. But it was in vain. He could not even compel himself.

Tonight, however, he was still serene, though little tremors of unreasonable exasperation ran through him. He had to handle the razor very carefully, as he shaved, for it was not at one with him, he was afraid of it. His hearing also was too much sharpened. He heard the woman lighting the lamps on the corridor, and attending to the fire in the visitor's room. And then, as he went to his room, he heard the trap arrive. Then came Isabel's voice, lifted and calling, like a bell ringing:

"Is it you, Bertie? Have you come?"

And a man's voice answered out of the wind:

"Hello, Isabel! There you are."

"Have you had a miserable drive? I'm so sorry we couldn't send a closed carriage. I can't see you at all, you know."

"I'm coming. No, I liked the drive—it was like Porthshire. Well, how are you? You're looking fit as ever, as far as I can see."

"Oh, yes," said Isabel. "I'm wonderfully well. How are you? Rather thin, I think—"

"Worked to death—everybody's old cry. But I'm all right, Ciss. How's Pervin?—isn't he here?"

"Oh, yes, he's upstairs changing. Yes, he's awfully well. Take off your wet things; I'll send them to be dried."

"And how are you both, in spirits? He doesn't fret?"

"No—no, not at all. No, on the contrary, really. We've been wonderfully happy, incredibly. It's more than I can understand—so wonderful: the nearness, and the peace—"

"Ah! Well, that's awfully good news—"

They moved away. Pervin heard no more. But a childish sense of desolation had come over him, as he heard their brisk voices. He seemed shut out—like a child that is left out. He was aimless and excluded, he did not know what to do with himself. The helpless desolation came over him. He fumbled nervously as he dressed himself, in a state almost of childishness. He disliked the Scotch accent in Bertie's speech, and the slight response it found on Isabel's tongue. He disliked the slight purr of complacency in the Scottish speech. He disliked intensely the glib way in which Isabel spoke of their happiness and nearness. It made him recoil. He was fretful and beside himself like a child, he had almost a childish nostalgia to be included in the life circle. And at the same time he was a man, dark and powerful and infuriated by his own weakness. By some fatal flaw, he could not be by himself, he had to depend on the support of another. And this very dependence enraged him. He hated Bertie Reid, and at the same time he knew the hatred was nonsense, he knew it was the outcome of his own weakness.

He went downstairs. Isabel was alone in the dining-room. She watched him enter, head erect, his feet tentative. He looked so strong-blooded and healthy and, at the same time, cancelled. Cancelled—that was the word that flew across her mind. Perhaps it was his scar suggested it.

"You heard Bertie come, Maurice?" she said.

"Yes—isn't he here?"

"He's in his room. He looks very thin and worn."

"I suppose he works himself to death."

A woman came in with a tray—and after a few minutes Bertie came down. He was a little dark man, with a very big forehead, thin, wispy hair, and sad, large eyes. His expression was inordinately sad—almost funny. He had odd, short legs.

Isabel watched him hesitate under the door, and glance nervously at her husband. Pervin heard him and turned.

"Here you are, now," said Isabel. "Come, let us eat."

Bertie went across to Maurice.

"How are you, Pervin?" he said, as he advanced.

The blind man stuck his hand out into space, and Bertie took it.

"Very fit. Glad you've come," said Maurice.

Isabel glanced at them, and glanced away, as if she could not bear to see them.

"Come," she said. "Come to table. Aren't you both awfully hungry? I am tremendously."

"I'm afraid you waited for me," said Bertie, as they sat down.

Maurice had a curious monolithic way of sitting in a chair, erect and distant. Isabel's heart always beat when she caught sight of him thus.

"No," she replied to Bertie. "We're very little later than usual. We're having a sort of high tea, not dinner. Do you mind? It gives us such a nice long evening, uninterrupted."

"I like it," said Bertie.

Maurice was feeling, with curious little movements, almost like a cat kneading her bed, for his plate, his knife and fork, his napkin. He was getting the whole geography of his cover into his consciousness. He sat erect and inscrutable, remote-seeming. Bertie watched the static figure of the blind man, the delicate tactile discernment of the large, ruddy hands, and the curious mindless silence of the brow, above the scar. With difficulty he looked away, and without knowing what he did, picked up a little crystal bowl of violets from the table, and held them to his nose.

"They are sweet-scented," he said. "Where do they come from?"

"From the garden—under the windows," said Isabel.

"So late in the year—and so fragrant! Do you remember the violets under Aunt Bell's south wall?"

The two friends looked at each other and exchanged a smile, Isabel's eyes lighting up.

"Don't I?" she replied. "*Wasn't* she queer!"

"A curious old girl," laughed Bertie. "There's a streak of freakishness in the family, Isabel."

"Ah—but not in you and me, Bertie," said Isabel. "Give them to Maurice, will you?" she added, as Bertie was putting down the flowers. "Have you smelled the violets, dear? Do!—they are so scented."

Maurice held out his hand, and Bertie placed the tiny bowl against his large, warm-looking fingers. Maurice's hand closed over the thin white fingers of the barrister. Bertie carefully extricated himself. Then the two watched the blind man smelling the violets. He bent his head and seemed to be thinking. Isabel waited.

"Aren't they sweet, Maurice?" she said at last, anxiously.

"Very," he said. And he held out the bowl. Bertie took it. Both he and Isabel were a little afraid, and deeply disturbed.

The meal continued. Isabel and Bertie chatted spasmodically. The blind man was silent. He touched his food repeatedly, with quick, delicate touches of his knife-point, then cut irregular bits. He could not bear to be helped. Both Isabel and Bertie suffered: Isabel wondered why. She did not suffer when she was alone with Maurice. Bertie made her conscious of a strangeness.

After the meal the three drew their chairs to the fire, and sat down to talk. The decanters were put on a table near at hand. Isabel knocked the logs on the fire, and clouds of brilliant sparks went up the chimney. Bertie noticed a slight weariness in her bearing.

"You will be glad when your child comes now, Isabel?" he said.

She looked up to him with a quick wan smile.

"Yes, I shall be glad," she answered. "It begins to seem long. Yes, I shall be very glad. So will you, Maurice, won't you?" she added.

"Yes, I shall," replied her husband.

"We are both looking forward so much to having it," she said.

"Yes, of course," said Bertie.

He was a bachelor, three or four years older than Isabel. He lived in beautiful rooms overlooking the river, guarded by a faithful Scottish man-servant. And he had his friends among the fair sex—not lovers, friends. So long as he could avoid any danger of courtship or marriage, he adored a few good women with constant and unfailing homage, and he was chivalrously fond of quite a number. But if they seemed to encroach on him, he withdrew and detested them.

Isabel knew him very well, knew his beautiful constancy, and kindness, also his incurable weakness, which made him unable ever to enter into close contact of any sort. He was ashamed of himself because he could not marry, could not approach women physically. He wanted to do so. But he could not. At the center of him he was afraid, helplessly and even brutally afraid. He had given up hope, had ceased to expect any more that he could escape his own weakness. Hence he was a brilliant and successful barrister, also a *littérateur* of high repute, a rich man, and a great social success. At the center he felt himself neuter, nothing.

Isabel knew him well. She despised him even while she admired him. She looked at his sad face, his little short legs, and felt contempt of him. She looked at his dark gray eyes, with their uncanny, almost childlike, intuition, and she loved him. He understood amazingly—but she had no fear of his understanding. As a man she patronized him.

And she turned to the impassive, silent figure of her husband. He sat leaning back, with folded arms, and face a little uptilted. His knees were straight and massive. She sighed, picked up the poker, and again began to prod the fire, to rouse the clouds of soft brilliant sparks.

"Isabel tells me," Bertie began suddenly, "that you have not suffered unbearably from the loss of sight."

Maurice straightened himself to attend but kept his arms folded.

"No," he said, "not unbearably. Now and again one struggles against it, you know. But there are compensations."

"They say it is much worse to be stone deaf," said Isabel.

"I believe it is," said Bertie. "Are there compensations?" he added, to Maurice.

"Yes. You cease to bother about a great many things." Again Maurice stretched his figure, stretched the strong muscles of his back, and leaned backwards, with uplifted face.

"And that is a relief," said Bertie. "But what is there in place of the bothering? What replaces the activity?"

There was a pause. At length the blind man replied, as out of a negligent, unattentive thinking:

"Oh, I don't know. There's a good deal when you're not active."

"Is there?" said Bertie. "What, exactly? It always seems to me that when there is no thought and no action, there is nothing."

Again Maurice was slow in replying.

"There is something," he replied. "I couldn't tell you what it is."

And the talk lapsed once more, Isabel and Bertie chatting gossip and reminiscence, the blind man silent.

At length Maurice rose restlessly, a big obtrusive figure. He felt tight and hampered. He wanted to go away.

"Do you mind," he said, "if I go and speak to Wernham?"

"No—go along dear," said Isabel.

And he went out. A silence came over the two friends. At length Bertie said:

"Nevertheless, it is a great deprivation, Cissie."

"It is, Bertie. I know it is."

"Something lacking all the time," said Bertie.

"Yes, I know. And yet—and yet—Maurice is right. There is something else, something *there*, which you never knew was there, and which you can't express."

"What is there?" asked Bertie.

"I don't know—it's awfully hard to define it—but something strong and immediate. There's something strange in Maurice's presence—indefinable—but I couldn't do without it. I agree that it seems to put one's mind to sleep. But when we're alone I miss nothing; it seems awfully rich, almost splendid, you know."

"I'm afraid I don't follow," said Bertie.

They talked desultorily. The wind blew loudly outside, rain chattered on the window-panes, making a sharp drum-sound because of the closed, mellow-golden shutters inside. The logs burned slowly, with hot, almost invisible small flames. Bertie seemed uneasy, there were dark circles round his eyes. Isabel, rich with her approaching maternity, leaned looking into the fire. Her hair curled in odd, loose strands, very pleasing to the man. But she had a curious feeling of old woe in her heart, old, timeless night-woe.

"I suppose we're all deficient somewhere," said Bertie.

"I suppose so," said Isabel wearily.

"Damned, sooner or later."

"I don't know," she said, rousing herself. "I feel quite all right, you know. The child coming seems to make me indifferent to everything, just placid. I can't feel that there's anything to trouble about, you know."

"A good thing, I should say," he replied slowly.

"Well, there it is. I suppose it's just Nature. If only I felt I needn't trouble about Maurice, I should be perfectly content—"

"But you feel you must trouble about him?"

"Well—I don't know—" She even resented this much effort.

The night passed slowly. Isabel looked at the clock. "I say," she said,

"It's nearly ten o'clock. Where can Maurice be? I'm sure they're all in bed at the back. Excuse me a moment."

She went out, returning almost immediately.

"It's all shut up and in darkness," she said. "I wonder where he is. He must have gone out to the farm—"

Bertie looked at her.

"I suppose he'll come in," he said.

"I suppose so," she said. "But it's unusual for him to be out now."

"Would you like me to go out and see?"

"Well—if you wouldn't mind. I'd go, but—" She did not want to make the physical effort.

Bertie put on an old overcoat and took a lantern. He went out from the side door. He shrank from the wet and roaring night. Such weather had a nervous effect on him: too much moisture everywhere made him feel almost imbecile. Unwilling, he went through it all. A dog barked violently at him. He peered in all the buildings. At last, as he opened the upper door of a sort of intermediate barn, he heard a grinding noise, and looking in, holding up his lantern, saw Maurice, in his shirtsleeves, standing listening, holding the handle of a turnip-pulper. He had been pulping sweet roots, a pile of which lay dimly heaped in a corner behind him.

"That you, Wernham?" said Maurice, listening.

"No, it's me," said Bertie.

A large, half-wild gray cat was rubbing at Maurice's leg. The blind man stooped to rub its sides. Bertie watched the scene, then unconsciously entered and shut the door behind him. He was in a high sort of barn-place, from which, right and left, ran off the corridors in front of the stalled cattle. He watched the slow, stooping motion of the other man, as he caressed the great cat.

Maurice straightened himself.

"You come to look for me?" he said.

"Isabel was a little uneasy," said Bertie.

"I'll come in. I like messing about doing these jobs."

The cat had reared her sinister, feline length against his leg, clawing at his thigh affectionately. He lifted her claws out of his flesh.

"I hope I'm not in your way at all at the Grange here," said Bertie, rather shy and stiff.

"My way? No, not a bit. I'm glad Isabel has somebody to talk to. I'm afraid it's I who am in the way. I know I'm not very lively company. Isabel's all right, don't you think? She's not unhappy, is she?"

"I don't think so."

"What does she say?"

"She says she's very content—only a little troubled about you."

"Why me?"

"Perhaps afraid that you might brood," said Bertie, cautiously.

"She needn't be afraid of that." He continued to caress the flattened gray head of the cat with his fingers. "What I am afraid of," he resumed, "is that she'll find me a dead weight, always alone with me down here."

"I don't think you need think that," said Bertie, though this was what he feared himself.

"I don't know," said Maurice. "Sometimes I feel it isn't fair that she's saddled with me." Then he dropped his voice curiously. "I say," he asked, secretly struggling, "is my face much disfigured? Do you mind telling me?"

"There is the scar," said Bertie, wondering. "Yes, it is a disfigurement. But more pitiable than shocking."

"A pretty bad scar, though," said Maurice.

"Oh, yes."

There was a pause.

"Sometimes I feel I am horrible," said Maurice, in a low voice, talking as if to himself. And Bertie actually felt a quiver of horror.

"That's nonsense," he said.

Maurice again straightened himself, leaving the cat.

"There's no telling," he said. Then again, in an odd tone, he added: "I don't really know you, do I?"

"Probably not," said Bertie.

"Do you mind if I touch you?"

The lawyer shrank away instinctively. And yet, out of very philanthropy, he said, in a small voice: "Not at all."

But he suffered as the blind man stretched out a strong, naked hand to him. Maurice accidently knocked off Bertie's hat.

"I thought you were taller," he said, starting. Then he laid his hand on Bertie Reid's head, closing the dome of the skull in a soft, firm grasp, gathering it, as it were; then, shifting his grasp and softly closing again, with a fine, close pressure, till he had covered the skull and the face of the smaller man, tracing the brows, and touching the full, closed eyes, touching the small nose and the nostrils, the rough, short moustache, the mouth, the rather strong chin. The hand of the blind man grasped the shoulder, the arm, the hand of the other man. He seemed to take him, in the soft, traveling grasp.

"You seem young," he said quietly, at last.

The lawyer stood almost annihilated, unable to answer.

"Your head seems tender, as if you were young," Maurice repeated. "So do your hands. Touch my eyes, will you?—touch my scar."

Now Bertie quivered with revulsion. Yet he was under the power of the blind man, as if hypnotized. He lifted his hand, and laid the fingers on the scar, on the scarred eyes. Maurice suddenly covered them with his own hand, pressed the fingers of the other man upon his disfigured eyesockets, trembling in every fiber, and rocking slightly, slowly, from side to side. He remained thus for a minute or more, whilst Bertie stood as if in a swoon, unconscious, imprisoned.

Then suddenly Maurice removed the hand of the other man from his brow, and stood holding it in his own.

"Oh, my God," he said, "we shall know each other now, shan't we? We shall know each other now."

Bertie could not answer. He gazed mute and terror-struck, overcome by his own weakness. He knew he could not answer. He had an unreasonable fear, lest the other man should suddenly destroy him. Whereas Maurice was actually filled with hot, poignant love, the passion of friendship. Perhaps it was this very passion of friendship which Bertie shrank from most.

"We're all right together now, aren't we?" said Maurice. "It's all right now, as long as we live, so far as we're concerned?"

"Yes," said Bertie, trying by any means to escape.

Maurice stood with head lifted, as if listening. The new delicate fulfillment of mortal friendship had come as a revelation and surprise to him, something exquisite and unhoped-for. He seemed to be listening to hear if it were real.

Then he turned for his coat.

"Come," he said, "we'll go to Isabel."

Bertie took the lantern and opened the door. The cat disappeared. The two men went in silence along the causeways. Isabel, as they came, thought their footsteps sounded strange. She looked up pathetically and anxiously for their entrance. There seemed a curious elation about Maurice. Bertie was haggard, with sunken eyes.

"What is it?" she asked.

"We've become friends," said Maurice, standing with his feet apart, like a strange colossus.

"Friends!" re-echoed Isabel. And she looked again at Bertie. He met her eyes with a furtive, haggard look; his eyes were as if glazed with misery.

"I'm so glad," she said, in sheer perplexity.

"Yes," said Maurice.

He was indeed so glad. Isabel took his hand with both hers, and held it fast.

"You'll be happier now, dear," she said.

But she was watching Bertie. She knew that he had one desire—to escape from this intimacy, this friendship, which had been thrust upon him. He could not bear it that he had been touched by the blind man, his insane reserve broken in. He was like a mollusc whose shell is broken.

Wilbur Daniel Steele

1886–1970

THE BODY OF THE CRIME

THE HOUSE in which Daniel was born was the kind of which we say, as we drive past it in the elm-pillared margin of some New England village: "What a monstrosity!" One day, when the Antique has caught up with the Eighties, perhaps we shall say: "What a beauty! What noble bays and airy cupolas and richness of brown scrollwork! They knew how to build their houses in those days."

Perhaps, too, we shall have matured enough to say of men like Dan Kinsman, who was Daniel's father: "They knew how to build their lives."

When the young Daniel came home from his first year away to prep school and saw with his changed eyes the unchanging house, the weighing cornices and flying towers, squared bays, rounded bays, portecochere, all cocoa brown in the shadows of the chestnuts—

"That's it," he thought, "it's not like other fellows' houses."

And when he studied this man, his father, it seemed for a while he had found the answer to the riddle as old in its secret wretchedness as the very beginnings of his memory. "And he, he's not like other fellows' fathers."

Other fellows' fathers, Daniel had found in his year, were men who arrived cheerfully from lifting their incomes and departed grimly to lower their medal scores. Forward-moving, tomorrow-thinking young elders, eager, industrious, mobile fellows fearful of nothing but of seeming to stand still.

But here was a father apparently content to be one year where he had been the year before, possessed of but the same possessions, the same small-town friendships, the same leisurely, half-patriarchal judgeship, the same pedestrian pleasures, books and dogs, pruning hooks and garden hoes and fishing rods. And he a strong, straight man alive, not yet fifty, with black hair thick on his head, and lungs to laugh with when he wanted. Strange!

Now it came to Daniel it must be because his father was so wanting in—that's to say, so strange this way—that he had always seemed to his son so—so—Daniel groped for a word for a thing he'd never been able to give a shape or name, and had to finish lamely—seemed so "strange."

Daniel could have laughed for joy to discover, now he was grown up, that the trouble about his father was so little a one as this. For all the weight of his fifteen years, he could have skipped for lightness, to know that here was a difference from other fathers he now could grasp, even learn to condone, yes, even admire, even fight for, with fellows with more—well—say—money-grabbing dads.

Yes, Daniel could have skipped for lightness on the deep cave-green turf of the hydrangea alley, where they walked and talked that first June afternoon at home, he and his father, while Mother watched them with her pale smile from her long chair in her high window.

It was curious; Daniel had always loved his ailing, beautiful mother, easily, and been near her and told her everything tellable, easily, and not thought much about it. The one he would have given his life to be able to love as easily, to be close to, friends with, whole of heart, was this other, this darkly handsome man whom he himself was so absurdly like to look at, his father.

So today it was as if the year of forgetting had worked a good miracle. It was a dream come true to find himself sauntering and chatting with Dan Kinsman as affectionately at ease as though they had been but two fellows gravely estimating the apple yield in the west yard and the hay chances in the back mowing, chuckling together over the antics of Spot's pups on the barn floor, waving answer to the view halloo of Doc Martin racketing by in the antique twin-six, and, wonder of wonders at last, arm in arm, man and man, marching indoors prepared to mount and demand of Mother if supper were ever to be ready—as if she, poor fragile chatelaine, could know anything about that.

But, day of marvels! An elixir must have run in the air. For here in their sight came Mother down the stairs to meet them, walking by herself, suddenly, subtly revivified, the flush on her cheeks and the shine in her eyes not more for their astonishment than for her own.

So tonight there were three at table in place of two, and it was like the sort of dream in which one wakes from an interior nightmare to find everything finished that was horrid, and everything at its beginning that is right and bright. Nor did it end with the supper table; afterward she would go out abroad with them, as if greedy to share in the marvel of those two men of hers who walked of a sudden as one, and by their walking so, seemed so suddenly to have made her walk again.

What a sight it was for the evening sun to see, level and bloody rose beneath the eaves of the chestnuts! Dan Kinsman, bemused, commencing words and swallowing their ends on half-choked chuckles, even as his eyes, quick for once, kept slant track of Vivian's every oddly exuberant gesture. Daniel, beatified, accepting wonders with a new omnivorous trust. And Vivian Kinsman, unbelievable, a princess freed from some evil enchantment in exile, returned to her kingdom, leading them.

In the east yard, hidden for years, the low, excited laugh was on her lips continuously. For this border, it was: "They're too gorgeous, Dan; I love them!" For that bed: "But there never *were* such flowers!" When she came in view of Father's season's pride, the bastion of man-high crimson poppies, all she could do was put her hands to her heart.

Only when she caught sight of Spot and her puppies taking the last of the sun at the barn door was there a shadow of change in the exclamation of discovery.

"You're going to keep them all, Dan!" She drew Father's eyes. "All, Dan!"

He would have temporized, laughingly: "Spot got away this time, and—"

"You're not going to drown them, Dan. I couldn't bear to think—"

The sharpness in her voice brought quickness to his.

"Why, no, of course not, Vivian. I shall keep them, of course—unless someone should want them very much—who'd give them a good home."

The sun touched distant woods. Father dared worry aloud at last.

"It'll be chilly in another second now, Vivian."

She turned back with a queer, mercurial docility, asking only, when they came to the porch steps, that she might have some of the crimson poppies for her room tonight.

"I should so love to see them in the morning, Dan, just three or four."

"You'll have an armful, that's what you'll have, dear; I'll go and get them now."

Daniel took her in on his arm, feeling tall, now his father was gone. She would go only as far as the living room for the moment, where a slender summer fire was laid, ready for the match. When Daniel had lighted it he studied the white figure lying back deep in Dan Kinsman's chair. He said: "You're happy tonight, Mother."

She needn't answer. Her eyes, fixed on the fire, were alight with all its beginning, playing flames. And before he knew why, "Have you always been happy here with Father," he demanded, "and with me?"

This must have seemed to need no answer, at first. But then she sat up and fixed the boy with her straight gaze. "Always, yes!" From vehemence it changed to mirth. "What ever put it in your head, sonny?— yes, yes, yes!" And sinking back, with a little gasp at the end of her laughter: "He's an angel, sonny, your father is, but he's an awful slowpoke; won't you go and hurry him along?"

Father had meant it when he said an armful; he had gathered a whole great sheaf of the poppies, and rather a pity, for the blooms were closed. But what matter if Vivian wanted them; they'd open again at day. So he seemed to be thinking as he stood there, laden and bemused, in the falling night.

And so it was that Daniel, his son, came upon him, deep in a preoccupation of his own, halted a rod away, and, without lifting his gaze from the ground, said: "Has Mother liked it here in Kennelbridge, Father?"

Dan Kinsman had had a day of astonishments. Without turning anything but his head, and that slowly, he studied his dim questioner.

"It has liked your mother here," he said quietly.

The boy, given a riddle, raised his eyes to the man, who was no more than a shadow shape in the dusk now—and, as shadows may be, something distorted and magnified—between the blackening blood of the poppies he carried and the dike he had torn them from. And Daniel forgot his riddle and widened his eyes. The father knew the sign of old. All afternoon he had been waiting for it, pulled between dread and the beginnings of an incredible hope. Now he wheeled, cried, "Ah, Daniel, son!" and held out his arms, careless of their sanguinary burden. And his son turned and ran.

What good is it to be fifteen and a man, instead of ten and a boy, or five and a child? When Daniel, fleeing, needles in his legs and an icicle up his backbone, reached the firelight where he had left his mother sitting, it was on the knees of veriest childhood he tumbled down, to hide his face in the chair bottom beside her, wind his fingers in her skirts, and sob it out in words aloud, at last:

"Mother—why am I—why am I sometimes—sometimes so fr-fr-frightened of my—my fa-fa-father?"

Mother had always answered his questions, till he asked this question. Her failure now, her complete, unstirring silence, doubled the magnitude of a terror till now his own shamed secret. And the doubled was redoubled by the sound of that man's feet on the piazza, coming toward the door.

He groveled. "Mother, please, hurry—hurry and tell me, tell me, Mother! What—what's there about my father—what's he done that's such a—a horror?"

Still, for answer, no word, no gesture. And it was too late; a quiet door had opened and the feet were in the room. As Daniel scrambled up and wheeled, a defending courage suffused him. He stood his ground, and, not knowing why, spread his arms across the man's way, and not knowing what, cried: "No! Don't! Don't come!"

Through the water in his eyes he began to see his father's face hung there before him, oddly gray, the stare of it fixed, not on him, but on her behind him. And he grew aware of two things fighting in that stare, the greater one like a stunned sorrow, the lesser like a reawakening hope.

As sometimes in crisis, it was of the lesser one the man spoke now.

"This, then, Daniel, is why you said what you said out there, and sobbed, and ran away back here? It wasn't that old queerness of yours coming back then, after all?"

The husband's shock was gentler than the son's, for all evening he had had in his mind as he watched Vivian the thought of a candle when it gutters, how it will flame to its old brightness for an instant at the last.

Not so with Daniel. When he turned and knew that the reason his mother had sat there and not answered him was that all the while she had sat there in the deep chair dead, he fainted.

Doc Martin had to mop his bald head with a troubled handkerchief many times in the following days. On the third, the afternoon after the funeral, stopping in at the Kinsmans' by right of the oldest and closest friend and finding Dan there all alone, he asked: "Where's Daniel hiding himself?" And if it sounded casual, and was meant to, already in the soil of the doctor's mind uneasy little roots of wonder had begun to set.

"Don't know; not far off, I guess." The answer was given with an averted face.

Why shouldn't it be? Men's faces, when they've just buried their wives of twenty years—why may they not wish to keep what's written on them to themselves? The physician mocked himself for a worrying idiot as he went on home.

But he had his head to mop again when he got to his own house and found Daniel fidgeting up and down the piazza, inarticulate and miserably mantling. It was all mysterious and awkward. He didn't know what he was to do or say, and especially was this so when the boy's dumbness, laboring, brought forth some mouse of words about the weather or the baseball standings. But finally, "Dr. Martin," it came at a rush, "was my mother happy, living here in Kennelbridge, with Father—and me?"

It is unfortunate that at such moments men seem to think they have to speak in the manner of oracles. As Dan Kinsman, three days before, now Doc Martin:

"Well, son, she *lived* here in Kennelbridge, with you and your father, almost exactly ten years longer than I gave her to live. Does that mean anything?"

And thereafter he wondered why the boy's eyes, savagely troubled, followed him slantwise everywhere. He wondered more. Seeing the sun go and the dusk come, he wondered why the sensitive, naturally unobtrusive lad stayed on, apparently aimless and plainly wretched, and stayed, and made no move to go. It was after dark when Doc Martin appeared at the Kinsman place, to find Dan out in the east yard, standing, chin down, hands locked behind him.

"I thought, Dan, you might wonder where the kid was. He's over at my house. I'm afraid I've been—uh—keeping him."

Dan listened, stock-still, without comment. It became an ordeal.

"I don't know just how to say it, Dan. The boy seems badly upset. He has a lot of his mother in him, Dan—a lot of the thing that made us all love her—and—want to spank her, sometimes. That sentimental defenselessness—it went with her ailment, I've no doubt. That making a mountain of emotion out of a molehill of—not that I mean this is a molehill—but—damn it, old man! The boy—this house—this night after the funeral—I've a hunch he'd more than half like to stay over with me. Thought I'd ask you."

"Yes."

The one syllable, it sounded rough in the throat. As he went away the doctor turned twice to study the figure posted there in darkness, head heavy, face hidden. Anger? Sorrow? What? Headless, tailless business! He told himself he wished he were dead and well out of it.

He wasn't. After that night, any half plans there may have been of father and son going off for a summer of travel together were dropped. There was a camp in the Green Mountains where Daniel's school went, and he was packed for it by the second morning. Dan came to Doc Martin, unhappy, unused to lying.

"I wonder if you'll do something for me, old man? Drive Daniel over to the main line this noon. I shall be busy."

The doctor did it. What their parting was he never knew, for the boy had his bags out at the gate when he drove by, and the father was "busy." If the friend of them both was profanely troubled he kept it quiet and set himself for a gallant hour of cheer and small talk. The problem of a book for the journey seemed a godsend. They went over the newsstand's library with a mutual pretense of care, but as if it were not bad enough that all the novels were detective novels, Daniel discovered after brief browsings that there was none he could be certain he hadn't read. As he accepted one at last—entitled *Murder!*—the physician had to stare.

"Lord, son! To look at you anybody'd think you were as mild as a lamb. And here you turn out a glutton for crime. Don't you ever read anything else?"

Daniel went red—even redder, the doctor thought, than was asked for.

"Oh, I forget 'em faster'n I read 'em. If you asked me one single thing that had happened, a week after, I couldn't any more remember it than I could—"

He got no further. He had touched by chance on a pet dogma of the other's; and Doc Martin, figuratively, squared off.

"Couldn't remember? Bosh! Ever tried?"

"Tried?" Daniel was confused by this vehemence.

"*Really* tried, I mean. Rolled up your mental sleeves and taken pick and spade to the humus of memory, to try and turn up some one particular thing that's buried there? It's surprising. There are authenticated records of long-term prisoners, men in solitary confinement, who, simply for something for their minds to do . . ."

And here they came, the classic cases, served up with a zealot's gusto; the aged criminals reconstructing verbatim the nursery tales of infanthood; the old fellows repainting in minutest detail places passed through as children and thereafter wholly forgotten. And so forth. And so on.

The man with a hobby is not to be held accountable. Doc Martin, who had toiled to make talk—now his one fear was that the belated train would make up time.

"Can't remember! Actually, you can't *forget!* Nothing you've ever felt, heard, seen, no matter how tiny—you may mislay the record, but you can't lose it. No matter how dim, it's here in your cranium somewhere, indelible, forever."

The bent ear and big eye of his audience it was cruel to give up. The train was in, but there was still the moment on the platform.

"Theoretically, Daniel, you ought to be able to remember the day of your birth. But it would probably take you as many as a thousand years, in a dark cell, and after all—"

After all, after the boy was up the step Doc Martin recollected something he had been two days thinking on.

"Daniel, listen! Your mother *was* happy. Her life here was a clear, quiet, happy life, with those she loved deeply. Believe me, Daniel."

It was good for Daniel he had the book called *Murder!* At the end of his emotional tether he must have escape, and the surest escape was here between these covers; he knew the taste of it beforehand, as the eater of drugs knows the taste of his drug. Escape, yes. And a curious, helpless, rather horrid surrender.

Never remember? "Bosh!" For a little while yet he left the book unopened, and thought of the mild old doctor and his ferocious expletive. But was it true, even a half of what he had claimed, about digging up buried things? . . . If you tried hard enough? . . . Took a pick and spade . . . to buried things?

There were five hours to ride, more than enough for the book. Let it wait.

To remember things forgotten! By dim footprints in the mold of old fantasies, by broken twigs of sensation—this sort of sound disliked for no reason, that odor as inexplicably agreeable—by clues so thinner-than-air to be able to track back relentlessly—what?

"Bosh!" It was Daniel's own bosh this time. But the light in the deeps of his abstracted eyes burned no less steadily, nor did the color of a strange excitation retreat from his cheeks and temples.

There was a station. Express, the train only slowed, going through. On the flickering platform stood an elderly woman, back to, a stoutish figure glimpsed for a split second, gray-clad, with a purple hat with a tulle quill.

"Emma!"

But then the boy lay back and derided himself. It was that purple, forward-tilted hat. Emma, his old nurse, had been dead three—no, two—years. It was three years ago she came to see him, from Albany, and that was the year before she died.

Yes, yes. She came in her nephew's car and brought Daniel a sweater she had knitted for him. He could see her now, when he tried to get into it, there on the big circular side piazza, and her chagrin. "Mercy, when I was here last I never looked to see you grow so in two years. Remember when I was here last time, Dannie?"

"Course I do; what d'you think? And you said I used to be a caution when I was little, and you hoped I'd got over it."

"Bless you, Dannie, and have you?"

Had he? Got over what? Three years ago he'd known what, because three years ago he'd remembered what she'd said two years before that. Something about: "I declare, you always were a caution, Dannie. The first day ever I saw you . . . saw you . . . first day ever I saw you . . ."

Concentrate on it! Try harder!

". . . first day ever I saw you, do you know what you said . . . what you . . ."

In the Pullman, but unconscious of the Pullman, Dannie knotted his brows.

Don't give up. Go at it some other way. . . .

Well, they'd been in his room; he was ready for bed, and Emma had come up—she'd stayed overnight that next-to-last visit—and she'd sat there in the blue rocker and talked and talked. Talked so long that Mother had called: "Daniel, Emma's tired, so you must stop asking her so many . . ."

But now he *had* it—the other thing—it was "question."

It wasn't "what you said." It was, complete: "First day ever I saw you, do you know *the question you asked me?* Well, most three-years-olds, they'll ask you like, 'What's a zebra?' or 'What's a airplane?' But the first thing you asked me was . . . thing you asked me was . . ."

No, after all, not quite complete. Why did the light of recollection close again, just there? Especially when, by thinking on it, that bedtime visit of Emma's had grown as vivid as a thing today.

The expression of the boy in seat No. 5 was a set scowl. A flush colored it, like anger. A "Bosh!" trembled on his lips. He had a book to read, and, by hang, he'd read it now. A book called *Murder!*

"Murder!"

Why, now he'd got that too!

"The first thing you asked me—I was trying to get you to go into the summerhouse and you were howling and pulling—and you asked me, 'What is murder?' And if you don't call that funny for a three-year-old to be asking . . ."

Murder? Three-year-old? Funny? . . . But leave those, for the moment.

Summerhouse! Latticework, probably. Light through it in squares or diamonds, probably. Unless—ugh, it was chilly in the Pullman—there were vines. Vines?

The train carried the corporeal weight of Daniel Kinsman to the White River Junction that summer afternoon. But the part of him that weighed nothing at all had started on an immensely longer journey, an incalculably stranger quest.

At camp, for the first while, they let him go his own gait, without nagging him or themselves. Aware of his shocking loss, they even let down the rules a little—rules, fundamentally, of good fellowship—in his case. Daniel, with his shut mouth, little appetite, and eyes fixed habitually on nothing, was no good fellow for anyone.

This was all right for a certain period. But when a week and another week had gone, and a normal youngster should have been getting some hold on healthy life, and Daniel was still not less separate, but if anything more so, physically torpid, colorless of expression, unmistakably

if incomprehensibly not among those present, the responsible began to
think of doing something about it.

At length the Head sat down and wrote a letter to the boy's father,
who had shut up house on Doc Martin's plea and gone off with him to
the Canadian woods. But that letter was destined not to be posted. Before a stamp was on it, word came in that young Kinsman had not been
seen since lights-out the night before. At the end of a day and night of
combing the woods, beating the hills, a telegram was despatched to
Canada.

Locked, bolted, and shuttered though the house was, Daniel knew a
boy's way into it. One of the cellar windows was loose enough to let a
lock-pick wire in.

Of all that Daniel had done, of all he was yet to undertake, this one
act was the hardest. That he could, in the night, enter into that sealed,
empty, pitch-black habitation, of which anyone might be nervous—and
he, with his mother dead and his imagination whipped keen by a fortnight's flagellation, was horribly, icily afraid—gives the measure of the
thing that was stronger than the house's terror, its pull.

If he were only in the house, only on the scene there, only at home!
Day by day, night by night, the brown house of home had kept the drag-
line taut on him, by innuendo, by promise, by command. Whenever a
peephole, opened in memory, had closed again before the glimpsed stage
could set itself with half the properties of old actuality, "Ah, yes, but
if you were *there* it might be different," something had seemed to
whisper.

And now that he was here? Now that he was actually in, his feet
weighing on sightless stairs, hands guiding him along blind walls? Now
what was he to do?

Nothing. When he had reached his own room, at the end of gropings
that brought sweat out of his neck, he pawed for his bed, found it, and
laid himself down along the middle of the mattress. There, inert—almost
as inert for hours at a time as a cataleptic—he remained. How long?

By calendar it came to four days. In his consciousness the lapse of
time was not measurable, it was as well a dream's forty winks as a
dungeon's forty years.

Of his rare actual moves he was to all intents unconscious. Luckily it
was summer, and the water not turned off; from time to time he drank.
Once he bolted raw oatmeal from a box in the pantry and was ill with it.
The electric current was cut, but there was the oil lantern he might have
lighted long before he did, had he cared. Rather, perhaps, had he dared.
Perhaps, more simply, had he felt the need. After all, his eyes were no
longer concerned with this shuttered Here and Now.

They were concerned with the half-open door of a summerhouse.

Relatively, it may have been little more than a scratching of the top-
soil; actually, in that blank-eyed fortnight away at camp, he had pene-

trated a surprising depth into the leaf mold of his fallen memories. Most important, he had caught the trick of it, learned the heft and balance of his tools, pick and spade, a dogged mental concentration working at one with a reserveless mental surrender.

So it had become child's play, literally, by fastening on some fag end of sensuous recollection—a barked shin of escapade, sting of a punishment, taste of the sweetmeat of some reward—to restore the outlines of whole episodes in the comparatively recent years of his sixes, fives, even his fours; to relive whole days, repeople whole scenes with shapes which began by having no names, or with names wanting shapes, and watch these phantasmal beings take on identities and lineaments—and lo! Auntie Prichard, of course, the doughnut woman! Or Mary Belle— who could forget the girl with wire on her teeth!

He had learned a lot about the creature of pranks and bush beatings that is the mind. He learned, at a price, that no lead can be too paltry to follow. So it was, retrieving a boy's face plastered with freckles and banged with red hair, he had given three long hours of his last camp morning to trying to find the face a name. A dozen times he nearly had it; the muscles of his tongue knew the feel of it, yet couldn't get the sound. It made him mad. "I won't give it up, not if it takes all day!"

And, "day," there it was. Georgie Day! Who could forget Georgie Day?

Accident? In the weird business Daniel was about, there's no such thing.

Georgie Day. Well, well! Immediately, fruitless hours fruited magically. A house suddenly sprang up around the freckled rascal, and around the house a tin-can-littered yard, and in the yard a tumbling barn, and in the barn, rabbits.

Rabbits? What about rabbits? Look! Here's a rabbit running, bounding high in fright across a greensward in sunshine. No, none of Georgie's; he and his have vanished from the scene. This is a wild one, cottontail, surprised among berry bushes behind the home garden, retreat cut off, scuttling across the west lawn for all it's worth, and Daniel running after it.

Run, cottontail! Run, boy! Bounce, bunny! Whoop, Dannie!

"Here, Daisy! Where are you, Daisy? Where's that dog?"

Daisy? Why, Spot's mother, of course, elderly, sleepy, all setter-red.

Yellow sunshine, green grass, little wild blue shadow, hunting, praying, for some hole. And a hole, a hole at last! Squarish aperture among massed leaves. Dive for it, bunny! Stop, boy! Into it, rabbit! Boy, stop dead! Don't go near there, youngster! Frown if you please, stamp, mutter; yes, you know you don't want to go near there. You know you don't.

Why not?

Pandemonium. Out comes rabbit, out comes Daisy, the lazy, surprised asleep in there. And the two of them, fleeing, pursuing, flicker past the transfixed Dannie, and away, into limbo. For it's the squarish aperture in massed woodbine leaves, crosshatch of lattice in their gaps, lattice door ajar—it's this he's staring at.

So it was, by uttering the irrelevant words "if it takes all day," Daniel had found the way back to the summerhouse.

Two weeks it had taken him to reach its viny exterior, those two weeks away at camp. Had he had a hundred years, real ones, in place of the hundred hours he could command, who knows but that he might actually have succeeded in covering the rest of the journey—might have crept or leaped at last across that one remaining rod of grass, gravel, and doorsill, and been inside?

Now he started sanguinely. Only a rod left—the last dash—home stretch. Pooh! Thrown back from it, confused, he started again with the same assurance, only again to be set on his heels by a wall, impalpable as air, but impenetrable as glass. How many times did he relaunch the attack? In one hour of the clock he could live a score in recollection, a hundred toward the end, when hunger and fever had whipped the pace. No longer sanguinely, but desperately, he tried one breach after another.

For now there were several; he had multiplied his points of attack. To the rabbit day he had added quickly the Emma day. It was no task by now to reconstruct that episode entire. He could commence with the breakfast table, where the new nurse was first introduced into the scheme of his cosmos. He could mount then to his room with her, suffer the change into denim play pants, come down, come out, and go towing around the yard at her arm's end, dazzled by the sudden wealth of her "What shall we play? Anything on earth you like, Dannie?"

So, not once, but dozens of times, he came to the spot where something in him balked, he began to howl, cleared Emma's grasp, let her go on. He could see her face in all its mystification now—and see it, more was the wonder, across the width of the rod he couldn't cross—in the doorway of the summerhouse. And he could hear her expostulating still:

"What is it, Dannie? Nothing but a toad here. You're not afraid of a toad!"

And he could feel something in his stomach's pit, that came up, and was words.

"What is murder, Emma?"

Why on earth that? What was it in him, cold and hot—not shame, not rage, not terror, alone, but like a misery of all three compounded? Or like the feeling Daniel had to this day, immensely diluted, whenever anyone in his hearing spoke of cycles or sickles or Seckles.

And, coming to that, why on earth that? Did it all come from "Seckle"? And did that come from the pear tree, down past the east corner of the barn, which, since he was recollecting, he recollected he had never liked? Recollected, in fact, that when they used to play hide-and-seek at his house, and Daniel himself was "it," and one of the boys hid behind that Seckle pear below the barn, he wouldn't go there to spy him, not if he stayed "it" forever.

So? Why wouldn't he? Time and time again he made an effort to follow that trace, but it was of no use; there was nothing there that was important, he had to tell himself; much better buckle down to business with the shovel day.

The shovel day he had added to the rabbit day and the Emma day now. Where it came in the chronology he couldn't say; though he judged from the longer time it had taken him to dig it out it must have been earlier. At any rate, it was the farthest back he could remember being frightened by his father.

He had to work on it. Again, again, stubbornly again, he would stand in a flushed twilight on the perimeter of that arc whose radius was a rod, and watch the woodbine leaves put aside, and see his father emerge from the dark interior, carrying a spade.

Well, what about it? What so fearful was his father doing? Going gardening, probably, in the evening's cool; tools may have been kept in the summerhouse. So, what? Look more deeply into this! But try as Daniel would, he couldn't. Each time, at sight of man and shovel, the child gulped, turned, ran, with goblins grabbing after him, for the house and Mother.

Why? Why, oh, why, oh, why?

And now at last, time lost all count of—grown to months and years, it seemed, in the black house—now at last, let down by the caving of the body beneath it, Daniel's mind began to surrender to exhaustion. Daylight—what was actually the fourth daylight—creeping through the shutter cracks in slim fans of grayness, did not waken him for a long time from the sleep into which he had sunk near midnight.

When it did he failed to fall immediately, as his habit was, into his reminiscent reverie. Lying supine, staring at the ceiling, it was the ceiling he saw this morning. He raised himself on the mattress, intending to go downstairs, but with the act a dizziness took hold of him. He lay back again and listened to his teeth knocking together. It is one thing for a man, adult and idle, to starve himself for a while; for a growing boy it is another thing.

It was the first time there had been room in Daniel's brain for a thought of failure. Was it not possible that the end of the time he could hide and have solitude was approaching? No sooner the idea than he repelled it. With a strength of panic he drove himself back to his task. Dig or die, now!

But the pick and spade, till now so docile, developed the balkings and crotchets of a curious sabotage. Today, when he summoned the old face of a playmate, straightway the features began to twist in the weirdest fashion, magnify, diminish, like the grotesque faces that dissolve in dreams. Or, coming on a new trail of old adventure unexplored, he found it leading him into extraordinary places, out of all color with the rest of his past—and realized with a start that it was something he had read, not lived.

And presently, frustrated, he slept again.

Each other day had been an age; this was but a dozen blinks long, a day wasted. How could Daniel know the incalculable value of that day his mind lay fallow?

It was night once more when he arose, went into his mother's room, and lay down on the bed there. It was nearly, if not quite, somnambulism. Certainly he was unaware of any reason for the move. Whether he fell asleep and woke up, whether he slept at all, or waked at all, whether at any time he was actually, bodily, in the summerhouse, it would be now impossible to say. It can only be said that the thing till the end had all the stigmata of true nightmare.

The will to terror, to begin with. Terror sprung of its own seed, an effect wanting a cause, a shadow condemned to create the object that casts it. And with this, alternately, a weightless, boundless mobility, and a sense of being held from moving, arms pinioned, legs bound.

Nothing was ever clear. Such moments as were lighted—less than pictures; mere rags of sight vignetted on the dark—were whisked away too quickly to be comprehended whole. Nor were these many. The pervading scene was a blackness in which blacknesses moved, giving forth but muffled sounds. Acts witnessed and no more, shadowy, separate, retreating rather than ever coming nearer.

"They're going away from the summerhouse, ma'am," or, "carrying him away"—that adverb, "away," was forever recurring. And generally, somewhere near it, whether before or after, blacknesses moved on blackness with a black burden; heavy breathing, soft feet.

It must be understood there was never an attempt at sequence. No act revealed itself whole at any one time; at divers times divers fractions of it would repeat themselves, mingled with stray fractions of other acts or utterances.

Take the one set of sounds. Sometimes it ran, out there—door creak, oath, blow, scuffle. Sometimes quite reversed. Sometimes—oath, blow, scuffle, door creak.

And that querying cry, coming from close above, thrown down—out of a window?—into the dark, now it would be, "Dan, what are you doing? *Tom!*" Then, like as not, next time it would be: "Tom, what are you doing? *Dan!*"

It is impossible to tell it, by a tenth, adequately. For by the very mechanics of telling, nine tenths of the formlessness is lost; fragments, released from the peculiar bedevilment of nightmare, inevitably fly together. Detached words, fractional phrases, flickering by, flitting back again; before they can be written here they must needs have formed themselves by some degree into sentences, no matter if the sentences are forever changing something of the forms. As, for instance, in the one, "Dan (Tom), what are you doing?" followed by, "*Tom! (Dan!)*"

There's the other sentence, into which at last the word "murder" has come. By the time it has crystallized itself into the sequence, "It was murder, Dan; I saw it; murder in cold blood!"—by that time the light around it has crystallized, too, in a pattern, a pattern of diamond-shaped pencils striking in through gaps of latticework. And the strait jacket of nightmare around one's limbs has taken the shape of the arms of the crier-out. And the crier-out is Mother.

"Don't come in that door; I'm afraid of you, Dan! The blood on your hands is blood of brutal murder. Why? Don't tell me. Was it because I loved him? I love my child, here in my arms. Must I be afraid for *him* then? Must he be afraid of his father, now, as long as the two of you live?"

And this cry, too, vibrant with hysteria, has a vision to go with it, a peephole vision of a close lantern, a red-flecked hand, a spade with earth spots on it, and the tight, white, terrible mask of Father's face.

So, in telling, already this big, close lantern light has extricated itself from the little lantern light at a distance. But in the dream, if it was a dream, this very separation of the two became from the first the thing, intuitively, the dreamer fought for. Wrestled for with tied hands, run after with hobbled feet; cried to with stopped mouth.

In the beginning it was equally the one or the other that might start it; toward the end of an aeon a kind of rule was established; it was the little light far off that began, and the big one then, too soon, that came and swallowed it, only to be swallowed in its turn by that blackness with black things moving in it, or the door-creak sequence, containing the scuffle, the oath, and the blow.

Perhaps it was because of this that the desire of the boy's dread centered more and more fiercely on that weakling spark, and he told himself it was there that whatever was hidden was hidden, and awaited its recurrence impatient of the other shadow plays. And when it came, and the voice of the second woman in the bedroom—a nurse?—began, "It's digging they are, ma'am, down there—," and with that the light began to swell, irresistibly, and stripe itself in the pattern that meant the summerhouse, Daniel fought with all his bitter, puny power against the re-enwrapping arms, the relifting hysteria of Mother's "Don't come in that door! I'm afraid of you!" and the reopening peepshow of the red hand and the white face.

And he cried: "Yes, but go on with the other! Digging down *where*, down *where?*" till in the nightmare the lees of the sweat of his exhaustion ran in icy dribbles down his skin.

It was not till he gave up, beaten by weariness, that it suddenly gave in.

"It's digging they are, ma'am, down there under—"

"Under *what?*"

"—under that pear tree—"

"Pear tree?"

"—with the little pears, below the barn. By the light of the lantern, ma'am—"

Lantern! By the way, where is a lantern? Now, quick!

"—they're digging in the—"

Digging! Pick and spade? Where are they?

"—ground, burying something—"

A thing that is buried!

"—under the pear tree, ma'am."

Ever tried? Rolled up your sleeves, taken pick and spade—to turn up something that is buried there?

When Dan Kinsman and Doc Martin reached the house late that night, and found it black, the one last hope, which neither had dared to confess to, seemed to have followed all its fellows. Red-lidded with sleeplessness, jaws ill-shaven, clothing long worn, they looked the men they felt now, as, unlocking the front door, they went in.

"What's the good?"

It was the doctor that saw it, through one of the living-room windows.

"Hey! What's up out there? Somebody with a lantern, down there behind the barn."

They started out of the door at a walk, but then ran.

They found a lantern, a spade, and a garden mattock under the Seckle-pear tree, and a sprawling trench dug, and a weazen-faced, wide-eyed boy to his knees in it, holding out toward them two brown bones.

Dan spoke. "For God's sake, what are you doing here?"

Daniel spoke. "For God's sake, what are *these* doing here?"

Doc Martin spoke. "For God's sake!" That was all.

It wasn't that Dan was obstinate; it was simply that he was dazed.

"What are you doing here, son? Tell me!"

It wasn't that Daniel was sullen; it was simply that his legs were going to go out from under him at any moment now.

"What are these, Father? You tell me!"

"Son—sonny—you're sick."

"I am sick. Who was Tom?"

"Good lord alive! Dan, look here! Be quiet, Daniel; wait till I get through with him. Dan, how long ago was it—I mean, how old would this kid have been, that night?"

"What night do you mean?"

"Come out of it, man! That night when you heard where Tom had been the week before, and called me, and I brought the chloroform over, thinking maybe, perhaps, the dog might—"

"Dog!" High in the roof of a boy's mouth, the one syllable, echoing.

"—and you, Dan, no maybe or perhaps about it, you got him in the

head with the spade, thank God, in time. What I asked you—how old
was Daniel then?"

"Not old enough to remember anything. . . . Daniel, who's been
telling you—"

But Doc Martin wouldn't have it. "No, man, you talk to me. How
old?"

"Two, perhaps. Not three. A baby. A babe in arms, actually, come
to think of it. Vivian had him there in her arms."

"Where?"

"There in the summerhouse."

"Vivian—in the summerhouse?"

"Afterward. She—she had come there."

"You've never told me."

"No. I—it's something I—Look here, Daniel, son, you'd best be—"

"No you don't, Dan. Talk! What's this about Vivian, and Daniel,
and the summerhouse afterward? Tell it, and tell it straight."

"She was ill, that's all. Frightened. And—and you know how she was
about animals and things—and she didn't understand. Couldn't expect her
to, not knowing anything. Hysterical. Went to the summerhouse to see
—and bolted herself in."

"But when you explained?"

"That's it. I was a fool, I suppose. I tried to lie, at first. The mastiff
was hers, from a pup; she adored him; it was all so sudden; I couldn't
bring myself to say the word—hydrophobia. A fool."

"Yes, and a damned one."

"She said she was afraid of me, Doc. She said it was—it was—"

"She said it was murder, Father. And—it was only—*Father!*"

"Son! Lord! What's the—Hey! Catch him, Doc, or he'll fall."

"Catch him yourself, he's yours. Pick him up, fool. Starvation; don't
worry too much. Bring him along."

"But if he should come to, and me carrying him. I'm afraid—"

"Don't be. Not any more."

Katherine Anne Porter

1890–

THE FIG TREE

OLD Aunt Nannie had a habit of gripping with her knees to hold
Miranda while she brushed her hair or buttoned her dress down
the back. When Miranda wriggled, Aunt Nannie squeezed still harder,
and Miranda wriggled more, but never enough to get away. Aunt Nannie gathered up Miranda's scalp lock firmly, snapped a rubber band

around it, jammed a freshly starched white chambray bonnet over her ears and forehead, fastened the crown to the lock with a large safety pin, and said: "Got to hold you still someways. Here now, don't you take this off your head till the sun go down."

"I didn't want a bonnet, it's too hot, I wanted a hat," said Miranda.

"You not goin' to get a hat, you goin' to get just what you got," said Aunt Nannie in the bossy voice she used for washing and dressing time, "and mo'over some of these days I'm goin' to *sew* this bonnet to your topknot. Your daddy says if you get freckles he blame me. Now, you're all ready to set out."

"Where are we going, Aunty?" Miranda could never find out about anything until the last minute. She was always being surprised. Once she went to sleep in her bed with her kitten curled on the pillow purring, and woke up in a stuffy tight bed in a train, hugging a hot-water bottle; and there was Grandmother stretched out beside her in her McLeod tartan dressing-gown, her eyes wide open. Miranda thought something wonderful had happened. "My goodness, Grandmother, where are we going?" And it was only for another trip to El Paso to see Uncle Bill.

Now Tom and Dick were hitched to the carry-all standing outside the gate with boxes and baskets tied on everywhere. Grandmother was walking alone through the house very slowly, taking a last look at everything. Now and then she put something else in the big leather portmoney[1] on her arm until it was pretty bulgy. She carried a long black mohair skirt on her other arm, the one she put on over her other skirt when she rode horseback. Her son Harry, Miranda's father, followed her saying: "I can't see the sense in rushing off to Halifax on five minutes' notice."

Grandmother said, walking on: "It's five hours exactly." Halifax wasn't the name of Grandmother's farm at all, it was Cedar Grove, but Father always called it Halifax. "Hot as Halifax," he would say when he wanted to describe something very hot. Cedar Grove was very hot, but they went there every summer because Grandmother loved it. "I went to Cedar Grove for fifty summers before you were born," she told Miranda, who remembered last summer very well, and the summer before a little. Miranda liked it for watermelons and grasshoppers and the long rows of blooming chinaberry trees where the hounds flattened themselves out and slept. They whined and winked their eyelids and worked their feet and barked faintly in their sleep, and Uncle Jimbilly said it was because dogs always dreamed they were chasing something. In the middle of the day when Miranda looked down over the thick green fields towards the spring she could simply see it being hot: everything blue and sleepy and the mourning doves calling.

"Are we going to Halifax, Aunty?"

"Now just ask your dad if you wanta know so much."

"Are we going to Halifax, Dad?"

[1] Anglicized form of French *porte-monnaie*, purse

Her father twitched her bonnet straight and pulled her hair forward so it would show. "You mustn't get sunburned. No, let it alone. Show the pretty curls. You'll be wading in Whirlypool before supper this evening."

Grandmother said, "Don't say Halifax, child, say Cedar Grove. Call things by their right names."

"Yes, ma'am," said Miranda. Grandmother said again, to her son, "It's five hours, exactly, and your Aunt Eliza has had plenty of time to pack up her telescope, and take my saddle horse. She's been there three hours by now. I imagine she's got the telescope already set up on the hen-house roof. I hope nothing happens."

"You worry too much, Mammy," said her son, trying to conceal his impatience.

"I'm not worrying," said Grandmother, shifting her riding skirt to the arm carrying the portmoney. "It will scarcely be any good taking this," she said; "I might in fact as well throw it away for this summer."

"Never mind, Mammy, we'll send to the Black Farm for Pompey, he's a good easy saddler."

"You may ride him yourself," said Grandmother. "I'll never mount Pompey while Fiddler is alive. Fiddler is my horse, and I hate having his mouth spoiled by a careless rider. Eliza never could ride, and she never will. . . ."

Miranda gave a little skip and ran away. So they were going to Cedar Grove. Miranda never got over being surprised at the way grown-up people simply did not seem able to give anyone a straight answer to any question, unless the answer was "No." Then it popped out with no trouble at all. At a little distance, she heard her grandmother say, "Harry, have you seen my riding crop lately?" and her father answered, at least maybe he thought it was an answer, "Now, Mammy, for God's sake let's get this thing over with." That was it, exactly.

Another strange way her father had of talking was calling Grandmother "Mammy." Aunt Jane was Mammy. Sometimes he called Grandmother "Mama," but she wasn't Mama either, she was really Grandmother. Mama was dead. Dead meant gone away forever. Dying was something that happened all the time, to people and everything else. Somebody died, and there was a long string of carriages going at a slow walk over the rocky ridge of the hill towards the river while the bell tolled and tolled, and that person was never seen again by anybody. Kittens and chickens and specially little turkeys died much oftener, and sometimes calves, but hardly ever cows or horses. Lizards on rocks turned into shells, with no lizard inside at all. If caterpillars all curled up and furry didn't move when you poked them with a stick, that meant they were dead—it was a sure sign.

When Miranda found any creature that didn't move or make a noise, or looked somehow different from the live ones, she always buried it in a little grave with flowers on top and a smooth stone at the head. Even grasshoppers. Everything dead had to be treated this way. "This way and no other!" Grandmother always said when she was laying down the law about all kinds of things. "It must be done *this* way, and no other!"

Miranda went down the crooked flat-stone walk hopping zigzag between the grass tufts. First there were pomegranate and cape jessamine bushes mixed together; then it got very dark and shady and that was the fig grove. She went to her favorite fig tree where the deep branches bowed down level with her chin, and she could gather figs without having to climb and skin her knees. Grandmother hadn't remembered to take any figs to the country the last time, she said there were plenty of them at Cedar Grove. But the ones at Cedar Grove were big soft greenish white ones, and these at home were black and sugary. It was strange that Grandmother did not seem to notice the difference. The air was sweet among the fig trees, and chickens were always getting out of the run and rushing there to eat the figs off the ground. One mother hen was scurrying around scratching and clucking. She would scratch around a fig lying there in plain sight and cluck to her children as if it was a worm and she had dug it up for them.

"Old smarty," said Miranda, "you're just pretending."

When the little chickens all ran to their mother under Miranda's fig tree, one little chicken did not move. He was spread out on his side with his eyes shut and his mouth open. He was yellow fur in spots and pinfeathers in spots, and the rest of him was naked and sunburned. "Lazy," said Miranda, poking him with her toe. Then she saw that he was dead.

Oh, and in no time at all they'd be setting out for Halifax. Grandmother never went away, she always set out for somewhere. She'd have to hurry like anything to get him buried properly. Back into the house she went on tiptoe hoping not to be seen, for Grandmother always asked: "Where are you going, child? What are you doing? What is that you're carrying? Where did you get it? Who gave you permission?" and after Miranda had explained all that, even if there turned out not to be anything wrong in it, nothing ever seemed so nice any more. Besides it took forever to get away.

Miranda slid open her bureau drawer, third down, left-hand side where her new shoes were still wrapped in tissue paper in a nice white box the right size for a chicken with pinfeathers. She pushed the rustling white folded things and the lavender bags out of the way and trembled a little. Down in front the carry-all wheels screeched and crunched on the gravel, with Old Uncle Jimbilly yelling like a foghorn, "Hiyi, thar, back up, you steeds! Back up thar, you!" and of course, that meant he was turning Tom and Dick around so they would be pointing towards Halifax. They'd be after her, calling and hurrying her, and she wouldn't have time for anything and they wouldn't listen to a word.

It wasn't hard work digging a hole with her little spade in the loose dry soil. Miranda wrapped the slimpsy chicken in tissue paper, trying to make it look pretty, laid it in the box carefully, and covered it up with a nice mound, just like people's. She had hardly got it piled up grave shape, kneeling and leaning to smooth it over, when a strange sound came from somewhere, a very sad little crying sound. It said Weep, weep, weep, three times like that slowly, and it seemed to come from the mound of dirt. "My goodness," Miranda asked herself aloud, "what's that?" She pushed her bonnet off her ears and listened hard. "Weep, weep," said the tiny sad voice. And People began calling and urging her, their voices coming nearer. She began to clamor, too.

"Yes, Aunty, wait a minute, Aunty!"

"You come right on here this minute, we're goin'!"

"You *have* to wait, Aunty!"

Her father was coming along the edge of the fig trees. "Hurry up, Baby, you'll get left!"

Miranda felt she couldn't bear to be left. She ran all shaking with fright. Her father gave her the annoyed look he always gave her when he said something to upset her and then saw that she was upset. His words were kind but his voice scolded: "Stop getting so excited, Baby, you know we wouldn't leave you for anything." Miranda wanted to talk back: "Then why did you say so?" but she was still listening for that tiny sound: "Weep, weep." She lagged and pulled backward, looking over her shoulder, but her father hurried her towards the carry-all. But things didn't make sounds if they were dead. They couldn't. That was one of the signs. Oh, but she had heard it.

Her father sat in front and drove, and old Uncle Jimbilly didn't do anything but get down and open gates. Grandmother and Aunt Nannie sat in the back seat, with Miranda between them. She loved setting out somewhere, with everybody smiling and settling down and looking up at the weather, with the horses bouncing and pulling on the reins, the springs jolting and swaying with a creaky noise that made you feel sure you were traveling. That evening she would go wading with Maria and Paul and Uncle Jimbilly, and that very night she would lie out on the grass in her nightgown to cool off, and they would all drink lemonade before going to bed. Sister Maria and Brother Paul would already be burned like muffins because they were sent on ahead the minute school was out. Sister Maria had got freckled and Father was furious. "Keep your bonnet on," he said to Miranda, sternly. "Now remember. I'm not going to have that face ruined, too." But oh, what had made that funny sound? Miranda's ears buzzed and she had a dull round pain in her just under her front ribs. She had to go back and let him out. He'd never get out by himself, all tangled up in tissue paper and that shoebox. He'd never get out without her.

"Grandmother, I've got to go back. Oh, I've *got* to go back!"

Grandmother turned Miranda's face around by the chin and looked at her closely, the way grown folks did. Grandmother's eyes were always the same. They never looked kind or sad or angry or tired or anything. They just looked, blue and still. "What is the matter with you, Miranda, what happened?"

"Oh, I've got to go back—I forg-got something important."

"Stop that silly crying and tell me what you want."

Miranda couldn't stop. Her father looked very anxious. "Mammy, maybe the Baby's sick." He reached out his handkerchief to her face. "What's the matter with my honey? Did you eat something?"

Miranda had to stand up to cry as hard as she wanted to. The wheels went grinding round in the road, the carry-all wobbled so that Grandmother had to take her by one arm, and her father by the other. They stared at each other over Miranda's head with a moveless gaze that Miranda had seen often, and their eyes looked exactly alike. Miranda blinked up at them, waiting to see who would win. Then Grandmother's hand fell away, and Miranda was handed over to her father. He gave the reins to Uncle Jimbilly, and lifted her over the top of the seat. She sprawled against his chest and knees as if he were an armchair and stopped crying at once. "We can't go back just for notions," he told her in the reasoning tone he always talked in when Grandmother scolded, and held the muffly handkerchief for her. "Now, blow hard. What did you forget, honey? We'll find another. Was it your doll?"

Miranda hated dolls. She never played with them. She always pulled the wigs off and tied them on the kittens, like hats. The kittens pulled them off instantly. It was fun. She put the doll clothes on the kittens and it took any one of them just half a minute to get them all off again. Kittens had sense. Miranda wailed suddenly, "Oh, I want my doll!" and cried again, trying to drown out the strange little sound, "Weep, weep"—

"Well now, if that's all," said her father comfortably, "there's a raft of dolls at Cedar Grove, and about forty fresh kittens. How'd you like that?"

"Forty?" asked Miranda.

"About," said Father.

Old Aunt Nannie leaned and held out her hand. "Look, honey, I toted you some nice black figs."

Her face was wrinkled and black and it looked like a fig upside down with a white ruffled cap. Miranda clenched her eyes tight and shook her head.

"Is that a pretty way to behave when Aunt Nannie offers you something nice?" asked Grandmother in her gentle reminding tone of voice.

"No, ma'am," said Miranda meekly. "Thank you, Aunt Nannie." But she did not accept the figs.

Great-Aunt Eliza, half way up a stepladder pitched against the flat-roofed chicken house, was telling Hinry just how to set up her telescope. "For a fellow who never saw or heard of a telescope," Great-Aunt Eliza said to Grandmother, who was really her sister Sophia Jane, "he doesn't do so badly so long as I tell him."

"I do wish you'd stop clambering up stepladders, Eliza," said Grandmother, "at your time of life."

"You're nothing but a nervous wreck, Sophia, I declare. When did you ever know me to get hurt?"

"Even so," said Grandmother tartly, "there is such a thing as appropriate behavior at your time of . . ."

Great-Aunt Eliza seized a fold of her heavy brown pleated skirt with one hand, with the other she grasped the ladder one rung higher and ascended another step. "Now Hinry," she called, "just swing it around facing west and leave it level. I'll fix it the way I want when I'm ready. You can come on down now." She came down then herself, and said to her sister: "So long as you can go bouncing off on that horse of yours, Sophia Jane, I s'pose I can climb ladders. I'm three years younger than you, and *at your time of life* that makes all the difference!"

Grandmother turned pink as the inside of a seashell, the one on her sewing table that had the sound of the sea in it; Miranda knew that she had always been the pretty one, and she was pretty still, but Great-Aunt Eliza was not pretty now and never had been. Miranda, watching and listening—for everything in the world was strange to her and something she had to know about—saw two old women, who were proud of being grandmothers, who spoke to children always as if they knew best about everything and children knew nothing, and they told children all day long to come here, go there, do this, do not do that, and they were always right and children never were except when they did anything they were told right away without a word. And here they were bickering like two little girls at school, or even the way Miranda and her sister Maria bickered and nagged and picked on each other and said things on purpose to hurt each other's feelings. Miranda felt sad and strange and a little frightened. She began edging away.

"Where are you going, Miranda?" asked Grandmother in her everyday voice.

"Just to the house," said Miranda, her heart sinking.

"Wait and walk with us," said Grandmother. She was very thin and pale and had white hair. Beside her, Great-Aunt Eliza loomed like a mountain with her grizzled iron-colored hair like a curly wig, her steel-rimmed spectacles over her snuff-colored eyes, and snuff-colored woolen skirts billowing about her, and her smell of snuff. When she came through the door she quite filled it up. When she sat down the chair disappeared under her, and she seemed to be sitting solidly on herself from her waistband to the floor.

Now with Grandmother sitting across the room rummaging in her work basket and pretending not to see anything, Great-Aunt Eliza took a small brown bottle out of her pocket, opened it, took a pinch of snuff in each nostril, sneezed loudly, wiped her nose with a big white starchy-looking handkerchief, pushed her spectacles up on her forehead, took a little twig chewed into a brush at one end, dipped and twisted it around in the little bottle, and placed it firmly between her teeth. Miranda had heard of this shameful habit in women of the lower classes, but no lady had been known to "dip snuff," and surely not in the family. Yet here was Great-Aunt Eliza, a lady even if not a very pretty one, dipping snuff. Miranda knew how her grandmother felt about it; she stared fascinated at Great-Aunt Eliza until her eyes watered. Great-Aunt Eliza stared back in turn.

"Look here, young one, d'ye s'pose if I gave you a gumdrop you'd get out from underfoot?"

She reached in the other pocket and took out a roundish, rather crushed-looking pink gumdrop with the sugar coating pretty badly crackled. "Now take this, and don't let me lay eyes on you any more today."

Miranda hurried away, clenching the gumdrop in her palm. When she reached the kitchen it was oozing through her fingers. She went to the tap and held her hand under the water and tried to wash off the snuffy smell. After this crime she did not really dare go near Great-Aunt Eliza again soon. "What did you do with that gumdrop so quickly, child?" she could almost hear her asking.

Yet Miranda almost forgot her usual interests, such as kittens and other little animals on the place, pigs, chickens, rabbits, anything at all so it was a baby and would let her pet and feed it, for Great-Aunt Eliza's ways and habits kept Miranda following her about, gazing, or sitting across the dining-table, gazing, for when Great-Aunt Eliza was not on the roof before her telescope, always just before daylight or just after dark, she was walking about with a microscope and a burning glass, peering closely at something she saw on a tree trunk, something she found in the grass; now and then she collected fragments that looked like dried leaves or bits of bark, brought them in the house, spread them out on a sheet of white paper, and sat there, poring, as still as if she were saying her prayers. At table she would dissect a scrap of potato peeling or anything else she might be eating, and sit there, bowed over, saying, "Hum," from time to time. Grandmother, who did not allow the children to bring anything to the table to play with and who forbade them to do anything but eat while they were there, ignored her sister's manners as long as she could, then remarked one day, when Great-Aunt Eliza was humming like a bee to herself over what her microscope had found in a raisin, "Eliza, if it is interesting save it for me to look at after dinner. Or tell me what it is."

"You wouldn't know if I told you," said Great-Aunt Eliza, coolly, putting her microscope away and finishing off her pudding.

When at last, just before they were all going back to town again, Great-Aunt Eliza invited the children to climb the ladder with her and see the stars through her telescope, they were so awed they looked at each other like strangers, and did not exchange a word. Miranda saw only a great pale flaring disk of cold light, but she knew it was the moon and called out in pure rapture, "Oh, it's like another world!"

"Why, of course, child," said Great-Aunt Eliza, in her growling voice, but kindly, "other worlds, a million other worlds."

"Like this one?" asked Miranda, timidly.

"Nobody knows, child. . . ."

"Nobody knows, nobody knows," Miranda sang to a tune in her head, and when the others walked on, she was so dazzled with joy she fell back by herself, walking a little distance behind Great-Aunt Eliza's swinging lantern and her wide-swinging skirts. They took the dewy path through the fig grove, much like the one in town, with the early dew bringing out the sweet smell of the milky leaves. They passed a fig tree with low hanging branches, and Miranda reached up by habit and touched it with her fingers for luck. From the earth beneath her feet came a terrible, faint troubled sound. "Weep weep, weep weep . . ." murmured a little crying voice from the smothering earth, the grave.

Miranda bounded like a startled pony against the back of Great-Aunt Eliza's knees, crying out, "Oh, oh, oh, wait . . ."

"What on earth's the matter, child?"

Miranda seized the warm snuffy hand held out to her and hung on hard. "Oh, there's something saying 'weep weep' out of the ground!"

Great-Aunt Eliza stooped, put her arm around Miranda and listened carefully, for a moment. "Hear them?" she said. "They're not in the ground at all. They are the first tree frogs, means it's going to rain," she said, "weep weep—hear them?"

Miranda took a deep trembling breath and heard them. They were in the trees. They walked on again, Miranda holding Great-Aunt Eliza's hand.

"Just think," said Great-Aunt Eliza, in her most scientific voice, "when tree frogs shed their skins, they pull them off over their heads like little shirts, and they eat them. Can you imagine? They have the prettiest little shapes you ever saw—I'll show you one some time under the microscope."

"Thank you, ma'am," Miranda remembered finally to say through her fog of bliss at hearing the tree frogs sing, "Weep weep . . ."

Ryūnosuke Akutagawa
1892–1927
IN A GROVE

THE TESTIMONY OF A WOODCUTTER QUESTIONED
BY A HIGH POLICE COMMISSIONER

YES, SIR. Certainly, it was I who found the body. This morning, as usual, I went to cut my daily quota of cedars, when I found the body in a grove in a hollow in the mountains. The exact location? About 150 meters off the Yamashina stage road. It's an out-of-the-way grove of bamboo and cedars.

The body was lying flat on its back dressed in a bluish silk kimono and a wrinkled head-dress of the Kyoto[1] style. A single sword-stroke had pierced the breast. The fallen bamboo blades around it were stained with bloody blossoms. No, the blood was no longer running. The wound had dried up, I believe. And also, a gad-fly was stuck fast there, hardly noticing my footsteps.

You ask me if I saw a sword or any such thing?

No, nothing, sir. I found only a rope at the root of a cedar near by. And . . . well, in addition to a rope, I found a comb. That was all. Apparently he must have made a battle of it before he was murdered, because the grass and fallen bamboo-blades had been trampled down all around.

"A horse was near by?"

No, sir. It's hard enough for a man to enter, let alone a horse.

THE TESTIMONY OF A TRAVELING BUDDHIST
PRIEST QUESTIONED BY A HIGH POLICE
COMMISSIONER

The time? Certainly, it was about noon yesterday, sir. The unfortunate man was on the road from Sekiyama to Yamashina. He was walking toward Sekiyama with a woman accompanying him on horseback, who I have since learned was his wife. A scarf hanging from her head hid her face from view. All I saw was the color of her clothes, a lilac-colored suit. Her horse was a sorrel with a fine mane. The lady's height? Oh, about four feet five inches. Since I am a Buddhist priest, I took little notice about her details. Well, the man was armed with a sword as well as a bow and arrows. And I remember that he carried some twenty odd arrows in his quiver.

Little did I expect that he would meet such a fate. Truly, human life is as evanescent as the morning dew or a flash of lightning. My words are inadequate to express my sympathy for him.

[1] a major Japanese city

THE TESTIMONY OF A POLICEMAN QUESTIONED BY A HIGH POLICE COMMISSIONER

The man that I arrested? He is a notorious brigand called Tajomaru. When I arrested him, he had fallen off his horse. He was groaning on the bridge at Awataguchi. The time? It was in the early hours of last night. For the record, I might say that the other day I tried to arrest him, but unfortunately he escaped. He was wearing a dark blue silk kimono and a large plain sword. And, as you see, he got a bow and arrows somewhere. You say that this bow and these arrows look like the ones owned by the dead man? Then Tajomaru must be the murderer. The bow wound with leather strips, the black lacquered quiver, the seventeen arrows with hawk feathers—these were all in his possession, I believe. Yes, sir, the horse is, as you say, a sorrel with a fine mane. A little beyond the stone bridge I found the horse grazing by the roadside, with his long rein dangling. Surely there is some providence in his having been thrown by the horse.

Of all the robbers prowling around Kyoto, this Tajomaru has given the most grief to the women in town. Last autumn a wife who came to the mountain back of the Pindora of the Toribe Temple, presumably to pay a visit, was murdered, along with a girl. It has been suspected that it was his doing. If this criminal murdered the man, you cannot tell what he may have done with the man's wife. May it please your honor to look into this problem as well.

THE TESTIMONY OF AN OLD WOMAN QUESTIONED BY A HIGH POLICE COMMISSIONER

Yes sir, that corpse is the man who married my daughter. He does not come from Kyoto. He was a samurai[2] in the town of Kokufu in the province of Wakasa. His name was Kanazawa no Takehiko, and his age was twenty-six. He was of a gentle disposition, so I am sure he did nothing to provoke the anger of others.

My daughter? Her name is Masago, and her age is nineteen. She is a spirited, fun-loving girl, but I am sure she has never known any man except Takehiko. She has a small, oval, dark-complected face with a mole at the corner of her left eye.

Yesterday Takehiko left for Wakasa with my daughter. What bad luck it is that things should have come to such a sad end! What has become of my daughter? I am resigned to giving up my son-in-law as lost, but the fate of my daughter worries me sick. For heaven's sake leave no stone unturned to find her. I hate that robber Tajomaru, or whatever his name is. Not only my son-in-law, but my daughter . . . (Her later words were drowned in tears.)

---

[2] a military retainer ranking as a lesser nobleman

TAJOMARU'S CONFESSION

I killed him, but not her. Where's she gone? I can't tell. Oh, wait a
minute. No torture can make me confess what I don't know. Now things
have come to such a head, I won't keep anything from you.

Yesterday a little past noon I met that couple. Just then a puff of wind
blew, and raised her hanging scarf, so that I caught a glimpse of her face.
Instantly it was again covered from my view. That may have been one
reason; she looked like a Bodhisattva.[3] At that moment I made up my
mind to capture her even if I had to kill her man.

Why? To me killing isn't a matter of such great consequence as you
might think. When a woman is captured, her man has to be killed anyway. In killing, I use the sword I wear at my side. Am I the only one who
kills people? You, you don't use your swords. You kill people with your
power, with your money. Sometimes you kill them on the pretext of
working for their good. It's true they don't bleed. They are in the best
of health, but all the same you've killed them. It's hard to say who is a
greater sinner, you or me. (An ironical smile.)

But it would be good if I could capture a woman without killing her
man. So, I made up my mind to capture her, and do my best not to kill
him. But it's out of the question on the Yamashina stage road. So I managed to lure the couple into the mountains.

It was quite easy. I became their traveling companion, and I told them
there was an old mound in the mountain over there, and that I had dug it
open and found many mirrors and swords. I went on to tell them I'd buried the things in a grove behind the mountain, and that I'd like to sell them
at a low price to anyone who would care to have them. Then . . . you
see, isn't greed terrible? He was beginning to be moved by my talk before he knew it. In less than half an hour they were driving their horse
toward the mountain with me.

When he came in front of the grove, I told them that the treasures
were buried in it, and I asked them to come and see. The man had no
objection—he was blinded by greed. The woman said she would wait
on horseback. It was natural for her to say so, at the sight of a thick
grove. To tell you the truth, my plan worked just as I wished, so I went
into the grove with him, leaving her behind alone.

The grove is only bamboo for some distance. About fifty yards ahead
there's a rather open clump of cedars. It was a convenient spot for my
purpose. Pushing my way through the grove, I told him a plausible lie
that the treasures were buried under the cedars. When I told him this,
he pushed his laborious way toward the slender cedar visible through the
grove. After a while the bamboo thinned out, and we came to where a
number of cedars grew in a row. As soon as we got there, I seized him
from behind. Because he was a trained, sword-bearing warrior, he was

[3] a compassionate being destined to become a Buddha

quite strong, but he was taken by surprise, so there was no help for him. I soon tied him up to the root of a cedar. Where did I get a rope? Thank heaven, being a robber, I had a rope with me, since I might have to scale a wall at any moment. Of course it was easy to stop him from calling out by gagging his mouth with fallen bamboo leaves.

When I disposed of him, I went to his woman and asked her to come and see him, because he seemed to have been suddenly taken sick. It's needless to say that this plan also worked well. The woman, her sedge hat off, came into the depths of the grove, where I led her by the hand. The instant she caught sight of her husband, she drew a small sword. I've never seen a woman of such violent temper. If I'd been off guard, I'd have got a thrust in my side. I dodged, but she kept on slashing at me. She might have wounded me deeply or killed me. But I'm Tajomaru. I managed to strike down her small sword without drawing my own. The most spirited woman is defenseless without a weapon. At least I could satisfy my desire for her without taking her husband's life.

Yes, . . . without taking his life. I had no wish to kill him. I was about to run away from the grove, leaving the woman behind in tears, when she frantically clung to my arm. In broken fragments of words, she asked that either her husband or I die. She said it was more trying than death to have her shame known to two men. She gasped out that she wanted to be the wife of whichever survived. Then a furious desire to kill him seized me. (Gloomy excitement.)

Telling you in this way, no doubt I seem a crueler man than you. But that's because you didn't see her face. Especially her burning eyes at that moment. As I saw her eye to eye, I wanted to make her my wife even if I were to be struck by lightning. I wanted to make her my wife . . . this single desire filled my mind. This was not only lust, as you might think. At that time if I'd had no other desire than lust, I'd surely not have minded knocking her down and running away. Then I wouldn't have stained my sword with his blood. But the moment I gazed at her face in the dark grove, I decided not to leave there without killing him.

But I didn't like to resort to unfair means to kill him. I untied him and told him to cross swords with me. (The rope that was found at the root of the cedar is the rope I dropped at the time.) Furious with anger, he drew his thick sword. And quick as thought, he sprang at me ferociously, without speaking a word. I needn't tell you how our fight turned out. The twenty-third stroke . . . please remember this. I'm impressed with this fact still. Nobody under the sun has ever clashed swords with me twenty strokes. (A cheerful smile.)

When he fell, I turned toward her, lowering my blood-stained sword. But to my great astonishment she was gone. I wondered to where she had run away. I looked for her in the clump of cedars. I listened, but heard only a groaning sound from the throat of the dying man.

As soon as we started to cross swords, she may have run away through the grove to call for help. When I thought of that, I decided it was a matter of life and death to me. So, robbing him of his sword, and bow and arrows, I ran out to the mountain road. There I found her horse still grazing quietly. It would be a mere waste of words to tell you the later details, but before I entered town I had already parted with the sword. That's all my confession. I know that my head will be hung in chains anyway, so put me down for the maximum penalty. (A defiant attitude.)

THE CONFESSION OF A WOMAN WHO HAS COME TO THE "SHIMIZU" TEMPLE

That man in the blue silk kimono, after forcing me to yield to him, laughed mockingly as he looked at my bound husband. How horrified my husband must have been! But no matter how hard he struggled in agony, the rope cut into him all the more tightly. In spite of myself I ran stumblingly toward his side. Or rather I tried to run toward him, but the man instantly knocked me down. Just at that moment I saw an indescribable light in my husband's eyes. Something beyond expression . . . his eyes make me shudder even now. That instantaneous look of my husband, who couldn't speak a word, told me all his heart. The flash in his eyes was neither anger nor sorrow . . . only a cold light, a look of loathing. More struck by the look in his eyes than by the blow of the thief, I called out in spite of myself and fell unconscious.

In the course of time I came to, and found that the man in blue silk was gone. I saw only my husband still bound to the root of the cedar. I raised myself from the bamboo-blades with difficulty, and looked into his face; but the expression in his eyes was just the same as before.

Beneath the cold contempt in his eyes, there was hatred. Shame, grief, and anger . . . I didn't know how to express my heart at that time. Reeling to my feet, I went up to my husband.

"Takejiro," I said to him, "since things have come to this pass, I cannot live with you, I'm determined to die, . . . but you must die, too. You saw my shame. I can't leave you alive as you are."

This was all I could say. Still he went on gazing at me with loathing and contempt. My heart breaking, I looked for his sword. It must have been taken by the robber. Neither his sword nor his bow and arrows were to be seen in the grove. But fortunately my small sword was lying at my feet. Raising it over head, once more I said, "Now give me your life. I'll follow you right away."

When he heard these words, he moved his lips with difficulty. Since his mouth was stuffed with leaves, of course his voice could not be heard at all. But at a glance I understood his words. Despising me, his look said only, "Kill me." Neither conscious nor unconscious, I stabbed the small sword through the lilac-colored kimono into his breast.

Again at this time I must have fainted. By the time I managed to look up, he had already breathed his last—still in bonds. A streak of sinking sunlight streamed through the clump of cedars and bamboos, and shone on his pale face. Gulping down my sobs, I untied the rope from his dead body. And . . . and what has become of me since I have no more strength to tell you. Anyway I hadn't the strength to die. I stabbed my own throat with the small sword, I threw myself into a pond at the foot of the mountain, and I tried to kill myself in many ways. Unable to end my life, I am still living in dishonor. (A lonely smile.) Worthless as I am, I must have been forsaken even by the most merciful Kwannon.[4] I killed my own husband. I was violated by the robber. Whatever can I do? Whatever can I . . . I . . . (Gradually, violent sobbing.)

THE STORY OF THE MURDERED MAN, AS TOLD
THROUGH A MEDIUM

After violating my wife, the robber, sitting there, began to speak comforting words to her. Of course I couldn't speak. My whole body was tied fast to the root of a cedar. But meanwhile I winked at her many times, as much as to say "Don't believe the robber." I wanted to convey some such meaning to her. But my wife, sitting dejectedly on the bamboo leaves, was looking hard at her lap. To all appearances, she was listening to his words. I was agonized by jealousy. In the meantime the robber went on with his clever talk, from one subject to another. The robber finally made his bold, brazen proposal. "Once your virtue is stained, you won't get along well with your husband, so won't you be my wife instead? It's my love for you that made me be violent toward you."

While the criminal talked, my wife raised her face as if in a trance. She had never looked so beautiful as at that moment. What did my beautiful wife say in answer to him while I was sitting bound there? I am lost in space, but I have never thought of her answer without burning with anger and jealousy. Truly she said, . . . "Then take me away with you wherever you go."

This is not the whole of her sin. If that were all, I would not be tormented so much in the dark. When she was going out of the grove as if in a dream, her hand in the robber's, she suddenly turned pale, and pointed at me tied to the root of the cedar, and said, "Kill him! I cannot marry you as long as he lives." "Kill him!" she cried many times, as if she had gone crazy. Even now these words threaten to blow me headlong into the bottomless abyss of darkness. Has such a hateful thing come out of a human mouth ever before? Have such cursed words ever struck a human ear, even once? Even once such a . . . (A sudden cry of scorn.) At these words the robber himself turned pale. "Kill him," she cried, clinging to his arms. Looking hard at her, he answered neither yes or no . . . but hardly had I thought about his answer before she had been knocked down into the bamboo leaves. (Again a cry of scorn.) Quietly

[4] Buddhist goddess of mercy

folding his arms, he looked at me and said, "What will you do with her? Kill her or save her? You have only to nod. Kill her?" For these words alone I would like to pardon his crime.

While I hesitated, she shrieked and ran into the depths of the grove. The robber instantly snatched at her, but he failed even to grasp her sleeve.

After she ran away, he took up my sword, and my bow and arrows. With a single stroke he cut one of my bonds. I remember his mumbling, "My fate is next." Then he disappeared from the grove. All was silent after that. No, I heard someone crying. Untying the rest of my bonds, I listened carefully, and I noticed that it was my own crying. (Long silence.)

I raised my exhausted body from the root of the cedar. In front of me there was shining the small sword which my wife had dropped. I took it up and stabbed my breast. A bloody lump rose to my mouth, but I didn't feel any pain. When my breast grew cold, everything was as silent as the dead in their graves. What profound silence! Not a single bird-note was heard in the sky over this grove in the hollow of the mountains. Only a lonely light lingered on the cedars and mountains. By and by the light gradually grew fainter, till the cedars and bamboo were lost to view. Lying there, I was enveloped in deep silence.

Then someone crept up to me. I tried to see who it was. But darkness had already been gathering round me. Someone . . . that someone drew the small sword softly out of my breast in its invisible hand. At the same time once more blood flowed into my mouth. And once and for all I sank down into the darkness of space.

Translated by Takashi Kojima

F. Scott Fitzgerald
1896–1940
THE JELLY-BEAN

JIM POWELL was a Jelly-bean. Much as I desire to make him an appealing character, I feel that it would be unscrupulous to deceive you on that point. He was a bred-in-the-bone, dyed-in-the-wool, ninety-nine three-quarters per cent Jelly-bean and he grew lazily all during Jelly-bean season, which is every season, down in the land of the Jelly-beans well below the Mason-Dixon line.

Now if you call a Memphis man a Jelly-bean he will quite possibly pull a long sinewy rope from his pocket and hang you to a convenient telegraph-pole. If you call a New Orleans man a Jelly-bean he will probably grin and ask you who is taking your girl to the Mardi Gras ball. The particular Jelly-bean patch which produced the protagonist of this history lies somewhere between the two—a little city of forty thousand that has dozed sleepily for forty thousand years in southern Georgia, occasionally stirring in its slumbers and muttering something about a war that took place sometime, somewhere, and that everyone else has forgotten long ago.

Jim was a Jelly-bean. I write that again because it has such a pleasant sound—rather like the beginning of a fairy story—as if Jim were nice. It somehow gives me a picture of him with a round, appetizing face and all sorts of leaves and vegetables growing out of his cap. But Jim was long and thin and bent at the waist from stooping over pooltables, and he was what might have been known in the indiscriminating North as a corner loafer. "Jelly-bean" is the name throughout the undissolved Confederacy for one who spends his life conjugating the verb *to idle* in the first person singular—I am idling, I have idled, I will idle.

Jim was born in a white house on a green corner. It had four weather-beaten pillars in front and a great amount of lattice-work in the rear that made a cheerful criss-cross background for a flowery sun-drenched lawn. Originally the dwellers in the white house had owned the ground next door and next door to that and next door to that, but this had been so long ago that even Jim's father scarcely remembered it. He had, in fact, thought it a matter of so little moment that when he was dying from a pistol wound got in a brawl he neglected even to tell little Jim, who was five years old and miserably frightened. The white house became a boarding-house run by a tight-lipped lady from Macon, whom Jim called Aunt Mamie and detested with all his soul.

He became fifteen, went to high school, wore his hair in black snarls, and was afraid of girls. He hated his home where four women and one old man prolonged an interminable chatter from summer to summer about what lots the Powell place had originally included and what sort of flowers would be out next. Sometimes the parents of little girls in town, remembering Jim's mother and fancying a resemblance in the dark eyes and hair, invited him to parties, but parties made him shy and he much preferred sitting on a disconnected axle in Tilly's Garage, rolling the bones or exploring his mouth endlessly with a long straw. For pocket money, he picked up odd jobs, and it was due to this that he stopped going to parties. At his third party little Marjorie Haight had whispered indiscreetly and within hearing distance that he was a boy who brought the groceries sometimes. So instead of the two-step and polka, Jim had learned to throw any number he desired on the dice and had listened to spicy tales of all the shootings that had occurred in the surrounding country during the past fifty years.

He became eighteen. The war[1] broke out and he enlisted as a gob and polished brass in the Charleston Navy-yard for a year. Then by way of

[1] World War I

variety, he went North and polished brass in the Brooklyn Navy-yard for a year.

When the war was over he came home. He was twenty-one, his trousers were too short and too tight. His buttoned shoes were long and narrow. His tie was an alarming conspiracy of purple and pink marvelously scrolled, and over it were two blue eyes faded like a piece of very good old cloth long exposed to the sun.

In the twilight of one April evening when a soft gray had drifted down along the cottonfields and over the sultry town, he was a vague figure leaning against a board fence, whistling and gazing at the moon's rim above the lights of Jackson Street. His mind was working persistently on a problem that had held his attention for an hour. The Jelly-bean had been invited to a party.

Back in the days when all the boys had detested all the girls, Clark Darrow and Jim had sat side by side in school. But, while Jim's social aspirations had died in the oily air of the garage, Clark had alternately fallen in and out of love, gone to college, taken to drink, given it up, and, in short, become one of the best beaux of the town. Nevertheless Clark and Jim had retained a friendship that, though casual, was perfectly definite. That afternoon Clark's ancient Ford had slowed up beside Jim, who was on the sidewalk and, out of a clear sky, Clark had invited him to a party at the country club. The impulse that made him do this was no stranger than the impulse which made Jim accept. The latter was probably an unconscious ennui, a half-frightened sense of adventure. And now Jim was soberly thinking it over.

He began to sing, drumming his long foot idly on a stone block in the side-walk till it wobbled up and down in time to the low throaty tune:

> *One mile from Home in Jelly-bean town,*
> *Lives Jeanne, the Jelly-bean Queen.*
> *She loves her dice and treats 'em nice;*
> *No dice would treat her mean.*

He broke off and agitated the sidewalk to a bumpy gallop.

"Daggone!" he muttered, half aloud.

They would all be there—the old crowd, the crowd to which, by right of the white house, sold long since, and the portrait of the officer in gray over the mantel, Jim should have belonged. But that crowd had grown up together into a tight little set as gradually as the girls' dresses had lengthened inch by inch, as definitely as the boys' trousers had dropped suddenly to their ankles. And to that society of first names and dead puppy-loves Jim was an outsider—a running mate of poor whites. Most of the men knew him, condescendingly; he tipped his hat to three or four girls. That was all.

When the dusk had thickened into a blue setting for the moon, he walked through the hot, pleasantly pungent town to Jackson Street. The stores were closing and the last shoppers were drifting homeward, as if borne on the dreamy revolution of a slow merry-go-round. A street-fair farther down made a brilliant alley of vari-colored booths and contributed a blend of music to the night—an oriental dance on a calliope, a melancholy bugle in front of a freak show, a cheerful rendition of "Back Home in Tennessee" on a hand-organ.

The Jelly-bean stopped in a store and bought a collar. Then he sauntered along toward Soda Sam's, where he found the usual three or four cars of a summer evening parked in front and the little darkies running back and forth with sundaes and lemonades.

"Hello, Jim."

It was a voice at his elbow—Joe Ewing sitting in an automobile with Marylyn Wade. Nancy Lamar and a strange man were in the back seat.

The Jelly-bean tipped his hat quickly.

"Hi, Ben—" then, after an almost imperceptible pause—"How y' all?"

Passing, he ambled on toward the garage where he had a room upstairs. His "How y' all?" had been said to Nancy Lamar, to whom he had not spoken in fifteen years.

Nancy had a mouth like a remembered kiss and shadowy eyes and blue-black hair inherited from her mother who had been born in Budapest. Jim passed her often in the street, walking small-boy fashion with her hands in her pockets, and he knew that with her inseparable Sally Carrol Hopper she had left a trail of broken hearts from Atlanta to New Orleans.

For a few fleeting moments Jim wished he could dance. Then he laughed and as he reached his door began to sing softly to himself:

> *Her Jelly Roll can twist your soul,*
> *Her eyes are big and brown,*
> *She's the Queen of the Queens of the Jelly-beans—*
> *My Jeanne of Jelly-bean town.*

2

At nine-thirty Jim and Clark met in front of Soda Sam's and started for the Country Club in Clark's Ford.

"Jim," asked Clark casually, as they rattled through the jasmine-scented night, "how do you keep alive?"

The Jelly-bean paused, considered.

"Well," he said finally, "I got a room over Tilly's Garage. I help him some with the cars in the afternoon an' he gives it to me free. Sometimes I drive one of his taxies and pick up a little thataway. I get fed up doin' that regular though."

"That's all?"

"Well, when there's a lot of work I help him by the day—Saturdays usually—and then there's one main source of revenue I don't generally mention. Maybe you don't recollect I'm about the champion crap-shooter of this town. They make me shoot from a cup now because once I get the feel of a pair of dice they just roll for me."

Clark grinned appreciatively.

"I never could learn to set 'em so's they'd do what I wanted. Wish you'd shoot with Nancy Lamar some day and take all her money away from her. She *will* roll 'em with the boys and she loses more than her daddy can afford to give her. I happen to know she sold a good ring last month to pay a debt."

The Jelly-bean was non-committal.

"The white house on Elm Street still belong to you?"

Jim shook his head.

"Sold. Got a pretty good price, seein' it wasn't in a good part of town no more. Lawyer told me to put it into Liberty bonds. But Aunt Mamie got so she didn't have no sense, so it takes all the interest to keep her up at Great Farms Sanitarium."

"H'm."

"I got an old uncle up-state an' I reckon I kin go up there if ever I get sure enough pore. Nice farm, but not enough niggers around to work it. He's asked me to come up and help him, but I don't guess I'd take much to it. Too doggone lonesome—" He broke off suddenly, "Clark, I want to tell you I'm much obliged to you for askin' me out, but I'd be a lot happier if you'd just stop the car right here an' let me walk back into town."

"Shucks!" Clark grunted. "Do you good to step out. You don't have to dance—just get out there on the floor and shake."

"Hold on," exclaimed Jim uneasily. "Don't you go leadin' me up to any girls and leavin' me there so I'll have to dance with 'em."

Clark laughed.

" 'Cause," continued Jim desperately, "without you swear you won't do that I'm agoin' to get out right here an' my good legs goin' carry me back to Jackson Street."

They agreed after some argument that Jim, unmolested by females, was to view the spectacle from a secluded settee in the corner where Clark would join him whenever he wasn't dancing.

So ten o'clock found the Jelly-bean with his legs crossed and his arms conservatively folded, trying to look casually at home and politely uninterested in the dancers. At heart he was torn between overwhelming self-consciousness and an intense curiosity as to all that went on around him. He saw the girls emerge one by one from the dressing-room, stretching and pluming themselves like bright birds, smiling over their powdered shoulders at the chaperones, casting a quick glance around to take in the room and, simultaneously, the room's reaction to their entrance—and then, again like birds, alighting and nestling in the sober arms of their waiting escorts. Sally Carrol Hopper, blonde and lazy-eyed, appeared clad in her favorite pink and blinking like an awakened rose. Marjorie Haight, Marylyn Wade, Harriet Cary, all the girls he had seen loitering down Jackson Street by noon, now, curled and brilliantined and delicately tinted for the overhead lights, were miraculously strange Dresden figures[2] of pink and blue and red and gold, fresh from the shop and not yet fully dried.

He had been there half an hour, totally uncheered by Clark's jovial visits which were each one accompanied by a "Hello, old boy, how you making out?" and a slap at his knee. A dozen males had spoken to him or stopped for a moment beside him, but he knew that they were each one surprised at finding him there and fancied that one or two were even slightly resentful. But at half past ten his embarrassment suddenly left him and a pull of breathless interest took him completely out of himself —Nancy Lamar had come out of the dressing-room.

She was dressed in yellow organdie, a costume of a hundred cool corners, with three tiers of ruffles and a big bow in back until she shed black and yellow around her in a sort of phosphorescent luster. The Jelly-bean's eyes opened wide and a lump arose in his throat. For a minute she stood beside the door until her partner hurried up. Jim recognized him as the stranger who had been with her in Joe Ewing's car that afternoon. He saw her set her arms akimbo and say something in a low voice, and laugh. The man laughed too and Jim experienced the quick pang of a weird new kind of pain. Some ray had passed between the pair, a shaft of beauty from that sun that had warmed him a moment since. The Jelly-bean felt suddenly like a weed in a shadow.

A minute later Clark approached him, bright-eyed and glowing.

"Hi, old man," he cried with some lack of originality. "How you making out?"

Jim replied that he was making out as well as could be expected.

"You come along with me," commanded Clark. "I've got something that'll put an edge on the evening."

Jim followed him awkwardly across the floor and up the stairs to the locker-room where Clark produced a flask of nameless yellow liquid.

"Good old corn."

Ginger ale arrived on a tray. Such potent nectar as "good old corn" needed some disguise beyond seltzer.

"Say, boy," exclaimed Clark breathlessly, "doesn't Nancy Lamar look beautiful?"

Jim nodded.

"Mighty beautiful," he agreed.

"She's all dolled up to a fare-you-well to-night," continued Clark. "Notice that fellow she's with?"

"Big fella? White pants?"

"Yeah. Well, that's Ogden Merritt from Savannah. Old man Merritt makes the Merritt safety razors. This fella's crazy about her. Been chasing after her all year.

[2] china dolls

"She's a wild baby," continued Clark, "but I like her. So does everybody. But she sure does do crazy stunts. She usually gets out alive, but she's got scars all over her reputation from one thing or another she's done."

"That so?" Jim passed over his glass. "That's good corn."

"Not so bad. Oh, she's a wild one. Shoots craps, say, boy! And she do like her highball. Promised I'd give her one later on."

"She in love with this—Merritt?"

"Damned if I know. Seems like all the best girls around here marry fellas and go off somewhere."

He poured himself one more drink and carefully corked the bottle.

"Listen, Jim, I got to go dance and I'd be much obliged if you just stick this corn right on your hip as long as you're not dancing. If a man notices I've had a drink he'll come up and ask me and before I know it it's all gone and somebody else is having my good time."

So Nancy Lamar was going to marry. This toast of a town was to become the private property of an individual in white trousers—and all because white trousers' father had made a better razor than his neighbor. As they descended the stairs Jim found the idea inexplicably depressing. For the first time in his life he felt a vague and romantic yearning. A picture of her began to form in his imagination—Nancy walking boylike and debonnaire along the street, taking an orange as tithe from a worshipful fruit-dealer, charging a dope[3] on a mythical account at Soda Sam's, assembling a convoy of beaux and then driving off in triumphal state for an afternoon of splashing and singing.

The Jelly-bean walked out on the porch to a deserted corner, dark between the moon on the lawn and the single lighted door of the ballroom. There he found a chair and, lighting a cigarette, drifted into the thoughtless reverie that was his usual mood. Yet now it was a reverie made sensuous by the night and by the hot smell of damp powder puffs, tucked in the fronts of low dresses and distilling a thousand rich scents to float out through the open door. The music itself, blurred by a loud trombone, became hot and shadowy, a languorous overtone to the scraping of many shoes and slippers.

Suddenly the square of yellow light that fell through the door was obscured by a dark figure. A girl had come out of the dressing-room and was standing on the porch not more than ten feet away. Jim heard a low-breathed "doggone" and then she turned and saw him. It was Nancy Lamar.

Jim rose to his feet.

"Howdy?"

"Hello—" she paused, hesitated, and then approached. "Oh, it's—Jim Powell."

[3] a cola drink

He bowed slightly, tried to think of a casual remark.

"Do you suppose," she began quickly, "I mean—do you know anything about gum?"

"What?"

"I've got gum on my shoe. Some utter ass left his or her gum on the floor and of course I stepped in it."

Jim blushed, inappropriately.

"Do you know how to get it off?" she demanded petulantly. "I've tried every damn thing in the dressing-room. I've tried soap and water —and even perfume and I've ruined my powder-puff trying to make it stick to that."

Jim considered the question in some agitation.

"Why—I think maybe gasoline—"

The words had scarcely left his lips when she grasped his hand and pulled him at a run off the low veranda, over a flower bed and at a gallop toward a group of cars parked in the moonlight by the first hole of the golf course.

"Turn on the gasoline," she commanded breathlessly.

"What?"

"For the gum, of course. I've got to get it off. I can't dance with gum on."

Obediently Jim turned to the cars and began inspecting them with a view to obtaining the desired solvent. Had she demanded a cylinder he would have done his best to wrench one out.

"Here," he said after a moment's search. "Here's one that's easy. Got a handkerchief?"

"It's upstairs wet. I used it for the soap and water."

Jim laboriously explored his pockets.

"Don't believe I got one either."

"Doggone it! Well, we can turn it on and let it run on the ground."

He turned it on fuller. The dripping became a flow and formed an oily pool that glistened brightly, reflecting a dozen tremulous moons on its quivering bosom.

"Ah," she sighed contentedly, "let it all out. The only thing to do is to wade in it."

In desperation he turned on the tap full and the pool suddenly widened, sending tiny rivers and trickles in all directions.

"That's fine. That's something like."

Raising her skirts she stepped gracefully in.

"I know this'll take it off," she murmured.

Jim smiled.

"There's lots more cars."

She stepped daintily out of the gasoline and began scraping her slippers, side and bottom, on the running-board of the automobile. The Jelly-bean contained himself no longer. He bent double with explosive laughter and after a second she joined in.

"You're here with Clark Darrow, aren't you?" she asked as they walked back toward the veranda.

"Yes."

"You know where he is now?"

"Out dancin', I reckin."

"The deuce. He promised me a highball."

"Well," said Jim, "I guess that'll be all right. I got his bottle right here in my pocket."

She smiled at him radiantly.

"I guess maybe you'll need ginger ale though," he added.

"Not me. Just the bottle."

"Sure enough?"

She laughed scornfully.

"Try me. I can drink anything any man can. Let's sit down."

She perched herself on the side of a table and he dropped into one of the wicker chairs beside her. Taking out the cork, she held the flask to her lips and took a long drink. He watched her, fascinated.

"Like it?"

She shook her head breathlessly.

"No, but I like the way it makes me feel. I think most people are that way."

Jim agreed.

"My daddy liked it too well. It got him."

"American men," said Nancy gravely, "don't know how to drink."

"What?" Jim was startled.

"In fact," she went on carelessly, "they don't know how to do anything very well. The one thing I regret in my life is that I wasn't born in England."

"In England?"

"Yes. It's the one regret of my life that I wasn't."

"Do you like it over there?"

"Yes. Immensely. I've never been there in person, but I've met a lot of Englishmen who were over here in the army, Oxford and Cambridge men—you know, that's like Sewanee and University of Georgia are here—and of course I've read a lot of English novels."

Jim was interested, amazed.

"D' you ever hear of Lady Diana Manners?" she asked earnestly.

No, Jim had not.

"Well, she's what I'd like to be. Dark, you know, like me, and wild as sin. She's the girl who rode her horse up the steps of some cathedral or church or something and all the novelists made their heroines do it afterwards."

Jim nodded politely. He was out of his depths.

"Pass the bottle," suggested Nancy. "I'm going to take another little one. A little drink wouldn't hurt a baby."

"You see," she continued, again breathless after a draft. "People over there have style. Nobody has style here. I mean the boys here aren't really worth dressing up for or doing sensational things for. Don't you know?"

"I suppose so—I mean I suppose not," murmured Jim.

"And I'd like to do 'em an' all. I'm really the only girl in town that has style."

She stretched out her arms and yawned pleasantly.

"Pretty evening."

"Sure is," agreed Jim.

"Like to have boat," she suggested dreamily. "Like to sail out on a silver lake, say the Thames, for instance. Have champagne and caviare sandwiches along. Have about eight people. And one of the men would jump overboard to amuse the party and get drowned like a man did with Lady Diana Manners once."

"Did he do it to please her?"

"Didn't mean to drown himself to please her. He just meant to jump overboard and make everybody laugh."

"I reckin they just died laughin' when he drowned."

"Oh, I suppose they laughed a little," she admitted. "I imagine she did, anyway. She's pretty hard, I guess—like I am."

"You hard?"

"Like nails." She yawned again and added, "Give me a little more from that bottle."

Jim hesitated but she held out her hand defiantly.

"Don't treat me like a girl," she warned him. "I'm not like any girl *you* ever saw." She considered. "Still, perhaps you're right. You got—you got old head on young shoulders."

She jumped to her feet and moved toward the door. The Jelly-bean rose also.

"Good-bye," she said politely, "good-bye. Thanks, Jelly-bean."

Then she stepped inside and left him wide-eyed upon the porch.

3

At twelve o'clock a procession of cloaks issued single file from the women's dressing-room and, each one pairing with a coated beau like dancers meeting in a cotillion figure, drifted through the door with sleepy happy laughter—through the door into the dark where autos backed and snorted and parties called to one another and gathered around the water-cooler.

Jim, sitting in his corner, rose to look for Clark. They had met at eleven; then Clark had gone in to dance. So, seeking him, Jim wandered into the soft-drink stand that had once been a bar. The room was deserted except for a sleepy Negro dozing behind the counter and two boys lazily fingering a pair of dice at one of the tables. Jim was about to leave them when he saw Clark coming in. At the same moment Clark looked up.

"Hi, Jim!" he commanded. "C'mon over and help us with this bottle. I guess there's not much left, but there's one all around."

Nancy, the man from Savannah, Marylyn Wade, and Joe Ewing were lolling and laughing in the doorway. Nancy caught Jim's eye and winked at him humorously.

They drifted over to a table and arranging themselves around it waited for the waiter to bring ginger ale. Jim, faintly ill at ease, turned his eyes on Nancy, who had drifted into a nickel crap game with the two boys at the next table.

"Bring them over here," suggested Clark.

Joe looked around.

"We don't want to draw a crowd. It's against club rules."

"Nobody's around," insisted Clark, "except Mr. Taylor. He's walk-up and down like a wild-man trying to find out who let all the gasoline out of his car."

There was a general laugh.

"I bet a million Nancy got something on her shoe again. You can't park when she's around."

"O Nancy, Mr. Taylor's looking for you!"

Nancy's cheeks were glowing with excitement over the game. "I haven't seen his silly little flivver in two weeks."

Jim felt a sudden silence. He turned and saw an individual of uncertain age standing in the doorway.

Clark's voice punctuated the embarrassment.

"Won't you join us, Mr. Taylor?"

"Thanks."

Mr. Taylor spread his unwelcome presence over a chair. "Have to, I'm waiting till they dig me up some gasoline. Somebody got funny with my car."

His eyes narrowed and he looked quickly from one to the other. Jim wondered what he had heard from the doorway—tried to remember what had been said.

"I'm right tonight," Nancy sang out, "and my four bits is in the ring."

"Faded!" snapped Taylor suddenly.

"Why, Mr. Taylor, I didn't know you shot craps!" Nancy was over-joyed to find that he had seated himself and instantly covered her bet. They had openly disliked each other since the night she had definitely discouraged a series of rather pointed advances.

"All right, babies, do it for your mama. Just one little seven." Nancy was *cooing* to the dice. She rattled them with a brave underhand flourish, and rolled them out on the table.

"Ah-h! I suspected it. And now again with the dollar up."

Five passes to her credit found Taylor a bad loser. She was making it personal, and after each success Jim watched triumph flutter across her face. She was doubling with each throw—such luck could scarcely last.

"Better go easy," he cautioned her timidly.

"Ah, but watch this one," she whispered. It was eight on the dice and she called her number.

"Little Ada, this time we're going South."

Ada from Decatur rolled over the table. Nancy was flushed and half-hysterical, but her luck was holding. She drove the pot up and up, refusing to drag. Taylor was drumming with his fingers on the table, but he was in to stay.

Then Nancy tried for a ten and lost the dice. Taylor seized them avidly. He shot in silence, and in the hush of excitement the clatter of one pass after another on the table was the only sound.

Now Nancy had the dice again, but her luck had broken. An hour passed. Back and forth it went. Taylor had been at it again—and again and again. They were even at last—Nancy lost her ultimate five dollars.

"Will you take my check," she said quickly, "for fifty, and we'll shoot it all?" Her voice was a little unsteady and her hand shook as she reached to the money.

Clark exchanged an uncertain but alarmed glance with Joe Ewing. Taylor shot again. He had Nancy's check.

"How 'bout another?" she said wildly. "Jes' any bank'll do—money everywhere as a matter of fact."

Jim understood—the "good old corn" he had given her—the "good old corn" she had taken since. He wished he dared interfere—a girl of that age and position would hardly have two bank accounts. When the clock struck two he contained himself no longer.

"May I—can't you let me roll 'em for you?" he suggested, his low, lazy voice a little strained.

Suddenly sleepy and listless, Nancy flung the dice down before him.

"All right—old boy! As Lady Diana Manners says, 'Shoot 'em, Jelly-bean'—My luck's gone."

"Mr. Taylor," said Jim, carelessly, "we'll shoot for one of those there checks against the cash."

Half an hour later Nancy swayed forward and clapped him on the back.

"Stole my luck, you did." She was nodding her head sagely.

Jim swept up the last check and putting it with the others tore them into confetti and scattered them on the floor. Someone started singing, and Nancy, kicking her chair backward, rose to her feet.

"Ladies and gentlemen," she announced. "Ladies—that's you, Mary-lyn. I want to tell the world that Mr. Jim Powell, who is a well-known Jelly-bean of this city, is an exception to a great rule—'lucky in dice—unlucky in love.' He's lucky in dice, and as matter of fact I—I *love* him. Ladies and gentlemen, Nancy Lamar, famous dark-haired beauty often featured in the *Herald* as one th' most popular members of younger set as other girls are often featured in this particular case. Wish to announce—

wish to announce, anyway, gentlemen—" She tipped suddenly. Clark caught her and restored her balance.

"My error," she laughed, "she stoops to—stoops to—anyways— We'll drink to Jelly-bean . . . Mr. Jim Powell, King of the Jelly-beans."

And a few minutes later as Jim waited hat in hand for Clark in the darkness of that same corner of the porch where she had come searching for gasoline, she appeared suddenly beside him.

"Jelly-bean," she said, "are you here, Jelly-bean? I think—" and her slight unsteadiness seemed part of an enchanted dream—"I think you deserve one of my sweetest kisses for that, Jelly-bean."

For an instant her arms were around his neck—her lips were pressed to his.

"I'm a wild part of the world, Jelly-bean, but you did me a good turn."

Then she was gone, down the porch, over the cricket-loud lawn. Jim saw Merritt come out the front door and say something to her angrily— saw her laugh and, turning away, walk with averted eyes to his car. Marylyn and Joe followed, singing a drowsy song about a Jazz baby.

Clark came out and joined Jim on the steps. "All pretty lit, I guess," he yawned. "Merritt's in a mean mood. He's certainly off Nancy."

Over east along the golf course a faint rug of gray spread itself across the feet of the night. The party in the car began to chant a chorus as the engine warmed up.

"Good-night, everybody," called Clark.

"Good-night, Clark."

"Good-night."

There was a pause, and then a soft, happy voice added, "Good-night, Jelly-bean."

The car drove off to a burst of singing. A rooster on a farm across the way took up a solitary mournful crow, and behind them a last Negro waiter turned out the porch light. Jim and Clark strolled over toward the Ford, their shoes crunching raucously on the gravel drive.

"O boy!" sighed Clark softly, "how you can set those dice!"

It was still too dark for him to see the flush on Jim's thin cheeks—or to know that it was a flush of unfamiliar shame.

4

Over Tilly's Garage a bleak room echoed all day to the rumble and snorting down-stairs and the singing of the Negro washers as they turned the hose on the cars outside. It was a cheerless square of a room punctuated with a bed and a battered table on which lay half a dozen books— Joe Miller's "Slow Train Through Arkansas," "Lucile," in an old edition very much annotated in an old-fashioned hand; "The Eyes of the World," by Harold Bell Wright,[4] and an ancient prayer-book of the

---

[4] a work of rustic humor and two sentimental novels

Church of England with the name Alice Powell and the date 1831 written on the fly-leaf.

The East, gray when the Jelly-bean entered the garage, became a rich and vivid blue as he turned on his solitary electric light. He snapped it out again, and going to the window rested his elbows on the sill and stared into the deepening morning. With the awakening of his emotions, his first perception was a sense of futility, a dull ache at the utter grayness of his life. A wall had sprung up suddenly around him, hedging him in, a wall as definite and tangible as the white wall of his bare room. And with his perception of this wall all that had been the romance of his existence, the casualness, the light-hearted improvidence, the miraculous open-handedness of life faded out. The Jelly-bean strolling up Jackson Street humming a lazy song, known at every shop and street stand, cropful of easy greeting and local wit, sad sometimes for only the sake of sadness and the flight of time—that Jelly-bean was suddenly vanished. The very name was a reproach, a triviality. With a flood of insight he knew that Merritt must despise him, that even Nancy's kiss in the dawn would have awakened not jealousy but only a contempt for Nancy so lowering herself. And on his part the Jelly-bean had used for her a dingy subterfuge learned from the garage. He had been her moral laundry; the stains were his.

As the gray became blue, brightened and filled the room, he crossed to his bed and threw himself down on it, gripping the edges fiercely.

"I love her," he cried aloud. "God!"

As he said this something gave way within him like a lump melting in his throat. The air cleared and became radiant with dawn, and turning over on his face he began to sob dully into the pillow.

In the sunshine of three o'clock Clark Darrow chugging painfully along Jackson Street was hailed by the Jelly-bean, who stood on the curb with his fingers in his vest pockets.

"Hi!" called Clark, bringing his Ford to an astonishing stop alongside. "Just get up?"

The Jelly-bean shook his head.

"Never did go to bed. Felt sorta restless, so I took a long walk this morning out in the country. Just got into town this minute."

"Should think you *would* feel restless. I been feeling thataway all day—"

"I'm thinkin' of leavin' town," continued the Jelly-bean, absorbed by his own thoughts. "Been thinkin' of goin' up on the farm, and takin' a little that work off Uncle Dun. Reckin I been bummin' too long."

Clark was silent and the Jelly-bean continued:

"I reckin maybe after Aunt Mamie dies I could sink that money of mine in the farm and make somethin' out of it. All my people originally came from that part up there. Had a big place."

Clark looked at him curiously.

"That's funny," he said. "This—this sort of affected me the same way."

The Jelly-bean hesitated.

"I don't know," he began slowly, "somethin' about—about that girl last night talkin' about a lady named Diana Manners—an English lady, sorta got me thinkin'!" He drew himself up and looked oddly at Clark. "I had a family once," he said defiantly.

Clark nodded.

"I know."

"And I'm the last of 'em," continued the Jelly-bean, his voice rising slightly, "and I ain't worth shucks. Name they call me by means jell—weak and wobbly like. People who weren't nothin' when my folks was a lot turn up their noses when they pass me on the street."

Again Clark was silent.

"So I'm through. I'm goin' today. And when I come back to this town it's going to be like a gentleman."

Clark took out his handkerchief and wiped his damp brow.

"Reckon you're not the only one it shook up," he admitted gloomily. "All this thing of girls going round like they do is going to stop right quick. Too bad, too, but everybody'll have to see it thataway."

"Do you mean," demanded Jim in surprise, "that all that's leaked out?"

"Leaked out? How on earth could they keep it secret? It'll be announced in the papers tonight. Doctor Lamar's got to save his name somehow."

Jim put his hands on the sides of the car and tightened his long fingers on the metal.

"Do you mean Taylor investigated those checks?"

It was Clark's turn to be surprised.

"Haven't you heard what happened?"

Jim's startled eyes were answer enough.

"Why," announced Clark dramatically, "those four got another bottle of corn, got tight and decided to shock the town—so Nancy and that fella Merritt were married in Rockville at seven o'clock this morning."

A tiny indentation appeared in the metal under the Jelly-bean's fingers.

"Married?"

"Sure enough. Nancy sobered up and rushed back into town, crying and frightened to death—claimed it'd all been a mistake. First, Doctor Lamar went wild and was going to kill Merritt, but finally they got it patched up some way, and Nancy and Merritt went to Savannah on the two-thirty train."

Jim closed his eyes and with an effort overcame a sudden sickness.

"It's too bad," said Clark philosophically. "I don't mean the wedding—reckon that's all right, though I don't guess Nancy cared a darn about him. But it's a crime for a nice girl like that to hurt her family that way."

The Jelly-bean let go the car and turned away. Again something was going on inside him, some inexplicable but almost chemical change.

"Where you going?" asked Clark.

The Jelly-bean turned and looked dully back over his shoulder.

"Got to go," he muttered. "Been up too long; feelin' right sick."

"Oh."

The street was hot at three and hotter still at four, the April dust seeming to enmesh the sun and give it forth again as a world-old joke forever played on an eternity of afternoons. But at half past four a first layer of quiet fell and the shades lengthened under the awnings and heavy foliaged trees. In this heat nothing mattered. All life was weather, a waiting through the hot where events had no significance for the cool that was soft and caressing like a woman's hand on a tired forehead. Down in Georgia there is a feeling—perhaps inarticulate—that this is the greatest wisdom of the South—so after a while the Jelly-bean turned into a pool-hall on Jackson Street where he was sure to find a congenial crowd who would make all the old jokes—the ones he knew.

William Faulkner

1897–1962

BARN BURNING

THE STORE in which the Justice of the Peace's court was sitting smelled of cheese. The boy, crouched on his nail keg at the back of the crowded room, knew he smelled cheese, and more: from where he sat he could see the ranked shelves close-packed with the solid, squat, dynamic shapes of tin cans whose labels his stomach read, not from the lettering which meant nothing to his mind but from the scarlet devils and the silver curve of fish—this, the cheese which he knew he smelled and the hermetic meat which his intestines believed he smelled, came in intermittent gusts momentary and brief between the other constant one, the smell and sense just a little of fear because mostly of despair and grief, the old fierce pull of blood. He could not see the table where the Justice sat and before which his father and his father's enemy (*our enemy* he thought in that despair; *ourn! mine and hisn both! He's my father!*) stood, but he could hear them, the two of them that is, because his father had said no word yet:

"But what proof have you, Mr. Harris?"

"I told you. The hog got into my corn. I caught it up and sent it back to him. He had no fence that would hold it. I told him so, warned him. The next time I put the hog in my pen. When he came to get it I gave

him enough wire to patch up his pen. The next time I put the hog up and
kept it. I rode down to his house and saw the wire I gave him still rolled
on to the spool in his yard. I told him he could have the hog when he paid
me a dollar pound fee. That evening a nigger came with the dollar and
got the hog. He was a strange nigger. He said, 'He say to tell you wood
and hay kin burn.' I said, 'What?' 'That whut he say to tell you,' the
nigger said. 'Wood and hay kin burn.' That night my barn burned. I got
the stock out but I lost the barn."

"Where is the nigger? Have you got him?"

"He was a strange nigger, I tell you. I don't know what became of
him."

"But that's not proof. Don't you see that's not proof?"

"Get that boy up here. He knows." For a moment the boy thought too
that the man meant his older brother until Harris said, "Not him. The
little one. The boy," and, crouching, small for his age, small and wiry
like his father, in patched and faded jeans even too small for him, with
straight, uncombed brown hair and eyes gray and wild as storm scud, he
saw the men between himself and the table part and become a lane of
grim faces, at the end of which he saw the Justice, a shabby, collarless,
graying man in spectacles, beckoning him. He felt no floor under his bare
feet; he seemed to walk beneath the palpable weight of the grim turning
faces. His father, stiff in his black Sunday coat donned not for the trial
but for the moving, did not even look at him. *He aims for me to lie*, he
thought, again with that frantic grief and despair. *And I will have to do hit.*

"What's your name, boy?" the Justice said.

"Colonel Sartoris Snopes," the boy whispered.

"Hey?" the Justice said. "Talk louder. Colonel Sartoris? I reckon
anybody named for Colonel Sartoris in this country can't help but tell the
truth, can they?" The boy said nothing. *Enemy! Enemy!* he thought;
for a moment he could not even see, could not see that the Justice's face
was kindly nor discern that his voice was troubled when he spoke to the
man named Harris: "Do you want me to question this boy?" But he
could hear, and during those subsequent long seconds while there was
absolutely no sound in the crowded little room save that of quiet and
intent breathing it was as if he had swung outward at the end of a grape
vine, over a ravine, and at the top of the swing had been caught in a prolonged instant of mesmerized gravity, weightless in time.

"No!" Harris said violently, explosively. "Damnation! Send him out
of here!" Now time, the fluid world, rushed beneath him again, the
voices coming to him again through the smell of cheese and sealed meat,
the fear and despair and the old grief of blood:

"This case is closed. I can't find against you, Snopes, but I can give
you advice. Leave this country and don't come back to it."

His father spoke for the first time, his voice cold and harsh, level, without emphasis: "I aim to. I don't figure to stay in a country among people
who . . ." he said something unprintable and vile, addressed to no one.

"That'll do," the Justice said. "Take your wagon and get out of this country before dark. Case dismissed."

His father turned, and he followed the stiff black coat, the wiry figure walking a little stiffly from where a Confederate provost's man's musket ball had taken him in the heel on a stolen horse thirty years ago, followed the two backs now, since his older brother had appeared from somewhere in the crowd, no taller than the father but thicker, chewing tobacco steadily, between the two lines of grim-faced men and out of the store and across the worn gallery and down the sagging steps and among the dogs and half-grown boys in the mild May dust, where as he passed a voice hissed:

"Barn burner!"

Again he could not see, whirling; there was a face in a red haze, moonlike, bigger than the full moon, the owner of it half again his size, he leaping in the red haze toward the face, feeling no blow, feeling no shock when his head struck the earth, scrabbling up and leaping again, feeling no blow this time either and tasting no blood, scrabbling up to see the other boy in full flight and himself already leaping into pursuit as his father's hand jerked him back, the harsh, cold voice speaking above him: "Go get in the wagon."

It stood in a grove of locusts and mulberries across the road. His two hulking sisters in their Sunday dresses and his mother and her sister in calico and sunbonnets were already in it, sitting on and among the sorry residue of the dozen and more movings which even the boy could remember—the battered stove, the broken beds and chairs, the clock inlaid with mother-of-pearl, which would not run, stopped at some fourteen minutes past two o'clock of a dead and forgotten day and time, which had been his mother's dowry. She was crying, though when she saw him she drew her sleeve across her face and began to descend from the wagon. "Get back," the father said.

"He's hurt. I got to get some water and wash his . . . ."

"Get back in the wagon," his father said. He got in too, over the tailgate. His father mounted to the seat where the older brother already sat and struck the gaunt mules two savage blows with the peeled willow, but without heat. It was not even sadistic; it was exactly that same quality which in later years would cause his descendants to overrun the engine before putting a motor car into motion, striking and reining back in the same movement. The wagon went on, the store with its quiet crowd of grimly watching men dropped behind; a curve in the road hit it. *Forever* he thought. *Maybe he's done satisfied now, now that he has* . . . stopping himself, not to say it aloud even to himself. His mother's hand touched his shoulder.

"Does hit hurt?" she said.

"Naw," he said. "Hit don't hurt. Lemme be."

"Can't you wipe some of the blood off before hit dries?"

"I'll wash to-night," he said. "Lemme be, I tell you."

The wagon went on. He did not know where they were going. None of them ever did or ever asked, because it was always somewhere, always a house of sorts waiting for them a day or two days or even three days away. Likely his father had already arranged to make a crop on another farm before he . . . Again he had to stop himself. He (the father) always did. There was something about his wolflike independence and even courage when the advantage was at least neutral which impressed strangers, as if they got from his latent ravening ferocity not so much a sense of dependability as a feeling that his ferocious conviction in the rightness of his own actions would be of advantage to all whose interest lay with his.

That night they camped in a grove of oaks and beeches where a spring ran. The nights were still cool and they had a fire against it, of a rail lifted from a nearby fence and cut into lengths—a small fire, neat, niggard almost, a shrewd fire; such fires were his father's habit and custom always, even in freezing weather. Older, the boy might have remarked this and wondered why not a big one; why should not a man who had not only seen the waste and extravagance of war, but who had in his blood an inherent voracious prodigality with material not his own, have burned everything in sight? Then he might have gone a step farther and thought that that was the reason: that niggard blaze was the living fruit of nights passed during those four years in the woods hiding from all men, blue or gray, with his strings of horses (captured horses, he called them). And older still, he might have divined the true reason: that the element of fire spoke to some deep mainspring of his father's being, as the element of steel or of powder spoke to other men, as the one weapon for the preservation of integrity, else breath were not worth the breathing, and hence to be regarded with respect and used with discretion.

But he did not think this now and he had seen those same niggard blazes all his life. He merely ate his supper beside it and was already half asleep over his iron plate when his father called him, and once more he followed the stiff back, the stiff and ruthless limp, up the slope and on to the starlit road where, turning, he could see his father against the stars but without face or depth—a shape black, flat and bloodless as though cut from tin in the iron folds of the frockcoat which had not been made for him, the voice harsh like tin and without heat like tin:

"You were fixing to tell them. You would have told him." He didn't answer. His father struck him with the flat of his hand on the side of the head, hard but without heat, exactly as he had struck the two mules at the store, exactly as he would strike either of them with any stick in order to kill a horse fly, his voice still without heat or anger: "You're getting to be a man. You got to learn. You got to learn to stick to your own blood or you ain't going to have any blood to stick to you. Do you think either of them, any man there this morning, would? Don't you know all they wanted was a chance to get at me because they knew I had them beat? Eh?" Later, twenty years later, he was to tell himself, "If I

had said they wanted only truth, justice, he would have hit me again."
But now he said nothing. He was not crying. He just stood there. "Answer me," his father said.

"Yes," he whispered. His father turned.

"Get on to bed. We'll be there tomorrow."

Tomorrow they were there. In the early afternoon the wagon stopped before a paintless two-room house identical almost with the dozen others it had stopped before even in the boy's ten years, and again, as on the other dozen occasions, his mother and aunt got down and began to unload the wagon, although his two sisters and his father and brother had not moved.

"Likely hit ain't fitten for hawgs," one of the sisters said.

"Nevertheless, fit it will and you'll hog it and like it," his father said. "Get down out of them chairs and help your Ma unload."

The two sisters got down, big, bovine, in a flutter of cheap ribbons; one of them drew from the jumbled wagon bed a battered lantern, the other a worn broom. His father handed the reins to the older son and began to climb stiffly over the wheel. "When they get unloaded, take the team to the barn and feed them." Then he said, and at first the boy thought he was still speaking to his brother: "Come with me."

"Me?" he said.

"Yes," his father said. "You."

"Abner," his mother said. His father paused and looked back—the harsh level stare beneath the shaggy, graying, irascible brows.

"I reckon I'll have a word with the man that aims to begin tomorrow owning me body and soul for the next eight months."

They went back up the road. A week ago—or before last night, that is—he would have asked where they were going, but not now. His father had struck him before last night but never before had he paused afterward to explain why; it was as if the blow and the following calm, outrageous voice still rang, repercussed, divulging nothing to him save the terrible handicap of being young, the light weight of his few years, just heavy enough to prevent his soaring free of the world as it seemed to be ordered but not heavy enough to keep him footed solid in it, to resist it and try to change the course of its events.

Presently he could see the grove of oaks and cedars and the other flowering trees and shrubs where the house would be, though not the house yet. They walked beside a fence massed with honeysuckle and Cherokee roses and came to a gate swinging open between two brick pillars, and now, beyond a sweep of drive, he saw the house for the first time and at that instant he forgot his father and the terror and despair both, and even when he remembered his father again (who had not stopped) the terror and despair did not return. Because, for all the twelve movings, they had sojourned until now in a poor country, a land of small farms and fields and houses, and he had never seen a house like this before. *Hit's big as a courthouse* he thought quietly, with a surge of peace and joy whose reason he could not have thought into words, being too young for that: *They are safe from him. People whose lives are a part of this peace and dignity are beyond his touch, be no more to them than a buzzing wasp: capable of stinging for a little moment but that's all, the spell of this peace and dignity rendering even the barns and stable and cribs which belong to it impervious to the puny flames he might contrive . . .* this, the peace and joy, ebbing for an instant as he looked again at the stiff black back, the stiff and implacable limp of the figure which was not dwarfed by the house, for the reason that it had never looked big anywhere and which now, against the serene columned back-drop, had more than ever the impervious quality of something cut ruthlessly from tin, depthless, as though, sidewise to the sun, it would cast no shadow. Watching him, the boy remarked the absolutely undeviating course which his father held and saw the stiff foot come squarely down in a pile of fresh droppings where a horse had stood in the drive and which his father could have avoided by a simple change of stride. But it ebbed only for a moment, though he could not have thought this into words either, walking on in the spell of the house, which he could even want but without envy, without sorrow, certainly never with that ravening and jealous rage which unknown to him walked in the ironlike black coat before him. *Maybe he will feel it too. Maybe it will even change him now from what maybe he couldn't help but be.*

They crossed the portico. Now he could hear his father's stiff foot as it came down on the boards with clocklike finality, a sound out of all proportion to the displacement of the body it bore and which was not dwarfed either by the white door before it, as though it had attained to a sort of vicious and ravening minimum not to be dwarfed by anything— the flat, wide, black hat, the formal coat of broadcloth which had once been black but which had now the friction-glazed greenish cast of the bodies of old house flies, the lifted sleeve which was too large, the lifted hand like a curled claw. The door opened so promptly that the boy knew the Negro must have been watching them all the time, an old man with neat grizzled hair, in a linen jacket, who stood barring the door with his body, saying, "Wipe yo foots, white man, fo you come in here. Major ain't home nohow."

"Get out of my way, nigger," his father said, without heat too, flinging the door back and the Negro also and entering, his hat still on his head. And now the boy saw the prints of the stiff foot on the doorjamb and saw them appear on the pale rug behind the machinelike deliberation of the foot which seemed to bear (or transmit) twice the weight which the body compassed. The Negro was shouting "Miss Lula! Miss Lula!" somewhere behind them, then the boy, deluged as though by a warm wave by a suave turn of carpeted stair and a pendant glitter of chandeliers and a mute gleam of gold frames, heard the swift feet and saw her too, a lady—perhaps he had never seen her like before either—in a gray, smooth gown with lace at the throat and an apron tied at the waist and the sleeves turned back, wiping cake or biscuit dough from her hands with a towel as she came up the hall, looking not at his father at all but at the tracks on the blond rug with an expression of incredulous amazement.

"I tried," the Negro cried. "I tole him to . . ."

"Will you please go away?" she said in a shaking voice. "Major de Spain is not at home. Will you please go away?"

His father had not spoken again. He did not speak again. He did not even look at her. He just stood stiff in the center of the rug, in his hat, the shaggy iron-gray brows twitching slightly above the pebblecolored eyes as he appeared to examine the house with brief deliberation. Then with the same deliberation he turned; the boy watched him pivot on the good leg and saw the stiff foot drag round the arc of the turning, leaving a final long and fading smear. His father never looked at it, he never once looked down at the rug. The Negro held the door. It closed behind them, upon the hysteric and indistinguishable woman-wail. His father stopped at the top of the steps and scraped his boot clean on the edge of it. At the gate he stopped again. He stood for a moment, planted stiffly on the stiff foot, looking back at the house. "Pretty and white, ain't it?" he said. "That's sweat. Nigger sweat. Maybe it ain't white enough yet to suit him. Maybe he wants to mix some white sweat with it."

Two hours later the boy was chopping wood behind the house within which his mother and aunt and the two sisters (the mother and aunt, not the two girls, he knew that; even at this distance and muffled by walls the flat loud voices of the two girls emanated an incorrigible idle inertia) were setting up the stove to prepare a meal, when he heard the hooves and saw the linen-clad man on a fine sorrel mare, whom he recognized even before he saw the rolled rug in front of the Negro youth following on a fat bay carriage horse—a suffused, angry face vanishing, still at full gallop, beyond the corner of the house where his father and brother were sitting in the two tilted chairs; and a moment later, almost before he could have put the axe down, he heard the hooves again and watched the sorrel mare go back out of the yard, already galloping again. Then his father began to shout one of the sisters' names, who presently emerged backward from the kitchen door dragging the rolled rug along the ground by one end while the other sister walked behind it.

"If you ain't going to tote, go on and set up the wash pot," the first said.

"You, Sarty!" the second shouted, "Set up the wash pot!" His father appeared at the door, framed against that shabbiness, as he had been against that other bland perfection, impervious to either, the mother's anxious face at his shoulder.

"Go on," the father said. "Pick it up." The two sisters stooped, broad, lethargic; stooping, they presented an incredible expanse of pale cloth and a flutter of tawdry ribbons.

"If I thought enough of a rug to have to git hit all the way from France

I wouldn't keep hit where folks coming in would have to tromp on hit,"
the first said. They raised the rug.

"Abner," the mother said. "Let me do it."

"You go back and git dinner," his father said. "I'll tend to this."

From the woodpile through the rest of the afternoon the boy watched
them, the rug spread flat in the dust beside the bubbling wash-pot, the
two sisters stooping over it with that profound and lethargic reluctance,
while the father stood over them in turn, implacable and grim, driving
them though never raising his voice again. He could smell the harsh
homemade lye they were using; he saw his mother come to the door
once and look toward them with an expression not anxious now but very
like despair; he saw his father turn, and he fell to with the axe and saw
from the corner of his eye his father raise from the ground a flattish fragment of field stone and examine it and return to the pot, and this time his
mother actually spoke: "Abner. Abner. Please don't. Please, Abner."

Then he was done too. It was dusk; the whippoorwills had already
begun. He could smell coffee from the room where they would presently
eat the cold food remaining from the midafternoon meal, though when
he entered the house he realized they were having coffee again probably
because there was a fire on the hearth, before which the rug now lay
spread over the backs of the two chairs. The tracks of his father's foot
were gone. Where they had been were now long, water-cloudy scoria-
tions resembling the sporadic course of a lilliputian mowing machine.

It still hung there while they ate the cold food and then went to bed,
scattered without order or claim up and down the two rooms, his mother
in one bed, where his father would later lie, the older brother in the other,
himself, the aunt, and the two sisters on pallets on the floor. But his father was not in bed yet. The last thing the boy remembered was the
depthless, harsh silhouette of the hat and coat bending over the rug and
it seemed to him that he had not even closed his eyes when the silhouette
was standing over him, the fire almost dead behind it, the stiff foot prodding him awake. "Catch up the mule," his father said.

When he returned with the mule his father was standing in the black
door, the rolled rug over his shoulder. "Ain't you going to ride?" he said.

"No. Give me your foot."

He bent his knee into his father's hand, the wiry, surprising power
flowed smoothly, rising, he rising with it, on to the mule's bare back
(they had owned a saddle once; the boy could remember it though not
when or where) and with the same effortlessness his father swung the
rug up in front of him. Now in the starlight they retraced the afternoon's
path, up the dusty road rife with honeysuckle, through the gate and up
the black tunnel of the drive to the lightless house, where he sat on the
mule and felt the rough warp of the rug drag across his thighs and vanish.

"Don't you want me to help?" he whispered. His father did not answer and now he heard again that stiff foot striking the hollow portico
with that wooden and clocklike deliberation, that outrageous overstate-

ment of the weight it carried. The rug, hunched, not flung (the boy could tell that even in the darkness) from his father's shoulder struck the angle of wall and floor with a sound unbelievably loud, thunderous, then the foot again, unhurried and enormous; a light came on in the house and the boy sat, tense, breathing steadily and quietly and just a little fast, though the foot itself did not increase its beat at all, descending the steps now; now the boy could see him.

"Don't you want to ride now?" he whispered. "We kin both ride now," the light within the house altering now, flaring up and sinking. *He's coming down the stairs now*, he thought. He had already ridden the mule up beside the horse block; presently his father was up behind him and he doubled the reins over and slashed the mule across the neck, but before the animal could begin to trot the hard, thin arm came round him, the hard, knotted hand jerking the mule back to a walk.

In the first red rays of the sun they were in the lot, putting plow gear on the mules. This time the sorrel mare was in the lot before he heard it at all, the rider collarless and even bareheaded, trembling, speaking in a shaking voice as the woman in the house had done, his father merely looking up once before stooping again to the hame he was buckling, so that the man on the mare spoke to his stooping back:

"You must realize you have ruined that rug. Wasn't there anybody here, any of your women . . ." he ceased, shaking, the boy watching him, the older brother leaning now in the stable door, chewing, blinking slowly and steadily at nothing apparently. "It cost a hundred dollars. But you never had a hundred dollars. You never will. So I'm going to charge you twenty bushels of corn against your crop. I'll add it in your contract and when you come to the commissary you can sign it. That won't keep Mrs. de Spain quiet but maybe it will teach you to wipe your feet off before you enter her house again."

Then he was gone. The boy looked at his father, who still had not spoken or even looked up again, who was now adjusting the logger-head in the hame.

"Pap," he said. His father looked at him—the inscrutable face, the shaggy brows beneath which the gray eyes glinted coldly. Suddenly the boy went toward him, fast, stopping as suddenly. "You done the best you could!" he cried. "If he wanted hit done different why didn't he wait and tell you how? He won't git no twenty bushels! He won't git none! We'll gether hit and hide hit! I kin watch . . ."

"Did you put the cutter back in the straight stock like I told you?"

"No, sir," he said.

"Then go do it."

That was Wednesday. During the rest of that week he worked stead-ily, at what was within his scope and some which was beyond it, with an industry that did not need to be driven nor even commanded twice; he had this from his mother, with the difference that some at least of what he did he liked to do, such as splitting wood with the half-size axe which his mother and aunt had earned, or saved money somehow, to present him with at Christmas. In company with the two older women (and on one afternoon, even one of the sisters), he built pens for the shoat and the cow which were a part of his father's contract with the landlord, and one afternoon, his father being absent, gone somewhere on one of the mules, he went to the field.

They were running a middle buster now, his brother holding the plow straight while he handled the reins, and walking beside the straining mule, the rich black soil shearing cool and damp against his bare ankles, he thought *Maybe this is the end of it. Maybe even that twenty bushels that seems hard to have to pay for just a rug will be a cheap price for him to stop forever and always from being what he used to be;* thinking, dreaming now, so that his brother had to speak sharply to him to mind the mule: *Maybe he even won't collect the twenty bushels. Maybe it will all add up and balance and vanish—corn, rug, fire; the terror and grief, the being pulled two ways like between two teams of horses—gone, done with for ever and ever.*

Then it was Saturday; he looked up from beneath the mule he was harnessing and saw his father in the black coat and hat. "Not that," his father said. "The wagon gear." And then, two hours later, sitting in the wagon bed behind his father and brother on the seat, the wagon accomplished a final curve, and he saw the weathered paintless store with its tattered tobacco and patent-medicine posters and the tethered wagons and saddle animals below the gallery. He mounted the gnawed steps behind his father and brother, and there again was the lane of quiet, watching faces for the three of them to walk through. He saw the man in spectacles sitting at the plank table and he did not need to be told this was a Justice of the Peace; he sent one glare of fierce, exultant, partisan defiance at the man in collar and cravat now, whom he had seen but twice before in his life, and that on a galloping horse, who now wore on his face an expression not of rage but of amazed unbelief which the boy could not have known was at the incredible circumstance of being sued by one of his own tenants, and came and stood against his father and cried at the Justice: "He ain't done it! He ain't burnt . . . ."

"Go back to the wagon," his father said.

"Burnt?" the Justice said. "Do I understand this rug was burned too?"

"Does anybody here claim it was?" his father said. "Go back to the wagon." But he did not, he merely retreated to the rear of the room, crowded as that other had been, but not to sit down this time, instead, to stand pressing among the motionless bodies, listening to the voices:

"And you claim twenty bushels of corn is too high for the damage you did to the rug?"

"He brought the rug to me and said he wanted the tracks washed out of it. I washed the tracks out and took the rug back to him."

"But you didn't carry the rug back to him in the same condition it was in before you made the tracks on it."

His father did not answer, and now for perhaps half a minute there was no sound at all save that of breathing, the faint, steady suspiration of complete and intent listening.

"You decline to answer that, Mr. Snopes?" Again his father did not answer. "I'm going to find against you, Mr. Snopes. I'm going to find that you were responsible for the injury to Major de Spain's rug and hold you liable for it. But twenty bushels of corn seems a little high for a man in your circumstances to have to pay. Major de Spain claims it cost a hundred dollars. October corn will be worth about fifty cents. I figure that if Major de Spain can stand a ninety-five dollar loss on something he paid cash for, you can stand a five-dollar loss you haven't earned yet. I hold you in damages to Major de Spain to the amount of ten bushels of corn over and above your contract with him, to be paid to him out of your crop at gathering time. Court adjourned."

It had taken no time hardly, the morning was but half begun. He thought they would return home and perhaps back to the field, since they were late, far behind all other farmers. But instead his father passed on behind the wagon, merely indicating with his hand for the older brother to follow with it, and crossed the road toward the blacksmith shop opposite, pressing on after his father, overtaking him, speaking, whispering up at the harsh, calm face beneath the weathered hat: "He won't git no ten bushels neither. He won't git one. We'll . . ." until his father glanced for an instant down at him, the face absolutely calm, the grizzled eyebrows tangled above the cold eyes, the voice almost pleasant, almost gentle:

"You think so? Well, we'll wait till October anyway."

The matter of the wagon—the setting of a spoke or two and the tightening of the tires—did not take long either, the business of the tires accomplished by driving the wagon into the spring branch behind the shop and letting it stand there, the mules nuzzling into the water from time to time, and the boy on the seat with the idle reins, looking up the slope and through the sooty tunnel of the shed where the slow hammer rang and where his father sat on an upended cypress bolt, easily, either talking or listening, still sitting there when the boy brought the dripping wagon up out of the branch and halted it before the door.

"Take them on to the shade and hitch," his father said. He did so and returned. His father and the smith and a third man squatting on his heels inside the door were talking, about crops and animals; the boy, squatting too in the ammoniac dust and hoof-parings and scales of rust, heard his father tell a long and unhurried story out of the time before the birth of the older brother even when he had been a professional horsetrader. And then his father came up beside him where he stood before a tattered last year's circus poster on the other side of the store, gazing rapt and quiet at the scarlet horses, the incredible poisings and convolutions of tulle and tights and the painted leers of comedians, and said, "It's time to eat."

But not at home. Squatting beside his brother against the front wall, he watched his father emerge from the store and produce from a paper sack a segment of cheese and divide it carefully and deliberately into three with his pocket knife and produce crackers from the same sack. They all three squatted on the gallery and ate, slowly, without talking; then in the store again, they drank from a tin dipper tepid water smelling of the cedar bucket and of living beech trees. And still they did not go home. It was a horse lot this time, a tall rail fence upon and along which men stood and sat and out of which one by one horses were led, to be walked and trotted and then cantered back and forth along the road while the slow swapping and buying went on and the sun began to slant westward, they—the three of them—watching and listening, the older brother with his muddy eyes and his steady, inevitable tobacco, the father commenting now and then on certain of the animals, to no one in particular.

It was after sundown when they reached home. They ate supper by lamp-light, then, sitting on the doorstep, the boy watched the night fully accomplished, listening to the whippoorwills and the frogs, when he heard his mother's voice: "Abner! No! No! Oh, God. Oh, God. Abner!" and he rose, whirled, and saw the altered light through the door where a candle stub now burned in a bottle neck on the table and his father, still in the hat and coat, at once formal and burlesque as though dressed carefully for some shabby and ceremonial violence, emptying the reservoir of the lamp back into the five-gallon kerosene can from which it had been filled, while the mother tugged at his arm until he shifted the lamp to the other hand and flung her back, not savagely or viciously, just hard, into the wall, her hands flung out against the wall for balance, her mouth open and in her face the same quality of hopeless despair as had been in her voice. Then his father saw him standing in the door.

"Go to the barn and get the can of oil we were oiling the wagon with," he said. The boy did not move. Then he could speak.

"What . . ." he cried. "What are you . . ."

"Go get that oil," his father said. "Go."

Then he was moving, running, outside the house, toward the stable: this the old habit, the old blood which he had not been permitted to choose for himself, which had been bequeathed him willy nilly and which had run for so long (and who knew where, battening on what of outrage and savagery and lust) before it came to him. *I could keep on*, he thought. *I could run on and on and never look back, never need to see his face again. Only I can't. I can't*, the rusted can in his hand now, the liquid sploshing in it as he ran back to the house and into it, into the sound of his mother's weeping in the next room, and handed the can to his father.

"Ain't you going to even send a nigger?" he cried. "At least you sent a nigger before!"

This time his father didn't strike him. The hand came even faster than the blow had, the same hand which had set the can on the table with almost excruciating care flashing from the can toward him too quick for him to follow it, gripping him by the back of his shirt and on to tiptoe before he had seen it quit the can, the face stooping at him in breathless and frozen ferocity, the cold, dead voice speaking over him to the older brother who leaned against the table, chewing with that steady, curious, sidewise motion of cows:

"Empty the can into the big one and go on. I'll ketch up with you."

"Better tie him up to the bedpost," the brother said.

"Do like I told you," the father said. Then the boy was moving, his bunched shirt and the hard, bony hand between his shoulder-blades, his toes just touching the floor, across the room and into the other one, past the sisters sitting with spread heavy thighs in the two chairs over the cold hearth, and to where his mother and aunt sat side by side on the bed, the aunt's arms about his mother's shoulders.

"Hold him," the father said. The aunt made a startled movement. "Not you," the father said. "Lennie. Take hold of him. I want to see you do it." His mother took him by the wrist. "You'll hold him better than that. If he gets loose don't you know what he is going to do? He will go up yonder." He jerked his head toward the road. "Maybe I'd better tie him."

"I'll hold him," his mother whispered.

"See you do then." Then his father was gone, the stiff foot heavy and measured upon the boards, ceasing at last.

Then he began to struggle. His mother caught him in both arms, he jerking and wrenching at them. He would be stronger in the end, he knew that. But he had no time to wait for it. "Lemme go!" he cried. "I don't want to have to hit you!"

"Let him go!" the aunt said. "If he don't go, before God, I am going up there myself!"

"Don't you see I can't?" his mother cried. "Sarty! Sarty! No! No! Help me, Lizzie!"

Then he was free. His aunt grasped at him but it was too late. He whirled, running, his mother stumbled forward on to her knees behind him, crying to the nearer sister: "Catch him, Net! Catch him!" But that was too late too, the sister (the sisters were twins, born at the same time, yet either of them now gave the impression of being, encompassing as much living meat and volume and weight as any other two of the family) not yet having begun to rise from the chair, her head, face, alone merely turned, presenting to him in the flying instant an astonishing expanse of young female features untroubled by any surprise even, wearing only an expression of bovine interest. Then he was out of the room, out of the house, in the mild dust of the star-lit road and the heavy rifeness of honeysuckle, the pale ribbon unspooling with terrific slowness under his running feet, reaching the gate at last and turning in, running, his heart and lungs drumming, on up the drive toward the lighted house, the lighted door. He did not knock, he burst in, sobbing for breath, incapable for the moment of speech; he saw the astonished face of the Negro in the linen jacket without knowing when the Negro had appeared.

"De Spain!" he cried, panted. "Where's . . ." then he saw the white man too emerging from a white door down the hall. "Barn!" he cried "Barn!"

"What?" the white man said. "Barn?"

"Yes!" the boy cried. "Barn!"

"Catch him!" the white man shouted.

But it was too late this time too. The Negro grasped his shirt, but the entire sleeve, rotten with washing, carried away, and he was out that door too and in the drive again, and had actually never ceased to run even while he was screaming into the white man's face.

Behind him the white man was shouting, "My horse! Fetch my horse!" and he thought for an instant of cutting across the park and climbing the fence into the road, but he did not know the park nor how high the vine-massed fence might be and he dared not risk it. So he ran on down the drive, blood and breath roaring; presently he was in the road again though he could not see it. He could not hear either: the galloping mare was almost upon him before he heard her, and even then he held his course, as if the very urgency of his wild grief and need must in a moment more find him wings, waiting until the ultimate instant to hurl himself aside and into the weed-choked roadside ditch as the horse thundered past and on, for an instant in furious silhouette against the stars, the tranquil early summer night sky which, even before the shape of the horse and rider vanished, stained abruptly and violently upward: a long, swirling roar incredible and soundless, blotting the stars, and he springing up and into the road again, running again, knowing it was too late yet still running even after he heard the shot and, an instant later, two shots, pausing now without knowing he had ceased to run, crying "Pap! Pap!", running again before he knew he had begun to run, stumbling, tripping over something and scrabbling up again without ceasing to run, looking backward over his shoulder at the glare as he got up, running on among the invisible trees, panting, sobbing, "Father! Father!"

At midnight he was sitting on the crest of a hill. He did not know it was midnight and he did not know how far he had come. But there was no glare behind him now and he sat now, his back toward what he had called home for four days anyhow, his face toward the dark woods which he would enter when breath was strong again, small, shaking steadily in the chill darkness, hugging himself into the remainder of his thin, rotten shirt, the grief and despair now no longer terror and fear but just grief and despair. *Father. My father*, he thought. "He was brave!" he cried suddenly, aloud but not loud, no more than a whisper. "He was! He was in the war! He was in Colonel Sartoris' cav'ry!" not knowing that his father had gone to that war a private in the fine old European sense, wearing no uniform, admitting the authority of and giving fidelity to no man or army or flag, going to war as Malbrouck himself did: for booty—it meant nothing and less than nothing to him if it were enemy booty or his own.

The slow constellations wheeled on. It would be dawn and then sun-up after a while and he would be hungry. But that would be tomorrow and now he was only cold, and walking would cure that. His breathing was easier now and he decided to get up and go on, and then he found that he had been asleep because he knew it was almost dawn, the night almost over. He could tell that from the whippoorwills. They were everywhere now among the dark trees below him, constant and inflectioned and ceaseless, so that, as the instant for giving over to the day birds drew nearer and nearer, there was no interval at all between them. He got up. He was a little stiff, but walking would cure that too as it would the cold, and soon there would be the sun. He went on down the hill, toward the dark woods within which the liquid silver voices of the birds called unceasing—the rapid and urgent beating of the urgent and quiring heart of the late spring night. He did not look back.

Ernest Hemingway
1898–1961
THE UNDEFEATED

MANUEL GARCIA climbed the stairs to Don Miguel Retana's office. He set down his suitcase and knocked on the door. There was no answer. Manuel, standing in the hallway, felt there was some one in the room. He felt it through the door.

"Retana," he said, listening.

There was no answer.

He's there, all right, Manuel thought.

"Retana," he said and banged the door.

"Who's there?" said some one in the office.

"Me, Manolo," Manuel said.

"What do you want?" asked the voice.

"I want to work," Manuel said.

Something in the door clicked several times and it swung open. Manuel went in, carrying his suitcase.

A little man sat behind a desk at the far side of the room. Over his head was a bull's head, stuffed by a Madrid taxidermist; on the walls were framed photographs and bull-fight posters.

The little man sat looking at Manuel.

"I thought they'd killed you," he said.

Manuel knocked with his knuckles on the desk. The little man sat looking at him across the desk.

"How many corridas[1] you had this year?" Retana asked.

"One," he answered.

"Just that one?" the little man asked.

"That's all."

"I read about it in the papers," Retana said. He leaned back in the chair and looked at Manuel.

Manuel looked up at the stuffed bull. He had seen it often before. He felt a certain family interest in it. It had killed his brother, the promising one, about nine years ago. Manuel remembered the day. There was a brass plate on the oak shield the bull's head was mounted on. Manuel could not read it, but he imagined it was in memory of his brother. Well, he had been a good kid.

The plate said: "The Bull 'Mariposa' of the Duke of Veragua, which accepted 9 varas[2] for 7 caballos,[3] and caused the death of Antonio Garcia, Novillero, April 27, 1909."

Retana saw him looking at the stuffed bull's head.

"The lot the Duke sent me for Sunday will make a scandal," he said. "They're all bad in the legs. What do they say about them at the Café?"

"I don't know," Manuel said. "I just got in."

"Yes," Retana said. "You still have your bag."

He looked at Manuel, leaning back behind the big desk.

"Sit down," he said. "Take off your cap."

Manuel sat down; his cap off, his face was changed. He looked pale, and his coleta[4] pinned forward on his head, so that it would not show under the cap, gave him a strange look.

"You don't look well," Retana said.

"I just got out of the hospital," Manuel said.

"I heard they'd cut your leg off," Retana said.

"No," said Manuel. "It got all right."

Retana leaned forward across the desk and pushed a wooden box of cigarettes toward Manuel.

"Have a cigarette," he said.

"Thanks."

Manuel lit it.

"Smoke?" he said, offering the match to Retana.

"No," Retana waved his hand, "I never smoke."

Retana watched him smoking.

"Why don't you get a job and go to work?" he said.

"I don't want to work," Manuel said. "I am a bull-fighter."

"There aren't any bull-fighters any more," Retana said.

"I'm a bull-fighter," Manuel said.

"Yes, while you're in there," Retana said.

---

[1] corrida de toros, bullfight   [2] thrusts with the picador's goad   [3] horses
[4] bullfighter's pigtail

Manuel laughed.

Retana sat, saying nothing and looking at Manuel.

"I'll put you in a nocturnal if you want," Retana offered.

"When?" Manuel asked.

"Tomorrow night."

"I don't like to substitute for anybody," Manuel said. That was the way they all got killed. That was the way Salvador got killed. He tapped with his knuckles on the table.

"It's all I've got," Retana said.

"Why don't you put me on next week?" Manuel suggested.

"You wouldn't draw," Retana said. "All they want is Litri and Rubito and La Torre. Those kids are good."

"They'd come to see me get it," Manuel said, hopefully.

"No, they wouldn't. They don't know who you are any more."

"I've got a lot of stuff," Manuel said.

"I'm offering to put you on tomorrow night," Retana said. "You can work with young Hernandez and kill two novillos[5] after the Charlots."

"Whose novillos?" Manuel asked.

"I don't know. Whatever stuff they've got in the corrals. What the veterinaries won't pass in the daytime."

"I don't like to substitute," Manuel said.

"You can take it or leave it," Retana said. He leaned forward over the papers. He was no longer interested. The appeal that Manuel had made to him for a moment when he thought of the old days was gone. He would like to get him to substitute for Larita because he could get him cheaply. He could get others cheaply too. He would like to help him though. Still he had given him the chance. It was up to him.

"How much do I get?" Manuel asked. He was still playing with the idea of refusing. But he knew he could not refuse.

"Two hundred and fifty pesetas,[6]" Retana said. He had thought of five hundred, but when he opened his mouth it said two hundred and fifty.

"You pay Villalta seven thousand," Manuel said.

"You're not Villalta," Retana said.

"I know it," Manuel said.

"He draws it, Manolo," Retana said in explanation.

"Sure," said Manuel. He stood up. "Give me three hundred, Retana."

"All right," Retana agreed. He reached in the drawer for a paper.

"Can I have fifty now?" Manuel asked.

"Sure," said Retana. He took a fifty-peseta note out of his pocketbook and laid it, spread out flat, on the table.

Manuel picked it up and put it in his pocket.

"What about a cuadrilla[7]?" he asked.

---

[5] young bulls   [6] about twenty-five dollars   [7] crew

"There's the boys that always work for me nights," Retana said.
"They're all right."

"How about picadors[8]?" Manuel asked.

"They're not much," Retana admitted.

"I've got to have one good pic," Manuel said.

"Get him then," Retana said. "Go and get him."

"Not out of this," Manuel said. "I'm not paying for any cuadrilla out of sixty duros."

Retana said nothing but looked at Manuel across the big desk.

"You know I've got to have one good pic," Manuel said.

Retana said nothing but looked at Manuel from a long way off.

"It's isn't right," Manuel said.

Retana was still considering him, leaning back in his chair, considering him from a long way away.

"There're the regular pics," he offered.

"I know," Manuel said. "I know your regular pics."

Retana did not smile. Manuel knew it was over.

"All I want is an even break," Manuel said reasoningly.

"When I go out there I want to be able to call my shots on the bull. It only takes one good picador."

He was talking to a man who was no longer listening.

"If you want something extra," Retana said, "go and get it. There will be a regular cuadrilla out there. Bring as many of your own pics as you want. The charlotada is over by 10.30."

"All right," Manuel said. "If that's the way you feel about it."

"That's the way," Retana said.

"I'll see you tomorrow night," Manuel said.

"I'll be out there," Retana said.

Manuel picked up his suitcase and went out.

"Shut the door," Retana called.

Manuel looked back. Retana was sitting forward looking at some papers. Manuel pulled the door tight until it clicked.

He went down the stairs and out of the door into the hot brightness of the street. It was very hot in the street and the light on the white buildings was sudden and hard on his eyes. He walked down the shady side of the steep street toward the Puerta del Sol. The shade felt solid and cool as running water. The heat came suddenly as he crossed the intersecting streets. Manuel saw no one he knew in all the people he passed.

Just before the Puerta del Sol he turned into a café.

It was quiet in the café. There were a few men sitting at tables against the wall. At one table four men played cards. Most of the men sat against the wall smoking, empty coffee-cups and liqueur-glasses before them on the tables. Manuel went through the long room to a small room

---

[8] lancer, mounted on horseback, who goads the bull

in back. A man sat at a table in the corner asleep. Manuel sat down at one of the tables.

A waiter came in and stood beside Manuel's table.

"Have you seen Zurito?" Manuel asked him.

"He was in before lunch," the waiter answered. "He won't be back before five o'clock."

"Bring me some coffee and milk and a shot of the ordinary," Manuel said.

The waiter came back into the room carrying a tray with a big coffee-glass and a liqueur-glass on it. In his left hand he held a bottle of brandy. He swung these down to the table and a boy who had followed him poured coffee and milk into the glass from two shiny, spouted pots with long handles.

Manuel took off his cap and the waiter noticed his pigtail pinned forward on his head. He winked at the coffee-boy as he poured out the brandy into the little glass beside Manuel's coffee. The coffee-boy looked at Manuel's pale face curiously.

"You fighting here?" asked the waiter, corking up the bottle.

"Yes," Manuel said. "Tomorrow."

The waiter stood there, holding the bottle on one hip.

"You in the Charlie Chaplins?" he asked.

The coffee-boy looked away, embarrassed.

"No. In the ordinary."

"I thought they were going to have Chaves and Hernandez," the waiter said.

"No. Me and another."

"Who? Chaves or Hernandez?"

"Hernandez, I think."

"What's the matter with Chaves?"

"He got hurt."

"Where did you hear that?"

"Retana."

"Hey, Looie," the waiter called to the next room, "Chaves got cogida.⁹"

Manuel had taken the wrapper off the lumps of sugar and dropped them into his coffee. He stirred it and drank it down, sweet, hot, and warming in his empty stomach. He drank off the brandy.

"Give me another shot of that," he said to the waiter.

The waiter uncorked the bottle and poured the glass full, slopping another drink into the saucer. Another waiter had come up in front of the table. The coffee-boy was gone.

"Is Chaves hurt bad?" the second waiter asked Manuel.

"I don't know," Manuel said, "Retana didn't say."

⁹ caught

"A hell of a lot he cares," the tall waiter said. Manuel had not seen him before. He must have just come up.

"If you stand in with Retana in this town, you're a made man," the tall waiter said. "If you aren't in with him, you might just as well go out and shoot yourself."

"You said it," the other waiter who had come in said. "You said it then."

"You're right I said it," said the tall waiter. "I know what I'm talking about when I talk about that bird."

"Look what he's done for Villalta," the first waiter said.

"And that ain't all," the tall waiter said. "Look what he's done for Marcial Lalanda. Look what he's done for Nacional."

"You said it, kid," agreed the short waiter.

Manuel looked at them, standing talking in front of his table. He had drunk his second brandy. They had forgotten about him. They were not interested in him.

"Look at that bunch of camels," the tall waiter went on. "Did you ever see this Nacional II?"

"I seen him last Sunday didn't I?" the original waiter said.

"He's a giraffe," the short waiter said.

"What did I tell you?" the tall waiter said. "Those are Retana's boys."

"Say, give me another shot of that," Manuel said. He had poured the brandy the waiter had slopped over in the saucer into his glass and drank it while they were talking.

The original waiter poured his glass full mechanically, and the three of them went out of the room talking.

In the far corner the man was still asleep, snoring slightly on the intaking breath, his head back against the wall.

Manuel drank his brandy. He felt sleepy himself. It was too hot to go out into the town. Besides there was nothing to do. He wanted to see Zurito. He would go to sleep while he waited. He kicked his suitcase under the table to be sure it was there. Perhaps it would be better to put it back under the seat, against the wall. He leaned down and shoved it under. Then he leaned forward on the table and went to sleep.

When he woke there was some one sitting across the table from him. It was a big man with a heavy brown face like an Indian. He had been sitting there some time. He had waved the waiter away and sat reading the paper and occasionally looking down at Manuel, asleep, his head on the table. He read the paper laboriously, forming the words with his lips as he read. When it tired him he looked at Manuel. He sat heavily in the chair, his black Cordoba hat tipped forward.

Manuel sat up and looked at him.

"Hello, Zurito," he said.

"Hello, kid," the big man said.

"I've been asleep." Manuel rubbed his forehead with the back of his fist.

"I thought maybe you were."

"How's everything?"

"Good. How is everything with you?"

"Not so good."

They were both silent. Zurito, the picador, looked at Manuel's white face. Manuel looked down at the picador's enormous hands folding the paper to put away in his pocket.

"I got a favor to ask you, Manos," Manuel said.

Manosduros[10] was Zurito's nickname. He never heard it without thinking of his huge hands. He put them forward on the table self-consciously.

"Let's have a drink," he said.

"Sure," said Manuel.

The waiter came and went and came again. He went out of the room looking back at the two men at the table.

"What's the matter, Manolo?" Zurito set down his glass.

"Would you pic two bulls for me tomorrow night?" Manuel asked, looking up at Zurito across the table.

"No," said Zurito. "I'm not pic-ing."

Manuel looked down at his glass. He had expected that answer; now he had it. Well, he had it.

"I'm sorry, Manolo, but I'm not pic-ing." Zurito looked at his hands.

"That's all right," Manuel said.

"I'm too old," Zurito said.

"I just asked you," Manuel said.

"Is it the nocturnal tomorrow?"

"That's it. I figured if I had just one good pic, I could get away with it."

"How much are you getting?"

"Three hundred pesetas."

"I get more than that for pic-ing."

"I know," said Manuel. "I didn't have any right to ask you."

"What do you keep on doing it for?" Zurito asked. "Why don't you cut off your coleta, Manolo?"

"I don't know," Manuel said.

"You're pretty near as old as I am," Zurito said.

"I don't know," Manuel said. "I got to do it. If I can fix it so that I get an even break, that's all I want. I got to stick with it, Manos."

"No, you don't."

"Yes, I do. I've tried keeping away from it."

"I know how you feel. But it isn't right. You ought to get out and stay out."

10 "Strong Hands"

"I can't do it. Besides, I've been going good lately."

Zurito looked at his face.

"You've been in the hospital."

"But I was going great when I got hurt."

Zurito said nothing. He tipped the cognac out of his saucer into his glass.

"The papers said they never saw a better faena,[11]" Manuel said.

Zurito looked at him.

"You know when I get going I'm good," Manuel said.

"You're too old," the picador said.

"No," said Manuel. "You're ten years older than I am."

"With me it's different."

"I'm not too old," Manuel said.

They sat silent, Manuel watching the picador's face.

"I was going great till I got hurt," Manuel offered.

"You ought to have seen me, Manos," Manuel said, reproachfully.

"I don't want to see you," Zurito said. "It makes me nervous."

"You haven't seen me lately."

"I've seen you plenty."

Zurito looked at Manuel, avoiding his eyes.

"You ought to quit it, Manolo."

"I can't," Manuel said. "I'm going good now, I tell you."

Zurito leaned forward, his hands on the table.

"Listen. I'll pic for you and if you don't go big tomorrow night, you'll quit. See? Will you do that?"

"Sure."

Zurito leaned back, relieved.

"You got to quit," he said. "No monkey business. You got to cut the coleta."

"I won't have to quit," Manuel said. "You watch me. I've got the stuff."

Zurito stood up. He felt tired from arguing.

"You got to quit," he said. "I'll cut your coleta myself."

"No, you won't," Manuel said. "You won't have a chance."

Zurito called the waiter.

"Come on," said Zurito. "Come on up to the house."

Manuel reached under the seat for his suitcase. He was happy. He knew Zurito would pic for him. He was the best picador living. It was all simple now.

"Come on up to the house and we'll eat," Zurito said.

Manuel stood in the patio de caballos[12] waiting for the Charlie Chaplins to be over. Zurito stood beside him. Where they stood it was dark. The high door that led into the bull-ring was shut. Above them they

---

[11] final series of passes before the kill   [12] corral

heard a shout, then another shout of laughter. Then there was silence. Manuel liked the smell of the stables about the patio de caballos. It smelt good in the dark. There was another roar from the arena and then applause, prolonged applause, going on and on.

"You ever seen these fellows?" Zurito asked, big and looming beside Manuel in the dark.

"No," Manuel said.

"They're pretty funny," Zurito said. He smiled to himself in the dark.

The high, double, tight-fitting door into the bull-ring swung open and Manuel saw the ring in the hard light of the arc-lights, the plaza, dark all the way around, rising high; around the edge of the ring were running and bowing two men dressed like tramps, followed by a third in the uniform of a hotel bell-boy who stooped and picked up the hats and canes thrown down onto the sand and tossed them back up into the darkness.

The electric light went on in the patio.

"I'll climb onto one of those ponies while you collect the kids," Zurito said.

Behind them came the jingle of the mules, coming out to go into the arena and be hitched onto the dead bull.

The members of the cuadrilla, who had been watching the burlesque from the runway between the barrera and the seats, came walking back and stood in a group talking, under the electric light in the patio. A good-looking lad in a silver-and-orange suit came up to Manuel and smiled.

"I'm Hernandez," he said and put out his hand.

Manuel shook it.

"They're regular elephants we've got tonight," the boy said cheerfully.

"They're big ones with horns," Manuel agreed.

"You drew the worst lot," the boy said.

"That's all right," Manuel said. "The bigger they are, the more meat for the poor."

"Where did you get that one?" Hernandez grinned.

"That's an old one," Manuel said. "You line up your cuadrilla, so I can see what I've got."

"You've got some good kids," Hernandez said. He was very cheerful. He had been on twice before in nocturnals and was beginning to get a following in Madrid. He was happy the fight would start in a few minutes.

"Where are the pics?" Manuel asked.

"They're back in the corrals fighting about who gets the beautiful horses," Hernandez grinned.

The mules came through the gate in a rush, the whips snapping, bells jangling and the young bull ploughing a furrow of sand.

They formed up for the paseo[13] as soon as the bull had gone through.

---

[13] procession

Manuel and Hernandez stood in front. The youths of the cuadrillas were behind, their heavy capes furled over their arms. In back, the four picadors, mounted, holding their steel-tipped push-poles erect in the half-dark of the corral.

"It's a wonder Retana wouldn't give us enough light to see the horses by," one picador said.

"He knows we'll be happier if we don't get too good a look at these skins," another pic answered.

"This thing I'm on barely keeps me off the ground," the first picador said.

"Well, they're horses."

"Sure, they're horses."

They talked, sitting their gaunt horses in the dark.

Zurito said nothing. He had the only steady horse of the lot. He had tried him, wheeling him in the corrals and he responded to the bit and the spurs. He had taken the bandage off his right eye and cut the strings where they had tied his ears tight shut at the base. He was a good, solid horse, solid on his legs. That was all he needed. He intended to ride him all through the corrida. He had already, since he had mounted, sitting in the half-dark in the big, quilted saddle, waiting for the paseo, pic-ed through the whole corrida in his mind. The other picadors went on talking on both sides of him. He did not hear them.

The two matadors stood together in front of their three peones,[14] their capes furled over their left arms in the same fashion. Manuel was thinking about the three lads in back of him. They were all three Madrilenos, like Hernandez, boys about nineteen. One of them, a gypsy, serious, aloof, and dark-faced, he liked the look of. He turned.

"What's your name, kid?" he asked the gypsy.

"Fuentes," the gypsy said.

"That's a good name," Manuel said.

The gypsy smiled, showing his teeth.

"You take the bull and give him a little run when he comes out," Manuel said.

"All right," the gypsy said. His face was serious. He began to think about just what he would do.

"Here she goes," Manuel said to Hernandez.

"All right. We'll go."

Heads up, swinging with the music, their right arms swinging free, they stepped out, crossing the sanded arena under the arc-lights, the cuadrillas opening out behind, the picadors riding after, behind came the bull-ring servants and the jingling mules. The crowd applauded Hernandez as they marched across the arena. Arrogant, swinging, they looked straight ahead as they marched.

They bowed before the president, and the procession broke up into its

[14] assistants

component parts. The bull-fighters went over to the barrera[15] and changed their heavy mantles for the light fighting capes. The mules went out. The picadors galloped jerkily around the ring, and two rode out the gate they had come in by. The servants swept the sand smooth.

Manuel drank a glass of water poured for him by one of Retana's deputies, who was acting as his manager and sword-handler. Hernandez came over from speaking with his own manager.

"You got a good hand, kid," Manuel complimented him.

"They like me," Hernandez said happily.

"How did the paseo go?" Manuel asked Retana's man.

"Like a wedding," said the handler. "Fine. You came out like Joselito and Belmonte.[16]"

Zurito rode by, a bulky equestrian statue. He wheeled his horse and faced him toward the toril[17] on the far side of the ring where the bull would come out. It was strange under the arc-light. He pic-ed in the hot afternoon sun for big money. He didn't like this arc-light business. He wished they would get started.

Manuel went up to him.

"Pic him, Manos," he said. "Cut him down to size for me."

"I'll pic him, kid," Zurito spat on the sand. "I'll make him jump out of the ring."

"Lean on him, Manos," Manuel said.

"I'll lean on him," Zurito said. "What's holding it up?"

"He's coming now," Manuel said.

Zurito sat there, his feet in the box-stirrups, his great legs in the buck-skin-covered armor gripping the horse, the reins in his left hand, the long pic held in his right hand, his broad hat well down over his eyes to shade them from the lights, watching the distant door of the toril. His horse's ears quivered. Zurito patted him with his left hand.

The red door of the toril swung back and for a moment Zurito looked into the empty passageway far across the arena. Then the bull came out in a rush, skidding on his four legs as he came out under the lights, then charging in a gallop, moving softly in a fast gallop, silent except as he woofed through wide nostrils as he charged, glad to be free after the dark pen.

In the first row of seats, slightly bored, leaning forward to write on the cement wall in front of his knees, the substitute bull-fight critic of *El Heraldo* scribbled: "Campagnero, Negro, 42, came out at 90 miles an hour with plenty of gas—"

Manuel, leaning against the barrera, watching the bull, waved his hand and the gypsy ran out, trailing his cape. The bull, in full gallop, pivoted and charged the cape, his head down, his tail rising. The gypsy moved in a zigzag, and as he passed, the bull caught sight of him and

---

[15] barrier   [16] two of Spain's most famous bullfighters
[17] holding pen for bulls

abandoned the cape to charge the man. The gyp sprinted and vaulted the red fence of the barrera as the bull struck it with his horns. He tossed into it twice with his horns, banging into the wood blindly.

The critic of *El Heraldo* lit a cigarette and tossed the match at the bull, then wrote in his note-book, "large and with enough horns to satisfy the cash customers, Campagnero showed a tendency to cut into the terrain of the bull-fighters."

Manuel stepped out on the hard sand as the bull banged into the fence. Out of the corner of his eye he saw Zurito sitting the white horse close to the barrera, about a quarter of the way around the ring to the left. Manuel held the cape close in front of him, a fold in each hand, and shouted at the bull. "Huh! Huh!" The bull turned, seemed to brace against the fence as he charged in a scramble, driving into the cape as Manuel side-stepped, pivoted on his heels with the charge of the bull, and swung the cape just ahead of the horns. At the end of the swing he was facing the bull again and held the cape in the same position close in front of his body, and pivoted again as the bull recharged. Each time, as he swung, the crowd shouted.

Four times he swung with the bull, lifting the cape so it billowed full, and each time bringing the bull around to charge again. Then, at the end of the fifth swing, he held the cape against his hip and pivoted, so the cape swung out like a ballet dancer's skirt and wound the bull around himself like a belt, to step clear, leaving the bull facing Zurito on the white horse, come up and planted firm, the horse facing the bull, its ears forward, its lips nervous, Zurito, his hat over his eyes, leaning forward, the long pole sticking out before and behind in a sharp angle under his right arm, held half-way down, the triangular iron point facing the bull.

El Heraldo's second-string critic, drawing on his cigarette, his eyes on the bull, wrote: "the veteran Manolo designed a series of acceptable veronicas,[18] ending in a very Belmontistic recorte[19] that earned applause from the regulars, and we entered the tercio of the cavalry.[20]"

Zurito sat his horse, measuring the distance between the bull and the end of the pic. As he looked, the bull gathered himself together and charged, his eyes on the horse's chest. As he lowered his head to hook, Zurito sunk the point of the pic in the swelling hump of muscle above the bull's shoulder, leaned all his weight on the shaft, and with his left hand pulled the white horse into the air, front hoofs pawing, and swung him to the right as he pushed the bull under and through so the horns passed safely under the horse's belly and the horse came down, quivering, the bull's tail brushing his chest as he charged the cape Hernandez offered him.

---

[18] a pass with the cape to draw the bull past the bullfighter, who keeps his feet in one position
[19] a movement with the cape to turn the bull
[20] that third of the bullfight given over to the horsemen

Hernandez ran sideways, taking the bull out and away with the cape, toward the other picador. He fixed him with a swing of the cape, squarely facing the horse and rider, and stepped back. As the bull saw the horse he charged. The picador's lance slid along his back, and as the shock of the charge lifted the horse, the picador was already half-way out of the saddle, lifting his right leg clear as he missed with the lance and falling to the left side to keep the horse between him and the bull. The horse, lifted and gored, crashed over with the bull driving into him, the picador gave a shove with his boots against the horse and lay clear, waiting to be lifted and hauled away and put on his feet.

Manuel let the bull drive into the fallen horse; he was in no hurry, the picador was safe; besides, it did a picador like that good to worry. He'd stay on longer next time. Lousy pics! He looked across the sand at Zurito a little way out from the barrera, his horse rigid, waiting.

"Huh!" he called to the bull, "Tomar!" holding the cape in both hands so it would catch his eye. The bull detached himself from the horse and charged the cape, and Manuel, running sideways and holding the cape spread wide, stopped, swung on his heels, and brought the bull sharply around facing Zurito.

"Campagnero accepted a pair of varas for the death of one rosinante,[21] with Hernandez and Manolo at the quites,[22]" *El Heraldo's* critic wrote. "He pressed on the iron and clearly showed he was no horse-lover. The veteran Zurito resurrected some of his old stuff with the pike-pole, notably the suerte[23]—"

"Olé! Olé!" the man sitting beside him shouted. The shout was lost in the roar of the crowd, and he slapped the critic on the back. The critic looked up to see Zurito, directly below him, leaning far out over his horse, the length of the pic rising in a sharp angle under his armpit, holding the pic almost by the point, bearing down with all his weight, holding the bull off, the bull pushing and driving to get at the horse, and Zurito, far out, on top of him, holding him, holding him, and slowly pivoting the horse against the pressure, so that at last he was clear. Zurito felt the moment when the horse was clear and the bull could come past, and relaxed the absolute steel lock of his resistance, and the triangular steel point of the pic ripped in the bull's hump of shoulder muscle as he tore loose to find Hernandez's cape before his muzzle. He charged blindly into the cape and the boy took him out into the open arena.

Zurito sat patting his horse and looking at the bull charging the cape that Hernandez swung for him out under the bright light while the crowd shouted.

"You see that one?" he said to Manuel.

"It was a wonder," Manuel said.

[21] nag, in reference to Don Quixote's horse
[22] a series of passes to draw the bull away from the fallen picador
[23] skilled trick

"I got him that time," Zurito said. "Look at him now."

At the conclusion of a closely turned pass of the cape the bull slid to his knees. He was up at once, but far out across the sand Manuel and Zurito saw the shine of the pumping flow of blood, smooth against the black of the bull's shoulder.

"I got him that time," Zurito said.

"He's a good bull," Manuel said.

"If they gave me another shot at him, I'd kill him," Zurito said.

"They'll change the thirds on us," Manuel said.

"Look at him now," Zurito said.

"I got to go over there," Manuel said, and started on a run for the other side of the ring, where the monos[24] were leading a horse out by the bridle toward the bull, whacking him on the legs with rods and all, in a procession, trying to get him toward the bull, who stood, dropping his head, pawing, unable to make up his mind to charge.

Zurito, sitting his horse, walking him toward the scene, not missing any detail, scowled.

Finally the bull charged, the horse leaders ran for the barrera, the picador hit too far back, and the bull got under the horse, lifted him, threw him onto his back.

Zurito watched. The monos, in their red shirts, running out to drag the picador clear. The picador, now on his feet, swearing and flopping his arms. Manuel and Hernandez standing ready with their capes. And the bull, the great, black bull, with a horse on his back, hooves dangling, the bridle caught in the horns. Black bull with a horse on his back, staggering short-legged, then arching his neck and lifting, thrusting, charging to slide the horse off, horse sliding down. Then the bull into a lunging charge at the cape Manuel spread for him.

The bull was slower now, Manuel felt. He was bleeding badly. There was a sheen of blood all down his flank.

Manuel offered him the cape again. There he came, eyes open, ugly, watching the cape. Manuel stepped to the side and raised his arms, tightening the cape ahead of the bull for the veronica.

Now he was facing the bull. Yes, his head was going down a little. He was carrying it lower. That was Zurito.

Manuel flopped the cape; there he comes; he side-stepped and swung in another veronica. He's shooting awfully accurately, he thought. He's had enough fight, so he's watching now. He's hunting now. Got his eye on me. But I always give him the cape.

He shook the cape at the bull; there he comes; he side-stepped. Awful close that time. I don't want to work that close to him.

The edge of the cape was wet with blood where it had swept along the bull's back as he went by.

All right, here's the last one.

[24] monkeys—i.e., men on foot

Manuel, facing the bull, having turned with him each charge, offered the cape with his two hands. The bull looked at him. Eyes watching, horns straight forward, the bull looked at him, watching.

"Huh!" Manuel said, "Toro!" and leaning back, swung the cape forward. Here he comes. He side-stepped, swung the cape in back of him, and pivoted, so the bull followed a swirl of cape and then was left with nothing, fixed by the pass, dominated by the cape. Manuel swung the cape under his muzzle with one hand, to show the bull was fixed, and walked away.

There was no applause.

Manuel walked across the sand toward the barrera, while Zurito rode out of the ring. The trumpet had blown to change the act to the planting of the banderillos[25] while Manuel had been working with the bull. He had not consciously noticed it. The monos were spreading canvas over the two dead horses and sprinkling sawdust around them.

Manuel came up to the barrera for a drink of water. Retana's man handed him the heavy porous jug.

Fuentes, the tall gypsy, was standing holding a pair of banderillos, holding them together, slim, red sticks, fish-hook points out. He looked at Manuel.

"Go on out there," Manuel said.

The gypsy trotted out. Manuel set down the jug and watched. He wiped his face with his handkerchief.

The critic of *El Heraldo* reached for the bottle of warm champagne that stood between his feet, took a drink, and finished his paragraph.

"—the aged Manolo rated no applause for a vulgar series of lances with the cape and we entered the third of the palings."

Alone in the center of the ring the bull stood, still fixed. Fuentes, tall, flat-backed, walking toward him arrogantly, his arms spread out, the two slim, red sticks, one in each hand, held by the fingers, points straight forward. Fuentes walked forward. Back of him and to one side was a peon with a cape. The bull looked at him and was no longer fixed.

His eyes watched Fuentes, now standing still. Now he leaned back, calling to him. Fuentes twitched the two banderillos and the light on the steel points caught the bull's eye.

His tail went up and he charged.

He came straight, his eyes on the man. Fuentes stood still, leaning back, the banderillos pointing forward. As the bull lowered his head to hook, Fuentes leaned backward, his arms came together and rose, his two hands touching, the banderillos two descending red lines, and leaning forward drove the points into the bull's shoulder, leaning far in over the bull's horns and pivoting on the two upright sticks, his legs tight together, his body curving to one side to let the bull pass.

"Olé!" from the crowd.

[25] a dart with colored streamers

The bull was hooking wildly, jumping like a trout, all four feet off the ground. The red shaft of the banderillos tossed as he jumped.

Manuel, standing at the barrera, noticed that he looked always to the right.

"Tell him to drop the next pair on the right," he said to the kid who started to run out to Fuentes with the new banderillos.

A heavy hand fell on his shoulder. It was Zurito.

"How do you feel, kid?" he asked.

Manuel was watching the bull.

Zurito leaned forward on the barrera, leaning the weight of his body on his arms. Manuel turned to him.

"You're going good," Zurito said.

Manuel shook his head. He had nothing to do now until the next third. The gypsy was very good with the banderillos. The bull would come to him in the next third in good shape. He was a good bull. It had all been easy up to now. The final stuff with the sword was all he worried over. He did not really worry. He did not even think about it. But standing there he had a heavy sense of apprehension. He looked out at the bull, planning his faena, his work with the red cloth that was to reduce the bull, to make him manageable.

The gypsy was walking out toward the bull again, walking heel-and-toe, insultingly, like a ballroom dancer, the red shafts of the banderillos twitching with his walk. The bull watched him, not fixed now, hunting him, but waiting to get close enough so he could be sure of getting him, getting the horns into him.

As Fuentes walked forward the bull charged. Fuentes ran across the quarter of a circle as the bull charged and, as he passed running backward, stopped, swung forward, rose on his toes, arm straight out, and sunk the banderillos straight down into the tight of the big shoulder muscles as the bull missed him.

The crowd were wild about it.

"That kid won't stay in this night stuff long," Retana's man said to Zurito.

"He's good," Zurito said.

"Watch him now."

They watched.

Fuentes was standing with his back against the barrera. Two of the caudrilla were back of him, with their capes ready to flop over the fence to distract the bull.

The bull, with his tongue out, his barrel heaving, was watching the gypsy. He thought he had him now. Back against the red planks. Only a short charge away. The bull watched him.

The gypsy bent back, drew back his arms, the banderillos pointing at the bull. He called to the bull, stamped one foot. The bull was suspicious. He wanted the man. No more barbs in the shoulder.

Fuentes walked a little closer to the bull. Bent back. Called again. Somebody in the crowd shouted a warning.

"He's too damn close," Zurito said.

"Watch him," Retana's man said.

Leaning back, inciting the bull with the banderillos, Fuentes jumped, both feet off the ground. As he jumped the bull's tail rose and he charged. Fuentes came down on his toes, arms straight out, whole body arching forward, and drove the shafts straight down as he swung his body clear of the right horn.

The bull crashed into the barrera where the flopping capes had attracted his eye as he lost the man.

The gypsy came running along the barrera toward Manuel, taking the applause of the crowd. His vest was ripped where he had not quite cleared the point of the horn. He was happy about it, showing it to the spectators. He made the tour of the ring. Zurito saw him go by, smiling, pointing at his vest. He smiled.

Somebody else was planting the last pair of banderillos. Nobody was paying any attention.

Retana's man tucked a baton inside the red cloth of a muleta,[26] folded the cloth over it, and handed it over the barrera to Manuel. He reached in the leather sword-case, took out a sword, and holding it by its leather scabbard, reached it over the fence to Manuel. Manuel pulled the blade out by the red hilt and the scabbard fell limp.

He looked at Zurito. The big man saw he was sweating.

"Now you get him, kid," Zurito said.

Manuel nodded.

"He's in good shape," Zurito said.

"Just like you want him," Retana's man assured him.

Manuel nodded.

The trumpeter, up under the roof, blew for the final act, and Manuel walked across the arena toward where, up in the dark boxes, the president must be.

In the front row of seats the substitute bull-fight critic of *El Heraldo* took a long drink of the warm champagne. He had decided it was not worth while to write a running story and would write up the corrida back in the office. What the hell was it anyway? Only a nocturnal. If he missed anything he would get it out of the morning papers. He took another drink of the champagne. He had a date at Maxim's at twelve. Who were these bull-fighters anyway? Kids and bums. A bunch of bums. He put his pad of paper in his pocket and looked over toward Manuel, standing very much alone in the ring, gesturing with his hat in a salute toward a box he could not see high up in the dark plaza. Out in the ring the bull stood quiet, looking at nothing.

[26] smaller cloth used during the faena in place of the fighting cape

"I dedicate this bull to you, Mr. President, and to the public of Madrid, the most intelligent and generous of the world," was what Manuel was saying. It was a formula. He said it all. It was a little long for nocturnal use.

He bowed at the dark, straightened, tossed his hat over his shoulder, and, carrying the muleta in his left hand and the sword in his right, walked out toward the bull.

Manuel walked toward the bull. The bull looked at him; his eyes were quick. Manuel noticed the way the banderillos hung down on his left shoulder and the steady sheen of blood from Zurito's pic-ing. He noticed the way the bull's feet were. As he walked forward, holding the muleta in his left hand and the sword in his right, he watched the bull's feet. The bull could not charge without gathering his feet together. Now he stood square on them, dully.

Manuel walked toward him, watching his feet. This was all right. He could do this. He must work to get the bull's head down, so he could go in past the horns and kill him. He did not think about the sword, not about killing the bull. He thought about one thing at a time. The coming things oppressed him, though. Walking forward, watching the bull's feet, he saw successively his eyes, his wet muzzle, and the wide, forward-pointing spread of his horns. The bull had light circles about his eyes. His eyes watched Manuel. He felt he was going to get this little one with the white face.

Standing still now and spreading the red cloth of the muleta with the sword, pricking the point into the cloth so that the sword, now held in his left hand, spread the red flannel like the jib of a boat, Manuel noticed the points of the bull's horns. One of them was splintered from banging against the barrera. The other was sharp as a porcupine quill. Manuel noticed while spreading the muleta that the white base of the horn was stained red. While he noticed these things he did not lose sight of the bull's feet. The bull watched Manuel steadily.

He's on the defensive now, Manuel thought. He's reserving himself. I've got to bring him out of that and get his head down. Always get his head down. Zurito had his head down once, but he's come back. He'll bleed when I start him going and that will bring it down.

Holding the muleta, with the sword in his left hand widening it in front of him, he called to the bull.

The bull looked at him.

He leaned back insultingly and shook the wide-spread flannel.

The bull saw the muleta. It was a bright scarlet under the arc-light. The bull's legs tightened.

Here he comes. Whoosh! Manuel turned as the bull came and raised the muleta so that it passed over the bull's horns and swept down his broad back from head to tail. The bull had gone clean up in the air with the charge. Manuel had not moved.

At the end of the pass the bull turned like a cat coming around a corner and faced Manuel.

He was on the offensive again. His heaviness was gone. Manuel noted the fresh blood shining down the black shoulder and dripping down the bull's leg. He drew the sword out of the muleta and held it in his right hand. The muleta held low down in his left hand, leaning toward the left, he called to the bull. The bull's legs tightened, his eyes on the muleta. Here he comes, Manuel thought. Yuh!

He swung with the charge, sweeping the muleta ahead of the bull, his feet firm, the sword following the curve, a point of light under the arcs.

The bull recharged as the pase natural[27] finished and Manuel raised the muleta for a pase de pecho.[28] Firmly planted, the bull came by his chest under the raised muleta. Manuel leaned his head back to avoid the clattering banderillo shafts. The hot, black bull body touched his chest as it passed.

Too damn close, Manuel thought. Zurito, leaning on the barrera, spoke rapidly to the gypsy, who trotted out toward Manuel with a cape. Zurito pulled his hat down low and looked out across the arena at Manuel.

Manuel was facing the bull again, the muleta held low and to the left. The bull's head was down as he watched the muleta.

"If it was Belmonte doing that stuff, they'd go crazy," Retana's man said.

Zurito said nothing. He was watching Manuel out in the center of the arena.

"Where did the boss dig this fellow up?" Retana's man asked.

"Out of the hospital," Zurito said.

"That's where he's going damn quick," Retana's man said.

Zurito turned on him.

"Knock on that," he said, pointing to the barrera.

"I was just kidding, man," Retana's man said.

"Knock on the wood."

Retana's man leaned forward and knocked three times on the barrera.

"Watch the faena," Zurito said.

Out in the center of the ring, under the lights, Manuel was kneeling, facing the bull, and as he raised the muleta in both hands the bull charged, tail up.

Manuel swung his body clear and, as the bull recharged, brought around the muleta in a half-circle that pulled the bull to his knees.

"Why, that one's a great bull-fighter," Retana's man said.

"No, he's not," said Zurito.

Manuel stood up and, the muleta in his left hand, the sword in his right, acknowledged the applause from the dark plaza.

---

[27] a close pass with the muleta in the left hand   [28] a pass at the chest

The bull had humped himself up from his knees and stood waiting, his head hung low.

Zurito spoke to two of the other lads of the cuadrilla and they ran out to stand back of Manuel with their capes. There were four men back of him now. Hernandez had followed him since he first came out with the muleta. Fuentes stood watching, his cape held against his body, tall, in repose, watching lazy-eyed. Now the two came up. Hernandez motioned them to stand one at each side. Manuel stood alone, facing the bull.

Manuel waved back the men with the capes. Stepping back cautiously, they saw his face was white and sweating.

Didn't they know enough to keep back? Did they want to catch the bull's eye with the capes after he was fixed and ready? He had enough to worry about without that kind of thing.

The bull was standing, his four feet square, looking at the muleta. Manuel furled the muleta in his left hand. The bull's eyes watched it. His body was heavy on his feet. He carried his head low, but not too low.

Manuel lifted the muleta at him. The bull did not move. Only his eyes watched.

He's all lead, Manuel thought. He's all square. He's framed right. He'll take it.

He thought in bull-fight terms. Sometimes he had a thought and the particular piece of slang would not come into his mind and he could not realize the thought. His instincts and his knowledge worked automatically, and his brain worked slowly and in words. He knew all about bulls. He did not have to think about them. He just did the right thing. His eyes noted things and his body performed the necessary measures without thought. If he thought about it, he would be gone.

Now, facing the bull, he was conscious of many things at the same time. There were the horns, the one splintered, the other smoothly sharp, the need to profile himself toward the left horn, lance himself short and straight, lower the muleta so the bull would follow it, and, going in over the horns, put the sword all the way into a little spot about as big as a five-peseta piece straight in back of the neck, between the sharp pitch of the bull's shoulders. He must do all this and must then come out from between the horns. He was conscious he must do all this, but his only thought was in words: "Corto y derecho."

"Corto y derecho," he thought, furling the muleta. Short and straight. Corto y derecho, he drew the sword out of the muleta, profiled on the splintered left horn, dropped the muleta across his body, so his right hand with the sword on the level with his eye made the sign of the cross, and, rising on his toes, sighted along the dipping blade of the sword at the spot high up between the bull's shoulders.

Corto y derecho he launched himself on the bull.

There was a shock, and he felt himself go up in the air. He pushed on the sword as he went up and over, and it flew out of his hand. He hit the ground and the bull was on him. Manuel, lying on the ground, kicked at the bull's muzzle with his slippered feet. Kicking, kicking, the bull after him, missing him in his excitement, bumping him with his head, driving the horns into the sand. Kicking like a man keeping a ball in the air, Manuel kept the bull from getting a clean thrust at him.

Manuel felt the wind on his back from the capes flopping at the bull, and then the bull was gone, gone over him in a rush. Dark, as his belly went over. Not even stepped on.

Manuel stood up and picked up the muleta. Fuentes handed him the sword. It was bent where it had struck the shoulder-blade. Manuel straightened it on his knee and ran toward the bull, standing now beside one of the dead horses. As he ran, his jacket flopped where it had been ripped under his armpit.

"Get him out of there," Manuel shouted to the gypsy. The bull had smelled the blood of the dead horse and ripped into the canvas-cover with his horns. He charged Fuentes's cape, with the canvas hanging from his splintered horn, and the crowd laughed. Out in the ring, he tossed his head to rid himself of the canvas. Hernandez, running up from behind him, grabbed the end of the canvas and neatly lifted it off the horn.

The bull followed it in a half-charge and stopped still. He was on the defensive again. Manuel was walking toward him with the sword and muleta. Manuel swung the muleta before him. The bull would not charge.

Manuel profiled toward the bull, sighting along the dipping blade of the sword. The bull was motionless, seemingly dead on his feet, incapable of another charge.

Manuel rose to his toes, sighting along the steel, and charged.

Again there was the shock and he felt himself being borne back in a rush, to strike hard on the sand. There was no chance of kicking this time. The bull was on top of him. Manuel lay as though dead, his head on his arms, and the bull bumped him. Bumped his back, bumped his face in the sand. He felt the horn go into the sand between his folded arms. The bull hit him in the small of the back. His face drove into the sand. The horn drove through one of his sleeves and the bull ripped it off. Manuel was tossed clear and the bull followed the capes.

Manuel got up, found the sword and muleta, tried the point of the sword with his thumb, and then ran toward the barrera for a new sword.

Retana's man handed him the sword over the edge of the barrera.

"Wipe off your face," he said.

Manuel, running again toward the bull, wiped his bloody face with his handkerchief. He had not seen Zurito. Where was Zurito?

The cuadrilla had stepped away from the bull and waited with their capes. The bull stood, heavy and dull again after the action.

Manuel walked toward him with the muleta. He stopped and shook it. The bull did not respond. He passed it right and left, left and right before the bull's muzzle. The bull's eyes watched it and turned with the swing, but he would not charge. He was waiting for Manuel.

Manuel was worried. There was nothing to do but go in. Corto y derecho. He profiled close to the bull, crossed the muleta in front of his body and charged. As he pushed in the sword, he jerked his body to the left to clear the horn. The bull passed him and the sword shot up in the air, twinkling under the arc-lights, to fall red-hilted on the sand.

Manuel ran over and picked it up. It was bent and he straightened it over his knee.

As he came running toward the bull, fixed again now, he passed Hernandez standing with his cape.

"He's all bone," the boy said encouragingly.

Manuel nodded, wiping his face. He put the bloody handkerchief in his pocket.

There was the bull. He was close to the barrera now. Damn him. Maybe he was all bone. Maybe there was not any place for the sword to go in. The hell there wasn't! He'd show them.

He tried a pass with the muleta and the bull did not move. Manuel chopped the muleta back and forth in front of the bull. Nothing doing.

He furled the muleta, drew the sword out, profiled and drove in on the bull. He felt the sword buckle as he shoved it in, leaning his weight on it, and then it shot high in the air, end-over-ending into the crowd. Manuel had jerked clear as the sword jumped.

The first cushions thrown down out of the dark missed him. Then one hit him in the face, his bloody face looking toward the crowd. They were coming down fast. Spotting the sand. Somebody threw an empty champagne-bottle from close range. It hit Manuel on the foot. He stood there watching the dark, where the things were coming from. Then something whished through the air and struck by him. Manuel leaned over and picked it up. It was his sword. He straightened it over his knee and gestured with it to the crowd.

"Thank you," he said. "Thank you."

Oh, the dirty bastards! Dirty bastards! Oh, the lousy, dirty bastards! He kicked into a cushion as he ran.

There was the bull. The same as ever. All right, you dirty, lousy bastard!

Manuel passed the muleta in front of the bull's black muzzle.

Nothing doing.

You won't! All right. He stepped close and jammed the sharp peak of the muleta into the bull's damp muzzle.

The bull was on him as he jumped back and as he tripped on a cushion he felt the horn go into him, into his side. He grabbed the horn with his two hands and rode backward, holding tight onto the place. The bull tossed him and he was clear. He lay still. It was all right. The bull was gone.

He got up coughing and feeling broken and gone. The dirty bastards! "Give me the sword," he shouted. "Give me the stuff."

Fuentes came up with the muleta and the sword.

Hernandez put his arm around him.

"Go on to the infirmary, man," he said. "Don't be a damn fool."

"Get away from me," Manuel said. "Get to hell away from me."

He twisted free. Hernandez shrugged his shoulders. Manuel ran toward the bull.

There was the bull standing, heavy, firmly planted.

All right, you bastard! Manuel drew the sword out of the muleta, sighted with the same movement, and flung himself onto the bull. He felt the sword go in all the way. Right up to the guard. Four fingers and his thumb into the bull. The blood was hot on his knuckles, and he was on top of the bull.

The bull lurched with him as he lay on, and seemed to sink; then he was standing clear. He looked at the bull going down slowly over on his side, then suddenly four feet in the air.

Then he gestured at the crowd, his hand warm from the bull blood.

All right, you bastards! He wanted to say something, but he started to cough. It was hot and choking. He looked down for the muleta. He must go over and salute the president. President hell! He was sitting down looking at something. It was the bull. His four feet up. Thick tongue out. Things crawling around on his belly and under his legs. Crawling where the hair was thin. Dead bull. To hell with the bull! To hell with them all! He started to get to his feet and commenced to cough. He sat down again, coughing. Somebody came and pushed him up.

They carried him across the ring to the infirmary, running with him across the sand, standing blocked at the gate as the mules came in, then around under the dark passageway, men grunting as they took him up the stairway, and then laid him down.

The doctor and two men in white were waiting for him. They laid him out on the table. They were cutting away his shirt. Manuel felt tired. His whole chest felt scalding inside. He started to cough and they held something to his mouth. Everybody was very busy.

There was an electric light in his eyes. He shut his eyes.

He heard some one coming very heavily up the stairs. Then he did not hear it. Then he heard a noise far off. That was the crowd. Well, somebody would have to kill his other bull. They had cut away all his shirt. The doctor smiled at him. There was Retana.

"Hello, Retana!" Manuel said. He could not hear his voice.

Retana smiled at him and said something. Manuel could not hear it.

Zurito stood beside the table, bending over where the doctor was working. He was in his picador clothes, without his hat.

Zurito said something to him. Manuel could not hear it.

Zurito was speaking to Retana. One of the men in white smiled and handed Retana a pair of scissors. Retana gave them to Zurito. Zurito said something to Manuel. He could not hear it.

To hell with this operating-table. He'd been on plenty of operating-tables before. He was not going to die. There would be a priest if he was going to die.

Zurito was saying something to him. Holding up the scissors.

That was it. They were going to cut off his coleta. They were going to cut off his pigtail.

Manuel sat up on the operating-table. The doctor stepped back, angry. Some one grabbed him and held him.

"You couldn't do a thing like that, Manos," he said.

He heard suddenly, clearly, Zurito's voice.

"That's all right," Zurito said. "I won't do it. I was joking."

"I was going good," Manuel said. "I didn't have any luck. That was all."

Manuel lay back. They had put something over his face. It was all familiar. He inhaled deeply. He felt very tired. He was very, very tired. They took the thing away from his face.

"I was going good," Manuel said weakly. "I was going great."

Retana looked at Zurito and started for the door.

"I'll stay here with him," Zurito said.

Retana shrugged his shoulders.

Manuel opened his eyes and looked at Zurito.

"Wasn't I going good, Manos?" he asked, for confirmation.

"Sure," said Zurito. "You were going great."

The doctor's assistant put the cone over Manuel's face and he inhaled deeply. Zurito stood awkwardly, watching.

Elizabeth Bowen
1899–1973
JOINING CHARLES

E VERYBODY in the White House was awake early that morning, even the cat. At an unprecedented hour in the thick gray dusk Polyphemus slipped upstairs and began to yowl at young Mrs. Charles's door, under which came out a pale yellow line of candlelight. On an ordinary morning he could not have escaped from the kitchen so easily, but last night the basement door had been left unbolted; all the doors were open downstairs, for the household had gone to bed at a crisis of preparation for the morrow. Sleep was to be no more than an interim, and came to most of them thinly and interruptedly. The rooms were littered with objects that had an air of having been put down momentarily, corded boxes were stacked up in the hall, and a spectral breakfast table waiting all night in the parlor reappeared slowly as dawn came in through the curtains.

Young Mrs. Charles came across to the door on her bare feet and, shivering, let in Polyphemus. She was still in pajamas, but her two suitcases were packed to the brim, with tissue paper smoothed on the tops of them: she must have been moving about for hours. She was always, superstitiously, a little afraid of Polyphemus and made efforts to propitiate him on all occasions; his expression of omniscience had imposed upon her thoroughly. His coming in now made her a little conscious; she stood still, one hand on the knob of the dressing-table drawer, and put the other hand to her forehead—what must she do? Between the curtains, drawn a little apart, light kept coming in slowly, solidifying the objects round her, which till now had been uncertain, wavering silhouettes in candlelight. So night fears gave place to the realities of daytime.

Polyphemus continued to melt round the room, staring malignly at nothing. Presently Agatha tapped and came in in her dressing gown; her plaits hung down each side of her long, kind face, and she carried a cup of tea.

"Better drink this," said Agatha. "What can I do?" She drew back the curtains a little more in her comfortable, commonsense way to encourage the daylight. Leaning for a moment out of the window she breathed in critically the morning air; the bare upland country was sheathed but not hidden by mist. "You're going to have a beautiful day," said Agatha.

Mrs. Charles shivered, then began tugging a comb through her short hair. She had been awake a long time and felt differently from Agatha about the day; she looked at her sister-in-law haggardly. "I dreamed and dreamed," said Mrs. Charles. "I kept missing my boat, saw it sliding away from the quay; and when I turned to come back to you all England was sliding away too, in the other direction, and I don't know where I was left—and I dreamed, too, of course, about losing my passport."

"One would think you had never traveled before," said Agatha tranquilly. She sat down on the end of the narrow bed where Mrs. Charles had slept for the last time, and shaking out Mrs. Charles's garments, passed them to her one by one, watching her dress as though she had been a child. Mrs. Charles felt herself being marveled at; her own smallness and youth had become objective to her at the White House; a thing, all she had, to offer them over again every day to be softened and pleased by.

As she pulled on the clothes she was to wear for so long she began to feel formal and wary, the wife of a competent banker going to join him at Lyon. The expression of her feet in those new brogues was quite unfamiliar; the feet of a "nice little woman." Her hair, infected by this feeling of strangeness that flowed to her very extremities, lay in a different line against her head. For a moment the face of a ghost from the future stared at her out of the looking glass. She turned quickly to Agatha, but her sister-in-law had left her while she was buttoning her jumper at the neck and had gone downstairs to print some more labels. It had occurred to Agatha that there would be less chance of losing the luggage (a contingency by which this untraveled family seemed to be haunted) if Louise were to tie on new labels, with more explicit directions, at Paris, where she would have to reregister. Agatha was gone, and the cup of tea, untasted, grew cold on the dressing table.

The room looked bare without her possessions and withdrawn, as though it had already forgotten her. At this naked hour of parting she had forgotten it also; she supposed it would come back in retrospect so distinctly as to be a kind of torment. It was a smallish room with sloping ceilings, and a faded paper rambled over by roses. It had white curtains and was never entirely dark; it had so palpably a life of its own that she had been able to love it with intimacy and a sense of return, as one could never have loved an inanimate thing. Lying in bed one could see from the one window nothing but sky or sometimes a veil of rain; when one got up and looked out there were fields, wild and bare, and an unbroken sky-line to emphasize the security of the house.

The room was up on the top floor, in one of the gables; a big house-hold cannot afford a spare bedroom of any pretensions. To go downstairs one had to unlatch the nursery gate at the head of the top flight. Last time Charles was home it had been very unfortunate; he had barked his shins on the gate and shouted angrily to his mother to know what the thing was still there for. Louise fully realized that it was being kept for Charles's children.

During that first visit with Charles she had hardly been up to the second floor, where the younger girls slept in the old nursery. There had been no confidences; she and Charles occupied very connubially a room Mrs. Ray gave up to them that had been hers since her marriage. It was not till Louise came back here alone that the White House opened its arms to her and she began to be carried away by this fullness, this intimacy and queer seclusion of family life. She and the girls were in and out of each other's room; Doris told sagas of high school, Maisie was always just on the verge of a love affair, and large grave Agatha began to drop the formality with which she had greeted a married woman and sister-in-law. She thought Agatha would soon have forgotten she was anything but her own child if it had ever been possible for Agatha to forget Charles.

It would have been terrible if Louise had forgotten, as she so nearly had, to pack Charles's photograph. There it had stood these three months, propped up on the mantelpiece, a handsome convention in sepia, becomingly framed, from which the young wife, falling asleep or waking, had turned away her face instinctively. She folded back a layer of tissue paper before shutting her suitcase and poked down a finger to feel the edge of the frame and reassure herself. There it was, lying face down, wrapped up in her dressing gown, and she would have seen Charles before she looked again at his photograph. The son and brother dominating the White House would be waiting on the Lyon platform to enfold her materially.

Mrs. Charles glanced round the room once more, then went down-stairs slowly. Through the house she could hear doors opening and shutting and people running about because of her. She felt ashamed that her packing was finished and there was nothing for her to do. Whenever she had pictured herself leaving the White House it had been in the evening, with curtains drawn, and they had all just come out to the door for a minute to say good-bye to her, then gone back to the fire. It had been more painful but somehow easier. Now she felt lonely; they had all gone away from her, there was nobody there.

She went shyly into the morning room as though for the first time and knelt down on the rug in front of a young fire. There was a sharp smell of wood smoke; thin little flames twisted and spat through the kindling. A big looking glass, down to the ground, reflected her kneeling there; small and childish among the solemn mahogany furniture; more like somebody sent back to school than someone rejoining a virile and generous husband who loved her. Her cropped fair hair turned under against her cheek and was cut in a straight line over the eyebrows. She had never had a home before, and had been able to boast till quite lately that she had never been homesick. After she married there had been houses in which she lived with Charles, but still she had not known what it meant to be homesick.

She hoped that, after all, nobody would come in for a moment or two; she had turned her head and was looking out at the lawn with its fringe of trees not yet free from the mist, and at the three blackbirds hopping about on it. The blackbirds made her know all at once what it meant to be going away; she felt as though someone had stabbed her a long time ago but she were only just feeling the knife. She could not take her eyes from the blackbirds, till one with a wild fluty note skimmed off into the trees and the other two followed it. Polyphemus had come in after her and was looking out at them, pressing himself against the windowpane.

"Polyphemus," said Mrs. Charles in her oddly unchildish voice, "have you any illusions?" Polyphemus lashed his tail.

By midday (when she would be nearly at Dover) the fire would be streaming up briskly, but by that time the sun would be pouring in at the windows and no one would need a fire at all. The mornings were not cold yet, the girls were active, and it was only because of her going away that the fire had been lighted. Perhaps Agatha, who never hurt anything's feelings, would come in and sit not too far away from it with her basket of mending, making believe to be glad of the heat. "I don't suppose there'll be fires at Lyon," thought Mrs. Charles. Somewhere, in some foreign room, tomorrow evening when the endearments were over or there was a pause in them, Charles would lean back in his chair with a gusty sigh, arch his chest up, stretch out his legs and say: "Well, come on. Tell me about the family."

Then she would have to tell him about the White House. Her cheeks burned as she thought how it would all come out. There seemed no chance yet of Agatha or Maisie getting married. That was what Charles would want to know chiefly about his sisters. He had a wholesome contempt for virginity. He would want to know how Doris, whom he rather admired, was "coming along." Those sisters of Charles's always sounded rather dreadful young women, not the sort that Agatha, Maisie, or Doris would care to know. It seemed to Charles funny—he often referred to it—that Agatha wanted babies so badly and went all tender and conscious when babies were mentioned.

"She'll make no end of a fuss over our kids," Charles would say. The White House seemed to Charles, all the same, very proper as an institution; it was equally proper that he should have a contempt for it. He helped to support the girls and his mother, for one thing, and that did place them all at a disadvantage. But they were dear, good souls. Mrs. Charles knelt with her hands on her knees and the hands clenched slowly from anger and helplessness.

Mrs. Ray, the mother of Charles, suddenly knelt down by his wife and put an arm round her shoulders without saying a word. She did these impulsive things gracefully. Mrs. Charles relaxed and leaned sideways a little against the kind shoulder. She had nothing to say, so they watched the fire struggle and heard the hall clock counting away the seconds.

"Have you got enough clothes on?" said Mother after a minute. "It's cold in trains. I never do think you wear enough clothes."

Mrs. Charles, nodding, unbuttoned her coat and showed a ribbed sweater pulled on over her jumper. "Sensible of me!" she proudly remarked.

"You're learning to be quite a sensible little thing," Mother said lightly. "I expect Charles will notice a difference. Tell Charles not to let you go out in the damp in your evening shoes. But I expect he knows how to take care of you."

"Indeed, yes," said Mrs. Charles, nodding.

"You're precious, you see." Mother smoothed back the hair from against Mrs. Charles's cheek to look at her thoughtfully, like a gentle skeptic at some kind of miracle. "Remember to write me about the flat: I want to know everything: wallpapers, views from the windows, sizes of rooms—We'll be thinking about you both tomorrow."

"I'll be thinking of you."

"Oh, no, you won't," said Mother, with perfect finality.

"Perhaps not," Mrs. Charles quickly amended.

Mother's son Charles was generous, sensitive, gallant, and shrewd. The things he said, the things he had made, his imprint, were all over the White House. Sometimes he looked out at Louise with bright eyes from the family talk, so striking, so unfamiliar that she fell in love with the stranger for moments together as a married woman should not. He was quiet and never said very much, but he noticed; he had an infallible understanding and entered deeply, it seemed, into the sisters' lives. He was so good; he was so keen for them all to be happy. He had the strangest way of anticipating one's wishes. He was master of an inimitable drollery —to hear him chaff Agatha! Altogether he was a knightly person, transcending modern convention. His little wife had come to them all in a glow from her wonderful lover. No wonder she was so quiet; they used to try and read him from her secret, sensitive face.

A thought of their Charles without his Louise troubled them all with a pang when Louise was her dearest. Charles in Lyon, uncomplaining, lonely, tramping the town after business to look for a flat. The return of Louise to him, to the home he had found for her, her room upstairs already aghast and vacant, the emptiness that hung over them, gave them the sense of pouring out an oblation. The girls were heavy, with the faces of Flemish Madonnas; Doris achieved some resemblance to Charles, but without being handsome. They had cheerful dispositions, but were humble when they considered themselves; they thought Louise must have a great deal of love in her to give them so much when there was a Charles in her life.

Mrs. Ray, with a groan at her "old stiff bones," got up from the hearth-rug and sat on a chair. She thought of something to say, but was not quite ready to say it till she had taken up her knitting. She had hoped to have finished this pair of socks in time to send out by Louise with his others; she hadn't been able to—Mrs. Ray sighed. "You're making my boy very happy," she said, with signs in her manner of the difficulty one has in expressing these things.

Louise thought: "Oh, I love you!" There was something about the hands, the hair, the expression, the general being of Mother that possessed her entirely, that she did not think she could live without. She knelt staring at Mother, all in a tumult. Why be so lonely, why never escape? She was too lonely, it couldn't be borne; not even for the sake of the White House. Not this morning, so early, with the buffeting strangeness of travel before her, with her wrists so chilly and the anticipation of seasickness making her stomach ache. The incommunicableness of even these things, these little ills of the body, bore Mrs. Charles down. She was tired of being brave alone, she was going to give it up.

It is with mothers that understanding and comfort are found. She wanted to put down her head on a bosom, this bosom, and say: "I'm unhappy. Oh, help me! I can't go on. I don't love my husband. It's death to be with him. He's grand, but he's rotten all through—" She needed to be fortified.

"Mother—" said Louise.

"Mm-mm?"

"If things were not a success out there—If one weren't a good wife always—" Mother smoothed her knitting out and began to laugh; an impassable resolute chuckle.

"What a thing—" she said. "What an idea!"

Louise heard steps in the hall and began kneading her hands together, pulling the fingers helplessly. "Mother," she said, "I feel—"

Mother looked at her; out of the eyes looked Charles. The steady, gentle look, their interchange, lasted moments. Steps came hurrying over the flags of the hall.

"I can't go—"

Doris came in with the teapot. She wasn't grown up, her movements were clumsy and powerful, more like a boy's. She should have been Charles. Her heavy plait came tumbling over her shoulders as she bent to put down the teapot—round and brown with a bluish glaze on it. Sleep and tears in the dark had puffed up her eyelids, which seemed to open with difficulty: her small eyes dwindled into her face. "Breakfast," she said plaintively.

Rose, the servant, brought in a plate of boiled eggs—nice and light for the journey—and put them down compassionately.

"Even Rose," thought Mrs. Charles, getting up and coming to the table obediently because they all expected her to, "even Rose—" She looked at the breakfast cups with poppies scattered across them as though she had not seen them before or were learning an inventory. Doris had begun to eat as though nothing else mattered. She took no notice of Louise, pretending, perhaps, to make things easier for herself, that Louise were already gone.

"Oh, Doris, not the tussore[1] tie with the red shirt." Whatever White House might teach Mrs. Charles about common sense, it was her mission to teach them about clothes. "Not," said Mrs. Charles, with bravado rising to an exaggeration of pathos, "not on my last day!"

"I dressed in the dark; I couldn't see properly," said Doris.

"You won't get eggs for breakfast in France," said Maisie with a certain amount of triumph as she came in and sat down.

"I wonder what the flat'll be like?" said Maisie. "Do write and tell us about the flat—describe the wallpapers and everything."

"Just think," said Doris, "of Charles buying the furniture! '*Donnez-moi une chaise!*' '*Bien, Monsieur.*' '*Non. Ce n'est pas assez confortable pour ma femme.*'[2]"

"Fancy!" said Maisie, laughing very much. "And fancy if the flat's high up."

"There'll be central heating and stoves. Beautiful rug. She actually won't be chilly." Mrs. Charles was always chilly: this was a household joke.

"Central heating is stuffy—"

Doris broke away suddenly from the conversation. "Oh!" said she violently. "Oh, Louise, you are lucky!"

[1] a shade of pink
[2] "I'd like a chair." "Very well, sir." "No. It's not comfortable enough for my wife."

A glow on the streets and on the pale, tall houses: Louise walking with Charles. Frenchmen running in blousy overalls (Doris saw), French poodles, French girls in plaid skirts putting the shutters back, French ladies on iron balconies, leaning over, watching Charles go up the street with Louise and help Louise over the crossings; Charles and Louise together. A door, a lift, a flat, a room, a kiss! "Charles, Charles, you are so splendid! Mother loves you and the girls love you and I love you—" "Little woman!" A French curtain fluttering in the high, fresh wind, the city under the roofs—forgotten. All this Doris watched: Louise watched Doris.

"Yes," smiled Louise. "I am lucky."

"Even to be going to France," said Doris, and stared with her dog's eyes.

Louise wanted to take France in her two hands and make her a present of it. "You'll be coming out soon, Doris, someday." (It was not likely that Charles would have her—and did one, anyhow, dare let the White House into the flat?)

"Do you really think so?"

"Why not, if Mother can spare you?"

"Louise!" cried Maisie reproachfully—she had been sitting watching —"you aren't eating."

Agatha, sitting next her, covered up her confusion with gentle comforting noises, cut the top off an egg and advanced it coaxingly. That was the way one made a child eat; she was waiting to do the same for Charles's and Louise's baby when it was old enough. Louise now almost saw the baby sitting up between them, but it was nothing to do with her.

"You'll be home in less than the two years, I shouldn't be surprised," said Mother startlingly. It was strange, now one came to think of it, that any question of coming back to the White House had not been brought up before. They might know Mrs. Charles would be coming back, but they did not (she felt) believe it. So she smiled at Mother as though they were playing a game.

"Well, two years at the very least," Mother said with energy.

They all cast their minds forward. Louise saw herself in the strong pale light of the future walking up to the White House and (for some reason) ringing the bell like a stranger. She stood ringing and ringing and nobody answered or even looked out of a window. She began to feel that she had failed them somehow, that something was missing. Of course it was. When Louise came back next time she must bring them a baby. Directly she saw herself coming up the steps with a child in her arms she knew at once what was wanted. Wouldn't Agatha be delighted? Wouldn't Maisie "run on"? Wouldn't Doris hang awkwardly round and make jokes, poking her big finger now and then between the baby's curling pink ones? As for Mother—at the supreme moment of handing the baby to Mother, Louise had a spasm of horror and nearly dropped it. For the first time she looked at the baby's face and saw it was Charles's.

"It would do no good," thought Mrs. Charles, cold all of a sudden and hardened against them all, "to have a baby of Charles's."

They all sat looking not quite at each other, not quite at her. Maisie said (thinking perhaps of the love affair that never completely materialized) : "A great deal can happen in two years," and began to laugh confusedly in an emotional kind of way. Mother and Agatha looked across at each other. "Louise, don't forget to send us a wire," said Mother, as though she had been wondering all this time she had sat so quiet behind the teapot whether Louise would remember to do this.

"Or Charles might send the wire."

"Yes," said Louise, "that would be better."

Polyphemus, knowing his moment, sprang up on to Mrs. Charles's knee. His black tail, stretched out over the tablecloth, lashed sideways, knocking the knives and forks crooked. His one green eye sardonically penetrated her. He knew. He had been given to Charles as a dear little kitten. He pressed against her, treading her lap methodically and mewing soundlessly, showing the purple roof of his mouth. "Ask Charles," suggested Polyphemus, "what became of my other eye." "I know," returned Mrs. Charles silently. "They don't, they haven't been told; you've a voice, I haven't—what about it?" "Satan!" breathed Mrs. Charles, and caressed fascinatedly the fur just over his nose.

"Funny," mused Agatha, watching, "you never have cared for Polyphemus, and yet he likes you. He's a very transparent cat; he is wonderfully honest."

"He connects her with Charles," said Maisie, also enjoying this interchange between the wife and the cat. "He's sending some kind of a message—he's awfully clever."

"Too clever for me," said Mrs. Charles, and swept Polyphemus off her knee with finality. Agatha was going as far as the station; she went upstairs for her hat and coat. Mrs. Charles rose also, picked up her soft felt hat from a chair and pulled it on numbly, in front of the long glass, arranging two little bits of hair at the sides against her cheeks. "Either I am dreaming," she thought, "or someone is dreaming me."

Doris roamed round the room and came up to her. "A book left behind, Louise; *Framley Parsonage*,[3] one of your books."

"Keep it for me."

"For two years—all that time?"

"Yes, I'd like you to."

Doris sat down on the floor and began to read *Framley Parsonage*. She went into it deeply—she had to go somewhere; there was nothing to say; she was suddenly shy of Louise again as she had been at first, as though they had never known each other—perhaps they never had.

"Haven't you read it before?"

"No, never, I'll write and tell you, shall I, what I think of it?"

---

[3] a novel by Anthony Trollope

"I've quite forgotten what I think of it," said Louise, standing above her, laughing and pulling on her gloves. She laughed as though she were at a party, moving easily now under the smooth compulsion of Somebody's dreaming mind. Agatha had come in quietly. "Hush!" she said in a strained way to both of them, standing beside the window in hat and coat as though she were the traveler. "Hush!" She was listening for the taxi. Mother and Maisie had gone.

Wouldn't the taxi come, perhaps? What if it never came? An intolerable jar for Louise, to be deprived of going; a tear in the mesh of the dream that she could not endure. "Make the taxi come soon!" she thought, praying now for departure. "Make it come soon!"

Being listened for with such concentration must have frightened the taxi, for it didn't declare itself; there was not a sound to be heard on the road. If it were not for the hospitality of *Framley Parsonage* where, at this moment, would Doris have been? She bent to the pages absorbedly and did not look up; the leaves of the book were thin and turned over noisily. Louise fled from the morning room into the hall.

Out in the dark hall Mother was bending over the pile of boxes, reading and rereading the labels upside down and from all aspects. She often said that labels could not be printed clearly enough. As Louise hurried past she stood up, reached out an arm and caught hold of her. Only a little light came down from the staircase window; they could hardly see each other. They stood like two figures in a picture, without understanding, created to face one another.

"Louise," whispered Mother, "if things should be difficult—Marriage isn't easy. If you should be disappointed—I know, I feel—you do understand? If Charles—"

"Charles?"

"I do love you, I do. You would tell me?"

But Louise, kissing her coldly and gently, said: "Yes, I know. But there isn't really, Mother, anything to tell."

Jorge Luis Borges
1899–

TLÖN, UQBAR, ORBIS TERTIUS

I

I OWE the discovery of Uqbar to the conjunction of a mirror and an encyclopedia. The mirror troubled the depths of a corridor in a country house on Gaona Street in Ramos Mejía; the encyclopedia is fallaciously called *The Anglo-American Cyclopædia* (New York, 1917) and is a literal but delinquent reprint of the *Encyclopædia Britannica* of 1902. The event took place some five years ago. Bioy Casares had had dinner with me that evening and we became lengthily engaged in a vast polemic concerning the composition of a novel in the first person, whose narrator would omit or disfigure the facts and indulge in various contradictions which would permit a few readers—very few readers—to perceive an atrocious or banal reality. From the remote depths of the corridor, the mirror spied upon us. We discovered (such a discovery is inevitable in the late hours of the night) that mirrors have something monstrous about them. Then Bioy Casares recalled that one of the heresiarchs of Uqbar had declared that mirrors and copulation are abominable, because they increase the number of men. I asked him the origin of this memorable observation and he answered that it was reproduced in *The Anglo-American Cyclopædia*, in its article on Uqbar. The house (which we had rented furnished) had a set of this work. On the last pages of Volume XLVI we found an article on Upsala; on the first pages of Volume XLVII, one on Ural-Altaic Languages, but not a word about Uqbar. Bioy, a bit taken aback, consulted the volumes of the index. In vain he exhausted all of the imaginable spellings: Ukbar, Ucbar, Ooqbar, Ookbar, Oukbahr . . . Before leaving, he told me that it was a region of Iraq or of Asia Minor. I must confess that I agreed with some discomfort. I conjectured that this undocumented country and its anonymous heresiarch were a fiction devised by Bioy's modesty in order to justify a statement. The fruitless examination of one of Justus Perthes' atlases fortified my doubt.

The following day, Bioy called me from Buenos Aires. He told me he had before him the article on Uqbar, in Volume XLVI of the encyclopedia. The heresiarch's name was not forthcoming, but there was a note on his doctrine, formulated in words almost identical to those he had repeated, though perhaps literarily inferior. He had recalled: *Copulation and mirrors are abominable.* The text of the encyclopedia said: *For one of those gnostics, the visible universe was an illusion or (more precisely) a sophism. Mirrors and fatherhood are abominable because they multiply and disseminate that universe.* I told him, in all truthfulness, that I should like to see that article. A few days later he brought it. This surprised me, since the scrupulous cartographical indices of Ritter's *Erdkunde*[1] were plentifully ignorant of the name Uqbar.

The tome Bioy brought was, in fact, Volume XLVI of the *Anglo-American Cyclopædia*. On the half-title page and the spine, the alphabetical marking (Tor-Ups) was that of our copy, but, instead of 917, it contained 921 pages. These four additional pages made up the article on Uqbar, which (as the reader will have noticed) was not indicated by the alphabetical marking. We later determined that there was no other difference between the volumes. Both of them (as I believe I have indicated) are reprints of the tenth *Encyclopædia Britannica*. Bioy had acquired his copy at some sale or other.

[1] geography

We read the article with some care. The passage recalled by Bioy was perhaps the only surprising one. The rest of it seemed very plausible, quite in keeping with the general tone of the work and (as is natural) a bit boring. Reading it over again, we discovered beneath its rigorous prose a fundamental vagueness. Of the fourteen names which figured in the geographical part, we only recognized three—Khorasan, Armenia, Erzerum[2]—interpolated in the text in an ambiguous way. Of the historical names, only one: the impostor magician Smerdis,[3] invoked more as a metaphor. The note seemed to fix the boundaries of Uqbar, but its nebulous reference points were rivers and craters and mountain ranges of that same region. We read, for example, that the lowlands of Tsai Khaldun and the Axa Delta marked the southern frontier and that on the islands of the delta wild horses procreate. All this, on the first part of page 918. In the historical section (page 920) we learned that as a result of the religious persecutions of the thirteenth century, the orthodox believers sought refuge on these islands, where to this day their obelisks remain and where it is not uncommon to unearth their stone mirrors. The section on Language and Literature was brief. Only one trait is worthy of recollection: it noted that the literature of Uqbar was one of fantasy and that its epics and legends never referred to reality, but to the two imaginary regions of Mlejnas and Tlön . . . The bibliography enumerated four volumes which we have not yet found, though the third—Silas Haslam: *History of the Land Called Uqbar*, 1874—figures in the catalogues of Bernard Quaritch's book shop.[4] The first, *Lesbare und lesenswerthe Bemerkungen über das Land Ukkbar in Klein-Asien*, dates from 1641 and is the work of Johannes Valentinus Andreä.[5] This fact is significant; a few years later, I came upon that name in the unsuspected pages of De Quincey (*Writings*, Volume XIII) and learned that it belonged to a German theologian who, in the early seventeenth century, described the imaginary community of Rosae Crucis[6]—a community that others founded later, in imitation of what he had prefigured.

That night we visited the National Library. In vain we exhausted atlases, catalogues, annuals of geographical societies, travelers' and historians' memoirs: no one had ever been in Uqbar. Neither did the general index of Bioy's encyclopedia register that name. The following day, Carlos Mastronardi (to whom I had related the matter) noticed the black and gold covers of the *Anglo-American Cyclopædia* in a bookshop on

---

[2] place names in the Middle East

[3] one of two usurpers who ruled Persia briefly in the sixth century B.C., in the time of Cambyses and Darius

[4] Haslam has also published *A General History of Labyrinths*. (Borges's note) Quaritch, 1819–1899, was actually London's leading bookseller.

[5] *Readable and Valuable Observations on the Land of Uqbar in Asia Minor*. Andreä was a seventeenth-century theologian, but the work attributed to him here is apparently fictitious.

[6] a society of mystic philosophers alleged by Andrea to have been founded in the fifteenth century. Rosicrucian societies have existed at various later times.

Corrientes and Talcahuano . . . He entered and examined Volume
XLVI. Of course, he did not find the slightest indication of Uqbar.

2

Some limited and waning memory of Herbert Ashe, an engineer of the
southern railways, persists in the hotel at Adrogué, amongst the effusive
honeysuckles and in the illusory depths of the mirrors. In his lifetime, he
suffered from unreality, as do so many Englishmen; once dead, he is not
even the ghost he was then. He was tall and listless and his tired rectangular beard had once been red. I understand he was a widower, without children. Every few years he would go to England, to visit (I judge
from some photographs he showed us) a sundial and a few oaks. He and
my father had entered into one of those close (the adjective is excessive)
English friendships that begin by excluding confidences and very soon
dispense with dialogue. They used to carry out an exchange of books
and newspapers and engage in taciturn chess games . . . I remember
him in the hotel corridor, with a mathematics book in his hand, sometimes
looking at the irrecoverable colors of the sky. One afternoon, we spoke
of the duodecimal system of numbering (in which twelve is written as
10). Ashe said that he was converting some kind of tables from the duodecimal to the sexagesimal system (in which sixty is written as 10). He
added that the task had been entrusted to him by a Norwegian, in Rio
Grande do Sul. We had known him for eight years and he had never
mentioned his sojourn in that region . . . We talked of country life, of
the *capangas*,[7] of the Brazilian etymology of the word *gaucho*[8] (which
some old Uruguayans still pronounce *gaúcho*) and nothing more was
said—may God forgive me—of duodecimal functions. In September of
1937 (we were not at the hotel), Herbert Ashe died of a ruptured
aneurysm. A few days before, he had received a sealed and certified
package from Brazil. It was a book in large octavo. Ashe left it at the
bar, where—months later—I found it. I began to leaf through it and experienced an astonished and airy feeling of vertigo which I shall not describe, for this is not the story of my emotions but of Uqbar and Tlön
and Orbis Tertius. On one of the nights of Islam called the Night of
Nights, the secret doors of heaven open wide and the water in the jars
becomes sweeter; if those doors opened, I would not feel what I felt that
afternoon. The book was written in English and contained 1001 pages.
On the yellow leather back I read these curious words which were repeated on the title page: *A First Encyclopædia of Tlön, Vol. XI. Hlaer
to Jangn*. There was no indication of date or place. On the first page and
on a leaf of silk paper that covered one of the color plates there was
stamped a blue oval with this inscription: *Orbis Tertius*. Two years before I had discovered, in a volume of a certain pirated encyclopedia, a
superficial description of a nonexistent country; now chance afforded me

---

[7] thugs (Brazilian Portuguese)   [8] cowboy

something more precious and arduous. Now I held in my hands a vast methodical fragment of an unknown planet's entire history, with its architecture and its playing cards, with the dread of its mythologies and the murmur of its languages, with its emperors and its seas, with its minerals and its birds and its fish, with its algebra and its fire, with its theological and metaphysical controversy. And all of it articulated, coherent, with no visible doctrinal intent or tone of parody.

In the "Eleventh Volume" which I have mentioned, there are allusions to preceding and succeeding volumes. In an article in the *N. R. F.* which is now classic, Néstor Ibarra has denied the existence of those companion volumes; Ezequiel Martínez Estrada and Drieu La Rochelle have refuted that doubt, perhaps victoriously. The fact is that up to now the most diligent inquiries have been fruitless. In vain we have upended the libraries of the two Americas and of Europe. Alfonso Reyes, tired of these subordinate sleuthing procedures, proposes that we should all undertake the task of reconstructing the many and weighty tomes that are lacking: *ex ungue leonem.*[9] He calculates, half in earnest and half jokingly, that a generation of *tlönistas* should be sufficient. This venturesome computation brings us back to the fundamental problem: Who are the inventors of Tlön? The plural is inevitable, because the hypothesis of a lone inventor —an infinite Leibniz[10] laboring away darkly and modestly—has been unanimously discounted. It is conjectured that this brave new world is the work of a secret society of astronomers, biologists, engineers, metaphysicians, poets, chemists, algebraists, moralists, painters, geometers . . . directed by an obscure man of genius. Individuals mastering these diverse disciplines are abundant, but not so those capable of inventiveness and less so those capable of subordinating that inventiveness to a rigorous and systematic plan. This plan is so vast that each writer's contribution is infinitesimal. At first it was believed that Tlön was a mere chaos, an irresponsible license of the imagination; now it is known that it is a cosmos and that the intimate laws which govern it have been formulated, at least provisionally. Let it suffice for me to recall that the apparent contradictions of the Eleventh Volume are the fundamental basis for the proof that the other volumes exist, so lucid and exact is the order observed in it. The popular magazines, with pardonable excess, have spread news of the zoology and topography of Tlön; I think its transparent tigers and towers of blood perhaps do not merit the continued attention of *all* men. I shall venture to request a few minutes to expound its concept of the universe.

Hume noted for all time that Berkeley's arguments did not admit the slightest refutation nor did they cause the slightest conviction. This dictum is entirely correct in its application to the earth, but entirely false

---

[9] By the claw of the lion we know him.

[10] Gottfried Wilhelm Leibniz, 1646–1716, German mathematician and philosopher, one of two independent inventors (Newton was the other) of the infinitesimal calculus.

in Tlön. The nations of this planet are congenitally idealist. Their language and the derivations of their language—religion, letters, metaphysics—all presuppose idealism. The world for them is not a concourse of objects in space; it is a heterogeneous series of independent acts. It is successive and temporal, not spatial. There are no nouns in Tlön's conjectural *Ursprache*,[11] from which the "present" languages and the dialects are derived: there are impersonal verbs, modified by monosyllabic suffixes (or prefixes) with an adverbial value. For example: there is no word corresponding to the word "moon," but there is a verb which in English would be "to moon" or "to moonate." "The moon rose above the river" is *hlör u fang axaxaxas mlö*, or literally: "upward behind the on-streaming it mooned."

The preceding applies to the languages of the southern hemisphere. In those of the northern hemisphere (on whose *Ursprache* there is very little data in the Eleventh Volume) the prime unit is not the verb, but the monosyllabic adjective. The noun is formed by an accumulation of adjectives. They do not say "moon," but rather "round airy-light on dark" or "pale-orange-of-the-sky" or any other such combination. In the example selected the mass of adjectives refers to a real object, but this is purely fortuitous. The literature of this hemisphere (like Meinong's[12] subsistent world) abounds in ideal objects, which are convoked and dissolved in a moment, according to poetic needs. At times they are determined by mere simultaneity. There are objects composed of two terms, one of visual and another of auditory character: the color of the rising sun and the faraway cry of a bird. There are objects of many terms: the sun and the water on a swimmer's chest, the vague tremulous rose color we see with our eyes closed, the sensation of being carried along by a river and also by sleep. These second-degree objects can be combined with others; through the use of certain abbreviations, the process is practically infinite. There are famous poems made up of one enormous word. This word forms a *poetic object* created by the author. The fact that no one believes in the reality of nouns paradoxically causes their number to be unending. The languages of Tlön's northern hemisphere contain all the nouns of the Indo-European languages—and many others as well.

It is no exaggeration to state that the classic culture of Tlön comprises only one discipline: psychology. All others are subordinated to it. I have said that the men of this planet conceive the universe as a series of mental processes which do not develop in space but successively in time. Spinoza[13] ascribes to his inexhaustible divinity the attributes of extension and thought; no one in Tlön would understand the juxtaposition of the first (which is typical only of certain states) and the second—which is a perfect synonym of the cosmos. In other words, they do not conceive

11 original language
12 Alexius von Meinung, 1853–1930, Austrian philosopher
13 Baruch Spinoza, 1632–1677, Dutch-Jewish philosopher and theologian

that the spatial persists in time. The perception of a cloud of smoke on the horizon and then of the burning field and then of the half-extinguished cigarette that produced the blaze is considered an example of association of ideas.

This monism or complete idealism invalidates all science. If we explain (or judge) a fact, we connect it with another; such linking, in Tlön, is a later state of the subject which cannot affect or illuminate the previous state. Every mental state is irreducible: the mere fact of naming it—i.e., of classifying it—implies a falsification. From which it can be deduced that there are no sciences on Tlön, not even reasoning. The paradoxical truth is that they do exist, and in almost uncountable number. The same thing happens with philosophies as happens with nouns in the northern hemisphere. The fact that every philosophy is by definition a dialectical game, a *Philosophie des Als Ob*,[14] has caused them to multiply. There is an abundance of incredible systems of pleasing design or sensational type. The metaphysicians of Tlön do not seek for the truth or even for verisimilitude, but rather for the astounding. They judge that metaphysics is a branch of fantastic literature. They know that a system is nothing more than the subordination of all aspects of the universe to any one such aspect. Even the phrase "all aspects" is rejectable, for it supposes the impossible addition of the present and of all past moments. Neither is it licit to use the plural "past moments," since it supposes another impossible operation . . . One of the schools of Tlön goes so far as to negate time: it reasons that the present is indefinite, that the future has no reality other than as a present hope, that the past has no reality other than as a present memory.[15] Another school declares that *all time* has already transpired and that our life is only the crepuscular and no doubt falsified and mutilated memory or reflection of an irrecoverable process. Another, that the history of the universe—and in it our lives and the most tenuous detail of our lives—is the scripture produced by a subordinate god in order to communicate with a demon. Another, that the universe is comparable to those cryptographs in which not all the symbols are valid and that only what happens every three hundred nights is true. Another, that while we sleep here, we are awake elsewhere and that in this way every man is two men.

Amongst the doctrines of Tlön, none has merited the scandalous reception accorded to materialism. Some thinkers have formulated it with less clarity than fervor, as one might put forth a paradox. In order to facilitate the comprehension of this inconceivable thesis, a heresiarch of the eleventh century[16] devised the sophism of the nine copper coins,

---

[14] philosophy of the "as if"

[15] Russell (*The Analysis of Mind*, 1921, page 159) supposes that the planet has been created a few minutes ago, furnished with a humanity that "remembers" an illusory past. (Borges's note)

[16] A century, according to the duodecimal system, signifies a period of a hundred and forty-four years. (Borges's note)

whose scandalous renown is in Tlön equivalent to that of the Eleatic paradoxes. There are many versions of this "specious reasoning," which vary the number of coins and the number of discoveries; the following is the most common:

On Tuesday, X crosses a deserted road and loses nine copper coins. On Thursday, Y finds in the road four coins, somewhat rusted by Wednesday's rain. On Friday, Z discovers three coins in the road. On Friday morning, X finds two coins in the corridor of his house. The heresiarch would deduce from this story the reality—i.e., the continuity—of the nine coins which were recovered. It is absurd (he affirmed) to imagine that four of the coins have not existed between Tuesday and Thursday, three between Tuesday and Friday afternoon, two between Tuesday and Friday morning. It is logical to think that they have existed—at least in some secret way, hidden from the comprehension of men—at every moment of those three periods.

The language of Tlön resists the formulation of this paradox; most people did not even understand it. The defenders of common sense at first did no more than negate the veracity of the anecdote. They repeated that it was a verbal fallacy, based on the rash application of two neologisms not authorized by usage and alien to all rigorous thought: the verbs "find" and "lose," which beg the question, because they presuppose the identity of the first and of the last nine coins. They recalled that all nouns (man, coin, Thursday, Wednesday, rain) have only a metaphorical value. They denounced the treacherous circumstance "somewhat rusted by Wednesday's rain," which presupposes what is trying to be demonstrated: the persistence of the four coins from Tuesday to Thursday. They explained that equality is one thing and identity another, and formulated a kind of reductio ad absurdum: the hypothetical case of nine men who on nine successive nights suffer a severe pain. Would it not be ridiculous—they questioned—to pretend that this pain is one and the same?[17] They said that the heresiarch was prompted only by the blasphemous intention of attributing the divine category of being to some simple coins and that at times he negated plurality and at other times did not. They argued: if equality implies identity, one would also have to admit that the nine coins are one.

Unbelievably, these refutations were not definitive. A hundred years after the problem was stated, a thinker no less brilliant than the heresiarch but of orthodox tradition formulated a very daring hypothesis. This happy conjecture affirmed that there is only one subject, that this indivisible subject is every being in the universe and that these beings are the organs and masks of the divinity. X is Y and is Z. Z discovers three coins because he remembers that X lost them; X finds two in the corridor because he remembers that the others have been found . . . The

---

[17] Today, one of the churches of Tlön Platonically maintains that a certain pain, a certain greenish tint of yellow, a certain temperature, a certain sound, are the only reality. All men, in the vertiginous moment of coitus, are the same man. All men who repeat a line from Shakespeare are William Shakespeare. (Borges's note)

Eleventh Volume suggests that three prime reasons determined the complete victory of this idealist pantheism. The first, its repudiation of solipsism; the second, the possibility of preserving the psychological basis of the sciences; the third, the possibility of preserving the cult of the gods. Schopenhauer[18] (the passionate and lucid Schopenhauer) formulates a very similar doctrine in the first volume of *Parerga und Paralipomena*.

The geometry of Tlön comprises two somewhat different disciplines: the visual and the tactile. The latter corresponds to our own geometry and is subordinated to the first. The basis of visual geometry is the surface, not the point. This geometry disregards parallel lines and declares that man in his movement modifies the forms which surround him. The basis of its arithmetic is the notion of indefinite numbers. They emphasize the importance of the concepts of greater and lesser, which our mathematicians symbolize as $>$ and $<$. They maintain that the operation of counting modifies quantities and converts them from indefinite into definite sums. The fact that several individuals who count the same quantity should obtain the same result is, for the psychologists, an example of association of ideas or of a good exercise of memory. We already know that in Tlön the subject of knowledge is one and eternal.

In literary practices the idea of a single subject is also all-powerful. It is uncommon for books to be signed. The concept of plagiarism does not exist: it has been established that all works are the creation of one author, who is atemporal and anonymous. The critics often invent authors: they select two dissimilar works—the *Tao Te Ching* and the *1001 Nights*, say—attribute them to the same writer and then determine most scrupulously the psychology of this interesting *homme de lettres* . . .[19]

Their books are also different. Works of fiction contain a single plot, with all its imaginable permutations. Those of a philosophical nature invariably include both the thesis and the antithesis, the rigorous pro and con of a doctrine. A book which does not contain its counterbook is considered incomplete.

Centuries and centuries of idealism have not failed to influence reality. In the most ancient regions of Tlön, the duplication of lost objects is not infrequent. Two persons look for a pencil; the first finds it and says nothing; the second finds a second pencil, no less real, but closer to his expectations. These secondary objects are called *hrönir* and are, though awkward in form, somewhat longer. Until recently, the *hrönir* were the accidental products of distraction and forgetfulness. It seems unbelievable that their methodical production dates back scarcely a hundred years, but this is what the Eleventh Volume tells us. The first efforts were unsuccessful. However, the *modus operandi* merits description. The director of one of the state prisons told his inmates that there were certain tombs in an ancient river bed and promised freedom to whoever might make an

18 Artur Schopenhauer, 1788–1860, German philosopher   19 man of letters

important discovery. During the months preceding the excavation the inmates were shown photographs of what they were to find. This first effort proved that expectation and anxiety can be inhibitory; a week's work with pick and shovel did not manage to unearth anything in the way of a *hrön* except a rusty wheel of a period posterior to the experiment. But this was kept in secret and the process was repeated later in four schools. In three of them the failure was almost complete; in the fourth (whose director died accidentally during the first excavations) the students unearthed—or produced—a gold mask, an archaic sword, two or three clay urns and the moldy and mutilated torso of a king whose chest bore an inscription which it has not yet been possible to decipher. Thus was discovered the unreliability of witnesses who knew of the experimental nature of the search . . . Mass investigations produce contradictory objects; now individual and almost improvised jobs are preferred. The methodical fabrication of *hrönir* (says the Eleventh Volume) has performed prodigious services for archaeologists. It has made possible the interrogation and even the modification of the past, which is now no less plastic and docile than the future. Curiously, the *hrönir* of second and third degree—the *hrönir* derived from another *hrön*, those derived from the *hrön* of a *hrön*—exaggerate the aberrations of the initial one; those of fifth degree are almost uniform; those of ninth degree become confused with those of the second; in those of the eleventh there is a purity of line not found in the original. The process is cyclical: the *hrön* of twelfth degree begins to fall off in quality. Stranger and more pure than any *hrön* is, at times, the *ur* : the object produced through suggestion, educed by hope. The great golden mask I have mentioned is an illustrious example.

Things become duplicated in Tlön; they also tend to become effaced and lose their details when they are forgotten. A classic example is the doorway which survived so long as it was visited by a beggar and disappeared at his death. At times some birds, a horse, have saved the ruins of an amphitheater.

Postscript (*1947*). I reproduce the preceding article just as it appeared in the *Anthology of Fantastic Literature* (1940), with no omission other than that of a few metaphors and a kind of sarcastic summary which now seems frivolous. So many things have happened since then . . . I shall do no more than recall them here.

In March of 1941 a letter written by Gunnar Erfjord was discovered in a book by Hinton which had belonged to Herbert Ashe. The envelope bore a cancellation from Ouro Preto; the letter completely elucidated the mystery of Tlön. Its text corroborated the hypotheses of Martínez Estrada. One night in Lucerne or in London, in the early seventeenth century, the splendid history has its beginning. A secret and benevolent society (amongst whose members were Dalgarno and later George Berkeley) arose to invent a country. Its vague initial program included "hermetic studies," philanthropy and the cabala. From this first period dates the curious book by Andreä. After a few years of secret conclaves and premature syntheses it was understood that one generation was not sufficient to give articulate form to a country. They resolved that each of the masters should elect a disciple who would continue his work. This hereditary arrangement prevailed; after an interval of two centuries the persecuted fraternity sprang up again in America. In 1824, in Memphis (Tennessee), one of its affiliates conferred with the ascetic millionaire Ezra Buckley. The latter, somewhat disdainfully, let him speak—and laughed at the plan's modest scope. He told the agent that in America it was absurd to invent a country and proposed the invention of a planet. To this gigantic idea he added another, a product of his nihilism:[20] that of keeping the enormous enterprise secret. At that time the twenty volumes of the *Encyclopædia Britannica* were circulating in the United States; Buckley suggested that a methodical encyclopedia of the imaginary planet be written. He was to leave them his mountains of gold, his navigable rivers, his pasture lands roamed by cattle and buffalo, his Negroes, his brothels and his dollars, on one condition: "The work will make no pact with the impostor Jesus Christ." Buckley did not believe in God, but he wanted to demonstrate to this nonexistent God that mortal man was capable of conceiving a world. Buckely was poisoned in Baton Rouge in 1828; in 1914 the society delivered to its collaborators, some three hundred in number, the last volume of the First Encyclopedia of Tlön. The edition was a secret one; its forty volumes (the vastest undertaking ever carried out by man) would be the basis for another more detailed edition, written not in English but in one of the languages of Tlön. This revision of an illusory world, was called, provisionally, *Orbis Tertius* and one of its modest demiurgi was Herbert Ashe, whether as an agent of Gunnar Erfjord or as an affiliate, I do not know. His having received a copy of the Eleventh Volume would seem to favor the latter assumption. But what about the others?

In 1942 events became more intense. I recall one of the first of these with particular clarity and it seems that I perceived then something of its premonitory character. It happened in an apartment on Laprida Street, facing a high and light balcony which looked out toward the sunset. Princess Faucigny Lucinge had received her silverware from Poitiers. From the vast depths of a box embellished with foreign stamps, delicate immobile objects emerged: silver from Utrecht and Paris covered with hard heraldic fauna, and a samovar. Amongst them—with the perceptible and tenuous tremor of a sleeping bird—a compass vibrated mysteriously. The Princess did not recognize it. Its blue needle longed for magnetic north; its metal case was concave in shape; the letters around its edge corresponded to one of the alphabets of Tlön. Such was the first intrusion of this fantastic world into the world of reality.

---

[20] Buckley was a freethinker, a fatalist and a defender of slavery. (Borges's note)

I am still troubled by a stroke of chance which made me the witness of the second intrusion as well. It happened some months later, at a country store owned by a Brazilian in Cuchilla Negra. Amorim and I were returning from Sant' Anna. The River Tacuarembó had flooded and we were obliged to sample (and endure) the proprietor's rudimentary hospitality. He provided us with some creaking cots in a large room cluttered with barrels and hides. We went to bed, but were kept from sleeping until dawn by the drunken ravings of an unseen neighbor, who intermingled inextricable insults with snatches of *milongas*[21]—or rather with snatches of the same *milonga*. As might be supposed, we attributed this insistent uproar to the store owner's fiery cane liquor. By daybreak, the man was dead in the hallway. The roughness of his voice had deceived us: he was only a youth. In his delirium a few coins had fallen from his belt, along with a cone of bright metal, the size of a die. In vain a boy tried to pick up this cone. A man was scarcely able to raise it from the ground. I held it in my hand for a few minutes; I remember that its weight was intolerable and that after it was removed, the feeling of oppressiveness remained. I also remember the exact circle it pressed into my palm. This sensation of a very small and at the same time extremely heavy object produced a disagreeable impression of repugnance and fear. One of the local men suggested we throw it into the swollen river; Amorim acquired it for a few pesos. No one knew anything about the dead man, except that "he came from the border." These small, very heavy cones (made from a metal which is not of this world) are images of the divinity in certain regions of Tlön.

Here I bring the personal part of my narrative to a close. The rest is in the memory (if not in the hopes or fears) of all my readers. Let it suffice for me to recall or mention the following facts, with a mere brevity of words which the reflective recollection of all will enrich or amplify. Around 1944, a person doing research for the newspaper *The American* (of Nashville, Tennessee) brought to light in a Memphis library the forty volumes of the First Encyclopedia of Tlön. Even today there is a controversy over whether this discovery was accidental or whether it was permitted by the directors of the still nebulous *Orbis Tertius*. The latter is most likely. Some of the incredible aspects of the Eleventh Volume (for example, the multiplication of the *hrönir*) have been eliminated or attenuated in the Memphis copies; it is reasonable to imagine that these omissions follow the plan of exhibiting a world which is not too incompatible with the real world. The dissemination of objects from Tlön over different countries would complement this plan . . .[22] The fact is that the international press infinitely proclaimed the "find." Manuals, anthologies, summaries, literal versions, authorized re-editions

---

[21] dance music

[22] There remains, of course, the problem of the *material* of some objects. (Borges's note)

and pirated editions of the Greatest Work of Man flooded and still flood the earth. Almost immediately, reality yielded on more than one account. The truth is that it longed to yield. Ten years ago any symmetry with a semblance of order— dialectical materialism, anti-Semitism, Nazism—was sufficient to entrance the minds of men. How could one do other than submit to Tlön, to the minute and vast evidence of an orderly planet? It is useless to answer that reality is also orderly. Perhaps it is, but in accordance with divine laws—I translate: inhuman laws—which we never quite grasp. Tlön is surely a labyrinth, but it is a labyrinth devised by men, a labyrinth destined to be deciphered by men.

The contact and the habit of Tlön have disintegrated this world. Enchanted by its rigor, humanity forgets over and again that it is a rigor of chess masters, not of angels. Already the schools have been invaded by the (conjectural) "primitive language" of Tlön; already the teaching of its harmonious history (filled with moving episodes) has wiped out the one which governed in my childhood; already a fictitious past occupies in our memories the place of another, a past of which we know nothing with certainty—not even that it is false. Numismatology, pharmacology and archaeology have been reformed. I understand that biology and mathematics also await their avatars . . . A scattered dynasty of solitary men has changed the face of the world. Their task continues. If our forecasts are not in error, a hundred years from now someone will discover the hundred volumes of the Second Encyclopedia of Tlön.

Then English and French and mere Spanish will disappear from the globe. The world will be Tlön. I pay no attention to all this and go on revising, in the still days at the Adrogué hotel, an uncertain Quevedian translation (which I do not intend to publish) of Browne's *Urn Burial*.[23]

—*Translated by James E. Irby*

[23] Sir Thomas Browne, English essayist, 1605–1682, published this meditative and mystical work in 1658.

Graham Greene

1904–

THE DESTRUCTORS

I

I T W A S on the eve of August Bank Holiday[1] that the latest recruit became the leader of the Wormsley Common Gang. No one was surprised except Mike, but Mike at the age of nine was surprised by every-

[1] the first Monday in August, when banks in England are legally closed; also observed as a general holiday

thing. "If you don't shut your mouth," somebody once said to him, "you'll get a frog down it." After that Mike had kept his teeth tightly clamped except when the surprise was too great.

The new recruit had been with the gang since the beginning of the summer holidays, and there were possibilities about his brooding silence that all recognised. He never wasted a word even to tell his name until that was required of him by the rules. When he said "Trevor" it was a statement of fact, not as it would have been with the others a statement of shame or defiance. Nor did anyone laugh except Mike, who finding himself without support and meeting the dark gaze of the newcomer opened his mouth and was quiet again. There was every reason why T., as he was afterwards referred to, should have been an object of mockery—there was his name (and they substituted the initial because otherwise they had no excuse not to laugh at it), the fact that his father, a former architect and present clerk, had "come down in the world" and that his mother considered herself better than the neighbors. What but an odd quality of danger, of the unpredictable, established him in the gang without any ignoble ceremony of initiation?

The gang met every morning in an impromptu car-park, the site of the last bomb of the first blitz.[2] The leader, who was known as Blackie, claimed to have heard it fall, and no one was precise enough in his dates to point out that he would have been one year old and fast asleep on the down[3] platform of Wormsley Common Underground Station. On one side of the car-park leaned the first occupied house, No. 3, of the shattered Northwood Terrace—literally leaned, for it had suffered from the blast of the bomb and the side walls were supported on wooden struts. A smaller bomb and some incendiaries had fallen beyond, so that the house stuck up like a jagged tooth and carried on the further wall relics of its neighbor, a dado, the remains of a fireplace. T., whose words were almost confined to voting "Yes" or "No" to the plan of operations proposed each day by Blackie, once startled the whole gang by saying broodingly, "Wren[4] built that house, father says."

"Who's Wren?"

"The man who built St. Paul's."

"Who cares?" Blackie said. "It's only Old Misery's."

Old Misery—whose real name was Thomas—had once been a builder and decorator. He lived alone in the crippled house, doing for himself: once a week you could see him coming back across the common with

---

[2] bombardment of London by rockets launched from sites in Germany in World War II

[3] the platform for boarding trains going away from London

[4] Sir Christopher Wren (1631–1723), English neo-classic architect, whose greatest work was the design for a new St. Paul's Cathedral in the heart of London to replace an earlier building destroyed in the Great Fire of London in 1666. The Cathedral survived the blitz in World War II when much around it was destroyed; it became a symbol of Britain's resistance to Nazi terror.

bread and vegetables, and once as the boys played in the car-park he put his head over the smashed wall of his garden and looked at them.

"Been to the loo," one of the boys said, for it was common knowledge that since the bombs fell something had gone wrong with the pipes of the house and Old Misery was too mean to spend money on the property. He could do the redecorating himself at cost price, but he had never learnt plumbing. The loo was a wooden shed at the bottom of the narrow garden with a star-shaped hole in the door: it had escaped the blast which had smashed the house next door and sucked out the window-frames of No. 3.

The next time the gang became aware of Mr. Thomas was more surprising. Blackie, Mike and a thin yellow boy, who for some reason was called by his surname Summers, met him on the common coming back from the market. Mr. Thomas stopped them. He said glumly, "You belong to the lot that play in the car-park?"

Mike was about to answer when Blackie stopped him. As the leader he had responsibilities. "Suppose we are?" he said ambiguously.

"I got some chocolates," Mr. Thomas said. "Don't like 'em myself. Here you are. Not enough to go round, I don't suppose. There never is," he added with somber conviction. He handed over three packets of Smarties.

The gang were puzzled and perturbed by this action and tried to explain it away. "Bet someone dropped them and he picked 'em up," somebody suggested.

"Pinched 'em and then got in a bleeding funk," another thought aloud.

"It's a bribe," Summers said. "He wants us to stop bouncing balls on his wall."

"We'll show him we don't take bribes," Blackie said, and they sacrificed the whole morning to the game of bouncing that only Mike was young enough to enjoy. There was no sign from Mr. Thomas.

Next day T. astonished them all. He was late at the rendezvous, and the voting for that day's exploit took place without him. At Blackie's suggestion the gang was to disperse in pairs, take buses at random and see how many free rides could be snatched from unwary conductors (the operation was to be carried out in pairs to avoid cheating). They were drawing lots for their companions when T. arrived.

"Where you been, T.?" Blackie asked. "You can't vote now. You know the rules."

"I've been *there*," T. said. He looked at the ground, as though he had thoughts to hide.

"Where?"

"At Old Misery's." Mike's mouth opened and then hurriedly closed again with a click. He had remembered the frog.

"At Old Misery's?" Blackie said. There was nothing in the rules against it, but he had a sensation that T. was treading on dangerous ground. He asked hopefully, "Did you break in?"

"No. I rang the bell."

"And what did you say?"

"I said I wanted to see his house."

"What did he do?"

"He showed it me."

"Pinch anything?"

"No."

"What did you do it for then?"

The gang had gathered round: it was as though an impromptu court were about to form and to try some case of deviation. T. said, "It's a beautiful house," and still watching the ground, meeting no one's eyes, he licked his lips first one way, then the other.

"What do you mean, a beautiful house?" Blackie asked with scorn.

"It's got a staircase two hundred years old like a corkscrew. Nothing holds it up."

"What do you mean, nothing holds it up. Does it float?"

"It's to do with opposite forces, Old Misery said."

"What else?"

"There's paneling."

"Like in the Blue Boar?"

"Two hundred years old."

"Is Old Misery two hundred years old?"

Mike laughed suddenly and then was quiet again. The meeting was in a serious mood. For the first time since T. had strolled into the car-park on the first day of the holidays his position was in danger. It only needed a single use of his real name and the gang would be at his heels.

"What did you do it for?" Blackie asked. He was just, he had no jealousy, he was anxious to retain T. in the gang if he could. It was the word "beautiful" that worried him—that belonged to a class world that you could still see parodied at the Wormsley Common Empire by a man wearing a top hat and a monocle, with a haw-haw accent. He was tempted to say, "My dear Trevor, old chap," and unleash his hell hounds. "If you'd broken in," he said sadly—that indeed would have been an exploit worthy of the gang.

"This was better," T. said. "I found out things." He continued to stare at his feet, not meeting anybody's eye, as though he were ab-sorbed in some dream he was unwilling—or ashamed—to share.

"What things?"

"Old Misery's going to be away all tomorrow and Bank Holiday."

Blackie said with relief, "You mean we could break in?"

"And pinch things?" somebody asked.

Blackie said, "Nobody's going to pinch things. Breaking in—that's good enough, isn't it? We don't want any court stuff."

"I don't want to pinch anything," T. said. "I've got a better idea."

"What is it?"

T. raised eyes, as gray and disturbed as the drab August day. "We'll pull it down," he said. "We'll destroy it."

Blackie gave a single hoot of laughter and then, like Mike, fell quiet, daunted by the serious implacable gaze. "What'd the police be doing all the time?" he said.

"They'd never know. We'd do it from inside. I've found a way in." He said with a sort of intensity, "We'd be like worms, don't you see, in an apple. When we came out again there'd be nothing there, no staircase, no panels, nothing but just walls, and then we'd make the walls fall down—somehow."

"We'd go to jug," Blackie said.

"Who's to prove? and anyway we wouldn't have pinched anything." He added without the smallest flicker of glee, "There wouldn't be anything to pinch after we'd finished."

"I've never heard of going to prison for breaking things," Summers said.

"There wouldn't be time," Blackie said. "I've seen housebreakers at work."

"There are twelve of us," T. said. "We'd organize."

"None of us know how . . ."

"I know," T. said. He looked across at Blackie, "Have you got a better plan?"

"Today," Mike said tactlessly, "we're pinching free rides . . ."

"Free rides," T. said. "You can stand down, Blackie, if you'd rather. . . ."

"The gang's got to vote."

"Put it up then."

Blackie said uneasily, "It's proposed that tomorrow and Monday we destroy Old Misery's house."

"Here, here," said a fat boy called Joe.

"Who's in favor?"

T. said, "It's carried."

"How do we start?" Summers asked.

"He'll tell you," Blackie said. It was the end of his leadership. He went away to the back of the car-park and began to kick a stone, dribbling it this way and that. There was only one old Morris in the park, for few cars were left there except lorries: without an attendant there was no safety. He took a flying kick at the car and scraped a little paint off the rear mudguard. Beyond, paying no more attention to him than to a stranger, the gang had gathered round T.; Blackie was dimly aware of the fickleness of favor. He thought of going home, of never returning, of letting them all discover the hollowness of T.'s leadership, but suppose after all what T. proposed was possible—nothing like it had ever been done before. The fame of the Wormsley Common car-park gang would surely reach around London. There would be headlines in the papers. Even the grown-up gangs who ran the betting at the all-in wrestling and the barrow-boys[5] would hear with respect of how Old Misery's house had been destroyed. Driven by the pure, simple and altruistic ambition of fame for the gang, Blackie came back to where T. stood in the shadow of Misery's wall.

T. was giving his orders with decision: it was as though this plan had been with him all his life, pondered through the seasons, now in his fifteenth year crystallised with the pain of puberty. "You," he said to Mike, "bring some big nails, the biggest you can find, and a hammer. Anyone else who can better bring a hammer and a screwdriver. We'll need plenty of them. Chisels too. We can't have too many chisels. Can anybody bring a saw?"

"I can," Mike said.

"Not a child's saw," T. said. "A real saw."

Blackie realized he had raised his hand like any ordinary member of the gang.

"Right, you bring one, Blackie. But now there's a difficulty. We want a hacksaw."

"What's a hacksaw?" someone asked.

"You can get 'em at Woolworth's," Summers said.

The fat boy called Joe said gloomily, "I knew it would end in a collection."

"I'll get one myself," T. said. "I don't want your money. But I can't buy a sledge-hammer."

Blackie said, "They are working on No. 15. I know where they'll leave their stuff for Bank Holiday."

"Then that's all," T. said. "We meet here at nine sharp."

"I've got to go to church," Mike said.

"Come over the wall and whistle. We'll let you in."

2

On Sunday morning all were punctual except Blackie, even Mike. Mike had had a stroke of luck. His mother felt ill, his father was tired after Saturday night, and he was told to go to church alone with many warnings of what would happen if he strayed. Blackie had had difficulty in smuggling out the saw, and then in finding the sledge-hammer at the back of No. 15. He approached the house from a lane at the rear of the garden, for fear of the policeman's beat along the main road. The tired evergreens kept off a stormy sun: another wet Bank Holiday was being prepared over the Atlantic, beginning in swirls of dust under the trees. Blackie climbed the wall into Misery's garden.

There was no sign of anybody anywhere. The loo stood like a tomb in a neglected graveyard. The curtains were drawn. The house slept.

---

[5] wrestling with no holds barred, and men who sell produce or other goods from push-carts

Blackie lumbered nearer with the saw and the sledge-hammer. Perhaps after all nobody had turned up: the plan had been a wild invention: they had woken wiser. But when he came close to the back door he could hear a confusion of sound, hardly louder than a hive in swarm: a clickety-clack, a bang bang bang, a scraping, a creaking, a sudden painful crack. He thought: it's true, and whistled.

They opened the back door to him and he came in. He had at once the impression of organization, very different from the old happy-go-lucky ways under his leadership. For a while he wandered up and down stairs looking for T. Nobody addressed him: he had a sense of great urgency, and already he could begin to see the plan. The interior of the house was being carefully demolished without touching the outer walls. Summers with hammer and chisel was ripping out the skirting-boards [6] in the ground floor dining-room: he had already smashed the panels of the door. In the same room Joe was heaving up the parquet blocks, exposing the soft wood floor-boards over the cellar. Coils of wire came out of the damaged skirting and Mike sat happily on the floor, clipping the wires.

On the curved stairs two of the gang were working hard with an inadequate child's saw on the banisters—when they saw Blackie's big saw they signaled for it wordlessly. When he next saw them a quarter of the banisters had been dropped into the hall. He found T. at last in the bath-room—he sat moodily in the least cared-for room in the house, listening to the sounds coming up from below.

"You've really done it," Blackie said with awe. "What's going to happen?"

"We've only just begun," T. said. He looked at the sledge-hammer and gave his instructions. "You stay here and break the bath and the wash-basin. Don't bother about the pipes. They come later."

Mike appeared at the door. "I've finished the wire, T.," he said.

"Good. You've just got to go wandering round now. The kitchen's in the basement. Smash all the china and glass and bottles you can lay hold of. Don't turn on the taps—we don't want a flood—yet. Then go into all the rooms and turn out drawers. If they are locked get one of the others to break them open. Tear up any papers you find and smash all the ornaments. Better take a carving-knife with you from the kitchen. The bedroom's opposite here. Open the pillows and tear up the sheets. That's enough for the moment. And you, Blackie, when you've finished in here crack the plaster in the passage up with your sledge-hammer."

"What are you going to do?" Blackie asked.

"I'm looking for something special," T. said.

It was nearly lunch-time before Blackie had finished and went in search of T. Chaos had advanced. The kitchen was a shambles of broken glass and china. The dining-room was stripped of parquet, the skirting was up,

[6] baseboards

the door had been taken off its hinges, and the destroyers had moved up a floor. Streaks of light came in through the closed shutters where they worked with the seriousness of creators—and destruction after all is a form of creation. A kind of imagination had seen this house as it had now become.

Mike said, "I've got to go home for dinner."

"Who else?" T. asked, but all the others on one excuse or another had brought provisions with them.

They squatted in the ruins of the room and swapped unwanted sandwiches. Half an hour for lunch and they were at work again. By the time Mike returned, they were on the top floor, and by six the superficial damage was completed. The doors were all off, all the skirtings raised, the furniture pillaged and ripped and smashed—no one could have slept in the house except on a bed of broken plaster. T. gave his orders—eight o'clock next morning, and to escape notice they climbed singly over the garden wall, into the car-park. Only Blackie and T. were left: the light had nearly gone, and when they touched a switch, nothing worked—Mike had done his job thoroughly.

"Did you find anything special?" Blackie asked.

T. nodded. "Come over here," he said, "and look." Out of both pockets he drew bundles of pound notes. "Old Misery's savings," he said. "Mike ripped out the mattress, but he missed them."

"What are you going to do? Share them?"

"We aren't thieves," T. said. "Nobody's going to steal anything from this house. I kept these for you and me—a celebration." He knelt down on the floor and counted them out—there were seventy in all. "We'll burn them," he said, "one by one," and taking it in turns they held a note upwards and lit the top corner, so that the flame burnt slowly towards their fingers. The gray ash floated above them and fell on their heads like age. "I'd like to see Old Misery's face when we are through," T. said.

"You hate him a lot?" Blackie asked.

"Of course I don't hate him," T. said. "There'd be no fun if I hated him." The last burning note illuminated his brooding face. "All this hate and love," he said, "it's soft, it's hooey. There's only things, Blackie," and he looked round the room crowded with the unfamiliar shadows of half things, broken things, former things. "I'll race you home, Blackie," he said.

3

Next morning the serious destruction started. Two were missing—Mike and another boy whose parents were off to Southend and Brighton in spite of the slow warm drops that had begun to fall and the rumble of thunder in the estuary like the first guns of the old blitz. "We've got to hurry," T. said.

Summers was restive. "Haven't we done enough?" he said. "I've been given a bob[7] for slot machines. This is like work."

"We've hardly started," T. said. "Why, there's all the floors left, and the stairs. We haven't taken out a single window. You voted like the others. We are going to *destroy* this house. There won't be anything left when we've finished."

They began again on the first floor picking up the top floor-boards next the outer wall, leaving the joists exposed. Then they sawed through the joists and retreated into the hall, as what was left of the floor heeled and sank. They had learnt with practise, and the second floor collapsed more easily. By the evening an odd exhilaration seized them as they looked down the great hollow of the house. They ran risks and made mistakes: when they thought of the windows it was too late to reach them. "Cor," Joe said, and dropped a penny down into the dry rubble-filled well. It cracked and span among the broken glass.

"Why did we start this?" Summers asked with astonishment; T. was already on the ground, digging at the rubble, clearing a space along the outer wall. "Turn on the taps," he said. "It's too dark for anyone to see now, and in the morning it won't matter." The water overtook them on the stairs and fell through the floorless rooms.

It was then they heard Mike's whistle at the back. "Something's wrong," Blackie said. They could hear his urgent breathing as they unlocked the door.

"The bogies?" Summers asked.

"Old Misery," Mike said. "He's on his way." He put his head between his knees and retched. "Ran all the way," he said with pride.

"But why?" T. said. "He told me . . ." He protested with the fury of the child he had never been, "It isn't fair."

"He was down at Southend," Mike said, "and he was on the train coming back. Said it was too cold and wet." He paused and gazed at the water. "My, you've had a storm here. Is the roof leaking?"

"How long will he be?"

"Five minutes. I gave Ma the slip and ran."

"We better clear," Summers said. "We've done enough, anyway."

"Oh no, we haven't. Anybody could do this—" "this" was the shattered hollowed house with nothing left but the walls. Yet walls could be preserved. Façades were valuable. They could build inside again more beautifully than before. This could again be a home. He said angrily, "We've got to finish. Don't move. Let me think."

"There's no time," a boy said.

"There's got to be a way," T. said. "We couldn't have got thus far . . ."

"We've done a lot," Blackie said.

[7] shilling—a little more than a dime

"No. No, we haven't. Somebody watch the front."

"We can't do any more."

"He may come in at the back."

"Watch the back too." T. began to plead. "Just give me a minute and I'll fix it. I swear I'll fix it." But his authority had gone with his ambiguity. He was only one of the gang. "Please," he said.

"Please," Summers mimicked him, and then suddenly struck home with the fatal name. "Run along home, Trevor."

T. stood with his back to the rubble like a boxer knocked groggy against the ropes. He had no words as his dreams shook and slid. Then Blackie acted before the gang had time to laugh, pushing Summers backward. "I'll watch the front, T.," he said, and cautiously he opened the shutters of the hall. The gray wet common stretched ahead, and the lamps gleamed in the puddles. "Someone's coming, T. No, it's not him. What's your plan, T.?"

"Tell Mike to go out to the loo and hide close beside it. When he hears me whistle he's got to count ten and start to shout."

"Shout what?"

"Oh, 'Help,' anything."

"You hear, Mike," Blackie said. He was the leader again. He took a quick look between the shutters. "He's coming, T."

"Quick, Mike. The loo. Stay here, Blackie, all of you till I yell."

"Where are you going, T.?"

"Don't worry. I'll see to this. I said I would, didn't I?"

Old Misery came limping off the common. He had mud on his shoes and he stopped to scrape them on the pavement's edge. He didn't want to soil his house, which stood jagged and dark between the bomb-sites, saved so narrowly, as he believed, from destruction. Even the fanlight had been left unbroken by the bomb's blast. Somewhere somebody whistled. Old Misery looked sharply round. He didn't trust whistles. A child was shouting: it seemed to come from his own garden. Then a boy ran into the road from the car-park. "Mr. Thomas," he called, "Mr. Thomas."

"What is it?"

"I'm terribly sorry, Mr. Thomas. One of us got taken short, and we thought you wouldn't mind, and now he can't get out."

"What do you mean, boy?"

"He's got stuck in your loo."

"He'd no business . . . Haven't I seen you before?"

"You showed me your house."

"So I did. That doesn't give you the right to . . ."

"Do hurry, Mr. Thomas. He'll suffocate."

"Nonsense. He can't suffocate. Wait till I put my bag in."

"I'll carry your bag."

"Oh no, you don't. I carry my own."

"This way, Mr. Thomas."

"I can't get in the garden that way. I've got to go through the house."

"But you *can* get in the garden this way, Mr. Thomas. We often do."

"You often do?" He followed the boy with a scandalized fascination. "When? What right? . . ."

"Do you see . . . ? the wall's low."

"I'm not going to climb walls into my own garden. It's absurd."

"This is how we do it. One foot here, one foot there, and over." The boy's face peered down, an arm shot out, and Mr. Thomas found his bag taken and deposited on the other side of the wall.

"Give me back my bag," Mr. Thomas said. From the loo a boy yelled and yelled. "I'll call the police."

"Your bag's all right, Mr. Thomas. Look. One foot there. On your right. Now just above. To your left." Mr. Thomas climbed over his own garden wall. "Here's your bag, Mr. Thomas."

"I'll have the wall built up," Mr. Thomas said, "I'll not have you boys coming over here, using my loo." He stumbled on the path, but the boy caught his elbow and supported him. "Thank you, thank you, my boy," he murmured automatically. Somebody shouted again through the dark. "I'm coming, I'm coming," Mr. Thomas called. He said to the boy beside him, "I'm not unreasonable. Been a boy myself. As long as things are done regular. I don't mind you playing round the place Saturday mornings. Sometimes I like company. Only it's got to be regular. One of you asks leave and I say Yes. Sometimes I'll say No. Won't feel like it. And you come in at the front door and out at the back. No garden walls."

"Do get him out, Mr. Thomas."

"He won't come to any harm in my loo," Mr. Thomas said, stumbling slowly down the garden. "Oh, my rheumatics," he said. "Always get 'em on Bank Holiday. I've got to go careful. There's loose stones here. Give me your hand. Do you know what my horoscope said yesterday? 'Abstain from any dealings in first half of week. Danger of serious crash.' That might be on this path," Mr. Thomas said. "They speak in parables and double meanings." He paused at the door of the loo. "What's the matter in there?" he called. There was no reply.

"Perhaps he's fainted," the boy said.

"Not in my loo. Here, you, come out," Mr. Thomas said, and giving a great jerk at the door he nearly fell on his back when it swung easily open. A hand first supported him and then pushed him hard. His head hit the opposite wall and he sat heavily down. His bag hit his feet. A hand whipped the key out of the lock and the door slammed. "Let me out," he called, and heard the key turn in the lock. "A serious crash," he thought, and felt dithery and confused and old.

A voice spoke to him softly through the star-shaped hole in the door. "Don't worry, Mr. Thomas," it said, "we won't hurt you, not if you stay quiet."

Mr. Thomas put his head between his hands and pondered. He had noticed that there was only one lorry in the car-park, and he felt certain that the driver would not come for it before the morning. Nobody could hear him from the road in front, and the lane at the back was seldom used. Anyone who passed there would be hurrying home and would not pause for what they would certainly take to be drunken cries. And if he did call "Help," who, on a lonely Bank Holiday evening, would have the courage to investigate? Mr. Thomas sat on the loo and pondered with the wisdom of age.

After a while it seemed to him that there were sounds in the silence —they were faint and came from the direction of his house. He stood up and peered through the ventilation-hole—between the cracks in one of the shutters he saw a light, not the light of a lamp, but the wavering light that a candle might give. Then he thought he heard the sound of hammering and scraping and chipping. He thought of burglars—perhaps they had employed the boy as a scout, but why should burglars engage in what sounded more and more like a stealthy form of carpentry? Mr. Thomas let out an experimental yell, but nobody answered. The noise could not even have reached his enemies.

4

Mike had gone home to bed, but the rest stayed. The question of leadership no longer concerned the gang. With nails, chisels, screwdrivers, anything that was sharp and penetrating they moved around the inner walls worrying at the mortar between the bricks. They started too high, and it was Blackie who hit on the damp course and realised the work could be halved if they weakened the joints immediately above. It was a long, tiring, unamusing job, but at last it was finished. The gutted house stood there balanced on a few inches of mortar between the damp course and the bricks.

There remained the most dangerous task of all, out in the open at the edge of the bomb-site. Summers was sent to watch the road for passers-by, and Mr. Thomas, sitting on the loo, heard clearly now the sound of sawing. It no longer came from his house, and that a little reassured him. He felt less concerned. Perhaps the other noises too had no significance.

A voice spoke to him through the hole. "Mr. Thomas."

"Let me out," Mr. Thomas said sternly.

"Here's a blanket," the voice said, and a long gray sausage was worked through the hole and fell in swathes over Mr. Thomas's head.

"There's nothing personal," the voice said. "We want you to be comfortable tonight."

"Tonight," Mr. Thomas repeated incredulously.

"Catch," the voice said. "Penny buns—we've buttered them, and sausage-rolls. We don't want you to starve, Mr. Thomas."

Mr. Thomas pleaded desperately. "A joke's a joke, boy. Let me out and I won't say a thing. I've got rheumatics. I got to sleep comfortable."

"You wouldn't be comfortable, not in your house, you wouldn't. Not now."

"What do you mean, boy?" but the footsteps receded. There was only the silence of night: no sound of sawing. Mr. Thomas tried one more yell, but he was daunted and rebuked by the silence—a long way off an owl hooted and made away again on its muffled flight through the soundless world.

At seven next morning the driver came to fetch his lorry. He climbed into the seat and tried to start the engine. He was vaguely aware of a voice shouting, but it didn't concern him. At last the engine responded and he backed the lorry until it touched the great wooden shore that supported Mr. Thomas's house. That way he could drive right out and down the street without reversing. The lorry moved forward, was momentarily checked as though something were pulling it from behind, and then went on to the sound of a long rumbling crash. The driver was astonished to see bricks bouncing ahead of him, while stones hit the roof of his cab. He put on his brakes. When he climbed out the whole landscape had suddenly altered. There was no house beside the carpark, only a hill of rubble. He went round and examined the back of his car for damage, and found a rope tied there that was still twisted at the other end round part of a wooden strut.

The driver again became aware of somebody shouting. It came from the wooden erection which was the nearest thing to a house in that desolation of broken brick. The driver climbed the smashed wall and unlocked the door. Mr. Thomas came out of the loo. He was wearing a gray blanket to which flakes of pastry adhered. He gave a sobbing cry. "My house," he said. "Where's my house?"

"Search me," the driver said. His eye lit on the remains of a bath and what had once been a dresser and he began to laugh. There wasn't anything left anywhere.

"How dare you laugh," Mr. Thomas said. "It was my house. My house."

"I'm sorry," the driver said, making heroic efforts, but when he remembered the sudden check to his lorry, the crash of bricks falling, he became convulsed again. One moment the house had stood there with such dignity between the bomb-sites like a man in a top hat, and then, bang, crash, there wasn't anything left—not anything. He said, "I'm sorry. I can't help it, Mr. Thomas. There's nothing personal, but you got to admit it's funny."

Lionel Trilling
1905–1970

OF THIS TIME, OF THAT PLACE

I T W A S a fine September day. By noon it would be summer again, but now it was true autumn with a touch of chill in the air. As Joseph Howe stood on the porch of the house in which he lodged, ready to leave for his first class of the year, he thought with pleasure of the long indoor days that were coming. It was a moment when he could feel glad of his profession.

On the lawn the peach tree was still in fruit and young Hilda Aiken was taking a picture of it. She held the camera tight against her chest. She wanted the sun behind her, but she did not want her own long morning shadow in the foreground. She raised the camera, but that did not help, and she lowered it, but that made things worse. She twisted her body to the left, then to the right. In the end she had to step out of the direct line of the sun. At last she snapped the shutter and wound the film with intense care.

Howe, watching her from the porch, waited for her to finish and called good morning. She turned, startled, and almost sullenly lowered her glance. In the year Howe had lived at the Aikens', Hilda had accepted him as one of her family, but since his absence of the summer she had grown shy. Then suddenly she lifted her head and smiled at him, and the humorous smile confirmed his pleasure in the day. She picked up her bookbag and set off for school.

The handsome houses on the streets to the college were not yet fully awake, but they looked very friendly. Howe went by the Bradby house where he would be a guest this evening at the first dinner party of the year. When he had gone the length of the picket fence, the whitest in town, he turned back. Along the path there was a fine row of asters and he went through the gate and picked one for his buttonhole. The Bradbys would be pleased if they happened to see him invading their lawn and the knowledge of this made him even more comfortable.

He reached the campus as the hour was striking. The students were hurrying to their classes. He himself was in no hurry. He stopped at his dim cubicle of an office and lit a cigarette. The prospect of facing his class had suddenly presented itself to him and his hands were cold; the lawful seizure of power he was about to make seemed momentous. Waiting did not help. He put out his cigarette, picked up a pad of theme paper, and went to his classroom.

As he entered, the rattle of voices ceased, and the twenty-odd freshmen settled themselves and looked at him appraisingly. Their faces seemed gross, his heart sank at their massed impassivity, but he spoke briskly.

"My name is Howe," he said, and turned and wrote it on the blackboard. The carelessness of the scrawl confirmed his authority. He went on, "My office is 412 Slemp Hall, and my office-hours are Monday, Wednesday and Friday from eleven-thirty to twelve-thirty."

He wrote, "M.,W., F., 11:30—12:30." He said, "I'll be very glad to see any of you at that time. Or if you can't come then, you can arrange with me for some other time."

He turned again to the blackboard and spoke over his shoulder. "The text for the course is Jarman's *Modern Plays*, revised edition. The Co-op has it in stock." He wrote the name, underlined "revised edition" and waited for it to be taken down in the new notebooks.

When the bent heads were raised again he began his speech of prospectus. "It is hard to explain—" he said, and paused as they composed themselves. "It is hard to explain what a course like this is intended to do. We are going to try to learn something about modern literature and something about prose composition."

As he spoke, his hands warmed and he was able to look directly at the class. Last year on the first day the faces had seemed just as cloddish, but as the term wore on they became gradually alive and quite likable. It did not seem possible that the same thing could happen again.

"I shall not lecture in this course," he continued. "Our work will be carried on by discussion and we will try to learn by an exchange of opinion. But you will soon recognize that my opinion is worth more than anyone else's here."

He remained grave as he said it, but two boys understood and laughed. The rest took permission from them and laughed too. All Howe's private ironies protested the vulgarity of the joke, but the laughter made him feel benign and powerful.

When the little speech was finished, Howe picked up the pad of paper he had brought. He announced that they would write an extemporaneous theme. Its subject was traditional, "Who I am and why I came to Dwight College." By now the class was more at ease and it gave a ritualistic groan of protest. Then there was a stir as fountain pens were brought out and the writing-arms of the chairs were cleared, and the paper was passed about. At last, all the heads bent to work, and the room became still.

Howe sat idly at his desk. The sun shone through the tall clumsy windows. The cool of the morning was already passing. There was a scent of autumn and of varnish and the stillness of the room was deep and oddly touching. Now and then a student's head was raised and scratched in the old, elaborate students' pantomime that calls the teacher to witness honest intellectual effort.

Suddenly a tall boy stood within the frame of the open door. "Is this," he said, and thrust a large nose into a college catalogue, "is this the meeting place of English 1A? The section instructed by Dr. Joseph Howe?"

He stood on the very sill of the door, as if refusing to enter until he was perfectly sure of all his rights. The class looked up from work, found him absurd and gave a low mocking cheer.

The teacher and the new student, with equal pointedness, ignored the disturbance. Howe nodded to the boy, who pushed his head forward and then jerked it back in a wide elaborate arc to clear his brow of a heavy lock of hair. He advanced into the room and halted before Howe, almost at attention. In a loud, clear voice he announced, "I am Tertan, Ferdinand R., reporting at the direction of Head of Department Vincent."

The heraldic formality of this statement brought forth another cheer. Howe looked at the class with a sternness he could not really feel, for there was indeed something ridiculous about this boy. Under his displeased regard the rows of heads dropped to work again. Then he touched Tertan's elbow, led him up to the desk and stood so as to shield their conversation from the class.

"We are writing an extemporaneous theme," he said. "The subject is, 'Who I am and why I came to Dwight College.'"

He stripped a few sheets from the pad and offered them to the boy. Tertan hesitated and then took the paper, but he held it only tentatively. As if with the effort of making something clear, he gulped, and a slow smile fixed itself on his face. It was at once knowing and shy.

"Professor," he said, "to be perfectly fair to my classmates"—he made a large gesture over the room—"and to you"—he inclined his head to Howe—"this would not be for me an extemporaneous subject."

Howe tried to understand. "You mean you've already thought about it—you've heard we always give the same subject? That doesn't matter."

Again the boy ducked his head and gulped. It was the gesture of one who wishes to make a difficult explanation with perfect candor. "Sir," he said, and made the distinction with great care, "the topic I did not expect, but I have given much ratiocination to the subject."

Howe smiled and said, "I don't think that's an unfair advantage. Just go ahead and write."

Tertan narrowed his eyes and glanced sidewise at Howe. His strange mouth smiled. Then in quizzical acceptance, he ducked his head, threw back the heavy, dank lock, dropped into a seat with a great loose noise and began to write rapidly.

The room fell silent again and Howe resumed his idleness. When the bell rang, the students who had groaned when the task had been set now groaned again because they had not finished. Howe took up the papers, and held the class while he made the first assignment. When he dismissed it, Tertan bore down on him, his slack mouth held ready for speech.

"Some professors," he said, "are pedants. They are Dryasdusts. However, some professors are free souls and creative spirits. Kant, Hegel and Nietzsche were all professors." With this pronouncement he paused. "It is my opinion," he continued, "that you occupy the second category."

Howe looked at the boy in surprise and said with good-natured irony, "With Kant, Hegel and Nietzsche?"

Not only Tertan's hand and head but his whole awkward body waved away the stupidity. "It is the kind and not the quantity of the kind," he said sternly.

Rebuked, Howe said as simply and seriously as he could, "It would be nice to think so." He added, "Of course I am not a professor."

This was clearly a disappointment but Tertan met it. "In the French sense," he said with composure. "Generically, a teacher."

Suddenly he bowed. It was such a bow, Howe fancied, as a stage director might teach an actor playing a medieval student who takes leave of Abelard—stiff, solemn, with elbows close to the body and feet together. Then, quite as suddenly, he turned and left.

A queer fish, and as soon as Howe reached his office, he sifted through the batch of themes and drew out Tertan's. The boy had filled many sheets with his unformed headlong scrawl. "Who am I?" he had begun. "Here, in a mundane, not to say commercialized academe, is asked the question which from time long immemorably out of mind has accreted doubts and thoughts in the psyche of man to pester him as a nuisance. Whether in St. Augustine (or Austin as sometimes called) or Miss Bashkirtsieff or Frederic Amiel or Empedocles, or in less lights of the intellect than these, this posed question has been ineluctable."

Howe took out his pencil. He circled "academe" and wrote "vocab." in the margin. He underlined "time long immemorably out of mind" and wrote "Diction!" But this seemed inadequate for what was wrong. He put down his pencil and read ahead to discover the principle of error in the theme. "Today as ever, in spite of gloomy prophets of the dismal science (economics) the question is uninvalidated. Out of the starry depths of heaven hurtles this spear of query demanding to be caught on the shield of the mind ere it pierces the skull and the limbs be unstrung."

Baffled but quite caught, Howe read on. "Materialism, by which is meant the philosophic concept and not the moral idea, provides no aegis against the question which lies beyond the tangible (metaphysics). Existence without alloy is the question presented. Environment and heredity relegated aside, the rags and old clothes of practical life discarded, the name and the instrumentality of livelihood do not, as the prophets of the dismal science insist on in this connection, give solution to the interrogation which not from the professor merely but veritably from the cosmos is given. I think, therefore I am (cogito etc.) but who am I? Tertan I am, but what is Tertan? Of this time, of that place, of some parentage, what does it matter?"

Existence without alloy! the phrase established itself. Howe put aside Tertan's paper and at random picked up another. "I am Arthur J. Casebeer, Jr.," he read. "My father is Arthur J. Casebeer and my grandfather was Arthur J. Casebeer before him. My mother is Nina Wimble Casebeer. Both of them are college graduates and my father is in insurance. I was born in St. Louis eighteen years ago and we still make our residence there."

Arthur J. Casebeer, who knew who he was, was less interesting than Tertan, but more coherent. Howe picked up Tertan's paper again. It was clear that none of the routine marginal comments, no "sent. str." or "punct." or "vocab." could cope with this torrential rhetoric. He read ahead, contenting himself with underscoring the errors against the time when he should have the necessary "conference" with Tertan.

It was a busy and official day of cards and sheets, arrangements and small decisions, and it gave Howe pleasure. Even when it was time to attend the first of the weekly Convocations he felt the charm of the beginning of things when intention is still innocent and uncorrupted by effort. He sat among the young instructors on the platform, and joined in their humorous complaints at having to assist at the ceremony, but actually he got a clear satisfaction from the ritual of prayer and prosy speech, and even from wearing his academic gown. And when the Convocation was over the pleasure continued as he crossed the campus, exchanging greetings with men he had not seen since the spring. They were people who did not yet, and perhaps never would, mean much to him, but in a year they had grown amiably to be part of his life. They were his fellow-townsmen.

The day had cooled again at sunset, and there was a bright chill in the September twilight. Howe carried his voluminous gown over his arm, he swung his doctoral hood by its purple neckpiece, and on his head he wore his mortarboard with its heavy gold tassel bobbing just over his eye. These were the weighty and absurd symbols of his new profession and they pleased him. At twenty-six Joseph Howe had discovered that he was neither so well off nor so bohemian as he had once thought. A small income, adequate when supplemented by a sizable cash legacy, was genteel poverty when the cash was all spent. And the literary life—the room at the Lafayette, or the small apartment without a lease, the long summers on the Cape, the long afternoons and the social evenings—began to weary him. His writing filled his mornings and should perhaps have filled his life, yet it did not. To the amusement of his friends, and with a certain sense that he was betraying his own freedom, he had used the last of his legacy for a year at Harvard. The small but respectable reputation of his two volumes of verse had proved useful—he continued at Harvard on a fellowship and when he emerged as Doctor Howe he received an excellent appointment, with prospects, at Dwight.

He had his moments of fear when all that had ever been said of the dangers of the academic life had occurred to him. But after a year in which he had tested every possibility of corruption and seduction he was ready to rest easy. His third volume of verse, most of it written in his first year of teaching, was not only ampler but, he thought, better than its predecessors.

There was a clear hour before the Bradby dinner party, and Howe looked forward to it. But he was not to enjoy it, for lying with his mail on the hall table was a copy of this quarter's issue of *Life and Letters*, to which his landlord subscribed. Its severe cover announced that its editor, Frederic Woolley, had this month contributed an essay called "Two Poets," and Howe, picking it up, curious to see who the two poets might be, felt his own name start out at him with cabalistic power—Joseph Howe. As he continued to turn the pages his hand trembled.

Standing in the dark hall, holding the neat little magazine, Howe knew that his literary contempt for Frederic Woolley meant nothing, for he suddenly understood how he respected Woolley in the way of the world. He knew this by the trembling of his hand. And of the little world as well as the great, for although the literary groups of New York might dismiss Woolley, his name carried high authority in the academic world. At Dwight it was even a revered name, for it had been here at the college that Frederic Woolley had made the distinguished scholarly career from which he had gone on to literary journalism. In middle life he had been induced to take the editorship of *Life and Letters*, a literary monthly not widely read but heavily endowed, and in its pages he had carried on the defense of what he sometimes called the older values. He was not without wit, he had great knowledge and considerable taste, and even in the full movement of the "new" literature he had won a certain respect for his refusal to accept it. In France, even in England, he would have been connected with a more robust tradition of conservatism, but America gave him an audience not much better than genteel. It was known in the college that to the subsidy of *Life and Letters* the Bradbys contributed a great part.

As Howe read, he saw that he was involved in nothing less than an event. When the Fifth Series of *Studies in Order and Value* came to be collected, this latest issue of Frederic Woolley's essays would not be merely another step in the old direction. Clearly and unmistakably, it was a turning point. All his literary life Woolley had been concerned with the relation of literature to morality, religion, and the private and delicate pieties, and he had been unalterably opposed to all that he had called "inhuman humanitarianism." But here, suddenly, dramatically late, he had made an about-face, turning to the public life and to the humanitarian politics he had so long despised. This was the kind of incident the histories of literature make much of. Frederic Woolley was opening for himself a new career and winning a kind of new youth. He contrasted the two poets, Thomas Wormser, who was admirable, Joseph Howe, who was almost dangerous. He spoke of the "precious subjectivism" of Howe's verse. "In times like ours," he wrote, "with millions facing penury and want, one feels that the qualities of the *tour d'ivoire*[1] are well-nigh inhuman, nearly insulting. The *tour d'ivoire* becomes the *tour d'ivresse*,[2] and it is not self-intoxicated poets that our people need." The essay said more: "The problem is one of meaning. I am not ignorant that the creed of the esoteric poets declares that a poem does not and should

---

[1] ivory tower   [2] tower of drunkenness

not *mean* anything, that it *is* something. But poetry is what the poet makes it, and if he is a true poet he makes what his society needs. And what is needed now is the tradition in which Mr. Wormser writes, the true tradition of poetry. The Howes do no harm, but they do no good when positive good is demanded of all responsible men. Or do the Howes indeed do no harm? Perhaps Plato would have said they do, that in some ways theirs is the Phrygian music that turns men's minds from the struggle. Certainly it is true that Thomas Wormser writes in the lucid Dorian mode which sends men into battle with evil.[3]"

It was easy to understand why Woolley had chosen to praise Thomas Wormser. The long, lilting lines of *Corn Under Willows* hymned, as Woolley put it, the struggle for wheat in the Iowa fields, and expressed the real lives of real people. But why out of the dozen more notable examples he had chosen Howe's little volume as the example of "precious subjectivism" was hard to guess. In a way it was funny, this multiplication of himself into "the Howes." And yet this becoming the multiform political symbol by whose creation Frederic Woolley gave the sign of a sudden new life, this use of him as a sacrifice whose blood was necessary for the rites of rejuvenation, made him feel oddly unclean.

Nor could Howe get rid of a certain practical resentment. As a poet he had a special and respectable place in the college life. But it might be another thing to be marked as the poet of a wilful and selfish obscurity.

As he walked to the Bradby's, Howe was a little tense and defensive. It seemed to him that all the world knew of the "attack" and agreed with it. And, indeed, the Bradbys had read the essay but Professor Bradby, a kind and pretentious man, said, "I see my old friend knocked you about a bit, my boy," and his wife Eugenia looked at Howe with her child-like blue eyes and said, "I shall *scold* Frederic for the untrue things he wrote about you. You aren't the least obscure." They beamed at him. In their genial snobbery they seemed to feel that he had distinguished himself. He was the leader of Howeism. He enjoyed the dinner party as much as he had thought he would.

And in the following days, as he was more preoccupied with his duties, the incident was forgotten. His classes had ceased to be mere groups. Student after student detached himself from the mass and required or claimed a place in Howe's awareness. Of them all it was Tertan who first and most violently signaled his separate existence. A week after classes had begun Howe saw his silhouette on the frosted glass of his office door. It was motionless for a long time, perhaps stopped by the problem of whether or not to knock before entering. Howe called, "Come in!" and Tertan entered with his shambling stride.

He stood beside the desk, silent and at attention. When Howe asked him to sit down, he responded with a gesture of head and hand, as if to

---

[3] In ancient Greece the various modes of music, such as Phrygian, Lydian, Dorian, were believed to have particular effects upon the emotions and behavior of listeners.

say that such amenities were beside the point. Nevertheless, he did take the chair. He put his ragged, crammed briefcase between his legs. His face, which Howe now observed fully for the first time, was confusing, for it was made up of florid curves, the nose arched in the bone and voluted in the nostril, the mouth loose and soft and rather moist. Yet the face was so thin and narrow as to seem the very type of asceticism. Lashes of unusual length veiled the eyes and, indeed, it seemed as if there were a veil over the whole countenance. Before the words actually came, the face screwed itself into an attitude of preparation for them.

"You can confer with me now?" Tertan said.

"Yes, I'd be glad to. There are several things in your two themes I want to talk to you about." Howe reached for the packet of themes on his desk and sought for Tertan's. But the boy was waving them away.

"These are done perforce," he said. "Under the pressure of your requirement. They are not significant; mere duties." Again his great hand flapped vaguely to dismiss his themes. He leaned forward and gazed at his teacher.

"You are," he said, "a man of letters? You are a poet?" It was more declaration than question.

"I should like to think so," Howe said.

At first Tertan accepted the answer with a show of appreciation, as though the understatement made a secret between himself and Howe. Then he chose to misunderstand. With his shrewd and disconcerting control of expression, he presented to Howe a puzzled grimace. "What does that mean?" he said.

Howe retracted the irony. "Yes. I am a poet." It sounded strange to say.

"That," Tertan said, "is a wonder." He corrected himself with his ducking head. "I mean that is wonderful."

Suddenly, he dived at the miserable briefcase between his legs, put it on his knees, and began to fumble with the catch, all intent on the difficulty it presented. Howe noted that his suit was worn thin, his shirt almost unclean. He became aware, even, of a vague and musty odor of garments worn too long in unaired rooms. Tertan conquered the lock and began to concentrate upon a search into the interior. At last he held in his hand what he was after, a torn and crumpled copy of *Life and Letters*.

"I learned it from here," he said, holding it out.

Howe looked at him sharply, his hackles a little up. But the boy's face was not only perfectly innocent, it even shone with a conscious admiration. Apparently nothing of the import of the essay had touched him except the wonderful fact that his teacher was a "man of letters." Yet this seemed too stupid, and Howe, to test it, said, "The man who wrote that doesn't think it's wonderful."

Tertain made a moist hissing sound as he cleared his mouth of saliva. His head, oddly loose on his neck, wove a pattern of contempt in the air.

"A critic," he said, "who admits *prima facie* that he does not understand." Then he said grandly, "It is the inevitable fate."

It was absurd, yet Howe was not only aware of the absurdity but of a tension suddenly and wonderfully relaxed. Now that the "attack" was on the table between himself and this strange boy, and subject to the boy's funny and absolutely certain contempt, the hidden force of his feeling was revealed to him in the very moment that it vanished. All unsuspected, there had been a film over the world, a transparent but discoloring haze of danger. But he had no time to stop over the brightened aspect of things. Tertan was going on. "I also am a man of letters. Putative."

"You have written a good deal?" Howe meant to be no more than polite, and he was surprised at the tenderness he heard in his words.

Solemnly the boy nodded, threw back the dank lock, and sucked in a deep, anticipatory breath. "First, a word of homiletics, which is a defense of the principles of religious optimism against the pessimism of Schopenhauer and the humanism of Nietzsche."

"Humanism? Why do you call it humanism?"

"It is my nomenclature for making a deity of man," Tertan replied negligently. "Then three fictional works, novels. And numerous essays in science, combating materialism. Is it your duty to read these if I bring them to you?"

Howe answered simply, "No, it isn't exactly my duty, but I shall be happy to read them."

Tertan stood up and remained silent. He rested his bag on the chair. With a certain compunction—for it did not seem entirely proper that, of two men of letters, one should have the right to blue-pencil the other, to grade him or to question the quality of his "sentence structure"—Howe reached for Tertan's papers. But before he could take them up, the boy suddenly made his bow-to-Abelard, the stiff inclination of the body with the hands seeming to emerge from the scholar's gown. Then he was gone.

But after his departure something was still left of him. The timbre of his curious sentences, the downright finality of so quaint a phrase as "It is the inevitable fate" still rang in the air. Howe gave the warmth of his feeling to the new visitor who stood at the door announcing himself with a genteel clearing of the throat.

"Doctor Howe, I believe?" the student said. A large hand advanced into the room and grasped Howe's hand. "Blackburn, sir, Theodore Blackburn, vice-president of the Student Council. A great pleasure, sir."

Out of a pair of ruddy cheeks a pair of small eyes twinkled good-naturedly. The large face, the large body were not so much fat as beefy and suggested something "typical"—monk, politician, or innkeeper.

Blackburn took the seat beside Howe's desk. "I may have seemed to introduce myself in my public capacity, sir," he said. "But it is really as an individual that I came to see you. That is to say, as one of your students to be."

He spoke with an English intonation and he went on, "I was once an English major, sir."

For a moment Howe was startled, for the roast-beef look of the boy and the manner of his speech gave a second's credibility to one sense of his statement. Then the collegiate meaning of the phrase asserted itself, but some perversity made Howe say what was not really in good taste even with so forward a student, "Indeed? What regiment?"

Blackburn stared and then gave a little pouf-pouf of laughter. He waved the misapprehension away. "*Very* good, sir. It certainly is an ambiguous term." He chuckled in appreciation of Howe's joke, then cleared his throat to put it aside. "I look forward to taking your course in the romantic poets, sir," he said earnestly. "To me the romantic poets are the very crown of English literature."

Howe made a dry sound, and the boy, catching some meaning in it, said, "Little as I know them, of course. But even Shakespeare who is so dear to us of the Anglo-Saxon tradition is in a sense but the preparation for Shelley, Keats and Byron. And Wadsworth."

Almost sorry for him, Howe dropped his eyes. With some embarrassment, for the boy was not actually his student, he said softly "Wordsworth."

"Sir?"

"Wordsworth, not Wadsworth. You said Wadsworth."

"Did I, sir?" Gravely he shook his head to rebuke himself for the error. "Wordsworth, of course—slip of the tongue." Then, quite in command again, he went on. "I have a favor to ask of you, Doctor Howe. You see, I began my college course as an English major,"—"as I said."

"Yes?"

"But after my first year I shifted. I shifted to the social sciences. Sociology and government—I find them stimulating and very *real*." He paused, out of respect for reality. "But now I find that perhaps I have neglected the other side."

"The other side?" Howe said.

"Imagination, fancy, culture. A well-rounded man." He trailed off as if there were perfect understanding between them. "And so, sir, I have decided to end my senior year with your course in the romantic poets."

His voice was filled with an indulgence which Howe ignored as he said flatly and gravely, "But that course isn't given until the spring term."

"Yes, sir, and that is where the favor comes in. Would you let me take your romantic prose course? I can't take it for credit, sir, my program is full, but just for background it seems to me that I ought to take it. I do hope," he concluded in a manly way, "that you will consent."

"Well, it's no great favor, Mr. Blackburn. You can come if you wish, though there's not much point in it if you don't do the reading."

The bell rang for the hour and Howe got up.

"May I begin with this class, sir?" Blackburn's smile was candid and boyish.

Howe nodded carelessly and together, silently, they walked to the classroom down the hall. When they reached the door Howe stood back to let his student enter, but Blackburn moved adroitly behind him and grasped him by the arm to urge him over the threshold. They entered together with Blackburn's hand firmly on Howe's biceps, the student inducting the teacher into his own room. Howe felt a surge of temper rise in him and almost violently he disengaged his arm and walked to the desk, while Blackburn found a seat in the front row and smiled at him.

2

The question was, At whose door must the tragedy be laid?

All night the snow had fallen heavily and only now was abating in sparse little flurries. The windows were valanced high with white. It was very quiet; something of the quiet of the world had reached the class, and Howe found that everyone was glad to talk or listen. In the room there was a comfortable sense of pleasure in being human.

Casebeer believed that the blame for the tragedy rested with heredity. Picking up the book he read, "The sins of the fathers are visited on their children." This opinion was received with general favor. Nevertheless, Johnson ventured to say that the fault was all Pastor Manders' because the Pastor had made Mrs. Alving go back to her husband and was always hiding the truth. To this Hibbard objected with logic enough, "Well then, it was really all her husband's fault. He *did* all the bad things " De Witt, his face bright with an impatient idea, said that the fault was all society's. "By society I don't mean upper-crust society," he said. He looked around a little defiantly, taking in any members of the class who might be members of upper-crust society. "Not in that sense. I mean the social unit."

Howe nodded and said, "Yes, of course."

"If the society of the time had progressed far enough in science," De Witt went on, "then there would be no problem for Mr. Ibsen to write about. Captain Alving plays around a little, gives way to perfectly natural biological urges, and he gets a social disease, a venereal disease. If the disease is cured, no problem. Invent salvarsan and the disease is cured. The problem of heredity disappears and li'l Oswald just doesn't get paresis. No paresis, no problem—no problem, no play."

This was carrying the ark into battle, and the class looked at De Witt with respectful curiosity. It was his usual way and on the whole they were sympathetic with his struggle to prove to Howe that science was better than literature. Still, there was something in his reckless manner that alienated them a little.

"Or take birth-control, for instance," De Witt went on. "If Mrs. Alving had some knowledge of contraception, she wouldn't have had to have li'l Oswald at all. No li'l Oswald, no play."

The class was suddenly quieter. In the back row Stettenhover swung his great football shoulders in a righteous sulking gesture, first to the right, then to the left. He puckered his mouth ostentatiously. Intellect was always ending up by talking dirty.

Tertan's hand went up, and Howe said, "Mr. Tertan." The boy shambled to his feet and began his long characteristic gulp. Howe made a motion with his fingers, as small as possible, and Tertan ducked his head and smiled in apology. He sat down. The class laughed. With more than half the term gone, Tertan had not been able to remember that one did not rise to speak. He seemed unable to carry on the life of the intellect without this mark of respect for it. To Howe the boy's habit of rising seemed to accord with the formal shabbiness of his dress. He never wore the casual sweaters and jackets of his classmates. Into the free and comfortable air of the college classroom he brought the stuffy sordid strictness of some crowded, metropolitan high school.

"Speaking from one sense," Tertan began slowly, "there is no blame ascribable. From the sense of determinism, who can say where the blame lies? The preordained is the preordained and it cannot be said without rebellion against the universe, a palpable absurdity."

In the back row Stettenhover slumped suddenly in his seat, his heels held out before him, making a loud, dry, disgusted sound. His body sank until his neck rested on the back of his chair. He folded his hands across his belly and looked significantly out of the window, exasperated not only with Tertan, but with Howe, with the class, with the whole system designed to encourage this kind of thing. There was a certain insolence in the movement and Howe flushed. As Tertan continued to speak, Howe stalked casually toward the window and placed himself in the line of Stettenhover's vision. He stared at the great fellow, who pretended not to see him. There was so much power in the big body, so much contempt in the Greek-athlete face under the crisp Greek-athlete curls, that Howe felt almost physical fear. But at last Stettenhover admitted him to focus and under his disapproving gaze sat up with slow indifference. His eyebrows raised high in resignation, he began to examine his hands. Howe relaxed and turned his attention back to Tertan.

"Flux of existence," Tertan was saying, "produces all things, so that judgment wavers. Beyond the phenomena, what? But phenomena are adumbrated and to them we are limited."

Howe saw it for a moment as perhaps it existed in the boy's mind— the world of shadows which are cast by a great light upon a hidden reality as in the old myth of the Cave.[4] But the little brush with Stettenhover had tired him, and he said irritably, "But come to the point, Mr. Tertan."

---

[4] In Plato's Myth of the Cave, men are depicted as bound so that their shadows, cast on the wall of the cave by a fire behind them, constitute the only reality they can apprehend.

He said it so sharply that some of his class looked at him curiously. For three months he had gently carried Tertan through his verbosities, to the vaguely respectful surprise of the other students, who seemed to conceive that there existed between this strange classmate and their teacher some special understanding from which they were content to be excluded. Tertan looked at him mildly, and at once came brilliantly to the point. "This is the summation of the play," he said and took up his book and read, " 'Your poor father never found any outlet for the overmastering joy of life that was in him. And I brought no holiday into his home, either. Everything seemed to turn upon duty and I am afraid I made your poor father's home unbearable to him, Oswald.' Spoken by Mrs. Alving."

Yes that was surely the "summation" of the play and Tertan had hit it, as he hit, deviously and eventually, the literary point of almost everything. But now, as always, he was wrapping it away from sight, "For most mortals," he said, "there are only joys of biological urgings, gross and crass, such as the sensuous Captain Alving. For certain few there are the transmutations beyond these to a contemplation of the utter whole."

Oh, the boy was mad. And suddenly the word, used in hyperbole, intended almost for the expression of exasperated admiration, became literal. Now that the word was used, it became simply apparent to Howe that Tertan was mad.

It was a monstrous word and stood like a bestial thing in the room. Yet it so completely comprehended everything that had puzzled Howe, it so arranged and explained what for three months had been perplexing him that almost at once its horror became domesticated. With this word Howe was able to understand why he had never been able to communicate to Tertan the value of a single criticism or correction of his wild, verbose themes. Their conferences had been frequent and long but had done nothing to reduce to order the splendid confusion of the boy's ideas. Yet, impossible though its expression was, Tertan's incandescent mind could always strike for a moment into some dark corner of thought.

And now it was suddenly apparent that it was not a faulty rhetoric that Howe had to contend with. With his new knowledge he looked at Tertan's face and wondered how he could have so long deceived himself. Tertan was still talking, and the class had lapsed into a kind of patient unconsciousness, a coma of respect for words which, for all that most of them knew, might be profound. Almost with a suffusion of shame, Howe believed that in some dim way the class had long ago had some intimation of Tertan's madness. He reached out as decisively as he could to seize the thread of Tertan's discourse before it should be entangled further.

"Mr. Tertan says that the blame must be put upon whoever kills the joy of living in another. We have been assuming that Captain Alving was a wholly bad man, but what if we assume that he became bad only because Mrs. Alving, when they were first married, acted toward him in the prudish way she says she did?"

It was a ticklish idea to advance to freshmen and perhaps not profitable. Not all of them were following.

"That would put the blame on Mrs. Alving herself, whom most of you admire. And she herself seems to think so." He glanced at his watch. The hour was nearly over. "What do you think, Mr. De Witt?"

De Witt rose to the idea; he wanted to know if society couldn't be blamed for educating Mrs. Alving's temperament in the wrong way. Casebeer was puzzled, Stettenhover continued to look at his hands until the bell rang.

Tertan, his brows louring in thought, was making as always for a private word. Howe gathered his books and papers to leave quickly. At this moment of his discovery and with the knowledge still raw, he could not engage himself with Tertan. Tertan sucked in his breath to prepare for speech and Howe made ready for the pain and confusion. But at that moment Casebeer detached himself from the group with which he had been conferring and which he seemed to represent. His constituency remained at a tactful distance. The mission involved the time of an assigned essay. Casebeer's presentation of the plea—it was based on the freshmen's heavy duties at the fraternities during Carnival Week—cut across Tertan's preparations for speech. "And so some of us fellows thought," Casebeer concluded with heavy solemnity, "that we could do a better job, give our minds to it more, if we had more time."

Tertan regarded Casebeer with mingled curiosity and revulsion. Howe not only said that he would postpone the assignment but went on to talk about the Carnival, and even drew the waiting constituency into the conversation. He was conscious of Tertan's stern and astonished stare, then of his sudden departure.

Now that the fact was clear, Howe knew that he must act on it. His course was simple enough. He must lay the case before the Dean. Yet he hesitated. His feeling for Tertan must now, certainly, be in some way invalidated. Yet could he, because of a word, hurry to assign to official and reasonable solicitude what had been, until this moment, so various and warm? He could at least delay and, by moving slowly, lend a poor grace to the necessary, ugly act of making his report.

It was with some notion of keeping the matter in his own hands that he went to the Dean's office to look up Tertan's records. In the outer office the Dean's secretary greeted him brightly, and at his request brought him the manila folder with the small identifying photograph pasted in the corner. She laughed. "He was looking for the birdie in the wrong place," she said.

Howe leaned over her shoulder to look at the picture. It was as bad as all the Dean's-office photographs were, but it differed from all that Howe had ever seen. Tertan, instead of looking into the camera, as no doubt he had been bidden, had, at the moment of exposure, turned his eyes upward. His mouth, as though conscious of the trick played on the photographer, had the sly superior look that Howe knew.

The secretary was fascinated by the picture. "What a funny boy," she said. "He looks like Tartuffe!" [5]

And so he did, with the absurd piety of the eyes and the conscious slyness of the mouth and the whole face bloated by the bad lens.

"Is he *like* that?" the secretary said.

"Like Tartuffe? No."

From the photograph there was little enough comfort to be had. The records themselves gave no clue to madness, though they suggested sadness enough. Howe read of a father, Stanislaus Tertan, born in Budapest and trained in engineering in Berlin, once employed by the Hercules Chemical Corporation—this was one of the factories that dominated the south end of the town—but now without employment. He read of a mother Erminie (Youngfellow) Tertan, born in Manchester, educated at a Normal School at Leeds, now housewife by profession. The family lived on Greenbriar Street which Howe knew as a row of once elegant homes near what was now the factory district. The old mansion had long ago been divided into small and primitive apartments. Of Ferdinand himself there was little to learn. He lived with his parents, had attended a Detroit high school and had transferred to the local school in his last year. His rating for intelligence, as expressed in numbers, was high, his scholastic record was remarkable, he held a college scholarship for his tuition.

Howe laid the folder on the secretary's desk. "Did you find what you wanted to know?" she asked.

The phrases from Tertan's momentous first theme came back to him. "Tertan I am, but what is Tertan? Of this time, of that place, of some parentage, what does it matter?"

"No, I didn't find it," he said.

Now that he had consulted the sad, half-meaningless record he knew all the more firmly that he must not give the matter out of his own hands. He must not release Tertan to authority. Not that he anticipated from the Dean anything but the greatest kindness for Tertan. The Dean would have the experience and skill which he himself could not have. One way or another the Dean could answer the question, "What is Tertan?" Yet this was precisely what he feared. He alone could keep alive—not forever but for a somehow important time—the question, "What is Tertan?" He alone could keep it still a question. Some sure instinct told him that he must not surrender the question to a clean official desk in a clear official light to be dealt with, settled and closed.

He heard himself saying, "Is the Dean busy at the moment? I'd like to see him."

His request came thus unbidden, even forbidden, and it was one of the

---

[5] the hypocritical title character of a play by Moliere

surprising and startling incidents of his life. Later when he reviewed the events, so disconnected in themselves, or so merely odd, of the story that unfolded for him that year, it was over this moment, on its face the least notable, that he paused longest. It was frequently to be with fear and never without a certainty of its meaning in his own knowledge of himself that he would recall this simple, routine request, and the feeling of shame and freedom it gave him as he sent everything down the official chute. In the end, of course, no matter what he did to "protect" Tertan, he would have had to make the same request and lay the matter on the Dean's clean desk. But it would always be a landmark of his life that, at the very moment when he was rejecting the official way, he had been, without will or intention, so gladly drawn to it.

After the storm's last delicate flurry, the sun had come out. Reflected by the new snow, it filled the office with a golden light which was almost musical in the way it made all the commonplace objects of efficiency shine with a sudden sad and noble significance. And the light, now that he noticed it, made the utterance of his perverse and unwanted request even more momentous.

The secretary consulted the engagement pad. "He'll be free any minute. Don't you want to wait in the parlor?"

She threw open the door of the large and pleasant room in which the Dean held his Committee meetings, and in which his visitors waited. It was designed with a homely elegance on the masculine side of the eighteenth-century manner. There was a small coal fire in the grate and the handsome mahogany table was strewn with books and magazines. The large windows gave on the snowy lawn, and there was such a fine width of window that the white casements and walls seemed at this moment but a continuation of the snow, the snow but an extension of casement and walls. The outdoors seemed taken in and made safe, the indoors seemed luxuriously freshened and expanded.

Howe sat down by the fire and lighted a cigarette. The room had its intended effect upon him. He felt comfortable and relaxed, yet nicely organized, some young diplomatic agent of the eighteenth century, the newly fledged Swift carrying out Sir William Temple's business. The rawness of Tertan's case quite vanished. He crossed his legs and reached for a magazine.

It was that famous issue of *Life and Letters* that his idle hand had found and his blood raced as he sifted through it, and the shape of his own name, Joseph Howe, sprang out at him, still cabalistic in its power. He tossed the magazine back on the table as the door of the Dean's office opened and the Dean ushered out Theodore Blackburn.

"Ah, Joseph!" the Dean said.

Blackburn said, "Good morning, Doctor." Howe winced at the title and caught the flicker of amusement over the Dean's face. The Dean stood with his hand high on the door-jamb and Blackburn, still in the doorway, remained standing almost under the long arm.

Howe nodded briefly to Blackburn, snubbing his eager deference. "Can you give me a few minutes?" he said to the Dean.

"All the time you want. Come in." Before the two men could enter the office, Blackburn claimed their attention with a long full "er." As they turned to him, Blackburn said, "Can *you* give *me* a few minutes, Doctor Howe?" His eyes sparkled at the little audacity he had committed, the slightly impudent play with hierarchy. Of the three of them Blackburn kept himself the lowest, but he reminded Howe of his subaltern relation to the Dean.

"I mean, of course," Blackburn went on easily, "when you've finished with the Dean."

"I'll be in my office shortly," Howe said, turned his back on the ready "Thank you, sir," and followed the Dean into the inner room.

"Energetic boy," said the Dean. "A bit beyond himself but very energetic. Sit down."

The Dean lighted a cigarette, leaned back in his chair, sat easy and silent for a moment, giving Howe no signal to go ahead with business. He was a young Dean, not much beyond forty, a tall handsome man with sad, ambitious eyes. He had been a Rhodes scholar. His friends looked for great things from him, and it was generally said that he had notions of education which he was not yet ready to try to put into practice.

His relaxed silence was meant as a compliment to Howe. He smiled and said, "What's the business, Joseph?"

"Do you know Tertan—Ferdinand Tertan, a freshman?"

The Dean's cigarette was in his mouth and his hands were clasped behind his head. He did not seem to search his memory for the name. He said, "What about him?"

Clearly the Dean knew something, and he was waiting for Howe to tell him more. Howe moved only tentatively. Now that he was doing what he had resolved to do, he felt more guilty at having been so long deceived by Tertan and more need to be loyal to his error.

"He's a strange fellow," he ventured. He said stubbornly, "In a strange way he's very brilliant." He concluded, "But very strange."

The springs of the Dean's swivel chair creaked as he came out of his sprawl and leaned forward to Howe. "Do you mean he's so strange that it's something you could give a name to?"

Howe looked at him stupidly. "What do you mean?" he said.

"What's his trouble?" the Dean said more neutrally.

"He's very brilliant, in a way. I looked him up and he has a top intelligence rating. But somehow, and it's hard to explain just how, what he says is always on the edge of sense and doesn't quite make it."

The Dean looked at him and Howe flushed up. The Dean had surely read Woolley on the subject of "the Howes" and the *tour d'ivresse*. Was that quick glance ironical?

The Dean picked up some papers from his desk, and Howe could see that they were in Tertan's impatient scrawl. Perhaps the little gleam in the Dean's glance had come only from putting facts together.

"He sent me this yesterday," the Dean said "After an interview I had with him. I haven't been able to do more than glance at it. When you said what you did, I realized there was something wrong."

Twisting his mouth, the Dean looked over the letter. "You seem to be involved," he said without looking up. "By the way, what did you give him at mid-term?"

Flushing, setting his shoulders, Howe said firmly, "I gave him A-minus."

The Dean chuckled. "Might be a good idea if some of our nicer boys went crazy—just a little." He said, "Well," to conclude the matter and handed the papers to Howe. "See if this is the same thing you've been finding. Then we can go into the matter again."

Before the fire in the parlor, in the chair that Howe had been occupying, sat Blackburn. He sprang to his feet as Howe entered.

"I said my office, Mr. Blackburn." Howe's voice was sharp. Then he was almost sorry for the rebuke, so clearly and naively did Blackburn seem to relish his stay in the parlor, close to authority.

"I'm in a bit of a hurry, sir," he said, "and I did want to be sure to speak to you, sir."

He was really absurd, yet fifteen years from now he would have grown up to himself, to the assurance and mature beefiness. In banks, in consular offices, in brokerage firms, on the bench, more seriously affable, a little sterner, he would make use of his ability to be administered by his job. It was almost reassuring. Now he was exercising his too-great skill on Howe. "I owe you an apology, sir," he said.

Howe knew that he did, but he showed surprise.

"I mean, Doctor, after your having been so kind about letting me attend your class, I stopped coming." He smiled in deprecation. "Extracurricular activities take up so much of my time. I'm afraid I undertook more than I could perform."

Howe had noticed the absence and had been a little irritated by it after Blackburn's elaborate plea. It was an absence that might be interpreted as a comment on the teacher. But there was only one way for him to answer. "You've no need to apologize," he said. "It's wholly your affair."

Blackburn beamed. "I'm so glad you feel that way about it, sir. I was worried you might think I had stayed away because I was influenced by —" he stopped and lowered his eyes.

Astonished, Howe said, "Influenced by what?"

"Well, by—" Blackburn hesitated and for answer pointed to the table on which lay the copy of *Life and Letters*. Without looking at it, he knew where to direct his hand. "By the unfavorable publicity, sir." He hurried on. "And that brings me to another point, sir. I am vice president of Quill and Scroll, sir, the student literary society, and I wonder if you would address us. You could read your own poetry, sir, and defend your own point of view. It would be very interesting."

It was truly amazing. Howe looked long and cruelly into Blackburn's face, trying to catch the secret of the mind that could have conceived this way of manipulating him, this way so daring and inept—but not entirely inept—with its malice so without malignity. The face did not yield its secret. Howe smiled broadly and said, "Of course I don't think you were influenced by the unfavorable publicity."

"I'm still going to take—regularly, for credit—your romantic poets course next term," Blackburn said.

"Don't worry, my dear fellow, don't worry about it."

Howe started to leave and Blackburn stopped him with, "But about Quill, sir?"

"Suppose we wait until next term? I'll be less busy then."

And Blackburn said, "Very good, sir, and thank you."

In his office the little encounter seemed less funny to Howe, was even in some indeterminate way disturbing. He made an effort to put it from his mind by turning to what was sure to disturb him more, the Tertan letter read in the new interpretation. He found what he had always found, the same florid leaps beyond fact and meaning, the same headlong certainty. But as his eye passed over the familiar scrawl it caught his own name, and for the second time that hour he felt the race of his blood.

"The Paraclete," Tertan had written to the Dean, "from a Greek word meaning to stand in place of, but going beyond the primitive idea to mean traditionally the helper, the one who comforts and assists, cannot without fundamental loss be jettisoned. Even if taken no longer in the supernatural sense, the concept remains deeply in the human consciousness inevitably. Humanitarianism is no reply, for not every man stands in the place of every other man for this other comrade's comfort. But certain are chosen out of the human race to be the consoler of some other. Of these, for example, is Joseph Barker Howe, Ph.D. Of intellects not the first yet of true intellect and lambent instructions, given to that which is intuitive and irrational, not to what is logical in the strict word, what is judged by him is of the heart and not the head. Here is one chosen, in that he chooses himself to stand in the place of another for comfort and consolation. To him more than another I give my gratitude, with all respect to our Dean who reads this, a noble man, but merely dedicated not consecrated. But not in the aspect of the Paraclete only is Dr. Joseph Barker Howe established, for he must be the Paraclete to another aspect of himself, that which is driven and persecuted by the lack of understanding in the world at large, so that he in himself embodies the full history of man's tribulations and, overflowing upon others, notably the present writer, is the ultimate end."

This was love. There was no escape from it. Try as Howe might to remember that Tertan was mad and all his emotions invalidated, he could not destroy the effect upon him of his student's stern, affectionate regard. He had betrayed not only a power of mind but a power of love. And, however firmly he held before his attention the fact of Tertan's madness, he could do nothing to banish the physical sensation of gratitude he felt. He had never thought of himself as "driven and persecuted" and he did not now. But still he could not make meaningless his sensation of gratitude. The pitiable Tertan sternly pitied him, and comfort came from Tertan's never-to-be-comforted mind.

3

In an academic community, even an efficient one, official matters move slowly. The term drew to a close with no action in the case of Tertan, and Joseph Howe had to confront a curious problem. How should he grade his strange student, Tertan?

Tertan's final examination had been no different from all his other writing, and what did one "give" such a student? De Witt must have his A, that was clear. Johnson would get a B. With Casebeer it was a question of a B-minus or a C-plus, and Stettenhover, who had been crammed by the team tutor to fill half a blue-book with his thin feminine scrawl, would have his C-minus which he would accept with mingled indifference and resentment. But with Tertan it was not so easy.

The boy was still in the college process and his name could not be omitted from the grade sheet. Yet what should a mind under suspicion of madness be graded? Until the medical verdict was given, it was for Howe to continue as Tertan's teacher and to keep his judgment pedagogical. Impossible to give him an F: he had not failed. B was for Johnson's stolid mediocrity. He could not be put on the edge of passing with Stettenhover, for he exactly did not pass. In energy and richness of intellect he was perhaps even De Witt's superior, and Howe toyed grimly with the notion of giving him an A, but that would lower the value of the A De Witt had won with his beautiful and clear, if still arrogant, mind. There was a notation which the Registrar recognized—Inc., for Incomplete, and in the horrible comedy of the situation, Howe considered that. But really only a mark of M for Mad would serve.

In his perplexity, Howe sought the Dean, but the Dean was out of town. In the end, he decided to maintain the A-minus he had given Tertan at mid-term. After all, there had been no falling away from that quality. He entered it on the grade sheet with something like bravado.

Academic time moves quickly. A college year is not really a year, lacking as it does three months. And it is endlessly divided into units which, at their beginning, appear larger than they are—terms, half-terms, months, weeks. And the ultimate unit, the hour, is not really an hour, lacking as it does ten minutes. And so the new term advanced rapidly, and one day the fields about the town were all brown, cleared of even the few thin patches of snow which had lingered so long.

Howe, as he lectured on the romantic poets, became conscious of Blackburn emanating wrath. Blackburn did it well, did it with enormous dignity. He did not stir in his seat, he kept his eyes fixed on Howe in perfect attention, but he abstained from using his notebook, there was no mistaking what he proposed to himself as an attitude. His elbow on the writing-wing of the chair, his chin on the curled fingers of his hand, he was the embodiment of intellectual indignation. He was thinking his own thoughts, would give no public offense, yet would claim his due, was not to be intimidated. Howe knew that he would present himself at the end of the hour.

Blackburn entered the office without invitation. He did not smile; there was no cajolery about him. Without invitation he sat down beside Howe's desk. He did not speak until he had taken the blue-book from his pocket. He said, "What does this mean, sir?"

It was a sound and conservative student tactic. Said in the usual way it meant, "How could you have so misunderstood me?" or "What does this mean for my future in the course?" But there were none of the humbler tones in Blackburn's way of saying it.

Howe made the established reply, "I think that's for you to tell me."

Blackburn continued icy. "I'm sure I can't, sir."

There was a silence between them. Both dropped their eyes to the blue-book on the desk. On its cover Howe had penciled: "F. This is very poor work."

Howe picked up the blue-book. There was always the possibility of injustice. The teacher may be bored by the mass of papers and not wholly attentive. A phrase, even the student's handwriting, may irritate him unreasonably. "Well," said Howe. "Let's go through it."

He opened the first page, "Now here: you write, 'In *The Ancient Mariner*, Coleridge lives in and transports us to a honey-sweet world where all is rich and strange, a world of charm to which we can escape from the humdrum existence of our daily lives, the world of romance. Here, in this warm and honey-sweet land of charming dreams we can relax and enjoy ourselves.'"

Howe lowered the paper and waited with a neutral look for Blackburn to speak. Blackburn returned the look boldly, did not speak, sat stolid and lofty. At last Howe said, speaking gently, "Did you mean that, or were you just at a loss for something to say?"

"You imply that I was just 'bluffing'?" The quotation marks hung palpably in the air about the word.

"I'd like to know. I'd prefer believing that you were bluffing to believing that you really thought this."

Blackburn's eyebrows went up. From the height of a great and firm-based idea he looked at his teacher. He clasped the crags for a moment and then pounced, craftily, suavely. "Do you mean, Doctor Howe, that there aren't two opinions possible?"

It was superbly done in its air of putting all of Howe's intellectual life into the balance. Howe remained patient and simple. "Yes, many opinions are possible, but not this one. Whatever anyone believes of *The Ancient Mariner*, no one can in reason believe that it represents a—a honey-sweet world in which we can relax."

"But that is what I *feel*, sir."

This was well-done, too. Howe said, "Look, Mr. Blackburn. Do you really relax with hunger and thirst, the heat and the sea-serpents, the dead men with staring eyes, Life in Death and the skeletons? Come now, Mr. Blackburn."

Blackburn made no answer, and Howe pressed forward. "Now, you say of Wordsworth, 'Of peasant stock himself, he turned from the effete life of the salons and found in the peasant the hope of a flaming revolution which would sweep away all the old ideas. This is the subject of his best poems.' "

Beaming at his teacher with youthful eagerness, Blackburn said, "Yes, sir, a rebel, a bringer of light to suffering mankind. I see him as a kind of Prothemeus."

"A kind of what?"

"Prothemeus, sir."

"Think, Mr. Blackburn. We were talking about him only today and I mentioned his name a dozen times. You don't mean Prothemeus. You mean—" Howe waited, but there was no response.

"You mean Prometheus."

Blackburn gave no assent, and Howe took the reins. "You've done a bad job here, Mr. Blackburn, about as bad as could be done." He saw Blackburn stiffen and his genial face harden again. "It shows either a lack of preparation or a complete lack of understanding." He saw Blackburn's face begin to go to pieces and he stopped.

"Oh, sir," Blackburn burst out, "I've never had a mark like this before, never anything below a B, never. A thing like this has never happened to me before."

It must be true, it was a statement too easily verified. Could it be that other instructors accepted such flaunting nonsense? Howe wanted to end the interview. "I'll set it down to lack of preparation," he said. "I know you're busy. That's not an excuse, but it's an explanation. Now, suppose you really prepare, and then take another quiz in two weeks. We'll forget this one and count the other."

Blackburn squirmed with pleasure and gratitude. "Thank you, sir. You're really very kind, very kind."

Howe rose to conclude the visit. "All right, then—in two weeks."

It was that day that the Dean imparted to Howe the conclusion of the case of Tertan. It was simple and a little anticlimactic. A physician had been called in, and had said the word, given the name.

"A classic case, he called it," the Dean said. "Not a doubt in the world," he said. His eyes were full of miserable pity, and he clutched at a word. "A classic case, a classic case." To his aid and to Howe's there came the Parthenon and the form of the Greek drama, the Aristotelian logic, Racine and the Well-Tempered Clavichord, the blueness of the Aegean and its clear sky. Classic—that is to say, without a doubt, perfect in its way, a veritable model, and, as the Dean had been told, sure to take a perfectly predictable and inevitable course to a fore-known conclusion.

It was not only pity that stood in the Dean's eyes. For a moment there was fear too. "Terrible," he said, "it is simply terrible."

Then he went on briskly. "Naturally, we've told the boy nothing. And, naturally, we won't. His tuition's paid by his scholarship, and we'll continue him on the rolls until the end of the year. That will be kindest. After that the matter will be out of our control. We'll see, of course, that he gets into the proper hands. I'm told there will be no change, he'll go on like this, be as good as this, for four to six months. And so we'll just go along as usual."

So Tertan continued to sit in Section 5 of English 1A, to his classmates still a figure of curiously dignified fun, symbol to most of them of the respectable but absurd intellectual life. But to his teacher he was now very different. He had not changed—he was still the greyhound casting for the scent of ideas, and Howe could see that he was still the same Tertan, but he could not feel it. What he felt as he looked at the boy sitting in his accustomed place was the hard blank of a fact. The fact itself was formidable and depressing. But what Howe was chiefly aware of was that he had permitted the metamorphosis of Tertan from person to fact.

As much as possible he avoided seeing Tertan's upraised hand and eager eye. But the fact did not know of its mere factuality, it continued its existence as if it were Tertan, hand up and eye questioning, and one day it appeared in Howe's office with a document.

"Even the spirit who lives egregiously, above the herd, must have its relations with the fellowman." Tertan declared. He laid the document on Howe's desk. It was headed "Quill and Scroll Society of Dwight College. Application for Membership."

"In most ways these are crass minds," Tertan said, touching the paper. "Yet as a whole, bound together in their common love of letters, they transcend their intellectual lacks since it is not a paradox that the whole is greater than the sum of its parts."

"When are the elections?" Howe asked.

"They take place tomorrow."

"I certainly hope you will be successful."

"Thank you. Would you wish to implement that hope?" A rather dirty finger pointed to the bottom of the sheet. "A faculty recommender is necessary," Tertan said stiffly, and waited.

"And you wish me to recommend you?"

"It would be an honor."

"You may use my name."

Tertan's finger pointed again. "It must be a written sponsorship, signed by the sponsor." There was a large blank space on the form under the heading, "Opinion of Faculty Sponsor."

This was almost another thing and Howe hesitated. Yet there was nothing else to do and he took out his fountain pen. He wrote, "Mr. Ferdinand Tertan is marked by his intense devotion to letters and by his exceptional love of all things of the mind." To this he signed his name, which looked bold and assertive on the white page. It disturbed him, the strange affirming power of a name. With a business-like air, Tertan whipped up the paper, folding it with decision, and put it into his pocket. He bowed and took his departure, leaving Howe with the sense of having done something oddly momentous.

And so much now seemed odd and momentous to Howe that should not have seemed so. It was odd and momentous, he felt, when he sat with Blackburn's second quiz before him, and wrote in an excessively firm hand the grade of C-minus. The paper was a clear, an indisputable failure. He was carefully and consciously committing a cowardice. Blackburn had told the truth when he had pleaded his past record. Howe had consulted it in the Dean's office. It showed no grade lower than a B-minus. A canvass of some of Blackburn's previous instructors had brought vague attestations to the adequate powers of a student imperfectly remembered, and sometimes surprise that his abilities could be questioned at all.

As he wrote the grade, Howe told himself that his cowardice sprang from an unwillingness to have more dealings with a student he disliked. He knew it was simpler than that. He knew he feared Blackburn, that was the absurd truth. And cowardice did not solve the matter after all. Blackburn, flushed with a first success, attacked at once. The minimal passing grade had not assuaged his feelings and he sat at Howe's desk and again the blue-book lay between them. Blackburn said nothing. With an enormous impudence, he was waiting for Howe to speak and explain himself.

At last Howe said sharply and rudely, "Well?" His throat was tense and the blood was hammering in his head. His mouth was tight with anger at himself for his disturbance.

Blackburn's glance was almost baleful. "This is impossible, sir."

"But there it is," Howe answered.

"Sir?" Blackburn had not caught the meaning but his tone was still haughty.

Impatiently Howe said, "There it is, plain as day. Are you here to complain again?"

"Indeed I am, sir." There was surprise in Blackburn's voice that Howe should ask the question.

"I shouldn't complain if I were you. You did a thoroughly bad job on your first quiz. This one is a little, only a very little, better." This was not true. If anything, it was worse.

"That might be a matter of opinion, sir."

"It is a matter of opinion. Of my opinion."

"Another opinion might be different, sir."

"You really believe that?" Howe said.

"Yes." The omission of the "sir" was monumental.

"Whose, for example?"

"The Dean's, for example." Then the fleshy jaw came forward a little. "Or a certain literary critic's, for example."

It was colossal and almost too much for Blackburn himself to handle. The solidity of his face almost crumpled under it. But he withstood his own audacity and went on. "And the Dean's opinion might be guided by the knowledge that the person who gave me this mark is the man whom a famous critic, the most eminent judge of literature in this country, called a drunken man. The Dean might think twice about whether such a man is fit to teach Dwight students."

Howe said in quiet admonition, "Blackburn, you're mad," meaning no more than to check the boy's extravagance.

But Blackburn paid no heed. He had another shot in the locker. "And the Dean might be guided by the information, of which I have evidence, documentary evidence,"—he slapped his breast pocket twice—"that this same person personally recommended to the college literary society, the oldest in the country, that he personally recommended a student who is crazy, who threw the meeting into an uproar—a psychiatric case. The Dean might take that into account."

Howe was never to learn the details of that "uproar." He had always to content himself with the dim but passionate picture which at that moment sprang into his mind, of Tertan standing on some abstract height and madly denouncing the multitude of Quill and Scroll who howled him down.

He sat quiet a moment and looked at Blackburn. The ferocity had entirely gone from the student's face. He sat regarding his teacher almost benevolently. He had played a good card and now, scarcely at all unfriendly, he was waiting to see the effect. Howe took up the blue-book and negligently sifted through it. He read a page, closed the book, struck out the C-minus and wrote an F.

"Now you may take the paper to the Dean," he said. "You may tell him that after reconsidering it, I lowered the grade."

The gasp was audible. "Oh, sir!" Blackburn cried. "Please!" His face was agonized. "It means my graduation, my livelihood, my future. Don't do this to me."

"It's done already."

Blackburn stood up, "I spoke rashly, sir, hastily. I had no intention, no real intention, of seeing the Dean. It rests with you—entirely, entirely. I *hope* you will restore the first mark."

"Take the matter to the Dean or not, just as you choose. The grade is what you deserve and it stands."

Blackburn's head dropped. "And will I be failed at mid-term, sir?"
"Of course."

From deep out of Blackburn's great chest rose a cry of anguish. "Oh, sir, if you want me to go down on my knees to you, I will, I will."

Howe looked at him in amazement.

"I will, I will. On my knees, sir. This mustn't, mustn't happen."

He spoke so literally, meaning so very truly that his knees and exactly his knees were involved and seeming to think that he was offering something of tangible value to his teacher, that Howe, whose head had become icy clear in the nonsensical drama, thought, "The boy is mad," and began to speculate fantastically whether something in himself attracted or developed aberration. He could see himself standing absurdly before the Dean and saying, "I've found another. This time it's the Vice-president of the Council, the manager of the debating team and secretary of Quill and Scroll."

One more such discovery, he thought, and he himself would be discovered! And there, suddenly, Blackburn was on his knees with a thump, his huge thighs straining his trousers, his hand out-stretched in a great gesture of supplication.

With a cry, Howe shoved back his swivel chair and it rolled away on its casters half across the little room. Blackburn knelt for a moment to nothing at all, then got to his feet.

Howe rose abruptly. He said, "Blackburn, you will stop acting like an idiot. Dust your knees off, take your paper and get out. You've behaved like a fool and a malicious person. You have half a term to do a decent job. Keep your silly mouth shut and try to do it. Now get out."

Blackburn's head was low. He raised it and there was a pious light in his eyes. "Will you shake hands, sir?" he said. He thrust out his hand.

"I will not," Howe said.

Head and hand sank together. Blackburn picked up his blue-book and walked to the door. He turned and said, "Thank you, sir." His back, as he departed, was heavy with tragedy and stateliness.

4

After years of bad luck with the weather, the College had a perfect day for Commencement. It was wonderfully bright, the air so transparent, the wind so brisk that no one could resist talking about it.

As Howe set out for the campus he heard Hilda calling from the back yard. She called, "Professor, professor," and came running to him.

Howe said, "What's this 'professor' business?"

"Mother told me," Hilda said. "You've been promoted. And I want to take your picture."

"Next year," said Howe. "I won't be a professor until next year. And you know better than to call anybody 'professor.'"

"It was just in fun," Hilda said. She seemed disappointed.

"But you can take my picture if you want. I won't look much different next year." Still, it was frightening. It might mean that he was to stay in this town all his life.

Hilda brightened. "Can I take it in this?" she said, and touched the gown he carried over his arm.

Howe laughed. "Yes, you can take it in this."

"I'll get my things and meet you in front of Otis," Hilda said. "I have the background all picked out."

On the campus the Commencement crowd was already large. It stood about in eager, nervous little family groups. As he crossed, Howe was greeted by a student, capped and gowned, glad of the chance to make an event for his parents by introducing one of his teachers. It was while Howe stood there chatting that he saw Tertan.

He had never seen anyone quite so alone, as though a circle had been woven about him to separate him from the gay crowd on the campus. Not that Tertan was not gay, he was the gayest of all. Three weeks had passed since Howe had last seen him, the weeks of examination, the lazy week before Commencement, and this was now a different Tertan. On his head he wore a panama hat, broad-brimmed and fine, of the shape associated with South American planters. He wore a suit of raw silk, luxurious, but yellowed with age and much too tight, and he sported a whangee cane. He walked sedately, the hat tilted at a devastating angle, the stick coming up and down in time to his measured tread. He had, Howe guessed, outfitted himself to greet the day in the clothes of that ruined father whose existence was on record in the Dean's office. Gravely and arrogantly he surveyed the scene—in it, his whole bearing seemed to say, but not of it. With his haughty step, with his flashing eye, Tertan was coming nearer. Howe did not wish to be seen. He shifted his position slightly. When he looked again, Tertan was not in sight.

The chapel clock struck the quarter hour. Howe detached himself from his chat and hurried to Otis Hall at the far end of the campus. Hilda had not yet come. He went up into the high portico and, using the glass of the door for a mirror, put on his gown, adjusted the hood on his shoulders and set the mortarboard on his head. When he came down the steps, Hilda had arrived.

Nothing could have told him more forcibly that a year had passed than the development of Hilda's photographic possessions from the box camera of the previous fall. By a strap about her neck was hung a leather case, so thick and strong, so carefully stitched and so molded to its contents that it could only hold a costly camera. The appearance was deceptive, Howe knew, for he had been present at the Aikens' pre-Christmas conference about its purchase. It was only a fairly good domestic camera. Still, it looked very impressive. Hilda carried another leather case from which she drew a collapsible tripod. Decisively she extended each of its gleaming legs and set it up on the path. She removed the camera from its case and fixed it to the tripod. In its compact efficiency the camera almost had a life of its own, but Hilda treated it with easy familiarity, looked into its eye, glanced casually at its gauges. Then from a pocket she took still another leather case and drew from it a small instrument through which she looked first at Howe, who began to feel inanimate and lost, and then at the sky. She made some adjustment on the instrument, then some adjustment on the camera. She swept the scene with her eye, found a spot and pointed the camera in its direction. She walked to the spot, stood on it and beckoned to Howe. With each new leather case, with each new instrument, and with each new adjustment she had grown in ease and now she said, "Joe, will you stand here?"

Obediently Howe stood where he was bidden. She had yet another instrument. She took out a tape-measure on a mechanical spool. Kneeling down before Howe, she put the little metal ring of the tape under the tip of his shoe. At her request, Howe pressed it with his toe. When she had measured her distance, she nodded to Howe who released the tape. At a touch, it sprang back into the spool. "You have to be careful if you're going to get what you want," Hilda said. "I don't believe in all this snap-snap-snapping," she remarked loftily. Howe nodded in agreement, although he was beginning to think Hilda's care excessive.

Now at last the moment had come. Hilda squinted into the camera, moved the tripod slightly. She stood to the side, holding the plunger of the shutter-cable. "Ready," she said. "Will you relax, Joseph, please?" Howe realized that he was standing frozen. Hilda stood poised and precise as a setter, one hand holding the little cable, the other extended with curled dainty fingers like a dancer's, as if expressing to her subject the precarious delicacy of the moment. She pressed the plunger and there was the click. At once she stirred to action, got behind the camera, turned a new exposure. "Thank you," she said. "Would you stand under that tree and let me do a character study with light and shade?"

The childish absurdity of the remark restored Howe's ease. He went to the little tree. The pattern the leaves made on his gown was what Hilda was after. He had just taken a satisfactory position when he heard in the unmistakable voice, "Ah, Doctor! Having your picture taken?"

Howe gave up the pose and turned to Blackburn who stood on the walk, his hands behind his back, a little too large for his bachelor's gown. Annoyed that Blackburn should see him posing for a character study in light and shade, Howe said irritably, "Yes, having my picture taken."

Blackburn beamed at Hilda. "And the little photographer?" he said. Hilda fixed her eyes on the ground and stood closer to her brilliant and aggressive camera. Blackburn, teetering on his heels, his hands behind his back, wholly prelatical and benignly patient, was not abashed at the silence. At last Howe said, "If you'll excuse us, Mr. Blackburn, we'll go on with the picture."

"Go right ahead, sir. I'm running along." But he only came closer.

"Doctor Howe," he said fervently, "I want to tell you how glad I am that I was able to satisfy your standards at last."

Howe was surprised at the hard, insulting brightness of his own voice, and even Hilda looked up curiously as he said, "Nothing you have ever done has satisfied me, and nothing you could ever do would satisfy me, Blackburn."

With a glance at Hilda, Blackburn made a gesture as if to hush Howe —as though all his former bold malice had taken for granted a kind of understanding between himself and his teacher, a secret which must not be betrayed to a third person. "I only meant, sir," he said, "that I was able to pass your course after all."

Howe said, "You didn't pass my course. I passed you out of my course. I passed you without even reading your paper. I wanted to be sure the college would be rid of you. And when all the grades were in and I did read your paper, I saw I was right not to have read it first."

Blackburn presented a stricken face. "It was very bad, sir?"

But Howe had turned away. The paper had been fantastic. The paper had been, if he wished to see it so, mad. It was at this moment that the Dean came up behind Howe and caught his arm. "Hello, Joseph," he said. "We'd better be getting along, it's almost late."

He was not a familiar man, but when he saw Blackburn, who approached to greet him, he took Blackburn's arm, too. "Hello, Theodore," he said. Leaning forward on Howe's arm and on Blackburn's, he said, "Hello, Hilda dear." Hilda replied quietly, "Hello, Uncle George."

Still clinging to their arms, still linking Howe and Blackburn, the Dean said, "Another year gone, Joe, and we've turned out another crop. After you've been here a few years, you'll find it reasonably upsetting— you wonder how there can be so many graduating classes while you stay the same. But of course you don't stay the same." Then he said, "Well," sharply, to dismiss the thought. He pulled Blackburn's arm and swung him around to Howe. "Have you heard about Teddy Blackburn?" he asked. "He has a job already, before graduation—the first man of his class to be placed." Expectant of congratulations, Blackburn beamed at Howe. Howe remained silent.

"Isn't that good?" the Dean said. Still Howe did not answer and the Dean, puzzled and put out, turned to Hilda. "That's a very fine-looking camera, Hilda." She touched it with affectionate pride.

"Instruments of precision," said a voice. "Instruments of precision." Of the three with joined arms, Howe was the nearest to Tertan, whose gaze took in all the scene except the smile and the nod which Howe gave him. The boy leaned on his cane. The broad-brimmed hat, canting jauntily over his eye, confused the image of his face that Howe had established, suppressed the rigid lines of the ascetic and brought out the baroque curves. It made an effect of perverse majesty.

"Instruments of precision," said Tertan for the last time, addressing no one, making a casual comment to the universe. And it occurred to Howe that Tertan might not be referring to Hilda's equipment. The sense of the thrice-woven circle of the boy's loneliness smote him fiercely. Tertan stood in majestic jauntiness, superior to all the scene, but his isolation made Howe ache with a pity of which Tertan was more the cause than the object, so general and indiscriminate was it.

Whether in his sorrow he made some unintended movement toward Tertan which the Dean checked, or whether the suddenly tightened grip on his arm was the Dean's own sorrow and fear, he did not know. Tertan watched them in the incurious way people watch a photograph being taken, and suddenly the thought that, to the boy, it must seem that the three were posing for a picture together made Howe detach himself almost rudely from the Dean's grasp.

"I promised Hilda another picture," he announced—needlessly, for Tertan was no longer there, he had vanished in the last sudden flux of visitors who, now that the band had struck up, were rushing nervously to find seats.

"You'd better hurry," the Dean said. "I'll go along, it's getting late for me." He departed and Blackburn walked stately by his side.

Howe again took his position under the little tree which cast its shadow over his face and gown. "Just hurry, Hilda, won't you?" he said. Hilda held the cable at arm's length, her other arm crooked and her fingers crisped. She rose on her toes and said "Ready," and pressed the release. "Thank you," she said gravely and began to dismantle her camera as he hurried off to join the procession.

Richard Wright
1908–1960
BIG BOY LEAVES HOME

I

Y*o mama don wear no drawers . . .*
  Clearly, the voice rose out of the woods, and died away. Like an echo another voice caught it up:
Ah seena when she pulled em off . . .
Another, shrill, cracking, adolescent:
N she washed 'em in alcohol . . .
Then a quartet of voices, blending in harmony, floated high above the tree tops:
N she hung 'em out in the hall . . .
Laughing easily, four black boys came out of the woods into cleared pasture. They walked lollingly in bare feet, beating tangled vines and bushes with long sticks.

"Ah wished Ah knowed some mo lines t tha song."

"Me too."

"Yeah, when yuh gits t where she hangs em out in the hall yuh has t stop."

"Shucks, whut goes wid *hall?*"

"*Call.*"

"*Fall.*"

"*Wall.*"

"*Quall.*"

They threw themselves on the grass, laughing.

"Big Boy?"

"Huh?"

"Yuh know one thing?"

"Whut?"

"Yuh sho is crazy!"

"Crazy?"

"Yeah, yuh crazys a bed-bug!"

"Crazy bout whut?"

"Man, whoever hearda *quall?*"

"Yuh said yuh wanted something t go wid *hall*, didnt yuh?"

"Yeah, but whuts a *quall?*"

"Nigger, a *qualls* a *quall.*"

They laughed easily, catching and pulling long green blades of grass with their toes.

"Waal, ef a *qualls* a *quall*, whut IS a *quall?*"

"Oh, Ah know."

"Whut?"

"Tha ol song goes something like this:

> *Yo mama don wear no drawers,*
> *Ah seena when she pulled em off,*
> *N she washed em in alcohol,*
> *N she hung em out in the hall,*
> *N then she put em back on her* QUALL!"

They laughed again. Their shoulders were flat to the earth, their knees propped up, and their faces square to the sun.

"Big Boy, yuhs CRAZY!"

"Don ax me nothin else."

"Nigger, yuhs CRAZY!"

They fell silent, smiling, drooping the lids of their eyes softly against the sunlight.

"Man, don the groun feel warm?"

"Jus lika bed."

"Jeeesus, Ah could stay here ferever."

"Me too."

"Ah kin feel tha ol sun goin all thu me."
"Feels like mah bones is warm."
In the distance a train whistled mournfully.
"There goes number fo!"
"Hittin on all six!"
"Highballin it down the line!"
"Boun fer up Noth, Lawd, boun fer up Noth!"
They began to chant, pounding bare heels in the grass.

> *Dis train boun fo Glory*
> *Dis train, Oh Hallelujah*
> *Dis train boun fo Glory*
> *Dis train, Oh Hallelujah*
> *Dis train boun fo Glory*
> *Ef yuh ride no need fer fret er worry*
> *Dis train, Oh Hallelujah*
> *Dis train . . .*
>
> *Dis train don carry no gambler*
> *Dis train, Oh Hallelujah*
> *Dis train don carry no gambler*
> *Dis train, Oh Hallelujah*
> *Dis train don carry no gambler*
> *No fo day creeper er midnight rambler*
> *Dis train, Oh Hallelujah*
> *Dis train . . .*

When the song ended they burst out laughing, thinking of a train bound for Glory.
"Gee, thas a good ol song!"
"Huuuuummmmmmmmmman . . ."
"Whut?"
"Geeee whiiiiiiz . . ."
"Whut?"
"Somebody don let win! Das whut!"
Buck, Bobo and Lester jumped up. Big Boy stayed on the ground, feigning sleep.
"Jeeesus, tha sho stinks!"
"Big Boy!"
Big Boy feigned to snore.
"Big Boy!"
Big Boy stirred as though in sleep.
"Big Boy!"
"Hunh?"
"Yuh rotten inside!"
"Rotten?"

"Lawd, cant yuh smell it?"

"Smell whut?"

"Nigger, yuh mus gotta bad col!"

"*Smell whut?*"

"NIGGER, YUH BROKE WIN!"

Big Boy laughed and fell back on the grass, closing his eyes.

"The hen whut cackles is the hen whut laid the egg."

"We ain no hens."

"Yuh cackled, didnt yuh?"

The three moved off with noses turned up.

"C mon!"

"Where yuh-all goin?"

"T the creek fer a swim."

"Yeah, les swim."

"Naw buddy naw!" said Big Boy, slapping the air with a scornful palm.

"Aw, c mon! Don be a heel!"

"N git *lynched?* Hell naw!"

"He ain gonna see us."

"How yuh know?"

"Cause he ain."

"Yuh-all go on. Ahma stay right here," said Big Boy.

"Hell, let im stay! C mon, les go," said Buck.

The three walked off, swishing at grass and bushes with sticks. Big Boy looked lazily at their backs.

"Hey!"

Walking on, they glanced over their shoulders.

"Hey, niggers!"

"C mon!"

Big Boy grunted, picked up his stick, pulled to his feet, and stumbled off.

"Wait!"

"C mon!"

He ran, caught up with them, leaped upon their backs, bearing them to the ground.

"Quit, Big Boy!"

"Gawddam, nigger!"

"Git t hell offa me!"

Big Boy sprawled in the grass beside them, laughing and pounding his heels in the ground.

"Nigger, whut yuh think we is, hosses?"

"How come yuh always hoppin on us?"

"Lissen, wes gonna double-team on yuh one of these days n beat yo ol ass good."

Big Boy smiled.

"Sho nough?"

"Yeah, don yuh like it?"

"We gonna beat yuh sos yuh cant walk!"

"N dare yuh t do nothin erbout it!"

Big Boy bared his teeth.

"C mon! Try it now!"

The three circled around him.

"Say, Buck, yuh grab his feets!"

"N yuh git his head, Lester!"

"N Bobo, yuh git berhin n grab his arms!"

Keeping more than arm's length, they circled round and round Big Boy.

"C mon!" said Big Boy, feinting at one and then the other.

Round and round they circled, but could not seem to get any closer. Big Boy stopped and braced his hands on his hips.

"Is all three of yuh-all scareda me?"

"Les git im some other time," said Bobo, grinning.

"Yeah, we kin ketch yuh when yuh ain thinkin," said Lester.

"We kin trick yuh," said Buck.

They laughed and walked together.

Big Boy belched.

"Ahm hongry," he said.

"Me too."

"Ah wished Ah hada big hot pota bellybusters!"

"Cooked wid some good ol salty ribs . . ."

"N some good ol egg cornbread . . ."

"N some buttermilk . . ."

"N some hot peach cobbler swimmin in juice . . ."

"Nigger, hush!"

They began to chant, emphasizing the rhythm by cutting at grass with sticks.

> *Bye n bye*
> *Ah wanna piece of pie*
> *Pies too sweet*
> *Ah wanna piece of meat*
> *Meats too red*
> *Ah wanna piece of bread*
> *Breads too brown*
> *Ah wanna go t town*
> *Towns too far*
> *Ah wanna ketch a car*
> *Cars too fas*
> *Ah fall n break mah ass*
> *Ahll understan it better bye n bye . . .*

They climbed over a barbed-wire fence and entered a stretch of thick woods. Big Boy was whistling softly, his eyes half-closed.

"LES GIT IM!"

Buck, Lester, and Bobo whirled, grabbed Big Boy about the neck, arms, and legs, bearing him to the ground. He grunted and kicked wildly as he went back into weeds.

"Hol im tight!"

"Git his arms! Git his arms!"

"Set on his legs so he cant kick!"

Big Boy puffed heavily, trying to get loose.

"WE GOT YUH NOW, GAWDDAMMIT, WE GOT YUH NOW!"

"Thas a Gawddam lie!" said Big Boy. He kicked, twisted, and clutched for a hold on one and then the other.

"Say, yuh-all hep me hol his arms!" said Bobo.

"Aw, we got this bastard now!" said Lester.

"Thas a Gawddam lie!" said Big Boy again.

"Say, yuh-all hep me hol his arms!" called Bobo.

Big Boy managed to encircle the neck of Bobo with his left arm. He tightened his elbow scissorslike and hissed through his teeth:

"Yuh got me, ain yuh?"

"Hol im!"

"Les beat this bastard's ass!"

"Say, hep me hol his *arms!* Hes got aholda mah *neck!*" cried Bobo.

Big Boy squeezed Bobo's neck and twisted his head to the ground.

"Yuh got me, ain yuh?"

"Quit, Big Boy, yuh chokin me; yuh hurtin mah neck!" cried Bobo.

"Turn me loose!" said Big Boy.

"Ah ain got yuh! Its the others whut got yuh!" pleaded Bobo.

"Tell them others t git t hell offa me or Ahma break yo neck," said Big Boy.

"Ssssay, yyyuh-all gggit ooooffa Bbig Boy Hhhes got me," gurgled Bobo.

"Cant yuh hol im?"

"Nnaw, hhes ggot mmah nneck . . ."

Big Boy squeezed tighter.

"N Ahma break it too less yuh tell em t git t hell offa me!"

"Ttturn mmmeee llloose," panted Bobo, tears gushing.

"Cant yuh hol im, Bobo?" asked Buck.

"Nnaw, yuh-all tturn im lloose; hhhes got mah nnneck . . ."

"Grab his neck, Bobo . . ."

"Ah cant; yugurgur . . ."

To save Bobo, Lester and Buck got up and ran to a safe distance. Big Boy released Bobo, who staggered to his feet, slobbering and trying to stretch a crick out of his neck.

"Shucks, nigger, yuh almos broke mah neck," whimpered Bobo.

"Ahm gonna break yo ass nex time," said Big Boy.

"Ef Bobo coulda hel yuh we woulda had yuh," yelled Lester.

"Ah wuznt gonna let im do that," said Big Boy.

They walked together again, swishing sticks.

"Yuh see," began Big Boy, "when a ganga guys jump on yuh, all yuh gotta do is jus put the heat on one of them n make im tell the others t let up, see?"

"Gee, thas a good idee!"

"Yeah, thas a good idee!"

"But yuh almos broke mah neck, man," said Bobo.

"Ahma smart nigger," said Big Boy, thrusting out his chest.

2

They came to the swimming hole.

"Ah ain goin in," said Bobo.

"Done got scared?" asked Big Boy.

"Naw, Ah ain scared . . ."

"How come yuh ain goin in?"

"Yuh know ol man Harvey don erllow no niggers t swim in this hole."

"N jus las year he took a shot at Bob fer swimmin in here," said Lester.

"Shucks, ol man Harvey ain studyin bout us niggers," said Big Boy.

"Hes at home thinkin about his jelly-roll," said Buck.

They laughed.

"Buck, yo mins lowern a snakes belly," said Lester.

"Ol man Harveys too doggone ol t think erbout jelly-roll," said Big Boy.

"Hes dried up; all the saps done lef im," said Bobo.

"C mon, les go!" said Big Boy.

Bobo pointed.

"See tha sign over yonder?"

"Yeah."

"Whut it say?"

"NO TRESPASSIN," read Lester.

"Know whut tha mean?"

"Mean ain no dogs n niggers erllowed," said Buck.

"Waal, wes here now," said Big Boy. "Ef he ketched us even like this thered be trouble, so we just as waal go in . . ."

"Ahm wid the nex one!"

"Ahll go ef anybody else goes!"

Big Boy looked carefully in all directions. Seeing nobody, he began jerking off his overalls.

"LAS ONE INS A OL DEAD DOG!"

"THAS YO MA!"

"THAS YO PA!"

"THAS BOTH YO MA N YO PA!"

They jerked off their clothes and threw them in a pile under a tree.

Thirty seconds later they stood, black and naked, on the edge of the hole under a sloping embankment. Gingerly Big Boy touched the water with his foot.

"Man, this waters col," he said.

"Ahm gonna put mah cloes back on," said Bobo, withdrawing his foot.

Big Boy grabbed him about the waist.

"Like hell yuh is!"

"Git outta the way, nigger!" Bobo yelled.

"Throw im in!" said Lester.

"Duck im!"

Bobo crouched, spread his legs, and braced himself against Big Boy's body. Locked in each other's arms, they tussled on the edge of the hole, neither able to throw the other.

"C mon, les me n yuh push em in."

"O.K."

Laughing, Lester and Buck gave the two locked bodies a running push. Big Boy and Bobo splashed, sending up silver spray in the sunlight. When Big Boy's head came up he yelled:

"Yuh bastard!"

"Tha wuz yo ma yuh pushed!" said Bobo, shaking his head to clear the water from his eyes.

They did a surface dive, came up and struck out across the creek. The muddy water foamed. They swam back, waded into shallow water, breathing heavily and blinking eyes.

"C mon in!"

"Man, the waters fine!"

Lester and Buck hesitated.

"Les wet em," Big Boy whispered to Bobo.

Before Lester and Buck could back away, they were dripping wet from handsful of scooped water.

"Hey, quit!"

"Gawddam, nigger! Tha waters col!"

"C mon in!" called Big Boy.

"We jus as waal go on in now," said Buck.

"Look n see ef anybodys comin."

Kneeling, they squinted among the trees.

"Ain nobody."

"C mon, les go."

They waded in slowly, pausing each few steps to catch their breath. A desperate water battle began. Closing eyes and backing away, they shunted water into one another's faces with the flat palms of hands.

"Hey, cut it out!"

"Yeah, Ahm bout drownin!"

They came together in water up to their navels, blowing and blinking. Big Boy ducked, upsetting Bobo.

"Look out, nigger!"

"Don holler so loud!"

"Yeah, they kin hear yo ol big mouth a mile erway."

"This waters too col fer me."

"Thas cause it rained yistiddy."

They swam across and back again.

"Ah wish we hada bigger place t swim in."

"The white folks got plenty swimmin pools n we ain got none."

"Ah useta swim in the ol Missippi when we lived in Vicksburg."

Big Boy put his head under the water and blew his breath. A sound
came like that of a hippopotamus.

"C mon, les be hippos."

Each went to a corner of the creek and put his mouth just below the
surface and blew like a hippopotamus. Tiring, they came and sat under
the embankment.

"Look like Ah gotta chill."

"Me too."

"Les stay here n dry off."

"Jeeesus, Ahm col!"

They kept still in the sun, suppressing shivers. After some of the water had dried off their bodies they began to talk through clattering teeth.

"Whut would yuh do ef ol man Harveyd come erlong right now?"

"Run like hell!"

"Man, Ahd run so fas hed thinka black streaka lightnin shot pass im."

"But spose he hada gun?"

"Aw, nigger, shut up!"

They were silent. They ran their hands over wet, trembling legs,
brushing water away. Then their eyes watched the sun sparkling on the
restless creek.

Far away a train whistled.

"There goes number seven!"

"Headin fer up Noth!"

"Blazin it down the line!"

"Lawd, Ahm goin Noth some day."

"Me too, man."

"They say colored folks up Noth is got ekual rights."

They grew pensive. A black winged butterfly hovered at the water's
edge. A bee droned. From somewhere came the sweet scent of honeysuckles. Dimly they could hear sparrows twittering in the woods. They
rolled from side to side, letting sunshine dry their skins and warm their
blood. They plucked blades of grass and chewed them.

"Oh!"

They looked up, their lips parting.

"Oh!"

A white woman, poised on the edge of the opposite embankment, stood directly in front of them, her hat in her hand and her hair lit by the sun.

"Its a woman!" whispered Big Boy in an underbreath, "A *white* woman!"

They stared, their hands instinctively covering their groins. Then they scrambled to their feet. The white woman backed slowly out of sight. They stood for a moment, looking at one another.

"Les git outta here!" Big Boy whispered.

"Wait till she goes erway."

"Les run, theyll ketch us here naked like this!"

"Mabbe theres a man wid her."

"C mon, les git our cloes," said Big Boy.

They waited a moment longer, listening.

"Whut t hell! Ahma git mah cloes," said Big Boy.

Grabbing at short tufts of grass, he climbed the embankment.

"Don run out there now!"

"C mon back, fool!"

Bobo hesitated. He looked at Big Boy, and then at Buck and Lester.

"Ahm goin wid Big Boy n git mah cloes," he said.

"Don run out there naked like tha, fool!" said Buck. "Yuh don know whos out there!"

Big Boy was climbing over the edge of the embankment.

"C mon," he whispered.

Bobo climbed after. Twenty-five feet away the woman stood. She had one hand over her mouth. Hanging by fingers, Buck and Lester peeped over the edge.

"C mon back; that womans scared," said Lester.

Big Boy stopped, puzzled. He looked at the woman. He looked at the bundle of clothes. Then he looked at Buck and Lester.

"C mon, les git our cloes!"

He made a step.

"Jim!" the woman screamed.

Big Boy stopped and looked around. His hands hung loosely at his sides. The woman, her eyes wide, her hand over her mouth, backed away to the tree where their clothes lay in a heap.

"Big Boy, come back n wait till shes gone!"

Bobo ran to Big Boy's side.

"Les go home! Theyll ketch us here," he urged.

Big Boy's throat felt tight.

"Lady, we wanna git our cloes," he said.

Buck and Lester climbed the embankment and stood indecisively. Big Boy ran toward the tree.

"Jim!" the woman screamed. "Jim! Jim!"

Black and naked, Big Boy stopped three feet from her.

"We wanna git our cloes," he said again, his words coming mechanically.

He made a motion.

"You go away! You go away! I tell you, you go away!"

Big Boy stopped again, afraid. Bobo ran and snatched the clothes. Buck and Lester tried to grab theirs out of his hands.

"You go away! You go away! You go away!" the woman screamed.

"Les go!" said Bobo, running toward the woods.

CRACK!

Lester grunted, stiffened, and pitched forward. His forehead struck a toe of the woman's shoes.

Bobo stopped, clutching the clothes. Buck whirled. Big Boy stared at Lester, his lips moving.

"Hes gotta gun; hes gotta gun!" yelled Buck, running wildly.

CRACK!

Buck stopped at the edge of the embankment, his head jerked backward, his body arched stiffly to one side; he toppled head-long, sending up a shower of bright spray to the sunlight. The creek bubbled.

Big Boy and Bobo backed away, their eyes fastened fearfully on a white man who was running toward them. He had a rifle and wore an army officer's uniform. He ran to the woman's side and grabbed her hand.

"You hurt, Bertha, you hurt?"

She stared at him and did not answer.

The man turned quickly. His face was red. He raised the rifle and pointed it at Bobo. Bobo ran back, holding the clothes in front of his chest.

"Don shoot me, Mistah, don shoot me . . ."

Big Boy lunged for the rifle, grabbing the barrel.

"You black sonofabitch!"

Big Boy clung desperately.

"Let go, you black bastard!"

The barrel pointed skyward.

CRACK!

The white man, taller and heavier, flung Big Boy to the ground. Bobo dropped the clothes, ran up, and jumped onto the white man's back.

"You black sonsofbitches!"

The white man released the rifle, jerked Bobo to the ground, and began to batter the naked boy with his fists. Then Big Boy swung, striking the man in the mouth with the barrel. His teeth caved in, and he fell, dazed. Bobo was on his feet.

"C mon, Big Boy, les go!"

Breathing hard, the white man got up and faced Big Boy. His lips were trembling, his neck and chin wet with blood. He spoke quietly.

"Give me that gun, boy!"

Big Boy leveled the rifle and backed away.

The white man advanced.

"Boy, I say give me that gun!"

Bobo had the clothes in his arms.

"Run, Big Boy, run!"

The man came at Big Boy.

"Ahll kill yuh; Ahll kill yuh!" said Big Boy.

His fingers fumbled for the trigger.

The man stopped, blinked, spat blood. His eyes were bewildered. His face whitened. Suddenly, he lunged for the rifle, his hands outstretched.

CRACK!

He fell forward on his face.

"Jim!"

Big Boy and Bobo turned in surprise to look at the woman.

"Jim!" she screamed again, and fell weakly at the foot of the tree.

Big Boy dropped the rifle, his eyes wide. He looked around. Bobo was crying and clutching the clothes.

"Big Boy, Big Boy . . ."

Big Boy looked at the rifle, started to pick it up, but didn't. He seemed at a loss. He looked at Lester, then at the white man; his eyes followed a thin stream of blood that seeped to the ground.

"Yuh done killed im," mumbled Bobo.

"Les go home!"

Naked, they turned and ran toward the woods. When they reached the barbed-wire fence they stopped.

"Les git our cloes on," said Big Boy.

They slipped quickly into overalls. Bobo held Lester's and Buck's clothes.

"Whut we gonna do wid these?"

Big Boy stared. His hands twitched.

"Leave em."

They climbed the fence and ran through the woods. Vines and leaves switched their faces. Once Bobo tripped and fell.

"C mon!" said Big Boy.

Bobo started crying, blood streaming from his scratches.

"Ahm scared!"

"C mon! Don cry! We wanna git home fo they ketches us!"

"Ahm scared!" said Bobo again, his eyes full of tears.

Big Boy grabbed his hand and dragged him along.

"C mon!"

3

They stopped when they got to the end of the woods. They could see the open road leading home, home to ma and pa. But they hung back, afraid. The thick shadows cast from the trees were friendly and sheltering. But the wide glare of sun stretching out over the fields was pitiless. They crouched behind an old log.

"We gotta git home," said Big Boy.

"Theys gonna lynch us," said Bobo, half-questioningly.

Big Boy did not answer.

"Theys gonna lynch us," said Bobo again.

Big Boy shuddered.

"Hush!" he said. He did not want to think of it. He could not think of it; there was but one thought, and he clung to that one blindly. He had to get home, home to ma and pa.

Their heads jerked up. Their ears had caught the rhythmic jingle of a wagon. They fell to the ground and clung flat to the side of a log. Over the crest of the hill came the top of a hat. A white face. Then shoulders in a blue shirt. A wagon drawn by two horses pulled into full view.

Big Boy and Bobo held their breath, waiting. Their eyes followed the wagon till it was lost in dust around a bend of the road.

"We gotta git home," said Big Boy.

"Ahm scared," said Bobo.

"C mon! Les keep t the fields."

They ran till they came to the cornfields. Then they went slower, for last year's corn stubbles bruised their feet.

They came in sight of a brickyard.

"Wait a minute," gasped Big Boy.

They stopped.

"Ahm goin on t mah home n yuh better go on t yos."

Bobo's eyes grew round.

"Ahm scared!"

"Yuh better go on!"

"Lemme go wid yuh; theyll ketch me . . ."

"Ef yuh kin git home mabbe yo folks kin hep yuh t git erway."

Big Boy started off. Bobo grabbed him.

"Lemme go wid yuh!"

Big Boy shook free.

"Ef yuh stay here theys gonna lynch yuh!" he yelled, running.

After he had gone about twenty-five yards he turned and looked; Bobo was flying through the woods like the wind.

Big Boy slowed when he came to the railroad. He wondered if he ought to go through the streets or down the track. He decided on the tracks. He could dodge a train better than a mob.

He trotted along the ties, looking ahead and back. His cheek itched, and he felt it. His hand came away smeared with blood. He wiped it nervously on his overalls.

When he came to his back fence he heaved himself over. He landed among a flock of startled chickens. A bantam rooster tried to spur him. He slipped and fell in front of the kitchen steps, grunting heavily. The ground was slick with greasy dishwater.

Panting, he stumbled through the doorway.

"Lawd, Big Boy, whuts wrong wid yuh?"

His mother stood gaping in the middle of the floor. Big Boy flopped wordlessly onto a stool, almost toppling over. Pots simmered on the stove. The kitchen smelled of food cooking.

"Whuts the matter, Big Boy?"

Mutely, he looked at her. Then he burst into tears. She came and felt the scratches on his face.

"Whut happened t yuh, Big Boy? Somebody been botherin yuh?"

"They after me, Ma! They after me . . ."

"Who!"

"Ah . . . Ah . . . We . . ."

"Big Boy, whuts wrong wid yuh?"

"He killed Lester n Buck," he muttered simply.

"Killed!"

"Yessum."

"Lester n Buck!"

"Yessum, Ma!"

"How killed?"

"He shot em, Ma!"

"Lawd Gawd in Heaven, have mercy on us all! This is mo trouble, mo trouble," she moaned, wringing her hands.

"N Ah killed im, Ma . . ."

She stared, trying to understand.

"Whut happened, Big Boy?"

"We tried t git our cloes from the tree . . ."

"Whut tree?"

"We wuz swimmin, Ma. N the white woman . . ."

"*White* woman? . . ."

"Yessum. She wuz at the swimmin hole . . ."

"Lawd have mercy! Ah knowed yuh boys wuz gonna keep on till yuh got into somethin like this!"

She ran into the hall.

"Lucy!"

"Mam?"

"C mere!"

"Mam?"

"C mere, Ah say!"

"Whutcha wan, Ma? Ahm sewin."

"Chile, will yuh c mere like Ah ast yuh?"

Lucy came to the door holding an unfinished apron in her hands. When she saw Big Boy's face she looked wildly at her mother.

"Whuts the matter?"

"Wheres Pa?"

"Hes out front, Ah reckon."

"Git im, quick!"

"Whuts the matter, Ma?"

"Go git yo Pa, Ah say!"

Lucy ran out. The mother sank into a chair, holding a dish rag. Suddenly, she sat up.

"Big Boy, Ah thought yuh wuz at school?"

Big Boy looked at the floor.

"How come yuh didnt go t school?"

"We went t the woods."

She sighed.

"Ah done done all Ah kin fer yuh, Big Boy. Only Gawd kin hep yuh now."

"Ma, don let em git me; don let em git me . . ."

His father came into the doorway. He stared at Big Boy, then at his wife.

"Whuts Big Boy inter now?" he asked sternly.

"Saul, Big Boys done gone n got inter trouble wid the white folks."

The old man's mouth dropped, and he looked from one to the other.

"Saul, we gotta git im erway from here."

"Open yo mouth n talk! Whut yuh been doin?" The old man gripped Big Boy's shoulders and peered at the scratches on his face.

"Me n Lester n Buck n Bobo wuz out on ol man Harveys place swimmin . . ."

"Saul, its a *white* woman!"

Big Boy winced. The old man compressed his lips and stared at his wife. Lucy gaped at her brother as though she had never seen him before.

"Whut happened? Cant yuh-all talk?" the old man thundered, with a certain helplessness in his voice.

"We wuz swimmin," Big Boy began, "n then a white woman comes up t the hole. We got up right erway t git our cloes sos we could git erway, n she started screamin. Our cloes wuz right by the tree where she wuz standin, n when we started to git em she jus screamed. We tol her we wanted our cloes . . . Yuh see, Pa, she wuz standin right *by* our cloes; n when we went t git em she jus screamed . . . Bobo got the cloes, n then he shot Lester . . ."

"*Who* shot Lester?"

"The white man."

"Whut white man?"

"Ah dunno, Pa. He wuz a soljer, n he had a rifle."

"A soljer?"

"Yessuh."

"A *soljer?*"

"Yessuh, Pa. A soljer."

The old man frowned.

"N then whut yuh-all do?"

"Waal, Buck said, 'Hes gotta gun!' N we started runnin. N then he shot Buck, n he fell in the swimmin hole. We didnt see im no mo . . . He wuz close on us then. He looked at the white woman n then he started t shoot Bobo. Ah grabbed the gun, n we started fightin. Bobo jumped on his back. He started beatin Bobo. Then Ah hit im wid the gun. Then he started at me n Ah shot im. Then we run . . ."

"Who seen?"

"Nobody."

"Wheres Bobo?"

"He went home."

"Anybody run after yuh-all?"

"Nawsuh."

"Yuh see anybody?"

"Nawsuh. Nobody but a white man. But he didnt see us."

"How long fo yuh-all lef the swimmin hole?"

"Little while ergo."

The old man nervously brushed his hand across his eyes and walked to the door. His lips moved, but no words came.

"Saul, whut we gonna do?"

"Lucy," began the old man, "go t Brother Sanders n tell im Ah said c mere; n go t Brother Jenkins n tell im Ah said c mere; n go t Elder Peters n tell im Ah said c mere. N don say nothin t nobody but whut Ah tol yuh. N when yuh git thu come straight back. Now go!"

Lucy dropped her apron across the back of a chair and ran down the steps. The mother bent over, crying and praying. The old man walked slowly over to Big Boy.

"Big Boy?"

Big Boy swallowed.

"Ahm talkin t yuh!"

"Yessuh."

"How come yuh didnt go t school this mawnin?"

"We went t the woods."

"Didnt yo ma send yuh t school?"

"Yessuh."

"How come yuh didnt go?"

"We went t the woods."

"Don yuh know thas wrong?"

"Yessuh."

"How come yuh go?"

Big Boy looked at his fingers, knotted them, and squirmed in his seat. "AHM TALKIN T YUH!"

His wife straightened up and said reprovingly:

"Saul!"

The old man desisted, yanking nervously at the shoulder straps of his overalls.

"How long wuz the woman there?"

"Not long."

"Wuz she young?"

"Yessuh. Lika gal."

"Did yuh-all say anythin t her?"

"Nawsuh. We jus said we wanted our cloes."

"N whut she say?"

"Nothin, Pa. She jus backed erway t the tree n screamed."

The old man stared, his lips trying to form a question.

"Big Boy, did yuh-all bother her?"

"Nawsuh, Pa. We didnt *touch* her."

"How long fo the white man come up?"

"Right erway."

"Whut he say?"

"Nothin. He jus cussed us."

Abruptly the old man left the kitchen.

"Ma, cant Ah go fo they ketches me?"

"Sauls doin whut he kin."

"Ma, Ma, Ah don wan em t ketch me . . ."

"Sauls doin whut he kin. Nobody but the good Lawd kin hep us now."

The old man came back with a shotgun and leaned it in a corner. Fascinatedly, Big Boy looked at it.

There was a knock at the front door.

"Liz, see whos there."

She went. They were silent, listening. They could hear her talking.

"Who there?"

"Me."

"Who?"

"Me, Brother Sanders."

"C mon in. Sauls waitin fer yuh."

Sanders paused in the doorway, smiling.

"Yuh sent fer me, Brother Morrison?"

"Brother Sanders, wes in deep trouble here."

Sanders came all the way into the kitchen.

"Yeah?"

"Big Boy done gone n killed a white man."

Sanders stopped short, then came forward, his face thrust out, his mouth open. His lips moved several times before he could speak.

"A *white* man?"

"They gonna kill me; they gonna kill me!" Big Boy cried, running to the old man.

"Saul, cant we git im erway somewhere?"

"Here now, take it easy; take it easy," said Sanders, holding Big Boy's wrists.

"They gonna kill me; they gonna lynch me!"

Big Boy slipped to the floor. They lifted him to a stool. His mother held him closely, pressing his head to her bosom.

"Whut we gonna do?" asked Sanders.

"Ah done sent fer Brother Jenkins n Elder Peters."

Sanders leaned his shoulders against the wall. Then as the full meaning of it all came to him, he exclaimed:

"Theys gonna git a mob! . . ." His voice broke off and his eyes fell on the shotgun.

Feet came pounding on the steps. They turned toward the door. Lucy

ran in crying. Jenkins followed. The old man met him in the middle of
the room, taking his hand.

"Wes in bad trouble here, Brother Jenkins. Big Boy's done gone n
killed a white man. Yuh-alls gotta hep me . . ."

Jenkins looked hard at Big Boy.

"Elder Peters says hes comin," said Lucy.

"When all this happen?" asked Jenkins.

"Near bout a hour ergo, now," said the old man.

"Whut we gonna do?" asked Jenkins.

"Ah wanna wait till Elder Peters come," said the old man helplessly.

"But we gotta work fas ef we gonna do anythin," said Sanders. "Well
git in trouble jus standin here like this."

Big Boy pulled away from his mother.

"Pa, lemme go now! Lemme me go now!"

"Be still, Big Boy!"

"Where kin yuh go?"

"Ah could ketch a freight!"

"Thas *sho* death!" said Jenkins. "Theyll be watchin em all!"

"Kin yuh-all hep me wid some money?" the old man asked.

They shook their heads.

"Saul, whut kin we do? Big Boy cant stay here."

There was another knock at the door.

The old man backed stealthily to the shotgun.

"Lucy go!"

Lucy looked at him, hesitating.

"Ah better go," said Jenkins.

It was Elder Peters. He came in hurriedly.

"Good evenin, everbody!"

"How yuh, Elder?"

"Good evenin."

"How yuh today?"

Peters looked around the crowded kitchen.

"Whuts the matter?"

"Elder, wes in deep trouble," began the old man. "Big Boy n some
mo boys . . ."

". . . Lester n Buck n Bobo . . ."

". . . wuz over on ol man Harveys place swimmin . . ."

"N he don like us niggers *none*," said Peters emphatically. He widened
his legs and put his thumbs in the armholes of his vest.

". . . n some white woman . . ."

"Yeah?" said Peters, coming closer.

". . . comes erlong n the boys tries t git their cloes where they done
lef em under a tree. Waal, she started screamin n all, see? Reckon she
thought the boys wuz after her. Then a white man in a soljer suit shoots
two of em . . ."

". . . Lester n Buck . . ."

"Huummm," said Peters. "Tha wuz ol man Harveys son."

"Harveys son?"

"Yuh mean the one tha wuz in the Army?"

"Yuh mean Jim?"

"Yeah," said Peters. "The papers said he wuz here fer a vacation from his regiment. N tha woman the boys saw wuz jus erbout his wife . . ."

They stared at Peters. Now that they knew what white person had been killed, their fears became definite.

"N whut else happened?"

"Big Boy shot the man . . ."

"Harveys *son?*"

"He had t, Elder. He wuz gonna shoot im ef he didnt . . ."

"Lawd!" said Peters. He looked around and put his hat back on.

"How long ergo wuz this?"

"Mighty near an hour now, Ah reckon."

"Do the white folks know yit?"

"Don know, Elder."

"Yuh-all better git this boy outta here right now," said Peters. "Cause ef yuh don theres gonna be a lynchin . . ."

"Where kin Ah go, Elder?" Big Boy ran up to him.

They crowded around Peters. He stood with his legs wide apart, looking up at the ceiling.

"Maybe we kin hide im in the church till he kin git erway," said Jenkins.

Peters' lips flexed.

"Naw, Brother, thall never do! Theyll git im there sho. N anyhow, ef they ketch im there itll ruin us all. We gotta git the boy outta town . . ."

Sanders went up to the old man.

"Listen," he said in a whisper. "Mah son, Will, the one whut drives fer the Magnolia Express Comny, is taking a truck o goods t Chicawgo in the mawnin. If we kin hide Big Boy somewhere till then, we kin put im on the truck . . ."

"Pa, please, lemme go wid Will when he goes in the mawnin," Big Boy begged.

The old man stared at Sanders.

"Yuh reckon thas safe?"

"It's the only thing yuh *kin* do," said Peters.

"But where we gonna hide im till then?"

"Whut time you boy leavin out in the mawnin?"

"At six."

They were quiet, thinking. The water kettle on the stove sang.

"Pa, Ah knows where Will passes erlong wid the truck out on Bullards Road. Ah kin hide in one of them ol kilns . . ."

"Where?"

"In one of them kilns we built . . ."

"But theyll git yuh there," wailed the mother.

"But there ain no place else fer im t go."

"Theres some holes big ernough fer me t git in n stay till Will comes erlong," said Big Boy. "Please Pa, lemme go fo they ketches me . . ."

"Let im go!"

"Please, Pa . . ."

The old man breathed heavily.

"Lucy, git his things!"

"Saul, theyll git im out there!" wailed the mother, grabbing Big Boy. Peters pulled her away.

"Sister Morrison, ef yuh don let im go n git erway from here hes gonna be caught shos theres a Gawd in Heaven!"

Lucy came running with Big Boy's shoes and pulled them on his feet. The old man thrust a battered hat on his head. The mother went to the stove and dumped the skillet of corn pone into her apron. She wrapped it, and unbuttoning Big Boy's overalls, pushed it into his bosom.

"Heres somethin fer yuh t eat; n pray, Big Boy, cause thas all anybody kin do now . . ."

Big Boy pulled to the door, his mother clinging to him.

"Let im go, Sister Morrison!"

"Run fas, Big Boy!"

Big Boy raced across the yard, scattering the chickens. He paused at the fence and hollered back:

"Tell Bobo where Ahm hidin n tell im t c mon!"

4

He made for the railroad, running straight toward the sunset. He held his left hand tightly over his heart, holding the hot pone of corn bread there. At times he stumbled over the ties, for his shoes were tight and hurt his feet. His throat burned from thirst; he had had no water since noon.

He veered off the track and trotted over the crest of a hill, following Bullard's Road. His feet slipped and slid in the dust. He kept his eyes straight ahead, fearing every clump of shrubbery, every tree. He wished it were night. If he could only get to the kilns without meeting anyone. Suddenly a thought came to him like a blow. He recalled hearing the old folks tell tales of blood-hounds, and fear made him run slower. None of them had thought of that. Spose blood-houns wuz put on his trail? Lawd! Spose a whole pack of em, foamin n howlin, tore im t pieces? He went limp and his feet dragged. Yeah, thas whut they wuz gonna send after im, bloodhouns! N then thered be no way fer im t dodge! Why hadnt Pa let him take tha shotgun? He stopped. He oughta go back n git tha shotgun. And then when the mob came he would take some with him.

In the distance he heard the approach of a train. It jarred him back to a sharp sense of danger. He ran again, his big shoes sopping up and down in the dust. He was tired and his lungs were bursting from running. He wet his lips, wanting water. As he turned from the road across a plowed field he heard the train roaring at his heels. He ran faster, gripped in terror.

He was nearly there now. He could see the black clay on the sloping hillside. Once inside a kiln he would be safe. For a little while, at least. He thought of the shotgun again. If he only had something! Someone to talk to . . . Thas right! Bobo! Bobod be wid im. Hed almost fergot Bobo. Bobod bringa gun; he knowed he would. N tergether they could kill the whole mob. Then in the mawning theyd git inter Will's truck n go far erway, t Chicawgo . . .

He slowed to a walk, looking back and ahead. A light wind skipped over the grass. A beetle lit on his cheek and he brushed it off. Behind the dark pines hung a red sun. Two bats flapped against that sun. He shivered, for he was growing cold; the sweat on his body was drying.

He stopped at the foot of the hill, trying to choose between two patches of black kilns high above him. He went to the left, for there lay the ones he, Bobo, Lester, and Buck had dug only last week. He looked around again; the landscape was bare. He climbed the embankment and stood before a row of black pits sinking four and five feet deep into the earth. He went to the largest and peered in. He stiffened when his ears caught the sound of a whir. He ran back a few steps and poised on his toes. Six foot of snake slid out of the pit and went into coil. Big Boy looked around wildly for a stick. He ran down the slope, peering into the grass. He stumbled over a tree limb. He picked it up and tested it by striking it against the ground.

Warily, he crept back up the slope, his stick poised. When about seven feet from the snake he stopped and waved the stick. The coil grew tighter, the whir sounded louder, and a flat head reared to strike. He went to the right, and the flat head followed him, the blue-black tongue darting forth; he went to the left, and the flat head followed him there too.

He stopped, teeth clenched. He had to kill this snake. Jus had t kill im! This wuz the safest pit on the hillside. He waved the stick again, looking at the snake before, thinking of a mob behind. The flat head reared higher. With stick over shoulder, he jumped in, swinging: The stick sang through the air, catching the snake on the side of the head, sweeping him out of coil. There was a brown writhing mass. Then Big Boy was upon him, pounding blows home, one on top of the other. He fought viciously, his eyes red, his teeth bared in a snarl. He beat till the snake lay still; then he stomped it with his heel, grinding its head into the dirt.

He stopped, limp, wet. The corners of his lips were white with spittle. He spat and shuddered.

Cautiously, he went to the hole and peered. He longed for a match. He imagined whole nests of them in there waiting. He put the stick into the hole and waved it around. Stooping, he peered again. It mus be awright. He looked over the hillside, his eyes coming back to the dead snake. Then he got to his knees and backed slowly into the hole.

When inside he felt there must be snakes all about him, ready to strike. It seemed he could see and feel them there, waiting tensely in coil. In the dark he imagined long white fangs ready to sink into his neck, his side, his legs. He wanted to come out, but kept still. Shucks, he told himself, ef there wuz any snakes in here they sho woulda done bit me by now. Some of his fear left, and he relaxed.

With elbows on the ground and chin on palms, he settled. The clay was cold to his knees and thighs, but his bosom was kept warm by the hot pone of corn bread. His thirst returned and he longed for a drink. He was hungry, too. But he did not want to eat the corn pone. Naw, not now. Mabbe after erwhile, after Bobod came. Then theyd both eat the corn pone.

The view from his hole was fringed by the long tufts of grass. He could see all the way to Bullard's Road, and even beyond. The wind was blowing, and in the east the first touch of dusk was rising. Every now and then a bird floated past, a spot of wheeling black printed against the sky. Big Boy sighed, shifted his weight, and chewed at a blade of grass. A wasp droned. He heard number nine, far away and mournful.

The train made him remember how they had dug these kilns on long hot summer days, how they had made boilers out of big tin cans, filled them with water, fixed stoppers for steam, cemented them in holes with wet clay, and built fires under them. He recalled how they had danced and yelled when a stopper blew out of a boiler, letting out a big spout of steam and a shrill whistle. There were times when they had the whole hillside blazing and smoking. Yeah, yuh see, Big Boy wuz Casey Jones n wuz speedin it down the gleamin rails of the Southern Pacific. Bobo had number two on the Santa Fe. Buck wuz on the Illinoy Central. Lester the Nickel Plate. Lawd, how they shelved the wood in! The boiling water would almost jar the cans loose from the clay. More and more pineknots and dry leaves would be piled under the cans. Flames would grow so tall they would have to shield their eyes. Sweat would pour off their faces. Then, suddenly, a peg would shoot high into the air, and

Pssseeeezzzzzzzzzzzzzzzzzzzzzz . . .

Big Boy sighed and stretched out his arm, quenching the flames and scattering the smoke. Why didnt Bobo c mon? He looked over the fields; there was nothing but dying sunlight. His mind drifted back to the kilns. He remembered the day when Buck, jealous of his winning, had tried to smash his kiln. Yeah, that ol sonofabitch! Naw, Lawd! He didnt go t say that. Whut wuz he thinkin erbout? Cussin the dead! Yeah, po ol Buck wuz dead now. N Lester too. Yeah, it wuz awright fer Buck t smash his kiln. Sho. N he wished he hadnt socked ol Buck so hard tha day. He wuz sorry fer Buck now. N he sho wished he hadnt cussed po ol Bucks ma, neither. Tha wuz sinful! Mabbe Gawd would git im fer tha? But he didnt go t do it! Po Buck! Po Lester! Hed never treat anybody like tha ergin, never . . .

Dusk was slowly deepening. Somewhere, he could not tell exactly where, a cricket took up a fitful song. The air was growing soft and heavy. He looked over the fields, longing for Bobo . . .

He shifted his body to ease the cold damp of the ground, and thought back over the day. Yeah, hed been dam right erbout not wantin t go swimmin. N ef hed followed his right min hed neverve gone n got inter all this trouble. At first hed said naw. But shucks, somehow hed just went on wid the res. Yeah, he shoulda went on to school tha mawnin, like Ma told im t do. But, hell, who wouldnt git tireda awways drivin a guy t school! Tha wuz the big trou awways drivin a guy t school. He wouldnt be in all this trouble now ef it wuznt fer that Gawddam school! Impatiently, he took the grass out of his mouth and threw it away, demolishing the little red school house . . .

Yeah, ef they had all kept still n quiet when tha ol white woman showed-up, mabbe shedve went on off. But yuh never kin tell erabout these white folks. Mabbe she wouldntve went. Mabbe tha white man woulda killed all of em! All *fo* of em! Yeah, yuh never kin tell erbout white folks. Then, ergin, mabbe tha white woman woulda went on off n laffed. Yeah, mabbe tha white woman woulda said: *Yuh nigger bastards git t hell outta here! Yuh know Gawddam well yuh don berlong here!* N then they woulda grabbed their cloes n run like all hell . . . He blinked the white man away. Where wuz Bobo? Why didnt he hurry up n c mon?

He jerked another blade and chewed. Yeah, ef pa had only let im have tha shotgun! He could stan off a whole mob wid a shotgun. He looked at the ground as he turned a shotgun over in his hands. Then he leveled it at an advancing white man. *Boooom!* The man curled up. Another came. He reloaded quickly, and let him have what the other had got. He too curled up. Then another came. He got the same medicine. Then the whole mob swirled around him, and he blazed away, getting as many as he could. They closed in; but, by Gawd, he had done his part, hadnt he? N the newspapersd say: NIGGER KILLS DOZEN OF MOB BEFO LYNCHED! Er mabbe theyd say: TRAPPED NIGGER SLAYS TWENTY BEFO KILLED! He smiled a little. Tha wouldnt be so bad, would it? Blinking the newspaper away, he looked over the fields. Where wuz Bobo? Why didnt he hurry up n c mon?

He shifted, trying to get a crick out of his legs. Shucks, he wuz gittin tireda this. N it wuz almos dark now. Yeah, there wuz a little bittie star way over yonder in the eas. Mabbe tha white man wuznt dead? Mabbe they wuznt even lookin fer im? Mabbe he could go back home now? Naw, better wait erwhile. Thad be bes. But, Lawd, ef he only had some water! He could hardly swallow, his throat was so dry. Gawddam them white folks! Thas all they wuz good fer, t run a nigger down lika rabbit! Yeah, they git yuh in a corner n then they let yuh have it. A thousan of em! He shivered, for the cold of the clay was chilling his bones. Lawd, spose they foun im here in this hole? N wid nobody t hep im? . . . But ain no use thinkin erbout tha; wait till trouble come fo yuh start fightin it. But ef tha mob came one by one hed wipe em all out. Clean up the whole bunch. He caught one by the neck and choked him long and hard, choked him till his tongue and eyes popped out. Then he jumped upon his chest and stomped him like he had stomped that snake. When he had finished with one, another came. He choked him too. Choked till he sank slowly to the ground, gasping . . .

"Hoalo!"

Big Boy snatched his fingers from the white man's neck and looked over the fields. He saw nobody. Had someone spied him? He was sure that somebody had hollered. His heart pounded. But, shucks, nobody couldnt see im here in this hole . . . But mabbe they seen im when he wuz comin n had laid low n wuz now closin in on im! Praps they wuz signalin fer the others? Yeah, they wuz creepin up on im! Mabbe he oughta git up n run . . . Oh! Mabbe tha wuz Bobo! Yeah, Bobo! He oughta clim out n see ef Bobo wuz lookin fer im . . . He stiffened.

"Hoalo!"

"Hoalo!"

"Wheres yuh?"

"Over here on Bullards Road!"

"C mon over!"

"Awright!"

He heard footsteps. Then voices came again, low and far away this time.

"Seen anybody?"

"Naw. Yuh?"

"Naw."

"Yuh reckon they got erway?"

"Ah dunno. Its hard t tell."

"Gawddam them sonofabitchin niggers!"

"We oughta kill ever black bastard in this country!"

"Waal, Jim got two of em, anyhow."

"But Bertha said there wuz *fo!*"

"Where in hell they hidin?"

"She said one of em wuz named Big Boy or somethin like tha."

"We went t his shack lookin fer im."

"Yeah?"

"But we didnt fin im."

"These niggers stick tergether; they don never tell on each other."

"We looked all thu the shack n couldnt fin hide ner hair of im. Then we drove the ol woman n man out n set the shack on fire . . ."

"Jeesus! Ah wished Ah coulda been there!"

"Yuh shoulda heard the ol nigger woman howl . . ."

"Hoalo!"

"C mon over!"

Big Boy eased to the edge and peeped. He saw a white man with a gun slung over his shoulder running down the slope. Wuz they gonna searcli the hill? Lawd, there wuz no way fer im t git erway now; he wuz caught! He shoulda knowed theyd git im here. N he didnt hava thing, notta thing t fight wid. Yeah, soon as the blood-houns came theyd fin im. Lawd, have mercy! Theyd lynch im right here on the hill . . . Theyd git im n tie im t a stake n burn im erlive! Lawd! Nobody but the good Lawd could hep im now, nobody . . .

He heard more feet running. He nestled deeper. His chest ached. Nobody but the good Lawd could hep now. They wuz crowdin all round im n when they hada big crowd theyd close in on im. Then itd be over . . . The good Lawd would have t hep im, cause nobody could hep im now, nobody . . .

And then he went numb when he remembered Bobo. Spose Bobod come now? Hed be caught sho! Both of em would be caught! They'd make Bobo tell where he wuz! Bobo oughta not try to come now. Somebody oughta tell im . . . But there wuz nobody; there wuz no way . . .

He eased slowly back to the opening. There was a large group of men. More were coming. Many had guns. Some had coils of rope slung over shoulders.

"Ah tell yuh they still here, somewhere . . ."

"But we looked all over!"

"What t hell! Wouldnt do t let em git erway!"

"Naw. Ef they git erway notta woman in this town would be safe."

"Say, whuts tha yuh got?"

"Er pillar."

"Fer whut?"

"Feathers, fool!"

"Chris! Thisll be hot ef we kin ketch them niggers!"

"Ol Anderson said he wuz gonna bringa barrela tar!"

"Ah got some gasoline in mah car ef yuh need it."

Big Boy had no feelings now. He was waiting. He did not wonder if they were coming after him. He just waited. He did not wonder about Bobo. He rested his cheek against the cold clay, waiting.

A dog barked. He stiffened. It barked again. He balled himself into a knot at the bottom of the hole, waiting. Then he heard the patter of dog feet.

"Look!"

"Whuts he got?"

"It's a snake!"

"Yeah, the dogs foun a snake!"

"Gee, its a big one!"

"Shucks, Ah wish he could fin one of them sonofabitchin niggers!"

The voices sank to low murmurs. Then he heard number twelve, its bell tolling and whistle crying as it slid along the rails. He flattened himself against the clay. Someone was singing:

> "*We'll hang ever nigger t a sour apple tree . . .*"

When the song ended there was hard laughter. From the other side of the hill he heard the dog barking furiously. He listened. There was more than one dog now. There were many and they were barking their throats out.

"Hush, Ah hear them dogs!"

"When theys barkin like tha theys foun somethin!"

"Here they come over the hill!"

"WE GOT IM! WE GOT IM!"

There came a roar. Tha mus be Bobo! tha mus be Bobo . . . In spite of his fear, Big Boy looked. The road, and half of the hillside across the road, were covered with men. A few were at the top of the hill, stenciled against the sky. He could see dark forms moving up the slopes. They were yelling.

"By Gawd, we got im!"

"C mon!"

"Where is he?"

"Theyre bringin im over the hill!"

"Ah got a rope fer im!"

"Say, somebody go n git the others!"

"Where is he? Cant we see im, Mister?"

"They say Berthas comin, too."

"Jack! Jack! Don leave me! Ah wanna see im!"

"Theyre bringin im over the hill, sweetheart!"

"AH WANNA BE THE FIRST PUT A ROPE ON THA BLACK BASTARDS NECK!"

"Les start the fire!"

"Heat the tar!"

"Ah got some chains t chain im."

"Bring im over this way!"

"Chris, Ah wished Ah hada drink . . ."

Big Boy saw men moving over the hill. Among them was a long dark spot. Tha mus be Bobo; tha mus be Bobo theys carryin . . . They'll git im here. He oughta git up n run. He clamped his teeth and ran his hand across his forehead, bringing it away wet. He tried to swallow, but could not; his throat was dry.

They had started the song again:

> "*We'll hang ever nigger t a sour apple tree . . .*"

There were women singing now. Their voices made the song round and full. Song waves rolled over the top of pine trees. The sky sagged low, heavy with clouds. Wind was rising. Sometimes cricket cries cut surprisingly across the mob song. A dog had gone to the utmost top of the hill. At each lull of the song his howl floated full into the night.

Big Boy shrank when he saw the first tall flame light the hillside. Would they see im here? Then he remembered you could not see into the dark if you were standing in the light. As flames leaped higher he saw two men rolling a barrel up the slope.

"Say, gimme a han here, will yuh?"

"Awright, heave!"

"C mon! Straight up! Git t the other end!"

"Ah got the feathers here in this pillar!"

"BRING SOME MO WOOD!"

Big Boy could see the barrel surrounded by flames. The mob fell back, forming a dark circle. Theyd fin im here! He had a wild impulse to climb out and fly across the hills. But his legs would not move. He stared hard, trying to find Bobo. His eyes played over a long dark spot near the fire. Fanned by wind, flames leaped higher. He jumped. That dark spot had moved. Lawd, thas Bobo; thas Bobo . . .

He smelt the scent of tar, faint at first, then stronger. The wind brought it full into his face, then blew it away. His eyes burned and he rubbed them with his knuckles. He sneezed.

"LES GIT SOURVINEERS!"

He saw the mob close in around the fire. Their faces were hard and sharp in the light of the flames. More men and women were coming over the hill. The long dark spot was smudged out.

"Everybody git back!"

"Look! Hes gotta finger!"

"C MON! GIT THE GALS BACK FROM THE FIRE!"

"Hes got one of his ears, see?"

"Whuts the matter!"

"A woman fell out! Fainted, Ah reckon . . ."

The stench of tar permeated the hillside. The sky was black and the wind was blowing hard.

"HURRY UP N BURN THE NIGGER FO IT RAINS!"

Big Boy saw the mob fall back, leaving a small knot of men about the fire. Then, for the first time, he had a full glimpse of Bobo.

A black body flashed in the light. Bobo was struggling, twisting; they were binding his arms and legs.

When he saw them tilt the barrel he stiffened. A scream quivered. He knew the tar was on Bobo. The mob fell back. He saw a tardrenched body glistening and turning.

"THE BASTARDS GOT IT!"

There was a sudden quiet. Then he shrank violently as the wind carried, like a flurry of snow, a widening spiral of white feathers into the night. The flames leaped tall as the trees. The scream came again. Big Boy trembled and looked. The mob was running down the slopes, leaving the fire clear. Then he saw a writhing white mass cradled in yellow flame, and heard screams, one on top of the other, each shriller and shorter than the last. The mob was quiet now, standing still, looking up the slopes at the writhing white mass gradually growing black, growing black in a cradle of yellow flame.

"PO ON MO GAS!"

"Gimme a lif, will yuh!"

The men were struggling, carrying between them a heavy can. They set it down, tilted it, leaving it so that the gas would trickle down to the hollowed earth around the fire.

Big Boy slid back into the hole, his face buried in clay. He had no feelings now, no fears. He was numb, empty, as though all blood had been drawn from him. Then his muscles flexed taut when he heard a faint patter. A tiny stream of cold water seeped to his knees, making him push back to a drier spot. He looked up; rain was beating in the grass.

"Its rainin!"

"C mon, les git t town!"

". . . don worry, when the fire git thu wid im hell be gone . . ."

"Wait, Charles! Don leave me; its slippery here . . ."

"Ahll take some of yuh ladies back in mah car . . ."

Big Boy heard the dogs barking again, this time closer. Running feet pounded past. Cold water chilled his ankles. He could hear raindrops steadily hissing.

Now a dog was barking at the mouth of the hole, barking furiously, sensing a presence there. He balled himself into a knot and clung to the bottom, his knees and shins buried in water. The bark came louder. He heard paws scraping and felt the hot scent of dog breath on his face. Green eyes glowed and drew nearer as the barking, muffled by the closeness of the hole, beat upon his eardrums. Backing till his shoulders pressed against the clay, he held his breath. He pushed out his hands, his fingers stiff. The dog yawped louder, advancing, his bark rising sharp and thin. Big Boy rose to his knees, his hands before him. Then he flattened out still more against the bottom, breathing lungsful of hot dog scent, breathing it slowly, hard, but evenly. The dog came closer, bringing hotter dog scent. Big Boy could go back no more. His knees were slipping and slopping in the water. He braced himself, ready. Then, he never exactly knew how—he never knew whether he had lunged or the dog had lunged—they were together, rolling in the water. The green eyes were beneath him, between his legs. Dognails bit into his arms. His knees slipped backward and he landed full on the dog; the dog's breath left in a heavy gasp. Instinctively, he fumbled for the throat as he felt the dog twisting between his knees. The dog snarled, long and low, as though gathering strength. Big Boy's hands traveled swiftly over the dog's back, groping for the throat. He felt dognails again and saw green eyes, but his fingers had found the throat. He choked, feeling his fingers sink; he choked, throwing back his head and stiffening his arms. He felt the dog's body heave, felt dognails digging into his loins. With strength flowing from fear, he closed his fingers, pushing his full weight on the dog's throat. The dog heaved again, and lay still . . . Big Boy heard the sound of his own breathing filling the hole, and heard shouts and footsteps above him going past.

For a long, long time he held the dog, held it long after the last footstep had died out, long after the rain had stopped.

5

Morning found him still on his knees in a puddle of rainwater, staring at the stiff body of a dog. As the air brightened he came to himself slowly. He held still for a long time, as though waking from a dream, as though trying to remember.

The chug of a truck came over the hill. He tried to crawl to the opening. His knees were stiff and a thousand needle-like pains shot from the bottom of his feet to the calves of his legs. Giddiness made his eyes blur. He pulled up and looked. Through brackish light he saw Will's truck standing some twenty-five yards away, the engine running. Will stood on the runningboard, looking over the slopes of the hill.

Big Boy scuffled out, falling weakly in the wet grass. He tried to call to Will, but his dry throat would make no sound. He tried again.

"Will!"

Will heard, answering:

"Big Boy, c mon!"

He tried to run, and fell. Will came, meeting him in the tall grass.

"C mon," Will said, catching his arm.

They struggled to the truck.

"Hurry up!" said Will, pushing him onto the runningboard.

Will pushed back a square trapdoor which swung above the back of the driver's seat. Big Boy pulled through, landing with a thud on the bottom. On hands and knees he looked around in the semi-darkness.

"Wheres Bobo?"

Big Boy stared.

"Wheres Bobo?"

"They got im."

"When?"

"Las night."

"The mob?"

Big Boy pointed in the direction of a charred sapling on the slope of the opposite hill. Will looked. The trapdoor fell. The engine purred, the gears whined, and the truck lurched forward over the muddy road, sending Big Boy on his side.

For a while he lay as he had fallen, on his side, too weak to move. As he felt the truck swing around a curve he straightened up and rested his back against a stack of wooden boxes. Slowly, he began to make out objects in the darkness. Through two long cracks fell thin blades of daylight. The floor was of smooth steel, and cold to his thighs. Splinters and bits of sawdust danced with the rumble of the truck. Each time they swung around a curve he was pulled over the floor; he grabbed at corners of boxes to steady himself. Once he heard the crow of a rooster. It made him think of home, of ma and pa. He thought he remembered hearing somewhere that the house had burned, but could not remember where . . . It all seemed unreal now.

He was tired. He dozed, swaying with the lurch. Then he jumped awake. The truck was running smoothly, on gravel. Far away he heard two short blasts from the Buckeye Lumber Mill. Unconsciously, the thought sang through his mind: It six erclock . . .

The trapdoor swung in. Will spoke through a corner of his mouth.

"How yuh comin?"

"Awright."

"How they git Bobo?"

"He wuz comin over the hill."

"Whut they do?"

"They burnt im . . . Will, Ah wan some water; mah throats like fire . . .

"Well git some when we pass a fillin station."

Big Boy leaned back and dozed. He jerked awake when the truck stopped. He heard Will get out. He wanted to peep through the trapdoor, but was afraid. For a moment, the wild fear he had known in the hole came back. Spose theyd search n fin im? He quieted when he heard Will's footstep on the runningboard. The trapdoor pushed in. Will's hat came through, dripping.

"Take it, quick!"

Big Boy grabbed, spilling water into his face. The truck lurched. He drank. Hard cold lumps of brick rolled into his hot stomach. A dull pain made him bend over. His intestines seemed to be drawing into a tight knot. After a bit it eased, and he sat up, breathing softly.

The truck swerved. He blinked his eyes. The blades of daylight had turned brightly golden. The sun had risen.

The truck sped over the asphalt miles, sped northward, jolting him, shaking out of his bosom the crumbs of corn bread, making them dance with the splinters and sawdust in the golden blades of sunshine.

He turned on his side and slept.

Eudora Welty
1909–

KEELA, THE OUTCAST INDIAN MAIDEN

ONE MORNING in summertime, when all his sons and daughters were off picking plums and Little Lee Roy was all alone, sitting on the porch and only listening to the screech owls away down in the woods, he had a surprise.

First he heard white men talking. He heard two white men coming up the path from the highway. Little Lee Roy ducked his head and held his breath; then he patted all around back of him for his crutches. The chickens all came out from under the house and waited attentively on the steps.

The men came closer. It was the young man who was doing all the talking. But when they got through the fence, Max, the older man, interrupted him. He tapped him on the arm and pointed his thumb toward Little Lee Roy.

He said, "Bud? Yonder he is."

But the younger man kept straight on talking, in an explanatory voice.

"Bud?" said Max again. "Look, Bud, yonder's the only little club-footed nigger man was ever around Cane Springs. Is he the party?"

They came nearer and nearer to Little Lee Roy and then stopped and stood there in the middle of the yard. But the young man was so excited he did not seem to realize that they had arrived anywhere. He was only about twenty years old, very sunburned. He talked constantly, making only one gesture—raising his hand stiffly and then moving it a little to one side.

"They dressed it in a red dress, and it ate chickens alive," he said. "I sold tickets and I thought it was worth a dime, honest. They gimme a piece of paper with the thing wrote off I had to say. That was easy, 'Keela, the Outcast Indian Maiden!' I call it out through a pasteboard megaphone. Then ever' time it was fixin' to eat a live chicken, I blowed the sireen out front."

"Just tell me, Bud," said Max, resting back on the heels of his perforated tan-and-white sports shoes, "Is this nigger the one? Is that him sittin' there?"

Little Lee Roy sat huddled and blinking, a smile on his face. . . . But the young man did not look his way.

"Just took the job that time. I didn't mean to—I mean, I meant to go to Port Arthur because my brother was on a boat," he said. "My name is Steve, mister. But I worked with this show selling tickets for three months, and I never would have knowed it was like that if it hadn't been for that man." He arrested his gesture.

"Yeah, what man?" said Max in a hopeless voice.

Little Lee Roy was looking from one white man to the other, excited almost beyond respectful silence. He trembled all over, and a look of amazement and sudden life came into his eyes.

"Two years ago," Steve was saying impatiently. "And he was travelin' through Texas in those ole trucks.—See, the reason nobody ever come clost to it before was they give it a iron bar this long. And tole it if anybody come near, to shake the bar good at 'em, like this. But it couldn't say nothin'. Turned out they'd tole it it couldn't say nothin' to anybody ever, so it just kind of mumbled and growled, like a animal."

"Hee! hee!" This from Little Lee Roy, softly.

"Tell me again," said Max, and just from his look you could tell that everybody knew old Max. "Somehow I can't get it straight in my mind. Is this the boy? Is this little nigger boy the same as this Keela, the Outcast Indian Maiden?"

Up on the porch, above them, Little Lee Roy gave Max a glance full of hilarity, and then bent the other way to catch Steve's next words.

"Why, if anybody was to even come near it or even bresh their shoulder against the rope it'd growl and take on and shake its iron rod. When it would eat the live chickens it'd growl somethin' awful—you ought to heard it."

"Hee! hee!" It was a soft, almost incredulous laugh that began to escape from Little Lee Roy's tight lips, a little mew of delight.

"They'd throw it this chicken, and it would reach out an' grab it. Would sort of rub over the chicken's neck with its thumb an' press on it good, an' then it would bite its head off."

"O.K.," said Max.

"It skint back the feathers and stuff from the neck and sucked the the blood. But ever'body said it was still alive." Steve drew closer to Max and fastened his light-colored troubled eyes on his face.

"O.K."

"Then it would pull the feathers out easy and neat-like, awful fast, an' growl the whole time, kind of moan, an' then it would commence to eat all the white meat. I'd go in an' look at it. I reckon I seen it a thousand times."

"That was you, boy?" Max demanded of Little Lee Roy unexpectedly.

But Little Lee Roy could only say, "Hee! hee!" The little man at the head of the steps where the chickens sat, one on each step, and the two men facing each other below made a pyramid.

Steve stuck his hand out for silence. "They said—I mean, I said it, out front through the megaphone, I said it myself, that it wouldn't eat nothin' but only live meat. It was supposed to be a Indian woman, see, in this red dress an' stockin's. It didn't have on no shoes, so when it drug its foot ever'body could see. . . . When it come to the chicken's heart, it would eat that too, real fast, and the heart would still be jumpin'."

"Wait a second, Bud," said Max briefly. "Say, boy, is this white man here crazy?"

Little Lee Roy burst into hysterical, deprecatory giggles. He said, "Naw suh, don't think so." He tried to catch Steve's eye, seeking appreciation, crying, "Naw suh, don't think he crazy, mista."

Steve gripped Max's arm. "Wait! Wait!" he cried anxiously. "You ain't listenin'. I want to tell you about it. You didn't catch my name—Steve. You never did hear about that little nigger—all that happened to him? Lived in Cane Springs, Miss'ippi?"

"Bud," said Max, disengaging himself, "I don't hear anything. I got a juke box, see, so I don't have to listen."

"Look—I was really the one," said Steve more patiently, but nervously, as if he had been slowly breaking bad news. He walked up and down the bare-swept ground in front of Little Lee Roy's porch, along the row of princess feathers and snow-on-the-mountain. Little Lee Roy's turning head followed him. "I was the one—that's what I'm tellin' you."

"Suppose I was to listen to what every dope comes in Max's Place got to say, I'd be nuts," said Max.

"It's all me, see," said Steve. "I know that. I was the one was the cause for it goin' on an' on an' not bein' found out—such an awful thing. It was me, what I said out front through the megaphone."

He stopped still and stared at Max in despair.

"Look," said Max. He sat on the steps, and the chickens hopped off. "I know I ain't nobody but Max. I got Max's Place. I only run a place, understand, fifty yards down the highway, liquor buried twenty feet from the premises, and no trouble yet. I ain't ever been up here before. I don't claim to been anywhere. People come to my place. Now. You're the hitchhiker. You're tellin' me, see. You claim a lot of information. If I don't get it I don't get it and I ain't complainin' about it, see. But I think you're nuts, and did from the first. I only come up here with you because I figured you's crazy."

"Maybe you don't believe I remember every word of it even now," Steve was saying gently. "I think about it at night—that an' drums on the midway. You ever hear drums on the midway?" He paused and stared politely at Max and Little Lee Roy.

"Yeh," said Max.

"Don't it make you feel sad? I remember how the drums was goin' and I was yellin', 'Ladies and gents! Do not try to touch Keela, the Outcast Indian Maiden—she will only beat your brains out with her iron rod, and eat them alive!' " Steven waved his arm gently in the air, and Little Lee Roy drew back and squealed. " 'Do not go near her, ladies and gents! I'm warnin' you!' So nobody ever did. Nobody ever come near her. Until that man."

"Sure," said Max. "That fella." He shut his eyes.

"Afterwards when he come up so bold, I remembered seein' him walk up an' buy the ticket an' go in the tent. I'll never forget that man as long as I live. To me he's a sort of—well——"

"Hero," said Max.

"I wish I could remember what he looked like. Seem like he was a tallish man with a sort of white face. Seem like he had bad teeth, but I may be wrong. I remember he frowned a lot. Kept frownin'. Whenever he'd buy a ticket, why, he'd frown."

"Ever seen him since?" asked Max cautiously, still with his eyes closed. "Ever hunt him up?"

"No, never did," said Steve. Then he went on. "He'd frown an' buy a ticket ever' day we was in these two little smelly towns in Texas, sometimes three-four times a day, whether it was fixin' to eat a chicken or not."

"O.K., so he gets in the tent," said Max.

"Well, what the man finally done was, he walked right up to the lit-tle stand where it was tied up and laid his hand out open there and said, 'Come here,' real low and quick, that-a-way."

Steve laid his open hand on Little Lee Roy's porch and held it there, frowning in concentration.

"I get it," said Max. "He'd caught on it was a fake."

Steve straightened up. "So ever'body yelled to git away, git away," he continued, his voice rising, "because it was growlin' an' carryin' on an' shakin' its iron bar like they tole it. When I heard all that com-motion—boy! I was scared."

"You didn't know it was a fake."

Steve was silent for a moment, and Little Lee Roy held his breath, for fear everything was all over.

"Look," said Steve finally, his voice trembling. "I guess I was sup-posed to feel bad like this, and you wasn't. I wasn't supposed to ship out on that boat from Port Arthur and all like that. This other had to happen to me—not you all. Feelin' responsible. You'll be O.K., mister, but I won't. I feel awful about it. That poor little old thing."

"Look, you got him right here," said Max quickly. "See him? Use your eyes. He's O.K., ain't he? Looks O.K. to me. It's just you. You're nuts, is all."

"You know—when that man laid out his open hand on the boards, why, it just let go the iron bar," continued Steve, "let it fall down like that—bang—and act like it didn't know what to do. Then it drug itself over to where the fella was standin' an' leaned down an' grabbed holt onto that white man's hand as tight as it could an' cried like a baby. It didn't want to hit him!"

"Hee! hee! hee!"

"No sir, it didn't want to hit him. You know what it wanted?"

Max shook his head.

"It wanted him to help it. So the man said, 'Do you wanta get out of this place, whoever you are?' An' it never answered—none of us knowed it could talk—but it just wouldn't let that man's hand a-loose. It hung on, cryin' like a baby. So the man says, 'Well, wait here till I come back.' "

"Uh-huh?" said Max.

"Went off an' come back with the sheriff. Took us all to jail. But just the man owned the show and his son got took to the pen. They said I could go free. I kep' tellin' 'em I didn't know it wouldn't hit me with the iron bar an' kep' tellin' 'em I didn't know it could tell what you was sayin' to it."

"Yeh, guess you told 'em," said Max.

"By that time I felt bad. Been feelin' bad ever since. Can't hold onto a job or stay in one place for nothin' in the world. They made it stay in jail to see if it could talk or not, and the first night it wouldn't say nothin'. Some time it cried. And they undressed it an' found out it wasn't no outcast Indian woman a-tall. It was a little club-footed nigger man."

"Hee! hee!"

"You mean it was this boy here—yeh. It was him."

"Washed its face, and it was paint all over it made it look red. It all come off. And it could talk—as good as me or you. But they'd tole it not to, so it never did. They'd tole it if anybody was to come near it they was comin' to git it—and for it to hit 'em quick with that iron bar an' growl. So nobody ever came near it—until that man. I was yellin' outside, tellin' 'em to keep away, keep away. You could see where they'd whup it. They had to whip it some to make it eat all the chickens. It was awful dirty. They let it go back home free, to where they got it in the first place. They made them pay its ticket from Little Oil, Texas, to Cane Springs, Miss'ippi."

"You got a good memory," said Max.

"The way it started was," said Steve, in a wondering voice, "the show was just travelin' along in ole trucks through the country, and just seen this little deformed nigger man, sittin' on a fence, and just took it. It couldn't help it."

Little Lee Roy tossed his head back in a frenzy of amusement.

"I found it all out later. I was up on the Ferris wheel with one of the boys—got to talkin' up yonder in the peace an' quiet—an' said they just kind of happened up on it. Like a cyclone happens: it wasn't nothin' it could do. It was just took up." Steve suddenly paled through his sunburn. "An' they found out that back in Miss'ippi it had it a little bitty pair of crutches an' could just go runnin' on 'em!"

"And there they are," said Max.

Little Lee Roy held up a crutch and turned it about, and then snatched it back like a monkey.

"But if it hadn't been for that man, I wouldn't of knowed it till yet. If it wasn't for him bein' so bold. If he hadn't knowed what he was doin'."

"You remember that man this fella's talkin' about, boy?" asked Max, eying Little Lee Roy.

"Naw suh, I cain't say as I remembas that ve'y man, suh," he said softly, looking down where just then a sparrow alighted on his child's shoe. He added happily, as if on inspiration, "Now I remembas this man."

Steve did not look up, but when Max shook with silent laughter, alarm seemed to seize him like a spasm in his side. He walked painfully over and stood in the shade for a few minutes, leaning his head on a sycamore tree.

"Seemed like that man just studied it out an' knowed it was somethin' wrong," he said presently, his voice coming more remotely than ever. "But I didn't know. I can't look at nothin' an' be sure what it is. Then afterwards I know. Then I see how it was."

"Yeh, but you're nuts," said Max affably.

"You wouldn't of knowed it either!" cried Steve in sudden boyish, defensive anger. Then he came out from under the tree and stood again almost pleadingly in the sun, facing Max where he was sitting below Little Lee Roy on the steps. "You'd of let it go on an' on when they made it do those things—just like I did."

"Bet I could tell a man from a woman and an Indian from a nigger though," said Max.

Steve scuffed the dust into little puffs with his worn shoe. The chickens scattered, alarmed at last.

Little Lee Roy looked from one man to the other radiantly, his hands pressed over his grinning gums.

Then Steve sighed, and as if he did not know what else he could do, he reached out and without any warning hit Max in the jaw with his fist. Max fell off the steps.

Little Lee Roy suddenly sat as still and dark as a statue, looking on.

"Say! Say!" cried Steve. He pulled shyly at Max where he lay on the ground, with his lips pursed up like a whistler, and then stepped back. He looked horrified. "How you feel?"

"Lousy," said Max thoughtfully. "Let me alone." He raised up on one elbow and lay there looking all around, at the cabin, at Little Lee Roy sitting cross-legged on the porch, and at Steve with his hand out. Finally he got up.

"I can't figure out how I could of ever knocked down an athaletic guy like you. I had to do it," said Steve. "But I guess you don't understand. I had to hit you. First you didn't believe me, and then it didn't bother you."

"That's all O.K., only hush," said Max, and added, "Some dope is always giving me the lowdown on something, but this is the first time one of 'em ever got away with a thing like this. I got to watch out."

"I hope it don't stay black long," said Steve.

"I got to be going," said Max. But he waited. "What you want to transact with Keela? You come a long way to see him." He stared at Steve with his eyes wide open now, and interested.

"Well, I was goin' to give him some money or somethin', I guess, if I ever found him, only now I ain't got any," said Steve defiantly.

"O.K.," said Max. "Here's some change for you, boy. Just take it. Go on back in the house. Go on."

Little Lee Roy took the money speechlessly, and then fell upon his yellow crutches and hopped with miraculous rapidity away through the door. Max stared after him for a moment.

"As for you"—he brushed himself off, turned to Steve and then said, "When did you eat last?"

"Well, I'll tell you," said Steve.

"Not here," said Max. "I didn't go to ask you a question. Just follow me. We serve eats at Max's Place, and I want to play the juke box. You eat, and I'll listen to the juke box."

"Well . . ." said Steve. "But when it cools off I got to catch a ride some place."

"Today, while all you all was gone, and not a soul in de house," said Little Lee Roy at the supper table that night, "two white mens come heah to de house. Wouldn't come in. But talks to me about de ole times when I use to be wid de circus—"

"Hush up, Pappy," said the children.

Ann Petry

1911–

MISS MURIEL

Almost every day, Ruth Davis and I walk home from school together. We walk very slowly because we like to talk to each other and we don't get much chance in school or after school either. We are very much alike. We are both twelve years old and we are freshmen in high school and we never study—well, not very much, because we learn faster than the rest of the class. We laugh about the same things and we are curious about the same things. We even wear our hair in the same style—thick braids halfway down our backs. We are not alike in one respect. She is white and I am colored.

Yesterday when we reached the building that houses my father's drugstore, we sat down on the front steps—long wooden steps that go all the way across the front of the building. Ruth said, "I wish I lived here," and patted the steps though they are very splintery.

Aunt Sophronia must have heard our voices, because she came to the door and said, "I left my shoes at the shoemaker's this morning. Please go and get them for me," and she handed me a little cardboard ticket with a number on it.

"You want to come with me, Ruth?"

"I've got to go home. I'm sure my aunt will have things for me to do. Just like your aunt." She smiled at Aunt Sophronia.

I walked part way home with Ruth and then turned back and went up Petticoat Lane toward the shoemaker's shop. Mr. Bemish, the shoemaker, is a little man with gray hair. He has a glass eye. This eye is not the same color as his own eye. It is a deeper gray. If I stand too close to him I get a squeamish feeling because one eye moves in its socket and the other eye does not.

Mr. Bemish and I are friends. I am always taking shoes to his shop to be repaired. We do not own a horse and buggy and so we walk a great deal. In fact, there is a family rule that we must walk any distance under three miles. As a result, our shoes are in constant need of repair, the soles and heels have to be replaced, and we always seem to be in need of shoelaces. Quite often I snag the uppers on the bull briars in the woods and then the tears have to be stitched.

When I went to get Aunt Sophronia's shoes, Mr. Bemish was sitting near the window. It is a big window and he has a very nice view of the street. He had on his leather apron and his eyeglasses. His glasses are small and they have steel rims. He was sewing a shoe and he had a long length of waxed linen thread in his needle. He waxes the thread himself.

I handed him the ticket and he got up from his workbench to get the shoes. I saw that he had separated them from the other shoes. These are Aunt Sophronia's store shoes. They had been polished so that they shone like patent leather. They lay alone, near the front of the table where he keeps the shoes he has repaired. He leaned toward me and I moved away from him. I did not like being so close to his glass eye.

"The lady who brought these shoes in. Who is she?"

I looked at him and raised one eyebrow. It has taken me two months of constant practice in front of a mirror to master the art of lifting one eyebrow.

Mr. Bemish said, "What's the matter with you? Didn't you hear what I said? Who was that lady who brought these shoes in?"

I moved further away from him. He didn't know it but I was imitating Dottle Smith, my favorite person in all the world. Dottle tells the most wonderful stories and he can act and recite poetry. He visits our family every summer. Anyway, I bowed to Mr. Bemish and I bowed to an imaginary group of people seated somewhere on my right and I said, "Gentlemen, be seated. Mr. Bones, who was that lady I saw you with last night?" I lowered the pitch of my voice and said, "That wasn't no lady. That was my *wife*."

"Girlie—"

"Why do you keep calling me 'girlie'? I have a name."

"I cannot remember people's names. I'm too old. I've told you that before."

"How old are you, Mr. Bemish?"

"None of your business," he said pettishly. "Who—"

"Well, I only asked in order to decide whether to agree with you that you're old enough to be forgetful. Does the past seem more real to you than the present?"

Mr. Bemish scowled his annoyance. "The town is full of children," he said. "It's the children who bring the shoes and come and get them after I've fixed them. They run the errands. All those children look just alike to me. I can't remember their names. I don't even try. I don't plan to clutter up my mind with a lot of children's names. I don't see the same children that often. So I call the boys 'boy,' and I call the girls 'girlie.' I've told you this before. What's the matter with you today?"

"It's spring and the church green is filled with robins looking for worms. Don't you sometimes wish you were a robin looking for a worm?"

He sighed, "Now tell me, who was that lady that brought these shoes in?"

"My Aunt Sophronia."

"Sophronia?" he said. "What a funny name. And she's your aunt?"

"Yes."

"Does she live with you?"

Mr. Bemish's cat mewed at the door and I let her in. She is a very handsome creature, gray, with white feet, and really lovely fur. "May-a-ling, May-a-ling," I said, patting her, "where have you been?" I always have the feeling that if I wait, if I persist, she will answer me. She is a very intelligent cat and very responsive.

"Does your aunt live with you?"

"Yes."

"Has she been living with you very long?"

"About six months, I guess. She's a druggist."

"You mean she knows about medicine?"

"Yes, just like my father. They run the store together."

Mr. Bemish thrust his hands in Aunt Sophronia's shoes and held them up, studying them. Then he made the shoes walk along the edge of the table, in a mincing kind of walk, a caricature of the way a woman walks.

"She has small feet, hasn't she?"

"No." I tried to sound like my mother when she disapproves of something.

He flushed and wrapped the shoes in newspaper, making a very neat bundle.

"Is she married?"

"Who? Aunt Sophronia? No. She's not married."

Mr. Bemish took his cookie crock off the shelf. He lives in the shop. Against one wall he has a kitchen stove, a big black iron stove with nickel fenders and a tea kettle on it, and there is a black iron sink with a pump right near the stove. He cooks his meals himself, he bakes bread, and usually there is a stew bubbling in a pot on the stove. In winter the windows of his little shop frost over, so that I cannot see in and he cannot see out. He draws his red curtains just after dusk and lights his lamps, and the windows look pink because of the frost and the red curtains and the light shining from behind them.

Sometimes he forgets to draw the curtains that separate his sleeping quarters from the rest of the shop and I can see his bed. It is a brass bed. He evidently polishes it, because it shines like gold. It has a very intricate design on the headboard and the footboard. He has a little piece of flowered carpet in front of his bed. I can see his white china pot under the bed. A dark suit and some shirts hang on hooks on the wall. There is a chest of drawers with a small mirror in a gold frame over it, and a washbowl and pitcher on a washstand. The washbowl and pitcher are white with pink rosebuds painted on them.

Mr. Bemish offered me a cookie from the big stoneware crock.

"Have a cookie, girlie."

He makes big thick molasses cookies. I ate three of them without stopping. I was hungry and did not know it. I ate the fourth cookie very slowly and I talked to Mr. Bemish as I ate it.

"I don't think my Aunt Sophronia will ever get married."

"Why not?"

"Well, I never heard of a lady druggist before and I don't know who a lady druggist would marry. Would she marry another druggist? There aren't any around here anywhere except my father and certainly she couldn't marry him. He's already married to my mother."

"She looks like a gypsy," Mr. Bemish said dreamily.

"You mean my Aunt Sophronia?"

Mr. Bemish nodded.

"She does not. She looks like my mother and my Aunt Ellen. And my father and Uncle Johno say they look like Egyptian queens."

They are not very tall and they move quickly and their skins are brown and very smooth and their eyes are big and black and they stand up very straight. They are not alike though. My mother is business-minded. She likes to buy and sell things. She is a chiropodist and a hair-dresser. Life sometimes seems full of other people's hair and their toenails. She makes a hair tonic and sells it to her customers. She designs luncheon sets and banquet cloths and guest towels and sells them. Aunt Ellen and Uncle Johno provide culture. Aunt Ellen lectures at schools and colleges. She plays Bach and Beethoven on the piano and organ. She writes articles for newspapers and magazines.

I do not know very much about Aunt Sophronia. She works in the store. She fills prescriptions. She does embroidery. She reads a lot. She doesn't play the piano. She is very neat. The men who come in the store look at her out of the corner of their eyes. Even though she wears her hair skinned tight back from her forehead, and wears very plain clothes, dresses with long, tight sleeves and high necks, she still looks like—

well, like an Egyptian queen. She is young but she seems very quiet and
sober.

Mr. Bemish offered me another cookie. "I'll eat it on my way home to
keep my strength up. Thank you very much," I said primly.

When I gave the shoes to Aunt Sophronia, I said, "Mr. Bemish thinks
you look like a gypsy."

My mother frowned. "Did he tell you to repeat that?"

"No, he didn't. But I thought it was an interesting statement."

"I wish you wouldn't repeat the things you hear. It just causes trouble.
Now every time I look at Mr. Bemish I'll wonder about him—"

"What will you wonder—I mean—"

She said I must go and practice my music lesson and ignored my question. I wonder how old I will be before I can ask questions of an adult
and receive honest answers to the questions. My family always finds
something for me to do. Are they not using their power as adults to give
orders in order to evade the questions?

That evening, about five o'clock, Mr. Bemish came in the store. I was
sitting on the bench in the front. It is a very old bench. The customers
sit there while they wait for their prescriptions to be filled. The wood is
a beautiful color. It is a deep, reddish brown.

Mr. Bemish sat down beside me on the bench. His presence irritated
me. He kept moving his hand up and down the arms of the bench, up and
down, in a quick, nervous movement. It is as though he thought he had
an awl in his hand, and he is going in and out making holes in leather and
then sewing, slipping a needle in and out, as he mends a saddle or a pair
of boots.

My father looked at him over the top of his glasses and said, "Well,
Bemish, what can I do for you?"

"Nothing. Nothing at all. I just stopped in to pass the time of day, to
see how you all were—" His voice trailed away, softly.

He comes every evening. I find this very annoying. Quite often I have
to squeeze myself onto the bench. Pritchett, the sexton of the Congregational church—stout, red-faced, smelling of whiskey—rings the bell for
a service at seven o'clock and then he, too, sits in the front of the store,
watching the customers as they come and go until closing time. He eyed
Mr. Bemish rather doubtfully at first, but then ignored him. When the
sexton and Mr. Bemish were on the bench, there was just room enough
for me to squeeze in between them. I didn't especially mind the sexton,
because he usually went to sleep, nodding and dozing until it was time
to close the store. But Mr. Bemish doesn't sit still—and the movement of
his hands is distracting.

My mother finally spoke to my father about Mr. Bemish. They were
standing in the back room. "Why does Mr. Bemish sit out there in the
store so much?" she asked.

"Nothin' else to do."

She shook her head. "I think he's interested in Sophronia. He keeps looking around for someone."

My father laughed out loud. "That dried-up old white man?"

The laughter of my father is a wonderful sound—if you know anything about music you know he sings tenor and you know he sings in the Italian fashion with an open throat and you begin to smile, and if he laughs long enough, you laugh too, because you can't help it.

"Bemish?" he said. And he laughed so hard that he had to lean against the doorjamb in order to keep his balance.

Every night right after supper, Mr. Bemish sits in the store rubbing the arm of the bench with that quick, jerking motion of his hand, nodding to people who come in, sometimes talking to them, but mostly just sitting.

Two weeks later I walked past his shop. He came to the door and called me. "Girlie," he said, beckoning.

"Yes, Mr. Bemish?"

"Is your aunt with the peculiar name still here—that is, in town, living with you?"

"Yes, she is, Mr. Bemish."

"Don't she ever go in the drugstore?"

"Not after five o'clock, Mr. Bemish. My father doesn't approve of ladies working at night. At night we act just like other people's families. We sit around the table in the dining room and talk, and we play checkers, and we read and we—"

"Yes, yes," he said impatiently. "But don't your aunt ever go anywhere at night?"

"I don't think so. I go to bed early."

"Do you think—" And he shook his head. "Never mind, girlie, never mind," and he sighed. "Here—I just made up a fresh batch of those big cookies you like so well."

I walked down Petticoat Lane toward the drugstore eating one of Mr. Bemish's thick molasses cookies. I wished I had taken time to tell him how cozy our downstairs parlor is in the winter. We have turkey-red curtains at the windows too, and we pull the window shades and draw the curtains, and there is a very thick rug on the floor and it is a small room, so the rug completely covers the floor. The piano is in there and an old-fashioned sofa with a carved mahogany frame and a very handsome round stove and it is warm in winter; and in the summer when the windows are open, you can look right out into the back yard and smell the flowers and feel the cool air that comes from the garden.

The next afternoon, Mr. Bemish came in the drugstore about quarter past three. It was a cold, windy afternoon. I had just come from school and there was a big mug of hot cocoa for me. Aunt Sophronia had it ready and waiting for me in the back room. I had just tasted the first spoonful; it was much too hot to gulp down, and I leaned way over and blew on it gently, and inhaled the rich, chocolatey smell of it. I heard my aunt say, "Why, Mr. Bemish, what are you doing out at this hour?"

"I thought I'd like an ice-cream soda." Mr. Bemish's voice sounded breathless, lighter in weight, and the pitch was lower than normal.

I peeked out at him. He was sitting near the fountain in one of the ice-cream parlor chairs. He looked very stiff and prim and neater than usual. He seems to have flattened his hair closer to his skull. This makes his head appear smaller. He was holding his head a little to one side. He looked like a bird but I cannot decide what bird—perhaps a chickadee. He drank the soda neatly and daintily. He kept looking at Aunt Sophronia.

He comes every day now, in the middle of the afternoon. He should have been in his shop busily repairing shoes or making boots, or making stews and cookies. Instead he is in our store, and his light-gray eye, the one good eye, travels busily over Aunt Sophronia. His ears seem to waggle when he hears her voice, and he has taken to giggling in a very silly fashion.

He always arrives about the same time. Sometimes I sit in one of the ice-cream parlor chairs and talk to him. He smells faintly of leather, and of shoe polish, and of wax, and of dead flowers. It was quite a while before I could place that other smell—dead flowers. Each day he stays a little longer than he stayed the day before.

I have noticed that my father narrows his eyes a little when he looks at Mr. Bemish. I heard him say to my mother, "I don't like it. I don't want to tell him not to come in here. But I don't like it—an old white man in here every afternoon looking at Sophronia and licking his chops— well, I just don't like it."

Aunt Sophronia took a sudden interest in the garden. In the afternoon, after school, I help her set out plants and sow seed. Our yard is filled with flowers in the summer; and we have a vegetable garden that in some ways is as beautiful as the flowers—it is so neat and precise-looking. We keep chickens so that we can have fresh eggs. And we raise a pig and have him butchered in the fall.

When the weather is bad and we cannot work in the garden, Aunt Sophronia and I clean house. I do not like to clean house but I do like to sort out the contents of other people's bureau drawers. We started setting Aunt Sophronia's bureau in order. She showed me a picture of her graduating class from Pharmacy College. She was the only girl in a class of boys. She was colored and the boys were white. I did not say anything about this difference in color and neither did she. But I did try to find out what it was like to be the only member of the female sex in a class filled with males.

"Didn't you feel funny with all those boys?"

"They were very nice boys."

"Oh, I'm sure they were. But didn't you feel funny being the only girl with so many young men?"

"No. I never let them get overly friendly and we got along very well."

I looked at the picture and then I looked at her and said, "You are beautiful."

She put the picture back in her top drawer. She keeps her treasures in there. She has a collar made of real lace, and a pair of very long white kid gloves, and a necklace made of gold nuggets from Colorado that a friend of my mother's left to Aunt Sophronia in her will. The gloves and the collar smell like our garden in August when the flowers are in full bloom and the sun is shining on them.

Sometimes I forget that Aunt Sophronia is an adult and that she belongs in the enemy camp, and I make the mistake of saying what I have been thinking.

I leaned against the bureau and looked down into the drawer, at the picture, and said, "You know, this picture reminds me of the night last summer when there was a female moth, one of those huge night moths, on the inside of the screen door, and all the male moths for miles around came and clung on the outside of the screen, making their wings flutter, and you know, they didn't make any sound but it was kind of scary. Weren't you—"

Aunt Sophronia closed the drawer with a hard push. "You get a broom and a dustpan and begin to sweep in the hall," she said.

On Saturday morning, after I finished washing the breakfast dishes and scrubbing the kitchen floor, I paid a call on Mr. Bemish. He is cleaning his house, too. He has taken down the red curtains that hung at the windows all winter, and the red curtains that hung in front of his bed, separating his sleeping quarters from the rest of his shop, and he was washing these curtains in a big tub at the side of his house. He was making a terrific splashing and the soapsuds were pale pink. He had his sleeves rolled up. His arms are very white and stringy-looking.

"Too much red for summer, girlie. I've got to get out the green summer ones."

He hung them on the line and poured the wash water out on the ground. It was pink.

"Your curtains ran, didn't they?" I looked at a little pink puddle left on top of a stone. "If you keep washing them, they'll be pink instead ef red."

His own eye, the real one, moved away from me, and there was something secret, and rather sly, about his expression. He said, "I haven't seen your aunt in the store lately. Where is she?"

"She's been busy fixing the garden and cleaning the house. Everybody seems to be cleaning house."

"As soon as I get my green curtains put up, I'm going to ask your aunt to come have tea."

"Where would she have tea with you?"

"In my shop."

I shook my head. "Aunt Sophronia does not drink tea in people's bedrooms and you have only that one room for your shop and there's a bed in it and it would be just like—"

"I would like to have her look at some old jewelry that I have and I thought she might have tea."

"Mr. Bemish," I said, "do you like my Aunt Sophronia?"

"Now, girlie," he said, and he tittered. "Well, now, do you think your aunt likes me?"

"Not especially. Not any more than anybody else. I think you're too old for her and besides, well, you're white and I don't think she would be very much interested in an old white man, do you?"

He frowned and said, "You go home. You're a very rude girl."

"You asked me what I thought, Mr. Bemish. I don't see why you get mad when I tell you what I think. You did ask me, Mr. Bemish."

I followed him inside his shop. He settled himself near the window and started to work on a man's boot. It needed a new sole and he cut the sole out of leather. I looked out the front window. There is always enough breeze to make his sign move back and forth; it makes a sighing noise. In the winter if there's a wind, the sign seems to groan because it moves back and forth quickly. There is a high-laced shoe painted on the sign. The shoe must once have been a deep, dark red, but it has weathered to a soft rose color.

Mr. Bemish is my friend and I wanted to indicate that I am still fond of him though I disapprove of his interest in Aunt Sophronia. I searched for some topic that would indicate that I enjoy talking to him.

I said, "Why don't you have a picture of a man's boot on your sign?"

"I prefer ladies' shoes. More delicate, more graceful—" He made an airy gesture with his awl and simpered.

I went home and I told Aunt Sophronia that Mr. Bemish is going to ask her to have tea with him.

"Will you go?"

"Of course not," she said impatiently.

Aunt Sophronia did not have tea with Mr. Bemish. He sees her so rarely in the store that he finally came in search of her.

It is summer now and the Wheeling Inn is open for the season. The great houses along the waterfront are occupied by their rich owners. We are all very busy. At night after the store is closed, we sit in the back yard. On those warm June nights, the fireflies come out, and there is a kind of soft summer light, composed of moonlight and starlight. The grass is thick underfoot and the air is sweet. Almost every night my mother and my father and Aunt Sophronia and I, and sometimes Aunt Ellen and Uncle Johno, sit there in the quiet and in the sweetness and in that curious soft light.

Last night when we were sitting there, Mr. Bemish came around the side of the house. There was something tentative in the way he came

towards us. I had been lying on the grass and I sat up straight, wondering
what they would do and what they would say.

He sidled across the lawn. He didn't speak until he was practically
upon us. My mother was sitting in the hammock under the cherry tree,
rocking gently back and forth, and she didn't see him until he spoke. He
said, "Good evening." He sounded as though he was asking a question.

We all looked at him. I hoped that someone would say: What are
you doing in our back yard, our private place, our especially private
place? You are an intruder, go back to your waxed thread and your awl,
go back to your house and your cat. Nobody said anything.

He stood there for a while, waiting, hesitant, and then he bowed and
sat down, cross-legged, on the grass near Aunt Sophronia. She was sitting
on one of the benches. And he sat so close to her that her skirt was resting
on one of his trouser legs. I kept watching him. One of his hands reached
toward her skirt and he gently fingered the fabric. Either she felt this or
the motion attracted her attention, because she moved away from him,
and gathered her skirt about her, and then stood up and said, "The air
is making me sleepy. Good night."

The next afternoon I took a pair of my father's shoes to Mr. Bemish
to have the heels fixed. My father wears high-laced black shoes. I left
them on Mr. Bemish's work table.

"You can get them tomorrow."

I did not look right at him. I leaned over and patted May-a-ling. "She
has such a lovely name, Mr. Bemish. It seems to me a name especially
suited for a cat."

Mr. Bemish looked at me over the top of his little steel-rimmed glasses.
"You've got a nice back yard," he said.

"I don't think you should have been in it."

"Why not?" he asked sharply. "Did anybody say that I shouldn't
have been in it?"

"No. But the front part of the building, the part where the drugstore
is, belongs to everybody. The back part of the building, and upstairs in
the building, and the yard are ours. The yard is a private part of our lives.
You don't belong in it. You're not a part of our family."

"But I'd like to be a part of your family."

"You can't get to be a part of other people's families. You have to be
born into a family. The family part of our lives is just for us. Besides,
you don't seem to understand that you're the wrong color, Mr. Bemish."

He didn't answer this. He got up and got his cookie crock and silently
offered me a cookie.

After I returned from the shoeshop, I sat on the wooden steps that
run across the front of the drugstore. I was trying to decide how I really
feel about Mr. Bemish. I always sit at the far end of the steps with my
back against the tightboard fence. It is a very good place from which to
observe the street, the front of the store, the church green. People walk
past me not noticing that I am there. Sometimes their conversations are

very unusual. I can see a long way down the path that bisects the green. It is a dirt path and not too straight. The only straight paths in town are those in front of the homes of people who have gardeners.

From where I sat I could see a man approaching. He was strolling down the path that crosses the church green. This is a most unusual way for a man to walk in Wheeling in the summer. It is during the summer that the year-round residents earn their living. They mow lawns, and cut hedges, and weed gardens, and generally look after the summer people. Able-bodied men in Wheeling walked fast in summer.

This tall, broad-shouldered man was strolling down the path. He was wearing a white suit, the pants quite tight in the leg, and he had his hands in his hip pockets, and a stiff straw hat, a boater, on the back of his head.

I sat up very straight when I discovered that this was a very dark colored man. I could not imagine where he came from. He could not possibly be a butler or a waiter even if he wanted to and spent a whole lifetime in trying. He would never be able to walk properly—he would always swagger, and who ever heard of a swaggering butler or a waiter who strolled around a table?

As he came nearer, I saw that he had a beard, an untidy shaggy beard like the beard of a goat. His hair was long and shaggy and rough-looking too. Though he was tall, with wide shoulders, the thick rough hair on his head and the goat's beard made his head and face look too big, out of proportion to his body.

When he saw me, he came straight toward me. He bent over me, smiling, and I moved back away from him, pressing against the fence. His eyes alarmed me. Whenever I think about his eyes, I close mine, trying to shut his out. They are reddish brown and they look hot, and having looked into them, I cannot seem to look away. I have never seen anyone with eyes that color or with that strange quality, whatever it is. I described them as looking "hot," but that's not possible. It must be that they are the color of something that I associate with fire or heat. I do not know what it is.

"You lost?" he said.

"No. Are you?"

"Yup. All us colored folks is lost." He said this in a husky, unmusical voice, and turned away and went in the store.

I went in the store, too. If this unusual-looking man with the goat's beard got into a discussion of "all of us colored folks is lost" with my father, I wanted to hear it.

My father said, "How-de-do?" and he made it a question.

The bearded man nodded and said, "The druggist in?"

"I'm the druggist."

"This your store?"

"That's right."

"Nice place you got here. You been here long?"

My father grunted. I waited for him to make the next move in the game we called Stanley and Livingstone.[1] All colored strangers who came into our store were Livingstones—and it was up to the members of our family to find out which lost Mr. Livingstone or which lost Mrs. Livingstone we had encountered in the wilds of the all-white town of Wheeling. When you live in a town where there aren't any other colored people, naturally you're curious when another colored person shows up.

I sat down in the front of the store and waited for my father to find out which Mr. David Livingstone he was talking to and what he was doing in our town. But my father looked at him with no expression on his face and said, "And what did you want?"

The man with the goat's beard fished in the pocket of his tight white pants. In order to do this, he thrust his leg forward a little to ease the strain on the fabric, and thus he gave the impression that he was pawing the ground. He handed my father a piece of paper.

"I got a prescription for a lotion—"

"It'll take a few minutes," my father said, and went in the back room. The bearded man came and sat beside me.

"Do you live here in Wheeling?" I asked.

"I work at the Inn. I'm the piano player."

"You play the piano?"

"And sing. I'm the whole orchestra. I play for the dinner hour. I play for all those nice rich white folks to dance at night. I'll be here all summer."

"You will?"

"That's right. And I've never seen a deader town."

"What's your name?"

"Chink."

"Mr. Chink—"

"No," he said, and stood up. "Chink is my first name. Chink Johnson."

Mr. Johnson is a restless kind of man. He keeps moving around even when he is sitting still, moving his feet, his hands, his head. He crosses his legs, uncrosses them, clasps his hands together, unclasps them.

"Why are you having a prescription filled?"

"Hand lotion. I use it for my hands."

My father came out of the back room, wrapped up a bottle, said, "Here you are."

Chink Johnson paid him, said good-by to me, and I said, "Goodby, Chink."

---

[1] Sir Henry Morton Stanley, 1841–1904, British explorer, made a trek across Tanganyika (east-central Africa) in 1871 to find the lost missionary, David Livingstone, 1813–1873. Stanley was financed by James Gordon Bennett, Jr., managing editor of the New York *Herald*, which published sensational accounts of the adventure. The names of the two men remained household words for decades after, and Stanley's greeting, "Dr. Livingstone, I presume?" became a popular instance of nonchalance.

"What's his name?"

"Chink Johnson. He plays the piano at the Inn."

Chink Johnson seems to me a very interesting and unusual man. To my surprise, my father did not mention our newest Mr. Livingstone to the family. He said nothing about him at all. Neither did I.

Yet he comes in the drugstore fairly often. He buys cigarettes and throat lozenges. Sometimes he drives over from the Inn in a borrowed horse and carriage. Sometimes he walks over. My father has very little to say to him.

He doesn't linger in the store, because my father's manner is designed to discourage him from lingering or hanging around. But he does seem to be looking for something. He looks past the door of the prescription room, and on hot afternoons, the door in the very back is open and you can see our yard, with its beautiful little flower gardens, and he looks out into the yard, seems to search it. When he leaves he looks at the house, examining it. It is as though he is trying to see around a corner, see through the walls, because some sixth sense has told him that there exists on the premises something that will interest him, and if he looks hard enough, he will find it.

My mother finally caught a glimpse of him as he went out the front door. She saw what I saw—the goat's beard in silhouette, the forward thrust of his head, the thick shaggy hair—because we were standing in the prescription room looking toward the door.

"Who was that?" she asked, her voice sharp.

"That's the piano player at the Inn," my father said.

"You've never mentioned him. What is his name?"

"Jones," my father said.

I started to correct him but I was afraid to interrupt him because he started talking fast and in a very loud voice. "Lightfoot Jones," he said. "Shake Jones. Barrelhouse Jones." He started tapping on the glass case in front of him. I have never heard him do this before. He sings in the Congregational church choir. He has a pure, lyric tenor voice, and he sings all the tenor solos, the "Sanctus," "The Heavens Are Telling." You can tell from his speaking voice that he sings. He is always humming or singing or whistling. There he was with a pencil in his hand, tapping out a most peculiar rhythm on the glass of a showcase.

"Shake Jones," he repeated. "Rhythm in his feet. Rhythm in his blood. Rhythm in his feet. Rhythm in his blood. Beats out his life, beats out his lungs, beats out his liver, on a piano," and he began a different and louder rhythm with his foot. "On a pi-an-o. On a pi-an-o. On a pi—"

"Samuel, what is the matter with you? What are you talking about?"

"I'm talkin' about Tremblin' Shakefoot Jones. The piano player. The piano player who can't sit still, and comes in here lookin' around and lookin' around, prancin' and stampin' his hoofs, and sniffin' the air. Just like a stallion who smells a mare—a stallion who—"

"Samuel! How can you talk that way in front of this child?"

My father was silent.

I said, "His name is Chink Johnson."

My father roared, terrible in his anger, "His name is Duke. His name is Bubber. His name is Count, is Maharajah, is King of Lions. I don't give a good goddamn what he calls himself. I don't want him and his restless feet hangin' around. He can let his long feet slap somebody else's floor. But not mine. Not here—"

He glared at me and glared at my mother. His fury silenced us. At that moment his eyes were red-brown just like Chink Jones, no, Johnson. He is shorter, he has no beard, but he had at that moment a strong resemblance to Chink.

I added to his fury. I said, "You look just like Chink Johnson."

He said, "Ah!!! . . ." He was so angry I could not understand one word he said. I went out the front door, and across the street, and sat on the church steps and watched the world go by and listened to the faint hum it made as it went around and around.

I saw Mr. Bemish go in the drugstore. He stayed a long time. That gave me a certain pleasure because I knew he had come to eat his ice-cream soda, mouthful by mouthful, from one of our long-handled ice-cream-soda spoons, and to look at Aunt Sophronia as he nibbled at the ice cream. He looks at her out of the corners of his eyes, stealing sly little glances at her. I knew that Aunt Sophronia would not be in the store until much later and that he was wasting his time. It was my father's birthday and Aunt Sophronia was in the kitchen baking a great big cake for him.

If Mr. Bemish had known this, he might have dropped in on the birthday celebration, even though he hadn't been invited. After all, he had sidled into our back yard without being invited and our yard is completely enclosed by a tight-board fence, and there is a gate that you have to open to get in the yard, so that entering our yard is like walking into our living room. It is a very private place. Mr. Bemish is the only person that I know of who has come into our yard without being invited, and he keeps coming, too.

After Mr. Bemish left the store, I crossed the street and sat outside on the store steps. It was hot. It was very quiet. Old Lady Chimble crossed the church green carrying a black silk umbrella, and she opened it and used it as a sunshade. A boy went by on a bicycle. Frances Jackins (we called her Aunt Frank), the colored cook in the boardinghouse across the street, hurried across the street carrying something in a basket. She is always cross and usually drunk. She drinks gin. Mother says this is what has made Aunt Frank's lips look as though they were turned inside out and she says this is called a "gin lip." They are bright-red, almost like a red gash across the dark skin of her face. I want very much to ask Aunt Frank about this—how it feels, when it happened, etc.—and someday I will, but I have not as yet had a suitable opportunity. When she is drunk, she cannot give a sensible answer to a sensible question, and when she is sober, or partially sober, she is very irritable and constantly finds fault with me. She is absolutely no relation to us; it is just that my mother got in the habit of calling her "Aunt" Frank many years ago and so we all call her that. Because I am young, she tries to boss me and to order me around, and she calls me "Miss" in a very unpleasant, sarcastic way.

She is a very good cook when she is sober. But when she is drunk, she burns everything, and she is always staggering across the street and stumbling up our back steps, with bread pans filled with dough which would not rise because she has forgotten the yeast, and with burned cakes and pies and burned hams and roasts of beef. When she burns things, they are not just scorched; they are blackened and hardened until they are like charcoal.

Almost every night she scratches at our back door. I have sharper hearing than everybody else; I can hear people walking around the side of the house and no one else has heard them—anyway, I always hear her first. I open the door suddenly and very fast, and she almost falls into the kitchen and stands there swaying, and fouling our kitchen with the sweetish smell of gin and the dank and musty odor of her clothes.

She always has a dip of snuff under her upper lip and she talks around this obstruction, so that her voice is peculiar. She speaks quickly to keep the snuff in place, and sometimes she pauses and works her upper lip, obviously getting the snuff in some special spot. When she comes to the back door at night, she puts the basket of ruined food just inside the door, on the floor, and says to my mother, "Here, Mar-tha, throw this away. Throw it a-way for me. Give it to the hens. Feed it to the pig—"

She turns all two-syllable words into two separate one-syllable words. She doesn't say "Martha" all in one piece. She separates it, so that it becomes "Mar-tha"; she doesn't say "away," but "a-way." It is a very jerky kind of speech.

I am always given the job of burying the stuff in the backyard, way down in the back. I dig a hole and throw the blackened mess into it and then cover it with lime to hasten decomposition and discourage skunks and dogs.

Sometimes I hide behind the fence and yell at her on her way back across the street:

> *Ole Aunt Frankie*
> *Black as tar*
> *Tried to get to heaven*
> *In a 'lectric car.*
> *Car got stalled in an underpass,*
> *Threw Aunt Frankie right on her ass.*

Whenever I singsong this rhyme at her, she invariably tries to climb over the fence, a furious drunken old woman, threatening me with the man's umbrella that she carries. I should think she would remember from past performances that she cannot possibly reach me. But she always tries. After several futile efforts, she gives up and goes back to the boardinghouse across the street. A lot of old maids and widows live there. No gentlemen. Just ladies. They spend their spare time rocking on the front porch, and playing whist, and looking over at the drugstore. Aunt Frank spends her spare time in the kitchen of the boardinghouse, rocking and emptying bottle after bottle of gin.

But on the day of my father's birthday, she was sober; at least, she walked as though she were. She had a basket on her arm with a white napkin covering its contents. I decided she must have made something special for my father's supper. She went in the drugstore, and when she came out, she didn't have the basket. She saw me sitting on the steps but she ignored me.

Aunt Sophronia came and stood in the window. She had washed the glass globes that we keep filled with blue, red, and yellow liquid. She was wearing a dark skirt and a white blouse. Her hair was no longer skinned tight back from her forehead; it was curling around her forehead, perhaps because she had been working in the garden, bending over, and the hairpins that usually hold it so tightly in place had worked themselves loose. She didn't look real. The sun was shining in the window and it reflected the lights from the jars of colored water back on her face and her figure, and she looked golden and rose-colored and lavender and it was though there was a rainbow moving in the window.

Chink Johnson drove up in his borrowed horse and carriage. He stood and talked to me and then started to go in the store, saw Aunt Sophronia, and stood still. He took a deep breath. I could hear him. He took off the stiff straw hat that he wore way back on his head and bowed to her. She nodded, as though she really didn't want to, and turned away and acted as though she were very busy.

He grabbed my arm and actually pinched it.

"What are you doin'?" I said angrily. "What is the matter with you? Let go my arm."

"Shut up," he said impatiently, pinching harder. His fingers felt as though they were made of iron. "Who is that?"

I pried his fingers loose and rubbed my arm. "Where?"

"In the window. Who is that girl in the window?"

"That's my Aunt Sophronia."

"Your aunt? Your aunt?"

"Yes."

He went in the store. One moment he was standing beside me and the next moment he had practically leaped inside the store.

I went in too. He was leaning in the window, saying "Wouldn't you like to go for a walk with me this Sunday?" She shook her head. "Well, couldn't you go for a ride with me? I'll call for you—"

Aunt Sophronia said, "I work every day."

"Every day?" he said. "But that's not possible. Nobody works every day. I'll be back tomorrow—"

And he was gone. Aunt Sophronia looked startled. She didn't look angry, just sort of surprised.

I said, "Tomorrow and tomorrow and tomorrow—" And I thought, well, she's got two suitors now. There's this Shake Jones Livingstone, otherwise known as Chink Johnson, and there's Mr. Bemish. I do not think I would pick either one. Mr. Bemish is too old even though he is my friend. I think of Chink Johnson as my friend too, but I do not think he would make a good husband. I tried to decide why I do not approve of him as a husband for Aunt Sophronia. I think it is because Aunt Sophronia is a lady and Chink Johnson is—well—he is not a gentleman.

That night at supper we celebrated my father's birthday. At that hour nobody much came in the store. Pickett, the sexton, sat on the bench in the front and if anybody came in and wanted my father, he'd come to the back door and holler for him.

There was a white tablecloth on the big, oak dining-room table, and we used my mother's best Haviland china and the sterling-silver knives and forks with the rose pattern, and there was a pile of packages by my father's plate, and there were candles on the cake and we had ice cream for dessert. My old enemy, Aunt Frank, had delivered Parker House rolls for his birthday and had made him a milk-panful of rice pudding, because my father has always said that when he dies he hopes it will be because he drowns in a sea composed of rice pudding, that he could eat his weight in rice pudding, that he could eat rice pudding morning, noon, and night. Aunt Frank must have been sober when she made the pudding, for it was creamy and delicious and I ate two helpings of it right along with my ice cream.

I kept waiting for Aunt Sophronia to say something about Chink Johnson. He is a very unusual-looking man and we've never had a customer, colored or white, with that kind of beard. She did not mention him. Neither did I. My father has never mentioned him—at least not at the table. I wonder if my father hopes he will vanish. Perhaps they are afraid he will become a part of the family circle if they mention him.

Chink Johnson has become a part of the family circle and he used the same method that Mr. Bemish used. He just walked into the yard and into the house. I was upstairs, and I happened to look out of the window, and there was Chink Johnson walking up the street. He opened our gate, walked around the side of the house and into our back yard. I hurried to the back of the house and looked out the window and saw him open the screen door and go into the kitchen. He didn't knock on the door either, he just walked in.

For the longest time I didn't hear a sound. I listened and listened. I must have stood still for fifteen minutes. Then I heard someone playing our piano. I knew it must be Chink Johnson because this was not the kind of music anyone in our house would have been playing. I ran downstairs. My mother had been in the cellar, and she came running up out of the cellar, and my father came hurrying over from the drugstore. We all stood and looked and looked.

Chink was sitting at our piano. He had a cigarette dangling from his lower lip, and the smoke from the cigarette was like a cloud—a blue-gray, hazy kind of cloud around his face, his eyes, his beard—so that you could only catch glimpses of them through the smoke. He was playing some kind of fast, discordant-sounding music and he was slapping the floor with one of his long feet and he was slapping the keys with his long fingers.

Aunt Sophronia was leaning against the piano looking down at him. He did not use music when he played, and he never once looked at the keyboard, he just kept looking right into Aunt Sophronia's eyes. I thought my father would tell Chink to go slap somebody else's floor with his long feet, but my mother gave him one of those now-don't-say-a-word looks and he glared at Chink and went back to the drugstore.

Chink stayed a long time, he played the piano, he sang, or rather I guess you would say he talked to the music. It is a very peculiar kind of musical performance. He plays some chords, a whole series of them, and he makes peculiar changes in the chords as he plays, and then he says the words of a song—he doesn't really sing, but his voice does change in pitch to, in a sense, match the chords he is playing, and he does talk to a kind of rhythm which also matches the chords. I sat down beside him and watched what he was doing, and listened to the words he said, and though it is not exactly music as I am accustomed to hearing it, I found it very interesting. He told me that what he does with those songs is known as the "talkin' blues." Only he said "*talk*in' " and he made "blues" sound like it was two separate words, not just a two-syllable word, but two distinct words.

I have been trying to play the piano the way he does but I get nothing but terrible sounds. I pretend that I am blind and keep my eyes closed all the time while I feel for chords. He must have a special gift for this because it is an extremely difficult thing that he is doing and I don't know whether I will ever be able to do it. He has a much better ear for music than I have.

Chink Johnson comes to see Aunt Sophronia almost every day. Sometimes when I look out in the back yard, Mr. Bemish is out there too. He always sits on the ground, and at his age, I should think it might give him rheumatism. He must be a very brave little man or else his love for Aunt Sophronia has given him great courage. I say this because Chink Johnson is very rude to Mr. Bemish and he stares at him with a dreadfully cruel look on his face. If I were small and slender and old like Mr. Bemish, I would not sit in the same yard with a much bigger, much younger man who obviously did not want me there.

I have thought a great deal about Mr. Bemish. I like him. He is truly a friend. But I do not think he should be interested in Aunt Sophronia—at least not in a loving kind of way. The thing that bothers me is that I honestly cannot decide whether I object to him as a suitor for her because he is white or because he is old. Sometimes I think it is for both reasons. I am fairly certain it isn't just because he's old. This bothers me. If my objections to him are because he's white (and that's what I told him, but I often say things that I know people do not want to hear and that they particularly do not want to hear from someone very much younger than they are), then I have been trained on the subject of race just as I have been "trained" to be a Christian. I know how I was trained to be a Christian—Sunday school, prayers, etc. I do not know exactly how I've been "trained" on the subject of race. Then why do I feel like this about Mr. Bemish?

Shortly after I wrote that, I stopped puzzling about Mr. Bemish because summer officially started—at least for me. It is true that school had been out for a long time, and we are wearing our summer clothes, and the yard is filled with flowers—but summer never really gets under way for me until Dottle Smith comes for his yearly visit.

Dottle and Uncle Johno went to school together. They look sort of alike. They are big men and they are so light in color they look like white men. But something in them (Dottle says that it is a "cultivated and developed and carefully nourished hatred of white men") will not permit them to pass for white. Dottle teaches English and elocution and dramatics at a school for colored people in Georgia, and he gives lectures and readings during the summer to augment his income. Uncle Johno is the chief fund-raising agent for a colored school in Louisiana.

I believe that my attitude towards Mr. Bemish stems from Dottle Smith. And Johno. They are both what my father calls race-conscious. When they travel on trains in the South, they ride in Jim Crow coaches until the conductor threatens to have them arrested unless they sit in the sections of the train reserved for whites. They are always being put out of the colored sections of waiting rooms, and warned out of the colored sections of towns, and being refused lodgings in colored rooming houses on the grounds that they would be a source of embarrassment—nobody would be able to figure out why a white man wanted to live with colored people, and they would be suspected of being spies, but of what kind or to what purpose, they have never been able to determine.

I have just reread what I have written here, and I find that I've left out the reason why I am writing so much about Dottle. Yesterday afternoon when I came back from an errand, there was a large, heavy-looking bag—leather, but it was shaped like a carpet-bag—near the bench where the customers sit when they wait for prescriptions. I recognized it immediately. I have seen that bag every summer for as far back as I can remember. I wondered if Dottle had come alone this time or if he had a friend with him. Sometimes he brings a young man with him. These young men look very much alike—they are always slender, rather shy, have big dark eyes and very smooth skin just about the color of bamboo.

I looked at Dottle's big battered old bag sitting on the floor near the bench, and I could almost see him, with his long curly hair, and I could hear him reciting poetry in his rich, buttery voice. He can quote all the great speeches from *Hamlet*, *Macbeth*, *Richard II*, and he can recite the sonnets.

I loved him. He was lively and funny and unexpected. Sometimes he would grab my braid and shout in his best Shakespearean voice, "Seize on her Furies, take her to your torments!"

I looked at Dottle's battered bag and I said to my father, "Is he alone? Or has he got one of those pretty boys with him?"

My father looked at me over the top of his glasses. "Alone."

"How come he to leave his bag here?"

"Well, the Ecckles aren't home. Ellen's gone on vacation—"

"Why does Aunt Ellen always go on vacation when Dottle comes?"

My father ignored this and went on talking. "Johno's gone to Albany collecting money for the school."

"Where is Dottle now?"

"I'm right here, sugar," and Dottle Smith opened the screen door and came in. He looked bigger than he had the summer before. He hugged me. He smelled faintly of lavender.

"You went and grew, honey," he said, and took off his hat and bowed. It was a wide-brimmed panama, and he had on a starched white shirt, and a flowing Byronic kind of black tie, and I looked at him with absolute delight. He was being a Southern "cunnel" and he was such an actor—I thought I could see lace at his wrists, hear mockingbirds sing, see a white-columned mansion, hear hoofbeats in the distance, and hear a long line of slaves, suitably clad as footmen and coachmen and butlers and house-men, murmur, Yes, massah, Yes, massah. It was all there in his voice.

"Why, in another couple years I'll be recitin' poetry to you. How's your momma? This summer I'll have to teach you how to talk. These Yankah teachers you've got all talk through their noses. They got you doin' the same thing—"

For two whole days I forgot about Chink Johnson and Mr. Bemish and Aunt Sophronia. Dottle liked to go fishing and crabbing; he liked to play whist; and he could tell the most marvelous stories and act them out.

The very next day Dottle and Uncle Johno and I went crabbing. We set out early in the morning with our nets and our fishing lines and the rotten meat we used for bait, and our lunch and thermos bottles with lemonade in them. It was a two-mile walk from where we lived to the creek where we caught crabs.

There was a bridge across the creek, an old wooden bridge. Some of the planks were missing. We stood on this bridge or sat on it and threw our lines in the water. Once in a great while a horse and wagon would drive across and set the planks to vibrating. Johno and Dottle would hop off the bridge. But I stayed on and held to the railing. The bridge trembled under my feet, and the horse and wagon would thunder across, and the driver usually waved and hollered, "I gotta go fast or we'll all fall in."

The water in the creek was so clear I could see big crabs lurking way down on the bottom; I could see little pieces of white shells and beautiful stones. We didn't talk much while we were crabbing. Sometimes I lay flat on my stomach on the bridge and looked down into the water, watching the little eddies and whirlpools that formed after I threw my line in.

Before we ate our lunch, we went wading in the creek. Johno and Dottle rolled up the legs of their pants, and their legs were so white I wondered if they were that white all over, and if they were, how they could be colored. We sat on the bank of the creek and ate our lunch. Afterwards Dottle and Johno told stories, wonderful stories in which animals talk, and there are haunted houses and ghosts and demons, and old colored preachers who believe in heaven and hell.

They always started off the same way. Dottle said to Johno, "Mr. Bones, be seated."

Though I have heard some of these stories many, many times, Dottle and Johno never tell them exactly the same. They change their gestures, they vary their facial expressions and the pitch of their voices.

Dottle almost always tells the story about the colored man who goes in a store in a small town in the South and asks for Muriel cigars. The white man who owns the store says (and here Johno becomes an outraged Southern white man), "Nigger, what's the matter with you? Don't you see that picture of that beautiful white woman on the front of this box? When you ask for them cigars, you say *Miss* Muriel cigars!"

Though Uncle Johno is a good storyteller, he is not as good, not as funny or as dramatic as Dottle. When I listen to Dottle I can see the old colored preacher who spent the night in a haunted house. I see him approaching the house, the wind blowing his coattails, and finally he takes refuge inside because of the violence of the storm. He lights a fire in the fireplace and sits down by it and rubs his hands together, warming them. As he sits there, he hears heavy footsteps coming down the stairs (and Dottle makes his hand go thump, thump, thump on the bank of the creek) and the biggest cat the old man has ever seen comes in and sits down, looks at the old preacher, looks around, and says, "Has Martin got here yet?" The old man is too startled and too nervous to answer. He hears heavy footsteps again—thump, thump, thump. And a second cat, much bigger than the first one, comes in, and sits down right next to the old preacher. Both cats stare at him, and then the second cat says to the first cat, "Has Martin got here yet?" and the first cat shakes his head. There is something so speculative in their glance that the old man gets more and more uneasy. He wonders if they are deciding to eat him. The wind howls in the chimney, puffs of smoke blow back into the room. Then another and bigger cat thumps down the stairs. Finally there are six enormous cats, three on each side of him. Each one of these cats has asked the same question of the others—"Martin got here yet?" A stair-shaking tread begins at the top of the stairs, the cats all look at each other, and the old man grabs his hat, and says to the assembled cats, "You tell Martin ah been here but ah've gone."

I clapped when Dottle finished this story. I looked around thinking how glad I am he is here and what a wonderful place this is to listen to stories. The sun is warm but there is a breeze and it blows through the long marsh grass which borders the creek. The grass moves, seems to wave. Gulls fly high overhead. The only sound is the occasional cry of a gull and the lapping of water against the piling of the bridge.

Johno tells the next story. It is about an old colored preacher and a rabbit. The old man tries to outrun an overfriendly and very talkative rabbit. The rabbit keeps increasing in size. The old man runs away from him and the rabbit catches up with him. Each time the rabbit says, "That was some run we had, wasn't it, brother?" Finally the old man runs until he feels as though his lungs are going to burst and his legs will turn to rubber, and he looks back and doesn't see the rabbit anywhere in sight. He sits down on a stone to rest and catch his breath. He has just seated himself when he discovers the rabbit sitting right beside him, smiling. The rabbit is now the same size as the preacher. The rabbit rolls his eyes and lisps, "That wath thome run we had, wathn't it?" The old man stood up, got ready to run again, and said, "Yes, that was some run we had, brother, but"—he took a deep breath—"you ain't *seen* no runnin' yet."

After they finished telling stories, we all took naps. Dottle and Johno were wearing old straw hats, wide-brimmed panamas with crooked, floppy brims. Dottle had attached a piece of mosquito netting to his, and it hung down across his shoulders. From the back he looked like a woman who was wearing a veil.

When we woke up it was late in the afternoon and time to start for home. I ran part of the way. Then I sat down by the side of the road, in the shade, and waited until they caught up with me.

Dottle said, "Sugar, what are you in such a hurry for?"

I said, laughing, "Miss Muriel, you tell Martin I been here but I've gone and that he ain't *seen* no runnin' yet."

I got home first. Chink Johnson was in the store. When Dottle and Johno arrived, I introduced Chink to my uncles, Johno and Dottle. They didn't seem much impressed with each other. Johno nodded and Dottle smiled and left. Chink watched Dottle as he went toward the back room. Dottle has a very fat bottom and he sort of sways from side to side as he walks.

Chink said, "He seems kind of ladylike. He related on your mother's side?"

"He's not related at all. He's an old friend of Uncle Johno's. They

went to school together. In Atlanta, Georgia." I sounded very condescending. "Do you know where that is?"

"Yeah. Nigger, read this. Nigger, don't let sundown catch you here.
Nigger, if you can't read this, run anyway. If you can't run—then vanish.
Just vanish out. I know the place. I came from there."

My father was standing outside on the walk talking to Aunt Frank, so
I felt at liberty to speak freely and I said, "Nigger, what are you talkin
about you want Muriel cigars. You see this picture of this beautiful red-
headed white woman, nigger, you say *Miss* Muriel."

Chink stood up and he was frowning and his voice was harsh. "Little
girl, don't you talk that way. I talk that way if I feel like it but don't you
ever talk that way."

I felt as though I had been betrayed. One moment he was my friend
and we were speaking as equals and the next moment, without warning,
he is an adult who is scolding me in a loud, harsh voice. I was furious and
I could feel tears welling up in my eyes. This made me angrier. I
couldn't seem to control my weeping. Recently, and I do not know how
it happened, whenever I am furiously angry, I begin to cry.

Chink leaned over and put his hand under my chin, lifted my face, saw
the tears, and he kissed my cheek. His beard was rough and scratchy.
He smelled like the pine woods, and I could see pine needles in his hair
and in his beard, and I wondered if he and Aunt Sophronia had been in
the woods.

"Sugar," he said gently, "I don't like that Miss Muriel story. It ought
to be told the other way around. A colored man should be tellin' a white
man, 'White man, you see this picture of this beautiful colored woman?
White man, you say *Miss* Muriel!'"

He went out of the store through the back room into the yard just as
though he were a member of the family. It hadn't taken him very long to
reach this position. Almost every afternoon he goes for a walk with
Aunt Sophronia. I watch them when they leave the store. He walks so
close to her that he seems to surround her, and he has his head bent so
that his face is close to hers. Once I met them strolling up Petticoat Lane,
his dark face so close to hers that his goat's beard was touching her
smooth brown cheek.

My mother used to watch them too, as they walked side by side on the
dirt path that led to the woods—miles and miles of woods. Sometimes he
must have said things that Aunt Sophronia didn't like, because she would
turn her head sharply away from him.

I decided that once you got used to his beard and the peculiar color and
slant of his eyes, why you could say he had an interesting face. I do not
know what it is about his eyes that makes me think of heat. But I know
what color they are. They are the color of petrified wood after it's been
polished, it's a red brown, and that's what his eyes are like.

I like the way he plays the piano, though I do not like his voice. I cannot get my mother to talk about him. My father grunts when I mention

Chink's name and scowls so ferociously that it is obvious he does not like him.

I tried to find out what Aunt Sophronia thought of him. Later in the day I found her in the store alone and I said, "Do you like Chink Johnson?"

She said, "Run along and do the supper dishes."

"But do you?"

"Don't ask personal questions," she said, and her face and neck flushed.

She must have liked him though. She not only went walking with him in the afternoon, but on Sunday mornings he went to church with her. He wore a white linen suit and that same stiff straw hat way back on his head. He brought her presents—a tall bottle of violet Eau de Cologne, a bunch of Parma violets made of silk, but they looked real. On Sundays, Aunt Sophronia wore the violets pinned at her waist and they made her look elegant, like a picture in a book.

I said, "Oh, you look beautiful."

My mother said, dryly, "Very stylish."

We all crossed the street together on Sunday mornings. They went to church. I went to Sunday school. Sunday school was out first and I waited for them to come down the church steps. Aunt Sophronia came down the church steps and he would be so close behind her that he might have been dancing with her and matching his leg movements to hers. Suddenly he was in front of her and down on the path before she was and he turned and held out his hand. Even there on the sidewalk he wasn't standing still. It is as though his feet and his hands are more closely connected to his heart, to his central nervous system, than is true of other people, so that during every waking moment he moves, tapping his foot on the floor, tapping his fingers on a railing, on somebody's arm, on a table top. I wondered if he kept moving like that when he was asleep, tapping quarter notes with his foot, playing eighth notes with his right hand, half notes with his left hand. He attacked a piano when he played, violated it—violate a piano? I thought, violate Aunt Sophronia?

He stood on the dirt path and held out his hand to Aunt Sophronia, smiling, helping her down the church steps.

"Get your prayers said, sugar?" he said to me.

"Yes. I said one for you and one for the family. Aunt Sophronia, you smell delicious. Like violets—"

"She does, doesn't she?"

We walked across the street to the drugstore, hand in hand. Chink was in the middle and he held one of my hands and one of Aunt Sophronia's. He stays for dinner on Sundays. And on Sunday nights we close the store early and we all sit in the back yard, where it is cool. Mr. Bemish joined us in the yard. At dusk the fireflies come out, and then as the darkness deepens, bats swoop around us. Aunt Sophronia says

"Oooooh!" and holds on to her head, afraid one might get entangled in her hair.

Dottle took out one of his big white handkerchiefs and tied it around his head, and said in his richest, most buttery voice, " 'One of the nocturnal or crepuscular flying mammals constituting the order Chiroptera.' "

Dottle sprawled in a chair and recited poetry or told long stories about the South—stories that sometimes had so much of fear and terror and horror in them that we shivered even though the air was warm. Chink didn't spend the evening. He sat in one of the lawn chairs, tapping on the arm with his long, flexible fingers, and then left. Mr. Bemish always stays until we go in for the night. He takes no part in the conversation, but sits on the ground, huddled near Aunt Sophronia's skirts. Once when a bat swooped quite close, Aunt Sophronia clutched his arm.

Sometimes Dottle recites whole acts from *Macbeth* or *Hamlet* or all of the Song of Solomon, or sometimes he recited the loveliest of Shakespeare's sonnets. We forget the bats swooping over our heads, ignore the mosquitoes that sting our ankles and our legs, and sit mesmerized while he declaims, "Shall I compare thee to a summer's day?"

The summer is going faster and faster—perhaps because of the presence of Aunt Sophronia's suitors. I don't suppose Dottle is really a suitor, but he goes through the motions. He picks little bouquets for her— bachelor buttons and candytuft—and leaves them on the kitchen table. He always calls her "Miss Sophronia." If we are outdoors and she comes out to sit in the yard, he leaps to his feet, and bows and says, "Wait, wait. Befo' you sit on that bench, let me wipe it off," and he pulls out an enormous linen handkerchief and wipes off the bench. He is always bowing and kissing her hand.

By the middle of August it was very hot. My father had the store painted, and when the blinds were taken down, the painter found whole families of bats clinging together in back of the blinds. Evidently they lived there. I couldn't get hold of one, although I tried. They were the most peculiar-looking creatures. They looked almost like a person who wears glasses all the time and then suddenly goes without them, and they have a kind of peering look.

Chink Johnson is always in our house or in the store or in the yard or going for walks with Aunt Sophronia. Whenever he is not violating the piano at the Inn, he is with Aunt Sophronia—

He taught her how to dance—in the back yard, without any music, just his counting and clapping his hands. His feet made no sound on our thick grass. On two different sunny afternoons, he gave her dancing lessons, and on the third afternoon, he had her dancing. She was laughing and she was lively-looking and she looked young. He persuaded her to take off her shoes and she danced in her bare feet. Fortunately, nobody knows this but me.

He took her fishing. When they came back, she was quite sunburned but her eyes were shining as though they held the reflected light from the sun shining on water.

Just in that one short summer he seemed to take on all kinds of guises —fisherman, dancer, singer, churchgoer, even delivery boy.

One morning someone knocked at the back door and there was Chink Johnson with our grocery order, saying to my Aunt Sophronia, "Here's your meat, ma'am, and your vegetables," touching his hat, bowing, unloading the crate of groceries, and then sitting down at the kitchen table as though he owned it, drinking a cup of coffee that no one had offered him, just pouring it out of the enamel pot that stays on the stove, finding cream and sugar himself, and sitting there with his legs thrust way out in front of him, and those terribly tight pants he wears looking as though they were painted on his thighs.

Sometimes when he sits in our kitchen, he laughs. His laughter is not merry. When my father laughs, the sound makes you laugh, even when you don't know what he is laughing about.

When Chink Johnson laughs, I look away from him. The sound hurts my ears. It is like the ugly squawk of some big bird that you have disturbed in the woods and it flies right into your face, pecking at your eyes.

It has been a very interesting summer. I have begun to refer to it in the past tense because there isn't much left of a summer by the middle of August. On Thursday afternoon, Aunt Sophronia and I saw that other ladies liked Chink Johnson too.

Thursday afternoon is traditionally maids' day off and Chink Johnson drove the maids from the Inn into town, in a wagon, late in the day. He stopped in front of the store with a wagon full of girls in long skirts, giggling, leaning against him, a kind of panting excitement in that wagon, their arms around him; they whispered to him, they were seized by fits of laughter, shrieks of laughter.

They came in the store and bought hairnets and hairpins and shampoo and Vaseline and hair tonics and cough medicines and court plaster and a great many items that they did not need because it was a pleasure to be spending money, and to be free of the tyranny of the housekeepers' demands—or so my mother said—some young and attractive, some not so young, about ten of them.

Aunt Sophronia was in the store and she waited on them, studying them. Every once in a while one would go to the door, and yell, "We'll be out in a minute, Chink. Just a little while!" and wave at him and throw kisses at him.

Then they were gone, all at once, piling into the wagon, long full skirts in disarray. One of them sat in Chink's lap, laughing, looking up into his face, and saying, "Let's go in the woods. Chink, take us in the woods. I'll help drive."

Aunt Sophronia and I stood in the doorway and watched them as they drove off, going towards the pine woods. The wagon seemed to be filled with wide skirts, and ruffled petticoats, all suddenly upended because Chink said, "Giddup, there!" and hit the horse with the whip, cracked it over the horse's ears, and the horse started off as though he were a race horse.

It was late when they went past the store, going home. Sitting in the back yard, we could hear the horse racing, and the girls squealing and laughing, and Chink singing a ribald song, about "Strollin', and Strollin'."

Dottle stopped right in the middle of a poem and Mr. Bemish straightened up so that he was not quite so close to Aunt Sophronia's skirts. It was like having Chink Johnson right there in the back yard with us, the rough, atonal voice, the red-brown eyes that looked hot, literally hot, as though if you touched them you would have to withdraw your fingers immediately because they would be scorched or singed or burned, the jutting beard, the restless feet and hands.

We sat absolutely still. We could hear the rattling of the wagon, the clop-clop of the horses' hoofs and above it the laughter of the girls, and dominating that sound, Chink Johnson's voice lifted in song. Even after they were so far away we could not possibly hear them, these sounds seemed to linger in the air, faint, far-off.

It was a warm night, brilliant with light from the moon. I pictured the girls as sitting on top of Chink, all around him, on his arms, in his lap, on his shoulders, and I thought the prettiest one should be perched on his head.

Dottle lit a cigar and puffed out clouds of bluish smoke and said, "I never heard the mating call of the male so clearly sounded on a summer's night." He laughed so hard that he had to get out one of his big handkerchiefs and dab at his eyes with it.

Aunt Sophronia got up from the bench so fast that she brushed against Mr. Bemish, almost knocking him over. He lost his balance and regained it only because he supported himself with one hand on the ground. She must have known that she had very nearly upset him but she went marching toward the house, her back very straight and her head up in the air, and she never once looked back.

Dottle said, "Have I offended her?"

My mother said, "It's late. It's time we went in."

Mr. Bemish must have gone home when we went in the house, but he was back in the yard so early the next morning he might just as well have spent the night. Dottle and I were standing in the kitchen, looking down the back yard. He was drinking coffee out of a mug and I was eating a piece of bread and butter. Our back yard is a pretty sight on a summer morning. It is filled with flowers, and birds are singing, and the air is very cool, and there is a special smell, a summer smell compounded of grass and dew on the grass and flowers, and the suggestion of heat to come later in the day.

We looked out the door and there was Mr. Bemish down on his knees in front of Aunt Sophronia. She was sitting on the bench and she looked

horrified and she seemed to have been in the act of trying to stop him, one
hand extended in a thrusting-away motion. I thought: His pants legs will
be very damp because there's still dew on the grass, and how did he get
here so early, and did he know that she would be sitting on the bench almost before sunup?

"Ah, girlie, girlie!" he said, on his knees in our back yard, kneeling
on our thick, soft grass. "Will you marry me?"

"No!"

"Is it," he said, "because I am old?" and his voice went straight up
in pitch just like a scale. "I'm not old. I'm not old. Why, I can still jump
up in the air and click my heels together three times!"

And he did. He got up off his knees and he jumped up, straight up, and
clicked his heels together three times, and landed on the grass, and there
was just a slight thumping sound when he landed.

Aunt Sophronia said, "Mr. Bemish, Mr. Bemish. Don't do that—
don't do that—go away, go home—" And she ran toward the house and
he started after her and then he saw us standing in the door, watching
him, and he stood still. He shouted after her, "I'll put on my best coat
and my best hat and you won't know me—I'll be back—and you won't
know me—"

Dottle glared at him through the screen door and said, "You old fool
—you old fool—"

Mr. Bemish hurried around the side of the house, pretending that he
hadn't heard him.

I did not know when Mr. Bemish would be back, wearing his best coat
and his best hat, but I certainly wanted to see him and, if possible, to witness his next performance. I decided that whenever Aunt Sophronia was
in the store, I'd be in the store too.

When my father went to eat his dinner at twelve-thirty, Aunt Sophronia looked after the store. There weren't many people who came in
at that hour; it was the dinner hour and Aunt Sophronia sat in the prescription room, with the door open, and read the morning newspaper.
There was an old wooden chair, by the window, in the prescription room.
It had a faded painting across the back, a wooden seat and back and arms.
It was a very comfortable chair if you sat up straight, and Aunt Sophronia sat up very straight. She could look out of the window and see
the church green, see the path that went up Petticoat Lane toward the
pine woods, and she commanded a view of the interior of the store.

I don't think she saw Mr. Bemish when he entered. If she had, she
would have gotten out of the chair immediately to wait on him. But she
was reading the newspaper, and he came in very quietly. He was wearing a cutaway coat that was too long, and a pair of striped trousers, and
he was carrying a silk hat in his hand, a collapsed silk hat. He stopped
inside the door and put the hat in shape and then placed it carefully on his
head. He looked like a circus clown who is making fun of the ring-
master, mocking him, making his costume look silly.

Mr. Bemish went straight through the store, and stood in front of Aunt Sophronia, and he jumped straight up in the air, like a dancer, and clicked his heels together three times. The bottles on the shelves rattled and the back room was filled with a pinging sound.

"Oh, my goodness," Aunt Sophronia said, frowning. "Oh, my goodness, don't jump like that." And she stood up.

My father came in through the back door and he said, "What's going on in here? What's going on in here?"

Mr. Bemish said, "I was just showing Miss Sophronia that I can still jump up in the air and click my heels together three times before I come back down again."

My father made a noise that sounded like "Boooooh!" but wasn't quite, and Mr. Bemish retreated, talking very fast. "I had asked Miss Sophronia if she would marry me and she said no, and I thought perhaps it was because she thinks I'm too old and not stylish enough and so I got dressed up and I was showing her I could still jump—"

"Get out of here! Get out of here! Get out of here!"

My father's voice kept rising and increasing in volume, and his face looked as though he were about to burst. It seemed to darken and to swell, to get bigger.

Aunt Sophronia said, "Oh, you mustn't talk to him like that—"

My father was moving toward Mr. Bemish, and Mr. Bemish was retreating, retreating, and finally he turned and ran out of the store and ran up Petticoat Lane with his long coattails flapping about his legs.

My father said, "I shouldn't have let him hang around here all these months. I can't leave this store for five minutes that I don't find one of these no-goods hangin' around when I come back. Not one of 'em worth the powder and shot to blow 'em to hell and back. That piano player pawin' the ground and this old white man jumpin' up in the air, and that friend of Johno's, that poet or whatever he is, all he needs are some starched petticoats and a bonnet and he'd make a woman—he's practically one now—and he's tee-heein' around, and if they were all put together in one piece, it still wouldn't be a whole man." My father shook his fist in the air and glared at Aunt Sophronia.

"I guess it's all my fault—" Aunt Sophronia sounded choked-up and funny.

My father said, "No, no, no, I didn't mean that," and patted her arm. "It's all perfectly natural. It's just that we're the only colored people living in this little bit of town and there aren't any fine young colored men around, only this tramp piano player, and everytime I look at him I can hear him playing some rags and see a whole line of big-bosomed women done up in sequined dresses standin' over him, moanin' about wantin' somebody to turn their dampers down, and I can see poker games and crap games and—"

My mother came in through the back room. She said, "Samuel, why are you talking about gambling games?"

"I was trying to explain to Sophy how I feel about that piano player."

To my surprise, my mother said, "Has Sophronia asked you how you feel about Mr. Johnson?"

When my father shook his head, she said, "Then I don't think there is any reason for you to say anything about him. I need you in the garden. I want you to move one of my peonies."

I wonder what my mother would say if she knew how my father chased little Mr. Bemish out of his store. I wonder if Mr. Bemish will ever come back.

Mr. Bemish did come back. He came back the following Sunday. We were all in the store, Aunt Sophronia, and Dottle, and Chink and I.

Mr. Bemish sidled in through the door. He looked as though he expected someone to jump out at him and yell "Go home!" But he came in anyway and he sat down beside me on the bench near the front of the store.

Chink was leaning on the cigar case, talking to Aunt Sophronia, his face very close to hers. I couldn't hear what he was saying, but he seemed to be trying to persuade her to do something, go for a walk, or something, and she was obviously refusing, politely but definitely. Dottle was standing near the back of the store, watching Chink.

Aunt Frank opened the store door, and she stood in the doorway holding the screen door open. She has a cross, sharp way of speaking, very fast, and very unpleasant. She saw me and she said, "Where's Mar-tha?"

I wasn't expecting to see Aunt Frank in the store at that hour and I was so surprised that I didn't answer her.

"What's the mat-ter with you? Cat got your tongue? Didn't you hear what I said? Where's your moth-er?"

"She's over on the other side of the building, in the kitchen. She's having coffee with my father."

She scowled at Chink. "How long's that bearded man been in here talkin' to Sophy?"

Chink turned around and looked toward Aunt Frank, Aunt Sophronia started toward her, moving very fast out from behind the cigar case, saying, "Can I get something for you?"

As Aunt Frank stood there holding the door open, a whole flight of bats came in the store. I say a "flight" because I don't know what else to call a large-sized group of bats. They swooped down and up in a blind, fast flight.

Aunt Frank shrieked, "Ahhh! My hair, watch out for your hair! Ahhhhhh!" and stood up on the bench, and held her black fusty skirts close about her and then pulled them over her head. I decided she had confused mice and bats, that the technique for getting rid of mice was to stand on a chair and clutch one's skirts around one, that is, if you were a lady and pretended to be afraid of mice. I did learn that Aunt Frank was wearing carpet slippers made of dark-gray felt, black cotton stockings, and under the outside layer of skirts there seemed to be a great many layers of black petticoats.

Dottle ran into the back room and held the door tightly shut. There is a glass in the door and he could look out at the rest of us as we dodged the bats. I could see his large white face, and long hair, and I supposed he was as frightened as Aunt Frank that bats would get entangled in his hair, because he squealed, all the rich, buttery quality gone from his voice, just a high-pitched squealing.

Aunt Frank cautiously lowered the outer skirt, fumbled in a pocket, and took out a bottle, not a big bottle, but about the size of an eight-ounce cough-medicine bottle, and she took two or three swigs from it, recorked it, and then re-covered her head.

Chink grabbed a newspaper and slapped at the bats as they circled. "Got-cha. Hi-hi-gotcha —hi-hi-gotcha—hi-hi!" and he folded the newspaper and belted them as they swished past him.

Mr. Bemish stared. I decided that he'd lived with bats and spiders and mice, well, not lived with perhaps, but was so accustomed to them that he could not understand why they should cause all this noise and confusion and fear. He ignored the bats entirely and went to the rescue of his lady love. He clasped Aunt Sophronia to his bosom, covering her head with his hands and arms and he kept murmuring comforting words. "Now, now. I won't let anything hurt you. Nothing can harm you." He took a deep breath and said, quite distinctly, "I love you, my darling. I love you, love you—"

Aunt Sophronia seemed to nestle in his arms, to cuddle closer to him, to lean harder every time a bat swooped past them.

Father came through the back room—he had to wrestle Dottle out of the way before he could get through the door—and he very sensibly held the screen door open, and what with the impetus offered by Chink's folded newspaper, the bats swooped outside.

It was really very exciting while it lasted, what with all the shrieks and the swift movement of the bats. When I began to really look around, the first thing I noticed was that Aunt Sophronia was still huddled in the protective arms of Mr. Bemish. Dottle came out of the back room with his mouth pursed and his cheeks were puffed out a little and I wouldn't have been surprised if he had hissed at Mr. Bemish. He and Chink headed straight towards Mr. Bemish. They are very tall men and Mr. Bemish is short and slender, and as they converged on him, one from the rear and the other from the side, he looked smaller and older than ever.

Aunt Sophronia stepped away from Mr. Bemish. She moved toward Chink. One side of her face was red where it had been pressed hard against the wool of Mr. Bemish's coat.

All of a sudden my father's hand was resting on one of Chink's shoulders. He has large, heavy hands and his hand seemed to have descended suddenly and with great weight. He said, "You'll not start any trouble in my store."

Aunt Frank said, "Bats! Bats!" She indicated that my father was to help her down from the bench. She climbed down awkwardly, holding on to him. "Worse than bats," she said, and she made a wide all-inclusive gesture that took in Chink and Dottle and Mr. Bemish. "Where's Mar-tha?" she demanded. "She still in the kitchen?"

My father nodded. He held the door open for Mr. Bemish, and Mr. Bemish scuttled out. Dottle and Chink went out too.

I found a dead bat on the floor and sat down on the bench at the front of the store to examine it. It had a very unpleasant smell. But it was such an interesting creature that I ignored the odor. It had rather large, pointed ears that I thought were quite charming. It had very sharp little claws. I could see why the ladies had screamed and covered their heads, because if those claws got entangled in their long hair, someone would have had to cut their hair to get a bat out of it. Aunt Frank's hair isn't long; it is like a sheep's wool, tight-curled and close to the skin or scalp. But I suppose a bat's sharp little claws and peculiar wings snarled up in that might create more of a problem that it would if caught in longer and less tightly curled hair.

The wings of the bat were webbed like the feet of ducks with a thin membrane-like tissue that was attached to the body, reaching from the front legs or arms to the back legs and attached to the sides. The body was small in comparison to the wide sweep of those curious wings. I stretched its wings out and they looked like the inside of an opened umbrella, and I couldn't help admiring them. I began to think of all the things I'd heard said about bats, "blind as a bat," and the word "batty" meaning crazy, and I tried to figure out why "batty," probably because a bat's behavior didn't make sense to a human being—its fast, erratic flight would look senseless.

Then Aunt Frank's voice sounded right in my ear, and her horrible breath was in my nose, and she smelled worse than the bat. She said, "You throw that nasty thing away. You throw that nasty thing away."

I thrust the dead bat straight at her black and wrinkled face. "Look out," I yelled. "It'll suck your blood. It's still alive. Look out!"

She jumped away, absolutely furious. "You little vixen," she said, and squealed just like a pig. Then she saw my mother standing in the door of the prescription room. "Mar-tha," she commanded, "you come here and make her throw this nasty thing away. Make her throw it away. She's settin' here playin' with a dead bat."

My mother said, "If you want to look at the bat, take it outside or take it in the back room. You can't keep a dead bat here in the drugstore."

"This can't hurt her. It's dead."

She interrupted me. "Many people are afraid of bats. It doesn't make any difference whether the bats are dead or alive—they are still afraid of them."

I went outside and sat on the front steps and waited. There was a full moon and the light from it made the street and the houses and the church look as though they had been whitewashed. I put the bat beside me on the step. I was going to wait for Aunt Frank, and when she came out of the store and started down the steps, I was going to put the dead stinking bat in one of the big pockets in her skirt—the pocket where she kept her bottle of gin. And when she got home and reached for a drink, I hoped she would discover, encounter, touch with her bony fingers, the corpse of "one of the nocturnal or crepuscular flying mammals constituting the order Chiroptera" as a token of my affection.

I must have waited there on the steps for two hours. My father began putting out the lights in the store. I stayed right there, anticipating the moment when my ancient enemy, Aunt Frank, would come stumbling around the side of the building.

And then—one moment I was sitting on the splintery front steps of the store, and the next moment I was running up Petticoat Lane, going just as fast as I could, because it had suddenly occurred to me that Chink Johnson and Dottle Smith had gone out of the drugstore right behind Mr. Bemish and they hadn't returned.

By the time I reached Mr. Bemish's shop, I was panting. I couldn't catch my breath.

Mr. Bemish's wagon was drawn up close to the side of the shop. The horse was hitched to it. Mr. Bemish was loading the headboard of his beautiful brass bed on the wagon. He was obviously moving—leaving town, at night. He walked in a peculiar fashion as though he were lame. He was panting too, and making hiccuping noises like someone who has been crying a long time, so long that no real sound comes out, just a kind of hiccuping noise due to the contractions of the throat muscles and the heaving of the chest.

As I stood there, he got the headboard on the wagon, and then he struggled with his mattress, and then the springs, and then he brought out his cobbler's bench.

Dottle and Chink stood watching him, just like two guards or two sheriffs. None of us said anything.

I finally sat down on the enormous millstone that served as Mr. Bemish's front step. I sat way off to one side where I wouldn't interfere with his comings and goings.

May-a-ling, his cat, rubbed against me and then came and sat in my lap, with her back to me, facing towards Mr. Bemish.

It didn't take him very long to empty the shop of his belongings. I couldn't help thinking that if we ever moved, if would take us days to pack all the books and the pictures and the china, and all our clothes and furniture. We all collected things. Aunt Sophronia did beautiful embroidery and she collected embroidered fabrics, and mother collected old dishes and old furniture, and my father collected old glass bottles and old mortars, and they all collected books, and then all the rooms had furniture and there were all kinds of cooking pots. No one of us would ever get all of our belongings in one wagon.

Mr. Bemish came out of the shop and walked all around the little building with that peculiar stiff-legged gait. Apparently the only item he'd overlooked was his garden bench. He had trouble getting it in the wagon, and I dumped May-a-ling on the ground and went to help him.

One of Dottle's meaty hands gripped my braid. "He can manage."

I twisted away from him. "He's just a little old man and he's my friend and I'm going to help him."

Chink said, "Leave her alone."

Dottle let go of my hair. I helped put the bench in the wagon, and then went inside the shop with him, and helped him carry out the few items that were left. Each time I went inside the shop with Mr. Bemish I asked him questions. We both whispered.

"Where are you going, Mr. Bemish?"

"Massachusetts."

"Why?"

He didn't answer. His hiccups got worse.

I waited until we'd taken down the green summer curtains and carefully folded them, and put them in the little trunk that held some of his clothes, and put his broom and his dustpan and his tall kitchen cooking stool on the wagon, before I repeated my question. His hiccups had quieted down.

"Why are you leaving, Mr. Bemish?" I whispered.

"They were going to sew me up."

"Sew you up. Did you say—sew you up?"

"Yes."

"Where?" I said, staring at him, thinking: sew up? Sew up what—eyes, nostrils, mouth, ears, rectum? "They were trying to scare you, Mr. Bemish. Nobody would sew up a person, a human being, unless it was a surgeon—after an operation—"

He shook his head. "No," he whispered. "I thought so too, but—no, they meant it—with my own waxed thread—"

"Did they—"

"Hush! Hush!"

We used his little piece of flowered carpet to wrap his washbowl and pitcher in and then put the whole bulky package it made on the wagon. We went back inside to make sure that we hadn't forgotten anything. The inside of his shop looked very small and shabby and lonely. There wasn't anything left except his stove and he obviously couldn't take that. It was a very big, handsome stove and he kept it quite shiny and clean.

"Can you keep a secret?" he whispered, standing quite close to me. He smelled old and dusty and withered like dried flowers.

I nodded.

He handed me a small velvet bag. "Hide it, girlie," he whispered.
"It's some old jewelry that belonged to my mother. Give it to Miss
Sophronia at Christmas from me." He patted my arm.

We went outside and he took down the sign with the lady's high-
laced shoe painted on it, and put it on the wagon seat. He climbed in the
wagon, picked up the reins.

"May-a-ling, May-a-ling," he called. It was the most musical sound
I have ever heard used to call a cat. She answered him instantly. She
mewed and jumped up on the wagon seat beside him. He clucked to the
horse and they drove off.

I waited not only until they were out of sight, but until I could no
longer hear the creak of the wagon wheels and the clop-clop of the
horses hoofs, and then I turned and ran.

Chink said, "Wait a minute—"

Dottle said, "You don't understand—"

I stopped running just long enough to shout at them, "You both stink.
You stink like dead bats. You and your goddamn Miss Muriel—"

John Cheever
1912–
THE SWIMMER*

IT WAS one of those midsummer Sundays when everyone sits around
saying: "I *drank* too much last night." You might have heard it
whispered by the parishioners leaving church, heard it from the lips of
the priest himself, struggling with his cassock in the *vestiarium*,[1] heard
it from the golf links and the tennis courts, heard it from the wildlife
preserve where the leader of the Audubon group was suffering from a
terrible hangover. "I *drank* too much," said Donald Westerhazy. "We
all *drank* too much," said Lucinda Merrill. "It must have been the wine,"
said Helen Westerhazy. "I *drank* too much of that claret."

This was at the edge of the Westerhazys' pool. The pool, fed by an
artesian well with a high iron content, was a pale shade of green. It was
a fine day. In the west there was a massive stand of cumulus cloud so
like a city seen from the distance—from the bow of an approaching
ship—that it might have had a name. Lisbon. Hackensack. The sun was
hot. Neddy Merrill sat by the green water, one hand in it, one around a
glass of gin. He was a slender man—he seemed to have the especial
slenderness of youth—and while he was far from young he had slid

[1] robing room
* Reprinted by permission; © 1964 John Cheever. Originally in *The New Yorker*.

down his banister that morning and given the bronze backside of Aphrodite[2] on the hall table a smack, as he jogged toward the smell of coffee
in his dining room. He might have been compared to a summer's day,[3]
particularly the last hours of one, and while he lacked a tennis racket or
a sail bag the impression was definitely one of youth, sport, and clement
weather. He had been swimming and now he was breathing deeply,
stertorously as if he could gulp into his lungs the components of that
moment, the heat of the sun, the intenseness of his pleasure. It all seemed
to flow into his chest. His own house stood in Bullet Park, eight miles to
the south, where his four beautiful daughters would have had their lunch
and might be playing tennis. Then it occurred to him that by taking a
dogleg to the south-west he could reach his home by water.

His life was not confining and the delight he took in this observation
could not be explained by its suggestion of escape. He seemed to see,
with a cartographer's eye, that string of swimming pools, that quasi-
subterranean stream that curved across the county. He had made a discovery, a contribution to modern geography; he would name the stream
Lucinda after his wife. He was not a practical joker nor was he a fool
but he was determinedly original and had a vague and modest idea of
himself as a legendary figure. The day was beautiful and it seemed to
him that a long swim might enlarge and celebrate its beauty.

He took off a sweater that was hung over his shoulders and dove in.
He had an inexplicable contempt for men who did not hurl themselves
into pools. He swam a choppy crawl, breathing either with every stroke
or every fourth stroke and counting somewhere well in the back of his
mind the one-two one-two of a flutter kick. It was not a serviceable
stroke for long distances but the domestication of swimming had saddled
the sport with some customs and in his part of the world a crawl was
customary. To be embraced and sustained by the light green water was
less a pleasure, it seemed, than the resumption of a natural condition,
and he would have liked to swim without trunks, but this was not possible, considering his project. He hoisted himself up on the far curb—
he never used the ladder—and started across the lawn. When Lucinda
asked where he was going he said he was going to swim home.

The only maps and charts he had to go by were remembered or imaginary but these were clear enough. First there were the Grahams, the
Hammers, the Lears, the Howlands, and the Crosscups. He would cross
Ditmar Street to the Bunkers and come, after a short portage, to the
Levys, the Welchers, and the public pool in Lancaster. Then there were
the Hallorans, the Sachses, the Biswangers, Shirley Adams, the Gilmartins, and the Cludes. The day was lovely, and that he lived in a world
so generously supplied with water seemed like a clemency, a beneficence.
His heart was high and he ran across the grass. Making his way home by
an uncommon route gave him the feeling that he was a pilgrim, an ex-

[2] goddess of love   [3] Shakespeare, Sonnet XVIII

plorer, a man with a destiny, and he knew that he would find friends all along the way; friends would line the banks of the Lucinda River.

He went through a hedge that separated the Westerhazys' land from the Grahams', walked under some flowering apple trees, passed the shed that housed their pump and filter, and came out at the Grahams' pool. "Why, Neddy," Mrs. Graham said, "what a marvelous surprise. I've been trying to get you on the phone all morning. Here, let me get you a drink." He saw then, like any explorer, that the hospitable customs and traditions of the natives would have to be handled with diplomacy if he was ever going to reach his destination. He did not want to mystify or seem rude to the Grahams nor did he have the time to linger there. He swam the length of their pool and joined them in the sun and was rescued, a few minutes later, by the arrival of two carloads of friends from Connecticut. During the uproarious reunions he was able to slip away. He went down by the front of the Graham's house, stepped over a thorny hedge, and crossed a vacant lot to the Hammers'. Mrs. Hammer, looking up from her roses, saw him swim by although she wasn't quite sure who it was. The Lears heard him splashing past the open windows of their living room. The Howlands and the Crosscups were away. After leaving the Howlands' he crossed Ditmar Street and started for the Bunkers', where he could hear, even at that distance, the noise of a party.

The water refracted the sound of voices and laughter and seemed to suspend it in midair. The Bunkers' pool was on a rise and he climbed some stairs to a terrace where twenty-five or thirty men and women were drinking. The only person in the water was Rusty Towers, who floated there on a rubber raft. Oh how bonny and lush were the banks of the Lucinda River! Prosperous men and women gathered by the sapphire-colored waters while caterer's men in white coats passed them cold gin. Overhead a red de Haviland trainer was circling around and around and around in the sky with something like the glee of a child in a swing. Ned felt a passing affection for the scene, a tenderness for the gathering, as if it was something he might touch. In the distance he heard thunder. As soon as Enid Bunker saw him she began to scream: "Oh look who's here! What a marvelous surprise! When Lucinda said that you couldn't come I thought I'd *die*." She made her way to him through the crowd, and when they had finished kissing she led him to the bar, a progress that was slowed by the fact that he stopped to kiss eight or ten other women and shake the hands of as many men. A smiling bartender he had seen at a hundred parties gave him a gin and tonic and he stood by the bar for a moment, anxious not to get stuck in any conversation that would delay his voyage. When he seemed about to be surrounded he dove in and swam close to the side to avoid colliding with Rusty's raft. At the far end of the pool he bypassed the Tomlinsons with a broad smile and jogged up the garden path. The gravel cut his feet but this was the only unpleasantness. The party was confined to the pool, and as he went toward the house he heard the brilliant, watery sound of voices

fade, heard the noise of a radio from the Bunkers' kitchen, where someone was listening to a ballgame. Sunday afternoon. He made his way
through the parked cars and down the grassy border of their driveway to
Alewives' Lane. He did not want to be seen on the road in his bathing
trunks but there was no traffic and he made the short distance to the
Levys' driveway, marked with a private property sign and a green tube
for the *New York Times*. All the doors and windows of the big house
were open but there were no signs of life; not even a dog barked. He
went around the side of the house to the pool and saw that the Levys had
only recently left. Glasses and bottles and dishes of nuts were on a table
at the deep end, where there was a bathhouse or gazebo, hung with Japanese lanterns. After swimming the pool he got himself a glass and poured
a drink. It was his fourth or fifth drink and he had swum nearly half the
length of the Lucinda River. He felt tired, clean, and pleased at that moment to be alone; pleased with everything.

It would storm. The stand of cumulus cloud—that city—had risen
and darkened, and while he sat there he heard the percussiveness of
thunder again. The de Haviland trainer was still circling overhead and it
seemed to Ned that he could almost hear the pilot laugh with pleasure
in the afternoon; but when there was another peal of thunder he took off
for home. A train whistle blew and he wondered what time it had gotten
to be. Four? Five? He thought of the provincial station at that hour,
where a waiter, his tuxedo concealed by a raincoat, a dwarf with some
flowers wrapped in newspaper, and a woman who had been crying would
be waiting for the local. It was suddenly growing dark; it was that moment when the pin-headed birds seem to organize their song into some
acute and knowledgeable recognition of the storm's approach. Then
there was a fine noise of rushing water from the crown of an oak at his
back, as if a spigot there had been turned. Then the noise of fountains
came from the crowns of all the tall trees.Why did he love storms, what
was the meaning of his excitement when the door sprang open and the
rain wind fled rudely up the stairs, why had the simple task of shutting
the windows of an old house seemed fitting and urgent, why did the first
watery notes of a storm wind have for him the unmistakable sound of
good news, cheer, glad tidings? Then there was an explosion, a smell of
cordite, and rain lashed the Japanese lanterns that Mrs. Levy had bought
in Kyoto the year before last, or was it the year before that?

He stayed in the Levys' gazebo until the storm had passed. The rain
had cooled the air and he shivered. The force of the wind had stripped
a maple of its red and yellow leaves and scattered them over the grass
and the water. Since it was midsummer the tree must be blighted, and yet
he felt a peculiar sadness at this sign of autumn. He braced his shoulders,
emptied his glass, and started for the Welchers' pool. This meant crossing the Lindleys' riding ring and he was surprised to find it overgrown
with grass and all the jumps dismantled. He wondered if the Lindleys
had sold their horses or gone away for the summer and put them out to

board. He seemed to remember having heard something about the Lindleys and their horses but the memory was unclear. On he went, barefoot through the wet grass, to the Welchers', where he found their pool was dry.

This breach in his chain of water disappointed him absurdly, and he felt like some explorer who seeks a torrential headwater and finds a dead stream. He was disappointed and mystified. It was common enough to go away for the summer but no one ever drained his pool. The Welchers had definitely gone away. The pool furniture was folded, stacked, and covered with a tarpaulin. The bathhouse was locked. All the windows of the house were shut, and when he went around to the driveway in front he saw a for-sale sign nailed to a tree. When had he last heard from the Welchers—when, that is, had he and Lucinda last regretted an invitation to dine with them? It seemed only a week or so ago. Was his memory failing or had he so disciplined it in the repression of unpleasant facts that he had damaged his sense of the truth? Then in the distance he heard the sound of a tennis game. This cheered him, cleared away all his apprehensions and let him regard the overcast sky and the cold air with indifference. This was the day that Neddy Merrill swam across the county. That was the day! He started off then for his most difficult portage.

Had you gone for a Sunday afternoon ride that day you might have seen him, close to naked, standing on the shoulders of route 424, waiting for a chance to cross. You might have wondered if he was the victim of foul play, had his car broken down, or was he merely a fool. Standing barefoot in the deposits of the highway—beer cans, rags, and blowout patches—exposed to all kinds of ridicule, he seemed pitiful. He had known when he started that this was a part of his journey—it had been on his maps—but confronted with the lines of traffic, worming through the summery light, he found himself unprepared. He was laughed at, jeered at, a beer can was thrown at him, and he had no dignity or humor to bring to the situation. He could have gone back, back to the Westerhazys', where Lucinda would still be sitting in the sun. He had signed nothing, vowed nothing, pledged nothing, not even to himself. Why, believing as he did, that all human obduracy was susceptible to common sense, was he unable to turn back? Why was he determined to complete his journey even if it meant putting his life in danger? At what point had this prank, this joke, this piece of horseplay become serious? He could not go back, he could not even recall with any clearness the green water at the Westerhazys', the sense of inhaling the day's components, the friendly and relaxed voices saying that they had *drunk* too much. In the space of an hour, more or less, he had covered a distance that made his return impossible.

An old man, tooling down the highway at fifteen miles an hour, let him get to the middle of the road, where there was a grass divider. Here he was exposed to the ridicule of the northbound traffic, but after ten or fifteen minutes he was able to cross. From here he had only a short walk to the Recreation Center at the edge of the Village of Lancaster, where there were some handball courts and a public pool.

The effect of the water on voices, the illusion of brilliance and suspense, was the same here as it had been at the Bunkers' but the sounds here were louder, harsher, and more shrill, and as soon as he entered the crowded enclosure he was confronted with regimentation. "ALL SWIMMERS MUST TAKE A SHOWER BEFORE USING THE POOL. ALL SWIMMERS MUST USE THE FOOTBATH. ALL SWIMMERS MUST WEAR THEIR IDENTIFICATION DISKS." He took a shower, washed his feet in a cloudy and bitter solution and made his way to the edge of the water. It stank of chlorine and looked to him like a sink. A pair of lifeguards in a pair of towers blew police whistles at what seemed to be regular intervals and abused the swimmers through a public address system. Neddy remembered the sapphire water at the Bunkers' with longing and thought that he might contaminate himself—damage his own prosperousness and charm—by swimming in this murk, but he reminded himself that he was an explorer, a pilgrim, and that this was merely a stagnant bend in the Lucinda River. He dove, scowling with distaste, into the chlorine and had to swim with his head above water to avoid collisions, but even so he was bumped into, splashed and jostled. When he got to the shallow end both lifeguards were shouting at him: "Hey, you, you without the identification disk, get outa the water." He did, but they had no way of pursing him and he went through the reek of suntan oil and chlorine out through the hurricane fence and passed the handball courts. By crossing the road he entered the wooded part of the Halloran estate. The woods were not cleared and the footing was treacherous and difficult until he reached the lawn and the clipped beech hedge that encircled their pool.

The Hallorans were friends, an elderly couple of enormous wealth who seemed to bask in the suspicion that they might be Communists. They were zealous reformers but they were not Communists, and yet when they were accused, as they sometimes were, of subversion, it seemed to gratify and excite them. Their beech hedge was yellow and he guessed this had been blighted like the Levy's maple. He called hullo, hullo, to warn the Hallorans of his approach, to palliate his invasion of their privacy. The Hallorans, for reasons that had never been explained to him, did not wear bathing suits. No explanations were in order, really. Their nakedness was a detail in their uncompromising zeal for reform and he stepped politely out of his trunks before he went through the opening in the hedge.

Mrs. Halloran, a stout woman with white hair and a serene face, was reading the *Times*. Mr. Halloran was taking beech leaves out of the water with a scoop. They seemed not surprised or displeased to see him. Their pool was perhaps the oldest in the county, a fieldstone rectangle fed by a brook. It had no filter or pump and its waters were the opaque gold of the stream.

"I'm swimming across the country," Ned said.

"Why, I didn't know one could," exclaimed Mrs. Halloran.

"Well, I've made it from the Westerhazys'," Ned said. "That must be about four miles."

He left his trunks at the deep end, walked to the shallow end, and swam this stretch. As he was pulling himself out of the water he heard Mrs. Halloran say: "We've been *terribly* sorry to hear about all your misfortunes, Neddy."

"My misfortunes?" Ned asked. "I don't know what you mean."

"Why, we heard that you'd sold the house and that your poor children . . ."

"I don't recall having sold the house," Ned said, "and the girls are at home."

"Yes," Mrs. Halloran sighed, "Yes . . ." Her voice filled the air with an unseasonable melancholy and Ned spoke briskly. "Thank you for the swim."

"Well, have a nice trip," said Mrs. Halloran.

Beyond the hedge he pulled on his trunks and fastened them. They were loose and he wondered if, during the space of an afternoon, he could have lost some weight. He was cold and he was tired and the naked Hallorans and their dark water had depressed him. The swim was too much for his strength but how could he have guessed this, sliding down the banister that morning and sitting in the Westerhazys' sun? His arms were lame. His legs felt rubbery and ached at the joints. The worst of it was the cold in his bones and the feeling that he might never be warm again. Leaves were falling down around him and he smelled woodsmoke on the wind. Who would be burning wood at this time of year?

He needed a drink. Whiskey would warm him, pick him up, carry him through the last of his journey, refresh his feeling that it was original and valorous to swim across the county. Channel swimmers took brandy. He needed a stimulant. He crossed the lawn in front of the Hallorans' house and went down a little path to where they had built a house for their only daughter Helen and her husband Eric Sachs. The Sachses' pool was small and he found Helen and her husband there.

"Oh, *Neddy*," Helen said. "Did you lunch at Mother's?"

"Not *really*," Ned said. "I *did* stop to see your parents." This seemed to be explanation enough. "I'm terribly sorry to break in on you like this but I've taken a chill and I wonder if you'd give me a drink."

"Why, I'd *love* to," Helen said, "but there hasn't been anything in this house to drink since Eric's operation. That was three years ago."

Was he losing his memory, had his gift for concealing painful facts let him forget that he sold his house, that his children were in trouble, and that his friend had been ill? His eyes slipped from Eric's face to his abdomen, where he saw three pale, sutured scars, two of them at least a foot long. Gone was his navel, and what, Neddy thought, would the roving hand, bed-checking one's gifts at 3 A.M. make of a belly with no navel, no link to birth, this breach in the succession?

"I'm sure you can get a drink at the Biswangers'," Helen said. "They're having an enormous do. You can hear it from here. Listen!"

She raised her head and from across the road, the lawns, the gardens, the woods, the fields, he heard again, the brilliant noise of voices over water. "Well, I'll get wet," he said, still feeling that he had no freedom of choice about his means of travel. He dove into the Sachses' cold water and, gasping, close to drowning, made his way from one end of the pool to the other. "Lucinda and I want *terribly* to see you," he said over his shoulder, his face set toward the Biswangers'. "We're sorry it's been so long and we'll call you *very* soon."

He crossed some fields to the Biswangers' and the sounds of revelry there. They would be honored to give him a drink, they would be happy to give him a drink, they would in fact be lucky to give him a drink. The Biswangers invited him and Lucinda for dinner four times a year, six weeks in advance. They were always rebuffed and yet they continued to send out their invitations, unwilling to comprehend the rigid and un-democratic realities of their society. They were the sort of people who discussed the price of things at cocktails, exchanged market tips during dinner, and after dinner told dirty stories to mixed company. They did not belong to Neddy's set—they were not even on Lucinda's Christmas card list. He went toward their pool with feelings of indifference, charity, and some unease, since it seemed to be getting dark and these were the longest days of the year. The party when he joined it was noisy and large. Grace Biswanger was the kind of hostess who asked the optome-trist, the veterinarian, the real-estate dealer and the dentist. No one was swimming and the twilight, reflected on the water of the pool, had a wintry gleam. There was a bar and he started for this. When Grace Biswanger saw him she came toward him, not affectionately as he had every right to expect, but bellicosely.

"Why, this party has everything," she said loudly, "including a gate crasher."

She could not deal him a social blow—there was no question about this and he did not flinch. "As a gate crasher," he asked politely, "do I rate a drink?"

"Suit yourself," she said. "You don't seem to pay much attention to invitations."

She turned her back on him and joined some guests, and he went to the bar and ordered a whiskey. The bartender served him but he served him rudely. His was a world in which the caterer's men kept the social score and to be rebuffed by a part-time barkeep meant that he had suffered some loss of social esteem. Or perhaps the man was new and uninformed. Then he heard Grace at his back say: "They went for broke overnight—

nothing but income—and he showed up drunk one Sunday and asked us to loan him five thousand dollars. . . ." She was always talking about money. It was worse than eating your peas off a knife. He dove into the pool, swam its length and went away.

The next pool on his list, the last but two, belonged to his old mistress, Shirley Adams. If he had suffered any injuries at the Biswangers' they would be cured here. Love—sexual roughhouse in fact—was the supreme elixir, the painkiller, the brightly colored pill that would put the spring back into his step, the joy of life in his heart. They had had an affair last week, last month, last year. He couldn't remember. It was he who had broken it off, his was the upper hand, and he stepped through the gate of the wall that surrounded her pool with nothing so considered as self-confidence. It seemed in a way to be his pool as the lover, particularly the illicit lover, enjoys the possessions of his mistress with an authority unknown to holy matrimony. She was there, her hair the color of brass, but her figure, at the edge of the lighted, cerulean water, excited in him no profound memories. It had been, he thought, a lighthearted affair, although she had wept when he broke it off. She seemed confused to see him and he wondered if she was still wounded. Would she, God forbid, weep again?

"What do you want?" she asked.

"I'm swimming across the county."

"Good Christ. Will you ever grow up?"

"What's the matter?"

"If you've come here for money," she said, "I won't give you another cent."

"You could give me a drink."

"I could but I won't. I'm not alone."

"Well, I'm on my way."

He dove in and swam the pool, but when he tried to haul himself up onto the curb he found that the strength in his arms and his shoulders had gone, and he paddled to the ladder and climbed out. Looking over his shoulder he saw, in the lighted bathhouse, a young man. Going out onto the dark lawn he smelled chrysanthemums or marigolds—some stubborn autumnal fragrance—on the night air, strong as gas. Looking overhead he saw that the stars had come out, but why should he seem to see Andromeda, Cepheus, and Cassiopeia? What had become of the constellations of midsummer? He began to cry.

It was probably the first time in his adult life that he had ever cried, certainly the first time in his life that he had ever felt so miserable, cold, tired, and bewildered. He could not understand the rudeness of the caterer's barkeep or the rudeness of a mistress who had come to him on her knees and showered his trousers with tears. He had swum too long, he had been immersed too long, and his nose and his throat were sore from the water. What he needed then was a drink, some company, and some clean dry clothes, and while he could have cut directly across the road to his home he went on to the Gilmartins' pool. Here, for the first time in his life, he did not dive but went down the steps into the icy water and swam a hobbled side stroke that he might have learned as a youth. He staggered with fatigue on his way to the Clydes' and paddled the length of their pool, stopping again and again with his hand on the curb to rest. He climbed up the ladder and wondered if he had the strength to get home. He had done what he wanted, he had swum the county, but he was so stupefied with exhaustion that his triumph seemed vague. Stooped, holding onto the gateposts for support, he turned up the driveway of his own house.

The place was dark. Was it so late that they had all gone to bed? Had Lucinda stayed at the Westerhazys' for supper? Had the girls joined her there or gone someplace else? Hadn't they agreed, as they usually did on Sunday, to regret all their invitations and stay at home? He tried the garage doors to see what cars were in but the doors were locked and rust came off the handles onto his hands. Going toward the house, he saw that the force of the thunderstorm had knocked one of the rain gutters loose. It hung down over the front door like an umbrella rib, but it could be fixed in the morning. The house was locked, and he thought that the stupid cook or the stupid maid must have locked the place up until he remembered that it had been some time since they had employed a maid or a cook. He shouted, pounded on the door, tried to force it with his shoulder, and then, looking in at the windows, saw that the place was empty.

Bernard Malamud

1914–

THE LAST MOHICAN

FIDELMAN, a self-confessed failure as a painter, came to Italy to prepare a critical study of Giotto,[1] the opening chapter of which he had carried across the ocean in a new pigskin leather brief case, now gripped in his perspiring hand. Also new were his gum-soled oxblood shoes, a tweed suit he had on despite the late-September sun slanting hot in the Roman sky, although there was a lighter one in his bag; and a dacron shirt and set of cotton-dacron underwear, good for quick and easy washing for the traveler. His suitcase, a bulky two-strapped affair which embarrassed him slightly, he had borrowed from his sister Bessie. He planned, if he had any funds left at the end of the year, to buy a new one in Florence. Although he had been in not much of a mood when he had left the U.S.A., Fidelman picked up in Naples, and at the moment, as he

---

[1] Giotto di Bondone, 1276?–1337?, Florentine artist

stood in front of the Rome railroad station, after twenty minutes still absorbed in his first sight of the Eternal City, he was conscious of a certain exaltation that devolved on him after he had discovered that directly across the many-vehicled piazza stood the remains of the Baths of Diocletian.[2] Fidelman remembered having read that Michelangelo[3] had helped in converting the baths into a church and convent, the latter ultimately changed into the museum that presently was there. "Imagine," he muttered. "Imagine all that history."

In the midst of his imagining, Fidelman experienced the sensation of suddenly seeing himself as he was, to the pinpoint, outside and in, not without bittersweet pleasure; and as the well-known image of his face rose before him he was taken by the depth of pure feeling in his eyes, slightly magnified by glasses, and the sensitivity of his elongated nostrils and often tremulous lips, nose divided from lips by a mustache of recent vintage that looked, Fidelman thought, as if it had been sculptured there, adding to his dignified appearance although he was a little on the short side. Almost at the same moment, this unexpectedly intense sense of his being—it was more than appearance—faded, exaltation having gone where exaltation goes, and Fidelman became aware that there was an exterior source to the strange, almost tri-dimensional reflection of himself he had felt as well as seen. Behind him, a short distance to the right, he had noticed a stranger—give a skeleton a couple of pounds—loitering near a bronze statue on a stone pedestal of the heavy-dugged Etruscan wolf suckling the infant Romulus and Remus,[4] the man contemplating Fidelman already acquisitively so as to suggest to the traveler that he had been mirrored (lock, stock, barrel) in the other's gaze for some time, perhaps since he had stepped off the train. Casually studying him though pretending no, Fidelman beheld a person of about his own height, oddly dressed in brown knickers and black knee-length woolen socks drawn up over slightly bowed, broomstick legs, these grounded in small porous pointed shoes. His yellowed shirt was open at the gaunt throat, both sleeves rolled up over skinny, hairy arms. The stranger's high forehead was bronzed, his black hair thick behind small ears, the dark close-shaven beard tight on the face; his experienced nose was weighted at the tip, and the soft brown eyes, above all, wanted. Though his expression suggested humility he all but licked his lips as he approached the ex-painter.

"Shalom," he greeted Fidelman.

"Shalom," the other hesitantly replied, uttering the word—so far as he recalled—for the first time in his life. My God, he thought, a handout for sure. My first hello in Rome and it has to be a schnorrer.[5]

---

[2] Roman emperor, 284–305
[3] Michelangelo Buonarroti, 1475–1564, Italian architect, sculptor, and painter
[4] sculpture by an unknown artist of the legendary founders of Rome suckling their foster mother
[5] panhandler

The stranger extended a smiling hand. "Susskind," he said, "Shimon Susskind."

"Arthur Fidelman." Transferring his brief case to under his left arm while standing astride the big suitcase he shook hands with Susskind. A blue-smocked porter came by, glanced at Fidelman's bag, looked at him, then walked away.

Whether he knew it or not Susskind was rubbing his palms contemplatively together.

"Parla italiano?"

"Not with ease, although I read it fluently. You might say I need the practice."

"Yiddish?"

"I express myself best in English."

"Let it be English then." Susskind spoke with a slight British intonation. "I knew you were Jewish," he said, "the minute my eyes saw you." Fidelman chose to ignore the remark. "Where did you pick up your knowledge of English?"

"In Israel."

Israel interested Fidelman. "You live there?"

"Once, not now," Susskind answered vaguely. He seemed suddenly bored.

"How so?"

Susskind twitched a shoulder. "Too much heavy labor for a man of my modest health. Also I couldn't stand the suspense."

Fidelman nodded.

"Furthermore, the desert air makes me constipated. In Rome I am lighthearted."

"A Jewish refugee from Israel, no less," Fidelman said with good humor.

"I'm always running," Susskind answered mirthlessly. If he was lighthearted he had yet to show it.

"Where else from, if I may ask?"

"Where else but Germany, Hungary, Poland? Where not?"

"Ah, that's so long ago." Fidelman then noticed the gray in the man's hair. "Well, I'd better be going." He picked up his bag as two porters hovered uncertainly nearby.

But Susskind offered certain services. "You got a hotel?"

"All picked and reserved."

"How long are you staying?"

What business is it of his? However, Fidelman courteously replied, "Two weeks in Rome, the rest of the year in Florence, with a few side trips to Siena, Assisi, Padua and maybe also Venice."

"You wish a guide in Rome?"

"Are you a guide?"

"Why not?"

"No," said Fidelman. "I'll look as I go along to museums, libraries, et cetera."

This caught Susskind's attention. "What are you, a professor?"

Fidelman couldn't help blushing. "Not exactly, really just a student."

"From which institution?"

He coughed a little. "By that I mean professional student, you might say. Call me Trofimov, from Chekhov.[6] If there's something to learn I want to learn it."

"You have some kind of a project?" the other persisted. "A grant?"

"No grant. My money is hard earned. I worked and saved a long time to take a year in Italy. I made certain sacrifices. As for a project, I'm writing on the painter Giotto. He was one of the most important—"

"You don't have to tell me about Giotto," Susskind interrupted with a little smile.

"You've studied his work?"

"Who doesn't know Giotto?"

"That's interesting to me," said Fidelman, secretly irritated. "How do you happen to know him?"

"How do you?"

"I've given a good deal of time and study to his work."

"So I know him too."

I'd better get this over with before it begins to amount up to something, Fidelman thought. He set down his bag and fished with a finger in his leather coin purse. The two porters watched with interest, one taking a sandwich out of his pocket, unwrapping the newspaper and beginning to eat.

"This is for yourself," Fidelman said.

Susskind hardly glanced at the coin as he let it drop into his pants pocket. The porters then left.

The refugee had an odd way of standing motionless, like a cigar store Indian about to burst into flight. "In your luggage," he said vaguely, "would you maybe have a suit you can't use? I could use a suit."

At last he comes to the point. Fidelman, though annoyed, controlled himself. "All I have is a change from the one you now see me wearing. Don't get the wrong idea about me, Mr. Susskind. I'm not rich. In fact I'm poor. Don't let a few new clothes deceive you. I owe my sister money for them."

Susskind glanced down at his shabby baggy knickers. "I haven't had a suit for years. The one I was wearing when I ran away from Germany, fell apart. One day I was walking around naked."

"Isn't there a welfare organization that could help you out—some group in the Jewish community, interested in refugees?"

"The Jewish organizations wish to give me what they wish, not what

[6] in *The Cherry Orchard*

I wish," Susskind replied bitterly. "The only thing they offer me is a ticket back to Israel."

"Why don't you take it?"

"I told you already, here I feel free."

"Freedom is a relative term."

"Don't tell me about freedom."

He knows all about that too, Fidelman thought. "So you feel free," he said, "but how do you live?"

Susskind coughed, a brutal cough.

Fidelman was about to say something more on the subject of freedom but left it unsaid. Jesus, I'll be saddled with him all day if I don't watch out.

"I'd better be getting off to the hotel." He bent again for his bag.

Susskind touched him on the shoulder and when Fidelman exasperatedly straightened up, the half dollar he had given the man was staring him in the eye.

"On this we both lose money."

"How do you mean?"

"Today the lira sells six twenty-three on the dollar, but for specie they only give you five hundred."

"In that case give it here and I'll let you have a dollar." From his billfold Fidelman quickly extracted a crisp bill and handed it to the refugee.

"Not more?" Susskind sighed.

"Not more," the student answered emphatically.

"Maybe you would like to see Diocletian's bath? There are some enjoyable Roman coffins inside. I will guide you for another dollar."

"No, thanks." Fidelman said goodbye, and lifting the suitcase, lugged it to the curb. A porter appeared and the student, after some hesitation, let him carry it toward the line of small dark-green taxis on the piazza. The porter offered to carry the brief case too but Fidelman wouldn't part with it. He gave the cab driver the address of the hotel, and the taxi took off with a lurch. Fidelman at last relaxed. Susskind, he noticed, had disappeared. Gone with his breeze, he thought. But on the way to the hotel he had an uneasy feeling that the refugee, crouched low, might be clinging to the little tire on the back of the cab; however he didn't look out to see.

Fidelman had reserved a room in an inexpensive hotel not far from the station with its very convenient bus terminal. Then, as was his habit, he got himself quickly and tightly organized. He was always concerned with not wasting time, as if it were his only wealth—not true, of course, though Fidelman admitted he was an ambitious person—and he soon arranged a schedule that made the most of his working hours. Mornings he usually visited the Italian libraries, searching their catalogues and archives, read in poor light, and made profuse notes. He napped for an hour after lunch, then at four, when the churches and museums were reopening, hurried off to them with lists of frescoes and paintings he must see. He was anxious to get to Florence, at the same time a little unhappy at all he would not have time to take in in Rome. Fidelman promised himself to return if he could afford it, perhaps in the spring, and look at everything he pleased.

After dark he managed to unwind himself and relax. He ate as the Romans did, late, enjoyed a half liter of white wine and smoked a cigarette. Afterward he liked to wander—especially in the old sections near the Tiber. He had read that here, under his feet, were the ruins of Ancient Rome. It was an inspiring business, he, Arthur Fidelman, after all, born a Bronx boy, walking around in all this history. History was mysterious, the remembrance of things unknown, in a way burdensome, in a way a sensuous experience. It uplifted and depressed, why he did not know except that it excited his thoughts more than he thought good for him. This kind of excitement was all right up to a point, perfect maybe for a creative artist, but less so for a critic. A critic ought to live on beans. He walked for miles along the winding Tiber, gazing at the star-strewn skies. Once, after a couple of days in the Vatican Museum, he saw flights of angels—gold, blue, white—intermingled in the sky. "My God, I got to stop using my eyes so much," Fidelman said to himself. But back in his room he sometimes wrote till morning.

Late one night, about a week after his arrival in Rome, as Fidelman was writing a few notes on the Byzantine style mosaics he had seen during the day, there was a knock on the door, and though the student, immersed in his work, was not conscious he had said "Avanti," he must have, for the door opened, and instead of an angel, in came Susskind in his shirt and baggy knickers.

Fidelman, who had all but forgotten the refugee, certainly never thought of him, half rose in astonishment. "Susskind," he exclaimed, "how did you get in here?"

Susskind for a moment stood motionless, then answered with a weary smile, "I'll tell you the truth, I know the clerk."

"But how did you know where I live?"

"I saw you walking in the street so I followed you."

"You mean you saw me accidentally?"

"How else? Did you leave me your address?"

Fidelman resumed his seat. "What can I do for you, Susskind?" He spoke grimly.

The refugee cleared his throat. "Professor, the days are warm but the nights are cold. You see how I go around naked." He held forth bluish arms, goosefleshed. "I came to ask you to reconsider about giving away your old suit."

"And who says it's an old suit?" Fidelman's voice thickened.

"One suit is new, so the other's old."

"Not precisely. I am afraid I have no suit for you, Susskind. The one

I presently have hanging in the closet is a little more than a year old and I can't afford to give it away. Besides, it's gabardine, more like a summer suit."

"On me it will be for all seasons."

After a moment's reflection, Fidelman drew out his billfold and counted four single dollars. These he handed to Susskind.

"Buy yourself a warm sweater."

Susskind also counted the money, bill for bill. "If four," he said, "then why not five?"

Fidelman flushed. The man's warped nerve. "Because I happen to have four available," he answered. "That's twenty-five hundred lire. You should be able to buy a warm sweater and have something left over besides."

"I need a suit," Susskind said. "The days are warm but the nights are cold." He rubbed his arms. "What else I need I won't say."

"At least roll down your sleeves if you're so cold."

"That won't help me."

"Listen, Susskind," Fidelman said gently, "I would gladly give you the suit if I could afford to, but I can't. I have barely enough money to squeeze out a year for myself here. I've already told you I am indebted to my sister. Why don't you try to get yourself a job somewhere, no matter how menial? I'm sure that in a short time you'll work yourself up into a decent position."

"A job, he says," Susskind muttered gloomily. "Do you know what it means to get a job in Italy? Who will give me a job?"

"Who gives anybody a job? They have to go out and get it."

"You don't understand, professor. I am an Israeli citizen and this means I can only work for an Israeli company. How many Israeli companies are there here?—maybe two, El Al and Zim, and even if they had a job, they wouldn't give it to me because I have lost my passport. I would be better off now if I were stateless. A stateless person shows his laissez-passer and sometimes he can find a small job."

"But if you lost your passport why didn't you put in for a duplicate?"

"I did but did they give it to me?"

"Why not?"

"Why not? They say I sold it."

"Had they reason to think so?"

"I swear to you somebody stole it."

"Under such circumstances," Fidelman asked, "how do you live?"

"How do I live?" He chomped with his teeth. "I eat air."

"Seriously?"

"Seriously—on air. I also peddle," he confessed, "but to peddle you need a license and that the Italians won't give me. When they caught me peddling I was interned for six months in a work camp."

"Didn't they attempt to deport you?"

"They did but I sold my mother's old wedding ring that I kept in my pocket so many years. The Italians are a humane people. They took the money and let me go but they told me not to peddle more."

"So what do you do now?"

"I peddle. What should I do, beg?—I peddle. But last spring I got sick and gave my little money away to the doctors. I still have a bad cough." He coughed fruitily. "Now I have no capital to buy stock with. Listen, professor, maybe we can go in partnership together? Lend me twenty thousand lire and I will buy ladies' nylon stockings. After I sell them I will return you your money."

"I have no funds to invest, Susskind."

"You will get it back, with interest."

"I honestly am sorry for you," Fidelman said, "but why don't you at least do something practical? Why don't you go to the Joint Distribution Committee, for instance, and ask them to assist you? That's their business."

"I already told you why. They wish me to go back, I wish to stay here."

"I still think going back would be the best thing for you."

"No," cried Susskind angrily.

"If that's your decision, freely made, then why pick on me? Am I responsible for you then, Susskind?"

"Who else?" Susskind loudly replied.

"Lower your voice, please, people are sleeping around here," said Fidelman, beginning to perspire. "Why should I be?"

"You know what responsibility means?"

"I think so."

"Then you are responsible. Because you are a man. Because you are a Jew, aren't you?"

"Yes, goddamn it, but I'm not the only one in the whole wide world. Without prejudice, I refuse the obligation. I am a single individual and can't take on everybody's personal burden. I have the weight of my own to contend with."

He reached for his billfold and plucked out another dollar.

"This makes five. It's more than I can afford but take it and after this please leave me alone. I have made my contribution."

Susskind stood there, oddly motionless, an impassioned statue, and for a moment Fidelman wondered if he would stay all night, but at last the refugee thrust forth a stiff arm, took the fifth dollar and departed.

Early the next morning Fidelman moved out of the hotel into another, less convenient for him, but far away from Shimon Susskind and his endless demands.

This was Tuesday. On Wednesday, after a busy morning in the library, Fidelman entered a nearby trattoria and ordered a plate of spaghetti with tomato sauce. He was reading his *Messaggero*, anticipating the coming of the food, for he was unusually hungry, when he sensed a presence at the table. He looked up, expecting the waiter, but beheld instead Susskind standing there, alas, unchanged.

Is there no escape from him? thought Fidelman, severely vexed. Is this why I came to Rome?

"Shalom, professor," Susskind said, keeping his eyes off the table. "I was passing and saw you sitting here alone, so I came in to say shalom."

"Susskind," Fidelman said in anger, "have you been following me again?"

"How could I follow you?" asked the astonished Susskind. "Do I know where you live now?"

Though Fidelman blushed a little, he told himself he owed nobody an explanation. So he had found out he had moved—good.

"My feet are tired. Can I sit five minutes?"

"Sit."

Susskind drew out a chair. The spaghetti arrived steaming hot. Fidelman sprinkled it with cheese and wound his fork into several tender strands. One of the strings of spaghetti seemed to stretch for miles, so he stopped at a certain point and swallowed the forkful. Having foolishly neglected to cut the long string he was left sucking it, seemingly endlessly. This embarrassed him.

Susskind watched with rapt attention.

Fidelman at last reached the end of the long spaghetti, patted his mouth with a large napkin, and paused in his eating.

"Would you care for a plateful?"

Susskind, eyes hungry, hesitated. "Thanks," he said.

"Thanks yes or thanks no?"

"Thanks no." The eyes looked away.

Fidelman resumed eating, carefully winding his fork; he had had not much practice with this sort of thing and was soon involved in the same dilemma with the spaghetti. Seeing Susskind still watching him, he soon became tense.

"We are not Italians, professor," the refugee said. "Cut it in small pieces with your knife. Then you will swallow it easier."

"I'll handle it as I please," Fidelman responded testily. "This is my business. You attend to yours."

"My business," Susskind sighed, "don't exist. This morning I had to let a wonderful chance get away from me. I had a chance to buy ladies' stockngs at three hundred lire if I had money to buy half a gross. I could easily sell them for five hundred a pair. We would have made a nice profit."

"The news doesn't interest me."

"So, if not ladies' stockings, I can also get sweaters, scarves, men's socks, also cheap leather goods, ceramics—whatever would interest you."

"What interests me is what you did with the money I gave you for a sweater."

"It's getting cold, professor," Susskind said worriedly. "Soon comes the November rains, and in winter the tramontana. I thought I ought to save your money to buy a couple of kilos of chestnuts and a bag of charcoal for my burner. If you sit all day on a busy street corner you can sometimes make a thousand lire. Italians like hot chestnuts. But if I do this I will need some warm clothes, maybe a suit."

"A suit," Fidelman remarked sarcastically, "why not an overcoat?"

"I have a coat, poor that it is, but now I need a suit. How can anybody come in company without a suit?"

Fidelman's hand trembled as he laid down his fork. "To my mind you are irresponsible and I won't be saddled with you. I have the right to choose my own problems and the right to my privacy."

"Don't get excited, professor, it's bad for your digestion. Eat in peace." Susskind got up and left the trattoria.

Fidelman hadn't the appetite to finish his spaghetti. He paid the bill, waited ten minutes, then departed, glancing around from time to time to see if he were being followed. He headed down the sloping street to a small piazza where he saw a couple of cabs. Not that he could afford one, but he wanted to make sure Susskind didn't tail him back to his new hotel. He would warn the clerk at the desk never to allow anybody of the refugee's name or description even to make inquiries about him.

Susskind, however, stepped out from behind a plashing fountain at the center of the little piazza. Modestly addressing the speechless Fidelman, he said, "I don't wish to take only, professor. If I had something to give you, I would gladly give it to you."

"Thanks," snapped Fidelman, "just give me some peace of mind."

"That you have to find yourself," Susskind answered.

In the taxi Fidelman decided to leave for Florence the next day, rather than at the end of the week, and once and for all be done with the pest.

That night, after returning to his room from an unpleasurable walk in the Trastevere—he had a headache from too much wine at supper—Fidelman found his door ajar and at once recalled that he had forgotten to lock it, although he had as usual left the key with the desk clerk. He was at first frightened, but when he tried the armadio[7] in which he kept his clothes and suitcase, it was shut tight. Hastily unlocking it, he was relieved to see his blue gabardine suit—a one-button jacket affair, the trousers a little frayed on the cuffs but all in good shape and usable for years to come—hanging amid some shirts the maid had pressed for him; and when he examined the contents of the suitcase he found nothing missing, including, thank God, his passport and traveler's checks. Gazing around the room, Fidelman saw all in place. Satisfied, he picked up a book and read ten pages before he thought of his brief case. He jumped to his feet and began to search everywhere, remembering distinctly that it had been on the night table as he had lain on the bed that afternoon, re-

[7] wardrobe

reading his chapter. He searched under the bed and behind the night table, then again throughout the room, even on top of and behind the
armadio. Fidelman hopelessly opened every drawer, no matter how
small, but found neither the brief case, nor, what was far worse, the
chapter in it.

With a groan he sank down on the bed, insulting himself for not having
made a copy of the manuscript, for he had more than once warned himself that something like this might happen to it. But he hadn't because
there were some revisions he had contemplated making, and he had
planned to retype the entire chapter before beginning the next. He
thought now of complaining to the owner of the hotel, who lived on the
floor below, but it was already past midnight and he realized nothing
could be done until morning. Who could have taken it? The maid or hall
porter? It seemed unlikely they would risk their jobs to steal a piece of
leather goods that would bring them only a few thousand lire in a pawn
shop. Possibly a sneak thief? He would ask tomorrow if other persons
on the floor were missing something. He somehow doubted it. If a thief,
he would then and there have ditched the chapter and stuffed the brief
case with Fidelman's oxblood shoes, left by the bed, and the fifteen-
dollar R. H. Macy sweater that lay in full view on the desk. But if not
the maid or porter or a sneak thief, then who? Though Fidelman had not
the slightest shred of evidence to support his suspicions he could think of
only one person—Susskind. This thought stung him. But if Susskind,
why? Out of pique, perhaps, that he had not been given the suit he had
coveted, nor was able to pry it out of the armadio? Try as he would,
Fidelman could think of no one else and no other reason. Somehow the
peddler had followed him home (he had suspected their meeting at the
fountain) and had got into his room while he was out to supper.

Fidelman's sleep that night was wretched. He dreamed of pursuing the
refugee in the Jewish catacombs under the ancient Appian Way, threatening him a blow on the presumptuous head with a seven-flamed can-
delabrum he clutched in his hand; while Susskind, clever ghost, who
knew the ins and outs of all the crypts and alleys, eluded him at every
turn. Then Fidelman's candles all blew out, leaving him sightless and
alone in the cemeterial dark; but when the student arose in the morning
and wearily drew up the noisy blinds, the yellow Italian, somewhat
shrunken, sun winked him cheerfully in both bleary eyes.

Fidelman postponed going to Florence. He reported his loss to the
Questura, and though the police were polite and eager to help, they could
do nothing for him. On the form on which the inspector noted the complaint, he listed the brief case as worth ten thousand lire, and for "valore
del manoscritto"[8] he drew a line. Fidelman, after giving the matter a
good deal of thought, did not report Susskind, first, because he had abso-

---

[8] value of the manuscript

lutely no proof, for the desk cleark swore he had seen no stranger around in knickers; second, because he was afraid of the consequences for the refugee if he were written down "suspected thief" as well as "unlicensed peddler" and inverterate refugee. He tried instead to rewrite the chapter, which he felt sure he knew by heart, but when he sat down at the desk there were important thoughts, whole paragraphs, even pages that went blank in the mind. He considered sending to America for his notes for the chapter but they were in a barrel in his sister's attic in Levittown, among many notes for other projects. The thought of Bessie, a mother of five, poking around in his things, and the work entailed in sorting the cards, then getting them packaged and mailed to him across the ocean, wearied Fidelman unspeakably; he was certain she would send the wrong ones. He laid down his pen and went into the street, seeking Susskind. He searched for him in neighborhoods where he had seen him before, and though Fidelman spent hours looking, literally days, Susskind never appeared; or if he perhaps did, the sight of Fidelman caused him to vanish. And when the student inquired about him at the Israeli consulate, the clerk, a new man on the job, said he had no record of such a person or his lost passport; on the other hand, the refugee was known at the JDC, but by name and address only, an impossibility, Fidelman thought. They gave him a number to go to but the place had long since been torn down to make way for an apartment house.

Time went without work, without accomplishment. To put an end to this appalling waste Fidelman tried to force himself back into his routine research and picture viewing. He moved out of the hotel, which he now could not stand for the harm it had done him (leaving a telephone number and urging he be called if the slightest clue turned up), and he took a room in a small pensione[9] near the Stazione and here had breakfast and supper rather than go out. He was much concerned with expenditures and carefully recorded them in a notebook he had acquired for the purpose. Nights, instead of wandering in the city, feasting himself on its beauty and mystery, he kept his eyes glued to paper, sitting steadfastly at his desk in an attempt to re-create his initial chapter, because he was lost without a beginning. He had tried writing the second chapter from notes in his possession but it had come to nothing. Always Fidelman needed something solid behind him before he could advance, some worthwhile accomplishment upon which to build another. He worked late but his mood, or inspiration, or whatever it was, had deserted him, leaving him with growing anxiety, almost disorientation; of not knowing—it seemed to him for the first time in months—what he must do next, a feeling that was torture. Therefore he again took up his search for the refugee. He thought now that once he had settled it, knew that the man had or hadn't stolen his chapter—whether he recovered it or not seemed at the moment

[9] boarding house

immaterial—just the knowing of it would ease his mind and again he would feel like working, the crucial element.

Daily he combed the crowded streets, searching for Susskind wherever people peddled. On successive Sunday mornings he took the long ride to the Porta Portese market and hunted for hours among the piles of second-hand goods and junk lining the back streets, hoping his brief case would magically appear, though it never did. He visited the open market at Piazza Fontanella Borghese, and observed the ambulant vendors at Piazza Dante. He looked among fruit and vegetable stalls set up in the streets, whenever he chanced upon them, and dawdled on busy street corners after dark, among beggars and fly-by-night peddlers. After the first cold snap at the end of October, when the chestnut sellers appeared throughout the city, huddled over pails of glowing coals, he sought in their faces the missing Susskind. Where in all of modern and ancient Rome was he? The man lived in the open air—he had to appear somewhere. Sometimes when riding in a bus or tram, Fidelman thought he had glimpsed somebody in a crowd, dressed in the refugee's clothes, and he invariably got off to run after whoever it was—once a man standing in front of the Banco di Santo Spirito, gone when Fidelman breathlessly arrived; and another time he overtook a person in knickers but this one wore a monocle. Sir Ian Susskind?

In November it drearily rained. Fidelman wore a blue beret with his trench coat and a pair of black Italian shoes, smaller, despite their pointed toes, than his burly oxbloods which overheated his feet and whose color he detested. But instead of visiting museums he frequented movie houses, sitting in the cheapest seats and regretting the cost. He was, at odd hours in certain streets, several times solicited by prostitutes, some heartbreakingly pretty, one a slender, unhappy-looking girl with bags under her eyes whom he desired mightily, but Fidelman feared for his health. He had got to know the face of Rome and spoke Italian fairly fluently but his heart was burdened, and in his blood raged a murderous hatred of the bandy-legged refugee—although there were times when he thought he might be wrong—so Fidelman more than once cursed him to perdition.

One Friday night, as the first star glowed over the Tiber, Fidelman, walking aimlessly along the left riverbank, came upon a synagogue and wandered in among a crowd of Sephardim [10] with Italianate faces. One by one they paused before a sink in an antechamber to dip their hands under a flowing faucet, then in the house of worship touched with loose fingers their brows, mouths, and breasts as they bowed to the Ark, Fidelman doing likewise. Where in the world am I? Three rabbis rose from a bench and the service began, a long prayer, sometimes chanted, sometimes accompanied by invisible organ music, but no Susskind anywhere. Fidelman sat at a desk-like pew in the last row where he could inspect the

[10] Jews of Spanish or Portuguese ancestry

congregants yet keep an eye on the door. The synagogue was unheated
and the cold rose like an exudation from the marble floor. The student's
freezing nose burned like a lit candle. He got up to go but the beadle, a
stout man in a high hat and short caftan, wearing a long thick silver chain
around his neck, fixed the student with his powerful left eye.

"From New York?" he inquired, slowly approaching.

Half the congregation turned to see who.

"State, not city," answered Fidelman, nursing an active embarrassment for the attention he was attracting. Taking advantage of a pause,
he whispered, "Do you happen to know a man named Susskind? He
wears knickers."

"A relative?" The beadle gazed at him sadly.

"Not exactly."

"My own son—killed in the Ardeatine Caves." Tears stood forth in
his eyes.

"Ah, for that I'm sorry."

But the beadle had exhausted the subject. He wiped his wet lids with
pudgy fingers and the curious Sephardim turned back to their prayer
books.

"Which Susskind?" the beadle wanted to know.

"Shimon."

He scratched his ear. "Look in the ghetto."

"I looked."

"Look again."

The beadle walked slowly away and Fidelman sneaked out.

The ghetto lay behind the synagogue for several crooked well-packed
blocks, encompassing aristocratic palazzi ruined by age and unbearable
numbers, their discolored façades strung with lines of withered wet wash,
the fountains in the piazzas, dirt-laden, dry. And dark stone tenements,
built partly on centuries-old ghetto walls, inclined towards one another
across narrow, cobblestoned streets. In and among the impoverished
houses were the wholesale establishments of wealthy Jews, dark holes
ending in jeweled interiors, silks and silver of all colors. In the mazed
streets wandered the present-day poor, Fidelman among them, oppressed
by history although, he joked to himself, it added years to his life.

A white moon shone upon the ghetto, lighting it like dark day. Once he
thought he saw a ghost he knew by sight, and hastily followed him
through a thick stone passage to a blank wall where shone in white letters under a tiny electric bulb: VIETATO URINARE.[11] Here was a smell
but no Susskind.

For thirty lire the student bought a dwarfed blackened banana from a
street vendor (not S) on a bicycle and stopped to eat. A crowd of ra-
gazzi[12] gathered to watch.

"Anybody here know Susskind, a refugee wearing knickers?" Fidel-

---

[11] urinating forbidden   [12] boys

man announced, stooping to point with the banana where the pants went beneath the knees. He also made his legs a trifle bowed but nobody noticed.

There was no response until he had finished his fruit, then a thin-faced boy with brown liquescent eyes out of Murillo,[13] piped: "He sometimes works in the Campo Verano, the Jewish section."

There too? thought Fidelman. "Works in the cemetery?" he inquired. "With a shovel?"

"He prays for the dead," the boy answered, "for a small fee."

Fidelman bought him a quick banana and the others dispersed.

In the cemetery, deserted on the Sabbath—he should have come Sunday—Fidelman went among the graves, reading legends on tombstones, many topped with small brass candelabra, whilst withered yellow chrysanthemums lay on the stone tablets of other graves, dropped stealthily, he imagined, on All Souls' Day—a festival in another part of the cemetery—by renegade sons and daughters unable to bear the sight of their dead bereft of flowers whilst the crypts of the goyim[14] were lit and in bloom. Many were burial places, he read on the stained stones, of those who, for one reason or another, had died in the late large war. Among them was an empty place, it said on a marble slab lying on the ground, for "My beloved father/ Betrayed by the damned Fascists/ Murdered at Auschwitz by the barbarous Nazis/ O Crimine Orrible."

—But no Susskind.

Three months had gone by since Fidelman's arrival in Rome. Should he, he many times asked himself, leave the city and this foolish search? Why not off to Florence, and there, amid the art splendors of the world, be inspired to resume his work? But the loss of his first chapter was like a spell cast over him. There were times he scorned it as a man-made thing, like all such, replaceable; other times he feared it wasn't the chapter per se,[15] but that his volatile curiosity had become somehow entangled with Susskind's personality—Had he repaid generosity by stealing a man's life work? Was he so distorted? To satisfy himself, to know man, Fidelman had to know, though at what a cost in precious time and effort. Sometimes he smiled wryly at all this; ridiculous, the chapter grieved him for itself only—the precious thing he had created then lost—especially when he got to thinking of the long diligent labor, how painstakingly he had built each idea, how cleverly mastered problems of order, form, how impressive the finished product, Giotto reborn! It broke the heart. What else, if after months he was here, still seeking?

And Fidelman was unchangingly convinced that Susskind had taken it, or why would he still be hiding? He sighed much and gained weight. Mulling over his frustrated career, on the backs of envelopes containing unanswered letters from his sister Bessie he aimlessly sketched little

---

[13] Bartolome Murillo, 1617–1682, Spanish painter   [14] Gentiles   [15] as such

angels flying. Once, studying his minuscule drawings, it occurred to him that he might someday return to painting but the thought was more painful than Fidelman could bear.

One bright morning in mid-December, after a good night's sleep, his first in weeks, he vowed he would have another look at the Navicella[16] and then be off to Florence. Shortly before noon he visited the porch of St. Peter's, trying, from his remembrance of Giotto's sketch, to see the mosaic as it had been before its many restorations. He hazarded a note or two in shaky handwriting, then left the Church and was walking down the sweeping flight of stairs, when he beheld at the bottom—his heart misgave him, was he still seeing pictures, a sneaky apostle added to the overloaded boatful?—ecce,[17] Susskind! The refugee, in beret and long green G.I. raincoat, from under whose skirts showed his black-stockinged rooster's ankles—indicating knickers going on above though hidden— was selling black and white rosaries to all who would buy. He held several strands of beads in one hand, while in the palm of the other a few gilded medallions glinted in the winter sun. Despite his outer clothing, Susskind looked, it must be said, unchanged, not a pound more of meat or muscle, the face though aged, ageless. Gazing at him, the student ground his teeth in remembrance. He was tempted quickly to hide, and unobserved, observe the thief; but his impatience, after the long unhappy search, was too much for him. With controlled trepidation he approached Susskind on his left as the refugee was busily engaged on the right, urging a sale of beads upon a woman drenched in black.

"Beads, rosaries, say your prayers with holy beads."

"Greetings, Susskind," Fidelman said, coming shakily down the stairs, dissembling the Unified Man, all peace and contentment. "One looks for you everywhere and finds you here. Wie gehts?"[18]

Susskind, though his eyes flickered, showed no surprise to speak of. For a moment his expression seemed to say he had no idea who was this, had forgotten Fidelman's existence, but then at last remembered—somebody long ago from another country, whom you smiled on, then forgot.

"Still here?" he perhaps ironically joked.

"Still." Fidelman was embarrassed at his voice slipping.

"Rome holds you?"

"Rome," faltered the student, "—the air." He breathed deep and exhaled with emotion.

Noticing the refugee was not truly attentive, his eyes roving upon potential customers, Fidelman, girding himself, remarked. "By the way, Susskind, you didn't happen to notice—did you?—the brief case I was carrying with me around the time we met in September?"

---

[16] a mosaic, in the vestibule of St. Peter's Cathedral, of Christ saving St. Peter from the waves

[17] a parody of Pontius Pilate's "Ecce Homo"—Behold the man (Christ wearing the crown of thorns) John 19:5

[18] How are you?—literally, How goes it?

"Brief case—what kind?" This he said absently, his eyes on the church doors.

"Pigskin. I had in it—" here Fidelman's voice could be heard cracking, "—a chapter of a critical work on Giotto I was writing. You know, I'm sure, the Trecento[19] painter?"

"Who doesn't know Giotto?"

"Do you happen to recall whether you saw, if, that is—" He stopped, at a loss for words other than accusatory.

"Excuse me—business." Susskind broke away and bounced up the steps two at a time. A man he approached shied away. He had beads, didn't need others.

Fidelman had followed the refugee. "Reward," he muttered up close to his ear. "Fifteen thousand for the chapter, and who has it can keep the brand-new brief case. That's his business, no questions asked. Fair enough?"

Susskind spied a lady tourist, including camera and guide book. "Beads —holy beads." He held up both handsful, but she was just a Lutheran passing through.

"Slow today," Susskind complained as they walked down the stairs, "but maybe it's the items. Everybody has the same. If I had some big ceramics of the Holy Mother, they go like hot cakes—a good investment for somebody with a little cash."

"Use the reward for that," Fidelman cagily whispered, "buy Holy Mothers."

If he heard, Susskind gave no sign. At the sight of a family of nine emerging from the main portal above, the refugee, calling addio over his shoulder, fairly flew up the steps. But Fidelman uttered no response. I'll get the rat yet. He went off to hide behind a high fountain in the square. But the flying spume raised by the wind wet him, so he retreated behind a massive column and peeked out at short intervals to keep the peddler in sight.

At two o'clock, when St. Peter's closed to visitors, Susskind dumped his goods into his raincoat pockets and locked up shop. Fidelman followed him all the way home, indeed the ghetto, although along a street he had not consciously been on before, which led into an alley where the refugee pulled open a left-handed door, and without transition, was "home." Fidelman, sneaking up close, caught a dim glimpse of an overgrown closet containing bed and table. He found no address on wall or door, nor, to his surpise, any door lock. This for a moment depressed him. It meant Susskind had nothing worth stealing. Of his own, that is. The student promised himself to return tomorrow, when the occupant was elsewhere.

Return he did, in the morning, while the entrepreneur was out selling religious articles, glanced around once and was quickly inside. He shiv-

[19] fourteenth century

ered—a pitch-black freezing cave. Fidelman scratched up a thick match and confirmed bed and table, also a rickety chair, but no heat or light except a drippy candle stub in a saucer on the table. He lit the yellow candle and searched all over the place. In the table drawer a few eating implements plus safety razor, though where he shaved was a mystery, probably a public toilet. On a shelf above the thin-blanketed bed stood half a flask of red wine, part of a package of spaghetti, and a hard panino. Also an unexpected little fish bowl with a bony goldfish swimming around in Arctic seas. The fish, reflecting the candle flame, gulped repeatedly, threshing its frigid tail as Fidelman watched. He loves pets, thought the student. Under the bed he found a chamber pot, but nowhere a brief case with a fine critical chapter in it. The place was not more than an ice-box someone probably had lent the refugee to come in out of the rain. Alas, Fidelman sighed. Back in the pensione, it took a hot water bottle two hours to thaw him out; but from the visit he never fully recovered.

In this latest dream of Fidelman's he was spending the day in a cemetery all crowded with tombstones, when up out of an empty grave rose this long-nosed brown shade, Virgilio[20] Susskind, beckoning.

Fidelman hurried over.

"Have you read Tolstoy?"

"Sparingly."

"Why is art?" asked the shade, drifting off.

Fidelman, willy-nilly, followed, and the ghost, as it vanished, led him up steps going through the ghetto and into a marble synagogue.

The student, left alone, because he could not resist the impulse, lay down upon the stone floor, his shoulders keeping strangely warm as he stared at the sunlit vault above. The fresco therein revealed this saint in fading blue, the sky flowing from his head, handing an old knight in a thin red robe his gold cloak. Nearby stood a humble horse and two stone hills.

Giotto. San Francesco dona le vesti al cavaliere povero.[21]

Fidelman awoke running. He stuffed his blue gabardine into a paper bag, caught a bus, and knocked early on Susskind's heavy portal.

"Avanti." The refugee, already garbed in beret and raincoat (probably his pajamas), was standing at the table, lighting the candle with a flaming sheet of paper. To Fidelman the paper looked the underside of a typewritten page. Despite himself the student recalled in letters of fire his entire chapter.

"Here, Susskind," he said in a trembling voice, offering the bundle, "I bring you my suit. Wear it in good health."

---

[20] Virgil was Dante's guide through Hell in the *Inferno*.
[21] Saint Francis gives his cloak to the impoverished knight.

The refugee glanced at it without expression. "What do you wish for it?"

"Nothing at all." Fidelman laid the bag on the table, called goodbye and left.

He soon heard footsteps clattering after him across the cobblestones.

"Excuse me, I kept this under my mattress for you." Susskind thrust at him the pigskin brief case.

Fidelman savagely opened it, searching frantically in each compartment, but the bag was empty. The refugee was already in flight. With a bellow the student started after him. "You bastard, you burned my chapter!"

"Have mercy," cried Susskind, "I did you a favor."

"I'll do you one and cut your throat."

"The words were there but the spirit was missing."

In a towering rage Fidelman forced a burst of speed, but the refugee, light as the wind in his marvelous knickers, green coattails flying, rapidly gained ground.

The ghetto Jews, framed in amazement in their medieval windows, stared at the wild pursuit. But in the middle of it, Fidelman, stout and short of breath, moved by all he had lately learned, had a triumphant insight.

"Susskind, come back," he shouted, half sobbing. "The suit is yours. All is forgiven."

He came to a dead halt but the refugee ran on. When last seen he was still running.

Jean Stafford

1915–

BETWEEN THE PORCH AND THE ALTAR

AT FIVE in the morning in February, it is darker than at midnight. The streets are empty of automobiles; the latest readers have gone to bed and the earliest risers are only just opening their eyes. The few people abroad are swift and furtive, like creatures who must quit a place before the sun shines forth. At that hour, their business seems mysterious and even shady, although they are not cutthroats or thieves but only watchmen and charwomen and night waitresses on their way home to dine at sunrise. So uncluttered are the streets, so starkly direct is the walk of the people that anyone whose custom it is to get up much later, at the normal hour, feels when he goes out that he intrudes upon a scene of bare but important privacy. And a light, springing on abruptly to make a staring eye in a blackened building, may stir him with embarrassment and wonder as if this were an alarm or an esoteric signal of hostility.

It was cold and the girl was hungry. She paused in the vestibule of the apartment building and half turned to unlock the outer door again and go back to her warm bed. But as she lingered, she observed a bright blue star high over the houses opposite and the sight inexplicably gave her resolution, even though its color was so pure and frigid that it made her all the more conscious of the cold. She drew on her gloves and went out, shocked by a biting gust of wind which passed her by like a big rapid bird. She turned the corner and hurried along Sixth Avenue on her way to the first mass.

Although the star, which was now behind her, had had a decisive effect on her, it had not dispelled her apprehension and her distrust of the unfamiliar streets. While her feet were steady enough, her breath was erratic and her ears were fanciful, making her think she heard sinister noises behind the blank faces of the buildings. She looked straight ahead, fearful of what she might see in the dark doorways and even in the interiors of delicatessens and bakery shops whose cheerless windows were dimly silvered by the street lights. And still, discomforting as it was, she took a certain pleasure in her uneasiness, feeling that even the most accidental castigation was excellent at the beginning of Lent.

On the corner of Thirteenth Street, there was a large second-hand shop whose windows she had many times studied with an incredulous amusement, so dreadful were the objects shown there: funeral wreaths made of human hair, armadillo baskets, back-scratchers that looked like sets of bad teeth, ceramic vessels of an unimaginable function. The antelope with eaten ears and rubbed-off hide, the alabaster boar and the complacent Chinese philosopher made of porcelain stared out, looking, even at five in the morning, for someone to adopt them and give them a good home.

Within the doorway of the shop, a drunken beggar sprawled like a lumpy rug, his feet in ruptured tennis shoes thrust out onto the sidewalk. He was not asleep. Under a cap set raffishly at an angle on his head, he regarded the girl's approach with an eye made visible to her by the arc light at the intersection. Paradoxically, her pace slowed down as her terror rose, and the man had risen to his feet before she was abreast of him. The smell of whisky was so strong that it was like a taste in her mouth. He stretched forth his hand and whined, "Lady, I'm hungry, lady."

She did not carry a purse, but in her pocket were two dimes and a quarter. She intended to put the quarter into the poor box and the dimes in the candle offering, for she wished to light a candle for the repose of her mother's soul and another for the safe-keeping of two friends, captive in China by the Japanese. Although it was only a fraction of a minute that she debated, a succession of images with an individual emotion attending each revolved through her mind. She saw the poor box in the dim vestibule of the lower church and heard her quarter click upon the other coins. This box was stationed beside the holy-water font, near the statue of Our Lord between whose palely gleaming feet someone placed fresh flowers each day. Then she saw her mother lying in the limbo of her last hours, unsightly, unconsoled, and heard the sonorous matter-of-factness of her Protestant relatives to whom this transformation, so unbearable to her, was neither strange nor dreadful. It was not that they did not grieve their kinswoman, but it was that they had many times before known death and had learned, through its reiteration, that it was no wonder. She, still bedewed with baptism, had knelt and the blue beads of her rosary slipped through her fingers until her mother's soul abandoned its wrecked flesh. She had been, she remembered, in the middle of the fourth decade when her aunt, vigilant at the bedside, had whispered, "She is gone now." And she remembered how the odor of belladonna had obtruded so in her devotions that part of her mind pronounced the word over and over as if it belonged to a litany.

Then she tried to fancy her friends as they might be in prison and could not, could only see them before their fireplace on a winter day of the year before. She had come to tea and had stayed on for sherry. She sat on a maroon sofa; a little dog slept with his chin on her arm, whimpering once in a dream. There was shortbread to go with the wine and as she ate a piece she realized that it was the texture rather than the taste that made it her favorite pastry. In an easy silence that came in the conversation, she saw her reflection in the brass bedwarmer that hung beside the fireplace, and this blurred travesty of her face had the power, as the star had done this morning, to make her suddenly purposeful, and she told her friends goodbye that day, although they did not leave for another week.

In the early desolation of this present year, she felt tenderness muffling her like smoke and smaller, general pictures showed themselves to her: a clean room, a forced branch of apple blossoms, her mother's silver-backed hairbrush, her friends' passport pictures.

No time at all had passed. She saw the beggar's lips part again. She could not find her voice, and one bold self chided her for her nervousness, for this was no extraordinary occurrence. On the contrary, the rarest day in New York was the one on which one was not asked for money by a fellow like this or by a senile tart or by a belligerent child. She could pass by, or she could say she had no money. But mechanically she had paused—she was not yet a craftsman in the selection of experience and her days were often a chain of pauses—and the man took advantage of her hesitance, saying, with his vague face close to hers, "Lady, was you ever hungry?" Her fear of him was obliterated by an abstract but brilliant anger, for his question was beside the point, unfair, a contemptible trick. She almost spoke her indignation aloud and then her anger burnt itself out; she controlled herself stiffly like a soldier: on this grave day she should not presume to judge. And into the cold hand, she put the quarter and one of the dimes. The man muttered something but she did not hear what he said and she went on hastily. In the windows of a flower shop, she saw her shadow drift through pots of white azaleas. When she turned the corner at Sixteenth Street, she slowed down, for two nuns walked slowly ahead of her. Her hunger returned with savage force.

The entrance to the Jesuits' church was dark. Its black iron gates were open only a crack. A nightlike and velvety blackness stood solidly between the columns on the porch of the upper church. The stone steps leading downward seemed colder than the sidewalks, and the holy water was cold. It teemed with the ripples of fingers that had been dipped there before her own, and the touch of it on her forehead was icy. Today, between the wounded feet, were dark roses. One of the sisters touched the feet and then pressed her fingers to her lips.

The mass had not begun. The girl said her prayers, but she could not concentrate, for her mind was occupied with what she would do with her last dime. Who was the neediest, she questioned: the poor, the dead, or the oppressed? Truly, she had to admit that she loved the poor less than her mother and her friends, and yet, for this very reason—for a willful sacrifice—should she not put the dime into the poor box? Then she thought, but I have given already to the poor. Lout, wastrel that he was, he was poor and it is not the duty, nor even the right, of the almsgiver to distinguish between degrees of poverty. But between her mother and her friends, how should she choose? Should one pray for someone's long life here or for someone else's shortened term in Purgatory? It occurred to her to offer her mass for her mother and light the candle for the prisoners. This seemed like a compromise and did not satisfy her, yet there was no alternative.

Four nuns were in the pew ahead of her and, finishing their prayers, they sat back and simultaneously opened their missals. On the right hand of one, she saw a wedding ring. She had never before been close enough to a nun to notice this, and she wondered when it was that the badge of their eternal marriage was placed upon them and if they really did feel unity with God at that moment or felt, instead, hushed isolation. The words of the Gospel today were: *Lay up to yourselves treasures in heaven: where neither the rust nor the moth doth consume, and where thieves do not break through nor steal. For where thy treasure is, there is thy heart also.* The words, now that she had seen the wedding ring, seemed richer and more profoundly exciting than they had done before, and for a moment she was almost idolatrous, worshipful, almost, of the fair-skinned sisters in their tower of ivory and their house of gold. And then she recoiled, for under the coif of one she saw black stubble.

The church was full, principally of old people who slept so little that rising for the earliest mass on Ash Wednesday was no great hardship. Most of them were telling their beads and only a few had missals. An aged man behind her said his Aves aloud in a harsh, sibilant voice and his false teeth clicked on one another in counterpoint to the measured whispers of his wooden beads. A bald young seminarian entered the sanctuary to light the candles on the altar. He genuflected gracefully and liquidly like a dancer, and the hand with which he crossed himself was as long and white and as shapely as one painted by El Greco.[1] He was incongruously beautiful in his surroundings, for the lower church was ugly and in bad taste. The statues were gaudy, even in this shadowy light, and the crucifix was sentimental. In all the accouterments of the sanctuary, there was a mixture of modern leanness and Victorian laciness. The seminarian alone seemed a product of inspiration.

At last the bell rang and the celebrant with his altar boys entered the sanctuary. The girl prayed that nothing would mar the spirit of penance which she carried like a fragile light; she closed her eyes to the nun's neck and begged forgiveness for her fault-finding. All through the mass, while she fixed her attention on her mother—imagining her face, disembodied, hovering in a crowd of other faces in Purgatory, which she saw as an echoing marble hall—she wondered if she had not committed an act of betrayal, both to the beggar to whom she gave unwillingly and to the parish poor, deprived of her offering through her cowardice. Although she knew that her confusion would be understood and unraveled by the counsel of a confessor, she went, half dazed, to the communion rail and received, she felt, with an imperfect heart. Afterwards, her thanksgiving was more full of petition than of gratitude: I humbly beseech guidance and my whole heart desires wisdom and stern purpose. Reason reiterated to her that she had properly allocated her good will: money to the poor, a mass for the dead, a candle for the oppressed. Yet she was not assured in her heart and she prayed with a dry compulsion.

When she had received the cross of ashes on her forehead, she went directly to the altar of St. Francis Xavier at the back of the church. The cups for the candles were blood-red; the flames cast a sheen on the closed tabernacle. She knelt down to pray the saint to watch over her friends. As she stood up to take the taper to light her candle, she saw an old woman coming from the vestibule. She pretended not to see, for she recognized the old crone who was always there before the sun and the Jesuits discovered her. At later masses she begged on the sidewalk. The girl had already lighted the taper and was looking for a fresh cup when the woman reached the altar.

Blear-eyed, unctuous, crafty, she slithered to her knees. "God bless you, dearie," she began, her face touching the skirt of the girl's coat. The dime was in the pocket on that side, and it was as if the woman smelled it with her long nose or heard it with her ear beneath her sour gray hair or felt it on her furrowed cheek. It was impossible to ignore her, and the girl could think of no way to resolve this preposterous dilemma. Her hand still held the taper and her eyes still roved the tiers of candles seeking an unlighted one.

It seemed some time before the old woman spoke again. Behind them,

---

[1] Spanish painter, 1548?–1614? or 1625?, noted for elongated and sinuous figures

people were moving about, unconcerned with anything but the small devotional tasks they had set themselves. Some were making the stations of the cross, some prayed at the Lady altar, others gazed meditatively at the crucifix. The bald young beadle had come again into the sanctuary and was preparing the altar for the next mass. Everything happening in the church was pious and usual, save for the squalid commerce at St. Francis' altar. The ceiling seemed oppressively low; she was reminded of a dreary train shed.

When the woman spoke again, her voice was more eager and hopeful. She nodded toward the candles and said, "They're every one of them lit already and they won't bring the new ones round till after the eight o'clock." How well she knew the habits of this church's servants! She had probably studied them for months, huddling in shadows behind the grating that enclosed the baptismal font or in the corner where the statue of St. Ignatius stood. The girl saw that what she said was true and she blew out the taper and replaced it. But she was determined to make the offering and she stepped down to go to another altar. The old woman took hold of her coat and peered straight into her face, shamelessly. She said, "You're young and pretty, girlie." The oblique entreaty weakened her, embarrassed her movement like a web, and finally she put her hand into her pocket and took out the dime. Before the clever, metropolitan fingers had enclosed the alms, the girl had gone, running down Sixteenth Street to the corner of Sixth Avenue. The streets were lighter now, and the big star had begun to pale. Shopkeepers were putting trash on the sidewalks; news vendors were cutting the ropes that bound the morning papers; a melancholy white horse ambled down the street dragging a milk truck after him.

When the coffee was nearly ready and her rooms were full of its fragrance, the girl looked at her forehead in the bathroom mirror and saw that the Jesuit had marked her clearly. She washed away the ashes, leaving herself alone possessed of the knowledge of her penanace.

Heinrich Boll

1917–

CHRISTMAS EVERY DAY

SYMPTOMS of decline have become evident in our family. For a time we were at pains to disregard them, but now we have resolved to face the danger. I dare not, as yet, use the word breakdown, but disturbing facts are piling up at such a rate as to constitute a menace and to compel me to report things that will sound disagreeable to my contemporaries; no one, however, can dispute their reality. The minute fungi of

destruction have found lodgement beneath the hard, thick crust of respectability; colonies of deadly parasites that proclaim the end of a whole
tribe's irreproachable correctness. Today we must deplore our disregard
of Cousin Franz, who began long ago to warn us of the dreadful consequences that would result from an event that was harmless enough in
itself. So insignificant indeed was the event that the disproportion of the
consequences now terrifies us. Franz warned us betimes. Unfortunately
he had too little standing. He had chosen a calling that no member of the
family had ever followed before, and none ever should have: he was a
boxer. Melancholy even in youth and possessed by a devoutness that was
always described as "pious fiddle-faddle," he early adopted ways that
worried my Uncle Franz, that good, kind man. He was wont to neglect
his schoolwork to a quite abnormal degree. He used to meet disreputable
companions in the thickets and deserted parks of the suburbs, and there
practice the rough discipline of the prize fight, with no thought for his
neglected humanistic heritage. These youngsters early revealed the vices
of their generation, which, as has since become abundantly evident, is
really worthless. The exciting spiritual combats of earlier centuries simply did not interest them; they were far too concerned with the dubious
excitements of their own. At first I thought Franz's piety in contradiction
to his systematic exercises in passive and active brutality. But today I
begin to suspect a connection. This is a subject I shall have to return to.

And so it was Franz who warned us in good time, who refused above
all to have anything to do with certain celebrations, calling the whole
thing a folly and a disgrace, and later on declined to participate in those
measures that proved necessary for the continuance of what he considered evil. But, as I have said, he had too little standing to get a hearing in
the family circle.

Now, to be sure, things have gone so far that we stand helpless, not
knowing how to call a halt.

Franz has long since become a famous boxer, but today he rejects the
praises that the family lavishes on him with the same indifference he once
showed toward their criticism.

His brother, however—my Cousin Johannes, a man for whom I would
at any time have walked through fire, the successful lawyer and favorite
son of my Uncle—Johannes is said to have struck up relations with the
Communist Party, a rumor I stubbornly refuse to believe. My Cousin
Lucie, hitherto a normal woman, is said to frequent disreputable night-
clubs, accompanied by her helpless husband, and to engage in dances
that I can only describe as existential. Even Uncle Franz, that good, kind
man, is reported to have remarked that he is weary of life, he whom the
whole family considered a paragon of vitality and the very model of what
we were taught to call a Christian businessman.

Doctors' bills are piling up, psychiatrists and analysts are being called
in. Only my Aunt Milla, who must be considered the cause of it all, enjoys the best of health, smiling, well and cheerful, as she has been almost

all her life. Her liveliness and cheerfulness are slowly beginning to get on our nerves after our very serious concern about the state of her health. For there was a crisis in her life that threatened to be serious. It is just this that I must explain.

2

In retrospect it is easy enough to determine the source of a disquieting series of events, but only now, when I regard the matter dispassionately, do the things that have been taking place in our family for almost two years appear out of the ordinary.

We might have surmised earlier that something was not quite right. Something in fact was not, and if things ever were quite right—which I doubt—events are now taking place that fill me with consternation.

For a long time Aunt Milla has been famous in our family for her delight in decorating the Christmas tree, a harmless though particularized weakness which is fairly widespread in our country. This weakness of hers was indulgently smiled at by one and all, and the resistance that Franz showed from his earliest days to this "nonsense" was treated with indignation, especially since Franz was in other respects a disturbing young man. He refused to take part in the decoration of the tree. Up to a certain point all this was taken in stride. My aunt had become accustomed to Franz's staying away from the preparations at Advent and also from the celebration itself and only putting in an appearance for the meal. It was not even mentioned.

At the risk of making myself unpopular, I must here mention a fact in defense of which I can only say that it really is a fact. In the years 1939 to 1945 we were at war. In war there is singing, shooting, oratory, fighting, starvation and death—and bombs are dropped. These are thoroughly disagreeable subjects, and I have no desire to bore my contemporaries by dwelling on them. I must only mention them because the war had an influence on the story I am about to tell. For the war registered on my aunt simply as a force that, as early as Christmas 1939, began to threaten her Christmas tree. To be sure, this tree of hers was peculiarly sensitive.

As its principal attraction my Aunt Milla's Christmas tree was furnished with glass gnomes that held cork hammers in their upraised hands. At their feet were bell-shaped anvils, and under their feet candles were fastened. When the heat rose to a certain degree, a hidden mechanism went into operation, imparting a hectic movement to the gnomes' arms; a dozen in number, they beat like mad on the bell-shaped anvils with their cork hammers, thus producing a concerted, high-pitched, elfin tinkling. And at the top of the tree stood a red-cheeked angel, dressed in silver, who at certain intervals opened his lips and whispered "Peace, peace." The mechanical secret of the angel was strictly guarded, and I only learned about it later, when as it happened I had the opportunity of admiring it almost weekly. Naturally in addition to this my aunt's Christmas tree was decorated with sugar rings, cookies, angel hair, marzipan figures and, not to be forgotten, strands of tinsel. I still remember that the proper preparation of these varied decorations cost a good deal of trouble, demanding the help of all, and the whole family on Christmas Eve was too nervous to be hungry. The mood, as people say, was simply terrible, and the one exception was my Cousin Franz, who of course had taken no part in the preparations and was the only one to enjoy the roasts, asparagus, creams and ices. If after that we came for a call on the day after Christmas and ventured the bold conjecture that the secret of the speaking angel resided in the same sort of mechanism that makes certain dolls say "Mama" or "Papa," we were simply greeted by derisive laughter.

Now it is easy to understand that in the neighborhood of falling bombs such a sensitive tree would be in great danger. There were terrible times when the gnomes pitched down from the tree, and once even the angel fell. My aunt was inconsolable. She went to endless pains to restore the tree completely after each air raid so as to preserve it at least through the Christmas holidays. But by 1940 it was out of the question. Once more at the risk of making myself unpopular I must briefly mention here that the number of air raids on our city was considerable, to say nothing of their severity. In any case my aunt's Christmas tree fell victim to the modern art of war (regulations forbid me to say anything about other victims); foreign ballistics experts temporarily extinguished it.

We all sympathized with our aunt, who was an amiable and charming woman, and pretty into the bargain. It pained us that she was compelled, after bitter struggles, endless disputes, scenes and tears, to agree to forego her tree for the duration.

Fortunately—or should I say unfortunately?—this was almost the only aspect of the war that was brought home to my aunt. The bunker my uncle built was really bombproof; in addition a car was always ready to whisk my Aunt Milla away to places where nothing was to be seen of the immediate effects of war. Everything was done to spare her the sight of the horrible ruins. My two cousins had the good fortune not to see military service in its harshest form. Johannes at once entered my uncle's firm, which played an essential part in the wholesale grocery business of our city. Besides, he suffered from gall bladder trouble. Franz on the other hand became a soldier, but he was only engaged in guarding prisoners, a post which he exploited to the extent of making himself unpopular with his military superiors by treating Russians and Poles like human beings. My Cousin Lucie was not yet married at that time and helped with the business. One afternoon a week she did voluntary war work, embroidering swastikas. But this is not the place to recite the political sins of my relations.

On the whole, then, there was no lack of money or food or reasonable safety, and my aunt's only sorrow was the absence of her tree. My Uncle Franz, that good, kind man, had for almost fifty years rendered invaluable service by purchasing oranges and lemons in tropical and subtropical countries and selling them at an appropriate profit. During the war he extended his business to less valuable fruits and to vegetables. After the war, however, the principal objects of his interest became popular once more under the name of citrus fruits and caused sharp competition in business circles. Here Uncle Franz succeeded once more in playing a decisive role by introducing the populace to a taste for vitamins and himself to a sizable fortune. He was almost seventy by that time, however, and wanted to retire and leave the business to his son-in-law. It was then that the event took place which made us smile at the time but which we now recognize as the cause of the whole affair.

My Aunt Milla began again with her Christmas tree. That was harmless in itself; even the tenacity with which she insisted that everything should be "as it used to be" only caused us to smile. At first there was really no reason to take the matter too seriously. To be sure, the war had caused much havoc which it was our duty to put right, but why—so we asked ourselves—deprive a charming old lady of this small joy?

Everyone knows how hard it was at that time to get butter and bacon. And even for my Uncle Franz, who had the best connections, it was impossible in the year 1945 to procure marzipan figures and chocolate rings. It was not until 1946 that everything could be made ready. Fortunately a complete set of gnomes and anvils as well as an angel had been preserved.

I still clearly remember the day on which we were invited. It was in January '47 and it was cold outside. But at my uncle's it was warm and there was no lack of delicacies. When the lights were turned out and the candles lighted, when the gnomes began to hammer and the angel whispered "Peace, peace," I had a vivid feeling of being restored to a time that I had assumed was gone forever.

This experience, however, though surprising was not extraordinary. The extraordinary thing was what happened three months later. My mother—it was now the middle of March—sent me over to find out whether "there was anything doing" with Uncle Franz. She needed fruit. I wandered into the neighboring quarter—the air was mild and it was twilight. Unsuspecting, I walked past the overgrown piles of ruins and the untended parks, turned in at the gate to my uncle's garden and suddenly stopped in amazement. In the evening quiet I could distinctly hear someone singing in my uncle's living room. Singing is a good old German custom, and there are lots of spring songs—but here I clearly heard:

> *Unto us a child is born!*
> *The King of all creation . . .*

I must admit I was confused. Slowly I approached and waited for the end of the song. The curtains were drawn and so I bent down to the keyhole. At that moment the tinkling of gnomes' bells reached my ear, and I distinctly heard the angel whispering.

I did not have the courage to intrude, and walked slowly home. My

report caused general merriment in the family, and it was not until Franz
turned up and told us the details that we discovered what had happened.

In our region Christmas trees are dismantled at Candlemas[1] and are
then thrown on the rubbish heap where good-for-nothing children pick
them up, drag them through ashes and other debris and play all sorts of
games with them. This was the time when the dreadful thing happened.
On Candlemas Eve after the tree had been lighted for the last time, and
Cousin Johannes began to unfasten the gnomes from their clamps, my
aunt who had hitherto been so gentle set up a dreadful screaming, so loud
and sudden that my cousin was startled, lost control of the swaying tree,
and in an instant it was all over; there was a tinkling and ringing;
gnomes and bells, anvils and angel, everything pitched down; and my
aunt screamed.

She screamed for almost a week. Neurologists were summoned by
telegram, psychiatrists came rushing up in taxicabs—but all of them,
even the specialists, left with a shrug of the shoulders and a faint expression of dread.

No one could put an end to this shrill and maddening concert. Only
the strongest drugs provided a few hours' rest, and the dose of Luminal
that one can daily prescribe for a woman in her sixties without endanger-
ing her life is, alas, slight. But it is anguish to have a woman in the house
screaming with all her might: on the second day the family was completely disorganized. Even the consolation of the priest, who was accustomed to attend the celebration on Holy Eve, remained unavailing:
my aunt screamed.

Franz made himself particularly unpopular by advising that a regular
exorcism be performed. The minister rebuked him, the family was
alarmed by his medieval views, and his reputation for brutality eclipsed
for several weeks his reputation as a boxer.

Meanwhile everything was tried to cure my aunt's ailment. She refused nourishment, did not speak, did not sleep; cold water was tried,
hot water, foot baths, alternate cold and hot baths; the doctors searched
the lexicons for the name of this complex but could not find it. And my
aunt screamed. She screamed until my Uncle Franz—that really kind,
good man—hit on the idea of putting up a new Christmas tree.

3

The idea was excellent, but to carry it out proved extremely hard. It was
now almost the middle of February, and to find a presentable fir tree in
the market at that time is naturally difficult. The whole business world
has long since turned with happy alacrity to other things. Carnival time
is near: masks, pistols, cowboy hats and fanciful gypsy headgear fill the
shop windows where angels and angel hair, candles and mangers, were

[1] a feast on February 2, celebrating the Purification of the Virgin

formerly on view. In the candy stores Christmas items have long since gone back to the storeroom, while fireworks now adorn the windows. Nowhere in the regular market is a fir tree to be found.

Finally an expedition of rapacious grandchildren was fitted out with pocket money and a sharp hatchet. They rode to the state forest and came back toward evening, obviously in the best of spirits, with a silver fir. But meanwhile it was discovered that four gnomes, six bell-shaped anvils and the crowning angel had been completely destroyed. The marzipan figures and the cookies had fallen victim to the rapacious grand-children. This coming generation, too, is worthless, and if any generation was ever of any worth—which I doubt—I am slowly coming to the be-lief that it was the generation of our fathers.

Although there was no lack of cash or the necessary connections, it took four days more before the decorations were complete. Meanwhile my aunt screamed uninterruptedly. Messages to the German centers of the toy business, which were just then resuming operations, were dis-patched by wireless, hurried telephone conversations were carried on, packages were delivered in the night by heated young postal employees, an import license from Czechoslovakia was obtained, by bribery, with-out delay.

These days will stand out in the chronicle of my uncle's family by reason of the extraordinary consumption of coffee, cigarettes and nerv-ous energy. Meanwhile my aunt fell into a decline: her round face became harsh and angular, her expression of kindliness changed to one of unalterable severity, she did not eat, she did not drink, she screamed constantly, she was attended by two nurses, and the dose of Luminal had to be increased daily.

Franz told us that the whole family was in the grip of a morbid tension when finally, on the twelfth of February, the decoration of the Christmas tree was at last completed. The candles were lighted, the curtains were drawn, my aunt was brought out from her sickroom, and in the family circle there was only the sound of sobs and giggles. My aunt's expression relaxed at sight of the candles, and when the heat had reached the proper point and the glass gnomes began to pound like mad and finally the angel, too, whispered "Peace, peace," a beautiful smile illuminated her face. Shortly thereafter everyone began to sing "O Tannenbaum." To complete the picture, they had invited the minister, whose custom it was to spend Christmas Eve at my Uncle Franz's; he, too, smiled, he too was relieved and joined in the singing.

What no test, no psychological opinion, no expert search for hidden traumas had succeeded in doing, my uncle's sympathetic heart had ac-complished. This good, kind man's Christmas-tree therapy had saved the situation.

My aunt was reassured and almost—so they hoped at the time— cured. After more songs had been sung and several plates of cookies had been emptied, everyone was tired and went to bed. And, imagine, my aunt slept without sedatives. The two nurses were dismissed, the doctors shrugged their shoulders, and everything seemed in order. My aunt ate again, drank again, was once more kind and amiable.

But the following evening at twilight, when my uncle was reading his newspaper beside his wife under the tree, she suddenly touched him gently on the arm and said: "Now we will call the children for the celebration. I think it's time." My uncle admitted to us later that he was startled, but he got up and hastily summoned his children and grandchildren and dispatched a messenger for the minister. The latter appeared, somewhat distraught and amazed; the candles were lighted, the gnomes hammered away, the angel whispered, there was singing and eating—and everything seemed in order.

Now all vegetation is subject to certain biological laws, and fir trees torn from the soil have a well-known tendency to wilt and lose their needles, especially if they are kept in a warm room, and in my uncle's house it was warm. The life of the silver fir is somewhat longer than that of the common variety, as the well-known work *Abies Vulgaris and Abies Nobilis* by Doctor Hergenring has shown. But even the life of the silver fir is not unlimited. As Carnival approached it became clear that my aunt would have to be prepared for a new sorrow: the tree was rapidly losing its needles, and at the evening singing a slight frown appeared on her forehead. On the advice of a really outstanding psychologist an attempt was made in light, casual conversation to warn her of the possible end of the Christmas season, especially as the trees outside were now covered with leaves, which is generally taken as a sign of approaching spring whereas in our latitudes the word Christmas connotes wintry scenes. My resourceful uncle proposed one evening that the songs "All the Birds Are Now Assembled" and "Come, Lovely May" should be sung, but at the first verse of the former such a scowl appeared on my aunt's face that the singers quickly broke off and intoned "O Tannenbaum." Three days later my cousin Johannes was instructed to undertake a quiet dismantling operation, but as soon as he stretched out his hand and took the cork hammer from one of the gnomes my aunt broke into such violent screaming that the gnome was immediately given back his implement, the candles were lighted and somewhat hastily but very loudly everyone began to sing "Silent Night."

But the nights were no longer silent; groups of singing, youthful revelers streamed through the city with trumpets and drums, everything was covered with streamers and confetti, masked children crowded the streets, fired guns, screamed, some sang as well, and a private investigation showed that there were at least sixty thousand cowboys and forty thousand gypsy princesses in our city; in short it was Carnival, a holiday that is celebrated in our neighborhood with as much enthusiasm as Christmas or even more. But my aunt seemed blind and deaf: she deplored the carnival costumes that inevitably appeared at this time in the wardrobes of our household; in a sad voice she lamented the decline of morals that caused people even at Christmas to indulge in such disgraceful practices, and when she discovered a toy balloon in Lucie's bedroom, a balloon that had, to be sure, collapsed but nevertheless clearly showed a white fool's cap painted on it, she broke into tears and besought my uncle to put an end to these unholy activities.

They were forced to realize with horror that my aunt actually believed it was still Christmas Eve. My uncle called a family council, requested consideration for his wife in view of her extraordinary state of mind, and at once got together an expedition to insure that at least the evening celebration would be peacefully maintained.

While my aunt slept the decorations were taken down from the old tree and placed on a new one, and her state of health continued to be satisfactory.

Carnival, too, went by, spring came for fair; instead of "Come Lovely May" one might properly have sung "Lovely May, Thou Art Here." June arrived. Four Christmas trees had already been discarded and none of the newly summoned doctors could hold out hope of improvement. My aunt remained firm. Even that internationally famous authority, Doctor Bless, had returned to his study, shrugging his shoulders, after having pocketed an honorarium in the sum of 1365 marks, thereby demonstrating once more his complete unworldliness. A few tentative attempts to put an end to the celebration or to intermit it were greeted with such outcries from my aunt that these sacrileges had to be abandoned once and for all.

The dreadful thing was that my aunt insisted that all those closest to her must be present. Among these were the minister and the grandchildren. Even the members of the family could only be compelled by extreme severity to appear punctually; with the minister it was even more difficult. For some weeks he kept it up without protest, out of consideration for his aged pensioner, but then he attempted, clearing his throat in embarrassment, to make it clear to my uncle that this could not go on. The actual celebration was short—it lasted only about thirty-eight minutes—but even this brief ceremonial, the minister maintained, could not be kept up indefinitely. He had other obligations, evening conferences with his confratres, duties connected with his cure of souls, not to mention his regular Saturday confessional. He agreed, however, to some weeks' continuance; but toward the end of May, he began energetic attempts to escape. Franz stormed about, seeking accomplices in the family for his plan to have his mother put in an institution. Everyone turned him down.

And yet difficulties continued. One evening the minister was missing and could not be located either telephonically or by messenger, and it became evident that he had simply skipped out. My uncle swore horribly and took the occasion to describe the servants of the Church in words I must decline to repeat. In this extremity one of the chaplains, a man of humble origin, was requested to help out. He did so, but behaved so abominably that it almost resulted in a catastrophe. However, one must bear in mind that it was June and therefore hot; nevertheless the curtains were drawn to give at least an illusion of wintry twilight and in addition the candles had been lighted. Then the celebration began. The chaplain had, to be sure, heard of this extraordinary event but had no proper idea of it. There was general apprehension when he was presented to my aunt as the minister's substitute. Unexpectedly she accepted this change in the program. Well then, the gnomes hammered, the angel whispered, "O Tannenbaum" was sung, then there was the eating of cookies, more singing, and suddenly the chaplain was overcome by a paroxysm of laughter. Later he admitted that it was the line ". . . in winter, too, when snow is falling" that had been too much for him to endure without laughing. He burst out with clerical tactlessness, left the room and was seen no more. All looked at my aunt apprehensively, but she only murmured resignedly something about "proletarians in priest's robes" and put a piece of marzipan in her mouth. We too deplored this event at the time—but today I am inclined to regard it as an outbreak of quite natural hilarity.

Here I must remark, if I am to be true to the facts, that my uncle exploited his connection with the highest Church authorities to lodge a complaint against both the minister and the chaplain. The matter was taken up with utmost correctness, proceedings were instituted on the grounds of neglect of pastoral duty, and in the first instance the two clergymen were exonerated. Further proceedings are in preparation.

Fortunately a pensioned prelate was found in the neighborhood. This charming old gentleman agreed, with amiable matter-of-factness, to hold himself in readiness daily for the evening celebration. But I am anticipating. My uncle Franz, who was sensible enough to realize that no medical aid would be of avail and who stubbornly refused to try exorcism, was also a good enough businessman to plan economies for the long haul. First of all, by mid-June, the grandchildren's expeditions were stopped because they proved too expensive. My resourceful Cousin Johannes, who was on good terms with all branches of the business world, discovered that Söderbaum and Company were in a position to provide fresh fir trees. For almost two years now this firm has done noble service in sparing my relations' nerves. At the end of six months Söderbaum and Company substantially reduced their charges and agreed to have the period of delivery determined most precisely by their conifer specialist Doctor Alfast, so that three days before the old tree became unpresentable a new one would be delivered and could be decorated at leisure. As an additional precaution two dozen gnomes and three crowning angels were kept constantly in reserve.

To this day the candles remain a sore point. They show a disturbing tendency to melt and drip down from the tree more quickly and completely than wax, at any rate in the summer months. Every effort to preserve them by carefully concealed refrigeration has thus far come to grief, as has a series of attempts to substitute artificial decorations. The family remains, however, gratefully receptive toward any proposal that might result in reducing the costs of this continuing festival.

4

Meanwhile the daily celebrations in my uncle's house have taken on an almost professional regularity. People assemble under the tree or around the tree. My aunt comes in, the candles are lighted, the gnomes begin to hammer and the angel whispers "Peace, peace," songs are sung, cookies nibbled, there is a little conversation and then everyone retires, yawning and murmuring "Merry Christmas to you, too." The young people turn to the forms of diversion dictated by the season, while my good, kind Uncle Franz goes to bed when Aunt Milla does. The smoke of the candles lingers in the room, there is the mild aroma of heated fir needles and the smell of spices. The gnomes, slightly phosphorescent, remain motionless in the darkness, their arms raised threateningly, and the angel can be seen in his silvery robes which are obviously phosphorescent too.

Perhaps it is superfluous to state that in our whole family circle the enjoyment of the real Christmas Eve has suffered a considerable diminution: we can, if we like, admire a classical Christmas tree at our uncle's at any time—and it often happens when we are sitting on the veranda in summertime after the toil and trouble of the day, pouring my uncle's mild orange punch down our throats, that the soft tinkling of glass bells comes to us and we can see in the twilight the gnomes hammering away like spry little devils while the angel whispers "Peace, peace." And it is still disconcerting to hear my uncle in mid-summer suddenly whisper to his children: "Please light the tree, Mother will be right out." Then, usually on the dot, the prelate enters, a kindly old gentleman whom we have all taken to our hearts because he plays his role so admirably, if indeed he knows that he is playing one. But no matter: he plays it, white-haired, smiling, with the violet band beneath his collar giving his appearance the final touch of distinction. And it gives one an extraordinary feeling on a mild summer evening to hear the excited cry: "The snuffer, quick, where is the snuffer?" It has even happened during severe thunderstorms that the gnomes have been suddenly impelled to lift their arms without the agency of heat and swing them wildly as though giving a special performance—a phenomenon that people have tried, rather unimaginatively, to explain by the prosaic word "electricity."

A by no means inessential aspect of this arrangement is the financial one. Even though in general our family suffers no lack of cash, such extraordinary expenses upset all calculations. For naturally, despite precautions, the breakage of gnomes, anvils, and hammers is enormous, and the delicate mechanism that causes the angel to speak requires constant

care and attention and must now and again be replaced. I have, incidentally, discovered its secret: the angel is connected by a cable with a
microphone in the adjoining room, in front of whose metal snout there is
a constantly rotating phonograph record which, at proper intervals,
whispers "Peace, peace." All these things are the more costly because
they are designed for use on only a few occasions during the year,
whereas with us they are subjected to daily wear and tear. I was astounded when my uncle told me one day that the gnomes actually had
to be replaced every three months, and that a complete set of them cost
no less than 128 marks. He said he had requested an engineering friend
of his to try strengthening them by a rubber covering without spoiling
the beauty of the tone. This experiment was unsuccessful. The consumption of candles, butter-and-almond cookies, marzipan, the regular
payments for the trees, doctor's bills and the quarterly honorarium that
has to be given to the prelate, altogether, said my uncle, come to an
average daily expense of 11 marks, not to mention the nervous wear
and tear and other disturbances of health that began to appear in the fall
of the first year. These upsets were generally ascribed, at the time, to
that autumnal sensibility that is always noticeable.

The real Christmas celebration went off quite normally. Something
like a sigh of relief ran through my uncle's family when other families
could be seen gathered under Christmas trees, others too had to sing
and eat butter-and-almond cookies. But the relief lasted only as long as
the Christmas holidays. By the middle of January my Cousin Lucie began to suffer from a strange ailment: at the sight of Christmas trees lying
on the streets and on rubbish heaps she broke into hysterical sobs. Then
she had a real attack of insanity which the family tried to discount as a
nervous breakdown. At a coffee party in a friend's house she struck a
dish out of her hostess' hand as the latter was smilingly offering her
butter-and-almond cookies. My cousin is, to be sure, what is called a
temperamental woman: and so she struck the dish from her friend's
hand, went up to the Christmas tree, tore it from its stand and trampled
on the glass balls, the artificial mushrooms, the candles and the stars, the
while emitting a continuous roar. The assembled ladies fled, including
the hostess. They let Lucie rage, and stood waiting for the doctor in the
vestibule, forced to give ear to the sound of crashing china within. Painful though it is for me, I must report that Lucie was taken away in a
straitjacket.

Sustained hypnotic treatment checked her illness, but the actual cure
proceeded very slowly. Above all, release from the evening celebration,
which the doctor demanded, seemed to do her visible good; after a few
days she began to brighten. At the end of ten days the doctor could risk
at least talking to her about butter-and-almond cookies, although she
stubbornly persisted in refusing to eat them. The doctor then struck on
the inspired idea of feeding her some sour pickles and offering her salads
and nourishing meat dishes. That was poor Lucie's real salvation. She

laughed once more and began to interject ironic observations into the endless therapeutic interviews she had with her doctor.

To be sure, the vacancy caused by her absence from the evening celebration was painful to my aunt, but it was explained to her by a circumstance that is an adequate excuse in any woman's eyes— pregnancy.

But Lucie had created what is called a precedent: she had proved that although my aunt suffered when someone was absent, she did not immediately begin to scream, and now my Cousin Johannes and his brother-in-law Carl attempted to infringe on the severe regulations, giving sickness as excuse or business appointments or some other quite transparent pretext. But here my uncle remained astonishingly inflexible: with iron severity he decreed that only in exceptional cases upon presentation of acceptable evidence could very short leaves of absence be permitted. For my aunt noticed every further dereliction at once and broke into silent but continuing tears, which gave rise to the most serious apprehensions.

At the end of four weeks Lucie, too, returned and said she was ready to take part once more in the daily ceremony, but her doctor had insisted that a jar of pickles and a platter of nourishing sandwiches should be held in readiness, since her butter-and-almond trauma had proved incurable. Thus for a time, through my uncle's unexpected severity, all breaches of discipline were suppressed.

Shortly after the first anniversary of the daily Christmas celebration, disquieting rumors began to circulate: my Cousin Johannes was said to have consulted a doctor friend of his about my aunt's life expectancy, a truly sinister rumor which throws a disturbing light on a peaceful family's evening gatherings. The doctor's opinion is said to have been crushing for Johannes. All my aunt's vital organs, which had always been sound, were in perfect condition; her father's age at the time of his death had been seventy-eight, and her mother's eighty-six. My aunt herself is sixty-two, and so there is no reason to prophesy an early passing. Still less reason, I consider, to wish for one. After this when my aunt fell ill in midsummer—the poor woman suffered from vomiting and diarrhea—it was hinted that she had been poisoned, but I expressly declare here and now that this rumor was simply the invention of evil-minded relations. The trouble was clearly shown to have been caused by an infection brought into the house by one of the grandchildren. Moreover, analyses that were made of my aunt's stools showed not the slightest trace of poison.

That same summer Johannes gave the first evidences of anti-social inclinations: he resigned from the singing circle and gave notice in writing that he planned to take no further part in the cultivation of the German song. It is only fair for me to add, however, that, despite the academic distinctions he had won, he was always an uncultivated man. For the "Virhymnia" the loss of his bass voice was a serious matter.

My brother-in-law Carl began secretly to consult travel agencies. The land of his dreams had to have unusual characteristics: no fir trees must grow there and their importation must be forbidden or rendered unfeasible by a high tariff; besides—on his wife's account—the secret of preparing butter-and-almond cookies must be unknown and the singing of German Christmas songs forbidden by law. Carl declared himself ready to undertake hard physical labor.

Since then he has been able to dispense with secrecy because of a complete and very sudden change which has taken place in my uncle. This happened at such a disagreeable level that we have really had cause to be disconcerted. That sober citizen, of whom it could be said that he was as stubborn as he was good and kind, was observed performing actions that are neither more nor less than immoral and will remain so as long as the world endures. Things became known about him, testified to by witnesses, that can only be described by the word adultery. And the most dreadful thing is that he no longer denies them, but claims for himself the right to live in circumstances and in relationships that make special legislation seem justifiable. Awkwardly enough, this sudden change became evident just at the time when the second hearing of the two parish priests was called. My Uncle Franz seems to have made such a deplorable impression as a witness, as disguised plaintiff indeed, that it must be ascribed to him alone that the second hearing turned out favorably for the two priests. But in the meantime all this had become a matter of indifference to Uncle Franz: his downfall is complete, already accomplished.

He too was the first to hit upon the shocking idea of having himself represented by an actor at the evening celebration. He had found an unemployed *bon vivant*,[2] who for two weeks imitated him so admirably that not even his wife noticed the impersonation. Nor did his children notice it either. It was one of the grandchildren who, during a pause in the singing, suddenly shouted: "Grandpapa has on socks with rings," and triumphantly raised the *bon vivant's* trouser leg. This scene must have been terrifying for the poor artist; the family, too, was upset and to avoid disaster struck up a song, as they had done so often before in critical situations. After my aunt had gone to bed, the identity of the artist was quickly established. It was the signal for almost complete collapse.

However one must bear in mind that a year and a half is a long time, and it was mid-summer again, the time when participation in the play is hardest on my relations. Listless in the heat, they nibble at sand tarts and ginger cookies, smile vacantly while they crack dried-out nuts, listen to the indefatigable hammering of the gnomes and wince when the rosy-cheeked angel above their heads whispers "Peace, peace." But they carry on while, despite their summer clothing, sweat streams down their cheeks and necks and soaks their shirts. Or rather: they have carried on so far.

[2] a lover of good living

For the moment money plays no part—almost the reverse. People are beginning to whisper that Uncle Franz has adopted business methods, too, which can hardly be described as those of a "Christian business-man." He is determined not to allow any material lessening of the family fortune, a resolution that both calms and alarms us.

The unmasking of the *bon vivant* led to a regular mutiny, as a result of which a compromise was reached: Uncle Franz agreed to pay the ex-penses of a small theatrical troupe, which would replace him, Johannes, my brother-in-law Carl, and Lucie, and it was further understood that one of the four would always take part in person in the evening celebra-tion in order to keep the children in check. Up till now the prelate has not noticed this deception, which can hardly be described as pious. Aside from my aunt and the children, he is the only original figure still in the play.

An exact schedule has been worked out which, in the family circle, is known as the operational program, and thanks to the provision that one of them is always present in person, the actors too are allowed certain vacations. Meanwhile it was observed that the latter were not averse to the celebration and were glad to earn some additional money; thus it was possible to reduce their wages, since fortunately there is no lack of un-employed actors. Carl tells me that there is reason to hope that these "salaries" can be reduced still more, especially as the actors are given a meal and it is well known that art becomes cheaper when food is in-volved.

I have already briefly mentioned Lucie's unhappy history: now she spends almost all her time in night spots and, on those days when she is compelled to take part in the household celebration, she is beside herself. She wears corduroy britches, colored pullovers, runs around in sandals and she has cut off her splendid hair in order to wear unbecoming bangs and a coiffure that I only recently discovered was once considered mod-ern—it is known as a pony-tail. Although I have so far been unable to observe any overt immorality on her part, but only a kind of exaltation, which she herself describes as existentialism, nevertheless I cannot re-gard this development as desirable; I prefer quiet women, who move decorously to the rhythm of the waltz, know how to recite agreeable verses and whose nourishment is not exclusively sour pickles and gou-lash seasoned with paprika. My brother-in-law Carl's plans to emigrate seem on the point of becoming a reality: he has found a country, not far from the equator, which seems to answer his requirements, and Lucie is full of enthusiasm; in this country people wear clothes not unlike hers, they love sharp spices and they dance to those rhythms without which she maintains life is no longer possible for her. It is a little shocking that these two do not plan to obey the command "Abide in the land I have given you," but on the other hand I can understand their desire to flee.

Things are worse with Johannes. Unfortunately the evil rumor has proved true; he has become a Communist. He has broken off all relations with the family, pays no attention to anything and takes part in the evening celebration only in the person of his double. His eyes have taken on a fanatical expression, he makes public appearances behaving like a dervish at party meetings, neglects his practice and writes furious articles in the appropriate journals. Strangely enough he now sees more of Franz, who is vainly trying to convert him—and vice versa. Despite all their spiritual estrangement, they seem personally to have grown somewhat closer.

Franz I have not seen in a long time, but I have had news of him. He is said to have fallen into a profound depression, to spend his time in dim churches, and I believe that his piety can be fairly described as exaggerated. After the family misfortunes began he started to neglect his calling, and recently I saw on the wall of a ruined house a faded poster saying: "Last Battle of our Veteran Lenz against Lecoq. Lenz is Hanging up the Gloves." The date on the poster was March, and now we are well into August. Franz is said to have fallen on bad times. I believe he finds himself in a situation which has never before occurred in our family: he is poor. Fortunately he has remained single, and so the social consequences of his irresponsible piety harm only him. He has tried with amazing perseverance to have a guardian appointed for Lucie's children because he considers they are endangered by the daily celebration. But his efforts have remained fruitless; thank God, the children of wealthy people are not exposed to the interference of social institutions.

The one least removed from the rest of the family circle is, for all his deplorable actions, Uncle Franz. To be sure, despite his advanced years, he has a mistress. And his business practices, too, are of a sort that we admire, to be sure, but cannot at all approve. Recently he has appointed an unemployed stage manager to supervise the evening celebration and see that everything runs like clockwork. Everything does in fact run like clockwork.

5

Almost two years have now gone by—a long time. And I could not resist the temptation, during one of my evening strolls, to stop in at my uncle's house, where no true hospitality is any longer possible, since strange actors wander about every evening and the members of the family have devoted themselves to reprehensible pleasures. It was a mild summer evening, and as I turned into the avenue of chestnut trees I heard the verse:

The wintry woods are clad in snow . . .

A passing truck made the rest inaudible. Slowly and softly I approached the house and looked through a crack in the curtains. The similarity of the actors who were present to those of my relations whom they represented was so startling that for an instant I could not recognize which one this evening was the superintendent, as they called him. I could not see the gnomes but I could hear them. Their chirping tinkle has a wave length that can penetrate any wall. The whispering of the angel was inaudible. My aunt seemed to be really happy · she was chatting with the prelate, and it was only later that I recognized my brother-in-law as the one real person present—if that is the right word. I recognized him by the way he rounded and pointed his lips as he blew out a match. Apparently there are unchangeable individual traits. This led me to reflect that the actors, too, were obviously treated to cigars, cigarettes and wine—in addition there was asparagus every evening. If their appetites were shameless—and what artist's is not?—this meant a considerable additional expense for my uncle. The children were playing with dolls and wooden wagons in a corner of the room. They looked pale and tired. Perhaps one really ought to have some consideration for them. I was struck by the idea that they might perhaps be replaced by wax dolls of the kind one sees in the windows of drugstores as advertisements for powdered milk and skin lotions. It seems to me those look quite natural.

As a matter of fact I intend to call the family's attention to the possible effect on the children's temperament of this unnatural daily excitement. Although a certain amount of discipline does no harm, it seems to me that they are being subjected to excessive demands.

I left my observation post when the people inside began to sing: "Silent Night." I simply could not bear the song. The air was so mild—and for an instant I had the feeling that I was watching an assembly of ghosts. Suddenly I had a craving for sour pickles and this gave me some inkling of how very much Lucie must have suffered.

I have now succeeded in having the children replaced by wax dolls. Their procurement was costly—Uncle Franz hesitated for some time—but one really could not go on irresponsibly feeding the children on marzipan every day and making them sing songs which in the long run might cause them psychic injury. The procurement of the dolls proved to be useful because Carl and Lucie really emigrated and Johannes also withdrew his children from his father's household. I bade farewell to Carl and Lucie and the children as they stood amid large traveling trunks. They seemed happy, if a little worried. Johannes, too, has left our town. Somewhere or other he is engaged in reorganizing a Communist cell.

Uncle Franz is weary of life. Recently he complained to me that people are always forgetting to dust off the dolls. His servants in particular cause him difficulties, and the actors seem inclined to be undisciplined. They drink more than they ought, and some of them have been caught filling their pockets with cigars and cigarettes. I advised my uncle to provide them with colored water and cardboard cigars.

The only reliable ones are my aunt and the prelate. They chat together about the good old times, giggle and seem to enjoy themselves, interrupting their conversation only when a song is struck up.

In any event, the celebration goes on.

My cousin Franz has taken an amazing step. He has been accepted as a lay brother in a nearby monastery. When I saw him for the first time in a cowl I was startled: that large figure, with broken nose, thickened lips and melancholy expression, reminded me more of a prisoner than a monk. He seemed almost to have read my thoughts. "Life is a prison sentence," he said softly. I followed him into the interview room. We conversed haltingly, and he was obviously relieved when the bell summoned him to the chapel for prayers. I remained behind, thoughtful, as he departed: he went in a great hurry, and his haste seemed genuine.

Translated by Denver Lindley

James Baldwin
1924–
PREVIOUS CONDITION

I WOKE up shaking, alone in my room. I was clammy cold with sweat; under me the sheet and the mattress were soaked. The sheet was gray and twisted like a rope. I breathed like I had been running.

I couldn't move for the longest while. I just lay on my back, spread-eagled, looking up at the ceiling, listening to the sounds of people getting up in other parts of the house, alarm clocks ringing and water splashing and doors opening and shutting and feet on the stairs. I could tell when people left for work: the hall doorway downstairs whined and shuffled as it opened and gave a funny kind of double slam as it closed. One thud and then a louder thud and then a little final click. While the door was open I could hear the street sounds too, horses' hoofs and delivery wagons and people in the streets and big trucks and motor cars screaming on the asphalt.

I had been dreaming. At night I dreamed and woke up in the morning trembling, but not remembering the dream, except that in the dream I had been running. I could not remember when the dream—or dreams— had started; it had been long ago. For long periods maybe, I would have no dreams at all. And then they would come back, every night, I would try not to go to bed, I would go to sleep frightened and wake up frightened and have another day to get through with the nightmare at my shoulder. Now I was back from Chicago, busted, living off my friends in a dirty furnished room downtown. The show I had been with had folded in Chicago. It hadn't been much of a part—or much of a show either, to tell the truth. I played a kind of intellectual Uncle Tom, a young college student working for his race. The playwright had wanted to prove he was a liberal, I guess. But, as I say, the show had folded and here I was, back in New York and hating it. I knew that I should be getting another job, making the rounds, pounding the pavement. But I didn't. I couldn't face it. It was summer. I seemed to be fagged out. And every day I hated myself more. Acting's a rough life, even if you're white. I'm not tall and I'm not good looking and I can't sing or dance and I'm not white; so even at the best of times I wasn't in much demand.

The room I lived in was heavy ceilinged, perfectly square, with walls the color of chipped dry blood. Jules Weissman, a Jewboy, had got the room for me. It's a room to sleep in, he said, or maybe to die in but God knows it wasn't meant to live in. Perhaps because the room was so hideous it had a fantastic array of light fixtures : one on the ceiling, one on the left wall, two on the right wall, and a lamp on the table beside my bed. My bed was in front of the window through which nothing ever blew but dust. It was a furnished room and they'd thrown enough stuff in it to furnish three rooms its size. Two easy chairs and a desk, the bed, the table, a straight-backed chair, a bookcase, a cardboard wardrobe; and my books and my suitcase, both unpacked; and my dirty clothes flung in a corner. It was the kind of room that defeated you. It had a fireplace, too, and a heavy marble mantelpiece and a great gray mirror above the mantelpiece. It was hard to see anything in the mirror very clearly— which was perhaps just as well—and it would have been worth your life to have started a fire in the fireplace.
"Well, you won't have to stay here long," Jules told me the night I came. Jules smuggled me in, sort of, after dark, when everyone had gone to bed.
"Christ, I hope not."
"I'll be moving to a big place soon," Jules said. "You can move in with me." He turned all the lights on. "Think it'll be all right for a while?" He sounded apologetic, as though he had designed the room himself.
"Oh, sure. D'you think I'll have any trouble?"
"I don't think so. The rent's paid. She can't put you out."
I didn't say anything to that.
"Sort of stay undercover," Jules said. "You know."
"Roger," I said.
I had been living there for three days, timing it so I left after everyone else had gone, coming back late at night when everyone else was asleep. But I knew it wouldn't work. A couple of the tenants had seen me on the stairs, a woman had surprised me coming out of the john. Every morning I waited for the landlady to come banging on the door. I didn't know what would happen. It might be all right. It might not be. But the waiting was getting me.
The sweat on my body was turning cold. Downstairs a radio was tuned in to the Breakfast Symphony. They were playing Beethoven. I sat up and lit a cigarette. "Peter," I said, "don't let them scare you to

death. You're a man, too." I listened to Ludwig and I watched the smoke rise to the dirty ceiling. Under Ludwig's drums and horns I listened to hear footsteps on the stairs.

I'd done a lot of traveling in my time. I'd knocked about through St. Louis, Frisco, Seattle, Detroit, New Orleans, worked at just about everything. I'd run away from my old lady when I was about sixteen. She's never been able to handle me. You'll never be nothin' *but* a bum, she'd say. We lived in an old shack in a town in New Jersey in the nigger part of town, the kind of houses colored people live in all over the U.S. I hated my mother for living there. I hated all the people in my neighborhood. They went to church and they got drunk. They were nice to the white people. When the landlord came around they paid him and took his crap.

The first time I was ever called nigger I was seven years old. It was a little white girl with long black curls. I used to leave the front of my house and go wandering by myself through town. This little girl was playing ball alone and as I passed her the ball rolled out of her hands into the gutter.

I threw it back to her.

"Let's play catch," I said.

But she held the ball and made a face at me.

"My mother don't let me play with niggers," she told me.

I did not know what the word meant. But my skin grew warm. I stuck my tongue out at her.

"I don't care. Keep your old ball." I started down the street.

She screamed after me: "Nigger, nigger, nigger!"

I screamed back: "Your mother was a nigger!"

I asked my mother what a nigger was.

"Who called you that?"

"I heard somebody say it."

"Who?"

"Just somebody."

"Go wash your face," she said. "You dirty as sin. Your supper's on the table."

I went to the bathroom and splashed water on my face and wiped my face and hands on the towel.

"You call that clean?" my mother cried. "Come here, boy!"

She dragged me back to the bathroom and began to soap my face and neck.

"You run around dirty like you do all the time, everybody'll call you a little nigger, you hear?" She rinsed my face and looked at my hands and dried me. "Now, go on and eat your supper."

I didn't say anything. I went to the kitchen and sat down at the table. I remember I wanted to cry. My mother sat down across from me.

"Mama," I said. She looked at me. I started to cry.

She came around to my side of the table and took me in her arms.

"Baby, don't fret. Next time somebody calls you nigger tell them you'd rather be your color than be lowdown and nasty like some white folks is."

We formed gangs when I was older, my friends and I. We met white boys and their friends on the opposite sides of fences and we threw rocks and tin cans at each other.

I'd come home bleeding. My mother would slap me and scold me and cry.

"Boy, you wanna get killed? You wanna end up like your father?"

My father was a bum and I had never seen him. I was named for him: Peter.

I was always in trouble: truant officers, welfare workers, everybody else in town.

"You ain't never gonna be nothin' *but* a bum," my mother said.

By and by older kids I knew finished school and got jobs and got married and settled down. They were going to settle down and bring more black babies into the world and pay the same rents for the same old shacks and it would go on and on—

When I was sixteen I ran away. I left a note and told Mama not to worry, I'd come back one day and I'd be all right. But when I was twenty-two she died. I came back and put my mother in the ground. Everything was like it had been. Our house had not been painted and the porch floor sagged and there was somebody's raincoat stuffed in the broken window. Another family was moving in.

Their furniture was stacked along the walls and their children were running through the house and laughing and somebody was frying pork chops in the kitchen. The oldest boy was tacking up a mirror.

Last year Ida took me driving in her big car and we passed through a couple of towns upstate. We passed some crumbling houses on the left. The clothes on the line were flying in the wind.

"Are people living there?" asked Ida.

"Just darkies," I said.

Ida passed the car ahead, banging angrily on the horn. "D'you know you're becoming paranoiac, Peter?"

"All right. All right. I know a lot of white people are starving too."

"You're damn right they are. I know a little about poverty myself."

Ida had come from the kind of family called shanty Irish. She was raised in Boston. She's a very beautiful woman who married young and married for money—so now I can afford to support attractive young men, she'd giggle. Her husband was a ballet dancer who was forever on the road. Ida suspected that he went with boys. Not that I give a damn, she said, as long as he leaves me alone. When we met last year she was thirty and I was twenty-five. We had a pretty stormy relationship but we stuck. Whenever I got to town I called her; whenever I was stranded out of town I'd let her know. We never let it get too serious. She went her way and I went mine.

In all this running around I'd learned a few things. Like a prizefighter learns to take a blow or a dancer learns to fall, I'd learned how to get by. I'd learned never to be belligerent with policemen, for instance. No matter who was right, I was certain to be wrong. What might be accepted as just good old American independence in someone else would be insufferable arrogance in me. After the first few times I realized that I had to play smart, to act out the role I was expected to play. I only had one head and it was too easy to get it broken. When I faced a policeman I acted like I didn't know a thing. I let my jaw drop and I let my eyes get big, I didn't give him any smart answers, none of the crap about my rights. I figured out what answers he wanted and I gave them to him. I never let him think he wasn't king. If it was more than routine, if I was picked up on suspicion of robbery or murder in the neighborhood, I looked as humble as I could and kept my mouth shut and prayed. I took a couple of beatings but I stayed out of prison and I stayed off chain gangs. That was also due to luck, Ida pointed out once. "Maybe it would've been better for you if you'd been a little less lucky. Worse things have happened than chain gangs. Some of them have happened to you."

There was something in her voice. "What are you talking about?" I asked.

"Don't lose your temper. I said maybe."

"You mean you think I'm a coward?"

"I didn't say that, Peter."

"But you meant that. Didn't you?"

"No. I didn't mean that. I didn't mean anything. Let's not fight."

There are times and places when a Negro can use his color like a shield. He can trade on the subterranean Anglo-Saxon guilt and get what he wants that way; or some of what he wants. He can trade on his nuisance value, his value as forbidden fruit; he can use it like a knife, he can twist it and get his vengeance that way. I knew these things long before I realized that I knew them and in the beginning I used them, not knowing what I was doing. Then when I began to see it, I felt betrayed. I felt beaten as a person. I had no honest place to stand.

That was the year before I met Ida. I'd been acting in stock companies and little theaters; sometimes fairly good parts. People were nice to me. They told me I had talent. They said it sadly, as though they were thinking, What a pity, he'll never get anywhere. I had got to the point where I resented praise and I resented pity and I wondered what people were thinking when they shook my hand. In New York I met some pretty fine people; easygoing, hard-drinking, flotsam and jetsam; and they liked me; and I wondered if I trusted them; if I was able any longer to trust anybody. Not on top, where all the world could see, but underneath where everybody lives.

Soon I would have to get up. I listened to Ludwig. He shook the little room like the footsteps of a giant marching miles away. On summer evenings (and maybe we would go this summer) Jules and Ida and I would go up to the Stadium and sit beneath the pillars on the cold stone steps. There it seemed to me the sky was far away; and I was not myself, I was high and lifted up. We never talked, the three of us. We sat and watched the blue smoke curl in the air and watched the orange tips of cigarettes. Every once in a while the boys who sold popcorn and soda pop and ice cream climbed the steep steps chattering; and Ida shifted slightly and touched her blue-black hair; and Jules scowled. I sat with my knee up, watching the lighted half-moon below, the black-coated, straining conductor, the faceless men beneath him moving together in a rhythm like the sea. There were pauses in the music for the rushing, calling, halting piano. Everything would stop except the climbing soloist; he would reach a height and everything would join him, the violins first and then the horns; and then the deep blue bass and the flute and the bitter trampling drums; beating, beating and mounting together and stopping with a clash like daybreak. When I first heard the *Messiah* I was alone; my blood bubbled like fire and wine; I cried; like an infant crying for its mother's milk; or a sinner running to meet Jesus.

Now below the music I heard footsteps on the stairs. I put out my cigarette. My heart was beating so hard I thought it would tear my chest apart. Someone knocked on the door.

I thought: Don't answer. Maybe she'll go away.

But the knocking came again, harder this time.

Just a minute, I said. I sat on the edge of the bed and put on my bathrobe. I was trembling like a fool. For Christ's sake, Peter, you've been through this before. What's the worst that can happen? You won't have a room. The world's full of rooms.

When I opened the door the landlady stood there, red-and-whitefaced and hysterical.

"Who are you? I didn't rent this room to you."

My mouth was dry. I started to say something.

"I can't have no colored people here," she said. "All my tenants are complainin'. Women afraid to come home nights."

"They ain't gotta be afraid of me," I said. I couldn't get my voice up; it rasped and rattled in my throat; and I began to be angry. I wanted to kill her. "My friend rented this room for me," I said.

"Well, I'm sorry, he didn't have no right to do that, I don't have nothin' against you, but you gotta get out."

Her glasses blinked, opaque in the light on the landing. She was frightened to death. She was afraid of me but she was more afraid of losing her tenants. Her face was mottled with rage and fear, her breath came rushed and little bits of spittle gathered at the edges of her mouth; her breath smelled bad, like rotting hamburger on a July day.

"You can't put me out," I said. "This room was rented in my name."

I started to close the door, as though the matter was finished: "I live here, see, this is my room, you can't put me out."

"You get outa my house!" she screamed. "I got the right to know who's in my house! This is a white neighborhood, I don't rent to colored people. Why don't you go on uptown, like you belong?"

"I can't stand niggers," I told her. I started to close the door again but she moved and stuck her foot in the way. I wanted to kill her, I watched her stupid, wrinkled frightened white face and I wanted to take a club, a hatchet, and bring it down with all my weight, splitting her skull down the middle where she parted her iron-gray hair.

"Get out of the door," I said. "I want to get dressed."

But I knew that she had won, that I was already on my way. We stared at each other. Neither of us moved. From her came an emanation of fear and fury and something else. You maggot-eaten bitch, I thought. I said evilly, "You wanna come in and watch me?" Her face didn't change, she didn't take her foot away. My skin prickled, tiny hot needles punctured my flesh. I was aware of my body under the bathrobe; and it was as though I had done something wrong, something monstrous, years ago, which no one had forgotten and for which I would be killed.

"If you don't get out," she said, "I'll get a policeman to put you out."

I grabbed the door to keep from touching her. "All right. All right. You can have the goddamn room. Now get out and let me dress."

She turned away. I slammed the door. I heard her going down the stairs. I threw stuff into my suitcase. I tried to take as long as possible but I cut myself while shaving because I was afraid she would come back upstairs with a policeman.

Jules was making coffee when I walked in.

"Good morning, good morning! What happened to you?"

"No room at the inn," I said. "Pour a cup of coffee for the notorious son of man." I sat down and dropped my suitcase on the floor.

Jules looked at me. "Oh. Well. Coffee coming up."

He got out the coffee cups. I lit a cigarette and sat there. I couldn't think of anything to say. I knew that Jules felt bad and I wanted to tell him that it wasn't his fault.

He pushed coffee in front of me and sugar and cream.

"Cheer up, baby. The world's wide and life—life, she is very long."

"Shut up. I don't want to hear any of your bad philosophy."

"Sorry."

"I mean, let's not talk about the good, the true, and the beautiful."

"All right. But don't sit there holding onto your table manners. Scream if you want to."

"Screaming won't do any good. Besides I'm a big boy now."

I stirred my coffee. "Did you give her a fight?" Jules asked.

I shook my head. "No."

"Why the hell not?"

I shrugged; a little ashamed now. "I couldn't have won it. What the hell."

"You might have won it. You might have given her a couple of bad moments."

"Goddamit to hell, I'm sick of it. Can't I get a place to sleep without dragging it through the courts? I'm goddam tired of battling every Tom, Dick, and Harry for what everybody else takes for granted. I'm tired, man, tired! Have you ever been sick to death of something? Well, I'm sick to death. And I'm scared. I've been fighting so goddamn long I'm not a person any more. I'm not Booker T. Washington. I've got no vision of emancipating anybody. I want to emancipate myself. If this goes on much longer, they'll send me to Bellevue, I'll blow my top, I'll break somebody's head. I'm not worried about that miserable little room. I'm worried about what's happening to me, *to me*, inside. I don't walk the streets, I crawl. I've never been like this before. Now when I go to a strange place I wonder what will happen, will I be accepted, if I'm accepted, can I accept?—"

"Take it easy," Jules said.

"Jules, I'm beaten."

"I don't think you are. Drink your coffee."

"Oh," I cried, "I know you think I'm making it dramatic, that I'm paranoiac and just inventing trouble! Maybe I think so sometimes, how can I tell? You get so used to being hit you find you're always waiting for it. Oh, I know, you're Jewish, you get kicked around, too, but you can walk into a bar and nobody *knows* you're Jewish and if you go looking for a job you'll get a better job than mine! How can I say what it feels like? I don't know. I know everybody's in trouble and nothing is easy, but how can I explain to you what it feels like to be black when I don't understand it and don't want to and spend all my time trying to forget it? I don't want to hate anybody—but now maybe, I can't love anybody either—are we friends? Can we be really friends?"

"We're friends," Jules said, "don't worry about it." He scowled. "If I wasn't Jewish I'd ask you why you don't live in Harlem." I looked at him. He raised his hand and smiled—"But I'm Jewish, so I didn't ask you. Ah Peter," he said, "I can't help you—take a walk, get drunk, we're all in this together."

I stood up. "I'll be around later. I'm sorry."

"Don't be sorry. I'll leave my door open. Bunk here for awhile."

"Thanks," I said.

I felt that I was drowning; that hatred had corrupted me like cancer in the bone.

I saw Ida for dinner. We met in a restaurant in the Village, an Italian place in a gloomy cellar with candles on the tables.

It was not a busy night, for which I was grateful. When I came in there were only two other couples on the other side of the room. No one looked at me. I sat down in a corner booth and ordered a Scotch old-fashioned. Ida was late and I had three of them before she came.

She was very fine in black, a high-necked dress with a pearl choker; and her hair was combed page-boy style, falling just below her ears.

"You look real sweet, baby."

"Thank you. It took fifteen extra minutes but I hoped it would be worth it."

"It was worth it. What're you drinking?"

"Oh—what're you drinking?"

"Old-fashioneds."

She sniffed and looked at me. "How many?"

I laughed. "Three."

"Well," she said, "I suppose you had to do something." The waiter came over. We decided on one Manhattan and one lasagna and one spaghetti with clam sauce and another old-fashioned for me.

"Did you have a constructive day, sweetheart? Find a job?"

"Not today," I said. I lit her cigarette. "Metro offered me a fortune to come to the coast and do the lead in *Native Son*[1] but I turned it down. Type casting, you know. It's so difficult to find a decent part."

"Well, if they don't come up with a decent offer soon tell them you'll go back to Selznick. *He'll* find you a part with guts—the very *idea* of offering you *Native Son!* I wouldn't stand for it."

"You ain't gotta tell me. I told them if they didn't find me a decent script in two weeks I was through, that's all."

"Now that's talking, Peter my lad."

The drinks came and we sat in silence for a minute or two. I finished half of my drink at a swallow and played with the toothpicks on the table. I felt Ida watching me.

"Peter, you're going to be awfully drunk."

"Honeychile, the first thing a southern gentleman learns is how to hold his liquor."

"That myth is older than the rock of ages. And anyway you come from Jersey."

I finished my drink and snarled at her: "That's just as good as the South."

Across the table from me I could see that she was readying herself for trouble: her mouth tightened slightly, setting her chin so that the faint cleft showed: "What happened to you today?"

I resented her concern; I resented my need. "Nothing worth talking about," I muttered, "just a mood."

And I tried to smile at her, to wipe away the bitterness.

"Now I know something's the matter. Please tell me."

It sounded trivial as hell: "You know the room Jules found for me? Well, the landlady kicked me out of it today."

---

[1] a powerful naturalistic novel by the Afro-American writer, Richard Wright

"God save the American republic," Ida said. "D'you want to waste some of my husband's money? We can sue her."

"Forget it. I'll end up with lawsuits in every state in the union."

"Still, as a gesture—"

"The devil with the gesture. I'll get by."

The food came. I didn't want to eat. The first mouthful hit my belly like a gong. Ida began cutting up lasagna.

"Peter," she said, "try not to feel so badly. We're all in this together the whole world. Don't let it throw you. What can't be helped you have to learn to live with."

"That's easy for you to say," I told her.

She looked at me quickly and looked away. "I'm not pretending that it's easy to do," she said.

I didn't believe that she could really understand it; and there was nothing I could say. I sat like a child being scolded, looking down at my plate, not eating, not saying anything. I wanted her to stop talking, to stop being intelligent about it, to stop being calm and grown-up about it; good Lord, none of us has ever grown up, we never will.

"It's no better anywhere else," she was saying. "In all of Europe there's famine and disease, in France and England they hate the Jews— nothing's going to change, baby, people are too empty-headed, too empty-hearted—it's always been like that, people always try to destroy what they don't understand—and they hate almost everything because they understand so little—"

I began to sweat in my side of the booth. I wanted to stop her voice. I wanted her to eat and be quiet and leave me alone. I looked around for the waiter so I could order another drink. But he was on the far side of the restaurant, waiting on some people who had just come in; a lot of people had come in since we had been sitting there.

"Peter," Ida said, "Peter please don't look like that."

I grinned: the painted grin of the professional clown. "Don't worry, baby, I'm all right. I know what I'm going to do. I'm gonna go back to my people where I belong and find me a nice, black nigger wench and raise me a flock of babies."

Ida had an old maternal trick; the grin tricked her into using it now. She raised her fork and rapped me with it across the knuckles. "Now, stop that. You're too old for that."

I screamed and stood up screaming and knocked the candle over: "Don't *do* that, you bitch, don't *ever* do that!"

She grabbed the candle and set it up and glared at me. Her face had turned perfectly white: "Sit down! Sit *down!*"

I fell back into my seat. My stomach felt like water. Everyone was looking at us. I turned cold, seeing what they were seeing: a black boy and a white woman, alone together. I knew it would take nothing to have them at my throat.

"I'm sorry," I muttered, "I'm sorry, I'm sorry."

The waiter was at my elbow. "Is everything all right, miss?"

"Yes, quite, thank you." She sounded like a princess dismissing a slave. I didn't look up. The shadow of the waiter moved away from me.

"Baby," Ida said, "forgive me, please forgive me."

I stared at the tablecloth. She put her hand on mine, brightness and blackness.

"Let's go," I said, "I'm terribly sorry."

She motioned for the check. When it came she handed the waiter a ten dollar bill without looking. She picked up her bag.

"Shall we go to a nightclub or a movie or something?"

"No, honey, not tonight." I looked at her. "I'm tired, I think I'll go on over to Jules's place. I'm gonna sleep on his floor for a while. Don't worry about me. I'm all right."

She looked at me steadily. She said: "I'll come see you tomorrow?"

"Yes, baby, please."

The waiter brought the change and she tipped him. We stood up; as we passed the tables (not looking at the people) the ground under me seemed falling, the doorway seemed impossibly far away. All my muscles tensed; I seemed ready to spring; I was waiting for the blow.

I put my hands in my pockets and we walked to the end of the block. The lights were green and red, the lights from the theater across the street exploded blue and yellow, off and on.

"Peter?"

"Yes?"

"I'll see you tomorrow?"

"Yeah. Come by Jules's. I'll wait for you."

"Goodnight, darling."

"Goodnight."

I started to walk away. I felt her eyes on my back. I kicked a bottle-top on the sidewalk.

God save the American republic.

I dropped into the subway and got on an uptown train, not knowing where it was going and not caring. Anonymous, islanded people surrounded me, behind newspapers, behind make-up, fat, fleshy masks and flat eyes. I watched the empty faces. (No one looked at me.) I looked at the ads, unreal women and pink-cheeked men selling cigarettes, candy, shaving cream, nightgowns, chewing gum, movies, sex; sex without organs, drier than sand and more secret than death. The train stopped. A white boy and a white girl got on. She was nice, short, svelte. Nice legs. She was hanging on his arm. He was the football type, blond, ruddy. They were dressed in summer clothes. The wind from the doors blew her print dress. She squealed, holding the dress at the knees and giggled and looked at him. He said something I didn't catch and she looked at me and the smile died. She stood so that she faced him and had her back to me. I looked back at the ads. Then I hated them. I wanted to do something to make them hurt, something that would crack the pink-cheeked mask. The white boy and I did not look at each other again. They got off at the next stop.

I wanted to keep on drinking. I got off in Harlem and went to a run-down bar on Seventh Avenue. My people, my people. Sharpies stood on the corner, waiting. Women in summer dresses pranced by on wavering heels. Click clack. Click clack. There were white mounted policemen in the streets. On every block there was another policeman on foot. I saw a black cop.

God save the American republic.

The juke box was letting loose with "Hamps' Boogie." The place was jumping, I walked over to the man.

"Rye," I said.

I was standing next to somebody's grandmother. "Hello, papa. What you puttin' down?"

"Baby, you can't pick it up," I told her. My rye came and I drank.

"Nigger," she said, "you must think you's somebody."

I didn't answer. She turned away, back to her beer, keeping time to the juke box, her face sullen and heavy and aggrieved. I watched her out of the side of my eye. She had been good looking once, pretty even, before she hit the bottle and started crawling into too many beds. She was flabby now, flesh heaved all over in her thin dress. I wondered what she'd be like in bed; then I realized that I was a little excited by her; I laughed and set my glass down.

"The same," I said. "And a beer chaser."

The juke box was playing something else now, something brassy and commercial which I didn't like. I kept on drinking, listening to the voices of my people, watching the faces of my people. (God pity us, the terrified republic.) Now I was sorry to have angered the woman who still sat next to me, now deep in conversation with another, younger woman. I longed for some opening, some sign, something to make me a part of the life around me. But there was nothing except my color. A white outsider coming in would have seen a young Negro drinking in a Negro bar, perfectly in his element, in his place, as the saying goes. But the people here knew differently, as I did. I didn't seem to have a place.

So I kept on drinking by myself, saying to myself after each drink, Now I'll go. But I was afraid; I didn't want to sleep on Jules's floor; I didn't want to go to sleep. I kept on drinking and listening to the juke box. They were playing Ella Fitzgerald, "Cow-Cow Boogie."

"Let me buy you a drink," I said to the woman.

She looked at me, startled, suspicious, ready to blow her top.

"On the level," I said. I tried to smile. "Both of you."

"I'll take a beer," the young one said.

I was shaking like a baby. I finished my drink.

"Fine," I said. I turned to the bar.

"Baby," said the old one, "what's your story?"

The man put three beers on the counter.
"I got no story, Ma," I said.

Flannery O'Connor
1925–1964
GOOD COUNTRY PEOPLE

BESIDES the neutral expression that she wore when she was alone,
Mrs. Freeman had two others, forward and reverse, that she used
for all her human dealings. Her forward expression was steady and driving like the advance of a heavy truck. Her eyes never swerved to left or
right but turned as the story turned as if they followed a yellow line
down the center of it. She seldom used the other expression because it
was not often necessary for her to retract a statement, but when she did,
her face came to a complete stop, there was an almost imperceptible
movement of her black eyes, during which they seemed to be receding,
and then the observer would see that Mrs. Freeman, though she might
stand there as real as several grain sacks thrown on top of each other, was
no longer there in spirit. As for getting anything across to her when this
was the case, Mrs. Hopewell had given it up. She might talk her head off.
Mrs. Freeman could never be brought to admit herself wrong on any
point. She would stand there and if she could be brought to say anything,
it was something like, "Well, I wouldn't of said it was and I wouldn't of
said it wasn't" or letting her gaze range over the top kitchen shelf where
there was an assortment of dusty bottles, she might remark, "I see you
ain't ate many of them figs you put up last summer."

They carried on their most important business in the kitchen at breakfast. Every morning Mrs. Hopewell got up at seven o'clock and lit her
gas heater and Joy's. Joy was her daughter, a large blonde girl who had an
artificial leg. Mrs. Hopewell thought of her as a child though she was
thirty-two years old and highly educated. Joy would get up while her
mother was eating and lumber into the bathroom and slam the door, and
before long, Mrs. Freeman would arrive at the back door. Joy would
hear her mother call, "Come on in," and then they would talk for a while
in low voices that were indistinguishable in the bathroom. By the time
Joy came in, they had usually finished the weather report and were on
one or the other of Mrs. Freeman's daughters, Glynese or Carramae.
Joy called them Glycerin and Caramel. Glynese, a redhead, was eighteen
and had many admirers; Carramae, a blonde, was only fifteen but already
married and pregnant. She could not keep anything on her stomach. Every
morning Mrs. Freeman told Mrs. Hopewell how many times she had
vomited since the last report.

Mrs. Hopewell liked to tell people that Glynese and Carramae were two of the finest girls she knew and that Mrs. Freeman was a *lady* and that she was never ashamed to take her anywhere or introduce her to anybody they might meet. Then she would tell how she had happened to hire the Freemans in the first place and how they were a godsend to her and how she had had them four years. The reason for her keeping them so long was that they were not trash. They were good country people. She had telephoned the man whose name they had given as reference and he had told her that Mr. Freeman was a good farmer but that his wife was the nosiest woman ever to walk the earth. "She's got to be into everything," the man said. "If she don't get there before the dust settles, you can bet she's dead, that's all. She'll want to know all your business. I can stand him real good," he had said, "but me nor my wife neither could have stood that woman one more minute on this place." That had put Mrs. Hopewell off for a few days.

She had hired them in the end because there were no other applicants but she had made up her mind beforehand exactly how she would handle the woman. Since she was the type who had to be into everything, then, Mrs. Hopewell had decided, she would not only let her be into everything, she would *see to it* that she was into everything—she would give her the responsibility of everything, she would put her in charge. Mrs. Hopewell had no bad qualities of her own but she was able to use other people's in such a constructive way that she had kept them four years.

Nothing is perfect. This was one of Mrs. Hopewell's favorite sayings. Another was: that is life! And still another, the most important, was: well, other people have their opinions too. She would make these statements, usually at the table, in a tone of gentle insistence as if no one held them but her, and the large hulking Joy, whose constant outrage had obliterated every expression from her face, would stare just a little to the side of her, her eyes icy blue, with the look of someone who has achieved blindness by an act of will and means to keep it.

When Mrs. Hopewell said to Mrs. Freeman that life was like that, Mrs. Freeman would say, "I always said so myself." Nothing had been arrived at by anyone that had not first been arrived at by her. She was quicker than Mr. Freeman. When Mrs. Hopewell said to her after they had been on the place a while, "You know, you're the wheel behind the wheel," and winked, Mrs. Freeman had said, "I know it. I've always been quick. It's some that are quicker than others."

"Everybody is different," Mrs. Hopewell said.

"Yes, most people is," Mrs. Freeman said.

"It takes all kinds to make the world."

"I always said it did myself."

The girl was used to this kind of dialogue for breakfast and more of it for dinner; sometimes they had it for supper too. When they had no guest they ate in the kitchen because that was easier. Mrs. Freeman always managed to arrive at some point during the meal and to watch them finish it. She would stand in the doorway if it were summer but in the winter she would stand with one elbow on top of the refrigerator and look down on them, or she would stand by the gas heater, lifting the back of her skirt slightly. Occasionally she would stand against the wall and roll her head from side to side. At no time was she in any hurry to leave. All this was very trying on Mrs. Hopewell but she was a woman of great patience. She realized that nothing is perfect and that in the Freemans she had good country people and that if, in this day and age, you get good country people, you had better hang onto them.

She had had plenty of experience with trash. Before the Freemans she had averaged one tenant family a year. The wives of these farmers were not the kind you would want to be around you for very long. Mrs. Hopewell, who had divorced her husband long ago, needed someone to walk over the fields with her; and when Joy had to be impressed for these services, her remarks were usually so ugly and her face so glum that Mrs. Hopewell would say, "If you can't come pleasantly, I don't want you at all," to which the girl, standing square and rigid-shouldered with her neck thrust slightly forward, would reply, "If you want me, here I am—LIKE I AM."

Mrs. Hopewell excused this attitude because of the leg (which had been shot off in a hunting accident when Joy was ten). It was hard for Mrs. Hopewell to realize that her child was thirty-two now and that for more than twenty years she had had only one leg. She thought of her still as a child because it tore her heart to think instead of the poor stout girl in her thirites who had never danced a step or had any *normal* good times. Her name was really Joy but as soon as she was twenty-one and away from home, she had had it legally changed. Mrs. Hopewell was certain that she had thought and thought until she had hit upon the ugliest name in any language. Then she had gone and had the beautiful name, Joy, changed without telling her mother until after she had done it. Her legal name was Hulga.

When Mrs. Hopewell thought the name, Hulga, she thought of the broad blank hull of a battleship. She would not use it. She continued to call her Joy to which the girl responded but in a purely mechanical way.

Hulga had learned to tolerate Mrs. Freeman who saved her from taking walks with her mother. Even Glynese and Carramae were useful when they occupied attention that might otherwise have been directed at her. At first she had thought she could not stand Mrs. Freeman for she had found that it was not possible to be rude to her. Mrs. Freeman would take on strange resentments and for days together she would be sullen but the source of her displeasure was always obscure; a direct attack, a positive leer, blatant ugliness to her face—these never touched her. And without warning one day, she began calling her Hulga.

She did not call her that in front of Mrs. Hopewell who would have been incensed but when she and the girl happened to be out of the house together, she would say something and add the name Hulga to the end of it, and the big spectacled Joy-Hulga would scowl and redden as if her privacy had been intruded upon. She considered the name her personal affair. She had arrived at it first purely on the basis of its ugly sound and then the full genius of its fitness had struck her. She had a vision of the name working like the ugly sweating Vulcan who stayed in the furnace and to whom, presumably, the goddess had to come when called. She saw it as the name of her highest creative act. One of her major triumphs was that her mother had not been able to turn her dust into Joy, but the greater one was that she had been able to turn it herself into Hulga. However, Mrs. Freeman's relish for using the name only irritated her. It was as if Mrs. Freeman's beady steel-pointed eyes had penetrated far enough behind her face to reach some secret fact. Something about her seemed to fascinate Mrs. Freeman and then one day Hulga realized that it was the artificial leg. Mrs. Freeman had a special fondness for the details of secret infections, hidden deformities, assaults upon children. Of diseases, she preferred the lingering or incurable. Hulga had heard Mrs. Hopewell give her the details of the hunting accident, how the leg had been literally blasted off, how she had never lost consciousness. Mrs. Freeman could listen to it any time as if it had happened an hour ago.

When Hulga stumped into the kitchen in the morning (she could walk without making the awful noise but she made it—Mrs. Hopewell was certain—because it was ugly-sounding), she glanced at them and did not speak. Mrs. Hopewell would be in her red kimono with her hair tied around her head in rags. She would be sitting at the table, finishing her breakfast and Mrs. Freeman would be hanging by her elbow outward from the refrigerator, looking down at the table. Hulga always put her eggs on the stove to boil and then stood over them with her arms folded, and Mrs. Hopewell would look at her—a kind of indirect gaze divided between her and Mrs. Freeman—and would think that if she would only keep herself up a little, she wouldn't be so bad looking. There was nothing wrong with her face that a pleasant expression wouldn't help. Mrs. Hopewell said that people who looked on the bright side of things would be beautiful even if they were not.

Whenever she looked at Joy this way, she could not help but feel that it would have been better if the child had not taken the Ph.D. It had certainly not brought her out any and now that she had it, there was no more excuse for her to go to school again. Mrs. Hopewell thought it was nice for girls to go to school to have a good time but Joy had "gone through." Anyhow, she would not have been strong enough to go again. The doctors had told Mrs. Hopewell that with the best of care, Joy might see forty-five. She had a weak heart. Joy had made it plain that if it had not been for this condition, she would be far from these red hills and good country people. She would be in a university lecturing to people who knew what she was talking about. And Mrs. Hopewell could very well picture her there, looking like a scarecrow and lecturing to more of the same. Here she went about all day in a six-year-old skirt and a yellow sweat shirt with a faded cowboy on a horse embossed on it. She thought this was funny; Mrs. Hopewell thought it was idiotic and showed simply that she was still a child. She was brilliant but she didn't have a grain of sense. It seemed to Mrs. Hopewell that every year she grew less like other people and more like herself—bloated, rude, and squint-eyed. And she said such strange things! To her own mother she had said—without warning, without excuse, standing up in the middle of a meal with her her face purple and her mouth half full—"Woman! do you ever look inside? Do you ever look inside and see what you are *not?* God!" she had cried sinking down again and staring at her plate, "Malebranche[1] was right: we are not our own light. We are not our own light!" Mrs. Hopewell had no idea to this day what brought that on. She had only made the remark, hoping Joy would take it in, that a smile never hurt anyone.

The girl had taken the Ph.D. in philosophy and this left Mrs. Hopewell at a complete loss. You could say, "My daughter is a nurse," or "My daughter is a school teacher," or even, "My daughter is a chemical engineer." You could not say, "My daughter is a philosopher." That was something that had ended with the Greeks and Romans. All day Joy sat on her neck in a deep chair, reading. Sometimes she went for walks but she didn't like dogs or cats or birds or flowers or nature or nice young men. She looked at nice young men as if she could smell their stupidity.

One day Mrs. Hopewell had picked up one of the books the girl had just put down and opening it at random, she read, "Science, on the other hand, has to assert its soberness and seriousness afresh and declare that it is concerned solely with what-is. Nothing—how can it be for science anything but a horror and a phantasm? If science is right, then one thing stands firm: science wishes to know nothing of nothing. Such is after all the strictly scientific approach to Nothing. We know it by wishing to know nothing of Nothing." These words had been underlined with a blue pencil and they worked on Mrs. Hopewell like some evil incantation in gibberish. She shut the book quickly and went out of the room as if she were having a chill.

This morning when the girl came in, Mrs. Freeman was on Carramae. "She thrown up four times after supper," she said, "and was up twict in the night after three o'clock. Yesterday she didn't do nothing but ramble in the bureau drawer. All she did. Stand up there and see what she could run up on."

"She's got to eat," Mrs. Hopewell muttered, sipping her coffee, while she watched Joy's back at the stove. She was wondering what the child had said to the Bible salesman. She could not imagine what kind of a conversation she could possibly have had with him.

He was a tall gaunt hatless youth who had called yesterday to sell them a Bible. He had appeared at the door, carrying a large black suitcase that weighted him so heavily on one side that he had to brace himself

[1] Nicolas Malebranche, 1638-1715, French philosopher

against the door facing. He seemed on the point of collapse but he said in a cheerful voice, "Good morning, Mrs. Cedars!" and set the suitcase down on the mat. He was not a bad-looking young man though he had on a bright blue suit and yellow socks that were not pulled up far enough. He had prominent face bones and a streak of sticky-looking brown hair falling across his forehead.

"I'm Mrs. Hopewell," she said.

"Oh!" he said, pretending to look puzzled but with his eyes sparkling, "I saw it said "The Cedars," on the mailbox so I thought you was Mrs. Cedars!" and he burst out in a pleasant laugh. He picked up the satchel and under cover of a pant, he fell forward into her hall. It was rather as if the suitcase had moved first, jerking him after it. "Mrs. Hopewell!" he said and grabbed her hand. "I hope you are well!" and he laughed again and then all at once his face sobered completely. He paused and gave her a straight earnest look and said, "Lady, I've come to speak of serious things."

"Well, come in," she muttered, none too pleased because her dinner was almost ready. He came into the parlor and sat down on the edge of a straight chair and put the suitcase between his feet and glanced around the room as if he were sizing her up by it. Her silver gleamed on the two sideboards; she decided he had never been in a room as elegant as this.

"Mrs. Hopewell," he began, using her name in a way that sounded almost intimate, "I know you believe in Chrustian service."

"Well yes," she murmured.

"I know," he said and paused, looking very wise with his head cocked on one side, "that you're a good woman. Friends have told me."

Mrs. Hopewell never liked to be taken for a fool. "What are you selling?" she asked.

"Bibles," the young man said and his eye raced around the room before he added, "I see you have no family Bible in your parlor, I see that is the one lack you got!"

Mrs. Hopewell could not say, "My daughter is an atheist and won't let me keep the Bible in the parlor." She said, stiffening slightly, "I keep my Bible by my bedside." This was not the truth. It was in the attic somewhere.

"Lady," he said, "the word of God ought to be in the parlor."

"Well, I think that's a matter of taste," she began. "I think . . ."

"Lady," he said, "for a Chrustian, the word of God ought to be in every room in the house besides in his heart. I know you're a Chrustian because I can see it in every line of your face."

She stood up and said, "Well, young man, I don't want to buy a Bible and I smell my dinner burning."

He didn't get up. He began to twist his hands and looking down at them, he said softly, "Well lady, I'll tell you the truth—not many people want to buy one nowadays and besides, I know I'm real simple. I don't know how to say a thing but to say it. I'm just a country boy." He glanced up into her unfriendly face. "People like you don't like to fool with country people like me!"

"Why!" she cried, "good country people are the salt of the earth! Besides, we all have different ways of doing, it takes all kinds to make the world go 'round. That's life!"

"You said a mouthful," he said.

"Why, I think there aren't enough good country people in the world!" she said, stirred. "I think that's what's wrong with it!"

His face had brightened. "I didn't inraduce myself," he said. "I'm Manley Pointer from out in the country around Willohobie, not even from a place, just from near a place."

"You wait a minute," she said. "I have to see about my dinner." She went out to the kitchen and found Joy standing near the door where she had been listening.

"Get rid of the salt of the earth," she said, "and let's eat."

Mrs. Hopewell gave her a pained look and turned the heat down under the vegetables. "*I* can't be rude to anybody," she murmured and went back into the parlor.

He had opened the suitcase and was sitting with a Bible on each knee.

"You might as well put those up," she told him. "I don't want one."

"I appreciate your honesty," he said. "You don't see any more real honest people unless you go way out in the country."

"I know," she said, "real genuine folks!" Through the crack in the door she heard a groan.

"I guess a lot of boys come telling you they're working their way through college," he said, "but I'm not going to tell you that. Somehow," he said, "I don't want to go to college. I want to devote my life to Chrustian service. See," he said, lowering his voice, "I got this heart condition. I may not live long. When you know it's something wrong with you and you may not live long, well then, lady . . ." He paused, with his mouth open, and stared at her.

He and Joy had the same condition! She knew that her eyes were filling with tears but she collected herself quickly and murmured, "Won't you stay for dinner? We'd love to have you!" and was sorry the instant she heard herself say it.

"Yes mam," he said in an abashed voice, "I would sher love to do that!"

Joy had given him one look on being introduced to him and then throughout the meal had not glanced at him again. He had addressed several remarks to her, which she had pretended not to hear. Mrs. Hopewell could not understand deliberate rudeness, although she lived with it, and she felt she had always to overflow with hospitality to make up for Joy's lack of courtesy. She urged him to talk about himself and he did. He said he was the seventh child of twelve and that his father had been crushed under a tree when he himself was eight year old. He had been crushed very badly, in fact, almost cut in two and was practically not recognizable. His mother had got along the best she could by hard work-ing and she had always seen that her children went to Sunday School and that they read the Bible every evening. He was now nineteen years old and he had been selling Bibles for four months. In that time he had sold seventy-seven Bibles and had the promise of two more sales. He wanted to become a missionary because he thought that was the way you could do most for people. "He who losest his life shall find it," he said simply and he was so sincere, so genuine and earnest that Mrs. Hopewell would not for the world have smiled. He prevented his peas from sliding onto the table by blocking them with a piece of bread which he later cleaned his plate with. She could see Joy observing sidewise how he handled his knife and fork and she saw too that every few minutes, the boy would dart a keen appraising glance at the girl as if he were trying to attract her attention.

After dinner Joy cleared the dishes off the table and disappeared and Mrs. Hopewell was left to talk with him. He told her again about his childhood and his father's accident and about various things that had hap-pened to him. Every five minutes or so she would stifle a yawn. He sat for two hours until finally she told him she must go because she had an appointment in town. He packed his Bibles and thanked her and pre-pared to leave, but in the doorway he stopped and wrung her hand and said that not on any of his trips had he met a lady as nice as her and he asked if he could come again. She had said she would always be happy to see him.

Joy had been standing in the road, apparently looking at something in the distance, when he came down the steps toward her, bent to the side with his heavy valise. He stopped where she was standing and con-fronted her directly. Mrs. Hopewell could not hear what he said but she trembled to think what Joy would say to him. She could see that after a minute Joy said something and that then the boy began to speak again, making an excited gesture with his free hand. After a minute Joy said something else at which the boy began to speak once more. Then to her amazement, Mrs. Hopewell saw the two of them walk off together, to-ward the gate. Joy had walked all the way to the gate with him and Mrs. Hopewell could not imagine what they had said to each other, and she had not yet dared to ask.

Mrs. Freeman was insisting upon her attention. She had moved from the refrigerator to the heater so that Mrs. Hopewell had to turn and face her in order to seem to be listening. "Glynese gone out with Harvey Hill again last night," she said. "She had this sty."

"Hill," Mrs. Hopewell said absently, "is that the one who works in the garage?"

"Nome, he's the one that goes to chiropracter school," Mrs. Freeman said. "She had this sty. Been had it two days. So she says when he brought her in the other night he says, 'Lemme get rid of that sty for you,' and she says, 'How?' and he says, 'You just lay yourself down acrost the seat of that car and I'll show you.' So she done it and he popped her neck. Kept on a-popping it several times until she made him quit. This morning," Mrs. Freeman said, "she ain't got no sty. She ain't got no traces of a sty."

"I never heard of that before," Mrs. Hopewell said.

"He ast her to marry him before the Ordinary."[2] Mrs. Freeman went on, "and she told him she wasn't going to be married in no *office*."

"Well, Glynese is a fine girl," Mrs. Hopewell said. "Glynese and Carramae are both fine girls."

"Carramae said when her and Lyman was married Lyman said it sure felt sacred to him. She said he said he wouldn't take five hundred dollars for being married by a preacher."

"How much would he take?" the girl asked from the stove.

"He said he wouldn't take five hundred dollars," Mrs. Freeman repeated.

"Well we all have work to do," Mrs. Hopewell said.

"Lyman said it just felt more sacred to him," Mrs. Freeman said. "The doctor wants Carramae to eat prunes. Says instead of medicine. Says them cramps is coming from pressure. You know where I think it is?"

"She'll be better in a few weeks," Mrs. Hopewell said.

"In the tube," Mrs. Freeman said. "Else she wouldn't be as sick as she is."

Hulga had cracked her two eggs into a saucer and was bringing them to the table along with a cup of coffee that she had filled too full. She sat down carefully and began to eat, meaning to keep Mrs. Freeman there by questions if for any reason she showed an inclination to leave. She could perceive her mother's eye on her. The first round-about question would be about the Bible salesman and she did not wish to bring it on. "How did he pop her neck?" she asked.

Mrs. Freeman went into a description of how he had popped her neck. She said he owned a '55 Mercury but that Glynese said she would rather marry a man with only a '36 Plymouth who would be married by a preacher. The girl asked what if he had a '32 Plymouth and Mrs. Freeman said what Glynese had said was a '36 Plymouth.

Mrs. Hopewell said there were not many girls with Glynese's common sense. She said what she admired in those girls was their common sense. She said that reminded her that they had had a nice visitor yesterday, a young man selling Bibles. "Lord," she said, "he bored me to death but he was so sincere and genuine I couldn't be rude to him. He was just good country people, you know," she said, "—just the salt of the earth."

"I seen him walk up," Mrs. Freeman said, "and then later—I seen him walk off," and Hulga could feel the slight shift in her voice, the slight insinuation, that he had not walked off alone, had he? Her face

---

[2] judge of probate

remained expressionless but the color rose into her neck and she seemed to swallow it down with the next spoonful of egg. Mrs. Freeman was looking at her as if they had a secret together.

"Well, it takes all kinds of people to make the world go 'round," Mrs. Hopewell said, "It's very good we aren't all alike."

"Some people are more alike than others," Mrs. Freeman said.

Hulga got up and stumped, with about twice the noise that was necessary, into her room and locked the door. She was to meet the Bible salesman at ten o'clock at the gate. She had thought about it half the night. She had started thinking of it as a great joke and then she had begun to see profound implications in it. She had lain in bed imagining dialogues for them that were insane on the surface but that reached below to depths that no Bible salesman would be aware of. Their conversation yesterday had been of this kind.

He had stopped in front of her and had simply stood there. His face was bony and sweaty and bright, with a little pointed nose in the center of it, and his look was different from what it had been at the dinner table. He was gazing at her with open curiosity, with fascination, like a child watching a new fantastic animal at the zoo, and he was breathing as if he had run a great distance to reach her. His gaze seemed somehow familiar but she could not think where she had been regarded with it before. For almost a minute he didn't say anything. Then on what seemed an insuck of breath, he whispered, "You ever ate a chicken that was two days old?"

The girl looked at him stonily. He might have just put this question up for consideration at the meeting of a philosophical association. "Yes," she presently replied as if she had considered it from all angles.

"It must have been mighty small!" he said triumphantly and shook all over with little nervous giggles, getting very red in the face, and subsiding finally into his gaze of complete admiration, while the girl's expression remained exactly the same.

"How old are you?" he asked softly.

She waited some time before she answered. Then in a flat voice she said, "Seventeen."

His smiles came in succession like waves breaking on the surface of a little lake. "I see you got a wooden leg," he said. "I think you're real brave. I think you're real sweet."

The girl stood blank and solid and silent.

"Walk to the gate with me," he said. "You're a brave sweet little thing and I liked you the minute I seen you walk in the door."

Hulga began to move forward.

"What's your name?" he asked, smiling down on the top of her head.

"Hulga," she said.

"Hulga," he murmured, "Hulga. Hulga. I never heard of anybody name Hulga before. You're shy, aren't you, Hulga?" he asked.

She nodded, watching his large red hand on the handle of the giant valise.

"I like girls that wear glasses," he said. "I think a lot. I'm not like these people that a serious thought don't ever enter their heads. It's because I may die."

"I may die too," she said suddenly and looked up at him. His eyes were very small and brown, glittering feverishly.

"Listen," he said, "don't you think some people was meant to meet on account of what all they got in common and all? Like they both think serious thoughts and all?" He shifted the valise to his other hand so that the hand nearest her was free. He caught hold of her elbow and shook it a little. "I don't work on Saturday," he said. "I like to walk in the woods and see what Mother Nature is wearing. O'er the hills and far away. Picnics and things. Couldn't we go on a picnic tomorrow? Say yes, Hulga," he said and gave her a dying look as if he felt his insides about to drop out of him. He had even seemed to sway slightly toward her.

During the night she had imagined that she seduced him. She imagined that the two of them walked on the place until they came to the storage barn beyond the two back fields and there, she imagined, that things came to such a pass that she very easily seduced him and that then, of course, she had to reckon with his remorse. True genius can get an idea across even to an inferior mind. She imagined that she took his remorse in hand and changed it into a deeper understanding of life. She took all his shame away and turned it into something useful.

She set off for the gate at exactly ten o'clock, escaping without drawing Mrs. Hopewell's attention. She didn't take anything to eat, forgetting that food is usually taken on a picnic. She wore a pair of slacks and a dirty white shirt, and as an afterthought, she had put some Vapex on the collar of it since she did not own any perfume. When she reached the gate no one was there.

She looked up and down the empty highway and had the furious feeling that she had been tricked, that he had only meant to make her walk to the gate after the idea of him. Then suddenly he stood up, very tall, from behind a bush on the opposite embankment. Smiling, he lifted his hat which was new and wide-brimmed. He had not worn it yesterday and she wondered if he had bought it for the occasion. It was toast-colored with a red and white band around it and was slightly too large for him. He stepped from behind the bush still carrying the black valise. He had on the same suit and the same yellow socks sucked down in his shoes from walking. He crossed the highway and said, "I knew you'd come!"

The girl wondered acidly how he had known this. She pointed to the valise and asked, "Why did you bring your Bibles?"

He took her elbow, smiling down on her as if he could not stop. "You can never tell when you'll need the word of God, Hulga," he said. She had a moment in which she doubted that this was actually happening and then they began to climb the embankment. They went down into the pasture toward the woods. The boy walked lightly by her side, bouncing on his toes. The valise did not seem to be heavy today; he even swung it. They crossed half the pasture without saying anything and then, putting his hand easily on the small of her back, he asked softly, "Where does your wooden leg join on?"

She turned an ugly red and glared at him and for an instant the boy looked abashed. "I didn't mean you no harm," he said. "I only meant you're so brave and all. I guess God takes care of you."

"No," she said, looking forward and walking fast, "I don't even believe in God."

At this he stopped and whistled. "No!" he exclaimed as if he were too astonished to say anything else.

She walked on and in a second he was bouncing at her side, fanning with his hat. "That's very unusual for a girl," he remarked, watching her out of the corner of his eye. When they reached the edge of the wood, he put his hand on her back again and drew her against him without a word and kissed her heavily.

The kiss, which had more pressure than feeling behind it, produced that extra surge of adrenalin in the girl that enables one to carry a packed trunk out of a burning house, but in her, the power went at once to the brain. Even before he released her, her mind, clear and detached and ironic anyway, was regarding him from a great distance, with amusement but with pity. She had never been kissed before and she was pleased to discover that it was an unexceptional experience and all a matter of the mind's control. Some people might enjoy drain water if they were told it was vodka. When the boy, looking expectant but uncertain, pushed her gently away, she turned and walked on, saying nothing as if such business, for her, were common enough.

He came along panting at her side, trying to help her when he saw a root that she might trip over. He caught and held back the long swaying blades of thorn vine until she had passed beyond them. She led the way and he came breathing heavily behind her. Then they came out on a sun-lit hillside, sloping softly into another one a little smaller. Beyond, they could see the rusted top of the old barn where the extra hay was stored.

The hill was sprinkled with small pink weeds. "Then you ain't saved?" he asked suddenly, stopping.

The girl smiled. It was the first time she had smiled at him at all. "In my economy," she said, "I'm saved and you are damned but I told you I didn't believe in God."

Nothing seemed to destroy the boy's look of admiration. He gazed at her now as if the fantastic animal at the zoo had put its paw through the bars and given him a loving poke. She thought he looked as if he wanted to kiss her again and she walked on before he had the chance.

"Ain't there somewheres we can sit down sometime?" he murmured, his voice softening toward the end of the sentence.

"In that barn," she said.

They made for it rapidly as if it might slide away like a train. It was a large two-story barn, cool and dark inside. The boy pointed up the ladder that led into the loft and said, "It's too bad we can't go up there."

"Why can't we?" she asked.

"Yer leg," he said reverently.

The girl gave him a contemptuous look and putting both hands on the ladder. she climbed it while he stood below, apparently awestruck. She pulled herself expertly through the opening and then looked down at him and said. "Well, come on if you're coming," and he began to climb the ladder, awkwardly bringing the suitcase with him.

"We won't need the Bible," she observed.

"You never can tell," he said, panting. After he had got into the loft, he was a few seconds catching his breath. She had sat down in a pile of straw. A wide sheath of sunlight, filled with dust particles, slanted over her. She lay back against a bale, her face turned away, looking out the front opening of the barn where hay was thrown from a wagon into the loft. The two pink-speckled hillsides lay back against a dark ridge of woods. The sky was cloudless and cold blue. The boy dropped down by her side and put one arm under her and the other over her and began methodically kissing her face, making little noises like a fish. He did not remove his hat but it was pushed far enough back not to interfere. When her glasses got in his way, he took them off of her and slipped them into his pocket.

The girl at first did not return any of the kisses but presently she began to and after she had put several on his cheek, she reached his lips and remained there, kissing him again and again as if she were trying to draw all the breath out of him. His breath was clear and sweet like a child's and the kisses were sticky like a child's. He mumbled about loving her and about knowing when he first seen her that he loved her, but the mumbling was like the sleepy fretting of a child being put to sleep by his mother. Her mind, throughout this, never stopped or lost itself for a second to her feelings. "You ain't said you loved me none," he whispered finally, pulling back from her. "You got to say that."

She looked away from him off into the hollow sky and then down at a black ridge and then down farther into what appeared to be two green swelling lakes. She didn't realize he had taken her glasses but this landscape could not seem exceptional to her for she seldom paid any close attention to her surroundings.

"You got to say it," he repeated. "You got to say you love me."

She was always careful how she committed herself. "In a sense," she began, "if you use the word loosely, you might say that. But it's not a word I use. I don't have illusions. I'm one of those people who see *through* to nothing."

The boy was frowning. "You got to say it. I said it and you got to say it," he said.

The girl looked at him almost tenderly. "You poor baby," she murmured. "It's just as well you don't understand," and she pulled him by the neck, face-down, against her. "We are all damned," she said, "but some of us have taken off our blindfolds and see that there's nothing to see. It's a kind of salvation."

The boy's astonished eyes looked blankly through the ends of her hair. "Okay," he almost whined, "but do you love me or don'tcher?"

"Yes," she said and added, "in a sense. But I must tell you something. There mustn't be anything dishonest between us." She lifted his head and looked him in the eye. "I am thirty years old," she said. "I have a number of degrees."

The boy's look was irritated but dogged. "I don't care," he said. "I don't care a thing about what all you done. I just want to know if you love me or don'tcher?" and he caught her to him and wildly planted her face with kisses until she said, "Yes, yes."

"Okay then," he said, letting her go. "Prove it."

She smiled, looking dreamily out on the shifty landscape. She had seduced him without even making up her mind to try. "How?" she asked, feeling that he should be delayed a little.

He leaned over and put his lips to her ear. "Show me where your wooden leg joins on," he whispered.

The girl uttered a sharp little cry and her face instantly drained of color. The obscenity of the suggestion was not what shocked her. As a child she had sometimes been subject to feelings of shame but education had removed the last traces of that as a good surgeon scrapes for cancer; she would no more have felt it over what he was asking than she would have believed in his Bible. But she was as sensitive about the artificial leg as a peacock about his tail. No one ever touched it but her. She took care of it as someone else would his soul, in private and almost with her own eyes turned away. "No," she said.

"I known it," he muttered, sitting up. "You're just playing me for a sucker."

"Oh no no!" she cried. "It joins on at the knee. Only at the knee. Why do you want to see it?"

The boy gave her a long penetrating look. "Because," he said, "it's what makes you different. You ain't like anybody else."

She sat staring at him. There was nothing about her face or her round freezing-blue eyes to indicate that this had moved her; but she felt as if her heart had stopped and left her mind to pump her blood. She decided that for the first time in her life she was face to face with real innocence. This boy, with an instinct that came from beyond wisdom, had touched the truth about her. When after a minute, she said in a hoarse high voice, "All right," it was like surrendering to him completely. It was like losing her own life and finding it again, miraculously, in his.

Very gently he began to roll the slack leg up. The artificial limb, in a white sock and brown flat shoe, was bound in a heavy material like canvas and ended in an ugly jointure where it was attached to the stump. The boy's face and his voice were entirely reverent as he uncovered it and said, "Now show me how to take it off and on."

She took it off for him and put it back on again and then he took it off himself, handling it as tenderly as if it were a real one. "See!" he said with a delighted child's face. "Now I can do it myself!"

"Put it back on," she said. She was thinking that she would run away with him and that every night he would take the leg off and every morning put it back on again. "Put it back on," she said.

"Not yet," he murmured, setting it on its foot out of her reach. "Leave it off for awhile. You got me instead."

She gave a little cry of alarm but he pushed her down and began to kiss her again. Without the leg she felt entirely dependent on him. Her brain seemed to have stopped thinking altogether and to be about some other function that it was not very good at. Different expressions raced back and forth over her face. Every now and then the boy, his eyes like two steel spikes, would glance behind him, where the leg stood. Finally she pushed him off and said, "Put it back on me now."

"Wait," he said. He leaned the other way and pulled the valise toward him and opened it. It had a pale blue spotted lining and there were only two Bibles in it. He took one of these out and opened the cover of it. It was hollow and contained a pocket flask of whiskey, a pack of cards, and a small blue box with printing on it. He laid these out in front of her one at a time in an evenly-spaced row, like one presenting offerings at the shrine of a goddess. He put the blue box in her hand. THIS PRODUCT TO BE USED ONLY FOR THE PREVENTION OF DISEASE, she read, and dropped it. The boy was unscrewing the top of the flask. He stopped and pointed, with a smile, to the deck of cards. It was not an ordinary deck but one with an obscene picture on the back of each card. "Take a swig," he said, offering her the bottle first. He held it in front of her, but like one mesmerized, she did not move.

Her voice when she spoke had an almost pleading sound. "Aren't you," she murmured, "aren't you just good country people?"

The boy cocked his head. He looked as if he were just beginning to understand that she might be trying to insult him. "Yeah," he said, curling his lip slightly, "but it ain't held me back none. I'm as good as you any day in the week."

"Give me my leg," she said.

He pushed it farther away with his foot. "Come on now, let's begin to have us a good time," he said coaxingly. "We ain't got to know one another good yet."

"Give me my leg!" she screamed and tried to lunge for it but he pushed her down easily.

"What's the matter with you all of a sudden?" he asked, frowning as he screwed the top on the flask and put it quickly back inside the Bible. "You just a while ago said you didn't believe in nothing. I thought you was some girl!"

Her face was almost purple. "You're a Christian!" she hissed. "You're a fine Christian! You're just like them all—say one thing and do another. You're a perfect Christian, you're . . ."

The boy's mouth was set angrily. "I hope you don't think," he said in a lofty indignant tone, "that I believe in that crap! I may sell Bibles but I know which end is up and I wasn't born yesterday and I know where I'm going!"

"Give me my leg!" she screeched. He jumped up so quickly that she barely saw him sweep the cards and the blue box back into the Bible and throw the Bible into the valise. She saw him grab the leg and then she saw it for an instant slanted forlornly across the inside of the suitcase with a Bible at either side of its opposite ends. He slammed the lid shut and snatched up the valise and swung it down the hole and then stepped through himself.

When all of him had passed but his head, he turned and regarded her with a look that no longer had any admiration in it. "I've gotten a lot of interesting things," he said. "One time I got a woman's glass eye this way. And you needn't to think you'll catch me because Pointer ain't really my name. I use a different name at every house I call at and don't stay nowhere long. And I'll tell you another thing, Hulga," he said, using the name as if he didn't think much of it, "you ain't so smart. I been believing in nothing ever since I was born!" and then the toast-colored hat disappeared down the hole and the girl was left, sitting on the straw in the dusty sunlight. When she turned her churning face toward the opening, she saw his blue figure struggling successfully over the green speckled lake.

Mrs. Hopewell and Mrs. Freeman, who were in the back pasture, digging up onions, saw him emerge a little later from the woods and head across the meadow toward the highway. "Why, that looks like that nice dull young man that tried to sell me a Bible yesterday," Mrs. Hopewell said, squinting. "He must have been selling them to the Negroes back in there. He was so simple," she said, "but I guess the world would be better off if we were all that simple."

Mrs. Freeman's gaze drove forward and just touched him before he disappeared under the hill. Then she returned her attention to the evil-smelling onion shoot she was lifting from the ground. "Some can't be that simple," she said. "I know I never could."

John Updike

1932–

FLIGHT

AT THE age of seventeen I was poorly dressed and funny-looking, and went around thinking about myself in the third person. "Allen Dow strode down the street and home." "Allen Dow smiled a thin sardonic smile." Consciousness of a special destiny made me both arrogant and shy. Years before, when I was eleven or twelve, just on the brink of ceasing to be a little boy, my mother and I, one Sunday afternoon—my father was busy, or asleep—hiked up to the top of Shale Hill, a child's mountain that formed one side of the valley that held our town. There the town lay under us, Olinger, perhaps a thousand homes, the best and biggest of them climbing Shale Hill toward us, and beyond them the blocks of brick houses, one- and two-family, the homes of my friends, sloping down to the pale thread of the Alton Pike, which strung together the high school, the tennis courts, the movie theater, the town's few stores and gasoline stations, the elementary school, the Lutheran church. On the other side lay more homes, including our own, a tiny white patch placed just where the land began to rise toward the opposite mountain, Cedar Top. There were rims and rims of hills beyond Cedar Top, and looking south we could see the pike dissolving in other towns and turning out of sight amid the patches of green and brown farmland, and it seemed the entire county was lying exposed under a thin veil of haze. I was old enough to feel embarrassment at standing there alone with my mother, beside a wind-stunted spruce tree, on a long spine of shale. Suddenly she dug her fingers into the hair on my head and announced, "There we all are, and there we'll all be forever." She hesitated before the word "forever," and hesitated again before adding, "Except you, Allen. You're going to fly." A few birds were hung far out over the valley, at the level of our eyes, and in her impulsive way she had just plucked the image from them, but it felt like the clue I had been waiting all my childhood for. My most secret self had been made to respond, and I was intensely embarrassed, and irritably ducked my head out from under her melodramatic hand.

She was impulsive and romantic and inconsistent. I was never able to develop this spurt of reassurance into a steady theme between us. That she continued to treat me like an ordinary child seemed a betrayal of the vision she had made me share. I was captive to a hope she had tossed off and forgotten. My shy attempts to justify irregularities in my conduct—reading late at night or not coming back from school on time—by appealing to the image of flight were received with a startled blank look, as if I were talking nonsense. It seemed outrageously unjust. Yes, but, I wanted to say, yes, but it's *your* nonsense. And of course it was just

this that made my appeal ineffective: her knowing that I had not made
it mine, that I cynically intended to exploit both the privileges of being
extraordinary and the pleasures of being ordinary. She feared my wish to
be ordinary; once she did respond to my protest that I was learning to
fly, by crying with red-faced ferocity, "You'll never learn, you'll stick
and die in the dirt just like I'm doing. Why should you be better than
your mother?"

She had been born ten miles to the south, on a farm she and her mother
had loved. Her mother, a small fierce woman who looked more like an
Arab than a German, worked in the fields with the men, and drove the
wagon to market ten miles away every Friday. When still a tiny girl,
my mother rode with her, and my impression of those rides is of fear—
the little girl's fear of the gross and beery men who grabbed and hugged
her, her fear of the wagon breaking, of the produce not selling, fear of
her mother's possible humiliation and of her father's condition when at
nightfall they returned. Friday was his holiday, and he drank. His drinking is impossible for me to picture; for I never knew him except as an
enduring, didactic, almost Biblical old man, whose one passion was reading the newspapers and whose one hatred was of the Republican Party.
There was something public about him; now that he is dead I keep seeing bits of him attached to famous politicians—his watch chain and his
plump square stomach in old films of Theodore Roosevelt, his high-top
shoes and the tilt of his head in a photograph of Alfalfa Bill Murray.[1]
Alfalfa Bill is turning his head to talk, and holds his hat by the crown,
pinching it between two fingers and a thumb, a gentle and courtly grip
that reminded me so keenly of my grandfather that I tore the picture out
of *Life* and put it in a drawer.

Laboring in the soil had never been congenial to my grandfather,
though with his wife's help he prospered by it. Then, in an era when success was hard to avoid, he began to invest in stocks. In 1922 he bought
our large white home in the town—its fashionable section had not yet
shifted to the Shale Hill side of the valley—and settled in to reap his
dividends. He believed to his death that women were foolish, and the
broken hearts of his two must have seemed specially so. The dignity of
finance for the indignity of farming must have struck him as an eminently
advantageous exchange. It strikes me that way, too, and how to reconcile
my idea of those fear-ridden wagon rides with the grief that my mother
insists she and her mother felt at being taken from the farm? Perhaps
prolonged fear is a ground of love. Or perhaps, and likelier, the equation
is long and complex, and the few factors I know—the middle-aged
woman's mannish pride of land, the adolescent girl's pleasure in riding
horses across the fields, their common feeling of rejection in Olinger—
are enclosed in brackets and heightened by coefficients that I cannot see.
Or perhaps it is not love of land but its absence that needs explaining, in

[1] a picturesque Democratic politician, Governor of Oklahoma during the 1930s

my grandfather's fastidiousness and pride. He believed that as a boy he had been abused, and bore his father a grudge that my mother could never understand. Her grandfather to her was a saintly slender giant, over six feet tall when this was a prodigy, who knew the names of everything, like Adam in Eden. In his old age he was blind. When he came out of the house, the dogs rushed forward to lick his hands. When he lay dying, he requested a Gravenstein apple from the tree on the far edge of the meadow, and his son brought him a Krauser from the orchard near the house. The old man refused it, and my grandfather made a second trip, but in my mother's eyes the outrage had been committed, a savage insult insanely without provocation. What had his father done to him? The only specific complaint I ever heard my grandfather make was that when he was a boy and had to fetch water for the men in the fields, his father would tell him sarcastically, "Pick up your feet; they'll come down themselves." How incongruous! As if each generation of parents commits atrocities against their children which by God's decree remain invisible to the rest of the world.

I remember my grandmother as a little dark-eyed woman who talked seldom and who tried to feed me too much, and then as a hook-nosed profile pink against the lemon cushions of the casket. She died when I was seven. All the rest I know about her is that she was the baby of thirteen children, that while she was alive she made our yard one of the most beautiful in town, and that I am supposed to resemble her brother Pete.

My mother was precocious; she was fourteen when they moved, and for three years had been attending the county normal school. She graduated from Lake College, near Philadelphia, when she was only twenty, a tall handsome girl with a deprecatory smile, to judge from one of the curling photographs kept in a shoebox that I was always opening as a child, as if it might contain the clue to the quarrels in my house. My mother stands at the end of our brick walk, beside the elaborately trimmed end of our privet hedge—in shape a thick square column mounted by a rough ball of leaf. The ragged arc of a lilac bush in flower cuts into the right edge of the photograph, and behind my mother I can see a vacant lot where there has been a house ever since I can remember. She poses with a kind of country grace in a long fur-trimmed coat, unbuttoned to expose her beads and a short yet somehow demure flapper dress. Her hands are in her coat pockets, a beret sits on one side of her bangs, and there is a swank about her that seemed incongruous to me, examining this picture on the stained carpet of an ill-lit old house in the evening years of the thirties and in the dark of the warring forties. The costume and the girl in it look so up-to-date, so formidable. It was my grandfather's pleasure, in his prosperity, to give her a generous clothes allowance. My father, the penniless younger son of a Presbyterian minister in Passaic, had worked his way through Lake College by waiting on tables, and still speaks with mild resentment of the beautiful clothes that

Lillian Baer wore. This aspect of my mother caused me some pain in high school; she was a fabric snob, and insisted on buying my slacks and sports shirts at the best store in Alton, and since we had little money, she bought me few, when of course what I needed was what my classmates had—a wide variety of cheap clothes.

At the time the photograph was taken, my mother wanted to go to New York. What she would have done there, or exactly what she wanted to do, I don't know; but her father forbade her. "Forbid" is a husk of a word today, but at that time, in that quaint province, in the mouth of an "indulgent father," it apparently was still viable, for the great moist weight of that forbidding continued to be felt in the house for years, and when I was a child, as one of my mother's endless harangues to my grandfather screamed toward its weeping peak, I could feel it around and above me, like a huge root encountered by an earthworm.

Perhaps in a reaction of anger my mother married my father, Victor Dow, who at least took her as far away as Wilmington, where he had made a beginning with an engineering firm. But the depression hit, my father was laid off, and the couple came to the white house in Olinger, where my grandfather sat reading the newspapers that traced his stocks' cautious decline into worthlessness. I was born. My grandmother went around as a cleaning lady, and grew things in our quarter-acre yard to sell. We kept chickens, and there was a large plot of asparagus. After she had died, in a frightened way I used to seek her in the asparagus patch. By midsummer it would be a forest of dainty green trees, some as tall as I was, and in their frothy touch a spirit seemed to speak, and in the soft thick net of their intermingling branches a promise seemed to be caught, as well as a menace. The asparagus trees were frightening; in the center of the patch, far from the house and the alley, I would fall under a spell, and become tiny, and wander among the great smooth green trunks expecting to find a little house with a smoking chimney, and in it my grandmother. She herself had believed in ghosts, which made her own ghost potent. Even now, sitting alone in my own house, a board creaks in the kitchen and I look up fearing she will come through the doorway. And at night, just before I fall asleep, her voice calls my name in a penetrating whisper, or calls, "*Pete.*"

My mother went to work in an Alton department store, selling inferior fabric for $14 a week. During the daytime of my first year of life it was my father who took care of me. He has said since, flattering me as he always does, that it was having me on his hands that kept him from going insane. It may have been this that has made my affection for him so inarticulate, as if I were still a wordless infant looking up into the mothering blur of his man's face. And that same shared year helps account, perhaps, for his gentleness with me, for his willingness to praise, as if everything I do has something sad and crippled in it. He feels sorry for me; my birth coincided with the birth of a great misery, a national misery—only recently has he stopped calling me by the nickname "Young America." Around my first birthday he acquired a position teaching arithmetic and algebra in the Olinger high school, and though he was so kind and humorous he couldn't enter a classroom without creating uproarious problems of discipline, he endured it day by day and year by year, and eventually came to occupy a place in this alien town, so that I believe there are now one or two dozen ex-students, men and women nearing middle age, who carry around with them some piece of encouragement my father gave them, or remember some sentence of his that helped shape them. Certainly there are many who remember the antics with which he burlesqued his discomfort in the classroom. He kept a confiscated cap pistol in his desk, and upon getting an especially stupid answer, he would take it out and, wearing a preoccupied, regretful expression, shoot himself in the head.

My grandfather was the last to go to work, and the most degraded by it. He was hired by the borough crew, men who went around the streets shoveling stones and spreading tar. Bulky and ominous in their overalls, wreathed in steam, and associated with dramatic and portentous equipment, these men had grandeur in the eyes of a child, and it puzzled me, as I walked to and from elementary school, that my grandfather refused to wave to me or confess his presence in any way. Curiously strong for a fastidious man, he kept at it well into his seventies, when his sight failed. It was my task then to read his beloved newspapers to him as he sat in his chair by the bay window, twiddling his high-top shoes in the sunshine. I teased him, reading too fast, then maddeningly slow, skipping from column to column to create one long chaotic story; I read him the sports page, which did not interest him, and mumbled the editorials. Only the speed of his feet's twiddling betrayed vexation. When I'd stop, he would plead mildly in his rather beautiful, old-fashioned, elocutionary voice, "Now just the obituaries, Allen. Just the names to see if anyone I know is there." I imagined, as I viciously barked at him the list of names that might contain the name of a friend, that I was avenging my mother; I believed that she hated him, and for her sake I tried to hate him also. From her incessant resurrection of mysterious grievances buried far back in the confused sunless earth of the time before I was born, I had been able to deduce only that he was an evil man, who had ruined her life, that fair creature in the beret. I did not understand. She fought with him not because she wanted to fight but because *she could not bear to leave him alone.*

Sometimes, glancing up from the sheet of print where our armies swarmed in retreat like harried insects, I would catch the old man's head in the act of lifting slightly to receive the warm sunshine on his face, a dry frail face ennobled by its thick crown of combed corn-silk hair. It would dawn on me then that his sins as a father were likely no worse than any father's. But my mother's genius was to give the people closest to her mythic immensity. I was the phoenix. My father and grandmother were legendary invader-saints, she springing out of some narrow vein of Arab blood in the German race and he crossing over from the Protestant wastes of New Jersey, both of them serving and enslaving their mates with their prodigious powers of endurance and labor. For my mother felt that she and her father alike had been destroyed by marriage, been made captive by people better yet less than they. It was true, my father had loved Mom Baer, and her death made him seem more of an alien than ever. He, and her ghost, stood to one side, in the shadows but separate from the house's dark core, the inheritance of frustration and folly that had descended from my grandfather to my mother to me, and that I, with a few beats of my grown wings, was destined to reverse and redeem.

At the age of seventeen, in the fall of my senior year, I went with three girls to debate at a high school over a hundred miles away. They were, all three, bright girls, A students; they were disfigured by A's as if by acne. Yet even so it excited me to be mounting a train with them early on a Friday morning, at an hour when our schoolmates miles away were slumping into the seats of their first class. Sunshine spread broad bars of dust down the length of the half-empty car, and through the windows Pennsylvania unravelled in a long brown scroll scribbled with industry. Black pipes raced beside the tracks for miles. At rhythmic intervals one of them looped upward, like the Greek letter Ω. "Why does it do that?" I asked. "Is it sick?"

"Condensation?" Judith Potteiger suggested in her shy, transparent voice. She loved science.

"No," I said. "It's in pain. It's writhing! It's going to grab the train! Look out!" I ducked, honestly a little scared. All the girls laughed.

Judith and Catharine Miller were in my class, and expected me to be amusing; the third girl, a plump small junior named Molly Bingaman, had not known what to expect. It was her fresh audience I was playing to. She was the best dressed of us four, and the most poised; this made me suspect that she was the least bright. She had been substituted at the last moment for a sick member of the debating team; I knew her just by seeing her in the halls and in assembly. From a distance she seemed dumpy and prematurely adult. But up close she was gently fragrant, and against the weary purple cloth of the train seats her skin seemed luminous. She had beautiful skin a pencil dot would have marred, and large blue eyes equally clear. Except for a double chin, and a mouth too large and thick, she would have been perfectly pretty, in a little woman's compact and cocky way. She and I sat side by side, facing the two senior girls, who more and more took on the wan slyness of matchmakers. It was they who had forced the seating arrangements.

We debated in the afternoon, and won. Yes, the German Federal Republic *should* be freed of all Allied control. The school, a posh castle on the edge of a miserable coal city, was the site of a statewide cycle of debates that was to continue into Saturday. There was a dance Friday night in the gym. I danced with Molly mostly, though to my annoyance she got in with a set of Harrisburg boys while I conscientiously pushed Judith and Catharine around the floor. We were stiff dancers, the three of us; only Molly made me seem good, floating backward from my feet fearlessly as her cheek rumpled my moist shirt. The gym was hung with orange and black crepe paper in honor of Hallowe'en, and the pennants of all the competing schools were fastened to the walls, and a twelve-piece band pumped away blissfully on the year's sad tunes—"Heartaches," "Near You," "That's My Desire." A great cloud of balloons gathered in the steel girders was released. There was pink punch, and a local girl sang.

Judith and Catharine decided to leave before the dance was over, and I made Molly come too, though she was in a literal sweat of pleasure; her perfect skin in the oval above her neckline was flushed and glazed. I realized, with a little shock of possessiveness and pity, that she was unused to attention back home, in competition with the gorgeous Olinger ignorant.

We walked together to the house where the four of us had been boarded, a large white frame owned by an old couple and standing with lonely decency in a semi-slum. Judith and Catharine turned up the walk, but Molly and I, with a diffident decision that I believe came from her initiative, continued, "to walk around the block." We walked miles, stopping off after midnight at a trolley-car-shaped diner. I got a hamburger, and she impressed me by ordering coffee. We walked back to the house and let ourselves in with the key we had been given; but instead of going upstairs to our rooms we sat downstairs in the dark living room and talked softly for more hours.

What did we say? I talked about myself. It is hard to hear, much less remember, what we ourselves say, just as it might be hard for a movie projector, given life, to see the shadows its eye of light is casting. A transcript, could I produce it, of my monologue through the wide turning point of that night, with all its word-by-word conceit, would distort the picture: this living room miles from home, the street light piercing the chinks in the curtains and erecting on the wallpaper rods of light the size of yardsticks, our hosts and companions asleep upstairs, the incessant sigh of my voice, coffee-primed Molly on the floor beside my chair, her stockinged legs stretched out on the rug; and this odd sense in the room, a tasteless and odorless aura unfamiliar to me, as a pool of water widening.

I remember one exchange. I must have been describing the steep waves of fearing death that had come over me ever since early childhood, about one every three years, and I ended by supposing that it would take great courage to be an atheist. "But I bet you'll become one," Molly said. "Just to show yourself that you're brave enough." I felt she overestimated me, and was flattered. Within a few years, while I still remembered many of her words, I realized how touchingly gauche our assumption was that an atheist is a lonely rebel; for mobs of men are united in atheism, and oblivion—the dense lead-like sea that would occasionally sweep over me—is to them a weight as negligible as the faint pressure of their wallets in their hip pockets. This grotesque and tender mis-estimate of the world flares in my memory of our conversation like one of the innumerable matches we struck.

The room filled with smoke. Too weary to sit, I lay down on the floor beside her, and stroked her silver arm in silence, yet still was too timid to act on the wide and negative aura that I did not understand was of compliance. On the upstairs landing, as I went to turn into my room, Molly came forward with a prim look and kissed me. With clumsy force I entered the negative space that had been waiting. Her lipstick smeared in little unflattering flecks into the skin around her mouth; it was as if I had been given a face to eat, and the presence of bone—skull under skin, teeth behind lips—impeded me. We stood for a long time under the burning hall light, until my neck began to ache from bowing. My legs were trembling when we finally parted and sneaked into our rooms. In bed I thought, "Allen Dow tossed restlessly," and realized it was the first time that day I had thought of myself in the third person.

On Saturday morning, we lost our debate. I was sleepy and verbose and haughty, and some of the students in the audience began to boo whenever I opened my mouth. The principal came up on the stage and made a scolding speech, which finished me and my cause, untrammeled Germany. On the train back, Catharine and Judith arranged the seating so that they sat behind Molly and me, and spied on only the tops of our heads. For the first time, on that ride home, I felt what it was to bury a humiliation in the body of a woman. Nothing but the friction of my face against hers drowned out the echo of those boos. When we kissed, a red shadow would well under my lids and eclipse the hostile hooting faces of the debate audience, and when our lips parted, the bright inner sea would ebb, and there the faces would be again, more intense than ever. With a shudder of shame I'd hide my face on her shoulder and in the warm darkness there, while a frill of her prissy collar gently scratched my nose, I felt united with Hitler and all the villains, traitors, madmen, and failures who had managed to keep, up to the moment of capture or death, a woman with them. This had puzzled me. In high school females were proud and remote; in the newspapers they were fantastic monsters of submission. And now Molly administered reassurance to me with small motions and bodily adjustments that had about them a strange flavor of the practical.

Our parents met us at the station. I was startled at how tired my mother looked. There were deep blue dents on either side of her nose, and her hair seemed somehow dissociated from her head, as if it were a ragged, half-gray wig she had put on carelessly. She was a heavy woman and her weight, which she usually carried upright, like a kind of wealth, had slumped away from her ownership and seemed, in the sullen light of the railway platform, to weigh on the world. I asked, "How's Grandpa?" He had taken to bed several months before with pains in his chest.

"He still sings," she said rather sharply. For entertainment in his increasing blindness my grandfather had long ago begun to sing, and his shapely old voice would pour forth hymns, forgotten comic ballads, and camp-meeting songs at any hour. His memory seemed to improve the longer he lived.

My mother's irritability was more manifest in the private cavity of the car; her heavy silence oppressed me. "You look so tired, Mother," I said, trying to take the offensive.

"That's nothing to how you look," she answered. "What happened up there? You stoop like an old married man."

"Nothing happened," I lied. My cheeks were parched, as if her high steady anger had the power of giving sunburn.

"I remember that Bingaman girl's mother when we first moved to town. She was the smuggest little snip south of the pike. They're real old Olinger stock, you know. They have no use for hillbillies."

My father tried to change the subject. "Well, you won one debate, Allen, and that's more than I would have done. I don't see how you do it."

"Why, he gets it from you, Victor. I've never won a debate with you."

"He gets it from Pop Baer. If that man had gone into politics, Lillian, all the misery of his life would have been avoided."

"Dad was never a debater. He was a bully. Don't go with little women, Allen. It puts you too close to the ground."

"I'm not *going* with *any*body, Mother. Really, you're so fanciful."

"Why, when she stepped off the train from the way her chins bounced I thought she had eaten a canary. And then making my poor son, all skin and bones, carry her bag. When she walked by me I honestly was afraid she'd spit in my eye."

"I had to carry somebody's bag. I'm sure she doesn't know who you are." Though it was true I had talked a good deal about my family the night before.

My mother turned away from me. "You see, Victor—he defends her. When I was his age that girl's mother gave me a cut I'm still bleeding from, and my own son attacks me on behalf of her fat little daughter. I wonder if her mother put her up to catching him."

"Molly's a nice girl," my father interceded. "She never gave me any trouble in class like some of those smug bastards." But he was curiously listless, for so Christian a man, in pronouncing this endorsement.

I discovered that nobody wanted me to go with Molly Bingaman. My friends—for on the strength of being funny I did have some friends, classmates whose love affairs went on over my head but whom I could

accompany, as clown, on communal outings—never talked with me
about Molly, and when I brought her to their parties gave the impression
of ignoring her, so that I stopped taking her. Teachers at school would
smile an odd tight smile when they saw us leaning by her locker or hanging around in the stairways. The eleventh-grade English instructor—one
of my "boosters" on the faculty, a man who was always trying to "challenge" me, to "exploit" my "potential"—took me aside and told me
how stupid she was. She just couldn't grasp the logical principals of syn-
tax. He confided her parsing mistakes to me as if they betrayed—as
indeed in a way they did—an obtuseness her social manner cleverly concealed. Even the Fabers, an ultra-Republican couple who ran a luncheon-
ette near the high school, showed malicious delight whenever Molly and
I broke up, and persistently treated my attachment as being a witty piece
of play, like my pretense with Mr. Faber of being a Communist. The
entire town seemed ensnarled in my mother's myth, that escape was my
proper fate. It was as if I were a sport that the ghostly elders of Olinger
had segregated from the rest of the livestock and agreed to donate in
time to the air; this fitted with the ambiguous sensation I had always
had in the town, of being simultaneously flattered and rejected.

Molly's parents disapproved because in their eyes my family was vir-
tually white trash. It was so persistently hammered into me that I was
too good for Molly that I scarcely considered the proposition that, by
another scale, she was too good for me. Further, Molly herself shielded
me. Only once, exasperated by some tedious, condescending confession
of mine, did she state that her mother didn't like me. "Why not?" I
asked, genuinely surprised. I admired Mrs. Bingaman—she was beautifully preserved—and I always felt gay in her house, with its white
woodwork and matching furniture and vases of iris posing before polished
mirrors.

"Oh, I don't know. She thinks you're flippant."

"But that's not true. Nobody takes himself more seriously than I
do."

While Molly protected me from the Bingaman side of the ugliness, I
conveyed the Dow side more or less directly to her. It infuriated me
that nobody allowed me to be proud of her. I kept, in effect, asking her,
Why was she stupid in English? Why didn't she get along with my
friends? Why did she look so dumpy and smug?—this last despite the
fact that she often, especially in intimate moments, looked beautiful to
me. I was especially angry with her because this affair had brought out
an ignoble, hysterical, brutal aspect of my mother that I might never
have had to see otherwise. I had hoped to keep things secret from her,
but even if her intuition had not been relentless, my father, at school,
knew everything. Sometimes, indeed, my mother said that she didn't
care if I went with Molly; it was my father who was upset. Like a
frantic dog tied by one leg, she snapped in any direction, mouthing ridiculous fancies—such as that Mrs. Bingaman had sicked Molly on me just

to keep me from going to college and giving the Dows something to be proud of—that would make us both suddenly start laughing. Laughter in that house that winter had a guilty sound. My grandfather was dying, and lay upstairs singing and coughing and weeping as the mood came to him, and we were too poor to hire a nurse, and too kind and cowardly to send him to a "home." It was still his house, after all. Any noise he made seemed to slash my mother's heart, and she was unable to sleep upstairs near him, and waited the nights out on the sofa downstairs. In her desperate state she would say unforgivable things to me even while the tears streamed down her face. I've never seen so many tears as I saw that winter.

Every time I saw my mother cry, it seemed I had to make Molly cry. I developed a skill at it; it came naturally to an only child who had been surrounded all his life by adults ransacking each other for the truth. Even in the heart of intimacy, half-naked each of us, I would say something to humiliate her. We never made love in the final, coital sense. My reason was a mixture of idealism and superstition; I felt that if I took her virginity she would be mine forever. I depended overmuch on a technicality; she gave herself to me anyway, and I had her anyway, and have her still, for the longer I travel in a direction I could not have taken with her, the more clearly she seems the one person who loved me without advantage. I was a homely, comically ambitious hillbilly, and I even refused to tell her I loved her, to pronounce the word "love"—an icy piece of pedantry that shocks me now that I have almost forgotten the context of confusion in which it seemed wise.

In addition to my grandfather's illness, and my mother's grief, and my waiting to hear if I had won a scholarship to the one college that seemed good enough for me, I was burdened with managing too many petty affairs of my graduating class. I was in charge of yearbook writeups, art editor of the school paper, chairman of the Class Gift Committee, director of the Senior Assembly, and teachers' workhorse. Frightened by my father's tales of nervous breakdowns he had seen, I kept listening for the sounds of my brain snapping, and the image of that gray, infinitely interconnected mass seemed to extend outward, to become my whole world, one dense organic dungeon, and I felt I had to get out; if I could just get out of this, into June, it would be blue sky, and I would be all right for life.

One Friday night in spring, after trying for over an hour to write thirty-five affectionate words for the yearbook about a null girl in the Secretarial Course I had never spoken a word to, I heard my grandfather begin coughing upstairs with a sound like dry membrane tearing, and I panicked. I called up the stairs, "Mother! I must go out."

"It's nine-thirty."

"I know, but I have to. I'm going insane."

Without waiting to hear her answer or to find a coat, I left the house

and got our old car out of the garage. The weekend before, I had broken
up with Molly again. All week I hadn't spoken to her, though I had seen
her once in Faber's, with a boy in her class, averting her face while I,
hanging by the side of the pinball machine, made wisecracks in her direction. I didn't dare go up to her door and knock so late at night; I just
parked across the street and watched the lit windows of her house.
Through their living-room window I could see one of Mrs. Bingaman's
vases of hothouse iris standing on a white mantel, and my open car window admitted the spring air, which delicately smelled of wet ashes.
Molly was probably out on a date with that moron in her class. But then
the Bingaman's door opened, and her figure appeared in the rectangle of
light. Her back was toward me, a coat was on her arm, and her mother
seemed to be screaming. Molly closed the door and ran down off the
porch and across the street and quickly got into the car, her eyes downcast in their sockets of shadow. *She came.* When I have finally forgotten
everything else, her powdery fragrance, her lucid cool skin, the way her
lower lip was like a curved pillow of two cloths, the dusty red outer and
wet pink inner, I'll still be grieved by this about Molly, that she came
to me.

After I returned her to her house—she told me not to worry, her
mother enjoyed shouting—I went to the all-night diner just beyond the
Olinger town line and ate three hamburgers, ordering them one at a
time, and drank two glasses of milk. It was close to two o'clock when
I got home, but my mother was still awake. She lay on the sofa in the
dark, with the radio sitting on the floor murmuring Dixieland piped up
from New Orleans by way of Philadelphia. Radio music was a steady
feature of her insomniac life; not only did it help drown out the noise
of her father upstairs but she seemed to enjoy it in itself. She would resist
my father's pleas to come to bed by saying that the New Orleans program was not over yet. The radio was an old Philco we had always had;
I had once drawn a fish on the orange disc of its celluloid dial, which
looked to my child's eyes like a fishbowl.

Her loneliness caught at me; I went into the living room and sat on a
chair with my back to the window. For a long time she looked at me
tensely out of the darkness. "Well," she said at last, "how was little
hotpants?" The vulgarity this affair had brought out in her language
appalled me.

"I made her cry," I told her.

"Why do you torment the girl?"

"To please you."

"It doesn't please me."

"Well, then, stop nagging me."

"I'll stop nagging you if you'll solemnly tell me you're willing to
marry her."

I said nothing to this, and after waiting she went on in a different voice, "Isn't it funny, that you should show this weakness?"

"Weakness is a funny way to put it when it's the only thing that gives me strength."

"Does it really, Allen? Well. It may be. I forget, you were born here."

Upstairs, close to our heads, my grandfather, in a voice frail but still melodious, began to sing, "There is a happy land, far, far away, where saints in glory stand, bright, bright as day." We listened; and his voice broke into coughing, a terrible rending cough growing in fury, struggling to escape, and loud with fear he called my mother's name. She didn't stir. His voice grew enormous, a bully's voice, as he repeated, "Lillian! Lillian!" and I saw my mother's shape quiver with the force coming down the stairs into her; she was like a dam; and then the power, as my grandfather fell momentarily silent, flowed toward me in the darkness, and I felt intensely angry, and hated that black mass of suffering, even while I realized, with a rapid, light calculation, that I was too weak to withstand it.

In a dry tone of certainty and dislike—how hard my heart had become!—I told her, "All right. You'll win this one, Mother; but it'll be the last one you'll win."

My pang of fright following this unprecedently cold insolence seemed to blot my senses; the chair ceased to be felt under me, and the walls and furniture of the room fell away—there was only the dim orange glow of the radio dial down below. In a husky voice that seemed to come across a great distance my mother said, with typical melodrama, "Goodbye, Allen."

Joyce Carol Oates

1938–

WHERE ARE YOU GOING, WHERE HAVE YOU BEEN?

FOR BOB DYLAN

HER NAME was Connie. She was fifteen and she had a quick nervous giggling habit of craning her neck to glance into mirrors, or checking other people's faces to make sure her own was all right. Her mother, who noticed everything and knew everything and who hadn't much reason any longer to look at her own face, always scolded Connie about it. "Stop gawking at yourself, who are you? You think you're so pretty?" she would say. Connie would raise her eyebrows at these familiar complaints and look right through her mother, into a shadowy vision of herself as she was right at that moment: she knew she was pretty and that was everything. Her mother had been pretty once too, if you could believe those old snapshots in the album, but now her looks were gone and that was why she was always after Connie.

"Why don't you keep your room clean like your sister? How've you got your hair fixed—what the hell stinks? Hair spray? You don't see your sister using that junk."

Her sister June was twenty-four and still lived at home. She was a secretary in the high school Connie attended, and if that wasn't bad enough—with her in the same building—she was so plain and chunky and steady that Connie had to hear her praised all the time by her mother and her mother's sisters. June did this, June did that, she saved money and helped clean the house and cooked and Connie couldn't do a thing, her mind was all filled with trashy daydreams. Their father was away at work most of the time and when he came home he wanted supper and he read the newspaper at supper and after supper he went to bed. He didn't bother talking much to them, but around his bent head Connie's mother kept picking at her until Connie wished her mother was dead and she herself was dead and it was all over. "She makes me want to throw up sometimes," she complained to her friends. She had a high, breathless, amused voice which made everything she said sound a little forced, whether it was sincere or not.

There was one good thing: June went places with girl friends of hers, girls who were just as plain and steady as she, and so when Connie wanted to do that her mother had no objections. The father of Connie's best girl friend drove the girls the three miles to town and left them off at a shopping plaza, so that they could walk through the stores or go to a movie, and when he came to pick them up again at eleven he never bothered to ask what they had done.

They must have been familiar sights, walking around that shopping plaza in their shorts and flat ballerina slippers that always scuffed the sidewalk, with charm bracelets jingling on their thin wrists; they would lean together to whisper and laugh secretly if someone passed by who amused or interested them. Connie had long dark blond hair that drew anyone's eye to it, and she wore part of it pulled up on her head and puffed out and the rest of it she let fall down her back. She wore a pullover jersey blouse that looked one way when she was at home and another way when she was away from home. Everything about her had two sides to it, one for home and one for anywhere that was not home: her walk that could be childlike and bobbing, or languid enough to make anyone think she was hearing music in her head, her mouth which was pale and smirking most of the time, but bright and pink on these evenings out, her laugh which was cynical and drawling at home—"Ha, ha, very funny"—but high-pitched and nervous anywhere else, like the jingling of the charms on her bracelet.

Sometimes they did go shopping or to a movie, but sometimes they went across the highway, ducking fast across the busy road, to a drive-in restaurant where older kids hung out. The restaurant was shaped like a big bottle, though squatter than a real bottle, and on its cap was a revolving figure of a grinning boy who held a hamburger aloft. One night in mid-summer they ran across, breathless with daring, and right away someone leaned out a car window and invited them over, but it was just a boy from high school they didn't like. It made them feel good to be able to ignore him. They went up through the maze of parked and cruising cars to the bright-lit, fly-infested restaurant, their faces pleased and expectant as if they were entering a sacred building that loomed out of the night to give them what haven and what blessing they yearned for. They sat at the counter and crossed their legs at the ankles, their thin shoulders rigid with excitement, and listened to the music that made everything so good : the music was always in the background like music at a church service, it was something to depend upon.

A boy named Eddie came in to talk with them. He sat backwards on his stool, turning himself jerkily around in semi-circles and then stopping and turning again, and after a while he asked Connie if she would like something to eat. She said she did and so she tapped her friend's arm on her way out—her friend pulled her face up into a brave droll look—and Connie said she would meet her at eleven, across the way. "I just hate to leave her like that," Connie said earnestly, but the boy said that she wouldn't be alone for long. So they went out to his car and on the way Connie couldn't help but let her eyes wander over the windshields and faces all around her, her face gleaming with a joy that had nothing to do with Eddie or even this place; it might have been the music. She drew her shoulders up and sucked in her breath with the pure pleasure of being alive, and just at that moment she happened to glance at a face just a few feet from hers. It was a boy with shaggy black hair, in a convertible jalopy painted gold. He stared at her and then his lips widened into a grin. Connie slit her eyes at him and turned away, but she couldn't help glancing back and there he was still watching her. He wagged a finger and laughed and said, "Gonna get you, baby," and Connie turned away again without Eddie noticing anything.

She spent three hours with him, at the restaurant where they ate hamburgers and drank Cokes in wax cups that were always sweating, and then down an alley a mile or so away, and when he left her off at five to eleven only the movie house was still open at the plaza. Her girl friend was there, talking with a boy. When Connie came up the two girls smiled at each other and Connie said, "How was the movie?" and the girl said, "*You* should know." They rode off with the girl's father, sleepy and pleased, and Connie couldn't help but look at the darkened shopping plaza with its big empty parking lot and its signs that were faded and ghostly now, and over at the drive-in restaurant where cars were still circling tirelessly. She couldn't hear the music at this distance.

Next morning June asked her how the movie was and Connie said, "So-so."

She and that girl and occasionally another girl went out several times a week that way, and the rest of the time Connie spent around the house —it was summer vacation—getting in her mother's way and thinking, dreaming, about the boys she met. But all the boys fell back and dissolved into a single face that was not even a face, but an idea, a feeling, mixed up with the urgent insistent pounding of the music and the humid night air of July. Connie's mother kept dragging her back to the daylight by finding things for her to do or saying, suddenly, "What's this about the Pettinger girl?"

And Connie would say nervously, "Oh, her. That dope." She always drew thick clear lines between herself and such girls, and her mother was simple and kindly enough to believe her. Her mother was so simple, Connie thought, that it was maybe cruel to fool her so much. Her mother went scuffling around the house in old bedroom slippers and complained over the telephone to one sister about the other, then the other called up and the two of them complained about the third one. If June's name was mentioned her mother's tone was approving, and if Connie's name was mentioned it was disapproving. This did not really mean she disliked Connie and actually Connie thought that her mother preferred her to June because she was prettier, but the two of them kept up a pretense of exasperation, a sense that they were tugging and struggling over something of little value to either of them. Sometimes, over coffee, they were almost friends, but something would come up— some vexation that was like a fly buzzing suddenly around their heads— and their faces went hard with contempt.

One Sunday Connie got up at eleven—none of them bothered with church—and washed her hair so that it could dry all day long, in the sun. Her parents and sister were going to a barbecue at an aunt's house and Connie said no, she wasn't interested, rolling her eyes to let mother know just what she thought of it. "Stay home alone then," her mother said sharply. Connie sat out back in a lawn chair and watched them drive away, her father quiet and bald, hunched around so that he could back the car out, her mother with a look that was still angry and not at all softened through the windshield, and in the back seat poor old June all dressed up as if she didn't know what a barbecue was, with all the running yelling kids and the flies. Connie sat with her eyes closed in the sun, dreaming and dazed with the warmth about her as if this were a kind of love, the caresses of love, and her mind slipped over onto thoughts of the boy she had been with the night before and how nice he had been, how sweet it always was, not the way someone like June would suppose but sweet, gentle, the way it was in movies and promised in songs; and when she opened her eyes she hardly knew where she was, the back yard ran off into weeds and a fence-line of trees and behind it the sky was perfectly blue and still. The asbestos "ranch house" that was now three years old startled her—it looked small. She shook her head as if to get awake.

It was too hot. She went inside the house and turned on the radio to drown out the quiet. She sat on the edge of her bed, barefoot, and listened for an hour and a half to a program called XYZ Sunday Jamboree, record after record of hard, fast, shrieking songs she sang along with, interspersed by exclamations from "Bobby King": "An' look here you girls at Napoleon's—Son and Charley want you to pay real close attention to this song coming up!"

And Connie paid close attention herself, bathed in a glow of slow-pulsed joy that seemed to rise mysteriously out of the music itself and lay languidly about the airless little room, breathed in and breathed out with each gentle rise and fall of her chest.

After a while she heard a car coming up the drive. She sat up at once, startled, because it couldn't be her father so soon. The gravel kept crunching all the way in from the road—the driveway was long—and Connie ran to the window. It was a car she didn't know. It was an open jalopy, painted a bright gold that caught the sunlight opaquely. Her heart began to pound and her fingers snatched at her hair, checking it, and she whispered "Christ. Christ," wondering how bad she looked. The car came to a stop at the side door and the horn sounded four short taps as if this were a signal Connie knew.

She went into the kitchen and approached the door slowly, then hung out the screen door, her bare toes curling down off the step. There were two boys in the car and now she recognized the driver: he had shaggy, shabby black hair that looked crazy as a wig and he was grinning at her.

"I ain't late, am I?" he said.

"Who the hell do you think you are?" Connie said.

"Toldja I'd be out, didn't I?"

"I don't even know who you are."

She spoke sullenly, careful to show no interest or pleasure, and he spoke in a fast bright monotone. Connie looked past him to the other boy, taking her time. He had fair brown hair, with a lock that fell onto his forehead. His sideburns gave him a fierce, embarrassed look, but so far he hadn't even bothered to glance at her. Both boys wore sunglasses. The driver's glasses were metallic and mirrored everything in miniature.

"You wanta come for a ride?" he said.

Connie smirked and let her hair fall loose over one shoulder.

"Don'tcha like my car? New paint job," he said. "Hey."

"What?"

"You're cute."

She pretended to fidget, chasing flies away from the door.

"Don'tcha believe me, or what?" he said.

"Look, I don't even know who you are," Connie said in disgust.

"Hey, Ellie's got a radio, see. Mine's broke down." He lifted his friend's arm and showed her the little transistor the boy was holding, and now Connie began to hear the music. It was the same program that was playing inside the house.

"Bobby King?" she said.

"I listen to him all the time. I think he's great."

"He's kind of great," Connie said reluctantly.

"Listen, that guy's *great*. He knows where the action is."

Connie blushed a little, because the glasses made it impossible for her to see just what this boy was looking at. She couldn't decide if she liked him or if he was just a jerk, and so she dawdled in the doorway and wouldn't come down or go back inside. She said, "What's all that stuff painted on your car?"

"Can'tcha read it?" He opened the door very carefully, as if he was afraid it might fall off. He slid out just as carefully, planting his feet firmly on the ground, the tiny metallic world in his glasses slowing down like gelatine hardening and in the midst of it Connie's bright green blouse. "This here is my name, to begin with," he said. ARNOLD FRIEND was written in tar-like black letters on the side, with a drawing of a round grinning face that reminded Connie of a pumpkin, except it wore sunglasses. "I wanta introduce myself, I'm Arnold Friend and that's my real name and I'm gonna be your friend, honey, and inside the car's Ellie Oscar, he's kinda shy." Ellie brought his transistor radio up to his shoulder and balanced it there. "Now these numbers are a secret code, honey," Arnold Friend explained. He read off the numbers 33, 19, 17 and raised his eyebrows at her to see what she thought of that, but she didn't think much of it. The left rear fender had been smashed and around it was written, on the gleaming gold background: DONE BY CRAZY WOMAN DRIVER. Connie had to laugh at that. Arnold Friend was pleased at her laughter and looked up at her. "Around the other side's a lot more—you wanta come and see them?"

"No."

"Why not?"

"Why should I?"

"Don'tcha wanta see what's on the car? Don'tcha wanta go for a ride?"

"I don't know."

"Why not?"

"I got things to do."

"Like what?"

"Things."

He laughed as if she had said something funny. He slapped his thighs. He was standing in a strange way, leaning back against the car as if he were balancing himself. He wasn't tall, only an inch or so taller than she would be if she came down to him. Connie liked the way he was dressed, which was the way all of them dressed: tight faded jeans stuffed into black, scuffed boots, a belt that pulled his waist in and showed how lean he was, and a white pull-over shirt that was a little soiled and showed the hard small muscles of his arms and shoulders. He looked as if he probably did hard work, lifting and carrying things. Even his neck looked muscular. And his face was a familiar face, somehow: the jaw and chin and cheeks slightly darkened, because he hadn't shaved for a day or two, and the nose long and hawk-like, sniffing as if she were a treat he was going to gobble up and it was all a joke.

"Connie, you ain't telling the truth. This is your day set aside for a ride with me and you know it," he said, still laughing. The way he straightened and recovered from his fit of laughing showed that it had been all fake.

"How do you know what my name is?" she said suspiciously.

"It's Connie."

"Maybe and maybe not."

"I know my Connie," he said, wagging his finger. Now she remembered him even better, back at the restaurant, and her cheeks warmed at the thought of how she sucked in her breath just at the moment she passed him—how she must have looked to him. And he had remembered her. "Ellie and I come out here especially for you," he said. "Ellie can sit in back. How about it?"

"Where?"

"Where what?"

"Where're we going?"

He looked at her. He took off the sunglasses and she saw how pale the skin around his eyes was, like holes that were not in shadow but instead in light. His eyes were like chips of broken glass that catch the light in an amiable way. He smiled. It was as if the idea of going for a ride somewhere, to some place, was a new idea to him.

"Just for a ride, Connie sweetheart."

"I never said my name was Connie," she said.

"But I know what it is. I know your name and all about you, lots of things," Arnold Friend said. He had not moved yet but stood still leaning back against the side of his jalopy. "I took a special interest in you, such a pretty girl, and found out all about you like I know your parents and sister are gone somewheres and I know where and how long they're going to be gone, and I know who you were with last night, and your best girl friend's name is Betty. Right?"

He spoke in a simple lilting voice, exactly as if he were reciting the words to a song. His smile assured her that everything was fine. In the car Ellie turned up the volume on his radio and did not bother to look around at them.

"Ellie can sit in the back seat," Arnold Friend said. He indicated his friend with a casual jerk of his chin, as if Ellie did not count and she should not bother with him.

"How'd you find out all that stuff?" Connie said.

"Listen: Betty Schultz and Tony Fitch and Jimmy Pettinger and Nancy Pettinger," he said, in a chant. "Raymond Stanley and Bob Hutter—"

"Do you know all those kids?"

"I know everybody."

"Look, you're kidding. You're not from around here."

"Sure."

"But—how come we never saw you before?"

"Sure you saw me before," he said. He looked down at his boots, as if he were a little offended. "You just don't remember."

"I guess I'd remember you," Connie said.

"Yeah?" He looked up at this, beaming. He was pleased. He began to mark time with the music from Ellie's radio, tapping his fists lightly together. Connie looked away from his smile to the car, which was painted so bright it almost hurt her eyes to look at it. She looked at that name, ARNOLD FRIEND. And up at the front fender was an expression that was familiar—MAN THE FLYING SAUCERS. It was an expression kids had used the year before, but didn't use this year. She looked at it for a while as if the words meant something to her that she did not yet know.

"What're you thinking about? Huh?" Arnold Friend demanded. "Not worried about your hair blowing around in the car, are you?"

"No."

"Think I maybe can't drive good?"

"How do I know?"

"You're a hard girl to handle. How come?" he said. "Don't you know I'm your friend? Didn't you see me put my sign in the air when you walked by?"

"What sign?"

"My sign." And he drew an X in the air, leaning out toward her. They were maybe ten feet apart. After his hand fell back to his side the X was still in the air, almost visible. Connie let the screen door close and stood perfectly still inside it, listening to the music from her radio and the boy's blend together. She stared at Arnold Friend. He stood there so stiffly relaxed, pretending to be relaxed, with one hand idly on the door handle as if he were keeping himself up that way and had no intention of ever moving again. She recognized most things about him, the tight jeans that showed his thighs and buttocks and the greasy leather boots and the tight shirt, and even that slippery friendly smile of his, that sleepy dreamy smile that all the boys used to get across ideas they didn't want to put into words. She recognized all this and also the singsong way he talked, slightly mocking, kidding, but serious and a little melancholy, and she recognized the way he tapped one fist against the other in homage to the perpetual music behind him. But all these things did not come together.

She said suddenly, "Hey, how old are you?"

His smile faded. She could see then that he wasn't a kid, he was much older—thirty, maybe more. At this knowledge her heart began to pound faster.

"That's a crazy thing to ask. Can'tcha see I'm your own age?"

"Like hell you are."

"Or maybe a coupla years older, I'm eighteen."

"Eighteen?" she said doubtfully.

He grinned to reassure her and lines appeared at the corners of his mouth. His teeth were big and white. He grinned so broadly his eyes became slits and she saw how thick the lashes were, thick and black as if painted with a black tar-like material. Then he seemed to become embarrassed, abruptly, and looked over his shoulder at Ellie. "*Him*, he's crazy," he said. "Ain't he a riot, he's a nut, a real character." Ellie was still listening to the music. His sunglasses told nothing about what he was thinking. He wore a bright orange shirt unbuttoned halfway to show his chest, which was a pale, bluish chest and not muscular like Arnold Friend's. His shirt collar was turned up all around and the very tips of the collar pointed out past his chin as if they were protecting him. He was pressing the transistor radio up against his ear and sat there in a kind of daze, right in the sun.

"He's kinda strange," Connie said.

"Hey, she says you're kinda strange! Kinda strange!" Arnold Friend cried. He pounded on the car to get Ellie's attention. Ellie turned for the first time and Connie saw with shock that he wasn't a kid either—he had a fair, hairless face, cheeks reddened slightly as if the veins grew too close to the surface of his skin, the face of a forty-year-old baby. Connie felt a wave of dizziness rise in her at this sight and she stared at him as if waiting for something to change the shock of the moment, make it all right again. Ellie's lips kept shaping words, mumbling along with the words blasting in his ear.

"Maybe you two better go away," Connie said faintly.

"What? How come?" Arnold Friend cried. "We come out here to take you for a ride. It's Sunday." He had the voice of the man on the radio now. It was the same voice, Connie thought. "Don'tcha know it's Sunday all day and honey, no matter who you were with last night today you're with Arnold Friend and don't you forget it!—Maybe you better step out here," He said, and this last was in a different voice. It was a little flatter, as if the heat was finally getting to him.

"No. I got things to do."

"Hey."

"You two better leave."

"We ain't leaving until you come with us."

"Like hell I am—"

"Connie, don't fool around with me. I mean, I mean, don't fool *around*," he said, shaking his head. He laughed incredulously. He placed his sunglasses on top of his head, carefully, as if he were indeed wearing a wig, and brought the stems down behind his ears. Connie stared at him, another wave of dizziness and fear rising in her so that for a moment he wasn't even in focus but was just a blur, standing there against his gold car, and she had the idea that he had driven up the driveway all right but had come from nowhere before that and belonged nowhere and that everything about him and even about the music that was so familiar to her was only half real.

"If my father comes and sees you—"

"He ain't coming. He's at a barbecue."

"How do you know that?"

"Aunt Tillie's. Right now they're—uh—they're drinking. Sitting around," he said vaguely, squinting as if he were staring all the way to town and over to Aunt Tillie's back yard. Then the vision seemed to get clear and he nodded energetically. "Yeah. Sitting around. There's your sister in a blue dress, huh? And high heels, the poor sad bitch—nothing like you, sweetheart! And your mother's helping some fat woman with the corn, they're cleaning the corn—husking the corn—"

"What fat woman?" Connie cried.

"How do I know what fat woman. I don't know every goddam fat woman in the world!" Arnold Friend laughed.

"Oh, that's Mrs. Hornby. . . . Who invited her?" Connie said. She felt a little light-headed. Her breath was coming quickly.

"She's too fat. I don't like them fat. I like them the way you are, honey," he said, smiling sleepily at her. They stared at each other for a while, through the screen door. He said softly, "Now what you're going to do is this: you're going to come out that door. You're going to sit up front with me and Ellie's going to sit in the back, the hell with Ellie, right? This isn't Ellie's date. You're my date. I'm your lover, honey."

"What? You're crazy—"

"Yes, I'm your lover. You don't know what that is but you will," he said. "I know that too. I know all about you. But look: it's real nice and you couldn't ask for nobody better than me, or more polite. I always keep my word. I'll tell you how it is, I'm always nice at first, the first time. I'll hold you so tight you won't think you have to try to get away or pretend anything because you'll know you can't. And I'll come inside you where it's all secret and you'll give in to me and you'll love me—"

"Shut up! You're crazy!" Connie said. She backed away from the door. She put her hands against her ears as if she'd heard something terrible, something not meant for her. "People don't talk like that, you're crazy," she muttered. Her heart was almost too big now for her chest and its pumping made sweat break out all over her. She looked out to see Arnold Friend pause and then take a step toward the porch lurching. He almost fell. But, like a clever drunken man, he managed to catch his balance. He wobbled in his high boots and grabbed hold of one of the porch posts.

"Honey?" he said. "You still listening?"

"Get the hell out of here!"

"Be nice, honey. Listen."

"I'm going to call the police—"

He wobbled again and out of the side of his mouth came a fast spat curse, an aside not meant for her to hear. But even this "Christ!" sounded forced. Then he began to smile again. She watched this smile come, awkward as if he were smiling from inside a mask. His whole face was a mask, she thought wildly, tanned down onto his throat but then running out as if he had plastered make-up on his face but had forgotten about his throat.

"Honey—? Listen, here's how it is. I always tell the truth and I promise you this: I ain't coming in that house after you."

"You better not! I'm going to call the police if you—if you don't—"

"Honey," he said, talking right through her voice, "honey, I'm not coming in there but you are coming out here. You know why?"

She was panting. The kitchen looked like a place she had never seen before, some room she had run inside but which wasn't good enough, wasn't going to help her. The kitchen window had never had a curtain, after three years, and there were dishes in the sink for her to do—probably—and if you ran your hand across the table you'd probably feel something sticky there.

"You listening, honey? Hey?"

"—going to call the police—"

"Soon as you touch the phone I don't need to keep my promise and can come inside. You won't want that."

She rushed forward and tried to lock the door. Her fingers were shaking. "But why lock it," Arnold Friend said gently, talking right into her face. "It's just a screen door. It's just nothing." One of his boots was at a strange angle, as if his foot wasn't in it. It pointed out to the left, bent at the ankle. "I mean, anybody can break through a screen door and glass and wood and iron or anything else if he needs to, anybody at all and specially Arnold Friend. If the place got lit up with a fire honey you'd come running out into my arms, right into my arms and safe at home— like you knew I was your lover and'd stopped fooling around. I don't mind a nice shy girl but I don't like no fooling around." Part of those words were spoken with a slight rhythmic lilt, and Connie somehow recognized them—the echo of a song from last year, about a girl rushing into her boy friend's arms and coming home again—

Connie stood barefoot on the linoleum floor, staring at him. "What do you want?" she whispered.

"I want you," he said.

"What?"

"Seen you that night and thought, that's the one, yes sir. I never needed to look any more."

"But my father's coming back. He's coming to get me. I had to wash my hair first—" She spoke in a dry, rapid voice, hardly raising it for him to hear.

"No, your daddy is not coming and yes, you had to wash your hair and you washed it for me. It's nice and shining and all for me, I thank you, sweetheart," he said, with a mock bow, but again he almost lost his balance. He had to bend and adjust his boots. Evidently his feet did not go all the way down; the boots must have been stuffed with something so that he would seem taller. Connie stared out at him and behind him Ellie in the car, who seemed to be looking off toward Connie's right, into nothing. This Ellie said, pulling the words out of the air one after another as if he were just discovering them, "You want me to pull out the phone?"

"Shut your mouth and keep it shut," Arnold Friend said, his face red from bending over or maybe from embarrassment because Connie had seen his boots. "This ain't none of your business."

"What—what are you doing? What do you want?" Connie said. "If I call the police they'll get you, they'll arrest you—"

"Promise was not to come in unless you touch that phone, and I'll keep that promise," he said. He resumed his erect position and tried to force his shoulders back. He sounded like a hero in a movie, declaring something important. He spoke too loudly and it was as if he were speaking to someone behind Connie. "I ain't made plans for coming in that house where I don't belong but just for you to come out to me, the way you should. Don't you know who I am?"

"You're crazy," she whispered. She backed away from the door but did not want to go into another part of the house, as if this would give him permission to come through the door. "What do you. . . . You're crazy, you . . ."

"Huh? What're you saying, honey?"

Her eyes darted everywhere in the kitchen. She could not remember what it was, this room.

"This is how it is, honey: you come out and we'll drive away, have a nice ride. But if you don't come out we're gonna wait till your people come home and then they're all going to get it."

"You want that telephone pulled out?" Ellie said. He held the radio away from his ear and grimaced, as if without the radio the air was too much for him.

"I toldja shut up, Ellie," Arnold Friend said, "you're deaf, get a hearing aid, right? Fix yourself up. This little girl's no trouble and's gonna be nice to me, so Ellie keep to yourself, this ain't your date—right? Don't hem in on me. Don't hog. Don't crush. Don't bird dog. Don't trail me," he said in a rapid meaningless voice, as if he were running through all the expressions he'd learned but was no longer sure which one of them was in style, then rushing on to new ones, making them up with his eyes closed, "Don't crawl under my fence, don't squeeze in my chipmunk hole, don't sniff my glue, suck my popsicle, keep your own greasy fingers on yourself!" He shaded his eyes and peered in at Connie, who was backed against the kitchen table. "Don't mind him honey he's just a creep. He's a dope. Right? I'm the boy for you and like I said you come out here nice like a lady and give me your hand, and nobody else gets hurt, I mean, your nice old bald-headed daddy and your mummy and your sister in her high heels. Because listen: why bring them in this?"

"Leave me alone," Connie whispered.

"Hey, you know that old woman down the road, the one with the chickens and stuff—you know her?"

"She's dead!"

"Dead? What? You know her?" Arnold Friend said.

"She's dead—"

"Don't you like her?"

"She's dead—she's—she isn't here any more—"

"But don't you like her, I mean, you got something against her? Some grudge or something?" Then his voice dipped as if he were conscious of a rudeness. He touched the sunglasses perched on top of his head as if to make sure they were still there. "Now you be a good girl."

"What are you going to do?"

"Just two things, or maybe three," Arnold Friend said. "But I promise it won't last long and you'll like me that way you get to like people you're close to. You will. It's all over for you here, so come on out. You don't want your people in any trouble, do you?"

She turned and bumped against a chair or something, hurting her leg, but she ran into the back room and picked up the telephone. Something roared in her ear, a tiny roaring, and she was so sick with fear that she could do nothing but listen to it—the telephone was clammy and very heavy and her fingers groped down to the dial but were too weak to touch it. She began to scream into the phone, into the roaring. She cried out, she cried for her mother, she felt her breath start jerking back and forth in her lungs as if it were something Arnold Friend were stabbing her with again and again with no tenderness. A noisy sorrowful wailing rose all about her and she was locked inside it the way she was locked inside this house.

After a while she could hear again. She was sitting on the floor with her wet back against the wall.

Arnold Friend was saying from the door, "That's a good girl. Put the phone back."

She kicked the phone away from her.

"No, honey. Pick it up. Put it back right."

She picked it up and put it back. The dial tone stopped.

"That's a good girl. Now you come outside."

She was hollow with what had been fear, but what was now just an emptiness. All that screaming had blasted it out of her. She sat, one leg cramped under her, and deep inside her brain was something like a pin-point of light that kept going and would not let her relax. She thought, I'm not going to see my mother again. She thought, I'm not going to sleep in my bed again. Her bright green blouse was all wet.

Arnold Friend said, in a gentle-loud voice that was like a stage voice, "The place where you came from ain't there any more, and where you had in mind to go is cancelled out. This place you are now—inside your daddy's house—is nothing but a cardboard box I can knock down any time. You know that and always did know it. You hear me?"

She thought, I have got to think. I have to know what to do.

"We'll go out to a nice field, out in the country here where it smells so nice and it's sunny," Arnold Friend said. "I'll have my arms tight around you so you won't need to try to get away and I'll show you what love is like, what it does. The hell with this house! It looks solid all right," he said. He ran a fingernail down the screen and the noise did not make Connie shiver, as it would have the day before. "Now put your hand on your heart, honey. Feel that? That feels solid too but we know better, be nice to me, be sweet like you can because what else is there for a girl like you but to be sweet and pretty and give in?—and get away before her people come back?"

She felt her pounding heart. Her hand seemed to enclose it. She thought for the first time in her life that it was nothing that was hers, that be-longed to her, but just a pounding, living thing inside this body that wasn't really hers either.

"You don't want them to get hurt," Arnold Friend went on. "Now get up, honey. Get up all by yourself."

She stood.

"Now turn this way. That's right. Come over here to me—Ellie, put that away, didn't I tell you? You dope. You miserable creepy dope," Arnold Friend said. His words were not angry but only part of an in-cantation. The incantation was kindly. "Now come out through the kitchen to me honey and let's see a smile, try it, you're a brave sweet little girl and now they're eating corn and hotdogs cooked to bursting over an outdoor fire, and they don't know one thing about you and never did and honey you're better than them because not a one of them would have done this for you."

Connie felt the linoleum under her feet; it was cool. She brushed her hair back out of her eyes. Arnold Friend let go of the post tentatively and opened his arms for her, his elbows pointing in toward each other and his wrists limp, to show that this was an embarrassed embrace and a little mocking, he didn't want to make her self-conscious.

She put out her hand against the screen. She watched herself push the door slowly open as if she were safe back somewhere in the other door-way, watching this body and this head of long hair moving out into the sunlight where Arnold Friend waited.

"My sweet little blue-eyed girl," he said, in a half-sung sigh that had nothing to do with her brown eyes but was taken up just the same by the vast sunlit reaches of the land behind him and on all sides of him, so much land that Connie had never seen before and did not recognize except to know that she was going to it.

Poetry

Poem

Anonymous Lyrics

SUMER IS ICUMEN IN

Sing cuccu nu![1] *Sing cuccu!*
Sing cuccu! Sing cuccu nu!

Sumer is icumen in,
  Lhude[2] sing cuccu;
Groweth sed and bloweth med[3]
  And springth the wde[4] nu.
    Sing cuccu!
Awe[5] bleteth after lomb,
  Lhouth[6] after calve cu;
Bulluc sterteth,[7] bucke verteth;[8]   10
  Murie[9] sing cuccu.
    Cuccu, cuccu,
  Wel singes thu, cuccu,
    Ne swik[10] thu naver nu.

[c. 1240]

[1] now
[2] loudly. The final *e* here and elsewhere in Middle English is pronounced as an unaccented neutral vowel (approximately *uh*), so that such words as *wde*, *calve*, and *singes* have two syllables.
[3] mead, meadow   [4] wood   [5] ewe   [6] lows   [7] leaps   [8] breaks wind
[9] merrily   [10] cease

UBI SUNT QUI ANTE NOS FUERUNT?[1]

Were beth they biforen us weren,
  Houndes ladden and havekes beren[2]
And hadden feld and wode?
The riche levedies[3] in hoere bour,
That wereden gold in hoere tressour,[4]
  With hoere brightte rode?[5]

[1] Where Are Those Who Were Before Us?   [2] led hounds and bore hawks
[3] ladies   [4] tresses   [5] complexion

Eten and drounken, and maden hem glad;
Hoere lif was al with gamen ilad; [6]
   Men kneleden hem biforen;
They beren hem wel swithe heye; [7]   10
And, in a twincling of an eye,
   Hoere soules were forloren. [8]

Were is that lawing [9] and that song,
That trayling and that proude gong, [10]
   Tho havekes and tho houndes?
Al that joye is went away,
That wele is comen to "Weylaway!"—
   To manie harde stoundes. [11]

Hoere paradis they nomen [12] here,
And nou they lien in helle ifere; [13]
   The fuir hit brennes [14] hevere. [15]   20
Long is ay, and long is o,
Long is wy, and long is wo;
   Thennes [16] ne cometh they nevere.

[c. 1275]

[6] led	[7] very high	[8] lost	[9] laughing	[10] going	[11] hours, times
[12] took	[13] together	[14] burns	[15] ever	[16] thence	

ADAM LAY I-BOWNDYN

ADAM lay i-bowndyn,
   Bowndyn is a bond;
Fowre thowsand wynter
   Thowt he not to long;
And al was for an appil,
   An appil that he tok,
As clerkes [1] fyndyn wretyn
   In here [2] book.

Ne hadde the appil take ben,
   The appil taken ben,   10
Ne hadde never our lady
   A ben hevene qwen.
Blyssid be the tyme
   That appil take was.
Therefore we mown [3] syngyn
   Deo gracias.

[1] scholars	[2] their	[3] may

BRING US IN GOOD ALE

BRING us in good ale, and bring us in good ale,
For our blesséd Lady's sake, bring us in good ale.

Bring us in no brown bread, for that is made of brane,
Nor bring us in no white bread, for therein is no game;
But bring us in good ale.

Bring us in no beef, for there is many bones;
But bring us in good ale, for that goth down at ones,
And bring us in good ale.

Bring us in no bacon, for that is passing fat;
But bring us in good ale, and give us enough of that,   10
And bring us in good ale.

Bring us in no mutton, for that is often lean,
Nor bring us in no tripes, for they be seldom clean;
But bring us in good ale.

Bring us in no egges, for there are many shelles,
But bring us in good ale, and give us nothing elles;
And bring us in good ale.

Bring us in no butter, for therein are many hairs,
Nor bring us in no pigges flesh, for that will make us boars;
But bring us in good ale.   20

Bring us in no puddings, for therein is all goats' blood,
Nor bring us in no venison, for that is not for our good;
But bring us in good ale.

Bring us in no capon's flesh, for that is often dear,
Nor bring us in duck's flesh, for they slobber in the meer;[1]
But bring us in good ale.

---

[1] pond

I MUST GO WALK THE WOOD SO WILD

I MUST go walk the wood so wild
And wander here and there
In dread and deadly fear,
For where I trusted I am beguiled,
And all for one.

Thus am I banished from my bliss
By craft and false pretense,
Faultless, without offense,
As of return no certain[1] is,
And all for fear of one.   10

My bed shall be under the greenwood tree,
A tuft of brakes[2] under my head,
As one from joy were fled.
Thus from my life day by day I flee,
And all for one.

The running streams shall be my drink,
Acorns shall be my food.
Nothing may do me good,
But when of your beauty I do think,
And all for love of one.   20

[1] certainty   [2] ferns

WESTERN WIND

WESTERN wind, when will thou blow,
    The small rain down can rain?
Christ, if my love were in my arms
And I in my bed again!

Geoffrey Chaucer
1340?–1400
◊
F R O M
THE CANTERBURY TALES
◊
THE GENERAL PROLOGUE

WHAN that Aprille with his shoures soote[1]
    The droghte of March hath perced to the rote,
And bathed every veyne in swich licour[2]
Of which vertu[3] engendred is the flour;
Whan Zephirus eek with his swete breeth
Inspired hath in every holt and heeth

[1] sweet   [2] such moisture   [3] power

The tendre croppes, and the yonge sonne
Hath in the Ram[4] his halve cours yronne,
And smale fowelcs maken melodye,
That slepen al the nyght with open ye   10
(So priketh[5] hem nature in hir corages) :[6]
Than longen folk to goon on pilgrymages,
And palmers for to seken straunge strondes,
To ferne halwes,[7] kouthe[8] in sondry londes ;
And specially from every shires ende
Of Engelond to Caunterbury they wende,
The holy blisful martir[9] for to seke,
That hem hath holpen whan that they were seke.

   Bifel that, in that seson on a day,
In Southwerk at the Tabard as I lay   20
Redy to wenden on my pilgrimage
To Caunterbury with ful devout corage,
At nyght was come into that hostelrye
Wel nyne and twenty in a companye,
Of sondry folk, by aventure[10] yfalle
In felaweshipe, and pilgrymes were they alle,
That toward Caunterbury wolden ryde.
The chambres and the stables weren wyde,
And wel we weren esed atte beste.[11]
And shortly, whan the sonne was to reste,   30
So hadde I spoken with hem everichon,
That I was of hir felaweshipe anon,
And made forward erly for to ryse,
To take our wey there as I yow devyse.[12]

   But natheles, whil I have tyme and space,
Er that I ferther in this tale pace,
Me thynketh it acordant to resoun
To telle yow al the condicioun
Of ech of hem, so as it semed me,
And whiche they weren, and of what degree,   40
And eek in what array that they were inne :
And at a knight than wol I first biginne.

   A Knight ther was, and that a worthy man,
That fro the tyme that he first bigan

---

[4] Aries, the constellation in the Zodiac through which the sun travels from March 21 to April 19
[5] influences   [6] feelings   [7] distant hallowed places ; shrines   [8] known
[9] St. Thomas à Becket   [10] by chance
[11] entertained in the best possible manner   [12] narrate

To riden out, he loved chivalrye,
Trouthe and honour, fredom[13] and curteisye.
Ful worthy was he in his lordes werre,
And ther-to hadde he riden, no man ferre,[14]
As wel in Christendom as in hethenesse,
And ever honoured for his worthynesse.   50
    At Alisaundre he was whan it was wonne.
Ful ofte tyme he hadde the bord bigonne[15]
Aboven alle nacions in Pruce.[16]
In Lettow[17] hadde he reysed and in Ruce,[18]
No Cristen man so ofte of his degree.
In Gernade at the seege eek hadde he be
Of Algezir, and riden in Belmarye.
At Lyeys was he and at Satalye,
Whan they were wonne; and in the Grete See[19]
At many a noble armee hadde he be.   60
At mortal batailles hadde he been fiftene,
And foghten for our feith at Tramyssene[20]
In lystes thries, and ay slayn his foo.
This ilke worthy knight hadde been also
Som-tyme with the lord of Palatye,
Agayn another hethen in Turkye.
    And evere-moore he hadde a sovereyn prys;[21]
And though that he were worthy, he was wys,
And of his port as meke as is a mayde.
He nevere yet no vileynye ne sayde   70
In al his lyf un-to no manner wight.
He was a verray[22] parfit gentil knight.
    But for to tellen yow of his array,
Hise hors were goode, but he was nat gay.[23]
Of fustian he wered a gypoun[24]
Al bismotered with his habergeoun,[25]
For he was late ycome from his viage,
And wente for to doon his pilgrymage.

    With hym ther was his sone, a young Squyer,
A lovere and a lusty bachelor,   80
With lokkes crulle,[26] as they were leyd in presse.
Of twenty yeer of age he was, I gesse.

---

[13] liberality   [14] farther   [15] sat at the head of the table   [16] Prussia
[17] Lithuania   [18] Russia   [19] the Mediterranian
[20] Granada, Algeciras, Benmarin, Lyas, Atalia, Tlemcen—all sites of fourteenth-
century battles
[21] worth   [22] true   [23] showy   [24] vest
[25] stained from contact with his coat of mail   [26] curled

Of his stature he was of evene lengthe,
And wonderly delyvere,[27] and of greet strengthe.
And he hadde been som-tyme in chivachye[28]
In Flaundres, in Artoys, and Picardye,
And born hym wel, as of so litel space,[29]
In hope to stonden in his lady grace.
Embrouded was he, as it were a meede
Al ful of fresshe floures, white and reede.   90
Syngynge he was, or floytynge,[30] al the day;
He was as fressh as is the monthe of May.
Short was his gowne, with sleves longe and wyde.
Wel koude he sitte on hors and faire ryde.
He koude songes make and wel endite,
Juste and eek daunce, and wel purtreye and write,
So hoote he lovede, that by nyghtertale
He slepte namoore than dooth a nyghtyngale.
Curteys he was, lowely, and servysable,
And carf biforn his fader at the table.   100

· · · · · · · · · ·

Ther was also a nonne, a Prioresse,
That of hir smylyng was ful symple and coy;
Hir gretteste ooth was but by Seint Loy;
And she was cleped [31] Madame Eglentyne.
Ful wel she soong the servyce dyvyne,
Entuned in hir nose ful semely,
And Frensh she spak ful faire and fetisly,[32]
After the scole of Stratford-atte-Bowe,[33]
For Frensch of Parys was to hire unknowe.
At mete wel ytaught was she with alle: 110
She let no morsel from hir lippes falle,
Ne wette hir fyngres in hir sauce depe.
Wel koude she carie a morsel and wel kepe
That no drope ne fille up-on hir brest.
In curteisie was set ful muche hir lest.[34]
· Hir over lippe wyped she so clene
That in hir coppe ther was no ferthyng [35] sene
Of grece, whan she dronken hadde hir draughte.
Ful semely after hir mete she raughte. [36]
And sikerly [37] she was of greet desport,[38]   120
And ful plesaunt, and amyable of port,

[27] agile   [28] cavalry attacks   [29] considering his short apprenticeship
[30] playing the flute   [31] called   [32] fastidiously
[33] the inferior French of an English nunnery
[34] She greatly esteemed good deportment.   [35] bit   [36] reached
[37] certainly   [38] good humor

And peyned hire to countrefete cheere
Of court,[39] and to been estatlich of manere,
And to been holden digne of reverence.
  But, for to speken of hir conscience,
She was so charitable and so pitous
She wolde wepe, if that she saw a mous
Caught in a trappe, if it were deed or bledde.
Of smale houndes hadde she, that she fedde
With rosted flessh, or mylk and wastel breed.   130
But soore wept she if oon of hem were deed,
Or if men[40] smoot it with a yerde[41] smerte;[42]
And al was conscience and tendre herte.
  Ful semely hir wympel pynched[43] was;
Hir nose tretys,[44] hir eyen greye as glas,
Hir mouth ful smal, and ther-to softe and reed;
But sikerly she hadde a fair forheed:
It was almoost a spanne brood, I trowe;
For, hardily, she was nat undergrowe.
Ful fetys was hir cloke, as I was war.   140
Of smal coral aboute hir arm she bar
A peyre of bedes, gauded al with grene,
And there-on heng a brooch of gold ful shene,
On which ther was first writ a crowned A,
And after *Amor vincit omnia.*[45]
  Another Nonne with hire hadde she,
That was hir chapeleyne, and preestes thre.

. . . .

  A good Wyf was ther of biside Bathe,
But she was somdel deef, and that was scathe.[46]
  Of clooth makyng she hadde swich an haunt,[47]   150
She passed hem of Ypres and of Gaunt.
In al the parisshe wyf ne was ther noon
That to the offrynge bifore hire sholde goon;
And if ther dide, certeyn so wrooth was she,
That she was out of alle charitee.
Hir coverchiefs ful fyne were of ground;[48]
I dorste swere they weyeden ten pound
That on a Sonday weren up-on hir heed.
Hir hosen weren of fyn scarlet reed,
Ful streite yteyd, and shoes ful moyste and newe.   160
Boold was hir face, and fair, and reed of hewe.

---

[39] took pains to imitate courtly manners   [40] one   [41] stick   [42] smartly
[43] pleated   [44] well-formed   [45] love conquers all   [46] a pity   [47] skill
[48] texture

She was a worthy womman al hir lyve;
Housbondes at chirche dore she hadde fyve,
With-outen oother[49] compaignye in youthe—
But ther-of nedeth nat to speke as nouthe.[50]
    And thries hadde she been at Jerusalem;
She hadde passed many a straunge strem;
At Rome she hadde been, and at Boloyne,
In Galice at Seint Jame, and at Coloyne.
She koude muche of wandrynge by the weye.   170
Gat tothed[51] was she, soothly for to seye.
    Upon an amblere esily she sat,
Ywympled wel, and on hir heed an hat
As brood as is a bokeler or a targe;
A foot mantel aboute hir hipes large,
And on hir feet a peyre of spores sharpe.
In felawshipe wel koude she laughe and carpe.[52]
Of remedies of love she knew par chaunce,
For she koude of that art the olde daunce.

.   .   .   .

    The Miller was a stout carl[53] for the nones,   180
Ful big he was of brawn, and eek of bones;
That proved wel, for over-al ther he cam,
At wrastlynge he wolde have alwey the ram.
He was short sholdred, brood, a thikke knarre;[54]
Ther was no dore that he nolde heve of harre,[55]
Or breke it at a rennyng, with his heed.
His berd as any sowe or fox was reed,
And ther-to brood as though it were a spade.
Upon the cop[56] right of his nose he hade
A werte, and ther-on stood a tuft of herys,   190
Reed as the bristles of a sowes erys;
His nosethirles[57] blake were and wyde
A swerd and a bokeler bar he by his syde.
His mouth as greet was as a greet fourneys.
He was a jangler[58] and a goliardeys,[59]
And that was moost of synne and harlotries.
Wel koude he stelen corn and tollen thries;[60]
And yet he hadde a thombe of gold, pardee.
A whit cote and a blew hood wered hee.

---

[49] without counting others   [50] at present
[51] with teeth widely spaced; hence supposedly amorous   [52] talk
[53] churl; fellow   [54] gnarled fellow   [55] off hinge   [56] top   [57] nostrils
[58] prattler   [59] coarse jokester   [60] charge three prices for grinding grain

A baggepipe wel koude he blowe and sowne,   200
And therwithal he broghte us out of towne.

[c. 1387]

Anonymous Ballads

LORD RANDAL

"O WHERE hae ye been, Lord Randal, my son?
O where hae ye been, my handsome young man?"
"I hae been to the wild wood; mother, make my bed soon,
For I'm weary wi hunting, and fain wald lie down."

"Where gat ye your dinner, Lord Randal, my son?
Where gat ye your dinner, my handsome young man?"
"I dined wi my true-love; mother, make my bed soon,
For I'm weary wi hunting and fain wald lie down."

"What get ye to your dinner, Lord Randal, my son?
What gat ye to your dinner, my handsome young man?"   10
"I gat eels boiled in broo; mother, make my bed soon,
For I'm weary wi hunting, and fain wald lie down."

"What became of your bloodhounds, Lord Randal, my son?
What became of your bloodhounds, my handsome young man?"
"O they swelld and they died; mother, make my bed soon,
For I'm weary wi hunting and fain wald lie down."

"O I fear ye are poisond, Lord Randal, my son!
O I fear ye are poisond, my handsome young man!"
"O yes! I am poisond; mother, make my bed soon,
For I'm sick at the heart, and I fain wald lie down."   20

THE WIFE OF USHER'S WELL

THERE lived a wife at Usher's Well,
    And a wealthy wife was she;
She had three stout and stalwart sons,
    And sent them o'er the sea.

They hadna been a week from her,
    A week but barely ane,
Whan word came to the carlin wife[1]
    That her three sons were gane.

_____
[1] old woman

They hadna been a week from her,
    A week but barely three,   10
Whan word came to the carlin wife
    That her sons she'd never see.

"I wish the wind may never cease,
    Nor fashes[2] in the flood,
Till my three sons come hame to me,
    In earthly flesh and blood."

It fell about the Martinmass,
    When nights are lang and mirk,
The carlin wife's three sons came hame,
    And their hats were o the birk.[3]   20

It neither grew in syke[4] nor ditch,
    Not yet in ony sheugh;[5]
But at the gates o Paradise,
    That birk grew fair eneugh.

"Blow up the fire, my maidens,
    Bring water from the well;
For a' my house shall feast this night,
    Since my three sons are well."

And she has made to them a bed,
    She's made it large and wide,   30
And she's taen her mantle her about,
    Sat down at the bed-side.

Up then crew the red, red cock,
    And up and crew the gray;
The eldest to the youngest said,
    " 'Tis time we were away."

The cock he hadna crawd but once,
    And clappd his wings at a',
When the youngest to the eldest said,
    "Brother, we must awa.   40

"The cock doth craw, the day doth daw,
    The channerin[6] worm doth chide;
Gin we be mist out o our place,
    A sair pain we maun bide.

---

[2] troubles   [3] birch (bark)   [4] gully   [5] trench   [6] devouring

"Fare ye weel, my mother dear!
    Fareweel to barn and byre!
And fare ye weel, the bonny lass
    That kindles my mother's fire!"

JOHNNY, I HARDLY KNEW YE

WHILE going the road to sweet Athy,
        Hurroo! hurroo!
While going the road to sweet Athy,
        Hurroo! hurroo!
While going the road to sweet Athy,
A stick in my hand and a drop in my eye,
A doleful damsel I heard cry:
    "Och, Johnny, I hardly knew ye!
        With drums and guns, and guns and drums,
        The enemy nearly slew ye;   10
        My darling dear, you look so queer,
        Och, Johnny, I hardly knew ye!

"Where are your eyes that looked so mild?
        Hurroo! hurroo!
Where are your eyes that looked so mild?
        Hurroo! hurroo!
Where are your eyes that looked so mild?
When my poor heart you first beguiled?
Why did you run from me and the child?
    Och, Johnny, I hardly knew ye!   20
        With drums, etc.

"Where are the legs with which you run?
        Hurroo! hurroo!
Where are the legs with which you run?
        Hurroo! hurroo!
Where are the legs with which you run?
When first you went to carry a gun?
Indeed, your dancing days are done;
    Och, Johnny, I hardly knew ye!
        With drums, etc.   30

"It grieved my heart to see you sail,
        Hurroo! hurroo!
It grieved my heart to see you sail,
        Hurroo! hurroo!

It grieved my heart to see you sail,
Though from my heart you took leg-bail;
Like a cod you're doubled up head and tail,
   Och, Johnny, I hardly knew ye!
     With drums, etc.

"You haven't an arm and you haven't a leg,   40
    Hurroo! hurroo!
You haven't an arm and you haven't a leg,
    Hurroo! hurroo!
You haven't an arm and you haven't a leg,
You're an eyeless, noseless, chickenless egg;
You'll have to be put with a bowl to beg:
   Och, Johnny, I hardly knew ye!
     With drums, etc.

"I'm happy for to see you home,
    Hurroo! hurroo!   50
I'm happy for to see you home,
    Hurroo! hurroo!
I'm happy for to see you home,
All from the Island of Sulloon;
So low in flesh, so high in bone;
   Och, Johnny, I hardly knew ye!
     With drums, etc.

"But sad it is to see you so,
    Hurroo! hurroo!
But sad it is to see you so,   60
    Hurroo! hurroo!
But sad it is to see you so,
And to think of you now as an object of woe,
Your Peggy'll still keep ye on as her beau;
   Och, Johnny, I hardly knew ye!
    With drums and guns, and guns and drums,
    The enemy nearly slew ye;
    My darling dear, you look so queer,
     Och, Johnny, I hardly knew ye!"

Sir Thomas Wyatt
1503?–1542

THE LONG LOVE

THE long love that in my thought doth harbor,
And in mine heart doth keep his residence,
Into my face presseth with bold pretense,
And therein campeth, spreading his banner.
She that me learneth to love and suffer,
And wills that my trust and lust's negligence
Be reined by reason, shame, and reverence,
With his hardiness taketh displeasure.
Wherewithal, unto the heart's forest he fleeth,
Leaving his enterprise with pain and cry;   10
And there him hideth, and not appeareth.
What may I do when my master feareth
But in the field with him to live and die?
For good is the life ending faithfully.

[1557]

MY GALLEY

MY GALLEY, chargéd with forgetfulness,
Thorough sharp seas in winter nights doth pass
'Tween rock and rock; and eke mine enemy, alas!
That is my Lord, steereth with cruelness;
And every oar a thought in readiness,
As though that death were light in such a case.
An endless wind doth tear the sail apace
Of forcéd sighs, and trusty fearfulness;
A rain of tears, a cloud of dark disdain,
Hath done the wearéd cords great hinderance,   10
Wreathéd with error and eke with ignorance.
The stars be hid that led me to this pain.
Drownéd is reason that should me comfort,
And I remain despairing of the port.

[1557]

WHOSO LIST TO HUNT

Whoso list to hunt, I know where is an hind,[1]
  But as for me—alas, I may no more.
The vain travail hath wearied me so sore,
I am of them that farthest come behind.
Yet may I, by no means, my wearied mind
Draw from the deer; but as she fleeth afore,
Fainting I follow. I leave off therefore,
Since in a net I seek to hold the wind.
Who list her hunt, I put him out of doubt,
As well as I, may spend his time in vain.   10
And graven with diamonds in letters plain
There is written her fair neck round about:
Noli me tangere,[2] for Caesar's I am,
And wild for to hold, though I seem tame.

[1557]

_____

[1] doe; usually supposed to refer to Anne Boleyn.   [2] touch me not

MY LUTE, AWAKE!

My lute, awake! perform the last
  Labor that thou and I shall waste,
And end that I have now begun;
For when this song is sung and past,
  My lute, be still, for I have done.

As to be heard where ear is none,
As lead to grave in marble stone,
  My song may pierce her heart as soon.
Should we then sigh, or sing, or moan?
  No, no, my lute, for I have done.   10

The rocks do not so cruelly
Repulse the waves continually,
  As she my suit and affection;
So that I am past remedy,
  Whereby my lute and I have done.

Proud of the spoil that thou hast got
Of simple hearts thorough love's shot,
  By whom, unkind, thou hast them won,
Think not he hath his bow forgot,
  Although my lute and I have done.   20

Vengeance shall fall on thy disdain,
That makest but game on earnest pain;
  Think not alone under the sun
Unquit[1] to cause thy lovers plain,[2]
  Although my lute and I have done.

Perchance thee lie withered and old,
The winter nights that are so cold,
  Plaining in vain unto the moon;
Thy wishes then dare not be told.
  Care then who list, for I have done.   30

And then may chance thee to repent
The time that thou hast lost and spent
  To cause thy lovers sigh and swoon;
Then shalt thou know beauty but lent,
  And wish and want as I have done.

Now cease, my lute! this is the last
Labor that thou and I shall waste,
  And ended is that we begun;
Now is this song both sung and past.
  My lute, be still, for I have done.   40
                                     [1557]

[1] with impunity   [2] (to) complain, i.e., give expression to grief

THEY FLEE FROM ME

THEY flee from me, that sometime did me seek,
  With naked foot, stalking in my chamber:
I have seen them gentle, tame, and meek,
That now are wild, and do not remember
That sometime they put themselves in danger
To take bread at my hand; and now they range,
Busily seeking with a continual change.

Thankèd be fortune, it hath been otherwise
Twenty times better; but once, in special,
In thin array, after a pleasant guise,   10
When her loose gown from her shoulders did fall,
And she me caught in her arms long and small,
Therewithal sweetly did me kiss,
And softly said, "Dear heart, how like you this?"

It was no dream; I lay broad waking.
But all is turned, thorough my gentleness,
Into a strange fashion of forsaking;
And I have leave to go of her goodness,
And she also to use new-fangleness.
But since that I so kindely am servéd,   20
I would fain know what she hath deservéd.

[1557]

Henry Howard, Earl of Surrey
1517?–1547
LOVE THAT DOTH REIGN

Love, that doth reign and live within my thought,
And built his seat within my captive breast,
Clad in the arms wherein with me he fought,
Oft in my face he doth his banner rest.
But she that taught me love and suffer pain,
My doubtful hope and eke my hot desire
With shamefast look to shadow and refrain,
Her smiling grace converteth straight to ire.
And coward Love, then, to the heart apace
Takerth his flight, where he doth lurk and plain,[1]   10
His purpose lost, and dare not show his face.
For my lord's guilt thus faultless bide I pain,
Yet from my lord shall not my foot remove:
Sweet is the death that taketh end by love.

[1557]

[1] complain; express grief

WYATT RESTETH HERE

Wyatt resteth here, that quick[1] could never rest;
Whose heavenly gifts increaséd by disdain,[2]
And virtue sank the deeper in his breast;
Such profit he of envy could obtain.
A head where wisdom mysteries did frame;
Whose hammers beat still in that lively brain
As on a stithy,[3] where some work of fame
Was daily wrought, to turn to Britain's gain.

[1] alive   [2] humility   [3] forge

A visage stern and mild; where both did grow,
Vice to condemn, in virtues to rejoice;   10
Amid great storms, whom grace assuréd so,
To live upright, and smile at fortune's choice.
A hand that taught what might be said in rhyme;
That reft Chaucer the glory of his wit;
A mark, the which—unperfited,[4] for time—
Some may approach, but never none shall hit.
A tongue that served in foreign realms his king;
Whose courteous talk to virtue did enflame
Each noble heart; a worthy guide to bring
Our English youth, by travail, unto fame.   20
An eye whose judgment no affect[5] could blind,
Friends to allure, and foes to reconcile;
Whose piercing look did represent a mind
With virtue fraught, reposéd, void of guile.
A heart where dread yet never so impressed
To hide the thought that might the truth advance;
In neither fortune,[6] nor so repressed,
To swell in wealth, nor yield unto mischance.
A valiant corpse,[7] where force and beauty met,
Happy, alas! too happy, but for foes,   30
Lived, and ran the race that nature set;
Of manhood's shape, where she the mold did lose.
But to the heavens that simple soul is fled;
Which left with such as covet Christ to know
Witness of faith that never shall be dead;
Sent for our health, but not receivéd so.
Thus for our guilt, this jewel have we lost;
The earth his bones, the heavens possess his ghost.

[1557]

[4] unperfected   [5] emotion   [6] lifted   [7] (living) body

Edmund Spenser
1552 1599

◇

F R O M

AMORETTI

◇

XIX

THE merry Cuckow, messenger of Spring,
His trompet shrill hath thrise already sounded :
That warnes al lovers wayt upon their king,
Who now is comming forth with girland crounéd.
With noyse whereof the quyre of Byrds resounded
Their anthemes sweet, devizéd of Loves prayse,
That all the woods theyr ecchoes back rebounded,
As if they knew the meaning of their layes.
But mongst them all, which did Loves honor rayse,
No word was heard of her that most it ought,   10
But she his precept proudly disobayes,
And doth his ydle message set at nought.
Therefore, O Love, unlesse she turne to thee,
Ere Cuckow end, let her a rebell be.

XXVI

SWEET is the Rose, but growes upon a brere ;
Sweet is the Junipere, but sharpe his bough ;
Sweet is the Eglantine, but pricketh nere ;
Sweet is the firbloome, but his braunches rough.
Sweet is the Cypresse, but his rynd is tough,
Sweet is the nut, but bitter is his pill ;
Sweet is the broome-flowre, but yet sowre enough ;
And sweet is Moly, but his root is ill.
So every sweet with soure is tempred still,
That maketh it be coveted the more :   10
For easie things that may be got at will,
Most sorts of men doe set but little store.
Why then should I accoumpt of little paine,
That endlesse pleasure shall unto me gaine.

XXXIV

LYKE as a ship that through the Ocean wyde,
By conduct of some star doth make her way,
Whenas a storme hath dimd her trusty guyde
Out of her course doth wander far astray.

So I whose star, that wont with her bright ray,
Me to direct, with cloudes is overcast,
Doe wander now in darknesse and dismay,
Through hidden perils round about me plast.
Yet hope I well, that when this storme is past
My *Helice* the lodestar of my lyfe   10
Will shine again, and looke on me at last,
With lovely light to clear my cloudy grief.
Till then I wander carefull comfortlesse,
In secret sorrow and sad pensivenesse.

LXXV

ONE day I wrote her name upon the strand,
But came the waves and washéd it away :
Agayne I wrote it with a second hand,
But came the tyde, and made my paynes his pray.
Vayne man, sayd she, that doest in vaine assay,
A mortell thing so to immortalize,
For I my selve shall lyke to this decay,
And eek my name bee wypéd out lykewize.
Not so, (quod I) let baser things devize
To dy in dust, but you shall live by fame :   10
My verse your vertues rare shall eternize,
And in the hevens wryte your glorious name.
Where whenas death shall all the world subdew,
Our love shall live, and later life renew.

[1595]

EPITHALAMION[1]

YE learnéd sisters, which have oftentimes
Beene to me ayding, others to adorne,
Whom ye thought worthy of your gracefull rymes,
That even the greatest did not greatly scorne
To heare theyr names sung in your simple layes,
    But joyéd in theyr praise ;
And when ye list your owne mishaps to mourne,
Which death, or love, or fortunes wreck did rayse,
Your string could soone to sadder tenor turne,
And teach the woods and waters to lament   10
    Your dolefull dreriment :
Now lay those sorrowful complaints aside,

---

[1] a song in celebration of a wedding

And having all your heads with girland crownd,
Helpe me mine owne loves prayses to resound;
Ne let the same of any be envide:
So Orpheus did for his owne bride:
So I unto my selfe alone will sing;
The woods shall to me answer, and my eccho ring.

Early, before the worlds light giving lampe
His golden beame upon the hils doth spred,   20
Having disperst the nights unchearefull dampe,
Doe ye awake, and, with fresh lustyhed,
Go to the bowre of my belovéd love,
    My truest turtle dove:
Bid her awake; for Hymen is awake,
And long since ready forth his maske to move,
With his bright tead[2] that flames with many a flake,
And many a bachelor to waite on him,
    In theyr fresh garments trim.
Bid her awake therefore, and soone her dight,   30
For lo! the wishéd day is come at last,
That shall, for all the paynes and sorrowes past,
Pay to her usury of long delight:
    And whylest she doth her dight,[3]
Doe ye to her of joy and solace sing,
That all the woods may answer, and your eccho ring.

Bring with you all the nymphes that you can heare,
Both of the rivers and the forrests greene,
And of the sea that neighbours to her neare,
Al with gay girlands goodly wel beseene.   40
And let them also with them bring in hand
    Another gay girland,
For my fayre love, of lillyes and of roses,
Bound truelove wize with a blew silke riband.
And let them make great store of bridale poses,
And let them eeke bring store of other flowers,
    To deck the bridale bowers.
And let the ground whereas her foot shall tread,
For feare the stones her tender foot should wrong,
Be strewed with fragrant flowers all along,   50
And diapred[4] lyke the discolored mead.
Which done, doe at her chamber dore awayt,
    For she will waken strayt;

---

[2] torch   [3] dress (v.)   [4] decorated

The whiles doe ye this song unto her sing,
The woods shall to you answer, and your eccho ring.

Ye nymphes of Mulla, which with carefull heed
The silver scaly trouts doe tend full well,
And greedy pikes which use therein to feed,
(Those trouts and pikes all others doo excel)
And ye likewise which keepe the rushy lake,   60
    Where none doo fishes take,
Bynde up the locks the which hang scattered light,
And in his waters, which your mirror make,
Behold your faces as the christall bright,
That when you come whereas my love doth lie,
    No blemish she may spie.
And eke ye lightfoot mayds which keepe the dere
That on the hoary mountayne use to towre,
And the wylde wolves, which seeke them to devoure,
With your steele darts doo chace from coming neer,   70
    Be also present heere,
To helpe to decke her, and to help to sing,
That all the woods may answer, and your eccho ring.

Wake now, my love, awake! for it is time:
The rosy Morne long since left Tithonés bed,
All ready to her silver coche to clyme,
And Phœbus gins to shew his glorious hed.
Hark how the cheerefull birds do chaunt theyr laies,
    And caroll of loves praise!
The merry larke hir mattins sings aloft,   80
The thrush replyes, the mavis descant playes,
The ouzell[5] shrills, the ruddock[6] warbles soft,
So goodly all agree, with sweet consent,
    To this dayes merriment.
Ah! my deere love, why doe ye sleepe thus long,
When meeter were that ye should now awake,
T'awayt the comming of your joyous make,
And hearken to the birds love-learnéd song,
    The deawy leaves among?
For they of joy and pleasance to you sing,   90
That all the woods them answer, and theyr eccho ring.

My love is now awake out of her dreame,
And her fayre eyes, like stars that dimméd were
With darksome cloud, now shew theyr goodly beams
More bright then Hesperus his head doth rere.

---

[5] blackbird   [6] robin

Come now, ye damzels, daughters of delight,
   Helpe quickly to her dight.
But first come ye, fayre Houres, which were begot,
In Joves sweet paradice, ot Day and Night,
Which doe the seasons of the year allot,   100
And al that ever in this world is fayre
   Do make and still repayre.
And ye three handmayds of the Cyprian Queene,
The which doe still adorne her beauties pride,
Helpe to addorne my beautifullest bride :
And as ye her array, still throw betweene
   Some graces to be seene :
And as ye use to Venus, to her sing,
The whiles the woods shal answer, and your eccho ring.

Now is my love all ready forth to come :   110
Let all the virgins therefore well awayt,
And ye fresh boyes, that tend upon her groome,
Prepare your selves, for he is comming strayt.
Set all your things in seemely good aray,
   Fit for so joyfull day,
The joyfulst day that ever sunne did see.
Faire Sun, shew forth thy favourable ray,
And let thy lifull heat not fervent be,
For feare of burning her sunshyny face,
   Her beauty to disgrace.   120
O fayrest Phœbus, father of the Muse,
If ever I did honour thee aright,
Or sing the thing that mote thy mind delight,
Doe not thy servants simple boone refuse,
But let this day, let this one day be myne,
   Let all the rest be thine.
Then I thy soverayne prayses loud wil sing,
That all the woods shal answer, and theyr eccho ring.

Hark how the minstels gin to shrill aloud
Their merry musick that resounds from far,   130
The pipe, the tabor, and the trembling croud,[7]
That well agree withouten breach or jar.
But most of all the damzels doe delite,
   When they their tymbrels smyte,
And thereunto doe daunce and carrol sweet,
That all the sences they doe ravish quite,
The whyles the boyes run up and downe the street,

[7] an instrument resembling a violin

Crying aloud with strong confuséd noyce,
   As if it were one voyce.
"Hymen, Iö Hymen, Hymen," they do shout,   140
That even to the heavens theyr shouting shrill
Doth reach, and all the firmament doth fill;
To which the people, standing all about,
As in approvance doe thereto applaud,
   And loud advaunce her laud,
And evermore they "Hymen, Hymen" sing,
That al the woods them answer, and theyr eccho ring.

Loe! where she comes along with portly pace,
Lyke Phœbe, from her chamber of the east,
Arysing forth to run her mighty race,   150
Clad all in white, that seemes a virgin best.
So well it her beseemes, that ye would weene
   Some angell she had beene.
Her long loose yellow locks lyke golden wyre,
Sprinckled with perle, and perling flowres atweene,
Doe lyke a golden mantle her attyre,
And being crownéd with a girland greene,
   Seeme lyke some mayden queene.
Her modest eyes, abashéd to behold
So many gazers as on her do stare,   160
Upon the lowly ground affixéd are;
Ne dare lift up her countenance too bold,
But blush to heare her prayses sung so loud,
   So farre from being proud.
Nathlesse doe ye still loud her prayses sing,
That all the woods may answer, and your eccho ring.

Tell me, ye merchants daughters, did ye see
So fayre a creature in your towne before,
So sweet, so lovely, and so mild as she,
Adorned with beautyes grace and vertues store?   170
Her goodly eyes lyke saphyres shining bright,
Her forehead yvory white,
Her cheekes lyke apples which the sun hath rudded,
Her lips lyke cherryes charming men to byte,
Her breast like to a bowle of creame uncrudded,[8]
   Her paps lyke lyllies budded,
Her snowie necke lyk to a marble towre,
And all her body like a pallace fayre,

---

[8] not curdled

Ascending uppe, with many a stately stayre,
To honors seat and chastities sweet bowre.   180
Why stand ye still, ye virgins, in amaze,
　　Upon her so to gaze,
Whiles ye forget your former lay to sing,
To which the woods did answer, and your eccho ring.

But if ye saw that which no eyes can see,
The inward beauty of her lively spright,[9]
Garnisht with heavenly guifts of high degree,
Much more then would ye wonder at that sight,
And stand astonisht lyke to those which red[10]
　　Medusaes mazeful hed.   190
There dwels sweet Love and constant Chastity,
Unspotted Fayth, and comely Womanhood,
Regard of Honour, and mild Modesty;
There Vertue raynes as queene in royal throne,
　　And giveth lawes alone,
The which the base affections doe obay,
And yeeld theyr services unto her will;
Ne thought of thing uncomely ever may
Thereto approch to tempt her mind to ill.
Had ye once seene these her celestial threasures,   200
　　And unrevealéd pleasures,
Then would ye wonder, and her prayses sing,
That al the woods should answer, and your eccho ring.

Open the temple gates unto my love,
Open them wide that she may enter in,
And all the postes adorne as doth behove,
And all the pillours deck with girlands trim,
For to receyve this saynt with honour dew,
　　That commeth in to you.
With trembling steps and humble reverence,   210
She commeth in before th' Almighties view:
Of her, ye virgins, learne obedience,
When so ye come into those holy places,
　　To humble your proud faces.
Bring her up to th' high altar, that she may
The sacred ceremonies there partake,
The which do endlesse matrimony make;
And let the roring organs loudly play
The praises of the Lord in lively notes,
　　The whiles with hollow throates

[9] spirit　　[10] saw

The choristers the joyous antheme sing,
That al the woods may answere, and their eccho ring.

Behold, whiles she before the altar stands,
Hearing the holy priest that to her speakes,
And blesseth her with his two happy hands,
How the red roses flush up in her cheekes,
And the pure snow with goodly vermill[11] stayne,
   Like crimson dyde in grayne:[12]
That even th' angels, which continually
About the sacred altare doe remaine,   230
Forget their service and about her fly,
Ofte peeping in her face, that seemes more fayre,
   The more they on it stare.
But her sad eyes, still fastened on the ground,
Are governéd with goodly modesty,
That suffers not one looke to glaunce awry,
Which may let in a little thought unsownd.
Why blush ye, love, to give to me your hand,
   The pledge of all our band?
Sing, ye sweet angels, Alleluya sing,   240
That all the woods may answere, and your eccho ring.

Now al is done; bring home the bride againe,
Bring home the triumph of our victory,
Bring home with you the glory of her gaine,
With joyance bring her and with jollity.
Never had man more joyfull day then this,
   Whom heaven would heape with blis.
Make feast therefore now all this live long day;
This day for ever to me holy is;
Poure out the wine without restraint or stay,   250
Poure not by cups, but by the belly full,
   Poure out to all that wull,
And sprinkle all the postes and wals with wine,
That they may sweat, and drunken be withall.
Crowne ye God Bacchus with a coronall.
And Hymen also crowne with wreathes of vine;
And let the Graces daunce unto the rest,
   For they can doo it best:
The whiles the maydens doe theyr carroll sing,
The which the woods shal answer, and theyr eccho ring,   260

Ring ye the bels, ye yong men of the towne,
And leave your wonted labors for this day:

---

[11] bright red   [12] in a fast color

This day is holy; doe ye write it downe,
That ye for ever it remember may.
This day the sunne is in his chiefest hight,
   With Barnaby [13] the bright,
From whence declining daily by degrees,
He somewhat loseth of his heat and light,
When once the Crab behind his back he sees.
But for this time it ill ordainéd was,   270
To chose the longest day in all the yeare,
And shortest night, when longest fitter weare:
Yet never day so long, but late would passe.
Ring ye the bels, to make it weare away,
   And bonefires make all day,
And daunce about them, and about them sing:
That all the woods may answer, and your eccho ring.

Ah! when will this long weary day have end,
And lende me leave to come unto my love?
How slowly do the houres theyr numbers spend!   280
How slowly does sad Time his feathers move!
Hast thee, O fayrest planet, to thy home
   Within the westerne foame:
Thy tyréd steedes long since have need of rest.
Long though it be, at last I see it gloome,
And the bright evening star with golden creast
   Appeare out of the east.
Fayre childe of beauty, glorious lampe of love,
That all the host of heaven in rankes doost lead,
And guydest lovers through the nightes dread,   290
How chearefully thou lookest from above,
And seemst to laugh atweene thy twinkling light,
   As joying in the sight
Of these glad many, which for joy doe sing,
That all the woods them answer, and their eccho ring!

Now ceasse, ye damsels, your delights forepast;
Enough is it that all the day was youres:
Now day is doen, and night is nighing fast:
Now bring the bryde into the brydall boures
The night is come, now soone her disaray,   300
   And in her bed her lay;

[13] St. Barnabas's Day was July 11, the longest day of the year in the old-style calendar.

Lay her in lillies and in violets,
And silken courteins over her display,
And odoured sheetes, and Arras coverlets.
Behold how goodly my faire love does ly,
    In proud humility!
Like unto Maia, when as Jove her tooke
In Tempe, lying on the flowry gras,
Twixt sleepe and wake, after she weary was
With bathing in the Acidalian brooke.   310
Now it is night, ye damsels may be gon,
    And leave my love alone.
And leave likwise your former lay to sing:
The woods no more shal answere, nor your echo ring.

And all my cares, which cruell Love collected,
Hast sumd in one, and cancelléd for aye:
Spread thy broad wing over my love and me,
    That no man may us see,   320
And in thy sable mantle us enwrap,
From feare of perrill and foule horror free.
Let no false treason seeke us to entrap,
Nor any dread disquiet once annoy
    The safety of our joy:
But let the night be calme and quietsome,
Without tempestuous storms or sad afray:
Lyke as when Jove with fayre Alcmena lay,
When he begot the great Tirynthian groome:
Or lyke as when he with thy selfe did lie,   330
    And begot Majesty.
And let the mayds and yongmen cease to sing:
Ne let the woods them answer, nor theyr eccho ring.

Let no lamenting cryes, nor dolefull teares,
Be heard all night within, nor yet without:
Ne let false whispers, breeding hidden feares,
Breake gentle sleepe with misconceivéd dout.
Let no deluding dreames, nor dreadful sights,
    Make sudden sad affrights;
Ne let house-fyres, nor lightnings helplesse harmes,   340
Ne let the Pouke, nor other evill sprights,
Ne let mischivous witches with theyr charmes,
Ne let hob goblins, names whose sense we see not,
    Fray us with things that be not.
Let not the shriech oule, nor the storke be heard,
Nor the night raven that still deadly yels,
Nor damnéd ghosts cald up with mighty spels,

Nor griesly vultures make us once affeard :
Ne let th' unpleasant quyre of frogs still croking
   Make us to wish theyr choking.
Let none of these theyr drery accents sing ;   350
Ne let the woods them answer, nor theyr eccho ring.

But let stil Silence trew night watches keepe,
That sacred Peace may in assurance rayne,
And tymely Sleep, when it is tyme to sleepe,
May poure his limbs forth on your pleasant playne,
The whiles an hundred little wingéd loves,
   Like divers fethered doves,
Shall fly and flutter round about our bed,
And in the secret darke, that none reproves,   360
Their prety stealthes shall worke, and snares shal spread
To filch away sweet snatches of delight,
   Conceald through covert night.
Ye sonnes of Venus, play your sports at will :
For greedy Pleasure, careless of your toyes,
Thinks more upon her paradise of joyes,
Then what ye do, albe it good or ill.
All night therefore attend your merry play,
   For it will soone be day :
Now none doth hinder you, that say or sing,   370
Ne will the woods now answer, nor your eccho ring.

Who is the same which at my window peepes ?
Or whose is that faire face that shines so bright ?
Is it not Cinthia, she that never sleepes,
But walkes about high heaven al the night ?
O fayrest goddesse, do thou not envy
   My love with me to spy :
For thou likewise didst love, though now unthought,
And for a fleece of woll, which privily
The Latmian shephard once unto thee brought,   380
   His pleasures with thee wrought.
Therefore to us be favorable now ;
And sith of wemens labours thou hast charge,
And generation goodly dost enlarge,
Encline thy will t' effect our wishful vow,
And the chast wombe informe with timely seed,
   That may our comfort breed :
Till which we cease our hopefull hap to sing,
Ne let the woods us answere, nor our eccho ring.

And thou, great Juno, which with awful might   390
The lawes of wedlock still dost patronize,
And the religion of the faith first plight
With sacred rites hast taught to solemnize,
And eeke for comfort often calléd art
    Of women in their smart,
Eternally bind thou this lovely band,
And all thy blessings unto us impart,
And thou, glad Genius, in whose gentle hand
The bridal bowre and geniall bed remaine,
    Without blemish or staine,   400
And the sweet pleasures of theyr loves delight
With secret ayde doest succour and supply,
Till they bring forth the fruitfull progeny,
Send us the timely fruit of this same night.
And thou, fayre Hebe, and thou, Hymen free,
    Grant that it may so be.
Til which we cease your further prayse to sing,
Ne any woods shal answer, nor your eccho ring.

And ye high heavens, the temple of the gods,
In which a thousand torches flaming bright   410
Doe burne, that to us wretched earthly clods
In dreadful darknesse lend desiréd light,
And all ye powers which in the same remayne,
    More then we men can fayne,
Poure out youre blessing on us plentiously,
And happy influence upon us raine,
That we may raise a large posterity,
Which from the earth, which they may long possesse
    With lasting happinesse,
Up to your haughty pallaces may mount,   420
And for the guerdon of theyr glorious merit,
May heavenly tabernacles there inherit,
Of blessed saints for to increase the count.
So let us rest, sweet love, in hope of this,
And cease till then our tymely joyes to sing:
The woods no more us answer, nor our eccho ring.

Song, made in lieu of many ornaments
With which my love should duly have bene dect,
Which cutting off through hasty accidents,
Ye would not stay your dew time to expect,   430
    But promist both to recompens,
Be unto her a goodly ornament,
And for short time an endlesse moniment.

                                                                [1594]

Sir Walter Ralegh
1552?–1618

FAREWELL, FALSE LOVE

FAREWELL, false love, the oracle of lies,
  A mortal foe and enemy to rest;
An envious boy, from whom all cares arise,
A bastard vile, a beast with rage possessed;
A way of error, a temple full of treason,
In all effects contrary unto reason.

A poisoned serpent covered all with flowers,
Mother of sighs and murderer of repose,
A sea of sorrows from whence are drawn such showers
As moisture lends to every grief that grows;   10
A school of guile, a net of deep deceit,
A gilded hook that holds a poisoned bait.

A fortress foiled which reason did defend,
A siren song, a fever of the mind,
A maze wherein affection finds no end,
A raging cloud that runs before the wind,
A substance like the shadow of the sun,
A goal of grief for which the wisest run.
A quenchless fire, a nurse of trembling fear,
A path that leads to peril and mishap;   20
A true retreat of sorrow and despair,
An idle boy that sleeps in pleasure's lap,
A deep distrust of that which certain seems,
A hope of that which reason doubtful deems.

Sith then thy trains[1] my younger years betrayed,
And for my faith ingratitude I find,
And sith repentance hath my wrongs bewrayed[2]
Whose course was ever contrary to kind[3]—
False love, desire, and beauty frail, adieu!
Dead is the root whence all these fancies grew.   30
                                                      [1588]

¹ deceits   ² exposed   ³ nature

THE NYMPH'S REPLY TO THE SHEPHERD[1]

If all the world and love were young,
And truth in every shepherd's tongue,
These pretty pleasures might me move,
To live with thee, and be thy love.

Time drives the flocks from field to fold,
When rivers rage, and rocks grow cold,
And Philomel becometh dumb,
The rest complains of cares to come.

The flowers do fade, and wanton fields,
To wayward winter reckoning yields,   10
A honey tongue, a heart of gall,
Is fancy's spring, but sorrow's fall.

Thy gowns, thy shoes, thy beds of roses,
Thy cap, thy kirtle, and thy posies,
Soon break, soon wither, soon forgotten:
In folly ripe, in reason rotten.

Thy belt of straw and ivy buds,
Thy coral clasps and amber studs,
All these in me no means can move,
To come to thee, and be thy love.   20

But could youth last, and love still breed,
Had joys no date, nor age no need,
Then these delights my mind might move,
To live with thee and be thy love.

[1600]

---

[1] Ralegh's poem is a reply to Marlowe's "The Passionate Shepherd to His Love,"
page 651. See also Donne's "The Bait," page 661, C. Day Lewis's "Come Live with
Me and Be My Love," page 932, and Robert Frost's "A Line-Storm Song," p. 884.

Sir Philip Sidney
1554 1586
◊
FROM
ASTROPHEL AND STELLA
◊

I

Loving in truth, and fain in verse my love to show,
That she, dear she, might take some pleasure of my pain,
Pleasure might cause her read, reading might make her know,
Knowledge might pity win, and pity grace obtain,
I sought fit words to paint the blackest face of woe;
Studying inventions fine, her wits to entertain.
Oft turning others' leaves to see if thence would flow
Some fresh and fruitful showers upon my sun-burned brain.
But words came halting forth, wanting Invention's stay;
Invention, Nature's child, fled step-dame Study's blows,   10
And others' feet still seemed but strangers in my way.
Thus, great with child to speak, and helpless in my throes,
Biting my truant pen, beating myself for spite,
"Fool," said my Muse to me, "look in thy heart and write."

XXVIII

You that with allegory's curious frame
Of others' children changelings use to make,
With me those pains, for God's sake, do not take;
I list not dig so deep for brazen fame.
When I say Stella, I do mean the same
Princess of beauty, for whose only sake
The reins of Love I love, though never slack,
And joy therein, though nations count it shame.
I beg no subject to use eloquence,
Nor in hid ways do guide philosophy;   10
Look at my hands for no such quintessence;
But know that I in pure simplicity
Breathe out the flames which burn within my heart,
Love only reading unto me this art.

XLI

Having this day my horse, my hand, my lance
Guided so well that I obtained the prize,
Both by the judgment of the English eyes
And of some sent from that sweet enemy, France,

Horsemen my skill in horsemanship advance,
Town-folks strength; a daintier judge applies
His praise to sleight which from good use doth rise;
Some lucky wits impute it but to chance;
Others, because of both sides I do take
My blood from them who did excel in this,   10
Think nature me a man-at-arms did make.
How far they shoot awry! The true cause is,
Stella looked on, and from her heavenly face
Sent forth the beams which made so fair my race.

[1591]

MY TRUE LOVE HATH MY HEART

MY true Love hath my heart, and I have his,
By just exchange one for the other given:
I hold his dear, and mine he cannot miss;
There never was a better bargain driven.
His heart in me keeps me and him in one,
My heart in him his thoughts and senses guides:
He loves my heart, for once it was his own;
I cherish his because in me it bides.
His heart his wound receivéd from my sight,
My heart was wounded with his wounded heart;   10
For as from me, on him his hurt did light,
So still methought in me his hurt did smart.
Both, equal hurt, in this change sought our bliss:
My true Love hath my heart, and I have his.

[1593]

Robert Southwell
1561?–1595
THE BURNING BABE

As I in hoary winter's night stood shivering in the snow,
Surprised I was with sudden heat, which made my heart to glow;
And lifting up a fearful eye to view what fire was near,
A pretty Babe all burning bright, did in the air appear,
Who scorchéd with excessive heat, such floods of tears did shed,
As though His floods should quench His flames which with His tears
    were fed;

Alas! quoth He, but newly born, in fiery heats I fry,
Yet none approach to warm their hearts or feel my fire but I!
My faultless breast the furnace is, the fuel wounding thorns,
Love is the fire, and sighs the smoke, the ashes shame and scorns;   10
The fuel Justice layeth on, and Mercy blows the coals,
The metal in this furnace wrought are men's defiléd souls,
For which, as now on fire I am to work them to their good,
So will I melt into a bath to wash them in My blood:
With this He vanished out of sight, and swiftly shrank away,
And straight I calléd unto mind that it was Christmas-day.

[1595?]

Christopher Marlowe
1564–1593

THE PASSIONATE SHEPHERD TO HIS LOVE

COME live with me and be my love,
  And we will all the pleasures prove,
That valleys, groves, hills and fields,
Woods, or steepy mountain yields.

And we will sit upon the rocks,
And see the shepherds feed their flocks,
By shallow rivers to whose falls
Melodious birds sing madrigals.

And I will make thee beds of roses
With a thousand fragrant posies,   10
A cap of flowers, and a kirtle
Embroidered all with leaves of myrtle;

A gown made of the finest wool
Which from our pretty lambs we pull;
Fair linéd slippers for the cold,
With buckles of the purest gold;

A belt of straw and ivy buds,
With coral clasps and amber studs:
And if these pleasures may thee move,
Come live with me and be my love.   20

The shepherds' swains shall dance and sing
For thy delight each May morning:
If these delights thy mind may move,
Then live with me and be my love.

[1600]

William Shakespeare
1564–1616

❖

SONGS FROM THE PLAYS

❖

FROM

THE TWO GENTLEMEN OF VERONA

SILVIA

W HO is Silvia? what is she,
     That all our swains commend her?
Holy, fair, and wise is she;
     The heaven such grace did lend her,
That she might admiréd be.

Is she kind as she is fair?
     For beauty lives with kindness.
Love doth to her eyes repair,
     To help him of his blindness;
And, being helped, inhabits there.   10

Then to Silvia let us sing,
     That Silvia is excelling;
She excels each mortal thing
     Upon the dull earth dwelling;
To her let us garlands bring.

[1591]

FROM

LOVE'S LABOR'S LOST

SPRING

W HEN daisies pied and violets blue
     And lady-smocks all silver-white
And cuckoo-buds of yellow hue
     Do paint the meadows with delight,

The cuckoo then, on every tree,
Mocks married men; for thus sings he,
   Cuckoo!
Cuckoo, cuckoo! O, word of fear,
Unpleasing to a married ear!

When shepherds pipe on oaten straws,   10
 And merry larks are ploughmen's clocks,
When turtles tread, and rooks, and daws,
 And maidens bleach their summer smocks,
The cuckoo then, on every tree,
Mocks married men; for thus sings he,
   Cuckoo!
Cuckoo, cuckoo! O, word of fear,
Unpleasing to a married ear!

    WINTER

WHEN icicles hang by the wall,
  And Dick the shepherd blows his nail,
And Tom bears logs into the hall,
 And milk comes frozen home in pail,
When blood is nipped, and ways be foul,
Then nightly sings the staring owl,
   To-whit!
To-who!—a merry note,
While greasy Joan doth keel[1] the pot.

When all aloud the wind doth blow,   10
 And coughing drowns the parson's saw,
And birds sit brooding in the snow,
 And Marian's nose looks red and raw,
When roasted crabs hiss in the bowl,
Then nightly sings the staring owl,
   To-whit!
To-who!—a merry note,
While greasy Joan doth keel the pot.

       [1593]

[1] stir, to prevent boiling over

F R O M

AS YOU LIKE IT

Blow, blow, thou winter wind,
  Thou are not so unkind
    As man's ingratitude;
Thy tooth is not so keen,
Because thou art not seen,
    Although thy breath be rude.
Heigh-ho! sing, heigh-ho! unto the green holly:
Most friendship is feigning, most loving mere folly.
    Then heigh-ho! the holly!
    This life is most jolly.   10

Freeze, freeze, thou bitter sky,
  That dost not bite so nigh
    As benefits forgot:
Though thou the water warp,
Thy sting is not so sharp
    As friend remembered not.
Heigh-ho! sing, heigh-ho! unto the green holly:
Most friendship is feigning, most loving mere folly.
    Then heigh-ho! the holly!
    This life is most jolly.   20
                                                        [1600]

F R O M

TWELFTH NIGHT

Come away, come away, Death!
  And in sad cypress[1] let me be laid;
Fly away, fly away, breath;
  I am slain by a fair cruel maid.
My shroud of white, stuck all with yew,
    O, prepare it!
My part of death, no one so true
    Did share it.

Not a flower, not a flower sweet,
  On my black coffin let there be strown;   10
Not a friend, not a friend greet
  My poor corpse, where my bones shall be thrown

[1] cypress lawn, a filmy black fabric used for burial robes

A thousand thousand sighs to save
Lay me, O, where
Sad true lover never find my grave,
To weep there!

[1601]

FROM
CYMBELINE

Hark, hark! the lark at heaven's gate sings,
    And Phœbus 'gins arise,
His steeds to water at those springs
    On chaliced flowers that lies;
And winking Mary-buds begin
    To ope their golden eyes:
With every thing that pretty is,
    My lady sweet, arise!
        Arise, arise!

*

Fear no more the heat o' the sun,
    Nor the furious winter's rages;
Thou thy worldly task hast done,
    Home art gone, and ta'en thy wages;
Golden lads and girls all must,
As chimney-sweepers, come to dust.

Fear no more the frown o' the great,
    Thou art past the tyrant's stroke:
Care no more to clothe and eat;
    To thee the reed is as the oak: 10
The scepter, learning, physic, must
All follow this, and come to dust.

Fear no more the lightning-flash,
    Nor the all-dread thunder-stone;
Fear no slander, censure rash;
    Thou hast finished joy and moan;
All lovers young, all lovers must
Consign to thee, and come to dust.

No exorciser harm thee!
    Nor no witchcraft charm thee!   20

Ghost unlaid forbear thee!
Nothing ill come near thee!
Quiet consummation have;
And renownéd be thy grave!

[1609]

F R O M

THE SONNETS

XVIII

SHALL I compare thee to a summer's day?
Thou art more lovely and more temperate:
Rough winds do shake the darling buds of May,
And summer's lease hath all too short a date:
Sometimes too hot the eye of heaven shines,
And often is his gold complexion dimmed;
And every fair from fair sometime declines,
By chance, or nature's changing course untrimmed;
But thy eternal summer shall not fade,
Nor lose possession of that fair thou owest,   10
Nor shall Death brag thou wander'st in his shade,
When in eternal lines to time thou growest;
So long as men can breathe, or eyes can see,
So long lives this, and this gives life to thee.

XXIX

WHEN in disgrace with fortune and men's eyes
I all alone beweep my outcast state,
And trouble deaf heaven with my bootless cries,
And look upon myself, and curse my fate,
Wishing me like to one more rich in hope,
Featured like him, like him with friends possessed,
Desiring this man's art, and that man's scope,
With what I most enjoy contented least;
Yet in these thoughts myself almost despising,
Haply I think on thee, and then my state,   10
Like to the lark at break of day arising
From sullen earth, sings hymns at heaven's gate;
For thy sweet love remembered such wealth brings
That then I scorn to change my state with kings.

XXX

WHEN to the sessions of sweet silent thought
I summon up remembrance of things past,
I sigh the lack of many a thing I sought,
And with old woes new wail my dear time's waste:

Then can I drown an eye, unused to flow,
For precious friends hid in death's dateless night,
And weep afresh love's long since cancelled woe,
And moan the expense of many a vanished sight:
Then can I grieve at grievances foregone,
And heavily from woe to woe tell o'er   10
The sad account of fore-bemoanèd moan,
Which I new pay as if not paid before.
But if the while I think on thee, dear friend,
All losses are restored and sorrows end.

XXXIII

FULL many a glorious morning have I seen
Flatter the mountain-tops with sovereign eye,
Kissing with golden face the meadows green,
Gilding pale streams with heavenly alchemy;
Anon permit the basest clouds to ride
With ugly rack on his celestial face,
And from the forlorn world his visage hide,
Stealing unseen to west with this disgrace:
Even so my sun one early morn did shine,
With all-triumphant splendor on my brow;   10
But out! alack! he was but one hour mine,
The region cloud hath masked him from me now.
Yet him for this my love no whit disdaineth;
Suns of the world may stain when heaven's sun staineth.

LV

NOT marble, nor the gilded monuments
Of princes, shall outlive this powerful rhyme;
But you shall shine more bright in these contents
Than unswept stone, besmeared with sluttish time.
When wasteful war shall statues overturn,
And broils root out the work of masonry,
Nor Mars his sword nor war's quick fire shall burn
The living record of your memory.
'Gainst death and all oblivious enmity
Shall you pace forth; your praise shall still find room   10
Even in the eyes of all posterity
That wear this world out to the ending doom.
So, till the judgment that yourself arise,
You live in this, and dwell in lovers' eyes.

LXXI

No longer mourn for me when I am dead,
Than you shall hear the surly sullen bell
Give warning to the world that I am fled
From this vile world, with vilest worms to dwell:
Nay, if you read this line, remember not
The hand that writ it; for I love you so,
That I in your sweet thoughts would be forgot,
If thinking on me then should make you woe.
O! if, I say, you look upon this verse,
When I perhaps compounded am with clay,   10
Do not so much as my poor name rehearse,
But let your love even with my life decay;
Lest the wise world should look into your moan,
And mock you with me after I am gone.

LXXIII

That time of year thou may'st in me behold
When yellow leaves, or none, or few, do hang
Upon those boughs which shake against the cold,
Bare ruined choirs, where late the sweet birds sang.
In me thou see'st the twilight of such day
As after sunset fadeth in the west,
Which by and by black night doth take away,
Death's second self that seals up all in rest.
In me thou see'st the glowing of such fire,
That on the ashes of his youth doth lie,   10
As the death-bed, whereon it must expire
Consumed with that which it was nourished by.
This thou perceiv'st, which makes thy love more strong
To love that well, which thou must leave ere long.

CXVI

Let me not to the marriage of true minds
Admit impediments. Love is not love
Which alters when it alteration finds,
Or bends with the remover to remove:
O, no! it is an ever-fixéd mark
That looks on tempests and is never shaken;
It is the star to every wand'ring bark,
Whose worth's unknown, although his height be taken.
Love's not Time's fool, though rosy lips and cheeks
Within his bending sickle's compass come;
Love alters not with his brief hours and weeks,   10
But bears it out even to the edge of doom.
If this be error and upon me proved,
I never writ, nor no man ever loved.

CXXX

M Y mistress' eyes are nothing like the sun;
Coral is far more red than her lips' red;
If snow be white, why then her breasts are dun;
If hairs be wires, black wires grow on her head.
I have seen roses damasked, red and white,
But no such roses see I in her cheeks,
And in some perfumes there is more delight
Than in the breath that from my mistress reeks.
I love to hear her speak, yet well I know
That music hath a far more pleasing sound.   10
I grant I never saw a goddess go;
My mistress, when she walks, treads on the ground:
And yet, by heaven, I think my love as rare
As any she belied with false compare.

[1609]

John Donne
1572–1631

SONG

Go AND catch a falling star,
   Get with child a mandrake root,
Tell me where all past years are,
   Or who cleft the devil's foot,
Teach me to hear mermaids singing,
Or to keep off envy's stinging,
      And find
      What wind
Serves to advance an honest mind.

If thou be'st born to strange sights,   10
   Things invisible to see,
Ride ten thousand days and nights,
   Till age snow white hairs on thee.
Thou, when thou return'st, wilt tell me,
All strange wonders that befell thee,
      And swear,
      No where
Lives a woman true and fair.

If thou find'st one, let me know;
   Such a pilgrimage were sweet.   20
Yet do not, I would not go,
   Though at next door we might meet:
Though she were true when you met her,
And last till you write your letter,
      Yet she
      Will be
False, ere I come, to two or three.

[1633]

THE BAIT

COME live with me, and be my love,
And we will some new pleasures prove,[1]
Of golden sands, and crystal brooks,
With silken lines, and silver hooks.

There will the river whispering run,
Warmed by thy eyes more than the sun.
And there th' enamored fish will stay,
Begging themselves they may betray.

When thou wilt swim in that live bath,
Each fish, which every channel hath,   10
Will amorously to thee swim,
Gladder to catch thee, than thou him.

If thou, to be so seen, be'st loath,
By sun or moon, thou dark'nest both;
And if myself have leave to see,
I need not their light, having thee.

Let others freeze with angling reeds,
And cut their legs with shells and weeds,
Or treacherously poor fish beset
With strangling snare, or windowy
    net.   20

Let coarse bold hands from slimy nest
The bedded fish in banks out-wrest,
Or curious traitors, sleave-silk[2] flies,
Bewitch poor fishes' wandering eyes.

For thee, thou need'st no such deceit,
For thou thyself art thine own bait;
That fish that is not catched thereby,
Alas, is wiser far than I.

                                                    [1633]

[1] test   [2] loosely twisted floss

A VALEDICTION: FORBIDDING MOURNING

AS VIRTUOUS men pass mildly away,
And whisper to their souls, to go,
Whilst some of their sad friends do say,
    The breath goes now, and some say, no:

So let us melt, and make no noise,
   No tear-floods, nor sigh-tempests move,
T'were profanation of our joys
   To tell the laity our love.

Moving of th' earth brings harms and fears,
   Men reckon what it did and meant,   10
But trepidation of the spheres,
   Though greater far, is innocent.

Dull sublunary lovers' love
   (Whose soul is sense) cannot admit
Absence, because it doth remove
   Those things which elemented it.

But we by a love, so much refined
   That our selves know not what it is,
Inter-assuréd of the mind,
   Care less, eyes, lips, and hands to miss.   20

Our two souls therefore, which are one,
   Though I must go, endure not yet
A breach, but an expansion,
   Like gold to airy thinness beat.

If they be two, they are two so
   As stiff twin compasses are two,
Thy soul, the fixed foot, makes no show
   To move, but doth, if th' other do.

And though it in the center sit,
   Yet when the other far doth roam,   30
It leans, and hearkens after it,
   And grows erect, as that comes home.

Such wilt thou be to me, who must
   Like th' other foot, obliquely run;
Thy firmness makes my circle just,
   And makes me end, where I begun.

                           [1633]

THE RELIC

W HEN my grave is broke up again
    Some second guest to entertain
(For graves have learned that woman-head
To be to more than one a bed),
    And he that digs it, spies
A bracelet of bright hair about the bone,
    Will he not let'us alone,
And think that there a loving couple lies,
Who thought that this device might be some way
To make their souls, at the last busy day,   10
Meet at this grave, and make a little stay?

    If this fall in a time, or land,
    Where mis devotion doth command,
Then, he that digs us up, will bring
Us to the bishop, and the king,
    To make us relics; then
Thou shalt be a Mary Magdalen, and I
    A something else thereby;
All women shall adore us, and some men;
And since at such time, miracles are sought,   20
I would have that age by this paper taught
What miracles we harmless lovers wrought.

    First, we loved well and faithfully,
    Yet knew not what we loved, nor why,
Difference of sex no more we knew,
Than our Guardian Angels do;
    Coming and going, we
Perchance might kiss, but not between those meals;
    Our hands ne'er touched the seals,
Which nature, injured by late law, sets free: 30
These miracles we did; but now alas,
All measure, and all language, I should pass,
Should I tell what a miracle she was.

                        [1633]

HOLY SONNETS

VII

At the round earth's imagined corners blow
Your trumpets, angels, and arise, arise
From death, you numberless infinities
Of souls, and to your scattered bodies go,
All whom the flood did, and fire shall o'erthrow,
All whom war, dearth, age, agues, tyrannies,
Despair, law, chance, hath slain, and you whose eyes
Shall behold God, and never taste death's woe.
But let them sleep, Lord, and me mourn a space;
For, if above all these my sins abound,   10
'Tis late to ask abundance of Thy grace,
When we are there. Here on this lowly ground,
Teach me how to repent, for that's as good
As if Thou hadst sealed my pardon with Thy blood.

X

Death, be not proud, though some have calléd thee
Mighty and dreadful, for thou art not so,
For those whom thou think'st thou dost overthrow
Die not, poor Death, nor yet canst thou kill me.
From rest and sleep, which but thy pictures be,
Much pleasure, then from thee much more must flow;
And soonest our best men with thee do go—
Rest of their bones and souls' delivery!
Thou'rt slave to fate, kings and desperate men,
And dost with poison, war, and sickness dwell,   10
And poppy or charms can make us sleep as well,
And better than thy stroke; why swell'st thou then?
One short sleep past, we wake eternally,
And death shall be no more: Death, thou shalt die!

XIV

Batter my heart, three-personed God; for you
As yet but knock, breathe, shine, and seek to mend;
That I may rise and stand, o'erthrow me and bend
Your force to break, blow, burn and make me new.
I, like an usurped town, to another due,
Labor to admit you, but oh, to no end;
Reason, your viceroy in me, me should defend,
But is captived and proves weak or untrue.

Yet dearly I love you and would be loved fain,
But am betrothed unto your enemy: 10
Divorce me, untie or break that knot again,
Take me to you, imprison me, for I
Except you enthrall me, never shall be free,
Nor ever chaste, except you ravish me.

[1633]

THE CANONIZATION

FOR God's sake hold your tongue, and let me love,
  Or chide my palsy, or my gout,
My five gray hairs, or ruined fortune flout,
    With wealth your state, your mind with arts improve
      Take you a course, get you a place,
      Observe His Honor, or His Grace,
Or the King's real, or his stampéd face
    Contemplate; what you will, approve,[1]
    So you will let me love.

Alas, alas, who's injured by my love?   10
  What merchant's ships have my sighs drowned?
Who says my tears have overflowed his ground?
    When did my colds a forward spring remove?
      When did the heats which my veins fill
      Add one more to the plaguy bill?[2]
Soldiers find wars, and lawyers find out still
    Litigious men, which quarrels move,
    Though she and I do love.

Call us what you will, we are made such by love;
  Call her one, me anothèr fly,   20
We're tapers too, and at our own cost die,
    And we in us find the eagle and the dove.
      The phoenix[3] riddle hath more wit
      By us: we two being one, are it.
So, to one neutral thing both sexes fit.
    We die and rise the same, and prove
    Mysterious by this love.

---

[1] try   [2] the list of those dead from the plague
  [3] Only one of these legendary birds exists at one time. It lights its own funeral fire and then rises from the ashes to live for another thousand years before repeating the process.

We can die by it, if not live by love,
  And if unfit for tombs and hearse
Our legend be, it will be fit for verse;   30
  And if no piece of chronicle we prove,
    We'll build in sonnets pretty rooms;
    As well as well-wrought urn becomes
The greatest ashes, as half-acre tombs,
  And by these hymns, all shall approve
  Us canonized for love:

And thus invoke us: You whom reverend love
  Made one another's hermitage;
You, to whom love was peace, that now is rage;
  Who did the whole world's soul contract, and drove   40
    Into the glasses of your eyes
    (So made such mirrors, and such spies,
That they did all to you epitomize)
  Countries, towns, courts: Beg from above
  A pattern of your love!

                                                         [1633]

HYMN TO GOD MY GOD, IN MY SICKNESS

SINCE I am coming to that holy room
  Where, with Thy choir of saints for evermore,
I shall be made Thy music; as I come
  I tune the instrument here at the door,
  And what I must do then, think here before.

Whilst my physicians by their love are grown
  Cosmographers, and I their map, who lie
Flat on this bed, that by them may be shown
  That this is my southwest discovery
  Per fretum febris,[1] by these straits to die,   10

I joy, that in these straits, I see my West;
  For, though their currents yield return to none,
What shall my West hurt me? As West and East
  In all flat maps (and I am one) are one,
  So death doth touch the resurrection.

___
[1] via the straits of fever

Is the Pacific Sea my home? Or are
  The Eastern riches? Is Jerusalem?
Anyan,[2] and Magellan, and Gibraltar,
  All straits, and none but straits, are ways to them,
  Whether where Japhet dwelt, or Cham, or Shem.[3]   20

We think that Paradise and Calvary,
  Christ's cross, and Adam's tree, stood in one place;
Look, Lord, and find both Adams[4] met in me;
  As the first Adam's sweat surrounds my face,
  May the last Adam's blood my soul embrace.

So, in his purple wrapped, receive me, Lord
  By these his thorns give me his other crown;
And, as to others' souls I preached Thy word,
  Be this my text, my sermon to mine own;
  Therefore that he may raise the Lord throws down.   30
                                                        [1635]

---

[2] the Bering Straits
[3] the sons of Noah, who after the Flood peopled, respectively, Europe, Africa, and Asia
[4] In Christian typology, Adam prefigures Christ.

Ben Jonson
1572-1637

FROM

CYNTHIA'S REVELS

Slow, slow, fresh fount, keep time with my salt tears;
  Yet slow, yet, O, faintly gentle springs:
List to the heavy part the music bears,
  Woe weeps out her division,[1] when she sings.
    Droop herbs, and flowers;
    Fall grief in showers;
    Our beauties are not ours:
      Oh, I could still
(Like melting snow upon some craggy hill)
      Drop, drop, drop, drop,   10
Since nature's pride is, now, a withered daffodil.
                                                        [1600]

---

[1] part in part-singing

SONG: TO CELIA

Drink to me only with thine eyes,
  And I will pledge with mine;
Or leave a kiss but in the cup
  And I'll not look for wine.
The thirst that from the soul doth rise
  Doth ask a drink divine;
But might I of Jove's nectar sup,
  I would not change for thine.

I sent thee late a rosy wreath,
  Not so much honoring thee   10
As giving it a hope that there
  It could not withered be;
But thou thereon didst only breathe,
  And sent'st it back to me;
Since when it grows, and smells, I swear,
  Not of itself, but thee!

                                                                    [1606]

INVITING A FRIEND TO SUPPER

Tonight, grave sir, both my poor house and I
  Do equally desire your company;
Not that we think us worthy such a guest,
  But that your worth will dignify our feast,
With those that come; whose grace may make that seem
  Something, which else could hope for no esteem.
It is the fair acceptance, Sir, creates
  The entertainment perfect, not the cates.[1]
Yet shall you have, to rectify your palate,
  An olive, capers, or some better salad   10
Ush'ring the mutton; with a short-legg'd hen,
  If we can get her, full of eggs, and then,
Lemons, and wine for sauce: to these a coney[2]
  Is not to be despaired of, for our money;
And, though fowl now be scarce, yet there be clerks,
  The sky not falling, think we may have larks.
I'll tell you of more, and lie, so you will come;
  Of partridge, pheasant, woodcock, of which some

---

[1] viands   [2] rabbit

May yet be there; and godwit if we can:
    Knot, rail,[3] and ruff[4] too. How so ere, my man   20
Shall read a piece of Virgil, Tacitus,
    Livy, or of some better book to us,
Of which we'll speak our minds, amidst our meat;
    And I'll profess no verses to repeat;
To this, if aught appear, which I know not of,
    That will the pastry, not the paper, show of.
Digestive cheese and fruit there sure will be;
    But that which most doth take my muse, and me,
Is a pure cup of rich Canary wine,
    Which is the Mermaid's[5] now, but shall be mine;   30
Of which had Horace or Anacreon tasted,
    Their lives, as do their lines, till now had lasted.
Tobacco, nectar, or the Thespian spring
    Are all but Luther's beer to this I sing.
Of this we will sup free, but moderately,
    And we will have no Pooly or Parrot[6] by;
Nor shall our cups make any guilty men:
    But at our parting we will be as when
We innocently met. No simple word
    That shall be uttered at our mirthful board   40
Shall make us sad next morning or affright
    The liberty that we'll enjoy tonight.

                [1616]

[3] three more game birds   [4] a fish
[5] Jonson and his cronies foregathered at the Mermaid Tavern.
[6] two government informers

TO THE MEMORY OF MY BELOVED,
THE AUTHOR
MASTER WILLIAM SHAKESPEARE

To DRAW no envy, Shakespeare, on thy name,
    Am I thus ample to thy book and fame;
While I confess thy writings to be such
As neither man nor Muse can praise too much.
'Tis true, and all men's suffrage. But these ways
Were not the paths I meant unto thy praise;
For silliest ignorance on these may light,
Which, when it sounds at best, but echoes right;
Or blind affection, which doth ne'er advance
The truth, but gropes, and urgeth all by chance;   10

Or crafty malice might pretend this praise,
And think to ruin, where it seemed to raise.
These are, as some infamous bawd or whore
Should praise a matron. What could hurt her more?
But thou art proof against them, and indeed,
Above the ill fortune of them, or the need.
I therefore will begin. Soul of the age!
The applause, delight, the wonder of our stage!
My Shakespeare, rise! I will not lodge thee by
Chaucer, or Spenser, or bid Beaumont lie   20
A little further, to make thee a room;
Thou art a monument without a tomb,
And art alive still while thy book doth live
And we have wits to read and praise to give.
That I not mix thee so, my brain excuses,
I mean with great, but disproportioned Muses;
For if I thought my judgment were of years,
I should commit thee surely with thy peers,
And tell how far thou didst our Lyly outshine,
Or sporting Kyd, or Marlowe's mighty line.   30
And though thou hadst small Latin and less Greek,
From thence to honor thee I would not seek
For names; but call forth thundering Aeschylus,
Euripides, and Sophocles to us;
Pacuvius, Accius,[1] him of Cordova[2] dead,
To life again, to hear thy buskin tread,
And shake a stage; or, when thy socks were on,
Leave thee alone for the comparison
Of all that insolent Greece or haughty Rome
Sent forth, or since did from their ashes come.   40
Triumph, my Britain, thou hast one to show
To whom all scenes of Europe homage owe.
He was not of an age, but for all time!
And all the Muses still were in their prime,
When, like Apollo, he came forth to warm
Our ears, or like a Mercury to charm!
Nature herself was proud of his designs
And joyed to wear the dressing of his lines,
Which were so richly spun, and woven so fit,
As, since, she will vouchsafe no other wit.   50
The merry Greek, tart Aristophanes,
Neat Terence, witty Plautus, now not please,
But antiquated and deserted lie,
As they were not of Nature's family.

[1] Roman poets of the second century B.C.
[2] Seneca, Roman philosoper, statesman, and tragedian of the first century

Yet must I not give Nature all; thy art,
My gentle Shakespeare, must enjoy a part.
For though the poet's matter Nature be,
His art doth give the fashion; and, that he
Who casts to write a living line, must sweat
(Such as thine are) and strike the second heat 60
Upon the Muses' anvil; turn the same
(And himself with it) that he thinks to frame,
Or, for the laurel, he may gain a scorn;
For a good poet's made, as well as born.
And such wert thou! Look how the father's face
Lives in his issue; even so the race
Of Shakespeare's mind and manners brightly shines
In his well-turnèd, and true-filèd lines;
In each of which he seems to shake a lance,
As brandished at the eyes of ignorance. 70
Sweet Swan of Avon! what a sight it were
To see thee in our waters yet appear,
And make those flights upon the banks of Thames,
That so did take Eliza,[3] and our James!
But stay, I see thee in the hemisphere
Advanced, and made a constellation there!
Shine forth, thou star of poets, and with rage
Or influence, chide or cheer the drooping stage,
Which, since thy flight from hence, hath mourned like night,
And despairs day, but for thy volume's light. 80
[1623]

[3] Queen Elizabeth; James: King James I

AN ODE TO HIMSELF

WHERE dost thou careless lie,
  Buried in ease and sloth?
Knowledge that sleeps doth die;
  And this security,
   It is the common moth
That eats on wits and arts, and destroys them both.

  Are all the Aonian springs[1]
  Dried up? Lies Thespia[2] waste?

[1] a spring at the foot of Mt. Helicon, which was a source of poetic inspiration
[2] a center of the worship of the Muses

Doth Clarius'[3] harp want strings,
That not a nymph now sings?   10
    Or droop they as disgraced,
To see their seats and bowers by chattering pies defaced?

If hence thy silence be,
    As 'tis too just a cause,
Let this thought quicken thee:
Minds that are great and free
    Should not on fortune pause;
'Tis crown enough to virtue still, her own applause.

What though the greedy fry
    Be taken with false baits   20
Of worded balladry,
And think it poesy?
    They die with their conceits,
And only piteous scorn upon their folly waits.

Then take in hand thy lyre;
    Strike in thy proper strain;
With Japhet's line[4] aspire
Sol's chariot for new fire
    To give the world again;
Who aided him will thee, the issue of Jove's brain.   30

And, since our dainty age
    Cannot endure reproof,
Make not thyself a page
To that strumpet the stage;
    But sing high and aloof,
Safe from the wolf's black jaw, and the dull ass's hoof.

                                                              [1640]

[3] an oracle of Apollo
[4] the descendants of one of the sons of Noah, who peopled Europe after the Flood

Robert Herrick

1591–1674

DELIGHT IN DISORDER

A sweet disorder in the dress
    Kindles in clothes a wantonness:
A lawn about the shoulders thrown
Into a fine distraction,

An erring lace, which here and there
Enthralls the crimson stomacher,
A cuff neglectful, and thereby
Ribbands to flow confusedly,
A winning wave (deserving note)
In the tempestuous petticoat, 10
A careless shoe-string, in whose tie
I see a wild civility,
Do more bewitch me, than when art
Is too precise in every part.

[1648]

THE NIGHT-PIECE, TO JULIA

Her eyes the glow-worm lend thee,
The shooting stars attend thee·
And the elves also,
Whose little eyes glow
Like the sparks of fire, befriend thee.

No will-o'-th'-wisp mislight thee;
Nor snake, or slow-worm bite thee:
But on, on thy way,
Not making a stay,
Since ghost there's none to affright thee. 10

Let not the dark thee cumber;
What though the moon does slumber:
The stars of the night
Will lend thee their light,
Like tapers clear without number.

Then, Julia, let me woo thee,
Thus, thus to come unto me:
And when I shall meet
Thy silv'ry feet,
My soul I'll pour into thee. 20

[1648]

UPON JULIA'S CLOTHES

WHENAS in silks my Julia goes
    Then, then (methinks) how sweetly flows
That liquefaction of her clothes.

Next, when I cast mine eyes and see
That brave vibration each way free;
O how that glittering taketh me!

[1648]

THE RESURRECTION POSSIBLE AND PROBABLE

FOR each one body that i' th' earth is sown
    There's an uprising but of one for one,
But for each grain that in the ground is thrown
Three score of fourscore springs up thence for one;
So that the wonder is not half so great
Of ours, as is the rising of the wheat.

[1648]

George Herbert
1593–1633

THE COLLAR

I STRUCK the board, and cried, No more.
    I will abroad.
What? shall I ever sigh and pine?
My lines and life are free; free as the road,
    Loose as the wind, as large as store.
        Shall I be still in suit?
Have I no harvest but a thorn
        To let me blood, and not restore
What I have lost with cordial fruit?
        Sure there was wine   10
Before my sighs did dry it: there was corn
    Before my tears did drown it.
    Is the year only lost to me?
        Have I no bays to crown it?

No flowers, no garlands gay? all blasted?
     All wasted?
  Not so, my heart: but there is fruit,
    And thou hast hands.
Recover all thy sigh-blown age
On double pleasures: leave thy cold dispute   20
Of what is fit, and not. Forsake thy cage,
    Thy rope of sands,
Which petty thoughts have made, and made to thee
Good cable, to enforce and draw,
    And be thy law,
Whilst thou didst wink and wouldst not see.
    Away; take heed:
  I will abroad.
Call in thy death's head there: tie up thy fears.
    He that forbears   30
  To suit and serve his need,
  Deserves his load.
But as I raved and grew more fierce and wild
    At every word,
Methought I heard one calling, *Child.*
And I replied, *My Lord.*

                [1633]

THE PULLEY

WHEN God at first made man,
  Having a glass of blessings standing by,
Let us (said He) pour on him all we can.
Let the world's riches, which dispersèd lie,
  Contract into a span.

  So strength first made a way,
Then beauty flowed, then wisdom, honor, pleasure.
  When almost all was out, God made a stay,
Perceiving that alone of all His treasure
  Rest in the bottom lay.   10

  For if I should (said He)
Bestow this jewel also on My creature,
  He would adore My gifts instead of Me,
And rest in Nature, not the God of Nature.
  So both should losers be.

Yet let him keep the rest,
But keep them with repining restlessness.
   Let him be rich and weary, that at least,
If goodness lead him not, yet weariness
         May toss him to My breast.   20

[1633]

TO HIS MOTHER

MY God, where is that ancient heat towards thee
      Wherewith whole shoals of martyrs once did burn,
Besides their other flames? Doth poetry
Wear Venus' livery, only serve her turn?
Why are not sonnets made of thee, and lays
Upon thine altar burnt? Cannot thy love
Heighten a spirit to sound out thy praise
As well as any she? Cannot thy dove
Outstrip their Cupid easily in flight?
Or, since thy ways are deep and still the same,   10
Will not a verse run smooth that bears thy name?
Why doth that fire, which by thy power and might
Each breast does feel, no braver fuel choose
Than that which one day worms may chance refuse?

[1633]

THE WINDOWS

LORD, how can man preach thy eternal word?
      He is a brittle crazy glass,
Yet in thy temple thou dost him afford
   This glorious and transcendent place
   To be a window, through thy grace.

But when thou dost anneal in glass thy story,
   Making thy life to shine within
The holy preacher's, then the light and glory
   More reverend grows, and doth more win;
   Which else shows wat'rish, bleak, and thin.   10

Doctrine and life, colors and light in one,
   When they combine and mingle, bring
A strong regard and awe; but speech alone
   Doth vanish like a flaring thing,
   And in the ear, not conscience, ring.

[1633]

John Milton
1608–1674

ON SHAKESPEARE

Wʜᴀᴛ needs my Shakespeare for his honored bones
⠀⠀The labor of an age in piléd stones,
Or that his hallowed relics should be hid
Under a star-ypointing pyramid?
Dear son of memory, great heir of fame,
What need'st thou such weak witness of thy name?
Thou in our wonder and astonishment
Hast built thyself a livelong monument.
For whilst to the shame of slow-endeavoring art
Thy easy numbers flow, and that each heart⠀⠀⠀⠀⠀⠀10
Hath from the leaves of thy unvalued[1] book
Those Delphic[2] lines with deep impression took,
Then thou, our fancy of itself bereaving,
Dost make us marble with too much conceiving,
And so sepúlchered in such pomp dost lie,
That kings for such a tomb would wish to die.

⠀⠀⠀⠀⠀⠀⠀⠀⠀⠀⠀⠀⠀⠀⠀⠀⠀⠀⠀⠀[1630]

---

[1] invaluable⠀⠀⠀[2] oracular

L'ALLEGRO

Hᴇɴᴄᴇ, loathéd Melancholy
⠀⠀Of Cerberus[1] and blackest Midnight born,
In Stygian[2] cave forlorn
⠀⠀'Mongst horrid shapes, and shrieks, and sights unholy!
Find out some uncouth cell,
⠀⠀Where brooding Darkness spreads his jealous wings.
And the night-raven sings;
⠀⠀There under ebon shades, and low-browed rocks
As ragged as thy locks,
⠀⠀In dark Cimmerian[3] desert ever dwell.⠀⠀⠀⠀⠀⠀10

⠀⠀⠀But come, thou Goddess fair and free,
In heaven yclept[4] Euphrosyne,

---

[1] the three-headed dog that guarded the gate of hell
[2] of the river Styx in Hades, over which Charon ferried dead souls
[3] The Cimmerians lived in eternal darkness at the outer edge of the world.
[4] called

And by men, heart-easing Mirth,
Whom lovely Venus at a birth
With two sister Graces[5] more
To ivy-crownéd Bacchus[6] bore;
Or whether (as some sager sing)
The frolic wind that breathes the spring
Zephyr,[7] with Aurora[8] playing,
As he met her once a-Maying,   20
There on beds of violets blue
And fresh-blown roses washed in dew
Filled her with thee, a daughter fair,
So buxom, blithe, and debonair.
    Haste thee, Nymph, and bring with thee
Jest, and youthful jollity,
Quips, and cranks, and wanton wiles,
Nods, and becks, and wreathéd smiles,
Such as hang on Hebe's[9] cheek,
And love to live in dimple sleek;   30
Sport that wrinkled Care derides,
And Laughter holding both his sides.
Come, and trip it as you go
On the light fantastic toe;
And in thy right hand lead with thee,
The mountain-nymph, sweet Liberty;
And if I give thee honor due,
Mirth, admit me of thy crew,
To live with her, and live with thee,
In unreprovéd pleasures free;   40
To hear the lark begin his flight,
And singing startle the dull night
From his watch-tower in the skies,
Till the dappled dawn doth rise;
Then to come, in spite of sorrow,
And at my window bid good-morrow
Through the sweetbriar, or the vine,
Or the twisted eglantine:
While the cock with lively din,
Scatters the rear of darkness thin,   50
And to the stack, or the barn-door,
Stoutly struts his dames before;
Oft listening how the hounds and horn
Cheerly rouse the slumbering morn,

---

[5] The Graces, Euphrosyne, Aglaia, and Thalia, were personifications of grace and beauty.
[6] god of wine   [7] god of the west wind   [8] the dawn
[9] cupbearer to the gods

From the side of some hoar hill,
Through the high wood echoing shrill.
Sometime walking not unseen,
By hedge-row elms, on hillocks green,
Right against the eastern gate,
Where the great Sun begins his state   60
Robed in flames and amber light,
The clouds in thousand liveries dight;
While the ploughman, near at hand,
Whistles o'er the furrowed land,
And the milkmaid singeth blithe,
And the mower whets his scythe,
And every shepherd tells his tale
Under the hawthorn in the dale.
　　Straight mine eye hath caught new pleasures
Whilst the landscape round it measures;   70
Russet lawns, and fallows gray,
Where the nibbling flocks do stray;
Mountains, on whose barren breast
The laboring clouds do often rest;
Meadows trim with daisies pied,
Shallow brooks, and rivers wide;
Towers and battlements it sees
Bosomed high in tufted trees,
Where perhaps some beauty lies,
The cynosure of neighboring eyes.   80
　　Hard by, a cottage chimney smokes,
From betwixt two agéd oaks,
Where Corydon and Thyris, met,
Are at their savory dinner set
Of herbs and other country messes,
Which the neat-handed Phillis dresses;
And then in haste her bower she leaves,
With Thestylis[10] to bind the sheaves;
Of, if the earlier season lead
To the tanned haycock in the mead.   90
　　Sometimes with secure delight
The upland hamlets will invite,
When the merry bells ring round,
And the jocund rebecks[11] sound
To many a youth and many a maid,
Dancing in the checkered shade;
And young and old come forth to play
On a sun-shine holyday,

----

[10] conventional pastoral names　　　[11] a small viol

Till the live-long day-light fail:
Then to the spicy nut-brown ale,   100
With stories told of many a feat,
How Faery Mab[12] the junkets eat,
She was pinched, and pulled, she said,
And he, by friar's lantern[13] led;
Tells how the drudging goblin sweat
To earn his cream-bowl duly set,
When in one night, ere glimpse of morn,
His shadowy flail hath threshed the corn
That ten day-laborers could not end;
Then lies him down the lubber fiend,   110
And, stretched out all the chimney's length,
Basks at the fire his hairy strength;
And crop-full out of doors he flings,
Ere the first cock his matin rings.
    Thus done the tales, to bed they creep,
By whispering winds soon lulled asleep.
    Towered cities please us then,
And the busy hum of men,
Where throngs of knights and barons bold,
In weeds of peace, high triumphs hold,   120
With store of ladies, whose bright eyes
Rain influence, and judge the prize
Of wit or arms, while both contend
To win her grace, whom all commend,
There let Hymen[14] oft appear
In saffron robe, with taper clear,
And pomp, and feast, and revelry,
With mask, and antique pageantry;
Such sighs as youthful poets dream
On summer eves by haunted stream.   130
Then to the well-trod stage anon,
If Jonson's learned sock be on,
Or sweetest Shakespeare, Fancy's child,
Warble his native wood-notes wild.
    And ever against eating cares,
Lap me in soft Lydían[15] airs,
Married to immortal verse
Such as the meeting soul may pierce
In notes with many a winding bout
Of linkéd sweetness long drawn out,   140

---

[12] queen of the fairies   [13] will o' the wisp   [14] god of marriage
[15] an effeminate or voluptuous mode in music

With wanton heed and giddy cunning,
The melting voice through mazes running,
Untwisting all the chains that tie
The hidden soul of harmony;
That Orpheus' self may heave his head
From golden slumber, on a bed
Of heaped Elysian flowers and hear
Such strains as would have won the ear
Of Pluto, to have quite set free
His half-regained Eurydice.[16]   150
These delights, if thou canst give,
Mirth, with thee I mean to live.

[1631?]

[16] Orpheus followed his wife, Eurydice, into Hades when she died. His music so moved Pluto, the god of the underworld, that he agreed to release Eurydice from death if Orpheus would precede her out of Hades and not look back to see if she was following. Orpheus complied until the last moment, but then looked back, only to see Eurydice snatched back into Hades.

IL PENSEROSO

HENCE, vain deluding Joys,
    The brood of Folly without father bred!
How little you bestead
    Or fill the fixéd mind with all your toys!
Dwell in some idle brain,
    And fancies fond with gaudy shapes possess
As thick and numberless
    As the gay motes that people the sunbeams,
Or likest hovering dreams,
    The fickle pensioners of Morpheus' train.   10

But hail, thou goddess sage and holy,
Hail, divinest Melancholy!
Whose saintly visage is too bright
To hit the sense of human sight;
And therefore to our weaker view,
O'erlaid with black, staid Wisdom's hue;
Black, but such as in esteem
Prince Memnon's sister[1] might beseem,
Or that starred Ethiop queen[2] that strove
To set her beauty's praise above   20

[1] Hemera. Prince Memmon, an Ethiopian, fought in the Trojan War.
[2] Cassiopeia, proud of her beauty, was placed among the stars after her death.

The sea-nymphs, and their powers offended.
Yet thou art higher far descended:
Thee bright-haired Vesta,[3] long of yore,
To solitary Saturn[4] bore;
His daughter she (in Saturn's reign
Such mixture was not held a stain).
Oft in glimmering bowers and glades
He met her, and in secret shades
Of woody Ida's[5] inmost grove,
While yet there was no fear of Jove.   30
   Come, pensive Nun, devout and pure
Sober, steadfast, and demure,
All in a robe of darkest grain,[6]
Flowing with majestic train,
And sable stole of cypress lawn,[7]
Over thy decent shoulders drawn.
Come, but keep thy wonted state,
With even step, and musing gait,
And looks commercing with the skies,
Thy rapt soul sitting in thine eyes: 40
There, held in holy passion still,
Forget thyself to marble, till
With a sad leaden downward cast,
Thou fix them on the earth as fast.
And join with thee calm Peace, and Quiet,
Spare Fast, that oft with gods doth diet,
And hears the Muses in a ring
Aye round about Jove's altar sing.
And add to these retired Leisure
That in trim gardens takes his pleasure;   50
But first and chiefest, with thee bring,
Him that yon soars on golden wing
Guiding the fiery-wheeléd throne,
The cherub Contemplation;
And the mute Silence hist along,
'Less Philomel[8] will deign a song
In her sweetest saddest plight,
Smoothing the rugged brow of Night,
While Cynthia[9] checks her dragon yoke,
Gently o'er the accustomed oak.   60
—Sweet bird, that shunn'st the noise of folly,
Most musical, most melancholy!

---

[3] goddess of the hearth   [4] mythical king of Italy's golden age
[5] sacred mountain in Crete   [6] dye   [7] a filmy black cloth
[8] the nightingale   [9] goddess of the moon, who drove a team of dragons

Thee, chauntress, oft, the woods among,
I woo, to hear thy even-song;
And missing thee, I walk unseen
On the dry smooth-shaven green,
To behold the wandering Moon,
Riding near her highest noon,
Like one that had been led astray
Through the heaven's wide pathless way;   70
And oft, as if her head she bowed,
Stooping through a fleecy cloud.
   Oft, on a plat of rising ground,
I hear the far-off curfew sound,
Over some wide-watered shore,
Swinging slow with sullen roar;
Or, if the air will not permit,
Some still removéd place will fit,
Where glowing embers through the room
Teach light to counterfeit a gloom,   80
Far from all resort of mirth,
Save the cricket on the hearth,
Or the bellman's drowsy charm
To bless the doors from nightly harm:
   Or let my lamp at midnight hour,
Be seen in some high lonely tower,
Where I may oft out-watch the Bear,[10]
With thrice-great Hermes,[11] or unsphere[12]
The spirit of Plato, to unfold
What worlds or what vast regions hold   90
The immortal mind, that hath forsook
Her mansion in this fleshly nook:
And of those demons that are found
In fire, air, flood, or under ground,
Whose power hath a true consent
With planet, or with element.
Sometime let gorgeous Tragedy
In sceptered pall come sweeping by,
Presenting Thebes,[13] or Pelop's line,
Or the tale of Troy divine;   100
Or what (though rare) of later age
Ennobled hath the buskined stage.
   But, O sad Virgin, that thy power
Might raise Musaeus[14] from his bower,

[10] the Big Dipper, a constellation which never sets at England's latitude
[11] Hermes Trismegistus, allegedly the author of books of secret lore
[12] recall from immortality   [13] legendary capital of Boeotia
[14] sixth-century Greek poet

Or bid the soul of Orpheus sing
Such notes as, warbled to the string,
Drew iron tears down Pluto's cheek
And made Hell grant what Love did seek.
Or call up him that left half-told
The story of Cambuscan bold,   110
Of Camball, and of Algarsife,
And who had Canacé to wife
That owned the virtuous ring and glass;
And of the wondrous horses of brass,
On which the Tartar king did ride; [15]
And if aught else great bards beside,
In sage and solemn tunes have sung,
Of tourneys, and of trophies hung;
Of forests, and enchantments drear,
Where more is meant that meets the ear.   120
    Thus, Night, oft see me in thy pale career,
Till civil-suited Morn [16] appear,
Not tricked and frounced as she was wont
With the Attic Boy [17] to hunt,
But kerchiefed in a comely cloud,
While rocking winds are piping loud,
Or ushered with a shower still,
When the gust hath blown his fill,
Ending on the rustling leaves,
With minute drops from off the eaves.   130
And when the sun begins to fling
His flaring beams, me, goddess, bring
To archéd walks of twilight groves,
And shadows brown, that Sylvan [18] loves,
Of pine, or monumental oak,
Where the rude axe, with heavéd stroke,
Was never heard the nymphs to daunt,
Or fright them from their hallowed haunt.
There in close covert by some brook,
Where no profaner eye may look,   140
Hide me from day's garish eye,
While the bee with honeyed thigh,
That at her flowery work doth sing,
And the waters murmuring,
With such consort as they keep,
Entice the dewy-feathered Sleep;
And let some strange mysterious dream
Wave at his wings in airy stream

[15] references to Chaucer's unfinished "Squire's Tale"   [16] Aurora
[17] Cephalus, beloved of Aurora   [18] god of the woods

Of lively portraiture displayed,
Softly on my eyelids laid.   150
And, as I wake, sweet music breathe
Above, about, or underneath,
Sent by some Spirit to mortals good,
Or the unseen Genius of the wood.
   But let my due feet never fail
To walk the studious cloister's pale,
And love the high-embowéd roof,
With antique pillars massy proof,
And storied windows richly dight,
Casting a dim religious light.   160
There let the pealing organ blow
To the full-voiced choir below,
In service high and anthems clear,
As may with sweetness, through mine ear,
Dissolve me into ecstasies,
And bring all Heaven before mine eyes.
   And may at last my weary age
Find out the peaceful hermitage,
The hairy gown and mossy cell,
Where I may sit and rightly spell   170
Of every star that heaven doth shew,
And every herb that sips the dew;
Till old experience do attain
To something like prophetic strain.
   These pleasures, Melancholy, give,
And I with thee will choose to live.

[1631?]

HOW SOON HATH TIME

How soon hath Time, the subtle thief of youth,
  Stol'n on his wing my three-and-twentieth year!
My hasting days fly on with full career,
But my late spring no bud or blossom shew'th.
Perhaps my semblance might deceive the truth,
That I to manhood am arrived so near,
And inward ripeness doth much less appear,
That some more timely-happy spirits endu'th.

Yet it be less or more, or soon or slow,
It shall be still in strictest measure even   10
To that same lot, however mean or high,
Toward Time leads me, and the will of Heaven;
All is, if I have grace to use it so,
As ever in my great Taskmaster's eye.

[1631]

WHEN I CONSIDER HOW MY LIGHT IS SPENT

WHEN I consider how my light is spent
Ere half my days in this dark world and wide,
And that one talent which is death to hide
Lodged with me useless, though my soul more bent
To serve therewith my Maker, and present
My true account, lest He returning chide,
"Doth God exact day-labor, light denied?"
I fondly ask. But Patience, to prevent
That murmur, soon replies, "God doth not need
Either man's work or his own gifts. Who best   10
Bear His mild yoke, they serve Him best. His state
Is kingly: thousands at His bidding speed,
And post o'er land and ocean without rest;
They also serve who only stand and wait."

[1652?]

METHOUGHT I SAW MY LATE ESPOUSÉD SAINT

METHOUGHT I saw my late espoused Saint
Brought to me like Alcestis¹ from the grave,
Whom Jove's great son to her glad husband gave,
Rescued from death by force though pale and faint.
Mine as whom washed from spot of child-bed taint,
Purification in the old Law² did save,
And such, as yet once more I trust to have
Full sight of her in Heaven without restraint,
Came vested all in white, pure as her mind:
Her face was veiled; yet to my fancied sight,   10
Love, sweetness, goodness, in her person shined
So clear, as in no face with more delight.
But O as to embrace me she enclined
I waked, she fled, and day brought back my night.

[1658?]

¹ the wife of Admetus, returned from death by Hercules
² rules for purification of women after childbirth, set forth in Leviticus, 12

Richard Crashaw
1612–1649

AN EPITAPH UPON A YOUNG MARRIED COUPLE DEAD AND BURIED TOGETHER

To THESE, whom death again did wed,
This grave's their second marriage-bed.
For though the hand of fate could force
'Twixt soul and body a divorce,
It could not sunder man and wife,
'Cause they both livéd but one life.
Peace, good reader. Do not weep.
Peace, the lovers are asleep.
They, sweet turtles, folded lie
In the last knot love could tie. 10
And though they lie as they were dead,
Their pillow stone, their sheets of lead,
(Pillow hard, and sheets not warm)
Love made the bed; they'll take no harm;
Let them sleep; let them sleep on.
Till this stormy night be gone,
Till th'eternal morrow dawn;
Then the curtains will be drawn
And they wake into a light,
Whose day shall never die in night. 20

[1646]

UPON THE BODY OF OUR BLESSÉD LORD, NAKED AND BLOODY

They have left thee naked, Lord; O that they had!
This garment too I would they had denied.

Thee with thyself they have too richly clad,
Opening the purple wardrobe in thy side.

O never could there be garment too good
For thee to wear, but this, of thine own blood.

[1652]

Andrew Marvell
1621–1678

ON A DROP OF DEW

S EE how the orient[1] dew,
   Shed from the bosom of the morn
Into the blowing roses,
Yet careless of its mansion new ;
For the clear region where 'twas born
   Round in itself encloses :
   And in its little globe's extent,
Frames as it can its native element.
   How it the purple flower does slight,
     Scarce touching where it lies,   10
   But gazing back upon the skies,
     Shines with a mournful light ;
   Like its own tear,
Because so long divided from the sphere.
   Restless it rolls and unsecure,
     Trembling lest it grow impure :
Till the warm sun pity its pain,
And to the skies exhale it back again.
   So the soul, that drop, that ray
Of the clear fountain of eternal day,   20
Could it within the human flower be seen,
     Rememb'ring still its former height,
     Shuns the sweet leaves and blossoms green ;
     And, recollecting its own light,
Does, in its pure and circling thoughts, express
The greater heaven in a heaven less.
     In how coy a figure wound,
     Every way it turns away :
     So the world excluding round,
     Yet receiving in the day.   30
     Dark beneath, but bright above :
     Here disdaining, there in love.
How loose and easy hence to go :
How girt and ready to ascend.
Moving but on a point below,
It all about does upwards bend.

[1] bright and lustrous, like a pearl

Such did the manna's[2] sacred dew distill :
White, and entire, though congealed and chill.
Congealed on earth : but does, dissolving, run
Into the glories of the almighty sun.   40
[1681]

[2] a food (perhaps a fungus) that appeared by a miracle to sustain the Israelites in
their flight from Egypt. The manna appeared in the night, and melted in the sun.

THE GARDEN

How vainly men themselves amaze
To win the palm, the oak, or bays ;
And their incessant labors see
Crowned from some single herb, or tree,
Whose short and narrow-vergéd shade
Does prudently their toils upbraid ;
While all flowers and all trees do close
To weave the garlands of repose !

Fair Quiet, have I found thee here,
And Innocence, thy sister dear ?   10
Mistaken long, I sought you then
In busy companies of men.
Your sacred plants, if here below,
Only among the plants will grow ;
Society is all but rude
To this delicious solitude.

No white nor red was ever seen
So amorous as this lovely green.
Fond lovers, cruel as their flame,
Cut in these trees their mistress' name :   20
Little, alas ! they know or heed
How far these beauties hers exceed !
Fair trees ! wheres'e'er your barks I wound
No name shall but your own be found.

When we have run our passion's heat,
Love hither makes his best retreat.
The gods, that mortal beauty chase,
Still in a tree did end their race ;
Apollo hunted Daphne so,[1]
Only that she might laurel grow ;   30

[1] Daphne prayed for help when Apollo had almost overtaken her ; she was transformed into a laurel tree.

And Pan did after Syrinx speed,[2]
Not as a nymph, but for a reed.

What wondrous life is this I lead!
Ripe apples drop about my head;
The luscious clusters of the vine
Upon my mouth do crush their wine;
The nectarine, and curious peach,
Into my hands themselves do reach;
Stumbling on melons, as I pass,
Ensnared with flowers, I fall on grass.   40

Meanwhile, the mind, from pleasure less,
Withdraws into its happiness:
The mind, that ocean where each kind
Does straight its own resemblance find;
Yet it creates, transcending these,
Far other worlds, and other seas;
Annihilating all that's made
To a green thought in a green shade.

Here at the fountain's sliding foot,
Or at some fruit-tree's mossy root,   50
Casting the body's vest aside,
My soul into the boughs does glide:
There like a bird it sits, and sings,
Then whets and combs its silver wings;
And, till prepared for longer flight,
Waves in its plumes the various light.

Such was that happy garden-state,
While man there walked without a mate:
After a place so pure and sweet,
What other help could yet be meet?   60
But 'twas beyond a mortal's share
To wander solitary there:
Two paradises 'twere in one,
To live in paradise alone.

How well the skillful gardener drew
Of flowers, and herbs, this dial new;
Where, from above, the milder sun
Does through a fragrant zodiac run;

---

[2] Under similar circumstances, Syrinx was metamorphosed into a reed, from which
Pan then made a flute.

And, as it works, the industrious bee
Computes its time as well as we. 70
How could such sweet and wholesome hours
Be reckoned but with herbs and flowers!

[1681]

BERMUDAS

WHERE the remote Bermudas ride
In th' ocean's bosom unespied,
From a small boat, that rowed along,
The list'ning winds received this song.
  What should we do but sing His praise
That led us through the wat'ry maze,
Unto an isle so long unknown,
And yet far kinder than our own?
Where He the huge sea-monsters wracks,
That lift the deep upon their backs; 10
He lands us on a grassy stage,
Safe from the storms, and prelate's rage.
He gives us this eternal spring,
Which here enamels everything;
And sends the fowls to us in care,
On daily visits through the air.
He hangs in shades the orange bright,
Like golden lamps in a green night,
And does in the pomegrantes close
Jewels more rich than Ormus[1] shows. 20
He makes the figs our mouths to meet,
And throws the melons at our feet;
But apples plants of such a price,
No tree could ever bear them twice.
With cedars, chosen by His hand,
From Lebanon, He stores the land;
And makes the hollow seas, that roar,
Proclaim the ambergris on shore.
He cast (of which we rather boast)
The gospel's pearl upon our coast; 30
And in these rocks for us did frame
A temple, where to sound His name.
Oh let our voice His praise exalt,
Till it arrive at Heaven's vault:

[1] Ormuz, a Portuguese port in the Middle East, of fabled wealth

Which thence (perhaps) rebounding, may
Echo beyond the Mexique Bay.
  Thus sung they, in the English boat,
An holy and a cheerful note,
And all the way, to guide their chime,
With falling oars they kept the time.   40
                                                        [1681]

TO HIS COY MISTRESS

HAD we but world enough, and time,
  This coyness, lady, were no crime.
We would sit down, and think which way
To walk, and pass our long love's day.
Thou by the Indian Ganges' side
Shouldst rubies find : I by the tide
Of Humber[1] would complain. I would
Love you ten years before the Flood :
And you should if you please refuse
Till the conversion of the Jews.   10
My vegetable love should grow
Vaster than empires, and more slow.
An hundred years should go to praise
Thine eyes, and on thy forehead gaze.
Two hundred to adore each breast :
But thirty thousand to the rest.
An age at least to every part,
And the last age should show your heart.
For, lady, you deserve this state ;
Nor would I love at lower rate.   20
   But at my back I always hear
Time's wingèd chariot hurrying near :
And yonder all before us lie
Deserts of vast eternity.
Thy beauty shall no more be found,
Nor, in thy marble vault, shall sound
My echoing song ; then worms shall try
That long preserved virginity :
And your quaint honor turn to dust ;
And into ashes all my lust.   30
The grave's a fine and private place,
But none, I think, do there embrace.

---

[1] a rather commonplace English river

Now therefore, while the youthful hue
Sits on thy skin like morning dew,
And while thy willing soul transpires
At every pore with instant fires,
Now let us sport us while we may;
And now, like am'rous birds of prey,
Rather at once our time devour,
Than languish in his slow-chapped[2] pow'r.   40
Let us roll all our strength, and all
Our sweetness, up into one ball:
And tear our pleasures with rough strife,
Through the iron gates of life.
Thus, though we cannot make our sun
Stand still, yet we will make him run.

[1681]

---

[2] slow-jawed

Later Ballads

EDWARD

"WHY dois your brand sae drap wi bluid,
  Edward, Edward,
Why dois your brand sae drap wi bluid,
  And why sae sad gang¹ yee O ?"
"O I hae killed my hauke sae guid,
  Mither, mither,
O I hae killed my hauke sae guid,
  And I had nae mair bot hee O."

"Your haukis bluid was nevir sae reid,
  Edward, Edward,   10
Your haukis bluid was nevir sae reid,
  My deir son I tell thee O."
"O I hae killed my reid-roan steid,
  Mither, mither,
O I hae killed my reid-roan steid,
  That erst was sae fair and frie O."

"Your steid was auld, and ye hae got mair,
  Edward, Edward,
Your steid was auld, and ye hae got mair,
  Sum other dule² ye drie³ O."   20
"O I hae killed my fadir deir,
  Mither, mither,
Oh I hae killed my fadir deir,
  Alas, and wae is mee O !"

"And whatten penance wul ye drie for that,
  Edward, Edward,
And whatten penance will ye drie for that?
  My deir son, now tell me O."
"Ile set my feit in yonder boat,
  Mither, mither,   30
Ile set my feit in yonder boat,
  And Ile fare ovir the sea O."

¹ go ² woe ³ suffer

"And what wul ye doe wi your towirs and your ha,[4]
  Edward, Edward?
And what wul ye doe wi your towirs and your ha,
  That were sae fair to see O?"
"Ile let thame stand tul they doun fa,
  Mither, mither,
Ile let thame stand tul they doun fa,
  For here nevir mair maun I bee O."   40

"And what wul ye leive to your bairns and your wife,
  Edward, Edward?
And what wul ye leive to your bairns and your wife,
  Whan ye gang ovir the Sea O?"
"The warldis room, late them beg thrae life,
  Mither, mither,
The warldis room, late them beg thrae life,
  For thame nevir mair wul I see O."

"And what wul ye leive to your ain mither deir,
  Edward, Edward,   50
And what wul ye leive to your ain mither deir?
  My deir son, now tell me O."
"The curse of hell frae me sall ye beir,
  Mither, mither,
The curse of hell frae me sall ye beir,
  Sic counseils ye gave to me O."

[4] hall

SIR PATRICK SPENS

THE king sits in Dumferling toune,
  Drinking the blude-reid wine:
"O whar will I get guid sailor,
  To sail this schip of mine?"

Up and spak an eldern knicht,
  Sat at the kings richt kne:
"Sir Patrick Spens is the best sailor,
  That sails upon the se."

The king has written a braid letter,
  And signd it wi his hand,   10
And sent it to Sir Patrick Spens,
  Was walking on the sand.

The first line that Sir Patrick red,
  A loud lauch lauchéd[1] he ;
The next line that Sir Patrick red,
  The teir blinded his ee.

"O wha is this has don this deid,
  This ill deid don to me,
To send me out this time o' the yeir,
  To sail upon the se !   20

"Mak hast, make hast, my mirry men all
  Our guid schip sails the morne : "
"O say na sae, my master deir,
  For I feir a deadlie storme.

"Late, late yestreen I saw the new moone,
  Wi the auld moone in hir arme,
And I feir, I feir, my deir master,
  That we will cum to harme."

O our Scots nobles wer richt laith[2]
  To weet their cork-heild schoone,[3]   30
Bot lang owre[4] a' the play wer playd,
  Their hats they swam aboone.

O lang, lang may their ladies sit,
  Wi thair fans into their hand,
Or eir they se Sir Patrick Spens
  Cum sailing to the land.

O lang, lang may the ladies stand,
  Wi thair gold kems in their hair
Waiting for thar ain deir lords,
  For they'll se thame na mair.   40

Half owre,[5] half owre to Aberdour,
  It's fiftie fadom deip,
And thair lies guid Sir Patrick Spens,
  Wi the Scots lords at his feit.

---

[1] laughed   [2] loath   [3] shoes   [4] ere   [5] over

Jonathan Swift
1667–1745

A DESCRIPTION OF THE MORNING

Now hardly here and there a hackney-coach
Appearing, showed the ruddy morn's approach.
Now Betty from her master's bed had flown,
And softly stole to discompose her own;
The slip-shod 'prentice from his master's door
Had pared the dirt, and sprinkled round the floor.
Now Moll had whirled her mop with dext'rous airs,
Prepared to scrub the entry and the stairs.
The youth with broomy stumps began to trace
The kennel-edge where wheels had worn the place.   10
The small-coal man was heard with cadence deep,
Till drowned in shriller notes of chimney-sweep:
Duns at his lordship's gate began to meet;
And brick-dust Moll had screamed through half the street.
The turnkey now his flock returning sees,
Duly let out a-nights to steal for fees:
The watchful bailiffs take their silent stands,
And schoolboys lag with satchels in their hands.

[1709]

CLEVER TOM CLINCH GOING TO BE HANGED

As clever Tom Clinch, while the rabble was bawling,
Rode stately through Holborn, to die in his calling;
He stopped at the George for a bottle of sack,
And promised to pay for it when he'd come back.
His waistcoat and stockings and breeches were white,
His cap had a new cherry ribbon to tie't.
The maids to the doors and the balconies ran,
And said, "Lack-a-day! He's a proper young man."
But as from the windows the ladies he spied,
Like a beau in a box, he bowed low on each side;   10
And when his last speech the loud hawkers did cry,
He swore from his cart, it was all a damned lie.
The hangman for pardon fell down on his knee;
Tom gave him a kick in the guts for his fee.
Then said, "I must speak to the people a little,
But I'll see you all damned before I will whittle.[1]

[1] a cant word for confessing at the gallows

My honest friend Wild,[2] may he long hold his place,
He lengthened my life with a whole year of grace.
Take courage, dear comrades, and be not afraid,
Nor slip this occasion to follow your trade.
My conscience is clear, and my spirits are calm,
And thus I go off without prayerbook or psalm."
Then follow the practice of clever Tom Clinch,
Who hung like a hero and never would flinch.

[1726–27]

[2] the noted thief-catcher (Swift's notes)

Alexander Pope
1688–1744
THE RAPE OF THE LOCK
AN HEROI-COMICAL POEM

Nolueram, Belinda, tuos violare capillos;
Sed juvat, hoc precibus me tribuisse tuis.
—MARTIAL, *Epigrams XII, 84.*[1]

CANTO I

WHAT dire offense from am'rous causes springs,
What mighty contests rise from trivial things,
I sing—This verse to *Caryl*,[2] Muse! is due:
This, even Belinda may vouchsafe to view:
Slight is the subject, but not so the praise,
If she inspire, and he approve my lays.
    Say what strange motive, Goddess! could compel
A well-bred lord t' assault a gentle belle?
O say what stranger cause, yet unexplored,
Could make a gentle belle reject a lord?   10
In tasks so bold, can little men engage,
And in soft bosoms dwells such mighty rage?
    Sol through white curtains shot a tim'rous ray,
And oped those eyes that must eclipse the day:
Now lap-dogs give themselves the rousing shake,
And sleepless lovers, just at twelve, awake:

[1] "I did not wish, Belinda, to profane your locks, but I am delighted to yield this to your beseeching."
[2] John Caryll, a close friend, who suggested the subject of the poem to Pope

Thrice rung the bell, the slipper knocked the ground,
And the pressed watch[3] returned a silver sound.
Belinda still her downy pillow pressed,
Her guardian sylph prolonged the balmy rest: 20
'Twas he had summoned to her silent bed
The morning-dream that hovered o'er her head;
A youth more glitt'ring than a birth-night beau,[4]
(That even in slumber caused her cheek to glow)
Seemed to her ear his winning lips to lay,
And thus in whispers said, or seemed to say:
    "Fairest of mortals, thou distinguished care
Of thousand bright inhabitants of air!
If e'er one vision touched thy infant thought,
Of all the nurse and all the priest have taught;   30
Of airy elves by moonlight shadows seen,
The silver token, and the circled green,
Or virgins visited by angel-powers,
With golden crowns and wreaths of heav'nly flowers;
Hear and believe! thy own importance know,
Nor bound thy narrow views to things below.
Some secret truths, from learnéd pride concealed,
To maids alone and children are revealed:
What though no credit doubting wits may give?
The fair and innocent shall still believe.
Know, then, unnumbered spirits round thee fly,   40
The light militia of the lower sky:
These, though unseen, are ever on the wing,
Hang o'er the box,[5] and hover round the Ring.[6]
Think what an equipage thou hast in air,
And view with scorn two pages and a chair.[7]
As now your own our beings were of old,
And once inclosed in woman's beauteous mold;
Thence, by a soft transition, we repair
From earthly vehicles to these of air.   50
Think not, when woman's transient breath is fled,
That all her vanities at once are dead;
Succeeding vanities she still regards,
And though she plays no more, o'erlooks the cards.
Her joy in gilded chariots, when alive,
And love of ombre,[8] after death survive.

[3] Pressing the stem makes the watch chime the hour.
[4] young man dressed in brilliant costume for a royal birthday   [5] at the theater
[6] the drive in Hyde Park   [7] sedan chair
[8] the card game that Belinda plays with the Baron in Canto III

For when the fair in all their pride expire,
To their first elements their souls retire :
The sprites of fiery termagants [9] in flame
Mount up, and take a salamander's [10] name.   60
Soft yielding minds to water glide away,
And sip, with nymphs, their elemental tea.
The graver prude sinks downward to a gnome,
In search of mischief still on earth to roam.
The light coquettes in sylphs aloft repair,
And sport and flutter in the fields of air.
    "Know further yet; whoever fair and chaste
Rejects mankind, is by some sylph embraced :
For spirits, freed from mortal laws, with ease
Assume what sexes and what shapes they please.   70
What guards the purity of melting maids,
In courtly balls, and midnight masquerades,
Safe from the treach'rous friend, the daring spark,
The glance by day, the whisper in the dark,
When kind occasion prompts their warm desires,
When music softens, and when dancing fires?
'Tis but their sylph, the wise celestials know,
Though honor is the word with men below.
    "Some nymphs there are, too conscious of their face,
For life predestined to the gnomes' embrace.   80
These swell their prospects and exalt their pride,
When offers are disdained, and love denied :
Then gay ideas crowd the vacant brain,
While peers, and dukes, and all their sweeping train,
And garters, stars, and coronets appear,
And in soft sounds, 'Your Grace' salutes their ear.
'Tis these that early taint the female soul,
Instruct the eyes of young coquettes to roll,
Teach infant-cheeks a bidden blush to know,
And little hearts to flutter at a beau.   90
    "Oft, when the world imagine women stray,
The sylphs through mystic mazes guide their way,
Through all the giddy circle they pursue,
And old impertinence expel by new.
What tender maid but must a victim fall
To one man's treat, but for another's ball?
When Florio what virgin could withstand,
If gentle Damon [11] did not squeeze her hand?

---

[9] shrewish women
[10] a lizard-like creature, once believed capable of living in fire
[11] conventional names in pastoral poetry

With varying vanities, from every part,
They shift the moving toyshop of their heart;   100
Where wigs with wigs, with sword-knots sword-knots strive,
Beaux banish beaux, and coaches coaches drive.
This erring mortals levity may call;
Oh blind to truth! the sylphs contrive it all.
    "Oh these am I, who thy protection claim,
A watchful sprite, and Ariel is my name.
Late, as I ranged the crystal wilds of air,
In the clear mirror of thy ruling star
I saw, alas! some dread event impend,
Ere to the main this morning sun descend,   110
But heaven reveals not what, or how, or where:
Warned by the sylph, oh pious maid, beware!
This to disclose is all thy guardian can:
Beware of all, but most beware of man!"
    He said; when Shock,[12] who thought she slept too long,
Leaped up, and waked his mistress with his tongue.
'Twas then, Belinda, if report say true,
Thy eyes first opened on a billet-doux;
Wounds, charms, and ardors were no sooner read,
But all the vision vanished from thy head.   120
    And now, unveiled, the toilet stands displayed,
Each silver vase in mystic order laid.
First, robed in white, the nymph intent adores,
With head uncovered, the cosmetic powers.
A heav'nly image in the glass appears,
To that she bends, to that her eyes she rears;
Th' inferior priestess,[13] at her altar's side,
Trembling begins the sacred rites of pride.
Unnumbered treasures ope at once, and here
The various off'rings of the world appear;   130
From each she nicely culls with curious[14] toil,
And decks the goddess with the glitt'ring spoil.
This casket India's glowing gems unlocks,
And all Arabia breathes from yonder box.
The tortoise here and elephant unite,
Transformed to combs, the speckled, and the white.
Here files of pins extend their shining rows,
Puffs, powders, patches, bibles,[15] billet-doux.
Now awful Beauty puts on all its arms;
The fair each moment rises in her charms,   140

---

[12] Belinda's lap dog   [13] Betty, Belinda's lady's maid   [14] painstaking
[15] perhaps curling papers

Repairs her smiles, awakens every grace,
And calls forth all the wonders of her face;
Sees by degrees a purer blush arise,
And keener lightnings quicken in her eyes.
The busy sylphs surround their darling care,
These set the head, and those divide the hair,
Some fold the sleeve, whilst others plait the gown;
And Betty's praised for labors not her own.

CANTO II

Not with more glories, in th' ethereal plain,
The sun first rises o'er the purpled main,
Than, issuing forth, the rival of his beams
Launched on the bosom of the silver Thames.
Fair nymphs, and well-dressed youths around her shone,
But every eye was fixed on her alone.
On her white breast a sparkling cross she wore,
Which Jews might kiss, and infidels adore.
Her lively looks a sprightly mind disclose,
Quick as her eyes, and as unfixed as those: 10
Favors to one, to all she smiles extends;
Oft she rejects, but never once offends.
Bright as the sun, her eyes the gazers strike,
And, like the sun, they shine on all alike.
Yet graceful ease, and sweetness void of pride,
Might hide her faults, if belles had faults to hide:
If to her share some female errors fall,
Look on her face, and you'll forget 'em all.
        This nymph, to the destruction of mankind,
Nourished two locks, which graceful hung behind   20
In equal curls, and well conspired to deck
With shining ringlets the smooth iv'ry neck.
Love in these labyrinths his slaves detains,
And mighty hearts are held in slender chains.
With hairy springes we the birds betray,
Slight lines of hair surprise the finny prey,
Fair tresses man's imperial race ensnare,
And beauty draws us with a single hair.
        Th' advent'rous Baron the bright locks admired;
He saw, he wished, and to the prize aspired.   30
Resolved to win, he meditates the way,
By force to ravish, or by fraud betray;
For when success a lover's toil attends,
Few ask, if fraud or force attained his ends.
        For this, ere Phœbus rose, he had implored
Propitious heaven, and every power adored,

But chiefly Love—to Love an altar built,
Of twelve vast French romances, neatly gilt.
There lay three garters, half a pair of gloves;
And all the trophies of his former loves;   40
With tender billet-doux he lights the pyre,
And breathes three am'rous sighs to raise the fire.
Then prostrate falls, and begs with ardent eyes
Soon to obtain, and long possess the prize:
The powers gave ear, and granted half his prayer,
The rest, the winds dispersed in empty air.
    But now secure the painted vessel glides,
The sun-beams trembling on the floating tides:
While melting music steals upon the sky,
And softened sounds along the waters die;   50
Smooth flow the waves, the zephyrs gently play,
Belinda smiled, and all the world was gay.
All but the sylph—with careful thoughts oppressed,
Th' impending woe sat heavy on his breast.
He summons straight his denizens of air;
The lucid squadrons round the sails repair:
Soft o'er the shrouds aërial whispers breathe,
That seemed but zephyrs to the train beneath.
Some to the sun their insect-wings unfold,
Waft on the breeze, or sink in clouds of gold;   60
Transparent forms, too fine for mortal sight,
Their fluid bodies half dissolved in light.
Loose to the wind their airy garments flew,
Thin glitt'ring textures of the filmy dew,
Dipped in the richest tincture of the skies,
Where light disports in ever-mingling dyes,
While every beam new transient colors flings,
Colors that change whene'er they wave their wings.
Amid the circle, on the gilded mast,
Superior by the head, was Ariel placed;   70
His purple pinions opening to the sun,
He raised his azure wand, and thus begun.
    "Ye sylphs and sylphids, to your chief give ear!
Fays, fairies, genii, elves, and dæmons, hear!
Ye know the spheres and various tasks assigned
By laws eternal to th' aërial kind.
Some in the fields of purest ether play,
And bask and whiten in the blaze of day.
Some guide the course of wand'ring orbs on high,
Or roll the planets through the boundless sky.   80
Some less refined, beneath the moon's pale light
Pursue the stars that shoot athwart the night,

Or suck the mists in grosser air below,
Or dip their pinions in the painted bow,
Or brew fierce tempests on the wintry main,
Or o'er the glebe[16] distil the kindly rain.
Others on earth o'er human race preside,
Watch all their ways, and all their actions guide:
Of these the chief the care of nations own,
And guard with arms divine the British throne.   90
    "Our humbler province is to tend the fair,
Not a less pleasing, though less glorious care;
To save the powder from too rude a gale,
Nor let th' imprisoned essences exhale;
To draw fresh colors from the vernal flowers;
To steal from rainbows ere they drop in showers
A brighter wash; to curl their waving hairs,
Assist their blushes, and inspire their airs;
Nay oft, in dreams, invention we bestow,
To change a flounce, or add a furbelow.   100
    "This day, black omens threat the brightest fair,
That e'er deserved a watchful spirit's care;
Some dire disaster, or by force, or sleight;
But what, or where, the fates have wrapped in night.
Whether the nymphs shall break Diana's law,[17]
Or some frail China jar receive a flaw;
Or stain her honor or her new brocade;
Forget her prayers, or miss a masquerade;
Or lose her heart, or necklace, at a ball;
Or whether Heaven has doomed that Shock must fall.   110
Haste, then, ye spirits! to your charge repair:
The flutt'ring fan be Zephyretta's care;
The drops[18] to thee, Brillante, we consign;
And, Momentilla, let the watch be thine;
Do thou, Crispissa, tend her fav'rite lock;
Ariel himself shall be the guard of Shock.
    "To fifty chosen sylphs, of special note,
We trust th' important charge, the petticoat:
Oft have we known that seven-fold fence to fail,
Though stiff with hoops, and armed with ribs of whale;   120
Form a strong line about the silver bound,
And guard the wide circumference around.
    "Whatever spirit, careless of his charge,
His post neglects, or leaves the fair at large,
Shall feel sharp vengeance soon o'ertake his sins,
Be stopped in vials, or transfixed with pins;

---

[16] cultivated land   [17] the law of chastity   [18] pendant earrings

Or plunged in lakes of bitter washes lie,
Or wedged whole ages in a bodkin's eye :
Gums and pomatums shall his flight restrain,
While clogged he beats his silken wings in vain ;   130
Or alum styptics with contracting power
Shrink his thin essence like a riveled flower :
Or, as Ixion[19] fixed, the wretch shall feel
The giddy motion of the whirling mill,
In fumes of burning chocolate shall glow,
And tremble at the sea that froths below ! "
   He spoke ; the spirits from the sails descend ;
Some, orb in orb, around the nymph extend ;
Some thrid the mazy ringlets of her hair ;
Some hang upon the pendants of her ear :   140
With beating hearts the dire event they wait,
Anxious, and trembling for the birth of Fate.

CANTO III

CLOSE by those meads, forever crowned with flowers,
Where Thames with pride surveys his rising towers,
There stands a structure[20] of majestic frame,
Which from the neighb'ring Hampton takes its name.
Here Britain's statesmen oft the fall foredoom
Of foreign tyrants and of nymphs at home ;
Here thou, great Anna ![21] whom three realms obey,
Dost sometimes counsel take—and sometimes tea.
   Hither the heroes and the nymphs resort,
To taste awhile the pleasures of a court ;   10
In various talk th' instructive hours they passed,
Who gave the ball, or paid the visit last ;
One speaks the glory of the British queen,
And one describes a charming Indian screen ;
A third interprets motions, looks, and eyes ;
At every word a reputation dies.
Snuff, or the fan, supply each pause of chat,
With singing, laughing, ogling, and all that.
   Meanwhile, declining from the noon of day,
The sun obliquely shoots his burning ray ;   20
The hungry judges soon the sentence sign,
And wretches hang that jury-men may dine ;
The merchant from th' Exchange returns in peace,
And the long labors of the toilet cease.

[19] punished by being chained to a wheel that rolled eternally through the air
[20] Hampton Court, a royal palace
[21] Queen Anne, ruler of "three realms" : England, Scotland, and Wales

Belinda now, whom thirst of fame invites,
Burns to encounter two advent'rous knights,
At ombre[22] singly to decide their doom;
And swells her breast with conquests yet to come.
Straight the three bands prepare in arms to join,
Each band the number of the sacred nine.[23]   30
Soon as she spreads her hand, th' aërial guard
Descend, and sit on each important card:
First Ariel perched upon a matadore,
Then each, according to the rank they bore;
For sylphs, yet mindful of their ancient race,
Are, as when women, wondrous fond of place.

  Behold, four kings in majesty revered,
With hoary whiskers and a forky beard;
And four fair queens whose hands sustain a flower,
Th' expressive emblem of their softer power;   40
Four knaves in garbs succinct, a trusty band,
Caps on their heads, and halberts in their hand;
And particolored troops, a shining train,
Draw forth to combat on the velvet plain.
  The skilful nymph reviews her force with care:
Let spades be trumps! she said, and trumps they were.
  Now move to war her sable matadores,
In show like leaders of the swarthy Moors.
Spadillio first, unconquerable lord!
Led off two captive trumps, and swept the board.   50
As many more Manillio forced to yield,
And marched a victor from the verdant field.
Him Basto followed, but his fate more hard
Gained but one trump and one plebian card.
With his broad sabre next, a chief in years,
Puts forth one manly leg, to sight revealed,
The rest, his many-colored robe concealed.
The rebel knave, who dares his prince engage,
Proves the just victim of his royal rage.   60
Even mighty Pam,[24] that kings and queens o'erthrew
And mowed down armies in the fights of loo,
Sad chance of war! now destitute of aid,
Falls undistinguished by the victor spade!

---

[22] The card game is played out accurately. The three "matadores" or high cards are called "Spadillio," "Manillio," and "Basto," but the cards which carry these names vary with the trump suit. Belinda's matadores are "sable" (1. 47) because she declares spades trumps.

[23] the Muses. A player's hand consists of nine cards.

[24] in loo, the highest card, the jack (knave) of clubs

Thus far both armies to Belinda yield;
Now to the Baron fate inclines the field.
His warlike Amazon[25] her host invades,
Th' imperial consort of the crown of spades.
The club's black tyrant first her victim died,
Spite of his haughty mien, and barb'rous pride: 70
What boots the regal circle on his head,
His giant limbs, in state unwieldy spread;
That long behind he trails his pompous robe,
And, of all monarchs, only grasps the globe?
     The Baron now his diamonds pours apace;
Th'embroidered king who shows but half his face,
And his refulgent queen, with powers combined
Of broken troops an easy conquest find.
Clubs, diamonds, hearts, in wild disorder seen,
With throngs promiscuous strow the level green.   80
Thus when dispersed a routed army runs,
Of Asia's troops, and Afric's sable sons,
With like confusion different nations fly,
Of various habit, and of various dye,
The pierced battalions disunited fall,
In heaps on heaps; one fate o'erwhelms them all.
     The knave of diamonds tries his wily arts,
And wins (oh shameful chance!) the queen of hearts.
At this, the blood the virgin's cheek forsook,
A livid paleness spreads o'er all her look;   90
She sees, and trembles at th' approaching ill,
Just in the jaws of ruin, and codille.[26]
And now (as oft in some distempered state)
On one nice trick depends the general fate.
An ace of hearts steps forth: The king unseen
Lurked in her hand, and mourned his captive queen:
He springs to vengeance with an eager pace,
And falls like thunder on the prostrate ace.
The nymph exulting fills with shouts the sky;
The walls, the woods, and long canals reply.   100
     Oh thoughtless mortals! ever blind to fate,
Too soon dejected, and too soon elate.
Sudden, these honors shall be snatched away,
And cursed for ever this victorious day.
     For lo! the board with cups and spoons is crowned,
The berries crackle,[27] and the mill turns round;

[25] in Greek mythology, one of a tribe of female warriors; here, the queen of spades
[26] failure to make one's bid   [27] Coffee is ground at the table.

On shining altars of Japan[28] they raise
The silver lamp; the fiery spirits blaze:
From silver spouts the grateful liquors glide,
While China's earth receives the smoking tide: 110
At once they gratify their scent and taste,
And frequent cups prolong the rich repast.
Straight hover round the fair her airy band;
Some, as she sipped, the fuming liquor fanned,
Some o'er her lap their careful plumes displayed,
Trembling, and conscious of the rich brocade.
Coffee (which makes the politician wise,
And see through all things with his half-shut eyes)
Sent up in vapors to the Baron's brain
New stratagems, the radiant lock to gain.   120
Ah cease, rash youth! desist ere 'tis too late,
Fear the just gods, and think of Scylla's[29] fate!
Changed to a bird, and sent to flit in air,
She dearly pays for Nisis' injured hair!
     But when to mischief mortals bend their will,
How soon they find fit instruments of ill!
Just then, Clarissa drew with tempting grace
A two-edged weapon from her shining case:
So ladies in romance assist their knight,
Present the spear, and arm him for the fight.   130
He takes the gift with rev'rence, and extends
The little engine on his fingers' ends;
This just behind Belinda's neck he spread,
As o'er the fragrant steams she bends her head.
Swift to the lock a thousand sprites repair,
A thousand wings, by turns, blow back the hair;
And thrice they twitched the diamond in her ear;
Thrice she looked back, and thrice the foe drew near.
Just in that instant, anxious Ariel sought
The close recesses of the virgin's thought;   140
As on the nosegay in her breast reclined,
He watched th' ideas rising in her mind,
Sudden he viewed, in spite of all her art,
An earthly lover lurking at her heart.
Amazed, confused, he found his power expired,
Resigned to fate, and with a sigh retired.

[28] japanned (lacquered) tables
[29] daughter of King Nisus of Megara. She fell in love with an enemy besieging the
the city, and pulled out of her father's head the golden hair on which the safety of the
city depended. When Nisus, metamorphosed into a sea eagle, pounced upon Scylla,
she was changed into a bird.

The peer now spreads the glitt'ring forfex wide,
T' inclose the lock; now joins it, to divide.
Even then, before the fatal engine closed,
A wretched sylph too fondly interposed;   150
Fate urged the shears, and cut the sylph in twain,
(But airy substance soon unites again)
The meeting points the sacred hair dissever
From the fair head, forever, and forever!
Then flashed the living lightning from her eyes,
And screams of horror rend th' affrightened skies.
Not louder shrieks to pitying heaven are cast,
When husbands, or when lap-dogs breathe their last;
Or when rich China vessels fall'n from high,
In glitt'ring dust and painted fragments lie!   160
"Let wreaths of triumph now my temples twine,"
(The victor cried); "the glorious prize is mine!
While fish in streams, or birds delight in air,
Or in a coach and six the British fair,
As long as *Atalantis*[30] shall be read,
Or the small pillow grace a lady's bed,
While visits shall be paid on solemn days,
When num'rous wax-lights in bright order blaze,
While nymphs take treats, or assignations give,
So long my honor, name, and praise shall live!"   170
What time would spare, from steel receives its date,
And monuments, like men, submit to fate!
Steel could the labor of the gods destroy,
And strike to dust th' imperial towers of Troy;
Steel could the works of mortal pride confound,
And hew triumphal arches to the ground.
What wonder then, fair nymph! thy hairs should feel,
The conq'ring of unresisted steel?

CANTO IV

B UT anxious cares the pensive nymph oppressed,
And secret passions labored in her breast.
Not youthful kings in battle seized alive,
Not scornful virgins who their charms survive,
Not ardent lovers robbed of all their bliss,
Not ancient ladies when refused a kiss,
Not tyrants fierce that unrepenting die,
Not Cynthia[31] when her manteau's pinned awry,

---

[30] a contemporary book filled with fashionable gossip
[31] Diana, goddess of chastity

E'er felt such rage, resentment, and despair,   10
As thou, sad virgin! for thy ravished hair.
   For, that sad moment, when the sylphs withdrew
And Ariel weeping from Belinda flew,
Umbriel, a dusky, melancholy sprite,
As ever sullied the fair face of light,
Down to the central earth, his proper scene,
Repaired to search the gloomy Cave of Spleen.[32]
   Swift on his sooty pinions flits the gnome,
And in a vapor reached the dismal dome.
No cheerful breeze this sullen region knows,
The dreaded east is all the wind that blows.   20
Here in a grotto, sheltered close from air,
And screened in shades from day's detested glare,
She sighs forever on her pensive bed,
Pain at her side, and Megrim[33] at her head.
   Two handmaids wait the throne: alike in place,
But diff'ring far in figure and in face.
Here stood Ill-nature like an ancient maid,
Her wrinkled form in black and white arrayed;
With store of prayers, for mornings, nights, and noons,
Her hand is filled; her bosom with lampoons.   30
   There Affectation, with a sickly mien,
Shows in her cheek the roses of eighteen,
Practised to lisp, and hang the head aside,
Faints into airs, and languishes with pride,
On the rich quilt sinks with becoming woe,
Wrapped in a gown, for sickness, and for show.
The fair ones feel such maladies as these,
When each new night-dress gives a new disease.
   A constant vapor o'er the palace flies;
Strange phantoms rising as the mists arise;   40
Dreadful, as hermit's dreams in haunted shades,
Or bright, as visions of expiring maids.
Now glaring fiends, and snakes on rolling spires,[34]
Pale specters, gaping tombs, and purple fires:
Now lakes of liquid gold, Elysian scenes,
And crystal domes, and angels in machines.
   Unnumbered throngs on every side are seen,
Of bodies changed to various forms by Spleen.
Here living tea-pots stand, one arm held out,
One bent; the handle this, and that the spout: 50
A pipkin[35] there, like Homer's tripod[36] walks;
Here sighs a jar, and there a goose-pie talks;

[32] bad temper; malice   [33] low spirits   [34] coils   [35] earthen jar
[36] three-legged stool

Men prove with child, as powerful fancy works,
And maids turned bottles, call aloud for corks.
        Safe past the gnome through this fantastic band,
A branch of healing spleenwort [37] in his hand.
Then thus addressed the power: "Hail, wayward Queen!
Who rule the sex to fifty from fifteen:
Parent of vapors [38] and of female wit,
Who give th' hysteric or poetic fit,   60
On various tempers act by various ways,
Make some take physic, others scribble plays;
Who cause the proud their visits to delay,
And send the godly in a pet to pray.
A nymph there is, that all thy power disdains,
And thousands more in equal mirth maintains.
But oh! if e'er thy gnome could spoil a grace,
Or raise a pimple on a beauteous face,
Like citron-waters [39] matrons' checks inflame,
Or change complexions at a losing game;   70
If e'er with airy horns [40] I planted heads,
Or rumpled petticoats, or tumbled beds,
Or caus'd suspicion when no soul was rude,
Or discomposed the head-dress of a prude,
Or e'er to costive lap-dog gave disease,
Which not the tears of brightest eyes could ease:
Hear me, and touch Belinda with chagrin,
That single act gives half the world the spleen."
        The goddess with a discontented air
Seems to reject him though she grants his prayer.   80
A wondrous bag with both her hands she binds,
Like that where once Ulysses held the winds; [41]
There she collects the force of female lungs,
Sighs, sobs, and passions, and the war of tongues.
A vial next she fills with fainting fears,
Soft sorrows, melting griefs, and flowing tears.
The gnome rejoicing bears her gifts away,
Spreads his black wings, and slowly mounts to day.
        Sunk in Thalestris' [42] arms the nymph he found,
Her eyes dejected and her hair unbound.   90

---

[37] a fern formerly believed effective in relieving spleen
[38] affected emotional depression
[39] a liquor prepared with citrus rinds, believed good for the complexion
[40] The man whose wife is unfaithful is traditionally pictured as growing horns; "airy" here would mean imaginary.
[41] In the Odyssey, Ulysses visits Aeolus, god of winds, who gives the wanderer a bag containing all the winds that might hinder his sailing.
[42] Pope gives this supporter of Belinda the name of a queen of the warlike Amazons.

Full o'er their heads the swelling bag he rent,
And all the furies issued at the vent.
Belinda burns with more than mortal ire,
And fierce Thalestris fans the rising fire.
"Oh wretched maid!" she spread her hands, and cried,
(While Hampton's echoes, "Wretched maid!" replied)
"Was it for this you took such constant care
The bodkin, comb, and essence to prepare?
For this your locks in paper durance bound,
For this with torturing irons wreathed around?   100
For this with fillets strained your tender head,
And bravely bore the double loads of lead?
Gods! shall the ravisher display your hair,
While the fops envy, and the ladies stare!
Honor forbid! at whose unrivaled shrine
Ease, pleasure, virtue, all our sex resign.
Methinks already I your tears survey,
Already hear the horrid things they say,
Already see you a degraded toast,
And all your honor in a whisper lost!   110
How shall I, then, your helpless fame defend?
'Twill then be infamy to seem your friend!
And shall this prize, th' inestimable prize,
Exposed through crystal to the gazing eyes,
And heightened by the diamond's circling rays,
On that rapacious hand forever blaze?
Sooner shall grass in Hyde Park Circus grow,
And wits take lodgings in the sound of Bow,[43]
Sooner let earth, air, sea, to chaos fall,
Men, monkeys, lap-dogs, parrots, perish all!"   120
    She said; then raging to Sir Plume repairs,
And bids her Beau demand the precious hairs:
(Sir Plume of amber snuff-box justly vain,
And the nice conduct of a clouded cane)
With earnest eyes, and round unthinking face,
He first the snuff-box opened, then the case,
And thus broke out—"My Lord, why, what the devil?
Z——ds! damn the lock! 'fore Gad, you must be civil!
Plague on't! 'tis past a jest—nay prithee, pox!
Give her the hair"—he spoke, and rapped his box.   130
    "It grieves me much" (replied the Peer again)
"Who speaks so well should ever speak in vain.
But by this lock, this sacred lock I swear,
(Which never more shall join its parted hair;

[43] "Within sound of Bow bells"—the bells of the church of St. Mary-le-Bow—is the cockney region of London; hence lower class and unfashionable.

Which never more its honors shall renew,
Clipped from the lovely head where late it grew)
That while my nostrils draw the vital air,
This hand, which won it, shall for ever wear."
He spoke, and speaking, in proud triumph spread
The long-contended honors of her head.   140
 But Umbriel, hateful gnome! forbears not so;
He breaks the vial whence the sorrows flow.
Then see! the nymph in beauteous grief appears,
Her eyes half-languishing, half-drowned in tears;
On her heaved bosom hung her drooping head,
Which, with a sigh, she raised; and thus she said.
 "Forever cursed be this detested day,
Which snatched my best, my fav'rite curl away!
Happy! ah ten times happy had I been,
If Hampton Court these eyes had never seen!   150
Yet am not I the first mistaken maid,
By love of courts to numerous ills betrayed.
Oh had I rather unadmired remained
In some lone isle, or distant northern land;
Where the gilt chariot never marks the way,
Where none learn ombre, none e'er taste bohea![44]
There kept my charms concealed from mortal eye,
Like roses, that in deserts bloom and die.
What moved my mind with youthful lords to roam?
Oh had I stayed, and said my prayers at home!   160
'Twas this, the morning omens seemed to tell,
Thrice from my trembling hand the patch-box[45] fell;
The tott'ring china shook without a wind,
Nay, Poll sat mute, and Shock was most unkind!
A sylph too warned me of the threats of fate,
In mystic visions, now believèd too late!
See the poor remnants of these slighted hairs!
My hands shall rend what even thy rapine spares:
These in two sable ringlets taught to break,
Once gave new beauties to the snowy neck;   170
The sister-lock now sits uncouth, alone,
And in its fellow's fate foresees its own;
Uncurled it hangs, the fatal shears demands,
And tempts once more, thy sacrilegious hands.
Oh hadst thou, cruel! been content to seize
Hairs less in sight, or any hairs but these!"

[44] a kind of tea
[45] a box for "beauty spots": bits of court plaster (a forerunner of adhesive tape)
used to ornament the face

CANTO V

S HE said: the pitying audience melt in tears.
But Fate and Jove had stopped the Baron's ears.
In vain Thalestris with reproach assails,
For who can move when fair Belinda fails?
Not half so fixed the Trojan could remain,
While Anna begged and Dido[46] raged in vain.
Then grave Clarissa graceful waved her fan;
Silence ensued, and thus the nymph began.
    "Say why are beauties praised and honored most,
The wise man's passion, and the vain man's toast?   10
Why decked with all that land and sea afford,
Why angels called, and angel-like adored?
Why round our coaches crowd the white-gloved beaux,
Why bows the side-box from its inmost rows;
How vain are all these glories, all our pains,
Unless good sense preserve what beauty gains:
That men may say, when we the front-box grace:
'Behold the first in virtue as in face!'
Of! if to dance all night, and dress all day,
Charmed the small-pox, or chased old age away;   20
Who would not scorn what housewife's cares produce,
Or who would learn one earthly thing of use?
To patch, nay ogle, might become a saint,
Nor could it sure be such a sin to paint.
But since, alas! frail beauty must decay.
Curled or uncurled, since locks will turn to gray;
Since painted, or not painted, all shall fade,
And she who scorns a man, must die a maid;
What then remains but well our power to use,
And keep good-humor still whate'er we lose?   30
And trust me, dear! good-humor can prevail,
When airs, and flights, and screams, and scolding fail.
Beauties in vain their pretty eyes may roll;
Charms strike the sight, but merit wins the soul."
    So spoke the dame, but no applause ensued;
Belinda frowned, Thalestris called her prude.
"To arms, to arms!" the fierce virago cries,
And swift as lightning to the combat flies.
All side in parties, and begin th' attack;
Fans clap, silks rustle, and tough whalebones crack;   40
Heroes' and heroines' shouts confus'dly rise,
And bass and treble voices strike the skies.

___

[46] Aeneas was unmoved by the reproaches of his wife, Dido, and her sister, Anna, when he proposed to leave Carthage for further wanderings.

No common weapons in their hands are found,
Like gods they fight, nor dread a mortal wound.
   So when bold Homer makes the gods engage,
And heavenly breasts with human passions rage;
'Gainst Pallas, Mars, Latona, Hermes arms ; [47]
And all Olympus rings with loud alarms :
Jove's thunder roars, heaven trembles all around,
Blue Neptune storms, the bellowing deeps resound :   50
Earth shakes her nodding towers, the ground gives way,
And the pale ghosts start at the flash of day !
   Triumphant Umbriel on a sconce's height
Clapped his glad wings, and sat to view the fight :
Propped on their bodkin spears, the sprites survey
The growing combat, or assist the fray.
   While through the press enraged Thalestris flies,
And scatters death around from both her eyes,
A beau and witling perished in the throng,
One died in metaphor, and one in song.   60
"O cruel nymph ! a living death I bear,"
Cried Dapperwit, and sunk beside his chair.
A mournful glance Sir Fopling upwards cast,
"Those eyes are made so killing"—was his last.
Thus on Meander's [48] flowery margin lies
Th' expiring swan, and as he sings he dies. [49]
   When bold Sir Plume had drawn Clarissa down,
Chloe stepped in, and killed him with a frown ;
She smiled to see the doughty hero slain,
But, at her smile, the beau revived again.   70
   Now Jove suspends his golden scales in air,
Weighs the men's wits against the lady's hair ;
The doubtful beam long nods from side to side ;
At length the wits mount up, the hairs subside.
   See, fierce Belinda on the Baron flies,
With more than usual lightning in her eyes :
Nor feared the chief th' unequal fight to try,
Who sought no more than on his foe to die.
But this bold lord with manly strength endued,
She with one finger and a thumb subdued :   80
Just where the breath of life his nostrils drew,
A charge of snuff the wily virgin threw ;
The gnomes direct, to every atom just,
The pungent grains of titillating dust.

---

[47] The specific identifications are less important than the comparison of the brawl to a battle of goddesses against gods.
[48] a wandering river in Phrygia
[49] According to legend the swan, normally mute, sings just once before it dies.

Sudden, with starting tears each eye o'erflows,
And the high dome re-echoes to his nose.
"Now meet thy fate," incensed Belinda cried,
And drew a deadly bodkin from her side.
(The same, his ancient personage to deck,
Her great grandsire wore about his neck,   90
In three seal-rings; which after, melted down,
Formed a vast buckle for his widow's gown:
Her infant grandame's whistle next it grew,
The bells she jingled, and the whistle blew;
Then in a bodkin graced her mother's hairs,
Which long she wore, and now Belinda wears.)
   "Boast not my fall" (he cried) "insulting foe!
Thou by some other shalt be laid as low,
Nor think, to die dejects my lofty mind:
All that I dread is leaving you behind!   100
Rather than so, ah let me still survive,
And burn in Cupid's flames—but burn alive."
   "Restore the lock!" she cries; and all around
"Restore the lock!" the vaulted roofs rebound.
Not fierce Othello in so loud a strain
Roared for the handkerchief that caused his pain.[50]
But see how oft ambitious aims are crossed,
And chiefs contend till all the prize is lost!
The lock, obtained with guilt, and kept with pain,
In every place is sought, but sought in vain: 110
With such a prize no mortal must be blest,
So heaven decrees! with heaven who can contest?
   Some thought it mounted to the lunar sphere,
Since all things lost on earth are treasured there.
There heroes' wits are kept in pond'rous vases,
And beaux' in snuff-boxes and tweezer-cases.
There broken vows and death-bed alms are found,
And lovers' hearts with ends of riband bound,
The courtier's promises, and sick man's prayers,
The smiles of harlots, and the tears of heirs,   120
Cages for gnats, and chains to yoke a flea,
Dried butterflies, and tomes of casuistry.
   But trust the Muse—she saw it upward rise,
Though marked by none but quick, poetic eyes:
(So Rome's great founder to the heavens withdrew,
To Proculus alone confessed in view) [51]

[50] Othello suspects that his wife, Desdemona, has given a prized handkerchief to
her supposed lover and demands that she produce it. (Shakespeare, *Othello*, III, iv.)
[51] Romulus was translated to heaven in a storm cloud; he later appeared to Proculus, a Senator.

A sudden star, it shot through liquid air,
And drew behind a radiant trail of hair.
Not Berenice's Locks[52] first rose so bright,
The heavens bespangling with disheveled light.   130
The sylphs behold it kindling as it flies,
And pleased pursue its progress through the skies.
   This the beau monde shall from the Mall[53] survey,
And hail with music its propitious ray.
This the blest lover shall for Venus take,
And send up vows from Rosamonda's lake.[54]
This Partridge[55] soon shall view in cloudless skies,
When next he looks through Galileo's eyes,[56]
And hence th' egregious wizard shall foredoom
The fate of Louis, and the fall of Rome.   140
   Then cease, bright nymph! to mourn thy ravished hair,
Which adds new glory to the shining sphere!
Not all the tresses that fair head can boast,
Shall draw such envy as the lock you lost.
For, after all the murders of your eye,
When, after millions slain, yourself shall die:
When those fair suns shall set, as set they must,
And all those tresses shall be laid in dust,
This lock, the Muse shall consecrate to fame,
And 'midst the stars inscribe Belinda's name.   150

[1714]

[52] A constellation (*Coma Berenicia*) is said to have been formed from the hair that Berenice, an Egyptian queen, dedicated to the gods in exchange for her husband's return from war.
[53] a fashionable walk in St. James's Park   [54] a pond in St. James's Park
[55] John Partridge (1644–1715), a foolish stargazer and prognosticator, who is also the butt of Swift's "Bickerstaff" joke
[56] a telescope

Thomas Gray

1716–1771

ODE ON THE DEATH OF A FAVORITE CAT, DROWNED IN A TUB OF GOLD FISHES

'TWAS on a lofty vase's side,
  Where China's gayest art had dyed
    The azure flowers, that blow;
Demurest of the tabby kind,
The pensive Selima reclined,
    Gazed on the lake below.

Her conscious tail her joy declared;
The fair round face, the snowy beard,
   The velvet of her paws,
Her coat, that with the tortoise vies,   10
Her ears of jet, and emerald eyes,
   She saw; and purred applause.

Still had she gazed; but 'midst the tide
Two angel forms were seen to glide,
   The Genii of the stream:
Their scaly armor's Tyrian hue[1]
Through richest purple to the view
   Betrayed a golden gleam.

The hapless nymph with wonder saw:
A whisker first and then a claw,   20
   With many an ardent wish,
She stretched in vain to reach the prize.
What female heart can gold despise?
   What cat's averse to fish?

Presumptuous maid! with looks intent
Again she stretched, again she bent,
   Nor knew the gulf between.
Malignant Fate sat by, and smiled!
The slippery verge her feet beguiled,
   She tumbled headlong in.   30

Eight times emerging from the flood
She mewed to every wat'ry god,
   Some speedy aid to send.
No dolphin came, no nereid[2] stirred:
Nor cruel Tom nor Susan heard.
   A favorite has no friend!

From hence, ye beauties, undeceived,
Know, one false step is ne'er retrieved,
   And be with caution bold.
Not all that tempts your wandering eyes   40
And heedless hearts is lawful prize;
   Nor all that glisters, gold.

          [1747]

---

[1] purple, the color of royal vestments   [2] sea nymph

ELEGY
WRITTEN IN A COUNTRY CHURCHYARD

THE curfew tolls the knell of parting day,
The lowing herd wind slowly o'er the lea,
The plowman homeward plods his weary way,
And leaves the world to darkness and to me.

Now fades the glimmering landscape on the sight,
And all the air a solemn stillness holds,
Save where the beetle wheels his droning flight,
And drowsy tinklings lull the distant folds;

Save that from yonder ivy-mantled tow'r
The moping owl does to the moon complain   10
Of such, as wand'ring near her secret bow'r,
Molest her ancient solitary reign.

Beneath those rugged elms, that yew-tree's shade,
Where heaves the turf in many a mold'ring heap,
Each in his narrow cell for ever laid,
The rude forefathers of the hamlet sleep.

The breezy call of incense-breathing morn,
The swallow twitt'ring from the straw-built shed,
The cock's shrill clarion, or the echoing horn,
No more shall rouse them from their lowly bed.   20

For them no more the blazing hearth shall burn,
Or busy housewife ply her evening care:
No children run to lisp their sire's return,
Or climb his knees the envied kiss to share.

Oft did the harvest to their sickle yield,
Their furrow oft the stubborn glebe[1] has broke;
How jocund did they drive their team afield!
How bowed the woods beneath their sturdy stroke!

Let not Ambition mock their useful toil,
Their homely joys, and destiny obscure;   30
Nor Grandeur hear with a disdainful smile,
The short and simple annals of the poor.

[1] sod

The boast of heraldry, the pomp of pow'r,
And all that beauty, all that wealth e'er gave
Awaits alike th' inevitable hour.
The paths of glory lead but to the grave.

Nor you, ye Proud, impute to these the fault,
If Mem'ry o'er their tomb no trophies raise,
Where through the long-drawn aisle and fretted vault
The pealing anthem swells the note of praise.   40

Can storied urn or animated bust
Back to its mansion call the fleeting breath?
Can Honor's voice provoke the silent dust,
Or Flatt'ry soothe the full cold ear of Death?

Perhaps in this neglected spot is laid
Some heart once pregnant with celestial fire;
Hands that the rod of empire might have swayed,
Or waked to ecstasy the living lyre.

But Knowledge to their eyes her ample page
Rich with the spoils of time did ne'er unroll: 50
Chill Penury repressed their noble rage,
And froze the genial current of the soul.

Full many a gem of purest ray serene,
The dark unfathomed caves of ocean bear:
Full many a flower is born to blush unseen,
And waste its sweetness on the desert air.

Some village Hampden,[2] that with dauntless breast
The little tyrant of his fields withstood;
Some mute inglorious Milton here may rest,
Some Cromwell guiltless of his country's blood.   60

Th' applause of list'ning senates to command,
The threats of pain and ruin to despise.
To scatter plenty o'er a smiling land,
And read their hist'ry in a nation's eyes,

Their lot forbade: nor circumscribed alone
Their growing virtues, but their crimes confined;
Forbade to wade through slaughter to a throne,
And shut the gates of mercy on mankind,

---

[2] John Hampden (1594–1643) was a leader of the opposition to Charles I that led to the Civil War of 1642–1649.

The struggling pangs of conscious truth to hide,
To quench the blushes of ingenuous shame,   70
Or heap the shrine of luxury and Pride
With incense kindled at the Muse's flame.

Far from the madding crowd's ignoble strife,
Their sober wishes never learned to stray;
Along the cool sequestered vale of life
They kept the noiseless tenor of their way.

Yet ev'n these bones from insult to protect
Some frail memorial still erected nigh,
With uncouth rhymes and shapeless sculpture decked,
Implores the passing tribute of a sigh.   80

Their name, their years, spelt by th' unlettered muse,
The place of fame and elegy supply:
And many a holy text around she strews,
That teach the rustic moralist to die.

For who to dumb forgetfulness a prey,
This pleasing anxious being e'er resigned,
Left the warm precincts of the cheerful day,
Nor cast one longing ling'ring look behind?

On some fond breast the parting soul relies,
Some pious drops the closing eye requires;   90
Ev'n from the tomb the voice of Nature cries,
Ev'n in our ashes live their wonted fires.

For thee, who mindful of th' unhonored dead
Dost in these lines their artless tale relate;
If chance, by lonely contemplation led,
Some kindred spirit shall inquire thy fate,

Haply some hoary-headed swain may say,
"Oft have we seen him at the peep of dawn
Brushing with hasty steps the dews away
To meet the sun upon the upland lawn.   100

"There at the foot of yonder nodding beech
That wreathes its old fantastic roots so high,
His listless length at noontide would he stretch,
And pore upon the brook that babbles by.

"Hard by yon wood, now smiling as in scorn,
    Mutt'ring his wayward fancies he would rove,
Now drooping, woeful wan, like one forlorn,
    Or crazed with care, or crossed in hopeless love.

"One morn I missed him on the customed hill,
    Along the heath and near his fav'rite tree;   110
Another came; nor yet beside the rill,
    Nor up the lawn, nor at the wood was he;

"The next with dirges due in sad array
    Slow through the church-way path we saw him borne.
Approach and read (for thou canst read) the lay,
    Graved on the stone beneath yon agéd thorn."

THE EPITAPH

*H*ERE *rests his head upon the lap of Earth
    A Youth to Fortune and to Fame unknown.
Fair Science frowned not on his humble birth,
    And Melancholy marked him for her own.*   120

*Large was his bounty, and his soul sincere,
    Heav'n did a recompense as largely send:
He gave to Mis'ry all he had, a tear,
    He gained from Heav'n ('twas all he wished) a friend.*

*No farther seek his merits to disclose,
    Or draw his frailties from their dread abode,
(There they alike in trembling hope repose,)
    The bosom of his Father and his God.*

[1751]

William Blake
1757–1827
THE LAMB

LITTLE Lamb, who made thee?
Dost thou know who made thee?
Gave thee life, and bid thee feed
By the stream and o'er the mead;
Gave thee clothing of delight,
Softest clothing, wooly, bright;
Gave thee such a tender voice,
Making all the vales rejoice?
  Little Lamb, who made thee?
  Dost thou know who made thee?   10
  Little Lamb, I'll tell thee,
  Little Lamb, I'll tell thee:
He is calléd by thy name,
For he calls himself a Lamb.
He is meek, and he is mild;
He became a little child.
I a child, and thou a lamb,
We are calléd by his name.
  Little Lamb, God bless thee!
  Little Lamb, God bless thee!   20
[1789]

THE CHIMNEY SWEEPER

WHEN my mother died I was very young,
And my father sold me while yet my tongue
Could scarcely cry " 'weep! 'weep! 'weep! 'weep!"
So your chimneys I sweep, and in soot I sleep.

There's little Tom Dacre, who cried when his head,
That curled like a lamb's back, was shaved: so I said
"Hush, Tom! never mind it, for when your head's bare
You know that the soot cannot spoil your white hair."

And so he was quiet, and that very night,
As Tom was a-sleeping, he had such a sight!   10
That thousands of sweepers, Dick, Joe, Ned, and Jack,
Were all of them locked up in coffins of black.

And by came an Angel who had a bright key,
And he opened the coffins and set them all free;
Then down a green plain leaping, laughing, they run,
And wash in a river, and shine in the Sun.

Then naked and white, all their bags left behind,
They rise upon clouds and sport in the wind;
And the Angel told Tom, if he'd be a good boy,
He'd have God for his father, and never want joy.   20

And so Tom awoke; and we rose in the dark,
And got with our bags and our brushes to work.
Though the morning was cold, Tom was happy and warm;
So if all do their duty they need not fear harm.

[1789]

THE TYGER

TYGER! Tyger! burning bright
   In the forests of the night,
What immortal hand or eye
Could frame thy fearful symmetry?

In what distant deeps or skies
Burnt the fire of thine eyes?
On what wings dare he aspire?
What the hand dare seize the fire?

And what shoulder, and what art,
Could twist the sinews of thy heart?   10
And when thy heart began to beat,
What dread hand? and what dread feet?

What the hammer? what the chain?
In what furnace was thy brain?
What the anvil? what dread grasp
Dare its deadly terrors clasp?

When the stars threw down their spears,
And watered heaven with their tears,
Did he smile his work to see?
Did he who made the Lamb make thee?   20

Tyger! Tyger! burning bright
In the forests of the night,
What immortal hand or eye,
Dare frame thy fearful symmetry?

[1794]

THE SICK ROSE

O ROSE, thou art sick!
The invisible worm
That flies in the night,
In the howling storm,

Has found out thy bed
Of crimson joy,
And his dark secret love
Does thy life destroy.

[1794]

LONDON

I WANDER through each chartered street,
Near where the chartered Thames does flow,
And mark in every face I meet
Marks of weakness, marks of woe.

In every cry of every man,
In every infant's cry of fear,
In every voice, in every ban,
The mind-forged manacles I hear.

How the Chimney-sweeper's cry
Every black'ning church appalls;   10
And the hapless soldier's sigh
Runs in blood down palace walls.

But most through midnight streets I hear
How the youthful harlot's curse
Blasts the new-born infant's tear,
And blights with plagues the marriage hearse.

[1794]

MOCK ON, MOCK ON, VOLTAIRE, ROUSSEAU

MOCK on, mock on, Voltaire,[1] Rousseau :[2]
Mock on, mock on : 'tis all in vain !
You throw the sand against the wind,
And the wind blows it back again.

And every sand becomes a gem
Reflected in the beams divine ;
Blown back they blind the mocking eye,
But still in Israel's paths they shine.

The atoms of Democritus[3]
And Newton's[4] particles of light   10
Are sands upon the Red Sea shore,
Where Israel's tents do shine so bright.

[1800 ?]

[1] François Marie Arouet de Voltaire (1694–1778), French philosopher of the Enlightenment
[2] Jean Jacques Rousseau (1712–1778), a Swiss-born rationalist philosopher
[3] Greek philosopher of the fifth century B.C. who postulated an infinite number of atoms in which resided the ultimate explanation of nature
[4] Sir Isaac Newton (1642–1727), English scientist whose particle theory of light was one more materialistic explanation of natural phenomena

Robert Burns
1759–1796
TO A MOUSE
ON TURNING HER UP IN HER NEST
WITH THE PLOUGH, NOVEMBER, 1785

WEE, sleekit, cowrin, tim'rous beastie,
O, what a panic's in thy breastie !
Thou need na start awa sae hasty,
        Wi' bickering brattle ![1]
I wad be laith to rin an' chase thee
        Wi' murd'ring pattle ![2]

[1] hurrying scramble   [2] a long-handled spade

I'm truly sorry Man's dominion
Has broken Nature's social union,
An' justifies that ill opinion
   Which makes thee startle 10
At me, thy poor, earth-born companion,
   An' fellow-mortal!

I doubt na, whyles, but thou may thieve;
What then? poor beastie, thou maun live!
A daimen icker in a thrave[3]
   'S a sma' request.
I'll get a blessin wi' the lave,[4]
   And never miss't!

Thy wee bit housie, too, in ruin!
Its silly wa's the win's are strewin! 20
An' naething, now, to big[5] a new ane,
   O' foggage[6] green!
An' bleak December's winds ensuin,
   Baith snell[7] and keen!

Thou saw the fields laid bare an' waste,
An' weary Winter comin fast,
An' cozie here, beneath the blast,
   Thou thought to dwell,
Till crash! the cruel coulter past
   Out thro' they cell. 30

That wee bit heap o' leaves an' stibble,
Has cost thee mony a weary nibble!
Now thou's turned out, for a' thy trouble,
   But[8] house or hald,[9]
To thole[10] the Winter's sleety dribble,
   An' cranreuch[11] cauld!

But, Mousie, thou are no thy lane,[12]
In proving foresight may be vain:
The best-laid schemes o' Mice an' Men,
   Gang aft a-gley,[13]
An' lae'e us nought but grief and pain,
   For promised joy.

---

[3] an occasional head of grain out of twenty-four sheaves [4] remainder
[5] build [6] vegetation [7] harsh [8] without
[9] dwelling—redundant, but alliterative with *house* [10] suffer [11] hoarfrost
[12] not alone [13] amiss

Still thou art blest, compared wi' me !
The present only toucheth thee ;
But, Och ! I backward cast my e'e,
    On prospects drear !
An' forward, tho' I canna see,
    I guess an' fear !

[1786]

AFTON WATER

FLOW gently, sweet Afton, among thy green braes,[1]
   Flow gently, I'll sing thee a song in thy praise ;
My Mary's asleep by thy murmuring stream,
Flow gently, sweet Afton, disturb not her dream.

Thou stock dove whose echo resounds through the glen,
Ye wild whistling blackbirds in yon thorny den,
Thou green-crested lapwing thy screaming forbear,
I charge you disturb not my slumbering fair.

How lofty, sweet Afton, thy neighboring hills,
Far marked with the courses of clear, winding rills ;   10
There daily I wander as noon rises high,
My flocks and my Mary's sweet cot in my eye.

How pleasant thy banks and green valleys below,
Where wild in the woodlands the primroses blow ;
There oft as mild evening weeps over the lea,
The sweet-scented birk[2] shades my Mary and me.

Thy crystal stream, Afton, how lovely it glides,
And winds by the cot where my Mary resides ;
How wanton thy waters her snowy feet lave,
As gathering sweet flowerets she stems thy clear wave.   20

Flow gently, sweet Afton, among thy green braes,
Flow gently, sweet river, the theme of my lays ;
My Mary's asleep by thy murmuring stream,
Flow gently, sweet Afton, disturb not her dream.

[1792]

[1] banks   [2] birch

FOR A' THAT AND A' THAT

Is THERE, for honest poverty,
  That hangs his head, and a' that;
The coward-slave, we pass him by,
  We dare be poor for a' that!
    For a' that, and a' that,
      Our toils obscure, and a' that,
    The rank is but the guinea's stamp,
      The man's the gowd[1] for a' that.

What though on hamely fare we dine,
  Wear hoddin[2] grey, and a' that;   10
Gie fools their silks, and knaves their wine,
  A man's a man for a' that:
    For a' that, and a' that,
      Their tinsel show, and a' that;
    The honest man, though e'er sae poor,
      Is king o' men for a' that.

Ye see yon birkie,[3] ca'd a lord,
  Wha struts, and stares, and a' that;
Though hundreds worship at his word,
  He's but a coof[4] for a' that: 20
    For a' that, and a' that:
      His ribband, star, and a' that,
    The man of independent mind,
      He looks and laughs at a' that.

A prince can mak a belted knight,
  A marquis, duke, and a' that;
But an honest man's aboon his might,
  Guid faith, he maunna fa'[5] that!
    For a' that, and a' that,
      Their dignities, and a' that,   30
    The pith o' sense and pride o' worth,
      Are higher ranks than a' that.

Then let us pray that come it may,
  As come it will for a' that,
That sense and worth, o'er a' the earth,
  May bear the gree,[6] and a' that.

[1] gold [2] coarse woolen [3] fop [4] fool [5] must not claim
[6] win the reward

For a' that, and a' that,
    It's comin' yet for a' that,
That man to man, the warld o'er,
    Shall brothers be for a' that.

                                                                40
                                                            [1795]

A RED, RED ROSE

O, MY luve is like a red red rose
    That's newly sprung in June:
O, my luve is like the melodie
    That's sweetly played in tune.

As fair art thou, my bonie lass,
    So deep in luve am I;
And I will luve thee still, my dear,
    Till a' the seas gang dry.

Till a' the seas gang dry, my dear,
    And the rocks melt wi' the sun;   10
And I will luve thee still, my dear,
    While the sands o' life shall run.

And fare thee weel, my only luve!
    And fare thee weel a while!
And I will come again, my luve,
    Tho' it were ten thousand mile.

                                                            [1796]

William Wordsworth
1770–1850
LINES

COMPOSED A FEW MILES ABOVE TINTERN
ABBEY, ON REVISITING THE BANKS OF THE
WYE DURING A TOUR. JULY 13, 1798

FIVE years have passed; five summers, with the length
    Of five long winters! and again I hear
These waters, rolling from their mountain-springs
With a soft inland murmur.—Once again
Do I behold these steep and lofty cliffs,
That on a wild secluded scene impress
Thoughts of more deep seclusion; and connect

The landscape with the quiet of the sky.
The day is come when I again repose
Here, under this dark sycamore, and view   10
These plots of cottage-ground, these orchard-tufts,
Which at this season, with their unripe fruits,
Are clad in one green hue, and lose themselves
'Mid groves and copses. Once again I see
These hedge-rows, hardly hedge-rows, little lines
Of sportive wood run wild : these pastoral farms,
Green to the very door ; and wreaths of smoke
Sent up, in silence, from among the trees !
With some uncertain notice, as might seem
Of vagrant dwellers in the houseless woods,   20
Or of some hermit's cave, where by his fire
The hermit sits alone.
                              These beauteous forms,
Through a long absence, have not been to me
As is a landscape to a blind man's eye :
But oft, in lonely rooms, and 'mid the din
Of towns and cities, I have owed to them
In hours of weariness, sensations sweet,
Felt in the blood, and felt along the heart ;
And passing even into my purer mind,
With tranquil restoration :—feelings too   30
Of unremembered pleasure : such, perhaps,
As have no slight or trivial influence
On that best portion of a good man's life,
His little, nameless, unremembered, acts
Of kindness and of love. Nor less, I trust,
To them I may have owed another gift,
Of aspect more sublime ; that blessèd mood,
In which the burthen of the mystery,
In which the heavy and the weary weight
Of all this unintelligible world,   40
Is lightened :—that serene and blessèd mood,
In which the affections gently lead us on,—
Until, the breath of this corporeal frame
And even the motion of our human blood
Almost suspended, we are laid asleep
In body, and become a living soul :
While with an eye made quiet by the power
Of harmony, and the deep power of joy,
We see into the life of things.
                              If this
Be but a vain belief, yet, oh ! how oft—   50
In darkness and amid the many shapes

Of joyless daylight; when the fretful stir
Unprofitable, and the fever of the world,
Have hung upon the beatings of my heart—
How oft, in spirit, have I turned to thee,
O sylvan Wye! thou wanderer through the woods,
How often has my spirit turned to thee!
    And now, with gleams of half-extinguished thought,
With many recognitions dim and faint,
And somewhat of a sad perplexity,   60
The picture of the mind revives again:
While here I stand, not only with the sense
Of present pleasure, but with pleasing thoughts
That in this moment there is life and food
For future years. And so I dare to hope,
Though changed, no doubt, from what I was when first
I came among these hills; when like a roe
I bounded o'er the mountains, by the sides
Of the deep rivers, and the lonely streams,
Wherever nature led: more like a man   70
Flying from something that he dreads, than one
Who sought the thing he loved. For nature then
(The coarser pleasures of my boyish days,
And their glad animal movements all gone by)
To me was all in all. I cannot paint
What then I was. The sounding cataract
Haunted me like a passion: the tall rock,
The mountain, and the deep and gloomy wood,
Their colors and their forms, were then to me
An appetite; a feeling and a love,   80
That had no need of a remoter charm,
By thought supplied, nor any interest
Unborrowed from the eye.—That time is past,
And all its aching joys are now no more,
And all its dizzy raptures. Not for this
Faint I, nor mourn nor murmur; other gifts
Have followed; for such loss, I would believe
Abundant recompense. For I have learned
To look on nature, not as in the hour
Of thoughtless youth; but hearing oftentimes   90
The still, sad music of humanity,
Nor harsh nor grating, though of ample power
To chasten and subdue. And I have felt
A presence that disturbs me with the joy
Of elevated thoughts; a sense sublime
Of something far more deeply interfused,
Whose dwelling is the light of setting suns,

And the round ocean and the living air,
And the blue sky, and in the mind of man ;
A motion and a spirit, that impels   100
All thinking things, all objects of all thought,
And rolls through all things. Therefore am I still
A lover of the meadows and the woods,
And mountains ; and of all that we behold
From this green earth ; of all the mighty world
Of eye, and ear,—both what they half create,
And what perceive ; well pleased to recognize
In nature and the language of the sense,
The anchor of my purest thoughts, the nurse,
The guide, the guardian of my heart, and soul   110
Of all my moral being.
       Nor perchance,
If I were not thus taught, should I the more
Suffer my genial spirits to decay :
For thou art with me here upon the banks
Of this fair river ; thou my dearest friend,
My dear, dear friend ; and in thy voice I catch
The language of my former heart, and read
My former pleasures in the shooting lights
Of thy wild eyes. Oh ! yet a little while
May I behold in thee what I was once,   120
My dear, dear Sister ! and this prayer I make,
Knowing that Nature never did betray
The heart that loved her ; 't is her privilege,
Through all the years of this our life, to lead
From joy to joy : for she can so inform
The mind that is within us, so impress
With quietness and beauty, and so feed
With lofty thoughts, that neither evil tongues,
Rash judgments, nor the sneers of selfish men,
Nor greetings where no kindness is, nor all   130
The dreary intercourse of daily life,
Shall e'er prevail against us, or disturb
Our cheerful faith, that all which we behold
Is full of blessings. Therefore let the moon
Shine on thee in thy solitary walk ;
And let the misty mountain-winds be free
To blow against thee : and, in after years,
When these wild ecstasies shall be matured
Into a sober pleasure ; when thy mind
Shall be a mansion for all lovely forms,   140
Thy memory be as a dwelling-place
For all sweet sounds and harmonies ; oh ! then,

If solitude, or fear, or pain, or grief,
Should be thy portion, with what healing thoughts
Of tender joy wilt thou remember me,
And these my exhortations! Nor, perchance—
If I should be where I no more can hear
Thy voice, nor catch from thy wild eyes these gleams
Of past existence—wilt thou then forget
That on the banks of this delightful stream   150
We stood together; and that I, so long
A worshipper of Nature, hither came
Unwearied in that service; rather say
With warmer love—oh! with far deeper zeal
Of holier love. Nor wilt thou then forget,
That after many wanderings, many years
Of absence, these steep woods and lofty cliffs,
And this green pastoral landscape, were to me
More dear, both for themselves and for thy sake!

                                                    [1798]

SHE DWELT AMONG THE
UNTRODDEN WAYS

SHE dwelt among the untrodden ways
    Beside the springs of Dove,
A maid whom there were none to praise,
    And very few to love.

A violet by a mossy stone
    Half-hidden from the eye!
—Fair as a star, when only one
    Is shining in the sky.

She lived unknown, and few could know
    When Lucy ceased to be;   10
But she is in her grave, and, oh,
    The difference to me!

                                                    [1799]

I TRAVELED AMONG UNKNOWN MEN

I TRAVELED among unknown men,
    In lands beyond the sea;
Nor, England! did I know till then
    What love I bore to thee.

'T is past, that melancholy dream!
   Nor will I quit thy shore
A second time; for still I seem
   To love thee more and more.

Among thy mountains did I feel
   The joy of my desire;   10
And she I cherished turned her wheel
   Beside an English fire.

Thy mornings showed, thy nights concealed
   The bowers where Lucy played;
And thine too is the last green field
   That Lucy's eyes surveyed.

                      [1799]

THREE YEARS SHE GREW IN SUN AND SHOWER

THREE years she grew in sun and shower,
   Then Nature said, "A lovelier flower
On earth was never sown;
This child I to myself will take;
She shall be mine, and I will make
   A lady of my own.

"Myself will to my darling be
Both law and impulse: and with me
   The girl, in rock and plain,
In earth and heaven, in glade and bower,   10
Shall feel an overseeing power
   To kindle or restrain.

"She shall be sportive as the fawn
   That wild with glee across the lawn,
Or up the mountain springs;
And hers shall be the breathing balm,
And hers the silence and the calm
   Of mute insensate things.

"The floating clouds their state shall lend
To her; for her the willow bend;   20
   Nor shall she fail to see
Even in the motions of the storm
Grace that shall mold the maiden's form
   By silent sympathy.

"The stars of midnight shall be dear
To her ; and she shall lean her ear
In many a secret place
Where rivulets dance their wayward round,
And beauty born of murmuring sound
Shall pass into her face.   30

"And vital feelings of delight
Shall rear her form to stately height,
Her virgin bosom swell ;
Such thoughts to Lucy I will give
While she and I together live
Here in this happy dell."

Thus Nature spake—The work was done—
How soon my Lucy's race was run !
She died, and left to me
This heath, this calm, and quiet scene ;   40
The memory of what has been,
And never more will be.

[1799]

A SLUMBER DID MY SPIRIT SEAL

A SLUMBER did my spirit seal ;
I had no human fears :
She seemed a thing that could not feel
The touch of earthly years.

No motion has she now, no force ;
She neither hears nor sees ;
Rolled round in earth's diurnal course,
With rocks, and stones, and trees.

[1799]

MY HEART LEAPS UP WHEN I BEHOLD

MY HEART leaps up when I behold
A rainbow in the sky :
So was it when my life began ;
So is it now I am a man ;
So be it when I shall grow old,
Or let me die !
The Child is father of the Man ;
And I could wish my days to be
Bound each to each by natural piety.

[1802]

COMPOSED UPON WESTMINSTER BRIDGE

SEPT. 3, 1802

EARTH has not anything to show more fair:
Dull would he be of soul who could pass by
A sight so touching in its majesty:
This city now doth, like a garment, wear
The beauty of the morning; silent, bare,
Ships, towers, domes, theaters, and temples lie
Open unto the fields, and to the sky;
All bright and glittering in the smokeless air.
Never did sun more beautifully steep
In his first splendor, valley, rock, or hill;   10
Ne'er saw I, never felt, a calm so deep!
The river glideth at his own sweet will:
Dear God! the very houses seem asleep;
And all that mighty heart is lying still!

[1802]

LONDON, 1802

MILTON! thou should'st be living at this hour:
England hath need of thee: she is a fen
Of stagnant waters: altar, sword, and pen,
Fireside, the heroic wealth of hall and bower,
Have forfeited their ancient English dower
Of inward happiness. We are selfish men;
Oh! raise us up, return to us again;
And give us manners, virtue, freedom, power.
Thy soul was like a star, and dwelt apart:
Thou hadst a voice whose sound was like the sea: 10
Pure as the naked heavens, majestic, free,
So didst thou travel on life's common way,
In cheerful godliness; and yet thy heart
The lowliest duties on herself did lay.

[1802]

THE SOLITARY REAPER

BEHOLD her, single in the field,
Yon solitary Highland Lass!
Reaping and singing by herself;
Stop here, or gently pass!

Alone she cuts and binds the grain,
And sings a melancholy strain;
O listen! for the vale profound
Is overflowing with the sound.

No nightingale did ever chaunt
More welcome notes to weary bands   10
Of travelers in some shady haunt,
Among Arabian sands:
A voice so thrilling ne'er was heard
In spring-time from the cuckoo-bird,
Breaking the silence of the seas
Among the farthest Hebrides.

Will no one tell me what she sings?—
Perhaps the plaintive numbers flow
For old, unhappy, far-off things,
And battles long ago: 20
Or is it some more humble lay,
Familiar matter of to-day?
Some natural sorrow, loss, or pain,
That has been, and may be again?

Whate'er the theme, the maiden sang
As if her song could have no ending;
I saw her singing at her work,
And o'er the sickle bending;—
I listened, motionless and still;
And, as I mounted up the hill,   30
The music in my heart I bore,
Long after it was heard no more.

[1803]

ODE

INTIMATIONS OF IMMORTALITY FROM
RECOLLECTIONS OF EARLY CHILDHOOD

THERE was a time when meadow, grove, and stream,
    The earth, and every common sight,
            To me did seem
        Apparelled in celestial light,
The glory and the freshness of a dream.
It is not now as it hath been of yore;—
        Turn wheresoe'er I may,
            By night or day,
The things which I have seen I now can see no more.

The rainbow comes and goes, 10
And lovely is the rose,
The moon doth with delight
Look round her when the heavens are bare,
Waters on a starry night
Are beautiful and fair;
The sunshine is a glorious birth;
But yet I know, where'er I go,
That there hath past away a glory from the earth.

Now, while the birds thus sing a joyous song,
And while the young lambs bound 20
As to the tabor's sound,
To me alone there came a thought of grief:
A timely utterance gave that thought relief,
And I again am strong:
The cataracts blow their trumpets from the steep;
No more shall grief of mine the season wrong;
I hear the echoes through the mountains throng,
The winds come to me from the fields of sleep,
And all the earth is gay;
Land and sea 30
Give themselves up to jollity,
And with the heart of May
Doth every beast keep holiday;—
Thou child of joy,
Shout round me, let me hear thy shouts, thou happy
Shepherd-boy!

Ye blessèd creatures, I have heard the call
Ye to each other make; I see
The heavens laugh with you in your jubilee;
My heart is at your festival,
My head hath its coronal, 40
The fulness of your bliss, I feel—I feel it all.
Oh, evil day! if I were sullen
While earth herself is adorning,
This sweet May-morning,
And the children are culling
On every side,
In a thousand valleys far and wide,
Fresh flowers; while the sun shines warm,
And the babe leaps up on his mother's arm:—
I hear, I hear, with joy I hear! 50
—But there's a tree, of many, one,

A single field which I have looked upon,
Both of them speak of something that is gone:
    The pansy at my feet
    Doth the same tale repeat:
Whither is fled the visionary gleam?
Where is it now, the glory and the dream?

Our birth is but a sleep and a forgetting;
The soul that rises with us, our life's star,
    Hath had elsewhere its setting,   60
        And cometh from afar:
    Not in entire forgetfulness,
    And not in utter nakedness,
But trailing clouds of glory do we come
    From God, who is our home:
Heaven lies about us in our infancy!
Shades of the prison-house begin to close
    Upon the growing boy,
But he beholds the light, and whence it flows,
    He sees it in his joy;   70
The youth, who daily farther from the east
    Must travel, still is Nature's priest,
    And by the vision splendid
    Is on his way attended;
At length the man perceives it die away,
And fade into the light of common day.

Earth fills her lap with pleasures of her own;
Yearnings she hath in her own natural kind,
And, even with something of a mother's mind,
    And no unworthy aim,   80
    The homely nurse doth all she can
To make her foster-child, her inmate man,
    Forget the glories he hath known,
And that imperial palace whence he came.

Behold the child among his new-born blisses,
A six years' darling of a pigmy size!
See, where 'mid work of his own hand he lies,
Fretted by sallies of his mother's kisses,
With light upon him from his father's eyes!
See, at his feet, some little plan or chart,   90
Some fragment from his dream of human life,
Shaped by himself with newly-learnéd art;
    A wedding or a festival,
    A mourning or a funeral;

And this hath now his heart,
And unto this he frames his song:
　　Then will he fit his tongue
To dialogues of business, love, or strife;
　　But it will not be long
　　Ere this be thrown aside,   100
　　And with new joy and pride
The little actor cons another part;
Filling from time to time his "humorous stage"
With all the persons, down to palsied Age,
That life brings with her in her equipage;
　　As if his whole vocation
　　Were endless imitation.

Thou, whose exterior semblance doth belie
　　Thy soul's immensity;
Thou best philosopher, who yet dost keep   110
Thy heritage, thou eye among the blind,
That, deaf and silent, read'st the eternal deep,
Haunted for ever by the eternal mind,—
　　Mighty prophet! Seer blest!
　　On whom those truths do rest,
Which we are toiling all our lives to find,
In darkness lost, the darkness of the grave;
Thou, over whom thy immortality
Broods like the day, a master o'er a slave,
A presence which is not to be put by: 120
Thou little child, yet glorious in the might
Of heaven-born freedom on thy being's height,
Why with such earnest pains dost thou provoke
The years to bring the inevitable yoke,
Thus blindly with thy blessedness at strife?
Full soon thy soul shall have her earthly freight,
And custom lie upon thee with a weight,
Heavy as frost, and deep almost as life!

　　O joy! that in our embers
　　Is something that doth live,   130
　　That nature yet remembers
　　What was so fugitive!
The thought of our past years in me doth breed
Perpetual benediction: not indeed
For that which is most worthy to be blest—
Delight and liberty, the simple creed
Of childhood, whether busy or at rest,
With new-fledged hope still fluttering in his breast:—

    Not for these I raise
     The song of thanks and praise;   140
   But for those obstinate questionings
   Of sense and outward things,
   Fallings from us, vanishings;
   Blank misgivings of a creature
Moving about in worlds not realized,
High instincts before which our mortal nature
Did tremble like a guilty thing surprised:
    But for those first affections,
    Those shadowy recollections,
   Which, be they what they may,   150
Are yet the fountain light of all our day,
Are yet a master light of all our seeing;
   Uphold us, cherish, and have power to make
Our noisy years seem moments in the being
Of the eternal silence: truths that wake,
    To perish never;
Which neither listlessness, nor mad endeavor,
    Nor man nor boy,
Nor all that is at enmity with joy,
Can utterly abolish or destroy!   160
    Hence in a season of calm weather
    Though inland far we be,
Our souls have sight of that immortal sea
    Which brought us hither,
    Can in a moment travel thither,
And see the children sport upon the shore,
And hear the mighty waters rolling evermore.

  Then sing, ye birds, sing, sing a joyous song!
    And let the young lambs bound
    As to the tabor's sound!   170
We in thought will join your throng,
    Ye that pipe and ye that play,
    Ye that through your hearts today
    Feel the gladness of the May!
What though the radiance which was once so bright
Be now forever taken from my sight,
    Though nothing can bring back the hour
Of splendor in the grass, of glory in the flower;
    We will grieve not, rather find
    Strength in what remains behind;   180
    In the primal sympathy
    Which having been must ever be;

In the soothing thoughts that spring
Out of human suffering;
In the faith that looks through death,
In years that bring the philosophic mind.

And O, ye fountains, meadows, hills, and groves,
Forbode not any severing of our loves!
Yet in my heart of hearts I feel your might;
I only have relinquished one delight   190
To live beneath your more habitual sway.
I love the brooks which down their channels fret,
Even more than when I tripped lightly as they;
The innocent brightness of a new-born day
      Is lovely yet;
The clouds that gather round the setting sun
Do take a sober coloring from an eye
That hath kept watch o'er man's mortality;
Another race hath been, and other palms are won.
Thanks to the human heart by which we live,   200
Thanks to its tenderness, its joys, and fears,
To me the meanest flower that blows can give
Thoughts that do often lie too deep for tears.

[1803]

SHE WAS A PHANTOM OF DELIGHT

S HE was a phantom of delight
  When first she gleamed upon my sight;
A lovely apparition, sent
To be a moment's ornament;
Her eyes as stars of twilight fair;
Like twilight's, too, her dusky hair;
But all things else about her drawn
From May-time and the cheerful dawn;
A dancing shape, an image gay,
To haunt, to startle, and waylay.   10

I saw her upon nearer view,
A spirit, yet a woman too!
Her household motions light and free,
And steps of virgin-liberty;
A countenance in which did meet
Sweet records, promises as sweet;

A creature not too bright or good
For human nature's daily food;
For transient sorrows, simple wiles,
Praise, blame, love, kisses, tears, and
    smiles.   20

And now I see with eye serene
The very pulse of the machine;
A being breathing thoughtful breath,
A traveler between life and death;
The reason firm, the temperate will,
Endurance, foresight, strength, and skill;
A perfect woman, nobly planned,
To warn, to comfort, and command;
And yet a spirit still, and bright
With something of angelic light.   30
                                                                    [1804]

THE WORLD IS TOO MUCH WITH US

THE world is too much with us; late and soon,
    Getting and spending, we lay waste our powers:
Little we see in Nature that is ours;
We have given our hearts away, a sordid boon!
The sea that bares her bosom to the moon;
The winds that will be howling at all hours,
And are up-gathered now like sleeping flowers;
For this, for everything, we are out of tune;
It moves us not.—Great God! I'd rather be
A pagan suckled in a creed outworn;   10
So might I, standing on this pleasant lea,
Have glimpses that would make me less forlorn;
Have sight of Proteus rising from the sea;
Or hear old Triton blow his wreathéd horn.

                                                                    [1806]

Samuel Taylor Coleridge

1772-1834

THE RIME OF THE ANCIENT MARINER

PART I

An ancient Mariner
meeteth three Gallants
bidden to a wedding-feast,
and detaineth one.

It is an ancient Mariner,
And he stoppeth one of three.
"By thy long gray beard and glittering eye,
Now wherefore stopp'st thou me?

The Bridegroom's doors are opened wide,
And I am next of kin;
The guests are met, the feast is set:
May'st hear the merry din."

He holds him with his skinny hand,
"There was a ship," quoth he.   10
"Hold off! unhand me, gray-beard loon!"
Eftsoons his hand dropped he.

The Wedding-Guest is
spellbound by the eye of the
old seafaring man, and constrained to hear his tale.

He holds him with his glittering eye—
The Wedding-Guest stood still,
And listens like a three years' child:
The Mariner hath his will.

The Wedding-Guest sat on a stone:
He cannot choose but hear;
And thus spake on that ancient man,
The bright-eyed Mariner.   20

"The ship was cheered, the harbor cleared,
Merrily did we drop
Below the kirk, below the hill,
Below the lighthouse top.

The Mariner tells how the
ship sailed southward with
a good wind and fair
weather, till it reached
the Line.

The Sun came up upon the left,
Out of the sea came he!
And he shone bright, and on the right
Went down into the sea.

Higher and higher every day,
Till over the mast at noon—"   30
The Wedding-Guest here beat his breast,
For he heard the loud bassoon.

The Wedding-Guest heareth
the bridal music; but the
Mariner continueth his tale.

The bride hath paced into the hall,
Red as a rose is she;
Nodding their heads before her goes
The merry minstrelsy.

The Wedding-Guest he beat his breast,
Yet he cannot choose but hear;
And thus spake on that ancient man,
The bright-eyed Mariner.   40

The ship driven by a storm
toward the south pole.

"And now the storm-blast came, and he
Was tyrannous and strong:
He struck with his o'ertaking wings,
And chased us south along.

With sloping masts and dipping prow,
As who pursued with yell and blow
Still treads the shadow of his foe,
And forward bends his head,
The ship drove fast, loud roared the blast,
And southward aye we fled.   50

And now there came both mist and snow,
And it grew wondrous cold:
And ice, mast high, came floating by,
As green as emerald.

The land of ice, and of fearful sounds where no living
thing was to be seen.

And through the drifts the snowy clifts
Did send a dismal sheen:
Nor shapes of men nor beasts we ken—
The ice was all between.

The ice was here, the ice was there,
The ice was all around: 60
It cracked and growled, and roared and
        howled,
Like noises in a swound!

Till a great sea-bird, called
the Albatross, came through
the snow-fog, and was re-
ceived with great joy and
hospitality.

At length did cross an Albatross,
Thorough the fog it came;
As if it had been a Christian soul,
We hailed it in God's name.

It ate the food it ne'er had eat,
And round and round it flew.
The ice did split with a thunder-fit;
The helmsman steered us through!   70

And lo! the Albatross proveth a bird of good omen, and followeth the ship as it returned northward through fog and floating ice.

And a good south wind sprung up behind;
The Albatross did follow,
And every day, for food or play,
Came to the mariners' hollo!

In mist or cloud, on mast or shroud,
It perched for vespers nine;
Whiles all the night, through fog-smoke
    white,
Glimmered the white moon-shine."

The ancient Mariner inhospitably killeth the pious bird of good omen.

"God save thee, ancient Mariner!
From the fiends, that plague thee thus!— 80
Why look'st thou so?"—"With my
    crossbow
I shot the Albatross."

PART II

THE Sun now rose upon the right:
    Out of the sea came he,
Still hid in mist, and on the left
Went down into the sea.

And the good south wind still blew behind
But no sweet bird did follow,
Nor any day for food or play
Came to the mariners' hollo!   90

His shipmates cry out against the ancient Mariner, for killing the bird of good luck.

And I had done a hellish thing,
And it would work 'em woe:
For all averred, I had killed the bird
That made the breeze to blow.
'Ah wretch!' said they, 'the bird to slay,
That made the breeze to blow!'

But when the fog cleared off, they justify the same, and thus make themselves accomplices in the crime.

Nor dim nor red, like God's own head,
The glorious Sun uprist:
Then all averred, I had killed the bird
That brought the fog and mist.   100
' 'Twas right,' said they, 'such birds to
    slay,
That bring the fog and mist.'

The fair breeze continues; the ship enters the Pacific Ocean, and sails northward, even till it reaches the Line. The ship hath been suddenly becalmed.

The fair breeze blew, the white foam flew,
The furrow followed free;
We were the first that ever burst
Into that silent sea.

Down dropped the breeze, the sails
  dropped down,
'Twas sad as sad could be;
And we did speak only to break
The silence of the sea!   110

All in a hot and copper sky,
The bloody Sun, at noon,
Right up above the mast did stand,
No bigger than the Moon.

Day after day, day after day,
We stuck, nor breath nor motion;
As idle as a painted ship
Upon a painted ocean.

And the Albatross begins to
be avenged.

Water, water, everywhere,
And all the boards did shrink;   120
Water, water, everywhere
Nor any drop to drink.

The very deep did rot: O Christ!
That ever this should be!
Yea, slimy things did crawl with legs
Upon the slimy sea.

A Spirit had followed them;
one of the invisible inhabitants of this planet, neither
departed souls nor angels;
concerning whom the learned
Jew, Josephus, and the Platonic Constantinopolitan,
Michael Psellus, may be
consulted. They are very
numerous, and there is no
climate or element without
one or more.

About, about, in reel and rout
The death-fires danced at night;
The water, like a witch's oils,
Burnt green, and blue, and white.   130

And some in dreams assuréd were
Of the Spirit that plagued us so:
Nine fathom deep he had followed us
From the land of mist and snow.

And every tongue, through utter drought,
Was withered at the root;
We could not speak, no more than if
We had been choked with soot.

The ship-mates, in their
sore distress, would fain
throw the whole guilt on the
ancient Mariner: in sign
whereof they hang the dead
sea-bird round his neck.

Ah! well a-day! what evil looks
Had I from old and young!   140
Instead of the cross, the Albatross
About my neck was hung."

PART III

The ancient Mariner be-
holdeth a sign in the element afar off.

THERE passed a weary time. Each throat
  Was parched, and glazed each eye.
A weary time! a weary time!
How glazed each weary eye,
When looking westward, I beheld
A something in the sky.

At first it seemed a little speck,
And then it seemed a mist;   150
It moved and moved, and took at last
A certain shape, I wist.

A speck, a mist, a shape, I wist!
And still it neared and neared:
As if it dodged a water-sprite,
It plunged and tacked and veered.

At its nearer approach, it
seemeth him to be a ship;
and at a dear ransom he
freeth his speech from the
bonds of thirst.

With throats unslaked, with black lips
  baked,
We could nor laugh nor wail;
Through utter drought all dumb we stood!
I bit my arm, I sucked the blood,   160
And cried, 'A sail! a sail!'

A flash of joy;

With throats unslaked, with black lips
  baked,
Agape they heard me call;
Gramercy! they for joy did grin,
And all at once their breath drew in,
As they were drinking all.

And horror follows. For can
it be a ship that comes onward without wind or tide?

'See! see! (I cried) she tacks no more!
Hither to work us weal;
Without a breeze, without a tide,
She steadies with upright keel!'   170

The western wave was all a-flame;
The day was well nigh done!
Almost upon the western wave
Rested the broad bright Sun;
When that strange shape drove suddenly
Betwixt us and the Sun.

It seemeth him but the
skeleton of a ship:

And straight the Sun was flecked with bars
(Heaven's Mother send us grace!)
As if through a dungeon-grate he peered
With broad and burning face.   180

Alas! (thought I, and my heart beat loud)
How fast she nears and nears!
Are those her sails that glance in the Sun,
Like restless gossameres?

And its ribs are seen as bars
on the face of the setting
Sun. The Specter-Woman
and her Death-mate, and
no other on board the
skeleton-ship. Like vessel,
like crew!

Are those her ribs through which the Sun
Did peer, as through a grate?
And is that Woman all her crew?
Is that a Death? and are there two?
Is Death that woman's mate?

Her lips were red, her looks were free,   190
Her locks were yellow as gold:
Her skin was a white leprosy,
The nightmare Life-in-Death was she,
Who thicks man's blood with cold.

Death and Life-in-Death
have diced for the ship's
crew, and she (the latter)
winneth the ancient
Mariner.

The naked hulk alongside came,
And the twain were casting dice;
'The game is done! I've won! I've won!'
Quoth she and whistles thrice.

No twilight within the courts
of the Sun.

The Sun's rim dips; the stars rush out:
At one stride comes the dark;   200
With far-heard whisper, o'er the sea,
Off shot the specter-bark.

At the rising of the Moon,

We listened and looked sideways up!
Fear at my heart, as at a cup,
My life-blood seemed to sip!
The stars were dim, and thick the night,
The steersman's face by his lamp gleamed
          white;
From the sails the dew did drip—
Till clomb above the eastern bar
The hornéd Moon, with one bright star   210
Within the nether tip.

One after another,

One after one, by the star-dogged Moon,
Too quick for groan or sigh,
Each turned his face with a ghastly pang,
And cursed me with his eye.

His ship-mates drop down dead.

Four times fifty living men
(And I heard nor sigh nor groan)
With heavy thump, a lifeless lump,
They dropped down one by one.

But Life-in-Death begins her work on the ancient Mariner.

The souls did from their bodies fly— 220
They fled to bliss or woe!
And every soul, it passed me by,
Like the whizz of my cross-bow!"

PART IV

The Wedding-Guest feareth that a Spirit is talking to him;

I FEAR thee, ancient Mariner!
I fear thy skinny hand!
And thou art long, and lank, and brown,
As is the ribbed sea-sand.

But the ancient Mariner assureth him of his bodily life, and proceedeth to relate his horrible penance.

I fear thee and thy glittering eye,
And thy skinny hand, so brown."—
"Fear not, fear not, thou Wedding-Guest! 230
This body dropped not down.

Alone, alone, all, all alone,
Alone on a wide, wide sea!
And never a saint took pity on
My soul in agony.

He despiseth the creatures of the calm.

The many men, so beautiful!
And they all dead did lie:
And a thousand thousand slimy things
Lived on; and so did I.

And envieth that they should live, and so many lie dead.

I looked upon the rotting sea, 240
And drew my eyes away;
I looked upon the rotting deck,
And there the dead men lay.

I looked to heaven, and tried to pray;
But or ever a prayer had gushed,
A wicked whisper came, and made
My heart as dry as dust.

I closed my lids, and kept them close,
And the balls like pulses beat;
For the sky and the sea, and the sea and
the sky 250
Lay like a load on my weary eye,
And the dead were at my feet.

But the curse liveth for him
in the eye of the dead men.

The cold sweat melted from their limbs,
Nor rot nor reek did they :
The look with which they looked on me
Had never passed away.

An orphan's curse would drag to hell
A spirit from on high ;
But oh ! more horrible than that
Is the curse in a dead man's eye !   260
Seven days, seven nights, I saw that curse,
And yet I could not die.

In his loneliness and fixedness
he yearneth toward the
ourneying Moon, and the
stars that still sojourn, yet
still more onward; and
everywhere the blue sky
belongs to them, and is their
appointed rest, and their
native country and their
own natural homes, which
they enter unannounced, as
lords that are certainly
expected and yet there is a
silent joy at their arrival.

The moving Moon went up the sky,
And nowhere did abide :
Softly she was going up,
And a star or two beside—

Her beams bemocked the sultry main,
Like April hoar-frost spread ;
But where the ship's huge shadow lay,
The charméd water burnt alway   270
A still and awful red.

Beyond the shadow of the ship,
I watched the water-snakes :
They moved in tracks of shining white,
And when they reared, the elfish light
Fell off in hoary flakes.

By the light of the Moon he
beholdeth God's creatures
of the great calm.

Within the shadow of the ship
I watched their rich attire :
Blue, glossy green, and velvet black,
They coiled and swam ; and every track   280
Was a flash of golden fire.

Their beauty and their
happiness.

O happy living things ! no tongue
Their beauty might declare :
A spring of love gushed from my heart,
And I blessed them unaware :
Sure my kind saint took pity on me,
And I blessed them unaware.

He blesseth them in his
heart.

The spell begins to break.

The selfsame moment I could pray ;
And from my neck so free
The Albatross fell off, and sank   290
Like lead into the sea.''

PART V

Oh, sleep! it is a gentle thing,
  Beloved from pole to pole!
To Mary Queen the praise be given!
She sent the gentle sleep from Heaven,
  That slid into my soul.

By grace of the holy Mother,
the ancient Mariner is
refreshed with rain.

The silly[1] buckets on the deck,
  That had so long remained,
I dreamt that they were filled with dew;
  And when I awoke, it rained.   300

My lips were wet, my throat was cold,
  My garments all were dank;
Sure I had drunken in my dreams,
  And still my body drank.

I moved, and could not feel my limbs;
  I was so light—almost
I thought that I had died in sleep,
  And was a blessèd ghost.

He heareth sounds and
seeth strange sights
and commotions in the
sky and the element.

And soon I heard a roaring wind:
  It did not come anear;   310
But with its sound it shook the sails,
  That were so thin and sere.

The upper air burst into life!
  And a hundred fire-flags sheen,
To and fro they were hurried about!
  And to and fro, and in and out,
  The wan stars danced between.

And the coming wind did roar more loud,
  And the sails did sigh like sedge;
And the rain poured down from one
        black cloud;   320
  The moon was at its edge.

The thick black cloud was cleft, and still
  The Moon was at its side:
Like waters shot from some high crag,
The lightning fell with never a jag,
  A river steep and wide.

[1] empty

The loud wind never reached the ship,
Yet now the ship moved on!
Beneath the lightning and the Moon
The dead men gave a groan.   330

The bodies of the ship's
crew are inspired and the
ship moves on;

They groaned, they stirred, they all uprose,
nor spake, nor moved their eyes;
It had been strange, even in a dream,
To have seen those dead men rise.

The helmsman steered, the ship moved on;
Yet never a breeze up blew;
The mariners all 'gan work the ropes,
Where they were wont to do;
They raised their limbs like lifeless tools—
We were a ghastly crew.   340

The body of my brother's son
Stood by me, knee to knee:
The body and I pulled at one rope
But he said nought to me."

But not by the souls of the
men, nor by dæmons of
earth or middle air, but by
a blessed troop of angelic
spirits, sent down by the
invocation of the guardian
saint.

"I fear thee, ancient Mariner!"
"Be calm, thou Wedding-Guest!
'Twas not those souls that fled in pain,
Which to their corses came again,
But a troop of spirits blest:

For when it dawned—they dropped
    their arms,   350
And clustered round the mast;
Sweet sounds rose slowly through their
    mouths,
And from their bodies passed.

Around, around, flew each sweet sound,
Then darted to the Sun;
Slowly the sounds came back again,
Now mixed, now one by one.

Sometimes a-dropping from the sky
I heard the sky-lark sing;
Sometimes all little birds that are,   360
How they seemed to fill the sea and air
With their sweet jargoning!

And now 'twas like all instruments,
Now like a lonely flute;
And now it is an angel's song,
That makes the heavens be mute.

It ceased; yet still the sails made on
A pleasant noise till noon,
A noise like of a hidden brook
In the leafy month of June,   370
That to the sleeping woods all night
Singeth a quiet tune.

Till noon we quietly sailed on,
Yet never a breeze did breathe:
Slowly and smoothly went the ship
Moved onward from beneath.

The lonesome Spirit from
the south pole carries on
the ship as far as the Line,
in obedience to the angelic
troop, but still requireth
vengeance.

Under the keel nine fathom deep,
From the land of mist and snow,
The Spirit slid: and it was he
That made the ship to go.   380
The sails at noon left off their tune,
And the ship stood still also.

The Sun, right up above the mast,
Had fixed her to the ocean:
But in a minute she 'gan stir,
With a short uneasy motion—
Backwards and forwards half her length
With a short uneasy motion.

Then like a pawing horse let go,
She made a sudden bound: 390
It flung the blood into my head,
And I fell down in a swound.

The Polar Spirit's fellow-
dæmons, the invisible
inhabitants of the element,
take part in his wrong; and
two of them relate one to
the other, that penance long
and heavy for the ancient
Mariner hath been accorded
to the Polar Spirit, who
returneth southward.

How long in that same fit I lay,
I have not to declare;
But ere my living life returned,
I heard and in my soul discerned
Two voices in the air.

'Is it he?' quoth one, 'Is this the man?
By Him who died on cross,
With his cruel bow he laid full low   400
The harmless Albatross.

The Spirit who bideth by himself
In the land of mist and snow,
He loved the bird that loved the man
Who shot him with his bow.'

The other was a softer voice,
As soft as honey-dew:
Quoth he, 'The man hath penance done,
And penance more will do.' "

PART VI

First Voice

Bᴜᴛ tell me, tell me! speak again,   410
Thy soft response renewing—
What makes that ship drive on so fast?
What is the ocean doing?'

Second Voice
'Still as a slave before his lord,
The ocean hath no blast;
His great bright eye most silently
Up to the Moon is cast—

If he may know which way to go;
For she guides him smooth or grim.
See, brother, see! how graciously   420
She looketh down on him.'

First Voice

The Mariner hath been cast into a trance; for the angelic power causeth the vessel to drive northward faster than human life could endure.

'But why drives on that ship so fast,
Without or wave or wind?'

Second Voice
'The air is cut away before,
And closes from behind.

Fly, brother, fly, more high, more high!
Or we shall be belated:
For slow and slow that ship will go,
When the Mariner's trance is abated.'

The supernatural motion is retarded; the Mariner awakes, and his penance begins anew.

I woke, and we were sailing on   430
As in a gentle weather:
'Twas night, calm night, the Moon was high,
The dead men stood together.

All stood together on the deck,
For a charnel-dungeon fitter:
All fixed on me their stony eyes,
That in the Moon did glitter.

The pang, the curse, with which they died,
Had never passed away:
I could not draw my eyes from theirs,   440
Nor turn them up to pray.

The curse is finally expiated.

And now this spell was snapped: once more
I viewed the ocean green,
And looked far forth, yet little saw
Of what had else been seen—

Like one, that on a lonesome road
Doth walk in fear and dread,
And having once turned round walks on,
And turns no more his head;
Because he knows a frightful fiend   450
Doth close behind him tread.

But soon there breathed a wind on me,
Nor sound nor motion made:
Its path was not upon the sea,
In ripple or in shade.

It raised my hair, it fanned my cheek
Like a meadow-gale of spring—
It mingled strangely with my fears,
Yet it felt like a welcoming.

Swiftly, swiftly flew the ship   460
Yet she sailed softly too:
Sweetly, sweetly blew the breeze—
On me alone it blew.

And the ancient Mariner
beholdeth his native country.

Oh! dream of joy! is this indeed
The light-house top I see?
Is this the hill? is this the kirk?
Is this mine own countree?

We drifted o'er the harbor-bar,
And I with sobs did pray—
O let me be awake, my God!   470
Or let me sleep alway.

The harbor-bay was clear as glass,
So smoothly it was strewn!
And on the bay the moonlight lay,
And the shadow of the Moon.

The rock shone bright, the kirk no less,
That stands above the rock :
The moonlight steeped in silentness
The steady weathercock.

And the bay was white with silent light   480
Till rising from the same,
Full many shapes, that shadows were,
In crimson colors came.

The angelic spirits leave the dead bodies,

A little distance from the prow
Those crimson shadows were :
I turned my eyes upon the deck—
Oh, Christ, what saw I there!

And appear in their own forms of light.

Each corse lay flat, lifeless and flat,
And, by the holy rood!
A man all light, a seraph-man,   490
On every corse there stood.

This seraph-band, each waved his hand;
It was a heavenly sight!
They stood as signals to the land
Each one a lovely light;

This seraph-band, each waved his hand,
No voice did they impart—
No voice; but oh! the silence sank
Like music on my heart.

But soon I heard the dash of oars,   500
I heard the Pilot's cheer;
My head was turned perforce away,
And I saw a boat appear.

The Pilot and the Pilot's boy,
I heard them coming fast :
Dear Lord in Heaven! it was a joy
The dead men could not blast.

I saw a third—I heard his voice:
It is the Hermit good!
He singeth loudly his godly hymns 510
That he makes in the wood.
He'll shrieve my soul; he'll wash away
The Albatross's blood."

PART VII

The Hermit of the Wood,

THIS Hermit good lives in that wood
    Which slopes down to the sea.
How loudly his sweet voice he rears!
He loves to talk with marineres
That come from a far countree.

He kneels at morn, and noon, and eve—
He hath a cushion plump: 520
It is the moss that wholly hides
The rotted old oak-stump.

The skiff-boat neared: I heard them talk,
'Why, this is strange, I trow!
Where are those lights so many and fair,
That signal made but now!'

Approacheth the ship with
wonder.

'Strange, by my faith!' the Hermit said—
'And they answered not our cheer!
The planks looked warped! and see those
    sails,
How thin they are and sere! 530
I never saw aught like to them,
Unless perchance it were

Brown skeletons of leaves that lag
My forest-brook along;
When the ivy-tod is heavy with snow,
And the owlet whoops to the wolf below,
That eats the she-wolf's young.'

'Dear Lord! it hath a fiendish look—
(The Pilot made reply)
I am a-feared'—'Push on, push on!' 540
Said the Hermit cheerily.

The boat came closer to the ship,
But I nor spake nor stirred;
The boat came close beneath the ship,
And straight a sound was heard.

The ship suddenly sinketh.

Under the water it rumbled on,
Still louder and more dread :
It reached the ship, it split the bay ;
The ship went down like lead.

The ancient Mariner is
saved in the Pilot's boat.

Stunned by that loud and dreadful sound,   550
Which sky and ocean smote,
Like one that hath been seven days drowned
My body lay afloat ;
But swift as dreams, myself I found
Within the Pilot's boat.

Upon the whirl, where sank the ship,
The boat spun round and round ;
And all was still, save that the hill
Was telling of the sound.

I moved my lips—the Pilot shrieked   560
And fell down in a fit ;
The holy Hermit raised his eyes,
And prayed where he did sit.

I took the oars : the Pilot's boy,
Who now doth crazy go,
Laughed loud and long, and all the while
His eyes went to and fro.
'Ha ! ha !' quoth he, 'full plain I see,
The Devil knows how to row.'

And now, all in my own countree,   570
I stood on the firm land !
The Hermit stepped forth from the boat,
And scarcely he could stand.

The ancient Mariner
earnestly entreateth the
Hermit to shrieve him ;
and the penance of life
falls on him.

'O shrieve me, shrieve me, holy man !'
The Hermit crossed his brow.
'Say quick,' quoth he, 'I bid thee say—
What manner of man art thou ?'

Forthwith this frame of mine was wrenched
With a woeful agony,
Which forced me to begin my tale ;   580
And then it left me free.

And ever and anon throughout his future life an agony
constraineth him to travel
from land to land,

Since then, at an uncertain hour,
That agony returns :
And till my ghastly tale is told,
This heart within me burns.

I pass, like night, from land to land;
I have strange power of speech;
That moment that his face I see,
I know the man that must hear me:
To him my tale I teach. 590

What loud uproar bursts from that door!
The wedding-guests are there:
But in the garden-bower the bride
And bride-maids singing are:
And hark the little vesper bell
Which biddeth me to prayer!

O Wedding-Guest! this soul hath been
Alone on a wide, wide sea;
So lonely 'twas, that God himself
Scarce seeméd there to be. 600

O sweeter than the marriage-feast,
'Tis sweeter to me,
To walk together to the kirk
With a goodly company!—

To walk together to the kirk,
And all together pray,
While each to his great Father bends,
Old men, and babes, and loving friends,
And youths and maidens gay!

And to teach, by his own
example, love and reverence
to all things that God made
and loveth.

Farewell, farewell! but this I tell 610
To thee, thou Wedding-Guest!
He prayeth well, who loveth well
Both man and bird and beast.

He prayeth best, who loveth best
All things both great and small;
For the dear God who loveth us,
He made and loveth all."

The Mariner, whose eye is bright,
Whose beard with age is hoar,
Is gone: and now the Wedding-Guest 620
Turned from the Bridegroom's door.

He went like one that hath been stunned,
And is of sense forlorn:
A sadder and a wiser man,
He rose the morrow morn.

[1798]

FROST AT MIDNIGHT

THE frost performs its secret ministry,
  Unhelped by any wind. The owlet's cry
Came loud—and hark, again! loud as before.
The inmates of my cottage, all at rest,
Have left me to that solitude, which suits
Abtruser musings : save that at my side
My cradled infant slumbers peacefully.
'Tis calm indeed! so calm, that it disturbs
And vexes meditation with its strange
And extreme silentness. Sea, hill, and wood,   10
This populous village! Sea, and hill, and wood,
With all the numberless goings-on of life,
Inaudible as dreams! the thin blue flame
Lies on my low-burnt fire, and quivers not;
Only that film, which fluttered on the grate,
Still flutters there, the sole unquiet thing.[1]
Methinks, its motion in this hush of nature
Gives it dim sympathies with me who live,
Making it a companionable form,
Whose puny flaps and freaks the idling Spirit   20
By its own moods interprets, everywhere
Echo or mirror seeking of itself,
And makes a toy of Thought.
                      But O! how oft,
How oft, at school, with most believing mind,
Presageful, have I gazed upon the bars,
To watch that fluttering *stranger!* and as oft
With unclosed lids, already had I dreamt
Of my sweet birth-place, and the old church-tower,
Whose bells, the poor man's only music, rang
From morn to evening, all the hot Fair-day,   30
So sweetly, that they stirred and haunted me
With a wild pleasure, falling on mine ear
Most like articulate sounds of things to come!
So gazed I, till the soothing things, I dreamt,
Lulled me to sleep, and sleep prolonged my dreams!
And so I brooded all the following morn,
Awed by the stern preceptor's face, mine eye
Fixed with mock study on my swimming book :
Save if the door half opened, and I snatched

---

[1] a fluttering flake of soot, called a *stranger*, believed to presage the arrival of an unforeseen visitor ; see also lines 26 and 41.

A hasty glance, and still my heart leaped up, 40
For still I hoped to see the *stranger's* face,
Townsman, or aunt, or sister more beloved,
My playmate when we both were clothed alike!

Dear Babe, that sleepest cradled by my side,
Whose gentle breathing, heard in this deep calm,
Fill up the interspersèd vacancies
And momentary pauses of the thought!
My babe so beautiful! it thrills my heart
With tender gladness, thus to look at thee,
And think that thou shalt learn far other lore, 50
And in far other scenes! For I was reared
In the great city, pent 'mid cloisters dim,
And saw nought lovely but the sky and stars.
But *thou*, my babe! shalt wander like a breeze
By lakes and sandy shores, beneath the crags
Of ancient mountain, and beneath the clouds,
Which image in their bulk both lakes and shores
And mountain crags: so shalt thou see and hear
The lovely shapes and sounds intelligible
Of that eternal language, which thy God 60
Utters, who from eternity doth teach
Himself in all, and all things in himself.
Great universal Teacher! he shall mold
Thy spirit, and by giving make it ask.

Therefore all seasons shall be sweet to thee,
Whether the summer clothe the general earth
With greenness, or the redbreast sit and sing
Betwixt the tufts of snow on the bare branch
Of mossy apple-tree, while the nigh thatch
Smokes in the sun-thaw; whether the eavedrops fall 70
Heard only in the trances of the blast,
Or if the secret ministry of frost
Shall hang them up in silent icicles,
Quietly shining to the quiet Moon.

[1798]

KUBLA KHAN

IN XANADU did Kubla Khan
A stately pleasure-dome decree:
Where Alph, the sacred river, ran
Through caverns measureless to man
Down to a sunless sea.

So twice five miles of fertile ground
With walls and towers were girdled round :
And here were gardens bright with sinuous rills,
Where blossomed many an incense-bearing tree,
And here were forests ancient as the hills,   10
Enfolding sunny spots of greenery.

But oh ! that deep romantic chasm which slanted
Down the green hill athwart a cedarn cover !
A savage place ! as holy and enchanted
As e'er beneath a waning moon was haunted
By woman wailing for her demon-lover !
And from this chasm, with ceaseless turmoil seething,
As if this earth in fast thick pants were breathing,
A mighty fountain momently was forced,
Amid whose swift half-intermitted burst   20
Huge fragments vaulted like rebounding hail,
Or chaffy grain beneath the thresher's flail :
And 'mid these dancing rocks at once and ever
It flung up momently the sacred river.
Five miles meandering with a mazy motion
Through wood and dale the sacred river ran,
Then reached the caverns measureless to man,
And sank in tumult to a lifeless ocean :
And 'mid this tumult Kubla heard from far
Ancestral voices prophesying war !   30
    The shadow of the dome of pleasure
    Floated midway on the waves ;
    Where was heard the mingled measure
    From the fountain and the caves.
It was a miracle of rare device,
A sunny pleasure-dome with caves of ice !

    A damsel with a dulcimer
    In a vision once I saw :
    It was an Abyssinian maid,
    And on her dulcimer she played,   40
    Singing of Mount Abora.
Could I revive within me
Her symphony and song,
To such a deep delight 'twould win me,
That with music loud and long,
I would build that dome in air,
That sunny dome ! those caves of ice !
And all who heard should see them there,
And all should cry, Beware ! Beware !

His flashing eyes, his floating hair! 50
Weave a circle round him thrice,
And close your eyes with holy dread,
For he on honey-dew hath fed,
And drunk the milk of Paradise.

[1798]

WORK WITHOUT HOPE
LINES COMPOSED 21ST FEBRUARY 1825

ALL nature seems at work. Slugs leave their lair—
The bees are stirring—birds are on the wing—
And winter slumbering in the open air,
Wears on his smiling face a dream of spring!
And I the while, the sole unbusy thing,
Nor honey make, nor pair, nor build, nor sing.

Yet well I ken the banks where amaranths blow,
Have traced the fount whence streams of nectar flow.
Bloom, O ye amaranths! bloom for whom ye may,
For me ye bloom not! Glide, rich streams, away! 10
With lips unbrightened, wreathless brow, I stroll:
And would you learn the spells that drowse my soul?
Work without hope draws nectar in a sieve,
And hope without an object cannot live.

[1825]

George Gordon, Lord Byron
1788–1824

SHE WALKS IN BEAUTY

SHE walks in Beauty, like the night
Of cloudless climes and starry skies;
And all that's best of dark and bright
Meet in her aspect and her eyes:
Thus mellowed to that tender light
Which Heaven to gaudy day denies.

One shade the more, one ray the less,
Had half impaired the nameless grace
Which waves in every raven tress,
Or softly lightens o'er her face; 10
Where thoughts serenely sweet express,
How pure, how dear their dwelling-place.

And on that cheek, and o'er that brow,
So soft, so calm, yet eloquent,
The smiles that win, the tints that glow,
But tell of days in goodness spent,
A mind at peace with all below,
A heart whose love is innocent!

[1814]

THE DESTRUCTION OF SENNACHARIB

THE Assyrian[1] came down like a wolf on the fold,
And his cohorts were gleaming in purple and gold;
And the sheen of their spears was like stars on the sea,
When the blue wave rolls nightly on deep Galilee.

Like the leaves of the forest when summer is green,
That host with their banners at sunset were seen:
Like the leaves of the forest when autumn hath blown,
That host on the morrow lay withered and strown.

For the Angel of Death spread his wings on the blast,
And breathed in the face of the foe as he passed;   10
And the eyes of the sleepers waxed deadly and chill,
And their hearts but once heaved, and forever grew still!

And there lay the steed with his nostril all wide,
But through it there rolled not the breath of his pride;
And the foam of his gasping lay white on the turf,
And cold as the spray of the rock-beating surf.

And there lay the rider distorted and pale,
With the dew on his brow, and the rust on his mail:
And the tents were all silent, the banners alone,
The lances unlifted, the trumpet unblown.   20

And the widows of Ashur[2] are loud in their wail,
And the idols are broke in the temple of Baal;
And the might of the Gentile, unsmote by the sword,
Hath melted like snow in the glance of the Lord!

[1815]

---

[1] King of Assyria; see II Kings, xviii–xix.   [2] Assyria

SONNET ON CHILLON

ETERNAL spirit of the chainless Mind!
Brightest in dungeons, Liberty! thou art,
For there thy habitation is the heart—
The heart which love of thee alone can bind;
And when thy sons to fetters are consigned—
To fetters, and the damp vault's dayless gloom,
Their country conquers with their martyrdom,
And Freedom's fame finds wings on every wind.
Chillon! thy prison is a holy place,
And thy sad floor an altar—for 'twas trod,   10
Until his very steps have left a trace
Worn, as if thy cold pavement were a sod,
By Bonnivard[1]—May none those marks efface!
For they appeal from tyranny to God.

[1816]

[1] Francois Bonivard [*sic*], a Swiss cleric and political leader who was imprisoned by the Duke of Savoy in the Castle of Chillon on Lake Geneva, 1532–36, and who became a symbol of resistance to tyranny in popular ballads

ON THIS DAY I COMPLETE MY THIRTY-SIXTH YEAR

MISSOLONGHI,[1] JAN. 22, 1824

TIS time this heart should be unmoved,
Since others it hath ceased to move:
Yet, though I cannot be beloved,
Still let me love!

My days are in the yellow leaf;
The flowers and fruits of love are gone;
The worm, the canker, and the grief
Are mine alone!

The fire that on my bosom preys
Is lone as some volcanic isle;   10
No torch is kindled at its blaze—
A funeral pile.

[1] Byron volunteered to train troops for the Greeks in their war for independence from Turkey. He succumbed to fever at Missolonghi shortly after he wrote this poem.

The hope, the fear, the jealous care,
    The exalted portion of the pain
And power of love, I cannot share,
    But wear the chain.

But 'tis not *thus*—and 'tis not *here*—
    Such thoughts should shake my soul, nor *now*,
Where glory decks the hero's bier,
    Or binds his brow.   20

The sword, the banner, and the field,
    Glory and Greece, around me see!
The Spartan, borne upon his shield,
    Was not more free.

Awake! (not Greece—she *is* awake!)
    Awake, my spirit! Think through *whom*
Thy life-blood tracks its parent lake,
    And then strike home!

Tread those reviving passions down,
    Unworthy manhood!—unto thee   30
Indifferent should the smile or frown
    Of beauty be.

If thou regrett'st thy youth, *why live?*
    The land of honorable death
Is here:—up to the field, and give
    Away thy breath!

Seek out—less often sought than found—
    A soldier's grave, for thee the best;
Then look around, and choose thy ground
    And take thy rest.   40
                                                    [1824]

Percy Bysshe Shelley
1792–1822

OZYMANDIAS

I MET a traveler from an antique land
Who said: Two vast and trunkless legs of stone
Stand in the desert . . . Near them, on the sand,
Half sunk, a shattered visage lies, whose frown,

And wrinkled lip, and sneer of cold command,
Tell that its sculptor well those passions read
Which yet survive, stamped on these lifeless things,
The hand that mocked them, and the heart that fed :
And on the pedestal these words appear :
"My name is Ozymandias, king of kings :   10
Look on my works, ye Mighty, and despair !"
Nothing beside remains. Round the decay
Of that colossal wreck, boundless and bare
The lone and level sands stretch far away.

[1817]

ODE TO THE WEST WIND

I

O WILD West Wind, thou breath of Autumn's being,
  Thou, from whose unseen presence the leaves dead
Are driven, like ghosts from an enchanter fleeing,

Yellow, and black, and pale, and hectic red,
Pestilence-stricken multitudes : O thou,
Who chariotest to their dark wintry bed

The wingéd seeds, where they lie cold and low,
Each like a corpse within its grave, until
Thine azure sister of the Spring shall blow

Her clarion o'er the dreaming earth, and fill   10
(Driving sweet buds like flocks to feed in air)
With living hues and odors plain and hill :

Wild Spirit, which art moving everywhere ;
Destroyer and preserver ; hear, oh hear !

II

Thou on whose stream, mid the steep sky's commotion,
Loose clouds like earth's decaying leaves are shed,
Shook from the tangled boughs of Heaven and Ocean,

Angels of rain and lightning : there are spread
On the blue surface of thine aëry surge,
Like the bright hair uplifted from the head   20

Of some fierce Maenad,[1] even from the dim verge
Of the horizon to the zenith's height,
The locks of the approaching storm. Thou dirge

[1] a frenetic female worshiper of Dionysus, god of wine and fertility

Of the dying year, to which this closing night
Will be the dome of a vast sepulcher,
Vaulted with all thy congregated might

Of vapors, from whose solid atmosphere
Black rain, and fire, and hail will burst : oh, hear !

III

Thou who didst waken from his summer dreams
The blue Mediterranean, where he lay,   30
Lulled by the coil of his crystálline streams,

Beside a pumice isle in Baiae's bay,[2]
And saw in sleep old palaces and towers
Quivering within the wave's intenser day,

All overgrown with azure moss and flowers
So sweet, the sense faints picturing them ! Thou
For whose path the Atlantic's level powers

Cleave themselves into chasms, while far below
The sea-blooms and the oozy woods which wear
The sapless foliage of the ocean, know   40

Thy voice, and suddenly grow gray with fear,
And tremble and despoil themselves : oh, hear !

IV

If I were a dead leaf thou mightest bear ;
If I were a swift cloud to fly with thee ;
A wave to pant beneath thy power, and share

The impulse of thy strength, only less free
Than thou, O uncontrollable ! If even
I were as in my boyhood, and could be

The comrade of thy wanderings over Heaven,
As then, when to outstrip thy skiey speed   50
Scarce seemed a vision ; I would ne'er have striven

As thus with thee in prayer in my sore need.
O, lift me as a wave, a leaf, a cloud !
I fall upon the thorns of life ! I bleed !

[2] on the west coast of Italy

A heavy weight of hours has chained and bowed
One too like thee : tameless, and swift, and proud.

v

Make my thy lyre, even as the forest is :
What if my leaves are falling like its own !
The tumult of thy mighty harmonies

Will take from both a deep, autumnal tone,   60
Sweet though in sadness. Be thou, Spirit fierce,
My spirit ! Be thou me, impetuous one !

Drive my dead thoughts over the universe
Like withered leaves to quicken a new birth !
And, by the incantation of this verse,

Scatter, as from an unextinguished hearth
Ashes and sparks, my words among mankind !
Be through my lips to unawakened earth

The trumpet of a prophecy ! O, Wind,
If Winter comes, can Spring be far behind ?   70
                                                          [1819]

TO A SKYLARK

HAIL to thee, blithe Spirit !
     Bird thou never wert,
That from Heaven, or near it,
     Pourest thy full heart
In profuse strains of unpremediated art.

Higher still and higher
     From the earth thou springest
Like a cloud of fire ;
     The blue deep thou wingest,
And singing still dost soar, and soaring ever singest.   10

In the golden lightning
     Of the sunken sun,
O'er which clouds are bright'ning,
     Thou dost float and run ;
Like an unbodied joy whose race is just begun.

The pale purple even
   Melts around thy flight;
Like a star of Heaven,
   In the broad daylight
Thou art unseen, but yet I hear thy shrill delight,   20

Keen as are the arrows
   Of that silver sphere,
Whose intense lamp narrows
   In the white dawn clear
Until we hardly see—we feel that it is there.

All the earth and air
   With thy voice is loud.
As, when night is bare,
   From one lonely cloud
The moon rains out her beams, and Heaven is overflowed. 30

What thou art we know not;
   What is most like thee?
From rainbow clouds there flow not
   Drops so bright to see
As from thy presence showers a rain of melody.

Like a Poet hidden
   In the light of thought,
Singing hymns unbidden,
   Till the world is wrought
To sympathy with hopes and fears it heeded not: 40

Like a high-born maiden
   In a palace tower,
Soothing her love-laden
   Soul in secret hour
With music sweet as love, which overflows her bower:

Like a glowworm golden
   In a dell of dew,
Scattering unbeholden
   Its aërial hue
Among the flowers and grass, which screen it from the view!
    51

Like a rose embowered
   In its own green leaves,
By warm winds deflowered,

Till the scent it gives
Makes faint with too much sweet those heavy-wingéd thieves :

Sound of vernal showers
    On the twinkling grass,
Rain-awakened flowers,
    All that ever was
Joyous, and clear, and fresh, thy music doth surpass :   60

Teach us, Sprite or Bird,
    What sweet thoughts are thine :
I have never heard
    Praise of love or wine
That panted forth a flood of rapture so divine.

Chorus Hymeneal,
    Or triumphal chant,
Matched with thine would be all
    But an empty vaunt,
A thing wherein we feel there is some hidden want.   70

What objects are the fountains
    Of thy happy strain ?
What fields, or waves, or mountains ?
    What shapes of sky or plain ?
What love of thine own kind ? what ignorance of pain ?

With thy clear keen joyance
    Languor cannot be :
Shadow of annoyance
    Never came near thee :
Thou lovest—but ne'er knew love's sad satiety.   80

Waking or asleep,
    Thou of death must deem
Things more true and deep
    Than we mortals dream,
Or how could thy notes flow in such a crystal stream ?

We look before and after,
    And pine for what is not
Our sincerest laughter
    With some pain is fraught ;
Our sweetest songs are those that tell of saddest thought.   90

Yet if we could scorn
Hate, and pride, and fear;
If we were things born
Not to shed a tear,
I know not how thy joy we ever should come near.

Better than all measures
Of delightful sound,
Better than all treasures
That in books are found,
Thy skill to poet were, thou scorner of the ground!   100

Teach me half the gladness
That thy brain must know,
Such harmonious madness
From my lips would flow
The world should listen then—as I am listening now.

[1820]

TO——

MUSIC, when soft voices die,
Vibrates in the memory—
Odors, when sweet violets sicken,
Live within the sense they quicken.

Rose leaves, when the rose is dead,
Are heaped for the belovéd's bed;
And so thy thoughts, when thou art gone,
Love itself shall slumber on.

[1821]

William Cullen Bryant
1794–1878
THANATOPSIS

To HIM who in the love of Nature holds
Communion with her visible forms, she speaks
A various language; for his gayer hours
She has a voice of gladness, and a smile
And eloquence of beauty, and she glides
Into his darker musings, with a mild

And healing sympathy, that steals away
Their sharpness, ere he is aware. When thoughts
Of the last bitter hour come like a blight
Over thy spirit, and sad images   10
Of the stern agony, and shroud, and pall,
And breathless darkness, and the narrow house,
Make thee to shudder, and grow sick at heart;—
Go forth, under the open sky, and list
To Nature's teachings, while from all around—
Earth and her waters, and the depths of air—
Comes a still voice—Yet a few days, and thee
The all-beholding sun shall see no more
In all his course; nor yet in the cold ground,
Where thy pale form was laid, with many tears,   20
Nor in the embrace of ocean, shall exist
Thy image. Earth, that nourished thee, shall claim
Thy growth, to be resolved to earth again,
And, lost each human trace, surrendering up
Thine individual being, shalt thou go
To mix for ever with the elements,
To be a brother to the insensible rock
And to the sluggish clod, which the rude swain
Turns with his share, and treads upon. The oak
Shall send his roots abroad, and pierce thy mold. 30

     Yet not to thine eternal resting-place
Shalt thou retire alone, nor couldst thou wish
Couch more magnificent. Thou shalt lie down
With patriarchs of the infant world—with kings,
The powerful of the earth—the wise, the good,
Fair forms, and hoary seers of ages past,
All in one mighty sepulchre. The hills
Rock-ribbed and ancient as the sun—the vales
Stretching in pensive quietness between;
The venerable woods—rivers that move   40
In majesty, and the complaining brooks
That make the meadows green; and, poured round all,
Old Ocean's gray and melancholy waste,—
Are but the solemn decorations all
Of the great tomb of man. The golden sun,
The planets, all the infinite host of heaven,
Are shining on the sad abodes of death,
Through the still lapse of ages. All that tread
The globe are but a handful to the tribes
That slumber in its bosom.—Take the wings   50

Of morning, pierce the Barcan[1] wilderness,
Or lose thyself in the continuous woods
Where rolls the Oregon, and hears no sound,
Save his own dashings—yet the dead are there:
And millions in those solitudes, since first
The flight of years began, have laid them down
In their last sleep—the dead reign there alone.
So shalt thou rest, and what if thou withdraw
In silence from the living, and no friend
Take note of thy departure? All that breathe   60
Will share thy destiny. The gay will laugh
When thou art gone, the solemn brood of care
Plod on, and each one as before will chase
His favorite phantom; yet all these shall leave
Their mirth and their employments, and shall come,
And make their bed with thee. As the long train
Of ages glide away, the sons of men,
The youth in life's green spring, and he who goes
In the full strength of years, matron and maid,
The speechless babe, and the gray-headed man—   70
Shall one by one be gathered to thy side,
By those, who in their turn shall follow them.

     So live, that when thy summons comes to join
The innumerable caravan, which moves
To that mysterious realm, where each shall take
His chamber in the silent halls of death,
Thou go not, like the quarry-slave at night,
Scourged to his dungeon, but, sustained and soothed
By an unfaltering trust, approach thy grave,
Like one who wraps the drapery of his couch   80
About him, and lies down to pleasant dreams.

                                                                  [1811]

¹ of Barca, a region on the south shore of the Mediterranian in what is now Libya

TO A WATERFOWL

WHITHER, 'midst falling dew,
     While glow the heavens with the last steps of day,
Far, through their rosy depths, dost thou pursue
     Thy solitary way?

     Vainly the fowler's eye
Might mark thy distant flight, to do thee wrong,
As, darkly seen against the crimson sky,
     Thy figure floats along.

Seek'st thou the plashy brink
Of weedy lake, or marge of river wide,   10
Or where the rocking billows rise and sink
    On the chaféd ocean side?

There is a Power, whose care
Teaches thy way along that pathless coast,
The desert and illimitable air,
    Lone wandering, but not lost,

All day thy wings have fanned,
At that far height, the cold thin atmosphere;
Yet stoop not, weary, to the welcome land,
    Though the dark night is near.   20

And soon that toil shall end,
Soon shalt thou find a summer home, and rest,
And scream among thy fellows; reeds shall bend,
    Soon, o'er thy sheltered nest.

Thou'rt gone, the abyss of heaven
Hath swallowed up thy form, yet, on my heart
Deeply hath sunk the lesson thou hast given,
    And shall not soon depart.

He, who, from zone to zone,
Guides through the boundless sky thy certain flight,   30
In the long way that I must trace alone,
    Will lead my steps aright.

[1815]

John Keats
1795–1821

ON FIRST LOOKING INTO
CHAPMAN'S HOMER[1]

MUCH have I traveled in the realms of gold,
    And many goodly states and kingdoms seen:
Round many western islands have I been
Which bards in fealty to Apollo[2] hold.

---

[1] George Chapman (c. 1559–1634) published translations of *The Iliad* (1611) and *The Odyssey* (1616).
[2] god of poetry

Oft of one wide expanse had I been told
That deep-browed Homer ruled as his demesne;[3]
Yet did I never breathe its pure serene
Till I heard Chapman speak out loud and bold:
Then felt I like some watcher of the skies
When a new planet swims into his ken;   10
Or like stout Cortez[4] when with eagle eyes
He stared at the Pacific—and all his men
Looked at each other with a wild surmise—
Silent, upon a peak in Darien.

[1816]

[3] estate
[4] Hernando Cortez (1485–1547), Spanish conqueror of Mexico. Actually it was
Vasco Nuñez de Balboa (1475–1517) who first sighted the Pacific from a mountain
in Darien, a region in eastern Panama.

TO HOMER

STANDING aloof in giant ignorance,[1]
Of thee I hear and of the Cyclades,[2]
As one who sits ashore and longs perchance
To visit dolphin-coral in deep seas.
So thou wast blind!—but then the veil was rent,
For Jove uncurtained Heaven to let thee live,
And Neptune made for thee a spumy tent,
And Pan made sing for thee his forest-hive;
Aye, on the shores of darkness there is light,
And precipices show untrodden green;   10
There is a budding morrow in midnight;
There is a triple sight in blindness keen;
Such seeing hadst thou, as it once befell
To Dian,[3] Queen of Earth, and Heaven, and Hell.

[1818]

[1] Keats could not read Homer in the original Greek; see "On First Looking into
Chapman's Homer," above.
[2] cluster of Greek islands in the Aegean Sea
[3] the moon goddess, who ruled over the three realms

WHEN I HAVE FEARS THAT
I MAY CEASE TO BE

WHEN I have fears that I may cease to be
Before my pen has gleaned my teeming brain,
Before high-piléd books, in charactery,
Hold like rich garners the full-ripened grain;

When I behold, upon the night's starred face,
Huge cloudy symbols of a high romance,
And think that I may never live to trace
Their shadows, with the magic hand of chance;
And when I feel, fair creature of an hour,
That I shall never look upon thee more,   10
Never have relish in the faery power
Of unreflecting love;—then on the shore
Of the wide world I stand alone, and think
Till love and fame to nothingness do sink.

[1818]

LA BELLE DAME SANS MERCI

I

O WHAT can ail thee, knight-at-arms,
    Alone and palely loitering?
The sedge has withered from the lake,
    And no birds sing.

II

O what can ail thee, knight-at-arms,
    So haggard and so woe-begone?
The squirrel's granary is full,
    And the harvest's done.

III

I see a lily on thy brow
    With anguish moist and fever dew,   10
And on thy cheek a fading rose
    Fast withereth too.

IV

I met a lady in the meads,
    Full beautiful—a faery's child,
Her hair was long, her foot was light,
    And her eyes were wild.

V

I made a garland for her head,
    And bracelets too, and fragrant zone;
She looked at me as she did love,
    And made sweet moan.   20

VI

I set her on my pacing steed,
   And nothing else saw all day long,
For sidelong would she bend, and sing
   A faery's song.

VII

She found me roots of relish sweet,
   And honey wild, and manna dew,
And sure in language strange she said—
   "I love thee true."

VIII

She took me to her elfin grot,
   And there she wept, and sighed full sore.   30
And there I shut her wild wild eyes
   With kisses four.

IX

And there she lulléd me asleep,
   And there I dreamed—Ah! woe betide!
The latest dream I ever dreamed
   On the cold hill side.

X

I saw pale kings and princes too,
   Pale warriors, death-pale were they all;
They cried—"La Belle Dame sans Merci
   Hath thee in thrall!"   40

XI

I saw their starved lips in the gloam,
   With horrid warning gapéd wide,
And I awoke and found me here,
   On the cold hill's side.

XII

And this is why I sojourn here,
   Alone and palely loitering,
Though the sedge is withered from the
     lake,
   And no birds sing.

[1819]

ODE ON A GRECIAN URN

I

Thou still unravished bride of quietness,
  Thou foster-child of silence and slow time,
Sylvan historian, who canst thus express
  A flowery tale more sweetly than our rhyme:
What leaf-fringed legend haunts about thy shape
  Of deities or mortals, or of both,
    In Tempe[1] or the dales of Arcady?[2]
What men or gods are these? What maidens loth?
  What mad pursuit? What struggle to escape?
    What pipes and timbrels? What wild ecstasy?   10

II

Heard melodies are sweet, but those unheard
  Are sweeter; therefore, ye soft pipes, play on;
Not to the sensual ear, but, more endeared,
  Pipe to the spirit ditties of no tone:
Fair youth, beneath the trees, thou canst not leave
  Thy song, nor ever can those trees be bare;
    Bold Lover, never, never canst thou kiss,
Though winning near the goal—yet, do not grieve;
  She cannot fade, though thou hast not thy bliss,
    Forever wilt thou love, and she be fair!   20

III

Ah, happy, happy boughs! that cannot shed
  Your leaves, nor ever bid the spring adieu;
And, happy melodist, unwearièd,
  Forever piping songs for ever new;
More happy love! more happy, happy love!
  Forever warm and still to be enjoyed,
    Forever panting, and forever young;
All breathing human passion far above,
  That leaves a heart high-sorrowful and cloyed,
    A burning forehead, and a parching tongue.   30

IV

Who are these coming to the sacrifice?
  To what green altar, O mysterious priest,
Lead'st thou that heifer lowing at the skies,
  And all her silken flanks with garlands dressed?

[1] valley in Thessaly, noted for natural beauty
[2] Arcadia, a region in Peloponnesus which is usually the setting for pastoral poetry

What little town by river or sea shore,
   Or mountain-built with peaceful citadel,
      Is emptied of this folk, this pious morn?
And, little town, thy streets for evermore
   Will silent be; and not a soul to tell
      Why thou art desolate, can e'er return.   40

V

O Attic[3] shape! Fair attitude! with brede[4]
   Of marble men and maidens overwrought,
      With forest branches and the trodden weed;
   Thou, silent form, dost tease us out of thought
As doth eternity: Cold Pastoral!
   When old age shall this generation waste,
      Thou shalt remain, in midst of other woe
Than ours, a friend to man, to whom thou say'st,
   "Beauty is truth, truth beauty,"—that is all
      Ye know on earth, and all ye need to know.   50

[1819]

---

[3] of Attica; hence, "classic"   [4] embroidery

ODE ON MELANCHOLY

I

No, no, go not to Lethe,[1] neither twist
   Wolf's bane,[2] tight-rooted, for its poisonous wine;
Nor suffer thy pale forehead to be kissed
   By nightshade, ruby grape of Proserpine;[3]
Make not your rosary of yew berries,[4]
   Nor let the bettle, nor the death-moth be
      Your mournful Psyche,[5] nor the downy owl
A partner in your sorrow's mysteries;
   For shade to shade will come too drowsily,
      And drown the wakeful anguish of the soul.   10

II

But when the melancholy fit shall fall
   Sudden from heaven like a weeping cloud,
That fosters the droop-headed flowers all,
   And hides the green hill in an April shroud;

---

[1] river of forgetfulness in Hades   [2] like nightshade, poisonous herb
[3] queen of the underworld   [4] Yew is associated with death and funerals.
[5] the soul

Then glut thy sorrow on a morning rose,
  Or on the rainbow of the salt sand-wave,
  Or on the wealth of globéd peonies;
Or if thy mistress some rich anger shows,
  Emprison her soft hand, and let her rave,
    And feed deep, deep upon her peerless eyes. 20

III

She dwells with Beauty—Beauty that must die;
  And Joy, whose hand is ever at his lips
Bidding adieu; and aching Pleasure nigh,
  Turning to poison while the bee-mouth sips:
Ay, in the very temple of Delight
  Veiled Melancholy has her sovereign shrine,
    Though seen of none save him whose strenuous tongue
Can burst Joy's grape against his palate fine;
  His soul shall taste the sadness of her might,
    And be among her cloudy trophies hung. 30
[1819]

ODE TO A NIGHTINGALE

I

My heart aches, and a drowsy numbness pains
  My sense, as though of hemlock[1] I had drunk,
Or emptied some dull opiate to the drains
  One minute past, and Lethe-wards[2] had sunk:
'Tis not through envy of thy happy lot,
  But being too happy in thine happiness,—
    That thou, light-wingéd Dryad[3] of the trees,
      In some melodious plot
Of beechen green, and shadows numberless,
  Singest of summer in full-throated ease. 10

II

O, for a draft of vintage! that hath been
  Cooled a long age in the deep-delvéd earth,
Tasting of Flora[4] and the country green,
  Dance, and Provençal[5] song, and sunburnt mirth!

---

[1] a poisonous herb administered as a liquid
[2] toward Lethe, the river of forgetfulness in Hades   [3] wood nymph
[4] goddess of flowers; hence, flowers
[5] of Provence, a province of France noted for its minstrelsy

O for a beaker full of the warm South,
  Full of the true, the blushful Hippocrene,[6]
    With beaded bubbles winking at the brim,
      And purple-stainéd mouth;
That I might drink, and leave the world unseen,
  And with thee fade away into the forest dim: 20

III

Fade far away, dissolve, and quite forget
  What thou among the leaves hast never known,
The weariness, the fever, and the fret
  Here, where men sit and hear each other groan;
Where palsy shakes a few, sad, last gray hairs,
  Where youth grows pale, and specter-thin, and dies;
    Where but to think is to be full of sorrow
      And leaden-eyed despairs,
Where Beauty cannot keep her lustrous eyes,
  Or new Love pine at them beyond to-morrow.   30

IV

Away! away! for I will fly to thee,
  Not charioted by Bacchus[7] and his pards,[8]
But on the viewless wings of Poesy,
  Though the dull brain perplexes and retards:
Already with thee! tender is the night,
  And haply the Queen-Moon is on her throne,
    Clustered around by all her starry Fays;[9]
      But here there is no light,
Save what from heaven is with the breezes blown
  Through verdurous glooms and winding mossy ways.   40

V

I cannot see what flowers are at my feet,
  Nor what soft incense hangs upon the boughs,
But, in embalméd darkness, guess each sweet
  Wherewith the seasonable month endows
The grass, the thicket, and the fruit-tree wild;
  White hawthorn, and the pastoral eglantine;
    Fast fading violets covered up in leaves;
      And mid-May's eldest child,
The coming musk-rose, full of dewy wine,
  The murmurous haunt of flies on summer eves.   50

---

[6] a fountain on Mt. Helicon, sacred to the Muses   [7] god of wine
[8] leopards   [9] fairies

VI

Darkling I listen; and, for many a time
   I have been half in love with easeful Death,
Called him soft names in many a muséd rhyme,
   To take into the air my quiet breath;
Now more than ever seems it rich to die,
   To cease upon the midnight with no pain,
      While thou art pouring forth thy soul abroad
         In such an ecstasy!
   Still wouldst thou sing, and I have ears in vain—
      To thy high requiem become a sod.   60

VII

Thou wast not born for death, immortal Bird!
   No hungry generations tread thee down;
The voice I hear this passing night was heard
   In ancient days by emperor and clown:[10]
Perhaps the self-same song that found a path
   Through the sad heart of Ruth,[11] when, sick for home,
      She stood in tears amid the alien corn;
         The same that oft-tmes hath
   Charmed magic casements, opening on the foam
      Of perilous seas, in faery lands forlorn.   70

VIII

Forlorn! the very word is like a bell
   To toll me back from thee to my sole self!
Adieu! the fancy cannot cheat so well
   As she is famed to do, deceiving elf.
Adieu! adieu! thy plaintive anthem fades
   Past the near meadows, over the still stream,
      Up the hill-side; and now 'tis buried deep
         In the next valley-glades:
   Was it a vision, or a waking dream?
      Fled is that music:—Do I wake or sleep?   80
                                                        [1819]

---

[10] farm hand
[11] heroine of the Old Testament Book of Ruth, who went with her mother-in-law to an alien land

TO AUTUMN

I

SEASON of mists and mellow fruitfulness,
   Close bosom-friend of the maturing sun;
Conspiring with him how to load and bless
   With fruit the vines that round the thatch-eaves run;
To bend with apples the mossed cottage-trees,
   And fill all fruit with ripeness to the core;
      To swell the gourd, and plump the hazel shells
With a sweet kernel; to set budding more,
   And still more, later flowers for the bees,
   Until they think warm days will never cease,   10
      For Summer has o'er-brimmed their clammy cells.

II

Who hath not seen thee oft amid thy store?
   Sometimes whoever seeks abroad may find
Thee sitting careless on a granary floor,
   Thy hair soft-lifted by the winnowing wind;
Or on a half-reaped furrow sound asleep,
   Drowsed with the fume of poppies, while thy hook
      Spares the next swath and all its twinéd flowers:
And sometimes like a gleaner thou dost keep
   Steady thy laden head across a brook;   20
   Or by a cider-press, with patient look,
      Thou watchest the last oozings hours by hours.

III

Where are the songs of Spring? Ay, where are they?
   Think not of them, thou hast thy music too,—
While barred clouds bloom the soft-dying day,
   And touch the stubble-plains with rosy hue;
Then in a wailful choir the small gnats mourn
   Among the river sallows[1] borne aloft
      Or sinking as the light wind lives or dies;
And full-grown lambs loud bleat from hilly bourn;[2]   30
   Hedge-crickets sing; and now with treble soft
   The red-breast whistles from a garden-croft;[3]
      And gathering swallows twitter in the skies.

[1819]

___

[1] willows   [2] field   [3] enclosed garden

Ralph Waldo Emerson
1803–1882

THE RHODORA[1]
ON BEING ASKED, WHENCE IS THE FLOWER?

IN MAY, when sea-winds pierced our solitudes,
I found the fresh Rhodora in the woods,
Spreading its leafless blooms in a damp nook,
To please the desert and the sluggish brook.
The purple petals, fallen in the pool,
Made the black water with their beauty gay;
Here might the red-bird come his plumes to cool,
And court the flower that cheapens his array.
Rhodora! if the sages ask thee why
This charm is wasted on the earth and sky,   10
Tell them, dear, that if eyes were made for seeing,
Then Beauty is its own excuse for being:
Why thou wert there, O rival of the rose!
I never thought to ask, I never knew:
But, in my simple ignorance, suppose
The self-same Power that brought me there brought you.

[1834]

[1] a small shrub related to the rhododendron

EACH AND ALL

LITTLE thinks, in the field, yon red-cloaked clown[1]
Of thee from the hill-top looking down;
The heifer that lows in the upland farm,
Far-heard, lows not thine ear to charm;
The sexton, tolling his bell at noon,
Deems not that great Napoleon
Stops his horse, and lists with delight,
Whilst his files sweep round yon Alpine height;
Nor knowest thou what argument   10
Thy life to thy neighbor's creed has lent.
Are all needed by each one;
Nothing is fair or good alone.

[1] farm laborer

I thought the sparrow's note from heaven,
Singing at dawn on the alder bough;
I brought him home, in his nest, at even;
He sings the song, but it cheers not now,
For I did not bring home the river and sky;
He sang to my ear,—they sang to my eye.
The delicate shells lay on the shore;
The bubbles of the latest wave   20
Fresh pearls to their enamel gave,
And the bellowing of the savage sea
Greeted their safe escape to me.
I wiped away the weeds and foam,
I fetched my sea-born treasures home;
But the poor, unsightly, noisome things
Had left their beauty on the shore
With the sun and the sand and the wild uproar.
The lover watched his graceful maid,
As 'mid the virgin train she strayed,   30
Nor knew her beauty's best attire
Was woven still by the snow-white choir.
As last she came to his hermitage,
Like the bird from the woodlands to the cage;—
The gay enchantment was undone,
A gentle wife, but fairy none.
Then I said, "I covet truth;
Beauty is unripe childhood's cheat;
I leave it behind with the games of youth:"—
As I spoke, beneath my feet   40
The ground-pine curled its pretty wreath,
Running over the club-moss[2] burrs;
I inhaled the violet's breath;
Around me stood the oaks and firs;
Pine-cones and acorns lay on the ground;
Over me soared the eternal sky,
Full of light and of deity;
Again I saw, again I heard,
The rolling river, the morning bird;—
Beauty through my senses stole;   50
I yielded myself to the perfect whole.

[1834]

[2] low-growing, ground-cover plants

THE SNOW-STORM

ANNOUNCED by all the trumpets of the sky,
Arrives the snow, and, driving o'er the fields,
Seems nowhere to alight: the whited air
Hides hills and woods, the river, and the heaven,
And veils the farm-house at the garden's end.
The sled and traveler stopped, the courier's feet
Delayed, all friends shut out, the housemates sit
Around the radiant fireplace, enclosed
In a tumultuous privacy of storm.

Come see the north wind's masonry.   10
Out of an unseen quarry evermore
Furnished with tile, the fierce artificer
Curves his white bastions with projected roof
Round every windward stake, or tree, or door.
Speeding, the myriad-handed, his wild work
So fanciful, so savage, nought cares he
For number or proportion. Mockingly,
On coop or kennel he hangs Parian[1] wreaths;
A swan-like form invests the hidden thorn;
Fills up the farmer's lane from wall to wall,   20
Maugre[2] the farmer's sighs; and at the gate
A tapering turret overtops the work.
And when his hours are numbered, and the world
Is all his own, retiring, as he were not,
Leaves, when the sun appears, astonished Art
To mimic in slow structures, stone by stone,
Built in an age, the mad wind's night-work,
The frolic architecture of the snow.

[1835]

[1] of Paros, one of the Cyclades islands in the Aegean noted for its beautiful marble
[2] despite

ODE

INSCRIBED TO W. H. CHANNING

THOUGH loathe to grieve
The evil time's sole patriot,
I cannot leave
My honied thought

For the priest's cant,
Or the statesman's rant.

If I refuse
My study for their politique,
Which at the best is trick,
The angry Muse   10
Puts confusion in my brain.

But who is he that prates
Of the culture of mankind,
Of better arts and life?
Go, blindworm, go,
Behold the famous States
Harrying Mexico
With rifle and with knife![1]

Or who, with accent bolder,
Dare praise the freedom-loving
    mountaineer?   20
I found by thee, O rushing Contoocook![2]
And in thy valleys, Agiochook![3]
The jackals of the negro-holder.

The God who made New Hampshire
Taunted the lofty land
With little men;—
Small bat and wren
House in the oak:—
If earth-fire cleave
The upheaved land, and bury the folk,   30
The southern crocodile would grieve.
Virtue palters; Right is hence;
Freedom praised, but hid;
Funeral eloquence
Rattles the coffin-lid.

What boots thy zeal,
O glowing friend,
That would indignant rend
The northland from the south?

[1] the Mexican War (1846–48), which Emerson, like many others, opposed as an effort to extend slave territory. Channing had urged Emerson to take an active part in opposition to the war.
[2] river in New Hampshire   [3] the White Mountains

Wherefore? to what good end?   40
Boston Bay and Bunker Hill
Would serve things still;
Things are of the snake.

The horseman serves the horse,
The neatherd serves the neat,
The merchant serves the purse,
The eater serves his meat;
'Tis the day of the chattel,
Web to weave, and corn to grind;
Things are in the saddle,   50
And ride mankind.

There are two laws discrete,
Not reconciled,—
Law for man, and law for thing;
The last builds town and fleet,
But it runs wild,
And doth the man unking.

'Tis fit the forest fall,
The steep be graded,
The mountain tunneled,   60
The sand shaded,
The orchard planted,
The glebe tilled,
The prairie granted,
The steamer built.

Let man serve law for man;
Live for friendship, live for love,
For truth's and harmony's behoof;
The state may follow how it can,
As Olympus[4] follows Jove.[5]   70

Yet do not I implore
The wrinkled shopman to my sounding woods,
Nor bid the unwilling senator
Ask votes of thrushes in the solitudes.
Every one to his chosen work;—

---

[4] dwelling place of the god, Jove   [5] king of the gods

Foolish hands may mix and mar;
Wise and sure the issues are.
Round they roll till dark is light,
Sex to sex, and even to odd;—
The over-god   80
Who marries Right to Might,
Who peoples, unpeoples,—
He who exterminates
Races by stronger races,
Black by white faces,—
Knows to bring honey
Out of the lion; [6]
Grafts gentlest scion
On pirate and Turk.

The Cossack eats Poland,   90
Like stolen fruit;
Her last noble is ruined,
Her last poet mute:
Straight, into double band
The victors divide;
Half for freedom strike and stand; [7]—
The astonished Muse finds thousands at
        her side.

                                                                [1846]

[6] Samson killed a lion and left it exposed; after a time bees had built honeycomb in the putrefying carcass (Judges 14:5–9).
[7] After decades of Russian oppression, Polish patriots carried out an uprising in 1830.

HAMATREYA

BULKELEY, Hunt, Willard, Hosmer, Meriam, Flint,
Possessed the land which rendered to their toil
Hay, corn, roots, hemp, flax, apples, wool and wood.
Each of these landlords walked amidst his farm,
Saying, " 'Tis mine, my children's and my name's.
How sweet the west wind sounds in my own trees!
How graceful climb those shadows on my hill!
I fancy these pure waters and the flags
Know me, as does my dog: we sympathize;
And, I affirm, my actions smack of the soil."   10

Where are these men ? Asleep beneath their grounds :
And strangers, fond as they, their furrows plough.
Earth laughs in flowers, to see her boastful boys
Earth-proud, proud of the earth which is not theirs ;
Who steer the plough, but cannot steer their feet
Clear of the grave.
They added ridge to valley, brook to pond,
And sighed for all that bounded their domain ;
"This suits me for a pasture ; that's my park ;
We must have clay, lime, gravel, granite-ledge,   20
And misty lowland, where to go for peat.
The land is well,—lies fairly to the south.
'T is good, when you have crossed the sea and back,
To find the sitfast acres where you left them."
Ah ! the hot owner sees not Death, who adds
Him to his land, a lump of mold the more.
Hear what the Earth says :—

EARTH-SONG

"Mine and yours ;
Mine, not yours.   30
Earth endures ;
Stars abide—
Shine down in the old sea ;
Old are the shores ;
But where are old men ?
I who have seen much,
Such have I never seen.
"The lawyer's deed
Ran sure,
In tail,
To them, and to their heirs   40
Who shall succeed,
Without fail,
Forevermore.

"Here is the land,
Shaggy with wood,
With its old valley,
Mound and flood.
But the heritors ?—
Fled like the flood's foam.
The lawyer, and the laws,   50

And the kingdom,
Clean swept herefrom.

"They called me theirs,
Who so controlled me;
Yet every one
Wished to stay, and is gone,
How am I theirs,
If they cannot hold me,
But I hold them?"

When I heard the Earth-song   60
I was no longer brave;
My avarice cooled
Like lust in the chill of the grave.

[1847]

Henry Wadsworth Longfellow
1807–1882
MEZZO CAMMIN[1]

HALF of my life is gone, and I have let
The years slip from me and have not fulfilled
The aspiration of my youth, to build
Some tower of song with lofty parapet.
Not indolence, nor pleasure, nor the fret
Of restless passions that would not be stilled,
But sorrow,[2] and a care that almost killed,
Kept me from what I may accomplish yet;
Though, half-way up the hill, I see the Past
Lying beneath me with its sounds and sights,—   10
A city in the twilight dim and vast,
With smoking roofs, soft bells, and gleaming lights,—
And hear above me on the autumnal blast
The cataract of Death far thundering from the heights.

[1842]

[1] the middle of the journey. Longfellow was thirty-five when he wrote this sonnet; he had lived half of the "three score years and ten" allotted in the Bible. The Italian phrase is from the opening line of Dante's *Divine Comedy*.
[2] Longfellow's first wife died in 1835.

THE ARSENAL AT SPRINGFIELD

THIS is the Arsenal. From floor to ceiling,
 Like a huge organ, rise the burnished arms;
But from their silent pipes no anthem pealing
 Startles the villages with strange alarms.

Ah! what a sound will rise, how wild and dreary,
 When the death-angel touches those swift keys!
What loud lament and dismal Miserere
 Will mingle with their awful symphonies!

I hear even now the infinite fierce chorus,
 The cries of agony, the endless groan,   10
Which, through the ages that have gone before us,
 In long reverberations reach our own.

On helm and harness rings the Saxon hammer,
 Through Cimbric forest roars the Norseman's song,
And loud, amid the universal clamor,
 O'er distant deserts sounds the Tartar gong.

I hear the Florentine, who from his palace
 Wheels out his battle-bell with dreadful din,
And Aztec priests upon their teocallis[1]
 Beat the wild war-drums made of serpent's skin;   20

The tumult of each sacked and burning village;
 The shout that every prayer for mercy drowns;
The soldiers' revels in the midst of pillage;
 The wail of famine in beleaguered towns;

The bursting shell, the gateway wrenched asunder,
 The rattling musketry, the clashing blade;
And ever and anon, in tones of thunder
 The diapason of the cannonade.

Is it, O man, with such discordant noises,
 With such accursèd instruments as these,   30
Thou drownest Nature's sweet and kindly voices,
 And jarrest the celestial harmonies?

---

[1] temple mounds

Were half the power that fills the world with terror,
  Were half the wealth bestowed on camps and courts,
Given to redeem the human mind from error,
  There were no need of arsenals or forts :

The warrior's name would be a name abhorréd !
  And every nation, that should lift again
Its hand against a brother, on its forehead
  Would wear forevermore the curse of Cain !   40

Down the dark future, through long generations,
  The echoing sounds grow fainter and then cease ;
And like a bell, with solemn, sweet vibrations,
  I hear once more the voice of Christ say, "Peace !"

Peace ! and no longer from its brazen portals
  The blast of War's great organ shakes the skies !
But beautiful as songs of the immortals,
  The holy melodies of love arise.

                                                        [1846]

MY LOST YOUTH

OFTEN I think of the beautiful town
    That is seated by the sea ;
Often in thought go up and down
The pleasant streets of that dear old town,
    And my youth comes back to me.
      And a verse of a Lapland song
      Is haunting my memory still :
    "A boy's will is the wind's will,
And the thoughts of youth are long, long thoughts."

I can see the shadowy lines of its trees,   10
    And catch, in sudden gleams,
The sheen of the far-surrounding seas,
And islands that were the Hesperides[1]
    Of all my boyish dreams.
      And the burden of that old song,
      It murmurs and whispers still :
    "A boy's will is the wind's will,
And the thoughts of youth are long, long thoughts."

---

[1] in Greek myth, paradise islands where golden apples were grown

I remember the black wharves and the slips,
　　And the sea-tides tossing free;
And Spanish sailors with bearded lips,
And the beauty and mystery of the ships,
　　And the magic of the sea.
　　　　And the voice of that wayward song
　　　　Is singing and saying still:
　　"A boy's will is the wind's will,
And the thoughts of youth are long, long thoughts."

I remember the bulwarks by the shore,
　　And the fort upon the hill;
The sunrise gun, with its hollow roar,
The drum-beat repeated o'er and o'er,
　　And the bugle wild and shrill.
　　　　And the music of that old song
　　　　Throbs in my memory still:
　　"A boy's will is the wind's will,
And the thoughts of youth are long, long thoughts."

I remember the sea-fight far away,
　　How it thundered o'er the tide!
And the dead captains, as they lay
In their graves, o'erlooking the tranquil bay
　　Where they in battle died.
　　　　And the sound of that mournful song
　　　　Goes through me with a thrill:
　　"A boy's will is the wind's will,
And the thoughts of youth are long, long thoughts."

I can see the breezy dome of groves,
　　The shadows of Deering's Woods;
And the friendships old and the early loves
Come back with a Sabbath sound, as of doves
　　In quiet neighborhoods.
　　　　And the verse of that sweet old song,
　　　　It flutters and murmurs still:
　　"A boy's will is the wind's will,
And the thoughts of youth are long, long thoughts."

I remember the gleams and glooms that dart
　　Across the school-boy's brain;
The song and the silence in the heart,
That in part are prophecies, and in part
　　Are longings wild and vain.
　　　　And the voice of that fitful song

20

30

40

50

60

Sings on, and is never still :
"A boy's will is the wind's will,
And the thoughts of youth are long, long thoughts."

There are things of which I may not speak ;
   There are dreams that cannot die ;
There are thoughts that make the strong heart weak,
And bring a pallor into the cheek,
   And a mist before the eye.
     And the words of that fatal song
     Come over me like a chill :   70
"A boy's will is the wind's will,
And the thoughts of youth are long, long thoughts."

Strange to me now are the forms I meet
   When I visit the dear old town ;
But the native air is pure and sweet,
And the trees that o'ershadow each well-known street,
   As they balance up and down,
     Are singing the beautiful song,
     Are sighing and whispering still :
"A boy's will is the wind's will,   80
And the thoughts of youth are long, long thoughts."

And Deering's Woods are fresh and fair,
   And with joy that is almost pain
My heart goes back to wander there,
And among the dreams of the days that were,
   I find my lost youth again.
     And the strange and beautiful song,
     The groves are repeating it still :
"A boy's will is the wind's will,
And the thoughts of youth are long, long thoughts."   90
                       [1858]

THE TIDE RISES, THE TIDE FALLS

THE tide rises, the tide falls,
   The twilight darkens, the curlew calls ;
Along the sea-sands damp and brown
The traveler hastens toward the town,
   And the tide rises, the tide falls.

Darkness settles on roofs and walls,
But the sea, the sea in the darkness calls,
The little waves, with their soft, white hands,
Efface the footprints in the sands,
    And the tide rises, the tide falls.   10

The morning breaks; the steeds in their stalls
Stamp and neigh, as the hostler calls;
The day returns, but nevermore
Returns the traveler to the shore,
    And the tide rises, the tide falls.

               [1880]

THE CROSS OF SNOW

IN THE long, sleepless watches of the night,
A gentle face—the face of one long dead—
Looks at me from the wall, where round its head
The night-lamp casts a halo of pale light.
Here in this room she died; and soul more white
Never through martyrdom of fire was led
To its repose; nor can in books be read
The legend of a life more benedight.
There is a mountain in the distant West
That, sun-defying, in its deep ravines   10
Displays a cross of snow upon its side.
Such is the cross I wear upon my breast
These eighteen years, through all the changing scenes
And seasons, changeless since the day she died.

               [1886]

John Greenleaf Whittier
1807–1892

SKIPPER IRESON'S RIDE

OF ALL the rides since the birth of time,
   Told in story or sung in rhyme,—
On Apuleius's Golden Ass,[1]
Or one-eyed Calender's horse of brass,[2]

---

[1] Lucius Apuleius, a Roman writer of the second century A.D., wrote *The Golden Ass*, a romance of transformation.

[2] "The Tale of the Third Kalandar" in *The Thousand Nights and a Night* (i.e., the *Arabian Nights*) tells of a wandering dervish's adventure with a brass horse.

Witch astride of a human back,
Islam's prophet on Al-Borak,[3]—
The strangest ride that ever was sped
Was Ireson's, out from Marblehead![4]
    Old Floyd Ireson, for his hard heart,
    Tarred and feathered and carried in a cart   10
    By the women of Marblehead!

Body of turkey, head of owl,
Wings a-droop like a rained-on fowl,
Feathered and ruffled in every part,
Skipper Ireson stood in the cart.
Scores of women, old and young,
Strong of muscle, and glib of tongue,
Pushed and pulled up the rocky lane,
Shouting and singing the shrill refrain:
    "Here's Flud Oirson, fur his horrd horrt,   20
    Torr'd an' futherr'd an' corr'd in a corrt
    By the women o' Morble'ead!"

Wrinkled scolds with hands on hips,
Girls in bloom of cheek and lips,
Wild-eyed, free-limbed, such as chase
Bacchus[5] round some antique vase,
Brief of skirt, with ankles bare,
Loose of kerchief and loose of hair,
With conch-shells blowing and fish-horns' twang,
Over and over the Mænads[6] sang: 30
    "Here's Flud Oirson, fur his horrd horrt,
    Torr'd an' futherr'd an' corr'd in a corrt
    By the women o' Morble'ead!"

Small pity for him!—He sailed away
From a leaking ship in Chaleur Bay,[7]—
Sailed away from a sinking wreck,
With his own town's people on her deck!
"Lay by! lay by!" they called to him.
Back he answered, "Sink or swim!
Brag of your catch of fish again!"   40
And off he sailed through the fog and rain!

---

[3] the horse that carried Mohammed to the seventh heaven
[4] The poem is based on an actual incident in the history of a Massachusetts sea-coast town.
[5] the Greek god of wine   [6] female votaries of Bacchus
[7] on the Gulf of St. Lawrence between Quebec and New Brunswick

Old Floyd Ireson, for his hard heart,
Tarred and feathered and carried in a cart
By the women of Marblehead!

Fathoms deep in dark Chaleur
That wreck shall lie forevermore.
Mother and sister, wife and maid,
Looked from the rocks of Marblehead
Over the moaning and rainy sea,—
Looked for the coming that might not be!   50
What did the winds and the sea-birds say
Of the cruel captain who sailed away?—
Old Floyd Ireson, for his hard heart,
Tarred and feathered and carried in a cart
By the women of Marblehead!

Through the street, on either side,
Up flew windows, doors swung wide;
Sharp-tongued spinsters, old wives gray,
Treble lent the fish-horn's bray.
Sea-worn grandsires, cripple-bound,   60
Hulks of old sailors run aground,
Shook head, and fist, and hat, and cane,
And cracked with curses the hoarse refrain:
"Here's Flud Oirson, fur his horrd horrt,
Torr'd an' futherr'd an' corr'd in a corrt
By the women o' Morble'ead!"

Sweetly along the Salem road
Bloom of orchard and lilac showed.
Little the wicked skipper knew
Of the fields so green and the sky so blue.   70
Riding there in his sorry trim,
Like an Indian idol glum and grim,
Scarcely he seemed the sound to hear
Of voices shouting, far and near:
"Here's Flud Oirson, fur his horrd horrt,
Torr'd an' futherr'd an' corr'd in a corrt
By the women o' Morble'ead!"

"Hear me, neighbors!" at last he cried,—
"What to me is this noisy ride?
What is the shame that clothes the skin   80
To the nameless horror that lives within?
Waking or sleeping, I see a wreck,
And hear a cry from a reeling deck!

Hate me and curse me,—I only dread
The hand of God and the face of the dead!"
Said old Floyd Ireson, for his hard heart,
Tarred and feathered and carried in a cart
    By the women of Marblehead!

Then the wife of the skipper lost at sea
Said, "God has touched him! why should we!"   90
Said an old wife mourning her only son,
"Cut the rogue's tether and let him run!"
So with soft relentings and rude excuse,
Half scorn, half pity, they cut him loose,
And gave him a cloak to hide him in,
And left him alone with his shame and sin.
    Poor Floyd Ireson, for his hard heart,
Tarred and feathered and carried in a cart
    By the women of Marblehead!

                                           [1860]

ABRAHAM DAVENPORT

IN THE old days (a custom laid aside
With breeches and cocked hats) the people sent
Their wisest men to make the public laws.
And so, from a brown homestead, where the Sound
Drinks the small tribute of the Mianas,
Waved over by the woods of Rippowams,
And hallowed by pure lives and tranquil deaths,
Stamford[1] sent up to the councils of the State
Wisdom and grace in Abraham Davenport.

  'Twas on a May-day of the far old year   10
Seventeen hundred eighty, that there fell
Over the bloom and sweet life of the Spring,
Over the fresh earth and the heaven of noon,
A horror of great darkness, like the night
In day of which the Norland sagas tell,
The Twilight of the Gods. The low-hung sky
Was black with ominous clouds, save where its rim
Was fringed with a dull glow, like that which climbs
The crater's sides from the red hell below.
Birds ceased to sing, and all the barnyard fowls   20

---

[1] place names in western Connecticut

Roosted; the cattle at the pasture bars
Lowed, and looked homeward; bats on leathern wings
Flitted abroad; the sounds of labor died;
Men prayed, and women wept, all ears grew sharp
To hear the doom-blast of the trumpet shatter
The black sky, that the dreadful face of Christ
Might look from the rent clouds, not as He looked
A loving guest at Bethany,[2] but stern
As Justice and inexorable Law.

Meanwhile in the old State House, dim as ghosts,   30
Sat the lawgivers of Connecticut,
Trembling beneath their legislative robes.
"It is the Lord's Great Day! Let us adjourn."
Some said; and then, as if with one accord,
All eyes were turned to Abraham Davenport.
He rose, slow cleaving with his steady voice
The intolerable hush. "This well may be
The Day of Judgment which the world awaits;
But be it so or not, I only know
My present duty, and my Lord's command   40
To occupy till He come. So at the post
Where He hath set me in His providence,
I choose, for one, to meet Him face to face,
No faithless servant frightened from my task,
But ready when the Lord of the harvest calls;
And therefore, with all reverence, I would say,
Let God do His work, we will see to ours.
Bring in the candles." And they brought them in.

Then by the flaring lights the Speaker read,
Albeit with husky voice and shaking hands,   50
An act to amend an act to regulate
The shad and alewive fisheries. Whereupon
Wisely and well spake Abraham Davenport,
Straight to the question, with no figures of speech
Save the ten Arab signs, yet not without
The shrewd dry humor natural to the man:
His awe-struck colleagues listening all the while,
Between the pauses of his argument,
To hear the thunder of the wrath of God
Break from the hollow trumpet of the cloud.   60

---

[2] where Jesus raised Lazarus from death, out of love for him and his sisters, Mary
and Martha. John 11:1–46

And there he stands in memory to this day,
Erect, self-poised, a rugged face, half seen
Against the background of unnatural dark,
A witness to the ages as they pass,
That simple duty hath no place for fear.

[1866]

LAUS DEO![1]

IT IS done!
Clang of bell and roar of gun
Send the tidings up and down.
How the belfries rock and reel!
How the great guns, peal on peal,
Fling the joy from town to town!

Ring, O bells!
Every stroke exulting tells
Of the burial hour of crime.
Loud and long, that all may hear,   10
Ring for every listening ear
Of Eternity and Time!

Let us kneel:
God's own voice is in that peal,
And this spot is holy ground.
Lord, forgive us! What are we,
That our eyes this glory see,
That our ears have heard the sound!

For the Lord
On the whirlwind is abroad;   20
In the earthquake He has spoken;
He has smitten with His thunder
The iron walls asunder,
And the gates of brass are broken!

Loud and long
Lift the old exulting song;
Sing with Miriam by the sea,
He has cast the mighty down;
Horse and rider sink and drown;
"He hath triumphed gloriously!"[2]   30

---

[1] Praise Be to God. The poem celebrates the adoption of the constitutional amendment abolishing slavery.
[2] Exodus 15:20-21

Did we dare,
In our agony of prayer,
Ask for more than He has done?
When was ever His right hand
Over any time or land
Stretched as now beneath the sun?

How they pale,
Ancient myth and song and tale,
In this wonder of our days,
When the cruel rod of war   40
Blossoms white with righteous law,
And the wrath of man is praise!

Blotted out!
All within and all about
Shall a fresher life begin;
Freer breathe the universe
As it rolls its heavy curse
On the dead and buried sin!

It is done!
In the circuit of the sun   50
Shall the sound thereof go forth.
It shall bid the sad rejoice,
It shall give the dumb a voice,
It shall belt with joy the earth!

Ring and swing,
Bells of joy! On morning's wing
Send the song of praise abroad!
With a sound of broken chains
Tell the nations that He reigns,
Who alone is Lord and God!   60
[1867]

Edgar Allan Poe

1809–1849

ROMANCE

Romance, who loves to nod and sing,
  With drowsy head and folded wing,
Among the green leaves as they shake
Far down within some shadowy lake,

To me a painted paroquet
Hath been—a most familiar bird—
Taught me my alphabet to say—
To lisp my very earliest word
While in the wild wood I did lie,
A child—with a most knowing eye.   10

Of late, eternal Condor years
So shake the very Heaven on high
With tumult as they thunder by,
I have no time for idle cares
Through gazing on the unquiet sky.
And when an hour with calmer wings
Its down upon my spirit flings—
That little time with lyre and rhyme
To while away—forbidden things!
My heart would feel to be a crime   20
Unless it trembled with the strings.

[1829]

SONNET: TO SCIENCE

Science! true daughter of Old Time thou art!
Who alterest all things with thy peering eyes.
Why preyest thou thus upon the poet's heart,
Vulture, whose wings are dull realities?
How should he love thee? or how deem thee wise,
Who wouldst not leave him in his wandering
To seek for treasure in the jeweled skies,
Albeit he soared with an undaunted wing?
Hast thou not dragged Diana[1] from her car?
And driven the Hamadryad[2] from the wood   10
To seek a shelter in some happier star?
Hast thou not torn the Naiad[3] from her flood,
The Elfin[4] from the green grass, and from me
The summer dream beneath the tamarind tree?[5]

[1829]

[1] a fertility goddess later identified as a huntress and as goddess of the moon
[2] a wood nymph   [3] a fresh-water nymph   [4] elf
[5] a tropical tree, here representing the exotic

THE CITY IN THE SEA

Lo! Death has reared himself a throne
In a strange city lying alone
Far down within the dim West,
Where the good and the bad and the worst and the best
Have gone to their eternal rest.
There shrines and palaces and towers
(Time-eaten towers that tremble not!)
Resemble nothing that is ours.
Around, by lifting winds forgot,
Resignedly beneath the sky   10
The melancholy waters lie.

No rays from the holy heaven come down
On the long night-time of that town;
But light from out the lurid sea
Streams up the turrets silently—
Gleams up the pinnacles far and free—
Up domes—up spires—up kingly halls—
Up fanes—up Babylon-like walls—
Up shadowy long-forgotten bowers
Of sculptured ivy and stone flowers—   20
Up many and many a marvellous shrine
Whose wreathéd friezes intertwine
The viol, the violet, and the vine.
Resignedly beneath the sky
The melancholy waters lie.
So blend the turrets and shadows there
That all seem pendulous in air,
While from a proud tower in the town
Death looks gigantically down.

There open fanes and gaping graves   30
Yawn level with the luminous waves;
But not the riches there that lie
In each idol's diamond eye—
Not the gayly-jeweled dead
Tempt the waters from their bed;
For no ripples curl, alas!
Along that wilderness of glass—
No swellings tell that winds may be
Upon some far-off happier sea—
No heavings hint that winds have been   40
On seas less hideously serene.

But lo, a stir is in the air!
The wave—there is a movement there!
As if the towers had thrust aside,
In slightly sinking, the dull tide—
As if their tops had feebly given
A void within the filmy Heaven.
The waves have now a redder glow—
The hours are breathing faint and low—
And when, amid no earthly moans,   50
Down, down that town shall settle hence,
Hell, rising from a thousand thrones,
Shall do it reverence.

[1831]

TO HELEN

HELEN,[1] thy beauty is to me
          Like those Nicéan[2] barks of yore,
That gently, o'er a perfumed sea,
     The weary, way-worn wanderer bore
     To his own native shore.

On desperate seas long wont to roam,
     Thy hyacinth[3] hair, thy classic face,
Thy Naiad airs[4] have brought me home
     To the glory that was Greece
And the grandeur that was Rome.   10

Lo! in yon brilliant window-niche
     How statue-like I see thee stand,
     The agate lamp within thy hand!
Ah, Psyche,[5] from the regions which
     Are Holy Land!

[1831]

[1] probably Helen of Troy   [2] pertaining to Nicea, a city in Asia Minor
[3] a classical epithet frequently applied to hair, probably in reference to curliness
[4] the graceful manner of a fresh-water nymph   [5] the soul

Oliver Wendell Holmes
1809 1894
THE CHAMBERED NAUTILUS[1]

THIS is the ship of pearl, which, poets feign,
    Sails the unshadowed main,—
    The venturous bark that flings
On the sweet summer wind its purpled wings
In gulfs enchanted, where the Siren[2] sings.
    And coral reefs lie bare,
Where the cold sea-maids rise to sun their streaming hair.

Its webs of living gauze no more unfurl;
    Wrecked is the ship of pearl!
    And every chambered cell,   10
Where its dim dreaming life was wont to dwell,
As the frail tenant shaped his growing shell,
    Before thee lies revealed,—
Its irised ceiling rent, its sunless crypt unsealed!

Year after year beheld the silent toil
    That spread his lustrous coil;
    Still, as the spiral grew,
He left the past year's dwelling for the new,
Stole with soft step its shining archway through,
    Built up its idle door,   20
Stretched in his last-found home, and knew the old no more.

Thanks for the heavenly message brought by thee,
    Child of the wandering sea,
    Cast from her lap, forlorn!
From thy dead lips a clearer note is born
Than ever Triton[3] blew from wreathéd horn!
    While on mine ear it rings,
Through the deep caves of thought I hear a voice that sings:—

Build thee more stately mansions, O my soul,
    As the swift seasons roll!   30
    Leave thy low-vaulted past!

[1] a shellfish which develops a spiral shell in which each year's growth is divided from earlier portions by a septum
[2] sea nymph whose song enthralled passing voyagers
[3] sea god who blew his horn to calm the waves

Let each new temple, nobler than the last,
Shut thee from heaven with a dome more vast,
    Till thou at length art free,
Leaving thine outgrown shell by life's unresting sea!

                            [1858]

THE DEACON'S MASTERPIECE
OR, THE WONDERFUL "ONE-HOSS SHAY"
A LOGICAL STORY

HAVE you heard of the wonderful one-hoss shay,[1]
   That was built in such a logical way
It ran a hundred years to a day,
And then, of a sudden, it—ah, but stay,
I'll tell you what happened without delay,
Scaring the parson into fits,
Frightening people out of their wits,—
Have you ever heard of that, I say?

Seventeen hundred and fifty-five,
Georgius Secundus was then alive,—   10
Snuffy old drone from the German hive.[2]
That was the year when Lisbon-town
Saw the earth open and gulp her down,[3]
And Braddock's army was done so brown,
Left without a scalp to its crown.[4]
It was on the terrible Earthquake-day
That the Deacon finished the one-hoss shay.

Now in building of chaises, I tell you what,
There is always *somewhere* a weakest spot,—
In hub, tire; felloe,[5] in spring or thill,[6]   20
In panel, or crossbar, or floor, or sill,

[1] chaise, a two-wheeled carriage, here representing the tightly logical system of New England Calvinism, which Holmes controverted and ridiculed in a number of works
[2] German-born king of England from 1727 to 1760
[3] This most famous of earthquakes is estimated to have killed 30,000 people. The event raised prolonged controversy about the benevolence of God.
[4] General Edward Braddock was defeated and mortally wounded in July 1755 at the Battle of the Wilderness in western Pennsylvania during the French and Indian War.
[5] segment of a wheel rim
[6] the shaft or shafts by which the horse draws the vehicle

In screw, bolt, thoroughbrace,[7]—lurking still,
Find it somewhere you must and will,—
Above or below, or within or without,—
And that's the reason, beyond a doubt,
That a chaise *breaks down*, but doesn't *wear out*.

But the Deacon swore (as Deacons do,
With an "I dew vum," or an "I tell *yeou*")
He would build one shay to beat the taown
'N' the keounty 'n' all the kentry raoun';   30
It should be so built that it *couldn'* break daown :
"Fur," said the Deacon, " 't's mighty plain
Thut the weakes' places mus' stan' the strain ;
'N' the way t' fix it, uz I maintain,
                Is only jest
T' make that place uz strong uz the rest."

So the Deacon inquired of the village folk
Where he could find the strongest oak,
That couldn't be split nor bent nor broke,—
That was for spokes and floor and sills ;   40
He sent for lancewood[8] to make the thills ;
The crossbars were ash, from the straightest trees,
The panels of white-wood,[9] that cuts like cheese,
But lasts like iron for things like these ;
The hubs of logs from the "Settler's ellum,"—
Last of its timber,—they couldn't sell 'em,
Never an axe had seen their chips,
And the wedges flew from between their lips,
Their blunt ends frizzled like celery-tips ;
Step and prop-iron, bolt and screw,   50
Spring, tire, axle, and linchpin[10] too,
Steel of the finest, bright and blue ;
Thoroughbrace bison-skin, thick and wide ;
Boot, top, dasher, from tough old hide
Found in the pit when the tanner died.
That was the way he "put her through."
"There !" said the Deacon, "naow she'll dew !"

Do ! I tell you, I rather guess
She was a wonder, and nothing less !

---

[7] one of two or more leather straps suspending the body of the carriage and cushioning it from road shock
[8] a hard tropical American wood
[9] either tulip tree or linden
[10] a hardened pin joining two parts, as the wheel on the axle

Colts grew horses, beards turned gray,   60
Deacon and deaconess dropped away,
Children and grandchildren—where were they?
But there stood the stout old one-hoss shay
As fresh as on Lisbon-earthquake-day!

EIGHTEEN HUNDRED;—it came and found
The Deacon's masterpiece strong and sound.
Eighteen hundred increased by ten;—
"Hahnsum kerridge" they called it then.
Eighteen hundred and twenty came;—
Running as usual; much the same.   70
Thirty and forty at last arrive,
And then come fifty, and FIFTY-FIVE.

Little of all we value here
Wakes on the morn of its hundredth year
Without both feeling and looking queer.
In fact, there's nothing that keeps its youth,
So far as I know, but a tree and truth.
(This is a moral that runs at large;
Take it.—You're welcome.—No extra charge.)

FIRST OF NOVEMBER,—the Earthquake-day,—   80
There are traces of age in the one-hoss shay,
A general flavor of mild decay,
But nothing local, as one may say.
There couldn't be,—for the Deacon's art
Had made it so like in every part
That there wasn't a chance for one to start.
For the wheels were just as strong as the thills,
And the floor was just as strong as the sills,
And the panels just as strong as the floor,
And the whipple-tree neither less nor more,   90
And the back-crossbar as strong as the fore,
And spring and axle and hub *encore*.
And yet, *as a whole*, it is past a doubt
In another hour it will be *worn out!*

First of November, 'Fifty-five!
This morning the parson takes a drive.
Now, small boys, get out of the way!
Here comes the wonderful one-hoss shay,
Drawn by a rat-tailed, ewe-necked bay.
"Huddup!" said the parson.—Off went they.   100

The parson was working his Sunday's text,—
Had got to *fifthly*, and stopped perplexed
At what the—Moses—was coming next.
All at once the horse stood still,
Close by the meet'n'-house on the hill.
First a shiver, and then a thrill,
Then something decidedly like a spill,—
And the parson was sitting upon a rock,
At half past nine by the meet'n'-house clock,—
Just the hour of the Earthquake shock!   110
What do you think the parson found,
When he got up and stared around?
The poor old chaise in a heap or mound,
As if it had been to the mill and ground!
You see, of course, if you're not a dunce,
How it went to pieces all at once,—
All at once, and nothing first,—
Just as bubbles do when they burst.

End of the wonderful one-hoss shay.
Logic is logic. That's all I say.   120
[1858]

Walt Whitman

1819–1892

OUT OF THE CRADLE ENDLESSLY ROCKING

Out of the cradle endlessly rocking,
  Out of the mocking-bird's throat, the musical shuttle,
Out of the Ninth-month midnight,
Over the sterile sands and the fields beyond, where the child leaving his
  bed wandered alone, bareheaded, barefoot,
Down from the showered halo,
Up from the mystic play of shadows twining and twisting as if they were
  alive,
Out from the patches of briers and blackberries,
From the memories of the bird that chanted to me,
From your memories sad brother, from the fitful risings and fallings I
  heard,
From under that yellow half-moon late-risen and swollen as if with tears,
From those beginning notes of yearning and love there in the mist,   10
From the thousand responses of my heart never to cease,

From the myriad thence-aroused words,
From the word stronger and more delicious than any,
From such as now they start the scene revisiting,
As a flock, twittering, rising, or overhead passing,
Borne hither, ere all eludes me, hurriedly,
A man, yet by these tears a little boy again,
Throwing myself on the sand, confronting the waves,
I, chanter of pains and joys, uniter of here and hereafter,   20
Taking all hints to use them, but swiftly leaping beyond them,
A reminiscence sing.[1]

Once Paumanock,[2]
When the lilac-scent was in the air and Fifth-month grass was growing,
Up this seashore in some briers,
Two feathered guests from Alabama, two together,
And their nest, and four light-green eggs spotted with brown,
And every day the he-bird to and fro near at hand,
And every day the she-bird crouched on her nest, silent, with bright eyes,
And every day I, curious boy, never too close, never disturbing them,   30
Cautiously peering, absorbing, translating.

Shine! shine! shine!
Pour down your warmth, great sun!
While we bask, we two together,

Two together!
Winds blow south, or winds blow north,
Day come white, or night come black,
Home, or rivers and mountains from home,
Singing all time, minding no time,
While we two keep together.   40

Till of a sudden,
May-be killed, unknown to her mate,
One forenoon the she-bird crouched not on the nest,
Nor returned that afternoon, nor the next,
Nor ever appeared again.

And thenceforward all summer in the sound of the sea,
And at night under the full of the moon in calmer weather,
Over the hoarse surging of the sea,
Or flitting from brier to brier by day,
I saw, I heard at intervals the remaining one, the he-bird,   50
The solitary guest from Alabama.

[1] Whitman echoes the epic formula of Virgil's *Aeneid* (as translated by John Dryden) : "Arms and the man I sing."
[2] Long Island

Blow! blow! blow!
Blow up sea-winds along Paumanok's shore;
I wait and I wait till you blow my mate to me.

Yes, when the stars glistened,
All night long on the prong of a moss-scalloped stake,
Down almost amid the slapping waves,
Sat the lone singer wonderful causing tears.
He called on his mate,
He poured forth the meanings which I of all men know. 60

Yes my brother I know,
The rest might not, but I have treasured every note,
For more than once dimly down to the beach gliding,
Silent, avoiding the moonbeams, blending myself with the shadows,
Recalling now the obscure shapes, the echoes, the sounds and sights after
   their sorts,
The white arms out in the breakers tirelessly tossing,
I, with bare feet, a child, the wind wafting my hair,
Listened long and long.
Listened to keep, to sing, now translating the notes,
Following you my brother. 70

Soothe! soothe! soothe!
Close on its wave soothes the wave behind,
And again another behind embracing and lapping, every one close,
But my love soothes not me, not me.

Low hangs the moon, it rose late,
It is lagging—O I think it is heavy with love, with love.

O madly the sea pushes upon the land,
With love, with love.

O night! do I not see my love fluttering out among the breakers?
What is that little black thing I see there in the white? 80

Loud! loud! loud!
Loud I call to you, my love!
High and clear I shoot my voice over the waves,
Surely you must know who is here, is here,
You must know who I am, my love.

Low-hanging moon!
What is that dusky spot in your brown yellow?

O it is the shape, the shape of my mate!
O moon do not keep her from me any longer.

Land! land! O land!
Whichever way I turn, O I think you could give me my mate back again if you
  only would,
For I am almost sure I see her dimly whichever way I look.

O rising stars!
Perhaps the one I want so much will rise, will rise with some of you.

O throat! O trembling throat!
Sound clearer through the atmosphere!
Pierce the woods, the earth,
Somewhere listening to catch you must be the one I want.

Shake out carols!   100
Solitary here, the night's carols!
Carols of lonesome love! death's carols!
Carols under that lagging, yellow, waning moon!
O under that moon where she droops down into the sea!
O reckless despairing carols.

But soft! sink low!
Soft! let me just murmur,
And do you wait a moment you husky-noised sea,
For somewhere I believe I heard my mate responding to me,
So faint, I must be still, be still to listen,
But not altogether still, for then she might not come immediately to me.   110

Hither my love!
Here I am! here!
With this just-sustained note I announce myself to you,
This gentle call is for you my love, for you.

Do not be decoyed elsewhere,
That is the whistle of the wind, it is not my voice,
That is the fluttering, the fluttering of the spray,
Those are the shadows of leaves.

O darkness! O in vain!
O I am very sick and sorrowful.   120

O brown halo in the sky near the moon, drooping upon the sea!
O troubled reflection in the sea!
O throat! O throbbing heart!
And I singing uselessly, uselessly all the night.

O past! O happy life! O song of joy!
In the air, in the woods, over fields,
Loved! loved! loved! loved!
But my mate no more, no more with me!
We two together no more.

The aria sinking, 130
All else continuing, the stars shining,
The winds blowing, the notes of the birds continuous echoing,
With angry moans the fierce old mother incessantly moaning,
On the sands of Paumanok's shore gray and rustling,
The yellow half-moon enlarged, sagging down, drooping, the face of the
  sea almost touching,
The boy ecstatic, with his bare feet the waves, with his hair the atmos-
  phere dallying,
The love in the heart long pent, now loose, now at last tumultuously
  bursting,
The aria's meaning, the ears, the soul, swiftly depositing,
The strange tears down the cheeks coursing,
The colloquy there, the trio, each uttering, 140
The undertone, the savage old mother incessantly crying,
To the boy's soul's questions sullenly timing, some drowned secret
  hissing,
To the outsetting bard.

Demon or bird! (said the boy's soul,)
Is it indeed toward your mate you sing? or is it really to me?
For I, that was a child, my tongue's use sleeping, now I have heard you,
Now in a moment I know what I am for, I awake,
And already a thousand singers, a thousand songs, clearer, louder and
  more sorrowful than yours,
A thousand warbling echoes have started to life within me, never to die.

O you singer, solitary, singing by yourself, projecting me, 150
O solitary me listening, never more shall I cease perpetuating you,
Never more shall I escape, never more the reverberations,
Never more the cries of unsatisfied love be absent from me,
Never again leave me to be the peaceful child I was before what there in
  the night,
By the sea under the yellow and sagging moon,
The messenger there aroused, the fire, the sweet hell within,
The unknown want, the destiny of me.

O give me the clue! (it lurks in the night here somewhere,)
O if I am to have so much, let me have more!

A word then, (for I will conquer it,)   160
The word final, superior to all,
Subtle, sent up—what is it?—I listen;
Are you whispering it, and have been all the time, you sea waves?
Is that it from your liquid rims and wet sands?

Whereto answering, the sea,
Delaying not, hurrying not,
Whispered me through the night, and very plainly before daybreak,
Lisped to me the low and delicious word death,
And again death, death, death, death,
Hissing melodious, neither like the bird nor like my aroused child's
    heart,   170
But edging near as privately for me rustling at my feet,
Creeping thence steadily up to my ears and laving me softly all over.
Death, death, death, death, death.

Which I do not forget,
But fuse the song of my dusky demon and brother,

That he sang to me in the moonlight on Paumanok's gray beach,
With the thousand responsive songs at random,
My own songs awaked from that hour,
And with them the key, the word up from the waves,
The word of the sweetest song and all songs,   180
That strong and delicious word which, creeping to my feet,
(Or like some old crone rocking the cradle, swathed in sweet garments,
    bending aside,)
The sea whispered me.

                                                          [1859; 1881]

A NOISELESS PATIENT SPIDER

A NOISELESS patient spider,
I marked where on a little promontory it stood isolated,
Marked how to explore the vacant vast surrounding,
It launched forth filament, filament, filament, out of itself,
Ever unreeling them, ever tirelessly speeding them.

And you O my soul where you stand,
Surrounded, detached, in measureless oceans of space,
Ceaselessly musing, venturing, throwing, seeking the spheres to connect
    them,
Till the bridge you will need be formed, till the ductile anchor hold,
Till the gossamer thread you fling catch somewhere, O my soul.   10
                                                          [1863?]

CAVALRY CROSSING A FORD

A LINE in long array where they wind betwixt green islands,
    They take a serpentine course, their arms flash in the sun —hark to
the musical clank,
Behold the silvery river, in it the splashing horses loitering stop to drink,
Behold the brown-faced men, each group, each person a picture, the negli-
    gent rest on the saddles,
Some emerge on the opposite bank, others are just entering the ford—
    while,
Scarlet and blue and snowy white,
The guidon flags flutter gayly in the wind.

[1865]

THERE WAS A CHILD WENT FORTH

T HERE was a child went forth every day,
    And the first object he looked upon, that object he became,
And that object became part of him for the day or a certain part of the
    day,
Or for many years or stretching cycles of years.

The early lilacs became part of this child,
And grass and white and red morning-glories, and white and red clover,
    and the song of the phoebe-bird,
And the Third-month lambs and the sow's pink-faint litter, and the
    mare's foal and the cow's calf,
And the noisy brood of the barnyard or by the mire of the pond-side,
And the fish suspending themselves so curiously below there, and the
    beautiful curious liquid,
And the water-plants with their graceful flat heads, all became part of
    him.   10

The field-sprouts of Fourth-month and Fifth-month became part of him,
Winter-grain sprouts and those of the light-yellow corn, and the esculent
    roots of the garden,
And the apple-trees covered with blossoms and the fruit afterward, and
    woodberries, and the commonest weeds by the road,
And the old drunkard staggering home from the outhouse of the tavern
    whence he had lately risen,
And the schoolmistress that passed on her way to the school,
And the friendly boys that passed, and the quarrelsome boys,
And the tidy and fresh-cheeked girls, and the barefoot Negro boy and girl,
And all the changes of city and country wherever he went.

His own parents, he that had fathered him and she that had conceived him
    in her womb and birthed him,
They gave this child more of themselves than that,   20
They gave him afterward every day, they became part of him.

The mother at home quietly placing the dishes on the supper-table,
The mother with mild words, clean her cap and gown, a wholesome odor
    falling off her person and clothes as she walks by,
The father, strong, self-sufficient, manly, mean, angered, unjust,
The blow, the quick loud word, the tight bargain, the crafty lure,
The family usages, the language, the company, the furniture, the yearn-
    ing and swelling heart,
Affection that will not be gainsaid, the sense of what is real, the thought
    if after all it should prove unreal,
The doubts of day-time and the doubts of night-time, the curious whether
    and how,
Whether that which appears so is so, or is it all flashes and specks?
Men and women crowding fast in the streets, if they are not flashes and
    specks what are they?   30
The streets themselves and the facades of houses, and goods in the
    windows,
Vehicles, teams, the heavy-planked wharves, the huge crossing at the
    ferries,
The village on the highland seen from afar at sunset, the river between,
Shadows, aureola and mist, the light falling on roofs and gables of white
    or brown two miles off,
The schooner nearby sleepily dropping down the tide, the little boat
    slack-towed astern,
The hurrying tumbling waves, quick-broken crests, slapping,
The strata of colored clouds, the long bar of maroon-tint away solitary
    by itself, the spread of purity it lies motionless in,
The horizon's edge, the flying sea-crow, the fragrance of salt marsh and
    shore mud,
These became part of that child who went forth every day, and who now
    goes, and will always go forth every day.

                                    [1855]

TO A LOCOMOTIVE IN WINTER

THEE for my recitative,
    Thee in the driving storm even as now, the snow, the winter-day
    declining,
Thee in thy panoply, thy measured dual throbbing and thy beat convul-
    sive,
Thy black cylindric body, golden brass and silvery steel,

Thy ponderous side-bars, parallel and connecting rods, gyrating, shut-
　　tling at thy sides,
Thy metrical, now swelling pant and roar, now tapering in the distance,
Thy great protruding head-light fixed in front,
Thy long, pale, floating vapor-pennants, tinged with delicate purple,
The dense and murky clouds out-belching from thy smoke-stack,
Thy knitted frame, thy springs and valves, the tremulous twinkle of thy
　　wheels,　　　　　　　　　　　　　　　　　　　　　　　　　　　　10
Thy train of cars behind, obedient, merrily following,
Through gale or calm, now swift, now slack, yet steadily careering;
Type of the modern—emblem of motion and power—pulse of the conti-
　　nent,
For once come serve the Muse and merge in verse, even as here I see thee,
With storm and buffeting gusts of wind and falling snow,
By day thy warning ringing bell to sound its notes,
By night thy silent signal lamps to swing.

Fierce-throated beauty!
Roll though my chant with all thy lawless music, thy swinging lamps at
　　night,
Thy madly-whistled laughter, echoing, rumbling like an earthquake,
　　rousing all,　　　　　　　　　　　　　　　　　　　　　　　　　20
Law of thyself complete thine own track firmly holding,
(No sweetness debonair of tearful harp or glib piano thine,)
Thy trills of shrieks by rocks and hills returned,
Launched o'er the prairies wide, across the lakes,
To the free skies unpent and glad and strong.

　　　　　　　　　　　　　　　　　　　　　　　　　　　　　　[1876]

Elizabeth Barrett Browning
1806–1861

A MUSICAL INSTRUMENT

WHAT was he doing, the great god Pan,
    Down in the reeds by the river?
Spreading ruin and scattering ban,
Splashing and paddling with hoofs of a goat,
And breaking the golden lilies afloat
    With the dragon-fly on the river?

He tore out a reed, the great god Pan,
    From the deep cool bed of the river.
The limpid water turbidly ran,
And the broken lilies a-dying lay,
And the dragon-fly had fled away,   10
    Ere he brought it out of the river.

High on the shore sat the great god Pan,
    While turbidly flowed the river,
And hacked and hewed as a great god can,
With his hard bleak steel at the patient reed,
Till there was not a sign of a leaf indeed
    To prove it fresh from the river.

He cut it short did the great god Pan,
    (How tall it stood in the river!)   20
Then drew the pith like the heart of a man,
Steadily from the outside ring,
Then notched the poor dry empty thing
    In holes as he sat by the river.

"This is the say," laughed the great god Pan,
    (Laughed while he sat by the river!)
"The only way since gods began
To make sweet music, they could succeed,"
Then dropping his mouth to a hole in the reed,
    He blew in power by the river.   30

Sweet, sweet, sweet, O Pan,
  Piercing sweet by the river!
Blinding sweet, O great god Pan!
The sun on the hill forgot to die,
And the lilies revived, and the dragon-fly
Came back to dream on the river.

Yet half a beast is the great god Pan
  To laugh, as he sits by the river,
Making a poet out of a man.
The true gods sigh for the cost and the pain—   40
For the reed that grows never more again
  As a reed with the reeds of the river.

[1860]

Alfred, Lord Tennyson
1809–1892

ULYSSES[1]

IT LITTLE profits that an idle king,
By this still hearth, among these barren crags,
Matched with an agéd wife,[2] I mete and dole
Unequal laws unto a savage race,
That hoard, and sleep, and feed, and know not me.
I cannot rest from travel; I will drink
Life to the lees. All times I have enjoyed
Greatly, have suffered greatly, both with those
That loved me, and alone; on shore, and when
Through scudding drifts the rainy Hyades[3]   10
Vexed the dim sea. I am become a name;
For always roaming with a hungry heart
Much have I seen and known,—cities of men
And manners, climates, councils, governments,
Myself not least, but honored of them all,—
And drunk delight of battle with my peers,
Far on the ringing plains of windy Troy.
I am a part of all that I have met;

[1] Tennyson takes his theme from Dante, who, in *The Inferno*, depicts the hero of *The Odyssey* as restless and eager to continue the search for knowledge and virtue.
[2] Penelope
[3] a constellation whose rising at the same time as the sun was anciently believed to bring rain

Yet all experience is an arch wherethrough
Gleams that untraveled world whose margin fades   20
For ever and for ever when I move.
How dull it is to pause, to make an end,
To rust unburnished, not to shine in use!
As though to breathe were life! Life piled on life
Were all too little, and of one to me
Little remains; but every hour is saved
From that eternal silence, something more,
A bringer of new things; and vile it were
For some three suns to store and hoard myself,
And this gray spirit yearning in desire   30
To follow knowledge like a sinking star,
Beyond the utmost bound of human thought.
　　This is my son, mine own Telemachus,
To whom I leave the scepter and the isle,[4]
Well-loved of me, discerning to fulfill
This labor, by slow prudence to make mild
A rugged people, and through soft degrees
Subdue them to the useful and the good.
Most blameless is he, centerd in the sphere
Of common duties, decent not to fail   40
In offices of tenderness, and pay
Meet adoration to my household gods,
When I am gone. He works his work, I mine.
　　There lies the port; the vessel puffs her sail;
There gloom the dark, broad seas. My mariners,
Souls that have toiled, and wrought, and thought with me,—
That ever with a frolic welcome took
The thunder and the sunshine, and opposed
Free hearts, free foreheads,—you and I are old;
Old age hath yet his honor and his toil.   50
Death closes all; but something ere the end,
Some work of noble note, may yet be done,
Not unbecoming men that strove with Gods.
The lights begin to twinkle from the rocks;
The long day wanes; the slow moon climbs; the deep
Moans round with many voices. Come, my friends.
'T is not too late to seek a newer world.
Push off, and sitting well in order smite
The sounding furrows; for my purpose holds
To sail beyond the sunset, and the baths   60
Of all the western stars, until I die.

[4] Ithaca

It may be that the gulfs will wash us down;
It may be we shall touch the Happy Isles,[5]
And see the great Achilles,[6] whom we knew.
Though much is taken, much abides; and though
We are not now that strength which in old days
Moved earth and heaven, that which we are, we are,—
One equal temper of heroic hearts,
Made weak by time and fate, but strong in will
To strive, to seek, to find, and not to yield.   70
                                                            [1842]

[5] the Islands of the Blessed in the western extremity of the ocean
[6] the major hero of the Trojan War, in which he was killed

BREAK, BREAK, BREAK

BREAK, break, break,
    On thy cold gray stones, O Sea!
And I would that my tongue could utter
    The thoughts that arise in me.

O well for the fisherman's boy,
    That he shouts with his sister at play!
O well for the sailor lad,
    That he sings in his boat on the bay!

And the stately ships go on
    To their haven under the hill;   10
But O for the touch of a vanished hand,
    And the sound of a voice that is still!

Break, break, break,
    At the foot of thy crags, O Sea!
But the tender grace of a day that is dead
    Will never come back to me.

                                                            [1842]

◇

SONGS FROM

THE PRINCESS

◇

SWEET AND LOW

Sweet and low, sweet and low,
 Wind of the western sea,
Low, low, breathe and blow,
 Wind of the western sea!
Over the rolling waters go,
Come from the dying moon, and blow,
 Blow him again to me;
While my little one, while my pretty one sleeps.

Sleep and rest, sleep and rest,
 Father will come to thee soon;   10
Rest, rest, on mother's breast,
 Father will come to thee soon;
Father will come to his babe in the nest,
Silver sails all out of the west
 Under the silver moon;
Sleep, my little one, sleep, my pretty one, sleep.

THE SPLENDOR FALLS ON CASTLE WALLS

The splendor falls on castle walls
 And snowy summits old in story:
The long light shakes across the lakes,
 And the wild cataract leaps in glory.
Blow, bugle, blow, set the wild echoes flying,
Blow, bugle, answer, echoes, dying, dying, dying.

O hark, O hear; how thin and clear,
 And thinner, clearer, farther going!
O sweet and far from cliff and scar
 The horns of Elfland faintly blowing!
Blow, let us hear the purple glens replying:
Blow, bugle; answer, echoes, dying, dying, dying.

O love, they die in yon rich sky,
　　They faint on hill or field or river:
Our echoes roll from soul to soul,
　　And grow for ever and ever.
Blow, bugle, blow, set the wild echoes flying,
And answer, echoes, answer, dying, dying, dying.

NOW SLEEPS THE CRIMSON PETAL

Now sleeps the crimson petal, now the white;
　　Nor waves the cypress in the palace walk;
Nor winks the gold fin in the porphyry font.
The fire-fly wakens; waken thou with me.

　　Now droops the milk-white peacock like a ghost,
And like a ghost she glimmers on to me.

　　Now lies the Earth all Danaë[1] to the stars,
And all thy heart lies open unto me.

　　Now slides the silent meteor on, and leaves
A shining furrow, as thy thoughts in me.　　　　　　　　10

　　Now folds the lily all her sweetness up,
And slips into the bosom of the lake.
So fold thyself, my dearest, thou, and slip
Into my bosom and be lost in me.

　　　　　　　　　　　　　　　　　　　[1850]

---

[1] a princess of Greek mythology who was impregnated by Zeus disguised as a golden shower

THE EAGLE

He clasps the crag with crooked hands;
　　Close to the sun in lonely lands,
Ringed with the azure world he stands.

The wrinkled sea beneath him crawls;
He watches from his mountain walls,
And like a thunderbolt he falls.

　　　　　　　　　　　　　　　　　　　[1851]

CROSSING THE BAR[1]

Sunset and evening star,
    And one clear call for me!
And may there be no moaning of the bar,
    When I put out to sea,

But such a tide as moving seems asleep,
    Too full for sound and foam,
When that which drew from out the boundless deep
    Turns again home.

Twilight and evening bell,
    And after that the dark!   10
And may there be no sadness of farewell,
    When I embark;

For though from out our bourne[2] of Time and Place
    The flood may bear me far,
I hope to see my Pilot face to face
    When I have crossed the bar.

[1889]

[1] sandbar partly enclosing a harbor   [2] realm

Robert Browning
1812–1889

SOLILOQUY OF THE SPANISH CLOISTER

Gr-r-r—there go, my heart's abhorrence!
    Water your damned flower-pots, do!
If hate killed men, Brother Lawrence,
    God's blood, would not mine kill you!
What? your myrtle-bush wants trimming?
    Oh, that rose has prior claims—
Needs its leaden vase filled brimming?
    Hell dry you up with its flames!

At the meal we sit together;
    Salve tibi![1] I must hear   10
Wise talk of the kind of weather,
    Sort of season, time of year:

[1] hail to thee

Not a plenteous cork-crop : scarcely
　　Dare we hope oak-galls,[2] I doubt;
What's the Latin name for "parsley"?
　　What's the Greek name for Swine's Snout?

Whew! We'll have our platter burnished,
　　Laid with care on our own shelf!
With a fire-new spoon we're furnished,
　　And a goblet for ourself,　　　　　　　　　　20
Rinsed like something sacrificial
　　Ere 'tis fit to touch our chaps—
Marked with L for our initial!
　　(He-he! There his lily snaps!)

Saint, forsooth! While brown Dolores
　　Squats outside the Convent bank
With Sanchicha, telling stories,
　　Steeping tresses in the tank,
Blue-black, lustrous, thick like horsehairs,
　　—Can't I see his dead eye glow,　　　　　　30
Bright as 'twere a Barbary corsair's?
　　(That is, if he'd let it show!)

When he finishes refection,
　　Knife and fork he never lays
Cross-wise, to my recollection,
　　As do I, in Jesu's praise.
I the Trinity illustrate,
　　Drinking watered orange-pulp—
In three sips the Arian[3] frustrate;
　　While he drains his at one gulp!　　　　　　40

Oh, those melons? If he's able
　　We're to have a feast! so nice!
One goes to the Abbot's table,
　　All of us get each a slice.
How go on your flowers? None double?
　　Not one fruit-sort can you spy?
Strange!—And I, too, at such trouble,
　　Keep them close-nipped on the sly!

[2] source of a dye used in writing ink
[3] one who accepts the doctrine of Arius (c. A.D. 260–336), which denies the trinitarian concept of the Deity

There's a great text in Galatians,
   Once you trip on it, entails   50
Twenty-nine distinct damnations,
   One sure, if another fails:
If I trip him just a-dying,
   Sure of heaven as sure can be,
Spin him round and send him flying
   Off to hell, a Manichee?[4]

Or, my scrofulous French novel
   On grey paper with blunt type!
Simply glance at it, you grovel
   Hand and foot in Belial's gripe: 60
If I double down its pages
   At the woeful sixteenth print,
When he gathers his greengages,
   Ope a sieve and slip it in't?

Or, there's Satan!—one might venture
   Pledge one's soul to him, yet leave
Such a flaw in the indenture
   As he'd miss till, past retrieve,
Blasted lay that rose-acacia
   We're so proud of! *Hy, Zy, Hine.* . . .
'St, there's Vespers! *Plena gratiâ*
   Ave, Virgo![5] Gr-r-r—you swine!

                                              [1842]

    [4] a believer in the heresy of Manes (*c.* A.D. 216–*c.* 276), which holds that good and evil are thoroughly mingled, and which denies the primacy of God
    [5] Hail, Mary, full of grace

MY LAST DUCHESS

FERRARA

Tʜᴀᴛ's my last Duchess painted on the wall,
  Looking as if she were alive; I call
That piece a wonder, now: Frà Pandolf's[1] hands
Worked busily a day, and there she stands.
Will't please you sit and look at her? I said
"Frà Pandolf" by design, for never read

    [1] an imaginary artist, as is Claus of Innsbruck of line 56

Strangers like you that pictured countenance,
The depth and passion of its earnest glance,
But to myself they turned (since none puts by
The curtain I have drawn for you, but I)   10
And seemed as they would ask me, if they durst,
How such a glance came there; so, not the first
Are you to turn and ask thus. Sir, 'twas not
Her husband's presence only, called that spot
Of joy into the Duchess' cheek: perhaps
Frà Pandolf chanced to say "Her mantle laps
Over my Lady's wrist too much," or "Paint
Must never hope to reproduce the faint
Half-flush that dies along her throat": such stuff
Was courtesy, she thought, and cause enough   20
For calling up that spot of joy. She had
A heart—how shall I say?—too soon made glad,
Too easily impressed; she liked whate'er
She looked on, and her looks went everywhere.
Sir, 'twas all one! My favor at her breast,
The dropping of the daylight in the West.
The bough of cherries some officious fool
Broke in the orchard for her, the white mule
She rode with round the terrace—all and each
Would draw from her alike the approving speech,   30
Or blush, at least. She thanked men,—good; but thanked
Somehow—I know not how—as if she ranked
My gift of a nine-hundred-years-old name
With anybody's gift. Who'd stoop to blame
This sort of trifling? Even had you skill
In speech—(which I have not)—to make your will
Quite clear to such an one, and say, "Just this
Or that in you disgusts me; here you miss,
Or there exceed the mark"—and if she let
Herself be lessoned so, nor plainly set   40
Her wits to yours, forsooth, and made excuse,
—E'en then would be some stooping, and I choose
Never to stoop. Oh, Sir, she smiled, no doubt,
Whene'er I passed her; but who passed without
Much the same smile? This grew; I gave commands;
Then all smiles stopped together. There she stands
As if alive. Will't please you rise? We'll meet
The company below, then. I repeat,
The Count your Master's known munificence
Is ample warrant that no just pretence   50
Of mine for dowry will be disallowed;
Though his fair daughter's self, as I avowed

At starting, is my object. Nay, we'll go
Together down, Sir! Notice Neptune, though,
Taming a sea-horse, thought a rarity,
Which Claus of Innsbruck cast in bronze for me.

[1842]

MEETING AT NIGHT

THE gray sea and the long black land;
    And the yellow half-moon large and low;
And the startled little waves that leap
In fiery ringlets from their sleep,
As I gain the cove with pushing prow,
And quench its speed i' the slushy sand.

Then a mile of warm sea-scented beach;
Three fields to cross till a farm appears;
A tap at the pane, the quick sharp scratch
And blue spurt of a lighted match,   10
And a voice less loud, through its joys and fears,
Than the two hearts beating each to each!

[1845]

PARTING AT MORNING

ROUND the cape of a sudden came the sea,
    And the sun looked over the mountain's rim:
And straight was a path of gold for him,
And the need of a world of men for me.

[1845]

HOME-THOUGHTS, FROM ABROAD

OH, TO BE in England
    Now that April's there,
And whoever wakes in England
Sees, some morning, unaware,
That the lowest boughs and the brushwood sheaf
Round the elm-tree bole are in tiny leaf,
While the chaffinch sings on the orchard bough
In England—now!

And after April, when May follows,
And the whitethroat builds, and all the swallows !   10
Hark, where my blossomed pear-tree in the hedge
Leans to the field and scatters on the clover
Blossoms and dewdrops—at the bent spray's edge
That's the wise thrush ; he sings each song twice over,
Lest you should think he never could recapture
The first fine careless rapture !
And though the fields look rough with hoary dew
All will be gay when noontide wakes anew
The buttercups, the little children's dower—
Far brighter than this gaudy melon-flower.   20

[1845]

HOME-THOUGHTS, FROM THE SEA

Nobly, nobly Cape Saint Vincent to the north-west died away ;
Sunset ran, one glorious blood-red, reeking into Cadiz Bay ;
Bluish 'mid the burning water, full in face Trafalgar lay ;
In the dimmest north-east distance, dawned Gibraltar grand and gray ;
"Here and here did England help me : how can I help England ?"—say,
Whoso turns as I, this evening, turn to God to praise and pray,
While Jove's planet rises yonder, silent over Africa.

[1845]

THE BISHOP ORDERS HIS TOMB AT
SAINT PRAXED'S CHURCH
(ROME, 15-.)

Vanity, saith the preacher, vanity !
Draw round my bed : is Anslem keeping back ?
Nephews—sons mine . . . ah God, I know not ! Well—
She, men would have to be your mother once,
Old Gandolf envied me, so fair she was !
What's done is done, and she is dead beside,
Dead long ago, and I am Bishop since,
And as she died so must we die ourselves,
And thence ye may perceive the world's a dream.
Life, how and what is it ? As here I lie   10
In this state-chamber, dying by degrees,
Hours and long hours in the dead night, I ask
"Do I live, am I dead ? " Peace, peace seems all.
Saint Praxed's ever was the church for peace ;
And so, about this tomb of mine. I fought

With tooth and nail to save my niche, ye know :
—Old Gandolf cozened me, despite my care ;
Shrewd was that snatch from out the corner South
He graced his carrion with, God curse the same !
Yet still my niche is not so cramped but thence   20
One sees the pulpit o' the epistle-side,[1]
And somewhat of the choir, those silent seats,
And up into the aery dome where live
The angels, and a sunbeam's sure to lurk :
And I shall fill my slab of basalt there,
And 'neath my tabernacle[2] take my rest,
With those nine columns round me, two and two,
The odd one at my feet where Anselm stands :
Peach-blossom marble all, the rare, the ripe
As fresh-poured red wine of a mighty pulse   30
—Old Gandolf with his paltry onion-stone,
Put me where I may look at him ! True peach,
Rosy and flawless : how I earned the prize !
Draw close : that conflagration of my church
—What then ? So much was saved if aught were missed !
My sons, ye would not be my death ? Go dig
The white-grape vineyard where the oil-press stood,
Drop water gently till the surface sinks,
And if ye find . . . Ah, God I know not, I ! . . .
Bedded in store of rotten figleaves soft,   40
And corded up in a tight olive-frail,[3]
Some lump, ah God, of lapis lazuli,
Big as a Jew's head cut off at the nape,
Blue as a vein o'er the Madonna's breast . . .
Sons, all have I bequeathed you, villas, all,
That brave Frascati villa with its bath,
So, let the blue lump poise between my knees,
Like God the Father's globe on both His hands
Ye worship in the Jesu Church so gay,
For Gandolf shall not choose but see and burst !   50
Swift as a weaver's shuttle fleet our years :
Man goeth to the grave, and where is he ?
Did I say basalt for my slab, sons ? Black—
'Twas ever antique-black I meant ! How else
Shall ye contrast my frieze to come beneath ?
The bas-relief in bronze ye promised me,
Those Pans and Nymphs ye wot of, and perchance
Some tripod, thyrsus,[4] with a vase or so,

---

[1] the right side as one faces the altar. The epistle is read from this side.
[2] the canopy which the Bishop imagines over his tomb   [3] a basket of rushes
[4] a staff decorated with vine leaves and denoting pagan revelry

The Savior at his sermon on the mount,
Saint Praxed in a glory, and one Pan   60
Ready to twitch the Nymph's last garment off,
And Moses with the tables . . . but I know
Ye mark me not! What do they whisper thee,
Child of my bowels, Anselm? Ah, ye hope
To revel down my villas while I gasp
Bricked o'er with beggar's moldy travertine
Which Gandolf from his tomb-top chuckles at!
Nay, boys, ye love me—all of jasper, then!
'Tis jasper ye stand pledged to, lest I grieve
My bath must needs be left behind, alas!   70
One block, pure green as a pistachio-nut,
There's plenty jasper somewhere in the world—
And have I not Saint Praxed's ear to pray
Horses for ye, and brown Greek manuscripts,
And mistresses with great smooth marbly limbs?
—That's if ye carve my epitaph aright,
Choice Latin, picked phrase, Tully's[5] every word,
No gaudy ware like Gandolf's second line—
Tully, my masters? Ulpian[6] serves his need!
And then how I shall lie through centuries,   80
And hear the blessèd mutter of the mass,
And see God made and eaten all day long,
And feel the steady candle-flame, and taste
Good strong thick stupefying incense-smoke!
For as I lie here, hours of the dead night,
Dying in state and by such slow degrees,
I fold my arms as if they clasped a crook,
And stretch my feet forth straight as stone can point
And let the bedclothes for a mortcloth drop
Into great laps and folds of sculptor's-work: 90
And as yon tapers dwindle, and strange thoughts
Grow, with a certain humming in my ears,
About the life before I lived this life,
And this life too, popes, cardinals and priests,
Saint Praxed at his sermon on the mount,
Your tall pale mother with her talking eyes,
And new-found agate urns as fresh as day,
And marble's language, Latin pure, discreet,
—Aha, ELUCESCEBAT[7] quoth our friend?

[5] Marcus Tullius Cicero (106–43 B.C.), noted for the eloquence and purity of his Latin style

[6] Domitius Ulpianus (c. A.D. 170–228), a prolific writer whose works are known chiefly through Justinian's *Digest*

[7] He was renowned; but the form of the word is that of decadent Latin.

No Tully, said I, Ulpian at the best!   100
Evil and brief hath been my pilgrimage.
All lapis, all, sons! Else I give the Pope
My villas: will ye ever eat my heart?
Ever your eyes were as a lizard's quick,
They glitter like your mother's for my soul,
Or ye would heighten my impoverished frieze,
Piece out its starved design, and fill my vase
With grapes, and add a vizor and a Term,[8]
And to the tripod ye would tie a lynx
That in his struggle throws the thyrsus down,   110
To comfort me on my entablature
Whereon I am to lie till I must ask
"Do I live, am I dead?" There, leave me, there!
For ye have stabbed me with ingratitude
To death—ye wish it—God, ye wish it! Stone—
Gritstone, a-crumble! Clammy squares which sweat
As if the corpse they keep were oozing through—
And no more lapis to delight the world!
Well, go! I bless ye. Fewer tapers there,
But in a row: and, going, turn your backs   120
—Ay, like departing altar-ministrants,
And leave me in my church, the church for peace,
That I may watch at leisure if he leers—
Old Gandolf, at me, from his onion-stone,
As still he envied me, so fair she was!

                                                                [1845]

[8] a commemorative bust on a pedestal

PROSPICE[1]

Fear death?—to feel the fog in my throat,
     The mist in my face,
When the snows begin, and the blasts denote
     I am nearing the place,
The power of the night, the press of the storm,
     The post of the foe;
Where he stands, the Arch Fear in a visible form,
     Yet the strong man must go:
For the journey is done and the summit attained,
     And the barriers fall,   10

[1] look ahead; pronounced prŏs'pis

Though a battle's to fight ere the guerdon be gained,
    The reward of it all.
I was ever a fighter, so—one fight more,
    The best and the last!
I would hate that death bandaged my eyes, and forbore,
    And bade me creep past.
No! let me taste the whole of it, fare like my peers,
    The heroes of old,
Bear the brunt, in a minute pay glad life's arrears
    Of pain, darkness, and cold.   20
For sudden the worst turns the best to the brave,
    The black minute's at end,
And the elements' rage, the fiend-voices that rave,
    Shall dwindle, shall blend,
Shall change, shall become first a peace out of pain,
    Then a light, then thy breast,
O thou soul of my soul! I shall clasp thee again,
    And with God be the rest!

                            [1861]

Emily Brontë

1818–1848

REMEMBRANCE

COLD in the earth—and the deep snow piled above thee,
  Far, far removed, cold in the dreary grave!
Have I forgot, my only Love, to love thee,
  Severed at last by Time's all-severing wave?

Now, when alone, do my thoughts no longer hover
  Over the mountains, on that northern shore,
Resting their wings where heath and fern-leaves cover
  Thy noble heart for ever, ever more?

Cold in the earth—and fifteen wild Decembers,
  From those brown hills, have melted into spring: 10
Faithful, indeed, is the spirit that remembers
  After such years of change and suffering!

Sweet Love of youth, forgive, if I forgot thee,
  While the world's tide is bearing me along;
Other desires and other hopes beset me,
  Hopes which obscure, but cannot do thee wrong!

No later light has lightened up my heaven,
No second morn has ever shone for me;
All my life's bliss from thy dear life was given,
All my life's bliss is in the grace with thee.   20

But, when the days of golden dreams had perished,
And even Despair was powerless to destroy;
Then did I learn how existence could be cherished,
Strengthened and fed without the aid of joy.

Then did I check the tears of useless passion—
Weaned my young soul from yearning after thine;
Sternly denied its burning wish to hasten
Down to that tomb already more than mine,

And, even yet, I dare not let it languish,
Dare not indulge in memory's rapturous pain;   30
Once drinking deep of that divinest anguish,
How could I seek the empty world again?

                                                        [1845]

TO IMAGINATION

WHEN weary with the long day's care,
    And earthly change from pain to pain,
And lost, and ready to despair
    Thy kind voice calls me back again
Oh, my true friend! I am not lone,
While thou canst speak with such a tone!

So hopeless is the world without,
    The world within I doubly prize;
Thy world, where guile and hate and doubt
    And cold suspicion never rise;   10
Where thou and I and Liberty
Have undisputed sovereignty.

What matters it, that all around
    Danger and guilt and darkness lie,
If but within our bosom's bound
    We hold a bright, untroubled sky,
Warm with ten thousand mingled rays
Of suns that know no winter days?

Reason, indeed, may oft complain
   For Nature's sad reality,   20
And tell the suffering heart how vain
   Its cherished dreams must always be;
And Truth may rudely trample down
The flowers of Fancy, newly-blown:

But thou art ever there, to bring
   The hovering vision back, and breathe
New glories o'er the blighted spring,
   And call a lovelier Life from Death,
And whisper, with a voice divine,
Of real worlds, as bright as thine.   30

I trust not to thy phantom bliss,
   Yet, still, in evening's quiet hour,
With never-failing thankfulness,
   I welcome thee, Benignant Power,
Sure solacer of human cares,
And sweeter hope, when hope despairs!

                           [1846]

Matthew Arnold
1822–1888

TO MARGUERITE

Yes! in the sea of life enisled,
   With echoing straits between us thrown,
Dotting the shoreless watery wild,
We mortal millions live *alone*.
The islands feel the enclasping flow,
And then their endless bounds they know.

But when the moon their hollows lights,
And they are swept by balms of spring,
And in their glens, on starry nights
The nightingales divinely sing;   10
And lovely notes, from shore to shore,
Across the sounds and channels pour—

Oh! then a longing like despair
Is to their farthest caverns sent;
For surely once, they feel, we were

Parts of a single continent!
Now round us spreads the watery plain—
Oh might our marges meet again!

Who ordered, that their longing's fire
Should be, as soon as kindled, cooled?   20
Who renders vain their deep desire?—
A God, a God their severance ruled!
And bade betwixt their shores to be
The unplumbed, salt, estranging sea.

[1852]

PHILOMELA[1]

Hark, ah, the nightingale—
    The tawny-throated!
Hark, from that moonlit cedar what a burst!
What triumph! hark!—what pain!
O wanderer from a Grecian shore,
Still, after many years, in distant lands,
Still nourishing in thy bewildered brain
That wild, unquenched, deep-sunken, old-world pain—
Say, will it never heal?
And can this fragrant lawn   10
With its cool trees, and night,
And the sweet, tranquil Thames,
And moonshine, and the dew,
To thy racked heart and brain
Afford no balm?

Dost thou tonight behold,
Here, through the moonlight on this English grass,
The unfriendly palace in the Thracian wild?
Dost thou again peruse
With hot cheeks and seared eyes   20
The too clear web, and thy dumb sister's shame?
Dost thou once more assay
Thy flight, and feel come over thee,
Poor fugitive, the feathery change

[1] King Tereus of Thrace married Philomela, but later raped her sister, Procne, and cut out her tongue. Procne wove a tapestry ("the too clear web"—l. 21) revealing the story and sent it to Philomela. The sisters killed Tereus' son Itylus and served the flesh to the king. When Tereus discovered the crime, he pursued the sisters, so that they called upon the gods for help. Philomela was transformed into the nightingale, Procne into the swallow, and Tereus into the hawk.

Once more, and once more seem to make resound
With love and hate, triumph and agony,
Lone Daulis,[2] and the high Cephissian vale?[3]
Listen, Eugenia[4]—
How thick the bursts come crowding through the leaves!
Again—thou hearest?   30
Eternal passion!
Eternal pain!

[1853]

[2] site of the transformation   [3] valley in Phocis, home of Tereus
[4] imaginary listener

DOVER BEACH

THE sea is calm to-night,
   The tide is full, the moon lies fair
Upon the Straits;—on the French coast, the light
Gleams, and is gone; the cliffs of England stand,
Glimmering and vast, out in the tranquil bay.
Come to the window, sweet is the night air!
Only, from the long line of spray
Where the ebb meets the moon-blanched sand,
Listen! you hear the grating roar
Of pebbles which the waves suck back, and fling,   10
At their return, up the high strand,
Begin, and cease, and then again begin,
With tremulous cadence slow, and bring
The eternal note of sadness in.

    Sophocles[1] long ago
Heard it on the Ægean, and it brought
Into his mind the turbid ebb and flow
Of human misery; we
Find also in the sound a thought,
Hearing it by this distant northern sea.

The sea of faith
Was once, too, at the full, and round earth's shore
Lay like the folds of a bright girdle furled;
But now I only hear
Its melancholy, long, withdrawing roar,
Retreating to the breath

[1] Greek tragedian (*c.* 496–*c.* 405 B.C.). In *Antigone* he likens the curse of heaven to the ebb and flow of the sea.

Of the night-wind down the vast edges drear
And naked shingles[2] of the world.

Ah, love, let us be true
To one another ! for the world, which seems   30
To lie before us like a land of dreams,
So various, so beautiful, so new,
Hath really neither joy, nor love, nor light,
Nor certitude, nor peace, nor help for pain ;
And we are here as on a darkling plain
Swept with confused alarms of struggle and flight,
Where ignorant armies clash by night.

[1867]

[2] beaches covered with coarse gravel

Emily Dickinson
1830–1886

67[1]

SUCCESS is counted sweetest
By those who ne'er succeed.
To comprehend a nectar
Requires sorest need.

Not one of all the purple Host
Who took the Flag today
Can tell the definition
So clear of Victory

As he defeated—dying—
On whose forbidden ear   10
The distant strains of triumph
Burst agonized and clear !

[1859]

[1] The numbers and dates attached to Dickinson's poems are those supplied by
Thomas H. Johnson (ed.), *The Complete Poems of Emily Dickinson* (Boston: Little,
Brown, 1960).

214

I TASTE a liquor never brewed—
From Tankards scooped in Pearl—
Not all the Vats upon the Rhine
Yield such an alcohol!

Inebriate of Air—am I—
And Debauchee of Dew—
Reeling—thro endless summer days—
From inns of Molten Blue—

When "Landlords" turn the drunken Bee
Out of the Foxglove's door—   10
When Butterflies—renounce their "drams"—
I shall but drink the more!

Till Seraphs swing their snowy Hats—
And Saints—to windows run—
To see the little Tippler
Leaning against the—Sun—

[*c.* 1860]

258

T HERE'S a certain Slant of light,
Winter Afternoons—
That oppresses, like the Heft
Of Cathedral Tunes—

Heavenly Hurt, it gives us—
We can find no scar,
But internal difference,
Where the Meanings, are—

None may teach it—Any—
'Tis the Seal Despair—   10
An imperial affliction
Sent us of the Air—

When it comes, the Landscape listens—
Shadows—hold their breath—
When it goes, 'tis like the Distance
On the look of Death—

[*c.* 1861]

303

THE Soul selects her own Society—
    Then—shuts the Door—
To her divine Majority—
Present no more—

Unmoved—she notes the Chariots—pausing—
At her low Gate—
Unmoved—an Emperor be kneeling
Upon her Mat—

I've known her—from an ample nation—
Choose One—   10
Then—close the Valves of her attention—
Like Stone—

                                                          [1862]

318

I'LL tell you how the Sun rose—
    A Ribbon at a time—
The Steeples swam in Amethyst—
The news, like Squirrels, ran—
The Hills untied their Bonnets—
The Bobolinks—begun—
Then I said softly to myself—
"That must have been the Sun"!
But how he set—I know not—
There seemed a purple stile   10
That little Yellow boys and girls
Were climbing all the while—
Till when they reached the other side,
A Dominie in Gray—
Put gently up the evening Bars—
And led the flock away—

                                                          [c. 1860]

328

A BIRD came down the Walk—
    He did not know I saw—
He bit an Angleworm in halves
And ate the fellow, raw,

And then he drank a Dew
From a convenient Grass—
And then hopped sidewise to the Wall
To let a Beetle pass—

He glanced with rapid eyes
That hurried all around—
They looked like frightened Beads, I thought—
He stirred his Velvet Head

Like one in danger, Cautious,
I offered him a Crumb
And he unrolled his feathers
And rowed him softer home—

Than Oars divide the Ocean,
Too silver for a seam—
Or Butterflies, off Banks of Noon
Leap, plashless as they swim.   20
                                              [1862]

341

AFTER great pain a formal feeling comes—
The Nerves sit ceremonious, like Tombs—
The stiff Heart questions was it He, that bore,
And Yesterday, or Centuries before?

The Feet, mechanical, go round—
Of Ground, or Air, or Ought—
A Wooden way
Regardless grown,
A Quartz contentment, like a stone

This is the Hour of Lead—
Remembered, if outlived,   10
As Freezing persons, recollect the Snow—
First—Chill—then Stupor—then the letting go.
                                              [*c.* 1862]

435

M uch Madness is divinest Sense—
To a discerning Eye—
Much Sense—the starkest Madness—
'Tis the Majority
In this, as All, prevail—
Assent—and you are sane—
Demur—you're straightway dangerous—
And handled with a Chain—

[*c.* 1862]

449

I died for Beauty—but was scarce
Adjusted in the Tomb
When One who died for Truth, was lain
In an adjoining Room—

He questioned softly "Why I failed"?
"For Beauty", I replied—
"And I—for Truth—Themself are One—
We Brethren, are", He said—

And so, as Kinsmen, met a Night—
We talked between the Rooms—   10
Until the Moss had reached our lips—
And covered up—our names—

[*c.* 1862]

712

B ecause I could not stop for Death—
He kindly stopped for me—
The Carriage held but just Ourselves—
And Immortality.

We slowly drove—He knew not haste
And I had put away
My labor and my leisure too,
For His Civility—

We passed the School, where Children strove
At Recess—in the Ring— 10
We passed the Fields of Gazing Grain—
We passed the Setting Sun—

Or rather—He passed Us—
The Dews drew quivering and chill—
For only Gossamer,[1] my Gown—
My Tippet[2]—only Tulle[3]—

We paused before a House that seemed
A Swelling of the Ground—
The Roof was scarcely visible—
The Cornice—in the Ground— 20

Since then—'tis Centuries—and yet
Feels shorter than the Day
I first surmised the Horses' Heads
Were toward Eternity—

[c. 1863]

---

[1] the filmiest of fabrics   [2] a scarf   [3] a thin netted fabric

754

M Y L I F E had stood—a Loaded Gun—
In Corners—till a Day
The Owner passed—identified—
And carried Me away—

And now We roam in Sovereign Woods—
And now We hunt the Doe—
And every time I speak for Him—
The Mountains straight reply—

And do I smile, such cordial light
Upon the Valley glow— 10
It is as a Vesuvian face
Had let its pleasure through—

And when at Night—Our good Day done—
I guard My Master's Head—
'Tis better than the Eider-Duck's
Deep Pillow—to have shared—

To foe of His—I'm deadly foe—
None stir the second time—
On whom I lay a Yellow Eye—
Or an emphatic Thumb—   20

Though I than He—may longer live
He longer must—than I—
For I have but the power to kill,
Without—the power to die—

[1863?]

764

PRESENTIMENT—is that long Shadow—on
    the Lawn—
Indicative that Suns go down—

The Notice to the startled Grass
That Darkness—is about to pass—

[c. 1863]

861

SPLIT the Lark—and you'll find the Music—
  Bulb after Bulb, in Silver rolled—
Scantily dealt to the Summer Morning
Saved for your Ear when Lutes be old.

Loose the Flood—you shall find it patent—
Gush after Gush, reserved for you—
Scarlet Experiment! Sceptic Thomas!
Now, do you doubt that your Bird was true?

[1864?]

875

I STEPPED from Plank to Plank
  A slow and cautious way
The Stars about my Head I felt
About my Feet the Sea.

I knew not but the next
Would be my final inch—
This gave me that precarious Gait
Some call Experience.

[1864?]

986

A NARROW Fellow in the Grass
    Occasionally rides—
You may have met Him—did you not
His notice sudden is—

The Grass divides as with a Comb—
A spotted shaft is seen—
And then it closes at your feet
And opens further on—

He likes a Boggy Acre
A Floor too cool for Corn—   10
Yet when a Boy, and Barefoot—
I more than once at Noon
Have passed, I thought, a Whip lash
Unbraiding in the Sun
When stooping to secure it
It wrinkled, and was gone—

Several of Nature's People
I know, and they know me—
I feel for them a transport
Of cordiality—   20

But never met this Fellow
Attended, or alone
Without a tighter breathing
And Zero at the Bone—

                                        [c. 1865]

1078

THE Bustle in a House
    The Morning after Death
Is solemnest of industries
Enacted upon Earth—

The Sweeping up the Heart
And putting Love away
We shall not want to use again
Until Eternity.

                                        [c. 1866]

1129

TELL all the Truth but tell it slant—
Success in Circuit lies
Too bright for our infirm Delight
The Truth's superb surprise

As Lightning to the Children eased
With explanation kind
The Truth must dazzle gradually
Or every man be blind—

[1868?]

Christina Rossetti
1830–1894

THREE SEASONS

"A CUP for hope!" she said,
In springtime ere the bloom was old;
The crimson wine was poor and cold
    By her mouth's richer red.

"A cup for love!" how low,
How soft the words; and all the while
Her blush was rippling with a smile
    Like summer after snow.

"A cup for memory!"
Cold cup that one must drain alone: 10
While autumn winds are up and moan
    Across the barren sea.

Hope, memory, love:
Hope for fair morn, and love for day,
And memory for the evening gray
    And solitary dove.

[1853]

AFTER DEATH

THE curtains were half drawn, the floor was swept
And strewn with rushes, rosemary and may[1]
Lay thick upon the bed on which I lay,
Where through the lattice ivy-shadows crept.
He leaned above me, thinking that I slept
And could not hear him; but I heard him say:
"Poor child, poor child": and as he turned away
Came a deep silence, and I knew he wept.
He did not touch the shroud, or raise the fold
That hid my face, or take my hand in his,   10
Or ruffle the smooth pillows for my head:
He did not love me living; but once dead
He pitied me; and very sweet it is
To know he still is warm though I am cold.

[1849]

[1] hawthorn blossoms

A BIRTHDAY

MY HEART is like a singing bird
Whose nest is in a watered shoot;
My heart is like an apple-tree
Whose boughs are bent with thickset fruit;
My heart is like a rainbow shell
That paddles in a halcyon sea;
My heart is gladder than all these,
Because my love is come to me.

Raise me a daïs of silk and down;
Hang it with vair[1] and purple dyes;   10
Carve it in doves and pomegranates,
And peacocks with a hundred eyes;
Work it in gold and silver grapes,
In leaves and silver fleur-de-lys;
Because the birthday of my life
Is come, my love is come to me.

[1857]

[1] costly fur

Lewis Carroll
1832–1898

◇

F R O M

THROUGH THE LOOKING-GLASS

◇

JABBERWOCKY

'Twas brillig,[1] and the slithy toves
   Did gyre and gimble in the wabe;
All mimsy were the borogoves,
   And the mome raths outgrabe.

"Beware the Jabberwock, my son!
   The jaws that bite, the claws that catch!
Beware the Jubjub bird, and shun
   The frumious Bandersnatch!"

He took his vorpal sword in hand;
   Long time the manxome foe he sought—   10
So rested he by the Tumtum tree,
   And stood awhile in thought.

And, as in uffish thought he stood,
   The Jabberwock, with eyes of flame,
Came whiffling through the tulgey wood,
   And burbled as it came!

[1] In *Through the Looking-Glass*, where "Jabberwocky" appears, Carroll offers the following explanations of some of the words in the poem:

brillig: four o' clock in the afternoon, when you begin broiling things for dinner
slithy: lithe and slimy; a "portmanteau word" which packs up two meanings into
   one word
toves: something like badgers, something like lizards, something like corkscrews
gyre: to go round and round like a gyroscope
gimble: to make holes like a gimlet
wabe: the grass plot around a sundial: it goes a long way before it, a long way behind it, and a long way beyond it on each side
mimsy: flimsy and miserable
borogove: a thin shabby-looking bird with its feathers sticking out all round, something like a live mop
mome: perhaps short for "from home," meaning that they had lost their way
rath: a sort of green pig
outgrabe: past tense of "outgribe," something between to bellow and to whistle,
   with a kind of sneeze in the middle

One, two! One, two! And through and through
  The vorpal blade went snicker-snack!
He left it dead, and with its head
  He went galumphing back.   20

"And hast thou slain the Jabberwock?
  Come to my arms, my beamish boy!
O frabjous day! Callooh! Callay!"
  He chortled in his joy.

'Twas brillig, and the slithy toves
  Did gyre and gimble in the wabe;
All mimsy were the borogoves,
  And the mome raths outgrabe.

[1855]

Thomas Hardy

1840–1928

HAP

IF BUT some vengeful god would call to me
From up the sky, and laugh: "Thou suffering thing,
Know that thy sorrow is my ecstasy,
That thy love's loss is my hate's profiting!"
Then would I bear it, clench myself, and die,
Steeled by the sense of ire unmerited;
Half-eased in that a Powerfuller than I
Had willed and meted me the tears I shed.

But not so. How arrives it joy lies slain,
And why unblooms the best hope ever sown?   10
—Crass Casualty obstructs the sun and rain,
And dicing Time for gladness casts a moan. . . .
These purblind Doomsters had as readily strown
Blisses about my pilgrimage as pain.

[1866]

NEUTRAL TONES

WE STOOD by a pond that winter day,
And the sun was white, as though chidden of God,
And a few leaves lay on the starving sod;
—They had fallen from an ash, and were gray.

Your eyes on me were as eyes that rove
Over tedious riddles of years ago;
And some words played between us to and fro
On which lost the more by our love.

The smile on your mouth was the deadest thing
Alive enough to have strength to die;   10
And a grin of bitterness swept thereby
Like an ominous bird a-wing. . . .

Since then, keen lessons that love deceives,
And wrings with wrong, have shaped to me
Your face, and the God curst sun, and a tree,
And a pond edge with grayish leaves.

[1867]

DRUMMER HODGE

THEY throw in Drummer Hodge, to rest
    Uncoffined—just as found:
His landmark is a kopje-crest[1]
    That breaks the veldt around:
And foreign constellations west
    Each night above his mound.

Young Hodge the Drummer never knew—
    Fresh from his Wessex home—
The meaning of the broad Karoo,[2]
    The Bush, the dusty loam,   10
And why uprose to nightly view
    Strange stars amid the gloam.

Yet portion of that unknown plain
    Will Hodge forever be;
His homely Northern breast and brain
    Grow to some Southern tree,
And strange-eyed constellations reign
    His stars eternally.

[1902]

[1] hillock (pron. kŏp′ĭ)   [2] a dry plateau in South Africa

THE DARKLING THRUSH
DECEMBER 31, 1900

I LEANT upon a coppice[1] gate
    When Frost was specter-gray,
And Winter's dregs made desolate
    The weakening eye of day.
The tangled bine-stems[2] scored the sky
    Like strings of broken lyres,
And all mankind that haunted nigh
    Had sought their household fires.

[1] a small thicket   [2] the wirelike shoots of a climbing plant

The land's sharp features seemed to be
    The Century's corpse outleant,   10
His crypt the cloudy canopy,
    The wind his death-lament.
The ancient pulse of germ and birth
    Was shrunken hard and dry,
And every spirit upon earth
    Seemed fervorless as I.

At once a voice arose among
    The bleak twigs overhead
In a full-hearted evensong
    Of joy illimited;   20
An agéd thrush, frail, gaunt, and small,
    In blast-beruffled plume,
Had chosen thus to fling his soul
    Upon the growing gloom.

So little cause for carolings
    Of such ecstatic sound
Was written on terrestrial things
    Afar or nigh around,
That I could think there trembled through
    His happy good-night air   30
Some blessed Hope, whereof he knew
    And I was unaware.

                                  [1902]

THE MAN HE KILLED

H<small>AD</small> he and I but met
    By some old ancient inn,
We should have sat us down to wet
    Right many a nipperkin![1]

"But ranged as infantry,
    And staring face to face,
I shot at him as he at me,
    And killed him in his place.

"I shot him dead because—
    Because he was my foe,   10
Just so: my foe of course he was;
    That's clear enough; although

[1] a half-pint glass for beer or ale

"He thought he'd 'list, perhaps,
Offhand like—just as I—
Was out of work—had sold his traps—
No other reason why.

"Yes; quaint and curious war is!
You shoot a fellow down
You'd treat if met where any bar is,
Or help to half-a-crown."   20

[1902]

AH, ARE YOU DIGGING ON MY GRAVE?

"Ah, are you digging on my grave
      My loved one?—planting rue?"
—"*No : yesterday he went to wed
One of the brightest wealth has bred.
'It cannot hurt her now,' he said,
      'That I should not be true.'*"

"Then who is digging on my grave?
      My nearest, dearest kin?"
—"*Ah, no : they sit and think, 'What use!
What good will planting flowers produce   10
No tendance of her mound can loose
      Her spirit from Death's gin.*[1]*'*"

"But someone digs upon my grave?
      My enemy?—prodding sly?"
—"*Nay : when she heard you had passed the Gate
That shuts on all flesh soon or late,
She thought you no more worth her hate,
      She cares not where you lie.*"

"Then, who is digging on my grave?
      Say—since I have not guessed!"   20
—"*O it is I, my mistress dear,
Your little dog, who still lives near,
And much I hope my movements here
      Have not disturbed your rest?*"

"Ah, yes! *You* dig upon my grave. . . .
      Why flashed it not on me

[1] snare

That one true heart was left behind!
What feeling do we ever find
To equal among human kind
    A dog's fidelity!"   30

    "Mistress, I dug upon your grave
       To bury a bone, in case
    I should be hungry near this spot
    When passing on my daily trot.
    I am sorry, but I quite forgot
       It was your resting-place."

[1914]

CHANNEL FIRING

THAT night your great guns, unawares,
  Shook all our coffins as we lay,
And broke the chancel window squares,
We thought it was the Judgment-day

And sat upright. While drearisome
Arose the howl of wakened hounds:
The mouse let fall the altar-crumb,
The worms drew back into the mounds,

The glebe cow drooled. Till God called, "No;
It's gunnery practice out at sea   10
Just as before you went below;
The world is as it used to be:

"All nations striving strong to make
Red war yet redder. Mad as hatters
They do no more for Christés sake
Than you who are helpless in such matters.

"That this is not the judgment-hour
For some of them's a blesséd thing,
For if it were they'd have to scour
Hell's floor for so much threatening . . .   20

"Ha, ha. It will be warmer when
I blow the trumpet (if indeed
I ever do; for you are men,
And rest eternal sorely need)."

So down we lay again. "I wonder,
Will the world ever saner be,"
Said one, "than when He sent us under
In our indifferent century!"

And many a skeleton shook his head.
"Instead of preaching forty years,"   30
My neighbor Parson Thirdly said,
"I wish I had stuck to pipes and beer."

Again the guns disturbed the hour,
Roaring their readiness to avenge,
As far inland as Stourton Tower,[1]
And Camelot,[2] and starlit Stonehenge.[3]

[1914]

---

[1] memorial to King Alfred   [2] legendary capital of King Arthur
[3] ancient temple of massive upright stones on Salisbury Plain

Gerard Manley Hopkins
1844–1889

HEAVEN-HAVEN

A NUN TAKES THE VEIL

I HAVE desired to go
        Where springs not fail,
To fields where flies no sharp and sided hail
    And a few lilies blow.

And I have asked to be
        Where no storms come,
Where the green swell is in the havens dumb,
    And out of the swing of the sea.

[1865]

GOD'S GRANDEUR

THE world is charged with the grandeur of God.
    It will flame out, like shining from shook foil;
It gathers to a greatness, like the ooze of oil
Crushed. Why do men then now not reck his rod?

Generations have trod, have trod, have trod;
And all is seared with trade; bleared, smeared with toil;
And wears man's smudge and shares man's smell: the soil
Is bare now, nor can foot feel, being shod.
And for all this, nature is never spent;
There lives the dearest freshness deep down things;   10
And though the last lights off the black West went
Oh, morning, at the brown brink eastward, springs—
Because the Holy Ghost over the bent
World broods with warm breast and with ah! bright wings.

[1877]

THE STARLIGHT NIGHT

LOOK at the stars! look, look up at the skies!
O look at all the fire-folk sitting in the air!
The bright boroughs, the circle-citadels there!
Down in dim woods the diamond delves![1] the elves'-eyes!
The gray lawns cold where gold, where quickgold lies!
Wind-beat whitebeam! airy abeles[2] set on a flare!
Flake-doves sent floating forth at a farmyard scare!—
Ah well! it is all a purchase, all is a prize.
Buy then! bid then!—What?—Prayer, patience, alms, vows.
Look, look: a May-mess, like on orchard boughs!   10
Look! March-bloom, like on mealed-with-yellow sallows![3]
These are indeed the barn; withindoors house
The shocks. This piece-bright[4] paling shuts the spouse
Christ home, Christ and his mother and all his hallows.[5]

[1877]

[1] pits or mines   [2] white poplars   [3] willows   [4] gleaming like a coin
[5] saints

SPRING

NOTHING is so beautiful as spring—
When weeds, in wheels, shoot long and lovely and lush;
Thrush's eggs look little low heavens, and thrush
Through the echoing timber does so rinse and wring
The ear, it strikes like lightnings to hear him sing;
The glassy peartree leaves and blooms, they brush
The descending blue; that blue is all in a rush
With richness; the racing lambs too have fair their fling.

What is all this juice and all this joy?
A strain of the earth's sweet being in the beginning   10
In Eden garden. —Have, get, before it cloy,
Before it cloud, Christ, lord, and sour with sinning,
Innocent mind and Mayday in girl and boy,
Most, O maid's child, thy choice and worthy the winning.

[1877]

THE WINDHOVER:

TO CHRIST OUR LORD

I CAUGHT this morning morning's minion, king-
    dom of daylight's dauphin, dapple-dawn-drawn Falcon, in his
    riding Of the rolling level underneath him steady air, and striding
High there, how he rung upon the rein of a wimpling wing
In his ecstasy! then off, off forth on swing,
    As a skate's heel sweeps smooth on a bow-bend: the hurl and
        gliding
    Rebuffed the big wind. My heart in hiding
Stirred for a bird,—the achieve of, the mastery of the thing!

Brute beauty and valor and act, oh, air, pride, plume, here
    Buckle! AND the fire that breaks from thee then, a billion   10
Times told lovelier, more dangerous, O my chevalier!

    No wonder of it: sheer plod makes plow down sillion[1]
Shine, and blue-bleak embers, ah my dear,
    Fall, gall themselves, and gash gold-vermillion.

[1877]

[1] the ridge between two furrows

PIED BEAUTY

GLORY be to God for dappled things—
    For skies of couple-color as a brinded[1] cow;
        For rose-moles all in stipple[2] upon trout that swim;
Fresh-firecoal chestnut-falls;[3] finches' wings;
    Landscape plotted and pieced—fold, fallow, and plow;
        And áll trádes, their gear and tackle and trim.

[1] streaked or spotted   [2] shading with small dots
[3] fallen chestnuts as bright as coals of fire

All things counter, original, spare, strange;
  Whatever is fickle, freckled (who knows how?)
    With swift, slow; sweet, sour; adazzle, dim;
He fathers-forth whose beauty is past change: 10
        Praise him.

[1877]

THE CANDLE INDOORS

Some candle clear burns somewhere I come by.
  I muse at how its being puts blissful back
With yellowy moisture mild night's blear-all black,
Or to-fro tender trambeams truckle at the eye.

By that window what task what fingers ply,
  I plod wondering, a-wanting, just for lack
Of answer the eagerer a-wanting Jessy or Jack
There / God to aggrándise, God to glorify.—

Come you indoors, come home; your fading fire
  Mend first and vital candle in close heart's vault: 10
You there are master, do your own desire;

What hinders? Are you beam-blind, yet to a fault
  In a neighbor deft-handed? are you that liar
And, cast by conscience out, spendsavor salt?

[1879]

"I WAKE AND FEEL THE FELL OF DARK"

I wake and feel the fell of dark, not day.
  What hours, O what black hoürs we have spent
This night! what sights you, heart, saw; ways you went
And more must, in yet longer light's delay.

With witness I speak this. But where I say
  Hours I mean years, mean life. And my lament
Is cries countless, cries like dead letters sent
To dearest him that lives alas! away.

I am gall, I am heartburn. God's most deep decree
  Bitter would have me taste: my taste was me;   10
Bones built in me, flesh filled, blood brimmed the curse.

Selfyeast of spirit a dull dough sours, I see
The lost are like this, and their scourge to be
As I am mine, their sweating selves; but worse.

[1885]

A. E. Housman
1859–1936
LOVELIEST OF TREES

LOVELIEST of trees, the cherry now
Is hung with bloom along the bough,
And stands about the woodland ride,
Wearing white for Eastertide.

Now, of my threescore years and ten,
Twenty will not come again,
And take from seventy springs a score,
It only leaves me fifty more.

And since to look at things in bloom
Fifty springs are little room,   10
About the woodlands I will go
To see the cherry hung with snow.

[1896]

WHEN I WAS ONE-AND-TWENTY

WHEN I was one-and-twenty
I heard a wise man say,
"Give crowns and pounds and guineas
But not your heart away;
Give pearls away and rubies
But keep your fancy free."
But I was one-and-twenty,
No use to talk to me.

When I was one-and-twenty
I heard him say again,   10
"The heart out of the bosom
Was never given in vain;

'Tis paid with sighs a plenty
        And sold for endless rue."
And I am two-and-twenty,
        And oh, 'tis true, 'tis true.

[1896]

ON THE IDLE HILL OF SUMMER

ON the idle hill of summer,
        Sleepy with the flow of streams,
Far I hear the steady drummer
        Drumming like a noise in dreams.

Far and near and low and louder
        On the roads of earth go by,
Dear to friends and food for powder,
        Soldiers marching, all to die.

East and west on fields forgotten
        Bleach the bones of comrades slain,   10
Lovely lads and dead and rotten;
        None that go return again.

Far the calling bugles hollo,
        High the screaming fife replies,
Gay the files of scarlet follow:
        Woman bore me, I will rise.

[1896]

ON WENLOCK EDGE

ON Wenlock Edge[1] the wood's in trouble;
        His forest fleece the Wrekin[2] heaves;
The gale, it plies the saplings double,
And thick on Severn[3] snow the leaves.

'Twould blow like this through holt[4] and hangar[5]
When Uricon[6] the city stood:
'Tis the old wind in the old anger,
But then it threshed another wood.

[1] a long ridge in Shropshire   [2] a hill
[3] river flowing through Shropshire for a part of its course
[4] woods   [5] shelter, such as a shed   [6] Roman fortress town

Then, 'twas before my time, the Roman
At yonder heaving hill would stare: 10
The blood that warms an English yeoman,
The thoughts that hurt him, they were there.

There, like the wind through woods in riot,
Through him the gale of life blew high;
The tree of man was never quiet:
Then 'twas the Roman, now 'tis I.

The gale, it plies the saplings double,
It blows so hard, 'twill soon be gone:
Today the Roman and his trouble
Are ashes under Uricon.   20
                                                    [1896]

TO AN ATHLETE DYING YOUNG

THE time you won your town the race
We chaired you through the market-place;
Man and boy stood cheering by,
And home we brought you shoulder-high.

Today, the road all runners come,
Shoulder-high we bring you home,
And set you at your threshold down,
Townsman of a stiller town.

Smart lad, to slip betimes away
From fields where glory does not stay,   10
And early though the laurel grows
It withers quicker than the rose.

Eyes the shady night has shut
Cannot see the record cut,
And silence sounds no worse than cheers
After earth has stopped the ears.

Now you will not swell the rout
Of lads that wore their honors out,
Runners whom renown outran
And the name died before the man.   20

So set, before its echoes fade,
The fleet foot on the sill of shade,
And hold to the low lintel up
The still-defended challenge-cup.

And round that early-laurelled head
Will flock to gaze the strengthless dead,
And find unwithered on its curls
The garland briefer than a girl's.

[1896]

1887

FROM Clee to heaven the beacon burns,
    The shires have seen it plain,
From north and south the sign returns
    And beacons burn again.

Look left, look right, the hills are bright,
    The dales are light between,
Because 'tis fifty years tonight[1]
    That God has saved the Queen.

Now, when the flame they watch not towers
    About the soil they trod,   10
Lads, we'll remember friends of ours
    Who shared the work with God.

To skies that knit their heartstrings right,
    To fields that bred them brave,
The saviors come not home to-night :
    Themselves they could not save.[2]

It dawns in Asia, tombstones show
    And Shropshire names are read ;
And the Nile spills his overflow
    Beside the Severn's dead.   20

We pledge in peace by farm and town
    The Queen they served in war,
And fire the beacons up and down
    The land they perished for.

[1] Queen Victoria succeeded to the throne on June 20, 1837.   [2] Matthew 27:42

> "God save the Queen" we living sing,
>   From height to height 'tis heard;
> And with the rest your voices ring,
>   Lads of the Fifty-third.
>
> Oh, God will save her, fear you not:
>   Be you the men you've been,   30
> Get you the sons your fathers got,
>   And God will save the Queen.

[1896]

Rudyard Kipling
1865–1936

DANNY DEEVER

"WHAT are the bugles blowin' for?" said Files-on-Parade.
    "To turn you out, to turn you out," the Color-Sergeant said.
"What makes you look so white, so white?" said Files-on-Parade.
"I'm dreadin' what I've got to watch," the Color-Sergeant said.
    For they're hangin' Danny Deever, you can 'ear the Dead March
        play,
    The regiment's in 'ollow square— they're hangin' him today;
    They've taken of his buttons off an' cut his stripes away,
    An' they're hangin' Danny Deever in the mornin'.

"What makes the rear-rank breathe so 'ard?" said Files-on-Parade.
"It's bitter cold, it's bitter cold," the Color-Sergeant said.   10
"What makes that front-rank man fall down?" says Files-on-Parade.
"A touch of sun, a touch of sun," the Color-Sergeant said.
    They are hangin' Danny Deever, they are marchin' of 'im round.
    They 'ave 'alted Danny Deever by 'is coffin on the ground;
    An 'e'll swing in 'arf a minute for a sneakin', shootin' hound—
    O they're hangin' Danny Deever in the mornin'!

" 'Is cot was right-' and cot to mine," said Files-on-Parade.
" 'E's sleepin' out an' far tonight," the Color-Sergeant said.
"I've drunk 'is beer a score o' times," said Files-on-Parade.
" 'E's drinkin' bitter beer alone," the Color-Sergeant said.   20
    They are hangin' Danny Deever, you must mark 'im to 'is place,
    For 'e shot a comrade sleepin'—you must look 'im in the face;
    Nine 'undred of 'is county an' the regiment's disgrace,
    While they're hangin' Danny Deever in the mornin'.'

"What's that so black agin the sun?" said Files-on-Parade.
"It's Danny fightin' 'ard for life," the Color-Sergeant said.
"What's that that whimpers over'ead?" said Files-on-Parade.
"It's Danny's soul that's passin' now," the Color-Sergeant said.
  For they're done with Danny Deever, you can 'ear the quickstep
    play,
  The regiment's in column, an' they're marchin' us away;   30
  Ho! the young recruits are shakin', an' they'll want their beer today,
  After hangin' Danny Deever in the mornin'.

                                                                    [1890]

L'ENVOI

WHEN Earth's last picture is painted, and the tubes are twisted and
    dried,
When the oldest colors have faded, and the youngest critic has died,
We shall rest, and, faith, we shall need it—lie down for an æon or two,
Till the Master of All Good Workmen shall set us to work anew!

And those that were good shall be happy: they shall sit in a golden chair;
They shall splash at a ten-league canvas with brushes of comet's hair;
They shall find real saints to draw from—Magdalene, Peter, and Paul;
They shall work for an age at a sitting and never be tired at all!

And only the Master shall praise us, and only the Master shall blame;
And no one shall work for money, and no one shall work for fame;   10
But each for the joy of the working, and each, in his separate star,
Shall draw the Thing as he sees It for the God of Things as They are!

                                                                    [1892]

RECESSIONAL

GOD of our fathers, known of old,
    Lord of our far-flung battle-line,
Beneath whose awful Hand we hold
    Dominion over palm and pine—
Lord God of Hosts, be with us yet,
Lest we forget—lest we forget!

The tumult and the shouting dies;
    The captains and the kings depart:
Still stands Thine ancient sacrifice,
    An humble and a contrite heart.   10
Lord God of Hosts, be with us yet,
Lest we forget—lest we forget!

Far-called, our navies melt away;
  On dune and headland sinks the fire:
Lo, all our pomp of yesterday
  Is one with Nineveh and Tyre!
Judge of the Nations, spare us yet,
Lest we forget—lest we forget!

If, drunk with sight of power, we loose
  Wild tongues that have not Thee in awe,   20
Such boastings as the Gentiles use,
  Or lesser breeds without the Law—
Lord God of Hosts, be with us yet,
Lest we forget—lest we forget!

For heathen heart that puts her trust
  In reeking tube and iron shard,
All valiant dust that builds on dust,
  And guarding, calls not Thee to guard,
For frantic boast and foolish word—
They mercy on Thy people, Lord!   30
                                                [1897]

THE WAY THROUGH THE WOODS

THEY shut the road through the woods
    Seventy years ago.
Weather and rain have undone it again,
And now you would never know
There was once a road through the woods
Before they planted the trees.
It is underneath the coppice and heath
And the thin anemones.
Only the keeper sees
That, where the ring-dove broods,   10
And the badgers roll at ease,
There was once a road through the woods.
Yet, if you enter the woods
Of a summer evening late,
When the night-air cools on the trout-ringed pools
Where the otter whistles his mate,
(They fear not men in the woods,
Because they see so few.)
You will hear the beat of a horse's feet,
And the swish of a skirt in the dew,   20
Steadily cantering through

The misty solitudes,
As though they perfectly knew
The old lost road through the woods. . . .
But there is no road through the woods.

William Butler Yeats
1865–1939

THE LAKE ISLE OF INNISFREE

I WILL arise and go now, and go to Innisfree,
And a small cabin build there, of clay and wattles made :
Nine bean-rows will I have there, a hive for the honey bee,
And live alone in the bee-loud glade.

And I shall have some peace there, for peace comes dropping slow,
Dropping from the veils of the morning to where the cricket sings ;
There midnight's all a glimmer, and noon a purple glow,
And evening full of the linnet's wings.

I will arise and go now, for always night and day
I hear lake water lapping with low sounds by the shore ;   10
While I stand on the roadway, or on the pavements gray,
I hear it in the deep heart's core.

THE WILD SWANS AT COOLE[1]

THE trees are in their autumn beauty,
The woodland paths are dry,
Under the October twilight the water
Mirrors a still sky ;
Upon the brimming water among the stones
Are nine-and-fifty swans.

The nineteenth autumn has come upon me
Since I first made my count ;
I saw, before I had well finished,
All suddenly mount   10
And scatter wheeling in great broken rings
Upon their clamorous wings.

[1] Coole Park in Galway was the estate of Lady Augusta Gregory. Yeats spent a number of summers as her guest.

I have looked upon those brilliant creatures,
And now my heart is sore.
All's changed since I, hearing at twilight,
The first time on this shore,
The bell-beat of their wings above my head,
Trod with a lighter tread.

Unwearied still, lover by lover,
They paddle in the cold   20
Companionable streams or climb the air;
Their hearts have not grown old;
Passion or conquest, wander where they will,
Attend upon them still.

But now they drift on the still water,
Mysterious, beautiful;
Among what rushes will they build,
By what lake's edge or pool
Delight men's eyes when I awake some day
To find they have flown away?   30
[1916]

THE SECOND COMING

TURNING and turning in the widening gyre[1]
The falcon cannot hear the falconer;
Things fall apart; the center cannot hold;
Mere anarchy is loosed upon the world,
The blood-dimmed tide is loosed, and everywhere
The ceremony of innocence is drowned;
The best lack all conviction, while the worst
Are full of passionate intensity.

Surely some revelation is at hand;
Surely the Second Coming is at hand.   10
The Second Coming! Hardly are those words out
When a vast image out of *Spiritus Mundi*[2]
Troubles my sight: somewhere in sands of the desert
A shape with lion body and the head of a man,
A gaze blank and pitiless as the sun,
Is moving its slow thighs, while all about it

[1] a centrifugal motion which Yeats associates with the conclusion of a cycle of history
[2] the soul of the world, a reservoir of the racial memory

Reel shadows of the indignant desert birds.
The darkness drops again; but now I know
That twenty centuries of stony sleep
Were vexed to nightmare by a rocking cradle,   20
And what rough beast, its hour come round at last,
Slouches towards Bethlehem to be born?

[1921]

SAILING TO BYZANTIUM[1]

THAT is no country for old men. The young
     In one another's arms, birds in the trees
—Those dying generations—at their song,
The salmon-falls, the mackerel-crowded seas,
Fish, flesh, or fowl, commend all summer long
Whatever is begotten, born, and dies.
Caught in that sensual music all neglect
Monuments of unageing intellect.

An agéd man is but a paltry thing,
A tattered coat upon a stick, unless   10
Soul clap its hands and sing, and louder sing
For every tatter in its mortal dress,
Nor is there singing school but studying
Monuments of its own magnificence;
And therefore I have sailed the seas and come
To the holy city of Byzantium.

O sages standing in God's holy fire
As in the gold mosaic of a wall,
Come from the holy fire, perne in a gyre,[2]
And be the singing-masters of my soul.   20
Consume my heart away; sick with desire
And fastened to a dying animal
It knows not what it is; and gather me
Into the artifice of eternity.

Once out of nature I shall never take
My bodily form from any natural thing,
But such a form as Grecian goldsmiths make
Of hammered gold and gold enamelling
To keep a drowsy Emperor awake;

[1] for Yeats, a symbol of the integrity of life perfected by art, and "out of nature"
—i.e., the realm of "the artifice of eternity"
[2] turn in the helix of fate

Or set upon a golden bough to sing   30
To lords and ladies of Byzantium
Of what is past, or passing, or to come.

[1928]

LEDA[1] AND THE SWAN

A SUDDEN blow: the great wings beating still
  Above the staggering girl, her thighs caressed
By the dark web, her nape caught in his bill,
He holds her helpless breast upon his breast.

How can those terrified vague fingers push
The feathered glory from her loosening thighs?
And how can body, laid in that white rush,
But feel the strange heart beating where it lies?

A shudder in the loins engenders there
The broken wall, the burning roof and tower   10
And Agamemnon dead.
                 Being so caught up,
So mastered by the brute blood of the air,
Did she put on his knowledge with his power
Before the indifferent beak could let her drop?

[1928]

[1] Ravished by Zeus in the form of a swan, she gave birth to Helen of Troy and to Clytemnestra, who murdered her husband Agamemnon, after his return from the Trojan War.

CRAZY JANE TALKS WITH THE BISHOP

I MET the Bishop on the road
  And much said he and I.
"Those breasts are flat and fallen now,
  Those veins must soon be dry;
Live in a heavenly mansion,
  Not in some foul sty."

"Fair and foul are near of kin,
  And fair needs foul," I cried.
"My friends are gone, but that's a truth
  Nor grave nor bed denied,   10
Learned in bodily lowliness
  And in the heart's pride.

"A woman can be proud and stiff
When on love intent;
But Love has pitched his mansion in
The place of excrement;
For nothing can be sole or whole
That has not been rent."

[1933]

BEAUTIFUL LOFTY THINGS

BEAUTIFUL lofty things: O'Leary's[1] noble head;
My father upon the Abbey[2] stage, before him a raging crowd:
"This Land of Saints," and then as the applause died out,
"Of plaster Saints"; his beautiful mischievous head thrown back.
Standish O'Grady[3] supporting himself between the tables
Speaking to a drunken audience high nonsensical words;
Augusta Gregory[4] seated at her great ormolu table,
Her eightieth winter approaching: "Yesterday he threatened my life.
I told him that nightly from six to seven I sat at this table,
The blinds drawn up"; Maud Gonne[5] at Howth station waiting a train,
Pallas Athene in that straight back and arrogant head: 11
All the Olympians; a thing never known again.

[1939]

[1] John O'Leary, Irish nationalist leader in politics and the literary revival
[2] The Abbey Theatre, Dublin, home of the Irish National Theatre company, which Yeats managed for a time, and which produced his early plays
[3] Irish nationalist historian and associate of Yeats in the Irish literary revival of the early twentieth century
[4] playwright, associate of Yeats in the management of the Abbey Theatre, and his long-time friend and patron
[5] actress and Irish nationalist, whom Yeats loved and wooed unsuccessfully for many years

HOUND VOICE

BECAUSE we love bare hills and stunted trees
And were the last to choose the settled ground,
Its boredom of the desk or of the spade, because
So many years companioned by a hound,
Our voices carry; and though slumber-bound,
Some few half wake and half renew their choice,
Give tongue, proclaim their hidden name—"Hound Voice."

The women that I picked spoke sweet and low
And yet gave tongue. "Hound Voices" were they all.
We picked each other from afar and knew   10
What hour of terror comes to test the soul,
And in that terror's name obeyed the call,
And understood, what none have understood,
Those images that waken in the blood.

Some day we shall get up before the dawn
And find our ancient hounds before the door,
And wide awake know that the hunt is on;
Stumbling upon the blood-dark track once more,
Then stumbling to the kill beside the shore;
Then cleaning out and bandaging of wounds,   20
And chants of victory amid the encircling hounds.

[1939]

Edwin Arlington Robinson
1869–1935

LUKE HAVERGAL

Go to the western gate, Luke Havergal,
There where the vines cling crimson on the wall,
And in the twilight wait for what will come.
The leaves will whisper there of her, and some,
Like flying words, will strike you as they fall;
But go, and if you listen she will call.
Go to the western gate, Luke Havergal—
Luke Havergal.

No, there is not a dawn in eastern skies
To rift the fiery night that's in your eyes;   10
But there, where western glooms are gathering,
The dark will end the dark, if anything:
God slays Himself with every leaf that flies,
And hell is more than half of paradise.
No, there is not a dawn in eastern skies—
In eastern skies.

Out of a grave I come to tell you this,
Out of a grave I come to quench the kiss
That flames upon your forehead with a glow
That blinds you to the way that you must go.   20

Yes, there is yet one way to where she is,
Bitter, but one that faith may never miss.
Out of a grave I come to tell you this—
To tell you this.

There is the western gate, Luke Havergal,
There are the crimson leaves upon the wall.
Go, for the winds are tearing them away,—
Nor think to riddle the dead words they say,
Nor any more to feel them as they fall;
But go, and if you trust her she will call.   30
There is the western gate, Luke Havergal—
Luke Havergal.

[1896]

RICHARD CORY

WHENEVER Richard Cory went down town,
        We people on the pavement looked at him:
He was a gentleman from sole to crown,
Clean favored, and imperially slim.

And he was always quietly arrayed,
And he was always human when he talked;
But still he fluttered pulses when he said,
"Good-morning," and he glittered when he walked.

And he was rich—yes, richer than a king—
And admirably schooled in every grace: 10
In fine, we thought that he was everything
To make us wish that we were in his place.

So on we worked, and waited for the light,
And went without the meat, and cursed the bread;
And Richard Cory, one calm summer night,
Went home and put a bullet through his head.

[1897]

HOW ANNANDALE WENT OUT

THEY called it Annandale—and I was there
       To flourish, to find words, and to attend:
Liar, physician, hypocrite, and friend,
I watched him; and the sight was not so fair

As one or two that I had seen elsewhere :
An apparatus not for me to mend—
A wreck, with hell between him and the end,
Remained of Annandale ; and I was there.
I knew the ruin as I knew the man ;
So put the two together, if you can,   10
Remembering the worst you know of me.
Now view yourself as I was, on the spot—
With a slight kind of engine. Do you see?
Like this. . . . You wouldn't hang me? I thought not."

[1910]

THE DARK HILLS

Dᴀʀᴋ hills at evening in the west,
   Where sunset hovers like a sound
Of golden horns that sang to rest
Old bones of warriors under ground,

Far now from all the bannered ways
Where flash the legions of the sun,
You fade—as if the last of days
Were fading, and all wars were done.

[1920]

MR. FLOOD'S PARTY

Oʟᴅ Eben Flood, climbing alone one night
   Over the hill between the town below
And the forsaken upland hermitage
That held as much as he should ever know
On earth again of home, paused warily.
The road was his with not a native near ;
And Eben, having leisure, said aloud,
For no man else in Tilbury Town[1] to hear :

"Well, Mr. Flood, we have the harvest moon
Again, and we may not have many more ;   10
The bird is on the wing, the poet says,
And you and I have said it here before.
Drink to the bird." He raised up to the light
The jug that he had gone so far to fill,
And answered huskily : "Well, Mr. Flood,
Since you propose it, I believe I will."

[1] the fictional site of several of Robinson's poems

Alone, as if enduring to the end
A valiant armor of scarred hopes outworn,
He stood there in the middle of the road
Like Roland's[2] ghost winding a silent horn.   20
Below him, in the town among the trees,
Where friends of other days had honored him,
A phantom salutation of the dead
Rang thinly till old Eben's eyes were dim.

Then, as a mother lays her sleeping child
Down tenderly, fearing it may awake,
He set the jug down slowly at his feet
With trembling care, knowing that most things break ;
And only when assured that on firm earth
It stood, as the uncertain lives of men   30
Assuredly did not, he paced away,
And with his hand extended paused again :

"Well, Mr. Flood, we have not met like this
In a long time ; and many a change has come
To both of us, I fear, since last it was
We had a drop together. Welcome home !"
Convivially returning with himself,
Again he raised the jug up to the light ;
And with an acquiescent quaver said :
"Well, Mr. Flood, if you insist, I might.   40

"Only a very little, Mr. Flood—
For auld lang syne. No more, sir ; that will do."
So, for the time, apparently it did,
And Eben evidently thought so too ;
For soon amid the silver loneliness
Of night he lifted up his voice and sang,
Secure, with only two moons listening,
Until the whole harmonious landscape rang—

"For auld lang syne." The weary throat gave out,
The last word wavered ; and the song being done,   50
He raised again the jug regretfully
And shook his head, and was again alone.
There was not much that was ahead of him,
And there was nothing in the town below—

[2] hero of the medieval French *Song of Roland*, who blew three mighty blasts on his horn to summon aid for his rearguard, who were ambushed at Roncevalles as they covered Charlemagne's retreat from Spain

Where strangers would have shut the many doors
That many friends had opened long ago.

[1921]

THE MILL

THE miller's wife had waited long,
　　The tea was cold, the fire was dead;
And there might yet be nothing wrong
　　In how he went and what he said:
"There are no millers any more,"
　　Was all that she had heard him say;
And he had lingered at the door
　　So long that it seemed yesterday.

Sick with a fear that had no form
　　She knew that she was there at last;　　　10
And in the mill there was a warm
　　And mealy fragrance of the past.
What else there was would only seem
　　To say again what he had meant;
And what was hanging from a beam
　　Would not have heeded where she went.

And if she thought it followed her,
　　She may have reasoned in the dark
That one way of the few there were
　　Would hide her and would leave no mark:　　　20
Black water, smooth above the weir
　　Like starry velvet in the night,
Though ruffled once, would soon appear
　　The same as ever to the sight.

[1920]

Paul Laurence Dunbar
1872–1906

SYMPATHY

I KNOW what the caged bird feels, alas!
　　When the sun is bright on the upland slopes;
When the wind stirs soft through the springing grass,
And the river flows like a stream of glass;
　　When the first bird sings and the first bud opes,
And the faint perfume from its chalice steals—
I know what the caged bird feels!

I know why the caged bird beats his wing
   Till its blood is red on the cruel bars;
For he must fly back to his perch and cling   10
When he fain would be on the bough a-swing;
   And a pain still throbs in the old, old scars
And they pulse again with a keener sting—
I know why he beats his wing!

I know why the caged bird sings, ah me,
   When his wing is bruised and his bosom sore,—
When he beats his bars and would be free;
It is not a carol of joy or glee,
   But a prayer that he sends from his heart's deep core,
But a plea, that upward to Heaven, he flings—   20
I know why the caged bird sings!

WHEN MALINDY SINGS

G'WAY an' quit dat noise, Miss Lucy—
   Put dat music book away;
What's de use to keep on tryin'?
   Ef you practise twell you're gray,
You cain't sta't no notes a-flyin'
   Lak de ones dat rants and rings
F'om de kitchen to de big woods
   When Malindy sings.

You ain't got de nachel o'gans
   Fu' to make de soun' come right,   10
You ain't got de tu'ns an' twistin's
   Fu' to make it sweet an' light.
Tell you one thing now, Miss Lucy,
   An' I'm tellin' you fu' true,
When hit comes to raal right singin',
   'T ain't no easy thing to do.

Easy 'nough fu' folks to hollah,
   Lookin' at de lines an' dots,
When dey ain't no one kin sence it,
   An' de chune comes in, in spots;   20
But fu' real melojous music,
   Dat jes' strikes yo' hea't and clings,
Jes' you stan' an' listen wif me
   When Malindy sings.

Ain't you nevah hyeahd Malindy?
    Blesséd soul, tek up de cross!
Look hyeah, ain't you jokin', honey?
    Well, you don't know whut you los'.
Y' ought to hyeah dat gal a-wa'blin'.
    Robins, la'ks, an' all dem things   30
Heish dey moufs an' hides dey faces
    When Malindy sings.

Fiddlin' man jes' stop his fiddlin'.
    Lay his fiddle on de she'f;
Mockin'-bird quit tryin' to whistle,
    'Cause he jes' so shamed hisse'f.
Folks a-playin' on de banjo
    Drap dey fingahs on de strings—
Bless yo' soul—fu'gits to move em,
    When Malindy sings.   40

She jes' spreads huh mouf and hollahs,
    "Come to Jesus," twell you hyeah
Sinnahs' tremblin' steps and voices
    Timid-lak a-drawin' neah;
Den she tu'ns to "Rock of Ages,"
    Simply to de cross she clings;
An' you fin' yo' teahs a-drappin'
    When Malindy sings.

Who dat says dat humble praises
    Wif de Master nevah counts?   50
Heish yo' mouf, I hyeah dat music,
    Ez hit rises up an' mounts—
Floatin' by de hills an' valleys,
    Way above dis buryin' sod,
Ez hit makes its way in glory
    To de very gates of God!

Oh, hit's sweetah dan de music
    Of an edicated band;
An hit's dearah dan de battle's
    Song o' triumph in de lan'.   60
It seems holier dan evenin'
    When de solemn chu'ch bell rings,
Ez I sit an' ca'mly listen
    While Malindy sings.

Towsah, stop dat ba'kin', hyeah me!
  Mandy, mek dat chile keep still;
Don't you hyeah de echoes callin'
  F'om de valley to de hill?
Let me listen, I can hyeah it,
  Th'oo de bresh of angels' wings,
Sof' an' sweet, "Swing Low, Sweet Chariot,"   70
  Ez Malindy sings.

Walter de la Mare
1873-1956

THE LISTENERS

"Is there anybody there?" said the Traveler,
  Knocking on the moonlit door;
And his horse in the silence champed the grasses
  Of the forest's ferny floor:
And a bird flew up out of the turret,
  Above the Traveler's head:
And he smote upon the door again a second time;
  "Is there anybody there?" he said.
But no one descended to the Traveler;
  No head from the leaf-fringed sill   10
Leaned over and looked into his gray eyes,
  Where he stood perplexed and still.
But only a host of phantom listeners
  That dwelt in the lone house then
Stood listening in the quiet of the moonlight
  To that voice from the world of men:
Stood thronging the faint moonbeams on the dark stair,
  That goes down to the empty hall,
Hearkening in an air stirred and shaken
  By the lonely Traveler's call.   20
And he felt in his heart their strangeness,
  Their stillness answering his cry,
While his horse moved, cropping the dark turf,
  'Neath the starred and leafy sky;
For he suddenly smote on the door, even
  Louder, and lifted his head:—
"Tell them I came, and no one answered,
  That I kept my word," he said.
Never the least stir made the listeners,
  Though every word he spake   30

Fell echoing through the shadowiness of the still house
    From the one man left awake:
Ay, they heard his foot upon the stirrup,
    And the sound of iron on stone,
And how the silence surged softly backward,
    When the plunging hoofs were gone.

[1912]

SILVER

Slowly, silently, now the moon
Walks the night in her silver shoon;
This way, and that, she peers, and sees
Silver fruit upon silver trees;
One by one the casements catch
Her beams beneath the silvery thatch;
Crouched in his kennel, like a log,
With paws of silver sleeps the dog;
From their shadowy cote the white breasts peep
Of doves in a silver-feathered sleep;   10
A harvest mouse goes scampering by,
With silver claws, and silver eye;
And moveless fish in the water gleam,
By silver reeds in a silver stream.

[1913]

THE DREAMER

O thou who giving helm and sword,
    Gav'st to the rusting rain,
And starry dark's all tender dews
    To blunt and stain:

Out of the battle I am sped,
    Unharmed, yet stricken sore;
A living shape amid whispering shades
    On Lethe's[1] shore.

No trophy in my hands I bring,
    To this sad, sighing stream,   10
The neighings and the trumps and cries
    Were but a dream.

[1] In classic myth the shades of the departed drank the waters of the River Lethe and forgot their earthly lives.

Traitor to life, of life betrayed
    O, of thy mercy deep,
A dream my all, the all I ask
    Is sleep.

[1918]

PEACE

NIGHT is o'er England, and the winds are still;
    Jasmine and honeysuckle steep the air;
Softly the stars that are all Europe's fill
Her heaven-wide dark with radiancy fair;
That shadowed moon now waxing in the west
Stirs not a rumor in her tranquil seas;
Mysterious sleep has lulled her heart to rest,
Deep even as theirs beneath her churchyard trees.
Secure, serene; dumb now the night-hawk's threat;
The guns' low thunder drumming o'er the tide;   10
The anguish pulsing in her stricken side. . . .
All is at peace. Ah, never, heart, forget
For this her youngest, best, and bravest died,
These bright dews once were mixed with bloody sweat.

Robert Frost
1874–1963
A LINE-STORM SONG

THE line-storm clouds fly tattered and swift.
    The road is forlorn all day,
Where a myriad snowy quartz-stones lift,
    And the hoofprints vanish away.
The roadside flowers, too wet for the bee,
    Expend their bloom in vain.
Come over the hills and far with me,
    And be my love in the rain.

The birds have less to say for themselves
    In the wood-world's torn despair   10
Than now these numberless years the elves,
    Although they are no less there:

All song of the woods is crushed like some
　　Wild, easily shattered rose.
Come, be my love in the wet woods, come,
　　Where the boughs rain when it blows.

There is the gale to urge behind
　　And bruit our singing down,
And the shallow waters aflutter with wind
　　From which to gather your gown.　　　　　　　20
What matter if we go clear to the west,
　　And come not through dry-shod?
For wilding brooch, shall wet your breast
　　The rain-fresh goldenrod.

Oh, never this whelming east wind swells
　　But it seems like the sea's return
To the ancient lands where it left the shells
　　Before the age of the fern;
And it seems like the time when, after doubt,
　　Our love came back amain.　　　　　　　　30
Oh, come forth into the storm and rout
　　And be my love in the rain.

　　　　　　　　　　　　　　　　　　[1907]

THE ROAD NOT TAKEN

Two roads diverged in a yellow wood,
　　And sorry I could not travel both
And be one traveler, long I stood
And looked down one as far as I could
To where it bent in the undergrowth;

Then took the other, as just as fair,
And having perhaps the better claim,
Because it was grassy and wanted wear;
Though as for that, the passing there
Had worn them really about the same,　　　　　10

And both that morning equally lay
In leaves no step had trodden black.
Oh, I kept the first for another day!
Yet knowing how way leads on to way,
I doubted if I should ever come back.

I shall be telling this with a sigh
Somewhere ages and ages hence :
Two roads diverged in a wood, and I—
I took the one less traveled by,
And that has made all the difference.   20

[1915]

BIRCHES

WHEN I see birches bend to left and right
Across the lines of straighter darker trees,
I like to think some boy's been swinging them.
But swinging doesn't bend them down to stay
As ice storms do. Often you must have seen them
Loaded with ice a sunny winter morning
After a rain. They click upon themselves
As the breeze rises, and turn many-colored
As the stir cracks and crazes their enamel.
Soon the sun's warmth makes them shed crystal shells   10
Shattering and avalanching on the snow crust—
Such heaps of broken glass to sweep away
You'd think the inner dome of heaven had fallen.
They are dragged to the withered bracken by the load,
And they seem not to break ; though once they are bowed
So low for long, they never right themselves :
You may see their trunks arching in the woods
Years afterwards, trailing their leaves on the ground
Like girls on hands and knees that throw their hair
Before them over their heads to dry in the sun.   20
But I was going to say when Truth broke in
With all her matter of fact about the ice storm,
I should prefer to have some boy bend them
As he went out and in to fetch the cows—
Some boy too far from town to learn baseball,
Whose only play was what he found himself,
Summer or winter, and could play alone.

One by one he subdued his father's trees
By riding them down over and over again
Until he took the stiffness out of them,   30
And not one but hung limp, not one was left
For him to conquer. He learned all there was
To learn about not launching out too soon
And so not carrying the tree away
Clear to the ground. He always kept his poise

To the top branches, climbing carefully
With the same pains you use to fill a cup
Up to the brim, and even above the brim.
Then he flung outward, feet first, with a swish,
Kicking his way down through the air to the ground.   40
So was I once myself a swinger of birches.
And so I dream of going back to be.
It's when I'm weary of considerations,
And life is too much like a pathless wood
Where your face burns and tickles with the cobwebs
Broken across it, and one eye is weeping
From a twig's having lashed across it open.
I'd like to get away from earth awhile
And then come back to it and begin over.
May no fate willfully misunderstand me   50
And half grant what I wish and snatch me away
Not to return. Earth's the right place for love:
I don't know where it's likely to go better.
I'd like to go by climbing a birch tree,
And climb black branches up a snow-white trunk
Toward heaven, till the tree could bear no more,
But dipped its top and set me down again
That would be good both going and coming back.
One could do worse than be a swinger of birches.

[1915]

STOPPING BY WOODS ON A
SNOWY EVENING

WHOSE woods these are I think I know.
His house is in the village, though;
He will not see me stopping here
To watch his woods fill up with snow.

My little horse must think it queer
To stop without a farmhouse near
Between the woods and frozen lake
The darkest evening of the year.

He gives his harness bells a shake
To ask if there is some mistake.   10
The only other sound's the sweep
Of easy wind and downy flake.

The woods are lovely, dark, and deep,
But I have promises to keep,
And miles to go before I sleep,
And miles to go before I sleep.

[1923]

FOR ONCE, THEN, SOMETHING

OTHERS taunt me with having knelt at well-curbs
Always wrong to the light, so never seeing
Deeper down in the well than where the water
Gives me back in a shining surface picture
Me myself in the summer heaven, godlike,
Looking out of a wreath of fern and cloud puffs.
Once, when trying with chin against a well-curb,
I discerned, as I thought, beyond the picture,
Through the picture, a something white, uncertain,
Something more of the depths—and then I lost it.   10
Water came to rebuke the too clear water.
One drop fell from a fern, and lo, a ripple
Shook whatever it was lay there at bottom,
Blurred it, blotted it out. What was that whiteness?
Truth? A pebble of quartz? For once, then, something.

[1923]

THE ONSET

ALWAYS the same, when on a fated night
At last the gathered snow lets down as white
As may be in dark woods, and with a song
It shall not make again all winter long
Of hissing on the yet uncovered ground,
I almost stumble looking up and round,
As one who overtaken by the end
Gives up his errand, and lets death descend
Upon him where he is, with nothing done
To evil, no important triumph won,   10
More than if life had never been begun.

Yet all the precedent is on my side:
I know that winter death has never tried
The earth but it has failed: the snow may heap
In long storms an undrifted four feet deep

As measured against maple, birch and oak,
It cannot check the peeper's silver croak;
And I shall see the snow all go down hill
In water of a slender April rill
That flashes tail through last year's withered brake   20
And dead weeds, like a disappearing snake.
Nothing will be left white but here a birch,
And there a clump of houses with a church.

[1923]

SPRING POOLS

THESE pools that, though in forests, still reflect
The total sky almost without defect,
And like the flowers beside them, chill and shiver,
Will like the flowers beside them soon be gone,
And yet not out by any brook or river,
But up by roots to bring dark foliage on.

The trees that have it in their pent-up buds
To darken nature and be summer woods—
Let them think twice before they use their powers
To blot out and drink up and sweep away   10
These flowery waters and these watery flowers
From snow that melted only yesterday.

[1928]

DESERT PLACES

SNOW falling and night falling fast, oh, fast
In a field I looked into going past,
And the ground almost covered smooth in snow,
But a few weeds and stubble showing last.

The woods around it have it—it is theirs.
All animals are smothered in their lairs.
I am too absent-spirited to count;
The loneliness includes me unawares.

And lonely as it is, that loneliness
Will be more lonely ere it will be less—   10
A blanker whiteness of benighted snow
With no expression, nothing to express.

They cannot scare me with their empty spaces
Between stars—on stars where no human race is.
I have it in me so much nearer home
To scare myself with my own desert places.

[1934]

DESIGN

I FOUND a dimpled spider, fat and white,
On a white heal-all, holding up a moth
Like a white piece of rigid satin cloth—
Assorted characters of death and blight
Mixed ready to begin the morning right,
Like the ingredients of a witches' broth—
A snow-drop spider, a flower like a froth,
And dead wings carried like a paper kite.

What had that flower to do with being white,
The wayside blue and innocent heal-all?   10
What brought the kindred spider to that height,
Then steered the white moth thither in the night?
What but design of darkness to appall?—
If design govern in a thing so small.

[1936]

THE SILKEN TENT

SHE is as in a field a silken tent
At midday when a sunny summer breeze
Has dried the dew and all its ropes relent,
So that in guys it gently sways at ease,
And its supporting central cedar pole,
That is its pinnacle to heavenward
And signifies the sureness of the soul,
Seems to owe naught to any single cord,
But strictly held by none, is loosely bound
By countless silken ties of love and thought   10
To everything on earth the compass round,
And only by one's going slightly taut
In the capriciousness of summer air
Is of the slightest bondage made aware.

[1942]

Carl Sandburg
1878–1967
CHICAGO

Hog Butcher for the World,
Tool Maker, Stacker of Wheat,
Player with Railroads and the Nation's Freight Handler;
Stormy, husky, brawling,
City of the Big Shoulders:

They tell me you are wicked and I believe them, for I have seen your
painted women under the gas lamps luring the farm boys.
And they tell me you are crooked and I answer: Yes, it is true I have seen
the gunman kill and go free to kill again.
And they tell me you are brutal and my reply is: On the faces of women
and children I have seen the marks of wanton hunger.
And having answered so I turn once more to those who sneer at this my
city, and I give them back the sneer and say to them:
Come and show me another city with lifted head singing so proud to be
alive and coarse and strong and cunning.   10
Flinging magnetic curses amid the toil of piling job on job, here is a tall
bold slugger set vivid against the little soft cities;
Fierce as a dog with tongue lapping for action, cunning as a savage pitted
against the wilderness,
Bareheaded,
Shoveling,
Wrecking,
Planning,
Building, breaking, rebuilding,
Under the smoke, dust all over his mouth, laughing with white teeth,
Under the terrible burden of destiny laughing as a young man laughs,
Laughing even as an ignorant fighter laughs who has never lost a battle, 20
Bragging and laughing that under his wrist is the pulse, and under his ribs
the heart of the people,
          Laughing!
Laughing the stormy, husky, brawling laughter of Youth, half-naked,
sweating, proud to be Hog Butcher, Tool Maker, Stacker of Wheat,
Player with Railroads and Freight Handler to the Nation.

                                                            [1916]

FOG

THE fog comes
on little cat feet.

It sits looking
over harbor and city
on silent haunches
and then moves on.

[1916]

NOCTURNE IN A DESERTED BRICKYARD

STUFF of the moon
Runs on the lapping sand
Out to the longest shadows.
Under the curving willows,
And round the creep of the wave line,
Fluxions of yellow and dusk on the waters
Make a wide dreaming pansy of an old pond in the night.

COOL TOMBS

WHEN Abraham Lincoln was shoveled into the tombs, he forgot
the copperheads[1] and the assassin . . . in the dust, in the cool
tombs.

And Ulysses Grant[2] lost all thought of con men and Wall Street, cash
and collateral turned ashes . . . in the dust, in the cool tombs.

Pocahontas'[3] body, lovely as a poplar, sweet as a red haw in November
or a pawpaw in May, did she wonder? does she remember? . . . in
the dust, in the cool tombs?

Take any streetful of people buying clothes and groceries, cheering a
hero or throwing confetti and blowing tin horns . . . tell me if the
lovers are losers . . . tell me if any get more than the lovers . . .
in the dust . . . in the cool tombs.

[1] Northern sympathizers of the Confederacy during the American Civil War
[2] leading Union general during the Civil War and eighteenth President of the
United States, whose administration was marked by unprecedented corruption
[3] Indian princess who, according to John Smith, saved him from execution by her
father's warriors

SKYSCRAPERS STAND PROUD

THE skyscrapers stand proud.
They seem to say they have sought the absolute and made it their own.

Yet they are blameless, innocent as dumb steel and the dumber concrete of their bastions.

"Man made us," they murmur. "We are proud only as man is proud and we have no more found the absolute than has man."

Wallace Stevens
1879–1955

DOMINATION OF BLACK

AT NIGHT, by the fire,
The colors of the bushes
And of the fallen leaves,
Repeating themselves,
Turned in the room,
Like the leaves themselves
Turning in the wind.
Yes : but the color of the heavy hemlocks
Came striding.
And I remembered the cry of the peacocks.   10

The colors of their tails
Were like the leaves themselves
Turning in the wind,
In the twilight wind.
They swept over the room,
Just as they flew from the boughs of the hemlocks
Down to the ground.
I heard them cry—the peacocks.
Was it a cry against the twilight
Or against the leaves themselves   20
Turning in the wind,
Turning as the flames
Turned in the fire,
Turning as the tails of the peacocks
Turned in the loud fire,

Loud as the hemlocks
Full of the cry of the peacocks?
Or was it a cry against the hemlocks?

Out of the window,
I saw how the planets gathered   30
Like the leaves themselves
Turning in the wind.
I saw how the night came,
Came striding like the color of the heavy hemlocks
I felt afraid.
And I remembered the cry of the peacocks.

[1923]

THE SNOW MAN

ONE must have a mind of winter
To regard the frost and the boughs
Of the pine-trees crusted with snow;

And have been cold a long time,
To behold the junipers shagged with ice,
The spruces rough in the distant glitter

Of the January sun; and not to think
Of any misery in the sound of the wind,
In the sound of a few leaves,

Which is the sound of the land   10
Full of the same wind
That is blowing in the same bare place

For the listener, who listens in the snow,
And, nothing himself, beholds
Nothing that is not there and the nothing that is.

[1923]

THE DEATH OF A SOLDIER

LIFE contracts and death is expected,
As in a season of autumn.
The soldier falls.

He does not become a three-days personage,
Imposing his separation,
Calling for pomp.

Death is absolute and without memorial,
As in a season of autumn,
When the wind stops,

When the wind stops and, over the heavens,   10
The clouds go, nevertheless,
In their direction.

[1923]

A POSTCARD FROM THE VOLCANO

CHILDREN picking up our bones
  Will never know that these were once
As quick as foxes on the hill;

And that in autumn, when the grapes
Made sharp air sharper by their smell
These had a being, breathing frost;

And least will guess that with our bones
We left much more, left what still is
The look of things, left what we felt

At what we saw. The spring clouds blow   10
Above the shuttered mansion-house,
Beyond our gate and the windy sky

Cries out a literate despair.
We knew for long the mansion's look
And what we said of it became

A part of what it is . . . Children,
Still weaving budded aureoles,
Will speak our speech and never know,

Will say of the mansion that it seems
As if he that lived there left behind   20
A spirit storming in blank walls,

A dirty house in a gutted world,
A tatter of shadows peaked to white,
Smeared with the gold of the opulent sun.

[1935]

STUDY OF TWO PEARS

OPUSCULUM paedagogum.[1]
The pears are not viols,
Nudes or bottles.
They resemble nothing else.

They are yellow forms
Composed of curves
Bulging toward the base.
They are touched red.

They are not flat surfaces
Having curved outlines.   10
They are round
Tapering toward the top.

In the way they are modelled
There are bits of blue.
A hard dry leaf hangs
From the stem.

The yellow glistens.
It glistens with various yellows,
Citrons, oranges and greens
Flowering over the skin.   20

The shadows of the pears
Are blobs on the green cloth.
The pears are not seen
As the observer wills.

[1942]

[1] a little work of instruction

THE HOUSE WAS QUIET AND
THE WORLD WAS CALM

THE house was quiet and the world was calm.
The reader became the book ; and summer night

Was like the conscious being of the book.
The house was quiet and the world was calm.

The words were spoken as if there was no book,
Except that the reader leaned above the page,

Wanted to lean, wanted much most to be
The scholar to whom his book is true, to whom

The summer night is like a perfection of thought.
The house was quiet because it had to be.   10

The quiet was part of the meaning, part of the mind :
The access of perfection to the page.

And the world was calm. The truth in a calm world,
In which there is no other meaning, itself

Is calm, itself is summer and night, itself
Is the reader leaning late and reading there.

[1947]

William Carlos Williams
1883–1963

DAWN

Ecstatic bird songs pound
  the hollow vastness of the sky
with metallic clinkings—
beating color up into it
at a far edge,—beating it, beating it
with rising, triumphant ardor,—
stirring it into warmth,
quickening in it a spreading change,—
bursting wildly against it as
dividing the horizon, a heavy sun   10
lifts himself—is lifted—
bit by bit above the edge
of things,—runs free at last
out into the open—! lumbering
glorified in full release upward—
                              songs cease.

THE POOR

I T ' s the anarchy of poverty
  delights me, the old
yellow wooden house indented
among the new brick tenements

Or a cast iron balcony
with panels showing oak branches
in full leaf. It fits
the dress of the children

reflecting every stage and
custom of necessity—   10
Chimneys, roofs, fences of
wood and metal in an unfenced

age and enclosing next to
nothing at all : the old man
in a sweater and soft black
hat who sweeps the sidewalk—

his own ten feet of it—
in a wind that fitfully
turning his corner has   19
overwhelmed the entire city

                                                                  [1917]

SPRING AND ALL

B Y T H E road to the contagious hospital
  under the surge of the blue
mottled clouds driven from the
northeast—a cold wind. Beyond, the
waste of broad, muddy fields
brown with dried weeds, standing and fallen

patches of standing water
the scattering of tall trees

All along the road the reddish
purplish, forked, upstanding, twiggy   10
stuff of bushes and small trees
with dead, brown leaves under them
leafless vines—

Lifeless in appearance, sluggish
dazed spring approaches—

They enter the new world naked,
cold, uncertain of all
save that they enter. All about them
the cold, familiar wind—

Now the grass, tomorrow   20
the stiff curl of wildcarrot leaf
One by one objects are defined—
It quickens: clarity, outline of leaf

But now the stark dignity of
entrance—Still, the profound change
has come upon them: rooted, they
grip down and begin to awaken

[1923]

THE YACHTS

contend in a sea which the land partly encloses
shielding them from the too heavy blows
of an ungoverned ocean which when it chooses

tortures the biggest hulls, the best man knows
to pit against its beating, and sinks them pitilessly.
Mothlike in mists, scintillant in the minute

brilliance of cloudless days, with broad bellying sails
they glide to the wind tossing green water
from their sharp prows while over them the crew crawls

ant-like, solicitously grooming them, releasing,   10
making fast as they turn, lean far over and having
caught the wind again, side by side, head for the mark.

In a well guarded arena of open water surrounded by
lesser and greater craft which, sycophant, lumbering
and flittering follow them, they appear youthful, rare

as the light of a happy eye, live with the grace
of all that in the mind is feckless, free and
naturally to be desired. Now the sea which holds them

is moody, lapping their glossy sides, as if feeling
for some slightest flaw but fails completely.   20
Today no race. Then the wind comes again. The yachts

move, jockeying for a start, the signal is set and they
are off. Now the waves strike at them but they are too
well made, they slip through, though they take in canvas.

Arms with hands grasping seek to clutch at the prows.
Bodies thrown recklessly in the way are cut aside.
It is a sea of faces about them in agony, in despair

until the horror of the race dawns staggering the mind,
the whole sea become an entanglement of watery bodies
lost to the world bearing what they cannot hold.   30
   Broken,

beaten, desolate, reaching from the dead to be taken up
they cry out, failing, failing! their cries rising
in waves still as the skillful yachts pass over.

                                                    [1935]

RALEIGH WAS RIGHT

W E CANNOT go to the country[1]
      for the country will bring us no peace
What can the small violets tell us
that grow on furry stems in
the long grass among lance shaped leaves?

   Though you praise us
   and call to mind the poets
   who sung of our loveliness
   it was long ago!
   long ago! when country people   10
   would plow and sow with
   flowering minds and pockets at ease—
   if ever this were true.

   Not now, Love itself a flower
   with roots in a parched ground.

_____

[1] See Christopher Marlowe, "The Passionate Shepherd to His Love," p. 651, and
Sir Walter Ralegh, "The Nymph's Reply to the Shepherd," p. 648.

Empty pockets make empty heads.
Cure it if you can but
do not believe that we can live
today in the country
for the country will bring us no peace.   20

[1941]

LANDSCAPE WITH THE FALL OF ICARUS

ACCORDING to Brueghel[1]
when Icarus fell
it was spring

a farmer was ploughing
his field
the whole pageantry

of the year was
awake tingling
near

the edge of the sea   10
concerned
with itself

sweating in the sun
that melted
the wings' wax

unsignificantly
off the coast
there was

a splash quite unnoticed
this was   20
Icarus drowning

[1950]

---

[1] Pieter Brueghel, Flemish painter, c. 1520–1569, depicted an ancient myth in his
Icarus. He showed Icarus falling into the sea after having flown too close to the sun
with wings attached to his shoulders with wax. See also W. H. Auden, "Musée des
Beaux Arts," p. 935.

D. H. Lawrence
1885–1930

GLOIRE DE DIJON

WHEN she rises in the morning
   I linger to watch her;
Spreads the bath-cloth underneath the window
And the sunbeams catch her
Glistening white on the shoulders,
While down her sides the mellow
Golden shadow glows as
She stoops to the sponge, and the swung breasts
Sway like full-blown yellow
Gloire de Dijon roses.   10

She drips herself with water, and the shoulders
Glisten as silver, they crumple up
Like wet and falling roses, and I listen
For the sluicing of their rain-dishevelled petals.
In the window full of sunlight
Concentrates her golden shadow
Fold on fold, until it glows as
Mellow as the glory roses.

                                                 [1917]

PIANO

SOFTLY, in the dusk, a woman is singing to me;
  Taking me back down the vista of years, till I see
A child sitting under the piano, in the boom of the tingling strings
And pressing the small, poised feet of a mother who smiles as she sings.

In spite of myself, the insidious mastery of song
Betrays me back, till the heart of me weeps to belong
To the old Sunday evenings at home, with winter outside
And hymns in the cozy parlor, the tinkling piano our guide.

So now it is vain for the singer to burst into clamor
With the great black piano appassionato. The glamor   10
Of childish days is upon me, my manhood is cast
Down in the flood of remembrance, I weep like a child for the past.

                                                 [1918]

SNAKE

A SNAKE came to my water-trough
On a hot, hot day, and I in pyjamas for the heat,
To drink there.

In the deep, strange-scented shade of the great dark carob tree
I came down the steps with my pitcher
And must wait, must stand and wait, for there he was at the trough before
  me.

He reached down from a fissure in the earth-wall in the gloom
And trailed his yellow-brown slackness soft-bellied down, over the edge
  of the stone trough
And rested his throat upon the stone bottom,
And where the water had dripped from the tap, in a small clearness,   10
He sipped with his straight mouth,
Softly drank through his straight gums, into his slack long body,
Silently.

Someone was before me at my water-trough,
And I, like a second comer, waiting.

He lifted his head from his drinking, as cattle do,
And looked at me vaguely, as drinking cattle do,
And flickered his two-forked tongue from his lips, and mused a moment,
And stooped and drank a little more,
Being earth-brown, earth-golden from the burning bowels of the earth   20
On the day of Sicilian July, with Etna smoking.

The voice of my education said to me
He must be killed,
For in Sicily the black, black snakes are innocent, the gold are venomous.
And voices in me said, If you were a man
You would take a stick and break him now, and finish him off.

But must I confess how I liked him,
How glad I was he had come like a guest in quiet, to drink at my water-
  trough
And depart peaceful, pacified, and thankless,
Into the burning bowels of this earth?   30

Was it cowardice, that I dared not kill him?
Was it perversity, that I longed to talk to him?

Was it humility, to feel so honored?
I felt so honored.

And yet those voices:
If you were not afraid, you would kill him!

And truly I was afraid, I was most afraid,
But even so, honored still more
That he should seek my hospitality
From out the dark door of the secret earth.   40

He drank enough
And lifted his head, dreamily, as one who has drunken,
And flickered his tongue like a forked night on the air, so black,
Seeming to lick his lips,
And looked around like a god, unseeing, into the air,
And slowly turned his head,
And slowly, very slowly, as if thrice adream,
Proceeded to draw his slow length curving round
And climb again the broken bank of my wall-face.

And as he put his head into that dreadful hole,   50
And as he slowly drew up, snake-easing his shoulders, and entered
        farther,
A sort of horror, a sort of protest again his withdrawing into that horrid
        black hole,
Deliberately going into the blackness, and slowly drawing himself after,
Overcame me now his back was turned.

I looked around, I put down my pitcher,
I picked up a clumsy log
And threw it at the water-trough with a clatter.

I think I did not hit him,
But suddenly that part of him that was left behind convulsed in undigni-
        fied haste,
Writhed like lightning, and was gone   60
Into the black hole, the earth-lipped fissure in the wall-front,
At which, in the intense still noon, I stared with fascination.

And immediately I regretted it.
I thought how paltry, how vulgar, what a mean act!
I despised myself and the voices of my accursed human education.

And I thought of the albatross,
And I wished he would come back, my snake.

For he seemed to me again like a king,
Like a king in exile, uncrowned in the underworld,
Now due to be crowned again.   70

And so, I missed my chance with one of the lords
Of life.
And I have something to expiate;
A pettiness.

[1923]

BAVARIAN GENTIANS

Nот every man has gentians in his house
In soft September, at slow, sad Michaelmas.

Bavarian gentians, tall and dark, but dark
Darkening the day-time torch-like with the smoking blueness of Pluto's
    gloom
Ribbed hellish flowers erect, with their blaze of darkness spread blue
Blown into points, by the heavy white draft of the day.

Torch-flowers of the blue-smoking darkness, Pluto's[1] dark blue haze
Black lamps from the halls of Dis, smoking dark blue
Giving off darkness, blue darkness, upon Demeter's yellow-pale day
Reach me a gentian, give me a torch!   10
Let me guide myself with the blue, forked torch of a flower
Down the darker and darker stairs, where blue is darkened on blueness
Down the way Persephone goes, just now, in first-frosted September
To the sightless realm where darkness is married to dark
And Persephone herself is but a voice, as a bride
A gloom invisible enfolded in the deeper dark
Of the arms of Pluto as he ravishes her once again
And pierces her once more with his passion of the utter dark.
Among the splendor of black-blue torches, shedding fathomless darkness
    on the nuptials.

Give me a flower on a tall stem, and three dark flames,   20
For I will go to the wedding, and be wedding-guest
At the marriage of the living dark.

[1932]

---

[1] Pluto (or Dis) abducted Persephone and made her Queen of the Underworld
despite efforts by Demeter, her mother, to rescue her.

Robinson Jeffers
1887–1962

TO THE STONE-CUTTERS

STONE-CUTTERS fighting time with marble, you fore-defeated
Challengers of oblivion
Eat cynical earnings, knowing rock splits, records fall down,
The square-limbed Roman letters
Scale in the thaws, wear in the rain. The poet as well
Builds his monument mockingly;
For man will be blotted out, the blithe earth die, the brave sun
Die blind and blacken to the heart:
Yet stones have stood for a thousand years, and pained thoughts found
The honey of peace in old poems.   10

[c.1922]

SHINE, PERISHING REPUBLIC

WHILE this America settles in the mold of its vulgarity, heavily
thickening to empire,
And protest, only a bubble in the molten mass, pops and sighs out, and the
mass hardens,

I sadly smiling remember that the flower fades to make fruit, the fruit
rots to make earth.
Out of the mother; and through the spring exultances, ripeness and
decadence; and home to the mother.

You making haste haste on decay: not blameworthy; life is good, be it
stubbornly long or suddenly
A mortal splendor: meteors are not needed less than mountains: shine,
perishing republic.

But for my children, I would have them keep their distance from the
thickening center; corruption
Never has been compulsory, when the cities lie at the monster's feet
there are left the mountains.

And boys, be in nothing so moderate as in love of man, a clever servant,
insufferable master.
There is the trap that catches noblest spirits, that caught—they say,—
God, when he walked on earth.   10

[1925]

HURT HAWKS

I

THE broken pillar of the wing jags from the clotted shoulder,
　The wing trails like a banner in defeat,
No more to use the sky forever but live with famine
And pain a few days : cat nor coyote
Will shorten the week of waiting for death, there is game without talons.
He stands under the oak-bush and waits
The lame feet of salvation ; at night he remembers freedom
And flies in a dream, the dawns ruin it.
He is strong and pain is worse to the strong, incapacity is worse.
The curs of the day come and torment him　　　　　　　　10
At distance, no one but death the redeemer will humble that head,
The intrepid readiness, the terrible eyes.
The wild God of the world is sometimes merciful to those
That ask mercy, not often to the arrogant.
You do not know him, you communal people, or you have forgotten him ;
Intemperate and savage, the hawk remembers him ;
Beautiful and wild, the hawks, and men that are dying, remember him.

II

I'd sooner, except the penalties, kill a man than a hawk, but the great
　redtail
Had nothing left but unable misery
From the bone too shattered for mending, the wing that trailed under his
　talons when he moved.
We had fed him six weeks, I gave him freedom,
He wandered over the foreland hill and returned in the evening, asking
　for death,
Not like a beggar, still eyed with the old
Implacable arrogance. I gave him the lead gift in the twilight. What fell
　was relaxed,
Owl-downy, soft feminine feathers ; but what　　　　　　20
Soared : the fierce rush : the night-herons by the flooded river cried fear
　at its rising
Before it was quite unsheathed from reality.

[1928]

THE EYE

THE Atlantic is a stormy moat ; and the Mediterranean,
　The blue pool in the old garden,
More than five thousand years has drunk sacrifice

Of ships and blood, and shines in the sun; but here the Pacific—
Our ships, planes, wars are perfectly irrelevant.
Neither our present blood-feud with the brave dwarfs
Nor any future world-quarrel of westering
And eastering man, the bloody migrations, greed of power, clash of
    faiths—
Is a speck of dust on the great scale-pan.
Here from this mountain shore, headland beyond stormy headland plung-
    ing like dolphins through the blue sea-smoke   10
Into pale sea—look west at the hill of water: it is half the planet: this
    dome, this half-globe, this bulging
Eyeball of water, arched over to Asia,
Australia and white Antarctica: those are the eyelids that never close;
    this is the staring unsleeping
Eye of the earth; and what it watches is not our wars.

[1948]

ORIGINAL SIN

THE man-brained and man-handed ground-ape, physically
    The most repulsive of all hot-blooded animals
Up to that time of the world: they had dug a pitfall
And caught a mammoth, but how could their sticks and stones
Reach the life in that hide? They danced around the pit, shrieking
With ape excitement, flinging sharp flints in vain, and the stench of their
    bodies
Stained the white air of dawn; but presently one of them
Remembered the yellow dancer, wood-eating fire
That guards the cave-mouth: he ran and fetched him, and others
Gathered sticks at the wood's edge; they made a blaze   10
And pushed it into the pit, and they fed it high, around the mired sides
Of their huge prey. They watched the long hairy trunk
Waver over the stifle-trumpeting pain,
And they were happy.
                    Meanwhile the intense color and nobility of sun-
    rise,
Rose and gold and amber, flowed up the sky. Wet rocks were shining, a
    little wind   20
Stirred the leaves of the forest and the marsh flag-flowers; the soft valley
    between the low hills
Became as beautiful as the sky; while in its midst, hour after hour, the
    happy hunters
Roasted their living meat slowly to death.
                    These are the people.
This is the human dawn. As for me, I would rather

Be a worm in a wild apple than a son of man.
But we are what we are, and we might remember
Not to hate any person, for all are vicious;
And not be astonished at any evil, all are deserved;
And not fear death; it is the only way to be cleansed.

[1948]

CARMEL POINT

THE extraordinary patience of things!
This beautiful place defaced with a crop of suburban houses—
How beautiful when we first beheld it,
Unbroken field of poppy and lupin walled with clean cliffs;
No intrusion but two or three horses pasturing,
Or a few milch cows rubbing their flanks on the outcrop rock-heads—
Now the spoiler has come: does it care?
Not faintly. It has all time. It knows the people are a tide
That swells and in time will ebb, and all
Their works dissolve. Meanwhile the image of the pristine beauty   10
Lives in the very grain of the granite,
Safe as the endless ocean that climbs our cliff.—As for us:
We must uncenter our minds from ourselves;
We must unhumanize our views a little, and become confident
As the rock and ocean that we were made from.

[1954]

Marianne Moore
1887–1972
POETRY

I TOO, dislike it: there are things that are important beyond all this
fiddle.
Reading it, however, with a perfect contempt for it, one discovers in
it after all, a place for the genuine.
Hands that can grasp, eyes
that can dilate, hair that can rise
if it must, these things are important not because a

high-sounding interpretation can be put upon them but because they are
useful. When they become so derivative as to become unintelligible,
the same thing may be said for all of us, that we
do not admire what   10
we cannot understand: the bat
holding on upside down or in quest of something to

eat, elephants pushing, a wild horse taking a roll, a tireless wolf under
  a tree, the immovable critic twitching his skin like a horse that feels a
    flea, the base-
  ball fan, the statistician—
    nor is it valid
      to discriminate against "business documents and

school-books"; [1] all these phenomena are important. One must make a
  distinction
  however: when dragged into prominence by half poets, the result is not
    poetry,
  nor till the poets among us can be   20
    "literalists of
    the imagination" [2]—above
      insolence and triviality and can present

for inspection, "imaginary gardens with real toads in them" shall we
  have it. In the meantime, if you demand on the one hand,
  the raw material of poetry in
    all its rawness and
    that which is on the other hand
      genuine, you are interested in poetry.

                                                                [1921]

  [1] a quotation from Tolstoi, who had written, ". . . poetry is everything with
the exception of business documents and school-books"
  [2] a quotation from Yeats, who characterizes Blake as a "too literal realist of the
imagination"

TO A STEAM ROLLER

THE illustration
  is nothing to you without the application.
    You lack half wit. You crush all the particles down
      into close conformity, and then walk back and forth on them.

Sparkling chips of rock
  are crushed down to the level of the parent block.
    Were not "impersonal judgment in aesthetic
      matters, a metaphysical impossibility," you

might fairly achieve
  it. As for butterflies, I can hardly conceive   10
    of one's attending upon you, but to question
      the congruence of the complement is vain, if it exists.

                                                                [1924]

THE STEEPLE-JACK

Dürer[1] would have seen a reason for living
    in a town like this, with eight stranded whales
to look at; with the sweet sea air coming into your house
on a fine day, from water etched
    with waves as formal as the scales
on a fish.

One by one, in two's, in three's, the seagulls keep
    flying back and forth over the town clock,
or sailing around the lighthouse without moving their wings—
rising steadily with a slight   10
    quiver of the body—or flock
mewing where

a sea the purple of the peacock's neck is
    paled to greenish azure as Dürer changed
the pine green of the Tyrol to peacock blue and guinea
grey. You can see a twenty-five-
    pound lobster and fishnets arranged
to dry. The

whirlwind fife-and-drum of the storm bends the salt
    marsh grass, disturbs stars in the sky and the   20
star on the steeple; it is a privilege to see so
much confusion.

          A steeple-jack in red, has let
    a rope down as a spider spins a thread;
he might be part of a novel, but on the sidewalk a
sign says C. J. Poole, Steeple-Jack,
    in black and white; and one in red
and white says

Danger. The church portico has four fluted
    columns, each a single piece of stone, made   30
modester by white-wash. This would be a fit haven for
waifs, children, animals, prisoners,
    and presidents who have repaid
sin-driven

---

[1] Albrecht Dürer (1471–1528), German artist in oils, woodcuts, and etchings, noted for meticulous detail

senators by not thinking about them. One
     sees a school-house, a post-office in a
store, fish-houses, hen-houses, a three-masted schooner on
the stocks. The hero, the student,
     the steeple-jack, each in his way,
is at home.   40

It scarcely could be dangerous to be living
     in a town like this, of simple people
who have a steeple-jack placing danger-signs by the
     church
when he is gilding the solid-
     pointed star, which on a steeple
stands for hope.

                                                                    [1935]

GRANITE AND STEEL

ENFRANCHISING cable,[1] silvered by the sea,
     of woven wire, grayed by the mist,
and Liberty[2] dominate the Bay—
her feet as one on shattered chains,
once whole links wrought by Tyranny.

Caged Circe of steel and stone,
her parent German ingenuity.[3]
"O catenary curve"[4] from tower to pier,
implacable enemy of the mind's deformity,
of man's uncompunctious greed,   10
his crass love of crass priority
     just recently
obstructing acquiescent feet
about to step ashore when darkness fell
     without a cause,
as if probity had not joined our cities
     in the sea.

"O path amid the stars
crossed by the seagull's wing!"
"O radiance that doth inherit me!"   20
—affirming inter-acting harmony!

[1] the suspension cables of the Brooklyn Bridge
[2] the Statue of Liberty, a gift of France to the United States
[3] John Roebling, a German engineer, developed the process of fabricating endless
steel cable and supervised the construction of the Brooklyn Bridge.
[4] the curve naturally assumed by a flexible filament such as a chain, rope, or cable
when it hangs free between fixed points

Untried expedient, untried; then tried;
way out; way in; romantic passageway
first seen by the eye of the mind,
then by the eye. O steel! O stone!
Climactic ornament, double rainbow,
as if inverted by French perspicacity,
    John Roebling's monument,
German tenacity's also;
composite span—an actuality.   30

[1966]

T. S. Eliot

1888–1965

THE LOVE SONG OF J. ALFRED PRUFROCK

*S'io credesse che mia risposta fosse
A.persona che mai tornasse al mondo,
Questa fiamma staria senza piu scosse.
Ma perciocche giammai di questo fondo
Non torno vivo alcun, s'i'odo il vero,
Senza tema d'infamia ti rispondo.*[1]

LET US go then, you and I,
When the evening is spread out against the sky
Like a patient etherised upon a table;
Let us go, through certain half-deserted streets,
The muttering retreats
Of restless nights in one-night cheap hotels
And sawdust restaurants with oyster-shells:
Streets that follow like a tedious argument
Of insidious intent
To lead you to an overwhelming question . . .   10
Oh, do not ask, "What is it?"
Let us go and make our visit.
In the room the women come and go
Talking of Michelangelo.

The yellow fog that rubs its back upon the window-panes,
The yellow smoke that rubs its muzzle on the window-panes
Licked its tongue into the corners of the evening,
Lingered upon the pools that stand in drains,

[1] Dante, *Inferno*, XXVII, ll. 61–66: "If I thought that my answer were directed to anyone who could ever return to the world, this flame would quiver no longer; but because, as I hear, no one ever returns alive from this depth, I reply to you without fear of infamy."

Let fall upon its back the soot that falls from chimneys,
Slipped by the terrace, made a sudden leap,   20
And seeing that it was a soft October night,
Curled once about the house, and fell asleep.

And indeed there will be time
For the yellow smoke that slides along the street
Rubbing its back upon the window-panes;
There will be time, there will be time
To prepare a face to meet the faces that you meet;
There will be time to murder and create,
And time for all the works and days of hands
That lift and drop a question on your plate;   30
Time for you and time for me,
And time yet for a hundred indecisions,
And for a hundred visions and revisions,
Before the taking of a toast and tea.

In the room the women come and go
Talking of Michelangelo.

And indeed there will be time
To wonder, "Do I dare?" and, "Do I dare?"
Time to turn back and descend the stair,
With a bald spot in the middle of my hair—   40
(They will say: "How his hair is growing thin!")
My morning coat, my collar mounting firmly to the chin,
My necktie rich and modest, but asserted by a simple pin—
(They will say: "But how his arms and legs are thin!")
Do I dare
Disturb the universe?
In a minute there is time
For decisions and revisions which a minute will reverse.

For I have known them all already, known them all—
Have known the evenings, mornings, afternoons,
I have measured out my life with coffee spoons;   50
I know the voices dying with a dying fall
Beneath the music from a farther room.
     So how should I presume?

And I have known the eyes already, known them all—
The eyes that fix you in a formulated phrase,
And when I am formulated, sprawling on a pin,
When I am pinned and wriggling on the wall,
Then how should I begin

To spit out all the butt-ends of my days and ways?   60
   And how should I presume?

And I have known the arms already, known them all—
Arms that are braceleted and white and bare
(But in the lamplight, downed with light brown hair!)
Is it perfume from a dress
That makes me so digress?
Arms that lie along a table, or wrap about a shawl.
   And should I then presume?
   And how should I begin?

.   .   .

Shall I say, I have gone at dusk through narrow streets   70
And watched the smoke that rises from the pipes
Of lonely men in shirt-sleeves, leaning out of windows? . . .

I should have been a pair of ragged claws
Scuttling across the floors of silent seas.

.   .   .

And the afternoon, the evening, sleep so peacefully!
Smoothed by long fingers,
Asleep . . . tired . . . or it malingers,
Stretched on the floor, here beside you and me.
Should I, after tea and cakes and ices,
Have the strength to force the moment to its crisis?   80
But though I have wept and fasted, wept and prayed,
Though I have seen my head (grown slightly bald) brought in upon a
    platter,[2]
I am no prophet—and here's no great matter;
I have seen the moment of my greatness flicker,
And I have seen the eternal Footman hold my coat, and snicker,
And in short, I was afraid.

And would it have been worth it, after all,
After the cups, the marmalade, the tea,
Among the porcelain, among some talk of you and me,
Would it have been worth while,   90
To have bitten off the matter with a smile,
To have squeezed the universe into a ball

---

  [2] John the Baptist was beheaded at the insistence of Salome, to whom his head was delivered on a platter. See Matthew 14:3–11 or Mark 6:16–28.

To roll it toward some overwhelming question,
To say: "I am Lazarus,[3] come from the dead,
Come back to tell you all, I shall tell you all"—
If one, settling a pillow by her head,
 Should say: "That is not what I meant at all;
 That is not it, at all."

And would it have been worth it, after all,
Would it have been worth while,   100
After the sunsets and the dooryards and the sprinkled streets,
After the novels, after the teacups, after the skirts that trail along
  the floor—
And this, and so much more?—
It is impossible to say just what I mean!
But as if a magic lantern threw the nerves in patterns on a screen:
Would it have been worth while
If one, settling a pillow or throwing off a shawl,
And turning toward the window, should say:
  "That is not it at all,
  That is not what I meant, at all."   110

     . . .

No! I am not Prince Hamlet, nor was meant to be;
Am an attendant lord, one that will do
To swell a progress, start a scene or two,
Advise the prince; no doubt, an easy tool,
Deferential, glad to be of use,
Politic, cautious, and meticulous;
Full of high sentence,[4] but a bit obtuse;
At times, indeed, almost ridiculous—
Almost, at times, the Fool.

I grow old . . . I grow old . . .
I shall wear the bottoms of my trousers rolled.

Shall I part my hair behind? Do I dare to eat a peach?
I shall wear white flannel trousers, and walk upon the beach.
I have heard the mermaids singing, each to each.

I do not think that they will sing to me.

 [3] One of the miracles of Jesus was the raising of Lazarus from the dead after he
had lain in the grave four days. See John 11:1–44.
 [4] *sententia,* wise sayings

I have seen them riding seaward on the waves
Combing the white hair of the waves blown back
When the wind blows the water white and black.

We have lingered in the chambers of the sea
By sea-girls wreathed with seaweed red and brown   130
Till human voices wake us, and we drown.

[1917]

EYES THAT LAST I SAW IN TEARS

EYES that last I saw in tears
Through division
Here in death's dream kingdom
The golden vision reappears
I see the eyes but not the tears
This is my affliction

This is my affliction
Eyes I shall not see again
Eyes of decision
Eyes I shall not see unless   10
At the door of death's other kingdom
Where, as in this,
The eyes outlast a little while
A little while outlast the tears
And hold us in derision.

[1924]

THE WIND SPRANG UP AT FOUR O'CLOCK

THE wind sprang up at four o'clock
The wind sprang up and broke the bells
Swinging between life and death
Here, in death's dream kingdom
The waking echo of confusing strife
Is it a dream or something else
When the surface of the blackened river
Is a face that sweats with tears?
I saw across the blackened river
The camp fire shake with alien spears.   10
Here, across death's other river
The Tartar horsemen shake their spears.

[1924]

JOURNEY OF THE MAGI

"A COLD coming we had of it,
Just the worst time of the year
For a journey, and such a long journey:
The ways deep and the weather sharp,
The very dead of winter."
And the camels galled, sore-footed, refractory,
Lying down in the melting snow.
There were times we regretted
The summer palaces on slopes, the terraces,
And the silken girls bringing sherbet.   10
Then the camel men cursing and grumbling
And running away, and wanting their liquor and women,
And the night-fires going out, and the lack of shelters,
And the cities hostile and the towns unfriendly
And the villages dirty and charging high prices:
A hard time we had of it.
At the end we preferred to travel all night,
Sleeping in snatches,
With the voices singing in our ears, saying
That this was all folly.   20

Then at dawn we came down to a temperate valley,
Wet, below the snow line, smelling of vegetation;
With a running stream and a water-mill beating the darkness,
And three trees on the low sky,
And an old white horse galloped away in the meadow.
Then we came to a tavern with vine-leaves over the lintel,
Six hands at an open door dicing for pieces of silver,
And feet kicking the empty wine-skins.
But there was no information, and so we continued
And arrived at evening, not a moment too soon   30
Finding the place; it was (you may say) satisfactory.

All this was a long time ago, I remember,
And I would do it again, but set down
This set down
This: were we led all that way for
Birth or Death? There was a Birth, certainly,
We had evidence and no doubt. I had seen birth and death,
But had thought they were different; this Birth was
Hard and bitter agony for us, like Death, our death.
We returned to our places, these Kingdoms,   40
But no longer at ease here, in the old dispensation,

With an alien people clutching their gods.
I should be glad of another death.

[1927]

Claude McKay
1890–1948

THE HARLEM DANCER

APPLAUDING youths laughed with young prostitutes
And watched her perfect, half-clothed body sway;
Her voice was like the sound of blended flutes
Blown by black players upon a picnic day.
She sang and danced on gracefully and calm,
The light gauze hanging loose about her form;
To me she seemed a proudly-swaying palm
Grown lovelier for passing through a storm.
Upon her swarthy neck black shiny curls
Luxuriant fell; and tossing coins in praise,   10
The wine-flushed, bold-eyed boys, and even the girls,
Devoured her shape with eager, passionate gaze;
But looking at her falsely-smiling face,
I knew her self was not in that strange place.

[1917]

AMERICA

ALTHOUGH she feeds me bread of bitterness,
And sinks into my throat her tiger's tooth,
Stealing my breath of life, I will confess
I love this cultured hell that tests my youth!
Her vigor flows like tides into my blood,
Giving me strength erect against her hate.
Her bigness sweeps my being like a flood,
Yet as a rebel fronts a king in state,
I stand within her walls with not a shred
Of terror, malice, not a word of jeer.   10
Darkly I gaze into the days ahead,
And see her might and granite wonders there,
Beneath the touch of Time's unerring hand,
Like priceless treasures sinking in the sand.

[1920]

FLAME-HEART

So MUCH I have forgotten in ten years,
So much in ten brief years! I have forgot
What time the purple apples come to juice,
And what month brings the shy forget-me-not.
I have forgot the special, startling season
Of the pimento's flowering and fruiting;
What time of year the ground doves brown the fields
And fill the noonday with their curious fluting.
I have forgotten much, but still remember
The poinsettia's red, blood-red, in warm December.   10

I still recall the honey-fever grass,
But cannot recollect the high days when
We rooted them out of the ping-wing[1] path
To stop the mad bees in the rabbit pen.
I often try to think in what sweet month
The languid painted ladies used to dapple
The yellow by-road mazing from the main,
Sweet with the golden threads of the rose-apple.
I have forgotten—strange—but quite remember
The poinsettia's red, blood-red, in warm December.   20

What weeks, what months, what time of the mild year
We cheated school to have our fling at tops?
What days our wine-thrilled bodies pulsed with joy
Feasting upon blackberries in the copse?
Oh some I know! I have embalmed the days,
Even the sacred moments when we played,
All innocent of passion, uncorrupt,
At noon and evening in the flame-heart's shade.
We were so happy, happy, I remember,
Beneath the poinsettia's red in warm December.   30

[1920]

[1] pinguin, a West Indian plant with spiny leaves

e. e. cummings
1894–1962

in Just-

in Just-
spring   when the world is mud-
luscious the little
lame balloonman

whistles   far   and wee

and eddieandbill come
running from marbles and
piracies and it's
spring

when the world is puddle-wonderful   10

the queer
old balloonman whistles
far   and   wee
and bettyandisbel come dancing

from hop-scotch and jump-rope and

it's
spring
and
    the

            goat-footed   20

balloonMan   whistles
far
and
wee

[1923]

a wind has blown the rain away

a wind has blown the rain away and blown
the sky away and all the leaves away,
and the trees stand. I think i too have known
autumn too long

(and what have you to say,
wind wind wind—did you love somebody
and have you the petal of somewhere in your heart
pinched from dumb summer?
                              O crazy daddy
of death dance cruelly for us and start

the last leaf whirling in the final brain
of air!) Let us as we have seen see   10
doom's integration . . . . a wind has blown the rain

away and the leaves and the sky and the
trees stand:
                    the trees stand. The trees,
suddenly wait against the moon's face.

                                                        [1923]

next to of course god america i

"next to of course god america i
love you land of the pilgrims' and so forth oh
say can you see by the dawn's early my
country 'tis of centuries come and go
and are no more what of it we should worry
in every language even deafanddumb
thy sons acclaim your glorious name by gorry
by jingo by gee by gosh by gum
why talk of beauty what could be more beaut-
iful than these heroic happy dead   10
who rushed like lions to the roaring slaughter
they did not stop to think they died instead
then shall the voice of liberty be mute?"

He spoke. And drank rapidly a glass of water

                                                        [1926]

anyone lived in a pretty how town

anyone lived in a pretty how town
(with up so floating many bells down)
spring summer autumn winter
he sang his didn't he danced his did

Women and men (both little and small)
cared for anyone not at all
they sowed their isn't they reaped their same
sun moon stars rain.

children guessed (but only a few
and down they forgot as up they grew   10
autumn winter spring summer)
that noone loved him more by more

when by now and tree by leaf
she laughed his joy she cried his grief
bird by snow and stir by still
anone's any was all to her

someones married their everyones
laughed their cryings and did their dance
(sleep wake hope and then) they
said their nevers they slept their dream   20

stars rain sun moon
(and only the snow can begin to explain
how children are apt to forget to remember
with up so floating many bells down)

one day anyone died i guess
(and noone stooped to kiss his face)
busy folk buried them side by side
little by little and was by was

all by all and deep by deep
and more by more they dream their sleep   30
noone and anyone earth by april
wish by spirit and if by yes.

Women and men (both dong and ding)
summer autumn winter spring
reaped their sowing and went their came
sun moon stars rain

[1940]

Hart Crane
1899–1932

REPOSE OF RIVERS

THE willows carried a slow sound,
  A sarabande the wind mowed on the mead.
I could never remember
That seething, steady leveling of the marshes
Till age had brought me to the sea.

Flags, weeds. And remembrance of steep alcoves
Where cypresses shared the noon's
Tyranny; they drew me into hades almost.
And mammoth turtles climbing sulphur dreams
Yielded, while sun-silt rippled them   10
Asunder . . .

How much I would have bartered! the black gorge
And all the singular nestings in the hills
Where beavers learn stitch and tooth.
The pond I entered once and quickly fled—
I remember now its singing willow rim.

And finally, in that memory all things nurse;
After the city that I finally passed
With scalding unguents spread and smoking darts
The monsoon cut across the delta   20
At gulf gates . . . There, beyond the dykes
I heard wind flaking sapphire, like this summer,
And willows could not hold more steady sound.

[1926]

PROEM: TO BROOKLYN BRIDGE

How many dawns, chill from his rippling rest
  The seagull's wings shall dip and pivot him,
Shedding white rings of tumult, building high
Over the chained bay waters Liberty—

Then, with inviolate curve, forsake our eyes
As apparitional as sails that cross
Some page of figures to be filed away;
—Till elevators drop us from our day . . .

I think of cinemas, panoramic sleights
With multitudes bent toward some flashing scene   10
Never disclosed, but hastened to again,
Foretold to other eyes on the same screen;

And Thee, across the harbor, silver-paced
As though the sun took step of thee, yet left
Some motion ever unspent in thy stride,—
Implicitly thy freedom staying thee!

Out of some subway scuttle, cell or loft
A bedlamite speeds to thy parapets,
Tilting there momently, shrill shirt ballooning,
A jest falls from the speechless caravan.   20

Down Wall, from girder into street noon leaks,
A rip-tooth of the sky's acetylene;
All afternoon the cloud-flown derricks turn . . .
Thy cables breathe the North Atlantic still.

And obscure as that heaven of the Jews,
Thy guerdon¹ . . . Accolade thou dost bestow
Of anonymity time cannot raise:
Vibrant reprieve and pardon thou dost show.

O harp and altar, of the fury fused,
(How could mere toil align thy choiring strings!)   30
Terrific threshold of the prophet's pledge,
Prayer of pariah,² and the lover's cry,—

Again the traffic lights that skim thy swift
Unfractioned idiom, immaculate sigh of stars,
Beading thy path—condense eternity:
And we have seen night lifted in thine arms.

Under thy shadow by the piers I waited;
Only in darkness is thy shadow clear.
The City's fiery parcels all undone,
Already snow submerges an iron year . . .   40

O Sleepless as the river under thee,
Vaulting the sea, the prairies' dreaming sod,
Unto us lowliest sometime sweep, descend
And of the curveship lend a myth to God.

[1930]

¹ reward   ² outcast

Langston Hughes
1902–1967

THE NEGRO SPEAKS OF RIVERS
(To W. E. B. DuBois) [1]

I'VE known rivers:
I've known rivers ancient as the world and older than the flow
of human blood in human veins.

My soul has grown deep like the rivers.

I bathed in the Euphrates when dawns were young.
I built my hut near the Congo and it lulled me to sleep.
I looked upon the Nile and raised the pyramids above it.
I heard the singing of the Mississippi when Abe Lincoln went
      down to New Orleans, and I've seen its muddy bosom
      turn all golden in the sunset.

I've known rivers:
Ancient, dusky rivers.

My soul has grown deep like the rivers.   10
                                                                [1926]

[1] Black social scientist, historian, and political activist

THE WEARY BLUES

DRONING a drowsy syncopated tune,
      Rocking back and forth to a mellow croon,
      I heard a Negro play.
Down on Lenox Avenue the other night
By the pale dull pallor of an old gas light
      He did a lazy sway. . . .
      He did a lazy sway. . . .
To the tune o' those Weary Blues.
With his ebony hands on each ivory key
He made that poor piano moan with melody.   10
      O Blues!
Swaying to and fro on his rickety stool
He played that sad raggy tune like a musical fool.
      Sweet Blues!

Coming from a black man's soul.
O Blues!
In a deep song voice with a melancholy tone
I heard that Negro sing, that old piano moan—
   "Ain't got nobody in all this world,
   Ain't got nobody but ma self.   20
   I's gwine to quit ma frownin'
   And put ma troubles on the shelf."
Thump, thump, thump, went his foot on the floor.
He played a few chords then he sang some more—
   "I got the Weary Blues
   And I can't be satisfied.
   Got the Weary Blues
   And can't be satisfied
   I ain't happy no mo'
   And I wish that I had died."   30
And far into the night he crooned that tune.
The stars went out and so did the moon.
The singer stopped playing and went to bed
While the Weary Blues echoed through his head
He slept like a rock or a man that's dead.

[1926]

THEME FOR ENGLISH B

THE instructor said,

     Go home and write
     a page tonight.
     And let that page come out of you—
     Then, it will be true.

I wonder if it's that simple?
I am twenty-two, colored, born in Winston-Salem.
I went to school there, then Durham, then here
to this college on the hill above Harlem.
I am the only colored student in my class.   10
The steps from the hill lead down into Harlem,
through a park, then I cross St. Nicholas,
Eight Avenue, Seventh, and I come to the Y,
the Harlem Branch Y, where I take the elevator
up to my room, sit down, and write this page:

It's not easy to know what is true for you or me
at twenty-two, my age. But I guess I'm what

I feel and see and hear. Harlem, I hear you:
hear you, hear me—we two—you, me talk on this page.
(I hear New York, too.) Me—who?   20
Well, I like to eat, sleep, drink, and be in love.
I like to work, read, learn, and understand life.
I like a pipe for a Christmas present,
or records—Bessie, bop, or Bach.

I guess being colored doesn't make me not like
the same things other folks like who are other races.
So will my page be colored that I write?
Being me, it will not be white.
But it will be
a part of you, instructor.   30
You are white—
yet a part of me, as I am a part of you.
That's American.
Sometimes perhaps you don't want to be a part of me.
Nor do I often want to be a part of you.
But we are, that's true!
As I learn from you,
I guess you learn from me—
although you're older—and white—
and somewhat more free.   40

This is my page for English B.

                                                      [1951]

DREAM VARIATION

To fling my arms wide
    In some place of the sun,
To whirl and to dance
Till the white day is done.
Then rest at cool evening
Beneath a tall tree
While night comes on gently,
    Dark like me—
That is my dream!
To fling my arms wide   10
In the face of the sun,
Dance! Whirl! Whirl!
Till the quick day is done.
Rest at pale evening . . .
A tall, slim tree . . .

Night coming tenderly
Black like me.

[1959]

I, TOO

I, TOO, sing America.
I am the darker brother.
They send me to eat in the kitchen
When company comes,
But I laugh,
And eat well,
And grow strong.

Tomorrow,
I'll be at the table
When company comes.
Nobody'll dare
Say to me,
"Eat in the kitchen,"
Then.

Besides,
They'll see how beautiful I am
And be ashamed—

I, too, am America.

[1959]

Ogden Nash

1902–

LISTEN . . .

THERE is a knocking in the skull,
An endless silent shout
Of something beating on a wall,
And crying, Let me out.

That solitary prisoner
Will never hear reply,
No comrade in eternity
Can hear the frantic cry.

No heart can share the terror
That haunts his monstrous dark;   10
The light that filters through the chinks
No other eye can mark.

When flesh is linked with eager flesh,
And words run warm and full,
I think that he is loneliest then,
The captive in the skull.

Caught in a mesh of living veins,
In cell of padded bone,
He loneliest is when he pretends
That he is not alone.   20

We'd free the incarcerate race of man
That such a doom endures
Could only you unlock my skull,
Or I creep into yours.

[1945]

VERY LIKE A WHALE

ONE thing that literature would be greatly the better for
    Would be a more restricted employment by authors of simile and
  metaphor.
Authors of all races, be they Greeks, Romans, Teutons or Celts,
Can't seem just to say that anything is the thing it is but have to go out of
  their way to say that it is like something else.
What does it mean when we are told
That the Assyrian came down like a wolf on the fold?
In the first place, George Gordon Byron had had enough experience
To know that it probably wasn't just one Assyrian, it was a lot of Assyr-
  ians.
However, as too many arguments are apt to induce apoplexy and thus
  hinder longevity,
We'll let it pass as one Assyrian for the sake of brevity.
Now then, this particular Assyrian, the one whose cohorts were gleam-
  ing in purple and gold,
Just what does the poet mean when he says he came down like a wolf on
  the fold?
In heaven and earth more than is dreamed of in our philosophy there are
  a great many things,
But I don't imagine that among them there is a wolf with purple and gold
  cohorts or purple and gold anythings.

No, no, Lord Byron, before I'll believe that this Assyrian was actually
    like a wolf I must have some kind of proof;
Did he run on all fours and did he have a hairy tail and a big red mouth
    and big white teeth and did he say Woof woof?
Frankly I think it very unlikely, and all you were entitled to say, at the
    very most,
Was that the Assyrian cohorts came down like a lot of Assyrian cohorts
    about to destroy the Hebrew host.
But that wasn't fancy enough for Lord Byron, oh dear me no, he had to
    invent a lot of figures of speech and then interpolate them,
With the result that whenever you mention Old Testament soldiers to
    people they say Oh yes, they're the ones that a lot of wolves dressed
    up in gold and purple ate them.   20
That's the kind of thing that's being done all the time by poets, from
    Homer to Tennyson;
They're always comparing ladies to lilies and veal to venison,
And they always say things like that the snow is a white blanket after a
    winter storm.
Oh it is, is it, all right then, you sleep under a six-inch blanket of snow
    and I'll sleep under a half-inch blanket of unpoetical blanket material
    and we'll see which one keeps warm,
And after that maybe you'll begin to comprehend dimly
What I mean by too much metaphor and simile.

[1945]

THE GERM

A MIGHTY creature is the germ,
  Though smaller than the pachyderm.
His customary dwelling place
Is deep within the human race.
His childish pride he often pleases
By giving people strange diseases.
Do you, my poppet, feel infirm?
You probably contain a germ.

[1945]

C. Day Lewis
1904–1972

COME, LIVE WITH ME AND BE MY LOVE

COME, live with me and be my love,
And we will all the pleasures prove
Of peace and plenty, bed and board,
That chance employment may afford.

I'll handle dainties on the docks
And thou shalt read of summer frocks :
At evening by the sour canals
We'll hope to hear some madrigals.

Care on thy maiden brow shall put
A wreath of wrinkles, and thy foot   10
Be shod with pain : not silken dress
But toil shall tire thy loveliness.

Hunger shall make thy modest zone
And cheat fond death of all but bone—
If these delights thy mind may move,
Then live with me and be my love.

[1935]

NEWSREEL

ENTER the dream-house, brothers and sisters, leaving
Your debts asleep, your history at the door :
This is the home for heroes, and this loving
Darkness a fur you can afford.

Fish in their tank electrically heated
Nose with envy the glass wall : for them
Clerk, spy, nurse, killer, prince, the great and the defeated,
Move in a mute day-dream.

Bathed in this common source, you gape incurious
At what your active hours have willed—   10
Sleep-walking on that silver wall, the furious
Sick shapes and pregnant fancies of your world.

There is the mayor opening the oyster season :
A society wedding : the autumn hats look swell :
An old crocks' race, and a politician
In fishing-waders to prove that all is well.

Oh, look at the warplanes ! Screaming hysteric treble
In the long power-dive, like gannets they fall steep.
But what are they to trouble—
These silver shadows to trouble your watery, womb-deep sleep ?   20

See the big guns, rising, groping, erected
To plant death in your world's soft womb.
Fire-bud, smoke-blossom, iron seed projected—
Are these exotics ? They will grow nearer home :

Grow nearer home—and out of the dream-house stumbling
One night into a strangling air and the flung
Rags of children and thunder of stone niagaras tumbling,
You'll know you slept too long.

[1935]

ALMOST HUMAN

THE man you know, assured and kind,
     Wearing fame like an old tweed suit—
You would not think he has an incurable
Sickness upon his mind.

Finely that tongue, for the listening people,
Articulates love, enlivens clay ;
While under his valued skin there crawls
An outlaw and a cripple.

Unenviable the renown he bears
When all's awry within ? But a soul   10
Divinely sick may be immunized
From the scourge of common cares.

A woman weeps, a friend's betrayed,
Civilization plays with fire—
His grief or guilt is easily purged
In a rush of words to the head.

The newly dead, and their waxwork faces
With the look of things that could never have lived,
He'll use to prime his cold, strange heart
And prompt the immortal phrases.   20

Before you condemn this eminent freak
As an outrage upon mankind,
Reflect : something there is in him
That must for ever seek

To share the condition it glorifies,
To shed the skin that keeps it apart,
To bury its grace in a human bed—
And it walks on knives, on knives.

                                                              [1957]

W. H. Auden
1907–1973
WHO'S WHO

A SHILLING life will give you all the facts :
How Father beat him, how he ran away,
What were the struggles of his youth, what acts
Made him the greatest figure of his day :
Of how he fought, fished, hunted, worked all night,
Though giddy, climbed new mountains ; named a sea :
Some of the last researchers even write
Love made him weep his pints like you and me.
With all his honors on, he sighed for one
Who, say astonished critics, lived at home ;   10
Did little jobs about the house with skill
And nothing else ; could whistle ; would sit still
Or potter round the garden ; answered some
Of his long marvelous letters but kept none.

                                                              [1934]

LULLABY

LAY your sleeping head, my love,
Human on my faithless arm ;
Time and fevers burn away
Individual beauty from
Thoughtful children, and the grave

Proves the child ephemeral:
But in my arms till break of day
Let the living creature lie,
Mortal, guilty, but to me
The entirely beautiful.   10

Soul and body have no bounds:
To lovers as they lie upon
Her tolerant enchanted slope
In their ordinary swoon,
Grave the vision Venus sends
Of supernatural sympathy,
Universal love and hope;
While an abstract insight wakes
Among the glaciers and the rocks
The hermit's carnal ecstasy.   20

Certainty, fidelity
On the stroke of midnight pass
Like vibrations of a bell
And fashionable madmen raise
Their pedantic boring cry:
Every farthing of the cost,
All the dreaded cards foretell,
Shall be paid, but from this night
Not a whisper, not a thought,
Not a kiss nor look be lost.   30

Beauty, midnight, vision dies:
Let the winds of dawn that blow
Softly round your dreaming head
Such a day of welcome show
Eye and knocking heart may bless,
Find our mortal world enough;
Noons of dryness find you fed
By the involuntary powers,
Nights of insult let you pass
Watched by every human love.   40
                                         [1937]

MUSÉE DES BEAUX ARTS

ABOUT suffering they were never wrong,
  The Old Masters: how well they understood
Its human position; how it takes place

While someone else is eating or opening a window or just walking dully
    along;
How, when the agéd are reverently, passionately waiting
For the miraculous birth, there always must be
Children who did not specially want it to happen, skating
On a pond at the edge of the wood:
They never forget
That even the dreadful martyrdom must run its course   10
Anyhow in a corner, some untidy spot
Where the dogs go on with their doggy life and the torturer's horse
Scratches its innocent behind on a tree.

In Brueghel's[1] *Icarus*, for instance: how everything turns away
Quite leisurely from the disaster; the ploughman may
Have heard the splash, the forsaken cry,
But for him it was not an important failure; the sun shone
As it had to on the white legs disappearing into the green
Water; and the expensive delicate ship that must have seen
Something amazing, a boy falling out of the sky,   20
Had somewhere to get to and sailed calmly on.

[1940]

[1] Pieter Brueghel, Flemish painter, *c.* 1520–1569. Icarus and his father, Dædalus, fashioned wings and attached them to their shoulders with wax. Icarus flew too close to the sun; he fell from the sky when the sun melted the wax.
See also W. C. Williams, "Landscape with the Fall of Icarus," p. 901.

THE UNKNOWN CITIZEN
(TO JS/07/M/378)
THIS MARBLE MONUMENT
IS ERECTED BY THE STATE

HE WAS found by the Bureau of Statistics to be
One against whom there was no official complaint,
And all the reports on his conduct agree
That, in the modern sense of an old-fashioned word, he was a saint,
For in everything he did he served the Greater Community.
Except for the War till the day he retired
He worked in a factory and never got fired,
But satisfied his employers, Fudge Motors Inc.
Yet he wasn't a scab or odd in his views,
For his Union reports that he paid his dues,   10
(Our report on his Union shows it was sound)
And our Social Psychology workers found

That he was popular with his mates and liked a drink.
The Press are convinced that he bought a paper every day
And that his reactions to advertisements were normal in every way.
Policies taken out in his name prove that he was fully insured,
And his Health-card shows he was once in hospital but left it cured.
Both Producers Research and High-Grade Living declare
He was fully sensible to the advantages of the Instalment Plan
And had everything necessary to the Modern Man,   20
A phonograph, a radio, a car and a frigidaire.
Our researchers into Public Opinion are content
That he held the proper opinions for the time of year;
When there was peace, he was for peace; when there was war, he
    went.
He was married and added five children to the population,
Which our Eugenist says was the right number for a parent of his
    generation,
And our teachers report that he never interfered with their educa-
    tion.
Was he free? Was he happy? The question is absurd:
Had anything been wrong, we should certainly have heard.

                                        [1939]

THE SHIELD OF ACHILLES

S H E looked over his shoulder
    For vines and olive trees,
Marble well-governed cities
    And ships upon untamed seas,
But there on the shining metal
    His hands had put instead
An artificial wilderness
    And a sky like lead.

A plain without a feature, bare and brown,
    No blade of grass, no sign of neighborhood,   10
Nothing to eat and nowhere to sit down,
    Yet, congregated on its blankness, stood
    An unintelligible multitude,
A million eyes, a million boots in line,
Without expression, waiting for a sign.

Out of the air a voice without a face
    Proved by statistics that some cause was just
In tones as dry and level as the place:

No one was cheered and nothing was discussed;
Column by column in a cloud of dust   20
They marched away enduring a belief
Whose logic brought them, somewhere else, to grief.

    She looked over his shoulder
      For ritual pieties,
    White flower-garlanded heifers,
      Libation and sacrifice,
    But there on the shining metal
      Where the altar should have been,
    She saw by his flickering forge-light
      Quite another scene.   30

Barbed wire enclosed an arbitrary spot
    Where bored officials lounged (one cracked a joke)
And sentries sweated for the day was hot:
    A crowd of ordinary decent folk
    Watched from without and neither moved nor spoke
As three pale figures were led forth and bound
To three posts driven upright in the ground.

The mass and majesty of this world, all
    That carries weight and always weighs the same
Lay in the hands of others; they were small   40
    And could not hope for help and no help came:
    What their foes liked to do was done, their shame
Was all the worst could wish; they lost their pride
And died as men before their bodies died.

    She looked over his shoulder
      For athletes at their games,
    Men and women in a dance
      Moving their sweet limbs
    Quick, quick, to music,
      But there on the shining shield   50
    His hands had set no dancing-floor
      But a weed-choked field.

A ragged urchin, aimless and alone,
    Loitered about that vacancy, a bird
Flew up to safety from his well-aimed stone:
    That girls are raped, that two boys knife a third,
    Were axioms to him, who'd never heard
Of any world where promises were kept,
Or one could weep because another wept.

The thin-lipped armorer,   60
  Hephæstos hobbled away,
Thetis of the shining breasts
  Cried out in dismay
At what the god had wrought
  To please her son, the strong
Iron-hearted man-slaying Achilles
  Who would not live long.

[1955]

Theodore Roethke

1908–1963

MOSS-GATHERING

To loosen with all ten fingers held wide and limber
  And lift up a patch, dark-green, the kind for lining cemetery baskets,
Thick and cushiony, like an old-fashioned door-mat,
The crumbling small hollow sticks on the underside mixed with roots,
And wintergreen berries and leaves still stuck to the top,—
That was moss-gathering.

But something always went out of me when I dug loose those carpets
Of green, or plunged to my elbows in the spongy yellowish moss of the
  marshes:
And afterwards I always felt mean, jogging back over the logging road,
As if I had broken the natural order of things in that swampland;   10
Disturbed some rhythm, old and of vast importance,
By pulling off flesh from the living planet;
As if I had committed, against the whole scheme of life, a desecration.

[1948]

MY PAPA'S WALTZ

THE whiskey on your breath
  Could make a small boy dizzy;
But I held on like death:
Such waltzing was not easy.

We romped until the pans
Slid from the kitchen shelf;
My mother's countenance
Could not unfrown itself.

The hand that held my wrist
Was battered on one knuckle;   10
At every step I missed
My right ear scraped a buckle.

You beat time on my head
With a palm caked hard by dirt,
Then waltzed me off to bed
Still clinging to your shirt.

[1948]

ELEGY FOR JANE

(MY STUDENT, THROWN BY A HORSE)

I REMEMBER the neckcurls, limp and damp as tendrils,
And her quick look, a sidelong pickerel smile;
And how, once startled into talk, the light syllables leaped for her,
And she balanced in the delight of her thought,
A wren, happy, tail into the wind,
Her song trembling the twigs and small branches.
The shade sang with her;
The leaves, their whispers turned to kissing;
And the mold sang in the bleached valleys under the rose.

Oh, when she was sad, she cast herself down into such a pure depth,   10
Even a father could not find her;
Scraping her cheek against straw;
Stirring the clearest water.

My sparrow, you are not here,
Waiting like a fern, making a spiny shadow.
The sides of wet stones cannot console me,
Nor the moss, wound with the last light.

If only I could nudge you from this sleep,
My maimed darling, my skittery pigeon.
Over this damp grave I speak the words of my love: 20
I, with no rights in this matter,
Neither father nor lover.

[1953]

THE WAKING

I WAKE to sleep, and take my waking slow.
I feel my fate in what I cannot fear.
I learn by going where I have to go.

We think by feeling. What is there to know?
I hear my being dance from ear to ear.
I wake to sleep, and take my waking slow.

Of those so close beside me, which are you?
God bless the Ground! I shall walk softly there,
And learn by going where I have to go.

Light takes the Tree; but who can tell us how?   10
The lowly worm climbs up a winding stair;
I wake to sleep, and take my waking slow.

Great Nature has another thing to do.
To you and me; so take the lively air,
And, lovely, learn by going where to go.

This shaking keeps me steady. I should know.
What falls away is always. And is near.
I wake to sleep, and take my waking slow.
I learn by going where I have to go.

[1953]

I KNEW A WOMAN

I KNEW a woman, lovely in her bones,
When small birds sighed, she would sigh back at them;
Ah, when she moved, she moved more ways than one:
The shapes a bright container can contain!
Of her choice virtues only gods should speak,
Or English poets who grew up on Greek
(I'd have them sing in chorus, cheek to cheek).

How well her wishes went! She stroked my chin,
She taught me Turn, and Counter-turn, and Stand;
She taught me Touch, that undulant white skin;   10
I nibbled meekly from her proffered hand;
She was the sickle; I, poor I, the rake,
Coming behind her for her pretty sake
(But what prodigious mowing we did make).

Love likes a gander, and adores a goose:
Her full lips pursed, the errant note to seize;
She played it quick, she played it light and loose;
My eyes, they dazzled at her flowing knees;
Her several parts could keep a pure repose,
Or one hip quiver with a mobile nose   20
(She moved in circles, and those circles moved).

Let seed be grass, and grass turn into hay:
I'm martyr to a motion not my own;
What's freedom for? To know eternity.
I swear she cast a shadow white as stone.
But who would count eternity in days?
These old bones live to learn her wanton ways:
(I measure time by how a body sways).

                                                        [1958]

IN A DARK TIME

In a dark time, the eye begins to see,
     I meet my shadow in the deepening shade;
I hear my echo in the echoing wood—
A lord of nature weeping to a tree.
I live between the heron and the wren,
Beasts of the hill and serpents of the den.

What's madness but nobility of soul
At odds with circumstance? The day's on fire!
I know the purity of pure despair,
My shadow pinned against a sweating wall.[1]   10
That place among the rocks—is it a cave,
Or winding path? The edge is what I have.

A steady storm of correspondences![2]
A night flowing with birds, a ragged moon,
And in broad day the midnight come again!
A man goes far to find out what he is—
Death of the self in a long, tearless night,
All natural shapes blazing unnatural light.

---

[1] Plato's Myth of the Cave compares man's limited knowledge of reality to that of a person so bound that he can see only his own shadow cast on a cave wall by a fire behind him.

[2] The transcendental doctrine of correspondences, essentially Platonic in origin, holds that earthly actualities are imperfect reflections of perfect divine ideas.

Dark, dark my light, and darker my desire.
My soul, like some heat-maddened summer fly,   20
Keeps buzzing at the sill. Which I is *I*?
A fallen man, I climb out of my fear.
The mind enters itself, and God the mind,
And one is One, free in the tearing wind.

[1964]

Elizabeth Bishop
1911–
THE MAN-MOTH[1]

H ERE, above,
cracks in the buildings are filled with battered moonlight.
The whole shadow of Man is only as big as his hat.
It lies at his feet like a circle for a doll to stand on,
and he makes an inverted pin, the point magnetized to the moon.
He does not see the moon; he observes only her vast properties,
feeling the queer light on his hands, neither warm nor cold,
of a temperature impossible to record in thermometers.

But when the Man-Moth
pays his rare, although occasional, visits to the surface,   10
the moon looks rather different to him. He emerges
from an opening under the edge of one of the sidewalks
and nervously begins to scale the faces of the buildings.
He thinks the moon is a small hole at the top of the sky,
proving the sky quite useless for protection.
He trembles, but must investigate as high as he can climb.

Up the façades,
his shadow dragging like a photographers' cloth behind him,
he climbs fearfully, thinking that this time he will manage
to push his small head through that round clean opening   20
and be forced through, as from a tube, in black scrolls on the light.
(Man, standing below him, has no such illusions.)
But what the Man-Moth fears most he must do, although
he fails, of course, and falls back scared but quite unhurt.

[1] Bishop notes that the title and subject were suggested by a newspaper misprint for "mammoth."

     Then he returns
to the pale subways of cement he calls his home. He flits,
he flutters, and cannot get aboard the silent trains
fast enough to suit him. The doors close swiftly.
The Man-Moth always seats himself facing the wrong way
and the train starts at once at its full, terrible speed,   30
without a shift in gears or a gradation of any sort.
He cannot tell the rate at which he travels backwards.

     Each night he must
be carried through artificial tunnels and dream recurrent dreams.
Just as the ties recur beneath his train, these underlie
his rushing brain. He does not dare look out the window,
for the third rail, the unbroken draft of poison,
runs there beside him. He regards it as a disease
he has inherited the susceptibility to. He has to keep
his hands in his pockets, as others must wear mufflers.   40

     If you catch him,
hold up a flashlight to his eye. It's all dark pupil,
an entire night itself, whose haired horizon tightens
as he stares back, and closes up the eye. Then from the lids
one tear, his only possession, like the bee's sting, slips.
Slyly he palms it, and if you're not paying attention
he'll swallow it. However, if you watch, he'll hand it over,
cool as from underground springs and pure enough to drink.

                                   [1948]

SANDPIPER

THE roaring alongside he takes for granted,
  and that every so often the world is bound to shake.
He runs, he runs to the south, finical, awkward,
in a state of controlled panic, a student of Blake.

The beach hisses like fat. On his left, a sheet
of interrupting water comes and goes
and glazes over his dark and brittle feet.
He runs, he runs straight through it, watching his toes.

—Watching, rather, the spaces of sand between them,
where (no detail too small) the Atlantic drains   10
rapidly backwards and downwards. As he runs,
he stares at the dragging grains.

The world is a mist. And then the world is
minute and vast and clear. The tide
is higher or lower. He couldn't tell you which.
His beak is focussed ; he is preoccupied,

looking for something, something, something.
Poor bird, he is obsessed !
The millions of grains are black, white, tan, and gray,
mixed with quartz grains, rose and amethyst.   20

[1965]

Josephine Miles
1911–

ON INHABITING AN ORANGE

ALL our roads go nowhere.
Maps are curled
To keep the pavement definitely
On the world.

All our footsteps, set to make
Metric advance,
Lapse into arcs in deference
To circumstance.

All our journeys nearing Space
Skirt it with care,   10
Shying at the distances
Present in air.

Blithely travel-stained and worn,
Erect and sure,
All our travelers go forth,
Making down the roads of Earth
Endless detour.

[1935]

BELIEF

MOTHER said to call her if the H bomb exploded
And I said I would, and it about did
When Louis my brother robbed a service station
And lay cursing on the oily cement in handcuffs.

But by that time it was too late to tell Mother,
She was too sick to worry the life out of her
Over *why why*. Causation is sequence
And everything is one thing after another.

Besides, my other brother, Eddie, had got to be President,
And you can't ask too much of one family.   10
The chances were as good for a good future
As bad for a bad one.

Therefore it was surprising that, as we kept the newspapers
    from Mother,
She died feeling responsible for a disaster unverified,
Murmuring, in her sleep as it seemed, the ancient slogan
Noblesse oblige.[1]

                                                            [1955]

---

[1] Nobility imposes obligations (on the noble).

REASON

SAID, Pull her up a bit will you, Mac, I want to unload there.
Said, Pull her up my rear end, first come first serve.
Said, Give her the gun, Bud, he needs a taste of his own bumper.
Then the usher came out and got into the act :

Said, Pull her up, pull her up a bit, we need this space, sir.
Said, For God's sake, is this still a free country or what ?
You go back and take care of Gary Cooper's horse
And leave me handle my own car.

Saw them unloading the lame old lady,
Ducked out under the wheel and gave her an elbow,   10
Said, All you needed to do was just explain ;
Reason, Reason is my middle name.

                                                            [1955]

Robert Hayden
1913–

THE BALLAD OF SUE ELLEN WESTERFIELD
(FOR CLYDE)

SHE grew up in bedeviled southern wilderness,
but had not been a slave, she said,
because her father wept and set her mother free.
She hardened in perilous rivertowns
and after The Surrender,
went as maid upon the tarnished Floating Palaces.
Rivermen reviled her for the rankling cold
sardonic pride
that gave a knife-edge to her comeliness.

When she was old, her back still straight,   10
her hair still glossy black,
she'd talk sometimes
of dangers lived through on the rivers.
But never told of him,
whose name she'd vowed she would not speak again
till after Jordan.
Oh, he was nearer nearer now
than wearisome kith and kin.
His blue eyes followed her
as she moved about her tasks upon the *Memphis Rose*.   20
He smiled and joshed, his voice quickening her.
She cursed the circumstance. . . .

The crazing horrors of that summer night,
the swifting flames, he fought his way to her,
the savaging panic, and helped her swim to shore.
The steamer like besieged Atlanta blazing,
the cries, the smoke and bellowing flames,
the flamelit thrashing forms in hellmouth water,
and he swimming out to them,
leaving her dazed and lost.   30
A woman screaming under the raddled trees—
Sue Ellen felt it was herself who screamed.
The moaning of the hurt, the terrified—
she held off shuddering despair
and went to comfort whom she could.
Wagons torches bells
and whimpering dusk of morning

and blankness lostness nothingness for her
until his arms had lifted her
into wild and secret dark.   40

How long how long was it they wandered,
loving fearing loving,
fugitives whose dangerous only hidingplace
was love?
How long was it before she knew
she could not forfeit what she was,
even for him—could not, even for him,
forswear her pride?
They kissed and said farewell at last.
He wept as had her father once.   50
They kissed and said farewell.
Until her dying-bed,
she cursed the circumstance.

                                                                          [1962]

RUNAGATE RUNAGATE

I

Runs falls rises stumbles on from darkness into darkness
and the darkness thicketed with shapes of terror
and the hunters pursuing and the hounds pursuing
and the night cold and the night long and the river
to cross and the jack-muh-lanterns beckoning beckoning
and blackness ahead and when shall I reach that somewhere
morning and keep on going and never turn back and keep on going

                Runagate
                        Runagate
                                Runagate   10
Many thousands rise and go
many thousands crossing over

                        O mythic North
                O star-shaped yonder Bible city

Some go weeping and some rejoicing
some in coffins and some in carriages
some in silks and some in shackles

                Rise and go or fare you well

No more auction block for me
no more driver's lash for me   20

    If you see my Pompey, 30 yrs of age,
    new breeches, plain stockings, negro shoes;
    if you see my Anna, likely young mulatto
    branded E on the right cheek, R on the left,
    catch them if you can and notify subscriber.
    Catch them if you can, but it won't be easy.
    They'll dart underground when you try to catch them,
    plunge into quicksand, whirlpools, mazes,
    turn into scorpions when you try to catch them.

And before I'll be a slave   30
I'll be buried in my grave

    North star and bonanza gold
    I'm bound for the freedom, freedom bound
    and oh Susyanna don't you cry for me

        Runagate

            Runagate

         II
Rises from their anguish and their power,

    Harriet Tubman,[1]
    woman of earth, whipscarred,
    a summoning, a shining   40

    Mean to be free

And this was the way of it, brethren brethren,
way we journeyed from Can't to Can.
Moon so bright and no place to hide,
the cry up and the patterollers[2] riding.
hound dogs belling in bladed air.
And fear starts a-murbling, Never make it,
we'll never make it. *Hush that now,*
and she's turned upon us, levelled pistol
glinting in the moonlight: 50
Dead folks can't jaybird-talk, she says;
you keep on going now or die, she says.

  [1] freed slave who aided other fugitives, and who supported abolition, women's rights, and education for Blacks
  [2] slave hunters

Wanted   Harriet Tubman   alias The General
alias Moses   Stealer of Slaves

In league with Garrison   Alcott   Emerson
Garrett   Douglass   Thoreau   John Brown[3]

Armed and known to be Dangerous

Wanted   Reward   Dead or Alive

   Tell me, Ezekiel, oh tell me do you see
   mailed Jehovah coming to deliver me?   60

Hoot-owl calling in the ghosted air,
five times calling to the hants in the air.
Shadow of a face in the scary leaves,
shadow of a voice in the talking leaves :

   Come ride-a my train

   Oh that train, ghost-story train
   through swamp and savanna movering movering,
   over trestles of dew, through caves of the wish,
   Midnight special on a saber track movering movering,
   first stop Mercy and the last Hallelujah.   70

   Come ride-a my train

     Mean mean mean to be free.

                            [1966]

[3] leaders, both black and white, who supported the antislavery cause in various
ways and with greater or less fervor

Karl Shapiro
1913–
AUTO WRECK

Iᴛs quick soft silver bell beating, beating,
And down the dark one ruby flare
Pulsing out red light like an artery,
The ambulance at top speed floating down
Past beacons and illuminated clocks
Wings in a heavy curve, dips down,

And brakes speed, entering the crowd.
The doors leap open, emptying light;
Stretchers are laid out, the mangled lifted
And stowed into the little hospital.   10
Then the bell, breaking the hush, tolls once,
And the ambulance with its terrible cargo
Rocking, slightly rocking moves away,
As the doors, an afterthought, are closed.
We are deranged, walking among the cops
Who sweep glass and are large and composed.
One is still making notes under the light.
One with a bucket douches ponds of blood
Into the street and gutter.
One hangs lanterns on the wrecks that cling,   20
Empty husks of locusts, to iron poles.
Our throats were tight as tourniquets,
Our feet were bound with splints, but now,
Like convalescents intimate and gauche,
We speak through sickly smiles and warn
With the stubborn saw of common sense,
The grim joke and the banal resolution.
The traffic moves around with care,
But we remain, touching a wound
That opens to our richest horror.   30
Already old, the question Who shall die?
Becomes unspoken Who is innocent?
For death in war is done by hands;
Suicide has cause and stillbirth, logic;
And cancer, simple as a flower, blooms.
But this invites the occult mind,
Cancels our physics with a sneer,
And spatters all we knew of denouement
Across the expedient and wicked stones.

[1942]

DRUG STORE

I do remember an apothecary
And hereabouts 'a dwells[1]

I T B A F F L E S the foreigner like an idiom,
And he is right to adopt it as a form
Less serious than the living-room or bar;
For it disestablishes the cafe,
Is a collective, and on basic country.

---

[1] *Romeo and Juliet*, V, i, 37-38

Not that it praises hygiene and corrupts
The ice-cream parlor and the tobacconist's
Is it a center; but that the attractive symbols
    Watch over puberty and leer
Like rubber bottles waiting for sick-use.   10

Youth comes to jingle nickles and crack wise;
The baseball scores are his, the magazines
Devoted to lust, the jazz, the Coca-Cola,
    The lending-library of love's latest.
He is the customer; he is heroized.

And every nook and cranny of the flesh
Is spoken to by packages with wiles.
"Buy me, buy me," they whimper and cajole;
    The hectic range of lipstick pouts,
Revealing the wicked and the simple mouth.   20

With scarcely any evasion in their eye
They smoke, undress their girls, exact a stance;
But only for a moment. The clock goes round;
    Crude fellowships are made and lost;
They slump in booths like rags, not even drunk.

                             [1942]

THE LEG

Among the iodoform, in twilight-sleep,
What have I lost? he first inquires,
Peers in the middle distance where a pain,
Ghost of a nurse, hastily moves, and day,
Her blinding presence pressing in his eyes
And now his ears. They are handling him
With rubber hands. He wants to get up.

One day beside some flowers near his nose
He will be thinking, *When will I look at it?*
And pain, still in the middle distance, will reply   10
At what? and he will know it's gone,
O where! and begin to tremble and cry.
He will begin to cry as a child cries
Whose puppy is mangled under a screaming wheel.

Later, as if deliberately, his fingers
Begin to explore the stump. He learns a shape

That is comfortable and tucked in like a sock.
This has a sense of humor, this can despise
The finest surgical limb, the dignity of limping,
The nonsense of wheel-chairs. Now he smiles to the wall: 20
The amputation becomes an acquisition.

For the leg is wondering where he is (all is not lost)
And surely he has a duty to the leg;
He is its injury, the leg is his orphan,
He must cultivate the mind of the leg,
Pray for the part that is missing, pray for peace
In the image of man, pray, pray for its safety,
And after a little it will die quietly.

The body, what is it, Father, but a sign
To love the force that grows us, to give back   30
What in Thy palm is senselessness and mud?
Knead, knead the substance of our understanding
That if Thou take me angrily in hand
And hurl me to the shark, I shall not die!

[1944]

Dylan Thomas
1914–1953

THE FORCE THAT THROUGH THE GREEN FUSE DRIVES THE FLOWER

THE force that through the green fuse drives the flower
Drives my green age; that blasts the roots of trees
Is my destroyer.
And I am dumb to tell the crooked rose
My youth is bent by the same wintry fever.

The force that drives the water through the rocks
Drives my red blood; that dries the mouthing streams
Turns mine to wax.
And I am dumb to mouth unto my veins
How at the mountain spring the same mouth sucks.   10

The hand that whirls the water in the pool
Stirs the quicksand; that ropes the blowing wind
Hauls my shroud sail.
And I am dumb to tell the hanging man
How of my clay is made the hangman's line.

The lips of time leech to the fountain head;
Love drips and gathers, but the fallen blood
Shall calm her sores.
And I am dumb to tell a weather's wind
How time has ticked a heaven round the stars.   20

And I am dumb to tell the lover's tomb
How at my sheet goes the same crooked worm.

[1934]

WHEN ALL MY FIVE AND COUNTRY
SENSES SEE

WHEN all my five and country senses see,
The fingers will forget green thumbs and mark
How, through the halfmoon's vegetable eye,
Husk of young stars and handfull zodiac,
Love in the frost is pared and wintered by,
The whispering ears will watch love drummed away
Down breeze and shell to a discordant beach,
And, lashed to syllables, the lynx tongue cry
That her fond wounds are mended bitterly.
My nostrils see her breath turn like a bush.   10

My one and noble heart has witnesses
In all love's countries, that will grope awake;
And when blind sleep drops on the spying senses,
The heart is sensual, though five eyes break.

[1939]

IN MY CRAFT OR SULLEN ART

In my craft or sullen art
Exercised in the still night
When only the moon rages
And the lovers lie abed
With all their griefs in their arms,
I labor by singing light
Not for ambition or bread
Or the strut and trade of charms
On the ivory stages
But for the common wages   10
Of their most secret heart.

Not for the proud man apart
From the raging moon I write
On these spindrift pages
Nor for the towering dead
With their nightingales and psalms
But for the lovers, their arms
Round the griefs of the ages,
Who pay no praise or wages
Nor heed my craft or art.   20

[1945]

FERN HILL

Now as I was young and easy under the apple boughs
About the lilting house and happy as the grass was green,
    The night above the dingle starry,
        Time let me hail and climb
    Golden in the heydays of his eyes,
And honored among wagons I was prince of the apple towns
And once below a time I lordly had the trees and leaves
        Trail with daisies and barley
    Down the rivers of the windfall light.

And as I was green and carefree, famous among the barns   10
About the happy yard and singing as the farm was home,
    In the sun that is young once only,
        Time let me play and be
    Golden in the mercy of his means,
And green and golden I was huntsman and herdsman, the calves
Sang to my horn, the foxes on the hills barked clear and cold,
        And the sabbath rang slowly
    In the pebbles of the holy streams.

All the sun long it was running, it was lovely, the hay
Fields high as the house, the tunes from the chimneys, it was air   20
        And playing, lovely and watery
            And fire green as grass.
        And nightly under the simple stars
As I rode to sleep the owls were bearing the farm away,
All the moon long I heard, blessed among stables, the night-jars
        Flying with the ricks, and the horses
            Flashing into the dark.

And then to awake, and the farm, like a wanderer white
With the dew, come back, the cock on his shoulder : it was all
    Shining, it was Adam and maiden,   30
        The sky gathered again
    And the sun grew round that very day.
So it must have been after the birth of the simple light
In the first, spinning place, the spellbound horses walking warm
    Out of the whinnying green stable
        On to the fields of praise.

And honored among foxes and pheasants by the gay house
Under the new made clouds and happy as the heart was long,
    In the sun born over and over,
        I ran my heedless ways,   40
    My wishes raced through the house high hay
And nothing I cared, at my sky blue trades, that time allows
In all his tuneful turning so few and such morning songs
    Before the children green and golden
        Follow him out of grace,

Nothing I cared, in the lamb white days, that time would take me
Up to the swallow thronged loft by the shadow of my hand,
    In the moon that is always rising,
        Nor that riding to sleep
    I should hear him fly with the high fields   50
And wake to the farm forever fled from the childless land.
Oh as I was young and easy in the mercy of his means,
        Time held me green and dying
    Though I sang in my chains like the sea.

                            [1946]

Gwendolyn Brooks

1917–

WE REAL COOL

THE POOL PLAYERS.
SEVEN AT THE GOLDEN SHOVEL

W E real cool. We
  Left school. We

Lurk late. We
Strike straight. We

> Sing sin. We
> Thin gin. We
>
> Jazz June. We
> Die soon.

[1960]

THE CHICAGO *DEFENDER* SENDS A MAN TO LITTLE ROCK

FALL, 1957[1]

IN Little Rock the people bear
Babes, and comb and part their hair
And watch the want ads, put repair
To roof and latch. While wheat toast burns
A woman waters multiferns.

Time upholds or overturns
The many, tight, and small concerns.

In Little Rock the people sing
Sunday hymns like anything
Through Sunday pomp and polishing.   10

And after testament and tunes,
Some soften Sunday afternoons
With lemon tea and Lorna Doones.

I forecast
And I believe
Come Christmas Little Rock will cleave
To Christmas tree and trifle, weave,
From laugh and tinsel, texture fast.

In Little Rock is baseball; Barcarolle.
That hotness in July . . . the uniformed figures raw and implacable   20
And not intellectual,
Batting the hotness or clawing the suffering dust.
The Open Air Concert, on the special twilight green. . . .
When Beethoven is brutal or whispers to lady-like air.
Blanket-sitters are solemn, as Johann troubles to lean
To tell them what to mean. . . .

[1] National Guard troops were called out in Little Rock, Arkansas, to protect black pupils from jeering crowds of white protesters following one of the earliest court orders directing school integration.

There is love, too, in Little Rock. Soft women softly
Opening themselves in kindness,
Or, pitying one's blindness,
Awaiting one's pleasure   30
In azure
Glory with anguished rose at the root. . . .
To wash away old semi-discomfitures.
They re-teach purple and unsullen blue.
The wispy soils go. And uncertain
Half-havings have they clarified to sures.

In Little Rock they know
Not answering the telephone is a way of rejecting life,
That it is our business to be bothered, is our business
To cherish bores or boredom, be polite   40
To lies and love and many-faceted fuzziness.

I scratch my head, massage the hate-I-had.
I blink across my prim and pencilled pad.
The saga I was sent for is not down.
Because there is a puzzle in this town.
The biggest News I do not dare
Telegraph to the Editor's chair:
"They are like people everywhere."

The angry Editor would reply
In hundred harryings of Why.   50

And true, they are hurling spittle, rock,
Garbage and fruit in Little Rock.
And I saw coiling storm a-writhe
On bright madonnas. And a scythe
Of men harassing brownish girls.
(The bows and barettes in the curls
And braids declined away from joy.)

I saw a bleeding brownish boy. . . .

The lariat lynch-wish I deplored.

The loveliest lynchee was our Lord.   60
                                                           [1960]

WAY-OUT MORGAN

Way-out Morgan is collecting guns
      in a tiny fourth-floor room.
He is not hungry, ever, though sinfully lean.
He flourishes, ever, on porridge or pat of bean
pudding or wiener soup—fills fearsomely
on visions of Death-to-the-Hordes-of-the-White-Men!
Death!
(This is the Maxim painted in big black
above a bed bought at a Champlain rummage sale.)
Remembering three local-and-legal beatings, he
rubs his hands in glee,
does Way-out Morgan. Remembering his Sister
mob-raped in Mississippi, Way-out Morgan
smacks sweet his lips and adds another gun
and listens to Blackness stern and blunt and beautiful,
organ-rich Blackness telling a terrible story.
Way-out Morgan
predicts the Day of Debt-pay shall begin,
the Day of Demon-diamond,
of blood in mouths and body-mouths,   20
of flesh-rip in the Forum of Justice at last!
Remembering mates in the Mississippi River,
mates with black bodies once majestic, Way-out
postpones a yellow woman in his bed, postpones
wetness and little cries and stomachings—
to consider Ruin.

                                                    [1960]

Robert Lowell

1917–

GRANDPARENTS

They're altogether otherworldly now,
      those adults champing for their ritual Friday spin
to pharmacist and five-and-ten in Brockton.
Back in my throw-away and shaggy span
of adolescence, Grandpa still waves his stick
like a policeman;
Grandmother, like a Mohammedan, still wears her thick
lavender mourning and touring veil;

the Pierce Arrow clears its throat in a horse-stall.
Then the dry road dust rises to whiten   10
the fatigued elm leaves—
the nineteenth century, tired of children, is gone.
They're all gone into a world of light ; [1] the farm's my own.

The farm's my own !
Back there alone,
I keep indoors, and spoil another season.
I hear the rattley little country gramophone
racking its five foot horn :
"O Summer Time ! "
Even at noon here the formidable   20
Ancien Régime [2] still keeps nature at a distance. Five
green shaded light bulbs spider the billiards-table ;
no field is greener than its cloth,
where Grandpa, dipping sugar for us both,
once spilled his demitasse.
His favorite ball, the number three,
still hides the coffee stain.

Never again
to walk there, chalk our cues,
insist on shooting for us both.   30
Grandpa ! Have me, hold me, cherish me !
Tears smut my fingers. There
half my life-lease later,
I hold an *Illustrated London News*—;
disloyal still,
I doodle handlebar
mustaches on the last Russian Czar.

                                                                     [1959]

[1] an echo of Henry Vaughan, "They Are All Gone into the World of Light"
(1655)
[2] the old order, before the French Revolution of 1789

FOR THE UNION DEAD

" *Relinquunt Omnia Servare Rem Publicam.*" [1]

THE old South Boston Aquarium stands
in a Sahara of snow now. Its broken windows are boarded.
The bronze weathervane cod has lost half its scales.
The airy tanks are dry.

[1] He gives up all to serve the nation.

Once my nose crawled like a snail on the glass;
my hand tingled
to burst the bubbles
drifting from the noses of the cowed, compliant fish.

My hand draws back. I often sigh still
for the dark downward and vegetating kingdom   10
of the fish and reptile. One morning last March,
I pressed against the new barbed and galvanized

fence on the Boston Common. Behind their cage,
yellow dinosaur steamshovels were grunting
as they cropped up tons of mush and grass
to gouge their underworld garage.

Parking spaces luxuriate like civic
sandpiles in the heart of Boston.
A girdle of orange, Puritan-pumpkin colored girders
braces the tingling Statehouse,   20

shaking over the excavations, as it faces Colonel Shaw[2]
and his bell-cheeked Negro infantry
on St. Gaudens'[3] shaking Civil War relief,
propped by a plank split against the garage's earthquake.

Two months after marching through Boston,
half the regiment was dead;
at the dedication,
William James[4] could almost hear the bronze Negroes breathe.

Their monument sticks like a fishbone
in the city's throat.   30
Its Colonel is as lean
as a compass-needle.

He has an angry wrenlike vigilance,
a greyhound's gentle tautness;
he seems to wince at pleasure,
and suffocate for privacy.

---

[2] Robert Gould Shaw led the 54th Massachusetts, the first black regiment to fight for the Union in the Civil War.

[3] Augustus St. Gaudens, a leading sculptor of the later nineteenth century, combined neo-classic style with American subjects.

[4] eminent physiologist, psychologist, and philosopher, who taught at Harvard for many years

He is out of bounds now. He rejoices in man's lovely,
peculiar power to choose life and die—
when he leads his black soldiers to death,
he cannot bend his back.   40

On a thousand small town New England greens,
the old white church holds their air
of sparse, sincere rebellion; frayed flags
quilt the graveyards of the Grand Army of the Republic.

The stone statues of the abstract Union Soldier
grow slimmer and younger each year—
wasp-waisted, they doze over muskets
and muse through their sideburns . . .

Shaw's father wanted no monument
except the ditch,   50
where his son's body was thrown
and lost with his "niggers."

The ditch is nearer.
There are no statues for the last war here;
on Boyleston Street, a commercial photograph
shows Hiroshima [5] boiling

over a Mosler Safe, the "Rock of Ages"
that survived the blast. Space is nearer.
When I crouch to my television set,
the drained faces of Negro school-children rise like balloons.

Colonel Shaw
is riding on his bubble;
he waits
for the blесséd break.

The Aquarium *is* gone. Everywhere,
giant finned cars nose forward like fish;
a savage servility
slides by on grease.

                                                                  [1959]

[5] target of the first atomic bomb, dropped by the United States in 1945

NEMEROV: *Make Love Not War* [963

THE MOUTH OF THE HUDSON
(FOR ESTHER BROOKS)

A SINGLE man stands like a bird-watcher,
and scuffles the pepper and salt snow
from a discarded, gray
Westinghouse Electric cable drum.
He cannot discover America by counting
the chains of condemned freight-trains
from thirty states. They jolt and jar
and junk in the siding below him.
He has trouble with his balance.
His eyes drop,   10
and he drifts with the wild ice
ticking seaward down the Hudson,
like the blank sides of a jig-saw puzzle.

The ice ticks seaward like a clock.
A Negro toasts
Wheat-seeds over the coke-fumes
of a punctured barrel.
Chemical air
sweeps in from New Jersey,
and smells of coffee.   20

Across the river,
ledges of suburban factories tan
in the sulphur-yellow sun
of the unforgivable landscape.

[1964]

Howard Nemerov
1920–

MAKE LOVE NOT WAR

LOVERS everywhere are bringing babies into the world.
Lovers with stars in their eyes are turning the stars
Into babies, lovers reading the instructions in comic books
Are turning out babies according to the instructions; this
Progression is said by demographers to be geometric and
Accelerating the rate of its acceleration. Lovers abed
Read up the demographers' reports, and accordingly produce

Babies with contact lenses and babies diapered in the flags
Of new and underdeveloped nations. Some experts contend
That bayonets are being put into the hands of babies   10
Not old enough to understand their use. And in the U.S.,
Treasury officials have expressed their grave concern about
The unauthorized entry of stateless babies without
Passports and knowing no English : these "wetbacks,"
As they are called from the circumstance of their swimming
Into this country, are to be reported to the proper
Authority wherever they occur and put through channels
For deportation to Abysmo the equatorial paradise
Believed to be their country of origin—"where,"
According to one of our usually informed sorcerers,   20
"The bounteous foison of untilled Nature alone
Will rain upon the heads of these homeless, unhappy
And helpless beings apples, melons, honey, nuts, and gum
Sufficient to preserve them in their prelapsarian state
Under the benign stare of Our Lord Et Cetera forevermore."

Meanwhile I forgot to tell you, back at the ranch,
The lovers are growing older, becoming more responsible.
Beginning with the mortal courtship of the Emerald Goddess
By Doctor Wasp—both of them twelve feet high
And insatiable ; he wins her love by scientific means   30
And she has him immolated in a specially designed mole—
They have now settled down in an L-shaped ranch-type home
Where they are running a baby ranch and bringing up
Powerful babies able to defend their Way of Life
To the death if necessary. Of such breeding pairs
The average he owns seven and a half pair of pants,
While she generally has three girdles and a stove.
They keep a small pump-action repeater in the closet,
And it will not go off in the last act of this epic.

To sum up, it was for all the world as if one had said   40
Increase ! Be fruitful ! Multiply ! Divide !
Be as the sands of the sea, the stars in the firmament,
The moral law within, the number of molecules
In the unabridged dictionary. BVD. Amen. Ahem.
                                                        AUM.
(Or, roughly, the peace that passeth understanding.)
                                                          [1967]

THE TOWN DUMP

"The art of our necessities is strange
That can make vile things precious." [1]

A MILE out in the marshes, under a sky
Which seems to be always going away
In a hurry, on that Venetian land threaded
With hidden canals, you will find the city
Which seconds ours (so cemeteries, too,
Reflect a town from hillsides out of town),
Where Being most Becomingly ends up
Becoming some more. From cardboard tenements,
Windowed with cellophane, or simply tenting
In paper bags, the angry mackerel eyes
Glare at you out of stove-in, sunken heads   10
Far from the sea; the lobster, also, lifts
An empty claw in his most minatory
Of gestures; oyster, crab, and mussel shells
Lie here in heaps, savage as money hurled
Away at the gate of hell. If you want results,
These are results.
                    Objects of value or virtue,
However, are also to be picked up here,
Though rarely, lying with bones and rotten meat,
Eggshells and moldy bread, banana peels   20
No one will skid on, apple cores that caused
Neither the fall of man nor a theory
Of gravitation. People do throw out
The family pearls by accident, sometimes,
Not often; I've known dealers in antiques
To prowl this place by night, with flashlights, on
The off-chance of somebody's having left
Derelict chairs which will turn out to be
By Hepplewhite, a perfect set of six
Going to show, I guess, that in any sty   30
Someone's heaven may open and shower down
Riches responsive to the right dream; though
It is a small chance, certainly, that sends
The ghostly dealer, heavy with fly-netting
Over his head, across these hills in darkness,
Stumbling in cut-glass goblets, lacquered cups,
And other products of his dreamy midden
Pencilled with light and guarded by the flies.

[1] *King Lear*, III, ii, 70–71

For there are flies, of course. A dynamo
Composed, by thousands, of our ancient black   40
Retainers, hums here day and night, steady
As someone telling beads, the hum becoming
A high whine at any disturbance; then,
Settled again, they shine under the sun
Like oil-drops, or are invisible as night,
By night.
          All this continually smolders,
Crackles, and smokes with mostly invisible fires
Which, working deep, rarely flash out and flare,
And never finish. Nothing finishes;
The flies, feeling the heat, keep on the move.   50

Among the flies, the purifying fires,
The hunters by night, acquainted with the art
Of our necessities, and the new deposits
That each day wastes with treasure, you may say
There should be ratios. You may sum up
The results, if you want results. But I will add
That wild birds, drawn to the carrion and flies,
Assemble in some numbers here, their wings
Shining with light, their flight enviably free,
Their music marvelous, though sad, and strange.   60
                                 [1958]

Richard Wilbur

1921–

THE PARDON

M Y DOG lay dead five days without a grave
    In the thick of summer, hid in a clump of pine
And a jungle of grass and honeysuckle-vine.
I who had loved him while he kept alive

Went only close enough to where he was
To sniff the heavy honeysuckle-smell
Twined with another odor heavier still
And hear the flies' intolerable buzz.

Well, I was ten and very much afraid.
In my kind world the dead were out of range   10
And I could not forgive the sad or strange
In beast or man. My father took the spade

And buried him. Last night I saw the grass
Slowly divide (it was the same scene
But now it glowed a fierce and mortal green)
And saw the dog emerging. I confess

I felt afraid again, but still he came
In the carnal sun, clothed in a hymn of flies,
And death was breeding in his lively eyes.
I started in to cry and call his name,   20

Asking forgiveness of his tongueless head.
. . . I dreamt the past was never past redeeming:
But whether this was false or honest dreaming
I beg death's pardon now. And mourn the dead.

[1950]

DIGGING FOR CHINA

F AR enough down is China," somebody said.
    "Dig deep enough and you might see the sky
As clear as at the bottom of a well.
Except it would be real—a different sky.
Then you could burrow down until you came
To China! Oh, it's nothing like New Jersey.
There's people, trees, and houses, and all that,
But much, much different. Nothing looks the same."

I went and got the trowel out of the shed
And sweated like a coolie all that morning,   10
Digging a hole beside the lilac-bush,
Down on my hands and knees. It was a sort
Of praying, I suspect. I watched my hand
Dig deep and darker, and I tried and tried
To dream a place where nothing was the same.
The trowel never did break through to blue.

Before the dream could weary of itself
My eyes were tired of looking into darkness,
My sunbaked head of hanging down a hole.

I stood up in a place I had forgotten,   20
Blinking and staggering while the earth went round
And showed me silver barns, the fields dozing
In palls of brightness, patens[1] growing and gone
In the tides of leaves, and the whole sky china blue.
Until I got my balance back again
All that I saw was China, China, China.

[1956]

[1] discs of brightness, like the plates used to hold the Eucharist

MIND

MIND in the purest play is like some bat
That beats about in caverns all alone,
Contriving by a kind of senseless wit
Not to conclude against a wall of stone.

It has no need to falter or explore;
Darkly it knows what obstacles are there,
And so may weave and flitter, dip and soar
In perfect courses through the blackest air.

And has this simile a like perfection?
The mind is like a bat. Precisely. Save   10
That in the very happiest intellection
A graceful error may correct the cave.

[1956]

ADVICE TO A PROPHET

WHEN you come, as you soon must, to the streets of our city,
Mad-eyed from stating the obvious,
Not proclaiming our fall but begging us
In God's name to have self-pity,

Spare us all word of the weapons, their force and range,
The long numbers that rocket the mind;
Our slow, unreckoning hearts will be left behind,
Unable to fear what is too strange.

Nor shall you scare us with talk of the death of the race.
How should we dream of this place without us?—
The sun mere fire, the leaves untroubled about us,   10
A stone look on the stone's face?

Speak of the world's own change. Though we cannot conceive
Of an undreamt thing, we know to our cost
How the dreamt cloud crumbles, the vines are blackened by frost,
How the view alters. We could believe,

If you told us so, that the white-tailed deer will slip
Into perfect shade, grown perfectly shy,
The lark avoid the reaches of our eye,   20
The jack-pine lose its knuckled grip

On the cold ledge, and every torrent burn
As Xanthus[1] once, its gliding trout
Stunned in a twinkling. What should we be without
The dolphin's arc, the dove's return,

These things in which we have seen ourselves and spoken?
Ask us, prophet, how we shall call
Our natures forth when that live tongue is all
Dispelled, that glass obscured or broken

In which we have said the rose of our love and the clean
Horse of our courage, in which beheld   30
The singing locust of the soul unshelled,
And all we mean or wish to mean.

Ask us, ask us whether with the worldless rose
Our hearts shall fail us; come demanding
Whether there shall be lofty or long standing
When the bronze annals of the oak-tree close.

[1959]

[1] The river Xanthus assaulted Achilles to defend Troy against him, but the goddess Hera rescued the Achaian hero by having her son Hephæstus blast the river with fire. (*Iliad*, XXI)

James Dickey

1923–

THE HEAVEN OF ANIMALS

HERE they are. The soft eyes open.
If they have lived in a wood
It is a wood.
If they have lived on plains

It is grass rolling
Under their feet forever.

Having no souls, they have come,
Anyway, beyond their knowing.
Their instincts wholly bloom
And they rise.   10
The soft eyes open

To match them, the landscape flowers,
Outdoing, desperately
Outdoing what is required :
The richest wood,
The deepest field.

For some of these,
It could not be the place
It is, without blood.
These hunt, as they have done,   20
But with teeth and claws grown perfect.

More deadly than they can believe.
They stalk more silently,
And crouch on the limbs of trees,
And their descent
Upon the bright backs of their prey

May take years
In a sovereign floating of joy.
And those that are hunted
Know this as their life,   30
Their reward : to walk

Under such trees in full knowledge
Of what is in glory above them,
And to feel no fear,
But acceptance, compliance.
Fulfilling themselves without pain

At the cycle's center,
They tremble, they walk
Under the tree,
They fall, they are torn,   40
They rise, they walk again.

[1961]

THE BEHOLDERS

FAR away under us, they are mowing on the green steps
 Of the valley, taking long, unending swings
Among the ripe wheat.
It is something about them growing,
Growing smaller, that makes us look up and see
That what has come over them is a storm.

It is a blue-black storm the shape of this valley,
And includes, perhaps, in its darkness,
Three men in the air
Taking long, limber swings, cutting water.   10
Swaths start to fall and, on earth,
The men come closer together as they mow.

Now in the last stand of wheat they bend.
From above, we watch over them like gods,
Our chins on our hands,
Our great eyes staring, our throats dry
And aching to cry down on their heads
Some curse or blessing,

Some word we have never known, but we feel
That when the right time arrives, and more stillness,   20
Lightning will leap
From our mouths in reasonless justice
As they arc their scythes more slowly, taking care
Not to look up.

As darkness increases there comes
A dancing into each of their swings,
A dancing like men in a cloud.
We two are coming together
Also, along the wall.
No lightning yet falls from us   30

Where their long hooks catch on the last of the sun
And the color of the wheat passes upward,
Drawn off like standing water
Into the cloud, turning green;
The field becomes whiter and darker,
And fire in us gathers and gathers

Not to call down death to touch brightly
The only metal for miles
In the hands of judged, innocent men,
But for our use only, who in the first sheaves of rain   40
Sit thunderstruck, having now the power to speak
With deadly intent of love.

[1962]

Allen Ginsberg
1926–

A SUPERMARKET IN CALIFORNIA

WHAT thoughts I have of you tonight, Walt Whitman, for I walked down the sidestreets under the trees with a headache self-conscious looking at the full moon.

In my hungry fatigue, and shopping for images, I went into the neon fruit supermarket, dreaming of your enumerations!

What peaches and what penumbras! Whole families shopping at night! Aisles full of husbands! Wives in the avocados, babies in the tomatoes!—and you, Garcia Lorca,[1] what were you doing down by the watermelons?

I saw you, Walt Whitman, childless, lonely old grubber, poking among the meats in the refrigerator and eyeing the grocery boys.

I heard you asking questions of each: Who killed the pork chops? What price bananas? Are you my Angel?

I wandered in and out of the brilliant stacks of cans following you, and followed in my imagination by the store detective.

We strode down the open corridors together in our solitary fancy tasting artichokes, possessing every frozen delicacy, and never passing the cashier.

Where are we going, Walt Whitman? The doors close in an hour. Which way does your beard point tonight?

(I touch your book and dream of our odyssey in the supermarket and feel absurd.)

Will we walk all night through solitary streets? The trees add shade to shade, lights out in the houses, we'll both be lonely.   10

Will we stroll dreaming of the lost America of love past blue automobiles in driveways, home to our silent cottage?

[1] Spanish poet and playwright of primitivist tendencies, murdered by the Fascists in 1936

Ah, dear father, graybeard, lonely old courage-teacher, what America did you have when Charon[2] quit poling his ferry and you got out on a smoking bank and stood watching the boat disappear on the black waters of Lethe?

[1956]

[2] boatman who ferried dead souls across a river, usually identified as Acheron or Styx, into Hades

MY SAD SELF

TO FRANK O'HARA[1]

Sometimes when my eyes are red
    I go up on top of the RCA Building
        and gaze at my world, Manhattan—
            my buildings, streets I've done feats in,
                lofts, beds, coldwater flats
    —on Fifth Ave below which I also bear in mind,
        its ant cars, little yellow taxis, men
            walking the size of specks of wool—
        Panorama of the bridges, sunrise over Brooklyn machine,
            sun go down over New Jersey where I was born   10
                & Paterson where I played with ants—
    my later loves on 15th Street,
        my greatest loves of Lower East Side,
            my once fabulous amours in the Bronx
                faraway—
    paths crossing in these hidden streets,
        my history summed up, my absences
            and ecstasies in Harlem—
        —sun shining down on all I own
            in one eyeblink to the horizon   20
                in my last eternity—
                    matter is water.
Sad,
    I take the elevator and go
        down, pondering,
    and walk on the pavements staring into all man's
                plateglass, faces,
        questioning after who loves,
    and stop, bemused
        in front of an automobile shopwindow   30
    standing lost in calm thought,
        traffic moving up & down 5th Avenue blocks
            behind me

[1] a poet contemporary with Ginsberg

waiting for a moment when. . . .
Time to go home & cook supper & listen to
              the romantic war news on the radio

                              . . . all movement stops
& I walk in the timeless sadness of existence,
        tenderness flowing thru the buildings,
              my finger tips touching reality's face,   40
my own face streaked with tears in the mirror
        of some window—at dusk—
                      where I have no desire—
for bonbons—or to own the dresses or Japanese
        lampshades of intellection—

Confused by the spectacle around me,
        Man struggling up the street
              with packages, newspapers,
                      ties, beautiful suits
              toward his desire   50
        Man, woman, streaming over the pavements
              red lights clocking hurried watches &
                      movements at the curb—

And all these streets leading
        so crosswise, honking, lengthily,
                      by avenues
        stalked by high buildings or crusted into slums
                      thru such halting traffic
                              screaming cars and engines
so painfully to this   60
        countryside, this graveyard
              this stillness
                              on deathbed or mountain
        once seen
                      never regained or desired
                              in the mind to come
where all Manhattan that I've seen must disappear.
                                                    [1963]

James Wright
1927–

A PRESENTATION OF TWO BIRDS
TO MY SON

CHICKEN. How shall I tell you what it is,
     And why it does not float with tanagers?
Its ecstasy is dead, it does not care.
Its children huddle underneath its wings,
And altogether lounge against the shack,
Warm in the slick tarpaulin, smug and soft.

You must not fumble in your mind
The genuine ecstasy of climbing birds
With that dull fowl.
When your grandfather held it by the feet   10
And laid the skinny neck across
The ragged chopping block,
The flop of wings, the jerk of the red comb
Were a dumb agony,
Stupid and meaningless. It was no joy
To leave the body beaten underfoot;
Life was a flick of corn, a steady roost.
Chicken. The sound is plain.

Look up and see the swift above the trees.
How shall I tell you why he always veers   20
And banks around the shaken sleeve of air,
Away from ground? He hardly flies on brains;
Pockets of air impale his hollow bones.
He leans against the rainfall or the sun.

You must not mix this pair of birds
Together in your mind before you know
That both are clods.
What makes the chimney swift approach the sky
Is ecstasy, a kind of fire
That beats the bones apart   30
And lets the fragile feathers close with air.
Flight too is agony,
Stupid and meaningless. Why should it be joy
To leave the body beaten underfoot,
To mold the limbs against the wind, and join
Those clean dark glides of Dionysian birds?
The flight is deeper than your father, boy.

[1957]

A BLESSING

JUST off the highway to Rochester, Minnesota,
Twilight bounds softly forth on the grass.
And the eyes of those two Indian ponies
Darken with kindness.
They have come gladly out of the willows
To welcome my friend and me.
We step over the barbed wire into the pasture
Where they have been grazing all day, alone.
They ripple tensely, they can hardly contain their happiness
That we have come.   10
They bow shyly as wet swans. They love each other.
There is no loneliness like theirs.
At home once more,
They begin munching the young tufts of spring in the darkness.
I would like to hold the slenderer one in my arms,
For she has walked over to me
And nuzzled my left hand.
She is black and white,
Her mane falls wild on her forehead,
And the light breeze moves me to caress her long ear   20
That is delicate as the skin over a girl's wrist.
Suddenly I realize
That if I stepped out of my body I would break
Into blossom.

                                                                [1961]

Anne Sexton
1928–1974

UNKNOWN GIRL IN THE
MATERNITY WARD

CHILD, the current of your breath is six days long.
You lie, a small knuckle on my white bed;
lie, fisted like a snail, so small and strong
at my breast. Your lips are animals; you are fed
with love. At first hunger is not wrong.
The nurses nod their caps; you are shepherded
down starch halls with the other unnested throng
in wheeling baskets. You tip like a cup; your head
moving to my touch. You sense the way we belong.

But this is an institution bed.   10
You will not know me very long.

The doctors are enamel. They want to know
the facts. They guess about the man who left me,
some pendulum soul, going the way men go
and leave you full of child. But our case history
stays blank. All I did was let you grow.
Now we are here for all the ward to see.
They thought I was strange, although
I never spoke a word. I burst empty
of you, letting you learn how the air is so.   20
The doctors chart the riddle they ask of me
and I turn my head away. I do not know.

Yours is the only face I recognize.
Bone at my bone, you drink my answers in.
Six times a day I prize
your need, the animals of your lips, your skin
growing warm and plump. I see your eyes
lifting their tents. They are blue stones, they begin
to outgrow their moss. You blink in surprise
and I wonder what you can see, my funny kin,   30
as you trouble my silence. I am a shelter of lies.
Should I learn to speak again, or hopeless in
such sanity will I touch some face I recognize?

Down the hall the baskets start back. My arms
fit you like a sleeve, they hold
catkins of your willows, the wild bee farms
of your nerves, each muscle and fold
of your first days. Your old man's face disarms
the nurses. But the doctors return to scold
me. I speak. It is you my silence harms.   40
I should have known; I should have told
them something to write down. My voice alarms
my throat. 'Name of father—none.' I hold
you and name you bastard in my arms.

And now that's that. There is nothing more
that I can say or lose.
Others have traded life before
and could not speak. I tighten to refuse
your owling eyes, my fragile visitor.
I touch your cheeks, like flowers. You bruise   50
against me. We unlearn. I am a shore

rocking you off. You break from me. I choose
your only way, my small inheritor
and hand you off, trembling the selves we lose.
Go child, who is my sin and nothing more.

[1960]

RINGING THE BELLS

A ND this is the way they ring
the bells in Bedlam
and this is the bell-lady
who comes each Tuesday morning
to give us a music lesson
and because the attendants make you go
and because we mind by instinct,
like bees caught in the wrong hive,
we are the circle of the crazy ladies
who sit in the lounge of the mental house   10
and smile at the smiling woman
who passes us each a bell,
who points at my hand
that holds my bell, E flat,
and this is the gray dress next to me
who grumbles as if it were special
to be old, to be old,
and this is the small hunched squirrel girl
on the other side of me
who picks at the hairs over her lip,   20
who picks at the hairs over her lip all day,
and this is how the bells really sound,
as untroubled and clean
as a workable kitchen,
and this is always my bell responding
to my hand that responds to the lady
who points at me, E flat;
and although we are no better for it,
they tell you to go. And you do.

[1960]

Adrienne Rich

1929–

THE KNIGHT

A KNIGHT rides into the noon,
and his helmet points to the sun,
and a thousand splintered suns
are the gaiety of his mail.
The soles of his feet glitter
and his palms flash in reply,
and under his crackling banner
he rides like a ship in sail.

A knight rides into the noon,
and only his eye is living,   10
a lump of bitter jelly
set in a metal mask,
betraying rags and tatters
that cling to the flesh beneath
and wear his nerves to ribbons
under the radiant casque.

Who will unhorse this rider
and free him from between
the walls of iron, the emblems
crushing his chest with their weight?   20
Will they defeat him gently,
or leave him hurled on the green,
his rags and wounds still hidden
under the great breastplate?

[1963]

THE TREES

THE trees inside are moving out into the forest,
the forest that was empty all these days
where no bird could sit
no insect hide
no sun bury its feet in shadow
the forest that was empty all these nights
will be full of trees by morning.

All night the roots work
to disengage themselves from the cracks
in the veranda floor.   10
The leaves strain toward the glass
small twigs stiff with exertion
long-cramped boughs shuffling under the roof
like newly discharged patients
half-dazed, moving
to the clinic doors.

I sit inside, doors open to the veranda
writing long letters
in which I scarcely mention the departure
of the forest from the house.   20
The night is fresh, the whole moon shines
in a sky still open
the smell of leaves and lichen
still reaches like a voice into the rooms.
My head is full of whispers
which tomorrow will be silent.

Listen. The glass is breaking.
The trees are stumbling forward
into the night. Winds rush to meet them.
The moon is broken like a mirror,   30
its pieces flash now in the crown
of the tallest oak.

[1966]

DIVING INTO THE WRECK

FIRST having read the book of myths,
    and loaded the camera,
and checked the edge of the knife-blade,
I put on
the body-armor of black rubber
the absurd flippers
the grave and awkward mask.
I am having to do this
not like Cousteau[1] with his
assiduous team   10
aboard the sun-flooded schooner
but here alone.

1 Jacques Cousteau, contemporary French marine biologist

There is a ladder.
The ladder is always there
hanging innocently
close to the side of the schooner.
We know what it is for,
we who have used it.
otherwise
it is a piece of maritime floss   20
some sundry equipment.

I go down.
Rung after rung and still
the oxygen immerses me
the blue light
the clear atoms
of our human air.
I go down.
My flippers cripple me,
I crawl like an insect down the ladder   30
and there is no one
to tell me when the ocean
will begin.

First the air is blue and then
it is bluer and then green and then
black I am blacking out and yet
my mask is powerful
it pumps my blood with power
the sea is another story
the sea is not a question of power   40
I have to learn alone
to turn my body without force
in the deep element.

And now : it is easy to forget
what I came for
among so many who have always
lived here
swaying their crenellated fans
between the reefs
and besides   50
you breathe differently down here.

I came to explore the wreck.
The words are purposes.
The words are maps.

I came to see the damage that was done
and the treasures that prevail.
I stroke the beam of my lamp
slowly along the flank
of something more permanent
than fish or weed   60

the thing I came for :
the wreck and not the story of the wreck
the thing itself and not the myth
the drowned face always staring
toward the sun
the evidence of damage
worn by salt and sway into this threadbare beauty
the ribs of the disaster
curving their assertion
among the tentative haunters.   70

This is the place.
And I am here, the mermaid whose dark hair
streams black, the merman in his armored body.
We circle silently
about the wreck
we dive into the hold.
I am she : I am he

whose drowned face sleeps with open eyes
whose breasts still bear the stress
whose silver, copper, vermeil cargo lies   80
obscurely inside barrels
half-wedged and left to rot
we are the half-destroyed instruments
that once held to a course
the water-eaten log
the fouled compass

We are, I am, you are
by cowardice or courage
the one who find our way
back to this scene   90
carrying a knife, a camera
a book of myths
in which
our names do not appear.

[1973]

Sylvia Plath
1932–1963

MORNING SONG

Love set you going like a fat gold watch.
The midwife slapped your footsoles, and your bald cry
Took its place among the elements.

Our voices echo, magnifying your arrival. New statue.
In a drafty museum, your nakedness
Shadows our safety. We stand round blankly as walls.

I'm no more your mother
Than the cloud that distils a mirror to reflect its own slow
Effacement at the wind's hand.

All night your moth-breath   10
Flickers among the flat pink roses. I wake to listen:
A far sea moves in my ear.

One cry, and I stumble from bed, cow-heavy and floral
In my Victorian nightgown.
Your mouth opens clean as a cat's. The window square

Whitens and swallows its dull stars. And now you try
Your handful of notes;
The clear vowels rise like balloons.

                                                        [1962]

TULIPS

The tulips are too excitable, it is winter here.
Look how white everything is, how quiet, how snowed-in.
I am learning peacefulness, lying by myself quietly
As the light lies on these white walls, this bed, these hands.
I am nobody; I have nothing to do with explosions.
I have given my name and my day-clothes up to the nurses
And my history to the anaesthetist and my body to surgeons.

They have propped my head between the pillow and the sheet-cuff
Like an eye between two white lids that will not shut.
Stupid pupil, it has to take everything in.   10
The nurses pass and pass, they are no trouble,
They pass the way gulls pass inland in their white caps,
Doing things with their hands, one just the same as another,
So it is impossible to tell how many there are.

My body is a pebble to them, they tend it as water
Tends to the pebbles it must run over, smoothing them gently.
They bring me numbness in their bright needles, they bring me sleep.
Now I have lost myself I am sick of baggage—
My patent leather overnight case like a black pillbox,
My husband and child smiling out of the family photo;   20
Their smiles catch onto my skin, little smiling hooks.

I have let things slip, a thirty-year-old cargo boat
Stubbornly hanging on to my name and address.
They have swabbed me clear of my loving associations.
Scared and bare on the green plastic-pillowed trolley
I watched my tea-set, my bureaus of linen, my books
Sink out of sight, and the water went over my head.
I am a nun now, I have never been so pure.

I didn't want any flowers, I only wanted
To lie with my hands turned up and be utterly empty.   30
How free it is, you have no idea how free—
The peacefulness is so big it dazes you,
And it asks nothing, a name tag, a few trinkets.
It is what the dead close on, finally; I imagine them
Shutting their mouths on it, like a Communion tablet.

The tulips are too red in the first place, they hurt me.
Even through the gift paper I could hear them breathe
Lightly, through their white swaddlings, like an awful baby.
Their redness talks to my wound, it corresponds.
They are subtle: they seem to float, though they weigh me down,   40
Upsetting me with their sudden tongues and their color,
A dozen red lead sinkers round my neck.

Nobody watched me before, now I am watched.
The tulips turn to me, and the window behind me
Where once a day the light slowly widens and slowly thins,
And I see myself, flat, ridiculous, a cut-paper shadow
Between the eye of the sun and the eyes of the tulips,
And I have no face, I have wanted to efface myself.
The vivid tulips eat my oxygen.

Before they came the air was calm enough,   50
Coming and going, breath by breath, without any fuss.
Then the tulips filled it up like a loud noise.
Now the air snags and eddies round them the way a river
Snags and eddies round a sunken rust-red engine.
They concentrate my attention, that was happy
Playing and resting without committing itself.

The walls, also, seem to be warming themselves.
The tulips should be behind bars like dangerous animals;
They are opening like the mouth of some great African cat,
And I am aware of my heart: it opens and closes   60
Its bowl of red blooms out of sheer love of me.
The water I taste is warm and salt, like the sea,
And comes from a country far away as health.

[1962]

LITTLE FUGUE

The yew's black fingers wag;
Cold clouds go over.
So the deaf and dumb
Signal the blind, and are ignored.

I like black statements.
The featurelessness of that cloud, now!
White as an eye all over!
The eye of the blind pianist

At my table on the ship.
He felt for his food.   10
His fingers had the noses of weasels.
I couldn't stop looking.

He could hear Beethoven:
Black yew, white cloud,
The horrific complications.
Finger-traps—a tumult of keys.

Empty and silly as plates,
So the blind smile.
I envy the big noises,
The yew hedge of the Grosse Fuge.[1]   20

[1] Beethoven's Opus 133 for string quartet

Deafness is something else.
Such a dark funnel, my father!
I see your voice
Black and leafy, as in my childhood,

A yew hedge of orders,
Gothic and barbarous, pure German.
Dead men cry from it.
I am guilty of nothing.

The yew my Christ, then.
Is it not as tortured?   30
And you, during the Great War
In the California delicatessen

Lopping the sausages!
They color my sleep,
Red, mottled, like cut necks.
There was a silence!

Great silence of another order.
I was seven, I knew nothing.
The world occurred.
You had one leg, and a Prussian mind.   40

Now similar clouds
Are spreading their vacuous sheets.
Do you say nothing?
I am lame in the memory.

I remember a blue eye,
A briefcase of tangerines.
This was a man, then!
Death opened, like a black tree, blackly.

I survive the while,
Arranging my morning.   50
These are my fingers, this my baby.
The clouds are a marriage dress, of that pallor.

                                                                              [1962]

THE ARRIVAL OF THE BEE BOX

I ORDERED this, this clean wood box
Square as a chair and almost too heavy to lift.
I would say it was the coffin of a midget
Or a square baby
Were there not such a din in it.

The box is locked, it is dangerous.
I have to live with it overnight
And I can't keep away from it.
There are no windows, so I can't see what is in there.
There is only a little grid, no exit.   10

I put my eye to the grid.
It is dark, dark,
With the swarmy feeling of African hands
Minute and shrunk for export,
Black on black, angrily clambering.

How can I let them out?
It is the noise that appalls me most of all,
The unintelligible syllables.
It is like a Roman mob,
Small, taken one by one, but my god, together!   20

I lay my ear to furious Latin.
I am not a Caesar.
I have simply ordered a box of maniacs.
They can be sent back.
They can die, I need feed them nothing, I am the owner.

I wonder how hungry they are.
I wonder if they would forget me
If I just undid the locks and stood back and turned into a tree.
There is the laburnum, its blond colonnades,
And the petticoats of the cherry.   30

They might ignore me immediately
In my moon suit and funeral veil.
I am no source of honey
So why should they turn on me?
Tomorrow I will be sweet God, I will set them free.

The box is only temporary.   [1966]

Imamu Amiri Baraka

1934–

PREFACE TO A TWENTY VOLUME
SUICIDE NOTE

FOR KELLIE JONES, BORN 16 MAY 1959

LATELY, I've become accustomed to the way
    The ground opens up and envelopes me
Each time I go out to walk the dog.
Or the broad edged silly music the wind
Makes when I run for a bus . . .

Things have come to that.

And now, each night I count the stars,
And each night I get the same number.
And when they will not come to be counted,
I count the holes they leave.   10

Nobody sings anymore.

And then last night, I tiptoed up
To my daughter's room and heard her
Talking to someone, and when I opened
The door, there was no one there . . .
Only she on her knees, peeking into

Her own clasped hands.

[1961]

A POEM FOR BLACK HEARTS

FOR Malcolm's eyes, when they broke
    the face of some dumb white man, For
Malcolm's hands raised to bless us
all black and strong in his image
of ourselves, For Malcolm's words
fire darts, the victor's tireless
thrusts, words hung above the world
change as it may, he said it, and
for this he was killed, for saying

and feeling, and being/ change, all   10
collected hot in his heart, For Malcolm's
heart, raising us above our filthy cities,
for his stride, and his beat, and his address
to the gray monsters of the world, For Malcolm's
pleas for your dignity, black men, for your life,
black men, for the filling of your minds
with righteousness, For all of him dead and
gone and vanished from us, and all of him which
clings to our speech black god of our time.
For all of him, and all of yourself, look up,   20
black man, quit stuttering and shuffling, look up,
black man, quit whining and stooping, for all of him,
For Great Malcolm a prince of the earth, let nothing in us rest
until we avenge ourselves for his death, stupid animals
that killed him, let us never breathe a pure breath if
we fail, and white men call us faggots till the end of
the earth.

[1961]

KA 'BA

A CLOSED window looks down
on a dirty courtyard, and black people
call across or scream across or walk across
defying physics in the stream of their will

Our world is full of sound
Our world is more lovely than anyone's
tho we suffer, and kill each other
and sometimes fail to walk the air

We are beautiful people
with african imaginations   10
full of masks and dances and swelling chants
with african eyes, and noses, and arms,
though we sprawl in gray chains in a place
full of winters, when what we want is sun.

We have been captured,
brothers. And we labor
to make our getaway, into
the ancient image, into a new

correspondence with ourselves
and our black family. We need magic   20
now we need the spells, to raise up
return, destroy, and create. What will be

the sacred words?

                                                         [1969]

Laurence Lieberman
1935-
SONG OF THE THRUSH

IN TERROR of my typewriter's greed for profit,
Tethered to business letters
Bleeding out of my hand, I hasten, a guest
Trespasser my beckoning neighbor

Halts, half out of my clothes half in, my face coloring
Before I can think *shame*, how much of me is showing

I cannot check now, but I feel cool
In two or three wrong skin
Places. Decoyed, I quit the public walk,
Prancing to the lawn, obedient   10

To her pointing finger, her lips including me in a message
I cannot hear over traffic, her husband beside her

Sighting directly on a branch at eye-level
Tail feathers: the first thrush
Of spring. Oh happy transport! I'm severed
By a cadence from the ambition magnet

Pulling my letters to the corner mailbox. Her face
Wound in its mystery, her arms folded for warmth

In the morning chill shift to a cradling
Motion as she explains how   20
Important the thrush music was each morning
Last spring when the nursing baby

Woke her at four. The thrush rescued her from petty
Anger, lifted her spirit, and deadened the worst

Acids of postpartum orneriness, her fifth
Offspring a boy at last,
Their last try taking more nerve than hope
After twin girls. Both past thirty-five.

Both saved. It is a joy to them for me to share their plunder
Of the bird they love. I bow to charities of the thrush.   30

[1972]

INSIDE THE GYROSCOPE
(FOR DEBRA)

DAUGHTER, this is our laughing-box:
a gyroscope orbiting us
two ways at once—
top to bottom, left to right. I try to relax
and enjoy the scares, to roll
with the machine's laughing gears—the computerized gentle
terrors, but shock kills my cackles:

I freeze like a funnybone
when the bumped elbow's burning nerve tickles
the length of your arm, and the skin—   10
pricked with a thousand
pins—tingles. As we sail
through the wider arc of the tilting Great Wheel,
our eggshell cage, an ellipsoid

spinning on its axis, hurtles me
upon you; my weight—
stone in a sling—pinning you sideways against our satellite's
grillewire, your legs tangled under,
frail wings flapping: "Daddy,
you take the steering bar,   20
give us a rough ride, make us twist

and twist." Now we halt,
trapped in the middle of a reverse somersault,
careening, heels over heads,
rocking on the base of our skulls. We are staring straight
up, fifty feet to the ground,
into three ovoids—family faces—high overhead
and directly below us:

mother and sister O-mouth gapes, the wailing face
of your brother, whose helium   30
balloon has fallen
up, up, up (I nearly capture the string,
its lifeline, poking
two fingers through the wiremesh
grate) and drops skyward

under our legs, shrinking
to an agate, a green pea, a pinhead
trailing a hair; it sails into a cloud, vanishing. . . .
I waken from a whacky dream. Stepping from bed
in the dark, I slip on the soft   40
bumps of my daughter's hips and head.
Must I walk on walls to spare her pain? When I lift

her to carry her back
to bed, the chill of the floor
passes from belly to belly. She is winning her war
with sleep—a rage to stay awake!
A little past midnight, she embarks on nocturnal tours:
I hear a soft pitter-patter with a mouse
under floorboards. She cartwheels

from room to room—practices   50
handsprings, headstands for Saturday tumbling class.
Like a wind-up toy, its spring coiled to the snapping point,
she never unwinds.
She rummages about the great toy-bin
of our house, moony-eyed, alchemizing our leaden nights
into goldened lonely second

days. She never lies down.
Sleep must overtake her in mid-play, standing up.
I find her in odd corners at sunup:
on the second shelf of the linen closet, half-awake,   60
buried in washcloths, towels; under the sofa,
the face of the lion rug curled over her ear, its sunflower
yellow whiskers licking her cheek.

[1972]

Drama

Drama

Sophocles

c.496–c.405 B.C.

ANTIGONE

An English Version by Dudley Fitts and Robert Fitzgerald

◊

THE CHARACTERS

ANTIGONE, *daughter of Œdipus, former banished king.*

ISMENE, *her elder sister.*

CREON, *their maternal uncle, now King of Thebes.*

HAIMON, *Creon's son, beloved of Antigone.*

EURYDICE, *the Queen, his mother,*

whose other son has just been killed defending Thebes from attack.

TEIRESIAS, *the old and blind seer or prophet.*

A SENTRY *and* A MESSENGER

THE CHORUS *of fifteen Thebans, elder citizens, among whom the* CHORAGOS *is the leader.*

TIME: *The legendary past of Ancient Greece.*
PLACE: *The walled city of Thebes with its seven gates.*

PROLOGUE

Scene: Before the palace of CREON, *King of Thebes. A central double door, and two lateral doors. A platform extends the length of the façade, and from this platform three steps lead down into the "orchestra," or chorus-ground. Time: Dawn of the day after the repulse of the Argive army from the assault on Thebes.*

> ANTIGONE *and* ISMENE *enter from the central door of the Palace.*

ANTIGONE. Ismenê, dear sister,
  You would think that we had already suffered enough
  For the curse on Œdipus:
  I cannot imagine any grief
  That you and I have not gone through. And now—
  Have they told you of the new decree of our King Creon?
ISMENE. I have heard nothing: I know
  That two sisters lost two brothers, a double death
  In a single hour; and I know that the Argive army
  Fled in the night; but beyond this, nothing.   10
ANTIGONE. I thought so. And that is why I wanted you
  To come out here with me. There is something we must do.
ISMENE. Why do you speak so strangely?
ANTIGONE. Listen, Ismenê:
  Creon buried our brother Eteoclês

995

With military honors, gave him a soldier's funeral,
And it was right that he should ; but Polyneicês,
Who fought as bravely and died as miserably,—
They say that Creon has sworn
No one shall bury him, no one mourn for him,   20
But his body must lie in the fields, a sweet treasure
For carrion birds to find as they search for food.
That is what they say, and our good Creon is coming here
To announce it publicly ; and the penalty—
Stoning to death in the public square ! There it is,
And now you can prove what you are :
A true sister, or a traitor to your family.

ISMENE. Antigonê, you are mad ! What could I possibly do ?
ANTIGONE. You must decide whether you will help me or not.
ISMENE. I do not understand you. Help you in what ?   30
ANTIGONE. Ismenê, I am going to bury him. Will you come ?
ISMENE. Bury him ! You have just said the new law forbids it.
ANTIGONE. He is my brother. And he is your brother, too.
ISMENE. But think of the danger ! Think what Creon will do !
ANTIGONE. Creon is not strong enough to stand in my way.
ISMENE. Ah sister !
Œdipus died, everyone hating him
For what his own search brought to light, his eyes
Ripped out by his own hand ; and Iocastê died,
His mother and wife at once : she twisted the cords   40
That strangled her life ; and our two brothers died,
Each killed by the other's sword. And we are left : [1]
But oh, Antigonê,
Think how much more terrible than these
Our own death would be if we should go against Creon
And do what he has forbidden ! We are only women,
We cannot fight with men, Antigonê !
The law is strong, we must give in to the law
In this thing, and in worse. I beg the Dead
To forgive me, but I am helpless : I must yield   50
To those in authority. And I think it is dangerous business
To be always meddling.

[1] Antigonê and Ismenê were the daughters and Eteoclês and Polyneicês the sons of
Oedipus. In attempting to flee from a fate predicted by the Oracle of Delphi, Oedipus
fulfilled it by killing his father, Laïus, and marrying his own mother, Iocastê, by
whom he had these four children. After he had reigned in Thebes for twenty years, his
sins were revealed to him and the world by Teiresias. Oedipus jabbed out his eyes,
and Iocastê hanged herself. These events are dealt with in Sophocles' *Oedipus Rex*.
  Eteoclês and Polyneicês assumed the throne jointly, but Eteoclês shortly banished
Polyneicês. The latter fled to Argos, where he raised an army and attacked Thebes.
(Aeschylus, *Seven Against Thebes*) The army was routed, but the brothers killed
each other. Their uncle, Creon, succeeded to the throne.

ANTIGONE.   If that is what you think,
 I should not want you, even if you asked to come.
 You have made your choice, you can be what you want to be.
 But I will bury him; and if I must die,
 I say that this crime is holy: I shall lie down
 With him in death, and I shall be as dear
 To him as he to me.
      It is the dead,
 Not the living, who make the longest demands:
 We die for ever . . .
        You may do as you like,   60
 Since apparently the laws of the gods mean nothing to you.
ISMENE. They mean a great deal to me; but I have no strength
 To break laws that were made for the public good.
ANTIGONE. That must be your excuse, I suppose. But as for me,
 I will bury the brother I love.
ISMENE.   Antigonê,
 I am so afraid for you!
ANTIGONE.   You need not be:
 You have yourself to consider, after all.
ISMENE. But no one must hear of this, you must tell no one!
 I will keep it a secret, I promise!
ANTIGONE. Oh, tell it! Tell everyone!   70
 Think how they'll hate you when it all comes out
 If they learn that you knew about it all the time!
ISMENE. So fiery! You should be cold with fear.
ANTIGONE. Perhaps. But I am doing only what I must.
ISMENE. But can you do it? I say that you cannot.
ANTIGONE. Very well: when my strength gives out, I shall do no
  more.
ISMENE. Impossible things should not be tried at all.
ANTIGONE. Go away, Ismenê:
 I shall be hating you soon, and the dead will too,
 For your words are hateful. Leave me my foolish plan: 80
 I am not afraid of the danger; if it means death,
 It will not be the worst of deaths—death without honor.
ISMENE. Go then, if you feel that you must.
 You are unwise,
 But a loyal friend indeed to those who love you.
      [*Exit into the Palace.* ANTIGONE *goes off, L.*]
     Enter the CHORUS.

PÁRODOS

              [*strophe 1*]
CHORUS. Now the long blade of the sun, lying
 Level east to west, touches with glory

Thebes of the Seven Gates. Open, unlidded
Eye of golden day ! O marching light
Across the eddy and rush of Dircê's stream,
Striking the white shields of the enemy
Thrown headlong backward from the blaze of morning !

CHORAGOS. Polyneicês their commander
Roused them with windy phrases,
He the wild eagle screaming   10
Insults above our land,
His wings their shields of snow,
His crest their marshaled helms.

                                                          [*antistrophe 1*]

CHORUS. Against our seven gates in a yawning ring
The famished spears came onward in the night ;
But before his jaws were sated with our blood,
Or pinefire took the garland of our towers,
He was thrown back ; and as he turned, great Thebes—
No tender victim for his noisy power—
Rose like a dragon behind him, shouting war.   20

CHORAGOS. For God hates utterly
The bray of bragging tongues ;
And when he beheld their smiling,
Their swagger of golden helms,
The frown of his thunder blasted
Their first man from our walls.

                                                            [*strophe 2*]

CHORUS. We heard his shout of triumph high in the air
Turn to a scream ; far out in a flaming arc
He fell with his windy torch, and the earth struck him.
And others storming in fury no less than his   30
Found shock of death in the dusty joy of battle.

CHORAGOS. Seven captains at seven gates
Yielded their clanging arms to the god
That bends the battle-line and breaks it.
These two only, brothers in blood,
Face to face in matchless rage,
Mirroring each the other's death,
Clashed in long combat.

                                                        [*antistrophe 2*]

CHORUS. But now in the beautiful morning of victory
Let Thebes of the many chariots sing for joy !   40

With hearts dancing we'll take leave of war:
Our temples shall be sweet with hymns of praise,
And the long night shall echo with our chorus.

SCENE I

CHORAGOS. But now at last our new King is coming:
Creon of Thebes, Menoiceus' son.
In this auspicious dawn of his reign
What are the new complexities
That shifting Fate has woven for him?
What is his counsel? Why has he summoned
The old men to hear him?

Enter CREON *from the Palace, C. He addresses the* CHORUS
from the top step.

CREON. Gentlemen: I have the honor to inform you that our Ship of
State, which recent storms have threatened to destroy, has come safely
to harbor at last, guided by the merciful wisdom of Heaven. I have   10
summoned you here this morning because I know that I can depend
upon you: your devotion to King Laïos was absolute; you never
hesitated in your duty to our late ruler Œdipus; and when Œdipus
died, your loyalty was transferred to his children. Unfortunately, as
you know, his two sons, the princes Eteoclês and Polyneicês, have
killed each other in battle; and I, as the next in blood, have succeeded
to the full power of the throne.

I am aware, of course, that no Ruler can expect complete loyalty
from his subjects until he has been tested in office. Nevertheless, I say
to you at the very outset that I have nothing but contempt for the   20
kind of Governor who is afraid, for whatever reason, to follow the
course that he knows is best for the State; and as for the man who sets
private friendship above the public welfare,—I have no use for him,
either. I call God to witness that if I saw my country headed for ruin,
I should not be afraid to speak out plainly; and I need hardly remind
you that I would never have any dealings with an enemy of the people.
No one values friendship more highly than I; but we must remember
that friends made at the risk of wrecking our Ship are not real friends
at all.

These are my principles, at any rate, and that is why I have   30
made the following decision concerning the sons of Œdipus: Eteoclês,
who died as a man should die, fighting for his country, is to be buried
with full military honors, with all the ceremony that is usual when
the greatest heroes die; but his brother Polyneicês, who broke his
exile to come back with fire and sword against his native city and the
shrines of his fathers' gods, whose one idea was to spill the blood of
his blood and sell his own people into slavery—Polyneicês, I say, is
to have no burial: no man is to touch him or say the least prayer for

him; he shall lie on the plain, unburied; and the birds and the scav-
enging dogs can do with him whatever they like.   40
    This is my command, and you can see the wisdom behind it. As long
as I am King, no traitor is going to be honored with the loyal man.
But whoever shows by word and deed that he is on the side of the
State,—he shall have my respect while he is living, and my reverence
when he is dead.

CHORAGOS. If that is your will, Creon son of Menoiceus,
    You have the right to enforce it: we are yours.
CREON. That is my will. Take care that you do your part.
CHORAGOS. We are old men: let the younger ones carry it out.
CREON. I do not mean that: the sentries have been appointed.   50
CHORAGOS. Then what is it that you would have us do?
CREON. You will give no support to whoever breaks this law.
CHORAGOS. Only a crazy man is in love with death!
CREON. And death it is; yet money talks, and the wisest
    Have sometimes been known to count a few coins too many.

                      Enter SENTRY *from* L.

SENTRY. I'll not say that I'm out of breath from running, King, be-
    cause every time I stopped to think about what I have to tell you, I
    felt like going back. And all the time a voice kept saying, "You fool,
    don't you know you're walking straight into trouble?"; and then an-
    other voice: "Yes, but if you let somebody else get the news to   60
    Creon first, it will be even worse than that for you!" But good sense
    won out, at least I hope it was good sense, and here I am with a story
    that makes no sense at all; but I'll tell it anyhow, because, as they say,
    what's going to happen's going to happen, and—

CREON. Come to the point. What have you to say?
SENTRY. I did not do it. I did not see who did it. You must not punish
    me for what someone else has done.
CREON. A comprehensive defense! More effective, perhaps,
    If I knew its purpose. Come: what is it?
SENTRY. A dreadful thing . . . I don't know how to put it—   70
CREON. Out with it!
SENTRY.   Well, then;
    The dead man—
                          Polyneicês—
Pause. The SENTRY *is overcome, fumbles for words.* CREON *waits
impassively.*
                          out there—
                                    someone,—
New dust on the slimy flesh!
Pause. No sign from CREON.

Someone has given it burial that way, and
Gone . . .
Long pause. CREON *finally speaks with deadly control.*
CREON.　　　And the man who dared do this?
SENTRY.　　　　　　　　　　　　　　　　I swear I
Do not know! You must believe me!
　　　　　　　　　　　　　　Listen:
The ground was dry, not a sign of digging, no,
Not a wheeltrack in the dust, no trace of anyone.
It was when they relieved us this morning: and one of them,
The corporal, pointed to it.
　　　　　　　　　　There it was,　　　　　　　　　　80
The strangest—
　　　　　　　Look:
The body, just mounded over with light dust: you see?
Not buried really, but as if they'd covered it
Just enough for the ghost's peace. And no sign
Of dogs or any wild animal that had been there.
And then what a scene there was! Every man of us
Accusing the other: we all proved the other man did it,
We all had proof that we could not have done it.
We were ready to take hot iron in our hands,
Walk through fire, swear by all the gods,　　　　　　　90
It was not I!
I do not know who it was, but it was not I!
CREON'S *rage has been mounting steadily, but the* SENTRY *is too intent
upon his story to notice it.*
And then, when this came to nothing, someone said
A thing that silenced us and made us stare
Down at the ground: you had to be told the news,
And one of us had to do it! We threw the dice,
And the bad luck fell to me. So here I am,
No happier to be here than you are to have me:
Nobody likes the man who brings bad news.
CHORAGOS. I have been wondering, King: can it be that the gods have
　　done this?
CREON [*furiously*]. Stop.　　　　　　　　　　　　　　　　100
Must you doddering wrecks
Go out of your heads entirely? "The gods!"
Intolerable!
The gods favor this corpse? Why? How had he served them?
Tried to loot their temples, burn their images,
Yes, and the whole State, and its laws with it!
Is it your senile opinion that the gods love to honor bad men?
A pious thought!—
　　　　　　　No, from the very beginning

There have been those who have whispered together,
Stiff-necked anarchists, putting their heads together,   110
Scheming against me in alleys. These are the men,
And they have bribed my own guard to do this thing.
[*Sententiously*]   Money!
There's nothing in the world so demoralising as money.
Down go your cities,
Homes gone, men gone, honest hearts corrupted,
Crookedness of all kinds, and all for money!
[*To* SENTRY]   But you—!
I swear by God and by the throne of God,
The man who has done this thing shall pay for it!
Find that man, bring him here to me, or your death
Will be the least of your problems: I'll string you up   120
Alive, and there will be certain ways to make you
Discover your employer before you die;
And the process may teach you a lesson you seem to have missed:
The dearest profit is sometimes all too dear:
That depends on the source. Do you understand me?
A fortune won is often misfortune.
SENTRY. King, may I speak?
CREON.   Your very voice distresses me.
SENTRY. Are you sure that it is my voice, and not your conscience?
CREON. By God, he wants to analyse me now!
SENTRY. It is not what I say, but what has been done, that hurts you. 130
CREON. You talk too much.
SENTRY. Maybe; but I've done nothing.
CREON. Sold your soul for some silver: that's all you've done.
SENTRY. How dreadful it is when the right judge judges wrong!
CREON. Your figures of speech
    May entertain you now; but unless you bring me the man,
    You will get little profit from them in the end.
                                        [*Exit* CREON *into the Palace.*]
SENTRY. "Bring me the man"—!
    I'd like nothing better than bringing him the man!
    But bring him or not, you have seen the last of me here.   140
    At any rate, I am safe!
                                                          [*Exit* SENTRY.]

ODE I

                                                              [*strophe 1*]
CHORUS. Numberless are the world's wonders, but none
    More wonderful than man; the stormgray sea
    Yields to his prows, the huge crests bear him high;
    Earth, holy and inexhaustible, is graven

With shining furrows where his plows have gone
Year after year, the timeless labor of stallions.

[*antistrophe 1*]

The lightboned birds and beasts that cling to cover,
The lithe fish lighting their reaches of dim water,
All are taken, tamed in the net of his mind;
The lion on the hill, the wild horse windy-maned,   10
Resign to him; and his blunt yoke has broken
The sultry shoulders of the mountain bull.

[*strophe 2*]

Words also, and thought as rapid as air,
He fashions to his good use; statecraft is his,
And his the skill that deflects the arrows of snow,
The spears of winter rain: from every wind
He has made himself secure—from all but one:
In the late wind of death he cannot stand.

[*antistrophe 2*]

O clear intelligence, force beyond all measure!
O fate of man, working both good and evil!   20
When the laws are kept, how proudly his city stands!
When the laws are broken, what of his city then?
Never may the anarchic man find rest at my hearth,
Never be it said that my thoughts are his thoughts.

SCENE II

Re-enter SENTRY *leading* ANTIGONE.

CHORAGOS. What does this mean? Surely this captive woman
Is the Princess, Antigonê. Why should she be taken?
SENTRY. Here is the one who did it! We caught her
In the very act of burying him.—Where is Creon?
CHORAGOS. Just coming from the house.

Enter CREON, *C.*

CREON.   What has happened?
Why have you come back so soon?
SENTRY [*expansively*].   O King,
A man should never be too sure of anything:
I would have sworn
That you'd not see me here again: your anger
Frightened me so, and the things you threatened me with;   10

But how could I tell then
That I'd be able to solve the case so soon?
No dice-throwing this time: I was only too glad to come!
Here is this woman. She is the guilty one:
We found her trying to bury him.
Take her, then; question her; judge her as you will.
I am through with the whole thing now, and glád óf it.
CREON. But this is Antigonê! Why have you brought her here?
SENTRY. She was burying him, I tell you!
CREON [*severely*].   Is this the truth?
SENTRY. I saw her with my own eyes. Can I say more?   20
CREON. The details: come, tell me quickly!
SENTRY.   It was like this:
After those terrible threats of yours, King,
We went back and brushed the dust away from the body.
The flesh was soft by now, and stinking,
So we sat on a hill to windward and kept guard.
No napping this time! We kept each other awake.
But nothing happened until the white round sun
Whirled in the center of the round sky over us:
Then, suddenly,
A storm of dust roared up from the earth, and the sky   30
Went out, the plain vanished with all its trees
In the stinging dark. We closed our eyes and endured it.
The whirlwind lasted a long time, but it passed;
And then we looked, and there was Antigonê!
I have seen
A mother bird come back to a stripped nest, heard
Her crying bitterly a broken note or two
For the young ones stolen. Just so, when this girl
Found the bare corpse, and all her love's work wasted,
She wept, and cried on heaven to damn the hands   40
That had done this thing.
                          And then she brought more dust
And sprinkled wine three times for her brother's ghost.
We ran and took her at once. She was not afraid,
Not even when we charged her with what she had done.
She denied nothing.
                    And this was a comfort to me,
And some uneasiness: for it is a good thing
To escape from death, but it is no great pleasure
To bring death to a friend.
                          Yet I always say
There is nothing so comfortable as your own safe skin!
CREON [*slowly, dangerously*]. And you, Antigonê?   50

You with your head hanging,—do you confess this thing?
ANTIGONE. I do. I deny nothing.
CREON [*to* SENTRY]. You may go.

[*Exit* SENTRY.]

[*To* ANTIGONE.] Tell me, tell me briefly:
Had you heard my proclamation touching this matter?
ANTIGONE. It was public. Could I help hearing it?
CREON. And yet you dared defy the law.
ANTIGONE. I dared.
  It was not God's proclamation. That final Justice
  That rules the world below makes no such laws.
  Your edict, King, was strong,
  But all your strength is weakness itself against   60
  The immortal unrecorded laws of God.
  They are not merely now: they were, and shall be,
  Operative for ever, beyond man utterly.
  I knew I must die, even without your decree:
  I am only mortal. And if I must die
  Now, before it is my time to die,
  Surely this is no hardship: can anyone
  Living, as I live, with evil all about me,
  Think Death less than a friend? This death of mine
  Is of no importance; but if I had left my brother   70
  Lying in death unburied, I should have suffered.
  Now I do not.
              You smile at me. Ah Creon,
  Think me a fool, if you like; but it may well be
  That a fool convicts me of folly.
CHORAGOS. Like father, like daughter: both headstrong, deaf to reason!
  She has never learned to yield.
CREON. She has much to learn.
  The inflexible heart breaks first, the toughest iron
  Cracks first, and the wildest horses bend their necks
  At the pull of the smallest curb.
                          Pride? In a slave?
  This girl is guilty of a double insolence,   80
  Breaking the given laws and boasting of it.
  Who is the man here,
  She or I, if this crime goes unpunished?
  Sister's child, or more than sister's child,
  Or closer yet in blood—she and her sister
  Win bitter death for this!
  [*To* SERVANTS.] Go, some of you,
  Arrest Ismenê. I accuse her equally.
  Bring her: you will find her sniffling in the house there.

Her mind's a traitor: crimes kept in the dark
Cry for light, and the guardian brain shudders;   90
But how much worse than this
Is brazen boasting of barefaced anarchy!
ANTIGONE. Creon, what more do you want than my death?
CREON.   Nothing.
That gives me everything.
ANTIGONE. Then I beg you: kill me.
This talking is a great weariness: your words
Are distasteful to me, and I am sure that mine
Seem so to you. And yet they should not seem so:
I should have praise and honor for what I have done.
All these men here would praise me   100
Were their lips not frozen shut with fear of you.
[Bitterly.] Ah the good fortune of kings,
Licensed to say and do whatever they please!
CREON. You are alone here in that opinion.
ANTIGONE. No, they are with me.
But they keep their tongues in leash.
CREON. Maybe. But you are guilty, and they are not.
ANTIGONE. There is no guilt in reverence for the dead.
CREON. But Eteoclês—was he not your brother too?
ANTIGONE. My brother too.
CREON.   And you insult his memory?   110
ANTIGONE [softly]. The dead man would not say that I insult it.
CREON. He would: for you honor a traitor as much as him.
ANTIGONE. His own brother, traitor or not, and equal in blood.
CREON. He made war on his country.
Eteoclês defended it.
ANTIGONE. Nevertheless, there are honors due all the dead.
CREON. But not the same for the wicked as for the just.
ANTIGONE. Ah Creon, Creon.
Which of us can say what the gods hold wicked?
CREON. An enemy is an enemy, even dead.   120
ANTIGONE. It is my nature to join in love, not hate.
CREON [finally losing patience]. Go join them, then; if you must have
your love,
Find it in hell!
CHORAGOS.   But see, Ismenê comes:

Enter ISMENE, *guarded.*

Those tears are sisterly, the cloud
That shadows her eyes rains down gentle sorrow.
CREON. You too, Ismenê,
Snake in my ordered house, sucking my blood

Stealthily—and all the time I never knew
That these two sisters were aiming at my throne!
Ismenê,
Do you confess your share in this crime, or deny it? 130
Answer me.
ISMENE. Yes, if she will let me say so. I am guilty.
ANTIGONE [*coldly*]. No, Ismenê. You have no right to say so.
You would not help me, and I will not have you help me.
ISMENE. But now I know what you meant; and I am here
To join you, to take my share of punishment.
ANTIGONE. The dead man and the gods who rule the dead
Know whose act this was. Words are not friends.
ISMENE. Do you refuse me, Antigonê? I want to die with you:
I too have a duty that I must discharge to the dead. 140
ANTIGONE. You shall not lessen my death by sharing it.
ISMENE. What do I care for life when you are dead?
ANTIGONE. Ask Creon. You're always hanging on his opinions.
ISMENE. You are laughing at me. Why Antigone?
ANTIGONE. It's a joyless laughter, Ismenê.
ISMENE.   But can I do nothing?
ANTIGONE. Yes. Save yourself. I shall not envy you.
There are those who will praise you; I shall have honor, too.
ISMENE. But we are equally guilty!
ANTIGONE.   No more, Ismenê.
You are alive, but I belong to Death.
CREON [*to the* CHORUS]. Gentlemen, I beg you to observe these
  girls: 150
One has just now lost her mind; the other,
It seems, has never had a mind at all.
ISMENE. Grief teaches the steadiest minds to waver, King.
CREON. Yours certainly did, when you assumed guilt with the guilty!
ISMENE. But how could I go on living without her?
CREON.   You are.
She is already dead.
ISMENE.   But, your own son's bride!
CREON. There are places enough for him to push his plow.
I want no wicked women for my sons!
ANTIGONE. O dearest Haimon, how your father wrongs you!
CREON. I've had enough of your childish talk of marriage! 160
CHORAGOS. Do you really intend to steal this girl from your son?
CREON. No; Death will do that for me.
CHORAGOS.   Then she must die?
CREON [*ironically*]. You dazzle me.
—But enough of this talk!
[*To* GUARDS.] You, there, take them away and guard them well:

For they are but women, and even brave men run
When they see Death coming.

                    [*Exeunt* ISMENE, ANTIGONE *and* GUARDS.]

ODE II

                    [*strophe 1*]
CHORUS. Fortunate is the man who has never tasted God's vengeance!
  Where once the anger of heaven has struck, that house is shaken
  For ever : damnation rises behind each child
  Like a wave cresting out of the black northeast,
  When the long darkness under sea roars up
  And bursts drumming death upon the windwhipped sand.

                    [*antistrophe 1*]
  I have seen this gathering sorrow from time long past
  Loom upon Œdipus' children : generation from generation
  Takes the compulsive rage of the enemy god.
  So lately this last flower of Œdipus' line   10
  Drank the sunlight ! but now a passionate word
  And a handful of dust have closed up all its beauty.

                    [*strophe 2*]
    What mortal arrogance
    Transcends the wrath of Zeus ?
  Sleep cannot lull him, nor the effortless long months
  Of the timeless gods : but he is young for ever,
  And his house is the shining day of high Olympos.
    All that is and shall be,
    And all the past, is his.
  No pride on earth is free of the curse of heaven.   20

                    [*antistrophe 2*]
    The straying dreams of men
    May bring them ghosts of joy :
  But as they drowse, the waking embers burn them ;
  Or they walk with fixed éyes, as blind men walk.
  But the ancient wisdom speaks for our own time :
    Fate works most for woe
    With Folly's fairest show.
  Man's little pleasure is the spring of sorrow.

SCENE III

CHORAGOS. But here is Haimon, King, the last of all your sons.
  Is it grief for Antigonê that brings him here,
  And bitterness at being robbed of his bride ?

                  Enter HAIMON.

CREON. We shall soon see, and no need of diviners.

                           —Son,

  You have heard my final judgment on that girl:
  Have you come here hating me, or have you come
  With deference and with love, whatever I do?
HAIMON. I am your son, father. You are my guide.
  You make things clear for me, and I obey you.
  No marriage means more to me than your continuing wisdom.   10
CREON. Good. That is the way to behave: subordinate
  Everything else, my son, to your father's will.
  This is what a man prays for, that he may get
  Sons attentive and dutiful in his house,
  Each one hating his father's enemies,
  Honoring his father's friends. But if his sons
  Fail him, if they turn out unprofitably,
  What has he fathered but trouble for himself
  And amusement for the malicious?

                    So you are right
  Not to lose your head over this woman.   20
  Your pleasure with her would soon grow cold, Haimon,
  And then you'd have a hellcat in bed and elsewhere.
  Let her find her husband in Hell!
  Of all the people in this city, only she
  Has had contempt for my law and broken it.
  Do you want me to show myself weak before the people?
  Or to break my sworn word? No, and I will not.
  The woman dies.
  I suppose she'll plead "family ties." Well, let her.
  If I permit my own family to rebel,   30
  How shall I earn the world's obedience?
  Show me the man who keeps his house in hand,
  He's fit for public authority.

                  I'll have no dealings
  With law-breakers, critics of the government:
  Whoever is chosen to govern should be obeyed—
  Must be obeyed, in all things, great and small,
  Just and unjust! O Haimon,
  The man who knows how to obey, and that man only,
  Knows how to give commands when the time comes.
  You can depend on him, no matter how fast   40
  The spears come: he's a good soldier, he'll stick it out.
  Anarchy, anarchy! Show me a greater evil!
  This is why cities tumble and the great houses rain down,
  This is what scatters armies!
  No, no: good lives are made so by discipline.
  We keep the laws then, and the lawmakers,

And no woman shall seduce us. If we must lose,
Let's lose to a man, at least! Is a woman stronger than we?
CHORAGOS. Unless time has rusted my wits,
What you say, King, is said with point and dignity.
HAIMON [*boyishly earnest*].   Father.   50
Reason is God's crowning gift to man, and you are right
To warn me against losing mine. I cannot say—
I hope that I shall never want to say—that you
Have reasoned badly. Yet there are other men
Who can reason, too; and their opinions might be helpful.
You are not in a position to know everything
That people say or do, or what they feel:
Your temper terrifies them—everyone
Will tell you only what you like to hear.
But I, at any rate, can listen; and I have heard them   60
Muttering and whispering in the dark about this girl.
They say no woman has ever, so unreasonably,
Died so shameful a death for a generous act:
"She covered her brother's body. Is this indecent?
"She kept him from dogs and vultures. Is this a crime?
"Death?—She should have all the honor that we can give her!"
This is the way they talk out there in the city.
You must believe me:
Nothing is closer to me than your happiness.
What could be closer? Must not any son   70
Value his father's fortune as his father does his?
I beg you, do not be unchangeable:
Do not believe that you alone can be right.
The man who thinks that,
The man who maintains that only he has the power
To reason correctly, the gift to speak, the soul—
A man like that, when you know him, turns out empty.
It is not reason never to yield to reason!
In flood time you can see how some trees bend,
And because they bend, even their twigs are safe,   80
While stubborn trees are torn up, roots and all.
And the same thing happens in sailing:
Make your sheet fast, never slacken,—and over you go,
Head over heels and under: and there's your voyage.
Forget you are angry! Let yourself be moved!
I know I am young; but please let me say this:
The ideal condition
Would be, I admit, that men should be right by instinct;
But since we are all too likely to go astray,
The reasonable thing is to learn from those who can teach.   90
CHORAGOS. You will do well to listen to him, King,

If what he says is sensible. And you, Haimon,
Must listen to your father.—Both speak well.
CREON. You consider it right for a man of my years and experience
To go to school to a boy?
HAIMON.   It is not right
If I am wrong. But if I am young, and right,
What does my age matter?
CREON. You think it right to stand up for an anarchist?
HAIMON. Not at all. I pay no respect to criminals.
CREON. Then she is not a criminal?   100
HAIMON. The City would deny it, to a man.
CREON. And the City proposes to teach me how to rule?
HAIMON. Ah. Who is it that's talking like a boy now?
CREON. My voice is the one voice giving orders in this City!
HAIMON. It is no City if it takes orders from one voice.
CREON. The State is the King!
HAIMON. Yes, if the State is a desert.

                                                                [*Pause.*]

CREON. This boy, it seems, has sold out to a woman.
HAIMON. If you are a woman: my concern is only for you.
CREON. So? Your "concern"! In a public brawl with your father!   110
HAIMON. How about you, in a public brawl with justice?
CREON. With justice, when all that I do is within my rights?
HAIMON. You have no right to trample on God's right.
CREON [*completely out of control*]. Fool, adolescent fool! Taken in by a
    woman!
HAIMON. You'll never see me taken in by anything vile.
CREON. Every word you say is for her!
HAIMON [*quietly, darkly*]. And for you.
    And for me. And for the gods under the earth.
CREON. You'll never marry her while she lives.
HAIMON. Then she must die.—But her death will cause another.   120
CREON. Another?
    Have you lost your senses? Is this an open threat?
HAIMON. There is no threat in speaking to emptiness.
CREON. I swear you'll regret this superior tone of yours!
    You are the empty one!
HAIMON. If you were not my father, I'd say you were perverse.
CREON. You girlstruck fool, don't play at words with me!
HAIMON. I am sorry. You prefer silence.
CREON.   Now, by God—!
    I swear, by all the gods in heaven above us,
    You'll watch it, I swear you shall!
    [*To the* SERVANTS]   Bring her out!   130
    Bring the woman out! Let her die before his eyes!
    Here, this instant, with her bridegroom beside her!

HAIMON. Not here, no; she will not die here, King.
  And you will never see my face again.
  Go on raving as long as you've a friend to endure you.

[Exit HAIMON.]

CHORAGOS.   Gone, gone.
  Creon, a young man in a rage is dangerous!
CREON. Let him do, or dream to do, more than a man can.
  He shall not save these girls from death.
CHORAGOS.   These girls?
  You have sentenced them both?
CREON.   No, you are right.
  I will not kill the one whose hands are clean.   140
CHORAGOS. But Antigonê?
CREON [*somberly*].   I will carry her far away
  Out there in the wilderness, and lock her
  Living in a vault of stone. She shall have food,
  As the custom is, to absolve the State of her death.
  And there let her pray to the gods of hell:
  They are her only gods:
  Perhaps they will show her an escape from death,
  Or she may learn, though late,
  That piety shown the dead is piety in vain.

[Exit CREON.]

ODE III

[strophe]

CHORUS. Love, unconquerable
  Waster of rich men, keeper
  Of warm lights and all-night vigil
  In the soft face of a girl:
  Sea-wanderer, forest-visitor!
  Even the pure Immortals cannot escape you,
  And mortal man, in his one day's dusk,
  Trembles before your glory.

[antistrophe]

Surely you swerve upon ruin
  The just man's consenting heart,   10
  As here you have made bright anger
  Strike between father and son—
  And none has conquered but Love!
  A girl's glánce wórking the will of heaven:
  Pleasure to her alone who mocks us,
  Merciless Aphroditê.

SCENE IV

ANTIGONE *enters guarded.*

CHORAGOS. But I can no longer stand in awe of this,
Nor, seeing what I see, keep back my tears.
Here is Antigonê, passing to that chamber
Where all find sleep at last.

[*strophe 1*]

ANTIGONE. Look upon me, friends, and pity me
Turning back at the night's edge to say
Goodbye to the sun that shines for me no longer;
Now sleepy Death
Summons me down to Acheron,[2] that cold shore:
There is no bridesong there, nor any music.   10

CHORUS. Yet not unpraised, not without a kind of honor.
You walk at last into the underworld;
Untouched by sickness, broken by no sword.
What woman has ever found your way to death?

[*antistrophe 1*]

ANTIGONE. How often I have heard the story of Niobê,
Tantalos' wretched daughter, how the stone
Clung fast about her, ivy-close: and they say
The rain falls endlessly
And sifting soft snow; her tears are never done.[3]
I feel the loneliness of her death in mine.   20

CHORUS. But she was born of heaven, and you
Are woman, woman-born. If her death is yours,
A mortal woman's, is this not for you
Glory in our world and in the world beyond?

[*strophe 2*]

ANTIGONE. You laugh at me. Ah, friends, friends,
Can you not wait until I am dead? O Thebes,
O men many-charioted, in love with Fortune,
Dear springs of Dircê, sacred Theban grove,[4]
Be witness for me, denied all pity,
Unjustly judged! and think a word of love   30

---

[2] the river dividing the world of the living from the underworld
[3] Niobê boasted that her children were better than Leto's. Apollo and Artemis, Leto's children, avenged the insult by killing Niobê's children. The bereaved mother wept ceaselessly and was eventually turned to stone.
[4] Dionysus caused a spring to flow from the spot near Thebes where Dircê was killed when a bull threw her to the ground.

For her whose path turns
Under dark earth, where there are no more tears.

CHORUS. You have passed beyond human daring and come at last
Into a place of stone where Justice sits.
I cannot tell
What shape of your father's guilt appears in this.

[*antistrophe 2*]

ANTIGONE. You have touched it at last : that bridal bed
Unspeakable, horror of son and mother mingling :
Their crime, infection of all our family !
O Œdipus, father and brother !   40
Your marriage strikes from the grave to murder mine.
I have been a stranger here in my own land :
All my life
The blasphemy of my birth has followed me.

CHORUS. Reverence is a virtue, but strength
Lives in established law : that must prevail.
You have made your choice,
Your death is the doing of your conscious hand.

[*epode*]

ANTIGONE. Then let me go, since all your words are bitter,
And the very light of the sun is cold to me.   50
Lead me to my vigil, where I must have
Neither love nor lamentation ; no song, but silence.

CREON *interrupts impatiently.*

CREON. If dirges and planned lamentations could put off death,
Men would be singing for ever.
[*To the* SERVANTS]   Take her, go !
You know your orders : take her to the vault
And leave her alone there. And if she lives or dies,
That's her affair, not ours : our hands are clean.
ANTIGONE. O tomb, vaulted bridebed in eternal rock,
Soon I shall be with my own again
Where Persephonê[5] welcomes the thin ghosts underground :   60
And I shall see my father again, and you, mother,
And dearest Polyneicês—
                              dearest indeed
To me, since it was my hand
That washed him clean and poured the ritual wine :
And my reward is death before my time !

[5] queen of the underworld

And yet, as men's hearts know, I have done no wrong,
I have not sinned before God. Or if I have,
I shall know the truth in death. But if the guilt
Lies upon Creon who judged me, then, I pray,
May his punishment equal my own.
CHORAGOS.   O passionate heart,   70
Unyielding, tormented still by the same winds!
CREON. Her guards shall have good cause to regret their delaying.
ANTIGONE. Ah! That voice is like the voice of death!
CREON. I can give you no reason to think you are mistaken.
ANTIGONE. Thebes, and you my fathers' gods,
And rulers of Thebes, you see me now, the last
Unhappy daughter of a line of kings,
Your kings led away to death. You will remember
What things I suffer, and at what men's hands,
Because I would not transgress the laws of heaven.   80
[*To the* GUARDS, *simply*] Come: let us wait no longer.
                              [*Exit* ANTIGONE, *L., guarded*]

ODE IV

[*strophe 1*]

CHORUS. All Danaê's beauty was locked away
In a brazen cell where the sunlight could not come:
A small room, still as any grave, enclosed her.
Yet she was a princess too,
And Zeus in a rain of gold poured love upon her.[6]
O child, child,
No power in wealth or war
Or tough sea-blackened ships
Can prevail against untiring Destiny!

[*antistrophe 1*]

And Dryas' son also, that furious king,   10
Bore the god's prisoning anger for his bride:
Sealed up by Dionysos in deaf stone,
His madness died among echoes.
So at the last he learned what dreadful power
His tongue had mocked:
For he had profaned the revels,
And fired the wrath of the nine
Implacable Sisters that love the sound of the flute.[7]

---

[6] Acrisius, king of Argos, imprisoned his daughter Danaê in a bronze tower because an oracle had foretold that a son of hers would kill the king. Zeus disguised himself as a golden shower and impregnated Danaê, who bore Perseus—who did indeed accidentally kill Acrisius with a discus.

[7] Lycurgus opposed Dionysus and was punished by madness and imprisonment.

[strophe 2]

And old men tell a half-remembered tale
Of horror done where a dark ledge splits the sea   20
And a double surf beats on the gráy shóres :
How a king's new woman, sick
With hatred for the queen he had imprisoned,
Ripped out his two sons' eyes with her bloody hands
While grinning Arês watched the shuttle plunge
Four times : four blind wounds crying for revenge,

[antistrophe 2]

Crying, tears and blood mingled.—Piteously born,
Those sons whose mother was of heavenly birth !
Her father was the god of the North Wind
And she was cradled by gales,   30
She raced with young colts on the glittering hills
And walked untrammeled in the open light :
But in her marriage deathless Fate found means
To build a tomb like yours for all her joy.[8]

Scene V

Enter blind Teiresias,[9] *led by a boy. The opening speeches of* Teiresias
should be in singsong contrast to the realistic lines of Creon.

Teiresias. This is the way the blind man comes, Princess, Princess,
  Lock-step, two heads lit by the eyes of one.
Creon. What new thing have you to tell us, old Teiresias ?
Teiresias. I have much to tell you : listen to the prophet, Creon.
Creon. I am not aware that I have ever failed to listen.
Teiresias. Then you have done wisely, King, and ruled well.
Creon. I admit my debt to you. But what have you to say ?
Teiresias. This, Creon : you stand once more on the edge of fate.
Creon. What do you mean ? Your words are a kind of dread.
Teiresias. Listen, Creon :   10
  I was sitting in my chair of augury, at the place
  Where the birds gather about me. They were all a-chatter,
  As is their habit, when suddenly I heard
  A strange note in their jangling, a scream, a
  Whirring fury ; I knew that they were fighting,
  Tearing each other, dying
  In a whirlwind of wings clashing. And I was afraid.

---

[8] This third instance of imprisonment involves the blinding with a weaving shuttle
of the sons of Phineus, king of Salmydessus, by their stepmother. Ares, known as
Mars to the Romans, was the god of war.
  [9] a blind, long-lived prophet, chiefly associated with Thebes, who appears in a
number of Greek writings

I began the rites of burnt-offering at the altar,
But Hephaistos[10] failed me : instead of bright flame,
There was only the sputtering slime of the fat thigh-flesh   20
Melting : the entrails dissolved in gray smoke,
The bare bone burst from the welter. And no blaze !
This was a sign from heaven. My boy described it,
Seeing for me as I see for others.
I tell you, Creon, you yourself have brought
This new calamity upon us. Our hearths and altars
Are stained with the corruption of dogs and carrion birds
That glut themselves on the corpse of Œdipus' son.
The gods are deaf when we pray to them, their fire
Recoils from our offering, their birds of omen   30
Have no cry of comfort, for they are gorged
With the thick blood of the dead.
                    O my son,
These are no trifles ! Think : all men make mistakes,
But a good man yields when he knows his course is wrong,
And repairs the evil. The only crime is pride.
Give in to the dead man, then : do not fight with a corpse—
What glory is it to kill a man who is dead ?
Think, I beg you :
It is for your own good that I speak as I do.
You should be able to yield for your own good.   40
CREON. It seems that prophets have made me their especial province.
All my life long
I have been a kind of butt for the dull arrows
Of doddering fortune-tellers !
                    No, Teiresias :
If your birds—if the great eagles of God himself
Should carry him stinking bit by bit to heaven,
I would not yield. I am not afraid of pollution :
No man can defile the gods.
                    Do what you will,
Go into business, make money, speculate
In India gold or that synthetic gold from Sardis,   50
Get rich otherwise than by my consent to bury him.
Teiresias, it is a sorry thing when a wise man
Sells his wisdom, lets out his words for hire !
TEIRESIAS. Ah Creon ! Is there no man left in the world—
CREON. To do what—Come, let's have the aphorism !
TEIRESIAS. No man who knows that wisdom outweighs any wealth ?
CREON. As surely as bribes are baser than any baseness.
TEIRESIAS. You are sick, Creon ! You are deathly sick !

[10] artisan of the gods

CREON. As you say : it is not my place to challenge a prophet.
TEIRESIAS. Yet you have said my prophecy is for sale.   60
CREON. The generation of prophets has always loved gold.
TEIRESIAS. The generation of kings has always loved brass.
CREON. You forget yourself! You are speaking to your King.
TEIRESIAS. I know it. You are a king because of me.
CREON. You have a certain skill ; but you have sold out.
TEIRESIAS. King, you will drive me to words that—
CREON.   Say them, say them!
   Only remember : I will not pay you for them.
TEIRESIAS. No, you will find them too costly.
CREON.   No doubt. Speak :
   Whatever you say, you will not change my will.
TEIRESIAS. Then take this, and take it to heart !   70
   The time is not far off when you shall pay back
   Corpse for corpse, flesh of your own flesh.
   You have thrust the child of this world into living night,
   You have kept from the gods below the child that is theirs :
   The one in a grave before her death, the other,
   Dead, denied the grave. This is your crime :
   And the Furies[11] and the dark gods of Hell
   Are swift with terrible punishment for you.
   Do you want to buy me now, Creon ?
                      Not many days,
   And your house will be full of men and women weeping,   80
   And curses will be hurled at you from far
   Cities grieving for sons unburied, left to rot
   Before the walls of Thebes.
   These are my arrows, Creon : they are all for you.
   [*To* BOY] But come, child : lead me home
   Let him waste his fine anger upon younger men.
   Maybe he will learn at last
   To control a wiser tongue in a better head.
                             [*Exit* TEIRESIAS.]
CHORAGOS. The old man has gone, King, but his words
   Remain to plague us. I am old, too,   90
   But I cannot remember that he was ever false.
CREON. That is true. . . . It troubles me.
   Oh it is hard to give in ! but it is worse
   To risk everything for stubborn pride.
CHORAGOS. Creon : take my advice.
CREON.   What shall I do ?
CHORAGOS. Go quickly : free Antigonê from her vault
   And build a tomb for the body of Polyneicês.

   [11] the three avenging spirits

CREON. You would have me do this?

CHORAGOS.   Creon, yes!
  And it must be done at once: God moves
  Swiftly to cancel the folly of stubborn men.   100

CREON. It is hard to deny the heart! But I
  Will do it: I will not fight with destiny.

CHORAGOS. You must go yourself, you cannot leave it to others.

CREON. I will go.
            —Bring axes, servants:
  Come with me to the tomb. I buried her, I
  Will set her free.
            Oh, quickly!
  My mind misgives—
  The laws of the gods are mighty, and a man must serve them
  To the last day of his life!

                                        [*Exit* CREON.]

PAEAN

                                        [*strophe 1*]

CHORAGOS. God of many names

CHORUS.   O Iacchos
                              son
  of Cadmeian Sémelê
                        O born of the Thunder!
  Guardian of the West
                        Regent
  of Eleusis' plain
                  O Prince of mænad Thebes
  and the Dragon Field by rippling Ismenos:

                                        [*antistrophe 1*]

CHORAGOS. God of many names [12]

CHORUS.   the flame of torches
  flares on our hills
                  the nymphs of Iacchos
  dance at the spring of Castalia:
  from the vine-close mountain
                              come ah come in ivy:
  Evohé evohé! sings through the streets of Thebes   10

                                        [*strophe 2*]

CHORAGOS. God of many names

CHORUS.   Iacchos of Thebes

[12] Dionysus, god of wine and vegetation, associated with revelry and debauchery, and much honored in Thebes, was also known as Bacchus and under these names and epithets.

heavenly Child
            of Sémelê bride of the Thunderer!
The shadow of plague is upon us:
                              come
with clement feet
            oh come from Parnasos
down the long slopes
                  across the lamenting water

                                          [antistrophe 2]

CHORAGOS. Iô Fire! Chorister of the throbbing stars!
    O purest among the voices of the night!
    Thou son of God, blaze for us!
CHORUS. Come with choric rapture of circling Mænads[13]
    Who cry *Iô Iacche!*
            God of many names!   20

                        ÉXODOS

                  Enter MESSENGER, *L.*

MESSENGER. Men of the line of Cadmos, you who live
    Near Amphion's citadel:
                        I cannot say
Of any condition of human life "This is fixed,
This is clearly good, or bad." Fate raises up,
And Fate casts down the happy and unhappy alike:
No man can foretell his Fate.
                        Take the case of Creon:
Creon was happy once, as I count happiness:
Victorious in battle, sole governor of the land,
Fortunate father of children nobly born.
And now it has all gone from him! Who can say   10
That a man is still alive when his life's joy fails?
He is a walking dead man. Grant him rich,
Let him live like a king in his great house:
If his pleasure is gone, I would not give
So much as the shadow of smoke for all he owns.
CHORAGOS. Your words hint at sorrow: what is your news for us?
MESSENGER. They are dead. The living are guilty of their death.
CHORAGOS. Who is guilty? Who is dead? Speak!
MESSENGER.   Haimon.
    Haimon is dead; and the hand that killed him
    Is his own hand.
CHORAGOS.   His father's? or his own?   20
MESSENGER. His own, driven mad by the murder his father had done.
CHORAGOS. Teiresias, how clearly you saw it all!

    [13] female devotees of Dionysus

MESSENGER. This is my news: you must draw what conclusions you
can from it.

CHORAGOS. But look: Eurydicê, our Queen:
Has she overheard us?

Enter EURYDICE *from the Palace, C.*

EURYDICE. I have heard something, friends:
As I was unlocking the gate of Pallas' shrine,
For I needed her help today, I heard a voice
Telling of some new sorrow. And I fainted
There at the temple with all my maidens about me.   30
But speak again: whatever it is, I can bear it:
Grief and I are no strangers.

MESSENGER.   Dearest Lady,
I will tell you plainly all that I have seen.
I shall not try to comfort you: what is the use,
Since comfort could lie only in what is not true?
The truth is always best.

                    I went with Creon
To the outer plain where Polyneicês was lying,
No friend to pity him, his body shredded by dogs.
We made our prayers in that place to Hecatê
And Pluto, that they would be merciful. And we bathed   40
The corpse with holy water, and we brought
Fresh-broken branches to burn what was left of it,
And upon the urn we heaped up a towering barrow
Of the earth of his own land.

                  When we were done, we ran
To the vault where Antigonê lay on her couch of stone.
One of the servants had gone ahead,
And while he was yet far off he heard a voice
Grieving within the chamber, and he came back
And told Creon. And as the King went closer,
The air was full of wailing, the words lost,   50
And he begged us to make all haste. "Am I a prophet?"
He said, weeping, "And must I walk this road,
"The saddest of all that I have gone before?
"My son's voice calls me on. Oh quickly, quickly!
"Look through the crevice there, and tell me
"If it is Haimon, or some deception of the gods!"
We obeyed; and in the cavern's farthest corner
We saw her lying:
She had made a noose of her fine linen veil
And hanged herself. Haimon lay beside her,   60
His arms about her waist, lamenting her,
His love lost under ground, crying out

That his father had stolen her away from him.
When Creon saw him the tears rushed to his eyes
And he called to him : "What have you done, child? Speak to me.
"What are you thinking that makes your eyes so strange?
"O my son, my son, I come to you on my knees!"
But Haimon spat in his face. He said not a word,
Staring—
           And suddenly drew his sword
And lunged. Creon shrank back, the blade missed; and the boy,   70
Desperate against himself, drove it half its length
Into his own side, and fell. And as he died
He gathered Antigonê close in his arms again,
Choking, his blood bright red on her white cheek.
And now he lies dead with the dead, and she is his
At last, his bride in the houses of the dead.

                                [*Exit* EURYDICE *into the Palace.*]

CHORAGOS. She has left us without a word. What can this mean?
MESSENGER. It troubles me, too; yet she knows what is best,
   Her grief is too great for public lamentation,
   And doubtless she has gone to her chamber to weep   80
   For her dead son, leading her maidens in his dirge.
CHORAGOS. It may be so: but I fear this deep silence.   [*Pause.*]
MESSENGER. I will see what she is doing. I will go in.

                        [*Exit* MESSENGER *into the Palace.*]

    Enter CREON *with attendants, bearing* HAIMON'S *body.*

CHORAGOS. But here is the King himself: oh look at him,
   Bearing his own damnation in his arms.
CREON. Nothing you say can touch me any more.
   My own blind heart has brought me
   From darkness to final darkness. Here you see
   The father murdering, the murdered son—
   And all my civic wisdom!   90
   Haimon my son, so young, so young to die,
   I was the fool, not you; and you died for me.
CHORAGOS. That is the truth; but you were late in learning it.
CREON. This truth is hard to bear. Surely a god
   Has crushed me beneath the hugest weight of heaven,
   And driven me headlong a barbaric way
   To trample out the thing I held most dear.
   The pains that men will take to come to pain!

              Enter MESSENGER *from the Palace.*

MESSENGER. The burden you carry in your hands is heavy,
   But it is not all: you will find more in your house.   100
CREON. What burden worse than this shall I find there?

MESSENGER. The Queen is dead.

CREON. O port of death, deaf world,
Is there no pity for me? And you, Angel of evil,
I was dead, and your words are death again.
Is it true, boy? Can it be true?
Is my life dead? Has death bred death?

MESSENGER. You can see for yourself.

The doors are opened, and the body of EURYDICE *is disclosed within.*

CREON. Oh pity!
All true, all true, and more than I can bear!
O my wife, my son!

MESSENGER. She stood before the altar, and her heart   110
Welcomed the knife her own hand guided,
And a great cry burst from her lips for Megareus dead,
And for Haimon dead, her sons; and her last breath
Was a curse for their father, the murderer of her sons.
And she fell, and the dark flowed in through her closing eyes.

CREON. O God, I am sick with fear.
Are there no swords here? Has no one a blow for me?

MESSENGER. Her curse is upon you for the deaths of both.

CREON. It is right that it should be. I alone am guilty.
I know it, and I say it. Lead me in,   130
Quickly, friends.
I have neither life nor substance. Lead me in.

CHORAGOS. You are right, if there can be right in so much wrong.
The briefest way is best in a world of sorrow.

CREON. Let it come,
Let death come quickly, and be kind to me.
I would not ever see the sun again.

CHORAGOS. All that will come when it will; but we, meanwhile,
Have much to do. Leave the future to itself.

CREON. All my heart was in that prayer!   130

CHORAGOS. Then do not pray any more: the sky is deaf.

CREON. Lead me away. I have been rash and foolish.
I have killed my son and my wife.
I look for comfort; my comfort lies here dead.
Whatever my hands have touched has come to nothing.
Fate has brought all my pride to a thought of dust.

As CREON *is being led into the house, the* CHORAGOS *advances and speaks
directly to the audience.*

CHORAGOS. There is no happiness where there is no wisdom;
No wisdom but in submission to the gods.
Big words are always punished,
And proud men in old age learn to be wise.   140

William Shakespeare

1564–1616

OTHELLO, THE MOOR OF VENICE

◇

DRAMATIS PERSONAE

DUKE OF VENICE.
BRABANTIO, *a senator.*
Other senators.
GRATIANO, *brother to Brabantio.*
LODOVICO, *kinsman to Brabantio.*
OTHELLO, *a noble Moor in the service of the Venetian state.*
CASSIO, *his lieutenant.*
IAGO, *his ancient.*
RODERIGO, *a Venetian gentleman.*
MONTANO, *Othello's predecessor in the government of Cyprus.*

CLOWN, *servant to Othello.*
DESDEMONA, *daughter to Brabantio and wife to Othello.*
EMILIA, *wife to Iago.*
BIANCA, *mistress to Cassio.*
SAILOR, MESSENGER, HERALD, OFFICERS, GENTLEMEN, MUSICIANS, *and* ATTENDANTS.

SCENE: *Venice; then a seaport in Cyprus.*

◇

ACT I

SCENE I
Venice. A street.

Enter RODERIGO *and* IAGO.

RODERIGO. Tush! never tell me; I take it much unkindly
    That thou, Iago, who hast had my purse
    As if the strings were thine, shouldst know of this.
IAGO. 'Sblood, but you will not hear me:
    If ever I did dream of such a matter,
    Abhor me.
RODERIGO. Thou told'st me thou didst hold him in thy hate.
IAGO. Despise me, if I do not. Three great ones of the city,
    In personal suit to make me his lieutenant,
    Off-capped to him: and, by the faith of man,
    I know my price, I am worth no worse a place:
    But he, as loving his own pride and purposes,   10

Evades them, with a bombast circumstance[1]
Horribly stuffed with epithets of war;
And, in conclusion,
Nonsuits[2] my mediators; for, "Certes," says he,
"I have already chose my officer."
And what was he?
Forsooth, a great arithmetician,
One Michael Cassio, a Florentine,   20
A fellow almost damned in a fair wife;[3]
That never set a squadron in the field,
Nor the division of a battle knows
More than a spinster;[4] unless the bookish theoric,
Wherein the togéd consuls[5] can propose
As masterly as he: mere prattle, without practice,
Is all his soldiership. But he, sir, had the election:
And I, of whom his eyes had seen the proof
At Rhodes, at Cyprus[6] and on other grounds
Christian and heathen, must be be-lee'd and calmed   30
By debitor and creditor: this counter-caster,[7]
He, in good time, must his lieutenant be,
And I—God bless the mark!—his Moorship's ancient.[8]
RODERIGO. By heaven, I rather would have been his hangman.
IAGO. Why, there's no remedy; 'tis the curse of service,
Preferment goes by letter and affection;
And not by old gradation, where each second
Stood heir to the first. Now, sir, be judge yourself,
Whether I in any just term am affined[9]
To love the Moor.
RODERIGO.   I would not follow him then.   40
IAGO. O, sir, content you;
I follow him to serve my turn upon him:
We cannot all be masters, nor all masters
Cannot be truly followed. You shall mark
Many a duteous and knee-crooking knave,
That, doting on his own obsequious bondage,
Wears out his time, much like his master's ass,
For nought but provender, and when he's old, cashiered:

---

[1] high-sounding circumlocution. Bombast is cotton padding.
[2] rejects the petition of
[3] Iago scorns Cassio as one whose knowledge of military tactics is derived only from a book (arithmetician), and who is fit only for commerce (Florentine). Wife here means woman; Cassio is not married.
[4] a man whose occupation is spinning   [5] senators wearing togas
[6] outposts of Venice in her war with the Turks   [7] bookkeeper
[8] ensign; i.e., standard bearer   [9] bound

Whip me such honest knaves. Others there are
Who, trimmed in forms and visages'of duty,   50
Keep yet their hearts attending on themselves,
And, throwing but shows of service on their lords,
Do well thrive by them and when they have lined their coats
Do themselves homage : these fellows have some soul ;
And such a one do I profess myself. For, sir,
It is as sure as you are Roderigo,
Were I the Moor, I would not be Iago :
In following him, I follow but myself ;
Heaven is my judge, not I for love and duty,
But seeming so, for my peculiar end :   60
For when my outward action doth demonstrate
The native act and figure of my heart
In compliment extern, 'tis not long after
But I will wear my heart upon my sleeve
For daws to peck at : I am not what I am.
RODERIGO. What a full fortune does the thicklips owe,[10]
   If he can carry 't thus !
IAGO.   Call up her father,
   Rouse him : make after him, poison his delight,
   Proclaim him in the streets ; incense her kinsmen,
   And, though he in a fertile climate dwell,   70
   Plague him with flies : though that his joy be joy,
   Yet throw such changes of vexation on 't,
   As it may lose some color.
RODERIGO. Here is her father's house ; I'll call aloud.
IAGO. Do, with like timorous[11] accent and dire yell
   As when, by night and negligence, the fire
   Is spied in populous cities.
RODERIGO. What, ho, Brabantio ! Signior Brabantio, ho !
IAGO. Awake ! what, ho, Brabantio ! thieves ! thieves ! thieves !
   Look to your house, your daughter and your bags !   80
   Thieves ! thieves !

BRABANTIO *appears above, at a window.*

BRABANTIO. What is the reason of this terrible summons ?
   What is the matter there ?
RODERIGO. Signior, is all your family within ?
IAGO. Are your doors locked ?
BRABANTIO.   Why, wherefore ask you this ?
IAGO. 'Zounds, sir, you're robbed ; for shame, put on your gown ;
   Your heart is burst, you have lost half your soul ;

---

[10] own   [11] terrifying

Even now, now, very now, an old black ram
Is tupping your white ewe. Arise, arise;
Awake the snorting citizens with the bell,   90
Or else the Devil will make a grandsire of you:
Arise, I say.
BRABANTIO. What, have you lost your wits?
RODERIGO. Most reverend signior, do you know my voice?
BRABANTIO. Not I: what are you?
RODERIGO. My name is Roderigo.
BRABANTIO.   The worser welcome:
I have charged thee not to haunt about my doors:
In honest plainness thou hast heard me say
My daughter is not for thee; and now, in madness,
Being full of supper and distempering drafts,   100
Upon malicious bravery, dost thou come
To start my quiet.
RODERIGO. Sir, sir, sir,—
BRABANTIO.   But thou must needs be sure
My spirit and my place have in them power
To make this bitter to thee.
RODERIGO.   Patience, good sir.
BRABANTIO. What tell'st thou me of robbing? this is Venice;
My house is not a grange.[12]
RODERIGO.   Most grave Brabantio,
In simple and pure soul I come to you.
IAGO. 'Zounds, sir, you are one of those that will not serve God, if the
devil bid you. Because we come to do you service and you think   110
we are ruffians, you'll have your daughter covered with a Barbary
horse; you'll have your nephews neigh to you; you'll have coursers
for cousins and gennets for germans.[13]
BRABANTIO. What profane wretch art thou?
IAGO. I am one, sir, that comes to tell you your daughter and the Moor
are now making the beast with two backs.
BRABANTIO. Thou art a villain.
IAGO.   You are—a senator.
BRABANTIO. This thou shalt answer; I know thee, Roderigo.
RODERIGO. Sir, I will answer any thing. But, I beseech you,
If't be your pleasure and most wise consent,   120
As partly I find it is, that your fair daughter,
At this odd-even[14] and dull watch o' the night,
Transported, with no worse nor better guard
But with a knave of common hire, a gondolier,
To the gross clasps of a lascivious Moor,—

---

[12] farmhouse   [13] Moorish horses for relatives   [14] the turn of midnight

If this be known to you and your allowance,
We then have done you bold and saucy wrongs;
But if you know not this, my manners tell me
We have your wrong rebuke. Do not believe
That, from [15] the sense of all civility,   130
I thus would play, and trifle with your reverence:
Your daughter, if you have not given her leave,
I say again, hath made a gross revolt;
Tying her duty, beauty, wit and fortunes
In an extravagant and wheeling stranger
Of here and every where. Straight satisfy yourself:
If she be in her chamber or your house,
Let loose on me the justice of the state
For thus deluding you.

BRABANTIO.   Strike on the tinder, ho!
Give me a taper! call up all my people!   140
This accident is not unlike my dream:
Belief of it oppresses me already.
Light, I say! light!

                                                        [*Exit above.*]

IAGO.   Farewell; for I must leave you:
It seems not meet, nor wholesome to my place,
To be produced—as, if I stay, I shall—
Against the Moor: for, I do know, the state,
However this may gall him with some check,
Cannot with safety cast him, for he's embarked
With such loud reason to the Cyprus wars,
Which even now stand in act, that, for their souls,   150
Another of his fathom they have none,
To lead their business: in which regard,
Though I do hate him as I do hell-pains,
Yet, for necessity of present life,
I must show out a flag and sign of love,
Which is indeed but sign. That you shall surely find him,
Lead to the Sagittary [16] the raiséd search;
And there will I be with him. So, farewell.

                                                        [*Exit.*]

Enter, below, BRABANTIO, *and* SERVANTS *with torches.*

BRABANTIO. It is too true an evil: gone she is;
And what's to come of my despiséd time   160
Is nought but bitterness. Now, Roderigo,
Where didst thou see her? O unhappy girl!

---

[15] contrary to
[16] either an inn or the company officers' residence at the Arsenal

With the Moor, say'st thou? Who would be a father!
How didst thou know 'twas she? O, she deceives me
Past thought! What said she to you? Get more tapers:
Raise all my kindred. Are they married, think you?
RODERIGO. Truly, I think they are.
BRABANTIO. O heaven! How got she out? O treason of the blood!
Fathers, from hence trust not your daughters' minds
By what you see them act. Is there not charms　　　　170
By which the property of youth and maidhood
May be abused? Have you not read, Roderigo,
Of some such thing?
RODERIGO.　　　　Yes, sir, I have indeed.
BRABANTIO. Call up my brother. O, would you had had her!
Some one way, some another. Do you know
Where we may apprehend her and the Moor?
RODERIGO. I think I can discover him, if you please
To get good guard and go along with me.
BRABANTIO. Pray you, lead on. At every house I'll call;
I may command at most. Get weapons, ho!　　　　180
And raise some special officers of night.
On, good Roderigo: I'll deserve your pains.

　　　　　　　　　　　　　　　　[Exeunt.]

SCENE II
Another street.

Enter OTHELLO, IAGO, *and* ATTENDANTS *with torches.*

IAGO. Though in the trade of war I have slain men,
Yet do I hold it very stuff o' the conscience
To do no contrived murder: I lack iniquity
Sometimes to do me service: nine or ten times
I had thought to have yerked [17] him here under the ribs.
OTHELLO. 'Tis better as it is.
IAGO.　　　　　　　　　Nay, but he prated,
And spoke such scurvy and provoking terms
Against your honor
That, with the little godliness I have,
I did full hard forbear him. But, I pray you, sir,　　　　10
Are you fast married? Be assured of this,
That the magnifico is much beloved,
And hath in his effect a voice potential
As double as the duke's: he will divorce you;
Or put upon you what restraint and grievance

---

[17] stabbed

The law, with all his might to enforce it on,
Will give him cable.
OTHELLO.   Let him do his spite;
My services which I have done the signiory[18]
Shall out-tongue his complaints. 'Tis yet to know,—
Which, when I know that boasting is an honor,   20
I shall promulgate—I fetch my life and being
From men of royal siege, and my demerits
May speak unbonneted to as proud a fortune
As this that I have reached: for know, Iago,
But that I love the gentle Desdemona,
I would not my unhoused free condition
Put into circumscription and confine
For the sea's worth.[19] But, look! what lights come yond?
IAGO. Those are the raised father and his friends:
You were best go in.
OTHELLO.   Not I; I must be found: 30
My parts, my title and my perfect soul
Shall manifest me rightly. Is it they?
IAGO. By Janus, I think no.

> *Enter* CASSIO, *and certain* OFFICERS *with torches.*

OTHELLO. The servants of the duke, and my lieutenant.
The goodness of the night upon you, friends!
What is the news?
CASSIO. The duke does greet you, general,
And he requires your haste-post-haste appearance,
Even on the instant.
OTHELLO.   What is the matter, think you?
CASSIO. Something from Cyprus, as I may divine: 40
It is a business of some heat: the galleys
Have sent a dozen sequent messengers
This very night at one another's heels,
And many of the consuls, raised and met,
Are at the duke's already: you have been hotly called for;
When, being not at your lodging to be found,
The senate hath sent about three several quests
To search you out.
OTHELLO.   'Tis well I am found by you.
I will but spend a word here in the house,
And go with you.
                                                              [*Exit.*]

---

[18] Venetian senate
[19] Treasures of gold and precious stones were thought to be buried in the bottom
of the sea.

CASSIO.   Ancient, what makes he here?   50
IAGO. 'Faith, he to-night hath boarded a land carack: [20]
  If it prove lawful prize, he's made for ever.
CASSIO. I do not understand.
IAGO.   He's married.
CASSIO.   To who?

Re-enter OTHELLO.

IAGO. Marry, to—Come, captain, will you go?
OTHELLO.   Have with you.
CASSIO. Here comes another troop to seek for you.
IAGO. It is Brabantio. General, be advised;
  He comes to bad intent.

Enter BRABANTIO, RODERIGO, *and* OFFICERS
with torches and weapons.

OTHELLO.   Holla! stand there!
RODERIGO. Signior, it is the Moor.
BRABANTIO.   Down with him, thief!
                         [*They draw on both sides.*]
IAGO. You, Roderigo! come, sir, I am for you.
OTHELLO. Keep up your bright swords, for the dew will rust them.   60
  Good signior, you shall more command with years
  Than with your weapons.
BRABANTIO. O thou foul thief, where hast thou stowed my daughter?
  Damned as thou art, thou hast enchanted her;
  For I'll refer me to all things of sense,
  If she in chains of magic were not bound,
  Whether a maid so tender, fair and happy,
  So opposite to marriage that she shunned
  The wealthy curléd darlings of our nation,
  Would ever have, to incur a general mock,   70
  Run from her guardage to the sooty bosom
  Of such a thing as thou, to fear, not to delight.
  Judge me the world, if 'tis not gross in sense [21]
  That thou hast practised on her with foul charms,
  Abused her delicate youth with drugs or minerals
  That weaken motion: I'll have't disputed on;
  'Tis probable and palpable to thinking.
  I therefore apprehend and do attach thee
  For an abuser of the world, a practiser
  Of arts inhibited and out of warrant.   80

[20] large vessel   [21] obvious to perception

Lay hold upon him : if he do resist,
Subdue him at his peril.
OTHELLO.   Hold your hands,
Both you of my inclining, and the rest :
Were it my cue to fight, I should have known it
Without a prompter. Where will you that I go
To answer this your charge ?
BRABANTIO.   To prison, till fit time
Of law and course of direct session
Call thee to answer.
OTHELLO.   What if I do obey ?
How may the duke be therewith satisfied,
Whose messengers are here about my side,   90
Upon some present business of the state
To bring me to him ?
FIRST OFFICER.   'Tis true, most worthy signior ;
The duke's in council, and your noble self,
I am sure, is sent for.
BRABANTIO.   How ! the duke in council !
In this time of the night ! Bring him away :
Mine's not an idle cause : the duke himself,
Or any of my brothers of the state,
Cannot but feel this wrong as 'twere their own ;
For if such actions may have passage free,
Bond-slaves and pagans shall our statesmen be.   100
                                        [*Exeunt.*]

                          SCENE III
                     A council-chamber.

The DUKE *and* SENATORS *sitting at a table;* OFFICERS *attending.*

DUKE. There is no composition in these news
That gives them credit.
FIRST SENATOR.   Indeed, they are disproportioned ;
My letters say a hundred and seven galleys.
DUKE. And mine, a hundred and forty.
SECOND SENATOR.   And mine, two hundred :
But though they jump not on a just account,—
As in these cases, where the aim reports,
'Tis oft with difference—yet do they all confirm
A Turkish fleet, and bearing up to Cyprus.
DUKE. Nay, it is possible enough to judgment :
I do not so secure me in the error,   10
But the main article I do approve

In fearful sense.[22]

SAILOR [*Within*]. What, ho! what, ho! what, ho!

FIRST OFFICER. A messenger from the galleys.

Enter a SAILOR.

DUKE.   Now, what's the

   business?

SAILOR. The Turkish preparation makes for Rhodes;

   So was I bid report here to the state

   By Signior Angelo.

DUKE. How say you by this change?

FIRST SENATOR.   This cannot be,

   By no assay of reason: 'tis a pageant,

   To keep us in false gaze.[23] When we consider   20

   The importancy of Cyprus to the Turk,

   And let ourselves again but understand,

   That as it more concerns the Turk than Rhodes,

   So may he with more facile question bear it,

   For that it stands not in such warlike brace,

   But altogether lacks the abilities

   That Rhodes is dressed in: if we make thought of this,

   We must not think the Turk is so unskillful

   To leave that latest which concerns him first,

   Neglecting an attempt of ease and gain,   30

   To wake and wage a danger profitless.

DUKE. Nay, in all confidence, he's not for Rhodes.

FIRST OFFICER. Here is more news.

Enter a MESSENGER.

MESSENGER. The Ottomites,[24] reverend and gracious,

   Steering with due course towards the isle of Rhodes,

   Have there injointed them with an after fleet.

FIRST SENATOR. Ay, so I thought. How many, as you guess?

MESSENGER. Of thirty sail: and now they do restem

   Their backward course, bearing with frank appearance

   Their purposes toward Cyprus. Signior Montano,   40

   Your trusty and most valiant servitor,

   With his free duty[25] recommends you thus,

   And prays you to believe him.

DUKE. 'Tis certain, then, for Cyprus.

   Marcus Luccicos, is not he in town?

---

[22] I do not feel myself so secure because of the discrepancy as not to believe the essential fact.

[23] looking in the wrong direction   [24] Turks   [25] willing deference

FIRST SENATOR. He's now in Florence.
DUKE. Write from us to him; post-post-haste dispatch.
FIRST SENATOR. Here comes Brabantio and the valiant Moor.

Enter BRABANTIO, OTHELLO, IAGO,
RODERIGO, *and* OFFICERS.

DUKE. Valiant Othello, we must straight employ you
  Against the general enemy Ottoman.   50
  [*To* BRABANTIO] I did not see you; welcome, gentle signior;
  We lacked your counsel and your help tonight.
BRABANTIO. So did I yours. Good your grace, pardon me;
  Neither my place nor aught I heard of business
  Hath raised me from my bed, nor doth the general care
  Take hold on me, for my particular grief
  Is of so flood-gate and o'erbearing nature
  That it engluts and swallows other sorrows
  And it is still itself.
DUKE.   Why, what's the matter?
BRABANTIO. My daughter! O, my daughter!
DUKE AND SENATOR.   Dead?
BRABANTIO.   Ay, to me;   60
  She is abused, stol'n from me, and corrupted
  By spells and medicines bought of mountebanks;
  For nature so preposterously to err,
  Being not deficient, blind, or lame of sense,
  Sans witchcraft could not.
DUKE. Who'er he be that in this foul proceeding
  Hath thus beguiled your daughter of herself
  And you of her, the bloody book of law
  You shall yourself read in the bitter letter
  After your own sense, yea, though our proper son   70
  Stood in your action.
BRABANTIO.   Humbly I thank your grace.
  Here is the man, this Moor, whom now, it seems,
  Your special mandate for the state-affairs
  Hath hither brought.
DUKE AND SENATOR. We are very sorry for 't.
DUKE [*to* OTHELLO]. What, in your own part, can you say to this?
BRABANTIO. Nothing, but this is so.
OTHELLO. Most potent, grave, and reverend signiors,
  My very noble and approved good masters,
  That I have ta'en away this old man's daughter,   80
  It is most true; true, I have married her:
  The very head and front of my offending
  Hath this extent, no more. Rude am I in my speech,
  And little blessed with the soft phrase of peace;

For since these arms of mine had seven years' pith,
Till now some nine moons wasted, they have used
Their dearest action in the tented field,
And little of this great world can I speak,
More than pertains to feats of broil and battle,
And therefore little shall I grace my cause   90
In speaking for myself. Yet, by your gracious patience,
I will a round²⁶ unvarnished tale deliver
Of my whole course of love; what drugs, what charms,
What conjuration and what mighty magic,
For such proceeding I am charged withal,
I won his daughter.
BRABANTIO.   A maiden never bold;
Of spirit so still and quiet, that her motion
Blushed at herself; and she, in spite of nature,
Of years, of country, credit, every thing,
To fall in love with what she feared to look on!   100
It is a judgment maimed and most imperfect
That will confess perfection so could err
Against all rules of nature, and must be driven
To find out practices of cunning hell,
Why this should be. I therefore vouch again
That with some mixtures powerful o'er the blood,
Or with some dram conjured to this effect
He wrought upon her.
DUKE.   To vouch this, is no proof,
Without more wider and more overt test
Than these thin habits and poor likelihoods   110
Of modern seeming²⁷ do prefer against him.
FIRST SENATOR. But, Othello, speak:
Did you by indirect and forcéd courses
Subdue and poison this young maid's affections?
Or came it by request and such fair question
As soul to soul affordeth?
OTHELLO.   I do beseech you,
Send for the lady to the Sagittary,
And let her speak of me before her father:
If you do find me foul in her report,
The trust, the office I do hold of you,   120
Not only take away, but let your sentence
Even fall upon my life.
DUKE.   Fetch Desdemona hither.

²⁶ straightforward
²⁷ superficial appearances and improbable charges of slight suspicion

OTHELLO. Ancient, conduct them; you best know the place.

                            [Exeunt IAGO *and* ATTENDANTS.]

    And, till she come, as truly as to heaven
    I do confess the vices of my blood,
    So justly to your grave ears I'll present
    How I did thrive in this fair lady's love,
    And she in mine.

DUKE. Say it, Othello.

OTHELLO. Her father loved me; oft invited me;   130
    Still questioned me the story of my life,
    From year to year, the battles, sieges, fortunes,
    That I have passed.
    I ran it through, even from my boyish days,
    To the very moment that he bade me tell it;
    Wherein I spake of most disastrous chances,
    Of moving accidents by flood and field,
    Of hair-breadth scapes i' the imminent deadly breach,
    Of being taken by the insolent foe
    And sold to slavery, of my redemption thence   140
    And portance [28] in my travels' history:
    Wherein of antres [29] vast and deserts idle,
    Rough quarries, rocks and hills whose heads touch heaven,
    It was my hint to speak,—such was the process.
    And of the Cannibals that each other eat,
    The Anthropophagi [30] and men whose heads
    Do grow beneath their shoulders. This to hear
    Would Desdemona seriously incline:
    But still the house-affairs would draw her thence:
    Which ever as she could with haste dispatch,   150
    She'd come again, and with a greedy ear
    Devour up my discourse: which I observing,
    Took once a pliant hour, and found good means
    To draw from her a prayer of earnest heart
    That I would all my pilgrimage dilate,
    Whereof by parcels she had something heard,
    But not intentively: I did consent,
    And often did beguile her of her tears,
    When I did speak of some distressful stroke
    That my youth suffered. My story being done,   160
    She gave me for my pains a world of sighs:
    She swore, in faith, 'twas strange, 'twas passing strange,
    'Twas pitiful, 'twas wondrous pitiful:
    She wished she had not heard it, yet she wished

---

[28] behavior   [29] caves   [30] man-eaters

That heaven had made her [31] such a man : she thanked me,
And bade me, if I had a friend that loved her,
I should but teach him how to tell my story,
And that would woo her. Upon this hint I spake :
She loved me for the dangers I had passed,
And I loved her that she did pity them.   170
This only is the witchcraft I have used :
Here comes the lady ; let her witness it.

Enter DESDEMONA, IAGO, *and* ATTENDANTS.

DUKE. I think this tale would win my daughter too.
  Good Brabantio,
  Take up this mangled matter at the best : [32]
  Men do their broken weapons rather use
  Than their bare hands.
BRABANTIO.   I pray you, hear her speak :
  If she confess that she was half the wooer
  Destruction on my head, if my bad blame
  Light on the man ! Come hither, gentle mistress :   180
  Do you perceive in all this noble company
  Where most you owe obedience ?
DESDEMONA.   My noble father,
  I do perceive here a divided duty :
  To you I am bound for life and education ;
  My life and education both do learn me
  How to respect you ; you are the lord of duty ;
  I am hitherto your daughter : but here's my husband,
  And so much duty as my mother showed
  To you, preferring you before her father,
  So much I challenge that I may profess   190
  Due to the Moor my lord.
BRABANTIO.   God be wi' you ! I have done.
  Please it your grace, on to the state-affairs :
  I had rather to adopt a child than get it.
  Come hither, Moor :
  I here do give thee that with all my heart
  Which, but thou hast already, with all my heart
  I would keep from thee. For your sake, jewel,
  I am glad at soul I have no other child ;
  For thy escape would teach me tyranny,
  To hang clogs on them. I have done, my lord.   200
DUKE. Let me speak like yourself,[33] and lay a sentence,

---

[31] for her   [32] make the best of it   [33] as you ought

Which, as a grise³⁴ or step, may help these lovers
Into your favor.
When remedies are past, the griefs are ended
By seeing the worst, which late on hopes depended.
To mourn a mischief that is past and gone
Is the next way to draw new mischief on.
What cannot be preserved when fortune takes,
Patience her injury a mockery makes.
The robbed that smiles steals something from the thief;   210
He robs himself that spends a bootless grief.
BRABANTIO. So let the Turk of Cyprus us beguile;
We lost it not, so long as we can smile.
He bears the sentence well that nothing bears
But the free comfort which from thence he hears,³⁵
But he bears both the sentence and the sorrow
That, to pay grief, must of poor patience borrow.³⁶
These sentences, to sugar, or to gall,
Being strong on both sides, are equivocal:
But words are words; I never yet did hear   220
That the bruised heart was piercéd through the ear.
I humbly beseech you, proceed to the affairs of state.
DUKE. The Turk with a most mighty preparation makes for Cyprus.
Othello, the fortitude of the place is best known to you; and though
we have there a substitute of most allowed sufficiency, yet opinion, a
sovereign mistress of effects, throws a more safer voice on you: you
must therefore be content to slubber³⁷ the gloss of your new fortunes
with this more stubborn and boisterous expedition.
OTHELLO. The tyrant custom, most grave senators,
Hath made the flinty and steel couch of war   230
My thrice-driven bed of down: I do agnize³⁸
A natural and prompt alacrity
I find in hardness, and do undertake
These present wars against the Ottomites.
Most humbly therefore bending to your state,
I crave fit disposition for my wife,
Due reference of place and exhibition,³⁹
With such accommodation and besort⁴⁰
As levels with her breeding.
DUKE.   If you please,
Be 't at her father's.
BRABANTIO.   I'll not have it so.   240

---

³⁴ one step in a flight
³⁵ He bears advice well who pays attention to nothing more than the easy comfort in the wisdom offered.
³⁶ But the man who has to endure both that sort of consolation and the sorrow
must be very patient.   ³⁷ soil   ³⁸ acknowledge   ³⁹ allowance   ⁴⁰ retinue

OTHELLO. Nor I.

DESDEMONA.   Nor I; I would not there reside,
To put my father in impatient thoughts
By being in his eye. Most gracious duke,
To my unfolding lend your prosperous ear;
And let me find a charter in your voice,
To assist my simpleness.

DUKE. What would you, Desdemona?

DESDEMONA. That I did love the Moor to live with him,
My downright violence and storm of fortunes
May trumpet to the world: my heart's subdued   250
Even to the very quality[41] of my lord:
I saw Othello's visage in his mind,
And to his honors and his valiant parts
Did I my soul and fortunes consecrate.
So that, dear lords, if I be left behind,
A moth of peace, and he go to the war,
The rites for which I love him are bereft me,
And I a heavy interim shall support
By his dear[42] absence. Let me go with him.

OTHELLO. Let her have your voices.   260
Vouch with me, heaven, I therefore beg it not,
To please the palate of my appetite,
Nor to comply with heat[43]—the young affects[44]
In me defunct—and proper satisfaction,
But to be free and bounteous to her mind:
And heaven defend your good souls, that you think
I will your serious and great business scant
For she is with me: no, when light-winged toys
Of feathered Cupid seel[45] with wanton dullness
My speculative and officed instruments,   270
That my disports corrupt and taint my business,
Let housewives make a skillet of my helm,
And all indign[46] and base adversities
Make head against my estimation!

DUKE. Be it as you shall privately determine,
Either for her stay or going: the affair cries haste,
And speed must answer it.

FIRST SENATOR. You must away to-night.

OTHELLO.   With all my heart.

DUKE. At nine i' the morning here we'll meet again.
Othello, leave some officer behind,   280

---

[41] distinctive characteristic; i.e., his color   [42] deeply felt   [43] passion
[44] youthful desires   [45] sew up the eyes (as of a falcon)
[46] unworthy; disgraceful

And he shall our commission bring to you;
With such things else of quality and respect
As doth import you.

OTHELLO.   So please your grace, my ancient;
A man he is of honesty and trust:
To his conveyance I assign my wife,
With what else needful your good grace shall think
To be sent after me.

DUKE.   Let it be so.
Good night to every one. [*To* BRABANTIO] And, noble signior,
If virtue no delighted beauty lack,[47]
Your son-in-law is far more fair than black.   290

FIRST SENATOR. Adieu, brave Moor; use Desdemona well.

BRABANTIO. Look to her, Moor, if thou hast eyes to see:
She has deceived her father, and may thee.

                 [*Exeunt* DUKE, SENATORS, OFFICERS, *&c.*]

OTHELLO. My life upon her faith! Honest Iago,
My Desdemona must I leave to thee:
I prithee, let thy wife attend on her;
And bring them after in the best advantage.
Come, Desdemona; I have but an hour
Of love, of worldly matters and direction,[48]
To spend with thee: we must obey the time.   300

                       [*Exeunt* OTHELLO *and* DESDEMONA.]

RODERIGO. Iago,—

IAGO. What say'st thou, noble heart?

RODERIGO. What will I do, thinkest thou?

IAGO. Why, go to bed, and sleep.

RODERIGO. I will incontinently drown myself.

IAGO. If thou dost, I shall never love thee after. Why, thou silly
gentleman!

RODERIGO. It is silliness to live when to live is torment; and then have
we a prescription to die when death is our physician.

IAGO. O villanous! I have looked upon the world for four times   310
seven years; and since I could distinguish betwixt a benefit and an injury, I never found man that knew how to love himself. Ere I would
say, I would drown myself for the love of a guinea-hen,[49] I would
change my humanity with a baboon.

RODERIGO. What should I do? I confess it is my shame to be so fond;
but it is not in my virtue[50] to amend it.

IAGO. Virtue! a fig! 'tis in ourselves that we are thus or thus. Our
bodies are our gardens, to the which our wills are gardeners; so that if
we will plant nettles, or sow lettuce, hyssop and weed up thyme, sup-

---

[47] if worth is in itself beautiful   [48] for the management of private affairs
[49] cant name for a harlot   [50] manhood

ply it with one gender of herbs, or distract it with many, either to 320
have it sterile with idleness, or manured with industry, why, the power
and corrigible authority[51] of this lies in our wills. If the balance of
our lives had not one scale of reason to poise another of sensuality,
the blood and baseness of our natures would conduct us to most pre-
pósterous conclusions: but we have reason to cool our raging motions,
our carnal stings, our unbitted lusts, whereof I take this that you call
love to be a sect or scion.

RODERIGO. It cannot be.

IAGO. It is merely a lust of the blood and a permission of the will.[52]
Come, be a man. Drown thyself! drown cats and blind puppies. I 330
have professed me thy friend and I confess me knit to thy deserving
with cables of perdurable toughness; I could never better stand thee
than now. Put money in thy purse; follow thou the wars; defeat thy
favor[53] with an usurped[54] beard; I say, put money in thy purse. It
cannot be that Desdemona should long continue her love to the Moor,
—put money in thy purse,—nor he his to her: it was a violent commencement, and thou shalt see an answerable sequestration:[55]—put
but money in thy purse. These Moors are changeable in their wills:—
fill thy purse with money:—the food that to him now is as luscious as
locusts,[56] shall be to him shortly as bitter as coloquintida.[57] She 340
must change for youth: when she is sated with his body, she will find
the error of her choice: she must have change, she must: therefore
put money in thy purse. If thou wilt needs damn thyself, do it a more
delicate way than drowning. Make all the money thou canst: if sanc-
timony and a frail vow betwixt an erring[58] barbarian and a super-
subtle Venetian be not too hard for my wits and all the tribe of hell,
thou shalt enjoy her; therefore make money. A pox of drowning thyself! it is clean out of the way: seek thou rather to be hanged in compassing[59] thy joy than to be drowned and go without her.

RODERIGO. Wilt thou be fast to my hopes, if I depend on the 350
issue?

IAGO. Thou art sure of me:—go, make money:—I have told thee often, and I re-tell thee again and again, I hate the Moor: my cause is
hearted; thine hath no less reason. Let us be conjunctive in our revenge
against him; if thou canst cuckold him, thou dost thyself a pleasure,
me a sport. There are many events in the womb of time which will be
delivered. Transverse![60] go, provide thy money. We will have more
of this tomorrow. Adieu.

RODERIGO. Where shall we meet i' the morning?

IAGO. At my lodging. 360

RODERIGO. I'll be with thee betimes.

---

[51] corrective control   [52] sexual license   [53] disguise your face
[54] assumed; i.e., grown for the purpose   [55] corresponding rupture
[56] fruit of the carob tree   [57] bitter apple   [58] vagabond   [59] obtaining
[60] a military term, "Forward march!"

IAGO. Go, to, farewell. Do you hear, Roderigo?
RODERIGO. What say you?
IAGO. No more of drowning, do you hear?
RODERIGO. I am changed: I'll go sell all my land.

[Exit.]

IAGO. Thus do I ever make my fool my purse;
    For I mine own gained knowledge should profane,
    If I would time expend with such a snipe,⁶¹
    But for my sport and profit. I hate the Moor;
    And it is thought abroad, that 'twixt my sheets   370
    He has done my office: I know not if 't be true;
    But I, for mere suspicion in that kind,
    Will do as if for surety. He holds me well;
    The better shall my purpose work on him.
    Cassio's a proper⁶² man: let me see now:
    To get his place and to plume up my will
    In double knavery—How, how?—Let's see:—
    After some time, to abuse⁶³ Othello's ear
    That he is too familiar with his wife.
    He hath a person and a smooth dispose   380
    To be suspected, framed to make women false.
    The Moor is of a free and open nature,
    That thinks men honest that but seem to be so,
    And will as tenderly be led by the nose
    As asses are.
    I have 't. It is engendered. Hell and night
    Must bring this monstrous birth to the world's light.

[Exit.]

ACT II

SCENE I
A Seaport in Cyprus. An open place near the quay.

Enter MONTANO *and two* GENTLEMEN.

MONTANO. What from the cape can you discern at sea?
FIRST GENTLEMAN. Nothing at all: it is a high-wrought flood;
    I cannot, 'twixt the heaven and the main,
    Descry a sail.
MONTANO. Methinks the wind hath spoke aloud at land;
    A fuller blast ne'er shook our battlements:
    If it hath ruffianed so upon the sea,
    What ribs of oak, when mountains melt on them,
    Can hold the mortise? What shall we hear of this?

---

⁶¹ a proverbially silly bird   ⁶² handsome   ⁶³ deceive

SECOND GENTLEMAN. A segregation[64] of the Turkish fleet: 10
    For do but stand upon the foaming shore,
    The chidden billow seems to pelt the clouds;
    The wind-shaked surge, with high and monstrous mane,
    Seems to cast water on the burning bear,[65]
    And quench the guards of the ever-fixéd pole:[66]
    I never did like molestation view
    On the enchaféd flood.
MONTANO.   If that the Turkish fleet
    Be not ensheltered and embayed, they are drowned;
    It is impossible they bear it out.

Enter a third GENTLEMAN.

THIRD GENTLEMAN. News, lads! our wars are done. 20
    The desperate tempest hath so banged the Turks,
    That their designment halts: a noble ship of Venice
    Hath seen a grievous wreck and sufferance
    On most part of their fleet.
MONTANO. How! is this true?
THIRD GENTLEMAN.   The ship is here put in,
    A Veronesa;[67] Michael Cassio,
    Lieutenant to the warlike Moor Othello,
    Is come on shore: the Moor himself at sea,
    And is in full commission here for Cyprus.
MONTANO. I am glad on 't; 'tis a worthy governor. 30
THIRD GENTLEMAN. But this same Cassio, though he speak of
        comfort
    Touching the Turkish loss, yet he looks sadly,
    And prays the Moor be safe; for they were parted
    With foul and violent tempest.
MONTANO.   Pray heavens he be;
    For I have served him, and the man commands
    Like a full soldier. Let's to the seaside, ho!
    As well to see the vessel that's come in
    As to throw out our eyes for brave Othello,
    Even till we make the main and the aerial blue
    An indistinct regard.[68]   40
THIRD GENTLEMAN. Come, let's do so;
    For every minute is expectancy
    Of more arrivance.

---

[64] dispersion   [65] the constellation of Ursa major, the Big Dipper
[66] two stars called pointers in the constellation Boötes, regarded as guards of the North Star
[67] from Verona, a dependency of Venice
[68] until the line between the sea and the sky becomes indistinct

Enter CASSIO.

CASSIO. Thanks, you the valiant of this warlike isle,
   That so approve the Moor! O, let the heavens
   Give him defense against the elements,
   For I have lost him on a dangerous sea.
MONTANO. Is he well shipped?
CASSIO. His bark is stoutly timbered, and his pilot
   Of very expert and approved allowance;   50
   Therefore my hopes, not surfeited to death,
   Stand in bold cure.
                           [*A cry within:* "A sail, a sail a sail!"]

Enter a fourth GENTLEMAN.

CASSIO. What noise?
FOURTH GENTLEMAN. The town is empty; on the brow o' the sea
   Stand ranks of people, and they cry "A sail!"
CASSIO. My hopes do shape him for[69] the governor.
                                                    [*Guns heard.*]
SECOND GENTLEMAN. They do discharge their shot of courtesy:
   Our friends at least.
CASSIO.   I pray you, sir, go forth,
   And give us truth who 'tis that is arrived.
SECOND GENTLEMAN. I shall.   60
                                                    [*Exit.*]
MONTANO. But, good lieutenant, is your general wived?
CASSIO. Most fortunately: he hath achieved a maid
   That paragons description and wild fame;
   One that excels the quirks of blazoning pens,
   And in the essential vesture of creation[70]
   Does tire the ingener.[71]

Re-enter second GENTLEMAN.

   How now! who has put in?
SECOND GENTLEMAN. 'Tis one Iago, ancient to the general.
CASSIO. Has had most favorable and happy speed:
   Tempests themselves, high seas and howling winds,
   The guttered[72] rocks and congregated sands,—   70
   Traitors ensteeped[73] to clog the guiltless keel,—
   As having sense of beauty, do omit
   Their mortal natures, letting go safely by
   The divine Desdemona.
MONTANO.   What is she?

---

[69] imagine him to be   [70] natural endowments   [71] inventor   [72] jagged
[73] submerged

CASSIO. She that I spake of, our great captain's captain,
  Left in the conduct of the bold Iago,
  Whose footing[74] here anticipates our thoughts
  A se'nnight's speed. Great Jove, Othello guard,
  And swell his sail with thine own powerful breath,
  That he may bless this bay with his tall ship,   80
  Make love's quick pants in Desdemona's arms,
  Give renewed fire to our extincted spirits,
  And bring all Cyprus comfort!

> *Enter* DESDEMONA, EMILIA, IAGO,
>   RODERIGO, *and* ATTENDANTS.

                                          O, behold,
  The riches of the ship is come on shore!
  Ye men of Cyprus, let her have your knees.
  Hail to thee, lady! and the grace of heaven,
  Before, behind thee and on every hand,
  Enwheel thee round!
DESDEMONA.   I thank you, valiant Cassio.
  What tidings can you tell me of my lord?
CASSIO. He is not yet arrived: nor know I aught   90
  But that he's well and will be shortly here.
DESDEMONA. O, but I fear—How lost you company?
CASSIO. The great contention of the sea and skies
  Parted our fellowship—but, hark! a sail.
                [*Within:* "A sail, a sail!" *Guns heard.*]
SECOND GENTLEMAN. They give their greeting to the citadel:
  This likewise is a friend.
CASSIO.   See for the news.
                                [*Exit* GENTLEMAN.]
  [*To* EMILIA] Good ancient, you are welcome. Welcome, mistress:
  Let it not gall your patience, good Iago,
  That I extend my manners; 'tis my breeding[75]
  That gives me this bold show of courtesy.   100
                                          [*Kissing her.*]
IAGO. Sir, would she give you so much of her lips
  As of her tongue she oft bestows on me,
  You'ld have enough.
DESDEMONA.   Alas, she has no speech.
IAGO. In faith, too much;
  I find it still, when I have list[76] to sleep:

---

[74] landing
[75] bringing up; i.e., as a gentleman, which makes it proper to me to kiss the wife of a social inferior
[76] inclination

Marry, before your ladyship, I grant,
She puts her tongue a little in her heart,
And chides with thinking.
EMILIA. You have little cause to say so.
IAGO. Come on, come on; you are pictures[77] out of doors,   110
Bells in your parlors, wild-cats in your kitchens,
Saints in your injuries,[78] devils being offended,
Players[79] in your housewifery, and housewives[80] in your beds.
DESDEMONA. O, fie upon thee, slanderer!
IAGO. Nay, it is true, or else I am a Turk:
You rise to play and go to bed to work.
EMILIA. You shall not write my praise.
IAGO.   No, let me not.
DESDEMONA. What wouldst thou write of me, if thou shouldst praise
me?
IAGO. O gentle lady, do not put me to 't;
For I am nothing, if not critical.   120
DESDEMONA. Come on, assay. There's one gone to the harbor?
IAGO. Ay, madam.
DESDEMONA. I am not merry, but I do beguile
The thing I am, by seeming otherwise.
Come, how wouldst thou praise me?
IAGO. I am about it; but indeed my invention
Comes from my pate as birdlime does from frize;[81]
It plucks out brains and all: but my Muse labors,
And thus she is delivered.
If she be fair and wise, fairness and wit,   130
The one's for use, the other useth it.
DESDEMONA. Well praised! How if she be black and witty?
IAGO. If she be black,[82] and thereto have a wit,
She'll find a white[83] that shall her blackness fit.
DESDEMONA. Worse and worse.
EMILIA. How if fair and foolish?
IAGO. She never yet was foolish that was fair;
For even her folly helped her to an heir.
DESDEMONA. These are old fond[84] paradoxes to make fools laugh i' the
alehouse. What miserable praise hast thou for her that's foul and fool-
ish?   141
IAGO. There's none so foul and foolish thereunto,
But does foul pranks which fair and wise ones do.

---

[77] i.e., painted and speechless   [78] say insulting things with a sanctimonious air
[79] triflers   [80] hussies; wanton creatures
[81] as the sticky substance spread on limbs for catching birds pulls away from coarse
woolen cloth
[82] a brunette and hence ugly   [83] a fair person; a wight (a person)   [84] silly

DESDEMONA. O heavy ignorance! thou praisest the worst best. But what praise couldst thou bestow on a deserving woman indeed, one that, in the authority of her merit, did justly put on the vouch[85] of very malice itself?

IAGO. She that was ever fair and never proud,
   Had tongue at will and yet was never loud,
   Never lacked gold and yet went never gay,   150
   Fled from her wish and yet said "Now I may,"
   She that being angered, her revenge being nigh,
   Bade her wrong stay and her displeasure fly,
   She that in wisdom never was so frail
   To change the cod's head for the salmon's tail,[86]
   She that could think and ne'er disclose her mind,
   See suitors following and not look behind,
   She was a wight, if ever such wight were,—

DESDEMONA. To do what?

IAGO. To suckle fools and chronicle small beer.[87]   160

DESDEMONA. O most lame and impotent conclusion! Do not learn of him, Emilia, though he be thy husband. How say you, Cassio? is he not a most profane and liberal[88] counsellor?

CASSIO. He speaks home, madam: you may relish him more in the soldier than in the scholar.

IAGO [*Aside*]. He takes her by the palm: ay, well said, whisper: with as little a web as this will I ensnare as great a fly as Cassio. Ay, smile upon her, do; I will gyve[89] thee in thine own courtship.[90] You say true; 'tis so, indeed: if such tricks as these strip you out of your lieu- 170 tenantry, it had been better you had not kissed your three fin- gers[91] so oft, which now again you are most apt to play the sir[92] in. Very good; well kissed! an excellent courtesy! 'tis so, indeed. Yet again your fingers to your lips? would they were clyster-pipes[93] for your sake!

                                        [*Trumpet within.*]

   The Moor! I know his trumpet.

CASSIO. 'Tis truly so.

DESDEMONA. Let's meet him and receive him.

CASSIO. Lo, where he comes!

              Enter OTHELLO *and* ATTENDANTS.

OTHELLO. O my fair warrior!

DESDEMONA.   My dear Othello!

OTHELLO. It gives me wonder great as my content   180
   To see you here before me. O my soul's joy!

---

[85] challenge the testimony   [86] to exchange a delicacy for refuse
[87] keep petty household accounts   [88] coarse and licentious   [89] fetter
[90] courtesy   [91] as a piece of gallantry to Desdemona   [92] gallant
[93] tubes used for enemas

If after every tempest come such calms,
May the winds blow till they have wakened death!
And let the laboring bark climb hills of seas
Olympus-high and duck again as low
As hell's from heaven! If it were now to die,
'Twere now to be most happy; for, I fear,
My soul hath her content so absolute
That not another comfort like to this
Succeeds in unknown fate.
DESDEMONA.   The heavens forbid   190
But that our loves and comforts should increase,
Even as our days do grow!
OTHELLO.   Amen to that, sweet powers!
I cannot speak enough of this content;
It stops me here; 94 it is too much of joy:
And this, and this, the greatest discords be
                                                          [Kissing her.]
That e'er our hearts shall make!
IAGO [Aside].   O, you are well tuned now!
But I'll set down the pegs 95 that make this music,
As honest as I am.
OTHELLO.   Come, let us to the castle.
News, friends; our wars are done, the Turks are drowned.
How does my old acquaintance of this isle?   200
Honey, you shall be well desired 96 in Cyprus;
I have found great love amongst them. O my sweet,
I prattle out of fashion,97 and I dote
In mine own comforts. I prithee, good Iago,
Go to the bay and disembark my coffers:
Bring thou the master to the citadel;
He is a good one, and his worthiness
Does challenge much respect. Come, Desdemona,
Once more, well met at Cyprus.
              [Exeunt OTHELLO, DESDEMONA, and ATTENDANTS.]
IAGO. Do thou meet me presently 98 at the harbor. Come hither. If   210
thou be'st valiant,—as, they say, base men being in love have then a
nobility in their natures more than is native to them,—list me. The
lieutenant tonight watches on the court of guard:—first, I must tell
thee this—Desdemona is directly in love with him.
RODERIGO. With him! why, 'tis not possible.
IAGO. Lay thy finger thus,99 and let thy soul be instructed. Mark me
with what violence she first loved the Moor, but for bragging and

---

94 i.e., in the heart   95 loosen the pegs and so untune the instrument
96 well loved   97 unconventionally   98 immediately
99 i.e., on your lips (while in silence you listen to me)

telling her fantastical lies: and will she love him still for prating? let
not thy discreet heart think it. Her eye must be fed; and what delight
shall she have to look on the devil? When the blood is made dull   220
with the act of sport, there should be, again to inflame it and to give
satiety a fresh appetite, loveliness in favor,[100] sympathy in years, manners and beauties; all which the Moor is defective in: now, for want of
these required conveniences, her delicate tenderness will find itself
abused, begin to heave the gorge, disrelish and abhor the Moor; very
nature will instruct her in it and compel her to some second choice.
Now, sir, this granted,—as it is a most pregnant and unforced position[101]—who stands so eminent in the degree of this fortune as Cassio
does? a knave very voluble;[102] no further conscionable than in putting
on the mere form of civil and humane seeming, for the better   230
compassing of his salt[103] and most hidden loose affection? why, none;
why, none: a slipper[104] and subtle knave, a finder of occasions, that
has an eye can stamp and counterfeit advantages, though true advantage never present itself; a devilish knave. Besides, the knave is
handsome, young, and hath all those requisites in him that folly and
green minds look after: a pestilent complete knave: and the woman
hath found him already.

RODERIGO. I cannot believe that in her; she's full of most blesséd condition.

IAGO. Blesséd fig's-end! the wine she drinks is made of grapes: if   240
she had been blessed, she could never have loved the Moor. Blesséd
pudding! Didst thou not see her paddle with the palm of his hand?
didst not mark that?

RODERIGO. Yes, that I did; but that was but courtesy.

IAGO. Lechery, by this hand; an index and obscure prologue to the
history of lust and foul thoughts. They met so near with their lips that
their breaths embraced together. Villainous thoughts, Roderigo! when
these mutualities so marshal[105] the way, hard at hand comes the master
and main exercise, the incorporate[106] conclusion, Pish! But, sir, be you
ruled by me: I have brought you from Venice. Watch you to-   250
night; for the command, I'll lay 't upon you. Cassio knows you not,
I'll not be far from you: do you find some occasion to anger Cassio,
either by speaking too loud, or tainting[107] his discipline; or from what
other course you please, which the time shall more favorably minister.

RODERIGO. Well.

IAGO. Sir, he is rash and very sudden in choler, and haply may strike at
you: provoke him, that he may; for even out of that will I cause these
of Cyprus to mutiny; whose qualification[108] shall come into no true
taste again but by the displanting of Cassio. So shall you have a shorter

---

[100] countenance   [101] a significant and convincing argument   [102] unstable
[103] salacious; licentious   [104] slippery   [105] lead   [106] intimately united
[107] disparaging   [108] appeasement

journey to your desires by the means I shall then have to prefer[109] them; and the impediment most profitably removed, without the which there were no expectation of our prosperity.   262

RODERIGO. I will do this, if I can bring it to any opportunity.

IAGO. I warrant thee. Meet me by and by at the citadel: I must fetch his necessaries ashore. Farewell.

RODERIGO. Adieu.

[*Exit.*]

IAGO. That Cassio loves her, I do well believe it;
  That she loves him, 'tis apt and of great credit:[110]
  The Moor, howbeit that I endure him not,
  Is of a constant, loving, noble nature,   270
  And I dare think he'll prove to Desdemona
  A most dear husband. Now, I do love her too;
  Not out of absolute lust, though peradventure
  I stand accountant for as great a sin,
  But partly led to diet my revenge,
  For that I do suspect the lusty Moor
  Hath leaped into my seat; the thought whereof
  Doth, like a poisonous mineral, gnaw my inwards;
  And nothing can or shall content my soul
  Till I am evened with him, wife for wife,   280
  Or failing so, yet that I put the Moor
  At least into a jealousy so strong
  That judgment cannot cure. Which thing to do,
  If this poor trash[111] of Venice, whom I trash[112]
  For his quick hunting, stand the putting on,
  I'll have our Michael Cassio on the hip,
  Abuse him to the Moor in the rank garb[113]—
  For I fear Cassio with my night-cap too—
  Make the Moor thank me, love me and reward me,
  For making him egregiously an ass   290
  And practising upon his peace and quiet
  Even to madness. 'Tis here, but yet confused:
  Knavery's plain face is never seen till used.

[*Exit.*]

SCENE II
A street.

Enter a HERALD *with a proclamation:* PEOPLE *following.*

HERALD. It is Othello's pleasure, our noble and valiant general, that, upon certain tidings now arrived, importing the mere perdition[114] of

---

[109] promote   [110] natural and very credible
[111] rubbish; worthless fellow   [112] check; hold back (a hunting term)
[113] coarse fashion   [114] complete loss

the Turkish fleet, every man put himself into triumph; some to dance some to make bonfires, each man to what sport and revels his addiction[115] leads him: for, besides these beneficial news, it is the celebration of his nuptial. So much was his pleasure should be proclaimed. All offices[116] are open, and there is full liberty of feasting from this present hour of five till the bell have told eleven. Heaven bless the isle of Cyprus and our noble general Othello!

[Exeunt.]

SCENE III
A hall in the castle.

Enter OTHELLO, DESDEMONA, CASSIO, *and* ATTENDANTS.

OTHELLO. Good Michael, look you to the guard tonight:
Let's teach ourselves that honorable stop,[117]
Not to outsport discretion.
CASSIO. Iago hath direction what to do;
But, notwithstanding, with my personal eye
Will I look to 't.
OTHELLO.   Iago is most honest.
Michael, good night: tomorrow with your earliest
Let me have speech with you. [*To* DESDEMONA] Come, my dear
    love,
The purchase made, the fruits are to ensue;
That profit's yet to come 'tween me and you.   10
Good night.

[Exeunt OTHELLO, DESDEMONA, *and* ATTENDANTS.]

Enter IAGO.

CASSIO. Welcome, Iago; we must to the watch.
IAGO. Not this hour, lieutenant; 'tis not yet ten o' the clock. Our general cast us thus early for the love of his Desdemona; who let us not therefore blame: he hath not yet made wanton the night with her; and she is sport for Jove.
CASSIO. She's a most exquisite lady.
IAGO. And, I'll warrant her, full of game.
CASSIO. Indeed, she's a most fresh and delicate creature.   19
IAGO. What an eye she has! methinks it sounds a parley of provocation.
CASSIO. An inviting eye; and yet methinks right modest.
IAGO. And when she speaks, is it not an alarum to love?
CASSIO. She is indeed perfection.
IAGO. Well, happiness to their sheets! Come, lieutenant, I have a

---

115 inclination   116 rooms in which food and drink were prepared and served
117 restraint

stoup[118] of wine; and here without are a brace of Cyprus gallants
that would fain have a measure to the health of black Othello.

CASSIO. Not tonight, good Iago: I have very poor and unhappy brains
for drinking: I could well wish courtesy would invent some other custom of entertainment.

IAGO. O, they are our friends; but one cup: I'll drink for you.   30

CASSIO. I have drunk but one cup tonight, and that was craftily quali-
fied[119] too, and, behold, what innovation it makes here:[120] I am unfortunate in the infirmity, and dare not task my weakness with any more.

IAGO. What, man! 'tis a night of revels: the gallants desire it.

CASSIO. Where are they?

IAGO. Here at the door; I pray you, call them in.

CASSIO. I'll do 't; but it dislikes me.

                                                                 [*Exit.*]

IAGO. If I can fasten but one cup upon him,
    With that which he hath drunk tonight already,
    He'll be as full of quarrel and offence   40
    As my young mistress' dog. Now, my sick fool Roderigo,
    Whom love hath turned almost the wrong side out,
    To Desdemona hath tonight caroused
    Potations pottle-deep;[121] and he's to watch:
    Three lads of Cyprus, noble swelling spirits,
    That hold their honors in a wary distance,[122]
    The very elements[123] of this warlike isle,
    Have I tonight flustered with flowing cups,
    And they watch[124] too. Now, 'mongst this flock of drunkards,
    Am I to put our Cassio in some action   50
    That may offend the isle.—But here they come:
    If consequence do but approve my dream,[125]
    My boat sails freely, both with wind and stream.

        Re-enter CASSIO; *with him* MONTANO *and* GENTLEMEN
             SERVANTS *following with wine.*

CASSIO. 'Fore God, they have given me a rouse[126] already.

MONTANO. Good faith, a little one; not past a pint, as I am a soldier.

IAGO. Some wine, ho!

    [*Sings*]   *And let me the canakin clink, clink;*
                       And let me the canakin clink:

---

[118] large flagon   [119] slyly diluted (by Cassio)
[120] what disturbance it makes in my head
[121] to the bottom of the pottle or tankard; i.e., "bottoms up"
[122] are very sensitive about their honor   [123] perfect specimens
[124] are on guard duty   [125] if the result confirms my expectations
[126] full bumper

> *A soldier's a man;*
> *A life's but a span;*[127]   60
> *Why, then, let a soldier drink.*

Some wine, boys!

CASSIO. 'Fore God, an excellent song.

IAGO. I learned it in England, where, indeed, they are most potent in potting: your Dane, your German, and your swag-bellied Hollander— Drink, ho!—are nothing to your English.

CASSIO. Is your Englishman so expert in his drinking?

IAGO. Why, he drinks you, with facility, your Dane drunk; he sweats not to overthrow your Almain;[128] he gives your Hollander a vomit, ere the next pottle can be filled.   70

CASSIO. To the health of our general!

MONTANO. I am for it, lieutenant; and I'll do you justice.[129]

IAGO [*Sings*].

> *O sweet England!*
> *King Stephen was a worthy peer,*
> *His breeches cost him but a crown;*
> *He held them sixpence all too dear,*
> *With that he called the tailor lown.*[130]
> *He was a wight of high renown,*
> *And thou art but of low degree:*
> *'Tis pride that pulls the country down;*   80
> *Then take thine auld cloak about thee.*

Some wine, ho!

CASSIO. Why, this is a more exquisite song than the other.

IAGO. Will you hear 't again?

CASSIO. No; for I hold him to be unworthy of his place that does those things. Well, God's above all; and there be souls must be saved, and there be souls must not be saved.

IAGO. It's true, good lieutenant.

CASSIO. For mine own part,—no offence to the general, nor any man of quality,—I hope to be saved.   90

IAGO. And so do I too, lieutenant.

CASSIO. Ay, but, by your leave, not before me; the lieutenant is to be saved before the ancient. Let's have no more of this; let's to our affairs.— Forgive us our sins!—Gentlemen, let's look to our business. Do not think, gentlemen, I am drunk: this is my ancient; this is my right hand, and this is my left: I am not drunk now; I can stand well enough, and speak well enough.

ALL. Excellent well.

[127] the distance between the little finger and thumb of the outstretched hand
[128] German   [129] I'll drink as much as you do.   [130] lout

CASSIO. Why, very well then; you must not think then that I am
   drunk.   100
                                                                          [*Exit.*]
MONTANO. To the platform, masters; come, let's set the watch.
IAGO. You see this fellow that is gone before;
   He is a soldier fit to stand by Cæsar
   And give direction: and do but see his vice;
   'Tis to his virtue a just equinox,[131]
   The one as long as the other: 'tis pity of him.
   I fear the trust Othello puts him in,
   On some odd time of his infirmity,
   Will shake this island.
MONTANO.   But is he often thus?
IAGO. 'Tis evermore the prologue to his sleep: 110
   He'll watch the horologe a double set,[132]
   If drink rock not his cradle.
MONTANO.   It were well
   The general were put in mind of it.
   Perhaps he sees it not; or his good nature
   Prizes the virtue that appears in Cassio,
   And looks not on his evils: is not this true?

                         Enter RODERIGO.

IAGO [*Aside to him*]. How now, Roderigo! I pray you, after the lieuten-
   ant; go.
                                                        [*Exit* RODERIGO.]
MONTANO. And 'tis great pity that the noble Moor
   Should hazard such a place as his own second   120
   With one of an ingraft[133] infirmity:
   It were an honest action to say
   So to the Moor.
IAGO.   Not I, for this fair island:
   I do love Cassio well; and would do much
   To cure him of this evil—But, hark! what noise?
                                      [*Cry within:* "Help! help!"]

            Re-enter CASSIO, *driving in* RODERIGO.

CASSIO. You rogue! you rascal!
MONTANO.   What's the matter, lieutenant?
CASSIO. A knave teach me my duty!
   I'll beat the knave into a twiggen bottle.[134]
RODERIGO. Beat me!
CASSIO.   Dost thou prate, rogue?
                                          [*Striking* RODERIGO.]

---

[131] exact counterpart   [132] stay awake twice around the clock
[133] deeply rooted   [134] bottle enclosed in wicker

MONTANO.   Nay, good lieutenant;
                                                [Staying him.]
  I pray you, sir, hold your hand.
CASSIO.   Let me go, sir,   130
  Or I'll knock you o'er the mazzard.[135]
MONTANO.   Come, come, you're drunk.
CASSIO. Drunk!
                                                [They fight.]
IAGO *[Aside to* RODERIGO]. Away, I say; go out, and cry a mutiny.
                                                [Exit RODERIGO.]
  Nay, good lieutenant,—alas, gentlemen;—
  Help, ho!—Lieutenant,—sir,—Montano,—sir;—
  Help, masters!—Here's a goodly watch indeed!
                                                [Bell rings.]
  Who's that which rings the bell?—Diablo,[136] ho!
  The town will rise: God's will, lieutenant, hold!
  You will be shamed for ever.

        Re-enter OTHELLO *and* ATTENDANTS.

OTHELLO.   What is the matter here?
MONTANO. 'Zounds, I bleed still; I am hurt to the death.   140
                                                [Faints.]
OTHELLO. Hold, for your lives!
IAGO. Hold, ho! Lieutenant,—sir,—Montano,—gentlemen,—
  Have you forgot all sense of place and duty?
  Hold! the general speaks to you; hold, hold, for shame!
OTHELLO. Why, how now, ho! from whence ariseth this?
  Are we turned Turks, and to ourselves do that
  Which heaven hath forbid the Ottomites?
  For Christian shame, put by this barbarous brawl:
  He that stirs next to carve for his own rage[137]
  Holds his soul light; he dies upon his motion.   150
  Silence that dreadful bell: it frights the isle
  From her propriety. What is the matter, masters?
  Honest Iago, that look'st dead with grieving,
  Speak, who began this? on thy love, I charge thee.
IAGO. I do not know: friends all but now, even now,
  In quarter, and in terms like bride and groom
  Devesting them for bed; and then, but now—
  As if some planet had unwitted men—
  Swords out, and tilting one at other's breast,
  In opposition bloody. I cannot speak   160
  Any beginning to this peevish odds;

---

[135] head   [136] the Devil   [137] indulge his appetite for rage

And would in action glorious I had lost
Those legs that brought me to a part of it!
OTHELLO. How comes it, Michael, you are thus forgot?
CASSIO. I pray you, pardon me; I cannot speak.
OTHELLO. Worthy Montano, you were wont be civil;
The gravity and stillness of your youth
The world hath noted, and your name is great
In mouths of wisest censure: what's the matter,
That you unlace your reputation thus   170
And spend your rich opinion for the name
Of a night-brawler? give me answer to it.
MONTANO. Worthy Othello, I am hurt to danger:
Your officer, Iago, can inform you,—
While I spare speech, which something now offends me,—
Of all that I do know: nor know I aught
By me that's said or done amiss this night;
Unless self-charity be sometimes a vice,
And to defend ourselves it be a sin
When violence assails us.
OTHELLO.   Now, by heaven,   180
My blood begins my safer guides to rule;
And passion, having my best judgment collied,[138]
Assays to lead the way: if I once stir,
Or do but lift this arm, the best of you
Shall sink in my rebuke. Give me to know
How this foul rout began, who set it on;
And he that is approved in this offence,
Though he had twinned with me, both at a birth,
Shall lose me. What! in a town of war,
Yet wild, the people's hearts brimful of fear,   190
To manage private and domestic quarrel,
In night, and on the court and guard of safety!
'Tis monstrous. Iago, who began 't?
MONTANO. If partially affined,[139] or leagued in office,
Thou art no solider.
IAGO.   Touch me not so near:
I had rather have this tongue cut from my mouth
Than it should do offence to Michael Cassio;
Yet, I persuade myself, to speak the truth
Shall nothing wrong him. Thus it is, general.
Montano and myself being in speech,   200
There comes a fellow crying out for help;
And Cassio following him with determined sword,
To execute upon him. Sir, this gentleman

---

[138] blackened; obscured   [139] made partial by near relationship

Steps in to Cassio, and entreats his pause:
Myself the crying fellow did pursue,
Lest by his clamor—as it so fell out—
The town might fall in fright: he, swift of foot,
Outran my purpose; and I returned the rather
For that I heard the clink and fall of swords,
And Cassio high in oath; which till tonight   210
I ne'er might say before. When I came back—
For this was brief—I found them close together,
At blow and thrust; even as again they were
When you yourself did part them.
More of this matter cannot I report:
But men are men; the best sometimes forget:
Though Cassio did some little wrong to him,
As men in rage strike those that wish them best,
Yet surely Cassio, I believe, received
From him that fled some strange indignity,   220
Which patience could not pass.
OTHELLO.   I know, Iago,
Thy honesty and love doth mince this matter,
Making it light to Cassio. Cassio, I love thee;
But never more be officer of mine.

Re-enter DESDEMONA, *attended.*

Look, if my gentle love be not raised up!
I'll make thee an example.
DESDEMONA.   What's the matter?
OTHELLO. All's well now, sweeting; come away to bed.
Sir, for your hurts, myself will be your surgeon:
Lead him off.

                              [*To* MONTANO, *who is led off.*]
Iago, look with care about the town,   230
And silence those whom this vile brawl distracted.
Come, Desdemona: 'tis the soldiers' life
To have their balmy slumbers waked with strife.
                              [*Exeunt all but* IAGO *and* CASSIO.]
IAGO. What, art you hurt, lieutenant?
CASSIO. Ay, past all surgery.
IAGO. Marry, heaven forbid!
CASSIO. Reputation, reputation, reputation! O I have lost my reputa-
tion! I have lost the immortal part of myself, and what remains is
bestial. My reputation, Iago, my reputation!
IAGO. As I am an honest man, I thought you had received some   240
bodily wound; there is more sense[140] in that than in reputation. Reputa-

---

[140] feeling

tion is an idle and most false imposition; oft got without merit, and lost without deserving: you have lost no reputation at all, unless you repute yourself such a loser. What, man! there are ways to recover the general again: you are but now cast in his mood,[141] a punishment more in policy than in malice; even so as one would beat his offenseless dog to affright an imperious lion: sue to him again, and he's yours.

CASSIO. I will rather sue to be despised than to deceive so good a commander with so slight, so drunken, and so indiscreet an officer. Drunk? and speak parrot? and squabble? swagger? swear? and discourse fustian[142] with one's own shadow? O thou invisible spirit of wine, if thou hast no name to be known by, let us call thee devil!   252

IAGO. What was he that you followed with your sword? What had he done to you?

CASSIO. I know not.

IAGO. Is 't possible?

CASSIO. I remember a mass of things, but nothing distinctly; a quarrel, but nothing wherefore. O God, that men should put an enemy in their mouths to steal away their brains! that we should, with joy, pleasance, revel and applause, transform ourselves into beasts!   260

IAGO. Why, but you are now well enough: how came you thus recovered?

CASSIO. It hath pleased the devil drunkenness to give place to the devil wrath: one unperfectness shows me another, to make me frankly despise myself.

IAGO. Come, you are too severe a moraler: as the time, the place, and the condition of this country stands, I could heartily wish this had not befallen; but, since it is as it is, mend it for your own good.

CASSIO. I will ask him for my place again; he shall tell me I am a drunkard! Had I as many mouths as Hydra,[143] such an answer   270 would stop them all. To be now a sensible man, by and by a fool, and presently a beast! O strange! Every inordinate cup is unblessed and the ingredient is a devil.

IAGO. Come, come, good wine is a good familiar creature, if it be well used: exclaim no more against it. And, good lieutenant, I think you think I love you.

CASSIO. I have well approved it, sir. I drunk!

IAGO. You or any man living may be drunk at a time, man. I'll tell you what you shall do. Our general's wife is now the general: I may say so in this respect, for that he hath devoted and given up himself to   280 the contemplation, mark, and denotement of her parts[144] and graces: confess yourself freely to her; importune her help to put you in your place again: she is of so free,[145] so kind, so apt, so blessed a disposi-

---

[141] dismissed in his anger   [142] high-sounding bombast
[143] a fabulous monster with nine heads, slain by Hercules   [144] qualities
[145] innocent

tion, she holds it a vice in her goodness not to do more than she is requested: this broken joint between you and her husband entreat her to
splinter;[146] and, my fortunes against any lay worth naming, this crack
of your love shall grow stronger than it was before.

CASSIO. You advise me well.

IAGO. I protest, in the sincerity of love and honest kindness.   289

CASSIO. I think it freely; and betimes in the morning I will beseech the
virtuous Desdemona to undertake for me: I am desperate of my fortunes if they check me here.

IAGO. You are in the right. Good night, lieutenant; I must to the watch.

CASSIO. Good night, honest Iago.

                                                                    [*Exit.*]

IAGO. And what's he then that says I play the villain?
When this advice is free I give and honest,
Probal[147] to thinking and indeed the course
To win the Moor again? For 'tis most easy
The inclining Desdemona to subdue
In any honest suit: she's framed as fruitful[148]   300
As the free elements. And then for her
To win the Moor —were 't to renounce his baptism,
All seals and symbols of redeeméd sin,
His soul is so enfettered to her love,
That she may make, unmake, do what she list,
Even as her appetite shall play the god
With his weak function.[149] How am I then a villain
To counsel Cassio to this parallel course,
Directly to his good? Divinity of hell!
When devils will the blackest sins put on,   310
They do suggest at first with heavenly shows,
As I do now: for whiles this honest fool
Plies Desdemona to repair his fortunes
And she for him pleads strongly to the Moor,
I'll pour this pestilence into his ear,
That she repeals him[150] for her body's lust;
And by how much she strives to do him good,
She shall undo her credit with the Moor.
So will I turn her virtue into pitch,
And out of her own goodness make the net   320
That shall enmesh them all.

                    Re-enter RODERIGO.

                    How now, Roderigo!

RODERIGO. I do follow here in the chase, not like a hound that hunts,

---

[146] bind with splints   [147] probable   [148] bountiful
[149] operation of his mind   [150] tries to have him restored to his place

but one that fills up the cry.[151] My money is almost spent; I have been
tonight exceedingly well cudgelled; and I think the issue will be, I
shall have so much experience for my pains, and so, with no money at
all and a little more wit, return again to Venice.

IAGO. How poor are they that have not patience!
What wound did ever heal but by degrees?
Thou know'st we work by wit, and not by witchcraft;
And wit depends on dilatory time.   330
Does 't not go well? Cassio hath beaten thee,
And thou, by that small hurt, hast cashierd Cassio:
Though other things grow fair against the sun,
Yet fruits that blossom first will first be ripe:
Content thyself awhile. By the mass, 'tis morning;
Pleasure and action make the hours seem short.
Retire thee; go where thou art billeted:
Away, I say; thou shalt know more hereafter:
Nay, get thee gone.
                                                    [Exit RODERIGO.]
                Two things are to be done:
My wife must move for Cassio to her mistress;   340
I'll set her on;
Myself the while to draw the Moor apart,
And bring him jump[152] when he may Cassio find
Soliciting his wife: ay, that's the way:
Dull not device by coldness and delay.
                                                                [Exit.]

ACT III

SCENE I
Before the castle.

Enter CASSIO *and some* MUSICIANS.

CASSIO. Masters, play here; I will content your pains;
Something that's brief; and bid "Good morrow, general."
                                                              [Music.]

Enter CLOWN.

CLOWN. Why, masters, have your instruments been in Naples, that
they speak i' the nose thus?
FIRST MUSICIAN. How, sir, how!
CLOWN. Are these, I pray you, wind-instruments?
FIRST MUSICIAN. Ay, marry, are they, sir.

151 pack   152 exactly

CLOWN. O, thereby hangs a tail.

FIRST MUSICIAN. Whereby hangs a tale, sir?   9

CLOWN. Marry, sir, by many a wind-instrument that I know. But, masters, here's money for you: and the general so likes your music, that he desires you, for love's sake, to make no more noise with it.

FIRST MUSICIAN. Well, sir, we will not.

CLOWN. If you have any music that may not be heard, to 't again: but, as they say, to hear music the general does not greatly care.

FIRST MUSICIAN. We have none such, sir.

CLOWN. Then put up your pipes in your bag, for I'll away: go, vanish into air; away!

> [*Exeunt* MUSICIANS.]

CASSIO. Dost thou hear, my honest friend?

CLOWN. No, I hear not your honest friend; I hear you.   20

CASSIO. Prithee, keep up thy quillets.[153] There's a poor piece of gold for thee: if the gentlewoman that attends the general's wife be stirring, tell her there's one Cassio entreats her a little favor of speech: wilt thou do this?

CLOWN. She is stirring, sir: if she will stir hither, I shall seem to notify unto her.

CASSIO. Do, good my friend.

> [*Exit* CLOWN.]

> *Enter* IAGO.

> In happy time, Iago.

IAGO. You have not been a-bed, then?

CASSIO. Why, no; the day had broke
Before we parted. I have made bold, Iago,   30
To send in to your wife: my suit to her
Is, that she will to virtuous Desdemona
Procure me some access.

IAGO.   I'll send her to you presently;[154]
And I'll devise a mean to draw the Moor
Out of the way, that your converse and business
May be more free.

CASSIO. I humbly thank you for 't.
                      I never knew
A Florentine more kind and honest.

> [*Exit* IAGO.]

> *Enter* EMILIA.

EMILIA. Good morrow, good lieutenant: I am sorry
For your displeasure;[155] but all will sure be well.   40
The general and his wife are talking of it;

---

[153] wise cracks   [154] at once   [155] i.e., Othello's displeasure with you

And she speaks for you stoutly : the Moor replies,
That he you hurt is of great fame in Cyprus
And great affinity [156] and that in wholesome wisdom
He might not but refuse you, but he protests he loves you
And needs no other suitor but his likings
To take the safest occasion by the front
To bring you in again.
CASSIO.   Yet, I beseech you,
If you think fit, or that it may be done,
Give me advantage of some brief discourse   50
With Desdemona alone.
EMILIA.   Pray you, come in :
I will bestow you where you shall have time
To speak your bosom freely.
CASSIO. I am much bound to you.

                                                          [*Exeunt.*]

SCENE II
A room in the castle.

Enter OTHELLO, IAGO, *and* GENTLEMEN.

OTHELLO. These letters give, Iago, to the pilot ;
And by him do my duties to the senate :
That done, I will be walking on the works ; [157]
Repair there to me.
IAGO.   Well, my good lord, I'll do 't.
OTHELLO. This fortification, gentlemen, shall we see 't?
GENTLEMEN. We'll wait upon your lordship.

                                                          [*Exeunt.*]

SCENE III
The garden of the castle.

Enter DESDEMONA, CASSIO, *and* EMILIA.

DESDEMONA. Be thou assured, good Cassio, I will do
All my abilities in thy behalf.
EMILIA. Good madam, do : I warrant it grieves my husband,
As if the case were his.
DESDEMONA. O, that's an honest fellow. Do not doubt, Cassio,
But I will have my lord and you again
As friendly as you were.
CASSIO.   Bounteous madam,
Whatever shall become of Michael Cassio,
He's never any thing but your true servant.

---

[156] family connections   [157] fortifications

DESDEMONA. I know 't; I thank you. You do love my lord: 10
    You have known him long; and be you well assured
    He shall in strangeness stand no further off
    Than in a politic distance.
CASSIO.   Ay, but, lady,
    That policy may either last so long,
    Or feed upon such nice and waterish diet,
    Or breed itself so out of circumstance,
    That, I being absent and my place supplied,
    My general will forget my love and service.
DESDEMONA. Do not doubt[158] that; before Emilia here
    I give thee warrant of thy place: assure thee, 20
    If I do vow a friendship, I'll perform it
    To the last article: my lord shall never rest;
    I'll watch him tame[159] and talk him out of patience;
    His bed shall seem a school, his board a shrift;
    I'll intermingle every thing he does
    With Cassio's suit: therefore be merry, Cassio;
    For thy solicitor shall rather die
    Than give thy cause away.
EMILIA. Madam, here comes my lord.
CASSIO. Madam, I'll take my leave. 30
DESDEMONA. Why, stay, and hear me speak.
CASSIO. Madam, not now: I am very ill at ease,
    Unfit for mine own purposes.
DESDEMONA. Well, do your discretion.

                         [*Exit* CASSIO.]

Enter OTHELLO *and* IAGO.

IAGO. Ha! I like not that.
OTHELLO.   What dost thou say?
IAGO. Nothing, my lord: or if—I know not what.
OTHELLO. Was not that Cassio parted from my wife?
IAGO. Cassio, my lord! No, sure, I cannot think it,
    That he would steal away so guilty-like,
    Seeing you coming.
OTHELLO.   I do believe 'twas he. 40
DESDEMONA. How now, my lord!
    I have been talking with a suitor here,
    A man that languishes in your displeasure.
OTHELLO. Who is 't you mean?
DESDEMONA. Why, your lieutenant, Cassio. Good my lord,
    If I have any grace or power to move you,

---

[158] suspect
[159] tame him by keeping him awake (a method of training falcons)

His present reconciliation take;
For if he be not one that truly loves you,
That errs in ignorance and not in cunning,[160]
I have no judgment in an honest face: 50
I prithee, call him back.

OTHELLO.   Went he hence now?

DESDEMONA. Ay, sooth; so humbled
That he hath left part of his grief with me,
To suffer with him. Good love, call him back.

OTHELLO. Not now, sweet Desdemona; some other time.

DESDEMONA. But shall 't be shortly?

OTHELLO.   The sooner, sweet, for you.

DESDEMONA. Shall 't be tonight at supper?

OTHELLO.   No, not tonight.

DESDEMONA. Tomorrow dinner, then?

OTHELLO.   I shall not dine at home;
I meet the captains at the citadel.

DESDEMONA. Why, then, tomorrow night; or Tuesday morn;   60
On Tuesday noon, or night; on Wednesday morn:
I prithee, name the time, but let it not
Exceed three days: in faith, he's penitent;
And yet his trespass, in our common reason—
Save that, they say, the wars must make examples
Out of their best—is not almost a fault
To incur a private check. When shall he come?
Tell me, Othello: I wonder in my soul,
What you would ask me, that I should deny,
Or stand so mammering[161] on. What! Michael Cassio,   70
That came a-wooing with you, and so many a time,
When I have spoke of you dispraisingly,
Hath ta'en your part; to have so much to do
To bring him in! Trust me, I could do much,—

OTHELLO. Prithee, no more: let him come when he will;
I will deny thee nothing.

DESDEMONA.   Why, this is not a boon;
'Tis as I should entreat you wear your gloves,
Or feed on nourishing dishes, or keep you warm,
Or sue to you to do a peculiar profit
To your own person: nay, when I have a suit   80
Wherein I mean to touch your love indeed,
It shall be full of poise[162] and difficult weight
And fearful to be granted.

OTHELLO.   I will deny thee nothing:

---

[160] knowingly; intentionally   [161] hesitatingly; originally "stammering"
[162] importance

Whereon, I do beseech thee, grant me this,
To leave me but a little to myself.
DESDEMONA. Shall I deny you? no: farewell, my lord.
OTHELLO. Farewell, my Desdemona: I'll come to thee straight.
DESDEMONA. Emilia, come. Be as your fancies teach you: [163]
Whate'er you be, I am obedient.

[*Exeunt* DESDEMONA *and* EMILIA.]

OTHELLO. Excellent wretch! [164] Perdition catch my soul, 90
But I do love thee! and when I love thee not,
Chaos is come again.
IAGO. My noble lord,—
OTHELLO.   What dost thou say, Iago?
IAGO. Did Michael Cassio, when you wooed my lady,
Know of your love?
OTHELLO. He did, from first to last: why dost thou ask?
IAGO. But for a satisfaction of my thought;
No further harm.
OTHELLO.   Why of thy thought, Iago?
IAGO. I did not think he had been acquainted with her.
OTHELLO. O, yes; and went between us very oft.   100
IAGO. Indeed!
OTHELLO. Indeed! ay, indeed: discern'st thou aught in that?
Is he not honest?
IAGO.   Honest, my lord!
OTHELLO.   Honest! ay, honest.
IAGO. My lord, for aught I know.
OTHELLO. What dost thou think?
IAGO.   Think, my lord!
OTHELLO.   Think, my lord!
By heaven, he echoes me,
As if there were some monster in his thought
Too hideous to be shown. Thou dost mean something:
I heard thee say even now, thou likedst not that,
When Cassio left my wife: what didst not like?   110
And when I told thee he was of my counsel
In my whole course of wooing, thou criedst "Indeed!"
And didst contract and purse thy brow together,
As if thou then hadst shut up in thy brain
Some horrible conceit: if thou dost love me,
Show me thy thought.
IAGO. My lord, you know I love you.
OTHELLO.   I think thou dost;
And, for I know thou'rt full of love and honesty,
And weigh'st thy words before thou givest them breath,

---

[163] please yourself   [164] term of mingled tenderness and pity

Therefore these stops of thine fright me the more: 120
For such things in a false disloyal knave
Are tricks of custom, but in a man that's just
They are close delations,[165] working from the heart
That passion cannot rule.[166]

IAGO.   For Michael Cassio,
I dare be sworn I think that he is honest.

OTHELLO. I think so too.

IAGO.   Men should be what they seem;
Or those that be not, would they might seem none![167]

OTHELLO. Certain, men should be what they seem.

IAGO. Why, then, I think Cassio's an honest man.

OTHELLO. Nay, there's more in this: 130
I prithee, speak to me as to thy thinkings,
As thou dost ruminate, and give thy worst of thoughts
The worst of words.

IAGO.   Good my lord, pardon me:
Though I am bound to every act of duty,
I am not bound to that all slaves are free to.
Utter my thoughts? Why, say they are vile and false;
As where's that palace whereinto foul things
Sometimes intrude not? who has a breast so pure,
But some uncleanly apprehensions
Keep leets[168] and law-days and in session sit   140
With meditations lawful?

OTHELLO. Thou dost conspire against thy friend, Iago,
If thou but think'st him wronged and makest his ear
A stranger to thy thoughts.

IAGO.   I do beseech you—
Though I perchance am vicious in my guess,
As, I confess, it is my nature's plague
To spy into abuses, and oft my jealousy
Shapes faults that are not—that your wisdom yet,
From one that so imperfectly conceits,
Would take no notice, nor build yourself a trouble   150
Out of his scattering and unsure observance.
It were not for your quiet nor your good,
Nor for my manhood, honesty, or wisdom,
To let you know my thoughts.

OTHELLO.   What dost thou mean?

IAGO. Good name in man and woman, dear my lord,
Is the immediate jewel of their souls:
Who steals my purse steals trash; 'tis something, nothing;

---

[165] secret accusations   [166] that cannot control its indignation
[167] not seem to be honorable men   [168] days on which courts are in session

'Twas mine, 'tis his, and has been slave to thousands;
But he that filches from me my good name
Robs me of that which not enriches him 160
And makes me poor indeed.

OTHELLO. By heaven, I'll know thy thoughts.

IAGO. You cannot, if my heart were in your hand;
Nor shall not, whilst 'tis in my custody.

OTHELLO. Ha!

IAGO. O, beware, my lord, of jealousy;
It is the green-eyed monster which doth mock
The meat it feeds on: that cuckold lives in bliss
Who, certain of his fate, loves not his wronger;
But, O, what damnéd minutes tells[169] he o'er
Who dotes, yet doubts, suspects, yet strongly loves! 170

OTHELLO. O misery!

IAGO. Poor and content is rich and rich enough,
But riches fineless[170] is as poor as winter
To him that ever fears he shall be poor.
Good heaven, the souls of all my tribe defend
From jealousy!

OTHELLO. Why, why is this?
Think'st thou I'ld make a life of jealousy,
To follow still the changes of the moon
With fresh suspicions? No; to be once in doubt
Is once to be resolved: exchange me for a goat, 180
When I shall turn the business of my soul
To such exsufflicate and blown[171] surmises,
Matching thy inference. 'Tis not to make me jealous
To say my wife is fair, feeds well, loves company,
Is free of speech, sings, plays and dances well;
Where virtue is, these are more virtuous:
Nor from mine own weak merits will I draw
The smallest fear or doubt[172] of her revolt;
For she had eyes, and chose me. No, Iago;
I'll see before I doubt; when I doubt, prove; 190
And on the proof, there is no more but this,—
Away at once with love or jealousy!

IAGO. I am glad of it; for now I shall have reason
To show the love and duty that I bear you
With franker spirit: therefore, as I am bound,
Receive it from me. I speak not yet of proof.
Look to your wife; observe her well with Cassio;
Wear your eye thus, not jealous nor secure:[173]

---

[169] counts [170] boundless [171] insubstantial and inflated [172] suspicion
[173] free from suspicion

I would not have your free and noble nature,
Out of self-bounty, be abused; look to 't: 200
I know our country disposition[174] well;
In Venice they do let heaven see the pranks
They dare not show their husbands; their best conscience
Is not to leave 't undone, but keep 't unknown.

OTHELLO. Dost thou say so?

IAGO. She did deceive her father, marrying you;
And when she seemed to shake and fear your looks,
She loved them most.

OTHELLO.   And so she did.

IAGO.   Why, go to then;
She that, so young, could give out such a seeming,
To seel[175] her father's eyes up close as oak—   210
He thought 'twas witchcraft—but I am much to blame;
I humbly do beseech you of your pardon
For too much loving you.

OTHELLO.   I am bound to thee for ever.

IAGO. I see this hath a little dashed your spirits.

OTHELLO. Not a jot, not a jot.

IAGO.   I' faith, I fear it has.
I hope you will consider what is spoke
Comes from my love. But I do see you're moved:
I am to pray you not to strain my speech
To grosser issues[176] nor to larger reach
Than to suspicion.   220

OTHELLO. I will not.

IAGO.   Should you do so, my lord,
My speech should fall into such vile success
As my thoughts aim not at. Cassio's my worthy friend—
My lord, I see you're moved.

OTHELLO.   No, not much moved:
I do not think but Desdemona's honest.[177]

IAGO. Long live she so! and long live you to think so!

OTHELLO. And yet, how nature erring from itself,—

IAGO. Ay, there's the point: as—to be bold with you—
Not to affect[178] many proposed matches
Of her own clime, complexion,[179] and degree,   230
Whereto we see in all things nature tends—
Foh! one may smell in such a will[180] most rank,
Foul disproportion, thoughts unnatural.

---

[174] prevailing spirit of our country   [175] sew up (as the eyes of a falcon)
[176] to more obvious conclusions   [177] chaste   [178] like
[179] temperament; perhaps also a reference to her fair skin in contrast to the dark
Moorish Othello
[180] sexual desire

But pardon me; I do not in position
Distinctly speak of her; though I may fear
Her will, recoiling to her better judgment,
May fall to match you with her country forms [181]
And happily [182] repent.

OTHELLO.   Farewell, farewell:
If more thou dost perceive, let me know more;
Set on thy wife to observe: leave me, Iago.   240

IAGO [*going*]. My lord, I take my leave.

OTHELLO. Why did I marry? This honest creature doubtless
Sees and knows more, much more, than he unfolds.

IAGO [*returning*]. My Lord, I would I might entreat your honor
To scan this thing no further; leave it to time:
Though it be fit that Cassio have his place,
For, sure, he fills it up with great ability,
Yet, if you please to hold him off awhile,
You shall by that perceive him and his means: [183]
Note, if your lady strain his entertainment [184]   250
With any strong or vehement importunity;
Much will be seen in that. In the mean time,
Let me be thought too busy in my fears—
As worthy cause I have to fear I am—
And hold her free, I do beseech your honor.

OTHELLO. Fear not my government. [185]

IAGO. I once more take my leave.

                    [*Exit.*]

OTHELLO. This fellow's of exceeding honesty,
And knows all qualities, with a learnèd spirit,
Of human dealings. If I do prove her haggard, [186]   260
Though that her jesses [187] were my dear heartstrings,
I'ld whistle her off and let her down the wind, [188]
To prey at fortune. [189] Haply, for I am black [190]
And have not those soft parts of conversation
That chamberers have, or for I am declined
Into the vale of years,—yet that's not much—
She's gone. I am abused; [191] and my relief
Must be to loathe her. O curse of marriage,
That we can call these delicate creatures ours,
And not their appetites! I had rather be a toad,   270

---

[181] the appearance of his white countrymen   [182] haply; perhaps
[183] the means he adopts to regain your favor   [184] overurge his reinstatement
[185] self-control   [186] an untamed falcon
[187] restraining straps attached to the bird's feet   [188] go free   [189] at random
[190] of dark complexion; in Elizabethan speech used as the opposite of fair
[191] deceived

And live upon the vapor of a dungeon,
Than keep a corner in the thing I love
For others' uses. Yet, 'tis the plague of great ones;
Prerogatived are they less than the base;
'Tis destiny unshunnable, like death :
Even then this forkéd plague[192] is fated to us
When we do quicken.[193] Desdemona comes :

Re-enter DESDEMONA *and* EMILIA.

If she be false, O, then heaven mocks itself!
I'll not believe 't.
DESDEMONA.   How now, my dear Othello!
Your dinner, and the generous[194] islanders   280
By you invited, do attend your presence.
OTHELLO. I am to blame.
DESDEMONA.   Why do you speak so faintly?
Are you not well?
OTHELLO. I have a pain upon my forehead here.
DESDEMONA. Faith, that's with watching;[195] 'twill away again :
Let me but bind it hard, within this hour
It will be well.
OTHELLO.   Your napkin[196] is too little :
                    [*He puts the handkerchief from him; and it drops.*]
Let it alone. Come, I'll go in with you.
DESDEMONA. I am very sorry that you are not well.
                              [*Exeunt* OTHELLO *and* DESDEMONA.]
EMILIA. I am glad I have found this napkin :   290
This was her first remembrance from the Moor :
My wayward husband hath a hundred times
Wooed me to steal it; but she so loves the token,
For he conjured her she should ever keep it,
That she reserves it evermore about her
To kiss and talk to. I'll have the work ta'en out,[197]
And give 't Iago : what he will do with it
Heaven knows, not I;
I nothing but to please his fantasy.[198]

Re-enter IAGO.

IAGO. How now! what do you here alone?   300
EMILIA. Do not you chide; I have a thing for you.
IAGO. A thing for me? it is a common thing—
EMILIA. Ha!

---

[192] the horns of a cuckold   [193] begin to stir in our mothers' wombs
[194] noble   [195] lying awake   [196] handkerchief   [197] embroidery copied
[198] whim

IAGO. To have a foolish wife.

EMILIA. O, is that all? What will you give me now
For that same handkerchief?

IAGO.   What handkerchief?

EMILIA. What handkerchief!
Why, that the Moor first gave to Desdemona;
That which so often you did bid me steal.

IAGO. Hast stol'n it from her?   310

EMILIA. No, 'faith; she let it drop by negligence,
And, to the advantage, I, being here, took 't up.
Look, here it is.

IAGO.   A good wench; give it me.

EMILIA. What will you do with 't, that you have been so earnest
To have me filch it?

                              [*Iago snatches the handkerchief.*]

IAGO.   Why, what's that to you?

EMILIA. If it be not for some purpose of import,
Give 't me again: poor lady, she'll run mad
When she shall lack it.

IAGO. Be not acknown on 't; [199] I have use for it.
Go, leave me.   320

                              [*Exit* EMILIA.]

I will in Cassio's lodging lose this napkin,
And let him find it. Trifles light as air
Are to the jealous confirmations strong
As proofs of holy writ: this may do something.
The Moor already changes with my poison:
Dangerous conceits are, in their natures, poisons,
Which at the first are scarce found to distaste,
But with a little act upon the blood,
Burn like the mines of sulphur. I did say so:
Look, where he comes!

                    Re-enter OTHELLO.

                    Not poppy, nor mandragora, [200]   330
Nor all the drowsy syrups of the world,
Shall ever medicine thee to that sweet sleep
Which thou owedst [201] yesterday.

OTHELLO.   Ha! ha! false to me?

IAGO. Why, how now, general! no more of that.

OTHELLO. Avaunt! be gone! thou hast set me on the rack:
I swear 'tis better to be much abused
Than but to know 't a little.

IAGO.   How now, my lord!

[199] Do not admit any knowledge of it.   [200] sleeping potions   [201] had

OTHELLO. What sense had I of her stol'n hours of lust?
  I saw't not, thought it not, it harmed not me :
  I slept the next night well, was free and merry ;   340
  I found not Cassio's kisses on her lips :
  He that is robbed, not wanting what is stol'n,
  Let him not know 't, and he's not robbed at all.
IAGO. I am sorry to hear this.
OTHELLO. I had been happy, if the general camp,
  Pioners[202] and all, had tasted her sweet body,
  So I had nothing known. O, now, for ever
  Farewell the tranquil mind! farewell content!
  Farewell the pluméd troop, and the big wars,
  That make ambition virtue! O, farewell!   350
  Farewell the neighing steed, and the shrill trump,
  The spirit-stirring drum, the ear-piercing fife,
  The royal banner, and all quality,
  Pride, pomp and circumstance of glorious war!
  And, O you mortal engines,[203] whose rude throats
  The immortal Jove's dread clamors counterfeit,
  Farewell! Othello's occupation's gone!
IAGO. Is 't possible, my lord?
OTHELLO. Villain, be sure thou prove my love a whore,
  Be sure of it; give me the ocular proof;   360
  Or, by the worth of man's eternal soul,
  Thou hadst been better have been born a dog
  Than answer my waked wrath!
IAGO.   Is 't come to this?
OTHELLO. Make me to see 't; or, at the least, so prove it,
  That the probation[204] bear no hinge nor loop
  To hang a doubt on; or woe upon thy life!
IAGO. My noble lord,—
OTHELLO. If thou dost slander her and torture me,
  Never pray more; abandon all remorse;[205]
  On horror's head horrors accumulate;   370
  Do deeds to make heaven weep, all earth amazed;
  For nothing canst thou to damnation add
  Greater than that.
IAGO.   O grace! O heaven forgive me!
  Are you a man? have you a soul or sense?
  God be wi' you; take mine office. O wretched fool,
  That livest to make thine honesty a vice!
  O monstrous world! Take note, take note, O world,
  To be direct and honest is not safe.

---

[202] sappers; the vilest men in the army   [203] deadly cannon   [204] proof
[205] hope for pity

I thank you for this profit; [206] and from hence
I'll love no friend, sith love breeds such offence.   380
OTHELLO. Nay, stay: thou shouldst be honest.
IAGO. I should be wise, for honesty's a fool
And loses that it works for.
OTHELLO.   By the world,
I think my wife be honest and think she is not;
I think that thou art just and think thou art not.
I'll have some proof. Her name, that was as fresh
As Dian's [207] visage, is now begrimed and black
As mine own face. If there be cords, or knives,
Poison, or fire, or suffocating streams,
I'll not endure it. Would I were satisfied!   390
IAGO. I see, sir, you are eaten up with passion:
I do repent me that I put it to you.
You would be satisfied?
OTHELLO.   Would! nay, I will.
IAGO. And may: but, how? how satisfied, my lord?
Would you, the supervisor, grossly gape on—
Behold her topped?
OTHELLO.   Death and damnation! O!
IAGO. It were a tedious difficulty, I think,
To bring them to that prospect: damn them then,
If ever mortal eyes do see them bolster [208]
More than their own! What then? how then?   400
What shall I say? Where's satisfaction?
It is impossible you should see this,
Were they as prime as goats, as hot as monkeys,
As salt as wolves in pride, [209] and fools as gross
As ignorance made drunk. But yet, I say,
If imputation [210] and strong circumstances,
Which lead directly to the door of truth,
Will give you satisfaction, you may have 't.
OTHELLO. Give me a living [211] reason she's disloyal.
IAGO. I do not like the office: 410
But, sith I am entered in this cause so far,
Prickd [212] to 't by foolish honesty and love,
I will go on. I lay with Cassio lately;
And, being troubled with a raging tooth,
I could not sleep.
There are a kind of men so loose of soul,
That in their sleeps will mutter their affairs:

---

[206] profitable lesson   [207] goddess of chastity   [208] lie together   [209] in heat
[210] opinion based on circumstantial evidence   [211] not founded on surmise
[212] spurred on

One of this kind is Cassio:
In sleep I heard him say "Sweet Desdemona,
Let us be wary, let us hide our loves;"   420
And then, sir, would he gripe and wring my hand,
Cry "O sweet creature!" and then kiss me hard,
As if he pluckd up kisses by the roots
That grew upon my lips: then laid his leg
Over my thigh, and sighd, and kissd; and then
Cried "Cursed fate that gave thee to the Moor!"

OTHELLO. O monstrous! monstrous!

IAGO.   Nay, this was but his dream.

OTHELLO. But this denoted a foregone conclusion: [213]
'Tis a shrewd doubt, though it be but a dream.

IAGO. And this may help to thicken other proofs   430
That do demonstrate thinly.

OTHELLO.   I'll tear her all to pieces.

IAGO. Nay, but be wise: yet we see nothing done;
She may be honest yet. Tell me but this,
Have you not sometimes seen a handkerchief
Spotted with strawberries in your wife's hand?

OTHELLO. I gave her such a one; 'twas my first gift.

IAGO. I know not that: but such a handkerchief—
I am sure it was your wife's—did I today
See Cassio wipe his beard with.

OTHELLO.   If it be that,—

IAGO. If it be that, or any that was hers,   440
It speaks against her with the other proofs.

OTHELLO. O, that the slave had forty thousand lives!
One is too poor, too weak for my revenge.
Now do I see 'tis true. Look here, Iago;
All my fond [214] love thus do I blow to heaven.
'Tis gone.
Arise, black vengeance, from thy hollow cell!
Yield up, O love, thy crown and hearted throne
To tyrannous hate! Swell, bosom, with thy fraught, [215]
For 'tis of aspics' [216] tongues!

IAGO.   Yet be content.   450

OTHELLO. O, blood, blood, blood!

IAGO. Patience, I say; your mind perhaps may change.

OTHELLO. Never, Iago. Like to the Pontic sea,
Whose icy current and compulsive course
Ne'er feels retiring ebb, but keeps due on
To the Propontic and the Hellespont, [217]

---

[213] previous experience   [214] foolish   [215] freight   [216] asps'
[217] Black Sea, Sea of Marmora, and the Dardanelles

Even so my bloody thoughts, with violent pace,
Shall ne'er look back, ne'er ebb to humble love,
Till that a capable²¹⁸ and wide revenge
Swallow them up. Now, by yond marble heaven,　　　　460
　　　　　　　　　　　　　　　　　　　　[Kneels.]

In the due reverence of a sacred vow
I here engage my words.
IAGO.　　　　　　　　　Do not rise yet.
　　　　　　　　　　　　　　　　　　　　　[Kneels.]

Witness, you ever-burning lights above,
You elements that clip us round about,
Witness that here Iago doth give up
The execution of his wit,²¹⁹ hands, heart,
To wronged Othello's service! Let him command,
And to obey shall be in me remorse,²²⁰
What bloody business ever.
　　　　　　　　　　　　　　　　　　　　[They rise.]
OTHELLO.　　　　　　　I greet thy love,
Not with vain thanks, but with acceptance bounteous,　　470
And will upon the instant put thee to 't:
Within these three days let me hear thee say
That Cassio's not alive.
IAGO. My friend is dead; 'tis done at your request.
But let her live.
OTHELLO. Damn her, lewd minx! O, damn her!
Come, go with me apart; I will withdraw,
To furnish me with some swift means of death
For the fair devil. Now art thou my lieutenant.
IAGO. I am your own for ever.　　　　　　　　　480
　　　　　　　　　　　　　　　　　　　　[Exeunt.]

SCENE IV
Before the castle.

Enter DESDEMONA, EMILIA, *and* CLOWN.

DESDEMONA. Do you know, sirrah, where Lieutenant Cassio lies?²²¹
CLOWN. I dare not say he lies any where.
DESDEMONA. Why, man?
CLOWN. He's a soldier, and for one to say a soldier lies, is stabbing.
DESDEMONA. Go to: where lodges he?
CLOWN. To tell you where he lodges, is to tell you where I lie.
DESDEMONA. Can any thing be made of this?
CLOWN. I know not where he lodges, and for me to devise a lodging

---

²¹⁸ comprehensive　　²¹⁹ exercise of his intelligence
²²⁰ obedience will be an act of pity　　²²¹ dwells

and say he lies here or he lies there, were to lie in mine own throat.

DESDEMONA. Can you inquire him out, and be edified by report?   10

CLOWN. I will catechize the world for him; that is, make questions, and by them answer.

DESDEMONA. Seek him, bid him come hither: tell him I have moved my lord on his behalf, and hope all will be well.

CLOWN. To do this is within the compass of man's wit; and therefore I will attempt the doing it.

[Exit.]

DESDEMONA. Where should I lose that handkerchief, Emilia?

EMILIA. I know not, madam.

DESDEMONA. Believe me, I had rather have lost my purse
Full of crusadoes: [222] and, but my noble Moor   20
Is true of mind and made of no such baseness
As jealous creatures are, it were enough
To put him to ill thinking.

EMILIA.   Is he not jealous?

DESDEMONA. Who, he? I think the sun where he was born
Drew all such humors from him.

EMILIA.   Look, where he comes.

DESDEMONA. I will not leave him now till Cassio
Be called to him.

Enter OTHELLO.

How is 't with you, my lord?

OTHELLO. Well, my good lady. *[Aside]* O, hardness to dissemble!—
How do you, Desdemona?

DESDEMONA.   Well, my good lord.

OTHELLO. Give me your hand: this hand is moist, [223] my lady.   30

DESDEMONA. It yet hath felt no age nor known no sorrow.

OTHELLO. This argues fruitfulness and liberal [224] heart:
Hot, hot, and moist: this hand of yours requires
A sequester [225] from liberty, fasting and prayer,
Much castigation, exercise devout;
For here's a young and sweating devil here,
That commonly rebels. 'Tis a good hand,
A frank one.

DESDEMONA. You may, indeed, say so;
For 'twas that hand that gave away my heart.   40

OTHELLO. A liberal hand: the hearts of old gave hands;
But our new heraldry is hands, not hearts. [226]

DESDEMONA. I cannot speak of this. Come now, your promise.

[222] Portuguese gold coins, stamped with a cross
[223] a moist hand was believed to be a sign of sexual arousal
[224] too generous; yielding   [225] separation   [226] i.e., loveless marriages

OTHELLO. What promise, chuck?

DESDEMONA. I have sent to bid Cassio come speak with you.

OTHELLO. I have a salt and sorry rheum[227] offends me;
Lend me thy handkerchief.

DESDEMONA. Here, my lord.

OTHELLO. That which I gave you.

DESDEMONA. I have it not about me.

OTHELLO. Not?

DESDEMONA. No, indeed, my lord.

OTHELLO. That is a fault.
That handkerchief 50
Did an Egyptian[228] to my mother give;
She was a charmer,[229] and could almost read
The thoughts of people: she told her, while she kept it,
'Twould make her amiable and subdue my father
Entirely to her love, but if she lost it
Or made a gift of it, my father's eye
Should hold her loathed and his spirits should hunt
After new fancies: she, dying, gave it me;
And bid me, when my fate would have me wive,
To give it her. I did so: and take heed on 't; 60
Make it a darling like your precious eye;
To lose 't or give 't away were such perdition[230]
As nothing else could match.

DESDEMONA. Is 't possible?

OTHELLO. 'Tis true: there's magic in the web of it:
A sibyl,[231] that had numbered in the world
The sun to course two hundred compasses,
In her prophetic fury sewed the work;
The worms were hallowed that did breed the silk;
And it was dyed in mummy which the skilful
Conserved of maidens' hearts.[232]

DESDEMONA. Indeed! is 't true? 70

OTHELLO. Most veritable; therefore look to 't well.

DESDEMONA. Then would to God that I had never seen 't!

OTHELLO. Ha! wherefore?

DESDEMONA. Why do you speak so startingly and rash?

OTHELLO. Is 't lost? is 't gone? speak, is it out o' the way?

DESDEMONA. Heaven bless us!

OTHELLO. Say you?

DESDEMONA. It is not lost; but what an if it were?

OTHELLO. How!

---

[227] watery and painful head cold   [228] gypsy   [229] enchantress
[230] such a loss   [231] prophetess
[232] medicinal fluid extracted from mummies; here, from the hearts of maidens

DESDEMONA. I say, it is not lost.
OTHELLO.   Fetch 't, let me see 't.   80
DESDEMONA. Why, so I can, sir, but I will not now.
    This is a trick to put me from my suit :
    Pray you, let Cassio be received again.
OTHELLO. Fetch me the handkerchief : my mind misgives.
DESDEMONA. Come, come ;
    You'll never meet a more sufficient [233] man.
OTHELLO. The handkerchief !
DESDEMONA.   I pray, talk me of Cassio.
OTHELLO. The handkerchief !
DESDEMONA.   A man that all his time
    Hath founded his good fortunes on your love,
    Shared dangers with you,—   90
OTHELLO. The handkerchief !
DESDEMONA. In sooth, you are to blame.
OTHELLO. Away !

                                                                  [Exit.]

EMILIA. Is not this man jealous ?
DESDEMONA. I ne'er saw this before.
    Sure, there's some wonder in this handkerchief :
    I am most unhappy in the loss of it.
EMILIA. 'Tis not a year or two shows us a man :
    They are all but stomachs, and we all but food ;
    They eat us hungerly, and when they are full,   100
    They belch us. Look you, Cassio and my husband !

                      Enter CASSIO *and* IAGO.

IAGO. There is no other way ; 'tis she must do 't :
    And, lo, the happiness ! go, and importune her.
DESDEMONA. How now, good Cassio ! what's the news with you ?
CASSIO. Madam, my former suit : I do beseech you
    That by your virtuous means I may again
    Exist, and be a member of his love
    Whom I with all the office [234] of my heart
    Entirely honor : I would not be delayed.
    If my offence be of such mortal kind   110
    That nor my service past, nor present sorrows,
    Nor purposed merit in futurity,
    Can ransom me into his love again,
    But to know so must be my benefit ;
    So shall I clothe me in a forced content,
    And shut myself up in [235] some other course,
    To fortune's alms. [236]

---

[233] competent   [234] services   [235] confine myself to
[236] to whatever fortune is willing to bestow upon you

DESDEMONA.   Alas, thrice-gentle Cassio!
My advocation is not now in tune;
My lord is not my lord; nor should I know him,
Were he in favor [237] as in humor altered.   120
So help me every spirit sanctified,
As I have spoken for you all my best
And stood within the blank [238] of his displeasure
For my free speech! you must awhile be patient:
What I can do I will; and more I will
Than for myself I dare: let that suffice you.

IAGO. Is my lord angry?

EMILIA.   He went hence but now,
And certainly in strange unquietness.

IAGO. Can he be angry? I have seen the cannon,
When it hath blown his ranks into the air,   130
And, like the devil, from his very arm
Puffed his own brother:—and can he be angry?
Something of moment then: I will go meet him:
There's matter in't indeed, if he be angry.

DESDEMONA. I prithee, do so.

                              [*Exit* IAGO.]

                    Something, sure, of state,
Either from Venice, or some unhatched practice [239]
Made demonstrable here in Cyprus to him,
Hath puddled his clear spirit; and in such cases
Men's natures wrangle with inferior things,
Though great ones are their object. 'Tis even so;   140
For let our finger ache, and it indues
Our other healthful members even to that sense
Of pain: nay, we must think men are not gods,
Nor of them look for such observances
As fit the bridal. Beshrew me much, Emilia,
I was, unhandsome [240] warrior as I am,
Arraigning his unkindness with my soul;
But now I find I had suborned [241] the witness,
And he's indicted falsely.

EMILIA. Pray heaven it be state-matters, as you think,   150
And no conception nor no jealous toy
Concerning you.

DESDEMONA. Alas the day! I never gave him cause

EMILIA. But jealous souls will not be answered so;
They are not ever jealous for the cause,

---

[237] face   [238] white spot at the center of a target   [239] unrevealed plot
[240] unfair   [241] procured to commit perjury

But jealous for they are jealous : 'tis a monster
Begot upon itself, born on itself.
DESDEMONA. Heaven keep that monster from Othello's mind !
EMILIA. Lady, amen.
DESDEMONA. I will go seek him, Cassio, walk here about :   160
If I do find him fit, I'll move your suit
And seek to effect it to my uttermost.
CASSIO. I humbly thank your ladyship.

[Exeunt DESDEMONA and EMILIA.]

Enter BIANCA.

BIANCA. Save you, friend Cassio !
CASSIO.   What make you from home ?
How is it with you, my most fair Bianca ?
I' faith, sweet love, I was coming to your house.
BIANCA. And I was going to your lodging, Cassio.
What, keep a week away ? seven days and nights ?
Eight score eight hours ? and lovers' absent hours,
More tedious than the dial eight score times ?   170
O weary reckoning !
CASSIO.   Pardon me, Bianca :
I have this while with leaden thoughts been pressed ;
But I shall, in a more continuate[242] time,
Strike off this score of absence. Sweet Bianca,

[Giving her DESDEMONA's handkerchief.]

Take me this work out.[243]
BIANCA.   O Cassio, whence came this ?
This is some token from a newer friend :
To the felt absence now I feel a cause :
Is 't come to this ? Well, well.
CASSIO.   Go to, woman !
Throw your vile guesses in the devil's teeth,
From whence you have them. You are jealous now   180
That this is from some mistress, some remembrance :
No, in good troth, Bianca.
BIANCA.   Why, whose is it ?
CASSIO. I know not, sweet : I found it in my chamber.
I like the work well : ere it be demanded—
As like enough it will—I'ld have it copied :
Take it, and do 't ; and leave me for this time.
BIANCA. Leave you ! wherefore ?
CASSIO. I do attend here on the general ;
And think it no addition, nor my wish,
To have him see me womaned.

---

[242] uninterrupted   [243] copy the pattern of this embroidery

BIANCA. Why, I pray you? 190
CASSIO. Not that I love you not.
BIANCA. But that you do not love me.
  I pray you, bring me on the way a little,
  And say if I shall see you soon at night.
CASSIO. 'Tis but a little way that I can bring you;
  For I attend here: but I'll see you soon.
BIANCA. 'Tis very good; I must be circumstanced.[244]

                                 [Exeunt.]

ACT IV

SCENE I
Cyprus. Before the castle.

Enter OTHELLO *and* IAGO.

IAGO. Will you think so?
OTHELLO. Think so, Iago!
IAGO. What,
  To kiss in private?
OTHELLO. An unauthorized kiss.
IAGO. Or to be naked with her friend in bed
  An hour or more, not meaning any harm?
OTHELLO. Naked in bed, Iago, and not mean harm!
  It is hypocrisy against the Devil:[245]
  They that mean virtuously, and yet do so,
  The Devil their virtue tempts, and they tempt heaven.
IAGO. So they do nothing, 'tis a venial slip:
  But if I give my wife a handkerchief,— 10
OTHELLO. What then?
IAGO. Why, then, 'tis hers, my lord; and, being hers,
  She may, I think, bestow 't on any man.
OTHELLO. She is protectress of her honor too:
  May she give that?
IAGO. Her honor is an essence that's not seen:
  They have it very oft that have it not:
  But, for the handkerchief,—
OTHELLO. By heaven, I would most gladly have forgot it.
  Thou said'st—O, it comes o'er my memory, 20
  As doth the raven o'er the infected house,[246]
  Boding to all—he had my handkerchief.

[244] yield to circumstance   [245] in the presence of the Devil
[246] The raven was thought to hover over a house in which there was sickness or infection.

IAGO. Ay, what of that?
OTHELLO.   That's not so good now.
IAGO.   What,
   If I had said I had seen him do you wrong?
   Or heard him say,—as knaves be such abroad,
   Who having, by their own importunate suit,
   Or voluntary dotage of²⁴⁷ some mistress,
   Convinced or supplied them,²⁴⁸ cannot choose
   But they must blab—
OTHELLO.   Hath he said any thing?
IAGO. He hath, my lord; but be you well assured,   30
   No more than he'll unswear.
OTHELLO.   What hath he said?
IAGO. 'Faith, that he did—I know not what he did.
OTHELLO. What? what?
IAGO.   Lie—
OTHELLO.   With her?
IAGO.   With her, on her; what you
   will.
OTHELLO. Lie with her! lie on her! We say lie on her, when they belie
   her. Lie with her! that's fulsome.²⁴⁹—Handkerchief—confessions—
   handkerchief!—To confess, and be hanged for his labor;—first, to be
   hanged, and then to confess.—I tremble at it. Nature would not invest
   herself in such shadowing passion without some instruction.²⁵⁰ It is not
   words that shake me thus. Pish! Noses, ears, and lips.—Is 't possible?
   —Confess—handkerchief!—O devil!   40
                                        [Falls in a trance.]
IAGO. Work on,
   My medicine, work! Thus credulous fools are caught;
   And many worthy and chaste dames even thus,
   All guiltless, meet reproach. What, ho! my lord!
   My lord, I say! Othello!

                        Enter CASSIO.

                    How now, Cassio!
CASSIO. What's the matter?
IAGO. My lord is fall'n into an epilepsy:
   This is his second fit; he had one yesterday.
CASSIO. Rub him about the temples.
IAGO.   No, forbear;
   The lethargy²⁵¹ must have his quiet course: 50

---

²⁴⁷ doting upon   ²⁴⁸ won by importunity or gratified the desire of
²⁴⁹ disgusting
²⁵⁰ Natural imagination would not arouse such darkening (blinding) passion in me
unless it was based on fact.
²⁵¹ fit

If not, he foams at mouth and by and by
Breaks out to savage madness. Look, he stirs:
Do you withdraw yourself a little while,
He will recover straight: when he is gone,
I would on great occasion²⁵² speak with you.

[*Exit* CASSIO.]

How is it, general? have you not hurt your head?
OTHELLO. Dost thou mock me?
IAGO.   I mock you! no, by heaven.
Would you would bear your fortune like a man!
OTHELLO. A hornéd man's²⁵³ a monster and a beast.
IAGO. There's many a beast then in a populous city,   60
And many a civil²⁵⁴ monster.
OTHELLO. Did he confess it?
IAGO.   Good sir, be a man;
Think every bearded fellow that's but yoked
May draw with you: there's millions now alive
That nightly lie in those unproper²⁵⁵ beds
Which they dare swear peculiar:²⁵⁶ your case is better.
O, 'tis the spite of hell, the fiend's arch-mock,
To lip²⁵⁷ a wanton in a secure²⁵⁸ couch,
And to suppose her chaste! No, let me know;
And knowing what I am, I know what she shall be.   70
OTHELLO. O, thou art wise; 'tis certain.
IAGO.   Stand you awhile apart;
Confine yourself but in a patient list.²⁵⁹
Whilst you were here o'erwhelmed with your grief—
A passion most unsuiting such a man—
Cassio came hither: I shifted him away,
And laid good 'scuse upon your ecstasy,
Bade him anon return and here speak with me;
The which he promised. Do but encave yourself,
And mark the fleers,²⁶⁰ the gibes, and notable scorns,
That dwell in every region of his face;   80
For I will make him tell the tale anew,
Where, how, how oft, how long ago, and when
He hath, and is again to cope your wife:
I say, but mark his gesture. Marry, patience;
Or I shall say you are all in all in spleen,²⁶¹
And nothing of a man.
OTHELLO.   Dost thou hear, Iago?

---

²⁵² about a very urgent matter   ²⁵³ a cuckold   ²⁵⁴ in civilized life
²⁵⁵ not their own   ²⁵⁶ their own   ²⁵⁷ kiss   ²⁵⁸ free from suspicion
²⁵⁹ within the bounds of patience   ²⁶⁰ sneers   ²⁶¹ anger

I will be found most cunning in my patience ; [262]
But—dost thou hear ?—most bloody.
IAGO.   That's not amiss ;
But yet keep time [263] in all. Will you withdraw ?

[OTHELLO *retires*.]

Now will I question Cassio of Bianca,   90
A housewife [264] that by selling her desires
Buys herself bread and clothes : it is a creature
That dotes on Cassio ; as 'tis the strumpet's plague
To beguile many and be beguiled by one :
He, when he hears of her, cannot refrain
From the excess of laughter. Here he comes :

Re-enter CASSIO.

As he shall smile, Othello shall go mad ;
And his unbookish [265] jealousy must construe
Poor Cassio's smiles, gestures and light behavior,
Quite in the wrong. How do you now, lieutenant ?   100
CASSIO. The worser that you give me the addition [266]
Whose want even kills me.
IAGO. Ply Desdemona well, and you are sure on 't.
[*Speaking lower*] Now, if this suit lay in Bianca's power.
How quickly should you speed !
CASSIO.   Alas, poor caitiff ! [267]
OTHELLO. Look, how he laughs already !
IAGO. I never knew a woman love man so.
CASSIO. Alas, poor rogue ! I think, i' faith, she loves me.
OTHELLO. Now he denies it faintly, and laughs it out.
IAGO. Do you hear, Cassio ?
OTHELLO.   Now he importunes him   110
To tell it o'er : go to ; well said, well said.
IAGO. She gives it out that you shall marry her :
Do you intend it ?
CASSIO. Ha, ha, ha !
OTHELLO. Do you triumph, Roman ? [268] do you triumph ?
CASSIO. I marry her ! what ? a customer ! [269] Prithee, bear some charity
to my wit ; do not think it so unwholesome. Ha, ha, ha !
OTHELLO. So, so, so, so : they laugh that win.
IAGO. 'Faith, the cry goes [270] that you shall marry her.
CASSIO. Prithee, say true.   120
IAGO. I am a very villain else.
OTHELLO. Have you scored me ? [271] Well.

---

[262] crafty in my self control   [263] obscure judgment   [264] hussy
[265] ignorant   [266] title   [267] wretch
[268] OTHELLO associates Romans with the idea of triumph.   [269] harlot
[270] common report is   [271] settled my fate

CASSIO. This is the monkey's own giving out: she is persuaded I will marry her, out of her own love and flattery,[272] not out of my promise.

OTHELLO. Iago beckons me; now he begins the story.

CASSIO. She was here even now; she haunts me in every place. I was the other day talking on the sea-bank with certain Venetians; and thither comes the bauble, and, by this hand, she falls me thus about my neck— 129

OTHELLO. Crying, "O dear Cassio!" as it were: his gesture imports it.

CASSIO. So hangs, and lolls, and weeps upon me; so hales,[273] and pulls me: ha, ha, ha!

OTHELLO. Now he tells how she plucked him to my chamber. O, I see that nose of yours, but not that dog I shall throw it to.

CASSIO. Well, I must leave her company.

IAGO. Before me![274] look, where she comes.

CASSIO. 'Tis such another fitchew![275] marry, a perfumed one.

Enter BIANCA.

What do you mean by this haunting of me?

BIANCA. Let the devil and his dam haunt you! What did you mean by that same handkerchief you gave me even now? I was a fine fool 140 to take it. I must take out the work?—A likely piece of work, that you should find it in your chamber, and not know who left it there! This is some minx's token, and I must take out the work? There; give it your hobbyhorse:[276] wheresoever you had it, I'll take out no work on 't.

CASSIO. How now, my sweet Bianca! how now! how now!

OTHELLO. By heaven, that should be my handkerchief!

BIANCA. An you'll come to supper tonight, you may; an you will not, come when you are next prepared for.

[*Exit.*]

IAGO. After her, after her. 150

CASSIO. Faith, I must; she'll rail in the street else.

IAGO. Will you sup there?

CASSIO. 'Faith, I intend so.

IAGO. Well, I may chance to see you; for I would very fain speak with you.

CASSIO. Prithee, come; will you?

IAGO. Go to; say no more.

[*Exit* CASSIO.]

OTHELLO *advances.*

OTHELLO. How shall I murder him, Iago?

IAGO. Did you perceive how he laughed at his vice?

---

[272] self-flattery   [273] harasses   [274] Upon my life!
[275] one of these polecats that are eager when in heat   [276] whore

OTHELLO. O Iago!   160

IAGO. And did you see the handkerchief?

OTHELLO. Was that mine?

IAGO. Yours, by this hand: and to see how he prizes the foolish woman
your wife! she gave it him, and he hath given it his whore.

OTHELLO. I would have him nine years a-killing. A fine woman! a fair
woman! a sweet woman!

IAGO. Nay, you must forget that.

OTHELLO. Ay, let her rot, and perish, and be damned tonight; for she
shall not live: no, my heart is turned to stone; I strike it, and it hurts
my hand. O, the world hath not a sweeter creature: she might   170
lie by an emperor's side and command him tasks.

IAGO. Nay, that's not your way.[277]

OTHELLO. Hang her! I do but say what she is: so delicate with her
needle: an admirable musician: O! she will sing the savageness out of
a bear: of so high and plenteous wit and invention:—

IAGO. She's the worse for all this.

OTHELLO. O, a thousand thousand times: and then, of so gentle a condition!

IAGO. Ay, too gentle.   179

OTHELLO. Nay, that's certain: but yet the pity of it, Iago! O Iago, the
pity of it, Iago!

IAGO. If you are so fond over her iniquity, give her patent to offend;
for, if it touch not you, it comes near nobody.

OTHELLO. I will chop her into messes:[278] cuckold me!

IAGO. O, 'tis foul in her.

OTHELLO. With mine officer!

IAGO. That's fouler.

OTHELLO. Get me some poison, Iago; this night: I'll not expostulate
with her, lest her body and beauty unprovide my mind again: this
night, Iago.   190

IAGO. Do it not with poison, strangle her in her bed, even the bed she
hath contaminated.

OTHELLO. Good, good: the justice of it pleases: very good.

IAGO. And for Cassio, let me be his undertaker: you shall hear more by
midnight.

OTHELLO. Excellent good.

                                                                    [*A trumpet within.*]
                         What trumpet is that same?

IAGO. Something from Venice, sure, 'tis Lodovico
Come from the duke: and, see, your wife is with him.

             Enter LODOVICO, DESDEMONA, *and* ATTENDANTS.

LODOVICO. Save you, worthy general!

---

[277] not the way you should be thinking about her   [278] small pieces of food

OTHELLO.   With all my heart, sir.
LODOVICO. The duke and senators of Venice greet you.   200
                              [*Gives him a letter.*]
OTHELLO. I kiss the instrument of their pleasures.
                              [*Opens the letter, and reads.*]
DESDEMONA. And what's the news, good cousin Lodovico?
IAGO. I am very glad to see you, signior; Welcome to Cyprus.
LODOVICO. I thank you. How does Lieutenant Cassio?
IAGO. Lives, sir.
DESDEMONA. Cousin, there's fall'n between him and my lord
    An unkind[279] breach: but you shall make all well.
OTHELLO. Are you sure of that?
DESDEMONA. My lord?
OTHELLO [*Reads*]. "This fail you not to do, as you will—"   210
LODOVICO. He did not call; he's busy in the paper.
    Is there division 'twixt my lord and Cassio?
DESDEMONA. A most unhappy one: I would do much
    To atone them, for the love I bear to Cassio.
OTHELLO. Fire and brimstone!
DESDEMONA.   My lord?
OTHELLO.   Are you wise?
DESDEMONA. What, is he angry?
LODOVICO.   May be the letter moved him;
    For, as I think, they do command him home,
    Deputing Cassio in his government.
DESDEMONA. Trust me, I am glad on 't.
OTHELLO.   Indeed!
DESDEMONA.   My lord?
OTHELLO. I am glad to see you mad.
DESDEMONA.   Why, sweet Othello,—   220
                              [OTHELLO *strikes* DESDEMONA.]
OTHELLO. Devil!
DESDEMONA. I have not deserved this.
LODOVICO. My lord, this would not be believed in Venice,
    Though I should swear I saw 't: 'tis very much:
    Make her amends; she weeps.
OTHELLO.   O devil, devil!
    If that the earth could teem with woman's tears,[280]
    Each drop she falls would prove a crocodile.[281]
    Out of my sight!
DESDEMONA.   I will not stay to offend you.
                              [*Going.*]

[279] unnatural   [280] if women's tears could impregnate the earth
[281] which was supposed to shed tears over the man it devours

LODOVICO. Truly, an obedient lady:
  I do beseech your lordship, call her back.   230
OTHELLO. Mistress!
DESDEMONA.   My lord?
OTHELLO.   What would you with her, sir?
LODOVICO. Who, I, my lord?
OTHELLO. Ay; you did wish that I would make her turn:
  Sir, she can turn, and turn, and yet go on,
  And turn again; and she can weep, sir, weep;
  And she's obedient, as you say, obedient,
  Very obedient. Proceed you in your tears.
  Concerning this, sir,—O well-painted passion!—
  I am commanded home. Get you away;
  I'll send for you anon. Sir, I obey the mandate,   240
  And will return to Venice. Hence, avaunt!

                          [Exit DESDEMONA.]

  Cassio shall have my place. And, sir, tonight,
  I do entreat that we may sup together:
  You are welcome, sir, to Cyprus.—Goats and monkeys!

                                  [Exit.]

LODOVICO. Is this the noble Moor whom our full senate
  Call all in all sufficient? Is this the nature
  Whom passion could not shake? whose solid virtue
  The shot of accident, nor dart of chance,
  Could neither graze nor pierce?
IAGO.   He is much changed.
LODOVICO. Are his wits safe? is he not light of brain?   250
IAGO. He's that he is: I may not breathe my censure[282]
  What he might be: if what he might he is not,
  I would to heaven he were!
LODOVICO.   What, strike his wife!
IAGO. 'Faith, that was not so well; yet would I knew
  That stroke would prove the worst!
LODOVICO.   Is it his use?[283]
  Or did the letters work upon his blood,
  And new-create this fault?
IAGO.   Alas, alas!
  It is not honesty[284] in me to speak
  What I have seen and known. You shall observe him,
  And his own courses will denote him so   260
  That I may save my speech: do but go after,
  And mark how he continues.

---

[282] opinion   [283] habit   [284] proper

LODOVICO. I am sorry that I am deceived in him.

[Exeunt.]

SCENE II
A room in the castle.

Enter OTHELLO *and* EMILIA.

OTHELLO. You have seen nothing then?
EMILIA. Nor ever heard, nor ever did suspect.
OTHELLO. Yes, you have seen Cassio and she together.
EMILIA. But then I saw no harm, and then I heard
Each syllable that breath made up between them.
OTHELLO. What, did they never whisper?
EMILIA.   Never, my lord.
OTHELLO. Nor send you out o' the way?
EMILIA. Never.
OTHELLO. To fetch her fan, her gloves, her mask, nor nothing?
EMILIA. Never, my lord.   10
OTHELLO. That's strange.
EMILIA. I durst, my lord, to wager she is honest,[285]
Lay down my soul at stake: if you think other,
Remove your thought; it doth abuse your bosom.
If any wretch have put this in your head,
Let heaven requite it with the serpent's curse![286]
For, if she be not honest, chaste, and true,
There's no man happy; the purest of their wives
Is foul as slander.
OTHELLO.   Bid her come hither: go.

[Exit EMILIA.*]*

She says enough; yet she's a simple bawd   20
That cannot say as much. This is a subtle whore,
A closet lock and key of villainous secrets:
And yet she'll kneel and pray; I have seen her do 't.

Enter DESDEMONA *with* EMILIA.

DESDEMONA. My lord, what is your will?
OTHELLO.   Pray, chuck, come hither.
DESDEMONA. What is your pleasure?
OTHELLO.   Let me see your eyes;
Look in my face.
DESDEMONA.   What horrible fancy 's this?

---

[285] chaste
[286] God's curse on the serpent in the Garden of Eden. Genesis 3:14

OTHELLO [*To* EMILIA]. Some of your function,[287] mistress;
  Leave procreants alone and shut the door;
  Cough, or cry "hem," if any body come:
  Your mystery, your mystery:[288] nay, dispatch.   30
                             [*Exit* EMILIA.]
DESDEMONA. Upon my knees, what doth your speech import?
  I understand a fury in your words,
  But not the words.
OTHELLO. Why, what art thou?
DESDEMONA.   Your wife, my lord; your true
  And loyal wife.
OTHELLO.   Come, swear it, damn thyself;
  Lest, being like one of heaven, the devils themselves
  Should fear to seize thee: therefore be double damned:
  Swear thou art honest.
DESDEMONA.   Heaven doth truly know it.
OTHELLO. Heaven truly knows that thou art false as hell.
DESDEMONA. To whom, my lord? with whom? how am I false?
OTHELLO. O Desdemona! away! away! away!   40
DESDEMONA. Alas the heavy day! Why do you weep?
  Am I the motive of these tears, my lord?
  If haply you my father do suspect
  An instrument of this your calling back,
  Lay not your blame on me: if you have lost him,
  Why, I have lost him too.
OTHELLO.   Had it pleased heaven
  To try me with affliction; had they rained
  All kinds of sores and shames on my bare head,
  Steeped me in poverty to the very lips,
  Given to captivity me and my utmost hopes,   50
  I should have found in some place of my soul
  A drop of patience: but, alas, to make me
  A fixéd figure for the time of scorn
  To point his slow unmoving finger at!
  Yet could I bear that too; well, very well:
  But there, where I have garnered up my heart,
  Where either I must live, or bear no life;
  The fountain from the which my current runs,
  Or else dries up; to be discarded thence!
  Or keep it as a cistern for foul toads   60
  To knot and gender in! Turn thy complexion there,
  Patience, thou young and rose-lipped cherubin,—
  Ay, there, look grim as hell!
DESDEMONA. I hope my noble lord esteems me honest.

---

[287] perform your duties (as bawd)   [288] trade; craft

OTHELLO. O, ay; as summer flies are in the shambles,[289]
That quicken even with blowing.[290] O thou weed,
Who art so lovely fair and smell'st so sweet
That the sense aches at thee, would thou hadst ne'er been born!
DESDEMONA. Alas, what ignorant sin have I committed?
OTHELLO. Was this fair paper, this most goodly book,   70
Made to write "whore" upon? What committed!
Committed! O thou public commoner![291]
I should make very forges of my cheeks,
That would to cinders burn up modesty,
Did I but speak thy deeds. What committed!
Heaven stops the nose at it and the moon winks,
The bawdy wind that kisses all it meets
Is hushed within the hollow mine of earth,
And will not hear it. What committed!
Impudent strumpet!
DESDEMONA.   By heaven, you do me wrong.   80
OTHELLO. Are not you a strumpet?
DESDEMONA.   No, as I am a Christian:
If to preserve this vessel[292] for my lord
From any other foul unlawful touch
Be not to be a strumpet, I am none.
OTHELLO. What, not a whore?
DESDEMONA.   No, as I shall be saved.
OTHELLO. Is 't possible?
DESDEMONA. O, heaven forgive us!
OTHELLO.   I cry you mercy, then:
I took you for that cunning whore of Venice
That married with Othello.

                                        [*Raising his voice.*]
                    You, mistress,
That have the office opposite to Saint Peter,   90
And keep the gate of hell!

                    Re-enter EMILIA.

                    You, you, ay, you!
We have done our course; there's money for your pains:
I pray you, turn the key and keep our counsel.

                                        [*Exit.*]

EMILIA. Alas, what does this gentleman conceive?
How do you, madam? how do you, my good lady?
DESDEMONA. 'Faith, half asleep.
EMILIA. Good madam, what's the matter with my lord?

---

[289] slaughter-house
[290] that are impregnated again as soon as they lay their eggs
[291] harlot   [292] body of mine

DESDEMONA. With who?

EMILIA. Why, with my lord, madam.

DESDEMONA. Who is thy lord?

EMILIA.   He that is yours, sweet lady.   100

DESDEMONA. I have none: do not talk to me, Emilia;
    I cannot weep; nor answer have I none,
    But what should go by water.[293] Prithee, tonight
    Lay on my bed my wedding sheets: remember;
    And call thy husband hither.

EMILIA.   Here's a change indeed!

                                  [Exit.]

DESDEMONA. 'Tis meet I should be used so, very meet.
    How have I been behaved, that he might stick
    The small'st opinion on my least misuse?

Re-enter EMILIA *with* IAGO.

IAGO. What is your pleasure, madam? How is 't with you?

DESDEMONA. I cannot tell. Those that do teach young babes   110
    Do it with gentle means and easy tasks:
    He might have chid me so; for, in good faith,
    I am a child to chiding.

IAGO.   What's the matter, lady?

EMILIA. Iago, my lord hath so bewhored her,
    Thrown such despite and heavy terms upon her,
    As true hearts cannot bear.

DESDEMONA. Am I that name, Iago?

IAGO.   What name, fair lady?

DESDEMONA. Such as she says my lord did say I was.

EMILIA. He called her whore: a beggar in his drink
    Could not have laid such terms upon his callet.[294]   120

IAGO. Why did he so?

DESDEMONA. I do not know; I am sure I am none such.

IAGO. Do not weep, do not weep. Alas the day!

EMILIA. Hath she forsook so many noble matches,
    Her father and her country and her friends,
    To be called whore? would it not make one weep?

DESDEMONA. It is my wretched fortune.

IAGO.   Beshrew[295] him for 't!
    How comes this trick upon him?

DESDEMONA.   Nay, heaven doth know.

EMILIA. I will be hanged, if some eternal villian,
    Some busy and insinuating rogue,   130
    Some cogging, cozening[296] slave, to get some office,

---

[293] be expressed by tears   [294] whore   [295] curse
[296] deceiving and cheating

Have not devised this slander ; I'll be hanged else.

IAGO. Fie, there is no such man ; it is impossible.

DESDEMONA. If any such there be, heaven pardon him !

EMILIA. A halter pardon him ! and hell gnaw his bones !
Why should he call her whore ? who keeps her company ?
What place ? what time ? what form ? what likelihood ?
The Moor's abused by some most villainous knave,
Some base notorious knave, some scurvy fellow.
O heaven, that such companions thou'ldst unfold,   140
And put in every honest hand a whip
To lash the rascals naked through the world
Even from the east to the west !

IAGO.   Speak within door.[297]

EMILIA. O, fie upon them ! Some such squire[298] he was
That turned your wit the seamy side without,
And made you to suspect me with the Moor.

IAGO. You are a fool ; go to.

DESDEMONA.   O good Iago,
What shall I do to win my lord again ?
Good friend, go to him ; for, by this light of heaven,
I know not how I lost him. Here I kneel :   150
If e'er my will did trespass 'gainst his love,
Either in discourse of thought or actual deed,
Or that mine eyes, mine ears, or any sense,
Delighted them in any other form ;
Or that I do not yet, and ever did,
And ever will—though he do shake me off
To beggarly divorcement—love him dearly,
Comfort forswear me ! Unkindness may do much ;
And his unkindness may defeat my life,
But never taint my love. I cannot say "whore."   160
It doth abhor me now I speak the word ;
To do the act that might the addition[299] earn
Not the world's mass of vanity could make me.

IAGO. I pray you, be content ; 'tis but his humor :
The business of the state does him offense,
And he does chide with you.

DESDEMONA. If 'twere no other,—

IAGO.   'Tis but so, I warrant.
                              [*Trumpets within.*]
Hark, how these instruments summon to supper !
The messengers of Venice stay the meat :[300]

---

[297] Don't talk so loud.   [298] contemptuous for person   [299] name
[300] are waiting for supper

Go in, and weep not; all things shall be well.   170
[Exeunt DESDEMONA and EMILIA.]

Enter RODERIGO.

How now, Roderigo!

RODERIGO. I do not find that thou dealest justly with me.

IAGO. What in the contrary?

RODERIGO. Every day thou daffest me[301] with some device, Iago; and rather, as it seems to me now, keepest from me all conveniency than suppliest me with the least advantage of hope. I will indeed no longer endure it, nor am I yet persuaded to put up in peace what already I have foolishly suffered.

IAGO. Will you hear me, Roderigo?

RODERIGO. 'Faith, I have heard too much, for your words and performances are no kin together.   180

IAGO. You charge me most unjustly.

RODERIGO. With nought but truth. I have wasted myself out of my means. The jewels you have had from me to deliver to Desdemona would half have corrupted a votarist: [302] you have told me she hath received them and returned me expectations and comforts of sudden respect and acquaintance, but I find none.

IAGO. Well; go to; very well.

RODERIGO. Very well! go to! I cannot go to, man; nor 'tis not very well: nay, I think it is scurvy, and begin to find myself fopped[303]   190 in it.

IAGO. Very well.

RODERIGO. I tell you 'tis not very well. I will make myself known to Desdemona: if she will return me my jewels, I will give over my suit and repent my unlawful solicitation; if not, assure yourself I will seek satisfaction of you.

IAGO. You have said now.[304]

RODERIGO. Ay, and said nothing but what I protest intendment of doing.

IAGO. Why, now I see there's mettle in thee, and even from this instant do build on thee a better opinion than ever before. Give me thy   200 hand, Roderigo: thou hast taken against me a most just exception; but yet, I protest, I have dealt more directly in thy affair.

RODERIGO. It hath not appeared.

IAGO. I grant indeed it hath not appeared, and your suspicion is not without wit and judgment. But, Roderigo, if thou hast that in thee indeed, which I have greater reason to believe now than ever, I mean purpose, courage and valor, this night show it: if thou the next night following enjoy not Desdemona, take me from this world with treachery and devise engines for my life.

---

[301] put me off   [302] nun   [303] duped   [304] Really!

RODERIGO. Well, what is it? is it within reason and compass?   210
IAGO. Sir, there is especial commission come from Venice to depute
  Cassio in Othello's place.
RODERIGO. Is that true? why, then Othello and Desdemona return
  again to Venice.
IAGO. O, no; he goes into Mauritania[305] and takes away with him the
  fair Desdemona, unless his abode be lingered here by some accident:
  wherein none can be so determinate as the removing of Cassio.
RODERIGO. How do you mean, removing of him?
IAGO. Why, by making him uncapable of Othello's place; knocking out
  his brains.   220
RODERIGO. And that you would have me to do?
IAGO. Ay, if you dare do yourself a profit and a right. He sups tonight
  with a harlotry, and thither will I go to him: he knows not yet of his
  honorable fortune. If you will watch his going thence, which I will
  fashion to fall out between twelve and one, you may take him at your
  pleasure: I will be near to second your attempt, and he shall fall between us. Come, stand not amazed at it, but go along with me; I will
  show you such a necessity in his death that you shall think yourself
  bound to put it on him. It is now high supper-time, and the night grows
  to waste: about it.   230
RODERIGO. I will hear further reason for this.
IAGO. And you shall be satisfied.

                                                    [*Exeunt.*]

SCENE III
Another room in the castle.

Enter OTHELLO, LODOVICO, DESDEMONA,
EMILIA, *and* ATTENDANTS.

LODOVICO. I do beseech you, sir, trouble yourself no further.
OTHELLO. O, pardon me; 'twill do me good to walk.
LODOVICO. Madam, good night; I humbly thank your ladyship.
DESDEMONA. Your honor is most welcome.
OTHELLO.   Will you walk, sir?
  O,—Desdemona—
DESDEMONA. My lord?
OTHELLO. Get you to bed on the instant; I will be returned forthwith:
  dismiss your attendant there: look it be done.
DESDEMONA. I will, my lord.
            [*Exeunt* OTHELLO, LODOVICO, *and* ATTENDANTS.]
EMILIA. How goes it now? he looks gentler than he did.   10
DESDEMONA. He says he will return incontinent:[306]
  He hath commanded me to go to bed,
  And bade me to dismiss you.

305 Morocco and western Algeria   306 immediately

EMILIA.   Dismiss me!
DESDEMONA. It was his bidding; therefore, good Emilia,
    Give me my nightly wearing, and adieu:
    We must not now displease him.
EMILIA. I would you had never seen him!
DESDEMONA. So would not I: my love doth so approve him,
    That even his stubbornness, his checks, his frowns,—
    Prithee, unpin me—have grace and favor in them.   20
EMILIA. I have laid those sheets you bade me on the bed.
DESDEMONA. All's one. Good faith, how foolish are our minds!
    If I do die before thee, prithee, shroud me
    In one of those same sheets.
EMILIA.   Come, come, you talk.
DESDEMONA. My mother had a maid called Barbara:
    She was in love, and he she loved proved mad
    And did forsake her: she had a song of "willow";
    An old thing 'twas, but it expressed her fortune,
    And she died singing it: that song tonight
    Will not go from my mind; I have much to do,   30
    But to go hang my head all at one side,
    And sing it like poor Barbara. Prithee, dispatch.
EMILIA. Shall I go fetch your night-gown?
DESDEMONA.   No, unpin me here.
    This Lodovico is a proper man.
EMILIA. A very handsome man.
DESDEMONA. He speaks well.
EMILIA. I know a lady in Venice would have walked barefoot to Pale-
    stine for a touch of his nether lip.
DESDEMONA [Singing].

> The poor soul sat sighing by a sycamore tree,
>   Sing all a green willow;   40
> Her hand on her bosom, her head on her knee,
>   Sing willow, willow, willow:
> The fresh streams ran by her, and murmured her moans;
>   Sing willow, willow, willow;
> Her salt tears fell from her, and softened the stones;—

Lay by these:
[Singing]

> Sing willow, willow, willow;

Prithee, hie thee; he'll come anon:—
[Singing]

> Sing all a green willow must be my garland.
> Let nobody blame him; his scorn I approve,—   50

Nay, that's not next.—Hark! who is 't that knocks?

EMILIA. It's the wind.

DESDEMONA [*Singing*].

> *I called my love false love;*
> *but what said he then*
> *Sing willow, willow, willow :*
> *If I court moe women, you'll couch with*
> *moe men.—*

So, get thee gone; good night. Mine eyes do itch;
Doth that bode weeping?

EMILIA.   'Tis neither here nor there.

DESDEMONA. I have heard it said so. O, these men, these men!   60
Dost thou in conscience think,—tell me, Emilia,—
That there be women do abuse their husbands
In such gross kind?

EMILIA.   There be some such, no question.

DESDEMONA. Wouldst thou do such a deed for all the world?

EMILIA. Why, would not you?

DESDEMONA.   No, by this heavenly light!

EMILIA. Nor I neither by this heavenly light; I might do 't as well i'
the dark.

DESDEMONA. Wouldst thou do such a deed for all the world?

EMILIA. The world's a huge thing: it is a great price
For a small vice.   70

DESDEMONA. In troth, I think thou wouldst not.

EMILIA. In troth, I think I should: and undo 't when I had done. Marry,
I would not do such a thing for a joint-ring,[307] nor for measures of
lawn,[308] nor for gowns, petticoats, nor caps, nor any petty exhibition[309]
but, for the whole world,—why, who would not make her husband a
cuckold to make him a monarch? I should venture purgatory for 't.

DESDEMONA. Beshrew me, if I would do such a wrong
For the whole world.

EMILIA. Why, the wrong is but a wrong i' the world; and having the
world for your labor, 'tis a wrong in your own world, and you might
quickly make it right.   81

DESDEMONA. I do not think there is any such woman.

EMILIA. Yes, a dozen; and as many to the vantage as would store the
world they played for.
But I do think it is their husbands' faults
If wives do fall: say that they slack their duties,
And pour our treasures into foreign laps,
Or else break out in peevish jealousies,

---

[307] a ring made in interlocked halves as a lover's token
[308] yards of sheer linen fabric   [309] allowance of money

Throwing restraint upon us; or say they strike us,
Or scant our former having in despite;   90
Why, we have galls,[310] and though we have some grace,[311]
Yet have we some revenge. Let husbands know
Their wives have sense like them: they see and smell
And have their palates both for sweet and sour,
As husbands have. What is it that they do
When they change us for others? Is it sport?
I think it is: and doth affection breed it?
I think it doth: is 't frailty that thus errs?
It is so too: and have not we affections,
Desires for sport, and frailty, as men have?   100
Then let them use us well: else let them know,
The ills we do, their ills instruct us so.

DESDEMONA. Good night, good night: heaven me such uses send,
Not to pick bad from bad, but by bad mend!

                                                                [*Exeunt.*]

ACT V

SCENE I
Cyprus. A street.

Enter IAGO *and* RODERIGO.

IAGO. Here, stand behind this bulk;[312] straight will he come:
Wear thy good rapier bare, and put it home:
Quick, quick; fear nothing; I'll be at thy elbow:
It makes us, or it mars us; think on that,
And fix most firm thy resolution.

RODERIGO. Be near at hand; I may miscarry in 't.

IAGO. Here, at thy hand: be bold, and take thy stand.

                                                                [*Retires.*]

RODERIGO. I have no great devotion to the deed;
And yet he hath given me satisfying reasons:
'Tis but a man gone. Forth, my sword: he dies.   10

IAGO. I have rubbed this young quat[313] almost to the sense,[314]
And he grows angry. Now, whether he kill Cassio,
Or Cassio him, or each do kill the other,
Every way makes my gain: live Roderigo,
He calls me to a restitution large
Of gold and jewels that I bobbed from him,[315]

---

[310] feelings of resentment   [311] disposition to forgive
[312] projecting part of a building   [313] pimple   [314] quick
[315] cheated him of

As gifts to Desdemona;
It must not be : if Cassio do remain,
He hath a daily beauty in his life
That makes me ugly ; and, besides, the Moor   20
May unfold me to him ; there stand I in much peril :
No, he must die. But so : I hear him coming.

Enter CASSIO.

RODERIGO. I know his gait, 'tis he.—Villain, thou diest!
[*Makes a pass at* CASSIO.]
CASSIO. That thrust had been mine enemy indeed,
But that my coat[316] is better than thou know'st :
I will make proof of thine.
[*Draws, and wounds* RODERIGO.]
RODERIGO.   O, I am slain!
[IAGO *from behind wounds* CASSIO *in the leg, and exit.*]
CASSIO. I am maimed for ever. Help, ho! murder! murder!
[*Falls.*]

Enter OTHELLO.

OTHELLO. The voice of Cassio : Iago keeps his word.
RODERIGO. O, villain that I am!
OTHELLO.   It is even so.
CASSIO. O, help, ho! light! a surgeon!   30
OTHELLO. 'Tis he :—O brave Iago, honest and just,
That hast such noble sense of thy friend's wrong!
Thou teachest me. Minion,[317] your dear lies dead,
And your unblest fate hies : [318] strumpet, I come.
Forth of my heart those charms, thine eyes, are blotted ;
Thy bed, lust-stained, shall with lust's blood be spotted.
[*Exit.*]

Enter LODOVICO *and* GRATIANO.

CASSIO. What, ho! no watch? no passage? [319] murder! murder!
GRATIANO. 'Tis some mischance ; the cry is very direful.
CASSIO. O, help!
LODOVICO. Hark!   40
RODERIGO. O wretched villain!
LODOVICO. Two or three groan : it is a heavy night :
These may be counterfeits : let's think 't unsafe
To come in to the cry[320] without more help.
RODERIGO. Nobody come? then shall I bleed to death.

---

[316] coat of mail   [317] lady-love (used contemptuously)
[318] hurries toward you   [319] No sentry? No passers-by?
[320] answer the appeal

LODOVICO. Hark!

Re-enter IAGO, *with a light.*

GRATIANO. Here's one comes in his shirt, with light and weapons.
IAGO. Who's there? whose noise is this that cries on murder?
LODOVICO. We do not know.
IAGO.   Did not you hear a cry?
CASSIO. Here, here! for heaven's sake, help me!
IAGO.   What's the matter? 50
GRATIANO. This is Othello's ancient, as I take it.
LODOVICO. The same indeed; a very valiant fellow.
IAGO. What are you here that cry so grievously?
CASSIO. Iago? O, I am spoiled, undone by villains!
    Give me some help.
IAGO. O me, lieutenant! what villains have done this?
CASSIO. I think that one of them is hereabout,
    And cannot make away.
IAGO.   O treacherous villains!
    What are you there? come in, and give some help.
                                    [*To* LODOVICO *and* GRATIANO.]
RODERIGO. O, help me here!   60
CASSIO. That's one of them.
IAGO.   O murderous slave! O villain!
                                        [*Stabs* RODERIGO.]
RODERIGO. O damned Iago! O inhuman dog!
IAGO. Kill men i' the dark!—Where be these bloody thieves?—
    How silent is this town!—Ho! murder! murder!—
    What may you be? are you of good or evil?
LODOVICO. As you shall prove [321] us, praise us.
IAGO. Signior Lodovico?
LODOVICO. He, sir.
IAGO. I cry you mercy. Here's Cassio hurt by villains.
GRATIANO. Cassio!   70
IAGO. How is 't, brother!
CASSIO. My leg is cut in two.
IAGO.   Marry, heaven forbid!
    Light, gentlemen: I'll bind it with my shirt.

Enter BIANCA.

BIANCA. What is the matter, ho? who is 't that cried?
IAGO. Who is 't that cried?
BIANCA. O my dear Cassio! my sweet Cassio!
    O Cassio, Cassio, Cassio!

---

[321] test

IAGO. O notable strumpet! Cassio, may you suspect
　Who they should be that have thus mangled you?
CASSIO. No.　　　　　　　　　　　　　　　　　　80
GRATIANO. I am sorry to find you thus: I have been to seek you.
IAGO. Lend me a garter. So. O, for a chair,[322]
　To bear him easily hence!
BIANCA. Alas, he faints! O Cassio, Cassio, Cassio!
IAGO. Gentlemen all, I do suspect this trash[323]
　To be a party in this injury.
　Patience awhile, good Cassio. Come, come;
　Lend me a light. Know we this face or no?
　Alas, my friend and my dear countryman
　Roderigo! no:—yes, sure:—O heaven! Roderigo.　　90
GRATIANO. What, of Venice?
IAGO. Even he, sir: did you know him?
GRATIANO.　　　　　　　　　　　　Know him! ay.
IAGO. Signior Gratiano? I cry you gentle pardon;
　These bloody accidents must excuse my manners,
　That so neglected you.
GRATIANO.　　　　　　　　I am glad to see you.
IAGO. How do you, Cassio? O, a chair, a chair!
GRATIANO. Roderigo!
IAGO. He, he, 'tis he.

　　　　　　　　　　　　　　　　[*A chair brought in.*]
　　　　　　　O, that's well said; the chair.
　Some good man bear him carefully from hence;
　I'll fetch the general's surgeon. [*To* BIANCA] For you, mistress,　100
　Save you your labor. He that lies slain here, Cassio,
　Was my dear friend: what malice was between you?
CASSIO. None in the world; nor do I know the man.
IAGO [*To* BIANCA]. What, look you pale? O, bear him out o' the air.
　　　　　　　　　　　[CASSIO *and* RODERIGO *are borne off.*]
　Stay you, good gentlemen. Look you pale, mistress?
　Do you perceive the gastness[324] of her eye?
　Nay, if you stare, we shall hear more anon.
　Behold her well; I pray you, look upon her:
　Do you see, gentlemen? nay, guiltiness will speak,
　Though tongues were out of use.　　　　　　　　　110

　　　　　　　　　　　Enter EMILIA.

EMILIA. 'Las, what's the matter? what's the matter, husband?
IAGO. Cassio hath here been set on in the dark
　By Roderigo and fellows that are scaped:
　He's almost slain, and Roderigo dead.

---

[322] sedan-chair　　[323] BIANCA　　[324] ghastliness

EMILIA. Alas, good gentleman! alas, good Cassio!
IAGO. This is the fruit of whoring. Prithee, Emilia,
  Go know of Cassio where he supped tonight.
  [*To* BIANCA] What, do you shake at that?
BIANCA. He supped at my house; but I therefore shake not.
IAGO. O, did he so? I charge you, go with me.   120
EMILIA. Fie, fie upon thee, strumpet!
BIANCA. I am no strumpet; but of life as honest
  As you that thus abuse me.
EMILIA.   As I! foh! fie upon thee!
IAGO. Kind gentlemen, let's go see poor Cassio dressed.
  Come, mistress, you must tell 's another tale.
  Emilia, run you to the citadel,
  And tell my lord and lady what hath happed.
  Will you go on? I pray. [*Aside*] This is the night
  That either makes me or fordoes me quite.

                                                    [*Exeunt.*]

SCENE II

A bedchamber in the castle: DESDEMONA *in bed asleep;
a light burning.*

Enter OTHELLO.

OTHELLO. It is the cause,[325] it is the cause, my soul,—
  Let me not name it to you, you chaste [326] stars!—
  It is the cause. Yet I'll not shed her blood;
  Nor scar that whiter skin of hers than snow,
  And smooth as monumental alabaster.
  Yet she must die, else she'll betray more men.
  Put out the light, and then put out the light:
  If I quench thee, thou flaming minister,[327]
  I can again thy former light restore,
  Should I repent me: but once put out thy light,   10
  Thou cunning'st pattern of excelling nature,
  I know not where is that Promethean heat [328]
  That can thy light relume. When I have plucked the rose,
  I cannot give it vital growth again,
  It must needs wither: I'll smell it on the tree.

                                                    [*Kissing her.*]

  Ah, balmy breath, that dost almost persuade
  Justice to break her sword! One more, one more.
  Be thus when thou art dead, and I will kill thee,

[325] the great provocation, with some suggestion of ground for legal action
[326] The stars in classical poetry were the virgin attendants of the moon, Diana,
the goddess of chastity.
[327] servant   [328] the divine creative fire stolen from Heaven by Prometheus

And love thee after. One more, and this the last:
So sweet was ne'er so fatal. I must weep,   20
But they are cruel tears: this sorrow's heavenly; [329]
It strikes where it doth love. She wakes.

DESDEMONA. Who's there? Othello?

OTHELLO.   Ay, Desdemona.

DESDEMONA. Will you come to bed, my lord?

OTHELLO. Have you prayed tonight, Desdemona?

DESDEMONA.   Ay, my lord.

OTHELLO. If you bethink yourself of any crime
   Unreconciled as yet to heaven and grace,
   Solicit for it straight.

DESDEMONA. Alas, my lord, what do you mean by that?

OTHELLO. Well, do it, and be brief; I will walk by: 30
   I would not kill thy unprepared spirit;
   No; heaven forfend! I would not kill thy soul.

DESDEMONA. Talk you of killing?

OTHELLO.   Ay, I do.

DESDEMONA.   Then heaven
   Have mercy on me!

OTHELLO.   Amen, with all my heart!

DESDEMONA. If you say so, I hope you will not kill me.

OTHELLO. Hum!

DESDEMONA. And yet I fear you; for you are fatal [330] then
   When your eyes roll so: why I should fear I know not,
   Since guiltiness I know not; but yet I feel I fear.

OTHELLO. Think on thy sins.

DESDEMONA.   They are loves I bear to you.   40

OTHELLO. Ay, and for that thou diest.

DESDEMONA. That death's unnatural that kills for loving.
   Alas, why gnaw you so your nether lip?
   Some bloody passion shakes your very frame:
   These are portents; but yet I hope, I hope,
   They do not point on me.

OTHELLO.   Peace, and be still!

DESDEMONA. I will so. What's the matter?

OTHELLO. That handkerchief which I so loved and gave thee
   Thou gavest to Cassio.

DESDEMONA.   No, by my life and soul!
   Send for the man, and ask him.

OTHELLO.   Sweet soul, take heed,   50
   Take heed of perjury; thou art on thy deathbed.

DESDEMONA. Ay, but not yet to die.

---

[329] because it is grief for doing an act of divine justice   [330] ominous

OTHELLO.   Yes, presently : [331]
  Therefore confess thee freely of thy sin ;
  For to deny each article with oath
  Cannot remove nor choke the strong conception
  That I do groan withal. Thou art to die.
DESDEMONA. Then Lord have mercy on me !
OTHELLO.   I say, amen.
DESDEMONA. And have you mercy too ! I never did
  Offend you in my life ; never loved Cassio
  But with such general warranty of heaven   60
  As I might love ; I never gave him token.
OTHELLO. By heaven, I saw my handkerchief in 's hand.
  O perjured woman ! thou dost stone [332] my heart,
  And makest me call what I intend to do
  A murder, which I thought a sacrifice :
  I saw the handkerchief.
DESDEMONA.   He found it then ;
  I never gave it him : send for him hither ;
  Let him confess a truth.
OTHELLO.   He hath confessed.
DESDEMONA. What, my lord ?
OTHELLO. That he hath used thee.
DESDEMONA.   How ? unlawfully ?
OTHELLO.   Ay.   70
DESDEMONA. He will not say so.
OTHELLO.   No, his mouth is stopped ;
  Honest Iago hath ta'en order for 't.
DESDEMONA. O ! my fear interprets : what, is he dead ?
OTHELLO. Had all his hairs been lives, my great revenge
  Had stomach for them all.
DESDEMONA. Alas ! he is betrayed and I undone.
OTHELLO. Out, strumpet ! weep'st thou for him to my face ?
DESDEMONA. O, banish me, my lord, but kill me not !
OTHELLO. Down, strumpet !
DESDEMONA. Kill me tomorrow : let me live tonight !   80
OTHELLO. Nay, if you strive,—
DESDEMONA. But half an hour !
OTHELLO.   Being done, there is no pause.[333]
DESDEMONA. But while I say one prayer !
OTHELLO.   It is too late.
                               [He stifles her.]

EMILIA [*Within*]. My lord, my lord ! what, ho ! my lord, my lord !
OTHELLO. What noise is this ? Not dead ? not yet quite dead ?

---

[331] at once   [332] turn to stone
[333] Now that execution of the retribution has begun, there can be no delay.

I that am cruel am yet merciful;
I would not have thee linger in thy pain:
So, so.
EMILIA [*Within*]. What, ho! my lord, my lord!
OTHELLO.   Who's there?
EMILIA [*Within*]. O, good my lord, I would speak a word with you!   90
OTHELLO. Yes: 'tis Emilia. By and by. She's dead.
  'Tis like she comes to speak of Cassio's death.—
  The noise was here. Ha! no more moving?
  Still as the grave. Shall she come in? were 't good?—
  I think she stirs again:—no. What's best to do?
  If she come in, she'll sure speak to my wife:
  My wife! my wife! what wife? I have no wife.
  O, insupportable! O heavy hour!
  Methinks it should be now a huge eclipse
  Of sun and moon, and that the affrighted globe   100
  Should yawn at alteration.[334]
EMILIA [*Within*].   I do beseech you
  That I may speak with you, O, good my lord!
OTHELLO. I had forgot thee: O, come in, Emilia:
  Soft; by and by. Let me the curtains draw.
  Where art thou?

                                      [Unlocks the door.]

Enter EMILIA.

                What's the matter with thee now?
EMILIA. O, my good lord, yonder's foul murders done!
OTHELLO. What, now?
EMILIA. But now, my lord.
OTHELLO. It is the very error of the moon;
  She comes more nearer earth than she was wont,   110
  And makes men mad.
EMILIA. Cassio, my lord, hath killed a young Venetian
  Called Roderigo.
OTHELLO.   Roderigo killed!
  And Cassio killed!
EMILIA.   No, Cassio is not killed.
OTHELLO. Not Cassio killed! then murder's out of tune,
  And sweet revenge grows harsh.
DESDEMONA. O, falsely, falsely murdered!
EMILIA.   Alas, what cry is that?
OTHELLO. That! what?
EMILIA. Out, and alas! that was my lady's voice.
  Help! help, ho! help! O lady, speak again!   120

---

[334] gape in astonishment at the change. Earthquakes were believed to accompany eclipses of the sun.

Sweet Desdemona! O sweet mistress, speak!

DESDEMONA. A guiltless death I die.

EMILIA. O, who hath done this deed?

DESDEMONA. Nobody; I myself. Farewell:
Commend me to my kind lord: O, farewell!

[*Dies.*]

OTHELLO. Why, how should she be murdered?

EMILIA.   Alas, who knows?

OTHELLO. You heard her say herself, it was not I.

EMILIA. She said so: I must needs report the truth.

OTHELLO. She's like a liar, gone to burning hell:
'Twas I that killed her.

EMILIA.   O, the more angel she,   130
And you the blacker devil!

OTHELLO. She turned to folly, and she was a whore.

EMILIA. Thou dost belie her, and thou art a devil.

OTHELLO. She was false as water.

EMILIA.   Thou art rash as fire, to say
That she was false: O, she was heavenly true!

OTHELLO. Cassio did top her; ask thy husband else.
O, I were damned beneath all depth in hell.
But that I did proceed upon just grounds
To this extremity. Thy husband knew it all

EMILIA. My husband!   140

OTHELLO. Thy husband.

EMILIA. That she was false to wedlock?

OTHELLO. Ay, with Cassio. Nay, had she been true,
If heaven would make me such another world
Of one entire and perfect chrysolite,[335]
I'ld not have sold her for it.

EMILIA. My husband!

OTHELLO.   Ay, 'twas he that told me first:
An honest man he is, and hates the slime
That sticks on filthy deeds.

EMILIA.   My husband!

OTHELLO. What needs this iteration, woman?   150
I say thy husband.

EMILIA. O mistress, villainy hath made mocks with love!
My husband say that she was false!

OTHELLO.   He, woman;
I say thy husband: dost understand the word?
My friend, thy husband, honest, honest Iago.

EMILIA. If he say so, may his pernicious soul
Rot half a grain a day! he lies to the heart:

[335] believed to be one of the largest and most precious stones

She was too fond of her most filthy bargain.
OTHELLO. Ha!
EMILIA. Do thy worst: 160
This deed of thine is no more worthy heaven
Than thou wast worthy her.
OTHELLO. Peace, you were best.
EMILIA. Thou hast not half that power to do me harm
As I have to be hurt. O gull! O dolt!
As ignorant as dirt! thou has done a deed—
I care not for thy sword; I'll make thee known,
Though I lost twenty lives.—Help! help, ho! help!
The Moor hath killed my mistress! Murder! murder!

Enter MONTANO, GRATIANO, IAGO, *and others.*

MONTANO. What is the matter? How now, general!
EMILIA. O, are you come, Iago? you have done well, 170
That men must lay their murders on your neck.
GRATIANO. What is the matter?
EMILIA. Disprove this villain, if thou be'st a man:
He says thou told'st him that his wife was false:
I know thou didst not, thou'rt not such a villain:
Speak, for my heart is full.
IAGO. I told him what I thought, and told no more
Than what he found himself was apt and true.
EMILIA. But did you ever tell him she was false?
IAGO. I did. 180
EMILIA. You told a lie; an odious, damnéd lie;
Upon my soul, a lie, a wicked lie.
She false with Cassio!—did you say with Cassio?
IAGO. With Cassio, mistress. Go to, charm your tongue.
EMILIA. I will not charm my tongue; I am bound to speak:
My mistress here lies murdered in her bed,—
ALL. O heavens forfend!
EMILIA. And your reports have set the murder on.
OTHELLO. Nay, stare not, masters: it is true, indeed.
GRATIANO. 'Tis a strange truth. 190
MONTANO. O monstrous act!
EMILIA. Villainy, villainy, villainy!
I think upon 't, I think: I smell 't: O villainy!—
I thought so then: [336]—I'll kill myself for grief:—
O villainy, villainy!
IAGO. What, are you mad? I charge you, get you home.
EMILIA. Good gentlemen, let me have leave to speak:

[336] when she believed some cozening slave had slandered Desdemona (IV, ii,
130ff)

     'Tis proper I obey him, but not now.
     Perchance, Iago, I will ne'er go home.
OTHELLO. O! O! O!

[He falls on the bed.]

EMILIA.   Nay, lay thee down and roar;
     For thou hast killed the sweetest innocent   200
     That e'er did lift up eye.

*[*OTHELLO *rises.]*

OTHELLO.   O, she was foul!
     I scarce did know you, uncle : there lies your niece,
     Whose breath, indeed, these hands have newly stopped :
     I know this act shows horrible and grim.
GRATIANO. Poor Desdemona! I am glad thy father's dead :
     Thy match was mortal to him, and pure grief
     Shore his old thread in twain : [337] did he live now,
     This sight would make him do a desperate turn,
     Yea, curse his better angel from his side,
     And fall to reprobation.   210
OTHELLO. 'Tis pitiful; but yet Iago knows
     That she with Cassio hath the act of shame
     A thousand times committed; Cassio confessed it :
     And she did gratify his amorous works
     With that recognizance and pledge of love
     Which I first gave her; I saw it in his hand :
     It was a handkerchief, an antique token
     My father gave my mother.
EMILIA. O heaven! O heavenly powers!
IAGO. Come, hold your peace.
EMILIA.   'Twill out, 'twill out : I peace!   220
     No, I will speak as liberal as the north : [338]
     Let heaven and men and devils, let them all,
     All, all, cry shame against me, yet I'll speak.
IAGO. Be wise, and get you home.
EMILIA.   I will not.

*[*IAGO *offers to stab* EMILIA.]*

GRATIANO.   Fie!
     Your sword upon a woman?
EMILIA. O thou dull Moor! that handkerchief thou speak'st of
     I found by fortune and did give my husband;
     For often, with a solemn earnestness,
     More than indeed belonged to such a trifle,
     He begged of me to steal it.

---

[337] sheared the thread of life in two ; a reference to Atropos, one of the Fates, who
carried the shears and cut the thread of life
[338] i.e., as the north wind

IAGO.   Villanous whore!   230
EMILIA. She give it Cassio! no, alas! I found it,
  And I did give 't my husband.
IAGO.   Filth, thou liest!
EMILIA. By heaven, I do not, I do not, gentlemen.
  O murderous coxcomb! what should such a fool
  Do with so good a woman?
OTHELLO.   Are there no stones in heaven
  But what serve for the thunder? [339]—Precious villain!
    [*He runs at* IAGO: IAGO, *from behind, stabs* EMILIA, *and exit.*]
GRATIANO. The woman falls; sure, he hath killed his wife.
EMILIA. Ay, ay: O, lay me by my mistress' side.
GRATIANO. He's gone, but his wife's killed.
MONTANO. 'Tis a notorious villain. Take you this weapon,   240
  Which I have here recovered from the Moor:
  Come, guard the door without; let him not pass,
  But kill him rather. I'll after that same villain,
  For 'tis a damned slave.
                          [*Exeunt* MONTANO *and* GRATIANO.]
OTHELLO.   I am not valiant neither.
  But every puny whipster gets my sword:
  But why should honor outlive honesty?
  Let it go all.
EMILIA. What did thy song bode, lady?
  Hark, canst thou hear me? I will play the swan,
  And die in music. [*Singing*] *Willow, willow, willow.*—   250
  Moor, she was chaste; she loved thee, cruel Moor;
  So come my soul to bliss, as I speak true;
  So speaking as I think, I die, I die.
                                          [*Dies.*]
OTHELLO. I have another weapon in this chamber;
  It is a sword of Spain, the ice-brook's temper: [340]—
  O, here it is. Uncle, I must come forth.
GRATIANO [*Within*]. If thou attempt it, it will cost thee dear:
  Thou hast no weapon, and perforce must suffer.
OTHELLO. Look in upon me then and speak with me,
  Or, naked as I am, I will assault thee.   260

                  Re-enter GRATIANO.

GRATIANO. What is the matter?
OTHELLO.   Behold, I have a weapon;
  A better never did itself sustain
  Upon a soldier's thigh: I have seen the day,

---

[339] It was thought that stones fell when it thundered.
[340] tempered in ice-cold water

That, with this little arm and this good sword,
I have made my way through more impediments
Than twenty times your stop: but, O vain boast!
Who can control his fate? 'tis not so now.
Be not afraid, though you do see me weaponed;
Here is my journey's end, here is my butt,[341]
And very sea-mark[342] of my utmost sail.   270
Do you go back dismayed? 'tis a lost fear;
Man but a rush against Othello's breast,
And he retires. Where should Othello go?
Now, how dost thou look now? O ill-starred wench!
Pale as thy smock! when we shall meet at compt,[343]
This look of thine will hurl my soul from heaven,
And fiends will snatch it. Cold, cold, my girl!
Even like thy chastity. O cursèd slave!
Whip me, ye devils,
From the possession of this heavenly sight!   280
Blow me about in winds! roast me in sulphur!
Wash me in steep-down gulfs of liquid fire!
O Desdemona! Desdemona! dead!
Oh! Oh! Oh!

Enter LODOVICO, MONTANO, CASSIO *carried in a chair,*
and OFFICERS *with* IAGO, *prisoner.*

LODOVICO. Where is this rash and most unfortunate man?
OTHELLO. That's he that was Othello: here I am.
LODOVICO. Where is that viper? bring the villain forth.
OTHELLO. I look down towards his feet;[344] but that's a fable.
If that thou be'st a devil, I cannot kill thee.

                                              [*Wounds* IAGO.]

LODOVICO. Wrench his sword from him.
IAGO.   I bleed, sir; but not killed. 290
OTHELLO. I am not sorry neither: I'ld have thee live;
For, in my sense, 'tis happiness to die.
LODOVICO. O thou Othello, that wert once so good,
Fall'n in the practice of a damnèd slave,
What shall be said to thee?
OTHELLO.   Why, any thing:
An honorable murderer, if you will;
For nought I did in hate, but all in honor.
LODOVICO. This wretch hath part confessed his villainy:
Did you and he consent in Cassio's death?
OTHELLO. Ay.   300

[341] target   [342] limit   [343] the last reckoning on Judgment Day
[344] to see if they are cloven like the Devil's

CASSIO. Dear general, I never gave you cause.
OTHELLO. I do believe it, and I ask your pardon.
  Will you, I pray, demand that demi-devil
  Why he hath thus ensnared my soul and body?
IAGO. Demand me nothing: what you know, you know:
  From this time forth I never will speak word.
LODOVICO. What, not to pray?
GRATIANO.   Torments will ope your lips.
OTHELLO. Well, thou dost best.
LODOVICO. Sir, you shall understand what hath befall'n,
  Which, as I think, you know not. Here is a letter   310
  Found in the pocket of the slain Roderigo;
  And here another: the one of them imports
  The death of Cassio to be undertook
  By Roderigo.
OTHELLO. O villain!
CASSIO.   Most heathenish and most gross!
LODOVICO. Now here's another discounted [345] paper,
  Found in his pocket too; and this, it seems,
  Roderigo meant to have sent this damnéd villain;
  But that belike Iago in the interim
  Came in and satisfied him.
OTHELLO.   O the pernicious caitiff!   320
  How came you, Cassio, by that handkerchief
  That was my wife's?
CASSIO.   I found it in my chamber:
  And he himself confessed but even now
  That there he dropped it for a special purpose
  Which wrought to his desire.
OTHELLO.   O fool! fool! fool!
CASSIO. There is besides in Roderigo's letter,
  How he upbraids Iago, that he made him
  Brave me upon the watch; [346] whereon it came
  That I was cast: and even but now he spake,
  After long seeming dead, Iago hurt him,   330
  Iago set him on.
LODOVICO. You must forsake this room, and go with us:
  Your power and your command is taken off,
  And Cassio rules in Cyprus. For this slave,
  If there be any cunning cruelty
  That can torment him much and hold him long,
  It shall be his. You shall close prisoner rest,
  Till that the nature of your fault be known
  To the Venetian state. Come, bring him away.

---

[345] expressing dissatisfaction   [346] when I was on sentry duty

OTHELLO. Soft you; a word or two before you go.   340
I have done the state some service, and they know 't.
No more of that. I pray you, in your letters,
When you shall these unlucky deeds relate,
Speak of me as I am; nothing extenuate,
Nor set down aught in malice: then must you speak
Of one that loved not wisely but too well;
Of one not easily jealous, but being wrought
Perplexed in the extreme; of one whose hand,
Like the base Indian,[347] threw a pearl away
Richer than all his tribe; of one whose subdued eyes,   350
Albeit unused to the melting mood,
Drop tears as fast as the Arabian trees
Their medicinal gum. Set you down this;
And say besides, that in Aleppo[348] once,
Where a malignant and a turbaned Turk
Beat a Venetian and traduced the state,
I took by the throat the circumcisèd dog,
And smote him, thus.

                                             [Stabs himself.]

LODOVICO. O bloody period!
GRATIANO.   All that's spoke is marred.[349]
OTHELLO. I kissed thee ere I killed thee: no way but this;   360
Killing myself, to die upon a kiss.

                                     [Falls on the bed, and dies.]

CASSIO. This did I fear, but thought he had no weapon;
For he was great of heart.
LODOVICO [*To* IAGO].   O Spartan dog,[350]
More fell[351] than anguish, hunger, or the sea!
Look on the tragic loading of this bed;
This is thy work: the object poisons sight;
Let it be hid. Gratiano, keep the house,
And seize upon the fortunes of the Moor,
For they succeed on you. To you, lord governor,
Remains the censure of this hellish villain;   370
The time, the place, the torture: O, enforce it!
Myself will straight aboard; and to the state
This heavy act with heavy heart relate.

                                            [Exeunt.]

---

[347] American Indians, regarded as ignorant savages.
[348] a Syrian town where Venice had special trading privileges. In Aleppo it was death for a Christian to strike a Turk.
[349] All that we have said has proved useless.
[350] Spartan dogs were noted for their ferocity.   [351] cruel

William Shakespeare
1564–1616
THE TEMPEST

❖

DRAMATIS PERSONAE

ALONSO, *King of Naples.*
SEBASTIAN, *his brother.*
PROSPERO, *the right Duke of Milan.*
ANTONIO, *his brother, the usurping Duke of Milan.*
FERDINAND, *son to the King of Naples.*
GONZALO, *an honest old Counsellor.*
ADRIAN,
FRANCISCO, } *Lords.*
CALIBAN, *a savage and deformed Slave.*

TRINCULO, *a Jester.*
STEPHANO, *a drunken Butler.*
MASTER *of a Ship.*
BOATSWAIN.
MARINERS.
MIRANDA, *daughter to Prospero.*
ARIEL, *an airy Spirit.*
IRIS,
CERES,
JUNO,   } *presented by* SPIRITS.
NYMPHS,
REAPERS,
Other SPIRITS *attending on Prospero.*

SCENE—*A ship at sea : an island.*

❖

ACT I

SCENE I
*On a ship at sea : a tempestuous noise
of thunder and lightning heard.*

Enter a SHIP-MASTER *and a* BOATSWAIN.

MASTER. Boatswain!
BOATSWAIN. Here, master: what cheer?
MASTER. Good, speak to the mariners: fall to 't, yarely,[1] or we run ourselves aground: bestir, bestir.

[*Exit.*]

Enter MARINERS.

BOATSWAIN. Heigh, my hearts! cheerly, cheerly, my hearts! yare,

---

[1] promptly

yare! Take in the topsail. Tend to the master's whistle. Blow, till thou
burst thy wind, if room enough![2]

>   *Enter* ALONSO, SEBASTIAN, ANTONIO, FERDINAND,
>   GONZALO, *and others.*

ALONSO. Good boatswain, have care. Where's the master? Play the[3]
men.

BOATSWAIN. I pray now, keep below.   10

ANTONIO. Where is the master, boatswain?

BOATSWAIN. Do you not hear him? You mar our labor: keep your
cabins: you do assist the storm.

GONZALO. Nay, good,[4] be patient.

BOATSWAIN. When the sea is. Hence! What cares these roarers[5] for
the name of king? To cabin: silence! trouble us not.

GONZALO. Good, yet remember whom thou hast aboard.

BOATSWAIN. None that I more love than myself. You are a counselor;
if you can command these elements to silence, and work the peace of
the present, we will not hand a rope more; use your authority: if you
cannot, give thanks you have lived so long, and make yourself ready
in your cabin for the mischance of the hour, if it so hap. Cheerly,
good hearts! Out of our way, I say.   23
                                                                [Exit.]

GONZALO. I have great comfort from this fellow: methinks he hath
no drowning mark upon him; his complexion[6] is perfect gallows.[7]
Stand fast, good Fate, to his hanging: make the rope of his destiny our
cable, for our own doth little advantage. If he be not born to be hanged,
our case is miserable.

                                                              [Exeunt.]

>   *Re-enter* BOATSWAIN.

BOATSWAIN. Down with the topmast! yare! lower, lower! Bring her
to try with maincourse.[8] *[A cry within.]* A plague upon this howling!
they are louder than the weather or our office.[9]   31

>   *Re-enter* SEBASTIAN, ANTONIO, *and* GONZALO.

Yet again! what do you here? Shall we give o'er and drown? Have
you a mind to sink?

SEBASTIAN. A pox o' your throat, you bawling, blasphemous, in-
charitable dog!

BOATSWAIN. Work you then.

ANTONIO. Hang, cur! hang, you whoreson, insolent noisemaker! We
are less afraid to be drowned than thou art.

---

[2] if there is open sea   [3] behave as   [4] good fellow
[5] i.e., the winds and the waves   [6] face
[7] an allusion to the proverb, "He who is born to be hanged will never be drowned."
[8] Bring her close to the wind under mainsail.   [9] the noise of our orders

GONZALO. I'll warrant him for[10] drowning; though the ship were no
stronger than a nutshell and as leaky as an unstanched wench.   40
BOATSWAIN. Lay her a-hold, a-hold![11] set her two courses off to sea
again; lay her off.[12]

Enter MARINERS *wet.*

MARINERS. All lost! to prayers, to prayers! all lost!
BOATSWAIN. What, must our mouths be cold?[13]
GONZALO. The king and prince at prayers! let's assist them,
For our case is as theirs.
SEBASTIAN.   I'm out of patience.
ANTONIO. We are merely[14] cheated of our lives by drunkards:
This wide-chapped[15] rascal—would thou mightst lie drowning
The washing of ten tides![16]
GONZALO.   He'll be hanged yet,
Though every drop of water swear against it   50
And gape at widest to glut[17] him.
[*A confused noise within :* "Mercy on us!"—
"We split, we split!"—"Farewell my wife and children!"—
"Farewell, brother!"—"We split, we split, we split!"]
ANTONIO. Let's all sink with the king.
SEBASTIAN. Let's take leave of him.
                              [*Exeunt* ANTONIO *and* SEBASTIAN.]
GONZALO. Now would I give a thousand furlongs of sea for an acre of
barren ground, long heath, brown furze, any thing. The wills above be
done! but I would fain die a dry death.
                                                    [*Exeunt.*]

SCENE II
The island. Before PROSPERO'S *cell.*

Enter PROSPERO *and* MIRANDA.

MIRANDA. If by your art, my dearest father, you have
Put the wild waters in this roar, allay them.
The sky, it seems, would pour down stinking pitch,
But that the sea, mounting to the welkin's[18] cheek,
Dashes the fire out. O, I have suffered
With those that I saw suffer: a brave[19] vessel,
Who had, no doubt, some noble creature in her,
Dashed all to pieces. O, the cry did knock

---

[10] guarantee him against   [11] close to the wind
[12] two points of the compass (22½ degrees) away from the shore
[13] The boatswain here takes to drink.   [14] completely
[15] wide-mouthed; i.e., insolent
[16] The punishment of a pirate was to be hanged on shore and left until three tides
had washed over him.
[17] swallow   [18] sky's   [19] gallant

Against my very heart. Poor souls, they perished.
Had I been any god of power, I would   10
Have sunk the sea within the earth or ere
It should the good ship so have swallowed and
The fraughting[20] souls within her.
PROSPERO.   Be collected:
No more amazement:[21] tell your piteous heart
There's no harm done.
MIRANDA.   O, woe the day!
PROSPERO.   No harm.
I have done nothing but in care of thee,
Of thee, my dear one, thee, my daughter, who
Art ignorant of what thou art, nought knowing
Of whence I am, nor that I am more better
Than Prospero, master of a full poor cell,   20
And thy no greater father.
MIRANDA.   More to know
Did never meddle[22] with my thoughts.
PROSPERO.   'Tis time
I should inform thee farther. Lend thy hand,
And pluck my magic garment from me. So:

                                      [*Lays down his mantle.*]

Lie there, my art. Wipe thou thine eyes; have comfort.
The direful spectacle of the wreck, which touched
The very virtue of compassion in thee,
I have with such provision in mine art
So safely ordered that there is no soul—
No, not so much perdition[23] as an hair   30
Betid[24] to any creature in the vessel
Which thou heard'st cry, which thou saw'st sink. Sit down;
For thou must now know farther.
MIRANDA.   You have often
Begun to tell me what I am, but stopped
And left me to a bootless inquisition,
Concluding "Stay: not yet."
PROSPERO.   The hour's now come;
The very minute bids thee ope thine ear;
Obey and be attentive. Canst thou remember
A time before we came unto this cell?
I do not think thou canst, for then thou wast not   40
Out[25] three years old.
MIRANDA.   Certainly, sir, I can.
PROSPERO. By what? by any other house or person?

---

[20] forming her cargo   [21] alarm   [22] mingle   [23] loss   [24] happened
[25] fully

Of any thing the image tell me that
Hath kept with thy remembrance.
MIRANDA.   'Tis far off
And rather like a dream than an assurance
That my remembrance warrants. Had I not
Four or five women once that tended me?
PROSPERO. Thou hadst, and more, Miranda. But how is it
That this lives in thy mind? What seest thou else
In the dark backward and abysm of time?   50
If thou remember'st aught ere thou camest here,
How thou camest here thou mayst.
MIRANDA.   But that I do not.
PROSPERO. Twelve year since, Miranda, twelve year since,
Thy father was the Duke of Milan and
A prince of power.
MIRANDA.   Sir, are not you my father?
PROSPERO. Thy mother was a piece[26] of virtue, and
She said thou wast my daughter; and thy father
Was Duke of Milan; and thou his only heir
And princess no worse issued.[27]
MIRANDA.   O the heavens!
What foul play had we, that we came from thence?   60
Or blessed was 't we did?
PROSPERO.   Both, both, my girl:
By foul play, as thou say'st, were we heaved thence,
But blessedly holp hither.
MIRANDA.   O, my heart bleeds
To think o' the teen that I have turned you to,[28]
Which is from my remembrance! Please you, farther.
PROSPERO. My brother and thy uncle, called Antonio—
I pray thee, mark me—that a brother should
Be so perfidious!—he whom next thyself
Of all the world I loved and to him put
The manage of my state; as at that time   70
Through all the signories it was the first
And Prospero the prime duke, being so reputed
In dignity, and for the liberal arts
Without a parallel; those being all my study,
The government I cast upon my brother
And to my state[29] grew stranger, being transported
And rapt in secret[30] studies. Thy false uncle—
Dost thou attend me?
MIRANDA.   Sir, most heedfully.

---

[26] masterpiece   [27] descended from no lower stock
[28] sorrow I have forced you to recall   [29] duties of government   [30] occult

PROSPERO. Being once perfected how to grant suits,
    How to deny them, who to advance and who   80
    To trash for over-topping,[31] new created
    The creatures that were mine, I say, or changed 'em,
    Or else new formed 'em; having both the key[32]
    Of officer and office, set all hearts i' the state
    To what tune pleased his ear; that now he was
    The ivy which had hid my princely trunk,
    And sucked my verdure out on 't. Thou attend'st not.
MIRANDA. O, good sir, I do.
PROSPERO.   I pray thee, mark me.
    I, thus neglecting worldly ends, all dedicated
    To closeness[33] and the bettering of my mind   90
    With that which, but by being so retired,
    O'er-prized all popular rate,[34] in my false brother
    Awaked an evil nature; and my trust,
    Like a good parent, did beget of him
    A falsehood[35] in its contrary as great
    As my trust was; which had indeed no limit,
    A confidence sans[36] bound. He being thus lorded,[37]
    Not only with what my revénue yielded,
    But what my power might else exact, like one
    Who having into truth, by telling of it,   100
    Made such a sinner of his memory,
    To credit his own lie,[38] he did believe
    He was indeed the duke; out o' the substitution,[39]
    And executing the outward face of royalty,
    With all prerogative: hence his ambition growing—
    Dost thou hear?
MIRANDA.   Your tale, sir, would cure deafness.
PROSPERO. To have no screen between this part he played
    And him he played it for, he needs will be
    Absolute Milan. Me, poor man, my library
    Was dukedom large enough: of temporal royalties[40]   110
    He thinks me now incapable; confederates—
    So dry he was for sway—wi' the King of Naples
    To give him annual tribute, do him homage,
    Subject his coronet to his crown and bend
    The dukedom yet unbowed—alas, poor Milan!—

[31] to restrain from becoming too ambitious   [32] the tuning key   [33] privacy
[34] (would have) surpassed in value all popular estimate   [35] treachery
[36] without   [37] made supreme ruler of the state
[38] who, by telling a lie often, has so corrupted his memory as to mistake his lie
for the truth
[39] by reason of acting as my substitute
[40] earthly (as contrasted to spiritual) royal prerogatives

To most ignoble stooping.
MIRANDA.   O the heavens!
PROSPERO. Mark his condition[41] and the event; then tell me
  If this might be a brother.
MIRANDA.   I should sin
  To think but nobly of my grandmother:
  Good wombs have borne bad sons.
PROSPERO.   Now the condition.   120
  This King of Naples, being an enemy
  To me inveterate, hearkens my brother's suit;
  Which was, that he, in lieu o' the premises[42]
  Of homage and I know not how much tribute,
  Should presently extirpate[43] me and mine
  Out of the dukedom and confer fair Milan
  With all the honors on my brother: whereon,
  A treacherous army levied, one midnight
  Fated to the purpose did Antonio open
  The gates of Milan, and, i' the dead of darkness,   130
  The ministers for the purpose hurried thence
  Me and thy crying self.
MIRANDA.   Alack, for pity!
  I, not remembering how I cried out then,
  Will cry it o'er again: it is a hint
  That wrings mine eyes to 't.
PROSPERO.   Hear a little further
  And then I'll bring thee to the present business
  Which now 's upon 's; without the which this story
  Were most impertinent.[44]
MIRANDA.   Wherefore did they not
  That hour destroy us?
PROSPERO.   Well demanded, wench:
  My tale provokes that question. Dear, they durst not,   140
  So dear the love my people bore me, nor set
  A mark so bloody on the business, but
  With colors[45] fairer painted their foul ends.
  In few, they hurried us aboard a bark,
  Bore us some leagues to sea; where they prepared
  A rotten carcass of a boat, not rigged,
  Nor tackle, sail, nor mast; the very rats
  Instinctively have quit it: there they hoist us,
  To cry to the sea that roared to us, to sigh
  To the winds whose pity, sighing back again,   150
  Did us but loving wrong.

---

[41] terms of his agreement   [42] in return for the stipulation
[43] at once uproot   [44] irrelevant   [45] pretexts

MIRANDA.   Alack, what trouble
Was I then to you!
PROSPERO.   O, a cherubin
Thou wast that did preserve me. Thou didst smile,
Infuséd with a fortitude from heaven,
When I have decked[46] the sea with drops full salt,
Under my burthen groaned; which raised in me
An undergoing stomach,[47] to bear up
Against what should ensue.
MIRANDA.   How came we ashore?
PROSPERO. By Providence divine.
Some food we had and some fresh water that   160
A noble Neapolitan, Gonzalo,
Out of his charity, who being then appointed
Master of this design, did give us, with
Rich garments, linens, stuffs and necessaries,
Which since have steaded much; so, of his gentleness,
Knowing I loved my books, he furnished me
From mine own library with volumes that
I prize above my dukedom.
MIRANDA.   Would I might
But ever see that man!
PROSPERO.   Now I arise:

                              [*Resumes his mantle.*]

Sit still, and hear the last of our sea-sorrow.   170
Here in this island we arrived; and here
Have I, thy schoolmaster, made thee more profit
Than other princesses can that have more time
For vainer hours and tutors not so careful.
MIRANDA. Heavens thank you for 't! And now, I pray you, sir,
For still 'tis beating in my mind, your reason
For raising this sea-storm?
PROSPERO.   Know thus far forth.
By accident most strange, bountiful Fortune,
Now my dear lady,[48] hath mine enemies
Brought to this shore; and by my prescience   180
I find my zenith doth depend upon
A most auspicious star, whose influence
If now I court not but omit, my fortunes
Will ever after droop. Here cease more questions:
Thou art inclined to sleep; 'tis a good dulness,
And give it way: I know thou canst not choose.

                              [MIRANDA *sleeps.*]

---

[46] covered   [47] courage to endure   [48] kind patroness

Come away, servant, come. I am ready now.
Approach, my Ariel, come.

Enter ARIEL.

ARIEL. All hail, great master! grave sir, hail! I come
  To answer thy best pleasure; be 't to fly,   190
  To swim, to dive into the fire, to ride
  On the curled clouds, to thy strong bidding task[49]
  Ariel and all his quality.[50]
PROSPERO.   Hast thou, spirit,
  Performed to point[51] the tempest that I bade thee?
ARIEL. To every article.
  I boarded the king's ship; now on the beak,[52]
  Now in the waist, the deck, in every cabin,
  I flamed amazement:[53] sometime I 'ld divide,
  And burn in many places; on the topmast,
  The yards and bowsprit, would I flame distinctly,[54]   200
  Then meet and join. Jove's lightnings, the precursors
  O' the dreadful thunder-claps, more momentary[55]
  And sight-outrunning were not; the fire and cracks
  Of sulphurous roaring the most mighty Neptune
  Seem to besiege and make his bold waves tremble,
  Yea, his dread trident shake.
PROSPERO.   My brave spirit!
  Who was so firm, so constant, that this coil[56]
  Would not infect his reason?
ARIEL.   Not a soul
  But felt a fever of the mad[57] and played
  Some tricks of desperation. All but mariners   210
  Plunged in the foaming brine and quit the vessel,
  Then all afire with me: the king's son, Ferdinand,
  With hair up-staring,—then like reeds, not hair,—
  Was the first man that leaped; cried, "Hell is empty,
  And all the devils are here."
PROSPERO.   Why, that's my spirit!
  But was not this nigh shore?
ARIEL.   Close by, my master.
PROSPERO. But are they, Ariel, safe?
ARIEL.   Not a hair perished;
  On their sustaining[58] garments not a blemish,
  But fresher than before: and, as thou badest me,
  In troops I have dispersed them 'bout the isle.   220

---

[49] put to the test   [50] skill   [51] to the most exact detail   [52] prow
[53] caused terror by becoming St. Elmo's fire   [54] in several places at once
[55] instantaneous   [56] turmoil   [57] such fever as madmen feel
[58] holding them up

The king's son have I landed by himself;
Whom I left cooling of the air with sighs
In an odd angle of the isle and sitting,
His arms in this sad knot.

PROSPERO.   Of the king's ship
The mariners say how thou hast disposed
And all the rest o' the fleet.

ARIEL.   Safely in harbor
Is the king's ship; in the deep nook, where once
Thou call'dst me up at midnight to fetch dew
From the still-vexed Bermoothes,[59] there she's hid:
The mariners all under hatches stowed;   230
Who, with a charm joined to their suffered labor,
I have left asleep: and for the rest o' the fleet
Which I dispersed, they all have met again
And are upon the Mediterranean flote,[60]
Bound sadly home for Naples,
Supposing that they saw the king's ship wrecked
And his great person perish.

PROSPERO.   Ariel, thy charge
Exactly is performed: but there's more work.
What is the time o' the day?

ARIEL.   Past the mid season.

PROSPERO. At least two glasses.[61] The time 'twixt six and now   240
Must by us both be spent most preciously.

ARIEL. Is there more toil? Since thou dost give me pains,
Let me remember thee what thou hast promised,
Which is not yet performed me.

PROSPERO.   How now? moody?
What is 't thou canst demand?

ARIEL.   My liberty.

PROSPERO. Before the time be out? no more!

ARIEL.   I prithee,
Remember I have done thee worthy service;
Told thee no lies, made thee no mistakings, served
Without or grudge or grumblings: thou didst promise
To bate me[62] a full year.

PROSPERO.   Dost thou forget   250
From what a torment I did free thee?

ARIEL.   No.

PROSPERO. Thou dost, and think'st it much to tread the ooze
Of the salt deep,
To run upon the sharp wind of the north,

---

[59] ever storm-beaten Bermuda   [60] sea   [61] hourglasses; hours
[62] reduce my term by

To do me business in the veins o' the earth
When it is baked with frost.
ARIEL.   I do not, sir.
PROSPERO. Thou liest, malignant thing! Hast thou forgot
  The foul witch Sycorax, who with age and envy [63]
  Was grown into a hoop? hast thou forgot her?
ARIEL. No, sir.
PROSPERO.   Thou hast. Where was she born? speak; tell me.   260
ARIEL. Sir, in Argier. [64]
PROSPERO.   O, was she so? I must
  Once in a month recount what thou hast been,
  Which thou forget'st. This damned witch Sycorax,
  For mischiefs manifold and sorceries terrible
  To enter human hearing, from Argier,
  Thou know'st, was banished: for one thing [65] she did
  They would not take her life. Is not this true?
ARIEL. Ay, sir.
PROSPERO. This blue-eyed [66] hag was hither brought with child
  And here was left by the sailors. Thou, my slave,   270
  As thou report'st thyself, wast then her servant;
  And, for thou wast a spirit too delicate
  To act her earthly and abhorred commands,
  Refusing her grand hests, she did confine thee,
  By help of her more potent ministers
  And in her most unmitigable rage,
  Into a cloven pine; within which rift
  Imprisoned thou didst painfully remain
  A dozen years; within which space she died
  And left thee there; where thou did'st vent thy groans   280
  As fast as mill-wheels strike. Then was this island—
  Save for the son that she did litter here,
  A freckled whelp hag-born—not honored with
  A human shape.
ARIEL.   Yes, Caliban her son.
PROSPERO. Dull thing, I say so; he, that Caliban
  Whom now I keep in service. Thou best know'st
  What torment I did find thee in; thy groans
  Did make wolves howl and penetrate the breasts
  Of ever angry bears: it was a torment
  To lay upon the damned, which Sycorax   290
  Could not again undo: it was mine art,
  When I arrived and heard thee, that made gape
  The pine and let thee out.

[63] malice   [64] Algeria   [65] one good deed
[66] with dark circles under her eyes

ARIEL.   I thank thee, master.
PROSPERO. If thou more murmur'st, I will rend an oak
  And peg thee in his knotty entrails till
  Thou hast howled away twelve winters.
ARIEL.   Pardon, master;
  I will be correspondent[67] to command
  And do my spiriting gently.
PROSPERO.   Do so, and after two days
  I will discharge thee.
ARIEL.   That's my noble master!
  What shall I do? say what; what shall I do?   300
PROSPERO. Go make thyself like a nymph o' the sea : be subject
  To no sight but thine and mine, invisible
  To every eyeball else. Go take this shape
  And hither come in 't : go, hence with diligence!
                                          [Exit ARIEL.]

  Awake, dear heart, awake! thou hast slept well;
  Awake!
MIRANDA. The strangeness of your story put
  Heaviness in me.
PROSPERO.   Shake it off. Come on;
  We'll visit Caliban my slave, who never
  Yields us kind answer.
MIRANDA.   'Tis a villain, sir,   310
  I do not love to look on.
PROSPERO.   But, as 'tis,
  We cannot miss him : he does make our fire,
  Fetch in our wood and serves in offices
  That profit us. What, ho! slave! Caliban!
  Thou earth, thou! speak.
CALIBAN [Within].   There's wood enough within.
PROSPERO. Come forth, I say! there's other business for thee :
  Come, thou tortoise! when?[68]

              Re-enter ARIEL *like a water-nymph.*

  Fine apparition! My quaint[69] Ariel,
  Hark in thine ear.
ARIEL.   My lord, it shall be done.
                                                    [Exit.]
PROSPERO. Thou poisonous slave, got by the devil himself   320
  Upon thy wicked dam, come forth!

                    Enter CALIBAN.

  ⁶⁷ obedient   ⁶⁸ an exclamation of impatience   ⁶⁹ ingenious

CALIBAN. As wicked dew as e'er my mother brushed
  With raven's feather from unwholesome fen
  Drop on you both! a south-west[70] blow on ye
  And blister you all o'er!
PROSPERO. For this, be sure, to-night thou shalt have cramps,
  Side-stitches that shall pen thy breath up; urchins[71]
  Shall, for that vast[72] of night that they may work,
  All exercise on thee; thou shalt be pinched
  As thick as honeycomb, each pinch more stinging   330
  Than bees that made 'em.
CALIBAN.   I must eat my dinner.
  This island's mine, by Sycorax my mother,
  Which thou takest from me. When thou camest first,
  Thou strokedst me and madest much of me, wouldst give me
  Water with berries in 't, and teach me how
  To name the bigger light, and how the less,
  That burn by day and night: and then I loved thee
  And showed thee all the qualities o' the isle,
  The fresh springs, brine-pits, barren place and fertile:
  Cursed be I that did so! All the charms   340
  Of Sycorax, toads, beetles, bats, light on you!
  For I am all the subjects that you have,
  Which first was mine own king: and here you sty me
  In this hard rock, whiles you do keep from me
  The rest o' the island.
PROSPERO.   Thou most lying slave,
  Whom stripes may move, not kindness! I have used thee,
  Filth as thou art, with human care, and lodged thee
  In mine own cell, till thou didst seek to violate
  The honor of my child.
CALIBAN. O ho, O ho! would't had been done!   350
  Thou didst prevent me; I had peopled else
  This isle with Calibans.
PROSPERO.   Abhorréd slave,
  Which any print of goodness wilt not take,
  Being capable of all ill! I pitied thee,
  Took pains to make thee speak, taught thee each hour
  One thing or other: when thou didst not, savage,
  Know thine own meaning, but wouldst gabble like
  A thing most brutish, I endowed thy purposes
  With words that made them known. But thy vile race,
  Though thou didst learn, had that in 't which good natures 360

[70] A southwest wind in England was supposed to bring infection with its fog.
[71] imps in the shape of hedgehogs   [72] abyss

Could not abide to be with; therefore wast thou
Deservedly confined into this rock,
Who hadst deserved more than a prison.

CALIBAN. You taught me language; and my profit on 't
Is, I know how to curse. The red plague rid you[73]
For learning me your language!

PROSPERO.   Hag-seed, hence!
Fetch us in fuel; and be quick, thou'rt best,
To answer other business. Shrug'st thou, malice?
If thou neglect'st or dost unwillingly
What I command, I'll rack thee with old cramps,   370
Fill all thy bones with aches, make thee roar
That beasts shall tremble at thy din.

CALIBAN.   No, pray thee.
[Aside] I must obey: his art is of such power,
It would control my dam's god, Setebos,[74]
And make a vassal of him.

PROSPERO. So, slave; hence!

                                                    [Exit CALIBAN.]

        Re-enter ARIEL, invisible, playing and singing;
                FERDINAND following.

                    ARIEL'S SONG.

        Come unto these yellow sands,
            And then take hands:
        Courtesied when you have and kissed
            The wild waves whist,[75]   380
        Foot it featly[76] here and there;
        And, sweet sprites, the burthen[77] bear.

BURTHEN [dispersedly[78]]. Hark, hark!
                                    Bow-wow.
        The watch-dogs bark:
                                    Bow-wow.
ARIEL.   Hark, hark! I hear
            The strain of strutting chanticleer
            Cry, Cock-a-diddle-dow.

FERDINAND. Where should this music be? i' the air or the earth?
It sounds no more: and, sure, it waits upon
Some god o' the island. Sitting on a bank,   390
Weeping again the king my father's wreck,

---

[73] the bubonic plague destroy you
[74] a god or devil thought to be worshipped by American Indians
[75] being hushed   [76] gracefully   [77] refrain
[78] coming from various directions

This music crept by me upon the waters,
Allaying both their fury and my passion
With its sweet air : thence I have followed it,
Or it hath drawn me rather. But 'tis gone.
No, it begins again.

ARIEL SINGS.

> *Full fathom five thy father lies;*
> *Of his bones are coral made;*
> *Those are pearls that were his eyes:*
> *Nothing of him that doth fade*   400
> *But doth suffer a sea-change*
> *Into something rich and strange.*
> *Sea-nymphs hourly ring his knell:*

BURTHEN.   *Ding-dong.*

ARIEL. Hark! now I hear them,—Ding-dong, bell.
FERDINAND. The ditty[79] does remember my drowned father.
This is no mortal business, nor no sound
That the earth owes.[80] I hear it now above me.
PROSPERO. The fringéd curtains of thine eye advance[81]
And say what thou seest yond.
MIRANDA.   What is 't? a spirit?   410
Lord, how it looks about! Believe me, sir
It carries a brave[82] form. But 'tis a spirit.
PROSPERO. No, wench; it eats and sleeps and hath such senses
As we have, such. This gallant which thou seest
Was in the wreck; and, but he's something stained
With grief that's beauty's canker,[83] thou mightst call him
A goodly[84] person: he hath lost his fellows
And strays about to find 'em.
MIRANDA.   I might call him
A thing divine, for nothing natural
I ever saw so noble.   420
PROSPERO [*Aside*]. It goes on, I see,
As my soul prompts it. Spirit, fine spirit! I'll free thee
Within two days for this.
FERDINAND.   Most sure, the goddess
On whom these airs attend! Vouchsafe my prayer
May know[85] if you remain[86] upon this island;
And that you will some good instruction give

---

[79] words to the song   [80] possesses   [81] lift up   [82] handsome; gallant
[83] canker-worm or caterpillar that eats rosebuds   [84] handsome
[85] may gain the knowledge from you   [86] dwell

How I may bear me here : my prime request,
Which I do last pronounce, is, O you wonder !
If you be maid or no ?[87]
MIRANDA.   No wonder, sir ;
But certainly a maid.
FERDINAND.   My language ! heavens !   430
I am the best of them that speak this speech,
Were I but where 'tis spoken.
PROSPERO.   How ? the best ?
What wert thou, if the King of Naples heard thee ?
FERDINAND. A single[88] thing, as I am now, that wonders
To hear thee speak of Naples. He does hear me ;
And that he does I weep : myself am Naples,[89]
Who with mine eyes, never since at ebb, beheld
The king my father wrecked.
MIRANDA.   Alack, for mercy !
FERDINAND. Yes, faith, and all his lords ; the Duke of Milan
And his brave son being twain.
PROSPERO [*Aside*].   The Duke of Milan   440
And his more braver daughter could control[90] thee,
If now 'twere fit to do 't. At the first sight
They have changed eyes.[91] Delicate Ariel,
I'll set thee free for this. [*To* FERDINAND.] A word, good sir ;
I fear you have done yourself some wrong :[92] a word.
MIRANDA. Why speaks my father so ungently ? This
Is the third man that e'er I saw, the first
That e'er I sighed for : pity move my father
To be inclined my way !
FERDINAND.   O, if a virgin,
And your affection not gone forth, I'll make you   450
The queen of Naples.
PROSPERO.   Soft, sir ! one word more.
[*Aside*] They are both in either's powers ; but this swift business
I must uneasy make, lest too light winning
Make the prize light. [*To* FERDINAND.] One word more ; I charge
    thee
That thou attend me : thou dost here usurp
The name thou owest[93] not ; and hast put thyself
Upon this island as a spy, to win it
From me, the lord on 't.
FERDINAND.   No, as I am a man.

---

[87] i.e., or a spirit   [88] solitary and hence helpless   [89] King of Naples
[90] confute   [91] have exchanged loving looks
[92] been untrue to your better nature   [93] ownest

MIRANDA. There's nothing ill can dwell in such a temple: 460
  If the ill spirit have so fair a house,
  Good things will strive to dwell with 't.[94]
PROSPERO.   Follow me.
  Speak not you for him; he's a traitor. Come;
  I'll manacle thy neck and feet together:
  Sea-water shalt thou drink; thy food shall be
  The fresh-brook mussels, withered roots and husks
  Wherein the acorn cradled. Follow.
FERDINAND.   No;
  I will resist such entertainment till
  Mine enemy has more power.

                   [*Draws, and is charmed from moving.*]
MIRANDA.   O dear father,
  Make not too rash a trial of him, for   470
  He's gentle and not fearful.[95]
PROSPERO.   What? I say,
  My foot[96] my tutor? Put thy sword up, traitor;
  Who makest a show but darest not strike, thy conscience
  Is so possessed with guilt: come from thy ward,[97]
  For I can here disarm thee with this stick[98]
  And make thy weapon drop.
MIRANDA.   Beseech you, father.
PROSPERO. Hence! hang not on my garments.
MIRANDA.   Sir, have pity;
  I'll be his surety.
PROSPERO.   Silence! one word more
  Shall make me chide thee, if not hate thee. What!
  An advocate for an imposter! hush!   480
  Thou think'st there is no more such shapes as he,
  Having seen but him and Caliban: foolish wench!
  To[99] the most of men this is a Caliban
  And they to him are angels.
MIRANDA.   My affections
  Are then most humble; I have no ambition
  To see a goodlier man.
PROSPERO.   Come on; obey:
  Thy nerves[100] are in their infancy again
  And have no vigor in them.
FERDINAND.   So they are;
  My spirits, as in a dream, are all bound up.

---

[94] i.e., to crowd it out   [95] well born and no coward
[96] an inferior part; i.e., Miranda   [97] abandon your posture of defense
[98] Prospero's magic wand   [99] in comparison with   [100] sinews

My father's loss, the weakness which I feel,   490
The wreck of all my friends, nor this man's threats,
To whom I am subdued, are but light to me,
Might I but through my prison once a day
Behold this maid : all corners else o' the earth
Let liberty make use of ; [101] space enough
Have I in such a prison.
PROSPERO [*Aside*].   It works. [*To* FERDINAND.] Come on.
Thou hast done well, fine Ariel ! [*To* FERDINAND.] Follow me.
[*To* ARIEL.] Hark what thou else shalt do me.
MIRANDA.   Be of comfort ;
My father's of a better nature, sir,
Than he appears by speech : this is unwonted   500
Which now came from him.
PROSPERO.   Thou shalt be as free
As mountain winds : but then exactly do
All points of my command.
ARIEL.   To the syllable.
PROSPERO. Come, follow. Speak not for him.

                                                        [*Exeunt.*]

ACT II

Scene I
Another part of the island.

Enter ALONSO, SEBASTIAN, ANTONIO, GONZALO,
ADRIAN, FRANCISCO, *and others.*

GONZALO. Beseech you, sir, be merry ; you have cause,
So have we all, of joy ; for our escape
Is much beyond our loss. Our hint [102] of woe
Is common ; every day some sailor's wife,
The masters of some merchant [103] and the merchant
Have just our theme of woe ; but [104] for the miracle,
I mean our preservation, few in millions
Can speak like us : then wisely, good sir, weigh
Our sorrow with our comfort.
ALONSO.   Prithee, peace.
SEBASTIAN. He receives comfort like cold porridge.   10

---

[101] Let those who are free have all the rest of the world.   [102] occasion for
[103] merchantman ; commercial ship   [104] as for

ANTONIO. The visitor[105] will not give him o'er so.

SEBASTIAN. Look, he's winding up the watch of his wit; by and by it will strike.

GONZALO. Sir,—

SEBASTIAN. One: tell.[106]

GONZALO. When every grief is entertained[107] that 's offered,
    Comes to the entertainer—

SEBASTIAN. A dollar.

GONZALO. Dolor comes to him, indeed: you have spoken truer than
    you purposed.   20

SEBASTIAN. You have taken it wiselier than I meant you should.

GONZALO. Therefore, my lord,—

ANTONIO. Fie, what a spendthrift is he of his tongue!

ALONSO. I prithee, spare.

GONZALO. Well, I have done: but yet,—

SEBASTIAN. He will be talking.

ANTONIO. Which, of he or Adrian, for a good wager, first begins to
    crow?

SEBASTIAN. The old cock.

ANTONIO. The cockerel.[108]   30

SEBASTIAN. Done. The wager?

ANTONIO. A laughter.

SEBASTIAN. A match!

ADRIAN. Though this island seem to be desert,—

SEBASTIAN. Ha, ha, ha! So, you're paid.

ADRIAN. Uninhabitable and almost inaccessible,—

SEBASTIAN. Yet,—

ADRIAN. Yet,—

ANTONIO. He could not miss 't.   39

ADRIAN. It must needs be of subtle, tender and delicate temperance.[109]

ANTONIO. Temperance[110] was a delicate wench.

SEBASTIAN. Ay, and a subtle; as he most learnedly delivered.

ADRIAN. The air breathes upon us here most sweetly.

SEBASTIAN. As if it had lungs and rotten ones.

ANTONIO. Or as 'twere perfumed by a fen.

GONZALO. Here is every thing advantageous to life.

ANTONIO. True; save means to live.

SEBASTIAN. Of that there's none, or little.

GONZALO. How lush and lusty the grass looks! how green!

ANTONIO. The ground indeed is tawny.   50

SEBASTIAN. With an eye of green in 't.

---

[105] spiritual counselor   [106] count   [107] accepted   [108] Gonzalo and Adrian
[109] temperature   [110] a character in a morality play

ANTONIO. He misses not much.

SEBASTIAN. No; he doth but mistake the truth totally.

GONZALO. But the rarity of it is,—which is indeed almost beyond credit,—

SEBASTIAN. As many vouched rarities[111] are.

GONZALO. That our garments, being, as they were, drenched in the sea, hold notwithstanding their freshness and glosses, being rather new-dyed than stained with salt water.   59

ANTONIO. If but one of his pockets could speak, would it not say he lies?

SEBASTIAN. Ay, or very falsely pocket up his report.

GONZALO. Methinks our garments are now as fresh as when we put them on first in Afric, at the marriage of the king's fair daughter Claribel to the King of Tunis.

SEBASTIAN. 'Twas a sweet marriage, and we prosper well in our return.

ADRIAN. Tunis was never graced before with such a paragon to their queen.

GONZALO. Not since widow Dido's[112] time.   70

ANTONIO. Widow! a pox o' that! How came that widow in? widow Dido!

SEBASTIAN. What if he had said "widower Æneas" too? Good Lord, how you take it!

ADRIAN. "Widow Dido" said you? you make me study of that: she was of Carthage, not of Tunis.

GONZALO. This Tunis, sir, was Carthage.

ADRIAN. Carthage?

GONZALO. I assure you, Carthage.   79

SEBASTIAN. His word is more than the miraculous harp; he hath raised the wall and houses too.[113]

ANTONIO. What impossible matter will he make easy next?

SEBASTIAN. I think he will carry this island home in his pocket and give it his son for an apple.

ANTONIO. And, sowing the kernels of it in the sea, bring forth more islands.

GONZALO. Ay.

ANTONIO. Why, in good time.

GONZALO. Sir, we were talking that our garments seem now as fresh as when we were at Tunis at the marriage of your daughter, who is now queen.   91

[111] strange tales vouched for by their narrators

[112] After the murder of her husband, Sichæus, Dido went from Greece to Africa and founded Carthage. Later she fell in love with Æneas.

[113] Amphion is said to have made the walls of Thebes rise by playing on his harp. Here Sebastian jests that Gonzalo has raised the wall and houses of Carthage, long destroyed, by identifying it with modern Thebes.

ANTONIO. And the rarest that e'er came there.

SEBASTIAN. Bate,[114] I beseech you, widow Dido.

ANTONIO. O, widow Dido! ay, widow Dido.

GONZALO. Is not, sir, my doublet as fresh as the first day I wore it? I
mean, in a sort.

ANTONIO. That sort was well fished for.[115]

GONZALO. When I wore it at your daughter's marriage?

ALONSO. You cram these words into mine ears against
  The stomach of my sense. Would I had never   100
  Married my daughter there! for, coming thence,
  My son is lost and, in my rate,[116] she too,
  Who is so far from Italy removed
  I ne'er again shall see her. O thou mine heir
  Of Naples and of Milan, what strange fish
  Hath made his meal on thee?

FRANCISCO.   Sir, he may live:
  I saw him beat the surges under him,
  And ride upon their backs; he trod the water,
  Whose enmity he flung aside, and breasted
  The surge most swoln that met him; his bold head   110
  'Bove the contentious waves he kept, and oared
  Himself with his good arms in lusty stroke
  To the shore, that o'er his wave-torn basis[117] bowed,
  As stooping to relieve him: I not doubt
  He came alive to land.

ALONSO.   No, no, he's gone.

SEBASTIAN. Sir, you may thank yourself for this great loss,
  That would not bless our Europe with your daughter,
  But rather lose her to an African;
  Where she at least is banished from your eye,
  Who[118] hath cause to wet the grief on 't.

ALONSO.   Prithee, peace.   120

SEBASTIAN. You were kneeled to and importuned otherwise
  By all of us, and the fair soul herself
  Weighed between loathness and obedience, at
  Which end o' the beam should bow. We have lost your son,
  I fear, for ever: Milan and Naples have
  Moe[119] widows in them of this business' making
  Than we bring men to comfort them:
  The fault's your own.

ALONSO.   So is the dear'st[120] o' the loss.

GONZALO. My lord Sebastian,
  The truth you speak doth lack some gentleness   130

---

[114] except   [115] The word "sort" was a lucky catch.   [116] estimation
[117] its . . . base   [118] your eye   [119] more   [120] worst; most costly

And time to speak it in : you rub the sore,
When you should bring the plaster.

SEBASTIAN.   Very well.

ANTONIO. And most chirurgeonly.[121]

GONZALO. It is foul weather in us all, good sir,
When you are cloudy.

SEBASTIAN.   Foul weather?

ANTONIO.   Very foul.

GONZALO. Had I plantation of this isle, my lord,—

ANTONIO. He 'ld sow 't with nettle-seed.

SEBASTIAN.   Or docks, or mallows.

GONZALO. And were the king on 't, what would I do?

SEBASTIAN. 'Scape being drunk for want of wine.

GONZALO. I' the commonwealth I would by contraries   140
Execute all things ; for no kind of traffic
Would I admit ; no name of magistrate ;
Letters should not be known ; riches, poverty,
And use of service,[122] none ; contract, succession,
Bourn,[123] bound of land, tilth,[124] vineyard, none ;
No use of metal, corn, or wine, or oil ;
No occupation ; all men idle, all ;
And women too, but innocent and pure ;
No sovereignty ;—

SEBASTIAN.   Yet he would be king on 't.   149

ANTONIO. The latter end of his commonwealth forgets the beginning.

GONZALO. All things in common nature should produce
Without sweat or endeavor : treason, felony,
Sword, pike, knife, gun, or need of any engine,[125]
Would I not have ; but nature should bring forth,
Of it[126] own kind, all foison,[127] all abundance,
To feed my innocent people.

SEBASTIAN. No marrying 'mong his subjects?

ANTONIO. None, man ; all idle :[128] whores and knaves.

GONZALO. I would with such perfection govern, sir,
To excel the golden age.

SEBASTIAN.   God save his majesty!   160

ANTONIO. Long live Gonzalo!

GONZALO.   And,—do you mark me, sir?

ALONZO. Prithee, no more : thou dost talk nothing to me.

GONZALO. I do well believe your highness ; and did it to minister occasion to these gentlemen, who are of such sensible[129] and nimble lungs that they always use to laugh at nothing.

---

121 like a surgeon   122 ceremony   123 boundary   124 tillage
125 military machine   126 its   127 plenty   128 worthless   129 sensitive

ANTONIO. 'Twas you we laughed at.

GONZALO. Who in this kind of merry fooling am nothing to you: so you may continue and laugh at nothing still.

ANTONIO. What a blow was there given!

SEBASTIAN. An it had not fallen flat-long.   170

GONZALO. You are gentlemen of brave mettle; you would lift the moon out of her sphere, if she would continue in it five weeks without changing.[130]

Enter ARIEL, *invisible, playing solemn music.*

SEBASTIAN. We would so, and then go a batfowling.[131]

ANTONIO. Nay, good my lord, be not angry.

GONZALO. No, I warrant you; I will not adventure[132] my discretion so weakly. Will you laugh me asleep, for I am very heavy?

ANTONIO. Go sleep, and hear us.

    [All sleep except ALONSO, SEBASTIAN, *and* ANTONIO.]

ALONZO. What, all so soon asleep! I wish mine eyes
Would, with themselves, shut up my thoughts: I find   180
They are inclined to do so.

SEBASTIAN.   Please you, sir,
Do not omit[133] the heavy offer[134] of it:
It seldom visits sorrow; when it doth,
It is a comforter.

ANTONIO.   We two, my lord,
Will guard your person while you take your rest,
And watch your safety.

ALONZO.   Thank you. Wondrous heavy.

                  *[*ALONSO *sleeps. Exit* ARIEL.]

SEBASTIAN. What a strange drowsiness possesses them!

ANTONIO. It is the quality o' the climate.

SEBASTIAN.   Why
Doth it not then our eyelids sink? I find not
Myself disposed to sleep.

ANTONIO.   Nor I; my spirits are nimble.[135]   190
They fell together all, as by consent;
They dropped, as by a thunder-stroke. What might,
Worthy Sebastian? O, what might?—No more:—
And yet methinks I see it in thy face,
What thou shouldst be: the occasion speaks thee,[136] and
My strong imagination sees a crown
Dropping upon thy head.

---

[130] undertake to correct the moon if she did not follow her normal course of waxing and waning
[131] bird-hunting at night with a light and a stick (bat)   [132] risk
[133] fail to accept   [134] the invitation which your drowsiness extends
[135] alert   [136] proclaims thee (king)

SEBASTIAN.   What, art thou waking?
ANTONIO. Do you not hear me speak?
SEBASTIAN.   I do; and surely
   It is a sleepy language and thou speak'st
   Out of thy sleep. What is it thou didst say?   200
   This is a strange repose, to be asleep
   With eyes wide open; standing, speaking, moving,
   And yet so fast asleep.
ANTONIO.   Noble Sebastian,
   Thou let'st thy fortune sleep—die, rather; wink'st
   Whiles thou art waking.
SEBASTIAN.   Thou dost snore distinctly;
   There's meaning in thy snores.
ANTONIO.   I am more serious than my custom: you
   Must be so too, if heed me; which to do
   Trebles thee o'er.
SEBASTIAN.   Well, I am standing water.[137]
ANTONIO. I'll teach you how to flow.
SEBASTIAN.   Do so: to ebb   210
   Hereditary sloth instructs me.
ANTONIO.   O,
   If you but knew how you the purpose[138] cherish
   Whiles thus you mock it! how, in stripping[139] it,
   You more invest it! Ebbing men, indeed,
   Most often do so near the bottom run
   By their own fear or sloth.
SEBASTIAN.   Prithee, say on:
   The setting[140] of thine eye and cheek proclaim
   A matter from thee, and a birth indeed
   Which throes thee much to yield.
ANTONIO.   Thus, sir:
   Although this lord of weak remembrance, this,   220
   Who shall be of as little memory
   When he is earthed,[141] hath here almost persuaded,—
   For he's a spirit of persuasion, only
   Professes to persuade,—the king his son's alive,
   'Tis as impossible that he's undrowned
   As he that sleeps here swims.
SEBASTIAN.   I have no hope
   That he's undrowned.
ANTONIO.   O, out of that "no hope"
   What great hope have you! no hope that way is

---

[137] i.e., when the tide neither ebbs nor flows   [138] i.e., to be king
[139] i.e., of pretense   [140] fixed expression
[141] The memory of him after he is buried will be as short as his own.

Another way so high a hope that even
Ambition cannot pierce a wink beyond,   230
But doubt discovery there.[142] Will you grant with me
That Ferdinand is drowned?

SEBASTIAN.   He's gone.

ANTONIO.   Then, tell me,
Who's the next heir of Naples?

SEBASTIAN.   Claribel.

ANTONIO. She that is queen of Tunis; she that dwells
Ten leagues beyond man's life; she that from Naples
Can have no note,[143] unless the sun were post—
The man i' the moon's too slow—till newborn chins
Be rough and razorable; she that—from whom?
We all were sea-swallowed, though some cast[144] again,
And by that destiny to perform an act   240
Whereof what's past is prologue, what to come
In yours and my discharge.[145]

SEBASTIAN.   What stuff is this! how say you?
'Tis true, my brother's daughter's queen of Tunis;
So is she heir of Naples; 'twixt which regions
There is some space.

ANTONIO.   A space whose every cubit
Seems to cry out, "How shall that Claribel
Measure us back to Naples?[146] Keep in Tunis,
And let Sebastian wake." Say, this were death
That now hath seized them;[147] why, they were no worse
Than now they are. There be that can rule Naples   250
As well as he that sleeps; lords that can prate
As amply and unnecessarily
As this Gonzalo; I myself could make
A chough of as deep chat.[148] O, that you bore
The mind that I do! what a sleep were this
For your advancement! Do you understand me?

SEBASTIAN. Methinks I do.

ANTONIO.   And how does your content
Tender your own good fortune?[149]

SEBASTIAN.   I remember
You did supplant your brother Prospero.

ANTONIO.   True:
And look how well my garments sit upon me;   260

---

[142] must doubt the truth of what it sees there   [143] information
[144] vomited up; or assigned a role in a play   [145] yours and mine to perform
[146] find her way back to us   [147] all the sleepers
[148] a crow talk as deep stuff
[149] With how much pleasure do you regard your good fortune?

Much feater[150] than before : my brother's servants
Were then my fellows ; now they are my men.
SEBASTIAN. But, for[151] your conscience?
ANTONIO. Ay, sir ; where lies that ? if 'twere a kibe,[152]
'Twould put me to my slipper : but I feel not
This deity in my bosom : twenty consciences,
That stand 'twixt me and Milan, candied be they
And melt ere they molest ![153] Here lies your brother,
No better than the earth he lies upon,
If he were that which now he's like, that's dead ;   270
Whom I, with this obedient steel, three inches of it,
Can lay to bed for ever ; whiles you, doing thus,
To the perpetual wink[154] for aye might put
This ancient morsel, this Sir Prudence, who
Should not upbraid our course. For all the rest,
They'll take suggestion as a cat laps milk ;
They'll tell the clock to[155] any business that
We say befits the hour.
SEBASTIAN.   Thy case, dear friend,
Shall be my precedent ; as thou got'st Milan.
I'll come by Naples. Draw thy sword : one stroke   280
Shall free thee from the tribute which thou payest ;
And I the king shall love thee.
ANTONIO.   Draw together ;
And when I rear my hand, do you the like,
To fall it on Gonzalo.
SEBASTIAN.   O, but one word.

                                                    [*They talk apart.*]

                        Re-enter ARIEL, *invisible.*

ARIEL. My master through his art foresees the danger
That you, his friend,[156] are in ; and sends me forth—
For else his project dies[157]—to keep them living
                                          [*Sings in* GONZALO'S *ear.*]

                    While you here do snoring lie,
                    Open-eyed conspiracy
                          His time doth take.   290
                    If of life you keep a care,
                    Shake off slumber, and beware :
                          Awake, awake!

[150] more becomingly   [151] as to   [152] sore heel
  [153] Let the twenty consciences that stand between me and the duchy of Milan be
crystallized and then melt rather than disturb me.
    [154] everlasting sleep   [155] count the strokes and agree that it's time for
    [156] Gonzalo   [157] plan miscarries

ANTONIO. Then let us both be sudden.
GONZALO.   Now, good angels
  Preserve the king.

                                        [*They wake.*]

ALONSO. Why, how now? ho, awake! Why are you drawn?
  Wherefore this ghastly looking?
GONZALO.   What's the matter?
SEBASTIAN. Whiles we stood here securing your repose,
  Even now, we heard a hollow burst of bellowing
  Like bulls, or rather lions: did 't not wake you?   300
  It struck mine ear most terribly.
ALONSO.   I heard nothing.
ANTONIO. O, 'twas a din to fright a monster's ear,
  To make an earthquake! sure, it was the roar
  Of a whole herd of lions.
ALONSO.   Heard you this, Gonzalo?
GONZALO. Upon mine honor, sir, I heard a humming,[158]
  And that a strange one too, which did awake me:
  I shaked you, sir, and cried: as mine eyes opened,
  I saw their weapons drawn: there was a noise,
  That's verily. 'Tis best we stand upon our guard,
  Or that we quit this place: let's draw our weapons.   310
ALONSO. Lead off this ground; and let's make further search
  For my poor son.
GONZALO. Heavens keep him from these beasts!
  For he is, sure, i' the island.
ALONSO.   Lead away.
ARIEL. Prospero my lord shall know what I have done:
  So, king, go safely on to seek thy son.

                                        [*Exeunt.*]

SCENE II
Another part of the island.

Enter CALIBAN *with a burden of wood. A noise of thunder heard.*

CALIBAN. All the infections that the sun sucks up
  From bogs, fens, flats, on Prosper fall and make him
  By inch-meal[159] a disease! His spirits hear me
  And yet I needs must curse. But they'll nor pinch,
  Fright me with urchin-shows,[160] pitch me i' the mire,
  Nor lead me, like a firebrand,[161] in the dark
  Out of my way, unless he bid 'em; but
  For every trifle are they set upon me;

---

[158] i.e., Ariel's song   [159] inch by inch; cf. *piecemeal*
[160] apparitions of goblins   [161] will-'o-the-wisp

Sometime like apes that mow[162] and chatter at me
And after bite me, then like hedgehogs which   10
Lie tumbling in my barefoot way and mount
Their pricks at my footfall; sometime am I
All wound with adders who with cloven tongues
Do hiss me into madness.

Enter TRINCULO.

Lo, now, lo!
Here comes a spirit of his, and to torment me
For bringing wood in slowly. I'll fall flat;
Perchance he will not mind me.

TRINCULO. Here's neither bush nor shrub, to bear off any weather at
all, and another storm brewing; I hear it sing i' the wind: yond same
black cloud, yond huge one, looks like a foul bombard[163] that   20
would shed his liquor. If it should thunder as it did before, I know not
where to hide my head: yond same cloud cannot choose but fall by
pailfuls. What have we here? a man or a fish? dead or alive? A fish:
he smells like a fish; a very ancient and fish-like smell; a kind of not of
the newest Poor-John.[164] A strange fish! Were I in England now, as
once I was, and had but this fish painted, not a holiday fool there but
would give a piece of silver: there would this monster make a man;[165]
any strange beast there makes a man: when they will not give a doit[166]
to relieve a lame beggar, they will lay out ten to see a dead Indian.
Legged like a man! and his fins like arms! Warm o' my troth! I   30
do now let loose my opinion; hold it no longer: this is no fish, but an
islander, that hath lately suffered by a thunderbolt.

[*Thunder.*]

Alas, the storm is come again! my best way is to creep under his
gaberdine;[167] there is no other shelter hereabout: misery acquaints a
man with strange bed-fellows. I will here shroud till the dregs of the
storm be past.

Enter STEPHANO, *singing: a bottle in his hand.*

STEPHANO.

I shall no more to sea, to sea,
Here shall I die ashore—

---

[162] make faces
[163] a wine jug made of black leather; so called because of its fancied resemblance
to a cannon
[164] salted hake; a kind of codfish   [165] make a man's fortune
[166] a very small Dutch coin, worth half an English farthing
[167] a long cloak

This is a very scurvy[168] tune to sing at a man's funeral: well, here's my comfort. 40

[*Drinks. Sings.*]

> The master, the swabber, the boatswain and I,
>   The gunner and his mate
> Loved Mall, Meg and Marian and Margery,
>   But none of us cared for Kate;
> For she had a tongue with a tang,
>   Would cry to a sailor, Go hang!
> She loved not the savor of tar nor of pitch,
> Yet a tailor might scratch her where'er she did itch:
>   Then to sea, boys, and let her go hang!

This is a scurvy tune too: but here's my comfort. 50

[*Drinks.*]

CALIBAN. Do not torment me: Oh!

STEPHANO. What's the matter? Have we devils here? Do you put tricks upon 's with savages and men of Ind,[169] ha? I have not 'scaped drowning to be afeard now of your four legs;[170] for it hath been said, As proper a man as ever went on four legs cannot make him give ground; and it shall be said so again while Stephano breathes at nostrils.

CALIBAN. The spirit torments me; Oh! 58

STEPHANO. This is some monster of the isle with four legs, who hath got, as I take it, an ague. Where the devil should he learn our language? I will give him some relief, if it be but for that. If I can recover[171] him and keep him tame and get to Naples with him, he's a present for any emperor that ever trod on neat's-leather.[172]

CALIBAN. Do not torment me, prithee; I'll bring my wood home faster.

STEPHANO. He's in his fit now and does not talk after the wisest. He shall taste of my bottle: if he have never drunk wine afore, it will go near to remove his fit. If I can recover him and keep him tame, I will not take too much[173] for him; he shall pay for him that hath him, and that soundly. 70

CALIBAN. Thou dost me yet but little hurt; thou wilt anon, I know it by thy trembling:[174] now Prosper works upon thee.

STEPHANO. Come on your ways;[175] open your mouth; here is that which will give language to you, cat:[176] open your mouth; this will

---

[168] mean; "lousy"   [169] the Indies, either east or west
[170] any four-legged creature   [171] cure   [172] cowhide
[173] no price will be too high   [174] a sign of being possessed by a devil
[175] an expression of encouragement
[176] an allusion to the proverb, "Good liquor will make a cat speak."

shake your shaking, I can tell you, and that soundly: you cannot tell
who's your friend: open your chaps[177] again.

TRINCULO. I should know that voice: it should be—but he is drowned;
and these are devils: O defend[178] me!   78

STEPHANO. Four legs and two voices: a most delicate monster! His
forward voice now is to speak well of his friend; his backward voice
is to utter foul speeches and to detract.[179] If all the wine in my bottle
will recover him, I will help his ague. Come. Amen! I will pour some
in thy other mouth.

TRINCULO. Stephano!

STEPHANO. Doth thy other mouth call me? Mercy, mercy! This is a
devil, and no monster: I will leave him; I have no long spoon.[180]

TRINCULO. Stephano! If thou beest Stephano, touch me and speak to
me; for I am Trinculo—be not afeard—thy good friend Trinculo.

STEPHANO. If thou beest Trinculo, come forth: I'll pull thee by the
lesser legs: if any be Trinculo's legs, these are they. Thou art   90
very Trinculo indeed! How camest thou to be the siege[181] of this
mooncalf?[182] can he vent Trinculos?

TRINCULO. I took him to be killed with a thunder-stroke. But art
thou not drowned, Stephano? I hope now thou art not drowned. Is
the storm overblown? I hid me under the dead moon-calf's gaberdine
for fear of the storm. And art thou living, Stephano? O Stephano,
two Neapolitans 'scaped!

STEPHANO. Prithee, do not turn me about; my stomach is not constant.

CALIBAN [Aside]. These be fine things, an if they be not sprites.   99
That's a brave[183] god and bears celestial liquor. I will kneel to him.

STEPHANO. How didst thou 'scape? How camest thou hither? swear
by this bottle how thou camest hither. I escaped upon a butt of sack[184]
which the sailors heaved o'erboard, by this bottle! which I made of
the bark of a tree with mine own hands since I was cast ashore.

CALIBAN. I'll swear upon that bottle to be thy true subject; for the
liquor is not earthy.

STEPHANO. Here; swear then how thou escapedst.

TRINCULO. Swum ashore, man, like a duck: I can swim like a duck,
I'll be sworn.   109

STEPHANO. Here, kiss the book.[185] Though thou canst swim like a
duck, thou art made like a goose.

TRINCULO. O Stephano, hast any more of this?

STEPHANO. The whole butt, man: my cellar is in a rock by the seaside where my wine is hid. How now, moon-calf! how does thine
ague?

---

[177] jaws   [178] God defend   [179] slander
[180] an allusion to the proverb, "He that sups with the Devil hath need of a long
spoon."
[181] excrement   [182] idiotic monster   [183] fine   [184] a large cask of wine
[185] He gives him the bottle instead of the Bible on which to take an oath.

CALIBAN. Hast thou not dropped from heaven?

STEPHANO. Out o' the moon, I do assure thee: I was the man i' the moon when time was.[186]

CALIBAN. I have seen thee in her and I do adore thee:
My mistress showed me thee and thy dog and thy bush.[187]   120

STEPHANO. Come, swear to that; kiss the book: I will furnish it anon with new contents: swear.

TRINCULO. By this good light, this is a very shallow monster! I afeard of him! A very weak monster! The man i' the moon! A most poor credulous monster! Well drawn,[188] monster, in good sooth!

CALIBAN. I'll show thee every fertile inch o' th' island;
And I will kiss thy foot: I prithee, be my god.

TRINCULO. By this light, a most perfidious and drunken monster! when 's god's asleep, he'll rob his bottle.

CALIBAN. I'll kiss thy foot; I'll swear myself thy subject.   130

STEPHANO. Come on then; down, and swear.

TRINCULO. I shall laugh myself to death at this puppy-headed monster. A most scurvy monster! I could find in my heart to beat him,—

STEPHANO. Come, kiss.

TRINCULO. But that the poor monster's in drink: an abominable monster!

CALIBAN. I'll show thee the best springs; I'll pluck thee berries;
I'll fish for thee and get thee wood enough.
A plague upon the tyrant that I serve!
I'll bear him no more sticks, but follow thee,   140
Thou wondrous man.

TRINCULO. A most ridiculous monster, to make a wonder of a poor drunkard!

CALIBAN. I prithee, let me bring thee where crabs[189] grow;
And I with my long nails will dig thee pignuts;
Show thee a jay's nest and instruct thee how
To snare the nimble marmoset;[190] I'll bring thee
To clustering filberts and sometimes I'll get thee
Young scamels[191] from the rock. Wilt thou go with me?   149

STEPHANO. I prithee now, lead the way without any more talking. Trinculo, the king and all our company else being drowned, we will inherit here: here; bear my bottle: fellow Trinculo, we'll fill him by and by[192] again.

CALIBAN. [*Sings drunkenly*]

Farewell, master; farewell, farewell!

---

[186] once upon a time
[187] There was a folk tradition that a peasant was banished to the moon for gathering brush on Sunday. The last bush he cut and his dog went with him.
[188] That was a good swig!   [189] crab-apples   [190] a small monkey
[191] perhaps sea-gulls; perhaps female godwits, long-billed wading birds
[192] right away

TRINCULO. A howling monster; a drunken monster!
CALIBAN. [*Sings*]

> *No more dams I'll make for fish;*
> *Nor fetch in firing*
> *At requiring;*
> *Nor scrape trencher,*[193] *nor wash dish:*
> *'Ban, 'Ban, Ca-Caliban*   160
> *Has a new master: get a new man.*

Freedom, hey-day! hey-day, freedom! freedom, hey-day, freedom!
STEPHANO. O brave monster! Lead the way.

                                                        [*Exeunt.*]

ACT III

SCENE I
Before PROSPERO'S *cell.*

Enter FERDINAND, *bearing a log.*

FERDINAND. There be some sports are painful, and their labor[194]
    Delight in them sets off:[195] some kinds of baseness
    Are nobly undergone and most poor matters
    Point to rich ends. This my mean task
    Would be as heavy to me as odious, but
    The mistress which I serve quickens what's dead
    And makes my labors pleasures: O, she is
    Ten times more gentle than her father's crabbed,
    And he's composed of harshness. I must remove
    Some thousands of these logs and pile them up,   10
    Upon a sore injunction:[196] my sweet mistress
    Weeps when she sees me work, and says, such baseness
    Had never like executor. I forget:[197]
    But these sweet thoughts do even refresh my labors,
    Most busy lest,[198] when I do it.[199]

        Enter MIRANDA; *and* PROSPERO *at a distance, unseen.*

MIRANDA.   Alas, now, pray you,
    Work not so hard: I would the lightning had
    Burnt up those logs that you are enjoined to pile!

---

193 wooden plate   194 fatigue   195 cancels
196 an order implying severe penalties
197 i.e., to work, in thinking about my sweet mistress
198 least; i.e., when I seem least busy   199 think such sweet thoughts

Pray, set it down and rest you : when this burns,
'Twill weep[200] for having wearied you. My father
Is hard at study ; pray now, rest yourself ;   20
He's safe for these three hours.
FERDINAND.   O most dear mistress,
  The sun will set before I shall discharge
  What I must strive to do.
MIRANDA.   If you'll sit down,
  I'll bear your logs the while : pray, give me that ;
  I'll carry it to the pile.
FERDINAND.   No, precious creature ;
  I had rather crack my sinews, break my back,
  Than you should such dishonor undergo,
  While I sit lazy by.
MIRANDA.   It would become me
  As well as it does you : and I should do it
  With much more ease ; for my good will is to it,   30
  And yours it is against.
PROSPERO.   Poor worm, thou art infected !
  This visitation[201] shows it.
MIRANDA.   You look wearily,
FERDINAND. No, noble mistress : 'tis fresh morning with me
  When you are by at night. I do beseech you —
  Chiefly that I might set it in my prayers—
  What is your name ?
MIRANDA.   Miranda.—O my father,
  I have broke your hest[202] to say so !
FERDINAND.   Admired Miranda !
  Indeed the top of admiration ! worth
  What's dearest to the world ! Full many a lady
  I have eyed with best regard and many a time   40
  The harmony of their tongues hath into bondage
  Brought my too diligent ear : for several virtues
  Have I liked several women ; never any
  With so full soul, but some defect in her
  Did quarrel with the noblest grace she owed[203]
  And put it to the foil :[204] but you, O you,
  So perfect and so peerless, are created
  Of every creature's best !
MIRANDA.   I do not know
  One of my sex ; no woman's face remember,
  Save, from my glass, mine own ; nor have I seen   50
  More that I may call men than you, good friend,

---

[200] exude sap   [201] visit (to Ferdinand)   [202] command   [203] owned
[204] rendered it ineffective

And my dear father : how features are abroad,[205]
I am skilless of; but, by my modesty,
The jewel in my dower, I would not wish
Any companion in the world but you,
Nor can imagination form a shape,
Besides yourself, to like of. But I prattle
Something too wildly and my father's precepts
I therein do forget.
FERDINAND.   I am in my condition[206]
A prince, Miranda; I do think, a king;   60
I would, not so!—and would no more endure
This wooden slavery than to suffer
The flesh-fly blow my mouth.[207] Hear my soul speak :
The very instant that I saw you, did
My heart fly to your service; there resides,
To make me slave to it; and for your sake
Am I this patient log-man.
MIRANDA.   Do you love me?
FERDINAND. O heaven, O earth, bear witness to this sound
And crown what I profess with kind event[208]
If I speak true! if hollowly, invert   70
What best is boded me to mischief! I
Beyond all limit of what else i' the world
Do love, prize, honor you.
MIRANDA.   I am a fool
To weep at what I am glad of.
PROSPERO.   Fair[209] encounter
Of two most rare affections![210] Heavens rain grace
On that which breeds between 'em!
FERDINAND.   Wherefore weep you?
MIRANDA. At mine unworthiness that dare not offer
What I desire to give and much less take
What I shall die to want. But this is trifling;
And all the more it seeks to hide itself,   80
The bigger bulk it shows. Hence, bashful cunning!
And prompt me, plain and holy innocence!
I am your wife, if you will marry me;
If not, I'll die your maid : [211] to be your fellow[212]
You may deny me; but I'll be your servant,
Whether you will or no.
FERDINAND.   My mistress, dearest;
And I thus humble ever.
MIRANDA.   My husband, then?

205 what beauty is like out in the world   206 rank   207 deposit eggs on
208 outcome   209 fortunate   210 dispositions   211 maidservant
212 wife

FERDINAND. Ay, with a heart as willing
  As bondage e'er of freedom: here's my hand.
MIRANDA. And mine, with my heart in 't: and now farewell   90
  Till half an hour hence.
FERDINAND.   A thousand thousand!
          [*Exeunt* FERDINAND *and* MIRANDA *severally.*]
PROSPERO. So glad of this as they I cannot be,
  Who are surprised withal; but my rejoicing
  At nothing can be more. I'll to my book,
  For yet ere supper-time must I perform
  Much business appertaining.²¹³

          [*Exit.*]

                    SCENE II
              Another part of the island.

        Enter CALIBAN, STEPHANO, *and* TRINCULO.

STEPHANO. Tell not me; when the butt is out, we will drink water;
  not a drop before: therefore bear²¹⁴ up, and board 'em. Servant-
  monster, drink to me.
TRINCULO. Servant-monster! the folly of this island! They say there's
  but five upon this isle: we are three of them; if th' other two be
  brained like us, the state totters.
STEPHANO. Drink, servant-monster, when I bid thee: thy eyes are almost set²¹⁵ in thy head.
TRINCULO. Where should they be set else? he were a brave monster
  indeed, if they were set in his tail.   10
STEPHANO. My man-monster hath drowned his tongue in sack: for my
  part, the sea cannot drown me; I swam, ere I could recover the shore,
  five and thirty leagues off and on. By this light, thou shalt be my lieu-
  tenant, monster, or my standard.²¹⁶
TRINCULO. Your lieutenant, if you list; he's no standard.
STEPHANO. We'll not run, Monsieur Monster.
TRINCULO. Nor go²¹⁷ neither; but you'll lie like dogs and yet say
  nothing neither.
STEPHANO. Moon-calf, speak once in thy life, if thou beest a good
  moon-calf.   20
CALIBAN. How does thy honor? Let me lick thy shoe.
  I'll not serve him; he is not valiant.
TRINCULO. Thou liest, most ignorant monster: I am in case to justle²¹⁸
  a constable. Why, thou deboshed²¹⁹ fish, thou, was there ever man a
  coward that hath drunk so much sack as I today? Wilt thou tell a
  monstrous lie, being but half a fish and half a monster?

---

²¹³ i.e., to the marriage   ²¹⁴ sail   ²¹⁵ fixed; i.e, in a drunken stare
²¹⁶ ensign; standard-bearer   ²¹⁷ walk   ²¹⁸ in a condition to wrestle
²¹⁹ debauched

CALIBAN. Lo, how he mocks me! wilt thou let him, my lord?

TRINCULO. "Lord" quoth he. That a monster should be such a natural! [220]

CALIBAN. Lo, lo, again! bite him to death, I prithee.   30

STEPHANO. Trinculo, keep a good tongue in your head: if you prove a mutineer,—the next tree! The poor monster's my subject and he shall not suffer indignity.

CALIBAN. I thank my noble lord. Wilt thou be pleased to hearken once again to the suit I made to thee?

STEPHANO. Marry, will I: kneel and repeat it; I will stand, and so shall Trinculo.

Enter ARIEL, *invisible.*

CALIBAN. As I told thee before, I am subject to a tyrant, a sorcerer, that by his cunning hath cheated me of the island.

ARIEL. Thou liest.   40

CALIBAN. Thou liest, thou jesting monkey, thou: I would my valiant master would destroy thee! I do not lie.

STEPHANO. Trinculo, if you trouble him any more in 's tale, by this hand, I will supplant some of your teeth.

TRINCULO. Why, I said nothing.

STEPHANO. Mum, then, and no more. Proceed.

CALIBAN. I say, by sorcery he got this isle;
From me he got it. If thy greatness will
Revenge it on him,—for I know thou darest,
But this thing dare not,—   50

STEPHANO. That's most certain.

CALIBAN. Thou shalt be lord of it and I'll serve thee.

STEPHANO. How now shall this be compassed? [221]
Canst thou bring me to the party?

CALIBAN. Yea, yea, my lord: I'll yield him thee asleep,
Where thou mayst knock a nail into his head.

ARIEL. Thou liest; thou canst not.

CALIBAN. What a pied [222] ninny's this! Thou scurvy patch! [223]
I do beseech thy greatness, give him blows
And take his bottle from him: when that's gone   60
He shall drink nought but brine; for I'll not show him
Where the quick freshes [224] are.

STEPHANO. Trinculo, run into no further danger: interrupt the monster one word further, and, by this hand, I'll turn my mercy out o' doors and make a stock-fish [225] of thee.

TRINCULO. Why, what did I? I did nothing. I'll go farther off.

[220] idiot   [221] brought to pass   [222] parti-colored; i.e., clad in jester's motley
[223] fool   [224] springs of running fresh water
[225] cod, because it was beaten to make it soft enough for cooking

STEPHANO. Didst thou not say he lied?

ARIEL. Thou liest.

STEPHANO. Do I so? take thou that.

                                            [*Beats* TRINCULO.]

As you like this, give me the lie another time.   70

TRINCULO. I did not give the lie. Out o' your wits and hearing too? A pox o' your bottle! this can sack and drinking do. A murrain[226] on your monster, and the devil take your fingers!

CALIBAN. Ha, ha, ha!

STEPHANO. Now, forward with your tale. Prithee, stand farther off.

CALIBAN. Beat him enough: after a little time
    I'll beat him too.

STEPHANO.   Stand farther. Come, proceed.

CALIBAN. Why, as I told thee, 'tis a custom with him,
    I' th' afternoon to sleep: there thou mayst brain him,
    Having first seized his books, or with a log   80
    Batter his skull, or paunch[227] him with a stake,
    Or cut his wezand[228] with thy knife. Remember
    First to possess his books; for without them
    He's but a sot,[229] as I am, nor hath not
    One spirit to command: they all do hate him
    As rootedly as I. Burn but his books.
    He has brave utensils,[230]   for so he calls them,
    Which, when he has a house, he'll deck withal.
    And that most deeply to consider is
    The beauty of his daughter; he himself   90
    Calls her a nonpareil:[231] I never saw a woman,
    But only Sycorax my dam and she;
    But she as far surpasseth Sycorax
    As great'st does least.

STEPHANO.   Is it so brave a lass?

CALIBAN. Ay, lord; she will become thy bed, I warrant,
    And bring thee forth brave brood.

STEPHANO. Monster, I will kill this man: his daughter and I will be king and queen,—save our graces!—and Trinculo and thyself shall be viceroys. Dost thou like the plot, Trinculo?

TRINCULO. Excellent.   100

STEPHANO. Give me thy hand: I am sorry I beat thee; but, while thou livest, keep a good tongue in thy head.

CALIBAN. Within this half hour will he be asleep:
    Wilt thou destroy him then?

STEPHANO.   Ay, on mine honor.

---

[226] a pestilence attacking cattle   [227] disembowel   [228] windpipe
[229] simpleton   [230] fine ornaments   [231] one without rival

ARIEL. This will I tell my master.

CALIBAN. Thou makest me merry; I am full of pleasure:
Let us be jocund: will you troll the catch [232]
You taught me but while-ere?

STEPHANO. At thy request, monster, I will do reason, any reason. [233]
Come on, Trinculo, let us sing.   110

[*Sings.*]

*Flout 'em and scout 'em
And scout 'em and flout 'em;
Thought is free.*

CALIBAN. That's not the tune.

[ARIEL *plays the tune on a tabor* [234] *and pipe.*]

STEPHANO. What is this same?

TRINCULO. This is the tune of our catch, played by the picture of
Nobody. [235]

STEPHANO. If thou beest a man, show thyself in thy likeness: if thou
beest a devil, take 't as thou list.

TRINCULO. O, forgive me my sins!   120

STEPHANO. He that dies pays all debts: I defy thee.
Mercy upon us!

CALIBAN. Art thou afeard?

STEPHANO. No, monster, not I.

CALIBAN. Be not afeard; the isle is full of noises,
Sounds and sweet airs, that give delight and hurt not.
Sometimes a thousand twangling instruments
Will hum about mine ears, and sometime voices
That, if I then had waked after long sleep,
Will make me sleep again: and then, in dreaming,   130
The clouds methought would open and show riches
Ready to drop upon me, that, when I waked,
I cried to dream again.

STEPHANO. This will prove a brave kingdom to me, where I shall have
my music for nothing.

CALIBAN. When Prospero is destroyed.

STEPHANO. That shall be by and by: I remember the story.

TRINCULO. The sound is going away; let's follow it, and after do our
work.   139

STEPHANO. Lead, monster; we'll follow. I would I could see this
taborer; he lays it on.

TRINCULO. Wilt come? I'll follow, Stephano.

[*Exeunt.*]

---

[232] sing the three-part round   [233] anything reasonable   [234] a small drum
[235] A picture on the title-page of a play, *No-body and Some-body* (1606), is all
head, neck, arms, legs, and particularly nose, and so has no body.

SCENE III

Another part of the island.

Enter ALONSO, SEBASTIAN, ANTONIO, GONZALO,
ADRIAN, FRANCISCO, *and others.*

GONZALO. By 'r lakin,[236] I can go no further, sir;
  My old bones ache: here's a maze trod indeed
  Through forth-rights and meanders![237] By your patience,
  I needs must rest me.
ALONSO.   Old lord, I cannot blame thee,
  Who am myself attached[238] with weariness,
  To the dulling of my spirits: sit down, and rest.
  Even here I will put off my hope and keep it
  No longer for my flatterer: he is drowned
  Whom thus we stray to find, and the sea mocks
  Our frustrate search on land. Well, let him go.   10
ANTONIO [*Aside to* SEBASTIAN]. I am right glad that he's so out of
  hope.
  Do not, for one repulse, forego the purpose
  That you resolved to effect.
SEBASTIAN [*Aside to* ANTONIO]. The next advantage
  Will we take throughly.
ANTONIO [*Aside to* SEBASTIAN]. Let it be tonight;
  For, now they are oppressed with travel, they
  Will not, nor cannot, use such vigilance
  As when they are fresh.
SEBASTIAN [*Aside to* ANTONIO]. I say, tonight: no more.
                          [*Solemn and strange music.*]
ALONSO. What harmony is this? My good friends, hark!
GONZALO. Marvelous sweet music!   20

Enter PROSPERO *above, invisible. Enter several strange* SHAPES, *bringing
in a banquet; they dance about it with gentle actions of salutation; and, inviting
the* KING, *etc. to eat, they depart.*

ALONSO. Give us kind keepers,[239] heavens! What were these?
SEBASTIAN. A living drollery.[240] Now I will believe
  That there are unicorns, that in Arabia
  There is one tree, the phœnix' throne, one phœnix
  At this hour reigning there.
ANTONIO.   I'll believe both;
  And what does else want credit,[241] come to me,
  And I'll be sworn 'tis true: travelers ne'er did lie,
  Though fools at home condemn 'em.

---

[236] by our Lady   [237] straight paths and winding paths   [238] seized
[239] guardian angels   [240] puppet show   [241] is incredible

GONZALO.   If in Naples
 I should report this now, would they believe me?
 If I should say, I saw such islanders—   30
 For, certes, these are people of the island—
 Who, though they are of monstrous shape, yet, note,
 Their manners are more gentle-kind than of
 Our human generation you shall find
 Many, nay, almost any.
PROSPERO [*Aside*].   Honest lord,
 Thou hast said well; for some of you there present
 Are worse than devils.
ALONSO.   I cannot too much muse[242]
 Such shapes, such gesture and such sound, expressing,
 Although they want the use of tongue, a kind
 Of excellent dumb discourse.
PROSPERO [*Aside*].   Praise in departing.   40
FRANCISCO. They vanished strangely.
SEBASTIAN.   No matter, since
 They have left their viands behind; for we have stomachs.[243]
 Will 't please you taste of what is here?
ALONSO.   Not I.
GONZALO. Faith, sir, you need not fear. When we were boys,
 Who would believe that there were mountaineers
 Dew-lapped[244] like bulls, whose throats had hanging at 'em
 Wallets of flesh? or that there were such men
 Whose heads stood in their breasts? which now we find
 Each putter-out of five for one[245] will bring us
 Good warrant of.
ALONSO.   I will stand to[246] and feed,   50
 Although my last: no matter, since I feel
 The best is past. Brother, my lord the duke,
 Stand to and do as we.

Thunder and lightning. Enter ARIEL, *like a harpy;*[247] *claps his wings upon
the table; and, with a quaint device,*[248] *the banquet vanishes.*

ARIEL. You are three men of sin, whom Destiny,
 That hath to instrument this lower world
 And what is in 't, the never-surfeited sea
 Hath caused to belch up you; and on this island
 Where man doth not inhabit; you 'mongst men
 Being most unfit to live. I have made you mad;
 And even with such-like valor[249] men hang and drown   60

242 wonder at   243 appetites   244 having a fold of skin under the neck
245 a traveler who wagers on his safe return   246 takes the risk
247 foul creature, half bird, half man   248 by an ingenious stage contrivance
249 the courage of madness

Their proper selves.

              [ALONSO, SEBASTIAN, *etc. draw their swords.*]

          You fools! I and my fellows

Are ministers of Fate: the elements,

Of whom your swords are tempered, may as well

Wound the loud winds, or with bemocked-at stabs

Kill the still-closing waters, as diminish

One dowle[250] that's in my plume: my fellow—ministers

Are like[251] invulnerable. If you could hurt,

Your swords are now too massy[252] for your strengths

And will not be uplifted. But remember—

For that's my business to you—that you three   70

From Milan did supplant good Prospero;

Exposed unto the sea, which hath requit it,[253]

Him and his innocent child: for which foul deed

The powers, delaying, not forgetting, have

Incensed the seas and shores, yea, all the creatures,

Against your peace. Thee of thy son, Alonso,

They have bereft; and do pronounce by me

Lingering perdition, worse than any death

Can be at once, shall step by step attend

You and your ways; whose wraths to guard you from—   80

Which here, in this most desolate isle, else falls

Upon your heads—is nothing but heart-sorrow

And a clear life ensuing.

He vanishes in thunder; then, to soft music, enter the SHAPES *again, and dance, with mocks and mows, and carrying out the table.*

PROSPERO. Bravely the figure of this harpy hast thou

   Performed, my Ariel; a grace it had, devouring:[254]

   Of my instruction hast thou nothing bated[255]

   In what thou hadst to say: so, with good life[256]

   And observation strange,[257] my meaner ministers

   Their several kinds have done. My high charms work

   And these mine enemies are all knit up   90

   In their distractions; they now are in my power;

   And in these fits I leave them, while I visit

   Young Ferdinand, whom they suppose is drowned,

   And his and mine loved darling.

                             [*Exit above.*]

GONZALO. I' the name of something holy, sir, why stand you

   In this strange stare?

---

[250] a tiny downy feather   [251] likewise   [252] heavy

[253] requited the crime against Prospero

[254] even while you were devouring the banquet   [255] left undone

[256] in a lifelike manner   [257] careful attention (to my commands)

ALONSO.   O, it is monstrous, monstrous!
  Methought the billows spoke and told me of it;
  The winds did sing it to me, and the thunder,
  That deep and dreadful organ-pipe, pronounced
  The name of Prosper: it did bass my trespass.[258]   100
  Therefore my son i' the ooze is bedded, and
  I'll seek him deeper than e'er plummet sounded
  And with him there lie mudded.

                                                    [*Exit.*]

SEBASTIAN.   But one fiend at a time,
  I'll fight their legions o'er.
ANTONIO.   I'll be thy second.

                  [*Exeunt* SEBASTIAN *and* ANTONIO.]

GONZALO. All three of them are desperate: their great guilt,
  Like poison given to work a great time after,
  Now 'gins to bite the spirits. I do beseech you
  That are of suppler joints, follow them swiftly
  And hinder them from what this ecstasy[259]
  May now provoke them to.
ADRIAN.   Follow, I pray you.   110

                                                  [*Exeunt.*]

ACT IV

SCENE I
Before PROSPERO'S *cell.*

Enter PROSPERO, FERDINAND, *and* MIRANDA.

PROSPERO. If I have too austerely punished you,
  Your compensation makes amends, for I
  Have given you here a third[260] of mine own life,
  Or that for which I live; who once again
  I tender to thy hand: all thy vexations
  Were but my trials of thy love, and thou
  Hast strangely[261] stood the test: here, afore Heaven,
  I ratify this my rich gift. O Ferdinand,
  Do not smile at me that I boast her off,[262]
  For thou shalt find she will outstrip all praise   10
  And make it halt behind her.
FERDINAND.   I do believe it
  Against an oracle.
PROSPERO. Then, as my gift and thine own acquisition
  Worthily purchased,[263] take my daughter: but

---

[258] publish my guilt in a bass voice   [259] frenzy
[260] Miranda; the other thirds are himself and his kingdom   [261] unusually well
[262] exhibit her virtues by boasting   [263] won

If thou dost break her virgin-knot before
All sanctimonious ceremonies may
With full and holy rite be ministered,
No sweet aspersion [264] shall the heavens let fall
To make this contract grow; but barren hate,
Sour-eyed disdain and discord shall bestrew   20
The union of your bed with weeds so loathly
That you shall hate it both: therefore take heed,
As Hymen's [265] lamps shall light you.
FERDINAND.   As I hope
For quiet days, fair issue and long life,
With such love as 'tis now, the murkiest den,
The most oppórtune place, the strong'st suggestion
Our worser genius can, shall never melt
Mine honor into lust, to take away
The edge of that day's celebration
When I shall think, or Phœbus' steeds are foundered,   30
Or Night kept chained below.
PROSPERO.   Fairly spoke.
Sit then and talk with her; she is thine own.
What, Ariel! my industrious servant, Ariel!

Enter ARIEL.

ARIEL. What would my potent master? here I am.
PROSPERO. Thou and thy meaner fellows your last service
Did worthily perform; and I must use you
In such another trick. Go bring the rabble,
O'er whom I give thee power, here to this place:
Incite them to quick motion; for I must
Bestow upon the eyes of this young couple   40
Some vanity of mine art: it is my promise,
And they expect it from me.
ARIEL.   Presently?
PROSPERO. Ay, with a twink.
ARIEL.

Before you can say "come" and "go,"
And breathe twice and cry "so, so,"
Each one, tripping on his toe,
Will be here with mop and mow.
Do you love me, master? no?

PROSPERO. Dearly, my delicate Ariel. Do not approach   50
Till thou dost hear me call.
ARIEL.   Well, I conceive. [266]

[*Exit.*]

[264] sprinkling (of dew as holy water)   [265] in classic myth, the god of marriage
[266] understand

PROSPERO. Look thou be true; do not give dalliance
  Too much the rein : the strongest oaths are straw
  To the fire i' the blood : be more abstemious,
  Or else, good night your vow!
FERDINAND.   I warrant you, sir ;
  The white cold virgin snow upon my heart
  Abates the ardor of my liver.[267]
PROSPERO.   Well.
  Now come, my Ariel! bring a corollary,[268]
  Rather than want a spirit : appear, and pertly!
  No tongue! all eyes! be silent.   60
                                          [*Soft music.*]

                          Enter IRIS.[269]

IRIS. Ceres, most bounteous lady, thy rich leas
  Of wheat, rye, barley, vetches,[270] oats and pease ;
  Thy turfy mountains, where live nibbling sheep,
  And flat meads thatchd with stover,[270] them to keep ;
  Thy banks with pionéd and twilléd brims,[271]
  Which spongy April at thy hest betrims,
  To make cold nymphs chaste crowns ; and thy broom-groves,
  Whose shadow the dismissed bachelor loves,
  Being lass-lorn ; thy pole-clipt vineyard ; [272]
  And thy sea-marge, sterile and rocky-hard,   70
  Where thou thyself dost air ;—the queen o' the sky,
  Whose watery arch [273] and messenger am I,
  Bids thee leave these, and with her sovereign grace,
  Here on this grass-plot, in this very place,
  To come and sport : her peacocks fly amain :
  Approach, rich Ceres,[274] her to entertain.

                         Enter CERES.

CERES. Hail, many-colored messenger, that ne'er
  Dost disobey the wife of Jupiter ; [275]
  Who with thy saffron wings upon my flowers
  Diffusest honey-drops, refreshing showers,   80
  And with each end of thy blue bow dost crown
  My bosky [276] acres and my unshrubbed down,
  Rich scarf to my proud earth ; why hath thy queen
  Summoned me hither, to this short-grassed green?

---

[267] the supposed seat of the passions   [268] surplus (of spirits)
[269] goddess of the rainbow   [270] leguminous fodder plants
[271] furrowed and ridged edges   [272] with vines clinging to poles
[273] rainbow   [274] goddess of agriculture
[275] Juno, goddess of women and childbirth   [276] covered with bushes

IRIS. A contract of true love to celebrate;
And some donation freely to estate
On the blest lovers.

CERES.   Tell me, heavenly bow,
If Venus or her son,[277] as thou dost know,
Do now attend the queen? Since they did plot
The means that dusky Dis my daughter got,[278]   90
Her and her blind boy's scandaled company
I have forsworn.

IRIS.   Of her society
Be not afraid: I met her deity
Cutting the clouds towards Paphos[279] and her son
Dove-drawn with her. Here thought they to have done
Some wanton charm upon this man and maid,
Whose vows are, that no bed-right shall be paid
Till Hymen's torch be lighted: but in vain;
Mars's hot minion is returned again;
Her waspish-headed son[280] has broke his arrows,   100
Swears he will shoot no more but play with sparrows
And be a boy right out.

CERES.   Highest queen of state,
Great Juno, comes; I know her by her gait.

       Enter JUNO.

JUNO. How does my bounteous sister? Go with me
To bless this twain, that they may prosperous be
And honored in their issue.

              [They sing.]

JUNO.   *Honor, riches, marriage-blessing,*
      Long continuance, and increasing,
      Hourly joys be still[281] *upon you!*
      Juno sings her blessings on you.   110

CERES.   *Earth's increase, foison plenty,*[282]
      Barns and garners never empty,
      Vines with clustering bunches growing,
      Plants with goodly burthen bowing;

      Spring come to you at the farthest
      In the very end of harvest!
      Scarcity and want shall shun you;
      Ceres' blessing so is on you.

[277] goddess of love and her son, Cupid
[278] Pluto carried off Proserpine, Ceres' daughter, to make her queen of hell.
[279] a town in Cyprus sacred to Venus [280] Venus and Cupid
[281] always [282] rich harvest

FERDINAND. This is a most majestic vision, and
  Harmonious charmingly. May I be bold   120
  To think these spirits?
PROSPERO.   Spirits, which by mine art
  I have from their confines called to enact
  My present fancies.
FERDINAND.   Let me live here ever;
  So rare a wondered father and a wife
  Makes this place Paradise.

            [JUNO and CERES whisper, and send
                      IRIS on employment.]

PROSPERO.   Sweet, now, silence!
  Juno and Ceres whisper seriously;
  There's something else to do: hush, and be mute,
  Or else our spell is marred.
IRIS. You nymphs, called Naiads, of the windring brooks,
  With your sedged crowns and ever-harmless looks,   130
  Leave your crisp[283] channels and on this green land
  Answer your summons; Juno does command:
  Come, temperate[284] nymphs, and help to celebrate
  A contract of true love; be not too late.

            Enter certain NYMPHS.

  You sunburnt sicklemen, of August weary,
  Come hither from the furrow and be merry:
  Make holiday; your rye-straw hats put on
  And these fresh nymphs encounter every one
  In country footing.

Enter certain REAPERS, *properly habited: they join with the* NYMPHS *in
a graceful dance; towards the end whereof* PROSPERO *starts suddenly, and
speaks; after which, to a strange, hollow, and confused noise, they heavily
vanish.*[285]

PROSPERO [*Aside*]. I had forgot that foul conspiracy   140
  Of the beast Caliban and his confederates
  Against my life: the minute of their plot
  Is almost come. [*To the* SPIRITS] Well done! avoid;[286] no more!
FERDINAND. This is strange: your father's in some passion
  That works him strongly.
MIRANDA.   Never till this day
  Saw I him touched with anger so distempered.[287]
PROSPERO. You do look, my son, in a movéd sort,
  As if you were dismayed: be cheerful, sir.

---

[283] rippling   [284] chaste   [285] vanish slowly and reluctantly   [286] begone
[287] violent

Our revels now are ended. These our actors,
As I foretold you, were all spirits and   150
Are melted into air, into thin air :
And, like the baseless fabric [288] of this vision,
The cloud-capped towers, the gorgeous palaces,
The solemn temples, the great globe itself,
Yea, all which it inherit, shall dissolve
And, like this insubstantial pageant faded,
Leave not a rack [289] behind. We are such stuff
As dreams are made on, and our little life
Is rounded with a sleep. Sir, I am vexed ;
Bear with my weakness ; my old brain is troubled :   160
Be not disturbed with my infirmity :
If you be pleased, retire into my cell
And there repose : a turn or two I'll walk,
To still my beating mind.
FERDINAND.   We wish your peace.

                                                            [*Exeunt.*]

PROSPERO. Come with a thought.[290] I thank thee, Ariel : come.

                            Enter ARIEL.

ARIEL. Thy thoughts I cleave to. What's thy pleasure ?
PROSPERO.   Spirit,
We must prepare to meet with Caliban.
ARIEL. Aye, my commander : when I presented Ceres,
I thought to have told thee of it, but I feared
Lest I might anger thee.   170
PROSPERO. Say again, where didst thou leave these varlets ? [291]
ARIEL. I told you, sir, they were red-hot with drinking ;
So full of valor that they smote the air
For breathing in their faces ; beat the ground
For kissing of their feet ; yet always bending
Towards their project.[292] Then I beat my tabor ;
At which, like unbacked [293] colts, they pricked their ears,
Advanced their eyelids, lifted up their noses
As they smelt music : so I charmed their ears
That calf-like they my lowing followed through   180
Toothed briers, sharp furzes, pricking goss [294] and thorns,
Which entered their frail shins : at last I left them
I' the filthy-mantled pool beyond your cell,
There dancing up to the chins, that the foul lake
O'erstunk their feet.

---

[288] structure lacking a foundation   [289] vestige   [290] on the instant
[291] scoundrels   [292] directing their course toward the murder of Prospero
[293] unbroken   [294] gorse

PROSPERO.   This was well done, my bird.
Thy shape invisible retain thou still:
The trumpery[295] in my house, go bring it hither,
For stale[296] to catch these thieves.
ARIEL.   I go, I go.

                                                                              [*Exit.*]

PROSPERO. A devil, a born devil, on whose nature
Nurture[297] can never stick; on whom my pains,   190
Humanely taken, all, all lost, quite lost;
And as with age his body uglier grows,
So his mind cankers. I will plague them all,
Even to roaring.

          Re-enter ARIEL, *loaden with glistering apparel, &c.*

          Come, hang them on this line.[298]

     PROSPERO *and* ARIEL *remain, invisible. Enter* CALIBAN,
          STEPHANO, *and* TRINCULO, *all wet.*

CALIBAN. Pray you, tread softly, that the blind mole may not
Hear a foot fall: we now are near his cell.
STEPHANO. Monster, your fairy, which you say is a harmless fairy,
has done little better than played the Jack[299] with us.
TRINCULO. Monster, I do smell all horse-piss; at which my nose is in
great indignation.   200
STEPHANO. So is mine. Do you hear, monster? If I should take a dis-
pleasure against you, look you,—
TRINCULO. Thou wert but a lost monster.
CALIBAN. Good my lord, give me thy favor still.
Be patient, for the prize I'll bring thee to
Shall hoodwink[300] this mischance: therefore speak softly.
All's hushed as midnight yet.
TRINCULO. Ay, but to lose our bottles in the pool,—
STEPHANO. There is not only disgrace and dishonor in that, monster,
but an infinite loss.   210
TRINCULO. That's more to me than my wetting: yet this is your
harmless fairy, monster.
STEPHANO. I will fetch off my bottle, though I be o'er ears for my
labor.
CALIBAN. Prithee, my king, be quiet. See'st thou here,
This is the mouth o' the cell: no noise, and enter.
Do that good mischief which may make this island
Thine own for ever, and I, thy Caliban,
For aye thy foot-licker.
STEPHANO. Give me thy hand. I do begin to have bloody thoughts. 220

----

295 showy stuff   296 decoy   297 education   298 perhaps lime; linden tree
299 knave   300 blind you to

TRINCULO. O king Stephano! O peer!³⁰¹ O worthy Stephano! look what a wardrobe here is for thee!

CALIBAN. Let it alone, thou fool; it is but trash.

TRINCULO. O, ho, monster! we know what belongs to a frippery.³⁰² O king Stephano!

STEPHANO. Put off that gown, Trinculo; by this hand, I'll have that gown.

TRINCULO. Thy grace shall have it.

CALIBAN. The dropsy drown this fool! what do you mean
To dote thus on such luggage? Let's alone³⁰³   230
And do the murder first: if he awake,
From toe to crown he'll fill our skins with pinches,
Make us strange stuff.

STEPHANO. Be you quiet, monster. Mistress line, is not this my jerkin? Now is the jerkin under the line: now, jerkin, you are like to lose your hair and prove a bald jerkin.³⁰⁴

TRINCULO. Do, do: we steal by line and level,³⁰⁵ an't like your grace.

STEPHANO. I thank thee for that jest; here's a garment for 't: wit shall not go unrewarded while I am king of this country. "Steal by   239 line and level" is an excellent pass of pate; ³⁰⁶ there's another garment for 't.

TRINCULO. Monster, come, put some lime³⁰⁷ upon your fingers, and away with the rest.

CALIBAN. I will have none on 't: we shall lose our time,
And all be turned to barnacles,³⁰⁸ or to apes
With foreheads villanous low.

STEPHANO. Monster, lay to your fingers: help to bear this away where my hogshead of wine is, or I'll turn you out of my kingdom: go to, carry this.

TRINCULO. And this.   250

STEPHANO. Ay, and this.

A noise of hunters heard. Enter divers SPIRITS, *in shape of dogs and hounds and hunt them about,* PROSPERO *and* ARIEL *setting them on.*

PROSPERO. Hey, Mountain, hey!

³⁰¹ TRINCULO refers to an old ballad, the first lines of which were,

> King Stephen was a worthy peer,
> His breeches cost him but a crown.

³⁰² a second-hand clothing shop   ³⁰³ let it alone

³⁰⁴ a short jacket. Stephano gets off a string of puns here: "Under the line" means not only "beneath the lime tree," but also "at the equator." Hence the jerkin could lose its hair as a result of a tropical fever. "Bald jerkin" may be an ironic reference to *baldachin*, a richly embroidered fabric.

³⁰⁵ the carpenter's or mason's line and spirit level; i.e., skillfully; by the use of instruments

³⁰⁶ sally of wit   ³⁰⁷ bird-lime; a very sticky substance

³⁰⁸ geese, that were thought to develop from barnacles

ARIEL. Silver! there it goes, Silver!

PROSPERO. Fury, Fury! there, Tyrant, there! hark! hark!
        [CALIBAN, STEPHANO, *and* TRINCULO *are driven out.*]
    Go charge my goblins that they grind their joints
    With dry convulsions, shorten up their sinews
    With agéd cramps, and more pinch-spotted [309] make them
    Than pard or cat o' mountain.

ARIEL.   Hark, they roar!

PROSPERO. Let them be hunted soundly. At this hour
    Lie at my mercy all mine enemies :   260
    Shortly shall all my labors end, and thou
    Shalt have the air at freedom : for a little
    Follow, and do me service.

                                                        [*Exeunt.*]

                            ACT V

                            SCENE I
                    Before PROSPERO's *cell.*

            Enter PROSPERO *in his magic robes, and* ARIEL.

PROSPERO. Now does my project gather to a head :
    My charms crack not ; [310] my spirits obey ; and time
    Goes upright [311] with his carriage. How's the day?

ARIEL. On the sixth hour ; at which time, my lord,
    You said our work should cease.

PROSPERO.   I did say so,
    When first I raised the tempest. Say, my spirit,
    How fares the king and 's followers?

ARIEL.   Confined together
    In the same fashion as you gave in charge,
    Just as you left them ; all prisoners, sir,
    In the line-grove [312] which weather-fends your cell ;   10
    They cannot budge till your release. The king,
    His brother and yours, abide all three distracted
    And the remainder mourning over them,
    Brimful of sorrow and dismay ; but chiefly
    Him that you termed, sir, "The good old lord, Gonzalo" ;
    His tears run down his beard, like winter's drops
    From eaves of reeds. [313] Your charm so strongly works 'em
    That if you now beheld them, your affections [314]
    Would become tender.

PROSPERO.   Dost thou think so, spirit?

───────────────

[309] spotted with bruises caused by pinching   [310] show no flaw
[311] does not stoop (because his burden is so light)   [312] lime-tree (linden) grove
[313] thatch   [314] feelings

ARIEL. Mine would, sir, were I human.

PROSPERO.   And mine shall.   20
Hast thou, which art but air, a touch, a feeling
Of their afflictions, and shall not myself
One of their kind, that relish all as sharply,
Passion as they, be kindlier moved than thou art?
Though with their high wrongs I am struck to the quick,
Yet with my nobler reason 'gainst my fury
Do I take part: the rarer action is
In virtue than in vengeance: they being penitent,
The sole drift of my purpose doth extend
Not a frown further. Go release them, Ariel: 30
My charms I'll break, their senses I'll restore,
And they shall be themselves.

ARIEL.   I'll fetch them, sir.

                                                                [*Exit.*]

PROSPERO. Ye elves of hills, brooks, standing lakes and groves,
And ye that on the sands with printless foot
Do chase the ebbing Neptune[315] and do fly him
When he comes back; you demi-puppets[316] that
By moonshine do the green sour ringlets[317] make,
Whereof the ewe not bites, and you whose pastime
Is to make midnight mushrooms,[318] that rejoice
To hear the solemn curfew;[319] by whose aid,   40
Weak masters though ye be, I have bedimmed
The noontide sun, called forth the mutinous winds,
And 'twixt the green sea and the azured vault
Set roaring war: to the dread rattling thunder
Have I given fire and rifted Jove's stout oak[320]
With his own bolt; the strong-based promontory
Have I made shake and by the spurs plucked up
The pine and cedar: graves at my command
Have waked their sleepers, oped, and let 'em forth
By my so potent art. But this rough magic   50
I here abjure, and, when I have required
Some heavenly music, which even now I do,
To work mine end upon their senses that
This airy charm is for, I'll break my staff,[321]

[315] outgoing tide   [316] half-size puppets
[317] circles of dark green grass supposed to be made by fairies dancing in a ring
[318] produced by fairy art at midnight
[319] because after it has sounded at 9 P.M. fairy creatures may wander where they
will
[320] Jove was pictured as having come down from heaven to live among humans,
but inside an oak tree. The blasting of the tree by lightning marked the death of the
god.
[321] magic wand

Bury it certain fathoms in the earth,
And deeper than did ever plummet sound
I'll drown my book.

[Solemn music.]

Re-enter ARIEL *before*: *then* ALONSO, *with a frantic gesture, attended by*
GONZALO; SEBASTIAN *and* ANTONIO *in like manner, attended by*
ADRIAN *and* FRANCISCO: *they all enter the circle which* PROSPERO *had
made, and there stand charmed*: *which* PROSPERO *observing, speaks*:

A solemn air and the best comforter
To an unsettled fancy cure thy brains,
Now useless, boiled within thy skull! There stand,   60
For you are spell-stopped.
Holy Gonzalo, honorable man,
Mine eyes, even sociable [322] to the show of thine,
Fall fellowly drops.[323] The charm dissolves apace,
And as the morning steals upon the night,
Melting the darkness, so their rising senses
Begin to chase the ignorant fumes that mantle
Their clearer reason. O good Gonzalo,
My true preserver, and a loyal sir
To him thou follow'st! I will pay thy graces   70
Home both in word and deed. Most cruelly
Didst thou, Alonso, use me and my daughter:
Thy brother was a furtherer in the act.
Thou art pinched for 't now, Sebastian. Flesh and blood,
You, brother mine, that entertained ambition,
Expelled remorse and nature; who, with Sebastian,
Whose inward pinches therefore are most strong,
Would here have killed your king; I do forgive thee,
Unnatural though thou art. Their understanding
Begins to swell, and the approaching tide   80
Will shortly fill the reasonable shore [324]
That now lies foul and muddy. Not one of them
That yet looks on me, or would know me: Ariel,
Fetch me the hat and rapier in my cell:
I will discase me, and myself present
As I was sometime Milan: quickly, spirit;
Thou shalt ere long be free.

[ARIEL sings and helps to attire him.]

[ARIEL]   *Where the bee sucks, there suck I*:
                 In a cowslip's bell I lie;
                 There I couch when owls do cry.   90
                 On the bat's back I do fly

---

[322] sympathetic   [323] shed sympathetic tears   [324] shore of reason

> *After summer merrily.*
> *Merrily, merrily shall I live now*
> *Under the blossom that hangs on the bough.*

PROSPERO. Why, that's my dainty Ariel! I shall miss thee;
But yet thou shalt have freedom: so, so, so.
To the king's ship; invisible as thou art:
There shalt thou find the mariners asleep
Under the hatches; the master and the boatswain
Being awake, enforce them to this place,   100
And presently,[325] I prithee.
ARIEL. I drink the air before me, and return
Or ere your pulse twice beat.

                                                        [*Exit.*]

GONZALO. All torment, trouble, wonder and amazement
Inhabits here: some heavenly power guide us
Out of this fearful country!
PROSPERO.   Behold, sir king,
The wrongéd Duke of Milan, Prospero:
For more assurance that a living prince
Does now speak to thee, I embrace thy body;
And to thee and thy company I bid   110
A hearty welcome.
ALONSO.   Whether thou be'st he or no,
Or some enchanted trifle to abuse me,
As late I have been, I not know: thy pulse
Beats as of flesh and blood; and, since I saw thee,
The affliction of my mind amends, with which,
I fear, a madness held me: this must crave,
An if this be at all, a most strange story.
Thy dukedom I resign and do entreat
Thou pardon me my wrongs. But how should Prospero
Be living and be here?
PROSPERO.   First, noble friend,   120
Let me embrace thine age, whose honor cannot
Be measured or confined.
GONZALO.   Whether this be
Or be not, I'll not swear.
PROSPERO.   You do yet taste
Some subtelties o' the isle, that will not let you
Believe things certain. Welcome, my friends all!

          [*Aside to* SEBASTIAN *and* ANTONIO.]

But you, my brace of lords, were I so minded,
I here could pluck [326] his highness' frown upon you

[325] at once   [326] bring down

And justify [327] you traitors : at this time
I will tell no tales.

SEBASTIAN [*Aside*]. The devil speaks in him.

PROSPERO.   No.
For you, most wicked sir, whom to call brother   130
Would even infect my mouth, I do forgive
Thy rankest fault ; all of them ; and require
My dukedom of thee, which perforce, I know,
Thou must restore.

ALONSO.   If thou be'st Prospero,
Give us particulars of thy preservation ;
How thou hast met us here, who three hours since
Were wrecked upon this shore ; where I have lost—
How sharp the point of this remembrance is !—
My dear son Ferdinand.

PROSPERO.   I am woe for 't, sir.

ALONSO. Irreparable is the loss, and patience   140
Says it is past her cure.

PROSPERO.   I rather think
You have not sought her help, of whose soft grace
For the like loss I have her sovereign aid
And rest myself content.

ALONSO.   You the like loss !

PROSPERO. As great to me as late ; and, supportable
To make the dear loss, have I means much weaker
Than you may call to comfort you, for I
Have lost my daughter.

ALONSO.   A daughter ?
O heavens, that they were living both in Naples,
The king and queen there ! that they were, I wish   150
Myself were mudded in that oozy bed
Where my son lies. When did you lose your daughter ?

PROSPERO. In this last tempest. I perceive, these lords
At this encounter do so much admire
That they devour their reason and scarce think
Their eyes do offices of truth, their words
Are natural breath : but, howsoe'er you have
Been justled from your senses, know for certain
That I am Prospero and that very duke
Which was thrust forth of Milan, who most strangely   160
Upon this shore, where you were wrecked, was landed,
To be the lord on 't. No more yet of this ;
For 'tis a chronicle of day by day,
Not a relation for a breakfast nor

[327] prove you to be

Befitting this first meeting. Welcome, sir;
This cell's my court: here have I few attendants
And subjects none abroad: pray you, look in.
My dukedom since you have given me again,
I will requite you with as good a thing;
At least bring forth a wonder, to content ye 170
As much as me my dukedom.

      [*Here* PROSPERO *discovers*[328] FERDINAND *and*
      MIRANDA *playing at chess.*]

MIRANDA. Sweet lord, you play me false.
FERDINAND.   No, my dear'st love,
  I would not for the world.
MIRANDA. Yes, for a score of kingdoms you should wrangle,
  And I would call it fair play.
ALONSO.   If this prove
  A vision of the island, one dear son
  Shall I twice lose.
SEBASTIAN.   A most high miracle!
FERDINAND. Though the seas threaten, they are merciful;
  I have cursed them without cause.

                    [*Kneels.*]

ALONSO.   Now all the blessings
  Of a glad father compass thee about! 180
  Arise, and say how thou camest here.
MIRANDA.   O, wonder!
  How many goodly creatures are there here!
  How beauteous mankind is! O brave[329] new world,
  That has such people in 't!
PROSPERO.   'Tis new to thee.
ALONSO. What is this maid with whom thou wast at play?
  Your eld'st acquaintance cannot be three hours:
  Is she the goddess that hath severed us,
  And brought us thus together?
FERDINAND.   Sir, she is mortal;
  But by immortal Providence she's mine:
  I chose her when I could not ask my father 190
  For his advice, nor thought I had one. She
  Is daughter to this famous Duke of Milan,
  Of whom so often I have heard renown,
  But never saw before; of whom I have
  Received a second life; and second father
  This lady makes him to me.
ALONSO.   I am hers:[330]

---

[328] reveals (by drawing back the curtain of the inner stage)   [329] splendid
[330] her father; i.e., I accept her as my daughter

But, O, how oddly will it sound that I
Must ask my child forgiveness!
PROSPERO.   There, sir, stop:
Let us not burthen our remembrance with
A heaviness that's gone.
GONZALO.   I have inly wept   200
Or should have spoke ere this. Look down, you gods,
And on this couple drop a blessèd crown!
For it is you that have chalked forth the way
Which brought us hither.
ALONSO.   I say, Amen, Gonzalo!
GONZALO. Was Milan thrust from Milan, that his issue
Should become kings of Naples? O, rejoice
Beyond a common joy, and set it down
With gold on lasting pillars: In one voyage
Did Claribel her husband find at Tunis
And Ferdinand, her brother, found a wife   210
Where he himself was lost, Prospero his dukedom
In a poor isle and all of us ourselves
When no man was his own.[331]
ALONSO [to FERDINAND and MIRANDA.]
                              Give me your hands:
Let grief and sorrow still embrace his heart
That doth not wish you joy!
GONZALO.   Be it so! Amen!

Re-enter ARIEL *with the* MASTER *and* BOATSWAIN
amazedly following.

O, look, sir, look, sir! here is more of us:
I prophesied, if a gallows were on land,
This fellow could not drown. Now, blasphemy,
That swear'st grace o'erboard,[332] not an oath on shore?
Hast thou no mouth by land? What is the news?   220
BOATSWAIN. The best news is, that we have safely found
Our king and company; the next, our ship—
Which, but three glasses[333] since, we gave out split—
Is tight and yare[334] and bravely rigged as when
We first put out to sea.
ARIEL [*Aside to* PROSPERO]. Sir, all this service
Have I done since I went.
PROSPERO [*Aside to* ARIEL]. My tricksy spirit!
ALONSO. These are not natural events; they strengthen
From strange to stranger. Say, how came you hither?

[331] when no one was in his right wits (because of the enchantment)
[332] drives God's protection away from the ship by swearing
[333] hours   [334] seaworthy

BOATSWAIN. If I did think, sir, I were well awake,
I 'ld strive to tell you. We were dead of sleep, 230
And—how we know not   all clapped under hatches;
Where but even now with strange and several noises
Of roaring, shrieking, howling, jingling chains,
And moe diversity of sounds, all horrible,
We were awaked; straightway, at liberty;
Where we, in all her trim,[335] freshly beheld
Our royal, good and gallant ship, our master
Capering to eye her: on a trice, so please you,
Even in a dream, were we divided from them
And were brought moping hither.

ARIEL [*Aside to* PROSPERO]. Was't well done? 240

PROSPERO [*Aside to* ARIEL]. Bravely,[336] my diligence. Thou shalt be free.

ALONSO. This is as strange a maze as e'er men trod;
And there is in this business more than nature
Was ever conduct of: some oracle
Must rectify our knowledge.

PROSPERO.   Sir, my liege,
Do not infest your mind with beating on
The strangeness of this business; at picked leisure
Which shall be shortly, single[337] I'll resolve you,
Which to you shall seem probable, of every 250
These happened accidents; till when, be cheerful
And think of each thing well. [*Aside to* ARIEL.] Come hither, spirit:
Set Caliban and his companions free;
Untie the spell.

                              [*Exit* ARIEL.]

How fares my gracious sir?[338]
There are yet missing of your company
Some few odd lads that you remember not.

Re-enter ARIEL *driving in* CALIBAN, STEPHANO
and TRINCULO *in their stolen apparel.*

STEPHANO. Every man shift for all the rest, and let no man take care
for himself; for all is but fortune. Coragio, bully-monster, coragio![339]

TRINCULO. If these be true spies which I wear in my head, here's a
goodly sight. 261

CALIBAN. O Setebos, these be brave spirits indeed!
How fine my master is! I am afraid
He will chastise me.

---

[335] rigging   [336] splendidly   [337] when we are alone   [338] Alonso
[339] courage

SEBASTIAN.   Ha, ha!
What things are these, my lord Antonio?
Will money buy 'em?
ANTONIO.   Very like; one of them
Is a plain fish, and, no doubt, marketable.
PROSPERO. Mark but the badges [340] of these men, my lords,
Then say if they be true. This mis-shapen knave,
His mother was a witch, and one so strong   270
That could control the moon, make flows and ebbs,
And deal in her command without her power.[341]
These three have robbed me; and this demi–devil—
For he's a bastard one—had plotted with them
To take my life. Two of these fellows you
Must know and own; [342] this thing of darkness I
Acknowledge mine.
CALIBAN.   I shall be pinched to death.
ALONSO. Is not this Stephano, my drunken butler?
SEBASTIAN. He is drunk now: where had he wine?
ALONSO. And Trinculo is reeling ripe: where should they   280
Find this grand liquor that hath gilded 'em?
How camest thou in this pickle?
TRINCULO. I have been in such a pickle since I saw you last that, I fear
me, will never out of my bones: I shall not fear fly-blowing.[343]
SEBASTIAN. Why, how now, Stephano!
STEPHANO. O, touch me not; I am not Stephano, but a cramp.
PROSPERO. You'll be king o' the isle, sirrah?
STEPHANO. I should have been a sore one then.
ALONSO. This is a strange thing as e'er I looked on.
                            [*Pointing to* CALIBAN.]
PROSPERO. He is as disproportioned in his manners   290
As in his shape. Go, sirrah, to my cell;
Take with you your companions; as you look
To have my pardon, trim it handsomely.
CALIBAN. Ay, that I will; and I'll be wise hereafter
And seek for grace. What a thrice-double ass
Was I, to take this drunkard for a god
And worship this dull fool!
PROSPERO.   Go to; away!
ALONSO. Hence, and bestow your luggage where you found it.
SEBASTIAN. Or stole it, rather.
                    [*Exeunt* CALIBAN, STEPHANO, *and* TRINCULO.]
PROSPERO. Sir, I invite your highness and your train   300

[340] emblems worn on the sleeves of servants to show to what family they belonged
[341] act in the area of the moon's authority with power greater than hers
[342] admit to be your servants   [343] because pickled meat is never flyblown

To my poor cell, where you shall take your rest
For this one night; which, part of it, I'll waste [344]
With such discourse as, I not doubt, shall make it
Go quick away; the story of my life
And the particular accidents [345] gone by
Since I came to this isle: and in the morn
I'll bring you to your ship and so to Naples,
Where I have hope to see the nuptial
Of these our dear-belovéd solemnized;
And thence retire me to my Milan, where   310
Every third thought shall be my grave.

ALONSO.   I long
To hear the story of your life, which must
Take the ear strangely.

PROSPERO.   I'll deliver all; [346]
And promise you calm seas, auspicious gales
And sail so expeditious that shall catch
Your royal fleet far off.
               [*Aside to* ARIEL.] My Ariel, chick,
That is thy charge: then to the elements
Be free, and fare thou well! Please you, draw near.

                               [*Exeunt.*]

EPILOGUE

SPOKEN BY PROSPERO.

Now my charms are all o'erthrown,
And what strength I have 's mine own,
Which is most faint: now, 'tis true,
I must be here confined by you,
Or sent to Naples. Let me not,
Since I have my dukedom got
And pardoned the deceiver, dwell
In this bare island by your spell;
But release me from my bands
With the help of your good hands: [347]   10
Gentle breath [348] of yours my sails
Must fill, or else my project fails,
Which was to please. Now I want
Spirits to enforce, art to enchant,
And my ending is despair,
Unless I be relieved by prayer,

---

[344] spend   [345] events   [346] tell everything   [347] applause
[348] favorable comment

Which pierces so that it assaults
Mercy itself and frees [349] all faults.
As you from crimes would pardoned be,
Let your indulgence set me free.   20

[Exit.]

[349] gains forgiveness for

Richard Brinsley Sheridan

1751–1816

THE RIVALS

❖

CHARACTERS

CAPTAIN ABSOLUTE.
LYDIA LANGUISH.
SIR ANTHONY ABSOLUTE, *father of Captain Absolute.*
MRS. MALAPROP, *aunt of Lydia Languish.*
FAULKLAND.
JULIA MELVILLE, *cousin of Lydia Languish.*
BOB ACRES.

SIR LUCIUS O'TRIGGER.
FAG, *valet of Captain Absolute.*
LUCY, *lady's maid of Lydia Languish.*
DAVID, *valet of Bob Acres.*
COACHMAN.
MAID.
BOY.
SERVANT.

SCENE. *Bath.*[1]
TIME OF ACTION. *Within one day.*

❖

ACT I

SCENE I
A street in Bath.

COACHMAN *crosses the stage.—Enter* FAG, *looking after him.*

FAG. What!—Thomas!—Sure, 'tis he?—What!—Thomas!—Thomas!

COACHMAN. Hey!—Odd's life![2]—Mr. Fag!—give us your hand, my old fellow-servant.

FAG. Excuse my glove, Thomas:—I'm dev'lish glad to see you, my lad: why, my prince of charioteers, you look as hearty!—but who the deuce thought of seeing you in Bath!

COACHMAN. Sure, Master, Madam Julia, Harry, Mrs. Kate, and the postilion be all come!

FAG. Indeed!

---

[1] city in the southwest of England, noted as a health resort and rallying place for the fashionable

[2] God's life: a euphemistic form of oath

COACHMAN. Aye! Master thought another fit of the gout was coming to make him a visit: so he'd a mind to gi't the slip, and whip! we were all off at an hour's warning.

FAG. Aye, aye! hasty in everything, or it would not be Sir Anthony Absolute!

COACHMAN. But tell us, Mr. Fag, how does young master? Odd! Sir Anthony will stare to see the Captain here!

FAG. I do not serve Captain Absolute now.

COACHMAN. Why sure!

FAG. At present I am employed by Ensign Beverley.

COACHMAN. I doubt, Mr. Fag, you ha'n't changed for the better.

FAG. I have not changed, Thomas.

COACHMAN. No! why, didn't you say you had left young master?

FAG. No.——Well, honest Thomas, I must puzzle you no farther: briefly then—Captain Absolute and Ensign Beverley are one and the same person.

COACHMAN. The devil they are!

FAG. So it is indeed, Thomas; and the *Ensign*-half of my master being on guard at present—the *Captain* has nothing to do with me.

COACHMAN. So, so!—What, this is some freak, I warrant!——Do tell us, Mr. Fag, the meaning o't—you know I ha' trusted you.

FAG. You'll be secret, Thomas?

COACHMAN. As a coach-horse.

FAG. Why then the cause of all this is—LOVE —Love, Thomas, who (as you may get read to you) has been a masquerader ever since the days of Jupiter.

COACHMAN. Aye, aye;—I guessed there was a lady in the case: but pray, why does your master pass only for *Ensign?* Now if he had shammed *General*, indeed——

FAG. Ah! Thomas, there lies the mystery o' the matter. Hark'ee, Thomas, my master is in love with a lady of a very singular taste: a lady who likes him better as a *half-pay Ensign* than if she knew he was son and heir to Sir Anthony Absolute, a baronet of three thousand a year!

COACHMAN. That is an odd taste indeed!—but has she got the stuff, Mr. Fag? is she rich, hey?

FAG. Rich—why, I believe she owns half the stocks—Z——ds![3] Thomas, she could pay the national debt as easily as I could my washerwoman! She has a lap-dog that eats out of gold—she feeds her parrot with small pearls—and all her thread-papers are made of bank-notes!

COACHMAN. Bravo!—Faith!—Odd! I warrant she has a set of thousands[4] at least. But does she draw kindly with the Captain?

---

[3] Zounds!: euphemism for God's (i.e., Christ's) wounds
[4] a costly team of horses

FAG. As fond as pigeons.

COACHMAN. May one hear her name?

FAG. Miss Lydia Languish. But there is an old tough aunt in the way; though, by the bye, she has never seen my master, for he got acquainted with Miss while on a visit in Gloucestershire.

COACHMAN. Well—I wish they were once harnessed together in matrimony.——But pray, Mr. Fag, what kind of a place is this Bath? I ha' heard a deal of it—here's a mort[5] o' merry-making, hey?

FAG. Pretty well, Thomas, pretty well—'tis a good lounge. In the morning we go to the Pump-room[6] (though neither my master nor I drink the waters); after breakfast we saunter on the Parades, or play a game at billiards; at night we dance: but d——n the place, I'm tired of it: their regular hours stupefy me—not a fiddle nor a card after eleven! However, Mr. Faulkland's gentleman and I keep it up a little in private parties—I'll introduce you there, Thomas: you'll like him much.

COACHMAN. Sure I know Mr. Du-Peigne—you know his master is to marry Madam Julia.

FAG. I had forgot.—But Thomas, you must polish a little—indeed you must. Here now—this wig! what the devil do you do with a *wig*, Thomas?—none of the London whips of any degree of *ton* wear *wigs* now.

COACHMAN. More's the pity! more's the pity, I say—Odd's life! when I heard how the lawyers and doctors had took to their own hair, I thought how 'twould go next:—Odd rabbit it! when the fashion had got foot on the Bar, I guessed 'twould mount to the Box![7] But 'tis all out of character, believe me, Mr. Fag: and look'ee, I'll never gi' up mine—the lawyers and doctors may do as they will.

FAG. Well, Thomas, we'll not quarrel about that.

COACHMAN. Why, bless you, the gentlemen of they professions ben't all of a mind—for in our village now, tho' ff *Jack Gauge*, the *exciseman*, has ta'en to his carrots,[8] there's little Dick, the farrier,[9] swears he'll never forsake his *bob*,[10] tho' all the college should appear with their own heads!

FAG. Indeed! well said, Dick! But hold—mark! mark! Thomas.

COACHMAN. Zooks![11] 'tis the Captain!—Is that the lady with him?

FAG. No! no! that is Madam Lucy—my master's mistress's maid. They lodge at that house—but I must after him to tell him the news.

COACHMAN. Odd! he's giving her money!——Well, Mr. Fag——

---

[5] a great deal [6] a salon where the supposedly beneficial waters were served
[7] driver's seat; i.e., coachmen have taken up the fad started by the lawyers.
[8] lets his red hair show
[9] one who cares for horses; specifically, one who shoes them
[10] bobwig, with the ends turned up in short curls
[11] Gadzooks: God's hooks; the nails of the Cross

FAG. Good-bye, Thomas.—I have an appointment in Gyde's Porch this evening at eight; meet me there, and we'll make a little party.

[*Exeunt severally.*]

SCENE II

A dressing room in MRS. MALAPROP'S *lodgings.*

LYDIA *sitting on a sofa, with a book in her hand.* LUCY, *as just returned from a message.*

LUCY. Indeed, Ma'am, I traversed half the town in search of it: I don't believe there's a circulating library in Bath I ha'n't been at.

LYDIA. And could not you get *The Reward of Constancy?*

LUCY. No, indeed, Ma'am.

LYDIA. Nor *The Fatal Connection?*

LUCY. No, indeed, Ma'am.

LYDIA. Nor *The Mistakes of the Heart?*

LUCY. Ma'am, as ill-luck would have it, Mr. Bull said Miss Sukey Saunter had just fetched it away.

LYDIA. Heigh-ho! Did you inquire for *The Delicate Distress?*

LUCY. Or *The Memoirs of Lady Woodford?* Yes, indeed, Ma'am. I asked everywhere for it; and I might have brought if from Mr. Frederick's, but Lady Slattern Lounger, who had just sent it home, had so soiled and dog's-eared it, it wa'n't fit for a Christian to read.

LYDIA. Heigh-ho!—Yes, I always know when Lady Slattern has been before me. She has a most observing thumb; and I believe cherishes her nails for the convenience of making marginal notes.——Well, child, what *have* you brought me?

LUCY. Oh! here, Ma'am. [*taking books from under her cloak, and from her pockets*] This is *The Gordian Knot*, and this *Peregrine Pickle*. Here are *The Tears of Sensibility* and *Humphry Clinker*. This is *The Memoirs of a Lady of Quality, written by herself*, and here the second volume of *The Sentimental Journey.*

LYDIA. Heigh-ho!—What are those books by the glass?

LUCY. The great one is only *The Whole Duty of Man*—where I press a few blonds,[12] Ma'am.

LYDIA. Very well—give me the *sal volatile.*

LUCY. Is it in a blue cover, Ma'am?

LYDIA. My smelling bottle, you simpleton!

LUCY. Oh, the drops!—Here, Ma'am.

LYDIA. Hold!—here's some one coming——quick! see who it is.

[*Exit* LUCY.]

Surely I heard my cousin Julia's voice!

Re-enter LUCY.

---

[12] silk bobbin lace

LUCY. Lud! Ma'am, here is Miss Melville.
LYDIA. Is it possible!——

Enter JULIA.

My dearest Julia, how delighted am I!—[*Embrace.*] How unexpected was this happiness!

JULIA. True, Lydia—and our pleasure is the greater; but what has been the matter?—you were denied to me at first!

LYDIA. Ah! Julia, I have a thousand things to tell you! But first inform me what has conjured you to Bath? Is Sir Anthony here?

JULIA. He is—we are arrived within this hour, and I suppose he will be here to wait on Mrs. Malaprop as soon as he is dressed.

LYDIA. Then, before we are interrupted, let me impart to you some of my distress! I know your gentle nature will sympathize with me, though your prudence may condemn me! My letters have informed you of my whole connection with Beverley—but I have lost him, Julia! My aunt has discovered our intercourse by a note she intercepted, and has confined me ever since! Yet, would you believe it? she has fallen absolutely in love with a tall Irish baronet she met one night since we have been here, at Lady Macshuffle's rout.

JULIA. You jest, Lydia!

LYDIA. No, upon my word. She really carries on a kind of correspondence with him, under a feigned name though, till she chooses to be known to him; but it is a *Delia* or a *Celia*, I assure you.

JULIA. Then surely she is now more indulgent to her niece.

LYDIA. Quite the contrary. Since she has discovered her own frailty she is become more suspicious of mine. Then I must inform you of another plague! That odious Acres is to be in Bath today; so that I protest I shall be teased out of all spirits!

JULIA. Come, come, Lydia, hope the best. Sir Anthony shall use his interest with Mrs. Malaprop.

LYDIA. But you have not heard the worst. Unfortunately I had quarreled with my poor Beverley just before my aunt made the discovery, and I have not seen him since to make it up.

JULIA. What was his offence?

LYDIA. Nothing at all! But, I don't know how it was, as often as we had been together we had never had a quarrel! And, somehow, I was afraid he would never give me an opportunity. So last Thursday I wrote a letter to myself to inform myself that Beverley was at that time paying his addresses to another woman. I signed it *your friend unknown*, showed it to Beverley, charged him with his falsehood, put myself in a violent passion, and vowed I'd never see him more.

JULIA. And you let him depart so, and have not seen him since?

LYDIA. 'Twas the next day my aunt found the matter out. I intended only to have teased him three days and a half, and now I've lost him forever!

JULIA. If he is as deserving and sincere as you have represented him to me, he will never give you up so. Yet consider, Lydia, you tell me he is but an ensign, and you have thirty thousand pounds!

LYDIA. But you know I lose most of my fortune if I marry without my aunt's consent, till of age; and that is what I have determined to do ever since I knew the penalty. Nor could I love the man who would wish to wait a day for the alternative.

JULIA. Nay, this is caprice!

LYDIA. What, does Julia tax me with caprice? I thought her lover Faulkland had inured her to it.

JULIA. I do not love even *his* faults.

LYDIA. But a-propos—you have sent to him, I suppose?

JULIA. Not yet, upon my word, nor has he the least idea of my being in Bath. Sir Anthony's resolution was so sudden I could not inform of it.

LYDIA. Well, Julia, you are your own mistress (though under the protection of Sir Anthony), yet have you for this long year been a slave to the caprice, the whim, the jealousy of this ungrateful Faulkland, who will ever delay assuming the right of a husband, while you suffer him to be equally imperious as a lover.

JULIA. Nay, you are wrong entirely. We were contracted before my father's death. That, and some consequent embarrassments, have delayed what I know to be my Faulkland's most ardent wish. He is too generous to trifle on such a point. And for his character, you wrong him there too. No, Lydia, he is too proud, too noble to be jealous: if he is captious, 'tis without dissembling; if fretful, without rudeness. Unused to the fopperies of love, he is negligent of the little duties expected from a lover—but being unhackneyed in the passion, his affection is ardent and sincere; and as it engrosses his whole soul, he expects every thought and emotion of his mistress to move in unison with his. Yet, though his pride calls for this full return, his humility makes him undervalue those qualities in him which would entitle him to it; and not feeling why he should be loved to the degree he wishes, he still suspects that he is not loved enough. This temper, I must own, has cost me many unhappy hours; but I have learned to think myself his debtor for those imperfections which arise from the ardor of his attachment.

LYDIA. Well, I cannot blame you for defending him. But tell me candidly, Julia, had he never saved your life, do you think you should have been attached to him as you are? Believe me, the rude blast that overset your boat was a prosperous gale of love to him.

JULIA. Gratitude may have strengthened my attachment to Mr. Faulkland, but I loved him before he had preserved me; yet surely that alone were an obligation sufficient——

LYDIA. Obligation! Why, a water-spaniel would have done as much!

Well, I should never think of giving my heart to a man because he could swim!

JULIA. Come, Lydia, you are too inconsiderate.

LYDIA. Nay, I do but jest.—— What's here?

Enter LUCY *in a hurry.*

LUCY. O Ma'am, here is Sir Anthony Absolute just come home with your aunt.

LYDIA. They'll not come here.——Lucy, do you watch.

[*Exit* LUCY.]

JULIA. Yet I must go. Sir Anthony does not know I am here, and if we meet, he'll detain me, to show me the town. I'll take another opportunity of paying my respects to Mrs. Malaprop, when she shall treat me, as long as she chooses, with her select words so ingeniously *misapplied*, without being *mispronounced*.

Re-enter LUCY.

LUCY. O lud! Ma'am, they are both coming upstairs.

LYDIA. Well, I'll not detain you, coz. Adieu, my dear Julia. I'm sure you are in haste to send to Faulkland. There—through my room you'll find another stair-case.

JULIA. Adieu.—— [*Embrace.*] [*Exit* JULIA.]

LYDIA. Here, my dear Lucy, hide these books. Quick, quick! Fling *Peregrine Pickle* under the toilet[13]—throw *Roderick Random* into the closet—put *The Innocent Adultery* into *The Whole Duty of Man*—thrust *Lord Aimworth* under the sofa—cram *Ovid* behind the bolster —there—put *The Man of Feeling* into your pocket—so, so,—now lay *Mrs. Chapone* in sight, and leave *Fordyce's Sermons* open on the table.

LUCY. Oh burn it, Ma'am! the hair-dresser has torn away as far as *Proper Pride*.[14]

LYDIA. Never mind—open at *Sobriety*.—Fling me *Lord Chesterfield's Letters*.—Now for 'em.

Enter MRS. MALAPROP, *and* SIR ANTHONY ABSOLUTE.

MRS. MALAPROP. There, Sir Anthony, there sits the deliberate simpleton who wants to disgrace her family, and lavish herself on a fellow not worth a shilling!

LYDIA. Madam. I thought you once——

MRS. MALAPROP. You thought, Miss! I don't know any business you have to think at all. Thought does not become a young woman. But the point we would request of you is, that you will promise to forget this fellow—to illiterate him, I say, quite from your memory.

---

[13] dressing table   [14] to get papers to use with the curling iron

LYDIA. Ah! Madam! our memories are independent of our wills. It is not so easy to forget.

MRS. MALAPROP. But I say it is, Miss; there is nothing on earth so easy as to *forget*, if a person chooses to set about it. I'm sure I have as much forgot your poor dear uncle as if he had never existed—and I thought it my duty so to do; and let me tell you, Lydia, these violent memories don't become a young woman.

SIR ANTHONY. Why sure she won't pretend to remember what she's ordered not!—aye, this comes of her reading!

LYDIA. What crime, Madam, have I committed to be treated thus?

MRS. MALAPROP. Now don't attempt to extirpate yourself from the matter; you know I have proof controvertible of it. But tell me, will you promise to do as you're bid? Will you take a husband of your friend's choosing?

LYDIA. Madam, I must tell you plainly, that had I no preference for anyone else, the choice you have made would be my aversion.

MRS. MALAPROP. What business have you, Miss, with *preference* and *aversion?* They don't become a young woman; and you ought to know, that as both always wear off, 'tis safest in matrimony to begin with a little *aversion.* I am sure I hated your poor dear uncle before marriage as if he'd been a blackamoor—and yet, Miss, you are sensible what a wife I made!—and when it pleased heaven to release me from him, 'tis unknown what tears I shed! But suppose we were going to give you another choice, will you promise us to give up this Beverley?

LYDIA. Could I belie my thoughts so far as to give that promise, my actions would certainly as far belie my words.

MRS. MALAPROP. Take yourself to your room. You are fit company for nothing but your own ill-humors.

LYDIA. Willingly, Ma'am—I cannot change for the worse.

[*Exit* LYDIA.]

MRS. MALAPROP. There's a little intricate hussy for you!

SIR ANTHONY. It is not to be wondered at, Ma'am—all this is the natural consequence of teaching girls to read. Had I a thousand daughters, by heaven! I'd as soon have them taught the black art as their alphabet!

MRS. MALAPROP. Nay, nay, Sir Anthony, you are an absolute misanthropy.

SIR ANTHONY. In my way hither, Mrs. Malaprop, I observed your niece's maid coming forth from a circulating library! She had a book in each hand—they were half-bound volumes, with marble covers! From that moment I guessed how full of duty I should see her mistress!

MRS. MALAPROP. Those are vile places, indeed!

SIR ANTHONY. Madam, a circulating library in a town is as an evergreen tree of diabolical knowledge! It blossoms through the year! And depend on it, Mrs. Malaprop, that they who are so found of handling the leaves, will long for the fruit at last.

MRS. MALAPROP. Fie, fie, Sir Anthony, you surely speak laconically!

SIR ANTHONY. Why, Mrs. Malaprop, in moderation, now, what would you have a woman know?

MRS. MALAPROP. Observe me, Sir Anthony. I would by no means wish a daughter of mine to be a progeny of learning; I don't think so much learning becomes a young woman; for instance—I would never let her meddle with Greek, or Hebrew, or Algebra, or Simony, or Fluxions, or Paradoxes, or such inflammatory branches of learning—neither would it be necessary for her to handle any of your mathematical, astronomical, diabolical instruments;—but, Sir Anthony, I would send her, at nine years old, to a boarding-school, in order to learn a little ingenuity and artifice. Then, Sir, she should have a supercilious knowledge in accounts—and as she grew up, I would have her instructed in geometry, that she might know something of the contagious countries—but above all, Sir Anthony, she should be mistress of orthodoxy, that she might not misspell, and mispronounce words so shamefully as girls usually do; and likewise that she might reprehend the true meaning of what she is saying. This, Sir Anthony, is what I would have a woman know—and I don't think there is a superstitious article in it.

SIR ANTHONY. Well, well, Mrs. Malaprop, I will dispute the point no further with you; though I must confess that you are a truly moderate and polite arguer, for almost every third word you say is on my side of the question. But, Mrs. Malaprop, to the more important point in debate—you say you have no objection to my proposal.

MRS. MALAPROP. None, I assure you. I am under no positive engagement with Mr. Acres, and as Lydia is so obstinate against him, perhaps your son may have better success.

SIR ANTHONY. Well, Madam, I will write for the boy directly. He knows not a syllable of this yet, though I have for some time had the proposal in my head. He is at present with his regiment.

MRS. MALAPROP. We have never seen your son, Sir Anthony; but I hope no objection on his side.

SIR ANTHONY. Objection!—let him object if he dare! No, no, Mrs. Malaprop, Jack knows that the least demur puts me in a frenzy directly. My process was always very simple—in their young days, 'twas "Jack do this";—if he demurred—I knocked him down—and if he grumbled at that—I always sent him out of the room.

MRS. MALAPROP. Aye, and the properest way, o' my conscience! —nothing is so conciliating to young people as severity. Well, Sir Anthony, I shall give Mr. Acres his discharge, and prepare Lydia to receive your son's invocations; and I hope you will represent *her* to the Captain as an object not altogether illegible.

SIR ANTHONY. Madam, I will handle the subject prudently. Well, I must leave you—and let me beg you, Mrs. Malaprop, to enforce this matter roundly to the girl; take my advice—keep a tight hand; if she rejects this proposal—clap her under lock and key—and if you were just to let the servants forget to bring her dinner for three or four days, you can't conceive how she'd come about!

[*Exit* SIR ANTHONY.]

MRS. MALAPROP. Well, at any rate I shall be glad to get her from under my intuition. She has somehow discovered my partiality for Sir Lucius O'Trigger—sure, Lucy can't have betrayed me! No, the girl is such a simpleton, I should have made her confess it.——[*Calls.*] Lucy!—Lucy—Had she been one of your artificial ones, I should never have trusted her.

Enter LUCY.

LUCY. Did you call, Ma'am?

MRS. MALAPROP. Yes, girl. Did you see Sir Lucius while you was out?

LUCY. No, indeed, Ma'am, not a glimpse of him.

MRS. MALAPROP. You are sure, Lucy, that you never mentioned——

LUCY. O Gemini! I'd sooner cut my tongue out.

MRS. MALAPROP. Well, don't let your simplicity be imposed on.

LUCY. No, Ma'am.

MRS. MALAPROP. So, come to me presently, and I'll give you another letter to Sir Lucius; but mind, Lucy—if ever you betray what you are intrusted with (unless it be other people's secret to me) you forfeit my malevolence forever, and your being a simpleton shall be no excuse for your locality. [*Exit* MRS. MALAPROP.]

LUCY. Ha! ha! ha!—So, my dear *simplicity*, let me give you a little respite—[*altering her manner*]—let girls in my station be as fond as they please of appearing expert, and knowing in their trusts—commend me to a mask of *silliness*, and a pair of sharp eyes for my own interest under it! Let me see to what account have I turned my *simplicity* lately—[*Looks at a paper.*] For *abetting Miss Lydia Languish in a design of running away with an Ensign!—in money—sundry times—twelve pound twelve—gowns, five—hats, ruffles, cups, &c., &c.—numberless! From the said Ensign, within this last month, six guineas and a half.—* About a quarter's pay!—Item, *from Mrs. Malaprop, for betraying the young people to her*—when I found matters were likely to be discovered —*two guineas, and a black paduasoy.*[15]—Item, *from Mr. Acres, for carrying divers letters*—which I never delivered—*two guineas, and a pair of buckles.*—Item, *from Sir Lucius O'Trigger—three crowns—two gold pocket-pieces—and a silver snuff-box!*—Well done, *simplicity!*—Yet I was forced to make my Hibernian[16] believe that he was corresponding, not with the *aunt*, but with the *niece*: for, though not overrich, I

---

[15] a garment made of a rich corded silk fabric   [16] Irishman

found he had too much pride and delicacy to sacrifice the feelings of a gentleman to the necessities of his fortune.

[*Exit.*]

ACT II

Scene I
CAPTAIN ABSOLUTE's *lodgings.*

CAPTAIN ABSOLUTE *and* FAG.

FAG. Sir, while I was there Sir Anthony came in: I told him you had sent me to inquire after his health, and to know if he was at leisure to see you.

ABSOLUTE. And what did he say on hearing I was at Bath?

FAG. Sir, in my life I never saw an elderly gentleman more astonished! He started back two or three paces, rapped out a dozen interjectoral oaths, and asked what the devil had brought you here!

ABSOLUTE. Well, Sir, and what did you say?

FAG. Oh, I lied, Sir—I forget the precise lie; but you may depend on't, he got no truth from me. Yet, with submission, for fear of blunders in future, I should be glad to fix what *has* brought us to Bath, in order that we may lie a little consistently. Sir Anthony's servants were curious, Sir, very curious indeed.

ABSOLUTE. You have said nothing to them?

FAG. Oh, not a word, Sir—not a word. Mr. Thomas, indeed, the coachman (whom I take to be the discreetest of whips)——

ABSOLUTE. 'Sdeath![17]—you rascal! you have not trusted him!

FAG. Oh, *no*, Sir!—no—no—not a syllable, upon my veracity! He was, indeed, a little inquisitive; but I was sly, Sir—devilish sly!—My master (said I), honest Thomas (you know, Sir, one says *honest* to one's inferiors), is come to Bath to *recruit*—yes, Sir—I said, *to recruit*—and whether for men, money, or constitution, you know, Sir, is nothing to him, nor anyone else.

ABSOLUTE. Well—*recruit* will do—let it be so——

FAG. Oh, Sir, recruit will do surprisingly—indeed, to give the thing an air, I told Thomas that your Honour had already enlisted five disbanded chairmen, seven minority waiters, and thirteen billiard markers.[18]

ABSOLUTE. You blockhead, never say more than is necessary.

FAG. I beg pardon, Sir—I beg pardon—— But with submission, a lie is nothing unless one supports it. Sir, whenever I draw on my invention

[17] God's death!
[18] five discharged sedan-chair carriers, seven unemployed waiters, and thirteen scorekeepers from billiard rooms

for a good current lie, I always forge indorsements, as well as the bill.

ABSOLUTE. Well, take care you don't hurt your credit by offering too much security. Is Mr. Faulkland returned?

FAG. He is above, Sir, changing his dress.

ABSOLUTE. Can you tell whether he has been informed of Sir Anthony's and Miss Melville's arrival?

FAG. I fancy not, Sir; he has seen no one since he came in but his gentleman, who was with him at Bristol.——I think, Sir, I hear Mr. Faulkland coming down——

ABSOLUTE. Go tell him I am here.

FAG. Yes, Sir [*going*]. I beg pardon, Sir, but should Sir Anthony call, you will do me the favor to remember that we are *recruiting*, if you please.

ABSOLUTE. Well, well.

FAG. And in tenderness to my character, if your Honor could bring in the chairmen and waiters, I shall esteem it as an obligation; for though I never scruple a lie to serve my master, yet it hurts one's conscience to be found out.   [*Exit.*]

ABSOLUTE. Now for my whimsical friend—if he does not know that his mistress is here, I'll tease him a little before I tell him——

Enter FAULKLAND.

Faulkland, you're welcome to Bath again; you are punctual in your return.

FAULKLAND. Yes; I had nothing to detain me when I had finished the business I went on. Well, what news since I left you? How stand matters between you and Lydia?

ABSOLUTE. Faith, much as they were; I have not seen her since our quarrel; however, I expect to be recalled every hour.

FAULKLAND. Why don't you persuade her to go off with you at once?

ABSOLUTE. What, and lose two-thirds of her fortune? You forget that, my friend. No, no, I could have brought her to that long ago.

FAULKLAND. Nay then, you trifle too long—if you are sure of *her*, propose to the aunt *in your own character*, and write to Sir Anthony for his consent.

ABSOLUTE. Softly, softly, for though I am convinced my little Lydia would elope with me as Ensign Beverley, yet am I by no means certain that she would take me with the impediment of our friend's consent, a regular hundrum wedding, and the reversion[19] of a good fortune on my side; no, no, I must prepare her gradually for the discovery, and make myself necessary to her, before I risk it.——Well, but Faulkland, you'll dine with us today at the hotel?

FAULKLAND. Indeed, I cannot: I am not in spirits to be of such a party.

19 inheritance

ABSOLUTE. By heavens! I shall forswear your company. You are the most teasing, captious, incorrigible lover! Do love like a man!

FAULKLAND. I own I am unfit for company.

ABSOLUTE. Am not *I* a lover; aye, and a romantic one too? Yet do I carry everywhere with me such a confounded farrago of doubts, fears, hopes, wishes, and all the flimsy furniture of a country miss's brain!

FAULKLAND. Ah! Jack, your heart and soul are not, like mine, fixed immutably on one only object. You throw for a large stake, but losing —you could stake, and throw again. But I have set my sum of happiness on this cast, and not to succeed were to be stripped of all.

ABSOLUTE. But, for heaven's sake! what grounds for apprehension can your whimsical brain conjure up at present?

FAULKLAND. What grounds for apprehension did you say? Heavens! are there not a thousand! I fear for her spirits—her health—her life. My absence may fret her; her anxiety for my return, her fears for me, may oppress her gentle temper. And for her health—does not every hour bring me cause to be alarmed? If it rains, some shower may even then have chilled her delicate frame! If the wind be keen, some rude blast may have affected her! The heat of noon, the dews of the evening, may endanger the life of her, for whom only I value mine. O! Jack, when delicate and feeling souls are separated, there is not a feature in the sky, not a movement of the elements, not an aspiration of the breeze, but hints some cause for a lover's apprehension!

ABSOLUTE. Aye, but we may choose whether we will take the hint or not. So then, Faulkland, if you were convinced that Julia were well and in spirits, you would be entirely content?

FAULKLAND. I should be happy beyond measure—I am anxious only for that.

ABSOLUTE. Then to cure your anxiety at once—Miss Melville is in perfect health, and is at this moment in Bath!

FAULKLAND. Nay, Jack—don't trifle with me.

ABSOLUTE. She is arrived here with my father within this hour.

FAULKLAND. Can you be serious?

ABSOLUTE. I thought you knew Sir Anthony better than to be surprised at a sudden whim of this kind. Seriously then, it is as I tell you —upon my honor.

FAULKLAND. My dear friend!—Hollo, Du-Peigne! my hat—my dear Jack—now nothing on earth can give me a moment's uneasiness.

Enter FAG.

FAG. Sir, Mr. Acres just arrived is below.

ABSOLUTE. Stay, Faulkland, this Acres lives within a mile of Sir Anthony, and he shall tell you how your mistress has been ever since you left her.—— Fag, show the gentleman up. [*Exit* FAG.]

FAULKLAND. What, is he much acquainted in the family?

ABSOLUTE. Oh, very intimate. I insist on your not going: besides, his character will divert you.

FAULKLAND. Well, I should like to ask him a few questions.

ABSOLUTE. He is likewise a rival of mine—that is of my *other self's*, for he does not think his friend Captain Absolute ever saw the lady in question; and it is ridiculous enough to hear him complain to me of *one Beverley*, a concealed skulking rival, who——

FAULKLAND. Hush! He's here.

Enter ACRES.

ACRES. Hah! my dear friend, noble captain, and honest Jack, how dost thou? Just arrived, faith, as you see. Sir, your humble servant. Warm work on the roads, Jack!—Odds whips and wheels! I've traveled like a comet, with a tail of dust all the way as long as the Mall.

ABSOLUTE. Ah! Bob, you are indeed an eccentric planet, but we know your attraction hither. Give me leave to introduce Mr. Faulkland to you; Mr. Faulkland, Mr. Acres.

ACRES. Sir, I am most heartily glad to see you: Sir, I solicit your connections.——Hey, Jack—what—this is Mr. Faulkland, who——?

ABSOLUTE. Aye, Bob, Miss Melville's Mr. Faulkland.

ACRES. Odd so! she and your father can be but just arrived before me —I suppose you have seen them. Ah! Mr. Faulkland, you are indeed a happy man.

FAULKLAND. I have not seen Miss Melville yet, Sir. I hope she enjoyed full health and spirits in Devonshire?

ACRES. Never knew her better in my life, Sir—never better. Odds blushes and blooms! she has been as healthy as the German Spa.

FAULKLAND. Indeed! I did hear that she had been a little indisposed.

ACRES. False, false, Sir—only said to vex you: quite the reverse, I assure you.

FAULKLAND. There, Jack, you see she has the advantage of me; I had almost fretted myself ill.

ABSOLUTE. Now are you angry with your mistress for not having been sick.

FAULKLAND. No, no, you misunderstand me: yet surely a little trifling indisposition is not an unnatural consequence of absence from those we love. Now confess—isn't there something unkind in this violent, robust, unfeeling health?

ABSOLUTE. Oh, it was very unkind of her to be well in your absence, to be sure!

ACRES. Good apartments, Jack.

FAULKLAND. Well, Sir, but you were saying that Miss Melville has been so *exceedingly* well—what, then she has been merry and gay, I suppose? Always in spirits—hey?

ACRES. Merry! Odds crickets! she has been the belle and spirit of the company wherever she has been—so lively and entertaining! so full of wit and humor!

FAULKLAND. There, Jack, there! Oh, by my soul! there is an innate levity in woman, that nothing can overcome. What! happy, and I away!

ABSOLUTE. Have done—how foolish this is! Just now you were only apprehensive for your mistress's *spirits*.

FAULKLAND. Why, Jack, have I been the joy and spirit of the company?

ABSOLUTE. No, indeed, you have not.

FAULKLAND. Have I been lively and entertaining?

ABSOLUTE. Oh, upon my word, I acquit you.

FAULKLAND. Have I been full of wit and humor?

ABSOLUTE. No, faith; to do you justice, you have been confoundedly stupid indeed.

ACRES. What's the matter with the gentleman?

ABSOLUTE. He is only expressing his great satisfaction at hearing that Julia has been so well and happy—that's all—hey, Faulkland?

FAULKLAND. Oh! I am rejoiced to hear it—yes, yes, she has a *happy* disposition!

ACRES. That she has indeed. Then she is so accomplished—so sweet a voice—so expert at her harpsichord—such a mistress of flat and sharp squallante, rumblante, and quiverante! There was this time month—Odds minims and crotchets![20] how she did chirrup at Mrs. Piano's concert!

FAULKLAND. There again, what say you to this? You see she has been all mirth and song—not a thought of me!

ABSOLUTE. Pho! man, is not music the food of love?[21]

FAULKLAND. Well, well, it may be so.——Pray, Mr.—— what's his d——d name? Do you remember what songs Miss Melville sung?

ACRES. Not I, indeed.

ABSOLUTE. Stay now, they were some pretty, melancholy, purling-stream airs, I warrant; perhaps you may recollect; did she sing *"When absent from my soul's delight"*?

ACRES. No, that wa'n't it.

ABSOLUTE. Or *"Go, gentle gales"* —*"Go, gentle gales!"* [*Sings.*]

ACRES. Oh no! nothing like it. Odds! now I recollect one of them— *"My heart's my own, my will is free."* [*Sings.*]

FAULKLAND. Fool! fool that I am! to fix all my happiness on such a trifler! 'Sdeath! to make herself the pipe and ballad-monger of a circle! to soothe her light heart with catches and glees! What can you say to this, Sir?

---

[20] a mixture of actual and imaginary musical terms
[21] "If music be the food of love, play on"—Shakespeare, *Twelfth Night*, I, i, 1

ABSOLUTE. Why, that I should be glad to hear my mistress had been
so merry, *Sir*.

FAULKLAND. Nay, nay, nay—I am not sorry that she has been happy
—no, no, I am glad of that—I would not have had her sad or sick—yet
surely a sympathetic heart would have shown itself even in the choice
of a song: she might have been temperately healthy, and, somehow,
plaintively gay; but she has been dancing too, I doubt not!

ACRES. What does the gentleman say about dancing?

ABSOLUTE. He says the lady we speak of dances as well as she sings.

ACRES. Aye, truly, does she—there was at our last race-ball——

FAULKLAND. Hell and the devil! There! there!—I told you so! I told
you so! Oh! she thrives in my absence! Dancing! But her whole feelings have been in opposition with mine! I have been anxious, silent,
pensive, sedentary—my days have been hours of care, my nights of
watchfulness. She has been all Health! Spirit! Laugh! Song! Dance!
Oh! d——n'd, d——n'd levity!

ABSOLUTE. For heaven's sake! Faulkland, don't expose yourself so.
Suppose she has danced, what then? Does not the ceremony of society
often oblige——

FAULKLAND. Well, well, I'll contain myself. Perhaps, as you say,
for form sake. What, Mr. Acres, you were praising Miss Melville's
manner of dancing a *minuet*—hey?

ACRES. Oh I dare insure her for that—but what I was going to speak
of was her *country dancing*. Odds swimmings! she has such an air
with her!

FAULKLAND. Now disappointment on her! Defend this, Absolute,
why don't you defend this? Country-dances! jigs, and reels! Am I to
blame now? A minuet I could have forgiven—I should not have
minded that—I say I should not have regarded a minuet—but *country-
dances!* Z——ds! had she made one in a cotillion—I believe I could
have forgiven even that—but to be monkey-led for a night! to run the
gauntlet through a string of amorous palming[22] puppies! to show paces
like a managed filly! O Jack, there never can be but *one* man in the
world whom a truly modest and delicate woman ought to pair with in
a *country-dance;* and even then, the rest of the couples should be her
great uncles and aunts!

ABSOLUTE. Aye, to be sure!—grandfathers and grandmothers!

FAULKLAND. If there be but one vicious mind in the Set, 'twill spread
like a contagion—the action of their pulse beats to the lascivious movement of the jig—their quivering, warm-breathed sighs impregnate the
very air—the atmosphere becomes electrical to love, and each amorous
spark darts through every link of the chain! I must leave you—I own
I am somewhat flurried—and that confounded looby[23] has perceived
it. [*going*]

---

[22] touching; caressing   [23] lout

ABSOLUTE. Nay, but stay, Faulkland, and thank Mr. Acres for his good news.

FAULKLAND. D——n his news! [*Exit* FAULKLAND.]

ABSOLUTE. Ha! ha! ha! Poor Faulkland! Five minutes since—"nothing on earth could give him a moment's uneasiness!"

ACRES. The gentleman wa'n't angry at my praising his mistress, was he?

ABSOLUTE. A little jealous, I believe, Bob.

ACRES. You don't say so? Ha! ha! jealous of me?—that's a good joke.

ABSOLUTE. There's nothing strange in that, Bob: let me tell you, that sprightly grace and insinuating manner of yours will do some mischief among the girls here.

ACRES. Ah! you joke—ha! ha!—mischief—ha! ha! But you know I am not my own property; my dear Lydia has forestalled me. She could never abide me in the country, because I used to dress so badly— but odds frogs and tambours![24] I shan't take matters so here—now ancient madam has no voice in it. I'll make my old clothes know who's master. I shall straightway cashier the hunting-frock, and render my leather breeches incapable. My hair has been in training some time.

ABSOLUTE. Indeed!

ACRES. Aye—and tho'ff the side-curls are a little restive, my hindpart takes to it very kindly.

ABSOLUTE. O, you'll polish, I doubt not.

ACRES. Absolutely I propose so. Then if I can find out this Ensign Beverley, odds triggers and flints! I'll make him know the difference o't.

ABSOLUTE. Spoke like a man—but pray, Bob, I observe you have got an odd kind of a new method of swearing——

ACRES. Ha! ha! you've taken notice of it? 'Tis genteel, isn't it? I didn't invent it myself, though; but a commander in our militia—a great scholar, I assure you—says that there is no meaning in the common oaths, and that nothing but their antiquity makes them respectable, because, he says, the ancients would never stick to an oath or two, but would say, by Jove! or by Bacchus! or by Mars! or by Venus! or by Pallas! according to the sentiment; so that to swear with propriety, says my little major, the "oath should be an echo to the sense";[25] and this we call the *oath referential*, or *sentimental swearing*—ha! ha! ha! 'tis genteel, isn't it?

ABSOLUTE. Very genteel, and very new, indeed—and I dare say will supplant all other figures of imprecation.

ACRES. Aye, aye, the best terms will grow obsolete. Damns have had their day.

---

[24] ornamental embroidery

[25] "The sound must seem an echo to the sense"—Pope, *An Essay on Criticism*, 1,365

Enter FAG.

FAG. Sir, there is a gentleman below desires to see you. Shall I show
him into the parlor?

ABSOLUTE. Aye—you may.

ACRES. Well, I must be gone——

ABSOLUTE. Stay; who is it, Fag?

FAG. Your father, Sir.

ABSOLUTE. You puppy, why didn't you show him up directly?

[*Exit* FAG.]

ACRES. You have business with Sir Anthony. I expect a message from
Mrs. Malaprop at my lodgings. I have sent also to my dear friend,
Sir Lucius O'Trigger. Adieu, Jack! We must meet at night, when you
shall give me a dozen bumpers [26] to little Lydia.

ABSOLUTE. That I will, with all my heart.   [*Exit* ACRES.]
Now for a parental lecture. I hope he has heard nothing of the business
that has brought me here. I wish the gout had held him fast in Devonshire, with all my soul!

Enter SIR ANTHONY.

Sir, I am delighted to see you here; and looking so well! Your sudden
arrival at Bath made me apprehensive for your health.

SIR ANTHONY. Very apprehensive, I dare say, Jack. What, you are
recruiting here, hey?

ABSOLUTE. Yes, Sir, I am on duty.

SIR ANTHONY. Well, Jack, I am glad to see you, though I did not
expect it, for I was going to write to you on a little matter of business.
Jack, I have been considering that I grow old and infirm, and shall
probably not trouble you long.

ABSOLUTE. Pardon me, Sir, I never saw you look more strong and
hearty; and I pray frequently that you may continue so.

SIR ANTHONY. I hope your prayers may be heard with all my heart.
Well then, Jack, I have been considering that I am so strong and
hearty, I may continue to plague you a long time. Now, Jack, I am
sensible that the income of your commission, and what I have hitherto
allowed you, is but a small pittance for a lad of your spirit.

ABSOLUTE. Sir, you are very good.

SIR ANTHONY. And it is my wish, while yet I live, to have my boy
make some figure in the world. I have resolved, therefore, to fix you
at once in a noble independence.

ABSOLUTE. Sir, your kindness overpowers me—such generosity makes
the gratitude of reason more lively than the sensations even of filial
affection.

[26] drink a dozen toasts

SIR ANTHONY. I am glad you are so sensible of my attention—and you shall be master of a large estate in a few weeks.

ABSOLUTE. Let my future life, Sir, speak my gratitude: I cannot express the sense I have of your munificence. Yet, Sir, I presume you would not wish me to quit the army?

SIR ANTHONY. Oh, that shall be as your wife chooses.

ABSOLUTE. My wife, Sir!

SIR ANTHONY. Aye, aye—settle that between you—settle that between you.

ABSOLUTE. A *wife*, Sir, did you say?

SIR ANTHONY. Aye, a wife—why; did not I mention her before?

ABSOLUTE. Not a word of her, Sir.

SIR ANTHONY. Odd so!—I mus'n't forget *her*, though. Yes, Jack, the independence I was talking of is by a marriage—the fortune is saddled with a wife—but I suppose that makes no difference.

ABSOLUTE. Sir! Sir!—you amaze me!

SIR ANTHONY. Why, what the devil's the matter with the fool? Just now you were all gratitude and duty.

ABSOLUTE. I was, Sir—you talked to me of independence and a fortune, but not a word of a wife.

SIR ANTHONY. Why—what difference does that make? Odd's life, Sir! if you have the estate, you must take it with the live stock on it, as it stands.

ABSOLUTE. If my happiness is to be the price, I must beg leave to decline the purchase. Pray, Sir, who is the lady?

SIR ANTHONY. What's that to you, Sir? Come, give me your promise to love, and to marry her directly.

ABSOLUTE. Sure, Sir, this is not very reasonable, to summon my affections for a lady I know nothing of!

SIR ANTHONY. I am sure, Sir, 'tis more unreasonable in you to *object* to a lady you know nothing of.

ABSOLUTE. Then, Sir, I must tell you plainly that my inclinations are fixed on another—my heart is engaged to an angel.

SIR ANTHONY. Then pray let it send an excuse. It is very sorry—but *business* prevents its waiting on her.

ABSOLUTE. But my vows are pledged to her.

SIR ANTHONY. Let her foreclose, Jack; let her foreclose; they are not worth redeeming: besides, you have the angel's vows in exchange, I suppose; so there can be no loss there.

ABSOLUTE. You must excuse me, Sir, if I tell you, once for all, that in this point I cannot obey you.

SIR ANTHONY. Hark'ee, Jack: I have heard you for some time with patience—I have been cool—quite cool; but take care—you know I am compliance itself when I am not thwarted—no one more easily led when I have my own way; but don't put me in a frenzy.

ABSOLUTE. Sir, I must repeat it—in this I cannot obey you.

SIR ANTHONY. Now, d——n me! if ever I call you *Jack* again while I live!

ABSOLUTE. Nay, Sir, but hear me.

SIR ANTHONY. Sir, I won't hear a word—not a word! not one word! so give me your promise by a nod—and I'll tell you what, Jack—I mean, you dog—if you don't, by——

ABSOLUTE. What, Sir, promise to link myself to some mass of ugliness! to——

SIR ANTHONY. Z——ds! Sirrah! the lady shall be as ugly as I choose: she shall have a hump on each shoulder; she shall be as crooked as the Crescent; [27] her one eye shall roll like the Bull's in Cox's Museum—she shall have a skin like a mummy, and the beard of a Jew—she shall be all this, Sirrah!—yet I'll make you ogle her all day, and sit up all night to write sonnets on her beauty.

ABSOLUTE. This is reason and moderation indeed!

SIR ANTHONY. None of your sneering, puppy! no grinning, jackanapes!

ABSOLUTE. Indeed, Sir, I never was in a worse humor for mirth in my life.

SIR ANTHONY. 'Tis false, Sir! I know you are laughing in your sleeve; I know you'll grin when I am gone, Sirrah!

ABSOLUTE. Sir, I hope I know my duty better.

SIR ANTHONY. None of your passion, Sir! none of your violence! if you please. It won't do with me, I promise you.

ABSOLUTE. Indeed, Sir, I never was cooler in my life.

SIR ANTHONY. 'Tis a confounded lie!—I know you are in a passion in your heart; I know you are, you hypocritical young dog! But it won't do.

ABSOLUTE. Nay, Sir, upon my word.

SIR ANTHONY. So you will fly out! Can't you be cool, like me? What the devil good can *passion* do! *Passion* is of no service, you impudent, insolent, overbearing reprobate!—There you sneer again! don't provoke me! But you rely upon the mildness of my temper—you do, you dog! you play upon the meekness of my disposition! Yet take care—the patience of a saint may be overcome at last!—but mark! I give you six hours and a half to consider of this: if you then agree, without any condition, to do everything on earth that I choose, why—confound you! I may in time forgive you. If not, z——ds! don't enter the same hemisphere with me! don't dare to breathe the same air, or use the same light with me; but get an atmosphere and a sun of your own! I'll strip you of your commission; I'll lodge a five-and-threepence in the hands of trustees, and you shall live on the interest.

[27] a semicircular street of fashionable town-houses in Bath

I'll disown you, I'll disinherit you, I'll unget you! and—d——n me, if ever I call you Jack again! [*Exit* SIR ANTHONY.]

ABSOLUTE solus.

ABSOLUTE. Mild, gentle, considerate Father—I kiss your hands. What a tender method of giving his opinion in these matters Sir Anthony has! I dare not trust him with the truth. I wonder what old wealthy hag it is that he wants to bestow on me! Yet he married himself for love! and was in his youth a bold intriguer, and a gay companion!

Enter FAG.

FAG. Assuredly, Sir, our father is wrath to a degree; he comes downstairs eight or ten steps at a time—muttering, growling, and thumping the bannisters all the way: I, and the cook's dog, stand bowing at the door—rap! he gives me a stroke on the head with his cane; bids me carry that to my master; then kicking the poor turnspit into the area,[28] d——ns us all for a puppy triumvirate! Upon my credit, Sir, were I in your place, and found my father such very bad company, I should certainly drop his acquaintance.

ABSOLUTE. Cease your impertinence, Sir, at present. Did you come in for nothing more? Stand out of the way!

[Pushes him aside, and exit.]

FAG solus.

FAG. Soh! Sir Anthony trims my master. He is afraid to reply to his father—then vents his spleen on poor Fag! When one is vexed by one person, to revenge one's self on another who happens to come in the way is the vilest injustice. Ah! it shows the worst temper—the basest——

Enter ERRAND-BOY.

BOY. Mr. Fag! Mr. Fag! your master calls you.

FAG. Well, you little dirty puppy, you need not bawl so!——The meanest disposition! the——

BOY. Quick, quick, Mr. Fag!

FAG. *Quick, quick,* you impudent jackanapes! am I to be commanded by you too? you little, impertinent, insolent, kitchen-bred——

[Exit, kicking and beating him.]

---

[28] kicking a menial servant (originally a boy who turned the spit at the fireplace to roast meat evenly) into the entrance from the street into the servants' hall in the basement

SCENE II
The North Parade.[29]
Enter LUCY

LUCY. So—I shall have another rival to add to my mistress's list—
Captain Absolute. However, I shall not enter his name till my purse
has received notice in form. Poor Acres is dismissed! Well, I have
done him a last friendly office in letting him know that Beverley was
here before him. Sir Lucius is generally more punctual when he expects to hear from his *dear Dalia*, as he calls her: I wonder he's not
here! I have a little scruple of conscience from this deceit; though I
should not be paid so well, if my hero knew that *Delia* was near fifty,
and her own mistress.

Enter SIR LUCIUS O'TRIGGER.

SIR LUCIUS. Hah! my little embassadress—upon my conscience, I
have been looking for you; I have been on the South Parade this half-
hour.
LUCY [*speaking simply*]. O Gemini! and I have been waiting for your
worship here on the North.
SIR LUCIUS. Faith!—maybe that was the reason we did not meet;
and it is very comical, too, how you could go out and I not see you—
for I was only taking a nap at the Parade Coffee-house, and I chose
the *window* on purpose that I might not miss you.
LUCY. My stars! Now I'd wager a sixpence I went by while you were
asleep.
SIR LUCIUS. Sure enough it must have been so—and I never dreamt it
so late, till I waked. Well, but my little girl, have you got nothing for
me?
LUCY. Yes, but I have: I've got a letter for you in my pocket.
SIR LUCIUS. Oh, faith! I guessed you weren't come empty-handed—
well—let me see what the dear creature says.
LUCY. There, Sir Lucius.

[*Gives him a letter.*]

SIR LUCIUS [*reads*]. *Sir—there is often a sudden incentive impulse in
love, that has a greater induction than years of domestic combination: such
was the commotion I felt at the first superfluous view of Sir Lucius
O'Trigger.*—Very pretty, upon my word.—*Female punctuation forbids
me to say more; yet let me add, that it will give me joy infallible to find
Sir Lucius worthy the last criterion of my affections.* DELIA. Upon my
conscience! Lucy, your lady is a great mistress of language. Faith,
she's quite the queen of the dictionary!—for the devil a word dare
refuse coming at her call—though one would think it was quite out of
hearing.

---

[29] one of two fashionable promenades

LUCY. Aye, Sir, a lady of her experience——

SIR LUCIUS. Experience! what, at seventeen?

LUCY. O true, Sir—but then she reads so—my stars! how she will read off-hand!

SIR LUCIUS. Faith, she must be very deep read to write this way— though she is rather an arbitrary writer too—for here are a great many poor words pressed into the service of this note, that would get their *habeas corpus*[30] from any court in Christendom.

LUCY. Ah! Sir Lucius, if you were to hear how she talks of you!

SIR LUCIUS. Oh tell her I'll make her the best husband in the world, and Lady O'Trigger into the bargain! But we must get the old gentlewoman's consent—and do everything fairly.

LUCY. Nay, Sir Lucius, I thought you wa'n't rich enough to be so nice![31]

SIR LUCIUS. Upon my word, young woman, you have hit it: I am so poor that I can't afford to do a dirty action. If I did not want money I'd steal your mistress and her fortune with a great deal of pleasure.
[*Gives her money.*]
However, my pretty girl here's a little something to buy you a ribband; and meet me in the evening, and I'll give you an answer to this. So, hussy, take a kiss beforehand to put you in mind.
[*Kisses her.*]

LUCY. O lud! Sir Lucius—I never seed such a gemman! My lady won't like you if you're so impudent.

SIR LUCIUS. Faith she will, Lucy——That same—pho! what's the name of it?—*Modesty!*—is a quality in a lover more praised by the women than liked; so, if your mistress asks you whether Sir Lucius ever gave you a kiss, tell her *fifty*—my dear.

LUCY. What, would you have me tell her a lie?

SIR LUCIUS. Ah, then, you baggage! I'll make it a truth presently.

LUCY. For shame now; here is someone coming.

SIR LUCIUS. Oh faith, I'll quiet your conscience.
[*Sees* FAG.—*Exit, humming a tune.*]

Enter FAG.

FAG. So, so, Ma'am. I humbly beg pardon.

LUCY. O lud!—now, Mr. Fag, you flurry one so.

FAG. Come, come, Lucy, here's no one by—so a little less simplicity, with a grain or two more sincerity, if you please. You play false with us, Madam. I saw you give the baronet a letter. My master shall know this, and if he don't call him out—I will.

LUCY. Ha! ha! ha! you gentlemen's gentlemen are so hasty. That letter was from Mrs. Malaprop, simpleton. She is taken with Sir Lucius's address.

[30] a court order challenging the lawfulness of detaining a person
[31] discriminating

FAG. How! what tastes some people have! Why, I suppose I have walked by her window an hundred times. But what says our young lady? Any message to my master?

LUCY. Sad news, Mr. Fag! A worse rival than Acres! Sir Anthony Absolute has proposed his son.

FAG. What, Captain Absolute?

LUCY. Even so. I overheard it all.

FAG. Ha! ha! ha!—very good, faith. Good-bye, Lucy, I must away with this news.

LUCY. Well—you may laugh, but it is true, I assure you. [going] But—Mr. Fag—tell your master not to be cast down by this.

FAG. Oh, he'll be so disconsolate!

LUCY. And charge him not to think of quarreling with young Absolute.

FAG. Never fear!—never fear!

LUCY. Be sure—bid him keep up his spirits.

FAG. We will—we will.

[*Exeunt severally.*]

ACT III

SCENE I
The North Parade.

Enter ABSOLUTE.

ABSOLUTE. 'Tis just as Fag told me, indeed. Whimsical enough, faith, My father wants to *force* me to marry the very girl I am plotting to run away with! He must not know of my connection with her yet awhile. He has too summary a method of proceeding in these matters. However, I'll read my recantation instantly. My conversion is something sudden, indeed, but I can assure him it is very *sincere.*——So, so—here he comes. He looks plaguy gruff.   [*Steps aside.*]

Enter SIR ANTHONY.

SIR ANTHONY. No—I'll die sooner than forgive him. *Die*, did I say? I'll live these fifty years to plague him. At our last meeting, his impudence had almost put me out of temper. An obstinate, passionate, self-willed boy! Who can he take after? This is my return for getting him before all his brothers and sisters!—for putting him, at twelve years old, into a marching regiment, and allowing him fifty pounds a year, beside his pay ever since! But I have done with him; he's anybody's son for me. I never will see him more—never—never—never—never!

ABSOLUTE. Now for a penitential face.

SIR ANTHONY. Fellow, get out of my way.

ABSOLUTE. Sir, you see a penitent before you.

SIR ANTHONY. I see an impudent scoundrel before me.

ABSOLUTE. A sincere penitent. I am come, Sir, to acknowledge my error, and to submit entry to your will.

SIR ANTHONY. What's that?

ABSOLUTE. I have been revolving, and reflecting, and considering on your past goodness, and kindness, and condescension to me.

SIR ANTHONY. Well, Sir?

ABSOLUTE. I have been likewise weighing and balancing what you were pleased to mention concerning duty, and obedience, and authority.

SIR ANTHONY. Well, puppy?

ABSOLUTE. Why, then, Sir, the result of my reflections is—a resolution to sacrifice every inclination of my own to your satisfaction.

SIR ANTHONY. Why, now you talk sense—absolute sense—I never heard anything more sensible in my life. Confound you, you shall be *Jack* again!

ABSOLUTE. I am happy in the appellation.

SIR ANTHONY. Why then, Jack, my dear Jack, I will now inform you who the lady really is. Nothing but your passion and violence, you silly fellow, prevented my telling you at first. Prepare, Jack, for wonder and rapture! prepare!—— What think you of Miss Lydia Languish?

ABSOLUTE. Languish! What, the Languishes of Worcestershire?

SIR ANTHONY. Worcestershire! No. Did you never meet Mrs. Malaprop and her niece, Miss Languish, who came into our country just before you were last ordered to your regiment?

ABSOLUTE. Malaprop! Languish! I don't remember ever to have heard the names before. Yet, stay—I think I do recollect something. ——*Languish! Languish!* She squints, don't she? A little, red-haired girl?

SIR ANTHONY. Squints? A red-haired girl! Z——ds, no!

ABSOLUTE. Then I must have forgot; it can't be the same person.

SIR ANTHONY. Jack! Jack! what think you of blooming, love-breathing seventeen?

ABSOLUTE. As to that, Sir, I am quite indifferent. If I can please you in the matter, 'tis all I desire.

SIR ANTHONY. Nay, but Jack, such eyes! such eyes! so innocently wild! so bashfully irresolute! Not a glance but speaks and kindles some thought of love! Then, Jack, her cheeks! her cheeks, Jack! so deeply blushing at the insinuations of her tell-tale eyes! Then, Jack, her lips!—O Jack, lips smiling at their own discretion; and if not smiling, more sweetly pouting, more lovely in sullenness!

ABSOLUTE [*aside*]. That's she, indeed. Well done, old gentleman!

SIR ANTHONY. Then, Jack, her neck!—O Jack! Jack!

ABSOLUTE. And which is to be mine, Sir, the niece or the aunt?

SIR ANTHONY. Why, you unfeeling, insensible puppy, I despise you! When I was of your age, such a description would have made me fly

like a rocket! The *aunt*, indeed! Odd's life! when I ran away with
your mother, I would not have touched anything old or ugly to gain an
empire.

ABSOLUTE. Not to please your father, Sir?

SIR ANTHONY. To please my father! Z——ds! not to please——
Oh, my father!—Odd so!—yes—yes!—if my father, indeed, had desired—that's quite another matter. Though he wa'n't the indulgent
father that I am, Jack.

ABSOLUTE. I dare say not, Sir.

SIR ANTHONY. But, Jack, you are not sorry to find your mistress is
so beautiful?

ABSOLUTE. Sir, I repeat it; if I please you in this affair, 'tis all I desire. Not that I think a woman the worse for being handsome; but,
Sir, if you please to recollect, you before hinted something about a
hump or two, one eye, and a few more graces of that kind. Now, without being very nice, I own I should rather choose a wife of mine to
have the usual number of limbs, and a limited quantity of back: and
though *one* eye may be very agreeable, yet as the prejudice has always
run in favor of *two*, I would not wish to affect a singularity in that
article.

SIR ANTHONY. What a phlegmatic sot it is! Why, Sirrah, you're
an anchorite! a vile, insensible stock. You a soldier! you're a walking
block, fit only to dust the company's regimentals on! Odd's life! I've
a great mind to marry the girl myself!

ABSOLUTE. I am entirely at your disposal, Sir; if you should think
of addressing Miss Languish yourself, I suppose you would have me
marry the *aunt;* or if you should change your mind, and take the old
lady—'tis the same to me—I'll marry the *niece*.

SIR ANTHONY. Upon my word, Jack, thou'rt either a very great
hypocrite, or——But come, I know your indifference on such a subject must be all a lie—I'm sure it must—come, now—damn your
demure face!—come, confess, Jack—you have been lying—ha'n't
you? you have been playing the hypocrite, hey?—I'll never forgive
you if you ha'n't been lying and playing the hypocrite.

ABSOLUTE. I'm sorry, Sir, that the respect and duty which I bear to
you should be so mistaken.

SIR ANTHONY. Hang your respect and duty! But come along with
me, I'll write a note to Mrs. Malaprop, and you shall visit the lady
directly. Her eyes shall be the Promethean torch[32] to you—come
along. I'll never forgive you if you don't come back stark mad with
rapture and impatience. If you don't, egad, I'll marry the girl myself!
                                                                    [*Exeunt.*]

---

[32] Prometheus stole fire from heaven to ignite the soul in humankind.

SCENE II
JULIA's *dressing-room.*

FAULKLAND *solus*

FAULKLAND. They told me Julia would return directly; I wonder she
is not yet come! How mean does this captious, unsatisfied temper of
mine appear to my cooler judgment! Yet I know not that I indulge it in
any other point: but on this one subject, and to this one subject, whom
I think I love beyond my life, I am ever ungenerously fretful, and
madly capricious! I am conscious of it—yet I cannot correct myself!
What tender, honest joy sparkled in her eyes when we met! How
delicate was the warmth of her expressions! I was ashamed to appear
less happy, though I had come resolved to wear a face of coolness and
upbraiding. Sir Anthony's presence prevented my proposed expostula-
tions, yet I must be satisfied that she has not been so *very* happy in my
absence. She is coming! Yes! I know the nimbleness of her tread
when she thinks her impatient Faulkland counts the moments of her
stay.

Enter JULIA.

JULIA. I had not hoped to see you again so soon.

FAULKLAND. Could I, Julia, be contented with my first welcome—
restrained as we were by the presence of a third person?

JULIA. O Faulkland, when your kindness can make me thus happy,
let me not think that I discovered something of coldness in your first
salutation.

FAULKLAND. 'Twas but your fancy, Julia. I *was* rejoiced to see you—
to see you in such health. Sure I had no cause for coldness?

JULIA. Nay then, I see you have taken something ill. You must not
conceal from me what it is.

FAULKLAND. When then—shall I own to you—that my joy at hearing of your health and arrival here, by your neighbor Acres, was
somewhat damped by his dwelling much on the high spirits you had
enjoyed in Devonshire—on your mirth, your singing, dancing, and I
know not what! For such is my temper, Julia, that I should regard
every mirthful moment in your absence as a treason to constancy. The
mutual tear that steals down the cheek of parting lovers is a compact
that no smile shall live there till they meet again.

JULIA. Must I never cease to tax my Faulkland with this teasing minute
caprice? Can the idle reports of a silly boor weigh in your breast
against my tried affection?

FAULKLAND. They have no weight with me, Julia: no, no—I am
happy if you have been so—yet only say that you did not sing with
mirth—say that you *thought* of Faulkland in the dance.

JULIA. I never can be happy in your absence. If I wear a countenance of content, it is to show that my mind holds no doubt of my Faulk-land's truth. If I seemed sad, it were to make malice triumph, and say that I had fixed my heart on one who left me to lament his roving, and my own credulity. Believe me, Faulkland, I mean not to upbraid you when I say that I have often dressed sorrow in smiles, lest my friends should guess whose unkindness had caused my tears.

FAULKLAND. You were ever all goodness to me. Oh, I am a brute when I but admit a doubt of your true constancy!

JULIA. If ever, without such cause from you, as I will not suppose possible, you find my affections veering but a point, may I become a proverbial scoff for levity and base ingratitude.

FAULKLAND. Ah! Julia, that last word is grating to me. I would I had no title to your *gratitude!* Search your heart, Julia; perhaps what you have mistaken for love, is but the warm effusion of a too thankful heart!

JULIA. For what quality must I love you?

FAULKLAND. For no quality! To regard me for any quality of mind or understanding were only to *esteem* me. And for person—I have often wished myself deformed, to be convinced that I owed no obligation *there* for any part of your affection.

JULIA. Where Nature has bestowed a show of nice attention in the features of a man, he should laugh at it as misplaced. I have seen men who in *this* vain article perhaps might rank above you; but my heart has never asked my eyes if it were so or not.

FAULKLAND. Now this is not well from *you*, Julia. I despise person in a man. Yet if you loved me as I wish, though I were an Æthiop, you'd think none so fair.

JULIA. I see you are determined to be unkind. The *contract* which my poor father bound us in gives you more than a lover's privilege.

FAULKLAND. Again, Julia, you raise ideas that feed and justify my doubts. I would not have been more free—no—I am proud of my restraint. Yet—yet—perhaps your high respect alone for this solemn compact has fettered your inclinations, which else had made a worthier choice. How shall I be sure, had you remained unbound in thought and promise, that I should still have been the object of your persevering love?

JULIA. Then try me now. Let us be free as strangers as to what is past: *my* heart will not feel more liberty!

FAULKLAND. There now! so hasty, Julia! so anxious to be free! If your love for me were fixed and ardent, you would not loose your hold, even though I wished it!

JULIA. Oh, you torture me to the heart! I cannot bear it.

FAULKLAND. I do not mean to distress you. If I loved you less I should never give you an uneasy moment. But hear me. All my fretful doubts arise from this: women are not used to weigh, and separate the motives of their affections; the cold dictates of prudence, gratitude, or filial duty, may sometimes be mistaken for the pleadings of the heart. I would not boast—yet let me say that I have neither age, person, or character to found dislike on; my fortune such as few ladies could be charged with *indiscretion* in the match. O Julia! when *Love* receives such countenance from *Prudence*, nice[33] minds will be suspicious of its birth.

JULIA. I know not whither your insinuations would tend, but as they seem pressing to insult me, I will spare you the regret of having done so. I have given you no cause for this!

[*Exit in tears.*]

FAULKLAND. In tears! Stay, Julia: stay but for a moment.——The door is fastened! Julia!—my soul—but for one moment. I hear her sobbing! 'Sdeath! what a brute am I to use her thus! Yet stay!—— Aye—she is coming now. How little resolution there is in woman! How a few soft words can turn them!——No, faith!—she is *not* coming either! Why, Julia—my love—say but that you forgive me—come but to tell me that. Now, this is being *too* resentful.——Stay! she is coming too—I thought she would—no *steadiness* in anything! her going away must have been a mere trick then. She sha'n't see that I was hurt by it. I'll affect indifference. [*Hums a tune: then listens.*]—— No—Z—ds! she's *not* coming!—nor don't intend it, I suppose. This is not *steadiness*, but *obstinacy!* Yet I deserve it. What, after so long an absence to quarrel with her tenderness!—'twas barbarous and unmanly! I should be ashamed to see her now. I'll wait till her just resentment is abated—and when I distress her so again, may I lose her forever, and be linked instead to some antique virago, whose gnawing passions, and long-hoarded spleen shall make me curse my folly half the day, and all the night!

[*Exit.*]

Scene III
Mrs. Malaprop's *lodgings.*

MRS. MALAPROP, *with a letter in her hand,*
and CAPTAIN ABSOLUTE.

MRS. MALAPROP. Your being Sir Anthony's son, Captain, would itself be a sufficient accommodation; but from the ingenuity of your appearance, I am convinced you deserve the character here given of you.

ABSOLUTE. Permit me to say, Madam, that as I never yet have had the pleasure of seeing Miss Languish, my principal inducement in this affair at present is the honor of being allied to Mrs. Malaprop; of whose intellectual accomplishments, elegant manners, and unaffected learning, no tongue is silent.

---

[33] precise

MRS. MALAPROP. Sir, you do me infinite honor! I beg, Captain, you'll be seated. [*Sit.*] Ah! few gentlemen now-a-days know how to value the ineffectual qualities in a woman! few think how a little knowledge becomes a gentlewoman! Men have no sense now but for the worthless flower of beauty!

ABSOLUTE. It is but too true, indeed, Ma'am. Yet I fear our ladies should share the blame—they think our admiration of *beauty* so great, that *knowledge* in *them* would be superfluous. Thus, like garden-trees, they seldom show fruit till time has robbed them of the more specious blossom. Few, like Mrs. Malaprop and the orange-tree, are rich in both at once!

MRS. MALAPROP. Sir—you overpower me with good-breeding. [*aside*] He is the very pineapple of politeness!—— You are not ignorant, Captain, that this giddy girl has somehow contrived to fix her affections on a beggarly, strolling, eaves-dropping Ensign, whom none of us have seen, and nobody knows anything of.

ABSOLUTE. Oh, I have heard the silly affair before. I'm not at all prejudiced against her on *that* account.

MRS. MALAPROP. You are very good, and very considerate, Captain. I am sure I have done everything in my power since I exploded the affair! Long ago I laid my positive conjunctions on her never to think on the fellow again; I have since laid Sir Anthony's preposition before her; but, I'm sorry to say, she seems resolved to decline every particle that I enjoin her.

ABSOLUTE. It must be very distressing, indeed, Ma'am.

MRS. MALAPROP. Oh! it gives me the hydrostatics to such a degree! I thought she had persisted from corresponding with him; but behold this very day I have interceded another letter from the fellow! I believe I have it in my pocket.

ABSOLUTE [*aside*]. Oh the devil! my last note.

MRS. MALAPROP. Aye, here it is.

ABSOLUTE [*aside.*] Aye, my note, indeed! Oh the little traitress Lucy!

MRS. MALAPROP. There, perhaps you may know the writing.
[*Gives him the letter.*]

ABSOLUTE. I think I have seen the hand before—yes, I certainly must have seen this hand before——

MRS. MALAPROP. Nay, but read it, Captain.

ABSOLUTE [*reads*]. "*My soul's idol, my adored Lydia!*"——Very tender, indeed!

MRS. MALAPROP. Tender! aye, and profane, too, o' my conscience!

ABSOLUTE. "*I am excessively alarmed at the intelligence you send me, the more so as my new rival*"——

MRS. MALAPROP. That's *you*, Sir.

ABSOLUTE. "*Has universally the character of being an accomplished gentleman, and a man of honor.*"—Well, that's handsome enough.

MRS. MALAPROP. Oh, the fellow had some design in writing so.

ABSOLUTE. That he had, I'll answer for him, Ma'am.

MRS. MALAPROP. But go on, Sir—you'll see presently.

ABSOLUTE. "*As for the old weather-beaten she-dragon who guards you*"
——Who can he mean by that?

MRS. MALAPROP. Me! Sir—*me!*—he means *me!* There—what do you think now? But go on a little further.

ABSOLUTE. Impudent scoundrel!—"*it shall go hard but I will elude her vigilance, as I am told that the same ridiculous vanity which makes her dress up her coarse features, and deck her dull chat with hard words which she don't understand*"——

MRS. MALAPROP. There, Sir! an attack upon my language! What do you think of that?—an aspersion upon my parts of speech! Was ever such a brute! Sure if I reprehend anything in this world, it is the use of my oracular tongue, and a nice derangement of epitaphs!

ABSOLUTE. He deserves to be hanged and quartered! Let me see— "*same ridiculous vanity*"——

MRS. MALAPROP. You need not read it again, Sir.

ABSOLUTE. I beg pardon, Ma'am—"*does also lay her open to the grossest deceptions from flattery and pretended admiration*"—an impudent coxcomb!—"*so that I have a scheme to see you shortly with the old harridan's consent, and even to make her a go-between in our interviews.*"—Was ever such assurance!

MRS. MALAPROP. Did you ever hear anything like it? He'll elude my vigilance, will he? Yes, yes! ha! ha! He's very likely to enter these doors! We'll try who can plot best!

ABSOLUTE. So we will, Ma'am—so we will. Ha! ha! ha! A conceited puppy, ha! ha! ha! Well, but Mrs. Malaprop, as the girl seems so infatuated by this fellow, suppose you were to wink at her corresponding with him for a little time—let her even plot an elopement with him—then do you connive at her escape—while *I*, just in the nick, will have the fellow laid by the heels, and fairly contrive to carry her off in his stead.

MRS. MALAPROP. I am delighted with the scheme; never was anything better perpetrated!

ABSOLUTE. But, pray, could not I see the lady for a few minutes now? I should like to try her temper a little.

MRS. MALAPROP. Why, I don't know—I doubt she is not prepared for a visit of this kind. There is a decorum in these matters.

ABSOLUTE. O Lord! she won't mind *me*—only tell her Beverley——

MRS. MALAPROP. Sir!——

ABSOLUTE [*aside.*] Gently, good tongue.

MRS. MALAPROP. What did you say of Beverley?

ABSOLUTE. Oh, I was going to propose that you should tell her, by way of jest, that it was Beverley who was below—she'd come down fast enough then—ha! ha! ha!

MRS. MALAPROP. 'Twould be a trick she well deserves. Besides, you know the fellow tells her he'll get my consent to see her—ha! ha! Let him if he can, I say again. [*calling*] Lydia, come down here!—— He'll make me a *go-between in their interviews!*—ha! ha! ha!—Come down, I say, Lydia!—I don't wonder at your laughing, ha! ha! ha!— his impudence is truly ridiculous.

ABSOLUTE. 'Tis very ridiculous, upon my soul, Ma'am, ha! ha! ha!

MRS. MALAPROP. The little hussy won't hear. Well, I'll go and tell her at once who it is. She shall know that Captain Absolute is come to wait on her. And I'll make her behave as becomes a young woman.

ABSOLUTE. As you please, Ma'am.

MRS. MALAPROP. For the present, Captain, your servant. Ah! you've not done laughing yet, I see—*elude my vigilance!*—yes, yes, ha! ha! ha!

[*Exit.*]

ABSOLUTE. Ha! ha! ha! one would think now that I might throw off all disguise at once, and seize my prize with security—but such is Lydia's caprice that to undeceive were probably to lose her. I'll see whether she knows me.   [*Walks aside, and seems engaged*
                                                              in looking at the pictures.]

Enter LYDIA.

LYDIA. What a scene am I now to go through! Surely nothing can be more dreadful than to be obliged to listen to the loathsome addresses of a stranger to one's heart. I have heard of girls persecuted as I am, who have appealed in behalf of their favored lover to the generosity of his rival: suppose I were to try it. There stands the hated rival— an officer, too!—but oh, how unlike my Beverley! I wonder he don't begin. Truly he seems a very negligent wooer! Quite at his ease, upon my word! I'll speak first. [*aloud*] Mr. Absolute.

ABSOLUTE. Madam.   [*Turns around.*]

LYDIA. O heavens! Beverley!

ABSOLUTE. Hush!—hush, my life! Softly! Be not surprised.

LYDIA. I am so astonished! and so terrified! and so overjoyed! For heaven's sake! how came you here?

ABSOLUTE. Briefly—I have deceived your aunt. I was informed that my new rival was to visit here this evening, and contriving to have him kept away, have passed myself on *her* for Captain Absolute.

LYDIA. Oh, charming! And she really takes you for young Absolute?

ABSOLUTE. Oh, she's convinced of it.

LYDIA. Ha! ha! ha! I can't forbear laughing to think how her sagacity is overreached!

ABSOLUTE. But we trifle with our precious moments. Such another opportunity may not occur. Then let me now conjure my kind, my condescending angel, to fix the time when I may rescue her from un- deserved persecution, and with a licensed warmth plead for my reward.

LYDIA. Will you then, Beverley, consent to forfeit that portion of my paltry wealth? that burden on the wings of love?

ABSOLUTE. Oh, come to me—rich only thus in loveliness. Bring no portion to me but thy love—'twill be generous in you, Lydia—for well you know, it is the only dower your poor Beverley can repay.

LYDIA. How persuasive are his words! How charming will poverty be with him!

ABSOLUTE. Ah! my soul, what a life will we then live! Love shall be our idol and support! We will worship him with a monastic strictness; abjuring all worldly toys, to center every thought and action there. Proud of calamity, we will enjoy the wreck of wealth; while the surrounding gloom of adversity shall make the flame of our pure love show doubly bright. By heavens! I would fling all goods of fortune from me with a prodigal hand to enjoy the scene where I might clasp my Lydia to my bosom, and say, the world affords no smile to me— but here. [*embracing her*]— —[*aside*] If she holds out now the devil is in it!

LYDIA [*aside*]. Now could I fly with him to the Antipodes! but my persecution is not yet come to a crisis.

Enter MRS. MALAPROP, *listening.*

MRS. MALAPROP [*aside*]. I am impatient to know how the little hussy deports herself.

ABSOLUTE. So pensive, Lydia!—is then your warmth abated?

MRS. MALAPROP [*aside*]. *Warmth abated!* So! she has been in a passion, I suppose.

LYDIA. No—nor ever can while I have life.

MRS. MALAPROP [*aside*]. An ill-tempered little devil! She'll be *in a passion all her life*—will she?

LYDIA. Think not the idle threats of my ridiculous aunt can ever have any weight with me.

MRS. MALAPROP [*aside*]. Very dutiful, upon my word!

LYDIA. Let her choice be Captain Absolute, but Beverley is mine.

MRS. MALAPROP [*aside*]. I am astonished at her assurance!—to his face—this is to his face!

ABSOLUTE. Thus then let me enforce my suit. [*kneeling*]

MRS. MALAPROP [*aside*]. Aye—poor young man! down on his knees entreating for pity! I can contain no longer.—[*aloud*] Why, thou vixen! I have overheard you.

ABSOLUTE. [*aside*]. Oh, confound her vigilance!

MRS. MALAPROP. Captain Absolute—I know not how to apologize for her shocking rudeness.

ABSOLUTE [*aside*]. So—all's safe, I find.—[*aloud*] I have hopes, Madam, that time will bring the young lady——

MRS. MALAPROP. Oh, there's nothing to be hoped for from her! She's as headstrong as an allegory on the banks of Nile.

LYDIA. Nay, Madam, what do you charge me with now?

MRS. MALAPROP. Why, thou unblushing rebel—didn't you tell this gentleman to his face that you loved another better?—didn't you say you never would be his?

LYDIA. No, Madam—I did not.

MRS. MALAPROP. Good heavens! what assurance! Lydia, Lydia, you ought to know that lying don't become a young woman! Didn't you boast that Beverley—that stroller Beverley—possessed your heart? Tell me that, I say.

LYDIA. 'Tis true, Ma'am, and none but Beverley——

MRS. MALAPROP. Hold—hold, Assurance! you shall not be so rude.

ABSOLUTE. Nay, pray Mrs. Malaprop, don't stop the young lady's speech: she's very welcome to talk thus—it does not hurt *me* in the least, I assure you.

MRS. MALAPROP. You are *too* good, Captain—*too* amiably patient —but come with me, Miss. Let us see you again soon, Captain. Remember what we have fixed.

ABSOLUTE. I shall, Ma'am.

MRS. MALAPROP. Come, take a graceful leave of the gentleman.

LYDIA. May every blessing wait on my Beverley, my loved Bev——

MRS. MALAPROP. Hussy! I'll choke the word in your throat!—come along—come along.

> [*Exeunt severally*, ABSOLUTE *kissing his hand to* LYDIA— MRS. MALAPROP *stopping her from speaking.*]

SCENE IV
ACRES'S *lodgings.*

ACRES *and* DAVID, ACRES *as just dressed.*

ACRES. Indeed, David—do you think I become it so?

DAVID. You are quite another creature, believe me, master, by the Mass! an' we've any luck we shall see the Devon monkeyrony[34] in all the print-shops in Bath!

ACRES. Dress *does* make a difference, David.

DAVID. 'Tis all in all, I think. Difference! why, an' you were to go now to Clod-Hall, I am certain the old lady wouldn't know you: Master Butler wouldn't believe his own eyes, and Mrs. Pickle would cry, "Lard presarve me!"—our dairy-maid would come giggling to the door, and I warrant Dolly Tester, your Honor's favorite, would blush like my waistcoat. Oons! I'll hold a gallon, there a'n't a dog in the house but would bark, and I question whether *Phillis* would wag a hair of her tail!

---

[34] macaroni—a fop who affects foreign manners. I.e., we shall see pictures of the dandified country bumpkin in all the art shops.

ACRES. Aye, David, there's nothing like polishing.

DAVID. So I says of your Honor's boots; but the boy never heeds me!

ACRES. But, David, has Mr. De-la-Grace been here? I must rub up my balancing, and chasing, and boring.[35]

DAVID. I'll call again, Sir.

ACRES. Do—and see if there are any letters for me at the post office.

DAVID. I will. By the Mass, I can't help looking at your head! If I hadn't been by at the cooking, I wish I may die if I should have known the dish again myself!

[*Exit.*]

ACRES *comes forward, practising a dancing step.*

ACRES. Sink, slide—coupee! Confound the first inventors of cotillions! say I—they are as bad as algebra to us country gentlemen. I can walk a minuet easy enough when I'm forced! and I have been accounted a good stick in a country-dance. Odds jigs and tabours! I never valued your cross-over to couple—figure in—right and left— and I'd foot it with e'er a captain in the county! But these outlandish heathen allemandes and cotillions are quite beyond me! I shall never prosper at 'em, that's sure. Mine are true-born English legs—they don't understand their curst French lingo! their *pas* this, and *pas* that, and *pas* t'other! D——n me! my feet don't like to be called paws! No, 'tis certain I have most anti-Gallican[36] toes!

Enter SERVANT.

SERVANT. Here is Sir Lucius O'Trigger to wait on you, Sir.

ACRES. Show him in.

Enter SIR LUCIUS.

SIR LUCIUS. Mr. Acres, I am delighted to embrace you.

ACRES. My dear Sir Lucius, I kiss your hands.

SIR LUCIUS. Pray, my friend, what has brought you so suddenly to Bath?

ACRES. Faith! I have followed Cupid's Jack-a-Lantern, and find myself in a quagmire at last. In short, I have been very ill-used, Sir Lucius. I don't choose to mention names, but look on me as on a very ill-used gentleman.

SIR LUCIUS. Pray, what is the case? I ask no names.

ACRES. Mark me, Sir Lucius, I fall as deep as need be in love with a young lady—her friends take my part—I follow her to Bath—send word of my arrival, and receive answer that the lady is to be otherwise disposed of. This, Sir Lucius, I call being ill-used.

SIR LUCIUS. Very ill, upon my conscience. Pray, can you divine the cause of it?

---

[35] corrupted forms of French dancing terms   [36] anti-French

ACRES. Why, there's the matter: she has another lover, one Beverley, who, I am told, is now in Bath. Odd slanders and lies! he must be at the bottom of it.

SIR LUCIUS. A rival in the case, is there? And you think he has supplanted you unfairly?

ACRES. Unfairly!—to be sure he has. He never could have done it fairly.

SIR LUCIUS. Then sure you know what is to be done!

ACRES. Not I, upon my soul!

SIR LUCIUS. We wear no swords here, but you understand me.

ACRES. What! fight him?

SIR LUCIUS. Aye, to be sure: what can I mean else?

ACRES. But he has given me no provocation.

SIR LUCIUS. Now, I think he has given you the greatest provocation in the world. Can a man commit a more heinous offence against another than to fall in love with the same woman? Oh, by my soul, it is the most unpardonable breach of friendship!

ACRES. Breach of friendship! Aye, aye; but I have no acquaintance with this man. I never saw him in my life.

SIR LUCIUS. That's no argument at all—he has the less right then to take such a liberty.

ACRES. 'Gad, that's true. I grow full of anger, Sir Lucius! I fire apace! Odd hilts and blades! I find a man may have a deal of valor in him and not know it! But couldn't I contrive to have a little right of my side?

SIR LUCIUS. What the devil signifies *right* when your *honor* is concerned? Do you think Achilles, or my little Alexander the Great ever inquired where the right lay? No, by my soul, they drew their broadswords, and left the lazy sons of peace to settle the justice of it.

ACRES. Your words are a grenadier's march to my heart! I believe courage must be catching! I certainly do feel a kind of valor rising, as it were—a kind of courage, as I may say. Odds flints, pans, and triggers! I'll challenge him directly.

SIR LUCIUS. Ah, my little friend! if we had Blunderbuss-Hall here —I could show you a range of ancestry, in the O'Trigger line, that would furnish the New Room, every one of whom had killed his man! For though the mansion-house and dirty acres have slipped through my fingers, I thank heaven our honor, and the family-pictures, are as fresh as ever.

ACRES. O Sir Lucius! I have had ancestors too! every man of 'em colonel or captain in the militia! Odds balls and barrels! say no more —I'm braced for it. The thunder of your words has soured the milk of human kindness in my breast! Z——ds! as the man in the play says, "I could do such deeds!"

SIR LUCIUS. Come, come, there must be no passion at all in the case— these things should always be done civilly.

ACRES. I must be in a passion, Sir Lucius—I must be in a rage. Dear

Sir Lucius, let me be in a rage, if you love me. Come, here's pen and paper. [*Sits down to write.*] I would the ink were red! Indite, I say, indite! How shall I begin? Odds bullets and blades! I'll write a good bold hand, however.

SIR LUCIUS. Pray compose yourself.

ACRES. Come now, shall I begin with an oath? Do, Sir Lucius, let me begin with a damme.

SIR LUCIUS. Pho! pho! do the thing decently and like a Christian. Begin now—"*Sir*"——

ACRES. That's too civil by half.

SIR LUCIUS. "*To prevent the confusion that might arise*"——

ACRES. Well——

SIR LUCIUS. "*From our both addressing the same lady*"——

ACRES. Aye—there's the reason—"*same lady*"—Well——

SIR LUCIUS. "*I shall expect the honor of your company*"——

ACRES. Z——ds! I'm not asking him to dinner.

SIR LUCIUS. Pray be easy.

ACRES. Well then—"*honor of your company*"——

SIR LUCIUS. "*To settle our pretensions*"——

ACRES. Well——

SIR LUCIUS. Let me see—aye, King's-Mead-Fields will do—"*In King's Mead-Fields,*"

ACRES. So that's done.——Well, I'll fold it up presently; my own crest—a hand and dagger shall be the seal.

SIR LUCIUS. You see now, this little explanation will put a stop at once to all confusion or misunderstanding that might arise between you.

ACRES. Aye, we fight to prevent any misunderstanding.

SIR LUCIUS. Now, I'll leave you to fix your own time. Take my advice, and you'll decide it this evening if you can; then let the worst come of it, 'twill be off your mind tomorrow.

ACRES. Very true.

SIR LUCIUS. So I shall see nothing more of you, unless it be by letter, till the evening. I would do myself the honor to carry your message; but, to tell you a secret, I believe I shall have just such another affair on my own hands. There is a gay captain here who put a jest on me lately at the expense of my country, and I only want to fall in with the gentleman to call him out.

ACRES. By my valor, I should like to see you fight first! Odd's life! I should like to see you kill him, if it was only to get a little lesson.

SIR LUCIUS. I shall be very proud of instructing you. Well for the present—but remember now, when you meet your antagonist, do everything in a mild and agreeable manner. Let your courage be as keen, but at the same time as polished, as your sword.

[*Exeunt severally.*]

ACT IV

SCENE I
ACRES'S *lodgings.*

ACRES *and* DAVID.

DAVID. Then, by the Mass, Sir! I would do no such thing—ne'er a
Sir Lucius O'Trigger in the kingdom should make me fight, when I
wa'n't so minded. Oons! what will the old lady say when she hears
o't!

ACRES. Ah! David, if you had heard Sir Lucius! Odds sparks and
flames! he would have roused your valor.

DAVID. Not he, indeed. I hates such bloodthirsty cormorants. Look'ee,
master, if you'd wanted a bout at boxing, quarterstaff, or shortstaff, I
should never be the man to bid you cry off: but for your curst sharps
and snaps,[37] I never knew any good come of 'em.

ACRES. But my honor, David, my honor! I must be very careful of
my honor.

DAVID. Aye, by the Mass! and I would be very careful of it; and I
think in return my *honor* couldn't do less than to be very careful of
me.

ACRES. Odds blades! David, no gentleman will ever risk the loss of
his honor!

DAVID. I say then, it would be but civil in *honor* never to risk the loss
of a *gentleman.* Look'ee, master, this *honor* seems to me to be a marvelous false friend; aye, truly, a very courtier-like servant. Put the
case, I was a gentleman (which, thank God, no one can say of me);
well—my honor makes me quarrel with another gentleman of my
acquaintance. So—we fight. (Pleasant enough that.) Boh!—I kill him
(the more's my luck). Now, pray who gets the profit of it? Why, my
honor. But put the case that he kills me!—by the Mass! I go to the
worms, and my honor whips over to my enemy!

ACRES. No, David—in that case—odds crowns and laurels!—your
honor follows you to the grave.

DAVID. Now, that's just the place where I could make a shift to do
without it.

ACRES. Z——ds, David, you're a coward! It doesn't become my valor
to listen to you. What, shall I disgrace my ancestors? Think of that,
David—think what it would be to disgrace my ancestors!

DAVID. Under favor, the surest way of not disgracing them is to keep
as long as you can out of their company. Look'ee now, master, to go

---

[37] swords and pistols

to them in such haste—with an ounce of lead in your brains—I should think might as well be let alone. Our ancestors are very good kind of folks, but they are the last people I should choose to have a visiting acquaintance with.

ACRES. But David, now, you don't think there is such very, very, *very* great danger, hey? Odd's life! people often fight without any mischief done!

DAVID. By the Mass, I think 'tis ten to one against you! Oons! here to meet some lion-headed fellow, I warrant, with his d——n'd double-barreled swords, and cut-and-thrust pistols! Lord bless us! it makes me tremble to think o't. Those be such desperate bloody-minded weapons! Well, I never could abide 'em! from a child I never could fancy 'em! I suppose there a'n't so merciless a beast in the world as your loaded pistol!

ACRES. Z——ds! I *won't* be afraid! Odds fire and fury! you sha'n't make me afraid! Here is the challenge, and I have sent for my dear friend Jack Absolute to carry it for me.

DAVID. Aye, i' the name of mischief, let *him* be the messenger. For my part, I wouldn't lend a hand to it for the best horse in your stable. By the Mass! it don't look like another letter! It is, as I may say, a designing and malicious-looking letter! and I warrant smells of gun-powder, like a soldier's pouch! Oons! I wouldn't swear it mayn't go off!

ACRES. Out, you poltroon! You ha'n't the valor of a grasshopper.

DAVID. Well, I say no more—'twill be sad news, to be sure, at Clod-Hall!—but I ha' done. How Phillis will howl when she hears of it! Aye, poor bitch, she little thinks what shooting her master's going after! And I warrant old Crop, who has carried your Honor, field and road, these ten years, will curse the hour he was born. [*whimpering*]

ACRES. It won't do, David—I am determined to fight—so get along, you coward, while I'm in the mind.

Enter SERVANT.

SERVANT. Captain Absolute, Sir.

ACRES. Oh! show him up.

[*Exit* SERVANT.]

DAVID. Well, heaven send we be all alive this time tomorrow.

ACRES. What's that! Don't provoke me, David!

DAVID [*whimpering*]. Good-bye, master.

ACRES. Get along, you cowardly, dastardly, croaking raven.

[*Exit* DAVID.]

Enter ABSOLUTE.

ABSOLUTE. What's the matter, Bob?

ACRES. A vile, sheep-hearted blockhead! If I hadn't the valor of St.
George and the dragon[38] to boot——
ABSOLUTE. But what did you want with me, Bob?
ACRES. Oh! There——

[Gives him the challenge.]

ABSOLUTE. "*To Ensign Beverley.*" [*aside*] So—what's going on now?
[*aloud*] Well, what's this?
ACRES. A challenge!
ABSOLUTE. Indeed! Why, you won't fight him, will you, Bob?
ACRES. 'Egad, but I will, Jack. Sir Lucius has wrought me to it. He
has left me full of rage, and I'll fight this evening, that so much good
passion mayn't be wasted.
ABSOLUTE. But what have I to do with this?
ACRES. Why, as I think you know something of this fellow, I want
you to find him out for me, and give him this mortal defiance.
ABSOLUTE. Well, give it to me, and trust me he gets it.
ACRES. Thank you, my dear friend, my dear Jack; but it is giving you
a great deal of trouble.
ABSOLUTE. Not in the least—I beg you won't mention it. No trouble
in the world, I assure you.
ACRES. You are very kind. What it is to have a friend! You couldn't
be my second—could you, Jack?
ABSOLUTE. Why no, Bob—not in *this* affair. It would not be quite so
proper.
ACRES. Well then, I must get my friend Sir Lucius. I shall have your
good wishes, however, Jack.
ABSOLUTE. Whenever he meets you, believe me.

Enter SERVANT.

SERVANT. Sir Anthony Absolute is below, inquiring for the Captain.
ABSOLUTE. I'll come instantly. Well, my little hero, success attend
you. [*going*]
ACRES. Stay—stay, Jack. If Beverley should ask you what kind of a
man your friend Acres is, do tell him I am a devil of a fellow—will
you, Jack?
ABSOLUTE. To be sure I shall. I'll say you are a determined dog—
hey, Bob?
ACRES. Aye, do, do—and if that frightens him, 'egad, perhaps he
mayn't come. So tell him I generally kill a man a week—will you,
Jack?
ABSOLUTE. I will, I will; I'll say you are called in the country "*Fighting Bob!*"

---

[38] the patron saint of England, represented as triumphing over evil by slaying a
dragon

ACRES. Right, right—'tis all to prevent mischief; for I don't want to take his life if I clear my honor.

ABSOLUTE. No!—that's very kind of you.

ACRES. Why, you don't wish me to kill him—do you, Jack?

ABSOLUTE. No, upon my soul, I do not. But a devil of a fellow, hey? [*going*]

ACRES. True, true—but stay—stay, Jack. You may add that you never saw me in such a rage before—a most devouring rage!

ABSOLUTE. I will, I will.

ACRES. Remember, Jack—a determined dog!

ABSOLUTE. Aye, aye, "*Fighting Bob!*"

[*Exeunt severally.*]

SCENE II
MRS. MALAPROP's *lodgings.*
MRS. MALAPROP *and* LYDIA.

MRS. MALAPROP. Why, thou perverse one! tell me what you can object to him? Isn't he a handsome man? tell me that. A genteel man? a pretty figure of a man?

LYDIA [*aside*]. She little thinks whom she is praising!—[*aloud*] So is Beverley, Ma'am.

MRS. MALAPROP. No caparisons, Miss, if you please! Caparisons don't become a young woman. No! Captain Absolute is indeed a fine gentleman!

LYDIA [*aside*]. Aye, the Captain Absolute *you* have seen.

MRS. MALAPROP. Then he's *so* well bred; *so* full of alacrity, and adulation! and has *so much* to say for himself—in such good language, too! His physiognomy so grammatical! Then his presence is so noble! I protest, when I saw him, I thought of what Hamlet says in the play: "Hesperian curls!—the front of *Job* himself! An eye, like *March*, to threaten at command—a station, like Harry Mercury, new"[39]— something about kissing on a hill—however, the similitude struck me directly.

LYDIA [*aside*]. How enraged she'll be presently when she discovers her mistake!

Enter SERVANT.

SERVANT. Sir Anthony and Captain Absolute are below, Ma'am.

MRS. MALAPROP. Show them up here.

[*Exit SERVANT.*]

---

[39] "Hyperion's curls; the front of Jove himself;/ An eye like Mars, to threaten and command;/ A station like the herald Mercury/New-lighted on a heaven-kissing hill (III, iv, 56–59)

Now, Lydia, I insist on your behaving as becomes a young woman.
Show your good breeding at least, though you have forgot your duty.
LYDIA. Madam, I have told you my resolution; I shall not only give
him no encouragement, but I won't even speak to, or look at him.
[*Flings herself into a chair with her face from the door.*]

Enter SIR ANTHONY *and* ABSOLUTE.

SIR ANTHONY. Here we are, Mrs. Malaprop, come to mitigate the
frowns of unrelenting beauty—and difficulty enough I had to bring
this fellow. I don't know what's the matter; but if I hadn't held him
by force, he'd have given me the slip.
MRS. MALAPROP. You have infinite trouble, Sir Anthony, in the
affair. I am ashamed for the cause!—[*aside to her*] Lydia, Lydia, rise,
I beseech you!—pay your respects!
SIR ANTHONY. I hope, Madam, that Miss Languish has reflected on
the worth of this gentleman, and the regard due to her aunt's choice,
and *my* alliance.—[*aside to him*] Now, Jack, speak to her!
ABSOLUTE [*aside*]. What the devil shall I do!—[*aloud*] You see, Sir,
she won't even look at me whilst you are here. I knew she wouldn't!
I told you so. Let me entreat you, Sir, to leave us together!
[ABSOLUTE *seems to expostulate with his father.*]
LYDIA [*aside*]. I wonder I ha'n't heard my aunt exclaim yet! Sure she
can't have looked at him! Perhaps their regimentals [40] are alike, and
she is something blind.
SIR ANTHONY. I say, Sir, I won't stir a foot yet!
MRS. MALAPROP. I am sorry to say, Sir Anthony, that my affluence
over my niece is very small.—[*aside to her*] Turn round, Lydia; I
blush for you!
SIR ANTHONY. May I not flatter myself that Miss Languish will
assign what cause of dislike she can have to my son! Why don't you
begin, Jack?—[*aside to him*] Speak, you puppy—speak!
MRS. MALAPROP. It is impossible, Sir Anthony, she can have any.
She will not *say* she has.—[*aside to her*] Answer, hussy! why don't
you answer?
SIR ANTHONY. Then, Madam, I trust that a childish and hasty predilection will be no bar to Jack's happiness.—[*aside to him*] Z——ds!
Sirrah! why don't you speak?
LYDIA [*aside*]. I think my lover seems as little inclined to conversation
as myself. How strangely blind my aunt must be!
ABSOLUTE. Hem! hem!—Madam—hem!—[ABSOLUTE *attempts to
speak, then returns to* SIR ANTHONY.]—Faith! Sir, I am so confounded! and so—so—confused! I told you I should be so, Sir, I knew
it. The—the—tremor of my passion entirely takes away my presence
of mind.

[40] uniforms

SIR ANTHONY. But it don't take away your voice, fool, does it? Go up, and speak to her directly!

[ABSOLUTE *makes signs to* MRS. MALAPROP *to leave them together.*]

MRS. MALAPROP. Sir Anthony, shall we leave them together?—[*aside to her*] Ah! you stubborn little vixen!

SIR ANTHONY. Not yet, Ma'am, not yet!—[*aside to him*] What the devil are you at? Unlock your jaws, Sirrah, or——

[ABSOLUTE *draws near* LYDIA.]

ABSOLUTE [*aside*]. Now heaven send she may be too sullen to look round! I must disguise my voice.—[*Speaks in a low hoarse tone.*] Will not Miss Languish lend an ear to the mild accents of true love? Will not——

SIR ANTHONY. What the devil ails the fellow? Why don't you speak out?—not stand croaking like a frog in a quinsy!

ABSOLUTE. The—the—excess of my awe, and my—my—my modesty quite choke me!

SIR ANTHONY. Ah! your *modesty* again! I'll tell you what, Jack, if you don't speak out directly, and glibly, too, I shall be in such a rage! Mrs. Malaprop, I wish the lady would favor us with something more than a side-front!

[MRS. MALAPROP *seems to chide* LYDIA.]

ABSOLUTE. So! All will out I see! [*Goes up to* LYDIA, *speaks softly.*] Be not surprised, my Lydia; suppress all surprise at present.

LYDIA [*aside*]. Heavens! 'tis Beverley's voice! Sure he can't have imposed on Sir Anthony, too!—[*Looks round by degrees, then starts up*]. Is this possible—my Beverley!— how can this be?—my Beverley?

ABSOLUTE [*aside*]. Ah! 'tis all over.

SIR ANTHONY. Beverley!—the devil! Beverley! What can the girl mean? This is my son, Jack Absolute!

MRS. MALAPROP. For shame, hussy! for shame! your head runs so on that fellow that you have him always in your eyes! Beg Captain Absolute's pardon directly.

LYDIA. I see no Captain Absolute, but my loved Beverley!

SIR ANTHONY. Z——ds! the girl's mad!—her brain's turned by reading!

MRS. MALAPROP. O' my conscience, I believe so! What do you mean by Beverley, hussy? You saw Captain Absolute before to-day; there he is—your husband that shall be.

LYDIA. With all my soul, Ma'am. When I refuse my Beverley——

SIR ANTHONY. Oh! she's as mad as Bedlam! Or has this fellow been playing us a rogue's trick! Come here, Sirrah!—who the devil are you?

ABSOLUTE. Faith, Sir, I am not quite clear myself, but I'll endeavor to recollect.

SIR ANTHONY. Are you my son, or not? Answer for your mother, you dog, if you won't for me.

MRS. MALAPROP. Aye, Sir, who are you? Oh mercy! I begin to suspect!——

ABSOLUTE [*aside*]. Ye Powers of Impudence befriend me!—[*aloud*] Sir Anthony, most assuredly I am your wife's son; and that I sincerely believe myself to be *yours* also, I hope my duty has always shown.—— Mrs. Malaprop, I am your most respectful admirer—and shall be proud to add *affectionate nephew*.——I need not tell my Lydia, that she sees her faithful Beverley, who, knowing the singular generosity of her temper, assumed that name, and a station which has proved a test of the most disinterested love, which he now hopes to enjoy in a more elevated character.

LYDIA [*sullenly*]. So!—there will be no elopement after all!

SIR ANTHONY. Upon my soul, Jack, thou art a very impudent fellow! to do you justice, I think I never saw a piece of more consummate assurance!

ABSOLUTE. Oh you flatter me, Sir—you compliment—'tis my *modesty* you know, Sir—my *modesty* that has stood in my way.

SIR ANTHONY. Well, I am glad you are not the dull, insensible varlet you pretended to be, however! I'm glad you have made a fool of your father, you dog—I am. So this was your *penitence*, your *duty*, and *obedience!* I thought it was d——d sudden! You *never heard their names before*, not you! *What! The Languishes of Worcestershire, hey?—if you could please me in the affair, 'twas all you desired!*—Ah! you dissembling villain! What!—[*pointing to* LYDIA] *she squints, don't she?— a little red-haired girl!*—hey? Why, you hypocritical young rascal! I wonder you a'n't ashamed to hold up your head!

ABSOLUTE. 'Tis with difficulty, Sir. I *am* confused—very much confused, as you must perceive.

MRS. MALAPROP. O lud! Sir Anthony!—a new light breaks in upon me! Hey! how! what! Captain, did *you* write the letters then? What! —am I to thank *you* for the elegant compilation of "*an old weatherbeaten she-dragon*"—hey? O mercy! was it *you* that reflected on my parts of speech?

ABSOLUTE. Dear Sir! my modesty will be overpowered at last, if you don't assist me. I shall certainly not be able to stand it!

SIR ANTHONY. Come, come, Mrs. Malaprop, we must forget and forgive. Odd's life! matters have taken so clever a turn all of a sudden, that I could find in my heart to be so good-humored! and so gallant!— hey! Mrs. Malaprop!

MRS. MALAPROP. Well, Sir Anthony, since *you* desire it, we will not anticipate the past; so mind, young people: our retrospection will now be all to the future.

SIR ANTHONY. Come, we must leave them together; Mrs. Malaprop, they long to fly into each other's arms. I warrant!—[*aside*] Jack— isn't the cheek as I said, hey?—and the eye, you rogue!—and the lip—hey? Come, Mrs. Malaprop, we'll not disturb their tenderness—theirs is the time of life for happiness!—[*Sings.*] "*Youth's the season made for joy*"—hey! Odd's life! I'm in such spirits, I don't know what I couldn't do! Permit me, Ma'am—[*Gives his hand to* MRS. MALA-PROP *Sings.*] Tol-de-rol!—'gad, I should like a little fooling myself. Tol-de-rol! de-rol!

[*Exit singing, and handing* MRS. MALAPROP.]
[LYDIA *sits sullenly in her chair.*]

ABSOLUTE [*aside*]. So much thought bodes me no good.——[*aloud*] So grave, Lydia!

LYDIA. Sir!

ABSOLUTE [*aside*]. So!—cgad! I thought as much! That d——d monosyllable has froze me!——[*aloud*] What, Lydia, now that we are as happy in our friends' consent, as in our mutual vows——

LYDIA [*peevishly*]. Friends' consent, indeed!

ABSOLUTE. Come, come, we must lay aside some of our romance—a little *wealth* and *comfort* may be endured after all. And for your fortune, the lawyers shall make such settlements as——

LYDIA. Lawyers! I hate lawyers!

ABSOLUTE. Nay then, we will not wait for their lingering forms but instantly procure the license, and——

LYDIA. The *license!* I *hate* license!

ABSOLUTE. O my love! be not so unkind! Thus let me intreat——
[*kneeling*]

LYDIA. Pshaw! what signifies kneeling when you know I *must* have you?

ABSOLUTE [*rising*]. Nay, Madam, there shall be no constraint upon your inclinations, I promise you. If I have lost your heart, I resign the rest.—[*aside*] 'Gad, I must try what a little *spirit* will do.

LYDIA [*rising*]. Then, Sir, let me tell you, the interest you had there was acquired by a mean, unmanly imposition, and deserves the punishment of fraud. What, you have been treating *me* like a child!—humoring my romance! and laughing, I suppose, at your success!

ABSOLUTE. You wrong me, Lydia, you wrong me. Only hear——

LYDIA. So, while *I* fondly imagined we were deceiving my relations, and flattered myself that I should outwit and incense them all—behold! my hopes are to be crushed at once, by my aunt's consent and approbation!—and *I* am myself the only dupe at last! [*walking about in heat*] But here, Sir, here is the picture—Beverley's picture! [*taking a miniature from her bosom*] which I have worn, night and day, in spite of threats and entreaties! There, Sir [*Flings it to him.*]—and be assured I throw the original from my heart as easily.

ABSOLUTE. Nay, nay, Ma'am, we will not differ as to that. Here [*taking out a picture*], here is Miss Lydia Languish. What a difference! Aye, *there* is the heavenly assenting smile that first gave soul and spirit to my hopes!—those are the lips which sealed a vow, as yet scarce dry in Cupid's calendar!—and *there*, the half resentful blush that *would* have checked the ardor of my thanks. Well, all that's past—all over indeed! There, Madam, in beauty, that copy is not equal to you, but in my mind its merit over the original, in being still the same, is such—that—I cannot find in my heart to part with it.   [*Puts it up again.*]

LYDIA [*softening*]. 'Tis *your own* doing, Sir. I—I—I suppose you are perfectly satisfied.

ABSOLUTE. Oh, most certainly. Sure now this is much better than being in love! Ha! ha! ha!—there's some spirit in *this!* What signifies breaking some scores of solemn promises, half an hundred vows, under one's hand, with the marks of a dozen or two angels to witness! —all that's of no consequence, you know. To be sure, people will say that Miss didn't know her own mind—but never mind that: or perhaps they may be ill-natured enough to hint that the gentleman grew tired of the lady and forsook her—but don't let that fret you.

LYDIA. There's no bearing his insolence.   [*Bursts into tears.*]

Enter MRS. MALAPROP *and* SIR ANTHONY.

MRS. MALAPROP [*entering*]. Come, we must interrupt your billing and cooing a while.

LYDIA [*sobbing*]. This is worse than your treachery and deceit, you base ingrate!

SIR ANTHONY. What the devil's the matter now! Z——ds! Mrs. Malaprop, this is the *oddest billing* and *cooing* I ever heard! But what the deuce is the meaning of it? I'm quite astonished!

ABSOLUTE. Ask the lady, Sir.

MRS. MALAPROP. Oh mercy! I'm quite analyzed, for my part! Why, Lydia, what is the reason of this?

LYDIA. Ask the *gentleman*, Ma'am.

SIR ANTHONY. Z——ds! I shall be in a frenzy!—— Why, Jack, you are not come out to be anyone else, are you?

MRS. MALAPROP. Aye, Sir, there's no more *trick*, is there? You are not like Cerberus, *three* gentlemen at once, are you?

ABSOLUTE. You'll not let me speak. I say the lady can account for this much better than I can.

LYDIA. Ma'am, you once commanded me never to think of Beverley again. There is the man—I now obey you:—for, from this moment, I renounce him forever.   [*Exit* LYDIA.]

MRS. MALAPROP. Oh mercy! and miracles! what a turn here is! Why, sure, Captain, you haven't behaved disrespectfully to my niece?

SIR ANTHONY. Ha! ha! ha!—ha! ha! ha!—now I see it—ha! ha! ha! —now I see it—you have been too lively, Jack.

ABSOLUTE. Nay, Sir, upon my word——

SIR ANTHONY. Come, no lying, Jack—I'm sure 'twas so.

MRS. MALAPROP. O lud! Sir Anthony! Oh fie, Captain!

ABSOLUTE. Upon my soul, Ma'am——

SIR ANTHONY. Come, no excuses, Jack; why, your father, you rogue, was so before you: the blood of the Absolutes was always impatient. Ha! ha! ha! poor little Lydia!—why, you've frightened her, you dog, you have.

ABSOLUTE. By all that's good, Sir——

SIR ANTHONY. Z——ds! say no more, I tell you. Mrs. Malaprop shall make your peace.——You must make his peace, Mrs. Malaprop; you must tell her 'tis Jack's way—tell her 'tis all our ways—it runs in the blood of our family! Come, away, Jack—ha! ha! ha! Mrs. Malaprop—a young villain! [*Pushes him out.*]

MRS. MALAPROP. Oh, Sir Anthony! Oh fie, Captain!

[*Exeunt severally.*]

SCENE III
The North Parade.

Enter SIR LUCIUS O'TRIGGER.

SIR LUCIUS. I wonder where this Captain Absolute hides himself. Upon my conscience! these officers are always in one's way in love-affairs. I remember I might have married Lady Dorothy Carmine, if it had not been for a little rogue of a major, who ran away with her before she could get a sight of me! And I wonder too what it is the ladies can see in them to be so fond of them—unless it be a touch of the old serpent in 'em, that makes the little creatures be caught, like vipers, with a bit of red cloth.— Hah!—isn't this the Captain coming?—faith it is! There is a probability of succeeding about that fellow that is mighty provoking! Who the devil is he talking to? [*Steps aside.*]

Enter CAPTAIN ABSOLUTE.

ABSOLUTE. To what fine purpose I have been plotting! A noble reward for all my schemes, upon my soul! A little gypsy! I did not think her romance could have made her so d——d absurd either. 'Sdeath, I never was in a worse humor in my life! I could cut my own throat, or any other person's, with the greatest pleasure in the world!

SIR LUCIUS. Oh, faith! I'm in the luck of it—I never could have found him in a sweeter temper for my purpose—to be sure I'm just come in the nick! Now to enter into conversation with him, and so quarrel genteelly. [SIR LUCIUS *goes up to* ABSOLUTE.]—With regard to that matter, Captain, I must beg leave to differ in opinion with you.

ABSOLUTE. Upon my word then, you must be a very subtle disputant, because, Sir, I happened just then to be giving no opinion at all.

SIR LUCIUS. That's no reason. For give me leave to tell you, a man may *think* an untruth as well as *speak* one.

ABSOLUTE. Very true, Sir, but if a man never utters his thoughts I should think they might stand a chance of escaping controversy.

SIR LUCIUS. Then, Sir, you differ in opinion with me, which amounts to the same thing.

ABSOLUTE. Hark'ee, Sir Lucius—if I had not before known you to be a gentleman, upon my soul, I should not have discovered it at this interview, for what you can drive at, unless you mean to quarrel with me, I cannot conceive!

SIR LUCIUS. I humbly thank you, Sir, for the quickness of your apprehension. [*bowing*] You have named the very thing I would be at.

ABSOLUTE. Very well, Sir—I shall certainly not balk your inclinations—but I should be glad you would please to explain your motives.

SIR LUCIUS. Pray, Sir, be easy: the quarrel is a very pretty quarrel as it stands—we should only spoil it by trying to explain it. However, your memory is very short or you could not have forgot an affront you passed on me within this week. So no more, but name your time and place.

ABSOLUTE. Well, Sir, since you are so bent on it, the sooner the better; let it be this evening—here, by the Spring-Gardens. We shall scarcely be interrupted.

SIR LUCIUS. Faith! that same interruption in affairs of this nature shows very great ill-breeding. I don't know what's the reason, but in England, if a thing of this kind gets wind, people make such a pother that a gentleman can never fight in peace and quietness. However, if it's the same to you, Captain, I should take it as a particular kindness if you'd let us meet in King's-Mead-Fields, as a little business will call me there about six o'clock, and I may dispatch both matters at once.

ABSOLUTE. 'Tis the same to me exactly. A little after six, then, we will discuss this matter more seriously.

SIR LUCIUS. If you please, Sir, there will be very pretty smallsword light, though it won't do for a long shot. So that matter's settled! and my mind's at ease!   [*Exit* SIR LUCIUS.]

Enter FAULKLAND, *meeting* ABSOLUTE.

ABSOLUTE. Well met. I was going to look for you. O Faulkland! all the demons of spite and disappointment have conspired against me! I'm so vexed that if I had not the prospect of a resource in being knocked o' the head by and by, I should scarce have spirits to tell you the cause.

FAULKLAND. What can you mean? Has Lydia changed her mind? I should have thought her duty and inclination would now have pointed to the same object.

ABSOLUTE. Aye, just as the eyes do of a person who squints: when her love-eye was fixed on me—t'other—her eye of duty, was finely obliqued:—but when duty bid her point that the same way—off t'other turned on a swivel, and secured its retreat with a frown!

FAULKLAND. But what's the resource you——

ABSOLUTE. Oh, to wind up the whole, a good-natured Irishman here has [*mimicking* SIR LUCIUS] begged leave to have the pleasure of cutting my throat, and I mean to indulge him—that's all.

FAULKLAND. Prithee, be serious.

ABSOLUTE. 'Tis fact, upon my soul. Sir Lucius O'Trigger—you know him by sight—for some affront, which I am sure I never intended, has obliged me to meet him this evening at six o'clock: 'tis on that account I wished to see you—you must go with me.

FAULKLAND. Nay, there must be some mistake, sure. Sir Lucius shall explain himself—and I dare say matters may be accommodated. But this evening, did you say? I wish it had been any other time.

ABSOLUTE. Why? there will be light enough. There will (as Sir Lucius says) "be very pretty small-sword light, though it won't do for a long shot." Confound his long shots!

FAULKLAND. But I am myself a good deal ruffled by a difference I have had with Julia. My vile tormenting temper has made me treat her so cruelly that I shall not be myself till we are reconciled.

ABSOLUTE. By heavens, Faulkland, you don't deserve her.

Enter SERVANT, *gives* FAULKLAND *a letter.*

FAULKLAND. O Jack! this is from Julia. I dread to open it. I fear it may be to take a last leave—perhaps to bid me return her letters and restore—— Oh! how I suffer for my folly!

ABSOLUTE. Here—let me see. [*Takes the letter and opens it.*] Aye, a final sentence indeed!—'tis all over with you, faith!

FAULKLAND. Nay, Jack—don't keep me in suspense.

ABSOLUTE. Hear then.—"*As I am convinced that my dear* Faulkland's *own reflections have already upbraided him for his last unkindness to me, I will not add a word on the subject. I wish to speak with you as soon as possible.—Yours ever and truly,* JULIA."—There's stubbornness and resentment for you! [*Gives him the letter.*] Why, man, you don't seem one whit happier at this.

FAULKLAND. Oh, yes, I am—but—but——

ABSOLUTE. Confound your *buts.* You never hear anything that would make another man bless himself, but you immediately d——n it with a *but.*

FAULKLAND. Now, Jack, as you are my friend, own honestly—don't you think there is something forward, something indelicate, in this haste to forgive? Women should never sue for reconciliation: that should always come from us. They should retain their coldness till

wooed to kindness—and their *pardon*, like their *love*, should "not un-
sought be won."

ABSOLUTE. I have not patience to listen to you—thou'rt incorrigible!
—so say no more on the subject. I must go to settle a few matters. Let
me see you before six—remember—at my lodgings. A poor industrious
devil like me, who have toiled, and drudged, and plotted to gain my
ends, and am at last disappointed by other people's folly, may in pity
be allowed to swear and grumble a little; but a captious skeptic in
love, a slave to fretfulness and whim, who has no difficulties but of
his own creating, is a subject more fit for ridicule than compassion!
[*Exit* ABSOLUTE.]

FAULKLAND. I feel his reproaches, yet I would not change this too exquisite nicety for the gross content with which *he* tramples on the
thorns of love. His engaging me in this duel has started an idea in my
head, which I will instantly pursue. I'll use it as the touchstone of
Julia's sincerity and disinterestedness. If her love prove pure and
sterling ore, my name will rest on it with honor!—and once I've
stamped it there, I lay aside my doubts forever—; but if the dross of
selfishness, the alloy of pride predominate, 'twill be best to leave her
as a toy for some less cautious fool to sigh for.
[*Exit* FAULKLAND.]

ACT V

SCENE I
JULIA's *dressing-room.*

JULIA *sola.*

JULIA. How this message has alarmed me! What dreadful accident
can he mean? why such charge to be alone? O Faulkland! how many
unhappy moments, how many tears, have you cost me!

Enter FAULKLAND.

JULIA. What means this?—why this caution, Faulkland?
FAULKLAND. Alas! Julia, I am come to take a long farewell.
JULIA. Heavens! what do you mean?
FAULKLAND. You see before you a wretch whose life is forfeited.
Nay, start not! the infirmity of my temper has drawn all this misery
on me. I left you fretful and passionate—an untoward accident drew
me into a quarrel—the event is that I must fly this kingdom instantly.
O Julia, had I been so fortunate as to have called you mine entirely
before this mischance had fallen on me, I should not so deeply dread
my banishment!

JULIA. My soul is oppressed with sorrow at the nature of your misfortune: had these adverse circumstances arisen from a less fatal cause, I should have felt strong comfort in the thought that I could now chase from your bosom every doubt of the warm sincerity of my love. My heart has long known no other guardian. I now entrust my person to your honor—we will fly together. When safe from pursuit, my father's will may be fulfilled, and I receive a legal claim to be the partner of your sorrows, and tenderest comforter. Then on the bosom of your wedded Julia, you may lull your keen regret to slumbering; while virtuous love, with a cherub's hand, shall smooth the brow of upbraiding thought, and pluck the thorn from compunction.

FAULKLAND. O Julia! I am bankrupt in gratitude! But the time is so pressing, it calls on you for so hasty a resolution—would you not wish some hours to weigh the advantages you forego, and what little compensation poor Faulkland can make you beside his solitary love?

JULIA. I ask not a moment. No, Faulkland, I have loved you for yourself: and if I now, more than ever, prize the solemn engagement which so long has pledged us to each other, it is because it leaves no room for hard aspersions on my fame, and puts the seal of duty to an act of love.—— But let us not linger. Perhaps this delay——

FAULKLAND. 'Twill be better I should not venture out again till dark. Yet am I grieved to think what numberless distresses will press heavy on your gentle disposition!

JULIA. Perhaps your fortune may be forfeited by this unhappy act. I know not whether 'tis so, but sure that alone can never make us unhappy. The little I have will be sufficient to support us; and exile never should be splendid.

FAULKLAND. Aye, but in such an abject state of life, my wounded pride perhaps may increase the natural fretfulness of my temper, till I become a rude, morose companion, beyond your patience to endure. Perhaps the recollection of a deed my conscience cannot justify may haunt me in such gloomy and unsocial fits that I shall hate the tenderness that would relieve me, break from your arms, and quarrel with your fondness!

JULIA. If your thoughts should assume so unhappy a bent, you will the more want some mild and affectionate spirit to watch over and console you, one who, by bearing *your* infirmities with gentleness and resignation, may teach you *so* to bear the evils of your fortune.

FAULKLAND. Julia, I have proved you to the quick! and with this useless device I throw away all my doubts. How shall I plead to be forgiven this last unworthy effect of my restless, unsatisfied disposition?

JULIA. Has no such disaster happened as you related?

FAULKLAND. I am ashamed to own that it was all pretended; yet in pity, Julia, do not kill me with resenting a fault which never can be repeated, but sealing, this once, my pardon, let me to-morrow, in the

face of heaven, receive my future guide and monitress, and expiate my
past folly by years of tender adoration.

JULIA. Hold, Faulkland! That you are free from a crime which I before
feared to name, heaven knows how sincerely I rejoice! These are tears
of thankfulness for that! But that your cruel doubts should have urged
you to an imposition that has wrung my heart, gives me now a pang
more keen than I can express!

FAULKLAND. By heavens! Julia——

JULIA. Yet hear me. My father loved you, Faulkland! and you preserved the life that tender parent gave me; in his presence I pledged
my hand—joyfully pledged it—where before I had given my heart.
When, soon after, I lost that parent, it seemed to me that Providence
had, in Faulkland, shown me whither to transfer without a pause my
grateful duty, as well as my affection: hence I have been content to
bear from you what pride and delicacy would have forbid me from
another. I will not upbraid you by repeating how you have trifled with
my sincerity.

FAULKLAND. I confess it all! yet hear——

JULIA. After such a year of trial, I might have flattered myself that I
should not have been insulted with a new probation of my sincerity,
as cruel as unnecessary! I now see it is not in your nature to be content or confident in love. With this conviction, I never will be yours.
While I had hopes that my persevering attention and unreproaching
kindness might in time reform your temper, I should have been happy
to have gained a dearer influence over you; but I will not furnish you
with a licensed power to keep alive an incorrigible fault, at the expense
of one who never would contend with you.

FAULKLAND. Nay, but Julia, by my soul and honor, if after this——

JULIA. But one word more. As my faith has once been given to you,
I never will barter it with another. I shall pray for your happiness with
the truest sincerity; and the dearest blessing I can ask of heaven to
send you will be to charm you from that unhappy temper which alone
has prevented the performance of our solemn engagement. All I request of *you* is that you will yourself reflect upon this infirmity, and
when you number up the many true delights it has deprived you of,
let it not be your *least* regret that it lost you the love of one, who would
have followed you in beggary through the world!   [*Exit.*]

FAULKLAND. She's gone!—forever! There was an awful resolution
in her manner, that riveted me to my place. O fool!—dolt!—barbarian! Cursed as I am with more imperfections than my fellow-
wretches, kind Fortune sent a heaven-gifted cherub to my aid, and,
like a ruffian, I have driven her from my side! I must now haste to
my appointment. Well, my mind is tuned for such a scene. I shall
wish only to become a principal in it, and reverse the tale my cursed
folly put me upon forging here. O love!—tormentor!—fiend! whose
influence, like the moon's, acting on men of dull souls, makes idiots of

them, but meeting subtler spirits, betrays their course, and urges sensibility to madness![41] [*Exit.*]

Enter MAID *and* LYDIA.

MAID. My mistress, Ma'am, I know, was here just now—perhaps she is only in the next room. [*Exit* MAID.]

LYDIA. Heigh-ho! Though he has used me so, this fellow runs strangely in my head. I believe one lecture from my grave cousin will make me recall him.

Enter JULIA.

LYDIA. O Julia, I am come to you with such an appetite for consolation.—Lud! child, what's the matter with you? You have been crying! I'll be hanged if that Faulkland has not been tormenting you!

JULIA. You mistake the cause of my uneasiness. Something *has* flurried me a little. Nothing that you can guess at —[*aside*] I would not accuse Faulkland to a sister!

LYDIA. Ah! whatever vexations you may have, I can assure you mine surpass them.— You know who Beverley proves to be?

JULIA. I will now own to you, Lydia, that Mr. Faulkland had before informed me of the whole affair. Had young Absolute been the person you took him for, I should not have accepted your confidence on the subject without a serious endeavor to counteract your caprice.

LYDIA. So, then, I see I have been deceived by everyone! But I don't care—I'll never have him.

JULIA. Nay, Lydia——

LYDIA. Why, is it not provoking? when I thought we were coming to the prettiest distress imaginable, to find myself made a mere Smithfield[42] bargain of at last! There had I projected one of the most sentimental elopements! so becoming a disguise! so amiable a ladder of ropes! Conscious moon—four horses—Scotch parson—with such surprise to Mrs. Malaprop, and such paragraphs in the newspapers! Oh, I shall die with disappointment!

JULIA. I don't wonder at it!

LYDIA. Now—sad reverse!—what have I to expect, but, after a deal of flimsy preparation, with a bishop's license,[43] and my aunt's blessing, to go simpering up to the altar; or perhaps be cried three times in a country-church, and have an unmannerly fat clerk ask the consent of every butcher in the parish to join John Absolute and Lydia Languish, Spinster! Oh, that I should live to hear myself called Spinster!

JULIA. Melancholy, indeed!

---

[41] The moon was traditionally regarded as the source of lunacy.

[42] the site of Bartholomew Fair

[43] The law normally required the publishing of banns (announcing the intention to marry) at church services on three successive Sundays. A bishop could issue a license for marrying without the publishing of banns.

LYDIA. How mortifying to remember the dear delicious shifts I used to be put to, to gain half a minute's conversation with this fellow! How often have I stole forth in the coldest night in January, and found him in the garden, stuck like a dripping statue! There would he kneel to me in the snow, and sneeze and cough so pathetically! he shivering with cold, and I with apprehension! and while the freezing blast numbed our joints, how warmly would he press me to pity his flame, and glow with mutual ardor! Ah, Julia, that was something like being in love!

JULIA. If I were in spirits, Lydia, I should chide you only by laughing heartily at you: but it suits more the situation of my mind, at present, earnestly to entreat you not to let a man, who loves you with sincerity, suffer that unhappiness from your caprice, which I know too well caprice can inflict.

LYDIA. O lud! what has brought my aunt here?

Enter MRS. MALAPROP, FAG, *and* DAVID.

MRS. MALAPROP. So! so! here's fine work!—here's fine suicide, parricide, and simulation going on in the fields! and Sir Anthony not to be found to prevent the antistrophe!

JULIA. For heaven's sake, Madam, what's the meaning of this?

MRS. MALAPROP. That gentleman can tell you—'twas he enveloped the affair to me.

LYDIA [*to* FAG]. Do, Sir, will you, inform us.

FAG. Ma'am, I should hold myself very deficient in every requisite that forms the man of breeding if I delayed a moment to give all the information in my power to a lady so deeply interested in the affair as you are.

LYDIA. But quick! quick, Sir!

FAG. True, Ma'am, as you say, one should be quick in divulging matters of this nature; for should we be tedious, perhaps while we are flourishing on the subject, two or three lives may be lost!

LYDIA. O patience! Do, Ma'am, for heaven's sake! tell us what is the matter!

MRS. MALAPROP. Why, murder's the matter! slaughter's the matter! killing's the matter! But he can tell you the perpendiculars.

LYDIA. Then, prithee, Sir, be brief.

FAG. Why then, Ma'am—as to murder, I cannot take upon me to say —and as to slaughter, or manslaughter, that will be as the jury finds it.

LYDIA. But who, Sir—who are engaged in this?

FAG. Faith, Ma'am, one is a young gentleman whom I should be very sorry anything was to happen to—a very pretty behaved gentleman! We have lived much together, and always on terms.

LYDIA. But who is this? who! who! who!

FAG. My master, Ma'am, my master—I speak of my master.

LYDIA. Heavens! What, Captain Absolute!

MRS. MALAPROP. Oh, to be sure, you are frightened now!

JULIA. But who are with him, Sir?

FAG. As to the rest, Ma'am, this gentleman can inform you better than I.

JULIA [*to* DAVID]. Do speak, friend.

DAVID. Look'ee, my lady—by the Mass! there's mischief going on. Folks don't use to meet for amusement with fire-arms, fire-locks, fire-engines, fire-screens, fire-office, and the devil knows what other crackers beside! This, my lady, I say, has an angry favor.

JULIA. But who is there beside Captain Absolute, friend?

DAVID. My poor master—under favor, for mentioning him first. You know me, my lady—I am David, and my master, of course, is, or *was*, Squire Acres. Then comes Squire Faulkland.

JULIA. Do, Ma'am, let us instantly endeavor to prevent mischief.

MRS. MALAPROP. Oh fie—it would be very inelegant in us: we should only participate things.

DAVID. Ah! do, Mrs. Aunt, save a few lives. They are desperately given, believe me. Above all, there is that bloodthirsty Philistine, Sir Lucius O'Trigger.

MRS. MALAPROP. Sir Lucius O'Trigger! O mercy! have they drawn poor little dear Sir Lucius into the scrape? Why, how you stand, girl! you have no more feeling than one of the Derbyshire putrefactions!

LYDIA. What are we to do, Madam?

MRS. MALAPROP. Why, fly with the utmost felicity, to be sure, to prevent mischief. Here, friend—you can show us the place?

FAG. If you please, Ma'am, I will conduct you.—— David, do you look for Sir Anthony.   [*Exit* DAVID.]

MRS. MALAPROP. Come, girls!— this gentleman will exhort us.—— Come, Sir, you're our envoy—lead the way, and we'll precede.

FAG. Not a step before the ladies for the world!

MRS. MALAPROP. You're sure you know the spot?

FAG. I think I can find it, Ma'am; and one good thing is we shall hear the report of the pistols as we draw near, so we can't well miss them; never fear, Ma'am, never fear.   [*Exeunt, he talking.*]

SCENE II
South Parade.

Enter ABSOLUTE, *putting his sword under his greatcoat.*

ABSOLUTE. A sword seen in the streets of Bath would raise as great an alarm as a mad dog. How provoking this is in Faulkland! never punctual! I shall be obliged to go without him at last. Oh, the devil! here's Sir Anthony! How shall I escape him?   [*Muffles up his face, and takes a circle to go off.*]

Enter SIR ANTHONY.

SIR ANTHONY. How one may be deceived at a little distance! Only that I see he don't know me, I could have sworn that was Jack!—— Hey! 'Gad's life! it is. Why, Jack!—what are you afraid of, hey!— Sure I'm right.—Why, Jack!—Jack Absolute! [*Goes up to him.*]

ABSOLUTE. Really, Sir, you have the advantage of me: I don't re- member ever to have had the honor. My name is Saunderson, at your service.

SIR ANTHONY. Sir, I beg your pardon—I took you—hey!—why, z——ds! it is—stay—[*Looks up to his face.*] So, so—your humble servant, Mr. Saunderson! Why, you scoundrel, what tricks are you after now?

ABSOLUTE. Oh! a joke, Sir, a joke! I came here on purpose to look for you, Sir.

SIR ANTHONY. You did! Well, I am glad you were so lucky. But what are you muffled up so for? What's this for?—hey?

ABSOLUTE. 'Tis cool, Sir; isn't it?—rather chilly, somehow. But I shall be late—I have a particular engagement.

SIR ANTHONY. Stay. Why, I thought you were looking for me? Pray, Jack, where is't you are going?

ABSOLUTE. Going, Sir!

SIR ANTHONY. Aye—where are you going?

ABSOLUTE. Where am I going?

SIR ANTHONY. You unmannerly puppy!

ABSOLUTE. I was going, Sir, to—to—to—to Lydia—Sir, to Lydia, to make matters up if I could; and I was looking for you, Sir, to— to——

SIR ANTHONY. To go with you, I suppose. Well, come along.

ABSOLUTE. Oh! z——ds! no, Sir, not for the world! I wished to meet with you, Sir—to—to—to—— You find it cool, I'm sure, Sir—you'd better not stay out.

SIR ANTHONY. Cool!—not at all. Well, Jack—and what will you say to Lydia?

ABSOLUTE. O, Sir, beg her pardon, humor her, promise and vow. But I detain you, Sir—consider the cold air on your gout.

SIR ANTHONY. Oh, not at all!—not at all! I'm in no hurry. Ah! Jack, you youngsters, when once you are wounded here—[*putting his hand to* ABSOLUTE'*s breast*] Hey! what the deuce have you got here?

ABSOLUTE. Nothing, Sir—nothing.

SIR ANTHONY. What's this? here's something d——d hard!

ABSOLUTE. Oh, trinkets, Sir! trinkets—a bauble for Lydia!

SIR ANTHONY. Nay, let me see your taste. [*Pulls his coat open, the sword falls.*] Trinkets!—a bauble for Lydia! Z——ds! Sirrah, you are not going to cut her throat, are you?

ABSOLUTE. Ha! ha! ha! I thought it would divert you, Sir; though I didn't mean to tell you till afterwards.

SIR ANTHONY. You didn't? Yes, this is a very diverting trinket, truly!

ABSOLUTE. Sir, I'll explain to you. You know, Sir, Lydia is romantic, dev'lish romantic, and very absurd of course. Now, Sir, I intend, if she refuses to forgive me, to unsheathe this sword and swear I'll fall upon its point, and expire at her feet!

SIR ANTHONY. Fall upon a fiddle-stick's end! Why, I suppose it is the very thing that would please her. Get along, you fool.

ABSOLUTE. Well, Sir, you shall hear of my success—you shall hear. "O Lydia!—forgive me, or this pointed steel"—says I.

SIR ANTHONY. "O, booby! stab away and welcome"—says she. Get along!—and d——n your trinkets! [*Exit* ABSOLUTE.]

Enter DAVID, *running.*

DAVID. Stop him! Stop him! Murder! Thief! Fire! Stop fire! Stop fire! O! Sir Anthony—call! call! bid 'em stop! Murder! Fire!

SIR ANTHONY. Fire! Murder! Where?

DAVID. Oons! he's out of sight! and I'm out of breath, for my part! O, Sir Anthony, why didn't you stop him? why didn't you stop him?

SIR ANTHONY. Z——ds! the fellow's mad! Stop whom? Stop Jack?

DAVID. Aye, the Captain, Sir! there's murder and slaughter——

SIR ANTHONY. Murder!

DAVID. Aye, please you, Sir Anthony, there's all kinds of murder, all sorts of slaughter to be seen in the fields: there's fighting going on, Sir—bloody sword-and-gun fighting!

SIR ANTHONY. Who are going to fight, dunce?

DAVID. Everybody that I know of, Sir Anthony—everybody is going to fight; my poor master, Sir Lucius O'Trigger, your son, the Captain——

SIR ANTHONY. Oh, the dog! I see his tricks.—— Do you know the place?

DAVID. King's-Mead-Fields.

SIR ANTHONY. You know the way?

DAVID. Not an inch; but I'll call the mayor—aldermen—constables —church-wardens—and beadles—we can't be too many to part them.

SIR ANTHONY. Come along—give me your shoulder! we'll get assistance as we go. The lying villain! Well, I shall be in such a frenzy! So—this was the history of his trinkets! I'll bauble him! [*Exeunt.*]

SCENE III
King's-Mead-Fields.

SIR LUCIUS *and* ACRES, *with pistols.*

ACRES. By my valor! then, Sir Lucius, forty yards is a good distance. Odds levels and aims! I say it is a good distance.

SIR LUCIUS. Is it for muskets or small field-pieces? Upon my conscience, Mr. Acres, you must leave those things to me. Stay now—
I'll show you. [*Measures paces along the stage.*] There now, that is a
very pretty distance—a pretty gentleman's distance.

ACRES. Z——ds! we might as well fight in a sentry-box! I tell you,
Sir Lucius, the farther he is off, the cooler I shall take my aim.

SIR LUCIUS. Faith! then I suppose you would aim at him best of all
if he was out of sight!

ACRES. No, Sir Lucius, but I should think forty, or eight and thirty
yards——

SIR LUCIUS. Pho! pho! nonsense! Three or four feet between the
mouths of your pistols is as good as a mile.

ACRES. Odds bullets, no! By my valor! there is no merit in killing
him so near: do, my dear Sir Lucius, let me bring him down at a long
shot—a long shot, Sir Lucius, if you love me!

SIR LUCIUS. Well—the gentleman's friend and I must settle that. But
tell me now, Mr. Acres, in case of an accident, is there any little will
or commission I could execute for you?

ACRES. I am much obliged to you, Sir Lucius, but I don't understand——

SIR LUCIUS. Why, you may think there's no being shot at without
a little risk, and if an unlucky bullet should carry a *quietus* with it—
I say it will be no time then to be bothering you about family matters.

ACRES. A *quietus!*

SIR LUCIUS. For instance, now—if that should be the case—would
you choose to be pickled and sent home? or would it be the same to you
to lie here in the Abbey? I'm told there is very snug lying in the
Abbey.

ACRES. Pickled! Snug lying in the Abbey! Odds tremors! Sir Lucius,
don't talk so!

SIR LUCIUS. I suppose, Mr. Acres, you never were engaged in an
affair of this kind before?

ACRES. No, Sir Lucius, never before.

SIR LUCIUS. Ah! that's a pity! there's nothing like being used to a
thing. Pray now, how would you receive the gentleman's shot?

ACRES. Odds files! I've practised that. There, Sir Lucius—there [*Puts
himself in an attitude.*]—a side-front, hey? Odd! I'll make myself
small enough: I'll stand edge-ways.

SIR LUCIUS. Now—you're quite out, for if you stand so when I take
my aim—— [*leveling at him*]

ACRES. Z——ds! Sir Lucius—are you sure it is not cocked?

SIR LUCIUS. Never fear.

ACRES. But—but—you don't know—it may go off of its own head!

SIR LUCIUS. Pho! be easy. Well, now if I hit you in the body, my
bullet has a double chance, for if it misses a vital part on your right
side, 'twill be very hard if it don't succeed on the left!

ACRES. A vital part!

SIR LUCIUS. But, there—fix yourself so. [*placing him*] Let him see the broad side of your full front—there now a ball or two may pass clean through your body, and never do any harm at all.

ACRES. Clean through me! a ball or two clean through me!

SIR LUCIUS. Aye, may they; and it is much the genteelest attitude into the bargain.

ACRES. Look'ee! Sir Lucius—I'd just as lieve be shot in an awkward posture as a genteel one—so, by my valor! I will stand edge-ways.

SIR LUCIUS [*looking at his watch*]. Sure they don't mean to disappoint us. Hah? No, faith—I think I see them coming.

ACRES. Hey! what!—coming!——

SIR LUCIUS. Aye. Who are those yonder getting over the stile?

ACRES. There are two of them indeed! Well—let them come—hey, Sir Lucius? We—we—we—we—won't run.

SIR LUCIUS. Run!

ACRES. No—I say—we *won't* run, by my valor!

SIR LUCIUS. What the devil's the matter with you?

ACRES. Nothing—nothing—my dear friend—my dear Sir Lucius— but—I—I—I don't feel quite so bold, somehow—as I did.

SIR LUCIUS. Oh fie! consider your honor.

ACRES. Aye—true—my honor, Do, Sir Lucius, edge in a word or two every now and then about my honor.

SIR LUCIUS [*looking*]. Well, here they're coming.

ACRES. Sir Lucius—if I wa'n't with you, I should almost think I was afraid. If my valor should leave me! Valor will come and go.

SIR LUCIUS. Then, pray, keep it fast while you have it.

ACRES. Sir Lucius—I doubt it is going—yes— my valor is certainly going! it is sneaking off! I feel it oozing out as it were at the palms of my hands!

SIR LUCIUS. Your honor—your honor. Here they are.

ACRES. Oh mercy! now that I were safe at Clod-Hall! or could be shot before I was aware!

Enter FAULKLAND *and* ABSOLUTE.

SIR LUCIUS. Gentlemen, your most obedient—hah!—what—Captain Absolute! So, I suppose, Sir, you are come here, just like myself— to do a kind office, first for your friend—then to proceed to business on your own account.

ACRES. What, Jack! my dear Jack! my dear friend!

ABSOLUTE. Hark'ee, Bob, Beverley's at hand.

SIR LUCIUS. Well, Mr. Acres, I don't blame your saluting the gentleman civilly. So, Mr. Beverley [*to* FAULKLAND], if you'll choose your weapons, the Captain and I will measure the ground.

FAULKLAND. *My* weapons, Sir!

ACRES. Odd's life! Sir Lucius, I'm not going to fight Mr. Faulkland; these are my particular friends.

SIR LUCIUS. What, Sir, did not you come here to fight Mr. Acres?

FAULKLAND. Not I, upon my word, Sir.

SIR LUCIUS. Well, now, that's mighty provoking! But I hope, Mr. Faulkland, as there are three of us come on purpose for the game, you won't be so cantankerous as to spoil the party by sitting out.

ABSOLUTE. Oh pray, Faulkland, fight to oblige Sir Lucius.

FAULKLAND. Nay, if Mr. Acres is so bent on the matter——

ACRES. No, no, Mr. Faulkland—I'll bear my disappointment like a Christian. Look'ee, Sir Lucius, there's no occasion at all for me to fight; and if it is the same to you, I'd as lieve let it alone.

SIR LUCIUS. Observe me, Mr. Acres—I must not be trifled with. You have certainly challenged somebody, and you came here to fight him. Now, if that gentleman is willing to represent him, I can't see, for my soul, why it isn't just the same thing.

ACRES. Why no, Sir Lucius—I tell you, 'tis one Beverley I've challenged—a fellow you see, that dare not show his face! If *he* were here, I'd make him give up his pretensions directly!

ABSOLUTE. Hold, Bob—let me set you right. There is no such man as Beverley in the case. The person who assumed that name is before you; and as his pretensions are the same in both characters, he is ready to support them in whatever way you please.

SIR LUCIUS. Well, this is lucky! Now you have an opportunity——

ACRES. What, quarrel with my dear friend Jack Absolute? Not if he were fifty Beverleys! Z——ds! Sir Lucius, you would not have me be so unnatural.

SIR LUCIUS. Upon my conscience, Mr. Acres, your valor has *oozed* away with a vengeance!

ACRES. Not in the least! Odds backs and abettors! I'll be your second with all my heart, and if you should get a *quietus*, you may command me entirely, I'll get you *snug lying* in the *Abbey here;* or *pickle* you, and send you over to Blunderbuss-Hall, or anything of the kind, with the greatest pleasure.

SIR LUCIUS. Pho! pho! you are little better than a coward.

ACRES. Mind, gentlemen, he calls me a *coward;* coward was the word, by my valor!

SIR LUCIUS. Well, Sir?

ACRES. Look'ee, Sir Lucius, 'tisn't that I mind the word coward—*coward* may be said in joke. But if you had called me a *poltroon*, odds daggers and balls!——

SIR LUCIUS. Well, Sir?

ACRES. ——I should have thought you a very ill-bred man.

SIR LUCIUS. Pho! you are beneath my notice.

ABSOLUTE. Nay, Sir Lucius, you can't have a better second than my friend Acres. He is a most *determined dog*, called in the country, *Fighting Bob*. He generally *kills a man a week;* don't you, Bob?

ACRES. Aye—at home!

SIR LUCIUS. Well then, Captain, 'tis we must begin. So come out, my little counselor, [*Draws his sword.*] and ask the gentleman whether he will resign the lady without forcing you to proceed against him.

ABSOLUTE. Come on then, Sir; [*Draws.*] since you won't let it be an amicable suit, here's my reply.

Enter SIR ANTHONY, DAVID, *and the Women.*

DAVID. Knock 'em all down, sweet Sir Anthony; knock down my master in particular, and bind his hands over to their good behavior!

SIR ANTHONY. Put up, Jack, put up, or I shall be in a frenzy. How came you in a duel, Sir?

ABSOLUTE. Faith, Sir, that gentleman can tell you better than I; 'twas he called on me, and you know, Sir, I serve his Majesty.

SIR ANTHONY. Here's a pretty fellow! I catch him going to cut a man's throat, and he tells me he serves his Majesty! Z——ds! Sirrah, then how durst you draw the King's sword against one of his subjects?

ABSOLUTE. Sir, I tell you! That gentleman called me out, without explaining his reasons.

SIR ANTHONY. Gad! Sir, how came you to call my son out, without explaining your reasons?

SIR LUCIUS. Your son, Sir, insulted me in a manner which my honor could not brook.

SIR ANTHONY. Z——ds! Jack, how durst you insult the gentleman in a manner which his honor could not brook?

MRS. MALAPROP. Come, come, let's have no honor before ladies. Captain Absolute, come here. How could you intimidate us so? Here's Lydia has been terrified to death for you.

ABSOLUTE. For fear I should be killed, or escape, Ma'am?

MRS. MALAPROP. Nay, no delusions to the past. Lydia is convinced; speak, child.

SIR LUCIUS. With your leave, Ma'am, I must put in a word here. I believe I could interpret the young lady's silence. Now mark ——

LYDIA. What is it you mean, Sir?

SIR LUCIUS. Come, come, Delia, we must be serious now—this is no time for trifling.

LYDIA. 'Tis true, Sir; and your reproof bids me offer this gentleman my hand, and solicit the return of his affections.

ABSOLUTE. O! my little angel, say you so? Sir Lucius, I perceive there must be some mistake here. With regard to the affront which you affirm I have given you, I can only say that it could not have been intentional. And as you must be convinced that I should not fear to support a real injury, you shall now see that I am not ashamed to atone for an inadvertency. I ask your pardon. But for this lady, while honored with her approbation, I will support my claim against any man whatever.

SIR ANTHONY. Well said, Jack! and I'll stand by you, my boy.

ACRES. Mind, I give up all my claim—I make no pretensions to anything in the world—and if I can't get a wife without fighting for her, by my valor! I'll live a bachelor.

SIR LUCIUS. Captain, give me your hand—an affront handsomely acknowledged becomes an obligation—and as for the lady, if she chooses to deny her own handwriting here——   [*Takes out letters.*]

MRS. MALAPROP. Oh, he will dissolve my mystery! Sir Lucius, perhaps there's some mistake—perhaps, I can illuminate——

SIR LUCIUS. Pray, old gentlewoman, don't interfere where you have no business. Miss Languish, are you my Delia, or not?

LYDIA. Indeed, Sir Lucius, I am not.

[LYDIA *and* ABSOLUTE *walk aside.*]

MRS. MALAPROP. Sir Lucius O'Trigger, ungrateful as you are, I own the soft impeachment—pardon my blushes, I am Delia.

SIR LUCIUS. You Delia!—pho! pho! be easy.

MRS. MALAPROP. Why, thou barbarous Vandyke!—those letters are mine. When you are more sensible of my benignity, perhaps I may be brought to encourage your addresses.

SIR LUCIUS. Mrs. Malaprop, I am extremely sensible of your condescension; and whether you or Lucy have put this trick upon me, I am equally beholden to you. And to show you I'm not ungrateful —— Captain Absolute! since you have taken that lady from me, I'll give you my Delia into the bargain.

ABSOLUTE. I am much obliged to you, Sir Lucius; but here's our friend, Fighting Bob, unprovided for.

SIR LUCIUS. Hah! little Valor—here, will you make your fortune?

ACRES. Odds wrinkles! No. But give me your hand, Sir Lucius; forget and forgive; but if ever I give you a chance of *pickling* me again, say Bob Acres is a dunce, that's all.

SIR ANTHONY. Come, Mrs. Malaprop, don't be cast down—you are in your bloom yet.

MRS. MALAPROP. O Sir Anthony!—men are all barbarians——

[*All retire but* JULIA *and* FAULKLAND.]

JULIA [*aside*]. He seems dejected and unhappy—not sullen. There was some foundation, however, for the tale he told me. O woman! how true should be your judgment, when your resolution is so weak!

FAULKLAND. Julia! how can I sue for what I so little deserve? I dare not presume—yet Hope is the child of Penitence.

JULIA. Oh! Faulkland, you have not been more faulty in your unkind treatment of me than I am now in wanting inclination to resent it. As my heart honestly bids me place my weakness to the account of love, I should be ungenerous not to admit the same plea for yours.

FAULKLAND. Now I shall be blest indeed!

[SIR ANTHONY *comes forward.*]

SIR ANTHONY. What's going on here? So you have been quarrelling too, I warrant. Come, Julia, I never interfered before; but let me have a hand in the matter at last. All the faults I have ever seen in my friend Faulkland seemed to proceed from what he calls the *delicacy* and *warmth* of his affection for you. There, marry him directly, Julia; you'll find he'll mend surprisingly!

[*The rest come forward.*]

SIR LUCIUS. Come now, I hope there is no dissatisfied person but what is content; for as I have been disappointed myself, it will be very hard if I have not the satisfaction of seeing other people succeed better——

ACRES. You are right, Sir Lucius. So, Jack, I wish you joy—Mr. Faulkland the same.—— Ladies,—come now, to show you I'm neither vexed nor angry, odds tabours and pipes! I'll order the fiddles in half an hour to the New Rooms, and I insist on your all meeting me there.

SIR ANTHONY. Gad! Sir, I like your spirit; and at night we single lads will drink a health to the young couples, and a husband to Mrs. Malaprop.

FAULKLAND. Our partners are stolen from us, Jack—I hope to be congratulated by each other—*yours* for having checked in time the errors of an ill-directed imagination, which might have betrayed an innocent heart; and *mine*, for having, by her gentleness and candor, reformed the unhappy temper of one who by it made wretched whom he loved most, and tortured the heart he ought to have adored.

ABSOLUTE. Well, Faulkland, we have both tasted the bitters, as well as the sweets, of love—with this difference only, that *you* always prepared the bitter cup for yourself, while *I*——

LYDIA. Was always obliged to *me* for it, hey! Mr. Modesty?—— But come, no more of that: our happiness is now as unalloyed as general.

JULIA. Then let us study to preserve it so; and while Hope pictures to us a flattering scene of future Bliss, let us deny its pencil those colors which are too bright to be lasting. When Hearts deserving Happiness would unite their fortunes, Virtue would crown them with an unfading garland of modest, hurtless flowers; but ill-judging Passion will force the gaudier Rose into the wreath, whose thorn offends them, when its leaves are dropped! [*Exeunt omnes.*]

Henrik Ibsen

1828–1906

A DOLL'S HOUSE

Translated and edited by James Walter McFarlane

◇

CHARACTERS

TORVALD HELMER, *a lawyer*
NORA, *his wife.*
DR. RANK.
MRS. KRISTINE LINDE.
NILS KROGSTAD.

ANNE MARIE, *the nursemaid.*
HELENE, *the maid.*
The Helmers' three children.
A porter.

The action takes place in the Helmers' flat.

◇

ACT ONE

A pleasant room, tastefully but not expensively furnished. On the back wall, one door on the right leads to the entrance hall, a second door on the left leads to HELMER'S *study. Between these two doors, a piano. In the middle of the left wall, a door; and downstage from it, a window. Near the window a round table with armchairs and a small sofa. In the right wall, upstage, a door; and on the same wall downstage, a porcelain stove with a couple of armchairs and a rockingchair. Between the stove and the door a small table. Etchings on the walls. A whatnot with china and other small objets d' art; a small bookcase with books in handsome bindings. Carpet on the floor; a fire burns in the stove. A winter's day.*

The front door-bell rings in the hall; a moment later, there is the sound of the front door being opened. NORA *comes into the room, happily humming to herself. She is dressed in her outdoor things, and is carrying lots of parcels which she then puts down on the table, right. She leaves the door into the hall standing open; a* PORTER *can be seen outside holding a Christmas tree and a basket; he hands them to the* MAID *who has opened the door for them.*

NORA. Hide the Christmas tree away carefully, Helene. The children mustn't see it till this evening when it's decorated. [*To the* PORTER, *taking out her purse.*] How much?
PORTER. Fifty öre.
NORA. There's a crown. Keep the change.
[*The* PORTER *thanks her and goes.* NORA *shuts the door. She continues to laugh quietly and happily to herself as she takes off her things. She takes a*

bag of macaroons out of her pocket and eats one or two; then she walks stealthily across and listens at her husband's door.]

NORA. Yes, he's in.

[*She begins humming again as she walks over to the table, right.*]

HELMER [*in his study*]. Is that my little sky-lark chirruping out there?

NORA [*busy opening some of the parcels*]. Yes, it is.

HELMER. Is that my little squirrel frisking about?

NORA. Yes!

HELMER. When did my little squirrel get home?

NORA. Just this minute. [*She stuffs the bag of macaroons in her pocket and wipes her mouth.*] Come on out, Torvald, and see what I've bought.

HELMER. I don't want to be disturbed! [*A moment later, he opens the door and looks out, his pen in his hand.*] "Bought," did you say? All that? Has my little spendthrift been out squandering money again?

NORA. But, Torvald, surely this year we can spread ourselves just a little. This is the first Christmas we haven't had to go carefully.

HELMER. Ah, but that doesn't mean we can afford to be extravagant, you know.

NORA. Oh yes, Torvald, surely we can afford to be just a little bit extravagant now, can't we? Just a teeny-weeny bit. You are getting quite a good salary now, and you are going to earn lots and lots of money.

HELMER. Yes, after the New Year. But it's going to be three whole months before the first pay check comes in.

NORA. Pooh! We can always borrow in the meantime.

HELMER. Nora! [*Crosses to her and takes her playfully by the ear.*] Here we go again, you and your frivolous ideas! Suppose I went and borrowed a thousand crowns today, and you went and spent it all over Christmas, then on New Year's Eve a slate fell and hit me on the head and there I was. . . .

NORA [*putting her hand over his mouth*]. Sh! Don't say such horrid things.

HELMER. Yes, but supposing something like that did happen . . . what then?

NORA. If anything as awful as that did happen, I wouldn't care if I owed anybody anything or not.

HELMER. Yes, but what about the people I'd borrowed from?

NORA. Them? Who cares about them! They are only strangers!

HELMER. Nora, Nora! Just like a woman! Seriously though, Nora, you know what I think about these things. No debts! Never borrow! There's always something inhibited, something unpleasant, about a home built on credit and borrowed money. We two have managed to stick it out so far, and that's the way we'll go on for the little time that remains.

NORA [*walks over to the stove*]. Very well, just as you say, Torvald.

HELMER [*following her*]. There, there! My little singing bird mustn't go drooping her wings, eh? Has it got the sulks, that little squirrel of mine? [*Takes out his wallet.*] Nora, what do you think I've got here?

NORA [*quickly turning round*]. Money!

HELMER. There! [*He hands her some notes.*] Good heavens, I know only too well how Christmas runs away with the housekeeping.

NORA [*counts*]. Ten, twenty, thirty, forty. Oh, thank you, thank you, Torvald! This will see me quite a long way.

HELMER. Yes, it'll have to.

NORA. Yes, yes, I'll see that it does. But come over here, I want to show you all the things I've bought. And so cheap! Look, some new clothes for Ivar . . . and a little sword. There's a horse and a trumpet for Bob. And a doll and a doll's cot for Emmy. They are not very grand but she'll have them all broken before long anyway. And I've got some dress material and some handkerchiefs for the maids. Though, really, dear old Anne Marie should have had something better.

HELMER. And what's in this parcel here?

NORA [*shrieking*]. No, Torvald! You mustn't see that till tonight!

HELMER. All right. But tell me now, what did my little spendthrift fancy for herself?

NORA. For me? Puh, I don't really want anything.

HELMER. Of course you do. Anything reasonable that you think you might like, just tell me.

NORA. Well, I don't really know. As a matter of fact, though, Torvald . . .

HELMER. Well?

NORA [*toying with his coat buttons, and without looking at him*]. If you did want to give me something, you could . . . you could always . . .

HELMER. Well, well, out with it!

NORA [*quickly*]. You could always give me money, Torvald. Only what you think you could spare. And then I could buy myself something with it later on.

HELMER. But Nora. . . .

NORA. Oh, please, Torvald dear! Please! I beg you. Then I'd wrap the money up in some pretty gilt paper and hang it on the Christmas tree. Wouldn't that be fun?

HELMER. What do we call my pretty little pet when it runs away with all the money?

NORA. I know, I know, we call it a spendthrift. But please let's do what I said, Torvald. Then I'll have a bit of time to think about what I need most. Isn't that awfully sensible, now, eh?

HELMER [*smiling*]. Yes, it is indeed—that is, if only you really could hold on to the money I gave you, and really did buy something for yourself with it. But it just gets mixed up with the housekeeping and frittered away on all sorts of useless things, and then I have to dig into my pocket all over again.

NORA. Oh but, Torvald. . . .

HELMER. You can't deny it, Nora dear. [*Puts his arm round her waist.*] My pretty little pet is very sweet, but it runs away with an awful lot of money. It's incredible how expensive it is for a man to keep such a pet.

NORA. For shame! How can you say such a thing? As a matter of fact I save everything I can.

HELMER [*laughs*]. Yes, you are right there. Everything you *can*. But you simply can't.

NORA [*hums and smiles quietly and happily*]. Ah, if you only knew how many expenses the likes of us sky-larks and squirrels have, Torvald!

HELMER. What a funny little one you are! Just like your father. Always on the look-out for money, wherever you can lay your hands on it; but as soon as you've got it, it just seems to slip through your fingers. You never seem to know what you've done with it. Well, one must accept you as you are. It's in the blood. Oh yes, it is, Nora. That sort of thing is hereditary.

NORA. Oh, I only wish I'd inherited a few more of Daddy's qualities.

HELMER. And I wouldn't want my pretty little song-bird to be the least bit different from what she is now. But come to think of it, you look rather . . . rather . . . how shall I put it? . . . rather guilty today. . . .

NORA. Do I?

HELMER. Yes, you do indeed. Look me straight in the eye.

NORA [*looks at him*]. Well?

HELMER [*wagging his finger at her*]. My little sweet-tooth surely didn't forget herself in town today?

NORA. No, whatever makes you think that?

HELMER. She didn't just pop into the confectioner's for a moment?

NORA. No, I assure you, Torvald. . . !

HELMER. Didn't try sampling the preserves?

NORA. No, really I didn't.

HELMER. Didn't go nibbling a macaroon or two?

NORA. No, Torvald, honestly, you must believe me. . . !

HELMER. All right then! It's really just my little joke. . . .

NORA [*crosses to the table*]. I would never dream of doing anything you didn't want me to.

HELMER. Of course not, I know that. And then you've given me your word. . . . [*Crosses to her.*] Well then, Nora dearest, you shall keep your little Christmas secrets. They'll all come out tonight, I dare say, when we light the tree.

NORA. Did you remember to invite Dr. Rank?

HELMER. No. But there's really no need. Of course he'll come and have dinner with us. Anyway, I can ask him when he looks in this morning. I've ordered some good wine. Nora, you can't imagine how I am looking forward to this evening.

NORA. So am I. And won't the children enjoy it, Torvald!

HELMER. Oh, what a glorious feeling it is, knowing you've got a nice, safe job, and a good fat income. Don't you agree? Isn't it wonderful, just thinking about it?

NORA. Oh, it's marvelous!

HELMER. Do you remember last Christmas? Three whole weeks beforehand you shut yourself up every evening till after midnight making flowers for the Christmas tree and all the other splendid things you wanted to surprise us with. Ugh, I never felt so bored in all my life.

NORA. I wasn't the least bit bored.

HELMER [smiling]. But it turned out a bit of an anticlimax, Nora.

NORA. Oh, you are not going to tease me about that again! How was I to know the cat would get in and pull everything to bits?

HELMER. No, of course you weren't. Poor little Nora! All you wanted was for us to have a nice time—and it's the thought behind it that counts, after all. All the same, it's a good thing we've seen the back of those lean times.

NORA. Yes, really it's marvelous.

HELMER. Now there's no need for me to sit here all on my own, bored to tears. And you don't have to strain your dear little eyes, and work those dainty little fingers to the bone. . . .

NORA [clapping her hands]. No, Torvald, I don't, do I? Not any more. Oh, how marvelous it is to hear that! [Takes his arm.] Now I want to tell you how I've been thinking we might arrange things, Torvald. As soon as Christmas is over. . . . [The door-bell rings in the hall.] Oh, there's the bell. [Tidies one or two things in the room.] It's probably a visitor. What a nuisance!

HELMER. Remember I'm not at home to callers.

MAID [in the doorway]. There's a lady to see you, ma'am.

NORA. Show her in, please.

MAID [to HELMER]. And the doctor's just arrived, too, sir.

HELMER. Did he go straight into my room?

MAID. Yes, he did, sir.

[HELMER goes into his study. The MAID shows in MRS. LINDE, who is in traveling clothes, and closes the door after her.]

MRS. LINDE [subdued and rather hesitantly]. How do you do, Nora?

NORA [uncertainly]. How do you do?

MRS. LINDE. I'm afraid you don't recognize me.

NORA. No, I don't think I . . . And yet I seem to. . . . [Bursts out suddenly.] Why! Kristine! Is it really you?

MRS. LINDE. Yes, it's me.

NORA. Kristine! Fancy not recognizing you again! But how was I to, when . . . [Gently.] How you've changed, Kristine!

MRS. LINDE. I dare say I have. In nine . . . ten years. . . .

NORA. Is it so long since we last saw each other? Yes, it must be. Oh, believe me these last eight years have been such a happy time. And now you've come up to town, too? All that long journey in winter-time. That took courage.

MRS. LINDE. I just arrived this morning on the steamer.

NORA. To enjoy yourself over Christmas, of course. How lovely! Oh, we'll have such fun, you'll see. Do take off your things. You are not cold, are you? [*Helps her.*] There now! Now let's sit down here in comfort beside the stove. No, here, you take the armchair, I'll sit here on the rocking-chair. [*Takes her hands.*] Ah, now you look a bit more like your old self again. It was just that when I first saw you. . . . But you are a little paler, Kristine . . . and perhaps even a bit thin-ner!

MRS. LINDE. And much, much older, Nora.

NORA. Yes, perhaps a little older . . . very, very little, not really very much. [*Stops suddenly and looks serious.*] Oh, what a thoughtless crea-ture I am, sitting here chattering on like this! Dear, sweet Kristine, can you forgive me?

MRS. LINDE. What do you mean, Nora?

NORA [*gently*]. Poor Kristine, of course you're a widow now.

MRS. LINDE. Yes, my husband died three years ago.

NORA. Oh, I remember now. I read about it in the papers. Oh, Kristine, believe me I often thought at the time of writing to you. But I kept putting it off, something always seemed to crop up.

MRS. LINDE. My dear Nora, I understand so well.

NORA. No, it wasn't very nice of me, Kristine. Oh, you poor thing, what you must have gone through. And didn't he leave you anything?

MRS. LINDE. No.

NORA. And no children?

MRS. LINDE. No.

NORA. Absolutely nothing?

MRS. LINDE. Nothing at all . . . not even a broken heart to grieve over.

NORA [*looks at her incredulously*]. But, Kristine, is that possible?

MRS. LINDE [*smiles sadly and strokes* NORA'*s hair*]. Oh, it sometimes happens, Nora.

NORA. So utterly alone. How terribly sad that must be for you. I have three lovely children. You can't see them for the moment, because they're out with their nanny. But now you must tell me all about yourself. . . .

MRS. LINDE. No, no, I want to hear about you.

NORA. No, you start. I won't be selfish today. I must think only about your affairs today. But there's just one thing I really must tell you. Have you heard about the great stroke of luck we've had in the last few days?

MRS. LINDE. No. What is it?

NORA. What do you think? My husband has just been made Bank Manager!

MRS. LINDE. Your husband? How splendid!

NORA. Isn't it tremendous! It's not a very steady way of making a living, you know, being a lawyer, especially if he refuses to take on anything that's the least bit shady—which of course is what Torvald does, and I think he's quite right. You can imagine how pleased we are! He starts at the Bank straight after New Year, and he's getting a big salary and lots of commission. From now on we'll be able to live quite differently . . . we'll do just what we want. Oh, Kristine, I'm so happy and relieved. I must say it's lovely to have plenty of money and not have to worry. Isn't it?

MRS. LINDE. Yes. It must be nice to have enough, at any rate.

NORA. No, not just enough, but pots and pots of money.

MRS. LINDE [smiles]. Nora, Nora, haven't you learned any sense yet? At school you used to be an awful spendthrift.

NORA. Yes, Torvald still says I am. [Wags her finger.] But little Nora isn't as stupid as everybody thinks. Oh, we haven't really been in a position where I could afford to spend a lot of money. We've both had to work.

MRS. LINDE. You too?

NORA. Yes, odd jobs—sewing, crochet-work, embroidery and things like that. [Casually.] And one or two other things, besides. I suppose you know that Torvald left the Ministry when we got married. There weren't any prospects of promotion in his department, and of course he needed to earn more money than he had before. But the first year he wore himself out completely. He had to take on all kinds of extra jobs, you know, and he found himself working all hours of the day and night. But he couldn't go on like that; and he became seriously ill. The doctors said it was essential for him to go South.

MRS. LINDE. Yes, I believe you spent a whole year in Italy, didn't you?

NORA. That's right. It wasn't easy to get away, I can tell you. It was just after I'd had Ivar. But of course we had to go. Oh, it was an absolutely marvelous trip. And it saved Torvald's life. But it cost an awful lot of money, Kristine.

MRS. LINDE. That I can well imagine.

NORA. Twelve hundred dollars. Four thousand eight hundred crowns. That's a lot of money, Kristine.

MRS. LINDE. Yes, but in such circumstances, one is very lucky if one has it.

NORA. Well, we got it from Daddy, you see.

MRS. LINDE. Ah, that was it. It was just about then your father died, I believe, wasn't it?

NORA. Yes, Kristine, just about then. And do you know, I couldn't even go and look after him. Here was I expecting Ivar any day. And I also had poor Torvald, gravely ill, on my hands. Dear, kind Daddy! I never saw him again, Kristine. Oh, that's the saddest thing that has happened to me in all my married life.

MRS. LINDE. I know you were very fond of him. But after that you left for Italy?

NORA. Yes, we had the money then, and the doctors said it was urgent. We left a month later.

MRS. LINDE. And your husband came back completely cured?

NORA. Fit as a fiddle!

MRS. LINDE. But . . . what about the doctor?

NORA. How do you mean?

MRS. LINDE. I thought the maid said something about the gentleman who came at the same time as me being a doctor.

NORA. Yes, that was Dr. Rank. But this isn't a professional visit. He's our best friend and he always looks in at least once a day. No, Torvald has never had a day's illness since. And the children are fit and healthy, and so am I. [*Jumps up and claps her hands.*] Oh God, oh God, isn't it marvelous to be alive, and to be happy, Kristine! . . . Oh but I ought to be ashamed of myself . . . Here I go on talking about nothing but myself. [*She sits on a low stool near* MRS. LINDE *and lays her arms on her lap.*] Oh, please, you mustn't be angry with me! Tell me, is it really true that you didn't love your husband? What made you marry him, then?

MRS. LINDE. My mother was still alive; she was bedridden and helpless. And then I had my two young brothers to look after as well. I didn't think I would be justified in refusing him.

NORA. No, I dare say you are right. I suppose he was fairly wealthy then?

MRS. LINDE. He was quite well off, I believe. But the business was shaky. When he died, it went all to pieces, and there just wasn't anything left.

NORA. What then?

MRS. LINDE. Well, I had to fend for myself, opening a little shop, running a little school, anything I could turn my hand to. These last three years have been one long relentless drudge. But now it's finished, Nora. My poor dear mother doesn't need me any more, she's passed away. Nor the boys either; they're at work now, they can look after themselves.

NORA. What a relief you must find it. . . .

MRS. LINDE. No, Nora! Just unutterably empty. Nobody to live for any more. [*Stands up restlessly.*] That's why I couldn't stand it any longer being cut off up there. Surely it must be a bit easier here to find something to occupy your mind. If only I could manage to find a steady job of some kind, in an office perhaps. . . .

NORA. But, Kristine, that's terribly exhausting; and you look so worn out even before you start. The best thing for you would be a little holiday at some quiet little resort.

MRS. LINDE [*crosses to the window*]. I haven't any father I can fall back on for the money, Nora.

NORA [*rises*]. Oh, please, you mustn't be angry with me!

MRS. LINDE [*goes to her*]. My dear Nora, you mustn't be angry with me either. That's the worst thing about people in my position, they become so bitter. One has nobody to work for, yet one has to be on the look-out all the time. Life has to go on, and one starts thinking only of oneself. Believe it or not, when you told me the good news about your step up, I was pleased not so much for your sake as for mine.

NORA. How do you mean? Ah, I see. You think Torvald might be able to do something for you.

MRS. LINDE. Yes, that's exactly what I thought.

NORA. And so he shall, Kristine. Just leave things to me. I'll bring it up so cleverly . . . I'll think up something to put him in a good mood. Oh, I do so much want to help you.

MRS. LINDE. It is awfully kind of you, Nora, offering to do all this for me, particularly in your case, where you haven't known much trouble or hardship in your own life.

NORA. When I . . . ? I haven't known much . . . ?

MRS. LINDE [*smiling*]. Well, good heavens, a little bit of sewing to do and a few things like that. What a child you are, Nora!

NORA [*tosses her head and walks across the room*]. I wouldn't be too sure of that, if I were you.

MRS. LINDE. Oh?

NORA. You're just like the rest of them. You all think I'm useless when it comes to anything really serious. . . .

MRS. LINDE. Come, come. . . .

NORA. You think I've never had anything much to contend with in this hard world.

MRS. LINDE. Nora dear, you've only just been telling me all the things you've had to put up with.

NORA. Pooh! They were just trivialities! [*Softly.*] I haven't told you about the really big thing.

MRS. LINDE. What big thing? What do you mean?

NORA. I know you rather tend to look down on me, Kristine. But you shouldn't, you know. You are proud of having worked so hard and so long for your mother.

MRS. LINDE. I'm sure I don't look down on anybody. But it's true what you say: I am both proud and happy when I think of how I was able to make Mother's life a little easier towards the end.

NORA. And you are proud when you think of what you have done for your brothers, too.

MRS. LINDE. I think I have every right to be.

NORA. I think so too. But now I'm going to tell you something, Kristine. I too have something to be proud and happy about.

MRS. LINDE. I don't doubt that. But what is it you mean?

NORA. Not so loud. Imagine if Torvald were to hear! He must never on any account . . . nobody must know about it, Kristine, nobody but you.

MRS. LINDE. But what is it?

NORA. Come over here. [*She pulls her down on the sofa beside her.*] Yes, Kristine, I too have something to be proud and happy about. I was the one who saved Torvald's life.

MRS. LINDE. Saved . . . ? How . . . ?

NORA. I told you about our trip to Italy. Torvald would never have recovered but for that. . . .

MRS. LINDE. Well? Your father gave you what money was necessary. . . .

NORA [*smiles*]. That's what Torvald thinks, and everybody else. But . . .

MRS. LINDE. But . . . ?

NORA. Daddy never gave us a penny. I was the one who raised the money.

MRS. LINDE. You? All that money?

NORA. Twelve hundred dollars. Four thousand eight hundred crowns. What do you say to that!

MRS. LINDE. But, Nora, how was it possible? Had you won a sweepstake or something?

NORA [*contemptuously*]. A sweepstake? Pooh! There would have been nothing to it then.

MRS. LINDE. Where did you get it from, then?

NORA [*hums and smiles secretively*]. H'm, tra-la-la!

MRS. LINDE. Because what you couldn't do was borrow it.

NORA. Oh? Why not?

MRS. LINDE. Well, a wife can't borrow without her husband's consent.

NORA [*tossing her head*]. Ah, but when it happens to be a wife with a bit of a sense for business . . . a wife who knows her way about things, then. . . .

MRS. LINDE. But, Nora, I just don't understand. . . .

NORA. You don't have to. I haven't said I did borrow the money. I might have got it some other way. [*Throws herself back on the sofa.*] I might even have got it from some admirer. Anyone as reasonably attractive as I am. . . .

MRS. LINDE. Don't be so silly!

NORA. Now you must be dying of curiosity, Kristine.

MRS. LINDE. Listen to me now, Nora dear—you haven't done anything rash, have you?

NORA [*sitting up again*]. Is it rash to save your husband's life?

MRS. LINDE. I think it was rash to do anything without telling him. . . .

NORA. But the whole point was that he mustn't know anything. Good heavens, can't you see! He wasn't even supposed to know how desperately ill he was. It was me the doctors came and told his life was in danger, that the only way to save him was to go South for a while. Do you think I didn't try talking him into it first? I began dropping hints about how nice it would be if I could be taken on a little trip abroad, like other young wives. I wept, I pleaded. I told him he ought to show some consideration for my condition, and let me have a bit of my own way. And then I suggested he might take out a loan. But at that he nearly lost his temper, Kristine. He said I was being frivolous, that it was his duty as a husband not to give in to all these whims and fancies of mine—as I do believe he called them. All right, I thought, somehow you've got to be saved. And it was then I found a way. . . .

MRS. LINDE. Did your husband never find out from your father that the money hadn't come from him?

NORA. No, never. It was just about the time Daddy died. I'd intended letting him into the secret and asking him not to give me away. But when he was so ill . . . I'm sorry to say it never became necessary.

MRS. LINDE. And you never confided in your husband?

NORA. Good heavens, how could you ever imagine such a thing! When he's so strict about such matters! Besides, Torvald is a man with a good deal of pride—it would be terribly embarrassing and humiliating for him if he thought he owed anything to me. It would spoil everything between us; this happy home of ours would never be the same again.

MRS. LINDE. Are you never going to tell him?

NORA [*reflectively, half-smiling*]. Oh yes, some day perhaps . . . in many years time, when I'm no longer as pretty as I am now. You mustn't laugh! What I mean of course is when Torvald isn't quite so much in love with me as he is now, when he's lost interest in watching me dance, or get dressed up, or recite. Then it might be a good thing to have something in reserve. . . . [*Breaks off.*] What nonsense! That day will never come. Well, what have you got to say to my big secret, Kristine? Still think I'm not much good for anything? One thing, though, it's meant a lot of worry for me, I can tell you. It hasn't always been easy to meet my obligations when the time came. You know in business there is something called quarterly interest, and other things called installments, and these are always terribly difficult things to cope with. So what I've had to do is save a little here and there, you see, wherever I could. I couldn't really save anything out of the housekeeping, because Torvald has to live in decent style. I couldn't let the children go about badly dressed either—I felt any money I got for them had to go on them alone. Such sweet little things!

MRS. LINDE. Poor Nora! So it had to come out of your own allowance?

NORA. Of course. After all, I was the one it concerned most. Whenever Torvald gave me money for new clothes and such-like, I never spent more than half. And always I bought the simplest and cheapest things. It's a blessing most things look well on me, so Torvald never noticed anything. But sometimes I did feel it was a bit hard, Kristine, because it is nice to be well dressed, isn't it?

MRS. LINDE. Yes, I suppose it is.

NORA. I have had some other sources of income, of course. Last winter I was lucky enough to get quite a bit of copying to do. So I shut myself up every night and sat and wrote through to the small hours of the morning. Oh, sometimes I was so tired, so tired. But it was tremendous fun all the same, sitting there working and earning money like that. It was almost like being a man.

MRS. LINDE. And how much have you been able to pay off like this?

NORA. Well, I can't tell exactly. It's not easy to know where you are with transactions of this kind, you understand. All I know is I've paid off just as much as I could scrape together. Many's the time I was at my wit's end. [*Smiles.*] Then I used to sit here and pretend that some rich old gentleman had fallen in love with me. . . .

MRS. LINDE. What! What gentleman?

NORA. Oh, rubbish! . . . and that now he had died, and when they opened his will, there in big letters were the words: "My entire fortune is to be paid over, immediately and in cash, to charming Mrs. Nora Helmer."

MRS. LINDE. But my dear Nora—who *is* this man?

NORA. Good heavens, don't you understand? There never was any old gentleman; it was just something I used to sit here pretending, time and time again, when I didn't know where to turn next for money. But it doesn't make very much difference; as far as I'm concerned the old boy can do what he likes, I'm tired of him; I can't be bothered any more with him or his will. Because now all my worries are over. [*Jumping up.*] Oh God, what a glorious thought, Kristine! No more worries! Just think of being without a care in the world . . . being able to romp with the children, and making the house nice and attractive, and having things just as Torvald likes to have them! And then spring will soon be here, and blue skies. And maybe we can go away somewhere. I might even see something of the sea again. Oh yes! When you're happy, life is a wonderful thing!

[*The door-bell is heard in the hall.*]

MRS. LINDE [*gets up*]. There's the bell. Perhaps I'd better go.

NORA. No, do stay, please. I don't suppose it's for me; it's probably somebody for Torvald. . . .

MAID [*in the doorway*]. Excuse me, ma'am, but there's a gentleman here wants to see Mr. Helmer, and I didn't quite know . . . because the Doctor is in there. . . .

NORA. Who is the gentleman?

KROGSTAD [*in the doorway*]. It's me, Mrs. Helmer.

[MRS. LINDE *starts, then turns away to the window.*]

NORA [*tense, takes a step towards him and speaks in a low voice*]. You? What is it? What do you want to talk to my husband about?

KROGSTAD. Bank matters . . . in a manner of speaking. I work at the bank, and I hear your husband is to be the new manager. . . .

NORA. So it's . . .

KROGSTAD. Just routine business matters, Mrs. Helmer. Absolutely nothing else.

[*She nods impassively and shuts the hall door behind him; then she walks across and sees to the stove.*]

MRS. LINDE. Nora . . . who was that man?

NORA. His name is Krogstad.

MRS. LINDE. So it really was him.

NORA. Do you know the man?

MRS. LINDE. I used to know him . . . a good many years ago. He was a solicitor's clerk in our district for a while.

NORA. Yes, so he was.

MRS. LINDE. How he's changed!

NORA. His marriage wasn't a very happy one, I believe.

MRS. LINDE. He's a widower now, isn't he?

NORA. With a lot of children. There, it'll burn better now.

[*She closes the stove door and moves the rocking chair a little to one side.*]

MRS. LINDE. He does a certain amount of business on the side, they say?

NORA. Oh? Yes, it's always possible. I just don't know. . . . But let's not think about business . . . it's all so dull.

[DR. RANK *comes in from* HELMER'*s study.*]

DR. RANK [*still in the doorway*]. No, no, Torvald, I won't intrude. I'll just look in on your wife for a moment. [*Shuts the door and notices* MRS. LINDE.] Oh, I beg your pardon. I'm afraid I'm intruding here as well.

NORA. No, not at all! [*Introduces them.*] Dr. Rank . . . Mrs. Linde.

RANK. Ah! A name I've often heard mentioned in this house. I believe I came past you on the stairs as I came in.

MRS. LINDE. I have to take things slowly going upstairs. I find it rather a trial.

NORA. Ah, some little disability somewhere, eh?

MRS. LINDE. Just a bit run down, I think, actually.

RANK. Is that all? Then I suppose you've come to town for a good rest —doing the rounds of the parties?

MRS. LINDE. I have come to look for work.

RANK. Is that supposed to be some kind of sovereign remedy for being run down?

MRS. LINDE. One must live, Doctor.

RANK. Yes, it's generally thought to be necessary.

NORA. Come, come, Dr. Rank. You are quite as keen to live as anybody.

RANK. Quite keen, yes. Miserable as I am, I'm quite ready to let things drag on as long as possible. All my patients are the same. Even those with a moral affliction are no different. As a matter of fact, there's a bad case of that kind in talking with Helmer at this very moment. . . .

MRS. LINDE [*softly*]. Ah!

NORA. Whom do you mean?

RANK. A person called Krogstad—nobody you would know. He's rotten to the core. But even he began talking about having to *live*, as though it were something terribly important.

NORA. Oh? And what did he want to talk to Torvald about?

RANK. I honestly don't know. All I heard was something about the Bank.

NORA. I didn't know that Krog . . . that this Mr. Krogstad had anything to do with the Bank.

RANK. Oh yes, he's got some kind of job down there. [*To* MRS. LINDE.] I wonder if you've got people in your part of the country too who go rushing round sniffing out cases of moral corruption, and then installing the individuals concerned in nice, well-paid jobs where they can keep them under observation. Sound, decent people have to be content to stay out in the cold.

MRS. LINDE. Yet surely it's the sick who most need to be brought in.

RANK [*shrugs his shoulders*]. Well, there we have it. It's that attitude that's turning society into a clinic.

[NORA, *lost in her own thoughts, breaks into smothered laughter and claps her hands.*]

RANK. Why are you laughing at that? Do you know in fact what society is?

NORA. What do I care about your silly old society? I was laughing about something quite different . . . something frightfully funny. Tell me, Dr. Rank, are all the people who work at the Bank dependent on Torvald now?

RANK. Is *that* what you find so frightfully funny?

NORA [*smiles and hums*]. Never you mind! Never you mind! [*Walks about the room.*] Yes, it really is terrible amusing to think that we . . .

that Torvald now has power over so many people. [*She takes the bag out of her pocket.*] Dr. Rank, what about a little macaroon?

RANK. Look at this, eh? Macaroons. I thought they were forbidden here.

NORA. Yes, but these are some Kristine gave me.

MRS. LINDE. What? I . . . ?

NORA. Now, now, you needn't be alarmed. You weren't to know that Torvald had forbidden them. He's worried in case they ruin my teeth, you know. Still . . . what's it matter once in a while! Don't you think so, Dr. Rank? Here! [*She pops a macaroon into his mouth.*] And you too, Kristine. And I shall have one as well; just a little one . . . or two at the most. [*She walks about the room again.*] Really I am so happy. There's just one little thing I'd love to do now.

RANK. What's that?

NORA. Something I'd love to say in front of Torvald.

RANK. Then why can't you?

NORA. No, I daren't. It's not very nice.

MRS. LINDE. Not very nice?

RANK. Well, in that case it might not be wise. But to us, I don't see why. . . . What is this you would love to say in front of Helmer?

NORA. I would simply love to say: "Damn."

RANK. Are you mad!

MRS. LINDE. Good gracious, Nora . . . !

RANK. Say it! Here he is!

NORA [*hiding the bag of macaroons*]. Sh! Sh!

[HELMER *comes out of his room, his overcoat over his arm and his hat in his hand.*]

NORA [*going over to him*]. Well, Torvald dear, did you get rid of him?

HELMER. Yes, he's just gone.

NORA. Let me introduce you. This is Kristine, who has just arrived in town. . . .

HELMER. Kristine . . . ? You must forgive me, but I don't think I know . . .

NORA. Mrs. Linde, Torvald dear. Kristine Linde.

HELMER. Ah, indeed. A school-friend of my wife's, presumably.

MRS. LINDE. Yes, we were girls together.

NORA. Fancy, Torvald, she's come all this long way just to have a word with you.

HELMER. How is that?

MRS. LINDE. Well, it wasn't really. . . .

NORA. The thing is, Kristine is terribly clever at office work, and she's frightfully keen on finding a job with some efficient man, so that she can learn even more. . . .

HELMER. Very sensible, Mrs. Linde.

NORA. And then when she heard you'd been made Bank Manager—

there was a bit in the paper about it—she set off at once. Torvald please! You *will* try and do something for Kristine, won't you? For my sake?

HELMER. Well, that's not altogether impossible. You are a widow, I presume?

MRS. LINDE. Yes.

HELMER. And you've had some experience in business?

MRS. LINDE. A fair amount.

HELMER. Well, it's quite probable I can find you a job, I think. . . .

NORA [*clapping her hands*]. There, you see!

HELMER. You have come at a fortunate moment. Mrs. Linde. . . .

MRS. LINDE. Oh, how can I ever thank you . . . ?

HELMER. Not a bit. [*He puts on his overcoat.*] But for the present I must ask you to excuse me. . . .

RANK. Wait. I'm coming with you.

[*He fetches his fur coat from the hall and warms it at the stove.*]

NORA. Don't be long, Torvald dear.

HELMER. Not more than an hour, that's all.

NORA. Are you leaving too, Kristine?

MRS. LINDE [*putting on her things*]. Yes, I must go and see if I can't find myself a room.

HELMER. Perhaps we can all walk down the road together.

NORA [*helping her*]. What a nuisance we are so limited for space here. I'm afraid it just isn't possible. . . .

MRS. LINDE. Oh, you mustn't dream of it! Goodbye, Nora dear, and thanks for everything.

NORA. Goodbye for the present. But . . . you'll be coming back this evening, of course. And you too, Dr. Rank? What's that? If you are up to it? Of course you'll be up to it. Just wrap yourself up well.

[*They go out, talking, into the hall; children's voices can be heard on the stairs.*]

NORA. Here they are! Here they are! [*She runs to the front door and opens it.* ANNE MARIE, *the nursemaid, enters with the children.*] Come in! Come in! [*She bends down and kisses them.*] Ah! my sweet little darlings. . . . You see them, Kristine? Aren't they lovely!

RANK. Don't stand here chattering in this draft!

HELMER. Come along, Mrs. Linde. The place now becomes unbearable for anybody except mothers.

[DR. RANK, HELMER *and* MRS. LINDE *go down the stairs: the* NURSEMAID *comes into the room with the children, then* NORA, *shutting the door behind her.*]

NORA. How fresh and bright you look! My, what red cheeks you've got! Like apples and roses. [*During the following, the children keep chattering away to her.*] Have you had a nice time? That's splendid. And you gave Emmy and Bob a ride on your sledge? Did you now!

Both together! Fancy that! There's a clever boy, Ivar. Oh, let me take her a little while, Anne Marie. There's my sweet little baby-doll! [*She takes the youngest of the children from the nursemaid and dances with her.*] All right, Mummy will dance with Bobby too. What? You've been throwing snowballs? Oh, I wish I'd been there. No, don't bother, Anne Marie, I'll help them off with their things. No, please, let me—I like doing it. You go on in, you look frozen. You'll find some hot coffee on the stove. [*The nursemaid goes into the room, left.* NORA *takes off the children's coats and hats and throws them down anywhere, while the children all talk at once.*] Really! A great big dog came running after you? But he didn't bite. No, the doggies wouldn't bite my pretty little dollies. You mustn't touch the parcels, Ivar! What are they? Wouldn't you like to know! No, no, that's nasty. Now? Shall we play something? What shall we play? Hide and seek? Yes, let's play hide and seek. Bob can hide first. Me first? All right, let me hide first.

[*She and the children play, laughing and shrieking, in this room and in the adjacent room on the right. Finally* NORA *hides under the table; the children come rushing in to look for her but cannot find her; they hear her stifled laughter, rush to the table, lift up the tablecloth and find her. Tremendous shouts of delight. She creeps out and pretends to frighten them. More shouts. Meanwhile there has been a knock at the front door, which nobody has heard. The door half opens, and* KROGSTAD *can be seen. He waits a little; the game continues.*]

KROGSTAD. I beg your pardon, Mrs. Helmer. . . .

NORA [*turns with a stifled cry and half jumps up*]. Ah! What do you want?

KROGSTAD. Excuse me. The front door was standing open. Somebody must have forgotten to shut it. . . .

NORA [*standing up*]. My husband isn't at home, Mr. Krogstad.

KROGSTAD. I know.

NORA. Well . . . what are you doing here?

KROGSTAD. I want a word with you.

NORA. With . . . ? [*Quietly, to the children.*] Go to Anne Marie. What? No, the strange man won't do anything to Mummy. When he's gone we'll have another game. [*She leads the children into the room, left, and shuts the door after them; tense and uneasy.*] You want to speak to me?

KROGSTAD. Yes, I do.

NORA. Today? But it isn't the first of the month yet. . . .

KROGSTAD. No, it's Christmas Eve. It depends entirely on you what sort of Christmas you have.

NORA. What do you want? Today I can't possibly . . .

KROGSTAD. Let's not talk about that for the moment. It's something else. You've got a moment to spare?

NORA. Yes, I suppose so, though . . .

KROGSTAD. Good. I was sitting in Olsen's café, and I saw your husband go down the road . . .

NORA. Did you?

KROGSTAD. . . . with a lady.

NORA. Well?

KROGSTAD. May I be so bold as to ask whether that lady was a Mrs. Linde?

NORA. Yes.

KROGSTAD. Just arrived in town?

NORA. Yes, today.

KROGSTAD. And she's a good friend of yours?

NORA. Yes, she is. But I can't see . . .

KROGSTAD. I also knew her once.

NORA. I know.

KROGSTAD. Oh? So you know all about it. I thought as much. Well, I want to ask you straight: is Mrs. Linde getting a job in the Bank?

NORA. How dare you cross-examine me like this, Mr. Krogstad? You, one of my husband's subordinates? But since you've asked me, I'll tell you. Yes, Mrs. Linde *has* got a job. And I'm the one who got it for her, Mr. Krogstad. Now you know.

KROGSTAD. So my guess was right.

NORA [*walking up and down*]. Oh, I think I can say that some of us have a little influence now and again. Just because one happens to be a woman, that doesn't mean. . . . People in subordinate positions, ought to take care they don't offend anybody . . . who . . . hm . . .

KROGSTAD. . . . has influence?

NORA. Exactly.

KROGSTAD [*changing his tone*]. Mrs. Helmer, will you have the goodness to use your influence on my behalf?

NORA. What? What do you mean?

KROGSTAD. Will you be so good as to see that I keep my modest little job at the Bank?

NORA. What do you mean? Who wants to take it away from you?

KROGSTAD. Oh, you needn't try and pretend to me you don't know. I can quite see that this friend of yours isn't particularly anxious to bump up against me. And I can also see now whom I can thank for being given the sack.

NORA. But I assure you. . . .

KROGSTAD. All right, all right. But to come to the point: there's still time. And I advise you to use your influence to stop it.

NORA. But, Mr. Krogstad, I *have* no influence.

KROGSTAD. Haven't you? I thought just now you said yourself . . .

NORA. I didn't mean it that way, of course. Me? What makes you think I've got any influence of that kind over my husband?

KROGSTAD. I know your husband from our student days. I don't suppose he is any more steadfast than other married men.

NORA. You speak disrespectfully of my husband like that and I'll show you the door.

KROGSTAD. So the lady's got courage.

NORA. I'm not frightened of you any more. After New Year I'll soon be finished with the whole business.

KROGSTAD [*controlling himself*]. Listen to me, Mrs. Helmer. If necessary I shall fight for my little job in the Bank as if I were fighting for my life.

NORA. So it seems.

KROGSTAD. It's not just for the money, that's the last thing I care about. There's something else . . . well, I might as well out with it. You see it's like this. You know as well as anybody that some years ago I got myself mixed up in a bit of trouble.

NORA. I believe I've heard something of the sort.

KROGSTAD. It never got as far as the courts; but immediately it was as if all paths were barred to me. So I started going in for the sort of business you know about. I had to do something, and I think I can say I haven't been one of the worst. But now I have to get out of it. My sons are growing up; for their sake I must try and win back what respectability I can. That job in the Bank was like the first step on the ladder for me. And now your husband wants to kick me off the ladder again, back into the mud.

NORA. But in God's name, Mr. Krogstad, it's quite beyond my power to help you.

KROGSTAD. That's because you haven't the will to help me. But I have ways of making you.

NORA. You wouldn't go and tell my husband I owe you money?

KROGSTAD. Suppose I did tell him?

NORA. It would be a rotten shame. [*Half choking with tears.*] That secret is all my pride and joy—why should he have to hear about it in this nasty, horrid way . . . hear about it from *you*. You would make things horribly unpleasant for me. . . .

KROGSTAD. Merely unpleasant?

NORA [*vehemently*]. Go on, do it then! It'll be all the worse for you. Because then my husband will see for himself what a bad man you are, and then you certainly won't be able to keep your job.

KROGSTAD. I asked whether it was only a bit of domestic unpleasantness you were afraid of?

NORA. If my husband gets to know about it, he'll pay off what's owing at once. And then we'd have nothing more to do with you.

KROGSTAD [*taking a pace towards her*]. Listen, Mrs. Helmer, either you haven't a very good memory, or else you don't understand much about business. I'd better make the position a little bit clearer for you.

NORA. How do you mean?

KROGSTAD. When your husband was ill, you came to me for the loan of twelve hundred dollars.

NORA. I didn't know of anybody else.

KROGSTAD. I promised to find you the money. . . .

NORA. And you did find it.

KROGSTAD. I promised to find you the money on certain conditions. At the time you were so concerned about your husband's illness, and so anxious to get the money for going away with, that I don't think you paid very much attention to all the incidentals. So there is perhaps some point in reminding you of them. Well, I promised to find you the money against an IOU which I drew up for you.

NORA. Yes, and which I signed.

KROGSTAD. Very good. But below that I added a few lines, by which your father was to stand security. This your father was to sign.

NORA. Was to . . . ? He did sign it.

KROGSTAD. I had left the date blank. The idea was that your father was to add the date himself when he signed it. Remember?

NORA. Yes, I think. . . .

KROGSTAD. I then gave you the IOU to post to your father. Wasn't that so?

NORA. Yes.

KROGSTAD. Which of course you did at once. Because only about five or six days later you brought it back to me with your father's signature. I then paid out the money.

NORA. Well? Haven't I paid the installments regularly?

KROGSTAD. Yes, fairly. But . . . coming back to what we were talking about . . . that was a pretty bad period you were going through then, Mrs. Helmer.

NORA. Yes, it was.

KROGSTAD. Your father was seriously ill, I believe.

NORA. He was very near the end.

KROGSTAD. And died shortly afterwards?

NORA. Yes.

KROGSTAD. Tell me, Mrs. Helmer, do you happen to remember which day your father died? The exact date, I mean.

NORA. Daddy died on 29 September.

KROGSTAD. Quite correct. I made some inquiries. Which brings up a rather curious point [*takes out a paper*] which I simply cannot explain.

NORA. Curious . . . ? I don't know . . .

KROGSTAD. The curious thing is, Mrs. Helmer, that your father signed this document three days after his death.

NORA. What? I don't understand. . . .

KROGSTAD. Your father died on 29 September. But look here. Your father has dated his signature 2 October. Isn't that rather curious, Mrs. Helmer? [NORA *remains silent.*] It's also remarkable that the words "2 October" and the year are not in your father's handwriting, but in a handwriting I rather think I recognize. Well, perhaps that could be explained. Your father might have forgotten to date his signature, and then somebody else might have made a guess at the date later, before the fact of your father's death was known. There is nothing wrong in that. What really matters is the signature. And *that* is of course genuine, Mrs. Helmer? It really was your father who wrote his name here?

NORA [*after a moment's silence, throws her head back and looks at him defiantly*]. No, it wasn't. It was me who signed father's name.

KROGSTAD. Listen to me. I suppose you realize that that is a very dangerous confession?

NORA. Why? You'll soon have all your money back.

KROGSTAD. Let me ask you a question: why didn't you send that document to your father?

NORA. It was impossible. Daddy was ill. If I'd asked him for his signature, I'd have had to tell him what the money was for. Don't you see, when he was as ill as that I couldn't go and tell him that my husband's life was in danger. It was simply impossible.

KROGSTAD. It would have been better for you if you had abandoned the whole trip.

NORA. No, that was impossible. This was the thing that was to save my husband's life. I couldn't give it up.

KROGSTAD. But did it never strike you that this was fraudulent . . . ?

NORA. That wouldn't have meant anything to me. Why should I worry about you? I couldn't stand you, not when you insisted on going through with all those cold-blooded formalities, knowing all the time what a critical state my husband was in.

KROGSTAD. Mrs. Helmer, it's quite clear you still haven't the faintest idea what it is you've committed. But let me tell you, my own offense was no more and no worse than that, and it ruined my entire reputation.

NORA. You? Are you trying to tell me that you once risked everything to save your wife's life?

KROGSTAD. The law takes no account of motives.

NORA. Then they must be very bad laws.

KROGSTAD. Bad or not, if I produce this document in court, you'll be condemned according to them.

NORA. I don't believe it. Isn't a daughter entitled to try and save her father from worry and anxiety on his deathbed? Isn't a wife entitled to save her husband's life? I might not know very much about the law, but I feel sure of one thing: it must say somewhere that things like this are allowed. You mean to say you don't know that—you, when it's your job? You must be a rotten lawyer, Mr. Krogstad.

KROGSTAD. That may be. But when it comes to business transactions—like the sort between us two—perhaps you'll admit I know something about *them?* Good. Now you must please yourself. But I tell you this: if I'm pitched out a second time, you are going to keep me company.

[*He bows and goes out through the hall.*]

NORA [*stands thoughtfully for a moment, then tosses her head*]. Rubbish! He's just trying to scare me. I'm not such a fool as all that. [*Begins gathering up the children's clothes; after a moment she stops.*] Yet . . . ? No, it's impossible! I did it for love, didn't I?

THE CHILDREN [*in the doorway, left*]. Mummy, the gentleman's just gone out of the gate.

NORA. Yes, I know. But you mustn't say anything to anybody about that gentleman. You hear? Not even to Daddy!

THE CHILDREN. All right, Mummy. Are you going to play again?

NORA. No, not just now.

THE CHILDREN. But Mummy, you promised!

NORA. Yes, but I can't just now. Off you go now, I have a lot to do. Off you go, my darlings. [*She herds them carefully into the other room and shuts the door behind them. She sits down on the sofa, picks up her embroidery and works a few stitches, but soon stops.*] No! [*She flings her work down, stands up, goes to the hall door and calls out.*] Helene! Fetch the tree in for me, please. [*She walks across to the table, left, and opens the drawer; again pauses.*] No, really, it's quite impossible!

MAID [*with the Christmas tree*]. Where shall I put it, ma'am?

NORA. On the floor there, in the middle.

MAID. Anything else you want me to bring?

NORA. No, thank you. I've got what I want.

[*The maid has put the tree down and goes out.*]

NORA [*busy decorating the tree*]. Candles here . . . and flowers here.— Revolting man! It's all nonsense! There's nothing to worry about. We'll have a lovely Christmas tree. And I'll do anything you want me to, Torvald; I'll sing for you, dance for you. . . .

[HELMER, *with a bundle of documents under his arm, comes in by the hall door.*]

NORA. Ah, back again already?

HELMER. Yes. Anybody been?

NORA. Here? No.

HELMER. That's funny. I just saw Krogstad leave the house.

NORA. Oh? O yes, that's right. Krogstad was here a minute.

HELMER. Nora, I can tell by your face he's been asking you to put a good word in for him.

NORA. Yes.

HELMER. And you were to pretend it was your own idea? You were to keep quiet about his having been here. He asked you to do that as well, didn't he?

NORA. Yes, Torvald. But . . .

HELMER. Nora, Nora, what possessed you to do a thing like that? Talking to a person like him, making him promises? And then on top of everything, to tell me a lie!

NORA. A lie . . . ?

HELMER. Didn't you say that nobody had been here? [*Wagging his finger at her.*] Never again must my little song-bird do a thing like that! Little song-birds must keep their pretty little beaks out of mischief; no chirruping out of tune! [*Puts his arm round her waist.*] Isn't that the way we want things to be? Yes, of course it is. [*Lets her go.*] So let's say no more about it. [*Sits down by the stove.*] Ah, nice and cozy here!

[*He glances through his papers.*]

NORA [*busy with the Christmas tree, after a short pause*]. Torvald!

HELMER. Yes.

NORA. I'm so looking forward to the fancy dress ball at the Stenborgs' on Boxing Day.[1]

HELMER. And I'm terribly curious to see what sort of surprise you've got for me.

NORA. Oh, it's too silly.

HELMER. Oh?

NORA. I just can't think of anything suitable. Everything seems so absurd, so pointless.

HELMER. Has my little Nora come to *that* conclusion?

NORA [*behind his chair, her arms on the chairback*]. Are you very busy, Torvald?

HELMER. Oh. . . .

NORA. What are all those papers?

HELMER. Bank matters.

NORA. Already?

HELMER. I have persuaded the retiring manager to give me authority to make any changes in organization or personnel I think necessary. I have to work on it over the Christmas week. I want everything straight by the New Year.

NORA. So that was why that poor Krogstad. . . .

HELMER. Hm!

NORA [*still leaning against the back of the chair, running her fingers through his hair*]. If you hadn't been so busy, Torvald, I'd have asked you to do me an awfully big favor.

HELMER. Let me hear it. What's it to be?

---

[1] the first weekday after Christmas

NORA. Nobody's got such good taste as you. And the thing is I do so want to look my best at the fancy dress ball. Torvald, couldn't you give me some advice and tell me what you think I ought to go as, and how I should arrange my costume?

HELMER. Aha! So my impulsive little woman is asking for somebody to come to her rescue, eh?

NORA. Please, Torvald, I never get anywhere without your help.

HELMER. Very well, I'll think about it. We'll find something.

NORA. That's sweet of you. [*She goes across to the tree again; pause.*] How pretty these red flowers look.—Tell me, was it really something terribly wrong this man Krogstad did?

HELMER. Forgery. Have you any idea what that means?

NORA. Perhaps circumstances left him no choice?

HELMER. Maybe. Or perhaps, like so many others, he just didn't think. I am not so heartless that I would necessarily want to condemn a man for a single mistake like that.

NORA. Oh no, Torvald, of course not!

HELMER. Many a man might be able to redeem himself, if he honestly confessed his guilt and took his punishment.

NORA. Punishment?

HELMER. But that wasn't the way Krogstad chose. He dodged what was due to him by a cunning trick. And that's what has been the cause of his corruption.

NORA. Do you think it would . . . ?

HELMER. Just think how a man with a thing like that on his conscience will always be having to lie and cheat and dissemble; he can never drop the mask, not even with his own wife and children. And the children—*that's* the most terrible part of it, Nora.

NORA. Why?

HELMER. A fog of lies like that in a household, and it spreads disease and infection to every part of it. Every breath the children take in that kind of house is reeking with evil germs.

NORA [*closer behind him*]. Are you sure of that?

HELMER. My dear Nora, as a lawyer I know what I'm talking about. Practically all juvenile delinquents come from homes where the mother is dishonest.

NORA. Why mothers particularly?

HELMER. It's generally traceable to the mothers, but of course fathers can have the same influence. Every lawyer knows that only too well. And yet there's Krogstad been poisoning his own children for years with lies and deceit. That's the reason I call him morally depraved. [*Holds out his hands to her.*] That's why my sweet little Nora must promise me not to try putting in any more good words for him. Shake hands on it. Well? What's this? Give me your hand. There now! That's settled. I assure you I would have found it impossible to work with him. I quite literally feel physically sick in the presence of such people.

NORA [*draws her hand away and walks over to the other side of the Christmas tree*]. How hot it is in here! And I still have such a lot to do.

HELMER [*stands up and collects his papers together*]. Yes, I'd better think of getting some of this read before dinner. I must also think about your costume. And I might even be able to lay my hands on something to wrap in gold paper and hang on the Christmas tree. [*He lays his hand on her head.*] My precious little singing bird.

[*He goes into his study and shuts the door behind him.*]

NORA [*quietly, after a pause*]. Nonsense! It can't be. It's impossible. It *must* be impossible.

MAID [*in the doorway, left*]. The children keep asking so nicely if they can come in and see Mummy.

NORA. No, no, don't let them in! You stay with them, Anne Marie.

MAID. Very well, ma'am.

[*She shuts the door.*]

NORA [*pale with terror*]. Corrupt my children. . . ! Poison my home? [*Short pause; she throws back her head.*] It's not true! It could never, never be true!

ACT TWO

The same room. In the corner beside the piano stands the Christmas tree, stripped, bedraggled and with its candles burnt out. Nora's outdoor things lie on the sofa. NORA, alone there, walks about restlessly; at last she stops by the sofa and picks up her coat.

NORA [*putting her coat down again*]. Somebody's coming! [*Crosses to the door, listens.*] No, it's nobody. Nobody will come today, of course, Christmas Day—nor tomorrow, either. But perhaps. . . . [*She opens the door and looks out.*] No, nothing in the letter box; quite empty. [*Comes forward.*] Oh, nonsense! He didn't mean it seriously. Things like that *can't* happen. It's impossible. Why, I have three small children.

[*The* NURSEMAID *comes from the room, left, carrying a big cardboard box.*]

NURSEMAID. I finally found it, the box with the fancy dress costumes.

NORA. Thank you. Put it on the table, please.

NURSEMAID [*does this*]. But I'm afraid they are in an awful mess.

NORA. Oh, if only I could rip them up into a thousand pieces!

NURSEMAID. Good heavens, they can be mended all right, with a bit of patience.

NORA. Yes, I'll go over and get Mrs. Linde to help me.

NURSEMAID. Out again? In this terrible weather? You'll catch your death of cold, Ma'am.

NORA. Oh, worse things might happen.—How are the children?

NURSEMAID. Playing with their Christmas presents, poor little things, but . . .

NORA. Do they keep asking for me?

NURSEMAID. They are so used to being with their Mummy.

NORA. Yes, Anne Marie, from now on I can't be with them as often as I was before.

NURSEMAID. Ah well, children get used to anything in time.

NORA. Do you think so? Do you think they would forget their Mummy if she went away for good?

NURSEMAID. Good gracious—for good?

NORA. Tell me, Anne Marie—I've often wondered—how on earth could you bear to hand your child over to strangers?

NURSEMAID. Well, there was nothing else for it when I had to come and nurse my little Nora.

NORA. Yes but . . . how could you *bring* yourself to do it?

NURSEMAID. When I had the chance of such a good place? When a poor girl's been in trouble she must make the best of things. Because *he* didn't help, the rotter.

NORA. But your daughter will have forgotten you.

NURSEMAID. Oh no, she hasn't. She wrote to me when she got confirmed, and again when she got married.

NORA [*putting her arms round her neck*]. Dear old Anne Marie, you were a good mother to me when I was little.

NURSEMAID. My poor little Nora never had any other mother but me.

NORA. And if my little ones only had you, I know you would. . . . Oh, what am I talking about! [*She opens the box.*] Go in to them. I must . . . Tomorrow I'll let you see how pretty I am going to look. [*She goes into the room, left.*]

NORA [*begins unpacking the box, but soon throws it down*]. Oh, if only I dare go out. If only I could be sure nobody would come. And that nothing would happen in the meantime here at home. Rubbish—nobody's going to come. I mustn't think about it. Brush this muff. Pretty gloves, pretty gloves! I'll put it right out of my mind. One, two, three, four, five, six. . . . [*Screams.*] Ah, they are coming. . . . [*She starts towards the door, but stops irresolute.* MRS. LINDE *comes from the hall, where she has taken off her things.*] Oh, it's you, Kristine. There's nobody else out there, is there? I'm so glad you've come.

MRS. LINDE. I heard you'd been over looking for me.

NORA. Yes, I was just passing. There's something you must help me with. Come and sit beside me on the sofa here. You see, the Stenborgs

are having a fancy dress party upstairs tomorrow evening, and now
Torvald wants me to go as a Neapolitan fisher lass and dance the
tarantella. I learned it in Capri, you know.

MRS. LINDE. Well, well! So you are going to do a party piece?

NORA. Torvald says I should. Look, here's the costume, Torvald had it
made for me down there. But it's got all torn and I simply don't
know. . . .

MRS. LINDE. We'll soon have that put right. It's only the trimming
come away here and there. Got a needle and thread? Ah, here's what
we are after.

NORA. It's awfully kind of you.

MRS. LINDE. So you are going to be all dressed up tomorrow, Nora?
Tell you what—I'll pop over for a minute to see you in all your
finery. But I'm quite forgetting to thank you for the pleasant time we
had last night.

NORA [gets up and walks across the room]. Somehow I didn't think yesterday was as nice as things generally are.—You should have come to
town a little earlier, Kristine.—Yes, Torvald certainly knows how to
make things pleasant about the place.

MRS. LINDE. You too, I should say. You are not your father's daughter for nothing. But tell me, is Dr. Rank always as depressed as he was
last night?

NORA. No, last night it was rather obvious. He's got something seriously wrong with him, you know. Tuberculosis of the spine, poor
fellow. His father was a horrible man, who used to have mistresses
and things like that. That's why the son was always ailing, right from
being a child.

MRS. LINDE [lowering her sewing]. But my dear Nora, how do you
come to know about things like that?

NORA [walking about the room]. Huh! When you've got three children,
you get these visits from . . . women who have had a certain amount
of medical training. And you hear all sorts of things from them.

MRS. LINDE [begins sewing again; short silence]. Does Dr. Rank call in
every day?

NORA. Every single day. He was Torvald's best friend as a boy, and
he's a good friend of mine, too. Dr. Rank is almost like one of the
family.

MRS. LINDE. But tell me—is he really genuine? What I mean is:
doesn't he sometimes rather turn on the charm?

NORA. No, on the contrary. What makes you think that?

MRS. LINDE. When you introduced me yesterday, he claimed he'd
often heard my name in this house. But afterwards I noticed your husband hadn't the faintest idea who I was. Then how is it that Dr. Rank
should. . . .

NORA. Oh yes, it was quite right what he said, Kristine. You see
Torvald is so terribly in love with me that he says he wants me all to

himself. When we were first married, it even used to make him sort of jealous if I only as much as mentioned any of my old friends from back home. So of course I stopped doing it. But I often talk to Dr. Rank about such things. He likes hearing about them.

MRS. LINDE. Listen, Nora! In lots of ways you are still a child. Now, I'm a good deal older than you, and a bit more experienced. I'll tell you something: I think you ought to give up all this business with Dr. Rank.

NORA. Give up what business?

MRS. LINDE. The whole thing, I should say. Weren't you saying yesterday something about a rich admirer who was to provide you with money. . . .

NORA. One who's never existed, I regret to say. But what of it?

MRS. LINDE. Has Dr. Rank money?

NORA. Yes, he has.

MRS. LINDE. And no dependents?

NORA. No, nobody. But . . . ?

MRS. LINDE. And he comes to the house every day?

NORA. Yes, I told you.

MRS. LINDE. But how can a man of his position want to pester you like this?

NORA. I simply don't understand.

MRS. LINDE. Don't pretend, Nora. Do you think I don't see now who you borrowed the twelve hundred from?

NORA. Are you out of your mind? Do you really think that? A friend of ours who comes here every day? The whole situation would have been absolutely intolerable.

MRS. LINDE. It *really* isn't him?

NORA. No, I give you my word. It would never have occurred to me for one moment. . . . Anyway, he didn't have the money to lend then. He didn't inherit it till later.

MRS. LINDE. Just as well for you, I'd say, my dear Nora.

NORA. No, it would never have occurred to me to ask Dr. Rank. . . . All the same I'm pretty certain if I were to ask him. . . .

MRS. LINDE. But of course you won't.

NORA. No, of course not. I can't ever imagine it being necessary. But I'm quite certain if ever I were to mention it to Dr. Rank. . . .

MRS. LINDE. Behind your husband's back?

NORA. I have to get myself out of that other business. That's also behind his back. I *must* get myself out of that.

MRS. LINDE. Yes, that's what I said yesterday. But . . .

NORA [*walking up and down*]. A man's better at coping with these things than a woman. . . .

MRS. LINDE. Your own husband, yes.

NORA. Nonsense! [*Stops.*] When you've paid everything you owe, you do get your IOU back again, don't you?

MRS. LINDE. Of course.

NORA. And you can tear it up into a thousand pieces and burn it—the nasty, filthy thing!

MRS. LINDE [*looking fixedly at her, puts down her sewing and slowly rises*]. Nora, you are hiding something from me.

NORA. Is it so obvious?

MRS. LINDE. Something has happened to you since yesterday morning. Nora, what is it?

NORA [*going towards her*]. Kristine! [*Listens.*] Hush! There's Torvald back. Look, you go and sit in there beside the children for the time being. Torvald can't stand the sight of mending lying about. Get Anne Marie to help you.

MRS. LINDE [*gathering a lot of the things together*]. All right, but I'm not leaving until we have thrashed this thing out.

[*She goes into the room, left; at the same time* HELMER *comes in from the hall.*]

NORA [*goes to meet him*]. I've been longing for you to be back, Torvald, dear.

HELMER. Was that the dressmaker . . . ?

NORA. No, it was Kristine; she's helping me with my costume. I think it's going to look very nice . . .

HELMER. Wasn't that a good idea of mine, now?

NORA. Wonderful! But wasn't it also nice of me to let you have your way?

HELMER [*taking her under the chin*]. Nice of you—because you let your husband have his way? All right, you little rogue, I know you didn't mean it that way. But I don't want to disturb you. You'll be wanting to try the costume on, I suppose.

NORA. And I dare say you've got work to do?

HELMER. Yes. [*Shows her a bundle of papers.*] Look at this. I've been down at the Bank. . . .

[*He turns to go into his study.*]

NORA. Torvald!

HELMER [*stopping*]. Yes.

NORA. If a little squirrel were to ask ever so nicely . . . ?

HELMER. Well?

NORA. Would you do something for it?

HELMER. Naturally I would first have to know what it is.

NORA. Please, if only you would let it have its way, and do what it wants, it'd scamper about and do all sorts of marvelous tricks.

HELMER. What is it?

NORA. And the pretty little sky-lark would sing all day long. . . .

HELMER. Huh! It does that anyway.

NORA. I'd pretend I was an elfin child and dance a moonlight dance for you, Torvald.

HELMER. Nora—I hope it's not that business you started on this morning?

NORA [*coming closer*]. Yes, it is, Torvald, I implore you!

HELMER. You have the nerve to bring that up again?

NORA. Yes, yes, you *must* listen to me. You must let Krogstad keep his job at the Bank.

HELMER. My dear Nora, I'm giving his job to Mrs. Linde.

NORA. Yes, it's awfully sweet of you. But couldn't you get rid of somebody else in the office instead of Krogstad?

HELMER. This really is the most incredible obstinacy! Just because you go and make some thoughtless promise to put in a good word for him, you expect me . . .

NORA. It's not that, Torvald. It's for your own sake. That man writes in all the nastiest papers, you told me that yourself. He can do you no end of harm. He terrifies me to death. . . .

HELMER. Aha, now I see. It's your memories of what happened before that are frightening you.

NORA. What do you mean?

HELMER. It's your father you are thinking of.

NORA. Yes . . . yes, that's right. You remember all the nasty insinuations those wicked people put in the papers about Daddy? I honestly think they would have had him dismissed if the Ministry hadn't sent you down to investigate, and you hadn't been so kind and helpful.

HELMER. My dear little Nora, there is a considerable difference between your father and me. Your father's professional conduct was not entirely above suspicion. Mine is. And I hope it's going to stay that way as long as I hold this position.

NORA. But nobody knows what some of these evil people are capable of. Things could be so nice and pleasant for us here, in the peace and quiet of our home—you and me and the children, Torvald! That's why I implore you. . . .

HELMER. The more you plead for him, the more impossible you make it for me to keep him on. It's already known down at the Bank that I am going to give Krogstad his notice. If it ever got around that the new manager had been talked over by his wife. . . .

NORA. What of it?

HELMER. Oh, nothing! As long as the little woman gets her own stubborn way. . . . ! Do you want me to make myself a laughing stock in the office? . . . Give people the idea that I am susceptible to any kind of outside pressure? You can imagine how soon I'd feel the consequences of that! Anyway, there's one other consideration that makes it impossible to have Krogstad in the Bank as long as I am manager.

NORA. What's that?

HELMER. At a pinch I might have overlooked his past lapses. . . .

NORA. Of course you could, Torvald!

HELMER. And I'm told he's not bad at his job, either. But we knew each other rather well when we were younger. It was one of those rather rash friendships that prove embarrassing in later life. There's no reason why you shouldn't know we were once on terms of some familiarity. And he, in his tactless way, makes no attempt to hide the fact, particularly when other people are present. On the contrary, he thinks he has every right to treat me as an equal, with his "Torvald this" and "Torvald that" every time he opens his mouth. I find it extremely irritating, I can tell you. He would make my position at the Bank absolutely intolerable.

NORA. Torvald, surely you aren't serious?

HELMER. Oh? Why not?

NORA. Well, it's all so petty.

HELMER. What's that you say? Petty? Do you think I'm petty?

NORA. No, not at all, Torvald dear! And that's why . . .

HELMER. Doesn't make any difference! . . . You call my motives petty; so I must be petty too. Petty! Indeed! Well, we'll put a stop to that, once and for all. [*He opens the hall door and calls.*] Helene!

NORA. What are you going to do?

HELMER [*searching among his papers*]. Settle things. [THE MAID *comes in.*] See this letter? I want you to take it down at once. Get hold of a messenger and get him to deliver it. Quickly. The address is on the outside. There's the money.

MAID. Very good, sir.

[*She goes with the letter.*]

HELMER [*putting his papers together*]. There now, my stubborn little miss.

NORA [*breathless*]. Torvald . . . what was that letter?

HELMER. Krogstad's notice.

NORA. Get it back, Torvald! There's still time! Oh, Torvald, get it back! Please for my sake, for your sake, for the sake of the children! Listen, Torvald, please! You don't realize what it can do to us.

HELMER. Too late.

NORA. Yes, too late.

HELMER. My dear Nora, I forgive you this anxiety of yours, although it is actually a bit of an insult. Oh, but it is, I tell you! It's hardly flattering to suppose that anything this miserable pen-pusher wrote could frighten *me!* But I forgive you all the same, because it is rather a sweet way of showing how much you love me. [*He takes her in his arms.*] This is how things must be, my own darling Nora. When it comes to the point, I've enough strength and enough courage, believe me, for whatever happens. You'll find I'm man enough to take everything on myself.

NORA [*terrified*]. What do you mean?

HELMER. Everything, I said. . . .

NORA [*in command of herself*]. That is something you shall never, never do.

HELMER. All right, then we'll share it, Nora—as man and wife. That's what we'll do. [*Caressing her.*] Does that make you happy now? There, there, don't look at me with those eyes, like a little frightened dove. The whole thing is sheer imagination.—Why don't you run through the tarantella and try out the tambourine? I'll go into my study and shut both the doors, then I won't hear anything. You can make all the noise you want. [*Turns in the doorway.*] And when Rank comes, tell him where he can find me.

[*He nods to her, goes with his papers into his room, and shuts the door behind him.*]

NORA [*wild-eyed with terror, stands as though transfixed*]. He's quite capable of doing it! He would do it! No matter what, he'd do it.— No, never in this world! Anything but that! Help? Some way out . . . ? [*The door-bell rings in the hall.*] Dr. Rank . . . ! Anything but that, *anything!* [*She brushes her hands over her face, pulls herself together and opens the door into the hall.* DR. RANK *is standing outside hanging up his fur coat. During what follows it begins to grow dark.*] Hello, Dr. Rank. I recognized your ring. Do you mind not going in to Torvald just yet, I think he's busy.

RANK. And you?

[DR. RANK *comes into the room and she closes the door behind him.*]

NORA. Oh, you know very well I've always got time for you.

RANK. Thank you. A privilege I shall take advantage of as long as I am able.

NORA. What do you mean—as long as you are able?

RANK. Does that frighten you?

NORA. Well, it's just that it sounds so strange. Is anything likely to happen?

RANK. Only what I have long expected. But I didn't think it would come quite so soon.

NORA [*catching at his arm*]. What have you found out? Dr. Rank, you must tell me!

RANK. I'm slowly sinking. There's nothing to be done about it.

NORA [*with a sigh of relief*]. Oh, it's *you* you're . . . ?

RANK. Who else? No point in deceiving oneself. I am the most wretched of all my patients, Mrs. Helmer. These last few days I've made a careful analysis of my internal economy. Bankrupt! Within a month I shall probably be lying rotting up there in the churchyard.

NORA. Come now, what a ghastly thing to say!

RANK. The whole damned thing is ghastly. But the worst thing is all the ghastliness that has to be gone through first. I only have one more test to make; and when that's done I'll know pretty well when the final disintegration will start. There's something I want to ask you. Helmer is a sensitive soul; he loathes anything that's ugly. I don't want him visiting me. . . .

NORA. But Dr. Rank. . . .

RANK. On no account must he. I won't have it. I'll lock the door on him.—As soon as I'm absolutely certain of the worst, I'll send you my visiting card with a black cross on it. You'll know then the final horrible disintegration has begun.

NORA. Really, you are being quite absurd today. And here I was hoping you would be in a thoroughly good mood.

RANK. With death staring me in the face? Why should I suffer for another man's sins? What justice is there in that? Somewhere, somehow, every single family must be suffering some such cruel retribution. . . .

NORA [stopping up her ears]. Rubbish! Do cheer up!

RANK. Yes, really the whole thing's nothing but a huge joke. My poor innocent spine must do penance for my father's gay subaltern life.

NORA [by the table, left]. Wasn't he rather partial to asparagus and pâté de foie gras?

RANK. Yes, he was. And truffles.

NORA. Trufflles, yes. And oysters, too, I believe?

RANK. Yes, oysters, oysters, of course.

NORA. And all the port and champagne that goes with them. It does seem a pity all these delicious things should attack the spine.

RANK. Especially when they attack a poor spine that never had any fun out of them.

NORA. Yes, that is an awful pity.

RANK [looks at her sharply]. Hm. . . .

NORA [after a pause]. Why did you smile?

RANK. No, it was you who laughed.

NORA. No, it was you who smiled, Dr. Rank!

RANK [getting up]. You are a bigger rascal than I thought you were.

NORA. I feel full of mischief today.

RANK. So it seems.

NORA [putting her hands on his shoulders]. Dear, dear Dr. Rank, you mustn't go and die on Torvald and me.

RANK. You wouldn't miss me for long. When you are gone, you are soon forgotten.

NORA [looking at him anxiously]. Do you think so?

RANK. People make new contacts, then . . .

NORA. Who make new contacts?

RANK. Both you and Helmer will, when I'm gone. You yourself are already well on the way, it seems to me. What was this Mrs. Linde doing here last night?

NORA. Surely you aren't jealous of poor Kristine?

RANK. Yes, I am. She'll be my successor in this house. When I'm done
for, I can see this woman. . . .

NORA. Hush! Don't talk so loud, she's in there.

RANK. Today as well? There you are, you see!

NORA. Just to do some sewing on my dress. Good Lord, how absurd
you are! [*She sits down on the sofa.*] Now Dr. Rank, cheer up. You'll
see tomorrow how nicely I can dance. And you can pretend I'm doing
it just for you—and for Torvald as well, of course. [*She takes various
things out of the box.*] Come here, Dr. Rank. I want to show you something.

RANK [*sits*]. What is it?

NORA. Look!

RANK. Silk stockings.

NORA. Flesh-colored! Aren't they lovely! Of course, it's dark here
now, but tomorrow. . . . No, no, no, you can only look at the feet.
Oh well, you might as well see a bit higher up, too.

RANK. Hm. . . .

NORA. Why are you looking so critical? Don't you think they'll fit?

RANK. I couldn't possibly offer any informed opinion about that.

NORA [*looks at him for a moment*]. Shame on you. [*Hits him lightly across
the ear with the stockings.*] Take that! [*Folds them up again.*]

RANK. And what other delights am I to be allowed to see?

NORA. Not another thing. You are too naughty. [*She hums a little and
searches among her things.*]

RANK [*after a short pause*]. Sitting here so intimately like this with you,
I can't imagine . . . I simply cannot conceive what would have become of me if I had never come to this house.

NORA [*smiles*]. Yes, I rather think you do enjoy coming here.

RANK [*in a low voice, looking fixedly ahead*]. And the thought of having
to leave it all . . .

NORA. Nonsense. You aren't leaving.

RANK [*in the same tone*]. . . . without being able to leave behind even
the slightest token of gratitude, hardly a fleeting regret even . . .
nothing but an empty place to be filled by the first person that comes
along.

NORA. Supposing I were to ask you to . . . ? No . . .

RANK. What?

NORA. . . . to show me the extent of your friendship . . .

RANK. Yes?

NORA. I mean . . . to do me a tremendous favor. . . .

RANK. Would you really, for once, give me that pleasure?

NORA. You have no idea what it is.

RANK. All right, tell me.

NORA. No, really I can't, Dr. Rank. It's altogether too much to ask
. . . because I need your advice and help as well. . . .

RANK. The more the better. I cannot imagine what you have in mind. But tell me anyway. You do trust me, don't you?

NORA. Yes, I trust you more than anybody I know. You are my best and my most faithful friend. I know that. So I will tell you. Well then, Dr. Rank, there is something you must help me to prevent. You know how deeply, how passionately Torvald is in love with me. He would never hesitate for a moment to sacrifice his life for my sake.

RANK [*bending towards her*]. Nora . . . do you think he's the only one who . . . ?

NORA [*stiffening slightly*]. Who . . . ?

RANK. Who wouldn't gladly give his life for your sake.

NORA [*sadly*]. Oh!

RANK. I swore to myself you would know before I went. I'll never have a better opportunity. Well, Nora! Now you know. And now you know too that you can confide in me as in nobody else.

NORA [*rises and speaks evenly and calmly*]. Let me past.

RANK [*makes way for her, but remains seated*]. Nora. . . .

NORA [*in the hall doorway*]. Helene, bring the lamp in, please. [*Walks over to the stove.*] Oh, my dear Dr. Rank, that really was rather horrid of you.

RANK [*getting up*]. That I have loved you every bit as much as anybody? Is *that* horrid?

NORA. No, but that you had to go and tell me. When it was all so unnecessary. . . .

RANK. What do you mean? Did you know. . . ?

[THE MAID *comes in with the lamp, puts it on the table, and goes out again.*]

RANK. Nora . . . Mrs. Helmer . . . I'm asking you if you knew?

NORA. How can I tell whether I did or didn't. I simply can't tell you. . . . Oh, how could you be so clumsy, Dr. Rank! When everything was so nice.

RANK. Anyway, you know now that I'm at your service, body and soul. So you can speak out.

NORA [*looking at him*]. After this?

RANK. I beg you to tell me what it is.

NORA. I can tell you nothing now.

RANK. You must. You can't torment me like this. Give me a chance—I'll do anything that's humanly possible.

NORA. You can do nothing for me now. Actually, I don't really need any help. It's all just my imagination, really it is. Of course! [*She sits down in the rocking-chair, looks at him and smiles.*] I must say, you are a nice one, Dr. Rank! Don't you feel ashamed of yourself, now the lamp's been brought in?

RANK. No, not exactly. But perhaps I ought to go—for good?

NORA. No, you mustn't do that. You must keep coming just as you've always done. You know very well Torvald would miss you terribly.

RANK. And *you?*

NORA. I always think it's tremendous fun having you.

RANK. That's exactly what gave me wrong ideas. I just can't puzzle you out. I often used to feel you'd just as soon be with me as with Helmer.

NORA. Well, you see, there are those people you love and those people you'd almost rather *be* with.

RANK. Yes, there's something in that.

NORA. When I was a girl at home, I loved Daddy best, of course. But I also thought it great fun if I could slip into the maids' room. For one thing they never preached at me. And they always talked about such exciting things.

RANK. Aha! So it's their role I've taken over!

NORA [*jumps up and crosses to him*]. Oh, my dear, kind Dr. Rank, I didn't mean that at all. But you can see how it's a bit with Torvald as it was with Daddy. . . .

[THE MAID *comes in from the hall.*]

MAID. Please, ma'am. . . . !

[*She whispers and hands her a card.*]

NORA [*glances at the card*]. Ah!

[*She puts it in her pocket.*]

RANK. Anything wrong?

NORA. No, no, not at all. It's just . . . it's my new costume. . . .

RANK. How is that? There's your costume in there.

NORA. That one, yes. But this is another one. I've ordered it. Torvald mustn't hear about it. . . .

RANK. Ah, so that's the big secret, is it!

NORA. Yes, that's right. Just go in and see him, will you? He's in the study. Keep him occupied for the time being. . . .

RANK. Don't worry. He shan't escape me.

[*He goes into Helmer's study.*]

NORA [*to the maid*]. Is he waiting in the kitchen?

RANK. Yes, he came up the back stairs. . . .

NORA. But didn't you tell him somebody was here?

RANK. Yes, but it was no good.

NORA. Won't he go?

RANK. No, he won't till he's seen you.

NORA. Let him in, then. But quietly. Helene, you mustn't tell anybody about this. It's a surprise for my husband.

MAID. I understand, ma'am. . . .

[*She goes out.*]

NORA. Here it comes! What I've been dreading! No, no, it can't happen, it *can't* happen.

[*She walks over and bolts Helmer's door. The maid opens the hall door for*

KROGSTAD *and shuts it again behind him. He is wearing a fur coat, over-shoes, and a fur cap.*]

NORA [*goes towards him*]. Keep your voice down, my husband is at home.

KROGSTAD. What if he is?

NORA. What do you want with me?

KROGSTAD. To find out something.

NORA. Hurry, then. What is it?

KROGSTAD. You know I've been given notice.

NORA. I couldn't prevent it, Mr. Krogstad, I did my utmost for you, but it was no use.

KROGSTAD. Has your husband so little affection for you? He knows what I can do to you, yet he dares. . . .

NORA. You don't imagine he knows about it!

KROGSTAD. No, I didn't imagine he did. It didn't seem a bit like my good friend Torvald Helmer to show that much courage. . . .

NORA. Mr. Krogstad, I must ask you to show some respect for my husband.

KROGSTAD. Oh, sure! All due respect! But since you are so anxious to keep this business quiet, Mrs. Helmer, I take it you now have a rather clearer idea of just what it is you've done, than you had yesterday.

NORA. Clearer than *you* could ever have given me.

KROGSTAD. Yes, being as I am such a rotten lawyer. . . .

NORA. What do you want with me?

KROGSTAD. I just wanted to see how things stood, Mrs. Helmer. I've been thinking about you all day. Even a mere money-lender, a hack journalist, a—well, even somebody like me has a bit of what you might call feeling.

NORA. Show it then. Think of my little children.

KROGSTAD. Did you or your husband think of mine? But what does it matter now? There was just one thing I wanted to say: you needn't take this business too seriously. I shan't start any proceedings, for the present.

NORA. Ah, I knew you wouldn't.

KROGSTAD. The whole thing can be arranged quite amicably. Nobody need know. Just the three of us.

NORA. My husband must never know.

KROGSTAD. How can you prevent it? Can you pay off the balance?

NORA. No, not immediately.

KROGSTAD. Perhaps you've some way of getting hold of the money in the next few days.

NORA. None I want to make use of.

KROGSTAD. Well, it wouldn't have been very much help to you if you had. Even if you stood there with the cash in your hand and to spare, you still wouldn't get your IOU back from me now.

NORA. What are you going to do with it?

KROGSTAD. Just keep it—have it in my possession. Nobody who isn't implicated need know about it. So if you are thinking of trying any desperate remedies . . .

NORA. Which I am. . . .

KROGSTAD. . . . if you happen to be thinking of running away . . .

NORA. Which I am!

KROGSTAD. . . . or anything worse . . .

NORA. How did you know?

KROGSTAD. . . . forget it!

NORA. How did you know I was thinking of *that?*

KROGSTAD. Most of us think of *that*, to begin with. I did, too; but I didn't have the courage. . . .

NORA [*tonelessly*]. I haven't either.

KROGSTAD [*relieved*]. So you haven't the courage either, eh?

NORA. No, I haven't! I haven't!

KROGSTAD. It would also be very stupid. There'd only be the first domestic storm to get over. . . . I've got a letter to your husband in my pocket here. . . .

NORA. And it's all in there?

KROGSTAD. In as tactful a way as possible.

NORA [*quickly*]. He must never read that letter. Tear it up. I'll find the money somehow.

KROGSTAD. Excuse me, Mrs. Helmer, but I've just told you. . . .

NORA. I'm not talking about the money I owe you. I want to know how much you are demanding from my husband, and I'll get the money.

KROGSTAD. I want no money from your husband.

NORA. What do you want?

KROGSTAD. I'll tell you. I want to get on my feet again, Mrs. Helmer; I want to get to the top. And your husband is going to help me. For the last eighteen months I've gone straight; all that time it's been hard going; I was content to work my way up, step by step. Now I'm being kicked out, and I won't stand for being taken back again as an act of charity. I'm going to get to the top, I tell you. I'm going back into that Bank—with a better job. Your husband is going to create a new vacancy, just for me. . . .

NORA. He'll never do that!

KROGSTAD. He will do it. I know him. He'll do it without so much as a whimper. And once I'm in there with him, you'll see what's what. In less than a year I'll be his right-hand man. It'll be Nils Krogstad, not Torvald Helmer, who'll be running that Bank.

NORA. You'll never live to see that day!

KROGSTAD. You mean you . . . ?

NORA. Now I have the courage.

KROGSTAD. You can't frighten me! A precious pampered little thing like you. . . .

NORA. I'll show you! I'll show you!

KROGSTAD. Under the ice, maybe? Down in the cold, black water? Then being washed up in the spring, bloated, hairless, unrecognizable. . . .

NORA. You can't frighten me.

KROGSTAD. You can't frighten me, either. People don't do that sort of thing, Mrs. Helmer. There wouldn't be any point to it, anyway, I'd still have him right in my pocket.

NORA. Afterwards? When I'm no longer . . .

KROGSTAD. Aren't you forgetting that your reputation would then be entirely in my hands? [NORA stands looking at him, speechless.] Well, I've warned you. Don't do anything silly. When Helmer gets my letter, I expect to hear from him. And don't forget: it's him who is forcing me off the straight and narrow again, your own husband! That's something I'll never forgive him for. Goodbye, Mrs. Helmer. [He goes out through the hall. NORA crosses to the door, opens it slightly, and listens.]

NORA. He's going. He hasn't left the letter. No, no, that would be impossible! [Opens the door further and further.] What's he doing? He's stopped outside. He's not going down the stairs. Has he changed his mind? Is he . . . ? [A letter falls into the letter-box. Then KROG-STAD's footsteps are heard receding as he walks downstairs. NORA gives a stifled cry, runs across the room to the sofa table; pause.] In the letter-box! [She creeps stealthily across to the hall door.] There it is! Torvald, Torvald! It's hopeless now!

MRS. LINDE [comes into the room, left, carrying the costume]. There, I think that's everything. Shall we try it on?

NORA [in a low, hoarse voice]. Kristine, come here.

MRS. LINDE [throws the dress down on the sofa]. What's wrong with you? You look upset.

NORA. Come here. Do you see that letter? There, look! Through the glass in the letter-box.

MRS. LINDE. Yes, yes, I can see it.

NORA. It's a letter from Krogstad.

MRS. LINDE. Nora! It was Krogstad who lent you the money!

NORA. Yes. And now Torvald will get to know everything.

MRS. LINDE. Believe me, Nora, it's best for you both.

NORA. But there's more to it than that. I forged a signature. . . .

MRS. LINDE. Heavens above!

NORA. Listen, I want to tell you something, Kristine, so you can be my witness.

MRS. LINDE. What do you mean "witness"? What do you want me to . . . ?

NORA. If I should go mad . . . which might easily happen . . .

MRS. LINDE. Nora!

NORA. Or if anything happened to me . . . which meant I couldn't be here.

MRS. LINDE. Nora, Nora! Are you out of your mind?

NORA. And if somebody else wanted to take it all upon himself, the whole blame, you understand. . . .

MRS. LINDE. Yes, yes. But what makes you think . . . ?

NORA. Then you must testify that it isn't true, Kristine. I'm not out of my mind; I'm quite sane now. And I tell you this: nobody else knew anything, I alone was responsible for the whole thing. Remember that!

MRS. LINDE. I will. But I don't understand a word of it.

NORA. Why should you? You see something miraculous is going to happen.

MRS. LINDE. Something miraculous?

NORA. Yes, a miracle. But something so terrible as well, Kristine— oh, it must *never* happen, not for anything.

MRS. LINDE. I'm going straight over to talk to Krogstad.

NORA. Don't go. He'll only do you harm.

MRS. LINDE. There was a time when he would have done anything for me.

NORA. Him!

MRS. LINDE. Where does he live?

NORA. How do I know. . . ? Wait a minute. [*She feels in her pocket.*] Here's his card. But the letter, the letter. . . !

HELMER [*from his study, knocking on the door*]. Nora!

NORA [*cries out in terror*]. What's that? What do you want?

HELMER. Don't be frightened. We're not coming in. You've locked the door. Are you trying on?

NORA. Yes, yes, I'm trying on. It looks so nice on me, Torvald.

MRS. LINDE [*who has read the card*]. He lives just round the corner.

NORA. It's no use. It's hopeless. The letter is there in the box.

MRS. LINDE. Your husband keeps the key?

NORA. Always.

MRS. LINDE. Krogstad must ask for his letter back unread, he must find some sort of excuse. . . .

NORA. But this is just the time that Torvald generally . . .

MRS. LINDE. Put him off! Go in and keep him busy. I'll be back as soon as I can.

[*She goes out hastily by the hall door.* NORA *walks over to Helmer's door, opens it and peeps in.*]

NORA. Torvald!

HELMER [*in the study*]. Well, can a man get into his own living-room again now? Come along, Rank, now we'll see . . . [*In the doorway.*] But what's this?

NORA. What, Torvald dear?

HELMER. Rank led me to expect some kind of marvelous transformation.

RANK [*in the doorway*]. That's what I thought too, but I must have been mistaken.

NORA. I'm not showing myself off to anybody before tomorrow.

HELMER. Nora dear, you look tired. You haven't been practicing too hard?

NORA. No, I haven't practiced at all yet.

HELMER. You'll have to, though.

NORA. Yes, I certainly must, Torvald. But I just can't get anywhere without your help: I've completely forgotten it.

HELMER. We'll soon polish it up.

NORA. Yes, do help me, Torvald. Promise? I'm so nervous. All those people. . . . You must devote yourself exclusively to me this evening. Pens away! Forget all about the office! Promise me, Torvald dear!

HELMER. I promise. This evening I am wholly and entirely at your service . . . helpless little thing that you are. Oh, but while I remember, I'll just look first . . .

[*He goes towards the hall door.*]

NORA. What do you want out there?

HELMER. Just want to see if there are any letters.

NORA. No, don't, Torvald!

HELMER. Why not?

NORA. Torvald, *please!* There aren't any.

HELMER. Just let me see.

[*He starts to go.* NORA, *at the piano, plays the opening bars of the tarantella.*]

HELMER [*at the door, stops*]. Aha!

NORA. I shan't be able to dance tomorrow if I don't rehearse it with you.

HELMER [*walks to her*]. Are you really so nervous, Nora dear?

NORA. Terribly nervous. Let me run through it now. There's still time before supper. Come and sit here and play for me, Torvald dear. Tell me what to do, keep me right—as you always do.

HELMER. Certainly, with pleasure, if that's what you want.

[*He sits at the piano.* NORA *snatches the tambourine out of the box, and also a long gaily-colored shawl which she drapes round herself, then with a bound she leaps forward.*]

NORA [*shouts*]. Now play for me! Now I'll dance!

[HELMER *plays and* NORA *dances;* DR. RANK *stands at the piano behind Helmer and looks on.*]

HELMER [*playing*]. Not so fast! Not so fast!

NORA. I can't help it.

HELMER. Not so wild, Nora!

NORA. This is how it has to be.

HELMER [*stops*]. No, no, that won't do at all.

NORA [*laughs and swings the tambourine*]. Didn't I tell you?

RANK. Let me play for her.

HELMER [*gets up*]. Yes, do. Then I'll be better able to tell her what to do.

[RANK *sits down at the piano and plays.* NORA *dances more and more wildly.* HELMER *stands by the stove giving her repeated directions as she dances; she does not seem to hear them. Her hair comes undone and falls about her shoulders; she pays no attention and goes on dancing.* MRS. LINDE *enters.*]

MRS. LINDE [*standing as though spellbound in the doorway*]. Ah. . . !

NORA [*dancing*]. See what fun we are having, Kristine.

HELMER. But my dear darling Nora, you are dancing as though your life depended on it.

NORA. It does.

HELMER. Stop, Rank! This is sheer madness. Stop, I say.

[RANK *stops playing and* NORA *comes to a sudden halt.*]

HELMER [*crosses to her*]. I would never have believed it. You have forgotten everything I ever taught you.

NORA [*throwing away the tambourine*]. There you are, you see.

HELMER. Well, some more instruction is certainly needed there.

NORA. Yes, you see how necessary it is. You must go on coaching me right up to the last minute. Promise me, Torvald?

HELMER. You can rely on me.

NORA. You mustn't think about anything else but me until after tomorrow . . . mustn't open any letters . . . mustn't touch the letter-box.

HELMER. Ah, you are still frightened of what that man might . . .

NORA. Yes, yes, I am.

HELMER. I can see from your face there's already a letter there from him.

NORA. I don't know. I think so. But you mustn't read anything like that now. We don't want anything horrid coming between us until all this is over.

RANK [*softly to* HELMER]. I shouldn't cross her.

HELMER [*puts his arm round her*]. The child must have her way. But tomorrow night, when your dance is done. . . .

NORA. Then you are free.

MAID [*in the doorway, right*]. Dinner is served, madam.

NORA. We'll have champagne, Helene.

MAID. Very good, madam.

[*She goes.*]

HELMER. Aha! It's to be quite a banquet, eh?

NORA. With champagne flowing until dawn. [*Shouts.*] And some maca-roons, Helene . . . lots of them, for once in a while.

HELMER [*seizing her hands*]. Now, now, not so wild and excitable! Let me see you being my own little singing bird again.

NORA. Oh yes, I will. And if you'll just go in . . . you, too, Dr. Rank. Kristine, you must help me to do my hair.

RANK [*softly, as they leave*]. There isn't anything . . . anything as it were, impending, is there?

HELMER. No, not at all, my dear fellow. It's nothing but these childish fears I was telling you about.

[*They go out to the right.*]

NORA. Well?

MRS. LINDE. He's left town.

NORA. I saw it in your face.

MRS. LINDE. He's coming back tomorrow evening. I left a note for him.

NORA. You shouldn't have done that. You must let things take their course. Because really it's a case for rejoicing, waiting like this for the miracle.

MRS. LINDE. What is it you are waiting for?

NORA. Oh, you wouldn't understand. Go and join the other two. I'll be there in a minute.

[MRS. LINDE *goes into the dining-room.* NORA *stands for a moment as though to collect herself, then looks at her watch.*]

NORA. Five. Seven hours to midnight. Then twenty-four hours till the next midnight. Then the tarantella will be over. Twenty-four and seven? Thirty-one hours to live.

HELMER [*in the doorway, right*]. What's happened to our little sky-lark?

NORA [*running towards him with open arms*]. Here she is!

ACT THREE

The same room. The round table has been moved to the center of the room, and the chairs placed round it. A lamp is burning on the table. The door to the hall stands open. Dance music can be heard coming from the floor above. MRS. LINDE *is sitting by the table, idly turning over the pages of a book; she tries to read, but does not seem able to concentrate. Once or twice she listens, tensely, for a sound at the front door.*

MRS. LINDE [*looking at her watch*]. Still not here. There isn't much time left. I only hope he hasn't . . . [*She listens again.*] Ah, there he is. [*She goes out into the hall, and cautiously opens the front door. Soft footsteps can be heard on the stairs. She whispers.*] Come in. There's nobody here.

KROGSTAD [*in the doorway*]. I found a note from you at home. What does it all mean?

MRS. LINDE. I *had* to talk to you.

KROGSTAD. Oh? And did it have to be here, in this house?

MRS. LINDE. It wasn't possible over at my place, it hasn't a separate entrance. Come in. We are quite alone. The maid's asleep and the Helmers are at a party upstairs.

KROGSTAD [*comes into the room*]. Well, well! So the Helmers are out dancing tonight! Really?

MRS. LINDE. Yes, why not?

KROGSTAD. Why not indeed!

MRS. LINDE. Well then, Nils. Let's talk.

KROGSTAD. Have we two anything more to talk about?

MRS. LINDE. We have a great deal to talk about.

KROGSTAD. I shouldn't have thought so.

MRS. LINDE. That's because you never really understood me.

KROGSTAD. What else was there to understand, apart from the old, old story? A heartless woman throws a man over the moment something more profitable offers itself.

MRS. LINDE. Do you really think I'm so heartless? Do you think I found it easy to break it off?

KROGSTAD. Didn't you?

MRS. LINDE. You didn't really believe that?

KROGSTAD. If that wasn't the case, why did you write to me as you did?

MRS. LINDE. There was nothing else I could do. If I had to make the break, I felt in duty bound to destroy any feeling that you had for me.

KROGSTAD [*clenching his hands*]. So that's how it was. And all that . . . was for money!

MRS. LINDE. You mustn't forget I had a helpless mother and two young brothers. We couldn't wait for you, Nils. At that time you hadn't much immediate prospect of anything.

KROGSTAD. That may be. But you had no right to throw me over for somebody else.

MRS. LINDE. Well, I don't know. Many's the time I've asked myself whether I was justified.

KROGSTAD [*more quietly*]. When I lost you, it was just as if the ground had slipped away from under my feet. Look at me now: a broken man clinging to the wreck of his life.

MRS. LINDE. Help might be near.

KROGSTAD. It was near. Then you came along and got in the way.

MRS. LINDE. Quite without knowing, Nils. I only heard today it's you I'm supposed to be replacing at the Bank.

KROGSTAD. If you say so, I believe you. But now you do know, aren't you going to withdraw?

MRS. LINDE. No, that wouldn't benefit you in the slightest.

KROGSTAD. Benefit, benefit. . . . ! I would do it just the same.

Mrs. Linde. I have learned to go carefully. Life and hard, bitter necessity have taught me that.

Krogstad. And life has taught me not to believe in pretty speeches.

Mrs. Linde. Then life has taught you a very sensible thing. But deeds are something you surely must believe in?

Krogstad. How do you mean?

Mrs. Linde. You said you were like a broken man clinging to the wreck of his life.

Krogstad. And I said it with good reason.

Mrs. Linde. And I am like a broken woman clinging to the wreck of her life. Nobody to care about, and nobody to care for.

Krogstad. It was your own choice.

Mrs. Linde. At the time there was no other choice.

Krogstad. Well, what of it?

Mrs. Linde. Nils, what about us two castaways joining forces?

Krogstad. What's that you say?

Mrs. Linde. Two of us on *one* wreck surely stand a better chance than each on his own.

Krogstad. Kristine!

Mrs. Linde. Why do you suppose I came to town?

Krogstad. You mean, you thought of me?

Mrs. Linde. Without work I couldn't live. All my life I have worked, for as long as I can remember; that has always been my one great joy. But now I'm completely alone in the world, and feeling horribly empty and forlorn. There's no pleasure in working only for yourself. Nils, give me somebody and something to work for.

Krogstad. I don't believe all this. It's only a woman's hysteria, wanting to be all magnanimous and self-sacrificing.

Mrs. Linde. Have you ever known me hysterical before?

Krogstad. Would you really do this? Tell me—do you know all about my past?

Mrs. Linde. Yes.

Krogstad. And you know what people think about me?

Mrs. Linde. Just now you hinted you thought you might have been a different person with me.

Krogstad. I'm convinced I would.

Mrs. Linde. Couldn't it still happen?

Krogstad. Kristine! You know what you are saying, don't you? Yes, you do. I can see you do. Have you really the courage . . . ?

Mrs. Linde. I need someone to mother, and your children need a mother. We two need each other. Nils, I have faith in what, deep down, you are. With you I can face anything.

Krogstad [*seizing her hands*]. Thank you, thank you, Kristine. And I'll soon have everybody looking up to me, or I'll know the reason why. Ah, but I was forgetting. . . .

Mrs. Linde. Hush! The tarantella! You must go!

KROGSTAD. Why? What is it?

MRS. LINDE. You hear that dance upstairs? When it's finished they'll be coming.

KROGSTAD. Yes, I'll go. It's too late to do anything. Of course, you know nothing about what steps I've taken against the Helmers.

MRS. LINDE. Yes, Nils, I do know.

KROGSTAD. Yet you still want to go on. . . .

MRS. LINDE. I know how far a man like you can be driven by despair.

KROGSTAD. Oh, if only I could undo what I've done!

MRS. LINDE. You still can. Your letter is still there in the box.

KROGSTAD. Are you sure?

MRS. LINDE. Quite sure. But . . .

KROGSTAD [*regards her searching*]. Is that how things are? You want to save your friend at any price? Tell me straight. Is that it?

MRS. LINDE. When you've sold yourself *once* for other people's sake, you don't do it again.

KROGSTAD. I shall demand my letter back.

MRS. LINDE. No, no.

KROGSTAD. Of course I will, I'll wait here till Helmer comes. I'll tell him he has to give me my letter back . . . that it's only about my notice . . . that he mustn't read it. . . .

MRS. LINDE. No, Nils, don't ask for it back.

KROGSTAD. But wasn't that the very reason you got me here?

MRS. LINDE. Yes, that was my first terrified reaction. But that was yesterday, and it's quite incredible the things I've witnessed in this house in the last twenty-four hours. Helmer must know everything. This unhappy secret must come out. Those two must have the whole thing out between them. All this secrecy and deception, it just can't go on.

KROGSTAD. Well, if you want to risk it. . . . But one thing I can do, and I'll do it at once. . . .

MRS. LINDE [*listening*]. Hurry! Go, go! The dance has stopped. We aren't safe a moment longer.

KROGSTAD. I'll wait for you downstairs.

MRS. LINDE. Yes, do. You must see me home.

KROGSTAD. I've never been so incredibly happy before.

[*He goes out by the front door. The door out into the hall remains standing open.*]

MRS. LINDE [*tidies the room a little and gets her hat and coat ready*]. How things change! How things change! Somebody to work for . . . to live for. A home to bring happiness into. Just let me get down to it. . . . I wish they'd come. . . . [*Listens.*] Ah, there they are. . . . Get my things.

[*She takes her coat and hat. The voices of* HELMER *and* NORA *are heard outside. A key is turned and* HELMER *pushes* NORA *almost forcibly into the hall. She is dressed in the Italian costume, with a big black shawl over it. He is in evening dress, and over it a black cloak, open.*]

NORA [*still in the doorway, reluctantly*]. No, no, not in here! I want to go back up again. I don't want to leave so early.

HELMER. But my dearest Nora . . .

NORA. Oh, please, Torvald, I beg you. . . . *Please*, just for another hour.

HELMER. Not another minute, Nora my sweet. You remember what we agreed. There now, come along in. You'll catch cold standing there.

[*He leads her, in spite of her resistance, gently but firmly into the room.*]

MRS. LINDE. Good evening.

NORA. Kristine!

HELMER. Why, Mrs. Linde. You here so late?

MRS. LINDE. Yes. You must forgive me but I did so want to see Nora all dressed up.

NORA. Have you been sitting here waiting for me?

MRS. LINDE. Yes, I'm afraid I wasn't in time to catch you before you went upstairs. And I felt I couldn't leave again without seeing you.

HELMER [*removing* NORA'S *shawl*]. Well take a good look at her. I think I can say she's worth looking at. Isn't she lovely, Mrs. Linde?

MRS. LINDE. Yes, I must say. . . .

HELMER. Isn't she quite extraordinarily lovely? That's what every-body at the party thought, too. But she's dreadfully stubborn . . . the sweet little thing! And what shall we do about that? Would you believe it, I nearly had to use force to get her away.

NORA. Oh Torvald, you'll be sorry you didn't let me stay, even for half an hour.

HELMER. You hear that, Mrs. Linde? She dances her tarantella, there's wild applause—which was well deserved, although the performance was perhaps rather realistic . . . I mean, rather more so than was strictly necessary from the artistic point of view. But anyway! The main thing is she was a success, a tremendous success. Was I sup-posed to let her stay after that? Spoil the effect? No thank you! I took my lovely little Capri girl—my capricious little Capri girl, I might say—by the arm, whished her once round the room, a curtsey all round, and then—as they say in novels—the beautiful vision vanished. An exit should always be effective, Mrs. Linde. But I just can't get Nora to see that. Phew! It's warm in here. [*He throws his cloak over a chair and opens the door to his study.*] What? It's dark. Oh yes, of course. Excuse me. . . .

[*He goes in and lights a few candles.*]

NORA [*quickly, in a breathless whisper*]. Well?

MRS. LINDE [*softly*]. I've spoken to him.

NORA. And . . . ?

MRS. LINDE. Nora . . . you must tell your husband everything.

NORA [*tonelessly*]. I knew it.

MRS. LINDE. You've got nothing to fear from Krogstad. But you must speak.

NORA. I won't.

MRS. LINDE. Then the letter will.

NORA. Thank you, Kristine. Now I know what's to be done. Hush . . . !

HELMER [*comes in again*]. Well, Mrs. Linde, have you finished admiring her?

MRS. LINDE. Yes. And now I must say good night.

HELMER. Oh, already? Is this yours, this knitting?

MRS. LINDE [*takes it*]. Yes, thank you. I nearly forgot it.

HELMER. So you knit, eh?

MRS. LINDE. Yes.

HELMER. You should embroider instead, you know.

MRS. LINDE. Oh? Why?

HELMER. So much prettier. Watch! You hold the embroidery like this in the left hand, and then you take the needle in the right hand, like this, and you describe a long, graceful curve. Isn't that right?

MRS. LINDE. Yes, I suppose so. . . .

HELMER. Whereas knitting on the other hand just can't help being ugly. Look! Arms pressed into the sides, the knitting needles going up and down—there's something Chinese about it. . . . Ah, that was marvelous champagne they served tonight.

MRS. LINDE. Well, good night, Nora! And stop being so stubborn.

HELMER. Well said, Mrs. Linde!

MRS. LINDE. Good night, Mr. Helmer.

HELMER [*accompanying her to the door*]. Good night, good night! You'll get home all right, I hope? I'd be only too pleased to . . . But you haven't far to walk. Good night, good night! [*She goes; he shuts the door behind her and comes in again.*] There we are, got rid of her at last. She's a frightful bore, that woman.

NORA. Aren't you very tired, Torvald?

HELMER. Not in the least.

NORA. Not sleepy?

HELMER. Not at all. On the contrary, I feel extremely lively. What about you? Yes, you look quite tired and sleepy.

NORA. Yes, I'm very tired. I just want to fall straight off to sleep.

HELMER. There you are, you see! Wasn't I right in thinking we shouldn't stay any longer.

NORA. Oh, everything you do is right.

HELMER [*kissing her forehead*]. There's my little sky-lark talking common sense. Did you notice how gay Rank was this evening?

NORA. Oh, was he? I didn't get a chance to talk to him.

HELMER. I hardly did either. But it's a long time since I saw him in such a good mood. [*Looks at* NORA *for a moment or two, then comes nearer her.*] Ah, it's wonderful to be back in our own home again, and quite alone with you. How irresistibly lovely you are, Nora!

NORA. Don't look at me like that, Torvald!

HELMER. Can't I look at my most treasured possession? At all this loveliness that's mine and mine alone, completely and utterly mine.

NORA [*walks round to the other side of the table*]. You mustn't talk to me like that tonight.

HELMER [*following her*]. You still have the tarantella in your blood, I see. And that makes you even more desirable. Listen! The guests are beginning to leave now. [*Softly.*] Nora . . . soon the whole house will be silent.

NORA. I should hope so.

HELMER. Of course you do, don't you, Nora my darling? You know, whenever I'm out at a party with you . . . do you know why I never talk to you very much, why I always stand away from you and only steal a quick glance at you now and then . . . do you know why I do that? It's because I'm pretending we are secretly in love, secretly engaged and nobody suspects there is anything between us.

NORA. Yes, yes. I know your thoughts are always with me, of course.

HELMER. And when it's time to go, and I lay your shawl round those shapely, young shoulders, round the exquisite curve of your neck . . . I pretend that you are my young bride, that we are just leaving our wedding, that I am taking you to our new home for the first time . . . to be alone with you for the first time . . . quite alone with your young and trembling loveliness! All evening I've been longing for you, and nothing else. And as I watched you darting and swaying in the tarantella, my blood was on fire . . . I couldn't bear it any longer . . . and that's why I brought you down here with me so early. . . .

NORA. Go away, Torvald! Please leave me alone. I won't have it.

HELMER. What's this? It's just your little game isn't it, my little Nora. Won't! Won't! Am I not your husband . . . ?

[*There is a knock on the front door.*]

NORA [*startled*]. Listen . . . !

HELMER [*going towards the hall*]. Who's there?

RANK [*outside*]. It's me. Can I come in for a minute?

HELMER [*in a low voice, annoyed*]. Oh, what does he want now? [*Aloud.*] Wait a moment. [*He walks across and opens the door.*] How nice of you to look in on your way out.

RANK. I fancied I heard your voice and I thought I would just look in. [*He takes a quick glance round.*] Ah yes, this dear, familiar old place! How cozy and comfortable you've got things here, you two.

HELMER. You seemed to be having a pretty good time upstairs your-self.

RANK. Capital! Why shouldn't I? Why not make the most of things in this world? At least as much as one can, and for as long as one can. The wine was excellent. . . .

HELMER. Especially the champagne.

RANK. You noticed that too, did you? It's incredible the amount I was able to put away.

NORA. Torvald also drank a lot of champagne this evening.

RANK. Oh?

NORA. Yes, and that always makes him quite merry.

RANK. Well, why shouldn't a man allow himself a jolly evening after a day well spent?

HELMER. Well spent? I'm afraid I can't exactly claim that.

RANK [clapping him on the shoulder]. But I can, you see!

NORA. Dr. Rank, am I right in thinking you carried out a certain laboratory test today?

RANK. Exactly.

HELMER. Look at our little Nora talking about laboratory tests!

NORA. And may I congratulate you on the result?

RANK. You may indeed.

NORA. So it was good?

RANK. The best possible, for both doctor and patient—certainty!

NORA [quickly and searchingly]. Certainty?

RANK. Absolute certainty. So why shouldn't I allow myself a jolly evening after that?

NORA. Quite right, Dr. Rank.

HELMER. I quite agree. As long as you don't suffer for it in the morning.

RANK. Well, you never get anything for nothing in this life.

NORA. Dr. Rank . . . you are very fond of masquerades, aren't you?

RANK. Yes, when there are plenty of amusing disguises. . . .

NORA. Tell me, what shall we two go as next time?

HELMER. There's frivolity for you . . . thinking about the next time already!

RANK. We two? I'll tell you. You must go as Lady Luck. . . .

HELMER. Yes, but how do you find a costume to suggest *that?*

RANK. Your wife could simply go in her everyday clothes. . . .

HELMER. That was nicely said. But don't you know what you would be?

RANK. Yes, my dear friend, I know exactly what I shall be.

HELMER. Well?

RANK. At the next masquerade, I shall be invisible.

HELMER. That's a funny idea!

RANK. There's a big black cloak . . . haven't you heard of the cloak of invisibility? That comes right down over you, and then nobody can see you.

HELMER [suppressing a smile]. Of course, that's right.

RANK. But I'm clean forgetting what I came for. Helmer, give me a cigar, one of the dark Havanas.

HELMER. With the greatest of pleasure.

[*He offers his case.*]

RANK [*takes one and cuts the end off*]. Thanks.

NORA [*strikes a match*]. Let me give you a light.

RANK. Thank you. [*She holds out the match and he lights his cigar.*] And now, goodbye!

HELMER. Goodbye, goodbye, my dear fellow!

NORA. Sleep well, Dr. Rank.

RANK. Thank you for that wish.

NORA. Wish me the same.

RANK. You? All right, if you want me to. . . . Sleep well. And thanks for the light.

[*He nods to them both, and goes.*]

HELMER [*subdued*]. He's had a lot to drink.

NORA [*absently*]. Very likely.

[HELMER *takes a bunch of keys out of his pocket and goes out into the hall.*]

NORA. Torvald . . . what do you want there?

HELMER. I must empty the letter-box, it's quite full. There'll be no room for the papers in the morning. . . .

NORA. Are you going to work tonight?

HELMER. You know very well I'm not. Hello, what's this? Somebody's been at the lock.

NORA. At the lock?

HELMER. Yes, I'm sure of it. Why should that be? I'd hardly have thought the maids . . . ? Here's a broken hair-pin. Nora, it's one of yours. . . .

NORA [*quickly*]. It must have been the children. . . .

HELMER. Then you'd better tell them not to. Ah . . . there . . . I've managed to get it open. [*He takes the things out and shouts into the kitchen.*] Helene! . . . Helene, put the light out in the hall. [*He comes into the room again with the letters in his hand and shuts the hall door.*] Look how it all mounts up. [*Runs through them.*] What's this?

NORA. The letter! Oh no, Torvald, no!

HELMER. Two visiting cards . . . from Dr. Rank.

NORA. From Dr. Rank?

HELMER [*looking at them*]. Dr. Rank, Medical Practitioner. They were on top. He must have put them in as he left.

NORA. Is there anything on them?

HELMER. There's a black cross above his name. Look. What an uncanny idea. It's just as if he were announcing his own death.

NORA. He is.

HELMER. What? What do you know about it? Has he said anything to you?

NORA. Yes. He said when these cards came, he would have taken his last leave of us. He was going to shut himself up and die.

HELMER. Poor fellow! Of course I knew we couldn't keep him with us very long. But so soon. . . . And hiding himself away like a wounded animal.

NORA. When it has to happen, it's best that it should happen without words. Don't you think so, Torvald?

HELMER [*walking up and down*]. He had grown so close to us. I don't think I can imagine him gone. His suffering and his loneliness seemed almost to provide a background of dark cloud to the sunshine of our lives. Well, perhaps it's all for the best. For him at any rate. [*Pauses.*] And maybe for us as well, Nora. Now there's just the two of us. [*Puts his arms round her.*] Oh, my darling wife, I can't hold you close enough. You know, Nora . . . many's the time I wish you were threatened by some terrible danger so I could risk everything, body and soul, for your sake.

NORA [*tears herself free and says firmly and decisively*]. Now you must read your letters, Torvald.

HELMER. No, no, not tonight. I want to be with you, my darling wife.

NORA. Knowing all the time your friend is dying . . . ?

HELMER. You are right. It's been a shock to both of us. This ugly thing has come between us . . . thoughts of death and decay. We must try to free ourselves from it. Until then . . . we shall go our separate ways.

NORA [*her arms round his neck*]. Torvald . . . good night! Good night!

HELMER [*kisses her forehead*]. Goodnight, my little singing bird. Sleep well, Nora, I'll just read through my letters.

[*He takes the letters into his room and shuts the door behind him.*]

NORA [*gropes around her, wild-eyed, seizes Helmer's cloak, wraps it round herself, and whispers quickly, hoarsely, spasmodically*]. Never see him again. Never, never, never. [*Throws her shawl over her head.*] And never see the children again either. Never, never. Oh, that black icy water. Oh, that bottomless . . . ! If only it were all over! He's got it now. Now he's reading it. Oh no, no! Not yet! Torvald, goodbye . . . and my children. . . .

[*She rushes out in the direction of the hall; at the same moment* HELMER *flings open his door and stands there with an open letter in his hand.*]

HELMER. Nora!

NORA [*shrieks*]. Ah!

HELMER. What is this? Do you know what is in this letter?

NORA. Yes, I know. Let me go! Let me out!

HELMER [*holds her back*]. Where are you going?

NORA [*trying to tear herself free*]. You mustn't try to save me, Torvald!

HELMER [*reels back*]. True! Is it true what he writes? How dreadful! no, no, it can't possibly be true.

NORA. It *is* true. I loved you more than anything else in the world.

HELMER. Don't come to me with a lot of paltry excuses!

NORA [*taking a step towards him*]. Torvald . . . !

HELMER. Miserable woman . . . what is this you have done?

NORA. Let me go. I won't have you taking the blame for me. You mustn't take it on yourself.

HELMER. Stop play-acting! [*Locks the front door.*] You are staying here to give an account of yourself. Do you understand what you have done? Answer me! Do you understand?

NORA [*looking fixedly at him, her face hardening*]. Yes, now I'm really beginning to understand.

HELMER [*walking up and down*]. Oh, what a terrible awakening this is. All these eight years . . . this woman who was my pride and joy . . . a hypocrite, a liar, worse than that, a criminal! Oh, how utterly squalid it all is! Ugh! Ugh! [NORA *remains silent and looks fixedly at him.*] I should have realized something like this would happen. I should have seen it coming. All your father's irresponsible ways. . . . Quiet! All your father's irresponsible ways are coming out in you. No religion, no morals, no sense of duty. . . . Oh, this is my punishment for turning a blind eye to him. It was for your sake I did it, and this is what I get for it.

NORA. Yes, this.

HELMER. Now you have ruined my entire happiness, jeopardized my whole future. It's terrible to think of. Here I am, at the mercy of a thoroughly unscrupulous person; he can do whatever he likes with me, demand anything he wants, order me about just as he chooses . . . and I daren't even whimper. I'm done for, a miserable failure, and it's all the fault of a feather-brained woman!

NORA. When I've left this world behind, you will be free.

HELMER. Oh, stop pretending! Your father was just the same, always ready with fine phrases. What good would it do me if you left this world behind, as you put it? Not the slightest bit of good. He can still let it all come out, if he likes; and if he does, people might even suspect me of being an accomplice in these criminal acts of yours, they might even think I was the one behind it all, that it was I who pushed you into it! And it's you I have to thank for this . . . and when I've taken such good care of you, all our married life. Now do you understand what you have done to me?

NORA [*coldly and calmly*]. Yes.

HELMER. I just can't understand it, it's so incredible. But we must see about putting things right. Take that shawl off. Take it off, I tell you! I must see if I can't find some way or other of appeasing him. The thing must be hushed up at all costs. And as far as you and I are concerned, things must appear to go on exactly as before. But only in the eyes of the world, of course. In other words you'll go on living here;

that's understood. But you will not be allowed to bring up the children, I can't trust you with them. . . . Oh, that I should have to say this to the woman I loved so dearly, the woman I still. . . . Well, that must be all over and done with. From now on, there can be no question of happiness. All we can do is save the bits and pieces from the wreck, preserve appearances. . . . [*The front door-bell rings.* HELMER *gives a start.*] What's that? So late? How terrible, supposing. . . . If he should . . . ? Hide, Nora! Say you are not well.

[NORA *stands motionless.* HELMER *walks across and opens the door into the hall.*]

MAID [*half dressed, in the hall*]. It's a note for Mrs. Helmer.

HELMER. Give it to me. [*He snatches the note and shuts the door.*] Yes, it's from him. You can't have it. I want to read it myself.

NORA. You read it then.

HELMER [*by the lamp*]. I hardly dare. Perhaps this is the end, for both of us. Well, I *must* know. [*He opens the note hurriedly, reads a few lines, looks at another enclosed sheet, and gives a cry of joy.*] Nora! [NORA *looks at him inquiringly.*] Nora! I must read it again. Yes, yes, it's true! I am saved! Nora, I am saved!

NORA. And me?

HELMER. You too, of course, we are both saved, you as well as me. Look, he's sent your IOU back. He sends his regrets and apologies for what he has done. . . . His luck has changed. . . . Oh, what does it matter what he says. We are saved, Nora! Nobody can do anything to you now. Oh, Nora, Nora . . . but let's get rid of this disgusting thing first. Let me see. . . . [*He glances at the IOU.*] No, I don't want to see it. I don't want it to be anything but a dream. [*He tears up the IOU and both letters, throws all the pieces into the stove and watches them burn.*] Well, that's the end of that. He said in his note you'd known since Christmas Eve. . . . You must have had three terrible days of it, Nora.

NORA. These three days haven't been easy.

HELMER. The agonies you must have gone through! When the only way out seemed to be. . . . No, let's forget the whole ghastly thing. We can rejoice and say: It's all over! It's all over! Listen to me, Nora! You don't seem to understand: it's all over! Why this grim look on your face? Oh, poor little Nora, of course I understand. You can't bring yourself to believe I've forgiven you. But I have, Nora, I swear it. I forgive you everything. I know you did what you did because you loved me.

NORA. That's true.

HELMER. You loved me as a wife should love her husband. It was simply that you didn't have the experience to judge what was the best way of going about things. But do you think I love you any the less for that; just because you don't know how to act on your own responsibility?

No, no, you just lean on me, I shall give you all the advice and guidance you need. I wouldn't be a proper man if I didn't find a woman doubly attractive for being so obviously helpless. You mustn't dwell on the harsh things I said in that first moment of horror, when I thought everything was going to come crashing down about my ears. I have forgiven you, Nora, I swear it! I have forgiven you!

NORA. Thank you for your forgiveness.

[*She goes out through the door, right.*]

HELMER. No, don't go! [*He looks through the doorway.*] What are you doing in the spare room?

NORA. Taking off this fancy dress.

HELMER [*standing at the open door*]. Yes, do. You try and get some rest, and set your mind at peace again, my frightened little song-bird. Have a good long sleep; you know you are safe and sound under my wing. [*Walks up and down near the door.*] What a nice, cozy little home we have here, Nora! Here you can find refuge. Here I shall hold you like a hunted dove I have rescued unscathed from the cruel talons of the hawk, and calm your poor beating heart. And that will come, gradually, Nora, believe me. Tomorrow you'll see everything quite differently. Soon everything will be just as it was before. You won't need me to keep on telling you I've forgiven you; you'll feel convinced of it in your own heart. You don't really imagine me ever thinking of turning you out, or even of reproaching you? Oh, a real man isn't made that way, you know, Nora. For a man, there's something indescribably moving and very satisfying in knowing that he has forgiven his wife—forgiven her, completely and genuinely, from the depths of his heart. It's as though it made her his property in a double sense: he has, as it were, given her a new life, and she becomes in a way both his wife and at the same time his child. That is how you will seem to me after today, helpless, perplexed little thing that you are. Don't you worry your pretty little head about anything, Nora. Just you be frank with me, and I'll take all the decisions for you. . . . What's this? Not in bed? You've changed your things?

NORA [*in her everyday dress*]. Yes, Torvald, I've changed.

HELMER. What for? It's late.

NORA. I shan't sleep tonight.

HELMER. But my dear Nora. . . .

NORA [*looks at her watch*]. It's not so terribly late. Sit down. Torvald. We two have a lot to talk about.

[*She sits down at one side of the table.*]

HELMER. Nora, what is all this? Why so grim?

NORA. Sit down. It'll take some time. I have a lot to say to you.

HELMER [*sits down at the table opposite her*]. You frighten me, Nora. I don't understand you.

NORA. Exactly. You don't understand me. And I have never understood

you, either—until tonight. No, don't interrupt. I just want you to listen to what I have to say. We are going to have things out, Torvald.

HELMER. What do you mean?

NORA. Isn't there anything that strikes you about the way we two are
sitting here?

HELMER. What's that?

NORA. We have now been married eight years. Hasn't it struck you
this is the first time you and I, man and wife, have had a serious talk
together?

HELMER. Depends what you mean by "serious."

NORA. Eight whole years—no, more, ever since we first knew each
other—and never have we exchanged one serious word about serious
things.

HELMER. What did you want me to do? Get you involved in worries
that you couldn't possibly help me to bear?

NORA. I'm not talking about worries. I say we've never once sat down
together and seriously tried to get to the bottom of anything.

HELMER. But, my dear Nora, would that have been a thing for you?

NORA. That's just it. You have never understood me . . . I've been
greatly wronged, Torvald. First by my father, and then by you.

HELMER. What! Us two! The two people who loved you more than
anybody?

NORA [*shakes her head*]. You two never loved me. You only thought how
nice it was to be in love with me.

HELMER. But, Nora, what's this you are saying?

NORA. It's right, you know, Torvald. At home, Daddy used to tell me
what he thought, then I thought the same. And if I thought differently,
I kept quiet about it, because he wouldn't have liked it. He used to call
me his baby doll, and he played with me as I used to play with my
dolls. Then I came to live in your house. . . .

HELMER. What way is that to talk about our marriage?

NORA [*imperturbably*]. What I mean is: I passed out of Daddy's hands
into yours. You arranged everything to your tastes, and I acquired
the same tastes. Or I pretended to . . . I don't really know . . . I
think it was a bit of both, sometimes one thing and sometimes the
other. When I look back, it seems to me I have been living here like a
beggar, from hand to mouth. I lived by doing tricks for you, Torvald.
But that's the way you wanted it. You and Daddy did me a great
wrong. It's your fault that I've never made anything of my life.

HELMER. Nora, how unreasonable . . . how ungrateful you are!
Haven't you been happy here?

NORA. No, never. I thought I was, but I wasn't really.

HELMER. Not . . . not happy!

NORA. No, just gay. And you've always been so kind to me. But our
house has never been anything but a play-room. I have been your doll

wife, just as at home I was Daddy's doll child. And the children in turn
have been my dolls. I thought it was fun when you came and played
with me, just as they thought it was fun when I went and played with
them. That's been our marriage, Torvald.

HELMER. There is some truth in what you say, exaggerated and hysterical though it is. But from now on it will be different. Play-time is
over; now comes the time for lessons.

NORA. Whose lessons? Mine or the children's?

HELMER. Both yours and the children's, my dear Nora.

NORA. Ah, Torvald, you are not the man to teach me to be a good wife
for you.

HELMER. How can you say that?

NORA. And what sort of qualifications have I to teach the children?

HELMER. Nora!

NORA. Didn't you say yourself, a minute or two ago, that you couldn't
trust me with that job.

HELMER. In the heat of the moment! You shouldn't pay any attention
to that.

NORA. On the contrary, you were quite right. I'm not up to it. There's
another problem needs solving first. I must take steps to educate myself. You are not the man to help me there. That's something I must
do on my own. That's why I'm leaving you.

HELMER [jumps up]. What did you say?

NORA. If I'm ever to reach any understanding of myself and the things
around me, I must learn to stand alone. That's why I can't stay here
with you any longer.

HELMER. Nora! Nora!

NORA. I'm leaving here at once. I dare say Kristine will put me up for
tonight. . . .

HELMER. You are out of your mind! I won't let you! I forbid you!

NORA. It's no use forbidding me anything now. I'm taking with me my
own personal belongings. I don't want anything of yours, either now
or later.

HELMER. This is madness!

NORA. Tomorrow I'm going home—to what used to be my home, I
mean. It will be easier for me to find something to do there.

HELMER. Oh, you blind, inexperienced . . .

NORA. I must set about *getting* experience, Torvald.

HELMER. And leave your home, your husband and your children?
Don't you care what people will say?

NORA. That's no concern of mine. All I know is that this is necessary
for *me*.

HELMER. This is outrageous! You are betraying your most sacred
duty.

NORA. And what do you consider to be my most sacred duty?

HELMER. Does it take me to tell you that? Isn't it your duty to your husband and your children?

NORA. I have another duty equally sacred.

HELMER. You have not. What duty might *that* be?

NORA. My duty to myself.

HELMER. First and foremost, you are a wife and mother.

NORA. That I don't believe any more. I believe that first and foremost I am an individual, just as much as you are—or at least I'm going to try to be. I know most people agree with you, Torvald, and that's also what it says in books. But I'm not content any more with what most people say, or with what it says in books. I have to think things out for myself, and get things clear.

HELMER. Surely you are clear about your position in your own home? Haven't you an infallible guide in questions like these? Haven't you your religion?

NORA. Oh, Torvald, I don't really know what religion is.

HELMER. What do you say!

NORA. All I know is what Pastor Hansen said when I was confirmed. He said religion was this, that and the other. When I'm away from all this and on my own, I'll go into that, too. I want to find out whether what Pastor Hansen told me was right—or at least whether it's right for *me*.

HELMER. This is incredible talk from a young woman! But if religion cannot keep you on the right path, let me at least stir your conscience. I suppose you do have some moral sense? Or tell me—perhaps you don't?

NORA. Well, Torvald, that's not easy to say. I simply don't know. I'm really confused about such things. All I know is my ideas about such things are very different from yours. I've also learned that the law is different from what I thought; but I simply can't get it into my head that that particular law is right. Apparently a woman has no right to spare her old father on his death-bed, or to save her husband's life, even. I just don't believe it.

HELMER. You are talking like a child. You understand nothing about the society you live in.

NORA. No, I don't. But I shall go into that too. I must try to discover who is right, society or me.

HELMER. You are ill, Nora. You are delirious. I'm half inclined to think you are out of your mind.

NORA. Never have I felt so calm and collected as I do tonight.

HELMER. Calm and collected enough to leave your husband and children?

NORA. Yes.

HELMER. Then only one explanation is possible.

NORA. And that is?

HELMER. You don't love me any more.

NORA. Exactly.

HELMER. Nora! Can you say that!

NORA. I'm desperately sorry, Torvald. Because you have always been so kind to me. But I can't help it. I don't love you any more.

HELMER [*struggling to keep his composure*]. Is that also a "calm and collected" decision you've made?

NORA. Yes, absolutely calm and collected. That's why I don't want to stay here.

HELMER. And can you also account for how I forfeited your love?

NORA. Yes, very easily. It was tonight, when the miracle didn't happen. It was then I realized you weren't the man I thought you were.

HELMER. Explain yourself more clearly. I don't understand.

NORA. For eight years I have been patiently waiting. Because, heavens, I knew miracles didn't happen every day. Then this devastating business started, and I became absolutely convinced the miracle *would* happen. All the time Krogstad's letter lay there, it never so much as crossed my mind that you would ever submit to that man's conditions. I was absolutely convinced you would say to him : Tell the whole wide world if you like. And when that was done . . .

HELMER. Yes, then what? After I had exposed my own wife to dishonor and shame . . . !

NORA. When that was done, I was absolutely convinced you would come forward and take everything on yourself, and say : I am the guilty one.

HELMER. Nora!

NORA. You mean I'd never let you make such a sacrifice for my sake? Of course not. But what would my story have counted for against yours?—That was the miracle I went in hope and dread of. It was to prevent it that I was ready to end my life.

HELMER. I would gladly toil day and night for you, Nora, enduring all manner of sorrow and distress. But nobody sacrifices his *honor* for the one he loves.

NORA. Hundreds and thousands of women have.

HELMER. Oh, you think and talk like a stupid child.

NORA. All right. But you neither think nor talk like the man I would want to share my life with. When you had got over your fright—and you weren't concerned about me but only about what might happen to you—and when all danger was past, you acted as though nothing had happened. I was your little sky-lark again, your little doll, exactly as before; except you would have to protect it twice as carefully as before, now that it had shown itself to be so weak and fragile. [*Rises.*] Torvald, that was the moment I realized that for eight years I'd been living with a stranger, and had borne him three children. . . . Oh, I can't bear to think about it! I could tear myself to shreds.

HELMER [*sadly*]. I see. I see. There is a tremendous gulf dividing us. But, Nora, is there no way we might bridge it?

NORA. As I am now, I am no wife for you.

HELMER. I still have it in me to change.

NORA. Perhaps . . . if you have your doll taken away.

HELMER. And be separated from you! No, no, Nora, the very thought of it is inconceivable.

NORA [*goes into the room, right*]. All the more reason why it must be done.

[*She comes back with her outdoor things and a small traveling bag which she puts on the chair beside the table.*]

HELMER. Nora, Nora, not now! Wait till the morning.

NORA [*putting on her coat*]. I can't spend the night in a strange man's room.

HELMER. Couldn't we go on living here like brother and sister. . . . ?

NORA [*tying on her hat*]. You know very well that wouldn't last. [*She draws the shawl round her.*] Goodbye, Torvald. I don't want to see the children. I know they are in better hands than mine. As I am now, I can never be anything to them.

HELMER. But some day, Nora, some day . . . ?

NORA. How should I know? I've no idea what I might turn out to be.

HELMER. But you are my wife, whatever you are.

NORA. Listen, Torvald, from what I've heard, when a wife leaves her husband's house as I am doing now, he is absolved by law of all responsibility for her. I can at any rate free you from all responsibility. You must not feel in any way bound, any more than I shall. There must be full freedom on both sides. Look, here's your ring back. Give me mine.

HELMER. That too?

NORA. That too.

HELMER. There it is.

NORA. Well, that's the end of that. I'll put the keys down here. The maids know where everything is in the house—better than I do, in fact. Kristine will come in the morning after I've left to pack up the few things I brought with me from home. I want them sent on.

HELMER. The end! Nora, will you never think of me?

NORA. I dare say I'll often think about you and the children and this house.

HELMER. May I write to you, Nora?

NORA. No, never. I won't let you.

HELMER. But surely I can send you . . .

NORA. Nothing, nothing.

HELMER. Can't I help you if ever you need it?

NORA. I said "no." I don't accept things from strangers.

HELMER. Nora, can I never be anything more to you than a stranger?

NORA [*takes her bag*]. Ah, Torvald, only by a miracle of miracles. . . .

HELMER. Name it, this miracle of miracles!

NORA. Both you and I would have to change to the point where . . .
Oh, Torvald, I don't believe in miracles any more.

HELMER. But I *will* believe. Name it! Change to the point
where . . . ?

NORA. Where we could make a real marriage of our lives together.
Goodbye!

[*She goes out through the hall door.*]

HELMER [*sinks down on a chair near the door, and covers his face with his
hands*]. Nora! Nora! [*He rises and looks round.*] Empty! She's gone!
[*With sudden hope.*] The miracle of miracles . . . ?

[*The heavy sound of a door being slammed is heard from below.*]

THE ALTERNATIVE "GERMAN" ENDING

UNDER STRONG PRESSURE, AND VERY RELUCTANTLY,
IBSEN WROTE AN ALTERNATIVE ENDING FOR THE
GERMAN THEATER. BOTH MAURICE IN HAMBURG AND
LAUBE IN VIENNA PRESSED FOR A "CONCILIATORY"
ENDING, AS ALSO DID FRAU HEDWIG NIEMANN-RAABE,
WHO WAS TO PLAY NORA ON TOUR. IN THE END, IBSEN
HIMSELF PROVIDED THE FOLLOWING ADDITIONAL DIA-
LOGUE:

NORA. . . . Where we could make a real marriage out of our lives together. Goodbye. [*Begins to go.*]

HELMER. Go then! [*Seizes her arm.*] But first you shall see your children for the last time!

NORA. Let me go! I will not see them! I cannot!

HELMER [*draws her over to the door, left*]. You shall see them. [*Opens
the door and says softly.*] Look, there they are asleep, peaceful and
carefree. Tomorrow, when they wake up and call for their mother,
they will be—motherless.

NORA [*trembling*]. Motherless . . . !

HELMER. As you once were.

NORA. Motherless! [*Struggles with herself, lets her traveling bag fall, and
says.*] Oh, this is a sin against myself, but I cannot leave them. [*Half
sinks down by the door.*]

HELMER [*joyfully, but softly*]. Nora!

[*The curtain falls.*]

Oscar Wilde

1854–1900

THE IMPORTANCE OF BEING EARNEST

❖

CHARACTERS

JOHN WORTHING, J.P.
ALGERNON MONCRIEFF
REV. CANON CHASUBLE, D.D.
MERRIMAN, *Butler*.
LANE, *Manservant*.

LADY BRACKNELL.
HON. GWENDOLEN
FAIRFAX.
CECILY CARDEW.
MISS PRISM, *Governess*.

THE SCENES OF THE PLAY.

ACT I.
Algernon Moncrieff's Flat in Half-Moon Street, W.

ACT II.
The Garden at the Manor House, Woolton.

ACT III.
Drawing-Room of the Manor House, Woolton.

Time—The Present.
Place—London.

❖

ACT I

SCENE

Morning-room in ALGERNON'S *flat in Half-Moon Street. The room is luxuriously and artistically furnished. The sound of a piano is heard in the adjoining room.*

[LANE *is arranging afternoon tea on the table, and after the music has ceased,* ALGERNON *enters.*]

ALGERNON. Did you hear what I was playing, Lane?

LANE. I didn't think it polite to listen, sir.

ALGERNON. I'm sorry for that, for your sake. I don't play accurately—anyone can play accurately—but I play with wonderful expression. As far as the piano is concerned, sentiment is my forte. I keep science for Life.

LANE. Yes, sir.

ALGERNON. And, speaking of the science of Life, have you got the cucumber sandwiches cut for Lady Bracknell?

LANE. Yes, sir. [*Hands them on a salver.*]

ALGERNON [*inspects them, takes two, and sits down on the sofa*]. Oh! . . . by the way, Lane, I see from your book that on Thursday night, when Lord Shoreman and Mr. Worthing were dining with me, eight bottles of champagne are entered as having been consumed.

LANE. Yes, sir; eight bottles and a pint.

ALGERNON. Why is it that in a bachelor's establishment the servants invariably drink the champagne? I ask merely for information.

LANE. I attribute it to the superior quality of the wine, sir. I have often observed that in married households the champagne is rarely of a first-rate brand.

ALGERNON. Good Heavens! Is marriage so demoralizing as that?

LANE. I believe it *is* a very pleasant state, sir. I have had very little experience of it myself up to the present. I have only been married once. That was in consequence of a misunderstanding between myself and a young woman.

ALGERNON [*languidly*]. I don't know that I am much interested in your family life, Lane.

LANE. No, sir; it is not a very interesting subject. I never think of it myself.

ALGERNON. Very natural, I am sure. That will do, Lane, thank you.

LANE. Thank you, sir. [LANE *goes out.*]

ALGERNON. Lane's views on marriage seem somewhat lax. Really, if the lower orders don't set us a good example, what on earth is the use of them? They seem, as a class, to have absolutely no sense of moral responsibility.

[*Enter* LANE.]

LANE. Mr. Ernest Worthing.

[*Enter* JACK. LANE *goes out.*]

ALGERNON. How are you, my dear Ernest? What brings you up to town?

JACK. Oh, pleasure, pleasure! What else should bring one anywhere? Eating as usual, I see, Algy!

ALGERNON [*stiffly*]. I believe it is customary in good society to take some slight refreshment at five o'clock. Where have you been since last Thursday?

JACK [*sitting down on the sofa*]. In the country.

ALGERNON. What on earth do you do there?

JACK [*pulling off his gloves*]. When one is in town one amuses oneself. When one is in the country one amuses other people. It is excessively boring.

ALGERNON. And who are the people you amuse?

JACK [*airily*]. Oh, neighbors, neighbors.

ALGERNON. Got nice neighbors in your part of Shropshire?

JACK. Perfectly horrid! Never speak to one of them.

ALGERNON. How immensely you must amuse them! [*Goes over and takes sandwich.*] By the way, Shropshire is your county, is it not?

JACK. Eh? Shropshire? Yes, of course. Hallo! Why all these cups? Why cucumber sandwiches? Why such reckless extravagance in one so young? Who is coming to tea?

ALGERNON. Oh! merely Aunt Augusta and Gwendolen.

JACK. How perfectly delightful!

ALGERNON. Yes, that is all very well; but I am afraid Aunt Augusta won't quite approve of your being here.

JACK. May I ask why?

ALGERNON. My dear fellow, the way you flirt with Gwendolen is perfectly disgraceful. It is almost as bad as the way Gwendolen flirts with you.

JACK. I am in love with Gwendolen. I have come up to town expressly to propose to her.

ALGERNON. I thought you had come for pleasure? . . . I call that business.

JACK. How utterly unromantic you are!

ALGERNON. I really don't see anything romantic in proposing. It is very romantic to be in love. But there is nothing romantic about a definite proposal. Why, one may be accepted. One usually is, I believe. Then the excitement is all over. The very essence of romance is uncertainty. If ever I get married, I'll certainly try to forget the fact.

JACK. I have no doubt about that, dear Algy. The Divorce Court was specially invented for people whose memories are so curiously constituted.

ALGERNON. Oh! there is no use speculating on that subject. Divorces are made in Heaven—[JACK *puts out his hand to take a sandwich.* ALGERNON *at once interferes.*] Please don't touch the cucumber sandwiches. They are ordered specially for Aunt Augusta. [*Takes one and eats it.*]

JACK. Well, you have been eating them all the time.

ALGERNON. That is quite a different matter. She is my aunt. [*Takes plate from below.*] Have some bread and butter. The bread and butter is for Gwendolen. Gwendolen is devoted to bread and butter.

JACK [*advancing to table and helping himself*]. And very good bread and butter it is, too.

ALGERNON. Well, my dear fellow, you need not eat as if you were going to eat it all. You behave as if you were married to her already. You are not married to her already, and I don't think you will ever be.

JACK. Why on earth do you say that?

ALGERNON. Well, in the first place girls never marry the men they flirt with. Girls don't think it right.

JACK. Oh, that is nonsense!

ALGERNON. It isn't. It is a great truth. It accounts for the extraordinary number of bachelors that one sees all over the place. In the second place, I don't give my consent.

JACK. Your consent!

ALGERNON. My dear fellow, Gwendolen is my first cousin. And before I allow you to marry her, you will have to clear up the whole question of Cecily. [*Rings bell.*]

JACK. Cecily! What on earth do you mean? What do you mean, Algy, by Cecily? I don't know anyone of the name of Cecily.
[*Enter* LANE.]

ALGERNON. Bring me that cigarette case Mr. Worthing left in the smoking-room the last time he dined here.

LANE. Yes, sir. [LANE *goes out.*]

JACK. Do you mean to say you have had my cigarette case all this time? I wish to goodness you had let me know. I have been writing frantic letters to Scotland Yard about it. I was very nearly offering a large reward.

ALGERNON. Well, I wish you would offer one. I happen to be more than usually hard up.

JACK. There is no good offering a large reward now that the thing is found.
[*Enter* LANE *with the cigarette case on a salver.* ALGERNON *takes it at once.* LANE *goes out.*]

ALGERNON. I think that is rather mean of you, Ernest, I must say. [*Opens case and examines it.*] However, it makes no matter, for, now that I look at the inscription, I find that the thing isn't yours after all.

JACK. Of course it's mine. [*Moving to him.*] You have seen me with it a hundred times, and you have no right whatsoever to read what is written inside. It is a very ungentlemanly thing to read a private cigarette case.

ALGERNON. Oh! it is absurd to have a hard-and-fast rule about what one should read and what one shouldn't. More than half of modern culture depends on what one shouldn't read.

JACK. I am quite aware of the fact, and I don't propose to discuss modern culture. It isn't the sort of thing one should talk of in private. I simply want my cigarette case back.

ALGERNON. Yes; but this isn't your cigarette case. This cigarette case is a present from someone of the name of Cecily, and you said you didn't know anyone of that name.

JACK. Well, if you want to know, Cecily happens to be my aunt.

ALGERNON. Your aunt!

JACK. Yes. Charming old lady she is, too. Lives at Tunbridge Wells. Just give it back to me, Algy.

ALGERNON [*retreating to back of sofa*]. But why does she call herself little Cecily if she is your aunt and lives at Tunbridge Wells? [*Reading.*] "From little Cecily with her fondest love."

JACK [*moving to sofa and kneeling upon it*]. My dear fellow, what on earth is there in that? Some aunts are tall, some aunts are not tall. That is a matter that surely an aunt may be allowed to decide for herself. You seem to think that every aunt should be exactly like your aunt! That is absurd! For Heaven's sake give me back my cigarette case. [*Follows* ALGERNON *round the room.*]

ALGERNON. Yes. But why does your aunt call you her uncle? "From little Cecily, with her fondest love to her dear Uncle Jack." There is no objection, I admit, to an aunt being a small aunt, but why an aunt, no matter what her size may be, should call her own nephew her uncle, I can't quite make out. Besides, your name isn't Jack at all; it's Ernest.

JACK. It isn't Ernest; it's Jack.

ALGERNON. You have always told me it was Ernest. I have introduced you to everyone as Ernest. You answer to the name of Ernest. You look as if your name was Ernest. You are the most earnest-looking person I ever saw in my life. It is perfectly absurd your saying that your name isn't Ernest. It's on your cards. Here is one of them. [*Taking it from case.*] "Mr. Ernest Worthing, B 4, The Albany." I'll keep this as a proof your name is Ernest if ever you attempt to deny it to me, or to Gwendolen, or to anyone else. [*Puts the card in his pocket.*]

JACK. Well, my name is Ernest in town and Jack in the country, and the cigarette case was given to me in the country.

ALGERNON. Yes, but that does not account for the fact that your small Aunt Cecily, who lives at Tunbridge Wells, calls you her dear uncle. Come, old boy, you had much better have the thing out at once.

JACK. My dear Algy, you talk exactly as if you were a dentist. It is very vulgar to talk like a dentist when one isn't a dentist. It produces a false impression.

ALGERNON. Well, that is exactly what dentists always do. Now, go on! Tell me the whole thing. I may mention that I have always suspected you of being a confirmed and secret Bunburyist; and I am quite sure of it now.

JACK. Bunburyist? What on earth do you mean by a Bunburyist?

ALGERNON. I'll reveal to you the meaning of that incomparable expression as soon as you are kind enough to inform me why you are Ernest in town and Jack in the country.

JACK. Well, produce my cigarette case first.

ALGERNON. Here it is. [*Hands cigarette case.*] Now produce your explanation, and pray make it improbable. [*Sits on sofa.*]

JACK. My dear fellow, there is nothing improbable about my explanation at all. In fact it's perfectly ordinary. Old Mr. Thomas Cardew, who adopted me when I was a little boy, made me in his will guardian to his grand-daughter, Miss Cecily Cardew. Cecily, who addresses

me as her uncle from motives of respect that you could not possibly
appreciate, lives at my place in the country under the charge of her admirable governess, Miss Prism.

ALGERNON. Where is that place in the country, by the way?

JACK. That is nothing to you, dear boy. You are not going to be invited. . . . I may tell you candidly that the place is not in Shropshire.

ALGERNON. I suspected that, my dear fellow! I have Bunburyed all
over Shropshire on two separate occasions. Now, go on. Why are you
Ernest in town and Jack in the country?

JACK. My dear Algy, I don't know whether you will be able to understand my real motives. You are hardly serious enough. When one is
placed in the position of guardian, one has to adopt a very high moral
tone on all subjects. It's one's duty to do so. And as a high moral tone
can hardly be said to conduce very much to either one's health or one's
happiness, in order to get up to town I have always pretended to have a
younger brother of the name of Ernest, who lives in the Albany, and
gets into the most dreadful scrapes. That, my dear Algy, is the whole
truth pure and simple.

ALGERNON. The truth is rarely pure and never simple. Modern life
would be very tedious if it were either, and modern literature a complete impossibility!

JACK. That wouldn't be at all a bad thing.

ALGERNON. Literary criticism is not your forte, my dear fellow. Don't
try it. You should leave that to people who haven't been at a University. They do it so well in the daily papers. What you really are is a
Bunburyist. I was quite right in saying you were a Bunburyist. You
are one of the most advanced Bunburyists I know.

JACK. What on earth do you mean?

ALGERNON. You have invented a very useful younger brother called
Ernest, in order that you may be able to come up to town as often as
you like. I have invented an invaluable permanent invalid called Bunbury, in order that I may be able to go down into the country whenever I choose. Bunbury is perfectly invaluable. If it wasn't for Bunbury's extraordinary bad health, for instance, I wouldn't be able to
dine with you at Willis' tonight, for I have been really engaged to
Aunt Augusta for more than a week.

JACK. I haven't asked you to dine with me anywhere tonight.

ALGERNON. I know. You are absolutely careless about sending out invitations. It is very foolish of you. Nothing annoys people so much as
not receiving invitations.

JACK. You had much better dine with your Aunt Augusta.

ALGERNON. I haven't the smallest intention of doing anything of the
kind. To begin with, I dined there on Monday, and once a week is
quite enough to dine with one's own relatives. In the second place,
whenever I do dine there I am always treated as a member of the fam-

ily, and sent down with either no woman at all, or two. In the third place, I know perfectly well whom she will place me next, tonight. She will place me next Mary Farquhar, who always flirts with her own husband across the dinnertable. That is not very pleasant. Indeed, it is not even decent . . . and that sort of thing is enormously on the increase. The amount of women in London who flirt with their own husbands is perfectly scandalous. It looks so bad. It is simply washing one's clean linen in public. Besides, now that I know you to be a confirmed Bunburyist I naturally want to talk to you about Bunburying. I want to tell you the rules.

JACK. I'm not a Bunburyist at all. If Gwendolen accepts me, I am going to kill my brother, indeed I think I'll kill him in any case. Cecily is a little too much interested in him. It is rather a bore. So I am going to get rid of Ernest. And I strongly advise you to do the same with Mr. . . . with your invalid friend who has the absurd name.

ALGERNON. Nothing will induce me to part with Bunbury, and if you ever get married, which seems to me extremely problematic, you will be very glad to know Bunbury. A man who marries without knowing Bunbury has a very tedious time of it.

JACK. That is nonsense. If I marry a charming girl like Gwendolen, and she is the only girl I ever saw in my life that I would marry, I certainly won't want to know Bunbury.

ALGERNON. Then your wife will. You don't seem to realize, that in married life three is company and two is none.

JACK [*sententiously*]. That, my dear young friend, is the theory that the corrupt French Drama has been propounding for the last fifty years.

ALGERNON. Yes; and that the happy English home has proved in half the time.

JACK. For heaven's sake, don't try to be cynical. It's perfectly easy to be cynical.

ALGERNON. My dear fellow, it isn't easy to be anything now-a-days. There's such a lot of beastly competition about. [*The sound of an electric bell is heard.*] Ah! that must be Aunt Augusta. Only relatives, or creditors, ever ring in that Wagnerian manner. Now, if I get her out of the way for ten minutes, so that you can have an opportunity for proposing to Gwendolen, may I dine with you to-night at Willis'?

JACK. I suppose so, if you want to.

ALGERNON. Yes, but you must be serious about it. I hate people who are not serious about meals. It is so shallow of them.

[*Enter* LANE.]

LANE. Lady Bracknell and Miss Fairfax.

[ALGERNON *goes forward to meet them. Enter* LADY BRACKNELL *and* GWENDOLEN.]

LADY BRACKNELL. Good afternoon, dear Algernon, I hope you are behaving very well.

ALGERNON. I'm feeling very well, Aunt Augusta.

LADY BRACKNELL. That's not quite the same thing. In face the two things rarely go together. [*Sees* JACK *and bows to him with icy coldness.*]

ALGERNON [*to* GWENDOLEN]. Dear me, you are smart!

GWENDOLEN. I am always smart! Aren't I, Mr. Worthing?

JACK. You're quite perfect, Miss Fairfax.

GWENDOLEN. Oh! I hope I am not that. It would leave no room for developments, and I intend to develop in *many directions*. [GWENDOLEN *and* JACK *sit down together in the corner.*]

LADY BRACKNELL. I'm sorry if we are a little late, Algernon, but I was obliged to call on dear Lady Harbury. I hadn't been there since her poor husband's death. I never saw a woman so altered; she looks quite twenty years younger. And now I'll have a cup of tea, and one of those nice cucumber sandwiches you promised me.

ALGERNON. Certainly, Aunt Augusta. [*Goes over to tea-table.*]

LADY BRACKNELL. Won't you come and sit here, Gwendolen?

GWENDOLEN. Thanks, mamma, I'm quite comfortable where I am.

ALGERNON [*picking up empty plate in horror*]. Good heavens! Lane! Why are there no cucumber sandwiches? I ordered them specially.

LANE [*gravely*]. There were no cucumbers in the market this morning, sir. I went down twice.

ALGERNON. No cucumbers!

LANE. No, sir. Not even for ready money.

ALGERNON. That will do, Lane, thank you.

LANE. Thank you, sir. [*Goes out.*]

ALGERNON. I am greatly distressed, Aunt Augusta, about there being no cucumbers, not even for ready money.

LADY BRACKNELL. It really makes no matter, Algernon. I had some crumpets with Lady Harbury, who seems to me to be living entirely for pleasure now.

ALGERNON. I hear her hair has turned quite gold from grief.

LADY BRACKNELL. It certainly has changed its color. From what cause I, of course, cannot say. [ALGERNON *crosses and hands tea.*] Thank you. I've quite a treat for you tonight, Algernon. I am going to send you down with Mary Farquhar. She is such a nice woman, and so attentive to her husband. It's delightful to watch them.

ALGERNON. I am afraid, Aunt Augusta, I shall have to give up the pleasure of dining with you tonight after all.

LADY BRACKNELL [*frowning*]. I hope not, Algernon. It would put my table completely out. Your uncle would have to dine upstairs. Fortunately he is accustomed to that.

ALGERNON. It is a great bore, and, I need hardly say, a terrible disappointment to me, but the fact is I have just had a telegram to say that my poor friend Bunbury is very ill again. [*Exchanges glances with* JACK.] They seem to think I should be with him.

LADY BRACKNELL. It is very strange. This Mr. Bunbury seems to suffer from curiously bad health.

ALGERNON. Yes, poor Bunbury is a dreadful invalid.

LADY BRACKNELL. Well, I must say, Algernon, that I think it is high time that Mr. Bunbury made up his mind whether he was going to live or to die. This shilly-shallying with the question is absurd. Nor do I in any way approve of the modern sympathy with invalids. I consider it morbid. Illness of any kind is hardly a thing to be encouraged in others. Health is the primary duty of life. I am always telling that to your poor uncle, but he never seems to take much notice . . . as far as any improvement in his ailment goes. I should be much obliged if you would ask Mr. Bunbury, from me, to be kind enough not to have a relapse on Saturday, for I rely on you to arrange my music for me. It is my last reception and one wants something that will encourage conversation, particularly at the end of the season when everyone has practically said whatever they had to say, which, in most cases, was probably not much.

ALGERNON. I'll speak to Bunbury, Aunt Augusta, if he is still conscious, and I think I can promise you he'll be all right by Saturday. You see, if one plays good music, people don't listen, and if one plays bad music people don't talk. But I'll run over the program I've drawn out, if you will kindly come into the next room for a moment.

LADY BRACKNELL. Thank you, Algernon. It is very thoughtful of you. [*Rising, and following* ALGERNON.] I'm sure the program will be delightful, after a few expurgations. French songs I cannot possibly allow. People always seem to think that they are improper, and either look shocked, which is vulgar, or laugh, which is worse. But German sounds a thoroughly respectable language, and indeed, I believe is so. Gwendolen, you will accompany me.

GWENDOLEN. Certainly, mamma.

[LADY BRACKNELL *and* ALGERNON *go into the music-room,* GWENDOLEN *remains behind.*]

JACK. Charming day it has been, Miss Fairfax.

GWENDOLEN. Pray don't talk to me about the weather, Mr. Worthing. Whenever people talk to me about the weather, I always feel quite certain that they mean something else. And that makes me so nervous.

JACK. I do mean something else.

GWENDOLEN. I thought so. In fact, I am never wrong.

JACK. And I would like to be allowed to take advantage of Lady Bracknell's temporary absence . . .

GWENDOLEN. I would certainly advise you to do so. Mamma has a way of coming back suddenly into a room that I have often had to speak to her about.

JACK [*nervously*]. Miss Fairfax, ever since I met you I have admired you more than any girl . . . I have ever met since . . . I met you.

GWENDOLEN. Yes, I am quite aware of the fact. And I often wish that in public, at any rate, you had been more demonstrative. For me you have always had an irresistible fascination. Even before I met you I was far from indifferent to you. [JACK *looks at her in amazement.*] We live, as I hope you know, Mr. Worthing, in an age of ideals. The fact is constantly mentioned in the more expensive monthly magazines, and has reached the provincial pulpits I am told : and my ideal has always been to love some one of the name of Ernest. There is something in that name that inspires absolute confidence. The moment Algernon first mentioned to me that he had a friend called Ernest, I knew I was destined to love you.

JACK. You really love me, Gwendolen?

GWENDOLEN. Passionately!

JACK. Darling! You don't know how happy you've made me.

GWENDOLEN. My own Ernest!

JACK. But you don't really mean to say that you couldn't love me if my name wasn't Ernest?

GWENDOLEN. But your name is Ernest.

JACK. Yes, I know it is. But supposing it was something else? Do you mean to say you couldn't love me then?

GWENDOLEN [*glibly*]. Ah! that is clearly a metaphysical speculation, and like most metaphysical speculations has very little reference at all to the actual facts of real life, as we know them.

JACK. Personally, darling, to speak quite candidly, I don't much care about the name of Ernest . . . I don't think that name suits me at all.

GWENDOLEN. It suits you perfectly. It is a divine name. It has a music of its own. It produces vibrations.

JACK. Well, really, Gwendolen, I must say that I think there are lots of other much nicer names. I think, Jack, for instance, a charming name.

GWENDOLEN. Jack? . . . No, there is very little music in the name Jack, if any at all, indeed. It does not thrill. It produces absolutely no vibrations. . . . I have known several Jacks, and they all, without exception, were more than usually plain. Besides, Jack is a notorious domesticity for John! And I pity any woman who is married to a man called John. She would probably never be allowed to know the entrancing pleasure of a single moment's solitude. The only really safe name is Ernest.

JACK. Gwendolen, I must get christened at once—I mean we must get married at once. There is no time to be lost.

GWENDOLEN. Married, Mr. Worthing?

JACK [*astounded*]. Well . . . surely. You know that I love you, and you led me to believe, Miss Fairfax, that you were not absolutely indifferent to me.

GWENDOLEN. I adore you. But you haven't proposed to me yet. Nothing has been said at all about marriage. The subject has not even been touched on.

JACK. Well . . . may I propose to you now?

GWENDOLEN. I think it would be an admirable opportunity. And to spare you any possible disappointment, Mr. Worthing, I think it only fair to tell you quite frankly beforehand that I am fully determined to accept you.

JACK. Gwendolen!

GWENDOLEN. Yes, Mr. Worthing, what have you got to say to me?

JACK. You know what I have got to say to you.

GWENDOLEN. Yes, but you don't say it.

JACK. Gwendolen, will you marry me? [*Goes on his knees.*]

GWENDOLEN. Of course I will, darling. How long you have been about it! I am afraid you have had very little experience in how to propose.

JACK. My own one, I have never loved anyone in the world but you.

GWENDOLEN. Yes, but men often propose for practice. I know my brother Gerald does. All my girl-friends tell me so. What wonderfully blue eyes you have, Ernest! They are quite, quite blue. I hope you will always look at me just like that, especially when there are other people present.

[*Enter* LADY BRACKNELL.]

LADY BRACKNELL. Mr. Worthing! Rise, sir, from this semi-recumbent posture. It is most indecorous.

GWENDOLEN. Mamma! [*He tries to rise; she restrains him.*] I must beg you to retire. This is no place for you. Besides, Mr. Worthing has not quite finished yet.

LADY BRACKNELL. Finished what, may I ask?

GWENDOLEN. I am engaged to Mr. Worthing, mamma. [*They rise together.*]

LADY BRACKNELL. Pardon me, you are not engaged to anyone. When you do become engaged to some one, I, or your father, should his health permit him, will inform you of the fact. An engagement should come on a young girl as a surprise, pleasant or unpleasant, as the case may be. It is hardly a matter that she could be allowed to arrange for herself. . . . And now I have a few questions to put to you, Mr. Worthing. While I am making these inquiries, you, Gwendolen, will wait for me below in the carriage

GWENDOLEN [*reproachfully*]. Mamma!

LADY BRACKNELL. In the carriage, Gwendolen! [GWENDOLEN *goes to the door. She and* JACK *blow kisses to each other behind* LADY BRACKNELL'S *back.* LADY BRACKNELL *looks vaguely about as if she could not understand what the noise was. Finally turns round.*] Gwendolen, the carriage!

GWENDOLEN. Yes, mamma. [*Goes out, looking back at* JACK.]

LADY BRACKNELL [*sitting down*]. You can take a seat, Mr. Worthing. [*Looks in her pocket for note-book and pencil.*]

JACK. Thank you, Lady Bracknell, I prefer standing.

LADY BRACKNELL [*pencil and note-book in hand*]. I feel bound to tell you that you are not down on my list of eligible young men, although I have the same list as the dear Duchess of Bolton has. We work together, in fact. However, I am quite ready to enter your name, should your answers be what a really affectionate mother requires. Do you smoke?

JACK. Well, yes, I must admit I smoke.

LADY BRACKNELL. I am glad to hear it. A man should always have an occupation of some kind. There are far too many idle men in London as it is. How old are you?

JACK. Twenty-nine.

LADY BRACKNELL. A very good age to be married at. I have always been of opinion that a man who desires to get married should know either everything or nothing. Which do you know?

JACK [*after some hesitation*]. I know nothing, Lady Bracknell.

LADY BRACKNELL. I am pleased to hear it. I do not approve of anything that tampers with natural ignorance. Ignorance is like a delicate exotic fruit; touch it and the bloom is gone. The whole theory of modern education is radically unsound. Fortunately in England, at any rate, education produces no effect whatsoever. If it did, it would prove a serious danger to the upper classes, and probably lead to acts of violence in Grosvenor Square. What is your income?

JACK. Between seven and eight thousand a year.

LADY BRACKNELL [*makes a note in her book*]. In land, or in investments?

JACK. In investments, chiefly.

LADY BRACKNELL. That is satisfactory. What between the duties expected of one during one's life-time, and the duties exacted from one after one's death, land has ceased to be either a profit or a pleasure. It gives one position, and prevents one from keeping it up. That's all that can be said about land.

JACK. I have a country house with some land, of course, attached to it, about fifteen hundred acres, I believe; but I don't depend on that for my real income. In fact, as far as I can make out, the poachers are the only people who make anything out of it.

LADY BRACKNELL. A country house! How many bedrooms? Well, that point can be cleared up afterwards. You have a town house, I hope? A girl with a simple, unspoiled nature, like Gwendolen, could hardly be expected to reside in the country.

JACK. Well, I own a house in Belgrave Square, but it is let by the year to Lady Bloxham. Of course, I can get it back whenever I like, at six months' notice.

LADY BRACKNELL. Lady Bloxham? I don't know her.

JACK. Oh, she goes about very little. She is a lady considerably advanced in years.

LADY BRACKNELL. Ah, now-a-days that is no guarantee of respectability of character. What number in Belgrave Square?

JACK. 149.

LADY BLACKNELL [*shaking her head*]. The unfashionable side. I thought there was something. However, that could easily be altered.

JACK. Do you mean the fashion, or the side?

LADY BLACKNELL [*sternly*]. Both, if necessary, I presume. What are your politics?

JACK. Well, I am afraid I really have none. I am a Liberal Unionist.

LADY BRACKNELL. Oh, they count as Tories. They dine with us. Or come in the evening, at any rate. Now to minor matters. Are your parents living?

JACK. I have lost both my parents.

LADY BRACKNELL. Both? . . . That seems like carelessness. Who was your father? He was evidently a man of some wealth. Was he born in what the Radical papers call the purple of commerce, or did he rise from the ranks of the aristocracy?

JACK. I am afraid I really don't know. The fact is, Lady Bracknell, I said I had lost my parents. It would be nearer the truth to say that my parents seem to have lost me . . . I don't actually know who I am by birth. I was . . . well, I was found.

LADY BRACKNELL. Found!

JACK. The late Mr. Thomas Cardew, an old gentleman of a very charitable and kindly disposition, found me, and gave me the name of Worthing, because he happened to have a first-class ticket for Worthing in his pocket at the time. Worthing is a place in Sussex. It is a seaside resort.

LADY BRACKNELL. Where did the charitable gentleman who had a first-class ticket for this seaside resort find you?

JACK [*gravely*]. In a hand-bag.

LADY BRACKNELL. A hand-bag?

JACK [*very seriously*]. Yes, Lady Bracknell. I was in a hand-bag—a somewhat large, black leather hand-bag, with handles to it—an ordinary hand-bag in fact.

LADY BRACKNELL. In what locality did this Mr. James, or Thomas, Cardew come across this ordinary hand-bag?

JACK. In the cloak-room at Victoria Station. It was given to him in mistake for his own.

LADY BRACKNELL. The cloak-room at Victoria Station?

JACK. Yes. The Brighton line.

LADY BRACKNELL. The line is immaterial. Mr. Worthing, I confess I feel somewhat bewildered by what you have just told me. To be born, or at any rate bred, in a hand-bag, whether it had handles or not,

seems to me to display a contempt for the ordinary decencies of family
life that remind one of the worst excesses of the French Revolution.
And I presume you know what that unfortunate movement led to? As
for the particular locality in which the handbag was found, a cloak-
room at a railway station might serve to conceal a social indiscretion
—has probably, indeed, been used for that purpose before now—but it
could hardly be regarded as an assured basis for a recognized position
in good society.

JACK. May I ask you then what you would advise me to do? I need
hardly say I would do anything in the world to ensure Gwendolen's
happiness.

LADY BRACKNELL. I would strongly advise you, Mr. Worthing, to
try and acquire some relations as soon as possible, and to make a
definite effort to produce at any rate one parent, of either sex, before
the season is quite over.

JACK. Well, I don't see how I could possibly manage to do that. I can
produce the hand-bag at any moment. It is in my dressing-room at
home. I really think that should satisfy you, Lady Bracknell.

LADY BRACKNELL. Me, sir! What has it to do with me? You can
hardly imagine that I and Lord Bracknell would dream of allowing our
only daughter—a girl brought up with the utmost care—to marry into
a cloakroom, and form an alliance with a parcel? Good morning, Mr.
Worthing!

[LADY BRACKNELL *sweeps out in majestic indignation.*]

JACK. Good morning! [ALGERNON, *from the other room, strikes up the
Wedding March.* JACK *looks perfectly furious, and goes to the door.*] For
goodness' sake don't play that ghastly tune, Algy! How idiotic you are!
[*The music stops, and* ALGERNON *enters cheerily.*]

ALGERNON. Didn't it go off all right, old boy? You don't mean to say
Gwendolen refused you? I know it is a way she has. She is always refusing people. I think it is most ill-natured of her.

JACK. Oh, Gwendolen is as right as a trivet. As far as she is concerned,
we are engaged. Her mother is perfectly unbearable. Never met such
a Gorgon . . . I don't really know what a Gorgon is like, but I am
quite sure that Lady Bracknell is one. In any case, she is a monster,
without being a myth, which is rather unfair. . . . I beg your pardon,
Algy, I suppose I shouldn't talk about your own aunt in that way before you.

ALGERNON. My dear boy, I love hearing my relations abused. It is the
only thing that makes me put up with them at all. Relations are simply
a tedious pack of people, who haven't got the remotest knowledge of
how to live, nor the smallest instinct about when to die.

JACK. Oh, that is nonsense!

ALGERNON. It isn't!

JACK. Well, I won't argue about the matter. You always want to argue
about things.

ALGERNON. That is exactly what things were originally made for.

JACK. Upon my word, if I thought that, I'd shoot myself. . . . [*A pause.*] You don't think there is any chance of Gwendolen becoming like her mother in about a hundred and fifty years, do you, Algy?

ALGERNON. All women become like their mothers. That is their tragedy. No man does. That's his.

JACK. Is that clever?

ALGERNON. It is perfectly phrased! and quite as true as any observation in civilized life should be.

JACK. I am sick to death of cleverness. Everybody is clever now-a-days. you can't go anywhere without meeting clever people. The thing has become an absolute public nuisance. I wish to goodness we had a few fools left.

ALGERNON. We have.

JACK. I should extremely like to meet them. What do they talk about?

ALGERNON. The fools? Oh! about the clever people, of course.

JACK. What fools!

ALGERNON. By the way, did you tell Gwendolen the truth about your being Ernest in town, and Jack in the country?

JACK [*in a very patronizing manner*]. My dear fellow, the truth isn't quite the sort of thing one tells to a nice, sweet, refined girl. What extraordinary ideas you have about the way to behave to a woman!

ALGERNON. The only way to behave to a woman is to make love to her, if she is pretty, and to someone else if she is plain.

JACK. Oh, that is nonsense.

ALGERNON. What about your brother? What about the profligate Ernest?

JACK. Oh, before the end of the week I shall have got rid of him. I'll say he died in Paris of apoplexy. Lots of people die of apoplexy, quite suddenly, don't they?

ALGERNON. Yes, but it's hereditary, my dear fellow. It's a sort of thing that runs in families. You had much better say a severe chill.

JACK. You are sure a severe chill isn't hereditary, or anything of that kind?

ALGERNON. Of course it isn't!

JACK. Very well, then. My poor brother Ernest is carried off suddenly in Paris, by a severe chill. That gets rid of him.

ALGERNON. But I thought you said that . . . Miss Cardew was a little too much interested in your poor brother Ernest? Won't she feel his loss a good deal?

JACK. Oh, that is all right. Cecily is not a silly, romantic girl, I am glad to say. She has got a capital appetite, goes for long walks, and pays no attention at all to her lessons.

ALGERNON. I would rather like to see Cecily.

JACK. I will take very good care you never do. She is excessively pretty, and she is only just eighteen.

ALGERNON. Have you told Gwendolen yet that you have an excessively pretty ward who is only just eighteen?

JACK. Oh! one doesn't blurt these things out to people. Cecily and Gwendolen are perfectly certain to be extremely great friends. I'll bet you anything you like that half an hour after they have met, they will be calling each other sister.

ALGERNON. Women only do that when they have called each other a lot of other things first. Now, my dear boy, if we want to get a good table at Willis', we really must go and dress. Do you know it is nearly seven?

JACK [*irritably*]. Oh! it always is nearly seven.

ALGERNON. Well, I'm hungry.

JACK. I never knew you when you weren't. . . .

ALGERNON. What shall we do after dinner? Go to a theater?

JACK. Oh, no! I loathe listening.

ALGERNON. Well, let us go to the Club?

JACK. Oh, no! I hate talking.

ALGERNON. Well, we might trot round to the Empire at ten?

JACK. Oh, no! I can't bear looking at things. It is so silly.

ALGERNON. Well, what shall we do?

JACK. Nothing!

ALGERNON. It is awfully hard work doing nothing. However, I don't mind hard work where there is no definite object of any kind.
    [*Enter* LANE.]

LANE. Miss Fairfax.
    [*Enter* GWENDOLEN. LANE *goes out.*]

ALGERNON. Gwendolen, upon my word!

GWENDOLEN. Algy, kindly turn your back. I have something very particular to say to Mr. Worthing.

ALGERNON. Really, Gwendolen, I don't think I can allow this at all.

GWENDOLEN. Algy, you always adopt a strictly immoral attitude towards life. You are not quite old enough to do that. [ALGERNON *retires to the fireplace.*]

JACK. My own darling!

GWENDOLEN. Ernest, we may never be married. From the expression on mamma's face I fear we never shall. Few parents now-a-days pay any regard to what their children say to them. The old-fashioned respect for the young is fast dying out. Whatever influence I ever had over mamma, I lost at the age of three. But although she may prevent us from becoming man and wife, and I may marry someone else, and marry often, nothing that she can possibly do can alter my eternal devotion to you.

JACK. Dear Gwendolen.

GWENDOLEN. The story of your romantic origin, as related to me by mamma, with unpleasing comments, has naturally stirred the deeper fibers of my nature. Your Christian name has an irresistible fascination. The simplicity of your character makes you exquisitely incomprehensible to me. Your town address at the Albany I have. What is your address in the country?

JACK. The Manor House, Woolton, Hertfordshire.

[ALGERNON, *who has been carefully listening, smiles to himself, and writes the address on his shirt-cuff. Then picks up the Railway Guide.*]

GWENDOLEN. There is a good postal service, I suppose? It may be necessary to do something desperate. That, of course, will require serious consideration. I will communicate with you daily.

JACK. My own one!

GWENDOLEN. How long do you remain in town?

JACK. Till Monday.

GWENDOLEN. Good! Algy, you may turn round now.

ALGERNON. Thanks, I've turned round already.

GWENDOLEN. You may also ring the bell.

JACK. You will let me see you to your carriage, my own darling?

GWENDOLEN. Certainly.

JACK [*to* LANE, *who now enters*]. I will see Miss Fairfax out.

LANE. Yes, sir.

[JACK *and* GWENDOLEN *go off*. LANE *presents several letters on a salver to* ALGERNON. *It is to be surmised that they are bills, as* ALGERNON, *after looking at the envelopes, tears them up.*]

ALGERNON. A glass of sherry, Lane.

LANE. Yes, sir.

ALGERNON. Tomorrow, Lane, I'm going Bunburying.

LANE. Yes, sir.

ALGERNON. I shall probably not be back till Monday. You can put up my dress clothes, my smoking jacket, and all the Bunbury suits . . .

LANE. Yes, sir. [*Handing sherry.*]

ALGERNON. I hope tomorrow will be a fine day, Lane.

LANE. It never is, sir.

ALGERNON. Lane, you're a perfect pessimist.

LANE. I do my best to give satisfaction, sir.

[*Enter* JACK. LANE *goes off.*]

JACK. There's a sensible, intellectual girl! the only girl I ever cared for in my life. [ALGERNON *is laughing immoderately.*] What on earth are you so amused at?

ALGERNON. Oh, I'm a little anxious about poor Bunbury, that's all.

JACK. If you don't take care, your friend Bunbury will get you into a serious scrape some day.

ALGERNON. I love scrapes. They are the only things that are never serious.

JACK. Oh, that's nonsense, Algy. You never talk anything but nonsense.

ALGERNON. Nobody ever does.

[JACK *looks indignantly at him, and leaves the room.* ALGERNON *lights a cigarette, reads his shirt-cuff, and smiles.*]

ACT DROP

ACT II

SCENE

Garden at the Manor House. A flight of gray stone steps leads up to the house. The garden, an old-fashioned one, full of roses. Time of year, July. Basket chairs, and a table covered with books, are set under a large yew tree.

[MISS PRISM *discovered seated at the table.* CECILY *is at the back watering flowers.*]

MISS PRISM [*calling*]. Cecily, Cecily! Surely such a utilitarian occupation as the watering of flowers is rather Moulton's duty than yours? Especially at a moment when intellectual pleasures await you. Your German grammar is on the table. Pray open it at page fifteen. We will repeat yesterday's lesson.

CECILY [*coming over very slowly*]. But I don't like German. It isn't at all a becoming language. I know perfectly well that I look quite plain after my German lesson.

MISS PRISM. Child, you know how anxious your guardian is that you should improve yourself in every way. He laid particular stress on your German, as he was leaving for town yesterday. Indeed, he always lays stress on your German when he is leaving for town.

CECILY. Dear Uncle Jack is so very serious! Sometimes he is so serious that I think he cannot be quite well.

MISS PRISM [*drawing herself up*]. Your guardian enjoys the best of health, and his gravity of demeanor is especially to be commended in one so comparatively young as he is. I know no one who has a higher sense of duty and responsibility.

CECILY. I suppose that is why he often looks a little bored when we three are together.

MISS PRISM. Cecily! I am surprised at you. Mr. Worthing has many troubles in his life. Idle merriment and triviality would be out of place in his conversation. You must remember his constant anxiety about that unfortunate young man, his brother.

CECILY. I wish Uncle Jack would allow that unfortunate young man, his brother, to come down here sometimes. We might have a good influence over him, Miss Prism. I am sure you certainly would. You know German, and geology, and things of that kind influence a man very much. [CECILY *begins to write in her diary.*]

MISS PRISM [*shaking her head*]. I do not think that even I could produce any effect on a character that, according to his own brother's admission, is irretrievably weak and vacillating. Indeed, I am not sure that I would desire to reclaim him. I am not in favor of this modern mania for turning bad people into good people at a moment's notice. As a man sows so let him reap. You must put away your diary, Cecily. I really don't see why you should keep a diary at all.

CECILY. I keep a dairy in order to enter the wonderful secrets of my life. If I didn't write them down I should probably forget all about them.

MISS PRISM. Memory, my dear Cecily, is the diary that we all carry about with us.

CECILY. Yes, but it usually chronicles the things that have never happened, and couldn't possibly have happened. I believe that Memory is responsible for nearly all the three-volume novels that Mudie[1] sends us.

MISS PRISM. Do not speak slightingly of the three-volume novel, Cecily. I wrote one myself in earlier days.

CECILY. Did you really, Miss Prism? How wonderfully clever you are! I hope it did not end happily? I don't like novels that end happily. They depress me so much.

MISS PRISM. The good ended happily, and the bad unhappily. That is what Fiction means.

CECILY. I suppose so. But it seems very unfair. And was your novel ever published?

MISS PRISM. Alas! no. The manuscript unfortunately was abandoned. I use the word in the sense of lost or mislaid. To your work, child, these speculations are profitless.

CECILY [*smiling*]. But I see dear Dr. Chasuble coming up through the garden.

MISS PRISM [*rising and advancing*]. Dr. Chasuble! This is indeed a pleasure.

[*Enter* CANON CHASUBLE.]

CHASUBLE. And how are we this morning? Miss Prism, you are, I trust, well?

CECILY. Miss Prism has just been complaining of a slight headache. I think it would do her so much good to have a short stroll with you in the park, Dr. Chasuble.

MISS PRISM. Cecily, I have not mentioned anything about a headache.

---

[1] Mudie's Lending Library

CECILY. No, dear Miss Prism, I know that, but I felt instinctively that you had a headache. Indeed I was thinking about that, and not about my German lesson when the Rector came in.

CHASUBLE. I hope, Cecily, you are not inattentive.

CECILY. Oh, I am afraid I am.

CHASUBLE. That is strange. Were I fortunate enough to be Miss Prism's pupil, I would hang upon her lips. [MISS PRISM *glares*.] I spoke metaphorically.—My metaphor was drawn from bees. Ahem! Mr. Worthing, I suppose, has not returned from town yet?

MISS PRISM. We do not expect him till Monday afternoon.

CHASUBLE. Ah yes, he usually likes to spend his Sunday in London. He is not one of those whose sole aim is enjoyment, as, by all accounts, that unfortunate young man, his brother, seems to be. But I must not disturb Egeria[2] and her pupil any longer.

MISS PRISM. Egeria? My name is Lætitia, Doctor.

CHASUBLE [*bowing*]. A classical allusion merely, drawn from the Pagan authors. I shall see you both no doubt at Evensong.

MISS PRISM. I think, dear Doctor, I will have a stroll with you. I find I have a headache after all, and a walk might do it good.

CHASUBLE. With pleasure, Miss Prism, with pleasure. We might go as far as the schools and back.

MISS PRISM. That would be delightful. Cecily, you will read your Political Economy in my absence. The chapter on the Fall of the Rupee you may omit. It is somewhat too sensational. Even these metallic problems have their melodramatic side.

[*Goes down the garden with* DR. CHASUBLE.]

CECILY [*picks up books and throws them back on table*]. Horrid Political Economy! Horrid Geography! Horrid, horrid German!

[*Enter* MERRIMAN *with a card on a salver*.]

MERRIMAN. Mr. Ernest Worthing has just driven over from the station. He has brought his luggage with him.

CECILY [*takes the card and reads it*]. "Mr. Ernest Worthing, B 4 The Albany, W." Uncle Jack's brother! Did you tell him Mr. Worthing was in town?

MERRIMAN. Yes, Miss. He seemed very much disappointed. I mentioned that you and Miss Prism were in the garden. He said he was anxious to speak to you privately for a moment.

CECILY. Ask Mr. Ernest Worthing to come here. I suppose you had better talk to the housekeeper about a room for him.

MERRIMAN. Yes, Miss. [MERRIMAN *goes off*.]

CECILY. I have never met any really wicked person before. I feel rather frightened. I am so afraid he will look just like everyone else.

[*Enter* ALGERNON, *very gay and debonair*.]

[2] a Roman nymph noted for wisdom

He does!

ALGERNON [*raising his hat*]. You are my little Cousin Cecily, I'm sure.

CECILY. You are under some strange mistake. I am not little. In fact, I am more than usually tall for my age. [ALGERNON *is rather taken aback.*] But I am your Cousin Cecily. You, I see from your card, are Uncle Jack's brother, my Cousin Ernest, my wicked Cousin Ernest.

ALGERNON. Oh! I am not really wicked at all, Cousin Cecily. You mustn't think that I am wicked.

CECILY. If you are not, then you have certainly been deceiving us all in a very inexcusable manner. I hope you have not been leading a double life, pretending to be wicked and being really good all the time. That would be hypocrisy.

ALGERNON [*looks at her in amazement*]. Oh! of course I have been rather reckless.

CECILY. I am glad to hear it.

ALGERNON. In fact, now you mention the subject, I have been very bad in my own small way.

CECILY. I don't think you should be so proud of that, though I am sure it must have been very pleasant.

ALGERNON. It is much pleasanter being here with you.

CECILY. I can't understand how you are here at all. Uncle Jack won't be back till Monday afternoon.

ALGERNON. That is a great disappointment. I am obliged to go up by the first train on Monday morning. I have a business appointment that I am anxious . . . to miss.

CECILY. Couldn't you miss it anywhere but in London?

ALGERNON. No; the appointment is in London.

CECILY. Well, I know, of course, how important it is not to keep a business engagement, if one wants to retain any sense of the beauty of life, but still I think you had better wait till Uncle Jack arrives. I know he wants to speak to you about your emigrating.

ALGERNON. About my what?

CECILY. Your emigrating. He has gone up to buy your outfit.

ALGERNON. I certainly wouldn't let Jack buy my outfit. He has no taste in neckties at all.

CECILY. I don't think you will require neckties. Uncle Jack is sending you to Australia.

ALGERNON. Australia! I'd sooner die.

CECILY. Well, he said at dinner on Wednesday night, that you would have to choose between this world, the next world, and Australia.

ALGERNON. Oh, well! The accounts I have received of Australia and the next world, are not particularly encouraging. This world is good enough for me, Cousin Cecily.

CECILY. Yes, but are you good enough for it?

ALGERNON. I'm afraid I'm not that. That is why I want you to reform me. You might make that your mission, if you don't mind, Cousin Cecily.

CECILY. I'm afraid I've not time, this afternoon.

ALGERNON. Well, would you mind my reforming myself this afternoon?

CECILY. That is rather Quixotic of you. But I think you should try.

ALGERNON. I will. I feel better already.

CECILY. You are looking a little worse.

ALGERNON. That is because I am hungry.

CECILY. How thoughtless of me. I should have remembered that when one is going to lead an entirely new life, one requires regular and wholesome meals. Won't you come in?

ALGERNON. Thank you. Might I have a button-hole first? I never have any appetite unless I have a button-hole first.

CECILY. A Maréchal Niel? [*Picks up scissors.*]

ALGERNON. No, I'd sooner have a pink rose.

CECILY. Why? [*Cuts a flower.*]

ALGERNON. Because you are like a pink rose, Cousin Cecily.

CECILY. I don't think it can be right for you to talk to me like that. Miss Prism never says such things to me.

ALGERNON. Then Miss Prism is a short-sighted old lady. [CECILY *puts the rose in his button-hole.*] You are the prettiest girl I ever saw.

CECILY. Miss Prism says that all good looks are a snare.

ALGERNON. They are a snare that every sensible man would like to be caught in.

CECILY. Oh! I don't think I would care to catch a sensible man. I shouldn't know what to talk to him about.

[*They pass into the house.* MISS PRISM *and* DR. CHAUSABLE *return.*]

MISS PRISM. You are too much alone, dear Dr. Chausable. You should get married. A misanthrope I can understand—a womanthrope, never!

CHAUSABLE [*with a scholar's shudder*]. Believe me, I do not deserve so neologistic a phrase. The precept as well as the practice of the Primitive Church was distinctly against matrimony.

MISS PRISM [*sententiously*]. That is obviously the reason why the Primitive Church has not lasted up to the present day. And you do not seem to realize, dear Doctor, that by persistently remaining single, a man converts himself into a permanent public temptation. Men should be careful; this very celibacy leads weaker vessels astray.

CHAUSABLE. But is a man not equally attractive when married?

MISS PRISM. No married man is ever attractive except to his wife.

CHAUSABLE. And often, I've been told, not even to her.

MISS PRISM. That depends on the intellectual sympathies of the woman. Maturity can always be depended on. Ripeness can be trusted. Young women are green. [DR. CHAUSABLE *starts.*] I spoke horticulturally. My metaphor was drawn from fruits. But where is Cecily?

CHASUBLE. Perhaps she followed us to the schools.

[*Enter* JACK *slowly from the back of the garden. He is dressed in the deepest mourning, with crape hat-band and black gloves.*]

MISS PRISM. Mr. Worthing!

CHASUBLE. Mr. Worthing?

MISS PRISM. This is indeed a surprise. We did not look for you till Monday afternoon.

JACK [*shakes* MISS PRISM'S *hand in a tragic manner*]. I have returned sooner than I expected. Dr. Chasuble, I hope you are well?

CHASUBLE. Dear Mr. Worthing, I trust this garb of woe does not betoken some terrible calamity?

JACK. My brother.

MISS PRISM. More shameful debts and extravagance?

CHASUBLE. Still leading his life of pleasure?

JACK [*shaking his head*]. Dead.

CHASUBLE. Your brother Ernest dead?

JACK. Quite dead.

MISS PRISM. What a lesson for him! I trust he will profit by it.

CHASUBLE. Mr. Worthing, I offer you my sincere condolence. You have at least the consolation of knowing that you were always the most generous and forgiving of brothers.

JACK. Poor Ernest! He had many faults, but it is a sad, sad blow.

CHASUBLE. Very sad indeed. Were you with him at the end?

JACK. No. He died abroad; in Paris, in fact. I had a telegram last night from the manager of the Grand Hotel.

CHASUBLE. Was the cause of death mentioned?

JACK. A severe chill, it seems.

MISS PRISM. As a man sows, so shall he reap.

CHASUBLE [*raising his hand*]. Charity, dear Miss Prism, charity! None of us are perfect. I myself am peculiarly susceptible to drafts. Will the interment take place here?

JACK. No. He seems to have expressed a desire to be buried in Paris.

CHASUBLE. In Paris! [*Shakes his head.*] I fear that hardly points to any very serious state of mind at the last. You would no doubt wish me to make some slight allusion to this tragic domestic affliction next Sunday. [JACK *presses his hand convulsively.*] My sermon on the meaning of the manna in the wilderness can be adapted to almost any occasion, joyful, or, as in the present case, distressing. [*All sigh.*] I have preached it at harvest celebrations, christenings, confirmations, on days of humiliation and festal days. The last time I delivered it was in the Cathedral, as a charity sermon on behalf of the Society for the Prevention of Discontentment among the Upper Orders. The Bishop, who was present, was much struck by some of the analogies I drew.

JACK. Ah, that reminds me, you mentioned christenings I think, Dr.

Chasuble? I suppose you know how to christen all right? [DR.
CHASUBLE *looks astounded.*] I mean, of course, you are continually
christening, aren't you?

MISS PRISM. It is, I regret to say, one of the Rector's most constant
duties in this parish. I have often spoken to the poorer classes on the
subject. But they don't seem to know what thrift is.

CHASUBLE. But is there any particular infant in whom you are interested, Mr. Worthing? Your brother was, I believe, unmarried, was
he not?

JACK. Oh, yes.

MISS PRISM [*bitterly*]. People who live entirely for pleasure usually
are.

JACK. But it is not for any child, dear Doctor. I am very fond of children. No! the fact is, I would like to be christened myself, this afternoon, if you have nothing better to do.

CHASUBLE. But surely, Mr. Worthing, you have been christened already?

JACK. I don't remember anything about it.

CHASUBLE. But have you any grave doubts on the subject?

JACK. I certainly intend to have. Of course. I don't know if the thing
would bother you in any way, or if you think I am a little too old
now.

CHASUBLE. Not at all. The sprinkling, and, indeed, the immersion of
adults is a perfectly canonical practice.

JACK. Immersion!

CHASUBLE. You need have no apprehensions. Sprinkling is all that is
necessary, or indeed I think advisable. Our weather is so changeable.
At what hour would you wish the ceremony performed?

JACK. Oh, I might trot around about five if that would suit you.

CHASUBLE. Perfectly, perfectly! In fact I have two similar ceremonies
to perform at that time. A case of twins that occurred recently in one
of the outlying cottages on your own estate. Poor Jenkins the carter,
a most hard-working man.

JACK. Oh! I don't see much fun in being christened along with other
babies. It would be childish. Would half-past five do?

CHASUBLE. Admirably! Admirably! Admirably! [*Takes out watch.*]
And now, dear Mr. Worthing, I will not intrude any longer into a
house of sorrow. I would merely beg you not to be too much bowed
down by grief. What seem to us bitter trials at the moment are often
blessings in disguise.

MISS PRISM. This seems to me a blessing of an extremely obvious
kind.

[*Enter* CECILY *from the house.*]

CECILY. Uncle Jack! Oh, I am pleased to see you back. But what horrid clothes you have on! Do go and change them.

MISS PRISM. Cecily!

CHASUBLE. My child! my child! [CECILY *goes towards* JACK; *he kisses her brow in a melancholy manner.*]

CECILY. What is the matter, Uncle Jack? Do look happy! You look as if you had a toothache and I have a surprise for you. Who do you think is in the dining-room? Your brother!

JACK. Who?

CECILY. Your brother Ernest. He arrived about half an hour ago.

JACK. What nonsense! I haven't got a brother.

CECILY. Oh, don't say that. However badly he may have behaved to you in the past he is still your brother. You couldn't be so heartless as to disown him. I'll tell him to come out. And you will shake hands with him, won't you, Uncle Jack? [*Runs back into the house.*]

CHASUBLE. These are very joyful tidings.

MISS PRISM. After we had all been resigned to his loss, his sudden returns seems to me peculiarly distressing.

JACK. My brother is in the dining-room? I don't know what it all means. I think it is perfectly absurd.

[*Enter* ALGERNON *and* CECILY *hand in hand. They come slowly up to* JACK.]

JACK. Good heavens! [*Motions* ALGERNON *away.*]

ALGERNON. Brother John, I have come down from town to tell you that I am very sorry for all the trouble I have given you, and that I intend to lead a better life in the future. [JACK *glares at him and does not take his hand.*]

CECILY. Uncle Jack, you are not going to refuse your own brother's hand?

JACK. Nothing will induce me to take his hand. I think his coming down here disgraceful. He knows perfectly well why.

CECILY. Uncle Jack, do be nice. There is some good in everyone. Ernest has just been telling me about his poor invalid friend, Mr. Bunbury, whom he goes to visit so often. And surely there must be much good in one who is kind to an invalid, and leaves the pleasures of London to sit by a bed of pain.

JACK. Oh, he has been talking about Bunbury, has he?

CECILY. Yes, he has told me all about poor Mr. Bunbury, and his terrible state of health.

JACK. Bunbury! Well, I won't have him talk to you about Bunbury or about anything else. It is enough to drive one perfectly frantic.

ALGERNON. Of course I admit that the faults were all on my side. But I must say that I think that Brother John's coldness to me is peculiarly painful. I expected a more enthusiastic welcome, especially considering it is the first time I have come here.

CECILY. Uncle Jack, if you don't shake hands with Ernest I will never forgive you.

JACK. Never forgive me?

CECILY. Never, never, never!

JACK. Well, this is the last time I shall ever do it. [*Shakes hands with* ALGERNON *and glares.*]

CHASUBLE. It's pleasant, is it not, to see so perfect a reconciliation? I think we might leave the two brothers together.

MISS PRISM. Cecily, you will come with us.

CECILY. Certainly, Miss Prism. My little task of reconciliation is over.

CHASUBLE. You have done a beautiful action today, dear child.

MISS PRISM. We must not be premature in our judgments.

CECILY. I feel very happy. [*They all go off.*]

JACK. You young scoundrel, Algy, you must get out of this place as soon as possible. I don't allow any Bunburying here.

[*Enter* MERRIMAN.]

MERRIMAN. I have put Mr. Ernest's things in the room next to yours, sir. I suppose that is all right?

JACK. What?

MERRIMAN. Mr. Ernest's luggage, sir. I have unpacked it and put it in the room next to your own.

JACK. His luggage?

MERRIMAN. Yes, sir. Three portmanteaus, a dressing-case, two hat-boxes, and a large luncheon-basket.

ALGERNON. I am afraid I can't stay more than a week this time.

JACK. Merriman, order the dog-cart at once. Mr. Ernest has been suddenly called back to town.

MERRIMAN. Yes, sir. [*Goes back into the house.*]

ALGERNON. What a fearful liar you are, Jack. I have not been called back to town at all.

JACK. Yes, you have.

ALGERNON. I haven't heard anyone call me.

JACK. Your duty as a gentleman calls you back.

ALGERNON. My duty as a gentleman has never interfered with my pleasures in the smallest degree.

JACK. I can quite understand that.

ALGERNON. Well, Cecily is a darling.

JACK. You are not to talk of Miss Cardew like that. I don't like it.

ALGERNON. Well, I don't like your clothes. You look perfectly ridiculous in them. Why on earth don't you go up and change? It is perfectly childish to be in deep mourning for a man who is actually staying for a whole week with you in your house as a guest. I call it grotesque.

JACK. You are certainly not staying with me for a whole week as a guest or anything else. You have got to leave . . . by the four-five train.

ALGERNON. I certainly won't leave you so long as you are in mourning. It would be most unfriendly. If I were in mourning you would stay with me, I suppose. I should think it very unkind if you didn't.

JACK. Well, will you go if I change my clothes?

ALGERNON. Yes, if you are not too long. I never saw anybody take so long to dress, and with such little result.

JACK. Well, at any rate, that is better than being always over-dressed as you are.

ALGERNON. If I am occasionally a little over-dressed, I make up for it by being always immensely over-educated.

JACK. Your vanity is ridiculous, your conduct an outrage, and your presence in my garden utterly absurd. However, you have got to catch the four-five, and I hope you will have a pleasant journey back to town. This Bunburying, as you call it, has not been a great success for you. [*Goes into the house.*]

ALGERNON. I think it has been a great success. I'm in love with Cecily, and that is everything.

[*Enter* CECILY *at the back of the garden. She picks up the can and begins to water the flowers.*]

But I must see her before I go, and make arrangements for another Bunbury. Ah, there she is.

CECILY. Oh, I merely came back to water the roses. I thought you were with Uncle Jack.

ALGERNON. He's gone to order the dog-cart for me.

CECILY. Oh, is he going to take you for a nice drive?

ALGERNON. He's going to send me away.

CECILY. Then have we got to part?

ALGERNON. I am afraid so. It's a very painful parting.

CECILY. It is always painful to part from people whom one has known for a very brief space of time. The absence of old friends one can endure with equanimity. But even a momentary separation from anyone to whom one has just been introduced is almost unbearable.

ALGERNON. Thank you.

[*Enter* MERRIMAN.]

MERRIMAN. The dog-cart is at the door, sir. [ALGERNON *looks appealingly at* CECILY.]

CECILY. It can wait, Merriman . . . for . . . five minutes.

MERRIMAN. Yes, miss. [*Exit* MERRIMAN.]

ALGERNON. I hope, Cecily, I shall not offend you if I state quite frankly and openly that you seem to me to be in every way the visible personification of absolute perfection.

CECILY. I think your frankness does you great credit, Ernest. If you will allow me I will copy your remarks into my diary. [*Goes over to table and begins writing in diary.*]

ALGERNON. Do you really keep a diary? I'd give anything to look at it. May I?

CECILY. Oh, no. [*Puts her hand over it.*] You see, it is simply a very young girl's record of her own thoughts and impressions, and consequently meant for publication. When it appears in volume form I hope you will order a copy. But pray, Ernest, don't stop. I delight in taking down from dictation. I have reached "absolute perfection." You can go on. I am quite ready for more.

ALGERNON [*somewhat taken aback*]. Ahem! Ahem!

CECILY. Oh, don't cough, Ernest. When one is dictating one should speak fluently and not cough. Besides, I don't know how to spell a cough. [*Writes as* ALGERNON *speaks.*]

ALGERNON [*speaking very rapidly*]. Cecily, ever since I first looked upon your wonderful and incomparable beauty, I have dared to love you wildly, passionately, devotedly, hopelessly.

CECILY. I don't think that you should tell me that you love me wildly, passionately, devotedly, hopelessly. Hopelessly doesn't seem to make much sense, does it?

ALGERNON. Cecily!

[*Enter* MERRIMAN.]

MERRIMAN. The dog-cart is waiting, sir.

ALGERNON. Tell it to come round next week, at the same hour.

MERRIMAN [*looks at* CECILY, *who makes no sign*]. Yes, sir. [MERRIMAN *retires.*]

CECILY. Uncle Jack would be very much annoyed if he knew you were staying on till next week, at the same hour.

ALGERNON. Oh, I don't care about Jack. I don't care for anybody in the whole world but you. I love you, Cecily. You will marry me, won't you?

CECILY. You silly you! Of course. Why, we have been engaged for the last three months.

ALGERNON. For the last three months?

CECILY. Yes, it will be exactly three months on Thursday.

ALGERNON. But how did we become engaged?

CECILY. Well, ever since dear Uncle Jack first confessed to us that he had a younger brother who was very wicked and bad, you of course have formed the chief topic of conversation between myself and Miss Prism. And of course a man who is much talked about is always very attractive. One feels there must be something in him after all. I daresay it was foolish of me, but I fell in love with you, Ernest.

ALGERNON. Darling! And when was the engagement actually settled?

CECILY. On the 4th of February last. Worn out by your entire ignorance of my existence, I determined to end the matter one way or the other, and after a long struggle with myself I accepted you under this dear old tree here. The next day I bought this little ring in your name, and this is the little bangle with the true lovers' knot I promised you always to wear.

ALGERNON. Did I give you this? It's very pretty, isn't it?

CECILY. Yes, you've wonderfully good taste, Ernest. It's the excuse I've always given for your leading such a bad life. And this is the box in which I keep all your dear letters. [*Kneels at table, opens box, and produces letters tied up with blue ribbon.*]

ALGERNON. My letters! But my own sweet Cecily, I have never written you any letters.

CECILY. You need hardly remind me of that, Ernest. I remember only too well that I was forced to write your letters for you. I wrote always three times a week, and sometimes oftener.

ALGERNON. Oh, do let me read them, Cecily?

CECILY. Oh, I couldn't possibly. They would make you far too conceited. [*Replaces box.*] The three you wrote me after I had broken off the engagement are so beautiful, and so badly spelled, that even now I can hardly read them without crying a little.

ALGERNON. But was our engagement ever broken off?

CECILY. Of course it was. On the 22nd of last March. You can see the entry if you like. [*Shows diary.*] "Today I broke off my engagement with Ernest. I feel it is better to do so. The weather still continues charming."

ALGERNON. But why on earth did you break it off? What had I done? I had done nothing at all. Cecily, I am very much hurt indeed to hear you broke it off. Particularly when the weather was so charming.

CECILY. It would hardly have been a really serious engagement if it hadn't been broken off at least once. But I forgave you before the week was out.

ALGERNON [*crossing to her, and kneeling*]. What a perfect angel you are, Cecily.

CECILY. You dear romantic boy. [*He kisses her, she puts her fingers through his hair.*] I hope your hair curls naturally, does it?

ALGERNON. Yes, darling, with a little help from others.

CECILY. I am so glad.

ALGERNON. You'll never break off our engagement again, Cecily?

CECILY. I don't think I could break it off now that I have actually met you. Besides, of course, there is the question of your name.

ALGERNON. Yes, of course. [*Nervously.*]

CECILY. You must not laugh at me, darling, but it had always been a girlish dream of mine to love some one whose name was Ernest. [ALGERNON *rises,* CECILY *also.*] There is something in that name that seems to inspire absolute confidence. I pity any poor married woman whose husband is not called Ernest.

ALGERNON. But, my dear child, do you mean to say you could not love me if I had some other name?

CECILY. But what name?

ALGERNON. Oh, any name you like—Algernon, for instance. . . .

CECILY. But I don't like the name of Algernon.

ALGERNON. Well, my own dear, sweet, loving little darling, I really can't see why you should object to the name of Algernon. It is not at all a bad name. In fact, it is rather an aristocratic name. Half of the chaps who get into the Bankruptcy Court are called Algernon. But seriously, Cecily . . . [*moving to her*] . . . if my name was Algy, couldn't you love me?

CECILY. [*rising*]. I might respect you, Ernest, I might admire your character, but I fear that I should not be able to give you my undivided attention.

ALGERNON. Ahem! Cecily! [*Picking up hat.*] Your Rector here is, I suppose, thoroughly experienced in the practice of all the rites and ceremonials of the church?

CECILY. Oh, yes. Dr. Chasuble is a most learned man. He has never written a single book, so you can imagine how much he knows.

ALGERNON. I must see him at once on a most important christening— I mean on most important business.

CECILY. Oh!

ALGERNON. I sha'n't be away more than half an hour.

CECILY. Considering that we have been engaged since February the 14th, and that I only met you to-day for the first time, I think it is rather hard that you should leave me for so long a period as half an hour. Couldn't you make it twenty minutes?

ALGERNON. I'll be back in no time. [*Kisses her and rushes down the garden.*]

CECILY. What an impetuous boy he is. I like his hair so much. I must enter his proposal in my diary.

[*Enter* MERRIMAN.]

MERRIMAN. A Miss Fairfax has just called to see Mr. Worthing. On very important business, Miss Fairfax states.

CECILY. Isn't Mr. Worthing in his library?

MERRIMAN. Mr. Worthing went over in the direction of the Rectory some time ago.

CECILY. Pray ask the lady to come out here; Mr. Worthing is sure to be back soon. And you can bring tea.

MERRIMAN. Yes, miss. [*Goes out.*]

CECILY. Miss Fairfax! I suppose one of the many good elderly women who are associated with Uncle Jack in some of his philanthropic work in London. I don't quite like women who are interested in philanthropic work. I think it is so forward of them.

[*Enter* MERRIMAN.]

MERRIMAN: Miss Fairfax.

[*Enter* GWENDOLEN. *Exit* MERRIMAN.]

CECILY [*advancing to meet her*]. Pray let me introduce myself to you. My name is Cecily Cardew.

GWENDOLEN. Cecily Cardew? [*Moving to her and shaking hands.*] What a very sweet name! Something tells me that we are going to be great friends. I like you already more than I can say. My first impressions of people are never wrong.

CECILY. How nice of you to like me so much after we have known each other such a comparatively short time. Pray sit down.

GWENDOLEN [*still standing up*]. I may call you Cecily, may I not?

CECILY. With pleasure!

GWENDOLEN. And you will always call me Gwendolen, won't you?

CECILY. If you wish.

GWENDOLEN. Then that is all quite settled, is it not?

CECILY. I hope so. [*A pause. They both sit down together.*]

GWENDOLEN. Perhaps this might be a favorable opportunity for my mentioning who I am. My father is Lord Bracknell. You have never heard of papa, I suppose?

CECILY. I don't think so.

GWENDOLEN. Outside the family circle, papa, I am glad to say, is entirely unknown. I think that is quite as it should be. The home seems to me to be the proper sphere for the man. And certainly once a man begins to neglect his domestic duties he becomes painfully effeminate, does he not? And I don't like that. It makes men so very attractive. Cecily, mamma, whose views on education are remarkably strict, has brought me up to be extremely short-sighted; it is part of her system; so do you mind my looking at you through my glasses?

CECILY. Oh, not at all, Gwendolen. I am very fond of being looked at.

GWENDOLEN [*after examining* CECILY *carefully through a lorgnette*]. You are here on a short visit, I suppose.

CECILY. Oh, no, I live here.

GWENDOLEN [*severely*]. Really? Your mother, no doubt, or some female relative of advanced years, resides here also?

CECILY. Oh, no. I have no mother, nor, in fact, any relations.

GWENDOLEN. Indeed?

CECILY. My dear guardian, with the assistance of Miss Prism, has the arduous task of looking after me.

GWENDOLEN. Your guardian?

CECILY. Yes, I am Mr. Worthing's ward.

GWENDOLEN. Oh! It is strange he never mentioned to me that he had a ward. How secretive of him! He grows more interesting hourly. I am not sure, however, that the news inspires me with feelings of unmixed delight. [*Rising and going to her.*] I am very fond of you, Cecily. I have liked you ever since I met you. But I am bound to state that now that I know that you are Mr. Worthing's ward, I cannot help expressing a wish you were—well, just a little older than you seem to be —and not quite so very alluring in appearance. In fact, if I may speak candidly——

CECILY. Pray do! I think that whenever one has anything unpleasant to say, one should always be quite candid.

GWENDOLEN. Well, to speak with perfect candor, Cecily, I wish that you were fully forty-two, and more than usually plain for your age. Ernest has a strong upright nature. He is the very soul of truth and honor. Disloyalty would be as impossible to him as deception. But even men of the noblest possible moral character are extremely susceptible to the influence of the physical charms of others. Modern, no less than Ancient History, supplies us with many most painful examples of what I refer to. If it were not so, indeed, History would be quite unreadable.

CECILY. I beg your pardon, Gwendolen, did you say Ernest?

GWENDOLEN. Yes.

CECILY. Oh, but it is not Mr. Ernest Worthing who is my guardian. It is his brother—his elder brother.

GWENDOLEN [*sitting down again*]. Ernest never mentioned to me that he had a brother.

CECILY. I am sorry to say they have not been on good terms for a long time.

GWENDOLEN. Ah! that accounts for it. And now that I think of it I have never heard any man mention his brother. The subject seems distasteful to most men. Cecily, you have lifted a load from my mind. I was growing almost anxious. It would have been terrible if any cloud had come across a friendship like ours, would it not? Of course you are quite, quite sure that it is not Mr. Ernest Worthing who is your guardian?

CECILY. Quite sure. [*A pause.*] In fact, I am going to be his.

GWENDOLEN [*enquiringly*]. I beg your pardon?

CECILY [*rather shy and confidingly*]. Dearest Gwendolen, there is no reason why I should make a secret of it to you. Our little county newspaper is sure to chronicle the fact next week. Mr. Ernest Worthing and I are engaged to be married.

GWENDOLEN [*quite politely, rising*]. My darling Cecily, I think there must be some slight error. Mr. Ernest Worthing is engaged to me. The announcement will appear in the *Morning Post* on Saturday at the latest.

CECILY [*very politely, rising*]. I am afraid you must be under some misconception. Ernest proposed to me exactly ten minutes ago. [*Shows diary.*]

GWENDOLEN [*examines diary through her lorgnette carefully*]. It is certainly very curious, for he asked me to be his wife yesterday afternoon at 5.30. If you would care to verify the incident, pray do so. [*Produces diary of her own.*] I never travel without my diary. One should always have something sensational to read in the train. I am so sorry, dear Cecily, if it is any disappointment to you, but I am afraid *I* have the prior claim.

CECILY. It would distress me more than I can tell you, dear Gwendolen, if it caused you any mental or physical anguish, but I feel bound to point out that since Ernest proposed to you he clearly has changed his mind.

GWENDOLEN [*meditatively*]. If the poor fellow has been entrapped into any foolish promise I shall consider it my duty to rescue him at once, and with a firm hand.

CECILY [*thoughtfully and sadly*]. Whatever unfortunate entanglement my dear boy may have got into, I will never reproach him with it after we are married.

GWENDOLEN. Do you allude to me, Miss Cardew, as an entanglement? You are presumptuous. On an occasion of this kind it becomes more than a moral duty to speak one's mind. It becomes a pleasure.

CECILY. Do you suggest, Miss Fairfax, that I entrapped Ernest into an engagement? How dare you? This is no time for wearing the shallow mask of manners. When I see a spade I call it a spade.

GWENDOLEN [*satirically*]. I am glad to say that I have never seen a spade. It is obvious that our social spheres have been widely different. [*Enter* MERRIMAN, *followed by the footman. He carries a salver, table-cloth, and plate-stand.* CECILY *is about to retort. The presence of the servants exercises a restraining influence, under which both girls chafe.*]

MERRIMAN. Shall I lay tea here as usual, miss?

CECILY [*sternly, in a calm voice*]. Yes, as usual. [MERRIMAN *begins to clear and lay cloth. A long pause.* CECILY *and* GWENDOLEN *glare at each other.*]

GWENDOLEN. Are there many interesting walks in the vicinity, Miss Cardew?

CECILY. Oh, yes, a great many. From the top of one of the hills quite close one can see five counties.

GWENDOLEN. Five counties! I don't think I should like that. I hate crowds.

CECILY [*sweetly*]. I suppose that is why you live in town? [GWENDOLEN *bites her lip, and beats her foot nervously with her parasol.*]

GWENDOLEN [*looking round*]. Quite a well-kept garden this is, Miss Cardew.

CECILY. So glad you like it, Miss Fairfax.

GWENDOLEN. I had no idea there were any flowers in the country.

CECILY. Oh, flowers are as common here, Miss Fairfax, as people are in London.

GWENDOLEN. Personally I cannot understand how anybody manages to exist in the country, if anybody who is anybody does. The country always bores me to death.

CECILY. Ah! This is what the newspapers call agricultural depression, is it not? I believe the aristocracy are suffering very much from it just at present. It is almost an epidemic amongst them, I have been told. May I offer you some tea, Miss Fairfax?

GWENDOLEN [*with elaborate politeness*]. Thank you. [*Aside.*] Detestable girl! But I require tea!

CECILY [*sweetly*]. Sugar?

GWENDOLEN [*superciliously*]. No, thank you. Sugar is not fashionable any more. [CECILY *looks angrily at her, takes up the tongs and puts four lumps of sugar into the cup.*]

CECILY [*severely*]. Cake or bread and butter?

GWENDOLEN [*in a bored manner*]. Bread and butter, please. Cake is rarely seen at the best houses nowadays.

CECILY [*cuts a very large slice of cake, and puts it on the tray*]. Hand that to MISS FAIRFAX. [MERRIMAN *does so, and goes out with footman.* GWENDOLEN *drinks the tea and makes a grimace. Puts down cup at once, reaches out her hand to the bread and butter, looks at it, and finds it is cake. Rises in indignation.*]

GWENDOLEN. You have filled my tea with lumps of sugar, and though I asked most distinctly for bread and butter, you have given me cake. I am known for the gentleness of my disposition, and the extraordinary sweetness of my nature, but I warn you, Miss Cardew, you may go too far.

CECILY [*rising*]. To save my poor, innocent, trusting boy from the machinations of any other girl there are no lengths to which I would not go.

GWENDOLEN. From the moment I saw you I distrusted you. I felt that you were false and deceitful. I am never deceived in such matters. My first impression of people are invariably right.

CECILY. It seems to me, Miss Fairfax, that I am trespassing on your valuable time. No doubt you have many other calls of a similar character to make in the neighborhood.

[*Enter* JACK.]

GWENDOLEN [*catching sight of him*]. Ernest! My own Ernest!

JACK. Gwendolen! Darling! [*Offers to kiss her.*]

GWENDOLEN [*drawing back*]. A moment! May I ask if you are engaged to be married to this young lady? [*Points to* CECILY.]

JACK [*laughing*]. To dear little Cecily! Of course not! What could have put such an idea into your pretty little head?

GWENDOLEN. Thank you. You may. [*Offers her cheek.*]

CECILY [*very sweetly*]. I knew there must be some misunderstanding, Miss Fairfax. The gentleman whose arm is at present around your waist is my dear guardian, Mr. John Worthing.

GWENDOLEN. I beg your pardon?

CECILY. This is Uncle Jack.

GWENDOLEN [*receding*]. Jack! Oh!

[*Enter* ALGERNON.]

CECILY. Here is Ernest.

ALGERNON [*goes straight over to* CECILY *without noticing anyone else*]. My own love! [*Offers to kiss her.*]

CECILY [*drawing back*]. A moment, Ernest! May I ask you—are you engaged to be married to this young lady?

ALGERNON [*looking round*]. To what young lady? Good heavens! Gwendolen!

CECILY. Yes, to good heavens, Gwendolen, I mean to Gwendolen.

ALGERNON [*laughing*]. Of course not! What could have put such an idea into your pretty little head?

CECILY. Thank you. [*Presenting her cheek to be kissed.*] You may. [ALGERNON *kisses her.*]

GWENDOLEN. I felt there was some slight error, Miss Cardew. The gentleman who is now embracing you is my cousin, Mr. Algernon Moncrieff.

CECILY [*breaking away from* ALGERNON]. Algernon Moncrieff! Oh! [*The two girls move towards each other and put their arms round each other's waists as if for protection.*]

CECILY. Are you called Algernon?

ALGERNON. I cannot deny it.

CECILY. Oh!

GWENDOLEN. Is your name really John?

JACK [*standing rather proudly*]. I could deny it if I liked. I could deny anything if I liked. But my name certainly is John. It has been John for years.

CECILY [*to* GWENDOLEN]. A gross deception has been practised on both of us.

GWENDOLEN. My poor wounded Cecily!

CECILY. My sweet, wronged Gwendolen!

GWENDOLEN [*slowly and seriously*]. You will call me sister, will you not? [*They embrace.* JACK *and* ALGERNON *groan and walk up and down.*]

CECILY [*rather brightly*]. There is just one question I would like to be allowed to ask my guardian.

GWENDOLEN. An admirable idea! Mr. Worthing, there is just one question I would like to be permitted to put to you. Where is your brother Ernest? We are both engaged to be married to your brother Ernest, so it is a matter of some importance to us to know where your brother Ernest is at present.

JACK [*slowly and hesitatingly*]. Gwendolen—Cecily—it is very painful for me to be forced to speak the truth. It is the first time in my life that I have ever been reduced to such a painful position, and I am really quite inexperienced in doing anything of the kind. However I will tell you quite frankly that I have no brother Ernest. I have no brother at all. I never had a brother in my life, and I certainly have not the smallest intention of ever having one in the future.

CECILY [*surprised*]. No brother at all?

JACK [*cheerily*]. None!

GWENDOLEN [*severely*]. Had you never a brother of any kind?

JACK [*pleasantly*]. Never. Not even of any kind.

GWENDOLEN. I am afraid it is quite clear, Cecily, that neither of us is engaged to be married to anyone.

CECILY. It is not a very pleasant position for a young girl suddenly to find herself in. Is it?

GWENDOLEN. Let us go into the house. They will hardly venture to come after us there.

CECILY. No, men are so cowardly, aren't they? [*They retire into the house with scornful looks.*]

JACK. This ghastly state of things is what you call Bunburying, I suppose?

ALGERNON. Yes, and a perfectly wonderful Bunbury it is. The most wonderful Bunbury I have ever had in my life.

JACK. Well, you've no right whatsoever to Bunbury here.

ALGERNON. That is absurd. One has a right to Bunbury anywhere one chooses. Every serious Bunburyist knows that.

JACK. Serious Bunburyist! Good heavens!

ALGERNON. Well, one must be serious about something, if one wants to have any amusement in life. I happen to be serious about Bunburying. What on earth you are serious about I haven't got the remotest idea. About everything, I should fancy. You have such an absolutely trivial nature.

JACK. Well, the only small satisfaction I have in the whole of this wretched business is that your friend Bunbury is quite exploded. You won't be able to run down to the country quite so often as you used to do, dear Algy. And a very good thing, too.

ALGERNON. Your brother is a little off color, isn't he, dear Jack? You won't be able to disappear to London quite so frequently as your wicked custom was. And not a bad thing, either.

JACK. As for your conduct towards Miss Cardew, I must say that your taking in a sweet, simple, innocent girl like that is quite inexcusable. To say nothing of the fact that she is my ward.

ALGERNON. I can see no possible defense at all for your deceiving a brilliant, clever, thoroughly experienced young lady like Miss Fairfax. To say nothing of the fact that she is my cousin.

JACK. I wanted to be engaged to Gwendolen, that is all. I love her.

ALGERNON. Well, I simply wanted to be engaged to Cecily. I adore her.

JACK. There is certainly no chance of your marrying Miss Cardew.

ALGERNON. I don't think there is much likelihood, Jack, of you and Miss Fairfax being united.

JACK. Well, that is no business of yours.

ALGERNON. If it was my business, I wouldn't talk about it. [*Begins to eat muffins.*] It is very vulgar to talk about one's business. Only people like stockbrokers do that, and then merely at dinner parties.

JACK. How you can sit there, calmly eating muffins, when we are in this horrible trouble, I can't make out. You seem to me to be perfectly heartless.

ALGERNON. Well, I can't eat muffins in an agitated manner. The butter would probably get on my cuffs. One should always eat muffins quite calmly. It is the only way to eat them.

JACK. I say it's perfectly heartless your eating muffins at all, under the circumstances.

ALGERNON. When I am in trouble, eating is the only thing that consoles me. Indeed, when I am in really great trouble, as anyone who knows me intimately will tell you, I refuse everything except food and drink. At the present moment I am eating muffins because I am unhappy. Besides, I am particularly fond of muffins. [*Rising.*]

JACK [*rising*]. Well, that is no reason why you should eat them all in that greedy way. [*Takes muffins from* ALGERNON.]

ALGERNON [*offering tea-cake*]. I wish you would have tea-cake instead. I don't like tea-cake.

JACK. Good heavens! I suppose a man may eat his own muffins in his own garden.

ALGERNON. But you have just said it was perfectly heartless to eat muffins.

JACK. I said it was perfectly heartless of you, under the circumstances. That is a very different thing.

ALGERNON. That may be. But the muffins are the same. [*He seizes the muffin-dish from* JACK.]

JACK. Algy, I wish to goodness you would go.

ALGERNON. You can't possibly ask me to go without having some dinner. It's absurd. I never go without my dinner. No one ever does, except vegetarians and people like that. Besides I have just made arrangements with Dr. Chasuble to be christened at a quarter to six under the name of Ernest.

JACK. My dear fellow, the sooner you give up that nonsense the better. I made arrangements this morning with Dr. Chasuble to be christened myself at 5.30, and I naturally will take the name of Ernest. Gwendolen would wish it. We can't both be christened Ernest. It's absurd. Besides, I have a perfect right to be christened if I like. There is no evidence at all that I ever have been christened by anybody. I should think it extremely probable I never was, and so does Dr. Chasuble. It is entirely different in your case. You have been christened already.

ALGERNON. Yes, but I have not been christened for years.

JACK. Yes, but you have been christened. That is the important thing.

ALGERNON. Quite so. So I know my constitution can stand it. If you are not quite sure about your ever having been christened, I must say I think it rather dangerous your venturing on it now. It might make you very unwell. You can hardly have forgotten that someone very closely connected with you was very nearly carried off this week in Paris by a severe chill.

JACK. Yes, but you said yourself that a severe chill was not hereditary.

ALGERNON. It usedn't to be, I know—but I daresay it is now. Science is always making wonderful improvements in things.

JACK [*picking up the muffin-dish*]. Oh, that is nonsense; you are always talking nonsense.

ALGERNON. Jack, you are at the muffins again! I wish you wouldn't. There are only two left. [*Takes them.*] I told you I was particularly fond of muffins.

JACK. But I hate tea-cake.

ALGERNON. Why on earth then do you allow tea-cake to be served up for your guests? What ideas you have of hospitality!

JACK. Algernon! I have already told you to go. I don't want you here. Why don't you go?

ALGERNON. I haven't quite finished my tea yet, and there is still one muffin left. [JACK *groans, and sinks into a chair.* ALGERNON *still continues eating.*]

ACT DROP

ACT III

SCENE

Morning-room at the Manor House.

[GWENDOLEN *and* CECILY *are at the window, looking out into the garden.*]

GWENDOLEN. The fact that they did not follow us at once into the house, as anyone else would have done, seems to me to show that they have some sense of shame left.

CECILY. They have been eating muffins. That looks like repentance.

GWENDOLEN [*after a pause*]. They don't seem to notice us at all. Couldn't you cough?

GWENDOLEN. They're looking at us. What effrontery!

CECILY. They're approaching. That's very forward of them.

GWENDOLEN. Let us preserve a dignified silence.

CECILY. Certainly. It's the only thing to do now.

[*Enter* JACK, *followed by* ALGERNON. *They whistle some dreadful popular air from a British opera.*]

GWENDOLEN. This dignified silence seems to produce an unpleasant effect.

CECILY. A most distasteful one.

GWENDOLEN. But we will not be the first to speak.

CECILY. Certainly not.

GWENDOLEN. Mr. Worthing, I have something very particular to ask you. Much depends on your reply.

CECILY. Gwendolen, your common sense is invaluable. Mr. Moncrieff, kindly answer me the following question. Why did you pretend to be my guardian's brother?

ALGERNON. In order that I might have an opportunity of meeting you.

CECILY [*to* GWENDOLEN]. That certainly seems a satisfactory explanation, does it not?

GWENDOLEN. Yes, dear, if you can believe him.

CECILY. I don't. But that does not affect the wonderful beauty of his answer.

GWENDOLEN. True. In matters of grave importance, style, not sincerity, is the vital thing. Mr. Worthing, what explanation can you offer to me for pretending to have a brother? Was it in order that you might have an opportunity of coming up to town to see me as often as possible?

JACK. Can you doubt it, Miss Fairfax?

GWENDOLEN. I have the gravest doubts upon the subject. But I intend to crush them. This is not the moment for German scepticism. [*Moving to* CECILY.] Their explanations appear to be quite satisfactory, especially Mr. Worthing's. That seems to me to have the stamp of truth upon it.

CECILY. I am more than content with what Mr. Moncrieff said. His voice alone inspires one with absolute credulity.

GWENDOLEN. Then you think we should forgive them?

CECILY. Yes. I mean no.

GWENDOLEN. True! I had forgotten. There are principles at stake that one cannot surrender. Which of us should tell them? The task is not a pleasant one.

CECILY. Could we not both speak at the same time?

GWENDOLEN. An excellent idea! I nearly always speak at the same time as other people. Will you take the time from me?

CECILY. Certainly. [GWENDOLEN *beats time with uplifted finger.*]

GWENDOLEN AND CECILY [*speaking together*]. Your Christian names are still an insuperable barrier. That is all!

JACK AND ALGERNON [*speaking together*]. Our Christian names! Is that all? But we are going to be christened this afternoon.

GWENDOLEN [*to* JACK]. For my sake you are prepared to do this terrible thing?

JACK. I am.

CECILY [*to* ALGERNON]. To please me you are ready to face this fearful ordeal?

ALGERNON. I am!

GWENDOLEN. How absurd to talk of the equality of the sexes! Where questions of self-sacrifice are concerned, men are infinitely beyond us.

JACK. We are. [*Clasps hands with* ALGERNON.]

CECILY. They have moments of physical courage of which we women know absolutely nothing.

GWENDOLEN [*to* JACK]. Darling!

ALGERNON [*to* CECILY]. Darling! [*They fall into each other's arms.*]

[*Enter* MERRIMAN. *When he enters he coughs loudly, seeing the situation.*]

MERRIMAN. Ahem! Ahem! Lady Bracknell!

JACK. Good heavens!

[*Enter* LADY BRACKNELL. *The couples separate in alarm. Exit* MERRIMAN.]

LADY BRACKNELL. Gwendolen! What does this mean?

GWENDOLEN. Merely that I am engaged to be married to Mr. Worthing, Mamma.

LADY BRACKNELL. Come here. Sit down. Sit down immediately. Hesitation of any kind is a sign of mental decay in the young, of physical weakness in the old. [*Turns to* JACK.] Apprised, sir, of my daughter's sudden flight by her trusty maid, whose confidence I purchased by means of a small coin, I followed her at once by a luggage train. Her unhappy father is, I am glad to say, under the impression that she is attending a more than usually lengthy lecture by the University Extension Scheme on the Influence of a Permanent Income Tax on Thought. I do not propose to undeceive him. Indeed I have never undeceived him on any question. I would consider it wrong. But of course, you will clearly understand that all communication between yourself and my daughter must cease immediately from this moment. On this point, as indeed on all points, I am firm.

JACK. I am engaged to be married to Gwendolen, Lady Bracknell!

LADY BRACKNELL. You are nothing of the kind, sir. And now, as regards Algernon! . . . Algernon!

ALGERNON. Yes, Aunt Augusta.

LADY BRACKNELL. May I ask if it is in this house that your invalid friend Mr. Bunbury resides?

ALGERNON [*stammering*]. Oh, no! Bunbury doesn't live here. Bunbury is somewhere else at present. In fact, Bunbury is dead.

LADY BRACKNELL. Dead! When did Mr. Bunbury die? His death must have been extremely sudden.

ALGERNON [*airily*]. Oh, I killed Bunbury this afternoon. I mean poor Bunbury died this afternoon.

LADY BRACKNELL. What did he die of?

ALGERNON. Bunbury? Oh, he was quite exploded.

LADY BRACKNELL. Exploded! Was he the victim of a revolutionary outrage? I was not aware that Mr. Bunbury was interested in social legislation. If so, he is well punished for his morbidity.

ALGERNON. My dear Aunt Augusta, I mean he was found out! The doctors found out that Bunbury could not live, that is what I mean—so Bunbury died.

LADY BRACKNELL. He seems to have had great confidence in the opinion of his physicians. I am glad, however, that he made up his mind at the last to some definite course of action, and acted under proper medical advice. And now that we have finally got rid of this Mr. Bunbury, may I ask, Mr. Worthing, who is that young person whose hand my nephew Algernon is now holding in what seems to me a peculiarly unnecessary manner?

JACK. That lady is Miss Cecily Cardew, my ward. [LADY BRACKNELL *bows coldly to* CECILY.]

ALGERNON. I am engaged to be married to Cecily, Aunt Augusta.

LADY BRACKNELL. I beg your pardon?

CECILY. Mr. Moncrieff and I are engaged to be married, Lady Bracknell.

LADY BRACKNELL [*with a shiver, crossing to the sofa and sitting down*]. I do not know whether there is anything peculiarly exciting in the air in this particular part of Hertfordshire, but the number of engagements that go on seems to me considerably above the proper average that statistics have laid down for our guidance. I think some preliminary enquiry on my part would not be out of place. Mr. Worthing, is Miss Cardew at all connected with any of the larger railway stations in London? I merely desire information. Until yesterday I had no idea that there were any families or persons whose origin was a Terminus. [JACK *looks perfectly furious, but restrains himself.*]

JACK [*in a clear, cold voice*]. Miss Cardew is the granddaughter of the late Mr. Thomas Cardew of 149, Belgrave Square, S.W.; Gervase Park, Dorking, Surrey; and the Sporran, Fifeshire, N.B.

LADY BRACKNELL. That sounds not unsatisfactory. Three addresses always inspire confidence, even in tradesmen. But what proof have I of their authenticity?

JACK. I have carefully preserved the Court Guide of the period. They are open to your inspection, Lady Bracknell.

LADY BRACKNELL [*grimly*]. I have known strange errors in that publication.

JACK. Miss Cardew's family solicitors are Messrs. Markby, Markby, and Markby.

LADY BRACKNELL. Markby, Markby and Markby? A firm of the very highest position in their profession. Indeed I am told that one of the Markbys is occasionally to be seen at dinner parties. So far I am satisfied.

JACK [*very irritably*]. How extremely kind of you, Lady Bracknell! I have also in my possession, you will be pleased to hear, certificates of Miss Cardew's birth, baptism, whooping cough registration, vaccination, confirmation, and the measles—both the German and the English variety.

LADY BRACKNELL. Ah! A life crowded with incident, I see; though perhaps somewhat too exciting for a young girl. I am not myself in favor of premature experiences. [*Rises, looks at her watch.*] Gwendolen! the time approaches for our departure. We have not a moment to lose. As a matter of form, Mr. Worthing, I had better ask you if Miss Cardew has any little fortune?

JACK. Oh, about a hundred and thirty thousand pounds in the Funds. That is all. Good-bye, Lady Bracknell. So pleased to have seen you.

LADY BRACKNELL [*sitting down again*]. A moment, Mr. Worthing. A hundred and thirty thousand pounds! And in the Funds! Miss Cardew seems to me a most attractive young lady, now that I look at her. Few girls of the present day have any really solid qualities, any of the qualities that last, and improve with time. We live, I regret to say, in an age of surfaces. [*To* CECILY.] Come over here, dear. [CECILY *goes across.*] Pretty child! your dress is sadly simple, and your hair seems almost as Nature might have left it. But we can soon alter all that. A thoroughly experienced French maid produces a really marvelous result in a very brief space of time. I remember recommending one to young Lady Lancing, and after three months her own husband did not know her.

JACK [*aside*]. And after six months nobody knew her.

LADY BRACKNELL [*glares at* JACK *for a few moments. Then bends, with a practised smile, to* CECILY]. Kindly turn round, sweet child. [CECILY *turns completely round.*] No, the side view is what I want. [CECILY *presents her profile.*] Yes, quite as I expected. There are distinct social possibilities in your profile. The two weak points in our age are its want of principle and its want of profile. The chin a little higher, dear. Style largely depends on the way the chin is worn. They are worn very high, just at present. Algernon!

ALGERNON. Yes, Aunt Augusta!

LADY BRACKNELL. There are distinct social possibilities in Miss Cardew's profile.

ALGERNON. Cecily is the sweetest, dearest, prettiest girl in the whole world. And I don't care twopence about social possibilities.

LADY BRACKNELL. Never speak disrespectfully of society, Algernon. Only people who can't get into it do that. [*To* CECILY.] Dear child, of course you know that Algernon has nothing but his debts to depend upon. But I do not approve of mercenary marriages. When I married Lord Bracknell I had no fortune of any kind. But I never dreamed for a moment of allowing that to stand in my way. Well, I suppose I must give my consent.

ALGERNON. Thank you, Aunt Augusta.

LADY BRACKNELL. Cecily, you may kiss me!

CECILY [*kisses her*]. Thank you, Lady Bracknell.

LADY BRACKNELL. You may also address me as Aunt Augusta for the future.

CECILY. Thank you, Aunt Augusta.

LADY BRACKNELL. The marriage, I think, had better take place quite soon.

ALGERNON. Thank you, Aunt Augusta.

CECILY. Thank you, Aunt Augusta.

LADY BRACKNELL. To speak frankly, I am not in favor of long engagements. They give people the opportunity of finding out each other's character before marriage, which I think is never advisable.

JACK. I beg your pardon for interrupting you, Lady Bracknell, but this engagement is quite out of the question. I am Miss Cardew's guardian, and she cannot marry without my consent until she comes of age. That consent I absolutely decline to give.

LADY BRACKNELL. Upon what grounds, may I ask? Algernon is an extremely, I may almost say an ostentatiously, eligible young man. He has nothing, but he looks everything. What more can one desire?

JACK. It pains me very much to have to speak frankly to you, Lady Bracknell, about your nephew, but the fact is that I do not approve at all of his moral character. I suspect him of being untruthful. [AL-GERNON *and* CECILY *look at him in indignant amazement.*]

LADY BRACKNELL. Untruthful! My nephew Algernon? Impossible! He is an Oxonian.

JACK. I fear there can be no possible doubt about the matter. This afternoon, during my temporary absence in London on an important question of romance, he obtained admission to my house by means of the false pretense of being my brother. Under an assumed name he drank, I've just been informed by my butler, an entire pint bottle of my Perrier-Jouet, Brut, '89, a wine I was specially reserving for myself. Continuing his disgraceful deception, he succeeded in the course of the afternoon in alienating the affections of my only ward. He subsequently stayed to tea, and devoured every single muffin. And what makes his conduct all the more heartless is, that he was perfectly well aware from the first that I have no brother, that I never had a brother, and that I don't intend to have a brother, not even of any kind. I distinctly told him so myself yesterday afternoon.

LADY BRACKNELL. Ahem! Mr. Worthing, after careful consideration I have decided entirely to overlook my nephew's conduct to you.

JACK. That is very generous of you, Lady Bracknell. My own decision, however, is unalterable. I decline to give my consent.

LADY BRACKNELL [*to* CECILY]. Come here, sweet child. [CECILY *goes over.*] How old are you, dear?

CECILY. Well, I am really only eighteen, but I always admit to twenty when I go to evening parties.

LADY BRACKNELL. You are perfectly right in making some slight alteration. Indeed, no woman should ever be quite accurate about her age. It looks so calculating. . . . [*In a meditative manner.*] Eighteen, but admitting to twenty at evening parties. Well, it will not be very long before you are of age and free from the restraints of tutelage. So I don't think your guardian's consent is, after all, a matter of any importance.

JACK. Pray excuse me, Lady Bracknell, for interrupting you again, but it is only fair to tell you that according to the terms of her grandfather's will Miss Cardew does not come legally of age till she is thirty-five.

LADY BRACKNELL. That does not seem to me to be a grave objection. Thirty-five is a very attractive age. London society is full of women of the very highest birth who have, of their own free choice, remained thirty-five for years. Lady Dumbleton is an instance in point. To my own knowledge she has been thirty-five ever since she arrived at the age of forty, which was many years ago now. I see no reason why our dear Cecily should not be even still more attractive at the age you mention than she is at present. There will be a large accumulation of property.

CECILY. Algy, could you wait for me till I was thirty-five?

ALGERNON. Of course I could, Cecily. You know I could.

CECILY. Yes, I felt it instinctively, but I couldn't wait all that time. I hate waiting even five minutes for anybody. It always makes me rather cross. I am not punctual myself, I know, but I do like punctuality in others, and waiting, even to be married, is quite out of the question.

ALGERNON. Then what is to be done, Cecily?

CECILY. I don't know, Mr. Moncrieff.

LADY BRACKNELL. My dear Mr. Worthing, as Miss Cardew states positively that she cannot wait till she is thirty-five—a remark which I am bound to say seems to me to show a somewhat impatient nature —I would beg of you to reconsider your decision.

JACK. But my dear Lady Bracknell, the matter is entirely in your own hands. The moment you consent to my marriage with Gwendolen, I will most gladly allow your nephew to form an alliance with my ward.

LADY BRACKNELL [rising and drawing herself up]. You must be quite aware that what you propose is out of the question.

JACK. Then a passionate celibacy is all that any of us can look forward to.

LADY BRACKNELL. That is not the destiny I propose for Gwendolen. Algernon, of course, can choose for himself. [Pulls out her watch.] Come, dear, [GWENDOLEN rises.] we have already missed five, if not six, trains. To miss any more might expose us to comment on the platform.

[Enter DR. CHASUBLE.]

CHASUBLE. Everything is quite ready for the christenings.

LADY BRACKNELL. The christenings, sir! Is not that somewhat premature?

CHASUBLE [*looking rather puzzled, and pointing to* JACK *and* ALGERNON]. Both these gentlemen have expressed a desire for immediate baptism.

LADY BRACKNELL. At their age? The idea is grotesque and irreligious! Algernon, I forbid you to be baptized. I will not hear of such excesses. Lord Bracknell would be highly displeased if he learned that that was the way in which you wasted your time and money.

CHASUBLE. Am I to understand then that there are to be no christenings at all this afternoon?

JACK. I don't think that, as things are now, it would be of much practical value to either of us, Dr. Chasuble.

CHASUBLE. I am grieved to hear such sentiments from you, Mr. Worthing. They savor of the heretical views of the Anabaptists, views that I have completely refuted in four of my unpublished sermons. However, as your present mood seems to be one peculiarly secular, I will return to the church at once. Indeed, I have just been informed by the pew-opener that for the last hour and a half Miss Prism has been waiting for me in the vestry.

LADY BRACKNELL [*starting*]. Miss Prism! Did I hear you mention a Miss Prism?

CHASUBLE. Yes, Lady Bracknell. I am on my way to join her.

LADY BRACKNELL. Pray allow me to detain you for a moment. This matter may prove to be one of vital importance to Lord Bracknell and myself. Is this Miss Prism a female of repellent aspect, remotely connected with education?

CHASUBLE [*somewhat indignantly*]. She is the most cultivated of ladies, and the very picture of respectability.

LADY BRACKNELL. It is obviously the same person. May I ask what position she holds in your household?

CHASUBLE [*severely*]. I am a celibate, madam.

JACK [*interposing*]. Miss Prism, Lady Bracknell, has been for the last three years Miss Cardew's esteemed governess and valued companion.

LADY BRACKNELL. In spite of what I hear of her, I must see her at once. Let her be sent for.

CHASUBLE [*looking off*]. She approaches; she is nigh.

[*Enter* MISS PRISM *hurriedly.*]

MISS PRISM. I was told you expected me in the vestry, dear Canon. I have been waiting for you there for an hour and three-quarters. [*Catches sight of* LADY BRACKNELL, *who has fixed her with a stony glare.* MISS PRISM *grows pale and quails. She looks anxiously round as if desirous to escape.*]

LADY BRACKNELL [*in a severe, judicial voice*]. Prism! [MISS PRISM *bows her head in shame.*] Come here, Prism! [MISS PRISM *approaches in a humble manner.*] Prism! Where is that baby? [*General consternation.*

The CANON *starts back in horror.* ALGERNON *and* JACK *pretend to be anxious to shield* CECILY *and* GWENDOLEN *from hearing the details of a terrible public scandal.*] Twenty-eight years ago, Prism, you left Lord Bracknell's house, Number 104, Upper Grosvenor Street, in charge of a perambulator that contained a baby, of the male sex. You never returned. A few weeks later, through the elaborate investigations of the Metropolitan police, the perambulator was discovered at midnight, standing by itself in a remote corner of Bayswater. It contained the manuscript of a three-volume novel of more than usually revolting sentimentality. [MISS PRISM *starts in involuntary indignation.*] But the baby was not there! [*Everyone looks at* MISS PRISM.] Prism, where is that baby? [*A pause.*]

MISS PRISM. Lady Bracknell, I admit with shame that I do not know. I only wish I did. The plain facts of the case are these. On the morning of the day you mention, a day that is forever branded on my memory, I prepared as usual to take the baby out in its perambulator. I had also with me a somewhat old but capacious handbag in which I had intended to place the manuscript of a work of fiction that I had written during my few unoccupied hours. In a moment of mental abstraction, for which I never can forgive myself, I deposited the manuscript in the bassinette, and placed the baby in the handbag.

JACK [*who has been listening attentively*]. But where did you deposit the handbag?

MISS PRISM. Do not ask me, Mr. Worthing.

JACK. Miss Prism, this is a matter of no small importance to me. I insist on knowing where you deposited the handbag that contained that infant.

MISS PRISM. I left it in the cloak-room of one of the larger railway stations in London.

JACK. What railway station?

MISS PRISM [*quite crushed*]. Victoria. The Brighton line. [*Sinks into a chair.*]

JACK. I must retire to my room for a moment. Gwendolen, wait here for me.

GWENDOLEN. If you are not too long, I will wait here for you all my life.

[*Exit* JACK *in great excitement.*]

CHASUBLE. What do you think this means, Lady Bracknell?

LADY BRACKNELL. I dare not even suspect, Dr. Chasuble. I need hardly tell you that in families of high position strange coincidences are not supposed to occur. They are hardly considered the thing. [*Noises heard overhead as if someone was throwing trunks about. Everybody looks up.*]

CECILY. Uncle Jack seems strangely agitated.

CHASUBLE. Your guardian has a very emotional nature.

LADY BRACKNELL. This noise is extremely unpleasant. It sounds as if he was having an argument. I dislike arguments of any kind. They are always vulgar, and often convincing.

CHASUBLE [*looking up*]. It has stopped now. [*The noise is redoubled.*]

LADY BRACKNELL. I wish he would arrive at some conclusion.

GWENDOLEN. This suspense is terrible. I hope it will last.

[*Enter* JACK *with a handbag of black leather in his hand.*]

JACK [*rushing over to* MISS PRISM]. Is this the handbag, Miss Prism? Examine it carefully before you speak. The happiness of more than one life depends on your answer.

MISS PRISM [*calmly*]. It seems to be mine. Yes, here is the injury it received through the upsetting of a Gower Street omnibus in younger and happier days. Here is the stain on the lining caused by the explosion of a temperance beverage, an incident that occurred at Leamington. And here, on the lock, are my initials. I had forgotten that in an extravagant mood I had had them placed there. The bag is undoubtedly mine. I am delighted to have it so unexpectedly restored to me. It has been a great inconvenience being without it all these years.

JACK [*in a pathetic voice*]. Miss Prism, more is restored to you than this handbag. I was the baby you placed in it.

MISS PRISM [*amazed*]. You?

JACK [*embracing her*]. Yes . . . mother!

MISS PRISM [*recoiling in indignant astonishment*]. Mr. Worthing! I am unmarried!

JACK. Unmarried! I do not deny that is a serious blow. But after all, who has the right to cast a stone against one who has suffered? Cannot repentance wipe out an act of folly? Why should there be one law for men and another for women? Mother, I forgive you. [*Tries to embrace her again.*]

MISS PRISM [*still more indignant*]. Mr. Worthing, there is some error. [*Pointing to* LADY BRACKNELL.] There is the lady who can tell you who you really are.

JACK [*after a pause*]. Lady Bracknell, I hate to seem inquisitive, but would you kindly inform me who I am?

LADY BRACKNELL. I am afraid that the news I have to give you will not altogether please you. You are the son of my poor sister, Mrs. Moncrieff, and consequently Algernon's elder brother.

JACK. Algy's elder brother! Then I have a brother after all. I knew I had a brother! I always said I had a brother! Cecily—how could you have ever doubted that I had a brother? [*Seizes hold of* ALGERNON.] Dr. Chasuble, my unfortunate brother. Miss Prism, my unfortunate brother. Gwendolen, my unfortunate brother. Algy, you young scoundrel, you will have to treat me with more respect in the future. You have never behaved to me like a brother in all your life.

ALGERNON. Well, not till today, old boy, I admit. I did my best, however, though I was out of practice. [*Shakes hands.*]

GWENDOLEN [*to* JACK]. My own! But what own are you? What is your Christian name, now that you have become someone else?

JACK. Good heavens! . . . I had quite forgotten that point. Your decision on the subject of my name is irrevocable, I suppose?

GWENDOLEN. I never change, except in my affections.

CECILY. What a noble nature you have, Gwendolen!

JACK. Then the question had better be cleared up at once. Aunt Augusta, a moment. At the time when Miss Prism left me in the handbag, had I been christened already?

LADY BRACKNELL. Every luxury that money could buy, including christening, had been lavished on you by your fond and doting parents.

JACK. Then I was christened! That is settled. Now, what name was I given? Let me know the worst.

LADY BRACKNELL. Being the eldest son you were naturally christened after your father.

JACK [*irritably*]. Yes, but what was my father's Christian name?

LADY BRACKNELL [*meditatively*]. I cannot at the present moment recall what the General's Christian name was. But I have no doubt he had one. He was eccentric, I admit. But only in later years. And that was the result of the Indian climate, and marriage, and indigestion, and other things of that kind.

JACK. Algy! Can't you recollect what our father's Christian name was?

ALGERNON. My dear boy, we were never even on speaking terms. He died before I was a year old.

JACK. His name would appear in the Army Lists of the period, I suppose, Aunt Augusta?

LADY BRACKNELL. The General was essentially a man of peace, except in his domestic life. But I have no doubt his name would appear in any military directory.

JACK. The Army Lists of the last forty years are here. These delightful records should have been my constant study. [*Rushes to bookcase and tears the books out.*] M. Generals . . . Mallam, Maxbohm, Magley, what ghastly names they have—Marksby, Migsby, Mobbs, Moncrieff! Lieutenant 1840, Captain, Lieutenant-Colonel, Colonel, General 1869, Christian names, Ernest John. [*Puts book very quietly down and speaks quite calmly.*] I always told you, Gwendolen, my name was Ernest, didn't I? Well, it is Ernest after all. I mean it naturally is Ernest.

LADY BRACKNELL. Yes, I remember that the General was called Ernest. I knew I had some particular reason for disliking the name.

GWENDOLEN. Ernest! My own Ernest! I felt from the first that you could have no other name!

JACK. Gwendolen, it is a terrible thing for a man to find out suddenly that all his life he has been speaking nothing but the truth. Can you forgive me?

GWENDOLEN. I can. For I feel that you are sure to change.

JACK. My own one!

CHASUBLE [*to* MISS PRISM]. Lætitia! [*Embraces her.*]

MISS PRISM [*enthusiastically*]. Frederick! At last!

ALGERNON. Cecily [*embraces her.*] At last!

JACK. Gwendolen! [*embraces her.*] At last!

LADY BRACKNELL. My nephew, you seem to be displaying signs of triviality.

JACK. On the contrary, Aunt Augusta, I've now realized for the first time in my life the vital Importance of Being Ernest.

TABLEAU
CURTAIN

George Bernard Shaw

1856–1950

ARMS AND THE MAN

ACT I

NIGHT. *A lady's bedchamber in Bulgaria, in a small town near the Dragoman Pass, late in November in the year 1885.*[1] *Through an open window with a little balcony a peak of the Balkans, wonderfully white and beautiful in the starlit snow, seems quite close at hand, though it is really miles away. The interior of the room is not like anything to be seen in the west of Europe. It is half rich Bulgarian, half cheap Viennese. Above the head of the bed, which stands against a little wall cutting off the left hand corner of the room, is a painted wooden shrine, blue and gold, with an ivory image of Christ, and a light hanging before it in a pierced metal ball suspended by three chains. The principal seat, placed towards the other side of the room and opposite the window, is a Turkish ottoman. The counterpane and hangings of the bed, the window curtains, the little carpet, and all the ornamental textile fabrics in the room are oriental and gorgeous : the paper on the walls is occidental and paltry. The washstand, against the wall on the side nearest the ottoman and window, consists of an enamelled iron basin with a pail beneath it in a painted metal frame, and a single towel on the rail at the side. The dressing table, between the bed and the window, is a common pine table, covered with a cloth of many colors, with an expensive toilet mirror on it. The door is on the side nearest the bed; and there is a chest of drawers between. This chest of drawers is also covered by a variegated native cloth; and on it there is a pile of paper backed novels, a box of chocolate creams, and a miniature easel with a large photograph of an extremely handsome officer, whose lofty bearing and magnetic glance can be felt even from the portrait. The room is lighted by a candle on the chest of drawers, and another on the dressing table with a box of matches beside it.*

The window is hinged doorwise and stands wide open. Outside, a pair of wooden shutters, opening outwards, also stand open. On the balcony a young lady, intensely conscious of the romantic beauty of the night, and of the fact that her own youth and beauty are part of it, is gazing at the snowy Balkans. She is in her nightgown, well covered by a long mantle of furs, worth, on a moderate estimate, about three times the furniture of her room.

---

[1] Serbia declared war on Bulgaria but was defeated in the Battle of Slivnitza, November 17–19, 1885.

The peculiarities of spelling and punctuation in this edition are Shaw's and are retained at the request of the copyright holder. Shaw, following the Continental practice, replaces *italics* with h a l f - s p a c i n g for emphasis.

Her reverie is interrupted by her mother, CATHERINE PETKOFF, *a woman over forty, imperiously energetic, with magnificent black hair and eyes, who might be a very splendid specimen of the wife of a mountain farmer, but is determined to be a Viennese lady, and to that end wears a fashionable tea gown on all occasions.*

CATHERINE [*entering hastily, full of good news*] Raina! [*She pronounces it* RAH-EENA, *with the stress on the ee*]. Raina! [*She goes to the bed, expecting to find* RAINA *there*]. Why, where—? [RAINA *looks into the room*]. Heavens, child! are you out in the night air instead of in your bed? Youll catch your death. Louka told me you were asleep.

RAINA [*dreamily*] I sent her away. I wanted to be alone. The stars are so beautiful! What is the matter?

CATHERINE. Such news! There has been a battle.

RAINA [*her eyes dilating*] Ah! [*She comes eagerly to* CATHERINE].

CATHERINE. A great battle at Slivnitza! A victory! And it was won by Sergius.

RAINA [*with a cry of delight*] Ah! [*They embrace rapturously*]. Oh, mother! [*Then, with sudden anxiety*] Is father safe?

CATHERINE. Of course: he sends me the news. Sergius is the hero of the hour, the idol of the regiment.

RAINA. Tell me, tell me. How was it? [*Ecstatically*] Oh, mother! mother! mother! [*She pulls her mother down on the ottoman; and they kiss one another frantically*].

CATHERINE [*with surging enthusiasm*] You cant guess how splendid it is. A cavalry charge! think of that! He defied our Russian commanders—acted without orders—led a charge on his own responsibility—headed it himself—was the first man to sweep through their guns. Cant you see it, Raina: our gallant splendid Bulgarians with their swords and eyes flashing, thundering down like an avalanche and scattering the wretched Serbs and their dandified Austrian officers like chaff. And you! you kept Sergius waiting a year before you would be betrothed to him. Oh, if you have a drop of Bulgarian blood in your veins, you will worship him when he comes back.

RAINA. What will he care for my poor little worship after the acclamations of a whole army of heroes? But no matter: I am so happy! so proud! [*She rises and walks about excitedly*]. It proves that all our ideas were real after all.

CATHERINE [*indignantly*] Our ideas real! What do you mean?

RAINA. Our ideas of what Sergius would do. Our patriotism. Our heroic ideals. I sometimes used to doubt whether they were anything but dreams. Oh, what faithless little creatures girls are! When I buckled on Sergius's sword he looked so noble: it was treason to think of disillusion or humiliation or failure. And yet—and yet—[*She sits down again suddenly*]. Promise me youll never tell him.

CATHERINE. Dont ask me for promises until I know what I'm promising.

RAINA. Well, it came into my head just as he was holding me in his arms and looking into my eyes, that perhaps we only had our heroic ideas because we are so fond of reading Byron and Pushkin, and because we were so delighted with the opera that season at Bucharest. Real life is so seldom like that! indeed never, as far as I knew it then. [*Remorsefully*] Only think, mother: I doubted him: I wondered whether all his heroic qualities and his soldiership might not prove mere imagination when he went into a real battle. I had an uneasy fear that he might cut a poor figure there beside all those clever officers from the Tsar's court.

CATHERINE. A poor figure! Shame on you! The Serbs have Austrian officers who are just as clever as the Russians; but we have beaten them in every battle for all that.

RAINA [*laughing and snuggling against her mother*] Yes: I was only a prosaic little coward. Oh, to think that it was all true! that Sergius is just as splendid and noble as he looks! that the world is really a glorious world for women who can see its glory and men who can act its romance! What happiness! what unspeakable fulfilment!

> *They are interrupted by the entry of* LOUKA, *a handsome proud girl in a pretty Bulgarian peasant's dress with double apron, so defiant that her servility to* RAINA *is almost insolent. She is afraid of* CATHERINE, *but even with her goes as far as she dares.*

LOUKA. If you please, madam, all the windows are to be closed and the shutters made fast. They say there may be shooting in the streets. [RAINA *and* CATHERINE *rise together, alarmed*]. The Serbs are being chased right back through the pass; and they say they may run into the town. Our cavalry will be after them; and our people will be ready for them, you may be sure, now theyre running away. [*She goes out on the balcony, and pulls the outside shutters to; then steps back into the room*].

CATHERINE [*businesslike, her housekeeping instincts aroused*] I must see that everything is made safe downstairs.

RAINA. I wish our people were not so cruel. What glory is there in killing wretched fugitives?

CATHERINE. Cruel! Do you suppose they would hesitate to kill y o u —or worse?

RAINA [*to* LOUKA] Leave the shutters so that I can just close them if I hear any noise.

CATHERINE [*authoritatively, turning on her way to the door*] Oh no, dear: you must keep them fastened. You would be sure to drop off to sleep and leave them open. Make them fast, Louka.

LOUKA. Yes, madam. [*She fastens them*].

RAINA. Don't be anxious about m e. The moment I hear a shot, I shall blow out the candles and roll myself up in bed with my ears well covered.

CATHERINE. Quite the wisest thing you can do, my love. Goodnight.

RAINA. Goodnight. [*Her emotion comes back for a moment*]. Wish me joy.

[*They kiss*]. This is the happiest night of my life—if only there are no fugitives.

CATHERINE. Go to bed, dear; and dont think of them. [*She goes out*].

LOUKA [*secretly, to* RAINA] If you would like the shutters open, just give them a push like this [*she pushes them: they open: she pulls them to again*]. One of them ought to be bolted at the bottom; but the bolt's gone.

RAINA [*with dignity, reproving her*] Thanks, Louka; but we must do what we are told. [LOUKA *makes a grimace*]. Goodnight.

LOUKA [*carelessly*] Goodnight. [*She goes out, swaggering*].

RAINA, *left alone, takes off her fur cloak and throws it on the ottoman. Then she goes to the chest of drawers, and adores the portrait there with feelings that are beyond all expression. She does not kiss it or press it to her breast, or shew it any mark of bodily affection; but she takes it in her hands and elevates it, like a priestess.*

RAINA [*looking up at the picture*] Oh, I shall never be unworthy of you any more, my soul's hero: never, never, never. [*She replaces it reverently. Then she selects a novel from the little pile of books. She turns over the leaves dreamily; finds her page; turns the book inside out at it; and, with a happy sigh, gets into bed and prepares to read herself to sleep. But before abandoning herself to fiction, she raises her eyes once more, thinking of the blessed reality, and murmurs*] My hero! my hero!

A distant shot breaks the quiet of the night. She starts, listening; and two more shots, much nearer, follow, startling her so that she scrambles out of bed, and hastily blows out the candle on the chest of drawers. Then, putting her fingers in her ears, she runs to the dressing table, blows out the light there, and hurries back to bed in the dark, nothing being visible but the glimmer of the light in the pierced ball before the image, and the starlight seen through the slits at the top of the shutters. The firing breaks out again: there is a startling fusillade quite close at hand. Whilst it is still echoing, the shutters disappear, pulled open from without; and for an instant the rectangle of snowy starlight flashes out with the figure of a man silhouetted in black upon it. The shutters close immediately; and the room is dark again. But the silence is now broken by the sound of panting. Then there is a scratch; and the flame of a match is seen in the middle of the room.

RAINA [*crouching on the bed*] Who's there? [*The match is out instantly*]. Who's there? Who is that?

A MAN'S VOICE [*in the darkness, subduedly, but threateningly*] Sh—sh! Dont call out; or youll be shot. Be good; and no harm will happen to you. [*She is heard leaving her bed, and making for the door*]. Take care: it's no use trying to run away.

RAINA. But who—

THE VOICE [*warning*] Remember: if you raise your voice my revolver will go off. [*Commandingly*]. Strike a light and let me see you. Do you hear. [*Another moment of silence and darkness as she retreats to the chest of drawers. Then she lights a candle; and the mystery is at an end. He is a man of about 35, in a deplorable plight, bespattered with mud and blood and*

*snow, his belt and the strap of his revolver-case keeping together the torn
ruins of the blue tunic of a Serbian artillery officer. All that the candlelight
and his unwashed unkempt condition make it possible to discern is that he is
of middling stature and undistinguished appearance, with strong neck and
shoulders, roundish obstinate looking head covered with short crisp bronze
curls, clear quick eyes and good brows and mouth, hopelessly prosaic nose
like that of a strong minded baby, trim soldierlike carriage and energetic
manner, and with all his wits about him in spite of his desperate predicament : even with a sense of the humor of it, without, however, the least intention of trifling with it or throwing away a chance. Reckoning up what
he can guess about* RAINA : *her age, her social position, her character, and
the extent to which she is frightened, he continues, more politely but still
most determinedly*] Excuse my disturbing you; but you recognize my
uniform? Serb! If I'm caught I shall be killed. [*Menacingly*]. Do you
understand that?

RAINA. Yes.

THE MAN. Well, I dont intend to get killed if I can help it. [*Still more
formidably*]. Do you understand t h a t? [*He locks the door quickly but
quietly*].

RAINA [*disdainfully*] I suppose not. [*She draws herself up superbly, and
looks him straight in the face, adding, with cutting emphasis*] S o m e
soldiers, I know, are a f r a i d to die.

THE MAN [*with grim goodhumor*] All of them, dear lady, all of them,
believe me. It is our duty to live as long as we can. Now, if you raise
an alarm—

RAINA [*cutting him short*] You will shoot me. How do you know that *I*
am afraid to die?

THE MAN [*cunningly*] Ah; but suppose I dont shoot you, what will
happen then? A lot of your cavalry will burst into this pretty room of
yours and slaughter me here like a pig; for I'll fight like a demon : they
shant get m e into the street to amuse themselves with : I know what
they are. Are you prepared to receive that sort of company in your
present undress? [RAINA, *suddenly conscious of her nightgown, instinctively shrinks, and gathers it more closely about her neck. He watches her,
and adds, pitilessly*] Hardly presentable, eh? [*She turns to the ottoman.
He raises his pistol instantly, and cries*] Stop! [*She stops*]. Where are you
going?

RAINA [*with dignified patience*] Only to get my cloak.

THE MAN [*passing swiftly to the ottoman and snatching the cloak*] A good
idea! I ' l l keep the cloak; and y o u l l take care that nobody comes
in and sees you without it. This is a better weapon than the revolver :
eh? [*He throws the pistol down on the ottoman*].

RAINA [*revolted*] It is not the weapon of a gentleman!

THE MAN. It's good enough for a man with only you to stand between
him and death. [*As they look at one another for a moment,* RAINA *hardly
able to believe that even a Serbian officer can be so cynically and selfishly*

unchivalrous, they are startled by a sharp fusillade in the street. The chill of imminent death hushes the man's voice as he adds] Do you hear? If you are going to bring those blackguards in on me you shall receive them as you are.

Clamor and disturbance. The pursuers in the street batter at the house door, shouting Open the door! Open the door! Wake up, will you! *A man servant's voice calls to them angrily from within* This is Major Petkoff's house: you cant come in here; *but a renewal of the clamor, and a torrent of blows on the door, end with his letting a chain down with a clank, followed by a rush of heavy footsteps and a din of triumphant yells, dominated at last by the voice of* CATHERINE, *indignantly addressing an officer with* What does this mean, sir? Do you know where you are? *The noise subsides suddenly.*

LOUKA [*outside, knocking at the bedroom door*] My lady! my lady! get up quick and open the door. If you dont they will break it down.

The fugitive throws up his head with the gesture of a man who sees that it is all over with him, and drops the manner he has been assuming to intimidate RAINA.

THE MAN [*sincerely and kindly*] No use, dear: I'm done for. [*Flinging the cloak to her*] Quick! wrap yourself up: theyre coming.

RAINA. Oh, thank you. [*She wraps herself up with intense relief*].

THE MAN [*between his teeth*] Dont mention it.

RAINA [*anxiously*] What will you do?

THE MAN [*grimly*] The first man in will find out. Keep out of the way; and dont look. It wont last long; but it will not be nice. [*He draws his sabre and faces the door, waiting*].

RAINA [*impulsively*] I'll help you. I'll save you.

THE MAN. You cant.

RAINA. I can. I'll hide you. [*She drags him towards the window*]. Here! behind the curtains.

THE MAN [*yielding to her*] Theres just half a chance, if you keep your head.

RAINA [*drawing the curtain before him*] S-sh! [*She makes for the ottoman*].

THE MAN [*putting out his head*] Remember—

RAINA [*running back to him*] Yes?

THE MAN. —nine soldiers out of ten are born fools.

RAINA. Oh! [*She draws the curtain angrily before him*].

THE MAN [*looking out at the other side*] If they find me, I promise you a fight: a devil of a fight.

She stamps at him. He disappears hastily. She takes off her cloak, and throws it across the foot of the bed. Then, with a sleepy, disturbed air, she opens the door. LOUKA *enters excitedly.*

LOUKA. One of those beasts of Serbs has been seen climbing up the waterpipe to your balcony. Our men want to search for him; and they are so wild and drunk and furious. [*She makes for the other side of the room to get as far from the door as possible*]. My lady says you are to dress at once, and to—[*She sees the revolver lying on the ottoman, and stops, petrified*].

RAINA [*as if annoyed at being disturbed*] They shall not search here. Why have they been let in?

CATHERINE [*coming in hastily*] Raina, darling: are you safe? Have you seen anyone or heard anything?

RAINA. I heard the shooting. Surely the soldiers will not dare come in here?

CATHERINE. I have found a Russian officer, thank Heaven: he knows Sergius. [*Speaking through the door to someone outside*] Sir: will you come in now. My daughter will receive you.

A young Russian officer, in Bulgarian uniform, enters, sword in hand.

OFFICER [*with soft feline politeness and stiff military carriage*] Good evening, gracious lady. I am sorry to intrude; but there is a Serb hiding on the balcony. Will you and the gracious lady your mother please to withdraw whilst we search?

RAINA [*petulantly*] Nonsense, sir: you can see that there is no one on the balcony. [*She throws the shutters wide open and stands with her back to the curtain where the man is hidden, pointing to the moonlit balcony. A couple of shots are fired right under the window; and a bullet shatters the glass opposite* RAINA, *who winks and gasps, but stands her ground; whilst* CATHERINE *screams, and the officer, with a cry of* Take care! *rushes to the balcony*].

THE OFFICER [*on the balcony, shouting savagely down to the street*] Cease firing there, you fools: do you hear? Cease firing, damn you! [*He glares down for a moment; then turns to* RAINA, *trying to resume his polite manner*]. Could anyone have got in without your knowledge? Were you asleep?

RAINA. No: I have not been to bed.

THE OFFICER [*impatiently, coming back into the room*] Your neighbors have their heads so full of runaway Serbs that they see them everywhere. [*Politely*] Gracious lady: a thousand pardons. Goodnight. [*Military bow, which* RAINA *returns coldly. Another to* CATHERINE, *who follows him out*].

RAINA *closes the shutters. She turns and sees* LOUKA, *who has been watching the scene curiously.*

RAINA. Dont leave my mother, Louka, until the soldiers go away.

LOUKA *glances at* RAINA, *at the ottoman, at the curtain; then purses her lips secretively, laughs insolently, and goes out.* RAINA, *highly offended by this demonstration, follows her to the door, and shuts it behind her with a slam, locking it violently. The man immediately steps out from behind the curtain, sheathing his sabre, and closes the shutters. Then, dismissing the danger from his mind in a businesslike way, he comes affably to* RAINA.

THE MAN. A narrow shave; but a miss is as good as a mile. Dear young lady: your servant to the death. I wish for your sake I had joined the Bulgarian army instead of the other one. I am not a native Serb.

RAINA [*haughtily*] No: you are one of the Austrians who set the Serbs on to rob us of our national liberty, and who officer their army for them. We hate them!

THE MAN. Austrian! not I. Dont hate me, dear young lady. I am a Swiss, fighting merely as a professional soldier. I joined the Serbs because they came first on the road from Switzerland. Be generous: youve beaten us hollow.

RAINA. Have I not been generous?

THE MAN. Noble! Heroic! But I'm not saved yet. This particular rush will soon pass through; but the pursuit will go on all night by fits and starts. I must take my chance to get off in a quiet interval. [*Pleasantly*] You dont mind my waiting just a minute or two, do you?

RAINA [*putting on her most genteel society manner*] Oh, not at all. Wont you sit down?

THE MAN. Thanks. [*He sits on the foot of the bed*].

RAINA *walks with studied elegance to the ottoman and sits down. Unfortunately she sits on the pistol, and jumps up with a shriek. The man, all nerves, shies like a frightened horse to the other side of the room.*

THE MAN [*irritably*] Dont frighten me like that. What is it?

RAINA. Your revolver! It was staring that officer in the face all the time. What an escape!

THE MAN [*vexed at being unnecessarily terrified*] Oh, is that all?

RAINA [*staring at him rather superciliously as she conceives a poorer and poorer opinion of him, and feels proportionately more and more at her ease*] I am sorry I frightened you. [*She takes up the pistol and hands it to him*]. Pray take it to protect yourself against me.

THE MAN [*grinning wearily at the sarcasm as he takes the pistol*] No use, dear young lady: theres nothing in it. It's not loaded. [*He makes a grimace at it, and drops it disparagingly into his revolver case*].

RAINA. Load it by all means.

THE MAN. Ive no ammunition. What use are cartridges in battle? I always carry chocolate instead; and I finished the last cake of that hours ago.

RAINA [*outraged in her most cherished ideals of manhood*] Chocolate! Do you stuff your pockets with s w e e t s—like a schoolboy—even in the field?

THE MAN [*grinning*] Yes: isnt it contemptible? [*Hungrily*] I wish I had some now.

RAINA. Allow me. [*She sails away scornfully to the chest of drawers, and returns with the box of confectionery in her hand*]. I am sorry I have eaten them all except these. [*She offers him the box*].

THE MAN [*ravenously*] Youre an angel! [*He gobbles the contents*]. Creams! Delicious! [*He looks anxiously to see whether there are any more. There are none: he can only scrape the box with his fingers and suck them. When that nourishment is exhausted he accepts the inevitable with pathetic goodhumor, and says, with grateful emotion*] Bless you, dear lady! You can always tell an old soldier by the inside of his holsters and cartridge boxes. The young ones carry pistols and cartridges : the old ones, grub. Thank you. [*He hands back the box. She snatches it contemptuously from him and throws it away. He shies again, as if she had meant to strike him*]. Ugh! Dont do things so suddenly, gracious lady. It's mean to revenge yourself because I frightened you just now.

RAINA [*loftily*] Frighten m e! Do you know, sir, that though I am only a woman, I think I am at heart as brave as you.

THE MAN. I should think so. You havnt been under fire for three days as I have. I can stand two days without shewing it much; but no man can stand three days: I'm as nervous as a mouse. [*He sits down on the ottoman, and takes his head in his hands*]. Would you like to see me cry?

RAINA [*alarmed*] No.

THE MAN. If you would, all you have to do is to scold me just as if I were a little boy and you my nurse. If I were in camp now, theyd play all sorts of tricks on me.

RAINA [*a little moved*]. I'm sorry. I wont scold you. [*Touched by the sympathy in her tone, he raises his head and looks gratefully at her : she immediately draws back and says stiffly*] You must excuse me : o u r soldiers are not like that. [*She moves away from the ottoman*].

THE MAN. Oh yes they are. There are only two sorts of soldiers: old ones and young ones. Ive served fourteen years : half of your fellows never smelt powder before. Why, how is it that youve just beaten us? Sheer ignorance of the art of war, nothing else. [*Indignantly*] I never saw anything so unprofessional.

RAINA [*ironically*] Oh! was it unprofessional to beat you?

THE MAN. Well, come! is it professional to throw a regiment of cavalry on a battery of machine guns, with the dead certainty that if the guns go off not a horse or man will ever get within fifty yards of the fire? I couldnt believe my eyes when I saw it.

RAINA [*eagerly turning to him, as all her enthusiasm and her dreams of glory rush back on her*] Did you see the great cavalry charge? Oh, tell me about it. Describe it to me.

THE MAN. You never saw a cavalry charge, did you?

RAINA. How could I?

THE MAN. Ah, perhaps not. No: of course not! Well, it's a funny sight. It's like slinging a handful of peas against a window pane : first one comes; then two or three close behind him; and then all the rest in a lump.

RAINA [*her eyes dilating as she raises her clasped hands ecstatically*] Yes, first One! the bravest of the brave!

THE MAN [*prosaically*] Hm! you should see the poor devil pulling at his horse.

RAINA. Why should he pull at his horse?

THE MAN [*impatient of so stupid a question*] It's running away with him, of course: do you suppose the fellow wants to get there before the others and be killed? Then they all come. You can tell the young ones

by their wildness and their slashing. The old ones come bunched up
under the number one guard: they know that theyre mere projectiles,
and that it's no use trying to fight. The wounds are mostly broken
knees, from the horses cannoning together.

RAINA. Ugh! But I dont believe the first man is a coward. I know he
is a hero!

THE MAN [*goodhumoredly*] Thats what youd have said if youd seen
the first man in the charge today.

RAINA [*breathless, forgiving him everything*] Ah, I knew it! Tell me.
Tell me about h i m.

THE MAN. He did it like an operatic tenor. A regular handsome fellow, with flashing eyes and lovely moustache, shouting his war-cry
and charging like Don Quixote at the windmills. We did laugh.

RAINA. You dared to laugh!

THE MAN. Yes; but when the sergeant ran up as white as a sheet, and
told us theyd sent us the wrong ammunition, and that we couldnt fire a
round for the next ten minutes, we laughed at the other side of our
mouths. I never felt so sick in my life; though Ive been in one or two
very tight places. And I hadnt even a revolver cartridge: only chocolate. We'd no bayonets: nothing. Of course, they just cut us to bits.
And there was Don Quixote flourishing like a drum major, thinking
he'd done the cleverest thing ever known, whereas he ought to be
courtmartialled for it. Of all the fools ever let loose on a field of battle,
that man must be the very maddest. He and his regiment simply committed suicide; only the pistol missed fire: thats all.

RAINA [*deeply wounded, but steadfastly loyal to her ideals*] Indeed! Would
you know him again if you saw him?

THE MAN. Shall I ever forget him!

*She again goes to the chest of drawers. He watches her with a vague hope
that she may have something more for him to eat. She takes the portrait from
its stand and brings it to him.*

RAINA. That is a photograph of the gentleman—the patriot and hero—
to whom I am betrothed.

THE MAN [*recognizing it with a shock*] I'm really very sorry. [*Looking
at her*] Was it fair to lead me on? [*He looks at the portrait again*] Yes:
thats Don Quixote: not a doubt of it. [*He stifles a laugh*].

RAINA [*quickly*] Why do you laugh?

THE MAN [*apologetic, but still greatly tickled*] I didnt laugh, I assure you.
At least I didnt mean to. But when I think of him charging the windmills and imagining he was doing the finest thing—[*He chokes with suppressed laughter*].

RAINA [*sternly*] Give me back the portrait, sir.

THE MAN [*with sincere remorse*] Of course. Certainly. I'm really very
sorry. [*He hands her the picture. She deliberately kisses it and looks him
straight in the face before returning to the chest of drawers to replace it. He
follows her, apologizing*]. Perhaps I'm quite wrong, you know: no

doubt I am. Most likely he had got wind of the cartridge business somehow, and knew it was a safe job.

RAINA. That is to say, he was a pretender and a coward! You did not dare say that before.

THE MAN [*with a comic gesture of despair*] It's no use, dear lady: I cant make you see it from the professional point of view. [*As he turns away to get back to the ottoman, a couple of distant shots threaten renewed trouble*].

RAINA [*sternly, as she sees him listening to the shots*] So much the better for you!

THE MAN [*turning*] How?

RAINA. You are my enemy; and you are at my mercy. What would I do if I were a professional soldier?

THE MAN. Ah, true, dear young lady: youre always right. I know how good youve been to me: to my last hour I shall remember those three chocolate creams. It was unsoldierly; but it was angelic.

RAINA [*coldly*] Thank you. And now I will do a soldierly thing. You cannot stay here after what you have just said about my future husband; but I will go out on the balcony and see whether it is safe for you to climb down into the street. [*She turns to the window*].

THE MAN [*changing countenance*] Down that waterpipe! Stop! Wait! I cant! I darent! The very thought of it makes me giddy. I came up it fast enough with death behind me. But to face it now in cold blood—! [*He sinks on the ottoman*]. It's no use: I give up: I'm beaten. Give the alarm. [*He drops his head on his hands in the deepest dejection*].

RAINA [*disarmed by pity*] Come: dont be disheartened. [*She stoops over him almost maternally: he shakes his head*]. Oh, you are a very poor soldier: a chocolate cream soldier! Come, cheer up! it takes less courage to climb down than to face capture: remember that.

THE MAN [*dreamily, lulled by her voice*] No: capture only means death; and death is sleep: oh, sleep, sleep, sleep, undisturbed sleep! Climbing down the pipe means doing something—exerting myself—thinking! Death ten times over first.

RAINA [*softly and wonderingly, catching the rhythm of his weariness*] Are you as sleepy as that?

THE MAN. Ive not had two hours undisturbed sleep since I joined. I havnt closed my eyes for forty-eight hours.

RAINA [*at her wit's end*] But what am I to do with you?

THE MAN [*staggering up, roused by her desperation*] Of course. I must do something. [*He shakes himself; pulls himself together; and speaks with rallied vigor and courage*]. You see, sleep or no sleep, hunger or no hunger, tired or not tired, you can always do a thing when you know it must be done. Well, that pipe m u s t be got down: [*he hits himself on the chest*] do you hear that, you chocolate cream soldier? [*He turns to the window*].

RAINA [*anxiously*] But if you fall?

THE MAN. I shall sleep as if the stones were a feather bed. Goodbye. [*He makes boldly for the window; and his hand is on the shutter when there is a terrible burst of firing in the street beneath*].

RAINA [*rushing to him*] Stop! [*She seizes him recklessly, and pulls him quite round*]. Theyll kill you.

THE MAN [*coolly, but attentively*] Never mind: this sort of thing is all in my day's work. I'm bound to take my chance. [*Decisively*] Now do what I tell you. Put out the candles; so that they shant see the light when I open the shutters. And keep away from the window, whatever you do. If they see me theyre sure to have a shot at me.

RAINA [*clinging to him*] Theyre sure to see you: it's bright moonlight. I'll save you. Oh, how can you be so indifferent! You want me to save you, dont you?

THE MAN. I really dont want to be troublesome. [*She shakes him in her impatience*]. I am not indifferent, dear young lady, I assure you. But how is it to be done?

RAINA. Come away from the window. [*She takes him firmly back to the middle of the room. The moment she releases him he turns mechanically towards the window again. She seizes him and turns him back, exclaiming*]. Please! [*He becomes motionless, like a hypnotized rabbit, his fatigue gaining fast on him. She releases him, and addresses him patronizingly*]. Now listen. You must trust to our hospitality. You do not yet know in whose house you are. I am a Petkoff.

THE MAN. A pet what?

RAINA [*rather indignantly*] I mean that I belong to the family of the Petkoffs, the richest and best known in our country.

THE MAN. Oh yes, of course. I beg your pardon. The Petkoffs, to be sure. How stupid of me!

RAINA. You know you never heard of them until this moment. How can you stoop to pretend!

THE MAN. Forgive me: I'm too tired to think; and the change of subject was too much for me. Dont scold me.

RAINA. I forgot. It might make you cry. [*He nods, quite seriously. She pouts and then resumes her patronizing tone*]. I must tell you that my father holds the highest command of any Bulgarian in our army. He is [*proudly*] a Major.

THE MAN [*pretending to be deeply impressed*] A Major! Bless me! Think of that!

RAINA. You shewed great ignorance in thinking that it was necessary to climb up to the balcony because ours is the only private house that has two rows of windows. There is a flight of stairs inside to get up and down by.

THE MAN. Stairs! How grand! You live in great luxury indeed, dear young lady.

RAINA. Do you know what a library is?

THE MAN. A library? A roomful of books?

RAINA. Yes. We have one, the only one in Bulgaria.

THE MAN. Actually a real library! I should like to see that.

RAINA [*affectedly*] I tell you these things to shew you that you are not in the house of ignorant country folk who would kill you the moment they saw your Serbian uniform, but among civilized people. We go to Bucharest every year for the opera season; and I have spent a whole month in Vienna.

THE MAN. I saw that, dear young lady. I saw at once that you knew the world.

RAINA. Have you ever seen the opera of Ernani?

THE MAN. Is that the one with the devil in it in red velvet, and a soldiers' chorus?[2]

RAINA [*contemptuously*] No!

THE MAN [*stifling a heavy sigh of weariness*] Then I dont know it.

RAINA. I thought you might have remembered the great scene where Ernani, flying from his foes just as you are tonight, takes refuge in the castle of his bitterest enemy, an old Castilian noble. The noble refuses to give him up. His guest is sacred to him.

THE MAN [*quickly, waking up a little*] Have your people got that notion?

RAINA [*with dignity*] My mother and I can understand that notion, as you call it. And if instead of threatening me with your pistol as you did you had simply thrown yourself as a fugitive on our hospitality, you would have been as safe as in your father's house.

THE MAN. Quite sure?

RAINA [*turning her back on him in disgust*] Oh, it is useless to try to make y o u understand.

THE MAN. Dont be angry: you see how awkward it would be for me if there was any mistake. My father is a very hospitable man: he keeps six hotels; but I couldnt trust him as far as that. What about y o u r father?

RAINA. He is away at Slivnitza fighting for his country. I answer for your safety. There is my hand in pledge of it. Will that reassure you? [*She offers him her hand*].

THE MAN [*looking dubiously at his own hand*] Better not touch my hand, dear young lady. I must have a wash first.

RAINA [*touched*] That is very nice of you. I see that you are a gentleman.

THE MAN [*puzzled*] Eh?

RAINA. You must not think I am surprised. Bulgarians of really good standing—people in o u r position—wash their hands nearly every day. So you see I can appreciate your delicacy. You may take my hand. [*She offers it again*].

---

[2] Giuseppi Verdi, *Ernani* (1844) and probably Charles Gounod, *Faust* (1859). The operas have little resemblance to each other.

THE MAN [*kissing it with his hands behind his back*] Thanks, gracious young lady: I feel safe at last. And now would you mind breaking the news to your mother? I had better not stay here secretly longer than is necessary.

RAINA. If you will be so good as to keep perfectly still whilst I am away.

THE MAN. Certainly. [*He sits down on the ottoman*].

RAINA *goes to the bed and wraps herself in the fur cloak. His eyes close. She goes to the door. Turning for a last look at him, she sees that he is dropping off to sleep.*

RAINA [*at the door*] You are not going asleep, are you? [*He murmurs inarticulately: she runs to him and shakes him*]. Do you hear? Wake up: you are falling asleep.

THE MAN. Eh? Falling aslee—? Oh no: not the least in the world: I was only thinking. It's all right: I'm wide awake.

RAINA [*severely*] Will you please stand up while I am away. [*He rises reluctantly*]. All the time, mind.

THE MAN [*standing unsteadily*] Certainly. Certainly: you may depend on me.

RAINA *looks doubtfully at him. He smiles weakly. She goes reluctantly, turning again at the door, and almost catching him in the act of yawning. She goes out.*

THE MAN [*drowsily*] Sleep, sleep, sleep, sleep, slee—[*The words trail off into a murmur. He wakes again with a shock on the point of falling*]. Where am I? Thats what I want to know: where am I? Must keep awake. Nothing keeps me awake except danger: remember that: [*intently*] danger, danger, danger, dan—[*trailing off again: another shock*] Wheres danger? Mus' find it. [*He starts off vaguely round the room in search of it*]. What am I looking for? Sleep—danger—dont know. [*He stumbles against the bed*]. Ah yes: now I know. All right now. I'm to go to bed, but not to sleep. Be sure not to sleep, because of danger. Not to lie down either, only sit down. [*He sits on the bed. A blissful expression comes into his face*]. Ah! [*With a happy sigh he sinks back at full length; lifts his boots into the bed with a final effort; and falls fast asleep instantly*].

CATHERINE *comes in, followed by* RAINA.

RAINA [*looking at the ottoman*] He's gone! I left him here.

CATHERINE. Here! Then he must have climbed down from the—

RAINA [*seeing him*] Oh! [*She points*].

CATHERINE [*scandalized*] Well! [*She strides to the bed*, RAINA *following until she is opposite her on the other side*]. He's fast asleep. The brute!

RAINA [*anxiously*] Sh!

CATHERINE [*shaking him*] Sir! [*Shaking him again, harder*] Sir!! [*Vehemently, shaking very hard*] Sir!!!

RAINA [*catching her arm*] Dont, mamma: the poor darling is worn out. Let him sleep.

CATHERINE [*letting him go, and turning amazed to* RAINA] The poor
darling! Raina!!! [*She looks sternly at her daughter*].
The man sleeps profoundly.

ACT II

THE *sixth of March,* 1886. *In the garden of Major Petkoff's house. It is a
fine spring morning : the garden looks fresh and pretty. Beyond the paling
the tops of a couple of minarets can be seen, shewing that there is a valley there,
with the little town in it. A few miles further the Balkan mountains rise and
shut in the landscape. Looking towards them from within the garden, the side
of the house is seen on the left, with a garden door reached by a little flight of
steps. On the right the stable yard, with its gateway, encroaches on the garden.
There are fruit bushes along the paling and house, covered with washing
spread out to dry. A path runs by the house, and rises by two steps at the corner, where it turns out of sight. In the middle, a small table, with two bent
wood chairs at it, is laid for breakfast with Turkish coffee pot, cups, rolls,
etc.; but the cups have been used and the bread broken. There is a wooden garden seat against the wall on the right.*

LOUKA, *smoking a cigaret, is standing between the table and the house,
turning her back with angry disdain on a man servant who is lecturing her.
He is a middle-aged man of cool temperament and low but clear and keen intelligence, with the complacency of the servant who values himself on his rank
in servitude, and the imperturbability of the accurate calculator who has no
illusions. He wears a white Bulgarian costume : jacket with embroidered border, sash, wide knickerbockers, and decorated gaiters. His head is shaved up
to the crown, giving him a high Japanese forehead. His name is* NICOLA.

NICOLA. Be warned in time, Louka: mend your manners. I know the
mistress. She is so grand that she never dreams that any servant could
dare be disrespectful to her; but if she once suspects that you are defying her, out you go.

LOUKA. I do defy her. I will defy her. What do I care for her?

NICOLA. If you quarrel with the family, I never can marry you. It's the
same as if you quarrelled with me!

LOUKA. You take her part against me, do you?

NICOLA [*sedately*] I shall always be dependent on the good will of the
family. When I leave their service and start a shop in Sofia, their custom will be half my capital: their bad word would ruin me.

LOUKA. You have no spirit. I should like to catch them saying a word
against me!

NICOLA [*pityingly*] I should have expected more sense from you, Louka.
But youre young: youre young:

LOUKA. Yes; and you like me the better for it, dont you? But I know

some family secrets they wouldnt care to have told, young as I am.
Let them quarrel with me if they dare!

NICOLA [*with compassionate superiority*] Do you know what they would
do if they heard you talk like that?

LOUKA. What could they do?

NICOLA. Discharge you for untruthfulness. Who would believe any
stories you told after that? Who would give you another situation?
Who in this house would dare be seen speaking to you ever again?
How long would your father be left on his little farm? [*She impatiently
throws away the end of her cigaret, and stamps on it*]. Child: you dont
know the power such high people have over the like of you and me
when we try to rise out of our poverty against them. [*He goes close to
her and lowers his voice*]. Look at me, ten years in their service. Do you
think I know no secrets? I know things about the mistress that she
wouldnt have the master know for a thousand levas. I know things
about him that she wouldnt let him hear the last of for six months if I
blabbed them to her. I know things about Raina that would break off
her match with Sergius if—

LOUKA [*turning on him quickly*] How do you know? I never told you!

NICOLA [*opening his eyes cunningly*] So thats your little secret, is it? I
thought it might be something like that. Well, you take my advice
and be respectful; and make the mistress feel that no matter what you
know or dont know, she can depend on you to hold your tongue and
serve the family faithfully. Thats what they like; and thats how youll
make most out of them.

LOUKA [*with searching scorn*] You have the soul of a servant, Nicola.

NICOLA [*complacently*] Yes: thats the secret of success in service.

*A loud knocking with a whip handle on a wooden door is heard from the
stable yard.*

MALE VOICE OUTSIDE. Hollo! Hollo there! Nicola!

LOUKA. Master! back from the war!

NICOLA [*quickly*] My word for it, Louka, the war's over. Off with you
and get some fresh coffee. [*He runs out into the stable yard*].

LOUKA [*as she collects the coffee pot and cups on the tray, and carries it into
the house*] Youll never put the soul of a servant into me.

MAJOR PETKOFF *comes from the stable yard, followed by* NICOLA.
*He is a cheerful, excitable, insignificant, unpolished man of about 50, natu-
rally unambitious except as to his income and his importance in local society
but just now greatly pleased with the military rank which the war has
thrust on him as a man of consequence in his town. The fever of plucky
patriotism which the Serbian attack roused in all the Bulgarians has pulled
him through the war; but he is obviously glad to be home again.*

PETKOFF [*pointing to the table with his whip*] Breakfast out here, eh?

NICOLA. Yes, sir. The mistress and Miss Raina have just gone in.

PETKOFF [*sitting down and taking a roll*] Go in and say Ive come; and
get me some fresh coffee.

NICOLA. It's coming, sir. [*He goes to the house door.* LOUKA, *with fresh coffee, a clean cup, and a brandy bottle on her tray, meets him*]. Have you told the mistress?

LOUKA. Yes: she's coming.

NICOLA *goes into the house.* LOUKA *brings the coffee to the table.*

PETKOFF. Well: the Serbs havnt run away with you, have they?

LOUKA. No, sir.

PETKOFF. Thats right. Have you brought me some cognac?

LOUKA [*putting the bottle on the table*] Here, sir.

PETKOFF. T h a t s right. [*He pours some into his coffee*].

CATHERINE, *who, having at this early hour made only a very perfunctory toilet, wears a Bulgarian apron over a once brilliant but now half worn-out dressing gown, and a colored handkerchief tied over her thick black hair, comes from the house with Turkish slippers on her bare feet, looking astonishingly handsome and stately under all the circumstances.* LOUKA *goes into the house.*

CATHERINE. My dear Paul: what a surprise for us! [*She stoops over the back of his chair to kiss him*]. Have they brought you fresh coffee?

PETKOFF. Yes: Louka's been looking after me. The war's over. The treaty was signed three days ago at Bucharest; and the decree for our army to demobilize was issued yesterday.

CATHERINE [*springing erect, with flashing eyes*] Paul: have you let the Austrians force you to make peace?

PETKOFF [*submissively*] My dear: they didnt consult me. What could *I* do? [*She sits down and turns away from him*]. But of course we saw to it that the treaty was an honorable one. It declares peace—

CATHERINE [*outraged*] Peace!

PETKOFF [*appeasing her*]—but not friendly relations: remember that. They wanted to put that in; but I insisted on its being struck out. What more could I do?

CATHERINE. You could have annexed Serbia and made Prince Alexander Emperor of the Balkans. Thats what I would have done.

PETKOFF. I dont doubt it in the least, my dear. But I should have had to subdue the whole Austrian Empire first; and that would have kept me too long away from you. I missed you greatly.

CATHERINE [*relenting*] Ah! [*She stretches her hand affectionately across the table to squeeze his*].

PETKOFF. And how have you been, my dear?

CATHERINE. Oh, my usual sore throats: thats all.

PETKOFF [*with conviction*] That comes from washing your neck every day. Ive often told you so.

CATHERINE. Nonsense, Paul!

PETKOFF [*over his coffee and cigaret*] I dont believe in going too far with these modern customs. All this washing cant be good for the health: it's not natural. There was an Englishman at Philippopolis who used to wet himself all over with cold water every morning when he got up. Disgusting! It all comes from the English: their climate makes them so dirty that they have to be perpetually washing themselves. Look at my father! he never had a bath in his life; and he lived to be ninety-eight, the healthiest man in Bulgaria. I dont mind a good wash once a week to keep up my position; but once a day is carrying the thing to a ridiculous extreme.

CATHERINE. You are a barbarian at heart still, Paul. I hope you behaved yourself before all those Russian officers.

PETKOFF. I did my best. I took care to let them know that we have a library.

CATHERINE. Ah; but you didnt tell them that we have an electric bell in it? I have had one put up.

PETKOFF. Whats an electric bell?

CATHERINE. You touch a button; something tinkles in the kitchen; and then Nicola comes up.

PETKOFF. Why not shout for him?

CATHERINE. Civilized people never shout for their servants. I ve learnt that while you were away.

PETKOFF. Well, I'll tell you something Ive learnt too. Civilized people dont hang out their washing to dry where visitors can see it; so youd better have all that [*indicating the clothes on the bushes*] put somewhere else.

CATHERINE. Oh, thats absurd, Paul: I dont believe really refined people notice such things.

SERGIUS [*knocking at the stable gates*] Gate, Nicola!

PETKOFF. Theres Sergius. [*Shouting*] Hollo, Nicola!

CATHERINE. Oh, dont shout, Paul: it really isnt nice.

PETKOFF. Bosh! [*He shouts louder than before*] Nicola!

NICOLA [*appearing at the house door*] Yes, sir.

PETKOFF. Are you deaf? Dont you hear Major Saranoff knocking? Bring him round this way. [*He pronounces the name with the stress on the second syllable: Sarahnoff*].

NICOLA. Yes, major. [*He goes into the stable yard*].

PETKOFF. You must talk to him, my dear, until Raina takes him off our hands. He bores my life out about our not promoting him. Over my head, if you please.

CATHERINE. He certainly ought to be promoted when he marries Raina. Besides, the country should insist on having at least one native general.

PETKOFF. Yes; so that he could throw away whole brigades instead of regiments. It's no use, my dear: he hasnt the slightest chance of promotion until we're quite sure that the peace will be a lasting one.

NICOLA [*at the gate, announcing*] Major Sergius Saranoff! [*He goes into the house and returns presently with a third chair, which he places at the table. He then withdraws*].

MAJOR SERGIUS SARANOFF, *the original of the portrait in*

RAINA'S *room, is a tall romantically handsome man, with the physical hardihood, the high spirit, and the susceptible imagination of an untamed mountaineer chieftain. But his remarkable personal distinction is of a characteristically civilized type. The ridges of his eyebrows, curving with an interrogative twist round the projections at the outer corners; his jealously observant eye; his nose, thin, keen, and apprehensive in spite of the pugnacious high bridge and large nostril; his assertive chin, would not be out of place in a Parisian salon, shewing that the clever imaginative barbarian has an acute critical faculty which has been thrown into intense activity by the arrival of western civilization in the Balkans. The result is precisely what the advent of nineteenth century thought first produced in England: to wit, Byronism.[3] By his brooding on the perpetual failure, not only of others, but of himself, to live up to his ideals; by his consequent cynical scorn for humanity; by his jejune credulity as to the absolute validity of his concepts and the unworthiness of the world in disregarding them; by his wincings and mockeries under the sting of the petty disillusions which every hour spent among men brings to his sensitive observation, he has acquired the half tragic, half ironic air, the mysterious moodiness, the suggestion of a strange and terrible history that has left nothing but undying remorse, by which Childe Harold fascinated the grandmothers of his English contemporaries. It is clear that here or nowhere is RAINA'S ideal hero. CATHERINE is hardly less enthusiastic about him than her daughter, and much less reserved in shewing her enthusiasm. As he enters from the stable gate, she rises effusively to greet him. PETKOFF, is distinctively less disposed to make a fuss about him.*

PETKOFF. Here already, Sergius! Glad to see you.

CATHERINE. My dear Sergius! [*She holds out both her hands*].

SERGIUS [*kissing them with scrupulous gallantry*] My dear mother, if I may call you so.

PETKOFF [*drily*] Mother-in-law, Sergius: mother-in-law! Sit down; and have some coffee.

SERGIUS. Thank you: none for me. [*He gets away from the table with a certain distaste for* PETKOFF'S *enjoyment of it, and posts himself with conscious dignity against the rail of the steps leading to the house*].

CATHERINE. You look superb. The campaign has improved you, Sergius. Everybody here is mad about you. We were all wild with enthusiasm about that magnificent cavalry charge.

SERGIUS [*with grave irony*] Madam: it was the cradle and the grave of my military reputation.

CATHERINE. How so?

SERGIUS. I won the battle the wrong way when our worthy Russian generals were losing it the right way. In short, I upset their plans, and wounded their self-esteem. Two Cossack colonels had their regiments

---

[3] Bold masculine individualism inspired by such works of Lord Byron as *Manfred* (1817) and *Childe Harold's Pilgrimage* (1812–1818).

routed on the most correct principles of scientific warfare. Two major-generals got killed strictly according to military etiquette. The two colonels are now major-generals; and I am still a simple major.

CATHERINE. You shall not remain so, Sergius. The women are on your side; and they will see that justice is done you.

SERGIUS. It is too late. I have only waited for the peace to send in my resignation.

PETKOFF [*dropping his cup in his amazement*] Your resignation!

CATHERINE. Oh, you must withdraw it!

SERGIUS [*with resolute measured emphasis, folding his arms*] I never withdraw.

PETKOFF [*vexed*] Now who could have supposed you were going to do such a thing?

SERGIUS [*with fire*] Everyone that knew me. But enough of myself and my affairs. How is Raina; and where is Raina?

RAINA [*suddenly coming round the corner of the house and standing at the top of the steps in the path*] Raina is here.

She makes a charming picture as they turn to look at her. She wears an underdress of pale green silk, draped with an overdress of thin ecru canvas embroidered with gold. She is crowned with a dainty eastern cap of gold tinsel. SERGIUS goes impulsively to meet her. Posing regally, she presents her hand: he drops chivalrously on one knee and kisses it.

PETKOFF [*aside to* CATHERINE, *beaming with parental pride*] Pretty, isn't it? She always appears at the right moment.

CATHERINE [*impatiently*] Yes: she listens for it. It is an abominable habit.

SERGIUS leads RAINA forward with splendid gallantry. When they arrive at the table, she turns to him with a bend of the head: he bows; and thus they separate, he coming to his place, and she going behind her father's chair.

RAINA [*stooping and kissing her father*] Dear father! Welcome home!

PETKOFF [*patting his cheek*] My little pet girl. [*He kisses her. She goes to the chair left by* NICOLA *for* SERGIUS, *and sits down*].

CATHERINE. And so youre no longer a soldier, Sergius.

SERGIUS. I am no longer a soldier. Soldiering, my dear madam, is the coward's art of attacking when you are strong, and keeping out of harm's way when you are weak. That is the whole secret of successful fighting. Get your enemy at a disadvantage; and never, on any account, fight him on equal terms.

PETKOFF. They wouldnt let us make a fair stand-up fight of it. However, I suppose soldiering has to be a trade like any other trade.

SERGIUS. Precisely. But I have no ambition to shine as a tradesman; so I have taken the advice of that bagman of a captain that settled the exchange of prisoners with us at Pirot, and given it up.

PETKOFF. What! that Swiss fellow? Sergius: Ive often thought of that exchange since. He over-reached us about those horses.

SERGIUS. Of course he over-reached us. His father was a hotel and livery stable keeper; and he owed his first step to his knowledge of horse-dealing. [*With mock enthusiasm*] Ah, he was a soldier: every inch a soldier! If only I had bought the horses for my regiment instead of foolishly leading it into danger, I should have been a field-marshal now!

CATHERINE. A Swiss? What was he doing in the Serbian army?

PETKOFF. A volunteer, of course: keen on picking up his profession. [*Chuckling*] We shouldnt have been able to begin fighting if these foreigners hadnt shewn us how to do it: we knew nothing about it; and neither did the Serbs. Egad, there'd have been no war without them!

RAINA. Are there many Swiss officers in the Serbian army?

PETKOFF. No. All Austrians, just as our officers were all Russians. This was the only Swiss I came across. I'll never trust a Swiss again. He humbugged us into giving him fifty ablebodied men for two hundred worn out chargers. They werent even eatable!

SERGIUS. We were two children in the hands of that consummate soldier, Major: simply two innocent little children.

RAINA. What was he like?

CATHERINE. Oh, Raina, what a silly question!

SERGIUS. He was like a commercial traveller in uniform. Bourgeois to his boots!

PETKOFF [*grinning*] Sergius: tell Catherine that queer story his friend told us about how he escaped after Slivnitza. You remember. About his being hid by two women.

SERGIUS [*with bitter irony*] Oh yes: quite a romance! He was serving in the very battery I so unprofessionally charged. Being a thorough soldier, he ran away like the rest of them, with our cavalry at his heels. To escape their sabres he climbed a waterpipe and made his way into the bedroom of a young Bulgarian lady. The young lady was enchanted by his persuasive commercial traveller's manners. She very modestly entertained him for an hour or so, and then called in her mother lest her conduct should appear unmaidenly. The old lady was equally fascinated; and the fugitive was sent on his way in the morning, disguised in an old coat belonging to the master of the house, who was away at the war.

RAINA [*rising with marked stateliness*] Your life in the camp has made you coarse, Sergius. I did not think you would have repeated such a story before me. [*She turns away coldly*].

CATHERINE [*also rising*] She is right, Sergius. If such women exist, we should be spared the knowledge of them.

PETKOFF. Pooh! nonsense! what does it matter?

SERGIUS [*ashamed*] No, Petkoff: I was wrong. [*To* RAINA, *with earnest humility*] I beg your pardon. I have behaved abominably. Forgive me, Raina. [*She bows reservedly*]. And you too, Madam. [CATHERINE *bows graciously and sits down. He proceeds solemnly, again addressing* RAINA] The glimpses I have had of the seamy side of life during the last few months have made me cynical; but I should not have brought my cynicism here: least of all into your presence, Raina. I—[*Here, turning to the others, he is evidently going to begin a long speech when the* MAJOR *interrupts him*].

PETKOFF. Stuff and nonsense, Sergius! Thats quite enough fuss about nothing: a soldier's daughter should be able to stand up without flinching to a little strong conversation. [*He rises*]. Come: it's time for us to get to business. We have to make up our minds how those three regiments are to get back to Philippopolis: theres no forage for them on the Sofia route. [*He goes towards the house*]. Come along. [SERGIUS *is about to follow him when* CATHERINE *rises and intervenes*].

CATHERINE. Oh, Paul, cant you spare Sergius for a few moments? Raina has hardly seen him yet. Perhaps I can help you to settle about the regiments.

SERGIUS [*protesting*] My dear madam, impossible: you—

CATHERINE [*stopping him playfully*] You stay here, my dear Sergius: [SERGIUS *instantly bows and steps back*]. Now, dear [*taking* PETKOFF'S *arm*]: come and see the electric bell.

PETKOFF. Oh, very well, very well.

They go into the house together affectionately. Sergius, left alone with Raina, looks anxiously at her, fearing that she is still offended. She smiles, and stretches out her arms to him.

SERGIUS [*hastening to her*] Am I forgiven?

RAINA [*placing her hands on his shoulders as she looks up at him with admiration and worship*] My hero! My king!

SERGIUS. My queen! [*He kisses her on the forehead*].

RAINA. How I have envied you, Sergius! You have been out in the world, on the field of battle, able to prove yourself there worthy of any woman in the world; whilst I have had to sit at home inactive—dreaming—useless—doing nothing that could give me the right to call myself worthy of any man.

SERGIUS. Dearest: all my deeds have been yours. You inspired me. I have gone through the war like a knight in a tournament with his lady looking down at him!

RAINA. And you have never been absent from my thoughts for a moment. [*Very solemnly*] Sergius: I think we two have found the higher love. When I think of you, I feel that I could never do a base deed or think an ignoble thought.

SERGIUS. My lady and my saint! [*He clasps her reverently*].

RAINA [*returning his embrace*] My lord and my—

SERGIUS. Sh—sh! Let me be the worshiper, dear. You little know how unworthy even the best man is of a girl's pure passion!

RAINA. I trust you. I love you. You will never disappoint me, Sergius. [*Louka is heard singing within the house. They quickly release each other*].

I cant pretend to talk indifferently before her: my heart is too full. [LOUKA *comes from the house with her tray. She goes to the table, and begins to clear it, with her back turned to them*]. I will get my hat; and then we can go out until lunch time. Wouldnt you like that?

SERGIUS. Be quick. If you are away five minutes, it will seem five hours. [RAINA *runs to the top of the steps, and turns there to exchange looks with him and wave him a kiss with both hands. He looks after her with emotion for a moment; then turns slowly away, his face radiant with the loftiest exaltation. The movement shifts his field of vision, into the corner of which there now comes the tail of* LOUKA's *double apron. His attention is arrested at once. He takes a stealthy look at her, and begins to twirl his moustache mischievously, with his left hand akimbo on his hip. Finally, striking the ground with his heels in something of a cavalry swagger, he strolls over to the other side of the table, opposite her, and says*] Louka: do you know what the higher love is?

LOUKA [*astonished*] No, sir.

SERGIUS. Very fatiguing thing to keep up for any length of time, Louka. One feels the need of some relief after it.

LOUKA [*innocently*] Perhaps you would like some coffee, sir? [*She stretches her hand across the table for the coffee pot*].

SERGIUS [*taking her hand*] Thank you, Louka.

LOUKA [*pretending to pull*] Oh, sir, you know I didnt mean that. I'm surprised at you!

SERGIUS [*coming clear of the table and drawing her with him*] I am surprised at myself, Louka. What would Sergius, the hero of Slivnitza, say if he saw me now? What would Sergius, the apostle of the higher love, say if he saw me now? What would the half dozen Sergiuses who keep popping in and out of this handsome figure of mine say if they caught us here? [*Letting go her hand and slipping his arm dexterously round her waist*] Do you consider my figure handsome, Louka?

LOUKA. Let me go, sir. I shall be disgraced. [*She struggles: he holds her inexorably*]. Oh, will you let go?

SERGIUS [*looking straight into her eyes*] No.

LOUKA. Then stand back where we cant be seen. Have you no common sense?

SERGIUS. Ah! thats reasonable. [*He takes her into the stableyard gateway, where they are hidden from the house*].

LOUKA [*plaintively*] I may have been seen from the windows: Miss Raina is sure to be spying about after you.

SERGIUS [*stung: letting her go*] Take care, Louka. I may be worthless enough to betray the higher love; but do not you insult it.

LOUKA [*demurely*] Not for the world, sir, I'm sure. May I go on with my work, please, now?

SERGIUS [*again putting his arm round her*] You are a provoking little witch, Louka. If you were in love with me, would you spy out of windows on me?

LOUKA. Well, you see, sir, since you say you are half a dozen different gentlemen all at once, I should have a great deal to look after.

SERGIUS [*charmed*] Witty as well as pretty. [*He tries to kiss her*].

LOUKA [*avoiding him*] No: I dont want your kisses. Gentlefolk are all alike: you making love to me behind Miss Raina's back; and she doing the same behind yours.

SERGIUS [*recoiling a step*] Louka!

LOUKA. It shews how little you really care.

SERGIUS [*dropping his familiarity, and speaking with freezing politeness*] If our conversation is to continue, Louka, you will please remember that a gentleman does not discuss the conduct of the lady he is engaged to with her maid.

LOUKA. It's so hard to know what a gentleman considers right. I thought from your trying to kiss me that you had given up being so particular.

SERGIUS [*turning from her and striking his forehead as he comes back into the garden from the gateway*] Devil! devil!

LOUKA. Ha! ha! I expect one of the six of you is very like me, sir; though I am only Miss Raina's maid. [*She goes back to her work at the table, taking no further notice of him*].

SERGIUS [*speaking to himself*] Which of the six is the real man? thats the question that torments me. One of them is a hero, another a buffoon, another a humbug, another perhaps a bit of a blackguard. [*He pauses, and looks furtively at Louka as he adds, with deep bitterness*] And one, at least, is a coward: jealous, like all cowards. [*He goes to the table*]. Louka.

LOUKA. Yes?

SERGIUS. Who is my rival?

LOUKA. You shall never get that out of me, for love or money.

SERGIUS. Why?

LOUKA. Never mind why. Besides, you would tell that I told you; and I should lose my place.

SERGIUS [*holding out his right hand in affirmation*] No! on the honor of a—[*He checks himself; and his hand drops, nerveless, as he concludes sardonically*]—of a man capable of behaving as I have been behaving for the last five minutes. Who is he?

LOUKA. I dont know. I never saw him. I only heard his voice through the door of her room.

SERGIUS. Damnation! How dare you?

LOUKA [*retreating*] Oh, I mean no harm: youve no right to take up my words like that. The mistress knows all about it. And I tell you that if that gentleman ever comes here again, Miss Raina will marry him, whether he likes it or not. I know the difference between the sort of manner you and she put on before one another and the real manner.

Sergius shivers as if she had stabbed him. Then, setting his face like iron, he strides grimly to her, and grips her above the elbows with both hands.

SERGIUS. Now listen you to me.

LOUKA [*wincing*] Not so tight: youre hurting me.

SERGIUS. That doesnt matter. You have stained my honor by making me a party to your eavesdropping. And you have betrayed your mistress.

LOUKA [*writhing*] Please—

SERGIUS. That shews that you are an abominable little clod of common clay, with the soul of a servant. [*He lets her go as if she were an unclean thing, and turns away, dusting his hands of her, to the bench by the wall, where he sits down with averted head, meditating gloomily*].

LOUKA [*whimpering angrily with her hands up her sleeves, feeling her bruised arms*] You know how to hurt with your tongue as well as with your hands. But I dont care, now Ive found out that whatever clay I'm made of, youre made of the same. As for her, she's a liar; and her fine airs are a cheat; and I'm worth six of her. [*She shakes the pain off hardily; tosses her head; and sets to work to put the things on the tray*].

He looks doubtfully at her. She finishes packing the tray, and laps the cloth over the edges, so as to carry all out together. As she stoops to lift it, he rises.

SERGIUS. Louka! [*She stops and looks defiantly at him*]. A gentleman has no right to hurt a woman under any circumstances. [*With profound humility, uncovering his head*] I beg your pardon.

LOUKA. That sort of apology may satisfy a lady. Of what use is it to a servant?

SERGIUS [*rudely crossed in his chivalry, throws it off with a bitter laugh, and says slightingly*] Oh! you wish to be paid for the hurt? [*He puts on his shako, and takes some money from his pocket*].

LOUKA [*her eyes filling with tears in spite of herself*] No: I want my hurt made well.

SERGIUS [*sobered by her tone*] How?

She rolls up her left sleeve; clasps her arm with the thumb and fingers of her right hand; and looks down at the bruise. Then she raises her head and looks straight at him. Finally, with a superb gesture, she presents her arm to be kissed. Amazed, he looks at her; at the arm; at her again; hesitates; and then, with shuddering intensity, exclaims Never! and gets away as far as possible from her.

Her arm drops. Without a word, and with unaffected dignity, she takes her tray, and is approaching the house when RAINA returns, wearing a hat and jacket in the height of the Vienna fashion of the previous year, 1885. LOUKA makes way proudly for her, and then goes into the house.

RAINA. I'm ready. Whats the matter? [*Gaily*] Have you been flirting with Louka?

SERGIUS [*hastily*] No, no. How can you think such a thing?

RAINA [*ashamed of herself*] Forgive me, dear: it was only a jest. I am so happy to-day.

He goes quickly to her, and kisses her hand remorsefully. CATHERINE *comes out and calls to them from the top of the steps.*

CATHERINE [*coming down to them*] I am sorry to disturb you, children; but Paul is distracted over those three regiments. He doesnt know how to send them to Philippopolis; and he objects to every suggestion of mine. You must go and help him, Sergius. He is in the library.

RAINA [*disappointed*] But we are just going out for a walk.

SERGIUS. I shall not be long. Wait for me just five minutes. [*He runs up the steps to the door*].

RAINA [*following him to the foot of the steps and looking up at him with timid coquetry*] I shall go round and wait in full view of the library windows. Be sure you draw father's attention to me. If you are a moment longer than five minutes, I shall go in and fetch you, regiments or no regiments.

SERGIUS [*laughing*] Very well. [*He goes in*].

Raina watches him until he is out of her sight. Then, with a perceptible relaxation of manner, she begins to pace up and down the garden in a brown study.

CATHERINE. Imagine their meeting that Swiss and hearing the whole story! The very first thing your father asked for was the old coat we sent him off in. A nice mess you have got us into!

RAINA [*gazing thoughtfully at the gravel as she walks*] The little beast!

CATHERINE. Little beast! What little beast?

RAINA. To go and tell! Oh, if I had him here, I'd cram him with chocolate creams til he couldnt ever speak again!

CATHERINE. Dont talk such stuff. Tell me the truth, Raina. How long was he in your room before you came to me?

RAINA [*whisking round and recommencing her march in the opposite direction*] Oh, I forget.

CATHERINE. You cannot forget! Did he really climb up after the soldiers were gone; or was he there when that officer searched the room?

RAINA. No. Yes: I think he must have been there then.

CATHERINE. You think! Oh, Raina! Raina! Will anything ever make you straightforward? If Sergius finds out, it will be all over between you.

RAINA [*with cool impertinence*] Oh, I know Sergius is your pet. I sometimes wish you could marry him instead of me. You would just suit him. You would pet him, and spoil him, and mother him to perfection.

CATHERINE [*opening her eyes very widely indeed*]. Well, upon my word!

RAINA [*capriciously: half to herself*] I always feel a longing to do or say something dreadful to him—to shock his propriety—to scandalize the five senses out of him. [*To Catherine, perversely*] I dont care whether he finds out about the chocolate cream soldier or not. I half hope he may. [*She again turns and strolls flippantly away up the path to the corner of the house*].

CATHERINE. And what should I be able to say to your father, pray?

RAINA [*over her shoulder, from the top of the two steps*] Oh, poor father! As if he could help himself! [*She turns the corner and passes out of sight*].

CATHERINE [*looking after her, her fingers itching*] Oh, if you were only ten years younger! [LOUKA *comes from the house with a salver, which she carries hanging down by her side*]. Well?

LOUKA. Theres a gentleman just called, madam. A Serbian officer.

CATHERINE [*flaming*] A Serb! And how dare he—[*checking herself bitterly*] Oh, I forgot. We are at peace now. I suppose we shall have them calling every day to pay their compliments. Well: if he is an officer why dont you tell your master? He is in the library with Major Saranoff. Why do you come to me?

LOUKA. But he asks for you, madam. And I dont think he knows who you are: he said the lady of the house. He gave me this little ticket for you. [*She takes a card out of her bosom; puts it on the salver; and offers it to Catherine*].

CATHERINE [*reading*] "Captain Bluntschli"? Thats a German name.

LOUKA. Swiss, madam, I think.

CATHERINE [*with a bound that makes* LOUKA *jump back*] Swiss! What is he like?

LOUKA [*timidly*] He has a big carpet bag, madam.

CATHERINE. Oh Heavens! he's come to return the coat. Send him away: say we're not at home: ask him to leave his address and I'll write to him. Oh stop: that will never do. Wait! [*She throws herself into a chair to think it out.* LOUKA *waits*]. The master and Major Saranoff are busy in the library, arnt they?

LOUKA. Yes, madam.

CATHERINE [*decisively*] Bring the gentleman out here at once. [*Peremptorily*] And be very polite to him. Dont delay. Here [*impatiently snatching the salver from her*] : leave that here; and go straight back to him.

LOUKA. Yes, madam [*going*].

CATHERINE. Louka!

LOUKA [*stopping*] Yes, madam.

CATHERINE. Is the library door shut?

LOUKA. I think so, madam.

CATHERINE. If not, shut it as you pass through.

LOUKA. Yes, madam [*going*].

CATHERINE. Stop! [*Louka stops*]. He will have to go that way [*indicating the gate of the stableyard*]. Tell Nicola to bring his bag here after him. Dont forget.

LOUKA [*surprised*] His bag?

CATHERINE. Yes: here: as soon as possible. [*Vehemently*] Be quick! [LOUKA *runs into the house.* CATHERINE *snatches her apron off and throws it behind a bush. She then takes up the salver and uses it as a mirror, with the result that the handkerchief tied round her head follows the apron.*

A touch to her hair and a shake to her dressing gown make her presentable].
Oh, how? how? how can a man be such a fool! Such a moment to select! [LOUKA *appears at the door of the house, announcing* Captain
Bluntschli. *She stands aside at the top of the steps to let him pass before she
goes in again. He is the man of the midnight adventure in* RAINA'*s room,
clean, well brushed, smartly uniformed, and out of trouble, but still unmistakably the same man. The moment* LOUKA'*s back is turned*, CATHE-
RINE *swoops on him with impetuous, urgent, coaxing appeal*]. Captain
Bluntschli: I am very glad to see you; but you must leave this house
at once. [*He raises his eyebrows*]. My husband has just returned with
my future son-in-law; and they know nothing. If they did, the consequences would be terrible. You are a foreigner: you do not feel our
national animosities as we do. We still hate the Serbs: the effect of
the peace on my husband has been to make him feel like a lion baulked
of his prey. If he discovers our secret, he will never forgive me; and
and my daughter's life will hardly be safe. Will you, like the chival-
rous gentleman and soldier you are, leave at once before he finds you
here?

BLUNTSCHLI [*disappointed, but philosophical*] At once, gracious lady. I
only came to thank you and return the coat you lent me. If you will
allow me to take it out of my bag and leave it with your servant as I
pass out, I need detain you no further. [*He turns to go into the house*].

CATHERINE [*catching him by the sleeve*] Oh, you must not think of going
back that way. [*Coaxing him across to the stable gates*] This is the shortest
way out. Many thanks. So glad to have been of service to you. Goodbye.

BLUNTSCHLI. But my bag?

CATHERINE. It shall be sent on. You will leave me your address.

BLUNTSCHLI. True. Allow me. [*He takes out his card-case, and stops to
write his address, keeping* CATHERINE *in an agony of impatience. As he
hands her the card*, PETKOFF, *hatless, rushes from the house in a fluster of
hospitality, followed by* SERGIUS].

PETKOFF [*as he hurries down the steps*] My dear Captain Bluntschli—

CATHERINE. Oh Heavens! [*She sinks on the seat against the wall*].

PETKOFF [*too preoccupied to notice her as he shakes* BLUNTSCHLI'*s hand
heartily*] Those stupid people of mine thought I was out here, instead
of in the—haw!—library [*he cannot mention the library without betraying how proud he is of it*]. I saw you through the window. I was
wondering why you didnt come in. Saranoff is with me: you remember
him, dont you?

SERGIUS [*saluting humorously, and then offering his hand with great charm
of manner*] Welcome, our friend the enemy!

PETKOFF. No longer the enemy, happily. [*Rather anxiously*] I hope
youve called as a friend, and not about horses or prisoners.

CATHERINE. Oh, quite as a friend, Paul. I was just asking Captain
Bluntschli to stay to lunch; but he declares he must go at once.

SERGIUS [*sardonically*] Impossible, Bluntschli. We want you here badly.

We have to send on three cavalry regiments to Philippopolis; and we dont in the least know how to do it.

BLUNTSCHLI [*suddenly attentive and businesslike*] Philippopolis? The forage is the trouble, I suppose.

PETKOFF [*eagerly*] Yes: thats it. [*To* SERGIUS] He sees the whole thing at once.

BLUNTSCHLI. I think I can shew you how to manage that.

SERGIUS. Invaluable man! Come along! [*Towering over* BLUNT-SCHLI, *he puts his hand on his shoulder and takes him to the steps,* PETKOFF *following*]. RAINA *comes from the house as* BLUNTSCHLI *puts his foot on the first step.*

RAINA. Oh! The chocolate cream soldier!

BLUNTSCHLI *stands rigid.* SERGIUS, *amazed, looks at* RAINA, *then at* PETKOFF, *who looks back at him and then at his wife.*

CATHERINE [*with commanding presence of mind*] My dear Raina, dont you see that we have a guest here? Captain Bluntschli: one of our new Serbian friends.

RAINA *bows:* BLUNTSCHLI *bows.*

RAINA. How silly of me! [*She comes down into the center of the group, between* BLUNTSCHLI *and* PETKOFF]. I made a beautiful ornament this morning for the ice pudding; and that stupid Nicola has just put down a pile of plates on it and spoilt it. [*To* BLUNTSCHLI, *winningly*] I hope you didnt think that you were the chocolate cream soldier, Captain Bluntschli.

BLUNTSCHLI [*laughing*] I assure you I did. [*Stealing a whimsical glance at her*] Your explanation was a relief.

PETKOFF [*suspiciously, to* RAINA] And since when, pray, have you taken to cooking?

CATHERINE. Oh, whilst you were away. It is her latest fancy.

PETKOFF [*testily*] And has Nicola taken to drinking? He used to be careful enough. First he shews Captain Bluntschli out here when he knew quite well I was in the library; and then he goes downstairs and breaks Raina's chocolate soldier. He must—[*Nicola appears at the top of the steps with the bag. He descends; places it respectfully before* BLUNT-SCHLI; *and waits for further orders. General amazement.* NICOLA, *unconscious of the effect he is producing, looks perfectly satisfied with himself. When* PETKOFF *recovers his power of speech, he breaks out at him with*] Are you mad, Nicola?

NICOLA [*taken aback*] Sir?

PETKOFF. What have you brought that for?

NICOLA. My lady's orders, major. Louka told me that—

CATHERINE [*interrupting him*] My orders! Why should I order you to bring Captain Bluntschli's luggage out here? What are you thinking of Nicola?

NICOLA [*after a moment's bewilderment, picking up the bag as he addresses* BLUNTSCHLI *with the very perfection of servile discretion*] I beg your pardon, captain, I am sure. [*To* CATHERINE] My fault, madam: I hope youll overlook it. [*He bows, and is going to the steps with the bag, when* PETKOFF *addresses him angrily*].

PETKOFF. Youd better go and slam that bag, too, down on Miss Raina's ice pudding! [*This is too much for* NICOLA. *The bag drops from his hand almost on his master's toes, eliciting a roar of*] Begone, you butter-fingered donkey.

NICOLA [*snatching up the bag, and escaping into the house*] Yes, major.

CATHERINE. Oh, never mind, Paul: dont be angry.

PETKOFF [*blustering*] Scoundrel! He's got out of hand while I was away. I'll teach him. Infernal blackguard! The sack next Saturday! I'll clear out the whole establishment—[*He is stifled by the caresses of his wife and daughter, who hang round his neck, petting him*].

CATHERINE ⎫ ⎧ Now, now, now, it mustnt be angry. He
RAINA ⎬ [*together*] ⎨ Wow, wow, wow: not on your first day at
⎩ meant no harm. Be good to please me, dear. Sh-sh-
home. I'll make another ice pudding. Tch-ch-ch.
sh-sh!

PETKOFF [*yielding*] Oh well, never mind. Come Bluntschli: let's have no more nonsense about going away. You know very well youre not going back to Switzerland yet. Until you do go back youll stay with us.

RAINA. Oh, do, Captain Bluntschli.

PETKOFF [*to* CATHERINE] Now, Catherine: it's of you he's afraid. Press him; and he'll stay.

CATHERINE. Of course I shall be only too delighted if [*appealingly*] Captain Bluntschli really wishes to stay. He knows my wishes.

BLUNTSCHLI [*in his driest military manner*] I am at madam's orders.

SERGIUS [*cordially*] That settles it!

PETKOFF [*heartily*] Of course!

RAINA. You see you must stay.

BLUNTSCHLI [*smiling*] Well, if I must, I must.

Gesture of despair from CATHERINE.

ACT III

IN *the library after lunch. It is not much of a library. Its literary equipment consists of a single fixed shelf stocked with old paper covered novels, broken backed, coffee stained, torn and thumbed; and a couple of little hanging shelves with a few gift books on them: the rest of the wall space being occupied by trophies of war and the chase. But it is a most comfortable sitting room. A row of three large windows shews a mountain panorama, just now seen in one of its friendliest aspects in the mellowing afternoon light. In the corner next the right hand window a square earthenware stove, a perfect tower of glistening pottery, rises nearly to the ceiling and guarantees plenty of warmth. The ottoman is like that in* RAINA'S *room, and similarly placed; and the window seats are luxurious with decorated cushions. There is one object, however, hopelessly out of keeping with its surroundings. This is a small kitchen table, much the worse for wear, fitted as a writing table with an old canister full of pens, an eggcup filled with ink, and a deplorable scrap of heavily used pink blotting paper.*

At the side of this table, which stands to the left of anyone facing the window, BLUNTSCHLI *is hard at work with a couple of maps before him, writing orders. At the head of it sits* SERGIUS, *who is supposed to be also at work, but is actually gnawing the feather of a pen, and contemplating* BLUNTSCHLI'S *quick, sure, businesslike progress with a mixture of envious irritation at his own incapacity and awestruck wonder at an ability which seems to him almost miraculous, though its prosaic character forbids him to esteem it. The* MAJOR *is comfortably established on the ottoman, with a newspaper in his hand and the tube of his hookah within easy reach.* CATHERINE *sits at the stove, with her back to them, embroidering.* RAINA, *reclining on the divan, is gazing in a day-dream out at the Balkan landscape, with a neglected novel in her lap.*

The door is on the same side as the stove, farther from the window. The button of the electric bell is at the opposite side, behind BLUNTSCHLI.

PETKOFF [*looking up from his paper to watch how they are getting on at the table*] Are you sure I cant help you in any way, Bluntschli?

BLUNTSCHLI [*without interrupting his writing or looking up*] Quite sure, thank you. Saranoff and I will manage it.

SERGIUS [*grimly*] Yes: we'll manage it. He finds out what to do; draws up the orders; and I sign em. Division of labor! [BLUNTSCHLI *passes him a paper*]. Another one? Thank you. [*He plants the paper squarely before him; sets his chair carefully parallel to it; and signs with his cheek on his elbow and his protruded tongue following the movements of his pen*]. This hand is more accustomed to the sword than to the pen.

PETKOFF. It's very good of you, Bluntschli: it is indeed, to let yourself be put upon in this way. Now are you quite sure I can do nothing?

CATHERINE [*in a low warning tone*] You can stop interrupting, Paul.

PETKOFF [*starting and looking round at her*] Eh? Oh! Quite right, my love: quite right. [*He takes his newspaper up again, but presently lets it drop*]. Ah, you havnt been campaigning, Catherine: you dont know how pleasant it is for us to sit here, after a good lunch, with nothing to do but enjoy ourselves. Theres only one thing I want to make me thoroughly comfortable.

CATHERINE. What is that?

PETKOFF. My old coat. I'm not at home in this one: I feel as if I were on parade.

CATHERINE. My dear Paul, how absurd you are about that old coat! It must be hanging in the blue closet where you left it.

PETKOFF. My dear Catherine, I tell you Ive looked there. Am I to believe my own eyes or not? [CATHERINE *rises and crosses the room to press the button of the electric bell*]. What are you shewing off that bell for? [*She looks at him majestically and silently resumes her chair and her needlework*]. My dear: if you think the obstinacy of your sex can make a coat out of two old dressing gowns of Raina's, your waterproof, and my mackintosh, youre mistaken. Thats exactly what the blue closet contains at present.

NICOLA *presents himself*.

CATHERINE. Nicola: go to the blue closet and bring your master's old coat here: the braided one he wears in the house.

NICOLA. Yes, madame. [*He goes out*].

PETKOFF. Catherine.

CATHERINE. Yes, Paul?

PETKOFF. I bet you any piece of jewellery you like to order from Sofia against a week's housekeeping money that the coat isnt there.

CATHERINE. Done, Paul!

PETKOFF [*excited by the prospect of a gamble*] Come: here's an opportunity for some sport. Wholl bet on it? Bluntschli: I'll give you six to one.

BLUNTSCHLI [*imperturbably*] It would be robbing you, major. Madame is sure to be right. [*Without looking up, he passes another batch of papers to* SERGIUS].

SERGIUS [*also excited*] Bravo, Switzerland! Major: I bet my best charger against an Arab mare for Raina that Nicola finds the coat in the blue closet.

PETKOFF [*eagerly*] Your best char—

CATHERINE [*hastily interrupting him*] Dont be foolish, Paul. An Arabian mare will cost you 50,000 levas.

RAINA [*suddenly coming out of her picturesque revery*] Really, mother, if you are going to take the jewellery, I dont see why you should grudge me my Arab.

NICOLA *comes back with the coat, and brings it to* PETKOFF, *who can hardly believe his eyes*.

CATHERINE. Where was it, Nicola?

NICOLA. Hanging in the blue closet, madame.

PETKOFF. Well, I am d—

CATHERINE [*stopping him*] Paul!

PETKOFF. I could have sworn it wasnt there. Age is beginning to tell on me. I'm getting hallucinations. [*To* NICOLA] Here: help me to change. Excuse me, Bluntschli. [*He begins changing coats,* NICOLA *acting as valet*]. Remember: I didnt take that bet of yours, Sergius. Youd better give Raina that Arab steed yourself, since youve roused her expectations. Eh, Raina? [*He looks round at her; but she is again rapt in the landscape. With a little gush of parental affection and pride, he points her out to them, and says*] She's dreaming, as usual.

SERGIUS. Assuredly she shall not be the loser.

PETKOFF. So much the better for her. I shant come off so cheaply, I expect. [*The change is now complete.* NICOLA *goes out with the discarded coat*]. Ah, now I feel at home at last. [*He sits down and takes his newspaper with a grunt of relief*].

BLUNTSCHLI [*to* SERGIUS, *handing a paper*] Thats the last order.

PETKOFF [*jumping up*] What! Finished?

BLUNTSCHLI. Finished.

PETKOFF [*with childlike envy*] Havnt you anything for me to sign?

BLUNTSCHLI. Not necessary. His signature will do.

PETKOFF [*inflating his chest and thumping it*] Ah well, I think weve done a thundering good day's work. Can I do anything more?

BLUNTSCHLI. You had better both see the fellows that are to take these. [SERGIUS *rises*] Pack them off at once; and shew them that Ive marked on the orders the time they should hand them in by. Tell them that if they stop to drink or tell stories—if theyre five minutes late, theyll have the skin taken off their backs.

SERGIUS [*stiffening indignantly*] I'll say so. [*He strides to the door*]. And if one of them is man enough to spit in my face for insulting him, I'll buy his discharge and give him a pension. [*He goes out*].

BLUNTSCHLI [*confidentially*] Just see that he talks to them properly, major, will you?

PETKOFF [*officiously*] Quite right, Bluntschli, quite right. I'll see to it. [*He goes to the door importantly, but hesitates on the threshold*]. By the bye, Catherine, you may as well come too. Theyll be far more frightened of you than of me.

CATHERINE [*putting down her embroidery*] I daresay I had better. You would only splutter at them. [*She goes out,* PETKOFF *holding the door for her and following her*].

BLUNTSCHLI. What an army! They make cannons out of cherry trees; and the officers send for their wives to keep discipline! [*He begins to fold and docket the papers*].

RAINA, *who has risen from the divan, marches slowly down the room with her hands clasped behind her, and looks mischievously at him.*

RAINA. You look ever so much nicer than when we last met. [*He looks up, surprised*]. What have you done to yourself?

BLUNTSCHLI. Washed; brushed; good night's sleep and breakfast. Thats all.

RAINA. Did you get back safely that morning?

BLUNTSCHLI. Quite, thanks.

RAINA. Were they angry with you for running away from Sergius's charge?

BLUNTSCHLI [*grinning*] No: they were glad; because theyd all just run away themselves.

RAINA [*going to the table, and leaning over it towards him*] It must have made a lovely story for them: all that about me and my room.

BLUNTSCHLI. Capital story. But I only told it to one of them: a particular friend.

RAINA. On whose discretion you could absolutely rely?

BLUNTSCHLI. Absolutely.

RAINA. Hm! He told it all to my father and Sergius the day you exchanged the prisoners. [*She turns away and strolls carelessly across to the other side of the room*].

BLUNTSCHLI [*deeply concerned, and half incredulous*] No! You dont mean that, do you?

RAINA [*turning, with sudden earnestness*] I do indeed. But they dont know that it was in this house you took refuge. If Sergius knew, he would challenge you and kill you in a duel.

BLUNTSCHLI. Bless me! then dont tell him.

RAINA. Please be serious, Captain Bluntschli. Can you not realize what it is to me to deceive him? I want to be quite perfect with Sergius: no meanness, no smallness, no deceit. My relation to him is the one really beautiful and noble part of my life. I hope you can understand that.

BLUNTSCHLI [*sceptically*] You mean that you wouldnt like him to find out that the story about the ice pudding was a—a—a—You know.

RAINA [*wincing*] Ah, dont talk of it in that flippant way. I lied: I know it. But I did it to save your life. He would have killed you. That was the second time I ever uttered a falsehood. [BLUNTSCHLI *rises quickly and looks doubtfully and somewhat severely at her*]. Do you remember the first time?

BLUNTSCHLI. I! No. Was I present?

RAINA. Yes; and I told the officer who was searching for you that you were not present.

BLUNTSCHLI. True. I should have remembered it.

RAINA [*greatly encouraged*] Ah, it is natural that you should forget it first. It cost you nothing: it cost me a lie! A lie!!

She sits down on the ottoman, looking straight before her with her hands clasped round her knee. BLUNTSCHLI, *quite touched, goes to the ottoman with a particularly reassuring and considerate air, and sits down beside her.*

BLUNTSCHLI. My dear young lady, dont let this worry you. Remember: I'm a soldier. Now what are the two things that happen to a soldier so often that he comes to think nothing of them? One is hearing people tell lies [RAINA *recoils*]: the other is getting his life saved in all sorts of ways by all sorts of people.

RAINA [*rising in indignant protest*] And so he becomes a creature incapable of faith and of gratitude.

BLUNTSCHLI [*making a wry face*] Do you like gratitude? I dont. If pity is akin to love, gratitude is akin to the other thing.

RAINA. Gratitude! [*Turning on him*] If you are incapable of gratitude you are incapable of any noble sentiment. Even animals are grateful. Oh, I see now exactly what you think of me! You were not surprised to hear me lie. To you it was something I probably did every day! every hour!! That is how men think of women. [*She paces the room tragically*].

BLUNTSCHLI [*dubiously*] Theres reason in everything. You said youd told only two lies in your whole life. Dear young lady: isnt that rather a short allowance? I'm quite a straightforward man myself; but it wouldnt last me a whole morning.

RAINA [*staring haughtily at him*] Do you know, sir, that you are insulting me?

BLUNTSCHLI. I cant help it. When you strike that noble attitude and speak in that thrilling voice, I admire you; but I find it impossible to believe a single word you say.

RAINA [*superbly*] Captain Bluntschli!

BLUNTSCHLI [*unmoved*] Yes?

RAINA [*standing over him, as if she could not believe her senses*] Do you mean what you said just now? Do you know what you said just now?

BLUNTSCHLI. I do.

RAINA [*gasping*] I! I!!! [*She points to herself incredulously, meaning "I, RAINA PETKOFF, tell lies!" He meets her gaze unflinchingly. She suddenly sits down beside him, and adds, with a complete change of manner from the heroic to a babyish familiarity*] How did you find me out?

BLUNTSCHLI [*promptly*] Instinct, dear young lady. Instinct, and experience of the world.

RAINA [*wonderingly*] Do you know, you are the first man I ever met who did not take me seriously?

BLUNTSCHLI. You mean, dont you, that I am the first man that has ever taken you quite seriously?

RAINA. Yes: I suppose I do mean that. [*Cosily, quite at her ease with him*] How strange it is to be talked to in such a way! You know, Ive always gone on like that.

BLUNTSCHLI. You mean the—?

RAINA. I mean the noble attitude and the thrilling voice. [*They laugh together*]. I did it when I was a tiny child to my nurse. She believed in it. I do it before my parents. They believe in it. I do it before Sergius. He believes in it.

BLUNTSCHLI. Yes: he's a little in that line himself, isnt he?

RAINA [*startled*] Oh! Do you think so?

BLUNTSCHLI. You know him better than I do.

RAINA. I wonder—I wonder is he? If I thought that—! [*Discouraged*] Ah, well: what does it matter? I suppose, now youve found me out, you despise me.

BLUNTSCHLI [*warmly, rising*] No, my dear young lady, no, no, no a thousand times. It's part of your youth: part of your charm. I'm like all the rest of them: the nurse, your parents, Sergius: I'm your infatuated admirer.

RAINA [*pleased*] Really?

BLUNTSCHLI [*slapping his breast smartly with his hand, German fashion*] Hand aufs Herz! Really and truly.

RAINA [*very happy*] But what did you think of me for giving you my portrait?

BLUNTSCHLI [*astonished*] Your portrait! You never gave me your portrait.

RAINA [*quickly*] Do you mean to say you never got it?

BLUNTSCHLI. No. [*He sits down beside her, with renewed interest, and says, with some complacency*] When did you send it to me?

RAINA [*indignantly*] I did not send it to you. [*She turns her head away, and adds, reluctantly*] It was in the pocket of that coat.

BLUNTSCHLI [*pursing his lips and rounding his eyes*] Oh-o-oh! I never found it. It must be there still.

RAINA [*springing up*] There still! for my father to find the first time he puts his hand in his pocket! Oh, how could you be so stupid?

BLUNTSCHLI [*rising also*] It doesnt matter: I suppose it's only a photograph: how can he tell who it was intended for? Tell him he put it there himself.

RAINA [*bitterly*] Yes: that is so clever! isnt it? [*Distractedly*] Oh! what shall I do?

BLUNTSCHLI. Ah, I see. You wrote something on it. That was rash.

RAINA [*vexed almost to tears*] Oh, to have done such a thing for you, who care no more—except to laugh at me—oh! Are you sure nobody has touched it?

BLUNTSCHLI. Well, I cant be quite sure. You see, I couldnt carry it about with me all the time: one cant take much luggage on active service.

RAINA. What did you do with it?

BLUNTSCHLI. When I got through to Pirot I had to put it in safe keeping somehow. I thought of the railway cloak room; but thats the surest place to get looted in modern warfare. So I pawned it.

RAINA. Pawned it!!!

BLUNTSCHLI. I know it doesnt sound nice; but it was much the safest plan. I redeemed it the day before yesterday. Heaven only knows whether the pawnbroker cleared out the pockets or not.

RAINA [*furious: throwing the words right into his face*] You have a low shopkeeping mind. You think of things that would never come into a gentleman's head.

BLUNTSCHLI [*phlegmatically*] Thats the Swiss national character, dear lady. [*He turns to the table*].

RAINA. Oh, I wish I had never met you. [*She flounces away, and sits at the window fuming*].

LOUKA *comes in with a heap of letters and telegrams on her salver, and crosses, with her bold free gait, to the table. Her left sleeve is looped up to the shoulder with a brooch, shewing her naked arm, with a broad gilt bracelet covering the bruise.*

LOUKA [*to* BLUNTSCHLI] For you. [*She empties the salver with a fling on to the table*]. The messenger is waiting. [*She is determined not to be civil to an enemy, even if she must bring him his letters*].

BLUNTSCHLI [*to* RAINA] Will you excuse me: the last postal delivery that reached me was three weeks ago. These are the subsequent accumulations. Four telegrams: a week old. [*He opens one*]. Oho! Bad news!

RAINA [*rising and advancing a little remorsefully*] Bad news?

BLUNTSCHLI. My father's dead. [*He looks at the telegram with his lips pursed, musing on the unexpected change in his arrangements.* LOUKA *crosses herself hastily*].

RAINA. Oh, how very sad!

BLUNTSCHLI. Yes: I shall have to start for home in an hour. He has left a lot of big hotels behind him to be looked after. [*He takes up a fat letter in a long blue envelope*]. Here's a whacking letter from the family solicitor. [*He pulls out the enclosures and glances over them*]. Great Heavens! Seventy! Two hundred! [*In a crescendo of dismay*] Four hundred! Four thousand!! Nine thousand six hundred!!! What on earth am I to do with them all?

RAINA [*timidly*] Nine thousand hotels?

BLUNTSCHLI. Hotels! nonsense. If you only knew! Oh, it's too ridiculous! Excuse me: I must give my fellow orders about starting. [*He leaves the room hastily, with the documents in his hand*].

LOUKA [*knowing instinctively that she can annoy* RAINA *by disparaging* BLUNTSCHLI] He has not much heart, that Swiss. He has not a word of grief for his poor father.

RAINA [*bitterly*] Grief! A man who has been doing nothing but killing people for years! What does he care? What does any soldier care? [*She goes to the door, restraining her tears with difficulty*].

LOUKA. Major Saranoff has been fighting too; and he has plenty of heart left. [RAINA, *at the door, draws herself up haughtily and goes out*]. Aha! I thought you wouldnt get much feeling out of your soldier. [*She is following* RAINA *when* NICOLA *enters with an armful of logs for the stove*].

NICOLA [*grinning amorously at her*] Ive been trying all the afternoon to get a minute alone with you, my girl. [*His countenance changes as he notices her arm*]. Why, what fashion is that of wearing your sleeve, child?

LOUKA [*proudly*] My own fashion.

NICOLA. Indeed! If the mistress catches you, she'll talk to you. [*He puts the logs down, and seats himself comfortably on the ottoman*].

LOUKA. Is that any reason why you should take it on yourself to talk to me?

NICOLA. Come! dont be so contrary with me. Ive some good news for you. [*She sits down beside him. He takes out some paper money.* LOUKA, *with an eager gleam in her eyes, tries to snatch it; but he shifts it quickly to his left hand, out of her reach*]. See! a twenty leva bill! Sergius gave me that, out of pure swagger. A fool and his money are soon parted. Theres ten levas more. The Swiss gave me that for backing up the mistress's and Raina's lies about him. He's no fool, he isnt. You should have heard old Catherine downstairs as polite as you please to me, telling me not to mind the Major being a little impatient; for they knew what a good servant I was—after making a fool and a liar of me before them all! The twenty will go to our savings; and you shall have the ten to spend if youll only talk to me so as to remind me I'm a human being. I get tired of being a servant occasionally.

LOUKA. Yes: sell your manhood for 30 levas, and buy me for 10! [*Rising scornfully*] Keep your money. You were born to be a servant. I was not. When you set up your shop you will only be everybody's servant instead of somebody's servant. [*She goes moodily to the table and seats herself regally in* SERGIUS'S *chair*].

NICOLA [*picking up his logs, and going to the stove*] Ah, wait til you see. We shall have our evenings to ourselves; and I shall be master in my own house, I promise you. [*He throws the logs down and kneels at the stove*].

LOUKA. You shall never be master in mine.

NICOLA [*turning, still on his knees, and squatting down rather forlornly on his calves, daunted by her implacable disdain*] You have a great ambition in you, Louka. Remember: if any luck comes to you, it was I that made a woman of you.

LOUKA. You!

NICOLA [*scrambling up and going at her*] Yes, me. Who was it made you give up wearing a couple of pounds of false black hair on your head and reddening your lips and cheeks like any other Bulgarian girl? I did. Who taught you to trim your nails, and keep your hands clean, and be dainty about yourself, like a fine Russian lady? Me: do you hear that? me! [*She tosses her head defiantly; and he turns away, adding, more coolly*] Ive often thought that if Raina were out of the way, and you just a little less of a fool and Sergius just a little more of one, you might come to be one of my grandest customers, instead of only being my wife and costing me money.

LOUKA. I believe you would rather be my servant than my husband. You would make more out of me. Oh, I know that soul of yours.

NICOLA [*going closer to her for greater emphasis*] Never you mind my soul; but just listen to my advice. If you want to be a lady, your present behavior to me wont do at all, unless when we're alone. It's too sharp and impudent; and impudence is a sort of familiarity: it shews affection for me. And dont you try being high and mighty with me, either. Youre like all country girls: you think it's genteel to treat a servant the way I treat a stableboy. Thats only your ignorance; and dont you forget it. And dont be so ready to defy everybody. Act as if you expected to have your own way, not as if you expected to be ordered about. The way to get on as a lady is the same as the way to get on as a servant: youve got to know your place: thats the secret of it. And you may depend on me to know my place if you get promoted. Think over it, my girl. I'll stand by you: one servant should always stand by another.

LOUKA [*rising impatiently*] Oh, I must behave in my own way. You take all the courage out of me with your cold-blooded wisdom. Go and put those logs on the fire: thats the sort of thing you understand.

Before NICOLA *can retort,* SERGIUS *comes in. He checks himself a moment on seeing* LOUKA; *then goes to the stove.*

SERGIUS [*to* NICOLA] I am not in the way of your work, I hope.

NICOLA [*in a smooth, elderly manner*] Oh no, sir: thank you kindly. I was only speaking to this foolish girl about her habit of running up here to the library whenever she gets a chance, to look at the books. Thats the worst of her education, sir: it gives her habits above her station. [*To* LOUKA] Make that table tidy, Louka, for the Major. [*He goes out sedately*].

LOUKA, *without looking at* SERGIUS, *pretends to arrange the papers on the table. He crosses slowly to her, and studies the arrangements of her sleeve reflectively.*

SERGIUS. Let me see: is there a mark there? [*He turns up the bracelet and sees the bruise made by his grasp. She stands motionless, not looking at him: fascinated, but on her guard*]. Ffff! Does it hurt?

LOUKA. Yes.

SERGIUS. Shall I cure it?

LOUKA [*instantly withdrawing herself proudly, but still not looking at him*] No. You cannot cure it now.

SERGIUS [*masterfully*] Quite sure? [*He makes a movement as if to take her in his arms*].

LOUKA. Dont trifle with me, please. An officer should not trifle with a servant.

SERGIUS [*indicating the bruise with a merciless stroke of his forefinger*] That was no trifle, Louka.

LOUKA [*flinching; then looking at him for the first time*] Are you sorry?

SERGIUS [*with measured emphasis, folding his arms*] I am never sorry.

LOUKA [*wistfully*] I wish I could believe a man could be as unlike a woman as that. I wonder are you really a brave man?

SERGIUS [*unaffectedly, relaxing his attitude*] Yes: I am a brave man. My heart jumped like a woman's at the first shot; but in the charge I found that I was brave. Yes: that at least is real about me.

LOUKA. Did you find in the charge that the men whose fathers are poor like mine were any less brave than the men who are rich like you?

SERGIUS [*with bitter levity*] Not a bit. They all slashed and cursed and yelled like heroes. Psha! the courage to rage and kill is cheap. I have an English bull terrier who has as much of that sort of courage as the whole Bulgarian nation, and the whole Russian nation at its back. But he lets my groom thrash him, all the same. Thats your soldier all over!

No, Louka: your poor men can cut throats; but they are afraid of their officers; they put up with insults and blows; they stand by and see one another punished like children: aye, and help to do it when they are ordered. And the officers!!! Well [*with a short harsh laugh*] I am an officer. Oh, [*fervently*] give me the man who will defy to the death any power on earth or in heaven that sets itself up against his own will and conscience: he alone is the brave man.

LOUKA. How easy it is to talk! Men never seem to me to grow up: they all have schoolboy's ideas. You dont know what true courage is.

SERGIUS [*ironically*] Indeed! I am willing to be instructed. [*He sits on the ottoman, sprawling magnificently*].

LOUKA. Look at me! how much am I allowed to have my own will? I have to get your room ready for you: to sweep and dust, to fetch and carry. How could that degrade me if it did not degrade you to have it done for you? But [*with subdued passion*] if I were Empress of Russia, above everyone in the world, then!! Ah then, though according to you I could shew no courage at all, you should see, you should see.

SERGIUS. What would you do, most noble Empress?

LOUKA. I would marry the man I loved, which no other queen in Europe has the courage to do. If I loved you, though you would be as far beneath me as I am beneath you, I would dare to be the equal of my inferior. Would you dare as much if you loved me? No: if you felt the beginnings of love for me you would not let it grow. You would not dare: you would marry a rich man's daughter because you would be afraid of what other people would say of you.

SERGIUS [*bounding up*] You lie: it is not so, by all the stars! If I loved you, and I were the Czar himself, I would set you on the throne by my side. You know that I love another woman, a woman as high above you as heaven is above earth. And you are jealous of her.

LOUKA. I have no reason to be. She will never marry you now. The man I told you of has come back. She will marry the Swiss.

SERGIUS [*recoiling*] The Swiss!

LOUKA. A man worth ten of you. Then you can come to me; and I will refuse you. You are not good enough for me. [*She turns to the door*].

SERGIUS [*springing after her and catching her fiercely in his arms*] I will kill the Swiss; and afterwards I will do as I please with you.

LOUKA [*in his arms, passive and steadfast*] The Swiss will kill you, perhaps. He has beaten you in love. He may beat you in war.

SERGIUS [*tormentedly*] Do you think I believe that she—she! whose worst thoughts are higher than your best ones, is capable of trifling with another man behind my back?

LOUKA. Do you think she would believe the Swiss if he told her now that I am in your arms?

SERGIUS [*releasing her in despair*] Damnation! Oh, damnation! Mockery! mockery everywhere! everything I think is mocked by everything I do. [*He strikes himself frantically on the breast*]. Coward! liar!

fool! Shall I kill myself like a man, or live and pretend to laugh at myself? [*She again turns to go*]. Louka! [*She stops near the door*]. Remember: you belong to me.

LOUKA [*turning*] What does that mean? An insult?

SERGIUS [*commandingly*] It means that you love me, and that I have had
you here in my arms, and will perhaps have you there again. Whether
that is an insult I neither know nor care: take it as you please. But
[*vehemently*] I will not be a coward and a trifler. If I choose to love
you, I dare marry you, in spite of all Bulgaria. If these hands ever
touch you again, they shall touch my affianced bride.

LOUKA. We shall see whether you dare keep your word. And take
care. I will not wait long.

SERGIUS [*again folding his arms and standing motionless in the middle of
the room*] Yes: we shall see. And you shall wait my pleasure.

BLUNTSCHLI, *much preoccupied, with his papers still in his hand,
enters, leaving the door open for* LOUKA *to go out. He goes across to the table, glancing at her as he passes.* SERGIUS, *without altering his resolute
attitude, watches him steadily.* LOUKA *goes out, leaving the door open.*

BLUNTSCHLI [*absently, sitting at the table as before, and putting down his
papers*] Thats a remarkable looking young woman.

SERGIUS [*gravely, without moving*] Captain Bluntschli.

BLUNTSCHLI. Eh?

SERGIUS. You have deceived me. You are my rival. I brook no rivals.
At six o'clock I shall be in the drilling-ground on the Klissoura road,
alone, on horseback, with my sabre. Do you understand?

BLUNTSCHLI [*staring, but sitting quite at his ease*] Oh, thank you: thats
a cavalry man's proposal. I'm in the artillery; and I have the choice of
weapons. If I go, I shall take a machine gun. And there shall be no mistake about the cartridges this time.

SERGIUS [*flushing, but with deadly coldness*] Take care, sir. It is not our
custom in Bulgaria to allow invitations of that kind to be trifled
with.

BLUNTSCHLI [*warmly*] Pooh! dont talk to me about Bulgaria. You
dont know what fighting is. But have it your own way. Bring your
sabre along. I'll meet you.

SERGIUS [*fiercely delighted to find his opponent a man of spirit*] Well said,
Switzer. Shall I lend you my best horse?

BLUNTSCHLI. No: damn your horse! thank you all the same, my dear
fellow. [RAINA *comes in, and hears the next sentence*]. I shall fight you
on foot. Horseback's too dangerous: I dont want to kill you if I can
help it.

RAINA [*hurrying forward anxiously*] I have heard what Captain Bluntschli said, Sergius. You are going to fight. Why? [SERGIUS *turns away
in silence, and goes to the stove, where he stands watching her as she continues, to* BLUNTSCHLI] What about?

BLUNTSCHLI. I dont know: he hasnt told me. Better not interfere, dear young lady. No harm will be done: Ive often acted as sword instructor. He wont be able to touch me; and I'll not hurt him. It will save explanations. In the morning I shall be off home; and youll never see me or hear of me again. You and he will then make it up and live happily ever after.

RAINA [*turning away deeply hurt, almost with a sob in her voice*] I never said I wanted to see you again.

SERGIUS [*striding forward*] Ha! That is a confession.

RAINA [*haughtily*] What do you mean?

SERGIUS. You love that man!

RAINA [*scandalized*] Sergius!

SERGIUS. You allow him to make love to you behind my back, just as you treat me as your affianced husband behind his. Bluntschli: you knew our relations; and you deceived me. It is for that that I call you to account, not for having received favors I never enjoyed.

BLUNTSCHLI [*jumping up indignantly*] Stuff! Rubbish! I have received no favors. Why, the young lady doesnt even know whether I'm married or not.

RAINA [*forgetting herself*] Oh! [*Collapsing on the ottoman*] Are you?

SERGIUS. You see the young lady's concern, Captain Bluntschli. Denial is useless. You have enjoyed the privilege of being received in her own room, late at night—

BLUNTSCHLI [*interrupting him pepperily*] Yes, you blockhead! she received me with a pistol at her head. Your cavalry were at my heels. I'd have blown out her brains if she'd uttered a cry.

SERGIUS [*taken aback*] Bluntschli! Raina: is this true?

RAINA [*rising in wrathful majesty*] Oh, how dare you, how dare you?

BLUNTSCHLI. Apologize, man: apologize. [*He resumes his seat at the table*].

SERGIUS [*with the old measured emphasis, folding his arms*]. I never apologize!

RAINA [*passionately*] This is the doing of that friend of yours, Captain Bluntschli. It is he who is spreading this horrible story about me. [*She walks about excitedly*].

BLUNTSCHLI. No: he's dead. Burnt alive.

RAINA [*stopping, shocked*] Burnt alive!

BLUNTSCHLI. Shot in the hip in a woodyard. Couldnt drag himself out. Your fellows' shells set the timber on fire and burnt him, with half a dozen other poor devils in the same predicament.

RAINA. How horrible!

SERGIUS. And how ridiculous! Oh, war! war! the dream of patriots and heroes! A fraud, Bluntschli. A hollow sham, like love.

RAINA [*outraged*] Like love! You say that before me!

BLUNTSCHLI. Come, Saranoff: that matter is explained.

SERGIUS. A hollow sham, I say. Would you have come back here if nothing had passed between you except at the muzzle of your pistol?

Raina is mistaken about your friend who was burnt. He was not my informant.

RAINA. Who then? [*Suddenly guessing the truth*] Ah, Louka! my maid! my servant! You were with her this morning all that time after—after—Oh, what sort of god is this I have been worshipping! [*He meets her gaze with sardonic enjoyment of her disenchantment. Angered all the more, she goes closer to him, and says, in a lower, intenser tone*] Do you know that I looked out of the window as I went upstairs, to have another sight of my hero; and I saw something I did not understand then. I know now that you were making love to her.

SERGIUS [*with grim humor*] You saw that?

RAINA. Only too well. [*She turns away, and throws herself on the divan under the centre window, quite overcome*].

SERGIUS [*cynically*] Raina: our romance is shattered. Life's a farce.

BLUNTSCHLI [*to Raina, whimsically*] You see: he's found himself out now.

SERGIUS [*going to him*] Bluntschli: I have allowed you to call me a blockhead. You may now call me a coward as well. I refuse to fight you. Do you know why?

BLUNTSCHLI. No; but it doesnt matter. I didnt ask the reason when you cried on; and I dont ask the reason now that you cry off. I'm a professional soldier: I fight when I have to, and am very glad to get out of it when I havnt to. Youre only an amateur: you think fighting's an amusement.

SERGIUS [*sitting down at the table, nose to nose with him*] You shall hear the reason all the same, my professional. The reason is that it takes two men—real men—men of heart, blood and honor—to make a genuine combat. I could no more fight with you than I could make love to an ugly woman. Youve no magnetism: youre not a man: youre a machine.

BLUNTSCHLI [*apologetically*] Quite true, quite true. I always was that sort of chap. I'm very sorry.

SERGIUS. Psha!

BLUNTSCHLI. But now that youve found that life isnt a farce, but something quite sensible and serious, what further obstacle is there to your happiness?

RAINA [*rising*] You are very solicitous about my happiness and his. Do you forget his new love—Louka? It is not you that he must fight now, but his rival, Nicola.

SERGIUS. Rival!! [*bounding half across the room*].

RAINA. Dont you know that theyre engaged?

SERGIUS. Nicola! Are fresh abysses opening? Nicola!!

RAINA [*sarcastically*] A shocking sacrifice, isnt it? Such beauty! such intellect! such modesty! wasted on a middle-aged servant man. Really, Sergius, you cannot stand by and allow such a thing. It would be unworthy of your chivalry.

SERGIUS [*losing all self-control*] Viper! Viper! [*He rushes to and fro, raging*].

BLUNTSCHLI. Look here, Saranoff: youre getting the worst of this.

RAINA [*getting angrier*] Do you realize what he has done, Captain Bluntschli? He has set this girl as a spy on us; and her reward is that he makes love to her.

SERGIUS. False! Monstrous!

RAINA. Monstrous! [*Confronting him*] Do you deny that she told you about Captain Bluntschli being in my room?

SERGIUS. No; but—

RAINA [*interrupting*] Do you deny that you were making love to her when she told you?

SERGIUS. No; but I tell you—

RAINA [*cutting him short contemptuously*] It is unnecessary to tell us anything more. That is quite enough for us. [*She turns away from him and sweeps majestically back to the window*].

BLUNTSCHLI [*quietly, as* SERGIUS, *in an agony of mortification, sinks on the ottoman, clutching his averted head between his fists*] I told you were getting the worst of it, Saranoff.

SERGIUS. Tiger cat!

RAINA [*running excitedly to* BLUNTSCHLI] You hear this man calling me names, Captain Bluntschli?

BLUNTSCHLI. What else can he do, dear lady? He must defend himself somehow. Come [*very persuasively*]: dont quarrel. What good does it do?

    RAINA, *with a gasp, sits down on the ottoman, and after a vain effort to look vexedly at* BLUNTSCHLI, *falls a victim to her sense of humor, and actually leans back babyishly against the writhing shoulder of* SERGIUS.

SERGIUS. Engaged to Nicola! Ha! ha! Ah well, Bluntschli, you are right to take this huge imposture of a world coolly.

RAINA [*quaintly to* BLUNTSCHLI, *with an intuitive guess at his state of mind*] I daresay you think us a couple of grown-up babies, dont you?

SERGIUS [*grinning savagely*] He does: he does. Swiss civilization nursetending Bulgarian barbarism, eh?

BLUNTSCHLI [*blushing*] Not at all, I assure you. I'm only very glad to get you two quieted. There! there! let's be pleasant and talk it over in a friendly way. Where is this other young lady?

RAINA. Listening at the door, probably.

SERGIUS [*shivering as if a bullet had struck him, and speaking with quiet but deep indignation*] I will prove that that, at least, is a calumny. [*He goes with dignity to the door and opens it. A yell of fury bursts from him as he looks out. He darts into the passage, and returns dragging in* LOUKA, *whom he flings violently against the table, exclaiming*] Judge her, Bluntschli. You, the cool impartial man: judge the eavesdropper.

    LOUKA *stands her ground, proud and silent.*

BLUNTSCHLI [*shaking his head*] I mustnt judge her. I once listened myself outside a tent when there was a mutiny brewing. It's all a question of the degree of provocation. My life was at stake.

LOUKA. My love was at stake. I am not ashamed.

RAINA [*contemptuously*] Your love! Your curiosity, you mean.

LOUKA [*facing her and retorting her contempt with interest*] My love, stronger than anything you can feel, even for your chocolate cream soldier.

SERGIUS [*with quick suspicion, to* LOUKA] What does that mean?

LOUKA [*fiercely*] It means—

SERGIUS [*interrupting her slightingly*] Oh, I remember: the ice pudding. A paltry taunt, girl!

MAJOR PETKOFF *enters, in his shirtsleeves.*

PETKOFF. Excuse my shirtsleeves, gentlemen. Raina: somebody has been wearing that coat of mine: I'll swear it. Somebody with a differently shaped back. It's all burst open at the sleeve. Your mother is mending it. I wish she'd make haste: I shall catch cold. [*He looks more attentively at them*]. Is anything the matter?

RAINA. No. [*She sits down at the stove, with a tranquil air*].

SERGIUS. Oh no. [*He sits down at the end of the table, as at first*].

BLUNTSCHLI [*who is already seated*] Nothing. Nothing.

PETKOFF [*sitting down on the ottoman in his old place*] Thats all right. [*He notices* LOUKA]. Anything the matter, Louka?

LOUKA. No, sir.

PETKOFF [*genially*] Thats all right. [*He sneezes*]. Go and ask your mistress for my coat, like a good girl, will you?

NICOLA *enters with the coat.* LOUKA *makes a pretence of having business in the room by taking the little table with the hookah away to the wall near the windows.*

RAINA [*rising quickly as she sees the coat on* NICOLA's *arm*] Here it is, papa. Give it to me, Nicola; and do you put some more wood on the fire. [*She takes the coat, and brings it to the* MAJOR, *who stands up to put it on.* NICOLA *attends to the fire*].

PETKOFF [*to* RAINA, *teasing her affectionately*] Aha! Going to be very good to poor old papa just one day after his return from the wars, eh?

RAINA [*with solemn reproach*] Ah, how can you say that to me, father?

PETKOFF. Well, well, only a joke, little one. Come: give me a kiss. [*She kisses him*]. Now give me the coat.

RAINA. No: I am going to put it on for you. Turn your back. [*He turns his back and feels behind him with his arms for the sleeves. She dexterously takes the photograph from the pocket and throws it on the table before* BLUNTSCHLI, *who covers it with a sheet of paper under the very nose of* SERGIUS, *who looks on amazed, with his suspicions roused in the highest degree. She then helps* PETKOFF *on with his coat*]. There, dear! Now are you comfortable?

PETKOFF. Quite, little love. Thanks. [*He sits down; and* RAINA *returns to her seat near the stove*]. Oh, by the bye, Ive found something funny

Whats the meaning of this? [*He puts his hand into the picked pocket*]. Eh? Hallo! [*He tries the other pocket*]. Well, I could have sworn—! [*Much puzzled, he tries the breast pocket*]. I wonder—[*trying the original pocket*] Where can it—? [*He rises, exclaiming*] Your mother's taken it!

RAINA [*very red*] Taken what?

PETKOFF. Your photograph, with the inscription: "Raina, to her Chocolate Cream Soldier: a Souvenir." Now you know theres something more in this than meets the eye; and I'm going to find it out. [*Shouting*] Nicola!

NICOLA [*coming to him*] Sir!

PETKOFF. Did you spoil any pastry of Miss Raina's this morning?

NICOLA. You heard Miss Raina say that I did, sir.

PETKOFF. I know that, you idiot. Was it true?

NICOLA. I am sure Miss Raina is incapable of saying anything that is not true, sir.

PETKOFF. Are you? Then I'm not. [*Turning to the others*] Come: do you think I dont see it all? [*He goes to* SERGIUS, *and slaps him on the shoulder*]. Sergius: youre the chocolate cream soldier, arnt you?

SERGIUS [*starting up*] I! A chocolate cream soldier! Certainly not.

PETKOFF. Not! [*He looks at them. They are all very serious and very conscious*]. Do you mean to tell me that Raina sends things like that to other men?

SERGIUS [*enigmatically*] The world is not such an innocent place as we used to think, Petkoff.

BLUNTSCHLI [*rising*] It's all right, Major. I'm the chocolate cream soldier. [PETKOFF *and* SERGIUS *are equally astonished*]. The gracious young lady saved my life by giving me chocolate creams when I was starving: shall I ever forget their flavour! My late friend Stolz told you the story at Pirot. I was the fugitive.

PETKOFF. You! [*He gasps*]. Sergius: do you remember how those two women went on this morning when we mentioned it? [SERGIUS *smiles cynically.* PETKOFF *confronts* RAINA *severely*]. Youre a nice young woman, arnt you?

RAINA [*bitterly*] Major Saranoff has changed his mind. And when I wrote that on the photograph, I did not know that Captain Bluntschli was married.

BLUNTSCHLI [*startled into vehement protest*] I'm not married.

RAINA [*with deep reproach*]. You said you were.

BLUNTSCHLI. I did not. I positively did not. I never was married in my life.

PETKOFF [*exasperated*] Raina: will you kindly inform me, if I am not asking too much, which of these gentlemen you are engaged to?

RAINA. To neither of them. This young lady [*introducing* LOUKA, *who faces them all proudly*] is the object of Major Saranoff's affections at present.

PETKOFF. Louka! Are you mad, Sergius? Why, this girl's engaged to Nicola.

NICOLA. I beg your pardon, sir. There is a mistake. Louka is not engaged to me.

PETKOFF. Not engaged to you, you scoundrel! Why, you had twenty-five levas from me on the day of your betrothal; and she had that gilt bracelet from Miss Raina.

NICOLA [*with cool unction*] We gave it out so, sir. But it was only to give Louka protection. She had a soul above her station; and I have been no more than her confidential servant. I intend, as you know, sir, to set up a shop later on in Sofia; and I look forward to her custom and recommendation should she marry into the nobility. [*He goes out with impressive discretion, leaving them all staring after him*].

PETKOFF [*breaking the silence*] Well, I am—hm!

SERGIUS. This is either the finest heroism or the most crawling baseness. Which is it, Bluntschli?

BLUNTSCHLI. Never mind whether it's heroism or baseness. Nicola's the ablest man Ive met in Bulgaria. I'll make him manager of a hotel if he can speak French and German.

LOUKA [*suddenly breaking out at* SERGIUS] I have been insulted by everyone here. You set them the example. You owe me an apology.

SERGIUS, *like a repeating clock of which the spring has been touched, immediately begins to fold his arms.*

BLUNTSCHLI [*before he can speak*] It's no use. He never apologizes.

LOUKA. Not to you, his equal and his enemy. To me, his poor servant, he will not refuse to apologize.

SERGIUS [*approvingly*] You are right. [*He bends his knee in his grandest manner*] Forgive me.

LOUKA. I forgive you. [*She timidly gives him her hand, which he kisses*]. That touch makes me your affianced wife.

SERGIUS [*springing up*] Ah! I forgot that.

LOUKA [*coldly*] You can withdraw if you like.

SERGIUS. Withdraw! Never! You belong to me. [*He puts his arm about her*].

CATHERINE *comes in and finds* LOUKA *in* SERGIUS'S *arms, with all the rest gazing at them in bewildered astonishment.*

CATHERINE. What does this mean?

SERGIUS *releases* LOUKA.

PETKOFF. Well, my dear, it appears that Sergius is going to marry Louka instead of Raina. [*She is about to break out indignantly at him: he stops her by exclaiming testily*] Dont blame me: Ive nothing to do with it. [*He retreats to the stove*].

CATHERINE. Marry Louka! Sergius: you are bound by your word to us!

SERGIUS [*folding his arms*] Nothing binds me.

BLUNTSCHLI [*much pleased by this piece of common sense*] Saranoff:

your hand. My congratulations. These heroics of yours have their practical side after all. [*To* LOUKA] Gracious young lady: the best wishes of a good Republican! [*He kisses her hand, to* RAINA's *great disgust, and returns to his seat*].

CATHERINE. Louka: you have been telling stories.

LOUKA. I have done Raina no harm.

CATHERINE [*haughtily*] Raina!

RAINA, *equally indignant, almost snorts at the liberty.*

LOUKA. I have a right to call her Raina: she calls me Louka. I told Major Saranoff she would never marry him if the Swiss gentleman came back.

BLUNTSCHLI [*rising, much surprised*] Hallo!

LOUKA [*turning to* RAINA] I thought you were fonder of him than of Sergius. You know best whether I was right.

BLUNTSCHLI. What nonsense! I assure you, my dear Major, my dear Madame, the gracious young lady simply saved my life, nothing else. She never cared two straws for me. Why, bless my heart and soul, look at the young lady and look at me. She, rich, young, beautiful, with her imagination full of fairy princes and noble natures and cavalry charges and goodness knows what! And I, a commonplace Swiss soldier who hardly knows what a decent life is after fifteen years of barracks and battles: a vagabond, a man who has spoiled all his chances in life through an incurably romantic disposition, a man—

SERGIUS [*starting as if a needle had pricked him and interrupting* BLUNT-SCHLI *in incredulous amazement*] Excuse me, Bluntschli: what did you say had spoiled your chances in life?

BLUNTSCHLI [*promptly*] An incurably romantic disposition. I ran away from home twice when I was a boy. I went into the army instead of into my father's business. I climbed the balcony of this house when a man of sense would have dived into the nearest cellar. I came sneaking back here to have another look at the young lady when any other man of my age would have sent the coat back—

PETKOFF. My coat!

BLUNTSCHLI. —yes: thats the coat I mean—would have sent it back and gone quietly home. Do you suppose I am the sort of fellow a young girl falls in love with? Why, look at our ages! I'm thirty-four: I dont suppose the young lady is much over seventeen. [*This estimate produces a marked sensation, all the rest turning and staring at one another. He proceeds innocently*] All that adventure which was life or death to me, was only a schoolgirl's game to her—chocolate creams and hide and seek. Heres the proof! [*He takes the photograph from the table*]. Now, I ask you, would a woman who took the affair seriously have sent me this and written on it "Raina, to her Chocolate Cream Soldier: a Souvenir"? [*He exhibits the photograph triumphantly, as if it settled the matter beyond all possibility of refutation*].

PETKOFF. Thats what I was looking for. How the deuce did it get there? [*He comes from the stove to look at it, and sits down on the otto-man*].

BLUNTSCHLI [*to* RAINA, *complacently*] I have put everything right, I hope, gracious young lady.

RAINA [*going to the table to face him*] I quite agree with your account of yourself. You are a romantic idiot. [BLUNTSCHLI *is unspeakably taken aback*]. Next time, I hope you will know the difference between a schoolgirl of seventeen and a woman of twenty-three.

BLUNTSCHLI [*stupefied*] Twenty-three!

RAINA *snaps the photograph contemptuously from his hand; tears it up; throws the pieces in his face; and sweeps back to her former place.*

SERGIUS [*with grim enjoyment of his rival's discomfiture*] Bluntschli: my one last belief is gone. Your sagacity is a fraud, like everything else. You have less sense than even I!

BLUNTSCHLI [*overwhelmed*] Twenty-three! Twenty-three!! [*He considers*]. Hm! [*Swiftly making up his mind and coming to his host*] In that case, Major Petkoff, I beg to propose formally to become a suitor for your daughter's hand, in place of Major Saranoff retired.

RAINA. You dare!

BLUNTSCHLI. If you were twenty-three when you said those things to me this afternoon, I shall take them seriously.

CATHERINE [*loftily polite*] I doubt, sir, whether you quite realize either my daughter's position or that of Major Sergius Saranoff, whose place you propose to take. The Petkoffs and the Saranoffs are known as the richest and most important families in the country. Our position is almost historical: we can go back for twenty years.

PETKOFF. Oh, never mind that, Catherine. [*To* BLUNTSCHLI] We should be most happy, Bluntschli, if it were only a question of your position; but hang it, you know, Raina is accustomed to a very comfortable establishment. Sergius keeps twenty horses.

BLUNTSCHLI. But who wants twenty horses? We're not going to keep a circus.

CATHERINE. [*severely*] My daughter, sir, is accustomed to a first-rate stable.

RAINA. Hush, mother: youre making me ridiculous.

BLUNTSCHLI. Oh well, if it comes to a question of an establishment, here goes! [*He darts impetuously to the table; seizes the papers in the blue envelope; and turns to Sergius*]. How many horses did you say?

SERGIUS. Twenty, noble Switzer.

BLUNTSCHLI. I have two hundred horses. [*They are amazed*]. How many carriages?

SERGIUS. Three.

BLUNTSCHLI. I have seventy. Twenty-four of them will hold twelve inside, besides two on the box, without counting the driver and conductor. How many tablecloths have you?

SERGIUS. How the deuce do I know?

BLUNTSCHLI. Have you four thousand?

SERGIUS. No.

BLUNTSCHLI. I have. I have nine thousand six hundred pairs of sheets and blankets, with two thousand four hundred eider-down quilts. I have ten thousand knives and forks, and the same quantity of dessert spoons. I have three hundred servants. I have six palatial establishments, besides two livery stables, a tea garden, and a private house. I have four medals for distinguished services; I have the rank of an officer and the standing of a gentleman; and I have three native languages. Shew me any man in Bulgaria that can offer as much!

PETKOFF [*with childish awe*] Are you Emperor of Switzerland?

BLUNTSCHLI. My rank is the highest known in Switzerland: I am a free citizen.

CATHERINE. Then, Captain Bluntschli, since you are my daughter's choice—

RAINA [*mutinously*] He's not.

CATHERINE [*ignoring her*]—I shall not stand in the way of her happiness. [*Petkoff is about to speak*] That is Major Petkoff's feeling also.

PETKOFF. Oh, I shall be only too glad. Two hundred horses! Whew!

SERGIUS. What says the lady?

RAINA [*pretending to sulk*] The lady says that he can keep his tablecloths and his omnibuses. I am not here to be sold to the highest bidder. [*She turns her back on him*].

BLUNTSCHLI. I wont take that answer. I appealed to you as a fugitive, a beggar, and a starving man. You accepted me. You gave me your hand to kiss, your bed to sleep in, and your roof to shelter me.

RAINA. I did not give them to the Emperor of Switzerland.

BLUNTSCHLI. Thats just what I say. [*He catches her by the shoulders and turns her face-to-face with him*]. Now tell us whom you did give them to.

RAINA [*succumbing with a shy smile*] To my chocolate cream soldier.

BLUNTSCHLI. [*with a boyish laugh of delight*] Thatll do. Thank you. [*He looks at his watch and suddenly becomes businesslike*]. Time's up, Major. Youve managed those regiments so well that youre sure to be asked to get rid of some of the infantry of the Timok division. Send them home by way of Lom Palanka. Saranoff: dont get married until I come back: I shall be here punctually at five in the evening on Tuesday fortnight. Gracious ladies [*his heels click*] good evening. [*He makes them a military bow, and goes*].

SERGIUS. What a man! Is he a man?

Eugene O'Neill

1888–1953

THE HAIRY APE

A COMEDY OF ANCIENT AND MODERN LIFE
IN EIGHT SCENES

❖

CHARACTERS

ROBERT SMITH, "YANK"   A GUARD
PADDY   A SECRETARY OF AN
LONG   ORGANIZATION
MILDRED DOUGLAS   STOKERS, LADIES,
HER AUNT   GENTLEMEN, ETC.
SECOND ENGINEER

SCENES

SCENE I: *The firemen's forecastle of an ocean liner—an hour after sailing from New York.* SCENE II: *Section of promenade deck, two days out— morning.* SCENE III: *The stokehole. A few minutes later.* SCENE IV: *Same as Scene I. Half an hour later.* SCENE V: *Fifth Avenue, New York. Three weeks later.* SCENE VI: *An island near the city. The next night.* SCENE VII: *In the city. About a month later.* SCENE VIII: *In the city. Twilight of the next day.*

❖

SCENE ONE

The firemen's forecastle of a transatlantic liner an hour after sailing from New York for the voyage across. Tiers of narrow, steel bunks, three deep, on all sides. An entrance in rear. Benches on the floor before the bunks. The room is crowded with men, shouting, cursing, laughing, singing—a confused, in- choate uproar swelling into a sort of unity, a meaning—the bewildered, furious, baffled defiance of a beast in a cage. Nearly all the men are drunk. Many bottles are passed from hand to hand. All are dressed in dungaree pants, heavy ugly shoes. Some wear singlets, but the majority are stripped to the waist.

The treatment of this scene, or of any other scene in the play, should by no means be naturalistic. The effect sought after is a cramped space in the bowels of a ship, imprisoned by white steel. The lines of bunks, the uprights support- ing them, cross each other like the steel framework of a cage. The ceiling crushes down upon the men's heads. They cannot stand upright. This accentuates the natural stooping posture which shoveling coal and the resultant over-develop- ment of back and shoulder muscles have given them. The men themselves should resemble those pictures in which the appearance of Neanderthal Man is guessed at. All are hairy-chested, with long arms of tremendous power, and low, receding brows above their small, fierce, resentful eyes. All the civilized white races are represented, but except for the slight differentiation in color of hair, skin, eyes, all these men are alike.

The curtain rises on a tumult of sound. YANK *is seated in the foreground. He seems broader, fiercer, more truculent, more powerful, more sure of himself than the rest. They respect his superior strength—the grudging respect of fear. Then, too, he represents to them a self-expression, the very last word in what they are, their most highly developed individual.*

VOICES. Gif me trink dere, you!
  'Ave a wet!
  Salute!
  Gesundheit!
  Skoal!
  Drunk as a lord, God stiffen you!
  Here's how!
  Luck!
  Pass back that bottle, damn you!
  Pourin' it down his neck!
  Ho, Froggy! Where the devil have you been?
  La Touraine.
  I hit him smash in yaw, py Gott!
  Jenkins—the First—he's a rotten swine—
  And the coppers nabbed him—and I run—
  I like peer better. It don't pig head gif you.
  A slut, I'm sayin'! She robbed me aslape—
  To hell with 'em all!
  You're a bloody liar!
  Say dot again! [*Commotion. Two men about to fight are pulled apart.*]
  No scrappin' now!
  Tonight—
  See who's the best man!
  Bloody Dutchman!
  Tonight on the for'ard square.
  I'll bet on Dutchy.
  He packa da wallop, I tella you!
  Shut up, Wop!
  No fightin', maties. We're all chums, ain't we?
    [*A voice starts bawling a song.*]

    "Beer, beer, glorious beer!
      Fill yourselves right up to here."

YANK [*for the first time seeming to take notice of the uproar about him, turns around threateningly—in a tone of contemptuous authority*]. Choke off dat noise! Where d'yuh get dat beer stuff? Beer, hell! Beer's for goils—and Dutchmen. Me for somep'n wit a kick to it! Gimme a drink, one of youse guys. [*Several bottles are eagerly offered. He takes a tremendous gulp at one of them; then, keeping the bottle in his hand, glares belligerently at the owner, who hastens to acquiesce in this robbery by saying*] All righto, Yank. Keep it and have another [YANK *contemptuously turns his back on the crowd again. For a second there is an embarrassed silence. Then—*]

VOICES. We must be passing the Hook.[1]
She's beginning to roll to it.
Six days in hell—and then Southampton.
Py Yesus, I vish somepody take my first vatch for me!
Gittin' seasick, Square-head?
Drink up and forget it!
What's in your bottle?
Gin.
Dot's nigger trink.
Absinthe? It's doped. You'll go off your chump, Froggy!
Cochon![2]
Whisky, that's the ticket!
Where's Paddy?
Going asleep.
Sing us that whisky song, Paddy. [*They all turn to an old, wizened Irishman who is dozing, very drunk, on the benches forward. His face is extremely monkey-like with all the sad, patient pathos of that animal in his small eyes.*]
Singa da song, Caruso[3] Pat!
He's gettin' old. The drink is too much for him.
He's too drunk.

PADDY [*blinking about him, starts to his feet resentfully, swaying, holding on to the edge of a bunk*]. I'm never too drunk to sing. 'Tis only when I'm dead to the world I'd be wishful to sing at all. [*With a sort of sad contempt*] "Whisky Johnny," ye want? A chanty, ye want? Now matther. [*He starts to sing in a thin, nasal, doleful tone*]:

> Oh, whisky is the life of man!
>   Whisky! O Johnny! [*They all join in on this.*]
> Oh, whisky is the life of man!
>   Whisky for my Johnny! [*Again chorus.*]

---

[1] Sandy Hook, the easternmost point of land passed by ships sailing from New York
[2] pig
[3] Enrico Caruso, 1873–1921, Italian operatic tenor, whose name was a household word

> *Oh, whisky drove my old man mad!*
> *Whisky! O Johnny!*
> *Oh, whisky drove my old man mad!*
> *Whisky for my Johnny!*

YANK [*again turning around scornfully*]. Aw hell! Nix on dat old sailing ship stuff! All dat bull's dead, see? And you're dead, too, yuh damned old Harp,[4] on'y yuh don't know it. Take it easy, see. Give us a rest. Nix on de loud noise. [*With a cynical grin*] Can't youse see I'm tryin' to t'ink?

ALL [*repeating the word after him as one with the same cynical amused mockery*]. Think! [*The chorused word has a brazen metallic quality as if their throats were phonograph horns. It is followed by a general uproar of hard, barking laughter.*]

VOICES. Don't be cracking your head wit ut, Yank.
You gat headache, py yingo!
One thing about it—it rhymes with drink!
Ha, ha, ha!
Drink, don't think!
Drink, don't think!
Drink, don't think! [*A whole chorus of voices has taken up this refrain, stamping on the floor, pounding on the benches with fists*]

YANK [*taking a gulp from his bottle—good-naturedly*]. Aw right. Can de noise. I got yuh de foist time. [*The uproar subsides. A very drunken sentimental tenor begins to sing*]:

> *Far away in Canada,*
> *Far across the sea,*
> *There's a lass who fondly waits*
> *Making a home for me—*

YANK [*fiercely contemptuous*]. Shut up, yuh lousy boob! Where d'yuh get dat tripe? Home? Home, hell! I'll make a home for yuh! I'll knock yuh dead. Home! T'hell wit home! Where d'yuh get dat tripe? Dis is home, see? What d'yuh want wit home? [*Proudly*] I runned away from mine when I was a kid. On'y too glad to beat it, dat was me. Home was lickings for me, dat's all. But yuh can bet your shoit no one ain't never licked me since! Wanter try it, any of youse? Huh! I guess not. [*In a more placated but still contemptuous tone*] Goils waitin' for yuh, huh? Aw, hell! Dat's all tripe. Dey don't wait for no one. Dey'd double-cross yuh for a nickel. Dey're all tarts, get me? Treat 'em rough, dat's me. To hell wit 'em. Tarts, dat's what, de whole bunch of 'em.

LONG [*very drunk, jumps on a bench excitedly, gesticulating with a bottle in his hand*]. Listen 'ere, Comrades! Yank 'ere is right. 'E says this 'ere

---

[4] Irishman

stinkin' ship is our 'ome. And 'e says as 'ome is 'ell. And 'e's right! This is 'ell. We lives in 'ell, Comrades—and right enough we'll die in it. [*Raging*] And who's ter blame, I arsks yer? We ain't. We wasn't born this rotten way. All men is born free and ekal. That's in the bleedin' Bible, maties. But what d'they care for the Bible—them lazy, bloated swine what travels first cabin? Them's the ones. They dragged us down 'til we're on'y wage slaves in the bowels of a bloody ship, sweatin', burnin' up, eatin' coal dust! Hit's them's ter blame—the damned Capitalist clarss! [*There had been a gradual murmur of contemptuous resentment rising among the men until now he is interrupted by a storm of catcalls, hisses, boos, hard laughter.*]

VOICES. Turn it off!
   Shut up!
   Sit down!
   Closa da face!
   Tamn fool! [*Etc.*]

YANK [*standing up and glaring at* LONG]. Sit down before I knock yuh down! [LONG *makes haste to efface himself.* YANK *goes on contemptuously*] De Bible, huh? De Cap'tlist class, huh? Aw nix on dat Salvation Army-Socialist bull. Git a soapbox! Hire a hall! Come and be saved, huh? Jerk us to Jesus, huh? Aw g'wan! I've listened to lots of guys like you, see. Yuh're all wrong. Wanter know what I t'ink? Yuh ain't no good for no one. Yuh're de bunk. Yuh ain't got no noive, get me? Yuh're yellow, dat's what. Yellow, dat's you. Say! What's dem slobs in de foist cabin got to do wit us? We're better men dan dey are, ain't we? Sure! One of us guys could clean up de whole mob wit one mit. Put one of 'em down here for one watch in de stokehole, what'd happen? Dey'd carry him off on a stretcher. Dem boids don't amount to nothin'. Dey're just baggage. Who makes dis old tub run? Ain't it us guys? Well den, we belong, don't we? We belong and dey don't. Dat's all. [*A loud chorus of approval.* YANK *goes on*] As for dis bein' hell—aw, nuts! Yuh lost your noive, dat's what. Dis is a man's job, get me? It belongs. It runs dis tub. No stiffs need apply.[5] But yuh're a stiff, see. Yuh're yellow, dat's you.

VOICES [*with a great hard pride in them*].
   Righto!
   A man's job!
   Talk is cheap, Long.
   He never could hold up his end.
   Divil take him!
   Yank's right. We make it go.
   Py Gott, Yank say right ting!
   We don't need no one cryin' over us.

---

[5] a parody of a line frequently seen in help-wanted ads in the nineteenth and early twentieth centuries: "No Irish need apply."

Makin' speeches.

Throw him out!

Yellow!

Chuck him overboard!

I'll break his jaw for him!

[*They crowd around* Long *threateningly.*]

Yank [*half good-natured again—contemptuously*]. Aw, take it easy. Leave him alone. He ain't woith a punch. Drink up. Here's how, whoever owns dis. [*He takes a long swallow from his bottle. All drink with him. In a flash all is hilarious amiability again, back-slapping, loud talk, etc.*]

Paddy [*who has been sitting in a blinking, melancholy daze—suddenly cries out in a voice full of old sorrow*]. We belong to this, you're saying? We make the ship to go, you're saying? Yerra then, that Almighty God have pity on us! [*His voice runs into the wail of a keen, he rocks back and forth on his bench. The men stare at him, startled and impressed in spite of themselves.*] Oh, to be back in the fine days of my youth, ochone![6] Oh, there was fine beautiful ships them days—clippers wid tall masts touching the sky—fine strong men in them—men that was sons of the sea as if 'twas the mother that bore them. Oh, the clean skins of them, and the clear eyes, the straight backs and full chests of them! Brave men they was, and bold men surely! We'd be sailing out, bound down round the Horn maybe. We'd be making sail in the dawn, with a fair breeze, singing a chanty song wid no care to it. And astern the land would be sinking low and dying out, but we'd give it no heed but a laugh, and never a look behind. For the day that was, was enough, for we was free men—and I'm thinking 'tis only slaves do be giving heed to the day that's gone or the day to come—until they're old like me. [*With a sort of religious exaltation*] Oh, to be scudding south again wid the power of the Trade Wind driving her on steady through the nights and the days! Full sail on her! Nights and days! Nights when the foam of the wake would be flaming wid fire, when the sky'd be blazing and winking wid stars. Or the full of the moon maybe. Then you'd see her driving through the gray night, her sails stretching aloft all silver and white, not a sound on the deck, the lot of us dreaming dreams, till you'd believe 'twas no real ship at all you was on but a ghost ship like the *Flying Dutchman* they say does be roaming the seas forevermore widout touching a port. And there was the days, too. A warm sun on the clean decks. Sun warming the blood of you, and wind over the miles of shiny green ocean like strong drink to your lungs. Work—aye, hard work—but who'd mind that at all? Sure, you worked under the sky and 'twas work wid skill and daring to it. And wid the day done, in the dog watch, smoking me pipe at ease, the lookout would be raising land maybe, and we'd see the mountains of South Americy wid the red fire of the setting sun painting their white tops

[6] alas

and the clouds floating by them! [*His tone of exaltation ceases. He goes on mournfully*] Yerra, what's the use of talking? 'Tis a dead man's whisper. [*To* YANK *resentfully*] 'Twas them days men belonged to ships, not now. 'Twas them days a ship was part of the sea, and a man was part of a ship, and the sea joined all together and made it one. [*Scornfully*] Is it one wid this you'd be, Yank—black smoke from the funnels smudging the sea, smudging the decks—the bloody engines pounding and throbbing and shaking—wid divil a sight of sun or a breath of clean air—choking our lungs wid coal dust—breaking our backs and hearts in the hell of the stokehole—feeding the bloody furnace—feeding our lives along wid the coal, I'm thinking—caged in by steel from a sight of the sky like bloody apes in the Zoo! [*With a harsh laugh*] Ho-ho, divil mend you! Is it to belong to that you're wishing? Is it a flesh and blood wheel of the engines you'd be?

YANK [*who has been listening with a contemptuous sneer, barks out the answer*]. Sure ting! Dat's me. What about it?

PADDY [*as if to himself—with great sorrows*]. Me time is past due. That a great wave wid sun in the heart of it may sweep me over the side sometime I'd be dreaming of the days that's gone!

YANK. Aw, yuh crazy Mick! [*He springs to his feet and advances on* PADDY *threateningly—then stops, fighting some queer struggle within himself—lets his hands fall to his sides—contemptuously*] Aw, take it easy. Yuh're aw right, at dat. Yuh're bugs, dat's all—nutty as a cuckoo. All dat tripe yuh been pullin'—Aw, dat's all right. On'y it's dead, get me? Yuh don't belong no more, see. Yuh don't get de stuff. Yuh're too old. [*Disgustedly*] But aw say, come up for air onct in a while, can't yuh? See what's happened since yuh croaked [*He suddenly bursts forth vehemently, growing more and more excited*] Say! Sure! Sure I meant it! What de hell—Say, lemme talk! Hey! Hey, you old Harp! Hey, youse guys! Say, listen to me—wait a moment—I gotter talk, see. I belong and he don't. He's dead but I'm livin'. Listen to me! Sure I'm part of de engines! Why de hell not! Dey move, don't dey? Dey're speed, ain't dey? Dey smash trou, don't dey? Twenty-five knots a hour! Dat's goin' some! Dat's new stuff! Dat belongs! But him, he's too old. He gets dizzy. Say, listen. All dat crazy tripe about nights and days; all dat crazy tripe about stars and moons; all dat crazy tripe about suns and winds, fresh air and de rest of it—Aw hell, dat's all a dope dream! Hittin' de pipe of de past, dat's what he's doin'. He's old and don't belong no more. But me, I'm young! I'm in de pink! I move wit it! It, get me! I mean de ting dat's de guts of all dis. It ploughs trou all de tripe he's been sayin'. It blows dat up! It knocks dat dead! It slams dat offen de face of de oith! It, get me! De engines and de coal and de smoke and all de rest of it! He can't breathe and swallow coal dust, but I kin, see? Dat's fresh air for me! Dat's food for me! I'm new, get me? Hell in de stokehole? Sure! It takes a man to work in hell. Hell, sure, dat's my fav'rite climate. I eat it up! I git fat on it! It's me makes it hot. It's me makes it roar! It's me makes it move! Sure, on'y for me everything stops. It all goes dead, get me? De noise and smoke and all de engines movin' de woild, dey stop. Dere ain't nothin' no more! Dat's what I'm sayin'. Everything else dat makes de woild move, somep'n makes it move. It can't move without somep'n else, see? Den yuh get down to me. I'm at de bottom, get me! Dere ain't nothin' foither. I'm de end! I'm de start! I start somep'n and de woild moves! It—dat's me!—de new dat's moiderin' de old! I'm de ting in coal dat makes it boin; I'm steam and oil for de engines; I'm de ting in noise dat makes yuh hear it; I'm smoke and express trains and steamers and factory whistles; I'm de ting in gold dat makes it money! And I'm what makes iron into steel! Steel, dat stands for de whole ting! And I'm steel—steel—steel! I'm de muscles in steel, de punch behind it! [*As he says this he pounds with his fist against the steel bunks. All the men, roused to a pitch of frenzied self-glorification by his speech, do likewise. There is a deafening metallic roar, through which* YANK's *voice can be heard bellowing*] Slaves, hell! We run de whole woiks. All de rich guys dat tink dey're somep'n, dey ain't nothin'! Dey don't belong. But us guys, we're in de move, we're at de bottom, de whole ting is us! [PADDY *from the start of* YANK's *speech has been taking one gulp after another from his bottle, at first frightenedly, as if he were afraid to listen, then desperately, as if to drown his senses, but finally has achieved complete indifferent, even amused, drunkenness.* YANK *sees his lips moving. He quells the uproar with a shout*] Hey, youse guys, take it easy! Wait a moment! De nutty Harp is sayin' somep'n.

PADDY [*is heard now—throws his head back with a mocking burst of laughter*]. Ho-ho-ho-ho-ho—

YANK [*drawing back his fist, with a snarl*]. Aw! Look out who yuh're givin' the bark!

PADDY [*begins to sing the "Miller of Dee" with enormous good nature*].

> I care for nobody, no, not I,
> And nobody cares for me.

YANK [*good-natured himself in a flash, interrupts* PADDY *with a slap on the bare back like a report*]. Dat's de stuff! Now yuh're gettin' wise to somep'n. Care for nobody, dat's de dope! To hell wit 'em all! And mix on nobody else carin'. I kin care for myself, get me! [*Eight bells sound, muffled, vibrating through the steel walls as if some enormous brazen gong were imbedded in the heart of the ship. All the men jump up mechanically, file through the door silently close upon each other's heels in what is very like a prisoners' lockstep.* YANK *slaps* PADDY *on the back.*] Our watch, yuh old Harp! [*Mockingly*] Come on down in hell. Eat up de coal dust. Drink in de heat. It's it, see! Act like yuh liked it, yuh better—or croak yuhself.

PADDY [*with jovial defiance*]. To the divil wid it! I'll not report this watch. Let him log me and be damned. I'm no slave the like of you.

I'll be sittin' here at me ease, and drinking, and thinking, and dreaming dreams.

YANK [*contemptuously*]. Tinkin' and dreamin', what'll that get yuh? What's tinkin' got to do wit it? We move, don't we? Speed ain't it? Fog, dat's all you stand for. But we drive trou dat, don't we? We split dat up and smash trou—twenty-five knots a hour! [*Turns his back on* PADDY *scornfully*] Aw, yuh make me sick! Yuh don't belong! [*He strides out the door in rear.* PADDY *hums to himself, blinking drowsily.*]

[*Curtain*]

SCENE TWO

Two days out. A section of the promenade deck. MILDRED DOUGLAS *and her aunt are discovered reclining in deck chairs. The former is a girl of twenty, slender, delicate, with a pale, pretty face marred by a self-conscious expression of disdainful superiority. She looks fretful, nervous and discontented, bored by her own anemia. Her aunt is a pompous and proud—and fat—old lady. She is a type even to the point of a double chin and lorgnettes. She is dressed pretentiously, as if afraid her face alone would never indicate her position in life.* MILDRED *is dressed all in white.*

The impression to be conveyed by this scene is one of the beautiful, vivid life of the sea all about—sunshine on the deck in a great flood, the fresh sea wind blowing across it. In the midst of this, these two incongruous, artificial figures, inert and disharmonious, the elder like a gray lump of dough touched up with rouge, the younger looking as if the vitality of her stock had been sapped before she was conceived, so that she is the expression not of its life energy but merely of the artificialities that energy had won for itself in the spending.

MILDRED [*looking up with affected dreaminess*]. How the black smoke swirls back against the sky! Is it not beautiful?

AUNT [*without looking up*]. I dislike smoke of any kind.

MILDRED. My great-grandmother smoked a pipe—a clay pipe.

AUNT [*ruffling*]. Vulgar!

MILDRED. She was too distant a relative to be vulgar. Time mellows pipes.

AUNT [*pretending boredom but irritated*]. Did the sociology you took up at college teach you that—to play the ghoul on every possible occasion, excavating old bones? Why not let your great-grandmother rest in her grave?

MILDRED [*dreamily*]. With her pipe beside her—puffing in Paradise.

AUNT [*with spite*]. Yes, you are a natural born ghoul. You are even getting to look like one, my dear.

MILDRED [*in a passionless tone*]. I detest you, Aunt. [*Looking at her critically*] Do you know what you remind me of? Of a cold pork pudding against a background of linoleum tablecloth in the kitchen of a—but the possibilities are wearisome. [*She closes her eyes.*]

AUNT [*with a bitter laugh*]. Merci for your candor. But since I am and must be your chaperon—in appearance, at least—let us patch up some sort of armed truce. For my part you are quite free to indulge any pose of eccentricity that beguiles you—as long as you observe the amenities—

MILDRED [*drawling*]. The inanities?

AUNT [*going on as if she hadn't heard*]. After exhausting the morbid thrills of social service work on New York's East Side—how they must have hated you, by the way, the poor that you made so much poorer in their own eyes!—you are now bent on making your slumming international. Well, I hope Whitechapel[7] will provide the needed nerve tonic. Do not ask me to chaperon you there, however. I told your father I would not. I loathe deformity. We will hire an army of detectives and you may investigate everything—they allow you to see.

MILDRED [*protesting with a trace of genuine earnestness*]. Please do not mock at my attempts to discover how the other half lives.[8] Give me credit for some sort of groping sincerity in that at least. I would like to help them. I would like to be some use in the world. Is it my fault I don't know how? I would like to be sincere, to touch life somewhere. [*With weary bitterness.*] But I'm afraid I have neither the vitality nor integrity. All that was burnt out in our stock before I was born. Grandfather's blast furnaces, flaming to the sky, melting steel, making millions—then father keeping those home fires burning, making more millions—and little me at the tail-end of it all. I'm a waste product in the Bessemer process[9]—like the millions. Or rather, I inherit the acquired trait of the by-product, wealth, but none of the energy, none of the strength of the steel that made it. I am sired by gold and damned by it, as they say at the race track;[10]—damned in more ways than one. [*She laughs mirthlessly.*]

AUNT [*unimpressed—superciliously*]. You seem to be going in for sincerity today. It isn't becoming to you, really—except as an obvious pose. Be as artificial as you are, I advise. There's a sort of sincerity in that, you know. And, after all, you must confess you like that better.

MILDRED [*again affected and bored*]. Yes, I suppose I do. Pardon me for my outburst. When a leopard complains of its spots, it must sound rather grotesque. [*In a mocking tone*] Purr, little leopard. Purr, scratch, tear, kill, gorge yourself and be happy—only stay in the jungle where your spots are camouflage. In a cage they make you conspicuous.

[7] a slum area of London
[8] Jacob Riis, *How the Other Half Lives* (1890) was a classic and shocking description of slum life in New York.
[9] for making steel   [10] sire and dam: the father and mother of a horse

AUNT. I don't know what you are talking about.

MILDRED. It would be rude to talk about anything to you. Let's just talk. [*She looks at her wrist watch.*] Well, thank goodness, it's about time for them to come for me. That ought to give me a new thrill, Aunt.

AUNT [*affectedly troubled*]. You don't mean to say you're really going? The dirt—the heat must be frightful—

MILDRED. Grandfather started as a puddler. I should have inherited an immunity to heat that would make a salamander[11] shiver. It will be fun to put it to the test.

AUNT. But don't you have to have the captain's—or someone's—permission to visit the stokehole?

MILDRED [*with a triumphant smile*]. I have it—both his and the chief engineer's. Oh, they didn't want to at first, in spite of my social service credentials. They didn't seem a bit anxious that I should investigate how the other half lives and works on a ship. So I had to tell them that my father, the president of Nazareth Steel, chairman of the board of directors of this line, had told me it would be all right.

AUNT. He didn't.

MILDRED. How naïve age makes one! But I said he did, Aunt. I even said he had given me a letter to them—which I had lost. And they were afraid to take the chance that I might be lying. [*Excitedly*] So it's ho! for the stokehole. The second engineer is to escort me. [*Looking at her watch again*] It's time. And here he comes, I think. [*The* SECOND ENGINEER *enters. He is a husky, fine-looking man of thirty-five or so. He stops before the two and tips his cap, visibly embarrassed and ill-at-ease.*]

SECOND ENGINEER. Miss Douglas?

MILDRED. Yes. [*Throwing off her rugs and getting to her feet*] Are we all ready to start?

SECOND ENGINEER. In just a second, ma'am. I'm waiting for the Fourth. He's coming along.

MILDRED [*with a scornful smile*]. You don't care to shoulder this responsibility alone, is that it?

SECOND ENGINEER [*forcing a smile*]. Two are better than one. [*Disturbed by her eyes, glances out to sea—blurts out*] A fine day we're having.

MILDRED. Is it?

SECOND ENGINEER. A nice warm breeze—

MILDRED. It feels cold to me.

SECOND ENGINEER. But it's hot enough in the sun—

MILDRED. Not hot enough for me. I don't like Nature. I was never athletic.

SECOND ENGINEER [*forcing a smile*]. Well, you'll find it hot enough where you're going.

---

[11] A puddler stirs the molten metal in a furnace to produce wrought iron. The salamander was a legendary lizard believed capable of living in fire.

MILDRED. Do you mean hell?

SECOND ENGINEER [*flabbergasted, decides to laugh*]. Ho-ho! No, I mean the stokehole.

MILDRED. My grandfather was a puddler. He played with boiling steel.

SECOND ENGINEER [*all at sea—uneasily*]. Is that so? Hum, you'll excuse me, ma'am, but are you intending to wear that dress?

MILDRED. Why not?

SECOND ENGINEER. You'll likely rub against oil and dirt. It can't be helped.

MILDRED. It doesn't matter. I have lots of white dresses.

SECOND ENGINEER. I have an old coat you might throw over—

MILDRED. I have fifty dresses like this. I will throw this one into the sea when I come back. That ought to wash it clean, don't you think?

SECOND ENGINEER [*doggedly*]. There's ladders to climb down that are none too clean—and dark alleyways—

MILDRED. I will wear this very dress and none other.

SECOND ENGINEER. No offense meant. It's none of my business. I was only warning you—

MILDRED. Warning? That sounds thrilling.

SECOND ENGINEER [*looking down the deck—with a sigh of relief*]. There's the Fourth now. He's waiting for us. If you'll come—

MILDRED. Go on. I'll follow you. [*He goes.* MILDRED *turns a mocking smile on her aunt*] An oaf—but a handsome, virile oaf.

AUNT [*scornfully*]. Poser!

MILDRED. Take care. He said there were dark alleyways—

AUNT [*in the same tone*]. Poser!

MILDRED [*biting her lips angrily*]. You are right. But would that my millions were not so anemically chaste!

AUNT. Yes, for a fresh pose I have no doubt you would drag the name of Douglas in the gutter!

MILDRED. From which it sprang. Good-by, Aunt. Don't pray too hard that I may fall into the fiery furnace.

AUNT. Poser!

MILDRED [*viciously*]. Old hag! [*She slaps her aunt insultingly across the face and walks off, laughing gaily.*]

AUNT [*screams after her*]. I said poser!

[*Curtain*]

SCENE THREE

The stokehole. In the rear, the dimly-outlined bulks of the furnaces and boilers. High overhead one hanging electric bulb sheds just enough light through the murky air laden with coal dust to pile up masses of shadows everywhere. A line of men, stripped to the waist, is before the furnace doors. They bend over, looking neither to right nor left, handling their shovels as if they were part of their bodies, with a strange, awkward, swinging rhythm. They use the shovels to throw open the furnace doors. Then from these fiery round holes in the black a flood of terrific light and heat pours full upon the men who are outlined in silhouette in the crouching, inhuman attitudes of chained gorillas. The men shovel with a rhythmic motion, swinging as on a pivot from the coal which lies in heaps on the floor behind to hurl it into the flaming mouths before them. There is a tumult of noise—the brazen clang of the furnace doors as they are flung open or slammed shut, the grating, teeth-gritting grind of steel against steel, of crunching coal. This clash of sounds stuns one's ears with its rending dissonance. But there is order in it, rhythm, a mechanical regulated recurrence, a tempo. And rising above all, making the air hum with the quiver of liberated energy, the roar of leaping flames in the furnaces, the monotonous throbbing beat of the engines.

As the curtain rises, the furnace doors are shut. The men are taking a breathing spell. One or two are arranging the coal behind them, pulling it into more accessible heaps. The others can be dimly made out leaning on their shovels in relaxed attitudes of exhaustion.

PADDY [*from somewhere in the line—plaintively*]. Yerra, will this divil's own watch nivir end? Me back is broke. I'm destroyed entirely.

YANK [*from the center of the line—with exuberant scorn*]. Aw, yuh make me sick! Lie down and croak, why don't yuh? Always beefin', dat's you! Say, dis is a cinch! Dis was made for me! It's my meat, get me! [*A whistle is blown—a thin, shrill note from somewhere overhead in the darkness. YANK curses without resentment*] Dere's de damn engineer crackin' de whip. He tinks we're loafin'.

PADDY [*vindictively*]. God stiffen him!

YANK [*in an exultant tone of command*]. Come on, youse guys! Git into de game! She's gittin' hungry! Pile some grub in her. Trow it into her belly! Come on now, all of youse! Open her up! [*At this last all the men, who have followed his movements of getting into position, throw open their furnace doors with a deafening clang. The fiery light floods over their shoulders as they bend round for the coal. Rivulets of sooty sweat have traced maps on their backs. The enlarged muscles form bunches of high light and shadow.*]

YANK [*chanting a count as he shovels without seeming effort*]. One—two—tree— [*His voice rising exultantly in the joy of battle*] Dat's de stuff! Let her have it! All togedder now! Sling it into her! Let her ride! Shoot de piece now! Call de toin on her! Drive her into it! Feel her move! Watch her smoke! Speed, dat's her middle name! Give her coal, youse guys! Coal, dat's her booze! Drink it up, baby! Let's see yuh sprint! Dig in and gain a lap! Dere she go-o-es. [*This last in the chanting formula of the gallery gods at the six-day bike race. He slams his furnace door shut. The others do likewise with as much unison as their wearied bodies will permit. The effect is of one fiery eye after another being blotted out with a series of accompanying bangs.*]

Paddy [*groaning*]. Me back is broke. I'm bate out—bate— [*There is a pause. Then the inexorable whistle sounds again from the dim regions above the electric light. There is a growl of cursing rage from all sides.*]

Yank [*shaking his fist upward—contemptuously*]. Take it easy dere, you! Who d'yuh tink's runnin' dis game, me or you? When I git ready, we move. Not before! When I git ready, git me!

Voices [*approvingly*]. That's the stuff!

Yank tal him, py golly!

Yank ain't affeerd.

Goot poy, Yank!

Give him hell!

Tell 'im 'e's a bloody swine!

Bloody slave-driver!

Yank [*contemptuously*]. He ain't got no noive. He's yellow, get me? All de engineers is yellow. Dey got streaks a mile wide. Aw, to hell wit him! Let's move, youse guys. We had a rest. Come on, she needs it! Give her pep! It ain't for him. Him and his whistle, dey don't belong. But we belong, see! We gotter feed de baby! Come on! [*He turns and flings his furnace door open. They all follow his lead. At this instant the* Second *and* Fourth Engineers *enter from the darkness on the left with* Mildred *between them. She starts, turns paler, her pose is crumbling, she shivers with fright in spite of the blazing heat, but forces herself to leave the* Engineers *and take a few steps nearer the men. She is right behind* Yank. *All this happens quickly while the men have their backs turned.*]

Yank. Come on, youse guys! [*He is turning to get coal when the whistle sounds again in a peremptory, irritating note. This drives* Yank *into a sudden fury. While the other men have turned full around and stopped dumfounded by the spectacle of* Mildred *standing there in her white dress,* Yank *does not turn far enough to see her. Besides, his head is thrown back, he blinks upward through the murk trying to find the owner of the whistle, he brandishes his shovel murderously over his head in one hand, pounding on his chest, gorilla-like, with the other, shouting*] Toin off dat whistle! Come down outa dere, yuh yellow, brass-buttoned, Belfast bum, yuh! Come down and I'll knock yer brains out! Yuh lousy, stinkin', yellow mut of a Catholic-moiderin' bastard! Come down and I'll moider yuh! Pullin' dat whistle on me, huh? I'll show yuh! I'll crash yer skull in! I'll drive yer teet' down yer troat! I'll slam yer nose trou de back of yer head! I'll cut yer guts out for a nickel, yuh lousy boob, yuh dirty, crummy, muck-eatin' son of a— [*Suddenly he becomes conscious of all the other men staring at something directly behind his back. He whirls defensively with a snarling, murderous growl, crouching to spring, his lips drawn back over his teeth, his small eyes gleaming ferociously. He sees* Mildred, *like a white apparition in the full light from the open furnace doors. He glares into her eyes, turned to stone. As for her, during his speech she has listened, paralyzed with horror, terror, her whole personality crushed, beaten in, collapsed, by the terrific impact of this unknown, abysmal brutality, naked and shameless. As she looks at his gorilla face, as his eyes bore into hers, she utters a low, choking cry and shrinks away from him, putting both hands up before her eyes to shut out the sight of his face, to protect her own. This startles* YANK *to a reaction. His mouth falls open, his eyes grow bewildered.*]

MILDRED [*about to faint—to the* ENGINEERS, *who now have her one by each arm—whimperingly*]. Take me away! Oh, the filthy beast! [*She faints. They carry her quickly back, disappearing in the darkness at the left, rear. An iron door clangs shut. Rage and bewildered fury rush back on* YANK. *He feels himself insulted in some unknown fashion in the very heart of his pride. He roars*] God damn yuh! [*And hurls his shovel after them at the door which has just closed. It hits the steel bulkhead with a clang and falls clattering on the steel floor. From overhead the whistle sounds again in a long, angry, insistent command.*]

[*Curtain*]

SCENE FOUR

The firemen's forecastle. YANK'S *watch has just come off duty and had dinner. Their faces and bodies shine from a soap and water scrubbing but around their eyes, where a hasty dousing does not touch, the coal dust sticks like black make-up, giving them a queer, sinister expression.* YANK *has not washed either face or body. He stands out in contrast to them, a blackened, brooding figure. He is seated forward on a bench in the exact attitude of Rodin's "The Thinker." The others, most of them smoking pipes, are staring at* YANK *half-apprehensively, as if fearing an outburst; half-amusedly, as if they saw a joke somewhere that tickled them.*

VOICES. He ain't ate nothin'.
  By golly, a fallar gat to gat grub in him.
  Divil a lie.
  Yank feeda da fire, no feeda da face.
  Ha-ha.
  He ain't even washed hisself.
  He's forgot.
  Hey, Yank, you forgot to wash.
YANK [*sullenly*]. Forgot nothin'! To hell wit washin'.
VOICES. It'll stick to you.
  It'll get under your skin.
  Give yer the bleedin' itch, that's wot.
  It makes spots on you—like a leopard.
  Like a piebald nigger, you mean.
  Better wash up, Yank.
  You sleep better.

Wash up, Yank.

Wash up! Wash up!

YANK [*resentfully*]. Aw say, youse guys. Lemme alone. Can't youse see I'm tryin' to tink?

ALL [*repeating the word after him as one with cynical mockery*]. Think!
[*The word has a brazen, metallic quality as if their throats were phonograph horns. It is followed by a chorus of hard, barking laughter.*]

YANK [*springing to his feet and glaring at them belligerently*]. Yes, tink!
Tink, dat's what I said! What about it? [*They are silent, puzzled by his sudden resentment at what used to be one of his jokes. YANK sits down again in the same attitude of "The Thinker."*]

VOICES. Leave him alone.

He's got a grouch on.

Why wouldn't he?

PADDY [*with a wink at the others*]. Sure I know what's the matther. 'Tis aisy to see. He's fallen in love, I'm telling you.

ALL [*repeating the word after him as one with cynical mockery*]. Love!
[*The word has a brazen, metallic quality as if their throats were phonograph horns. It is followed by a chorus of hard, barking laughter.*]

YANK [*with a contemptuous snort*]. Love, hell! Hate, dat's what. I've fallen in hate, get me?

PADDY [*philosophically*]. 'Twould take a wise man to tell one from the other. [*With a bitter, ironical scorn, increasing as he goes on*]. But I'm telling you it's love that's in it. Sure what else but love for us poor bastes in the stokehole would be bringing a fine lady, dressed like a white quane, down a mile of ladders and steps to be havin' a look at us? [*A growl of anger goes up from all sides.*]

LONG [*jumping on a bench—hectically*]. Hinsultin' us! Hinsultin' us, the bloody cow! And them bloody engineers! What right 'as they got to be exhibitin' us 's if we was bleedin' monkeys in a menagerie? Did we sign for hinsults to our dignity as 'onest workers? Is that in the ship's articles? You kin bloody well bet it ain't! But I knows why they done it. I arsked a deck steward 'o she was and 'e told me. 'Er old man's a bleedin' millionaire, a bloody Capitalist! 'E's got enuf bloody gold to sink this bleedin' ship! 'E makes arf the bloody steel in the world! 'E owns this bloody boat! And you and me, Comrades, we're 'is slaves! And the skipper and mates and engineers, they're 'is slaves! And she's 'is bloody daughter and we're all 'er slaves, too! And she gives 'er orders as 'ow she wants to see the bloody animals below decks and down they takes 'er! [*There is a roar of rage from all sides.*]

YANK [*blinking at him bewilderedly*]. Say! Wait a moment! Is all dat straight goods?

LONG. Straight as string! The bleedin' steward as waits on 'em, 'e told me about 'er. And what're we goin' ter do, I arsks yer? 'Ave we got ter swaller 'er hinsults like dogs? It ain't in the ship's articles. I tell yer we got a case. We kin go to law—

YANK [*with abysmal contempt*]. Hell! Law!

ALL [*repeating the word after him as one with cynical mockery*]. Law! [*The word has a brazen metallic quality as if their throats were phonograph horns. It is followed by a chorus of hard, barking laughter.*]

LONG [*feeling the ground slipping from under his feet—desperately*]. As voters and citizens we kin force the bloody governments—

YANK [*with abysmal contempt*]. Hell! Governments!

ALL [*repeating the word after him as one with cynical mockery*]. Governments! [*The word has a brazen metallic quality as if their throats were phonograph horns. It is followed by a chorus of hard, barking laughter.*]

LONG [*hysterically*]. We're free and equal in the sight of God—

YANK [*with abysmal contempt*]. Hell! God!

ALL [*repeating the word after him as one with cynical mockery*]. God! [*The word has a brazen metallic quality as if their throats were phonograph horns. It is followed by a chorus of hard, barking laughter.*]

YANK [*witheringly*]. Aw, join de Salvation Army!

ALL. Sit down! Shut up! Damn fool! Sea-lawyer! [LONG *slinks back out of sight.*]

PADDY [*continuing the trend of his thoughts as if he had never been interrupted—bitterly*]. And there she was standing behind us, and the Second pointing at us like a man you'd hear in a circus would be saying: In this cage is a queerer kind of baboon than ever you'd find in darkest Africy. We roast them in their own sweat—and be damned if you won't hear some of thim saying they like it! [*He glances scornfully at* YANK.]

YANK [*With a bewildered uncertain growl*]. Aw!

PADDY. And there was Yank roarin' curses and turning round wid his shovel to brain her—and she looked at him, and him at her—

YANK [*slowly*]. She was all white. I tought she was a ghost. Sure.

PADDY [*with heavy, biting sarcasm*]. 'Twas love at first sight, divil a doubt of it! If you'd seen the endearin' look on her pale mug when she shriveled away with her hands over her eyes to shut out the sight of him! Sure, 'twas as if she'd seen a great hairy ape escaped from the Zoo!

YANK [*stung—with a growl of rage*]. Aw!

PADDY. And the loving way Yank heaved his shovel at the skull of her, only she was out the door! [*A grin breaking over his face*] 'Twas touching, I'm telling you! It put the touch of home, swate home in the stokehole. [*There is a roar of laughter from all.*]

YANK [*glaring at* PADDY *menacingly*]. Aw, choke dat off, see!

PADDY [*not heeding him—to the others*]. And her grabbin' at the Second's arm for protection. [*With a grotesque imitation of a woman's voice*] Kiss me, Engineer dear, for it's dark down here and me old man's in Wall Street making money! Hug me tight, darlin', for I'm afeerd in the dark and me mother's on deck makin' eyes at the skipper! [*Another roar of laughter.*]

YANK [*threateningly*]. Say! What yuh tryin' to do, kid me, yuh old Harp?

PADDY. Divil a bit! Ain't I wishin' myself you'd brained her?

YANK [*fiercely*]. I'll brain her! I'll brain her yet, wait 'n' see! [*Coming over to* PADDY—*slowly*] Say, is dat what she called me—a hairy ape?

PADDY. She looked it at you if she didn't say the word itself.

YANK [*grinning horribly*]. Hairy ape, huh? Sure! Dat's de way she looked at me, aw right. Hairy ape! So dat's me, huh? [*Bursting into rage—as if she were still in front of him*] Yuh skinny tart! Yuh white-faced bum, yuh! I'll show yuh who's a ape! [*Turning to the others, bewilderment seizing him again*] Say, youse guys. I was bawlin' him out for pullin' de whistle on us. You heard me. And den I seen youse lookin' at somep'n and I tought he'd sneaked down to come up in back of me, and I hopped round to knock him dead wit de shovel. And dere she was wit de light on her! Christ, yuh coulda pushed me over with a finger! I was scared, get me? Sure! I tought she was a ghost, see? She was all in white like dey wrap around stiffs. You seen her. Kin yuh blame me? She didn't belong, dat's what. And den when I come to and seen it was a real skoit and seen de way she was lookin' at me —like Paddy said—Christ, I was sore, get me? I don't stand for dat stuff from nobody. And I flung de shovel—on'y she'd beat it. [*Furiously*] I wished it'd banged her! I wished it'd knocked her block off!

LONG. And be 'anged for murder or 'lectrocuted? She ain't bleedin' well worth it.

YANK. I don't give a damn what! I'd be square wit her, wouldn't I? Tink I wanter let her put somep'n over on me? Tink I'm goin' to let her git away wit dat stuff? Yuh don't know me! No one ain't never put nothin' over on me and got away wit it, see!—not dat kind of stuff—no guy and no skoit neither! I'll fix her! Maybe she'll come down again—

VOICE. No chance, Yank. You scared her out of a year's growth.

YANK. I scared her? Why de hell should I scare her? Who de hell is she? Ain't she de same as me? Hairy ape, huh? [*With his old confident bravado*] I'll show her I'm better'n her if she on'y knew it. I belong and she don't, see! I move and she's dead! Twenty-five knots a hour, dat's me! Dat carries her but I make dat. She's on'y baggage. Sure! [*Again bewilderedly*] But, Christ, she was funny lookin'! Did yuh pipe her hands? White and skinny. Yuh could see de bones through 'em. And her mush, dat was dead white, too. And her eyes, dey was like dey'd seen a ghost. Me, dat was! Sure! Hairy ape! Ghost, huh? Look at dat arm! [*He extends his right arm, swelling out the great muscles*] I coulda took her wit dat, wit just my little finger even, and broke her in two. [*Again bewilderedly*] Say, who is dat skoit, huh? What is she? What's she come from? Who made her? Who give her de noive to look at me like dat? Dis ting's got my goat right. I don't get her. She's new to me. What does a skoit like her mean, huh? She don't belong, get me! I can't see her. [*With growing anger*] But one ting I'm wise to, aw right, aw right! Youse all kin bet your shoits I'll git even wit her. I'll show her if she tinks she— She grinds de organ and I'm on de string, huh? I'll fix her! Let her come down again and I'll fling her in de furnace! She'll move den! She won't shiver at nothin', den! Speed, dat'll be her! She'll belong den! [*He grins horribly.*]

PADDY. She'll never come. She had her belly-full, I'm telling you. She'll be in bed now, I'm thinking, wid ten doctors and nurses feedin' her salts to clean the fear out of her.

YANK [*enraged*]. Yuh tink I made her sick, too, do yuh? Just lookin' at me, huh? Hairy ape, huh? [*In a frenzy of rage*] I'll fix her! I'll tell her where to git off! She'll git down on her knees and take it back or I'll bust de face offen her! [*Shaking one fist upward and beating on his chest with the other*] I'll find yuh! I'm comin', d'yuh hear? I'll fix yuh, God damn yuh! [*He makes a rush for the door.*]

VOICES. Stop him!
    He'll get shot!
    He'll murder her!
    Trip him up!
    Hold him!
    He's gone crazy!
    Gott, he's strong!
    Hold him down!
    Look out for a kick!
    Pin his arms!
    [*They have all piled on him and, after a fierce struggle, by sheer weight of numbers have borne him to the floor just inside the door.*]

PADDY [*who has remained detached*]. Kape him down till he's cooled off. [*Scornfully*] Yerra, Yank, you're a great fool. Is it payin' attention at all you are to the like of that skinny sow widout one drop of rale blood in her?

YANK [*frenziedly, from the bottom of the heap*]. She done me doit! She done me doit, didn't she? I'll git square wit her! I'll get her some way! Git offen me, youse guys! Lemme up! I'll show her who'a a ape!
                                        [*Curtain*]

SCENE FIVE

Three weeks later. A corner of Fifth Avenue in the Fifties on a fine Sunday morning. A general atmosphere of clean, well-tidied, wide street; a flood of mellow, tempered sunshine; gentle, genteel breezes. In the rear, the show windows of two shops, a jewelry establishment on the corner, a furrier's next to it. Here the adornments of extreme wealth are tantalizingly displayed. The jeweler's window is gaudy with glittering diamonds, emeralds, rubies, pearls, etc., fashioned in ornate tiaras, crowns, necklaces, collars, etc. From each piece hangs an enormous tag from which a dollar sign and numerals in intermittent electric lights wink out the incredible prices. The same in the furrier's. Rich furs of all varieties hang there bathed in a downpour of artificial light. The general effect is of a background of magnificence cheapened and made grotesque by commercialism, a background in tawdry disharmony with the clear light and sunshine on the street itself.

Up the side street YANK *and* LONG *come swaggering.* LONG *is dressed in shore clothes, wears a black Windsor tie, cloth cap.* YANK *is in his dirty dungarees. A fireman's cap with black peak is cocked defiantly on the side of his head. He has not shaved for days and around his fierce, resentful eyes—as around those of* LONG *to a lesser degree—the black smudge of coal dust still sticks like make-up. They hesitate and stand together at the corner, swaggering, looking about them with a forced, defiant contempt.*

LONG [*indicating it all with an oratorical gesture*]. Well, 'ere we are. Fif' Avenoo. This 'ere's their bleedin' private lane, as yer might say. [*Bitterly*] We're trespassers 'ere. Proletarians keep orf the grass!

YANK [*dully*]. I don't see no grass, yuh boob. [*Staring at the sidewalk*] Clean, ain't it? Yuh could eat a fried egg offen it. The white wings got some job sweepin' dis up. [*Looking up and down the avenue—surlily*] Where's all de white-collar stiffs yuh said was here—and de skoits— her kind?

LONG. In church, blarst 'em! Arskin' Jesus to give 'em more money.

YANK. Choich, huh? I useter to go to choich onct—sure—when I was a kid. Me old man and woman, dey made me. Dey never went demselves, dough. Always got too big a head on Sunday mornin', dat was dem. [*With a grin*] Dey was scrappers for fair, bot' of dem. On Satiday nights when dey bot' got a skinful dey could put up a bout oughter been staged at de Garden. When dey got trough dere wasn't a chair or table wit a leg under it. Or else dey bot' jumped on me for somep'n. Dat was where I loined to take punishment. [*With a grin and a swagger*] I'm a chip offen de old block, get me?

LONG. Did yer old man follow the sea?

YANK. Naw. Worked along shore. I runned away when me old lady croaked wit de tremens.[12] I helped at truckin' and in de market. Den I shipped in de stokehole. Sure. Dat belongs. De rest was nothin'. [*Looking around him*] I ain't never seen dis before. De Brooklyn waterfront, dat was where I was dragged up. [*Taking a deep breath*] Dis ain't so bad at dat, huh?

LONG. Not bad? Well, we pays for it wiv our bloody sweat, if yer wants to know!

YANK [*with sudden angry disgust*]. Aw, hell! I don't see no one, see —like her. All dis gives me a pain. It don't belong. Say, ain't dere a

---

[12] the violent delirium occasioned by acute alcoholism

back room around dis dump? Let's go shoot a ball. All dis is too clean
and quiet and dolled-up, get me! It gives me a pain.

LONG. Wait and yer'll bloody well see—

YANK. I don't wait for no one. I keep on de move. Say, what yuh drag
me up here for, anyway? Tryin' to kid me, yuh simp, yuh?

LONG. Yer wants to get back at 'er, don't yer? That's what yer been
sayin' every bloomin' hour since she hinsulted yer.

YANK [*vehemently*]. Sure ting I do! Didn't I try to get even wit her
in Southampton? Didn't I sneak on de dock and wait for her by de
gang-plank? I was goin' to spit in her pale mug, see! Sure, right in her
pop-eyes! Dat woulda made me even, see? But no chanct. Dere was a
whole army of plainclothes bulls around. Dey spotted me and gimme
de bum's rush. I never seen her. But I'll git square wit her yet, you
watch! [*Furiously*] De lousy tart! She tinks she kin get away with
moider—but not wit me! I'll fix her! I'll tink of a way!

LONG [*as disgusted as he dares to be*]. Ain't that why I brought yer up
'ere—to show yer? Yer been lookin' at this 'ere 'ole affair wrong. Yer
been actin' an' talkin' if it was all a bleedin' personal matter between
yer and that bloody cow. I wants to convince yer she was on'y a
representative of 'er clarss. I wants to awaken yer bloody clarss consciousness. Then yer'll see it's 'er clarss yer've got to fight, not 'er
alone. There's a 'ole mob of 'em like 'er, Gawd blind 'em!

YANK [*spitting on his hands—belligerently*]. De more de merrier when
I gits started. Bring on de gang!

LONG. Yer'll see 'em in arf a mo', when that church lets out.[*He turns
and sees the window display in the two stores for the first time.*] Blimey!
Look at that, will yer? [*They both walk back and stand looking in the
jeweler's.* LONG *flies into a fury*] Just look at this 'ere bloomin' mess!
Just look at it! Look at the bleedin' prices on 'em—more'n our 'ole
bloody stokehole makes in ten voyages sweatin' in 'ell! And they—
'er and 'er bloody clarss—buys 'em for toys to dangle on 'em! One of
these 'ere would buy scoff[13] for a starvin' family for a year!

YANK. Aw, cut de sob stuff! T' hell wit de starvin' family! Yuh'll be
passin' de hat to me next. [*With naïve admiration*] Say, dem tings is
pretty, huh? Bet yuh dey'd hock for a piece of change aw right. [*Then
turning away, bored*] But, aw hell, what good are dey? Let her have
'em. Dey don't belong no more'n she does. [*With a gesture of sweeping
the jeweler's into oblivion*] All dat don't count, get me?

LONG [*who has moved to the furrier's—indignantly*]. And I s'pose this
'ere don't count neither—skins of poor, 'armless animals slaughtered
so as 'er and 'ers can keep their bleedin' noses warm!

YANK [*who has been staring at something inside—with queer excitement*].
Take a slant at dat! Give it de once-over! Monkey fur—two thousand

---

[13] food

bucks! [*Bewilderedly*] Is dat straight goods—monkey fur? What de hell—?

LONG [*bitterly*]. It's straight enuf. [*With grim humor*] They wouldn't bloody well pay that for a 'airy ape's skin—no, nor for the 'ole livin' ape with all 'is 'ead, and body, and soul thrown in!

YANK [*clenching his fists, his face growing pale with rage as if the skin in the window were a personal insult*]. Trowin' it up in my face! Christ! I'll fix her!

LONG [*excitedly*]. Church is out. 'Ere they come, the bleedin' swine. [*After a glance at* YANK'S *lowering face—uneasily*] Easy goes, Comrade. Keep yer bloomin' temper. Remember force defeats itself. It ain't our weapon. We must impress our demands through peaceful means—the votes of the on-marching proletarians of the bloody world!

YANK [*with abysmal contempt*]. Votes, hell! Votes is a joke, see. Votes for women! Let dem do it!

LONG [*still more uneasily*]. Calm, now. Treat 'em wiv the proper contempt. Observe the bleedin' parasites but 'old yer 'orses.

YANK [*angrily*]. Git away from me! Yuh're yellow, dat's what. Force, dat's me! De punch, dat's me every time, see! [*The crowd from church enter from the right, sauntering slowly and affectedly, their heads held stiffly up, looking neither to right nor left, talking in toneless, simpering voices. The women are rouged, calcimined, dyed, overdressed to the nth degree. The men are in Prince Alberts, high hats, spats, canes, etc. A procession of gaudy marionettes, yet with something of the relentless horror of Frankensteins in their detached, mechanical unawareness.*]

VOICES. Dear Doctor Caiaphas![14] He is so sincere!

What was the sermon? I dozed off.

About the radicals, my dear—and the false doctrines that are being preached.

We must organize a hundred per cent American bazaar.

And let everyone contribute one one-hundredth per cent of their income tax.

What an original idea!

We can devote the proceeds to rehabilitating the veil of the temple.

But that has been done so many times.

YANK [*glaring from one to the other of them—with an insulting snort of scorn*]. Huh! Huh! [*Without seeming to see him, they make wide detours to avoid the spot where he stands in the middle of the sidewalk.*]

LONG [*frightenedly*]. Keep yer bloomin' mouth shut. I tells yer.

YANK [*viciously*]. G'wan! Tell it to Sweeney! [*He swaggers away and deliberately lurches into a top-hatted gentleman, then glares at him pugnaciously.*] Say, who d'yuh tink yuh're bumpin'? Tink yuh own de oith?

---

[14] Caiaphas was the high priest who prophesied that Christ would die for the nation (John 11:49–51). The name has become synonymous with hypocrisy.

GENTLEMAN [*coldly and affectedly*]. I beg your pardon. [*He has not looked at* YANK *and passes on without a glance, leaving him bewildered.*]

LONG [*rushing up and grabbing* YANK'*s arm*]. Ere! Come away! This wasn't what I meant. Yer'll 'ave the bloody coppers down on us.

YANK [*savagely—giving him a push that sends him sprawling*]. G'wan!

LONG [*picks himself up—hysterically*]. I'll pop orf then. This ain't what I meant. And whatever 'appens, yer can't blame me. [*He slinks off left.*]

YANK. T' hell wit youse! [*He approaches a lady—with a vicious grin and a smirking wink.*] Hello, Kiddo. How's every little ting? Got anything on for tonight? I know an old boiler down to de docks we kin crawl into. [*The lady stalks by without a look, without a change of pace.* YANK *turns to others—insultingly.*] Holy smokes, what a mug! Go hide yuhself before de horses shy at yuh. Gee, pipe de heine on dat one! Say, youse, yuh look like de stoin of a ferryboat. Paint and powder! All dolled up to kill! Yuh look like stiffs laid out for de boneyard! Aw, g'wan, de lot of youse! Yuh give me de eye-ache. Yuh don't belong, get me! Look at me, why don't youse dare? I belong, dat's me! [*Pointing to a skyscraper across the street which is in process of construction—with bravado*] See dat building goin' up dere? See de steel work? Steel, dat's me! Youse guys live on it and tink yuh're somep'n. But I'm *in* it, see! I'm de hoistin' engine dat makes it go up! I'm it— de inside and bottom of it! Sure! I'm steel and steam and smoke and de rest of it! It moves—speed—twenty-five stories up—and me at de top and bottom—movin'! Youse simps don't move. Yuh're on'y dolls I winds up to see 'm spin. Yuh're de garbage, get me—de leavin's—de ashes we dump over de side! Now, what 'a 'yuh gotta say? [*But as they seem neither to see nor hear him, he flies into a fury*] Bums! Pigs! Tarts! Bitches! [*He turns in a rage on the men, bumping viciously into them but not jarring them the least bit. Rather it is he who recoils after each collision. He keeps growling*] Git off de oith! G'wan, yuh bum! Look where yuh're goin', can't yuh? Git outa here! Fight, why don't yuh? Put up yer mits! Don't be a dog! Fight or I'll knock yuh dead! [*But, without seeming to see him, they all answer with mechanical affected politeness*] I beg your pardon. [*Then at a cry from one of the women, they all scurry to the furrier's window.*]

THE WOMAN [*ecstatically, with a gasp of delight*]. Monkey fur! [*The whole crowd of men and women chorus after her in the same tone of affected delight*] Monkey fur!

YANK [*with a jerk of his head back on his shoulders, as if he had received a punch full in the face—raging*]. I see yuh, all in white! I see yuh, yuh white-faced tart, yuh! Hairy ape, huh? I'll hairy ape yuh! [*He bends down and grips at the street curbing as if to pluck it out and hurl it. Foiled in this, snarling with passion, he leaps to the lamp-post on the corner and tries to pull it up for a club. Just at that moment a bus is heard rumbling up. A fat, high-hatted, spatted gentleman runs out from the side street.*]

He calls out plaintively] Bus! Bus! Stop there! [*And runs full tilt into the bending, straining* YANK, *who is bowled off his balance.*]

YANK [*seeing a fight—with a roar of joy as he springs to his feet*]. At last! Bus, huh? I'll bust yuh! [*He lets drive a terrific swing, his fist landing full on the fat gentleman's face. But the gentleman stands unmoved as if nothing had happened.*]

GENTLEMAN. I beg your pardon. [*Then irritably*] You have made me lose my bus. [*He clasps his hands and begins to scream*] Officer! Officer! [*Many police whistles shrill out on the instant and a whole platoon of policemen rush in on* YANK *from all sides. He tries to fight but is clubbed to the pavement and fallen upon. The crowd at the window have not moved or noticed this disturbance. The clanging gong of the patrol wagon approaches with a clamoring din.*]

[*Curtain*]

SCENE SIX

Night of the following day. A row of cells in the prison on Blackwells Island.[15] *The cells extend back diagonally from right front to left rear. They do not stop, but disappear in the dark background as if they ran on, numberless, into infinity. One electric bulb from the low ceiling of the narrow corridor sheds its light through the heavy steel bars of the cell at the extreme front and reveals part of the interior.* YANK *can be seen within, crouched on the edge of his cot in the attitude of Rodin's "The Thinker." His face is spotted with black and blue bruises. A blood-stained bandage is wrapped around his head.*

YANK [*suddenly starting as if awakening from a dream, reaches out and shakes the bars—aloud to himself, wonderingly*]. Steel. Dis is de Zoo, huh? [*A burst of hard, barking laughter comes from the unseen occupants of the cells, runs back down the tier, and abruptly ceases.*]

VOICES [*mockingly*]. The Zoo? That's a new name for this coop—a damn good name!

Steel, eh? You said a mouthful. This is the old iron house.

Who is that boob talkin'?

He's the bloke they brung in out of his head. The bulls had beat him up fierce.

YANK [*dully*]. I musta been dreamin'. I tought I was in a cage at de Zoo—but de apes don't talk, do dey?

VOICES [*with mocking laughter*]. You're in a cage aw right.

A coop!

A pen!

A sty!

A kennel! [*Hard laughter—a pause.*]

Say, guy! Who are you? No, never mind lying. What are you?

15 site of the city prison in New York

Yes, tell us your sad story. What's your game?

What did they jug yuh for?

YANK [*dully*]. I was a fireman—stokin' on de liners. [*Then with sudden rage, rattling his cell bars*] I'm a hairy ape, get me? And I'll bust youse all in de jaw if yuh don't lay off kiddin' me.

VOICES. Huh! You're a hard boiled duck, ain't you!

When you spit, it bounces! [*Laughter.*]

Aw, can it. He's a regular guy. Ain't you?

What did he say he was—a ape?

YANK [*defiantly*]. Sure ting! Ain't dat what youse all are—apes? [*A silence. Then a furious rattling of bars from down the corridor.*]

A VOICE [*thick with rage*]. I'll show yuh who's a ape, yuh bum!

VOICES. Ssshh! Nix!

Can de noise!

Piano![16]

You'll have the guard down on us!

YANK [*scornfully*]. De guard? Yuh mean de keeper, don't yuh? [*Angry exclamations from all the cells.*]

VOICE [*placatingly*]. Aw, don't pay no attention to him. He's off his nut from the beatin'-up he got. Say, you guy! We're waitin' to hear what they landed you for—or ain't yuh tellin'?

YANK. Sure. I'll tell youse. Sure! Why de hell not? On'y—youse won't get me. Nobody gets me but me, see? I started to tell de Judge and all he says was: "Toity days to tink it over." Tink it over! Christ, dat's all I been doin' for weeks! [*After a pause*] I was tryin' to git even wit someone, see?—someone dat done me doit.

VOICES [*cynically*]. De old stuff, I bet. Your goil, huh?

Give yuh the double-cross, huh?

That's them every time!

Did yuh beat up de odder guy?

YANK [*disgustedly*]. Aw, yuh're all wrong! Sure dere was a skoit in it —but not what youse mean, not dat old tripe. Dis was a new kind of skoit. She was dolled up all in white—in de stokehole. I tought she was a ghost. Sure. [*A pause.*]

VOICES [*whispering*]. Gee, he's still nutty.

Let him rave. It's fun listenin'.

YANK [*unheeding—groping in his thoughts*]. Her hands—dey was skinny and white like dey wasn't real but painted on somep'n. Dere was a million miles from me to her—twenty-five knots a hour. She was like some dead ting de cat brung in. Sure, dat's what. She didn't belong. She belonged in de window of a toy store, or on de top of a garbage can, see! Sure! [*He breaks out angrily*] But would yuh believe it, she

---

[16] quiet

had de noive to do me doit. She lamped me like she was seein' somep'n broke loose from de menagerie. Christ, yuh'd oughter seen her eyes! [*He rattles the bars of his cell furiously.*] But I'll get back at her yet, you watch! And if I can't find her I'll take it out on de gang she runs wit. I'm wise to where dey hangs out now. I'll show her who belongs! I'll show her who's in de move and who ain't. You watch my smoke!

VOICES [*serious and joking*]. Dat's de talkin'!

Take her for all she's got!

What was this dame, anyway? Who was she, eh?

YANK. I dunno. First cabin stiff. Her old man's a millionaire, dey says—name of Douglas.

VOICES. Douglas? That's the president of the Steel Trust, I bet. Sure, I seen his mug in de papers.

Sure, I seen his mug in de papers.

He's filthy with dough.

VOICE. Hey, feller, take a tip from me. If you want to get back at that dame, you better join the Wobblies.[17] You'll get some action then.

YANK. Wobblies? What de hell's dat?

VOICE. Ain't you ever heard of the IWW?

YANK. Naw. What is it?

VOICE. A gang of blokes—a tough gang. I been readin' about 'em today in the paper. The guard give me the *Sunday Times*. There's a long spiel about 'em. It's from a speech made in the Senate by a guy named Senator Queen. [*He is in the cell next to* YANK'S. *There is a rustling of paper*] Wait'll I see if I got light enough and I'll read you. Listen. [*He reads*]: "There is a menace existing in this country today which threatens the vitals of our fair Republic—as foul a menace against the very life-blood of the American Eagle as was the foul conspiracy of Cataline[18] against the eagles of ancient Rome!"

VOICE [*disgustedly*]. Aw, hell! Tell him to salt de tail of dat eagle!

VOICE [*reading*]. "I refer to that devil's brew of rascals, jailbirds, murderers and cutthroats who libel all honest working men by calling themselves the Industrial Workers of the World; but in the light of their nefarious plots, I call them the Industrious *Wreckers* of the World!"

YANK [*with vengeful satisfaction*]. Wreckers, dat's de right dope! Dat belongs! Me for dem!

VOICE. Sssshh! [*Reading*] "This fiendish organization is a foul ulcer on the fair body of our Democracy—"

VOICE. Democracy, hell! Give him the boid, fellers—the raspberry! [*They do.*]

---

[17] Industrial Workers of the World, a militant labor organization
[18] conspirator who attempted the overthrow of the government of Rome

VOICE. *Ssshh!* [*Reading*] "Like Cato I say to this Senate, the IWW must be destroyed![19] For they represent an ever-present dagger pointed at the heart of the greatest nation the world has ever known, where all men are born free and equal, with equal opportunities to all, where the Founding Fathers have guaranteed to each one happiness, where Truth, Honor, Liberty, Justice, and the Brotherhood of Man are a religion absorbed with one's mother's milk, taught at our father's knee, sealed, signed, and stamped upon in the glorious Constitution of these United States!" [*A perfect storm of hisses, catcalls, boos, and hard laughter.*]

VOICES [*scornfully*]. Hurrah for de Fort' of July!
        Pass de hat!
        Liberty!
        Justice!
        Honor!
        Opportunity!
        Brotherhood!

ALL [*with abysmal scorn*]. Aw, hell!

VOICE. Give that Queen Senator guy the bark! All togedder now— one—two—tree— [*A terrific chorus of barking and yapping.*]

GUARD [*from a distance*]. Quiet there, youse—or I'll git the hose. [*The noise subsides.*]

YANK [*with growling rage*]. I'd like to catch dat senator guy alone for a second. I'd loin him some trut'!

VOICE. Ssshh! Here's where he gits down to cases on the Wobblies. [*Reads*] They plot with fire in one hand and dynamite in the other. They stop not before murder to gain their ends, nor at the outraging of defenseless womanhood. They would tear down society, put the lowest scum in the seats of the mighty, turn Almighty God's revealed plan for the world topsy-turvy, and make of our sweet and lovely civilization a shambles, a desolation where man, God's masterpiece, would soon degenerate back to the ape!"

VOICE [*to* YANK]. Hey, you guy. There's your ape stuff again.

YANK [*with a growl of fury*]. I got him. So dey blow up tings, do dey? Dey turn tings round, do dey? Hey, lend me dat paper, will yuh?

VOICE. Sure. Give it to him. On'y keep it to yourself, see. We don't wanter listen to no more of that slop.

VOICE. Here you are. Hide it under your mattress.

YANK [*reaching out*]. Tanks. I can't read much but I kin manage. [*He sits, the paper in the hand at his side, in the attitude of Rodin's "The Thinker." A pause. Several snores from down the corridor. Suddenly* YANK *jumps to his feet with a furious groan as if some appalling thought had crashed on him—bewilderedly*] Sure—her old man—president of de

---

[19] Marcus Portius Cato, 234–149 B.C., Roman soldier and statesman, repeatedly ended his speeches in the Senate with, "Carthage must be destroyed."

Steel Trust—makes half de steel in de world—steel—where I tought
I belonged—drivin' trou—movin'—in dat—to make *her*—and cage me
in for her to spit on! Christ! [*He shakes the bars of his cell door till the
whole tier trembles. Irritated, protesting exclamations from those awakened
or trying to get to sleep*] He made dis—dis cage! Steel! *It* don't belong,
dat's what! Cages, cells, locks, bolts, bars—dat's what it means!—
holdin' me down wit him at de top! But I'll drive trou! Fire, dat melts
it! I'll be fire—under de heap—fire dat never goes out—hot as hell—
breakin' out in de night— [*While he has been saying this last he has
shaken his cell door to a clanging accompaniment. As he comes to the
"breakin' out" he seizes one bar with both hands and, putting his two
feet up against the others so that his position is parallel to the floor like a
monkey's, he gives a great wrench backwards. The bar bends like a licorice
stick under his tremendous strength. Just at this moment the* Prison
Guard *rushes in, dragging a hose behind him.*]

Guard [*angrily*]. I'll loin youse bums to wake me up! [*Sees* Yank]
Hello, it's you, huh? Got the D.1.'s,[20] hey? Well, I'll cure 'em. I'll
drown your snakes for yuh! [*Noticing the bar*] Hell, look at dat bar
bended! On'y a bug is strong enough for dat!

Yank [*glaring at him*]. Or a hairy ape, yuh big yellow bum! Look out!
Here I come! [*He grabs another bar.*]

Guard [*scared now—yelling off left*]. Toin de hose on, Ben!—full
pressure! And call de others—and a straitjacket! [*The curtain is falling.
As it hides* Yank *from view, there is a splattering smash as the stream of
water hits the steel of* Yank's *cell.*]

[*Curtain*]

Scene Seven

*Nearly a month later. An IWW local near the waterfront, showing the
interior of a front room on the ground floor, and the street outside. Moonlight on the narrow street, buildings massed in black shadow. The interior
of the room, which is general assembly room, office, and reading room,
resembles some dingy settlement boys' club. A desk and high stool are in
one corner. A table with papers, stacks of pamphlets, chairs about it, is at
center. The whole is decidedly cheap, banal, commonplace and unmysterious
as a room could well be. The secretary is perched on the stool making entries
in a large ledger. An eye shade casts his face into shadows. Eight or ten
men, longshoremen, iron workers, and the like, are grouped about the table.
Two are playing checkers. One is writing a letter. Most of them are smoking
pipes. A big signboard is on the wall at the rear, "Industrial Workers of the
World—Local No. 57."*

Yank *comes down the street outside. He is dressed as in Scene Five. He
moves cautiously, mysteriously. He comes to a point opposite the door; tip-*

[20] *Delirium tremens*

toes softly up to it, listens, is impressed by the silence within, knocks care-
fully, as if he were guessing at the password to some secret rite. Listens. No
answer. Knocks again a bit louder. No answer. Knocks impatiently, much
louder.

SECRETARY [*turning around on his stool*]. What the hell is that— someone knocking? [*Shouts*] Come in, why don't you? [*All the men in the*
room look up. YANK *opens the door slowly, gingerly, as if afraid of an*
ambush. He looks around for secret doors, mystery, is taken aback by the
commonplaceness of the room and the men in it, thinks he may have gotten
in the wrong place, then sees the signboard on the wall and is reassured.]
YANK [*blurts out*]. Hello.
MEN [*reservedly*]. Hello.
YANK [*more easily*]. I tought I'd bumped into de wrong dump.
SECRETARY [*scrutinizing him carefully*]. Maybe you have. Are you a
member?
YANK. Naw, not yet. Dat's what I come for—to join.
SECRETARY. That's easy. What's your job—longshore?
YANK. Naw. Fireman—stoker on de liners.
SECRETARY [*with satisfaction*]. Welcome to our city. Glad to know
you people are waking up at last. We haven't got many members in
your line.
YANK. Naw. Dey're all dead to de woild.
SECRETARY. Well, you can help to wake 'em. What's your name? I'll
make out your card.
YANK [*confused*]. Name? Lemme tink.
SECRETARY [*sharply*]. Don't you know your own name?
YANK. Sure; but I been just Yank for so long—Bob, dat's it—Bob
Smith.
SECRETARY [*writing*]. Robert Smith. [*Fills out the rest of card*] Here
you are. Cost you half a dollar.
YANK. Is dat all—four bits? Dat's easy. [*Gives the Secretary the money.*]
SECRETARY [*throwing it in drawer*]. Thanks. Well, make yourself at
home. No introductions needed. There's literature on the table. Take
some of those pamphlets with you to distribute aboard ship. They may
bring results. Sow the seed, only go about it right. Don't get caught
and fired. We got plenty out of work. What we need is men who can
hold their jobs—and work for us at the same time.
YANK. Sure. [*But he still stands, embarrassed and uneasy.*]
SECRETARY [*looking at him—curiously*]. What did you knock for?
Think we had a coon in uniform to open doors?
YANK. Naw. I tought it was locked—and dat yuh'd wanter give me the
once-over trou a peep-hole or somep'n to see if I was right.
SECRETARY [*alert and suspicious but with an easy laugh*]. Think we were
running a crap game? That door is never locked. What put that in
your nut?

YANK [*with a knowing grin, convinced that this is all camouflage, a part of the secrecy*]. Dis burg is full of bulls, ain't it?

SECRETARY [*sharply*]. What have the cops got to do with us? We're breaking no laws.

YANK [*with a knowing wink*]. Sure. Youse wouldn't for woilds. Sure. I'm wise to dat.

SECRETARY. You seem to be wise to a lot of stuff none of us knows about.

YANK [*with another wink*]. Aw, dat's aw right, see. [*Then made a bit resentful by the suspicious glances from all sides*] Aw, can it! Youse needn't put me trou de toid degree. Can't youse see I belong? Sure! I'm reg'lar. I'll stick, get me? I'll shoot de woiks for youse. Dat's why I wanted to join in.

SECRETARY [*breezily, feeling him out*]. That's the right spirit. Only are you sure you understand what you've joined? It's all plain and above board; still, some guys get a wrong slant on us. [*Sharply*] What's your notion of the purpose of the IWW?

YANK. Aw, I know all about it.

SECRETARY [*sarcastically*]. Well, give us some of your valuable information.

YANK [*cunningly*]. I know enough not to speak outa my toin. [*Then resentfully again*] Aw, say! I'm reg'lar. I'm wise to de game. I know yuh got to watch your step wit a stranger. For all youse know, I might be a plain-clothes dick, or somep'n, dat's what yuh're tinkin', huh? Aw, forget it! I belong, see? Ask any guy down to de docks if I don't.

SECRETARY. Who said you didn't?

YANK. After I'm 'nitiated, I'll show yuh.

SECRETARY [*astounded*]. Initiated? There's no initiation.

YANK [*disappointed*]. Ain't there no password—no grip nor nothin'?

SECRETARY. What'd you think this is—the Elks—or the Black Hand? [21]

YANK. De Elks, hell! De Black Hand, dey're a lot of yellow back-stickin' Ginees.[22] Naw. Dis is a man's gang, ain't it?

SECRETARY. You said it! That's why we stand on our two feet in the open. We got no secrets.

YANK [*surprised but admiringly*]. Yuh mean to say yuh always run wide open—like dis?

SECRETARY. Exactly.

YANK. Den yuh sure got your noive wit youse!

SECRETARY [*sharply*]. Just what was it made you want to join us? Come out with that straight.

YANK. Yuh call me? Well, I got noive, too! Here's my hand. Yuh wanter blow tings up, don't yuh? Well, dat's me! I belong!

SECRETARY [*with pretended carelessness*]. You mean change the unequal

---

[21] the Mafia   [22] Italian

conditions of society by legitimate direct action—or with dynamite?

YANK. Dynamite! Blow it offen de oith—steel—all de cages—all de factories, steamers, buildings, jails—de Steel Trust and all dat makes it go.

SECRETARY. So—that's your idea, eh? And did you have any special job in that line you wanted to propose to us? [*He makes a sign to the men, who get up cautiously one by one and group behind* YANK.]

YANK [*boldly*]. Sure, I'll come out wit it. I'll show youse I'm one of de gang. Dere's dat millionaire guy, Douglas—

SECRETARY. President of the Steel Trust, you mean? Do you want to assassinate him?

YANK. Naw, dat don't get yuh nothin'. I mean blow up de factory, de woiks, where he makes de steel. Dat's what I'm after— to blow up de steel, knock all de steel in de woild up to de moon. Dat'll fix tings! [*Eagerly, with a touch of bravado*] I'll do it by me lonesome! I'll show yuh! Tell me where his woiks is, how to git there, all de dope. Gimme de stuff, de old butter—and watch me do de rest! Watch de smoke and see it move! I don't give a damn if dey nab me—long as it's done! I'll soive life for it—and give 'em de laugh! [*Half to himself*] And I'll write her a letter and tell her de hairy ape done it. Dat'll square tings.

SECRETARY [*stepping away from* YANK]. Very interesting. [*He gives a signal. The men, huskies all, throw themselves on* YANK *and before he knows it they have his legs and arms pinioned. But he is too flabbergasted to make a struggle, anyway. They feel him over for weapons.*]

MAN. No gat, no knife. Shall we give him what's what and put the boots to him?

SECRETARY. No. He isn't worth the trouble we'd get into. He's too stupid. [*He comes closer and laughs mockingly in* YANK'*s face*] Ho-ho! By God, this is the biggest joke they've put up on us yet. Hey, you Joke! Who sent you—Burns or Pinkerton?[23] No, by God, you're such a bonehead I'll bet you're in the Secret Service! Well, you dirty spy, you rotten agent provocator,[24] you can go back and tell whatever skunk is paying you blood-money for betraying your brothers that he's wasting his coin. You couldn't catch a cold. And tell him that all he'll ever get on us, or ever has got, is just his own sneaking plots that he's framed up to put us in jail. We are what our manifesto says we are, neither more nor less—and we'll give him a copy of that any time he calls. And as for you—[*He glares scornfully at* YANK, *who is sunk in an oblivious stupor*] Oh, hell, what's the use of talking? You're a brainless ape.

YANK [*aroused by the word to fierce but futile struggles*]. What's dat, yuh Sheeny bum, yuh!

---

[23] private detective agencies sometimes used for strike-breaking or other anti-union activity

[24] man sent into a union to provoke violence or other illegal action

SECRETARY. Throw him out, boys. [*In spite of his struggles, this is done with gusto and éclat. Propelled by several parting kicks,* YANK *lands sprawling in the middle of the narrow cobbled street. With a growl he starts to get up and storm the closed door, but stops bewildered by the confusion in his brain, pathetically impotent. He sits there, brooding, in as near to the attitude of Rodin's "Thinker" as he can get in his position.*]

YANK [*bitterly*]. So dem boids don't tink I belong, neider. Aw, to hell wit 'em! Dey're in de wrong pew—de same old bull—soapboxes and Salvation Army—no guts! Cut out an hour offen de job a day and make me happy! Gimme a dollar more a day and make me happy! Tree square a day, and cauliflowers in de front yard—ekal rights—a woman and kids—a lousy vote—and I'm all fixed for Jesus, huh? Aw, hell! What does dat get yuh? Dis ting's in your inside, but it ain't your belly. Feedin' your face—sinkers and coffee—dat don't touch it. It's way down—at de bottom. Yuh can't grab it, and yuh can't stop it. It moves, and everything moves. It stops and de whole woild stops. Dat's me now—I don't tick, see?—I'm a busted Ingersoll,[25] dat's what. Steel was me, and I owned de woild. Now I ain't steel, and de woild owns me. Aw, hell! I can't see—it's all dark, get me? It's all wrong! [*He turns a bitter mocking face up like an ape gibbering at the moon*] Say, youse up dere, Man in de Moon, yuh look so wise, gimme de answer, huh? Slip me de inside dope, de information right from de stable—where do I get off at, huh?

A POLICEMAN [*who has come up the street in time to hear this last— with grim humor*]. You'll get off at the station, you boob, if you don't get up out of that and keep movin'.

YANK [*looking up at him—with a hard, bitter laugh*]. Sure! Lock me up! Put me in a cage! Dat's de on'y answer yuh know. G'wan, lock me up!

POLICEMAN. What you been doin'?

YANK. Enuf to gimme life for! I was born, see? Sure, dat's de charge. Write it in de blotter. I was born, get me!

POLICEMAN [*jocosely*]. God pity your old woman! [*Then matter-of-fact*] But I've no time for kidding. You're soused. I'd run you in but it's too long a walk to the station. Come on now, get up, or I'll fan your ears with this club. Beat it now! [*He hauls* YANK *to his feet.*]

YANK [*in a vague mocking tone*]. Say, where do I go from here?

POLICEMAN [*giving him a push—with a grin, indifferently*]. Go to hell.

[*Curtain*]

SCENE EIGHT

Twilight of the next day. The monkey house at the Zoo. One spot of clear gray light falls on the front of one cage so that the interior can be seen. The other cages are vague, shrouded in shadow from which chatterings pitched in

---

25 a cheap pocket watch

a conversational tone can be heard. On the one cage a sign from which the word
"gorilla" stands out. The gigantic animal himself is seen squatting on his
haunches on a bench in much the same attitude as Rodin's "Thinker." YANK
enters from the left. Immediately a chorus of angry chattering and screeching
breaks out. The gorilla turns his eyes but makes no sound or move.

YANK [*with a hard, bitter laugh*]. Welcome to your city, huh? Hail, hail,
de gang's all here! [*At the sound of his voice the chattering dies away into
an attentive silence.* YANK *walks up to the gorilla's cage and, leaning over the
railing, stares in at its occupant, who stares back at him, silent and motionless. There is a pause of dead stillness. Then* YANK *begins to talk in a
friendly confidential tone, half-mockingly, but with a deep undercurrent
of sympathy*] Say, yuh're some hard-lookin' guy, ain't yuh? I seen lots
of tough nuts dat de gang called gorillas, but yuh're de foist real one
I ever seen. Some chest yuh got, and shoulders, and dem arms and
mits! I bet yuh got a punch in eider fist dat'd knock 'em all silly! [*This
with genuine admiration. The gorilla, as if he understood, stands upright,
swelling out his chest and pounding on it with his fist.* YANK *grins sym-
pathetically*] Sure, I get yuh. Yuh challenge de whole woild, huh? Yuh
got what I was sayin' even if yuh muffed de woids. [*Then bitterness
creeping in*] And why wouldn't yuh get me? Ain't we both members of
de same club—de Hairy Apes? [*They stare at each other—a pause—then*
YANK *goes on slowly and bitterly*] So yuh're what she seen when she
looked at me, de white-faced tart! I was you to her, get me? On'y
outa de cage—broke out—free to moider her, see? Sure! Dat's what
she tought. She wasn't wise dat I was in a cage, too—worser'n yours
—sure—a damn sight—'cause you got some chanct to bust loose—
but me— [*He grows confused*] Aw, hell! It's all wrong, ain't it? [*A
pause*] I s'pose yuh wanter know what I'm doin' here, huh? I been
warmin' a bench down to de Battery²⁶—ever since last night. Sure.
I seen de sun come up. Dat was pretty, too—all red and pink and
green. I was lookin' at de skyscrapers—steel—and all de ships comin'
in, sailin' out, all over de oith—and dey was steel, too. De sun was
warm, dey wasn't no clouds, and dere was a breeze blowin'. Sure, it
was great stuff. I got it aw right—what Paddy said about dat bein' de
right dope—on'y I couldn't get *in* it, see? I couldn't belong in dat. It
was over my head. And I kept tinkin'—and den I beat it up here to see
what youse was like. And I waited till dey was all gone to git yuh
alone. Say, how d'yuh feel sittin' in dat pen all de time, havin' to stand
for 'em comin' and starin' at yuh—de white-faced, skinny tarts and
de boobs what marry 'em—makin' fun of yuh, laughin' at yuh, gittin'
scared of yuh—damn 'em! [*He pounds on the rail with his fist. The
gorilla rattles the bars of his cage and snarls. All the other monkeys set up*

²⁶ a park at the southern tip of Manhattan

an angry chattering in the darkness. YANK *goes on excitedly*] Sure! Dat's de way it hits me, too. On'y yuh're lucky, see? Yuh don't belong wit 'em and yuh know it. But me, I belong wit 'em—but I don't, see? Dey don't belong wit me, dat's what. Get me? Tinkin' is hard— [*He passes one hand across his forehead with a painful gesture. The gorilla growls impatiently.* YANK *goes on gropingly*] It's dis way, what I'm drivin' at. Youse can sit and dope dream in de past, green woods, de jungle and de rest of it. Den yuh belong and dey don't. Den yuh kin laugh at 'em, see? Yuh're de champ of de woild. But me—I ain't got no past to tink in, nor nothin' dat's comin', on'y what's now—and dat don't belong. Sure, you're de best off! Yuh can't tink, can yuh? Yuh can't talk neider. But I kin make a bluff at talkin' and tinkin'—a'most git away wit it—a'most!—and dat's where de joker comes in. [*He laughs*] I ain't on oith and I ain't in heaven, get me? I'm in de middle tryin' to separate 'em, takin' all de woist punches from bot' of 'em. Maybe dat's what dey call hell, huh? But you, yuh're at de bottom. You belong! Sure! Yuh're de on'y one in de woild dat does, yuh lucky stiff! [*The gorilla growls proudly*] And dat's why dey gotter put yuh in a cage, see? [*The gorilla roars angrily*] Sure! Yuh get me. It beats it when you try to tink it or talk it—it's way down—deep—behind— you 'n' me we feel it. Sure! Bot' members of dis club! [*He laughs— then in a savage tone*] What de hell! T' hell wit it! A little action, dat's our meat! Dat belongs! Knock 'em down and keep bustin' 'em till dey croaks yuh with a gat—with steel! Sure! Are yuh game? Dey've looked at youse, ain't dey—in a cage? Wanter git even? Wanter wind up like a sport 'stead of croakin' slow in dere? [*The gorilla roars an emphatic affirmative.* YANK *goes on with a sort of furious exaltation*] Sure! Yuh're reg'lar! Yuh'll stick to de finish! Me 'n' you, huh?—bot members of this club! We'll put up one last star bout dat'll knock 'em offen deir seats! Dey'll have to make de cages stronger after we're trou! [*The gorilla is straining at his bars, growling, hopping from one foot to the other.* YANK *takes a jimmy from under his coat and forces the lock on the cage door. He throws this open*] Pardon from de governor! Step out and shake hands. I'll take yuh for a walk down Fif' Avenoo. We'll knock 'em offen de oith and croak wit de band playin'. Come on, Brother. [*The gorilla scrambles gingerly out of his cage. Goes to* YANK *and stands looking at him.* YANK *keeps his mocking tone—holds out his hand*] Shake—de secret grip of our order. [*Something, the tone of mockery, perhaps, suddenly enrages the animal. With a spring he wraps his huge arms around* YANK *in a murderous hug. There is a crackling snap of crushed ribs—a gasping cry, still mocking, from* YANK] Hey, I didn't say kiss me! [*The gorilla lets the crushed body slip to the floor; stands over it uncertainly, considering; then picks it up, throws it in the cage, shuts the door, and shuffles off menacingly into the darkness at left. A great uproar of frightened chattering and whimpering comes from the other cages. Then*

YANK *moves, groaning, opening his eyes, and there is silence. He mutters painfully*] Say—dey oughter match him—wit Zybszko.[27] He got me, aw right. I'm trou. Even him didn't tink I belonged. [*Then, with sudden passionate despair*] Christ, where do I get off at? Where do I fit in? [*Checking himself as suddenly*] Aw, what de hell! No squawkin', see! No quittin', get me! Croak wit your boots on! [*He grabs hold of the bars of the cage and hauls himself painfully to his feet—looks around him bewilderedly—forces a mocking laugh*] In de cage, huh? [*In the strident tones of a circus barker*] Ladies and gents, step forward and take a slant at de one and only— [*His voice weakening*]—one and original—Hairy Ape from de wilds of— [*He slips in a heap on the floor and dies. The monkeys set up a chattering, whimpering wail. And, perhaps, the Hairy Ape at last belongs.*]

[*Curtain*]

27 a professional wrestler

Bertolt Brecht

1898–1956

MOTHER COURAGE AND
HER CHILDREN

A CHRONICLE OF THE THIRTY YEARS' WAR

English Version by Eric Bentley

❖

CHARACTERS
(In order of appearance)

There are 32 roles plus four "voices off" and three supers. But much doubling is possible; in fact, of all the actors, only the seven principals cannot double; these seven are Mother Courage, her three children, Cook, Chaplain, Yvette—even one of the children, Swiss Cheese, *could* double if absolutely necessary.

Prologue

MOTHER COURAGE
EILIF
SWISS CHEESE
CATHERINE

Scene One

RECRUITING OFFICER
SERGEANT

Scene Two

COOK
COMMANDER
CHAPLAIN

Scene Three

ORDNANCE OFFICER
YVETTE POTTIER
SOLDIER
SERGEANT
ONE EYE
COLONEL
(TWO SUPERS)

Scene Four

CLERK
OLDER SOLDIER
YOUNGER SOLDIER

Scene Five

FIRST SOLDIER
SECOND SOLDIER
PEASANT
PEASANT WOMAN

Scene Six

SOLDIER (*singing*)

Scene Seven

No new characters

Scene Eight

OLD WOMAN
YOUNG MAN
VOICES (*two*)
SOLDIER
(ONE SUPER)

Scene Nine	SECOND SOLDIER
VOICE	OLD PEASANT
	PEASANT WOMAN
Scene Ten	YOUNG PEASANT
VOICE (*girl singing*)	*Scene Twelve*
Scene Eleven	No new characters
LIEUTENANT	
FIRST SOLDIER	

THE TIME 1624–1636
THE PLACE *Sweden, Poland, Germany.*

❖

PROLOGUE

The wagon of a vivandière. MOTHER COURAGE *sitting on it, singing. Her dumb daughter* CATHERINE *beside her playing the mouth organ. The wagon is drawn by her two sons,* EILIF *and* SWISS CHEESE, *who join in the refrain.*

> *Here's Mother Courage and her wagon!*
> > *Hey, Captain, let them come and buy!*
> *Beer by the keg! Wine by the flagon!*
> > *Let your men drink before they die!*
> *Sabers and swords are hard to swallow:*
> > *First you must give them beer to drink.*
> *Then they can face what is to follow—*
> > *But let 'em swim before they sink!*
> > > *Christians, awake! The winter's gone!*
> > > *The snows depart. The dead sleep on.*
> > > *And though you may not long survive*
> > > *Get out of bed and look alive!*

> *Your men will march till they are dead, sir,*
> > *But cannot fight unless they eat.*
> *The blood they spill for you is red, sir,*
> > *What fires that blood is my red meat.*
> *For meat and soup and jam and jelly*
> > *In this old cart of mine are found:*
> *So fill the hole up in your belly*
> > *Before you fill one underground.*
> > > *Christians awake! The winter's gone!*
> > > *The snows depart. The dead sleep on.*
> > > *And though you may not long survive*
> > > *Get out of bed and look alive!*

SCENE ONE

SPRING, 1624. IN DALARNA, SWEDEN, KING GUSTAVUS
ADOLPHUS IS RECRUITING FOR THE CAMPAIGN IN PO-
LAND. THE PROVISIONER ANNA FIERLING, KNOWN AS
CANTEEN ANNA OR MOTHER COURAGE, LOSES A SON.[1]

A highway in the neighborhood of a town. A top SERGEANT *and a* RE-
CRUITING OFFICER *stand shivering.*

OFFICER. How the hell can you line up a squadron in *this* place? You
know what I keep thinking about, Sergeant? Suicide. I'm supposed to
slap four platoons together by the twelfth—four platoons the Chief's
asking for! And they're so friendly around here I'm scared to sleep
nights. Suppose I do get my hands on some character and squint at him
so I don't notice he's chicken breasted and has varicose veins. I get him
drunk and relaxed, he signs on the dotted line. I pay for the drinks, he
steps outside for a minute. I get a hunch I should follow him to the
door, and am I right! Off he's shot like a louse from a scratch. You
can't take a man's word any more, Sergeant. There's no loyalty left in
the world, no trust, no faith, no sense of honor. I'm losing my confidence in mankind, Sergeant.

SERGEANT. What they could use round here is a good war. What else
can you expect with peace running wild all over the place? You know
what the trouble with peace is? No organization. When do you get
organization? In a war. Peace is one big waste of equipment. Anything goes, no one gives a god damn. See the way they eat? Cheese on
rye, bacon on the cheese? Disgusting! How many horses they got in
this town? How many young men? Nobody knows! They haven't
bothered to count 'em!! That's peace for you!!! I been in places
where they haven't had a war in seventy years and you know what?
The people can't remember their own names! They don't know who
they are! It takes a war to fix all that. In a war everyone registers,
everybody's name's on a list, their shoes are stacked, their corn's in the
bag, you count it all up—cattle, men, et cetera—and take it away!
Yeah, that's the story—no organization, no war!

OFFICER. It's the God's truth.

SERGEANT. Course, a war's like every real good deal, hard to get going. But when it's on the road, it's a pisser—everybody's scared off
peace—like a crapshooter that keeps fading to cover his loss. Course,
until it gets going, they're just as scared of war—afraid to try anything new.

OFFICER. Look, a wagon! Two women and a couple of young punks.

---

[1] The scene headings in block capitals are projected on a front curtain. In the scene
itself the location is indicated by large black letters hanging from the flies (e.g.
SWEDEN in this first scene).

Stop the old lady, Sergeant. And if there's nothing doing this time, you won't catch *me* freezing my ass in the April wind!

MOTHER COURAGE [*entering with her three children as in the prologue*]. Good day to you, Sergeant!

SERGEANT [*barring the way*]. Good day! Who do you think you are?

MOTHER COURAGE. Tradespeople!

[*She prepares to go.*]

SERGEANT. Halt! Where are you riffraff from?

EILIF. The Second Protestant Regiment.

SERGEANT. Where are your papers?

MOTHER COURAGE. Papers?

SWISS CHEESE. But this is Mother Courage!

SERGEANT. Never heard of her. Where'd she get a name like that?

MOTHER COURAGE. They call me Mother Courage because I was afraid I'd be ruined, so I drove through the bombardment of Riga like a madwoman, with fifty loaves of bread in my cart. They were getting moldy, I couldn't please myself.

SERGEANT. No funny business! Where are your papers?

MOTHER COURAGE [*rummaging among a mass of papers in a tin box, and clambering down from her cart*]. Here, Sergeant! Here's a whole Bible I got in Altötting to wrap cucumbers in, and a map of Moravia, God knows if I'll ever get there, it's good enough for the cat if I don't. And here's a document to say my horse hasn't got hoof and mouth disease; too bad he died on us, he cost fifteen gilders, thank God I didn't pay it. Is that enough paper?

SERGEANT. Are you making a pass at me? Well, you got another guess coming. You got to have a license and you know it.

MOTHER COURAGE. Show a little respect for a lady and don't go telling these grown children of mine I'm making a pass at you, it's not proper, what would I want with *you?* My license in the Second Protestant Regiment is an honest face, even if *you* wouldn't know how to read it. I'll have no rubber stamp on it neither.

OFFICER. There's insubordination for you, my dear Sergeant! [*To* MOTHER COURAGE.] Do you know what we need in the army? [MOTHER COURAGE *starts to reply but he doesn't let her.*] Discipline!

MOTHER COURAGE. I'd have said frankfurters.

SERGEANT. Name?

MOTHER COURAGE. Anna Fierling.

SERGEANT. So you're all Fierlings?

MOTHER COURAGE. What do you mean? I was talking about me.

SERGEANT. And I was talking about your children!

MOTHER COURAGE. Must they all have the same name!

[*Indicating the elder son.*]

This boy, for instance, his name is Eilif Noyocki—for the good reason that his father always said his name was Koyocki or Moyocki. The boy remembers him to this day, only it's another one he remembers to this day, a Frenchman with a pointed beard. Anyhow he certainly has his father's brains—that man would have the pants off a farmer's behind before he knew what had happened. So we all have our own names.

SERGEANT. You're all called something different?

MOTHER COURAGE. Are you pretending you don't get it?

SERGEANT [*indicating* SWISS CHEESE]. He's Chinese, I suppose?

MOTHER COURAGE. Wrong again. A Swiss.

SERGEANT. After the Frenchman?

MOTHER COURAGE. Frenchman? I don't know any Frenchman. Don't confuse the issue or we'll be here all day, He's a Swiss but he happens to be called Feyos, a name that has nothing to do with his father, who was called something else; he was a military engineer, if you please, and a drunkard.

[SWISS CHEESE *nods, beaming, and even* CATHERINE *is amused.*]

SERGEANT. Then how come his name's Feyos?

MOTHER COURAGE. No harm meant, Sergeant, but you have no imagination. Of course he's called Feyos—when he came I was with a Hungarian, he didn't mind a bit, he had a floating kidney, though he never touched a drop, he was a very honest man. The boy takes after him.

SERGEANT. But he wasn't his father!

MOTHER COURAGE. I said he took after him. I call him Swiss Cheese because he's good at pulling the wagon.

[*Indicating her daughter.*]

She's called Catherine Haupt. Half German.

SERGEANT. A nice family I must say.

MOTHER COURAGE. We've seen the whole world together, my wagon and me.

SERGEANT [*writing*]. We'll need all that in writing. You are from Bamberg in Bavaria. How do you come to be in this place?

MOTHER COURAGE. I can't wait till the war decides to come to Bavaria.

OFFICER [*to* EILIF]. And you two oxen pull the cart. Jacob Ox and Esau Ox! Do you ever get out of harness?

EILIF. Can I smack him in the puss, Mother? I'd like to.

MOTHER COURAGE. No, you can't, you stay where you are. And now, gentlemen, what about a fine pair of pistols? Or a belt—yours is practically worn through, Sergeant.

SERGEANT. I'm after something else. I see these boys are straight as birch trees, broad in the chest, strong of limb—what are specimens like that doing out of the army I'd like to know?

MOTHER COURAGE [*rapidly*]. It's no use, Sergeant: the soldier's life is not for sons of mine!

OFFICER. Why not? It means money. It means fame. Peddling boots is woman's work.

[*To* EILIF.]
Just step up here and let me see if that's muscle or chicken fat.

MOTHER COURAGE. Chicken fat. Give him a good hard look and he'll fall over.

OFFICER. And kill a calf while he's falling if there's one in the way. [*He tries to hustle* EILIF *off*.]

MOTHER COURAGE. Will you let him alone? He's not for you!

OFFICER. He called my face a puss, that's an insult. The two of us will now go out in the field and settle this affair like men of honor.

EILIF. Don't worry, I can handle him, Mother.

MOTHER COURAGE. Stay here, you trouble maker! Never happy unless you're in a fight.
[*To the* OFFICER.]
He has a knife in his boot and he knows how to use it.

OFFICER. I'll draw it out of him like a milk tooth. Come on, young fellow!

MOTHER COURAGE. Officer, I'll report you to the colonel, he'll throw you in jail. The lieutenant is courting my daughter!

SERGEANT. Take it easy, brother.
[*To* MOTHER COURAGE.]
What have you got against the service? Wasn't his father a soldier? Didn't he die a soldier's death? You said so yourself.

MOTHER COURAGE. Yes, he's dead, but this one's just a baby, and you'll lead him to the slaughter for me, I know you. You'll get five gilders for him.

OFFICER. First thing you know, you'll have a new cap and knee boots, how about it?

EILIF. Not from you, thanks.

MOTHER COURAGE. "Come on, let's go fishing," said the angler to the worm.
[*To* SWISS CHEESE.]
Run and tell everybody they're trying to steal your brother!
[*She draws a knife.*]
Now try and steal him! And I'll let you have it, I'll cut you down like dogs! Using *him* in your war! We sell linen, we sell ham, we're peaceful people!

SERGEANT. You're peaceful all right, your knife proves it. Why, you should be ashamed of yourself. Give me that knife, you hag! You admit you live off the war, what else *would* you live off? Tell me: how can we have a war without soldiers?

MOTHER COURAGE. Do they have to be mine?

SERGEANT. So that's it. The war should swallow the pits and spit out the peach, huh? Your brood should get fat off the war, and the poor war shouldn't ask a thing in return; it can look after itself, huh? Call yourself Mother Courage and then get scared of the war—your bread-winner? Your sons aren't scared, I know that much.

EILIF. No war can scare me.

SERGEANT. Why should it? Look at me: the soldier's life hasn't done me any harm, has it? I enlisted at seventeen.

MOTHER COURAGE. You haven't reached seventy.

SERGEANT. I will, though.

MOTHER COURAGE. Above ground?

SERGEANT. Are you trying to rile me, telling me I'll die?

MOTHER COURAGE. Suppose it's the truth? Suppose I can see it's your fate? Suppose I know you're just a corpse on furlough?

SWISS CHEESE. She has second sight. Everyone says so. She can look into the future.

OFFICER. Then go look into the sergeant's future, it might amuse him.

SERGEANT. I don't believe in that stuff.

MOTHER COURAGE. Your helmet!

[*He gives her his helmet.*]

SERGEANT. It means about as much as a crap in the grass. But anything for a laugh.

MOTHER COURAGE [*takes a sheet of parchment and tears it in two pieces*]. Eilif, Swiss Cheese, and Catherine, so should we all be torn asunder if we let ourselves be drawn too deep into the war!

[*To the* SERGEANT.]

For you, I'll make an exception, and do it free. Death is black. I draw a black cross on this piece of paper.

SWISS CHEESE. And the other she leaves blank, see?

MOTHER COURAGE. Then I fold them, put them in the helmet, and shuffle them up—mixed up like we all are from our mother's womb on. And now you draw and find out the answer.

[*The* SERGEANT *hesitates.*]

OFFICER [*to* EILIF]. I don't take just anybody, I'm particular, they all say so. And you're full of punch, I like that.

SERGEANT [*fishing into the helmet*]. It's a lot of bunk. Hogwash!

SWISS CHEESE. He's drawn the black cross. His number's up!

OFFICER. Don't let them frighten you, there aren't enough bullets to go round.

SERGEANT [*hoarsely*]. You swindled me.

MOTHER COURAGE. You swindled yourself, the day you enlisted. And now we must drive on, there isn't a war every day in the week, we got to get to work.

SERGEANT. Hell and damnation, you're not getting away with this. We're taking that bastard of yours with us, we'll make a soldier of him.

EILIF. I'd like that, Mother.

MOTHER COURAGE. Shut up, you Finnish devil!

EILIF. And Swiss Cheese would like to be a soldier too.

MOTHER COURAGE. That's news to me. I see I'll have to draw lots for all three of you.

[*She goes to the back to draw crosses on the slips.*]

OFFICER [*to* EILIF]. People've been saying the Swedish soldier is religious. That's malicious gossip, I can't tell you how much damage it's done us. We only sing on Sunday. One verse of a hymn. And then only if you have a voice.

MOTHER COURAGE [*returns with the slips and throws them into the* SERGEANT'S *helmet*]. Run away from their mother would they, the devils, and off to war like a cat to cream? Just let me consult these slips and they'll see the world's no promised land with its "Join up, son, you're officer material!"

[*She thrusts the helmet at* EILIF.]

There, take yours, Eilif.

[*He does so. As he unfolds the paper she snatches it from him.*]

There you are, a cross! If he's a soldier, his number's up, that's for sure.

OFFICER [*still talking to* EILIF]. If you're wetting your pants, I'll try your brother.

MOTHER COURAGE. Now take yours, Swiss Cheese. You're a safer bet because you're my *good* boy.

[*He draws his lot.*]

Why do you look so strangely at it? It *must* be blank.

[*She takes it from him.*]

A cross? Oh, Swiss Cheese, there's no saving you either—unless you're a good boy through and through every minute of every day! Just look, Sergeant, a black cross, isn't it?

SERGEANT. Another cross. But I don't see why *I* got one, I always stay well in the rear.

[*To the* OFFICER.]

It can't be a trick, it gets her own children.

MOTHER COURAGE [*to* CATHERINE]. And now all I have left is you, you're a cross in yourself, but you have a kind heart.

[*She holds the helmet up but takes the paper herself.*]

Oh! I could give up in despair! I can't be right, I must have made a mistake. Don't be *too* kind, Catherine, don't be too kind, there's a cross in your path!

[*Breaking the mood.*]

So now you all know: always be very careful! And now we'll get in and drive on.

[*She climbs on to the wagon.*]

OFFICER [*to* SERGEANT]. Do something.

SERGEANT. I don't feel so well.

OFFICER. Maybe you caught a cold when you took your helmet off. Try doing business with her.

[*Aloud.*]

That belt, Sergeant, you could at least take a look at it, after all they live by trade, don't they, these good people? Hey, you! The sergeant will buy the belt!

MOTHER COURAGE. Half a gilder. Worth four times the price.

SERGEANT. It's not even a new one. But there's too much wind here, I'll go look at it behind your wagon.

MOTHER COURAGE. It doesn't seem windy to me.

SERGEANT. Hey, maybe it is worth half a gilder at that, there's silver on it.

MOTHER COURAGE [*following him back of the wagon*]. A solid six ounces worth.

OFFICER [*to* EILIF]. I can let you have some cash in advance, come on!

[EILIF *is undecided.*]

MOTHER COURAGE [*behind the wagon with the* SERGEANT]. Half a gilder then, quick.

SERGEANT. I still don't see why I had to draw a cross. I told you I always stay in the rear, it's the only place that's safe. You send the others on ahead to win the laurels of victory or the glory of heroic defeat as the case may be. You've ruined my afternoon.

MOTHER COURAGE. You mustn't take on so. Here, have a shot of brandy.
[*She gives him some.*]
And go right on staying in the rear. Half a gilder.

OFFICER [*has taken* EILIF *by the arm and is drawing him upstage*]. Ten gilders in advance and you're a soldier of the king, my lad, a stout fellow! The women'll be mad about you. And you can smack me in the puss because I insulted you.
[*Both leave.* CATHERINE *makes harsh noises.*]

MOTHER COURAGE. Coming, Catherine, coming! The sergeant's just paying his bill.
[*She bites the half gilder.*]
To me, Sergeant, all money is suspect, but your half gilder's okay. Now we'll be off. Where's Eilif?

SWISS CHEESE. Gone with the recruiting officer.

MOTHER COURAGE [*stops in her tracks, a pause, then*]. Oh, you simpleton!
[*To* CATHERINE.]
And you could do nothing about it, you're dumb.

SERGEANT. Take a shot yourself, Mother. That's how it goes. Your son's a soldier, he might do worse.

MOTHER COURAGE [*motions* CATHERINE *down from the wagon*]. You must help your brother now, Catherine.
[*Brother and sister get into harness together and pull the wagon,* MOTHER COURAGE *beside them.*]

SERGEANT [*looking after them*].

If from the war you'd like to borrow
Remember: the debt must be paid tomorrow!

Scene Two

Tent of the Swedish Commander. Kitchen next to it. Sound of cannon. The Cook *is quarreling with* Mother Courage *who is trying to sell him a capon.*

Cook [*who has a Dutch accent*]. Sixty hellers for that paltry poultry?

Mother Courage. Paltry poultry? Why, he's the fattest fowl you ever saw! I see no reason why I shouldn't get sixty hellers for him—this Commander can eat till the cows come home.

Cook. They're ten hellers a dozen on every street corner.

Mother Courage. A capon like this on every street corner! With a siege going on and people all skin and bones? Maybe you can get a field rat! I said maybe. Because we're all out of *them* too. Didn't you see the soldiers running five deep after one hungry little field rat? All right then, in a siege, my price for a giant capon is fifty hellers.

Cook. But we're not "in a siege," we're doing the besieging, it's the other side that's "in a siege" . . .

Mother Courage. A fat lot of difference that makes, *we* don't have a thing to eat either. They took everything in the town with them before all this started, and now they've nothing to do but eat and drink. It's us I'm worried about. Look at the farmers round here, they haven't a thing.

Cook. Sure they have. They hide it.

Mother Courage. They have not! They're ruined. They're so hungry I've seen 'em digging up roots to eat. I could boil your leather belt and make their mouths water with it. That's how things are round here. And I'm supposed to let a capon go for forty hellers!

Cook. Thirty. Not forty, I said thirty hellers.

Mother Courage. I say this is no ordinary chicken. It was a talented animal, so I hear. It would only feed when they played it some music. In fact, it had its own way of marching. It was so intelligent it could count. Forty hellers is too much for all this? I know *your* problem: if you don't find something to eat and quick, the Chief will—cut—your—fat—head—off!

Cook. All right, just watch.

[*He takes a piece of beef and lays his knife on it.*]

Here's a piece of beef, I'm going to roast it. I give you one more
chance.

MOTHER COURAGE. Roast it, go ahead, it's only one year old.

COOK. One *day* old! Yesterday it was a cow. I saw it running around.

MOTHER COURAGE. In that case it must have started stinking before
it died.

COOK. I don't care if I have to cook it five hours.
[*He cuts into it.*]

MOTHER COURAGE. Put plenty of pepper in.
[*The* SWEDISH COMMANDER, *a* CHAPLAIN *and* EILIF *enter the
tent.*]

COMMANDER [*clapping* EILIF *on the shoulder*]. In the Commander's
tent with you, Eilif my son! Sit at my right hand, you happy warrior!
You've played a hero's part, you've served the Lord in his own Holy
War, *that's* the thing! And you'll get a gold bracelet out of it when we
take the town if *I* have any say in the matter! We come to save their
souls and what do they do, the filthy, irreligious sons of bitches? Drive
their cattle away from *us*, while they stuff their priests with beef at
both ends! But you showed 'em. So here's a can of red wine for you,
we'll drink together!
[*They do so.*]
The chaplain gets the dregs, he's religious. Now what would you like
for dinner, my hearty?

EILIF. How about a slice of meat?

COOK. Nothing to eat, so he brings company to eat it.
[MOTHER COURAGE *makes him stop talking, she wants to listen.*]

COMMANDER. Cook, meat!

EILIF. Tires you out, skinny peasants. Gives you an appetite.

MOTHER COURAGE. Dear God, it's my Eilif!

COOK. Who?

MOTHER COURAGE. My eldest. It's two years since I saw him, he
was stolen from me right off the street. He must be in high favor if the
Commander's invited him to dinner. And what do you have to eat?
Nothing. You hear what the Commander's guest wants? Meat!
Better take my advice, buy the capon. The price is one gilder.

COMMANDER [*who has sat down with* EILIF *and the* CHAPLAIN,
roaring]. Cook! Dinner, you pig, or I'll have your head!

COOK. This is blackmail. Give me the damn thing!

MOTHER COURAGE. Paltry poultry like this?

COOK. You were right. Give it here. It's highway robbery, fifty hellers.

MOTHER COURAGE. I said one gilder. Nothing's too high for my
eldest, the Commander's guest of honor.

COOK. Well, you might at least pluck the damn thing till I have a fire
going.

MOTHER COURAGE [*sitting down to pluck the capon*]. I can't wait to see
his face when he sees me. This is my brave son. I also have a stupid

one but he's honest. The daughter is nothing. At least, she doesn't
talk; we must be thankful for small mercies.

COMMANDER. Have another glass, my son, it's my favorite Falernian.
There's only one cask left—two at the most—but it's worth it to
meet a soldier that still believes in God! Our chaplain here just looks
on, he only preaches, he hasn't a clue how anything gets done. So now,
Eilif my son, give us the details; tell us how you fixed the peasants and
grabbed the twenty bullocks.

EILIF. Well, it was like this. I found out that the peasants had hidden
their oxen and—on the sly and chiefly at night—had driven them into
a certain wood. The people from the town were to pick them up there.
I let them get their oxen in peace—they ought to know better than me
where they are, I said to myself. Meanwhile I made my men crazy
for meat. Their rations were short and I made sure they got shorter.
Their mouths'd water at the sound of any word beginning with M,
like mother.

COMMANDER. Smart kid.

EILIF. Not bad. The rest was a snap. Only the peasants had clubs and
outnumbered us three to one and made a murderous attack on us. Four
of them drove me into a clump of trees, knocked my good sword from
my hand, and yelled, "Surrender!" What now, I said to myself,
they'll make mincemeat of me.

COMMANDER. What did you do?

EILIF. I laughed.

COMMANDER. You what?

EILIF. I laughed. And so we got to talking. I came right down to business and said: "Twenty gilders an ox is too much, I bid fifteen."
Like I wanted to buy. That foxed 'em. So while they were scratching
their heads, I reached for my good sword and cut 'em to pieces. Necessity knows no law, huh?

COMMANDER. What do *you* say, keeper of souls?

CHAPLAIN. Strictly speaking, that saying is not in the Bible. Our Lord
made five hundred loaves out of five so that no such necessity would
arise. When he told men to love their neighbors, their bellies were full.
Nowadays things are different.

COMMANDER [*laughing*]. Quite different. A swallow of wine for those
wise words, you pharisee!

[*To* EILIF.]

You cut 'em to pieces in a good cause, our fellows were hungry and
you gave 'em to eat. Doesn't it say in the Bible "Whatsoever thou
doest to the least of these my children, thou doest unto me?" And
what *did* you do to 'em? You got 'em the best steak dinner they ever
tasted.

EILIF. I reached for my good sword and cut 'em to pieces.

COMMANDER. You have the markings of a Julius Caesar, why, you
should be presented to the King!

EILIF. I've seen him—from a distance of course. He seemed to shed a light all around. I must try to be like him!

COMMANDER. I think you're succeeding, my boy! Oh, Eilif, you don't know how I value a brave soldier like you!

[*He takes him to the map.*]

Take a look at our position, Eilif, it isn't all it might be, is it?

MOTHER COURAGE [*who has been listening and is now plucking angrily at her capon*]. He must be a very bad commander.

COOK. Just a greedy one. Why bad?

MOTHER COURAGE. Because he needs *brave* soldiers, that's why. If his plan of campaign was any good, why would he need *brave* soldiers, wouldn't plain, ordinary soldiers do? Whenever there are great virtues, it's a sure sign something's wrong.

COOK. You mean, it's a sure sign something's right.

MOTHER COURAGE. I mean what I say. Listen. When a king is a stupid king and leads his soldiers into a trap, they need this virtue of courage. When he's tight-fisted and hasn't enough soldiers, the few he does have need the heroism of Hercules—another virtue. And if he's a sloven and doesn't give a damn about anything, they have to fend for themselves and be wise as serpents or they're through. Loyalty's another virtue and you need plenty of it if the king's always asking too much of you. But in a good country the virtues wouldn't be necessary. Everybody could be quite ordinary, middling, and, for all of me, cowards.

COMMANDER. I bet your father was a soldier.

EILIF. I've heard he was a great soldier. My mother warned me. I know a song about that.

COMMANDER. Sing it to us.

[*Roaring.*]

Bring the meat!

EILIF. It's called THE SONG OF THE FISHWIFE AND THE SOLDIER.

[*He sings and at the same time does a war dance with his saber.*]

> To a soldier lad comes an old fishwife
>   And this old fishwife, says she:
> A gun will shoot, a knife will knife,
>   You will drown if you fall in the sea.
> Keep away from the ice if you want my advice,
>   Says the old fishwife, says she.
> The soldier laughs and loads his gun
> Then he grabs his knife and starts to run:
>   It's the life of a hero for me!
> From the north to the south I shall march through the land
> With a knife at my side and a gun in my hand!
>   Says the soldier lad, says he.

When the lad defies the fishwife's cries
  The old fishwife, says she:
The young are young, the old are wise,
  You will drown if you fall in the sea.
Don't ignore what I say or you'll rue it one day!
  Says the old fishwife, says she.
But gun in hand and knife at side
The soldier steps into the tide:
  It's the life of a hero for me!
When the new moon is shining on shingle roofs white
We are all coming back, go and pray for that night!
  Says the soldier lad, says he

And the fishwife old does what she's told:
  Down upon her knees drops she.
When the smoke is gone, the air is cold,
  Your heroic deeds won't warm me!
See the smoke, how it goes! May God scatter his foes!
  Down upon her knees drops she.
But gun in hand and knife at side
The lad is swept out by the tide:
  He floats with the ice to the sea.
And the new moon is shining on shingle roofs white
But the lad and his laughter are lost in the night:
  He floats with the ice to the sea.

COMMANDER. What a kitchen I've got! There's no end to the liberties
they take!

EILIF [*has entered the kitchen and embraced his mother*]. To see you again!
Where are the others?

MOTHER COURAGE [*in his arms*]. Happy as ducks in a pond. Swiss
Cheese is paymaster with the Second Protestant Regiment, so at least
he isn't in the fighting, I couldn't keep him out altogether.

EILIF. Are your feet holding up?

MOTHER COURAGE. I've a bit of trouble getting my shoes on in the
morning.

COMMANDER [*who has come over*]. So, you're his mother! I hope you
have more sons for me like this fellow.

EILIF. If I'm not the lucky one: you sit there in the kitchen and hear
your son being feasted!

MOTHER COURAGE. Yes. I heard all right.
[*Gives him a box on the ear.*]

EILIF. Because I took the oxen?

MOTHER COURAGE. No. Because you didn't surrender when the four
peasants let fly at you and tried to make mincemeat of you! Didn't
I teach you to take care of yourself? Finnish devil!

[*The* COMMANDER *and the* CHAPLAIN *stand laughing in the door-way.*]

SCENE THREE

THREE YEARS PASS AND MOTHER COURAGE, WITH
PARTS OF A FINNISH REGIMENT, IS TAKEN PRISONER.
HER DAUGHTER IS SAVED, HER WAGON LIKEWISE, BUT
HER HONEST SON DIES.

A camp. The regimental flag is flying from a pole. Afternoon. All sorts of wares hanging on the wagon. MOTHER COURAGE'S *clothes line is tied to the wagon at one end, to a cannon at the other. She and* CATHERINE *are folding the wash on the cannon. At the same time she is bargaining with an* ORDNANCE OFFICER *over a bag of bullets.* SWISS CHEESE, *in paymaster's uniform now, looks on.* YVETTE POTTIER, *a very good-looking young person, is sewing at a colored hat, a glass of brandy before her. She is in stocking feet. Her red boots are near by.*

OFFICER. I'm letting you have the bullets for two gilders. Dirt cheap. 'Cause I need the money. The Colonel's been drinking with the officers for three days and we're out of liquor.

MOTHER COURAGE. They're army property. If they find 'em on me, I'll be courtmartialed. You sell your bullets, you bastards, and send your men out to fight with nothing to shoot with.

OFFICER. Aw, come on, one good turn deserves another.

MOTHER COURAGE. I won't take army stuff. Not at *that* price.

OFFICER. You can resell 'em for five gilders, maybe eight, to the Ordnance Officer of the Fourth Regiment. All you have to do is give him a receipt for twelve. He hasn't a bullet left.

MOTHER COURAGE. Why don't you do it yourself?

OFFICER. I don't trust him. We're friends.

MOTHER COURAGE [*takes the bag*]. Give it here.
[*To* CATHERINE.]
Take it round the back and pay him a gilder and a half.
[*As the* OFFICER *protests.*]
I said a gilder and a half!
[CATHERINE *drags the bag away. The* OFFICER *follows.* MOTHER COURAGE *speaks to* SWISS CHEESE.]
Here's your underwear back, take care of it; it's October now, autumn may come at any time; I purposely don't say it must come, I've learnt from experience there's nothing that must come, not even the seasons. But your books *must* balance now you're the regimental paymaster. *Do* they balance?

SWISS CHEESE. Yes, Mother.

MOTHER COURAGE. Don't forget they made you paymaster because you're honest and so simple you'd never think of running off with the cash. Don't lose that underwear.

SWISS CHEESE. No, Mother. I'll put it under the mattress.

[*He starts to go.*]

OFFICER. I'll go with you, paymaster.

MOTHER COURAGE. Don't teach him how to finagle!

[*Without a good-by the* OFFICER *leaves with* SWISS CHEESE.]

YVETTE [*waving to him*]. You might at least say good-by!

MOTHER COURAGE [*to* YVETTE]. I don't like that. *He's* no sort of company for my Swiss Cheese. But the war's not making a bad start. Before all the different countries get into it, four of five years'll have gone by like nothing. If I look ahead and make no mistakes, business will be good. Don't you know you shouldn't drink in the morning with your illness?

YVETTE. Who says I'm ill? That's libel!

MOTHER COURAGE. They all say so.

YVETTE. They're all liars. I'm desperate, Mother Courage. They all avoid me like a stinking fish. Because of those lies. So what am I fixing my hat for?

[*She throws it down.*]

That's why I drink in the morning; I never used to, it gives you crow's feet, but now it's all one, every man in the regiment knows me. I should have stayed home when my first was unfaithful. But pride isn't for the likes of us, you eat dirt or down you go.

MOTHER COURAGE. Now don't you start in again with your friend Peter and how it all happened—in front of my innocent daughter.

YVETTE. She's the one that should hear it. So she'll get hardened against love.

MOTHER COURAGE. That's something no one ever gets hardened against.

YVETTE. He was an army cook, blond, a Dutchman, but thin. Catherine, beware of thin men! I didn't. I didn't even know he'd had another girl before me and she called him Peter Piper because he never took his pipe out of his mouth the whole time, it meant so little to him.

[*She sings* THE CAMP FOLLOWER'S SONG.]

> *Scarce seventeen was I when*
> *The foe came to our land*
> *And laid aside his saber*
> *And took me by the hand.*
> *And we performed by day*
> *The sacred rite of May*
> *And we performed by night*
> *Another sacred rite.*
> *The regiment, well exercised,*

> *Presented arms, then stood at ease,*
> *Then took us off behind the trees*
> *Where we fraternized.*
>
> *Each of us had her foe and*
> *A cook fell to my lot.*
> *I hated him by daylight*
> *But in the dark did not.*
> *So we perform by day*
> *The sacred rite of May*
> *And we perform by night*
> *That other sacred rite.*
> *The regiment, well exercised,*
> *Presents its arms, then stands at ease,*
> *Then takes us off behind the trees*
> *Where we fraternize.*
>
> *Ecstasy filled my heart, O*
> *My love seemed heaven-born!*
> *But why were people saying*
> *It was not love but scorn?*
> *The springtime's soft amour*
> *Through summer may endure*
> *But swiftly comes the fall*
> *And winter ends it all.*
> *December came. All of the men*
> *Filed past the trees where once we hid*
> *Then quickly marched away and did*
> *Not come back again.*

I made the mistake of running after him, I never found him. It's ten years ago now.

[*With swaying gait she goes behind the wagon.*]

MOTHER COURAGE. You're leaving your hat.

YVETTE. For the birds.

MOTHER COURAGE. Let this be a lesson to you, Catherine, never start anything with a soldier. Love *is* like a heavenly dove, so watch out! He tells you he'd like to kiss the ground under your feet—did you wash 'em yesterday, while we're on the subject? And then if you don't look out, your number's up, you're his slave for life. Be glad you're dumb, Catherine: you'll never contradict yourself, you'll never want to bite your tongue off because you spoke out of turn. Dumbness is a gift from God. Here comes the Commander's Cook, what's biting him?

[*Enter the* COOK *and the* CHAPLAIN.]

CHAPLAIN. I bring a message from your son Eilif. The Cook came with me. You've made, ahem, an impression on him.

COOK. I thought I'd get a little whiff of the balmy breeze.

MOTHER COURAGE. Get it then, and welcome. But what does Eilif want? I've no money to spare.

CHAPLAIN. Actually, I have something to tell his brother, the pay-master.

MOTHER COURAGE. He isn't here. And he isn't anywhere else either. He's not his brother's paymaster, and I won't have him led into temptation.

[She takes money from the purse at her belt.]

Give him this. It's a sin. He's speculating in mother love, he ought to be ashamed of himself.

COOK. Not for long. He has to go with his regiment now—to his death maybe. Send some more money, or you'll be sorry. You women are hard—and sorry afterward. A glass of brandy wouldn't cost very much, but you don't give it, and six feet under goes your man and you can't dig him up again.

CHAPLAIN. All very touching, my dear Cook, but to fall in this war is not a misfortune, it's a blessing. This is a holy war. Not just any old war but a religious one, and therefore pleasing unto God.

COOK. Sure. In one sense it's a war because there's fleecing, bribing, plundering, not to mention a little raping, but it's different from all other wars because it's a holy war. That's clear. All the same, it makes you thirsty.

CHAPLAIN [to MOTHER COURAGE, pointing at the COOK]. I tried to hold him off but he said you'd bewitched him. He dreams about you.

COOK [lighting a clay pipe]. Brandy from the fair hand of a lady, that's for me. And don't embarrass me any more: the stories the chaplain was telling on the way over still have me blushing.

MOTHER COURAGE. A man of his cloth! I must get you both some-thing to drink or you'll be making improper advances out of sheer boredom.

CHAPLAIN. That is indeed a temptation, said the Court Chaplain, and gave way to it.

[Turning toward CATHERINE as he strolls around.]

And who is this captivating young person?

MOTHER COURAGE. She's not a captivating young person, she's a respectable young person.

[The CHAPLAIN and the COOK go with MOTHER COURAGE behind the cart.]

MOTHER COURAGE. The trouble here in Poland is that the Poles would keep meddling. It's true our Swedish King moved in on them with man, beast, and wagon, but instead of maintaining the peace the Poles were always meddling in their own affairs. They attacked the Swedish King when he was in the act of peacefully withdrawing. So they were guilty of a breach of the peace and their blood is on their own heads.

CHAPLAIN. Anyway, our Gustavus Adolphus was thinking of nothing but their freedom. The German Kaiser enslaved them all, Poles and Germans alike, so our King *had* to liberate them.

COOK. Just what *I* think. Your health! Your brandy is first rate, I'm never mistaken in a face.

[CATHERINE *looks after them, leaves the washing, and goes to the hat, picks it up, sits down, and takes up the red boots.*]

And the war is a holy war.

[*Singing while* CATHERINE *puts the boots on.*]

"A mighty fortress is our God . . ." [*He sings a verse or so of Luther's hymn.*] And talking of King Gustavus, this freedom he tried to bring to Germany cost him a pretty penny. Back in Sweden he had to levy a salt tax, the poorer folks didn't like it a bit. Then, too, he had to lock up the Germans and even cut their heads off, they clung so to slavery and their Kaiser. Of course, if no one had *wanted* to be free, the King wouldn't have had any fun. First it was just Poland he tried to protect from bad men, specially the Kaiser, then his appetite grew with eating, and he ended protecting Germany too.

CHAPLAIN. He had one thing in his favor anyway: the Word of God. Or they could have said he did it all for himself and for profits. He has a clear conscience, that man.

COOK [*with heavy irony*]. Yes. He always put conscience first.

CHAPLAIN. It's plain you're no Swede, or you'd speak differently of the Hero King!

MOTHER COURAGE. What's more, you eat his bread.

COOK. I don't eat his bread. I bake his bread.

MOTHER COURAGE. He can never be conquered, and I'll tell you why: his men believe in him.

[*Earnestly.*]

To hear the big fellows talk, they wage the war from fear of God and for all things bright and beautiful, but just look into it, and you'll see they're not so silly: they want a good profit out of it, or else the little fellows like you and me wouldn't back 'em up.

COOK. Surely.

CHAPLAIN [*indicating the Protestant flag*]. And as a Dutchman you'd do well to see which flag's flying here before you express an opinion!

MOTHER COURAGE. All good Protestants for ever!

COOK. A health!

[CATHERINE *has begun to strut around with* YVETTE'S *hat on, copying* YVETTE'S *sexy walk.*
Suddenly cannon and shots. Drums. MOTHER COURAGE, *the* COOK, *and the* CHAPLAIN *rush round to the front of the cart, the two last with glasses in their hands. The* ORDNANCE OFFICER *and a* SOLDIER *come running to the cannon and try to push it along.*]

MOTHER COURAGE. What's the matter? Let me get my wash off
that gun, you slobs!
[*She tries to do so.*]
OFFICER. The Catholics! Surprise attack! We don't know if we can
get away!
[*To the* SOLDIER.]
Get that gun!
[*Runs off.*]
COOK. For heaven's sake! I must go to the Commander. Mother Cour-
age, I'll be back in a day or two—for a short conversation.
[*Rushes off.*]
MOTHER COURAGE. Hey, you're leaving your pipe!
COOK [*off*]. Keep it for me, I'll need it!
MOTHER COURAGE. This *would* happen when we were just making
money.
CHAPLAIN. Well, I must be going too. Yes, if the enemy's so close, it
can be dangerous. "Blessed are the peacemakers," a good slogan in
wartime! If only I had a cloak.
MOTHER COURAGE. I'm lending no cloaks. Not even to save a life
I'm not. I've had experience in that line.
CHAPLAIN. But I'm in special danger. Because of my religion!
MOTHER COURAGE [*brings him a cloak*]. It's against my better judg-
ment. Now run!
CHAPLAIN. I thank you, you're very generous, but maybe I'd better
stay and sit here. If I run, I might attract the enemy's attention. I
might arouse suspicion.
MOTHER COURAGE [*to the* SOLDIER]. Let it alone, you dope, who's
going to pay you for this? It'll cost you your life, let me hold it for
you.
SOLDIER [*running away*]. You're my witness: I tried!
MOTHER COURAGE. I'll swear to it!
[*Seeing* CATHERINE *with the hat.*]
What on earth are you up to—with a whore's hat! Take it off this
minute! Are you crazy? With the enemy coming?
[*She tears the hat off her head.*]
Do you want them to find you and make a whore of you? And she has
the boots on too, straight from Babylon, I'll soon fix that.
[*She tries to get them off.*]
Oh God, Chaplain, help me with these boots, I'll be right back!
[*She runs to the wagon.*]
YVETTE [*entering and powdering her face*]. What's that you say; the
Catholics are coming? Where's my hat? Who's been trampling on it?
I can't run around in that, what will they think of me? And I've no
mirror either.
[*To the* CHAPLAIN, *coming very close.*]
How do I look—too much powder?

CHAPLAIN. Just, er, right.

YVETTE. And where are my red boots?

[*She can't find them because* CATHERINE *is hiding her feet under her skirt.*]

I left them here! Now I've got to go barefoot to my tent, it's a scandal! [*Exit.*]

[SWISS CHEESE *comes running in carrying a cash box.*]

MOTHER COURAGE [*Enters with her hands covered with ashes*].

[*To* CATHERINE] Ashes!

[*To* SWISS CHEESE] What you got there?

SWISS CHEESE. The regimental cash box.

MOTHER COURAGE. Throw it away! Your paymastering days are over!

SWISS CHEESE. It's a trust!

[*He goes to the back.*]

MOTHER COURAGE [*to the* CHAPLAIN]. Off with your pastor's coat, Chaplain, or they'll recognize you, cloak or no cloak.

[*She is rubbing ashes into* CATHERINE'S *face.*]

Keep still. A little dirt, and you're safe. When a soldier sees a clean face, there's one more whore in the world. Specially a Catholic soldier. That should do, it looks like you've been rolling in muck. Don't tremble. Nothing can happen to you now.

[*To* SWISS CHEESE.]

Where have you left that cash?

SWISS CHEESE. I thought I'd just put it in the wagon.

MOTHER COURAGE [*horrified*]. What!? In my wagon? God punish you for a prize idiot! If I just look away for a moment! They'll hang all three of us!

SWISS CHEESE. Then I'll put it somewhere else. Or escape with it.

MOTHER COURAGE. You'll stay right here. It's too late.

CHAPLAIN [*still changing his clothes*]. For Heaven's sake: the Protestant flag!

MOTHER COURAGE [*taking down the flag*]. I don't notice it any more, I've had it twenty-five years.

[*The sound of cannon grows.*]

[*Three days later. Morning. The cannon is gone.* MOTHER COURAGE, CATHERINE, *the* CHAPLAIN *and* SWISS CHEESE *sit anxiously eating.*]

SWISS CHEESE. This is the third day I've been sitting here doing nothing, and the Sergeant, who's always been patient with me, may be slowly beginning to ask, "Where on earth is Swiss Cheese with that cash box?"

MOTHER COURAGE. Be glad they're not on the scent.

CHAPLAIN. What about me? I can't hold service here or I'll be in hot water. It is written, "Out of the abundance of the heart, the tongue speaketh." But woe is me if *my* tongue speaketh!

MOTHER COURAGE. That's how it is. Here you sit—one with his religion, the other with his cash box, I don't know which is more dangerous.

CHAPLAIN. We're in God's hands now!

MOTHER COURAGE. I hope we're not as desperate as *that*, but it *is* hard to sleep at night. 'Course it'd be easier if *you* weren't here, Swiss Cheese, all the same I've not done badly. When they questioned me, I always asked where I could buy holy candles a bit cheaper. I know these things because Swiss Cheese's father was a Catholic and made jokes about it. They didn't quite believe me but they needed a canteen, so they winked an eye. Maybe it's all for the best. We're prisoners. But so are lice in fur.

CHAPLAIN. The milk is good. As far as quantity goes, we may have to reduce our Swedish appetites somewhat. We are defeated.

MOTHER COURAGE. Who's defeated? The defeats and victories of the fellows at the top aren't always defeats and victories for the fellows at the bottom. Not at all. There've been cases where a defeat is a victory for the fellows at the bottom, it's only their honor that's lost, nothing serious. In Livonia once, our Chief took such a knock from the enemy, in the confusion I got a fine gray mare out of the baggage train, it pulled my wagon seven months—till we won and there was inventory. But in general both defeat and victory are a costly business for us that haven't got much. The best thing is for politics to kind of get stuck in the mud.

[*To* SWISS CHEESE.]

Eat!

SWISS CHEESE. I don't like it. How will the Sergeant pay his men?

MOTHER COURAGE. Soldiers in flight don't get paid.

SWISS CHEESE. Well, they could claim to be. No pay, no flight. They can refuse to budge.

MOTHER COURAGE. Swiss Cheese, your sense of duty worries me. I've brought you up to be honest because you're not very bright. But don't go too far! And now I'm going with the Chaplain to buy a Catholic flag and some meat. A good thing they let me continue in business. In business you ask what price, not what religion. Protestant pants keep you just as warm.

[*She disappears into the wagon.*]

CHAPLAIN. She's worried about the cash box. Up to now they've ignored us—as if we were part of the wagon—but can it last?

SWISS CHEESE. I can get rid of it.

CHAPLAIN. That's almost *more* dangerous. Suppose you're seen. They have spies. Yesterday morning one jumped out of the very hole I was relieving myself in. I was so off guard I almost broke out in prayer— *that* would have given me away all right! I believe their favorite way of finding a Protestant is smelling his, um, excrement. The spy was a little brute with a bandage over one eye.

MOTHER COURAGE [*clambering out of the wagon with a basket*]. I've found you out, you shameless hussy!

[*She holds up* YVETTE'S *red boots in triumph.*]

Yvette's red boots! She just snitched them—because you went and told her she was a captivating person.

[*She lays them in the basket.*]

Stealing Yvette's boots! But *she* disgraces herself for money, *you* do it for nothing—for pleasure! Save your proud peacock ways for peacetime!

CHAPLAIN. I don't find her proud.

MOTHER COURAGE. I like her when people say "I never noticed the poor thing." I like her when she's a stone in Dalarna where there's nothing but stones.

[*To* SWISS CHEESE.]

Leave the cash box where it is, do you hear? And pay attention to your sister, she needs it. Between the two of you, you'll be the death of me yet; I'd rather take care of a bag of fleas.

[*She leaves with the* CHAPLAIN.

CATHERINE *clears the dishes away.*]

SWISS CHEESE. Not many days more when you can sit in the sun in your shirtsleeves.

[CATHERINE *points to a tree.*]

Yes, the leaves are yellow already.

[*With gestures,* CATHERINE *asks if he wants a drink.*]

I'm not drinking, I'm thinking.

[*Pause.*]

She says she can't sleep. So I *should* take the cash box away. I've found a place for it. I'll keep it in the mole hole by the river till the time comes. I might get it tonight before sunrise and take it to the regiment. How far can they have fled in three days? The Sergeant's eyes'll pop out of his head. "You've disappointed me most pleasantly, Swiss Cheese," he'll say, "*I* trust you with the cash box and *you* bring it back!" Yes, Catherine, I *will* have a glass now!

[*When* CATHERINE *reappears behind the wagon two men confront her. One of them is a sergeant. The other doffs his hat and flourishes it in a shadowy greeting. He has a bandage over one eye.*]

THE MAN WITH THE BANDAGE. Good morning, young lady. Have you seen a staff officer from the Second Protestant Regiment?

[*Terrified,* CATHERINE *runs away, spilling her brandy. The two men look at each other and then withdraw after seeing* SWISS CHEESE.]

SWISS CHEESE [*starting up from his reflections*]. You're spilling it! What's the matter with you, can't you see where you're going? I don't understand you. Anyway, I must be off, I've decided it's the thing to do.

[*He stands up. She does all she can to make him aware of the danger he is in. He only pushes her away.*]

I'd like to know what you mean. I know you mean well, poor thing, you just can't get it out. And don't trouble yourself about the brandy; I'll live to drink so much of it, what's one glass?

[*He takes the cash box out of the wagon and puts it under his coat.*]

I'll be right back. But don't hold me up or I'll have to scold you. Yes, I know you mean well. If you only could speak!

[*When she tries to hold him back he kisses her and pulls himself free. Exit. She is desperate and runs up and down, emitting little sounds.* MOTHER COURAGE *and the* CHAPLAIN *return.* CATHERINE *rushes at her mother.*]

MOTHER COURAGE. What *is* it, what *is* it, Catherine? Control yourself! Has someone done something to you? Where is Swiss Cheese?

[*To the* CHAPLAIN.]

Don't stand around, get that Catholic flag up!

[*She takes a Catholic flag out of her basket and the* CHAPLAIN *runs it up the pole.*]

CHAPLAIN [*bitterly*]. All good Catholics forever!

MOTHER COURAGE. Now, Catherine, calm down and tell all about it, your mother understands. What, that little bastard of mine's taken the cash box away? I'll box his ears for him, the rascal! Now take your time and don't try to talk, use your hands. I don't like it when you howl like a dog, what'll the Chaplain think of you? See how shocked he looks. A man with one eye was here?

CHAPLAIN. That fellow with one eye is an informer! Have they caught Swiss Cheese?

[CATHERINE *shakes her head, shrugs her shoulders.*]

This is the end.

[*Voices off. The two men bring in* SWISS CHEESE.]

SWISS CHEESE. Let me go. I've nothing on me. You're breaking my shoulder! I am innocent.

SERGEANT. This is where he comes from. These are his friends.

MOTHER COURAGE. Us? Since when?

[*Putting things in her basket.*]

SWISS CHEESE. I don't even know 'em. I was just getting my lunch here. Ten hellers it cost me. Maybe you saw me sitting on that bench It was too salty.

SERGEANT. Who *are* you people, anyway?

MOTHER COURAGE. Law abiding citizens! It's true what he says. He bought his lunch here. And it was too salty.

SERGEANT. Are you pretending you don't know him?

MOTHER COURAGE. I can't know all of them, can I? *I* don't ask, "What's your name and are you a heathen?" If they pay up, they're not heathens to me. Are you a heathen?

SWISS CHEESE. Oh, no!

CHAPLAIN. He sat there like a law-abiding chap and never once opened his mouth. Except to eat. Which is necessary.

SERGEANT. Who do you think *you* are?

MOTHER COURAGE. Oh, he's my barman. And you're thirsty, I'll bring you a glass of brandy; you must be footsore and weary!

SERGEANT. No brandy on duty.

[*To* SWISS CHEESE.]

You were carrying something. You must have hidden it by the river. We saw the bulge in your shirt.

MOTHER COURAGE. Sure it was him?

SWISS CHEESE. I think you mean another fellow. There *was* a fellow with something under his shirt, I saw him. I'm the wrong man.

MOTHER COURAGE. I think so too. It's a misunderstanding. Could happen to anyone. Oh, I know what people are like, I'm Mother Courage, you've heard of me, everyone knows about me, and I can tell you this: he looks honest.

SERGEANT. We're after the regimental cash box. And we know what the man looks like who's been keeping it. We've been looking for him two days. It's you.

SWISS CHEESE. No, it's not!

SERGEANT. And if you don't shell out, you're dead, see? Where is it?

MOTHER COURAGE [*urgently*]. 'Course he'd give it to you to save his life. He'd up and say, I do have it, here it is, you're stronger than me. He's not *that* stupid. Speak, little stupid, the Sergeant's giving you a chance!

SWISS CHEESE. What if I don't have it?

SERGEANT. Come with us. We'll get it out of you.

[*They take him off.*]

MOTHER COURAGE [*shouting after them*]. He'd tell you! He's not *that* stupid! And leave his shoulder alone!!

[*She runs after them.*]

[*The same evening. The* CHAPLAIN *and* CATHERINE *are rinsing glasses and polishing knives.*]

CHAPLAIN. Cases of people getting caught like this are by no means unknown in the history of religion. I am reminded of the Passion of Our Lord and Savior. There's an old song about it. [*He sings* THE SONG OF THE HOURS.]

> *In the first hour of the day*
> *Simple Jesus Christ was*
> *Halèd as a murderer*
> *Before the heathen Pilate.*
>
> *Pilate found no fault in him*
> *No cause to condemn him*
> *So he sent the Lord away.*
> *Let King Herod see him!*

Hour the third: the Son of God
Was with scourges beaten
And they set a crown of thorns
On the head of Jesus.

And they dressed him as a king
Joked and jested at him
And the cross to die upon
He himself must carry.

Six: they stripped Lord Jesus bare.
To the cross they nailed him.
When the blood came gushing, he
Prayed and loud lamented.

From their neighbor crosses, thieves
Mocked him like the others.
And the bright sun crept away
Not to see such doings.

Nine: Lord Jesus cried aloud
That he was forsaken!
In a sponge upon a pole
Vinegar was fed him.

Then the Lord gave up the ghost
And the earth did tremble.
Temple curtain split in twain.
Cliffs fell in the ocean.

Evening: they broke the bones
Of the malefactors.
Then they took a spear and pierced
The side of gentle Jesus.

And the blood and water ran
And they laughed at Jesus.
Of this simple son of man
Such and more they tell us.

MOTHER COURAGE [*entering, excited*]. It's life and death. But the Sergeant will still listen to us. The only thing is, he mustn't know it's our Swiss Cheese, or they'll say we helped him. It's only a matter of money, but where can *we* get money? Wasn't Yvette here? I met her on the way over. She's picked up a Colonel! Maybe he'll buy her a canteen business!

CHAPLAIN. You'd sell the wagon, everything?

MOTHER COURAGE. Where else would I get the money for the
Sergeant?

CHAPLAIN. What are you to live off?

MOTHER COURAGE. That's just it.

[*Enter* YVETTE POTTIER *with a hoary old* COLONEL.]

YVETTE [*embracing* MOTHER COURAGE]. *Dear* Mistress Courage, we
meet again!

[*Whispering.*]

He didn't say no.

[*Aloud.*]

This is my friend, my, um, business adviser. I happened to hear you
might like to sell your wagon. Due to special circumstances. I'd like
to think about it.

MOTHER COURAGE. I want to pawn it, not sell it. And nothing
hasty. In war time you don't find another wagon like that so easy.

YVETTE [*disappointed*]. Only pawn it? I thought you wanted to sell,
I don't know if I'm interested.

[*To the* COLONEL.]

What do *you* think, my dear?

COLONEL. I quite agree with you, honey bun.

MOTHER COURAGE. It's only for pawn.

YVETTE. I thought you *had* to have the money.

MOTHER COURAGE [*firmly*]. I do have to have it. But I'd rather wear
my feet off looking for an offer than just sell. We live off the wagon.

COLONEL. Take it, take it!

YVETTE. My friend thinks I should go ahead, but I'm not sure—if it's
only for pawn. You think we should buy it outright, don't you?

COLONEL. I do, bunny, I do!

MOTHER COURAGE. Then you must find something that's for sale.

YVETTE. Yes, we can go around looking for something, I *love* going
around looking, I *love* going around with you, Poldy . . .

COLONEL. Really? You do?

YVETTE. Oh, it's *lovely!* I could take *weeks* of it!

COLONEL. Really? You could?

YVETTE. If you get the money, when are you thinking of paying it
back?

MOTHER COURAGE. In two weeks. Maybe in one.

YVETTE. I can't make up my mind. Poldy, advise me, *chéri!*

[*She takes the* COLONEL *to one side.*]

She'll *have* to sell, don't worry. That lieutenant—the blond one—you
know the one I mean—he'll lend me the money. He's *mad* about me,
he says I remind him of someone. What do you advise?

COLONEL. Oh, I have to warn you against *him*. He's no good. He'll
exploit the situation. I told you, bunny, I told you *I'd* buy you something, didn't I tell you that?

YVETTE. I simply can't let you!

COLONEL. Oh, please, please!

YVETTE. Well, if you think the lieutenant might exploit the situation I *will* let you!

COLONEL. I do think so.

YVETTE. So you advise me to?

COLONEL. I do, bunny, I do!

YVETTE [*returning to* MOTHER COURAGE]. My friend says all right. Write me out a receipt saying the wagon's mine when the two weeks are up—with everything in it. I'll just run through it all now, the two hundred gilders can wait.
[*To the* COLONEL.]
You go on ahead to the camp, I'll follow, I must go over all this so nothing'll be missing later from *my* wagon!

COLONEL. Wait, I'll help you up!
[*He does so.*]
Come soon, honey-bunny!
[*Exit.*]

MOTHER COURAGE. Yvette, Yvette!

YVETTE. There aren't many boots left!

MOTHER COURAGE. Yvette, this is no time to go through the wagon, yours or not yours. You promised you'd talk to the Sergeant about Swiss Cheese. There isn't a minute to lose. He's up before the court martial one hour from now.

YVETTE. I just want to check through these shirts.

MOTHER COURAGE [*dragging her down the steps by the skirt*]. You hyena, Swiss Cheese's life's at stake! And don't say who the money comes from. Pretend he's your sweetheart, for heaven's sake, or we'll all get it for helping him.

YVETTE. I've arranged to meet One Eye in the bushes. He must be there by now.

CHAPLAIN. And don't hand over all two hundred, a hundred and fifty's sure to be enough.

MOTHER COURAGE. I'll thank you to keep your nose out of this, I'm not doing *you* out of your porridge. Now run, and no haggling, remember his life's at stake.
[*She pushes* YVETTE *off.*]

CHAPLAIN. I didn't want to talk you into anything, but what are we going to live on? You have an unmarriageable daughter round your neck.

MOTHER COURAGE. I'm counting on that cash box, smart alec. They'll pay his expenses out of it.

CHAPLAIN. You think she can work it?

MOTHER COURAGE. It's to her interest: I pay out the two hundred and she gets the wagon. She knows what she's doing, she won't have her colonel on the string forever. Catherine, go and clean the knives, use pumice stone.

[*To the* CHAPLAIN.]

And don't *you* stand around like Jesus in Gethsemane. Get a move on, wash those glasses. There'll be over fifty cavalrymen here tonight, can't you just hear them grumbling, "Isn't walking terrible, oh my poor feet!" I think they'll let us have him. Thanks be to God they're corruptible. They're not wolves, they're human and after money. God is merciful, and men are bribable, that's how His will is done on earth as it is in Heaven. Corruption is our only hope. As long as there's corruption, there'll be merciful judges and even the innocent may get off!

YVETTE [*comes panting in*]. They'll do it for two hundred if you make it snappy, these things change from one minute to the next. I'd better take One Eye to my colonel right now. He confessed he had the cash box, they put the thumb screws on him. But he threw it in the river when he noticed them coming up behind him. So it's gone. Shall I run and get the money from my colonel?

MOTHER COURAGE. The cash box gone? How'll I ever get my two hundred back?

YVETTE. So you thought you could get it from the cash box? I *would* have been sunk. Not a hope, Mother Courage. If you want your Swiss Cheese, you'll have to pay. Or should I let the whole thing drop, so you can keep your wagon?

MOTHER COURAGE. What can I do? I can't pay two hundred. You *should* have haggled with them. I must hold on to something, or any passer-by can kick me in the ditch. Go and say I'll pay a hundred and twenty or the deal's off. Even at that I lose the wagon.

YVETTE. They won't do it. And anyway, One Eye's in a hurry. He looks over his shoulder the whole time, he's so worked up. Hadn't I better give them the whole two hundred?

MOTHER COURAGE [*desperate*]. I can't pay it! I've been working thirty years. She's twenty-five and still no husband, I have her to think of. So leave me alone, I know what I'm doing. A hundred and twenty or no deal.

YVETTE. You know best.

[*Runs off.*]

[MOTHER COURAGE *turns away and slowly walks a few paces to the rear. Then she turns round, looks neither at the* CHAPLAIN *nor her daughter, and sits down to help* CATHERINE *polish the knives.*]

MOTHER COURAGE. You'll have your brother back. I *will* pay two hundred—if I have to. With eighty gilders we could pack a hamper with goods and begin over. It wouldn't be the end of the world.

CHAPLAIN. The Bible says, the Lord will provide.

MOTHER COURAGE [*to* CATHERINE]. You must rub them dry.

YVETTE [*comes running on*]. They won't do it. I warned you. He said the drums would roll any second now and that's the sign a verdict has been pronounced. I offered a hundred and fifty, he didn't even shrug his shoulders. I could hardly get him to stay there while I came to you.

MOTHER COURAGE. Tell him, I'll pay two hundred. Run!

[YVETTE *runs.* MOTHER COURAGE *sits, silent. The* CHAPLAIN *has stopped doing the glasses.*]

I believe—I haggled too long.

[*In the distance, a roll of drums. The* CHAPLAIN *stands up and walks toward the rear.* MOTHER COURAGE *remains seated. It grows dark. It gets light again.* MOTHER COURAGE *has not moved.*]

YVETTE [*appears, pale*]. Now you've done it—with your haggling. You can keep the wagon now. He got eleven bullets, that's all. I don't know why I still bother about you, you don't deserve it, but I just happened to learn they don't think the cash box is really in the river. They suspect it's here, they think you're connected with him. I think they mean to bring him here to see if you give yourself away when you see him. I warn you not to know him or we're in for it. And I better tell you straight, they're right behind me. Shall I keep Catherine away?

[MOTHER COURAGE *shakes her head.*]

Does she know? Maybe she never heard the drums or didn't understand.

MOTHER COURAGE. She knows. Bring her.

[YVETTE *brings* CATHERINE, *who walks over to her mother and stands by her.* MOTHER COURAGE *takes her hand. Two men come on with a stretcher; there is a sheet on it and something underneath. Beside them, the* SERGEANT. *They put the stretcher down.*]

SERGEANT. Here's a man we don't know the name of. But he has to be registered to keep the records straight. He bought a meal from you. Look at him, see if you know him.

[*He pulls back the sheet.*]

Do you know him?

[MOTHER COURAGE *shakes her head.*]

What? You never saw him before he took that meal?

[MOTHER COURAGE *shakes her head.*]

Lift him up. Throw him on the junk heap. He has no one that knows him.

[*They carry him off.*]

SCENE FOUR

MOTHER COURAGE SINGS THE SONG OF THE GREAT CAPITULATION.

Outside an officer's tent, MOTHER COURAGE *waits. A* CLERK *looks out of the tent.*

CLERK. You want to speak to the captain? I know you. You had a

Protestant paymaster with you, he was hiding out. Better make no complaint here.

MOTHER COURAGE. I will too! I'm innocent and if I give up it'll look like I have a bad conscience. They cut everything in my wagon to ribbons with their sabers and then claimed a fine of five thalers for nothing and less than nothing.

CLERK. For your own good, keep your trap shut. We haven't many canteens, so we let you stay in business, especially if you've a bad conscience and have to pay a fine now and then.

MOTHER COURAGE. I'm going to lodge a complaint.

CLERK. As you wish. Wait here till the captain has time.

[*Withdraws into the tent.*]

YOUNG SOLDIER [*comes storming in*]. Screw the captain! Where *is* the son-of-a-bitch? Snitching my reward, spending it on brandy for his whores, I'll rip his belly open!

OLDER SOLDIER [*coming after him*]. Shut your hole, you'll wind up in the stocks.

YOUNG SOLDIER. Come out, you thief, I'll make lamb chops out of you! I was the only one in the squad who swam the river and *he* grabs my money, I can't even buy a beer. Come on out! And let me slice you up!

OLDER SOLDIER. Holy Christ, he'll destroy himself!

YOUNG SOLDIER. Let me go or I'll run *you* down too. This thing has got to be settled!

OLDER SOLDIER. Saved the colonel's horse and didn't get the reward. He's young, he hasn't been at it long.

MOTHER COURAGE. Let him go. He doesn't have to be chained, he's not a dog. Very reasonable to want a reward. Why else should he want to shine?

YOUNG SOLDIER. He's in there pouring it down! You're all chickens. I done something special, I want the reward!

MOTHER COURAGE. Young man, don't scream at *me*, I have my own troubles.

YOUNG SOLDIER. He's whoring on my money and I'm hungry! I'll murder him!

MOTHER COURAGE. I understand: you're hungry. You're angry: I understand that too.

YOUNG SOLDIER. It's no use you talking, I won't stand for injustice!

MOTHER COURAGE. You're quite right. But how long for? How long won't you stand injustice for? One hour? Or two? You haven't asked yourself that, have you? And yet it's the main thing. It's a misery to sit in the stocks. Especially if you leave it till then to decide you do stand for injustice.

YOUNG SOLDIER. I don't know why I listen to you. Screw that captain! Where is he?

MOTHER COURAGE. You listen because you know I'm right. Your

rage has calmed down already. It was a short one and you'd need a long one. But where would you find it?

YOUNG SOLDIER. Are you trying to say it's not right to ask for the money?

MOTHER COURAGE. Just the opposite. I only say, your rage won't last. You'll get nowhere with it, it's a pity. If your rage was a long one, I'd urge you on. Slice him up, I'd advise you. But what's the use if you *don't* slice him up because you feel your tail between your legs? You stand there and the captain lets you have it.

OLDER SOLDIER. You're quite right, he's nuts.

YOUNG SOLDIER. All right, we'll see whether I slice him up or not. [*Draws his sword.*]
When he comes out, I slice him up!

CLERK [*looking out*]. The captain will be right out.
[*In the tone of military command.*] Be seated!
[*The* YOUNG SOLDIER *sits.*]

MOTHER COURAGE. What did I tell you? They know us inside out, they know their business. Be seated! And we sit. Oh, you needn't be embarrassed in front of me, I'm no better. We don't stick our necks out, do we? We're too well paid to keep 'em in. Let me tell you about the Great Capitulation.
[*She sings* THE SONG OF THE GREAT CAPITULATION]

> *Long, long ago, a green beginner*
> *I thought myself a special case.*
> (*None of your ordinary, run of the mill girls, with my looks*
> *and my talent and my love of the higher things!*)
> *I picked a hair out of my dinner*
> *And put the waiter in his place.*
> (*All or nothing. Anyway, never the second best. I am the*
> *master of my fate. I'll take no orders from no one.*)
> *Then a little bird whispers!*
> *The bird says: "Wait a year or so*
> *And marching with the band you'll go*
> *Keeping in step, now fast, now slow,*
> *And piping out your little spiel.*
> *Then one day the battalions wheel*
> *And you go down upon your knees*
> *To God Almighty if you please!"*
>
> *My friend, before that year was over*
> *I'd learned to drink their cup of tea.*
> (*Two children round your neck and the price of bread and*
> *what all!*)
> *When they were through with me, moreover,*
> *They had me where they wanted me.*

(You must get in with people. If you scratch my back, I'll
scratch yours. Never stick your neck out!)
Then a little bird whispered!
  The bird says: "Scarce a year or so
  And marching with the band she'd go
  Keeping in step, now fast, now slow,
  And piping out her little spiel.
  Then one day the battalions wheel
  And she goes down upon her knees
  To God Almighty if you please!"

Our plans are big, our hopes colossal.
  We hitch our wagon to a star.
(Where there's a will, there's a way. You can't hold a good
  man down.)
"We can lift mountains," says the apostle.
  And yet: how heavy one cigar!
(You must cut your coat according to your cloth.)
That little bird whispers!
  The bird says: "Wait a year or so
  And marching with the band we go
  Keeping in step, now fast, now slow,
  And piping out our little spiel.
  Then one day the battalions wheel
And we go down upon our knees
To God Almighty if you please!"

MOTHER COURAGE. And so I think you should stay here with your
  sword drawn if you're set on it and your anger is big enough. You have
  good cause, I admit. But if your anger is a short one, you'd better go.
YOUNG SOLDIER. Aw, shove it!
[He stumbles off, the other soldier following him.]
CLERK *[sticks his head out]*. The captain is here. You can lodge your
  complaint.
MOTHER COURAGE. I've thought better of it. I'm not complaining.
[Exit. The CLERK looks after her, shaking his head.]

SCENE FIVE

TWO YEARS HAVE PASSED. THE WAR COVERS WIDER
AND WIDER TERRITORY. FOREVER ON THE MOVE THE
LITTLE WAGON CROSSES POLAND, MORAVIA, BAVARIA,
ITALY, AND AGAIN BAVARIA. 1631. TILLY'S VICTORY
AT LEIPZIG COSTS MOTHER COURAGE FOUR SHIRTS.

The wagon stands in a war-ruined village. Faint military music from the distance. Two soldiers are being served at a counter by CATHERINE *and* MOTHER COURAGE. *One of them has a woman's fur coat about his shoulders.*

MOTHER COURAGE. What, you can't pay? No money, no schnapps! They can play a victory march, they should pay their men.

FIRST SOLDIER. I want my schnapps! I arrived too late for plunder. The Chief allowed one hour to plunder the town, it's a swindle. He's not inhuman, he says. So I guess they bought him off.

CHAPLAIN [*staggering in*]. There are more in the farmhouse. A whole family of peasants. Help me someone, I need linen!

[*The* SECOND SOLDIER *goes with him.* CATHERINE *is getting very excited. She tries to get her mother to bring linen out.*]

MOTHER COURAGE. I have none. I sold all my bandages to the regiment. I'm not tearing up my officer's shirts for these people.

CHAPLAIN [*calling over his shoulder*]. I said I need linen!

MOTHER COURAGE [*stopping* CATHERINE *from entering the wagon*]. Not a thing! They have nothing and they pay nothing!

CHAPLAIN [*to a woman he is carrying in*]. Why did you stay out there in the line of fire?

WOMAN. Our farm——

MOTHER COURAGE. Think they'd ever let go of *anything*? And now I'm supposed to pay. Well, I won't!

FIRST SOLDIER. They're Protestants, why should they be Protestants?

MOTHER COURAGE. Protestant, Catholic, what do *they* care? Their farm's gone, that's what.

SECOND SOLDIER. They're not Protestants anyway, they're Catholics.

FIRST SOLDIER. In a bombardment we can't pick and choose.

PEASANT [*brought on by* CHAPLAIN]. My arm's gone.

CHAPLAIN. Where's that linen?

MOTHER COURAGE. I can't give you any. With all I have to pay out —taxes, duties, bribes . . .

[CATHERINE *takes up a board and threatens her mother with it, emitting gurgling sounds.*]

Are you out of your mind? Put that board down or I'll fetch you one, you lunatic! I'm giving nothing, I don't dare, I have myself to think of.

[*The* CHAPLAIN *lifts her bodily off the steps of the wagon and sets her down on the ground. He takes out shirts from the wagon and tears them in strips.*]

My shirts, my officer's shirts!

[*From the house comes the cry of a child in pain.*]

PEASANT. The child's still in there!

[CATHERINE *runs in.*]

MOTHER COURAGE. Hold her back, the roof may fall in!

CHAPLAIN. I'm not going back in there!

MOTHER COURAGE. My officer's shirts, half a gilder apiece! I'm ruined.

[CATHERINE *brings a baby out of the ruins.*]

MOTHER COURAGE. Another baby to drag around, you must be pleased with yourself. Give it to its mother this minute!

[CATHERINE *is rocking the child and half humming a lullaby.*]

CHAPLAIN [*bandaging*]. The blood's coming through.

MOTHER COURAGE. There she sits, happy as a lark in all this!

[*Shouting toward the music.*]

Stop that music, I can see your victory all right!

[*Seeing* FIRST SOLDIER *trying to make off with the bottle he's been drinking from.*]

Stop, you pig, if you want *another* victory you must pay for it!

FIRST SOLDIER. I'm broke.

MOTHER COURAGE [*tearing the fur coat off him*]. Then leave this, it's stolen goods anyhow.

[CATHERINE *rocks the child and raises it high above her head.*]

SCENE SIX

BEFORE THE CITY OF INGOLSTADT IN BAVARIA MOTHER COURAGE ATTENDS THE FUNERAL OF THE FALLEN COMMANDER, TILLY. CONVERSATIONS TAKE PLACE ABOUT WAR HEROES AND THE DURATION OF THE WAR. THE CHAPLAIN COMPLAINS THAT HIS TALENTS ARE LYING FALLOW AND CATHERINE GETS THE RED BOOTS. THE YEAR IS 1632.

The inside of a canteen tent. The inner side of a counter at the rear. Rain. In the distance, drums and funeral music. The CHAPLAIN *and the* REGIMENTAL CLERK *are playing checkers.* MOTHER COURAGE *and her* DAUGHTER *are taking inventory.*

CHAPLAIN. The funeral procession is just starting out.

MOTHER COURAGE. Pity about the Chief—twenty-two pairs, socks—getting killed that way. They say it was an accident. There was a fog over the fields that morning, and the fog was to blame. The Chief called up another regiment, told 'em to fight to the death, rode back again, missed his way in the fog, went forward instead of back, and ran straight into a bullet in the thick of the battle!

[*A whistle from the rear. She goes to the counter. To a soldier.*]

It's a disgrace the way you're all skipping your Commander's funeral!

[*She pours a drink.*]

CLERK. They shouldn't have handed the money out before the funeral. Now the men are all getting drunk instead of going to it.

CHAPLAIN [to the CLERK]. Don't you have to be there?

CLERK. I stayed away because of the rain.

MOTHER COURAGE. It's different for you, the rain might spoil your
uniform.

VOICE FROM THE COUNTER. Service! One brandy!

MOTHER COURAGE. Your money first. No, you *can't* come inside the
tent, not with those boots; you can drink outside, rain or no rain. I
only let officers in here.

[*To the* CLERK.]

The Chief had his troubles lately, I hear. There was unrest in the
second regiment because he didn't pay 'em but said it was a holy war
and they might fight it for free.

CHAPLAIN [*as music continues*]. Now they're filing past the body.

MOTHER COURAGE. I feel sorry for a commander or an emperor like
that—when maybe he had something special in mind, something
they'd talk about in times to come, something they'd raise a statue to
him for. The conquest of the world now, *that's* a goal for a commander, he couldn't do better than *that*, could he? . . . Lord, worms
have got into the biscuit. . . . In short he works his hands to the
bone and then it's all spoiled by the common riffraff that only wants
a jug of beer or a bit of company, not the higher things in life. The
finest plans have always been spoiled by the littleness of them that
should carry them out. Even emperors can't do it all by themselves.
They count on support from their soldiers and the people round about.
Am I right?

CHAPLAIN [*laughing*]. You're right, Mother Courage, till you come to
the soldiers. They do what they can. Those fellows outside, for example, drinking their brandy in the rain, I'd trust 'em to fight a hundred years, one war after another, two at once if necessary. And I
wasn't trained as a Commander.

MOTHER COURAGE. . . . Seventeen leather belts . . . Then you
don't think the war might end?

CHAPLAIN. Because a Commander's dead? Don't be childish, they're
a dime a dozen. There are always heroes.

MOTHER COURAGE. Well, I wasn't asking just for the sake of argument. I was wondering if I should buy up a lot of supplies. They happen to be cheap right now. But if the war ended, I might just as well
throw them away.

CHAPLAIN. I realize you are serious, Mother Courage. Well, there
have always been people going around saying someday the war will
end. I say, you can't be sure the war will *ever* end. Of course it may
have to pause occasionally—for breath, as it were—it can even meet
with an accident—nothing on this earth is perfect—a war of which we
could say it left nothing to be desired will probably never exist. A war
can come to a sudden halt—from unforeseen causes—you can't think
of everything—a little oversight, and the war's in the hole, and some-

one's got to pull it out again! The someone is the Emperor or the King or the Pope. They're such friends in need, the war has really nothing to worry about, it can look forward to a prosperous future.

A SOLDIER [*sings at the counter*].

> A schnapps, host, quick, make haste!
> A soldier's no time to waste,
> Must be for his Kaiser fighting!

Make it a double, this is a holiday.

MOTHER COURAGE. If I was sure you're right . . .

CHAPLAIN. Think it out for yourself, how *could* the war end?

SOLDIER.

> Your breast, girl, quick, make haste!
> A soldier's no time to waste,
> Must be to Moravia riding!

CLERK [*of a sudden*]. What about peace? Yes, peace. I'm from Bohemia, I'd like to get home once in a while.

CHAPLAIN. You would, would you? Dear old peace! What happens to the hole when the cheese is gone?

CLERK. In the long run you can't live without peace!

CHAPLAIN. Well, I'd say there's peace even in war, war has its . . . islands of peace. For war satisfies *all* needs, even those of peace, yes, they're provided for, or the war couldn't keep going. In war—as in the very thick of peace—you can take a crap, and between one battle and the next there's always a beer, and even on the march you can catch a nap—on your elbow maybe, in a gutter—something can always be managed. Of course you can't play cards during an attack, but neither can you while plowing the fields in peace-time; it's when the victory's won that there are possibilities. And can't you be fruitful and multiply in the very midst of slaughter—behind a barn or some place? Nothing can keep you from it very long in any event. And so the war has your offspring and can carry on. War is like love, it always finds a way. Why *should* it end?

[CATHERINE *has stopped working. She stares at the* CHAPLAIN.]

MOTHER COURAGE. Then I *will* buy those supplies, I'll rely on you.

[CATHERINE *suddenly bangs a basket of glasses down on the ground and runs out.* MOTHER COURAGE *laughs.*]

Lord, Catherine's still going to wait for peace. I promised her she'll get a husband—when it's peace.

[*Runs after her.*]

CLERK [*standing up*]. I win. You were talking. You pay.

MOTHER COURAGE [*returning with* CATHERINE]. Be sensible, the war'll go on a bit longer, and we'll make a bit more money, then peace'll be all the nicer. Now you go into the town, it's not ten minutes walk, and bring the things from the Golden Lion, just the more expensive ones, we can get the rest later in the wagon. It's all arranged, the clerk will go with you, most of the soldiers are at the funeral, nothing can happen to you. Do a good job, don't lose anything, Catherine, think of your trousseau!

[CATHERINE *ties a cloth round her head and leaves with the* CLERK.]

CHAPLAIN. You don't mind her going with the clerk?

MOTHER COURAGE. She's not so pretty anyone would want to ruin her.

CHAPLAIN. The way you run your business and always come through is nothing short of commendable, Mother Courage—I see how you got your name.

MOTHER COURAGE. Poorer people need courage. They're lost, that's why. That they even get up in the morning is something—in *their* plight. Or that they plow a field—in war time. Or that they have an Emperor and a Pope, what courage *that* takes, when you can lose your life by it! The poor! They hang each other one by one, they slaughter each other in the lump, so if they want to look each other in the face once in a while—well, it takes courage, that's all.

[*She sits, takes a small pipe from her pocket and smokes it.*]

You might chop me a bit of firewood.

CHAPLAIN [*reluctantly taking his coat off and preparing to chop wood*]. Properly speaking, I'm a pastor of souls, not a woodcutter.

MOTHER COURAGE. But I don't have a soul. And I do need wood.

CHAPLAIN. What's that little pipe you've got there?

MOTHER COURAGE. Just a pipe.

CHAPLAIN. I think it's a very particular pipe.

MOTHER COURAGE. Oh?

CHAPLAIN. The cook's pipe in fact. Our Swedish Commander's cook.

MOTHER COURAGE. If you know, why beat about the bush?

CHAPLAIN. Because I don't know if you've been *aware* that's what you've been smoking. It was possible you just rummaged among your belongings and your fingers just lit on a pipe and you just took it. In pure absent-mindedness.

MOTHER COURAGE. How do you know that's not it?

CHAPLAIN. It isn't. You *are* aware of it.

[*He brings the ax down on the block with a crash.*]

MOTHER COURAGE. What if I was?

CHAPLAIN. I must give you a warning, Mother Courage, it's my duty. You are unlikely ever again to see the gentleman but that's no pity, you're in luck. Mother Courage, he did not impress me as trustworthy. On the contrary.

MOTHER COURAGE. Really? He was such a nice man.

CHAPLAIN. Well! So that's what you call a nice man. I do not.

[*The ax falls again.*]

Far be it from me to wish him ill, but I cannot—cannot—describe him as nice. No, no, he's a Don Juan, a cunning Don Juan. Just look at that pipe if you don't believe me. You must admit it tells everything about him.

MOTHER COURAGE. I see nothing special in it. It's been, um, used.

CHAPLAIN. It's bitten half-way through! He's a man of great violence! It is the pipe of a man of great violence, you can see *that* if you've any judgment left!

[*He deals the block a tremendous blow.*]

MOTHER COURAGE. Don't bite my chopping block halfway through!

CHAPLAIN. I told you I had no training as a woodcutter. The care of souls was my field. Around here my gifts and capabilities are grossly misused. In physical labor my god-given talents find no—um—adequate expression—which is a sin. You haven't heard me preach. Why, I can put such spirit into a regiment with a single sermon that the enemy's a mere flock of sheep to them and their own lives no more than smelly old shoes to be thrown away at the thought of final victory! God has given me the gift of tongues. I can preach you out of your senses!

MOTHER COURAGE. I need my senses, what would I do without them?

CHAPLAIN. Mother Courage, I have often thought that—under a veil of plain speech—you conceal a heart. You are human, you need . . . warmth.

MOTHER COURAGE. The best way of warming this tent is to chop plenty of firewood.

CHAPLAIN. You're changing the subject. Seriously, my dear Courage, I sometimes ask myself how it would be if our relationship should be somewhat more firmly . . . cemented. I mean, now the wind of war has whirled us so strangely together.

MOTHER COURAGE. The cement's pretty firm already. I cook your meals. And you lend a hand—at chopping firewood, for instance.

CHAPLAIN [*going over to her, gesturing with the ax*]. You know what I mean by a close relationship. It has nothing to do with eating and woodcutting and such base necessities. Let your heart speak!

MOTHER COURAGE. Don't come at me like that with your ax, that'd be *too* close a relationship!

CHAPLAIN. This is no laughing matter, I am in earnest. I've thought it all over.

MOTHER COURAGE. Dear Chaplain, be a sensible fellow. I like you, and I don't want to heap coals of fire on your head. All I'm after is to bring me and my children through in that wagon. Now chop the firewood and we'll be warm of an evening, which is quite a lot these days. What's that?

[*She stands up.* CATHERINE *enters breathless with a nasty wound above her eye and brow. She is letting everything fall, parcels, leather goods, a drum, etc.*]

Catherine, what is it? Were you attacked? On the way back? It's
not serious, only a flesh wound, I'll bandage it up for you, and you'll
be better within the week. Didn't the clerk walk you back? That's because you're a good girl, he thought they'd leave you alone. The
wound really isn't deep, it won't show, though I wouldn't mind if it
did. The pretty girls have a bad time, they get dragged around till
they're finished off, and the other ones get left alone. I've seen so
many with pretty faces and they looked like something that would
scare a wolf in no time. They can't go behind a tree without getting
scared. They lead a horrible life. It's like with the trees: the straight
and tall ones are cut down for roof timber while the crooked ones are
left to enjoy life. That's it, now it's all bandaged. Now I've got something for you, I've been keeping it, just watch.
[*She digs* YVETTE POTTIER'*s red boots out of a bag.*]
You see? You always wanted 'em and now you have 'em. Put them on
before I think twice about it.
[*She helps her.*]
It won't show at all! The boots have kept well, I cleaned them good
before I put them away.
[CATHERINE *leaves the shoes and creeps into the wagon.*]
CHAPLAIN [*when she's gone*]. I hope she won't be disfigured?
MOTHER COURAGE. There'll be a scar. She needn't wait for peace
now.
CHAPLAIN. She didn't let them get any of the stuff from her.
MOTHER COURAGE. Maybe I shouldn't have been so strict with her.
If only I ever knew what went on inside her head. One time she stayed
out all night, once in all the years. I could never get out of her what
happened, I racked my brains for quite a while.
[*She picks up the things* CATHERINE *spilled and sorts them angrily.*]
This is war. A nice source of income to have!
[*Cannon shots.*]
CHAPLAIN. Now they're lowering the Commander in his grave! A
historic moment.
MOTHER COURAGE. It's a historic moment to me when they hit my
daughter over the eye. She's all but finished now, she'll get no husband,
and she's so crazy for children! Even her dumbness comes from the
war. A soldier stuck something in her mouth when she was little. I'll
not see Swiss Cheese again, and where my Eilif is the Good Lord
knows. Curse the war!

SCENE SEVEN

A highway. The CHAPLAIN *and* CATHERINE *are pulling the wagon. It
is dirty and neglected, though there are new goods hung round it.*

MOTHER COURAGE [*walking beside the wagon and drinking heavily
from a flask at her waist*]. I won't have my war all spoiled for me! It

destroys the weak, does it? Well, what does peace do for 'em? Huh?
[*She sings her song.*]

> So cheer up, boys, the rose is fading
> When victory comes you may be dead
> A war is just the same as trading
> But not with cheese—with steel and lead!
> Christians, awake! The winter's gone!
> The snows depart, the dead sleep on.
> And though you may not long survive
> Get out of bed and look alive!

[*And the wagon moves on.*]

SCENE EIGHT

1632. IN THIS SAME YEAR GUSTAVUS ADOLPHUS FELL
IN THE BATTLE OF LÜTZEN. THE PEACE THREATENS
MOTHER COURAGE WITH RUIN. HER BRAVE SON PER-
FORMS ONE HEROIC DEED TOO MANY AND COMES TO A
SHAMEFUL END.

A camp. A summer morning. In front of the wagon, an old woman and her son. The son is dragging a large bag of bedding.

MOTHER COURAGE [*from inside the wagon*]. Must you come at the crack of dawn?

YOUNG MAN. We've been walking all night, twenty miles it was, we have to be back today.

MOTHER COURAGE [*still inside*]. What do I want with bed feathers? Take 'em to the town!

YOUNG MAN. At least wait till you see 'em.

OLD WOMAN. Nothing doing here either, let's go.

YOUNG MAN. And let 'em sign away the roof over our heads for taxes? Maybe she'll pay three gilders if you throw in that bracelet. [*Bells start ringing.*]
You hear, Mother?

VOICES [*from the rear*]. It's peace! The King of Sweden's killed!

MOTHER COURAGE [*sticking her head out of the wagon. She hasn't done her hair yet*]. Bells! What are the bells for, middle of the week?

CHAPLAIN [*crawling out from under the wagon*]. What's that they're shouting?

YOUNG MAN. It's peace.

CHAPLAIN. Peace!?

MOTHER COURAGE. Don't tell me peace has broken out—when I've just gone and bought all these supplies!

CHAPLAIN [*calling, toward the rear*]. Is it peace?

VOICE [*from a distance*]. Yes, the war stopped three weeks ago!

CHAPLAIN [*to* MOTHER COURAGE]. Or why would they ring the bells?

VOICE. A great crowd of Lutherans have just arrived with wagons—they brought the news.

YOUNG MAN. It's peace, Mother.

[*The* OLD WOMAN *collapses*.] What's the matter?

MOTHER COURAGE [*back in the wagon*]. Catherine, it's peace! Put on your black dress, we're going to church, we owe it to Swiss Cheese!

YOUNG MAN. The people here say so too, the war's over.

[*The* OLD WOMAN *stands up, dazed*.] I'll get the harness shop going again now, I promise you. Everything'll be all right, father will get his bed back. . . . Can you walk?

[*To the* CHAPLAIN.] She felt sick, it was the news. She didn't believe there'd ever be peace again. Father always said there would. We're going home.

[*They leave*.]

MOTHER COURAGE [*off*]. Give her a schnapps!

CHAPLAIN. They've left already.

MOTHER COURAGE [*still off*]. What's going on in the camp over there?

CHAPLAIN. They're all getting together, I think I'll go over. Shall I put my pastor's clothes on again?

MOTHER COURAGE. Better get the exact news first, and not risk being taken for the antichrist. I'm glad about the peace even though I'm ruined. At least I've got two of my children through the war. Now I'll see my Eilif again.

CHAPLAIN. And who may this be coming down from the camp? Well, if it isn't our Swedish Commander's cook!

COOK [*somewhat bedraggled, carrying a bundle*]. Who's here? The Chaplain!

CHAPLAIN. Mother Courage, a visitor!

[MOTHER COURAGE *clambers out*.]

COOK. Well, I promised I'd come over for a brief conversation as soon as I had time. I didn't forget your brandy, Mrs. Fierling.

MOTHER COURAGE. Mr. Lamp, the Commander's cook! After all these years! Where is Eilif?

COOK. Isn't he here yet? He went on ahead yesterday, he was on his way over.

CHAPLAIN. I *will* put my pastor's clothes on.

[*He goes behind the wagon*.]

MOTHER COURAGE. He may be here any minute then.

[*Calls toward the wagon*.] Catherine, Eilif's coming! Bring a glass of brandy for the Cook, Catherine!

[CATHERINE *doesn't come.*]
Pull your hair over it and have done, the Cook's no stranger. She won't come out. Peace is nothing to her, it was too long coming. Well, one more schnapps!

COOK. Dear old peace!

[*He and* MOTHER COURAGE *sit.*]

MOTHER COURAGE. Cook, you come at a bad time: I'm ruined.

COOK. What? That's terrible!

MOTHER COURAGE. The peace has broken my neck. On the Chaplain's advice I've gone and bought a lot of supplies. Now everybody's leaving and I'm holding the bag.

COOK. How ever could you listen to the Chaplain? If I'd had time— but the Catholics were too quick—I'd have warned you against him. He's a windbag. Well, so now he's the big wheel round here!

MOTHER COURAGE. He's been doing the dishes for me and helping with the wagon.

COOK. I'll bet he has. And I'll bet he's told you a few of his jokes. He has a most unhealthy attitude to women. I tried to influence him but it was no good. He isn't sound.

MOTHER COURAGE. Are you sound?

COOK. If I'm nothing else, I'm sound. Your health!

MOTHER COURAGE. Sound! Only one person around here was ever sound, and I never had to slave as I did then. He sold the blankets off the children's beds in autumn. You aren't recommending yourself if you *admit* you're sound.

COOK. You fight tooth and nail, don't you? I like that.

MOTHER COURAGE. Don't tell me you dream of my teeth and nails.

COOK. Well, here we sit, while the bells of peace do ring, and you pour your famous brandy as only you know how.

MOTHER COURAGE. I don't think much of the bells of peace at the moment. I don't see how they can hand out all this pay that's in arrears. And then where shall I be with my famous brandy? Have you all been paid?

COOK [*hesitating*]. Not exactly. That's why we disbanded. In the circumstances, I thought, why stay? For the time being, I'll look up a couple of friends. So here I am.

MOTHER COURAGE. In other words, you're broke.

COOK [*annoyed by the bells*]. It's about time they stopped that racket! I'd like to set myself up in some business. I'm fed up with being their cook. I'm supposed to make do with tree roots and shoe leather, and then they throw the soup in my face. Being a cook nowadays is a dog's life. I'd sooner do war service, but of course it's peace now. We'll discuss it later.

MOTHER COURAGE. Oh, Cook, it's a dog's life.

COOK [*as the* CHAPLAIN *turns up, wearing his old costume*]. We'll discuss it.

CHAPLAIN. The coat's pretty good. Just a few moth holes.

COOK. I don't know why you take the trouble. You won't find another job. Who could you incite now to earn an honorable wage or risk his life for a cause? Besides I have a bone to pick with you.

CHAPLAIN. Have you?

COOK. I have. You advised a lady to buy superfluous goods on the pretext that the war would never end.

CHAPLAIN [hotly]. I'd like to know what business it is of yours?

COOK. It's unprincipled behavior! How can you give unwanted advice? And interfere with the conduct of other people's businesses?

CHAPLAIN. Who's interfering now, I'd like to know?
[Haughtily to MOTHER COURAGE.]
I had no idea you were such a close friend of this gentleman and had to account to him for everything.

MOTHER COURAGE. Now don't get excited. The Cook's giving his personal opinion. You can't deny your war was a lemon.

CHAPLAIN. You mustn't take the name of peace in vain. Remember, you're a hyena of the battlefield!

MOTHER COURAGE. A what!?

COOK. If you insult my girl friend, you'll have to reckon with me!

CHAPLAIN. I am not speaking to you, your intentions are only too transparent!
[To MOTHER COURAGE.]
But when I see you take peace between finger and thumb like a snotty old hanky, my humanity rebels! It shows that you want war, not peace, for what you get out of it. But don't forget the proverb: he who sups with the devil must use a long spoon!

MOTHER COURAGE. Remember what one fox said to another that was caught in a trap? "If you stay there, you're just asking for trouble!" There isn't much love lost between me and the war. And when it comes to calling me a hyena, you and I part company.

CHAPLAIN. Then why all this grumbling about the peace just as everyone's heaving a sigh of relief? Is it just for the junk in your wagon?

MOTHER COURAGE. My goods are not junk. I live off them.

CHAPLAIN. You live off war. Exactly.

COOK [to the CHAPLAIN]. As a grown man, you should know better than to go around advising people.
[To MOTHER COURAGE.]
Now, in your situation you'd be smart to get rid of certain goods at once—before the prices sink to zero. Get ready and get going, there isn't a moment to lose!

MOTHER COURAGE. That's sensible advice, I think I'll take it.

CHAPLAIN. Because the Cook says so.

MOTHER COURAGE. Why didn't you say so? He's right, I must get to the market.
[She climbs into the wagon.]

COOK. One up for me, Chaplain. You have no presence of mind. You should have said, "*I* gave *you* advice? Why, I was just talking politics!" And you shouldn't take me on as a rival. Cockfights are not becoming to your cloth.

CHAPLAIN. If you don't shut your trap, I'll murder you, whether it's becoming or not!

COOK [*taking his boots off and unwinding the wrappings on his feet*]. If you hadn't degenerated into a godless tramp, you could easily be quite a success these days. Cooks won't be needed, there's nothing to cook, but there's still plenty to believe, and people'll go right on believing it.

CHAPLAIN [*changing his tone*]. Cook, please don't drive me out! Since I became a tramp, I'm a somewhat better man. I couldn't preach to 'em any more. So where should I go?

[YVETTE POTTIER *enters, decked out in black, with a stick. She is much older, fatter, and heavily powdered. Behind her, a servant.*]

YVETTE. Hullo, everybody! Is this Mother Courage's establishment?

CHAPLAIN. Quite right. And with whom have we the pleasure?

YVETTE. I am Madame Colonel Starhemberg, good people. Where's Mother Courage?

CHAPLAIN [*calling to the wagon*]. Madame Colonel Starhemberg wants to speak with you!

MOTHER COURAGE [*from inside*]. Coming!

YVETTE [*calling*]. It's Yvette!

MOTHER COURAGE [*inside*]. Yvette!

YVETTE. Just to see how you're getting on!
[*As the* COOK *turns round in horror.*]
Peter!

COOK. Yvette!

YVETTE. Of all things! How did *you* get here?

COOK. On a cart.

CHAPLAIN. Well! You know each other? Intimately?

YVETTE. I'll say!
[*Scrutinizing the* COOK.]
You're fat.

COOK. For that matter, *you're* no beanpole.

YVETTE. Anyway, nice meeting you, tramp. Now I can tell you what I think of you.

CHAPLAIN. Do that, tell him all, but wait till Mother Courage comes out.

COOK. Now don't make a scene . . .

MOTHER COURAGE [*comes out, laden with goods*]. Yvette!
[*They embrace.*]
But why are you in mourning?

YVETTE. Doesn't it suit me? My husband, the colonel, died several years ago.

MOTHER COURAGE. The old fellow that nearly bought my wagon?

YVETTE. Naw, not him—his older brother!

MOTHER COURAGE. Good to see one person who got somewhere in the war.

YVETTE. I've had my ups and downs.

MOTHER COURAGE. Don't let's talk badly of Colonels. They make money like hay.

CHAPLAIN. If I were you, I'd put my shoes on again. You promised to give us your opinion of this gentleman.

COOK. Now, Yvette, don't make a stink!

MOTHER COURAGE. He's a friend of mine, Yvette.

YVETTE. He's—Peter Piper, that's what!

MOTHER COURAGE. What!?

COOK. Cut the nicknames. My name's Lamp.

MOTHER COURAGE [laughing]. Peter Piper? Who turned the women's heads? I'll have to sit down. And I've been keeping your pipe for you.

CHAPLAIN. And smoking it.

YVETTE. Lucky I can warn you against him. He's a bad lot. You won't find a worse on the whole coast of Flanders. He got more girls in trouble than . . .

COOK. That's a long time ago, it isn't true any more.

YVETTE. Stand up when you talk to a lady! Oh, how I loved that man! And all the time he was having a little bowlegged brunette. He got *her* in trouble too, of course.

COOK. I seem to have brought *you* luck!

YVETTE. Shut your trap, you hoary ruin! And you take care, Mother Courage, this type is still dangerous even in decay!

MOTHER COURAGE [to YVETTE]. Come with me, I must get rid of this stuff before the prices fall.

YVETTE [concentrating on COOK]. Miserable cur!

MOTHER COURAGE. Maybe you can help me at army headquarters, you have contacts.

YVETTE. Damnable whore hunter!

MOTHER COURAGE [shouting into the wagon]. Catherine, church is all off, I'm going to market!

YVETTE. Inveterate seducer!

MOTHER COURAGE [still to CATHERINE]. When Eilif comes, give him something to drink!

YVETTE. I've put an end to your tricks, Peter Piper, and one day—in a better life than this—the Lord God will reward me!
[She sniffs.]
Come, Mother Courage!
[Leaves with MOTHER COURAGE. Pause.]

CHAPLAIN. As our text this morning let us take the saying, the mills of God grind slowly. And you complain of my jokes!

COOK. I have no luck. I'll be frank, I was hoping for a good hot dinner, I'm starving. And now they'll be talking about me, and she'll get a completely wrong picture. I think I should go before she comes back.

CHAPLAIN. I think so too.

COOK. Chaplain, the peace makes me sick. Mankind must perish by fire and sword, we're born and bred in sin! Oh, how I wish I was roasting a great fat capon for the Commander—God knows where *he's* got to—with mustard sauce and those little yellow carrots. . . .

CHAPLAIN. Red cabbage—with capon, red cabbage.

COOK. You're right. But he always wanted yellow carrots.

CHAPLAIN. He never understood a thing.

COOK. You always put plenty away.

CHAPLAIN. Under protest.

COOK. Anyway, you must admit, those were the days.

CHAPLAIN. Yes, that I might admit.

COOK. Now you've called her a hyena, there's not much future for you here either. What are you staring at?

CHAPLAIN. It's Eilif!

[*Followed by two soldiers with halberds,* EILIF *enters. His hands are fettered. He is white as chalk.*]

What's happened to you?

EILIF. Where's Mother?

CHAPLAIN. Gone to town.

EILIF. They said she was here. I was allowed a last visit.

COOK [*to the soldiers*]. Where are you taking him?

SOLDIER. For a ride.

[*The other soldier makes the gesture of throat cutting.*]

CHAPLAIN. What has he done?

SOLDIER. He broke in on a peasant. The wife is dead.

CHAPLAIN. Eilif, how could you?

EILIF. It's no different. It's what I did before.

COOK. That was in wartime.

EILIF. Shut your hole. Can I sit down till she comes?

SOLDIER. No.

CHAPLAIN. It's true. In wartime they honored him for it. He sat at the Commander's right hand. It was bravery. Couldn't we speak with the provost?

SOLDIER. What's the use? Stealing cattle from a peasant, what's brave about that?

COOK. It was just dumb.

EILIF. If I'd been dumb, I'd have starved, smarty.

COOK. So you were bright and paid for it.

CHAPLAIN. At least we must bring Catherine out.

EILIF. Let her alone. Just give me some brandy.

SOLDIER. No.

CHAPLAIN. What shall we tell your mother?

EILIF. Tell her it was no different. Tell her it was the same. Aw, tell her nothing.

[*The soldiers take him away.*]

CHAPLAIN. I'll come with you, I'll . . .

EILIF. I don't need a priest!

CHAPLAIN. You don't know—yet.

[*Follows him.*]

COOK [*calling after him*]. I'll have to tell her, she'll want to see him!

CHAPLAIN. Better tell her nothing. Or maybe just that he was here, and he'll return, maybe tomorrow. Meantime I'll be back and can break the news.

[*Leaves quickly. The* COOK *looks after him, shakes his head, then walks uneasily around. Finally, he approaches the wagon.*]

COOK. Hi! Won't you come out? You want to run away from the peace, don't you? Well, so do I! I'm the Swedish Commander's cook, remember me? I was wondering if you got anything to eat in there—while we're waiting for your mother. I wouldn't mind a bit of bacon—or even bread—just to pass the time.

[*He looks in.*]

She's got a blanket over her head.

[*The thunder of cannon.*]

MOTHER COURAGE [*running, out of breath, still carrying the goods*]. Cook, the peace is over, the war's on again, has been for three days! I didn't get rid of this stuff after all, thank God! There's a shooting match in the town already—with the Lutherans. We must get away with the wagon. Pack, Catherine! What's on *your* mind? Something the matter?

COOK. Nothing.

MOTHER COURAGE. But there is, I see it in your face.

COOK. Eilif was here. Only he had to go away again.

MOTHER COURAGE. He was here? Then we'll see him on the march. I'll be with our side this time. How'd he look?

COOK. The same.

MOTHER COURAGE. He'll *never* change. And the war couldn't get *him*, he's bright. Help me with the packing.

[*She starts it.*]

Did he tell you anything? Is he in good with the captain? Did he tell you about his heroic deeds?

COOK [*darkly*]. He's done one of them over again.

MOTHER COURAGE. Tell me about it later.

[CATHERINE *appears.*]

Catherine, the peace is all through, we're on the move again.

[*To the* COOK.]

What *is* biting you?

COOK. I'll enlist.

MOTHER COURAGE. A good idea. Where's the Chaplain?

COOK. In the town. With Eilif.

MOTHER COURAGE. Stay with us a while, Mr. Lamp, I need a bit of help.

COOK. This Yvette thing . . .

MOTHER COURAGE. Hasn't done you any harm at all in my eyes. Just the opposite. Where there's smoke, there's fire, they say. You'll come?

COOK. I won't say no.

MOTHER COURAGE. The twelfth regiment's under way. Into harness with you! Maybe I'll see Eilif before the day is out, just think! Well, it wasn't such a long peace, we can't grumble. Let's go!

[*They move off.* MOTHER COURAGE *sings.*]

> *Up hill, down dale, past dome and steeple,*
> *My wagon always moves ahead.*
> *The war can care for all its people*
> *So long as there is steel and lead.*
> *Though steel and lead are stout supporters*
> *A war needs human beings too.*
> *Report today to your headquarters!*
> *If it's to last, this war needs you!*
> *Christians, awake! The winter's gone!*
> *The snows depart, the dead sleep on.*
> *And though you may not long survive*
> *Get out of bed and look alive!*

SCENE NINE

THE HOLY WAR HAS LASTED SIXTEEN YEARS AND GER-
MANY HAS LOST HALF ITS INHABITANTS. THOSE WHO
ARE SPARED IN BATTLE DIE BY PLAGUE. OVER ONCE
BLOOMING COUNTRYSIDE HUNGER RAGES. TOWNS ARE
BURNED DOWN. WOLVES PROWL THE EMPTY STREETS.
IN THE AUTUMN OF 1634 WE FIND MOTHER COURAGE
IN THE FICHTELGEBIRGE NOT FAR FROM THE ROAD
THE SWEDISH ARMY IS TAKING. WINTER HAS COME
EARLY AND IS HARD. BUSINESS IS BAD. ONLY BEGGING
REMAINS. THE COOK RECEIVES A LETTER FROM
UTRECHT AND IS SENT PACKING.

In front of a half-ruined parsonage. Early winter. A gray morning. Gusts of wind. MOTHER COURAGE *and the* COOK *at the wagon in shabby clothes.*

COOK. There are no lights on, no one's up.

MOTHER COURAGE. But it's a parsonage. the parson'll have to leave his feather bed and go ring the bells. Then he'll have himself a hot soup.

COOK. Where'll he get it from? The whole village is starving.

MOTHER COURAGE. The house is lived in. There was a dog barking.

COOK. If the parson has anything, he'll stick to it.

MOTHER COURAGE. Maybe if we sang him something . . .

COOK. I've had enough. Anna, I didn't tell you, a letter came from Utrecht. My mother died of cholera, the inn is mine. There's the letter, if you don't believe me.

MOTHER COURAGE [reading]. Mr. Lamp, I'm tired of wandering, too. I feel like a butcher's dog taking meat to my customers and getting none myself. I've nothing more to sell and people have nothing to pay for it. In Saxony someone tried to saddle me with a chestful of books in return for two eggs. And in Württemberg they would have let me have their plough for a bag of salt. Nothing grows any more, only thorn bushes. I hear they've even caught nuns committing robbery.

COOK. The world's dying out.

MOTHER COURAGE. Sometimes I see myself driving through hell with this wagon and selling brimstone. And sometimes I'm driving through heaven handing out provisions to wandering souls! If only we could find a place where there's no shooting, me and my children —what's left of 'em—we might rest up a while.

COOK. We could open this inn together. Think about it, Courage. My mind's made up. With or without you, I'm leaving for Utrecht. And today at that.

MOTHER COURAGE. I must talk to Catherine, it's sudden.

[CATHERINE emerges from the wagon.]

Catherine, I've something to tell you. The cook and I want to go to Utrecht, he's been left an inn. We'd be sure of our dinner: nice, hm? And you'd have a bed, what do you think of that? This is a dog's life, on the road, you might be killed any time, even now you're covered with lice. . . . I think we'll decide to go, Catherine.

COOK. Anna, I must have a word with you alone.

MOTHER COURAGE. Go back inside, Catherine.

[CATHERINE does so.]

COOK. I'm interrupting because there's a misunderstanding, Anna. I thought I wouldn't have to say it right out, but I see I must. If you're bringing her, it's all off.

[CATHERINE has her head out of the back of the wagon and is listening.]

MOTHER COURAGE. You mean I leave Catherine behind?

COOK. What do you think? There's no room in the inn, it isn't one of those places with three counters. If the two of us stand on our hindlegs we can earn a living, but three's too many. Let Catherine keep your wagon.

MOTHER COURAGE. I was thinking she might find a husband in Utrecht.

COOK. Don't make me laugh. With that scar? And old as she is? And dumb?

MOTHER COURAGE. Not so loud!

COOK. Loud or soft, what is, is. That's another reason I can't have her in the inn, the customers wouldn't like it.

MOTHER COURAGE. Not so loud, I said!

COOK. There's a light in the parsonage, we can sing now!

[*They go over toward the wall.*]

MOTHER COURAGE. How could she pull the wagon by herself? The war frightens her. She has terrible dreams. I hear her groan at night, especially after battles. What she sees in her dreams I don't know. The other day I found a hedgehog with her that we'd run over.

COOK. The inn's too small.

[*Calling.*]

Worthy Sir, menials, and all within! We now present the song of Solomon, Julius Caesar, and other great souls who came to no good, so you can see we're law-abiding folk too, and have a hard time getting by, especially in winter.

[*He sings:* THE SONG OF THE GREAT SOULS OF THIS EARTH.]

> *You've heard of wise old Solomon*
> *You know his history.*
> *He thought so little of this earth*
> *He cursed the hour of his birth*
> *Declaring: all is vanity.*
> *How very wise was Solomon!*
> *But ere night came and day did go*
> *This fact was clear to everyone:*
> *It was his wisdom that had brought him low.*
> Better for you if you have none.

For the virtues are dangerous in this world, as our fine song tells. You're better off without, you have a nice life, breakfast included—a good hot soup maybe. . . . I'm an example of a man who's not had any, and I'd like some, I'm a soldier, but what good did my bravery do me in all those battles? None at all. I might just as well have wet my pants like a coward and stayed home. For why?

> *And Julius Caesar, who was brave,*
> *You saw what came of him.*
> *He sat like God on an altar-piece*
> *And yet they tore him limb from limb*
> *While his prestige did still increase!*
> *"Et tu, Brute, I am undone!"*
> *And ere night came and day did go*
> *This fact was clear to everyone:*
> *It was his bravery that brought him low*
> Better for you if you have none.

[*Under his breath.*]
They don't even look out.
[*Aloud.*]
Worthy Sir, menials, and all within! You should say, no, courage isn't
the thing to fill a man's belly, try honesty, that should be worth a
dinner, at any rate it must have *some* effect. Let's see.

> *You all know honest Socrates*
> *Who always spoke the truth.*
> *They owed him thanks for that, you'd think,*
> *Yet they put hemlock in his drink*
> *And swore that he was bad for youth.*
> *How honest was the people's son!*
> *But ere night came and day did go*
> *This fact was clear to everyone:*
> *It was his honesty that brought him low.*
> Better for you if you have none.

Yes, we're told to be unselfish and share what we have but what if we
have nothing? And those who do share it don't have an easy time
either, for what's left when you're through sharing? Unselfishness is
a very rare virtue—it doesn't pay.

> *Unselfish Martin could not bear*
> *His fellow creature's woes.*
> *He met a beggar in the snows*
> *And gave him half his cloak to wear:*
> *So both of them fell down and froze.*
> *What an unselfish paragon!*
> *But ere night came and day did go*
> *This fact was clear to everyone:*
> *It was unselfishness that brought him low.*
> Better for you if you have none.

That's how it is with us. We're law-abiding folk, we keep to ourselves, don't steal, don't kill, don't burn the place down. And in this
way we sink lower and lower and the song proves true and there's no
soup going. And if we were different, if we were thieves and killers,
maybe we could eat our fill! For virtues bring no reward, only vices.
Such is the world, need it be so?

> *God's Ten Commandments we have kept*
> *And acted as we should.*
> *It has not done us any good.*
> *O you who sit beside a fire*
> *Please help us now: our need is dire!*

> *Strict godliness we've always shown*
> > *But ere night came and day did go*
> *This fact was clear to every one:*
> > *It was our godliness that brought us low.*
> Better for you if you have none.

VOICE [*from above*]. You there! Come up! There's some soup here for you!

MOTHER COURAGE. Lamp, I couldn't swallow a thing. Was that your last word?

COOK. Yes, Anna. Think it over.

MOTHER COURAGE. There's nothing to think over.

COOK. You're going to be silly, but what can I do? I'm not inhuman, it's just that the inn's a small one. And now we must go up, or it'll be no soap here too, and we've been singing in the cold for nothing.

MOTHER COURAGE. I'll get Catherine.

COOK. Better stick something in your pocket for her. If there are three of us, they won't like it.

[*Exeunt.*]

[CATHERINE *clambers out of the wagon with a bundle. She makes sure they're both gone. Then, on a wagon wheel, she lays out a skirt of her mother's and a pair of the* COOK's *pants side by side and easy to see. She has just finished, and has picked her bundle up, when* MOTHER COURAGE *returns.*]

MOTHER COURAGE [*with a plate of soup*]. Catherine! Stay where you are, Catherine! Where do you think you're going with that bundle?
[*She examines the bundle.*]
She's packed her things. Were you listening? I told him there was nothing doing, he can *have* Utrecht and his lousy inn, what would *we* want with a lousy inn?
[*She sees the skirt and pants.*]
Oh, you're a stupid girl, Catherine, what if I'd seen that and you gone?
[*She takes hold of* CATHERINE, *who's trying to leave.*]
And don't think I've sent him packing on your account. It was the wagon. You can't part us, I'm too used to it, *you* didn't come into it, it was the wagon. Now we're leaving, and we'll put the cook's things here where he'll find 'em, the stupid man.
[*She clambers up and throws a couple of things down to go with the pants.*]
There! He's fired! The last man I'll take into *this* business! Now let's you and me be going. Get into harness. This winter'll pass—like all the others.
[*They harness themselves to the wagon, turn it around, and start out. A gust of wind. Enter the* COOK, *still chewing. He sees his things.*]

SCENE TEN

On the highway. MOTHER COURAGE *and* CATHERINE *are pulling the wagon. They come to a prosperous farmhouse. Someone inside is singing* THE SONG OF SHELTER.

> In March a tree we planted
>   To make the garden gay.
> In June we were enchanted :
> A lovely rose was blooming
> The balmy air perfuming!
>   Blest of the gods are they
>   Who have a garden gay!
> In June we were enchanted.
>
> When snow falls helter-skelter
>   And loudly blows the storm
> Our farmhouse gives us shelter.
> The winter's in a hurry
> But we've no cause to worry.
>   Cosy are we and warm
>   Though loudly blows the storm
> Our farmhouse gives us shelter.

[MOTHER COURAGE *and* CATHERINE *have stopped to listen. Then they start out again.*]

SCENE ELEVEN

JANUARY, 1636. CATHOLIC TROOPS THREATEN THE
PROTESTANT TOWN OF HALLE. THE STONES BEGIN TO
TALK. MOTHER COURAGE LOSES HER DAUGHTER AND
JOURNEYS ONWARD ALONE. THE WAR IS NOT YET
NEAR ITS END.

The wagon, very far gone now, stands near a farmhouse with a straw roof. It is night. Out of the wood comes a LIEUTENANT *and three* SOLDIERS *in full armor.*

LIEUTENANT. And there mustn't be a sound. If anyone yells, cut him down.

FIRST SOLDIER. But we'll have to knock—if we want a guide.

LIEUTENANT. Knocking's a natural noise, it's all right, could be a cow hitting the wall of the cowshed.

[*The* SOLDIERS *knock at the farmhouse door. An old peasant woman opens. A hand is clapped over her mouth. Two* SOLDIERS *enter.*]

MAN'S VOICE. What is it?

[*The* SOLDIERS *bring out an old peasant and his son.*]

LIEUTENANT [*pointing to the wagon on which* CATHERINE *has appeared*]. There's one.
[*A soldier pulls her out.*]
Is this everybody that lives here?
PEASANTS [*alternating*]. That's our son. And that's a girl that can't talk. Her mother's in town buying up stocks because the shopkeepers are running away and selling cheap. They're canteen people.
LIEUTENANT. I'm warning you. Keep quiet. One sound and you'll have a sword in your ribs. And I need someone to show us the path to the town.
[*Points to the* YOUNG PEASANT.]
You! Come here!
YOUNG PEASANT. I don't know any path!
SECOND SOLDIER [*grinning*]. He don't know any path!
YOUNG PEASANT. I don't help Catholics.
LIEUTENANT [*to* SECOND SOLDIER]. Show him your sword.
YOUNG PEASANT [*forced to his knees, a sword at his throat*]. I'd rather die!
SECOND SOLDIER [*again mimicking*]. He'd rather die!
FIRST SOLDIER. I know how to change his mind.
[*Walks over to the cowshed.*]
Two cows and a bull. Listen, you. If you aren't going to be reasonable, I'll saber your cattle.
YOUNG PEASANT. Not the cattle!
PEASANT WOMAN [*weeping*]. Spare the cattle, Captain, or we'll starve!
LIEUTENANT. If he must be pigheaded!
FIRST SOLDIER. I think I'll start with the bull.
YOUNG PEASANT [*to the old one*]. Do I have to?
[*The* OLDER ONE *nods.*]
I'll do it.
PEASANT WOMAN. Thank you, thank you, Captain, for sparing us, for ever and ever, Amen.
[*The old man stops her going on thanking him.*]
FIRST SOLDIER. I knew the bull came first all right!
[*Led by the* YOUNG PEASANT, *the* LIEUTENANT *and the* SOLDIERS *go on their way.*]
OLD PEASANT. I wish we knew what it was. Nothing good, I guess.
PEASANT WOMAN. Maybe they're just scouts. What are you doing?
OLD PEASANT [*setting a ladder against the roof and climbing up*]. I'm seeing if they're alone.
[*On the roof.*]
Things are moving—all over. I can see armor. And a cannon. There must be more than a regiment. God have mercy on the town and all within!
PEASANT WOMAN. Are there lights in the town?

OLD PEASANT. No, they're all asleep.

[*He climbs down.*]

There'll be an attack, and they'll all be slaughtered in their beds.

PEASANT WOMAN. The watchman'll give warning.

OLD PEASANT. They must have killed the watchman in the tower on the hill or he'd have sounded his horn before this.

PEASANT WOMAN. If there were more of us . . .

OLD PEASANT. But being that we're alone with that cripple . . .

PEASANT WOMAN. There's nothing we can do, is there?

OLD PEASANT. Nothing.

PEASANT WOMAN. We can't get down there. In the dark.

OLD PEASANT. The whole hillside's swarming with 'em.

PEASANT WOMAN. We could give a sign?

OLD PEASANT. And be cut down for it?

PEASANT WOMAN. No, there's nothing we can do.

[*To* CATHERINE.]

Pray, poor thing, pray! There's nothing we can do to stop this bloodshed, so even if you can't talk, at least pray! He hears, if no one else does. I'll help you.

[ALL *kneel*, CATHERINE *behind.*]

Our Father, which art in Heaven, hear our prayer, let not the town perish with all that lie therein asleep and fearing nothing. Wake them, that they rise and go to the walls and see the foe that comes with fire and sword in the night down the hill and across the fields. God protect our mother and make the watchman not sleep but wake ere it's too late. And save our son-in-law too, O God, he's there with his four children, let them not perish, they're innocent, they know nothing, one of them's not two years old, the eldest is seven.

[CATHERINE *rises, troubled.*]

Heavenly Father, hear us, only Thou canst help us or we die, for we are weak and have no sword for nothing; we cannot trust our own strength but only Thine, O Lord; we are in Thy hands, our cattle, our farm, and the town too, we're all in Thy hands, and the foe is nigh unto the walls with all his power.

[CATHERINE *unperceived, has crept off to the wagon, has taken something out of it, put it under her skirt, and has climbed up the ladder to the roof.*]

Be mindful of the children in danger, especially the little ones, be mindful of the old folk who cannot move, and of all Christian souls O Lord.

OLD PEASANT. And forgive us our trespasses as we forgive them that trespass against us. Amen.

[*Sitting on the roof*, CATHERINE *takes a drum from under her skirt, and starts to beat it.*]

PEASANT WOMAN. Heavens, what's she doing?

OLD PEASANT. She's out of her mind!

PEASANT WOMAN. Bring her down, quick.

[*The* OLD PEASANT *runs to the ladder but* CATHERINE *pulls it up on the roof.*]
She'll get us in trouble.

OLD PEASANT. Stop it this minute, you silly cripple!

PEASANT WOMAN. The soldiers'll come!

OLD PEASANT [*looking for stones*]. I'll stone you!

PEASANT WOMAN. Have you no pity, don't you have a heart? We have relations there too, four grandchildren, but there's nothing we can do. If they find us now, it's the end, they'll stab us to death!
[CATHERINE *is staring into the far distance, toward the town. She goes on drumming.*]

PEASANT WOMAN [*to the* PEASANT]. I told you not to let that riff-raff in your farm. What do *they* care if we lose our cattle?

LIEUTENANT [*running back with* SOLDIERS *and* YOUNG PEASANT]. I'll cut you all to bits!

PEASANT WOMAN. We're innocent, sir, there's nothing we can do. She did it, a stranger!

LIEUTENANT. Where's the ladder?

OLD PEASANT. On the roof.

LIEUTENANT [*calling*]. Throw down the drum. I order you!
[*To* PEASANTS.]
You're all in this, but you won't live to tell the tale.

OLD PEASANT. They've been cutting down fir trees around here. If we bring a tall enough trunk we can knock her off the roof. . . .

FIRST SOLDIER [*to the* LIEUTENANT]. I beg leave to make a suggestion.
[*He whispers something to the* LIEUTENANT, *who nods. To* CATHERINE.]
Listen, you! We have an idea—for your own good.
Come down and go with us to the town. Show us your mother and we'll spare her.
[CATHERINE *replies with more drumming.*]

LIEUTENANT [*pushing him away*]. She doesn't trust you, no wonder with your face.
[*He calls up to* CATHERINE.]
Hey, you! Suppose I give you my word? I'm an officer, my word's my bond!
[CATHERINE *again replies with drumming—harder this time.*]
Nothing is sacred to her.

FIRST SOLDIER. This can't go on, they'll sure as hell hear it in the town.

LIEUTENANT. We must make another noise with something. Louder than that drum. What can we make a noise with?

FIRST SOLDIER. But we mustn't make a noise!

LIEUTENANT. A harmless noise, fool, a peacetime noise!

OLD PEASANT. I could start chopping wood.

LIEUTENANT. That's it!
[*The* PEASANT *brings his ax and chops away.*]
Chop! Chop harder! Chop for your life! It's not enough.
[*To* FIRST SOLDIER.]
You chop too!
OLD PEASANT. I've only one ax.
LIEUTENANT. We must set fire to the farm. Smoke her out.
OLD PEASANT. That's no good, Captain, when they see fire from the
town, they'll know everything.
[CATHERINE *is laughing now and drumming harder than ever.*]
LIEUTENANT. She's laughing at us, that's too much, I'll have her guts
if it's the last thing I do. Bring a musket!
[*Two* SOLDIERS *off.*]
PEASANT WOMAN. I have it, Captain. That's their wagon over there,
Captain. If we smash that, she'll stop. It's all they have, Captain.
LIEUTENANT [*to the* YOUNG PEASANT]. Smash it!
[*Calling.*]
If you don't stop that noise, we'll smash up your wagon!
[*The* YOUNG PEASANT *deals the wagon a couple of feeble blows with a
board.*]
PEASANT WOMAN [*to* CATHERINE]. Stop, you little beast!
[CATHERINE *stares at the wagon and pauses. Noises of distress come out of
her. She goes on drumming.*]
LIEUTENANT. Where are those sonsofbitches with that gun?
FIRST SOLDIER. They can't have heard anything in the town or we'd
heard their cannon.
LIEUTENANT [*calling*]. They don't hear you. And now we're going to
shoot you. I'll give you one more chance: throw down that drum!
YOUNG PEASANT [*dropping the board, screaming to* CATHERINE].
Don't stop now! Go on, go on, go on . . .
[*The* SOLDIER *knocks him down and stabs him.* CATHERINE *starts
crying but goes on drumming.*]
PEASANT WOMAN. Not in the back, you're killing him!
[*The* SOLDIERS *arrive with the musket.*]
LIEUTENANT. Set it up!
[*Calling while the musket is set up on forks.*]
Once for all: stop that drumming!
[*Still crying,* CATHERINE *is drumming as hard as she can.*]
Fire!
[*The* SOLDIERS *fire.* CATHERINE *is hit. She gives the drum another
feeble beat or two, then collapses.*]
LIEUTENANT. That's an end to the noise.
[*But the last beats of the drum are lost in the din of cannon from the town.
Mingled with the thunder of cannon, alarm-bells are heard in the distance.*]
FIRST SOLDIER. She made it.

SCENE TWELVE

Toward morning. The drums and pipes of troops on the march, receding. In front of the wagon MOTHER COURAGE *sits by* CATHERINE'S *body. The peasants of the last scene are standing near.*

PEASANTS [*one sentence apiece*]. You must leave. There's only one regiment to go. You can never get away by yourself.

MOTHER COURAGE. Maybe she's asleep.

[*She sings.*]

> *Lullay, lullay, what's that in the hay?*
> *The neighbor's kids cry but mine are gay.*
> *The neighbor's kids are dressed in dirt:*
> *Your silks were cut from an angel's skirt.*
> *They are all starving: you have a cake;*
> *If it's too stale, you need but speak.*
> *Lullay, lullay, what's rustling there?*
> *One lad fell in Poland. The other is where?*

You shouldn't have told her about the children.

PEASANTS. If you hadn't gone off to the town to get your cut, maybe it wouldn't have happened.

MOTHER COURAGE. I'm glad she can sleep.

PEASANT [*one sentence apiece*]. She's not asleep, it's time you realized. She's through. You must get away. There are wolves in these parts. And the bandits are worse.

MOTHER COURAGE [*standing up*]. That's right.

PEASANTS. Have you no one now?

MOTHER COURAGE. Yes. My son Eilif.

PEASANTS. Find him then. Leave *her* to us. We'll give her a proper burial. You needn't worry.

MOTHER COURAGE. Here's a little money for the expenses.

[*Harnessing herself to the wagon.*]

I hope I can pull the wagon by myself. Yes, I'll manage, there's not much in it now.

[*Another regiment passes with pipe and drum.*]

MOTHER COURAGE. Hey! Take me with you!!

[*She starts pulling the wagon. Soldiers are heard singing.*]

> *Dangers, surprises, devastations—*
> *The war takes hold and will not quit.*
> *But though it last three generations*
> *We shall get nothing out of it.*
> *Starvation, filth, and cold enslave us.*
> *The army robs us of our pay.*
> *Only a miracle can save us*

And miracles have had their day.
    Christians, awake! The winter's gone!
    The snows depart. The dead sleep on.
    And though you may not long survive
    Get out of bed and look alive!

Arthur Miller

1915–

DEATH OF A SALESMAN

CERTAIN PRIVATE CONVERSATIONS IN TWO ACTS AND
A REQUIEM

❖

C A S T

(In order of appearance)

WILLY LOMAN.
LINDA.
BIFF.
HAPPY.
BERNARD.
THE WOMAN (MISS
  FRANCIS).

CHARLEY.
UNCLE BEN.
HOWARD WAGNER.
JENNY.
STANLEY.
MISS FORSYTHE.
LETTA.

The action takes place in Willy Loman's house and yard and in various places he visits in the New York and Boston of today.

Throughout the play, in the stage directions, left and right mean stage left and stage right.

❖

ACT ONE

A melody is heard, played upon a flute. It is small and fine, telling of grass and trees and the horizon. The curtain rises.

Before us is the Salesman's house. We are aware of towering, angular shapes behind it, surrounding it on all sides. Only the blue light of the sky falls upon the house and forestage; the surrounding area shows an angry glow of orange. As more light appears, we see a solid vault of apartment houses around the small, fragile-seeming home. An air of the dream clings to the place, a dream rising out of reality. The kitchen at center seems actual enough, for there is a kitchen table with three chairs, and a refrigerator. But no other fixtures are seen. At the back of the kitchen there is a draped entrance, which leads to the living-room. To the right of the kitchen, on a level raised two feet, is a bedroom furnished only with a brass bedstead and a straight chair. On a shelf over the bed a silver athletic trophy stands. A window opens onto the apartment house at the side.

*Behind the kitchen, on a level raised six and a half feet, is the boys' bedroom,
at present barely visible. Two beds are dimly seen, and at the back of the
room a dormer window. (This bedroom is above the unseen living-room.)
At the left a stairway curves up to it from the kitchen.*

*The entire setting is wholly or, in some places, partially transparent. The
roof-line of the house is one-dimensional; under and over it we see the
apartment buildings. Before the house lies an apron, curving beyond the
forestage into the orchestra. This forward area serves as the back yard as
well as the locale of all WILLY's imaginings and of his city scenes.
Whenever the action is in the present the actors observe the imaginary wall-
lines, entering the house only through its door at the left. But in the scenes
of the past these boundaries are broken, and characters enter or leave a room
by stepping "through" a wall onto the forestage.*

*From the right, WILLY LOMAN, the Salesman, enters, carrying two
large sample cases. The flute plays on. He hears but is not aware of it. He
is past sixty years of age, dressed quietly. Even as he crosses the stage to the
doorway of the house, his exhaustion is apparent. He unlocks the door,
comes into the kitchen, and thankfully lets his burden down, feeling the
soreness of his palms. A word-sigh escapes his lips—it might be "Oh, boy,
oh, boy." He closes the door, then carries his cases out into the living-room,
through the draped kitchen doorway.*

*LINDA, his wife, has stirred in her bed at the right. She gets out and puts
on a robe, listening. Most often jovial, she has developed an iron repression
of her exceptions to WILLY's behavior—she more than loves him, she
admires him, as though his mercurial nature, his temper, his massive
dreams and little cruelties, served her only as sharp reminders of the turbu-
lent longings within him, longings which she shares but lacks the temperament to utter and follow to their end.*

LINDA [*hearing* WILLY *outside the bedroom, calls with some trepidation.*]
Willy!
WILLY. It's all right. I came back.
LINDA. Why? What happened? [*Slight pause.*] Did something happen,
Willy?
WILLY. No, nothing happened.
LINDA. You didn't smash the car, did you?
WILLY [*with casual irritation*]. I said nothing happened. Didn't you
hear me?
LINDA. Don't you feel well?
WILLY. I'm tired to the death. [*The flute has faded away. He sits on the
bed beside her, a little numb.*] I couldn't make it. I just couldn't make it,
Linda.
LINDA [*very carefully, delicately*]. Where were you all day? You look
terrible.

WILLY. I got as far as a little above Yonkers. I stopped for a cup of coffee. Maybe it was the coffee.

LINDA. What?

WILLY [*after a pause*]. I suddenly couldn't drive any more. The car kept going off onto the shoulder, y'know?

LINDA [*helpfully*]. Oh. Maybe it was the steering again. I don't think Angelo knows the Studebaker.

WILLY. No, it's me, it's me. Suddenly I realize I'm goin' sixty miles an hour and I don't remember the last five minutes. I'm—I can't seem to —keep my mind to it.

LINDA. Maybe it's your glasses. You never went for your new glasses.

WILLY. No, I see everything. I came back ten miles an hour. It took me nearly four hours from Yonkers.

LINDA [*resigned*]. Well, you'll just have to take a rest, Willy, you can't continue this way.

WILLY. I just got back from Florida.

LINDA. But you didn't rest your mind. Your mind is over-active, and the mind is what counts, dear.

WILLY. I'll start out in the morning. Maybe I'll feel better in the morning. [*She is taking off his shoes.*] These goddam arch supports are killing me.

LINDA. Take an aspirin. Should I get you an aspirin? It'll soothe you.

WILLY [*with wonder*]. I was driving along, you understand? And I was fine. I was even observing the scenery. You can imagine, me looking at scenery, on the road every week of my life. But it's so beautiful there, Linda, the trees are so thick, and the sun is warm. I opened the windshield and just let the warm air bathe over me. And then all of a sudden I'm goin' off the road! I'm tellin' ya, I absolutely forgot I was driving. If I'd've gone the other way over the white line I might've killed somebody. So I went on again—and five minutes later I'm dreamin' again, and I nearly—[*He presses two fingers against his eyes.*] I have such thoughts, I have such strange thoughts.

LINDA. Willy, dear. Talk to them again. There's no reason why you can't work in New York.

WILLY. They don't need me in New York. I'm the New England man. I'm vital in New England.

LINDA. But you're sixty years old. They can't expect you to keep traveling every week.

WILLY. I'll have to send a wire to Portland. I'm supposed to see Brown and Morrison tomorrow morning at ten o'clock to show the line. Goddammit, I could sell them! [*He starts putting on his jacket.*]

LINDA [*taking the jacket from him*]. Why don't you go down to the place tomorrow and tell Howard you've simply got to work in New York? You're too accommodating, dear.

WILLY. If old man Wagner was alive I'd a been in charge of New York now! That man was a prince, he was a masterful man. But that boy of his, that Howard, he don't appreciate. When I went north the first time, the Wagner Company didn't know where New England was!

LINDA. Why don't you tell those things to Howard, dear?

WILLY [*encouraged*]. I will, I definitely will. Is there any cheese?

LINDA. I'll make you a sandwich.

WILLY. No, go to sleep. I'll take some milk. I'll be up right away. The boys in?

LINDA. They're sleeping. Happy took Biff on a date tonight.

WILLY [*interested*]. That so?

LINDA. It was so nice to see them shaving together, one behind the other, in the bathroom. And going out together. You notice? The whole house smells of shaving lotion.

WILLY. Figure it out. Work a lifetime to pay off a house. You finally own it, and there's nobody to live in it.

LINDA. Well, dear, life is a casting off. It's always that way.

WILLY. No, no, some people—some people accomplish something. Did Biff say anything after I went this morning?

LINDA. You shouldn't have criticized him, Willy, especially after he just got off the train. You mustn't lose your temper with him.

WILLY. When the hell did I lose my temper? I simply asked him if he was making any money. Is that a criticism?

LINDA. But, dear, how could he make any money?

WILLY [*worried and angered*]. There's such an undercurrent in him. He became a moody man. Did he apologize when I left this morning?

LINDA. He was crestfallen, Willy. You know how he admires you. I think if he finds himself, then you'll both be happier and not fight any more.

WILLY. How can he find himself on a farm? Is that a life? A farm-hand? In the beginning, when he was young, I thought, well, a young man, it's good for him to tramp around, take a lot of different jobs. But it's more than ten years now and he has yet to make thirty-five dollars a week!

LINDA. He's finding himself, Willy.

WILLY. Not finding yourself at the age of thirty-four is a disgrace!

LINDA. Shh!

WILLY. The trouble is he's lazy, goddammit!

LINDA. Willy, please!

WILLY. Biff is a lazy bum!

LINDA. They're sleeping. Get something to eat. Go on down.

WILLY. Why did he come home? I would like to know what brought him home.

LINDA. I don't know. I think he's still lost, Willy. I think he's very lost.

WILLY. Biff Loman is lost. In the greatest country in the world a young man with such—personal attractiveness, gets lost. And such a hard worker. There's one thing about Biff—he's not lazy.

LINDA. Never.

WILLY [*with pity and resolve*]. I'll see him in the morning; I'll have a nice talk with him. I'll get him a job selling. He could be big in no time. My God! Remember how they used to follow him around in high school? When he smiled at one of them their faces lit up. When he walked down the street . . .

[*He loses himself in reminiscences.*]

LINDA [*trying to bring him out of it*]. Willy, dear, I got a new kind of American-type cheese today. It's whipped.

WILLY. Why do you get American when I like Swiss?

LINDA. I just thought you'd like a change—

WILLY. I don't want a change! I want Swiss cheese. Why am I always being contradicted?

LINDA [*with a covering laugh*]. I thought it would be a surprise.

WILLY Why don't you open a window in here, for God's sake?

LINDA [*with infinite patience*]. They're all open, dear.

WILLY. The way they boxed us in here. Bricks and windows, windows and bricks.

LINDA. We should've bought the land next door.

WILLY. The street is lined with cars. There's not a breath of fresh air in the neighborhood. The grass don't grow any more, you can't raise a carrot in the back yard. They should've had a law against apartment houses. Remember those two beautiful elm trees out there? When I and Biff hung the swing between them?

LINDA. Yeah, like being a million miles from the city.

WILLY. They should've arrested the builder for cutting those down. They massacred the neighborhood. [*Lost.*] More and more I think of those days, Linda. This time of year it was lilac and wisteria. And then the peonies would come out, and the daffodils. What fragrance in this room!

LINDA. Well, after all, people had to move somewhere.

WILLY. No, there's more people now.

LINDA. I don't think there's more people. I think—

WILLY. There's more people! That's what's ruining this country! Population is getting out of control. The competition is maddening! Smell the stink from that apartment house! And another one on the other side . . . How can they whip cheese?

[*On* WILLY'S *last line,* BIFF *and* HAPPY *raise themselves up in their beds, listening.*]

LINDA. Go down, try it. And be quiet.

WILLY [*turning to* LINDA, *guiltily*]. You're not worried about me, are you, sweetheart?

BIFF. What's the matter?

HAPPY. Listen!

LINDA. You've got too much on the ball to worry about.

WILLY. You're my foundation and my support, Linda.

LINDA. Just try to relax, dear. You make mountains out of molehills.

WILLY. I won't fight with him any more. If he wants to go back to Texas, let him go.

LINDA. He'll find his way.

WILLY. Sure. Certain men just don't get started till later in life. Like Thomas Edison, I think. Or B. F. Goodrich. One of them was deaf. [*He starts for the bedroom doorway.*] I'll put my money on Biff.

LINDA. And Willy—if it's warm Sunday, we'll drive in the country. And we'll open the windshield, and take lunch.

WILLY. No, the windshields don't open on the new cars.

LINDA. But you opened it today.

WILLY. Me? I didn't. [*He stops.*] Now isn't that peculiar! Isn't that a remarkable— [*He breaks off in amazement and fright as the flute is heard distantly.*]

LINDA. What, darling?

WILLY. That is the most remarkable thing.

LINDA. What, dear?

WILLY. I was thinking of the Chevvy. [*Slight pause.*] Nineteen twenty-eight . . . when I had that red Chevvy—[*Breaks off.*] That funny? I coulda sworn I was driving that Chevvy today.

LINDA. Well, that's nothing. Something must've reminded you.

WILLY. Remarkable. Ts. Remember those days? The way Biff used to simonize that car? The dealer refused to believe there was eighty thousand miles on it. [*He shakes his head.*] Heh! [*To* LINDA.] Close your eyes, I'll be right up. [*He walks out of the bedroom.*]

HAPPY [*to* BIFF]. Jesus, maybe he smashed up the car again!

LINDA [*calling after* WILLY]. Be careful on the stairs, dear! The cheese is on the middle shelf! [*She turns, goes over to the bed, takes his jacket, and goes out of the bedroom.*]

[*Light has risen on the boys' room. Unseen,* WILLY *is heard talking to himself, "Eighty thousand miles," and a little laugh.* BIFF *gets out of bed, comes downstage a bit, and stands attentively.* BIFF *is two years older than his brother* HAPPY, *well built, but in these days bears a worn air and seems less self-assured. He has succeeded less, and his dreams are stronger and less acceptable than* HAPPY'S. HAPPY *is tall, powerfully made. Sexuality is like a visible color on him, or a scent that many women have discovered. He, like his brother, is lost, but in a different way, for he has never allowed himself to turn his face toward defeat and is thus more confused and hard-skinned, although seemingly more content.*]

HAPPY [*getting out of bed*]. He's going to get his license taken away if he keeps that up. I'm getting nervous about him, y'know, Biff?

BIFF. His eyes are going.

HAPPY. No, I've driven with him. He sees all right. He just doesn't keep his mind on it. I drove into the city with him last week. He stops at a green light and then it turns red and he goes. [*He laughs.*]
BIFF. Maybe he's color-blind.
HAPPY. Pop? Why he's got the finest eye for color in the business. You know that.
BIFF [*sitting down on his bed*]. I'm going to sleep.
HAPPY. You're not still sour on Dad, are you, Biff?
BIFF. He's all right, I guess.
HAPPY [*underneath them, in the living-room*]. Yes, sir, eighty thousand miles—eighty-two thousand!
BIFF. You smoking?
HAPPY [*holding out a pack of cigarettes*]. Want one?
BIFF [*taking a cigarette*]. I can never sleep when I smell it.
WILLY. What a simonizing job, heh!
HAPPY [*with deep sentiment*]. Funny, Biff, y'know? Us sleeping in here again? The old beds. [*He pats his bed affectionately.*] All the talk that went across those two beds, huh? Our whole lives.
BIFF. Yeah. Lotta dreams and plans.
HAPPY [*with a deep and masculine laugh*]. About five hundred women would like to know what was said in this room.
[*They share a soft laugh.*]
BIFF. Remember that big Betsy something—what the hell was her name—over on Bushwick Avenue?
HAPPY [*combing his hair*]. With the collie dog!
BIFF. That's the one. I got you in there, remember?
HAPPY. Yeah, that was my first time—I think. Boy, there was a pig! [*They laugh, almost crudely.*] You taught me everything I know about women. Don't forget that.
BIFF. I bet you forgot how bashful you used to be. Especially with girls.
HAPPY. Oh, I still am, Biff.
BIFF. Oh, go on.
HAPPY. I just control it, that's all. I think I got less bashful and you got more so. What happened, Biff? Where's the old humor, the old confidence? [*He shakes* BIFF's *knee.* BIFF *gets up and moves restlessly about the room.*] What's the matter?
BIFF. Why does Dad mock me all the time?
HAPPY. He's not mocking you, he—
BIFF. Everything I say there's a twist of mockery on his face. I can't get near him.
HAPPY. He just wants you to make good, that's all. I wanted to talk to you about Dad for a long time, Biff. Something's—happening to him. He—talks to himself.
BIFF. I noticed that this morning. But he always mumbled.

HAPPY. But not so noticeable. It got so embarrassing I sent him to Florida. And you know something? Most of the time he's talking to you.

BIFF. What's he say about me?

HAPPY. I can't make it out.

BIFF. What's he say about me?

HAPPY. I think the fact that you're not settled, that you're still kind of up in the air . . .

BIFF. There's one or two other things depressing him, Happy.

HAPPY. What do you mean?

BIFF. Never mind. Just don't lay it all to me.

HAPPY. But I think if you just got started—I mean—is there any future for you out there?

BIFF. I tell ya, Hap, I don't know what the future is. I don't know—what I'm supposed to want.

HAPPY. What do you mean?

BIFF. Well, I spent six or seven years after high school trying to work myself up. Shipping clerk, salesman, business of one kind or another. And it's a measly manner of existence. To get on that subway on the hot mornings in summer. To devote your whole life to keeping stock, or making phone calls, or selling or buying. To suffer fifty weeks of the year for the sake of a two-week vacation, when all you really desire is to be outdoors, with your shirt off. And always to have to get ahead of the next fella. And still—that's how you build a future.

HAPPY. Well, you really enjoy it on a farm? Are you content out there?

BIFF [with rising agitation]. Hap, I've had twenty or thirty different kinds of jobs since I left home before the war, and it always turns out the same. I just realized it lately. In Nebraska when I herded cattle, and the Dakotas, and Arizona, and now in Texas. It's why I came home now, I guess, because I realized it. This farm I work on, it's spring there now, see? And they've got about fifteen new colts. There's nothing more inspiring or—beautiful than the sight of a mare and a new colt. And it's cool there now, see? Texas is cool now, and it's spring. And whenever spring comes to where I am, I suddenly get the feeling, my God, I'm not gettin' anywhere! What the hell am I doing, playing around with horses, twenty-eight dollars a week! I'm thirty-four years old, I oughta be makin' my future. That's when I come running home. And now, I get here, and I don't know what to do with myself. [After a pause.] I've always made a point of not wasting my life, and every time I come back here I know that all I've done is to waste my life.

HAPPY. You're a poet, you know that, Biff? You're a—you're an idealist!

BIFF. No, I'm mixed up very bad. Maybe I oughta get married. Maybe

I oughta get stuck into something. Maybe that's my trouble. I'm like a boy. I'm not married, I'm not in business, I just—I'm like a boy. Are you content, Hap? You're a success, aren't you? Are you content?

HAPPY. Hell, no!

BIFF. Why? You're making money, aren't you?

HAPPY [*moving about with energy, expressiveness*]. All I can do now is wait for the merchandise manager to die. And suppose I get to be merchandise manager? He's a good friend of mine, and he just built a terrific estate on Long Island. And he lived there about two months and sold it, and now he's building another one. He can't enjoy it once it's finished. And I know that's just what I would do. I don't know what the hell I'm workin' for. Sometimes I sit in my apartment—all alone. And I think of the rent I'm paying. And it's crazy. But then, it's what I always wanted. My own apartment, a car, and plenty of women. And still, goddammit, I'm lonely.

BIFF [*with enthusiasm*]. Listen, why don't you come out West with me?

HAPPY. You and I, heh?

BIFF. Sure, maybe we could buy a ranch. Raise cattle, use our muscles. Men built like we are should be working out in the open.

HAPPY [*avidly*]. The Loman Brothers, heh?

BIFF [*with vast affection*]. Sure, we'd be known all over the counties!

HAPPY [*enthralled*]. That's what I dream about, Biff. Sometimes I want to just rip my clothes off in the middle of the store and outbox that goddam merchandise manager. I mean I can outbox, outrun, and outlift anybody in that store, and I have to take orders from those common, petty sons-of-bitches till I can't stand it any more.

BIFF. I'm tellin' you, kid, if you were with me I'd be happy out there.

HAPPY [*enthused*]. See, Biff, everybody around me is so false that I'm constantly lowering my ideals . . .

BIFF. Baby, together we'd stand up for one another, we'd have someone to trust.

HAPPY. If I were around you—

BIFF. Hap, the trouble is we weren't brought up to grub for money. I don't know how to do it.

HAPPY. Neither can I!

BIFF. Then let's go!

HAPPY. The only thing is—what can you make out there?

BIFF. But look at your friend. Builds an estate and then hasn't the peace of mind to live in it.

HAPPY. Yeah, but when he walks into the store the waves part in front of him. That's fifty-two thousand dollars a year coming through the revolving door, and I got more in my pinky finger than he's got in his head.

BIFF. Yeah, but you just said—

HAPPY. I gotta show some of those pompous, self-important executives over there that Hap Loman can make the grade. I want to walk into the store the way he walks in. Then I'll go with you, Biff. We'll be together yet, I swear. But take those two we had tonight. Now weren't they gorgeous creatures?

BIFF. Yeah, yeah, most gorgeous I've had in years.

HAPPY. I get that any time I want, Biff. Whenever I feel disgusted. The only trouble is, it gets like bowling or something. I just keep knockin' them over and it doesn't mean anything. You still run around a lot?

BIFF. Naa. I'd like to find a girl—steady, somebody with substance.

HAPPY. That's what I long for.

BIFF. Go on! You'd never come home.

HAPPY. I would! Somebody with character, with resistance! Like Mom, y'know? You're gonna call me a bastard when I tell you this. That girl Charlotte I was with tonight is engaged to be married in five weeks. [*He tries on his new hat.*]

BIFF. No kiddin'!

HAPPY. Sure, the guy's in line for the vice-presidency of the store. I don't know what gets into me, maybe I just have an overdeveloped sense of competition or something, but I went and ruined her, and furthermore I can't get rid of her. And he's the third executive I've done that to. Isn't that a crummy characteristic? And to top it all, I go to their weddings! [*Indignantly, but laughing.*] Like I'm not supposed to take bribes. Manufacturers offer me a hundred-dollar bill now and then to throw an order their way. You know how honest I am, but it's like this girl, see. I hate myself for it. Because I don't want the girl, and, still, I take it and—I love it!

BIFF. Let's go to sleep.

HAPPY. I guess we didn't settle anything, heh?

BIFF. I just got one idea that I think I'm going to try.

HAPPY. What's that?

BIFF. Remember Bill Oliver?

HAPPY. Sure, Oliver is very big now. You want to work for him again?

BIFF. No, but when I quit he said something to me. He put his arm on my shoulder, and he said, "Biff, if you ever need anything, come to me."

HAPPY. I remember that. That sounds good.

BIFF. I think I'll go to see him. If I could get ten thousand or even seven or eight thousand dollars I could buy a beautiful ranch.

HAPPY. I bet he'd back you. 'Cause he thought highly of you, Biff. I mean, they all do. You're well liked, Biff. That's why I say to come back here, and we both have the apartment. And I'm tellin' you, Biff, any babe you want . . .

BIFF. No, with a ranch I could do the work I like and still be something. I just wonder, though. I wonder if Oliver still thinks I stole that carton of basketballs.

HAPPY. Oh, he probably forgot that long ago. It's almost ten years. You're too sensitive. Anyway, he didn't really fire you.

BIFF. Well, I think he was going to. I think that's why I quit. I was never sure whether he knew or not. I know he thought the world of me, though. I was the only one he'd let lock up the place.

WILLY [*below*]. You gonna wash the engine, Biff?

HAPPY. Shh!

[BIFF *looks at* HAPPY, *who is gazing down, listening.* WILLY *is mumbling in the parlor.*]

HAPPY. You hear that?

[*They listen.* WILLY *laughs warmly.*]

BIFF [*growing angry*]. Doesn't he know Mom can hear that?

WILLY. Don't get your sweater dirty, Biff!

[*A look of pain crosses* BIFF'*s face.*]

HAPPY. Isn't that terrible? Don't leave again, will you? You'll find a job here. You gotta stick around. I don't know what to do about him, it's getting embarrassing.

WILLY. What a simonizing job!

BIFF. Mom's hearing that!

WILLY. No kiddin', Biff, you got a date? Wonderful!

HAPPY. Go on to sleep. But talk to him in the morning, will you?

BIFF [*reluctantly getting into bed*]. With her in the house. Brother!

HAPPY [*getting into bed*]. I wish you'd have a good talk with him.

[*The light on their room begins to fade.*]

BIFF [*To himself in bed*]. That selfish, stupid . . .

HAPPY. Sh . . . Sleep, Biff.

[*Their light is out. Well before they have finished speaking,* WILLY'*s form is dimly seen below in the darkened kitchen. He opens the refrigerator, searches in there, and takes out a bottle of milk. The apartment houses are fading out, and the entire house and surroundings become covered with leaves. Music insinuates itself as the leaves appear.*]

WILLY. Just wanna be careful with those girls, Biff, that's all. Don't make any promises. No promises of any kind. Because a girl, y'know, they always believe what you tell 'em, and you're very young, Biff, you're too young to be talking seriously to girls.

[*Light rises on the kitchen.* WILLY, *talking, shuts the refrigerator door and comes downstage to the kitchen table. He pours milk into a glass. He is totally immersed in himself, smiling faintly.*]

WILLY. Too young entirely, Biff. You want to watch your schooling first. Then when you're all set, there'll be plenty of girls for a boy like you. [*He smiles broadly at a kitchen chair.*] That so? The girls pay for you? [*He laughs.*] Boy, you must really be makin' a hit.

[WILLY *is gradually addressing—physically—a point offstage, speaking through the wall of the kitchen, and his voice has been rising in volume to that of a normal conversation.*]

WILLY. I been wondering why you polish the car so careful. Ha! Don't leave the hubcaps, boys. Get the chamois to the hubcaps. Happy, use newspaper on the windows, it's the easiest thing. Show him how to do it, Biff! You see, Happy? Pad it up, use it like a pad. That's it, that's it, good work. You're doin' all right, Hap. [*He pauses, then nods in approbation for a few seconds, then looks upward.*] Biff, first thing we gotta do when we get time is clip that big branch over the house. Afraid it's gonna fall in a storm and hit the roof. Tell you what. We get a rope and sling her around, and then we climb up there with a couple of saws and take her down. Soon as you finish the car, boys, I wanna see ya. I got a surprise for you, boys.

BIFF [*offstage*]. Whatta ya got, Dad?

WILLY. No, you finish first. Never leave a job till you're finished— remember that. [*Looking toward the "big trees"*] Biff, up in Albany I saw a beautiful hammock. I think I'll buy it next trip, and we'll hang it right between those two elms. Wouldn't that be something? Just swingin' there under those branches. Boy, that would be . . .

[YOUNG BIFF *and* YOUNG HAPPY *appear from the direction* WILLY *was addressing.* HAPPY *carries rags and a pail of water.* BIFF, *wearing a sweater with a block "S," carries a football.*]

BIFF [*pointing in the direction of the car offstage*]. How's that, Pop, professional?

WILLY. Terrific. Terrific job, boys. Good work, Biff.

HAPPY. Where's the surprise, Pop?

WILLY. In the back seat of the car.

HAPPY. Boy! [*He runs off.*]

BIFF. What is it, Dad? Tell me, what'd you buy?

WILLY [*laughing, cuffs him*]. Never mind, something I want you to have.

BIFF [*turns and starts off*]. What is it, Hap?

HAPPY [*offstage*]. It's a punching bag!

BIFF. Oh, Pop!

WILLY. It's got Gene Tunney's signature on it!

[HAPPY *runs onstage with a punching bag.*]

BIFF. Gee, how'd you know we wanted a punching bag?

WILLY. Well, it's the finest thing for the timing.

HAPPY [*lies down on his back and pedals with his feet*]. I'm losing weight, you notice, Pop?

WILLY [*to* HAPPY]. Jumping rope is good too.

BIFF. Did you see the new football I got?

WILLY [*examining the ball*]. Where'd you get a new ball?

BIFF. The coach told me to practice my passing.

WILLY. That so? And he gave you the ball, heh?

BIFF. Well, I borrowed it from the locker room. [*He laughs confidentially.*]

WILLY [*laughing with him at the theft*]. I want you to return that.

HAPPY. I told you he wouldn't like it!

BIFF [*angrily*]. Well, I'm bringing it back!

WILLY [*stopping the incipient argument, to* HAPPY]. Sure, he's gotta practice with a regulation ball, doesn't he? [*To* BIFF] Coach'll probably congratulate you on your initiative!

BIFF. Oh, he keeps congratulating my initiative all the time, Pop.

WILLY. That's because he likes you. If somebody else took that ball there'd be an uproar. So what's the report, boys, what's the report?

BIFF. Where'd you go this time, Dad? Gee we were lonesome for you.

WILLY [*pleased, puts an arm around each boy and they come down to the apron*]. Lonesome, heh?

BIFF. Missed you every minute.

WILLY. Don't say? Tell you a secret, boys. Don't breathe it to a soul. Someday I'll have my own business, and I'll never have to leave home any more.

HAPPY. Like Uncle Charley, heh?

WILLY. Bigger than Uncle Charley! Because Charley is not—liked. He's liked, but he's not—well liked.

BIFF. Where'd you go this time, Dad?

WILLY. Well, I got on the road, and I went north to Providence. Met the Mayor.

BIFF. The Mayor of Providence!

WILLY. He was sitting in the hotel lobby.

BIFF. What'd he say?

WILLY. He said, "Morning!" And I said, "You got a fine city here, Mayor." And then he had coffee with me. And then I went to Waterbury. Waterbury is a fine city. Big clock city, the famous Waterbury clock. Sold a nice bill there. And then Boston—Boston is the cradle of the Revolution. A fine city. And a couple of other towns in Mass., and on to Portland and Bangor and straight home!

BIFF. Gee, I'd love to go with you sometime, Dad.

WILLY. Soon as summer comes.

HAPPY. Promise?

WILLY. You and Hap and I, and I'll show you all the towns. America is full of beautiful towns and fine, upstanding people. And they know me, boys, they know me up and down New England. The finest people. And when I bring you fellas up, there'll be open sesame for all of us, 'cause one thing, boys: I have friends. I can park my car in any street in New England, and the cops protect it like their own. This summer, heh?

BIFF *and* HAPPY, *together*. Yeah! You bet!

WILLY. We'll take our bathing suits.

HAPPY. We'll carry your bags, Pop!

WILLY. Oh, won't that be something! Me comin' into the Boston stores with you boys carryin' my bags. What a sensation!

[BIFF *is prancing around, practicing passing the ball.*]

WILLY. You nervous, Biff, about the game?

BIFF. Not if you're gonna be there.

WILLY. What do they say about you in school, now that they made you captain?

HAPPY. There's a crowd of girls behind him every time the classes change.

BIFF [*taking* WILLY's *hand*]. This Saturday, Pop, this Saturday—just for you, I'm going to break through for a touchdown.

HAPPY. You're supposed to pass.

BIFF. I'm takin' one play for Pop. You watch me, Pop, and when I take off my helmet, that means I'm breakin' out. Then you watch me crash through that line!

WILLY [*kisses* BIFF]. Oh, wait'll I tell this in Boston!

[BERNARD *enters in knickers. He is younger than* BIFF, *earnest and loyal, a worried boy.*]

BERNARD. Biff, where are you? You're supposed to study with me today.

WILLY. Hey, looka Bernard. What're you lookin' so anemic about, Bernard?

BERNARD. He's gotta study, Uncle Willy. He's got Regents next week.

HAPPY [*tauntingly, spinning* BERNARD *around*]. Let's box, Bernard!

BERNARD. Biff! [*He gets away from* HAPPY]. Listen, Biff, I heard Mr. Birnbaum say that if you don't start studyin' math he's gonna flunk you, and you won't graduate. I heard him!

WILLY. You better study with him, Biff. Go ahead now.

BERNARD. I heard him!

BIFF. Oh, Pop, you didn't see my sneakers! [*He holds up a foot for* WILLY *to look at*]

WILLY. Hey, that's a beautiful job of printing!

BERNARD [*wiping his glasses*]. Just because he printed University of Virginia on his sneakers doesn't mean they've got to graduate him, Uncle Willy!

WILLY [*angrily*]. What're you talking about? With scholarships to three universities they're gonna flunk him?

BERNARD. But I heard Mr. Birnbaum say—

WILLY. Don't be a pest, Bernard! [*To his boys*] What an anemic!

BERNARD. Okay, I'm waiting for you in my house, Biff.

[BERNARD *goes off. The* LOMANS *laugh.*]

WILLY. Bernard is not well liked, is he?

BIFF. He's liked, but he's not well liked.

HAPPY. That's right, Pop.

WILLY. That's just what I mean. Bernard can get the best marks in school, y'understand, but when he gets out in the business world, y'understand, you are going to be five times ahead of him. That's why I thank Almighty God you're both built like Adonises. Because the man who makes an appearance in the business world, the man who creates personal interest, is the man who gets ahead. Be liked and you will never want. You take me, for instance. I never have to wait in line to see a buyer. "Willy Loman is here!" That's all they have to know, and I go right through.

BIFF. Did you knock them dead, Pop?

WILLY. Knocked 'em cold in Providence, slaughtered 'em in Boston.

HAPPY [*on his back, pedaling again*]. I'm losing weight, you notice, Pop? [LINDA *enters, as of old, a ribbon in her hair, carrying a basket of washing.*]

LINDA [*with youthful energy*]. Hello, dear!

WILLY. Sweetheart!

LINDA. How'd the Chevvy run?

WILLY. Chevrolet, Linda, is greatest car ever built. [*To the boys*] Since when do you let your mother carry wash up the stairs?

BIFF. Grab hold there, boy!

HAPPY. Where to, Mom?

LINDA. Hang them up on the line. And you better go down to your friends, Biff. The cellar is full of boys. They don't know what to do with themselves.

BIFF. Ah, when Pop comes home they can wait!

WILLY [*laughs appreciatively*]. You better go down and tell them what to do, Biff.

BIFF. I think I'll have them sweep out the furnace room.

WILLY. Good work, Biff.

BIFF [*goes through wall-line of kitchen to doorway at back and calls down*]. Fellas! Everybody sweep out the furnace room! I'll be right down!

VOICES. All right! Okay, Biff.

BIFF. George and Sam and Frank, come out back! We're hangin' up the wash! Come on, Hap, on the double! [*He and* HAPPY *carry out the basket.*]

LINDA. The way they obey him!

WILLY. Well, that's training, the training. I'm tellin' you, I was sellin' thousands and thousands, but I had to come home.

LINDA. Oh, the whole block'll be at that game. Did you sell anything?

WILLY. I did five hundred gross in Providence and seven hundred gross in Boston.

LINDA. No! Wait a minute, I've got a pencil. [*She pulls pencil and paper out of her apron pocket.*] That makes your commission . . . two hundred—my God! Two hundred and twelve dollars!

WILLY. Well, I didn't figure it yet, but . . .

LINDA. How much did you do?

WILLY. Well, I—I did—about a hundred and eighty gross in Providence. Well, no—it came to—roughly two hundred gross on the whole trip.

LINDA [*without hesitation*]. Two hundred gross. That's . . . [*She figures.*]

WILLY. The trouble was that three of the stores were half closed for inventory in Boston. Otherwise I woulda broke records.

LINDA. Well, it makes seventy dollars and some pennies. That's very good.

WILLY. What do we owe?

LINDA. Well, on the first there's sixteen dollars on the refrigerator—

WILLY. Why sixteen?

LINDA. Well, the fan belt broke, so it was a dollar eighty.

WILLY. But it's brand new.

LINDA. Well, the man said that's the way it is. Till they work themselves in, y'know.

[*They move through the wall-line into the kitchen.*]

WILLY. I hope we didn't get stuck on that machine.

LINDA. They got the biggest ads of any of them!

WILLY. I know, it's a fine machine. What else?

LINDA. Well, there's nine-sixty for the washing machine. And for the vacuum cleaner there's three and a half due on the fifteenth. Then the roof, you got twenty-one dollars remaining.

WILLY. It don't leak, does it?

LINDA. No, they did a wonderful job. Then you owe Frank for the carburetor.

WILLY. I'm not going to pay that man! That goddam Chevrolet, they ought to prohibit the manufacture of that car!

LINDA. Well, you owe him three and a half. And odds and ends, comes to around a hundred and twenty dollars by the fifteenth.

WILLY. A hundred and twenty dollars! My God, if business don't pick up I don't know what I'm gonna do!

LINDA. Well, next week you'll do better.

WILLY. Oh, I'll knock 'em dead next week. I'll go to Hartford. I'm very well liked in Hartford. [*Pause*] You know, the trouble is, Linda, people don't seem to take to me.

[*They move onto the forestage.*]

LINDA. Oh, don't be foolish.

WILLY. I know it when I walk in. They seem to laugh at me.

LINDA. Why? Why would they laugh at you? Don't talk that way, Willy.

[WILLY *moves to the edge of the stage.* LINDA *goes into the kitchen and starts to darn stockings.*]

WILLY. I don't know the reason for it, but they just pass me by. I'm not noticed.

LINDA. But you're doing wonderful, dear. You're making seventy to a hundred dollars a week.

WILLY. But I gotta be at it ten, twelve hours a day. Other men—I don't know—they do it easier. I don't know why—I can't stop myself—I talk too much. A man oughta come in with a few words. One thing about Charley. He's a man of few words, and they respect him.

LINDA. You don't talk too much, you're just lively.

WILLY [*smiling*]. Well, I figure, what the hell, life is short, a couple of jokes. [*To himself*] I joke too much! [*The smile goes.*]

LINDA. Why? You're—

WILLY. I'm fat. I'm very—foolish to look at, Linda. I didn't tell you, but Christmas time I happened to be calling on F. H. Stewarts, and a salesman I know, as I was going in to see the buyer, I heard him say something about—walrus. And I—I cracked him right across the face. I won't take that. I simply will not take that. But they do laugh at me. I know that.

LINDA. Darling . . .

WILLY. I gotta overcome it. I know I gotta overcome it. I'm not dressing to advantage, maybe.

LINDA. Willy, darling, you're the handsomest man in the world—

WILLY. Oh, no, Linda.

LINDA. To me you are. [*Slight pause*] The handsomest.

[*From the darkness is heard the laughter of a woman.* WILLY *doesn't turn to it, but it continues through* LINDA'*s lines.*]

LINDA. And the boys, Willy. Few men are idolized by their children the way you are.

[*Music is heard as behind a scrim, to the left of the house,* THE WOMAN, *dimly seen, is dressing.*]

WILLY [*with great feeling*]. You're the best there is, Linda, you're a pal, you know that? On the road—on the road I want to grab you sometimes and just kiss the life outa you.

[*The laughter is loud now, and he moves into a brightening area at the left, where* THE WOMAN *has come from behind the scrim and is standing, putting on her hat, looking into a "mirror" and laughing.*]

WILLY. 'Cause I get so lonely—especially when business is bad and there's nobody to talk to. I get the feeling that I'll never sell anything again, that I won't make a living for you, or a business, a business for the boys. [*He talks through* THE WOMAN'*s subsiding laughter;* THE WOMAN *primps at the "mirror."*] There's so much I want to make for—

THE WOMAN. Me? You didn't make me, Willy. I picked you.

WILLY [*pleased*]. You picked me?

THE WOMAN [*who is quite proper-looking,* WILLY'*s age*]. I did. I've been sitting at that desk watching all the salesmen go by, day in, day out. But you've got such a sense of humor, and we do have such a good time together, don't we?

WILLY. Sure, sure. [*He takes her in his arms.*] Why do you have to go now?

THE WOMAN. It's two o'clock . . .

WILLY. No, come on in! [*He pulls her.*]

THE WOMAN. . . . my sisters'll be scandalized. When'll you be back?

WILLY. Oh, two weeks about. Will you come up again?

THE WOMAN. Sure thing. You do make me laugh. It's good for me. [*She squeezes his arm, kisses him.*] And I think you're a wonderful man.

WILLY. You picked me, heh?

THE WOMAN. Sure. Because you're so sweet. And such a kidder.

WILLY. Well, I'll see you next time I'm in Boston.

THE WOMAN. I'll put you right through to the buyers.

WILLY [*slapping her bottom*]. Right. Well, bottoms up!

THE WOMAN [*slaps him gently and laughs*]. You just kill me, Willy. [*He suddenly grabs her and kisses her roughly.*] You kill me. And thanks for the stockings. I love a lot of stockings. Well, good night.

WILLY. Good night. And keep your pores open!

THE WOMAN. Oh, Willy!

[THE WOMAN *bursts out laughing, and* LINDA's *laughter blends in.* THE WOMAN *disappears into the dark. Now the area at the kitchen table brightens.* LINDA *is sitting where she was at the kitchen table, but now is mending a pair of her silk stockings.*]

LINDA. You are, Willy. The handsomest man. You've got no reason to feel that—

WILLY [*coming out of* THE WOMAN's *dimming area and going over to* LINDA]. I'll make it all up to you, Linda, I'll—

LINDA. There's nothing to make up, dear. You're doing fine, better than—

WILLY [*noticing her mending*]. What's that?

LINDA. Just mending my stockings. They're so expensive—

WILLY [*angrily, taking them from her*]. I won't have you mending stockings in this house! Now throw them out!

[LINDA *puts the stockings in her pocket.*]

BERNARD [*entering on the run*]. Where is he? If he doesn't study!

WILLY [*moving to the forestage, with great agitation*]. You'll give him the answers!

BERNARD. I do, but I can't on a Regents! That's a state exam! They're liable to arrest me!

WILLY. Where is he? I'll whip him, I'll whip him!

LINDA. And he'd better give back that football, Willy, it's not nice.

WILLY. Biff! Where is he? Why is he taking everything?

LINDA. He's too rough with the girls, Willy. All the mothers are afraid of him!

WILLY. I'll whip him!

BERNARD. He's driving the car without a license!

[THE WOMAN'S *laugh is heard.*]

WILLY. Shut up!

LINDA. All the mothers—

WILLY. Shut up!

BERNARD [*backing quietly away and out*]. Mr. Birnbaum says he's stuck up.

WILLY. Get outa here!

BERNARD. If he doesn't buckle down he'll flunk math!

[*He goes off.*]

LINDA. He's right, Willy, you've gotta—

WILLY [*exploding at her*]. There's nothing the matter with him! You want him to be a worm like Bernard? He's got spirit, personality . . .

[*As he speaks,* LINDA, *almost in tears, exits into the living-room.* WILLY *is alone in the kitchen, wilting and staring. The leaves are gone. It is night again, and the apartment houses look down from behind.*]

WILLY. Loaded with it. Loaded! What is he stealing? He's giving it back, isn't he? Why is he stealing? What did I tell him? I never in my life told him anything but decent things.

[HAPPY *in pajamas has come down the stairs;* WILLY *suddenly becomes aware of* HAPPY'S *presence.*]

HAPPY. Let's go now, come on.

WILLY [*sitting down at the kitchen table*]. Huh! Why did she have to wax the floors herself? Every time she waxes the floors she keels over. She knows that!

HAPPY. Shh! Take it easy. What brought you back tonight?

WILLY. I got an awful scare. Nearly hit a kid in Yonkers. God! Why didn't I go to Alaska with my brother Ben that time! Ben! That man was a genius, that man was success incarnate! What a mistake! He begged me to go.

HAPPY. Well, there's no use in—

WILLY. You guys! There was a man started with the clothes on his back and ended up with diamond mines!

HAPPY. Boy, someday I'd like to know how he did it.

WILLY. What's the mystery? The man knew what he wanted and went out and got it! Walked into a jungle, and comes out, the age of twenty-one, and he's rich! The world is an oyster, but you don't crack it open on a mattress!

HAPPY. Pop, I told you I'm gonna retire you for life.

WILLY. You'll retire me for life on seventy goddam dollars a week? And your women and your car and your apartment, and you'll retire me for life! Christ's sake, I couldn't get past Yonkers today! Where

are you guys, where are you? The woods are burning! I can't drive
a car!

[CHARLEY *has appeared in the doorway. He is a large man, slow of speech,
laconic, immovable. In all he says, despite what he says, there is pity, and,
now, trepidation. He has a robe over pajamas, slippers on his feet. He enters
the kitchen.*]

CHARLEY. Everything all right?

HAPPY. Yeah, Charley, everything's . . .

WILLY. What's the matter?

CHARLEY. I heard some noise. I thought something happened. Can't
we do something about the walls? You sneeze in here, and in my
house hats blow off.

HAPPY. Let's go to bed, Dad. Come on.

[CHARLEY *signals to* HAPPY *to go.*]

WILLY. You go ahead, I'm not tired at the moment.

HAPPY [*to* WILLY]. Take it easy, huh? [*He exits.*]

WILLY. What're you doin' up?

CHARLEY [*sitting down at the kitchen table opposite* WILLY]. Couldn't
sleep good. I had a heartburn.

WILLY. Well, you don't know how to eat.

CHARLEY. I eat with my mouth.

WILLY. No, you're ignorant. You gotta know about vitamins and
things like that.

CHARLEY. Come on, let's shoot. Tire you out a little.

WILLY [*hesitantly*]. All right. You got cards?

CHARLEY [*taking a deck from his pocket*]. Yeah, I got them. Someplace.
What is it with those vitamins?

WILLY [*dealing*]. They build up your bones. Chemistry.

CHARLEY. Yeah, but there's no bones in a heartburn.

WILLY. What are you talkin' about? Do you know the first thing
about it?

CHARLEY. Don't get insulted.

WILLY. Don't talk about something you don't know anything about.
[*They are playing. Pause.*]

CHARLEY. What're you doin' home?

WILLY. A little trouble with the car.

CHARLEY. Oh. [*Pause*] I'd like to take a trip to California.

WILLY. Don't say.

CHARLEY. You want a job?

WILLY. I got a job, I told you that. [*After a slight pause*] What the hell
are you offering me a job for?

CHARLEY. Don't get insulted.

WILLY. Don't insult me.

CHARLEY. I don't see no sense in it. You don't have to go on this
way.

WILLY. I got a good job. [*Slight pause*] What do you keep comin' in here for?

CHARLEY. You want me to go?

WILLY [*after a pause, withering*]. I can't understand it. He's going back to Texas again. What the hell is that?

CHARLEY. Let him go.

WILLY. I got nothin' to give him, Charley, I'm clean, I'm clean.

CHARLEY. He won't starve. None a them starve. Forget about him.

WILLY. Then what have I got to remember?

CHARLEY. You take it too hard. To hell with it. When a deposit bottle is broken you don't get your nickel back.

WILLY. That's easy enough for you to say.

CHARLEY. That ain't easy for me to say.

WILLY. Did you see the ceiling I put up in the living-room?

CHARLEY. Yeah, that's a piece of work. To put up a ceiling is a mystery to me. How do you do it?

WILLY. What's the difference?

CHARLEY. Well, talk about it.

WILLY. You gonna put up a ceiling?

CHARLEY. How could I put up a ceiling?

WILLY. Then what the hell are you bothering me for?

CHARLEY. You're insulted again.

WILLY. A man who can't handle tools is not a man. You're disgusting.

CHARLEY. Don't call me disgusting, Willy.

[UNCLE BEN, *carrying a valise and an umbrella, enters the forestage from around the right corner of the house. He is a stolid man, in his sixties, with a mustache and an authoritative air. He is utterly certain of his destiny, and there is an aura of far places about him. He enters exactly as* WILLY *speaks.*]

WILLY. I'm getting awfully tired, Ben.

[BEN'S *music is heard.* BEN *looks around at everything.*]

CHARLEY. Good, keep playing; you'll sleep better. Did you call me Ben?

[BEN *looks at his watch.*]

WILLY. That's funny. For a second there you reminded me of my brother Ben.

BEN. I only have a few minutes.

[*He strolls, inspecting the place.* WILLY *and* CHARLEY *continue playing.*]

CHARLEY. You never heard from him again, heh? Since that time?

WILLY. Didn't Linda tell you? Couple of weeks ago we got a letter from his wife in Africa. He died.

CHARLEY. That so.

BEN [*chuckling*]. So this is Brooklyn, eh?

CHARLEY. Maybe you're in for some of his money.

WILLY. Naa, he had seven sons. There's just one opportunity I had with that man . . .

BEN. I must make a train, William. There are several properties I'm looking at in Alaska.

WILLY. Sure, sure! If I'd gone with him to Alaska that time, everything would've been totally different.

CHARLEY. Go on, you'd froze to death up there.

WILLY. What're you talking about?

BEN. Opportunity is tremendous in Alaska, William. Surprised you're not up there.

WILLY. Sure, tremendous.

CHARLEY. Heh?

WILLY. There was the only man I ever met who knew the answers.

CHARLEY. Who?

BEN. How are you all?

WILLY [taking a pot, smiling]. Fine, fine.

CHARLEY. Pretty sharp tonight.

BEN. Is Mother living with you?

WILLY. No, she died a long time ago.

CHARLEY. Who?

BEN. That's too bad. Fine specimen of a lady, Mother.

WILLY [to CHARLEY]. Heh?

BEN. I'd hoped to see the old girl.

CHARLEY. Who died?

BEN. Heard anything from Father, have you?

WILLY [unnerved]. What do you mean, who died?

CHARLEY [taking a pot]. What're you talkin' about?

BEN [looking at his watch]. William, it's half-past eight!

WILLY [as though to dispel his confusion he angrily stops CHARLEY'S hand]. That's my build!

CHARLEY. I put the ace—

WILLY. If you don't know how to play the game I'm not gonna throw my money away on you!

CHARLEY [rising]. It was my ace, for God's sake!

WILLY. I'm through, I'm through!

BEN. When did Mother die?

WILLY. Long ago. Since the beginning you never knew how to play cards.

CHARLEY [picks up the cards and goes to the door]. All right! Next time I'll bring a deck with five aces.

WILLY. I don't play that kind of game!

CHARLEY [turning to him]. You ought to be ashamed of yourself!

WILLY. Yeah?

CHARLEY. Yeah! [He goes out.]

WILLY [slamming the door after him]. Ignoramus!

BEN [as WILLY comes toward him through the wall-line of the kitchen]. So you're William.

WILLY [*shaking* BEN's *hand*]. Ben! I've been waiting for you so long! What's the answer? How did you do it?

BEN. Oh, there's a story in that.

[LINDA *enters the forestage, as of old, carrying the wash basket.*]

LINDA. Is this Ben?

BEN [*gallantly*]. How do you do, my dear.

LINDA. Where've you been all these years? Willy's always wondered why you—

WILLY [*pulling* BEN *away from her impatiently*]. Where is Dad? Didn't you follow him? How did you get started?

BEN. Well, I don't know how much you remember.

WILLY. Well, I was just a baby, of course, only three or four years old—

BEN. Three years and eleven months.

WILLY. What a memory, Ben!

BEN. I have many enterprises, William, and I have never kept books.

WILLY. I remember I was sitting under the wagon in—was it Nebraska?

BEN. It was South Dakota, and I gave you a bunch of wild flowers.

WILLY. I remember you walking away down some open road.

BEN [*laughing*]. I was going to find Father in Alaska.

WILLY. Where is he?

BEN. At that age I had a very faulty view of geography, William. I discovered after a few days that I was heading due south, so instead of Alaska, I ended up in Africa.

LINDA. Africa!

WILLY. The Gold Coast!

BEN. Principally diamond mines.

LINDA. Diamond mines!

BEN. Yes, my dear. But I've only a few minutes—

WILLY. No! Boys! Boys! [YOUNG BIFF *and* HAPPY *appear*.] Listen to this. This is your Uncle Ben, a great man! Tell my boys, Ben!

BEN. Why, boys, when I was seventeen I walked into the jungle, and when I was twenty-one I walked out. [*He laughs.*] And by God I was rich.

WILLY [*to the boys*]. You see what I been talking about? The greatest things can happen!

BEN [*glancing at his watch*]. I have an appointment in Ketchikan Tuesday week.

WILLY. No, Ben! Please tell about Dad. I want my boys to hear. I want them to know the kind of stock they spring from. All I remember is a man with a big beard, and I was in Mamma's lap, sitting around a fire, and some kind of high music.

BEN. His flute. He played the flute.

WILLY. Sure, the flute, that's right!

[*New music is heard, a high, rollicking tune.*]

BEN. Father was a very great and a very wild-hearted man. We would start in Boston, and he'd toss the whole family into the wagon, and then he'd drive the team right across the country; through Ohio, and Indiana, Michigan, Illinois, and all the Western states. And we'd stop in the towns and sell the flutes that he'd made on the way. Great inventor, Father. With one gadget he made more in a week than a man like you could make in a lifetime.

WILLY. That's just the way I'm bringing them up, Ben—rugged, well liked, all-around.

BEN. Yeah? [*To* BIFF.] Hit that, boy—hard as you can.

[*He pounds his stomach.*]

BIFF. Oh, no, sir!

BEN [*taking boxing stance*]. Come on, get to me! [*He laughs.*]

WILLY. Go to it, Biff! Go ahead, show him!

BIFF. Okay! [*He cocks his fists and starts in.*]

LINDA [*to* WILLY]. Why must he fight, dear?

BEN [*sparring with* BIFF]. Good boy! Good boy!

WILLY. How's that, Ben, heh?

HAPPY. Give him the left, Biff!

LINDA. Why are you fighting?

BEN. Good boy! [*Suddenly comes in, trips* BIFF, *and stands over him, the point of his umbrella poised over* BIFF'*s eye.*]

LINDA. Look out, Biff!

BIFF. Gee!

BEN [*patting* BIFF'*s knee*]. Never fight fair with a stranger, boy. You'll never get out of the jungle that way. [*Taking* LINDA'*s hand and bowing.*] It was an honor and a pleasure to meet you, Linda.

LINDA [*withdrawing her hand coldly, frightened*]. Have a nice—trip.

BEN [*to* WILLY]. And good luck with your—what do you do?

WILLY. Selling.

BEN. Yes. Well . . . [*He raises his hand in farewell to all.*]

WILLY. No, Ben, I don't want you to think . . . [*He takes* BEN'*s arm to show him.*] It's Brooklyn, I know, but we hunt too.

BEN. Really, now.

WILLY. Oh, sure, there's snakes and rabbits and—that's why I moved out here. Why, Biff can fell any one of these trees in no time! Boys! Go right over to where they're building the apartment house and get some sand. We're gonna rebuild the entire front stoop right now! Watch this, Ben!

BIFF. Yes, sir! On the double, Hap!

HAPPY [*as he and* BIFF *run off*]. I lost weight, Pop, you notice?

[CHARLEY *enters in knickers, even before the boys are gone.*]

CHARLEY. Listen, if they steal any more from that building the watchman'll put the cops on them!

LINDA [*to* WILLY]. Don't let Biff . . .

[BEN *laughs lustily*.]

WILLY. You shoulda seen the lumber they brought home last week. At least a dozen six-by-tens worth all kinds a money.

CHARLEY. Listen, if that watchman—

WILLY. I gave them hell, understand. But I got a couple of fearless characters there.

CHARLEY. Willy, the jails are full of fearless characters.

BEN [*clapping* WILLY *on the back, with a laugh at* CHARLEY]. And the stock exchange, friend!

WILLY [*joining in* BEN'S *laughter*]. Where are the rest of your pants?

CHARLEY. My wife bought them.

WILLY. Now all you need is a golf club and you can go upstairs and go to sleep. [*To* BEN] Great athlete! Between him and his son Bernard they can't hammer a nail!

BERNARD [*rushing in*]. The watchman's chasing Biff!

WILLY [*angrily*]. Shut up! He's not stealing anything!

LINDA [*alarmed, hurrying off left*]. Where is he? Biff, dear! [*She exits.*]

WILLY [*moving toward the left, away from* BEN]. There's nothing wrong. What's the matter with you?

BEN. Nervy boy. Good!

WILLY [*laughing*]. Oh, nerves of iron, that Biff!

CHARLEY. Don't know what it is. My New England man comes back and he's bleedin', they murdered him up there.

WILLY. It's contacts, Charley, I got important contacts!

CHARLEY [*sarcastically*]. Glad to hear it, Willy. Come in later, we'll shoot a little casino. It'll take some of your Portland money. [*He laughs at* WILLY *and exits.*]

WILLY [*turning to* BEN]. Business is bad, it's murderous. But not for me, of course.

BEN. I'll stop by on my way back to Africa.

WILLY [*longingly*]. Can't you stay a few days? You're just what I need, Ben, because I—I have a fine position here, but I—well, Dad left when I was such a baby and I never had a chance to talk to him and I still feel—kind of temporary about myself.

BEN. I'll be late for my train.

[*They are at opposite ends of the stage.*]

WILLY. Ben, my boys—can't we talk? They'd go into the jaws of hell for me, see, but I—

BEN. William, you're being first-rate with your boys. Outstanding, manly chaps!

WILLY [*hanging on to his words*]. Oh, Ben, that's good to hear! Because sometimes I'm afraid that I'm not teaching them the right kind of— Ben, how should I teach them?

BEN [*giving great weight to each word, and with a certain vicious audacity*]. William, when I walked into the jungle, I was seventeen. When I walked out I was twenty-one. And, by God, I was rich! [*He goes off into darkness around the right corner of the house.*]

WILLY. . . . . was rich! That's just the spirit I want to imbue them with! To walk into a jungle! I was right! I was right! I was right! [BEN *is gone, but* WILLY *is still speaking to him as* LINDA, *in nightgown and robe, enters the kitchen, glances around for* WILLY, *then goes to the door of the house, looks out and sees him. Comes down to his left. He looks at her.*]

LINDA. Willy, dear? Willy?

WILLY. I was right!

LINDA. Did you have some cheese? [*He can't answer.*] It's very late, darling. Come to bed, heh?

WILLY [*looking straight up*]. Gotta break your neck to see a star in this yard.

LINDA. You coming in?

WILLY. Whatever happened to that diamond watch fob? Remember? When Ben came from Africa that time? Didn't he give me a watch fob with a diamond in it?

LINDA. You pawned it, dear. Twelve, thirteen years ago. For Biff's radio correspondence course.

WILLY. Gee, that was a beautiful thing. I'll take a walk.

LINDA. But you're in your slippers.

WILLY [*starting to go around the house at the left*]. I was right! I was! [*Half to* LINDA, *as he goes, shaking his head*] What a man! There was a man worth talking to. I was right!

LINDA [*calling after* WILLY]. But in your slippers, Willy! [WILLY *is almost gone when* BIFF, *in his pajamas, comes down the stairs and enters the kitchen.*]

BIFF. What is he doing out there?

LINDA. Sh!

BIFF. God Almighty, Mom, how long has he been doing this?

LINDA. Don't, he'll hear you.

BIFF. What the hell is the matter with him?

LINDA. It'll pass by morning.

BIFF. Shouldn't we do anything?

LINDA. Oh, my dear, you should do a lot of things, but there's nothing to do, so go to sleep.

[HAPPY *comes down the stair and sits on the steps.*]

HAPPY. I never heard him so loud, Mom.

LINDA. Well, come around more often; you'll hear him.

[*She sits down at the table and mends the lining of* WILLY'*s jacket.*]

BIFF. Why didn't you ever write me about this, Mom?

LINDA. How would I write to you? For over three months you had no address.

BIFF. I was on the move. But you know I thought of you all the time. You know that, don't you, pal?

LINDA. I know, dear, I know. But he likes to have a letter. Just to know that there's still a possibility for better things.

BIFF. He's not like this all the time, is he?

LINDA. It's when you come home he's always the worst.

BIFF. When I come home?

LINDA. When you write you're coming, he's all smiles, and talks about the future, and—he's just wonderful. And then the closer you seem to come, the more shaky he gets, and then, by the time you get here, he's arguing, and he seems angry at you. I think it's just that maybe he can't bring himself to—to open up to you. Why are you so hateful to each other? Why is that?

BIFF [*evasively*]. I'm not hateful, Mom.

LINDA. But you no sooner come in the door than you're fighting!

BIFF. I don't know why. I mean to change. I'm tryin', Mom, you understand?

LINDA. Are you home to stay now?

BIFF. I don't know. I want to look around, see what's doin'.

LINDA. Biff, you can't look around all your life, can you?

BIFF. I just can't take hold, Mom. I can't take hold of some kind of a life.

LINDA. Biff, a man is not a bird, to come and go with the springtime.

BIFF. Your hair . . . [*He touches her hair.*] Your hair got so gray.

LINDA. Oh, it's been gray since you were in high school. I just stopped dyeing it, that's all.

BIFF. Dye it again, will ya? I don't want my pal looking old. [*He smiles.*]

LINDA. You're such a boy! You think you can go away for a year and . . . You've got to get it into your head now that one day you'll knock on this door and there'll be strange people here—

BIFF. What are you talking about? You're not even sixty, Mom.

LINDA. But what about your father?

BIFF [*lamely*]. Well, I meant him too.

HAPPY. He admires Pop.

LINDA. Biff, dear, if you don't have any feeling for him, then you can't have any feeling for me.

BIFF. Sure I can, Mom.

LINDA. No. You can't just come to see me, because I love him. [*With a threat, but only a threat, of tears*] He's the dearest man in the world to me, and I won't have anyone making him feel unwanted and low and blue. You've got to make up your mind now, darling, there's no lee-way any more. Either he's your father and you pay him that respect, or else you're not to come here. I know he's not easy to get along with—nobody knows that better than me—but . . .

WILLY [*from the left, with a laugh*]. Hey, hey, Biffo!

BIFF [*starting to go out after* WILLY]. What the hell is the matter with him? [HAPPY *stops him.*]

LINDA. Don't—don't go near him!

BIFF. Stop making excuses for him! He always, always wiped the floor with you. Never had an ounce of respect for you.

HAPPY. He's always had respect for—

BIFF. What the hell do you know about it?

HAPPY [*surlily*]. Just don't call him crazy!

BIFF. He's got no character— Charley wouldn't do this. Not in his own house—spewing out that vomit from his mind.

HAPPY. Charley never had to cope with what he's got to.

BIFF. People are worse off than Willy Loman. Believe me, I've seen them!

LINDA. Then make Charley your father, Biff. You can't do that, can you? I don't say he's a great man. Willy Loman never made a lot of money. His name was never in the paper. He's not the finest character that ever lived. But he's a human being, and a terrible thing is happening to him. So attention must be paid. He's not to be allowed to fall into his grave like an old dog. Attention, attention must be finally paid to such a person. You called him crazy—

BIFF. I didn't mean—

LINDA. No, a lot of people think he's lost his—balance. But you don't have to be very smart to know what his trouble is. The man is exhausted.

HAPPY. Sure!

LINDA. A small man can be just as exhausted as a great man. He works for a company thirty-six years this March, opens up unheard-of territories to their trademark, and now in his old age they take his salary away.

HAPPY [*indignantly*]. I didn't know that, Mom.

LINDA. You never asked, my dear! Now that you get your spending money someplace else you don't trouble your mind with him.

HAPPY. But I gave you money last—

LINDA. Christmas time, fifty dollars! To fix the hot water it cost ninety-seven fifty! For five weeks he's been on straight commission, like a beginner, an unknown!

BIFF. Those ungrateful bastards!

LINDA. Are they any worse than his sons? When he brought them business, when he was young, they were glad to see him. But now his old friends, the old buyers that loved him so and always found some order to hand him in a pinch—they're all dead, retired. He used to be able to make six, seven calls a day in Boston. Now he takes his valises out of the car and puts them back and takes them out again and he's exhausted. Instead of walking he talks now. He drives seven hundred miles, and when he gets there no one knows him any more, no one welcomes him. And what goes through a man's mind, driving seven hundred miles home without having earned a cent? Why shouldn't he talk to himself? Why? When he has to go to Charley and borrow fifty dollars a week and pretend to me that it's his pay? How long can that go on? How long? You see what I'm sitting here and waiting for? And you tell me he has no character? The man who never worked a day but for your benefit? When does he get the medal for that? Is this his reward—to turn around at the age of sixty-three and find his sons, who he loved better than his life, one a philandering bum—

HAPPY. Mom!

LINDA. That's all you are, my baby! [*To* BIFF] And you! What happened to the love you had for him? You were such pals! How you used to talk to him on the phone every night! How lonely he was till he could come home to you!

BIFF. All right, Mom. I'll live here in my room, and I'll get a job. I'll keep away from him, that's all.

LINDA. No, Biff. You can't stay here and fight all the time.

BIFF. He threw me out of this house, remember that.

LINDA. Why did he do that? I never knew why.

BIFF. Because I know he's a fake and he doesn't like anybody around who knows!

LINDA. Why a fake? In what way? What do you mean?

BIFF. Just don't lay it all at my feet. It's between me and him—that's all I have to say. I'll chip in from now on. He'll settle for half my pay check. He'll be all right. I'm going to bed. [*He starts for the stairs.*]

LINDA. He won't be all right.

BIFF [*turning on the stairs, furiously*]. I hate this city and I'll stay here. Now what do you want?

LINDA. He's dying, Biff.

[HAPPY *turns quickly to her, shocked.*]

BIFF [*after a pause*]. Why is he dying?

LINDA. He's been trying to kill himself.

BIFF [*with great horror*]. How?

LINDA. I live from day to day.

BIFF. What're you talking about?

LINDA. Remember I wrote you that he smashed up the car again? In February?

BIFF. Well?

LINDA. The insurance inspector came. He said that they have evidence. That all these accidents in the last year—weren't—weren't—accidents.

HAPPY. How can they tell that? That's a lie.

LINDA. It seems there's a woman . . . [*She takes a breath as*

{ BIFF [*sharply but contained*]. What woman?

{ LINDA [*simultaneously*] . . . and this woman . . .

LINDA. What?

BIFF. Nothing. Go ahead.

LINDA. What did you say?

BIFF. Nothing. I just said what woman?

HAPPY. What about her?

LINDA. Well, it seems she was walking down the road and saw his car. She says that he wasn't driving fast at all, and that he didn't skid. She says he came to that little bridge, and then deliberately smashed into the railing, and it was only the shallowness of the water that saved him.

BIFF. Oh, no, he probably just fell asleep again.

LINDA. I don't think he fell asleep.

BIFF. Why not?

LINDA. Last month . . . [*With great difficulty*] Oh, boys, it's so hard to say a thing like this! He's just a big stupid man to you, but I tell you there's more good in him than in many other people. [*She chokes, wipes her eyes.*] I was looking for a fuse. The lights blew out, and I went down the cellar. And behind the fuse box—it happened to fall out—was a length of rubber pipe—just short.

HAPPY. No kidding?

LINDA. There's a little attachment on the end of it. I knew right away. And sure enough, on the bottom of the water heater there's a new little nipple on the gas pipe.

HAPPY [*angrily*]. That—jerk.

BIFF. Did you have it taken off?

LINDA. I'm—I'm ashamed to. How can I mention it to him? Every day I go down and take away that little rubber pipe. But, when he comes home, I put it back where it was. How can I insult him that way? I don't know what to do. I live from day to day, boys. I tell you, I know every thought in his mind. It sounds so old-fashioned and silly, but I tell you he put his whole life into you and you've turned your backs on him. [*She is bent over in the chair, weeping, her face in her hands.*] Biff, I swear to God! Biff, his life is in your hands!

HAPPY [*to* BIFF]. How do you like that damned fool!

BIFF [*kissing her*]. All right, pal, all right. It's all settled now. I've been remiss. I know that, Mom. But now I'll stay, and I swear to you, I'll apply myself. [*Kneeling in front of her, in a fever of self-reproach*] It's just—you see, Mom, I don't fit in business. Not that I won't try. I'll try, and I'll make good.

HAPPY. Sure you will. The trouble with you in business was you never tried to please people.

BIFF. I know, I—

HAPPY. Like when you worked for Harrison's. Bob Harrison said you were tops, and then you go and do some damn fool thing like whistling whole songs in the elevator like a comedian.

BIFF [*against* HAPPY]. So what? I like to whistle sometimes.

HAPPY. You don't raise a guy to a responsible job who whistles in the elevator!

LINDA. Well, don't argue about it now.

HAPPY. Like when you'd go off and swim in the middle of the day instead of taking the line around.

BIFF [*his resentment rising*]. Well, don't you run off? You take off sometimes, don't you? On a nice summer day?

HAPPY. Yeah, but I cover myself!

LINDA. Boys!

HAPPY. If I'm going to take a fade the boss can call any number where I'm supposed to be and they'll swear to him that I just left. I'll tell you something that I hate to say, Biff, but in the business world some of them think you're crazy.

BIFF [*angered*]. Screw the business world!

HAPPY. All right, screw it! Great, but cover yourself!

LINDA. Hap, Hap!

BIFF. I don't care what they think! They've laughed at Dad for years, and you know why? Because we don't belong in this nuthouse of a city! We should be mixing cement on some open plain, or—or carpenters. A carpenter is allowed to whistle!

[WILLY *walks in from the entrance of the house, at left.*]

WILLY. Even your grandfather was better than a carpenter. [*Pause. They watch him.*] You never grew up. Bernard does not whistle in the elevator, I assure you.

BIFF [*as though to laugh* WILLY *out of it*]. Yeah, but you do, Pop.

WILLY. I never in my life whistled in an elevator! And who in the business world thinks I'm crazy?

BIFF. I didn't mean it like that, Pop. Now don't make a whole thing out of it, will ya?

WILLY. Go back to the West! Be a carpenter, a cowboy, enjoy yourself!

LINDA. Willy, he was just saying—

WILLY. I heard what he said!

HAPPY [*trying to quiet* WILLY]. Hey, Pop, come on now . . .

WILLY [*continuing over* HAPPY's *line*]. They laugh at me, heh? Go to Filene's, go to the Hub, go to Slattery's,[1] Boston. Call out the name Willy Loman and see what happens! Big shot!

BIFF. All right, Pop.

WILLY. Big!

BIFF. All right!

WILLY. Why do you always insult me?

BIFF. I didn't say a word. [*To* LINDA.] Did I say a word?

LINDA. He didn't say anything, Willy.

WILLY [*going to the doorway of the living-room*]. All right, good night, good night.

LINDA. Willy, dear, he just decided . . .

---

[1] Boston department stores

WILLY [*to* BIFF]. If you get tired hanging around tomorrow, paint the ceiling I put up in the living-room.

BIFF. I'm leaving early tomorrow.

HAPPY. He's going to see Bill Oliver, Pop.

WILLY [*interestedly*]. Oliver? For what?

BIFF [*with reserve, but trying, trying*]. He always said he'd stake me. I'd like to go into business, so maybe I can take him up on it.

LINDA. Isn't that wonderful?

WILLY. Don't interrupt. What's wonderful about it? There's fifty men in the City of New York who'd stake him. [*To* BIFF] Sporting goods?

BIFF. I guess so. I know something about it and—

WILLY. He knows something about it! You know sporting goods better than Spalding, for God's sake! How much is he giving you?

BIFF. I don't know, I didn't even see him yet, but—

WILLY. Then what're you talkin' about?

BIFF [*getting angry*]. Well, all I said was I'm gonna see him, that's all!

WILLY [*turning away*]. Ah, you're counting your chickens again.

BIFF [*starting left for the stairs*]. Oh, Jesus, I'm going to sleep!

WILLY [*calling after him*]. Don't curse in this house!

BIFF [*turning*]. Since when did you get so clean?

HAPPY [*trying to stop them*]. Wait a . . .

WILLY. Don't use that language to me! I won't have it!

HAPPY [*grabbing* BIFF, *shouts*]. Wait a minute! I got an idea. I got a feasible idea. Come here, Biff, let's talk this over now, let's talk some sense here. When I was down in Florida last time, I thought of a great idea to sell sporting goods. It just came back to me. You and I, Biff— we have a line, the Loman Line. We train a couple of weeks, and put on a couple of exhibitions, see?

WILLY. That's an idea!

HAPPY. Wait! We form two basketball teams, see? Two waterpolo teams. We play each other. It's a million dollars' worth of publicity. Two brothers, see? The Loman Brothers. Displays in the Royal Palms—all the hotels. And banners over the ring and the basketball court: "Loman Brothers." Baby, we could sell sporting goods!

WILLY. That is a one-million-dollar idea!

LINDA. Marvelous!

BIFF. I'm in great shape as far as that's concerned.

HAPPY. And the beauty of it is, Biff, it wouldn't be like a business. We'd be out playin' ball again . . .

BIFF [*enthused*]. Yeah, that's . . .

WILLY. Million-dollar . . .

HAPPY. And you wouldn't get fed up with it, Biff. It'd be the family again. There'd be the old honor, and comradeship, and if you wanted to go off for a swim or somethin'—well, you'd do it! Without some smart cooky gettin' up ahead of you!

WILLY. Lick the world! You guys together could absolutely lick the civilized world.

BIFF. I'll see Oliver tomorrow. Hap, if we could work that out . . .

LINDA. Maybe things are beginning to—

WILLY [*wildly enthused, to* LINDA]. Stop interrupting! [*To* BIFF] But don't wear sport jacket and slacks when you see Oliver.

BIFF. No, I'll—

WILLY. A business suit, and talk as little as possible, and don't crack any jokes.

BIFF. He did like me. Always liked me.

LINDA. He loved you!

WILLY [*to* LINDA]. Will you stop! [*To* BIFF] Walk in very serious. You are not applying for a boy's job. Money is to pass. Be quiet, fine, and serious. Everybody likes a kidder, but nobody lends him money.

HAPPY. I'll try to get some myself, Biff. I'm sure I can.

WILLY. I see great things for you kids, I think your troubles are over. But remember, start big and you'll end big. Ask for fifteen. How much you gonna ask for?

BIFF. Gee, I don't know—

WILLY. And don't say "Gee." "Gee" is a boy's word. A man walking in for fifteen thousand dollars does not say "Gee!"

BIFF. Ten, I think, would be top though.

WILLY. Don't be so modest. You always started too low. Walk in with a big laugh. Don't look worried. Start off with a couple of your good stories to lighten things up. It's not what you say, it's how you say it—because personality always wins the day.

LINDA. Oliver always thought the highest of him—

WILLY. Will you let me talk?

BIFF. Don't yell at her, Pop, will ya?

WILLY [*angrily*]. I was talking, wasn't I?

BIFF. I don't like you yelling at her all the time, and I'm tellin' you, that's all.

WILLY. What're you, takin' over this house?

LINDA. Willy—

WILLY [*turning on her*]. Don't take his side all the time, goddammit!

BIFF [*furiously*]. Stop yelling at her!

WILLY [*suddenly pulling on his cheek, beaten down, guilt-ridden*]. Give my best to Bill Oliver—he may remember me. [*He exits through the living-room doorway.*]

LINDA [*her voice subdued*]. What'd you have to start that for? [BIFF *turns away.*] You see now sweet he was as soon as you talked hopefully? [*She goes over to* BIFF.] Come up and say good night to him. Don't let him go to bed that way.

HAPPY. Come on, Biff, let's buck him up.

LINDA. Please, dear. Just say good night. It takes so little to make him happy. Come. [*She goes through the living-room doorway, calling upstairs from within the living-room.*] Your pajamas are hanging in the bathroom, Willy!

HAPPY [*looking toward where* LINDA *went out*]. What a woman! They broke the mold when they made her. You know that, Biff?

BIFF. He's off salary. My God, working on commission!

HAPPY. Well, let's face it: he's no hot-shot selling man. Except that sometimes, you have to admit, he's a sweet personality.

BIFF [*deciding*]. Lend me ten bucks, will ya? I want to buy some new ties.

HAPPY. I'll take you to a place I know. Beautiful stuff. Wear one of my striped shirts tomorrow.

BIFF. She got gray. Mom got awful old. Gee, I'm gonna go in to Oliver tomorrow and knock him for a—

HAPPY. Come on up. Tell that to Dad. Let's give him a whirl. Come on.

BIFF [*steamed up*]. You know, with ten thousand bucks, boy!

HAPPY [*as they go into the living-room*]. That's the talk, Biff, that's the first time I've heard the old confidence out of you! [*From within the living-room, fading off*] You're gonna live with me, kid, and any babe you want just say the word . . . [*The last lines are hardly heard. They are mounting the stairs to their parents' bedroom.*]

LINDA [*entering her bedroom and addressing* WILLY, *who is in the bathroom. She is straightening the bed for him*]. Can you do anything about the shower? It drips.

WILLY [*from the bathroom*]. All of a sudden everything falls to pieces! Goddam plumbing, oughta be sued, those people. I hardly finished putting it in and the thing . . . [*His words rumble off.*]

LINDA. I'm just wondering if Oliver will remember him. You think he might?

WILLY [*coming out of the bathroom in his pajamas*]. Remember him? What's the matter with you, you crazy? If he'd've stayed with Oliver he'd be on top by now! Wait'll Oliver gets a look at him. You don't know the average caliber any more. The average young man today— [*He is getting into bed*]—is got a caliber of zero. Greatest thing in the world for him was to bum around.

[BIFF *and* HAPPY *enter the bedroom. Slight pause.*]

WILLY [*stops short, looking at* BIFF]. Glad to hear it, boy.

HAPPY. He wanted to say good night to you, sport.

WILLY [*to* BIFF]. Yeah. Knock him dead, boy. What'd you want to tell me?

BIFF. Just take it easy, Pop. Good night. [*He turns to go.*]

WILLY [*unable to resist*]. And if anything falls off the desk while you're talking to him—like a package or something— don't you pick it up. They have office boys for that.

LINDA. I'll make a big breakfast—

WILLY. Will you let me finish? [*To* BIFF] Tell him you were in the business in the West. Not farm work.

BIFF. All right, Dad.

LINDA. I think everything

WILLY [*going right through her speech*]. And don't undersell yourself. No less than fifteen thousand dollars.

BIFF [*unable to bear him*]. Okay. Good night, Mom.
[*He starts moving.*]

WILLY. Because you got a greatness in you, Biff, remember that. You got all kinds a greatness . . .
[*He lies back, exhausted.* BIFF *walks out.*]

LINDA [*calling after* BIFF]. Sleep well, darling!

HAPPY. I'm gonna get married, Mom. I wanted to tell you.

LINDA. Go to sleep, dear.

HAPPY [*going*]. I just wanted to tell you.

WILLY. Keep up the good work. [HAPPY *exits.*] God . . . remember that Ebbets Field game? The championship of the city?

LINDA. Just rest. Should I sing to you?

WILLY. Yeah. Sing to me. [LINDA *hums a soft lullaby.*] When that team came out—he was the tallest, remember?

LINDA. Oh, yes. And in gold.
[BIFF *enters the darkened kitchen, takes a cigarette, and leaves the house. He comes downstage into a golden pool of light. He smokes, staring at the night.*]

WILLY. Like a young god. Hercules—something like that. And the sun, the sun all around him. Remember how he waved to me? Right up from the field, with the representatives of three colleges standing by? And the buyers I brought, and the cheers when he came out—Loman, Loman, Loman! God Almighty, he'll be great yet. A star like that, magnificent, can never really fade away!
[*The light on* WILLY *is fading. The gas heater begins to glow through the kitchen wall, near the stairs, a blue flame beneath red coils.*]

LINDA [*timidly*]. Willy dear, what has he got against you?

WILLY. I'm so tired. Don't talk any more.
[BIFF *slowly returns to the kitchen. He stops, stares toward the heater.*]

LINDA. Will you ask Howard to let you work in New York?

WILLY. First thing in the morning. Everything'll be all right.
[BIFF *reaches behind the heater and draws out a length of rubber tubing. He is horrified and turns his head toward* WILLY'*s room, still dimly lit, from which the strains of* LINDA'*s desperate but monotonous humming rise.*]

WILLY [*staring through the window into the moonlight*]. Gee, look at the moon moving between the buildings!
[BIFF *wraps the tubing around his hand and quickly goes up the stairs.*]
Curtain

ACT TWO

Music is heard, gay and bright. The curtain rises as the music fades away.
WILLY, *in shirt sleeves, is sitting at the kitchen table, sipping coffee, his hat
in his lap.* LINDA *is filling his cup when she can.*

WILLY. Wonderful coffee. Meal in itself.

LINDA. Can I make you some eggs?

WILLY. No. Take a breath.

LINDA. You look so rested, dear.

WILLY. I slept like a dead one. First time in months. Imagine, sleeping
till ten on a Tuesday morning. Boys left nice and early, heh?

LINDA. They were out of here by eight o'clock.

WILLY. Good work!

LINDA. It was so thrilling to see them leaving together. I can't get over
the shaving lotion in this house!

WILLY [*smiling*]. Mmm—

LINDA. Biff was very changed this morning. His whole attitude seemed
to be hopeful. He couldn't wait to get downtown to see Oliver.

WILLY. He's heading for a change. There's no question, there simply
are certain men that take longer to get—solidified. How did he dress?

LINDA. His blue suit. He's so handsome in that suit. He could be a—
anything in that suit!

[WILLY *gets up from the table.* LINDA *holds his jacket for him.*]

WILLY. There's no question, no question at all. Gee, on the way home
tonight I'd like to buy some seeds.

LINDA [*laughing*]. That'd be wonderful. But not enough sun gets back
there. Nothing'll grow any more.

WILLY. You wait, kid, before it's all over we're gonna get a little
place out in the country, and I'll raise some vegetables, a couple of
chickens . . .

LINDA. You'll do it yet, dear.

[WILLY *walks out of his jacket.* LINDA *follows him.*]

WILLY. And they'll get married, and come for a week-end. I'd build a
little guest house. 'Cause I got so many fine tools, all I'd need would
be a little lumber and some peace of mind.

LINDA [*joyfully*]. I sewed the lining . . .

WILLY. I could build two guest houses, so they'd both come. Did he
decide how much he's going to ask Oliver for?

LINDA [*getting him into the jacket*]. He didn't mention it, but I imagine
ten or fifteen thousand. You going to talk to Howard today?

WILLY. Yeah. I'll put it to him straight and simple. He'll just have to
take me off the road.

LINDA. And Willy, don't forget to ask for a little advance, because
we've got the insurance premium. It's the grace period now.

WILLY. That's a hundred . . . ?

LINDA. A hundred and eight, sixty-eight. Because we're a little short again.

WILLY. Why are we short?

LINDA. Well, you had the motor job on the car . . .

WILLY. That goddam Studebaker!

LINDA. And you got one more payment on the refrigerator . . .

WILLY. But it just broke again!

LINDA. Well, it's old, dear.

WILLY. I told you we should've bought a well-advertised machine. Charley bought a General Electric and it's twenty years old and it's still good, that son-of-a-bitch.

LINDA. But, Willy—

WILLY. Whoever heard of a Hastings refrigerator? Once in my life I would like to own something outright before it's broken! I'm always in a race with the junkyard! I just finished paying for the car and it's on its last legs. The refrigerator consumes belts like a goddam maniac. They time those things. They time them so when you finally paid for them, they're used up.

LINDA [*buttoning up his jacket as he unbuttons it*]. All told, about two hundred dollars would carry us, dear. But that includes the last payment on the mortgage. After this payment, Willy, the house belongs to us.

WILLY. It's twenty-five years!

LINDA. Biff was nine years old when we bought it.

WILLY. Well, that's a great thing. To weather a twenty-five year mortgage is—

LINDA. It's an accomplishment.

WILLY. All the cement, the lumber, the reconstruction I put in this house! There ain't a crack to be found in it any more.

LINDA. Well, it served its purpose.

WILLY. What purpose? Some stranger'll come along, move in, and that's that. If only Biff would take this house, and raise a family . . . [*He starts to go.*] Good-by, I'm late.

LINDA [*suddenly remembering*]. Oh, I forgot! You're supposed to meet them for dinner.

WILLY. Me?

LINDA. At Frank's Chop House on Forty-eighth near Sixth Avenue.

WILLY. Is that so! How about you?

LINDA. No, just the three of you. They're gonna blow you to a big meal!

WILLY. Don't say! Who thought of that?

LINDA. Biff came to me this morning, Willy, and he said, "Tell Dad, we want to blow him to a big meal." Be there six o'clock. You and your two boys are going to have dinner.

WILLY. Gee whiz! That's really somethin'. I'm gonna knock Howard for a loop, kid. I'll get an advance, and I'll come home with a New York job. Goddammit, now I'm gonna do it!

LINDA. Oh, that's the spirit, Willy!

WILLY. I will never get behind a wheel the rest of my life!

LINDA. It's changing, Willy, I can feel it changing!

WILLY. Beyond a question. G'by, I'm late. [*He starts to go again.*]

LINDA [*calling after him as she runs to the kitchen table for a handkerchief*]. You got your glasses?

WILLY [*feels for them, then comes back in*]. Yeah, yeah, got my glasses.

LINDA [*giving him the handkerchief*]. And a handkerchief.

WILLY. Yeah, handkerchief.

LINDA. And your saccharine?

WILLY. Yeah, my saccharine.

LINDA. Be careful on the subway stairs.

[*She kisses him, and a silk stocking is seen hanging from her hand.* WILLY *notices it.*]

WILLY. Will you stop mending stockings? At least while I'm in the house. It gets me nervous. I can't tell you. Please.

[LINDA *hides the stocking in her hand as she follows* WILLY *across the forestage in front of the house.*]

LINDA. Remember, Frank's Chop House.

WILLY [*passing the apron*]. Maybe beets would grow out there.

LINDA [*laughing*]. But you tried so many times.

WILLY. Yeah. Well, don't work hard today. [*He disappears around the right corner of the house.*]

LINDA. Be careful!

[*As* WILLY *vanishes,* LINDA *waves to him. Suddenly the phone rings. She runs across the stage and into the kitchen and lifts it.*]

LINDA. Hello? Oh, Biff! I'm so glad you called, I just . . . Yes, sure, I told him. Yes, he'll be there for dinner at six o'clock, I didn't forget. Listen, I was just dying to tell you. You know that little rubber pipe I told you about? That he connected to the gas heater? I finally decided to go down the cellar this morning and take it away and destroy it. But it's gone! Imagine? He took it away himself, it isn't there! [*She listens.*] When? Oh, then you took it. Oh—nothing, it's just that I'd hoped he'd taken it away himself. Oh, I'm not worried, darling, because this morning he left in such high spirits, it was like the old days! I'm not afraid any more. Did Mr. Oliver see you? . . . Well, you wait there then. And make a nice impression on him, darling. Just don't perspire too much before you see him. And have a nice time with Dad. He may have big news too! . . . That's right, a New York job. And be sweet to him tonight, dear. Be loving to him. Because he's only a little boat looking for a harbor. [*She is trembling with sorrow and joy.*] Oh, that's wonderful, Biff, you'll save his life. Thanks, darling. Just put your arm around him when he comes into the restau-

rant. Give him a smile. That's the boy . . . Good-by, dear. . . .
You got your comb? . . . That's fine. Good-by, Biff dear.

[*In the middle of her speech, Howard Wagner, thirty-six, wheels on a small typewriter table on which is a wire-recording machine and proceeds to plug it in. This is on the left forestage. Light slowly fades on* LINDA *as it rises on* HOWARD. HOWARD *is intent on threading the machine and only glances over his shoulder as* WILLY *appears.*]

WILLY. Pst! Pst!

HOWARD. Hello, Willy, come in.

WILLY. Like to have a little talk with you, Howard.

HOWARD. Sorry to keep you waiting. I'll be with you in a minute.

WILLY. What's that, Howard?

HOWARD. Didn't you ever see one of these? Wire recorder.

WILLY. Oh. Can we talk a minute?

HOWARD. Records things. Just got delivery yesterday. Been driving me crazy, the most terrific machine I ever saw in my life. I was up all night with it.

WILLY. What do you do with it?

HOWARD. I bought it for dictation, but you can do anything with it. Listen to this. I had it home last night. Listen to what I picked up. The first one is my daughter. Get this. [*He flicks the switch and "Roll out the Barrel" is heard being whistled.*] Listen to that kid whistle.

WILLY. That is lifelike, isn't it?

HOWARD. Seven years old. Get that tone.

WILLY. Ts, ts. Like to ask a little favor of you . . .

[*The whistling breaks off, and the voice of* HOWARD'S *daughter is heard.*]

HIS DAUGHTER. "Now you, Daddy."

HOWARD. She's crazy for me! [*Again the same song is whistled.*] That's me! Ha! [*He winks.*]

WILLY. You're very good!

[*The whistling breaks off again. The machine runs silent for a moment.*]

HOWARD. Sh! Get this now, this is my son.

HIS SON. "The capital of Alabama is Montgomery; the capital of Arizona is Phoenix; the capital of Arkansas is Little Rock; the capital of California is Sacramento . . ." [*And on, and on.*]

HOWARD [*holding up five fingers*]. Five years old, Willy!

WILLY. He'll make an announcer some day!

HIS SON [*continuing*]. "The capital . . ."

HOWARD. Get that—alphabetical order! [*The machine breaks off suddenly.*] Wait a minute. The maid kicked the plug out.

WILLY. It certainly is a—

HOWARD. Sh, for God's sake!

HIS SON. "It's nine o'clock, Bulova watch time. So I have to go to sleep."

WILLY. That really is—

HOWARD. Wait a minute! The next is my wife.
[*They wait.*]

HOWARD'S VOICE. "Go on, say something." [*Pause.*] "Well, you gonna talk?"

HIS WIFE. "I can't think of anything."

HOWARD'S VOICE. "Well, talk—it's turning."

HIS WIFE [*shyly, beaten*]. "Hello." [*Silence.*] "Oh, Howard, I can't talk into this . . ."

HOWARD [*snapping the machine off*]. That was my wife.

WILLY. That is a wonderful machine. Can we—

HOWARD. I tell you, Willy, I'm gonna take my camera, and my band-saw, and all my hobbies, and out they go. This is the most fascinating relaxation I ever found.

WILLY. I think I'll get one myself.

HOWARD. Sure, they're only a hundred and a half. You can't do without it. Supposing you wanna hear Jack Benny, see? But you can't be at home at that hour. So you tell the maid to turn the radio on when Jack Benny comes on, and this automatically goes on with the radio . . .

WILLY. And when you come home you . . .

HOWARD. You can come home twelve o'clock, one o'clock, any time you like, and you get yourself a Coke and sit yourself down, throw the switch, and there's Jack Benny's program in the middle of the night!

WILLY. I'm definitely going to get one. Because lots of time I'm on the road, and I think to myself, what I must be missing on the radio!

HOWARD. Don't you have a radio in the car?

WILLY. Well, yeah, but whoever thinks of turning it on?

HOWARD. Say, aren't you supposed to be in Boston?

WILLY. That's what I want to talk to you about, Howard. You got a minute? [*He draws a chair in from the wing.*]

HOWARD. What happened? What're you doing here?

WILLY. Well . . .

HOWARD. You didn't crack up again, did you?

WILLY. Oh, no. No . . .

HOWARD. Geez, you had me worried there for a minute. What's the trouble?

WILLY. Well, tell you the truth, Howard. I've come to the decision that I'd rather not travel any more.

HOWARD. Not travel! Well, what'll you do?

WILLY. Remember, Christmas time, when you had the party here? You said you'd try to think of some spot for me here in town.

HOWARD. With us?

WILLY. Well, sure.

HOWARD. Oh, yeah, yeah. I remember. Well, I couldn't think of anything for you, Willy.

WILLY. I tell ya, Howard. The kids are all grown up, y'know. I don't need much any more. If I could take home—well, sixty-five dollars a week, I could swing it.

HOWARD. Yeah, but Willy, see I—

WILLY. I tell ya why, Howard. Speaking frankly and between the two of us, y'know—I'm just a little tired.

HOWARD. Oh, I could understand that, Willy. But you're a road man, Willy, and we do a road business. We've only got a half-dozen salesmen on the floor here.

WILLY. God knows, Howard, I never asked a favor of any man. But I was with the firm when your father used to carry you in here in his arms.

HOWARD. I know that, Willy, but—

WILLY. Your father came to me the day you were born and asked me what I thought of the name of Howard, may he rest in peace.

HOWARD. I appreciate that, Willy, but there just is no spot here for you. If I had a spot I'd slam you right in, but I just don't have a single solitary spot.

[*He looks for his lighter. Willy has picked it up and gives it to him.*] [*Pause.*]

WILLY [*with increasing anger*]. Howard, all I need to set my table is fifty dollars a week.

HOWARD. But where am I going to put you, kid?

WILLY. Look, it isn't a question of whether I can sell merchandise, is it?

HOWARD. No, but it's business, kid, and everybody's gotta pull his own weight.

WILLY [*desperately*]. Just let me tell you a story, Howard—

HOWARD. 'Cause you gotta admit, business is business.

WILLY [*angrily*]. Business is definitely business, but just listen for a minute. You don't understand this. When I was a boy—eighteen, nineteen—I was already on the road. And there was a question in my mind as to whether selling had a future for me. Because in those days I had a yearning to go to Alaska. See, there were three gold strikes in one month in Alaska, and I felt like going out. Just for the ride, you might say.

HOWARD [*barely interested*]. Don't say.

WILLY. Oh, yeah, my father lived many years in Alaska. He was an adventurous man. We've got quite a little streak of self-reliance in our family. I thought I'd go out with my older brother and try to locate him, and maybe settle in the North with the old man. And I was almost decided to go, when I met a salesman in the Parker House. His name was Dave Singleman. And he was eighty-four years old, and he'd drummed merchandise in thirty-one states. And old Dave, he'd go up to his room, y'understand, put on his green velvet slippers—I'll never forget—and pick up his phone and call the buyers, and without ever leaving his room, at the age of eighty-four, he made his living. And when I saw that, I realized that selling was the greatest career a man could want. 'Cause what could be more satisfying than to be able to go, at the age of eighty-four, into twenty or thirty different cities, and pick up a phone, and be remembered and loved and helped by so many different people? Do you know? when he died—and by the way he died the death of a salesman, in his green velvet slippers in the smoker of the New York, New Haven and Hartford, going into Boston— when he died, hundreds of salesmen and buyers were at his funeral. Things were sad on a lotta trains for months after that. [*He stands up. HOWARD has not looked at him.*] In those days there was personality in it, Howard. There was respect, and comradeship, and gratitude in it. Today, it's all cut and dried, and there's no chance for bringing friendship to bear—or personality. You see what I mean? They don't know me any more.

HOWARD [*moving away, to the right*]. That's just the thing, Willy.

WILLY. If I had forty dollars a week—that's all I'd need. Forty dollars, Howard.

HOWARD. Kid, I can't take blood from a stone, I—

WILLY [*desperation is on him now*]. Howard, the year Al Smith was nominated, your father came to me and—

HOWARD [*starting to go off*]. I've got to see some people, kid.

WILLY [*stopping him*]. I'm talking about your father! There were promises made across this desk! You mustn't tell me you've got people to see—I put thirty-four years into this firm, Howard, and now I can't pay my insurance! You can't eat the orange and throw the peel away— a man is not a piece of fruit! [*After a pause*] Now pay attention. Your father—in 1928 I had a big year. I averaged a hundred and seventy dollars a week in commissions.

HOWARD [*impatiently*]. Now, Willy, you never averaged—

WILLY [*banging his hand on the desk*]. I averaged a hundred and seventy dollars a week in the year of 1928! And your father came to me—or rather, I was in the office here—it was right over this desk—and he put his hand on my shoulder—

HOWARD [*getting up*]. You'll have to excuse me, Willy, I gotta see some people. Pull yourself together. [*Going out.*] I'll be back in a little while.

[*On HOWARD's exit, the light on his chair grows very bright and strange.*]

WILLY. Pull myself together! What the hell did I say to him? My God, I was yelling at him! How could I! [*WILLY breaks off, staring at the light, which occupies the chair, animating it. He approaches this chair, standing across the desk from it.*] Frank, Frank, don't you remember what you told me that time? How you put your hand on my shoulder, and Frank . . . [*He leans on the desk and as he speaks the dead man's name he accidentally switches on the recorder, and instantly*]

HOWARD'S SON. ". . . of New York is Albany. The capital of Ohio, is Cincinnati, the capital of Rhode Island is . . ." [*The recitation continues.*]

WILLY. [*leaping away with fright, shouting*]. Ha! Howard! Howard! Howard!

HOWARD [*rushing in*]. What happened?

WILLY [*pointing at the machine, which continues nasally, childishly, with the capital cities*]. Shut it off! Shut it off!

HOWARD [*pulling the plug out*]. Look, Willy . . .

WILLY [*pressing his hands to his eyes*]. I gotta get myself some coffee. I'll get some coffee . . .

[WILLY *starts to walk out*. HOWARD *stops him.*]

HOWARD [*rolling up the cord*]. Willy, look . . .

WILLY. I'll go to Boston.

HOWARD. Willy, you can't go to Boston for us.

WILLY. Why can't I go?

HOWARD. I don't want you to represent us. I've been meaning to tell you for a long time now.

WILLY. Howard, are you firing me?

HOWARD. I think you need a good long rest, Willy.

WILLY. Howard—

HOWARD. And when you feel better, come back, and we'll see if we can work something out.

WILLY. But I gotta earn money, Howard. I'm in no position to—

HOWARD. Where are your sons? Why don't your sons give you a hand?

WILLY. They're working on a very big deal.

HOWARD. This is no time for false pride, Willy. You go to your sons and you tell them that you're tired. You've got two great boys, haven't you?

WILLY. Oh, no question, no question, but in the meantime . . .

HOWARD. Then that's that, heh?

WILLY. All right, I'll go to Boston tomorrow.

HOWARD. No, no.

WILLY. I can't throw myself on my sons. I'm not a cripple!

HOWARD. Look, kid, I'm busy this morning.

WILLY [*grasping* HOWARD's *arm*]. Howard, you've got to let me go to Boston!

HOWARD [*hard, keeping himself under control*]. I've got a line of people to see this morning. Sit down, take five minutes, and pull yourself together, and then go home, will ya? I need the office, Willy. [*He starts to go, turns, remembering the recorder, starts to push off the table holding the recorder.*] Oh, yeah. Whenever you can this week, stop by and drop off the samples. You'll feel better, Willy, and then come back and we'll talk. Pull yourself together, kid, there's people outside.

[HOWARD *exits, pushing the table off left*. WILLY *stares into space, ex-*

hausted. Now the music is heard—BEN's music—first distantly, then closer, closer. As WILLY speaks, BEN enters from the right. He carries valise and umbrella.]

WILLY. Oh, Ben, how did you do it? What is the answer? Did you wind up the Alaska deal already?

BEN. Doesn't take much time if you know what you're doing. Just a short business trip. Boarding ship in an hour. Wanted to say good-by.

WILLY. Ben, I've got to talk to you.

BEN [*glancing at his watch*]. Haven't the time, William.

WILLY [*crossing the apron to* BEN]. Ben, nothing's working out. I don't know what to do.

BEN. Now, look here, William. I've bought timberland in Alaska and I need a man to look after things for me.

WILLY. God, timberland! Me and my boys in those grand outdoors!

BEN. You've a new continent at your doorstep, William. Get out of these cities, they're full of talk and time payments and courts of law. Screw on your fists and you can fight for a fortune up there.

WILLY. Yes, yes! Linda, Linda!

[LINDA *enters as of old, with the wash.*]

LINDA. Oh, you're back?

BEN. I haven't much time.

WILLY. No, wait! Linda, he's got a proposition for me in Alaska.

LINDA. But you've got— [*To* BEN] He's got a beautiful job here.

WILLY. But in Alaska, kid, I could—

LINDA. You're doing well enough, Willy!

BEN [*to* LINDA]. Enough for what, my dear?

LINDA [*frightened of* BEN *and angry at him*]. Don't say those things to him! Enough to be happy right here, right now. [*To* WILLY, *while* BEN *laughs*] Why must everybody conquer the world? You're well liked, and the boys love you, and someday— [*To* BEN]—why, old man Wagner told him just the other day that if he keeps it up he'll be a member of the firm, didn't he, Willy?

WILLY. Sure, sure. I am building something with this firm, Ben, and if a man is building something he must be on the right track, mustn't he?

BEN. What are you building? Lay your hand on it. Where is it?

WILLY [*hesitantly*]. That's true, Linda, there's nothing.

LINDA. Why? [*To* BEN] There's a man eighty-four years old—

WILLY. That's right, Ben, that's right. When I look at that man I say, what is there to worry about?

BEN. Bah!

WILLY. It's true, Ben. All he has to do is go into any city, pick up the phone, and he's making his living and you know why?

BEN [*picking up his valise*]. I've got to go.

WILLY [*holding* BEN *back*]. Look at this boy!

[BIFF, *in his high school sweater, enters carrying suitcase.* HAPPY *carries* BIFF's *shoulder guards, gold helmet, and football pants.*]

WILLY. Without a penny to his name, three great universities are begging for him, and from there the sky's the limit, because it's not what you do, Ben. It's who you know and the smile on your face! It's contacts, Ben, contacts! The whole wealth of Alaska passes over the lunch table at the Commodore Hotel, and that's the wonder, the wonder of this country, that a man can end with diamonds here on the basis of being liked! [*He turns to* BIFF.] And that's why when you get out on that field today it's important. Because thousands of people will be rooting for you and loving you. [*To* BEN, *who has again begun to leave*] And Ben! when he walks into a business office his name will sound out like a bell and all the doors will open to him! I've seen it, Ben, I've seen it a thousand times! You can't feel it with your hand like timber, but it's there!

BEN. Good-by, William.

WILLY. Ben, am I right? Don't you think I'm right? I value your advice.

BEN. There's a new continent at your doorstep, William. You could walk out rich. Rich! [*He is gone.*]

WILLY. We'll do it here, Ben! You hear me? We're gonna do it here! [*Young* BERNARD *rushes in. The gay music of the* BOYS *is heard.*]

BERNARD. Oh, gee, I was afraid you left already!

WILLY. Why? What time is it?

BERNARD. It's half-past one!

WILLY. Well, come on, everybody! Ebbets Field next stop! Where's the pennants? [*He rushes through the wall-line of the kitchen and out into the living-room.*]

LINDA [*to* BIFF]. Did you pack fresh underwear?

BIFF [*who has been limbering up*]. I want to go!

BERNARD. Biff, I'm carrying your helmet, ain't I?

HAPPY. No, I'm carrying the helmet.

BERNARD. Oh, Biff, you promised me.

HAPPY. I'm carrying the helmet.

BERNARD. How am I going to get in the locker room?

LINDA. Let him carry the shoulder guards. [*She puts her coat and hat on in the kitchen.*]

BERNARD. Can I, Biff? 'Cause I told everybody I'm going to be in the locker room.

HAPPY. In Ebbets Field it's the clubhouse.

BERNARD. I meant the clubhouse. Biff!

HAPPY. Biff!

BIFF [*grandly, after a slight pause.*] Let him carry the shoulder guards.

HAPPY [*as he gives* BERNARD *the shoulder guards*]. Stay close to us now. [WILLY *rushes in with the pennants.*]

WILLY [*handing them out*]. Everybody wave when Biff comes out on
the field. [HAPPY *and* BERNARD *run off.*] You set now, boy?
[*The music has died away.*]

BIFF. Ready to go, Pop. Every muscle is ready.

WILLY [*at the edge of the apron*]. You realize what this means?

BIFF. That's right, Pop.

WILLY [*feeling* BIFF'S *muscles*]. You're comin' home this afternoon
captain of the All-Scholastic Championship Team of the City of New
York.

BIFF. I got it, Pop. And remember, pal, when I take off my helmet,
that touchdown is for you.

WILLY. Let's go! [*He is starting out, with his arm around* BIFF, *when*
CHARLEY *enters, as of old, in knickers.*] I got no room for you, Charley.

CHARLEY. Room? For what?

WILLY. In the car.

CHARLEY. You goin' for a ride? I wanted to shoot some casino.

WILLY [*furiously*]. Casino! [*Incredulously.*] Don't you realize what
today is?

LINDA. Oh, he knows, Willy. He's just kidding you.

WILLY. That's nothing to kid about!

CHARLEY. No, Linda, what's goin' on?

LINDA. He's playing in Ebbets Field.

CHARLEY. Baseball in this weather?

WILLY. Don't talk to him. Come on, come on! [*He is pushing them
out.*]

CHARLEY. Wait a minute, didn't you hear the news?

WILLY. What?

CHARLEY. Don't you listen to the radio? Ebbets Field just blew up.

WILLY. You go to hell! [CHARLEY *laughs. Pushing them out.*] Come
on, come on! We're late.

CHARLEY [*as they go*]. Knock a homer, Biff, knock a homer!

WILLY [*the last to leave, turning to* CHARLEY]. I don't think that was
funny, Charley. This is the greatest day of his life.

CHARLEY. Willy, when are you going to grow up?

WILLY. Yeah, heh? When this game is over, Charley, you'll be laughing out of the other side of your face. They'll be calling him another
Red Grange. Twenty-five thousand a year.

CHARLEY [*kidding*]. Is that so?

WILLY. Yeah, that's so.

CHARLEY. Well, then, I'm sorry, Willy. But tell me something.

WILLY. What?

CHARLEY. Who is Red Grange?

WILLY. Put up your hands. Goddam you, put up your hands!
[CHARLEY, *chuckling, shakes his head and walks away, around the left
corner of the stage.* WILLY *follows him. The music rises to a mocking
frenzy.*]

WILLY. Who the hell do you think you are, better than everybody else? You don't know everything, you big, ignorant, stupid . . . Put up your hands!

[*Light rises, on the right side of the forestage, on a small table in the reception room of* CHARLEY'S *office. Traffic sounds are heard.* BERNARD, *now mature, sits whistling to himself. A pair of tennis rackets and an overnight bag are on the floor beside him.*]

WILLY [*offstage*]. What are you walking away for? Don't walk away! If you're going to say something say it to my face! I know you laugh at me behind my back. You'll laugh out of the other side of your goddam face after this game. Touchdown! Touchdown! Eighty thousand people! Touchdown! Right between the goal posts.

[BERNARD *is a quiet, earnest, but self-assured young man.* WILLY'S *voice is coming from right upstage now.* BERNARD *lowers his feet off the table and listens.* JENNY, *his father's secretary, enters.*]

JENNY [*distressed*]. Say, Bernard, will you go out in the hall?

BERNARD. What is that noise? Who is it?

JENNY. Mr. Loman. He just got off the elevator.

BERNARD [*getting up*]. Who's he arguing with?

JENNY. Nobody. There's nobody with him. I can't deal with him any more, and your father gets all upset every time he comes. I've got a lot of typing to do, and your father's waiting to sign it. Will you see him?

WILLY [*entering*]. Touchdown! Touch— [*He sees* JENNY.] Jenny, Jenny, good to see you. How're ya? Workin'? Or still honest?

JENNY. Fine. How've you been feeling?

WILLY. Not much any more, Jenny. Ha, Ha! [*He is surprised to see the rackets.*]

BERNARD. Hello, Uncle Willy.

WILLY [*almost shocked*]. Bernard! Well, look who's here! [*He comes quickly, guiltily, to* BERNARD *and warmly shakes his hand.*]

BERNARD. How are you? Good to see you.

WILLY. What are you doing here?

BERNARD. Oh, just stopped by to see Pop. Get off my feet till my train leaves. I'm going to Washington in a few minutes.

WILLY. Is he in?

BERNARD. Yes, he's in his office with the accountant. Sit down.

WILLY [*sitting down*]. What're you going to do in Washington?

BERNARD. Oh, just a case I've got there, Willy.

WILLY. That so? [*Indicating the rackets*] You going to play tennis there?

BERNARD. I'm staying with a friend who's got a court.

WILLY. Don't say. His own tennis court. Must be fine people, I bet.

BERNARD. They are, very nice. Dad tells me Biff's in town.

WILLY [*with a big smile*]. Yeah, Biff's in. Working on a very big deal, Bernard.

BERNARD. What's Biff doing?

WILLY. Well, he's been doing very big things in the West. But he decided to establish himself here. Very big. We're having dinner. Did I hear your wife had a boy?

BERNARD. That's right. Our second.

WILLY. Two boys! What do you know!

BERNARD. What kind of a deal has Biff got?

WILLY. Well, Bill Oliver—very big sporting-goods man—he wants Biff very badly. Called him in from the West. Long distance, carte blanche, special deliveries. Your friends have their own private tennis court?

BERNARD. You still with the old firm, Willy?

WILLY [after a pause]. I'm—I'm overjoyed to see how you made the grade, Bernard, overjoyed. It's an encouraging thing to see a young man really—really—Looks very good for Biff—very—[He breaks off, then] Bernard— [He is so full of emotion, he breaks off again.]

BERNARD. What is it, Willy?

WILLY [small and alone]. What—what's the secret?

BERNARD. What secret?

WILLY. How—how did you? Why didn't he ever catch on?

BERNARD. I wouldn't know that, Willy.

WILLY [confidentially, desperately]. You were his friend, his boyhood friend. There's something I don't understand about it. His life ended after that Ebbets Field game. From the age of seventeen nothing good ever happened to him.

BERNARD. He never trained himself for anything.

WILLY. But he did, he did. After high school he took so many correspondence courses. Radio mechanics; television; God knows what, and never made the slightest mark.

BERNARD [taking off his glasses]. Willy, do you want to talk candidly?

WILLY [rising, faces BERNARD]. I regard you as a very brilliant man, Bernard. I value your advice.

BERNARD. Oh, the hell with the advice, Willy. I couldn't advise you. There's just one thing I've always wanted to ask you. When he was supposed to graduate, and the math teacher flunked him—

WILLY. Oh, that son-of-a-bitch ruined his life.

BERNARD. Yeah, but, Willy, all he had to do was go to summer school and make up that subject.

WILLY. That's right, that's right.

BERNARD. Did you tell him not to go to summer school?

WILLY. Me? I begged him to go. I ordered him to go!

BERNARD. Then why wouldn't he go?

WILLY. Why? Why! Bernard, that question has been trailing me like a ghost for the last fifteen years. He flunked the subject, and laid down and died like a hammer hit him!

BERNARD. Take it easy, kid.

WILLY. Let me talk to you—I got nobody to talk to. Bernard, Bernard, was it my fault? Y'see? It keeps going around in my mind, maybe I did something to him. I got nothing to give him.

BERNARD. Don't take it so hard.

WILLY Why did he lay down? What is the story there? You were his friend!

BERNARD. Willy, I remember, it was June, and our grades came out. And he'd flunked math.

WILLY. That son-of-a-bitch!

BERNARD. No, it wasn't right then. Biff just got very angry, I remember, and he was ready to enroll in summer school.

WILLY [*surprised*]. He was?

BERNARD. He wasn't beaten by it at all. But then, Willy, he disappeared from the block for almost a month. And I got the idea that he'd gone up to New England to see you. Did he have a talk with you then?

[WILLY *stares in silence.*]

BERNARD. Willy?

WILLY [*with a strong edge of resentment in his voice*]. Yeah, he came to Boston. What about it?

BERNARD. Well, just that when he came back—I'll never forget this, it always mystifies me. Because I'd thought so well of Biff, even though he'd always taken advantage of me. I loved him, Willy, y'know? And he came back after that month and took his sneakers— remember those sneakers with "University of Virginia" printed on them? He was so proud of those, wore them every day. And he took them down in the cellar, and burned them up in the furnace. We had a fist fight. It lasted at least half an hour. Just the two of us, punching each other down the cellar, and crying right through it. I've often thought of how strange it was that I knew he'd given up his life. What happened in Boston, Willy?

[WILLY *looks at him as at an intruder.*]

BERNARD. I just bring it up because you asked me.

WILLY [*angrily*]. Nothing. What do you mean, "What happened?" What's that got to do with anything?

BERNARD. Well, don't get sore.

WILLY. What are you trying to do, blame it on me? If a boy lays down is that my fault?

BERNARD. Now, Willy, don't get—

WILLY. Well, don't—don't talk to me that way! What does that mean, "What happened?"

[CHARLEY *enters. He is in his vest, and he carries a bottle of bourbon.*]

CHARLEY. Hey, you're going to miss that train. [*He waves the bottle.*]

BERNARD. Yeah, I'm going. [*He takes the bottle.*] Thanks, Pop. [*He picks up his rackets and bag.*] Good-by, Willy, and don't worry about it. You know, "If at first you don't succeed . . . ."

WILLY. Yes, I believe in that.

BERNARD. But sometimes, Willy, it's better for a man just to walk away.

WILLY. Walk away?

BERNARD. That's right.

WILLY. But if you can't walk away?

BERNARD [*after a slight pause*]. I guess that's when it's tough. [*Extending his hand*] Good-by, Willy.

WILLY [*shaking* BERNARD'S *hand*]. Good-by, boy.

CHARLEY [*an arm on* BERNARD'S *shoulder*]. How do you like this kid? Gonna argue a case in front of the Supreme Court.

BERNARD [*protesting*]. Pop!

WILLY [*genuinely shocked, pained, and happy*]. No! The Supreme Court!

BERNARD. I gotta run. 'By, Dad!

CHARLEY. Knock 'em dead, Bernard!

[BERNARD *goes off.*]

WILLY [*as* CHARLEY *takes out his wallet*]. The Supreme Court! And he didn't even mention it!

CHARLEY [*counting out money on the desk*]. He don't have to—he's gonna do it.

WILLY. And you never told him what to do, did you? You never took any interest in him.

CHARLEY. My salvation is that I never took any interest in anything. There's some money—fifty dollars. I got an accountant inside.

WILLY. Charley, look . . . [*With difficulty*] I got my insurance to pay. If you can manage it—I need a hundred and ten dollars.

[CHARLEY *doesn't reply for a moment; merely stops moving.*]

WILLY. I'd draw it from my bank but Linda would know, and I . . .

CHARLEY. Sit down, Willy.

WILLY [*moving toward the chair*]. I'm keeping an account of everything, remember. I'll pay every penny back. [*He sits.*]

CHARLEY. Now listen to me, Willy.

WILLY. I want you to know I appreciate . . .

CHARLEY [*sitting down on the table*]. Willy, what're you doin'? What the hell is goin' on in your head?

WILLY. Why? I'm simply . . .

CHARLEY. I offered you a job. You can make fifty dollars a week. And I won't send you on the road.

WILLY. I've got a job.

CHARLEY. Without pay? What kind of a job is a job without pay? [*He rises.*] Now, look, kid, enough is enough. I'm no genius but I know when I'm being insulted.

WILLY. Insulted!

CHARLEY. Why don't you want to work for me?

WILLY. What's the matter with you? I've got a job.

CHARLEY. Then what're you walkin' in here every week for?

WILLY [*getting up*]. Well, if you don't want me to walk in here—

CHARLEY. I am offering you a job.

WILLY. I don't want your goddam job!

CHARLEY. When the hell are you going to grow up?

WILLY [*furiously*]. You big ignoramus, if you say that to me again I'll rap you one! I don't care how big you are! [*He's ready to fight.*] [*Pause.*]

CHARLEY [*kindly, going to him*]. How much do you need, Willy?

WILLY. Charley, I'm strapped, I'm strapped. I don't know what to do. I was just fired.

CHARLEY. Howard fired you?

WILLY. That snotnose. Imagine that? I named him. I named him Howard.

CHARLEY. Willy, when're you gonna realize that them things don't mean anything? You named him Howard, but you can't sell that. The only thing you got in this world is what you can sell. And the funny thing is that you're a salesman, and you don't know that.

WILLY. I've always tried to think otherwise, I guess. I always felt that if a man was impressive, and well liked, that nothing—

CHARLEY. Why must everybody like you? Who liked J. P. Morgan? Was he impressive? In a Turkish bath he'd look like a butcher. But with his pockets on he was very well liked. Now listen, Willy, I know you don't like me, and nobody can say I'm in love with you, but I'll give you a job because—just for the hell of it, put it that way. Now what do you say?

WILLY. I—I just can't work for you, Charley.

CHARLEY. What're you, jealous of me?

WILLY. I can't work for you, that's all, don't ask me why.

CHARLEY [*angered, takes out more bills*]. You been jealous of me all your life, you damned fool! Here, pay your insurance. [*He puts the money in* WILLY's *hand.*]

WILLY. I'm keeping strict accounts.

CHARLEY. I've got some work to do. Take care of yourself. And pay your insurance.

WILLY [*moving to the right*]. Funny, y'know? After all the highways, and the trains, and the appointments, and the years, you end up worth more dead than alive.

CHARLEY. Willy, nobody's worth nothin' dead. [*After a slight pause*] Did you hear what I said?

[WILLY *stands still, dreaming.*]

CHARLEY. Willy!

WILLY. Apologize to Bernard for me when you see him. I didn't mean to argue with him. He's a fine boy. They're all fine boys, and they'll end up big—all of them. Someday they'll all play tennis together. Wish me luck, Charley. He saw Bill Oliver today.

CHARLEY. Good luck.

WILLY [*on the verge of tears*]. Charley, you're the only friend I got. Isn't that a remarkable thing? [*He goes out.*]

CHARLEY. Jesus!

[CHARLEY *stares after him a moment and follows. All light blacks out. Suddenly raucous music is heard, and a red glow rises behind the screen at right.* STANLEY, *a young waiter, appears, carrying a table, followed by* HAPPY, *who is carrying two chairs.*]

STANLEY [*putting the table down*]. That's all right, Mr. Loman, I can handle it myself. [*He turns and takes the chairs from* HAPPY *and places them at the table.*]

HAPPY [*glancing around*]. Oh, this is better.

STANLEY. Sure, in the front there you're in the middle of all kinds a noise. Whenever you got a party, Mr. Loman, you just tell me and I'll put you back here. Y'know, there's a lotta people they don't like it private, because when they go out they like to see a lotta action around them because they're sick and tired to stay in the house by theirself. But I know you, you ain't from Hackensack. You know what I mean?

HAPPY [*sitting down*]. So how's it coming, Stanley?

STANLEY. Ah, it's a dog's life. I only wish during the war they'd a took me in the Army. I coulda been dead by now.

HAPPY. My brother's back, Stanley.

STANLEY. Oh, he come back, heh? From the Far West.

HAPPY. Yeah, big cattle man, my brother, so treat him right. And my father's coming too.

STANLEY. Oh, your father too!

HAPPY. You got a couple of nice lobsters?

STANLEY. Hundred per cent, big.

HAPPY. I want them with the claws.

STANLEY. Don't worry, I don't give you no mice. [HAPPY *laughs.*] How about some wine? It'll put a head on the meal.

HAPPY. No. You remember, Stanley, that recipe I brought you from overseas? With the champagne in it?

STANLEY. Oh, yeah, sure. I still got it tacked up yet in the kitchen. But that'll have to cost a buck apiece anyways.

HAPPY. That's all right.

STANLEY. What'd you, hit a number or somethin'?

HAPPY. No, it's a little celebration. My brother is—I think he pulled off a big deal today. I think we're going into business together.

STANLEY. Great! That's the best for you. Because a family business, you know what I mean?—that's the best.

HAPPY. That's what I think.

STANLEY. 'Cause what's the difference? Somebody steals? It's in the family. Know what I mean? [*Sotto voce*] Like this bartender here. The boss is goin' crazy what kinda leak he's got in the cash register. You put it in but it don't come out.

HAPPY [*raising his head*]. Sh!

STANLEY. What?

HAPPY. You notice I wasn't lookin' right or left, was I?

STANLEY. No.

HAPPY. And my eyes are closed.

STANLEY. So what's the—?

HAPPY. Strudel's comin'.

STANLEY [*catching on, looks around*]. Ah, no, there's no—
[*He breaks off as a furred, lavishly dressed girl enters and sits at the next table. Both follow her with their eyes.*]

STANLEY. Geez, how'd ya know?

HAPPY. I got radar or something. [*Staring directly at her profile*] Oooooooo . . . Stanley.

STANLEY. I think that's for you, Mr. Loman.

HAPPY. Look at that mouth. Oh, God. And the binoculars.

STANLEY. Geez, you got a life, Mr. Loman.

HAPPY. Wait on her.

STANLEY [*going to the* GIRL'*s table*]. Would you like a menu, ma'am?

GIRL. I'm expecting someone, but I'd like a—

HAPPY. Why don't you bring her—excuse me, miss, do you mind? I sell champagne, and I'd like you to try my brand. Bring her a champagne, Stanley.

GIRL. That's awfully nice of you.

HAPPY. Don't mention it. It's all company money. [*He laughs.*]

GIRL. That's a charming product to be selling, isn't it?

HAPPY. Oh, gets to be like everything else. Selling is selling, y'know.

GIRL. I suppose.

HAPPY. You don't happen to sell, do you?

GIRL. No, I don't sell.

HAPPY. Would you object to a compliment from a stranger? You ought to be on a magazine cover.

GIRL [*looking at him a little archly*]. I have been.
[STANLEY *comes in with a glass of champagne.*]

HAPPY. What'd I say before, Stanley? You see? She's a cover girl.

STANLEY. Oh, I could see. I could see.

HAPPY [*to the* GIRL]. What magazine?

GIRL. Oh, a lot of them. [*She takes the drink.*] Thank you.

HAPPY. You know what they say in France, don't you? "Champagne is the drink of the complexion"—Hya, Biff!
[BIFF *has entered and sits with* HAPPY.]

BIFF. Hello, kid. Sorry I'm late.

HAPPY. I just got here. Uh, Miss—?

GIRL. Forsythe.

HAPPY. Miss Forsythe, this is my brother.

BIFF. Is Dad here?

HAPPY. His name is Biff. You might've heard of him. Great football player.

GIRL. Really? What team?

HAPPY. Are you familiar with football?

GIRL. No, I'm afraid I'm not.

HAPPY. Biff is quarterback with the New York Giants.

GIRL. Well, that is nice, isn't it? [*She drinks.*]

HAPPY. Good health.

GIRL. I'm happy to meet you.

HAPPY. That's my name. Hap. It's really Harold, but at West Point they call me Happy.

GIRL [*now really impressed*]. Oh, I see. How do you do? [*She turns her profile.*]

BIFF. Isn't Dad coming?

HAPPY. You want her?

BIFF. Oh, I could never make that.

HAPPY. I remember the time that idea would never come into your head. Where's the old confidence, Biff?

BIFF. I just saw Oliver—

HAPPY. Wait a minute. I've got to see that old confidence again. Do you want her? She's on call.

BIFF. Oh, no. [*He turns to look at the* GIRL.]

HAPPY. I'm telling you. Watch this. [*Turning to the* GIRL.] Honey? [*She turns to him.*] Are you busy?

GIRL. Well, I am . . . but I could make a phone call.

HAPPY. Do that, will you, honey? And see if you can get a friend. We'll be here for a while. Biff is one of the greatest football players in the country.

GIRL [*standing up*]. Well, I'm certainly happy to meet you.

HAPPY. Come back soon.

GIRL. I'll try.

HAPPY. Don't try, honey, try hard.

[*The* GIRL *exits.* STANLEY *follows, shaking his head in bewildered admiration.*]

HAPPY. Isn't that a shame now? A beautiful girl like that? That's why I can't get married. There's not a good woman in a thousand. New York is loaded with them, kid!

BIFF. Hap, look—

HAPPY. I told you she was on call!

BIFF [*strangely unnerved*]. Cut it out, will ya? I want to say something to you.

HAPPY. Did you see Oliver?

BIFF. I saw him all right. Now look, I want to tell Dad a couple of things and I want you to help me.

HAPPY. What? Is he going to back you?

BIFF. Are you crazy? You're out of your goddam head, you know that?

HAPPY. Why? What happened?

BIFF [*breathlessly*]. I did a terrible thing today, Hap. It's been the strangest day I ever went through. I'm all numb, I swear.

HAPPY. You mean he wouldn't see you?

BIFF. Well, I waited six hours for him, see? All day. Kept sending my name in. Even tried to date his secretary so she'd get me to him, but no soap.

HAPPY. Because you're not showin' the old confidence, Biff. He remembered you, didn't he?

BIFF [*stopping* HAPPY *with a gesture*]. Finally, about five o'clock, he comes out. Didn't remember who I was or anything. I felt like such an idiot, Hap.

HAPPY. Did you tell him my Florida idea?

BIFF. He walked away. I saw him for one minute. I got so mad I could've torn the walls down! How the hell did I ever get the idea I was a salesman there? I even believed myself that I'd been a salesman for him! And then he gave me one look and—I realized what a ridiculous lie my whole life has been! We've been talking in a dream for fifteen years. I was a shipping clerk.

HAPPY. What'd you do?

BIFF [*with great tension and wonder*]. Well, he left, see. And the secretary went out. I was all alone in the waiting-room. I don't know what came over me, Hap. The next thing I know I'm in his office—paneled walls, everything. I can't explain it. I—Hap, I took his fountain pen.

HAPPY. Geez, did he catch you?

BIFF. I ran out. I ran down all eleven flights. I ran and ran and ran.

HAPPY. That was an awful dumb—what'd you do that for?

BIFF [*agonized*]. I don't know, I just—wanted to take something, I don't know. You gotta help me, Hap, I'm gonna tell Pop.

HAPPY. You crazy? What for?

BIFF. Hap, he's got to understand that I'm not the man somebody lends that kind of money to. He thinks I've been spiting him all these years and it's eating him up.

HAPPY. That's just it. You tell him something nice.

BIFF. I can't.

HAPPY. Say you got a lunch date with Oliver tomorrow.

BIFF. So what do I do tomorrow?

HAPPY. You leave the house tomorrow and come back at night and say Oliver is thinking it over. And he thinks it over for a couple of weeks, and gradually it fades away and nobody's the worse.

BIFF. But it'll go on forever!

HAPPY. Dad is never so happy as when he's looking forward to something!

[WILLY *enters*.]

HAPPY. Hello, scout!

WILLY. Gee, I haven't been here in years!
[STANLEY *has followed* WILLY *in and sets a chair for him.* STANLEY
starts off but HAPPY *stops him.*]
HAPPY. Stanley!
[STANLEY *stands by, waiting for an order.*]
BIFF [*going to* WILLY *with guilt, as to an invalid*]. Sit down, Pop. You
want a drink?
WILLY. Sure, I don't mind.
BIFF. Let's get a load on.
WILLY. You look worried.
BIFF. N-no. [*To* STANLEY] Scotch all around. Make it doubles.
STANLEY. Doubles, right. [*He goes.*]
WILLY. You had a couple already, didn't you?
BIFF. Just a couple, yeah.
WILLY. Well, what happened, boy? [*Nodding affirmatively, with a
smile.*] Everything go all right?
BIFF [*takes a breath, then reaches out and grasps* WILLY's *hand*]. Pal
. . . [*He is smiling bravely, and* WILLY *is smiling too.*] I had an ex-
perience today.
HAPPY. Terrific, Pop.
WILLY. That so? What happened?
BIFF [*high, slightly alcoholic, above the earth*]. I'm going to tell you every-
thing from first to last. It's been a strange day. [*Silence. He looks around,
composes himself as best he can, but his breath keeps breaking the rhythm of
his voice.*] I had to wait quite a while for him, and—
WILLY. Oliver?
BIFF. Yeah, Oliver. All day, as a matter of cold fact. And a lot of—
instances—facts, Pop, facts about my life came back to me. Who was
it, Pop? Who ever said I was a salesman with Oliver?
WILLY. Well, you were.
BIFF. No, Dad, I was a shipping clerk.
WILLY. But you were practically—
BIFF [*with determination*]. Dad, I don't know who said it first, but I
was never a salesman for Bill Oliver.
WILLY. What're you talking about?
BIFF. Let's hold on to the facts tonight, Pop. We're not going to get
anywhere bullin' around. I was a shipping clerk.
WILLY [*angrily*]. All right, now listen to me—
BIFF. Why don't you let me finish?
WILLY. I'm not interested in stories about the past or any crap of that
kind because the woods are burning, boys, you understand? There's a
big blaze going on all around. I was fired today.
BIFF [*shocked*]. How could you be?
WILLY. I was fired, and I'm looking for a little good news to tell your
mother, because the woman has waited and the woman has suffered.

The gist of it is that I haven't got a story left in my head, Biff. So don't give me a lecture about facts and aspects. I am not interested. Now what've you got to say to me?

[STANLEY *enters with three drinks. They wait until he leaves.*]

WILLY. Did you see Oliver?

BIFF. Jesus, Dad!

WILLY. You mean you didn't go up there?

HAPPY. Sure he went up there.

BIFF. I did. I—saw him. How could they fire you?

WILLY [*on the edge of his chair*]. What kind of a welcome did he give you?

BIFF. He won't even let you work on commission?

WILLY. I'm out! [*Driving*] So tell me, he gave you a warm welcome?

HAPPY. Sure, Pop, sure!

BIFF [*driven*]. Well, it was kind of—

WILLY. I was wondering if he'd remember you. [*To* HAPPY] Imagine, man doesn't see him for ten, twelve years and gives him that kind of a welcome!

HAPPY. Damn right!

BIFF [*trying to return to the offensive*]. Pop, look—

WILLY. You know why he remembered you, don't you? Because you impressed him in those days.

BIFF. Let's talk quietly and get this down to the facts, huh?

WILLY [*as though* BIFF *had been interrupting*]. Well, what happened? It's great news, Biff. Did he take you into his office or'd you talk in the waiting-room?

BIFF. Well, he came in, see, and—

WILLY [*with a big smile*]. What'd he say? Betcha he threw his arm around you.

BIFF. Well, he kinda—

WILLY. He's a fine man. [*To* HAPPY] Very hard man to see, y'know.

HAPPY [*agreeing*]. Oh, I know.

WILLY [*to* BIFF]. Is that where you had the drinks?

BIFF. Yeah, he gave me a couple of—no, no!

HAPPY [*cutting in*]. He told him my Florida idea.

WILLY. Don't interrupt. [*To* BIFF] How'd he react to the Florida idea?

BIFF. Dad, will you give me a minute to explain?

WILLY. I've been waiting for you to explain since I sat down here! What happened? He took you into his office and what?

BIFF. Well—I talked. And—and he listened, see.

WILLY. Famous for the way he listens, y'know. What was his answer?

BIFF. His answer was— [*He breaks off, suddenly angry.*] Dad, you're not letting me tell you what I want to tell you!

WILLY [*accusing, angered*]. You didn't see him, did you?

1548]   DRAMA

BIFF. I did see him!

WILLY. What'd you insult him or something? You insulted him, didn't you?

BIFF. Listen, will you let me out of it, will you just let me out of it!

HAPPY. What the hell!

WILLY. Tell me what happened!

BIFF [to HAPPY]. I can't talk to him!

[*A single trumpet note jars the ear. The light of green leaves stains the house, which holds the air of night and a dream.* YOUNG BERNARD *enters and knocks on the door of the house.*]

YOUNG BERNARD [*frantically*]. Mrs. Loman, Mrs. Loman!

HAPPY. Tell him what happened!

BIFF [to HAPPY]. Shut up and leave me alone!

WILLY. No, no! You had to go and flunk math!

BIFF. What math? What're you talking about?

YOUNG BERNARD. Mrs. Loman, Mrs. Loman!

[LINDA *appears in the house, as of old.*]

WILLY [*wildly*]. Math, math, math!

BIFF. Take it easy, Pop!

YOUNG BERNARD. Mrs. Loman!

WILLY [*furiously*]. If you hadn't flunked you'd've been set by now!

BIFF. Now, look, I'm gonna tell you what happened, and you're going to listen to me.

YOUNG BERNARD. Mrs. Loman!

BIFF. I waited six hours—

HAPPY. What the hell are you saying?

BIFF. I kept sending in my name but he wouldn't see me. So finally he . . . [*He continues unheard as light fades low on the restaurant.*]

YOUNG BERNARD. Biff flunked math!

LINDA. No!

YOUNG BERNARD. Birnbaum flunked him! They won't graduate him!

LINDA. But they have to. He's gotta go to the university. Where is he? Biff! Biff!

YOUNG BERNARD. No, he left. He went to Grand Central.

LINDA. Grand— You mean he went to Boston!

YOUNG BERNARD. Is Uncle Willy in Boston?

LINDA. Oh, maybe Willy can talk to the teacher. Oh, the poor, poor boy!

[*Light on house area snaps out.*]

BIFF [*at the table, now audible, holding up a gold fountain pen*]. . . . so I'm washed up with Oliver, you understand? Are you listening to me?

WILLY [*at a loss*]. Yeah, sure. If you hadn't flunked—

BIFF. Flunked what? What're you talking about?

WILLY. Don't blame everything on me! I didn't flunk math—you did! What pen?

HAPPY. That was awful dumb, Biff, a pen like that is worth—
WILLY [*seeing the pen for the first time*]. You took Oliver's pen?
BIFF [*weakening*]. Dad, I just explained it to you.
WILLY. You stole Bill Oliver's fountain pen!
BIFF. I didn't exactly steal it! That's just what I've been explaining to you!
HAPPY. He had it in his hand and just then Oliver walked in, so he got nervous and stuck it in his pocket!
WILLY. My God, Biff!
BIFF. I never intended to do it, Dad!
OPERATOR'S VOICE. Standish Arms, good evening!
WILLY [*shouting*]. I'm not in my room!
BIFF [*frightened*]. Dad, what's the matter? [*He and* HAPPY *stand up.*]
OPERATOR. Ringing Mr. Loman for you!
WILLY. I'm not there, stop it!
BIFF [*horrified, gets down on one knee before* WILLY]. Dad, I'll make good, I'll make good. [WILLY *tries to get to his feet.* BIFF *holds him down.*] Sit down now.
WILLY. No, you're no good, you're no good for anything.
BIFF. I am, Dad, I'll find something else, you understand? Now don't worry about anything. [*He holds up* WILLY'*s face.*] Talk to me, Dad.
OPERATOR. Mr. Loman does not answer. Shall I page him?
WILLY [*attempting to stand, as though to rush and silence the* OPERATOR]. No, no, no!
HAPPY. He'll strike something, Pop.
WILLY. No, no . . .
BIFF [*desperately, standing over* WILLY]. Pop, listen! Listen to me! I'm telling you something good. Oliver talked to his partner about the Florida idea. You listening? He—he talked to his partner, and he came to me . . . I'm going to be all right, you hear? Dad, listen to me, he said it was just a question of the amount!
WILLY. Then you . . . got it?
HAPPY. He's gonna be terrific, Pop!
WILLY [*trying to stand*]. Then you got it, haven't you? You got it! You got it!
BIFF [*agonized, holds* WILLY *down*]. No, no. Look, Pop. I'm supposed to have lunch with them tomorrow. I'm just telling you this so you'll know that I can still make an impression, Pop. And I'll make good somewhere, but I can't go tomorrow, see?
WILLY. Why not? You simply—
BIFF. But the pen, Pop!
WILLY. You give it to him and tell him it was an oversight!
HAPPY. Sure, have lunch tomorrow!
BIFF. I can't say that—
WILLY. You were doing a crossword puzzle and accidentally used his pen!

BIFF. Listen, kid, I took those balls years ago, now I walk in with his
   fountain pen? That clinches it, don't you see? I can't face him like
   that! I'll try elsewhere.
PAGE'S VOICE. Paging Mr. Loman!
WILLY. Don't you want to be anything?
BIFF. Pop, how can I go back?
WILLY. You don't want to be anything, is that what's behind it?
BIFF [*now angry at* WILLY *for not crediting his sympathy*]. Don't take
   it that way! You think it was easy walking into that office after what
   I'd done to him? A team of horses couldn't have dragged me back to
   Bill Oliver!
WILLY. Then why'd you go?
BIFF. Why did I go? Why did I go! Look at you! Look at what's be-
   come of you!
   [*Off left,* THE WOMAN *laughs.*]
WILLY. Biff, you're going to go to that lunch tomorrow, or—
BIFF. I can't go. I've got no appointment!
HAPPY. Biff, for . . . !
WILLY. Are you spiting me?
BIFF. Don't take it that way! Goddammit!
WILLY [*strikes* BIFF *and falters away from the table*]. You rotten little
   louse! Are you spiting me?
THE WOMAN. Someone's at the door, Willy!
BIFF. I'm no good, can't you see what I am?
HAPPY [*separating them*]. Hey, you're in a restaurant! Now cut it out,
   both of you! [*The girls enter.*] Hello, girls, sit down.
   [THE WOMAN *laughs, off left.*]
MISS FORSYTHE. I guess we might as well. This is Letta.
THE WOMAN. Willy, are you going to wake up?
BIFF [*ignoring* WILLY]. How're ya, miss, sit down. What do you
   drink?
MISS FORSYTHE. Letta might not be able to stay long.
LETTA. I gotta get up very early tomorrow. I got jury duty. I'm so
   excited! Were you fellows ever on a jury?
BIFF. No, but I been in front of them! [*The girls laugh.*] This is my
   father.
LETTA. Isn't he cute? Sit down with us, Pop.
HAPPY. Sit him down, Biff!
BIFF [*going to him*]. Come on, slugger, drink us under the table. To hell
   with it! Come on, sit down, pal.
   [*On* BIFF'S *last insistence,* WILLY *is about to sit.*]
THE WOMAN [*now urgently*]. Willy, are you going to answer the
   door!
   [THE WOMAN'S *call pulls* WILLY *back. He starts right, befuddled.*]
BIFF. Hey, where are you going?
WILLY. Open the door.

BIFF. The door?

WILLY. The washroom . . . the door . . . where's the door?

BIFF [*leading* WILLY *to the left*]. Just go straight down.

[WILLY *moves left*]

THE WOMAN. Willy, Willy, are you going to get up, get up, get up, get up?

[WILLY *exits left*.]

LETTA. I think it's sweet you bring your daddy along.

MISS FORSYTHE. Oh, he isn't really your father!

BIFF [*at left, turning to her resentfully*]. Miss Forsythe, you've just seen a prince walk by. A fine, troubled prince. A hard-working, unappreciated prince. A pal, you understand? A good companion. Always for his boys.

LETTA. That's so sweet.

HAPPY. Well, girls, what's the program? We're wasting time. Come on, Biff. Gather round. Where would you like to go?

BIFF. Why don't you do something for him?

HAPPY. Me!

BIFF. Don't you give a damn for him, Hap?

HAPPY. What're you talking about? I'm the one who—

BIFF. I sense it, you don't give a good goddam about him. [*He takes the rolled-up hose from his pocket and puts it on the table in front of* HAPPY.] Look what I found in the cellar, for Christ's sake. How can you bear to let it go on?

HAPPY. Me? Who goes away? Who runs off and—

BIFF. Yeah, but he doesn't mean anything to you. You could help him— I can't! Don't you understand what I'm talking about? He's going to kill himself, don't you know that?

HAPPY. Don't I know it! Me!

BIFF. Hap, help him! Jesus . . . help him . . . Help me, help me, I can't bear to look at his face! [*Ready to weep he hurries out, up right.*]

HAPPY [*starting after him*]. Where are you going?

MISS FORSYTHE. What's he so mad about?

HAPPY. Come on, girls, we'll catch up with him.

MISS FORSYTHE [*as* HAPPY *pushes her out*]. Say, I don't like that temper of his!

HAPPY. He's just a little overstrung, he'll be all right!

WILLY [*off left, as* THE WOMAN *laughs*]. Don't answer! Don't answer!

LETTA. Don't you want to tell your father—

HAPPY. No, that's not my father. He's just a guy. Come on, we'll catch Biff, and, honey, we're going to paint this town! Stanley, where's the check! Hey, Stanley!

[*They exit.* STANLEY *looks toward left.*]

STANLEY [*calling to* HAPPY *indignantly*]. Mr. Loman! Mr. Loman!

[STANLEY *picks up a chair and follows them off. Knocking is heard off left.* THE WOMAN *enters, laughing,* WILLY *follows her. She is in a black slip; he is buttoning his shirt. Raw, sensuous music accompanies their speech.*]

WILLY. Will you stop laughing? Will you stop?

THE WOMAN. Aren't you going to answer the door? He'll wake the whole hotel.

WILLY. I'm not expecting anybody.

THE WOMAN. Whyn't you have another drink, honey, and stop being so damn self-centered?

WILLY. I'm so lonely.

THE WOMAN. You know you ruined me. Willy? From now on, whenever you come to the office, I'll see that you go right through to the buyers. No waiting at my desk any more, Willy. You ruined me.

WILLY. That's nice of you to say that.

THE WOMAN. Gee, you are self-centered! Why so sad? You are the saddest, self-centeredest soul I ever did see-saw. [*She laughs. He kisses her.*] Come on inside, drummer boy. It's silly to be dressing in the middle of the night. [*As knocking is heard.*] Aren't you going to answer the door?

WILLY. They're knocking on the wrong door.

THE WOMAN. But I felt the knocking. And he heard us talking in here. Maybe the hotel's on fire!

WILLY [*his terror rising*]. It's a mistake.

THE WOMAN. Then tell him to go away!

WILLY. There's nobody there.

THE WOMAN. It's getting on my nerves, Willy. There's somebody standing out there and it's getting on my nerves!

WILLY [*pushing her away from him*]. All right, stay in the bathroom here, and don't come out. I think there's a law in Massachusetts about it, so don't come out. It may be that new room clerk. He looked very mean. So don't come out. It's a mistake, there's no fire.

[*The knocking is heard again. He takes a few steps away from her, and she vanishes into the wing. The light follows him, and now he is facing* YOUNG BIFF, *who carries a suitcase.* BIFF *steps toward him. The music is gone.*]

BIFF. Why didn't you answer?

WILLY. Biff! What are you doing in Boston?

BIFF. Why didn't you answer? I've been knocking for five minutes, I called you on the phone—

WILLY. I just heard you. I was in the bathroom and had the door shut. Did anything happen home?

BIFF. Dad—I let you down.

WILLY. What do you mean?

BIFF. Dad . . .

WILLY. Biffo, what's this about? [*Putting his arm around* BIFF.] Come on, let's go downstairs and get you a malted.

BIFF. Dad, I flunked math.
WILLY. Not for the term?
BIFF. The term. I haven't got enough credits to graduate.
WILLY. You mean to say Bernard wouldn't give you the answers?
BIFF. He did, he tried, but I only got a sixty-one.
WILLY. And they wouldn't give you four points?
BIFF. Birnbaum refused absolutely. I begged him, Pop, but he won't give me those points. You gotta talk to him before they close the school. Because if he saw the kind of man you are, and you just talked to him in your way, I'm sure he'd come through for me. The class came right before practice, see, and I didn't go enough. Would you talk to him? He'd like you, Pop. You know the way you could talk.
WILLY. You're on. We'll drive right back.
BIFF. Oh, Dad, good work! I'm sure he'll change it for you!
WILLY. Go downstairs and tell the clerk I'm checkin' out. Go right down.
BIFF. Yes, sir! See, the reason he hates me, Pop—one day he was late for class so I got up at the blackboard and imitated him. I crossed my eyes and talked with a lithp.
WILLY [*laughing*]. You did? The kids like it?
BIFF. They nearly died laughing!
WILLY. Yeah! What'd you do?
BIFF. The thquare root of thixthy twee is . . . [WILLY *bursts out laughing; BIFF joins him.*] And in the middle of it he walked in!
[WILLY *laughs and* THE WOMAN *joins in offstage.*]
WILLY [*without hesitation*]. Hurry downstairs and—
BIFF. Somebody in there?
WILLY. No, that was next door.
[THE WOMAN *laughs offstage.*]
BIFF. Somebody got in your bathroom!
WILLY. No, it's the next room, there's a party—
THE WOMAN [*enters, laughing. She lisps this*]. Can I come in? There's something in the bathtub, Willy, and it's moving!
[WILLY *looks at* BIFF, *who is staring open-mouthed and horrified at* THE WOMAN.]
WILLY. Ah—you better go back to your room. They must be finished painting by now. They're painting her room so I let her take a shower here. Go back, go back . . . [*He pushes her.*]
THE WOMAN [*resisting*]. But I've got to get dressed, Willy, I can't—
WILLY. Get out of here! Go back, go back . . . [*Suddenly striving for the ordinary.*] This is Miss Francis, Biff, she's a buyer. They're painting her room. Go back, Miss Francis, go back . . .
THE WOMAN. But my clothes, I can't go out naked in the hall!
WILLY [*pushing her offstage*]. Get outa here! Go back, go back!
[BIFF *slowly sits down on his suitcase as the argument continues offstage.*]

THE WOMAN. Where's my stockings? You promised me stockings, Willy!

WILLY. I have no stockings here!

THE WOMAN. You had two boxes of size nine sheers for me, and I want them!

WILLY. Here, for God's sake, will you get outa here!

THE WOMAN [*enters holding a box of stockings*]. I just hope there's nobody in the hall. That's all I hope. [*To* BIFF.] Are you football or baseball?

BIFF. Football.

THE WOMAN [*angry, humiliated*]. That's me too. G'night. [*She snatches her clothes from* WILLY, *and walks out.*]

WILLY [*After a pause*]. Well, better get going. I want to get to the school first thing in the morning. Get my suits out of the closet. I'll get my valise. [BIFF *doesn't move.*] What's the matter? [BIFF *remains motionless, tears falling.*] She's a buyer. Buys for J. H. Simmons. She lives down the hall—they're painting. You don't imagine— [*He breaks off. After a pause.*] Now listen, pal, she's just a buyer. She sees merchandise in her room and they have to keep it looking just so . . . [*Pause. Assuming command.*] All right, get my suits. [BIFF *doesn't move.*] Now stop crying and do as I say. I gave you an order. Biff, I gave you an order! Is that what you do when I give you an order? How dare you cry! [*Putting his arm around* BIFF.] Now look, Biff, when you grow up you'll understand about these things. You mustn't —you mustn't overemphasize a thing like this. I'll see Birnbaum first thing in the morning.

BIFF. Never mind.

WILLY [*getting down beside* BIFF]. Never mind! He's going to give you those points. I'll see to it.

BIFF. He wouldn't listen to you.

WILLY. He certainly will listen to me. You need those points for the U. of Virginia.

BIFF. I'm not going there.

WILLY. Heh? If I can't get him to change that mark you'll make it up in summer school. You've got all summer to—

BIFF [*his weeping breaking from him*]. Dad . . .

WILLY [*infected by it*]. Oh, my boy . . .

BIFF. Dad . . .

WILLY. She's nothing to me, Biff. I was lonely, I was terribly lonely.

BIFF. You—you gave her Mama's stockings! [*His tears break through and he rises to go.*]

WILLY [*grabbing for* BIFF]. I gave you an order!

BIFF. Don't touch me, you—liar!

WILLY. Apologize for that!

BIFF. You fake! You phony little fake! You fake!

[*Overcome, he turns quickly and weeping fully goes out with his suitcase.*

WILLY *is left on the floor on his knees.*]

WILLY. I gave you an order! Biff, come back here or I'll beat you! Come back here! I'll whip you!

[STANLEY *comes quickly in from the right and stands in front of* WILLY.]

WILLY [*shouts at* STANLEY]. I gave you an order . . .

STANLEY. Hey, let's pick it up, pick it up, Mr. Loman. [*He helps* WILLY *to his feet.*] Your boys left with the chippies. They said they'll see you home.

[*A second waiter watches some distance away.*]

WILLY. But we were supposed to have dinner together.

[*Music is heard,* WILLY'*s theme.*]

STANLEY. Can you make it?

WILLY. I'll—sure, I can make it. [*Suddenly concerned about his clothes.*] Do I—I look all right?

STANLEY. Sure, you look all right. [*He flicks a speck off* WILLY'*s lapel.*]

WILLY. Here—here's a dollar.

STANLEY. Oh, your son paid me. It's all right.

WILLY [*putting it in* STANLEY'*s hand*]. No, take it. You're a good boy.

STANLEY. Oh, no, you don't have to . . .

WILLY. Here—here's some more, I don't need it any more. [*After a slight pause.*] Tell me—is there a seed store in the neighborhood?

STANLEY. Seeds? You mean like to plant?

[*As* WILLY *turns,* STANLEY *slips the money back into his jacket pocket.*]

WILLY. Yes. Carrots, peas . . .

STANLEY. Well, there's hardware stores on Sixth Avenue, but it may be too late now.

WILLY [*anxiously*]. Oh, I'd better hurry. I've got to get some seeds. [*He starts off to the right.*] I've got to get some seeds, right away. Nothing's planted. I don't have a thing in the ground.

[WILLY *hurries out as the light goes down.* STANLEY *moves over to the right after him, watches him off. The other waiter has been staring at* WILLY.]

STANLEY [*to the waiter*]. Well, whatta you looking at?

[*The waiter picks up the chairs and moves off right.* STANLEY *takes the table and follows him. The light fades on this area. There is a long pause, the sound of the flute coming over. The light gradually rises on the kitchen, which is empty.* HAPPY *appears at the door of the house, followed by* BIFF. HAPPY *is carrying a large bunch of long-stemmed roses. He enters the kitchen, looks around for* LINDA. *Not seeing her, he turns to* BIFF, *who is just outside the house door, and makes a gesture with his hands, indicating "Not here, I guess." He looks into the living-room and freezes. Inside,* LINDA, *unseen, is seated,* WILLY'*s coat on her lap. She rises ominously and quietly and moves toward* HAPPY, *who backs up into the kitchen, afraid.*]

HAPPY. Hey, what're you doing up? [LINDA *says nothing but moves toward him implacably.*] Where's Pop? [*He keeps backing to the right, and now* LINDA *is in full view in the doorway to the living-room.*] Is he sleeping?

LINDA. Where were you?

HAPPY [*trying to laugh it off*]. We met two girls, Mom, very fine types. Here, we brought you some flowers. [*Offering them to her.*] Put them in your room, Ma.

[*She knocks them to the floor at* BIFF's *feet. He has now come inside and closed the door behind him. She stares at* BIFF, *silent.*]

HAPPY. Now what'd you do that for? Mom, I want you to have some flowers—

LINDA [*cutting* HAPPY *off, violently to* BIFF]. Don't you care whether he lives or dies?

HAPPY [*going to the stairs*]. Come upstairs, Biff.

BIFF [*with a flare of disgust, to* HAPPY]. Go away from me! [*To* LINDA.] What do you mean, lives or dies? Nobody's dying around here, pal.

LINDA. Get out of my sight! Get out of here!

BIFF. I wanna see the boss.

LINDA. You're not going near him!

BIFF. Where is he? [*He moves into the living-room and* LINDA *follows.*]

LINDA [*shouting after* BIFF]. You invite him for dinner. He looks forward to it all day— [BIFF *appears in his parents' bedroom, looks around, and exits.*]—and then you desert him there. There's no stranger you'd do that to!

HAPPY. Why? He had a swell time with us. Listen, when I— [LINDA *comes back into the kitchen.*]—desert him I hope I don't outlive the day!

LINDA. Get out of here!

HAPPY. Now look, Mom . . .

LINDA. Did you have to go to women tonight? You and your lousy rotten whores!

[BIFF *re-enters the kitchen.*]

HAPPY. Mom, all we did was follow Biff around trying to cheer him up! [*To* BIFF] Boy, what a night you gave me!

LINDA. Get out of here, both of you, and don't come back! I don't want you tormenting him any more. Go on now, get your things together! [*To* BIFF] You can sleep in his apartment. [*She starts to pick up the flowers and stops herself.*] Pick up this stuff, I'm not your maid any more. Pick it up, you bum, you!

[HAPPY *turns his back to her in refusal.* BIFF *slowly moves over and gets down on his knees, picking up the flowers.*]

LINDA. You're a pair of animals! Not one, not another living soul would have had the cruelty to walk out on that man in a restaurant!

BIFF [*not looking at her*]. Is that what he said?

LINDA. He didn't have to say anything. He was so humiliated he nearly limped when he came in.

HAPPY. But, Mom, he had a great time with us—

BIFF [*cutting him off violently*]. Shut up!

[*Without another word,* HAPPY *goes upstairs.*]

LINDA. You! You didn't even go in to see if he was all right!

BIFF [*still on the floor in front of* LINDA, *the flowers in his hand; with self-loathing*]. No. Didn't. Didn't do a damned thing. How do you like that, heh? Left him babbling in a toilet.

LINDA. You louse. You . . .

BIFF. Now you hit it on the nose! [*He gets up, throws the flowers in the wastebasket.*] The scum of the earth, and you're looking at him!

LINDA. Get out of here!

BIFF. I gotta talk to the boss, Mom. Where is he?

LINDA. You're not going near him. Get out of this house!

BIFF [*with absolute assurance, determination*]. No. We're gonna have an abrupt conversation, him and me.

LINDA. You're not talking to him!

[*Hammering is heard from outside the house, off right.* BIFF *turns toward the noise.*]

LINDA [*suddenly pleading*]. Will you please leave him alone?

BIFF. What's he doing out there?

LINDA. He's planting the garden!

BIFF [*quietly*]. Now? Oh, my God!

[BIFF *moves outside,* LINDA *following. The light dies down on them and comes up on the center of the apron as* WILLY *walks into it. He is carrying a flashlight, a hoe, and a handful of seed packets. He raps the top of the hoe sharply to fix it firmly, and then moves to the left, measuring off the distance with his foot. He holds the flashlight to look at the seed packets, reading off the instructions. He is in the blue of night.*]

WILLY. Carrots . . . quarter-inch apart. Rows . . . one-foot rows. [*He measures it off.*] One foot. [*He puts down a package and measures off.*] Beets. [*He puts down another package and measures again.*] Lettuce. [*He reads the package, puts it down.*] One foot—[*He breaks off as* BEN *appears at the right and moves slowly down to him.*] What a proposition, ts, ts. Terrific, terrific. 'Cause she's suffered, Ben, the woman has suffered. You understand me? A man can't go out the way he came in, Ben, a man has got to add up to something. You can't, you can't [BEN *moves toward him as though to interrupt.*] You gotta consider, now. Don't answer so quick. Remember, it's a guaranteed twenty-thousand-dollar proposition. Now look, Ben, I want you to go through the ins and outs of this thing with me. I've got nobody to talk to, Ben, and the woman has suffered, you hear me?

BEN [*standing still, considering*]. What's the proposition?

WILLY. It's twenty thousand dollars on the barrelhead. Guaranteed, gilt-edged, you understand?

BEN. You don't want to make a fool of yourself. They might not honor the policy.

WILLY. How can they dare refuse? Didn't I work like a coolie to meet every premium on the nose? And now they don't pay off? Impossible!

BEN. It's called a cowardly thing, William.

WILLY. Why? Does it take more guts to stand here the rest of my life ringing up a zero?

BEN [*yielding*]. That's a point, William. [*He moves, thinking, turns.*] And twenty thousand—that *is* something one can feel with the hand, it is there.

WILLY [*now assured, with rising power*]. Oh, Ben, that's the whole beauty of it! I see it like a diamond, shining in the dark, hard and rough, that I can pick up and touch in my hand. Not like—like an appointment! This would not be another damned-fool appointment, Ben, and it changes all the aspects. Because he thinks I'm nothing, see, and so he spites me. But the funeral— [*Straightening up.*] Ben, that funeral will be massive! They'll come from Maine, Massachusetts, Vermont, New Hampshire! All the oldtimers with the strange license plates— that boy will be thunder-struck, Ben, because he never realized—I am known! Rhode Island, New York, New Jersey—I am known, Ben, and he'll see it with his eyes once and for all. He'll see what I am, Ben! He's in for a shock, that boy!

BEN [*coming down to the edge of the garden*]. He'll call you a coward.

WILLY [*suddenly fearful*]. No, that would be terrible.

BEN. Yes. And a damned fool.

WILLY. No, no, he mustn't, I won't have that! [*He is broken and desperate.*]

BEN. He'll hate you, William.

[*The gay music of the* BOYS *is heard.*]

WILLY. Oh, Ben, how do we get back to all the great times? Used to be so full of light, and comradeship, the sleigh-riding in winter, and the ruddiness on his cheeks. And always some kind of good news coming up, always something nice coming up ahead. And never even let me carry the valises in the house, and simonizing, simonizing that little red car! Why, why can't I give him something and not have him hate me?

BEN. Let me think about it. [*He glances at his watch.*] I still have a little time. Remarkable proposition, but you've got to be sure you're not making a fool of yourself.

[BEN *drifts off upstage and goes out of sight.* BIFF *comes down from the left.*]

WILLY [*suddenly conscious of* BIFF, *turns and looks up at him, then begins picking up the packages of seeds in confusion*]. Where the hell is that seed? [*Indignantly.*] You can't see nothing out here! They boxed in the whole goddam neighborhood!

BIFF. There are people all around here. Don't you realize that?

WILLY. I'm busy. Don't bother me.

BIFF [*taking the hoe from* WILLY]. I'm saying good-by to you, Pop.

[W ILLY *looks at him, silent, unable to move.*] I'm not coming back any more.

WILLY. You're not going to see Oliver tomorrow?

BIFF. I've got no appointment, Dad.

WILLY. He put his arm around you, and you've got no appointment?

BIFF. Pop, get this now, will you? Everytime I've left it's been a fight that sent me out of here. Today I realized something about myself and I tried to explain it to you and I—I think I'm just not smart enough to make any sense out of it for you. To hell with whose fault it is or anything like that. [*He takes* WILLY'*s arm.*] Let's just wrap it up, heh? Come on in, we'll tell Mom. [*He gently tries to pull* WILLY *to left.*]

WILLY [*frozen, immobile, with guilt in his voice*]. No, I don't want to see her.

BIFF. Come on! [*He pulls again, and* WILLY *tries to pull away.*]

WILLY [*highly nervous*]. No, no, I don't want to see her.

BIFF [*tries to look into* WILLY'*s face, as if to find the answer there*]. Why don't you want to see her?

WILLY [*more harshly now*]. Don't bother me, will you?

BIFF. What do you mean, you don't want to see her? You don't want them calling you yellow, do you? This isn't your fault; it's me, I'm a bum. Now come inside! [WILLY *strains to get away.*] Did you hear what I said to you?

[WILLY *pulls away and quickly goes by himself into the house.* BIFF *follows.*]

LINDA [*to* WILLY]. Did you plant, dear?

BIFF [*at the door, to* LINDA]. All right, we had it out. I'm going and I'm not writing any more.

LINDA [*going to* WILLY *in the kitchen*]. I think that's the best way, dear. 'Cause there's no use drawing it out, you'll just never get along. [WILLY *doesn't respond.*]

BIFF. People ask where I am and what I'm doing, you don't know, and you don't care. That way it'll be off your mind and you can start brightening up again. All right? That clears it, doesn't it? [WILLY *is silent, and* BIFF *goes to him.*] You gonna wish me luck, scout? [*He extends his hand.*] What do you say?

LINDA. Shake his hand, Willy.

WILLY [*turning to her, seething with hurt*]. There's no necessity to mention the pen at all, y'know.

BIFF [*gently*]. I've got no appointment, Dad.

WILLY [*erupting fiercely*]. He put his arm around . . . ?

BIFF. Dad, you're never going to see what I am, so what's the use of arguing? If I strike oil I'll send you a check. Meantime forget I'm alive.

WILLY [*to* LINDA]. Spite, see?

BIFF. Shake hands, Dad.

WILLY. Not my hand.

BIFF. I was hoping not to go this way.

WILLY. Well, this is the way you're going. Good-by.

[BIFF *looks at him a moment, then turns sharply and goes to the stairs.*]

WILLY [*stops him with*]. May you rot in hell if you leave this house!

BIFF [*turning*]. Exactly what is it that you want from me?

WILLY. I want you to know, on the train, in the mountains, in the valleys, wherever you go, that you cut down your life for spite!

BIFF. No, no.

WILLY. Spite, spite, is the word of your undoing! And when you're down and out, remember what did it. When you're rotting somewhere beside the railroad tracks, remember, and don't you dare blame it on me!

BIFF. I'm not blaming it on you!

WILLY. I won't take the rap for this, you hear?

[HAPPY *comes down the stairs and stands on the bottom step, watching.*]

BIFF. That's just what I'm telling you!

WILLY [*sinking into a chair at the table, with full accusation*]. You're trying to put a knife in me—don't think I don't know what you're doing!

BIFF. All right, phony! Then let's lay it on the line.

[*He whips the rubber tube out of his pocket and puts it on the table.*]

HAPPY. You crazy—

LINDA. Biff! [*She moves to grab the hose, but* BIFF *holds it down with his hand.*]

BIFF. Leave it there! Don't move it!

WILLY [*not looking at it*]. What is that?

BIFF. You know goddam well what that is.

WILLY [*caged, wanting to escape*]. I never saw that.

BIFF. You saw it. The mice didn't bring it into the cellar! What is this supposed to do, make a hero out of you? This supposed to make me sorry for you?

WILLY. Never heard of it.

BIFF. There'll be no pity for you, you hear it? No pity!

WILLY [*to* LINDA]. You hear the spite!

BIFF. No, you're going to hear the truth—what you are and what I am!

LINDA. Stop it!

WILLY. Spite!

HAPPY [*coming down toward* BIFF]. You cut it now!

BIFF [*to* HAPPY]. The man don't know who we are! The man is gonna know! [*To* WILLY.] We never told the truth for ten minutes in this house!

HAPPY. We always told the truth!

BIFF [*turning on him*]. You big blow, are you the assistant buyer? You're one of the two assistants to the assistant, aren't you?

HAPPY. Well, I'm practically—

BIFF. You're practically full of it! We all are! And I'm through with it. [*To* WILLY.] Now hear this, Willy, this is me.

WILLY. I know you!

BIFF. You know why I had no address for three months? I stole a suit in Kansas City and I was in jail. [*To* LINDA, *who is sobbing.*] Stop crying. I'm through with it.

[LINDA *turns away from them, her hands covering her face.*]

WILLY. I suppose that's my fault!

BIFF. I stole myself out of every good job since high school!

WILLY. And whose fault is that?

BIFF. And I never got anywhere because you blew me so full of hot air I could never stand taking orders from anybody! That's whose fault it is!

WILLY. I hear that!

LINDA. Don't, Biff!

BIFF. It's goddam time you heard that! I had to be boss big shot in two weeks, and I'm through with it!

WILLY. Then hang yourself! For spite, hang yourself!

BIFF. No! Nobody's hanging himself, Willy! I ran down eleven flights with a pen in my hand today. And suddenly I stopped, you hear me? And in the middle of that office building, do you hear this? I stopped in the middle of that building and I saw—the sky. I saw the things that I love in this world. The work and the food and time to sit and smoke. And I looked at the pen and said to myself, what the hell am I grabbing this for? Why am I trying to become what I don't want to be? What am I doing in an office, making a contemptuous, begging fool of myself, when all I want is out there, waiting for me the minute I say I know who I am! Why can't I say that, Willy? [*He tries to make* WILLY *face him, but* WILLY *pulls away and moves to the left.*]

WILLY [*with hatred, threateningly*]. The door of your life is wide open!

BIFF. Pop! I'm a dime a dozen, and so are you!

WILLY [*turning on him now in an uncontrolled outburst*]. I am not a dime a dozen! I am Willy Loman, and you are Biff Loman!

[BIFF *starts for* WILLY, *but is blocked by* HAPPY. *In his fury,* BIFF *seems on the verge of attacking his father.*]

BIFF. I am not a leader of men, Willy, and neither are you. You were never anything but a hard-working drummer who landed in the ash can like all the rest of them! I'm one dollar an hour, Willy! I tried seven states and couldn't raise it. A buck an hour! Do you gather my meaning? I'm not bringing home any prizes any more, and you're going to stop waiting for me to bring them home!

WILLY [*directly to* BIFF]. You vengeful, spiteful mutt!

[BIFF *breaks from* HAPPY. WILLY, *in fright, starts up the stairs.* BIFF *grabs him.*]

BIFF [*at the peak of his fury*]. Pop, I'm nothing! I'm nothing, Pop. Can't you understand that? There's no spite in it any more. I'm just what I am, that's all.

[BIFF's *fury has spent itself, and he breaks down, sobbing, holding on to* WILLY, *who dumbly fumbles for* BIFF's *face.*]

WILLY [*astonished*]. What're you doing? What're you doing? [*To* LINDA.] Why is he crying?

BIFF [*crying, broken*]. Will you let me go, for Christ's sake? Will you take that phony dream and burn it before something happens? [*Struggling to contain himself, he pulls away and moves to the stairs.*] I'll go in the morning. Put him—put him to bed. [*Exhausted,* BIFF *moves up the stairs to his room.*]

WILLY [*after a long pause, astonished, elevated*]. Isn't that—isn't that remarkable? Biff—he likes me!

LINDA. He loves you, Willy!

HAPPY [*deeply moved*]. Always did, Pop.

WILLY. Oh, Biff! [*Staring wildly.*] He cried! Cried to me. [*He is choking with his love, and now cries out his promise.*] That boy—that boy is going to be magnificent!

[BEN *appears in the light just outside the kitchen.*]

BEN. Yes, outstanding, with twenty thousand behind him.

LINDA [*sensing the racing of his mind, fearfully, carefully*]. Now come to bed, Willy. It's all settled now.

WILLY [*finding it difficult not to rush out of the house*]. Yes, we'll sleep. Come on. Go on to sleep, Hap.

BEN. And it does take a great kind of a man to crack the jungle.

[*In accents of dread,* BEN's *idyllic music starts up.*]

HAPPY [*his arm around* LINDA]. I'm getting married, Pop, don't forget it. I'm changing everything. I'm gonna run that department before the year is up. You'll see, Mom. [*He kisses her.*]

BEN. The jungle is dark but full of diamonds, Willy.

[WILLY *turns, moves, listening to* BEN.]

LINDA. Be good. You're both good boys, just act that way, that's all.

HAPPY. 'Night, Pop. [*He goes upstairs.*]

LINDA [*to* WILLY]. Come, dear.

BEN [*with greater force*]. One must go in to fetch a diamond out.

WILLY [*to* LINDA, *as he moves slowly along the edge of the kitchen, toward the door*]. I just want to get settled down, Linda. Let me sit alone for a little.

LINDA [*almost uttering her fear*]. I want you upstairs.

WILLY [*taking her in his arms*]. In a few minutes, Linda. I couldn't sleep right now. Go on, you look awful tired. [*He kisses her.*]

BEN. Not like an appointment at all. A diamond is rough and hard to the touch.

WILLY. Go on now. I'll be right up.

LINDA. I think this is the only way, Willy.

WILLY. Sure, it's the best thing.

BEN. Best thing!

WILLY. The only way. Everything is gonna be—go on, kid, get to bed. You look so tired.

LINDA. Come right up.

WILLY. Two minutes.

[LINDA *goes into the living-room, then reappears in her bedroom.* WILLY *moves just outside the kitchen door.*]

WILLY. Loves me. [*Wonderingly.*] Always loved me. Isn't that a remarkable thing? Ben, he'll worship me for it!

BEN [*with promise*]. It's dark there, but full of diamonds.

WILLY. Can you imagine that magnificence with twenty thousand dollars in his pocket?

LINDA [*calling from her room*]. Willy! Come up!

WILLY [*calling into the kitchen*]. Yes! Yes. Coming! It's very smart, you realize that, don't you, sweetheart? Even Ben sees it. I gotta go, baby. 'By! 'By! [*Going over to* BEN, *almost dancing.*] Imagine? When the mail comes he'll be ahead of Bernard again!

BEN. A perfect proposition all around.

WILLY. Did you see how he cried to me? Oh, if I could kiss him, Ben!

BEN. Time, William, time!

WILLY. Oh, Ben, I always knew one way or another we were gonna make it, Biff and I!

BEN [*looking at his watch*]. The boat. We'll be late.

[*He moves slowly off into the darkness.*]

WILLY [*elegiacally, turning to the house*]. Now when you kick off, boy, I want a seventy-yard boot, and get right down the field under the ball, and when you hit, hit low and hit hard, because it's important, boy. [*He swings around and faces the audience.*] There's all kinds of important people in the stands, and the first thing you know . . . [*Suddenly realizing he is alone.*] Ben! Ben, where do I . . . ? [*He makes a sudden movement of search.*] Ben, how do I . . . ?

LINDA [*calling*]. Willy, you coming up?

WILLY [*uttering a gasp of fear, whirling about as if to quiet her*]. Sh! [*He turns around as if to find his way; sounds, faces, voices, seem to be swarming in upon him and he flicks at them, crying.*] Sh! Sh! [*Suddenly music, faint and high, stops him. It rises in intensity, almost to an unbearable scream. He goes up and down on his toes, and rushes off around the house.*] Shhh!

LINDA. Willy?

[*There is no answer.* LINDA *waits.* BIFF *gets up off his bed. He is still in his clothes.* HAPPY *sits up.* BIFF *stands listening.*]

LINDA [*with real fear*]. Willy, answer me! Willy!

[*There is the sound of a car starting and moving away at full speed.*]

LINDA. No!

BIFF [*rushing down the stairs*]. Pop!

[*As the car speeds off, the music crashes down in a frenzy of sound, which becomes the soft pulsation of a single cello string.* BIFF *slowly returns to his bedroom. He and* HAPPY *gravely don their jackets.* LINDA *slowly walks out of her room. The music has developed into a dead march. The leaves of day are appearing over everything.* CHARLEY *and* BERNARD, *somberly dressed, appear and knock on the kitchen door.* BIFF *and* HAPPY *slowly descend the stairs to the kitchen as* CHARLEY *and* BERNARD *enter. All stop a moment when* LINDA, *in clothes of mourning, bearing a little bunch of roses, comes through the draped doorway into the kitchen. She goes to* CHARLEY *and takes his arm. Now all move toward the audience, through the wall-line of the kitchen. At the limit of the Apron,* LINDA *lays down the flowers, kneels, and sits back on her heels. All stare down at the grave.*]

REQUIEM

CHARLEY. It's getting dark, Linda.
 [LINDA *doesn't react. She stares at the grave.*]
BIFF. How about it, Mom? Better get some rest, heh? They'll be closing the gate soon.
 [LINDA *makes no move. Pause.*]
HAPPY [*deeply angered*]. He had no right to do that. There was no necessity for it. We would've helped him.
CHARLEY [*grunting*]. Hmmm.
BIFF. Come along, Mom.
LINDA. Why didn't anybody come?
CHARLEY. It was a very nice funeral.
LINDA. But where are all the people he knew? Maybe they blame him.
CHARLEY. Naa. It's a rough world, Linda. They wouldn't blame him.
LINDA. I can't understand it. At this time especially. First time in thirty-five years we were just about free and clear. He only needed a little salary. He was even finished with the dentist.
CHARLEY. No man only needs a little salary.
LINDA. I can't understand it.
BIFF. There were a lot of nice days. When he'd come home from a trip; or on Sundays, making the stoop; finishing the cellar; putting on the new porch; when he built the extra bathroom; and put up the garage. You know something, Charley, there's more of him in that front stoop than in all the sales he ever made.
CHARLEY. Yeah. He was a happy man with a batch of cement.
LINDA. He was so wonderful with his hands.
BIFF. He had the wrong dreams. All, all, wrong.
HAPPY [*almost ready to fight* BIFF]. Don't say that!
BIFF. He never knew who he was.
CHARLEY [*stopping* HAPPY'S *movement and reply. To* BIFF]. Nobody dast blame this man. You don't understand: Willy was a salesman.

And for a salesman, there is no rock bottom to the life. He don't put a bolt to a nut, he don't tell you the law or give you medicine. He's a man way out there in the blue, riding on a smile and a shoeshine. And when they start not smiling back—that's an earthquake. And then you get yourself a couple of spots on your hat, and you're finished. Nobody dast blame this man. A salesman is got to dream, boy. It comes with the territory.

BIFF. Charley, the man didn't know who he was.

HAPPY [*infuriated*]. Don't say that!

BIFF. Why don't you come with me, Happy?

HAPPY. I'm not licked that easily. I'm staying right in this city, and I'm gonna beat this racket! [*He looks at* BIFF, *his chin set.*] The Loman Brothers!

BIFF. I know who I am, kid.

HAPPY. All right, boy. I'm gonna show you and everybody else that Willy Loman did not die in vain. He had a good dream. It's the only dream you can have—to come out number-one man. He fought it out here, and this is where I'm gonna win it for him.

BIFF [*with a hopeless glance at* HAPPY, *bends toward his mother*]. Let's go, Mom.

LINDA. I'll be with you in a minute. Go on, Charley. [*He hesitates.*] I want to, just for a minute. I never had a chance to say good-by.

[CHARLEY *moves away, followed by* HAPPY. BIFF *remains a slight distance up and left of* LINDA. *She sits there, summoning herself. The flute begins, not far away, playing behind her speech.*]

LINDA. Forgive me, dear. I can't cry. I don't know what it is, but I can't cry. I don't understand it. Why did you ever do that? Help me, Willy, I can't cry. It seems to me that you're just on another trip. I keep expecting you. Willy, dear, I can't cry. Why did you do it? I search and search and I search, and I can't understand it, Willy. I made the last payment on the house today. Today, dear. And there'll be nobody home. [*A sob rises in her throat.*] We're free and clear. [*Sobbing more fully, released.*] We're free. [BIFF *comes slowly toward her.*] We're free . . . We're free . . .

BIFF *lifts her to her feet and moves out up right with her in his arms.* [LINDA *sobs quietly.* BERNARD *and* CHARLEY *come together and follow them, followed by* HAPPY. *Only the music of the flute is left on the darkening stage as over the house the hard towers of the apartment buildings rise into sharp focus, and The Curtain Falls.*]

Lorraine Hansberry

1931–1965

A RAISIN IN THE SUN

◇

CAST OF CHARACTERS
(In order of appearance)

RUTH YOUNGER.
TRAVIS YOUNGER.
WALTER LEE YOUNGER
 (*Brother*).
BENEATHA YOUNGER.
LENA YOUNGER (*Mama*).

JOSEPH ASAGAI.
GEORGE MURCHISON.
KARL LINDNER.
BOBO.
MOVING MEN.

SCENE: The action of the play is set in Chicago's Southside, sometime between World War II and the present.

ACT ONE

Scene 1. Friday morning.
Scene 2. The following morning.

ACT TWO

Scene 1. Later, the same day.
Scene 2. Friday night, a few weeks later.
Scene 3. Moving day, one week later.

ACT THREE

An hour later.

◇

ACT ONE

SCENE ONE

The YOUNGER *living room would be a comfortable and well-ordered room if it were not for a number of indestructible contradictions to this state of being. Its furnishings are typical and undistinguished and their primary feature now is that they have clearly had to accommodate the living of too many people for too many years—and they are tired. Still, we can see that at some time, a time probably no longer remembered by the family (except perhaps for* MAMA) *the furnishings of this room were actually selected with care and love and even hope—and brought to this apartment and arranged with taste and pride.*

That was a long time ago. Now the once loved pattern of the couch uphol-stery has to fight to show itself from under acres of crocheted doilies and couch covers which have themselves finally come to be more important than the up-holstery. And here a table or a chair has been moved to disguise the worn places in the carpet; but the carpet has fought back by showing its weariness, with depressing uniformity, elsewhere on its surface.

Weariness has, in fact, won in this room. Everything has been polished, washed, sat on, used, scrubbed too often. All pretenses but living itself have long since vanished from the very atmosphere of this room.

Moreover, a section of this room, for it is not really a room unto itself, though the landlord's lease would make it seem so, slopes backward to provide a small kitchen area, where the family prepares the meals that are eaten in the living room proper, which must also serve as dining room. The single win-dow that has been provided for these "two" rooms is located in this kitchen area. The sole natural light the family may enjoy in the course of a day is only that which fights its way through this little window.

At left, a door leads to a bedroom which is shared by MAMA *and her daughter,* BENEATHA. *At right, opposite, is a second room (which in the beginning of the life of this apartment was probably a breakfast room) which serves as a bedroom for* WALTER *and his wife,* RUTH.

Time: Sometime between World War II and the present.

Place: Chicago's Southside.

At Rise: It is morning dark in the living room. TRAVIS *is asleep on the make-down bed at center. An alarm clock sounds from within the bedroom at right, and presently* RUTH *enters from that room and closes the door behind her. She crosses sleepily toward the window. As she passes her sleeping son she reaches down and shakes him a little. At the window she raises the shade and a dusky Southside morning light comes in feebly. She fills a pot with water and puts it on to boil. She calls to the boy, between yawns, in a slightly muf-fled voice.*

RUTH is about thirty. We can see that she was a pretty girl, even exception-ally so, but now it is apparent that life has been little that she expected, and dis-appointment has already begun to hang in her face. In a few years, before thirty-five even, she will be known among her people as a "settled woman."

She crosses to her son and gives him a good, final, rousing shake.

RUTH. Come on now, boy, it's seven thirty! [*Her son sits up at last, in a stupor of sleepiness.*] I say hurry up, Travis! You ain't the only person in the world got to use a bathroom! [*The child, a sturdy, handsome little boy of ten or eleven, drags himself out of the bed and almost blindly takes his towels and "today's clothes" from the drawers and a closet and goes out to the bathroom, which is in an outside hall and which is shared by an-other family or families on the same floor.* RUTH *crosses to the bedroom door at right and opens it and calls in to her husband.*] Walter Lee! . . . It's after seven thirty! Lemme see you do some waking up in there now! [*She waits.*] You better get up from there, man! It's after seven thirty I tell you. [*She waits again.*] All right, you just go ahead and lay there and next thing you know Travis be finished and Mr. Johnson'll be in there and you'll be fussing and cussing round here like a mad man! And be late too! [*She waits, at the end of patience.*] Walter Lee— it's time for you to get up!

[*She waits another second and then starts to go into the bedroom, but is apparently satisfied that her husband has begun to get up. She stops, pulls the door to, and returns to the kitchen area. She wipes her face with a moist cloth and runs her fingers through her sleep-disheveled hair in a vain effort and ties an apron around her housecoat. The bedroom door at right opens and her husband stands in the doorway in his pajamas, which are rumpled and mismated. He is a lean, intense young man in his middle thirties, inclined to quick nervous movements and erratic speech habits—and always in his voice there is a quality of indictment.*]

WALTER. Is he out yet?

RUTH. What do you mean *out?* He ain't hardly got in there good yet.

WALTER [*wandering in, still more oriented to sleep than to a new day*]. Well, what was you doing all that yelling for if I can't even get in there yet? [*Stopping and thinking*] Check coming today?

RUTH. They *said* Saturday and this is just Friday and I hopes to God you ain't going to get up here first thing this morning and start talking to me 'bout no money—'cause I 'bout don't want to hear it.

WALTER. Something the matter with you this morning?

RUTH. No—I'm just sleepy as the devil. What kind eggs you want?

WALTER. Not scrambled. [RUTH *starts to scramble eggs.*] Paper come? [RUTH *points impatiently to the rolled up* Tribune *on the table, and he gets it and spreads it out and vaguely reads the front page.*] Set off another bomb yesterday.

RUTH [*maximum indifference*]. Did they?

WALTER [*looking up*]. What's the matter with you?

RUTH. Ain't nothing the matter with me. And don't keep asking me that this morning.

WALTER. Ain't nobody bothering you. [*Reading the news of the day absently again.*] Say Colonel McCormick is sick.

RUTH [*affecting tea-party interest*]. Is he now? Poor thing.

WALTER [*sighing and looking at his watch*]. Oh, me. [*He waits.*] Now what is that boy doing in that bathroom all this time? He just going to have to start getting up earlier. I can't be being late to work on account of him fooling around in there.

RUTH [*turning on him*]. Oh, no he ain't going to be getting up no earlier no such thing! It ain't his fault that he can't get to bed no earlier nights 'cause he got a bunch of crazy good-for-nothing clowns sitting up running their mouths in what is supposed to be his bedroom after ten o'clock at night . . .

WALTER. That's what you mad about, ain't it? The things I want to talk about with my friends just couldn't be important in your mind, could they?

[*He rises and finds a cigarette in her handbag on the table and crosses to the little window and looks out, smoking and deeply enjoying this first one.*]

RUTH [*almost matter of factly, a complaint too automatic to deserve emphasis*]. Why you always got to smoke before you eat in the morning?

WALTER [*at the window*]. Just look at 'em down there . . . Running and racing to work . . . [*He turns and faces his wife and watches her a moment at the stove, and then, suddenly,*] You look young this morning, baby.

RUTH [*indifferently*]. Yeah?

WALTER. Just for a second—stirring them eggs. It's gone now—just for a second it was—you looked real young again. [*Then, drily,*] It's gone now—you look like yourself again.

RUTH. Man, if you don't shut up and leave me alone.

WALTER [*looking out to the street again*]. First thing a man ought to learn in life is not to make love to no colored woman first thing in the morning. You all some evil people at eight o'clock in the morning.

[TRAVIS *appears in the hall doorway, almost fully dressed and quite wide awake now, his towels and pajamas across his shoulders. He opens the door and signals for his father to make the bathroom in a hurry.*]

TRAVIS [*watching the bathroom*]. Daddy, come on! [WALTER *gets his bathroom utensils and flies out to the bathroom.*]

RUTH. Sit down and have your breakfast, Travis.

TRAVIS. Mama, this is Friday. [*Gleefully.*] Check coming tomorrow, huh?

RUTH. You get your mind off money and eat your breakfast.

TRAVIS [*eating*]. This is the morning we supposed to bring the fifty cents to school.

RUTH. Well, I ain't got no fifty cents this morning.

TRAVIS. Teacher say we have to.

RUTH. I don't care what teacher say. I ain't got it. Eat your breakfast, Travis.

TRAVIS. I *am* eating.

RUTH. Hush up now and just eat!

[*The boy gives her an exasperated look for her lack of understanding, and eats grudgingly.*]

TRAVIS. You think Grandma would have it?

RUTH. No! And I want you to stop asking your grandmother for money, you hear me?

TRAVIS [*outraged*]. Gaaaleee! I don't ask her, she just gimme it sometimes!

RUTH. Travis Willard Younger—I got too much on me this morning to be—

TRAVIS. Maybe Daddy—

RUTH. *Travis!*

[*The boy hushes abruptly. They are both quiet and tense for several seconds.*]

TRAVIS [*presently*]. Could I maybe go carry some groceries in front of the supermarket for a little while after school then?

RUTH. Just hush, I said. [TRAVIS *jabs his spoon into his cereal bowl viciously, and rests his head in anger upon his fists.*] If you through eating, you can get over there and make up your bed.

[*The boy obeys stiffly and crosses the room, almost mechanically, to the bed and more or less carefully folds the covering. He carries the bedding into his mother's room and returns with his books and cap.*]

TRAVIS [*sulking and standing apart from her unnaturally*]. I'm gone.

RUTH [*looking up from the stove to inspect him automatically*]. Come here. [*He crosses to her and she studies his head.*] If you don't take this comb and fix this here head, you better! [TRAVIS *puts down his books with a great sigh of oppression, and crosses to the mirror. His mother mutters under her breath about his "slubbornness."*] 'Bout to march out of here with that head looking just like chickens slept in it! I just don't know where you get your stubborn ways . . . And get your jacket, too. Looks chilly out this morning.

TRAVIS [*with conspicuously brushed hair and jacket*]. I'm gone.

RUTH. Get carfare and milk money—[*waving one finger*]—and not a single penny for no caps, you hear me?

TRAVIS [*with sullen politeness*]. Yes'm.

[*He turns in outrage to leave. His mother watches after him as in his frustration he approaches the door almost comically. When she speaks to him, her voice has become a very gentle tease.*]

RUTH [*mocking; as she thinks he would say it*]. Oh, Mama makes me so mad sometimes, I don't know what to do! [*She waits and continues to his back as he stands stock-still in front of the door.*] I wouldn't kiss that woman good-bye for nothing in this world this morning! [*The boy finally turns around and rolls his eyes at her, knowing the mood has changed and he is vindicated; he does not, however, move toward her yet.*] Not for nothing in this world! [*She finally laughs aloud at him and holds out her arms to him and we see that it is a way between them, very old and practiced. He crosses to her and allows her to embrace him warmly but keeps his face fixed with masculine rigidity. She holds him back from her presently and looks at him and runs her fingers over the features of his face. With utter gentleness—*] Now—whose little old angry man are you?

TRAVIS [*the masculinity and gruffness start to fade at last*]. Aw gaalee— Mama . . .

RUTH [*mimicking*]. Aw—gaaaaalleeeee, Mama! [*She pushes him, with rough playfulness and finality, toward the door.*] Get on out of here or you going to be late.

TRAVIS [*in the face of love, new aggressiveness*]. Mama, could I *please* go carry groceries?

RUTH. Honey, it's starting to get so cold evenings.

WALTER [*coming in from the bathroom and drawing a make-believe gun*

from a make-believe holster and shooting at his son]. What is it he wants
to do?

RUTH. Go carry groceries after school at the supermarket.

WALTER. Well, let him go . . .

TRAVIS [*quickly, to the ally*]. I *have* to—she won't gimme the fifty
cents . . .

WALTER [*to his wife only*]. Why not?

RUTH [*simply, and with flavor*]. 'Cause we don't have it.

WALTER [*to RUTH only*]. What you tell the boy things like that for?
[*Reaching down into his pants with a rather important gesture.*] Here,
son—

[*He hands the boy the coin, but his eyes are directed to his wife's. TRAVIS
takes the money happily.*]

TRAVIS. Thanks, Daddy.

[*He starts out. RUTH watches both of them with murder in her eyes.
WALTER stands and stares back at her with defiance, and suddenly reaches
into his pocket again on an afterthought.*]

WALTER [*without even looking at his son, still staring hard at his wife*]. In
fact, here's another fifty cents . . . Buy yourself some fruit today—
or take a taxicab to school or something!

TRAVIS. Whoopee—

[*He leaps up and clasps his father around the middle with his legs, and they
face each other in mutual appreciation; slowly WALTER LEE peeks
around the boy to catch the violent rays from his wife's eyes and draws his
head back as if shot.*]

WALTER. You better get down now—and get to school, man.

TRAVIS [*at the door*]. O.K. Goodbye.

[*He exits.*]

WALTER [*after him, pointing with pride*]. That's *my* boy. [*She looks at
him in disgust and turns back to her work.*] You know what I was thinking 'bout in the bathroom this morning?

RUTH. No.

WALTER. How come you always try to be so pleasant!

RUTH. What is there to be pleasant 'bout!

WALTER. You want to know what I was thinking 'bout in the bathroom or not!

RUTH. I know what you thinking 'bout.

WALTER [*ignoring her*]. 'Bout what me and Willy Harris was talking
about last night.

RUTH [*immediately—a refrain*]. Willy Harris is a good-for-nothing
loud mouth.

WALTER. Anybody who talks to me has got to be a good-for-nothing
loud mouth, ain't he? And what you know about who is just a good-
for-nothing loud mouth? Charlie Atkins was just a "good-for-nothing
loud mouth" too, wasn't he! When he wanted me to go in the dry-
cleaning business with him. And now—he's grossing a hundred thou-

sand a year. A hundred thousand dollars a year! You still call *him* a loud mouth!

RUTH [*bitterly*]. Oh, Walter Lee . . .

[*She folds her head on her arms over the table.*]

WALTER [*rising and coming to her and standing over her*]. You tired, ain't you? Tired of everything. Me, the boy, the way we live—this beat-up hole—everything. Ain't you? [*She doesn't look up, doesn't answer.*] So tired—moaning and groaning all the time, but you wouldn't do nothing to help, would you? You couldn't be on my side that long for nothing, could you?

RUTH. Walter, please leave me alone.

WALTER. A man needs for a woman to back him up . . .

RUTH. Walter—

WALTER. Mama would listen to you. You know she listen to you more than she do me and Bennie. She think more of you. All you have to do is just sit down with her when you drinking your coffee one morning and talking 'bout things like you do and—[*He sits down beside her and demonstrates graphically what he thinks her methods and tone should be.*]—you just sip your coffee, see, and say easy like that you been thinking 'bout that deal Walter Lee is so interested in, 'bout the store and all, and sip some more coffee, like what you saying ain't really that important to you—And the next thing you know, she be listening good and asking you questions and when I come home—I can tell her the details. This ain't no fly-by-night proposition, baby. I mean we figured it out, me and Willy and Bobo.

RUTH [*with a frown*]. Bobo?

WALTER. Yeah. You see, this little liquor store we got in mind cost seventy-five thousand and we figured the initial investment on the place be 'bout thirty thousand, see. That be ten thousand each. Course, there's a couple of hundred you got to pay so's you don't spend your life just waiting for them clowns to let your license get approved—

RUTH. You mean graft?

WALTER [*frowning impatiently*]. Don't call it that. See there, that just goes to show you what women understand about the world. Baby, don't *nothing* happen for you in this world 'less you pay *somebody* off!

RUTH. Walter, leave me alone! [*She raises her head and stares at him vigorously—then says, more quietly,*] Eat your eggs, they gonna be cold.

WALTER [*straightening up from her and looking off*]. That's it. There you are. Man say to his woman: I got me a dream. His woman say: Eat your eggs. [*Sadly, but gaining in power.*] Man say: I got to take hold of this here world, baby! And a woman will say: Eat your eggs and go to work. [*Passionately now.*] Man say: I got to change my life, I'm choking to death, baby! And his woman say—[*in utter anguish as he brings his fists down on his thighs*]—Your eggs is getting cold!

RUTH [*softly*]. Walter, that ain't none of our money.

WALTER [*not listening at all or even looking at her*]. This morning, I was lookin' in the mirror and thinking about it . . . I'm thirty-five years old; I been married eleven years and I got a boy who sleeps in the living room—[*very, very quietly*]—and all I got to give him is stories about how rich white people live . . .

RUTH. Eat your eggs, Walter.

WALTER. *Damn my eggs . . . damn all the eggs that ever was!*

RUTH. Then go to work.

WALTER [*looking up at her*]. See—I'm trying to talk to you 'bout myself—[*shaking his head with the repetition*]—and all you can say is eat them eggs and go to work.

RUTH [*wearily*]. Honey, you never say nothing new. I listen to you every day, every night and every morning, and you never say nothing new. [*Shrugging.*] So you would rather *be* Mr. Arnold than be his chauffeur. So—I would *rather* be living in Buckingham Palace.

WALTER. That is just what is wrong with the colored woman in this world . . . Don't understand about building their men up and making 'em feel like they somebody. Like they can do something.

RUTH [*drily, but to hurt*]. There *are* colored men who do things.

WALTER. No thanks to the colored woman.

RUTH. Well, being a colored woman, I guess I can't help myself none. [*She rises and gets the ironing board and sets it up and attacks a huge pile of rough-dried clothes, sprinkling them in preparation for the ironing and then rolling them into tight fat balls.*]

WALTER [*mumbling*]. We one group of men tied to a race of women with small minds.

[*His sister* BENEATHA *enters. She is about twenty, as slim and intense as her brother. She is not as pretty as her sister-in-law, but her lean, almost intellectual face has a handsomeness of its own. She wears a bright-red flannel nightie, and her thick hair stands wildly about her head. Her speech is a mixture of many things; it is different from the rest of the family's insofar as education has permeated her sense of English—and perhaps the Midwest rather than the South has finally—at last—won out in her inflection; but not altogether, because over all of it is a soft slurring and transformed use of vowels which is the decided influence of the Southside. She passes through the room without looking at either* RUTH *or* WALTER *and goes to the outside door and looks, a little blindly, out to the bathroom. She sees that it has been lost to the Johnsons. She closes the door with a sleepy vengeance and crosses to the table and sits down a little defeated.*]

BENEATHA. I am going to start timing those people.

WALTER. You should get up earlier.

BENEATHA [*her face in her hands. She is still fighting the urge to go back to bed*]. Really—would you suggest dawn? Where's the paper?

WALTER [*pushing the paper across the table to her as he studies her almost clinically, as though he has never seen her before*]. You a horrible-looking chick at this hour.

BENEATHA [*dirty*]. Good morning, everybody.

WALTER [*senselessly*]. How is school coming?

BENEATHA [*in the same spirit*]. Lovely. Lovely. And you know, biology
is the greatest. [*Looking up at him.*] I dissected something that looked
just like you yesterday.

WALTER. I just wondered if you've made up your mind and everything.

BENEATHA [*gaining in sharpness and impatience*]. And what did I answer
yesterday morning—and the day before that?

RUTH [*from the ironing board, like someone disinterested and old*]. Don't
be so nasty, Bennie.

BENEATHA [*still to her brother*]. And the day before that and the day before that!

WALTER [*defensively*]. I'm interested in you. Something wrong with
that? Ain't many girls who decide—

WALTER *and* BENEATHA [*in unison*]. —"to be a doctor."
[*Silence.*]

WALTER. Have we figured out yet just exactly how much medical
school is going to cost?

RUTH. Walter Lee, why don't you leave that girl alone and get out of
here to work?

BENEATHA [*exits to the bathroom and bangs on the door*]. Come on out of
there, please!
[*She comes back into the room.*]

WALTER [*looking at his sister intently*]. You know the check is coming
tomorrow.

BENEATHA [*turning on him with a sharpness all her own*]. That money
belongs to Mama, Walter, and it's for her to decide how she wants to
use it. I don't care if she wants to buy a house or a rocket ship or just
nail it up somewhere and look at it. It's hers. Not ours—*hers.*

WALTER [*bitterly*]. Now ain't that fine! You just got your mother's interest at heart, ain't you, girl? You such a nice girl—but if Mama got
that money she can always take a few thousand and help you through
school too—can't she?

BENEATHA. I have never asked anyone around here to do anything
for me!

WALTER. No! And the line between asking and just accepting when
the time comes is big and wide—ain't it!

BENEATHA [*with fury*]. What do you want from me, Brother—that I
quit school or just drop dead, which!

WALTER. I don't want nothing but for you to stop acting holy 'round
here. Me and Ruth done made some sacrifices for you—why can't you
do something for the family?

RUTH. Walter, don't be dragging me in it.

WALTER. You are in it—Don't you get up and go work in somebody's
kitchen for the last three years to help put clothes on her back?

RUTH. Oh, Walter—that's not fair . . .

WALTER. It ain't that nobody expects you to get on your knees and say thank you, Brother; thank you, Ruth; thank you, Mama—and thank you, Travis, for wearing the same pair of shoes for two semesters—

BENEATHA [*dropping to her knees*]. Well—I *do*—all right?—thank everybody . . . and forgive me for ever wanting to be anything at all . . . forgive me, forgive me!

RUTH. Please stop it! Your mama'll hear you.

WALTER. Who the hell told you you had to be a doctor? If you so crazy 'bout messing 'round with sick people—then go be a nurse like other women—or just get married and be quiet . . .

BENEATHA. Well—you finally got it said . . . It took you three years but you finally got it said. Walter, give up; leave me alone—it's Mama's money.

WALTER. *He was my father, too!*

BENEATHA. So what? He was mine, too—and Travis' grandfather—but the insurance money belongs to Mama. Picking on me is not going to make her give it to you to invest in any liquor stores—[*underbreath, dropping into a chair*]—and I for one say, God bless Mama for that!

WALTER [*to* RUTH]. See—did you hear? Did you hear!

RUTH. Honey, please go to work.

WALTER. Nobody in this house is ever going to understand me.

BENEATHA. Because you're a nut.

WALTER. Who's a nut?

BENEATHA. You—you are a nut. Thee is mad, boy.

WALTER [*looking at his wife and his sister from the door, very sadly*]. The world's most backward race of people, and that's a fact.

BENEATHA [*turning slowly in her chair*]. And then there are all those prophets who would lead us out of the wilderness—[WALTER *slams out of the house.*]—into the swamps!

RUTH. Bennie, why you always gotta be pickin' on your brother? Can't you be a little sweeter sometimes? [*Door opens.* WALTER *walks in.*]

WALTER [*to* RUTH]. I need some money for carfare.

RUTH [*looks at him, then warms; teasing, but tenderly*]. Fifty cents? [*She goes to her bag and gets money.*] Here, take a taxi.

[WALTER *exits.* MAMA *enters. She is a woman in her early sixties, full-bodied and strong. She is one of those women of a certain grace and beauty who wear it so unobtrusively that it takes a while to notice. Her dark-brown face is surrounded by the total whiteness of her hair, and, being a woman who has adjusted to many things in life and overcome many more, her face is full of strength. She has, we can see, wit and faith of a kind that keep her eyes lit and full of interest and expectancy. She is, in a word, a beautiful woman. Her bearing is perhaps most like the noble bearing of the women of the Hereros of Southwest Africa—rather as if she imagines that as she walks*] *she still bears a basket or a vessel upon her head. Her speech, on the other hand, is as careless as her carriage is precise—she is inclined to slur everything—but her voice is perhaps not so much quiet as simply soft.*]

MAMA. Who that 'round here slamming doors at this hour?

[*She crosses through the room, goes to the window, opens it, and brings in a feeble little plant growing doggedly in a small pot on the window sill. She feels the dirt and puts it back out.*]

RUTH. That was Walter Lee. He and Bennie was at it again.

MAMA. My children and they tempers. Lord, if this little old plant don't get more sun than it's been getting it ain't never going to see spring again. [*She turns from the window.*] What's the matter with you this morning, Ruth? You looks right peaked. You aiming to iron all them things? Leave some for me. I'll get to 'em this afternoon. Bennie honey, it's too drafty for you to be sitting 'round half dressed. Where's your robe?

BENEATHA. In the cleaners.

MAMA. Well, go get mine and put it on.

BENEATHA. I'm not cold, Mama, honest.

MAMA. I know—but you so thin . . .

BENEATHA [*irritably*]. Mama, I'm not cold.

MAMA [*seeing the make-down bed as* TRAVIS *has left it*]. Lord have mercy, look at that poor bed. Bless his heart—he tries, don't he?

[*She moves to the bed* TRAVIS *has sloppily made up.*]

RUTH. No—he don't half try at all 'cause he knows you going to come along behind him and fix everything. That's just how come he don't know how to do nothing right now—you done spoiled that boy so.

MAMA. Well—he's a little boy. Ain't supposed to know 'bout housekeeping. My baby, that's what he is. What you fix for his breakfast this morning?

RUTH [*angrily*]. I feed my son, Lena!

MAMA. I ain't meddling—[*underbreath; busy-bodyish*]. I just noticed all last week he had cold cereal, and when it starts getting this chilly in the fall a child ought to have some hot grits or something when he goes out in the cold—

RUTH [*furious*]. I gave him hot oats—is that all right!

MAMA. I ain't meddling. [*Pause.*] Put a lot of nice butter on it? [RUTH *shoots her an angry look and does not reply.*] He likes lots of butter.

RUTH [*exasperated*]. Lena—

MAMA [*to* BENEATHA. MAMA *is inclined to wander conversationally sometimes*]. What was you and your brother fussing 'bout this morning?

BENEATHA. It's not important, Mama.

[*She gets up and goes to look out at the bathroom, which is apparently free, and she picks up her towels and rushes out.*]

MAMA. What was they fighting about?

RUTH. Now you know as well as I do.

MAMA [*shaking her head*]. Brother still worrying hisself sick about that money?

RUTH. You know he is.

MAMA. You had breakfast?

RUTH. Some coffee.

MAMA. Girl, you better start eating and looking after yourself better. You almost thin as Travis.

RUTH. Lena—

MAMA. Un-hunh?

RUTH. What are you going to do with it?

MAMA. Now don't you start, child. It's too early in the morning to be talking about money. It ain't Christian.

RUTH. It's just that he got his heart set on that store—

MAMA. You mean that liquor store that Willy Harris want him to invest in?

RUTH. Yes—

MAMA. We ain't no business people, Ruth. We just plain working folks.

RUTH. Ain't nobody business people till they go into business. Walter Lee say colored people ain't never going to start getting ahead till they start gambling on some different kinds of things in the world—investments and things.

MAMA. What done got into you, girl? Walter Lee done finally sold you on investing.

RUTH. No. Mama, something is happening between Walter and me. I don't know what it is—but he needs something—something I can't give him any more. He needs this chance, Lena.

MAMA [*frowning deeply*]. But liquor, honey—

RUTH. Well—like Walter say—I spec people going to always be drinking themselves some liquor.

MAMA. Well—whether they drinks it or not ain't none of my business. But whether I go into business selling it to 'em *is*, and I don't want that on my ledger this late in life. [*Stopping suddenly and studying her daughter-in-law.*] Ruth Younger, what's the matter with you today? You look like you could fall over right there.

RUTH. I'm tired.

MAMA. Then you better stay home from work today.

RUTH. I can't stay home. She'd be calling up the agency and screaming at them, "My girl didn't come in today—send me somebody! My girl didn't come in!" Oh, she just have a fit . . .

MAMA. Well, let her have it. I'll just call her up and say you got the flu—

RUTH [*laughing*]. Why the flu?

MAMA. 'Cause it sounds respectable to 'em. Something white people get, too. They know 'bout the flu. Otherwise they think you been cut up or something when you tell 'em you sick.

RUTH. I got to go in. We need the money.

MAMA. Somebody would of thought my children done all but starved to death the way they talk about money here late. Child, we got a great big old check coming tomorrow.

RUTH [*sincerely, but also self-righteously*]. Now that's your money. It ain't got nothing to do with me. We all feel like that—Walter and Bennie and me—even Travis.

MAMA [*thoughtfully, and suddenly very far away*]. Ten thousand dollars—

RUTH. Sure is wonderful.

MAMA. Ten thousand dollars.

RUTH. You know what you should do, Miss Lena? You should take yourself a trip somewhere. To Europe or South America or some-place—

MAMA [*throwing up her hands at the thought*]. Oh, child!

RUTH. I'm serious. Just pack up and leave! Go on away and enjoy yourself some. Forget about the family and have yourself a ball for once in your life—

MAMA [*drily*]. You sound like I'm just about ready to die. Who'd go with me? What I look like wandering 'round Europe by myself?

RUTH. Shoot—these here rich white women do it all the time. They don't think nothing of packing up they suitcases and piling on one of them big steamships and—swoosh!—they gone, child.

MAMA. Something always told me I wasn't no rich white woman.

RUTH. Well—what are you going to do with it then?

MAMA. I ain't rightly decided. [*Thinking. She speaks now with emphasis.*] Some of it got to be put away for Beneatha and her schoolin' —and ain't nothing going to touch that part of it. Nothing. [*She waits several seconds, trying to make up her mind about something, and looks at* RUTH *a little tentatively before going on.*] Been thinking that we maybe could meet the notes on a little old two-story somewhere, with a yard where Travis could play in the summertime, if we use part of the insurance for a down payment and everybody kind of pitch in. I could maybe take on a little day work again, few days a week—

RUTH [*studying her mother-in-law furtively and concentrating on her ironing, anxious to encourage without seeming to*]. Well, Lord knows, we've put enough rent into this here rat trap to pay for four houses by now . . .

MAMA [*looking up at the words "rat trap" and then looking around and leaning back and sighing—in a suddenly reflective mood—*]. "Rat trap" —yes, that's all it is. [*Smiling*] I remember just as well the day me and Big Walter moved in here. Hadn't been married but two weeks and wasn't planning on living here no more than a year. [*She shakes her head at the dissolved dream.*] We was going to set away, little by little, don't you know, and buy a little place out in Morgan Park. We had even picked out the house. [*Chuckling a little.*] Looks right dumpy today. But Lord, child, you should know all the dreams I had 'bout buying that house and fixing it up and making me a little garden in the back —[*She waits and stops smiling.*] And didn't none of it happen. [*Dropping her hands in a futile gesture.*]

RUTH [*keeps her head down, ironing*]. Yes, life can be a barrel of disappointments, sometimes.

MAMA. Honey, Big Walter would come in here some nights back then and slump down on that couch there and just look at the rug, and look at me and look at the rug and then back at me—and I'd know he was down then . . . really down. [*After a second very long and thoughtful pause; she is seeing back to times that only she can see.*] And then, Lord, when I lost that baby—little Claude—I almost thought I was going to lose Big Walter too. Oh, that man grieved hisself! He was one man to love his children.

RUTH. Ain't nothin' can tear at you like losin' your baby.

MAMA. I guess that's how come that man finally worked hisself to death like he done. Like he was fighting his own war with this here world that took his baby from him.

RUTH. He sure was a fine man, all right. I always liked Mr. Younger.

MAMA. Crazy 'bout his children! God knows there was plenty wrong with Walter Younger—hard-headed, mean, kind of wild with women —plenty wrong with him. But he sure loved his children. Always wanted them to have something—be something. That's where Brother gets all these notions, I reckon. Big Walter used to say, he'd get right wet in the eyes sometimes, lean his head back with the water standing in his eyes and say, "Seem like God didn't see fit to give the black man nothing but dreams—but He did give us children to make them dreams seem worth while." [*She smiles.*] He could talk like that, don't you know.

RUTH. Yes, he sure could. He was a good man, Mr. Younger.

MAMA. Yes, a fine man—just couldn't never catch up with his dreams, that's all.

[BENEATHA *comes in, brushing her hair and looking up to the ceiling where the sound of a vacuum cleaner has started up.*]

BENEATHA. What could be so dirty on that woman's rugs that she has to vacuum them every single day?

RUTH. I wish certain young women 'round here who I could name would take inspiration about certain rugs in a certain apartment I could also mention.

BENEATHA [*shrugging*]. How much cleaning can a house need, for Christ's sakes.

MAMA [*not liking the Lord's name used thus*]. Bennie!

RUTH. Just listen to her—just listen!

BENEATHA. Oh, God!

MAMA. If you use the Lord's name just one more time—

BENEATHA [*a bit of a whine*]. Oh, Mama—

RUTH. Fresh—just fresh as salt, this girl!

BENEATHA [drily]. Well—if the salt loses its savor—

MAMA. Now that will do. I just ain't going to have you 'round here reciting the scriptures in vain—you hear me?

BENEATHA. How did I manage to get on everybody's wrong side by just walking into a room?

RUTH. If you weren't so fresh—

BENEATHA. Ruth, I'm twenty years old.

MAMA. What time you be home from school today?

BENEATHA. Kind of late. [With enthusiasm.] Madeline is going to start my guitar lessons today.

[MAMA and RUTH look up with the same expression.]

MAMA. Your what kind of lessons?

BENEATHA. Guitar.

RUTH. Oh, Father!

MAMA. How come you done taken it in your mind to learn to play the guitar?

BENEATHA. I just want to, that's all.

MAMA [smiling]. Lord, child, don't you know what to do with yourself? How long it going to be before you get tired of this now—like you got tired of that little play-acting group you joined last year? [Looking at RUTH.] And what was it the year before that?

RUTH. The horseback-riding club for which she bought that fifty-five-dollar riding habit that's been hanging in the closet ever since!

MAMA [to BENEATHA]. Why you got to flit so from one thing to another, baby?

BENEATHA [sharply]. I just want to learn to play the guitar. Is there anything wrong with that?

MAMA. Ain't nobody trying to stop you. I just wonders sometimes why you has to flit so from one thing to another all the time. You ain't never done nothing with all that camera equipment you brought home—

BENEATHA. I don't flit! I—I experiment with different forms of expression—

RUTH. Like riding a horse?

BENEATHA. —People have to express themselves one way or another.

MAMA. What is it you want to express?

BENEATHA [angrily]. Me! [MAMA and RUTH look at each other and burst into raucous laughter.] Don't worry—I don't expect you to understand.

MAMA [to change the subject]. Who you going out with tomorrow night?

BENEATHA [with displeasure]. George Murchison again.

MAMA [pleased]. Oh—you getting a little sweet on him?

RUTH. You ask me, this child ain't sweet on nobody but herself—[underbreath]. Express herself!

[*They laugh.*]

BENEATHA. Oh—I like George all right, Mama. I mean I like him enough to go out with him and stuff, but—

RUTH [*for devilment*]. What does *and stuff* mean?

BENEATHA. Mind your own business.

MAMA. Stop picking at her now, Ruth. [*A thoughtful pause, and then a suspicious sudden look at her daughter as she turns in her chair for emphasis.*] What *does* it mean?

BENEATHA [*wearily*]. Oh, I just mean I couldn't ever really be serious about George. He's—he's so shallow.

RUTH. Shallow—what do you mean he's shallow? He's *rich!*

MAMA. Hush, Ruth.

BENEATHA. I know he's rich. He knows he's rich, too.

RUTH. Well—what other qualities a man got to have to satisfy you, little girl?

BENEATHA. You wouldn't even begin to understand. Anybody who married Walter could not possibly understand.

MAMA [*outraged*]. What kind of way is that to talk about your brother?

BENEATHA. Brother is a flip—let's face it.

MAMA [*to* RUTH, *helplessly*]. What's a flip?

RUTH [*glad to add kindling*]. She's saying he's crazy.

BENEATHA. Not crazy. Brother isn't really crazy yet—he—he's an elaborate neurotic.

MAMA. Hush your mouth!

BENEATHA. As for George. Well. George looks good—he's got a beautiful car and he takes me to nice places and, as my sister-in-law says, he is probably the richest boy I will ever get to know and I even like him sometimes—but if the Youngers are sitting around waiting to see if their little Bennie is going to tie up the family with the Murchisons, they are wasting their time.

RUTH. You mean you wouldn't marry George Murchison if he asked you someday? That pretty, rich thing? Honey, I knew you was odd—

BENEATHA. No I would not marry him if all I felt for him was what I feel now. Besides, George's family wouldn't really like it.

MAMA. Why not?

BENEATHA. Oh, Mama—The Murchisons are honest-to-God-real-*live*-rich colored people, and the only people in the world who are more snobbish than rich white people are rich colored people. I thought everybody knew that. I've met Mrs. Murchison. She's a scene!

MAMA. You must not dislike people 'cause they well off, honey.

BENEATHA. Why not? It makes just as much sense as disliking people 'cause they are poor, and lots of people do that.

RUTH [*a wisdom-of-the-ages manner. To* MAMA]. Well, she'll get over some of this—

BENEATHA. Get over it? What are you talking about, Ruth? Listen,
I'm going to be a doctor. I'm not worried about who I'm going to
marry yet—if I ever get married.
MAMA *and* RUTH. *If!*
MAMA. Now, Bennie—
BENEATHA. Oh, I probably will . . . but first I'm going to be a doc-
tor, and George, for one, still thinks that's pretty funny. I couldn't be
bothered with that. I am going to be a doctor and everybody around
here better understand that!
MAMA [*kindly*]. 'Course you going to be a doctor, honey, God willing.
BENEATHA [*drily*]. God hasn't got a thing to do with it.
MAMA. Beneatha—that just wasn't necessary.
BENEATHA. Well—neither is God. I get sick of hearing about God.
MAMA. Beneatha!
BENEATHA. I mean it! I'm just tired of hearing about God all the time.
What has He got to do with anything? Does he pay tuition?
MAMA. You 'bout to get your fresh little jaw slapped!
RUTH. That's just what she needs, all right!
BENEATHA. Why? Why can't I say what I want to around here, like
everybody else?
MAMA. It don't sound nice for a young girl to say things like that—you
wasn't brought up that way. Me and your father went to trouble to
get you and Brother to church every Sunday.
BENEATHA. Mama, you don't understand. It's all a matter of ideas, and
God is just one idea I don't accept. It's not important. I am not going
out and be immoral or commit crimes because I don't believe in God.
I don't even think about it. It's just that I get tired of Him getting
credit for all the things the human race achieves through its own stubborn effort. There simply is no blasted God—there is only man and it
is he who makes miracles!
[MAMA *absorbs this speech, studies her daughter and rises slowly and crosses
to* BENEATHA *and slaps her powerfully across the face. After, there is only
silence and the daughter drops her eyes from her mother's face, and* MAMA
is very tall before her.]
MAMA. Now—you say after me, in my mother's house there is still
God. [*There is a long pause and* BENEATHA *stares at the floor wordlessly.*
MAMA *repeats the phrase with precision and cool emotion.*] In my mother's
house there is still God.
BENEATHA. In my mother's house there is still God.
[*A long pause.*]
MAMA [*walking away from* BENEATHA, *too disturbed for triumphant pos-
ture. Stopping and turning back to her daughter*]. There are some ideas
we ain't going to have in this house. Not long as I am at the head of
this family.
BENEATHA. Yes, ma'am.
[MAMA *walks out of the room.*]

RUTH [*almost gently, with profound understanding*]. You think you a woman, Bennie—but you still a little girl. What you did was childish —so you got treated like a child.

BENEATHA. I see. [*Quietly.*] I also see that everybody thinks it's all right for Mama to be a tyrant. But all the tyranny in the world will never put a God in the heavens!

[*She picks up her books and goes out.*]

RUTH [*goes to* MAMA'*s door*]. She said she was sorry.

MAMA [*coming out, going to her plant*]. They frightens me, Ruth. My children.

RUTH. You got good children, Lena. They just a little off sometimes— but they're good.

MAMA. No—there's something come down between me and them that don't let us understand each other and I don't know what it is. One done almost lost his mind thinking 'bout money all the time and the other done commence to talk about things I can't seem to understand in no form or fashion. What is it that's changing, Ruth?

RUTH [*soothingly, older than her years*]. Now . . . you taking it all too seriously. You just got strong-willed children and it takes a strong woman like you to keep 'em in hand.

MAMA [*looking at her plant and sprinkling a little water on it*]. They spirited all right, my children. Got to admit they got spirit—Bennie and Walter. Like this little old plant that ain't never had enough sun- shine or nothing—and look at it . . .

[*She has her back to* RUTH, *who has had to stop ironing and lean against something and put the back of her hand to her forehead.*]

RUTH [*trying to keep* MAMA *from noticing*]. You . . . sure . . . loves that little old thing, don't you? . . .

MAMA. Well, I always wanted me a garden like I used to see some- times at the back of the houses down home. This plant is close as I ever got to having one. [*She looks out of the window as she replaces the plant.*] Lord, ain't nothing as dreary as the view from this window on a dreary day, is there? Why ain't you singing this morning, Ruth? Sing that "No Ways Tired." That song always lifts me up so—[*She turns at last to see that* RUTH *has slipped quietly into a chair, in a state of semi- consciousness.*] Ruth! Ruth honey—what's the matter with you . . . Ruth!

Curtain.

SCENE TWO

It is the following morning; a Saturday morning, and house cleaning is in progress at the YOUNGERS. *Furniture has been shoved hither and yon and* MAMA *is giving the kitchen-area walls a washing down.* BENEATHA, *in dungarees, with a handkerchief tied around her face, is spraying insecticide into the cracks in the walls. As they work, the radio is on and a Southside disk-*

jockey program is inappropriately filling the house with a rather exotic saxophone blues. TRAVIS, *the sole idle one, is leaning on his arms, looking out of the window.*

TRAVIS. Grandmama, that stuff Bennie is using smells awful. Can I go downstairs, please?

MAMA. Did you get all them chores done already? I ain't seen you doing much.

TRAVIS. Yes'm—finished early. Where did Mama go this morning?

MAMA [*looking at* BENEATHA]. She had to go on a little errand.

TRAVIS. Where?

MAMA. To tend to her business.

TRAVIS. Can I go outside then?

MAMA. Oh, I guess so. You better stay right in front of the house, though . . . and keep a good lookout for the postman.

TRAVIS. Yes'm. [*He starts out and decides to give his* AUNT BENEATHA *a good swat on the legs as he passes her.*] Leave them poor little old cockroaches alone, they ain't bothering you none.
[*He runs as she swings the spray gun at him both viciously and playfully.* WALTER *enters from the bedroom and goes to the phone.*]

MAMA. Look out there, girl, before you be spilling some of that stuff on that child!

TRAVIS [*teasing*]. That's right—look out now!
[*He exits.*]

BENEATHA [*drily*]. I can't imagine that it would hurt him—it has never hurt the roaches.

MAMA. Well, little boys' hides ain't as tough as Southside roaches.

WALTER [*into phone*]. Hello—Let me talk to Willy Harris.

MAMA. You better get over there behind the bureau. I seen one marching out of there like Napoleon yesterday.

WALTER. Hello, Willy? It ain't come yet. It'll be here in a few minutes. Did the lawyer give you the papers?

BENEATHA. There's really only one way to get rid of them, Mama—

MAMA. How?

BENEATHA. Set fire to this building.

WALTER. Good. Good. I'll be right over.

BENEATHA. Where did Ruth go, Walter?

WALTER. I don't know.
[*He exits abruptly.*]

BENEATHA. Mama, where did Ruth go?

MAMA [*looking at her with meaning*]. To the doctor, I think.

BENEATHA. The doctor? What's the matter? [*They exchange glances.*] You don't think—

MAMA [*with her sense of drama*]. Now I ain't saying what I think. But I ain't never been wrong 'bout a woman neither.
[*The phone rings.*]

BENEATHA [*at the phone*]. Hay-lo . . . [*pause, and a moment of recognition*]. Well—when did you get back! . . . And how was it? . . . Of course I've missed you—in my way . . . This morning? No . . . house cleaning and all that and Mama hates it if I let people come over when the house is like this . . . You *have?* Well, that's different . . . What is it—Oh, what the hell, come on over . . . Right, see you then.
[*She hangs up.*]

MAMA [*who has listened vigorously, as is her habit*]. Who is that you inviting over here with this house looking like this? You ain't got the pride you was born with!

BENEATHA. Asagai doesn't care how houses look, Mama—he's an intellectual.

MAMA. *Who?*

BENEATHA. Asagai—Joseph Asagai. He's an African boy I met on campus. He's been studying in Canada all summer.

MAMA. What's his name?

BENEATHA. Asagai, Joseph. Ah-sah-guy . . . He's from Nigeria.

MAMA. Oh, that's the little country that was founded by slaves way back . . .

BENEATHA. No, Mama—that's Liberia.

MAMA. I don't think I never met no African before.

BENEATHA. Well, do me a favor and don't ask him a whole lot of ignorant questions about Africans. I mean, do they wear clothes and all that—

MAMA. Well, now, I guess if you think we so ignorant 'round here maybe you shouldn't bring your friends here—

BENEATHA. It's just that people ask such crazy things. All anyone seems to know about when it comes to Africa is Tarzan—

MAMA [*indignantly*]. Why should I know anything about Africa?

BENEATHA. Why do you give money at church for the missionary work?

MAMA. Well, that's to help save people.

BENEATHA. You mean save them from *heathenism*—

MAMA [*innocently*]. Yes.

BENEATHA. I'm afraid they need more salvation from the British and the French.
[RUTH *comes in forlornly and pulls off her coat with dejection. They both turn to look at her.*]

RUTH [*dispiritedly*]. Well, I guess from all the happy faces—everybody knows.

BENEATHA. You pregnant?

MAMA. Lord have mercy, I sure hope it's a little old girl. Travis ought to have a sister.
[BENEATHA *and* RUTH *give her a hopeless look for this grandmotherly enthusiasm.*]

BENEATHA. How far along are you?

RUTH. Two months.

BENEATHA. Did you mean to? I mean did you plan it or was it an accident?

MAMA. What do you know about planning or not planning?

BENEATHA. Oh, Mama.

RUTH [*wearily*]. She's twenty years old, Lena.

BENEATHA. Did you plan it, Ruth?

RUTH. Mind your own business.

BENEATHA. It is my business—where is he going to live, on the *roof?* [*There is silence following the remark as the three women react to the sense of it.*] Gee—I didn't mean that, Ruth, honest. Gee, I don't feel like that at all. I—I think it is wonderful.

RUTH [*dully*]. Wonderful.

BENEATHA. Yes—really.

MAMA [*looking at* RUTH, *worried*]. Doctor say everything going to be all right?

RUTH [*far away*]. Yes—she says everything is going to be fine . . .

MAMA [*immediately suspicious*]. "She"—What doctor you went to? RUTH *folds over, near hysteria.*

MAMA [*worriedly hovering over* RUTH]. Ruth honey—what's the matter with you—you sick? [RUTH *has her fists clenched on her thighs and is fighting hard to suppress a scream that seems to be rising in her.*]

BENEATHA. What's the matter with her, Mama?

MAMA [*working her fingers in* RUTH'*s shoulder to relax her*]. She be all right. Women gets right depressed sometimes when they get her way. [*Speaking softly, expertly, rapidly.*] Now you just relax. That's right . . . just lean back, don't think 'bout nothing at all . . . nothing at all—

RUTH. I'm all right . . . [*The glassy-eyed look melts and then she collapses into a fit of heavy sobbing. The bell rings.*]

BENEATHA. Oh, my God—that must be Asagai.

MAMA [*to* RUTH]. Come on now, honey. You need to lie down and rest awhile . . . then have some nice hot food. [*They exit,* RUTH'*s weight on her mother-in-law.* BENEATHA, *herself profoundly disturbed, opens the door to admit a rather dramatic-looking young man with a large package.*]

ASAGAI. Hello, Alaiyo—

BENEATHA [*holding the door open and regarding him with pleasure*]. Hello . . . [*Long pause.*] Well—come in. And please excuse everything. My mother was very upset about my letting anyone come here with the place like this.

ASAGAI [*coming into the room*]. You look disturbed too . . . Is something wrong?

BENEATHA [*still at the door, absently*]. Yes . . . we've all got acute ghetto-itus. [*She smiles and comes toward him, finding a cigarette and sitting.*] So—sit down! How was Canada?

ASAGAI [*a sophisticate*]. Canadian.

BENEATHA [*looking at him*]. I'm very glad you are back.

ASAGAI [*looking back at her in turn*]. Are you really?

BENEATHA. Yes—very.

ASAGAI. Why—you were quite glad when I went away. What happened?

BENEATHA. You went away.

ASAGAI. Ahhhhhhhh.

BENEATHA. Before—you wanted to be so serious before there was time.

ASAGAI. How much time must there be before one knows what one feels?

BENEATHA [*stalling this particular conversation. Her hands pressed together, in a deliberately childish gesture*]. What did you bring me?

ASAGAI [*handing her the package*]. Open it and see.

BENEATHA [*eagerly opening the package and drawing out some records and the colorful robes of a Nigerian woman*]. Oh, Asagai! . . . You got them for me! . . . How beautiful! . . . and the records, too! [*She lifts out the robes and runs to the mirror with them and holds the drapery up in front of herself.*]

ASAGAI [*coming to her at the mirror*]. I shall have to teach you how to drape it properly. [*He flings the material about her for the moment and stands back to look at her.*] Ah—Oh-pay-gay-day, oh-ghah-mu-shay. [*A Yoruba exclamation for admiration.*] You wear it well . . . very well . . . mutilated hair and all.

BENEATHA [*turning suddenly*]. My hair—what's wrong with my hair?

ASAGAI [*shrugging*]. Were you born with it like that?

BENEATHA [*reaching up to touch it*]. No . . . of course not.
[*She looks back to the mirror, disturbed.*]

ASAGAI [*smiling*]. How then?

BENEATHA. You know perfectly well how . . . as crinkly as yours . . . that's how.

ASAGAI. And it is ugly to you that way?

BENEATHA [*quickly*]. Oh, no—not ugly . . . [*More slowly, apologetically.*] But it's so hard to manage when it's, well—raw.

ASAGAI. And so to accommodate that—you mutilate it every week?

BENEATHA. It's not mutilation!

ASAGAI [*laughing aloud at her seriousness*]. Oh . . . please! I am only teasing you because you are so very serious about these things. [*He stands back from her and folds his arms across his chest as he watches her pulling at her hair and frowning in the mirror.*] Do you remember the first time you met me at school? . . . [*He laughs.*] You came up to me and you said—and I thought you were the most serious little thing

I had ever seen—you said: [*He imitates her.*] "Mr. Asagai—I want very much to talk with you. About Africa. You see, Mr. Asagai, I am looking for my *identity!*"
[*He laughs.*]
BENEATHA [*turning to him, not laughing*]. Yes—
[*Her face is quizzical, profoundly disturbed.*]
ASAGAI [*still teasing and reaching out and taking her face in his hands and turning her profile to him*]. Well . . . it is true that this is not so much a profile of a Hollywood queen as perhaps a queen of the Nile—[*a mock dismissal of the importance of the question*]. But what does it matter? Assimilationism is so popular in your country.
BENEATHA [*wheeling, passionately, sharply*]. I am not an assimilationist!
ASAGAI [*The protest hangs in the room for a moment and* ASAGAI *studies her, his laughter fading*]. Such a serious one. [*There is a pause.*] So— you like the robes? You must take excellent care of them—they are from my sister's personal wardrobe.
BENEATHA [*with incredulity*]. You—you sent all the way home—for me?
ASAGAI [*with charm*]. For you—I would do much more . . . Well, that is what I came for. I must go.
BENEATHA. Will you call me Monday?
ASAGAI. Yes . . . We have a great deal to talk about. I mean about identity and time and all that.
BENEATHA. Time?
ASAGAI. Yes. About how much time one needs to know what one feels.
BENEATHA. You never understood that there is more than one kind of feeling which can exist between a man and a woman—or, at least, there should be.
ASAGAI [*shaking his head negatively but gently*]. No. Between a man and a woman there need be only one kind of feeling. I have that for you . . . Now even . . . right this moment . . .
BENEATHA. I know—and by itself—it won't do. I can find that any- where.
ASAGAI. For a woman it should be enough.
BENEATHA. I know—because that's what it says in all the novels that men write. But it isn't. Go ahead and laugh—but I'm not interested in being someone's little episode in America or—[*with feminine venge- ance*]—one of them! [ASAGAI *has burst into laughter again.*] That's funny as hell, huh!
ASAGAI. It's just that every American girl I have known has said that to me. White—black—in this you are all the same. And the same speech, too!
BENEATHA [*angrily*]. Yuk, yuk, yuk!
ASAGAI. It's how you can be sure that the world's most liberated women are not liberated at all. You all talk about it too much!

[MAMA *enters and is immediately all social charm because of the presence of a guest.*]

BENEATHA. Oh—Mama—this is Mr. Asagai.

MAMA. How do you do?

ASAGAI [*total politeness to an elder*]. How do you do, Mrs. Younger. Please forgive me for coming at such an outrageous hour on a Saturday.

MAMA. Well, you are quite welcome. I just hope you understand that our house don't always look like this. [*Chatterish.*] You must come again. I would love to hear all about—[*not sure of the name*]—your country. I think it's so sad the way our American Negroes don't know nothing about Africa 'cept Tarzan and all that. And all that money they pour into these churches when they ought to be helping you people over there drive out them French and Englishmen done taken away your land.

[*The mother flashes a slightly superior look at her daughter upon completion of the recitation.*]

ASAGAI [*taken aback by this sudden and acutely unrelated expression of sympathy*]. Yes . . . yes . . .

MAMA [*smiling at him suddenly and relaxing and looking him over*]. How many miles is it from here to where you come from?

ASAGAI. Many thousands.

MAMA [*looking at him as she would* WALTER]. I bet you don't half look after yourself, being away from your mama either. I spec you better come 'round here from time to time and get yourself some decent home-cooked meals . . .

ASAGAI [*moved*]. Thank you. Thank you very much. [*They are all quiet, then—*] Well . . . I must go. I will call you Monday, Alaiyo.

MAMA. What's that he call you?

ASAGAI. Oh—"Alaiyo." I hope you don't mind. It is what you would call a nickname, I think. It is a Yoruba word. I am a Yoruba.

MAMA [*looking at* BENEATHA]. I—I thought he was from—

ASAGAI [*understanding*]. Nigeria is my country. Yoruba is my tribal origin—

BENEATHA. You didn't tell us what Alaiyo means . . . for all I know, you might be calling me Little Idiot or something . . .

ASAGAI. Well . . . let me see . . . I do not know how just to explain it . . . The sense of a thing can be so different when it changes languages.

BENEATHA. You're evading.

ASAGAI. No—really it is difficult . . . [*Thinking.*] It means . . . it means One for Whom Bread—Food—Is Not Enough. [*He looks at her.*] Is that all right?

BENEATHA [*understanding, softly*]. Thank you.

MAMA [*looking from one to the other and not understanding any of it*].

Well . . . that's nice . . . You must come see us again—Mr.—

ASAGAI. Ah-sah-guy . . .

MAMA. Yes . . . Do come again.

ASAGAI. Good-bye.

[*He exits.*]

MAMA [*after him*]. Lord, that's a pretty thing just went out here! [*Insinuatingly, to her daughter.*] Yes, I guess I see why we done commence to get so interested in Africa 'round here. Missionaries my aunt Jenny!

[*She exits.*]

BENEATHA. Oh, Mama! . . .

[*She picks up the Nigerian dress and holds it up to her in front of the mirror again. She sets the headdress on haphazardly and then notices her hair again and clutches at it and then replaces the headdress and frowns at herself. Then she starts to wriggle in front of the mirror as she thinks a Nigerian woman might.* TRAVIS *enters and regards her.*]

TRAVIS. You cracking up?

BENEATHA. Shut up.

[*She pulls the headdress off and looks at herself in the mirror and clutches at her hair again and squinches her eyes as if trying to imagine something. Then, suddenly, she gets her raincoat and kerchief and hurriedly prepares for going out.*]

MAMA [*coming back into the room*]. She's resting now. Travis, baby, run next door and ask Miss Johnson to please let me have a little kitchen cleanser. This here can is empty as Jacob's kettle.

TRAVIS. I just came in.

MAMA. Do as you told. [*He exits and she looks at her daughter.*] Where you going?

BENEATHA [*halting at the door*]. To become a queen of the Nile!

[*She exits in a breathless blaze of glory.* RUTH *appears in the bedroom doorway.*]

MAMA. Who told you to get up?

RUTH. Ain't nothing wrong with me to be lying in no bed for. Where did Bennie go?

MAMA [*drumming her fingers*]. Far as I could make out—to Egypt. [RUTH *just looks at her.*] What time is it getting to?

RUTH. Ten twenty. And the mailman going to ring that bell this morning just like he done every morning for the last umpteen years.

[TRAVIS *comes in with the cleanser can.*]

TRAVIS. She say to tell you that she don't have much.

MAMA [*angrily*]. Lord, some people I could name sure is tight-fisted! [*Directing her grandson.*] Mark two cans of cleanser down on the list there. If she that hard up for kitchen cleanser, I sure don't want to forget to get her none!

RUTH. Lena—maybe the woman is just short on cleanser—

MAMA [*not listening*]. —Much baking powder as she done borrowed from me all these years, she could of done gone into the baking business!

[*The bell sounds suddenly and sharply and all three are stunned—serious and silent—mid-speech. In spite of all the other conversations and distractions of the morning, this is what they have been waiting for, even* TRAVIS, *who looks helplessly from his mother to his grandmother.* RUTH *is the first to come to life again.*]

RUTH [*to* TRAVIS]. Get down them steps, boy!

TRAVIS *snaps to life and flies out to get the mail.*

MAMA [*her eyes wide, her hand to her breast*]. You mean it done really come?

RUTH [*excited*]. Oh, Miss Lena!

MAMA [*collecting herself*]. Well . . . I don't know what we all so excited about 'round here for. We known it was coming for months.

RUTH. That's a whole lot different from having it come and being able to hold it in your hands . . . a piece of paper worth ten thousand dollars . . . [TRAVIS *bursts back into the room. He holds the envelope high above his head, like a little dancer, his face is radiant and he is breathless. He moves to his grandmother with sudden slow ceremony and puts the envelope into her hands. She accepts it, and then merely holds it and looks at it.*] Come on! Open it . . . Lord have mercy, I wish Walter Lee was here!

TRAVIS. Open it, Grandmama!

MAMA [*staring at it*]. Now you all be quiet. It's just a check.

RUTH. Open it . . .

MAMA [*still staring at it*]. Now don't act silly . . . We ain't never been no people to act silly 'bout no money—

RUTH [*swiftly*]. We ain't never had none before—*open it!*

[MAMA *finally makes a good strong tear and pulls out the thin blue slice of paper and inspects it closely. The boy and his mother study it raptly over* MAMA's *shoulders.*]

MAMA. Travis! [*She is counting off with doubt.*] Is that the right number of zeros.

TRAVIS. Yes'm . . . ten thousand dollars. Gaalee, Grandmama, you rich.

MAMA [*She holds the check away from her, still looking at it. Slowly her face sobers into a mask of unhappiness*]. Ten thousand dollars. [*She hands it to* RUTH.] Put it away somewhere, Ruth. [*She does not look at* RUTH; *her eyes seem to be seeing something somewhere very far off.*] Ten thousand dollars they give you. Ten thousand dollars.

TRAVIS [*to his mother, sincerely*]. What's the matter with Grandmama—don't she want to be rich?

RUTH [*distractedly*]. You go on out and play now, baby. [TRAVIS *exits.* MAMA *starts wiping dishes absently, humming intently to herself.* RUTH *turns to her, with kind exasperation.*] You've gone and got yourself upset.

MAMA [*not looking at her*]. I spec if it wasn't for you all . . . I would just put that money away or give it to the church or something.

RUTH. Now what kind of talk is that. Mr. Younger would just be plain mad if he could hear you talking foolish like that.

MAMA [*stopping and staring off*]. Yes . . . he sure would. [*Sighing.*] We got enough to do with that money, all right. [*She halts then, and turns and looks at her daughter-in-law hard; RUTH avoids her eyes and MAMA wipes her hands with finality and starts to speak firmly to RUTH.*] Where did you go today, girl?

RUTH. To the doctor.

MAMA [*impatiently*]. Now, Ruth . . . you know better than that. Old Doctor Jones is strange enough in his way but there ain't nothing 'bout him make somebody slip and call him "she"—like you done this morning.

RUTH. Well, that's what happened—my tongue slipped.

MAMA. You went to see that woman, didn't you?

RUTH [*defensively, giving herself away*]. What woman you talking about?

MAMA [*angrily*]. That woman who—
      [WALTER *enters in great excitement.*]

WALTER. Did it come?

MAMA [*quietly*]. Can't you give people a Christian greeting before you start asking about money?

WALTER [*to* RUTH]. Did it come? [RUTH *unfolds the check and lays it quietly before him, watching him intently with thoughts of her own.* WALTER *sits down and grasps it close and counts off the zeros.*] Ten thousand dollars—[*He turns suddenly, frantically to his mother and draws some papers out of his breast pocket.*] Mama—look. Old Willy Harris put everything on paper—

MAMA. Son—I think you ought to talk to your wife . . . I'll go on out and leave you alone if you want—

WALTER. I can talk to her later—Mama, look—

MAMA. Son—

WALTER. WILL SOMEBODY PLEASE LISTEN TO ME TODAY!

MAMA [*quietly*]. I don't 'low no yellin' in this house, Walter Lee, and you know it—[WALTER *stares at them in frustration and starts to speak several times.*] And there ain't going to be no investing in no liquor stores. I don't aim to have to speak on that again.
      [*A long pause.*]

WALTER. Oh—so you don't aim to have to speak on that again? So *you* have decided . . . [*Crumpling his papers.*] Well, *you* tell that to my boy tonight when you put him to sleep on the living-room couch . . . [*Turning to* MAMA *and speaking directly to her.*] Yeah—and tell it to my wife, Mama, tomorrow when she has to go out of here to look after somebody else's kids. And tell it to *me*, Mama, every time we

need a new pair of curtains and I have to watch *you* go out and work in somebody's kitchen. Yeah, you tell me then!
[WALTER *starts out.*]

RUTH. Where you going?

WALTER. I'm going out!

RUTH. Where?

WALTER. Just out of this house somewhere—

RUTH [*getting her coat*]. I'll come too.

WALTER. I don't want you to come!

RUTH. I got something to talk to you about, Walter.

WALTER. That's too bad.

MAMA [*still quietly*]. Walter Lee—[*She waits and he finally turns and looks at her.*] Sit down.

WALTER. I'm a grown man, Mama.

MAMA. Ain't nobody said you wasn't grown. But you still in my house and my presence. And as long as you are—you'll talk to your wife civil. Now sit down.

RUTH [*suddenly*]. Oh, let him go on out and drink himself to death! He makes me sick to my stomach! [*She flings her coat against him.*]

WALTER [*violently*]. And you turn mine too, baby! [RUTH *goes into their bedroom and slams the door behind her.*] That was my greatest mistake—

MAMA [*still quietly*]. Walter, what is the matter with you?

WALTER. Matter with me? Ain't nothing the matter with *me!*

MAMA. Yes there is. Something eating you up like a crazy man. Something more than me not giving you this money. The past few years I been watching it happen to you. You get all nervous acting and kind of wild in the eyes—[WALTER *jumps up impatiently at her words.*] I said sit there now, I'm talking to you!

WALTER. Mama—I don't need no nagging at me today.

MAMA. Seem like you getting to a place where you always tied up in some kind of knot about something. But if anybody ask you 'bout it you just yell at 'em and bust out the house and go out and drink somewheres. Walter Lee, people can't live with that. Ruth's a good, patient girl in her way—but you getting to be too much. Boy, don't make the mistake of driving that girl away from you.

WALTER. Why—what she do for me?

MAMA. She loves you.

WALTER. Mama—I'm going out. I want to go off somewhere and be by myself for a while.

MAMA. I'm sorry 'bout your liquor store, son. It just wasn't the thing for us to do. That's what I want to tell you about—

WALTER. I got to go out, Mama—
[*He rises.*]

MAMA. It's dangerous, son.

WALTER. What's dangerous?

MAMA. When a man goes outside his home to look for peace.

WALTER [*beseechingly*]. Then why can't there never be no peace in this house then?

MAMA. You done found it in some other house?

WALTER. No—there ain't no woman! Why do women always think there's a woman somewhere when a man gets restless. [*Coming to her.*] Mama—Mama—I want so many things . . .

MAMA. Yes, son—

WALTER. I want so many things that they are driving me kind of crazy. . . . Mama—look at me.

MAMA. I'm looking at you. You a good-looking boy. You got a job, a nice wife, a fine boy and—

WALTER. A job. [*Looks at her.*] Mama, a job? I open and close car doors all day long. I drive a man around in his limousine and I say, "Yes, sir; no, sir; very good, sir; shall I take the Drive, sir?" Mama, that ain't no kind of job . . . that ain't nothing at all. [*Very quietly.*] Mama, I don't know if I can make you understand.

MAMA. Understand what, baby?

WALTER [*quietly*]. Sometimes it's like I can see the future stretched out in front of me—just plain as day. The future, Mama. Hanging over there at the edge of my days. Just waiting for me—a big, looming blank space—full of *nothing*. Just waiting for *me*. [*Pause.*] Mama— sometimes when I'm downtown and I pass them cool, quiet-looking restaurants where them white boys are sitting back and talking 'bout things . . . sitting there turning deals worth millions of dollars . . . sometimes I see guys don't look much older than me—

MAMA. Son—how come you talk so much 'bout money?

WALTER [*with immense passion*]. Because it is life, Mama!

MAMA [*quietly*]. Oh—[*very quietly*]. So now it's life. Money is life. Once upon a time freedom used to be life—now it's money. I guess the world really do change . . .

WALTER. No—it was always money, Mama. We just didn't know about it.

MAMA. No . . . something has changed. [*She looks at him.*] You something new, boy. In my time we was worried about not being lynched and getting to the North if we could and how to stay alive and still have a pinch of dignity too . . . Now here come you and Beneatha— talking 'bout things we ain't never even thought about hardly, me and your daddy. You ain't satisfied or proud of nothing we done. I mean that you had a home; that we kept you out of trouble till you was grown; that you don't have to ride to work on the back of nobody's streetcar— You my children—but how different we done become.

WALTER. You just don't understand, Mama, you just don't under-stand.

MAMA. Son—do you know your wife is expecting another baby?

[WALTER *stands, stunned, and absorbs what his mother has said.*] That's what she wanted to talk to you about. [WALTER *sinks down into a chair.*] This ain't for me to be telling—but you ought to know. [*She waits.*] I think Ruth is thinking 'bout getting rid of that child.

WALTER [*slowly understanding*]. No—no—Ruth wouldn't do that.

MAMA. When the world gets ugly enough—a woman will do anything for her family. *The part that's already living.*

WALTER. You don't know Ruth, Mama, if you think she would do that.

[RUTH *opens the bedroom door and stands there a little limp.*]

RUTH [*beaten*]. Yes I would too, Walter. [*Pause.*] I gave her a five-dollar down payment.

[*There is a total silence as the man stares at his wife and the mother stares at her son.*]

MAMA [*presently*]. Well—[*tightly*]. Well—son, I'm waiting to hear you say something . . . I'm waiting to hear how you be your father's son. Be the man he was . . . [*Pause.*] Your wife say she going to destroy your child. And I'm waiting to hear you talk like him and say we a people who give children life, not who destroys them—[*She rises.*] I'm waiting to see you stand up and look like your daddy and say we done give up one baby to poverty and that we ain't going to give up nary another one . . . I'm waiting.

WALTER. Ruth—

MAMA. If you a son of mine, tell her! [WALTER *turns, looks at her and can say nothing. She continues, bitterly.*] You . . . you are a disgrace to your father's memory. Somebody get me my hat.

Curtain.

ACT TWO

SCENE ONE

Time: Later the same day.

At rise: RUTH *is ironing again. She has the radio going. Presently* BENEATHA'S *bedroom door opens and* RUTH'S *mouth falls and she puts down the iron in fascination.*

RUTH. What have we got on tonight!

BENEATHA [*emerging grandly from the doorway so that we can see her thoroughly robed in the costume Asagai brought*]. You are looking at what a well-dressed Nigerian woman wears—[*She parades for* RUTH. *her hair completely hidden by the headdress; she is coquettishly fanning herself with an ornate oriental fan, mistakenly more like Butterfly than any Nigerian that ever was.*] Isn't it beautiful? [*She promenades to the radio and, with an arrogant flourish, turns off the good loud blues that is playing.*]

Enough of this assimilationist junk! [RUTH *follows her with her eyes as she goes to the phonograph and puts on a record and turns and waits ceremoniously for the music to come up. Then, with a shout—*]
OCOMOGOSIAY!
[RUTH *jumps. The music comes up, a lovely Nigerian melody.* BENEATHA *listens, enraptured, her eyes far away—"back to the past." She begins to dance.* RUTH *is dumbfounded.*]

RUTH. What kind of dance is that?

BENEATHA. A folk dance.

RUTH [*Pearl Bailey*]. What kind of folks do that, honey?

BENEATHA. It's from Nigeria. It's a dance of welcome.

RUTH. Who you welcoming?

BENEATHA. The men back to the village.

RUTH. Where they been?

BENEATHA. How should I know—out hunting or something. Anyway, they are coming back now . . .

RUTH. Well, that's good.

BENEATHA [*with the record*].

> Alundi, alundi
> Alundi alunya
> Jop pu a jeepua
> Ang gu sooooooooooo
>
> Ai yai yae . . .
> Ayehaye—alundi . . .

[WALTER *comes in during this performance; he has obviously been drinking. He leans against the door heavily and watches his sister, at first with distaste. Then his eyes look off—"back to the past"—as he lifts both his fists to the roof, screaming.*]

WALTER. YEAH . . . AND ETHIOPIA STRETCH FORTH HER HANDS AGAIN! . . .

RUTH [*drily, looking at him*]. Yes—and Africa sure is claiming her own tonight. [*She gives them both up and starts ironing again.*]

WALTER [*all in a drunken, dramatic shout*]. Shut up! . . . I'm digging them drums . . . them drums move me! . . . [*He makes his weaving way to his wife's face and leans close to her.*] In my *heart of hearts*—[*He thumps his chest.*]—I am much warrior!

RUTH [*without even looking up*]. In your heart of hearts you are much drunkard.

WALTER [*coming away from her and starting to wander around the room, shouting*]. Me and Jomo . . . [*Intently, in his sister's face. She has stopped dancing to watch him in this unknown mood.*] That's my man, Kenyatta. [*Shouting and thumping his chest.*] FLAMING SPEAR! HOT DAMN! [*He is suddenly in possession of an imaginary spear and actively spearing enemies all over the room.*] OCOMOGOSIAY . . .

THE LION IS WAKING . . . OWIMIWEH! [*He pulls his shirt open and leaps up on a table and gestures with his spear. The bell rings.* RUTH *goes to answer.*]

BENEATHA [*to encourage* WALTER, *thoroughly caught up with this side of him*]. OCOMOGOSIAY, FLAMING SPEAR!

WALTER [*on the table, very far gone, his eyes pure glass sheets. He sees what we cannot, that he is a leader of his people, a great chief, a descendant of Chaka, and that the hour to march has come*]. Listen, my black brothers—

BENEATHA. OCOMOGOSIAY!

WALTER. —Do you hear the waters rushing against the shores of the coastlands—

BENEATHA. OCOMOGOSIAY!

WALTER. —Do you hear the screeching of the cocks in yonder hills beyond where the chiefs meet in council for the coming of the mighty war—

BENEATHA. OCOMOGOSIAY!

WALTER. —Do you hear the beating of the wings of the birds flying low over the mountains and the low places of our land—
[RUTH *opens the door.* GEORGE MURCHISON *enters.*]

BENEATHA. OCOMOGOSIAY!

WALTER. —Do you hear the singing of the women, singing the war songs of our fathers to the babies in the great houses . . . singing the sweet war songs? OH, DO YOU HEAR, MY BLACK BROTHERS!

BENEATHA [*completely gone*]. We hear you, Flaming Spear—

WALTER. Telling us to prepare for the greatness of the time— [*To* GEORGE,] Black Brother!
[*He extends his hand for the fraternal clasp.*]

GEORGE. Black Brother, hell!

RUTH [*having had enough, and embarrassed for the family*]. Beneatha, you got company—what's the matter with you? Walter Lee Younger, get down off that table and stop acting like a fool . . .
[WALTER *comes down off the table suddenly and makes a quick exit to the bathroom.*

RUTH. He's had a little to drink . . . I don't know what her excuse is.

GEORGE [*to* BENEATHA]. Look honey, we're going to the theatre— we're not going to be *in* it . . . so go change, huh?

RUTH. You expect this boy to go out with you looking like that?

BENEATHA [*looking at* GEORGE]. That's up to George. If he's ashamed of his heritage—

GEORGE. Oh, don't be so proud of yourself, Bennie—just because you look eccentric.

BENEATHA. How can something that's natural be eccentric?

GEORGE. That's what being eccentric means—being natural. Get dressed.

BENEATHA. I don't like that, George.

RUTH. Why must you and your brother make an argument out of everything people say?

BENEATHA. Because I hate assimilationist Negroes!

RUTH. Will somebody please tell me what assimila-whoever means!

GEORGE. Oh, it's just a college girl's way of calling people Uncle Toms —but that isn't what it means at all.

RUTH. Well, what does it mean?

BENEATHA [*cutting* GEORGE *off and staring at him as she replies to* RUTH]. It means someone who is willing to give up his own culture and submerge himself completely in the dominant, and in this case, *oppressive* culture!

GEORGE. Oh, dear, dear, dear! Here we go! A lecture on the African past! On our Great West African Heritage! In one second we will hear all about the great Ashanti empires; the great Songhay civilizations; and the great sculpture of Bénin—and then some poetry in the Bantu—and the whole monologue will end with the word *heritage!* [*Nastily.*] Let's face it, baby, your heritage is nothing but a bunch of raggedy-assed spirituals and some grass huts!

BENEATHA. *Grass huts!* [RUTH *crosses to her and forcibly pushes her toward the bedroom.*] See there . . . you are standing there in your splendid ignorance talking about people who were the first to smelt iron on the face of the earth! [RUTH *is pushing her through the door.*] The Ashanti were performing surgical operations when the English— [RUTH *pulls the door to, with* BENEATHA *on the other side, and smiles graciously at* GEORGE. BENEATHA *opens the door and shouts the end of the sentence defiantly at* GEORGE.]—were still tattooing themselves with blue dragons . . . [*She goes back inside.*]

RUTH. Have a seat, George. [*They both sit.* RUTH *folds her hands rather primly on her lap, determined to demonstrate the civilization of the family.*] Warm, ain't it? I mean for September. [*Pause.*] Just like they always say about Chicago weather: If it's too hot or cold for you, just wait a minute and it'll change. [*She smiles happily at this cliché of clichés.*] Everybody say it's got to do with them bombs and things they keep setting off. [*Pause.*] Would you like a nice cold beer?

GEORGE. No, thank you. I don't care for beer. [*He looks at his watch.*] I hope she hurries up.

RUTH. What time is the show?

GEORGE. It's an eight-thirty curtain. That's just Chicago, though. In New York standard curtain time is eight forty.

[*He is rather proud of this knowledge.*]

RUTH [*properly appreciating it*]. You get to New York a lot?

GEORGE [*offhand*]. Few times a year.

RUTH. Oh—that's nice. I've never been to New York.

[WALTER *enters. We feel he has relieved himself, but the edge of unreality is still with him.*]

WALTER. New York ain't got nothing Chicago ain't. Just a bunch of hustling people all squeezed up together—being "Eastern."
[*He turns his face into a screw of displeasure.*]

GEORGE. Oh—you've been?

WALTER. Plenty of times.

RUTH [*shocked at the lie*]. Walter Lee Younger!

WALTER [*staring her down*]. Plenty! [*Pause.*] What we got to drink in this house? Why don't you offer this man some refreshment. [*To* GEORGE.] They don't know how to entertain people in this house, man.

GEORGE. Thank you—I don't really care for anything.

WALTER [*feeling his head; sobriety coming*]. Where's Mama?

RUTH. She ain't come back yet.

WALTER [*looking* MURCHISON *over from head to toe, scrutinizing his carefully casual tweed sports jacket over cashmere V-neck sweater over soft eyelet shirt and tie, and soft slacks, finished off with white buckskin shoes*]. Why all you college boys wear them fairyish-looking white shoes?

RUTH. Walter Lee!

[GEORGE MURCHISON *ignores the remark.*]

WALTER [*to* RUTH]. Well, they look crazy as hell—white shoes, cold as it is.

RUTH [*crushed*]. You have to excuse him—

WALTER. No he don't! Excuse me for what? What you always excusing me for! I'll excuse myself when I needs to be excused! [*A pause.*] They look as funny as them black knee socks Beneatha wears out of here all the time.

RUTH. It's the college *style*, Walter.

WALTER. Style hell. She looks like she got burnt legs or something!

RUTH. Oh, Walter—

WALTER [*an irritable mimic*]. Oh, Walter! Oh, Walter! [*To* MURCHISON] How's your old man making out? I understand you all going to buy that big hotel on the Drive? [*He finds a beer in the refrigerator, wanders over to* MURCHISON, *sipping and wiping his lips with the back of his hand, and straddling a chair backwards to talk to the other man.*] Shrewd move. Your old man is all right, man. [*Tapping his head and half winking for emphasis.*] I mean he knows how to operate. I mean he thinks *big*, you know what I mean, I mean for a *home*, you know? But I think he's kind of running out of ideas now. I'd like to talk to him. Listen, man, I got some plans that could turn this city upside down. I mean I think like he does. *Big*. Invest big, gamble big, hell, lose *big* if you have to, you know what I mean. It's hard to find a man on this whole Southside who understands my kind of thinking—you dig? [*He scrutinizes* MURCHISON *again, drinks his beer, squints his eyes and leans in close, confidential, man to man.*] Me and you ought to sit down and talk sometimes, man. Man, I got me some ideas . . .

MURCHISON [*with boredom*]. Yeah—sometimes we'll have to do that, Walter.

WALTER [*understanding the indifference, and offended*]. Yeah—well, when you get the time, man. I know you a busy little boy.

RUTH. Walter, please—

WALTER [*bitterly, hurt*]. I know ain't nothing in this world as busy as you colored college boys with your fraternity pins and white shoes . . .

RUTH [*covering her face with humiliation*]. Oh, Walter Lee—

WALTER. I see you all all the time—with the books tucked under your arms—going to your [*British A—a mimic*] "clahsses." And for what! What the hell you learning over there? Filling up your heads—[*counting off on his fingers*]—with the sociology and the psychology—but they teaching you how to be a man? How to take over and run the world? They teaching you how to run a rubber plantation or a steel mill? Naw—just to talk proper and read books and wear white shoes . . .

GEORGE [*looking at him with distaste, a little above it all*]. You're all wacked up with bitterness, man.

WALTER [*intently, almost quietly, between the teeth, glaring at the boy*]. And you—ain't you bitter, man? Ain't you just about had it? Don't you see no stars gleaming that you can't reach out and grab? You happy?—You contented son-of-a-bitch—you happy? You got it made? Bitter? Man, I'm a volcano. Bitter? Here I am a giant—surrounded by ants! Ants who can't even understand what it is the giant is talking about.

RUTH [*passionately and suddenly*]. Oh, Walter—ain't you with nobody!

WALTER [*violently*]. No! 'Cause ain't nobody with me! Not even my own mother!

RUTH. Walter, that's a terrible thing to say!

[BENEATHA *enters, dressed for the evening in a cocktail dress and earrings.*]

GEORGE. Well—hey, you look great.

BENEATHA. Let's go, George. See you all later.

RUTH. Have a nice time.

GEORGE. Thanks. Good night. [*To* WALTER, *sarcastically,*] Good night, *Prometheus.*[1]

[BENEATHA *and* GEORGE *exit.*]

WALTER [*to* RUTH]. Who is Prometheus?

RUTH. I don't know. Don't worry about it.

WALTER [*in fury, pointing after* GEORGE]. See there—they get to a point where they can't insult you man to man—they got to go talk about something ain't nobody never heard of!

RUTH. How do you know it was an insult? [*To humor him,*] Maybe Prometheus is a nice fellow.

---

[1] a Giant who stole fire from heaven to ignite the soul in humans

WALTER. Prometheus! I bet there ain't even no such thing! I bet that simple-minded clown—

RUTH. Walter—

[*She stops what she is doing and looks at him.*]

WALTER [*yelling*]. Don't start!

RUTH. Start what?

WALTER. Your nagging! Where was I? Who was I with? How much money did I spend?

RUTH [*plaintively*]. Walter Lee—why don't we just try to talk about it . . .

WALTER [*not listening*]. I been out talking with people who understand me. People who care about the things I got on my mind.

RUTH [*wearily*]. I guess that means people like Willy Harris.

WALTER. Yes, people like Willy Harris.

RUTH [*with a sudden flash of impatience*]. Why don't you all hurry up and go into the banking business and stop talking about it!

WALTER. Why? You want to know why? 'Cause we all tied up in a race of people that don't know how to do nothing but moan, pray and have babies!

[*The line is too bitter even for him and he looks at her and sits down.*]

RUTH. Oh, Walter . . . [*Softly.*] Honey, why can't you stop fighting me?

WALTER [*without thinking*]. Who's fighting you? Who even cares about you?

[*This line begins the retardation of his mood.*]

RUTH. Well—[*She waits a long time, and then with resignation starts to put away her things.*] I guess I might as well go on to bed . . . [*More or less to herself,*] I don't know where we lost it . . . but we have . . . [*Then, to him,*] I—I'm sorry about this new baby, Walter. I guess maybe I better go on and do what I started . . . I guess I just didn't realize how bad things was with us . . . I guess I just didn't really realize— [*She starts out to the bedroom and stops.*] You want some hot milk?

WALTER. Hot milk?

RUTH. Yes—hot milk.

WALTER. Why hot milk?

RUTH. 'Cause after all that liquor you come home with you ought to have something hot in your stomach.

WALTER. I don't want no milk.

RUTH. You want some coffee then?

WALTER. No, I don't want no coffee. I don't want nothing hot to drink. [*Almost plaintively.*] Why you always trying to give me something to eat?

RUTH [*standing and looking at him helplessly*]. What else can I give you, Walter Lee Younger?

[*She stands and looks at him and presently turns to go out again. He lifts his head and watches her going away from him in a new mood which began to emerge when he asked her "Who cares about you?"*

WALTER. It's been rough, ain't it, baby? [*She hears and stops but does not turn around and he continues to her back.*] I guess between two people there ain't never as much understood as folks generally thinks there is. I mean like between me and you—[*She turns to face him.*] How we gets to the place where we scared to talk softness to each other. [*He waits, thinking hard himself.*] Why you think it got to be like that? [*He is thoughtful, almost as a child would be.*] Ruth, what is it gets into people ought to be close?

RUTH. I don't know, honey. I think about it a lot.

WALTER. On account of you and me, you mean? The way things are with us. The way something done come down between us.

RUTH. There ain't so much between us, Walter . . . Not when you come to me and try to talk to me. Try to be with me . . . a little even.

WALTER [*total honesty*]. Sometimes . . . sometimes . . . I don't even know how to try.

RUTH. Walter—

WALTER. Yes?

RUTH [*coming to him, gently and with misgiving, but coming to him*]. Honey . . . life don't have to be like this. I mean sometimes people can do things so that things are better . . . You remember how we used to talk when Travis was born . . . about the way we were going to live . . . the kind of house . . . [*She is stroking his head.*] Well, it's all starting to slip away from us . . .

[MAMA *enters, and* WALTER *jumps up and shouts at her.*]

WALTER. Mama, where have you been?

MAMA. My—them steps is longer than they used to be. Whew! [*She sits down and ignores him.*] How you feeling this evening, Ruth?

[RUTH *shrugs, disturbed some at having been prematurely interrupted and watching her husband knowingly.*]

WALTER. Mama, where have you been all day?

MAMA [*still ignoring him and leaning on the table and changing to more comfortable shoes*]. Where's Travis?

RUTH. I let him go out earlier and he ain't come back yet. Boy, is he going to get it!

WALTER. Mama!

MAMA [*as if she has heard him for the first time*]. Yes, son?

WALTER. Where did you go this afternoon?

MAMA. I went downtown to tend to some business that I had to tend to.

WALTER. What kind of business?

MAMA. You know better than to question me like a child, Brother.

WALTER [*rising and bending over the table*]. Where were you, Mama? [*Bringing his fists down and shouting.*] Mama, you didn't go do something with that insurance money, something crazy?

[*The front door opens slowly, interrupting him, and* TRAVIS *peeks his head in, less than hopefully.*]

TRAVIS [*to his mother*]. Mama, I—

RUTH. "Mama I" nothing! You're going to get it, boy! Get on in that bedroom and get yourself ready!

TRAVIS. But I—

MAMA. Why don't you all never let the child explain himself.

RUTH. Keep out of it now, Lena.

[MAMA *clamps her lips together, and* RUTH *advances toward her son menacingly.*]

RUTH. A thousand times I have told you not to go off like that—

MAMA [*holding out her arms to her grandson*]. Well—at least let me tell him something. I want him to be the first one to hear . . . Come here, Travis. [*The boy obeys, gladly.*] Travis—[*She takes him by the shoulder and looks into his face.*]—you know that money we got in the mail this morning?

TRAVIS. Yes'm—

MAMA. Well—what you think your grandmama gone and done with that money?

TRAVIS. I don't know, Grandmama.

MAMA [*putting her finger on his nose for emphasis*]. She went out and she bought you a house! [*The explosion comes from* WALTER *at the end of the revelation and he jumps up and turns away from all of them in a fury.* MAMA *continues, to* TRAVIS.] You glad about the house? It's going to be yours when you get to be a man.

TRAVIS. Yeah—I always wanted to live in a house.

MAMA. All right, gimme some sugar then—[TRAVIS *puts his arms around her neck as she watches her son over the boy's shoulder. Then, to* TRAVIS, *after the embrace.*] Now when you say your prayers tonight, you thank God and your grandfather—'cause it was him who give you the house—in his way.

RUTH [*taking the boy from* MAMA *and pushing him toward the bedroom*]. Now you get out of here and get ready for your beating.

TRAVIS. Aw, Mama—

RUTH. Get on in there— [*Closing the door behind him and turning radiantly to her mother-in-law*] So you went and did it!

MAMA [*quietly, looking at her son with pain*]. Yes, I did.

RUTH [*raising both arms classically*]. Praise God! [*Looks at* WALTER *a moment, who says nothing. She crosses rapidly to her husband.*] Please, honey—let me be glad . . . you be glad too. [*She has laid her hands on his shoulders, but he shakes himself free of her roughly, without turning to face her.*] Oh, Walter . . . a home . . . a home. [*She comes back to* MAMA.] Well—where is it? How big is it? How much it going to cost?

MAMA. Well—

RUTH. When we moving?

MAMA [*smiling at her*]. First of the month.

RUTH [*throwing back her head with jubilance*]. *Praise God!*

MAMA [*tentatively, still looking at her son's back turned against her and*
RUTH]. It's—it's a nice house too . . . [*She cannot help speaking
directly to him. An imploring quality in her voice, her manner, makes her
almost like a girl now.*] Three bedrooms—nice big one for you and
Ruth. . . . Me and Beneatha still have to share our room, but Travis
have one of his own—and [*with difficulty*] I figure if the—new baby—
is a boy, we could get one of them double-decker outfits . . . And
there's a yard with a little patch of dirt where I could maybe get to
grow me a few flowers . . . And a nice big basement . . .

RUTH. Walter honey, be glad—

MAMA [*still to his back, fingering things on the table*]. 'Course I don't
want to make it sound fancier than it is . . . It's just a plain little old
house—but it's made good and solid—and it will be *ours*. Walter Lee
—it makes a difference in a man when he can walk on floors that belong to *him* . . .

RUTH. Where is it?

MAMA [*frightened at this telling*]. Well—well—it's out there in Clybourne Park—

[RUTH's *radiance fades abruptly, and* WALTER *finally turns slowly to
face his mother with incredulity and hostility.*]

RUTH. Where?

MAMA [*matter-of-factly*]. Four o six Clybourne Street, Clybourne Park.

RUTH. Clybourne Park? Mama, there ain't no colored people living in
Clybourne Park.

MAMA [*almost idiotically*]. Well, I guess there's going to be some now.

WALTER [*bitterly*]. So that's the peace and comfort you went out and
bought for us today!

MAMA [*raising her eyes to meet his finally*]. Son—I just tried to find the
nicest place for the least amount of money for my family.

RUTH [*trying to recover from the shock*]. Well—well—'course I ain't one
never been 'fraid of no crackers, mind you—but—well, wasn't there
no other houses nowhere?

MAMA. Them houses they put up for colored in them areas way out all
seem to cost twice as much as other houses. I did the best I could.

RUTH [*struck senseless with the news, in its various degrees of goodness and
trouble, she sits a moment, her fists propping her chin in thought, and then
she starts to rise, bringing her fists down with vigor, the radiance spreading
from cheek to cheek again*]. Well—well!—All I can say is—if this is my
time in life—*my time*—to say good-bye—[*And she builds with mo-
mentum as she starts to circle the room with an exuberant, almost tearfully
happy release.*]—to these Goddamned cracking walls!—[*She pounds the
walls.*]—and these marching roaches!—[*She wipes at an imaginary
army of marching roaches.*]—and this cramped little closet which ain't
now or never was no kitchen! . . . then I say it loud and good,

Hallelujah! and goodbye misery . . . I don't never want to see your ugly face again! [*She laughs joyously, having practically destroyed the apartment, and flings her arms up and lets them come down happily, slowly, reflectively, over her abdomen, aware for the first time perhaps that the life therein pulses with happiness and not despair.*] Lena?

MAMA [*moved, watching her happiness*]. Yes, honey?

RUTH [*looking off*]. Is there—is there a whole lot of sunlight?

MAMA [*understanding*]. Yes, child, there's a whole lot of sunlight.

Long pause.

RUTH [*collecting herself and going to the door of the room* TRAVIS *is in*]. Well—I guess I better see 'bout Travis. [*To* MAMA] Lord, I sure don't feel like whipping nobody today!

[*She exits.*]

MAMA [*The mother and son are left alone now and the mother waits a long time, considering deeply, before she speaks*]. Son—you—you understand what I done, don't you? [WALTER *is silent and sullen.*] I—I just seen my family falling apart today . . . just falling to pieces in front of my eyes . . . We couldn't of gone on like we was today. We was going backwards 'stead of forwards—talking 'bout killing babies and wishing each other was dead . . . When it gets like that in life—you just got to do something different, push on out and do something bigger . . . [*She waits.*] I wish you say something, son . . . I wish you'd say how deep inside you you think I done the right thing—

WALTER [*crossing slowly to his bedroom door and finally turning there and speaking measuredly*]. What you need me to say you done right for? *You* the head of this family. You run our lives like you want to. It was your money and you did what you wanted with it. So what you need for me to say it was all right for? [*Bitterly, to hurt her as deeply as he knows is possible.*] So you butchered up a dream of mine—you—who always talking 'bout your children's dreams . . .

MAMA. Walter Lee—

[*He just closes the door behind him.* MAMA *sits alone, thinking heavily.*]

Curtain.

SCENE TWO

Time: Friday night. A few weeks later.
At rise: Packing crates mark the intention of the family to move. BENEATHA *and* GEORGE *come in, presumably from an evening out again.*

GEORGE. O.K. . . . O.K., whatever you say . . . [*They both sit on the couch. He tries to kiss her. She moves away.*] Look, we've had a nice evening; let's not spoil it, huh? . . .

[*He again turns her head and tries to nuzzle in and she turns away from him, not with distaste but with momentary lack of interest; in a mood to pursue what they were talking about.*]

BENEATHA. I'm *trying* to talk to you.

GEORGE. We always talk.

BENEATHA. Yes—and I love to talk.

GEORGE [*exasperated; rising*]. I know it and I don't mind it sometimes . . . I want you to cut it out, see—The moody stuff, I mean. I don't like it. You're a nice-looking girl . . . all over. That's all you need, honey, forget the atmosphere. Guys aren't going to go for the atmosphere—they're going to go for what they see. Be glad for that. Drop the Garbo routine. It doesn't go with you. As for myself, I want a nice—[*groping*]—simple [*thoughtfully*]—sophisticated girl . . . not a poet—O.K.?

[*She rebuffs him again and he starts to leave.*]

BENEATHA. Why are you angry?

GEORGE. Because this is stupid! I don't go out with you to discuss the nature of "quiet desperation" or to hear all about your thoughts—because the world will go on thinking what it thinks regardless—

BENEATHA. Then why read books? Why go to school?

GEORGE [*with artificial patience, counting on his fingers*]. It's simple. You read books—to learn facts—to get grades—to pass the course—to get a degree. That's all—it has nothing to do with thoughts.

[*A long pause.*]

BENEATHA. I see. [*A longer pause as she looks at him.*] Good night, George.

[GEORGE *looks at her a little oddly, and starts to exit. He meets* MAMA *coming in.*]

GEORGE. Oh—hello, Mrs. Younger.

MAMA. Hello, George, how you feeling?

GEORGE. Fine—fine, how are you?

MAMA. Oh, a little tired. You know them steps can get you after a day's work. You all have a nice time tonight?

GEORGE. Yes—a fine time. Well, good night.

MAMA. Good night. [*He exits.* MAMA *closes the door behind her.*] Hello, honey. What you sitting like that for?

BENEATHA. I'm just sitting.

MAMA. Didn't you have a nice time?

BENEATHA. No.

MAMA. No? What's the matter?

BENEATHA. Mama, George is a fool—honest. [*She rises.*]

MAMA [*hustling around unloading the packages she has entered with. She stops*]. Is he, baby?

BENEATHA. Yes.

[BENEATHA *makes up* TRAVIS' *bed as she talks.*]

MAMA. You sure?

BENEATHA. Yes.

MAMA. Well—I guess you better not waste your time with no fools.

[BENEATHA *looks up at her mother, watching her put groceries in the re-*

frigerator. Finally she gathers up her things and starts into the bedroom. At the door she stops and looks back at her mother.]

BENEATHA. Mama—

MAMA. Yes, baby—

BENEATHA. Thank you.

MAMA. For what?

BENEATHA. For understanding me this time.

[She exits quickly and the mother stands, smiling a little, looking at the place where BENEATHA *just stood.* RUTH *enters.]*

RUTH. Now don't you fool with any of this stuff, Lena—

MAMA. Oh, I just thought I'd sort a few things out.

[The phone rings. RUTH *answers.]*

RUTH *[at the phone]*. Hello—Just a minute. *[Goes to door.]* Walter, it's Mrs. Arnold. *[Waits. Goes back to the phone. Tense.]* Hello. Yes, this is his wife speaking . . . He's lying down now. Yes . . . well, he'll be in tomorrow. He's been very sick. Yes—I know we should have called, but we were so sure he'd be able to come in today. Yes—yes, I'm very sorry. Yes . . . Thank you very much. *[She hangs up.* WALTER *is standing in the doorway of the bedroom behind her.]* That was Mrs. Arnold.

WALTER *[indifferently]*. Was it?

RUTH. She said if you don't come in tomorrow that they are getting a new man . . .

WALTER. Ain't that sad—ain't that crying sad.

RUTH. She said Mr. Arnold has had to take a cab for three days . . . Walter, you ain't been to work for three days! *[This is a revelation to her.]* Where you been, Walter Lee Younger? *[*WALTER *looks at her and starts to laugh.]* You're going to lose your job.

WALTER. That's right . . .

RUTH. Oh, Walter, and with your mother working like a dog every day—

WALTER. That's sad too—Everything is sad.

MAMA. What you been doing for these three days, son?

WALTER. Mama—you don't know all the things a man what got leisure can find to do in this city . . . What's this—Friday night? Well— Wednesday I borrowed Willy Harris' car and I went for a drive . . . just me and myself and I drove and drove . . . Way out . . . way past South Chicago, and I parked the car and I sat and looked at the steel mills all day long. I just sat in the car and looked at them big black chimneys for hours. Then I drove back and I went to the Green Hat. *[Pause.]* And Thursday—Thursday I borrowed the car again and I got in it and I pointed it the other way and I drove the other way —for hours—way, way up to Wisconsin, and I looked at the farms. I just drove and looked at the farms. Then I drove back and I went to the Green Hat. *[Pause.]* And today—today I didn't get the car. Today I just walked. All over the Southside. And I looked at the Negroes and they looked at me and finally I just sat down on the curb at Thirty-ninth and South Parkway and I just sat there and watched the Negroes go by. And then I went to the Green Hat. You all sad? You all depressed? And you know where I am going right now— [RUTH *goes out quietly*.]

MAMA. Oh, Big Walter, is this the harvest of our days?

WALTER. You know what I like about the Green Hat? [*He turns the radio on and a steamy, deep blues pours into the room*.] I like this little cat they got there who blows a sax . . . He blows. He talks to me. He ain't but 'bout five feet tall and he's got a conked head and his eyes is always closed and he's all music—

MAMA [*rising and getting some papers out of her handbag*]. Walter—

WALTER. And there's this other guy who plays the piano . . . and they got a sound. I mean they can work on some music . . . They got the best little combo in the world in the Green Hat . . . You can just sit there and drink and listen to them three men play and you realize that don't nothing matter worth a damn, but just being there—

MAMA. I've helped do it to you, haven't I, son? Walter, I been wrong.

WALTER. Naw—you ain't never been wrong about nothing, Mama.

MAMA. Listen to me, now. I say I been wrong, son. That I been doing to you what the rest of the world been doing to you. [*She stops and he looks up slowly at her and she meets his eyes pleadingly*.] Walter—what you ain't never understood is that I ain't got nothing, don't own nothing, ain't never really wanted nothing that wasn't for you. There ain't nothing as precious to me . . . . There ain't nothing worth holding on to, money, dreams, nothing else—if it means—if it means it's going to destroy my boy. [*She puts her papers in front of him and he watches her without speaking or moving*.] I paid the man thirty-five hundred dollars down on the house. That leaves sixty-five hundred dollars. Monday morning I want you to take this money and take three thousand dollars and put it in a savings account for Beneatha's medical schooling. The rest you put in a checking account—with your name on it. And from now on any penny that come out of it or that go in it is for you to look after. For you to decide. [*She drops her hands a little helplessly*.] It ain't much, but it's all I got in the world and I'm putting it in your hands. I'm telling you to be the head of this family from now on like you supposed to be.

WALTER [*stares at the money*]. You trust me like that, Mama?

MAMA. I ain't never stop trusting you. Like I ain't never stop loving you. [*She goes out, and* WALTER *sits looking at the money on the table as the music continues in its idiom, pulsing in the room. Finally, in a decisive gesture, he gets up, and, in mingled joy and desperation, picks up the money. At the same moment,* TRAVIS *enters for bed*.]

TRAVIS. What's the matter, Daddy? You drunk?

WALTER [*sweetly, more sweetly than we have ever known him*]. No, Daddy ain't drunk. Daddy ain't going to never be drunk again. . . .

TRAVIS. Well, good night, Daddy.

[*The* FATHER *has come from behind the couch and leans over, embracing his son.*]

WALTER. Son, I feel like talking to you tonight.

TRAVIS. About what?

WALTER. Oh, about a lot of things. About you and what kind of man you going to be when you grow up. . . . Son—son, what do you want to be when you grow up?

TRAVIS. A bus driver.

WALTER [*laughing a little*]. A what? Man, that ain't nothing to want to be!

TRAVIS. Why not?

WALTER. 'Cause, man—it ain't big enough—you know what I mean.

TRAVIS. I don't know then. I can't make up my mind. Sometimes Mama asks me that too. And sometimes when I tell you I just want to be like you—she says she don't want me to be like that and sometimes she says she does. . . .

WALTER [*gathering him up in his arms*]. You know what, Travis? In seven years you going to be seventeen years old. And things is going to be very different with us in seven years, Travis. . . . One day when you are seventeen I'll come home—home from my office downtown somewhere—

TRAVIS. You don't work in no office, Daddy.

WALTER. No—but after tonight. After what your daddy gonna do tonight, there's going to be offices—a whole lot of offices. . . .

TRAVIS. What you gonna do tonight, Daddy?

WALTER. You wouldn't understand yet, son, but your daddy's gonna make a transaction . . . a business transaction that's going to change our lives. . . . That's how come one day when you 'bout seventeen years old I'll come home and I'll be pretty tired, you know what I mean, after a day of conferences and secretaries getting things wrong the way they do . . . 'cause an executive's life is hell, man—[*The more he talks the farther away he gets.*] And I'll pull the car up on the driveway . . . just a plain black Chrysler, I think, with white walls —no—black tires. More elegant. Rich people don't have to be flashy . . . though I'll have to get something a little sportier for Ruth— maybe a Cadillac convertible to do her shopping in. . . . And I'll come up the steps to the house and the gardener will be clipping away at the hedges and he'll say, "Good evening, Mr. Younger." And I'll say, "Hello, Jefferson, how are you this evening?" And I'll go inside and Ruth will come downstairs and meet me at the door and we'll kiss each other and she'll take my arm and we'll go up to your room to see you sitting on the floor with the catalogues of all the great schools in America around you. . . . All the great schools in the world! And— and I'll say, all right son—it's your seventeenth birthday, what is it you've decided? . . . Just tell me where you want to go to school

and you'll *go.* Just tell me, what it is you want to be—and you'll *be*
it. . . . Whatever you want to be—Yessir! [*He holds his arms open
for* TRAVIS.] You just name it, son . . . [TRAVIS *leaps into them.*]
and I hand you the world!

[WALTER'S *voice has risen in pitch and hysterical promise and on the last
line he lifts* TRAVIS *high.*]

Blackout.

SCENE THREE

Time : Saturday, moving day, one week later.
Before the curtain rises, RUTH'S *voice, a strident, dramatic church alto, cuts
through the silence.*

*It is, in the darkness, a triumphant surge, a penetrating statement of expecta-
tion :* "*Oh, Lord, I don't feel no ways tired! Children, oh, glory hallelujah!*"

As the curtain rises we see that RUTH *is alone in the living room, finishing
up the family's packing. It is moving day. She is nailing crates and tying car-
tons.* BENEATHA *enters, carrying a guitar case, and watches her exuberant
sister-in-law.*

RUTH. Hey!
BENEATHA [*putting away the case*]. Hi.
RUTH [*pointing at a package*]. Honey—look in that package there and
    see what I found on sale this morning at the South Center. [RUTH
    gets up and moves to the package and draws out some curtains.] Lookahere
    —hand-turned hems!
BENEATHA. How do you know the window size out there?
RUTH [*who hadn't thought of that*]. Oh—Well, they bound to fit some-
    thing in the whole house. Anyhow, they was too good a bargain to pass
    up. [RUTH *slaps her head, suddenly remembering something.*] Oh, Ben-
    nie—I meant to put a special note on that carton over there. That's
    your mama's good china and she wants 'em to be very careful with it.
BENEATHA. I'll do it.
BENEATHA *finds a piece of paper and starts to draw large letters on it.*
RUTH. You know what I'm going to do soon as I get in that new house?
BENEATHA. What?
RUTH. Honey—I'm going to run me a tub of water up to here . . .
    [*with her fingers practically up to her nostrils.*] And I'm going to get in
    it—and I am going to sit . . . and sit . . . and sit in that hot water
    and the first person who knocks to tell *me* to hurry up and come out—
BENEATHA. Gets shot at sunrise.
RUTH [*laughing happily*]. You said it, sister! [*Noticing how large*
    BENEATHA *is absent-mindedly making the note.*] Honey, they ain't
    going to read that from no airplane.
BENEATHA [*laughing herself*]. I guess I always think things have more
    emphasis if they are big, somehow.

RUTH [*looking up at her and smiling*]. You and your brother seem to have that as a philosophy of life. Lord, that man—done changed so 'round here. You know—you know what we did last night? Me and Walter Lee?

BENEATHA. What?

RUTH. [*smiling to herself*]. We went to the movies. [*Looking at* BENEATHA *to see if she understands*.] We went to the movies. You know the last time me and Walter went to the movies together?

BENEATHA. No.

RUTH. Me neither. That's how long it been. [*Smiling again*.] But we went last night. The picture wasn't much good, but that didn't seem to matter. We went—and we held hands.

BENEATHA. Oh, Lord!

RUTH. We held hands—and you know what?

BENEATHA. What?

RUTH. When we come out of the show it was late and dark and all the stores and things was closed up . . . and it was kind of chilly and there wasn't many people on the streets . . . and we was still holding hands, me and Walter.

BENEATHA. You're killing me.

[WALTER *enters with a large package. His happiness is deep in him; he cannot keep still with his new-found exuberance. He is singing and wiggling and snapping his fingers. He puts his package in a corner and puts a phonograph record, which he has brought in with him, on the record player. As the music comes up he dances over to* RUTH *and tries to get her to dance with him. She gives in at last to his raunchiness and in a fit of giggling allows herself to be drawn into his mood and together they deliberately burlesque an old social dance of their youth.*]

BENEATHA [*regarding them a long time as they dance, then drawing in her breath for a deeply exaggerated comment which she does not particularly mean*]. Talk about—olddddddddddd-fashionedddddddd—Negroes!

WALTER [*stopping momentarily*]. What kind of Negroes?

[*He says this in fun. He is not angry with her today, nor with anyone. He starts to dance with his wife again.*]

BENEATHA. Old-fashioned.

WALTER [*as he dances with* RUTH]. You know, when these *New Negroes* have their convention—[*pointing at his sister*]—that is going to be chairman of the Committee on Unending Agitation. [*He goes on dancing, then stops.*] Race, race, race! . . . Girl, I do believe you are the first person in the history of the entire human race to successfully brainwash yourself. [BENEATHA *breaks up and he goes on dancing. He stops again, enjoying his tease.*] Damn, even the N double A C P takes a holiday sometimes! [BENEATHA *and* RUTH *laugh. He dances with* RUTH *some more and starts to laugh and stops and pantomimes someone over an operating table.*] I can just see that chick someday looking down at some poor cat on an operating table before she starts to slice him.

saying . . . [*pulling his sleeves back maliciously,*] "By the way, what
are your views on civil rights down there? . . ."
[*He laughs at her again and starts to dance happily. The bell sounds.*]

BENEATHA. Sticks and stones may break my bones but . . . words
will never hurt me!

[BENEATHA *goes to the door and opens it as* WALTER *and* RUTH *go on
with the clowning.* BENEATHA *is somewhat surprised to see a quiet-
looking middle-aged white man in a business suit holding his hat and a
briefcase in his hand and consulting a small piece of paper.*]

MAN. Uh—how do you do, miss. I am looking for a Mrs.—[*He looks at
the slip of paper.*] Mrs. Lena Younger?

BENEATHA [*smoothing her hair with slight embarrassment*]. Oh—yes,
that's my mother. Excuse me [*She closes the door and turns to quiet the
other two.*] Ruth! Brother! Somebody's here. [*Then she opens the door.
The man casts a curious quick glance at all of them.*] Uh—come in please.

MAN [*coming in*]. Thank you.

BENEATHA. My mother isn't here just now. Is it business?

MAN. Yes . . . well, of a sort.

WALTER [*freely, the Man of the House*]. Have a seat. I'm Mrs. Younger's son. I look after most of her business matters.

[RUTH *and* BENEATHA *exchange amused glances.*]

MAN [*regarding* WALTER, *and sitting*]. Well—My name is Karl
Lindner . . .

WALTER [*stretching out his hand*]. Walter Younger. This is my wife—
[RUTH *nods politely.*]—and my sister.

LINDNER. How do you do.

WALTER [*amiably, as he sits himself easily on a chair, leaning with interest
forward on his knees and looking expectantly into the newcomer's face*].
What can we do for you, Mr. Lindner!

LINDNER [*some minor shuffling of the hat and briefcase on his knees*].
Well—I am a representative of the Clybourne Park Improvement
Association—

WALTER [*pointing*]. Why don't you sit your things on the floor?

LINDNER. Oh—yes, Thank you. [*He slides the briefcase and hat under
the chair.*] And as I was saying—I am from the Clybourne Park Improvement Association and we have had it brought to our attention at
the last meeting that you people—or at least your mother—has bought
a piece of residential property at—[*He digs for the slip of paper again.*]
—four o six Clybourne Street . . .

WALTER. That's right. Care for something to drink? Ruth, get Mr.
Lindner a beer.

LINDNER [*upset for some reason*]. Oh—no, really. I mean thank you very
much, but no thank you.

RUTH [*innocently*]. Some coffee?

LINDNER. Thank you, nothing at all.

[BENEATHA *is watching the man carefully.*]

LINDNER. Well, I don't know how much you folks know about our organization. [*He is a gentle man; thoughtful and somewhat labored in his manner.*] It is one of these community organizations set up to look after—oh, you know, things like block upkeep and special projects and we also have what we call our New Neighbors Orientation Committee . . .

BENEATHA [*drily*]. Yes—and what do they do?

LINDNER [*turning a little to her and then returning the main force to* WALTER]. Well—it's what you might call a sort of welcoming committee, I guess. I mean they, we, I'm the chairman of the committee—go around and see the new people who move into the neighborhood and sort of give them the lowdown on the way we do things out in Clybourne Park.

BENEATHA [*with appreciation of the two meanings, which escape* RUTH *and* WALTER]. Un-huh.

LINDNER. And we also have the category of what the association calls —[*He looks elsewhere.*]—uh—special community problems . . .

BENEATHA. Yes—and what are some of those?

WALTER. Girl, let the man talk.

LINDNER [*with understated relief*]. Thank you. I would sort of like to explain this thing in my own way. I mean I want to explain to you in a certain way.

WALTER. Go ahead.

LINDNER. Yes. Well. I'm going to try to get right to the point. I'm sure we'll all appreciate that in the long run.

BENEATHA. Yes.

WALTER. Be still now!

LINDNER. Well—

RUTH [*still innocently*]. Would you like another chair—you don't look comfortable.

LINDNER [*more frustrated than annoyed*]. No, thank you very much. Please. Well—to get right to the point I—[*A great breath, and he is off at last.*] I am sure you people must be aware of some of the incidents which have happened in various parts of the city when colored people have moved into certain areas—[BENEATHA *exhales heavily and starts tossing a piece of fruit up and down in the air.*] Well—because we have what I think is going to be a unique type of organization in American community life—not only do we deplore that kind of thing—but we are trying to do something about it. [BENEATHA *stops tossing and turns with a new and quizzical interest to the man.*] We feel—[*gaining confidence in his mission because of the interest in the faces of the people he is talking to*]—we feel that most of the trouble in this world, when you come right down to it—[*He hits his knee for emphasis.*]—most of the trouble exists because people just don't sit down and talk to each other.

RUTH [*nodding as she might in church, pleased with the remark*]. You can say that again, mister.

LINDNER [*more encouraged by such affirmation*]. That we don't try hard enough in this world to understand the other fellow's problem. The other guy's point of view.

RUTH. Now that's right.

BENEATHA and WALTER *merely watch and listen with genuine interest*.

LINDNER. Yes—that's the way we feel out in Clybourne Park. And that's why I was elected to come here this afternoon and talk to you people. Friendly like, you know, the way people should talk to each other and see if we couldn't find some way to work this thing out. As I say, the whole business is a matter of *caring* about the other fellow. Anybody can see that you are a nice family of folks, hard working and honest I'm sure. [BENEATHA *frowns slightly,* *quizzically, her head tilted regarding him.*] Today everybody knows what it means to be on the outside of *something*. And of course, there is always somebody who is out to take the advantage of people who don't always understand.

WALTER. What do you mean?

LINDNER. Well—you see our community is made up of people who've worked hard as the dickens for years to build up that little community. They're not rich and fancy people; just hard-working, honest people who don't really have much but those little homes and a dream of the kind of community they want to raise their children in. Now, I don't say we are perfect and there is a lot wrong in some of the things they want. But you've got to admit that a man, right or wrong, has the right to want to have the neighborhood he lives in a certain kind of way. And at the moment the overwhelming majority of our people out there feel that people get along better, take more of a common interest in the life of the community, when they share a common background. I want you to believe me when I tell you that race prejudice simply doesn't enter into it. It is a matter of the people of Clybourne Park believing, rightly or wrongly, as I say, that for the happiness of all concerned that our Negro families are happier when they live in their *own* communities.

BENEATHA [*with a grand and bitter gesture*]. This, friends, is the Welcoming Committee!

WALTER [*dumfounded, looking at* LINDNER]. Is this what you came marching all the way over here to tell us?

LINDNER. Well, now we've been having a fine conversation. I hope you'll hear me all the way through.

WALTER [*tightly*]. Go ahead, man.

LINDNER. You see—in the face of all the things I have said, we are prepared to make your family a very generous offer . . .

BENEATHA. Thirty pieces and not a coin less!

WALTER. Yeah?

LINDNER [*putting on his glasses and drawing a form out of the briefcase*].

Our association is prepared, through the collective effort of our people, to buy the house from you at a financial gain to your family.

RUTH. Lord have mercy, ain't this the living gall!

WALTER. All right, you through?

LINDNER. Well, I want to give you the exact terms of the financial arrangement—

WALTER. We don't want to hear no exact terms of no arrangements. I want to know if you got any more to tell us 'bout getting together?

LINDNER [*taking off his glasses*]. Well—I don't suppose that you feel . . .

WALTER. Never mind how I feel—you got any more to say 'bout how people ought to sit down and talk to each other? . . . Get out of my house, man.

[*He turns his back and walks to the door.*]

LINDNER [*looking around at the hostile faces and reaching and assembling his hat and briefcase*]. Well—I don't understand why you people are reacting this way. What do you think you are going to gain by moving into a neighborhood where you just aren't wanted and where some elements—well—people can get awful worked up when they feel that their whole way of life and everything they've ever worked for is threatened.

WALTER. Get out.

LINDNER [*at the door, holding a small card*]. Well—I'm sorry it went like this.

WALTER. Get out.

LINDNER [*almost sadly regarding* WALTER]. You just can't force people to change their hearts, son.

[*He turns and puts his card on a table and exits.* WALTER *pushes the door to with stinging hatred, and stands looking at it.* RUTH *just sits and* BENEATHA *just stands. They say nothing.* MAMA *and* TRAVIS *enter.*]

MAMA. Well—this all the packing got done since I left out of here this morning. I testify before God that my children got all the energy of the dead. What time the moving men due?

BENEATHA. Four o'clock. You had a caller, Mama.

[*She is smiling, teasingly.*]

MAMA. Sure enough—who?

BENEATHA [*her arms folded saucily*]. The Welcoming Committee.

[WALTER *and* RUTH *giggle.*]

MAMA [*innocently*]. Who?

BENEATHA. The Welcoming Committee. They said they're sure going to be glad to see you when you get there.

WALTER [*devilishly*]. Yeah, they said they can't hardly wait to see your face.

[*Laughter.*]

MAMA [*sensing their facetiousness*]. What's the matter with you all?

WALTER. Ain't nothing the matter with us. We just telling you 'bout the gentleman who came to see you this afternoon. From the Clybourne Park Improvement Association.

MAMA. What he want?

RUTH [*in the same mood as* BENEATHA *and* WALTER]. To welcome you, honey.

WALTER. He said they can't hardly wait. He said the one thing they don't have, that they just *dying* to have out there is a fine family of colored people! [*To* RUTH *and* BENEATHA.] Ain't that right!

RUTH *and* BENEATHA [*mockingly*]. Yeah! He left his card in case— [*They indicate the card, and* MAMA *picks it up and throws it on the floor— understanding and looking off as she draws her chair up to the table on which she has put her plant and some sticks and some cord.*]

MAMA. Father, give us strength. [*Knowingly—and without fun.*] Did he threaten us?

BENEATHA. Oh—Mama—they don't do it like that any more. He talked Brotherhood. He said everybody ought to learn how to sit down and hate each other with good Christian fellowship.

[*She and* WALTER *shake hands to ridicule the remark.*]

MAMA [*sadly*]. Lord, protect us . . .

RUTH. You should hear the money those folks raised to buy the house from us. All we paid and then some.

BENEATHA. What they think we going to do—eat 'em?

RUTH. No, honey, marry 'em.

MAMA [*shaking her head*]. Lord, Lord, Lord . . .

RUTH. Well—that's the way the crackers crumble. Joke.

BENEATHA [*laughingly noticing what her mother is doing*]. Mama, what are you doing?

MAMA. Fixing my plant so it won't get hurt none on the way . . .

BENEATHA. Mama, you going to take *that* to the new house?

MAMA. Un-huh—

BENEATHA. That raggedy-looking old thing?

MAMA [*stopping and looking at her*]. It expresses *me*.

RUTH [*with delight, to* BENEATHA]. So there, Miss Thing!

[WALTER *comes to* MAMA *suddenly and bends down behind her and squeezes her in his arms with all his strength. She is overwhelmed by the suddenness of it and, though delighted, her manner is like that of* RUTH *with* TRAVIS.]

MAMA. Look out now, boy! You make me mess up my thing here!

WALTER [*His face lit, he slips down on his knees beside her, his arms still about her*]. Mama . . . you know what it means to climb up in the chariot?

MAMA [*gruffly, very happy*]. Get on away from me now . . .

RUTH [*near the gift-wrapped package, trying to catch* WALTER'S *eye*]. Psst—

WALTER. What the old song say, Mama . . .

RUTH. Walter—Now?

[*She is pointing at the package.*]

WALTER [*speaking the lines, sweetly, playfully, in his mother's face*].

> *I got wings . . . . you got wings . . .*
> *All God's Children got wings . . .*

MAMA. Boy—get out of my face and do some work . . .

WALTER.

> *When I get to heaven gonna put on my wings,*
> *Gonna fly all over God's heaven . . .*

BENEATHA [*teasingly, from across the room*]. Everybody talking 'bout heaven ain't going there!

WALTER [*to* RUTH, *who is carrying the box across to them*]. I don't know, you think we ought to give her that . . . Seems to me she ain't been very appreciative around here.

MAMA [*eying the box, which is obviously a gift*]. What is that?

WALTER [*taking it from* RUTH *and putting it on the table in front of* MAMA]. Well—what you all think? Should we give it to her?

RUTH. Oh—she was pretty good today.

MAMA. I'll good you—

[*She turns her eyes to the box again.*]

BENEATHA. Open it, Mama.

[*She stands up, looks at it, turns and looks at all of them, and then presses her hands together and does not open the package.*]

WALTER [*sweetly*]. Open it, Mama. It's for you. [MAMA *looks in his eyes. It is the first present in her life without its being Christmas. Slowly she opens her package and lifts out, one by one, a brand-new sparkling set of gardening tools.* WALTER *continues, prodding.*] Ruth made up the note —read it . . .

MAMA [*picking up the card and adjusting her glasses*]. "To our own Mrs. Miniver—Love from Brother, Ruth and Beneatha." Ain't that lovely . . .

TRAVIS [*tugging at his father's sleeve*]. Daddy, can I give her mine now?

WALTER. All right, son. [TRAVIS *flies to get his gift.*] Travis didn't want to go in with the rest of us, Mama. He got his own. [*Somewhat amused.*] We don't know what it is . . .

TRAVIS [*racing back in the room with a large hatbox and putting it in front of his grandmother*]. Here!

MAMA. Lord have mercy, baby. You done gone and bought your grandmother a hat?

TRAVIS [*very proud*]. Open it!

[*She does and lifts out an elaborate, but very elaborate, wide gardening hat, and all the adults break up at the sight of it.*]

RUTH. Travis, honey, what is that?

TRAVIS [*who thinks it is beautiful and appropriate*]. It's a gardening hat!

Like the ladies always have on in the magazines when they work in their gardens.

BENEATHA [*giggling fiercely*]. Travis—we were trying to make Mama Mrs. Miniver—not Scarlett O'Hara!

MAMA [*indignantly*]. What's the matter with you all! This here is a beautiful hat! [*Absurdly*] I always wanted me one just like it!
[*She pops it on her head to prove it to her grandson, and the hat is ludicrous and considerably oversized.*]

RUTH. Hot dog! Go, Mama!

WALTER [*doubled over with laughter*]. I'm sorry, Mama—but you look like you ready to go out and chop you some cotton sure enough!
[*They all laugh except* MAMA, *out of deference to* TRAVIS' *feelings.*]

MAMA [*gathering the boy up to her*]. Bless your heart—this is the prettiest hat I ever owned—[WALTER, RUTH *and* BENEATHA *chime in—noisily, festively and insincerely congratulating* TRAVIS *on his gift.*] What are we all standing around here for? We ain't finished packin' yet. Bennie, you ain't packed one book.
[*The bell rings.*]

BENEATHA. That couldn't be the movers . . . it's not hardly two good yet—
[BENEATHA *goes into her room.* MAMA *starts for door.*]

WALTER [*turning, stiffening*]. Wait—wait—I'll get it.
[*He stands and looks at the door.*]

MAMA. You expecting company, son?

WALTER [*just looking at the door*]. Yeah—yeah . . .
[MAMA *looks at* RUTH, *and they exchange innocent and unfrightened glances.*]

MAMA [*not understanding*]. Well, let them in, son.

BENEATHA [*from her room*]. We need some more string.

MAMA. Travis—you run to the hardware and get me some string cord.
[MAMA *goes out and* WALTER *turns and looks at* RUTH. TRAVIS *goes to a dish for money.*]

RUTH. Why don't you answer the door, man?

WALTER [*suddenly bounding across the floor to her*]. 'Cause sometimes it hard to let the future begin! [*Stooping down in her face*]

> I got wings! You got wings!
> All God's children got wings! . . .

[*He crosses to the door and throws it open. Standing there is a very slight little man in a not too prosperous business suit and with haunted frightened eyes and a hat pulled down tightly, brim up, around his forehead.* TRAVIS *passes between the men and exits.* WALTER *leans deep in the man's face, still in his jubilance.*]

> When I get to heaven gonna put on my wings,
> Gonna fly all over God's heaven . . .

[*The little man just stares at him.*]

     Heaven—

[*Suddenly he stops and looks past the little man into the empty hallway.*]

Where's Willy, man?

BOBO. He ain't with me.

WALTER [*not disturbed*]. Oh—come on in. You know my wife.

BOBO [*dumbly, taking off his hat*]. Yes—h'you, Miss Ruth.

RUTH [*quietly, a mood apart from her husband already, seeing* BOBO]. Hello, Bobo.

WALTER. You right on time today . . . Right on time. That's the way! [*He slaps* BOBO *on his back.*] Sit down . . . lemme hear.

[RUTH *stands stiffly and quietly in back of them, as though somehow she senses death, her eyes fixed on her husband.*]

BOBO [*his frightened eyes on the floor, his hat in his hands*]. Could I please get a drink of water, before I tell you about it, Walter Lee?

[WALTER *does not take his eyes off the man.* RUTH *goes blindly to the tap and gets a glass of water and brings it to* BOBO.]

WALTER. There ain't nothing wrong, is there?

BOBO. Lemme tell you—

WALTER. Man—didn't nothing go wrong?

BOBO. Lemme tell you—Walter Lee. [*Looking at* RUTH *and talking to her more than to* WALTER.] You know how it was. I got to tell you how it was. I mean first I got to tell you how it was all the way . . . I mean about the money I put in, Walter Lee . . .

WALTER [*with taut agitation now*]. What about the money you put in?

BOBO. Well—it wasn't much as we told you—me and Willy—[*He stops.*] I'm sorry, Walter. I got a bad feeling about it. I got a real bad feeling about it . . .

WALTER. Man, what you telling me about all this for? . . . Tell me what happened in Springfield . . .

BOBO. Springfield.

RUTH [*like a dead woman*]. What was supposed to happen in Springfield?

BOBO [*to her*]. This deal that me and Walter went into with Willy— Me and Willy was going to go down to Springfield and spread some money 'round so's we wouldn't have to wait so long for the liquor license . . . That's what we were going to do. Everybody said that was the way you had to do, you understand, Miss Ruth?

WALTER. Man—what happened down there?

BOBO [*a pitiful man, near tears*]. I'm trying to tell you, Walter.

WALTER [*screaming at him suddenly*]. THEN TELL ME, GOD-DAMMIT . . . WHAT'S THE MATTER WITH YOU?

BOBO. Man . . . I didn't go to no Springfield, yesterday.

WALTER [*halted, life hanging in the moment*]. Why not?

BOBO [*the long way, the hard way to tell*]. 'Cause I didn't have no reasons
to . . .

WALTER. Man, what are you talking about!

BOBO. I'm talking about the fact that when I got to the train station
yesterday morning—eight o'clock like we planned . . . Man—
Willy didn't never show up.

WALTER. Why . . . where was he . . . where is he?

BOBO. That's what I'm trying to tell you . . . I don't know . . . I
waited six hours . . . I called his house . . . and I waited . . . six
hours . . . I waited in that train station six hours . . . [*Breaking into
tears.*] That was all the extra money I had in the world . . . [*Looking
up at* WALTER *with the tears running down his face.*] Man, *Willy is
gone.*

WALTER. Gone, what you mean Willy is gone? Gone where? You
mean he went by himself. You mean he went off to Springfield by
himself—to take care of getting the license—[*Turns and looks anxiously
at* RUTH.] You mean maybe he didn't want too many people in on the
business down there? [*Looks to* RUTH *again, as before.*] You know
Willy got his own ways. [*Looks back to* BOBO.] Maybe you was late
yesterday and he just went on down there without you. Maybe—
maybe—he's been callin' you at home tryin' to tell you what happened
or something. Maybe—maybe—he just got sick. He's somewhere—
he's got to be somewhere. We just got to find him—me and you got to
find him. [*Grabs* BOBO *senselessly by the collar and starts to shake him.*]
We got to!

BOBO [*in sudden angry, frightened agony*]. What's the matter with you,
Walter! *When a cat take off with your money he don't leave you no
maps!*

WALTER [*turning madly, as though he is looking for* WILLY *in the very
room*]. Willy! . . . Willy . . . don't do it . . . Please don't do
it . . . Man, not with that money . . . Man, please, not with that
money . . . Oh, God . . . Don't let it be true . . . [*He is wandering around, crying out for* WILLY *and looking for him or perhaps for
help from God.*] Man . . . I trusted you . . . Man, I put my life in
your hands . . . [*He starts to crumple down on the floor as* RUTH *just
covers her face in horror.* MAMA *opens the door and comes into the room,
with* BENEATHA *behind her.*] Man . . . [*He starts to pound the floor
with his fists, sobbing wildly.*] That money is made out of my father's
flesh . . .

BOBO [*standing over him helplessly*]. I'm sorry, Walter . . . [*Only*
WALTER'S *sobs reply.* BOBO *puts on his hat.*] I had my life staked on
this deal, too . . .
[*He exits.*]

MAMA [*to* WALTER]. Son—[*She goes to him, bends down to him, talks
to his bent head.*] Son . . . Is it gone? Son, I gave you sixty-five hundred dollars. Is it gone? All of it? Beneatha's money, too?

WALTER [*lifting his head slowly*]. Mama . . . I never . . . went to
the bank at all . . .
MAMA [*not wanting to believe him*]. You mean . . . your sister's school
money . . . you used that too . . . Walter? . . .
WALTER. Yessss! . . . All of it . . . It's all gone . . .

[*There is total silence.* RUTH *stands with her face covered with her hands;*
BENEATHA *leans forlornly against a wall, fingering a piece of red ribbon
from the mother's gift.* MAMA *stops and looks at her son without recognition and then, quite without thinking about it, starts to beat him senselessly
in the face.* BENEATHA *goes to them and stops it.*]

BENEATHA. Mama!

[MAMA *stops and looks at both of her children and rises slowly and wanders
vaguely, aimlessly away from them.*]

MAMA. I seen . . . him . . . night after night . . . come in . . .
and look at that rug . . . and then look at me . . . the red showing
in his eyes . . . the veins moving in his head . . . I seen him grow
thin and old before he was forty . . . working and working and
working like somebody's old horse . . . killing himself . . . and
you—you give it all away in a day . . .
BENEATHA. Mama—
MAMA. Oh, God . . . [*She looks up to Him.*] Look down here—and
show me the strength.
BENEATHA. Mama—
MAMA [*folding over*]. Strength . . .
BENEATHA [*plaintively*]. Mama . . .
MAMA. Strength!

Curtain.

ACT THREE

An hour later.
*At curtain, there is a sullen light of gloom in the living room, gray light not
unlike that which began the first scene of Act One. At left we can see*
WALTER *within his room, alone with himself. He is stretched out on the
bed, his shirt out and open, his arms under his head. He does not smoke, he
does not cry out, he merely lies there, looking up at the ceiling, much as if he
were alone in the world.*

In the living room BENEATHA *sits at the table, still surrounded by the now
almost ominous packing crates. She sits looking off. We feel that this is a mood
struck perhaps an hour before, and it lingers now, full of the empty sound of
profound disappointment. We see on a line from her brother's bedroom the
sameness of their attitudes. Presently the bell rings and* BENEATHA *rises
without ambition or interest in answering. It is* ASAGAI, *smiling broadly,
striding into the room with energy and happy expectation and conversation.*

ASAGAI. I came over . . . I had some free time. I thought I might help
with the packing. Ah, I like the look of packing crates! A household
in preparation for a journey! It depresses some people . . . but for
me . . . it is another feeling. Something full of the flow of life, do
you understand? Movement, progress . . . It makes me think of
Africa.

BENEATHA. Africa!

ASAGAI. What kind of a mood is this? Have I told you how deeply you
move me?

BENEATHA. He gave away the money, Asagai . . .

ASAGAI. Who gave away what money?

BENEATHA. The insurance money. My brother gave it away.

ASAGAI. Gave it away?

BENEATHA. He made an investment! With a man even Travis
wouldn't have trusted.

ASAGAI. And it's gone?

BENEATHA. Gone!

ASAGAI. I'm very sorry . . . And you, now?

BENEATHA. Me? . . . Me? . . . Me I'm nothing . . . Me. When
I was very small . . . we used to take our sleds out in the wintertime
and the only hills we had were the ice-covered stone steps of some
houses down the street. And we used to fill them in with snow and
make them smooth and slide down them all day . . . and it was very
dangerous you know . . . far too steep . . . and sure enough one
day a kid named Rufus came down too fast and hit the sidewalk . . .
and we saw his face just split open right there in front of us . . . And
I remember standing there looking at his bloody open face thinking
that was the end of Rufus. But the ambulance came and they took him
to the hospital and they fixed the broken bones and they sewed it all
up . . . and the next time I saw Rufus he just had a little line down
the middle of his face . . . I never got over that . . .

[WALTER sits up, listening on the bed. Throughout this scene it is important that we feel his reaction at all times, that he visibly respond to the words
of his sister and ASAGAI.]

ASAGAI. What?

BENEATHA. That that was what one person could do for another, fix
him up—sew up the problem, make him all right again. That was the
most marvelous thing in the world . . . I wanted to do that. I always
thought it was the one concrete thing in the world that a human being
could do. Fix up the sick, you know—and make them whole again.
This was truly being God . . .

ASAGAI. You wanted to be God?

BENEATHA. No—I wanted to cure. It used to be so important to me.
I wanted to cure. It used to matter. I used to care. I mean about people
and how their bodies hurt . . .

ASAGAI. And you've stopped caring?

BENEATHA. Yes—I think so.

ASAGAI. Why?

[WALTER *rises, goes to the door of his room and is about to open it, then stops and stands listening, leaning on the door jamb*]

BENEATHA. Because it doesn't seem deep enough, close enough to what ails mankind—I mean this thing of sewing up bodies or administering drugs. Don't you understand? It was a child's reaction to the world. I thought that doctors had the secret to all the hurts. . . . That's the way a child sees things—or an idealist.

ASAGAI. Children see things very well sometimes—and idealists even better.

BENEATHA. I know that's what you think. Because you are still where I left off—you still care. This is what you see for the world, for Africa. You with the dreams of the future will patch up all Africa—you are going to cure the Great Sore of colonialism with Independence—

ASAGAI. Yes!

BENEATHA. Yes—and you think that one word is the penicillin of the human spirit: "Independence!" But then what?

ASAGAI. That will be the problem for another time. First we must get there.

BENEATHA. And where does it end?

ASAGAI. End? Who even spoke of an end? To life? To living?

BENEATHA. An end to misery!

ASAGAI [*smiling*]. You sound like a French intellectual.

BENEATHA. No! I sound like a human being who just had her future taken right out of her hands! While I was sleeping in my bed in there, things were happening in this world that directly concerned me—and nobody asked me, consulted me—they just went out and did things— and changed my life. Don't you see there isn't any real progress, Asagai, there is only one large circle that we march in, around and around, each of us with our own little picture—in front of us—our own little mirage that we think is the future.

ASAGAI. That is the mistake.

BENEATHA. What?

ASAGAI. What you just said—about the circle. It isn't a circle—it is simply a long line—as in geometry, you know, one that reaches into infinity. And because we cannot see the end—we also cannot see how it changes. And it is very odd but those who see the changes are called "idealists"—and those who cannot, or refuse to think, they are the "realists." It is very strange, and amusing too, I think.

BENEATHA. You—you are almost religious.

ASAGAI. Yes . . . I think I have the religion of doing what is necessary in the world—and of worshipping man—because he is so marvelous, you see.

BENEATHA. Man is foul! And the human race deserves its misery!

ASAGAI. You see: *you* have become the religious one in the old sense.

Already, and after such a small defeat, you are worshipping despair.

BENEATHA. From now on, I worship the truth—and the truth is that people are puny, small and selfish. . . .

ASAGAI. Truth? Why is it that you despairing ones always think that only you have the truth? I never thought to see *you* like that. You! Your brother made a stupid, childish mistake—and you are grateful to him. So that now you can give up the ailing human race on account of it. You talk about what good is struggle; what good is anything? Where are we all going? And why are we bothering?

BENEATHA. *And you cannot answer it!* All your talk and dreams about Africa and Independence. Independence and then what? What about all the crooks and petty thieves and just plain idiots who will come into power to steal and plunder the same as before—only now they will be black and do it in the name of the new Independence—You cannot answer that.

ASAGAI [*shouting over her*]. *I live the answer!* [*Pause.*] In my village at home it is the exceptional man who can even read a newspaper . . . or who ever *sees* a book at all. I will go home and much of what I will have to say will seem strange to the people of my village . . . But I will teach and work and things will happen, slowly and swiftly. At times it will seem that nothing changes at all . . . and then again . . . the sudden dramatic events which make history leap into the future. And then quiet again. Retrogression even. Guns, murder, revolution. And I even will have moments when I wonder if the quiet was not better than all that death and hatred. But I will look about my village at the illiteracy and disease and ignorance and I will not wonder long. And perhaps . . . perhaps I will be a great man . . . I mean perhaps I will hold on to the substance of truth and find my way always with the right course . . . and perhaps for it I will be butchered in my bed some night by the servants of empire . . .

BENEATHA. *The martyr!*

ASAGAI. . . . or perhaps I shall live to be a very old man, respected and esteemed in my new nation . . . And perhaps I shall hold office and this is what I'm trying to tell you, Alaiyo; perhaps the things I believe now for my country will be wrong and outmoded, and I will not understand and do terrible things to have things my way or merely to keep my power. Don't you see that there will be young men and women, not British soldiers then, but my own black countrymen . . . to step out of the shadows some evening and slit my then useless throat? Don't you see they have always been there . . . that they always will be. And that such a thing as my own death will be an advance? They who might kill me even . . . actually replenish me!

BENEATHA. Oh, Asagai, I know all that.

ASAGAI. Good! Then stop moaning and groaning and tell me what you plan to do.

BENEATHA. Do?

ASAGAI. I have a bit of a suggestion.

BENEATHA. What?

ASAGAI [*rather quietly for him*]. That when it is all over—that you come home with me—

BENEATHA [*slapping herself on the forehead with exasperation born of misunderstanding*]. Oh—Asagai—at this moment you decide to be romantic!

ASAGAI [*quickly understanding the misunderstanding*]. My dear, young creature of the New World—I do not mean across the city—I mean across the ocean; home—to Africa.

BENEATHA [*slowly understanding and turning to him with murmured amazement*]. To—to Nigeria?

ASAGAI. Yes! . . . [*Smiling and lifting his arms playfully.*] Three hundred years later the African Prince rose up out of the seas and swept the maiden back across the middle passage over which her ancestors had come—

BENEATHA [*unable to play*]. Nigeria?

ASAGAI. Nigeria. Home. [*Coming to her with genuine romantic flippancy.*] I will show you our mountains and our stars; and give you cool drinks from gourds and teach you the old songs and the ways of our people—and, in time, we will pretend that—[*very softly*]—you have only been away for a day—

[*She turns her back to him, thinking. He swings her around and takes her full in his arms in a long embrace which proceeds to passion.*]

BENEATHA [*pulling away*]. You're getting me all mixed up—

ASAGAI. Why?

BENEATHA. Too many things—too many things have happened today. I must sit down and think. I don't know what I feel about anything right this minute.

[*She promptly sits down and props her chin on her fist.*]

ASAGAI [*charmed*]. All right, I shall leave you. No—don't get up. [*Touching her, gently, sweetly.*] Just sit awhile and think . . . Never be afraid to sit awhile and think. [*He goes to door and looks at her.*] How often I have looked at you and said, "Ah—so this is what the New World hath finally wrought . . ."

[*He exits.* BENEATHA *sits on alone. Presently* WALTER *enters from his room and starts to rummage through things, feverishly looking for something. She looks up and turns in her seat.*]

BENEATHA [*hissingly*]. Yes—just look at what the New World hath wrought! . . . Just look! [*She gestures with bitter disgust.*] There he is! *Monsieur le petit bourgeois noir*—himself! There he is—Symbol of a Rising Class! Entrepreneur! Titan of the system! [WALTER *ignores her completely and continues frantically and destructively looking for something and hurling things to floor and tearing things out of their place in his search.* BENEATHA *ignores the eccentricity of his actions and goes on with the monologue of insult.*] Did you dream of yachts on Lake Michigan,

Brother? Did you see yourself on that Great Day sitting down at the Conference Table, surrounded by all the mighty bald-headed men in America? All halted, waiting, breathless, waiting for your pronouncements on industry? Waiting for you—Chairman of the Board? [WALTER *finds what he is looking for—a small piece of white paper— and pushes it in his pocket and puts on his coat and rushes out without ever having looked at her. She shouts after him.*] I look at you and I see the final triumph of stupidity in the world!

[*The door slams and she returns to just sitting again.* RUTH *comes quickly out of* MAMA'S *room.*]

RUTH. Who was that?

BENEATHA. Your husband.

RUTH. Where did he go?

BENEATHA. Who knows—maybe he has an appointment at U.S. Steel.

RUTH [*anxiously, with frightened eyes*]. You didn't say nothing bad to him, did you?

BENEATHA. Bad? Say anything bad to him? No—I told him he was a sweet boy and full of dreams and everything is strictly peachy keen, as the ofay kids say!

[MAMA *enters from her bedroom. She is lost, vague, trying to catch hold, to make some sense of her former command of the world, but it still eludes her. A sense of waste overwhelms her gait; a measure of apology rides on her shoulders. She goes to her plant, which has remained on the table, looks at it, picks it up and takes it to the window sill and sets it outside, and she stands and looks at it a long moment. Then she closes the window, straightens her body with effort and turns around to her children.*]

MAMA. Well—ain't it a mess in here, though? [*A false cheerfulness, a beginning of something.*] I guess we all better stop moping around and get some work done. All this unpacking and everything we got to do. [RUTH *raises her head slowly in response to the sense of the line; and* BENEATHA *in similar manner turns very slowly to look at her mother.*] One of you all better call the moving people and tell 'em not to come.

RUTH. Tell 'em not to come?

MAMA. Of course, baby. Ain't no need in 'em coming all the way here and having to go back. They charges for that too. [*She sits down, fingers to her brow, thinking.*] Lord, ever since I was a little girl, I always remembers people saying, "Lena—Lena Eggleston, you aims too high all the time. You needs to slow down and see life a little more like it is. Just slow down some." That's what they always used to say down home—"Lord, that Lena Eggleston is a high-minded thing. She'll get her due one day!"

RUTH. No, Lena . . .

MAMA. Me and Big Walter just didn't never learn right.

RUTH. Lena, no! We gotta go. Bennie—tell her . . . [*She rises and crosses to* BENEATHA *with her arms outstretched.* BENEATHA *doesn't respond.*] Tell her we can still move . . . the notes ain't but a hundred

and twenty-five a month. We got four grown people in this house—
we can work . . .

MAMA [*to herself*]. Just aimed too high all the time—

RUTH [*turning and going to* MAMA *fast—the words pouring out with
urgency and desperation*]. Lena—I'll work . . . I'll work twenty
hours a day in all the kitchens in Chicago . . . I'll strap my baby on
my back if I have to and scrub all the floors in America and wash all
the sheets in America if I have to—but we got to move . . . We got
to get out of here . . .

[MAMA *reaches out absently and pats* RUTH's *hand.*]

MAMA. No—I sees things differently now. Been thinking 'bout some
of the things we could do to fix this place up some. I seen a second-
hand bureau over on Maxwell Street just the other day that could fit
right there. [*She points to where the new furniture might go.* RUTH *wanders away from her.*] Would need some new handles on it and then a
little varnish and then it look like something brand-new. And—we can
put up them new curtains in the kitchen . . . Why this place be looking fine. Cheer us all up so that we forget trouble ever came . . . [*To*
RUTH,] And you could get some nice screens to put up in your room
round the baby's bassinet . . . [*She looks at both of them, pleadingly.*]
Sometimes you just got to know when to give up some things . . .
and hold on to what you got.

[WALTER *enters from the outside, looking spent and leaning against the
door, his coat hanging from him.*]

MAMA. Where you been, son?

WALTER [*breathing hard*]. Made a call.

MAMA. To who, son?

WALTER. To The Man.

MAMA. What man, baby?

WALTER. The Man, Mama. Don't you know who The Man is?

RUTH. Walter Lee?

WALTER. *The Man.* Like the guys in the streets say—The Man. Captain Boss—Mistuh Charley . . . Old Captain Please Mr. Bossman . . .

BENEATHA [*suddenly*]. Lindner!

WALTER. That's right! That's good. I told him to come right over.

BENEATHA [*fiercely, understanding*]. For what? What do you want to
see him for!

WALTER [*looking at his sister*]. We going to do business with him.

MAMA. What you talking 'bout son?

WALTER. Talking 'bout life, Mama. You all always telling me to see
life like it is. Well—I laid in there on my back today . . . and I figured it out. Life just like it is. Who gets and who don't get. [*He sits
down with his coat on and laughs.*] Mama, you know it's all divided up.
Life is. Sure enough. Between the takers and the "tooken." [*He
laughs.*] I've figured it out finally. [*He looks around at them.*] Yeah.

Some of us always getting "tooken." [*He laughs.*] People like Willy
Harris, they don't never get "tooken." And you know why the rest
of us do? 'Cause we all mixed up. Mixed up bad. We get to looking
'round for the right and the wrong; and we worry about it and cry
about it and stay up nights trying to figure out 'bout the wrong and the
right of things all the time . . . And all the time, man, them takers is
out there operating, just taking and taking. Willy Harris? Shoot—
Willy Harris don't even count. He don't even count in the big scheme
of things. But I'll say one thing for old Willy Harris . . . he's taught
me something. He's taught me to keep my eye on what counts in this
world. Yeah—[*Shouting out a little.*] Thanks, Willy!

RUTH. What did you call that man for, Walter Lee?

WALTER. Called him to tell him to come on over to the show. Gonna
put on a show for the man. Just what he wants to see. You see, Mama,
the man came here today and he told us that them people out there
where you want us to move—well they so upset they willing to pay
us not to move out there. [*He laughs again.*] And—and oh, Mama—
you would of been proud of the way me and Ruth and Bennie acted.
We told him to get out . . . Lord have mercy! We told the man to
get out. Oh, we was some proud folks this afternoon, yeah. [*He lights
a cigarette.*] We were still full of that old-time stuff . . .

RUTH [*coming toward him slowly*]. You talking 'bout taking them people's money to keep us from moving in that house?

WALTER. I ain't just talking 'bout it, baby—I'm telling you that's
what's going to happen.

BENEATHA. Oh, God! Where is the bottom! Where is the real honest-
to-God bottom so he can't go any farther!

WALTER. See—that's the old stuff. You and that boy that was here
today. You all want everybody to carry a flag and a spear and sing
some marching songs, huh? You wanna spend your life looking into
things and trying to find the right and the wrong part, huh? Yeah. You
know what's going to happen to that boy someday—he'll find himself
sitting in a dungeon, locked in forever—and the takers will have the
key! Forget it, baby! There ain't no causes—there ain't nothing but
taking in this world, and he who takes most is smartest—and it don't
make a damn bit of difference *how.*

MAMA. You making something inside me cry, son. Some awful pain
inside me.

WALTER. Don't cry, Mama. Understand. That white man is going to
walk in that door able to write checks for more money than we ever
had. It's important to him and I'm going to help him . . . I'm going
to put on the show, Mama.

MAMA. Son—I come from five generations of people who was slaves
and sharecroppers—but ain't nobody in my family never let nobody
pay 'em no money that was a way of telling us we wasn't fit to walk

the earth. We ain't never been that poor. [*Raising her eyes and looking at him.*] We ain't never been that dead inside.

BENEATHA. Well—we are dead now. All the talk about dreams and sunlight that goes on in this house. All dead.

WALTER. What's the matter with you all! I didn't make this world! It was give to me this way! Hell, yes, I want me some yachts someday! Yes, I want to hang some real pearls 'round my wife's neck. Ain't she supposed to wear no pearls? Somebody tell me—tell me, who decides which women is suppose to wear pearls in this world. I tell you I am a *man*—and I think my wife should wear some pearls in this world!

[*This last line hangs a good while and* WALTER *begins to move about the room. The word "Man" has penetrated his consciousness; he mumbles it to himself repeatedly between strange agitated pauses as he moves about.*]

MAMA. Baby, how you going to feel on the inside?

WALTER. Fine! . . . Going to feel fine . . . a man . . .

MAMA. You won't have nothing left then, Walter Lee.

WALTER [*coming to her*]. I'm going to feel fine, Mama. I'm going to look that son-of-a-bitch in the eyes and say—[*He falters.*]—and say, "All right, Mr. Lindner—[*He falters even more.*]—that's your neighborhood out there. You got the right to keep it like you want. You got the right to have it like you want. Just write the check and—the house is yours." And, and I am going to say—[*His voice almost breaks.*] And you—you people just put the money in my hand and you won't have to live next to this bunch of stinking niggers! . . . [*He straightens up and moves away from his mother, walking around the room.*] Maybe—maybe I'll just get down on my black knees . . . [*He does so;* RUTH *and* BENNIE *and* MAMA *watch him in frozen horror.*] Captain, Mistuh, Bossman. [*He starts crying.*] A-hee-hee-hee! [*Wringing his hands in profoundly anguished imitation.*] Yasssssuh! Great White Father, just gi' ussen de money, fo' God's sake, and we's ain't gwine come out deh and dirty up yo' white folks neighborhood . . .

[*He breaks down completely, then gets up and goes into the bedroom.*]

BENEATHA. That is not a man. That is nothing but a toothless rat.

MAMA. Yes—death done come in this here house. [*She is nodding, slowly, reflectively.*] Done come walking in my house. On the lips of my children. You what supposed to be my beginning again. You— what supposed to be my harvest. [*To* BENEATHA.] You—you mourning your brother?

BENEATHA. He's no brother of mine.

MAMA. What you say?

BENEATHA. I said that that individual in that room is no brother of mine.

MAMA. That's what I thought you said. You feeling like you better than he is today? [BENEATHA *does not answer.*] Yes? What you tell

him a minute ago? That he wasn't a man? Yes? You give him up for
me? You done wrote his epitaph too—like the rest of the world?
Well, who give you the privilege?

BENEATHA. Be on my side for once! You saw what he just did, Mama!
You saw him—down on his knees. Wasn't it you who taught me—to
despise any man who would do that. Do what he's going to do.

MAMA. Yes—I taught you that. Me and your daddy. But I thought I
taught you something else too . . . I thought I taught you to love
him.

BENEATHA. Love him? There is nothing left to love.

MAMA. There is always something left to love. And if you ain't
learned that, you ain't learned nothing. [*Looking at her.*] Have you
cried for that boy today? I don't mean for yourself and for the family
'cause we lost the money. I mean for him; what he been through and
what it done to him. Child, when do you think is the time to love somebody the most; when they done good and made things easy for everybody? Well then, you ain't through learning—because that ain't the
time at all. It's when he's at his lowest and can't believe in hisself
'cause the world done whipped him so. When you starts measuring
somebody, measure him right, child, measure him right. Make sure
you done taken into account what hills and valleys he come through
before he got to wherever he is.

[TRAVIS *bursts into the room at the end of the speech, leaving the door
open.*]

TRAVIS. Grandmama—the moving men are downstairs! The truck
just pulled up.

MAMA [*turning and looking at him*]. Are they, baby? They downstairs?
[*She sighs and sits.* LINDNER *appears in the doorway. He peers in and
knocks lightly, to gain attention, and comes in. All turn to look at him.*]

LINDNER [*hat and briefcase in hand*]. Uh—hello . . .
[RUTH *crosses mechanically to the bedroom door and opens it and lets it
swing open freely and slowly as the lights come up on* WALTER *within,
still in his coat, sitting at the far corner of the room. He looks up and out
through the room to* LINDNER.]

RUTH. He's here.

[*A long minute passes and* WALTER *slowly gets up.*]

LINDNER [*coming to the table with efficiency, putting his briefcase on the
table and starting to unfold papers and unscrew fountain pens.*] Well, I
certainly was glad to hear from you people. [WALTER *has begun the
trek out of the room, slowly and awkwardly, rather like a small boy, passing
the back of his sleeve across his mouth from time to time.*] Life can really
be so much simpler than people let it be most of the time. Well—with
whom do I negotiate? You, Mrs. Younger, or your son here? [MAMA
sits with her hands folded on her lap and her eyes closed as WALTER
advances. TRAVIS *goes close to* LINDNER *and looks at the papers curiously.*] Just some official papers, sonny.

RUTH. Travis, you go downstairs.

MAMA [*opening her eyes and looking into* WALTER'S]. No. Travis, you stay right here. And you make him understand what you doing, Walter Lee. You teach him good. Like Willy Harris taught you. You show where our five generations done come to. Go ahead, son—

WALTER [*looks down into his boy's eyes.* TRAVIS *grins at him merrily and* WALTER *draws him beside him with his arm lightly around his shoulder*]. Well, Mr. Lindner. [BENEATHA *turns away.*] We called you— [*There is a profound, simple groping quality in his speech.*]—because, well, me and my family [*He looks around and shifts from one foot to the other.*] Well—we are very plain people . . .

LINDNER. Yes—

WALTER. I mean—I have worked as a chauffeur most of my life—and my wife here, she does domestic work in people's kitchens. So does my mother. I mean—we are plain people . . .

LINDNER. Yes, Mr. Younger—

WALTER [*really like a small boy, looking down at his shoes and then up at the man*]. And—uh—well, my father, well, he was a laborer most of his life.

LINDNER [*absolutely confused*]. Uh, yes—

WALTER [*looking down at his toes once again*]. My father almost beat a man to death once because this man called him a bad name or something, you know what I mean?

LINDNER. No, I'm afraid I don't.

WALTER [*finally straightening up*]. Well, what I mean is that we come from people who had a lot of pride. I mean—we are very proud people. And that's my sister over there and she's going to be a doctor—and we are very proud—

LINDNER. Well—I am sure that is very nice, but—

WALTER [*starting to cry and facing the man eye to eye*]. What I am telling you is that we called you over here to tell you that we are very proud and that this is—this is my son, who makes the sixth generation of our family in this country, and that we have all thought about your offer and we have decided to move into our house because my father—my father—he earned it. [MAMA *has her eyes closed and is rocking back and forth as though she were in church, with her head nodding the amen yes.*] We don't want to make no trouble for nobody or fight no causes—but we will try to be good neighbors. That's all we got to say. [*He looks the man absolutely in the eyes.*] We don't want your money. [*He turns and walks away from the man.*]

LINDNER [*looking around at all of them*]. I take it then that you have decided to occupy.

BENEATHA. That's what the man said.

LINDNER [*to* MAMA *in her reverie*]. Then I would like to appeal to you, Mrs. Younger. You are older and wiser and understand things better I am sure . . .

MAMA [*rising*]. I am afraid you don't understand. My son said we was going to move and there ain't nothing left for me to say. [*Shaking her head with double meaning.*] You know how these young folks is nowadays, mister. Can't do a thing with 'em. Good-bye.

LINDNER [*folding up his materials*]. Well—if you are that final about it . . . There is nothing left for me to say. [*He finishes. He is almost ignored by the family, who are concentrating on* WALTER LEE. *At the door* LINDNER *halts and looks around.*] I sure hope you people know what you're doing.

[*He shakes his head and exits.*]

RUTH [*looking around and coming to life*]. Well, for God's sake—if the moving men are here—LET'S GET THE HELL OUT OF HERE!

MAMA [*into action*]. Ain't it the truth! Look at all this here mess. Ruth, put Travis' good jacket on him . . . Walter Lee, fix your tie and tuck your shirt in, you look just like somebody's hoodlum. Lord have mercy, where is my plant? [*She flies to get it amid the general bustling of the family, who are deliberately trying to ignore the nobility of the past moment.*] You all start on down . . . Travis child, don't go empty-handed . . . Ruth, where did I put that box with my skillets in it? I want to be in charge of it myself . . . I'm going to make us the biggest dinner we ever ate tonight . . . Beneatha, what's the matter with them stockings? Pull them things up, girl . . .

[*The family starts to file out as two moving men appear and begin to carry out the heavier pieces of furniture, bumping into the family as they move about.*]

BENEATHA. Mama, Asagai—asked me to marry him today and go to Africa—

MAMA [*in the middle of her getting-ready activity*]. He did? You ain't old enough to marry nobody— [*Seeing the moving men lifting one of her chairs precariously.*] Darling, that ain't no bale of cotton, please handle it so we can sit in it again. I had that chair twenty-five years . . .

[*The movers sigh with exasperation and go on with their work.*]

BENEATHA [*girlishly and unreasonably trying to pursue the conversation*]. To go to Africa, Mama—be a doctor in Africa . . .

MAMA [*distracted*]. Yes, baby—

WALTER. Africa! What he want you to go to Africa for?

BENEATHA. To practice there . . .

WALTER. Girl, if you don't get all them silly ideas out your head! You better marry yourself a man with some loot . . .

BENEATHA [*angrily, precisely as in the first scene of the play*]. What have you got to do with who I marry!

WALTER. Plenty. Now I think George Murchison—

[*He and* BENEATHA *go out yelling at each other vigorously;* BENEATHA *is heard saying that she would not marry* GEORGE MURCHISON *if he were Adam and she were Eve, etc. The anger is loud and real till their voices diminish.* RUTH *stands at the door and turns to* MAMA *and smiles knowingly.*]

MAMA [*fixing her hat at last*]. Yeah—they something, all right, my children . . .

RUTH. Yeah—they're something. Let's go, Lena.

MAMA [*stalling, starting to look around at the house*]. Yes— I'm coming. Ruth—

RUTH. Yes?

MAMA [*quietly, woman to woman*]. He finally come into his manhood today, didn't he? Kind of like a rainbow after the rain . . .

RUTH [*biting her lip lest her own pride explode in front of* MAMA]. Yes, Lena.

[WALTER'S *voice calls for them raucously.*]

MAMA [*waving* RUTH *out vaguely*]. All right, honey—go on down. I be down directly.

[RUTH *hesitates, then exits.* MAMA *stands, at last alone in the living room, her plant on the table before her as the lights start to come down. She looks around at all the walls and ceilings and suddenly, despite herself, while the children call below, a great heaving thing rises in her and she puts her finger to her mouth, takes a final desperate look, pulls her coat about her, pats her hat and goes out. The lights dim down. The door opens and she comes back in, grabs her plant, and goes out for the last time.*]

Curtain.

Fernando Arrabal

1932–

PICNIC ON THE BATTLEFIELD

❖

CHARACTERS

ZAPO, *a soldier.*
MONSIEUR TÉPAN, *the soldier's father.*
MADAME TÉPAN, *the soldier's mother.*

ZÉPO, *an enemy soldier.*
FIRST STRETCHER BEARER.
SECOND STRETCHER BEARER.

❖

A battlefield. The stage is covered with barbed wire and sandbags.
The battle is at its height. Rifle shots, exploding bombs and machine guns can be heard.
Z APO is alone on the stage, flat on his stomach, hidden among the sandbags. He is very frightened. The sound of the fighting stops. Silence.
Z APO takes a ball of wool and some needles out of a canvas workbag and starts knitting a pullover, which is already quite far advanced. The field telephone, which is by his side, suddenly starts ringing.

ZAPO. Hallo, hallo . . . yes, Captain . . . yes, I'm the sentry of sector 47 . . ˙. Nothing new, Captain . . . Excuse me, Captain, but when's the fighting going to start again? And what am I supposed to do with the hand-grenades? Do I chuck them in front of me or behind me? . . . Don't get me wrong, I didn't mean to annoy you . . . Captain, I really feel terribly lonely, couldn't you send me someone to keep me company? . . . Even if it's only a nanny-goat? [*The Captain is obviously severely reprimanding him.*] Whatever you say, Captain, whatever you say.
[*Z APO hangs up. He mutters to himself. Silence. Enter* MONSIEUR *and* MADAME TÉPAN, *carrying baskets as if they are going to a picnic. They address their son, who has his back turned and doesn't see them come in.*]
MONS. TÉPAN [*ceremoniously*]. Stand up, my son, and kiss your mother on the brow. [*Z APO, surprised, gets up and kisses his mother very respectfully on the forehead. He is about to speak, but his father doesn't give him a chance.*] And now, kiss *me.*
ZAPO. But, dear Father and dear Mother, how did you dare to come all this way, to such a dangerous place? You must leave at once.
MONS. TÉPAN. So you think you've got something to teach your father about war and danger, do you? All this is just a game to me.

1634

How many times—to take the first example that comes to mind—
have I got off an underground train while it was still moving.

MME. TÉPAN. We thought you must be bored, so we came to pay
you a little visit. This war must be a bit tedious, after all.

ZAPO. It all depends.

MONS. TÉPAN. I know exactly what happens. To start with you're
attracted by the novelty of it all. It's fun to kill people, and throw
hand-grenades about, and wear uniforms—you feel smart, but in the
end you get bored stiff. You'd have found it much more interesting in
my day. Wars were much more lively, much more highly colored.
And then, the best thing was that there were horses, plenty of horses.
It was a real pleasure; if the Captain ordered us to attack, there we all
were immediately, on horseback, in our red uniforms. It was a sight to
be seen. And then there were the charges at the gallop, sword in hand,
and suddenly you found yourself face to face with the enemy, and he
was equal to the occasion too—with his horses—there were always
horses, lots of horses, with their well-rounded rumps—in his highly-
polished boots, and his green uniform.

MME. TÉPAN. No no, the enemy uniform wasn't green. It was blue.
I remember distinctly that it was blue.

MONS. TÉPAN. I tell you it was green.

MME. TÉPAN. When I was little, how many times did I go out on
to the balcony to watch the battle and say to the neighbor's little boy:
"I bet you a gum-drop the blues win." And the blues were our enemies.

MONS. TÉPAN. Oh well, you must be right, then.

MME. TÉPAN. I've always liked battles. As a child I always said
that when I grew up I wanted to be a Colonel of dragoons. But my
mother wouldn't hear of it, you know how she will stick to her principles at all costs.

MONS. TÉPAN. Your mother's just a half-wit.

ZAPO. I'm sorry, but you really must go. You can't come into a war
unless you're a soldier.

MONS. TÉPAN. I don't give a damn, we came here to have a picnic
with you in the country and to enjoy our Sunday.

MME. TÉPAN. And I've prepared an excellent meal, too. Sausage,
hard-boiled eggs—you know how you like them!—ham sandwiches,
red wine, salad, and cakes.

ZAPO. All right, let's have it your way. But if the Captain comes he'll
be absolutely furious. Because he isn't at all keen on us having visits
when we're at the front. He never stops telling us: "Discipline and
hand-grenades are what's wanted in a war, not visits."

MONS. TÉPAN. Don't worry, I'll have a few words to say to your
Captain.

ZAPO. And what if we have to start fighting again?

MONS. TÉPAN. You needn't think that'll frighten me, it won't be

the first fighting I've seen. Now if only it was battles on horseback!
Times have changed, you can't understand. [*Pause.*] We came by
motor bike. No one said a word to us.

ZAPO. They must have thought you were the referees.

MONS. TÉPAN. We had enough trouble getting through, though.
What with all the tanks and jeeps.

MME. TÉPAN. And do you remember the bottle-neck that cannon
caused, just when we got here?

MONS. TÉPAN. You mustn't be surprised at anything in wartime,
everyone knows that.

MME. TÉPAN. Good, let's start our meal.

MONS. TÉPAN. You're quite right, I feel as hungry as a hunter. It's
the smell of gunpowder.

MME. TÉPAN. We'll sit on the rug while we're eating.

ZAPO. Can I bring my rifle with me?

MME. TÉPAN. You leave your rifle alone. It's not good manners to
bring your rifle to table with you. [*Pause.*] But you're absolutely filthy,
my boy. How on earth did you get into such a state? Let's have a look
at your hands.

ZAPO [*ashamed, holding out his hands*]. I had to crawl about on the
ground during the maneuvers.

MME. TÉPAN. And what about your ears?

ZAPO. I washed them this morning.

MME. TÉPAN. Well that's all right, then. And your teeth? [*He shows
them.*] Very good. Who's going to give her little boy a great big kiss
for cleaning his teeth so nicely? [*To her husband.*] Well, go on, kiss
your son for cleaning his teeth so nicely. [M. TÉPAN *kisses his son.*]
Because, you know, there's one thing I *will* not have, and that's making fighting a war an excuse for not washing.

ZAPO. Yes, Mother.
    They eat.

MONS. TÉPAN. Well, my boy, did you make a good score?

ZAPO. When?

MONS. TÉPAN. In the last few days, of course.

ZAPO. Where?

MONS. TÉPAN. At the moment, since you're fighting a war.

ZAPO. No, nothing much. I didn't make a good score. Hardly ever
scored a bull.

MONS. TÉPAN. Which are you best at shooting, enemy horses or
soldiers?

ZAPO. No, not horses, there aren't any horses any more.

MONS. TÉPAN. Well, soldiers then?

ZAPO. Could be.

MONS. TÉPAN. Could be? Aren't you sure?

ZAPO. Well you see . . . I shoot without taking aim, [*pause*] and at
the same time I say a Pater Noster for the chap I've shot.

MONS. TÉPAN. You must be braver than that. Like your father.

MME. TÉPAN. I'm going to put a record on.

[*She puts a record on the gramophone—a pasodoble.*[1] *All three are sitting on the ground, listening.*]

MONS. TÉPAN. That really *is* music. Yes indeed, olé!

[*The music continues. Enter an enemy soldier:* ZÉPO. *He is dressed like* ZAPO. *The only difference is the color of their uniforms.* ZÉPO *is in green and* ZAPO *is in gray.* ZÉPO *listens to the music openmouthed. He is behind the family so they can't see him. The record ends. As he gets up* ZAPO *discovers* ZÉPO. *Both put their hands up.* M. *and* MME. TÉPAN *look at them in surprise.*]

What's going on?

[ZAPO *reacts—he hesitates. Finally, looking as if he's made up his mind, he points his rifle at* ZÉPO.]

ZAPO. Hands up!

[ZÉPO *puts his hands up even higher, looking even more terrified.* ZAPO *doesn't know what to do. Suddenly he goes quickly over to* ZÉPO *and touches him gently on the shoulder, like a child playing a game of "tag!"*]

Got you! [*To his father, very pleased*] There we are! A prisoner!

MONS. TÉPAN. Fine. And now what're you going to do with him?

ZAPO. I don't know, but, well, could be—they might make me a corporal.

MONS. TÉPAN. In the meantime you'd better tie him up.

ZAPO. Tie him up? Why?

MONS. TÉPAN. Prisoners always get tied up!

ZAPO. How?

MONS. TÉPAN. Tie up his hands.

MME. TÉPAN. Yes, there's no doubt about that, you must tie up his hands, I've always seen them do that.

ZAPO. Right. [*To the prisoner.*] Put your hands together, if you please.

ZÉPO. Don't hurt me too much.

ZAPO. I won't.

ZÉPO. Ow! You're hurting me.

MONS. TÉPAN. Now now, don't maltreat your prisoner.

MME. TÉPAN. Is that the way I brought you up? How many times have I told you that we must be considerate to our fellow-men?

ZAPO. I didn't do it on purpose. [*To* ZÉPO.] And like that, does it hurt?

ZÉPO. No, it's all right like that.

MONS. TÉPAN. Tell him straight out, say what you mean, don't mind us.

ZÉPO. It's all right like that.

MONS. TÉPAN. Now his feet.

ZAPO. His feet as well, whatever next?

---

[1] a march rhythm used at bullfights

MONS. TÉPAN. Didn't they teach you the rules?

ZAPO. Yes.

MONS. TÉPAN. Well then!

ZAPO [*very politely, to* ZÉPO]. Would you be good enough to sit on the
ground, please?

ZÉPO. Yes, but don't hurt me.

MME. TÉPAN. You'll see, he'll take a dislike to you.

ZAPO. No he won't, no he won't. I'm not hurting you, am I?

ZÉPO. No, that's perfect.

ZAPO. Papa, why don't you take a photo of the prisoner on the ground
and me with my foot on his stomach?

MONS. TÉPAN. Oh yes, that'd look good.

ZÉPO. Oh no, not that!

MME. TÉPAN. Say yes, don't be obstinate.

ZÉPO. No. I said no, and no it is.

MME. TÉPAN. But just a little teeny weeny photo, what harm could
that do you? And we could put it in the dining room, next to the life-
saving certificate my husband won thirteen years ago.

ZÉPO. No—you won't budge me.

ZAPO. But why won't you let us?

ZÉPO. I'm engaged. And if she sees the photo one day, she'll say I don't
know how to fight a war properly.

ZAPO. No she won't, all you'll need to say is that it isn't you, it's a
panther.

MME. TÉPAN. Come on, do say yes.

ZÉPO. All right then. But only to please you.

ZAPO. Lie down flat.

[ZÉPO *lies down.* ZAPO *puts a foot on his stomach and grabs his rifle with a
martial air.*]

MME. TÉPAN. Stick your chest out a bit further.

ZAPO. Like this?

MME. TÉPAN. Yes, like that, and don't breathe.

MONS. TÉPAN. Try and look like a hero.

ZAPO. What d'you mean, like a hero?

MONS. TÉPAN. It's quite simple; try and look like the butcher does
when he's boasting about his successes with the girls.

ZAPO. Like this?

MONS. TÉPAN. Yes, like that.

MME. TÉPAN. The most important thing is to puff your chest out
and not breathe.

ZÉPO. Have you nearly finished?

MONS. TÉPAN. Just be patient a moment. One . . . two . . . three.

ZAPO. I hope I'll come out well.

MME. TÉPAN. Yes, you looked very martial.

MONS. TÉPAN. You were fine.

MME. TÉPAN. It makes me want to have my photo taken with you.

MONS. TÉPAN. Now there's a good idea.

ZAPO. Right. I'll take it if you like.

MME. TÉPAN. Give me your helmet to make me look like a soldier.

ZÉPO. I don't want any more photos. Even one's far too many.

ZAPO. Don't take it like that. After all, what harm can it do you?

ZÉPO. It's my last word.

MONS. TÉPAN [*to his wife*]. Don't press the point, prisoners are always very sensitive. If we go on he'll get cross and spoil our fun.

ZAPO. Right, what're we going to do with him, then?

MME. TÉPAN. We could invite him to lunch. What do you say?

MONS. TÉPAN. I don't see why not.

ZAPO [*to* ZÉPO]. Well, will you have lunch with us, then?

ZÉPO. Er . . .

MONS. TÉPAN. We brought a good bottle with us.

ZÉPO. Oh well, all right then.

MME. TÉPAN. Make yourself at home, don't be afraid to ask for anything you want.

ZÉPO. All right.

MONS. TÉPAN. And what about you, did you make a good score?

ZÉPO. When?

MONS. TÉPAN. In the last few days, of course.

ZÉPO. Where?

MONS. TÉPAN. At the moment, since you're fighting a war.

ZÉPO. No, nothing much. I didn't make a good score, hardly ever scored a bull.

MONS. TÉPAN. Which are you best at shooting? Enemy horses or soldiers?

ZÉPO. No, not horses, there aren't any horses any more.

MONS. TÉPAN. Well, soldiers then?

ZÉPO. Could be.

MONS. TÉPAN. Could be? Aren't you sure?

ZÉPO. Well you see . . . I shoot without taking aim [*pause*], and at the same time I say an Ave Maria for the chap I've shot.

ZAPO. An Ave Maria? I'd have thought you'd have said a Pater Noster.

ZÉPO. No, always an Ave Maria. [*Pause.*] It's shorter.

MONS. TÉPAN. Come come, my dear fellow, you must be brave.

MME. TÉPAN. [*to* ZÉPO]. We can untie you if you like.

ZÉPO. No, don't bother, it doesn't matter.

MONS. TÉPAN. Don't start getting stand-offish with us now. If you'd like us to untie you, say so.

MME. TÉPAN. Make yourself comfortable.

ZÉPO. Well, if that's how you feel, you can untie my feet, but it's only to please you.

MONS. TÉPAN. Zapo, untie him.

ZAPO *unties him.*

MME. TÉPAN. Well, do you feel better?

ZÉPO. Yes, of course. I really am putting you to a lot of inconvenience.
MONS. TÉPAN. Not at all, just make yourself at home. And if you'd
  like us to untie your hands you only have to say so.
ZÉPO. No, not my hands, I don't want to impose upon you.
MONS. TÉPAN. No no, my dear chap, no no. I tell you, it's no trouble
  at all.
ZÉPO. Right . . . Well then, untie my hands too. But only for lunch,
  eh? I don't want you to think that you give me an inch and I take
  an ell.
MONS. TÉPAN. Untie his hands, son.
MME. TÉPAN. Well, since our distinguished prisoner is so charming,
  we're going to have a marvelous day in the country.
ZÉPO. Don't call me your distinguished prisoner, just call me your
  prisoner.
MME. TÉPAN. Won't that embarrass you?
ZÉPO. No no, not at all.
MONS. TÉPAN. Well, I must say you're modest.
  [*Noise of aeroplanes.*]
ZAPO. Aeroplanes. They're sure to be coming to bomb us.
  [ZAPO *and* ZÉPO *throw themselves on the sandbags and hide.*]
  [*To his parents*]. Take cover. The bombs will fall on you.
  [*The noise of the aeroplanes overpowers all the other noises. Bombs imme-
  diately start to fall. Shells explode very near the stage but not on it. A
  deafening noise.*
    ZAPO *and* ZÉPO *are cowering down between the sandbags.* MONS.
  TÉPAN *goes on talking calmly to his wife, and she answers in the same unruffled way. We can't hear what they are saying because of the bombing.*
  MME. TÉPAN *goes over to one of the baskets and takes an umbrella out
  of it. She opens it.* MONS. *and* MME. TÉPAN *shelter under it as if it
  were raining. They are standing up. They shift rhythmically from one foot
  to the other and talk about their personal affairs.*
    The bombing continues.
    Finally the aeroplanes go away. Silence.
    MONS. TÉPAN *stretches an arm outside the umbrella to make sure that
  nothing more is falling from the heavens.*]
MONS. TÉPAN [*to his wife*]. You can shut your umbrella.
  [MME. TÉPAN *does so. They both go over to their son and tap him lightly
  on the behind with the umbrella.*]
  Come on, out you come. The bombing's over.
  [ZAPO *and* ZÉPO *come out of their hiding place.*]
ZAPO. Didn't you get hit?
MONS. TÉPAN. What d'you think could happen to your father?
  [*Proudly.*] Little bombs like that! Don't make me laugh!
  [*Enter, left, two* RED CROSS SOLDIERS. *They are carrying a stretcher.*]
FIRST STRETCHER BEARER. Any dead here?
ZAPO. No, no one around these parts.

FIRST STRETCHER BEARER. Are you sure you've looked properly?
ZAPO. Sure.
FIRST STRETCHER BEARER. And there isn't a single person dead?
ZAPO. I've already told you there isn't.
FIRST STRETCHER BEARER. No one wounded, even?
ZAPO. Not even that.
SECOND STRETCHER BEARER [*to the* FIRST STRETCHER BEARER].
Well, now we're in a mess! [*To* ZAPO *persuasively*.] Just look again, search everywhere, and see if you can't find us a stiff.
FIRST STRETCHER BEARER. Don't keep on about it, they've told you quite clearly there aren't any.
SECOND STRETCHER BEARER. What a lousy trick!
ZAPO. I'm terribly sorry. I promise you I didn't do it on purpose.
SECOND STRETCHER BEARER. That's what they all say. That no one's dead and that they didn't do it on purpose.
FIRST STRETCHER BEARER. Oh, let the chap alone!
MONS. TÉPAN [*obligingly*]. We should be only too pleased to help you. At your service.
SECOND STRETCHER BEARER. Well, really, if things go on like this I don't know what the Captain will say to us.
MONS. TÉPAN. But what's it all about?
SECOND STRETCHER BEARER. Quite simply that the others' wrists are aching with carting so many corpses and wounded men about, and that we haven't found any yet. And it's not because we haven't looked!
MONS. TÉPAN. Well yes, that really is annoying. [*To* ZAPO.] Are you quite sure no one's dead?
ZAPO. Obviously, Papa.
MONS. TÉPAN. Have you looked under all the sandbags?
ZAPO. Yes, Papa.
MONS. TÉPAN [*angrily*]. Well then, you might as well say straight out that you don't want to lift a finger to help these gentlemen, when they're so nice, too!
FIRST STRETCHER BEARER. Don't be angry with him. Let him be. We must just hope we'll have more luck in another trench and that all the lot'll be dead.
MONS. TÉPAN. I should be delighted.
MME. TÉPAN. Me too. There's nothing I like more than people who put their hearts into their work.
MONS. TÉPAN [*indignantly, addressing his remarks to the wings*]. Then is no one going to do anything for these gentlemen?
ZAPO. If it only rested with me, it'd already be done.
ZÉPO. I can say the same.
MONS. TÉPAN. But look here, is neither of you even wounded?
ZAPO [*ashamed*]. No, not me.
MONS. TÉPAN [*to* ZÉPO]. What about you?
ZÉPO [*ashamed*]. Me neither. I never have any luck.

MME. TÉPAN [*pleased*]. Now I remember! This morning, when I was peeling the onions, I cut my finger. Will that do you?

MONS. TÉPAN. Of course it will! [*Enthusiastically.*] They'll take you off at once!

FIRST STRETCHER BEARER. No, that won't work. With ladies it doesn't work.

MONS. TÉPAN. We're no further advanced, then.

FIRST STRETCHER BEARER. Never mind.

SECOND STRETCHER BEARER. We may be able to make up for it in the other trenches.

[*They start to go off.*]

MONS. TÉPAN. Don't worry! If we find a dead man we'll keep him for you! No fear of us giving him to anyone else!

SECOND STRETCHER BEARER. Thank you very much, sir.

MONS. TÉPAN. Quite all right, old chap, think nothing of it.

[*The two* STRETCHER BEARERS *say goodbye. All four answer them. The* STRETCHER BEARERS *go out.*]

MME. TÉPAN. That's what's so pleasant about spending a Sunday in the country. You always meet such nice people. [*Pause.*] But why are you enemies?

ZÉPO. I don't know, I'm not very well educated.

MME. TÉPAN. Was it by birth, or did you become enemies afterwards?

ZÉPO. I don't know, I don't know anything about it.

MONS. TÉPAN. Well then, how did you come to be in the war?

ZÉPO. One day, at home, I was just mending my mother's iron, a man came and asked me: "Are you Zépo?" "Yes." "Right, you must come to the war." And so I asked him: "But what war?" and he said: "Don't you read the papers then? You're just a peasant!" I told him I did read the papers but not the war bits. . . .

ZAPO. Just how it was with me—exactly how it was with me.

MONS. TÉPAN. Yes, they came to fetch you too.

MME. TÉPAN. No, it wasn't quite the same; that day you weren't mending an iron, you were mending the car.

MONS. TÉPAN. I was talking about the rest of it. [*To* ZÉPO] Go on, what happened then?

ZÉPO. Then I told him I had a fiancée and that if I didn't take her to the pictures on Sundays she wouldn't like it. He said that that wasn't the least bit important.

ZAPO. Just how it was with me—exactly how it was with me.

ZÉPO. And then my father came down and he said I couldn't go to the war because I didn't have a horse.

ZAPO. Just what my father said.

ZÉPO. The man said you didn't need a horse any more, and I asked him if I could take my fiancée with me. He said no. Then I asked whether

I could take my aunt with me so that she could make me one of her custards on Thursdays; I'm very fond of them.

MME. TÉPAN [*realizing that she'd forgotten it*]. Oh! The custard!

ZÉPO. He said no again.

ZAPO. Same as with me.

ZÉPO. And ever since then I've been alone in the trench nearly all the time.

MME. TÉPAN. I think you and your distinguished prisoner might play together this afternoon, as you're so close to each other and so bored.

ZAPO. Oh no, Mother, I'm too afraid, he's an enemy.

MONS. TÉPAN. Now now, you mustn't be afraid.

ZAPO. If you only knew what the General was saying about the enemy!

MME. TÉPAN. What did he say?

ZAPO. He said the enemy are very nasty people. When they take prisoners they put little stones in their shoes so that it hurts them to walk.

MME. TÉPAN. How awful! What barbarians!

MONS TÉPAN [*indignantly, to* ZÉPO]. And aren't you ashamed to belong to an army of criminals?

ZÉPO. I haven't done anything. I don't do anybody any harm.

MME. TÉPAN. He was trying to take us in, pretending to be such a little saint!

MONS. TÉPAN. We oughtn't to have untied him. You never know, we only need to turn our backs and he'll be putting a stone in our shoes.

ZÉPO. Don't be so nasty to me.

MONS. TÉPAN. What d'you think we *should* be, then? I'm indignant. I know what I'll do. I'll go and find the Captain and ask him to let me fight in the war.

ZAPO. He won't let you, you're too old.

MONS. TÉPAN. Then I'll buy myself a horse and a sword and come and fight on my own account.

MME. TÉPAN. Bravo! If I were a man I'd do the same.

ZÉPO. Don't be like that with me, Madame. Anyway I'll tell you something—our General told us the same thing about you.

MME. TÉPAN. How could he dare tell such a lie!

ZAPO. No—but the same thing really?

ZÉPO. Yes, the same thing.

MONS. TÉPAN. Perhaps it was the same man who talked to you both?

MME. TÉPAN. Well if it was the same man he might at least have said something different. That's a fine thing—saying the same thing to everyone!

MONS. TÉPAN [*to* ZÉPO, *in a different tone of voice*]. Another little drink?

MME. TÉPAN. I hope you liked our lunch?

MONS. TÉPAN. In any case, it was better than last Sunday.

ZÉPO. What happened?

MONS. TÉPAN. Well, we went to the country and we put the food on the rug. While we'd got our backs turned a cow ate up all our lunch, and the napkins as well.

ZÉPO. What a greedy cow!

MONS. TÉPAN. Yes, but afterwards, to get our own back, we ate the cow.

[*They laugh.*]

ZAPO [*to* ZÉPO]. They couldn't have been very hungry after that!

MONS. TÉPAN. Cheers! [*They all drink.*]

MME. TÉPAN [*to* ZÉPO]. And what do you do to amuse yourself in the trench?

ZÉPO. I spend my time making flowers out of rags, to amuse myself. I get terribly bored.

MME. TÉPAN. And what do you do with the flowers?

ZÉPO. At the beginning I used to send them to my fiancée, but one day she told me that the greenhouse and the cellar were already full of them and that she didn't know what to do with them any more, and she asked me, if I didn't mind, to send her something else.

MME. TÉPAN. And what did you do?

ZÉPO. I tried to learn to make something else, but I couldn't. So I go on making rag flowers to pass the time.

MME. TÉPAN. Do you throw them away afterwards, then?

ZÉPO. No, I've found a way to use them now. I give one flower for each pal who dies. That way I know that even if I make an awful lot there'll never be enough.

MONS. TÉPAN. That's a good solution you've hit on.

ZÉPO [*shyly*]. Yes.

ZAPO. Well, what I do is knit, so as not to get bored.

MME. TÉPAN. But tell me, are all the soldiers as bored as you?

ZÉPO. It all depends on what they do to amuse themselves.

ZAPO. It's the same on our side.

MONS. TÉPAN. Then let's stop the war.

ZÉPO. How?

MONS. TÉPAN. It's very simple. [*To* ZAPO.] You just tell your pals that the enemy soldiers don't want to fight a war, and you [*to* ZÉPO] say the same to your comrades. And then everyone goes home.

ZAPO. Marvelous!

MME. TÉPAN. And then you'll be able to finish mending the iron.

ZAPO. How is it that no one thought of such a good idea before?

MME. TÉPAN. Your father is the only one who's capable of thinking up such ideas; don't forget he's a former student of the École Normale, *and* a philatelist.

ZÉPO. But what will the sergeant-majors and corporals do?

Mons. Tépan. We'll give them some guitars and castanets to keep them quiet!

Zépo. Very good idea.

Mons. Tépan. You see how easy it is. Everything's fixed.

Zépo. We shall have a tremendous success.

Zapo. My pals will be terribly pleased.

Mme. Tépan. What d'you say to putting on the pasodoble we were playing just now, to celebrate?

Zépo. Perfect.

Zapo. Yes, put the record on, Mother.

[Mme. Tépan *puts a record on. She turns the handle. She waits. Nothing can be heard.*]

Mons. Tépan. I can't hear a thing.

Mme. Tépan. Oh, how silly of me! Instead of putting a record on I put on a beret.

[*She puts the record on. A gay pasodoble is heard.* Zapo *dances with* Zépo, *and* Mme. Tépan *with her husband. They are all very gay. The field telephone rings. None of the four hears it. They go on dancing busily. The telephone rings again. The dance continues.*

The battle starts up again with a terrific din of bombs, shots and bursts of machine-gun fire. None of the four has seen anything and they go on dancing merrily. A burst of machine-gun fire mows them all down. They fall to the ground, stone dead. A shot must have grazed the gramophone; the record keeps repeating the same thing, like a scratched record. The music of the scratched record can be heard till the end of the play.

The two Stretcher Bearers *enter left. They are carrying the empty stretcher.*]

Sudden Curtain.

GLOSSARY OF
LITERARY TERMS

ABSTRACTION: a nonmaterial idea, as distinct from CONCRETE objects, persons, or actions.

ACCENT: the vocal emphasis or stress given a syllable in oral reading, or the mental emphasis in silent reading.

ACTION: in any NARRATIVE form, the sequence of events which constitute the STORY and convey the PLOT; in DRAMA, also the gestures, posture, and movement of an actor; BUSINESS.

ALEXANDRINE: an IAMBIC HEXAMETER line used as a variant in IAMBIC PENTAMETER verse; specifically the last line in a SPENSERIAN STANZA.

ALLEGORY: a form of NARRATIVE which acts out abstract ideas through characters PERSONIFYING qualities such as hope or justice. In one view, all literature is allegorical, because it dramatizes ideas, moral attitudes, or emotional tones through the manipulation of CONCRETE DRAMATIC SYMBOLS.

ALLITERATION: the repetition of consonant sounds, usually at the beginnings of successive words:

> In Xanadu did *K*ubla *K*han
> A *s*tately pleasure-*d*ome *d*ecree:
> Where *A*lph, the sacred *r*iver, *r*an
> Through caverns *m*easureless to *m*an
> Down to a *s*unless *s*ea.
> —Coleridge

ALLUSION: reference to literature, history, or contemporary affairs to add vividness, historical association, or IRONIC contrast to the text: "He was a veritable Caesar among the neighborhood children."

ALTER EGO: "the other I"; *doppelgänger;* a character representing a portion of a personality, usually paired with another character completing the depiction. Alternatively, a close CONFIDANT.

AMBIGUITY: doubleness of meaning, whether controlled or unintentional, which can enrich the significance of a passage, provide humor or IRONY, or manifest the elusiveness of truth.

ANAPEST: a trisyllabic METRIC FOOT consisting of two unaccented syllables followed by an accented one: dĭs·ŭ·níte.

ANTAGONIST: the person or force opposed to the PROTAGONIST in the CONFLICT at the heart of a PLOT or ACTION.

ANTICLIMAX: a deflation of interest or emotion when a trivial element follows a significant one. If controlled, anticlimax can produce an IRONIC effect.

ANTIREALISTIC STYLE: the technique of representing life as other than the logical, plausible sequence of events which realism presents. Fantastic fiction and absurdist drama are among the subgenres using such a style.

APOSTROPHE: an utterance, usually in poetry, addressed to a PERSONIFIED ABSTRACTION or to an absent person or character.

ARCHAISM: the use of archaic or obsolete language forms to evoke the atmosphere of an earlier time.

ARCHETYPE: a frequently recurrent MOTIF—THEME, character type, situation, IMAGE, or NARRATIVE—presumed by Jungian psychological critics to represent the survival in the collective unconscious or the racial memory of early experiences of the human race.

ARENA STAGING: the presentation of plays in an area surrounded by the audience. Also called THEATER IN THE ROUND.

ASIDE: in neo-classic drama, a speech representing a mental reflection of a character, though spoken aloud so as to be heard by the audience but supposedly not by the other characters on the stage.

ASSONANCE: the repetition, usually in poetry, of vowel sounds within syllables placed near each other: Time's scythe.

ATMOSPHERE: the emotional effect of a literary work on a reader. It may be produced by description, language sounds, ALLUSIONS, CONNOTATIONS, ACTION, and many other elements. See "The Fall of the House of Usher," in the first paragraph and indeed throughout.

AUTHORIAL INTRUSION: the author's expression, especially in fiction, of his opinions in his own voice. Sometimes apparent authorial intrusion is a device for developing the character of a fictional narrative PERSONA quite unlike the author.

BALLAD: a simple narrative form of verse of early folk origin, suitable for singing or recitation, concerned often with thwarted love, physical prowess, vengeance, or the supernatural, and frequently including a REFRAIN or INCREMENTAL REFRAIN. Art ballads are those written by sophisticated poets, e.g., Keats, "La Belle Dame sans Merci."

BALLAD STANZA: the frequent but not invariable stanza of ballads: four alternately eight- and six-syllable lines rhyming xaxa.

BUSINESS: in drama, the gesture, posture, and motion of an actor, especially the handling of PROPERTIES.

CACOPHONY: harsh, jangling sounds, in contrast to EUPHONY.

CAESURA: a logical pause in a line of verse, usually marked by punctuation:

By fools 'tis hated, and by knaves undone!

CATALOG: a listing, often in vivid terminology, of objects, qualities, or events. Used frequently in EPICS and in the poetry of Walt Whitman.

CATASTROPHE: the last phase of the DÉNOUEMENT of TRAGEDY, usually including the death of the hero.

CATHARSIS: the purging of the emotions, especially of pity and terror, as a result of perceiving a TRAGEDY.

CHARACTERIZATION: the means of depicting CHARACTERS: DRAMATIC CHARACTERIZATION reveals personal qualities through ACTION; EXPOSITORY CHARACTERIZATION uses description and analysis by the narrator or by another character.

CHARACTERS: literary representations of people. Characters may be DEVELOPING or STATIC; ROUND if the person is depicted in full detail or FLAT if only the major outlines are sketched in. Characters representative of a group are called TYPICAL; those representing recurrent conventional roles, such as the braggart soldier, the fair maiden disguised as a man, or the sententious (and foolish) counsellor are called STOCK CHARACTERS; those representing predictable and wholly unindividualized figures are called STEREOTYPES. See also the entries for the roles played by characters: PROTAGONIST, ANTAGONIST, CONFIDANT, FOIL, CHORUS.

CHORUS: in early classic drama, a group of singers and dancers whose songs constituted the major part of the drama; in later times the group (or an individual) commented on the action of the play. Also called *choragus*, the Greek form of the word.

CLICHÉ: a FIGURE OF SPEECH that has lost its METAPHORIC force and become entirely conventional. "We worked like Trojans" no longer has anything to do with the siege of Troy; it manifests an unimaginative and lazy mind.

CLIMAX: in an ACTION or PLOT, the highest point of CONFLICT, at which the contest turns finally for or against the PROTAGONIST.

COMEDY: a literary work, usually a play, intended to amuse by dealing with minor problems in a light manner. The work usually evokes laughter and ends with the PROTAGONIST triumphing over his difficulties. The COMEDY OF HUMORS deals with characters dominated by a single trait or "humor" such as sloth, irritability, or optimism. The COMEDY OF MANNERS deals with deviations from social convention. The COMEDY OF INTRIGUE or SITUATION emphasizes complication rather than character or moral problems. In Northrop Frye's classification of MODES, a low mimetic form.

COMPLICATION: the phase of PLOT development in which the conflicting characters or forces are brought into confrontation.

CONCEIT: a FIGURE OF SPEECH establishing an ingenious or strained parallel between two things highly dissimilar, as when Donne in "A Valediction: Forbidding Mourning" compares the souls of two lovers to "stiff twin compasses" tracing a circle. This very striking form, when used by the Metaphysical poets of the earlier seventeenth century, is called a METAPHYSICAL CONCEIT.

CONCRETE: the material quality of a visible, physical object (which may embody or represent an ABSTRACTION). DRAMATIC SYMBOLS are the concrete means of acting out an idea.

CONFIDANT (feminine form, CONFIDANTE): a lesser character in whom a major character confides, sometimes so that the reader may overhear the intimate thoughts of the characters.

CONFLICT: the motivating element in an ACTION or PLOT; the developing contest between the PROTAGONIST and the ANTAGONIST.

CONNOTATION: the intellectual and emotional associations clustered about a word or phrase. See, by contrast, DENOTATION.

CONSONANCE: the patterned repetition of consonant sounds associated with varying vowels:

> But swollen with wind . . .
> Rot inwardly

CONTEXT: the surrounding discourse in which a particular expression occurs, or the circumstances associated with a particular fact. In either sense the context affects the reader's understanding of the particular matter.

CONVENTION: an improbable device accepted by the tacit consent of the literate world, as when a SOLILOQUY heard by the audience is understood to represent the unspoken thoughts of a character.

COUPLET: two successive related lines of verse, usually rhyming. If the couplet is END-STOPPED (concluded by a semicolon or period) it is a CLOSED COUPLET; if the expression flows without impediment into the next couplet it is an OPEN COUPLET. The couplet in IAMBIC TETRAMETER is called an OCTOSYLLABIC COUPLET; the closed couplet in IAMBIC PENTAMETER is called a HEROIC COUPLET.

CRISIS: an intense moment of CONFLICT in PLOT development that precipitates the CLIMAX.

DACTYL: a FOOT in verse METER consisting of an accented syllable followed by two unaccented syllables: lóv·ĭng·lў.

DECORUM: in general, appropriateness; specifically, the just adaptation of STYLE to a speaker's character, the subject, and the occasion.

DENOTATION: the literal, impersonal meaning of a word, as contrasted with its CONNOTATION.

DÉNOUEMENT: "unknotting"; the resolution of CONFLICT at the end of the FALLING ACTION in an ACTION or PLOT.

DETERMINISM: the doctrine that human choices are determined (or at least strongly influenced) by an omnipotent deity, the environment, one's own character, or heredity.

DEUS EX MACHINA: "god out of a machine." In Greek drama a stage device was apparently used to lower an actor representing a god onto the stage to rescue a hero from difficulty. The term is now used derogatorily for any implausible plot device introduced to resolve problems.

DEVELOPING CHARACTER: see CHARACTERS.

DIALOGUE: the exchange of utterances between characters.

DICTION: the choice of language in any piece of speech or writing. The term is most often used in the discussion of poetry.

DIMETER: a verse line of two FEET—infrequently used, and oftenest for comic effect.

DISTANCE; AESTHETIC DISTANCE: the detachment, objectivity, and impersonality of a writer (and hence of the reader) from involvement in the affairs depicted in a work of literature. Thus detached the reader can contemplate the problems discussed without injecting his own attitudes or difficulties into the scene.

DOPPELGÄNGER: see ALTER EGO.

DRAMA: a visible, audible representation of life presented by actors moving and speaking, often on a stage set which represents a location, and acting out a plot, which is a NARRATIVE of altering human perceptions and relationships. Secondarily, drama is a literary GENRE to be read in the form of plays.

DRAMATIC METHOD: the characteristic procedure of literature as it acts out meanings through the use of DRAMATIC SYMBOLS. See also SCENIC METHOD.

DRAMATIC MONOLOGUE: a poem represented as spoken by a character to another (silent) character in a setting sketched in by suggestion and dealing with a crucial moment in the speaker's life. As developed by Robert Browning, the dramatic monologue is concerned chiefly with delineating the character of the speaker.

DRAMATIC SITUATION: the set of circumstances in which a NARRATIVE ACTION occurs.

DRAMATIC SYMBOL: a CHARACTER, SETTING, PROPERTY, or situation used as the visible means of dramatizing a THEME.

ECLOGUE: see PASTORAL.

ELEGY: a poem lamenting a death.

ELLIPSIS: the omission of sentence parts necessary for grammatical completeness but not essential to clarity.

EMOTION: the nonrational response to experience, including imaginative literature.

EMPATHY: the act of a reader who identifies himself with (places himself in the position of) a character in a work of literature. Empathy is usually based on a recognition of some similarity in personality or circumstances and implies that the reader sees the experience of the character as a possibility for himself.

ENJAMBMENT: the use of two run-on lines of verse; i.e., those that flow on without a pause marked by punctuation at the end of the first of the lines.

EPIC: a long, serious narrative poem dealing in a heightened STYLE with the adventures of a HERO whose destiny involves (or represents) the fate of a race or nation. Conventional aspects of the epic include the poet's plea for the assistance of the muse, a statement of epic purpose and THEME, beginning the action in the midst of things (IN MEDIAS RES), adventures chiefly in the form of warfare, the intervention of supernatural beings or forces, the hero's descent into the underworld, and the use of EPIC SIMILES and CATALOGS.

EPIC SIMILE: a comparison of events in the Bible, myth, or history with events in the foreground action of a work. The epic simile usually takes the form: "*As* a person in myth, history, or the Bible once did something, *so* now a character in the epic does something similar."

EPIGRAM: a brief, witty poem cleverly phrasing a single point:

> Damnation follows death in other men,
> But your damned poet lives and writes again.—Pope

EPIGRAPH: a quotation prefixed to a literary work to suggest its THEME or interpretation.

EPIPHANY: a moment of revelation in which the meaning of an experience or literary work becomes clear.

EPISODE: in Greek drama, a passage of action between choruses. In fiction, an uninterrupted sequence of ACTION.

EPITAPH: a motto, quotation, or short poem commemorating a death.

EPITHET: a word or phrase, usually an adjective, used repeatedly to characterize and identify a character: "Achilleus of the swift feet"—Richmond Lattimore's translation of Homer's *Iliad*.

EUPHONY: harmonious sounds, in contrast to CACOPHONY.

EXPOSITION: in a NARRATIVE work, explanation by the narrator or a character of necessary background information, or of the significance or THEME of a work.

EXPRESSIONISM: a stylized, nonrealistic manner in any literary genre, but especially prominent in the drama of the 1920s and 30s. SYMBOLIC SETTINGS, disruptions of the normal time sequence, and stylized speech and action are used to manifest the psychic states of the characters, who are sometimes disturbed or abnormal. See *The Hairy Ape*.

FALLING ACTION: the phase of diminishing intensity of CONFLICT from the CLIMAX to the DÉNOUEMENT of an ACTION or PLOT.

FARCE: a comic form of drama played for maximum laughter through fast pace, ludicrous situations, wisecracks, exaggerated reactions, and slapstick bordering on violence.

FICTION: a prose NARRATIVE of imaginary events which dramatize changes in human relationships.

FIGURES OF SPEECH: verbal formulations that relate two unlike things by suggesting their identity, similarity, or other relationship. See APOSTROPHE, CONCEIT, METAPHOR, METONYMY, PERSONIFICATION, SIMILE, SYNECHDOCHE. See also RHETORICAL DEVICES.

FLASHBACK: an interruption of a NARRATIVE (which has very likely begun IN MEDIAS RES) to dramatize antecedent events at a moment appropriate to the development of the story.

FLAT CHARACTER: see CHARACTERS.

FOCUS: the principal center of interest of a literary work.

FOIL: a minor character whose contrasting qualities emphasize the characteristics of the PROTAGONIST or other major figure.

FOLK DRAMA: plays which, though written by sophisticated dramatists, deal with the life of the people—their customs, language, closeness to the soil, and exposure to the environment. See Brecht's *Mother Courage*.

FOOT: a recurrent unit in lines of verse, consisting of a characteristic arrangement of two or three ACCENTED and unaccented syllables.

FORESHADOWING: anticipation by DIALOGUE, ACTION, or SYMBOLIC objects of the outcome of PLOT CONFLICT. It may stimulate SUSPENSE, or, if it prematurely reveals the ending, it may permit the reader to take an IRONIC view of events. An example is the crack in the structure of the House of Usher, which the NARRATOR sees before he enters the house.

FORM: the language, STRUCTURE, and STYLE of presentation of a literary work.

FREE VERSE: verse which does not employ regular METERS or STANZAS. The style is chiefly associated with Walt Whitman, but is now very widely practiced.

GENRE: one of the major forms of literature, as FICTION, POETRY, DRAMA, or nonfiction prose. Also sometimes called *types*. Innumerable subgenres, such as EPIC poetry and tragicomedy, have been identified.

HEPTAMETER: a seven-foot line of verse. A line of this length tends to break down in oral reading into two lines, one of TETRAMETER and one of TRIMETER, the order of these depending on the location of the CAESURA. Lines longer than heptameter are theoretically possible, but are rarely written.

HERO: a PROTAGONIST of admirable qualities, who embodies some popular ideals.

HEXAMETER: a six-foot line of verse.

HUBRIS; HYBRIS: in classic literature, the god-insulting pride of humans, particularly of TRAGIC HEROES.

HYPERBOLE: (pron. hy·pér·bo·lēe) exaggeration of facts and emotions by means of inflated language.

IAMB: a METRIC FOOT in verse consisting of an unaccented syllable followed by an ACCENTED one: to·dáy.

IDENTIFICATION: see EMPATHY.

IMAGE CLUSTERS: groups of related IMAGES that give a clue to meanings and attitudes.

IMAGERY: mental effects, resembling sensory impressions, produced by language. Mental pictures of visible objects are called VISUAL IMAGERY—the commonest type. Tactile, auditory, and other kinds of imagery are also sometimes used.

INCITING FORCE: a character or event that upsets the initial equilibrium between PROTAGONIST and ANTAGONIST in a NARRATIVE to begin the PLOT phase of RISING ACTION leading to the CRISIS and CLIMAX.

IN MEDIAS RES: "in the midst of things"—where NARRATIVES often begin in order to get off to a fast start, leaving necessary antecedent events to be filled in later by FLASHBACK or retrospective EXPOSITION.

INVERSION: the arrangement of sentence elements out of their usual subject-verb-complement order:

> Whose woods these are I think I know.—Frost

IRONY: a perception of discrepancy between expectations and actual outcomes. VERBAL IRONY rests on a discrepancy between two meanings of language:

> Get you the sons your fathers got,
> And God will save the Queen.—Housman

IRONY OF CIRCUMSTANCE recognizes the discrepancy between human aspiration and human weakness; thus Ozymandias, in the Shelley poem, builds what he hopes will be an enduring monument to his power, but natural forces turn it into a ruin that commemorates only human frailty. DRAMATIC IRONY results when viewers of a play (or readers of fiction) know some important thing, such as the outcome of the plot, that is unknown to all or some of the characters. The IRONIC MODE is one of Northrop Frye's categories.

LITOTES: (lў·tóe·tĕes). a RHETORICAL DEVICE that emphasizes a meaning by denying its opposite: "The proposal is not without merit" may mean that we had better pay attention.

LYRIC: originally to be sung to the accompaniment of a lyre. Now, poetry primarily expressive of emotion.

MACROCOSM: the actual full-scale world, which may be represented in little by a MICROCOSM.

MELODRAMA: sensational drama marked by violent action, simplified characterization, and the triumph of the virtuous.

METAPHOR: a FIGURE OF SPEECH asserting that one thing is equivalent to another, though the two are in literal fact dissimilar:

> All experience is an arch—Tennyson

An EXTENDED METAPHOR records the equivalence of parts or functions as well as of the whole. An IMPLICIT or SUBMERGED METAPHOR is implied rather than stated: "My winged thoughts" rather than "My thoughts were birds." A DEAD METAPHOR has lost its figurative force and become a CLICHÉ through long, customary use: "The head of the table."

METER: in verse, the ideal pattern of alternating ACCENTED and unaccented syllables. See ANAPEST, DACTYL, IAMB, SPONDEE, TROCHEE, SCANSION, RHYTHM.

METONYMY: substituting for the name of something the name of another thing with which it is associated: "He sets a good table" means "He serves good food." Compare with SYNECHDOCHE.

MICROCOSM: a limited and simplified SETTING in which the human relationships of the larger world, or MACROCOSM, are dramatized in simplified form.

MIME: an actor who uses gesture, facial expression, and posture to suggest events and emotions. See PANTOMIME.

MIRACLE PLAYS: see MYSTERY PLAYS.

MODE: a class of subject matter and an associated style of literary treatment, including ROMANCE, COMEDY, TRAGEDY, AND IRONY (Northrop Fry's list) and sometimes ALLEGORY, polemic, and SATIRE.

MONOLOGUE: a speech, usually lengthy, uninterrupted by other speakers, which may be part of a DRAMA or an independent performance.

MORAL: a principle of behavior deduced from a work of literature. The term is often used derogatorily for a simplistic admonition.

MORALITY, OR MORALITY PLAY: a late medieval form of DRAMA that succeeded the MYSTERY PLAY and dramatized an ABSTRACT conflict, such as good versus evil, by means of ALLEGORY.

MOTIF, OR MOTIVE: a recurrent THEME, situation, CHARACTER, or verbal formula.

MOTIVATION: the stimulus of the behavior or attitudes of characters. In realistic forms of literature, plausibility is the first requisite.

MYSTERY PLAYS: medieval English plays based on biblical themes and acted by craft guilds (mysteries; cf. mastery) on wagons in the streets or, later, in the courtyards of inns. Some authorities use the term *miracle play* for this subgenre; others reserve it for an earlier form based on saints' lives or miracles and acted in churches or churchyards.

MYTH: a NARRATIVE of the exploits of gods or heroes, dramatizing a people's beliefs about significant matters, such as the creation of the world, the nature of the universe, or the destiny of a nation. In recent criticism the term is also used for any system of belief or for a milieu and the drama acted out in it, such as Tolkien's *The Lord of the Rings* or Faulkner's Yoknapatawpha saga.

NARRATIVE: the telling of a sequence of events, or the sequence itself. In the latter sense, synonymous with ACTION.

NARRATOR: the story-teller in a work of literature, either a fictional character in the work, or an implied speaker who does not appear as a character.

NATURALISM: in DRAMA, a highly REALISTIC style of acting. In fiction, a variety of heightened REALISM based on a theory of DETERMINISM, or the theory that the impersonal universe is chaotic, or without purpose or meaning.

NOVEL: an extended prose FICTION, sometimes regarded as more REALISTIC and more exclusively concerned with the ordinary and probable in human affairs than the ROMANCE.

OBJECTIVITY: a method of presentation that excludes the author's attitudes and judgments of the events pictured.

OCTAVE: an eight-line STANZA; specifically, the first eight lines of an ITALIAN SONNET, though these are not normally set off by a stanza space.

ODE: a poem usually celebrating a specific occasion in an elevated STYLE. The line length, RHYME SCHEME, and STANZA form are highly variable.

ONOMATOPOEIA: the imitation of natural sounds by the sounds of words. The representations of animal sounds, for example, are conventional (and only approximately accurate) ONOMATOPOETIC WORDS.

ORGANIC FORM: a theory that the content of a work has its shape implicit within it, and that if such arbitrary devices as METER and STANZAS are not imposed on the material it will be expressed in its innate natural or organic form.

OTTAVA RIMA: a stanza of eight IAMBIC PENTAMETER lines rhyming abababcc.

OXYMORON: the paradoxical coupling of two apparently contradictory terms to express the AMBIGUITY of human experience: "Parting is such sweet sorrow"—Shakespeare.

PANTOMIME: a dramatic performance using no DIALOGUE, and hence relying on gesture and other motion to convey NARRATIVE and feeling. See MIME.

PARADOX: an apparently self-contradictory statement that expresses an unsuspected truth. The Metaphysical poets used paradox to express the mysteries of religious faith:

> . . . I
> Except you enthrall me, never shall be free,
> Nor ever chaste, except you ravish me.
> —Donne

PARAPHRASE: a summary of the substance of a literary work, especially a poem, in different words, in order to test one's comprehension of the original and to set forth singly the dual or several aspects of the work's AMBIGUITY. The paraphrase cannot be expected to improve upon or substitute for the original.

PARODY: the comic imitation of the style and substance of a literary work.

PASTORAL: a conventional kind of poetry using the life of shepherds as a means of discussing themes of interest to the urban audience to whom the sophisticated poet addresses the work. As an adjective denoting a manner this term is often coupled with nouns to form phrases denoting subgenres: *pastoral lyric* or *pastoral elegy.*

PATHETIC FALLACY: the depiction of nature as possessing and expressing the emotions of humans: "There was a terrible grace in the move of the waves, and they came in silence save for the snarl of the crests"—Stephen Crane. The term was devised by John Ruskin.

PENTAMETER: a five-FOOT line of verse, the most commonly used in English poetry.

PERSONA: the special character or voice which the author projects as the speaker of a poem, or as the NARRATOR in fiction.

PERSONIFICATION: the representation of ABSTRACT ideas (such as justice or hope) as persons or CHARACTERS in a NARRATIVE. The characters in the purest forms of ALLEGORY are personifications.

PLAIN SENSE: the ordinary, literal meaning of the sentences in a poem, without consideration of AMBIGUITIES, associations, or SYMBOLIC import. The term was devised by I. A. Richards.

PLAUSIBILITY: the likelihood that events could occur as depicted in a fictional narrative. Plausibility is appropriate to REALISM, but not necessarily to other kinds of writing.

PLOT: the sequence of changes in human relationships motivated by and revealed through the EPISODES of the ACTION. In this definition, action consists of CONCRETE events acted out by means of DRAMATIC SYMBOLS; plot is the series of ABSTRACT relationships thus manifested.

POETRY: imaginative discourse that gives powerful expression to experience, ideas, and emotion in heightened, patterned language.

POINT OF VIEW: in FICTION, the position from which events are observed and narrated. The point of view may be LIMITED to what can be observed by a particular character, and events may be related in the first or third person. Alternatively, the point of view may be OMNISCIENT (all-knowing), and may be EDITORIAL (told with the addition of interpretive comment) or OBJECTIVE (told without comment).

PRELIMINARY SITUATION: the state of equilibrium existing between the PROTAGONIST and ANTAGONIST before the INCITING FORCE instigates the RISING ACTION of a NARRATIVE.

PROBLEM PLAY: a play that depicts a social or moral problem without advancing a particular solution.

PROLOGUE: a prefatory passage, often a MONOLOGUE spoken (sometimes by a character called "prologue") before the ACTION of a play begins.

PROPERTIES (PROPS): in the staging of a play, the objects, such as letters, items of clothing, ladders, tools, or what not, used by the actors in the performance of their rôles.

PROSCENIUM: the arch near the forward edge of a stage, providing a psychological separation of the actual world of the spectators' lives and the illusory world of the DRAMA.

PROTAGONIST: in narrative forms, the chief character with whom the audience identify themselves. See EMPATHY.

PUN: a word of double meaning. In *Romeo and Juliet*, Mercutio says as he is dying, "Ask for me tomorrow, and you shall find me a grave man."

QUATRAIN: a four-line STANZA, occasionally unrhymed, or oftener rhymed in such patterns as abab, abba, xaxa, and aaxa.

REALISM: presentation of the actual and ordinary life of unexceptional people in an OBJECTIVE manner without idealization or sensationalizing, and often with little or no AUTHORIAL INTRUSION.

RECOGNITION SCENE: an incident in TRAGEDY in which a character (usually the HERO) resolves the PLOT complication by perceiving his own or another's true identity or the true nature of his situation.

REFRAIN: in poetry, a line repeated at the end of each STANZA. An INCREMENTAL REFRAIN is altered with each repetition by the addition of new material.

REPARTEE: rapid, witty exchange in DIALOGUE.

RESOLUTION: the outcome and unraveling of a PLOT or ACTION. See DÉNOUEMENT.

RHETORICAL DEVICES: intellectual stratagems for sharpening meaning. See
AMBIGUITY, ANTICLIMAX, HYPERBOLE, IRONY, LITOTES, OXYMO-
RON, PARADOX, PUN, and UNDERSTATEMENT.

RHYME: Words are said to rhyme when their sounds are identical from the
last pronounced vowel of the final syllable to the end. This form is called
PERFECT RHYME. IMPERFECT, OBLIQUE, WRENCHED, INEXACT,
NEAR, or SLANT RHYME occurs when the sounds approximate each other but
do not correspond exactly: room/become (Dickinson). EYE RHYME is not
strictly rhyme at all; the words look alike, but do not sound alike: bough/
cough. END RHYME involves the final words in the lines. INTERNAL RHYME
occurs when a word near the middle of a line rhymes with the final word of the
same line (and perhaps with other words nearby):

> For the moon never *beams* without bringing me *dreams*
> Of the beautiful Annabel Lee;
> And the stars never *rise* but I see the bright *eyes*
> Of the beautiful Annabel Lee.
> —Poe

The rhyming of final accented syllables is called MASCULINE RHYME. The
far less frequent rhyming of a final accented syllable and one unaccented syllable following it is DOUBLE FEMININE RHYME: education/conversation. The
very unusual rhyming of a final accented syllable followed by two unaccented
syllables—often used for comic effect—is TRIPLE FEMININE RHYME: in-
tellectual/hen-pecked you all—Byron. Rhyme gives pleasure in the fulfillment
of a pattern; it sometimes draws attention to relationships in the content of the
poem; it unifies stanzas; and it aids the memory. Rhyme is not invariable in
poetry, but it is an effective and frequently used device.

RHYTHM: in language, more or less regular recurrence of ACCENT or stress,
as it is also called, in phrases, sentences, or lines of verse. In poetry rhythm is
a compromise between the logical pattern of accents in the sentence and the
normal or ideal pattern of accents known as METER.

RIME ROYAL: a seven-line STANZA in IAMBIC PENTAMETER rhyming
ababbcc.

RISING ACTION: the phase of increasing intensity of CONFLICT from the IN-
CITING INCIDENT to the CRISIS of an ACTION or PLOT.

ROMANCE: a form of NARRATIVE dealing with the somewhat idealized adventures of characters above the ordinary level in social status or abilities, and
sometimes incorporating the marvelous in the form of fairies or the occult.
Contrasted by Hawthorne and others to the NOVEL. Along with COMEDY,
TRAGEDY, and IRONY, one of Northrop Frye's four MODES.

ROUND CHARACTER: see CHARACTERS.

SARCASM: harsh and often IRONIC scornful language.

SATIRE: a literary MODE which, through the use of witty ridicule and often
IRONY seeks to correct folly by contrasting it with an assumed standard of
conduct.

SCANSION: the act of determining the METER and RHYTHM of verse.

SCENIC METHOD: the dramatization or acting out of meanings, as against EX-

POSITION; what Henry James called "the march of an action." See DRA-
MATIC METHOD.

SENTIMENTALITY: expression of emotion in excess of what is warranted by
the conditions dramatized.

SESTET: the last six lines of an ITALIAN SONNET.

SETTING: the place, real or imagined, in which ACTION, speech, or meditation
occurs. In poetry, fiction, and printed plays, setting is presented by naming
and description. In stage spectacles the setting is represented by a STAGE SET,
a visible imitation, sometimes more and sometimes less REALISTIC, of a
location.

SHORT STORY: a relatively brief prose FICTION, distinguished from anecdote
or sketch by its fuller development, and from the NOVEL by its briefer, more
unified, and more sharply focused treatment.

SIGNIFICANT FORM: in any work of art, the means of presenting the SUB-
JECT MATTER and THEME is SIGNIFICANT; that is, it is part of the meaning
of the work.

SIMILE: a special form of METAPHOR that asserts the similarity of two things
largely unlike each other: "O, my love is like a red red rose"—Burns.

SOLILOQUY: in DRAMA, a speech representing the inner thoughts of the
speaker, usually delivered when no other actors are on stage.

SONNET: a fourteen-line poem in IAMBIC PENTAMETER. The ENGLISH or
SHAKESPEAREAN SONNET RHYMES abab, cdcd, efef, gg, and hence divides into three QUATRAINS, carrying forward a logical progression, and a
summarizing COUPLET. The SPENSERIAN SONNET RHYMES abab, bcbc,
cdcd, ee. The PETRARCHAN or ITALIAN SONNET, rhymed abba, abba,
cde, cde (or cd, cd, cd, or other variants), divides into an OCTAVE and a
SESTET. The octave poses a problem, depicts a situation, or offers an observation. The sestet resolves the challenge posed by the octave.

SPENSERIAN STANZA: a STANZA of eight IAMBIC PENTAMETER lines followed by an ALEXANDRINE, and rhyming ababbcbcc.

SPOKESMAN: a character who as NARRATOR or in DIALOGUE voices the
author's views.

SPONDEE: in verse, a metric FOOT consisting of two accented syllables:
lóok óut!

STANZA: a repeated unit of lines of verse bound together by a RHYME
SCHEME. Various stanzas are defined in this glossary under their adjectives or
subgroup nouns such as QUATRAIN.

STATIC CHARACTER: see CHARACTERS.

STEREOTYPE: see CHARACTERS.

STOCK CHARACTER: see CHARACTERS.

STOCK RESPONSE: a conventional reaction to various recurrent aspects of
literature, that may minimize or ignore the distinctive features of an individual
work.

STREAM OF CONSCIOUSNESS: a style of NARRATION that reproduces the unspoken reflections of a character.

STRESS: see ACCENT.

STRUCTURE: the division, proportion, arrangement, and articulation of the
parts of a literary composition.

STYLE: a strategy of literary presentation; the author's characteristic selection and disposition of language elements in accommodation to the occasion, purpose, audience, and substance of the work.

SUBJECTIVITY: the inclusion of interpretations and judgments, usually the author's, in a work of literature.

SUBJECT MATTER: the human experience depicted in literature; the DRAMATIC SYMBOLS—the CHARACTERS, ACTIONS, and PROPERTIES—employed in dramatizing a THEME.

SUMMARY NARRATION: EXPOSITION, rather than dramatization, of events by a NARRATOR or character.

SURPRISE ENDING: an unexpected outcome that may be LEGITIMATE if the writer has clearly prepared the circumstances leading to that DÉNOUEMENT, or ILLEGITIMATE if he belatedly introduces new elements to force a satisfactory outcome. See DEUS EX MACHINA.

SURREALISM: a non-realistic STYLE, stressing incongruity, dream fantasy, and alogical structure in order to penetrate the literal surface of experience and to manifest the irrationality of dreams.

SUSPENSION: a delay in completion of the logical structure of a sentence by the intrusion of subordinate elements between the subject and the predicate.

SYMBOL: an object, an action, a situation, or a verbal formula that represents an ABSTRACTION, an unseen object, or a complex phenomenon that cannot be dealt with directly or literally. The symbol often has a multiple significance, is naturally rather than arbitrarily related to what it represents, and arouses emotions appropriate to what it symbolizes.

SYMBOL, DRAMATIC: see DRAMATIC SYMBOL.

SYNECHDOCHE: a FIGURE OF SPEECH that substitutes a part for the whole: "He was a good *hand* at mowing." Synechdoche is sometimes regarded as a kind of METONYMY.

TABLEAU: in NARRATIVE, a moment of arrested ACTION in which the locations and postures of the characters represent their moral and psychological relationships at that moment.

TERCET: a three-line STANZA.

TERZA RIMA: a sequence of STANZAS of three IAMBIC PENTAMETER lines rhyming aba, bcb, etc.

TETRAMETER: a four-FOOT line of verse.

THEATER IN THE ROUND: see ARENA STAGING.

THEME: a general vision of life or an explicit proposition about human experience dramatized by a work of literature; loosely, the significance or "meaning" of the work. Also a problem dealt with, rather than a conclusion demonstrated.

TONE: the author's implicit attitude toward the subject matter of the work, such as playful, solemn, or IRONIC. In older writing the term denotes the ATMOSPHERE or emotional tonality of a work; thus Poe identifies the tone of "The Raven" as melancholy.

TRAGEDY: a subgenre of DRAMA presenting CHARACTERS of powerful moral natures defeated by the inescapable forces that shape human life. The PROTAGONIST is a HERO, beset by a TRAGIC FLAW (ambition, HUBRIS, avarice), who is overcome by the forces of society or the deity. The effect of the spectacle is said by Aristotle to be CATHARSIS.

TRIMETER: a three-FOOT line of verse.

TRIPLET: a set of three RHYMING lines interpolated into a sequence of COUPLETS.

TROCHEE: a METRIC FOOT consisting of an ACCENTED syllable followed by an unaccented one: súm·mer.

TROPE: in rhetoric, any FIGURE OF SPEECH. In drama, a brief DIALOGUE (e.g., *Quem Quaeritis*) sung during a church service; an important forerunner from which evolved MIRACLE and MYSTERY PLAYS.

TURNING POINT: the CLIMAX of an ACTION or PLOT.

TYPICAL CHARACTER: see CHARACTERS.

UNDERSTATEMENT: a RHETORICAL DEVICE in which mild language has the effect of magnifying the subject: "The recent unpleasantness" was the British term for World War I.

UNITIES: Aristotle described Greek drama as observing the UNITIES OF TIME, PLACE, AND ACTION, which limited the time of a play to one day, the setting to one city, and the action to one story-line.

VERISIMILITUDE: the apt and persuasive representation of actuality through literary means.

VERSE PARAGRAPH: in FREE VERSE, lines grouped by logic, in the absence of a RHYME SCHEME; analogous to the STANZA in rhymed verse.

VERSIFICATION: all the technical devices of verse, including sound qualities, RHYTHM, METER, and STANZA form.

NOTE: Terms in SMALL CAPITALS within an entry are treated more fully in other entries under those terms, or represent a variety of the main entry.

INDEX OF
AUTHORS AND TITLES

Titles of stories are in Roman type enclosed in quotation marks; titles of poems are in Roman type without quotation marks; titles of plays are italicized, without quotation marks.

XYZ